ROTHMANS
FOOTBALL
YEARBOOK
1993-94

EDITOR: JACK ROLLIN

HEADLINE

First published in 1993
by HEADLINE BOOK PUBLISHING LTD

10 9 8 7 6 5 4 3 2 1

Cover photograph Left: Dean Saunders (Aston Villa); right: Chris Fairclough (Leeds United) (*Action Images*)

British Library Cataloguing in Publication Data
Rothmans Football Yearbook.—1993–94
1. Association Football—Serials
796.334′05

ISBN 0 7472 0755 0 (hardback)
0 7472 7895 4 (softback)

Typeset by BPCC Whitefriars Ltd,
Tunbridge Wells

Printed and bound in Great Britain by
BPCC Hazell Books Ltd
Member of BPCC Ltd

HEADLINE BOOK PUBLISHING LTD
A Member of the Hodder Headline PLC Group
Headline House
79 Great Titchfield Street
London W1P 7FN

CONTENTS

INTRODUCTION

The 24th edition of Rothmans Football Yearbook marks a significant change in the presentation of players appearances for both English and Scottish League teams. The total number of appearances for each player is positioned at the top of the list of matches in which they have appeared and the indication of players substituted now features a light type figure and an italic number, replacing the * and +.

Once again six pages are devoted to each English club for FA Premier League and Barclays League competitions. As in recent editions, every one has a full page photograph of the 1992–93 squad and this includes the new addition to the Football League, Wycombe Wanderers.

Transfer fees are again listed, but there remains a wide variation in what can be determined as an accurate figure, when net fees, tribunal decisions and complicated additional payments are concerned. Also the date when a player is signed often varies from the one given as his registration. As an extra ingredient this year, players notified as being transferred between non-league clubs are also quoted without an indication of fees.

With the World Cup finals looming nearer for 1994, there are up-to-date teams, results and scorers of all European Group matches plus results from the rest of the world.

The Editor would like to thank Alan Elliott for the Scottish section, Norman Barrett for the Milestones Diary and Ian Vosper for the Obituaries. Thanks are also dues to John English who provided his usual painstaking and conscientious reading of the proofs. Appreciation, too, for the fine editorial assiatance of Glenda Meeson and Christine Forrest.

The Editor would also like to pay tribute to the various organisations who have helped to make this edition complete, especially Sheila Murphy of the Football League, Mike Foster of the FA Premier League and the secretaries of all the Football League and Scottish League clubs for their kind co-operation. The ready availability of Football League secretary David Dent and his staff to answer queries was as usual most appreciated especially Ian Cotton and Chris Hull and thanks are due in equal measure to the Scottish Football League as well as Adrian Cook and Jane Scott of the FA Premier League.

ACKNOWLEDGEMENTS

The Editor would also like to express his appreciation of the following individuals and organisations for their co-operation: Glynis Firth, Sandra Whiteside, Lorna Parnell, Debbie Birch (all from the Football League), David C. Thompson of the Scottish League, Malcolm Stammers (FA of Wales), Alan Dick, Malcolm Brodie, Bob Hennessy, Peter Hughes (English Schools FA), W.P. Goss (AFA), Ken Scott for GM Vauxhall Conference information, Rev. Nigel Sands, Edward Grayson, Ken Goldman, Andy Howland and Don Aldridge.

Special appreciation is due to Lorraine Jerram of Headline Book Publishing Ltd for her continuing patience, understanding, appreciation and support.

Finally sincere thanks to Allan Wyatt, Trevor Stevens and the production staff at BPCC Whitefriars for their efforts in the production of this book which was much appreciated throughout the year.

EDITORIAL

The FA Carling Premiership and the Endsleigh Insurance League will day by day become familiar names to us. By a similar measure one hopes that the nagging nightmare prospect of the kick-in taking the place of a throw-in may yet prove only a bad dream. One can only trust that wiser heads will ultimately dismiss the idea.

Presumably the change was designed to up the pace of the game, which is already threatening to exceed the speed limit. Surely to improve standards a concentrated effort at encouraging players at the highest level, who can only kick the ball with one foot to practise with both.

While the pirouettes of those who manouevre themselves to avoid having to strike the ball with their 'wrong' foot can be admired, for efficiency, the two-footed player must be worth double the value of the colleague with just one foot in the groove.

If those clamouring for a return to the ancient kick-in as a hark back to basics. there can be no more rudimentary knowledge than controlling the ball with both feet.

Trying to keep both feet on the ground is something which David Platt will have to do now that he has been handed the unwanted tag of the world's most expensive footballer in transfer terms. Fortunately he is a sensible man, but the fees which have been paid for him are breathtaking enough.

His first move took him from Crewe Alexandra to Aston Villa for a modest enough £200,000. Three years later he went to Italy for the first time when Bari paid £5.5 million for his services. A year later it was Juventus who topped this at £6.5 million and in the recent close season he switched to Sampdoria in a £5.2 million deal. Total: £17.4 million.

Of course transfer fees have to be taken at their reported value. If Freedom of Information ever reaches soccer, we may all be surprised at the revelations.

All this is a far cry from the latest piece of archive information affecting an international player of long ago, brought to our attention by Gareth M. Davies co-author of the Who's Who of Welsh International Soccer Players.

It appears that for years W. H. Hunter was thought to have been a player with North End Belfast, while making a solitary international appearance in 1886–87. It has since transpired that he was the then FA of Wales Secretary, who had little or no practical knowledge of the game at all, but was pressed into service in an emergency.

He did later become a referee for a time and obviously has a unique niche in footballing history.

Transfer fees were modest or non-existent at the time, professionalism having only just started to gain a foothold in the game. Whether Hunter was able to strike the ball with both feet or even one at all, has not been recorded to any great detail.

The two-handed throw dates back to 1882 and even Hunter might have been shaken to learn that it is being seriously discussed for a vanishing act in the near future.

On a more up-to-date note, attendances in the FA Premier League and Football League combined to a figure which represented a seventh season in succession of increased crowds.

The Premier League began slowly but rallied noticeably in the closing weeks of the season when aggregate attendances for the weekend of 1 May reached 276,709 and 253,940 for the last full programme of the season.

The Football League can also be pleased with the final figures for their truncated competition and full details of the season's crowds appear elsewhere in this edition.

ROTHMANS FOOTBALL AWARDS

Rothmans Football Awards are presented to clubs and players who have achieved success and enriched the game during the past season. They also reveal the wide ranging nature of the book itself.

ALDERSHOT TOWN FOOTBALL CLUB rose from the ashes of the former Football League club, reorganised themselves with largely local players and won the Diadora League Division Three Championship in style, averaging League gates of 2090 and attracting nearly 6000 for a Hampshire Senior Cup semi-final with neighbours Farnborough Town. Their away support was such that they achieved the best attendance of the season at each of their opponents' grounds. The determination of Chairman Terry Owens, backed by a board which is enabling the club to be run in a professional manner augers well for their future again.

GEORGE GRAHAM steered Arsenal to both domestic trophies, winning the Coca Cola Cup and then the FA Cup at the expense of Sheffield Wednesday in both finals. He became the first manager to have won both in the same season, having previously claimed to have achieved the distinction of being the first Arsenal man to win title medals with the club as a player and manager. In 1989 he had become the ninth to play in and later manage the League Championship-winning teams. His guidance of the team in 1992–93 was all the more impressive in cup competitions as the club's Premier League form was well below its best. He is one of Arsenal's most successful managers.

ALEX FERGUSON became the first Manchester United manager to win the championship for 26 years. The honour came in the first season of the FA Premier League. While all managers face exacting requirements by the needs of the modern game, there is little doubt that for the club with the most widespread support that Manchester United possess, the pressures to take the title are intense. Old Trafford has not had such a cause for celebration in terms of League football for a quarter of a century. He is a seasoned campaigner at the helm and becomes the first manager to win the League title in Scotland (with Aberdeen) and then England.

TEDDY SHERINGHAM established himself as the FA Premier League's ace goalscorer with 22 goals, including one goal for Nottingham Forest before his transfer to Tottenham Hotspur in the early weeks of the season. By achieving this figure he has set a target for others to aim at and in this respect he will have established a niche in his own. Towards the end of the season he was capped by England for the first time. This is his second Rothmans goalscoring award in the last three years, a tribute to a consistency of marksmanship during his career which began with Millwall. His average in all senior matches during is 2.34 matches per goal.

GUY WHITTINGHAM topped the 40-goal mark for Portsmouth, achieving the comparatively rare feat of scoring more than half the total number of goals registered by his club. His 42 in the League also broke the club scoring record held by Billy 'Farmer' Haines at Fratton Park since 1926-27. The former Army man came late to full-time professional football, but has shown ability and tenacity of purpose. He helped push Portsmouth towards promotion as serious challengers, though they just missed out on it in the play-offs. His overall total was an impressive 47 for all competitions.

WYCOMBE WANDERERS were pipped for the right to attain Football League status just over a year agao, but were convincing winners of the GM Vauxhall Conference this time round. They coupled this performance with winning the FA Trophy to rightly justify the title of the most successful club outside the FA Premier League and Football League. The level of the club's support—around 5000 for League games alone—their excellent facilities at their relatively new home and go ahead leadership through manager Martin O'Neill, should provide sufficient basis for further success.

MILESTONES DIARY 1992·93

June 1992
England flop out of the European Championships . . . Danes come out on top . . . Plans for a Scottish 'super league'

13   Graham Taylor dismisses speculation that he is about to drop England captain Gary Lineker. Injuries leave Keown, Merson and Palmer doubtful against France.

14   England and France play out a dull goalless draw in Malmo. Sweden chalk up the first win in the group, beating Denmark 1-0.

15   Scotland bow out of the European Championships outplaying Germany for most of the game but losing 2-0. Holland draw 0-0 with CIS. Sir John Quinton and Rick Parry are confirmed as chairman and chief executive of the FA Premier League, respectively. Liverpool dismiss reserve team coach Phil Thompson.

16   Liverpool sign Watford's England Under-21 keeper David James for a fee to be determined.

17   England are knocked out of the European Championships, losing 2-1 to Sweden after taking an early lead; Graham Taylor takes Gary Lineker off after 61 minutes of what proves to be his last chance of equalling Bobby Charlton's scoring record. France, too, are eliminated, losing 2-1 to unfancied Denmark.

18   Two fine displays enliven the European Championships – from holders and favourites Holland, who outplay Germany 3-1, and from already eliminated Scotland, whose 3-0 victory over CIS lets Germany through to the semi-finals.

21   Germany reach the European final with a 3-2 win over Sweden.

22   Denmark produce another shock, beating Holland on penalties to reach the European final, Peter Schmeichel saving Van Basten's spot-kick.

24   Don Howe resigns as Coventry manager because of the strain of travelling, and is replaced by joint manager Bobby Gould.

25   Sheffield Wednesday sign Chris Waddle from Olympique Marseille for £1m.

26   Battered and bruised after their semi-final, underdogs Denmark produce another remarkable performance to beat Germany 2-0 in the final of the European Championships. Five Scottish clubs – Aberdeen, Celtic, Dundee United, Hearts and Rangers – tender their resignations (in advance) to the League and announce plans for a 'super league' in 1994. Bert Millichip is re-elected for a four-year term on UEFA's executive committee.

30   The FA's 'Manifesto for Football', revealed to the Parliamentary All-Party Football Committee, calls for a further reduction in Pools betting duty and new legislation to outlaw ticket touting. Brazil's Jorginho is awarded FIFA's fair play prize. Fiorentina pay Bayern Munich £3.5m for Danish international Brian Laudrup.

July
£13 million transfer . . . Referees to wear green – and purple . . . South Africa back . . . 'Back-pass rule' is adjusted . . . Dalglish pays £3.6m for Alan Shearer . . . Coca-Cola to sponsor League Cup

1   The FA Premier League grant four clear week-ends before midweek World Cup qualifying matches. AC Milan pay Torino a world record £13m for left-winger Gianluigi Lentini, who will net a reported £16m over four years.

2   Referees in the Premier League will wear green, there will be a choice from three substitutes, one a goalkeeper, and a 15-minute half-time interval. Football League referees will wear purple, with yellow the first change. Michel Platini resigns as coach of France, who win the right to host the 1998 World Cup finals by 12 votes over Morocco (7) and Switzerland (0). FIFA award Sir Stanley Matthews their special merit order for outstanding services. Dave Sexton joins Aston Villa as coach.

3   South Africa are re-elected to FIFA after 18 years with a unanimous vote.

5   Chelsea appoint Don Howe as coach.

7   South Africa, playing their first international for over 30 years, beat Cameroon 1-0 at Durban.

8   Middlesbrough winger Stuart Ripley joins Blackburn for £1.3m. Harry Redknapp joins West Ham as manager Billy Bonds' assistant, while Phil Neal joins Coventry in a similar capacity under Bobby Gould.

10   The government rules that clubs in the two lower divisions will not be obliged to have all-seater stadiums after all. Terry Butcher will make a playing comeback with Sunderland on a two-month trial. The only nationwide competition in the United States, the indoor Major Soccer League, folds after 14 years.

11   The FA 'School of Excellence' at Lilleshall is set to close in 1994 after 10 years through lack of success. Former West Ham manager Ted Fenton, 77, dies following a car crash a week ago.

13   Barnet's first-team squad deliver a mass transfer request to chairman Stan Flashman over a pay dispute.

14   Arsenal pay Danish club Brondby £1.1m for midfielder John Jensen. Ipswich upgrade Mick McGiven to first-team manager to work alongside 'football manager' John Lyall.

15   Barnet players resolve their differences with chairman Flashman. QPR sign a one-year sponsorship deal with new radio station Classic FM.

17   Not for the first time, a new FIFA ruling is proving contentious, and the Premier League and Football League invite all managers and captains to a seminar in Birmingham on 4 August primarily to discuss interpretation of the 'back-pass' ruling.

18   Crystal Palace become the first foreign club side to play in South Africa since their readmittance to FIFA, beating Kaizer Chiefs 3-2 in Johannesburg.

21 FIFA are making last-minute adjustments to the new back-pass rule to close loopholes being exploited by German players, one of whom was sent off for kneeling down to knee the ball back to his keeper.
23 Leeds sign David Rocastle from Arsenal for £2m. Referees block BSkyB's plans to wire them for sound so that they can announce their decisions.
24 Everton announce a £2m loss for last season.
25 Trevor Steven returns to Rangers from Marseille for £2.4m, less than half what he cost.
26 Alan Shearer completes his move from Southampton to Blackburn for a British record fee of £3.6m, and Liverpool pay Spurs £2.3m for Paul Stewart.
27 The Premier League clubs block proposed sponsorship by Bass and Ford because of conflicting interests with individual club sponsors.
29 Manchester United's Bryan Robson is injured in a friendly and will miss the start of the season. Stoke manager Lou Macari is cleared of tax fraud while with Swindon, but the club's former chairman Brian Hillier and accountant Vivian Farrar are convicted of making secret payments to players.
30 The FA introduce compulsory random drug testing for next season.
31 Coca-Cola become new League Cup sponsors, with a £2.25m deal for two years and a three-year option.

August
Cantona hat-trick in Charity Shield . . . Season starts with home defeat for Premier favourites Arsenal . . . Ailing Maidstone resign from League . . . Shilton sent off . . . Norwich top League

1 The opening of the Scottish season is marked by the debut of Aberdeen's Duncan Shearer, newly signed from Blackburn, who scores two in their 3-0 defeat of Hibs. In Division One, Raith slam relegated St Mirren 7-0.
2 Sampdoria win the Makita Tournament, beating Leeds 1-0.
3 FIFA alter the 'back pass' law, ruling that a 'deliberate trick', such as flicking the ball up to head it back, will be punished by an indirect free-kick and a booking for ungentlemanly conduct. They also order referees to be stricter with time-wasters and to book players who encroach at free-kicks.
4 The meeting of referees, managers, coaches and players at Birmingham shows concern that there will be an increase in bookings and dismissals in the new season.
6 Cambridge striker Dion Dublin agrees to join Manchester United for £1m plus £300,000 if he plays for England.
8 Eric Cantona scores a hat-trick as Leeds beat a much weakened Liverpool (no Barnes, McManaman, Molby, Jones, Nicol or Thomas) 4-3 in an entertaining Charity Shield match at Wembley. In Scotland, Aberdeen go top on goal difference.
11 A tribunal rule that Liverpool must pay Watford £1.3m for keeper David James.
12 Chelsea sign their third player in a week, paying a club record £2.1m for Norwich striker Robert Fleck after earlier acquiring Mick Harford (Luton) and John Spencer (Rangers).
14 Celtic complete the £1.5m signing of Stuart Slater from West Ham. The FA fine Southampton £20,000 (£15,000 suspended) for their poor disciplinary record (80 cautions, 5 dismissals) last season. Troubled Maidstone are given till Monday to assure the League they can fulfil their fixtures, and tomorrow's game against Scunthorpe is called off. Managers Kenny Dalglish and Kevin Keegan are warned as to their future conduct after being found guilty of bringing the game into disrepute over comments to match officials last April.
15 The season opens with a shock as Premier League favourites Arsenal go down 4-2 at home to Norwich after leading 2-0, new signing Mark Robins scoring twice for the Canaries. In the new First Division, Portsmouth's Guy Whittingham hits three in a 3-3 draw at Southend. All three Scottish Premier leaders lose.
16 In the first BSkyB live televised match, Liverpool go down to a Teddy Sheringham goal at Nottingham Forest. South Africa play their first African Nations Cup match, but lose 4-1 to Zimbabwe for whom Bruce Grobbelaar plays his first match since 1984 and Coventry striker Peter Ndlovu scores two.
17 The first BSkyB evening fixture is a draw, QPR holding Manchester City 1-1 at Maine Road. Maidstone resign from the Football League, heavily in debt and unable to guarantee to fulfil their fixtures. Manchester United's Lee Sharpe has viral meningitis and will need at least two months' rest before he starts training again.
18 A late Alan Shearer goal gives Blackburn, who withdraw their £3m bid for Palace captain Geoff Thomas, a 1-0 win over Arsenal. Ipswich win 1-0 at Wimbledon to join Blackburn at the top of the table on 4 points. In Scotland, Kilmarnock shock Hibs 3-1 in the Skol Cup.
19 Norwich go top of the Premier League on goal difference from Coventry as the two unfancied clubs boast the only 100 per cent records after two games.
20 The FA rule than any player withdrawn from an England squad must provide a medical certificate or have his fitness assessed by the England team doctor. The League impose a transfer ban at Barnet after complaints by players about wages. A meeting in Scotland in response to proposals by the 8 leading clubs to secede agrees to create four divisions of 10 clubs.
21 Spurs complain to the FA over reported comments by referee Dermot Gallagher, who was quoted as saying that he booked Gordon Durie for feigning injury to get an opponent sent off.
22 Coventry win 2-1 at Wimbledon to go top of the Premier League, the only club with a 100 per cent record, while Wimbledon are bottom without a point. Champions Leeds crash 4-1 at Middlesbrough. In the Scottish Premier, Celtic draw 1-1 at Rangers but lose the leadership to Aberdeen.
23 Arsenal earn their first points with a 2-0 win at Liverpool.

24 A late winner from new signing Dion Dublin at Southampton gives Manchester United their first win of the season, while Manchester City sign Wimbledon's Terry Phelan for £2.5m, a British record for a full-back.

25 Leeds crush Spurs 5-0 to go third in the Premier League, helped by a Cantona hat-trick. The FA charge Tottenham's Gordon Durie with misconduct for feigning injury, the first case of its kind in England. Charlton beat Bristol Rovers 4-1 to lead Division One by 5 points. In the Coca-Cola Cup, Andy Cole, Bristol City's new signing from Arsenal, scores a hat-trick in their 5-1 defeat of Cardiff. Chester return home after three years' playing at Macclesfield, but lose to Stockport. The Scottish FA outlaw the proposed Super League.

26 QPR win 1-0 at Premier League leaders Coventry and go top.

28 Spurs sign Forest striker Teddy Sheringham for £2.1m. Peter Shilton is sent off for the first time in his career, in his 971st League game, for a 'professional foul'. Football League clubs sign a four-year deal with ITV guaranteeing £25m and up to £100,000 extra per match for as many as 70 live Sunday matches (many on a regional basis) per season plus the Coca-Cola Cup semi-finals and the First Division play-off final.

29 Unbeaten Blackburn go top of the Premier League with a 2-0 win at second-placed Coventry as leaders QPR go down 1-0 at Chelsea. In the Barclays First, Charlton, held at home by a Luton side winning their first point, lose their first point but stay top by 3. Newcastle, with the day's highest gate in England, beat West Ham 2-0 to maintain their 100 per cent record and have two games in hand. In Scotland, Rangers beat leaders Aberdeen 3-1 to go second, behind Dundee United. Partick's George Shaw scores 4 in their 6-3 win over Dundee.

30 A Spurs draw at Ipswich takes them off the bottom of the Premier League. Coventry assistant manager Phil Neal is to take over as an England coach from Exeter manager Alan Ball.

31 Norwich go to the top of the Premier League with a 3-1 victory over Forest, whose fourth successive defeat spells out their worst start in Brian Clough's 17 years as manager. Sheffield Wednesday striker David Hirst has his hairline ankle fracture, sustained against Arsenal on Saturday, confirmed, and will be out of the England squad to be announced tomorrow. The Scottish World Cup squad contains only one change from the European Championships, Rangers' Ian Durrant returning after a serious knee injury threatened to end his career.

September
Stuart Pearce new England captain . . . Ian Rush equals Welsh scoring record . . . Gascoigne plays again . . . Leeds and Manchester United out of Europe . . . Vinny Jones charged over controversial video

1 Graham Taylor appoints Forest's Stuart Pearce England captain in succession to Gary Lineker, and includes two uncapped players in the squad for the friendly in Spain, wingers David White (Manchester City) and Rod Wallace (Leeds). Millwall striker Chris Armstrong completes his £1m move to Crystal Palace. Liverpool open their £8m Centenary Stand, but are held 1-1 by Southampton, Kerry Dixon scoring his first goal for the visitors since signing from Chelsea and Mark Wright his first League goal for Liverpool. Birmingham make it four out of four in Division One, beating Southend 2-0 to go second, a point behind Charlton. In the only match in the Scottish Premier Division, Hearts win 3-1 at Dundee to go top.

2 Manchester United lose new striker Dion Dublin with a broken leg against Palace. Sheffield United keeper Simon Tracey is sent off at Spurs, and substitute keeper Alan Kelly goes on for outfield player Glyn Hodges. In Division One, Newcastle's 2-0 victory over Luton makes it four out of four – their best start for 84 years – and they go third. Ally McCoist hits another three for Rangers – taking his club tally past 250 – in their 4-1 win at Motherwell and they go top of the Scottish Premier on goal difference. Manchester City's Paul Lake, who returned this season after a two-year battle against a knee injury, has an exploratory op which reveals more serious ligament damage, putting his career in jeopardy again.

3 Below-average gates persuade Arsenal to ditch their all-ticket policy.

4 QPR's David Bardsley replaces the injured Rob Jones in the England squad.

5 The top three in the Premier League all win. The Scottish Premier programme is reduced to one match because of Scotland's World Cup commitments.

6 Last year's runners-up Manchester United beat champions Leeds 2-0 to go fifth in the Premier League. Northampton and Hereford draw 1-1 in an extraordinary match in Division Three, in which Hereford have a League record four players sent off, all in the last 18 minutes – in the middle of which both goals are scored.

7 Chelsea defender Paul Elliott could be out for a year after damaging cruciate knee ligaments at Anfield on Saturday. The Premier League's attempt to tie up a sponsorship deal with brewers Bass is thwarted by the votes of eight clubs, precipitating a possible constitutional crisis.

9 The Republic of Ireland, aided by a John Aldridge hat-trick, beat Latvia 4-0 to go top of their World Cup group, with Northern Ireland second after their 3-0 victory over Albania, in which Portsmouth's Colin Clarke breaks the scoring record with his 13th international goal. Scotland lose their first group match 3-1 in Switzerland and captain Richard Gough is sent off near the end for a pointless handball. Ian Rush scores 3 in Wales' 6-0 demolition of the Faeroes to equal the Welsh individual goalscoring record of 23, held jointly by Ivor Allchurch and Trevor Ford. England lose their friendly in Spain 1-0, while in their World Cup group Norway beat San Marino 10-0. Chelsea's Vinny Jones takes a pay cut and returns to Wimbledon.

10 After 10 days of negotiations, Dean Saunders moves from Liverpool to Aston Villa for £2.3m.

12 Norwich, with another 2 goals from Mark Robins, making it 6 in six games, come from two down to win 3-2 at Chelsea and go 2 points clear in the Premier League, with Blackburn second after beating Arsenal 1-0 at Highbury. At the other end of the table, Forest lose their sixth successive game, 2-1 at home to Sheffield Wednesday. Newcastle score their sixth successive win in Division

One to take over at the top from Charlton. Rangers win 4-1 at Partick to stay top of the Scottish Premier.

13 A late Steve Hodge goal for Leeds robs Villa of a win at Elland Road and saves the champions' long unbeaten home record.

14 Coventry complete the double over Spurs and move into second place, a point behind Premier Division leaders Norwich.

15 Celtic make a poor start in the UEFA Cup, going down 2-0 in Cologne, while Hibs are held at home 2-2 by Anderlecht. Blackburn miss their chance to go back on top of the Premier League, losing at home to Everton 3-2.

16 In the European Cup, Leeds crash at Stuttgart in the first round first leg to three goals in the last half hour, while Rangers beat Lyngby 2-0 at Ibrox. Liverpool, with Ian Rush scoring 4, beat Appollon 6-1 in the Cup-Winners' Cup. In the UEFA Cup, Sheffield Wednesday slaughter Spora Luxembourg 8-1, while Manchester United are held 0-0 at Old Trafford by Torpedo Moscow. Hearts lose 1-0 at Slavia Prague. Wednesday's Paul Warhurst, drafted in as an emergency striker, narrowly misses death after colliding with the keeper when scoring his second goal, and will need a precautionary brain scan. Notts County defender Craig Short chooses First Division Derby over Blackburn and signs for £2.5m.

17 Paul Warhurst gets a medical all-clear. A hamstring injury rules out Eric Cantona of Leeds for six weeks. Spurs announce a £2.9m trading profit compared with a £3.1m loss last year. Manchester United manager Alex Ferguson is furious at discovering that he had omitted Ryan Giggs in error from the UEFA Cup tie owing to ambiguous new rules. Diego Maradona, 31, announces his retirement after failing to negotiate his transfer from Napoli to Seville.

19 Norwich beat Sheffield Wednesday to go 4 points clear in the Premier League. Newcastle retain their 100 per cent record, beating Bristol City 5-0 to go 3 points clear in Division One. Rangers beat Hearts 2-0 to go 2 points ahead in the Scottish Premier.

21 Nottingham Forest stem their run of 6 defeats with a draw against Coventry.

22 The first leg of the Coca-Cola Cup second round throws up some shocks, possibly the most sensational being Liverpool's inability to beat Third Division Chesterfield at Anfield – they had to come from 3-0 and then 4-2 down to scrape a 4-4 draw, conceding more goals than in any home cup tie since 1898. In Scotland, Rangers beat St Johnstone 3-1 to reach the Skol Cup final. Barnet chairman Stan Flashman transfer-lists and fines two players for their comments in a newspaper. Diego Maradona signs for Seville from Napoli for £4m five days after 'retiring'.

23 Paul Gascoigne scores after only 10 minutes of his long-awaited comeback as Lazio beat his former club Spurs 3-0 in a friendly. In the Coca-Cola Cup first-leg, Second Division Rotherham beat Everton 1-0 and Bristol Rovers hold Manchester City 0-0 at Maine Road. Aberdeen beat Celtic 1-0 and will play Rangers in the final of the Skol Cup. In England's World Cup group, Norway beat Holland 2-1 in Oslo. The PFA overrule the Barnet chairman's sanction on captain Duncan Horton and Kenny Lowe and tell manager Barry Fry he can play them.

26 Blackburn beat Oldham 2-0 and cut Norwich's lead to 2 points as third-placed Coventry hold the leaders 1-1. Liverpool lose 3-2 at home to second-from-bottom Wimbledon. Ipswich are another side to replace a sent-off keeper with the sub keeper, withdrawing an outfield player. Newcastle's 1-0 win at Peterborough takes their opening run to 8 straight victories in Division One. Rangers go 4 points clear in the Scottish Premier.

27 Darren Roberts, playing his first full match for Wolves, scores a first-half hat-trick as they win 4-0 at Birmingham. Paul Gascoigne's Italian League debut lasts 45 minutes before he is forced off with a knee injury, although it is not serious.

28 Despite Carlisle's draw with Premier League leaders Norwich in the Coca-Cola Cup last week, Aidan McCaffery becomes the first managerial casualty of the season. Maradona makes a charismatic comeback to football in a friendly for Seville, while German striker Rudi Voeller announces his impending retirement from international football.

29 After another goalless draw with Torpedo Moscow, Manchester United are eliminated from the UEFA Cup on penalties after going two up, while Hibs' 1-1 draw at Anderlecht leaves them out on the away-goals rule. In the Cup-Winners' Cup, Liverpool have Paul Stewart sent off in their 2-1 win in Cyprus. Preston sack manager Les Chapman. Carlisle appoint David McCreery manager. Wimbledon owner Sam Hammam labels Vinny Jones a 'mosquito brain' for his involvement in a video glorifying cheating and violence in football.

30 A great comeback by Leeds is in vain, as they beat Stuttgart 4-1 at Elland Road but go out of the European Cup on away goals, while Rangers keep British interest alive with a 1-0 win at Lyngby and a 3-0 aggregate. In the UEFA Cup, Celtic overcome a two-goal deficit to beat Cologne 3-2 on aggregate and Hearts a goal deficit to beat Slavia Prague 4-3. The FA charge Vinny Jones with misconduct over his controversial video.

October

Leeds reinstated in Europe . . . Gascoigne back for England . . . Ian Rush breaks Roger Hunt's Liverpool record . . . Newcastle beaten after 11 straight wins . . . Rangers win Skol Cup . . . Holders out of Coca-Cola Cup

1 Leeds are back in the European Cup but might have to replay with Stuttgart, who are confirmed to have fielded four foreign players. Paul Gascoigne is in England's squad for the World Cup qualifier against Norway. John Salako of Crystal Palace is also recalled after a year out of the game through injury. But Graham Taylor omits Liverpool's out-of-form captain Mark Wright, including Richard Jobson (Oldham) and Gary Pallister as possible replacements. Vinny Jones apologizes for his controversial video, dissociating himself from the final edited version. Sheffield Wednesday

complete a 10-2 aggregate win in the UEFA Cup over Spora Luxembourg. Italy's captain Franco Baresi announces his retirement from international football.

3   Blackburn slam Premier League leaders Norwich 7-1 and go top themselves. Leeds go down 4-2 at Ipswich, and learn that their European tie will go to a replay on a neutral ground. Bryan Robson comes on as sub at Ayresome Park to make his Premier League debut, but Middlesbrough hold Manchester United 1-1. In Scotland, Rangers beat Falkirk 4-0, with last year's Golden Boot winner Ally McCoist scoring all 4 to take his League tally to 13.

4   Newcastle make it nine out of nine, winning 2-1 at Brentford to go 5 points clear in Division One. West Ham captain Julian Dicks is sent off for the second time this season in a bad-tempered goalless draw at Wolves. Paul Gascoigne, recovered from his knock, plays 67 minutes of Lazio's 5-2 win over Parma. Dutch star Ruud Gullit, playing his first League game of the season, helps Milan win 7-3 in Florence, scores twice and announces his retirement from international football.

6   In second-leg Coca-Cola ties, Huddersfield, bottom of Division Two, nearly topple Blackburn at Ewood Park, where a late Shearer equalizer saves the League leaders, who win it in extra time, and Ian Rush equals Roger Hunt's club scoring record of 286 goals as Liverpool come from behind again to win 4-1 at Chesterfield.

7   Third Division Scarborough score a remarkable Coca-Cola Cup win over high-flying Coventry, overturning a two-goal deficit with three goals in the last 18 minutes, the last two coming in the last minute. Other giant-killers from Division Three are Bury, who win at Charlton, and Crewe who beat West Ham. Unbeaten First Division leaders Newcastle beat Premier league neighbours Middlesbrough 3-1 at Ayresome Park. Millwall take Arsenal to penalties, but three saves by David Seaman take the Gunners through. Derby hit 7 against Southend. In the Scottish Premier Division, Ally McCoist scores another 2 in Rangers' 5-1 win at St Johnstone. Norway retain their 100 per cent record in the World Cup with a 2-0 win at San Marino.

9   Leeds beat Stuttgart 2-1 in Barcelona and will meet Rangers in the European Cup second round. Liverpool's Paul Stewart is banned for three matches in Europe for his sending-off in Limassol. Hibs are fined nearly £6,000 for crowd misbehaviour at their match against Anderlecht.

10 With no Premier League games because of the midweek internationals, Saturday's focus is on Newcastle, whose 10th win, 1-0 over Tranmere in front of 30,000, with another 7,000 shut out, takes them 8 points clear in Division One. Grimsby have two players sent off and another six booked in their 1-0 defeat at Notts County. There is little Premier League action in Scotland, but in Division Two, Stenhousemuir, smarting from a seven-goal 'slight' in a TV commercial, win 7-3 themselves at East Stirling. Aston Villa midfielder Garry Parker is called into the England squad for the first time to replace the injured Trevor Steven.

11 West Ham slam Sunderland 6-0 to move up into fifth place in Division One, but their gate, 10,326, is their lowest in the League since 1957. Paul Gascoigne is over the top when clowning in front of a Norwegian TV camera, and has to apologize for swearing.

12 Leeds and Rangers ban away fans from their forthcoming European tie.

13 Paul Gascoigne and Tony Adams are back as Graham Taylor selects a 4-4-2 formation for England, with Alan Shearer and Ian Wright up front.

14 Gascoigne inspires England at Wembley – and plays a full game – but Norway equalize David Platt's goal as England miss their chances. In other World Cup matches, Wales win 1-0 in Cyprus and Ireland hold European champions Denmark 0-0 in Copenhagen, while Scotland survive two plausible penalty appeals in their 0-0 draw with Portugal at Ibrox. Northern Ireland also draw 0-0 at home, to Spain. Former Scotland and Rangers winger Willie Waddell, 71, dies.

16 Spurs' Gordon Durie is the first player in English football to be found guilty of feigning injury (against Coventry on 18 August) and is suspended for three matches, but will appeal.

17 With Blackburn playing Monday, Norwich recover from their 7-goal drubbing to go back on top of the Premier League after beating QPR 2-1. In Scotland, Rangers need a late McCoist goal to beat Hibs and stay 5 points ahead of Celtic.

18 An Ian Rush goal at Old Trafford, his 287th for Liverpool, takes him past Roger Hunt's club record, but two late Mark Hughes goals earn Manchester United a point. Newcastle take their opening winning streak to 11 in Division One with a 2-1 win at Sunderland, their first at Roker Park for 36 years.

19 Barnet, second in Division Three, face a mass player walk-out in a dispute over wages, with manager Barry Fry also hinting at quitting.

20 Sheffield Wednesday go down 3-1 at Kaiserslautern in their first leg UEFA Cup tie, after David Hirst puts them ahead in 4 minutes but is later sent off. Celtic also lose in Germany, 1-0 to Borussia Dortmund. Chester sack manager Harry McNally after seven years, putting his assistant Graham Barrow in charge.

21 Rangers edge the first leg of the European showdown with Leeds 2-1 at Ibrox. Hearts go down 1-0 at home to Standard Liege in the UEFA Cup. An industrial tribunal rules that normal employment laws apply to football, awarding Alan Gillett, Plymouth Argyle's former assistant manager, undisclosed damages for his dismissal last May.

22 Disaster strikes Liverpool in their Cup-Winners' Cup tie in Moscow as keeper Grobbelaar is sent off for a 'professional foul' 8 minutes from time with the score 2-2, the Russians converting the resultant penalty and going on to win 4-2. Barclays announce their withdrawal from the sponsorship of the Football League when the contract expires in May. Cambridge manager John Beck, who rejected an offer from Preston earlier in the week, is sacked, along with assistant Gary Peters; youth team coach Gary Johnson is installed as caretaker.

24 Blackburn, held at Ewood Park 0-0 by Manchester United, still go top of the Premier League, as Norwich play tomorrow. Newcastle's fine run in Division One – 11 straight wins – comes to an end at last at the unlikely hands of lowly Grimsby, who win 1-0 at St James's Park, helped in no small part by keeper Dave Beasant, signed on loan from Chelsea only yesterday.

25 Wolves, the last unbeaten team in England, go down 2-0 at Millwall and stay fourth in Division One. Rangers win the Skol Cup for the 7th time in 10 years, in extra time, thanks to an own goal by Aberdeen's Gary Smith in the 114th minute. Celtic sack their £100,000-a-year chief executive Terry Cassidy.

26 Barnet players sign new contracts after a six-hour meeting between chairman Stan Flashman and representatives of the players, the PFA and the League. The Premier League is to defend a writ for £2.5m issued against chief executive Rick Parry by the Swiss Bank Corporation claiming commission owed for the BSkyB TV contract.

27 UEFA suspend Liverpool manager Graeme Souness for five matches as a result of the referee's report on his 'abusive words' after last week's defeat in Moscow. In third round Coca-Cola Cup matches, Sheffield Wednesday slam Leicester 7-1 and QPR's 2-0 victory at Bury is marred when Andy Sinton hobbles off after a controversial tackle from Lee Anderson.

28 Holders Manchester United are out of the Coca-Cola Cup, beaten 1-0 at Villa Park. Blackburn beat Norwich 2-0 in the battle of the top two Premier clubs. First Division leaders Newcastle suffer their second successive defeat, 2-1 at Stamford Bridge. The FL suspend Preston referee Jim Parker after allegations of swearing at a player.

29 Chairman Alan Sugar, defying Taylor Report stadium requirements, claims Spurs will not comply in full by the 1994 deadline.

31 Blackburn and Norwich stretch their lead at the top of the Premier League despite drawing, Blackburn away to Sheffield Wednesday, Norwich at home to Middlesbrough. The prolific Ally McCoist hits a hat-trick in Rangers' 4-2 win over Motherwell to take his season's tally to a remarkable 28.

November
Rangers beat Leeds in European Cup . . . Mass exit of other British clubs . . . Steve Bull breaks Wolves scoring record . . . Gascoigne inspires England . . . Barnes returns for Liverpool . . . Leeds sell Cantona to Manchester United

3 Celtic bow out of the UEFA Cup to Borussia Dortmund 3-1 on aggregate, after levelling the tie before half-time.

4 Rangers knock Leeds out of the European Cup with another 2-1 defeat, this time at Elland Road. They are joined in the last-eight league stage by AC Milan and CSKA Moscow, victors over holders Barcelona, who throw away a 2-0 advantage. In the Cup-Winners' Cup another Moscow club, Spartak, score two at Anfield to inflict a 6-2 defeat on Liverpool, their heaviest in Europe for 26 years, and Mike Marsh is sent off, Liverpool's third dismissal in successive European matches. England's last hope in the UEFA Cup, Sheffield Wednesday, also go out, unable to dent Kaiserslautern's two-goal lead from the first leg. Hearts also bow out, beaten 1-0 again by Standard Liege.

5 Barnet chairman Stan Flashman bans manager and players from talking to the media. Stoke manager Lou Macari, in court again, is cleared of illegally running a bookmakers. QPR striker Les Ferdinand is the only change in England's squad for the game against Turkey on the 18th, replacing the injured Trevor Steven. Former Newcastle chairman Stan Seymour dies at 76.

6 Birmingham City are up for sale following the collapse of chairman Samesh Kumar's business with its 84 per cent stake in the club. Liverpool call in the police to investigate an alleged ticket-office fraud. Dick Wragg, chairman of the FA International Committee for nearly 20 years and FA and FL vice-president, dies at 82.

7 Pre-season League favourites Arsenal notch their sixth League win on the trot, beating Coventry 3-0 and going top, thanks to Spurs' 2-0 victory at leaders Blackburn (Norwich play Monday). Liverpool recover from their European downfall with a 4-1 win over Middlesbrough in which Ian Rush scores his 200th League goal. Steve Bull scores twice for Wolves, taking his tally to 163 and breaking the club goalscoring record. Paul Groves scores a hat-trick in Grimsby's 4-1 win at Luton. Rangers win 1-0 at Celtic, their 16th successive victory, including the Skol Cup final and their European Cup triumphs over Leeds.

9 Norwich go back on top of the Premier League thanks to a Mark Robins hat-trick which gives them a last-minute 3-2 win at Oldham and a goals for/against record of 27/27.

10 Further grief for Leeds as they go out of the Coca-Cola Cup, beaten 2-1 by Watford. Malcolm Allison becomes caretaker manager of ailing Bristol Rovers.

11 In Coca-Cola Cup replays, Liverpool beat Sheffield United 3-0 and Third Division Scarborough beat Plymouth 2-1. In Scotland, two more McCoist goals help Rangers to a 3-1 win over Dundee. Four players are sent off at Birmingham in their Anglo-Italian Cup tie with Bari, two from each side.

12 An FA disciplinary committee find Wimbledon manager Joe Kinnear guilty of his third offence in three months and ban him from the touchline for a month for insulting comments made to the referee on 19 September in the game against Blackburn. Referee Jim Parker escapes with a warning after a hearing concerning alleged swearing during the Stoke-West Brom match the same day.

13 Nottingham Forest manager Brian Clough signs a 12-month extension to his contract. Chester appoint Graham Barrow player-manager.

14 With no Premier League matches because of the forthcoming World Cup qualifiers, the First Division share the limelight with the first round of the FA Cup. Newcastle's 3-1 win over Charlton, playing their last game as tenants at Upton Park, keeps them 9 points ahead of Swindon and Tranmere. John Durnin scores all Oxford's goals in their 4-0 defeat of Luton. There are some fine performances by non-League sides in the Cup, none better than perennial giant-killers Yeovil's 5-2 win at Torquay, with Paul Batty scoring a hat-trick in their 15th Cup victory over a League club. Marine, the Merseyside 'minnows' of the HFS Loans League, beat hapless Halifax 4-1 and Bath

win 3-2 at Cardiff. But Orient win a thriller at Dagenham and Redbridge 5-4 after twice being two goals down, and West Brom thrash Aylesbury 8-0. Last year's giant-killers Wrexham suffer a 6-1 humiliation at Crewe, Craig Hignett scoring 4.

15 First Division Birmingham have their fifth player – keeper Martin Thomas – sent off in three games as they go out of the Cup 1-0 at Second Division Reading, even though replacement Trevor Matthewson saves the resultant penalty.

17 The FA disciplinary committee impose a record £20,000 fine on Vinny Jones and hand him a six-month suspension, suspended for three years, for bringing the game into disrepute over his video 'Soccer's Hard Men'.

18 Paul Gascoigne sparks England to a 4-0 win over Turkey at Wembley in a World Cup qualifier, scoring twice himself in a fine team performance. At Ibrox, shaky Italian defending – despite the international 'comeback' of Franco Baresi – is matched only by poor Scottish finishing, and the Scots have to settle for a 0-0 draw. Northern Ireland also miss their chances and lose 1-0 to Denmark at Windsor Park, but the Republic stay top of Group 3 with a 0-0 draw in Spain. Belgium beat Wales 2-0 to make it five out of five in Group 4.

20 Sheffield Wednesday reject a record £3.5m bid for striker David Hirst from Manchester United, who sell Neil Webb back to Forest for £800,000.

21 Norwich go 4 points clear in the Premier League, beating Sheffield United 2-1. Arsenal's six-game winning streak comes to an end, with a 3-0 defeat at Leeds. In Scotland, leaders Rangers draw 1-1 at Hearts to stay 5 points above them.

23 After 6 months out, John Barnes returns for Liverpool, who win 1-0 at QPR. Barnet are fined £50,000 for breaches of League regulations and chairman Stan Flashman is involved in scuffles with photographers before and after the hearing.

24 Duncan Shearer hits 3 for Aberdeen, whose 7-0 win at Partick takes them into second place behind Rangers in the Scottish Premier.

25 In the first of the European Cup group matches, Rangers fight back from two down at Ibrox to salvage a draw with Marseille, while Marco Van Basten scores all of AC Milan's goals in their 4-0 victory over IFK Gothenburg. In FA Cup replays, non-Leaguers Altrincham and Stafford Rangers beat Second Division Chester and Third Division Lincoln 2-0 and 2-1 respectively, and Macclesfield win on penalties at Chesterfield thanks to keeper Steve Farrelly's three saves in the shoot-out. First Division Peterborough crush Kingstonian 9-1, with Philliskirk scoring 5, but the non-Leaguers appeal for a replay because their keeper Adrian Blake is hit by an object thrown from the crowd and has to be substituted with the score at 3-0. Bradford win a thriller 5-4 at Preston despite having a player sent off.

26 Manchester United make a sudden swoop for Eric Cantona, and Leeds let him go for £1.2m. David Platt has a cartilage removed and will be out for about a month.

27 Luton's Scottish Under-21 defender Darren Salton is seriously hurt in a car crash. England manager Graham Taylor launches a withering attack on TV's 'saturation coverage' of soccer.

28 Norwich are beginning to persuade the big clubs to take their title challenge seriously as they open up a 5-point gap at the head of the Premier League with a 3-2 win at Villa Park, Villa's first defeat for 13 games. David Kelly hits three for Newcastle who beat Cambridge 4-1 to open up a 12-point lead in Division One. Duncan Shearer hits his second hat-trick in five days for Aberdeen, who beat Hearts 6-2, but Rangers, without injured strikers McCoist and Hateley and captain Gough, stay 5 points ahead in the Scottish Premier with a 3-0 win over Partick.

30 Peterborough are ordered to replay their Cup tie with Kingstonian. Liverpool may find themselves reinstated in the European Cup-Winners' Cup as Spartak Moscow are accused of fielding an ineligible player against them and previous opponents Avenir Beggen (Luxembourg). UEFA confirm that in 1996 England will host the first 16-strong European Championships. Chelsea's Paul Elliott issues a writ against Dean Saunders over an injury incurred in Saunders' last game for Liverpool, in September, which has sidelined Elliott possibly for the season.

December
FA chief in storm over Blissett verdict . . . Lineker biography reveals rift with Graham Taylor . . . Prolific McCoist first to 200 Premier goals . . . Sao Paulo win World Club Championship . . . Gordon Durie wins appeal . . . Van Basten European Footballer of the Year again . . . Ted Croker dies

1 There are Coca-Cola Cup victories for Arsenal, 2-1 winners over Derby in their third round replay, breaking Derby's run of seven consecutive away wins, and First Division Cambridge, who beat Oldham 1-0 in the fourth round to reach the quarter-finals. Crystal Palace, after losing 5-0 at Anfield on Saturday, return to hold Liverpool 1-1 in a controversial tie. Liverpool manager Graeme Souness is angry at a tackle that leaves David Burrows out for perhaps three months. The Barnet saga continues, with chairman Stan Flashman yet again sacking manager Barry Fry, but this time officially, in writing. The players support Fry, whose last act before leaving is to persuade them not to strike. UEFA admit Armenia and Belarus, bringing membership up to 44 nations.

2 Nottingham Forest leave their League form behind to beat Spurs 2-0 in the Coca-Cola Cup, while Sheffield Wednesday stroll past QPR 4-0. Barnet's assistant manager Edwin Stein turns down chairman Flashman's offer of the manager's job, but will fill in as caretaker.

3 After a three-day trial at Salisbury Crown Court, Brentford's Gary Blissett is cleared of causing grievous bodily harm to Torquay's John Uzzell in an on-field incident on 14 December 1991, but Torquay chairman Mike Bateson ridicules the evidence of FA chief executive Graham Kelly that he sees fifty such challenges a game. Crystal Palace are to seek damages from the FA over John Salako, who broke down again in training with the England squad and has had to undergo further knee surgery in the USA. Exeter suspend Steve Williams after a dispute with manager Alan Ball and strip him of the assistant manager's job.

4   In their replayed first round FA Cup tie behind closed doors at Peterborough, Kingstonian are this time edged out by a single goal. John Aldridge scoes a hat-trick as second-placed Tranmere beat third-placed West Ham 5-2 in Division One. Torquay chairman Mike Bateson lodges an official complaint against Graham Kelly. Former Birmingham assistant manager Ian Atkins is appointed manager of Cambridge.

5   There's no stopping Norwich, who go 8 points clear in the Premier League, beating Wimbledon 2-1 after being down with 13 minutes left, as Blackburn lose 3-2 at Middlesbrough to a John Hendrie hat-trick. Bottom club Nottingham Forest beat Leeds 4-1 at Elland Road, the champions' first home defeat since 13 April 1991. In the First Division, Charlton celebrate their return to The Valley after seven years with a 1-0 win over Portsmouth, while Newcastle go 12 points clear after winning 2-0 at Notts County. In the first round of the Scottish Cup, non-League Huntly beat Stranraer 4-2, with Thomson notching a hat-trick.

6   In Division One, Derby, with only two wins at home and six losses, notch their sixth successive away League win, beating Swindon 4-2. In the Cup, non-League Wycombe come from two down to hold West Brom 2-2.

7   Preston, without a manager for 11 weeks, appoint John Beck 6 weeks after he lost his job at Cambridge.

8   Peterborough police charge a man in connection with the coin-throwing incident that caused their Cup tie with Kingstonian to be replayed, and the FA are not planning further action against the club. The Association of Referees and Linesmen call for an FA inquiry into Graham Kelly's court comments at the Blissett case. John McGrath resigns as manager of ailing Halifax, physio Mike Rathbone taking over temporarily.

9   Rangers chalk up a valuable two points in the European Cup with a 1-0 win over CSKA Moscow whose home tie is played in Germany because of the Russian winter. Marseille beat Bruges 3-0 to go top of the group on goal difference. Milan's 2-1 win at PSV Eindhoven confirms them as strong favourites in the other group. Blackburn hammer Watford 6-1 to reach the last eight of the Coca-Cola Cup. A biography of Gary Lineker to be published next week reveals a two-year bust-up between Lineker and England manager Graham Taylor, and Lineker himself is quoted as fiercely critical of Taylor.

12   Premier leaders Norwich lose 1-0 at Old Trafford and Manchester United go third. Barnet celebrate Barry Fry's return by going top of Division Three on goals. In Scotland, Ally McCoist becomes the first player to score 200 Premier Division goals, and Rangers' 2-1 win at Falkirk takes them 4 points clear of Aberdeen.

13   Sao Paulo win the Toyota World Club Championship in Tokyo, beating Barcelona 2-1. Two goals from Mark Walters spoil Kenny Dalglish's return to Anfield as Liverpool beat Blackburn 2-1. Hamilton retain the B & Q Scottish Cup for First and Second Division teams, beating Morton 3-2 at St Mirren.

14   St Johnstone sack manager Alex Totten, who took them from the foot of Division Two when he joined them in 1987 to a respectable Premier Division place. St Mirren dismiss club captain Chic Charnley for the 'culmination of increasingly serious cases of misconduct'.

15   Ipswich beat Villa 1-0 to reach the Coca-Cola Cup quarter-finals. In FA Cup replays, Wycombe hold Second Division West Brom for 80 minutes before finally succumbing 1-0, while Bath go out to three goals in the last 15 minutes at Northampton. Shrewsbury manager John Bond, under threat from Burnley fans, wears a steward's outfit to watch from the back of the stand as his side lose 2-1 to two goals in the last four minutes. Justice is done at Exeter, where Swansea win 5-2 after having the first game abandoned through floodlight failure when they were leading with 4 minutes to go. Chelsea chairman Ken Bates clinches a £16.5m deal that gives the club security after their 8-year battle, as the Royal Bank of Scotland buys Stamford Bridge and gives them a 20-year lease. Celtic manager Liam Brady is banned from the dug-out for 3 months and fined for a pitchside clash with Airdrie's coach and assistant manager, who receive similar sanctions.

16   Crystal Palace and Chelsea will meet in the Coca-Cola Cup quarter-finals after winning their home replays, Palace 2-1 over Liverpool after extra time, and Chelsea 1-0 over Everton. In FA Cup second round replays, Yeovil chalk up their 16th League scalp with a 2-1 win at Hereford and Marlow beat VS Rugby 2-0. In England's World Cup group, Ruud Gullit makes a successful international comeback with a goal as Holland win 3-1 in Turkey. Six more players are sent off in 8 Anglo-Italian Cup ties, making 18 dismissals in 32 matches. Brentford, with a 100 per cent record in their group, will meet Derby in the English semi-final. Spurs' Gordon Durie wins his appeal and is cleared of feigning injury in the game against Coventry on 19 August, while Arsenal's Ian Wright is charged with misconduct for allegedly aiming a punch at Spurs' David Howells on Saturday.

17   Lucozade Sport become a Premier League sponsor to the tune of £3m over 3 years.

19   Liverpool suffer their worst defeat for 16 years, going down 5-1 at Coventry, and have Jamie Redknapp sent off. In Division One, John Aldridge hits 3 as Tranmere beat Wolves 3-0 to go within 9 points of Newcastle, who play tomorrow. In Division Two, Stoke win 2-1 at Hartlepool to stretch their lead to 6 points. Division Three leaders York, hit by a Darren Foreman hat-trick, crash 4-2 at Scarborough, but go top on goals scored over Barnet, who play tomorrow. In Scotland, Rangers stay 4 points clear of Aberdeen, but Celtic lose 1-0 at Hearts, their first away defeat for 55 weeks and 24 League games. Italy have captain Franco Baresi sent off but scrape a 2-1 win in Malta to go 2 points clear of Scotland in their World Cup group.

20   Marco van Basten, of Holland and Milan, who goes into hospital for an operation tomorrow, is voted European Footballer of the Year for the third time in five seasons, equalling the record of Cruyff and Platini. Coventry's Peter Ndlovu and Liverpool's Bruce Grobbelaar shine in Zimbabwe's 2-1 victory over Egypt in an important World Cup qualifier. Former England coach Steve Harrison turns down a job at St Johnstone to take up a coaching post at Crystal Palace.

21   Norwich suffer their first home defeat, going down 2-0 to neighbours Ipswich, who move into sixth

place with only two League defeats, leaving Norwich top with a 34-34 goal record. Barnet beat Colchester 4-2 to go 3 points clear of York in Division Three, but have played 2 more games.

22 A cold spell hits midweek Cup replays.

23 AC Milan win 2-1 at Sampdoria to complete a calendar year unbeaten in the League.

24 Scottish League vice-president and Airdrie director Bobby Davidson dies at 64.

25 Former FA supremo Ted Croker dies at 68.

26 Twelve matches are postponed through frost in the Premier and Football Leagues. Leading League scorer Guy Whittingham hits 4 for Portsmouth, who beat Bristol Rovers 4-1, his third hat-trick of the season. The Scottish programme survives the frost, apart from one abandoned Second Division match and a postponed second-round Cup tie. Rangers win 3-1 at Dundee to retain their 4-point lead in the Premier Division.

28 Manchester United hammer form team Coventry 5-0 to go second in the Premier League, only 3 points behind Norwich, held 0-0 at Leeds. Andy Sinton hits his first hat-trick for QPR, who struggle to beat an Everton side reduced to nine men by 4-2. Guy Whittingham scores 2 to take his season's total to 29 as Portsmouth win 4-2 at Derby. Birmingham, without a game, go bottom, as the three clubs below them get results. Stoke make it seven consecutive League wins, beating Rotherham 2-0 to go 9 points clear in Division Two.

29 Four out of the six scheduled League matches are postponed through frost.

30 Thirties Arsenal and England wing-half, former manager Jack Crayston dies at 82.

31 Partick manager John Lambie is furious as free agent Frank McAvennie allegedly reneges on an agreement and rejoins Celtic.

January 1993
Strachan sent off in friendly...three-match ban for Ian Wright...Bolton humble Cup-holders Liverpool at Anfield...kick-in for throw-in experiments to go ahead

2 A third of the 3rd round FA Cup ties are called off as frost and fog abound around the country. Hartlepool are the only giant-killers, beating Crystal Palace 1-0, but Oldham and Sheffield United both have to come back from 2-0 deficits to earn replays, against Tranmere and Burnley, respectively, while Leeds and Manchester City both recover from a goal down to save their respective ties against Charlton and Reading. Blackburn beat Bournemouth 3-1 after going behind, and Villa are held at home by Bristol Rovers. Ian Wright prevents an upset at Yeovil with a hat-trick in Arsenal's 3-1 win, while Marlow go down 5-1 to Spurs in their home tie played at White Hart Lane. Rangers beat Celtic 1-0 at Ibrox to go 5 points ahead of Aberdeen, who are held at home by lowly Dundee.

3 In the Cup, a late Ian Rush goal at Bolton completes Liverpool's comeback from 2-0 down, while Forest beat Southampton 2-1.

4 In the Cup, QPR beat a prodigal Swindon 3-0. Non-League Huntly beat Queen of the South 2-1 in the Scottish Cup. Arsenal manager George Graham is charged with misconduct over remarks made to match officials after the game with Spurs last month.

5 Manchester United beat Bury 2-0 in the Cup. Ally McCoist's 35th goal of the season is the winner for Rangers who beat Dundee United 3-2 to stretch their lead in the Scottish Premier to 7 points.

6 In the Coca-Cola Cup, Blackburn and Palace reach the semi-finals with home wins over Cambridge United and Chelsea, respectively, the latter on a quagmire of a pitch, while Arsenal reach the quarter-finals with victory at Scarborough in the fog. Leeds' Gordon Strachan is sent off in a friendly tournament in Italy. Richard Money is the new manager of Scunthorpe, who sacked Bill Green earlier in the week.

7 The FA hand Arsenal's Ian Wright a 3-match ban on TV evidence showing he struck David Howells of Spurs, while manager George Graham is fined £500 for remarks made to referee Alf Buksh in the same match, on 12 December. Liverpool agree to pay former captain Phil Thompson £28,000 for dropping his claim for unfair dismissal as coach and staying silent on the issue for 2 years. Celtic withdraw their support for a Scottish 'super league', and will vote for the 3-division 14-12-12 format.

9 Eric Cantona inspires Manchester United with his usual goal and deft touches as they beat Spurs to top the Premier table for the first time, on goal difference from Norwich, who play tomorrow. Villa squeeze into 2nd place, also on 41 points, with a 2-1 win at Liverpool, Dean Saunders scoring the winner against his old club. Newcastle win 2-1 at Bristol City to lead Division 1 by 14 points. The only shock in the Scottish Cup is Premier League Partick's home defeat by Cowdenbeath, bottom of the 1st Division with only 5 points. Celtic are held by Clyde, while 1st Division leaders Raith are crushed 5-0 by 2nd-placed Kilmarnock.

10 Norwich lose 1-0 at Sheffield Wednesday and fail to return to the top. The first four clubs in the Premier League have 34 goals, although Norwich have conceded 35. In Division 1, West Ham retain their 15-minute 2-0 lead at Derby despite having Julian Dicks dismissed for the third time this season. QPR's Ray Wilkins, hurt in a freak training accident before yesterday's game, has a broken shin and is joined on the long-term injury list by Gary Penrice, who broke a leg in the match at Middlesbrough.

11 Dundee transfer their support to a Scottish 'super league', negating Celtic's withdrawal and virtually putting paid to the 3-division reconstruction. David Speedie is cleared of assaulting a fan after a play-off match last season when he was with Blackburn. Elton John quits the Watford board after 19 years because concert tours are taking so much of his time. Scottish international qualification is extended to grandparents.

12 Wimbledon win their Cup replay at Everton and Tranmere trounce Oldham 3-0, but Burnley fall to a Brian Deane first-half hat-trick as Sheffield United punish them 4-2. In postponed ties, last non-Leaguers Marine go down 3-1 at Crewe, while Sunderland win 2-0 at Notts County. Arsenal reach

the Coca-Cola Cup semi-finals, beating Forest 2-0, both goals from Ian Wright in his last game before suspension. Severe snowstorms wipe out all midweek football in Scotland.

13   With Rush, McManaman and Nicol missing from their FA Cup replay, holders Liverpool are humbled at Anfield as Bolton hit 2, this time without reply, but Leeds and Manchester City have no trouble in away replays. In postponed ties, Norwich score their first goal in 6 matches to beat Coventry, whose manager Bobby Gould is ordered from the dug-out, and Middlesbrough beat Chelsea 2-1. Former Scotland, Hearts and Chelsea inside-forward and Hearts manager Tommy Walker dies at 77.

14   Supporters of a Scottish 'super league' defeat proposals for the 14-12-12 divisional structure. Michael Thomas is out for the season, having snapped his Achilles tendon in Liverpool's Cup defeat last night. Notts County dismiss manager Neil Warnock, leaving coach Mick Walker in temporary charge.

15   Tranmere go back into second place in Division One with a 4-0 win over Oxford.

16   Norwich, with Villa and Manchester United playing tomorrow and Monday, are held at home by Coventry, but go top again despite a goal record of 35 against 36. Blackburn win at Oldham to go third. Liverpool's decline continues with a 2-0 defeat at lowly Wimbledon, while Arsenal's win at Manchester City comes after a run of eight League games without one, and Brian Deane's hat-trick as Sheffield United beat Ipswich 3-0 is his second in five days. Newcastle, Stoke and Barnet all win to consolidate their respective leads in the League divisions. Most of the Scottish programme is snowed off, but Aberdeen's 7-0 pasting of Airdrie, with Mika-Matti Paatelainen scoring 4, puts them well clear in second place.

17   Aston Villa take over at the top of the Premier League with a 5-1 mauling of Middlesbrough, and Millwall move into fourth place in Division One, level on points with Tranmere and West Ham, after thrashing Brentford 6-1.

18   Manchester United become the third new leaders of the Premier in three days as they win 3-1 at QPR. The FA's National School at Lilleshall gets a two-year reprieve.

19   Sheffield Wednesday draw their 5th-round Coca-Cola Cup tie at Ipswich. Over 70 brawling fans are arrested in Cardiff's streets before and after their Autoglass Trophy game against Swansea.

20   Villa win their 3rd-round FA Cup replay at Bristol Rovers 3-0, while Barnsley beat Leicester on penalties after a last-minute equalizer earns them a shoot-out. Celtic beat Clyde 1-0 in their Scottish Cup replay at Parkhead.

21   Bristol City sack manager Denis Smith after only 10 months, and put Russell Osman, who will continue to play, in charge until the end of the season. The DoE reject Spurs' application for a work permit for Dinamo Kiev striker Oleg Salenko.

22   Norwich put a ban on players leaving Carrow Road while the club are still in the running for Cup or League.

23   In the 4th round of the Cup, Villa are held at home by Wimbledon, Manchester United scrape a 1-0 win over Second Division Brighton at Old Trafford thanks to a late Giggs 25-yard free-kick, and Derby win 5-1 at Luton, with Mark Pembridge scoring 3 against his old club. Manchester City become the first club to win at QPR in the Cup since 1980. Stoke increase their lead in Division 2 to 10 points with a 2-1 win at West Brom, while Orient go 2nd as Robert Taylor hits 3 in their 5-0 defeat of Exeter.

24   Bolton march on in the Cup, winning 2-0 at Wolves, while Spurs do the same at Norwich. West Ham crash 4-1 at Barnsley, knocked back by an Andy Rammell hat-trick.

25   A late Merson strike clinches a two-goal Cup comeback for Arsenal against Leeds at Highbury. Paul Gascoigne incurs the wrath of an Italian MP for belching into a microphone. Birmingham chairman of four years Samesh Kumar and his two brothers are voted off the board at a meeting called by receivers controlling their collapsed business empire.

26   Blackburn crash 5-2 at home to Coventry and miss the chance of topping the table.

27   Premier League top three Manchester United, Villa and Norwich all have two-goal home wins. FIFA general secretary Sepp Blatter's controversial idea for replacing throw-ins with kick-ins is to have a trial in August's under-17 world championships in Tokyo.

28   The League Managers Association tell their members to make any criticisms of referees through the proper channel.

29   Former Derby player and manager Tim Ward dies at 75.

30   Norwich win 1-0 at Everton to go back on top of the Premier League as Manchester United and Villa lose at Ipswich and Southampton, respectively. Aberdeen keep up the pressure in Scotland with a 4-1 win at Falkirk, but Rangers stay 5 points ahead after their 4-3 win at Hibs.

31   After 7 games without a win, Liverpool move up from 17th to 12th as a Barnes penalty gives them a 1-0 win at Highbury, where Arsenal miss their 4th penalty of the season and have Nigel Winterburn sent off. Newcastle, held at home by away specialists Derby, take an 11-point lead in Division 1.

February
Sunderland sack Malcolm Crosby...Chelsea sack Ian Porterfield...concern about Gascoigne's fitness...Premier League go Carling...Bobby Moore dies

1   Arsenal pay Everton £2m for England defender Martin Keown, 26, having lost him to Villa in 1986 for a transfer tribunal fee of £200,000. Sunderland sack manager Malcolm Crosby, who got them to the FA Cup final last season. Holland and AC Milan striker Marco van Basten is named FIFA's World Player of the Year in a worldwide poll of 70 national coaches.

2   Rangers' 1-0 win at Aberdeen takes them 7 points clear of their rivals for the title. Palace's 2-1 win at Blackburn relieves their relegation worries and dents their opponents' title hopes.

3   Arsenal and Forest win their away Cup replays, Arsenal 3-2 at Leeds after extra time and Forest 3-0 at Middlesbrough, and will meet at Highbury in the 5th round. Wimbledon beat Villa 6-5 on

penalties after a 0-0 draw. Wednesday beat Ipswich 1-0 at Sheffield in their 5th-round Coca-Cola Cup replay. Ian Durrant of Rangers and Scotland agrees an out-of-court settlement for an estimated £200,000 and costs against Neil Simpson (now at Motherwell) and Aberdeen for an incident at Pittodrie on 8 October 1988 that put him out of the game for long periods and necessitated two major operations on knee ligaments.

5   Sunderland appoint Terry Butcher player-manager 13 months after his sacking at Coventry.

6   Home wins for Manchester United and Villa take them to top of the Premier League as Norwich are without a game. Outgoing champions Leeds lose their 8th away match on the trot in the League, 1-0 at Wimbledon, and are now only 4 points clear of the relegation zone. Everton keeper Neville Southall is sent off for the 2nd time in 6 weeks in their 3-1 defeat at Hillsborough, again for handling outside the box. Celtic are out of the Scottish Cup, beaten 2-0 at Falkirk.

7   Arsenal win 3-1 at Palace in the first leg of their Coca-Cola Cup semi-final. Spurs beat Southampton 4-2 in a record scoring spree of 4 goals in 4 min 44 sec of the second half.

8   Manchester United are held 0-0 at Elland Road, where the returning Eric Cantona gets a hostile reception, but go clear by a point in the Premier League. Graham Taylor restores John Barnes, the new Liverpool captain, to the England squad after his long injury. Manchester City's Steve McMahon is out for the season with a groin injury sustained against QPR on Saturday.

9   West Ham beat Peterborough 2-1 to move within 7 points of Division 1 leaders Newcastle, who suffer their first defeat of the year, 2-0 at Portsmouth. Rangers use their game in hand to beat Falkirk 5-0 and go 9 points clear of Aberdeen in the Scottish Premier.

10   Blackburn score first and last but lose 4-2 at home to Sheffield Wednesday in the first leg of their Coca-Cola Cup semi-final, all the goals coming in the first 37 minutes. Manchester United stay top of the Premier League as challengers Villa and Norwich lose, 1-0 at Palace and 3-0 at Southampton, respectively.

11   Referee Stephen Lodge reports himself to the FA for sending off the wrong Oxford player after seeing a video of their midweek match at Sunderland.

13   Home teams win all six 5th-round Cup ties, notably Arsenal in the only Premier League clash, 2-0 over Forest, with Ian Wright scoring both goals, and Blackburn 1-0 with a last-minute Wegerle goal over First Division leaders Newcastle, whose lead is now cut to 4 points by West Ham, 2-1 winners at Watford. Bolton's great Cup run comes to an end, 3-1 at Derby, and Bulgarian Bontcho Guentchev scores 3 in Ipswich's 4-0 defeat of Grimsby. Meanwhile Villa take over the Premier leadership with a 1-0 victory at Chelsea. In Scotland, Rangers lose only their second home point in the Premier, held 2-2 at Ibrox by bottom club Falkirk, but stay 9 points in front of Aberdeen who are held 1-1 by Celtic at Pittodrie.

14   The 100 per cent record for home teams in the FA Cup 5th round is completed by Sheffield United and Spurs, 2-1 and 3-2 victors, respectively, over Manchester United and Wimbledon.

15   Chelsea sack manager Ian Porterfield and former Stamford Bridge favourite David Webb takes over at least until the end of the season. Hartlepool's Alan Murray is replaced by his assistant Viv Busby. Inter Milan sign Ajax stars Dennis Bergkamp and Wim Jonk for a reported £6.3m and £4m, respectively.

17   Skipper David Platt scores 4 in England's 6-0 World Cup defeat of San Marino and misses a penalty that would have given him a share in the England record, while the Wembley crowd give John Barnes a disgraceful reception. In other qualifying matches, Scotland beat Malta 3-0 and Northern Ireland win 2-1 in Albania. Ireland beat Wales 2-1 in a friendly in Dublin, but David O'Leary, captain for the first time in 12 years, is stretchered off with concussion after 2 minutes. Chesterfield sack manager Chris McMenemy. Former England and Portsmouth outside-left Jack Froggatt dies at 71.

18   England manager Graham Taylor reveals he is concerned about Paul Gascoigne's level of fitness after his lack-lustre performance against San Marino yesterday. John Duncan is named new Chesterfield manager.

19   Bass Brewery will sponsor the Premier League as the Carling Premier League from next season, as a £12m deal over 4 years is finally agreed; Bass already sponsor the Scottish League (under the Tennents brand name) and the Charity Shield. Diego Maradona, 32, makes his international comeback for Argentina in a 1-1 draw with Brazil. 3rd Division leaders Barnet put their entire playing staff up for sale after players' salary cheques bounce.

20   The three Premier League title contenders Villa, Manchester United and Norwich all have 2-1 home wins, United's being the trickiest as they find themselves a goal down to Southampton after 77 minutes, but a Giggs double 5 minutes later sees them through. A Teddy Sheringham hat-trick at White Hart Lane helps Spurs to a 4-0 revenge over Leeds for their 5-0 thrashing at Elland Road in August. Forest climb off the bottom with a 2-1 win at Middlesbrough. In Division 1, Millwall lose their unbeaten home record as Barnsley thrash them 4-0, while Derby suffer a club-record 10th home defeat, 2-1 at the hands of Watford.

21   West Ham and Newcastle draw 0-0 at Upton Park in the 1st Division top of the table clash.

22   Sheffield United beat Oldham 2-0 in the relegation battle at Bramall Lane.

23   Sheffield Wednesday's 2-1 win at Maine Road is their 8th successive victory, taking them to 4th in the Premier League, with makeshift striker Paul Warhurst scoring for the 7th game running. Rangers win 4-0 at Motherwell to lead the Scottish Premier by 10 points.

24   Bobby Moore dies of cancer at 51 and the world of football mourns. Forest beat QPR 1-0 to move out of the relegation places. Newcastle are held at home by lowly Bristol Rovers and now lead West Ham by 5 points with no games in hand.

25   Spurs call off their attempt to keep Nick Barmby from playing for England in the World Youth Championship in Australia. Vinny Jones fails in his appeal against the FA's £20,000 fine for his 'Soccer's Hard Men' video.

27   The International Board pass a new law permitting coaching from a 'technical area', provided that

coaches 'conduct themselves at all times in a responsible manner'. A late Yorke goal for Villa keeps them 2 points ahead of Manchester United, who beat Middlesbrough 3-0. Hartlepool's 2-0 defeat at home to Bolton in Division 2 marks their 12th League and Cup game without scoring, a new English record. Arsenal captain Tony Adams needs 29 stitches after hurting his head in a fall down stairs and is doubtful for Monday's League match with Chelsea. Rangers beat Hearts 2-1, setting a club record of 39 games without defeat, and go 11 points clear in Scotland, Aberdeen's match being postponed.

28 Norwich, held 0-0 at home by Blackburn, fall behind in the title race. Newcastle return to form with a 3-0 victory at Tranmere, their first for 6 weeks, and go 7 points clear again in Division 1. Paul Gascoigne is sent off in Lazio's 3-2 win at Genoa.

March
Pitch invasion at Maine Road...Grobbelaar has brain scan...Rangers' 44-match and Milan's 58-match unbeaten runs end...Liverpool boss Souness sent off...England win 2-0 in Turkey

1 West Ham admit their bond scheme has been a flop, fewer than 600 having been sold out of 19,000. A group of Nottingham Forest shareholders, in the first extraordinary general meeting of the club for 23 years, fail in their bid to get more information about Brian Clough's day-to-day management, losing the vote by 126 to 41. Total weekend Premier League attendance, 269,489, beats season's previous best (28 December).

2 Relegation-threatened Sheffield United and Middlesbrough have good wins, United 6-0 over Spurs, Middlesbrough 1-0 at Ipswich. For Spurs, it ended a six-win run and was their worst defeat for 15 years. Hartlepool's lowest crowd of the season, 1,791, see them notch their 13th successive game without scoring, a 0-0 draw with Wigan.

3 A late goal by Pieter Huistra earns Rangers a draw at Bruges and keeps them abreast of Marseille, who are held at CSKA Moscow after leading at half-time. In the other group, a Papin goal gives Milan their third win out of three, keeping them 2 points ahead of Gothenburg, splendid 3-1 winners at PSV. Norwich lose more ground on the Premier League leaders as Arsenal snatch a point at Carrow Road. Graeme Souness turns down a £3.5m offer for John Barnes from Villa, having already sold the League leaders £4.3m worth of talent in Saunders, Houghton and Staunton.

5 UEFA president Lennart Johansson proposes merging the Champions and UEFA cups to create a 128-club tournament played on a league basis. David Sullivan, owner of *Sunday Sport* and *Daily Sport*, is confirmed as Birmingham's new owner.

6 Arsenal win 4-2 at Ipswich and Sheffield United draw at Blackburn in FA Cup quarter-finals. A 2-1 win at Anfield puts Manchester United back on top of the Premier League, a point ahead of Villa, who have no game, while Norwich's defeat at QPR virtually puts them out of the race. The defeat leaves Liverpool only 3 points above the relegation places. Good wins for Newcastle and West Ham consolidate their 1-2 positions in Division 1. Hartlepool end their goal famine after 20 hr 27 min with Andy Saville's 51st-minute goal at Blackpool in a 1-1 draw. Aberdeen, who lose Eoin Jess with a broken ankle, are held 1-1 at Pittodrie by Clydebank in the Scottish Cup quarter-finals, while Rangers, Hearts and Hibs go through to the semis.

7 Nayim scores a hat-trick as Spurs beat Manchester City 4-2 at Maine Road to book a Cup semi-final place against Arsenal, but a fine match is overshadowed by a pitch invasion near the end that holds the game up for 13 minutes and needs mounted police to clear it. England draw 1-1 with South Korea in the World Youth Cup in Australia.

8 In the third Cup quarter-final 6-goal thriller, Paul Warhurst scores his 2nd 5 minutes from time to earn Sheffield Wednesday a 3-3 draw with Derby. The Arsenal-Spurs semi-final will take place at Wembley – for the second time in 3 years. The FA charge Manchester City with misconduct and failure to control their supporters over yesterday's pitch invasion.

9 Premier League leaders Manchester United go down 1-0 at Oldham, who remain bottom. Villa, a point behind, now have a game in hand. West Ham win to close the 1st Division gap with Newcastle (no game) to 4 points. England beat USA 1-0 in the World Youth Cup.

10 Arsenal ease into the Coca-Cola Cup final with two more goals against Palace at Highbury for a 5-1 aggregate win. Spurs draw 0-0 at Villa to keep them behind Manchester United on goal difference in the Premier League, while Norwich, 1-0 winners at Bramall Lane, creep back to within 4 points. Liverpool steer clear of trouble with a 1-0 win over QPR. In Division 1, Newcastle are held 2-2 at home by Charlton. Sprinter Jason Livingstone, sent home from the Barcelona Olympics for a failed drugs test, fails to cut the mustard with Wigan after a week's trial. Bruce Grobbelaar has a brain scan after being hit on the head with a lump of concrete while on duty for Zimbabwe in Cairo. Barcelona win the European Super Cup. San Marino collect their first ever World Cup point in a 0-0 draw at home to Turkey.

11 England reach the World Youth Cup quarter-finals for the first time in 10 years with a 1-0 win over Turkey, heading their group. Fulham strike a deal with the Royal Bank of Scotland to lease Craven Cottage for 10 years.

12 Russell Osman takes over officially as manager of Bristol City and sells Andy Cole to Newcastle for £1.75m (of which Arsenal will get about £400,000), while John Ward becomes Bristol Rovers manager, after resigning from York, who place Alan Little in charge for the rest of the season. Cardiff take over the 3rd Division leadership from Barnet (2 games in hand) on goals scored with their 7th away victory on the trot, 4-2 at Colchester, but their fans twice invade the pitch. Fulham sign a sponsorship deal with 900,000-strong trade union GMB (General Municipal and Boilermakers). FIFA order Zimbabwe's World Cup tie with Egypt (who won 2-1) to be replayed in a neutral country because of the missiles thrown at the visiting players.

13 Norwich put themselves right back in the title race with a 1-0 win over bottom club Oldham, and

are now just a point behind the two leaders who play each other tomorrow. 1st Division leaders Newcastle and West Ham both lose away. Barnet, with the League giving them 7 days to sort out their financial irregularities and their still unpaid £50,000 fine, lose their unbeaten home record, crashing 1-5 to York and a Paul Barnes hat-trick. Rangers power on in Scotland, a 3-0 win over Hibs taking them 9 points clear of Aberdeen, who drop a home point to lowly Falkirk.

14 Villa hold Manchester United 1-1 at Old Trafford, which is good for Norwich, now 2 points behind the joint leaders, all three having played 33 games. Blackburn take a first-half lead in the Coca-Cola Cup semi-final second leg, but Wednesday score twice in the second half to ease through 6-3 on aggregate to a final against Arsenal. England make the semi-finals of the World Youth Cup, beating Mexico 4-3 on penalties after a 0-0 draw.

16 Sheffield United reach the semi-finals of the FA Cup, beating Blackburn 5-3 on penalties after a 2-2 draw in their replay at Bramall Lane. Aberdeen reach the Scottish Cup semis with a thrilling 4-3 replay win at Clydebank, after going 2-0 up and then 3-2 down. Defending champions Ajax are knocked out of the UEFA Cup in the quarter-finals by Auxerre.

17 Home wins for all four leading teams in the European Cup groups: Rangers scrape past Bruges 2-1 despite having Mark Hateley sent off shortly before the interval, while Marseille demolish CSKA Moscow 6-0; Milan are stretched by Porto, but Gothenburg cruise past PSV. Norwich remarkably go top again in the Premier League for the first time in two months with a 3-0 win at Nottingham that pushes Forest deeper into the relegation mire. Sheffield Wednesday beat Derby 1-0 in their Cup replay, and will meet neighbours United in the semi-finals, ensuring a Sheffield-North London final. Ghana beat England 2-1 in the World Youth Cup and will meet Brazil in the final.

19 The FA give in to pressure from the clubs and switch the all-Sheffield Cup semi-final from Elland Road to Wembley, and Wednesday's converted central defender Paul Warhurst, who has scored 12 goals in 12 games, is named in England's World Cup qualifying squad. Arsenal will release David O'Leary on a free transfer at the end of the season. Stoke striker Mark Stein is granted police bail after being charged with assault in respect of an incident at the end of the game with Stockport that left Jim Gannon injured.

20 Norwich's charge is halted at Wimbledon with a 3-0 defeat and Villa, 2-0 winners over Sheffield Wednesday, and Manchester United, who draw at Maine Road, overtake them. Palace's 1-0 win at Bramall Lane takes them 5 points clear of the relegation zone. Rangers' 44-match unbeaten run ends as they lose 2-1 at Celtic and have their Scottish Premier lead cut to 7 points by Aberdeen, 2-1 winners at Dundee. Brazil beat Ghana 2-1 in the final of the World Youth Cup, and England beat Australia 2-1 in the match for 3rd place but are condemned from many quarters for their long-ball tactics.

21 AC Milan's 58-match unbeaten League run is ended surprisingly with a 1-0 home defeat by Parma. Oldham's 3-2 win at fellow-strugglers Middlesbrough takes them off the bottom of the Premier League and out of the relegation places. Reserve team coach Sammy Lee, 34, is named in injury-hit Liverpool's squad for tomorrow's game with Palace.

23 Liverpool manager Graeme Souness, with a record of touchline bans in Scotland and Europe, goes for his hat-trick as he is sent off at Palace for allegedly swearing at a linesman. Newcastle and West Ham both lose 1-0 away, while Portsmouth move to within 3 points of the Hammers with a 2-0 victory at Tranmere, both goals coming from Guy Whittingham, who chalks up his 39th of the season. Division 3 leaders Cardiff lose their first League game of the year, 1-0 at Bury. Blackburn's Roy Wegerle and Coventry's Kevin Gallacher are swapped in a £1.5m deal, with a cash adjustment in favour of Coventry. Barnet are given 48 hours to resolve their financial difficulties.

24 Norwich beat Villa 1-0 and leapfrog into top Premier place as Arsenal hold Manchester United 0-0 at Old Trafford. Away wins for Sheffield United and Forest shake up the relegation zone. Wimbledon's John Fashanu is red-carded at Hillsborough as he is stretchered off after an off-the-ball incident with Wednesday captain Viv Anderson in the 1-1 draw. In a World Cup qualifier, a drastically depleted Holland side still beat San Marino 6-0 and go above England in Group 2, while Italy's 6-1 defeat of Malta takes them to the top of Scotland's group. Scotland with a virtual reserve side, lose a friendly with Germany 1-0 at Ibrox Park. Paul Warhurst pulls out of England's squad with a groin injury. Players in the Coca-Cola Cup final will wear their names on their shirt backs.

25 With first- to third-choice left-backs injured, Graham Taylor drafts Newcastle's John Beresford into the England squad, and Newcastle chairman Sir John Hall makes his private jet available to fly him to Turkey after their Sunday match. Exactly £1m exchanges hands in a remarkably quiet transfer deadline-day of only 9 cash deals, although Southend turn down Forest's increased bid of £2m for striker Stan Collymore.

26 UEFA fine Rangers £6,500 for their fans' 'unruly behaviour' at their match in Bruges on 3 March.

27 No Premier League matches because of England's midweek World Cup match. Portsmouth move above West Ham (no game) to 2nd in Division 1 with a 3-0 defeat of Oxford and Whittingham scores 40th goal of season. Swindon have two forwards sent off in first half but still draw 0-0 at Brentford. Derby lose the Anglo-Italian Cup final 3-1 to Cremonese at Wembley. After 3rd Division leaders Cardiff are held 1-1 by 2nd-placed Barnet at Ninian Park, chairman Rick Wright hands the unpaid visitors £1,000 for a drink and a meal on the way home. Ally McCoist scores his 50th goal of the season in Rangers' 3-0 defeat of Dundee.

28 Newcastle and West Ham are both held 2-2 at home, the leaders by struggling Birmingham, who are two up at half-time. West Ham's point against Millwall, however, puts them back in 2nd place as the fight for the automatic promotion places in Division 1 hots up. England's plane is struck by lightning on landing at Izmir, Turkey, but no one is hurt.

29 QPR's left-winger Andy Sinton is named as left-back for Wednesday's World Cup qualifier in Turkey. Vinny Jones fails to report on time for a disciplinary hearing and is banned indefinitely, i.e. until he attends another hearing: he apparently got the time wrong. Barnet chairman Stan Flashman threatens to fine the players two weeks' wages for complaining about not being paid.

QPR striker Gary Penrice is out for the rest of the season after breaking his leg in training, the same leg he broke in January.

30 In European Under-21 matches, England draw 0-0 in Turkey, Wales 0-0 with Belgium. Beleaguered Barnet earn a point at Scarborough. The FA put Liverpool manager Graeme Souness on a disrepute charge after receiving the referee's report from their match at Palace. Manchester United striker Eric Cantona is fined £1,000 for spitting at supporters of former club Leeds.

31 Tony Adams wins plaudits as England survive hostile opponents and crowd to beat Turkey 2-0, with first-half goals from Platt and Gascoigne, to go level on points with group leaders Norway and 3rd-placed Holland, who have played one more game. Ryan Giggs is the Welsh inspiration as they beat group leaders Belgium 2-0 at Cardiff Arms Park, scoring with a 20-yard free-kick before Ian Rush hits No.2, his 24th for Wales, to beat the 37-year-old record set by Trevor Ford and later equalled by Ivor Allchurch. The Republic of Ireland beat Northern Ireland 3-0, also scoring all their goals in the first half, to move within a point of Spain, who go down 1-0 to Denmark, now a point behind them; Spain have played two more games. In Scotland's group, leaders Switzerland are held at home by Portugal, offering the Scots a modicum of hope. In Division 2, Stoke win 2-0 at 2nd-placed Port Vale to go 10 points ahead. The Barnet soap opera gathers pace as manager Barry Fry is sacked officially for the eighth time, but is reinstated by new chairman Robert Woolfson after Stan Flashman resigns for health reasons. Team captain Duncan Horton and four other players are also reinstated after being sacked by Flashman, who fails to keep an appointment with PFA chairman Gordon Taylor. A 2-2 draw with Juventus puts Torino through to the Italian Cup final on 'away' goals, both ties being played at their shared stadium!

April
Fry leaves Barnet for Southend...Stuart Pearce out for season...Arsenal's Morrow dropped after scoring Coca-Cola Cup winner...Brian Clough retires...Portugal thrash Scotland ... Zambian air crash...Tommy Caton dies

1 Barry Fry, deciding not to remain with the new Barnet regime, accepts the manager's job at Southend, with a brief to keep them out of the 2nd Division.

2 The FA warn players and clubs that they may be charged with misconduct for overexuberant celebration of goals, even if the referee takes no action.

3 Wednesday win the battle of the Sheffields 2-1 in the FA Cup semi-final at Wembley with a Bright goal in extra time. Aberdeen and Rangers reach the Scottish Cup final with wins over Hibs (1-0) and Hearts (2-1) respectively, Rangers coming from behind with two late goals. Oldham blast their way out of the Premier League's relegation zone with a 6-2 defeat of Wimbledon, while Liverpool go down 4-1 at Blackburn. Bottom club Middlesbrough crash 4-0 at Chelsea. In Division 1 Barry Fry's first half-time pep-talk produces 3 goals and a 4-2 win for second-from-bottom Southend at Sunderland. At the top, Newcastle win 3-0 at Cambridge and West Ham 2-1 at Birmingham.

4 Arsenal book their second final date in a month with Sheffield Wednesday when an Adams header from a Merson free-kick gives them a 1-0 win over Spurs at Wembley in their FA Cup semi-final. Aston Villa's 1-0 win at Forest takes them back to the top of the Premier League and leaves Forest stuck in 21st place.

5 Manchester United, inspired by Giggs and Cantona, hit a breathtaking 3 goals in the first 21 minutes to win 3-1 at Carrow Road and jump over Norwich into 2nd, a point behind Villa. In Division 2, Hartlepool beat Plymouth 1-0, their first win in 21 matches.

6 Middlesbrough climb off the Premier League bottom spot with a 1-0 win over Arsenal, whose David Hillier is taken off with ligament injuries that might keep him out of the Coca-Cola Cup final. Guy Whittingham's hat-trick in Portsmouth's 4-0 win over Peterborough is his fourth of the season and takes his goal tally to 43, equalling the club record set by Billy 'Farmer' Haines in 1926-27, but he misses a late penalty; Portsmouth go 2nd in Division 1. A Kenny Irons hat-trick, his first goals for 4 months, in Tranmere's 3-1 defeat of Swindon takes them to within a point of the play-off zone. Argentine international Claudio Caniggia follows in Maradona's footsteps with a positive drug test (cocaine) confirmed following a Serie A match for AS Roma. England and Forest captain Stuart Pearce is out for the rest of the season with a groin injury.

7 A spectacular Ian Durrant equalizer soon after half-time earns Rangers a 1-1 draw in Marseille and takes their European Cup group to the last match. The winners will meet AC Milan in the final, after the Italian league leaders win 1-0 in Gothenburg to clinch the other group. Premier League strugglers Forest lose 3-1 at home to Blackburn and have full-back Gary Charles sent off in the 85th minute, while Oldham are held at home by Sheffield Wednesday. Arsenal's David Hillier will probably miss both their finals. In Division 1, new boy Andy Cole continues his scoring spree (6 now in 5 games) for Newcastle with 3 in their 6-0 demolition of Barnsley, and they increase their lead to 8 points as West Ham flop 1-0 at revitalized Southend. Diego Maradona is suspended for two games in Spain for his part in a brawl between his club Sevilla and Cadiz.

9 Norwich's title aspirations are surely over this time as Spurs blast them out of the title race with a 5-1 mauling at White Hart Lane. Palace's relegation worries are multiplied as they are crushed 4-0 'away' at Selhurst Park by tenants Wimbledon.

10 Two late headers from Bruce, the second well into injury time, give Manchester United a dramatic 2-1 win over Wednesday at Old Trafford and catapult them into a 1-point lead over Villa, who are held at home by Coventry. A Les Ferdinand hat-trick keeps Forest at the bottom as QPR beat them 4-3. Guy Whittingham's record 44th goal for Portsmouth helps them win 2-1 at Bristol Rovers and come within 5 points of Newcastle, 1-0 losers at Wolves. Troubled Barnet beat Scarborough and go top of Division 3 as Cardiff lose at York. A late Brown goal at Ibrox over struggling Motherwell edges Rangers 10 points clear in the Scottish Premier as Aberdeen are held at bottom club Airdrie.

11 West Ham chalk up an important 3-0 win over Leicester to keep up with 2nd-placed Portsmouth in Division 1. Rangers keeper Andy Goram is Scottish Footballer of the Year. Former Ipswich keeper Roy Bailey, 60, dies in Johannesburg. Former Argentina coach Carlos Bilardo, now with Sevilla, says drug-taking is rife among Argentine footballers.

12 Easter Monday sees United still top with a 1-0 win at Coventry, and again it's a defender, Irwin this time, who scores the goal. Villa keep pace with a 1-0 win at Highbury thanks to Tony Daley's first goal for a year and a half. Other Premier League games average nearly 5 goals apiece, notably at Goodison where Ferdinand scores his second hat-trick in 3 days as QPR beat Everton 5-3. Wednesday, resting many of their players for Sunday's Coca-Cola Cup final, still beat Southampton 5-2, Chris Bart-Williams scoring 3. Forest climb off the bottom with a 2-1 win over Spurs, Middlesbrough crashing 4-1 to Palace, who ease their relegation fears. Performance of the day goes to Swindon, in Division 1, coming back from 4-1 down after an hour at Birmingham to win 6-4, with Dave Mitchell hitting 3. Whittingham scores 2 more as Portsmouth move to within 2 points of Newcastle, whose match with Oxford is postponed. West Brom's automatic promotion hopes to Division 1 are dealt a blow when they crash 5-2 to Plymouth at the Hawthorns, Steve Castle scoring 3 for the West Country side. In Division 3, Barnet, without a game, are overtaken by Cardiff and York.

13 Sheffield United draw at Oldham in the Premier Division relegation battle. West Ham lose 2-0 at Luton to stay 3 points behind Portsmouth in Division 1. Battling Barnet win 1-0 at Torquay to go back on top of Division 3. Vinny Jones turns up early for his rescheduled FA hearing and is banned for 4 matches for reaching 41 disciplinary points and told to grow up.

14 A Chris Sutton hat-trick keeps Norwich's fading title hopes alive as they beat Leeds 4-2. Southend's 3-0 victory over Bristol Rovers takes them out of the Division 1 relegation zone on goals scored. Denmark's 2-0 win over Latvia takes them level on points with Spain in World Cup Group 3, a point ahead of Ireland. St Johnstone's caretaker manager John McClelland is appointed manager.

15 Graham Taylor ignores public opinion and the media campaign to recall Chris Waddle, but his England squad includes leading Premier League scorer Teddy Sheringham of Spurs and Villa's Earl Barrett. Coventry's Mick Quinn, sent off against Manchester United on Easter Monday for a second bookable offence, has had the dismissal cancelled after referee Rodger Gifford watched the video.

16 Manchester City escape with a suspended sentence – a £50,000 fine and a match played behind closed doors – for the pitch invasion last month in the Cup tie against Spurs.

17 Manchester United beat Chelsea 3-0 to go 4 points ahead of Villa, who play tomorrow. Mark Walters hits 3 in Liverpool's 4-0 win over Coventry. At the bottom, Oldham, Forest and Sheffield United all lose, while Palace gain a precious point at Leeds. Division 1 top three all win, Newcastle and Portsmouth away. Division 2 leaders Stoke suffer shock home defeat to Hartlepool, who leap 3 places out of the relegation zone, while Port Vale's 4-0 win at Wigan cuts Stoke's lead to 7 points. In Scotland, Rangers retain their 12-point lead over Aberdeen, both winning.

18 It's ecstasy and agony for Arsenal's midfield marker Steve Morrow, 22, who hits the Coca-Cola Cup winner against Sheffield Wednesday, his first goal for the club, and then breaks his arm as skipper Tony Adams drops him in the final-whistle celebrations. Villa keep the pressure on Manchester United in the Premier League, coming from behind to beat Manchester City 3-1, and are now a point behind with 3 games left.

19 Norwich finally bow out of the title race, beaten 3-1 by neighbours Ipswich, who virtually assure their Premier League safety.

20 Next season's Coca-Cola Cup is provisionally scheduled to start before the League fixtures, with a final in February, avoiding the clash with the League run-in. Middlesbrough keep their Premier League survival hopes alive with a 3-0 win over Spurs. Barnet are back on top of Division 3, their 1-0 win over Bury taking them a point clear of Cardiff with a game still in hand. Turkey escape with a £9,000 fine and a 6-month ban on internationals at Izmir after the crowd trouble at the recent match with England.

21 Rangers are held 0-0 at home by CSKA Moscow, but Marseille's 1-0 win at Bruges would have taken them through anyway to play AC Milan in the final of the European Cup. Milan finish with a 100 per cent record after beating PSV Eindhoven 2-0. Manchester United take a giant step towards the Premier League title with a 2-0 win at Palace to go 4 points clear of Villa, who crash 3-0 at Blackburn, with ony 2 games left.

22 A broken toe will keep Ian Wright out of England's World Cup qualifier with Holland and possibly out of the Cup final. Hereford player-coach Greg Downs becomes manager, with a contract till the end of the season.

23 There are worries that Paul Gascoigne's right knee may keep him out of the game with Holland. FIFA intervene in a club v country row and order Wales to release four of their squad to play for their clubs tomorrow. Dean Saunders is arrested for disorderly behaviour but released with a caution after an incident at an Essex nightclub. Southend beat Grimsby 1-0 to ease relegation pressure.

24 With no Premier League football because of the World Cup, Portsmouth steal the headlines – and 1st place in Division 1 – with a 2-0 victory over Wolves, and Newcastle, playing tomorrow, find themselves off the top for the first time since September. West Ham come back from a goal down to scrape a 2-1 home win over Bristol Rovers, who are relegated. Scoring feats in the lower divisions include 4 in the last 8 minutes by Bolton in their 5-0 win over the already relegated Chester; hat-tricks by Sean Farrell in Fulham's 4-0 win over Burnley and Mick Cecere in Walsall's 4-0 win at Halifax; and, the performance of the day, Tony Naylor's 5 in Crewe's 7-1 thrashing of Colchester. Barnet lose 2-0 at Scunthorpe, missing their chance to increase their lead in Division 3, but gaining promotion along with Cardiff, as York, the first club in the League to complete their programme, lose 1-0 at Rochdale.

25 Newcastle beat Sunderland 1-0 to go back on top of Division 1 and give their struggling neighbours more to worry about.
26 Brian Clough, 58, announces his retirement after 18 years as Nottingham Forest manager, sadly with the club facing relegation, and his solicitor announces that he will be suing a newspaper and a club director over defamatory remarks. Gascoigne will be fit to play against Holland.
27 In European Under-21 matches, England beat Holland 3-0, Wales draw, but Scotland and Ireland lose. Wrexham are promoted to Division 2 thanks to their 2-0 victory at Northampton. Liverpool manager Graeme Souness is fined £500 for misconduct and warned by the FA about his future behaviour.
28 In World Cup qualifying ties, England take a 2-0 lead through Barnes, with a superb free-kick, and Platt, but allow Holland back into the game for a draw, while both Norway and Poland win. Scotland are virtually out of the competition after their 5-0 thrashing in Portugal. Ireland are held at home by Denmark, while Northern Ireland lose 3-1 in Spain. These setbacks are put in perspective, however, by the news of the Zambian air crash, when all but 4 of the national squad are killed on their way to a World Cup match. All 30 people on the plane were killed when it crashed into the sea after a refuelling stop at Libreville, Gabon. Wales gain an excellent result, a 1-1 draw in Ostrava against the Representation of Czech and Slovak Republics (RCS). Stoke beat Plymouth 1-0 to clinch promotion to Division 1.
29 X-rays reveal Ally McCoist has a leg fracture, and is out for the rest of the season, and Paul Gascoigne a hairline cheek fracture, from Wouters' elbow, that is not thought to be serious.
30 Tommy Caton, former England Under-21 defender, dies at 30 of a heart attack. Middlesbrough chairman of 7 years Colin Henderson resigns, claiming another director, Steve Gibson, was trying to gain control.

May

Rangers' record 43rd League title...United champions at last...Hearts sack Joe Jordan...Halifax out of League...Souness stays at Anfield...Frank Clark new Forest manager...Sugar tries to oust Venables from Spurs...double Cup triumph for Arsenal...Steve Coppell resigns from relegated Palace...Marseille first French winners of European Cup...Rangers complete treble

1 Brian Clough is given a fond farewell from the fans at his last home match, although their 2-0 defeat by Sheffield United means certain relegation – for them as well as Middlesbrough, despite the latter's defiant 3-2 win at Hillsborough. Portsmouth, on the verge of automatic promotion, have two players sent off and crash 4-1 at Sunderland, their only bright spot being Guy Whittingham's club record 41st League goal. Sunderland are still struggling to escape a relegation zone in which any 2 of 7 clubs will join Bristol Rovers in the drop with only 1 or 2 matches left. Cambridge's 3-1 victory over Southend also complicates the issue. In Division 2, Swansea fans invade the Elm Park pitch before and during the match, won 2-0 by Reading, causing damage in and out of the ground. Cardiff beat Shrewsbury 2-1 to take over at the top of Division 3 from Barnet, held at home by Lincoln. Rangers clinch a record 43rd League title with a 1-0 win at Airdrie, without needing Aberdeen's defeat at Celtic. Falkirk's 6-0 thrashing of Hearts gives them a faint hope of survival at the other end of the table. Chris Waddle is voted Footballer of the Year by the football writers.
2 Manchester United are League champions for the first time in 26 years thanks to Oldham's 1-0 victory at Villa Park, and Alex Ferguson is the first manager to win the League north (with Aberdeen) and south of the border. West Ham's fine 3-1 win at Swindon puts them back in second place in Division 1, above Portsmouth on goals scored. Speculation is rife about Graeme Souness's chances of survival after a secret board meeting at Anfield in the middle of the Bank Holiday weekend.
3 Manchester United celebrate their title at Old Trafford with a 3-1 win over Blackburn. They will be joined in European Cup competition next season by Cwmbran Town, who clinch the inaugural Konica League of Wales with a 1-0 win at Llanelli. Hearts sack manager Joe Jordan.
4 Newcastle win 2-0 at Grimsby to clinch promotion and the 1st Division title. Sheffield United's 2-0 win at Everton keeps them out of the 1st Division. Bolton beat Stoke 1-0 to make themselves favourites to join them in Division 1 next season, as Port Vale can only scrape a draw at Exeter with a last-minute penalty that has Exeter manager Alan Ball fuming; referee Bob Hamer is bundled to the ground by irate fans for the decision that robs Exeter of safety from relegation. One club to ensure safety is Partick Thistle with a 3-0 triumph over Scottish champions Rangers.
5 Oldham's 3-2 win over Liverpool keeps them on course for a remarkable escape as Palace only draw at Maine Road. Don Hutchison is the 6th Liverpool player sent off this season, a fact not helping Souness's increasingly unlikely survival at Anfield. Barnsley manager Mel Machin resigns. Juventus win 3-1 at Borussia Dortmund in the first leg of the UEFA Cup final.
6 Forest chairman Fred Reacher again calls for the resignation of director Chris Wootton (who campaigned for manager Brian Clough's removal), following the refusal of other directors to work with him. Sheffield Wednesday beat Arsenal 1-0 in a Cup final 'rehearsal' missing most of the leading players. Newcastle celebrate their 1st Division title with a 2-1 win over Oxford in front of a near 30,000 crowd at St James's Park.
8 Most of the remaining issues are decided on the last full Saturday of the League season, notably Oldham's Premier League survival despite a Le Tissier hat-trick that threatened their 4-3 win over Southampton, as Palace old boy Ian Wright began the 3-0 destruction of his former club-mates at Highbury to condemn them to 1st Division football next season. Norwich's 3-3 draw at Middlesbrough secures them 3rd spot in the Premier League and a place in the UEFA Cup next season if Arsenal win the Cup. In a free-scoring last day, the Merseyside duo finish with flamboyant victories, Everton 5-2 at Maine Road and Liverpool 6-2 over Spurs to mark the end of the Kop at Anfield, where manager Souness was conspicuous by his absence and missed seeing Ian Rush score

his 300th goal for the club. A Rod Wallace hat-trick for Leeds, including 2 in the last 2 minutes, earns them a 3-3 draw at Coventry but not their first away win of the season. In Division 1, West Ham beat Cambridge 2-0 to send them down and win promotion themselves by a single goal scored – from Portsmouth, who can only beat Grimsby 2-1. In the scramble at the other end, Brentford also go down following their 4-1 defeat at Bristol City, Rosenior scoring 3, while Sunderland are lucky to survive after their 3-1 defeat at Notts County and wins by Birmingham and Southend. In Division 2, Port Vale's comeback to win 4-2 at Blackpool is in vain as Bolton clinch the second automatic promotion place with a 1-0 win over Preston, at the same time sending the old 'Invincibles' down to the bottom division. In Division 3, Cardiff clinch the title with a 3-0 win at Scunthorpe, while Halifax, beaten 1-0 at home by Hereford, go out of the League. Northampton's 3-2 win at Shrewsbury after being 2 down would have sealed their fate anyway; it also deprives Shrewsbury of a play-off place.

9   Liverpool call a news conference and announce, to everyone's surprise, that Graeme Souness is staying as manager for another 3 years, a boardroom triumph for chairman David Moores. Manchester United's 2-1 win at Wimbledon gives them a 10-point final margin over Villa, beaten 2-1 at QPR, but their celebrations are marred by a pitch invasion, with a fan arrested for hitting Vinny Jones. Newcastle tie up the Division 1 programme with a 7-1 win over Leicester, 6 goals coming in the first half and hat-tricks for Cole and Kelly. GM Vauxhall Conference champions Wycombe Wanderers beat Runcorn 4-1 at Wembley to add the Vauxhall FA Trophy to their season's haul.

10 Sandy Clark is Hearts' new manager.

11 David Webb, having done his job at Chelsea, is nevertheless sacked after his 3-month trial as manager. Relegated Brentford sack Phil Holder. The two Cup-finalists, fielding sub-strength teams, both lose 3-1, Arsenal at home to Spurs and Wednesday at QPR. Barnet are fined £25,000 by the FA for making an irregular payment to striker Paul Showler and warned that one more similar indiscretion could cost them their League status.

12 Frank Clark, 49, MD of Orient, is named as Forest's new manager, Wycombe manager Martin O'Neill having declined the job. Shrewsbury manager John Bond, 60, resigns. Parma beat Royal Antwerp 3-1 at Wembley to win the Cup-Winners' Cup. Norwich win the PFA Fair Play award.

13 Spurs chairman Alan Sugar calls an emergency board meeting for tomorrow in a sensational attempt to oust chief executive Terry Venables from the club. Leeds beat Manchester United 2-1 at Elland Road to win the FDA Youth Cup 4-1 on aggregate.

14 The Spurs board sacks Venables, but he is reinstated by a High Court ruling for 10 days pending further hearings.

15 Arsenal and Sheffield Wednesday draw a poor FA Cup final, David Hirst finding a second-half equalizer to Ian Wright's first-half goal for Arsenal. England manager Graham Taylor warns clubs that the FA will not allow any withdrawals from the upcoming US tour.

16 In play-offs, a late Joachim goal gives Leicester a slender lead over Portsmouth, but Swindon take a 3-1 lead into the second leg with Tranmere. The only comprehensive win is Crewe's 5-1 thrashing of Walsall. Cardiff beat Rhyl 5-0 in the Allbright Bitter Welsh Cup final. Wembley's fences will be replaced by a dry moat to improve sightlines for fans. Wednesday right-back Roland Nilsson joins the Swedish squad for an international on Wednesday, the night before the Cup final replay.

17 Brentford appoint David Webb manager. David O'Leary earns about £100,000 from his testimonial at Highbury, after 20 years with the club, and 22,000 see him score a late goal for an almost full-strength Arsenal to draw 4-4 with Manchester United. An Italian judge orders Diego Maradona and his ex-manager at Napoli, Guillermo Coppola, to stand trial in connection with 3 kg of cocaine allegedly shipped from Argentina to Naples before he left the club in 1991. Spurs board sack consultant Eddie Ashby, a Venables ally.

18 Arsenal plan to install two giant video screens at Highbury next season, although it is doubtful they will be able to show instant replays during matches.

19 Juventus win the UEFA Cup 6-1 on aggregate after beating Borussia Dortmund 3-0 in Turin. Poland win 3-0 in San Marino and are now a point behind England in World Cup Group 2 with a game in hand. Scotland win 3-0 in Estonia. Leicester and Swindon will meet in the Division 1 play-off final, Port Vale and West Brom in Division 2, and Crewe and York in Division 3, Crewe's 4-2 win at Walsall giving them a 9-3 aggregate, all the other ties being decided by a single goal.

20 Arsenal beat Sheffield Wednesday 2-1 with a goal by much-maligned Andy Linighan in the last minute of extra time at Wembley to win the FA Cup and become the first club to win both major domestic Cup trophies in the same season. Manager George Graham is the first to play in and manage teams to win all three major domestic trophies, all with Arsenal. Norwich benefit from their ex-player's winner with a place in next season's UEFA Cup. Steve Coppell comes back from holiday and announces his resignation as Palace manager after 9 years. The FA ban Glasgow Rangers from taking part in next season's Makita Tournament at White Hart Lane because of fears of trouble from Scottish fans, a 'pot calling the kettle black' attitude that has infuriated the Scottish club.

23 Greece draw 1-1 in Moscow to qualify for the World Cup finals for the first time. Port Vale beat Stockport 2-1 at Wembley in the final of the Autoglass Trophy.

24 Portsmouth manager Jim Smith is named in advance of the publication of the FA annual blacklist of people selling Cup final tickets at above face value and will receive a 5-year ban on getting tickets. Cardiff reinstate reserve keeper Mark Grew, who was originally sacked after admitting to selling Cup tickets. Edwin Stein signs a 3-year contract to remain as Barnet manager. John Barnes will go with England to the USA, instead of staying behind, as agreed, to build up his fitness. Paul McGrath withdraws mysteriously from Ireland's squad to play Albania, and David O'Leary, originally left out, is called in as cover.

25 Terry Venables is still in charge of Spurs as he and chairman Alan Sugar reach an agreement, after

2 hours in the High Court, on peaceful coexistence until their case returns to court. Northern Ireland win their World Cup tie 1-0 in Lithuania to lift them into 4th place in Group 3. Lazio insist Paul Gascoigne wear his protective 'Phantom' mask in England's upcoming World Cup qualifiers.

26 Marseille shock AC Milan in Munich with a goal headed by Basile Boli from a corner to become the first French winners of the European Cup. A late goal by sub Tony Cascarino completes Ireland's comeback in Tirana to beat Albania 2-1 and take them level with Spain on points at the top of World Cup Group 3 with a game in hand. After next season, Welsh clubs that play in England will no longer be eligible for the European Cup-Winners' Cup. There will be fewer referees in the Premier and Football Leagues next season, natural wastage being employed to ensure that officials get more games, and consequently more experience.

27 Wimbledon's John Fashanu, who donated £6,000 to the families of those who died in the recent Zambian air crash, has been asked to find the country a new national coach.

28 Graham Taylor gives Teddy Sheringham his first cap tomorrow in Poland in place of the injured Les Ferdinand. England Under-21s win 4-1 to wreck Poland's 100 per cent record and stay in with a slim chance of qualification themselves for the UEFA U-21 Championship. The FA charge Cup-finalists Arsenal and Sheffield Wednesday with fielding under-strength teams in the run-up to Wembley. Crewe's assistant manager Kenny Swain is named Wigan's new manager. Ruud Gullit, left out of Milan's European Cup final side, announces he will be leaving the club, while triumphant Marseille manager Raymond Goethals, 71, is to retire.

29 Sub Ian Wright chooses the right time to score his first goal for England, earning a 1-1 draw in Poland with 7 minutes left to keep them in contention in World Cup Group 2. Rangers beat Aberdeen 2-1 in the Scottish Cup final to bring off their first League/Cup/League Cup treble since 1978, while the Dons pick up their third runners-up medals of the season. York beat Crewe 5-3 on penalties at Wembley in the play-offs to win promotion to Division 2, after Crewe had forced the shoot-out with a penalty in the last minute of extra time. Arsenal – the women's side – completed the treble by adding the League Cup to their Premier Division title and FA Cup.

30 West Brom win promotion to Division 1 when they beat Port Vale 3-0 at Wembley, all their goals coming in the last half hour after opponent Peter Swan is sent off for a 'professional foul'.

31 In arguably the best game seen at Wembley this season, Swindon win promotion to the Premier League for the first time, beating Leicester 4-3 in a thrilling play-off with a penalty after Leicester had magnificently come back from 3 goals down. Scotland captain Richard Gough announces he is no longer prepared to play under manager Andy Roxburgh. Ireland manager Jack Charlton invites Paul McGrath to rejoin the squad despite his controversial withdrawal last week.

June
England crash in Oslo...Graham Taylor under pressure to go...Hoddle new Chelsea manager...Liverpool sign Nigel Clough for £2m plus...England beaten by USA...Brian Clough 'bung' allegation

1 Graham Taylor will not reveal the England side until just before kick-off in Oslo tomorrow, but it seems that Gascoigne, still short of full fitness, will be given another chance. Andy Cole gets a late equalizer for England Under-21s in Oslo.

2 Graham Taylor's lopsided England make Norway look good as they go down 2-0 in Oslo, with Des Walker needing stiches in a head would and having another nightmare match; England are now in serious danger of elimination from the World Cup as the calls for Taylor's head come inb from all sides. Scotland beat Estonia 3-1 at Pittodrie in Group 1 to cling on to their own slender hopes, while N. Ireland win 2-1 in Latvia.

3 Graham Taylor dismisses suggestions that he is about to resign. Alan Smith, formerly Steve Coppell's assistant, takes over as manager of Palace. Sheffield Wednesday's Viv Anderson is appointed player-manager of Barnsley.

4 Glenn Hoddle, fresh from taking Swindon into the Premier League, is appointed Chelsea player-manager and will be succeeded at Swindon by his assistant John Gorman. Liverpool sign Nigel Clough from Forest for £2m plus. Barnet players, owed 2 weeks' wages plus promotion bonuses, are told the club is on the brink of collapse. Ranger and Scotland keeper Andy Goram has knee operations that will keep him out of the game unto next year.

5 The FA plan to prevent managers profiting from transfer fees. England's party of 22 arrive in the USA for the US Cup '93, without four players from their World Cup squad, Arsenal's Tony Adams and David Seaman who are to undergo hernia operations, QPR's David Bardsley an ankle op, and Paul Gascoigne, who has been release too late after Lazio's Canadian tour was cancelled.

6 Ryan Giggs inspires Wales to a comfortable 3-0 win in the Faroes to give them every chance of qualifying for the World Cup with 3 games, all at home, remaining. Brazil beat the USA 2-0 in the US Cup '93 tournament.

7 With David Platt unfit, Graham Taylor names Manchester United midfielder Paul Ince, aged 25 with only 6 caps and a reputation as a hothead, as England captain for the game against the USA. England beat Portugal 2-0 in the Toulon Under-21 tournament.

8 Former England and Bristol City goalscorer John Atyeo dies at 61. England, without Gascoigne, look to Nigel Clough to provide the midfield penetration against the USA tomorrow. The financial crisis at Barnet deepens, and the PFA pay the players' outstanding wages and bonuses as company secretary Stanley Beller warns the club could be put into liquidation in 24 hours. The FA charge Exeter and manager Alan Ball with bringing the game into disrepute over incidents with the referee in the game with Port Vale. Ally McCoist (Rangers) wins the Adidas Golden Boot for the second season running, with 34 League goals, one more than Vasilis Dimitriadis of AEK Athens.

9 The good nes comes first: Norway draw 0-0 in Holland to boost England's chances of qualifying for the World Cup. The bad news is that they may find it difficult to win in San Marino after their debacle in Boston—a 2-0 defeat by the United States, which instead of restoring England's battered

pride, marks a new low in the fortunes of the 'country that gave football to the world'. No such setbacks for Jack Charlton's men in Latvia, goals by Aldridge and the reinstated McGrath giving Ireland the win that puts them up with Spain on top of Group 3, with an inferior goal difference but with a game in hand, a point in front of Denmark. Gary Bull's refusal to re-sign for Barnet may spell the end for the club, whose mystery backer has stipulated that no player leaves.

10 The Sugar-Venables saga at Spurs continues in the High Court with 2,500 pages of sworn statements, including the sensational implication that Forest manager Brian Clough expected a 'bung' (secret personal payment) to smooth through transfer deals, an allegation he immediately denies; the Premier League confirm they have asked to see affidavits from the hearing. FA chief executive Graham Kelly insists Graham Taylor will remain England manager for next season's World Cup climax. Germany come back from 3-0 down against the brilliant Brazilians to draw 3-3, with Brazil's old failure, the lack of safe goalkeeping, to the fore.

11 Kelly announces categorically that Taylor will remain in charge for the remainder of the World Cup campaign, with 100% FA backing. The Premier League's first annual meeting approves a plan for players to wear shirts with their names and squad numbers, teams to emerge side by side, and a proposal for keepers to wear shorts and socks of any colour, while a scheme for an under-21 league is scrapped. Barnet assure the Football League that they will be able to fulfil their fixtures next season, a 5-man consortium having stepped in to save the club.

12 Southampton keeper Tim Flowers will win his first England cap against Brazil tomorrow, and Nigel Clough will move up to partner Wright up front. Barrett and Sinton also come into the side, and Walker returns. Paul Gascoigne pledges his future to Lazio and declares his love for Rome.

Guy Whittingham (Portsmouth) is delighted with one of the 47 League and Cup goals he scored in the 1992–93 season. (Colorsport)

REVIEW OF THE SEASON

Manchester United ended 26 years of frustration by collecting the inaugural FA Premier League championship, finishing strongly with seven successive wins, though for a time it had seemed the title would again elude them.

Aston Villa provided a confident challenge and indeed, appeared capable of taking the prize themselves. That was until losing 3-0 at Blackburn on 21 April, a defeat which finally took the edge from them.

However, on 5 December Norwich City had established an eight point lead over Blackburn, Aston Villa and Chelsea. At the time, Manchester United were lying seventh, twelve points adrift, but with a game in hand.

Comparisons with earlier title-winning teams were inevitable, but different times require different requirements. Yet United contrived to be both effective and attractive. Moreover in Ryan Giggs, United possessed a player who might well be added to the club's illustrious list of outstanding discoveries in any era. He possessed the touch and flair of the gifted.

But it would be unfair to extract the performances of one player from what was essentially a smooth-running outfit in all departments. Defensively, in front of the towering Dane Peter Schmeichel the back four of Denis Irwin, Paul Parker, Gary Pallister and Steve Bruce were soundness itself, after a not-too-convincing start.

In midfield, the always industrious Brian McClair, Lee Sharpe recovered from lengthy illness and Paul Ince, who enjoyed his best season at Old Trafford -revealing hitherto latent maturity -provided the foraging and craft in the playmaking area.

The attacking roles finished in the hands of Mark Hughes and Alex Ferguson's ace signing of the season, the controversial Frenchman Eric Cantona, who apparently revels in short bursts of life with new clubs. Cantona gave United the panache which Leeds the previous season had enjoyed from him and the Frenchman was able to win championship medals in successive seasons with these clubs.

Andrei Kanchelskis had been used on the right side of midfield in the lengthy injury absence of Bryan Robson before Cantona's arrival in December.

It is interesting to note that United began the season trying to find the right playing formation to suit their abilities. They experimented with 4-5-1 in the early days of the season before settling to a more relaxed mixture of 4-3-3 and 4-4-2.

Norwich, commendably adhering to their policy of playing through midfield at all times, lacked punch in attack. They were still top on 30 January but had five games without scoring before the turn of the year and failed to capitalize on their advantages.

Villa won 1-0 at Chelsea on 13 February to go top but that late reverse at Blackburn affected them noticeably and signalled the end of their quest. Dean Saunders, who had been in fine scoring form, found the target only twice in the last fifteen matches.

Free-spending Blackburn suffered a severe blow when Alan Shearer was injured after scoring twice against Leeds on Boxing Day. Blackburn were then second but were never able to match that position again. After scoring seven against Norwich, they failed to score again in the next four matches.

Such are the traditions at Anfield that a finishing position of sixth for Liverpool was considered disappointing. But it was the manner of their performances which proved below previous standards. They achieved their highest position (fifth) on the last day of the season beating Tottenham 6-2.

Sheffield Wednesday had an outside thrust for the title but this became unrealistic after losing 2-0 to Aston Villa on 20 March. Instead, they had two opportunities of a place in Europe but lost both domestic cup competitions to Arsenal.

Queens Park Rangers striker Les Ferdinand staked a place in the new England team and came close to finishing as the Premier League's leading scorer. Neat, attractive at times, Rangers were never lower than ninth and a place in Europe was never entirely out of their reach for some months.

Manchester City suffered their heaviest defeat in the last game losing 5-2 at Everton, but generally, reverses came at well spaced out intervals, but for Arsenal, their best was reserved for the cup competitions.

However, in the League, only twice did an Arsenal player score more than one goal. Their total of 40 was one fewer than relegated Nottingham Forest. They failed to score at all in 19 matches but were top on 7 November after six successive wins.

Chelsea were fourth on 5 December when they won 2-0 at Tottenham. But this was to be their highest, and Spurs themselves showed irratic form; their best effort being five successive wins to the end of February. Darren Anderton, one of the most improved players in the country, was among 31 players used. Several local youngsters did well, particularly Nick Barmby.

Wimbledon's second half of the season improvement again kept them out of trouble and Dean Holdsworth had a late run of ten goals in eight games for them.

Everton, unbeaten in the first five matches including a 3-0 win at Old Trafford, never achieved anything better all season and Sheffield United's Christmas party in August designed to head off their annual relegation worries was ultimately a success, though they did hit bottom on 6 February after losing 2-0 at Manchester United.

Coventry won their first three matches to head the division and went back to fourth place early in February after Mick Quinn was signed from Newcastle, but they fell away. Ipswich beat Manchester United 2-1 on 30 January to move into fourth place but won only two more games; the East Anglian derby win over Norwich on 19 April proving crucial for both teams.

Leeds had a poor season and failed to win once away from home. They were never serious challengers to defending their title and called upon thirty players. However, the development of a number of youngsters who provided the backbone of their FA Youth Cup winning team, augers well for the future.

Southampton were occasionally involved in free-scoring games: 2-4 v Tottenham; 4-3 v Ipswich; 3-4 v Arsenal; 2-5 v Sheffield Wednesday and 3-4 v Oldham. They just escaped relegation. Oldham too were able to survive, but needed that victory over Southampton on the last day of the season to keep their status. They deserved this reward as they had beaten Manchester United 1-0 on 9 March when they were bottom and Aston Villa 1-0 away on 2 May.

The relegated trio were Crystal Palace, Middlesbrough and Nottingham Forest. Palace had four successive wins in December when they were fifteenth, but the turn of the year was disastrous for them. Middlesbrough's five successive defeats to the end of February sowed the seeds of relegation and despite scoring three goals in each of their last three games, found it was too little, too late.

Nottingham Forest, who sold Des Walker to Italy, Darren Wassall to Derby and then Teddy Sheringham to Tottenham after three matches, could hardly expect to survive. They were bottom for all but seven weeks of the season.

The Barclays League champions Newcastle United had a flying start with eleven straight wins. They wobbled a bit in the New Year but recovered to finish with five successive wins. Manager Kevin Keegan bought wisely before the transfer deadline bringing Andy Cole, Scott Sellars and Mark Robinson to St James' Park.

They were joined in automatic promotion by West Ham, never out of the top four after mid October and snatched second place by winning their last four games. The team who missed out were Portsmouth despite Guy Whittingham's 42 League goals. They were to rue a May Day disaster losing 4-1 at Sunderland.

Portsmouth were joined in the play-offs by Tranmere, Swindon and Leicester. John Aldridge scored 19 goals in the first 24 matches but missed out 16 games with injury. He returned and Tranmere were unbeaten in their last ten.

Swindon were involved in an incredible game at Birmingham on 12 April when they won 6-4 after being 4-1 down, but they failed to win another game and were robbed of an automatic promotion place. Leicester's best run gave them seven successive wins from late February to March but were beaten 7-1 at Newcastle when already assured of a play-off place.

Millwall had a late season slump winning only one of their last nine and Derby's wretched home form, which saw them lose 10 games at the Baseball Ground, robbed them of any chance of advancement.

Grimsby put together several promising runs which came to nothing and Peterborough had a middle of the table look throughout the season. Their roughest spell produced one win in nine.

Wolves were unbeaten in their first twelve and Steve Bull established himself as the club's overall leading League and Cup goalscorer but 11th place was all they had to show for it. Charlton returned to The Valley on 5 December and beat Portsmouth 1-0. This began an unsustained improvement featuring nine games without loss. Barnsley's Wayne Biggins, signed from Stoke, boosted the scoring rate for a time after a goalless first four games.

Oxford's John Durnin hit all four goals against Luton on 14 November and the team itself shared ten goals with Portsmouth during a spell when four of their matches yielded 25 goals. Bristol City sold Cole to Newcastle but retained sufficient fuel to survive.

Watford managed only eight goals in their last fourteen and sixteenth place was their lowest all season, though Notts County improved in the second half of the season under the managership of Mick Walker and Southend also benefited from a change at the helm when Barry Fry took over and enabled the team to win five and draw one of their last nine. But their salvation on the field came from Stan Collymore scoring 15 goals in thirty games.

Birmingham called upon thirty-seven players, won only two of their last nine, but still stayed up and Luton's annual struggle against relegation was brought about this time by their attack failing to match a reasonable defence. At one time, they went seven games without conceding a goal.

Sunderland sacked Malcolm Crosby and Terry Butcher found himself under as much pressure as his predecessor. They won only one of their last ten, significantly 4-1 against Portsmouth.

Brentford, Cambridge and Bristol Rovers all went down. Brentford were tenth on Boxing Day but won only four more games, Cambridge, who called upon thirty-one players only once managed two wins in a row. Bristol Rovers were never higher than ninteenth after the first month and bottom from 6 March.

In Division Two, Stoke were never headed after 21 November. From their 0-0 draw at home to Bolton on 5 September, they went twenty-five games without loss. Bolton joined

Ryan Giggs (left) in action for Manchester United the FA Premier League champions. He crowned a fine year by becoming Barclays Young Eagle of the season and the PFA's Young Player of the Year for the seond time. (Acion Images)

them in automatic promotion. Based on two outstanding runs: mid October to late December without loss and only one defeat in the last nineteen.

Port Vale just missed out despite a second half of the season which saw them win 17 of their last 25 and West Bromwich Albion's Bob Taylor broke a club post-war scoring record and was well supported in the later stages by Andy Hunt, on loan from Newcastle who scored 9 goals in 10 games.

Swansea's nine games without loss up to 24 October put them top, but they had to battle to reach the play-offs. Stockport owed much to 6ft 7in striker Kevin Francis but goals dried up for him at the wrong time and he failed to score in the last five games.

Leyton Orient looked a firm bet for the play-offs but they achieved only one point during March. Reading improved with eleven games without loss to the end of the same month.

For Brighton, Kurt Nogan signed after a trial, scored twenty goals in thirty games, but they lost three of their last four. Bradford City were top on 7 November but failed to maintain this performance. Rotherham looked well placed on 12 December when second, only to settle in mid-table.

Fulham were unbeaten in their last seven, their defence being the strong feature, letting in only eleven goals in seventeen matches.

Burnley's support continued at a higher level but seventh place was disappointingly the highest they managed all season, while Plymouth, castigated by the club chairman after losing 3-0 at home to neighbours Exeter, responded by winning 5-2 at West Bromwich, their best performance of an average season.

Huddersfield began with six successive defeats and were still bottom on 27 February before recovering. Hartlepool after knocking Crystal Palace out of the Cup, went 11 league games without scoring. Andy Saville the marksman against Palace, missed a penalty at Chester during this spell but later moved to Birmingham and helped them avoid relegation.

Bournemouth endured thirteen games without a win to mid-April yet it cost them only three places in the table. The return of Dave Bamber to the attack in January was the signal for a Blackpool revival and Exeter again escaped relegation even though they had just one win in the last nine.

Hull began well then searched in vain for a win in twelve matches as the defence let in twenty-eight goals, but Preston failed to escape relegation after losing their last five. They were joined by Mansfield, Wigan and Chester. The writing was on the wall for Mansfield as they were never out of the last four after the end of November. Wigan took one point from the last eight and Chester suffered two spells of seven successive defeats. The last of these ending the season.

Cardiff City enjoyed a second half in which they won seventeen of their last twenty-two matches and added the Welsh Cup for the second year to equal Wrexham's record. They were joined in promotion by Wrexham whose only defeat in the last thirteen was against Cardiff. Barnet, who looked at one time likely champions of Division Three, went six games without a win to the beginning of April.

But York had an even better chance until six successive draws to mid-January began a slump. In fact, one win in 13 threatened even the play-offs.

Walsall's ninth was their lowest placing after losing 2-1 at Chesterfield on 3 April but they were then undefeated. Crewe and Bury also made the play-offs. Tony Naylor of Crewe scored a club record five goals in a 7-1 win over Colchester and Bury owed their placing to a run of 11 games without defeat to March.

Lincoln had two wins in their last nine and this cost them a play-off place, while Shrewsbury failed to win on the last day -victory would have put them in the play-offs -after a wretched spell of one win in 13.

Colchester's first season back in the League produced defensive problems. They conceded a 7, a 5 and six 4's. Rochdale did not win a game while Andy Flounders was on loan to Rotherham and Chesterfield's similar outside bet for the play-offs failed when they were unable to win one of their last seven.

Any lingering hopes Scarborough had were dispelled when ten games produced just two points and Scunthorpe's ten without loss to Easter Monday raised unfulfilled hopes.

Darlington's ten matches without a win to the end of February consigned them to mid-table, Doncaster Rovers' spell of 11 without a win ended at Darlington on 12 April and goalscoring was also a problem for Hereford who registered just 13 in the last 15 matches.

Carlisle won only one of the last 12 and Torquay drew just seven games all season, four of them in the last nine. Northampton had a courageous 3-2 win at Shrewsbury on the last day after being 2-0 down, to save their League status and Gillingham required a change of manager with Glenn Roeder helping to scrape enough points to survive.

Unfortunately, it was Halifax who lost their status winning only four games in 1993. They had been as high as 10th on 24 October, ironically when beating Gillingham 2-0.

INTRODUCTION TO THE CLUB SECTION

The full page team photographs which appear on the first of each club's six pages in this section of the yearbook were taken at the beginning of the 1992–93 season, and therefore relate to the season covered by this edition's statistics.

The third and fourth pages of each club's section give a complete record of the League season for the club concerned, including date, venue, opponents, result, half-time score, League position, goalscorers, attendance and complete line-ups, including substitutes where used, for every League game in the 1992–93 season. These two pages also include consolidated lists of goalscorers for the club in League, Coca Cola and FA Cup matches and a summary of results in the two main domestic cups. The full League history of the club, a complete list of major honours won and best placings achieved, and a note of the team's first and second choice colours appears on the sixth page of this section. The colours are checked with the clubs, but please note that second choice colours may vary during the season.

Note also that the League position shown after each League result is recalculated as at every Saturday night plus full holiday programmes, but the position after mid-week fixtures will not normally be updated. Please be advised that the attendance figures quoted for each League game are those which appeared in the Press at the time, whereas the attendance statistics published on pages 610 and 611 are those issued officially by the FA Premier League and Football League after the season has been completed. However, the figures for each League game are those used by the Football League in its weekly bulletin, in conjunction with the *Daily Telegraph* and Jack Rollin's Monday morning statistics in that newspaper.

On the fourth page of each club's section, the total League appearances for the season are listed at the top of each player's column. Substitutes are inserted as numbers 12 and 14 where they actually came on to play. The players taken off are now respectively given a light type figure and an italic one, replacing the * and +. This has enabled more players to be listed in the columns available. Where only one substitute has been used, the number 12 is listed.

In the totals at the top of each column, substitute appearances are listed separately by the '+' sign, but have been amalgamated in the totals which feature in the player's historical section on the final page for each club. Thus these appearances include those as substitute.

The final pages for each club list all the players included on the FA Premier League and Football League's 'Retained' list, which is published at the end of May. Here you will find each player's height and weight, where known, plus birthplace, birthdate and source, together with total League appearances and goals for each club he has represented. Full names of all other players retained including trainees, non-contract players and schoolboys are also given. In addition more club information is added on these pages including items of interest from the club's history and a list of previous managers.

The player's details remain under the club which retained him at the end of the season. An asterisk * by a player's name on the fifth and sixth pages means that he was given a free transfer at the end of the 1992–93 season, a dagger † against a name means that he is a non-contract player, and a double dagger ‡ indicates that the player's registration was cancelled during the season. An § indicates either a Trainee or an Associated Schoolboy who has made Football League appearances.

The play-offs in the Football League are listed separately on pages 586 and 587. Appearances made by players in these play-offs will *not* be included in their career totals.

Two pages have been included for Wycombe Wanderers.

Editor's note: In the Scottish League, substitutes where used are listed as 12 and 14. The second player to be taken off is also picked out with a dagger.

ARSENAL 1992-93 Back row (left to right): Gary Lewin (Physio), Pat Rice (Youth Team Coach), Perry Groves, Steve Bould, David O'Leary, Alan Smith, Alan Miller, David Seaman, Andrew Linighan, Colin Pates, Tony Adams, Lee Dixon, Stewart Houston (First Team Coach), George Armstrong (Reserve Team Coach).
Front row: Nigel Winterburn, Paul Davis, Kevin Campbell, Pal Lydersen, Ian Wright, Ray Parlour, George Graham (Manager), Anders Limpar, Jimmy Carter, Neil Heaney, Paul Merson, John Jensen, David Hillier.

FA Premier

ARSENAL

Arsenal Stadium, Highbury, London N5. Telephone 071–226 0304. Box office direct line 071–354 5404. Commercial and Marketing 359 0808. Recorded information on 071–359 0131. Clubline: 0898 20 20 20. Mail Order 354 8397.

Ground capacity: 39,000 all seated by October 1993.

Record attendance: 73,295 v Sunderland, Div 1, 9 March 1935.

Record receipts: £233,595 v Everton, Littlewoods Cup semi-final, 24 February 1988.

Pitch measurements: 110yd × 71yd.

Chairman: P. D. Hill-Wood. *Vice-chairman:* D. Dein.

Directors: Sir Robert Bellinger CBE, DSC, R. G. Gibbs,C. E. B. L. Carr, R. C. S. Carr.

Managing Director: K. J. Friar.

Manager: George Graham. *Assistant Manager/Coach:* Stewart Houston.

Physio: Gary Lewin. *Reserve Coach:* George Armstrong. *Youth Coach:* Pat Rice.

Secretary: K. J. Friar. *Assistant Secretary:* David Miles. *Commercial Manager:* John Hazell. *Marketing Manager:* Phil Carling.

Year Formed: 1886. *Turned Professional:* 1891. *Ltd Co.:* 1893.

Previous Names: 1886, Dial Square; 1886–91, Royal Arsenal; 1891–1914, Woolwich Arsenal.

Club Nickname: 'Gunners'.

Previous Grounds: 1886–87, Plumstead Common; 1887–88, Sportsman Ground; 1888–90, Manor Ground; 1890–93, Invicta Ground; 1893–1913, Manor Ground; 1913, Highbury.

Record League Victory: 12–0 v Loughborough T, Division 2, 12 March 1900 – Orr; McNichol, Jackson; Moir, Dick (2), Anderson (1); Hunt, Cottrell (2), Main (2), Gaudie (3), Tennant (2).

Record Cup Victory: 11–1 v Darwen, FA Cup, 3rd rd, 9 January 1932 – Moss; Parker, Hapgood; Jones, Roberts, John; Hulme (2), Jack (3), Lambert (2), James, Bastin (4).

Record Defeat: 0–8 v Loughborough T, Division 2, 12 December 1896.

Most League Points (2 for a win): 66, Division 1, 1930–31.

Most League Points (3 for a win): 83, Division 1, 1990–91.

Most League Goals: 127, Division 1, 1930–31.

Highest League Scorer in Season: Ted Drake, 42, 1934–35.

Most League Goals in Total Aggregate: Cliff Bastin, 150, 1930–47.

Most Capped Player: Kenny Sansom, 77 (86), England.

Most League Appearances: David O'Leary, 558, 1975–93.

Record Transfer Fee Received: £2,000,000 from Leeds U for David Rocastle.

Record Transfer Fee Paid: £1,300,000 to QPR for David Seaman, May 1990.

Football League Record: 1893 Elected to Division 2; 1904–13 Division 1; 1913–19 Division 2; 1919–92 Division 1; 1992– FA Premier League.

Honours: Football League: Division 1 – Champions 1930–31, 1932–33, 1933–34, 1934–35, 1937–38, 1947–48, 1952–53, 1970–71, 1988–89, 1990–91; Runners-up 1925–26, 1931–32, 1972–73; Division 2 – Runners-up 1903–04. *FA Cup:* Winners 1929–30, 1935–36, 1949–50, 1970–71, 1978–79, 1992–93; Runners-up 1926–27, 1931–32, 1951–52, 1971–72, 1977–78, 1979–80. *Double Performed:* 1970–71. *Football League Cup:* Winners 1986–87, 1992–93; Runners-up 1967–68, 1968–69, 1987–88. **European Competitions:** *Fairs Cup:* 1963–64, 1969–70 (winners), 1970–71; *European Cup:* 1971–72, 1991–92; *UEFA Cup:* 1978–79, 1981–82, 1982–83; *European Cup-Winners' Cup:* 1979–80 (runners-up).

ARSENAL 1992—93 LEAGUE RECORD

Match No.	Date		Venue	Opponents	Result		H/T Score	Lg. Pos.	Goalscorers	Attendance
1	Aug	15	H	Norwich C	L	2-4	2-0	—	Bould, Campbell	24,030
2		18	A	Blackburn R	L	0-1	0-0	—		16,454
3		23	A	Liverpool	W	2-0	0-0	—	Limpar, Wright	34,961
4		26	H	Oldham Ath	W	2-0	2-0	—	Winterburn, Wright	20,796
5		29	H	Sheffield W	W	2-1	2-1	5	Parlour, Merson	23,389
6	Sept	2	A	QPR	D	0-0	0-0	—		20,868
7		5	A	Wimbledon	L	2-3	1-1	7	Wright 2	12,906
8		12	H	Blackburn R	L	0-1	0-0	9		28,643
9		19	A	Sheffield U	D	1-1	0-0	13	Wright	19,105
10		28	H	Manchester C	W	1-0	1-0	—	Wright	21,504
11	Oct	3	H	Chelsea	W	2-1	1-0	7	Merson, Wright	27,780
12		17	A	Nottingham F	W	1-0	1-0	5	Smith	24,862
13		24	H	Everton	W	2-0	1-0	4	Wright, Limpar	28,052
14	Nov	2	A	Crystal Palace	W	2-1	1-0	—	Merson, Wright	20,287
15		7	H	Coventry C	W	3-0	3-0	1	Smith, Wright, Campbell	27,693
16		21	A	Leeds U	L	0-3	0-0	2		30,516
17		28	H	Manchester U	L	0-1	0-1	3		29,739
18	Dec	5	A	Southampton	L	0-2	0-1	6		17,286
19		12	A	Tottenham H	L	0-1	0-1	8		33,707
20		19	H	Middlesbrough	D	1-1	0-1	6	Wright	23,197
21		26	H	Ipswich T	D	0-0	0-0	8		26,198
22		28	A	Aston Villa	L	0-1	0-1	9		35,170
23	Jan	9	H	Sheffield U	D	1-1	1-0	9	Hillier	23,818
24		16	A	Manchester C	W	1-0	0-0	7	Merson	25,041
25		31	H	Liverpool	L	0-1	0-0	—		27,580
26	Feb	10	H	Wimbledon	L	0-1	0-1	—		18,253
27		20	A	Oldham Ath	W	1-0	0-0	11	Linighan	12,311
28		24	H	Leeds U	D	0-0	0-0	—		21,061
29	Mar	1	A	Chelsea	L	0-1	0-0	—		17,725
30		3	A	Norwich C	D	1-1	0-1	—	Wright	14,802
31		13	A	Coventry C	W	2-0	2-0	12	Campbell, Wright	15,437
32		20	H	Southampton	W	4-3	3-2	9	Linighan, Merson, Carter 2	24,149
33		24	A	Manchester U	D	0-0	0-0	—		37,301
34	Apr	6	A	Middlesbrough	L	0-1	0-1	—		12,726
35		10	A	Ipswich T	W	2-1	1-1	10	Smith, Merson	20,358
36		12	H	Aston Villa	L	0-1	0-0	11		27,123
37		21	H	Nottingham F	D	1-1	0-0	—	Wright	19,024
38	May	1	A	Everton	D	0-0	0-0	12		19,044
39		4	H	QPR	D	0-0	0-0	—		18,817
40		6	A	Sheffield W	L	0-1	0-1	—		23,645
41		8	H	Crystal Palace	W	3-0	1-0	9	Wright, Dickov, Campbell	25,225
42		11	H	Tottenham H	L	1-3	0-1	—	Dickov	26,393

Final League Position: 10

GOALSCORERS

League (40): Wright 15, Merson 6, Campbell 4, Smith 3, Carter 2, Dickov 2, Limpar 2, Linighan 2, Bould 1, Hillier 1, Parlour 1, Winterburn 1.
Coca Cola Cup (15): Wright 5 (1 pen), Campbell 4, Smith 2, Linighan 1, Merson 1, Morrow 1, Winterburn 1.
FA Cup (18): Wright 10 (1 pen), Adams 2, Campbell 1, Linighan 1, Merson 1, Parlour 1, Smith 1, own goal 1.

Seaman 39	Dixon 29	Winterburn 29	Hillier 27 + 3	Bould 24	Adams 33 + 2	Jensen 29 + 3	Smith 27 + 4	Campbell 32 + 5	Merson 32 + 1	Limpar 12 + 11	Wright 30 + 1	Carter 11 + 5	Groves — + 1	Pates 2 + 5	Parlour 16 + 5	Morrow 13 + 3	O'Leary 6 + 5	Selley 9	Linighan 19 + 2	Flatts 6 + 4	Miller 3 + 1	Lydersen 7 + 1	Heaney 3 + 2	Keown 15 + 1	Davis 6	Dickov 1 + 2	Marshall 2	McGowan — + 2	Match No.
1	2	3	4	5	6	7	8	9	10	11	12																		1
1	2	3	4	5	6	7	8	9		11		10	12	14															2
1	2	3	4		6	7		9	12	11	8				5	10													3
1	2	3	4	5	6		12	9	10		8				14	7	11												4
1	2	3	4	5	6	7	12	9	10		8				11														5
1	2	3	4	5	6	7	12	9	10		8				14	11													6
1	2	3		5	6	7	12	9	10		8				4	11			14										7
1	2	3		5	6	7		9	12	10	8				11	14	4												8
1	2	3		5	6	7		9	10	11	8				4				12	14									9
1	2	3	4	5	6	7		9	11	10	12	8																	10
1	2	3	4	5	6	7		9	11	10	12	8																	11
1	2	3	4	5	6	7		9	11	10	12	8			14														12
1	2	3	4	5	6	7		9	11	10	12	8			14														13
1	2		4	5	6	7		9	11	10	12	8										3							14
1	2		4	5	6	7		9	11	10	12	8										3							15
1	2		4	5	6	7		9	10	11	8				12				14			3							16
1	2		4	5	6	7		9	10	11	8				12				14			3							17
1	2		4	5	6	14		9	10	12	8				7		11					3							18
1		3	4	5	6	7		9	10	12	8				11									2					19
1		3	4		6	14		9	12	10	8				11				5			7		2					20
1		3	4	5		7		9	10	12	8				14		6		11					2					21
1		3	4	5				9	10	12	8				11	7	6		14					2					22
1	2	3	4		6	7		9	10	11	8				12				5										23
1	2	3	4	5	6	7		9		8	10								11										24
1	2	3	4		6			9	8	10		7			11	12			5					14					25
1		3	4		6			9	11	10	8				12	14	7		5					2					26
1			4		6	7		9	10	11	12				3		8		5					2					27
1		3	4		6			9	12	10	11	8					7		5					2					28
1	2		4			7		9	8	10	12				3				5		11		14	6					29
1	2	3					7	12	11	8	10	9							5					6	4				30
1	2		14		6			9	10	12	8				7		11		5					3	4				31
1		3	14		6			9	10	11	7	8			5									2		4	12		32
1	2		14		6	7		9	10		8				11	12	4		5			3							33
1		3	4		6	7		9	11	8	10				14		2		5							12			34
1		3	12			7		9	8	10	11				14	4	2		5						6				35
1	2	3			6			9	11	10	8				14	7	4		12					5					36
1	2	3		12		7		9	14		8				11	10	4		5					6					37
1							6	12	9	10					11		2	8	5			3	14	7	4				38
	2						6	7	9	8	10	12					5				1	11	3	4					39
					6		7	9		11					5	8	14	1	2	10	3					4	12		40
1	2	3			6			9	10	8	7				11	14	5							4	12				41
					6			9	12		5	8	7				1	2	11	3				10	4	14			42

Coca Cola Cup	Second Round	Millwall (h)	1-1
		(a)	1-1
	Third Round	Derby Co (a)	1-1
		(h)	2-1
	Fourth Round	Scarborough (a)	1-0
	Fifth Round	Nottingham F (h)	2-0
	Semi-Final	Crystal Palace (a)	3-1
		(h)	2-0
	Final at Wembley	Sheffield W	2-1
FA Cup	Third Round	Yeovil (a)	3-1
	Fourth Round	Leeds U (h)	2-2
		(a)	3-2
	Fifth Round	Nottingham F (h)	2-0
	Sixth Round	Ipswich T (a)	4-2
	Semi-Final at Wembley	Tottenham H	1-0
	Final at Wembley	Sheffield W	1-1
	Replay		2-1

ARSENAL

Player and Position	Ht	Wt	Date	Birth Place	Source	Clubs	League App	Gls
Goalkeepers								
Allan Miller	6 3	14 07	29 3 70	Epping	Trainee	Arsenal	4	—
						Plymouth Arg (loan)	13	—
						WBA (loan)	3	—
						Birmingham C (loan)	15	—
David Seaman	6 4	14 10	19 9 63	Rotherham	Apprentice	Leeds U	—	—
						Peterborough U	91	—
						Birmingham C	75	—
						QPR	141	—
						Arsenal	119	—
James Will	6 2	13 13	7 10 72	Turiff	Trainee	Arsenal	—	—
						Sheffield U (loan)	—	—
Defenders								
Tony Adams	6 3	13 11	10 10 66	London	Apprentice	Arsenal	284	20
Stephen Bould	6 4	14 02	16 11 62	Stoke	Apprentice	Stoke C	183	6
						Torquay U (loan)	9	—
						Arsenal	136	4
Lee Dixon	5 8	11 08	17 3 64	Manchester	Local	Burnley	4	—
						Chester	57	1
						Bury	45	5
						Stoke C	71	5
						Arsenal	182	15
Craig Gaunt*	5 11	12 02	31 3 73	Nottingham	Trainee	Arsenal	—	—
Martin Keown	6 1	12 04	24 7 66	Oxford	Apprentice	Arsenal	22	—
						Brighton (loan)	16	—
						Brighton (loan)	7	1
						Aston Villa	112	3
						Everton	96	—
						Arsenal	16	—
Justin Lee*	5 6	11 05	19 9 73	Hereford	Trainee	Arsenal	—	—
Andy Linighan	6 4	13 10	18 6 62	Hartlepool	Smiths BC	Hartlepool U	110	4
						Leeds U	66	3
						Oldham Ath	87	6
						Norwich C	86	8
						Arsenal	48	2
Pal Lydersen	6 0	14 01	10 9 65	Odense	IK Start.	Arsenal	15	—
Gavin McGowan§			16 1 76	Blackheath	Trainee	Arsenal	2	—
Scott Marshall	6 1	12 05	1 5 73	Edinburgh	Trainee	Arsenal	2	—
Steve Morrow	5 11	12 02	2 7 70	Belfast	Trainee	Arsenal	18	—
						Reading (loan)	10	—
						Watford (loan)	8	—
						Reading (loan)	3	—
						Barnet (loan)	1	—
David O'Leary*	6 1	13 09	2 5 58	London	Apprentice	Arsenal	558	10
Colin Pates*	6 0	13 00	10 8 61	Mitcham	Apprentice	Chelsea	281	10
						Charlton Ath	38	—
						Arsenal	21	—
						Brighton (loan)	17	—
Ken Webster	5 8	13 02	2 3 73	Hammersmith	Trainee	Arsenal	—	—
Nigel Winterburn	5 8	11 04	11 12 63	Coventry	Local	Birmingham C	—	—
						Oxford U	—	—
						Wimbledon	165	8
						Arsenal	199	5
Midfield								
Jimmy Carter	5 10	11 01	9 11 65	London	Apprentice	Crystal Palace	—	—
						QPR	—	—
						Millwall	110	10
						Liverpool	5	—
						Arsenal	22	2

ARSENAL

Colours: Red shirts with white sleeves, white shorts, red stockings. **Change colours:** Yellow shirts, navy blue shorts, yellow stockings.

Foundation: Formed by workers at the Royal Arsenal, Woolwich in 1886 they began as Dial Square (name of one of the workshops) and included two former Nottingham Forest players Fred Beardsley and Morris Bates. Beardsley wrote to his old club seeking help and they provided the new club with a full set of red jerseys and a ball. The club became known as the "Woolwich Reds" although their official title soon after formation was Woolwich Arsenal.

First Football League game: 2 September, 1893, Division 2, v Newcastle U (h) D 2-2 – Williams; Powell, Jeffrey; Devine, Buist, Howat; Gemmell, Henderson, Shaw (1), Elliott (1), Booth.

Did you know: After weeks of negotiating with the London Passenger Transport Board, Herbert Chapman the Arsenal manager, was successful in persuading them to rename Gillespie Road Underground station. From 5 November 1932 it became known as Arsenal.

Managers (and Secretary-Managers)
Sam Hollis 1894–97, Tom Mitchell 1897–98, George Elcoat 1898–99, Harry Bradshaw 1899–1904, Phil Kelso 1904–08, George Morrell 1908–15, Leslie Knighton 1919–25, Herbert Chapman 1925–34, George Allison 1934–47, Tom Whittaker 1947–56, Jack Crayston 1956–58, George Swindin 1958–62, Billy Wright 1962–66, Bertie Mee 1966–76, Terry Neill 1976–83, Don Howe 1984–86, George Graham May 1986–   .

Player and Position	Ht	Wt	Date	Birth Place	Source	Clubs	League App	Gls
Steve Clements*	5 10	11 10	26 9 72	Slough	Trainee	Arsenal	—	—
Paul Davis	5 10	10 13	9 12 61	London	Apprentice	Arsenal	325	29
Mark Flatts	5 06	9 08	14 10 72	Haringay	Trainee	Arsenal	10	—
David Hillier	5 10	12 05	19 12 69	Blackheath	Trainee	Arsenal	73	2
John Jensen	5 10	12 06	3 5 65	Denmark	Brondby	Arsenal	32	—
Gary McKeown (To Dundee July 1992)	5 10	11 07	19 10 70	Oxford	Trainee	Arsenal	—	—
						Shrewsbury T (loan)	8	1
Ray Parlour	5 10	11 12	7 3 73	Romford	Trainee	Arsenal	27	2
Ian Selley	5 9	10 01	14 6 74	Chertsey	Trainee	Arsenal	9	—
Forwards								
John Bacon*	5 11	11 05	23 3 73	Dublin	Trainee	Arsenal	—	—
Kevin Campbell	6 1	13 08	4 2 70	Lambeth	Trainee	Arsenal	106	28
						Leyton Orient (loan)	16	9
						Leicester C (loan)	11	5
Paul Dickov	5 5	11 05	1 11 72	Glasgow	Trainee	Arsenal	3	2
Neil Heaney	5 9	11 09	3 11 71	Middlesbrough	Trainee	Arsenal	6	—
						Hartlepool U (loan)	3	—
						Cambridge U (loan)	13	2
Anders Limpar	5 8	11 07	24 9 65	Solna	Cremonese	Arsenal	86	17
Paul Merson	6 0	13 02	20 3 68	London	Apprentice	Arsenal	200	56
						Brentford (loan)	7	—
Paul Read	5 11	12 06	25 9 73	Harlow	Trainee	Arsenal	—	—
Paul Shaw	5 11	12 02	4 9 73	Burnham	Trainee	Arsenal	—	—
Alan Smith	6 3	12 13	21 11 62	Birmingham	Alvechurch	Leicester C	191	73
						Leicester C (loan)	9	3
						Arsenal	220	81
Ian Wright	5 9	11 08	3 11 63	Woolwich	Greenwich Borough	Crystal Palace	225	89
						Arsenal	61	39

Trainees
Brissett, Jason C; Campbell, Stuart J; Clarke, Adrian J; Connolly, Anthony; Hall, Graeme B; Harford, Paul R. T; Kirby, Ryan M; McArdle, Mark; McDonald, Christopher; McGowan, Gavin G; O'Brien, Roy J; Rawlins, Matthew; Rose, Matthew; Rust, Nicholas C. I; Swain, Joel T; Zumrutel, Soner.

Associated Schoolboys
Burgess, Danny; Hollingsworth, Orlando; Rankin, Isaiah; Richardson, Lee; Wynter, Jermaine.

Associated Schoolboys who have accepted the club's offer of a Traineeship/Contract
Black, Michael J; Clarke, Albert; Dennis, Kevin; Howell, Jamie; Hughes, Stephen J; Owen, Dafydd; Taylor, Ross E.

ASTON VILLA 1992-93 *Back row (left to right): Stefan Beinlich, Matthias Breitkreutz, Neil Cox, Mark Blake, Ugochuko Ehiogu, Earl Barrett, Stephen Froggatt, Bryan Small, David Farrell. Centre row: Jim Walker, Richard Money, Dean Saunders, Garry Parker, Nigel Spink, Mark Bosnich, Ray Houghton, Paul McGrath, Dave Sexton, Roger Spry. Front row: Cyrille Regis, Tony Daley, Dariusz Kubicki, Kevin Richardson, Ron Atkinson, Jim Barron, Dalian Atkinson, Shaun Teale, Steve Staunton, Dwight Yorke.*

FA Premier **ASTON VILLA**

Villa Park, Trinity Rd, Birmingham B6 6HE. Telephone 021–327 2299. Fax 021 322 2107. Commercial Dept. 021–327 5399. Clubcall: 0898 121148. Ticketline: 0898 121848. Ticket office: 021 327 5353. Club Shop: 021–327 2800.

Ground capacity: 39,406.

Record attendance: 76,588 v Derby Co, FA Cup 6th rd, 2 March 1946.

Record receipts: £385,678 Everton v Norwich C, FA Cup semi-final, 15 April 1989.

Pitch measurements: 115yd × 75yd.

President: H. J. Musgrove. *Chairman:* H. D. Ellis.

Directors: J. A. Alderson, Dr D. H. Targett, P. D. Ellis.

Manager: Ron Atkinson. *Assistant Manager:* Jim Barron. *First Team Coach:* Dave Sexton.

Secretary: Steven Stride. *Director of Youth:* Dave Richardson.

Physio: Jim Walker. *Youth Coach:* Colin Clarke. *Chief Scout:* Brian Whitehouse. *Fitness Consultant:* Roger Spry.

Commercial Manager: Abdul Rashid.

Year Formed: 1874. *Turned Professional:* 1885. *Ltd Co.:* 1896.

Previous Grounds: 1874–76, Aston Park; 1876–97, Perry Barr; 1897, Villa Park.

Club Nickname: 'The Villans'.

Record League Victory: 12–2 v Accrington S, Division 1, 12 March 1892 – Warner; Evans, Cox; Harry Devey, Jimmy Cowan, Baird; Athersmith (1), Dickson (2), John Devey (4), L. Campbell (4), Hodgetts (1).

Record Cup Victory: 13–0 v Wednesbury Old Ath, FA Cup, 1st rd, 30 October 1886 – Warner; Coulton, Simmonds; Yates, Robertson, Burton (2); R. Davis (1), A. Brown (3), Hunter (3), Loach (2), Hodgetts (2).

Record Defeat: 1–8 v Blackburn R, FA Cup, 3rd rd, 16 February 1889.

Most League Points (2 for a win): 70, Division 3, 1971–72.

Most League Points (3 for a win): 78, Division 2, 1987–88.

Most League Goals: 128, Division 1, 1930–31.

Highest League Scorer in Season: 'Pongo' Waring, 49, Division 1, 1930–31.

Most League Goals in Total Aggregate: Harry Hampton, 215, 1904–15.

Most Capped Player: Peter McParland, 33 (34), Northern Ireland.

Most League Appearances: Charlie Aitken, 561, 1961–76.

Record Transfer Fee Received: £5,500,000 from Bari for David Platt, August 1991.

Record Transfer Fee Paid: £2,300,000 to Liverpool for Dean Saunders, September 1992.

Football League Record: 1888 Founder Member of the League; 1936–38 Division 2; 1938–59 Division 1; 1959–60 Division 2; 1960–67 Division 1; 1967–70 Division 2; 1970–72 Division 3; 1972–75 Division 2; 1975–87 Division 1; 1987–88 Division 2; 1988–92 Division 1; 1992– FA Premier League.

Honours: FA Premier League: – Runners-up 1992–93. *Football League:* Division 1 – Champions 1893–94, 1895–96, 1896–97, 1898–99, 1899–1900, 1909–10, 1980–81; Runners-up 1888–89, 1902–03, 1907–08, 1910–11, 1912–13, 1913–14, 1930–31, 1932–33, 1989–90; Division 2 – Champions 1937–38, 1959–60; Runners-up 1974–75, 1987–88; Division 3 – Champions 1971–72. *FA Cup:* Winners 1887, 1895, 1897, 1905, 1913, 1920, 1957; Runners-up 1892, 1924. *Double Performed:* 1896–97. *Football League Cup:* Winners 1961, 1975, 1977; Runners-up 1963, 1971. **European Competitions:** *European Cup:* 1981–82 (winners), 1982–83; *UEFA Cup:* 1975–76, 1977–78, 1983–84, 1990–91. *World Club Championship:* 1982–83; *European Super Cup:* 1982–83 (winners).

ASTON VILLA 1992—93 LEAGUE RECORD

Match No.	Date		Venue	Opponents	Result	H/T Score	Lg. Pos.	Goalscorers	Attendance
1	Aug	15	A	Ipswich T	D	1-1	0-1	—	Atkinson	16,818
2		19	H	Leeds U	D	1-1	0-0	—	Atkinson	29,151
3		22	H	Southampton	D	1-1	0-0	12	Atkinson	17,894
4		25	A	Everton	L	0-1	0-0	—		22,372
5		29	A	Sheffield U	W	2-0	1-0	11	Parker 2	18,773
6	Sept	2	H	Chelsea	L	1-3	1-2	—	Richardson	19,125
7		5	H	Crystal Palace	W	3-0	2-0	11	Yorke, Staunton, Froggatt	17,120
8		13	A	Leeds U	D	1-1	1-0	—	Parker	27,817
9		19	H	Liverpool	W	4-2	1-1	7	Saunders 2, Atkinson, Parker	37,863
10		26	A	Middlesbrough	W	3-2	1-0	6	Saunders 2, Atkinson	20,905
11	Oct	3	A	Wimbledon	W	3-2	2-1	5	Saunders 2, Atkinson	6849
12		19	H	Blackburn R	D	0-0	0-0	—		30,398
13		24	A	Oldham Ath	D	1-1	0-1	6	Atkinson	13,457
14	Nov	1	H	QPR	W	2-0	1-0	—	Saunders, Atkinson	20,140
15		7	H	Manchester U	W	1-0	1-0	3	Atkinson	39,063
16		21	A	Tottenham H	D	0-0	0-0	3		32,852
17		28	H	Norwich C	L	2-3	1-2	4	Houghton, Parker	28,837
18	Dec	5	A	Sheffield W	W	2-1	1-1	3	Atkinson 2	29,964
19		12	H	Nottingham F	W	2-1	1-1	2	Regis, McGrath	29,015
20		19	A	Manchester C	D	1-1	1-0	2	Parker	23,525
21		26	A	Coventry C	L	0-3	0-0	4		24,245
22		28	H	Arsenal	W	1-0	1-0	3	Saunders (pen)	35,170
23	Jan	9	A	Liverpool	W	2-1	0-1	2	Parker, Saunders	40,826
24		17	H	Middlesbrough	W	5-1	3-0	—	Parker, McGrath, Yorke, Saunders, Teale	19,977
25		27	H	Sheffield U	W	3-1	0-0	—	McGrath, Saunders, Richardson	20,266
26		30	A	Southampton	L	0-2	0-1	3		19,087
27	Feb	6	H	Ipswich T	W	2-0	2-0	2	Yorke, Saunders	25,395
28		10	A	Crystal Palace	L	0-1	0-1	—		12,270
29		13	A	Chelsea	W	1-0	1-0	1	Houghton	20,081
30		20	H	Everton	W	2-1	2-1	1	Cox, Barrett	32,913
31		27	H	Wimbledon	W	1-0	0-0	1	Yorke	34,496
32	Mar	10	H	Tottenham H	D	0-0	0-0	—		37,727
33		14	A	Manchester U	D	1-1	0-0	—	Staunton	36,163
34		20	H	Sheffield W	W	2-0	1-0	1	Yorke 2	38,024
35		24	A	Norwich C	L	0-1	0-0	—		19,528
36	Apr	4	A	Nottingham F	W	1-0	0-0	—	McGrath	26,742
37		10	H	Coventry C	D	0-0	0-0	2		38,543
38		12	A	Arsenal	W	1-0	0-0	2	Daley	27,123
39		18	H	Manchester C	W	3-1	0-1	—	Saunders, Parker (pen), Houghton	33,108
40		21	A	Blackburn R	L	0-3	0-3	—		15,127
41	May	2	H	Oldham Ath	L	0-1	0-1	—		37,247
42		9	A	QPR	L	1-2	1-0	—	Daley	18,904

Final League Position: 2

GOALSCORERS

League (57): Saunders 13 (1 pen), Atkinson 11, Parker 9 (1 pen), Yorke 6, McGrath 4, Houghton 3, Daley 2, Richardson 2, Staunton 2, Barrett 1, Cox 1, Froggatt 1, Regis 1, Teale 1.
Coca Cola Cup (7): Atkinson 2, Saunders 2, McGrath 1, Richardson 1, Teale 1.
FA Cup (5): Saunders 2, Cox 1, Houghton 1, Yorke 1.

Spink 25	Barrett 42	Staunton 42	Teale 39	McGrath 42	Richardson 42	Daley 8 + 5	Parker 37	Houghton 39	Atkinson 28	Froggatt 16 + 1	Regis 7 + 6	Yorke 22 + 5	Ehiogu 1 + 3	McAvennie — + 3	Saunders 35	Blake — + 1	Small 10 + 4	Farrell 1 + 1	Bosnich 17	Cox 6 + 9	Breitkreutz 2 + 1	Beinlich 1 + 6	Carruthers — + 1	Match No.
1	2	3	4	5	6	7	8	9	10	11	12													1
1	2	3	4	5	6	7	8	9	10	12	11													2
1	2	3	4	5	6		8	7	10	11		9	12	14										3
1	2	3	4	5	6	7	8	9	10	11	12													4
1	2	3	4	5	6		8	7	10	11		9	12											5
1	2	3	4	5	6		8	7	10	11		9		12										6
1	2	3	4	5	6		8	7	10	11		9		12										7
1	2	3	4	5	6		8	7	10	11					9									8
1	2	3	4	5	6		8	7	10	11					9									9
1	2	3	4	5	6		8	7	10	11	12				9	14								10
1	2	3	4	5	6		8	7	10	11	12				9									11
1	2	3	4	5	6		8	7	10	11					9		12							12
1	2	3	4	5	6			7	10				8		9		11	12						13
1	2	3	4	5	6		8	7	10			14			9		12	11						14
1	2	3	4	5	6		8	7	10						9		11							15
1	2	3	*4*	5	6		8	7	10		12		14		9		11							16
1	2	3		5	6		8	7	10		12		4		9		11							17
	2	3		5	6		8		10				7		9		11		1	4				18
1	2	3	4	5	6		8	7			10				9		11							19
1	2	3	4	5	6		8	7	10			11			9					12				20
1	2	3	4	5	6		8	7			10				9		11			12	14			21
1	2	3	4	5	6		8	7		11	10				9					12				22
1	2	3	4	5	6		8	7	10	*14*	11				9					12				23
1	2	3	4	5	6		8	7		*11*	10				9					12	14			24
1	2	3	4	5	6		8					10			9		11			12	7	14		25
1	2	3	4	5	6		8					10			9			*11*		12	7	14		26
	2	3	4	5	6		8	7		11	*10*				9				1	12	14			27
	2	3	4	5	6		8	7		11	10				9				1		12			28
	2	3	4	5	6		8	7	10	11		14			9				1	12				29
	2	3	4	5	6			7				10			9				1	8		11		30
	2	3	4	5	6			7			11	10			9				1	8				31
	2	3	4	5	6	11	8	7		12	10				9				1					32
	2	3	4	5	6	12	8	7				10			9		11		1					33
	2	3	4	5	6		8	7		11	10				9				1					34
	2	3	4	5	6	12	8	7		11	10				9				1					35
	2	3	4	5	6	12	8	7	10			11			9				1					36
	2	3	4	5	6	12	8	7	10			11			9				1					37
	2	3	4	5	6	11		7				10			9		12		1	8				38
	2	3		5	6	11	8	7				10			9		12		1	4				39
	2	3	4	5	6	11		7			10	12			9				1	8				40
	2	3	4	5	6	12	8	7	10			11			9				1					41
	2	3	4	5	6	11	8	7	10						9				1	12		14		42

Coca Cola Cup	Second Round	Oxford U (a)	2-1
		(h)	2-1
	Third Round	Manchester U (h)	1-0
	Fourth Round	Ipswich T (h)	2-2
		(a)	0-1
FA Cup	Third Round	Bristol R (h)	1-1
		(a)	3-0
	Fourth Round	Wimbledon (h)	1-1
		(a)	0-0

ASTON VILLA

Player and Position	Ht	Wt	Date	Birth Place	Source	Clubs	League App	Gls
Goalkeepers								
Mark Bosnich	6 1	13 07	13 1 72	Fairfield	Croatia Sydney	Manchester U	3	—
						Aston Villa	18	—
Michael Oakes	6 1	12 07	30 10 73	Northwich	Trainee	Aston Villa	—	—
Nigel Spink	6 2	14 08	8 8 58	Chelmsford	Chelsmford C	Aston Villa	331	—
Defenders								
Earl Barrett	5 11	11 00	28 4 67	Rochdale	Apprentice	Manchester C	3	—
						Chester C (loan)	12	—
						Oldham Ath	183	7
						Aston Villa	55	1
Chris Boden	5 09	11 00	13 10 73	Wolverhampton	Trainee	Aston Villa	—	—
Tony Cullen‡			25 9 73	Salford	Blackburn R	Aston Villa	—	—
Ugo Ehiogu	6 2	13 03	3 11 72	London	Trainee	WBA	2	—
						Aston Villa	12	—
Dariusz Kubicki	5 10	11 07	6 6 63	Warsaw	Legia Warsaw	Aston Villa	23	—
Paul McGrath	6 2	14 00	4 12 59	Greenford	St Patrick's Ath	Manchester U	163	12
						Aston Villa	153	6
Bryan Small	5 9	11 09	15 11 71	Birmingham	Trainee	Aston Villa	22	—
Steve Staunton	6 0	12 04	19 1 69	Drogheda	Dundalk	Liverpool	65	—
						Bradford C (loan)	8	—
						Aston Villa	79	6
Shaun Teale	6 0	13 10	10 3 64	Southport	Weymouth	Bournemouth	100	4
						Aston Villa	81	1
Midfield								
Mark Blake	5 11	12 07	16 12 70	Nottingham	Trainee	Aston Villa	31	2
						Wolverhampton W (loan)	2	—
Matthias Breitkreutz	5 9	11 03	12 5 71	Crivitz	Bergmann Borsig	Aston Villa	11	—
Neil Cox	6 00	12 10	8 10 71	Scunthorpe	Trainee	Scunthorpe U	17	1
						Aston Villa	22	1
Richard Crisp	5 7	10 05	23 5 72	Wordsley	Trainee	Aston Villa	—	—
						Scunthorpe U (loan)	8	—
Gareth Farrelly	6 0	12 07	28 8 75	Dublin	Home Farm	Aston Villa	—	—
Steve Froggatt	5 10	11 00	9 3 73	Lincoln	Trainee	Aston Villa	26	1
Ray Houghton	5 7	10 10	9 1 62	Glasgow	Amateur	West Ham U	1	—
						Fulham	129	16
						Oxford U	83	10
						Liverpool	153	28
						Aston Villa	39	3
Garry Parker	5 11	12 05	7 9 65	Oxford	Apprentice	Luton T	42	3
						Hull C	84	8
						Nottingham F	103	17
						Aston Villa	62	10
Kevin Richardson	5 7	11 07	4 12 62	Newcastle	Apprentice	Everton	109	16
						Watford	39	2
						Arsenal	96	5
					Real Sociedad	Aston Villa	84	8
Lee Williams	5 7	11 00	3 2 73	Birmingham	Trainee	Aston Villa	—	—
						Shrewsbury T (loan)	3	—
Forwards								
Dalian Atkinson	6 0	13 10	21 3 68	Shrewsbury		Ipswich T	60	18
						Sheffield W	38	10
					Real Sociedad	Aston Villa	42	12

ASTON VILLA

Colours: Claret shirts, blue trim, white shorts, claret and blue trim, blue stockings, claret trim. **Change colours:** White shirts, purple/black trim, black shorts, white stockings.

Foundation: Cricketing enthusiasts of Villa Cross Wesleyan Chapel, Aston, Birmingham decided to form a football club during the winter of 1873–74. Football clubs were few and far between in the Birmingham area and in their first game against Aston Brook St. Mary's Rugby team they played one half rugby and the other soccer. In 1876 they were joined by a Scottish soccer enthusiast George Ramsay who was immediately appointed captain and went on to lead Aston Villa from obscurity to one of the country's top clubs in a period of less than 10 years.

First Football League game: 8 September, 1888, Football League, v Wolverhampton W, (a) D 1-1 – Warner; Cox, Coulton; Yates, H. Devey, Dawson; A. Brown, Green (1), Allen, Garvey, Hodgetts.

Did you know: Aston Villa were the first Football League club to play in as many as 100 League Cup games. They achieved this milestone in the 1980–81 season.

Managers (and Secretary-Managers)
George Ramsay 1884–1926*, W. J. Smith 1926–34*, Jimmy McMullan 1934–35, Jimmy Hogan 1936–44, Alex Massie 1945–50, George Martin 1950–53, Eric Houghton 1953–58, Joe Mercer 1958–64, Dick Taylor 1965–67, Tommy Cummings 1967–68, Tommy Docherty 1968–70, Vic Crowe 1970–74, Ron Saunders 1974–82, Tony Barton 1982–84, Graham Turner 1984–86, Billy McNeill 1986–87, Graham Taylor 1987–90, Dr. Jozef Venglos 1990–91, Ron Atkinson June 1991– .

Player and Position	Ht	Wt	Date	Birth Place	Source	Clubs	League App	Gls
Stefan Beinlich	5 11	11 02	13 1 72	Berlin	Bergmann Borsig	Aston Villa	9	—
Trevor Berry	5 07	10 08	1 8 74	Surrey	Bournemouth	Aston Villa	—	—
Martin Carruthers	5 11	11 07	7 8 72	Nottingham	Trainee	Aston Villa	4	—
						Hull C (loan)	13	6
Tony Daley	5 8	10 08	18 10 67	Birmingham	Apprentice	Aston Villa	206	30
Neil Davis	5 8	11 00	15 8 73	Bloxwich	Redditch U	Aston Villa	—	—
David Farrell	5 11	11 02	11 11 71	Birmingham	Redditch U	Aston Villa	2	—
						Scunthorpe U (loan)	5	1
Graham Fenton	5 10	11 03	22 5 74	Wallsend	Trainee	Aston Villa	—	—
Frank McAvennie (To Celtic December 1992)	5 9	11 0	22 11 59	Glasgow	Partick T	St Mirren	135	50
						West Ham U	85	33
						Celtic	55	27
						West Ham U	68	16
						Aston Villa	3	—
Mark Parrott*	5 11	11 00	14 3 71	Cheltenham	Trainee	Aston Villa	—	—
Cyrille Regis*	6 0	13 04	9 2 58	French Guyana	Hayes	WBA	237	82
						Coventry C	238	47
						Aston Villa	52	13
Dean Saunders	5 8	10 06	21 6 64	Swansea	Apprentice	Swansea C	49	12
						Cardiff C (loan)	4	—
						Brighton	72	21
						Oxford U	59	22
						Derby Co	106	42
						Liverpool	42	11
						Aston Villa	35	13
Dwight Yorke	5 11	11 13	3 12 71	Tobago	Tobago	Aston Villa	79	19

Trainees
Aston, Lee A; Blenkinship, Paul; Brown, Ian S; Browne, Paul; Cowe, Steven M; Evans, Darren; Harrison, Garry M; Henderson, Brian; King, Ian J; Murphy, John P; Pearce, Christopher J; Pearce, Dennis A; Pitcher, Steven; Scimeca, Riccardo.

Associated Schoolboys
Barrett, Neil R; Burgess, Richard D; Collins, Lee D; Deacon, Robert A; Hickman, John A; Jaszczun, Antony J; Jones, Jonathan B; King, Robert D; Miley, Jonathan H; Peet, David K; Petty, Ben J; Read, Lewis T; Walker, Richard M.

Associated Schoolboys who have accepted the club's offer of a Traineeship/Contract
Boxall, Michael K; Brock, Stuart A; Burchell, Lee A; Byfield, Darren; Hendrie, Lee A; Hines, Leslie D; Mitchell, Andrew B; Moore, David; Peters, Mark P; Rachel, Adam; Senior, Marc A.

44

BARNET 1992–93 *Back row (left to right)*: Tim Alexander, Mark Carter, Mark Flashman, Andy Pape, Gary Phillips, Nicky Evans, Hakan Hayrettin.
Centre row: Gordon Ogbourne (Kit Manager), Tony Lynch, Jonathan Hunt, Derek Payne, Dave Barnett, Mick Bodley, David Howell, Richard Huxford, Roger Willis, Carl Hoddle.
Front row: Dominic Naylor, Gary Bull, Gavin MacPherson, Duncan Horton, Barry Fry (Manager), Edwin Stein (Assistant Manager), Geoff Cooper, Paul Showler, Kenny Lowe.
(Photograph by kind permission of Colorsport)

Division 2   **BARNET**

Underhill Stadium, Barnet Lane, Barnet, Herts EN5 2BE.
Telephone 081–441 6932. Fax 081–447 0655. Clubcall: 0898
121544.

Ground capacity: 5363.

Record attendance: 11,026 v Wycombe Wanderers. FA
Amateur Cup 4th Round 1951–52.

Record Receipts: £31,202 v Portsmouth FA Cup 3rd Round 5th
January 1991.

Pitch measurements: 110yd × 72yd.

Chairman: R. Woolfson.

Directors: M. Ozin, A. Needleman.

Manager: Gary Phillips. *Physio:* Phil Edwards.

Secretary: Bryan Ayres. *Commercial Manager:* Mick Hooker.

Year Formed: 1888. *Turned Professional:* 1965. *Ltd Co:*

Club Nickname: The Bees.

Previous Names: 1906–19 Barnet Alston FC.

Previous Grounds: Queens Road (1888–1901) Totteridge Lane (1901–07).

Record League Victory: 6–0 v Lincoln C (away), Division 4, 4 September 1991 – Pape;
Poole, Naylor, Bodley, Howell, Evans (1), Willis (1), Murphy (1), Bull (2), Lowe, Showler
(1 og).

Record Defeat: 1–5 v York C, Division 3, 13 March 1993.

Most League Points (3 for a win): 79, Division 3, 1992–93.

Most League Goals: 81, Division 4, 1991–92.

Highest League Scorer in Season: Gary Bull, 20, Division 4, 1991–92.

Most League Goals in Total Aggregate: Gary Bull 37, 1991–93.

Most League Appearances: Gary Bull, 83, 1991–93.

Record Transfer Fee Received: £350,000 from Wimbledon for Andy Clarke, February 1991.

Record Transfer Fee Paid: £40,000 to Barrow for Kenny Lowe, January 1991 and £40,000
to Runcorn for Mark Carter, February 1991.

Football League Record: Promoted to Division 4 from GMVC 1991; 1991–92 Division 4;
1992–93 Division 3; 1993– Division 2.

Honours: Football League: best season 3rd, Division 3, 1992–93. *FA Amateur Cup:* Winners
1945–46. *GM Vauxhall Conference:* Winners 1990–91. *FA Cup:* best season; never past 3rd
rd. *League Cup:* never past 1st rd.

BARNET 1992—93 LEAGUE RECORD

Match No.	Date	Venue	Opponents	Result	H/T Score	Lg. Pos.	Goalscorers	Attendance
1	Aug 15	A	Chesterfield	W	2-1	1-0	—	Bull 2	3140
2	21	H	Colchester U	W	3-1	0-1	—	Willis, Bull, Hoddle	3600
3	29	A	Gillingham	D	1-1	1-0	2	Carter	3874
4	Sept 1	A	Doncaster R	L	1-2	0-2	—	Barnett	1747
5	5	H	Carlisle U	W	2-0	0-0	2	Carter, Bull	2733
6	12	A	Bury	D	0-0	0-0	4		3355
7	15	H	Northampton T	W	3-0	0-0	—	Carter, Stein, Showler	2885
8	19	H	Hereford U	W	2-0	1-0	2	Showler, Hoddle	2788
9	26	A	Wrexham	W	3-2	2-1	2	Bull 2, Carter	3078
10	Oct 3	H	Shrewsbury T	D	2-2	0-2	2	Bull 2	2913
11	17	H	Scunthorpe U	W	3-0	1-0	2	Carter, Payne, Showler	2924
12	24	A	Lincoln C	L	1-4	1-2	2	Payne	2955
13	31	H	Crewe Alex	W	3-2	1-0	2	Bull, Carter 2	3481
14	Nov 3	H	Walsall	W	3-0	2-0	—	Lowe 2, Smith (og)	2623
15	7	A	York C	L	0-2	0-1	2		6425
16	22	H	Cardiff C	W	2-1	0-0	—	Barnett, Payne	4181
17	28	A	Darlington	L	0-1	0-0	2		1763
18	Dec 5	A	Halifax T	W	2-1	1-1	2	Stein 2	1253
19	12	H	Rochdale	W	2-0	1-0	1	Showler, Carter	2778
20	28	H	Torquay U	W	5-4	0-1	1	Bull 2 (2 pens), Stein, Carter, Evans	3891
21	Jan 2	H	Darlington	D	0-0	0-0	1		3437
22	8	A	Northampton T	D	1-1	0-0	—	Bull (pen)	4266
23	16	A	Wrexham	W	3-1	3-1	1	Bodley, Payne, Carter	4079
24	23	A	Hereford U	D	1-1	0-1	1	Bull	2591
25	29	A	Colchester U	W	2-1	0-0	—	Bull, Payne	5609
26	Feb 6	H	Chesterfield	W	2-1	0-0	1	Stein, Huxford	3401
27	13	A	Carlisle U	W	1-0	1-0	1	Stein	4020
28	20	H	Doncaster R	W	2-0	1-0	1	Lynch, Bull	3458
29	Mar 2	H	Gillingham	W	2-0	1-0	—	Butler (og), Breen (og)	3446
30	6	A	Shrewsbury T	L	0-1	0-1	1		4518
31	13	H	York C	L	1-5	1-2	2	Bull	4985
32	20	A	Walsall	L	0-2	0-1	2		3418
33	27	A	Cardiff C	D	1-1	1-0	2	Evans	16,073
34	30	A	Scarborough	D	2-2	1-1	—	Bull, Evans	2301
35	Apr 3	H	Halifax T	D	0-0	0-0	2		3042
36	6	A	Rochdale	W	1-0	0-0	—	Stein	1661
37	10	H	Scarborough	W	3-1	2-0	1	Showler, Sorrell, Stein	3118
38	13	A	Torquay U	W	1-0	0-0	—	Sorrell	4090
39	20	H	Bury	W	1-0	0-0	—	Evans	3820
40	24	A	Scunthorpe U	L	0-2	0-1	1		2810
41	May 1	H	Lincoln C	D	1-1	0-0	2	Bodley	4422
42	8	A	Crewe Alex	L	1-4	1-3	3	Carter	4264

Final League Position: 3

GOALSCORERS

League (66): Bull 17 (3 pens), Carter 11, Stein B 8, Payne 5, Showler 5, Evans 4, Barnett 2, Bodley 2, Hoddle 2, Lowe 2, Sorrell 2, Huxford 1, Lynch 1, Willis 1, own goals 3.
Coca Cola Cup (2): Bull 2 (2 pens).
FA Cup (1): Carter.

Phillips 42	Huxford 33	Cooper 17	Bodley 33	Howell 23	Horton 28	Willis 6	Carter 26 + 15	Bull 41	Payne 37	Showler 30 + 2	Barnett 36	Stein B 17 + 23	Hoddle 1 + 4	Lowe 29 + 7	Hunt 10 + 9	Naylor 24 + 1	Lynch 6 + 2	Hayrettin — + 2	Evans 5 + 13	Wilson 9	Sorrell 8	Oxbrow 1	Match No.
1	2	3	4	5	6	7	8	9	10	11													1
1	2	3	4		6	7	8	9	*10*	11		5	12	14									2
1	2	3	4		6	7	8	9		11		5	12	*10*	14								3
1	2	3	4		6	7	8	9		11		5	12		14	*10*							4
1	2	3	4		6	7	8	9	*10*	11		5	12		14								5
1	2	3	4		6	*7*	8	9		11		5	12		10	14							6
1	2	3	4		6		8	9		11		5	12	14	10	*7*							7
1	2	3	4		6		8	9		11		5	12	14	10	*7*							8
1		3	4	2	6		8	9	7	*11*		5	12		10		14						9
1		3	4	2	6		8	9	*7*	11		5	12	14	10								10
1	2	3		4	6		8	9	7	11		5		10	12								11
1	2	3		4	6		8	9	7	11		5	12	*10*	14								12
1	*2*		4		6		8	9	7	11		5	12	10	14	3							13
1	*2*		4		6		8	9	7	11		5	12	10	14	3							14
1		*4*	2		6		8	9	7	11		5	12	10	14	3							15
1	2		4		6		8	9	7	11		5	12	*10*		3	14						16
1		3	4	5	6		8	9	7	11	*2*	12	10				14						17
1	2	3	4	5	6		12	9	7	14		8	*10*	11									18
1	2	*3*	4		6	*8*		7	11	5	9	10		14	12								19
1	2	*3*	4		6		12	9	7	11	5	8	10				14						20
1	2	3	4		6		12	9	7		5	8	*10*	11	14								21
1	2		4		6		12	9	7	11	5	8	*10*		14	3							22
1	2		4		6		8	9	7	*11*	5	12	10	14		3							23
1	2		4		*6*		8	9	7	11	5	12	10			3	14						24
1	2		4				*8*	9	7	11	5	12	10			3	14			6			25
1	2		4				*8*	9	7	11	5	12	10			3	14			6			26
1	2		4	6			12	9	7		5	8	*10*			3	11		14				27
1	2		4	6			12	9	7		5	8	*10*			3	11		14				28
1	2		4				12	9	7		5	8	*10*			3	11		14	6			29
1	2		4				12	9	7		5	8	10			3	*11*		14	6			30
1	2		4	6			8	9	7		5	12	10	14		*3*	11						31
1	2		4	5	*6*		8	9	7	11		12	10			3			14				32
1	2		4	5			9	7				8		11		3			10	6			33
1	2		4	5			12	9	7	14		8		6	11	3			10				34
1	2		4	5			12	9	7		8	14	11			3			*10*	6			35
1		4	2				12	9	7	11	5	8				3			10	6			36
1		4	2				12	9	7	11	5	8	14			3			10	*6*			37
1		4	*2*				12	9	7	11	5	8	14			3			10	6			38
1	2		*4*				12	9	7	11	5	8				3		14	10	6			39
1	2		4				12	9	7	11	5	8				3		14	*10*	6			40
1		4					8	9	7		5	12	14		11	3			10		*6*	2	41
1		4	2				8	9	7		5	12	*6*	14	3			11	10				42

Coca Cola Cup	First Round	Peterborough U (a)	0-4
		(h)	2-2
FA Cup	First Round	Bournemouth (a)	0-0
		(h)	1-2

BARNET

Player and Position	Ht	Wt	Date	Birth Place	Source	Clubs	League App	Gls
Goalkeepers								
Mark Flashman*			25 6 71	London		Barnet	—	—
Andy Pape†	6 0	12 00	22 3 62	London	Enfield	Barnet	36	—
Gary Phillips	6 0	14 00	20 9 61	St Albans		WBA	—	—
					Barnet	Brentford	143	—
						Reading	24	—
						Hereford U	6	—
						Barnet	48	—
Defenders								
Tim Alexander	6 0	12 00	29 3 74	Chertsey	Wimbledon	Barnet	—	—
Dave Barnett	6 0	12 08	16 4 67	London	Windsor & Eton	Colchester U	20	—
						WBA	—	—
						Walsall	5	—
					Kidderminster H	Barnet	40	2
Mick Bodley	5 11	12 00	14 9 67	Hayes	Apprentice	Chelsea	6	1
						Northampton T	20	—
						Barnet	69	3
David Howell	6 0	12 00	10 10 58	London	Enfield	Barnet	57	3
Richard Huxford	5 10	11 06	25 7 69	Scunthorpe	Kettering T	Barnet	33	1
Dominic Naylor	5 9	11 07	12 8 70	Watford	Trainee	Watford	—	—
						Halifax T	6	1
					Barnet	Barnet	51	—
Darren Oxbrow†	6 1	12 06	1 9 69	Ipswich	Trainee	Ipswich T	—	—
						Maidstone U	85	2
						Colchester U	16	4
						Barnet	1	—
Paul Wilson	5 9	11 04	26 9 64	London	Barking	Barnet	34	1
Midfield								
Geoff Cooper‡	5 10	11 00	27 12 60	Kingston	Bognor Regis	Brighton	7	—
					Barnet	Barnet	31	1
Nicky Evans	6 0	11 10	6 7 58	Bedford	Wycombe W	Barnet	27	5
Hakan Hayrettin‡	5 9	11 02	4 2 70	London	Trainee	Leyton Orient	—	—
					Barnet	Barnet	6	—
						Torquay U (loan)	4	—
Carl Hoddle*	6 4	11 00	8 3 67	Harlow	Bishop's Stortford	Leyton Orient	28	2
						Barnet	18	2
Duncan Horton	5 10	11 12	18 2 67	Maidstone	Welling U	Barnet	57	3
Kenny Lowe	6 1	11 04	6 11 64	Sedgefield	Apprentice	Hartlepool U	54	3
					Barrow	Scarborough	4	—
					Barrow	Barnet	72	5
Derek Payne	5 7	10 01	26 4 67	Edgware	Hayes	Barnet	51	6
Tony Sorrell‡	5 11	12 04	17 10 66	London	Bishop's Stortford	Maidstone U	55	8
						Peterborough U	—	—
						Colchester U	5	1
						Barnet	8	2
Edwin Stein‡	5 10	11 00	28 6 55	Cape Town	Dagenham	Barnet	1	—
Forwards								
Gary Bull	5 9	11 07	12 6 66	West Bromwich		Southampton	—	—
						Cambridge U	19	4
					Barnet	Barnet	83	37
Mark Carter	5 9	11 06	17 12 60	Liverpool	Runcorn	Barnet	77	30
Jonathan Hunt	5 10	11 00	2 11 71	London		Barnet	33	—

BARNET

Colours: Amber shirts, black shorts, amber stockings. **Change colours:** White shirts, red shorts, white stockings.

Foundation: Barnet Football Club was formed in 1888, disbanded in 1901. A club known as Alston Works FC was then formed and in 1906 changed its name to Barnet Alston FC. In 1912 it combined with The Avenue to become Barnet and Alston.

First Football League game: 17 August, 1991, Division 4, v Crewe Alex (h) L 4-7 – Phillips; Blackford, Cooper (Murphy), Horton, Bodley (Stein), Johnson, Showler, Carter (2), Bull (2), Lowe, Evans.

Managers: (since 1946) Lester Finch, George Wheeler, Dexter Adams, Tommy Coleman, Gerry Ward, Gordon Ferry, Brian Kelly, Bill Meadows, Barry Fry, Roger Thompson, Don McAllister, Barry Fry, Edwin Stein April 1993–.

Player and Position	Ht	Wt	Date	Birth Place	Source	Clubs	League App	Gls
Tony Lynch	5 8	10 08	20 1 66	Paddington	Maidstone U	Brentford	45	6
					Wealdstone	Barnet	14	1
Gavin MacPherson*	6 0	12 00	22 3 71	Watford		Barnet	—	—
Paul Showler	5 10	11 06	10 10 66	Doncaster	Altrincham	Barnet	71	12
Brian Stein‡	5 10	11 08	19 10 57	S. Africa	Edgware T	Luton T	388	128
					Caen	Luton T	39	3
						Barnet	40	8

**Non-Contract
Oxbrow, Darren W; Pape, Andrew M.

**Non-Contract Players who are retained must be re-signed before they are eligible to play in League matches.

BARNSLEY 1992–93 *Back row (left to right):* Gerry Taggart, Andy Rammell, Phil Gridelet, David Currie, Lee Butler, David Watson, Warren Godfrey, Steve Davis, Charlie Bishop, Mark Robinson.

Centre row: Mick Wadsworth (Coach), Eric Winstanley (Youth Team Coach), Mark Mercer, Wayne Bullimore, Mark Burton, Nicky Eaden, Jamie Robinson, Brendan O'Connell, John Pearson, John Benson (Chief Scout), Steve Stafford (Physio).

Front row: Dean Connelly, Greg Morgan, Deiniol Graham, Mark Smith, Mel Machin (Manager), Gary Fleming, Owen Archdeacon, Neil Redfearn, Andrew Liddell.

Division 1   **BARNSLEY**

Oakwell Ground, Grove St, Barnsley. Telephone Barnsley (0226) 295353. Clubcall: 0898 121152. Commercial Office: 0226 286718. Fax: 0226 201000.

Ground capacity: 26,586 (15,000 under cover).

Record attendance: 40,255 v Stoke C, FA Cup 5th rd, 15 February 1936.

Record receipts: Not disclosed.

Pitch measurements: 110yd × 75yd.

President: Arthur Raynor. *Vice-presidents: Chairman:* J. A. Dennis.

Directors: C. B. Taylor (Vice-chairman), C. H. Harrison, M. R. Hayselden, J. N. Kelly, S. Manley, I. D. Potter.

Player-Manager: Viv Anderson. *Assistant Manager:* Danny Wilson.

Coach: Michael Wadsworth. *Physio:* Steve Stafford.

Secretary: Michael Spinks. *Commercial Manager:* Gerry Whewall.

Year Formed: 1887. *Turned Professional:* 1888. *Ltd Co.:* 1899.

Previous Name: Barnsley St Peter's, 1887–97.

Club Nickname: 'The Tykes', 'Reds' or 'Colliers'.

Record League Victory: 9–0 v Loughborough T, Division 2, 28 January 1899 – Greaves; McCartney, Nixon; Porteous, Burleigh, Howard; Davis (4), Hepworth (1), Lees (1), McCullough (1), Jones (2). 9–0 v Accrington S, Division 3 (N), 3 February 1934 – Ellis; Cookson, Shotton; Harper, Henderson, Whitworth; Spence (2), Smith (1), Blight (4), Andrews (1), Ashton (1).

Record Cup Victory: 6–0 v Blackpool, FA Cup, 1st rd replay, 20 January 1910 – Mearns; Downs, Ness; Glendinning, Boyle (1), Utley; Bartrop, Gadsby (1), Lillycrop (2), Tufnell (2), Forman. 6–0 v Peterborough U, League Cup, 1st rd, 2nd leg, 15 September 1981 – Horn; Joyce, Chambers, Glavin (2), Banks, McCarthy, Evans, Parker (2), Aylott (1), McHale, Barrowclough (1).

Record Defeat: 0–9 v Notts Co, Division 2, 19 November 1927.

Most League Points (2 for a win): 67, Division 3 (N), 1938–39.

Most League Points (3 for a win): 74, Division 2, 1988–89.

Most League Goals: 118, Division 3 (N), 1933–34.

Highest League Scorer in Season: Cecil McCormack, 33, Division 2, 1950–51.

Most League Goals in Total Aggregate: Ernest Hine, 123, 1921–26 and 1934–38.

Most Capped Player: Gerry Taggart, 21, Northern Ireland.

Most League Appearances: Barry Murphy, 514, 1962–78.

Record Transfer Fee Received: £1,500,000 from Nottingham F for Carl Tiler, May 1991.

Record Transfer Fee Paid: £250,000 to Oldham Ath for David Currie, September 1991.

Football League Record: 1898 Elected to Division 2; 1932–34 Division 3 (N); 1934–38 Division 2; 1938–39 Division 3 (N); 1946–53 Division 2; 1953–55 Division 3 (N); 1955–59 Division 2; 1959–65 Division 3; 1965–68 Division 4; 1968–72 Division 3; 1972–79 Division 4; 1979–81 Division 3; 1981–92 Division 2; 1992– Division 1.

Honours: Football League: best season: 3rd, Division 2, 1914–15, 1921–22; Division 3 (N) – Champions 1933–34, 1938–39, 1954–55; Runners-up 1953–54; Division 3 – Runners-up 1980–81; Division 4 – Runners-up 1967–68; Promoted 1978–79. *FA Cup:* Winners 1912; Runners-up 1910. *Football League Cup:* best season: 5th rd, 1981–82.

BARNSLEY 1992—93 LEAGUE RECORD

Match No.	Date		Venue	Opponents	Result		H/T Score	Lg. Pos.	Goalscorers	Atten dance
1	Aug	16	H	West Ham U	L	0-1	0-1	—		6791
2		22	A	Portsmouth	L	0-1	0-0	23		11,473
3		29	H	Millwall	D	0-0	0-0	22		4795
4	Sept	1	H	Wolverhampton W	L	0-1	0-1	—		6906
5		5	A	Notts Co	W	3-1	3-0	18	Taggart, Liddell, Archdeacon	6205
6		12	H	Derby Co	D	1-1	0-0	19	Rammell	8412
7		19	H	Peterborough U	L	1-2	0-1	22	Liddell	5275
8		26	A	Bristol C	L	1-2	1-1	24	O'Connell	8049
9	Oct	3	A	Leicester C	L	1-2	1-0	24	Biggins	12,290
10		10	H	Luton T	W	3-0	3-0	22	Biggins 2, Pearson	5261
11		17	A	Oxford U	D	0-0	0-0	21		4422
12		24	H	Brentford	W	3-2	1-2	18	Biggins, Pearson 2	4928
13		31	A	Swindon T	L	0-1	0-1	20		7784
14	Nov	3	A	Bristol R	W	5-1	1-0	—	Rammell, Redfearn, O'Connell, Taggart, Robinson M	5019
15		7	H	Watford	L	0-1	0-0	19		6193
16		14	A	Cambridge U	W	2-1	2-0	18	Biggins 2	3971
17		21	H	Birmingham C	W	1-0	0-0	16	Currie	5603
18		28	H	Charlton Ath	W	1-0	1-0	14	Biggins	5851
19	Dec	5	A	Sunderland	L	1-2	0-2	16	Archdeacon	17,395
20		13	H	Newcastle U	W	1-0	0-0	—	O'Connell	13,263
21		19	A	Southend U	L	0-3	0-1	14		3629
22		26	A	Grimsby T	L	2-4	0-2	15	Taggart, Currie	8242
23		28	H	Tranmere R	W	3-1	2-0	15	Currie, Rammell, Redfearn	8204
24	Jan	9	A	Peterborough U	D	1-1	0-1	15	Rammell	6008
25		16	H	Bristol C	W	2-1	2-0	12	O'Connell 2	5423
26		27	A	Wolverhampton W	L	0-1	0-0	—		11,342
27		30	H	Portsmouth	D	1-1	0-0	12	Archdeacon (pen)	6551
28	Feb	6	A	West Ham U	D	1-1	1-1	—	Rammell	14,101
29		10	A	Derby Co	L	0-3	0-1	—		13,096
30		20	A	Millwall	W	4-0	3-0	13	Archdeacon 2, Biggins 2	8034
31		27	A	Luton T	D	2-2	0-1	14	O'Connell, Currie	7595
32	Mar	6	H	Leicester C	L	2-3	1-1	14	Rammell 2	9452
33		9	H	Cambridge U	W	2-0	1-0	—	Biggins, Redfearn	5445
34		13	A	Watford	W	2-1	1-0	13	Biggins 2	5785
35		16	H	Notts Co	D	0-0	0-0	—		6372
36		21	H	Sunderland	W	2-0	1-0	—	Biggins 2	7278
37		23	A	Birmingham C	L	0-3	0-1	—		12,664
38		27	H	Bristol R	W	2-1	1-0	9	Graham, Archdeacon	5220
39	Apr	3	A	Charlton Ath	D	0-0	0-0	10		6370
40		7	A	Newcastle U	L	0-6	0-2	—		29,460
41		10	H	Grimsby T	L	0-2	0-1	12		4958
42		12	A	Tranmere R	L	1-2	0-1	13	Taggart	6436
43		17	A	Southend U	W	3-1	1-1	12	Williams 3	3855
44		24	H	Oxford U	L	0-1	0-1	13		5523
45	May	1	A	Brentford	L	1-3	1-2	13	Williams	7958
46		8	H	Swindon T	W	1-0	1-0	13	Williams	6031

Final League Position: 13

GOALSCORERS

League (56): Biggins 14, Rammell 7, Archdeacon 6 (1 pen), O'Connell 6, Williams 5, Currie 4, Taggart 4, Pearson 3, Redfearn 3, Liddell 2, Graham 1, Robinson M 1.
Coca Cola Cup (2): Liddell 1, Redfearn 1.
FA Cup (7): Rammell 3, Redfearn 2, Archdeacon 1, own goal 1.

Butler 28	Robinson M 28 + 1	Taggart 44	Bishop 43	Fleming 46	Bullimore 10 + 7	Currie 23 + 12	Rammell 27 + 3	Pearson 21 + 1	Redfearn 46	Archdeacon 37 + 1	Liddell 16 + 5	Smith 3 + 1	Graham 9 + 6	Burton 5	O'Connell 35 + 5	Biggins 32 + 2	Robinson J 8	Godfrey 1 + 7	Connelly — + 1	Williams 4 + 4	Watson 5	Davis 10 + 1	Whitehead 13	Hendon 6	Jackson 1 + 2	Gridelet 2	Bennett 2	Feeney — + 2	Eaden 1 + 1	Match No.
1	2	3	4	5	6	7	8	9	10	11	12																			1
1	2	3	4	5	6	12	8	9	10	11	7	14																		2
1	2	3	4	5	6	8	12	9	10	11	7		14																	3
1	2	3	4	5	6	8	12	9	10	11	7		14																	4
1	14	3	4	5		12	8	9	10	11	7	2			6															5
1		3	4	5			8	9	10	11	7	2			6	12														6
1		3	4	5		12	8	9	10	11	7	2			6	14														7
1	2	3	4	5	14	12		9	10	11	7				6	8														8
1		5	4	2			8	9	10	11	12				6	14	7	3												9
1	2		4	5	6		8	9	10	11	12					7		3	14											10
1	2	5	4	3	6		8	9	10	11	12					7														11
1	2	5	4	3			8	9	10	11					6	7		12												12
1	2	5	4	3		12		9	10	11	8				6	7														13
1	2	5	4	3			8		10	11	9				6	7		12	14											14
1	2	5	4	3			8		10	11	9				6	7		12												15
1	2	5	4	3		12		9	10	11	8				6	7														16
1	2	5	4	3		12		9	10	11	8				6	7														17
1	2	5	4	3		12		9	10	11	8				6	7														18
1	2	5	4	3		12	8	9	10	11					6	7														19
1	2	5	4	3			8	9	10	11	12				6	7														20
1	2	5	4	3		12	8		10	11	9				6	7				14										21
1	2	5	4	3		7	8		10	11	9				6			12		14										22
1	2	5	4	3		9	8		10	11	12				6	7														23
1	2	5	4	3		9	8	12	10	11					6	7														24
1	2	5	4	3		9	8		10	11					6	7														25
1	2	5	4	3		7	8	9	10	11					6			12												26
1	2	5	4	3		7	8	9	10	11					6															27
1	2	5	4	3		7	8	9	10	11	12				6															28
	2	5	4	3		7	8		10	11					6	12	9						1							29
	2	5		3			9	8	10	11					6	7				4			1							30
	2	5		3			9	8	10	11					6	7				4			1							31
	2	5	4	3			9	8	10	11	12				6	7				14			1							32
		5		3			9	8	10	11	2				6	7		12		4			1							33
		5	2	3		12	9	8	10	11					6	7				4			1							34
		5	2	3			8	9	10	11					6	7				4			1							35
		5	2	3			9		10	11	12				6	7				4		8	1							36
		5	2	3		14	9		10	11					6	7		12		4		8	1							37
		5	4	3		14	9		10	11	8				6	7		12					1	2						38
		5	4	3			8	14	10	11	9				6	7		12					1	2						39
		5	4	3			8	9	10	11	12				6	7				14			1	2						40
		5	4	3		14	12	9	10	11					6	7						8	1	2						41
		5	4	3			8	9	10	11					6	7		12			1		14	2						42
			4	3		14		9	10	11						7					1	8		2	5		6	12		43
		5	4	3		12		9	10	11					6	7					1	8		2						44
		5	4	3			8	9	10	11					6	7					1			2				12	14	45
		5	4	3		14	8	9	10	11	12				6						1			2					7	46

Coca Cola Cup	First Round	Grimsby T (a)	1-1
		(h)	1-1
FA Cup	Third Round	Leicester C (a)	2-2
		(h)	1-1
	Fourth Round	West Ham U (h)	4-1
	Fifth Round	Manchester C (a)	0-2

BARNSLEY

Player and Position	Ht	Wt	Date	Birth Place	Source	Clubs	League App	Gls
Goalkeepers								
Lee Butler	6 2	14 02	30 5 66	Sheffield	Haworth Colliery	Lincoln C	30	—
						Aston Villa	8	—
						Hull C (loan)	4	—
						Barnsley	71	—
David Watson	5 11	12 00	10 11 73	Barnsley	Trainee	Barnsley	5	—
Philip Whitehead	6 3	13 07	17 12 69	Halifax	Trainee	Halifax T	42	—
						Barnsley	16	—
						Halifax T (loan)	9	—
						Scunthorpe U (loan)	8	—
						Scunthorpe U (loan)	8	—
						Bradford C (loan)	6	—
Defenders								
Charlie Bishop	6 0	12 01	16 2 68	Nottingham	Stoke C	Watford	—	—
						Bury	114	6
						Barnsley	71	—
Steve Davis	6 0	12 07	26 7 65	Birmingham	Stoke C	Crewe Alex	145	1
						Burnley	147	11
						Barnsley	20	—
Nicky Eaden	6 0	12 00	12 12 72	Sheffield	Trainee	Barnsley	2	—
Gary Fleming	5 9	11 03	17 2 67	Londonderry	Apprentice	Nottingham F	74	—
						Manchester C	14	—
						Notts Co (loan)	3	—
						Barnsley	144	—
Marvin Harriott			20 4 74	Dulwich	West Ham U	Oldham Ath	—	—
						Barnsley	—	—
Mark Mercer*	6 1	12 00	21 6 74	Barnsley	Trainee	Barnsley	—	—
Jamie Robinson	6 0	12 03	26 2 72	Liverpool	Trainee	Liverpool	—	—
						Barnsley	8	—
Gerry Taggart	6 1	12 03	18 10 70	Belfast	Trainee	Manchester C	12	1
						Barnsley	133	11
Midfield								
Troy Bennett§			25 12 75	Barnsley	Trainee	Barnsley	2	—
Wayne Bullimore	5 9	10 06	12 9 70	Sutton-in-Ashfield	Trainee	Manchester U	—	—
						Barnsley	35	1
Mark Burton	5 8	11 07	7 5 73	Barnsley	Trainee	Barnsley	5	—
Mark Feeney§			26 7 74	Derry	Trainee	Barnsley	2	—
Warren Godfrey	5 11	11 02	31 3 73	Liverpool	Trainee	Liverpool	—	—
						Barnsley	8	—
Phil Gridelet	5 11	12 00	30 4 67	Edgware	Barnet	Barnsley	6	—
						Rotherham U (loan)	9	—
Andrew Liddell	5 8	10.05	28 6 73	Leeds	Trainee	Barnsley	22	2
Gregory Morgan	5 7	10 00	12 10 73	Batley	Trainee	Barnsley	—	—
Neil Redfearn	5 10	12 09	20 6 65	Dewsbury	Nottingham F	Bolton W	35	1
						Lincoln C (loan)	10	1
						Lincoln C	90	12
						Doncaster R	46	14
						Crystal Palace	57	10
						Watford	24	3
						Oldham Ath	62	16
						Barnsley	82	7
Forwards								
Owen Archdeacon	5 9	10 08	4 3 66	Greenock	Gourock U	Celtic	76	7
						Barnsley	144	17

BARNSLEY

Colours: Red shirts, white trim, white shorts, red stockings. **Change colours:** Yellow shirts, black shorts, yellow stockings.

Foundation: Many clubs owe their inception to the church and Barnsley are among them, for they were formed in 1887 by the Rev. T. T. Preedy, curate of Barnsley St. Peter's and went under that name until it was dropped in 1897 a year before being admitted to the Second Division of the Football League.

First Football League game: 1 September, 1898, Division 2, v Lincoln C (a) L 0-1 – Fawcett; McArtney, Nixon; King, Burleigh, Porteous; Davis, Lees, Murray, McCullough, McGee.

Did you know: Barnsley fielded probably the lightest player to have appeared in the Football League in inside-right Walter Hepworth, who in the 1896–97 season weighed 7 st 5 lb (46.72 kg).

Managers (and Secretary-Managers)
Arthur Fairclough 1898–1901*, John McCartney 1901–04*, Arthur Fairclough 1904–12, John Hastie 1912–14, Percy Lewis 1914–19, Peter Sant 1919–26, John Commins 1926–29, Arthur Fairclough 1929–30, Brough Fletcher 1930–37, Angus Seed 1937–53, Tim Ward 1953–60, Johnny Steele 1960–71 (continued as GM), John McSeveney 1971–72, Johnny Steele (GM) 1972–73, Jim Iley 1973–78, Allan Clarke 1978–80, Norman Hunter 1980–84, Bobby Collins 1984–85, Allan Clarke 1985–89, Mel Machin 1989–93, Viv Anderson June 1993–.

Player and Position	Ht	Wt	Birth Date	Birth Place	Source	Clubs	League App	Gls
Wayne Biggins	5 10	11 00	20 11 61	Sheffield	Apprentice Matlock Town and King's Lynn	Lincoln C	8	1
						Burnley	78	29
						Norwich C	79	16
						Manchester C	32	9
						Stoke C	122	46
						Barnsley	34	14
David Currie	5 11	12 09	27 11 62	Stockton	Local	Middlesbrough	113	31
						Darlington	76	33
						Barnsley	80	30
						Nottingham F	8	1
						Oldham Ath	31	3
						Barnsley	72	11
						Rotherham U (loan)	5	2
Deniol Graham	5 10	10 05	4 10 69	Cannock	Trainee	Manchester U	2	—
						Barnsley	36	2
						Preston NE (loan)	8	—
Chris Jackson	6 0	12 00	16 1 76	Barnsley	Trainee	Barnsley	3	—
Brendan O'Connell	5 10	10 09	12 11 66	London		Portsmouth	—	—
						Exeter C	81	19
						Burnley	64	17
						Huddersfield T (loan)	11	1
						Barnsley	132	21
John Pearson*	6 3	13 00	1 9 63	Sheffield	Apprentice	Sheffield W	105	24
						Charlton Ath	61	15
						Leeds U	99	12
						Rotherham U (loan)	11	5
						Barnsley	32	4
						Hull C (loan)	15	—
Andy Rammell	5 10	11 07	10 2 67	Nuneaton	Atherstone U	Manchester U	—	—
						Barnsley	107	27
Gareth Williams	5 10	11 08	12 3 67	Isle of Wight	Gosport Borough	Aston Villa	12	—
						Barnsley	25	5
						Hull C (loan)	4	—

Trainees
Bennett, Troy; Bochenski, Simon; Brooke, David; Driver, Christopher; Feeney, Mark A; Gregg, John H; Hanby, Robert J; Jebson, Carl M; Jones, Scott; Lumb, Richard M; Peacock, Dennis J; Shelley, Steven P; Yates, Kevin.

Associated Schoolboys
Arkle, Paul I; Baker, Damian; Clayton, Steven; Fearon, Dean A; Green, Simon; Gregory, Andrew; Halstead, Peter; Hayes, Shaun A; Hughes, Russell; Hume, Mark A; Jackson, Darren; Jones, Dean S; McClare, Sean P; Morgan, Christopher P; Moses, Adrian P; Newsam, Andrew; Owen, Daniel J. M; Rawlin, Andrew C; Shaw, Ian; Sollitt, Adam; Standish, Mark A; Swallow, Christopher J; Thorpe, Andrew D; Townsend, Peter; Wainwright, Jonathan M; Webster, Stephen; Wragg, Jamie; Wright, Lee A.

BIRMINGHAM CITY 1992-93   Back row (left to right): Simon Sturridge, Louie Donowa, Paul Tait, Martin Thomas, Martin Hicks, John Gayle, Andy Gosney, Matthew Fox, Jason Beckford, Paul Holmes.

Centre row: Brian Caswell (Reserve Coach), Graham Potter, Trevor Matthewson, Nigel Gleghorn, Dean Peer, Paul Mardon, Ian Atkins (Assistant Manager), Mark Sale, Alan O'Neill, David Foy, Darren Rogers, David Rennie, Tony Taylor (Youth Coach).

Front row: Paul Heath (Physio), Ian Rodgerson, Carl Adams, Eric Hogan, Paul Jones, Darran Rowbotham, Mark Cooper, Ian Clarkson, John Frain, Terry Cooper (Manager).

Division 1   BIRMINGHAM CITY

St Andrews, Birmingham B9 4NH. Telephone 021–772 0101. Lottery office/Souvenir shop: 021 772 1245. Clubcall: 0891 121188. Fax: 021 766 7866. Club Soccer Shop: 021 766 8274.

Ground capacity: 28,235.

Record attendance: 66,844 v Everton, FA Cup 5th rd,11 February 1939.

Record receipts: £116,372.50 v Nottingham Forest, FA Cup 5th rd, 20 February 1988.

Pitch measurements: 115yd × 75yd.

Directors: J. F. Wiseman (Chairman), D. Sullivan, K. Brady, B. H. Slater, A. G. Jones, T. Cooper.

Manager: Terry Cooper. *Assistant Manager:* Trevor Morgan. *Coach:* Tony Taylor. *Physio:* Paul Heath. *Commercial Manager:* Mark Bowler.

Secretary: Alan Jones BA, MBA

Year Formed: 1875. *Turned Professional:* 1885. *Ltd Co.:* 1888.

Previous Names: 1875–88, Small Heath Alliance; 1888, dropped 'Alliance'; became Birmingham 1905; became Birmingham City 1945.

Club Nickname: 'Blues'.

Previous Grounds: 1875, waste ground near Arthur St; 1877, Muntz St, Small Heath; 1906, St Andrews.

Record League Victory: 12–0 v Walsall T Swifts, Division 2, 17 December 1892 – Charnley; Bayley, Jones; Ollis, Jenkyns, Devey; Hallam (2), Walton (3), Mobley (3), Wheldon (2), Hands (2). 12–0 v Doncaster R, Division 2, 11 April 1903 – Dorrington; Goldie, Wassell; Beer, Dougherty (1), Howard; Athersmith (1), Leonard (3), McRoberts (1), Wilcox (4), Field (1). Aston. (1 og).

Record Cup Victory: 9–2 v Burton W, FA Cup, 1st rd, 31 October 1885 – Hedges; Jones, Evetts (1); F. James, Felton, A. James (1); Davenport (2), Stanley (4), Simms, Figures, Morris (1).

Record Defeat: 1–9 v Sheffield W, Division 1, 13 December 1930 and v Blackburn R, Division 1, 5 January 1895.

Most League Points (2 for a win): 59, Division 2, 1947–48.

Most League Points (3 for a win): 82, Division 2, 1984–85.

Most League Goals: 103, Division 2, 1893–94 (only 28 games).

Highest League Scorer in Season: Joe Bradford, 29, Division 1, 1927–28.

Most League Goals in Total Aggregate: Joe Bradford, 249, 1920–35.

Most Capped Player: Malcolm Page, 28, Wales.

Most League Appearances: Frank Womack, 491, 1908–28.

Record Transfer Fee Received: £975,000 from Nottingham F for Trevor Francis, February 1979.

Record Transfer Fee Paid: £350,000 to Derby Co for David Langan, June 1980.

Football League Record: 1892 elected to Division 2; 1894–96 Division 1; 1896–1901 Division 2; 1901–02 Division 1; 1902–03 Division 2; 1903–08 Division 1; 1908–21 Division 2; 1921–39 Division 1; 1946–48 Division 2; 1948–50 Division 1; 1950–1955 Division 2; 1955–65 Division 1; 1965–72 Division 2; 1972–79 Division 1; 1979–80 Division 2; 1980–84 Division 1; 1984–1985 Division 2; 1985–86 Division 1; 1986–89 Division 2; 1989–92 Division 3; 1992– Division 1.

Honours: Football League: Division 1 best season: 6th, 1955–56; Division 2 – Champions 1892–93, 1920–21, 1947–48, 1954–55; Runners-up 1893–94, 1900–01, 1902–03, 1971–72, 1984–85. Division 3 Runners-up 1991–92. *FA Cup:* Runners-up 1931, 1956. *Football League Cup:* Winners 1963. *Leyland Data Cup:* Winners 1991. **European Competitions:** *European Fairs Cup:* 1955–58, 1958–60 (runners-up), 1960–61 (runners-up), 1961–62.

BIRMINGHAM CITY 1992—93 LEAGUE RECORD

Match No.	Date		Venue	Opponents	Result		H/T Score	Lg. Pos.	Goalscorers	Atten dance
1	Aug	16	H	Notts Co	W	1-0	1-0	—	Donowa	10,614
2		22	A	Cambridge U	W	3-0	2-0	5	Rennie 2, Donowa	5015
3		30	H	Grimsby T	W	2-1	1-1	—	Gleghorn, Rowbotham	6807
4	Sept	1	H	Southend U	W	2-0	1-0	—	Tait, Beckford	8234
5		5	A	Portsmouth	L	0-4	0-1	4		12,152
6		12	A	Millwall	D	0-0	0-0	4		8581
7		19	A	Luton T	D	1-1	0-1	4	Rowbotham	8481
8		27	H	Wolverhampton W	L	0-4	0-4	—		14,391
9	Oct	3	A	Oxford U	D	0-0	0-0	8		7096
10		10	H	Leicester C	L	0-2	0-1	8		13,443
11		17	A	Tranmere R	L	0-4	0-1	10		7901
12		24	H	Bristol R	W	2-1	1-0	10	Matthewson, Frain (pen)	9874
13	Nov	1	A	Charlton Ath	D	0-0	0-0	—		4445
14		4	H	Newcastle U	L	2-3	2-3	—	Speedie, Potter	14,376
15		7	A	Bristol C	L	0-3	0-1	17		10,008
16		21	A	Barnsley	L	0-1	0-0	18		5603
17		28	A	West Ham U	L	1-3	1-1	19	Rodgerson	15,004
18	Dec	5	H	Brentford	L	1-3	1-2	20	Frain	8582
19		12	A	Derby Co	L	1-3	1-0	21	Speedie	16,662
20		19	H	Watford	D	2-2	0-1	21	Peschisolido, Frain	7182
21	Jan	9	H	Luton T	W	2-1	1-1	19	Frain (pen), Gayle	9601
22		12	A	Swindon T	D	0-0	0-0	—		14,398
23		17	A	Wolverhampton W	L	1-2	1-0	—	Tait	13,560
24		22	H	Peterborough U	W	2-0	2-0	—	Gayle, Frain (pen)	10,277
25		27	A	Southend U	L	0-4	0-3	—		4065
26		30	H	Cambridge U	L	0-2	0-1	20		9425
27	Feb	6	A	Notts Co	L	1-3	0-2	22	Potter	8550
28		9	H	Millwall	D	0-0	0-0	—		8504
29		13	H	Portsmouth	L	2-3	0-1	22	Sturridge, Peschisolido	10,935
30		20	A	Grimsby T	D	1-1	0-1	22	Gayle	5237
31		28	A	Leicester C	L	1-2	1-1	—	Matthewson	10,284
32	Mar	6	H	Oxford U	W	1-0	1-0	22	Peschisolido	11,104
33		9	A	Peterborough U	L	1-2	1-1	—	Peschisolido	7600
34		13	H	Bristol C	L	0-1	0-1	23		15,611
35		16	H	Sunderland	W	1-0	0-0	—	Peschisolido	10,934
36		20	A	Brentford	W	2-0	0-0	21	Peschisolido 2	7532
37		23	H	Barnsley	W	3-0	1-0	—	Saville 2, Moulden	12,664
38		28	A	Newcastle U	D	2-2	2-0	—	Saville, Rodgerson	27,087
39	Apr	3	H	West Ham U	L	1-2	1-0	21	Saville	19,053
40		6	H	Derby Co	D	1-1	0-1	—	Moulden	15,424
41		10	A	Sunderland	W	2-1	1-1	19	Moulden, Saville	16,382
42		12	H	Swindon T	L	4-6	2-1	19	Peer, Frain, Moulden, Saville	17,903
43		17	A	Watford	L	0-1	0-1	22		9186
44		24	H	Tranmere R	D	0-0	0-0	20		14,600
45	May	1	A	Bristol R	D	3-3	0-2	23	Saville, Mardon, Smith	5150
46		8	H	Charlton Ath	W	1-0	0-0	19	Moulden	22,234

Final League Position: 19

GOALSCORERS

League (50): Peschisolido 7, Saville 7, Frain 6 (3 pens), Moulden 5, Gayle 3, Donowa 2, Matthewson 2, Potter 2, Rennie 2, Rodgerson 2, Rowbotham 2, Speedie 2, Tait 2, Beckford 1, Gleghorn 1, Mardon 1, Peer 1, Smith 1, Sturridge 1.
Coca Cola Cup (1): Sale 1.
FA Cup (0).

Gosney 21	Clarkson 25 + 3	Frain 45	Rennie 15 + 3	Rogers 14 + 3	Mardon 18 + 3	Donowa 18 + 3	Tait 28	Sale 9 + 6	Gleghorn 11	Sturridge 15 + 5	Rodgerson 24 + 7	Hicks 16 + 2	Cooper 3 + 3	Beckford 3	Rowbotham 10 + 4	Matthewson 40	Peer 13	Sealey 12	Holmes 12	Gayle 17 + 2	Speedie 10	Potter 16 + 2	Peschisolido 16 + 3	Fenwick 3 + 7	Fitzpatrick 7	Quinn 1 + 3	Foy 3	Thomas 5	Catlin 8	Hiley 7	Parris 13	Moulden 13	Smith 13	Dryden 11	Saville 10	Scott 1	Match No.
1	2	3	4	5	6	7	8	9	10	11	12																										1
1	2	3	4	5	6	7	8	9	10	11		12																									2
1	2	3		5	6	7	8	*9*	10		12		4	11	14																						3
1	2	3		5		7	8	9	10				4	11		6																					4
1	2	3		5	12	7	8	9	10				4	11	14	6																					5
1	2	3		5		7	8	9	10				4		11	6																					6
1	2	3		5		7	*8*	9	10		12		4	14	11	6																					7
1	2	3		5		7	8	14	10	9	12				11	6	4																				8
	2	3		5		9	8	12	10						7	6	11	4	1																		9
	2	3	14	5	11		*8*	12	10						7	6	9	4	1																		10
		3	8	5		11			10						7	6	9	4	1	2	12																11
		3	4			9									7	5	11	6	1	2	8	10															12
12		4		11			*8*	7	5	14	10				6		1	2	9	3																	13
	3	*4*		12	8	10	7	5	14						6	1	2	9	11																		14
	2	3	*4*	8	10	7	5	14	11						6	1		9	12																		15
	11	12	4	*10*	7	5									6	1	2	8	9	3	14																16
	10	5	11	4	12	7									6	1	2	8	9	3																	17
	5	6	10	8	12	11	7								2	1	9	3	4																		18
	2	5	11	10	12	7	6								1	8	9	3	14	*4*																	19
	2	11	4	12	*10*	7	5								6	1	8	9	3	14																	20
1	2	11	14	10	12	5									6	8	9	3	7	*4*																	21
1	2	11	9	10		5									6	8	3	7	4																		22
1	2	11	7	10		5									6	8	3	9	4	12																	23
1	2	11	7	10		5									6	8	3	9	4																		24
1	2	11	7	8	10	5									6		3	9	4	12																	25
1	2	11	14	5	10	7		8	12						6		*3*	9	4																		26
1	2	11		5	10	7	8								12	6	3	9	4																		27
1		11	4	5	10	12	7								6	2	*8*	3	9	14																	28
1		11	*4*	5	12	7									6	2	3	9	14	8	10																29
1		3	*4*	5	11										7	6	2	8	9	14	12	10															30
	3	12	5	7		*11*	14								6	2	8	9	4	10	1																31
	3		5	12	10	11	7								6	4	2	8	*9*	14	1																32
	3		5	12	10	11	7								6	4	2	8	*9*	14	1																33
	3		5	10		12									*6*	8	9	14	1	2	4	7	11														34
	3		5			12									6	10	8	9		1	2	4	7	11													35
12	3					8									6	*10*		9	14	1	2	4	7	11	5												36
	3					8									6	10				1	2	4	7	11	5	9											37
	3					8									6	10				1	2	4	7	11	5	9											38
	2	3				12	8								6	10				1		4	7	11	5	9											39
1		3	10	6		8											12					4	7	11	5	9	2										40
1	2	3				8									6	10						4	7	11	5	9											41
1	2	3		12		8									6	10						4	7	11	5	9											42
	2	3		12		8									6	10							4	7	11	5	9		1								43
	2	3		10		8									6			12					4	7	11	5	9		1								44
12	*3*			10		14									6		8						4	7	11	5	9		1		2						45
	3			6		8										10							4	7	11	5	9		1		2						46

Coca Cola Cup   First Round   Exeter C (a)   0-0
    (h)   1-4
FA Cup   First Round   Reading (a)   0-1

BIRMINGHAM CITY

Player and Position	Ht	Wt	Date	Birth Place	Source	Clubs	League App	Gls
Goalkeepers								
Andy Gosney	6 4	13 02	8 11 63	Southampton	Apprentice	Portsmouth	48	—
						York C (loan)	5	—
						Birmingham C	21	—
Martin Thomas*	6 1	13 00	28 11 59	Caerphilly	Apprentice	Bristol R	162	—
						Cardiff C (loan)	15	—
						Tottenham H (loan)	—	—
						Southend U (loan)	6	—
						Newcastle U (loan)	3	—
						Newcastle U	115	—
						Middlesbrough (loan)	4	—
						Birmingham C	144	—
						Crystal Palace (loan)	—	—
						Aston Villa (loan)	—	—
Defenders								
Ian Clarkson	5 11	12 00	4 12 70	Birmingham	Trainee	Birmingham C	136	—
Richard Dryden	6 0	11 02	14 6 69	Stroud		Bristol R	13	—
						Exeter C	51	7
						Manchester C (loan)	—	—
						Notts Co	31	1
						Plymouth Arg (loan)	5	—
						Birmingham C	11	—
Paul Fenwick			25 8 69	London	Winnipeg Fury	Birmingham C	10	—
Martin Hicks*	6 3	13 06	27 2 57	Stratford-on-Avon	Stratford T	Charlton Ath	—	—
						Reading	500	23
						Birmingham C	60	1
Paul Mardon	6 0	11 10	14 9 69	Bristol	Trainee	Bristol C	42	—
						Doncaster R (loan)	3	—
						Birmingham C	56	1
Trevor Matthewson	6 1	12 05	12 2 63	Sheffield	Apprentice	Sheffield W	3	—
						Newport Co	75	—
						Stockport Co	80	—
						Lincoln C	83	8
						Birmingham C	168	12
George Parris	5 9	13 00	11 9 64	Ilford	Apprentice	West Ham U	239	12
						Birmingham C	13	—
Graham Potter			20 5 75	Solihull	Trainee	Birmingham C	18	2
Darren Rogers	5 10	11 02	9 4 71	Birmingham	Trainee	WBA	14	1
						Birmingham C	17	—
Richard Scott§			29 9 74	Dudley	Trainee	Birmingham C	1	—
Midfield								
Carl Adams*	5 8	10 00	13 3 74	Marston Green	Trainee	Birmingham C	—	—
Jason Beckford	5 9	12 04	14 2 70	Manchester	Trainee	Manchester C	20	1
						Blackburn R (loan)	4	—
						Port Vale (loan)	5	1
						Birmingham C	7	2
Paul Fitzpatrick*	6 4	12 00	5 10 65	Liverpool		Tranmere R	—	—
						Liverpool	—	—
						Preston NE	—	—
						Bolton W	14	—
						Bristol C	44	7
						Carlisle U	109	4
						Preston NE (loan)	2	—
						Leicester C	27	4
						Birmingham C	7	—
						Bury (loan)	9	—
John Frain	5 7	11 10	8 10 68	Birmingham	Apprentice	Birmingham C	217	21
Scott Hiley	5 9	10 07	27 9 68	Plymouth	Trainee	Exeter C	210	12
						Birmingham C	7	—
Dean Peer	6 2	12 00	8 8 69	Dudley	Trainee	Birmingham C	120	8
						Mansfield T (loan)	10	—
Ian Rodgerson	5 10	10 07	9 4 66	Hereford	Pegasus Juniors	Hereford U	100	6
						Cardiff C	99	4
						Birmingham C	95	13
Darren Rowbotham	5 10	11 05	22 10 66	Cardiff	Trainee	Plymouth Arg	46	2
						Exeter C	118	47
						Torquay U	14	3
						Birmingham C	36	6
						Hereford U (loan)	8	2
						Mansfield T (loan)	4	—

BIRMINGHAM CITY

Colours: Royal blue and white shirts, white shorts, blue stockings with white trim. **Change colours:** All white.

Foundation: In 1875 cricketing enthusiasts who were largely members of Trinity Church, Bordesley, determined to continue their sporting relationships throughout the year by forming a football club which they called Small Heath Alliance. For their earliest games played on waste land in Arthur Street, the team included three Edden brothers and two James brothers.

First Football League game: 3 September, 1892, Division 2, v Burslem Port Vale (h) W5-1 – Charsley; Bayley, Speller; Ollis, Jenkyns, Devey; Hallam (1), Edwards (1), Short (1), Wheldon (2), Hands.

Did you know: Birmingham City were the first English club side to play in one of the three major European competitions. On 15 May 1956 they drew 0-0 away to Internazionale of Milan in a Group D, Fairs Cup match in the 1955–58 series.

Managers (and Secretary-Managers)
Alfred Jones 1892–1908*, Alec Watson 1908–1910, Bob McRoberts 1910–15, Frank chRichards 1915–23, Bill Beer 1923–27, Leslie Knighton 1928–33, George Liddell 1933–39, Harry Storer 1945–48, Bob Brocklebank 1949–54, Arthur Turner 1954–58, Pat Beasley 1959–60, Gil Merrick 1960–64, Joe Mallett 1965, Stan Cullis 1965–70, Fred Goodwin 1970–75, Willie Bell 1975–77, Jim Smith 1978–82, Ron Saunders 1982–86, John Bond 1986–87, Garry Pendrey 1987–89, Dave Mackay 1989–1991, Lou Macari 1991, Terry Cooper August 1991–.

Player and Position	Ht	Wt	Date	Birth Place	Source	Clubs	League App	Gls
David Smith	5 8	10 02	29 3 68	Gloucester		Coventry C	154	19
						Bournemouth (loan)	1	—
						Birmingham C	13	1
Paul Tait	6 1	10 00	31 1 71	Sutton Coldfield	Trainee	Birmingham C	82	7
Forwards								
Lou Donowa	5 9	11 00	24 9 64	Ipswich	Apprentice	Norwich C	62	11
						Stoke C (loan)	4	1
					Coruna, Willem	Ipswich T	23	1
					II Tilburg	Bristol C	24	3
						Birmingham C	47	4
						Crystal Palace (loan)	—	—
						Burnley (loan)	4	—
John Gayle	6 4	13 01	30 7 64	Birmingham	Burton Alb	Wimbledon	20	2
						Birmingham C	44	10
Paul Jones*			6 2 74	Solihull	Trainee	Birmingham C	1	
Paul Moulden	5 8	11 03	6 9 67	Farnworth	Apprentice	Manchester C	64	18
						Bournemouth	32	13
						Oldham Ath	38	4
						Brighton (loan)	11	5
						Birmingham C	13	5
Alan O'Neill			27 8 73	Cork	Cobh Ramblers	Birmingham C	4	—
Paul Peschisolido			25 5 71	Canada	Toronto Blizzards	Birmingham C	19	7
James Quinn§			15 12 74	Coventry	Trainee	Birmingham C	4	—
Andrew Saville	6 0	12 06	12 12 64	Hull	Local	Hull C	100	18
						Walsall	38	5
						Barnsley	82	21
						Hartlepool U	37	13
						Birmingham C	10	7
Simon Sturridge	5 5	10 07	9 12 69	Birmingham	Trainee	Birmingham C	150	30

Trainees
Aston, David E; Baker, Lewis M; Black, Simon A; Cross, Robert B; Fowkes, Graeme L; Lucas, Jay; McKeever, Scott J; Morley, Jamie D; Prince, Simon P; Quinn, Stephen J; Robinson, Steven E; Scott, Richard P; Steadman, Richard D; Wardle, Adam; Wratten, Adam P.

**Non-Contract
Morgan, Trevor J.

Associated Schoolboys
Archer, Paul D; Bass, Jonathan D. M; Bloxham, Robert S; Bryan, Simon M; Burden, Neil; Challinor, Paul D; Dandy, Richard; Dyer, Wayne; Fieldhouse, Sean P; Goode, Craig T; Marsh, Christopher D; McKenzie, Christy; Plant, Philip; Sandland, Paul N; Simcox, Neil R; Williams, Jamie P.

Associated Schoolboys who have accepted the club's offer of a Traineeship/Contract
Bunch, James; Evans, Richard J; Hiles, Paul; Hughes, Lee R; Jones, Ian; Rea, Simon; Round, Steven C; Sedgemore, Benjamin R; Weston, Richard.

**Non-Contract Players who are retained must be re-signed before they are eligible to play in League matches.

BLACKBURN ROVERS 1992–93 *Back row (left to right):* Nicky Reid, Craig Skinner, Wayne Burnett, David May, Frank Talia, Bobby Mimms, Matt Dickins, Darren Collier, Keith Hill, Jason Wilcox, Mark Atkins, Peter Thorne.

Centre row: Mike Pettigrew (Physio), Ray Harford (Assistant Manager), Tim Sherwood, Stuart Ripley, Mike Newell, Colin Hendry, Bob Dewhurst, Lee Richardson, Richard Brown, Steve Agnew, Darren Donnelly, Stuart Munro, Ian McGarry, Gordon Cowans, Tony Parkes, (First Team Coach), ASA Hartford (Reserve Team Manager).

Front row: Garry Tallon, Roy Wegerle, Alan Shearer, Chris Price, Alan Wright, Brendan O'Shaughnessy, Kenny Dalglish (Manager), Kevin Moran, Tony Dobson, Steve Livingstone, Jonathan Pickup, Scott Lindsay, Lee Makel.

FA Premier   **BLACKBURN ROVERS**

Ewood Park, Blackburn BB2 4JF. Telephone Blackburn (0254) 55432. Fax 0254 671042. Commercial Dept Fax 0254 67525.

Ground capacity: 15,537 (temporary).

Record attendance: 61,783 v Bolton W, FA Cup 6th rd, 2 March, 1929.

Record receipts: £156,000 v Newcastle U, FA Cup 5th rd, 13 February 1993.

Pitch measurements: 115yd × 76yd.

Chairman: R. D. Coar BSC. *Vice-chairman:* R. D. Coar BSC.

Directors: T. W. Ibbotson LL.B (Managing Director and Vice-Chairman), K. C. Lee, I. R. Stanners, G. R. Root FCMA, R. L. Matthewman.

Manager: Kenny Dalglish MBE. *Assistant Manager:* Ray Harford. *Reserve Team Manager:* Asa Hartford.

Physio: M. Pettigrew.

Commercial Manager: Ken Beamish.

Secretary: John W. Howarth FAAI.

Year Formed: 1875. *Turned Professional:* 1880. *Ltd Co.:* 1897.

Club Nickname: Rovers.

Previous Grounds: 1875/6, all matches played away; 1876, Oozehead Ground; 1877, Pleasington Cricket Ground; 1878, Alexandra Meadows; 1881, Leamington Road; 1890, Ewood Park.

Record League Victory: 9–0 v Middlesbrough, Division 2, 6 November 1954 – Elvy; Suart, Eckersley; Clayton, Kelly, Bell; Mooney (3), Crossan (2), Briggs, Quigley (3), Langton (1).

Record Cup Victory: 11–0 v Rossendale, FA Cup 1st rd, 13 October 1884 – Arthur; Hopwood, McIntyre; Forrest, Blenkhorn, Lofthouse; Sowerbutts (2), J. Brown (1), Fecitt (4), Barton (3), Birtwistle (1).

Record Defeat: 0–8 v Arsenal, Division 1, 25 February 1933.

Most League Points (2 for a win): 60, Division 3, 1974–75.

Most League Points (3 for a win): 77, Division 2, 1987–88, 1988–89.

Most League Goals: 114, Division 2, 1954–55.

Highest League Scorer in Season: Ted Harper, 43, Division 1, 1925–26.

Most League Goals in Total Aggregate: Simon Garner, 168, 1978–92.

Most Capped Player: Bob Crompton, 41, England.

Most League Appearances: Derek Fazackerley, 596, 1970–86.

Record Transfer Fee Received: £720,000 from Leeds U for Scott Sellars, September 1992.

Record Transfer Fee Paid: £3,300,000 to Southampton for Alan Shearer, July 1992.

Football League Record: 1888 Founder Member of the League; 1936–39 Division 2; 1946–48 Division 1; 1948–58 Division 2; 1958–66 Division 1; 1966–71 Division 2; 1971–75 Division 3; 1975–79 Division 2; 1979–80 Division 3; 1980–92 Division 2; 1992– FA Premier League.

Honours: Football League: Division 1 – Champions 1911–12, 1913–14; Division 2 – Champions 1938–39; Runners-up 1957–58; Division 3 – Champions 1974–75; Runners-up 1979–80. *FA Cup:* Winners 1884, 1885, 1886, 1890, 1891, 1928; Runners-up 1882, 1960. *Football League Cup:* Semi-final 1961–62, 1992–93. *Full Members' Cup:* Winners 1986–87.

BLACKBURN ROVERS 1992—93 LEAGUE RECORD

Match No.	Date		Venue	Opponents	Result	H/T Score	Lg. Pos.	Goalscorers	Atten dance
1	Aug	15	A	Crystal Palace	D 3-3	1-1	—	Ripley, Shearer 2	17,086
2		18	H	Arsenal	W 1-0	0-0	—	Shearer	16,454
3		22	H	Manchester City	W 1-0	0-0	4	Newell	19,433
4		26	A	Chelsea	D 0-0	0-0	—		19,575
5		29	A	Coventry C	W 2-0	0-0	1	Shearer (pen), Atkins	14,541
6	Sept	5	H	Nottingham F	W 4-1	1-1	3	Shearer 2 (1 pen), Atkins, Crossley (og)	16,180
7		12	A	Arsenal	W 1-0	0-0	2	Newell	28,643
8		15	H	Everton	L 2-3	1-2	—	Shearer 2 (1 pen)	19,563
9		19	A	Wimbledon	D 1-1	1-1	2	Shearer	6117
10		26	H	Oldham Ath	W 2-0	1-0	2	Shearer, Ripley	18,393
11	Oct	3	H	Norwich C	W 7-1	4-1	1	Wegerle 2, Sherwood, Shearer 2, Cowans, Ripley	16,312
12		19	A	Aston Villa	D 0-0	0-0	—		30,398
13		24	H	Manchester U	D 0-0	0-0	1		20,305
14		31	A	Sheffield W	D 0-0	0-0	1		31,044
15	Nov	7	H	Tottenham H	L 0-2	0-0	2		17,305
16		22	A	Southampton	D 1-1	1-1	—	Moran	16,626
17		28	H	QPR	W 1-0	1-0	2	Shearer	15,850
18	Dec	5	A	Middlesbrough	L 2-3	1-0	2	Wilcox, Phillips (og)	20,096
19		13	A	Liverpool	L 1-2	0-0	—	Shearer	43,668
20		19	H	Sheffield U	W 1-0	1-0	3	Moran	16,057
21		26	H	Leeds U	W 3-1	2-1	2	Wilcox, Shearer 2	19,910
22		28	A	Ipswich T	L 1-2	0-0	4	Wegerle	21,431
23	Jan	9	H	Wimbledon	D 0-0	0-0	4		14,504
24		16	A	Oldham Ath	W 1-0	0-0	3	Ripley	13,742
25		26	H	Coventry C	L 2-5	1-2	—	Newell, Hendry	15,215
26		30	A	Manchester C	L 2-3	2-1	5	Newell, Phelan (og)	29,122
27	Feb	2	A	Crystal Palace	L 1-2	1-1	—	Wegerle	14,163
28		21	H	Chelsea	W 2-0	1-0	—	Newell 2	14,780
29		28	A	Norwich C	D 0-0	0-0	—		15,821
30	Mar	9	A	Everton	L 1-2	1-0	—	May	18,086
31		9	H	Southampton	D 0-0	0-0	—		13,556
32		20	H	Middlesbrough	D 1-1	1-1	6	Atkins	14,041
33		24	A	QPR	W 3-0	1-0	—	Ripley, Moran, Atkins	10,677
34	Apr	3	H	Liverpool	W 4-1	3-0	4	Newell, Moran, Gallacher, Wilcox	15,032
35		7	A	Nottingham F	W 3-1	1-0	—	Wilcox, Ripley, Newell	20,467
36		10	A	Leeds U	L 2-5	0-2	4	Gallacher, Atkins	31,791
37		12	H	Ipswich T	W 2-1	2-0	4	Ripley, Whelan (og)	14,071
38		17	A	Sheffield U	W 3-1	1-1	4	Gallacher, Newell, Sherwood	18,186
39		21	H	Aston Villa	W 3-0	3-0	—	Newell 2, Gallacher	15,127
40	May	3	A	Manchester U	L 1-3	1-1	—	Gallacher	40,447
41		5	A	Tottenham H	W 2-1	1-0	—	Newell 2	23,097
42		8	H	Sheffield W	W 1-0	0-0	4	Sherwood	14,956

Final League Position: 4

GOALSCORERS

League (68): Shearer 16 (3 pens), Newell 13, Ripley 7, Atkins 5, Gallacher 5, Moran 4, Wegerle 4, Wilcox 4, Sherwood 3, Cowans 1, Hendry 1, May 1, own goals 4.
Coca Cola Cup (19): Shearer 6, Newell 5, Wegerle 4, Andersson 1, Atkins 1, May 1, own goal 1.
FA Cup (9): Newell 3, Ripley 2, Wegerle 2, Livingstone 1, Moran 1.

Mimms 42	May 34	Wright 24	Sherwood 38 + 1	Hendry 41	Moran 36	Ripley 38 + 2	Atkins 24 + 7	Shearer 21	Newell 40	Dobson 15 + 4	Price 2 + 4	Wilcox 31 + 2	Wegerle 11 + 11	Hill — + 1	Cowans 23 + 3	Marker 12 + 3	Brown 2	Andersson 6 + 5	Ireland — + 1	Berg 2 + 2	Livingstone 1 + 1	Makel 1	Le Saux 9	Gallacher 9	Match No.
1	2	3	4	5	6	7	8	9	10	11	12														1
1	2		4	5	6	7	8	9	10	3			11												2
1	2	3	4	5	6	7	8	9	10	11	12														3
1	2		4	5	6	7	8	9	10	3			11												4
1	2	11	4	5	6	7	8	9	10	3			12												5
1	2	11	4	5	6	7	8	9	10	3			12												6
1	2	11	4	5	6	7	8	9	10	3	12														7
1	2	11	4	5	6	7	8	9	10	*3*		14	12												8
1	2	11	4	5	6	7	8	9	10	3					12										9
1	2	3	4	5	6	7	8	9	10						11	12									10
1		3	4	5	6	7	8	9				14	10		11	12	2								11
1	2	3	4	5	6	7		9	10			11			8										12
1	2	3	4	5	6	7		9	10			11	12		8										13
1	2	3	4	5	6		*7*	9	10	14		11	12		8										14
1	*2*	3	4	5	6	11	7	9	10			14	12		8										15
1	2		4	5	6	7		9	10	3		11	12		8										16
1		3	4	5	6	7		9	10		2	*11*	12		8	14									17
1		3	4	5	6	7		9	10		2	11	12		8										18
1	2	3	7	5	6	14	4	9	10			*11*	12		8										19
1	2	3		5	6	7	4	9	10	12		11			8										20
1	2	3	12	5	6	7	4	9	10			11			8										21
1	2	3	7	5		12	4		10	14		*11*	9		8	6									22
1	2	3	4	5	6	7			10			11	9		8	12									23
1	2	3	4	5	6	7			10			11	9		8										24
1	2	*3*	4	5		7	14		10			11	9		8	6		12							25
1			4	5	6		8		10	3		11	9		2			7		12					26
1		3	4	5		7	2		10			11	9		*8*	6		12	14						27
1	2		4	5	6	7	12		10	3		11	9		8										28
1	2		4	5	6	7			10	3		11	9		8										29
1	2	3	4	5		7	12		10			11	*9*		6		8		14						30
1	2		4	5	6	7	8		10	3		11	9		12										31
1	2			5	6	7	8					11	12		10	3	9	4							32
1				5	6	7	9		10	3		8	11	2				4							33
1	2		4	5	6	7			10			11			8								3	9	34
1	2		4	5	6	*7*	12		10			11			8				14				3	9	35
1	2		4	5	6	7	12		10			11			8								3	9	36
1	2		4	5	6	7			10			11			8								3	9	37
1	2		4		6	7	12		10			11			8	5							3	9	38
1	2		4	5	6	7			10			11			8								3	9	39
1			4	5	6	7	8		10			11			14	*2*	12						3	9	40
1			4	5		7	8		10	12		11			6	2							3	9	41
1	2		4	5		7	12		10			11			8	6							3	9	42

Coca Cola Cup	Second Round	Huddersfield T (a)		1-1
		(h)		4-3
	Third Round	Norwich C (h)		2-0
	Fourth Round	Watford (h)		6-1
	Fifth Round	Cambridge U (h)		3-2
	Semi-Final	Sheffield W (h)		2-4
		(a)		1-2
FA Cup	Third Round	Bournemouth (h)		3-1
	Fourth Round	Crewe Alex (a)		3-0
	Fifth Round	Newcastle U (h)		1-0
	Sixth Round	Sheffield U (h)		0-0
		(a)		2-2

BLACKBURN ROVERS

Player and Position	Ht	Wt	Date	Birth Place	Source	Clubs	League App	Gls
Goalkeepers								
Darren Collier	5 11	11 09	1 12 67	Stockton	Middlesbrough	Blackburn R	27	—
Matt Dickins	6 4	14 00	3 9 70	Sheffield	Trainee	Sheffield U	—	—
						Leyton Orient (loan)	—	—
						Lincoln C	27	—
						Blackburn R	1	—
						Blackpool (loan)	19	—
Bobby Mimms	6 2	12 13	12 10 63	York	Halifax T	Rotherham U	83	—
						Everton	29	—
						Notts Co (loan)	2	—
						Sunderland (loan)	4	—
						Blackburn R (loan)	6	—
						Manchester C (loan)	3	—
						Tottenham H	37	—
						Aberdeen (loan)	6	—
						Blackburn R	109	—
Frank Talia			20 7 72	Melbourne	Sunshine George Cross	Blackburn R	—	—
						Hartlepool U (loan)	14	—
Defenders								
Patrik Andersson			18 8 71	Borgeby	Malmo	Blackburn R	11	—
Mark Atkins	6 1	12 00	14 8 68	Doncaster		Scunthorpe U	48	2
						Blackburn R	204	28
Henning Berg			1 9 69	Eidsvell	Lillestrom	Blackburn R	4	—
Richard Brown	5 10	11 02	13 1 67	Nottingham	Ilkeston T Kettering T	Sheffield W	—	—
						Blackburn R	28	—
						Maidstone U (loan)	3	—
Robert Dewhurst	6 3	13 01	10 9 71	Keighley	Trainee	Blackburn R	13	—
						Darlington R (loan)	11	1
						Huddersfield T (loan)	7	—
Tony Dobson	6 1	12 10	5 2 69	Coventry	Apprentice	Coventry C	54	1
						Blackburn R	41	—
Colin Hendry	6 1	12 00	7 12 65	Keith	Islavale	Dundee	41	2
						Blackburn R	102	22
						Manchester C	63	5
						Blackburn R	71	5
Graeme Le Saux	5 9	12 00	17 10 68	Jersey		Chelsea	90	8
						Blackburn R	9	—
Nick Marker	6 1	13 00	3 5 65	Exeter	Apprentice	Exeter C	202	3
						Plymouth Arg	202	13
						Blackburn R	15	—
David May	6 0	11 07	24 6 70	Oldham	Trainee	Blackburn R	83	2
Kevin Moran	5 11	12 09	29 4 56	Dublin	Pegasus Sporting Gijon	Manchester U	231	21
						Blackburn R	128	9
Andrew Scott			27 6 75	Manchester	Trainee	Blackburn R	—	—
Midfield								
Wayne Burnett	5 9	10 11	4 9 71	London	Trainee	Leyton Orient	40	—
						Blackburn R	—	—
Gordon Cowans	5 7	9 8	27 10 58	Durham	Apprentice	Aston Villa	286	42
						Bari	94	3
						Aston Villa	117	7
						Blackburn R	50	2
Ian McGarry‡			13 2 74	Darwen	Trainee	Blackburn R	—	—
Lee Makel	5 10	9 10	11 1 73	Sunderland	Trainee	Newcastle U	12	1
						Blackburn R	1	—
Jonathon Pickup*			24 8 74	Sydney	Trainee	Blackburn R	—	—
Lee Richardson (To Aberdeen September 1992)	5 11	11 00	12 3 69	Halifax		Halifax T	56	2
						Watford	41	1
						Blackburn R	62	3
Paul Shepstone (To Motherwell)	5 8	10 06	8 11 70	Coventry	FA Schools	Coventry C	—	—
						Birmingham C	—	—
						Blackburn R	26	1
					Atherstone U	York C (loan)	2	—
Tim Sherwood	6 1	11 04	6 2 69	St Albans	Trainee	Watford	32	2
						Norwich C	71	10
						Blackburn R	50	3
Alan Wright	5 4	9 04	28 9 71	Ashton-under-Lyme	Trainee	Blackpool	98	—
						Blackburn R	57	1

BLACKBURN ROVERS

Colours: Blue and white halved shirts, white shorts, blue stockings. **Change colours:** Black & red striped shirts, black shorts, black stockings with red turnovers.

Foundation: It was in 1875 that some Public School old boys called a meeting at which the Blackburn Rovers club was formed and the colours blue and white adopted. The leading light was John Lewis, later to become a founder of the Lancashire FA, a famous referee who was in charge of two FA Cup Finals, and a vice-president of both the FA and the Football League.

First Football League game: 15 September, 1888, Football League, v Accrington (h) D 5-5 – Arthur; Beverley, James Southworth; Douglas, Almond, Forrest; Beresford (1), Walton, John Southworth (1), Fecitt (1), Townley (2).

Did you know: Johnny McInytre scored four goals in five minutes for Blackburn Rovers against Everton in a Division 1 match on 16 September 1922. Rovers won 5-1 but scored only 47 goals that season.

Managers (and Secretary-Managers)
Thomas Mitchell 1884–96*, J. Walmsley 1896–1903*, R. B. Middleton 1903–25, Jack Carr 1922–26 (TM under Middleton to 1925), Bob Crompton 1926–30 (Hon. TM), Arthur Barritt 1931–36 (had been Sec. from 1927), Reg Taylor 1936–38, Bob Crompton 1938–41, Eddie Hapgood 1944–47, Will Scott 1947, Jack Bruton 1947–49, Jackie Bestall 1949–53, Johnny Carey 1953–58, Dally Duncan 1958–60, Jack Marshall 1960–67, Eddie Quigley 1967–70, Johnny Carey 1970–71, Ken Furphy 1971–73, Gordon Lee 1974–75, Jim Smith 1975–78, Jim Iley 1978, John Pickering 1978–79, Howard Kendall 1979–81, Bobby Saxton 1981–86, Don Mackay 1987–91, Kenny Dalglish October 1991–.

Player and Position	Ht	Wt	Date	Birth Place	Source	Clubs	League App	Gls
Forwards								
Darren Donnelly*	5 10	11 06	28 12 71	Liverpool	Trainee	Blackburn R	2	—
Kevin Gallacher	5 7	9 11	23 11 66	Clydebank	Duntocher BC	Dundee U	131	27
						Coventry C	100	28
						Blackburn R	9	5
Simon Ireland	5 11	11 12	23 11 71	Barnstaple	School	Huddersfield T	19	—
						Wrexham (loan)	5	—
						Blackburn R	1	—
Scott Lindsay‡			15 11 73	Preston	Trainee	Blackburn R	—	—
Mike Newell	6 1	11 00	27 1 65	Liverpool	Liverpool	Crewe Alex	3	—
						Wigan Ath	72	25
						Luton T	63	18
						Leicester C	81	21
						Everton	68	15
						Blackburn R	60	19
Brendan O'Shaughnessy*			20 9 73	Bury	Trainee	Blackburn R	—	—
Stuart Ripley	5 11	12 06	20 11 67	Middlesbrough	Apprentice	Middlesbrough	249	26
						Bolton W (loan)	5	1
						Blackburn R	40	7
Alan Shearer	5 11	11 03	13 8 70	Newcastle	Trainee	Southampton	118	23
						Blackburn R	21	16
Duncan Shearer (To Aberdeen July 1992)	5 10	10 09	28 8 62	Fort William	Inverness Clach	Chelsea	2	1
						Huddersfield T	83	38
						Swindon T	159	78
						Blackburn R	6	1
Gary Tallon	5 10	11 02	5 9 73	Drogheda	Trainee	Blackburn R	—	—
Peter Thorne	6 0	12 10	21 6 73	Manchester	Trainee	Blackburn R	—	—
Jason Wilcox	5 10	11 06	15 7 71	Bolton	Trainee	Blackburn R	90	8

Trainees
Ainscough, Paul B; Bardsley, Christopher J; Berry, Ian J; Berry, James S; Gifford, Andrew J; Gill, Wayne J; Goodall, Daniel J; Grassby, Darren P; Grunshaw, Steven J; Hitchen, Lee A; Metcalf, Joshua H; Moss, Lee A; Ridgway, Alec D; Sweeney, Damian; Thornton, Scott L.

Associated Schoolboys
Beattie, James S; Bingham, Stuart J; Bottomley, Lee; Hall, Stephen J; Lee, Barry; McLean, James L; Richards, James K; Rimmer, Martin J; Scaldwell, Kieron; Sherrington, Paul S; Stimpson, Richard C; Taylor, Philip M; Tierney, Darren; Watling, Christopher; Westworth, Mark J; Wojciechowicz, Alexander.

Associated Schoolboys who have accepted the club's offer of a Traineeship/Contract
Gaston, Karl S; Hitchen, Steven J; McCrone, Christopher P; Ormerod, Brett R; Sinnott, Adam J; Whealing, Anthony J.

BLACKPOOL 1992-93 *Back row (left to right):* Steven Redmond (Physio), Chris Speak, Gary Briggs, Jamie Murphy, Michael Davies, Steve McIharcey, Phil Horner, David Bamber, Paul Stoneman, Lee Martin, Steve Thornber, David Robinson, Andy Garner, Bill Ayre (Manager), Grant Leitch, Neil Bailey (Coach)
Front row: David Burgess, Mark Murray, Trevor Sinclair, Andy Gouck, Tony Rodwell, Peter Duffield, David Eyres, Mark Bonner.

Division 2   BLACKPOOL

Bloomfield Rd Ground, Blackpool FY1 6JJ. Telephone Blackpool (0253) 404331. Fax: 0253 405011.

Ground capacity: 10,337.

Record attendance: 38,098 v Wolverhampton W, Division 1, 17 September 1955.

Record receipts: £72,949 v Tottenham H, FA Cup 3rd rd, 5 January 1991.

Pitch measurements: 111yd × 73yd.

President: C. A. Sagar BEM.

Chairman: Owen J. Oyston. *Deputy chairman:* Mrs V. Oyston.

Managing Director: C. Melling.

Directors: W. Ayre, G. Warburton, J. Wilde MBE, W. Bingham MBE, Mrs R. Bingham.

Manager: Bill Ayre.

Secretary: D. J. Allan.

Commercial Manager: Geoffrey Warburton.

Coach: Neil Bailey. *Physio:* Stephen Redmond.

Year Formed: 1887. *Turned Professional:* 1887. *Ltd Co.:* 1896.

Previous Name: 'South Shore' combined with Blackpool in 1899, twelve years after the latter had been formed on the breaking up of the old 'Blackpool St John's' club.

Club Nickname: 'The Seasiders'.

Previous Grounds: 1887, Raikes Hall Gardens; 1897, Athletic Grounds; 1899, Raikes Hall Gardens; 1899, Bloomfield Road.

Record League Victory: 7–0 v Preston NE (away), Division 1, 1 May 1948 – Robinson; Shimwell, Crosland; Buchan, Hayward, Kelly; Hobson, Munro (1), McIntosh (5), McCall, Rickett (1).

Record Cup Victory: 7–1 v Charlton Ath, League Cup, 2nd rd, 25 September 1963 – Harvey; Armfield, Martin; Crawford, Gratrix, Cranston; Lea, Ball (1), Charnley (4), Durie (1), Oakes (1).

Record Defeat: 1–10 v Small Heath, Division 2, 2 March 1901 and v Huddersfield T, Division 1, 13 December 1930.

Most League Points (2 for a win): 58, Division 2, 1929–30.

Most League Points (3 for a win): 86, Division 4, 1984–85.

Most League Goals: 98, Division 2, 1929–30.

Highest League Scorer in Season: Jimmy Hampson, 45, Division 2, 1929–30.

Most League Goals in Total Aggregate: Jimmy Hampson, 247, 1927–38.

Most Capped Player: Jimmy Armfield, 43, England.

Most League Appearances: Jimmy Armfield, 568, 1952–71.

Record Transfer Fee Received: £633,333 from Manchester C for Paul Stewart, March 1987.

Record Transfer Fee Paid: £116,666 to Sunderland for Jack Ashurst, October 1979.

Football League Record: 1896 Elected to Division 2; 1899 Failed re-election; 1900 Re-elected; 1900–30 Division 2; 1930–33 Division 1; 1933–37 Division 2; 1937–67 Division 1; 1967–70 Division 2; 1970–71 Division 1; 1971–78 Division 2; 1978–81 Division 3; 1981–85 Division 4; 1985–90 Division 3; 1990–92 Division 4; 1992– Division 2.

Honours: Football League: Division 1 – Runners-up 1955–56; Division 2 – Champions 1929–30; Runners-up 1936–37, 1969–70; Division 4 – Runners-up 1984–85. *FA Cup:* Winners 1953; Runners-up 1948, 1951. *Football League Cup:* Semi-final 1962. *Anglo-Italian Cup:* Winners 1971; Runners-up 1972.

BLACKPOOL 1992—93 LEAGUE RECORD

Match No.	Date	Venue	Opponents	Result	H/T Score	Lg. Pos.	Goalscorers	Atten dance
1	Aug 15	A	WBA	L 1-3	1-2	—	Rodwell	16,527
2	22	H	Exeter C	W 2-0	2-0	12	Robinson, Sinclair	3999
3	29	A	Leyton Orient	L 0-1	0-1	17		4310
4	Sept 1	A	Bolton W	L 0-3	0-2	—		7291
5	5	H	Mansfield T	D 1-1	1-0	18	Duffield	4322
6	12	A	Swansea C	L 0-3	0-2	20		3861
7	15	H	Bournemouth	W 2-0	0-0	—	Eyres, Robinson	3455
8	19	H	Brighton & HA	D 2-2	1-0	19	Stringfellow, Sinclair	4618
9	26	A	Rotherham U	L 2-3	1-1	19	Horner, Sinclair	4408
10	Oct 2	A	Hartlepool U	L 0-1	0-0	—		2837
11	10	H	Preston NE	L 2-3	1-2	22	Sinclair, Briggs	7631
12	16	A	Stockport Co	D 0-0	0-0	—		5680
13	24	H	Burnley	L 1-3	1-3	22	Gouck	7942
14	31	A	Port Vale	L 1-2	0-0	23	Eyres	7057
15	Nov 3	H	Huddersfield T	D 2-2	1-1	—	Mitchell, Eyres	3441
16	7	A	Reading	D 0-0	0-0	24		4163
17	21	H	Stoke C	L 1-3	1-2	24	Ward	8028
18	28	A	Hull C	L 2-3	0-3	24	Eyres, Horner	3906
19	Dec 12	A	Wigan Ath	L 1-2	0-0	24	Gouck	2492
20	20	H	Fulham	D 1-1	0-1	—	Horner	3802
21	26	H	Bradford C	D 3-3	2-1	23	Gouck 2, Eyres (pen)	5448
22	28	A	Chester C	W 2-1	2-1	23	Sinclair, Eyres	3787
23	Jan 5	H	Swansea C	D 0-0	0-0	—		3417
24	9	A	Bournemouth	L 1-5	1-3	22	Bamber	3807
25	16	H	Rotherham U	W 2-0	0-0	22	Bamber, Horner	6144
26	26	H	Leyton Orient	W 3-1	3-0	—	Eyres, Bamber, Sinclair	3164
27	30	A	Exeter C	W 1-0	1-0	21	Bamber	3384
28	Feb 6	H	WBA	W 2-1	1-1	20	Horner 2	9386
29	13	A	Mansfield T	D 2-2	1-1	20	Eyres 2 (2 pens)	3593
30	20	H	Bolton W	D 1-1	0-0	21	Eyres (pen)	8054
31	27	A	Preston NE	D 3-3	1-1	20	Davies, Watson 2	10,403
32	Mar 6	H	Hartlepool U	D 1-1	0-0	20	Horner	4926
33	9	A	Plymouth Arg	L 1-2	0-1	—	Bamber	5959
34	13	H	Reading	L 0-1	0-0	21		4160
35	20	A	Huddersfield T	L 2-5	1-2	22	Bamber 2	6249
36	23	H	Hull C	W 5-1	2-1	—	Bamber 2, Sinclair, Eyres, Leitch	3515
37	27	A	Stoke C	W 1-0	0-0	20	Sinclair	17,918
38	31	A	Brighton & HA	D 1-1	0-0	—	Sinclair	5170
39	Apr 3	H	Plymouth Arg	D 1-1	1-0	20	Eyres	4397
40	6	H	Wigan Ath	W 2-1	0-1	—	Eyres 2 (1 pen)	5096
41	10	A	Bradford C	L 0-2	0-1	21		6191
42	13	H	Chester C	W 2-0	2-0	—	Eyres (pen), Bamber	5078
43	17	A	Fulham	L 0-1	0-1	20		4633
44	24	H	Stockport Co	W 2-0	1-0	17	Sinclair, Bamber	7205
45	May 1	A	Burnley	D 2-2	0-1	17	Sinclair, Bamber	12,475
46	8	H	Port Vale	L 2-4	2-1	18	Eyres, Bamber	9295

Final League Position: 18

GOALSCORERS

League (63): Eyres 16 (6 pens), Bamber 13, Sinclair 11, Horner 7, Gouck 4, Robinson 2, Watson 2, Briggs 1, Davies 1, Duffield 1, Leitch 1, Mitchell 1, Rodwell 1, Stringfellow 1, Ward 1.
Coca Cola Cup (4): Eyres 1, Murphy 1, Robinson 1, own goal 1.
FA Cup (1): Mitchell 1.

McIlhargey 3	Davies 30	Murphy 28+5	Horner 46	Briggs 33	Gouck 27+2	Rodwell 19+1	Sinclair 45	Duffield 3+2	Garner 4+1	Eyres 46	Robinson 12+2	Bonner 8+7	Martin 24	Burgess 20	Thornber 21+3	Mitchell 6+6	Murray 1	Speak —+1	Leitch 11+6	Stringfellow 3	Stoneman 8+2	Gore 30	Bond —+1	Harvey 4+1	Ward 2	Bamber 24	Dickins 19	Spooner 2	Watson 10+5	Cook 9	Bailey 7+1	Beech 1	Match No.
1	2	3	4	5	6	7	8	9	10	11	12	14																					1
	3		4	5		7	8		10	11	9	14	1	2	6	12																	2
	3		4	5		7	8	12	10	11	9		1	2	6																		3
	3		4			7	8	12	10	11	9		1	2	6					5													4
5	3		4			7	8	10	12	11	9		1	2	6	14																	5
9	3		4	5		7			10	11	12	8	1	2	6				14														6
	2	3	4	5		7	8			11	9	14	1		6	12			10														7
	2	3	4	5		7	8			11	9		1						10	6													8
	2	12	4	5	10	7	8			11			1						6		9	3											9
1	2		4	5	10	7	8			11	9										6	3											10
1	2	3	4	5	10	7	8			11				14					9		6	12											11
	3		4	5	10	7	8			11	9		1	2							6												12
	2		4		10	7	8			11	9		1			3			5		6												13
5			4		10	12	8			11	9	7	1	2							6			3									14
5			4		10	7	8			11	6		1	2							9			3									15
			4	5	10	7	8			11	6		1	2							9			3									16
		12	4	5	10	7	8			11	14		1	2							9			3	6								17
	3		4	5	10	7	8			11			1	2							6		12	9									18
	3		4	5	10	7	8			11			1	2							6			9									19
	3	12	4	5	10	7	8			11	9	6	1	2	14																		20
	3	7	4		10		8			11	9	6	1	2					14		12	5											21
	3	7	4		10		8			11	9		1	2					12		5	6											22
	3		4	5	10		8			11	7		1	2							6					9							23
	3		4	5	10		8			11	14		1	2	12				7		6					9							24
	2		4	5	10		8			11			1			3			7		6					9							25
	2		4	5	10		8			11						3			7		6					9	1						26
	2	10	4	5			8			11						3			7		6					9	1						27
	2	10	4				8			11						3			7		6					9	1		5	12			28
	2	3	4		10		8			11											6					9	1		5	7			29
	2		4		10		8			11									5		6					9	1			7	3		30
	2		4	5	10		8			11											6					9	1			7	3		31
	2		4	5	10		8			11						3			12		6					9	1			7			32
	2	12	4	5	10		8			11				14		3			7		6					9	1						33
	2	10	4	5			8			11						3			7		6					9	1						34
	2	10	4				8			11						3			5		6					9	1			7			35
	2	10	4	5			8			11						3			7		6					9	1		12	14			36
		10	4	5			8			11						3			7	12	6					9	1			2			37
		10	4	5			8			11				3		3			7		6					9	1			2			38
	2		4	5			8			11				3					7		6					9	1		12	10			39
	2		4	5	12		8			11									14		6					9	1		7	3	10		40
	2		4	5	12		8			11									7		6					9	1		14	3	10		41
	2		4	5	10		8			11									12	14	6					9	1		7	3			42
	2		4	5	10		8			11									12	14	6					9	1		7	3			43
	2		4	5	10		8			11									12		6					9	1		7	3			44
	2	12	4				8			11			1						10	14	6					9				7	3	5	45
	2		4				8			11			1						10		6					9			12	3	5	7	46

Coca Cola Cup	First Round	Tranmere R (a)	0-3
		(h)	4-0
	Second Round	Portsmouth (h)	0-4
		(a)	0-2
FA Cup	First Round	Rochdale (h)	1-1
		(a)	0-1

BLACKPOOL

Player and Position	Ht	Wt	Date	Birth Place	Source	Clubs	League App	Gls
Goalkeepers								
Steve McIlhargey	6 0	11 07	28 8 63	Ferryhill	Blantyre Celtic	Walsall	—	—
						Blackpool	97	—
Lee Martin	6 0	13 00	9 9 68	Huddersfield	Trainee	Huddersfield T	54	—
						Blackpool	24	—
Defenders								
Neil Bailey†			26 9 58	Wigan	Apprentice	Burnley	—	—
						Newport Co	134	7
						Wigan Ath	41	2
						Stockport Co	51	—
						Newport Co (loan)	9	1
					Retired	Blackpool	8	—
Gary Briggs	6 3	12 10	8 5 58	Leeds	Apprentice	Middlesbrough	—	—
						Oxford U	420	18
						Blackpool	104	3
Dave Burgess	5 10	11 04	20 1 60	Liverpool.	Local	Tranmere R	218	1
						Grimsby T	69	—
						Blackpool	101	1
						Carlisle U (loan)	6	—
Jamie Murphy	6 1	13 00	25 2 73	Manchester	Trainee	Blackpool	33	—
Mark Murray	5 8	10 12	13 6 73	Manchester	Trainee	Blackpool	3	—
Paul Stoneman	6 1	13 06	26 2 73	Whitley Bay	Trainee	Blackpool	29	—
Andy Watson	5 9	11 02	1 4 67	Huddersfield	Harrogate T	Halifax T	83	15
						Swansea C	14	1
						Carlisle U	56	22
						Blackpool	15	2
Midfield								
Mark Bonner	5 10	11 00	7 6 74	Ormskirk	Trainee	Blackpool	18	—
Mitch Cook	6 0	12 0	15 10 61	Scarborough	Scarborough	Darlington	34	4
						Middlesbrough	6	—
						Scarborough	81	10
						Halifax T	54	2
						Scarborough (loan)	9	1
						Darlington (loan)	9	—
						Darlington	27	3
						Blackpool	17	—
Michael Davies	5 8	10 07	19 1 66	Stretford	Apprentice	Blackpool	285	16
Ian Gore	5 11	12 04	10 1 68	Liverpool		Birmingham C	—	—
					Southport	Blackpool	167	—
Andy Gouck	5 9	11 02	8 6 72	Blackpool	Trainee	Blackpool	66	7
Neil Mitchell			7 11 74	Lytham	Trainee	Blackpool	13	1
Trevor Sinclair	5 10	11 02	2 3 73	Dulwich	Trainee	Blackpool	112	15
Steve Spooner	5 10	12 00	25 1 61	London	Apprentice	Derby Co	8	—
						Halifax T	72	13
						Chesterfield	93	14
						Hereford U	84	19
						York C	72	11
						Rotherham U	19	1
						Mansfield T	58	3
						Blackpool	2	—
Stephen Thornber*	5 10	11 02	11 10 65	Dewsbury	Local	Halifax T	104	4
						Swansea C	117	6
						Blackpool	24	—

BLACKPOOL

Colours: Tangerine shirts with navy and white trim, white shorts, tangerine stockings with white tops.
Change colours: Navy and sky blue stripes, navy shorts, navy stockings.

Foundation: Old boys of St. John's School who had formed themselves into a football club decided to establish a club bearing the name of their town and Blackpool FC came into being at a meeting at the Stanley Arms Hotel in the summer of 1887. In their first season playing at Raikes Hall Gardens, the club won both the Lancashire Junior Cup and the Fylde Cup.

First Football League game: 5 September, 1896, Division 2, v Lincoln C (a) L 1-3 – Douglas; Parr, Bowman; Stuart, Stirzaker, Norris; Clarkin, Donnelly, R. Parkinson, Mount (1), J. Parkinson.

Did you know: During 1966–67, Blackpool achieved only one home League victory, but it was a spectacular affair on 22 October and saw them put six goals past Newcastle United without reply.

Managers (and Secretary-Managers)
Tom Barcroft 1903–33* (Hon. Sec.), John Cox 1909–11, Bill Norman 1919–23, Maj. Frank Buckley 1923–27, Sid Beaumont 1927–28, Harry Evans 1928–33 (Hon. TM), Alex "Sandy" Macfarlane 1933–35, Joe Smith 1935–58, Ronnie Suart 1958–67, Stan Mortensen 1967–69, Les Shannon 1969–70, Bob Stokoe 1970–72, Harry Potts 1972–76, Allan Brown 1976–78, Bob Stokoe 1978–79, Stan Ternent 1979–80, Alan Ball 1980–81, Allan Brown 1981–82, Sam Ellis 1982–89, Jimmy Mullen 1989–90, Graham Carr 1990, Bill Ayre December 1990– .

Player and Position	Ht	Wt	Date	Birth Place	Source	Clubs	League App	Gls
Forwards								
Dave Bamber	6 3	13 10	1 2 59	St. Helens	Manchester Univ	Blackpool	86	29
						Coventry C	19	3
						Walsall	20	7
						Portsmouth	4	1
						Swindon T	106	31
						Watford	18	3
						Stoke C	43	8
						Hull C	28	5
						Blackpool	89	56
Chris Beech§			16 9 74	Blackpool	Trainee	Blackpool	1	—
Richie Bond*	5 11	11 06	27 10 65	Blyth	Blyth S	Blackpool	1	—
David Eyres	5 10	11 00	26 2 64	Liverpool	Rhyl	Blackpool	158	38
Andy Garner*	6 0	12 01	8 3 66	Chesterfield	Apprentice	Derby Co	71	17
						Blackpool	159	37
Philip Horner	6 1	12 07	10 11 66	Leeds	Lincoln C	Leicester C	10	—
						Rotherham U (loan)	4	—
						Halifax T	72	4
						Blackpool	112	18
Grant Leitch	6 1	12 05	31 10 72	South Africa		Blackpool	23	1
David Robinson	6 0	13 02	27 11 69	Newcastle	Trainee	Newcastle U	8	—
						Peterborough U (loan)	7	3
						Reading	8	—
						Blackpool	14	2
Tony Rodwell	5 11	11 02	26 8 62	Southport	Colne Dynamoes	Blackpool	105	16
Chris Speak	6 0	12 04	20 8 73	Preston	Trainee	Blackpool	1	—

Trainees
Beech, Christopher S; Birkman, Darren M; Craggs, Graham; Hutchinson, Andrew; Irvine, Jonathan A; Little, Glen; Lowery Ian; Maclean, Fraser R; Morris, Andrew; Sheppard, James H; Sunderland, Jonathan; Symons, Paul; Thompson, Paul D; Thorpe, Lee A; Trickett, Andrew; Wood, Timothy.

**Non-Contract
Bailey, Neil.

Associated Schoolboys
Birkman, Peter L; Blacow, Iain C; Carroll, David; Croasdale, Peter J; Day, David R; Gawthorpe, Neil J; Haddow, Paul A; Hall, Gary A; Hartley, Michael G; Hills, John D; Hunt, Kris; Kershaw, Steven L; Ramsdale, Stephen; Shaw, Richard E.

**Non-Contract Players who are retained must be re-signed before they are eligible to play in League matches.

74

BOLTON WANDERERS 1992–93 *Back row (left to right)*: Jason Lydiate, Mark Seagraves, Mark Winstanley, Mark Came, Alan Stubbs, Julian Darby, Nicky Spooner.
Third row: Andy Roscoe, Jason McAteer, David Reeves, Tony Philliskirk, Stuart Storer, Barry Smith, Craig Lewin.
Second row: Ewan Simpson, Darren Oliver, David Burke, Keith Branagan, Chris Clarke, Dave Felgate, Scott Green, Michael Brown, Dean Crombie.
Front row: Steve Carroll, Mark Patterson, Neil Fisher, Bruce Rioch (Manager), Phil Brown, Colin Todd (Assistant Manager), Andy Walker, Tony Kelly.

Division 1   **BOLTON WANDERERS**

Burnden Park, Bolton BL3 2QR. Telephone Bolton (0204) 389200. Fax (0204) 382334. Information Service: Bolton 21101. Commercial Dept. (0204) 24518.

Ground capacity: 24,772.

Record attendance: 69,912 v Manchester C, FA Cup 5th rd, 18 February 1933.

Record receipts: £150,860.50 v Liverpool, FA Cup 3rd rd, 3 January 1993.

Pitch measurements: 113yd × 76yd.

President: Nat Lofthouse.

Chairman: G. Hargreaves.

Directors: P. A. Gartside, G. Ball, G. Seymour, G. Warburton, W. B. Warburton.

Team Manager: Bruce Rioch. *Assistant Manager:* Colin Todd. *Physio:* E. Simpson.

Chief Executive & Secretary: Des McBain. *Commercial Manager:* T. Holland. *Assistant Commercial Manager:* G. Porter.

Year Formed: 1874. *Turned Professional:* 1880. *Ltd Co.:* 1895.

Previous Name: 1874–77, Christ Church FC; 1877 became Bolton Wanderers.

Club Nickname: 'The Trotters'.

Previous Grounds: Park Recreation Ground and Cockle's Field before moving to Pike's Lane ground 1881; 1895, Burnden Park.

Record League Victory: 8–0 v Barnsley, Division 2, 6 October 1934 – Jones; Smith, Finney; Goslin, Atkinson, George Taylor; George T. Taylor (2), Eastham, Milsom (1), Westwood (4), Cook. (1 og).

Record Cup Victory: 13–0 v Sheffield U, FA Cup, 2nd rd, 1 February 1890 – Parkinson; Robinson (1), Jones; Bullough, Davenport, Roberts; Rushton, Brogan (3), Cassidy (5), McNee, Weir (4).

Record Defeat: 1–9 v Preston NE, FA Cup 2nd rd, 10 December 1887.

Most League Points (2 for a win): 61, Division 3, 1972–73.

Most League Points (3 for a win): 90, Division 2, 1992–93.

Most League Goals: 96, Division 2, 1934–35.

Highest League Scorer in Season: Joe Smith, 38, Division 1, 1920–21.

Most League Goals in Total Aggregate: Nat Lofthouse, 255, 1946–61.

Most Capped Player: Nat Lofthouse, 33, England.

Most League Appearances: Eddie Hopkinson, 519, 1956–70.

Record Transfer Fee Received: £340,000 from Birmingham C for Neil Whatmore, August 1981.

Record Transfer Fee Paid: £350,000 to WBA for Len Cantello, May 1979.

Football League Record: 1888 Founder Member of the League; 1899–1900 Division 2; 1900–03 Division 1; 1903–05 Division 2; 1905–08 Division 1; 1908–09 Division 2; 1909–10 Division 1; 1910–11 Division 2; 1911–33 Division 1; 1933–35 Division 2; 1935–64 Division 1; 1964–71 Division 2; 1971–73 Division 3; 1973–78 Division 2; 1978–80 Division 1; 1980–83 Division 2; 1983–87 Division 3; 1987–88 Division 4; 1988–92 Division 3; 1992–93 Division 2; 1993– Division 1.

Honours: Football League: Division 1 best season: 3rd, 1891–92, 1920–21, 1924–25; Division 2 – Champions 1908–09, 1977–78; Runners-up 1899–1900, 1904–05, 1910–11, 1934–35, 1992–93; Division 3 – Champions 1972–73. *FA Cup:* Winners 1923, 1926, 1929, 1958; Runners-up 1894, 1904, 1953. *Football League Cup:* Semi-final 1976–77. *Freight Rover Trophy:* Runners-up 1986. *Sherpa Van Trophy:* Winners 1989.

BOLTON WANDERERS 1992—93 LEAGUE RECORD

Match No.	Date		Venue	Opponents	Result	H/T Score	Lg. Pos.	Goalscorers	Atten dance
1	Aug	15	H	Huddersfield T	W 2-0	1-0	—	Walker, Darby	7897
2		22	A	Brighton & HA	L 1-2	1-1	11	Walker	6205
3		29	H	Reading	W 2-1	1-0	7	Seagraves, Walker	4877
4	Sept	1	H	Blackpool	W 3-0	2-0	—	Philliskirk, Walker, Green	7291
5		5	A	Stoke C	D 0-0	0-0	7		14,252
6		12	A	Rotherham U	L 1-2	0-1	10	Brown P	5227
7		15	H	WBA	L 0-2	0-0	—		8531
8		19	H	Bournemouth	D 1-1	0-1	11	Philliskirk	4623
9		26	A	Plymouth Arg	L 1-2	0-2	15	Darby	6829
10	Oct	3	A	Leyton Orient	L 0-1	0-0	17		3946
11		10	H	Hartlepool U	L 1-2	1-1	18	Green	5097
12		17	A	Chester C	D 2-2	0-2·	18	Reeves, McGinlay	3394
13		24	H	Hull C	W 2-0	0-0	18	McGinlay, Patterson	4136
14		31	A	Preston NE	D 2-2	0-2	17	Green, Stubbs	7013
15	Nov	3	A	Exeter C	W 3-1	0-0	—	Spooner, Walker 2	2431
16		7	H	Port Vale	D 1-1	0-1	16	McGinlay	7349
17		21	A	Fulham	W 4-1	1-1	14	Walker 2, Stubbs, Lee	4049
18		28	H	Burnley	W 4-0	2-0	11	Lee, Walker 2 (1 pen), Brown P	11,438
19	Dec	19	H	Bradford C	W 5-0	0-0	11	Seagraves, McGinlay 2, Lee, Walker	6887
20		26	H	Wigan Ath	W 2-1	0-1	8	Walker 2	11,493
21		28	A	Swansea C	W 2-1	1-1	6	Brown P, McGinlay	7220
22	Jan	9	A	WBA	L 1-3	1-1	9	Walker (pen)	14,581
23		16	H	Plymouth Arg	W 3-1	3-1	6	Walker, Seagraves, Morrison (og)	8256
24		27	A	Reading	W 2-1	1-1	6	Walker, Lee	4640
25		30	H	Brighton & HA	L 0-1	0-0	6		8929
26	Feb	6	A	Huddersfield T	D 1-1	1-0	7	Walker	8858
27		9	A	Stockport Co	L 0-2	0-1	—		7363
28		20	A	Blackpool	D 1-1	0-0	8	McGinlay (pen)	8054
29		27	A	Hartlepool U	W 2-0	1-0	7	McGinlay, Green	2756
30	Mar	6	H	Leyton Orient	W 1-0	0-0	6	Walker	7763
31		9	H	Mansfield T	W 2-1	1-1	—	Walker 2	6557
32		13	A	Port Vale	D 0-0	0-0	6		11,055
33		20	H	Exeter C	W 4-1	2-1	5	McGinlay 2, Walker, Kelly	6819
34		23	A	Burnley	W 1-0	0-0	—	McGinlay	15,085
35		27	H	Fulham	W 1-0	0-0	5	Walker	8402
36		30	H	Rotherham U	W 2-0	1-0	—	Walker 2 (1 pen)	7985
37	Apr	3	A	Mansfield T	D 1-1	0-1	5	Seagraves	5366
38		6	H	Stockport Co	W 2-1	1-0	4	Walker, McGinlay	13,773
39		10	A	Wigan Ath	W 2-0	0-0	4	Kelly, Walker	5408
40		12	A	Swansea C	W 3-1	0-1	3	Green 2, Lee	10,854
41		17	A	Bradford C	L 1-2	0-1	4	McGinlay	9813
42		24	H	Chester C	W 5-0	0-0	4	Brown P, Seagraves, McGinlay, Patterson, Winstanley	8514
43		27	A	Bournemouth	W 2-1	1-0	—	Darby, Brown P	4434
44		30	A	Hull C	W 2-1	0-1	—	Windass (og), McGinlay	8785
45	May	4	A	Stoke C	W 1-0	1-0	—	Darby	19,238
46		8	H	Preston NE	W 1-0	0-0	2	McGinlay (pen)	21,270

Final League Position: 2

GOALSCORERS

League (80): Walker 26 (3 pens), McGinlay 16 (2 pens), Green 6, Brown P 5, Lee 5, Seagraves 5, Darby 4, Kelly 2, Patterson 2, Philliskirk 2, Stubbs 2, Reeves 1, Spooner 1, Winstanley 1, own goals 2.
Coca Cola Cup (5): Stubbs 2, Green 1, Philliskirk 1, Walker 1.
FA Cup (13): McGinlay 5, Walker 4, Green 1, McAteer 1, Reeves 1, Seagraves 1.

Branagan 46	Brown P 40	Burke 43	Darby 18 + 3	Seagraves 36 + 1	Winstanley 27 + 2	Brown M 4 + 2	Stubbs 37 + 5	Walker 31 + 1	Philliskirk 9 + 1	Patterson 35 + 2	Reeves 10 + 4	Green 33 + 8	Kelly 33 + 3	Came 3 + 1	Fisher 3 + 1	Oliver 3	McGinlay 31 + 3	Spooner 6	Lydiate 6	Lee 32	McAteer 19 + 2	Storer 1 + 2	Parkinson — + 2	Match No.
1	2	3	4	5	6		7	8	9	10	11	12	14											1
1	2	3	4	5	6	12	8	9	10	11			7											2
1	2	3	4	5	6		8	9	10	11		7	12											3
1	2	3	4	5	6		8	9	10			7	11											4
1	2	3	4	5	6	12	8	9	10			7	11											5
1	2	3	4	5	6		8	9	10		12	7	11	14										6
1	2	3	4		6		9	8		12	10	7	11				5							7
1	2	3	4		6		9	8		12	14	10	7				11			5				8
1	2	3	12		6		8	9	10	11		7	4				5					14		9
1	2		4		6		5		10	11		7					8	3		9				10
1			4		6				10			9	11			7	8	3	12	2	5			11
1					6				10		11	12	7		4		8	3	9	2	5			12
1		3			6		8				11	10	7		4		9			2	5			13
1		3	14		6	4	8	12			11	10	7				9			2	5			14
1		3		5	6		8	9			11	10	7							2	4			15
1		3		5	6		8	9			11	10	7				12			2	4			16
1	2	3		5	6		8	9			11	10	7	14			12				4			17
1	2	3		5	6			9			11	7	8				10				4	12		18
1	2	3		5	6			9			11	7	8				10				4			19
1	2	3		5	6		12	9			11	7	8				10				4			20
1	2	3		5	6			9			11	7	8				10				4			21
1	2	3		5	6		12	9			11	7	8				10				4	14		22
1	2	3		5	6		12	9			11	7	8				10				4			23
1	2	3		5	6			9			11	7	8				10				4			24
1	2	3		5			6	9			11	12	7	8			10				4			25
1	2	3	7	5	6		12	9			11	10		8							4	14		26
1	2	3		5	6		12				11	9	7	8			10				4	14		27
1	2	3					6			11		9	12				10	5		4	8	7		28
1	2	3					6	9			11		7				10	5		4	8			29
1	2	3		5			6	9			11		7				10			4	8			30
1	2	3	12	5			6	9			11	7	14				10			4	8			31
1	2	3	10	5			6	9			11	12	7							4	8			32
1	2	3		5			6	9			11		7				10			4	8			33
1	2	3		5			6	9			11		7				10			4	8			34
1	2	3		5			6	9			11	12	7				10			4	8			35
1	2	3	11	5			6	9					7				10			4	8			36
1	2	3	11	5			6	9				12	7				10			4	8			37
1	2	3		5			6	9				11	7				10			4	8	12		38
1	2	3		5			6	9				11	7				10			4	8			39
1	2	3		5	14		6	9				11	7				10			4	8	12		40
1	2	3		5	9		6					11	7				10			4	8			41
1	2	3	12	5	14		6				11	9	7				10			4	8			42
1	2	3	9	5			6			11		12	7				10			4	8			43
1	2	3	9	5			6			11			7				10			4	8			44
1	2	3	9	5			6			11		12	7				10			4	8			45
1	2	3	9	5			6			11		12	7				10			4	8			46

Coca Cola Cup	First Round	Port Vale (h)	2-1
		(a)	1-1
	Second Round	Wimbledon (h)	1-3
		(a)	1-0
FA Cup	First Round	Sutton Cd (h)	2-1
	Second Round	Rochdale (h)	4-0
	Third Round	Liverpool (h)	2-2
		(a)	2-0
	Fourth Round	Wolverhampton W (a)	2-0
	Fifth Round	Derby Co (a)	1-3

BOLTON WANDERERS

Player and Position	Ht	Wt	Date	Birth Place	Source	Clubs	League App	Gls
Goalkeepers								
Keith Branagan	6 1	13 00	10 7 66	Fulham		Cambridge U	110	—
						Millwall	46	—
						Brentford (loan)	2	—
						Gillingham (loan)	1	—
						Fulham (loan)	—	—
						Bolton W	46	—
Chris Clarke			1 5 74	Barnsley	Trainee	Bolton W	—	—
David Felgate*	6 2	13 06	4 3 60	Blaenau Ffestiniog	Blaenau Ffestiniog	Bolton W	—	—
						Rochdale (loan)	35	—
						Bradford C (loan)	—	—
						Crewe Alex (loan)	14	—
						Rochdale (loan)	12	—
						Lincoln C	198	—
						Cardiff C (loan)	4	—
						Grimsby T (loan)	12	—
						Grimsby T	12	—
						Bolton W	238	—
						Rotherham U (loan)	—	—
Defenders								
Phil Brown	5 11	11 06	30 5 59	South Shields	Local	Hartlepool U	217	8
						Halifax T	135	19
						Bolton W	214	12
David Burke	5 10	11 00	6 8 60	Liverpool	Apprentice	Bolton W	69	1
						Huddersfield T	189	3
						Crystal Palace	81	—
						Bolton W	94	—
Julian Darby	6 0	11 04	3 10 67	Bolton		Bolton W	265	36
Jason Lydiate	5 11	12 07	29 10 71	Manchester	Trainee	Manchester U	—	—
						Bolton W	7	—
Darren Oliver	5 8	10 05	1 11 71	Liverpool		Bolton W	3	—
Gary Parkinson	5 10	11 06	10 1 68	Middlesbrough	Everton	Middlesbrough	202	5
						Southend U (loan)	6	—
						Bolton W	2	—
Mark Seagraves	6 1	12 10	22 10 66	Bootle		Liverpool	—	—
						Norwich C (loan)	3	—
						Manchester C	42	—
						Bolton W	109	6
Nicky Spooner	5 8	11 00	5 6 71	Manchester	Trainee	Bolton W	21	2
Alan Stubbs	6 2	12 12	6 10 71	Kirkby	Trainee	Bolton W	97	3
Mark Winstanley	6 1	12 04	22 1 68	St. Helens	Trainee	Bolton W	199	3
Midfield								
Neil Fisher	5 8	11 00	7 11 70	St Helens	Trainee	Bolton W	11	1
Tony Kelly	5 10	11 09	1 10 64	Prescot	Liverpool	Derby Co	—	—
						Wigan Ath	101	15
						Stoke C	36	4
						WBA	26	1
						Chester C (loan)	5	—
						Colchester U (loan)	13	2
						Shrewsbury T	101	15
						Bolton W	67	4
Dave Lee	5 8	10 02	5 11 67	Manchester	Schools	Bury	208	35
						Southampton	20	—
						Bolton W	32	5
Jason McAteer	5 10	10 05	18 6 71	Liverpool	Marine	Bolton W	21	—
Andrew Roscoe	5 11	12 00	4 6 73	Liverpool	Trainee	Liverpool	—	—
						Bolton W	—	—
Barry Smith*			30 4 74	Liverpool	Trainee	Bolton W	—	—

BOLTON WANDERERS

Colours: White shirts, navy blue shorts, red stockings, blue and white tops. **Change colours:** Red and blue striped shirts, white shorts, red stockings.

Foundation: In 1874 boys of Christ Church Sunday School, Blackburn Street, led by their master Thomas Ogden, established a football club which went under the name of the school and whose president was Vicar of Christ Church. Membership was 6d (2cp). When their president began to lay down too many rules about the use of church premises, the club broke away and formed Bolton Wanderers in 1877, holding their earliest meetings at the Gladstone Hotel.

First Football League game: 8 September, 1888, Football League, v Derby C (h), L 3-6 – Harrison; Robinson, Mitchell; Roberts, Weir, Bullough, Davenport (2), Milne, Coupar, Barbour, Brogan (1).

Did you know: Bolton Wanderers are the only club to have won the FA Cup at least four times without conceding a goal in any of their final victories achieved in 1923, 1926, 1929 and 1958.

Managers (and Secretary-Managers)
Tom Rawthorne 1874–85*, J. J. Bentley 1885–86*, W. G. Struthers 1886–87*, Fitzroy Norris 1887*, J. J. Bentley 1887–95*, Harry Downs 1895–96*, Frank Brettell 1896–98*, John Somerville 1898–1910, Will Settle 1910–15, Tom Mather 1915–19, Charles Foweraker 1919–44, Walter Rowley 1944–50, Bill Ridding 1951–68, Nat Lofthouse 1968–70, Jimmy McIlroy 1970, Jimmy Meadows 1971, Nat Lofthouse 1971 (then admin. man. to 1972), Jimmy Armfield 1971–74, Ian Greaves 1974–80, Stan Anderson 1980–81, George Mulhall 1981–82, John McGovern 1982–85, Charlie Wright 1985, Phil Neal December 1985–92, Bruce Rioch May 1992–.

Player and Position	Ht	Wt	Date	Birth Place	Source	Clubs	League App	Gls
Forwards								
Scott Green	6 0	11 12	15 1 70	Walsall	Trainee	Derby Co	—	—
						Bolton W	124	16
Craig Lewin*			1 1 74	Whiston	Trainee	Bolton W	—	—
John McGinlay	5 9	11 06	8 4 64	Inverness	Elgin C	Shrewsbury T	60	27
						Bury	25	9
						Millwall	34	10
						Bolton W	34	16
Mark Patterson	5 6	10 10	24 5 65	Darwen	Apprentice	Blackburn R	101	20
						Preston NE	55	19
						Bury	42	10
						Bolton W	92	6
Andy Walker	5 8	10 07	6 4 65	Glasgow	Baillieston J	Motherwell	76	17
						Celtic	108	30
						Newcastle U (loan)	2	—
						Bolton W	56	41

Trainees
Antrobus, Wayne A; Fist, Dean T; Foster, Neil; Harrison, Craig A; Hassall, Jonathan; Hughes, Lee A; Jackson, Justin J; Mason, Andrew J; McKay, Andrew S; Osmand, Marc; Smith, Marcus; Strange, Stephen A; Wall, Ryan J.

Associated Schoolboys
Barron, Michael; Bowman, Matthew S; Doherty, Martin A; Done, John; Feeney, Gareth T; Glennon, Mathew W; Gradwell, Robert A; Gregory, Christopher; Harris, Neil; Irwin, Nicholas J; Lloyd, Steven M; Martin, Shaun A; Potter, Lee; Proctor, Daniel R; Purslow, David J; Westhead, Mark L.

Associated Schoolboys who have accepted the club's offer of a Traineeship/Contract
Evans, Robert T. D; Leather, Ian; Redmond, Brendan; Wiggans, Andrew.

AFC BOURNEMOUTH 1992–93 *Back row (left to right):* Sean O'Driscoll (Player/Community Officer), David Morris, Paul Wood, Scott Mean, Brian McGorry, Neil Masters, Denny Mundee, Peter Scott, Paul Mitchell, Mick Newman (Physio).

Centre row: Ken Sullivan (Youth Trainer), Adrian Pennock, Efan Ekoku, Alex Watson, Steven Fletcher, Sammy Bibbo, Vince Bartram, Mark Morris, Paul Morrell, Peter Shearer, Brett Phillips, Mike Trusson (Youth Manager).

Front row: Richard Cooke, Shaun Brooks, Keith Rowland, David Williams (Assistant Manager/Coach), Tony Pulis (Manager), John Kirk (Trainer), Danny Holmes, Paul Smith, David Puckett, Matthew Lovell.

Division 2   AFC BOURNEMOUTH

Dean Court Ground, Bournemouth. Telephone Bournemouth (0202) 395381. Fax: (0202) 309797.

Ground capacity: 11,880.

Record attendance: 28,799 v Manchester U, FA Cup 6th rd, 2 March 1957.

Record receipts: £33,723 v Manchester U, FA Cup 3rd rd, 7 January 1984.

Pitch measurements: 112yd × 75yd.

Chairman: N Hayward.

Directors: B. E. Willis (vice-chairman), E. G. Keep, G. M. C. Hayward, C. W. Legg, K. Gardiner.

Chief Executive: Annie Bassett.

Secretary: K. R. J. MacAlister.

Manager: Tony Pulis. *Assistant Manager:* David Williams. *Youth team coach:* Mike Trusson.

Trainer: J. Kirk. *Physio: Steve Hardwick.*

Year Formed: 1899. *Turned Professional:* 1912. *Ltd Co.:* 1914.

Previous Names: Boscombe St Johns, 1890–99; Boscombe FC, 1899–1923; Bournemouth & Boscombe Ath FC, 1923–71.

Club Nickname: 'Cherries'.

Previous Grounds: 1899–1910, Castlemain Road, Pokesdown; 1910, Dean Court.

Record League Victory: 7–0 v Swindon T, Division 3 (S), 22 September 1956 – Godwin; Cunningham, Keetley; Clayton, Crosland, Rushworth; Siddall (1), Norris (2), Arnott (1), Newsham (2), Cutler (1). 10–0 win v Northampton T at start of 1939–40 expunged from the records on outbreak of war.

Record Cup Victory: 11–0 v Margate, FA Cup, 1st rd, 20 November 1971 – Davies; Machin (1), Kitchener, Benson, Jones, Powell, Cave (1), Boyer, MacDougall (9 incl. 1p), Miller, Scott (De Garis).

Record Defeat: 0–9 v Lincoln C, Division 3, 18 December 1982.

Most League Points (2 for a win): 62, Division 3, 1971–72.

Most League Points (3 for a win): 97, Division 3, 1986–87.

Most League Goals: 88, Division 3 (S), 1956–57.

Highest League Scorer in Season: Ted MacDougall, 42, 1970–71.

Most League Goals in Total Aggregate: Ron Eyre, 202, 1924–33.

Most Capped Player: Gerry Peyton, 7 (33), Republic of Ireland.

Most League Appearances: Ray Bumstead, 412, 1958–70.

Record Transfer Fee Received: £765,000 from Norwich C for Efan Ekoku, March 1993.

Record Transfer Fee Paid: £210,000 to Gillingham for Gavin Peacock, August 1989.

Football League Record: 1923 Elected to Division 3 (S). Remained a Third Division club for record number of years until 1970; 1970–71 Division 4; 1971–75 Division 3; 1975–82 Division 4; 1982–87 Division 3; 1987–90 Division 2; 1990– 92 Division 3; 1992– Division 2.

Honours: Football League: Division 3 – Champions 1986–87; Division 3 (S) – Runners-up 1947–48. Promotion from Division 4 1970–71 (2nd), 1981–82 (4th). *FA Cup:* best season: 6th rd, 1956–57. *Football League Cup:* best season: 4th rd, 1962, 1964. *Associate Members' Cup:* Winners 1984.

BOURNEMOUTH 1992—93 LEAGUE RECORD

Match No.	Date		Venue	Opponents	Result		H/T Score	Lg. Pos.	Goalscorers	Atten dance
1	Aug	15	A	Preston NE	D	1-1	1-0	—	Rowland	4756
2		22	H	Port Vale	W	2-1	1-0	5	Fletcher, Watson	4825
3		29	A	WBA	L	1-2	0-1	12	Regis	12,563
4	Sept	1	A	Mansfield T	W	2-0	1-0	—	Regis, Fletcher	3031
5		5	H	Hartlepool U	L	0-2	0-0	11		4328
6		12	H	Fulham	W	2-1	1-1	11	McGorry 2	5398
7		15	A	Blackpool	L	0-2	0-0	—		3455
8		19	A	Bolton W	D	1-1	1-0	12	Morris	4623
9		26	H	Huddersfield T	D	1-1	0-0	12	Rowland	4447
10	Oct	3	A	Exeter C	D	1-1	0-1	15	Shearer	3653
11		10	H	Rotherham U	D	0-0	0-0	15		4761
12		17	A	Leyton Orient	L	0-1	0-0	16		4528
13		24	H	Stockport Co	W	1-0	0-0	15	Morgan	4058
14		31	A	Wigan Ath	D	0-0	0-0	16		1803
15	Nov	3	H	Brighton & HA	D	1-1	1-0	—	Mundee (pen)	4828
16		7	A	Stoke C	L	0-2	0-0	17		15,146
17		21	H	Reading	D	1-1	0-0	17	McGorry	4418
18		28	A	Plymouth Arg	L	1-2	0-1	18	Burrows (og)	6408
19	Dec	12	A	Bradford C	W	1-0	0-0	16	McGorry	5011
20		19	H	Hull C	D	0-0	0-0	16		4200
21		26	H	Swansea C	L	0-2	0-0	17		4995
22	Jan	9	H	Blackpool	W	5-1	3-1	17	Ekoku 2, Murray 2, Wood	3807
23		16	A	Huddersfield T	W	1-0	0-0	17	Ekoku	4316
24		26	H	WBA	L	0-1	0-1	—		5687
25		30	A	Port Vale	L	0-3	0-2	19		6834
26	Feb	6	H	Preston NE	W	2-1	2-0	16	Ekoku, McGorry	3601
27		13	A	Hartlepool U	W	1-0	1-0	16	Ekoku	2166
28		20	H	Mansfield T	W	4-1	3-0	14	McGorry, Fletcher, Ekoku, Wood	3987
29		26	A	Rotherham U	W	2-1	0-0	—	McGorry, Wood	4401
30	Mar	2	A	Fulham	D	1-1	1-0	—	Wood	3424
31		6	H	Exeter C	L	1-3	0-1	14	Pennock	4948
32		9	A	Chester C	L	0-1	0-1	—		1614
33		13	H	Stoke C	D	1-1	0-0	15	Ekoku	7129
34		16	A	Burnley	D	1-1	1-1	—	Mundee	8601
35		20	A	Brighton & HA	L	0-1	0-1	15		7059
36		23	H	Plymouth Arg	L	1-3	0-0	—	Fletcher	4150
37		27	A	Reading	L	2-3	0-2	15	Shearer, Beadle	5978
38	Apr	3	H	Chester C	D	0-0	0-0	15		2829
39		6	H	Bradford C	D	1-1	0-0	—	Murray	2851
40		10	A	Swansea C	L	1-2	0-1	17	Mean	5101
41		13	H	Burnley	D	1-1	1-0	—	Shearer	4456
42		17	A	Hull C	L	0-3	0-2	17		3442
43		24	H	Leyton Orient	W	3-0	2-0	16	McGorry, Shearer, Beadle	4595
44		27	H	Bolton W	L	1-2	0-1	—	Murray	4434
45	May	1	A	Stockport Co	D	0-0	0-0	16		5446
46		8	H	Wigan Ath	D	0-0	0-0	17		3838

Final League Position: 17

GOALSCORERS

League (45): McGorry 8, Ekoku 7, Fletcher 4, Murray 4, Shearer 4, Wood 4, Beadle 2, Mundee 2 (1 pen), Regis 2, Rowland 2, Mean 1, Morgan 1, Morris 1, Pennock 1, Watson 1, own goal 1.
Coca Cola Cup (1): Morris 1.
FA Cup (7): Mundee 2, Ekoku 1, Lovell 1, McGorry 1, Morgan 1, Shearer 1.

Bartram 45	O'Driscoll 38 + 4	Morrell 20 + 1	Watson 46	Pennock 43	Scott 9 + 1	Mean 6 + 9	Regis 6	Fletcher 29 + 2	McGorry 36 + 1	Rowland 31 + 4	Cooke 8 + 4	Mundee 23 + 3	Morris 43	Murray 5 + 20	Holmes — + 1	Shearer 34	Morgan 6	Masters 19 + 1	Lovell 3	Wood 27	Butler 1	Ekoku 14	Smith 1	Beadle 9	Mitchell 3 + 2	Moss 1	Williams — + 1	McElhatton — + 1	Match No.
1	2	3	4	5	6	7	8	9	10	11	12	14																	1
1	7	3	4	2	6	14	8	9	10	11	12			5															2
1	7	3	4	2		6	8	9	10	11	12			5															3
1	6	3	4	2		7	8	9	10	11	12			5															4
1	6	3	4	2			8	9	10	11	7	12		5															5
1	6	3	4	2	12		8	9	10	11	7			5															6
1	6		4	2			8	9	10	11	7	3	5	12		14													7
1	6		4	2				9	10	11	7	3	5			8													8
1	6		4	2	12			9	10	11	7	3	5			8													9
1	7	14	5	2			8	9	10	11	12	3	4			6													10
1		4	5	2		7	8	9	10	11		3				6													11
1	7		5	2	12		8	9	10	11		3	4			6													12
1	7		5	2			8	9		11		3	4			6		10											13
1	7	3	5	2			8	9		14	12		4			6		10		11									14
1	7	3	5	2	10		8	9			12		4	14		6		11											15
1	7	3	5			10	8			11		2	4	14		6		12						9					16
1	2	3	5	6	11			9					4			8		10		7									17
1	8	3	5	2	6					11	12		4	14				10				7		9					18
1			5	2				9		11		6	4			8		10		3		7							19
1	14		5	2						11	12	6	4			8		10		3		7		9					20
1	10		5	2				9		11	12	6	4	14		8		7		3									21
1			5	2				9				6	4	11		8				3		7		10					22
1			5	2				9		11	12	6	4	14		8				3		7		10					23
1			5	6	11			9				2	4	12		8				3		7		10					24
1	6		5	2				9					4			8				3		7		10	11				25
1	14		5	6	11			9				2	4	12		8				3		7		10					26
1	8		5	6	11			9				2	4							3		7		10					27
1	2		5	6	11			9					4	12		8				3		7		10					28
1	2		5	6	11			9	12				4			8				3		7		10					29
1	2		5	6				9		11			4	12		8				3		7		10					30
1	2		5	6				9		11			4	12		8				3		7		10					31
1	14		5	6	11			9				2	4	12		8				3		7		10					32
1	14		5	6	11			9				2	4	12		8				3		7		10					33
1	2		5	6	10			9		11			4	12		8				3		7							34
1	2		5	6				9		11			4	12		8				3		7		10					35
1	4		5	6				9		11		2		12		8				3		7		10					36
1	2		5	6	12						11	3	4	7		8		10						9	14				37
1	2		5	6				9				3	4	12				8		7				10	11				38
1	2	3	5	6				9		11			4	7				8						10	12				39
	2	10	5	6	12			9				3	4					8		7					11	1			40
1	2	3	5	6	11			9					4	12				8		7					10				41
1	2	3	5	6	11			9	12				4					8		7					10				42
1	2	3	5	6				9		11			4	12				8		7					10				43
1	2	3	5	6				9		11			4	12				8		7					10		14		44
1	2	3	5	6	11			9	12				4					8		7					10				45
1		3	5	6			8	9	12	11			4							7					10	2		14	46

Coca Cola Cup	First Round	Walsall (a)		1-1
		(h)		0-1
FA Cup	First Round	Barnet (h)		0-0
		(a)		2-1
	Second Round	Cheltenham T (a)		1-1
		(h)		3-0
	Third Round	Blackburn R (a)		1-3

AFC BOURNEMOUTH

Player and Position	Ht	Wt	Birth Date	Birth Place	Source	Clubs	League App	Gls
Goalkeepers								
Vince Bartram	6 2	13 04	7 8 68	Birmingham	Local	Wolverhampton W	5	—
						Blackpool (loan)	9	—
						WBA (loan)	—	—
						Bournemouth	91	—
Neil Moss	6 1	12 11	10 5 75	New Milton	Trainee	Bournemouth	1	—
Defenders								
Dan Holmes‡			13 6 72	Clophill	Middlesbrough	Bournemouth	1	—
Michael McElhatton§			16 4 75	Co.Kerry	Trainee	Bournemouth	1	—
Neil Masters	6 1	13 03	25 5 72	Lisburn	Trainee	Bournemouth	20	—
Paul Mitchell	5 10	12 00	20 10 71	Bournemouth	Trainee	Bournemouth	12	—
Paul Morrell	5 11	13 05	23 3 61	Poole	Weymouth	Bournemouth	343	8
Mark Morris	6 1	13 08	26 9 62	Morden	Apprentice	Wimbledon	168	9
						Aldershot (loan)	14	—
						Watford	41	1
						Sheffield U	56	3
						Bournemouth	86	4
Adrian Pennock	5 11	12 01	27 3 71	Ipswich	Trainee	Norwich C	1	—
						Bournemouth	43	1
Alex Watson	6 0	11 09	5 4 68	Liverpool	Apprentice	Liverpool	4	—
						Derby Co (loan)	5	—
						Bournemouth	84	4
Midfield								
Shaun Brooks*	5 7	11 00	9 10 62	London	Apprentice	Crystal Palace	54	4
						Orient	148	26
						Bournemouth	128	13
						Stockport Co (loan)	—	—
Brian McGorry	5 10	11 00	16 4 70	Liverpool	Weymouth	Bournemouth	45	8
Scott Mean	5 11	11 11	13 12 73	Crawley	Trainee	Bournemouth	15	1
Sean O'Driscoll	5 8	11 03	1 7 57	Wolverhampton	Alvechurch	Fulham	148	13
						Bournemouth (loan)	19	1
						Bournemouth	386	18
Tony Pulis	5 10	11 08	16 1 58	Newport	Apprentice	Bristol R	85	3
					Happy Valley	Bristol R	45	2
						Newport Co	77	—
						Bournemouth	74	3
						Gillingham	16	—
						Bournemouth	16	1
Keith Rowland	5 10	10 00	1 9 71	Portadown	Trainee	Bournemouth	72	2
						Coventry C (loan)	2	—
Peter Scott*	5 9	11 12	1 10 63	London	Apprentice	Fulham	277	27
						Bournemouth	10	—
David Williams†	5 10	11 08	11 3 55	Cardiff	Clifton Ath	Bristol R	352	66
						Norwich C	60	11
						Bournemouth	1	—
Forwards								
Richard Cooke‡	5 6	9 00	4 9 65	Islington	Apprentice	Tottenham H	11	2
						Birmingham C (loan)	5	—
						Bournemouth	72	16
						Luton T	17	1
						Bournemouth	53	2
Steve Fletcher	6 2	14 00	26 6 72	Hartlepool	Trainee	Hartlepool U	32	4
						Bournemouth	31	4

AFC BOURNEMOUTH

Colours: Red shirts with white V shape & reverse V shape 3″ pattern, black shorts with white piping, black stockings with red/white turnback. **Change colours:** Purple shirts with green & navy V shape & reverse V shape 3″ pattern, white shorts, white stockings.

Foundation: There was a Bournemouth FC as early as 1875, but the present club arose out of the remnants of the Boscombe St John's club (formed 1890). The meeting at which Boscombe FC came into being was held at a house in Gladstone Road in 1899. They began by playing in the Boscombe and District Junior League.

First Football League game: 25 August, 1923, Division 3(S), v Swindon T (a), L 1-3 – Heron; Wingham, Lamb; Butt, C. Smith, Voisey; Miller, Lister (1), Davey, Simpson, Robinson.

Did you know: AFC Bournemouth lost only one match in the second half of their Division 4 programme in 1981–82. Of the 23 games they won 12 and drew ten.

Managers (and Secretary-Managers)
Vincent Kitcher 1914–23*, Harry Kinghorn 1923–25, Leslie Knighton 1925–28, Frank Richards 1928–30, Billy Birrell 1930–35, Bob Crompton 1935–36, Charlie Bell 1936–39, Harry Kinghorn 1939–47, Harry Lowe 1947–50, Jack Bruton 1950–56, Fred Cox 1956–58, Don Welsh 1958–61, Bill McGarry 1961–63, Reg Flewin 1963–65, Fred Cox 1965–70, John Bond 1970–73, Trevor Hartley 1974–78, John Benson 1975–78, Alec Stock 1979–80, David Webb 1980–82, Don Megson 1983, Harry Redknapp 1983–92, Tony Pulis 1992–.

Player and Position	Ht	Wt	Date	Birth Place	Source	Clubs	League App	Gls
Steve Lovell‡	5 10	11 10	16 7 60	Swansea	Apprentice	Crystal Palace	74	3
						Stockport Co (loan)	12	—
						Millwall	146	44
						Swansea C (loan)	2	1
						Gillingham	233	94
						Bournemouth	3	—
Denny Mundee*	5 10	11 00	10 10 68	Swindon	Apprentice	QPR	—	—
						Swindon T	—	—
						Bournemouth	100	6
						Torquay U (loan)	9	—
Robert Murray	5 11	11 07	31 10 74	Hammersmith	Trainee	Bournemouth	25	4
Peter Shearer	6 0	11 06	4 2 67	Birmingham	Apprentice	Birmingham C	4	—
						Rochdale	1	—
					Cheltenham T	Bournemouth	85	10
Paul Wood	5 9	10 01	1 11 64	Middlesbrough	Apprentice	Portsmouth	47	6
						Brighton	92	8
						Sheffield U	28	3
						Bournemouth (loan)	21	—
						Bournemouth	62	13

Trainees
Barfoot, Stuart J; Champion, Neil B; Hearn, Matthew C; Jones, Mark D; Kerr, Stuart P; McElhatton, Michael; Morgan, Scott; Reeve, James M; Wake, Nathan; Walters, Jesse P.

**Non-Contract
Williams, David M.

Associated Schoolboys
Benson, David; Cox, Robin A; Dean, Michael J; Glavin, Michael; Howe, Edward J; Kydd, Peter R; Perry, Ashley G; Preston, Jonathan R; Richards, Carl D; Rothwell, Ryan J; Smith, Mark L; Stringer, William M; Strong, Steven G; Taylor, Robert A; Wells, David.

Associated Schoolboys who have accepted the club's offer of a Traineeship/Contract
Eastland, Robert L; Ferrett, Christopher A; Town, David E.

**Non-Contract Players who are retained must be re-signed before they are eligible to play in League matches.

86

BRADFORD CITY 1992–93 *Back row (left to right):* Lee Margerison, Dean Richards, Stephen Torpey, Noel Blake, Scott Bairstow, Brian Tinnion, Sean McCarthy.
Centre row: Steve Smith (Youth Development Officer), Andy Hanson (Chief Scout), Stuart Pearson (Assistant Manager), Paul West, Michael McHugh, Paul Tomlinson, Chris Pearce, Gary Williams, Paul Coy, Craig Lawford, Frank Stapleton (Manager), Bryan Edwards (Physio).
Front row: Paul Reid, Paul Jewell, Scott Partridge, Gavin Oliver, Jeremy Howe, Lee Duxbury, Mike Duxbury.

Division 2   **BRADFORD CITY**

Valley Parade Ground, Bradford BD8 7DY. Telephone Bradford (0274) 306062 (Office); (0274) 307050 (Ticket Office). Fax (0274) 307457.

Ground capacity: 14,387.

Record attendance: 39,146 v Burnley, FA Cup 4th rd, 11 March 1911.

Record receipts: £59,250 v Tottenham H, FA Cup 3rd rd, 7 January 1989.

Pitch measurements: 110yd × 76yd.

Chairman: David Simpson. *Vice-chairman:* D. Thompson FCA.

Directors: D. Taylor FCA, M. Woodhead, T. Goddard. *Chief Executive:* David Clayton.

Manager: Frank Stapleton. *Assistant Manager:* Stuart Pearson. *Chief Scout:* Andy Hanson.

Youth Coach: Steve Smith. *Physio:* Steve Foster.

Secretary: Angie Harrison. *Commercial Manager:* Russell Gaunt. *Year Formed:* 1903. *Turned Professional:* 1903. *Ltd Co.:* 1908.

Club Nickname: 'The Bantams'.

Record League Victory: 11–1 v Rotherham U, Division 3 (N), 25 August 1928 – Sherlaw; Russell, Watson; Burkinshaw (1), Summers, Bauld; Harvey (2), Edmunds (3), White (3), Cairns, Scriven (2).

Record Cup Victory: 11–3 v Walker Celtic, FA Cup, 1st rd (replay), 1 December 1937 – Parker; Rookes, McDermott; Murphy, Mackie, Moore; Bagley (1), Whittingham (1), Deakin (4 incl. 1p), Cooke (1), Bartholomew (4).

Record Defeat: 1–9 v Colchester U, Division 4, 30 December 1961.

Most League Points (2 for a win): 63, Division 3 (N), 1928–29.

Most League Points (3 for a win): 94, Division 3, 1984–85.

Most League Goals: 128, Division 3 (N), 1928–29.

Highest League Scorer in Season: David Layne, 34, Division 4, 1961–62.

Most League Goals in Total Aggregate: Bobby Campbell, 121, 1981–84, 1984–86.

Most Capped Player: Harry Hampton, 9, Northern Ireland.

Most League Appearances: Cec Podd, 502, 1970–84.

Record Transfer Fee Received: £850,000 from Everton for Stuart McCall, June 1988.

Record Transfer Fee Paid: £290,000 to Newcastle U for Peter Jackson, October 1988.

Football League Record: 1903 Elected to Division 2; 1908–22 Division 1; 1922–27 Division 2; 1927–29 Division 3 (N); 1929–37 Division 2; 1937–61 Division 3; 1961–69 Division 4; 1969–72 Division 3; 1972–77 Division 4; 1977–78 Division 3; 1978–82 Division 4; 1982–85 Division 3; 1985–90 Division 2; 1990–92 Division 3; 1992– Division 2.

Honours: Football League: Division 1 best season: 5th, 1910–11; Division 2 – Champions 1907–08; Division 3 – Champions 1984–85; Division 3 (N) – Champions 1928–29; Division 4 – Runners-up 1981–82. *FA Cup:* Winners 1911 (first holders of the present trophy). *Football League Cup:* best season: 5th rd, 1965, 1989.

BRADFORD CITY 1992—93 LEAGUE RECORD

Match No.	Date	Venue	Opponents	Result	H/T Score	Lg. Pos.	Goalscorers	Atten dance
1	Aug 15	H	Chester C	W 3-1	0-1	—	Jewell, Torpey, Tinnion	5780
2	22	A	Plymouth Arg	L 0-3	0-1	13		6504
3	29	H	Brighton & HA	D 1-1	0-0	14	McCarthy	5151
4	Sept 2	H	Stoke C	W 3-1	1-1	—	Jewell 2, Duxbury L	5959
5	6	A	Huddersfield T	W 2-1	0-1	—	Jewell, McCarthy	5883
6	12	A	Mansfield T	L 2-5	2-3	9	Blake, Jewell	3545
7	15	H	Stockport Co	L 2-3	0-0	—	Reid, Jewell	5070
8	19	H	Preston NE	W 4-0	1-0	7	McCarthy 3, Tinnion	5882
9	26	A	Swansea C	D 1-1	1-1	8	Jewell	4781
10	Oct 3	A	Hull C	W 2-0	1-0	6	Jewell 2	5340
11	11	H	Burnley	W 1-0	1-0	—	Williams	10,235
12	17	A	Reading	D 1-1	0-0	5	McCarthy	4348
13	24	H	Leyton Orient	W 1-0	0-0	2	Blake	7235
14	31	A	Hartlepool U	L 0-2	0-1	7		4349
15	Nov 3	A	Wigan Ath	W 2-1	1-0	—	McCarthy, Lawford	2070
16	7	H	Fulham	W 3-2	3-1	1	McCarthy 2, Oliver	7625
17	21	A	WBA	D 1-1	1-1	2	McCarthy	15,416
18	28	H	Rotherham U	L 0-3	0-2	5		9004
19	Dec 12	H	Bournemouth	L 0-1	0-0	6		5011
20	19	A	Bolton W	L 0-5	0-0	8		6887
21	26	A	Blackpool	D 3-3	1-2	10	McCarthy 2, Jewell	5448
22	28	H	Port Vale	W 3-2	0-0	8	McHugh, McCarthy, Jewell	8018
23	Jan 2	H	Mansfield T	D 0-0	0-0	4		6940
24	9	A	Stockport Co	D 2-2	0-1	6	Reid, McHugh	4999
25	16	H	Swansea C	D 0-0	0-0	7		5551
26	23	A	Preston NE	L 2-3	1-3	7	McHugh, Hoyle	5155
27	27	A	Brighton & HA	D 1-1	0-0	—	Tinnion (pen)	5141
28	30	H	Plymouth Arg	D 0-0	0-0	7		5528
29	Feb 6	A	Chester C	W 5-2	3-1	5	Reid, Torpey, Duxbury L 2, Williams	2594
30	14	H	Huddersfield T	L 0-1	0-0	—		8214
31	20	A	Stoke C	L 0-1	0-0	9		16,494
32	27	A	Burnley	D 2-2	2-1	10	Reid, Jewell	13,262
33	Mar 6	H	Hull C	L 1-2	0-2	11	Jewell	6245
34	10	H	Exeter C	W 3-1	2-0	—	McCarthy, Torpey, Duxbury L	3900
35	13	A	Fulham	D 1-1	1-0	12	Oliver	4343
36	20	H	Wigan Ath	W 2-1	0-0	11	McCarthy, Williams (pen)	4748
37	23	A	Rotherham U	L 0-2	0-1	—		4447
38	28	H	WBA	D 2-2	1-1	—	Jewell, Reid	6627
39	Apr 3	A	Exeter C	W 1-0	0-0	10	Torpey	2547
40	6	A	Bournemouth	D 1-1	0-0	—	Jewell	2851
41	10	H	Blackpool	W 2-0	1-0	9	Torpey, Jewell	6191
42	13	A	Port Vale	W 2-1	0-1	—	Stapleton, Reid	8743
43	17	H	Bolton W	W 2-1	1-0	8	McCarthy, McHugh	9813
44	24	H	Reading	W 3-0	1-0	6	Duxbury L, McCarthy, Stapleton	7042
45	May 1	A	Leyton Orient	L 2-4	0-1	8	Blake, Heseltine	5504
46	8	H	Hartlepool U	L 0-2	0-1	10		5612

Final League Position: 10

GOALSCORERS

League (69): McCarthy 17, Jewell 16, Reid 6, Duxbury L 5, Torpey 5, McHugh 4, Blake 3, Tinnion 3 (1 pen), Williams 3 (1 pen), Oliver 2, Stapleton 2, Heseltine 1, Hoyle 1, Lawford 1.
Coca Cola Cup (3): Jewell 1, McCarthy 1, Reid 1.
FA Cup (6): Jewell 2, McCarthy 2, Blake 1, Tinnion 1 (pen).

Pearce 9	Duxbury M 36	Heseltine 40 + 2	Duxbury L 42	Blake 31 + 1	Oliver 39 + 1	Jewell 45 + 1	McCarthy 40 + 2	Torpey 17 + 7	Tinnion 24 + 3	Reid 44	Partridge — + 4	Richards 1 + 2	Margerison 1 + 2	McDonald 7	Hoyle 33	Williams 31	Tomlinson 24	McHugh 10 + 6	Lawford 5 + 3	Jenkins 6	Whitehead 6	Stapleton 8 + 5	Bowling 7	Match No.
1	2	3	4	5	6	7	8	9	10	11	12													1
1	2		4	5	6	7	8	9	10	11	12	3	14											2
1	8	3	4	5		7		9	10	11					2	6								3
1	8	3	4	5		7		9	10	11					2	6								4
1	8	3	4	5		7		9	10	11					2	6								5
1		3	4	5	12	7		9	10	11					2	6	8							6
1			4	5	3	7		9	10	11					2	6	8							7
	14		4	5	3	7		9	10	11					2	6	8	1	12					8
			4	5	3	7		9	10	11					2	6	8	1						9
	2		4	5	3	7		9	12	10	11					6	8	1						10
	2		4	5	3	7		9	10	11						6	8	1						11
	6	2	4	5	3	7		9	12	10	11						8	1						12
	2		4	5	3	7		9	10	11							8	1	6					13
	4	2		5	3	7		9	12	10	11						8	1	6					14
	4	2		5	3	7		9	10	11							8	1	6					15
	4	2		5	3	7		9	10	11							8	1	6					16
11	12		4	5	3	7		9	10						8	6	1		2					17
11			4	5	8	7		9	12	10	2				6	3		1						18
2	8		4	5		7		9		11	12				6	3	1	10						19
8	3		4	5		7		9	10	11	12				6	2	1							20
2	3		4	5	6	7		9		10	11					1	8							21
2	3		4	5	6	7		9		11	12	8				1	10							22
2	3		4		6	7		9	12	11		8				1	10	5						23
8	3		4	14	5	7		9	12	11		6				10		2	1					24
8	3		4		5	7		9	12	11		6				10		2	1					25
8	3		4		5	7		9	12	11		6				1	10	2						26
8	3		4		5	12		9		10	11	6				7		2	1					27
8	3		4	5	6	7			12	10	11	9						2	1					28
8	3		4		5	7		9		11	12	6				2						1	10	29
8	3		4		5	7		9		11		6				2						1	10	30
8	3		4		5	7		9	10	11		6				2	1							31
8	3		4		5	7		9	10	11		6				2	1	12						32
8	3		4	5	5	7		9	12	11		6				2	1	10				14		33
8	3		4		5	7		9	10	11		6				2	1							34
8	3		4		5	7		9	10	11		6				2	1					12		35
8	3		4		5	7		9	10	11		6				2	1							36
8	3		4		5	7		9	10	11		6				2	1					12		37
8	3		4		5	7			10	11		6				2		12				9	1	38
8	3	4	5		7			9	10	11		6				2						12	1	39
8	3	4	5	6		7	12	9		11		2										10	1	40
8	3	4	5	6		7		9	10	11		2										12	1	41
8	3	4	5	6		7	12	9		11		2						14				10	1	42
8	3	4	5	6		7	11	9				2						14	12			10	1	43
	3	4	5	6		7	11	9		8		2										10	1	44
1	3	4	5	6		7	11	9		8		10	2					14	12					45
1	3		5	6		7	11	9		8	12	4	2					14				10		46

Coca Cola Cup	First Round	Scarborough (a)	0-3
		(h)	3-5
FA Cup	First Round	Preston NE (h)	1-1
		(a)	5-4
	Second Round	Huddersfield T (h)	0-2

BRADFORD CITY

Player and Position	Ht	Wt	Date	Birth Place	Source	Clubs	League App	Gls
Goalkeepers								
Chris Pearce*	6 0	11 04	7 8 61	Newport	Wolverhampton W	Blackburn R	—	—
						Rochdale (loan)	5	—
						Barnsley (loan)	—	—
						Rochdale	36	—
						Port Vale	48	—
						Wrexham	25	—
						Burnley	181	—
						Bradford C	9	—
Paul Tomlinson	6 2	13 12	22 2 64	Brierley Hill	Middlewood R	Sheffield U	37	—
						Birmingham C (loan)	11	—
						Bradford C	233	—
Defenders								
Scott Bairstow‡	6 1	12 07	1 6 72	Bradford		Bradford C	—	—
Noel Blake	6 0	13 11	12 1 62	Jamaica	Sutton Coldfield	Aston Villa	4	—
						Shrewsbury T (loan)	6	—
						Birmingham C	76	5
						Portsmouth	144	10
						Leeds U	51	4
						Stoke C	75	3
						Bradford C (loan)	6	—
						Bradford C	32	3
Paul Coy*			7 11 73	Huddersfield	Trainee	Bradford C	—	—
Mike Duxbury	5 9	11 02	1 9 59	Accrington	Apprentice	Manchester U	299	6
						Blackburn R	27	—
						Bradford C	52	—
Wayne Heseltine	5 9	11 06	3 12 69	Bradford	Trainee	Manchester U	—	—
						Oldham Ath	1	—
						Bradford C	42	1
Craig Lawford	5 10	11 10	25 11 72	Dewsbury	Trainee	Bradford C	9	1
Gavin Oliver	6 0	12 10	6 9 62	Felling	Apprentice	Sheffield W	20	—
						Tranmere R (loan)	17	1
						Brighton (loan)	16	—
						Bradford C	267	9
Dean Richards	6 0	12 00	9 6 74	Bradford	Trainee	Bradford C	10	1
Paul West*	5 11	11 00	22 6 70		Alcester T	Port Vale	—	—
						Bradford C	—	—
Gary Williams	5 9	11 12	17 6 60	Wolverhampton	Apprentice	Aston Villa	240	—
						Walsall (loan)	9	—
						Leeds U	39	3
						Watford	42	—
						Bradford C	53	3
Midfield								
Lee Duxbury‡	5 10	11 07	7 10 69	Skipton	Trainee	Bradford C	146	16
						Rochdale (loan)	10	—
Lee Margerison*			10 9 73	Bradford	Trainee	Bradford C	3	—
Forwards								
Jeremy Howe*			5 9 73	Stancliffe	Trainee	Bradford C	3	—
Colin Hoyle	5 11	12 03	15 1 72	Derby	Trainee	Arsenal	—	—
						Chesterfield (loan)	3	—
						Barnsley	—	—
						Bradford C	33	1
Paul Jewell	5 8	11 10	28 9 64	Liverpool	Apprentice	Liverpool	—	—
						Wigan Ath	137	35
						Bradford C	183	34

BRADFORD CITY

Colours: Claret and amber shirts, black shorts, amber stockings. **Change colours:** Dark and light blue shirts, blue shorts, light blue stockings.

Foundation: Bradford was a rugby stronghold around the turn of the century but after Manningham RFC held an archery contest to help them out of financial difficulties in 1903, they were persuaded to give up the handling code and turn to soccer. So they formed Bradford City and continued at Valley Parade. Recognising this as an opportunity of spreading the dribbling code in this part of Yorkshire, the Football League immediately accepted the new club's first application for membership of the Second Division.

First Football League game: 1 September, 1903, Division 2, v Grimsby T (a), L 0-2 – Seymour; Wilson, Halliday; Robinson, Millar, Farnall; Guy, Beckram, Forrest, McMillan, Graham.

Did you know: Jimmy Conlin was the first Bradford City player to receive international honours when he was selected to play at outside-left for England against Scotland on 7 April 1906.

Managers (and Secretary-Managers)
Robert Campbell 1903–05, Peter O'Rourke 1905–21, David Menzies 1921–26, Colin Veitch 1926–28, Peter O'Rourke 1928–30, Jack Peart 1930–35, Dick Ray 1935–37, Fred Westgarth 1938–43, Bob Sharp 1943–46, Jack Barker 1946–47, John Milburn 1947–48, David Steele 1948–52, Albert Harris 1952, Ivor Powell 1952–55, Peter Jackson 1955–61, Bob Brocklebank 1961–64, Bill Harris 1965–66, Willie Watson 1966–69, Grenville Hair 1967–68, Jimmy Wheeler 1968–71, Bryan Edwards 1971–75, Bobby Kennedy 1975–78, John Napier 1978, George Mulhall 1978–81, Roy McFarland 1981–82, Trevor Cherry 1982–87, Terry Dolan 1987–89, Terry Yorath 1989–90, John Docherty 1990–91, Frank Stapleton December 1991–.

Player and Position	Ht	Wt	Date	Birth Place	Source	Clubs	League App	Gls
Sean McCarthy	6 0	12 05	12 9 67	Bridgend	Bridgend	Swansea C	91	25
						Plymouth Arg	70	19
						Bradford C	113	46
Michael McHugh	5 11	11 00	3 4 71	Donegal		Bradford C	26	4
Scott Partridge	5 9	11 00	13 10 74	Grimsby	Trainee	Bradford C	4	—
Paul Reid	5 8	10 08	19 1 68	Warley	Apprentice	Leicester C	162	21
						Bradford C (loan)	7	—
						Bradford C	44	6
Frank Stapleton	6 0	13 01	10 7 56	Dublin	Apprentice	Arsenal	225	75
						Manchester U	223	60
						Ajax	4	—
						Derby Co	10	1
					Le Havre	Blackburn R	81	13
						Aldershot	—	—
						Huddersfield T	5	—
						Bradford C	40	2
Stephen Torpey	6 2	12 11	8 12 70	Islington	Trainee	Millwall	7	—
						Bradford C	96	22
Darren Treacy*	5 10	12 09	6 9 70	Lambeth	Trainee	Millwall	7	—
						Bradford C	16	2

Trainees
Benn, Wayne; Blair, David A; Carss, Anthony J; Dale, Michael; Grayston, Neil J; Hamilton, Derrik V; Hart, Aiden M; Lodge, Jason; Lynch, Michael; Owen, Gary; Stuttard, Andrew J; Summerscales, Lee J; Tomlinson, Graeme M; Wilson, Richard J.

Associated Schoolboys
Aldred, Andrew J; Brannan, Michael L; Briggs, Ian M; Calvert, Lee J; Crowther, Andrew J; Crowther, Mathew; Davey, Ben J. N; Davies, Robert A; Ellis, John; Gautrey, Paul J; Hague, Thomas A; Holmes, Richard M; Marshall, Jamie B; Mazurke, Shane; Megson, Daniel M. D; Morrell, Michael J; Nichols, Stuart J; Smith, Christopher P; Symonds, David K; Wardman, Paul J.

Associated Schoolboys who have accepted the club's offer of a Traineeship/Contract
Jackson, Scott; Lowe, Anthony; Proctor, James A; Richardson, Christopher; Stabb, Christopher J.

BRENTFORD 1992–93 *Back row (left to right):* Marcus Gayle, Danny Tripp, Murray Jones, Keith Millen, Ashley Bayes, Terry Evans, Graham Benstead, Bob Booker, Chris Sparks, Jamie Bates.
Centre row: Joe Gadston (Youth Team Manager), Micky Bennett, Detzi Kruszynski, Lee Luscombe, Gary Blissett, Simon Ratcliffe, Grant Chalmers, Kevin Godfrey, Robert Peters,
Roy Clare (Physio).
Front row: Wilf Rostron (Assistant Manager), Brian Statham, Billy Manuel, Chris Hughton, Phil Holder (Manager), Neil Smillie, Paul Buckle, Steve Bircham, Graham Pearce (First Team Coach).
(Photograph: Lee Doyle)

Division 2   **BRENTFORD**

Griffin Park, Braemar Rd, Brentford, Middlesex TW8 0NT.
Telephone 081–847 2511. Fax 081–568 9940. Commercial
Dept: 081–560 6062. Press Office: 081–574 3047. Clubcall: 0898
121108.

Ground capacity: 13,870.

Record attendance: 39,626 v Preston NE, FA Cup 6th rd,
5 March 1938.

Record receipts: £79,838 v Tottenham H, Coca Cola Cup 2nd
rd 2nd leg, 7 October 1992.

Pitch measurements: 111yd × 74yd.

President: W. Wheatley. *Life Vice-president:* F. Edwards.

Chairman: M. M. Lange. *Vice-chairman:* G. V. Potter.

Directors: R. J. J. Blindell LL.B, E. J. Radley-Smith MS, FRCS,
LRCP, D. Tana, J. F. Herting, B. Evans. *Managing Director:* Keith Loring. *Manager:* David
Webb. *Assistant Manager:* Kevin Lock. *Physio:* Roy Clare. *Youth Team Manager:* Joe
Gadston. *Community Liaison Officer:* Martyn Spong. *Secretary:* Polly Kates. *Press Officer/
Programme Editor:* Eric White (081–574 3047). *Promotions Manager:* Royce Dickinson.
Safety officer: Jill Dawson.

Year Formed: 1889. *Turned Professional:* 1899. *Ltd Co.:* 1901.

Club Nickname: 'The Bees'.

Previous Grounds: 1889–91, Clifden Road; 1891–95, Benns Fields, Little Ealing; 1895–98,
Shotters Field; 1898–1900, Cross Road, S. Ealing; 1900–04, Boston Park; 1904, Griffin
Park.

Record League Victory: 9–0 v Wrexham, Division 3, 15 October 1963 – Cakebread; Coote,
Jones; Slater, Scott, Higginson; Summers (1), Brooks (2), McAdams (2), Ward (2), Hales
(1). (1 og).

Record Cup Victory: 7–0 v Windsor & Eton (away), FA Cup, 1st rd, 20 November 1982 –
Roche; Rowe, Harris (Booker); McNichol (1), Whitehead, Hurlock (2), Kamara, Bowles,
Joseph (1), Mahoney (3), Roberts.

Record Defeat: 0–7 v Swansea T, Division 3 (S), 8 November 1924 and v Walsall, Division
3 (S), 19 January 1957.

Most League Points (2 for a win): 62, Division 3 (S), 1932–33 and Division 4, 1962–63.

Most League Points (3 for a win): 82, Division 3, 1991–92.

Most League Goals: 98, Division 4, 1962–63.

Highest League Scorer in Season: Jack Holliday, 38, Division 3 (S), 1932–33.

Most League Goals in Total Aggregate: Jim Towers, 153, 1954–61.

Most Capped Player: John Buttigieg, (44), Malta.

Most League Appearances: Ken Coote, 514, 1949–64.

Record Transfer Fee Received: £720,000 from Wimbledon for Dean Holdsworth, August
1992.

Record Transfer Fee Paid: £275,000 to Chelsea for Joe Allon, November 1992.

Football League Record: 1920 Original Member of Division 3; 1921–33 Division 3 (S);
1933–35 Division 2; 1935–47 Division 1; 1947–54 Division 2; 1954–62 Division 3 (S); 1962–
63 Division 4; 1963–66 Division 3; 1966–72 Division 4; 1972–73 Division 3; 1973–78
Division 4; 1978–92 Division 3; 1992–93 Division 1; 1993– Division 2.

Honours: Football League: Division 1 best season: 5th, 1935–36; Division 2 – Champions
1934–35; Division 3 – Champions 1991–92; Division 3 (S) – Champions 1932–33; Runners-
up 1929–30, 1957–58; Division 4 – Champions 1962–63. *FA Cup:* best season: 6th rd, 1938,
1946, 1949, 1989. *Football League Cup:* best season: 4th rd, 1982–83. *Freight Rover Trophy*
– Runners-up 1985.

BRENTFORD 1992—93 LEAGUE RECORD

Match No.	Date		Venue	Opponents	Result		H/T Score	Lg. Pos.	Goalscorers	Atten dance
1	Aug	15	H	Wolverhampton W	L	0-2	0-0	—		9069
2		22	A	Bristol R	L	1-2	0-2	21	Blissett (pen)	5779
3		29	H	Southend U	W	2-1	1-1	18	Bennett, Millen	6431
4	Sept	1	H	Portsmouth	W	4-1	1-1	—	Bennett, Smillie, Gayle, Blissett	8471
5		4	A	Cambridge U	L	0-1	0-0	—		5075
6		13	H	Luton T	L	1-2	0-0	—	Blissett	7310
7		19	A	Leicester C	D	0-0	0-0	17		12,972
8		26	H	Millwall	D	1-1	1-0	16	Ratcliffe	8823
9	Oct	4	H	Newcastle U	L	1-2	0-1	—	Blissett	10,131
10		10	A	Peterborough U	D	0-0	0-0	19		5818
11		17	H	Watford	D	1-1	1-0	20	Putney (og)	8490
12		24	A	Barnsley	L	2-3	2-1	21	Blissett 2	4928
13		31	H	Bristol C	W	5-1	2-1	19	Millen 2, Chalmers, Blissett 2	8726
14	Nov	3	A	Swindon T	W	2-0	2-0	—	Blissett, Luscombe	7832
15		7	H	Charlton Ath	W	2-0	1-0	16	Luscombe 2	9354
16		14	A	Tranmere R	L	2-3	2-0	16	Blissett, Gayle	7852
17		21	H	Grimsby T	L	1-3	0-2	17	Allon (pen)	7439
18		28	H	Oxford U	W	1-0	1-0	17	Allon (pen)	8017
19	Dec	5	A	Birmingham C	W	3-1	2-1	12	Blissett, Ratcliffe, Manuel	8582
20		12	A	Sunderland	W	3-1	1-1	11	Blissett 2, Bennett	16,972
21		20	H	West Ham U	D	0-0	0-0	—		11,912
22		26	H	Derby Co	W	2-1	2-0	10	Allon, Goulooze (og)	10,226
23		28	A	Notts Co	D	1-1	1-1	10	Westley	6892
24	Jan	9	H	Leicester C	L	1-3	1-1	12	Blissett	8517
25		17	A	Millwall	L	1-6	0-3	—	Blissett	7571
26		23	A	Portsmouth	L	0-1	0-0	13		10,267
27		30	H	Bristol R	L	0-3	0-1	16		7527
28	Feb	6	A	Wolverhampton W	W	2-1	0-0	14	Allon 2 (1 pen)	12,361
29		9	A	Luton T	D	0-0	0-0	—		7248
30		14	H	Cambridge U	L	0-1	0-1	—		7318
31		21	A	Southend U	L	0-3	0-1	—		4123
32		27	H	Peterborough U	L	0-1	0-1	17		6337
33	Mar	6	A	Newcastle U	L	1-5	0-1	17	Scott (og)	30,006
34		9	H	Tranmere R	L	0-1	0-0	—		7993
35		13	A	Charlton Ath	L	0-1	0-0	19		7194
36		20	H	Birmingham C	L	0-2	0-0	22		7532
37		23	A	Grimsby T	W	1-0	0-0	—	Blissett	4384
38		27	H	Swindon T	D	0-0	0-0	19		10,197
39	Apr	3	A	Oxford U	W	2-0	1-0	16	Blissett, Bennett	5466
40		6	H	Sunderland	D	1-1	1-0	—	Gayle	9302
41		10	A	Derby Co	L	2-3	1-1	20	Gayle, Millen	12,366
42		12	A	Notts Co	D	2-2	1-1	17	Dickens, Blissett	8045
43		17	A	West Ham U	L	0-4	0-1	20		16,522
44		24	A	Watford	L	0-1	0-1	22		9045
45	May	1	H	Barnsley	W	3-1	2-1	21	Blissett 2 (1 pen), Allon	7958
46		8	A	Bristol C	L	1-4	0-2	22	Blissett	12,659

Final League Position: 22

GOALSCORERS

League (52): Blissett 21 (2 pens), Allon 6 (3 pens), Bennett 4, Gayle 4, Millen 4, Luscombe 3, Ratcliffe 2, Chalmers 1, Dickens 1, Manuel 1, Smillie 1, Westley 1, own goals 3.
Coca Cola Cup (7): Blissett 4, Bates 1, Booker 1, Millen 1.
FA Cup (0):

Benstead 25	Statham 45	Hughton 20	Millen 43	Evans 11	Ratcliffe 25 + 5	Bennett 34 + 4	Rostron 1 + 1	Godfrey 9 + 12	Blissett 46	Smillie 18 + 3	Gayle 31 + 7	Jones 6 + 10	Bates 24	Booker 1 + 2	Kruszynski 5 + 1	Manuel 39 + 2	Bayes 2	Luscombe 19 + 10	Peyton 19	Chalmers 9 + 2	Buckle 4 + 1	Westley 15 + 2	Allon 17 + 7	Mortimer 6	Peters — + 1	Dickens 13 + 2	Stephenson 11	Sansom 8	Match No.
1	2	3	4	5	6	7	8	*9*	10	11	12	14																	1
1	2	3	4		6	7		*9*	10	11	12			5	8	14													2
1	2	3	4		6	7		14	10	11	12	*9*		5		8													3
	2	3	4		6	7			10	11	9			5		8	1												4
1	2	3	4		6	7	12	14	10	*11*	9			5		8													5
	2	3	4		6	7			10		*9*	11		5		8	1	12											6
	2	3	4		6	7			10	14	*9*			5	12	8		11	1										7
	2	3	4		6			14	10	7	*9*			5	12	8		11	1										8
	2	3	4		6	7		*9*	10	11	14			5		8		12	1										9
	2	3	4				*7*	14	10	11	9			5		8		12	1	6									10
	2	3	4				*7*		10	11	9			5		8		12	1	6									11
	2	3	4						10	11	9	14		5		8		12	1	6		*7*							12
	2	3	4		12				10	11	9			14		8		*7*	1	6		5							13
	2	3	4		6				10		9	14				8		*7*	1	11	12	5							14
	2	3	4		12				10	11	9					8		*7*	1	6		5							15
	2	3	4		6	7	12		10		9					8		11	1			5							16
	2	*3*	4		14				10	11	9					8		12	1	6		5	*7*						17
	2	3	4		8	*11*		14	10		9					6		12	1			5	*7*						18
	2	3	4		6	11	12		10		9					8			1			5	*7*						19
	2	*3*	4		6	11		14	10		9					8		12	1			5	*7*						20
1	2		4		6	7		14	10	12	11					3		*8*				5	9						21
1	2		4		6	3			10	11		14				8		9		*12*		5	*7*						22
1	2		4			3			10	11		6	12			8		9				5	*7*						23
1	2					9			10			3	4	8	6	11						5	7						24
1	2					9	12		10			3		5		8		11		6	4	7							25
1			4			9	*8*		10			3	14	5				12		6	2					7	11		26
1	2		4			8		9	10		12					6				14		*5*	7	3					27
1	2		4			8		9	10	11				5		*6*		12				14	7	3					28
1	2		4			8	12		10					5		6		11			9		7	3					29
1	2		4			8		9	10		12			5		6		11					7	3					30
1	2		4			8		9	10		7			5		6		11								3	12		31
1	2		4		3	8	*7*		10					9	5	6		11						12		14			32
1	2		4		3	8			10					5		6						9	7			12	11		33
1	2		4			3			10			9		5		8	7					12				6	11		34
1	2		4		14	3			10			9		5		6		*11*				12				8	7		35
1	2		4		6	3			10			12	14	5		11						*9*				8	7		36
1	2		4	5	6				10			12		3	14	11						9				8	*7*		37
1	2		4	5	6				10			9	12			11										8	7	3	38
1	2		4	5	6	14			10			9				11						12				8	7	3	39
1	2		4	5	6	12			10			9				11										8	7	3	40
1	2		4	5	*6*	3	12		10			9				11						14				8	7		41
	2		4	5	6	14			10			9				*11*				1		12				8	7	3	42
	2			5		11			10	12		9				6				1	4					8		3	43
	2		4	5		12			10	11		9				6		7	1							8		3	44
	2		4	5		7			10	11		*9*				6		14	1			*12*				8		3	45
	2		4	5	14	*7*			10	11		9				6				1		12				8		3	46

Coca Cola Cup	First Round	Fulham (a)	2-0
		(h)	2-0
	Second Round	Tottenham H (a)	1-3
		(h)	2-4
FA Cup	Third Round	Grimsby T (h)	0-2

BRENTFORD

Player and Position	Ht	Wt	Date	Birth Place	Source	Clubs	League App	Gls
Goalkeepers								
Ashley Bayes*	6 1	12 12	19 4 72	Lincoln	Trainee	Brentford	4	—
Graham Benstead	6 2	12 04	20 8 63	Aldershot	Apprentice	QPR	—	—
						Norwich C (loan)	1	—
						Norwich C	15	—
						Colchester U (loan)	18	—
						Sheffield U (loan)	8	—
						Sheffield U	39	—
						Brentford	107	—
Gerry Peyton	6 2	13 09	20 5 56	Birmingham	Atherstone T	Burnley	30	—
						Fulham	345	—
						Southend U (loan)	10	—
						Bournemouth	202	—
						Everton	—	—
						Bolton W (loan)	1	—
						Norwich C (loan)	—	—
						Chelsea (loan)	1	—
						Brentford	19	—
Defenders								
Jamie Bates	6 1	12 12	24 2 68	London	Trainee	Brentford	196	6
Terry Evans	6 5	15 01	12 4 65	London	Hillingdon B	Brentford	229	23
Chris Hughton‡	5 7	11 05	11 12 58	West Ham	Amateur	Tottenham H	297	12
						West Ham U	33	—
						Brentford	32	—
Billy Manuel	5 5	10 00	28 6 69	Hackney	Apprentice	Tottenham H	—	—
						Gillingham	87	5
						Brentford	76	1
Keith Millen	6 2	12 04	26 9 66	Croydon	Juniors	Brentford	305	17
Rob Peters	5 8	11 02	18 5 71	Kensington	Trainee	Brentford	18	1
Simon Ratcliffe	5 11	11 09	8 2 67	Davyhulme	Apprentice	Manchester U	—	—
						Norwich C	9	—
						Brentford	146	9
Wilf Rostron*	5 6	11 01	29 9 56	Sunderland		Arsenal	17	2
						Sunderland	76	17
						Watford	317	22
						Sheffield W	7	—
						Sheffield U	36	3
						Brentford	42	2
Kenny Sansom*	5 7	10 04	26 9 58	Camberwell	Apprentice	Crystal Palace	172	3
						Arsenal	314	6
						Newcastle U	20	—
						QPR	64	—
						Coventry C	51	—
						Everton	7	1
						Brentford	8	—
Chris Sparks*	6 1	13 00	28 12 73	London	Trainee	Brentford	—	—
Brian Statham	5 11	11 00	21 5 69	Zimbabwe	Apprentice	Tottenham H	24	—
						Reading (loan)	8	—
						Bournemouth (loan)	2	—
						Brentford (loan)	18	—
						Brentford	45	—
Danny Tripp*	5 10	11 05	11 8 74	Basildon	Trainee	Brentford	—	—
Shane Westley	6 2	13 08	16 6 65	Canterbury	Apprentice	Charlton Ath	8	—
						Southend U	144	10
						Norwich C (loan)	—	—
						Wolverhampton W	50	2
						Brentford	17	1
Midfield								
Mickey Bennett	5 10	11 11	27 7 69	London	Apprentice	Charlton Ath	35	2
						Wimbledon	18	2
						Brentford	38	4
Bob Booker	6 3	13 03	25 1 58	Watford	Bedmond Sports	Brentford	251	41
						Sheffield U	109	13
						Brentford	19	2
Paul Buckle	5 8	10 08	16 12 70	Hatfield	Trainee	Brentford	57	1
Grant Chalmers	5 10	11 10	12 9 69	Guernsey	Northerners	Brentford	11	1
Alan Dickens	5 11	12 05	3 9 64	Plaistow	Apprentice	West Ham U	192	23
						Chelsea	48	1
						WBA (loan)	3	1
						Brentford	15	1
Marcus Gayle	6 2	12 13	27 9 70	Hammersmith	Trainee	Brentford	121	16
Detsi Kruszynski	6 0	12 12	14 10 61	Divschav	Homburg	Wimbledon	71	4
						Brentford (loan)	8	—
						Brentford	6	—

BRENTFORD

Colours: Red and white vertical striped shirts, black shorts, red stockings. **Change colours:** Blue shirts, dark blue shorts, dark blue stockings.

Foundation: Formed as a small amateur concern in 1889 they were very successful in local circles. They won the championship of the West London Alliance in 1893 and a year later the West Middlesex Junior Cup before carrying off the Senior Cup in 1895. After winning both the London Senior Amateur Cup and the Middlesex Senior Cup in 1898 they were admitted to the Second Division of the Southern League.

First Football League game: 28 August, 1920, Division 3, v Exeter C (a), L 0-3 – Young; Rosier, Hodson; Amos, Levitt, Elliott; Henery, Morley, Spredbury, Thompson, Smith.

Did you know: In 1900–01 Brentford became champions of Division 2 of the Southern League without losing a match and conceding only 11 goals. They had to apply for election to Division 1 but were refused and only gained admission when Gravesend dropped out.

Managers (and Secretary-Managers)
Will Lewis 1900–03*, Dick Molyneux 1903–06, W. G. Brown 1906–08, Fred Halliday 1908–26 (only secretary to 1922), Ephraim Rhodes 1912–15, Archie Mitchell 1921–22, Harry Curtis 1926–49, Jackie Gibbons 1949–52, Jimmy Blain 1952–53, Tommy Lawton 1953, Bill Dodgin Snr 1953–57, Malcolm Macdonald 1957–65, Tommy Cavanagh 1965–66, Billy Gray 1966–67, Jimmy Sirrel 1967–69, Frank Blunstone 1969–73, Mike Everitt 1973–75, John Docherty 1975–76, Bill Dodgin Jnr 1976–80, Fred Callaghan 1980–84, Frank McLintock 1984–87, Steve Perryman 1987–90, Phil Holder 1990–93, David Webb May 1993–.

Player and Position	Ht	Wt	Date	Birth Place	Source	Clubs	League App	Gls
Forwards								
Joe Allon	5 10	11 12	12 11 66	Gateshead	England Youth	Newcastle U	9	2
						Swansea C	34	11
						Hartlepool U	112	50
						Chelsea	14	2
						Port Vale (loan)	6	—
						Brentford	24	6
Paul Birch	6 0	12 05	3 12 68	Reading	Trainee	Arsenal	—	—
						Portsmouth	—	—
						Brentford	18	2
Gary Blissett	6 1	11 13	29 6 64	Manchester	Altrincham	Crewe Alex	122	39
						Brentford	233	79
Kevin Godfrey*	5 10	10 11	24 2 60	Kennington	Apprentice	Orient	285	63
						Plymouth Arg (loan)	7	1
						Brentford	140	17
Murray Jones	6 4	14 00	7 10 64	Bexley	Carshalton	Crystal Palace	—	—
						Bristol C	—	—
						Doncaster R (loan)	—	—
						Exeter C	20	3
						Grimsby T	28	3
						Brentford	16	—
Lee Luscombe*	6 0	12 04	16 7 71	Guernsey	Trainee	Southampton	—	—
						Brentford	42	6
Neil Smillie	5 6	10 07	19 7 58	Barnsley	Apprentice	Crystal Palace	83	7
						Brentford (loan)	3	—
						Brighton	75	2
						Watford	16	3
						Reading	39	—
						Brentford	172	18
Paul Stephenson	5 10	12 02	2 1 68	Wallsend	Apprentice	Newcastle U	61	1
						Millwall	98	6
						Gillingham (loan)	12	2
						Brentford	11	—

Trainees
Aouf, Tamer H; Beer, Jamie T; Brady, Jon E. A; Bunce, Nathan; Fleet, Matthew J; Gibson, Robert W; Houghton, Anthony J; Hutchings, Carl E; Johnson, Michael S; Lacey, Scott A; Marskell, Ben; Miller, Barry S; North, Tyrone L; Potter, Andrew J; Ravenscroft, Craig; Udaw, Emem; Winyard, Alfred P.

Associated Schoolboys
Adams, Russell; Brown, Dominic; Brown, Stewart; Christophe, Stephen J; Daldy, Neil F; Doyle, Mark A; Genus, Marlon H; Green, Darren J; Hamblin, Leigh C; Kean, Robert J; Lecky, Marcus; Marsh, Simon T; O'Neill, Stephen M; Pelton, Daryl; Stockwell, Mark R; Waters, Stephen P; Whall, Scott T; Wright, Simon.

Associated Schoolboys who have accepted the club's offer of a Traineeship/Contract
Campbell, Corey A; Cleary, Kevin J; Edgeley, David C; Evans, Luke; Flitter, Mathew.

BRIGHTON AND HOVE ALBION 1992-93 *Back row (left to right):* Larry May (Reserve Team Coach), Stuart Myall, John Crumplin, Simon Funnell, Nicky Bissett, Gary O'Reilly, Paul McCarthy, Robert Codner, Ted Streeter (Youth Development Officer).

Centre row: Malcolm Stuart (Physio), Mark Farrington, Andy Polston, Perry Digweed, Gary Chivers, Mark Beeney, Mark Gall, Billy Logan, Martin Hinshelwood (Coach).

Front row: Dean Wilkins, Bernard Gallacher, John Robinson, Barry Lloyd (Managing Director), Clive Walker, Matthew Edwards, Ian Chapman.

Division 2   BRIGHTON & HOVE ALBION

Goldstone Ground, Old Shoreham Rd, Hove, Sussex BN3 7DE.
Telephone Brighton (0273) 739535. Fax (0273) 321095.
Commercial Dept: (0273) 778230. Ticket office (0273) 778855.
Shop (0273) 326412. Recorded information (team & ticket
news etc): Seagull Line 0898 800609.

Ground capacity: 17,607.

Record attendance: 36,747 v Fulham, Division 2, 27 December
1958.

Record receipts: £109,615.65 v Crawley T, FA Cup 3rd rd, 4
January 1992.

Pitch measurements: 112yd × 75yd.

Directors: B. D. Lloyd (Managing Director), G. A. Stanley (Chairman), R. Bloom, J. L.
Campbell, W. A. Archer.

Manager: Barry Lloyd.

Assistant Secretary: Amanda Stewart. *Chief Executive:* Ron Pavey.

Coach: Martin Hinshelwood. *Physio:* Malcolm Stuart.

Marketing Manager: Terry Gill.

Year Formed: 1900. *Turned Professional:* 1900. *Ltd Co.:* 1904.

Previous Name: Brighton & Hove Rangers. *Previous Grounds:* 1900, Withdean; 1901,
County Ground; 1902, Goldstone Ground.

Club Nickname: 'The Seagulls'.

Record League Victory: 9–1 v Newport C, Division 3 (S), 18 April 1951 – Ball; Tennant
(1p), Mansell (1p); Willard, McCoy, Wilson; Reed, McNichol (4), Garbutt, Bennett (2),
Keene (1). 9–1 v Southend U, Division 3, 27 November 1965 – Powney; Magill, Baxter;
Leck, Gall, Turner; Gould (1), Collins (1), Livesey (2), Smith (3), Goodchild (2).

Record Cup Victory: 10–1 v Wisbech, FA Cup, 1st rd, 13 November 1965 – Powney; Magill,
Baxter; Collins (1), Gall, Turner; Gould, Smith (2), Livesey (3), Cassidy (2), Goodchild (1).
(1 og).

Record Defeat: 0–9 v Middlesbrough, Division 2, 23 August 1958.

Most League Points (2 for a win): 65, Division 3 (S), 1955–56 and Division 3, 1971–72.

Most League Points (3 for a win): 84, Division 3, 1987–88.

Most League Goals: 112, Division 3 (S), 1955–56.

Highest League Scorer in Season: Peter Ward, 32, Division 3, 1976–77.

Most League Goals in Total Aggregate: Tommy Cook, 113, 1922–29.

Most Capped Player: Stefan Iovan, 34, Romania.

Most League Appearances: 'Tug' Wilson, 509, 1922–36.

Record Transfer Fee Received: £900,000 from Liverpool for Mark Lawrenson, August 1981.

Record Transfer Fee Paid: £500,000 to Manchester U for Andy Ritchie, October 1980.

Football League Record: 1920 Original Member of Division 3; 1921–58 Division 3 (S);
1958–62 Division 2; 1962–63 Division 3; 1963–65 Division 4; 1965–72 Division 3; 1972–73
Division 2; 1973–77 Division 3; 1977–79 Division 2; 1979–83 Division 1; 1983–87 Division
2; 1987–88 Division 3; 1988– Division 2.

Honours: Football League: Division 1 best season: 13th, 1981–82; Division 2 – Runners-up
1978–79; Division 3 (S) – Champions 1957–58; Runners-up 1953–54, 1955–56; Division 3 –
Runners-up 1971–72, 1976–77, 1987–88; Division 4 – Champions 1964–65. *FA Cup:*
Runners-up 1982–83. *Football League Cup:* best season: 5th rd, 1978–79.

BRIGHTON & HOVE ALBION 1992—93 LEAGUE RECORD

Match No.	Date		Venue	Opponents	Result		H/T Score	Lg. Pos.	Goalscorers	Atten dance
1	Aug	15	A	Leyton Orient	L	2-3	0-1	—	Moulden, Cotterill	5614
2		22	H	Bolton W	W	2-1	1-1	10	Cotterill, Chapman	6205
3		29	A	Bradford C	D	1-1	0-0	11	Foster	5151
4	Sept	1	A	Exeter C	W	3-2	2-2	—	Foster, Cotterill, Wilkinson	3035
5		5	H	Preston NE	W	2-0	0-0	5	Moulden 2	6026
6		12	H	Huddersfield T	W	2-1	1-1	3	Foster, Moulden	6141
7		16	A	Stoke C	D	1-1	0-1	—	Wilkins	10,867
8		19	A	Blackpool	D	2-2	0-1	5	Moulden, Codner	4618
9		26	H	Reading	L	0-1	0-1	7		7341
10	Oct	3	A	Port Vale	L	1-3	1-1	9	Wilkins	5731
11		10	H	Wigan Ath	W	1-0	1-0	6	Cotterill	5784
12		17	A	Rotherham U	L	0-1	0-1	10		4404
13		24	H	Hartlepool U	D	1-1	0-0	12	Foster	5918
14		31	A	Chester C	L	1-2	0-2	13	Edwards	2735
15	Nov	3	A	Bournemouth	D	1-1	0-1	—	Wilkins	4828
16		7	H	Stockport Co	W	2-0	1-0	12	Kennedy 2	5742
17		20	A	Swansea C	W	1-0	0-0	—	Kennedy	4645
18		28	H	Fulham	L	0-2	0-0	13		7894
19	Dec	12	A	Mansfield T	W	3-1	1-0	9	Kennedy, Gray (og), Wilkinson	2869
20		19	H	Plymouth Arg	W	2-1	1-0	7	Nogan, Codner	5872
21		26	H	Burnley	W	3-0	1-0	6	Nogan 2, Crumplin	8741
22		28	A	Hull C	L	0-1	0-0	9		4785
23	Jan	9	H	Stoke C	D	2-2	0-0	8	Nogan, Overson (og)	8622
24		16	A	Reading	L	0-3	0-2	9		4400
25		27	H	Bradford C	D	1-1	0-0	—	Walker	5141
26		30	A	Bolton W	W	1-0	0-0	8	Nogan	8929
27	Feb	6	H	Leyton Orient	L	1-3	0-2	9	Kennedy	7850
28		13	A	Preston NE	L	0-1	0-0	9		4334
29		20	H	Exeter C	W	3-0	0-0	10	Nogan, Kennedy, Walker	5585
30		27	A	Wigan Ath	W	2-1	1-0	8	Nogan 2	2033
31	Mar	3	A	Huddersfield T	W	2-1	1-0	—	Nogan, Walker	3563
32		6	H	Port Vale	L	0-2	0-0	7		7294
33		10	H	WBA	W	3-1	0-0	—	Nogan, Kennedy 2	7440
34		13	A	Stockport Co	D	0-0	0-0	7		5298
35		20	H	Bournemouth	W	1-0	1-0	7	Nogan	7059
36		23	A	Fulham	L	0-2	0-1	—		5402
37		27	H	Swansea C	L	0-2	0-1	9		7558
38		31	H	Blackpool	D	1-1	0-0	—	Nogan	5170
39	Apr	3	A	WBA	L	1-3	0-0	9	Codner	13,002
40		7	H	Mansfield T	W	3-1	2-0	—	Edwards, Nogan, Wilkinson	4731
41		10	A	Burnley	W	3-1	2-1	6	Nogan 2, Farrington	9424
42		14	H	Hull C	W	2-0	1-0	—	Nogan, Farrington	7776
43		17	A	Plymouth Arg	L	2-3	1-2	7	Nogan 2	4924
44		24	A	Rotherham U	L	1-2	0-0	9	Nogan	7841
45	May	1	A	Hartlepool U	L	0-2	0-0	10		2693
46		8	H	Chester C	W	3-2	2-2	9	Nogan, Byrne 2	6247

Final League Position: 9

GOALSCORERS

League (63): Nogan 20, Kennedy 8, Moulden 5, Cotterill 4, Foster 4, Codner 3, Walker 3, Wilkins 3, Wilkinson 3, Byrne 2, Edwards 2, Farrington 2, Chapman 1, Crumplin 1, own goals 2.
Coca Cola Cup (3): Wilkins 2, Edwards 1.
FA Cup (6): Codner 2, Kennedy 2, Crumplin 1, Edwards 1.

Beeney 42	Chivers 43	Chapman 32 + 2	Wilkins 32 + 3	Bissett 12	Foster 35	Robinson 6	Moulden 11	Cotterill 11	Codner 43	Walker 36 + 2	Funnell — + 2	Crumplin 27 + 5	Edwards 24 + 9	Wilkinson 26 + 1	Macciochi — + 2	McCarthy 30	Kennedy 26 + 4	Nogan 30	Farrington 3 + 5	Gallacher 14	Digweed 4	Munday 7	Byrne 5 + 2	Myall 7	Match No.
1	2	3	4	5	6	7	8	9	10	11	12														1
1	2	3	4		6	7	8	9	10	11		5	12												2
1	2	3			6	7	8	9	10	11		5		4											3
1	2	3			6	7	8	9	10	11		5	12	4											4
1	2	3			6	7	8	9	10	11		5		4											5
1	2	3			6	7	8	9	10	11		5	12	4											6
1	2	3	11		6		8	9	10			5	7	4	12										7
1		3	4		6		8	9	10	11		5	7		12	2									8
1	2	3	4		6		8	9	10	11		14	7			5	12								9
1		3	4		6		8	9	10	11		2	7	14		5	12								10
1	2	3	4		6		8	9	10	11			7			5									11
1	2	3	4		6				10	11		7	12			5	9	8	14						12
1	2	3	4		6					11		7	12	8		5	9	10							13
1	2	3	4		6					11		7	10	8		5		9							14
1	2	3	4		6					11		7	10	8		5	12	9							15
1	2	3	4		6				10	11		7	9			5	8								16
1	2	3	4		6				10	11		7	9			5	8								17
1	2	3	4		6				10	11		7	9			5	8	12							18
1	2		4		6				10	11			7			5	8	9	3						19
1	2	3	4		6				10	11		7	12			5	8	9							20
	2	3	4		6				10	11		7	12			5	8	9			1				21
1	2	3	4		6				10	11		7				5	8	9							22
1	2		4	5	6				10	11		7					8	9	3						23
1	2	12	4	5	6				10	11		7					8	9	3						24
1	2	3	4	5	6				10	11			12				8	9				7			25
1	2	3	4		6				10	11			12			5	8	9				7			26
1	2	3	4		6				10	11			12			5	8	9				7			27
1	2	3	4		6				10	11				8		5		9				7			28
1		3	4		6				10	11			7			5	8	9		2					29
1	2	3			6				10	11			7	4		5	8	9							30
1	2	3			6				10	11			7	4		5	8	9							31
1	2	3			6				10	11			7	4		5	8	9							32
1	2	12			6				10	11			7	4		5	8	9	3						33
1	2	11			6				10				7	4		5	8	9	3						34
1	2	11			6				10	12			7	4		5	8	9	3						35
1	2	11			6				10			7	12	4		5	8	9	3						36
1	6	3	11						10			7	12	4		5	8	9	2	14					37
1	6	3	11						10			7	12	4		5	8	9	2						38
1	6		11						10			7		4		5	8	9	3				12	2	39
1	2				6				10			7	11	4		5	8	9	12	3					40
1	6			5					10			7	11	4			9	8	3					2	41
1	6			5					10			7	11	4			9	12	3				8	2	42
1	6	14		5					10			7	11	4			9	12	3				8	2	43
	6			5					10	12		7	11	4			9		3		1		8	2	44
	6	12	14	5					10			7	11	4			9		3		1		8	2	45
	6	3	11	5					10			14	7	4			12	9			1		8	2	46

Coca Cola Cup	First Round	Colchester U (a)		1-1
		(h)		1-0
	Second Round	Manchester U (h)		1-1
		(a)		0-1
FA Cup	First Round	Hayes (h)		2-0
	Second Round	Woking (h)		1-1
		(a)		2-1
	Third Round	Portsmouth (h)		1-0
	Fourth Round	Manchester U (a)		0-1

BRIGHTON & HOVE ALBION

Player and Position	Ht	Wt	Date	Birth Place	Source	Clubs	League App	Gls
Goalkeepers								
Perry Digweed*	6 0	11 04	26 10 59	London	Apprentice	Fulham	15	—
						Brighton	179	—
						WBA (loan)	—	—
						Charlton Ath (loan)	—	—
						Newcastle U (loan)	—	—
						Chelsea (loan)	3	—
						Wimbledon (loan)	—	—
Defenders								
Nicky Bissett	6 2	12 10	5 4 64	Fulham	Barnet	Brighton	73	7
Ian Chapman	5 9	12 05	31 5 70	Brighton		Brighton	160	4
Gary Chivers*	5 11	11 05	15 5 60	Stockwell	Apprentice	Chelsea	133	4
						Swansea C	10	—
						QPR	60	—
						Watford	14	—
						Brighton	217	13
Steve Foster*	6 1	14 00	24 9 57	Portsmouth		Portsmouth	109	6
						Brighton	172	6
						Aston Villa	15	3
						Luton T	163	11
						Oxford U	95	9
						Brighton	35	4
Bernard Gallacher*	5 9	11 00	22 3 67	Johnstone	Apprentice	Aston Villa	57	—
						Blackburn R (loan)	4	—
						Doncaster R (loan)	2	—
						Brighton	45	1
Paul McCarthy	6 0	13 06	4 8 71	Cork	Trainee	Brighton	74	—
Stuart Munday	5 11	11 00	28 9 72	London	Trainee	Brighton	21	1
Stuart Myall§			12 11 74	Eastbourne	Trainee	Brighton	7	—
Midfield								
David Clarkson	5 9	10 00	1 2 68	Preston	Sunshine George Cross	Brighton	13	—
Robert Codner	5 11	11 08	23 1 65	Walthamstow	Barnet	Brighton	203	27
John Crumplin*	5 8	11 10	26 5 67	Bath	Bognor Regis	Brighton	175	5
Matthew Edwards	5 10	11 00	15 6 71	Hammersmith	Trainee	Tottenham H	—	—
						Reading (loan)	8	—
						Brighton	33	2
David Macciochi‡			14 1 72	Harlow	Trainee	QPR	—	—
						Brighton	2	—
Dean Wilkins	5 10	12 04	12 7 62	Hillingdon	Apprentice	QPR	6	—
						Brighton	2	—
						Orient (loan)	10	—
					PEC Zwolle	Brighton	240	20
Darron Wilkinson	5 11	12 08	24 11 69	Reading	Wokingham	Brighton	27	3
Forwards								
Mark Farrington	5 10	11 12	15 6 65	Liverpool	Everton	Norwich C	14	2
						Cambridge U	10	1
						Cardiff C	31	3
					Feyenoord	Brighton	22	3
Simon Funnell	6 0	12 08	8 8 74	Brighton	Trainee	Brighton	3	—

BRIGHTON & HOVE ALBION

Colours: Royal blue shirts with white pin stripe, royal blue sleeves, royal blue shorts with white and royal trim, royal blue stockings with red/white trim. **Change colours:** White shirts with red/royal trim, white shorts with royal trim, white stockings with royal and red band on turnover.

Foundation: After barely two seasons in existence, a professional club named Brighton United, consisting mostly of Scotsmen, was forced to disband in 1900. The club's manager John Jackson determined to keep the professional game alive in the town and initiated the movement which led to the formation of Brighton & Hove Rangers that same year.

First Football League game: 28 August, 1920, Division 3, v Southend U (a), L 0-2 – Hayes; Woodhouse, Little; Hall, Comber, Bentley; Longstaff, Ritchie, Doran, Rodgerson, March.

Did you know: When Brighton beat Liverpool 2-1 at Anfield on 20 February 1983 in an FA Cup fifth round tie, they were bottom of Division 1, their opponents top 37 points ahead of them. Brighton's manager was Jimmy Melia an ex-Liverpool player.

Managers (and Secretary-Managers)
John Jackson 1901–05, Frank Scott-Walford 1905–08, John Robson 1908–14, Charles Webb 1919–47, Tommy Cook 1947, Don Welsh 1947–51, Billy Lane 1951–61, George Curtis 1961–63, Archie Macaulay 1963–68, Fred Goodwin 1968–70, Pat Saward 1970–73, Brian Clough 1973–74, Peter Taylor 1974–76, Alan Mullery 1976–81, Mike Bailey 1981–82, Jimmy Melia 1982–83, Chris Cattlin 1983–86, Alan Mullery 1986–87, Barry Lloyd January 1987–.

Player and Position	Ht	Wt	Date	Birth Place	Source	Clubs	League App	Gls
Andy Kennedy	6 2	13 00	8 10 64	Stirling	Sauchie Ath	Rangers	15	3
						Birmingham C	76	18
						Sheffield U (loan)	9	1
						Blackburn R	59	23
						Watford	25	4
						Bolton W (loan)	1	—
						Brighton	30	8
Kurt Nogan	5 11	12 07	9 9 70	Cardiff	Trainee	Luton T	33	3
						Peterborough U	—	—
						Brighton	30	20
Clive Walker*	5 7	11 09	26 5 57	Oxford	Apprentice	Chelsea	198	60
						Sunderland	50	10
						QPR	21	1
						Fulham	109	29
						Brighton	106	8

Trainees
Fox, Mark S; Henderson, Nicolas J; Logan, William P; Macaulay, Lee; Moulding, Matthew A; Myall, Stuart T; Oliva, Umberto; Ormerod, Mark I; Pryce-Jones, Liam; Rogers, Sean T; Scott, Steven; Simmonds, Daniel B; Thompson, Ian; Tuck, Stuart G; Wood, David; Wosahlo, Bradley E; Yorke-Johnson, Ross.

Associated Schoolboys
Corlett, James; Deacon, Craig; Hill, Owen D; Lambert, Joseph A; Mayo, Kerry; Mutu, Tamer; Pickering, Jay T; Sallis, Steven A; Stepney, Damian E; Taylor, Paul D; Townsend, Kevin B. C.

Associated Schoolboys who have accepted the club's offer of a Traineeship/Contract
Andrews, Phillip D; Fox, Simon M; Kember, Paul M. J; McGarrigle, Kevin; Smith, Daniel K; Tilley, Anthony J; Whitehouse, Timothy J.

BRISTOL CITY FOOTBALL CLUB 1992–93 *Back row (left to right):* Micky Mellon, Nicky Morgan, Gerry Harrison, James McIntyre, Ray Atteveld, Mark Gavin, Terry Connor.
Middle row: Buster Footman (Physiotherapist), Denis Smith (Manager), Wayne Allison, Dariusz Dziekanowski, Rob Edwards, Gary Campbell, Andy Leaning, Keith Welch, David Thompson, Matt Bryant, Brian Mitchell, Leroy Rosenior, Steve Benton, Mark Harrison (YTS Coach), Alan Crawford (Youth Coach).
Front row: Deion Vernon, Andy Paterson, Shaun Rouse, Andy Cole, Russell Osman, Gary Shelton, Mark Aizlewood, Andy Llewellyn, Martin Scott, Junior Bent, Andy Hogg.

Division 1   BRISTOL CITY

Ashton Gate, Bristol BS3 2EJ. Telephone Bristol (0272) 632812 (5 lines). Fax 0272 639574. Commercial: 0272 633836. Shop: 0272 538566. Clubcall: 0898 121176.

Ground capacity: 23,636.

Record attendance: 43,335 v Preston NE, FA Cup 5th rd, 16 February 1935.

Record receipts: £129,071 v Bristol R, Division 2, 6 April 1993.

Pitch measurements: 115yd × 75yd.

Chairman: L. J. Kew. *Vice-chairmen:* W. I. Williams, K. Sage.

Directors: O. W. Newland, P. Manning, M. Fricker. *Commercial Manager:* John Cox.

Manager: Russell Osman. *Assistant Manager:*   *Coach:* Leroy Rosenior.

Physio: H. Footman. *Secretary:* Jean Harrison. *Commercial Manager:* John Cox.

Year Formed: 1894. *Turned Professional:* 1897. *Ltd Co.:* 1897. BCFC (1982) PLC.

Previous Name: Bristol South End 1894–97.

Club Nickname: 'Robins'.

Previous Grounds: 1894, St John's Lane; 1904, Ashton Gate.

Record League Victory: 9–0 v Aldershot, Division 3 (S), 28 December 1946 – Eddols; Morgan, Fox; Peacock, Roberts, Jones (1); Chilcott, Thomas, Clark (4 incl. 1p), Cyril Williams (1), Hargreaves (3).

Record Cup Victory: 11–0 v Chichester C, FA Cup, 1st rd, 5 November 1960 – Cook; Collinson, Thresher; Connor, Alan Williams, Etheridge; Tait (1), Bobby Williams (1), Atyeo (5), Adrian Williams (3), Derrick. (1 og).

Record Defeat: 0–9 v Coventry C, Division 3 (S), 28 April 1934.

Most League Points (2 for a win): 70, Division 3 (S), 1954–55.

Most League Points (3 for a win): 91, Division 3, 1989–90.

Most League Goals: 104, Division 3 (S), 1926–27.

Highest League Scorer in Season: Don Clark, 36, Division 3 (S), 1946–47.

Most League Goals in Total Aggregate: John Atyeo, 314, 1951–66.

Most Capped Player: Billy Wedlock, 26, England.

Most League Appearances: John Atyeo, 597, 1951–66.

Record Transfer Fee Received: £1,750,000 from Newcastle United for Andy Cole, March 1993.

Record Transfer Fee Paid: £500,000 to Arsenal for Andy Cole, July 1992.

Football League Record: 1901 Elected to Division 2; 1906–11 Division 1; 1911–22 Division 2; 1922–23 Division 3 (S); 1923–24 Division 2; 1924–27 Division 3 (S); 1927–32 Division 2; 1932–55 Division 3 (S); 1955–60 Division 2; 1960–65 Division 3; 1965–76 Division 2; 1976–80 Division 1; 1980–81 Division 2; 1981–82 Division 3; 1982–84 Division 4; 1984–90 Division 3; 1990–92 Division 2; 1992– Division 1.

Honours: Football League: Division 1 – Runners-up 1906–07; Division 2 – Champions 1905–06; Runners-up 1975–76; Division 3 (S) – Champions 1922–23, 1926–27, 1954–55; Runners-up 1937–38; Division 3 – Runners-up 1964–65, 1989–90. *FA Cup:* Runners-up 1909. *Football League Cup:* Semi-final 1970–71, 1988–89. *Welsh Cup:* Winners 1934. *Anglo-Scottish Cup:* Winners 1977–78. *Freight Rover Trophy:* Winners 1985–86; Runners-up 1986–87.

BRISTOL CITY 1992—93 LEAGUE RECORD

Match No.	Date	Venue	Opponents	Result		H/T Score	Lg. Pos.	Goalscorers	Atten dance
1	Aug 15	H	Portsmouth	D	3-3	2-2	—	Dziekanowski 2, Cole	15,301
2	22	A	Luton T	W	3-0	1-0	7	Mellon, Dreyer (og), Cole	7926
3	29	H	Sunderland	D	0-0	0-0	10		14,076
4	Sept 6	A	Derby Co	W	4-3	1-2	—	Scott (pen), Bent, Comyn (og), Allison	12,738
5	12	H	Southend U	L	0-1	0-0	8		9515
6	15	H	West Ham U	L	1-5	0-3	—	Scott	14,130
7	19	A	Newcastle U	L	0-5	0-2	12		29,465
8	26	H	Barnsley	W	2-1	1-1	10	Allison, Scott (pen)	8049
9	Oct 3	A	Tranmere R	L	0-3	0-1	13		5975
10	10	H	Charlton Ath	W	2-1	1-1	12	Dziekanowski, Harrison	9282
11	17	A	Cambridge U	L	1-2	0-1	11	Cole	3894
12	24	H	Leicester C	W	2-1	0-1	11	Cole, Grayson (og)	10,408
13	31	A	Brentford	L	1-5	1-2	15	Cole	8726
14	Nov 4	A	Millwall	L	1-4	1-4	—	Cole	5934
15	7	H	Birmingham C	W	3-0	1-0	14	Rosenior, Shelton, Cole	10,008
16	14	H	Grimsby T	L	1-2	0-0	15	Cole	5651
17	17	H	Swindon T	D	2-2	1-1	15	Shelton, Rosenior	14,066
18	28	H	Notts Co	W	1-0	0-0	13	Shelton	9065
19	Dec 5	A	Watford	D	0-0	0-0	13		6746
20	13	A	Bristol R	L	0-4	0-1	—		7106
21	19	H	Peterborough U	L	0-1	0-1	17		7309
22	26	H	Oxford U	D	1-1	1-1	17	Rosenior	10,737
23	28	A	Wolverhampton W	D	0-0	0-0	18		16,419
24	Jan 9	H	Newcastle U	L	1-2	1-2	18	Allison	15,446
25	16	A	Barnsley	L	1-2	0-2	18	Cole	5423
26	27	A	West Ham U	L	0-2	0-0	—		12,118
27	30	H	Luton T	D	0-0	0-0	19		8877
28	Feb 6	A	Portsmouth	W	3-2	1-1	17	Shelton, Bryant, Gavin	10,675
29	10	A	Southend U	D	1-1	1-1	—	Cole	3086
30	20	A	Sunderland	D	0-0	0-0	20		17,122
31	27	A	Charlton Ath	L	1-2	1-0	20	Cole	7351
32	Mar 6	H	Tranmere R	L	1-3	0-2	21	Cole	8810
33	9	H	Millwall	L	0-1	0-1	—		8771
34	13	A	Birmingham C	W	1-0	1-0	20	Morgan	15,611
35	20	H	Watford	W	2-1	1-1	20	Bent, Pennyfather	8265
36	24	A	Swindon T	L	1-2	0-1	—	Rosenior	13,157
37	28	H	Grimsby T	W	1-0	0-0	—	Morgan	6755
38	Apr 3	A	Notts Co	D	0-0	0-0	20		6633
39	6	H	Bristol R	W	2-1	1-0	—	Morgan, Tinnion (pen)	21,854
40	10	A	Oxford U	L	0-2	0-1	17		6145
41	12	H	Wolverhampton W	W	1-0	0-0	14	Bent	11,756
42	17	A	Peterborough U	D	1-1	0-0	15	Tinnion	5169
43	20	H	Derby Co	D	0-0	0-0	—		8869
44	24	H	Cambridge U	D	0-0	0-0	16		8995
45	May 1	A	Leicester C	D	0-0	0-0	16		19,294
46	8	H	Brentford	W	4-1	2-0	15	Rosenior 3, Allison	12,659

Final League Position: 15

GOALSCORERS

League (49): Cole 12, Rosenior 7, Allison 4, Shelton 4, Bent 3, Dziekanowski 3, Morgan 3, Scott 3 (2 pens), Tinnion 2 (1 pen), Bryant 1, Gavin 1, Harrison 1, Mellon 1, Pennyfather 1, own goals 3.
Coca Cola Cup (8): Cole 4, Allison 1, Edwards 1, Rosenior 1, Scott 1 (pen).
FA Cup (0).

Leaning 1	Mitchell 15 + 1	Scott 35	Thompson 17	Bryant 41	Osman 33 + 1	Mellon 7 + 3	Dziekanowski 24 + 2	Morgan 10	Cole 29	Shelton 42	Harrison 24 + 9	Welch 45	Rosenior 29 + 9	Edwards 14 + 4	Aizlewood 19 + 1	Allison 22 + 17	Bent 13 + 7	Llewellyn 12	Connor 2 + 3	Reid 3 + 1	Gavin 16 + 3	Kristensen 4	Atteveld 5 + 2	Munro 16	Pennyfather 14	Tinnion 11	Fowler — + 1	Shall 3 + 1	Match No.
1	2	3	4	5	6	7	8	9	10	11	12																		1
	2	3	4	5	6	7	8		10	*11*	12	1	9	14															2
	2	3	4	5		7	8		10	11		1	9		6	12													3
	2	3	4	5	6	7	8			11	10	1				9	12												4
	2	3	4	5	6	7	8			11		1	10			9	12												5
		3	4	5			8		10	*11*	7	1	9	6		12			2	14									6
		3	4	5			8			11		1	9	6	10	12		2	14	7									7
	2	3	4	5		10	8			14	1		6			9	12		7	11									8
	2	3	4	5			8		10	*11*	14	1	12			9			7	6									9
	2	3	4		5		8		10	*11*	7	1	9	6		12				14									10
	2		4	3	5		8		10	11	7	1	9	6		12													11
	2	3	4	5	6		8		10	*11*	7	1	9	14		12													12
	2	3	4		6		8		10		7	1	9	5		*11*		14		12									13
		3	4	2	*6*				10	8	7	1	9	5		12 14				11									14
		3	4	2	6				10	8	7	1	9	5						11									15
6		3	4	2		11			10	8	7	1	9	5															16
	2	3		5	6		8		10	7	12	1	9	11									4						17
		3		5	6		8		10	7	2	1	9	11		12							4						18
		3		5	6	14	*8*		10	7	2	1	9	11		12							4						19
		3		5	6		8		10	7	2	1	9	*11*		12						14	4						20
14		3		5	6				10	7	2	1	9	*4*		12	8				11								21
4		3		5	6				10	7	2	1	9			12	8				11								22
4		3		5	6		14		10	7	*2*	1	9			12	8				11								23
		3		5	6	14			10	7	2	1			12	9	*8*	4			11								24
				5	6				10	8	4	1	12		3	9	7	2			11								25
		3		5	6		14		10	7	8	1	12		4	9					*11*		2						26
		3		5	6	14	*8*		10	*7*	11	1	9		4	12		2											27
				5			8		10	7	*11*	1	12		4	9		2			14				3	6			28
				5			8		10	7		1	12		4	9		2			11				3	6			29
				5	11		8		10	7		1			4	9		2							3	6			30
				5	14		*8*		10	7		1	12		4	9		2			11				3	*6*			31
	9			5			8		10	7		1	12		4	14		*2*			11				3	6			32
		3		5	6		8		10	7	14	1	12		*4*	9					11		2						33
		3		5	4				10		7	1	9				8				11		2	6					34
		3		5	4				10		7	1	9	14	12	8	2				*11*			6					35
		3		5	4				10	7		1	9		12	8							2	6	11				36
		3		5	4				10	7		1	9			8							2	6	11				37
		3		5	4				10	7		1	9		12	8							2	6	11				38
				5	4				10	7		1	9		3	8							2	6	11				39
		3	5						10	7	14	1	9		4	8	12					*2*		6	11				40
		3		5	2				10	14	1		4	9	8			*7*			6	11	12						41
		3		5	6				10	7	8	1	4	9					12	2	11								42
				5	2					7	8	1	4	9	10				12	3	6 11			14					43
				5						7	2	1 12	14	4	9	10			*8*	3	11			6					44
			2							7		1	10	4	9				8	6	3	11		5					45
										7	14	1	10	3	4	9	12	2	8	6		11		5					46

Coca Cola Cup	First Round	Cardiff C (a)	0-1
		(h)	5-1
	Second Round	Sheffield U (h)	2-1
		(a)	1-4
FA Cup	Third Round	Luton T (a)	0-2

BRISTOL CITY

Player and Position	Ht	Wt	Date	Birth Place	Source	Clubs	League App	Gls
Goalkeepers								
Andy Leaning	6 1	14 07	18 5 63	York	Rowntree Mackintosh	York C	69	—
						Sheffield U	21	—
						Bristol C	75	—
Keith Welch	6 0	12 0	3 10 68	Bolton	Trainee	Bolton W	—	—
						Rochdale	205	—
						Bristol C	71	—
Defenders								
Stephen Benton	5 10	12 03	20 12 73	Bristol	Trainee	Bristol C	—	—
Matthew Bryant	6 1	12 11	21 9 70	Bristol	Trainee	Bristol C	106	4
						Walsall (loan)	13	—
Robert Edwards	6 0	11 06	1 7 73	Kendal		Carlisle U	48	5
						Bristol C	38	1
Andy Llewellyn	5 7	11 00	26 2 66	Bristol	Apprentice	Bristol C	286	3
Brian Mitchell*	6 1	13 01	16 7 63	Stonehaven	King St	Aberdeen	65	1
						Bradford C	178	9
						Bristol C	16	—
Stuart Munro	5 8	10 05	15 9 62	Falkirk	Bo'ness U	St Mirren	1	—
						Alloa	60	6
						Rangers	179	3
						Blackburn R	1	—
						Bristol C	16	—
Russell Osman	5 11	12 01	14 2 59	Repton	Apprentice	Ipswich	294	17
						Leicester C	108	8
						Southampton	96	6
						Bristol C	65	2
Mark Shail	6 1	13 03	15 10 63	Sweden	Yeovil	Bristol C	4	—
David Thompson	6 3	12 07	20 11 68	Ashington	Trainee	Millwall	92	6
						Bristol C	17	—
Brian Tinnion	5 11	11 05	23 2 68	Stanley	Apprentice	Newcastle U	32	2
						Bradford C	145	22
						Bristol C	11	2
Midfield								
Mark Aizlewood	6 0	13 03	1 10 59	Newport	Apprentice	Newport Co	38	1
						Luton T	98	3
						Charlton Ath	152	9
						Leeds U	70	3
						Bradford C	39	1
						Bristol C	96	3
Ray Atteveld	5 10	12 00	8 9 66	Amsterdam	Haarlem	Everton	51	1
						West Ham U (loan)	1	—
						Bristol C	14	1
Jason Fowler§	6 1	11 06	20 8 74	Bristol	Trainee	Bristol C	1	—
Mark Gavin	5 8	10 07	10 12 63	Bailleston	Apprentice	Leeds U	30	3
						Hartlepool U (loan)	7	—
						Carlisle U	13	1
						Bolton W	49	3
						Rochdale	23	6
						Hearts	9	—
						Bristol C	69	6
						Watford	13	—
						Bristol C	33	2
Gerry Harrison	5 10	12 12	15 4 72	Lambeth	Trainee	Watford	9	—
						Bristol C	37	1
						Cardiff C (loan)	10	1
Abdul Kamara	5 9	11 00	10 2 74	Southampton	Southampton	Bristol C	—	—
Glenn Pennyfather	5 8	11 05	11 2 63	Billericay	Apprentice	Southend U	238	36
						Crystal Palace	34	1
						Ipswich T	15	1
						Bristol C	14	1
Shaun Rouse*	5 9	11 02	28 2 72	Gt Yarmouth	Rangers	Bristol C	—	—
Martin Scott	5 8	10 10	7 1 68	Sheffield	Apprentice	Rotherham U	94	3
						Nottingham F (loan)	—	—
						Bristol C	108	7
Gary Shelton	5 7	10 12	21 3 58	Nottingham	Apprentice	Walsall	24	—
						Aston Villa	24	7
						Notts Co (loan)	8	—
						Sheffield W	198	18
						Oxford U	65	1
						Bristol C	147	24
Forwards								
Wayne Allison	6 1	12 06	16 10 68	Huddersfield		Halifax T	84	23
						Watford	7	—
						Bristol C	119	20

BRISTOL CITY

Colours: Red shirts, white shorts, red and white stockings. **Change colours:** Purple shirts, green shorts, white stockings with purple top.

Foundation: The name Bristol City came into being in 1897 when the Bristol South End club, formed three years earlier, decided to adopt professionalism and apply for admission to the Southern League after competing in the Western League. The historic meeting was held at The Albert Hall, Bedminster. Bristol City employed Sam Hollis from Woolwich Arsenal as manager and gave him £40 to buy players. In 1901 they merged with Bedminster, another leading Bristol club.

First Football League game: 7 September, 1901, Division 2, v Blackpool (a) W 2-0 – Moles; Tuft, Davies; Jones, McLean, Chambers; Bradbury, Connor, Boucher, O'Brien (2), Flynn.

Did you know: When Bristol City sold Andy Cole to Newcastle United in March 1993, he became the first graduate of the FA National School to command a seven-figure fee.

Managers (and Secretary-Managers)
Sam Hollis 1897–99, Bob Campbell 1899–1901, Sam Hollis 1901–05, Harry Thickett 1905–10, Sam Hollis 1911–13, George Hedley 1913–15, Jack Hamilton 1915–19, Joe Palmer 1919–21, Alex Raisbeck 1921–29, Joe Bradshaw 1929–32, Bob Hewison 1932–49 (under suspension 1938–39), Bob Wright 1949–50, Pat Beasley 1950–58, Peter Doherty 1958–60, Fred Ford 1960–67, Alan Dicks 1967–80, Bobby Houghton 1980–82, Roy Hodgson 1982, Terry Cooper 1982–88 (Director from 1983), Joe Jordan 1988–90, Jimmy Lumsden 1990–92, Denis Smith 1992–93, Russell Osman March 1993–.

Player and Position	Ht	Wt	Date	Birth Place	Source	Clubs	League App	Gls
Junior Bent	5 5	10 06	1 3 70	Huddersfield	Trainee	Huddersfield T	36	6
						Burnley (loan)	9	3
						Bristol C	58	7
						Stoke C (loan)	1	—
Ian Brown			11 9 65	Ipswich	Chelmsford C	Bristol C	—	—
Gary Campbell‡	6 0	11 08	25 8 72	Glasgow	Trainee	Bristol C	—	—
Steve Clifford‡			13 7 73	Telford	Trainee	Bristol C	—	—
Terry Connor*	5 9	11 08	9 11 62	Leeds	Apprentice	Leeds U	96	19
						Brighton	156	51
						Portsmouth	48	12
						Swansea C	39	6
						Bristol C	16	1
						Swansea C (loan)	3	—
Dariusz Dziekanowski	6 1	12 13	30 9 62	Warsaw	Legia Warsaw	Celtic	49	10
						Bristol C	43	7
Andrew Hogg*	5 10	11 03	25 3 74	Bristol	Trainee	Bristol C	—	—
James McIntyre	5 11	11 05	24 5 72	Dumbarton	Duntocher Boys	Bristol C	1	—
						Exeter C (loan)	15	3
Nicky Morgan	5 10	13 10	30 10 59	East Ham	Apprentice	West Ham U	21	2
						Portsmouth	95	32
						Stoke C	88	21
						Bristol C	80	23
						Bournemouth (loan)	6	1
Leroy Rosenior	6 1	11 10	24 3 64	London	School	Fulham	54	16
						QPR	38	7
						Fulham	34	20
						West Ham U	53	15
						Fulham (loan)	11	3
						Charlton Ath (loan)	3	—
						Bristol C	46	12
Deion Vernon‡	5 11	11 07	7 3 73	Bristol	Trainee	Bristol C	—	—

Trainees
De Ste Croix, Lee; Donaldson, Michael I; Durbin, Gary J; Fowler, Jason K. G; Hewlett, Matthew; Hicks, Nathan J; King, Ryan P; Licata, Guiseppe; Limna, James A; Lumsden, Jamie; Milsom, Paul J; Skidmore, Robert J; Steadman, Matthew; Westlake, Andrew E; Wyatt, Michael J.

Associated Schoolboys
Alderan, Scott; Anderson, Paul; Carey, Louis A; Carree, Nicholas W; Elsworthy, Leigh; Fowler, Paul; Harding, Richard; Jacobs, Kristen; Jones, Stuart C; Kentish, Neil A; Langan, Kevin; Lawrie, Benjamin; Perry, Richard; Plummer, Dwayne; Ponfield, Stuart; Royall, Kevin J. P; Simmonds, Dean; Turner, Chris.

Associated Schoolboys who have accepted the club's offer of a Traineeship/Contract
Barclay, Dominic A; Farrow, Marcus W; Gitsham, Scott; Haines, Daniel C; Huggins, Dean; Lewis, Kristian C; Parrott, Lee; Pettitt, David M.

BRISTOL ROVERS 1992–93 *Back row (left to right):* Gareth Taylor, Lee Maddison, David Mehew, Andy Gurney, Andy Reece, Carl Saunders, Marcus Stewart, Adie Boothroyd, Vaughan Jones, Richard Evans.
Centre row: Roy Dolling, Bill Clark, John Taylor, Gavin Kelly, Marcus Browning, Steve Yates, Brian Parkin, Geoff Twentyman, Justin Skinner, Ray Kendall.
Front row: Paul Tovey, Phil Purnell, Paul Chenoweth, Steve Cross, Dennis Rofe, Tony Gill, Tony Pounder, Paul Hardyman, Dave Wilson, Lee Archer.

Division 2   **BRISTOL ROVERS**

Twerton Park, Twerton, Bath. Telephone: 0272 352508. Training ground: 0272 861743. Match day ticket office: 0225 312327. Offices: 199 Two Mile Road, Kingswood, Bristol BS15 1AZ. 0272 352303. Pirates Hotline 0898 338345. Fax 0272 352303.

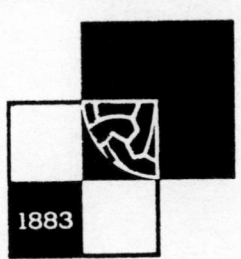

Ground capacity: 8880.

Record attendance: 9464 v Liverpool, FA Cup 4th rd, 8 February 1992 (Twerton Park). 38,472 v Preston NE, FA Cup 4th rd, 30 January 1960 (Eastville).

Record receipts: £62,480 v Liverpool, FA Cup 4th rd, 8 February 1992.

Pitch measurements: 110yd × 75yd.

President: Marquis of Worcester. *Vice-Presidents:* Dr W. T. Cussen, A. I. Seager, H. E. L. Brown, R. Redmond. *Chairman:* D. H. A. Dunford. *Vice-chairman:* G. M. H. Dunford. *Directors:* R. Craig, V. Stokes (managing director in charge of administration), R. Andrews. *Manager:* John Ward. *Assistant Manager:* Dennis Booth. *Coach:* Des Bulpin. *Physio:* Keith James *Youth team coach:* Tony Gill.. *Commercial Manager:* A. Wood. *Secretary:* R. C. Twyford. *Assistant Secretary:* I. I. Wilson. *Office Manager:* Mrs Angela Mann. *Year Formed:* 1883. *Turned Professional:* 1897. *Ltd Co.:* 1896.

Previous Names: 1883, Black Arabs; 1884, Eastville Rovers; 1897, Bristol Eastville Rovers; 1898, Bristol Rovers.

Club Nickname: 'Pirates'.

Previous Grounds: Purdown, Three Acres, Ashley Hill, Rudgeway, Eastville.

Record League Victory: 7–0 v Brighton & HA, Division 3 (S), 29 November 1952 – Hoyle; Bamford, Geoff Fox; Pitt, Warren, Sampson; McIlvenny, Roost (2), Lambden (1), Bradford (1), Peterbridge (2). (1 og). 7–0 v Swansea T, Division 2, 2 October 1954 – Radford; Bamford, Watkins; Pitt, Muir, Anderson; Petherbridge, Bradford (2), Meyer, Roost (1), Hooper (2). (2 og). 7–0 v Shrewsbury T, Division 3, 21 March 1964 – Hall; Hillard, Gwyn Jones; Oldfield, Stone (1), Mabbutt; Jarman (2), Brown (1), Biggs (1p), Hamilton, Bobby Jones (2).

Record Cup Victory: 6–0 v Merthyr Tydfil, FA Cup, 1st rd, 14 November 1987 – Martyn; Alexander (Dryden), Tanner, Hibbitt, Twentyman, Jones, Holloway, Meacham (1), White (2), Penrice (3) (Reece), Purnell.

Record Defeat: 0–12 v Luton T, Division 3 (S), 13 April 1936.

Most League Points (2 for a win): 64, Division 3 (S), 1952–53.

Most League Points (3 for a win): 93, Division 3, 1989–90.

Most League Goals: 92, Division 3 (S), 1952–53.

Highest League Scorer in Season: Geoff Bradford, 33, Division 3 (S), 1952–53.

Most League Goals in Total Aggregate: Geoff Bradford, 245, 1949–64.

Most Capped Player: Neil Slatter, 10 (22), Wales.

Most League Appearances: Stuart Taylor, 545, 1966–80.

Record Transfer Fee Received: £1,000,000 from Crystal Palace for Nigel Martyn, November 1989.

Record Transfer Fee Paid: £275,000 to QPR for Andy Tillson, November 1992.

Football League Record: 1920 Original Member of Division 3; 1921–53 Division 3 (S); 1953–62 Division 2; 1962–74 Division 3; 1974–81 Division 2; 1981–90 Division 3; 1990– 92 Division 2. 1992–93 Division 1; 1993– Division 2.

Honours: Football League: Division 2 best season: 6th, 1955–56, 1958–59; Division 3 (S) – Champions 1952–53; Division 3 – Champions 1989–90; Runners-up 1973–74. *FA Cup:* best season: 6th rd, 1950–51, 1957–58. *Football League Cup:* best season: 5th rd, 1970–71, 1971–72.

BRISTOL ROVERS 1992—93 LEAGUE RECORD

Match No.	Date	Venue	Opponents	Result	H/T Score	Lg. Pos.	Goalscorers	Atten dance
1	Aug 15	A	Oxford U	L 1-2	0-2	—	Taylor J	7333
2	19	H	Swindon T	L 3-4	1-3	—	Mehew, Stewart, Hardyman	6150
3	22	H	Brentford	W 2-1	2-0	10	Taylor J 2	5779
4	25	A	Charlton Ath	L 1-4	0-1	—	Reece	4719
5	28	A	Tranmere R	L 1-2	1-0	—	Stewart	5458
6	Sept 5	H	Newcastle U	L 1-2	1-1	20	Taylor J	7487
7	12	A	Swindon T	D 2-2	0-1	21	Stewart (pen), Taylor J	10,006
8	19	H	Grimsby T	L 0-3	0-0	23		5320
9	26	A	Sunderland	D 1-1	1-0	23	Stewart	15,593
10	Oct 3	H	Notts Co	D 3-3	3-2	23	Hardyman 2, Taylor J	5031
11	10	A	Watford	L 2-4	1-2	24	Stewart (pen), Saunders	7624
12	17	H	West Ham U	L 0-4	0-3	24		6187
13	24	A	Birmingham C	L 1-2	0-1	24	Moore	9874
14	Nov 31	H	Millwall	W 1-0	0-0	24	Saunders	5378
15	3	H	Barnsley	L 1-5	0-1	—	Mehew	5019
16	7	A	Wolverhampton W	L 1-5	1-2	24	Saunders	12,163
17	14	H	Derby Co	L 1-2	1-1	24	Taylor J	6668
18	21	A	Peterborough U	D 1-1	0-0	24	Saunders	6120
19	28	A	Leicester C	W 1-0	1-0	23	Channing	12,848
20	Dec 5	H	Luton T	W 2-0	2-0	21	Saunders, Channing	6245
21	13	H	Bristol C	W 4-0	1-0	—	Channing, Stewart, Saunders, Taylor J	7106
22	18	A	Cambridge U	W 1-0	0-0	—	Browning	4027
23	26	A	Portsmouth	L 1-4	1-2	19	Taylor J	14,288
24	28	H	Southend U	L 0-2	0-0	19		7707
25	Jan 9	A	Grimsby T	L 0-2	0-0	20		4922
26	16	H	Sunderland	D 2-2	1-2	21	Stewart, Hardyman	6140
27	27	H	Charlton Ath	L 0-2	0-1	—		5096
28	30	A	Brentford	W 3-0	1-0	21	Stewart 2, Alexander	7527
29	Feb 6	H	Oxford U	L 0-1	0-0	23		5593
30	20	H	Tranmere R	W 1-0	1-0	21	Saunders	5135
31	24	A	Newcastle U	D 0-0	0-0	—		29,372
32	27	H	Watford	L 0-3	0-1	23		5702
33	Mar 6	A	Notts Co	L 0-3	0-1	24		6445
34	10	A	Derby Co	L 1-3	1-3	—	Saunders (pen)	13,294
35	13	H	Wolverhampton W	D 1-1	0-1	24	Mehew	5982
36	20	A	Luton T	D 1-1	0-0	24	Taylor	7717
37	24	H	Peterborough U	W 3-1	2-0	—	Pounder, Saunders, Taylor	4855
38	27	A	Barnsley	L 1-2	0-1	24	Reece	5220
39	Apr 3	H	Leicester C	D 0-0	0-0	24		5270
40	6	A	Bristol C	L 1-2	0-1	—	Taylor	21,854
41	10	H	Portsmouth	L 1-2	0-1	24	Stewart	5377
42	14	A	Southend U	L 0-3	0-0	—		6154
43	17	H	Cambridge U	D 1-1	1-1	24	Saunders	3929
44	24	A	West Ham U	L 1-2	0-0	24	Clark	16,682
45	May 1	H	Birmingham C	D 3-3	2-0	24	Taylor 2, Saunders	5150
46	8	A	Millwall	W 3-0	1-0	24	Archer, Stewart, Davis	15,821

Final League Position: 24

GOALSCORERS

League (55): Taylor 14, Saunders 11 (1 pen), Stewart 11 (2 pens), Hardyman 4, Channing 3, Mehew 3, Reece 2, Alexander 1, Archer 1, Browning 1, Clark 1, Davis 1, Moore 1, Pounder 1.
Coca Cola Cup (1): Reece 1.
FA Cup (1): Browning 1.

Parkin 26	Alexander 41	Clark 19 + 5	Yates 44	Hardyman 36 + 1	Skinner 12	Mehew 14 + 10	Reece 22 + 4	Taylor J 39 + 3	Saunders 33 + 8	Pounder 17 + 1	Stewart 27 + 11	Cross 6 + 5	Twentyman 7 + 1	Maddison 12	Wilson 8	Kelly 19	Moore 4	Channing 23 + 2	Archer 1 + 1	Tillson 29	Waddock 31	Browning 17 + 2	Jones 12	Evans 6 + 5	Beasley 1	Davis — + 1	Match No.
1	2	3	4	5	6	7	8	9	10	11	12	14															1
1	2	3	4	5	6	7	8	9	10	11	12	14															2
1	2	3	4	5	6	7	8	9	10	11	12	14															3
1	2	3	4	5	6		8	9	10	11	12	7	14														4
1	2	14	4	5		8	9	12	11	10	7	3	6														5
1	2		4			8	9	12	11	10	7	3	6		5												6
1	2	6	4	5		8	9	12	14	10	7	3	11														7
1	2		4	11		8	9	12	7	10	14	3	5	6													8
1	2		4	11		8	12	9	10	7		3	5	6													9
1	2		4	11	14	8	9	12	7	10		3	5	6													10
1	2		4	11		7	8	9	12	10		3	5	6													11
	2	3	4	5	6	7	8	9	10	11						1											12
	2		4	5	6	12	8	9	10	11	14					1		3	7								13
1	2		4	5		12	8	9	10	11							6	3	7								14
1	2		4	5		12	8	9	10	11							6	3	7	14							15
1	2		4	5			8	9	10					12				3	7	6	11	14					16
1	2		4	5				9	10					12				7		3	11	8	6				17
1	2		4	5				9	10					12				7		3	11	8	6				18
1	2		4	5				9	10					12				7		3	11	8	6				19
1	2		4	5				9	10						8			7		3	11		6				20
1	2		4	5				9	10						8			7		3	11		6				21
1	2		4	5				9	10						8			7		3	11		6				22
1	2		4	5				9	10						8					3	11	7	6	12			23
	2		4	5				9	10					12	8	1				3	11	7	6				24
	2		4	5				9	10						8	1		6		3	11	7		12			25
			4	5				9	10						8	1	2			3	11	7	6				26
	2	3	4	5				9	10			14				1		8			11	7	6	12			27
	2	3	4	5				9	10							1		8			11	7	6				28
	2		4	5				9	10							1		8		3	11	7	6	12			29
	2		4	5	6			9	10					12		1		8		3	11	7					30
	2	14	4	5	6			9	10					12		1		8		3	11	7					31
	2	12	4	5			8	9	10							1				3	11	7	6				32
	2		4	5		7	8	9	10							1				3	11	12	6				33
1	2		4	5		7		9	10					12						3	11	8	6				34
	2		4	5		7		9	10					12		1				3	11	8	6				35
1	2	14	4			7		9	10					12			6	5		3	11	8					36
1	2		4			7	8	9	10					12			6	5		3	11						37
1	2		4	5		7	8	9	10								6	12		3	11						38
	2		4	5		7	8	9	10							1	6	12	14	3	11						39
	2		4	5		7	8	9	10								6		1	14	3	11		12			40
	2	14	4	5			8	9	10					12			6	7		3	11				1		41
	2		4	5	6		8	9	10					12		1		7		3	11						42
			4	5	6			9	10					12		1	2	7		3	11			8			43
			4	5	6	14		9	10					12		1	2	7		3	11			8			44
			4	5	6	14		9	10					12		1	2	7		3	11			8			45
1			4	5	6	14		9	10								2	7		3	11	8				12	46

Coca Cola Cup	Second Round	Manchester C (a)		0-0
		(h)		1-2
FA Cup	Third Round	Aston Villa (a)		1-1
		(h)		0-3

BRISTOL ROVERS

Player and Position	Ht	Wt	Date	Birth Place	Source	Clubs	League App	Gls
Goalkeepers								
Gavin Kelly	6 0	12 13	29 9 68	Beverley		Hull C	11	—
						Bristol R (loan)	—	—
						Bristol R	29	—
Brian Parkin	6 1	12 00	12 10 65	Birkenhead	Local	Oldham Ath	6	—
						Crewe Alex (loan)	12	—
						Crewe Alex	86	—
						Crystal Palace (loan)	—	—
						Crystal Palace	20	—
						Bristol R	138	—
Defenders								
Ian Alexander	5 8	10 07	26 1 63	Glasgow	Leicester J	Rotherham U	11	—
						Motherwell	24	2
						Morton	7	1
					Pezoporikos	Bristol R	273	6
Justin Channing	5 11	11 07	19 11 68	Reading	Apprentice	QPR	55	5
						Bristol R	25	3
Billy Clark	6 0	12 03	19 5 67	Christchurch	Local	Bournemouth	4	—
						Bristol R	104	4
Steve Cross	5 10	11 05	22 12 59	Wolverhampton	Apprentice	Shrewsbury T	262	34
						Derby Co	73	3
						Bristol R	43	2
Andrew Gurney	5 7	10 08	25 1 74	Bristol	Trainee	Bristol R	—	—
Paul Hardyman	5 8	11 07	11 3 64	Portsmouth	Local	Portsmouth	117	3
						Sunderland	106	9
						Bristol R	37	4
Vaughan Jones‡	5 8	11 11	2 9 59	Tonyrefail	Apprentice	Bristol R	101	3
						Newport Co	68	4
						Cardiff C	11	—
						Bristol R	280	9
Lee Maddison	5 11	11 00	5 10 72	Bristol	Trainee	Bristol R	22	—
Gareth Taylor	6 2	12 05	25 2 73	Weston-Super-Mare	Southampton	Bristol R	1	—
Andy Tillson	6 2	12 07	30 6 66	Huntingdon	Kettering T	Grimsby T	105	5
						QPR	29	2
						Grimsby T (loan)	4	—
						Bristol R	29	—
Geoff Twentyman‡	6 1	13 02	10 3 59	Liverpool	Chorley	Preston NE	98	4
						Bristol R	252	6
Steve Yates	5 11	11 00	29 1 70	Bristol	Trainee	Bristol R	196	—
Midfield								
Lee Archer	5 6	9 04	6 11 72	Bristol	Trainee	Bristol R	7	1
Paul Chenoweth*	5 4	8 0	5 2 73	Bristol	Trainee	Southampton	—	—
						Bristol R	—	—
Richard Evans	5 11	11 07	12 4 68	Ebbw Vale	Weymouth	Bristol R	13	1
						Exeter C (loan)	5	2
Andy Reece	5 11	12 04	5 9 62	Shrewsbury	Willenhall	Bristol R	239	17
						Walsall (loan)	9	1
Justin Skinner	6 0	11 03	30 1 69	London	Apprentice	Fulham	135	23
						Bristol R	54	3
Paul Tovey	5 8	11 07	5 12 73	Wokingham	Trainee	Bristol R	—	—
Gary Waddock	5 10	11 12	17 3 62	Alperton	Apprentice	QPR	203	8
					Charleroi	Millwall	58	2
						QPR	—	—
						Swindon T (loan)	6	—
						Bristol R	31	—

BRISTOL ROVERS

Colours: Blue and white quartered shirts, white shorts, blue stockings with two white rings on top.
Change colours: Green, black, white shadow striped shirts, black shorts, white stockings.

Foundation: Bristol Rovers were formed at a meeting in Stapleton Road, Eastville, in 1883. However, they first went under the name of the Black Arabs (wearing black shirts). Changing their name to Eastville Rovers in their second season, they won the Gloucestershire Senior Cup in 1888–89. Original members of the Bristol & District League in 1892, this eventually became the Western League and Eastville Rovers adopted professionalism in 1897.

First Football League game: 28 August, 1920, Division 3, v Millwall (a) L 0-2 – Stansfield; Bethune, Panes; Boxley, Kenny, Steele; Chance, Bird, Sims, Bell, Palmer.

Did you know: Non-league Bristol Rovers featured in ten FA Cup games in 1901–02 when their victims included neighbours City, Swindon Town, Millwall and Middlesbrough. They were beaten 1-0 by Stoke.

Managers (and Secretary-Managers)
Alfred Homer 1899–1920 (continued as secretary to 1928), Ben Hall 1920–21, Andy Wilson 1921–26, Joe Palmer 1926–29, Dave McLean 1929–30, Albert Prince-Cox 1930–36, Percy Smith 1936–37, Brough Fletcher 1938–49, Bert Tann 1950–68 (continued as GM to 1972), Fred Ford 1968–69, Bill Dodgin Snr 1969–72, Don Megson 1972–77, Bobby Campbell 1978–79, Harold Jarman 1979–80, Terry Cooper 1980–81, Bobby Gould 1981–83, David Williams 1983–85, Bobby Gould 1985–87, Gerry Francis 1987–91, Martin Dobson 1991, Dennis Rofe 1992, Malcolm Allison 1992–93, John Ward March 1993–.

Player and Position	Ht	Wt	Date	Birth Place	Source	Clubs	League App	Gls
David Wilson*	5 9	10 10	20 3 69	Burnley	Apprentice	Manchester U	4	—
						Charlton Ath (loan)	7	2
						Lincoln C (loan)	3	—
						Bristol R	11	—
Forwards								
Marcus Browning	5 11	12 00	22 4 71	Bristol	Trainee	Bristol R	31	1
						Hereford U (loan)	7	5
Mike Davis			19 10 74	Bristol	Yate T	Bristol R	1	1
David Mehew	5 11	12 06	29 10 67	Camberley		Leeds U	—	—
						Bristol R	222	63
Tony Pounder	5 8	11 00	11 3 66	Yeovil	Weymouth	Bristol R	103	8
Carl Saunders	5 8	11 02	26 11 64	Marston Green	Local	Stoke C	164	23
						Bristol R	135	42
Marcus Stewart	5 10	10 03	7 11 72	Bristol	Trainee	Bristol R	71	16
John Taylor	6 2	11 12	24 10 64	Norwich	Local	Colchester U	—	—
					Sudbury	Cambridge U	160	46
						Bristol R	50	21

Trainees
Bennett, Anthony P; Crossey, Scott; Harrington, Mark P; Hayfield, Matthew A; Impey, Scott; Law, Marcus W; Levett, Simon; Micciche, Marco; Paul, Martin L; Rofe, Daniel; Smith, Ian S; Stewart, Andrew W; White, Thomas M.

Associated Schoolboys
Cuff, Andrew T; Low, Joshua D; Morgan, Gavin S; Sage, Kris; Sanderson, Jonathan; Spring, Andrew J; Turner, David R.

Associated Schoolboys who have accepted the club's offer of a Traineeship/Contract
French, Jonathan; Parkinson, Matthew S.

116

BURNLEY 1992-93 *Back row (left to right):* Andy Farrell, Michael Conroy, Roger Eli, John Pender, Neil Howarth, John Deary, Paul Murray.
Centre row: Jamalur Rahman, Simon Wallace, Steve Penney, Ian Measham, David Williams, Graham Lancashire, Danny Sonner, Robbie Painter, Adrian Randall, Paul McKenzie.
Front row: Mark Yates, Steve Davis, Mark Monington, Paul McKay, Jimmy Mullen (Manager), Joe Jakub, Les Thompson, Steve Harper, Brian Welch.

Division 2   **BURNLEY**

Turf Moor, Burnley BB10 4BX. Telephone Burnley (0282) 427777. Fax (0282) 428938. Clubcall: 0891 121153.

Ground capacity: 22,085.

Record attendance: 54,775 v Huddersfield T, FA Cup 3rd rd, 23 February 1924.

Record receipts; £63,988 v Sheffield W, FA Cup 6th rd, 12 March 1983.

Pitch measurements: 115yd × 73yd.

Chairman: F. J. Teasdale.

Vice-chairman: Dr R. D. Iven MRCS (Eng), LRCP (Lond), MRCGP.

Directors: B. Dearing LLB, B. Rothwell JP, C. Holt,R. Blakeborough.

Manager: Jimmy Mullen. *Assistant Manager:* Clive Middlemass.

Secretary: Mark Blackbourne. *Youth Team Coach:* Harry Wilson.

Commercial Manager: T. Skelly. *Physio:* M. Leather.

Year Formed: 1882. *Turned Professional:* 1883. *Ltd Co.:* 1897.

Previous Name: 1881–82, Burnley Rovers.

Club Nickname: 'The Clarets'.

Previous Grounds: 1881, Calder Vale; 1882, Turf Moor.

Record League Victory: 9–0 v Darwen, Division 1, 9 January 1892 – Hillman; Walker, McFettridge, Lang, Matthews, Keenan, Nicol (3), Bowes, Espie (1), McLardie (3), Hill (2).

Record Cup Victory: 9–0 v Crystal Palace, FA Cup, 2nd rd (replay) 10 February 1909 – Dawson; Barron, McLean; Cretney (2), Leake, Moffat; Morley, Ogden, Smith (3), Abbott (2), Smethams (1). 9–0 v New Brighton, FA Cup, 4th rd, 26 January 1957 – Blacklaw; Angus, Winton; Seith, Adamson, Miller; Newlands (1), McIlroy (3), Lawson (3), Cheesebrough (1), Pilkington (1). 9–0 v Penrith FA Cup, 1st rd, 17 November 1984 – Hansbury; Miller, Hampton, Phelan, Overson (Kennedy), Hird (3 incl. 1p), Grewcock (1), Powell (2), Taylor (3), Biggins, Hutchison.

Record Defeat: 0–10 v Aston Villa, Division 1, 29 August 1925 and v Sheffield U, Division 1, 19 January 1929.

Most League Points (2 for a win): 62, Division 2, 1972–73.

Most League Points (3 for a win): 83, Division 4, 1991–92.

Most League Goals: 102, Division 1, 1960–61.

Highest League Scorer in Season: George Beel, 35, Division 1, 1927–28.

Most League Goals in Total Aggregate: George Beel, 178, 1923–32.

Most Capped Player: Jimmy McIlroy, 51 (55), Northern Ireland.

Most League Appearances: Jerry Dawson, 522, 1907–28.

Record Transfer Fee Received: £300,000 from Everton for Martin Dobson, August 1974, and from Derby Co for Leighton James, November 1975.

Record Transfer Fee Paid: £165,000 to QPR for Leighton James, September 1978.

Football League Record: 1888 Original Member of the Football League; 1897–98 Division 2; 1898–1900 Division 1; 1900–13 Division 2; 1913–30 Division 1; 1930–47 Division 2; 1947–71 Division 1; 1971–73 Division 2; 1973–76 Division 1; 1976–80 Division 2; 1980–82 Division 3; 1982–83 Division 2; 1983–85 Division 3; 1985–92 Division 4; 1992– Division 2.

Honours: Football League: Division 1 – Champions 1920–21, 1959–60; Runners-up 1919–20, 1961–62; Division 2 – Champions 1897–98, 1972–73; Runners-up 1912–13, 1946–47; Division 3 – Champions 1981–82. Division 4 – Champions 1991–92. Record 30 consecutive Division 1 games without defeat 1920–21. *FA Cup:* Winners 1913–14; Runners-up 1946–47, 1961–62. *Football League Cup:* semi-final 1960–61, 1968–69, 1982–83. *Anglo Scottish Cup:* Winners 1978–79. *Sherpa Van Trophy:* Runners-up 1988. **European Competitions;** *European Cup:* 1960–61. *European Fairs Cup:* 1966–67.

BURNLEY 1992—93 LEAGUE RECORD

Match No.	Date	Venue	Opponents	Result	H/T Score	Lg. Pos.	Goalscorers	Atten dance
1	Aug 15	H	Swansea C	W 1-0	0-0	—	Penney	10,913
2	22	A	Stockport Co	L 1-2	0-1	15	Heath	4953
3	29	H	Rotherham U	D 1-1	0-0	16	Deary	9684
4	Sept 5	A	Chester C	L 0-3	0-2	19		4981
5	12	A	Preston NE	L 0-2	0-0	21		7209
6	15	H	Port Vale	D 1-1	0-0	—	Monington	8556
7	19	H	Mansfield T	W 1-0	1-0	20	Monington	8613
8	26	A	Wigan Ath	D 1-1	0-0	18	Deary	4032
9	29	H	Plymouth Arg	D 0-0	0-0	—		8676
10	Oct 3	H	WBA	W 2-1	1-0	16	Harper, Conroy	14,796
11	11	A	Bradford C	L 0-1	0-1	—		10,235
12	17	H	Fulham	W 5-2	4-1	14	Harper, Farrell, Penney, Heath, Conroy	9881
13	24	A	Blackpool	W 3-1	3-1	13	Harper, Farrell, Penney	7942
14	31	H	Stoke C	L 0-2	0-2	14		16,667
15	Nov 3	H	Reading	D 1-1	1-1	—	Harper	8382
16	7	A	Hull C	W 2-0	1-0	13	Heath 2	5751
17	21	H	Huddersfield T	W 2-1	2-1	10	Deary, Clayton	10,615
18	28	A	Bolton W	L 0-4	0-2	14		11,438
19	Dec 12	H	Leyton Orient	W 2-0	1-0	10	Bellamy (og), Heath	8882
20	19	A	Exeter C	D 2-2	2-1	10	Heath 2	3179
21	26	A	Brighton & HA	L 0-3	0-1	13		8741
22	Jan 9	A	Port Vale	L 0-3	0-1	14		8815
23	16	H	Wigan Ath	L 0-1	0-0	15		9154
24	23	A	Mansfield T	D 1-1	1-0	13	Pender	3991
25	26	A	Rotherham U	W 1-0	0-0	—	Heath (pen)	4989
26	30	H	Stockport Co	D 1-1	0-0	13	Conroy	11,229
27	Feb 5	A	Swansea C	D 1-1	0-1	—	Farrell	4973
28	13	H	Chester C	W 5-0	4-0	10	Conroy, Abel (og), Heath, Pender, Harper	9434
29	16	H	Preston NE	W 2-0	1-0	—	Farrell, Heath	12,648
30	20	A	Plymouth Arg	W 2-1	1-1	7	Pender 2	5905
31	27	H	Bradford C	D 2-2	1-2	9	Slawson, McCarthy (og)	13,262
32	Mar 6	A	WBA	L 0-2	0-1	9		15,722
33	9	A	Hartlepool U	D 0-0	0-0	—		3021
34	13	H	Hull C	W 2-0	1-0	10	Heath, Slawson	9974
35	16	H	Bournemouth	D 1-1	1-1	—	Conroy	8601
36	20	A	Reading	L 0-1	0-0	12		6398
37	23	H	Bolton W	L 0-1	0-0	—		15,085
38	27	H	Huddersfield T	D 1-1	1-1	11	Heath	9411
39	Apr 3	H	Hartlepool U	W 3-0	1-0	12	Heath 2, Davis	8226
40	6	A	Leyton Orient	L 2-3	1-3	—	Heath 2 (1 pen)	4236
41	10	H	Brighton & HA	L 1-3	1-2	12	Conroy	9424
42	13	A	Bournemouth	D 1-1	0-1	—	Davis	4456
43	17	A	Exeter C	W 3-1	1-0	12	Heath 2, Daniels (og)	7332
44	24	A	Fulham	L 0-4	0-1	13		5531
45	May 1	H	Blackpool	D 2-2	1-0	13	Heath, Francis	12,475
46	8	A	Stoke C	D 1-1	1-0	13	Randall	21,840

Final League Position: 13

GOALSCORERS

League (57): Heath 19 (2 pens), Conroy 6, Harper 5, Farrell 4, Pender 4, Deary 3, Penney 3, Davis 2, Monington 2, Slawson 2, Clayton 1, Francis 1, Randall 1, own goals 4.
Coca Cola Cup (2): Pender 1, Sonner 1.
FA Cup (9): Conroy 3, Heath 3, Monington 1, Pender 1, own goal 1.

	Williams 2	Measham 39	Jakub 31 + 1	Randall 19 + 4	Pender 44	Farrell 40 + 2	Penney 10 + 1	Deary 32	Painter 7 + 10	Conroy 38 + 1	Harper 33 + 1	Monington 22 + 9	Heath 43	Clayton 3	Thompson 2 + 1	Beresford 44	Lancashire 2 + 1	Mooney 6	Davis 37	Sonner — + 1	Palin 1	Eli 2 + 9	Donowa 4	Yates — + 1	Wilson 20	Slawson 5	Campbell 7 + 1	Pickering 4	Francis 9	Match No.
	1	2	3	4	5	6	7	8	9	10	11																			1
	1	2	3	4	5			8	12	10			6	7	9	11														2
		2	3	4	5	12		8	7		11		6	10				1	9											3
		2	3	4	5			8	7		11		6	10			12	1	9											4
		2	3	4	5	10		8		12	6	9			11	1		7												5
		2	3	4	5	10		8			6	9			1		7	11	12											6
		2	3	6	5			8		11	9	10			1		7	4												7
		2	3	6	5			8		12	11	9	10		1		7	4												8
		2	3	6	5	8			10	11		9			1		7	4												9
		2	3	6	5	7			10	11	9	8			1			4												10
		2	3		5	6			10	11		8			1		7	4				9	12							11
		2	3		5	6	7	8		10	11	14	9		1			4				12								12
		2	3		5	6	7	8		10	11		9		1			4				12								13
		2	3			6	7	8		10	11	5	9		1			4				12								14
		2	3			6	7	8	14	10	11	5	9		1			4				12								15
		2	3		5	6	7	8		10	11		9		1			4												16
		2	3		5	6	7	8			11		9	10	1			4				12								17
		2	3		5	6	7	8			11		9	10	1			4				12								18
		2	3	6	5	14	7	8		10	11		9		1			4				12								19
		2	3		5	6	7	8		10	11	12	9		1			4												20
		2	3		5	6	12	8	14	10		7	9		1			4		11										21
		2	3	8	5	6		7	10	11		9			1			4		12										22
		2	3	8	5	6			10	11	9			1	12	4				7										23
		2	3	8	5	4		6	14	10	11			1			9	7	12											24
		2	3		5	8	6		10	11		9			1			4		7										25
		2	3		5	8	6		10	11		9			1			4		7										26
		2	7		5	8	6		10	11	12	9		1			4				3									27
		2			5	8	6		10	7		9		1			4				3	11								28
		2			5	8	6		10	7	12	9		1			4				3	11								29
					5	8		6	12	10	7	2	9	1			4				3	11								30
		2			5	8	6		10	7	12	9		1			4				3	11								31
		2	14		5	8	6	11	10	7	12	9	1			4				3										32
		2	6	11	5	8		14	10		12	9	1			4				3		7								33
		2			6	5	8		7	10		4	9	1							3	11	12							34
		2	7	12	5	8		11	10		4	9	1							3		6								35
		2	7	12	5	8		14	10		11	9	1			4				3		6								36
		2			7	5	8	12	10			9	1			4				3		6	11							37
		2		12	5	8		10		14	9	1			4				3		6	11	7							38
					5	8		10		2	9	1			4				3		6	11	7							39
			12		5	8		14	10		2	9	1			4				3		6	11	7						40
			6		5	8		10	11	2	9	1			4				3			7								41
					5	8	6	10	11	2	9	1			4				3			7								42
		6			5	8	11	10		2	9	1			4				3			7								43
		2			5	8	6	10	11		9	1			4				3			7								44
		2			5	8	6	10	11	12	9	1			4				3			7								45
			8		5	2	6	12	10	11	4	9	1							3			7							46

Coca Cola Cup	First Round	Carlisle U (a)	1-4
		(h)	1-1
FA Cup	First Round	Scarborough (h)	2-1
	Second Round	Shrewsbury T (h)	1-1
		(a)	2-1
	Third Round	Sheffield U (a)	2-2
		(h)	2-4

BURNLEY

Player and Position	Ht	Wt	Date	Birth Place	Source	Clubs	League App	Gls
Goalkeepers								
Marlon Beresford	6 1	12 06	2 9 69	Lincoln	Trainee	Sheffield W	—	—
						Bury (loan)	1	—
						Ipswich T (loan)	—	—
						Northampton T (loan)	13	—
						Crewe Alex (loan)	3	—
						Northampton T (loan)	15	—
						Burnley	44	—
David Williams	6 0	12 00	18 9 68	Liverpool	Trainee	Oldham Ath	—	—
						Burnley	24	—
						Rochdale (loan)	6	—
						Crewe Alex (loan)	—	—
Defenders								
Steve Davis	6 2	12 08	30 10 68	Hexham	Trainee	Southampton	7	—
						Burnley (loan)	9	—
						Notts Co (loan)	2	—
						Burnley	77	8
Wayne Dowell	5 10	11 02	28 12 73	Co Durham	Trainee	Burnley	—	—
Roger Eli	5 11	11 03	11 9 65	Bradford	Apprentice	Leeds U	2	—
						Wolverhampton W	18	—
						Cambridge U	—	—
						Crewe Alex	27	1
						York C	4	1
						Bury	2	—
					Northwich Vic	Burnley	99	11
Andy Farrell	6 0	11 00	7 10 65	Colchester	School	Colchester U	105	5
						Burnley	235	18
Paul McKay	5 8	10 05	28 1 71	Banbury	Trainee	Burnley	12	—
Ian Measham	5 11	11 08	14 12 64	Barnsley	Apprentice	Huddersfield T	17	—
						Lincoln C (loan)	6	—
						Rochdale (loan)	12	—
						Cambridge U	46	—
						Burnley	176	2
John Pender	6 0	12 03	19 11 63	Luton	Apprentice	Wolverhampton W	117	3
						Charlton Ath	41	—
						Bristol C	83	3
						Burnley	123	7
Paul Wilson	5 10	13 00	2 8 68	Bradford	Trainee	Huddersfield T	15	—
						Norwich C	—	—
						Northampton T	141	6
						Halifax T	45	7
						Burnley	20	—
Midfield								
Dave Campbell	5 10	11 02	2 6 65	Eglinton	Oxford BC	Nottingham F	41	3
						Notts Co (loan)	18	2
						Charlton Ath	30	1
						Plymouth Arg (loan)	1	—
						Bradford C	35	4
						Shamrock R (loan)	31	5
						WBA	—	—
						Rotherham U	1	—
						Burnley	8	—
John Deary	5 10	12 04	18 10 62	Ormskirk	Apprentice	Blackpool	303	43
						Burnley	156	18
Neil Howarth			15 11 71	Farnworth	Trainee	Burnley	1	—
Joe Jakub*	5 6	9 06	7 12 56	Falkirk	Apprentice	Burnley	42	—
						Bury	265	27
					AZ Alkmaar	Chester C	42	1
						Burnley	163	8
Paul McKenzie	5 9	11 10	4 10 69	Aberdeen	Peterhead	Burnley	4	—
Mark Monington	6 1	13 00	21 10 70	Bilsthorpe	Schoolboy	Burnley	64	4
Paul Murray (To Berwick R January 1993)	5 6	10 10	8 1 74	Berwick	Trainee	Burnley	—	—
Robert Painter	5 11	11 00	26 1 71	Ince	Trainee	Chester C	84	8
						Maidstone U	30	5
						Burnley	26	2
Steve Penney	5 8	10 07	16 1 64	Ballymena	Ballymena U	Brighton	138	15
						Hearts	9	—
						Burnley	11	3
Nick Pickering	6 0	11 10	4 8 63	Newcastle	Apprentice	Sunderland	179	18
						Coventry C	78	9
						Derby Co	45	3
						Darlington	57	7
						Burnley	4	—
Simon Wallace*	5 5	10 00	7 12 73	Liverpool	Trainee	Burnley	—	—
Brian Welch	5 08	11 11	17 7 73	South Shields	Hebburn	Burnley	—	—

BURNLEY

Colours: Claret shirts with sky blue sleeves, white shorts and stockings. **Change colours:** Jade/black halved shirts and shorts, jade stockings.

Foundation: The majority of those responsible for the formation of the Burnley club in 1881 were from the defunct rugby club Burnley Rovers. Indeed, they continued to play rugby for a year before changing to soccer and dropping "Rovers" from their name. The changes were decided at a meeting held in May 1882 at the Bull Hotel.

First Football League game: 8 September, 1888, Football League, v PNE (a), L 2–5 – Smith; Lang, Bury, Abrams, Friel, Keenan, Brady, Tait, Poland (1), Gallocher (1), Yates.

Did you know: On 2 May 1960 Burnley beat Manchester City 2-1 at Maine Road to go top of Division 1 for the first time in the season and become champions. Only two players cost transfer fees: Jimmy McIlroy and Alex Elder, both from Glentoran.

Managers (and Secretary-Managers)
Arthur F. Sutcliffe 1893–96*, Harry Bradshaw 1896–99*, Ernest Magnall 1899–1903*, Spen Whittaker 1903–10, R. H. Wadge 1910–11*, John Haworth 1911–25, Albert Pickles 1925–32, Tom Bromilow 1932–35, Alf Boland 1935–39*, Cliff Britton 1945–48, Frank Hill 1948–54, Alan Brown 1954–57, Billy Dougall 1957–58, Harry Potts 1958–70 (GM to 1972), Jimmy Adamson 1970–76, Joe Brown 1976–77, Harry Potts 1977–79, Brian Miller 1979–83, John Bond 1983–84, John Benson 1984–85, Martin Buchan 1985, Tommy Cavanagh 1985–86, Brian Miller 1986–89, Frank Casper 1989–91, Jimmy Mullen October 1991–.

Player and Position	Ht	Wt	Date	Birth Place	Source	Clubs	League App	Gls
Mark Yates	5 11	11 09	24 1 70	Birmingham	Trainee	Birmingham C	54	6
						Burnley	18	1
						Lincoln C (loan)	14	—
Forwards								
John Clayton	5 11	11 07	20 8 61	Elgin	Apprentice	Derby C	24	4
					Bulova, Hong Kong	Chesterfield	33	5
						Tranmere R	47	35
						Plymouth Arg	77	21
						Fortuna Sittard	47	16
						Volendam	61	18
						Burnley	3	1
Mike Conroy	6 0	11 00	31 12 65	Glasgow	Apprentice	Coventry C	—	—
						Clydebank	114	38
						St Mirren	10	1
						Reading	80	7
						Burnley	77	30
John Francis	5 8	11 02	21 11 63	Dewsbury	Emley	Halifax T	4	—
						Sheffield U	42	6
						Burnley	101	26
						Cambridge U	29	3
						Burnley	9	1
Steve Harper	5 10	11 05	3 2 69	Stoke	Trainee	Port Vale	28	2
						Preston NE	77	10
						Burnley	69	8
Adrian Heath	5 6	10 01	11 1 61	Stoke	Apprentice	Stoke C	95	16
						Everton	226	71
					Espanol	Aston Villa	9	—
						Manchester C	75	4
						Stoke C	6	—
						Burnley	43	19
Graham Lancashire	5 10	11 12	19 10 72	Blackpool	Trainee	Burnley	29	8
						Halifax T (loan)	2	—
Richard Livingstone	5 10	11 02	10 4 74	Aberdeen	Trainee	Burnley	—	—
John Mullin	6 0	11 05	11 8 75	Bury	School	Burnley	—	—
Jamalur Rahman*	5 4	10 00	1 11 73	Bangladesh	Trainee	Burnley	—	—
Adrian Randall	5 11	10 11	10 11 68	Amesbury	Apprentice	Bournemouth	3	—
						Aldershot	107	12
						Burnley	41	3
Danny Sonner*	5 10	11 00	9 1 72	Wigan	Wigan Ath	Burnley	6	—
						Bury (loan)	5	3
Les Thompson	5 10	11 00	23 9 68	Cleethorpes		Hull C	35	4
						Scarborough (loan)	3	1
						Maidstone U	38	—
						Burnley	3	—

Trainees
Allen, Nicholas S; Anderson, Stuart P; Arthur, Paul M; Atkinson, Paul; Bannister, Andrew P; Binningsley, David; Brass, Christopher P; Chadkirk, Paul G; Davies, Glen; Livesey, David; McCluskey, Anthony; Parry, Christopher M; Peake, Warren C; Smith, Ian P; Sutton, Liam R; Taylor, Matthew J; Weller, Paul.

Associated Schoolboys
Ciaraldi, Craig; Cotton, David P; Duerden, Ian C; Graville, Lee M; Heys, Anthony; Nutter, Paul N.

Associated Schoolboys who have accepted the club's offer of a Traineeship/Contract
Evers, Robert J.

BURY 1992–93 *Back row (left to right):* Mark Kearney, Alan Knill, Matthew Lambert, David Jones, Darren Lyons.
Centre row: Jack Chapman (Chief Scout), Ian Hughes, Darren Wilson, Gary Kelly, Andy Gorton, Mike Pollitt, Ian Stevens, Lawrence Greenhalgh, John King (Assistant Manager).
Front row: Paul Robertson, Lee Anderson, Kevin Hulme, Mike Walsh (Manager), Peter Valentine, Liam Robinson, Darren Emmett, Ian Scott.

Division 3   **BURY**

Gigg Lane, Bury BL9 9HR. Telephone 061–764 4881. Fax 061–764 5521. Commercial Dept. 061–705 2144. Clubcall: 0898 121197. Community Programme: 061–797 5423. Social Club: 061–764 6771.

Ground capacity: 12,000.

Record attendance: 35,000 v Bolton W, FA Cup 3rd rd, 9 January 1960.

Record receipts: £37,000 v Bolton W, Division 3 play-off, 19 May 1991.

Pitch measurements: 112yd × 72yd.

Chairman: T. Robinson. *Vice-chairman:* Canon J. R. Smith MA.

Directors: C. H. Eaves, J. Smith, A. Noonan, F. Mason.

Manager: Mike Walsh. *Assistant Manager:* John King.

Physio: Mandy Johnson.

Assistant Secretary: J. Neville. *Commercial Manager:* Neville Neville.

Year Formed: 1885. *Turned professional:* 1885. *Ltd Co.:* 1897. **Club Nickname:** 'Shakers'.

Club Sponsors: MacPherson Paints.

Record League Victory: 8–0 v Tranmere R, Division 3, 10 January 1970 – Forrest; Tinney, Saile; Anderson, Turner, McDermott; Hince (1), Arrowsmith (1), Jones (4), Kerr (1), Grundy. (1 og).

Record Cup Victory: 12–1 v Stockton, FA Cup, 1st rd (replay), 2 February 1897 – Montgomery; Darroch, Barbour; Hendry (1), Clegg, Ross (1); Wylie (3), Pangbourn, Millar (4), Henderson (2), Plant. (1 og).

Record Defeat: 0–10 v Blackburn R, FA Cup, preliminary round, 1 October 1887 and v West Ham U, Milk Cup, 2nd rd, 2nd leg, 25 October 1983.

Most League Points (2 for a win): 68, Division 3, 1960–61.

Most League Points (3 for a win): 84, Division 4, 1984–85.

Most League Goals: 108, Division 3, 1960–61.

Highest League Scorer in Season: Craig Madden, 35, Division 4, 1981–82.

Most League Goals in Total Aggregate: Craig Madden, 129, 1978–86.

Most Capped Player: Bill Gorman, 11 (13), Eire and (4), Northern Ireland.

Most League Appearances: Norman Bullock, 506, 1920–35.

Record Transfer Fee Received: £375,000 from Southampton for David Lee, October 1991.

Record Transfer Fee Paid: £175,000 to Shrewsbury T for John McGinlay, July 1990.

Football League Record: 1894 Elected to Division 2; 1895–1912 Division 1; 1912–24 Division 2; 1924–29 Division 1; 1929–57 Division 2; 1957–61 Division 3; 1961–67 Division 2; 1967–68 Division 3; 1968–69 Division 2; 1969–71 Division 3; 1971–74 Division 4; 1974–80 Division 3; 1980–85 Division 4; 1985– Division 3.

Honours: Football League: Division 1 best season: 4th, 1925–26; Division 2 – Champions 1894–95; Runners-up 1923–24; Division 3 – Champions 1960–61; Runners-up 1967–68. *FA Cup:* Winners 1900, 1903. *Football League Cup:* Semi-final 1963.

BURY 1992—93 LEAGUE RECORD

Match No.	Date	Venue	Opponents	Result	H/T Score	Lg. Pos.	Goalscorers	Attendance
1	Aug 15	A	Doncaster R	W 3-2	2-0	—	Valentine, Robinson, Scott	3350
2	22	H	Gillingham	W 1-0	0-0	2	Stevens	1806
3	29	A	Chesterfield	L 1-2	0-1	6	Valentine	2847
4	Sept 1	A	Carlisle U	L 1-5	0-2	—	Kilner	4650
5	5	H	Colchester U	W 3-2	1-0	6	Lyons, Robinson, Scott	2072
6	12	H	Barnet	D 0-0	0-0	5		3355
7	15	A	Walsall	L 3-4	2-0	—	Robinson 2, Hulme	3097
8	19	A	Shrewsbury T	L 0-2	0-2	10		2307
9	26	H	Torquay U	W 2-0	1-0	7	Robinson (pen), Knill (pen)	2199
10	Oct 3	H	Scarborough	L 0-2	0-1	8		2048
11	10	A	Wrexham	L 2-4	0-1	10	Knill (pen), Lyons	2829
12	17	H	Lincoln C	L 1-2	0-1	14	Mauge	2208
13	24	A	Crewe Alex	L 1-2	0-1	16	Valentine	3231
14	31	H	York C	D 1-1	0-1	16	Robinson	2763
15	Nov 7	A	Darlington	D 0-0	0-0	19		1895
16	21	H	Hereford U	W 2-0	0-0	17	Sonner, Branch	1739
17	28	A	Cardiff C	L 0-3	0-1	18		4348
18	Dec 12	H	Northampton T	D 3-3	3-1	18	Hulme 2, Terry (og)	1954
19	19	A	Halifax T	W 1-0	0-0	16	Sonner	1760
20	26	A	Gillingham	W 4-1	2-0	13	Hulme 3, Sonner	3632
21	Jan 9	H	Walsall	W 2-1	1-1	13	Stevens 2	2421
22	16	A	Torquay U	W 1-0	0-0	12	Stevens	1796
23	26	H	Chesterfield	W 3-0	0-0	—	Stevens 2, Adekola	1953
24	Feb 6	H	Doncaster R	W 3-0	2-0	10	Stevens, Hulme 2	2496
25	13	A	Colchester U	D 0-0	0-0	10		3264
26	20	H	Carlisle U	W 6-0	6-0	10	Adekola 2, Hulme, Knill, Stevens 2	2723
27	27	H	Wrexham	W 3-1	2-0	9	Stevens, Lyons, Adekola	4550
28	Mar 6	A	Scarborough	W 3-1	2-0	7	Adekola 3	2189
29	9	A	Scunthorpe U	L 0-2	0-0	—		2589
30	13	H	Darlington	D 1-1	0-0	10	Kearney	2879
31	16	H	Rochdale	D 2-2	0-0	—	Stevens, Daws	3315
32	20	A	York C	W 2-1	1-0	8	Rigby 2	3985
33	23	H	Cardiff C	W 1-0	0-0	—	Stevens	3574
34	27	A	Hereford U	L 1-3	1-2	5	Mike	2208
35	30	H	Shrewsbury T	D 0-0	0-0	—		2976
36	Apr 3	H	Scunthorpe U	D 0-0	0-0	5		2509
37	6	A	Northampton T	L 0-1	0-0	—		2878
38	13	A	Rochdale	W 2-1	0-0	—	Stevens 2	2905
39	17	H	Halifax T	L 1-2	0-1	6	Adekola	3069
40	20	A	Barnet	L 0-1	0-0	—		3820
41	24	A	Lincoln C	W 2-1	0-1	7	Kearney, Knill	3651
42	May 1	H	Crewe Alex	L 1-2	0-1	7	Knill	4411

Final League Position: 7

GOALSCORERS

League (63): Stevens 14, Hulme 9, Adekola 8, Robinson 6 (1 pen), Knill 5 (2 pens), Lyons 3, Sonner 3, Valentine 3, Kearney 2, Rigby 2, Scott 2, Branch 1, Daws 1, Kilner 1, Mauge 1, Mike 1, own goal 1.
Coca Cola Cup (6): Hulme 2, Valentine 2, Kearney 1, Robinson 1.
FA Cup (4): Hulme 1, Knill 1 (pen), Mauge 1, Robinson 1 (pen).

Kelly 42	Anderson 13	Robertson 3	Knill 38	Valentine 35 + 1	Hughes 11 + 4	Lyons 14 + 12	Robinson 14	Stevens 28 + 4	Kearney 37 + 2	Scott 7 + 2	Hulme 32	Daws 35 + 1	Greenhalgh 2	Kilner 4 + 1	Reid 25 + 4	Mauge 12 + 1	Ward 25	Stanislaus 23 + 1	Morris — + 1	Gardner 1	Norman 1 + 1	White 1 + 1	Sonner 5	Branch 3 + 1	McKee 2	Rigby 21	Adekola 14 + 2	Esdaille 1 + 5	Mike 5 + 2	Fitzpatrick 8 + 1	Match No.
1	2	3	4	5	6	7	8	9	10	11																					1
1	2	3	6	5	4	7	8	12	10	11		9	14																		2
1	2		6	5		7	8	9	10	11				4	3	12															3
1	2		6	5			12	8	9	10	11			4	3	7	14														4
1	2		6	5			12	8	9	10	14			4	11	3	7														5
1	2			5			12	8	10	6	9			4	11	3	7														6
1	2			5			12	8	10	6	9			4	11	3	7														7
1				5			11	8	10		9			4	6	7	2	3													8
1			6	5			12	8	10	14	9			4	11	7	2	3													9
1			6	5			12	8	10		9			4	11	7	2	3	14												10
1			6	5			12	8	10	3	9			4	11	7	2														11
1			6	5				10	8		9			4	11	7	2	3	12												12
1	2	3	6	5		10		12	14		9			4	11	7		8													13
1	2		6	5	10		8	11	3		9			4		7						12									14
1			6	5	2	12	8	11	3		9			4	10							7									15
1			6	5	2	7		3			9			4	10									8	11						16
1			6	5	2	7		3			9			4	10	12								8	11						17
1	2			5	3	7	12	14			9			4	6	10								8	11						18
1			6	5	2	7		3			9			4	10	11								8	12						19
1			6	5	2	7		14	3		9			4	10	11	12							8							20
1			6	5	7		8	2			4			12	10	11	3							9							21
1			6	5		10	2	9	4		12				11	3					7			8	14						22
1			6	5		10	2	9	4						11	3								8	7						23
1			6	5		10	2	9	4						11	3								8	7						24
1			6	5		10	2	9	4						11	3								8	7	12					25
1			6	5	12	10	2	9	4						11	3								8	7						26
1			6	5	9	10	2		4						11	3								8	7						27
1			6	5	12	10	2	9	4						11	3								8	7						28
1			6	5	12	10	2	9	4						11	3								8	7						29
1			6			10	2	9	4			5			11	3								8	7						30
1			6	5		10	2	9	4						11	3								8	7						31
1			6			10	2	9	4			5			11	3								8	7	12					32
1			6			10	2	9	4			5			11	3								8	7	12					33
1			6			10	2	9	4			5			11	3								8		7	12				34
1			6	12		10	2	9	4			5			11									8		7	3				35
1			6	5	12	10		9				11				2								8	14	4	7	3			36
1			6	5	12	10	11	9	4			2												8		14	7	3			37
1			6		4	10	9					5			2	3								8	7		12	11		38
1			6		14	10	9	4				5			2	3								8	7		12	11		39
1	2		6	5		7	10	4							3									8		12	9	11		40
1	2		6	5	14	7	10	4		9		12			3									8					11	41
1	2		6	5		12	10					9			4	3								8	7			11		42

Coca Cola Cup	First Round	Wrexham (a)	1-1
		(h)	4-3
	Second Round	Charlton Ath (h)	0-0
		(a)	1-0
	Third Round	QPR (h)	0-2
FA Cup	First Round	Witton Alb (h)	2-0
	Second Round	Wigan Ath (a)	1-1
		(h)	1-0
	Third Round	Manchester U (a)	0-2

BURY

Player and Position	Ht	Wt	Date	Birth Place	Source	Clubs	League App	Gls
Goalkeepers								
Andy Gorton	5 11	11 04	23 9 66	Salford		Oldham Ath	26	—
						Stockport Co (loan)	14	—
						Tranmere R (loan)	1	—
						Stockport Co	34	—
						Lincoln C	20	—
					Glossop	Oldham Ath	—	—
						Crewe Alex	3	—
						Bury	—	—
Gary Kelly	5 11	12 03	3 8 66	Fulwood	Apprentice	Newcastle U	53	—
						Blackpool (loan)	5	—
						Bury	172	—
Defenders								
Lee Anderson	5 9	10 07	4 10 73	Bury	Trainee	Bury	18	—
Steve Gardner*	5 11	12 06	3 7 68	Teeside	Apprentice	Manchester U	—	—
						Burnley	95	—
					Glossop	Bradford C	14	—
						Bury	1	—
Laurie Greenhalgh‡	5 10	11 00	2 4 74	Salford	Trainee	Bury	2	—
Ian Hughes	5 11	12 00	2 8 74	Bangor	Trainee	Bury	47	—
Alan Knill	6 2	11 07	8 10 64	Slough	Apprentice	Southampton	—	—
						Halifax T	118	6
						Swansea C	89	3
						Bury	136	8
Ron Mauge	5 10	10 06	10 3 69	Islington	Trainee	Charlton Ath	—	—
						Fulham	50	2
						Bury	64	7
						Manchester C (loan)	—	—
Paul Morris§			6 2 75	Bolton	Trainee	Bury	1	—
Paul Robertson‡	5 7	11 06	5 2 72	Stockport	York C	Stockport Co	10	—
						Bury	8	—
Roger Stanislaus	5 9	12 06	2 11 68	Hammersmith	Trainee	Arsenal	—	—
						Brentford	111	4
						Bury	108	5
Peter Valentine	5 10	12 00	16 6 63	Huddersfield	Apprentice	Huddersfield T	19	1
						Bolton W	68	1
						Bury	319	16
Darren Wilson*	5 11	12 07	30 9 71	Manchester		Manchester C	—	—
						Bury	32	1
Midfield								
Nick Daws	5 11	13 02	15 3 70	Manchester	Altrincham	Bury	36	1
Darren Emmett*	5 9	12 00	13 10 73	Liverpool	Trainee	Bury	—	—
David Esdaille†			22 7 63	Manchester		Wrexham	4	—
						Bury	6	—
Mark Kearney	5 10	11 00	12 6 62	Ormskirk	Marine	Everton	—	—
						Mansfield T	250	29
						Bury (loan)	13	1
						Bury	91	3
Matthew Lambert*	6 2	13 01	28 9 71	Morecambe	Trainee	Preston NE	16	2
						Bury	—	—
John Norman‡			26 6 71	Birkenhead		Bury	2	—
Andrew Reid	6 0	13 01	4 7 62	Manchester	Altrincham	Bury	29	—
Tony Rigby	5 10	12 01	10 8 72	Ormskirk	Barrow	Bury	21	2
Derek Ward	5 10	11 03	17 5 72	Birkenhead		Bury	25	—

BURY

Colours: White shirts, navy blue shorts, navy stockings. **Change colours:** Green/purple shirts, purple shorts, purple stockings.

Foundation: A meeting at the Waggon & Horses Hotel, attended largely by members of Bury Wesleyans and Bury Unitarians football clubs, decided to form a new Bury club. This was officially formed at a subsequent gathering at the Old White Horse Hotel, Fleet Street, Bury on April 24, 1885.

First Football League game: 1 September, 1894, Division 2, v Manchester C (h) W 4-2 – Lowe; Gillespie, Davies; White, Clegg, Ross; Wylie, Barbour (2), Millar (1), Ostler (1), Plant.

Did you know: Norman Bullock who held three Bury records – most League goals, most in a season and most League appearances – at one time, began as a centre-forward and ended just as successfully as a centre-half.

Managers (and Secretary-Managers)
 T. Hargreaves 1887*, H. S. Hamer 1887–1907*, Archie Montgomery 1907–15, William Cameron 1919–23, James Hunter Thompson 1923–27, Percy Smith 1927–30, Arthur Paine 1930–34, Norman Bullock 1934–38, Jim Porter 1944–45, Norman Bullock 1945–49, John McNeil 1950–53, Dave Russell 1953–61, Bob Stokoe 1961–65, Bert Head 1965–66, Les Shannon 1966–69, Jack Marshall 1969, Les Hart 1970, Tommy McAnearney 1970–72, Alan Brown 1972–73, Bobby Smith 1973–77, Bob Stokoe 1977–78, David Hatton 1978–79, Dave Connor 1979–80, Jim Iley 1980–84, Martin Dobson 1984–89, Sam Ellis 1989–90, 90, Mike Walsh December 1990–.

Player and Position	Ht	Wt	Birth Date	Birth Place	Source	Clubs	League App	Gls
Forwards								
David Adekola	6 0	12 02	18 5 68	Nigeria		Bury	16	8
Kevin Hulme	5 10	11 09	2 12 67	Farnworth	Radcliffe Borough	Bury	110	21
						Chester C (loan)	4	—
Andy Kilner‡	6 0	11 12	11 10 66	Bolton	Apprentice	Burnley	5	—
					Jonsered	Stockport Co	42	14
						Rochdale (loan)	3	—
						Bury	5	1
Darren Lyons	6 1	12 00	9 11 66	Manchester	Ashton U	Bury	36	7
Liam Robinson	5 7	11 05	29 12 65	Bradford	Nottingham F	Huddersfield T	21	2
						Tranmere R (loan)	4	3
						Bury	262	89
Ian Scott‡	5 9	11 04	20 9 67	Radcliffe	Apprentice	Manchester C	24	3
						Stoke C	30	2
						Crewe Alex (loan)	12	1
						Bury	9	2
Ian Stevens	5 9	12 00	21 10 66	Malta	Trainee	Preston NE	11	2
						Stockport Co	2	—
					Lancaster C	Bolton W	47	7
						Bury	77	31

Trainees
Adams, Daniel B; Byrne, Steven A; Dooner, Paul B; Doyle, Lee J; Higgens, Saul J; Morris, Paul I; Thornley, James D; Wallace, Richard E; Wilkinson, Lee; Williamson, Paul J.

**Non-Contract
Collings, Paul W; Curtis, Gary; Esdaille, David; Jackson, Robert G; Winter, Paul.

Associated Schoolboys
Nuttall, Mark; Rawlinson, Craig A; Stevens, Richard A; White, Christian P.

Associated Schoolboys who have accepted the club's offer of a Traineeship/Contract
Berry, Damian J; George, Lee J; Shuttleworth, Barry; Steele, Winfield J. J.

**Non-Contract Players who are retained must be re-signed before they are eligible to play in League matches.

CAMBRIDGE UNITED 1992–93 *Back row (left to right)*: Michael Cheetham, Richard Wilkins, Jamie Smeeth, Danny O'Shea, Gary Rowett, Steve Ball, Lee Philpott, Gary Clayton, Chris Leadbitter.

Centre row: Roger Parker (Kit Manager), Ken Steggles (Physio), Liam Daish, Michael Norbury, Mick Heathcote, Jon Sheffield, John Vaughan, Devon White, Warren Patmore, Phil Chapple, John Griffin (Chief Scout), Neil Lanham (Technical Adviser), Paul Ashworth (Youth Development Officer).

Front row: Andy Fensome, Phil Parkhill, Paul Raynor, Gary Peters (Assistant Manager), John Beck (Manager), Gary Johnson (Youth Manager), Gareth Ainsworth, Tony Dennis, Alan Kimble.

Division 2   **CAMBRIDGE UNITED**

CAMBRIDGE UNITED F.C.

Abbey Stadium, Newmarket Rd, Cambridge. Telephone (0223) 566500. Clubcall: 0898 121141. Fax 0223 566502.

Ground capacity: 10,206.

Record attendance; 14,000 v Chelsea, Friendly, 1 May 1970.

Record receipts: £86,308 v Manchester U, Rumbelows Cup 2nd rd 2nd leg, 9 October 1991.

Pitch measurements: 110yd × 74yd.

President: D. A. Ruston.

Chairman: R. H. Smart. *Vice-chairman:* D. A. Ruston. *Directors:* G. Harwood, J. Howard, C, Howlett, R. Hunt, G. Lowe, R. Smith.

Manager: Gary Johnson. *Assistant Manager:*

Physio: Ken Steggles. *Coach:* Graham Scarff.

Secretary: Steve Greenall. *Commercial Manager:* John Holmes. *Stadium Manager:* Ian Darler.

Year Formed: 1919. *Turned Professional:* 1946. *Ltd Co.:* 1948.

Club Nickname: The 'U's'.

Previous Name: Abbey United until 1949.

Record League Victory: 6–0 v Darlington, Division 4, 18 September 1971 – Roberts; Thompson, Akers, Guild, Eades, Foote, Collins (1p), Horrey, Hollett, Greenhalgh (4), Phillips. (1 og). 6–0 v Hartlepool, Division 4, 11 February 1989 – Vaughan; Beck, Kimble, Turner, Chapple, Daish, Clayton, Holmes, Taylor (3 incl. 1p), Bull (1), Leadbitter (1).

Record Cup Victory: 5–1 v Bristol C, FA Cup, 5th rd, second replay, 27 February 1990 – Vaughan; Fensome, Kimble, Bailie (O'Shea), Chapple, Daish, Cheetham (Robinson), Leadbitter (1), Dublin (2), Taylor (1), Philpott (1).

Record Defeat: 0–6 v Aldershot, Division 3, 13 April 1974 and v Darlington, Division 4, 28 September 1974 and v Chelsea, Division 2, 15 January 1983.

Most League Points (2 for a win): 65, Division 4, 1976–77.

Most League Points (3 for a win): 86, Division 3, 1990–91.

Most League Goals: 87, Division 4, 1976–77.

Highest League Scorer in Season: David Crown, 24, Division 4, 1985–86.

Most League Goals in Total Aggregate: Alan Biley, 74, 1975–80.

Most Capped Player: Tom Finney, 7 (15), Northern Ireland.

Most League Appearances: Steve Spriggs, 416, 1975–87.

Record Transfer Fee Received: £1,000,000 from Manchester U for Dion Dublin, August 1992.

Record Transfer Fee Paid: £190,000 to Luton T for Steve Claridge, November 1992.

Football League Record: 1970 Elected to Division 4; 1973–74 Division 3; 1974–77 Division 4; 1977–78 Division 3; 1978–84 Division 2; 1984–85 Division 3; 1985–90 Division 4; 1990–91 Division 3; 1991–92 Division 2; 1992–93 Division 1; 1993– Division 2.

Honours: Football League: Division 2 best season: 5th, 1991–92; Division 3 – Champions 1990–91; Runners-up 1977–78; Division 4 – Champions 1976–77. *FA Cup:* best season: 6th rd, 1989–90, 1990–91. *Football League Cup:* 5th rd, 1992–93.

CAMBRIDGE UNITED 1992—93 LEAGUE RECORD

Match No.	Date	Venue	Opponents	Result	H/T Score	Lg. Pos.	Goalscorers	Atten- dance
1	Aug 15	A	Tranmere R	L 0-2	0-0	—		5248
2	18	H	Charlton Ath	L 0-1	0-0	—		5094
3	22	H	Birmingham C	L 0-3	0-2	24		5015
4	29	A	Swindon T	L 1-4	0-2	24	Chapple	8134
5	Sept 4	H	Brentford	W 1-0	0-0	—	Francis	5075
6	12	A	Charlton Ath	D 0-0	0-0	22		5836
7	15	A	Oxford U	L 0-3	0-1	—		3785
8	19	H	Sunderland	W 2-1	1-0	19	Philpott, Chapple	5383
9	26	A	Grimsby T	D 1-1	0-0	18	Leadbitter	4848
10	Oct 3	H	Derby Co	L 1-3	0-0	20	White	6170
11	10	A	Millwall	D 2-2	2-2	21	White, Leadbitter	7096
12	17	H	Bristol C	W 2-1	1-0	18	Kimble (pen), Ainsworth	3894
13	25	A	Southend U	D 1-1	1-0	—	Rowett	3810
14	31	H	West Ham U	W 2-1	1-0	17	Norbury, White	7214
15	Nov 3	H	Luton T	D 3-3	0-1	—	Philpott, Francis 2	5716
16	7	A	Portsmouth	L 0-3	0-1	18		8956
17	14	H	Barnsley	L 1-2	0-2	19	Clayton	3971
18	21	A	Leicester C	D 2-2	1-1	19	Claridge, Heathcote	12,175
19	28	A	Newcastle U	L 1-4	0-1	20	Claridge	27,991
20	Dec 5	H	Wolverhampton W	D 1-1	0-0	19	White	6429
21	12	H	Notts Co	L 0-1	0-1	20		5037
22	18	H	Bristol R	L 0-1	0-0	—		4027
23	28	A	Watford	D 2-2	0-2	22	Soloman (og), Dennis	8147
24	Jan 9	A	Sunderland	D 3-3	1-2	23	Clayton, Claridge, Raynor	16,778
25	16	H	Grimsby T	W 2-0	2-0	19	Rowett, Butler	4137
26	23	H	Oxford U	D 2-2	2-2	20	Claridge, Kimble (pen)	4536
27	30	A	Birmingham C	W 2-0	1-0	18	Butler, Claridge	9425
28	Feb 6	H	Tranmere R	L 0-1	0-0	20		4802
29	14	A	Brentford	W 1-0	1-0	—	Butler	7318
30	20	H	Swindon T	W 1-0	0-0	18	Kimble (pen)	5437
31	27	H	Millwall	D 1-1	0-1	18	Butler	5144
32	Mar 3	A	Derby Co	D 0-0	0-0	—		14,106
33	9	A	Barnsley	L 0-2	0-1	—		5445
34	13	H	Portsmouth	L 0-1	0-1	21		5975
35	16	H	Peterborough U	D 2-2	2-0	—	Claridge, Heathcote	8077
36	20	A	Wolverhampton W	W 2-1	1-0	18	Butler, Leadbitter	11,473
37	23	H	Leicester C	L 1-3	0-0	—	Kimble (pen)	6836
38	27	A	Luton T	L 0-2	0-1	21		8077
39	Apr 3	H	Newcastle U	L 0-3	0-1	22		7925
40	6	H	Notts Co	W 3-0	1-0	—	Clayton, Bartlett, Leadbitter	4583
41	10	A	Peterborough U	L 0-1	0-1	23		10,235
42	13	A	Watford	D 1-1	0-1	—	Raynor	5106
43	17	A	Bristol R	D 1-1	1-1	23	Butler	3929
44	24	A	Bristol C	D 0-0	0-0	23		8995
45	May 1	H	Southend U	W 3-1	2-0	22	Claridge, Leadbitter 2	7137
46	8	A	West Ham U	L 0-2	0-0	23		27,399

Final League Position: 23

GOALSCORERS

League (48): Claridge 7, Butler 6, Leadbitter 6, Kimble 4 (4 pens), White 4, Clayton 3, Francis 3, Chapple 2, Heathcote 2, Philpott 2, Raynor 2, Rowett 2, Ainsworth 1, Bartlett 1, Dennis 1, Norbury 1, own goal 1.
Coca Cola Cup (10): Clayton 2, Chapple 1, Danzey 1, Fowler 1, Francis 1, Heathcote 1, Philpott 1, Rowett 1, White 1.
FA Cup (1): Heathcote 1.

Vaughan 27	Heathcote 42	Kimble 46	Raynor 41	O'Shea 37	Daish 15 + 1	Cheetham 16 + 1	Wilkins 1	Norbury 7 + 5	Francis 15 + 14	Philpott 16	White 14 + 6	Fowler 2 + 1	Fensome 27 + 3	Leadbitter 34 + 4	Chapple 16 + 2	Rowett 17 + 4	Sheffield 13	Dennis 12 + 4	Clayton 34 + 2	Ainsworth 1 + 3	Patmore 1	Danzey 1 + 1	Claridge 29	Atkins 1 + 1	Butler 23	Lyne 5 + 9	McGlashan — + 1	Rush 4 + 6	Bartlett 3 + 5	Filan 6	Match No.
1	2	3	4	5	6	7	8	9	10	11	12	14																			1
1	10	3	4	5	6	7		14	9	11	8		2	12																	2
1	10	3	4	5	6	7		8	9	11	12		2	14																	3
1	2	3	4		6			9	10	11	12		8	5	7																4
	2	3	4		6			9	10	11	12		8	5	7		1														5
	5	3	4			10		14	12	11	9		2	8	6	7	1														6
	5	3	4			10		14	7	11	9		2	8	6	12	1														7
1	2	3	4		6			9	10	11	12		8	5	7	14															8
		3	9		6				10	11	12		2	8	5	7	1	4		14											9
		3	7		6				10	11	12		9	8	5	2	1	4		14											10
	5	3	7		6				10	9	12		2	11	8		1	4		14											11
	5	3	7		6				10	9	12		2	11			1	4					8								12
	5	3	4		6						9		2	11		7	1		10				8								13
	5	3	4		6				8		9		2	11		7	1	12	10	14											14
	5	3	4		6				8	9	12		2	11		7	1		10	14											15
	5	3	4		6				8	9			2	11		7	1	12	10	14											16
	5	3	4	7	6				8		9	14	2	11			1	12	10												17
	5	3	4	7	6								2	11	8		1	12	10	14					9						18
1	5	3	4	7	6								2	11	8			12	10	14					9						19
1	5	3	4		6						9		2	11		7		12	10				8								20
1	5	3	4		6						9		2	11		7		12	10				8								21
1	5	3	4		6						9		2	11		7		12	10				8	2							22
1	5	3	4		6								2	11		7		12	10	14			8		9						23
1	5	3	4		6								2	11		7		12	10	14			8		9						24
1	5	3	4		6								2			7			10				8		9	11		12			25
1	5	3	4		6								2			7		12	10	14			8		9	11					26
1	5	3	4	7	6								2	11				12	10				8		9						27
1	5	3	4	7	6								2	11				12	10				8		9			14			28
1	5	3	4	7	6								2	11					10				8		9						29
1	5	3	4	7	6								2	11				12	10				8		9						30
1		3	4	5	6								2	11		7		12	10				8		9						31
1	5	3			6								2	11	4	7			10				8		9						32
1	5	3			6								2	11	4	7			10				8	12	9	14					33
1	5	3	7		6								2	11				4	10				8		9	14		12			34
1	5	3			6								2	11	12			4	10				8		9	14			7		35
1	5	3	4		6								2	11					10				8		9	12			7		36
1	5	3	4	2	6									11	12				10				8		9	14			7		37
1	5	3	4	2	6									11					10				8		9	14		12	7		38
	5	3	4	7	6								2						10				8		9	11		14	12	1	39
1	5	3	4		6								2	11					10				8		9	12			7		40
1	5	3	4		6								2	11	12				10				8		9	14			7		41
		3	4		6								2	11	5				10				8		9	12		14	7	1	42
	2	3	4		6									11	5			7	10				8		9			14	12	1	43
	2	3	4		6										5			7	10				8		9	11		14	12	1	44
	2	3	4		6									11	5	7		12	10				8		9					1	45
	2	3	4		6									11	5	7			10				8		9			12		1	46

Coca Cola Cup	Second Round	Stoke C (h)	2-2
		(a)	2-1
	Third Round	Notts Co (a)	3-2
	Fourth Round	Oldham Ath (h)	1-0
	Fifth Round	Blackburn R (a)	2-3
FA Cup	Third Round	Sheffield W (h)	1-2

CAMBRIDGE UNITED

Goalkeepers

Name				Birthplace	Source	Club	Apps	Goals
John Filan†	5 11	12 10	8 2 70	Sydney	Budapest St George	Cambridge U	6	—
Jon Sheffield	5 11	11 07	1 2 69	Bedworth		Norwich C	1	—
						Aldershot (loan)	11	—
						Ipswich T (loan)	—	—
						Aldershot (loan)	15	—
						Cambridge U (loan)	2	—
						Cambridge U	26	—
John Vaughan*	5 10	13 01	26 6 64	Isleworth	Apprentice	West Ham U		
						Charlton Ath (loan)	6	—
						Bristol R (loan)	6	—
						Wrexham (loan)	4	—
						Bristol C (loan)	2	—
						Fulham	44	—
						Bristol C (loan)	3	—
						Cambridge U	178	—

Defenders

Name				Birthplace	Source	Club	Apps	Goals
Phil Chapple	6 2	12 07	26 11 66	Norwich		Norwich C	—	—
						Cambridge U	187	19
Liam Daish	6 2	13 05	23 9 68	Portsmouth	Apprentice	Portsmouth	1	—
						Cambridge U	121	2
Mike Heathcote	6 2	12 05	10 9 65	Durham	Spennymoor U	Sunderland	9	—
						Halifax T (loan)	7	1
						York C (loan)	3	—
						Shrewsbury T	44	6
						Cambridge U	64	7
Alan Kimble	5 8	11 00	6 8 66	Poole		Charlton Ath	6	—
						Exeter C (loan)	1	—
						Cambridge U	299	24
Danny O'Shea	6 0	12 08	26 3 63	Kennington	Apprentice	Arsenal	6	—
						Charlton Ath (loan)	9	—
						Exeter C	45	2
						Southend U	118	12
						Cambridge U	134	1
Jamie Smeeth	6 1	13 00	7 9 74	Hackney		Cambridge U	—	—

Midfield

Name				Birthplace	Source	Club	Apps	Goals
Ian Atkins‡	6 0	12 03	16 1 57	Birmingham	Apprentice	Shrewsbury T	278	58
						Sunderland	77	6
						Everton	7	1
						Ipswich T	77	4
						Birmingham C	93	6
						Colchester U	—	—
						Birmingham C	8	—
						Cambridge U	2	—
Michael Cheetham	5 11	11 05	30 6 67	Amsterdam	Army	Ipswich T	4	—
						Cambridge U	119	20
Gary Clayton	5 11	12 08	2 2 63	Sheffield	Burton Alb	Doncaster R	35	5
						Cambridge U	154	13
						Peterborough U (loan)	4	—
Tony Dennis	5 7	10 02	1 12 63	Eton	Slough	Cambridge U	111	10
Andy Fensome	5 8	11 02	18 2 69	Northampton	Trainee	Norwich C	—	—
						Newcastle U (loan)	—	—
						Cambridge U	124	1
John Fowler	5 10	11 10	27 10 74	Preston	Trainee	Cambridge U	3	—
						Preston NE (loan)	6	—
Warren Patmore†			14 8 71	Kingsbury		Cambridge U	1	—
Richard Wilkins	6 0	12 00	28 5 65	London	Haverhill R	Colchester U	152	22
						Cambridge U	74	7

Forwards

Name				Birthplace	Source	Club	Apps	Goals
Kevin Bartlett	5 9	10 12	12 10 62	Portsmouth	Apprentice	Portsmouth	3	—
					Fareham	Cardiff C	82	25

CAMBRIDGE UNITED

Colours: Amber & black striped shirts, black shorts with amber & black trim, black & amber stockings.
Change colours: Patterned white & sky blue shirts, royal blue shorts, royal blue stockings.

Foundation: The football revival in Cambridge began soon after World War II when the Abbey United club (formed 1919) decided to turn professional and in 1949 changed their name to Cambridge United. They were competing in the United Counties League before graduating to the Eastern Counties League in 1951 and the Southern League in 1958.

First Football League game: 15 August, 1970, Division 4, v Lincoln C (h) D 1-1 – Roberts; Thompson, Meldrum (1), Slack, Eades, Hardy, Leggett, Cassidy, Lindsey, McKinven, Harris.

Did you know: Cambridge United staged the first FA Cup tie to be played on a Sunday. On 6 January 1974 they drew 2-2 with Oldham Athletic in the third round. A crowd of 8479 attended the morning kick-off.

Managers (and Secretary-Managers)
Bill Whittaker 1949–55, Gerald Williams 1955, Bert Johnson 1955–59, Bill Craig 1959–60, Alan Moore 1960–63, Roy Kirk 1964–66, Bill Leivers 1967–74, Ron Atkinson 1974–78, John Docherty 1978–83, John Ryan 1984–85, Ken Shellito 1985, Chris Turner 1985–90, John Beck 1990–1992, Ian Atkins 1992–93, Gary Johnson June 1993–.

Name	Ht	Wt	Born	Birthplace	Signed from	Club	Apps	Goals
						WBA	37	10
						Notts Co	99	33
						Port Vale (loan)	5	1
						Cambridge U	8	1
Steve Butler	6 2	13 00	27 1 62	Birmingham	Wokingham Maidstone U (1986)	Brentford	97	44
						Watford	62	9
						Bournemouth (loan)	1	—
						Cambridge U	23	6
Steve Claridge	5 11	11 08	10 4 66	Portsmouth	Fareham Weymouth	Bournemouth	7	1
						Crystal Palace	—	—
						Aldershot	62	19
						Cambridge U	79	28
						Luton T	16	2
						Cambridge U	29	7
Michael Danzey	6 1	12 00	8 2 71	Widnes	Trainee	Nottingham F	—	—
						Chester C (loan)	2	—
						Peterborough U	1	—
					St Albans	Cambridge U	2	—
Chris Leadbitter	5 9	10 07	17 10 67	Middlesbrough	Apprentice	Grimsby T	—	—
						Hereford U	36	1
						Cambridge U	176	18
Neil Lyne	6 1	12 04	4 4 70	Leicester	Leicester U	Nottingham F	—	—
						Walsall (loan)	7	—
						Shrewsbury T (loan)	16	6
						Shrewsbury T	64	11
						Cambridge U	14	—
Philip Parkhill			22 2 74	Harrogate		Cambridge U	—	—
Paul Raynor	6 0	11 04	29 4 66	Nottingham	Apprentice	Nottingham F	3	—
						Bristol R (loan)	8	—
						Huddersfield T	50	9
						Swansea C	191	27
						Wrexham (loan)	6	—
						Cambridge U	49	2
David Robinson*	5 11		27 9 71	Ely	Trainee	Cambridge U	—	—
Gary Rowett	6 0	12 10	6 3 74	Bromsgrove	Trainee	Cambridge U	34	4

Trainees
Beresford, Paul R; Clark, Paul D; Gibbens, Neil; Granville, Daniel P; Hunter, Alvin J; Hyde, Micah; Kilbane, Farrell N; Nyamah, Kofi; Parker, Scott J; Rattle, Jonathan P; Toombs, David J.

**Non-Contract
Filan, John R; Patmore, Warren J.

Associated Schoolboys
Akinylvre, Jide J; Archer, Aaron A; Beall, John H; Ferdinandi, Mark A; Hayes, Adrian M; Howes, Shaun; Pack, Lenny J; Price, Robert A; Sampaney, Kwame S; Thomas, Tyrone.

Associated Schoolboys who have accepted the club's offer of a Traineeship/Contract
Barry, Mark S; Collard, Allan; Gutzmore, Leon; Kyd, Michael R; Lake, Edward J; Stock, Russell J; Walker, Richard K; Williams, Stuart R.

**Non-Contract Players who are retained must be re-signed before they are eligible to play in League matches.

CARDIFF CITY 1992-93 *Back row (left to right):* Lee Baddeley, Chris Pike, Gareth Abraham, Paul Millar, Derek Brazil.
Centre row: Jason Donovan, Robbie James, Jason Perry, Gavin Ward, Mark Grew, Alan Lewis, Nick Richardson, Paul Ramsey.
Front row: Cohen Griffith, Damon Searle, Roger Gibbins (Player/Coach), Eddie May (First Team Coach), John Williams, Carl Dale, Nathan Blake.

Division 2   **CARDIFF CITY**

Ninian Park, Cardiff CF1 8SX. Telephone Cardiff (0222) 398636. Fax (0222) 341148. Newsline (0898) 888603.

Ground capacity: 20,284.

Record attendance: 61,566, Wales v England, 14 October 1961.

Club record: 57,893 v Arsenal, Division 1, 22 April 1953.

Record receipts: £81,338.54 v Shrewsbury T, Division 3, 1 May 1993.

Pitch measurements: 114yd × 78yd.

Directors: D. Henderson.

Secretary: Jim Finney.

Manager: Eddie May. *Commercial Manager:*

Physio: Jimmy Goodfellow. *Coach:* Eddie May.

Year Formed: 1899. *Turned Professional:* 1910. *Ltd Co.:* 1910.

Previous Names: 1899–1902, Riverside; 1902–08, Riverside Albion; 1908, Cardiff City.

Club Nickname: 'Bluebirds'.

Previous Grounds: Riverside, Sophia Gardens, Old Park and Fir Gardens. Moved to Ninian Park, 1910.

Record League Victory: 9–2 v Thames, Division 3 (S), 6 February 1932 – Farquharson; E. L. Morris, Roberts; Galbraith, Harris, Ronan; Emmerson (1), Keating (1), Jones (1), McCambridge (1), Robbins (5).

Record Cup Victory: 8–0 v Enfield, FA Cup, 1st rd, 28 November 1931 – Farquharson; Smith, Roberts; Harris (1), Galbraith, Ronan; Emmerson (2), Keating (3); O'Neill (2), Robbins, McCambridge.

Record Defeat: 2–11 v Sheffield U, Division 1, 1 January 1926.

Most League Points (2 for a win): 66, Division 3 (S), 1946–47.

Most League Points (3 for a win): 86, Division 3, 1982–83.

Most League Goals: 93, Division 3 (S), 1946–47.

Highest League Scorer in Season: Stan Richards, 30, Division 3 (S), 1946–47.

Most League Goals in Total Aggregate: Len Davies, 128, 1920–31.

Most Capped Player: Alf Sherwood, 39 (41), Wales.

Most League Appearances: Phil Dwyer, 471, 1972–85.

Record Transfer Fee Received: £215,000 from Portsmouth for Jimmy Gilligan, October 1989.

Record Transfer Fee Paid: £180,000 to San Jose Earthquakes for Godfrey Ingram, September 1982.

Football League Record: 1920 Elected to Division 2; 1921–29 Division 1; 1929–31 Division 2; 1931–47 Division 3 (S); 1947–52 Division 2; 1952–57 Division 1; 1957–60 Division 2; 1960–62 Division 1; 1962–75 Division 2; 1975–76 Division 3; 1976–82 Division 2; 1982–83 Division 3; 1983–85 Division 2; 1985–86 Division 3; 1986–88 Division 4; 1988–90 Division 3; 1990–92 Division 4; 1992–93 Division 3; 1993– Division 2.

Honours: Football League: Division 1 – Runners-up 1923–24; Division 2 – Runners-up 1920–21, 1951–52, 1959–60; Division 3 (S) – Champions 1946–47; Division 3 – Champions 1992–93. Runners-up 1975–76, 1982–83; Division 4 – Runners-up 1987–88. *FA Cup:* Winners 1926–27 (only occasion the Cup has been won by a club outside England); Runners-up 1925. *Football League Cup:* Semi-final 1965–66. *Welsh Cup:* Winners 21 times. *Charity Shield:* 1927. European Competitions: *European Cup-Winners' Cup:* 1964–65, 1965–66, 1967–68, 1968–69, 1969–70, 1970–71, 1971–72, 1973–74, 1974–75, 1976–77, 1977–78, 1988–89, 1991–92, 1992–93.

CARDIFF CITY 1992—93 LEAGUE RECORD

Match No.	Date		Venue	Opponents	Result	H/T Score	Lg. Pos.	Goalscorers	Atten dance
1	Aug	15	H	Darlington	D 0-0	0-0	—		8399
2		22	A	Walsall	W 3-2	2-0	4	Searle, Dale 2	4611
3		29	H	Halifax T	W 2-1	1-0	3	James, Dale	7692
4	Sept	1	H	Northampton T	W 2-1	0-1	—	Ramsey (pen), Dale	7494
5		5	A	Torquay U	L 1-2	0-1	3	Pike	2939
6		8	H	Carlisle U	D 2-2	1-0	—	Pike (pen), Perry	6859
7		13	A	Hereford U	D 1-1	0-1	—	Blake	4039
8		19	H	Gillingham	W 3-1	2-0	3	Blake, Pike 2	6356
9	Oct	3	H	Rochdale	D 1-1	1-1	5	Pike	6161
10		10	A	Crewe Alex	L 0-2	0-2	7		3638
11		24	A	Shrewsbury T	L 2-3	1-2	12	Dale, Pike (pen)	4161
12		31	H	Scunthorpe U	W 3-0	1-0	9	Blake, Kelly, Ramsey (pen)	6027
13	Nov	3	A	Chesterfield	L 1-2	0-2	—	James	2590
14		7	H	Colchester U	W 3-1	0-0	10	Dale, Blake, English (og)	5505
15		22	A	Barnet	L 1-2	0-0	—	Dale	4181
16		28	H	Bury	W 3-0	1-0	8	Kearney (og), Blake, Griffith	4348
17	Dec	11	A	Doncaster R	W 1-0	1-0	—	Millar	2023
18		18	H	Wrexham	L 1-2	1-1	—	Blake	6832
19		26	H	York C	D 3-3	3-0	8	Hall (og), Gorman, Stant	10,411
20		28	A	Lincoln C	L 2-3	0-0	8	Ramsey, Millar	4359
21	Jan	2	H	Hereford U	W 2-1	1-1	7	Stant, Richardson	6593
22		9	A	Carlisle U	W 2-1	1-0	5	Bird, Ratcliffe	3691
23		23	A	Gillingham	W 1-0	1-0	4	Griffith	4069
24		26	A	Halifax T	W 1-0	0-0	—	Stant	1339
25		30	H	Walsall	W 2-1	2-1	4	Stant, Griffith	9012
26	Feb	6	A	Darlington	W 2-0	0-0	4	Pike 2 (1 pen)	1775
27		13	H	Torquay U	W 4-0	1-0	2	Millar, Stant 2, Blake	7771
28		19	A	Northampton T	W 2-1	0-0	—	Stant, Pike	4519
29		27	A	Crewe Alex	D 1-1	1-1	2	Griffith	10,012
30	Mar	6	A	Rochdale	W 2-1	1-0	2	Blake, Griffith	2831
31		9	H	Scarborough	W 1-0	1-0	—	Stant	8583
32		12	A	Colchester U	W 4-2	3-1	—	Pike 2, Richardson, Matthews	4538
33		20	H	Chesterfield	W 2-1	1-0	1	Dale, Richardson	6756
34		23	A	Bury	L 0-1	0-0	—		3574
35		27	H	Barnet	D 1-1	0-1	1	Griffith	16,073
36	Apr	3	A	Scarborough	W 3-1	2-1	1	Pike (pen), Richardson, Stant	2223
37		6	D	Doncaster R	D 1-1	0-1	1	Perry	9938
38		10	H	York C	L 1-3	0-2	2	Griffith	6568
39		12	H	Lincoln C	W 3-1	2-0	1	Stant, Blake, Ramsey (pen)	11,257
40		17	A	Wrexham	W 2-0	2-0	1	Griffith, Blake	10,852
41	May	1	H	Shrewsbury T	W 2-1	1-1	1	Perry, Blake	17,253
42		8	A	Scunthorpe U	W 3-0	2-0	1	Griffith 2, Stant	7407

Final League Position: 1

GOALSCORERS

League (77): Pike 12 (4 pens), Blake 11, Stant 11, Griffith 10, Dale 8, Ramsey 4 (3 pens), Richardson 4, Millar 3, Perry 3, James 2, Bird 1, Gorman 1, Kelly 1, Matthews 1, Ratcliffe 1, Searle 1, own goals 3.
Coca Cola Cup (2): Dale 2.
FA Cup (2): Blake 1, Millar 1.

Grew 10	James 42	Searle 42	Richardson 36 + 3	Perry 38 + 1	Brazil 33 + 1	Ramsey 30	Griffith 28 + 6	Pike 20 + 8	Dale 19 + 1	Blake 30 + 4	Millar 30 + 3	Bird 3 + 6	Gibbins 1 + 7	Williams — + 1	Baddeley 7 + 1	Ward 32	Kelly 5	Matthews 12 + 2	Stant 24	Gorman 1	Ratcliffe 19	Match No.
1	2	3	4	5	6	7	8	9	10	11	12											1
1	2	3		5	6	7	8	9	10	11		4	12									2
1	2	3	8	5	6	7	12	9	10	11	4											3
1	2	3	4	5	6	7	8	12	10	11	9											4
1	2	3	4	5	6	7	8	9		11	10		12	14								5
1	2	3	14		6	7	8	9	10	11	4		12		5							6
1	2	3	4	5	6		8	9	10	11	7	14	12									7
1	2	3	4		6	7		9	10	11	8				5							8
1	2	3	12		6	7	8	9	10	11	4				5							9
	2	3			6	7	8	9	10	11	4		12		5					1		10
1	2	3	4	14	6	7	8	9	10	11	12				5							11
	2	3	4	5	6	7		12	10	9	11					1	8					12
	2	3	4	5	6			12	10	9	11					1	8	7				13
	4	3			6	7		10	9	11		2				1	8	5				14
	2	3	4	5	6	7		10	9	11			12			1	8					15
	2	3	4	5	6	7	14	12	10	9	11					1	8					16
	2	3	8	5	6	7			10	11	4					1			9			17
	2	3	8	5	6	7	14		10	11	4	12				1			9			18
	2	3	8	5	6	7	14			4	10				12	1			9		11	19
	2	3	8	5	6	7	11			10	12				4	1			9			20
6	3	8	2			7	11			4	10				5	1			9			21
	2	3	8	5		7	11			4	10					1			9		6	22
	2	3	8	5			11		10	7	12					1		4	9		6	23
	2	3	8	5			11		10	7						1		4	9		6	24
	2	3	8	5			11	12	10	7						1		4	9		6	25
	2	3	8	5	14		11	12	10	7						1		4	9		6	26
	2	3	8	5			11	10		12	7					1		4	9		6	27
	2	3	8	5	4		11	10		12	7					1			9		6	28
	2	3	8	5	4		11	10		12	7					1			9		6	29
	2	3	8	5	4		11	10		9	7					1					6	30
	2	3	8	5	4		10			11	7	12				1			9		6	31
	2	3	8	5	4		11	10								1		7	9		6	32
	2	3	8	5	4	7	12	10								1		11	9		6	33
	2	3	8	5	4	7	10						12			1		11	9		6	34
	2	3	12	5	4	7	14	10		11						1		8	9		6	35
	2	3	8	5	4	7	11	10				12				1		14	9		6	36
	2	3	8	5	4	7	12	10		11						1		6	9			37
	2	3	8	5	4	7	11	10				12				1		14	9		6	38
	2	3	8	5	4	7	11		10							1			9		6	39
	2	3	8	5	4	7	11	12	10							1			9		6	40
	2	3	8	5	4	7	11	12	10	9	14					1					6	41
	2	3	8	5	4	7	11		10	6						1			9			42

Coca Cola Cup	First Round	Bristol C (h)	1-0
		(a)	1-5
FA Cup	First Round	Bath C (h)	2-3

CARDIFF CITY

Player and Position	Ht	Wt	Date	Birth Place	Source	Clubs	League App	Gls
Goalkeepers								
Mark Grew	5 11	12 08	15 2 58	Bilston	Amateur	WBA	33	—
						Wigan Ath (loan)	4	—
						Notts Co (loan)	—	—
						Leicester C	5	—
						Oldham Ath (loan)	5	—
						Ipswich T	6	—
						Fulham (loan)	4	—
						WBA (loan)	1	—
						Derby Co (loan)	—	—
						Port Vale	184	—
						Blackburn R (loan)	13	—
						Cardiff C	10	—
Gavin Ward	6 2	12 12	30 6 70	Sutton Coldfield	Aston Villa	Shrewsbury T	—	—
						WBA	—	—
						Cardiff C	59	—
Defenders								
Lee Baddeley	6 1	12 10	12 7 74	Cardiff	Trainee	Cardiff C	28	—
Nathan Blake	5 10	12 00	27 1 72	Cardiff	Chelsea	Cardiff C	111	21
Derek Brazil	5 11	10 05	14 12 68	Dublin	Rivermount BC	Manchester U	2	—
						Oldham Ath (loan)	1	—
						Swansea C (loan)	12	1
						Cardiff C	34	—
Andy Gorman§	5 11	13 03	13 9 74	Cardiff		Cardiff C	12	1
Allan Lewis*	6 2	13 00	31 5 71	Pontypridd	Trainee	Cardiff C	50	—
Neil Matthews‡	6 0	11 07	3 12 67	Manchester	Apprentice	Blackpool	76	1
						Cardiff C	66	2
Jason Perry	5 11	10 04	2 4 70	Newport		Cardiff C	158	3
Paul Ramsey	5 11	13 00	3 9 62	Londonderry	Apprentice	Leicester C	290	13
						Cardiff C	69	7
Kevin Ratcliffe†	5 11	12 07	12 11 60	Mancot	Apprentice	Everton	359	2
						Dundee	4	—
						Everton	—	—
						Cardiff C	19	1
Damon Searle	5 11	10 04	26 10 71	Cardiff	Trainee	Cardiff C	119	2
John Williams	6 1	13 12	3 10 60	Liverpool	Amateur	Tranmere R	173	13
						Port Vale	50	2
						Bournemouth	117	9
						Wigan Ath (loan)	4	—
						Cardiff C	6	—
Midfield								
Nick Richardson	6 0	12 07	11 4 67	Halifax	Local	Halifax T	101	17
						Cardiff C	39	4
Forwards								
Anthony Bird§	5 10	11 09	1 9 74	Cardiff	Trainee	Cardiff C	9	1
Carl Dale	6 0	12 00	29 4 66	Colwyn Bay	Bangor C	Chester C	116	41
						Cardiff C	61	30
Roger Gibbins‡	5 10	11 09	6 9 55	Enfield	Apprentice	Tottenham H	—	—
						Oxford U	19	2
						Norwich C	48	12
					New England	Cambridge U	100	12
					Tea Men	Cardiff C	139	17
						Swansea C	35	6
						Newport Co	79	9
						Torquay U	33	5
					Newport Co	Cardiff C	142	7

CARDIFF CITY

Colours: All blue. **Change colours:** All red.

Foundation: Credit for the establishment of a first class professional football club in such a rugby stronghold as Cardiff, is due to members of the Riverside club formed in 1899 out of a cricket club of that name. Cardiff became a city in 1905 and in 1908 the local FA granted Riverside permission to call themselves Cardiff City.

First Football League game: 28 August, 1920, Division 2, v Stockport C (a) W 5-2 – Kneeshaw; Brittain, Leyton; Keenor (1), Smith, Hardy; Grimshaw (1), Gill (2), Cashmore, West, Evans (1).

Did you know: Three seasons before they beat Arsenal in the FA Cup final, Cardiff City succeeded in beating them on three successive Saturdays, twice in Division 1 and once in the FA Cup: 19 January 1924 (a) 2-1, 26 January (h) 4-0 and in the cup 2 February (h) 1-0.

Managers (and Secretary-Managers)
Davy McDougall 1910–11, Fred Stewart 1911–33, Bartley Wilson 1933–34, B. Watts-Jones 1934–37, Bill Jennings 1937–39, Cyril Spiers 1939–46, Billy McCandless 1946–48, Cyril Spiers 1948–54, Trevor Morris 1954–58, Bill Jones 1958–62, George Swindin 1962–64, Jimmy Scoular 1964–73, Frank O'Farrell 1973–74, Jimmy Andrews 1974–78, Richie Morgan 1978–82, Len Ashurst 1982–84, Jimmy Goodfellow 1984, Alan Durban 1984–86, Frank Burrows 1986–89, Len Ashurst 1989–91, Eddie May July 1991–.

Player and Position	Ht	Wt	Date	Birth Place	Source	Clubs	League App	Gls
Cohen Griffith	5 10	11 07	26 12 62	Georgetown	Kettering T	Cardiff C	154	29
Robbie James	5 11	13 0	23 3 57	Swansea	Apprentice	Swansea C	394	99
						Stoke C	48	6
						QPR	87	4
						Leicester C	23	—
						Swansea C	90	16
						Bradford C	89	6
						Cardiff C	42	2
Paul Millar	6 2	12 07	16 11 66	Belfast	Portadown	Port Vale	40	5
						Hereford U (loan)	5	2
						Cardiff C	48	3
Chris Pike*	6 2	13 07	19 10 61	Cardiff	Barry T	Fulham	42	4
						Cardiff C (loan)	6	2
						Cardiff C	148	65
Phil Stant	6 1	12 07	13 10 62	Bolton	Camberley Army	Reading	4	2
						Hereford U	89	38
						Notts Co	22	6
						Blackpool (loan)	12	5
						Lincoln C (loan)	4	—
						Huddersfield T (loan)	5	1
						Fulham	19	5
						Mansfield T	57	32
						Cardiff C	24	11

Trainees
Bartley, Kevin D; Bird, Anthony; Callaway, Nilsson A. D; Crocker, Mathew; Evans, Terry; Gorman, Andrew D; Graham, Benjamin; Hainsworth, Darren J; Parsons, Andrew K; Sime, Leighton R; Street, Daniel C; Walker, Lee; Young, Scott.

**Non-Contract
Ratcliffe, Kevin.

Associated Schoolboys
Jarman, Lee; McCarthy, James; Mountain, Patrick; Parsons, James; Pugh, Richard; Street, Lee J; Tobutt, Richard; Toole, Andrew; Vick, Leigh.

Associated Schoolboys who have accepted the club's offer of a Traineeship/Contract
Davies, Christopher; Haworth, Simon; Ingram, Chris; Jones, Ian; Keepin, Andrew W; Wigg, Nathan.

**Non-Contract Players who are retained must be re-signed before they are eligible to play in League matches.

CARLISLE UNITED 1992–93 *Back row (left to right):* Richard Sendall, Ricardo Gabbiadini, Simon Davey, Andy Barnsley, Jeff Thorpe, Craig Potts.
Centre row: Steve Holden, John Holliday, Warren Hawke, Derek Walsh, George Oghani, Kelham O'Hanlon, Darren Edmondson, Andy Watson.
Front row: Micky Holmes, Peter Hampton (Physio), Michael Knighton (Chairman/Chief Executive), David McCreery (Player/Coach), Ian Dalziel, Ian Arnold.

Division 3   CARLISLE UNITED

Brunton Park, Carlisle CA1 1LL. Telephone Carlisle (0228) 26237. Fax (0228) 30138. Promotions Dept: (0228) 24014. Commercial Dept: (0228) 24014.

Record attendance: 27,500 v Birmingham C, FA Cup 3rd rd, 5 January 1957 and v Middlesbrough, FA Cup 5th rd, 7 February 1970.

Record receipts: £75,988.50 v Liverpool, FA Cup 3rd 7 January 1989.

Ground capacity: 13,913.

Pitch measurements: 117yd × 78yd.

President: J. C. Monkhouse. *Vice-presidents:* H. A. Jenkins, R. S. Liddell, J. R. Sheffield, T. A. Bingley, T. L. Sibson, Dr. T. Gardner.

Directors: M Knighton (Chairman), B. Chaytow (Vice-chairman), R. McKnight, A. Doweck.

Player-coach: David McCreery. *Assistant Manager:* Peter Hampton.

Coach: . *Physio:* Peter Hampton.

Commercial Manager: Jim Thoburn.

Secretary: Phillip Vine.

Year Formed: 1903. *Ltd Co.:* 1921.

Previous Grounds: 1903–5, Milholme Bank; 1905–9, Devonshire Park; 1909– Brunton Park.

Previous Name: Shaddongate United.

Club Nickname: 'Cumbrians' or 'The Blues'.

Record League Victory: 8–0 v Hartlepools U, Division 3 (N), 1 September 1928 – Prout; Smiles, Cook; Robinson (1) Ross, Pigg; Agar (1), Hutchison (1), McConnell (4), Ward (1), Watson. 8–0 v Scunthorpe United, Division 3 (N), 25 December 1952 – MacLaren; Hill, Scott; Stokoe, Twentyman, Waters; Harrison (1), Whitehouse (5), Ashman (2), Duffett, Bond.

Record Cup Victory: 6–1 v Billingham Synthonia, FA Cup, 1st rd, 17 November 1956 – Fairley; Hill, Kenny; Johnston, Waters, Thompson; Mooney, Broadis (1), Ackerman (2), Garvie (3), Bond.

Record Defeat: 1–11 v Hull C, Division 3 (N), 14 January 1939.

Most League Points (2 for a win): 62, Division 3 (N), 1950–51.

Most League Points (3 for a win): 80, Division 3, 1981–82.

Most League Goals: 113, Division 4, 1963–64.

Highest League Scorer in Season: Jimmy McConnell, 42, Division 3 (N), 1928–29.

Most League Goals in Total Aggregate: Jimmy McConnell, 126, 1928–32.

Most Capped Player: Eric Welsh, 4, Northern Ireland.

Most League Appearances: Alan Ross, 466, 1963–79.

Record Transfer Fee Received: £275,000 from Vancouver Whitecaps for Peter Beardsley, April 1981.

Record Transfer Fee Paid: £120,000 to York C for Gordon Staniforth, October 1979.

Football League Record: 1928 Elected to Division 3 (N); 1958–62 Division 4; 1962–63 Division 3; 1963–64 Division 4; 1964–65 Division 3; 1965–74 Division 2; 1974–75 Division 1; 1975–77 Division 2; 1977–82 Division 3; 1982–86 Division 2; 1986–87 Division 3; 1987–92 Division 4; 1992– Division 3.

Honours: Football League: Division 1 best season: 22nd, 1974–75; Promoted from Division 2 (3rd) 1973–74; Division 3 – Champions 1964–65; Runners-up 1981–82; Division 4 – Runners-up 1963–64. *FA Cup:* 6th rd 1974–75. *Football League Cup:* Semi-final 1969–70.

CARLISLE UNITED 1992—93 LEAGUE RECORD

Match No.	Date		Venue	Opponents	Result		H/T Score	Lg. Pos.	Goalscorers	Atten dance
1	Aug	15	H	Walsall	L	3-4	1-1	—	Oghani, McDonald (og), Watson	4199
2		29	H	Lincoln C	W	2-0	0-0	13	Oghani, Watson	4023
3	Sept	1	H	Bury	W	5-1	2-0	—	Williams, Watson, Gabbiadini, Oghani 2	4650
4		5	A	Barnet	L	0-2	0-0	9		2733
5		8	A	Cardiff C	D	2-2	0-1	—	Watson, Gabbiadini	6859
6		12	H	York C	L	1-2	0-1	9	Sendall	5355
7		19	A	Chesterfield	L	0-1	0-0	15		3362
8		26	H	Scunthorpe U	L	0-2	0-1	18		4772
9	Oct	3	H	Halifax T	D	1-1	1-1	19	Watson	3824
10		10	A	Rochdale	D	2-2	2-1	19	Watson, Barnsley	2543
11		17	H	Wrexham	L	0-2	0-0	20		3520
12		24	A	Torquay U	W	2-0	1-0	18	Arnold, Gabbiadini	1960
13		31	H	Scarborough	D	2-2	0-1	19	Arnold, Hawke	3150
14	Nov	3	A	Colchester U	L	1-2	1-1	—	Barnsley (pen)	3263
15		7	H	Gillingham	W	1-0	1-0	18	Watson	3213
16		21	A	Doncaster R	W	2-1	1-0	15	Hicks (og), Proudlock	2159
17		28	H	Northampton T	W	2-0	1-0	12	Hawke, Davey	3603
18	Dec	12	H	Crewe Alex	L	1-3	1-1	15	Oghani	3487
19	Jan	9	H	Cardiff C	L	1-2	0-1	18	Arnold (pen)	3691
20		12	A	Darlington	D	1-1	1-1	—	Oghani	1596
21		16	A	Scunthorpe U	D	0-0	0-0	18		2570
22		19	A	York C	D	2-2	0-1	—	Oghani, Proudlock	3071
23		23	H	Chesterfield	W	3-1	1-1	14	Watson, Oghani, Walsh	3103
24		26	A	Lincoln C	L	1-2	0-0	—	Oghani	2947
25	Feb	6	A	Walsall	L	1-2	0-1	17	Oghani	2817
26		13	H	Barnet	L	0-1	0-1	17		4020
27		20	A	Bury	L	0-6	0-6	18		2723
28		27	H	Rochdale	W	3-0	1-0	15	Oghani 2, Arnold	3021
29	Mar	6	A	Halifax T	W	2-0	1-0	15	Oghani, Arnold (pen)	1309
30		9	H	Shrewsbury T	W	1-0	0-0	—	Davey	4022
31		13	A	Gillingham	L	0-1	0-0	14		3307
32		20	H	Colchester U	L	0-2	0-2	16		3003
33		23	H	Northampton T	L	0-2	0-2	—		2561
34		27	H	Doncaster R	D	1-1	1-1	16	Davey	2939
35	Apr	3	A	Shrewsbury T	W	3-2	1-1	15	Oghani 2, Davey	3100
36		6	A	Crewe Alex	L	0-4	0-0	—		3246
37		10	A	Darlington	D	2-2	2-1	16	Davey, Gallimore	3297
38		12	A	Hereford U	L	0-1	0-1	15		2457
39		17	H	Hereford U	D	0-0	0-0	16		2527
40		24	A	Wrexham	L	1-3	1-2	17	Holden	5912
41	May	1	H	Torquay U	L	0-1	0-0	17		2689
42		8	A	Scarborough	D	2-2	1-0	18	Arnold, Proudlock	2948

Final League Position: 18

GOALSCORERS

League (51): Oghani 15, Watson 8, Arnold 6 (2 pens), Davey 5, Gabbiadini 3, Proudlock 3, Barnsley 2 (1 pen), Hawke 2, Gallimore 1, Holden 1, Sendall 1, Walsh 1, Williams 1, own goals 2.
Coca Cola Cup (7): Barnsley 2 (2 pens), Gabbiadini 2, Edmondson 1, Oghani 1, Watson 1.
FA Cup (1): Arnold 1.

O'Hanlon 41	Williams 19	Thorpe 28	Holmes 18 + 1	Knight 1	Barnsley 25 + 2	Gabbiadini 18 + 6	Davey 38	Oghani 37 + 2	Watson 21	Proudlock 24 + 2	Walling 21 + 2	Edmondson 33 + 1	Connelly — + 3	Sendall — + 10	Walsh 20 + 4	Holliday 2	Dalziel 11 + 1	Caig 1	Potts 6 + 2	Hawke 8	McCreery 19 + 3	Arnold 26 + 3	Holden 21	Prins 2 + 7	Finley 1	Burgess 6	White 6	Gallimore 8	Hopper 1	Delap — + 1	Match No.
1	2	3	4	5	6	7	8	9	10	11	12	14																			1
1	2	3	4		6	7	8	9	10				5	11	12																2
1	2	3	4		6	7	8	9	10				5	11	12	14															3
1	2	3	4		6	7	8	9	10				5	11	12																4
1	2	3	4		6	7	8	9	10				5	11		14	12														5
1	2		4		6	7	8	9	10				5	11		12	3														6
1	2	3	4		6	11	7	9	10				5	8	12																7
1	2	3	4		6	7	8	9	10					11		12	5	14													8
	2	3	4			7	8	9	10		6		12	14	5			1	11												9
1	2	3	4	5			9	10			6		14				11	7	8	12											10
1		3	4		6		8	9	10		2						11	7	14	12	5										11
1	2				6		7	8	10								3				9	5	11	4							12
1	2				6		8	7	10							12	3				9	5	11	4							13
1	2				6		8	7	10							12	3				9	5	11	4							14
1	2	11								10	7		8	12	6		3				9	5		4							15
1	2	11				6				10	7				8	5	3				9			4							16
1	2	11				6	12	10	7					8	5	3				9	14		4								17
1	2		8	10		6	9		7	12					5		3				11	4	14								18
1	2				6	12	10	7		11			8		3					5	9			4							19
1	2				6		7	10		4	11		8		3					5	9										20
1	2	14			6		7	10		4	11	12	8		3					5	9										21
1	2	5			6		7	10	12	4	11		8		3						9										22
1		3	5		6		7	10	11	4	2		8								9										23
1		3	5		6		7	10	11	4	2		8								9										24
1		3	10		6		7		2	4	11		8								5	9	12								25
1		3	4	12	6		7		11	5	2		8		10					14	9										26
1		3	2	12	10		7		9	6	11		8							5		4									27
1		3					8	7		10	4	6									5	9				2	11				28
1		3			12		8	7		10	4										5	9	6			2	11				29
1		3	12				8	7		10	4										5	9	6			2	11				30
1		3			6	12	8	7		10	4										5	9				2	11				31
1		3	12				8	7		10	4	6									5	9				2	11				32
1			6	12			8	7		14	4				11		3				5	9				2	10				33
1			12	11			8	7		10	4	2									5	9	6					3			34
1			4	11			8	7		10		2	14								5	9	6	12				3			35
1			4	11			8	7		10		2	5		14							9	6	12				3			36
1			4	11			8	7		10		2	5									9	6	12				3			37
1			4				8	7			2		10				11				5	9	6	12				3			38
1			4				8	7		10		2	5									9	6	11				3			39
1	11	3	4				8	7		10		2	5				14				9	6	12								40
1			4	11			8	7		10		2					12				5	9	6					3			41
1	11		4				8	7		10		2										9	6					3	5	12	42

Coca Cola Cup	First Round	Burnley (h)	4-1
		(a)	1-1
	Second Round	Norwich C (h)	2-2
		(a)	0-2
FA Cup	First Round	Wigan Ath (a)	1-3

CARLISLE UNITED

Player and Position	Ht	Wt	Birth Date	Birth Place	Source	Clubs	League App	Gls
Goalkeepers								
Anthony Caig	6 1	13 05	11 4 74	Whitehaven	Trainee	Carlisle U	1	—
Kelham O'Hanlon	6 1	13 01	16 5 62	Saltburn	Apprentice	Middlesbrough	87	—
						Rotherham U	248	—
						Carlisle U	83	—
Defenders								
Andy Barnsley*	6 0	11 11	9 6 62	Sheffield	Denaby U	Rotherham U	28	—
						Sheffield U	77	1
						Rotherham U	83	3
						Carlisle U	55	5
Ian Dalziel‡	5 8	11 10	24 10 62	South Shields	Apprentice	Derby Co	22	4
						Hereford U	150	8
						Carlisle U	91	2
Darren Edmondson	6 0	12 02	4 11 71	Coniston	Trainee	Carlisle U	92	2
John Holliday‡	6 4	11 00	13 3 70	Penrith		Carlisle U	19	—
						Mansfield T	—	—
						Carlisle U	—	—
Tony Hopper§			31 5 76	Carlisle	Trainee	Carlisle U	1	—
Ian Knight‡	6 2	12 04	26 10 66	Hartlepool	Apprentice	Barnsley	—	—
						Sheffield W	21	—
						Scunthorpe U (loan)	2	—
						Grimsby T	21	2
						Carlisle U	1	—
Craig Potts	5 10	11 00	25 2 74	Carlisle	Trainee	Carlisle U	14	—
Dean Walling	6 0	12 00	17 4 69	Leeds		Leeds U	—	—
						Rochdale	65	8
					Guiseley	Carlisle U	60	5
Midfield								
Simon Davey	5 10	11 02	1 10 70	Swansea	Trainee	Swansea C	49	4
						Carlisle U	38	5
Rory Delap§			6 7 76	Coldfield	Trainee	Carlisle U	1	—
David McCreery	5 6	10 07	16 9 57	Belfast	Apprentice	Manchester U	87	7
						QPR	57	4
					Tulsa R	Newcastle U	243	2
						Hearts	29	—
						Hartlepool U	30	—
						Carlisle U	22	—
Jason Prins§			1 11 74	Wisbech		Carlisle U	13	—
Jeff Thorpe	5 10	12 06	17 11 72	Whitehaven	Trainee	Carlisle U	69	1
Derek Walsh	5 7	11 05	24 10 67	Hamilton	Apprentice	Everton	1	—
						Hamilton A.	2	—
						Carlisle U	121	7
Neil Williams*	5 11	11 04	23 10 64	Waltham Abbey	Apprentice	Watford	—	—
						Hull C	91	10
						Preston NE	121	6
						Carlisle U	19	1
Forwards								
Ian Arnold‡	5 9	11 00	4 7 72	Durham City	Trainee	Middlesbrough	3	—
						Carlisle U	29	6
Ricardo Gabbiadini*	5 11	13 06	11 3 70	Newport	Trainee	York C	1	—
						Sunderland	1	—
						Blackpool (loan)	5	3
						Brighton (loan)	1	—
						Grimsby T (loan)	3	1
						Crewe Alex (loan)	2	—
						Hartlepool U	14	2
						Scarborough	7	1
						Carlisle U	24	3

CARLISLE UNITED

Colours: Blue shirts, white shorts, blue stockings. **Change colours:** All yellow.

Foundation: Carlisle United came into being in 1903 through the amalgamation of Shaddongate United and Carlisle Red Rose. The new club was admitted to the Second Division of the Lancashire Combination in 1905–06, winning promotion the following season.

First Football League game: 25 August, 1928, Division 3(N), v Accrington S (a) W 3-2 – Prout; Coulthard, Cook; Harrison, Ross, Pigg; Agar, Hutchison, McConnell (1), Ward (1), Watson. 1 o.g.

Did you know: Carlisle United's record for appearances is held by goalkeeper Allan Ross, whose 466 League games includes one as an outfield player. This was as substitute v Portsmouth on 28 February 1970.

Managers (and Secretary-Managers)
H. Kirkbride 1904–05*, McCumiskey 1905–06*, J. Houston 1906–08*, Bert Stansfield 1908–10, J. Houston 1910–12, D. Graham 1912–13, George Bristow 1913–30, Billy Hampson 1930–33, Bill Clarke 1933–35, Robert Kelly 1935–36, Fred Westgarth 1936–38, David Taylor 1938–40, Howard Harkness 1940–45, Bill Clark 1945–46*, Ivor Broadis 1946–49, Bill Shankly 1949–51, Fred Emery 1951–58, Andy Beattie 1958–60, Ivor Powell 1960–63, Alan Ashman 1963–67, Tim Ward 1967–68, Bob Stokoe 1968–70, Ian MacFarlane 1970–72, Alan Ashman 1972–75, Dick Young 1975–76, Bobby Moncur 1976–80, Martin Harvey 1980, Bob Stokoe 1980–85, Bryan "Pop" Robson 1985, Bob Stokoe 1985–86, Harry Gregg 1986–87, Cliff Middlemass 1987–91, Aidan McCaffery 1991–92, David McCreery October 1992–.

Player and Position	Ht	Wt	Date	Birth Place	Source	Clubs	League App	Gls
Steve Holden	6 0	11 13	4 9 72	Luton	Trainee	Leicester C	1	—
						Carlisle U	21	1
George Oghani	5 11	12 01	2 9 60	Manchester	Hyde	Bolton W	99	27
						Wrexham (loan)	7	—
						Burnley	74	21
						Stockport Co	8	2
						Hereford U	8	2
						Scarborough	50	18
					Evagoras	Carlisle U	39	15
Paul Proudlock	5 10	11 00	25 10 65	Hartlepool	Local	Hartlepool U	15	—
						Middlesbrough	5	1
						Carlisle U	155	20
						Hartlepool U (loan)	6	—
Richard Sendall‡	5 10	11 06	10 7 67	Stamford	Watford	Blackpool	11	—
						Carlisle U	84	14
						Cardiff C (loan)	4	—

Trainees
Dalton, Neil J; Delap, Rory J; Fleming, William J; Fryer, Andrew M; Grainger, Christopher; Hopper, Tony; McKecknie, Michael F; Prins, Jason; Prokas, Richard; Scott, Alan P; Wilson, Graeme J.

**Non-Contract
Wilkes, David A.

Associated Schoolboys
Armstrong, Gavin; Bird, Shane L; Doswell, Lee A; Edwards, Richard; Green, Mark; Hewitt, Steven P; Hodgson, Michael; Holt, Steven; Jansen, Matthew B; Kirk, Nigel B. J; Lawson, Wayne; Lewis, Graeme; McMahon, Ronan J; Palmer, Daniel R; Sandwith, Kevin; Taylor, Lee R; Thurstan, Matthew.

Associated Schoolboys who have accepted the club's offer of a Traineeship/Contract
Murray, Paul; Varty, John W; Wilson, Darren L.

**Non-Contract Players who are retained must be re-signed before they are eligible to play in League matches.

146

CHARLTON ATHLETIC 1992-93 *Back row (left to right):* Danny Warden, Steve Brown, Carl Leaburn, Bob Bolder, Lee Harrison, Mike Salmon, Stuart Balmer, Linvoy Primus, Alan Pardew. *Centre row:* Gary Moss (Assistant Physio), Scott Minto, Alex Dyer, Paul Bacon, The Vinh Nguyen, Steve Gatting, Paul Gorman, Kim Grant, Jermaine Darlington, Jimmy Hendry (Physio). *Front row:* Garry Nelson, Darren Pitcher, Simon Webster, Steve Gritt (Player/Manager), Alan Curbishley (Player/Manager), Keith Peacock (Reseve Team Coach), Colin Walsh, Robert Lee, John Bumstead.

Photograph: Tom Morris.

Division 1   **CHARLTON ATHLETIC**

The Valley, Floyd Road, Charlton, London SE7 8BL.
Telephone 081–859 8888. Fax 081–293 5143. Clubcall (0891)
121146.

Ground: The Valley, London SE7 8BL.

Ground capacity: 8337.

Record attendance: 75,031 v Aston Villa, FA Cup 5th rd,
12 February 1938 (at The Valley).

Record receipts: £114,618.70 v Liverpool (at Selhurst Park),
Division 1, 23 January 1988.

Pitch measurements: 112yd × 73yd.

President: R. D. Collins.

Chairman: R. N. Alwen.

Directors: S. Clarke, R. D. Collins, R. A. Murray, M. A. Simons, M. Stevens, D. G. Ufton.

General Manager: Jonathan Fuller.

Managers: Steve Gritt and Alan Curbishley.

Reserve team manager: Keith Peacock. *Youth team manager:* John Cartwright. *Youth Development officer:* Neil Banfield. *Physio:* Jimmy Hendry.

Secretary: Chris Parkes.

Marketing Manager: Steve Dixon.

Year Formed: 1905. *Turned Professional:* 1920. *Ltd Co.:* 1919.

Club Nickname: 'Haddicks', 'Robins' or 'Valiants'.

Previous Grounds: 1906, Siemen's Meadow; 1907, Woolwich Common; 1909, Pound Park; 1913, Horn Lane; 1920, The Valley; 1923, Catford (The Mount); 1924, The Valley; 1985 Selhurst Park.

Record League Victory: 8–1 v Middlesbrough, Division 1, 12 September 1953 – Bartram; Campbell, Ellis; Fenton, Ufton, Hammond; Hurst (2), O'Linn (2), Leary (1), Firmani (3), Kiernan.

Record Cup Victory: 7–0 v Burton A, FA Cup, 3rd rd, 7 January 1956 – Bartram; Campbell, Townsend; Hewie, Ufton, Hammond; Hurst (1), Gauld (1), Leary (3), White, Kiernan (2).

Record Defeat: 1–11 v Aston Villa, Division 2, 14 November 1959.

Most League Points (2 for a win): 61, Division 3 (S), 1934–35.

Most League Points (3 for a win): 77, Division 2, 1985–86.

Most League Goals: 107, Division 2, 1957–58.

Highest League Scorer in Season: Ralph Allen, 32, Division 3 (S), 1934–35.

Most League Goals in Total Aggregate: Stuart Leary, 153, 1953–62.

Most Capped Player: John Hewie, 19, Scotland.

Most League Appearances: Sam Bartram, 583, 1934–56.

Record Transfer Fee Received: £650,000 from Crystal Palace for Mike Flanagan, August 1979.

Record Transfer Fee Paid: £600,000 to Chelsea for Joe McLaughlin, August 1989.

Football League Record: 1921 Elected to Division 3 (S); 1929–33 Division 2; 1933–35 Division 3 (S); 1935–36 Division 2; 1936–57 Division 1; 1957–72 Division 2; 1972–75 Division 3; 1975–80 Division 2; 1980–81 Division 3; 1981–86 Division 2; 1986–90 Division 1; 1990–92 Division 2; 1992– Division 1.

Honours: Football League: Division 1 – Runners-up 1936–37; Division 2 – Runners-up 1935–36, 1985–86; Division 3 (S) – Champions 1928–29, 1934–35; Promoted from Division 3 (3rd) 1974–75, 1980–81. *FA Cup:* Winners 1947; Runners-up 1946. *Football League Cup:* best season: 4th rd, 1962–63, 1965–66, 1978–79. *Full Members Cup:* Runners-up 1987.

CHARLTON ATHLETIC 1992—93 LEAGUE RECORD

Match No.	Date		Venue	Opponents	Result		H/T Score	Lg. Pos.	Goalscorers	Atten dance
1	Aug	15	H	Grimsby T	W	3-1	2-0	—	Nelson, Leaburn, Dyer	4823
2		18	A	Cambridge U	W	1-0	0-0	—	Pardew	5094
3		22	A	West Ham U	W	1-0	1-0	1	Pardew	17,054
4		25	H	Bristol R	W	4-1	1-0	—	Lee, Dyer, Pardew 2 (1 pen)	4719
5		29	H	Luton T	D	0-0	0-0	1		6302
6	Sept	5	A	Sunderland	W	2-0	0-0	1	Butcher (og), Bennett (og)	17,954
7		12	H	Cambridge U	D	0-0	0-0	2		5836
8		18	A	Tranmere R	D	0-0	0-0	—		6055
9		26	H	Swindon T	W	2-0	1-0	2	Minto, Grant	6742
10	Oct	3	H	Southend U	D	1-1	0-0	2	Grant	6399
11		10	A	Bristol C	L	1-2	1-1	2	Leaburn	9282
12		18	H	Millwall	L	0-2	0-1	—		7527
13		24	A	Derby Co	L	3-4	1-3	5	Pardew 2, Robinson	15,482
14	Nov	1	H	Birmingham C	D	0-0	0-0	—		4445
15		4	H	Leicester C	W	2-0	0-0	—	Nelson 2	4107
16		7	A	Brentford	L	0-2	0-1	6		9354
17		14	A	Newcastle U	L	1-3	0-2	7	Nelson	12,945
18		22	A	Wolverhampton W	L	1-2	1-1	—	Bumstead	10,593
19		28	A	Barnsley	L	0-1	0-1	10		5851
20	Dec	5	H	Portsmouth	W	1-0	1-0	9	Walsh	8337
21		13	A	Watford	D	1-1	1-0	—	Robinson	6541
22		19	H	Oxford U	D	1-1	0-1	9	Bumstead	7287
23		26	H	West Ham U	D	1-1	0-1	11	Bumstead	8337
24		28	A	Peterborough U	D	1-1	1-1	11	Garland	8931
25	Jan	9	H	Tranmere R	D	2-2	1-1	10	Balmer, Leaburn	8337
26		16	A	Swindon T	D	2-2	2-2	8	Nelson, Dyer	8605
27		27	A	Bristol R	W	2-0	1-0	—	Pardew 2	5096
28		30	H	Notts Co	W	2-1	0-0	8	Dyer, Pardew (pen)	8337
29	Feb	6	A	Grimsby T	L	0-1	0-0	9		5403
30		13	H	Sunderland	L	0-1	0-0	10		8151
31		20	A	Luton T	L	0-1	0-0	10		8443
32		27	A	Bristol C	W	2-1	0-1	10	Gorman, Gatting	7351
33	Mar	6	A	Southend U	W	2-0	0-0	9	Webster, Leaburn	5804
34		10	A	Newcastle U	D	2-2	1-2	—	Nelson, Leaburn	29,582
35		13	H	Brentford	W	1-0	0-0	9	Pitcher	7194
36		20	A	Portsmouth	L	0-1	0-1	9		12,854
37		23	H	Wolverhampton W	L	0-1	0-0	—		7852
38		27	A	Leicester C	L	1-3	0-2	12	Dyer	17,290
39	Apr	3	H	Barnsley	D	0-0	0-0	11		6370
40		6	H	Watford	W	3-1	2-1	—	Webster, Balmer, Gatting	6462
41		10	A	Notts Co	L	0-2	0-0	11		6206
42		12	H	Peterborough U	L	0-1	0-0	12		6721
43		17	A	Oxford U	W	1-0	1-0	11	Dyer	5121
44		24	A	Millwall	L	0-1	0-1	12		10,159
45	May	1	H	Derby Co	W	2-1	0-0	11	Pitcher, Gorman	7802
46		8	A	Birmingham C	L	0-1	0-0	12		22,234

Final League Position: 12

GOALSCORERS

League (49): Pardew 9 (2 pens), Dyer 6, Nelson 6, Leaburn 5, Bumstead 3, Balmer 2, Gatting 2, Gorman 2, Grant 2, Pitcher 2, Robinson 2, Webster 2, Garland 1, Lee 1, Minto 1, Walsh 1, own goals 2.
Coca Cola Cup (0).
FA Cup (2): Nelson 1, Pitcher 1 (pen).

Bolder 27	Pitcher 40 + 1	Barness 5	Pardew 29 + 1	Webster 43	Gatting 31 + 1	Lee 7	Bacon 14 + 4	Leaburn 28 + 11	Nelson 39 + 5	Walsh 42	Dyer 23 + 7	Balmer 42 + 3	Bumstead 18 + 2	Grant 11 + 10	Minto 34 + 2	Gritt 4 + 3	Warden 1 + 2	Robinson 15	Salmon 19	Primus 4	Power 5	Garland 10 + 3	Curbishley 1	Gorman 5 + 5	Houghton 6	Linger — + 2	Sturgess 1 + 3	Newton 2	Match No.
1	2	3	4	5	6	7	*8*	9	10	11	12	14																	1
1	2	3	4	5	6	7			10	11	9			8	12														2
1	*2*	3	4	5	6	*7*			10	11	9	14		8	12														3
1	*2*	3	4	5	6	7			10	11	9	12		8															4
1		3	4	5	6	7			10	11	9	2		8	12														5
1			4	5	6	7	14		10	11	*9*	2		8		3	12												6
1	5		4		6	7		12	10	11	9	2		8		3													7
1	7		4	5	*6*		14	12	10	11	9	2		8		3													8
1	6		4	5				7	*10*	11	9	2		8	12	3	14												9
1	6		4	5				7	10	11	9	2		8	12	3	14												10
1	6		4	5				7	10		9	2		8	11	3	12												11
1	6		4	5					10	11	8	2	12	9		3		7											12
1	8		4	5	6			9	12	11		2			10	3		7											13
			4		6			9	12	11		2		8	10	3		7	1	5									14
			4	5				9	12	11		2		8	10	3		7	1		6								15
1			4	5				9	10	11	12	2		8		3		7			6								16
1	14		4	5				9	10	11	12	2		*8*		3		7			6								17
1	6		4	5				9	10	11		2	8	12		3		*7*											18
1	2		4	5				12	10	9	14	6		*8*	11	3		7											19
1	2			5				9	10	11		6		12	3	4		7				8							20
1	2	10		5				9		11		6		12	3	4		7				8							21
1	2	10		5				9		11		6	14	12	3	4		*7*				8							22
1	2			5				9	10	11		6		4		3		7				8	12						23
1	2			5					10	11		6		4		3		7				8	9						24
1	2	12		5	3			8	10	11		6		4				7				9							25
1	2	8		5	4	3		10				9		6	12			7						11					26
1	2		4	5	3			8	12	10	11	9		6				7								14			27
1	2	8		5	4	3		12	10	11	9	6		7												14			28
1	2		4	5	3			*8*	12	10	11	9	6	7									14						29
	2		4	5	3			8	12	10	11	9	6	*7*	14				1										30
	2		4	5	3	14		9	10	11		6		8	*7*				1					12					31
	2		4	5	3			9	10	11		*6*		8	14				1					12	7				32
	2		4	5	3			9	10	11		6		8					1						7				33
	2			5	3			4	9	10	11	12	6	8					1						*7*				34
	2			5	3			4	9	10	11	12	6	8					1						*7*				35
	2			5	3			4	9	10	11	12	6	8					1						*7*				36
	2			5	3			4	9	10	11	6		8					1			12			*7*				37
	2			5	3			4	9	10	11	7	6						1			8	12						38
	2			5	3		14	9	10	11	7	6		4					1			*8*	12						39
	2			5	3	7	9	12	11		6		4						1			*8*	10		14				40
	2			5	3	*7*	*9*	12	11		6		4						1			8	10		14				41
	2			5	3		12	10	11		6		4						1			8	9		7				42
	2			5	3		9	10	11	7	6		4						1			8		12					43
	2			5	3	14	9	10	11	7	6		4	*8*					1				12						44
	2			*5*	14		12	10	11	7	6		3						1			8	9		4				45
	2			5			11	12	10		7	6		3					1			8	*9*		14	4			46

Coca Cola Cup	Second Round	Bury (a)	0-0
		(h)	0-1
FA Cup	Third Round	Leeds U (a)	1-1
		(h)	1-3

CHARLTON ATHLETIC

Player and Position	Ht	Wt	Date	Birth Place	Source	Clubs	League App	Gls
Goalkeepers								
Bob Bolder	6 3	14 06	2 10 58	Dover	Dover	Sheffield W	196	—
						Liverpool	—	—
						Sunderland	22	—
						Luton T (loan)	—	—
						Charlton Ath	249	—
Lee Harrison*	6 2	12 02	12 9 71	Billericay	Trainee	Charlton Ath	—	—
						Fulham (loan)	—	—
						Gillingham (loan)	2	—
						Fulham (loan)	—	—
Mike Salmon	6 2	13 00	14 7 64	Leyland	Local	Blackburn R	1	—
						Chester C (loan)	16	—
						Stockport Co	118	—
						Bolton W	26	—
						Wrexham (loan)	17	—
						Wrexham	83	—
						Charlton Ath	26	—
Defenders								
Stuart Balmer	6 1	12 04	20 6 69	Falkirk	Celtic BC	Celtic	—	—
						Charlton Ath	87	2
Steve Brown*	6 1	12 08	13 5 72	Brighton	Trainee	Charlton Ath	1	—
Steve Gatting*	5 11	11 11	29 5 59	Park Royal	Apprentice	Arsenal	58	5
						Brighton	316	19
						Charlton Ath	64	3
Paul Linger§			20 12 74	Tower Hamlets	Trainee	Charlton Ath	2	—
Scott Minto	5 10	10 00	6 8 71	Cheshire	Trainee	Charlton Ath	138	5
Darren Pitcher	5 9	12 02	12 10 69	London	Trainee	Charlton Ath	131	7
						Galway (loan)	—	—
Linvoy Primus	5 10	12 04	14 9 73	Stratford	Trainee	Charlton Ath	4	—
Simon Webster	6 0	11 07	20 1 64	Earl Shilton	Apprentice	Tottenham H	3	—
						Exeter C (loan)	26	—
						Norwich C (loan)	—	—
						Huddersfield T	118	4
						Sheffield U	37	3
						Charlton Ath	127	7
Midfield								
Paul Bacon*	5 9	10 04	20 12 70	London	Trainee	Charlton Ath	33	—
John Bumstead*	5 7	10 05	27 11 58	Rotherhithe	Apprentice	Chelsea	339	38
						Charlton Ath	56	3
Alan Curbishley	5 11	11 10	8 11 57	Forest Gate	Apprentice	West Ham U	85	5
						Birmingham C	130	11
						Aston Villa	36	1
						Charlton Ath	63	6
						Brighton	116	13
						Charlton Ath	27	—
Jermaine Darlington*	5 6	10 06	11 4 74	London	Trainee	Charlton Ath	2	—
Alex Dyer‡	5 11	11 12	14 11 65	West Ham	Watford	Blackpool	108	19
						Hull C	60	14
						Crystal Palace	17	2
						Charlton Ath	78	13
Peter Garland	5 9	12 00	20 1 71	Croydon	Trainee	Tottenham H	1	—
						Newcastle U	2	—
						Charlton Ath	13	1
Steve Gritt	5 9	10 10	31 10 57	Bournemouth	Apprentice	Bournemouth	6	3
						Charlton Ath	347	24
						Walsall	20	1
						Charlton Ath	33	1
Shaun Newton§	5 8	10 04	20 8 75	Camberwell	Trainee	Charlton Ath	2	—

CHARLTON ATHLETIC

Colours: Red shirts, white shorts, red stockings. **Change colours:** White shirts, red shorts, white stockings.

Foundation: Although formed in 1905 by members of such clubs as East Street Mission, Blundell Mission, and Charlton Reds, Charlton Athletic did not really make their presence felt until adopting professionalism and joining the Southern League in 1920. Before that, they had played in such competitions as the Lewisham, Southern Suburban and London Leagues.

First Football League game: 27 August, 1921, Division 3(S), v Exeter C (h) W 1-0 – Hughes; Mitchell, Goodman; Dowling (1), Hampson, Dunn; Castle, Bailey, Halse, Green, Wilson.

Did you know:

Managers (and Secretary-Managers)
Bill Rayner 1920–25, Alex McFarlane 1925–27, Albert Lindon 1928, Alex McFarlane 1928–32, Jimmy Seed 1933–56, Jimmy Trotter 1956–61, Frank Hill 1961–65, Bob Stokoe 1965–67, Eddie Firmani 1967–70, Theo Foley 1970–74, Andy Nelson 1974–79, Mike Bailey 1979–81, Alan Mullery 1981–82, Ken Craggs 1982, Lennie Lawrence 1982–91, Steve Gritt/Alan Curbishley July 1991–.

Player and Position	Ht	Wt	Date	Birth Place	Source	Clubs	League App	Gls
The Vinh Nguyen*	5 08	10 10	25 10 73	Vietnam	Trainee	Charlton Ath	—	—
Alan Pardew	5 10	11 00	18 7 61	Wimbledon	Yeovil	Crystal Palace	128	8
						Charlton Ath	54	11
John Robinson	5 10	11 05	29 8 71	Bulawayo, Rhodesia	Apprentice	Brighton	62	6
						Charlton Ath	15	2
Paul Sturgess§			4 8 75	Dartford	Trainee	Charlton Ath	-4	
Colin Walsh	5 9	10 11	22 7 62	Hamilton	Apprentice	Nottingham F	139	32
						Charlton Ath	173	16
						Peterborough U (loan)	5	1
						Middlesbrough (loan)	13	1
Forwards								
Paul Gorman	5 9	12 02	18 9 68	Macclesfield		Doncaster R	16	2
					Fisher Ath	Charlton Ath	26	7
Kim Grant	5 10	10 12	25 9 72	Ghana	Trainee	Charlton Ath	37	4
Carl Leaburn	6 3	11 03	30 3 69	Lewisham	Apprentice	Charlton Ath	158	20
						Northampton T (loan)	9	—
Garry Nelson	5 10	11 04	16 1 61	Braintree	Amateur	Southend U	129	17
						Swindon T	79	7
						Plymouth Arg	74	20
						Brighton	144	46
						Notts Co (loan)	2	—
						Charlton Ath	85	12
Danny Warden*	5 8	10 10	11 4 73	London	Arsenal	Charlton Ath	3	—

Trainees
Appiah, Sam K; Bakes, Sean; Bassey, Simon J; Chadwick, Neil; Chandler, Dean A. R; Gilfillian, Nathan G. R; Gray, Andrew J; Hodgson, Paul; Jackson, James T; Lawson, John W; Linger, Paul H; Magloire, Christopher; Mills, Daniel R; Newton, Shaun O; Rufus, Richard R; Sloan, Craig S; Sturgess, Paul C.

Associated Schoolboys
Blackburn, Darren S; Burridge, Matthew A; Foster, Daniel C; Kyte, Jamie R; Larkin, Andrew K; Lomakin, Justin A; Matthews, Patrick W; Mbuya, Modisa; Melville-Brown, Luke S. W; Nicholls, Kevin J. R; Notley, Jay; Oakey, Stephen R; Ponsford, Richard; Rowlinson, Matthew A. V; Tindall, Jason; Walsh, Paul D; Watkins, Jake A.

Associated Schoolboys who have accepted the club's offer of a Traineeship/Contract
Blain, Dean R; Burt, Leslie; Frampton, Stephen G; Lee, Dean J; Morley, Darren R; Ross, Leo K; Rufus, Marvin M; Stuart, Jamie C.

CHELSEA 1992-93 *Back row (left to right):* Dave Collyer; Eddie Niedzwiecki; David Lee; Mick Harford; Paul Elliott; Dave Beasant; Ken Monkov; Tony Cascarino; Erland Johnsen; Craig Burley; Gwynn Williams; Peter Nicholas.
Centre row: Bob Ward; Damien Matthew; Darren Barnard; Zeke Rowe; Andy Myers; Ian Pearce; Kevin Hitchcock; Alan Dickens; Steve Clarke; Joe Allon; Graeme Le Saux; Don Howe.
Front row: Eddie Newton; Gareth Hall; Graham Stuart; Dennis Wise; Vinnie Jones; Ian Porterfield; Andy Townsend; Mal Donaghy; Robert Fleck; John Spencer; Frank Sinclair.
(Photograph: Action Images)

FA Premier

CHELSEA

Stamford Bridge, London SW6. Telephone 071–385 5545. Clubcall: 0898 121159. Ticket News and Promotions: 0898 121011. Ticket credit card service: 071–386 7799. Fax: 071 381 4831.

Ground capacity: 36,965 (28,000 covered).

Record attendance: 82,905 v Arsenal, Division 1, 12 Oct 1935.

Record receipts: £412,656 v Manchester U, FA Premier League, 19 December 1992.

Pitch measurements: 110yd × 72yd.

President: G. M. Thomson.

Chairman: K. W. Bates. **Vice-chairman:**

Directors: C. Hutchinson (Managing), Y. S. Todd.

Team Manager: Glenn Hoddle. **Assistant Manager:** Peter Shreeves.

Physio: Bob Ward. **Reserve Team Manager:** Eddie Niedzwiecki.

Company Secretary/Director: Yvonne Todd. **Match Secretary:** Keith Lacy. **Commercial Manager:** John Shaw.

Year Formed: 1905. **Turned Professional:** 1905. **Ltd Co.:** 1905.

Club Nickname: 'The Blues'.

Record League Victory: 9–2 v Glossop N E, Division 2, 1 September 1906 – Byrne; Walton, Miller; Key (1), McRoberts, Henderson; Moran, McDermott (1), Hilsdon (5), Copeland (1), Kirwan (1).

Record Cup Victory: 13–0 v Jeunesse Hautcharage, ECWC, 1st rd 2nd leg, 29 September 1971 – Bonetti; Boyle, Harris (1), Hollins (1p), Webb (1), Hinton, Cooke, Baldwin (3), Osgood (5), Hudson (1), Houseman (1).

Record Defeat: 1–8 v Wolverhampton W, Division 1, 26 September 1953.

Most League Points (2 for a win): 57, Division 2, 1906–07.

Most League Points (3 for a win): 99, Division 2, 1988–89.

Most League Goals: 98, Division 1, 1960–61.

Highest League Scorer in Season: Jimmy Greaves, 41, 1960–61.

Most League Goals in Total Aggregate: Bobby Tambling, 164, 1958–70.

Most Capped Player: Ray Wilkins, 24 (84), England.

Most League Appearances: Ron Harris, 655, 1962–80.

Record Transfer Fee Received: £2,200,000 from Tottenham H for Gordon Durie, July 1991.

Record Transfer Fee Paid: £2,100,000 to Norwich C for Robert Fleck, July 1992.

Football League Record: 1905 Elected to Division 2; 1907–10 Division 1; 1910–12 Division 2; 1912–24 Division 1; 1924–30 Division 2; 1930–62 Division 1; 1962–63 Division 2; 1963–75 Division 1; 1975–77 Division 2; 1977–79 Division 1; 1979–84 Division 2; 1984–88 Division 1; 1988–89 Division 2; 1989–92 Division 1; 1992– FA Premier League.

Honours: *Football League: Division 1* – Champions 1954–55; *Division 2* – Champions 1983–84, 1988–89; Runners-up 1906–7, 1911–12, 1929–30, 1962–63, 1976–77. *FA Cup:* Winners 1970; Runners-up 1914–15, 1966–67. *Football League Cup:* Winners 1964–65; Runners-up 1971–72. *Full Members' Cup:* Winners 1985–86. *Zenith Data Systems Cup:* Winners 1989–90.**European Competitions:** *European Fairs Cup:* 1958–60, 1965–66, 1968–69; *European Cup-Winners' Cup:* 1970–71 (winners), 1971–72.

CHELSEA 1992—93 LEAGUE RECORD

Match No.	Date	Venue	Opponents	Result	H/T Score	Lg. Pos.	Goalscorers	Attendance
1	Aug 15	H	Oldham Ath	D 1-1	0-0	—	Harford	20,699
2	19	A	Norwich C	L 1-2	1-0	—	Stuart	15,164
3	22	A	Sheffield W	D 3-3	0-2	16	Jones, Stuart, Newton	26,338
4	26	H	Blackburn R	D 0-0	0-0	—		19,575
5	29	H	QPR	W 1-0	0-0	14	Harford	22,910
6	Sept 2	A	Aston Villa	W 3-1	2-1	—	Fleck, Newton, Wise	19,125
7	5	A	Liverpool	L 1-2	0-1	12	Harford	34,199
8	12	H	Norwich C	L 2-3	2-0	13	Harford, Townsend	16,880
9	20	A	Manchester C	W 1-0	1-0	—	Harford	22,420
10	26	H	Nottingham F	D 0-0	0-0	9		19,760
11	Oct 3	A	Arsenal	L 1-2	0-1	11	Wise	27,780
12	17	H	Ipswich T	W 2-1	1-0	11	Hall, Harford	16,707
13	24	A	Coventry C	W 2-1	1-0	8	Harford, Stuart	15,626
14	31	H	Sheffield U	L 1-2	1-1	10	Townsend	13,763
15	Nov 7	H	Crystal Palace	W 3-1	2-0	8	Shaw (og), Stuart, Harford	17,141
16	21	A	Everton	W 1-0	1-0	7	Fleck	17,418
17	29	H	Leeds U	W 1-0	0-0	—	Townsend	24,345
18	Dec 5	A	Tottenham H	W 2-1	0-0	4	Newton 2	31,540
19	11	A	Middlesbrough	D 0-0	0-0	—		15,599
20	19	H	Manchester U	D 1-1	0-0	5	Lee	34,464
21	26	H	Southampton	D 1-1	0-1	5	Newton	18,344
22	28	A	Wimbledon	D 0-0	0-0	6		14,687
23	Jan 9	H	Manchester C	L 2-4	0-2	7	Stuart, Spencer	15,939
24	16	A	Nottingham F	L 0-3	0-1	8		23,249
25	27	A	QPR	D 1-1	0-0	—	Spencer	15,806
26	30	H	Sheffield W	L 0-2	0-1	10		16,261
27	Feb 6	A	Oldham Ath	L 1-3	0-1	10	Harford	11,772
28	10	H	Liverpool	D 0-0	0-0	—		20,981
29	13	H	Aston Villa	L 0-1	0-1	11		20,081
30	21	A	Blackburn R	L 0-2	0-1	—		14,780
31	Mar 1	H	Arsenal	W 1-0	0-0	—	Stuart	17,725
32	10	H	Everton	W 2-1	1-1	—	Stuart, Spencer	12,739
33	15	A	Crystal Palace	D 1-1	1-1	—	Stuart	12,610
34	20	H	Tottenham H	D 1-1	0-1	15	Cascarino	25,157
35	24	A	Leeds U	D 1-1	0-1	—	Donaghy	28,135
36	Apr 3	H	Middlesbrough	W 4-0	0-0	9	Donaghy, Spencer, Stuart, Barnard	13,043
37	6	A	Ipswich T	D 1-1	0-1	—	Spencer	17,444
38	10	A	Southampton	L 0-1	0-0	11		15,135
39	12	H	Wimbledon	W 4-2	1-0	7	Wise (pen), Hall, Spencer, Shipperley	13,138
40	17	A	Manchester U	L 0-3	0-2	9		40,139
41	May 1	H	Coventry C	W 2-1	1-0	8	Spencer, Cascarino	14,186
42	8	A	Sheffield U	L 2-4	0-3	10	Lee, Townsend	24,850

Final League Position: 11

GOALSCORERS

League (51): Harford 9, Stuart 9, Spencer 7, Newton 5, Townsend 4, Wise 3 (1 pen), Cascarino 2, Donaghy 2, Fleck 2, Hall 2, Lee 2, Barnard 1, Jones 1, Shipperley 1, own goal 1.
Coca Cola Cup (10): Townsend 3, Harford 2, Fleck 1 (pen), Newton 1, Sinclair 1, Stuart 1, Wise 1.
FA Cup (1): own goal 1.

Beasant 17	Clarke 18 + 2	Hall 36 + 1	Jones 7	Elliott 7	Donaghy 39 + 1	Stuart 31 + 8	Fleck 28 + 3	Harford 27 + 1	Townsend 41	Matthew 3 + 1	Newton 32 + 2	Allon 1 + 2	Spencer 13 + 10	Wise 27	Lee 23 + 2	Pearce — + 1	Barness 2	Spackman 6	Hitchcock 20	Sinclair 32	Le Saux 10 + 4	Barnard 8 + 5	Burley 1 + 2	Myers 3	Johnsen 13	Kharine 5	Peyton — + 1	Hopkin 2 + 2	Cascarino 8 + 1	Shipperley 2 + 1	Livingstone — + 1	Match No.
1	2	3	4	5	6	7	8	9	10	11	12																					1
1	2	3	4	5	6	7		9	10	11	12		*8*		14																	2
1	2	3	4	5	6	7	8	9	10			11	12																			3
1	2	3	4	5	6	7	8	9	10						11																	4
1	2	3	4	5	6	7	8	9	10						11																	5
1	2	3	4	5	6		8	9	10				7	11	12																	6
1		3	4	5	6		8	9	10				7	11	2	12																7
		2			6	12	8	9	4		7			11	5					3	10											8
		2			6	12	*8*	9	4		7		14	11	5			10	1	3												9
		2			6	12	*8*	9	4		7		14	11	5			10	1	3												10
		2			6	12	8	9	4		7			11	5			10	1	3												11
		2			6	7	8	9	4		10			11	5				1	3	12											12
		2			6	7	8	9	4		10				5				1	3	12	11										13
		2			6	7	*8*	9	4		10	14		11	5				1	3	12											14
		2			6	7	8	9	4		10			11	5				1	3	12											15
		2			6	7	8	9	4		10			11	5				1	3												16
		2			6	7	8	9	4		10			11	5				1	3												17
		2			6	7	8		4		10			11	5				1	3	9		12									18
		2			6	7	8		4		10			11	5				1	3	9											19
		2			6	7	8	12	4		10			11	5				1	3	9											20
		2			6	7	*8*		4		10	14		11	5				1	3	9		12									21
		2			6	7	8		4		10			11	5				1	3				9								22
		2			6	7	8	9	4		10			11	5				1	3	11											23
		2			6	7	12	9	4		10				14				1	3	11	8		5								24
12		2			6	7		9	4		10		8							3	11				5	1						25
12		2			6	7		9	4		10		8							3	11				5	*1*	14					26
		2			6	*7*	12	9	4		10		8		5				1	3	*11*	14										27
		2			6	12	*8*	9	4		10		14	11	5				1	3	11						7					28
		2			*6*	12	8	9	4		10		14	11	5				1	3							7					29
		2			14	12		7	9	4		10			5	6			1	3	*11*								8			30
1		2			6	7	8	*9*	4	12	10		14							3	11				5							31
1	2				6	7	*8*	9	4		10		14		3						11			5					12			32
1	2				6	7			4		10		8							3	11			5					9			33
1	2				6	*7*			4		10		8	11						3	12			5					9			34
1	2				6	7			4		10		8	11						3				5					9			35
1	2	14			6	7	12		4		*10*		8							3	11			5					9			36
1	2	10			6	7			4				8	11						3				5					9			37
1	2	10			6	*7*	9		4				8	11						3	12			5					14			38
	2	10			6	7				4			8	11						3	12		5	1	14	9					39
1	2	10			6	7			4				8	11						3	12		5					*9*	14		40
	2	10							4				8	11	3		6				7		5	1		12	9				41
	2	10			14				4				*8*	11	12		6		3		7		5	1		9					42

Coca Cola Cup	Second Round	Walsall (a)		3-0
		(h)		1-0
	Third Round	Newcastle U (h)		2-1
	Fourth Round	Everton (a)		2-2
		(h)		1-0
	Fifth Round	Crystal Palace (a)		1-3
FA Cup	Third Round	Middlesbrough (a)		1-2

CHELSEA

Player and Position	Ht	Wt	Date	Birth Place	Source	Clubs	League App	Gls
Goalkeepers								
Dave Beasant	6 4	13 00	20 3 59	Willesden	Edgware T	Wimbledon	340	—
						Newcastle U	20	—
						Chelsea	133	—
						Grimsby T (loan)	6	—
						Wolverhampton W (loan)	4	—
Ian Chatfield‡	5 10	10 10	10 11 72	Redhill	Trainee	Chelsea	—	—
Nick Colgan	6 1	12 00	19 9 73	Eire	Drogheda	Chelsea	—	—
Kevin Hitchcock	6 1	12 02	5 10 62	Custom House	Barking	Nottingham F	—	—
						Mansfield T (loan)	14	—
						Mansfield T	168	—
						Chelsea	55	—
						Northampton T (loan)	17	—
						West Ham U (loan)	—	—
Dimitri Kharine	6 2	12 04	16 8 68	Moscow	CSKA Moscow	Chelsea	5	—
Defenders								
Darren Barnard	5 9	11 00	30 11 71	Rinteln	Wokingham	Chelsea	17	1
Anthony Barness	5 10	10 12	25 3 72	London	Trainee	Charlton Ath	27	1
						Chelsea	2	—
Stephen Clarke	5 10	10 02	29 8 63	Saltcoats	Beith J	St Mirren	151	6
						Chelsea	183	6
Mal Donaghy	5 9	10 00	13 9 57	Belfast	Larne	Luton T	410	16
						Manchester U	89	—
						Luton T (loan)	5	—
						Chelsea	40	2
Paul Elliott	6 2	11 11	18 3 64	London	Apprentice	Charlton Ath	63	1
						Luton T	66	4
						Aston Villa	57	7
					Bari	Celtic	54	2
						Chelsea	42	3
Gareth Hall	5 8	10 07	20 3 69	Croydon		Chelsea	120	3
Erland Johnsen	6 0	12 10	5 4 67	Fredrikstad (Norway)	Bayern Munich	Chelsea	44	—
David Lee	6 3	13 12	26 11 69	Kingswood	Trainee	Chelsea	97	8
						Reading (loan)	5	5
						Plymouth Arg (loan)	9	1
Ian Pearce	6 1	12 04	7 5 74	Bury St Edmunds	School	Chelsea	4	—
Frank Sinclair	5 8	11 02	3 12 71	Lambeth	Trainee	Chelsea	44	1
						WBA (loan)	6	1
Midfield								
Craig Burley	6 1	11 07	24 9 71	Ayr	Trainee	Chelsea	12	—
David Hopkin	5 9	10 03	21 8 70	Greenock	Pt Glasgow R BC	Morton	18	—
						Chelsea	4	—
Damian Matthew	5 11	10 10	23 9 70	Islington, London	Trainee	Chelsea	21	—
						Luton T (loan)	5	—
Andy Myers	5 8	9 10	3 11 73	Hounslow	Trainee	Chelsea	17	1
Zeke Rowe	5 6	9 08	30 10 73	Stoke Newington	Trainee	Chelsea	—	—
Nigel Spackman	6 1	13 02	2 12 60	Romsey	Andover	Bournemouth	119	10
						Chelsea	141	12
						Liverpool	51	—
						QPR	29	1
						Rangers	100	1
						Chelsea	6	—
Andy Townsend	5 11	12 13	23 7 63	Maidstone	Weymouth	Southampton	83	5
						Norwich C	71	8
						Chelsea	110	12

CHELSEA

Colours: Royal blue shirts and shorts, white stockings. **Change colours:** White shirts with red stripe, black shorts, black stockings.

Foundation: Chelsea may never have existed but for the fact that Fulham rejected an offer to rent the Stamford Bridge ground from Mr. H. A. Mears who had owned it since 1904. Fortunately he was determined to develop it as a football stadium rather than sell it to the Great Western Railway and got together with Frederick Parker, who persuaded Mears of the financial advantages of developing a major sporting venue. Chelsea FC was formed in 1905, and when admission to the Southern League was denied, they immediately gained admission to the Second Division of the Football League.

First Football League game: 2 September, 1905, Division 2, v Stockport C (a) L 0-1 – Foulke; Mackie, McEwan; Key, Harris, Miller; Moran, J.T. Robertson, Copeland, Windridge, Kirwan.

Did you know: Chelsea won an FA Cup fourth round replay at home to Preston North End in January 1969 by 2-1, despite going a goal down in the 90th minute. They scored twice in the two minutes added on for injuries.

Managers (and Secretary-Managers)
John Tait Robertson 1905–07, David Calderhead 1907–33, A. Leslie Knighton 1933–39, Billy Birrell 1939–52, Ted Drake 1952–61, Tommy Docherty 1962–67, Dave Sexton 1967–74, Ron Suart 1974–75, Eddie McCreadie 1975–77, Ken Shellito 1977–78, Danny Blanchflower 1978–79, Geoff Hurst 1979–81, John Neal 1981–85 (Director to 1986), John Hollins 1985–88, Bobby Campbell 1988–91, Ian Porterfield 1991–93, David Webb 1993, Glenn Hoddle June 1993–.

Player and Position	Ht	Wt	Birth Date	Birth Place	Source	Clubs	League App	Gls
Forwards								
Tony Cascarino	6 2	13 12	1 9 62	St Paul's Cray	Crockenhill	Gillingham	219	78
						Millwall	105	42
						Aston Villa	46	11
						Celtic	24	4
						Chelsea	20	4
Robert Fleck	5 10	10 03	11 8 65	Glasgow	Possil YM	Partick T	2	1
						Rangers	85	29
						Norwich C	143	40
						Chelsea	31	2
Steve Livingstone	6 1	11 04	8 9 69	Middlesbrough	Trainee	Coventry C	31	5
						Blackburn R	30	10
						Chelsea	1	—
Eddie Newton	5 11	11 02	13 12 71	Hammersmith	Trainee	Chelsea	35	6
						Cardiff C (loan)	18	4
Neil Shipperley			30 10 74	Chatham	Trainee	Chelsea	3	1
John Spencer	5 6	10 00	11 9 70	Glasgow	Rangers Am BC	Rangers	—	—
						Morton (loan)	4	1
					Lisburg, HK	Rangers	13	2
						Chelsea	23	7
Graham Stuart	5 8	11 06	24 10 70	Tooting, London	Trainee	Chelsea	87	14
Dennis Wise	5 6	9 05	15 12 66	Kensington	Southampton	Wimbledon	135	27
						Chelsea	98	23

Trainees
Bowder, Stanley R; Brown, Kevin; Christie, Terry W; Cumberbatch, Allan R; Duberry, Michael W; Izzet, Mustafa K; Martin, Steven M; McLennan, Jason D; Metcalfe, Christian W; Norman, Craig T; Sakala, Landilani; Skiverton, Terence J; Yates, Paul S.

Associated Schoolboys
Alfred, Ricky E; Allen, Kristian; Barr, Steven; Carlin, Philip L; Dennis, Daniel G; Dignam, Michael; Garrity, Greig S; Hall, Rudi C; Harrison, Gavin A; Healy, Stephen C; Hopkins, Nicholas S; Hughes, John P; Lazic, Vladimir; Limbert, Peter A; Mills, Ray; Morris, Jody; Pritchard, Justin; Ray, Damien L; Rouse, Mark; Schneider, Paul; Sharpe, Robert L; Thomas, Rhodri O; Ullah, Ainsley C; Wellington, Lee A; Williams, Gary L; Williams, Leon P; Wright, Robert A.

Associated Schoolboys who have accepted the club's offer of a Traineeship/Contract
Baker, Joseph P. J; Carroll, Lee G; Ellis, Clinton; Hall, David G; Hughes, Andrew J; McCann, Christian; Mendes, Hillyard A; Nicholls, Mark.

158

CHESTER CITY 1992-93 *Back row (left to right):* Tony Allan (Secretary), Eddie Bishop, Craig Goodwin, David Pugh, Paul Comstive, Billy Stewart, Alan Tyrrell, Graham Abel, Chris Lightfoot, Spencer Whelan, Barry Butler, Joe Hinnigan (Physio).

Centre row: Roger Preece, John Kelly, Graham Barrow (Manager), Harry McNally, Mr R. Crofts (Chairman), Stuart Rimmer, Neil Morton, Darren Ryan.

Front row: Andy Allan, Darren Barthrop, Mark Limbert, Scott Miller.

Division 3 — **CHESTER CITY**

The Deva Stadium, Bumpers Lane, Chester. Telephone Chester (0244) 371376, 371809. Cityline (Ticket and Travel Information) (0244) 373829.

Ground capacity: 6000.

Record attendance: 20,500 v Chelsea, FA Cup 3rd rd (replay), 16 January, 1952 (at Sealand Road).

Record receipts: £30,609 v Sheffield W, FA Cup 4th rd, 31 January 1987.

Pitch measurements: 115yd × 78yd.

Club Patron: Duke of Westminster.

President: Reg Rowlands.

Chairman: R. H. Crofts.

Directors:

Manager: Graham Barrow.

Secretary: R. A. Allan. *Physio:* Joe Hinnigan. *Commercial Manager:* Miss A. Walker

Year Formed: 1884. *Turned Professional:* 1902. *Ltd Co.:* 1909.

Previous Name: Chester until 1983.

Club Nickname: 'Blues'.

Previous Grounds: Faulkner Street; Old Showground; 1904, Whipcord Lane; 1906, Sealand Road; 1990, Moss Rose Ground, Macclesfield; 1992, The Stadium, Bumpers Lane.

Record League Victory: 12–0 v York C, Division 3 (N), 1 February 1936 – Middleton; Common, Hall; Wharton, Wilson, Howarth; Horsman (2), Hughes, Wrightson (4), Cresswell (2), Sargeant (4).

Record Cup Victory: 6–1 v Darlington, FA Cup, 1st rd, 25 November 1933 – Burke; Bennett, Little; Pitcairn, Skitt, Duckworth; Armes (3), Whittam, Mantle (2), Cresswell (1), McLachlan.

Record Defeat: 2–11 v Oldham Ath, Division 3 (N), 19 January 1952.

Most League Points (2 for a win): 56, Division 3 (N), 1946–47 and Division 4, 1964–65.

Most League Points (3 for a win): 84, Division 4, 1985–86.

Most League Goals: 119, Division 4, 1964–65.

Highest League Scorer in Season: Dick Yates, 36, Division 3 (N), 1946–47.

Most League Goals in Total Aggregate: Stuart Rimmer, 100, 1985–88, 1991–93.

Most Capped Player: Bill Lewis, 7 (30), Wales.

Most League Appearances: Ray Gill, 408, 1951–62.

Record Transfer Fee Received: £300,000 from Liverpool for Ian Rush, May 1980.

Record Transfer Fee Paid: £94,000 to Barnsley for Stuart Rimmer, August 1991.

Football League Record: 1931 Elected Division 3 (N); 1958–75 Division 4; 1975–82 Division 3; 1982–86 Division 4; 1986–92 Division 3; 1992–93 Division 2; 1993– Division 3.

Honours: Football League: Division 3 best season: 5th, 1977–78; Division 3 (N) – Runners-up 1935–36; Division 4 – Runners-up 1985–86. *FA Cup:* best season: 5th rd, 1976–77, 1979–80. *Football League Cup:* Semi-final 1974–75. *Welsh Cup:* Winners 1908, 1933, 1947. *Debenhams Cup:* Winners 1977.

CHESTER CITY 1992—93 LEAGUE RECORD

Match No.	Date		Venue	Opponents	Result	H/T Score	Lg. Pos.	Goalscorers	Atten dance
1	Aug	15	A	Bradford C	L 1-3	1-0	—	Bishop	5780
2		22	A	Hull C	D 1-1	0-0	19	Rimmer	4906
3		29	A	Preston NE	L 3-4	2-1	20	Bishop, Rimmer, Morton	4471
4	Sept	1	A	Hartlepool U	L 0-2	0-1	—		3061
5		5	H	Burnley	W 3-0	2-0	16	Morton, Lightfoot, Comstive	4981
6		12	A	Leyton Orient	L 3-4	1-1	18	Barrow, Rimmer, Ryan	4158
7		15	H	Mansfield T	L 1-2	1-1	—	Rimmer	3326
8		19	H	Stockport Co	L 0-3	0-0	23		3627
9		26	A	Port Vale	L 0-2	0-0	23		6392
10	Oct	3	H	Stoke C	D 1-1	0-0	23	Bishop	5237
11		10	A	Plymouth Arg	L 0-2	0-1	23		7182
12		17	A	Bolton W	D 2-2	2-0	24	Ryan, Comstive (pen)	3394
13		24	A	Fulham	L 0-1	0-0	24		3753
14		31	H	Brighton & HA	W 2-1	2-0	22	Rimmer, Morton	2735
15	Nov	3	A	Rotherham U	D 3-3	2-2	—	Rimmer, Pugh 2	4188
16		7	H	Swansea C	W 3-2	2-1	21	Lightfoot, Pugh 2	2861
17		21	A	Exeter C	L 0-2	0-0	22		2452
18		28	H	Wigan Ath	L 1-2	1-0	22	Rimmer (pen)	2395
19	Dec	12	H	Reading	L 0-3	0-1	22		2011
20		19	A	Huddersfield T	W 2-0	1-0	21	Rimmer, Kelly	4626
21		26	A	WBA	L 0-2	0-1	21		15,209
22		28	H	Blackpool	L 1-2	1-2	22	Barrow	3787
23	Jan	2	H	Leyton Orient	L 1-3	1-0	22	Bishop	2510
24		9	A	Mansfield T	L 0-2	0-0	23		2659
25		16	H	Port Vale	L 1-2	1-0	23	Pugh	4367
26		22	A	Stockport Co	L 0-2	0-2	—		4427
27		26	H	Preston NE	L 2-4	1-1	—	Rimmer 2 (1 pen)	2901
28		30	H	Hull C	W 3-0	3-0	23	Rimmer 2, Bishop	3232
29	Feb	6	A	Bradford C	L 2-5	1-3	23	Rimmer, Bishop	2594
30		13	A	Burnley	L 0-5	0-4	23		9434
31		20	H	Hartlepool U	W 1-0	1-0	23	Rimmer (pen)	1912
32		27	H	Plymouth Arg	L 1-2	0-0	23	Rimmer	2163
33	Mar	6	A	Stoke C	L 0-4	0-2	24		14,534
34		9	H	Bournemouth	W 1-0	1-0	—	Abel	1614
35		13	A	Swansea C	L 2-4	1-2	24	Rimmer 2	4056
36		19	H	Rotherham U	L 1-2	0-0	—	Thompson	2265
37		23	A	Wigan Ath	W 2-1	2-0	—	Comstive, Rimmer	1861
38		27	H	Exeter C	L 0-3	0-1	24		2047
39	Apr	3	A	Bournemouth	D 0-0	0-0	24		2829
40		7	A	Reading	L 0-1	0-0	—		3754
41		10	H	WBA	L 1-3	0-1	24	Morton	4812
42		13	A	Blackpool	L 0-2	0-2	—		5078
43		17	H	Huddersfield T	L 0-2	0-0	24		3019
44		24	A	Bolton W	L 0-5	0-0	24		8514
45	May	1	H	Fulham	L 2-3	0-1	24	Rimmer, Thompson	2016
46		8	A	Brighton & HA	L 2-3	2-2	24	Thompson, Rimmer	6247

Final League Position: 24

GOALSCORERS

League (49): Rimmer 20 (3 pens), Bishop 6, Pugh 5, Morton 4, Comstive 3 (1 pen), Thompson 3, Barrow 2, Lightfoot 2, Ryan 2, Abel 1, Kelly 1.
Coca Cola Cup (2): Bishop 1, Comstive 1.
FA Cup (1): Ryan 1.

Stewart 42	Preece 23	Comstive 27 + 2	Butler 30 + 1	Abel 28 + 5	Lightfoot 39	Kelly 24 + 7	Thompson 30 + 9	Rimmer 43	Bishop 25 + 4	Pugh 35	Ryan 5 + 12	Albiston 23 + 1	Morton 20 + 7	Keeley 4	Whelan 24 + 4	Goodwin 3 + 2	Barrow 32 + 1	Limbert 12 + 2	Garnett 9	Came 17	Wheeler 11 + 3	Match No.
1	2	3	4	5	6	7	8	9	10	11	12											1
1	2	3	4	5	6		8	9	10		11		12		7							2
	2	3			6	4	8	9	10	11		7	1	5								3
	2	3		4	11	7	9				12		10	1	5	6	8	14				4
	2	3		5	6	11	7	9					10	1	4		8					5
1		3		5	6	11	7	9			12		10	2	4		8					6
1		3		5	6	11	7	9	4				10	2			8					7
1		3		5		11	7	9	4	6	12		10	2			8					8
1	2	3		5	6	11	7		10		12	9	4				8	14				9
1	2		4	5		11	7	9	10		12				14	3	8		6			10
1	2		4	5		11	7	9	10							3	8		6			11
1	2	7	4	14		11			10	3	9	12			5		8		6			12
1	2	3	4		6	10	7	9		11	8		12		14		5					13
1	2	3	4		6	10	7	9		11	12				8	14	5					14
1	2	3			6		7	9		11	12				8	4	14	10	5			15
1	2	3			6	4	7	9		11	8				12	10	5					16
	2		4	8	6		7	9		11	12	3	1		10		5					17
1	2	8	6	4	7	9				11	12	3	10				5					18
1	2	10	8	6	4	7	12			11		3	9		14		5					19
1		8	12	6	4		9	10	11			3			2	7	5					20
1	2	8	14	6	4		9	10	11	12		3				7	5					21
1	2	8	14	6	4	12	9	10	11			3				7	5					22
1	2	14	8	6	4	12	9	10	11			3				7	5					23
1	3	8	6	4	7		9	10	11	12	14				2		5					24
1	3	4	6		7		9	10	11						2	8	5					25
1	3	4	14		6	12	7	9	10	11					2	8	5					26
1		3		5	6	12	7	9	10	11			14		2	4					8	27
1		3		5	6	12	7	9	10	11					2	4					8	28
1		3		5	6	12	7	9	10	11			14		2	4					8	29
1	2	3		5	6	12	7	9	10	11						4					8	30
1	2	10		5	6	7	12	9		11		3				4					8	31
1	2	12	4	5	6	7	9	10	11			3			14						8	32
1		4	10	5	6	7	12	9		11		3			2						8	33
1		8		5	6	7	9			11		3	10		12		2			4		34
1		10		5	6	7	9			11		3	8				2			4	12	35
1		8		5	6	12	9			11		3	10		7		2			4	14	36
1		6	8	5		12	9			11		3	10		7		2			4		37
1		6	8	5	14	12	9			11		3	10		7		2			4		38
1		8		5	6		9			11		3	10		7		2			4		39
1		8		5	6		9		14	11	12	3	10		7		2			4		40
1		8		5	6		9			11	12	3	10		7		2			4	14	41
1			4		6		9	10	11			3			5		2	7			8	42
1		7	4		6	12	9	10	11			3			5		2				8	43
1		14	4		6	12	9	10	11			3			5		2	7			8	44
1	2		4		6		9			11	12	3			14		5	7	10		8	45
1		8	4		6	7	9	10	11			3			2					5		46

Coca Cola Cup	First Round	Stockport Co (a)	1-1
		(h)	1-2
FA Cup	First Round	Altrincham (h)	1-1
		(a)	0-2

CHESTER CITY

Player and Position	Ht	Wt	Date	Birth Place	Source	Clubs	League App	Gls
Goalkeepers								
Billy Stewart	5 11	11 07	1 1 65	Liverpool	Apprentice	Liverpool	—	—
						Wigan Ath	14	—
						Chester C	265	—
Defenders								
Graham Abel*	6 2	13 00	17 9 60	Runcorn	Runcorn	Chester C	296	29
Arthur Albiston*	5 7	11 03	14 7 57	Edinburgh	Apprentice	Manchester U	379	6
						WBA	43	2
						Dundee	10	—
						Chesterfield	3	1
						Chester C	68	—
Barry Butler*	6 2	13 0	4 6 62	Farnworth	Atherton T	Chester C	268	15
Mark Came	6 0	12 13	14 9 61	Exeter	Winsford U	Bolton W	195	7
						Chester C	17	—
Craig Goodwin*			12 2 74	Wrexham	Aston Villa	Chester C	5	—
Joe Hinnigan	6 0	12 00	3 21 55	Liverpool	S Liverpool	Wigan Ath	66	10
						Sunderland	63	4
						Preston NE	52	8
						Gillingham	103	7
						Wrexham	29	1
						Chester C	54	2
Mark Limbert*			3 10 73	Hawarden	Trainee	Chester C	14	—
Spencer Whelan	6 1	11 13	17 9 71	Liverpool	Liverpool	Chester C	71	—
Midfield								
Graham Barrow	6 2	13 07	13 6 54	Chorley	Altrincham	Wigan Ath	179	36
						Chester C	235	17
Eddie Bishop	5 8	11 07	28 11 62	Liverpool	Runcorn	Tranmere R	76	19
						Chester C	69	17
						Crewe Alex (loan)	3	—
Paul Comstive*	6 1	12 07	25 11 61	Southport	Amateur	Blackburn R	6	—
						Rochdale (loan)	9	2
						Wigan Ath	35	2
						Wrexham	99	8
						Burnley	82	17
						Bolton W	49	3
						Chester C	57	6
Chris Lightfoot	6 1	12 00	1 4 70	Wimwick	Trainee	Chester C	212	18
Roger Preece	5 9	10 12	9 6 69	Much Wenlock	Coventry C	Wrexham	110	12
						Chester C	87	—
David Pugh	5 10	11 02	19 9 64	Liverpool	Runcorn	Chester C	142	11
Forwards								
John Kelly*	5 10	10 09	20 10 60	Bebbington	Cammell Laird	Tranmere R	64	9
						Preston NE	130	27
						Chester C	85	17
						Swindon T	7	1
						Oldham Ath	52	6
						Walsall	39	1
						Huddersfield T (loan)	10	—
						Huddersfield T	18	—
						Chester C	31	1
Neil Morton*	5 9	10 07	21 12 68	Congleton	Trainee	Crewe Alex	31	1
						Northwich Vic	Chester C	95	13

CHESTER CITY

Colours: Royal blue shirts, white shorts, blue stockings, white trim. **Change colours:** Gold shirts, black shorts, black stockings.

Foundation: All students of soccer history have read about the medieval games of football in Chester, but the present club was not formed until 1884 through the amalgamation of King's School Old Boys with Chester Rovers. For many years Chester were overshadowed in Cheshire by Northwich Victoria and Crewe Alexandra who had both won the Senior Cup several times before Chester's first success in 1894–95.

First Football League game: 2 September, 1931, Division 3(N), v Wrexham (a) D 1-1 – Johnson; Herod, Jones; Keeley, Skitt, Reilly; Thompson, Ranson, Jennings (1), Cresswell, Hedley.

Did you know: In 1974–75 Chester were promoted from Division 4 by having .03 of a better goal average than Lincoln City. They were the last of the then Football League clubs to achieve promotion.

Managers (and Secretary-Managers)
Charlie Hewitt 1930–36, Alex Raisbeck 1936–38, Frank Brown 1938–53, Louis Page 1953–56, John Harris 1956–59, Stan Pearson 1959–61, Bill Lambton 1962–63, Peter Hauser 1963–68, Ken Roberts 1968–76, Alan Oakes 1976–82, Cliff Sear 1982, John Sainty 1982–83, John McGrath 1984, Harry McNally 1985–92, Graham Barrow October 1992–.

Player and Position	Ht	Wt	Birth Date	Birth Place	Source	Clubs	League App	Gls
Stuart Rimmer	5 8	11 00	12 10 64	Southport	Apprentice	Everton	3	—
						Chester C	114	67
						Watford	10	1
						Notts Co	4	2
						Walsall	88	31
						Barnsley	15	1
						Chester C	87	33
David Thompson*	5 11	12 10	27 5 62	Manchester	Local	Rochdale	155	13
						Manchester U (loan)	—	—
						Notts Co	55	8
						Wigan Ath	108	14
						Preston NE	46	4
						Chester C	39	3
Paul Wheeler	5 9	11 00	3 1 65	Caerphilly	Apprentice Aberaman	Bristol R	—	—
						Cardiff C	101	10
						Hull C	5	—
						Hereford U	54	12
						Stockport Co	23	5
						Scarborough (loan)	7	1
						Chester C	14	—

Trainees
Allen, Andrew; Barthorpe, Darren J; Millar, Scott G; O'Hara, Paul J; Robinson, Neal B.

Associated Schoolboys
Holden, Richard G; Kopanski, Alan; Lewis, Ian P; Moss, Steven J; Pemberton, Michael A; Quinn, Phillip; Roberts, Daniel L; Sweeney, Roy J; Turner, David J.

CHESTERFIELD 1992–93 *Back row (left to right):* Mark Preston, Steve Williams, Tony Brien, Stuart Cash, Steve Norris.
Centre row: Lee Turnbull, Dave Lancaster, Mick Leonard, Andy Morris, Mark Goldring, Paul McGugan, Sean Dyche.
Front row: Cliff Carr, Lee Rogers, Trevor Hebberd, Steve Hetzke (Coach), Chris McMenemy (Manager), Dave Rushbury (Physio), Scott Whitehead, Paul Lemon, Mick Kennedy.

Division 3 **CHESTERFIELD**

Recreation Ground, Chesterfield S40 4SX. Telephone Chesterfield (0246) 209765. Fax 0246 556799. Commercial Dept: (0246) 231535.

Ground capacity: 11,279.

Record attendance: 30,968 v Newcastle U, Division 2, 7 April 1939.

Record receipts: £32,410 v Sheffield U, Division 3, 25 March 1989.

Pitch measurements: 113yd × 73yd.

President: His Grace the Duke of Devonshire MC, DL, JP.

Vice-president: P. C. J. T. Kirkman.

Chairman: J. N. Lea. *Vice-chairman:* B. W. Hubbard.

Associate Directors: J. A. Plant, R. F. Pepper.

Manager: John Duncan.

Physio: Dave Rushbury. *Assistant Manager:* Kevin Randall. *Coach* Kevin Randall.

Secretary: Miss N. J. Hodgson. *Commercial Manager:* Jim Brown.

Year Formed: 1866. *Turned Professional:* 1891. *Ltd Co:* 1871.

Previous Names: Chesterfield Town.

Club Nickname: 'Blues' or 'Spireites'.

Record League Victory: 10–0 v Glossop, Division 2, 17 January 1903 – Clutterbuck; Thorpe, Lerper; Haig, Banner, Thacker; Tomlinson (2), Newton (1), Milward (3), Munday (2), Steel (2).

Record Cup Victory: 5–0 v Wath Ath (away), FA Cup, 1st rd, 28 November 1925 – Birch; Saxby, Dennis; Wass, Abbott, Thompson; Fisher (1), Roseboom (1), Cookson (2), Whitfield (1), Hopkinson.

Record Defeat: 0–10 v Gillingham, Division 3, 5 September 1987.

Most League Points (2 for a win): 64, Division 4, 1969–70.

Most League Points (3 for a win): 91, Division 4, 1984–85.

Most League Goals: 102, Division 3 (N), 1930–31.

Highest League Scorer in Season: Jimmy Cookson, 44, Division 3 (N), 1925–26.

Most League Goals in Total Aggregate: Ernie Moss, 161, 1969–76, 1979–81 and 1984–86.

Most Capped Player: Walter McMillen, 4 (7), Northern Ireland.

Most League Appearances: Dave Blakey, 613, 1948–67.

Record Transfer Fee Received: £200,000 from Wolverhampton W for Alan Birch, August 1981.

Record Transfer Fee Paid: £150,000 to Carlisle U for Phil Bonnyman, March 1980.

Football League Record: 1899 Elected to Division 2; 1909 failed re-election; 1921–31 Division 3 (N); 1931–33 Division 2; 1933–36 Division 3 (N); 1936–51 Division 2; 1951–58 Division 3 (N); 1958–61 Division 3; 1961–70 Division 4; 1970–83 Division 3; 1983–85 Division 4; 1985–89 Division 3; 1989–92 Division 4; 1992– Division 3.

Honours: Football League: Division 2 best season: 4th, 1946–47; Division 3 (N) – Champions 1930–31, 1935–36; Runners-up 1933–34; Division 4 – Champions 1969–70, 1984–85. *FA Cup:* best season: 5th rd, 1932–33, 1937–38, 1949–50. *Football League Cup:* best season: 4th rd, 1964–65. *Anglo-Scottish Cup:* Winners 1980–81.

CHESTERFIELD 1992—93 LEAGUE RECORD

Match No.	Date	Venue	Opponents	Result	H/T Score	Lg. Pos.	Goalscorers	Attendance
1	Aug 15	H	Barnet	L	1-2	0-1	—	Huxford (og)	3140
2	29	H	Bury	W	2-1	1-0	16	Lancaster, Norris	2847
3	Sept 1	H	Darlington	W	2-0	1-0	—	Norris 2	2673
4	12	A	Gillingham	D	0-0	0-0	14		2853
5	15	H	Crewe Alex	W	2-1	1-0	—	Norris, McGugan	5452
6	19	H	Carlisle U	W	1-0	0-0	6	Norris	3362
7	26	A	Colchester U	L	0-3	0-1	8		3436
8	Oct 3	H	Scunthorpe U	L	1-2	1-1	9	Lancaster	3552
9	10	A	Torquay U	D	2-2	1-0	8	Morris, Turnbull (pen)	2354
10	13	A	Northampton T	W	1-0	1-0	—	Norris	1922
11	17	H	Shrewsbury T	L	2-4	2-1	7	Norris 2	3207
12	24	A	Scarborough	D	2-2	1-0	9	McGugan, Turnbull	1797
13	31	H	Rochdale	L	2-3	0-1	12	Turnbull, Carr	3094
14	Nov 3	H	Cardiff C	W	2-1	2-0	—	Kennedy, Turnbull	2590
15	7	A	Hereford U	W	3-1	1-1	7	Turnbull (pen), Lemon 2	1774
16	28	A	Halifax T	D	1-1	0-0	9	Lancaster	1432
17	Dec 12	A	York C	D	0-0	0-0	9		3382
18	19	H	Doncaster R	D	0-0	0-0	11		3319
19	28	A	Wrexham	L	4-5	1-2	11	Williams 2, Hebberd, Lancaster	5339
20	Jan 9	H	Crewe Alex	W	2-0	1-0	11	Lemon 2	2671
21	16	H	Colchester U	W	4-0	0-0	8	Williams 2, Lemon, Lancaster	3016
22	23	A	Carlisle U	L	1-3	1-1	11	Morris	3103
23	26	A	Bury	L	0-3	0-0	—		1953
24	30	A	Northampton T	L	1-3	0-1	12	Norris	3031
25	Feb 6	A	Barnet	L	1-2	0-0	13	Lancaster	3401
26	16	H	Gillingham	D	1-1	1-0	—	Williams	2721
27	20	A	Darlington	D	1-1	0-1	13	Morris	1366
28	27	H	Torquay U	W	1-0	0-0	13	Morris	2657
29	Mar 2	H	Lincoln C	W	2-1	1-0	—	Norris, Morris	2842
30	6	A	Scunthorpe U	W	1-0	1-0	11	Lancaster	2725
31	9	A	Walsall	L	2-3	1-1	—	Lancaster, Turnbull (pen)	2884
32	13	H	Hereford U	W	1-0	1-0	11	Morris	2834
33	20	H	Cardiff C	L	1-2	0-1	11	Lancaster	6756
34	23	A	Halifax T	W	2-1	1-1	—	Morris, Turnbull	2382
35	Apr 3	H	Walsall	W	2-1	1-1	10	Norris, Smith	3278
36	6	H	York C	D	1-1	1-0	—	Morris	3850
37	10	A	Lincoln C	D	1-1	0-1	10	Rogers	4271
38	12	H	Wrexham	L	2-3	1-1	10	Brien, Turnbull	5385
39	17	A	Doncaster R	L	1-2	1-1	10	Lemon	2441
40	24	A	Shrewsbury T	D	2-2	1-1	11	Morris 2	3473
41	May 1	H	Scarborough	L	0-3	0-1	11		2271
42	8	A	Rochdale	L	1-2	0-0	12	Dyche	1544

Final League Position: 12

GOALSCORERS

League (59): Norris 11, Morris 10, Lancaster 9, Turnbull 8 (3 pens), Lemon 6, Williams 5, McGugan 2, Brien 1, Carr 1, Dyche 1, Hebberd 1, Kennedy 1, Rogers 1, Smith 1, own goal 1.
Coca Cola Cup (7): Norris 3, Lancaster 2, Hebberd 1, Morris 1.
FA Cup (2): Turnbull 1, Williams 1 (pen).

Leonard 17	Lemon 28 + 3	Carr 42	Turnbull 27 + 6	Brien 39	McGugan 13	Cash 23	Norris 28 + 2	Morris 31 + 9	Lancaster 39 + 1	Hebberd 31 + 1	Williams 24 + 7	Kennedy 19 + 8	Rogers 29 + 6	Dyche 18 + 2	Fee 10	Whitehead 1 + 3	Marples 25	Clarke 7	Falana 4 + 1	Smith 6	Davidson — + 1	Kopel 1	Match No.
1	2	3	4	5	6	7	8	9	10	11	12												1
1	2	3		5	6	7	8	9	10	11	4												2
1	2	3		5	6	7	8	9	10	11	4												3
1	2	3		5	6	7	8	9	10	11	4	12											4
1	2	3		5	6	7	8	9	10	11	4	12	14										5
1	2	3		5	6	7	8	9	10	11	4		12										6
1	2	3	14	5		7	8	9	10	11	4	12	6										7
1	2	3		5		7	8	9	10	11	4	12	6										8
1	2	3	12	5	6	7	8	9	10		4		11										9
1	2	3	9	5	6	7	8	12	10		4		11	14									10
1	2	3	9	5	6	7	8	12	10		4		11	14									11
1	2	3	12	5	6	7	8	10	9	11	4												12
1	2	3	10	5	6	7	8		9	11	12		4										13
1	2	3	10	5	6	7		8	9	11	4												14
1	2	3	10	5	6	7		8	9	11	4	12											15
1	2	3	10	5			12	9	7	8	11	6	4										16
1	2	3	10	5		7	12	9		8	11	14	6	4									17
	2	3	10			7		12	9	4	8	11	5		6	14	1						18
	2	3	10			7		12	9	4	8	11	5	14	6		1						19
	2	3				7		12	9	4	8	11	5	10	6		1						20
	2	3	12	6		7		9		4	8	11	5	10			1						21
	2	3	12	6		7	14	8	9	4		11	5	10			1						22
	2	3		5		7	8	9	12	4		11	10		6		1						23
		3	10	5		7	8	12	9	4		11	2		6		1						24
	10	3	14	5			8	12	9	4		11	6	2	7		1						25
	10	3		5			8	11	9	4		12	6	2	7		1						26
		3	10	5		7	8	9	11	12			6	2	4		1						27
		3	10	5		7	8	9	11	6				2			1	4					28
		3	10	5		7	8	9	11	6				2		12	1	4					29
		3	10	5		7	8	9	11	6				12	2		1	4					30
		3	10	5		7	8	9	11	6				12	2		1	4					31
		3	10	5		7		9	11	6	12			2		14	1	4	8				32
	12	3	10	5		7		9	11	6	8			2		14	1	4					33
		3	10	5		7		9	11	6				2	8		1	4					34
		3	10	5		7	8	9	11	12				2	6		1		4				35
		3	10	5		7	8	9	11	12				2	6		1		4				36
		3	10	5		7	8	9	11	12				2	6		1		4				37
	12	3	10	5		7	8	9	11					2	6		1		14	4			38
	11	3	10	5		7	8							2	6		1		9	4	12		39
	11	3	10	5		7		9						2	6		1		8	4			40
	11	3	10	5		7	4	9	14	12				2	6		1			8			41
	12	3	10	5		7	14	9	11	4				2	6		1					8	42

Coca Cola Cup	First Round	York C (h)	2-0
		(a)	0-0
	Second Round	Liverpool (a)	4-4
		(h)	1-4
FA Cup	First Round	Macclesfield (a)	0-0
		(h)	2-2

CHESTERFIELD

Player and Position	Ht	Wt	Date	Birth Place	Source	Clubs	League App	Gls
Goalkeepers								
Mark Goldring*	6 2	13 00	17 9 72	Brighton	Trainee	Chesterfield	7	—
Mick Leonard	5 11	11 00	9 5 59	Carshalton	Epson & Ewell	Halifax T	69	—
						Notts Co	204	—
						Chesterfield	144	—
						Halifax T (loan)	3	—
Chris Marples	6 0	13 03	3 8 64	Chesterfield	Goole	Chesterfield	84	—
						Stockport Co	57	—
						York C	138	—
						Scunthorpe U (loan)	1	—
						Chesterfield	25	—
Defenders								
Tony Brien	5 11	11 09	10 2 69	Dublin	Apprentice	Leicester C	16	1
						Chesterfield	195	8
Stuart Cash	5 10	11 11	5 9 65	Tipton	Halesowen	Nottingham F	—	—
						Rotherham U (loan)	8	1
						Brentford (loan)	11	—
						Shrewsbury T (loan)	8	1
						Chesterfield	23	—
Paul McGugan	6 2	12 00	17 7 64	Glasgow	Eastercraigs	Celtic	49	2
						Barnsley	49	2
						Chesterfield	72	6
Lee Rogers	5 11	12 01	21 10 66	Doncaster	Doncaster R	Chesterfield	222	1
Midfield								
Cliff Carr	5 8	10 12	19 6 64	London	Apprentice	Fulham	145	14
						Stoke C	124	1
						Shrewsbury T	1	1
						Mansfield T	20	—
						Chesterfield	42	1
Sean Dyche	6 0	11 07	28 6 71	Kettering	Trainee	Nottingham F	—	—
						Chesterfield	112	8
Trevor Hebberd	6 0	11 04	19 6 58	Winchester	Apprentice	Southampton	97	7
						Bolton W (loan)	6	—
						Leicester C (loan)	4	1
						Oxford U	260	37
						Derby Co	81	10
						Portsmouth	4	—
						Chesterfield	56	1
Mick Kennedy	5 9	12 00	9 4 61	Salford	Apprentice	Halifax T	76	4
						Huddersfield T	81	9
						Middlesbrough	68	5
						Portsmouth	129	4
						Bradford C	45	2
						Leicester C	9	—
						Luton T	32	—
						Stoke C	52	3
						Chesterfield	27	1
Lee Turnbull	6 0	11 09	27 9 67	Teesside	Local	Middlesbrough	16	4
						Aston Villa	—	—
						Doncaster R	123	21
						Chesterfield	79	24
Scott Whitehead	5 9	11 10	20 4 74	Doncaster	Trainee	Chesterfield	9	—
Steven Williams	5 11	10 06	18 7 70	Mansfield	Trainee	Mansfield T	11	—
						Chesterfield	98	12
Forwards								
Wade Falana‡			7 1 70	London		Doncaster R	4	—
						Scarborough	—	—
						Chesterfield	5	—

CHESTERFIELD

Colours: Blue shirts, white shorts, blue stockings. **Change colours:** Yellow shirts, green shorts, yellow stockings.

Foundation: Chesterfield are fourth only to Stoke, Notts County and Nottingham Forest in age for they can trace their existence as far back as 1866, although it is fair to say that they were somewhat casual in the first few years of their history playing only a few friendlies a year. However, their rules of 1871 are still in existence showing an annual membership of 2s (10p), but it was not until 1891 that they won a trophy (the Barnes Cup) and followed this a year later by winning the Sheffield Cup, Barnes Cup and the Derbyshire Junior Cup.

First Football League game: 2 September, 1899, Division 2, v Sheffield W (a) L 1-5 – Hancock; Pilgrim, Fletcher; Ballantyne, Bell, Downie; Morley, Thacker, Gooing, Munday (1), Geary.

Did you know: Chesterfield established a record for a club outside the top two divisions by completing 65 matches in 1980–81. They comprised 46 League, four League Cup, six FA Cup and nine Anglo-Scottish games.

Managers (and Secretary-Managers)
E. Russell Timmeus 1891–95*, Gilbert Gillies 1895–1901, E. F. Hind 1901–1902, Jack Hoskin 1902–1906, W. Furness 1906–07, George Swift 1907–10, G. H. Jones 1911–13, R. L. Weston 1913–17, T. Callaghan 1919, J. J. Caffrey 1920–22, Harry Hadley 1922, Harry Parkes 1922–27, Alec Campbell 1927, Ted Davison 1927–32, Bill Harvey 1932–38, Norman Bullock 1938–45, Bob Brocklebank 1945–48, Bobby Marshall 1948–52, Ted Davison 1952–58, Duggie Livingstone 1958–62, Tony McShane 1962–67, Jimmy McGuigan 1967–73, Joe Shaw 1973–76, Arthur Cox 1976–80, Frank Barlow 1980–83, John Duncan 1983–87, Kevin Randall 1987–88, Paul Hart 1988–91, Chris McMenemy 1991–93, John Duncan February 1993–.

Player and Position	Ht	Wt	Birth Date	Birth Place	Source	Clubs	League App	Gls
Scott Kopel‡			25 2 70	Blackburn		Chesterfield	1	—
Dave Lancaster*	6 3	14 00	8 9 61	Preston	Colne Dynamoes	Blackpool	8	1
						Chesterfield (loan)	12	4
						Chesterfield	69	16
Paul Lemon*	5 11	11 06	3 6 66	Middlesbrough	Apprentice	Sunderland	107	15
						Carlisle U (loan)	2	—
						Walsall (loan)	2	—
						Reading (loan)	3	—
						Chesterfield	85	10
Andy Morris	6 4	15 07	17 11 67	Sheffield		Rotherham U	7	—
						Chesterfield	158	29
						Exeter C (loan)	7	2
Steve Norris	5 10	10 10	22 9 61	Coventry	Telford	Scarborough	45	13
						Notts Co (loan)	1	—
						Carlisle U	29	5
						Halifax T	56	35
						Chesterfield	51	21

Trainees
Aylward, Adam C; Bettney, Jamie D; Clarke, Robert I; Cooper, Damian R. W; Elson, Christopher B; Jones, Mark D; Meylan, Martin P; Smith, Mark; Smith, Paul; Sorrell, James A.

Associated Schoolboys
Pugh, Mark A.

Associated Schoolboys who have accepted the club's offer of a Traineeship/Contract
Davies, Kevin C; Otter, Nicholas A; Thacker, Jamie M.

COLCHESTER UNITED 1992–93   *Back row (left to right)*: Steve Foley (Youth Team Coach), Tony English (Captain), Martin Grainger, Nathan Munson, Steve McGavin, Paul Roberts, Roy McDonough (Manager).
Centre row: Chris Toulson (Physio), Robbie Deveraux, Nicky Smith, Julian Hazel, James Goodwin, Paul Abrahams, Eamon Mongan, Ian Phillips (Assistant Coach).
Front row: Gary Bennett, Warren Donald, Jason Cook, Mark Kinsella, Nicky Cropper.

Division 3 **COLCHESTER UNITED**

Layer Rd Ground, Colchester.

Telephone (0206) 574042. *Commercial Dept:* (0206) 574042.

Ground capacity: 7944.

Record attendance: 19,072 v Reading, FA Cup 1st rd, 27 Nov, 1948.

Record receipts: £26,330 v Barrow, GM Vauxhall Conference, 2 May 1992.

Pitch measurements: 110yd × 71yd.

Patron: Mrs Mary Frank, Mayor of Colchester.

Directors: Gordon Parker (Chairman), Peter Heard (vice-chairman), John Worsp, Peter Powell, Robert Jackson, James Bowdidge.

Player-coach: Roy McDonough. *Youth coach:* Steve Foley.

Physio: Brian Owen. *Consultant Physio:* C. Simpson.

Secretary: Sue Smith.

Commercial Manager: Marie Partner. *Lottery Manager:* Jackie McDonough.

Year Formed: 1937. *Turned Professional:* 1937. *Ltd Co.:* 1937.

Club Nickname: 'The U's'.

Record League Victory: 9–1 v Bradford C, Division 4, 30 December 1961 – Ames; Millar, Fowler; Harris, Abrey, Ron Hunt; Foster, Bobby Hunt (4), King (4), Hill (1), Wright.

Record Cup Victory: 7–1 v Yeovil T (away), FA Cup, 2nd rd (replay), 11 December 1958 – Ames; Fisher, Fowler; Parker, Milligan, Hammond; Williams (1), McLeod (2), Langman (4), Evans, Wright.

Record Defeat: 0–8 v Leyton Orient, Division 4, 15 October 1989.

Most League Points (2 for a win): 60, Division 4, 1973–74.

Most League Points (3 for a win): 81, Division 4, 1982–83.

Most League Goals: 104, Division 4, 1961–62.

Highest League Scorer in Season: Bobby Hunt, 37, Division 4, 1961–62.

Most League Goals in Total Aggregate: Martyn King, 131, 1959–65.

Most Capped Player: None.

Most League Appearances: Micky Cook, 613, 1969–84.

Record Transfer Fee Received: £90,000 from Gillingham for Trevor Lee, January 1981.

Record Transfer Fee Paid: £40,000 to Lokeren for Dale Tempest, August 1987.

Football League Record: 1950 Elected to Division 3(S); 1958–61 Division 3; 1961–62 Division 4; 1962–65 Division 3; 1965–66 Division 4; 1966–68 Division 3; 1968–74 Division 4; 1974–76 Division 3, 1976–77 Division 4; 1977–81 Division 3; 1981–90 Division 4; 1990–92 GM Vauxhall Conference; 1992– Division 3.

Honours: Football League: Division 3(S) best season: 3rd , 1956–57; Division 4 – Runners-up 1961–62. *FA Cup* best season: 1970–71, 6th rd (record for a Fourth Division club shared with Oxford United and Bradford City). *Football League Cup:* best season 5th rd 1974–75. *GM Vauxhall Conference winners* 1991–92. *FA Trophy winners* 1991–92.

COLCHESTER UNITED 1992—93 LEAGUE RECORD

Match No.	Date		Venue	Opponents		Result	H/T Score	Lg. Pos.	Goalscorers	Atten dance
1	Aug	15	H	Lincoln C	W	2-1	2-1	—	McDonough, Oxbrow	4131
2		21	A	Barnet	L	1-3	1-0	—	Kinsella	3600
3		29	H	Darlington	L	0-3	0-1	18		3524
4	Sept	1	H	Shrewsbury T	L	0-2	0-1			3530
5		5	A	Bury	L	2-3	0-1	22	Bennett, McDonough (pen)	2072
6		12	H	Walsall	W	3-1	2-0	18	Bennett, Smith, McDonough (pen)	3218
7		15	A	Doncaster R	L	0-1	0-1	—		1719
8		19	A	York C	L	0-2	0-1	20		3820
9		26	H	Chesterfield	W	3-0	1-0	14	Bennett 2, Kinsella	3436
10	Oct	10	A	Halifax T	W	4-2	2-0	15	Kinsella, Oxbrow, McDonough, Bennett	2445
11		16	H	Crewe Alex	W	3-2	2-1		Bennett, McDonough, Oxbrow	4524
12		24	A	Scunthorpe U	L	1-3	1-2	13	McGavin	2473
13		30	H	Wrexham	L	2-4	1-2	—	Ball, Kinsella	4423
14	Nov	3	H	Carlisle U	W	2-1	1-1	—	Roberts, Cawley	3263
15		7	A	Cardiff C	L	1-3	0-0	13	Kinsella	5505
16		21	H	Rochdale	D	4-4	2-2	14	Cawley, Ball, Sorrell, McDonough	3172
17		28	A	Hereford U	L	1-3	0-3	16	Oxbrow	1671
18	Dec	11	H	Torquay U	W	2-0	2-0	—	McDonough, Smith	2774
19		18	A	Gillingham	W	1-0	0-0	—	McGavin	2331
20		26	A	Northampton T	L	0-1	0-1	12		4861
21		29	H	Scarborough	W	1-0	1-0	—	McGavin	3640
22	Jan	2	A	Walsall	W	3-1	2-0	10	Martin, McGavin, Cawley	3669
23		8	A	Doncaster R	W	2-0	0-0	—	Grainger, McGavin	4402
24		16	A	Chesterfield	L	0-4	0-0	7		3016
25		22	H	York C	D	0-0	0-0	—		4528
26		29	H	Barnet	L	1-2	0-0	—	Bennett	5609
27	Feb	6	A	Lincoln C	D	1-1	0-0	11	Martin	3380
28		13	A	Bury	D	0-0	0-0	12		3264
29		20	A	Shrewsbury T	L	3-4	0-1	12	Hopkins, Grainger (pen), McGavin	2653
30		26	H	Halifax T	W	2-1	1-1	—	McGavin, Grainger	3007
31	Mar	12	H	Cardiff C	L	2-4	1-3	—	McDonough (pen), McGavin	4538
32		20	A	Carlisle U	W	2-0	2-0	13	Cook, Edmondson (og)	3003
33		23	H	Hereford U	W	3-1	1-0	—	Titterton (og), McDonough, Abrahams	3024
34		27	A	Rochdale	L	2-5	2-2	13	Smith, Abrahams	1783
35	Apr	6	A	Torquay U	D	2-2	1-0	—	McGavin, Ball	2915
36		13	A	Scarborough	W	1-0	1-0	—	Abrahams	1803
37		16	H	Gillingham	W	3-0	2-0	—	Clark (og), Smith, Abrahams	4695
38		20	H	Northampton T	W	2-0	0-0	—	Ball (pen), Abrahams	3519
39		24	A	Crewe Alex	L	1-7	1-4	10	English	3250
40	May	1	H	Scunthorpe U	W	1-0	1-0	10	Abrahams	3421
41		4	A	Darlington	L	0-1	0-1	—		2007
42		8	A	Wrexham	L	3-4	0-2	10	Hardy (og), Bennett, Kinsella	9705

Final League Position: 10

GOALSCORERS

League (67): McDonough 9 (3 pens), McGavin 9, Bennett 8, Abrahams 6, Kinsella 6, Ball 4 (1 pen), Oxbrow 4, Smith 4, Cawley 3, Grainger 3 (1 pen), Martin 2, Cook 1, English 1, Hopkins 1, Roberts 1, Sorrell 1, own goals 4.
Coca Cola Cup (1): English 1.
FA Cup (7): Ball 3, Bennett 2, McGavin 1, Sorrell 1.

Newell 14	Donald 8 + 2	Roberts 42	Kinsella 37 + 1	English 30 + 3	Oxbrow 12 + 4	Devereux 3 + 3	Bennett 30 + 8	McDonough 21 + 4	Grainger 28 + 3	Smith 42	Abrahams 9 + 14	Phillips — + 1	Cook 30 + 4	Hazel 2	McGavin 35 + 2	Ball 19 + 5	Cawley 22 + 2	Green 4	Sorrell 4 + 1	Emberson 13	Betts 23	Martin 8	Hopkins 13 + 1	Flowers 2 + 1	Partner — + 1	Barber 10	Munson 1	Match No.
1	2	3	4	5	6	7	8	9	10	11	12																	1
1	2	3	4	5	6	7	8	9	10	11	12	14																2
1	14	3	4	5	6	2	8	9		11	12		7		10													3
1	2	3	4	5	6		8	9		11	12		7		10													4
1	2	3	4	5	6		8	9	14	11	12		7		10													5
1	2	3	4	5	6		8	9	10	11			7															6
1	2	3	4	5	6		8	9		11			7		10													7
1	2	3	4	5	6	12	8	9		11	14		7		10													8
1		3	4	5	6	2	8	9		11			7		10													9
1	14	3	4		6	2	8	9		11	12		7		10		5											10
1		3	4		6	2	8	9		11	12		7		10	14	5											11
1		3	4		6	2	8	9		11	12		7		10	14	5											12
1		3	4		6	2	8	9		11	12		7		10	14	5											13
1		3	4		6	2	8	9		11	12		7		10		5											14
		3	4		6	2	8			11	12		7		10	14	5			1	9							15
		3	4		6		8	9		11	12		7		10	14	5			1		2						16
	2	3			6		8	9		11	12		7		10	14	5	4		1								17
		3	4		6	2		9		11	12		7		10	14	5			1	8							18
		3	4		6	2	8	9		11	12		7		10		5			1								19
		3	4		6	2	8	9		11	12		7		10		5			1								20
		3	4		6	2	8	9		11			7		10		5			1								21
		3	4			2	8			11			7		10		5			1	6		9					22
		3	4			2	8			11	12		7		10	14	5			1	6		9					23
		3	4			2	8			11			7		10		5			1	6		9					24
		3	4			2	8			11	12		7		10	14	5			1	6		9					25
		3	4		6	2	8			11	12		7		10		5			1	6		9					26
		3			6	2	8			11					10		5			1	7		9					27
		3			6	2	8			11	12		14		10		5	4		1	7		9					28
		3	14		6	2				11	12				10		5	4		1	7		9	8				29
		3	4		6	2		9		11	12				10		5			1	7		8					30
		3	4				8	9		11	12		7		10					1		2	6	5	14			31
		3	4				8	9		11	12		7		10	14				1		2	6	5				32
		3	14			2	8	9		11	12		7		10		5	4		1			6					33
		3	4			2	8	9	12	11					10	14	5			1	7		6					34
		3	4		6	2		9	12	11			7		10		5			1						8		35
		3	4		6	2		9	12	11			7		10		5			1						8		36
		3	4		6	2		9	12	11			7		10		5			1						8		37
		3	4		6	2	14	9	12	11			7		10					1						8		38
		3	4		6	2		9	12	11			7		10	14				1						8		39
		3	4		6	2	14	9	12	11			7		10		5			1						8		40
		3			6	2	14	9	12	11			7		10		5	4		1						8		41
		3	4			2	8	9		11	12		7		10	14	5			1			6				1	42

Coca Cola Cup	First Round	Brighton & HA (h)	1-1
		(a)	0-1
FA Cup	First Round	Slough (h)	4-0
	Second Round	Gillingham (a)	1-1
		(h)	2-3

COLCHESTER UNITED

Player and Position	Ht	Wt	Date	Birth Place	Source	Clubs	League App	Gls
Goalkeepers								
Alastair Monk*			8 11 72	Epsom	Everton	Colchester U	—	—
Nathan Munson§			10 11 74	Colchester	Trainee	Colchester U	1	—
Defenders								
Simon Betts†	5 8	10 07	3 3 73	Middlesbrough	Trainee	Ipswich T	—	—
						Scarborough	—	—
						Colchester U	23	—
Peter Cawley	6 4	13 00	15 9 65	London	Chertsey	Wimbledon	1	—
						Bristol R (loan)	10	—
						Fulham (loan)	5	—
						Bristol R	3	—
						Southend U	7	1
						Exeter C	7	—
						Barnet	3	—
						Colchester U	24	3
Tony English	6 0	12 04	19 10 66	Luton	Coventry C	Colchester U	255	36
Paul Flowers§	5 11	12 06	7 9 74	London	Trainee	Colchester U	3	—
James Goodwin‡			20 7 74	Colchester	Trainee	Colchester U	—	—
Martin Grainger	5 11	12 00	23 8 72	Enfield	Trainee	Colchester U	38	5
Andy Partner§	6 1	12 10	21 10 74	Colchester	Trainee	Colchester U	1	—
Ian Phillips‡	5	11 12	23 4 59	Edinburgh	Ipswich T	Mansfield T	23	—
						Peterborough U	97	3
						Northampton T	42	1
						Colchester U	150	10
						Aldershot	106	2
					Kettering T	Colchester U	1	—
Paul Roberts	5 9	11 13	27 4 62	London	Apprentice	Millwall	146	—
						Brentford	62	—
						Swindon T	27	—
						Southend U	38	—
						Aldershot	39	—
						Exeter C	3	—
						Southend U	54	—
					Fisher Ath	Colchester U	42	1
Midfield								
Steve Ball	6 0	12 01	2 9 69	Colchester	Trainee	Arsenal	—	—
						Colchester U	4	—
						Norwich C	2	—
						Colchester U	24	4
Gary Bennett	5 7	10 06	2 9 69	Enfield	Trainee	Colchester U	83	13
Jason Cook	5 7	10 06	29 12 69	Edmonton	Trainee	Tottenham H	—	—
						Southend U	30	1
						Colchester U	34	1
Robert Devereux‡	5 8	10 09	13 1 71	Gt Cornard	Ipswich T local	Colchester U	2	—
						Colchester U	6	—
Warren Donald	5 7	10 03	7 10 64	Hillingdon	Apprentice	West Ham U	2	—
						Northampton T (loan)	11	2
						Northampton T	177	11
						Colchester U	10	—
Robert Hopkins‡	5 7	10 07	25 10 61	Birmingham	Apprentice	Aston Villa	3	1
						Birmingham C	123	21
						Manchester C	7	1
						WBA	83	11
						Birmingham C	50	9
						Shrewsbury T	27	3
						Colchester U	14	1
Mark Kinsella	5 9	11 00	12 8 72	Dublin	Home Farm	Colchester U	44	6
Nicky Smith	5 7	10 00	28 1 69	Berkley		Southend U	60	6
						Colchester U	42	4

COLCHESTER UNITED

Colours: Blue shirts, white shorts with blue band, blue stockings with white band. **Change colours:** White shirts, black shorts white trim, black stockings white trim.

Foundation: Colchester United was formed in 1937 when a number of enthusiasts of the much older Colchester Town club decided to establish a professional concern as a limited liability company. The new club continued at Layer Road which had been the amateur club's home since 1909.

First Football League game: 19 August, 1950, Division 3(S), v Gillingham (a) D 0-0 – Wright; Kettle, Allen; Bearryman, Stewart, Elder; Jones, Curry, Turner, McKim, Church.

Did you know: Colchester United were the first Football League club to stage a commercially sponsored League game. In September 1973, their match with Crewe Alexandra was sponsored by a local newspaper who provided money for pre-match entertainment.

Managers (and Secretary-Managers)
Ted Fenton 1946–48, Jimmy Allen 1948–53, Jack Butler 1953–55, Benny Fenton 1955–63, Neil Franklin 1963–68, Dick Graham 1968–72, Jim Smith 1972–75, Bobby Roberts 1975–82, Allan Hunter 1982–83, Cyril Lea 1983–86, Mike Walker 1986–87, Roger Brown 1987–88, Jock Wallace 1989, Mick Mills 1990. Ian Atkins 1990–91, Roy McDonough July 1991–.

Player and Position	Ht	Wt	Birth Date	Birth Place	Source	Clubs	League App	Gls
Forwards								
Paul Abrahams†	5 8	10 06	31 10 73	Colchester	Trainee	Colchester U	23	6
Julian Hazel‡			25 9 73	Luton	Trainee	Colchester U	2	—
Roy McDonough	6 1	13 07	16 10 58	Solihull	Apprentice	Birmingham C	2	1
						Walsall	82	15
						Chelsea	—	—
						Colchester U	93	24
						Southend U	22	4
						Exeter C	20	1
						Cambridge U	32	5
						Southend U	186	30
						Colchester U	25	9
Steve McGavin	5 8	11 00	24 1 69	North Walsham	Sudbury	Colchester U	37	9

Trainees
Andress, Simon; Booty, Justin; Campbell, Sean M; Champ, Paul J; Dunsdon, Ian C; Flowers, Paul A; Hunt, Tyler C; Lawrence, Robert; Mongan, Eamon M; Munson, Nathan W; Partner, Andrew N; Partner, Lloyd; Ridgers, Scott; Roberts, Danny; Schultz, David H; Seal, Richard; Steggle, Jamie.

**Non-Contract
Abrahams, Paul; Betts, Simon R.

Associated Schoolboys
Appleford, Christian A; Dowdeswell, David J; Gilbert, Asa W; Matthews, Ashley M.

**Non-Contract Players who are retained must be re-signed before they are eligible to play in League matches.

COVENTRY CITY 1992–93 *Back row (left to right):* Terry Fleming, David Smith, Billy Woods, Paul Edwards, Stewart Robson, David Busst, John Williams, Andy Pearce, Robert Rosario, Phil Babb, Chris Greenman, Luke Chadwick, Ray Woods, Martyn Booty.

Centre row: Kevin Gallacher, Stewart Bowen, Barry Crews, Peter Ndlovu, Sean Flynn, Tony Sheridan, Lee Hurst, Martin Davies, Steve Ogrizovic, Jonathan Gould, Peter Billing, Craig Middleton, Gerard Carr, Michael Stephenson, Ricky Smith, Carl Wilson, Brian Borrows.

Front row: Kenny Sansom, Lloyd McGrath, John Gowens (Assistant Physio), Tim Exeter (Strength and Conditioning Coach), Ian Cockerill (Sport Psychologist), Roy Evans (Youth Development Officer), Phil Neal (Assistant Manager), Bobby Gould (Team Manager), Brian Roberts (Reserve Team Coach), Bert Edwards (Youth Team Manager), Peter Hill (Kit Supervisor), George Dalton (Physio), Michael Gynn, Peter Atherton.

FA Premier   COVENTRY CITY

Highfield Road Stadium, King Richard Street, Coventry CV2 4FW. Telephone (General Enquiries): (0203) 2223535. Ticket office: (0203) 225545. Fax: 0203 630318.

Ground capacity: 17,000.

Record attendance: 51,455 v Wolverhampton W, Division 2, 29 April 1967.

Record receipts: £177,271.55 v Nottingham F, Littlewoods Cup Semi-final 2nd leg, 25 February 1990.

Pitch measurements: 110yd × 75yd.

Life President: Derrick H. Robbins.

Chairman: P. D. H. Robins. *Vice-chairman:* B. A. Richardson.

Directors: J. F. W. Reason, A. M. Jepson, J. E. Clarke.

Managing Director: G. W. Curtis.

Secretary: Graham Hover.

Team Manager: Bobby Gould. *Assistant Manager:* Mike Kelly. *Physio:* George Dalton. *Sales & Marketing Manager:* Mark Jones.

Year Formed: 1883. *Turned Professional:* 1893. *Ltd Co.:* 1907.

Previous Names: 1883–98, Singers FC; 1898, Coventry City FC.

Club Nickname: 'Sky Blues'.

Previous Grounds: Binley Road, 1883–87; Stoke Road, 1887–99; Highfield Road, 1899–.

Record League Victory: 9–0 v Bristol C, Division 3 (S), 28 April 1934 – Pearson; Brown, Bisby; Perry, Davidson, Frith; White (2), Lauderdale Bourton (5), Jones (2), Lake.

Record Cup Victory: 7–0 v Scunthorpe U, FA Cup, 1st rd, 24 November 1934 – Pearson; Brown, Bisby; Mason, Davidson, Boileau; Birtley (2), Lauderdale (2), Bourton (1), Jones (1), Liddle (1).

Record Defeat: 2–10 v Norwich C, Division 3 (S), 15 March 1930.

Most League Points (2 for a win): 60, Division 4, 1958–59 and Division 3, 1963–64.

Most League Points (3 for a win): 63, Division 1, 1986–87.

Most League Goals: 108, Division 3 (S), 1931–32.

Highest League Scorer in Season: Clarrie Bourton, 49, Division 3 (S), 1931–32.

Most League Goals in Total Aggregate: Clarrie Bourton, 171, 1931–37.

Most Capped Player: Dave Clements, 21 (48), Northern Ireland.

Most League Appearances: George Curtis, 486, 1956–70.

Record Transfer Fee Received: £1,500,000 from Blackburn R for Kevin Gallacher, March 1993.

Record Transfer Fee Paid: £900,000 to Dundee U for Kevin Gallacher, January 1990.

Football League Record: 1919 Elected to Division 2; 1925–26 Division 3 (N); 1926–36 Division 3 (S); 1936–52 Division 2; 1952–58 Division 3 (S); 1958–59 Division 4; 1959–64 Division 3; 1964–67 Division 2; 1967–92 Division 1; 1992– FA Premier League.

Honours: Football League: Division 1 best season: 6th, 1969–70; Division 2 – Champions 1966–67; Division 3 – Champions 1963–64; Division 3 (S) – Champions 1935–36; Runners-up 1933–34; Division 4 – Runners-up 1958–59. *FA Cup:* Winners 1986–87. *Football League Cup:* best season: Semi-final 1980–81, 1989–90. **European Competitions:** *European Fairs Cup:* 1970–71.

COVENTRY CITY 1992—93 LEAGUE RECORD

Match No.	Date		Venue	Opponents	Result		H/T Score	Lg. Pos.	Goalscorers	Atten dance
1	Aug	15	H	Middlesbrough	W	2-1	1-0	—	Williams J, Smith	12,681
2		19	A	Tottenham H	W	2-0	2-0	—	Williams J 2	24,388
3		22	A	Wimbledon	W	2-1	1-0	1	Gynn, Rosario	3759
4		26	H	QPR	L	0-1	0-1	—		13,563
5		29	H	Blackburn R	L	0-2	0-0	6		14,541
6	Sept	2	H	Sheffield W	W	2-1	1-0	—	Ndlovu, Hurst	22,874
7		5	A	Oldham Ath	W	1-0	0-0	2	Gallacher	11,254
8		14	H	Tottenham H	W	1-0	0-0	—	Williams J	15,348
9		21	A	Nottingham F	D	1-1	1-0	—	Rosario	17,553
10		26	H	Norwich C	D	1-1	1-1	3	Ndlovu	16,436
11	Oct	3	H	Crystal Palace	D	2-2	2-2	3	Pearce, Gallacher	11,808
12		17	A	Everton	D	1-1	1-1	3	Ndlovu	17,587
13		24	H	Chelsea	L	1-2	0-1	5	Rosario	15,626
14		31	A	Leeds U	D	2-2	1-0	5	McAllister (og), Ndlovu	28,018
15	Nov	7	A	Arsenal	L	0-3	0-3	6		27,693
16		21	H	Manchester C	L	2-3	1-0	9	Quinn 2	14,590
17		28	A	Sheffield U	D	1-1	1-1	11	Quinn	15,625
18	Dec	5	H	Ipswich T	D	2-2	1-1	11	Gallacher, Quinn	11,294
19		12	A	Southampton	D	2-2	2-1	9	Quinn 2	12,306
20		19	H	Liverpool	W	5-1	1-0	8	Borrows 2 (1 pen), Gallacher, Quinn 2	19,779
21		26	A	Aston Villa	W	3-0	0-0	7	Quinn 2, Rosario	24,245
22		28	A	Manchester U	L	0-5	0-2	8		36,025
23	Jan	9	H	Nottingham F	L	0-1	0-0	10		15,264
24		16	A	Norwich C	D	1-1	0-1	11	Quinn	13,613
25		23	H	Oldham Ath	W	3-0	3-0	6	Gallacher 2, Ndlovu	10,544
26		26	A	Blackburn R	W	5-2	2-1	—	Hendry (og), Hurst, Williams, Quinn 2	15,215
27		30	H	Wimbledon	L	0-2	0-1	8		11,774
28	Feb	6	A	Middlesbrough	W	2-0	0-0	4	Ndlovu, Quinn	14,008
29		20	A	QPR	L	0-2	0-2	7		12,453
30		27	A	Crystal Palace	D	0-0	0-0	10		12,248
31	Mar	3	H	Sheffield W	W	1-0	1-0	—	Gynn	13,806
32		7	H	Everton	L	0-1	0-1	—		11,285
33		10	A	Manchester C	L	0-1	0-1	—		20,092
34		13	H	Arsenal	L	0-2	0-2	8		15,437
35		20	A	Ipswich T	D	0-0	0-0	8		16,698
36		24	H	Sheffield U	L	1-3	1-0	—	Williams	12,993
37	Apr	3	A	Southampton	W	2-0	1-0	7	Quinn (pen), Williams	10,463
38		10	A	Aston Villa	D	0-0	0-0	9		38,543
39		12	H	Manchester U	L	0-1	0-1	10		24,429
40		17	A	Liverpool	L	0-4	0-2	12		33,328
41	May	1	A	Chelsea	L	1-2	0-1	13	Quinn	14,186
42		8	H	Leeds U	D	3-3	2-1	15	Williams, Quinn, Ndlovu	19,591

Final League Position: 15

GOALSCORERS

League (52): Quinn 17 (1 pen), Williams 8, Ndlovu 7, Gallacher 6, Rosario 4, Borrows 2 (1 pen), Gynn 2, Hurst 2, Pearce 1, Smith 1, own goals 2.
Coca Cola Cup (2): Borrows 1 (pen), Ndlovu.
FA Cup (0).

Ogrizovic 33	Fleming 8 + 3	Sansom 21	Robson 14 + 1	Pearce 21 + 3	Atherton 39	Gynn 18 + 2	Hurst 35	Rosario 28	Williams J 38 + 3	Smith 6	Babb 27 + 7	Flynn 4 + 3	Ndlovu 27 + 5	McGrath 20 + 5	Borrows 36 + 2	Gallacher 19 + 1	Williams P 1 + 1	Billing 3	Sheridan 1	Middleton 1	Quinn 26	Gould 9	Busst 10	Greenman 1 + 1	Rowland — + 2	Rennie 9	Jenkinson 2 + 3	Wegerle 5 + 1	Boland — + 1	Match No.
1	2	3	4	5	6	7	8	9	10	11	12		14																	1
1	2	3	4	5	6	7	8	9	10	11			12																	2
1	2	3	4	5	6	7	8	9	10	11				12	14															3
1	2	3	4	5	6	7	8	9	10	11				12	14															4
1	2	3		5			8	9	12	11		14	4	7	6	10														5
1	2	3	4	5			8	9	11			14	6	7	12	10														6
1	12	3	4	5			8	9	11			14	6	7	2	10														7
1		3		5	4		8	9	11				6	7	2	10														8
1		3		5	4		8	9	11				6	7	2	10														9
1		3		5	4		8	9	11		12		6	7	2	10														10
1	12	3		5	4		8	9	11				6	7	2	10														11
1	9	3	10	5	4		8		11				6	7	2															12
1		3	10	5	4		8	9	11				6	7	2						12									13
1		3	10		4		8		11		12		6		2			9	5	7										14
1	12	3			4		8	9	11				10	6	2				5	7										15
1		3	7	5	4		8	9	11		12		6		2						10									16
1			7	5	4		8	9	12		3		6		2	11					10									17
1			7	5	4		8	9	12		3		6	14	2	11					10									18
1	5				4		8	9			3		6	7	2	11					10									19
	5				4		8	9	6		3			7	2	11					10	1								20
	5		14		4		8	9	6		3	12		7	2	11					10	1								21
	5				4		8	9	6		3	12		7	2	11					10	1								22
1	5	12			4		8	9	6		3			7	2	11					10									23
1					4		8	9	6		3				2	11					10		5	7	12					24
1					4		8	9	6		3			7	2	11					10		5	12						25
1					4		8	9	11		3		6	7	2						10		5							26
1					4		8	9	11		3		6	12	2		7				10		5							27
1		5			4		8	9	11		3		6	7	2						10									28
1	12	5			4		8	9	11		3		6	7	2						10									29
1		5	7		4		8	9	6	11	3	12			2						10									30
1	11	5			4		8		6		3		7	9	2						10									31
1		5			4		8		6		3	11	7	9	2	12					10									32
1					4				6		3	11	7	9	2	8					10		5	12						33
1					4	12			6		3	11	7	14	2	8							5			9	10			34
1					4			11	6		3			7	2	8					10		5			9				35
1					4	10	8		11		3			7	2											9	5	6		36
					4	12	8		11		3		7	14	2						9	1	5			6		10		37
					4	5	8		11		3			7	2						9	1				6	12	10		38
					4	5	8		11		3			7	2						9	1				6	12	10		39
	14				4	5	8		11		3			7	2						9	1				6	12	10		40
		2			4	7	8		11		3			12							9	1	5			6		10	14	41
					4		8		11		3		10	5	2						9	1				6	7	12		42

Coca Cola Cup	Second Round	Scarborough (h)	2-0
		(a)	0-3
FA Cup	Third Round	Norwich C (a)	0-1

COVENTRY CITY

Player and Position	Ht	Wt	Date	Birth Place	Source	Clubs	League App	Gls
Goalkeepers								
Martin Davies‡	6 2	13 07	28 6 74	Swansea	Trainee	Coventry C	—	—
Jonathan Gould	6 1	12 07	18 7 68	Paddington		Halifax T	32	—
						WBA	—	—
						Coventry C	9	—
Steve Ogrizovic	6 5	15 00	12 9 57	Mansfield	ONRYC	Chesterfield	16	—
						Liverpool	4	—
						Shrewsbury T	84	—
						Coventry C	349	1
Defenders								
Peter Atherton	5 11	12 03	6 4 70	Orrell	Trainee	Wigan Ath	149	1
						Coventry C	74	—
Peter Billing	6 2	13 00	24 10 64	Liverpool	South Liverpool	Everton	1	—
						Crewe Alex	88	1
						Coventry C	58	1
						Port Vale (loan)	12	—
Martyn Booty	5 8	12 01	30 5 71	Kirby Muxloe	Trainee	Coventry C	3	—
Brian Borrows	5 10	10 12	20 12 60	Liverpool	Amateur	Everton	27	—
						Bolton W	95	—
						Coventry C	301	11
Dave Busst	6 1	12 10	30 6 67	Birmingham	Moor Green	Coventry C	10	—
Gerard Carr*	5 11	12 04	23 12 75	Coventry	Trainee	Coventry C	—	—
Luke Chadwick‡			8 9 73	Birmingham	Trainee	Coventry C	—	—
Craig Melrose*	6 2	13 02	28 8 74	Newcastle	Trainee	Coventry C	—	—
Andy Pearce	6 4	13 00	20 4 66	Bradford	Halesowen	Coventry C	71	4
David Rennie	6 0	12 00	29 8 64	Edinburgh	Apprentice	Leicester C	21	1
						Leeds U	101	5
						Bristol C	104	8
						Birmingham C	35	4
						Coventry C	9	—
Brian Roberts	5 8	11 07	6 11 55	Manchester	Apprentice	Coventry C	215	1
						Hereford U (loan)	5	—
						Birmingham C	187	—
						Wolverhampton W	21	—
						Coventry C	—	—
Midfield								
Phil Babb	6 0	12 03	30 11 70	Lambeth		Millwall	—	—
						Bradford C	80	14
						Coventry C	34	—
Willie Boland	5 9	11 02	6 8 75	Ennis		Coventry C	1	—
Sean Flynn	5 8	11 08	13 3 68	Birmingham	Halesowen T	Coventry C	29	2
Mick Gynn*	5 5	10 10	19 8 61	Peterborough	Apprentice	Peterborough U	156	33
						Coventry C	241	32
Lee Hurst	6 0	11 09	21 9 70	Nuneaton	Trainee	Coventry C	49	2
Lloyd McGrath	5 5	11 06	24 2 65	Birmingham	Apprentice	Coventry C	203	4
Stewart Robson	5 11	12 04	6 11 64	Billericay	Apprentice	Arsenal	151	16
						West Ham U	69	4
						Coventry C (loan)	4	—
						Coventry C	52	3
John Williams	6 2	12 04	11 5 68	Birmingham	Cradley T	Swansea C	39	11
						Coventry C	41	8
Karl Wilson*	5 9	10 12	19 11 73	Dublin		Coventry C	—	—

COVENTRY CITY

Colours: All Sky blue. **Change colours:** Yellow shirts, blue shorts, yellow stockings.

Foundation: Workers at Singer's cycle factory formed a club in 1883. The first success of Singers' FC was to win the Birmingham Junior Cup in 1891 and this led in 1894 to their election to the Birmingham and District League. Four years later they changed their name to Coventry City and joined the Southern League in 1908 at which time they were playing in blue and white quarters.

First Football League game: 30 August, 1919, Division 2, v Tottenham H (h) L 0-5 – Lindon; Roberts, Chaplin, Allan, Hawley, Clarke, Sheldon, Mercer, Sambrooke, Lowes, Gibson.

Did you know: Coventry City staged the first closed-circuit TV soccer on 6 October 1965 when a crowd of over 10,000 watched the 2-1 win at Cardiff on four large screens.

Managers (and Secretary-Managers)
H. R. Buckle 1909–10, Robert Wallace 1910–13*, Frank Scott-Walford 1913–15, William Clayton 1917–19, H. Pollitt 1919–20, Albert Evans 1920–24, Jimmy Kerr 1924–28, James McIntyre 1928–31, Harry Storer 1931–45, Dick Bayliss 1945–47, Billy Frith 1947–48, Harry Storer 1948–53, Jack Fairbrother 1953–54, Charlie Elliott 1954–55, Jesse Carver 1955–56, Harry Warren 1956–57, Billy Frith 1957–61, Jimmy Hill 1961–67, Noel Cantwell 1967–72, Bob Dennison 1972, Joe Mercer 1972–75, Gordon Milne 1972–81, Dave Sexton 1981–83, Bobby Gould 1983–84, Don Mackay 1985–86, George Curtis 1986–87 (became MD), John Sillett 1987–90, Terry Butcher 1990–92, Don Howe 1992, Bobby Gould July 1992–.

Player and Position	Ht	Wt	Birth Date	Birth Place	Source	Clubs	League App	Gls
Forwards								
Kevin Drinkell (To Falkirk July 1992)	5 11	12 06	18 6 60	Grimsby	Apprentice	Grimsby T	270	89
						Norwich C	121	50
						Rangers	36	12
						Coventry C	41	5
						Birmingham C (loan)	5	2
Terry Fleming*	5 9	11 00	5 1 73	Marston Green	Trainee	Coventry C	13	—
Leigh Jenkinson	6 0	12 02	9 7 69	Thorne	Trainee	Hull C	130	13
						Rotherham U (loan)	7	—
						Coventry C	5	—
Craig Middleton*	5 9	11 00	10 9 70	Nuneaton	Trainee	Coventry C	3	—
Peter Ndlovu	5 8	10 02	25 2 73	Zimbabwe	Highlanders	Coventry C	55	9
Mick Quinn	5 9	13 00	2 5 62	Liverpool	Derby Co	Wigan Ath	69	19
						Stockport Co	63	39
						Oldham Ath	80	34
						Portsmouth	121	54
						Newcastle U	115	59
						Coventry C	26	17
Tony Sheridan	6 0	11 08	21 11 74	Dublin		Coventry C	1	—
Michael Stephenson	5 9	12 00	6 10 73	Coventry	Trainee	Coventry C	—	—
Roy Wegerle	5 11	11 00	19 3 64	South Africa	Tampa Bay R	Chelsea	23	3
						Swindon T (loan)	7	1
						Luton T	45	10
						QPR	75	29
						Blackburn R	34	6
						Coventry C	6	—
Billy Woods‡			24 10 73	Cork	Trainee	Coventry C	—	—
Ray Woods	5 11	10 00	7 6 65	Birkenhead	Apprentice Colne D.	Tranmere R	7	2
						Wigan Ath	28	3
						Coventry C	21	1
						Wigan Ath (loan)	13	—

Trainees
Barnwell-Edinboro, Jamie; Blake, Timothy A; Carmichael, David; Cleland, Jamie A; Coleman, Daniel J; Hall, Marcus T. J; Jones, Richard J; Kellings, Tommy L; O'Brien, Paul W; O'Toole, Gavin F; Rogers, Lee; Williams, Stephen D.

Associated Schoolboys
Field, Marc I; Gosling, Adam; Healy, Brett W; Nolan, Carl N; Robinson, Mark T.

Associated Schoolboys who have accepted the club's offer of a Traineeship/Contract
Christie, Iyseden; Lenton, Jamie; Lovelock, Andrew J; Williams, James D; Willis, Adam P; Wood, Simon.

182

CREWE ALEXANDRA 1992–93 *Back row (left to right):* Gus Wilson, Ahmed Mettioui, Steve Macauley, Dele Adebola, Anthony Hughes, Michael Jackson, Mark Gardiner.
Centre row: Dario Gradi (Manager), Jimmy Harvey, Phil Clarkson, Shaun Smith, Dean Greygoose, Dave McKearney, Gareth Whalley, Kenny Swain (Assistant Manager).
Front row: Rob Edwards, Richard Annan, Craig Hignett, Steve Garvey, Tony Naylor, Steve Walters.
(Photograph courtesy of Steve Finch L.R.P.S.)

Division 3   **CREWE ALEXANDRA**

Football Ground, Gresty Rd, Crewe. Telephone Crewe (0270) 213014. (0270) 55657.

Ground capacity: 7200.

Record attendance: 20,000 v Tottenham H, FA Cup 4th rd, 30 January 1960.

Record receipts: £41,093 v Liverpool, FA Cup 3rd rd, 6 January 1992.

Pitch measurements: 112yd × 74yd.

President: N. Rowlinson.

Chairman: J. Bowler. *Vice-chairman:* J. McMillan.

Directors: K. Potts, D. Rowlinson, R. Clayton, N. Hassall, E. Weetman, J. R. Holmes.

Manager: Dario Gradi. *Coach/Assistant Manager:*

Secretary/Commercial Manager: Mrs Gill Palin.

Year Formed: 1877. *Turned Professional:* 1893. *Ltd Co.:* 1892.

Club Nickname: 'Railwaymen'.

Record League Victory: 8–0 v Rotherham U, Division 3 (N), 1 October 1932 – Foster; Pringle, Dawson; Ward, Keenor (1), Turner (1); Gillespie, Swindells (1), McConnell (2), Deacon (2), Weale (1).

Record Cup Victory: 5–0 v Druids, FA Cup, 1st rd, 15 October 1887 – Hickton; Conde, Cope; Bayman, Halfpenny, Osborne (1); Pearson, Payne (1), Price (1), Tinsley, Ellis. (2 scorers unknown.)

Record Defeat: 2–13 v Tottenham H, FA Cup 4th rd replay, 3 February 1960.

Most League Points (2 for a win): 59, Division 4, 1962–63.

Most League Points (3 for a win): 78, Division 4, 1988–89.

Most League Goals: 95, Division 3 (N), 1931–32.

Highest League Scorer in Season: Terry Harkin, 35, Division 4, 1964–65.

Most League Goals in Total Aggregate: Bert Swindells, 126, 1928–37.

Most Capped Player: Bill Lewis, 12 (30), Wales.

Most League Appearances: Tommy Lowry, 436, 1966–78.

Record Transfer Fee Received: £600,000 from Liverpool for Rob Jones, October 1991.

Record Transfer Fee Paid: £80,000 to Barnsley for Darren Foreman, March 1990.

Football League Record: 1892 Original Member of Division 2; 1896 Failed re-election; 1921 Re-entered Division 3 (N); 1958–63 Division 4; 1963–64 Division 3; 1964–68 Division 4; 1968–69 Division 3; 1969–89 Division 4; 1989–91 Division 3; 1991–92 Division 4; 1992– Division 3.

Honours: Football League: Division 2 best season: 10th, 1892–93. *FA Cup:* best season: semi-final 1888. *Football League Cup:* best season: 3rd rd, 1974–75, 1975–76, 1978–79, 1992–93. *Welsh Cup:* Winners 1936, 1937.

CREWE ALEXANDRA 1992—93 LEAGUE RECORD

Match No.	Date	Venue	Opponents	Result	H/T Score	Lg. Pos.	Goalscorers	Attendance
1	Aug 15	H	Torquay U	W 4-2	2-0	—	Hignett 2, Clarkson 2	3096
2	22	A	Scarborough	L 0-1	0-0	9		1829
3	28	H	Northampton T	W 3-2	2-0	—	Hignett, Naylor 2	3603
4	Sept 1	H	Halifax T	W 2-1	2-0	—	Naylor 2	3228
5	5	A	Darlington	L 0-3	0-1	5		2037
6	12	H	Doncaster R	W 4-0	2-0	2	Hignett (pen), Garvey, Macauley, McKearney (pen)	3127
7	15	A	Chesterfield	L 1-2	0-1	—	Naylor	5452
8	19	A	Scunthorpe U	D 3-3	1-2	4	Naylor, Walters, Clarkson	2995
9	Oct 3	A	Gillingham	W 2-1	1-0	4	Smith, Macauley	2420
10	10	H	Cardiff C	W 2-0	2-0	3	Gardiner, Hignett	3638
11	16	A	Colchester U	L 2-3	1-2	—	Macauley, Naylor	4524
12	24	H	Bury	W 2-1	1-0	4	McKearney, Hignett	3231
13	31	A	Barnet	L 2-3	0-1	5	Naylor, Hignett	3481
14	Nov 7	A	Rochdale	W 1-0	0-0	5	Hignett	3058
15	21	H	Lincoln C	L 1-2	1-0	6	Walters	3208
16	28	A	York C	L 1-3	0-2	7	Clarkson	4190
17	Dec 12	A	Carlisle U	W 3-1	1-1	6	Lyons 2, Clarkson	3487
18	26	H	Wrexham	L 0-1	0-0	10		4481
19	28	A	Shrewsbury T	L 1-4	0-1	10	Williams (og)	4789
20	Jan 9	H	Chesterfield	L 0-2	0-1	12		2671
21	26	A	Northampton T	W 2-0	2-0	—	Clarkson, Edwards	2510
22	30	H	Scarborough	L 2-3	1-2	14	Edwards, Clarkson	3067
23	Feb 6	A	Torquay U	W 2-1	1-0	12	Clarkson, Naylor	1931
24	13	H	Darlington	W 1-0	0-0	11	Walters	2953
25	16	A	Doncaster R	D 1-1	1-1	—	Edwards	1844
26	20	A	Halifax T	W 2-1	1-1	11	Edwards, Carr	1604
27	27	A	Cardiff C	D 1-1	1-1	10	Clarkson	10,012
28	Mar 6	H	Gillingham	W 3-1	2-0	10	Smith, McKearney (pen), Clark (og)	3215
29	9	A	Hereford U	W 1-0	1-0	—	Carr	1872
30	12	H	Rochdale	D 1-1	0-0	—	Ward	3515
31	23	H	York C	W 3-1	2-1	—	Ward, Naylor, Smith	3381
32	27	A	Lincoln C	D 1-1	1-1	9	Evans	4235
33	Apr 2	H	Hereford U	D 1-1	0-1	—	Ward	3413
34	6	A	Carlisle U	W 4-0	0-0	—	Smith (pen), Edwards 2, Hughes	3246
35	10	A	Wrexham	L 0-2	0-2	6		8164
36	12	H	Shrewsbury T	D 2-2	1-0	6	Clarkson 2	4215
37	17	A	Walsall	L 0-1	0-0	7		4643
38	20	H	Scunthorpe U	W 1-0	1-0	—	McKearney	3006
39	24	H	Colchester U	W 7-1	4-1	5	Naylor 5, McKearney, Clarkson	3250
40	27	H	Walsall	L 0-1	0-1	—		4549
41	May 1	A	Bury	W 2-1	1-0	6	McKearney, Clarkson	4411
42	8	H	Barnet	W 4-1	3-1	6	Naylor, Whalley, Ward, Edwards	4264

Final League Position: 6

GOALSCORERS
League (75): Naylor 16, Clarkson 13, Hignett 8 (1 pen), Edwards 7, McKearney 6 (2 pens), Smith 4 (1 pen), Ward 4, Macauley 3, Walters 3, Carr 2, Lyons 2, Evans 1, Gardiner 1, Garvey 1, Hughes 1, Whalley 1, own goals 2.
Coca Cola Cup (8): Hignett 3, Naylor 2, Clarkson 1, Garvey 1, Harvey 1.
FA Cup (15): Hignett 4, McKearney 3 (1 pen), Clarkson 2, Naylor 2, Whalley 2, Carr 1, Edwards 1.

Greygoose 30	McKearney 28 + 1	Annan 8 + 1	Wilson 35	Hughes 14 + 3	Smith S 29 + 7	Hignett 14	Naylor 35	Clarkson 32 + 3	Harvey 16 + 1	Walters 23	Garvey 3 + 7	Adebola — + 6	Macauley 25	Whalley 22 + 3	Carr 31 + 1	Gardiner 11 + 2	Mettioui 1 + 2	Edwards 17 + 6	Lennon 23 + 1	Vaughan 3 + 4	Lyons 6 + 3	Kite 5	Evans 22 + 4	Ward 18 + 2	Jackson 4	Duffield — + 2	Smith M 7	Woodward — + 6	Tierney — + 1	Match No.
1	2	3	4	5	6	7	8	9	10	11	12	14																		1
1	2		4	5	3		7	8	9	10	11	12		6	14															2
1	2	3	4	5	12	7	8	9	10	11				6																3
1	2	3	4	5	14	7	8	9	10	11	12			6																4
1	2		4	5	3	7	8	12	10	11	9			6	14															5
1	2		4			7	8	9	10	11				6	3	5	12													6
1	2		4		12		8	9	10	11		14		6	3	5	7													7
1	2		4		3	7	8	9	10	11		14		6		5	12													8
1	2		4	12	3	7	8					14		6	11	5	10	9												9
1	2		4		12	7	8	9		11		14		6	3	5	10													10
1	2		4			7	8	9		11		12		6	3	5	10													11
1	2		4	14	3	7	8	12		11				6		5			9	10										12
1	2		4	6	3	7	8	12								5	10		9	11	14									13
1	2		4		3	7	8						12	6		5			9	11		10								14
1	2	12	4		5	7	8	9		11				6	3				10											15
	2		4				9	7		11				6	3	5	10	8	14			1	12							16
	2	3	4				8	7						6		5		10			11	1		9						17
	2	3	4		14		8	7						6	9	5	10				11	1	12							18
	2	3	4		14		8	7						6	9	5	10				11	1	12							19
	2		4		14		8	7		11					3	5	10				12	1	9		6					20
1	2		4	6			9							5	3	10		11	7		8		12	14						21
1	2		4	5			9		7					6		12	14	11	8		10		3							22
1	2	12	3				8	9	10					6		5		11	7				4		14					23
1	2		3				8	9	12	10				6		5		11	7				4	14						24
1			3				8	9	7	10				6		5		11	2		12		4	14						25
1			3				8	9		10				6		5		11	2				4	7						26
1	2		3				8	9						6		5		11	10		12		4	7						27
1	12	2	3				8	9				14		6		5		11	10				4	7						28
1	6	2	3				8	9								5		11	10				4	7						29
1	6	2	3				8	9				12				5		11	10				4	7						30
1	2		3				8		9					6		5	11		10		12		4	7						31
1	2	6	3				8		9					11		5			10		12		4	7						32
1	2	6	3				8		9					11		5		12	10				4	7						33
1	2	6	3				8		9					11		5		12	10	14			4	7						34
1		6	3				8		9			12		14		5		11	10	2			4	7						35
	2	6	3				8	9						11		5		12	10				4	7			1			36
	2		3				8	9						6		5		12	10	11			4	7			1	14		37
	2		3				8	9						6		5			10	11			4	7			1	12		38
	2		3				8	9		10				6		5		12					4	7	11		1	14		39
	2	5	3				8	9		10				6				12					4	7	11		1	14		40
	2	10	3				8	9						6			12	11					4	7	5		1	14		41
	2	5	3				8	9		10				6				11					4	7			1	14	12	42

Coca Cola Cup	First Round	Rochdale (h)	4-1
		(a)	2-1
	Second Round	West Ham U (a)	0-0
		(h)	2-0
	Third Round	Nottingham F (h)	0-1
FA Cup	First Round	Wrexham (h)	6-1
	Second Round	Accrington S (a)	6-1
	Third Round	Marine (h)	3-1
	Fourth Round	Blackburn R (h)	0-3

CREWE ALEXANDRA

Player and Position	Ht	Wt	Date	Birth Place	Source	Clubs	League App	Gls
Goalkeepers								
Dean Greygoose*	5 11	11 05	18 12 64	Thetford	Apprentice	Cambridge U	26	—
						Orient (loan)	—	—
						Lincoln C (loan)	6	—
						Orient	1	—
						C. Palace	—	—
						Crewe Alex	205	—
Mark Smith†	6 1	13 09	2 1 73	Birmingham	Trainee	Nottingham F	—	—
						Crewe Alex	7	—
Defenders								
Richard Annan	5 8	11 00	4 12 68	Leeds	Guiseley	Crewe Alex	9	—
Darren Carr	6 2	13 00	4 9 68	Bristol		Bristol R	30	—
						Newport Co	9	—
						Sheffield U	13	1
						Crewe Alex	104	5
Anthony Hughes	6 0	12 05	3 10 73	Liverpool	Trainee	Crewe Alex	17	1
Michael Jackson	5 11	11 10	4 12 73	West Cheshire	Trainee	Crewe Alex	5	—
Neil Lennon	5 9	11 06	25 6 71	Lurgan	Trainee	Manchester C	1	—
						Crewe Alex	58	3
Steve Macauley	6 1	12 00	4 3 69	Lytham	Fleetwood	Crewe Alex	34	4
Paul Rushton	5 10	11 10	25 1 74	Buckley	Trainee	Crewe Alex	—	—
Shaun Smith	5 10	11 00	9 4 71	Leeds	Trainee	Halifax T	7	—
						Crewe Alex	46	4
Danny Vaughan*	5 8	10 00	18 2 72	Liverpool		Crewe Alex	7	—
Gus Wilson	5 11	12 00	11 4 63	Manchester	Runcorn	Crewe Alex	76	—
Andy Woodward	5 10	10 12	23 9 73	Stockport	Trainee	Crewe Alex	6	—
Midfield								
Martin Clark			12 9 70	Accrington	Accrington S	Crewe Alex	—	—
Phil Clarkson	5 10	10 08	13 11 68	Hambleton	Fleetwood	Crewe Alex	63	19
Chris Duffy*	5 10	11 11	31 10 73	Manchester	Trainee	Crewe Alex	—	—
Jimmy Harvey*	5 9	11 04	2 5 58	Lurgan	Glenavon	Arsenal	3	—
						Hereford U (loan)	11	—
						Hereford U	267	39
						Bristol C	3	—
						Wrexham (loan)	6	—
						Tranmere R	184	18
						Crewe Alex	17	—
Francis Tierney	5 10	10 12	10 9 75	Liverpool	Trainee	Crewe Alex	1	—
Gareth Whalley	5 10	11 00	19 12 73	Manchester	Trainee	Crewe Alex	25	1
Forwards								
Dele Adebola§	6 3	11 08	23 6 75	Liverpool	Trainee	Crewe Alex	6	—
Robert Edwards	5 8	11 07	23 2 70	Manchester	Trainee	Crewe Alex	94	25
Stewart Evans	6 4	11 05	15 11 60	Maltby	Apprentice Gainsborough T	Rotherham U	—	—
						Sheffield U	—	—
						Wimbledon	175	50
						WBA	14	1
						Plymouth Arg	45	10
						Rotherham U	65	14
						Torquay U (loan)	15	5
						Crewe Alex	43	5
Mark Gardiner	5 10	10 07	25 12 66	Cirencester	Apprentice	Swindon T	10	—
						Torquay U	49	4
						Crewe Alex	148	32

CREWE ALEXANDRA

Colours: Red shirts, white shorts, red stockings. **Change colours:** Blue shirts, white shorts, blue stockings.

Foundation: Crewe Alexandra played cricket and probably rugby before they decided to form a football club in 1877. Whether they took the name "Alexandra" from a pub where they held their meetings, or whether it was after Princess Alexandra, is a matter of conjecture. Crewe's first trophy was the Crewe and District Cup in 1887 and it is worth noting that they reached the semi-finals of the FA Cup the following year.

First Football League game: 3 September, 1892, Division 2, v Burton Swifts (a) L 1-7 – Hickton; Moore, Cope; Linnell, Johnson, Osborne; Bennett, Pearson (1), Bailey, Barnett, Roberts.

Did you know: A local garage group offered a car worth £3500 to any Crewe Alexandra player who scored 30 League goals in 1982–83. Crewe's entire output in Division 4 during the previous season had been 29.

Managers (and Secretary-Managers)
W. C. McNeill 1892–94*, J. G. Hall 1895–96*, 1897 R. Roberts* (1st team sec.), J. B. Bromerley 1898–1911* (continued as Hon. Sec. to 1925), Tom Bailey 1925–38, George Lillicrop 1938–44, Frank Hill 1944–48, Arthur Turner 1948–51, Harry Catterick 1951–53, Ralph Ward 1953–55, Maurice Lindley 1955–58, Harry Ware 1958–60, Jimmy McGuigan 1960–64, Ernie Tagg 1964–71 (continued as secretary to 1972), Dennis Viollet 1971, Jimmy Melia 1972–73, Ernie Tagg 1974, Harry Gregg 1975–78, Warwick Rimmer 1978–79, Tony Waddington 1979–81, Arfon Griffiths 1981–82, Peter Morris 1982–83, Dario Gradi June 1983– .

Player and Position	Ht	Wt	Birth Date	Birth Place	Source	Clubs	League App	Gls
Steve Garvey	5 9	11 01	22 11 73	Tameside	Trainee	Crewe Alex	22	1
Andy Lyons	5 10	11 00	19 10 66	Blackpool	Fleetwood	Crewe Alex	9	2
David McKearney	5 10	11 02	20 6 68	Crosby		Bolton W	—	—
						Crewe Alex	108	12
Ahmed Mettioui‡	5 10	10 10	3 11 65	Tangier	Fath Union	Crewe Alex	3	—
Tony Naylor	5 8	10 08	29 3 67	Manchester	Droylsden	Crewe Alex	85	32
Steve Walters	5 10	11 08	9 1 72	Plymouth	Trainee	Crewe Alex	115	8
Ashley Ward	6 1	11 07	24 11 70	Manchester	Trainee	Manchester C	1	—
						Wrexham (loan)	4	2
						Leicester C	10	—
						Blackpool (loan)	2	1
						Crewe Alex	20	4

Trainees
Adebola, Dele; Byrne, Christopher; Chapman, Iain A; Fraser, Stuart A; Frawley, Andrew; Hawtin, Dale C; Hughes, Robert M; Meeson, Christopher; Ouslem, Joseph A; Rivers, Mark A; Watson, Melvin M; Williams, Carwyn.

**Non-Contract
McPhillips, Terence; Smith, Mark A.

Associated Schoolboys
Adams, Richard; Aimes, David; Bell, Christopher G; Bullock, Darren J; Challoner, Darren; Collins, James I; Connors, Christopher J; Critchely, Neil; Dungey, James A; Edwards, Gareth J; Gannon, Michael J; Hibbs, John R; Humphray, Darren J; Hyland, Mark J; Longman, David P; Mason, Philip; Morse, Peter R; Murray, David R; Owen, Gareth J; Parker, Justin N; Paylor, Richard; Percival, Christopher; Riley, Andrew S; Smith, Matthew; Smith, Peter L; Street, Kevin; Wainwright, Neil; Whittaker, David A; Wiggins, Nikolas; Williams, Geraint.

Associated Schoolboys who have accepted the club's offer of a Traineeship/Contract
Corcoran, Matthew L; Ellis, Duncan J; Murphy, Daniel B; Murray, Thomas O; Pope, Steven A; Simpson, Wesley L.

**Non-Contract Players who are retained must be re-signed before they are eligible to play in League matches.

CRYSTAL PALACE 1992-93 *Back row (left to right);* Darren Patterson, Paul Mortimer, Chris Coleman, Simon Osborn, John Humphrey.
Centre row: Chris Armstrong, Eric Young, Andy Woodman, Nigel Martyn, Andy Thorn, Lee Shinott.
Front row: Paul Williams, Eddie McGoldrick, Alan Smith, Steve Coppell, Richard Shaw, Gareth Southgate.

Division 1   CRYSTAL PALACE

Selhurst Park, London SE25 6PU. Telephone 081–653 1000. Lottery Office: 081–771 9502. Club Shop: 081–653 5584. Dial-A-Seat Ticketline 081 771 8841. Palace Publications: 081–771 8299. Fax: 081–653 6312. Palace clubline: 0891 400 333. Palace Ticket Line: 0891 400 334 (normal 0891 charges apply for these services).

Ground capacity: 29,225.

Record attendance: 51,482 v Burnley, Division 2, 11 May 1979.

Record receipts: £327,124 v Manchester U, FA Premier League, 21 April 1993 (League); £336,583 v Chelsea, Coca Cola Cup 5th rd, 6 January 1993.

Pitch measurements: 110yd × 74yd.

President: S. Stephenson.

Chairman: R. G. Noades.

Directors: R. G. Noades (Chairman and Managing), B. Coleman, A. S. C. De Souza, G. Geraghty, M. E. Lee, S. Hume-Kendall, P. H. J. Norman, R. E. Anderson, V. E. Murphy, C. L. Noades.

Team Manager: Alan Smith. *Coaches:* Steve Harrison, David Kemp and Dave Garland. *Physio:* David West. *Company Secretary:* Doug Miller. *Club Secretary:* Mike Hurst. *Assistant Secretary:* Terry Byfield. *Marketing Manager:* Tony Willis. *Year Formed:* 1905. *Turned Professional:* 1905. *Ltd Co.:* 1905. *Club Nickname:* 'The Eagles'. *Club Sponsor:* Tulip Computers. *Commercial Manager:* Graham Drew.

Previous Grounds: 1905, Crystal Palace; 1915, Herne Hill; 1918, The Nest; 1924, Selhurst Park.

Record League Victory: 9–0 v Barrow, Division 4, 10 October 1959 – Rouse; Long, Noakes; Truett, Evans, McNichol; Gavin (1), Summersby (4 incl. 1p), Sexton, Byrne (2), Colfar (2).

Record Cup Victory: 8–0 v Southend U, Rumbelows League Cup, 2nd rd (1st leg), 25 September 1990 – Martyn; Humphrey (Thompson (1)), Shaw, Pardew, Young, Thorn, McGoldrick, Thomas, Bright (3), Wright (3), Barber (Hodges (1)).

Record Defeat: 0–9 v Burnley, FA Cup, 2nd rd replay, 10 February 1909 and 0–9 v Liverpool, Division 1, 12 September 1990.

Most League Points (2 for a win): 64, Division 4, 1960–61.

Most League Points (3 for a win): 81, Division 2, 1988–89.

Most League Goals: 110, Division 4, 1960–61.

Highest League Scorer in Season: Peter Simpson, 46, Division 3 (S), 1930–31.

Most League Goals in Total Aggregate: Peter Simpson, 153, 1930–36.

Most Capped Player: Eric Young, 15 (16), Wales.

Most League Appearances: Jim Cannon, 571, 1973–88.

Record Transfer Fee Received: £2,500,000 from Arsenal for Ian Wright, September 1991.

Record Transfer Fee Paid: £1,800,000 to Sunderland for Marco Gabbiadini, September 1991.

Football League Record: 1920 Original Members of Division 3; 1921–25 Division 2; 1925–58 Division 3 (S); 1958–61 Division 4; 1961–64 Division 3; 1964–69 Division 2; 1969–73 Division 1; 1973–74 Division 2; 1974–77 Division 3; 1977–79 Division 2; 1979–81 Division 1; 1981–89 Division 2; 1989–92 Division 1; 1992–93 FA Premier League; 1993– Division 1.

Honours: Football League: Division 1 best season: 3rd 1990–91; Division 2 – Champions 1978–79; Runners-up 1968–69; Division 3 – Runners-up 1963–64; Division 3 (S) – Champions 1920–21; Runners-up 1928–29, 1930–31, 1938–39; Division 4 – Runners-up 1960–61. *FA Cup:* best season: Runners-up 1989–90. *Football League Cup:* best season; semi-final 1992–93. *Zenith Data System Cup:* Winners: 1991.

CRYSTAL PALACE 1992—93 LEAGUE RECORD

Match No.	Date	Venue	Opponents	Result	H/T Score	Lg. Pos.	Goalscorers	Attendance
1	Aug 15	H	Blackburn R	D 3-3	1-1	—	Bright, Southgate, Osborn	17,086
2	19	A	Oldham Ath	D 1-1	0-1	—	McGoldrick	11,063
3	22	A	Tottenham H	D 2-2	1-1	11	McGoldrick, Young	25,237
4	25	H	Sheffield W	D 1-1	1-0	—	Young	14,005
5	29	H	Norwich C	L 1-2	1-1	18	McGoldrick	12,033
6	Sept 2	A	Manchester U	L 0-1	0-0	—		29,736
7	5	A	Aston Villa	L 0-3	0-2	20		17,120
8	12	H	Oldham Ath	D 2-2	0-1	17	Armstrong 2	11,224
9	19	A	Everton	W 2-0	2-0	18	Armstrong 2	18,080
10	26	H	Southampton	L 1-2	0-1	21	Young	13,829
11	Oct 3	A	Coventry C	D 2-2	2-2	20	Coleman, McGoldrick	11,808
12	17	H	Manchester C	D 0-0	0-0	21		14,005
13	24	A	Ipswich T	D 2-2	0-0	18	Armstrong, Coleman	17,861
14	Nov 2	H	Arsenal	L 1-2	0-1	—	McGoldrick	20,287
15	7	A	Chelsea	L 1-3	0-2	21	Young	17,141
16	21	H	Nottingham F	D 1-1	1-0	21	Armstrong	15,330
17	28	A	Liverpool	L 0-5	0-3	21		36,380
18	Dec 5	H	Sheffield U	W 2-0	1-0	21	Armstrong, Southgate	12,361
19	12	H	QPR	W 3-1	0-1	21	McGoldrick 2, Armstrong	14,571
20	20	H	Leeds U	W 1-0	1-0	—	Thorn	14,462
21	26	H	Wimbledon	W 2-0	2-0	17	Coleman, Thomas	16,825
22	28	A	Middlesbrough	W 1-0	0-0	15	Osborn	21,123
23	Jan 9	H	Everton	L 0-2	0-0	16		13,227
24	16	A	Southampton	L 0-1	0-0	18		13,397
25	27	A	Norwich C	L 2-4	2-2	—	Armstrong, Thomas	13,543
26	30	H	Tottenham H	L 1-3	0-3	19	Ruddock (og)	20,937
27	Feb 2	A	Blackburn R	W 2-1	1-1	—	Armstrong, Rodger	14,163
28	10	A	Aston Villa	W 1-0	1-0	—	Bowry	12,270
29	20	A	Sheffield W	L 1-2	0-1	17	Armstrong	26,459
30	27	H	Coventry C	D 0-0	0-0	17		12,248
31	Mar 3	A	Nottingham F	D 1-1	1-1	—	Southgate	20,603
32	15	A	Chelsea	D 1-1	1-1	—	Armstrong	12,610
33	20	A	Sheffield U	W 1-0	1-0	18	Coleman	18,857
34	23	H	Liverpool	D 1-1	0-0	—	Armstrong	18,688
35	Apr 3	H	QPR	D 1-1	0-1	18	Bardsley (og)	14,705
36	9	A	Wimbledon	L 0-4	0-2	—		12,275
37	12	H	Middlesbrough	W 4-1	0-0	18	Rodger, Young, Armstrong, Coleman	15,123
38	17	A	Leeds U	D 0-0	0-0	18		27,545
39	21	H	Manchester U	L 0-2	0-0	—		30,115
40	May 1	H	Ipswich T	W 3-1	2-1	18	Young, Armstrong, McGoldrick	18,881
41	5	A	Manchester C	D 0-0	0-0	—		21,167
42	8	A	Arsenal	L 0-3	0-1	20		25,225

Final League Position: 20

GOALSCORERS

League (48): Armstrong 15, McGoldrick 8, Young 6, Coleman 5, Southgate 3, Osborn 2, Rodger 2, Thomas 2, Bowry 1, Bright 1, Thorn 1, own goals 2.
Coca Cola Cup (13): Coleman 2, McGoldrick 2, Salako 2, Southgate 2, Watts 2, Ndah 1, Osborn 1 (pen), Thorn 1.
FA Cup (0).

Martyn 42	Humphrey 28 + 4	Shaw 32 + 1	Southgate 33	Young 38	Thorn 34	Coleman 31 + 7	Thomas 28 + 1	Bright 5	Salako 12 + 1	McGoldrick 42	Rodger 22 + 1	Osborn 27 + 4	Sinnott 18 + 1	Gordon 6 + 4	Armstrong 35	Massey — + 1	Williams 15 + 3	Collymore — + 2	Mortimer 1	Ndah 4 + 9	Bowry 6 + 5	Watts 2 + 2	Newman 1 + 1	Match No.
1	2	3	4	5	6	7	8	9	10	11	12	14												1
1	2	3	4	5	6	7	8		10	11			9	12										2
1	2	3	4	5	6	7	8			11			9	10										3
1	2	3	4	5	6	7	8	9		11				10										4
1	2		4	5	6	7	8	9	12	11			14	3	10									5
1	12		4	5	6		8	9	10	11			2	3	7									6
1	2		4	5		12	8	9	10	11			6	3	7	14								7
1	2		4	5		12	8		10	11			6	3	9		7							8
1	2		4	5			8		10	11			6	3	9		7							9
1	2		4	5			8		10	11			6	3	9		7	12						10
1	2		4	5			8		10	11			6	3	9		7							11
1	2		4	5			8		10	11			6	3	9		7	12						12
1	2		4	5			8		10	11			6	3	9		7							13
1	2		4	5	6	14	12		10	11			7	3	9	8								14
1	2		4	5	6	12			10	11			7	3	9	8								15
1	2	3	4	5	6	12				11			7		9	8	10							16
1	2	3	4	5	6	12				11			7	8	9	10			14					17
1	2	3	4	5	6	10				11			7		9		8	12						18
1	2	3	4	5	6	10				11			7		9		8	12	14					19
1	2	3	4	5	6			8		11	10	7			9		12							20
1	2	3	4	5	6	7	8			11	10	12			9									21
1	2	3		5	6	4	8			11	10	7			9		12							22
1	2			5	6	4	8			11	10				9		14	3	7	12				23
1	2				6	4	8			11	10		3	14	9		7	12	5					24
1	2	3			6	4	8			11	10	7	5		9		12							25
1		3		5	6	4	8			11	10	7	2		9		12							26
1	2			5	6	4				11	10	7	3		9		8							27
1	12	3		5	6	4	8			11	10	7			9		14		2					28
1	2	3		5	6	12				11	10	7			9		8		4					29
1	2	3		5	6	4	8			11	10				9		12	7						30
1	12	2		5	6	4	8			11	10		3		9		14	7						31
1	2	12	3	5		4	8			11	10	7		6	9		14							32
1	2	3		5	6	4	8			11	10	7			9									33
1	2	3		5	6	4	8			11	10	7			9		12							34
1	2	3			6	4	8			11	10	7		12	9		5							35
1	12	2	3		6	4	8			11	10	7		5	9			14						36
1	7	2	3	5	6	4	8			11	10		12		9	14								37
1	7	2	3	5	6	4	8			11	10	12			9									38
1	7	2	3	5	6	4				11		10			9		12		8					39
1	7	2	3	5	6	4	8			11	10				9		12							40
1	7	2	3	5	6			8		11	10				9	4								41
1	7	2	3	5	6			8		11	10			12	9	4								42

Coca Cola Cup	Second Round	Lincoln C (h)	3-1	
		(a)	1-1	
	Third Round	Southampton (a)	2-0	
	Fourth Round	Liverpool (a)	1-1	
		(h)	2-1	
	Fifth Round	Chelsea (h)	3-1	
	Semi-Final	Arsenal (h)	1-3	
		(a)	0-2	
FA Cup	Third Round	Hartlepool U (a)	0-1	

CRYSTAL PALACE

Player and Position	Ht	Wt	Date	Birth Place	Source	Clubs	League App	Gls
Goalkeepers								
James Glass	6 01	11 10	1 8 73	Epsom	Trainee	Crystal Palace	—	—
Nigel Martyn	6 2	14 00	11 8 66	St Austell	St Blazey	Bristol R	101	—
						Crystal Palace	143	—
Andrew Woodman	6 1	12 04	11 8 71	Denmark Hill	Trainee	Crystal Palace	—	—
Defenders								
John Budden*	6 1	12 06	17 7 71	Croydon		Crystal Palace	—	—
Chris Coleman	6 2	12 10	10 6 70	Swansea	Apprentice	Swansea C	160	2
						Crystal Palace	56	9
Russell Edwards	6 2	12 07	21 12 73	Beckenham	Local	Crystal Palace	—	—
John Humphrey	5 10	11 03	31 1 61	Paddington	Apprentice	Wolverhampton W	149	3
						Charlton Ath	194	3
						Crystal Palace	107	1
Darren Patterson	6 2	11 10	15 10 69	Belfast	Trainee	WBA	—	—
						Wigan Ath	97	6
						Crystal Palace	—	—
Simon Rodger	5 9	11 07	3 10 71	Shoreham	Trainee	Crystal Palace	45	2
Richard Shaw	5 9	11 08	11 9 68	Brentford	Apprentice	Crystal Palace	117	1
						Hull C (loan)	4	—
Lee Sinnott	6 1	12 07	12 7 65	Pelsall	Apprentice	Walsall	40	2
						Watford	78	2
						Bradford C	173	6
						Crystal Palace	55	—
Eric Smith	6 2	12 08	20 10 75	Dublin	Trainee	Crystal Palace	—	—
Gareth Southgate	5 10	11 12	3 9 70	Watford	Trainee	Crystal Palace	64	3
Andy Thorn	6 0	11 05	12 11 66	Carshalton	Apprentice	Wimbledon	107	2
						Newcastle U	36	2
						Crystal Palace	118	3
Eric Young	6 2	13 00	25 3 60	Singapore	Slough T	Brighton	126	10
						Wimbledon	99	9
						Crystal Palace	102	10
Midfield								
Bobby Bowry	5 8	10 00	19 5 71	Croydon		Crystal Palace	11	1
Dean Gordon	6 0	11 05	10 2 73	Croydon		Crystal Palace	14	—
Mark Hawthorne	5 9	10 12	31 10 73	Glasgow	Trainee	Crystal Palace	—	—
Mark Holman	5 11	12 04	29 10 73	Croydon	Trainee	Crystal Palace	—	—
Eddie McGoldrick	5 10	12 00	30 4 65	London	Kettering T	Northampton T	107	9
						Crystal Palace	147	11
Stuart Massey	5 10	10 10	17 11 64	Crawley	Sutton U	Crystal Palace	1	—
Paul Mortimer	5 11	11 03	8 5 68	London	Fulham	Charlton Ath	113	17
						Aston Villa	12	1
						Crystal Palace	22	2
						Brentford (loan)	6	—
George Ndah	6 1	10 00	23 12 74	Camberwell	Trainee	Crystal Palace	13	—
Ricky Newman	5 10	11 00	5 8 70	Guildford		Crystal Palace	2	—
						Maidstone U (loan)	10	1
Martyn O'Connor	5 8	10 08	10 12 67	Walsall	Bromsgrove R	Crystal Palace	—	—
						Walsall (loan)	10	1
Simon Osborn	5 10	11 04	19 1 72	New Addington	Apprentice	Crystal Palace	49	4
Geoff Thomas	5 10	10 07	5 8 64	Manchester	Local	Rochdale	11	1
						Crewe Alex	125	20
						Crystal Palace	195	26

CRYSTAL PALACE

Colours: Red and blue shirts, red shorts, red stockings. **Change colours:** White shirts with red & royal random print on sleeve, white shorts with red & royal random print on seams, white stockings.

Foundation: There was a Crystal Palace club as early as 1861 but the present organisation was born in 1905 after the formation of a club by the company that controlled the Crystal Palace (the building that is), had been rejected by the FA who did not like the idea of the Cup Final hosts running their own club. A separate company had to be formed and they had their home on the old Cup Final ground until 1915.

First Football League game: 28 August, 1920, Division 3, v Merthyr T (a) L 1-2 – Alderson; Little, Rhodes; McCracken, Jones, Feebury; Bateman, Conner, Smith, Milligan (1), Whibley.

Did you know: Crystal Palace played Real Madrid in a friendly at Selhurst Park on 18 April 1962 to inaugurate the club's new floodlights. Despite heavy rain a crowd of 25,000 saw the Spaniards win 4-3.

Managers (and Secretary-Managers)
John T. Robson 1905–07, Edmund Goodman 1907–25 (had been secretary since 1905 and afterwards continued in this position to 1933). Alec Maley 1925–27, Fred Maven 1927–30, Jack Tresadern 1930–35, Tom Bromilow 1935–36, R. S. Moyes 1936, Tom Bromilow 1936–39, George Irwin 1939–47, Jack Butler 1947–49, Ronnie Rooke 1949–50, Charlie Slade and Fred Dawes (joint managers) 1950–51, Laurie Scott 1951–54, Cyril Spiers 1954–58, George Smith 1958–60, Arthur Rowe 1960–62, Dick Graham 1962–66, Bert Head 1966–72 (continued as GM to 1973), Malcolm Allison 1973–76, Terry Venables 1976–80, Ernie Walley 1980, Malcolm Allison 1980–81, Dario Gradi 1981, Steve Kember 1981–82, Alan Mullery 1982–84, Steve Coppell 1984–93, Alan Smith June 1993–.

Player and Position	Ht	Wt	Date	Birth Place	Source	Clubs	League App	Gls
Forwards								
Chris Armstrong	6 0	11 00	19 6 71	Newcastle		Wrexham	60	13
						Millwall	28	5
						Crystal Palace	35	15
Andy Barnes	5 11	12 06	31 3 67	Croydon	Sutton U	Crystal Palace	1	—
John Salako	5 9	11 00	11 2 69	Nigeria.	Trainee	Crystal Palace	138	10
						Swansea C (loan)	13	3
Niall Thompson	5 11	11 00	16 4 74	Birmingham	Trainee	Crystal Palace	—	—
Grant Watts	6 0	11 02	5 11 73	Croydon	Trainee	Crystal Palace	4	—
David Whyte	5 9	10 06	20 4 71	Greenwich		Crystal Palace	11	1
						Charlton Ath (loan)	8	2
Paul Williams	5 7	10 03	16 8 65	London	Woodford T	Charlton Ath	82	23
						Brentford (loan)	7	3
						Sheffield W	93	25
						Crystal Palace	18	—

Trainees
Charlton, Paul; Clark, Timothy J; Daly, Sean F; Dixon, Edward J; Hall, Kevin; Little, Glen; Roberts, Christopher; Rourke, Marcus P; Sparrow, Paul; Stokoe, Paul D; Vincent, Jamie R.

Associated Schoolboys
Barnard, Dean; Cowie, Stuart; Craze, Neil; Davies, Paul C; Field, Gary; Freeman, Andrew; Gilbert, Adam L; Hamilton, Brian; Henderson, Mark; Ivett, James G; Monger, Adam J; Neville, Ben A. W; Parry, David M; Robertson, Simon; Sherling, William; Smith, Rory D; Spencer, Marcus W; Williams, Ceri J.

Associated Schoolboys who have accepted the club's offer of a Traineeship/Contract
Bell, Stuart J; Harris, Jason A; Mannering, Peter C; Quinn, Robert J.

194

DARLINGTON 1992-93 *Back row (left to right):* Anthony Isaacs, Simon Shaw, Mark Prudhoe, Adrian Swan, Stephen Ball, Alan Dowson.
Centre row: Tim Parkin, Steve Tupling, Gary Hinchley, Sean Gregan, Kevan Smith, Steve O'Shaughnessy, Richard Cooper, Nick Pickering, Billy McEwan (Manager).
Front row: Clive Middlemass (Youth Team Coach), Andy Toman, Steve Mardenborough, Steve Gaughan, Mark Sunley, Lee Ellison, Mark Dobie, Nigel Carnell (Physio).

Division 3   **DARLINGTON**

Feethams Ground, Darlington. Telephone Darlington (0325) 465097. Fax (0325) 381377.

Ground capacity: 10,113.

Record attendance: 21,023 v Bolton W, League Cup 3rd rd, 14 November 1960.

Record receipts: £32,300 v Rochdale, Division 4, 11 May 1991.

Pitch measurements: 110yd × 74yd.

President: A. Noble.

Chairman: J. Brockbank. *Vice-chairman:* B. Lowery.

Directors: R. Tonks, S. Brockbank, G. Hampton, G. Hodgson, S. Weeks.

Manager: Billy McEwan. *Chief Executive:* T. D. Hughes.

Secretary: Brian Anderson. *Commercial Manager:* Keith Agar. *Physio:* Nigel Carnell.

Year Formed: 1883. *Turned Professional:* 1908. *Ltd Co.:* 1891.

Club Nickname: 'The Quakers'.

Record League Victory: 9–2 v Lincoln C, Division 3 (N), 7 January 1928 – Archibald; Brooks, Mellen; Kelly, Waugh, McKinnell; Cochrane (1), Gregg (1), Ruddy (3), Lees (3), McGiffen (1).

Record Cup Victory: 7–2 v Evenwood T, FA Cup, 1st rd, 17 November 1956 – Ward; Devlin, Henderson; Bell (1p), Greener, Furphy; Forster (1), Morton (3), Tulip (2), Davis, Moran.

Record Defeat: 0–10 v Doncaster R, Division 4, 25 January 1964.

Most League Points (2 for a win): 59, Division 4, 1965–66.

Most League Points (3 for a win): 85, Division 4, 1984–85.

Most League Goals: 108, Division 3 (N), 1929–30.

Highest League Scorer in Season: David Brown, 39, Division 3 (N), 1924–25.

Most League Goals in Total Aggregate: Alan Walsh, 90, 1978–84.

Most Capped Player: None.

Most League Appearances: Ron Greener, 442, 1955–68.

Record Transfer Fee Received: £200,000 from Leicester C for Jim Willis, December 1991.

Record Transfer Fee Paid: £95,000 to Motherwell for Nick Cusack, January 1992.

Football League Record: 1921 Original Member Division 3 (N); 1925–27 Division 2; 1927–58 Division 3 (N); 1958–66 Division 4; 1966–67 Division 3; 1967–85 Division 4; 1985–87 Division 3; 1987–89 Division 4; 1989–90 GM Vauxhall Conference; 1990–91 Division 4; 1991– Division 3.

Honours: Football League: Division 2 best season: 15th, 1925–26; Division 3 (N) – Champions 1924–25; Runners-up 1921–22; Division 4 Champions 1990–91 – Runners-up 1965–66. *FA Cup:* best season: 3rd rd, 1910–11, 5th rd, 1957–58. *Football League Cup:* best season: 5th rd, 1967–68. GM Vauxhall Conference Champions 1989–90.

DARLINGTON 1992—93 LEAGUE RECORD

Match No.	Date	Venue	Opponents	Result	H/T Score	Lg. Pos.	Goalscorers	Atten dance
1	Aug 15	A	Cardiff C	D 0-0	0-0	—		8399
2	21	H	Hereford U	L 0-1	0-0	—		1730
3	29	A	Colchester U	W 3-0	1-0	8	Shaw, Juryeff, Dobson	3524
4	Sept 1	A	Chesterfield	L 0-2	0-1	—		2673
5	5	H	Crewe Alex	W 3-0	1-0	7	Hinchley, Pickering, Juryeff	2037
6	15	A	Halifax T	L 0-1	0-1	—		1287
7	19	A	Rochdale	L 1-3	1-0	19	Mardenborough	1854
8	25	H	York C	L 0-1	0-0	—		3787
9	Oct 2	H	Torquay U	W 4-1	0-1	—	Dobie (pen), Parkin, Mardenborough, Toman	1423
10	10	A	Shrewsbury T	W 2-1	1-0	11	Ball, Mardenborough	2829
11	17	H	Scarborough	L 2-3	1-1	16	Dobie, Juryeff	2474
12	31	H	Lincoln C	L 1-3	0-3	20	Dobson	2051
13	Nov 3	A	Northampton T	W 2-1	1-0	—	Mardenborough, Ball	1991
14	7	H	Bury	D 0-0	0-0	16		1895
15	21	A	Gillingham	L 1-3	1-2	18	Green (og)	2563
16	28	H	Barnet	W 1-0	0-0	15	Juryeff	1763
17	Dec 12	A	Walsall	D 2-2	2-0	16	Methven (og), Mardenborough	3002
18	19	H	Scunthorpe U	D 2-2	1-0	17	Gregan, Dobie	1801
19	28	A	Doncaster R	W 1-0	0-0	15	Dobie	2878
20	Jan 2	A	Barnet	D 0-0	0-0	13		3437
21	9	H	Halifax T	L 0-3	0-1	15		1984
22	12	H	Carlisle U	D 1-1	1-1	—	Juryeff	1596
23	16	A	York C	D 0-0	0-0	15		3563
24	23	H	Rochdale	L 0-4	0-3	16		1710
25	30	A	Hereford U	D 1-1	1-1	16	Mardenborough	2000
26	Feb 6	H	Cardiff C	L 0-2	0-0	16		1775
27	13	A	Crewe Alex	L 0-1	0-0	16		2953
28	20	H	Chesterfield	D 1-1	0-0	16	Parkin	1366
29	27	H	Shrewsbury T	L 0-2	0-1	17		1422
30	Mar 6	A	Torquay U	W 2-0	1-0	16	O'Shaughnessy, Mardenborough	3147
31	9	H	Wrexham	D 1-1	1-0	—	Dobie	1597
32	13	A	Bury	D 1-1	0-0	16	Gaughan	2879
33	20	H	Northampton T	W 3-1	0-0	15	Isaacs, Pickering, Dobie	2106
34	27	H	Gillingham	D 1-1	0-0	15	Reed	2404
35	Apr 2	A	Wrexham	D 1-1	1-1	—	Shaw	6972
36	6	H	Walsall	L 1-2	0-1	—	Shaw	1739
37	10	A	Carlisle U	D 2-2	1-2	16	Dobie, Juryeff	3297
38	12	H	Doncaster R	L 1-2	1-0	18	Mardenborough	2218
39	17	A	Scunthorpe U	W 3-1	1-1	15	Shaw, Mardenborough 2	2774
40	24	A	Scarborough	W 3-0	2-0	15	Hirst (og), Dobie, Mardenborough	1733
41	May 4	H	Colchester U	W 1-0	1-0	—	Reed	2007
42	8	A	Lincoln C	L 0-2	0-2	15		3107

Final League Position: 15

GOALSCORERS

League (48): Mardenborough 11, Dobie 8 (1 pen), Juryeff 6, Shaw 4, Ball 2, Dobson 2, Parkin 2, Pickering 2, Reed 2, Gaughan 1, Gregan 1, Hinchley 1, Isaacs 1, O'Shaughnessy 1, Toman 1, own goals 3.
Coca Cola Cup (1): Mardenborough 1.
FA Cup (1): Dobie 1.

Prudhoe 42	Hinchley 7	Dowson 30 + 2	Gaughan 34 + 3	Parkin 40	Gregan 15 + 2	Pickering 28	Toman 22 + 7	Ellison 2 + 1	Dobie 35 + 1	Mardenborough 41 + 1	Ball 15 + 7	O'Shaughnessy 41	Shaw 19 + 4	Tupling 8 + 3	Isaacs 17 + 5	Juryeff 25 + 8	Dobson 4 + 10	Fickling 14	Sunley 2	Smith 13	Reed 8 + 2	Maddick — + 1	Match No.
1	2	3	4	5	6	7	8	9	10	11	12												1
1	2	3	4	5			8		10	9	11	6	7	12	14								2
1	2	11	4	5			8			7	3	6	10	12		9	14						3
1	2	11	4	5			8			7	3	6	10	12		9	14						4
1	2	11	4	5		3	8			7		6	12			9	10						5
1	2	11	4	5		3	8			7		6	12			9	10						6
1	2	11	4	5		3	8			7		6	10			9	12						7
1		11	4	5	7	3	8		10	14	12	6		2		9							8
1		11	4	5		3	8		10	14		6	7	2		9	12						9
1			4	5	11	3	8		10	14		6	7	2		9	12						10
1			4	5	11	3	8		10	14		6	7	2		9	12						11
1			4	5	14	3	8		12	7	11	6		2		9	10						12
1	12		4	5	7				10	11	3	6		2	8	9							13
1			4	5	7				10	11	3	6		2	8	9							14
1		8	5	4	3				10	7	11	6		2	14	9	12						15
1		11	5	4	3		8	9	10	7		6				12				2			16
1		11	5	4	3		8		10	7		6			14	9	12			2			17
1		11	5	4	3		8		10	7		6			14	9	12			2			18
1		11	12	5	4	3	8		10	7		6				9				2			19
1		11		5	4	3	8		10	7		6				9				2			20
1		11	14	5	4	3	8		10	7		6				9	12			2			21
1		11		5	4	3	8		10	7		6				9				2			22
1		11	4	5		3	8		10	7		6				9				2			23
1		11	8	5	4	3	14		10	7		6		12		9				2			24
1		11	4	5		3	8	9		7		6	10			12				2			25
1	12			5		3	14		10	7		6	8		11	9				2	4		26
1		11	9	5	14	3			10	7		6	8		4	12				2			27
1		8		5		3			10	7	12	6			11	9				2	4		28
1	14	8	5		3				10	7		6	12		11	9			2		4		29
1	11	8	5		3		12			7		6	2		10	9					4		30
1	11	8	5		3			9	7	14		6	2		10	12					4		31
1	11	8	5		3			9	7	12		6	2		10						4		32
1	11	8	5		3			9	7			6	2		10						4	12	33
1		2	5		8		9	10	3	6	11			4	12						7		34
1	10				8		9	11	3	6	2			4							5	7	35
1	10				8		9	11	3	6	2			4	12						5	7	36
1	11	10	4			9	7	3	6	2			8	12							5	14	37
1	3	2	4		8	10	7	14	6	12			9								5	11	38
1	3	11	4			10	9		6	2	8			5	7								39
1	11	2	4		14	10	9	3	6	8		12			5	7							40
1	3	11	4			10	9	12	6	2	8			5	7								41
1	3	11	4			10	9	12	6	2	8			5	7	14							42

Coca Cola Cup	First Round	Scunthorpe U (h)	1-1
		(a)	0-2
FA Cup	First Round	Hull C (h)	1-2

DARLINGTON

Player and Position	Ht	Wt	Date	Birth Place	Source	Clubs	League App	Gls
Goalkeepers								
Mark Prudhoe	6 0	13 00	8 11 63	Washington	Apprentice	Sunderland	7	—
						Hartlepool U (loan)	3	—
						Birmingham C	1	—
						Walsall	26	—
						Doncaster R (loan)	5	—
						Sheffield W (loan)	—	—
						Grimsby T (loan)	8	—
						Hartlepool U (loan)	13	—
						Bristol C (loan)	3	—
						Carlisle U	34	—
						Darlington	146	—
Adrian Swan*			31 7 73	Middlesbrough		Darlington	—	—
Defenders								
Steve Ball	5 7	11 00	22 11 73	Leeds	Leeds U	Darlington	22	2
Richard Cooper*	6 2	12 00	11 11 73	Middlesbrough	Trainee	Darlington	—	—
Alan Dowson	5 10	11 02	17 6 70	Gateshead	Trainee	Millwall	1	—
						Fulham (loan)	4	—
						Bradford C	18	—
						Darlington	32	—
Sean Gregan	6 2	13 7	29 3 74	Cleveland		Darlington	34	1
Gary Hinchley*	6 0	12 07	14 11 68	Guisborough		Darlington	14	—
					Guisborough	Darlington	13	1
Steve O'Shaughnessy	6 2	13 01	13 10 67	Wrexham		Leeds U	—	—
						Bradford C	1	—
						Rochdale	109	16
						Exeter C	3	—
						Darlington	56	2
Tim Parkin*	6 2	13 02	31 12 57	Penrith	Apprentice	Blackburn R	13	—
					Malmo and	Bristol R	206	12
					Almondsbury	Swindon T	110	6
					Greenway	Port Vale	48	1
						Shrewsbury T (loan)	5	—
						Darlington	40	2
Kevan Smith*	6 3	12 07	13 12 59	Eaglescliffe	Stockton	Darlington	245	11
						Rotherham U	59	4
						Coventry C	6	—
						York C	31	5
						Darlington	98	5
						Hereford U (loan)	6	—
Mark Sunley	6 1	12 07	13 10 71	Stockton		Middlesbrough	—	—
						Darlington	17	—
Midfield								
Steve Gaughan	5 11	11 02	14 4 70	Doncaster		Doncaster R	67	3
						Sunderland	—	—
						Darlington	57	1
Tony Isaacs	5 8	10 07	8 4 73	Middlesbrough		Darlington	31	1
Kevin Maddick‡			18 9 74	Newcastle	Trainee	Darlington	1	—
Simon Shaw	6 0	12 00	21 9 73	Teeside	Trainee	Darlington	24	4
Andy Toman	5 10	11 07	7 3 62	Northallerton	Bishop	Lincoln C	24	4
					Auckland	Hartlepool U	112	28
						Darlington	115	10
						Scarborough (loan)	6	—
Steve Tupling‡	6 0	11 03	11 7 64	Wensleydale	Apprentice	Middlesbrough	—	—
						Carlisle U (loan)	1	—
						Darlington	111	8
						Newport Co	33	2
						Cardiff C	5	—
						Torquay U (loan)	3	—
						Exeter C (loan)	9	1

DARLINGTON

Colours: Black and white. **Change colours:** All red.

Foundation: A football club was formed in Darlington as early as 1861 but the present club began in 1883 and reached the final of the Durham Senior Cup in their first season, losing to Sunderland in a replay after complaining that they had suffered from intimidation in the first. The following season Darlington won this trophy and for many years were one of the leading amateur clubs in their area.

First Football League game: 27 August, 1921, Division 3(N), v Halifax T (h) W 2-0 – Ward; Greaves, Barbour; Dickson (1), Sutcliffe, Malcolm; Dolphin, Hooper (1), Edmunds, Wolstenholme, Winship.

Did you know: Darlington won the championship of Division 3 (N) in 1924–25 with a team costing only £80 in transfer fees, which went on one player, David Brown from Kilmarnock who became their leading scorer.

Managers (and Secretary-Managers)
Tom McIntosh 1902–11, W. L. Lane 1911–12*, Dick Jackson 1912–19, Jack English 1919–28, Jack Fairless 1928–33, George Collins 1933–36, George Brown 1936–38, Jackie Carr 1938–42, Jack Surtees 1942, Jack English 1945–46, Bill Forrest 1946–50, George Irwin 1950–52, Bob Gurney 1952–57, Dick Duckworth 1957–60, Eddie Carr 1960–64, Lol Morgan 1964–66, Jimmy Greenhalgh 1966–68, Ray Yeoman 1968–70, Len Richley 1970–71, Frank Brennan 1971, Ken Hale 1971–72, Allan Jones 1972, Ralph Brand 1972–73, Dick Conner 1973–74, Billy Horner 1974–76, Peter Madden 1976–78, Len Walker 1978–79, Billy Elliott 1979–83, Cyril Knowles 1983–87, Dave Booth 1987–89, Brian Little 1989–91, Frank Gray 1991–92, Ray Hankin 1992, Billy McEwan July 1992–.

Player and Position	Ht	Wt	Date	Birth Place	Source	Clubs	League App	Gls
						Hartlepool U	89	3
						Darlington	11	—
Forwards								
Mark Dobie	5 11	11 07	8 11 63	Carlisle	Gretna	Cambridge U	—	—
						Torquay U	20	2
						Darlington	36	8
Paul Dobson‡	5 11	10 02	17 12 62	Hartlepool	Newcastle U Horden	Hartlepool U	111	32
						Torquay U	77	38
						Doncaster R	24	10
						Scarborough	61	22
						Halifax T (loan)	1	1
						Hereford U (loan)	6	1
						Lincoln C	21	5
						Darlington	14	2
Tony Ellison	6 0	12 00	13 1 73	Bishop Auckland	Trainee	Darlington	43	13
						Hartlepool U (loan)	4	1
Ian Juryeff	5 11	12 0	24 11 62	Gosport	Apprentice Sweden	Southampton	—	—
						Southampton	2	—
						Mansfield T (loan)	12	5
						Reading (loan)	7	1
						Orient	111	44
						Ipswich T (loan)	2	—
						Halifax T	17	7
						Hereford U	28	4
						Halifax T	72	13
						Darlington	33	6
Steve Mardenborough	5 8	11 09	11 9 64	Birmingham	Apprentice	Coventry C	—	—
						Wolverhampton W	9	1
						Cambridge U (loan)	6	—
						Swansea C	36	7
						Newport Co	64	11
						Cardiff C	32	1
						Hereford U	27	—
						Darlington	106	18

Trainees
Bean, Michael; Blake, Robert J; Carter, Stuart; Casey, Mark; Cimmermann, Mathew J; Cooper, Paul; Hack, Benjamin C; McGlynn, David; Middleton, James; Reed, Adam M; Ripley, Andrew I; Robinson, Carl; Scollett, Matthew; Scott, Ryan; Theakstone, Justin.

Associated Schoolboys
Key, Daniel C; Morgan, Lee; Taylor, Neil V.

Associated Schoolboys who have accepted the club's offer of a Traineeship/Contract
Trees, Steven R.

200

DERBY COUNTY 1992–93 *Back row (left to right):* Roy MacFarland (Assistant Manager), Mark Stallard, Ted McMinn, Michael Forsyth, Andy Comyn, Steven Sutton, Simon Coleman, Justin Phillips, Martin Taylor, Darren Wassall, Shane Nicholson, Paul Williams, Jason Kavanagh, Gordon Guthrie (Physio).
Front row: Paul Simpson, Gary Micklewhite, Craig Ramage, Marco Gabbiadini, Paul Kitson, Arthur Cox (Manager), Mark Pembridge, Tommy Johnson, Steve Hayward, Steve Round, Martyn Chalk.

Division 1   **DERBY COUNTY**

Baseball Ground, Shaftesbury Crescent, Derby DE3 8NB.
Telephone Derby (0332) 40105. Fax 0332 293514. Ramtique
Sports Shop: (0332) 292081. Clubcall: 0891 121187.

Ground capacity: 22,700 (15,000 seated).

Record attendance: 41,826 v Tottenham H, Division 1,
20 September 1969.

Record receipts: £146,651 v Aston Villa, FA Cup 4th rd, 5
February 1992.

Pitch measurements: 110yd × 71yd.

President:

Chairman: B. E. Fearn. ***Vice-chairman:*** L. V. Pickering.

Directors: C. W. McKerrow, W. Hart, J. N. Kirkland, A. Cox, M. Mills, M. Horton.

Manager: Arthur Cox. ***Assistant Manager:*** Roy McFarland.

Physio: Gordon Guthrie.

Secretary/General Manager: Michael Dunford. ***Commercial Manager:*** Colin Tunnicliffe.

Year Formed: 1884. ***Turned Professional:*** 1884. ***Ltd Co.:*** 1896.

Club Nickname: 'The Rams'.

Previous Grounds: 1884–95, Racecourse Ground; 1895, Baseball Ground.

Record League Victory: 9–0 v Wolverhampton W, Division 1, 10 January 1891 – Bunyan;
Archie Goodall, Roberts; Walker, Chalmers, Roulston (1); Bakewell, McLachlan, Johnny
Goodall (1), Holmes (2), McMillan (5). 9–0 v Sheffield W, Division 1, 21 January 1899 –
Fryer; Methven, Staley; Cox, Archie Goodall, May; Oakden (1), Bloomer (6), Boag,
McDonald (1), Allen. (1 og).

Record Cup Victory: 12–0 v Finn Harps, UEFA Cup, 1st rd 1st leg, 15 September 1976 –
Moseley; Thomas, Nish, Rioch (1), McFarland, Todd (King), Macken, Gemmill, Hector
(5), George (3), James (3).

Record Defeat: 2–11 v Everton, FA Cup 1st rd, 1889–90.

Most League Points (2 for a win): 63, Division 2, 1968–69 and Division 3 (N), 1955–56 and
1956–57.

Most League Points (3 for a win): 84, Division 3, 1985–86 and Division 3, 1986–87.

Most League Goals: 111, Division 3 (N), 1956–57.

Highest League Scorer in Season: Jack Bowers, 37, Division 1, 1930–31 and Ray Straw, 37
Division 3 (N), 1956–57.

Most League Goals in Total Aggregate: Steve Bloomer, 292, 1892–1906 and 1910–14.

Most Capped Player: Peter Shilton, 34 (125), England.

Most League Appearances: Kevin Hector, 486, 1966–78 and 1980–82.

Record Transfer Fee Received: £2,900,000 from Liverpool for Dean Saunders, July 1991.

Record Transfer Fee Paid: £2,500,000 to Notts Co for Craig Short, September 1992.

Football League Record: 1888 Founder Member of the Football League; 1907–12 Division
2; 1912–14 Division 1; 1914–15 Division 2; 1915–21 Division 1; 1921–26 Division 2; 1926–
53 Division 1; 1953–55 Division 2; 1955–57 Division 3 (N); 1957–69 Division 2; 1969–80
Division 1; 1980–84 Division 2; 1984–86 Division 3; 1986–87 Division 2; 1987–91 Division
1; 1991–92 Division 2; 1992– Division 1.

Honours: *Football League:* Division 1 – Champions 1971–72, 1974–75; Runners-up 1895–
96, 1929–30, 1935–36; Division 2 – Champions 1911–12, 1914–15, 1968–69, 1986–87;
Runners-up 1925–26; Division 3 (N) Champions 1956–57; Runners-up 1955–56. *FA Cup:*
Winners 1945–46; Runners-up 1897–98, 1898–99, 1902–03. *Football League Cup:* Semi-final
1967–68. *Texaco Cup:* 1971–72. **European Competitions:** *European Cup:* 1972–73, 1975–76;
UEFA Cup: 1974–75, 1976–77. *Anglo-Italian Cup:* Runners-up 1992–93.

DERBY COUNTY 1992—93 LEAGUE RECORD

Match No.	Date		Venue	Opponents	Result	H/T Score	Lg. Pos.	Goalscorers	Atten dance
1	Aug	15	A	Peterborough U	L 0-1	0-0	—		9955
2		22	H	Newcastle U	L 1-2	0-0	20	Pembridge	17,522
3		26	A	Leicester C	L 2-3	1-2	—	Simpson 2	17,739
4		29	A	Watford	D 0-0	0-0	20		9809
5	Sept	6	H	Bristol C	L 3-4	2-1		Simpson 3	12,738
6		12	A	Barnsley	D 1-1	0-0	23	Kitson	8412
7		20	A	West Ham U	D 1-1	1-0	—	Miklosko (og)	11,493
8		26	H	Southend U	W 2-0	0-0	22	Gabbiadini, Simpson (pen)	15,172
9	Oct	3	A	Cambridge U	W 3-1	0-0	16	Simpson 2 (1 pen), Gabbiadini	6170
10		11	H	Oxford U	L 0-1	0-0	—		14,249
11		17	A	Luton T	W 3-1	1-0	15	Kitson 2, Johnson	8848
12		24	H	Charlton Ath	W 4-3	3-1	14	Gabbiadini, Minto (og), Pembridge, Simpson	15,482
13		31	A	Wolverhampton W	W 2-0	1-0	10	Kitson, Short	17,270
14	Nov	3	A	Notts Co	W 2-0	2-0	—	Pembridge, Kitson	15,267
15		7	H	Millwall	L 1-2	1-0	13	Pembridge	17,087
16		14	A	Bristol R	W 2-1	1-1	9	Kitson, Johnson	6668
17		21	H	Sunderland	L 0-1	0-1	12		17,581
18		28	H	Tranmere R	L 1-2	1-0	12	Kitson	15,665
19	Dec	6	A	Swindon T	W 4-2	2-0	—	Johnson, Pembridge, Kuhl, McMinn	8924
20		12	H	Birmingham C	W 3-1	0-1	8	Johnson, Kitson, Williams	16,662
21		20	A	Grimsby T	W 2-0	1-0	—	Johnson, Kitson	6475
22		26	A	Brentford	L 1-2	0-2	8	Kitson	10,226
23		28	H	Portsmouth	L 2-4	1-1	8	Johnson, Kitson	21,478
24	Jan	10	H	West Ham U	L 0-2	0-2	—		13,737
25		16	A	Southend U	D 0-0	0-0	9		4243
26		31	A	Newcastle U	D 1-1	1-0	—	Johnson	27,285
27	Feb	6	H	Peterborough U	L 2-3	2-2	16	Kitson 2	16,062
28		10	H	Barnsley	W 3-0	1-0	—	Gabbiadini, Kitson, Williams	13,096
29		20	H	Watford	L 1-2	0-2	14	Pembridge (pen)	15,190
30		24	H	Leicester C	W 2-0	1-0	—	Forsyth, Gabbiadini	17,507
31		27	A	Oxford U	W 1-0	0-0	8	Williams	7456
32	Mar	3	H	Cambridge U	D 0-0	0-0	—		14,106
33		10	H	Bristol R	W 3-1	3-1	—	Short, Williams, Gabbiadini	13,294
34		13	A	Millwall	L 0-1	0-0	10		9365
35		21	H	Swindon T	W 2-1	0-0	—	Kitson, Pembridge (pen)	12,166
36		24	A	Sunderland	L 0-1	0-0	—		17,246
37	Apr	2	A	Tranmere R	L 1-2	1-1	—	Simpson	7774
38		6	A	Birmingham C	D 1-1	1-0	—	Johnson	15,424
39		10	H	Brentford	W 3-2	1-1	10	Kitson, Gabbiadini, Simpson	12,366
40		12	A	Portsmouth	L 0-3	0-2	11		23,805
41		17	H	Grimsby T	W 2-1	0-1	9	Simpson, Kitson	12,428
42		20	A	Bristol C	D 0-0	0-0	—		8869
43		24	H	Luton T	D 1-1	0-1	9	Short	13,741
44	May	1	A	Charlton Ath	L 1-2	0-0	12	Gabbiadini	7802
45		5	H	Notts Co	W 2-0	0-0	—	McMinn, Pembridge (pen)	13,326
46		8	H	Wolverhampton W	W 2-0	0-0	8	Gabbiadini, Hayward	15,083

Final League Position: 8

GOALSCORERS

League (68): Kitson 17, Simpson 12 (2 pens), Gabbiadini 9, Johnson 8, Pembridge 8 (3 pens), Williams 4, Short 3, McMinn 2, Forsyth 1, Hayward 1, Kuhl 1, own goals 2.
Coca Cola Cup (9): Simpson 3 (1 pen), Gabbiadini 2, Johnson 1, Kitson 1, Pembridge 1 (pen), own goals 1.
FA Cup (13): Short 4, Pembridge 3, Gabbiadini 2, Kitson 1, Nicholson 1, Williams 1, own goal 1.

Sutton 25	Kavanagh 10	Forsyth 41	Pembridge 42	Coleman 17 + 8	Wassall 24	Johnson 34 + 1	Kitson 44	Gabbiadini 42 + 2	Williams 19	Simpson 32 + 3	McMinn 6 + 13	Comyn 13 + 4	Micklewhite 4 + 2	Patterson 17 + 1	Taylor 21	Short 38	Sturidge 8 + 2	Kuhl 32	Goulooze 7 + 5	Hayward 6 + 1	Nicholson 17	Round 6	Stallard 1 + 4	Ramage — + 1	Match No.
1	2	3	4	5	6	7	8	9	10	11	12														1
1	2	3	4	5	6	7	8	9	10	11	12														2
1	2	3	4	5	6	9	8		10	11	7														3
1	2	3	4	5	6	9	8	12	10	11	7	14													4
1	2	3	4	5	6	9	8	7	10	11	14	12													5
1		3	4	5	6	7	8	9	10	11	12			2											6
		3			6	12	5	7	8	9	10	11		2		1		4	14						7
1		3			6	12	5	7	9	10	11			2				4	8						8
1		3			6	12	5	7	9	10	11			2				4	8	14					9
1		3			6		5	7	9	10	11			2				4	8	12					10
1		3			6		5	7	9	10	11	12		2				4	8						11
1		3			6		5	7	9	10	11	12		2				4	8	14					12
1		3			6		5	7	9	10	11			2				4	8						13
1		3			6		5	7	9	10	11	12		2				4	8						14
1		3			6	14	5	7	9	10	11	12		2				4	8						15
1		3			6		5	7	9	10	11			2				4	8						16
1		3			6		5	7	9	10	11	12		2				4	8	14					17
1		3			6		5	7	9	10	11			2				4	8						18
1		3			6		5	7	9	10	11	12					2	4	8						19
1	2	3			6		5	7	9	10	11							4	8						20
		3			6		5	7	9	10	11					1	2	4	8						21
1		3			6		5	7	9	10	11	12					2	4	8						22
1		3			6	14	5	7	9	10	11	12					2	4	8						23
1	2	3			6		5	10	9	12	11	7						4	8						24
1	2	3			6		5	7	9	10								4	8	11					25
1	2	3			6		5	7	9	10		12	11					4	8						26
1	2	3			6		5	7	9	10		12	11					4	8						27
		3			6		4	9	10		7		11		2	1	5	8							28
		3			6		4	9	10		7		11	12	2	1	5	8							29
		3			6		11	9	10		7		8		2	1	5		12		4				30
		3					11	9	10		7				2	1	5	6	8		4				31
		3					11	9	10		7		12		2	1	5	6	8		4				32
		3			6		11	9	10		7				2	1	5	8			4				33
		3			6			9	10		7		11		2	1	5	8			4				34
		3			6	14	11	9	10		7					1	5	8			4		2	12	35
		3		5	6		11	9	10			12	7			1		8			4		2		36
					6	12		9	10	11		14	7	2	1	5		8			4	3			37
					6				10	11			7	4	1	5	14	8	12		3	2	9		38
					6	4		9	10	11					1	5	7	8			3	2			39
					6	4		9	10	11				14	1	5	7	8			3	2	12		40
				5	6	14		9	10	11				4	2	1		7	8			3		12	41
			4		6			9	10	11				2	1	5	7	8			3				42
			4		6	12		9	10	11				2	1	5	7	8			3	14			43
			4		6			9	10	11	12			2	1	5	7	8			3				44
			4		6			9	10	11	12			2	1	5	7	8			3				45
					6		4		10	11		7		2	1	5	9				8	3	12		46

Coca Cola Cup	Second Round	Southend U (a)	0-1
		(h)	7-0
	Third Round	Arsenal (h)	1-1
		(a)	1-2
FA Cup	Third Round	Stockport C (h)	2-1
	Fourth Round	Luton T (a)	5-1
	Fifth Round	Bolton W (h)	3-1
	Sixth Round	Sheffield W (h)	3-3
		(a)	0-1

DERBY COUNTY

Player and Position	Ht	Wt	Birth Date	Birth Place	Source	Clubs	League App	Gls
Goalkeepers								
Simon Dunne*	6 1	12 08	9 9 73	Dublin		Derby Co	—	—
Steve Sutton	6 1	13 07	16 4 61	Hartington	Apprentice	Nottingham F	199	—
						Mansfield T (loan)	8	—
						Derby Co (loan)	14	—
						Coventry C (loan)	1	—
						Luton T (loan)	14	—
						Derby Co	35	—
Martin Taylor	5 11	12 04	9 12 66	Tamworth	Mile Oak R	Derby Co	36	—
						Carlisle U (loan)	10	—
						Scunthorpe U (loan)	8	—
Jon Thomson	5 10	12 00	23 12 73	Newcastle	Trainee	Derby Co	—	—
Defenders								
Lee Carsley	5 10	11 11	28 2 74	Birmingham	Trainee	Derby Co	—	—
Andy Comyn	6 1	12 00	2 6 68	Manchester	Alvechurch	Aston Villa	15	—
						Derby Co	63	1
Mike Forsyth	5 11	12 02	20 3 66	Liverpool	Apprentice	WBA	29	—
						Northampton T (loan)	—	—
						Derby Co	275	6
Richard Goulooze	5 11	13 06	16 11 67	Holland	SC Heerenveen	Derby Co	12	—
Shane Nicholson	5 10	11 00	3 6 70	Newark	Trainee	Lincoln C	133	6
						Derby Co	17	—
Mark Patterson	5 10	11 05	13 9 68	Leeds	Trainee	Carlisle U	22	—
						Derby Co	51	3
Justin Phillips	6 3	14 07	17 12 71	Derby	Trainee	Derby Co	3	—
Steve Round	5 10	11 00	9 11 70	Buxton	Trainee	Derby Co	9	—
Mel Sage	5 8	10 04	24 3 64	Gillingham	Apprentice	Gillingham	132	5
						Derby Co	140	4
Craig Short	6 2	12 03	25 6 68	Bridlington	Pickering T	Scarborough	63	7
						Notts Co	128	6
						Derby Co	38	3
Wayne Sutton			1 10 75	Derby	Trainee	Derby Co	—	—
Darren Wassall	5 11	11 09	27 6 68	Edgbaston		Nottingham F	27	—
						Hereford U (loan)	5	—
						Bury (loan)	7	1
						Derby Co	24	—
Midfield								
Simon Coleman	6 0	10 08	13 3 68	Worksop		Mansfield T	96	7
						Middlesbrough	55	2
						Derby Co	68	2
Tommy Curtis*	5 8	11 04	1 3 73	Exeter	School	Derby Co	—	—
Steve Hayward	5 10	11 07	8 9 71	Walsall	Trainee	Derby Co	18	1
Jason Kavanagh	5 9	11 00	23 11 71	Birmingham	Birmingham C	Derby Co	46	—
Martin Kuhl	5 11	11 13	10 1 65	Frimley	Apprentice	Birmingham C	111	5
						Sheffield U	38	4
						Watford	4	—
						Portsmouth	157	27
						Derby Co	32	1
Colin Loss‡	5 11	11 04	15 8 73	Brentwood	Trainee	Norwich C	—	—
						Derby Co	—	—
Mark Pembridge	5 7	11 01	29 11 70	Methyr Tydfil	Trainee	Luton T	60	6
						Derby Co	42	8
Steve Taylor*	5 8	10 04	10 1 70	Holbrook	Trainee	Derby Co	—	—
Peter Weston‡	5 7	10 12	13 2 74	Stoke	Trainee	Derby Co	—	—
Paul Williams	5 11	12 00	26 3 71	Burton	Trainee	Derby Co	89	22
						Lincoln C (loan)	3	—

DERBY COUNTY

Colours: White shirts, black shorts, white stockings. **Change colours:** Pale blue and black striped shirts, pale blue shorts, black stockings with pale blue tops.

Foundation: Derby County was formed by members of the Derbyshire County Cricket Club in 1884, when football was booming in the area and the cricketers thought that a football club would help boost finances for the summer game. To begin with, they sported the cricket club's colours of amber, chocolate and pale blue, and went into the game at the top immediately entering the FA Cup.

First Football League game: 8 September, 1888, Football League, v Bolton W (a) W 6-3 – Marshall; Latham, Ferguson, Williamson; Monks, W. Roulstone; Bakewell (2), Cooper (2), Higgins, H. Plackett, L. Plackett (2).

Did you know: On 2 April 1960 Derby County made ten changes for the visit of Huddersfield Town in a Division 2 match. Only centre-half Ray Young retained his place and Derby won 3-2.

Managers (and Secretary-Managers)
Harry Newbould 1896–1906, Jimmy Methven 1906–22, Cecil Potter 1922–25, George Jobey 1925–41, Ted Magner 1944–46, Stuart McMillan 1946–53, Jack Barker 1953–55, Harry Storer 1955–62, Tim Ward 1962–67, Brian Clough 1967–73, Dave Mackay 1973–76, Colin Murphy 1977, Tommy Docherty 1977–79, Colin Addison 1979–82, Johnny Newman 1982, Peter Taylor 1982–84, Roy McFarland 1984, Arthur Cox May 1984– .

Player and Position	Ht	Wt	Date	Birth Place	Source	Clubs	League App	Gls
Forwards								
Martyn Chalk	5 6	10 00	30 8 69	Louth	Louth U	Derby Co	7	1
Mark Clarke*	5 9	11 02	22 11 72	Birmingham	Trainee	Derby Co	—	—
Marco Gabbiadini	5 10	12 04	20 1 68	Nottingham	Apprentice	York C	60	14
						Sunderland	157	74
						Crystal Palace	15	5
						Derby Co	64	15
Stewart Hadley	6 0	13 02	30 12 73	Dudley	Halesowen	Derby Co	—	—
Tommy Johnson	5 10	11 02	15 1 71	Newcastle	Trainee	Notts Co	118	47
						Derby Co	47	10
Paul Kitson	5 11	10 12	9 1 71	Co Durham	Trainee	Leicester C	50	6
						Derby Co	56	21
Ted McMinn	5 11	11 02	28 9 62	Castle Douglas	Glenafton Athletic	Queen of the S	62	5
						Rangers	63	4
					Seville	Derby Co	123	9
Gary Micklewhite*	5 7	10 04	21 3 61	Southwark	Apprentice	Manchester U	—	—
						QPR	106	11
						Derby Co	240	31
Craig Ramage	5 9	11 08	30 3 70	Derby	Trainee	Derby Co	37	4
						Wigan Ath (loan)	10	2
Paul Simpson	5 7	11 04	26 7 66	Carlisle	Apprentice	Manchester C	121	18
						Oxford U	144	43
						Derby Co	51	19
Mark Stallard	6 0	12 06	24 10 74	Derby	Trainee	Derby Co	8	—
Robert Straw‡	5 9	11 08	4 11 70	Derby	Trainee	Derby Co	—	—
Dean Sturridge	5 7	10 10	26 7 73	Birmingham	Trainee	Derby Co	11	—

Trainees
Anderson, Wayne S; Cooper, Kevin L; Dakin, Simon M; Davies, William; Franklin, Nicholas; Geddis, Stewart R; Green, Mathew R; Henson, Christopher P; Johnson, Brian A; Matthews, Martin; McAra, Ian; McKeever, Nigel; Ward, Michael J; Warren, Matthew T. J; Wood, Mark A; Wrack, Darren; Wright, Nicholas J.

Associated Schoolboys
Baker, Mark A; Clarke, Bret; Giles, Damon P; Gittus, Mark G; Hardy, Jon; Lyons, Patrick M; Machin, Shaun; Marshall, Andrew J; McHugh, Edward T; McHugh, Philip; Murphy, Shaun P; Rowntree, Martyn E; Wright, Matthew R.

Associated Schoolboys who have accepted the club's offer of a Traineeship/Contract
Ashbee, Ian; Cunningham, Carl M; McGann, Thomas; Powell, Stephen R; Tretton, Andrew.

DONCASTER ROVERS 1992-93 *Back row (left to right):* Mark Hine, Craig Bennett, Grant Morrow, Eddie Gormley, Steve Prindiville, Mike Jeffrey. *Centre row:* Steve Beaglehole (Manager), Jamie Hewitt, Jon Cullen, Colin Douglas, Paul Crichton, Peter Heritage, Andy Crosby, John Bird (First Team Coach). *Front row:* Shane Reddish, Steve Hodder, Steve Richards, Jamie Roberts, Brian Rowe.

Division 3   **DONCASTER ROVERS**

Doncaster Rovers Football Club Ltd.

(Founded 1879)

Belle Vue Ground, Doncaster. Telephone Doncaster (0302) 539441. Fax (0302) 539679.

Ground capacity: 7794.

Record attendance: 37,149 v Hull C, Division 3 (N), 2 October 1948.

Record receipts: £22,000 v QPR, FA Cup 3rd rd, 5 January 1985.

Pitch measurements: 110yd × 76yd.

Chairman: J. J. Burke. *Vice-chairman:* K. Chappell.

Directors: M. Collett, J. Ryan, T. Nuttall.

Manager: Steve Beaglehole. *Coach:* John Bird.

Secretary: Mrs K. J. Oldale. *Physio:* Eric Brailsford. *Youth Team Coach:* Jim Golze.

Year Formed: 1879. *Turned Professional:* 1885. *Ltd Co.:* 1905 and 1920.

Club Nickname: 'Rovers'.

Previous Grounds: 1880–1916, Intake Ground; 1920–22, Benetthorpe Ground; 1922, Low Pasture, Belle Vue.

Record League Victory: 10–0 v Darlington, Division 4, 25 January 1964 – Potter; Raine, Meadows; Windross (1), White, Ripley (2); Robinson, Book (2), Hale (4), Jeffrey, Broadbent (1).

Record Cup Victory: 7–0 v Blyth Spartans, FA Cup, 1st rd, 27 November 1937 – Imrie; Shaw, Rodgers; McFarlane, Bycroft, Cyril Smith; Burton (1), Kilourhy (4), Morgan (2), Malam, Dutton.

Record Defeat: 0–12 v Small Heath, Division 2, 11 April 1903.

Most League Points (2 for a win): 72, Division 3 (N), 1946–47.

Most League Points (3 for a win): 85, Division 4, 1983–84.

Most League Goals: 123, Division 3 (N), 1946–47.

Highest League Scorer in Season: Clarrie Jordan, 42, Division 3 (N), 1946–47.

Most League Goals in Total Aggregate: Tom Keetley, 180, 1923–29.

Most Capped Player: Len Graham, 14, Northern Ireland.

Most League Appearances: Fred Emery, 417, 1925–36.

Record Transfer Fee Received: £250,000 from QPR for Rufus Brevett, February 1991.

Record Transfer Fee Paid: £60,000 to Stirling Albion for John Philliben, March 1984.

Football League Record: 1901 Elected to Division 2; 1903 Failed re-election; 1904 Re-elected; 1905 Failed re-election; 1923 Re-elected to Division 3 (N); 1935–37 Division 2; 1937–47 Division 3 (N); 1947–48 Division 2; 1948–50 Division 3 (N); 1950–58 Division 2; 1958–59 Division 3; 1959–66 Division 4; 1966–67 Division 3; 1967–69 Division 4; 1969–71 Division 3; 1971–81 Division 4; 1981–83 Division 3; 1983–84 Division 4; 1984–88 Division 3; 1988– 92 Division 4; 1992– Division 3.

Honours: Football League: Division 2 best season: 7th, 1901–02; Division 3 (N) Champions 1934–35, 1946–47, 1949–50; Runners-up 1937–38, 1938–39; Division 4 – Champions 1965–66, 1968–69; Runners-up 1983–84. Promoted 1980–81 (3rd). *FA Cup:* best season: 5th rd, 1951–52, 1953–54, 1954–55, 1955–56. *Football League Cup:* best season: 5th rd, 1975–76.

DONCASTER ROVERS 1992—93 LEAGUE RECORD

Match No.	Date		Venue	Opponents	Result	H/T Score	Lg. Pos.	Goalscorers	Atten dance
1	Aug	15	H	Bury	L 2-3	0-2	—	Jeffrey 2 (1 pen)	3350
2		22	A	Shrewsbury T	L 1-2	1-1	17	Jeffrey	1867
3		29	H	Torquay U	L 2-3	2-0	21	Gormley, Heritage	1969
4	Sept	1	H	Barnet	W 2-1	2-0	—	Gormley, Jeffrey	1747
5		5	A	Wrexham	D 1-1	1-1	17	Jeffrey	2389
6		12	A	Crewe Alex	L 0-4	0-2	21		3127
7		15	H	Colchester U	W 1-0	1-0	—	Jeffrey	1719
8		18	H	Lincoln C	D 0-0	0-0	—		2936
9		26	A	Scarborough	D 1-1	1-1	9	Jeffrey	1859
10	Oct	3	A	York C	D 1-1	0-0	15	Morrow	4611
11		10	H	Gillingham	W 1-0	0-0	12	Jeffrey	2477
12		17	A	Northampton T	W 1-0	0-0	9	Prindiville	2137
13		23	H	Hereford U	W 2-1	1-0	—	Morrow, Brady (pen)	2614
14		31	A	Walsall	L 1-3	0-1	10	Brady (pen)	3525
15	Nov	7	A	Scunthorpe U	W 1-0	0-0	11	Brady	4451
16		21	H	Carlisle U	L 1-2	0-1	11	Hine	2159
17		28	A	Rochdale	D 1-1	0-0	11	Morrow	2094
18	Dec	11	H	Cardiff C	L 0-1	0-1	—		2023
19		19	A	Chesterfield	D 0-0	0-0	14		3319
20		26	A	Halifax T	D 2-2	0-1	15	Richards 2	1854
21		28	H	Darlington	L 0-1	0-0	16		2878
22	Jan	2	H	Rochdale	D 1-1	1-0	15	Richards	2559
23		8	A	Colchester U	L 0-2	0-0	—		4402
24		16	A	Scarborough	W 4-3	2-1	13	Douglas, Prindiville, White W, Gormley	2009
25		23	A	Lincoln C	L 1-2	0-0	13	Gormley	3269
26		26	A	Torquay U	W 2-1	1-0	—	Gormley (pen), White W	1771
27		30	H	Shrewsbury T	L 0-1	0-1	—		2227
28	Feb	6	A	Bury	L 0-3	0-2	14		2496
29		13	H	Wrexham	D 1-1	1-0	14	Morrow	2693
30		16	H	Crewe Alex	D 1-1	1-1	—	Rowe	1844
31		20	A	Barnet	L 0-2	0-1	14		3458
32		27	A	Gillingham	D 1-1	1-0	14	O'Connor (og)	2975
33	Mar	5	H	York C	L 0-1	0-0	—		3188
34		13	H	Scunthorpe U	L 0-1	0-0	17		2760
35		27	A	Carlisle U	D 1-1	1-1	17	Moss	2939
36	Apr	6	H	Cardiff C	D 1-1	1-0	—	Jeffrey (pen)	9938
37		10	H	Halifax T	L 0-1	0-1	18		2160
38		12	A	Darlington	W 2-1	0-1	18	Moss, Jeffrey (pen)	2218
39		17	H	Chesterfield	W 2-1	1-1	17	Reddish, Heritage	2441
40		24	H	Northampton T	D 2-2	2-2	16	Moss, Jeffrey	2111
41	May	1	A	Hereford U	W 2-0	0-0	16	Gormley, Jeffrey	2352
42		8	H	Walsall	L 0-3	0-0	16		2900

Final League Position: 16

GOALSCORERS

League (42): Jeffrey 12 (3 pens), Gormley 6 (1 pen), Morrow 4, Brady 3 (2 pens), Richards 3, Moss 3, Heritage 2, Prindiville 2, White W 2, Douglas 1, Hine 1, Reddish 1, Rowe 1, own goal 1.
Coca Cola Cup (1): Hewitt 1.
FA Cup (1): Quinlan 1.

Crichton 41	Douglas 12 + 9	Prindiville 42	Hine 18 + 7	Crosby 26 + 3	Hicks 36	Hewitt 27	Gormley 41	Morrow 17 + 6	Jeffrey 29 + 1	Rowe 21 + 4	Richards 36 + 2	Quinlan 2 + 7	Hodder 1 + 1	Heritage 25 + 6	Hodson 15	Reece 1	Reddish 27 + 4	Brady 4	Falana 2 + 2	White C 6	White W 4	Kabia 5	Roberts 1 + 1	Gilzean 3	Masefield 8 + 1	Taylor 2	Bennett 1	Moss 9	Match No.
1	2	3	4	5	6	7	*8*	9	10	11	12	14																	1
1	2	3	12	4	6	7		14	10	11	5		*8*	9															2
1 14		3	12	4	6	2	8	*11*	10	7	5			9															3
1		3	8	4	6	7	11		10	2	5			9															4
1		3	8	4	6	7	11		10	2	5			9															5
1		3	*8*	4	6	7	11		10	2	5	14	12	9															6
1		3	8	4	6	7	11		10	2	5	12		9															7
1		3		4	6	7	11		10	2	5			9	8														8
		3		4	6	7	11	9	10	2	5			12	8	1													9
1		3			6	7	11	9	10	2	5				8		4												10
1		3			6	7	11	14	10	2	5	12		9	8		4												11
1		3			6	7	11	9	10	2	5	14		12	8		4												12
1		3 12			6	7	11	9			5	14		10	8		4	2											13
1 12		3			6	7	11	9			5			10	8		4	2											14
1		3			6	7	11				5	10		9	8		4	2											15
1		3 14			6	7	11	9			5	*10*		12	8		4	2											16
1		3	2		6	7	11	9			5	12		10	8		4												17
1		3	*2* 12		6	7	11	9			5			10	8		4		14										18
1		3	6		7	11	12				2	5		9	8		4		10										19
1		3 12	*6*		7	11	9				2	5		10	8		4		14										20
1		3 12			6	7	11			14	2	5		9	8		4		*10*										21
1		3	6		7	11	9	10			2	5			8		4												22
1	4	3	8		6	7	11	9	10		2	5					12												23
1	9	3	12	6	7	11			10	2	5									4	8								24
1	*9*	3 12	2	6	7	11	10			14	5			8			4												25
1 12		3	10	6	7	11			14	5				2						4	8	*9*							26
1 12		3	10	6	*7*	11			14	5				2						4	8	9							27
1	6	3	10		11	12			14	5		7		2						4	8	*9*							28
1	2	3			6		11	8	10	7	5										4	9							29
1	2	3			6		11	8	10	7	5	*12*					4						9	14					30
1	2	3	14	6			11		10	*7*	5	12					4						8	9					31
1	*2*	3	7		6		11	12	10		5			14										9	4	8			32
1	2	3	7		6		11	12	10		5			14										*9*	4	8			33
1	2	3	7	6			11	9	10		5	12		14												4	8		34
1 12		3	7	5	6		11		10					9			4								2			8	35
1		3	7	5	6		11		10					9			4								2			8	36
1 12		3	7	5	6		11		10					9			*4*								2			8	37
1 12		3	7	5			11		10	6				9			4								*2*			8	38
1		3	7	5	2		11		10	6				9			4											8	39
1 12		3	7	5	2		11		10	*6*				9			4								14			8	40
1		3	7	5			11		10					9			4								2			8	41
1 12		3	7	5	6		11		10	14				9			4								*2*			8	42

Coca Cola Cup	First Round	Lincoln C (h)		0-3
		(a)		1-1
FA Cup	First Round	Hartlepool U (h)		1-2

DONCASTER ROVERS

Player and Position	Ht	Wt	Date	Birth Place	Source	Clubs	League App	Gls
Goalkeepers								
Paul Crichton*	6 1	12 05	3 10 68	Pontefract	Apprentice	Nottingham F	—	—
						Notts Co (loan)	5	—
						Darlington (loan)	5	—
						Peterborough U (loan)	4	—
						Darlington (loan)	3	—
						Swindon T (loan)	4	—
						Rotherham U (loan)	6	—
						Torquay U (loan)	13	—
						Peterborough U	47	—
						Doncaster R	77	—
Defenders								
Andy Crosby	6 2	13 00	3 3 73	Rotherham	Leeds U	Doncaster R	51	—
Jon Cullen			10 1 73	Durham	Trainee	Doncaster R	9	—
Colin Douglas*	6 1	11 07	9 9 62	Hurlford	Celtic	Doncaster R	212	48
						Rotherham U	83	4
						Doncaster R	192	5
Jamie Hewitt	5 11	11 07	17 5 68	Chesterfield	School	Chesterfield	249	14
						Doncaster R	27	—
Stuart Hicks	6 1	13 00	30 5 67	Peterborough	Wisbech	Colchester U	64	—
						Scunthorpe U	67	1
						Doncaster R	36	—
Paul Masefield*	6 1	12 12	21 10 70	Birmingham	Trainee	Birmingham C	—	—
						Preston NE	—	—
						Exeter C	1	—
						Stockport Co	7	—
						Doncaster R	9	—
Steve Prindiville	5 9	11 07	26 12 68	Harlow	Apprentice	Leicester C	1	—
						Chesterfield	43	1
						Mansfield T	28	—
						Doncaster R	58	2
Steve Richards*	6 1	13 00	24 10 61	Dundee	Apprentice	Hull C	58	2
					Gainsborough T	York C	7	—
						Lincoln C	21	—
						Cambridge U	4	2
						Scarborough	164	13
						Halifax T	25	—
						Doncaster R	38	3
Midfield								
Eddie Gormley	5 7	10 07	23 10 68	Dublin	Bray W	Tottenham H	—	—
						Chesterfield (loan)	4	—
						Motherwell (loan)	—	—
						Shrewsbury T (loan)	—	—
						Doncaster R	118	16
Mark Hine	5 8	10 08	18 5 64	Middlesbrough	Local	Grimsby T	22	1
						Darlington	128	8
						Peterborough U	55	8
						Scunthorpe U	22	2
						Doncaster R	25	1
David Moss†			15 11 68	Doncaster	Boston U	Doncaster R	9	3
Shane Reddish*	5 10	11 10	5 5 71	Bolsover	Trainee	Doncaster R	60	3
Brian Rowe*	5 9	10 12	24 10 71	Sunderland	Trainee	Doncaster R	54	1
Forwards								
Craig Bennett	6 0	12 00	29 8 73	Doncaster	Trainee	Doncaster R	8	—
Ian Gilzean (on loan from Dundee)	6 1	12 10	10 12 69	London		Doncaster R	3	—

DONCASTER ROVERS

Colours: White shirts with red lightning stripes, red shorts, red stockings. **Change colours:** White shirts with red & green stripes over shoulder and above waist, green shorts, green stockings.

Foundation: In 1879 Mr. Albert Jenkins got together a team to play a game against the Yorkshire Institution for the Deaf. The players stuck together as Doncaster Rovers joining the Midland Alliance in 1889 and the Midland Counties League in 1891.

First Football League game: 7 September, 1901, Division 2, v Burslem Port Vale (h) D 3-3 – Eggett; Simpson, Layton; Longden, Jones, Wright; Langham, Murphy, Price, Goodson (2), Bailey (1).

Did you know: Doncaster Rovers were involved in the highest scoring League game of 1982-83 when they beat Reading 7-5 in a Division 3 match. The scores went: 1-0, 1-1, 2-1, 3-1, 3-2, 4-2, 4-3, 5-3 (at half-time), 5-4, 6-4, 6-5 and 7-5.

Managers (and Secretary-Managers)
Arthur Porter 1920–21*, Harry Tufnell 1921–22, Arthur Porter 1922–23, Dick Ray 1923–27, David Menzies 1928–36, Fred Emery 1936–40, Bill Marsden 1944–46, Jackie Bestall 1946–49, Peter Doherty 1949–58, Jack Hodgson and Sid Bycroft (joint managers) 1958, Jack Crayston 1958–59 (continued as Sec-Man to 1961), Jackie Bestall (TM) 1959–60, Norman Curtis 1960–61, Danny Malloy 1961–62, Oscar Hold 1962–64, Bill Leivers 1964–66, Keith Kettleborough 1966–67, George Raynor 1967–68, Lawrie McMenemy 1968–71, Maurice Setters 1971–74, Stan Anderson 1975–78, Billy Bremner 1978–85, Dave Cusack 1985–87, Dave Mackay 1987–89, Billy Bremner July 1989–91, Steve Beaglehole November 1991–.

Player and Position	Ht	Wt	Date	Birth Place	Source	Clubs	League App	Gls
Peter Heritage	6 1	13 00	8 11 60	Bexhill	Hythe Town	Gillingham	57	11
						Hereford U	57	9
						Doncaster R	31	2
Steve Hodder*	5 9	11 03	18 10 71	Sheffield	Nottingham F	Notts Co	—	—
						Doncaster R	2	—
Mike Jeffrey	5 11	11 06	11 8 71	Liverpool	Trainee	Bolton W	15	—
						Doncaster R (loan)	11	6
						Doncaster R	30	12
Grant Morrow*	5 10	11 07	4 10 70	Glasgow	Rowntree Mackintosh	Doncaster R	64	7
Paul Quinlan‡	5 7	10 02	17 4 71	Madrid	Trainee	Everton	—	—
						Huddersfield T (loan)	8	2
						Doncaster R	9	—
Jamie Roberts*			11 4 74	Doncaster	Trainee	Doncaster R	2	—

Trainees
Burton, Arron L; Flint, Carl; Maxfield, Scott; Sibson, Andrew; Soar, Mark; Sykes, Paul R; Taylor, James A; Taylor, James M; Thew, Lee; Wasilewski, Steven C.

**Non-Contract
Moss, David.

Associated Schoolboys
Abbotts, Scott P; Jones, David J; Nixon, Russell S; Tomes, Paul; Wilson, Martin I.

Associated Schoolboys who have accepted the club's offer of a Traineeship/Contract
Buxton, Nick G; Harmer, Russell; Pask, Darren L.

**Non-Contract Players who are retained must be re-signed before they are eligible to play in League matches.

EVERTON 1992-93 *Back row (left to right):* Kevin Ratcliffe, John Ebbrell, David Unsworth, Jason Kearton, Gerry Peyton, Neville Southall, Andy Hinchcliffe, Matthew Jackson, Gary Ablett. *Centre row:* Jimmy Martin (Kit Manager), Jimmy Gabriel (Reserve Team Coach), Peter Beardsley, Iain Jenkins, Stuart Barlow, Robert Warzycha, Ian Snodin, Alan Harper, Peter Beagrie, Colin Harvey (First Team Coach), Les Helm (Physio). *Front row:* Barry Horne, Mark Ward, Dave Watson, Howard Kendall (Manager), Martin Keown, Tony Cottee, Maurice Johnston.

FA Premier

EVERTON

Goodison Park, Liverpool L4 4EL. Telephone 051–521 2020.
Fax 051 523 9666. Ticket Infoline: 0898 121599. Clubcall 0898
121199. Dial-a-seat service: 051–525 1231.

Ground capacity: 38,578.

Record attendance: 78,299 v Liverpool, Division 1,
18 September 1948.

Record receipts: £207,780 v Liverpool, FA Cup, 5th rd,
21 February 1988.

Pitch measurements: 112yd × 78yd.

Chairman: Dr D. M. Marsh.

Directors: Sir Desmond Pitcher, A. W. Waterworth, K. M. Tamlin, Sir Philip Carter CBE,
D. A. B. Newton, W. Kenright.

Manager: Howard Kendall. ***Assistant Manager:*** Colin Harvey. ***Coach:*** Jimmy Gabriel.

Physio: Les Helm.

Chief Executive & Secretary: Jim Greenwood.

Commercial Manager: Derek Johnston. ***Sales Promotion Manager:*** Colum Whelan.

Year Formed: 1878. ***Turned Professional:*** 1885. ***Ltd Co.:*** 1892.

Previous Name: St Domingo FC, 1878–79.

Club Nickname: 'The Toffees'.

Previous Grounds: 1878, Stanley Park; 1882, Priory Road; 1884, Anfield Road; 1892,
Goodison Park.

Record League Victory: 9–1 v Manchester C, Division 1, 3 September 1906 – Scott; Balmer,
Crelley; Booth, Taylor (1), Abbott (1); Sharp, Bolton (1), Young (4), Settle (2), George
Wilson. 9–1 v Plymouth Arg, Division 2, 27 December 1930 – Coggins; Williams, Cresswell;
McPherson, Griffiths, Thomson; Critchley, Dunn, Dean (4), Johnson (1), Stein (4).

Record Cup Victory: 11–2 v Derby Co, FA Cup, 1st rd, 18 January 1890 – Smalley;
Hannah, Doyle; Kirkwood (3), Holt, Parry; Latta, Brady (3), Geary (2), Chadwick,
Millward (3).

Record Defeat: 4–10 v Tottenham H, Division 1, 11 October 1958.

Most League Points (2 for a win): 66, Division 1, 1969–70.

Most League Points (3 for a win): 90, Division 1, 1984–85.

Most League Goals: 121, Division 2, 1930–31.

Highest League Scorer in Season: William Ralph 'Dixie' Dean, 60, Division 1, 1927–28 (All-
time League record).

Most League Goals in Total Aggregate: William Ralph 'Dixie' Dean, 349, 1925–37.

Most Capped Player: Neville Southall, 68, Wales.

Most League Appearances: Ted Sagar, 465, 1929–53.

Record Transfer Fee Received: £2,750,000 from Barcelona for Gary Lineker, July 1986.

Record Transfer Fee Paid: £2,000,000 to West Ham U for Tony Cottee, July 1988.

Football League Record: 1888 Founder Member of the Football League; 1930–31 Division
2; 1931–51 Division 1; 1951–54 Division 2; 1954–92 Division 1; 1992– FA Premier League.

Honours: *Football League:* Division 1 – Champions 1890–91, 1914–15, 1927–28, 1931–32,
1938–39, 1962–63, 1969–70, 1984–85, 1986–87; Runners-up 1889–90, 1894–95, 1901–02,
1904–05, 1908–09, 1911–12, 1985–86; Division 2 Champions 1930–31; Runners-up 1953–54.
FA Cup: Winners 1906, 1933, 1966, 1984; Runners-up 1893, 1897, 1907, 1968, 1985, 1986,
1989. *Football League Cup:* Runners-up 1976–77, 1983–84. *League Super Cup:* Runners-up
1986. *Simod Cup:* Runners-up 1989. *Zenith Data System Cup:* Runner-up 1991. **European
Competitions:** *European Cup:* 1963–64, 1970–71. *European Cup-Winners' Cup:* 1966–67,
1984–85 (winners). *European Fairs Cup:* 1962–63, 1964–65, 1965–66. *UEFA Cup:* 1975–76,
1978–79, 1979–80.

EVERTON 1992—93 LEAGUE RECORD

Match No.	Date	Venue	Opponents	Result	H/T Score	Lg. Pos.	Goalscorers	Attendance
1	Aug 15	H	Sheffield W	D 1-1	1-1	—	Horne	27,687
2	19	A	Manchester U	W 3-0	1-0	—	Beardsley, Warzycha, Johnston	31,901
3	22	A	Norwich C	D 1-1	0-0	6	Beardsley	14,150
4	25	H	Aston Villa	W 1-0	0-0	—	Johnston	22,372
5	29	H	Wimbledon	D 0-0	0-0	4		18,118
6	Sept 5	A	Tottenham H	L 1-2	1-0	10	Beardsley	26,503
7	12	H	Manchester U	L 0-2	0-1	12		30,002
8	15	A	Blackburn R	W 3-2	2-1	—	Cottee 2, Ebbrell	19,563
9	19	H	Crystal Palace	L 0-2	0-2	9		18,080
10	26	A	Leeds U	L 0-2	0-0	11		27,915
11	Oct 4	A	Oldham Ath	L 0-1	0-1	—		13,013
12	17	H	Coventry C	D 1-1	1-1	15	Beagrie	17,587
13	24	A	Arsenal	L 0-2	0-1	16		28,052
14	31	H	Manchester C	L 1-3	0-2	20	Brightwell (og)	20,242
15	Nov 7	A	Nottingham F	W 1-0	0-0	17	Rideout	20,941
16	21	H	Chelsea	L 0-1	0-1	17		17,418
17	28	A	Ipswich T	L 0-1	0-0	19		18,034
18	Dec 7	H	Liverpool	W 2-1	0-0	—	Johnston, Beardsley	35,826
19	12	A	Sheffield U	L 0-1	0-1	18		16,266
20	19	H	Southampton	W 2-1	2-1	17	Beardsley (pen), Rideout	14,051
21	26	H	Middlesbrough	D 2-2	0-0	18	Rideout, Beardsley (pen)	24,391
22	28	A	QPR	L 2-4	0-1	18	Barlow 2	14,802
23	Jan 9	A	Crystal Palace	W 2-0	0-0	17	Jackson, Beardsley	13,227
24	16	H	Leeds U	W 2-0	1-0	13	Cottee 2	21,031
25	26	A	Wimbledon	W 3-1	0-0	—	Cottee 2, Snodin	3039
26	30	H	Norwich C	L 0-1	0-1	12		20,301
27	Feb 6	A	Sheffield W	L 1-3	0-2	13	Cottee	24,979
28	10	H	Tottenham H	L 1-2	1-1	—	Sansom	16,164
29	20	A	Aston Villa	L 1-2	1-2	18	Beardsley (pen)	32,913
30	27	H	Oldham Ath	D 2-2	1-0	18	Beardsley (pen), Barlow	18,025
31	Mar 3	H	Blackburn R	W 2-1	0-1	—	Hendry (og), Cottee	18,086
32	7	A	Coventry C	W 1-0	1-0	—	Ward	11,285
33	10	A	Chelsea	L 1-2	1-1	—	Kenny	12,739
34	13	H	Nottingham F	W 3-0	3-0	17	Cottee 2, Hinchcliffe	21,271
35	20	A	Liverpool	L 0-1	0-0	17		44,619
36	24	H	Ipswich T	W 3-0	1-0	—	Barlow, Jackson, Cottee	15,638
37	Apr 10	A	Middlesbrough	W 2-1	1-0	15	Watson, Radosavljevic	16,627
38	12	H	QPR	L 3-5	1-2	15	Cottee, Barlow, Radosavljevic	19,057
39	17	A	Southampton	D 0-0	0-0	15		16,911
40	May 1	H	Arsenal	D 0-0	0-0	14		19,044
41	4	H	Sheffield U	L 0-2	0-2	—		15,197
42	8	A	Manchester C	W 5-2	3-1	13	Jackson, Beagrie 2, Beardsley, Radosavljevic	25,180

Final League Position: 13

GOALSCORERS

League (53): Cottee 12, Beardsley 10 (4 pens), Barlow 5, Beagrie 3, Jackson 3, Johnston 3, Radosavljevic 3, Rideout 3, Ebbrell 1, Hinchcliffe 1, Horne 1, Kenny 1, Sansom 1, Snodin 1, Ward 1, Warzycha 1, Watson 1, own goals 2.
Coca Cola Cup: (6): Beardsley 2, Rideout 2, Barlow 1, Cottee 1 (pen).
FA Cup (1): Watson 1.

Southall 40	Jackson 25 + 2	Hinchcliffe 25	Ebbrell 24	Watson 40	Ablett 40	Ward 19	Beardsley 39	Rideout 17 + 7	Horne 34	Beagrie 11 + 11	Warzycha 15 + 5	Harper 16 + 2	Johnston 7 + 6	Barlow 8 + 18	Cottee 25 + 1	Unsworth 3	Radosavljevic 13 + 10	Keown 13	Kenny 16 + 1	Snodin 19 + 1	Jenkins 1	Kearton 2 + 3	Sansom 6 + 1	Holmes 4	Moore — + 1	Match No.
1	2	3	4	5	6	7	8	9	10	11	12															1
1		3	4	5	6	11	8	9	10	12		7	2	14												2
1		3	*4*	5	6	11	8	9	10	12		7	2	14												3
1		3	4	5	6	7	8	9	10	12			2	11												4
1		3	4	5	6	11	8	*9*	10	12		7	2	14												5
1		3	4	5	6	11	8		10	12		7	2	*9*	14											6
1		3	4	5	6	11	8		10	12		7	2	9												7
1	14	3	11	5	6		7	8	9	4		12	2		10											8
1	12	3	4	5	6		8	9	11	7			2	14	10											9
1		3	4	5	6		8	12	7	2	14				10		9	11								10
1		3	4	5	6		9	8	12	7	2	10			14			11								11
1		3		5	6		8		10	11	*2*				9		14	4	7	12						12
1		*3*		5	6		8	12	10	11	7	14			9			4				*2*				13
1	2			5	3		9	10	11	7					8		12		6	4						14
1	2	11		5	3		8	9	10	12	7								6	4						15
1	2	11		5	3		8	9	*10*	12	7				14				6	4						16
1		11		5	3		8	12					14	2	9		*10*		6	7	4					17
1				5	3		8	14	2	12					10		9	11	6	7	*4*					18
1	*2*			5	3		8	14	7	12					10		9	11	6		4					19
1				5	3		8	9	4	11	7					7			6	10				2		20
1				5	6		8	9	4	11	*7*				14	3	12			10				2		21
1				5	3		8	9	4	*11*	7				14				6	10		2	12			22
1	2	11		5	3		8	9							12				7	6	10	4				23
1	2	4		5	3		8		10	*11*				14			12	9	7	6						24
-1	2			5	3		8		10			7			12		9	11	6	4						25
1	2			5	6		8	14	10			3			12	9			7	11	*4*					26
1	2			5	6		8				*7*				12	9	*11*		10	4	14	3				27
1	4			5	6		8	10	11		*2*	14			9	12		7				3				28
	2			5	6		8		11		*7*	10	14		9	12			4			1	3			29
	2			5	6		8	12	10						11	9			7	4		1	3			30
1	2	11		5	6	7	8		10						12	9			4				3			31
1	2	11		5	6	7	8		10						9	12			4				3			32
1	2	3		5	6	7	8		10						11	9		12	4							33
1	2	3		5	6	7	8								12	9	*11*		10	4		14				34
1	2	3	11	5	6	7	8								14	9	12	*10*	4							35
1	6	3	10	5		7	8	14		12					11	9			4			2				36
1	2	3	11	5	6	7	8	*10*	4						14	9	12									37
1	*2*	3	11	5	6	7	8		4						14	9	12		10							38
1	6	3	4	5			11	8							10	9	7	12				2				39
1	2	3	10	5	6	11	8		4						12	9	7									40
1	5	3	4		6		8	*10*	11						12	9	7						2		14	41
1	5	3	4		6	7	8		11						12	9	10					14	2			42

Coca Cola Cup	Second Round	Rotherham U (a)		0-1
		(h)		3-0
	Third Round	Wimbledon (h)		0-0
		(a)		1-0
	Fourth Round	Chelsea (h)		2-2
		(a)		0-1
FA Cup	Third Round	Wimbledon (a)		0-0
		(h)		1-2

EVERTON

Player and Position	Ht	Wt	Date	Birth Place	Source	Clubs	League App	Gls
Goalkeepers								
Jason Kearton	6 1	11 10	9 7 69	Ipswich (Australia)	Brisbane Lions	Everton	5	—
						Stoke C (loan)	16	—
						Blackpool (loan)	14	—
Neville Southall	6 1	12 01	16 9 58	Llandudno	Winsford	Bury	39	—
						Everton	411	—
						Port Vale (loan)	9	—
Defenders								
Gary Ablett	6 0	11 04	19 11 65	Liverpool	Apprentice	Liverpool	109	1
						Derby Co (loan)	6	—
						Hull C (loan)	5	—
						Everton	57	1
John Doolan	5 11	11 09	7 5 73	Liverpool	Trainee	Everton	—	—
Alan Harper*	5 8	10 09	1 11 60	Liverpool	Apprentice	Liverpool	—	—
						Everton	127	4
						Sheffield W	35	—
						Manchester C	50	1
						Everton	51	—
Andy Hinchcliffe	5 10	12 10	5 2 69	Manchester	Apprentice	Manchester C	112	8
						Everton	64	2
Paul Holmes	5 10	11 03	18 2 68	Wortley	Apprentice	Doncaster R	47	1
						Torquay U	138	4
						Birmingham C	12	—
						Everton	4	—
Matthew Jackson	6 1	12 12	19 10 71	Leeds	School	Luton T	9	—
						Preston NE (loan)	4	—
						Everton	57	4
Iain Jenkins‡	5 11	11 07	24 11 72	Prescot	Trainee	Everton	5	—
						Bradford C (loan)	6	—
Eddie Langton*	5 10	12 00	30 7 74	Liverpool	Trainee	Everton	—	—
Neil Moore	6 1	12 02	21 9 72	Liverpool	Trainee	Everton	1	—
Dave Watson	6 0	11 12	20 11 61	Liverpool	Amateur	Liverpool	—	—
						Norwich C	212	11
						Everton	240	18
Midfield								
Peter Beagrie	5 8	9 10	28 11 65	Middlesbrough	Local	Middlesbrough	33	2
						Sheffield U	84	11
						Stoke C	54	7
						Everton	85	8
						Sunderland (loan)	5	1
John Ebbrell	5 7	9 12	1 10 69	Bromborough		Everton	120	5
Barry Horne	5 10	12 02	18 5 62	St Asaph	Rhyl	Wrexham	136	17
						Portsmouth	70	7
						Southampton	112	6
						Everton	34	1
William Kenny	5 07	10 10	19 9 73	Liverpool	Trainee	Everton	17	1
Chris Priest	5 9	10 10	18 10 73	Leigh	Trainee	Everton	—	—
Ian Snodin	5 7	9 01	15 8 63	Rotherham	Apprentice	Doncaster R	188	25
						Leeds U	51	6
						Everton	116	3
Mark Ward	5 6	9 12	10 10 62	Prescot	Northwich Vic	Oldham Ath	84	12
						West Ham U	165	12
						Manchester C	55	14
						Everton	56	5
Forwards								
Stuart Barlow	5 10	11 01	16 7 68	Liverpool		Everton	35	5
						Rotherham U (loan)	—	—

EVERTON

Colours: Royal blue shirts with white collar, white shorts, blue stockings. **Change colours:** Salmon and dark blue striped shirts, salmon shorts, salmon stockings.

Foundation: St. Domingo Church Sunday School formed a football club in 1878 which played at Stanley Park. Enthusiasm was so great that in November 1879 they decided to expand membership and changed the name to Everton playing in black shirts with a white sash and nicknamed the "Black Watch". After wearing several other colours, royal blue was adopted in 1901.

First Football League game: 8 September, 1888, Football League, v Accrington (h) W 2-1 – Smalley; Dick, Ross; Holt, Jones, Dobson; Fleming (2), Waugh, Lewis, E. Chadwick, Farmer.

Did you know: Everton became the first Football League club to reach 3000 matches in Division 1 when they visited Brighton on 7 October 1980. The Brighton directors presented their Everton counterparts with an engraved tray. Everton won 3-1.

Managers (and Secretary-Managers)
W. E. Barclay 1888–89*, Dick Molyneux 1889–1901*, William C. Cuff 1901–18*, W. J. Sawyer 1918–19*, Thomas H. McIntosh 1919–35*, Theo Kelly 1936–48, Cliff Britton 1948–56, Ian Buchan 1956–58, Johnny Carey 1958–61, Harry Catterick 1961–73, Billy Bingham 1973–77, Gordon Lee 1977–81, Howard Kendall 1981–87, Colin Harvey 1987–90, Howard Kendall November 1990– .

Player and Position	Ht	Wt	Birth Date	Birth Place	Source	Clubs	League App	Gls
Peter Beardsley	5 8	11 07	18 1 61	Newcastle	Wallsend BC	Carlisle U	102	22
					Vancouver Whitecaps	Manchester U	—	—
					Vancouver Whitecaps	Newcastle U	147	61
						Liverpool	131	46
						Everton	81	25
Tony Cottee	5 7	11 03	11 7 65	West Ham	Apprentice	West Ham U	212	92
						Everton	142	56
Mo Johnston	5 9	10 06	30 4 63	Glasgow	Milton Battlefield	Partick T	85	41
						Watford	38	23
						Celtic	99	52
						Nantes	66	22
						Rangers	76	31
						Everton	34	10
Predrag Radosavljevic	5 11	12 10	24 6 63	Belgrade	St Louis Storms	Everton	23	3
Paul Rideout	5 11	12 01	14 8 64	Bournemouth	Apprentice	Swindon T	95	38
						Aston Villa	54	19
						Bari	99	23
						Southampton	75	19
						Swindon T (loan)	9	1
						Notts Co	11	3
						Rangers	12	1
						Everton	24	3
David Unsworth	5 11	12 02	16 10 73	Preston	Trainee	Everton	5	1
Robert Warzycha	5 8	11 10	20 6 63	Poland	Gornik Zabrze	Everton	65	6
Kenny Woods*	5 10	11 07	15 4 74	Liverpool	Trainee	Everton	—	—

Trainees
Ashley, David P; Carridge, John J; Emery, Richard; Grant, Anthony J; Holcroft, Peter I; Jones, Terence P; McMahon, Alan D; Powell, Mark A; Price, Christopher; Reeves, Stephen T; Renforth, Glenn L; Roberts, Sean M; Ruffer, Carl J; Smith, Alex P; Smith, Dean A; Tait, Paul; Williams, Lee J.

Associated Schoolboys
Ali, Thomas A; Arnison, Paul S; Barton, Joseph S; Branch, Paul M; Davies, Paul; Denton, Adam M; Dilworth, Paul; Dreslin, John C; Hussin, Edward W; Hynes, Martin R; Johnson, Michael P; Knight, Christopher D; Leeming, Daniel J; Maguire, John; McCann, Gavin P; McHugh, Bartholomew; O'Toole, John; Owen, David J. M; Roscoe, Christopher J; Townsend, Richard P; West, Andrew; Wood, Robert D. M.

Associated Schoolboys who have accepted the club's offer of a Traineeship/Contract
Allen, Graham; Hayes, Phillip J; Hennigan, Gerard J; O'Connor, Jonathan; Quigley, James D; Singleton, Benjamin P; Speare, James P. V; Weathers, Andrew W; Woods, Matthew J.

EXETER CITY 1992–93 *Back row (left to right):* Steve Allen, Mark Hutchings, Scott Daniels, Kevin Maloy, Kevin Miller, Eamonn Dolan, Richard Pears, Philip Dafferty.
Third row: Mike Chapman (Physio), George Kent (Community Officer), Alan Tonge, Gary Chapman, David Cooper, Gary Marshall, Toby Redwood, Jon Brown, Craig Taylor, Tom Kelly,
Eamonn Collins, Mike Radford (Youth Development Officer), Alan Ball (Manager).
Second row: Andy Cook, Steve Moran, Scott Hiley, Peter Whiston (Team Captain), Steve Williams (Assistant Manager), Glen Sprod, Andy Harris, John Hodge.
Front row: Mark Brown, Anthony Thirlby, Martin Phillips, Kevin Darch, Marc Baines, Jimmy Ball, Gary Rice, Matthew Harris.

Division 2 **EXETER CITY**

St James Park, Exeter EX4 6PX. Telephone Exeter (0392) 54073. Fax (0392) 425885. Training Ground: 0395 232784.

Ground capacity: 8650.

Record attendance: 20,984 v Sunderland, FA Cup 6th rd (replay), 4 March 1931.

Record receipts: £32,007 v Newcastle U, FA Cup 5th rd replay, 18 February 1981.

Pitch measurements: 114yd × 73yd.

President: W. C. Hill.

Chairman:

Directors: L. G. Vallance, A. W. Gooch, S. Dawe, G. Vece, C. Hill, A. R. Trump.

Manager: Alan Ball. *Coach/Assistant Manager:*   *Physio:* Mike Chapman.

Secretary: Margaret Bond. *Company Secretary:* A. R. Trump.

Commercial Manager: Steve Birley.

Year Formed: 1904. *Turned Professional:* 1908. *Ltd Co.:* 1908.

Club Nickname: 'The Grecians'.

Record League Victory: 8–1 v Coventry C, Division 3 (S), 4 December 1926 – Bailey; Pollard, Charlton; Pullen, Pool, Garrett; Purcell (2), McDevitt, Blackmore (2), Dent (2), Compton (2). 8–1 v Aldershot, Division 3 (S), 4 May 1935 – Chesters; Gray, Miller; Risdon, Webb, Angus; Jack Scott (1), Wrightson (1), Poulter (3), McArthur (1), Dryden (1). (1 og).

Record Cup Victory: 9–1 v Aberdare, FA Cup 1st rd, 26 November 1927 – Holland; Pollard, Charlton; Phoenix, Pool, Gee; Purcell (2), McDevitt, Dent (4), Vaughan (2), Compton (1).

Record Defeat: 0–9 v Notts Co, Division 3 (S), 16 October 1948 and v Northampton T, Division 3 (S), 12 April 1958.

Most League Points (2 for a win): 62, Division 4, 1976–77.

Most League Points (3 for a win): 89, Division 4, 1989–90.

Most League Goals: 88, Division 3 (S), 1932–33.

Highest League Scorer in Season: Fred Whitlow, 33, Division 3 (S), 1932–33.

Most League Goals in Total Aggregate: Tony Kellow, 129, 1976–78, 1980–83, 1985–88.

Most Capped Player: Dermot Curtis, 1 (17), Eire.

Most League Appearances: Arnold Mitchell, 495, 1952–66.

Record Transfer Fee Received: £500,000 from Rangers for Chris Vinnicombe, November 1989.

Record Transfer Fee Paid: £65,000 to Blackpool for Tony Kellow, March 1980.

Football League Record: 1920 Elected Division 3; 1921–58 Division 3 (S); 1958–64 Division 4; 1964–66 Division 3; 1966–77 Division 4; 1977–84 Division 3; 1984–90 Division 4; 1990–92 Division 3; 1992– Division 2.

Honours: Football League: Division 3 best season: 8th, 1979–80; Division 3 (S) – Runners-up 1932–33; Division 4 – Champions 1989–90; Runners-up 1976–77. *FA Cup:* best season: 6th rd replay, 1931. *Football League Cup:* never beyond 4th rd. *Division 3 (S) Cup:* Winners 1934.

EXETER CITY 1992—93 LEAGUE RECORD

Match No.	Date		Venue	Opponents	Result	H/T Score	Lg. Pos.	Goalscorers	Attendance
1	Aug	15	H	Rotherham U	L 0-2	0-0	—		3362
2		22	A	Blackpool	L 0-2	0-2	24		3999
3		29	H	Stoke C	D 2-2	1-2	21	Jepson, Harris	4106
4	Sept	1	H	Brighton & HA	L 2-3	2-2	—	Chapman, Jepson	3035
5		5	A	Stockport Co	D 2-2	1-0	21	Hodge 2	3759
6		12	A	Port Vale	D 2-2	1-1	22	Moran, Hodge	5642
7		15	H	Wigan Ath	D 0-0	0-0	—		2393
8		19	H	Leyton Orient	W 1-0	0-0	21	Whiston	2788
9		26	A	WBA	L 0-2	0-1	21		14,676
10	Oct	3	H	Bournemouth	D 1-1	1-0	20	Evans	3653
11		10	A	Swansea C	D 0-0	0-0	21		4439
12		17	H	Mansfield T	W 2-0	2-0	20	Evans, Jepson	2820
13		24	A	Huddersfield T	D 0-0	0-0	19		4707
14		31	H	Fulham	L 1-2	1-2	20	Hodge	3284
15	Nov	3	H	Bolton W	L 1-3	0-0	—	Hodge	2431
16		7	H	Hartlepool U	W 3-1	1-0	18	Moran, Kelly, Jepson	2856
17		21	H	Chester C	W 2-0	0-0	18	Hodge, Dolan	2452
18		28	A	Reading	W 3-2	2-1	17	Hiley 3	4015
19	Dec	12	A	Hull C	L 0-4	0-4	19		3167
20		19	H	Burnley	D 2-2	1-2	18	Moran, Pender (og)	3179
21		26	H	Plymouth Arg	W 2-0	1-0	15	Whiston, Daniels	6534
22		28	A	Preston NE	D 2-2	1-2	15	Whiston, Moran	5796
23	Jan	9	A	Wigan Ath	W 1-0	0-0	13	Brown	1882
24		16	H	WBA	L 2-3	1-0	13	Moran, Raven (og)	5437
25		23	A	Leyton Orient	L 0-5	0-2	16		5247
26		27	A	Stoke C	D 1-1	1-1	—	Cook	14,181
27		30	H	Blackpool	L 0-1	0-1	16		3384
28	Feb	6	A	Rotherham U	D 1-1	0-1	17	Jepson	4210
29		13	H	Stockport Co	D 2-2	1-2	19	Tonge, McIntyre	2795
30		20	A	Brighton & HA	L 0-3	0-0	19		5585
31		27	H	Swansea C	L 0-2	0-0	19		3146
32	Mar	6	A	Bournemouth	W 3-1	1-0	19	Dolan 2, McIntyre	4948
33		10	H	Bradford C	L 1-3	0-2	—	Daniels	3900
34		13	H	Hartlepool U	W 3-1	1-1	18	Jepson, Hodge, Moran	2639
35		20	A	Bolton W	L 1-4	1-2	18	Moran	6819
36		23	H	Reading	D 0-0	0-0	—		2874
37		27	A	Chester C	W 3-0	1-0	16	Dolan, McIntyre, Storer	2047
38	Apr	3	H	Bradford C	L 0-1	0-0	16		2547
39		6	H	Hull C	D 1-1	1-0	—	Jepson	2415
40		10	A	Plymouth Arg	W 3-0	1-0	15	Storer, Hodge 2	9391
41		12	A	Preston NE	L 0-1	0-0	17		3410
42		17	A	Burnley	L 1-3	0-1	21	Jepson	7332
43		24	A	Mansfield T	D 0-0	0-0	19		2527
44	May	1	H	Huddersfield T	L 1-2	1-1	20	Storer	3271
45		4	H	Port Vale	D 1-1	0-0	—	Moran	3219
46		8	A	Fulham	D 1-1	0-0	19	Storer	6501

Final League Position: 19

GOALSCORERS

League (54): Hodge 9, Jepson 8, Moran 8, Dolan 4, Storer 4, Hiley 3, McIntyre 3, Whiston 3, Daniels 2, Evans 2, Brown 1, Chapman 1, Cook 1, Harris 1, Kelly 1, Tonge 1, own goals 2.
Coca Cola Cup (4): Dolan 2, Hodge 1, Kelly 1.
FA Cup (3): Moran 2, Cook 1.

O'Keefe 2	Hiley 33	Cooper 16 + 4	Bond 17 + 1	Brown 40	Whiston 27	Collins 8 + 3	Harris 23 + 5	Moran 19 + 4	Jepson 35 + 3	Kelly 20 + 2	Miller 44	Williams 8 + 4	Hodge 41 + 1	Chapman 3 + 1	Cook 32	Redwood 3 + 3	Loram 2 + 1	Dolan 10 + 9	Evans 5	Tonge 13 + 2	Taylor 2 + 3	Daniels 26	Bailey 27	Gallen 6	Phillips — + 6	McIntyre 12 + 3	Minett 11 + 1	White 11	Storer 10	Match No.
1	2	3	4	5	6	7	8	9	10	11																				1
	2	3	5	11	6	7	8	9	10	14	1	4	12																	2
	2	3		5	6	7	8	9		4	1	12	11	10																3
	2	3		5	6	7	8	9		4	1	12	11	10																4
	2	7		5	6	14	8	9		4	1	12	11	10		3														5
	2	3		5	6	7	8	10	9	4	1		11		12															6
	2	7		5	6	12	8	10	9	4	1		11		3															7
	2	12		5	6		8	9	7		1	4	11		3			10												8
	2	10	4	5	6		8		7		1	12	11		3		14	9												9
	2	12		5	6		8	9	14	4	1		11		3			10		7										10
	2	7		5	6	12	8	9		4	1		11		3			10												11
	2			5	6	7		9	8		1	4	11		3			10												12
	2			5	6		10	12	7		1	4	11		3			8	9											13
	2	14		5	6		8	12	9	7	1	4	11		3			10												14
	2	7		5	6		8	10	9	4	1		11		3			12												15
	2	7	4	5	6		12	10	9	8	1		11		3															16
	2		7	5	6		14	10	9	8	1	4	11		3			12												17
	2		4	5	6		8	9	10		1		11		3					7										18
	2			5		7		9			1	14	11		3	12		10				4				6			8	19
	2				6			9	7	4	1		11		3			12		14		5				8			10	20
	2				6			9	8		1		11		3			4				5					7		10	21
	2	12			6			9	8		1		11		3			4				5					7		10	22
	2			5	6			9	8		1		11		3			7					4			10			12	23
	2	8			6		7	9	12		1		11		3							5	4						10	24
	2	7			6		8	9			1		11		3							5	4		12				10	25
	2	8			6		7	9			1		11		3			10				5	4							26
1	2	8			6		7	9	10		11				3			14				5	4		12					27
	2	3			6		7	12	9		1		11					10		8	14	5	4							28
	2	3	5				7	9			1		11		6			12		8	14	4							10	29
	2	3			6			9			1		11					12		7	8	5	4		14				10	30
	2	12			6			9			1		11		3			10		7	14	5	4			8				31
	2				6		7	9			1		11		3			10				5	4			8				32
	2				6		7	9			1		11		3			10				5	4			8				33
					6		7	12	9		1		11		3	14		10			2	5	4			8				34
					6		14	10	9		1		11		3			12			2	5	4			8			7	35
		7			6		14	10	9		1				3			12				5	4		11	8		2		36
					6						1		11		3			10				5	4		12	8	7	2	9	37
					6		14	12			1		11		3			10				5	4			8	7	2	9	38
					6		4		9		1		11		3							5				8	7	2	10	39
		7			6			9			1		11		3							5	4			8		2	10	40
		7			6			9			1		11		3			12				5	4		14	8		2	10	41
		7			6			9			1		11		3			12				5	4		14	8		2	10	42
		3	7		6			9			1											5	4		12	11	8	2	10	43
		3	7		6		12	9			1		11									5	4		14	8		2	10	44
		7	3		6		8	9			1		11									5	4		12			2	10	45
		7			6			9			1		11		3							5	4			8		2	10	46

Coca Cola Cup	First Round	Birmingham C (h)	0-0
		(a)	4-1
	Second Round	Oldham Ath (h)	0-1
		(a)	0-0
FA Cup	First Round	Kidderminster H (h)	1-0
	Second Round	Swansea C (h)	2-5

EXETER CITY

Player and Position	Ht	Wt	Date	Birth Place	Source	Clubs	League App	Gls
Goalkeepers								
Kevin Miller	6 1	12 10	15 3 69	Falmouth	Newquay	Exeter C	163	—
Vince O'Keefe‡	6 2	13 00	2 4 57	Birmingham	Local	Birmingham C	—	—
						Peterborough U (loan)	—	—
						Walsall	—	—
					AP Leamington	Exeter C	53	—
						Torquay U	108	—
						Blackburn R	68	—
						Bury (loan)	2	—
						Blackpool (loan)	1	—
						Blackpool (loan)	6	—
						Wrexham	83	—
						Exeter C	2	—
Defenders								
Kevin Bond	6 2	13 10	22 6 57	London	Bournemouth	Norwich C	142	12
					Seattle S	Manchester C	110	11
						Southampton	140	6
						Bournemouth	126	4
						Exeter C	18	—
Jon Brown	5 10	11 03	8 9 66	Barnsley	Denaby U	Exeter C	104	1
Andy Cook	5 9	10 12	10 8 69	Romsey	Apprentice	Southampton	16	1
						Exeter C	70	1
David Cooper	6 0	12 00	7 3 73	Welwyn	Luton T	Exeter C	33	—
Scott Daniels	6 1	11 09	22 11 69	Benfleet	Trainee	Colchester U	73	—
						Exeter C	69	5
Martin Phillips§			13 3 76	Exeter	Trainee	Exeter C	6	—
Toby Redwood			7 10 73	Newton Abbot	Trainee	Exeter C	7	—
Craig Taylor	6 1	12 00	24 1 74	Plymouth	Trainee	Exeter C	5	—
Alan Tonge	5 8	11 11	25 2 72	Bury	Trainee	Manchester U	—	—
						Exeter C	18	1
Chris White	5 11	11 10	11 12 70	Chatham	Trainee	Portsmouth	—	—
						Peterborough U	13	—
						Doncaster R (loan)	6	—
						Exeter C	11	—
Midfield								
Danny Bailey†	5 7	12 07	21 5 64	Leyton	Apprentice	Bournemouth	2	—
					Local	Torquay U	1	—
					Wealdstone	Exeter C	64	2
						Reading	50	2
						Fulham (loan)	3	—
						Exeter C	27	—
Eamonn Collins‡	5 6	10 09	22 10 65	Dublin	Blackpool	Southampton	3	—
						Portsmouth	5	—
						Exeter C (loan)	9	—
						Colchester U	39	2
						Exeter C	11	—
Andy Harris	5 10	12 02	17 11 70	Birmingham	Trainee	Birmingham C	1	—
						Oxford U (loan)	1	—
						Exeter C	34	1
Steve Williams*	5 9	11 04	12 7 58	London	Apprentice	Southampton	278	18
						Arsenal	95	4
						Luton T	40	1
						Exeter C	48	—
Forwards								
Eamonn Dolan	5 10	12 01	20 9 67	Dagenham	Apprentice	West Ham U	15	3
						Bristol C (loan)	3	—
						Birmingham C	12	1
						Exeter C	26	4

EXETER CITY

Colours: Red and white striped shirts, black shorts, red stockings. **Change colours:** Navy blue shirts, yellow shorts.

Foundation: Exeter City was formed in 1904 by the amalgamation of St. Sidwell's United and Exeter United. The club first played in the East Devon League and then the Plymouth & District League. After an exhibition match between West Bromwich Albion and Woolwich Arsenal was held to test interest as Exeter was then a rugby stronghold, Exeter City decided at a meeting at the Red Lion Hotel to turn professional in 1908.

First Football League game: 28 August, 1920, Division 3, v Brentford (h) W 3-0 – Pym; Coleburne, Feebury (1p); Crawshaw, Carrick, Mitton; Appleton, Makin, Wright (1), Vowles (1), Dockray.

Did you know: Spectators at the last home game of the 1934–35 season watched a goalless first half between Exeter City and Aldershot. The final score was Exeter 8, Aldershot 1.

Managers (and Secretary-Managers)
Arthur Chadwick 1910–22, Fred Mavin 1923–27, Dave Wilson 1928–29, Billy McDevitt 1929–35, Jack English 1935–39, George Roughton 1945–52, Norman Kirkman 1952–53, Norman Dodgin 1953–57, Bill Thompson 1957–58, Frank Broome 1958–60, Glen Wilson 1960–62, Cyril Spiers 1962–63, Jack Edwards 1963–65, Ellis Stuttard 1965–66, Jock Basford 1966–67, Frank Broome 1967–69, Johnny Newman 1969–76, Bobby Saxton 1977–79, Brian Godfrey 1979–83, Gerry Francis 1983–84, Jim Iley 1984–85, Colin Appleton 1985–87, Terry Cooper 1988–91, Alan Ball August 1991–.

Player and Position	Ht	Wt	Date	Birth Place	Source	Clubs	League App	Gls
John Hodge	5 6	10 00	1 4 69	Ormskirk	Exmouth	Exeter C	65	10
Ron Jepson	6 1	13 02	12 5 63	Stoke	Nantwich	Port Vale	22	—
						Peterborough U (loan)	18	5
						Preston NE	38	8
						Exeter C	38	8
Steve Moran*	5 8	11 03	10 1 61	Croydon	Amateur	Southampton	180	78
						Leicester C	43	14
						Reading	116	30
						Exeter C	57	27
Stuart Storer	5 11	11 08	16 1 67	Harborough	Local	Mansfield T	1	—
						Birmingham C	8	—
						Everton	—	—
						Wigan Ath (loan)	12	—
						Bolton W	123	12
						Exeter C	10	4
Peter Whiston	6 0	11 06	4 1 68	Widnes		Plymouth Arg	10	—
						Torquay U (loan)	8	1
						Torquay U	32	—
						Exeter C	63	6

Trainees
Allen, Stephen J. A; Baines, Mark; Ball, James A; Brown, Mark J; Darch, Kevin J; Harris, Matthew; Hutchings, Mark; Lafferty, Philip R; Pears, Richard J; Phillips, Martin J; Rice, Gary J; Thirlby, Anthony D.

**Non-Contract
Bailey, Danny S.

Associated Schoolboys
Beavis, Ian J; Bell, Daniel A; Dodge, William J; Green, Brendan S; Grylls, Casey B. H. V; Harris, Nathan G; Littley, James M; Moxey, Matthew J; Page, Mark J; Parsons, Timothy J; Rodwell, Andrew; Shearer, Adam; Smith, Jason L; Thomas, Nigel W; Vittles, James M. S; Wright, Brett M.

Associated Schoolboys who have accepted the club's offer of a Traineeship/Contract
Hare, Matthew; McConnell, Barry; Medlin, Nicholas R. M; Rollason, Andrew.

**Non-Contract Players who are retained must be re-signed before they are eligible to play in League matches.

224

FULHAM 1992-93 *Back row (left to right):* Stacey North, Kelly Haag, Gavin Nebbeling, Glen Thomas, Martin Pike, Sean Farrell.
Third row: Junior Lewis, Alan Gough, Jim Stannard, Gus Hurdle, Terry Bullivant (Youth Coach).
Second row: Ray Lewington (Coach), Julian Hails, Paul Sheldrick, John Marshall, Leon Lewis, Jeff Eckhardt, Peter Baah, Martin Ferney, Jimmy Sugrue, Mark Tucker, Eric Deanus (Kit Manager).
Front row: Mark Newson, Lee Tierling, Udo Onwere, Don Mackay (Team Manager), Simon Morgan, Paul Kelly, Gary Brazil.

Division 2 **FULHAM**

Craven Cottage, Stevenage Rd, Fulham, London SW6.
Telephone 071–736 6561. Clubcall: 0898 121198.

Ground capacity: 16,815.

Record attendance: 49,335 v Millwall, Division 2, 8 October 1938.

Record receipts: £80,247 v Chelsea, Division 2, 8 October 1983.

Pitch measurements: 110yd × 75yd.

Chief Executive: R.J. Summers.

Chairman: Jimmy Hill.

Directors: W. F. Muddyman (Vice-chairman), C. A. Swain, A. Muddyman, T. Wilson, D. E. Shrimpton.

Manager: Don Mackay. *Assistant Manager:* Ray Lewington.

Physio: Chris Smith. *Commercial/Community Manager:* Tom Enefer. *Community Officer:* Gary Mulcahey.

Club Secretary: Mrs Janice O'Doherty.

Commercial Manager: Ken Myers.

Year Formed: 1879. *Turned Professional:* 1898. *Ltd Co.:* 1903. *Reformed:* 1987.

Club Nickname: 'Cottagers'.

Previous Name: 1879–88, Fulham St Andrew's.

Previous Grounds: 1879 Star Road, Fulham; c.1883 Eel Brook Common, 1884 Lillie Road; 1885 Putney Lower Common; 1886 Ranelagh House, Fulham; 1888 Barn Elms, Castelnau; 1889 Purser's Cross (Roskell's Field), Parsons Green Lane; 1891 Eel Brook Common; 1891 Half Moon, Putney; 1895 Captain James Field, West Brompton; 1896 Craven Cottage.

Record League Victory: 10–1 v Ipswich T, Division 1, 26 December 1963 – Macedo; Cohen, Langley; Mullery (1), Keetch, Robson (1); Key, Cook (1), Leggat (4), Haynes, Howfield (3).

Record Cup Victory: 6–0 v Wimbledon (away), FA Cup, 1st rd (replay), 3 December 1930 – Iceton; Gibbon, Lilley; Oliver, Dudley, Barrett; Temple, Hammond (1), Watkins (1), Gibbons (2), Penn (2). 6–0 v Bury, FA Cup, 3rd rd, 7 January 1938 – Turner; Bacuzzi, Keeping; Evans, Dennison, Tompkins; Higgins, Worsley, Rooke (6), O'Callaghan, Arnold.

Record Defeat: 0–10 v Liverpool, League Cup 2nd rd, 1st leg, 23 September 1986.

Most League Points (2 for a win): 60, Division 2, 1958–59 and Division 3, 1970–71.

Most League Points (3 for a win): 78, Division 3, 1981–82.

Most League Goals: 111, Division 3 (S), 1931–32.

Highest League Scorer in Season: Frank Newton, 43, Division 3 (S), 1931–32.

Most League Goals in Total Aggregate: Gordon Davies, 159, 1978–84, 1986–91.

Most Capped Player: Johnny Haynes, 56, England.

Most League Appearances: Johnny Haynes, 594, 1952–70.

Record Transfer Fee Received: £333,333 from Liverpool for Richard Money, May 1980.

Record Transfer Fee Paid: £150,000 to Orient for Peter Kitchen, February 1979, and to Brighton & HA for Teddy Maybank, December 1979.

Football League Record: 1907 Elected to Division 2; 1928–32 Division 3 (S); 1932–49 Division 2; 1949–52 Division 1; 1952–59 Division 2; 1959–68 Division 1; 1968–69 Division 2; 1969–71 Division 3; 1971–80 Division 2; 1980–82 Division 3; 1982–86 Division 2; 1986–92 Division 3; 1992– Division 2.

Honours: Football League: Division 1 best season: 10th, 1959–60; Division 2 – Champions 1948–49; Runners-up 1958–59; Division 3 (S) – Champions 1931–32; Division 3 – Runners-up 1970–71. *FA Cup:* Runners-up 1974–75. *Football League Cup:* best season: 5th rd, 1967–68, 1970–71.

FULHAM 1992—93 LEAGUE RECORD

Match No.	Date		Venue	Opponents	Result	H/T Score	Lg. Pos.	Goalscorers	Atten dance
1	Aug	15	A	Port Vale	D	0-0	0-0	—	6746
2		22	H	Preston NE	W	2-1	1-0	8	Eckhardt, Pike	3641
3		29	A	Mansfield T	W	3-2	1-0	2	Marshall, Farrell, Eckhardt	3228
4	Sept	1	A	Wigan Ath	W	3-1	3-1	—	Eckhardt, Marshall, Farrell	1591
5		5	H	WBA	D	1-1	0-1	3	Farrell	9143
6		12	A	Bournemouth	L	1-2	1-1	8	Pike	5398
7		15	H	Swansea C	D	1-1	1-0	—	Ferney	4268
8		19	H	Plymouth Arg	W	3-1	0-0	6	Brazil 2, Nebbeling	5439
9		25	A	Stockport Co	D	0-0	0-0	—		4755
10	Oct	2	A	Reading	L	0-3	0-2	—		7204
11		10	H	Hull C	D	3-3	1-3	11	Morgan, Brazil, Onwere	5247
12		17	A	Burnley	L	2-5	1-4	12	Farrell 2	9881
13		24	H	Chester C	W	1-0	0-0	10	Preece (og)	3753
14		31	A	Exeter C	W	2-1	2-1	10	Farrell 2	3284
15	Nov	3	H	Stoke C	D	0-0	0-0	—		5903
16		7	A	Bradford C	L	2-3	1-3	11	Pike, Blake (og)	7625
17		21	H	Bolton W	L	1-4	1-1	13	Eckhardt	4049
18		28	A	Brighton & HA	W	2-0	0-0	10	Hails, Pike	7894
19	Dec	5	H	Mansfield T	D	0-0	0-0	9		3285
20		12	H	Rotherham U	L	0-1	0-1	12		3629
21		20	A	Blackpool	D	1-1	1-0	—	McGlashan	3802
22		26	A	Leyton Orient	D	0-0	0-0	12		8431
23		28	H	Hartlepool U	L	1-3	1-1	12	Hails	4403
24	Jan	9	A	Swansea C	D	2-2	0-1	12	Morgan, Hails	5048
25		16	H	Stockport Co	W	2-1	1-0	11	Pike, Nebbeling	3516
26		23	A	Plymouth Arg	D	1-1	0-0	11	Morgan	5703
27		30	A	Preston NE	W	2-1	0-1	10	Hails, Morgan	5858
28	Feb	6	H	Port Vale	L	1-2	1-1	10	Eckhardt	4905
29		13	A	WBA	L	0-4	0-2	11		12,859
30		20	H	Wigan Ath	W	1-0	0-0	11	Eckhardt	3502
31		27	A	Hull C	D	1-1	0-1	12	Morgan	3645
32	Mar	2	H	Bournemouth	D	1-1	0-1	—	Pike (pen)	3424
33		6	H	Reading	D	0-0	0-0	12		4818
34		10	A	Huddersfield T	L	0-1	0-1	—		3670
35		13	H	Bradford C	D	1-1	0-1	14	Hails	4343
36		20	A	Stoke C	L	0-1	0-0	14		17,935
37		23	H	Brighton & HA	W	2-0	1-0	—	Farrell, Onwere	5402
38		27	A	Bolton W	L	0-1	0-0	14		8402
39	Apr	2	H	Huddersfield T	L	0-1	0-0	—		3611
40		6	A	Rotherham U	D	1-1	1-0	—	Hails	3065
41		10	H	Leyton Orient	W	1-0	0-0	13	Onwere	5976
42		12	A	Hartlepool U	W	3-0	0-0	13	Morgan 2, Brazil	2361
43		17	H	Blackpool	W	1-0	1-0	13	Brazil	4633
44		24	H	Burnley	W	4-0	1-0	12	Kelly, Farrell 3	5531
45	May	1	A	Chester C	W	3-2	1-0	11	Brazil 2, Morgan	2016
46		8	H	Exeter C	D	1-1	0-0	12	Farrell	6501

Final League Position: 12

GOALSCORERS

League (57): Farrell 12, Morgan 8, Brazil 7, Eckhardt 6, Hails 6, Pike 6 (1 pen), Onwere 3, Marshall 2, Nebbeling 2, Ferney 1, Kelly 1, McGlashan 1, own goals 2.
Coca Cola Cup (0).
FA Cup (1): Farrell 1.

Stannard 43	Morgan 38+1	Pike 46	Bailey 2+1	Nebbeling 28+2	Thomas 43	Halis 45+1	Marshall 40+1	Farrell 34+1	Eckhardt 30	Kelly M 19+6	Newson 26+3	Ferney 10+6	Baah 12+4	Onwere 22+7	Archibald 2	Gough 3	Brazil 27+3	Lewis J 4+2	Tierling 2+3	Cooper 8+1	McGlashan 5	Haag 5+5	Tucker 2	Bedrossian 7+2	Jupp 3	Match No.
1	2	3	4	5	6	7	8	9	10	11	12															1
1	2	3	4	5	6	7	8	9	10	11																2
1	2	3	14	5		7	8	9	10			6	*4*	*11*	12											3
1	2	3		5	6	7	8	9	10				4	11	12											4
1	2	3		5	6	7	8	9	4					11			10									5
	2	3		5	6	7	8	9			14		*4*	11			10	1	12							6
	2	3		5	6	7	8	9			12		4	11				1	10							7
1	2	3		5	6	7	8	9		11			4				10									8
1	2	3		5	6	7	8	9	4	11							10									9
1	2	3		5	6	7	8	9	4	11		12					10									10
1	2	3		5	6	7	8	9	4	*11*	12			14			10									11
1	2	3		5	6	7	8	9	4		12			*11*			10	14								12
1	2	3		5	6	7	8	9	4								10	11								13
1	2	3		5	6	7	8	9	4								10	11								14
1	2	3		5	6	7	8	9	4					12			10	11								15
1	2	3		5	6	7	8	9	4					12			*10*	11	14							16
1	2	3			6	7	8	9	4					11			10	12			5					17
1		3		2	6	7	8	9	4					11			10				5					18
1		3			6	7	8	9	4		*2*			11			10				5					19
1		3			6	7	8	9	4		*2*	12		11				14		5	10					20
1		3			6	7	8		4		*2*		9	11						5	10					21
1		3	5		6	12	8		4		*2*			11			9			7	10					22
1	12	3	5		6	7	8		4		*2*			11			14			9	10					23
1	2	3			6	7	8		4	5	12			11						9	10					24
1	2	3	9		6	7	8		4	5	12			11			10									25
1	2	3	5		6	7	8	14	9	4	12			*11*			10									26
1	2	3	5		6	7	8	11	9	4							10									27
1	2	3	11		6	7	8	9	4	5		12					10									28
1	2	3				7	8	9	4	11	5	*6*	12	10					14							29
1	2	3			6	7	8	9	4	11	5			10						12						30
1	2	3	4		6	7	8			11	5			10						9						31
1	2	3	4		6	7	8			11	5	10	12							9						32
1	2	3	4		6	7	8	9	10	11	5	14					12									33
1		3			7	*2*	9	6	11	5	4			12			10			14	8					34
1	2	3			6	7	8	9	4	11	5	12		10												35
1		3			6	7	8	9		11	5	12	4	10					2							36
1	2	3			6	7	8	9		11	5		4				10									37
	2	3			6	7	8	9		11	5		*4*	1	12		10	14								38
1	2	3	12		6	7	8			11	5		4	10						9	14					39
1	2	3	12		6	7	*8*			5	11		4	10						14	*9*					40
1	2	3	8		6	7			12	5	11		4	10						14	*9*					41
1	2	3	8		6	7			12	5	11		4	10						14	*9*					42
1	2	3			6	7	8		12		11		4				10							9	5	43
1	2	3			6	7	8		11	5			4				10							9		44
1	2	3			6	7	12	8	11				4				10							9	5	45
1	2	3			6	7		9	12			4		11			10							8	5	46

Coca Cola Cup	First Round	Brentford (h)	0-2
		(a)	0-2
FA Cup	First Round	Northampton T (a)	1-3

FULHAM

Player and Position	Ht	Wt	Date	Birth Place	Source	Clubs	League App	Gls
Goalkeepers								
Alan Gough	5 11	12 13	10 3 71	Watford	Shelbourne	Portsmouth	—	—
						Fulham	3	—
Jim Stannard	6 2	14 12	6 10 62	London	Local	Fulham	41	—
						Charlton Ath (loan)	1	—
						Southend U (loan)	17	—
						Southend U	92	—
						Fulham	266	1
Defenders								
Jeff Eckhardt	6 0	11 07	7 10 65	Sheffield		Sheffield U	74	2
						Fulham	214	20
Martin Ferney	5 11	12 04	8 11 71	Lambeth	Trainee	Fulham	30	1
Duncan Jupp§	6 0	12 02	25 1 75	Guildford	Trainee	Fulham	3	—
Leon Lewis*	5 9	11 04	9 12 73	London	Trainee	Fulham	—	—
John Marshall	5 10	12 01	18 8 64	Surrey	Apprentice	Fulham	347	25
Simon Morgan	5 10	11 07	5 9 66	Birmingham		Leicester C	160	3
						Fulham	107	11
Gavin Nebbeling*	6 0	12 10	15 5 63	Johannesburg	Arcadia Shepherds	Crystal Palace	151	8
						Northampton T (loan)	11	—
						Fulham	88	2
						Hereford U (loan)	3	—
Mark Newson*	5 10	12 06	7 12 60	Stepney	Apprentice Maidstone U	Charlton Ath	—	—
						Bournemouth	177	23
						Fulham	102	4
Martin Pike	5 11	11 07	21 10 64	South Shields	Apprentice	WBA	—	—
						Peterborough U	126	8
						Sheffield U	129	5
						Tranmere R (loan)	2	—
						Bolton W (loan)	5	1
						Fulham	157	13
Glen Thomas	6 1	12 07	6 10 67	Hackney	Apprentice	Fulham	207	6
Mark Tucker*	6 0	11 07	27 4 72	Woking	Trainee	Fulham	4	—
Midfield								
Ara Bedrossian†	5 9	10 00	2 6 67	Cyprus		Fulham	9	—
Mark Cooper	5 8	11 04	18 12 68	Wakefield	Trainee	Bristol C	—	—
						Exeter C	50	12
						Southend U (loan)	5	—
						Birmingham C	39	4
						Fulham	9	—
						Huddersfield T (loan)	10	4
Sean Farrell	6 1	12 08	28 2 69	Watford	Apprentice	Luton T	25	1
						Colchester U (loan)	9	1
						Northampton T (loan)	4	1
						Fulham	60	22
Mark Kelly*	5 9	10 05	7 10 66	Blackpool		Shrewsbury T	—	—
						Cardiff C	105	2
						Fulham	64	2
Paul Kelly	5 7	10 13	24 2 74	Hillingdon	Trainee	Fulham	3	—
Junior Lewis*	6 2	11 08	9 10 73	Middlesex	Trainee	Fulham	6	—
Udo Onwere	6 0	11 07	9 11 71	Hammersmith	Trainee	Fulham	63	7
Forwards								
Steve Archibald‡	5 10	11 02	27 9 56	Glasgow	Fernhill Ath	Clyde	65	7
						Aberdeen	76	29
						Tottenham H	131	58

FULHAM

Colours: White shirts, red and black trim, black shorts, white stockings red and black trim. **Change colours:** Red/black striped shirts, white shorts, red stockings.

Foundation: Churchgoers were responsible for the foundation of Fulham, which first saw the light of day as Fulham St. Andrew's Church Sunday School FC in 1879. They won the West London Amateur Cup in 1887 and the championship of the West London League in its initial season of 1892–93. The name Fulham had been adopted in 1888.

First Football League game: 3 September, 1907, Division 2, v Hull C (h) L 0-1 – Skene; Ross, Lindsay; Collins, Morrison, Goldie; Dalrymple, Freeman, Bevan, Hubbard, Threlfall.

Did you know: When Fulham won the Division 2 championship in 1948–49, all but eight of their 77 goals were scored by their regular forwards: Bob Thomas (23), Arthur Rowley (19), Arthur Stevens (12) plus Jack McDonald and Bedford Jezzard with 15 between them.

Managers (and Secretary-Managers)
Harry Bradshaw 1904–09, Phil Kelso 1909–24, Andy Ducat 1924–26, Joe Bradshaw 1926–29, Ned Liddell 1929–31, Jim MacIntyre 1931–34, Jim Hogan 1934–35, Jack Peart 1935–48, Frank Osborne 1948–64 (was secretary-manager or GM for most of this period), Bill Dodgin Snr 1949–53, Duggie Livingstone 1956–58, Bedford Jezzard 1958–64 (GM for last two months), Vic Buckingham 1965–68, Bobby Robson 1968, Bill Dodgin Jnr 1969–72, Alec Stock 1972–76, Bobby Campbell 1976–80, Malcolm Macdonald 1980–84, Ray Harford 1984–86, Ray Lewington 1986–90, Alan Dicks 1990–91, Don Mackay December 1991–.

Player and Position	Ht	Wt	Date	Birth Place	Source	Clubs	League App	Gls
					Barcelona	Blackburn R	20	6
						Hibernian	44	15
						St Mirren	16	2
						Reading	1	—
						Fulham	2	—
Peter Baah	5 9	10 04	1 5 73	Littleborough	Trainee	Blackburn R	1	—
						Fulham	16	—
Gary Brazil	5 11	10 02	19 9 62	Tunbridge Wells	Crystal Palace	Sheffield U	62	9
						Port Vale (loan)	6	3
						Preston NE	166	58
						Newcastle U	23	2
						Fulham	117	25
Kelly Haag*	6 0	12 03	6 10 70	Enfield	Trainee	Brentford	5	—
						Fulham	67	9
Julian Hails	5 10	11 01	20 11 67	Lincoln		Fulham	64	7
Lee Tierling	5 7	11 08	25 10 72	Wegberg	Trainee	Portsmouth	—	—
						Fulham	5	—

Trainees
Andrews, Nicholas T; Armitage, James A; Bolt, Daniel A; Carey, John D. T; Girdler, Stuart; Hawkins, Benjamin J; Haworth, Robert J; Hendricks, Alan W; Jupp, Duncan A; Mison, Michael; Munoz, Mark S; Murphy, Gary J; Omogbehin, Collin L; Power, James S; Power, Raymond O; Richards, Jonathan I; Whitaker, Andrew T; Wright, Stuart J.

**Non-Contract
Bedrossian, Ara.

Associated Schoolboys
Bascombe, Roland; Chapple, Kevin; Johns, Jason; Probets, Clayton; Scannell, David.

Associated Schoolboys who have accepted the club's offer of a Traineeship/Contract
Abbott, Stuart R. C; Bartley, Carl; Ray, Kevin P; Smith, David P; Williams, Carl.

**Non-Contract Players who are retained must be re-signed before they are eligible to play in League matches.

GILLINGHAM 1992-93   *Back row (left to right):* Richard Carpenter, Nick Forster, Mark Dempsey, Neil Smith, Eliot Martin, Mark O'Connor, Joe Dunne, David Crown.
Centre row: Pat Hilton (Youth Team Manager), Richard Breen, Tony Butler, Paul Hague, Scott Barrett, Trevor Aylott, Harvey Lim, Brian Clarke, Gary Breen, Andy Arnott, Javed Mughal (Physio).
Front row: Lawrence Osbourne, Steve Lovell, Liburd Henry, Damien Richardson (First Team Manager), Paul Clark, Ron Hillyard, Tony Eeles, Lee Palmer.

Division 3   **GILLINGHAM**

Priestfield Stadium, Gillingham. Telephone Medway (0634) 851854/576828. Fax (0634) 850986. Commercial Office: 851462.

Ground capacity: 10,412.

Record attendance: 23,002 v QPR, FA Cup 3rd rd 10 January 1948.

Record receipts: £49,377 v Swindon T, play-offs, 22 May 1987.

Pitch measurements: 114yd × 75yd.

President: J. W. Leech. *Vice-presidents:* G. B. Goodere, G. V. W. Lukehurst.

Chairman: B. R. Baker. *Vice-chairman:* Rt. Hon. Earl Henry Sondes.

Managing Director: A. Smith.

Directors: P. H. Giles FCA, M. G. Lukehurst, G. T. Carney.

Manager: Mike Flanagan.

Physio: Javed Mughal.

Chief Executive/Company Secretary: Barry Bright. *Commercial Manager:* Bill Williams.

Year Formed: 1893. *Turned Professional:* 1894. *Ltd Co.:* 1893.

Club Nickname: 'The Gills'.

Previous Name: New Brompton, 1893–1913.

Record League Victory: 10–0 v Chesterfield, Division 3, 5 September 1987 – Kite; Haylock, Pearce, Shipley (2) (Lillis), West, Greenall (1), Pritchard (2), Shearer (2), Lovell, Elsey (2), David Smith (1).

Record Cup Victory: 10–1 v Gorleston, FA Cup, 1st rd, 16 November 1957 – Brodie; Parry, Hannaway; Riggs, Boswell, Laing; Payne, Fletcher (2), Saunders (5), Morgan (1), Clark (2).

Record Defeat: 2–9 v Nottingham F, Division 3 (S), 18 November 1950.

Most League Points (2 for a win): 62, Division 4, 1973–74.

Most League Points (3 for a win): 83, Division 3, 1984–85.

Most League Goals: 90, Division 4, 1973–74.

Highest League Scorer in Season: Ernie Morgan, 31, Division 3 (S), 1954–55 and Brian Yeo, 31, Division 4, 1973–74.

Most League Goals in Total Aggregate: Brian Yeo, 135, 1963–75.

Most Capped Player: Tony Cascarino, 3 (43), Republic of Ireland.

Most League Appearances: John Simpson, 571, 1957–72.

Record Transfer Fee Received: £300,000 from Tottenham H for Peter Beadle, June 1992.

Record Transfer Fee Paid: £102,500 to Tottenham H for Mark Cooper, October 1987.

Football League Record: 1920 Original Member of Division 3; 1921 Division 3 (S); 1938 Failed re-election; Southern League 1938–44; Kent League 1944–46; Southern League 1946–50; 1950 Re-elected to Division 3 (S); 1958–64 Division 4; 1964–71 Division 3; 1971–74 Division 4; 1974–89 Division 3; 1989–92 Division 4; 1992– Division 3.

Honours: Football League: Division 3 best season: 4th, 1978–79, 1984–85; Division 4 – Champions 1963–64; Runners-up 1973–74. *FA Cup:* best season: 5th rd, 1969–70. *Football League Cup:* best season: 4th rd, 1964.

GILLINGHAM 1992—93 LEAGUE RECORD

Match No.	Date		Venue	Opponents	Result	H/T Score	Lg. Pos.	Goalscorers	Atten dance
1	Aug	15	H	Northampton T	L 2-3	1-2	—	Osborne, O'Connor	3863
2		22	A	Bury	L 0-1	0-0	19		1806
3		29	H	Barnet	D 1-1	0-1	20	Crown	3874
4	Sept	1	H	Wrexham	W 4-1	3-0	—	Aylott, Lovell 3 (1 pen)	2503
5		5	A	Scarborough	D 1-1	0-1	14	Aylott	1412
6		12	H	Chesterfield	D 0-0	0-0	15		2853
7		15	A	Rochdale	D 1-1	0-1	—	Henry	1879
8		19	A	Cardiff C	L 1-3	0-2	16	Forster	6356
9		26	H	Walsall	L 0-1	0-0	19		2821
10	Oct	3	H	Crewe Alex	L 1-2	0-1	21	Clark	2420
11		10	A	Doncaster R	L 0-1	0-0	22		2477
12		24	A	Halifax T	L 0-2	0-1	22		1216
13		31	H	Torquay U	L 0-2	0-0	22		3067
14	Nov	3	H	Hereford U	W 3-1	2-1	—	Forster 2, Arnott	2143
15		7	A	Carlisle U	L 0-1	0-1	22		3213
16		21	A	Darlington	W 3-1	2-1	22	Crown, Parkin (og), Forster	2563
17		28	A	Lincoln C	D 1-1	0-1	21	Arnott	3175
18	Dec	12	A	Shrewsbury T	L 1-2	0-1	22	Arnott	2442
19		18	H	Colchester U	L 0-1	0-0	—		2331
20		26	H	Bury	L 1-4	0-2	22	Smith	3632
21		28	A	Scunthorpe U	D 2-2	1-0	22	Arnott, Stephenson	2835
22	Jan	8	H	Rochdale	W 4-2	1-1	—	Arnott 2, Green, Baker	3052
23		16	A	Walsall	D 1-1	0-0	22	Smith	3253
24		23	H	Cardiff C	L 0-1	0-1	22		4069
25	Feb	6	A	Northampton T	D 2-2	2-1	22	Baker, Ritchie	3812
26		13	H	Scarborough	W 3-1	2-1	21	Ritchie 2, Stephenson	3022
27		16	A	Chesterfield	D 1-1	0-1	—	Green	2721
28		20	A	Wrexham	L 0-2	0-0	21		4415
29		27	H	Doncaster R	D 1-1	0-1	21	Crown	2975
30	Mar	2	A	Barnet	L 0-2	0-1	—		3446
31		6	A	Crewe Alex	L 1-3	0-2	21	Martin	3215
32		9	A	York C	D 1-1	0-1	—	Eeles	3327
33		13	H	Carlisle U	W 1-0	0-0	19	Smith	3307
34		20	A	Hereford U	L 1-3	0-2	21	Crown	2138
35		23	H	Lincoln C	W 3-1	0-0	—	Green, Forster	2906
36		27	A	Darlington	D 1-1	0-0	19	Crane	2404
37	Apr	2	H	York C	L 1-4	1-2	—	Baker	3912
38		6	H	Shrewsbury T	W 1-0	1-0	—	Crown	3086
39		12	H	Scunthorpe U	D 1-1	1-1	19	Baker	3859
40		16	A	Colchester U	L 0-3	0-2	—		4695
41	May	1	H	Halifax T	W 2-0	0-0	19	Eeles, Baker	7151
42		8	A	Torquay U	L 1-2	1-0	21	Baker	4645

Final League Position: 21

GOALSCORERS

League (48): Arnott 6, Baker 6, Forster 6, Crown 5, Green 3, Lovell 3 (1 pen), Ritchie 3, Smith 3, Aylott 2, Eeles 2, Stephenson 2, Clark 1, Crane 1, Henry 1, Martin 1, O'Connor 1, Osborne 1, own goal 1.
Coca Cola Cup (4): Crown 2, Aylott 1, Lovell 1.
FA Cup (8): Crown 2, Forster 2, Arnott 1, Clark 1, Green 1 (pen), Henry 1 (pen).

Barrett 34	Green 39	Palmer 9 + 1	Butler 41	Breen 25 + 4	Smith 37 + 2	Clark 34 + 1	Osborne 1	Aylott 8 + 2	O'Connor 16 + 5	Henry 25 + 3	Lovell 11 + 2	Dempsey 9 + 7	Crown 19 + 1	Arnott 13 + 2	Forster 19 + 7	Lim 8	Carpenter 25 + 3	Eeles 12 + 2	Martin 22	Hague 1	Stephenson 12	Houghton 3	Roeder 6	Baker 21	Ritchie 6	Dunne 3 + 1	Watson 1	Crane 2 + 5	Match No.
1	2	3	4	5	6	7	8	9	10	11	12	14																	1
1	2	3	4	5	6	7			10	11	9	14		8	12														2
1	2	3	4	5	6	7		9	10	11	12	14	8																3
1	2	3	4	5	6	7		9	10	12	11		8	14															4
	2	3	4	5	6	7		9	10	12	11		8	14		1													5
	2		4	5	6	7		9	10	3	11				12	8	1												6
	2		4	5	6	7				3	11	12		9	8		1	10											7
	2		4	5	6	7		9	10	3	11				8		1	12											8
1	2		4	5	6	7		9	10	3	11	14			8		12												9
1	12		4	5	6	7		9	10	3	11	8		14			2												10
1			4	5	6	7				3	11			9			12	2	8	10									11
	2		4	5	6	7				11	3	10		9			12	1	8										12
	2		4		6	7				5	11	10	9	14	1	12	8	3											13
1	2		4	5	6	7								11			9	8	10			3							14
1	2		4		6	7						12		11			9	8	10		5	3							15
1	2		4	5	6	7								8			9	10	3		11								16
1	2		4	5	6	7								8			9	10	3		11								17
1	2		4	5	6	7						12	14	8			9	10	3		11								18
1			4	5	6	7						12	10	2	9		3				11	8							19
	2		4	5	6	7							10	9	1		3				11	8							20
	2	3	4	14	6	7						12	10	9	1						11	8	5						21
1	2	3	4	5		7											8	9	6		11			10					22
1	2	3	4	5	6	7						12			9		8	9	8		11			10					23
1	2	3	4	5	6	7						12			9		8				11			10					24
1	2		4		6	7											8	3			11		5	10	9				25
1	2		4		6										7		8	3			11		5	10	9				26
1	2		4		6										7		8	3			11		5	10	9				27
1	2		4	14	6					12	11				7		8	3					5	10	9				28
1	2		4	5	6					11		12			7		8	3						10	9			14	29
1	2		4	5	6										8		10	3						9	11	7			30
1	2		4	5	6	14						12			8		10	7	3		11			9					31
1	2		4	5	6	7				10	12						8		3		11			9					32
1	5		4		6	7				3					8			2			11			10	9				33
1	5		4	14		7						12	2		8						11		6	10	9	3			34
1	2		4							3					11		8				10		5	6	9			12	35
1	2		4	14	12	7				3					11						10		5	6	9			8	36
1	2		4		12	7				3					11						10		5	6	9			8	37
1	2		4		6	7									11		8		3		10		5		9			12	38
1	2		4		6	7									11		8	12	3		10		5		9				39
1	2		4		6	7									11		8		3		10		5	14	9			12	40
1			4		6	7									8				3		11		5	10	9	2		12	41
1			4		6	7	8												3		11		5	10	9	2		12	42

GILLINGHAM

Player and Position	Ht	Wt	Date	Birth Place	Source	Clubs	League App	Gls
Goalkeepers								
Scott Barrett	5 10	14 02	2 4 63	Derby	Ilkeston T	Wolverhampton W	30	—
						Stoke C	51	—
						Colchester U (loan)	13	—
						Stockport Co (loan)	10	—
						Colchester U	—	—
						Gillingham	34	—
Harvey Lim*	6 0	13 07	30 8 67	Halesworth	Apprentice	Norwich C	—	—
						Plymouth Arg (loan)	—	—
					Kettering T	Gillingham	90	—
Defenders								
Gary Breen	6 1	12 07	12 12 73	London	Charlton Ath	Maidstone U	19	—
						Gillingham	29	—
Tony Butler	6 2	11 12	28 9 72	Stockport	Trainee	Gillingham	52	—
Richard Green	6 1	13 11	22 11 67	Wolverhampton		Shrewsbury T	125	5
						Swindon T	—	—
						Gillingham	51	7
Paul Hague	6 2	12 06	16 9 72	Durham	Trainee	Gillingham	8	—
Mark Leahy‡			22 1 73	Tenterden	Ashford T	Gillingham	—	—
Eliot Martin	5 6	10 00	27 9 72	Plumstead	Trainee	Gillingham	44	1
Lee Palmer	5 11	13 00	19 9 70	Gillingham	Trainee	Gillingham	82	4
Glenn Roeder†	6 2	13 09	13 12 55	Woodford	Apprentice	Orient	115	4
						QPR	157	17
						Notts Co (loan)	4	—
						Newcastle U	193	8
						Watford	78	2
						Leyton Orient	8	—
						Gillingham	6	—
Paul Watson	5 8	10 10	4 1 75	Hastings	Trainee	Gillingham	1	—
Midfield								
Paul Baker	6 1	13 06	5 1 63	Newcastle	Bishop Auckland	Southampton	—	—
						Carlisle U	71	11
						Hartlepool U	197	67
						Motherwell	9	1
						Gillingham	21	6
Richard Carpenter	5 10	13 00	30 9 72	Sheppey	Trainee	Gillingham	40	1
Paul Clark	5 9	13 07	14 9 58	Benfleet	Apprentice	Southend U	33	1
						Brighton	79	9
						Reading (loan)	2	—
						Southend U	276	3
						Gillingham	77	1
Mark Dempsey	5 8	11 02	10 12 72	Dublin	Trainee	Gillingham	48	2
Joe Dunne	5 8	11 06	25 5 73	Dublin	Trainee	Gillingham	41	—
Tony Eeles	5 6	10 08	15 11 70	Chatham	Trainee	Gillingham	73	5
Matthew Joseph‡			30 9 72	Bethnal Green	Trainee	Arsenal	—	—
						Gillingham	—	—
Mark O'Connor*	5 7	10 02	10 3 63	Rochdale	Apprentice	QPR	3	—
						Exeter C (loan)	38	1
						Bristol R	80	10
						Bournemouth	128	12
						Gillingham	116	8
Neil Smith	5 9	12 00	30 9 71	London	Trainee	Tottenham H	—	—
						Gillingham	65	5
Forwards								
Andy Arnott	5 11	12 07	18 10 73	Chatham	Trainee	Gillingham	34	8
						Manchester U (loan)	—	—
Trevor Aylott*	6 1	14 00	26 11 57	London	Apprentice	Chelsea	29	2
						QPR (loan)	—	—

GILLINGHAM

Colours: All Royal blue. **Change colours:** Black and white striped shirts, black shorts, black stockings.

Foundation: The success of the pioneering Royal Engineers of Chatham excited the interest of the residents of the Medway Towns and led to the formation of many clubs including Excelsior. After winning the Kent Junior Cup and the Chatham District League in 1893, Excelsior decided to go for bigger things and it was at a meeting in the Napier Arms, Brompton, in 1893 that New Brompton FC came into being as a professional concern, securing the use of a ground in Priestfield Road.

First Football League game: 28 August, 1920, Division 3, v Southampton (h) D 1-1 – Branfield; Robertson, Sissons; Battiste, Baxter, Wigmore; Holt, Hall, Gilbey (1), Roe, Gore.

Did you know: Gillingham inside-forward Jimmy Scarth scored three goals in two and a half minutes of a Division 3 (S) match against Leyton Orient on 1 November 1952. Gillingham won 3-2 after leading 3-0 at half-time.

Managers (and Secretary-Managers)
W. Ironside Groombridge 1896–1906* (previously financial secretary), Steve Smith 1906–08, W. I. Groombridge 1908–19*, George Collins 1919–20, John McMillan 1920–23, Harry Curtis 1923–26, Albert Hoskins 1926–29, Dick Hendrie 1929–31, Fred Maven 1932–37, Alan Ure 1937–38, Bill Harvey 1938–39, Archie Clark 1939–58, Harry Barratt 1958–62, Freddie Cox 1962–65, Basil Hayward 1966–71, Andy Nelson 1971–74, Len Ashurst 1974–75, Gerry Summers 1975–81, Keith Peacock 1981–87, Paul Taylor 1988, Keith Burkinshaw 1988–89, Damien Richardson 1989–93, Mike Flanagan July 1993–.

Player and Position	Ht	Wt	Date	Birth Place	Source	Clubs	League App	Gls
						Barnsley	96	26
						Millwall	32	5
						Luton T	32	10
						Crystal Palace	53	12
						Barnsley (loan)	9	—
						Bournemouth	147	27
						Birmingham C	27	—
						Oxford U	37	6
						Gillingham	10	2
Steve Crane	5 9	12 00	3 6 72	Essex	USA	Gillingham	7	1
David Crown	5 9	12 03	16 2 58	Enfield	Walthamstow Ave	Brentford	46	8
						Portsmouth	28	2
						Exeter C (loan)	7	3
						Reading	88	15
						Cambridge U	106	45
						Southend U	113	61
						Gillingham	86	38
Nick Forster	5 9	11 05	8 9 73	Oxted	Horley T	Gillingham	26	6
Liburd Henry	5 11	12 09	29 8 67	Dominica	Leytonstone/ Ilford	Watford	10	1
						Halifax T (loan)	5	—
						Maidstone U	67	9
						Gillingham	28	1
Lawrence Osborne	5 10	11 11	20 10 67	London	Apprentice	Arsenal	—	—
						Newport Co	15	—
					Redbridge Forest	Maidstone U	37	4
					Redbridge Forest	Maidstone U	53	8
						Gillingham	6	1
Robert Reinelt	5 10	11 13	11 3 74	Epping	Trainee	Aldershot	5	—
						Gillingham	—	—
Paul Ritchie (on loan from Dundee)	5 11	12 00	25 1 69	St Andrews		Gillingham	6	3

Trainees
Agutter, Andrew J; Aston, Wayne D; Christou, Christopher B; Hake, Kevin S; Hills, Marc; Hunt, kevin; Maxted, Daniel R; Newman, Terry R; Russell, Steven J; Smart, Matthew; Smith, Gary, J; Tekell, Lee D; Trott, Robin F; Verrall, Damon F.

**Non-Contract
Roeder, Glenn V.

Associated Schoolboys
Birchley, Warren J; Brooks, James; Clifford, Kevin D; Crowley, Robert T; Cullum, Andrew J; Dean, Sam; Dolan, Paul R; Friend, Shaun M; Lander, Daniel M; Loft, Graham D; Newman, Keir C; Parsons, Matthew; Roser, Craig M.

Associated Schoolboys who have accepted the club's offer of a Traineeship/Contract
Corbyn, Richard; Wilson, Paul A. F.

**Non-Contract Players who are retained must be re-signed before they are eligible to play in League matches.

GRIMSBY TOWN 1992–93 *Back row (left to right):* Paul Agnew, Tony Rees, Tony Ford, Paul Futcher, Paul Reece, Neil Woods, Mark Smith, Jim Dobbin. *Centre row:* Ken Reed (Physio), Ian Baraclough, Graham Rodger, Rhys Wilmot, Steve Sherwood, Mark Lever, John Cockerill, Arthur Mann (Reserve Coach). *Front row:* Chris Hargreaves, Kevin Jobling, John McDermott, Gary Childs, Alan Buckley (Manager), David Gilbert, Tommy Watson, Stuart Burns, Gary Croft.

Division 1   **GRIMSBY TOWN**

Blundell Park, Cleethorpes, South Humberside DN35 7PY. Telephone Cleethorpes (0472) 697111. Fax (0472) 693665. Clubcall: 0898 121576.

Ground capacity: 16,116.

Record attendance: 31,651 v Wolverhampton W, FA Cup 5th rd, 20 February 1937.

Record receipts: £96,636 v Tottenham H, Rumbelows Cup 3rd rd, 29 October 1991.

Pitch measurements: 111yd × 75yd.

Presidents: T. J. Lindley, T. Wilkinson.

Chairman: P. W. Furneaux. *Vice-chairman:* W. H. Carr.

Directors: T. Aspinall, G. W. Duffield, G. Lamming, J. Mager.

Manager: Alan Buckley. *Assistant Manager:* Arthur Mann.

Youth team coach: Richard O'Kelly.

Company Secretary: Ian Fleming. *Commercial Manager:* Anthony Richardson. *Lottery Director:* T. E. Harvey.

Physio: Ken Reed.

Year Formed. 1878. *Turned Professional:* 1890. *Ltd Co.:* 1890.

Previous Name: Grimsby Pelham.

Club Nickname: 'The Mariners'.

Previous Grounds: Clee Park; Abbey Park.

Record League Victory: 9–2 v Darwen, Division 2, 15 April 1899 – Bagshaw; Lockie, Nidd; Griffiths, Bell (1), Nelmes; Jenkinson (3), Richards (1), Cockshutt (3), Robinson, Chadburn (1).

Record Cup Victory: 8–0 v Darlington, FA Cup, 2nd rd, 21 November 1885 – G. Atkinson; J. H. Taylor, H. Taylor; Hall, Kimpson, Hopewell; H. Atkinson (1), Garnham, Seal (3), Sharman, Monument (4).

Record Defeat: 1–9 v Arsenal, Division 1, 28 January 1931.

Most League Points (2 for a win): 68, Division 3 (N), 1955–56.

Most League Points (3 for a win): 83, Division 3, 1990–91.

Most League Goals: 103, Division 2, 1933–34.

Highest League Scorer in Season: Pat Glover, 42, Division 2, 1933–34.

Most League Goals in Total Aggregate: Pat Glover, 182, 1930–39.

Most Capped Player: Pat Glover, 7, Wales.

Most League Appearances: Keith Jobling, 448, 1953–69.

Record Transfer Fee Received: £650,000 from Sunderland for Shaun Cunnington, July 1992.

Record Transfer Fee Paid: £150,000 to Blackpool for Paul Groves, August 1992.

Football League Record: 1892 Original Member Division 2; 1901–03 Division 1; 1903 Division 2; 1910 Failed re-election; 1911 re-elected Division 2; 1920–21 Division 3; 1921–26 Division 3 (N); 1926–29 Division 2; 1929–32 Division 1; 1932–34 Division 2; 1934–48 Division 1; 1948–51 Division 2; 1951–56 Division 3 (N); 1956–59 Division 2; 1959–62 Division 3; 1962–64 Division 2; 1964–68 Division 3; 1968–72 Division 4; 1972–77 Division 3; 1977–79 Division 4; 1979–80 Division 3; 1980–87 Division 2; 1987–88 Division 3; 1988–90 Division 4; 1990–91 Division 3; 1991–92 Division 2; 1992– Division 1.

Honours: Football League: Division 1 best season: 5th, 1934–35; Division 2 – Champions 1900–01, 1933–34; Runners-up 1928–29; Division 3 (N) – Champions 1925–26, 1955–56; Runners-up 1951–52; Division 3 – Champions 1979–80; Runners-up 1961–62; Division 4 – Champions 1971–72; Runners-up 1978–79; 1989–90. *FA Cup:* Semi-finals, 1936, 1939. *Football League Cup:* best season: 5th rd, 1979–80, 1984–85. *League Group Cup:* Winners 1981–82.

GRIMSBY TOWN 1992—93 LEAGUE RECORD

Match No.	Date		Venue	Opponents	Result		H/T Score	Lg. Pos.	Goalscorers	Atten dance
1	Aug	15	A	Charlton Ath	L	1-3	0-2	—	Dobbin	4823
2		22	H	Watford	W	3-2	2-2	13	Mendonca, Watson, Rodger	4772
3		30	A	Birmingham C	L	1-2	1-1	—	Mendonca	6807
4	Sept	5	H	Oxford U	D	1-1	0-0	16	Mendonca (pen)	4546
5		12	A	Tranmere R	D	1-1	0-1	18	Watson	5330
6		19	A	Bristol R	W	3-0	0-0	13	Rees, Woods 2	5320
7		26	H	Cambridge U	D	1-1	0-0	12	Rodger	4848
8		29	A	Swindon T	L	0-1	0-1	—		5759
9	Oct	3	H	Peterborough U	L	1-3	0-2	18	Rodger	5208
10		10	A	Notts Co	L	0-1	0-1	18		6442
11		17	H	Southend U	W	1-0	0-0	17	Rodger	4117
12		24	A	Newcastle U	W	1-0	0-0	15	Dobbin	30,088
13		31	H	Portsmouth	W	3-0	1-0	12	Gilbert, McDermott, Rees	5708
14	Nov	3	H	West Ham U	D	1-1	0-0	—	Mendonca	9119
15		7	A	Luton T	W	4-1	3-0	12	Groves 3, Rees	6928
16		14	H	Bristol C	W	2-1	0-0	8	Watson, Mendonca	5651
17		21	A	Brentford	W	3-1	2-0	6	Mendonca, Groves, Dobbin	7439
18		28	A	Wolverhampton W	L	1-2	0-2	8	Lever	14,240
19	Dec	5	H	Leicester C	L	1-3	0-2	10	Groves	7488
20		12	A	Millwall	L	1-2	0-1	12	McDermott	6900
21		20	A	Derby Co	L	0-2	0-1	—		6475
22		26	H	Barnsley	W	4-2	2-0	12	Gilbert 2, Groves, Watson	8242
23		28	A	Sunderland	L	0-2	0-1	12		20,771
24	Jan	9	H	Bristol R	W	2-0	0-0	8	Dobbin, Rees	4922
25		16	A	Cambridge U	L	0-2	0-2	10		4137
26		26	H	Swindon T	W	2-1	1-0	—	Rees, Groves	5207
27		30	A	Watford	W	3-2	0-1	9	Rodger, Mendonca, Groves	6613
28	Feb	6	H	Charlton Ath	W	1-0	0-0	7	Rodger	5403
29		20	A	Birmingham C	D	1-1	1-0	7	Rodger	5237
30		23	A	Oxford U	W	1-0	0-0	—	Gilbert	4944
31		27	H	Notts Co	D	3-3	1-2	7	Groves 3	5871
32	Mar	6	A	Peterborough U	L	0-1	0-1	8		6657
33		9	A	West Ham U	L	1-2	0-2	—	Groves	13,170
34		13	H	Luton T	W	3-1	1-0	8	Ford 2, Mendonca	5193
35		16	H	Tranmere R	D	0-0	0-0	—		5686
36		20	A	Leicester C	L	0-3	0-3	8		15,930
37		23	H	Brentford	L	0-1	0-0	—		4384
38		28	A	Bristol C	L	0-1	0-0	—		6755
39	Apr	3	H	Wolverhampton W	W	1-0	0-0	8	Dobbin	5080
40		6	H	Millwall	W	1-0	0-0	—	Mendonca (pen)	4445
41		10	A	Barnsley	W	2-0	1-0	8	Mendonca, Dobbin	4958
42		12	H	Sunderland	W	1-0	0-0	8	Woods	8090
43		17	A	Derby Co	L	1-2	1-0	8	Woods	12,428
44		23	A	Southend U	L	0-1	0-0	—		5807
45	May	4	H	Newcastle U	L	0-2	0-0	—		14,402
46		8	A	Portsmouth	L	1-2	1-0	9	Daws	24,955

Final League Position: 9

GOALSCORERS

League (58): Groves 12, Mendonca 10 (2 pens), Rodger 7, Dobbin 6, Rees 5, Gilbert 4, Watson 4, Woods 4, Ford 2, McDermott 2, Daws 1, Lever 1.
Coca Cola Cup (5): Mendonca 2, Watson 2, Woods 1.
FA Cup (4): Mendonca 2, Dobbin 1, Gilbert 1.

Wilmot 33	McDermott 38	Jobling 11 + 3	Baraclough 1	Rodger 27 + 3	Dobbin 39	Watson 24	Gilbert 41	Rees 24 + 7	Mendonca 38 + 4	Woods 21 + 9	Smith 8 + 18	Groves 45 + 1	Agnew 20 + 3	Handyside 11	Hargreaves — + 4	Ford 15 + 2	Croft 28 + 4	Futcher 35	Tillson 4	Childs 11 + 6	Lever 14	Beasant 6	Sherwood 7	Daws 5 + 1	Match No.
1	2	3	4	5	6	7	8	9	10	11	12	14													1
1	2	3		4	6	7	8		10	11			9	5											2
1	2	3			6	7			10	11	8	9	5	4	12										3
1	2	3			6	7		12	10	11		9		5				2							4
1		3		4	6	7	8	12	10	11		9		5				2							5
1				5	6	7	8	9		11		10					3	2	4	12					6
1	2			5	6	7	8	*9*		11	14	10					3		4	12					7
1				5	6	7	8	9		*11*	14	10					3	2	4	12					8
1		3		5	6	7	8	9		11	14	10						*2*	4	12					9
1				4	6	2		9	12	11	14	10					3	*8*		7	5				10
1	2			4	6		8	9	12	11		10					3			7	5				11
	2				6	7	8		10	11		9					3	4		5	1				12
	2				6	7	8	12	10	11		9					3	4		5	1				13
	2				6	7	8	11	10		12	9					3	4		5	1				14
	2		14		6	7	8	11	10		12	9					3	4		*5*	1				15
	2		14		6	7	8	11	10	12		9					3	4		*5*	1				16
	2				6	7	8	11	10	12		9					3	4		5	1				17
1	2		14		6	7	8	11	10	12		9					3	*4*		5					18
1	2			4	6		8	11	*10*		12	9			14		3			7	5				19
1	2			5	6	*7*	8	11	10	9	12				14		3	4							20
	2			5	6	7	8	9		*11*	12	10			14		3	4				1			21
	2			4	6	7	8	11	10	12		9					3			5		1			22
	2			4	6	7	8	11	10	12	14	9					3			*5*		1			23
1	2			5	6	7	8	11	10		12	9					3	4							24
1	2			5	6	*7*	8	11	10			9			12	14	3	4							25
1	2			5	6		8	11	10		12	9					3	4		7					26
1	2			5	6			11	10		8	9				12	3	4		*7*					27
1	2			5	6			11	10		8	9					3	4		*7*					28
	2	14		5	6		8	11	10		12	9					3	4		*7*		1			29
	2			5	6		8	11	10			9					3	4		7		1			30
		14		5	6		8	12	10	11		9					3	2	*4*	7		1			31
	2			*5*	6		8	12	10	11		9				14	3	*4*		7		1			32
1	2				6		*8*		10	12	11	9			14	7	3	4		5					33
1	2				6		8		10	11		9				7	3	4		5					34
1	2				6		8		10	11		9				7	3	4		5					35
1	2				6		8		10	*11*		9			14	7	3	4	12	5					36
1	2			5	*6*		8		10	11	12	9				7	3	4		14					37
1				5			8	11	10	12		9			3	6	*2*	4		7			14		38
1					6		8			12	11	10			2	7	3	4		5			9		39
1	2				6		8		10		11					7	3	4		5			9		40
1	2				6		8	14	*10*	12	11					7	3	4		5			9		41
1	2				6		8	14	10	12	11					7	3	4		5			*9*		42
1	2				6		8		10	12	11	9			14	7	*3*	4		5					43
1	2	14			6		8		10	12	11	9				7	3	4		*5*					44
1	2			5	6		8		10	11	12	9				7	3	*4*					14		45
1	2			5	6		8	14	*10*	12	11					7	3	4					9		46

Coca Cola Cup	First Round	Barnsley (h)		1-1
		(a)		1-1
	Second Round	QPR (a)		1-2
		(h)		2-1
FA Cup	Third Round	Brentford (a)		2-0
	Fourth Round	Swansea C (a)		0-0
		(h)		2-0
	Fifth Round	Ipswich T (a)		0-4

GRIMSBY TOWN

Player and Position	Ht	Wt	Date	Birth Place	Source	Clubs	League App	Gls
Goalkeepers								
Steve Sherwood*	6 4	14 07	10 12 53	Selby	Apprentice	Chelsea	16	—
						Brighton (loan)	—	—
						Millwall (loan)	1	—
						Brentford (loan)	16	—
						Brentford (loan)	46	—
						Watford	211	1
						Grimsby T	183	—
Rhys Wilmot	6 1	12 00	21 2 62	Newport	Apprentice	Arsenal	8	—
						Hereford U (loan)	9	—
						Orient (loan)	46	—
						Swansea C (loan)	16	—
						Plymouth Arg (loan)	17	—
						Plymouth Arg	116	—
						Grimsby T	33	—
Defenders								
Paul Agnew	5 9	10 07	15 8 65	Lisburn	Cliftonville	Grimsby T	208	3
Gary Croft	5 9	10 08	17 2 74	Burton-on-Trent	Trainee	Grimsby T	33	—
Paul Futcher	6 0	12 03	25 9 56	Chester	Apprentice	Chester	20	—
						Luton T	131	1
						Manchester C	37	—
						Oldham Ath	98	1
						Derby Co	35	—
						Barnsley	230	—
						Halifax T	15	—
						Grimsby T	86	—
Peter Handyside	6 1	12 03	31 7 74	Dumfries	Trainee	Grimsby T	11	—
Mark Lever	6 3	12 08	29 3 70	Beverley	Trainee	Grimsby T	166	7
John McDermott	5 7	10 00	3 2 69	Middlesbrough		Grimsby T	238	4
Graham Rodger	6 2	11 13	1 4 67	Glasgow	Apprentice	Wolverhampton W	1	—
						Coventry C	36	2
						Luton T	28	2
						Grimsby T	46	7
Midfield								
Stewart Burns*	5 4	10 02	23 1 74	Stranraer	Trainee	Grimsby T	—	—
Gary Childs	5 7	10 08	19 4 64	Birmingham	Apprentice	WBA	3	—
						Walsall	131	17
						Birmingham C	55	2
						Grimsby T	115	12
John Cockerill‡	6 0	12 07	12 7 61	Cleethorpes	Stafford R	Grimsby T	107	19
Jim Dobbin	5 9	10 07	17 9 63	Dunfermline	Whitburn BC	Celtic	2	—
						Motherwell (loan)	2	—
						Doncaster R	64	13
						Barnsley	129	12
						Grimsby T	71	12
David Gilbert	5 4	10 04	22 6 63	Lincoln	Apprentice	Lincoln C	30	1
						Scunthorpe U	1	—
					Boston U	Northampton T	120	21
						Grimsby T	182	31
Paul Groves	5 11	11 05	28 2 66	Derby	Burton Alb	Leicester C	16	1
						Lincoln C (loan)	8	1
						Blackpool	107	21
						Grimsby T	46	12
Kevin Jobling	5 9	10 11	1 1 68	Sunderland	Apprentice	Leicester C	9	—
						Grimsby T	175	8
Tommy Watson	5 8	10 10	29 9 69	Liverpool	Trainee	Grimsby T	138	20

GRIMSBY TOWN

Colours: Black and white vertical striped shirts, black shorts with red triangular panel on side, white stockings with red band on turnover. **Change colours:** All yellow.

Foundation: Grimsby Pelham FC as they were first known, came into being at a meeting held at the Wellington Arms in September 1878. Pelham is the family name of big landowners in the area, the Earls of Yarborough. The receipts for their first game amounted to 6s. 9d. (approx. 39p). After a year, the club name was changed to Grimsby Town.

First Football League game: 3 September, 1892, Division 2, v Northwich Victoria (h) W 2-1 – Whitehouse; Lundie, T. Frith; C. Frith, Walker, Murrell; Higgins, Henderson, Brayshaw, Riddoch (2), Ackroyd.

Did you know: Fred Smith scored four goals in seven minutes for Grimsby Town in a Division 3 (N) match against Hartlepools United on 15 November 1952. His goals came in the 14th, 17th, 19th and 21st minutes of a 7-0 win.

Managers (and Secretary-Managers)
H. N. Hickson 1902–20*, Haydn Price 1920, George Fraser 1921–24, Wilf Gillow 1924–32, Frank Womack 1932–36, Charles Spencer 1937–51, Bill Shankly 1951–53, Billy Walsh 1954–55, Allenby Chilton 1955–59, Tim Ward 1960–62, Tom Johnston 1962–64, Jimmy McGuigan 1964–67, Don McEvoy 1967–68, Bill Harvey 1968–69, Bobby Kennedy 1969–71, Lawrie McMenemy 1971–73, Ron Ashman 1973–75, Tom Casey 1975–76, Johnny Newman 1976–79, George Kerr 1979–82, David Booth 1982–85, Mike Lyons 1985–87, Bobby Roberts 1987–88, Alan Buckley June 1988–.

Forwards

Name				Birthplace	Signed	Club	Apps	Goals
Tony Daws	5 8	11 10	10 9 66	Sheffield	Apprentice	Notts Co	8	1
						Sheffield U	11	3
						Scunthorpe U	183	63
						Grimsby T	6	1
Tony Ford	5 9	12 02	14 5 59	Grimsby	Apprentice	Grimsby T	354	54
						Sunderland (loan)	9	1
						Stoke C	112	13
						WBA	114	14
						Grimsby T	39	3
Christian Hargreaves	5 1	11 00	12 5 72	Cleethorpes	Trainee	Grimsby T	51	5
						Scarborough (loan)	3	—
Clive Mendonca	5 10	10 07	9 9 68	Tullington	Apprentice	Sheffield U	13	4
						Doncaster R (loan)	2	—
						Rotherham U	84	27
						Sheffield U	10	1
						Grimsby T (loan)	10	3
						Grimsby T	42	10
Tony Rees	5 9	11 13	1 8 64	Merthyr Tydfil	Apprentice	Aston Villa	—	—
						Birmingham C	95	12
						Peterborough U (loan)	5	2
						Shrewsbury T (loan)	2	—
						Barnsley	31	3
						Grimsby T	125	33
Mark Smith	5 9	12 02	19 12 61	Sheffield	Worksop, Gainsborough T, Kettering	Sheffield U	—	—
						Scunthorpe U	1	—
						Rochdale	27	7
						Huddersfield T	96	11
						Grimsby T	77	4
Neil Woods	6 0	12 11	30 7 66	York	Apprentice	Doncaster R	65	16
						Rangers	3	—
						Ipswich T	27	5
						Bradford C	14	2
						Grimsby T	111	24

Trainees
Barratt, Mark A; Brookes, Mark; Buckley, Simon J; Clohessy, Mark J; Connelly, Martin J; Cook, John; Dunlop, Simon A; Gowshall, Joby; Harriott, Kevin A; Lambert, Darren K; Maddison, Craig; Madigan, Terrence G; Martin, Paul A; Miller, David; Neil, James D.

**Non-Contract
Trinder, Jason L.

Associated Schoolboys
Bell, Richard P; Bloomer, Matthew B; Burdon, Andrew J; Cox, Jonathan D; Davy, Jonathan P; Hamnett, John C; Harsley, Paul; Mundell, Andrew A; Savage, Christopher I; Welton, Guy E; Wilson, Peter E.

Associated Schoolboys who have accepted the club's offer of a Traineeship/Contract
Petchey, Stuart; Rushby, Mathew S; Wilkinson, David A.

**Non-Contract Players who are retained must be re-signed before they are eligible to play in League matches.

HALIFAX TOWN 1992–93 *Back Row (left to right):* Paul Wilson, Ian Juryeff, Nigel Greenwood, Chris Lucketti, Nick Richardson, Lee Bracey, Ian Thompstone, Russell Bradley, Neil Griffiths, Scott Longley, Billy Barr.
Front Row: Jamie Paterson, John Thomas, Greg Abbott, Kevin Megson, Alan Kamara, Mick Rathbone (Physio), Jimmy Case (Coach), David German, Jason Hardy, Ronnie Hildersley.

GM Vauxhall Conference   **HALIFAX TOWN**

Shay Ground, Halifax HX1 2YS. Offices: 7 Clare Road, Halifax HX1 2HX. Telephone Halifax (0422) 353423. Fax (0422) 349487. Ground: 0422 361582 (Match day only). Souvenir Shop: (0422) 363336.

Ground capacity: 8049.

Record attendance: 36,885 v Tottenham H, FA Cup 5th rd, 15 February 1953.

Record receipts: £27,000 v Manchester U, League Cup, 2nd rd, 1st leg, 26 September 1990.

Pitch measurements: 110yd × 70yd.

President: John S. Crowther. *Honorary Life Vice-president:* Frank Hinchliffe. *Vice-president:* R. Aspey.

Chairman: S. J. Brown. *Vice-chairman:* D. C. Greenwood.

Directors: B. J. Boulton, J. Stockwell, A. Hall, J. Rawson, C. Holland.

Manager: Peter Wragg. *Coach and Physio:* Mick Rathbone.

Youth Team Coach: Arthur Graham.

General Manager/Secretary: Bev Fielding. *Commercial Manager:* Nick Beaumont. *Lottery Manager:* Derek Newiss.

Year Formed: 1911. *Turned Professional:* 1911. *Ltd Co.:* 1911.

Club Nickname: 'The Shaymen'.

Previous Grounds: Sandhall and Exley.

Record League Victory: 6–0 v Bradford PA, Division 3 (N), 3 December 1955 – Johnson; Griffiths, Ferguson; Watson, Harris, Bell; Hampson (2), Baker (3), Watkinson (1), Capel, Lonsdale. 6–0 v Doncaster R, Division 4, 2 November 1976 – Gennoe; Trainer, Loska (Bradley), McGill, Dunleavy (1), Phelan, Hoy (2), Carroll (1), Bullock (1), Lawson (1), Johnston.

Record Cup Victory: 7–0 v Bishop Auckland, FA Cup 2nd rd (replay), 10 January 1967 – White; Russell, Bodell; Smith, Holt, Jeff Lee; Taylor (2), Hutchison (2), Parks (2), Atkins (1), McCarthy.

Record Defeat: 0–13 v Stockport Co, Division 3 (N), 6 January, 1934.

Most League Points (2 for a win): 57, Division 4, 1968–69.

Most League Points (3 for a win): 60, Division 4, 1982–83.

Most League Goals: 83, Division 3 (N), 1957–58.

Highest League Scorer in Season: Albert Valentine. 34, Division 3 (N), 1934–35.

Most League Goals in Total Aggregate: Ernest Dixon, 129, 1922–30.

Most Capped Player: None.

Most League Appearances: John Pickering, 367, 1965–74.

Record Transfer Fee Received: £250,000 from Watford for Wayne Allison, July 1989.

Record Transfer Fee Paid: £50,000 to Hereford U for Ian Juryeff, September 1990.

Football League Record: 1921 Original Member of Division 3 (N); 1958–63 Division 3; 1963–69 Division 4; 1969–76 Division 3; 1976–92 Division 4; 1992–93 Division 3; 1993– GM Vauxhall Conference.

Honours: Football League: Division 3 best season: 3rd, 1970–71; Division 3(N) – Runners-up 1934–35; Division 4 – Runners-up 1968–69. *FA Cup:* best season; 5th rd, 1932–33, 1952–53. *Football League Cup:* best season: 4th rd, 1964.

HALIFAX TOWN 1992—93 LEAGUE RECORD

Match No.	Date		Venue	Opponents	Result	H/T Score	Lg. Pos.	Goalscorers	Attendance
1	Aug	15	A	Rochdale	W 3-2	1-0	—	Hildersley 2, Wilson (pen)	2497
2		22	H	Scunthorpe U	D 0-0	0-0	5		1793
3		29	A	Cardiff C	L 1-2	0-1	7	Thompstone	7692
4	Sept	1	A	Crewe Alex	L 1-2	0-2	—	Wilson (og)	3228
5		12	A	Lincoln C	L 1-2	0-1	22	Lucketti	2689
6		15	H	Darlington	W 1-0	1-0	—	Greenwood	1287
7		19	H	Scarborough	L 3-4	1-3	17	Greenwood, Wilson (pen), Hirst (og)	1230
8		26	A	Northampton T	W 5-2	2-0	11	Thompstone 3, Lucketti, Greenwood	2021
9	Oct	3	A	Carlisle U	D 1-1	0-1	13	Bradley	3824
10		10	H	Colchester U	L 2-4	0-2	17	Matthews, German	2445
11		17	A	Walsall	W 2-1	1-0	13	Smith (og), Peake	3867
12		24	A	Gillingham	W 2-0	1-0	10	Matthews, Thompstone	1216
13		31	A	Hereford U	L 0-3	0-3	13		1936
14	Nov	3	A	Shrewsbury T	L 0-1	0-1	—		2704
15		7	H	Torquay U	L 0-2	0-2	15		1651
16		21	A	Wrexham	D 1-1	0-1	16	Hardy	1873
17		28	H	Chesterfield	D 1-1	0-0	17	Hardy	1432
18	Dec	5	H	Barnet	L 1-2	1-1	19	Greenwood	1253
19		19	H	Bury	L 0-1	0-0	18		1760
20		26	H	Doncaster R	D 2-2	1-0	18	Megson, Thompstone	1854
21		29	A	York C	D 1-1	0-1	—	Williams	4068
22	Jan	9	A	Darlington	W 3-0	1-0	17	Ridings 2, Thompstone	1984
23		16	H	Northampton T	D 2-2	0-0	17	Ridings 2	1323
24		23	A	Scarborough	L 0-2	0-1	18		1552
25		26	H	Cardiff C	L 0-1	0-0	—		1339
26		30	A	Scunthorpe U	L 1-4	0-3	18	Patterson	2460
27	Feb	6	H	Rochdale	L 2-3	2-2	18	Jones (og), Barr (pen)	1906
28		16	A	Lincoln C	W 2-1	2-1	—	Case, Greenwood	1260
29		20	A	Crewe Alex	L 1-2	1-1	17	Case	1604
30		26	A	Colchester U	L 1-2	1-1	—	Thompstone	3007
31	Mar	6	H	Carlisle U	L 0-2	0-1	18		1309
32		13	A	Torquay U	L 0-2	0-0	20		3345
33		20	H	Shrewsbury T	D 1-1	1-0	20	Barr	3872
34		23	A	Chesterfield	L 1-2	1-1	—	Thompstone	2382
35		26	H	Wrexham	L 0-1	0-0	—		3920
36	Apr	3	A	Barnet	D 0-0	0-0	22		3042
37		10	A	Doncaster R	W 1-0	1-0	21	Barr	2160
38		12	H	York C	L 0-1	0-0	21		3983
39		17	A	Bury	W 2-1	1-0	21	Patterson, German	3069
40		24	H	Walsall	L 0-4	0-1	22		2829
41	May	1	A	Gillingham	L 0-2	0-0	22		7151
42		8	H	Hereford U	L 0-1	0-0	22		7451

Final League Position: 22

GOALSCORERS

League (45): Thompstone 9, Greenwood 5, Ridings 4, Barr 3 (1 pen), Case 2, German 2, Hardy 2, Hildersley 2, Lucketti 2, Matthews 2, Patterson 2, Wilson 2 (2 pens), Bradley 1, Megson 1, Peake 1, Williams 1, own goals 4.
Coca Cola Cup (3): Lucketti 1, Megson 1, Thomas 1.
FA Cup (1): German 1.

Bracey 41	Megson 24 + 2	Wilson 22	Lucketti 42	Thompstone 31	Bradley 29 + 1	Matthews 23	Case 17 + 4	Thomas 10 + 2	Juryeff 1	Hildersley 7 + 6	Gayle 2 + 3	Greenwood 21 + 4	German 28 + 7	Peake 32 + 1	Lewis 10 + 3	Hardy 20 + 2	Kamara — + 1	Barr 28	Griffiths 1	Wright 1	Patterson 18 + 5	Lancashire 2	Edmonds — + 2	Williams 9	Brown L 3	Ridings 21	Christie 6 + 3	Peel 3	Everingham 2	Brown N 1	Craven 7	Circuit — + 1	Obebo — + 3	Match No.
1	2	3	4	5	6	7	8	9	10	11	12																							1
1	2	3	4	5	6	7	*8*	9				11	10	12	14																			2
1	2	3	*4*	5	6	7	8	9				10	14	11	12																			3
1	2	3	4		6	7	8	9				12	10	*11*	5	14																		4
1	2	3	4	5	6	7	*8*	9				12	10	11	14																			5
1	2	3	4	5	6	7	8	9				12		10	11																			6
1	2	3	4	5	6	7	*8*	9				10	14	11			12																	7
1	2	3	4	5	6	7	8				12	*10*	14	11		9																		8
1		3	4	5	6	7	*8*				12	10	14	11		9		2																9
1		3	4	5		7	8					10	12	11		9		2	6															10
1		3	4	5	6	7	12				9	*10*	8	11	14			2																11
1		3	4	5	6	7	12					8	11	9				2			10													12
1		3	4	5	6	7	12				*9*	8	11	10				2					14											13
1		3	4	5	6	7	8	9				10		11				2			12													14
1		3	4	5	6	7	8	9			12	10		11				2																15
1	2	3	4				8			*11*		7		5	14			6			9	10	12											16
1	12	3	4	2	6	7	8							5	11						9	10												17
1	2	3	4	5	6	7				9		10	14	*11*				8				12												18
1	2	3		5	9					11		4	8					6			12					7	10							19
1	2	3		5	9							4	8	11				6								7	10							20
1	2	3		5	9							4	8	11				6								7	10							21
1	2	3		5	9							4						6			10			7		8	11							22
1	2			5	9					12		4				3		6			10			7		8	11							23
1	*2*			5	9					12		4	14			3		6			10			7		8	11							24
1				5	9							2	4			3		6			10			7		8	11							25
1				5	9					12		2	4			3		6			10			7		8	11							26
1				5	9	12				4		10	2			3		6						7		8	11							27
1				5	9	6				4		10	2	7		3										8	11							28
1				5	9	6				4		10	2	*7*		3					12					8	14	11						29
1	7			5	9	6	4					10	2			3										8			11					30
1				5	9	6	4					10	2		*11*						12			7		8	14		3					31
12				5	*9*	6	4					14	2	11		3					7		10			8				1				32
1				5	6	4						9	2	7		3					10					8	11							33
1				5	11	6	4					9	2	7		3					10					8								34
1				5	6	*4*	12					9	2	7		3					10					8						11	14	35
1	6			5			12					9	2	7	4	3					10					8					11			36
1	6			5						9			2	7	4	3					10					8						11	12	37
1	2			5	6							9	11	7	3	4					10					8						12		38
1	9			5	6								2	7	4	3					10					8					11			39
1	9			5	6								2	7	*4*	3					10					8	14					11	12	40
1	9			5	6							12	2	7	4	3					10					8					11			41
1	9			5	6							12	2	7	4	3					10					8					11			42

Coca Cola Cup	First Round	Hartlepool U (h)	1-2
		(a)	2-3
FA Cup	First Round	Marine (a)	1-4

HALIFAX TOWN

Player and Position	Ht	Wt	Date	Birth Place	Source	Clubs	League App	Gls
Goalkeepers								
Lee Bracey	6 1	12 08	11 9 68	Ashford	Trainee	West Ham U	—	—
						Swansea C	99	—
						Halifax T	73	—
Nicky Brown	6 1	13 00	25 1 73	Northampton	Norwich C	Halifax T	2	—
Defenders								
Billy Barr	5 11	11 07	21 1 69	Halifax	Trainee	Halifax T	196	13
Steve Circuit†			11 4 72	Sheffield	Sheffield U	Halifax T	1	—
Nick Everingham‡			11 2 73	Hull	Oldham Ath	Halifax T	2	—
Neil Griffiths*	6 1	12 00	4 9 72	Halifax	Trainee	Halifax T	4	—
Alan Kamara*	5 9	10 12	15 7 58	Sheffield	Kiveton Park	York C	10	—
						Darlington	134	1
					York RI,	Scarborough	159	2
					Retford, Burton Alb	Halifax T	36	—
Chris Lucketti	6 0	12 10	28 9 71	Littleborough	Trainee	Rochdale	1	—
						Stockport Co	—	—
						Halifax T	78	2
Andrew Warnes*			5 9 73	Halifax	Trainee	Halifax T	—	—
Midfield								
Russell Bradley	6 0	12 05	28 3 66	Birmingham	Dudley T	Nottingham F	—	—
						Hereford U (loan)	12	1
						Hereford U	77	3
						Halifax T	56	3
Peter Craven†			30 6 68	Hanover	Park Avenue	Bury	—	—
						Halifax T	7	—
Darren Edmonds‡	5 9	11 06	12 4 71	Watford	Trainee	Leeds U	—	—
						Ipswich T	2	—
						Scarborough	1	—
						Halifax T	2	—
Howard Gayle‡	5 10	10 09	18 5 58	Liverpool	Local	Liverpool	4	1
						Fulham (loan)	14	—
						Birmingham C (loan)	13	1
						Newcastle U (loan)	8	2
						Birmingham C	33	8
						Sunderland	48	4
						Stoke C	6	2
						Blackburn R	116	29
						Halifax T	5	—
David German	5 10	11 07	16 10 73	Sheffield	Sheffield W	Halifax T	39	2
Jason Hardy	5 10	11 04	14 12 69	Burnley	Trainee	Burnley	43	1
						Halifax T (loan)	4	—
						Halifax T	22	2
Scott Longley			16 7 73	Wakefield	Trainee	Halifax T	1	—
Mike Matthews*	5 9	11 03	25 9 60	Hull	Apprentice	Wolverhampton W	76	7
						Scunthorpe U	58	5
						Halifax T	99	8
						Scarborough	7	1
						Stockport Co	35	3
						Scarborough	66	4
						Hull C	16	2
						Halifax T	23	2
Leigh Palin (To Partick T December 1992)	5 9	11 07	12 9 65	Worcester	Apprentice	Aston Villa	—	—
						Shrewsbury T (loan)	2	—
						Nottingham F	—	—
						Bradford C	71	10
						Stoke C	19	3
						Hull C	57	7
						Rochdale (loan)	3	—
						Burnley	1	—
						Halifax T	—	—
Jason Peake	5 9	11 05	29 9 71	Leicester	Trainee	Leicester C	8	1
						Hartlepool U (loan)	6	1
						Halifax T	33	1

HALIFAX TOWN

Colours: Blue and white vertical striped shirts, black shorts, black stockings. **Change colours:** White shirts with purple and green trim, green shorts, white stockings.

Foundation: The real pioneer behind the setting up of the club was Mr. A. E. Jones, who, using the *non de plume* 'Old Sport', wrote to the *The Halifax Evening Courier*. His letter suggesting a club be set up and inviting public opinion was published on 20 April 1911. A public meeting was held at the Saddle Hotel on 23 May 1911, whereafter Dr. A. H. Muir became the club's first president and Joe McClelland its first secretary.

First Football League game: 27 August, 1921, Division 3(N), v Darlington (a) L 0-2 – Haldane; Hawley, Mackrill; Hall, Wellock, Challinor; Pinkey, Hetherington, Woods, Dent, Phipps.

Did you know: Halifax Town, having been unable to play a home match since the previous 14 December because of frost and snow, made football history on 2 March 1963 when they opened their Shay ground to a paying public as an ice rink.

Managers (and Secretary-Managers)
A. M. Ricketts 1911–12*, Joe McClelland 1912–30, Alec Raisbeck 1930–36, Jimmy Thomson 1936–47, Jack Breedon 1947–50, William Wootton 1951–52, Gerald Henry 1952–54, Willie Watson 1954–56, Billy Burnikell 1956, Harry Hooper 1957–62, Willie Watson 1964–66, Vic Metcalfe 1966–67, Alan Ball Snr 1967–70, George Kirby 1970–71, Ray Henderson 11971–72, George Mulhall 1972–74, Johnny Quinn 1974–76, Alan Ball Snr 1976–77, Jimmy Lawson 1977–78, George Kirby 1978–81, Mick Bullock 1981–84, Mick Jones 1984–86, Bill Ayre 1986–90, Jim McCalliog 1990–91, John McGrath 1991–92, Peter Wragg December 1992–.

Player and Position	Ht	Wt	Date	Birth Place	Source	Clubs	League App	Gls
Forwards								
David Christie*	6 1	12 00	26 2 73	Salford	Trainee	Preston NE	4	—
						Halifax T	9	—
Nigel Greenwood	5 11	12 00	27 11 66	Preston	Apprentice	Preston NE	45	14
						Bury	110	25
						Preston NE	30	4
						Halifax T	25	5
Ron Hildersley‡	5 4	9 2	6 4 65	Fife	Apprentice	Manchester C	1	—
						Chester C (loan)	9	—
						Chester C	9	—
						Rochdale	16	—
						Preston NE	58	3
						Cambridge U (loan)	9	3
						Blackburn R	30	4
						Wigan Ath	4	—
						Halifax T	31	2
Kevin Megson	5 11	11 00	1 7 71	Halifax	Trainee	Bradford C	27	—
						Halifax T	41	1
Jonathan Niblo*			24 10 73	Newcastle	Trainee	Halifax T	—	—
Godfrey Obebo‡			16 4 66	Lagos		Halifax T	3	—
Jamie Patterson	5 5	9 07	26 4 73	Dumfries	Trainee	Halifax T	44	5
David Ridings			27 2 70	Farnworth	Cutzon Ashton	Halifax T	21	4
John Thomas*	5 8	11 03	5 8 58	Wednesbury		Everton	—	—
						Tranmere R (loan)	11	2
						Halifax T (loan)	5	—
						Bolton W	22	6
						Chester	44	20
						Lincoln C	67	20
						Preston NE	78	38
						Bolton W	73	31
						WBA	18	1
						Preston NE	27	6
						Hartlepool U	7	1
						Halifax T	12	—
Paul Wright‡			29 7 69	London		Halifax T	1	—

Trainees
Gray, Ryan P; Hook, Steven J; Issacs, Michael D.

**Non-Contract
Barr, Robert A; Circuit, Steven; Craven, Peter A.

Associated Schoolboys
Billington, Paul A; Brooks, Bryan P; Calland, Matthew W; Curran, James A. D; Hamer, Adam; King, Stephen J; Mucci, Carlo; Siddle, Paul A; Spencer, James A.

**Non-Contract Players who are retained must be re-signed before they are eligible to play in League matches.

HARTLEPOOL UNITED 1992-93 *Back row (left to right):* Ian McGuckin, John MacPhail, Martin Hodge, Ryan Cross, Steve Jones, Andy Saville, Mick Tait.
Centre row: Nicky Southall, Paul Proudlock, Paul Wratten, Lenny Johnrose, Paul Thompson, John Gallacher, Scott Garrett, Paul Olsson.
Front row: Gary Henderson (Physio), Paul Cross, Alan Murray (Manager), Dean Emerson, Eddie Kyle (Assistant Manager), Brian Honour, Tony McAndrew (Youth Team Coach).
(Photograph: Frank Reid)

Division 2   **HARTLEPOOL UNITED**

HUFC
1 9 0 8
HARTLEPOOL UNITED
FOOTBALL CLUB LTD
VICTORIA GROUND
HARTLEPOOL
CLEVELAND TS24 8BZ
TEL: 0429-272584
FAX: 0429-863007

The Victoria Ground, Clarence Road, Hartlepool. Telephone Hartlepool (0429) 272584. Commercial Dept: (0429) 222077. Fax: 0429 863007.

Ground capacity: 6721.

Record attendance: 17,426 v Manchester U, FA Cup 3rd rd, 5 January 1957.

Record receipts: £42,300 v Tottenham H, Rumbelows Cup, 2nd rd 2nd leg, 9 October 1990.

Pitch measurements: 110yd × 75yd.

President: E. Leadbitter.

Chairman: G. Gibson. *Vice-chairman:* A. Bamford.

Directors: D. Jukes, A. Elliott.

Manager: Viv Busby.

Youth/Reserve Coach: Eric Gates. *Physio:* Gary Henderson. *Commercial Manager:* G. McDonnell. *Assistant Secretary:* Lisa Charlton.

Year Formed: 1908. *Turned Professional:* 1908. *Ltd Co.:* 1908.

Club Nickname: 'The Pool'.

Previous Names: Hartlepools United until 1968; Hartlepool until 1977.

Record League Victory: 10–1 v Barrow, Division 4, 4 April 1959 – Oakley; Cameron, Waugh; Johnson, Moore, Anderson; Scott (1), Langland (1), Smith (3), Clark (2), Luke (2). (1 og).

Record Cup Victory: 6–0 v North Shields, FA Cup, 1st rd, 30 November 1946 – Heywood; Brown, Gregory; Spelman, Lambert, Jones; Price, Scott (2), Sloan (4), Moses, McMahon.

Record Defeat: 1–10 v Wrexham, Division 4, 3 March 1962.

Most League Points (2 for a win): 60, Division 4, 1967–68.

Most League Points (3 for a win): 82, Division 4, 1990–91.

Most League Goals: 90, Division 3 (N), 1956–57.

Highest League Scorer in Season: William Robinson, 28, Division 3 (N), 1927–28 and Joe Allon, 28, Division 4, 1990–91.

Most League Goals in Total Aggregate: Ken Johnson, 98, 1949–64.

Most Capped Player: Ambrose Fogarty, 1 (11), Eire.

Most League Appearances: Wattie Moore, 447, 1948–64.

Record Transfer Fee Received: £300,000 from Chelsea for Joe Allon, August 1991.

Record Transfer Fee Paid: £60,000 to Barnsley for Andy Saville, March 1992.

Football League Record: 1921 Original Member of Division 3 (N); 1958–68 Division 4; 1968–69 Division 3; 1969–91 Division 4; 1991–92 Division 3; 1992– Division 2.

Honours: Football League: Division 3 best season: 22nd, 1968–69; Division 3 (N) – Runners-up 1956–57. *FA Cup:* best season: 4th rd, 1954–55, 1977–78, 1988–89, 1992–93. *Football League Cup,* best season: 4th rd, 1974–75.

HARTLEPOOL UNITED 1992—93 LEAGUE RECORD

Match No.	Date	Venue	Opponents	Result	H/T Score	Lg. Pos.	Goalscorers	Atten dance
1	Aug 15	H	Reading	D	1-1	0-0	—	Saville (pen)	4149
2	22	A	Rotherham U	D	0-0	0-0	17		4355
3	29	H	Huddersfield T	W	1-0	1-0	9	Olsson	4120
4	Sept 1	H	Chester C	W	2-0	1-0	—	Cross R, Emerson	3061
5	5	A	Bournemouth	W	2-0	0-0	4	Cross R, Saville	4328
6	11	A	Wigan Ath	D	2-2	1-1	—	Saville 2	2073
7	15	H	Leyton Orient	L	0-2	0-1	—		3129
8	19	H	Port Vale	D	1-1	1-0	9	Olsson	2871
9	26	A	Preston NE	W	2-0	1-0	6	Gallacher, Johnrose	4347
10	Oct 2	H	Blackpool	W	1-0	0-0	—	Saville (pen)	2837
11	10	A	Bolton W	W	2-1	1-1	2	Johnrose, Saville	5097
12	17	H	Swansea C	L	0-1	0-0	4		4175
13	24	A	Brighton & HA	D	1-1	0-0	6	Honour	5918
14	31	H	Bradford C	W	2-0	1-0	4	Southall, Wratten	4349
15	Nov 3	A	WBA	L	1-3	1-1	—	Southall	13,046
16	7	A	Exeter C	L	1-3	0-1	9	Cross P	2856
17	28	H	Stockport Co	W	3-2	1-0	8	Johnrose, McGuckin, Saville	2814
18	Dec 12	A	Plymouth Arg	D	2-2	1-2	7	Johnrose, Saville	5996
19	19	H	Stoke C	L	1-2	0-1	9	Honour	4021
20	26	H	Hull C	W	1-0	1-0	7	Johnrose	4187
21	28	A	Fulham	W	3-1	1-1	4	Saville 2 (1 pen), Southall	4403
22	Jan 9	A	Leyton Orient	D	0-0	0-0	7		5539
23	16	H	Preston NE	D	0-0	0-0	8		2682
24	27	A	Huddersfield T	L	0-3	0-2	—		4153
25	30	H	Rotherham U	L	0-2	0-1	11		3992
26	Feb 6	A	Reading	L	0-2	0-0	11		3431
27	9	A	Port Vale	L	0-2	0-0	—		6629
28	13	H	Bournemouth	L	0-1	0-1	12		2166
29	16	A	Mansfield T	L	0-2	0-0	—		2655
30	20	A	Chester C	L	0-1	0-1	15		1912
31	27	H	Bolton W	L	0-2	0-1	16		2756
32	Mar 2	H	Wigan Ath	D	0-0	0-0	—		1791
33	6	A	Blackpool	D	1-1	0-0	16	Saville	4926
34	9	H	Burnley	D	0-0	0-0	—		3021
35	13	A	Exeter C	L	1-3	1-1	16	Tait	2639
36	20	H	WBA	D	2-2	1-1	17	Saville 2 (1 pen)	4174
37	23	A	Stockport Co	L	1-4	0-0	—	Southall	4154
38	27	H	Mansfield T	L	0-1	0-0	18		2292
39	Apr 3	A	Burnley	L	0-3	0-1	19		8226
40	5	H	Plymouth Arg	W	1-0	0-0	—	Honour	1822
41	10	A	Hull C	L	2-3	2-1	19	Ellison, Southall	3562
42	12	H	Fulham	L	0-3	0-0	20		2361
43	17	A	Stoke C	W	1-0	1-0	18	Johnrose	17,363
44	24	A	Swansea C	L	0-3	0-1	20		5310
45	May 1	H	Brighton & HA	W	2-0	0-0	18	Southall, Peverell	2693
46	8	A	Bradford C	W	2-0	1-0	16	MacPhail, Thompson	5612

Final League Position: 16

GOALSCORERS

League (42): Saville 13 (4 pens), Johnrose 6, Southall 6, Honour 3, Cross R 2, Olsson 2, Cross P 1, Ellison 1, Emerson 1, Gallacher 1, McGuckin 1, MacPhail 1, Peverell 1, Tait 1, Thompson 1, Wratten 1.
Coca Cola Cup (7): Johnrose 4, MacPhail 1, Saville 1 (pen), Southall 1.
FA Cup (7): Saville 5 (2 pens), Johnrose 1, Peverell 1.

Hodge 29	Cross R 32 + 1	Cross P 36 + 1	Tait 35	MacPhail 42	Olsson 39	Johnrose 35 + 3	Emerson 32	Saville 36	Honour 36 + 1	Gallacher 16 + 5	Southall 30 + 9	Nobbs 27	Proudlock 3 + 3	Wratten 10 + 5	Jones 3	McGuckin 12 + 2	Johnson 3	Gilchrist 24	Peverell 8 + 11	Talia 14	Thompson — + 2	Ellison 3 + 1	Skedd 1	Lynch — + 1	Match No.
1	2	3	4	5	6	7	8	9	10	11															1
1	2	3	4	5	8	7	6	9	10	11	12														2
1	2	3	4	5	8	7	6	9	10			11													3
1	2	3	4	5	8	7	6	9		11	10														4
1	2	3	4	5	8	7	6	9		11	10														5
1	2	3	4	5	8	7	6	9		11	10	12													6
1	2	3	4	5	8	7	6	9	14	11	10	12													7
1	14	3	4	5	8	7	6	9	11	12	10	2													8
1	2	3	4	5	8	7	6	9	11		10														9
1	2	3	4	5	8	7	6	9	14	11		10	12												10
1	2	3	4		8	7	6	9	11		12	10	5												11
1	2	3	4		8	7		9	11		12	10	5	6											12
1	2	3	4	5	8	7	6	9	11		12	10													13
1	2	3	4	5	8		6	9	10				7		11										14
1	2	3	4	5	8	12	6	9	10	14			7		11										15
	2	3	4		8	12	6	9	10				7		11	1		5							16
1	2	3		5	8	7	6	9	10									4	11						17
1	2	3		5	8	7	6	9	10									4	11						18
1	2	3		5	8	7	6	9	10				12			11		4	14						19
	2	3		5	8	7	6	9	10				11		1			4							20
	2	3		5	8	7	6	9	10				12	11	1			4							21
	2	3		5	8	7	6	9	10				11					4		1					22
	2	3		5	8	7	6	9	10				12		14			4	11	1					23
	2	3	6	5		7		9	10	11	8				14			4	12	1					24
		3	6	5		7		9	10	11					4	2		8		1	12				25
		3		5		7		9	10	11			12	6	8	2		4		1					26
	2	3		5		7		9	10	11				6	8	12		4		1					27
	2	3	6	5		7		9	10	11			12		8			4	14	1					28
	2	3	6	5		7		9	10	11					8			4		1					29
		3	6	5		7		9	10	11			2		8	12		4	14	1					30
			6	5	8	7		9	10	11			3	2				4		1					31
			6	5	8	7		9	10				11	2		3		4		1					32
			6	5	8	7		9	10				11	2		3		4	12	1					33
			6	5	8	7		9	10				11	2		3		4	12	1					34
			6	5	8			9	10				11	2	12	3		4	7	1					35
1		11		5	8		6	9	10				2		12	3		4	7						36
1		11		5	8		6		10		9		2		12	3		4	7						37
1	2	11		5	8		6		10	14			7	3				4	12			9			38
1	2	12	11	5	8		6			14			7	3	10			4				9			39
1	2	11		5	8		6		10		9		7	3				4	12						40
1	2	3	11		8	12	6		10				7	5				4	14			9			41
1		3	11	5	8		6		10		9		7	2				4	12						42
1	2	3	11	5	8	9			10				7	6				4	12						43
1		3		5	8	9	6		10				2	11				4	7		12				44
1		3	4	5	8	9	6		10				11	2					7						45
1	2	3		5	8	9	6						7	4				10			12	11		14	46

Coca Cola Cup	First Round	Halifax T (a)	2-1
		(h)	3-2
	Second Round	Sheffield W (a)	0-3
		(h)	2-2
FA Cup	First Round	Doncaster R (a)	2-1
	Second Round	Southport (h)	4-0
	Third Round	Crystal Palace (h)	1-0
	Fourth Round	Sheffield U (a)	0-1

HARTLEPOOL UNITED

Player and Position	Ht	Wt	Date	Birth Place	Source	Clubs	League App	Gls
Goalkeepers								
Martin Hodge	6 1	14 06	4 2 59	Southport	Apprentice	Plymouth Arg	43	—
						Everton	25	—
						Preston NE (loan)	28	—
						Oldham Ath (loan)	4	—
						Gillingham (loan)	4	—
						Preston NE (loan)	16	—
						Sheffield W	197	—
						Leicester C	75	—
						Hartlepool U	69	—
Steven Jones	5 11	12 03	31 1 74	Teeside	Trainee	Hartlepool U	9	—
Defenders								
Ryan Cross	6 1	13 06	11 10 72	Plymouth	Trainee	Plymouth Arg	19	—
						Hartlepool U	33	2
Scott Garrett			9 1 74	Gateshead	Trainee	Hartlepool	—	—
Philip Gilchrist	6 0	11 12	25 8 73	Stockton	Trainee	Nottingham F	—	—
						Middlesbrough	—	—
						Hartlepool U	24	—
Thomas McGuckin	6 2	12 02	24 4 73	Middlesbrough	Trainee	Hartlepool U	21	1
John MacPhail	6 0	12 03	7 12 55	Dundee	St. Columba's	Dundee	68	—
						Sheffield U	135	7
						York C	142	24
						Bristol C	26	1
						Sunderland	130	22
						Hartlepool U	125	3
Keith Nobbs	5 10	11 10	19 9 61	Bishop Auckland	Apprentice	Middlesbrough	1	—
						Halifax T	87	1
					Bishop Auckland	Hartlepool U	280	1
Midfield								
Paul Cross	5 7	9 06	31 10 65	Barnsley	Apprentice	Barnsley	118	—
						Preston NE (loan)	5	—
						Hartlepool U	58	1
Dean Emerson	5 9	12 11	27 12 62	Salford	Local	Stockport Co	156	7
						Rotherham U	55	8
						Coventry C	114	—
						Hartlepool U	32	1
Brian Honour	5 7	12 05	16 2 64	Horden	Apprentice Peterlee	Darlington	74	4
						Hartlepool U	301	22
Paul Olsson	5 8	10 11	24 12 65	Hull	Apprentice	Hull C	—	—
						Exeter C (loan)	8	—
						Exeter C	35	2
						Scarborough	48	5
						Hartlepool U	139	11
Tony Skedd§			19 5 75	North Cleveland	Trainee	Hartlepool U	1	—
Mick Tait	5 11	12 05	30 9 56	Wallsend	Apprentice	Oxford U	64	23
						Carlisle U	106	20
						Hull C	33	3
						Portsmouth	240	30
						Reading	99	9
						Darlington	79	2
						Hartlepool U	35	1
Paul Wratten	5 7	10 00	29 11 70	Middlesbrough	Trainee	Manchester U	2	—
						Hartlepool U	15	1

HARTLEPOOL UNITED

Colours: Navy/sky blue. **Change colours:** All yellow.

Foundation: The inspiration for the launching of Hartlepool United was the West Hartlepool club which won the FA Amateur Cup in 1904–05. They had been in existence since 1881 and their Cup success led in 1908 to the formation of the new professional concern which first joined the North-Eastern League. In those days they were Hartlepools United and won the Durham Senior Cup in their first two seasons.

First Football League game: 27 August, 1921, Division 3(N), v Wrexham (a) W 2-0 – Gill; Thomas, Crilly; Dougherty, Hopkins, Short; Kessler, Mulholland (1), Lister (1), Robertson, Donald.

Did you know: Johnny Wigham, a Jarrow schoolmaster, joined Hartlepools in 1931 and in eight seasons made more appearances between the wars than any other player for the club, with 263 League games and 96 goals to his credit as an inside-left.

Managers (and Secretary-Managers)
Alfred Priest 1908–12, Percy Humphreys 1912–13, Jack Manners 1913–20, Cecil Potter 1920–22, David Gordon 1922–24, Jack Manners 1924–27, Bill Norman 1927–31, Jack Carr 1932–35 (had been player-coach since 1931), Jimmy Hamilton 1935–43, Fred Westgarth 1943–57, Ray Middleton 1957–59, Bill Robinson 1959–62, Allenby Chilton 1962–63, Bob Gurney 1963–64, Alvan Williams 1964–65, Geoff Twentyman 1965, Brian Clough 1965–67, Angus McLean 1967–70, John Simpson 1970–71, Len Ashurst 1971–74, Ken Hale 1974–76, Billy Horner 1976–83, Johnny Duncan 1983, Mike Docherty 1983, Billy Horner 1984–86, John Bird 1986–88, Bobby Moncur 1988–89, Cyril Knowles 1989–91, Alan Murray 1991–93, Viv Busby February 1993–.

Player and Position	Ht	Wt	Date	Birth Place	Source	Clubs	League App	Gls
Forwards								
John Gallacher	5 10	10 08	26 1 69	Glasgow		Falkirk	18	5
						Newcastle U	29	6
						Hartlepool U	21	1
Lenny Johnrose	5 11	12 00	29 11 69	Preston	Trainee	Blackburn R	42	11
						Preston NE (loan)	3	1
						Hartlepool U	53	8
Chris Lynch§			18 11 74	Middlesbrough	Halifax T	Hartlepool U	1	—
Nick Peverell	5 11	11 10	28 4 73	Middlesbrough	Trainee	Middlesbrough	—	—
						Hartlepool U	19	1
Nicky Southall	5 10	11 02	28 1 72	Teeside		Hartlepool U	61	9
Paul Thompson	5 11	11 10	17 4 73	Newcastle	Trainee	Hartlepool U	2	1

Trainees
Anderson, Simon C; Chew, Paul; Grimes, Darren; Halliday, Stephen W; Hutchinson, Robert A; Hyson, Matthew A; Ingram, Stuart D; Leahy, Mark; Lowery, Paul A; Lynch, Christopher J; March, Anthony; Maughan, Neil G; Oliver, Keith; Porteous, Jason; Skedd, Anthony S; Strike, Anthony P; Wardle, Paul.

**Non-Contract
Cramman, Kenneth W; Hughes, David J; McBeth, Simon.

Associated Schoolboys
Andrews, Christopher J; Ashe, Robert L; Bogan, Darren J; Dunning, Richard W; Fisher, Benjamin M; Franks, Paul B; Gallagher, Ian; Hyson, Daniel J; Robinson, Paul; Watson, David S; Weighell, Paul.

Associated Schoolboys who have accepted the club's offer of a Traineeship/Contract
Dawkins, Mark A.

**Non-Contract Players who are retained must be re-signed before they are eligible to play in League matches.

254

HEREFORD UNITED 1992–93   *Back row (left to right):* Meshach Wade, Steve Devine, Gareth Davies, Paul Robinson, Alan Judge, Andy Theodosiou, Owen Pickard, David Titterton, Richard Jones.

Front Row: Chris Fry, Kentoine Jennings, Max Nicholson, Greg Downs, Simon Brain, Derek Hall, Colin Anderson.

Division 3   **HEREFORD UNITED**

Edgar Street, Hereford. Telephone Hereford (0432) 276666. Fax (0432) 341359. Commercial Dept: (0432) 273155.

Ground capacity: 13,777.

Record attendance: 18,114 v Sheffield W, FA Cup 3rd rd, 4 January 1958.

Record receipts: £72,840 v Manchester U, FA Cup 4th rd, 28 January 1990.

Pitch measurements: 111yd × 74yd.

Chairman: P. S. Hill FRICS. *Vice-chairman:* M. B. Roberts.

Directors: D. H. Vaughan, J. W. T. Duggan, D. A. Jones, R. A. Fry (Managing).

Manager: Greg Downs.

Physio: Colin Taylor.

Secretary: David Vaughan.

Year Formed: 1924. *Turned Professional:* 1924. *Ltd Co.:* 1939.

Club Nickname: 'United'.

Record League Victory: 6–0 v Burnley (away), Division 4, 24 January 1987 – Rose; Rodgerson, Devine, Halliday, Pejic, Dalziel, Harvey (1p), Wells, Phillips (3), Kearns (2), Spooner.

Record Cup Victory: 6–1 v QPR, FA Cup, 2nd rd, 7 December 1957 – Sewell; Tomkins, Wade; Masters, Niblett, Horton (2p); Reg Bowen (1), Clayton (1), Fidler, Williams (1), Cyril Beech (1).

Record Defeat: 0–6 v Rotherham U, Division 4, 29 April 1989.

Most League Points (2 for a win): 63, Division 3, 1975–76.

Most League Points (3 for a win): 77, Division 4, 1984–85.

Most League Goals: 86, Division 3, 1975–76.

Highest League Scorer in Season: Dixie McNeil, 35, 1975–76.

Most League Goals in Total Aggregate: Stewart Phillips, 93, 1980–88, 1990–1.

Most Capped Player: Brian Evans, 1 (7), Wales.

Most League Appearances: Mel Pejic, 412, 1980–92.

Record Transfer Fee Received: £200,000 from QPR for Darren Peacock, December 1990.

Record Transfer Fee Paid: £50,000 to Halifax T for Ian Juryeff, December 1989.

Football League Record: 1972 Elected to Division 4; 1973–76 Division 3; 1976–77 Division 2; 1977–78 Division 3; 1978–92 Division 4; 1992– Division 3.

Honours: Football League: Division 2 best season: 22nd, 1976–77; Division 3 – Champions 1975–76; Division 4 – Runners-up 1972–73. *FA Cup:* best season: 4th rd, 1971–72, 1976–77, 1981–82, 1989–90. *Football League Cup:* best season: 3rd rd, 1974–75. *Welsh Cup:* Winners, 1990.

HEREFORD UNITED 1992—93 LEAGUE RECORD

Match No.	Date	Venue	Opponents	Result		H/T Score	Lg. Pos.	Goalscorers	Attendance
1	Aug 15	H	Scarborough	D	1-1	1-1	—	Pickard	1836
2	21	A	Darlington	W	1-0	0-0	—	Pickard	1730
3	29	H	Walsall	L	1-3	1-2	10	Jones	2895
4	Sept 1	H	Lincoln C	L	0-2	0-2	—		1403
5	6	A	Northampton T	D	1-1	0-0	—	Brain	2668
6	13	H	Cardiff C	D	1-1	1-0	—	Fry	4039
7	15	A	York C	L	2-4	0-1	—	Pickard, McMillan (og)	3672
8	19	A	Barnet	L	0-2	0-1	21		2788
9	26	H	Rochdale	D	1-1	0-0	21	Fry	1834
10	Oct 3	H	Wrexham	D	1-1	0-0	20	Browning	2916
11	17	H	Torquay U	W	3-1	2-1	19	Hall, Browning, Pickard	1780
12	23	A	Doncaster R	L	1-2	0-1	—	Browning	2614
13	31	H	Halifax T	W	3-0	3-0	17	Browning 2, Davies	1936
14	Nov 3	A	Gillingham	L	1-3	1-2	—	Rowbotham J	2143
15	7	H	Chesterfield	L	1-3	1-1	20	Theodosiou	1774
16	21	A	Bury	L	0-2	0-0	20		1739
17	28	H	Colchester U	W	3-1	3-0	19	Pickard, Donald (og), Jones	1671
18	Dec 12	A	Scunthorpe U	L	1-3	1-1	19	Hall	1970
19	26	H	Shrewsbury T	D	1-1	0-0	20	Hall	3287
20	Jan 2	A	Cardiff C	L	1-2	1-1	20	Nicholson	6593
21	9	H	York C	D	1-1	1-1	20	Pickard	1975
22	16	A	Rochdale	W	3-1	1-1	19	Hall, Brian, Jones	1751
23	23	H	Barnet	D	1-1	1-0	19	Huxford (og)	2591
24	26	A	Walsall	D	1-1	0-0	—	Hall	2719
25	30	H	Darlington	D	1-1	1-1	19	May	2000
26	Feb 6	A	Scarborough	L	0-2	0-1	19		1467
27	13	H	Northampton T	W	3-2	1-1	18	Hall, Nicholson, Pickard	2352
28	20	A	Lincoln C	L	0-2	0-1	19		2875
29	Mar 6	A	Wrexham	L	0-2	0-2	19		5280
30	9	H	Crewe Alex	L	0-1	0-1	—		1872
31	13	A	Chesterfield	L	0-1	0-1	21		2834
32	20	H	Gillingham	W	3-1	2-0	18	May, Abraham, Hall	2138
33	23	A	Colchester U	L	1-3	0-1	—	Fry	3024
34	27	H	Bury	W	3-1	2-1	18	Ward (og), Rowbotham D, Hall (pen)	2208
35	Apr 2	A	Crewe Alex	D	1-1	1-0	—	Rowbotham D	3413
36	6	H	Scunthorpe U	D	2-2	0-1	—	Fry, Pickard	1740
37	10	A	Shrewsbury T	D	1-1	1-1	17	Pickard	3604
38	12	H	Carlisle U	W	1-0	1-0	17	Nicholson	2457
39	17	A	Carlisle U	D	0-0	0-0	16		2527
40	24	A	Torquay U	D	0-0	0-0	18		3414
41	May 1	H	Doncaster R	L	0-2	0-0	18		2352
42	8	A	Halifax T	W	1-0	0-0	17	Hall	7451

Final League Position: 17

GOALSCORERS

League (47): Hall 9 (1 pen), Pickard 9, Browning 5, Fry 4, Jones 3, Nicholson 3, Brain 2, May 2, Rowbotham D 2, Abraham 1, Davies 1, Rowbotham J 1, Theodosiou 1, own goals 4.
Coca Cola Cup (2): Pickard 2.
FA Cup (3): Pickard 2, own goal 1.

Judge 42	Fry 31 + 6	Downs 36 + 2	Jones 34 + 1	Devine 26 + 1	Theodosiou 8 + 1	Hall 41	Anderson 35	Brain 19 + 2	Pickard 36 + 1	Wade 3 + 4	Heathcock 1 + 1	Davies 31 + 1	Titterton 19 + 7	Nicholson 30 + 6	Jennings 2 + 3	Browning 7	Langford 1	Smith 6	Rowbotham J 3 + 2	Cousins 3	May 11 + 3	Abraham 19	Morris 10 + 1	Cross — + 1	Rowbotham D 8	Match No.
1	2	3	4	5	6	7	8	9	10	11																1
1	2	3	4	5	6	7	8	9	10			11	12													2
1	2	3	4	5	6	7	8	9	10			11	12	14												3
1	12	3	4	5	6	7	2	9	10	8				11												4
1		3	4	5	6	7	2	9		8			11	10												5
1	2	3	4	5		7	10	9	12			8		11		6										6
1	2	3	4	5		7	10	9	8					11		6										7
1	2	3	4	5		7	10	12	8			6	14	11		9										8
1	2		3			7	6	8	10	12		4		11		9		5								9
1	2	3	10	5		7	6	8				4		12	11	9										10
1	2	3	6			7	8	10				4		11		9		5								11
1	2	3	6	8		7		10				4		11		9		5								12
1	2	3	8	12	6	7		10				4				9		5	11							13
1	2	3	8	6		7		10				4		12		9		5	11							14
1	2	3	8	6	11	7		9	10			4		12				5	14							15
1	2	3	8	6		7		9	10			4						5	11							16
1	2	3	8	5		7	10	9				4	6	12					14	11						17
1	12	3	8	4	5	7	6	9						2		11					10					18
1	2	3	8			7	6	12	9			4	5	11							10					19
1	2		8	3		7	6	10	9	12		4	5	11	14											20
1	2		8	3		7	6	10	9			4	5	11							12					21
1	2	12	8	3		7	6	10	9			4	5	11												22
1	2	3	12	14		7	8	10	9			4	6								11	5				23
1	2	6		4		7	11	8	9			3	12								10	5				24
1	2	6		4		7	11	8	9			3	12								10	5				25
1		6				7	4	8	9	12		3		11	14						10	5	2			26
1	12	6				7	8	9				4	3	11							10	5	2			27
1	12		4	6		7	8	9				3		11	14						10	5	2			28
1	12	6	8			7	11	9				4	3	14							10	5	2			29
1	10	8				7	6	9		12		4	3	11								5	2			30
1		2	6			7	8	9				4	3	11							10	5				31
1	12	2	6			7	8	9				4	3	11							10	5				32
1	12	2	6	8		7		9				4	3	11							10	5	14			33
1	10	2	6	8		7	12					3		11								5	4		9	34
1	10	2	6			7	8					4	12	11								5	3		9	35
1	10	2	6			7	3	8				4		11								5			9	36
1	10	2	6			7	3	8				4	14	11							12	5			9	37
1	10	2	6			7	3	9				4		11							8	5			9	38
1	10	2	6	5		7	3	8				4		11											9	39
1	10	2				7	3	8				4		11							12	5	6		9	40
1	10	2				7	3	8				4	12	11								5	6	14	9	41
1		2	10			7	3	8				4		11								5	6		9	42

Coca Cola Cup	First Round	Torquay U (h)	2-2
		(a)	0-5
FA Cup	First Round	Sutton U (a)	2-1
	Second Round	Yeovil (a)	0-0
		(h)	1-2

HEREFORD UNITED

Player and Position	Ht	Wt	Date	Birth Place	Source	Clubs	League App	Gls
Goalkeepers								
Alan Judge	5 11	11 06	14 5 60	Kingsbury	Amateur	Luton T	11	—
						Reading (loan)	33	—
						Reading	44	—
						Oxford U	97	—
						Lincoln C (loan)	2	—
						Cardiff C (loan)	8	—
						Hereford U	66	—
Defenders								
Gareth Abraham	6 4	12 11	13 2 69	Merthyr Tydfil	Trainee	Cardiff C	87	4
						Hereford U	19	1
Gareth Davies			11 12 73	Hereford	Trainee	Hereford U	36	1
Greg Downs	5 9	10 07	13 12 58	Carlton	Apprentice	Norwich C	169	7
						Torquay U (loan)	1	1
						Coventry C	146	4
						Birmingham C	17	—
						Hereford U	78	2
Richard Jones*	5 11	11 01	26 4 69	Pontypool		Newport Co	41	1
						Hereford U	148	9
Craig Langford§			12 3 75	Solihull	Trainee	Hereford U	1	—
Andy Theodosiou*	6 0	12 10	30 10 70	Stoke Newington	Tottenham H	Norwich C	—	—
						Hereford U	42	2
Midfield								
Colin Anderson	5 8	10 08	26 4 62	Newcastle	Apprentice	Burnley	6	—
						Torquay U	109	11
						QPR (loan)	—	—
						WBA	140	10
						Walsall	26	2
						Hereford U	35	—
Steve Devine*	5 9	11 00	11 12 64	Strabane	Apprentice	Wolverhampton W	—	—
						Derby Co	11	—
						Stockport Co	2	—
						Hereford U	272	4
Derek Hall	5 8	12 03	5 1 65	Manchester	Apprentice	Coventry C	1	—
						Torquay U (loan)	10	2
						Torquay U	45	4
						Swindon T	10	—
						Southend U	123	15
						Halifax T	49	4
						Hereford U	61	9
Adrian Heathcock§			26 1 75	Dudley	Trainee	Hereford U	2	—
David Morris	5 11	12 00	19 11 71	Plumstead	Trainee	Bournemouth	1	—
						Hereford U	11	—
Jason Rowbotham‡	5 9	11 00	3 1 69	Cardiff	Trainee	Plymouth Arg	9	—
						Shrewsbury T	—	—
						Hereford U	5	1
David Titterton*	5 11	10 09	25 9 71	Hatton	Trainee	Coventry C	2	—
						Hereford U	51	1
Meashach Wade‡			23 1 73	Bermuda	Bermuda	Hereford U	17	—
Forwards								
Simon Brain	5 6	10 08	31 3 66	Evesham	Cheltenham T	Hereford U	84	20
Mark Cross§			6 5 76	Abergavenny	Trainee	Hereford U	1	—
Chris Fry	5 9	9 06	23 10 69	Cardiff	Trainee	Cardiff C	55	1
						Hereford U	74	7
Jedd Jennings‡			15 10 71	Bermuda	Bermuda	Hereford U	16	—

HEREFORD UNITED

Colours: White shirts, black shorts, white stockings. **Change colours:** All red.

Foundation: A number of local teams amalgamated in 1924 under the chairmanship of Dr. E. W. Maples to form Hereford United and joined the Birmingham Combination. They graduated to the Birmingham League four years later.

First Football League game: 12 August, 1972, Division 4, v Colchester U (a) L 0-1 – Potter; Mallender, Naylor; Jones, McLaughlin, Tucker; Slattery, Hollett, Owen, Radford, Wallace.

Did you know: In the days before they were elected to the Football League, Hereford United made FA Cup history by reaching the competition proper in 21 successive seasons.

Managers (and Secretary-Managers)
Eric Keen 1939, George Tranter 1948–49, Alex Massie 1952, George Tranter 1953–55, Joe Wade 1956–62, Ray Daniels 1962–63, Bob Dennison 1963–67, John Charles 1967–71, Colin Addison 1971–74, John Sillett 1974–78, Mike Bailey 1978–79, Frank Lord 1979–82, Tommy Hughes 1982–83, Johnny Newman 1983–87, Ian Bowyer 1987–90, Colin Addison 1990–91, John Sillett 1991–92, Greg Downs May 1992–.

Player and Position	Ht	Wt	Birth Date	Birth Place	Source	Clubs	League App	Gls
Leroy May	6 1	11 07	12 8 69	Wolverhampton	Tividale	Walsall	4	—
					Tividale	Hereford U	14	2
Max Nicholson	5 10	12 03	3 10 71	Leeds	Trainee	Doncaster R	27	2
						Hereford U	36	3
Owen Pickard	5 10	11 03	18 11 69	Barnstaple	Trainee	Plymouth Arg	16	1
						Hereford U	37	9
Paul Robinson*	6 4	14 07	21 2 71	Nottingham	Bury	Scarborough	20	3
						Plymouth Arg	11	3
						Hereford U	11	—

Trainees
Cross, Mark; Eversham, Paul J; Gambling, Benjamin R; Heathcock, Adrian N; Langford, Craig R; Lees, Michael J; Preedy, Phillip; Thomas, Brian; Tivey, Robert; Watkins, Andrew J; Watkins, Christopher W; Watkins, Edward J; Williams, Christopher J.

260

HUDDERSFIELD TOWN 1992–93 *Back row (left to right):* Mark Wright, Iwan Roberts, Tony Elliott, Tim Clarke, Ifem Onoura, Simon Trevitt. *Centre row:* Kevin Donovan, Graham Mitchell, Kieran O'Regan, Chris Billy, Kevin Lampkin, Thomas Mooney, Jonathan Dyson, Simon Ireland, John Dysart, Gary Barnett. *Front row:* Simon Collins, Chris Marsden, Simon Charlton, Peter Jackson, Ian Ross (Manager), Phil Starbuck, Andrew Booth, Anthony Brennan, Neil Parsley.

Division 2   HUDDERSFIELD TOWN

© 1973

Leeds Rd, Huddersfield HD1 6PE. Telephone (0484) 420335/6. Fax (0484) 515122. Recorded Information: (0898) 121635.

Ground capacity: 32,000.

Record attendance: 67,037 v Arsenal, FA Cup 6th rd, 27 February1932.

Record receipts: £52,607 v Newcastle U, Division 2, 7 May, 1984.

Pitch measurements: 115yd × 75yd.

Chairman: T. S. Fisher. *Vice-chairman:* D. G. Headey.

Directors: R. Whiteley, H. Asquith, D. A. Taylor, G. A. Leslie.

Associate Director: T. J. Cherry.

Manager: Neil Warnock. *Assistant Manager:* Mick Jones.

Secretary: Alan D. Sykes. *Commercial Manager:* Alan Stevenson. *Chief Executive:* Paul Fletcher.

Physio: George McAllister.

Year Formed: 1908. *Turned Professional:* 1908. *Ltd Co.:* 1908.

Club Nickname: 'The Terriers'.

Record League Victory: 10–1 v Blackpool, Division 1, 13 December 1930 – Turner; Goodall, Spencer; Redfern, Wilson, Campbell; Bob Kelly (1), McLean (4), Robson (3), Davies (1), Smailes (1).

Record Cup Victory: 7–1 v Chesterfield (away), FA Cup, 3rd rd, 12 January 1929 – Turvey; Goodall, Wadsworth; Evans, Wilson, Naylor: Jackson (1), Kelly, Brown (3), Cumming (2), Smith. (1 o.g).

Record Defeat: 1–10 v Manchester C, Division 2, 7 November 1987.

Most League Points (2 for a win): 66, Division 4, 1979–80.

Most League Points (3 for a win): 82, Division 3, 1982–83.

Most League Goals: 101, Division 4, 1979–80.

Highest League Scorer in Season: Sam Taylor, 35, Division 2, 1919–20; George Brown, 35, Division 1, 1925–26.

Most League Goals in Total Aggregate: George Brown, 142, 1921–29 and Jimmy Glazzard, 142, 1946–56.

Most Capped Player: Jimmy Nicholson, 31 (41), Northern Ireland.

Most League Appearances: Billy Smith, 520, 1914–34.

Record Transfer Fee Received: £250,000 from Reading for Craig Maskell, July 1990.

Record Transfer Fee Paid: £275,000 to Watford for Iwan Roberts, August 1990.

Football League Record: 1910 Elected to Division 2; 1920–52 Division 1; 1952–53 Division 2; 1953–56 Division 1; 1956–70 Division 2; 1970–72 Division 1; 1972–73 Division 2; 1973–75 Division 3; 1975–80 Division 4; 1980–83 Division 3; 1983–88 Division 2; 1988–92 Division 3; 1992– Division 2.

Honours: Football League: Division 1 – Champions 1923–24, 1924–25, 1925–26; Runners-up 1926–27, 1927–28, 1933–34; Division 2 – Champions 1969–70; Runners-up 1919–20, 1952–53; Division 4 – Champions 1979–80. *FA Cup:* Winners 1922; Runners-up 1920, 1928, 1930, 1938. *Football League Cup:* Semi-final, 1967–68.

HUDDERSFIELD TOWN 1992—93 LEAGUE RECORD

Match No.	Date		Venue	Opponents	Result		H/T Score	Lg. Pos.	Goalscorers	Atten dance
1	Aug 15	A		Bolton W	L	0-2	0-1	—		7897
2	22	H		WBA	L	0-1	0-1	23		7947
3	29	A		Hartlepool U	L	0-1	0-1	24		4120
4	Sept 1	A		Leyton Orient	L	1-4	0-1	—	Starbuck	3765
5	6	H		Bradford C	L	1-2	1-0	—	Barnett	5883
6	12	A		Brighton & HA	L	1-2	1-1	24	Roberts (pen)	6141
7	15	H		Plymouth Arg	W	2-1	1-1	—	Jackson, Roberts	4411
8	19	H		Swansea C	L	1-2	0-0	24	Roberts	4839
9	26	A		Bournemouth	D	1-1	0-0	24	Roberts	4447
10	Oct 3	A		Rotherham U	L	0-1	0-0	24		5459
11	10	H		Reading	D	0-0	0-0	24		5281
12	17	A		Hull C	W	3-2	1-1	23	Starbuck, Robinson, Roberts	4705
13	24	H		Exeter C	D	0-0	0-0	23		4707
14	30	A		Stockport Co	L	0-5	0-1	—		5405
15	Nov 3	A		Blackpool	D	2-2	1-1	—	Booth, Stuart	3441
16	7	H		Mansfield T	W	2-1	2-1	23	Booth, Stuart	4933
17	21	A		Burnley	L	1-2	1-2	23	Robinson	10,615
18	28	H		Port Vale	L	1-2	1-1	23	Robinson	5822
19	Dec 12	A		Stoke C	L	0-3	0-0	23		13,377
20	19	H		Chester C	L	0-2	0-1	23		4626
21	Jan 16	H		Bournemouth	L	0-1	0-0	24		4316
22	27	H		Hartlepool U	W	3-0	2-0	—	O'Regan (pen), Starbuck, Roberts	4153
23	30	A		WBA	D	2-2	0-0	24	Dunn, Starbuck	13,667
24	Feb 6	H		Bolton W	D	1-1	0-1	24	O'Regan (pen)	8858
25	14	A		Bradford C	W	1-0	0-0	—	Barnett	8214
26	16	A		Wigan Ath	L	0-1	0-1	—		2474
27	20	H		Leyton Orient	D	1-1	0-1	24	Stuart	5112
28	27	H		Reading	L	1-2	0-2	24	Roberts	3948
29	Mar 3	H		Brighton & HA	L	1-2	0-1	—	Starbuck	3563
30	6	H		Rotherham U	D	1-1	0-0	23	Roberts	5235
31	10	H		Fulham	W	1-0	1-0	—	O'Regan (pen)	3670
32	13	A		Mansfield T	W	2-1	0-1	23	Onuora, Barnett	3987
33	17	A		Preston NE	W	1-0	0-0	—	Onuora	4915
34	20	H		Blackpool	W	5-2	2-1	20	O'Regan (pen), Barnett, Starbuck, Onuora 2	6249
35	23	A		Port Vale	L	0-1	0-1	—		7747
36	27	H		Burnley	D	1-1	0-1	23	Starbuck	9411
37	30	A		Plymouth Arg	W	3-1	1-1	—	Onuora 2, Barnett	4986
38	Apr 2	A		Fulham	W	1-0	0-0	—	Roberts	3611
39	7	H		Stoke C	W	1-0	1-0	—	Dunn	11,089
40	10	A		Preston NE	L	1-2	0-1	18	Robinson	7647
41	12	H		Wigan Ath	W	2-1	1-0	15	Barnett, Starbuck	6822
42	17	A		Chester C	W	2-0	0-0	15	Dunn, Cooper	3019
43	20	A		Swansea C	L	0-3	0-1	—		5190
44	24	H		Hull C	W	3-0	1-0	15	O'Regan (pen), Charlton, Starbuck	6607
45	May 1	A		Exeter C	W	2-1	1-1	15	Cooper 2	3271
46	8	H		Stockport Co	W	2-1	1-1	15	Cooper, Barnett	7673

Final League Position: 15

GOALSCORERS

League (54): Roberts 9 (1 pen), Starbuck 9, Barnett 7, Onuora 6, O'Regan 5 (5 pens), Cooper 4, Robinson 4, Dunn 3, Stuart 3, Booth 2, Charlton 1, Jackson 1.
Coca Cola Cup (7): Roberts 2, Barnett 1, Ireland 1, Onuora 1, Parsley 1, Starbuck 1.
FA Cup (7): Barnett 2, Dunn 2, Mitchell 1, O'Regan 1 (pen), Robinson 1.

Clarke 31	Parsley 44	Charlton 46	Marsden 6 + 1	Wright 11 + 3	Jackson 39	Billy 4 + 9	Lampkin 13	Roberts 37	Starbuck 29 + 9	Onuora 30 + 9	Barnett 45 + 1	O'Regan 37 + 4	Robinson 35 + 1	Booth 3 + 2	Elliott 15	Dyson 15	Donovan 2 + 1	Dewhurst 7	Ireland 4	Stuart 9 + 6	Mooney 1	Mitchell 3 + 1	Dunn 25 + 3	Collins — + 1	Smith 5	Cooper 10	Match No.
1	2	3	4	5	6	7	8	9	10	11	12	14															1
1	2	3	4	5	6	12		9	10	11		7	8														2
1	2	3	4	5	6	12		9	10	11		7	8														3
1	2	3	4	5	6	12		9	10	11		7	8														4
1	2	3	4	5	6	10		9		11		7	8	12													5
	2	3	4		6	10	11	9	14			7	8		1	5	12										6
	2	3			6	10		9		11		7	8		1	5			4								7
	2	3	14		6	4		9	10	11	12	7	8		1	5											8
	2	3		5	6	10		9	12	11		7	8	14	1				4								9
1	2	3		12	6			9	10			7	8			4		5		11							10
	2	3	4					9	10	12		7	8	6	1			5		11							11
	2	3		12		4		9	10			7	8	6	1			5		11							12
	2	3			6			9	10	12		7	8		1	4		5		11							13
	2	3			6	12			10	11		7	8		1	4		5		9							14
1		3	8		6				12	11		7	14			4	2	5		9		10					15
1		3	10		6				12	11		7				4	2	5		9		8					16
1	2	3			6	10		9	12			7	8			4		5		11							17
1	2	3			6	10		9	14	11		7	8			4		5				12					18
1	2	3			6			9	12			7	8							11	4	5	10				19
1	2	3			6			9	12			7	8			4				11		5	10				20
	2	3			6			9	12	11		7	8		1	4						5	10				21
	2	3			6	12		9	10	11		7	8		1	4		5					14				22
	2	3			6			9	10	11		7	8		1	4		5				12	14				23
	2	3			6	12		9	10			7	8		1			5				11	4				24
	2	3			6			9	10			7	8		1			5				11	4				25
	2	3	14		6			9	10	12		7	8		1			5				11	4				26
	2	3			6			9	10	11		7	8		1			5				12	4	14			27
1	2	3						9	10	11		7	8			4		5				12	14		6		28
1	2	3			6			9	10	12		7	8			4							11		5		29
1	2	3		14			5	9	10	12		7	8			4							11		6		30
1	2	3		14			5	9	10	12		7	8			4							11		6		31
1	2	3			6		5	9	10			7	8			4							11				32
1	2	3			6		5	9	10			7	8			4							11				33
1	2	3			6		5	9	10			7	8			4						12	11				34
1	2	3			6			9	10			7	8			4						12	11		5		35
1	2	3			6			9	10			7	8			4							11		5		36
1	2	3			6			9	10			7	8			4							11		5		37
1	2	3			6		5	9	10			7	8			4							11				38
1	2	3			6			9	10			7	8			4							11		5		39
1	2	3			6			9	12	10		7	8			4							11		5		40
1	2	3			6			9	12	10		7	8			4							11		5		41
1	2	3			6			9	10			7	8			4						12	11		5		42
1	2	3			6			9	10			7	8			4							11		5		43
1	2	3			6			9	12	10		7	8			4							11		5		44
1	2	3			6			9	12	10		7	8			4						14	11		5		45
1	2	3	12		6			9	10			7	8			4							11		5		46

Coca Cola Cup	First Round	Sunderland (a)	3-2
		(h)	0-1
	Second Round	Blackburn R (h)	1-1
		(a)	3-4
FA Cup	First Round	Scunthorpe U (a)	0-0
		(h)	2-1
	Second Round	Bradford C (a)	2-0
	Third Round	Gillingham (a)	0-0
		(h)	2-1
	Fourth Round	Southend U (h)	1-2

HUDDERSFIELD TOWN

Player and Position	Ht	Wt	Date	Birth Place	Source	Clubs	League App	Gls
Goalkeepers								
Tim Clarke	6 3	13 07	19 9 68	Stourbridge	Halesowen	Coventry C	—	—
						Huddersfield T	70	—
						Rochdale (loan)	2	—
Tony Elliott‡	6 0	12 12	30 11 69	Nuneaton		Birmingham C	—	—
						Hereford U	75	—
						Huddersfield T	15	—
Defenders								
Simon Charlton	5 7	10 11	25 10 71	Huddersfield	Trainee	Huddersfield T	124	1
Jon Dyson	6 1	12 00	18 12 71	Mirfield	School	Huddersfield T	15	—
Peter Jackson	6 0	12 07	6 4 61	Bradford	Apprentice	Bradford C	278	24
						Newcastle U	60	3
						Bradford C	58	5
						Huddersfield T	122	3
Graham Mitchell	6 0	11 05	16 2 68	Shipley	Apprentice	Huddersfield T	210	2
Neil Parsley	5 10	10 11	25 4 66	Liverpool	Witton Alb	Leeds U	—	—
						Chester C (loan)	6	—
						Huddersfield T	57	—
						Doncaster R (loan)	3	—
Simon Trevitt	5 11	11 02	20 12 67	Dewsbury	Apprentice	Huddersfield T	173	2
Mark Wright*	5 11	10 12	29 1 70	Manchester	Trainee	Everton	1	—
						Blackpool (loan)	3	—
						Huddersfield T (loan)	10	1
						Huddersfield T	22	—
Midfield								
Anthony Brennan	5 7	10 12	1 12 73	Dublin	Trainee	Huddersfield T	—	—
Simon Collins	6 0	11 02	16 12 73	Pontefract	Trainee	Huddersfield T	1	—
John Dysart*	5 7	10 00	30 9 73	Huddersfield	Trainee	Huddersfield T	—	—
Kevin Lampkin	5 10	11 08	20 12 72	Liverpool	Trainee	Liverpool	—	—
						Huddersfield T	13	—
Chris Marsden	5 11	10 12	3 1 69	Sheffield	Trainee	Sheffield U	16	1
						Huddersfield T	119	9
Tom Mooney	5 11	11 02	14 12 73	Newry	Trainee	Huddersfield T	1	—
Kieran O'Regan	5 8	10 12	9 11 63	Cork	Tramore Ath	Brighton	86	2
						Swindon T	26	1
						Huddersfield T	199	25
Phil Robinson	5 10	10 10	6 1 67	Stafford	Apprentice	Aston Villa	3	1
						Wolverhampton W	71	8
						Notts Co	66	5
						Birmingham C (loan)	9	—
						Huddersfield T	36	4
Forwards								
Gary Barnett	5 6	9 13	11 3 63	Stratford	Apprentice	Coventry C	—	—
						Huddersfield T	22	1
						Oxford U	45	9
						Wimbledon (loan)	5	1
						Fulham (loan)	2	1
						Fulham	180	30
						Huddersfield T	99	11
Chris Billy	5 11	11 08	2 1 73	Huddersfield	Trainee	Huddersfield T	23	2
Andrew Booth	5 10	10 03	17 3 73	Huddersfield	Trainee	Huddersfield T	8	2
Iain Dunn	5 11	10 10	1 4 72	Derwent	School	York C	77	11
						Chesterfield	13	1
					Goole T	Huddersfield T	28	3

HUDDERSFIELD TOWN

Colours: Blue and white striped shirts, white shorts, white stockings. **Change colours:** Red/black hooped shirts, black shorts, black stockings.

Foundation: A meeting, attended largely by members of the Huddersfield & District FA, was held at the Imperial Hotel in 1906 to discuss the feasibility of establishing a football club in this rugby stronghold. However, it was not until a man with both the enthusiasm and the money to back the scheme came on the scene, that real progress was made. This benefactor was Mr. Hilton Crowther and it was at a meeting at the Albert Hotel in 1908, that the club formally came into existence with a capital of £2,000 and joined the North-Eastern League.

First Football League game: 3 September, 1910, Division 2, v Bradford PA (a) W 1-0 – Mutch; Taylor, Morris; Beaton, Hall, Bartlett; Blackburn, Wood, Hamilton (1), McCubbin, Jee.

Did you know: Jimmy Glazzard headed four goals for Huddersfield Town in an 8-2 win over Everton in Division 2 on 7 April 1953. All four came from centres by left-winger Vic Metcalfe.

Managers (and Secretary-Managers)
Fred Walker 1908–10, Richard Pudan 1910–12, Arthur Fairclough 1912–19, Ambrose Langley 1919–21, Herbert Chapman 1921–25, Cecil Potter 1925–26, Jack Chaplin 1926–29, Clem Stephenson 1929–42, David Steele 1943–47, George Stephenson 1947–52, Andy Beattie 1952–56, Bill Shankly 1956–59, Eddie Boot 1960–64, Tom Johnston 1964–68, Ian Greaves 1968–74, Bobby Collins 1974 1–75 (GM), Tom Johnston 1975–7/1977–78, Mike Buxton 1978–86, Steve Smith 1986–87, Malcolm Macdonald 1987–88, Eoin Hand 1988–92, Ian Ross 1992–93; Neil Warnock July 1993–.

Player and Position	Ht	Wt	Date	Birth Place	Source	Clubs	League App	Gls
Iffy Onuora	5 10	11 10	28 7 67	Glasgow	British Universities	Huddersfield T	143	24
Iwan Roberts	6 3	12 06	26 6 68	Bangor		Watford	63	9
						Huddersfield T	127	46
Philip Starbuck	5 10	10 13	24 11 68	Nottingham	Apprentice	Nottingham F	36	2
						Birmingham C (loan)	3	—
						Hereford U (loan)	6	—
						Blackburn R (loan)	6	1
						Huddersfield T	82	23
Mark Stuart*	5 10	11 03	15 12 66	Hammersmith	QPR	Charlton Ath	107	28
						Plymouth Arg	57	11
						Ipswich T (loan)	5	2
						Bradford C	29	5
						Huddersfield T	15	3

Trainees
Baldry, Simon; Crowther, Matthew J; Doherty, Gerald A; Donaldson, Stephen; McKenzie, Wayne; Midwood, Michael A; Payne, Stephen J; Rowe, Rodney C; Taylor, Craig L; Whitehead, Scot; Wood, Sean P. A.

Associated Schoolboys
Booth, Martin; Bullock, Richard M; Cooke, Peter J; Fearnley, Robert A; Fearnley, Thomas E; Halstead, Miles R; Hart, Andrew C; Heddon, Matthew P; Jones, Geoffrey A; Keighley, James H; Kitchin, Timothy; Lawson, Ian J; Mitchell, David P; Moorhouse, Robert J; Richardson, Ben; Roberts, Andrew; Stansfield, James E; Stokes, Andrew J; Stott, Michael J; Sweet, Benjamin J; Sykes, James A; Whitehead, Kristian M. J.

Associated Schoolboys who have accepted the club's offer of a Traineeship/Contract
Collins, Sam J; Crompton, Glen S; Crowther, Paul; Garside, Liam; Illingworth, Jeremy M; Wood, Nicholas I.

HULL CITY 1992-93 *Back row (left to right):* Leigh Jenkinson, Neil Allison, Darren France, Gary Hobson, Lee Warren, David Mail.
Centre row: David Hockaday, Mark Calvert, Stuart Young, Steve Wilson, Alan Fettis, Wayne Jacobs, Darren Cairns, Jeff Radcliffe (Physio).
Front row: Graeme Atkinson, Mick Matthews, Dean Windass, Jeff Lee (Assistant Manager), Martin Fish (Chairman), Terry Dolan (Manager), Russ Wilcox, Paul Hunter, Gareth Stoker, David Norton.

Division 2

HULL CITY

Boothferry Park, Hull HU4 6EU. Telephone Hull (0482) 51119. Commercial Manager: (0482) 566050. Football in the Community Office: 0482 565088. Fax: 0482 565752.

Ground capacity: 17,528.

Record attendance: 55,019 v Manchester U, FA Cup 6th rd, 26 February 1949.

Record receipts: £79,604 v Liverpool FA Cup, 5th rd, 18 February 1989.

Pitch measurements: 112yd × 73yd.

President: T. C. Waite FIMI, MIRTE.

Honorary Vice-president: D. Robinson, H. Bermitz, J. Johnson BA, DPA.

Vice-presidents: R. Beercock, K. Davis, N. Howe, R. Booth, A. Fetiveau, W. Law.

Chairman: M. W. Fish MCA. *Vice-chairman:* R. M. Chetham.

Directors: G. H. C. Needler MA, FCA, M. G. ST, Quinton BA, MBA.

Manager: Terry Dolan. *Assistant Manager:* Jeff Lee.

Secretary: Tom Wilson. *Physio:* Jeff Radcliffe MCSP, SRP.

Commercial Manager: Simon Cawkhill. *Stadium Manager:* John Cooper.

Ticket Office/Gate Manager: Wilf Rogerson. *Hon, Medical Officers:* G. Hoyle, MBCHB, FRCS, Dr. B. Kell, MBBS.

Year Formed: 1904. *Turned Professional:* 1905. *Ltd Co.:* 1905.

Club Nickname: 'The Tigers'.

Previous Grounds: 1904, Boulevard Ground (Hull RFC); 1905, Anlaby Road (Hull CC); 1944/5 Boulevard Ground; 1946, Boothferry Park.

Record League Victory: 11–1 v Carlisle U, Division 3 (N), 14 January 1939 – Ellis; Woodhead, Dowen; Robinson (1), Blyth, Hardy; Hubbard (2), Richardson (2), Dickinson (2), Davies (2), Cunliffe (2).

Record Cup Victory: 8–2 v Stalybridge Celtic (away), FA Cup, 1st rd, 26 November 1932 – Maddison; Goldsmith, Woodhead; Gardner, Hill (1), Denby; Forward (1), Duncan, McNaughton (1), Wainscoat (4), Sargeant (1).

Record Defeat: 0–8 v Wolverhampton W, Division 2, 4 November 1911.

Most League Points (2 for a win): 69, Division 3, 1965–66.

Most League Points (3 for a win): 90, Division 4, 1982–83.

Most League Goals: 109, Division 3, 1965–66.

Highest League Scorer in Season: Bill McNaughton, 39, Division 3 (N), 1932–33.

Most League Goals in Total Aggregate: Chris Chilton, 195, 1960–71.

Most Capped Player: Terry Neill, 15 (59), Northern Ireland.

Most League Appearances: Andy Davidson, 520, 1952–67.

Record Transfer Fee Received: £750,000 from Middlesbrough for Andy Payton, November 1991.

Record Transfer Fee Paid: £200,000 to Leeds U for Peter Swan, March 1989.

Football League Record: 1905 Elected to Division 2; 1930–33 Division 3 (N); 1933–36 Division 2; 1936–49 Division 3 (N); 1949–56 Division 2; 1956–58 Division 3 (N); 1958–59 Division 3; 1959–60 Division 2; 1960–66 Division 3; 1966–78 Division 2; 1978–81 Division 3; 1981–83 Division 4; 1983–85 Division 3; 1985–91 Division 2; 1991– 92 Division 3; 1992– Division 2.

Honours: Football League: Division 2 best season: 3rd, 1909–10; Division 3 (N) – Champions 1932–33, 1948–49; Division 3 – Champions 1965–66; Runners-up 1958–59; Division 4 – Runners-up 1982–83. *FA Cup:* best season: Semi-final, 1930. *Football League Cup:* best season: 4th, 1973–74, 1975–76, 1977–78. *Associate Members' Cup:* Runners-up 1984.

HULL CITY 1992—93 LEAGUE RECORD

Match No.	Date		Venue	Opponents	Result		H/T Score	Lg. Pos.	Goalscorers	Atten dance
1	Aug	15	H	Stoke C	W	1-0	0-0	—	Hunter	9088
2		22	H	Chester C	D	1-1	0-0	7	Atkinson	4906
3		28	H	Plymouth Arg	W	2-0	0-0	—	Hockaday, Lund	4194
4	Sept	1	H	Swansea C	W	1-0	0-0	—	Hunter	4408
5		5	A	Reading	W	2-1	1-1	2	Lund, Windass	3465
6		12	A	Stockport Co	L	3-5	2-4	4	Carstairs (og), Jenkinson, Hunter	4216
7		15	H	Preston NE	L	2-4	2-1	—	Flynn (og), Jenkinson	4463
8		19	H	Rotherham U	L	0-1	0-0	8		4780
9		26	A	Leyton Orient	D	0-0	0-0	10		4951
10	Oct	3	H	Bradford C	L	0-2	0-1	14		5340
11		10	A	Fulham	D	3-3	3-1	14	Atkinson, Jenkinson, Mohan	5247
12		17	H	Huddersfield T	L	2-3	1-1	15	Wilcox, Atkinson	4705
13		24	A	Bolton W	L	0-2	0-0	17		4136
14		31	H	WBA	L	1-2	0-1	18	Jenkinson	5443
15	Nov	3	A	Mansfield T	L	1-3	0-0	—	Carruthers	3038
16		7	H	Burnley	L	0-2	0-1	19		5751
17		21	A	Port Vale	D	1-1	1-0	19	Carruthers	6202
18		28	H	Blackpool	W	3-2	3-0	19	Atkinson, Windass, Carruthers	3906
19	Dec	12	H	Exeter C	W	4-0	4-0	18	Atkinson, Carruthers 2, Windass	3167
20		19	A	Bournemouth	D	0-0	0-0	17		4200
21		26	A	Hartlepool U	L	0-1	0-1	18		4187
22		28	H	Brighton & HA	W	1-0	0-0	17	Hunter	4785
23	Jan	9	A	Preston NE	W	2-1	1-1	16	Carruthers, Wilcox	4719
24		16	H	Leyton Orient	D	0-0	0-0	14		3897
25		26	A	Plymouth Arg	D	0-0	0-0	—		4612
26		30	A	Chester C	L	0-3	0-3	17		3232
27	Feb	6	A	Stoke C	L	0-3	0-2	18		15,391
28		9	A	Rotherham U	W	1-0	1-0	—	Lund	3660
29		13	H	Reading	D	1-1	0-0	17	Windass	3593
30		20	A	Swansea C	L	0-1	0-1	17		2656
31		27	H	Fulham	D	1-1	1-0	17	Atkinson	3645
32	Mar	6	A	Bradford C	W	2-1	2-0	17	Windass, Stapleton (og)	6245
33		9	H	Wigan Ath	D	0-0	0-0	—		3394
34		13	A	Burnley	L	0-2	0-1	17		9974
35		20	H	Mansfield T	W	1-0	1-0	16	Brown	3551
36		23	H	Blackpool	L	1-5	1-2	—	Abbott	3515
37		27	H	Port Vale	L	0-1	0-0	17		4558
38	Apr	3	A	Wigan Ath	L	0-2	0-2	17		1872
39		6	A	Exeter C	D	1-1	0-1	—	Hunter	2415
40		10	H	Hartlepool U	W	3-2	1-2	16	Windass, Jones, Norton	3562
41		14	A	Brighton & HA	L	0-2	0-1	—		7776
42		17	H	Bournemouth	W	3-0	2-0	16	Hunter, France 2	3442
43		24	A	Huddersfield T	L	0-3	0-1	18		6607
44		27	A	Stockport Co	L	0-2	0-0	—		4079
45		30	H	Bolton W	L	1-2	1-0	—	Windass (pen)	8785
46	May	8	A	WBA	L	1-3	0-1	20	France	20,122

Final League Position: 20

GOALSCORERS

League (46): Windass 7 (1 pen), Atkinson 6, Carruthers 6, Hunter 6, Jenkinson 4, France 3, Lund 3, Wilcox 2, Abbott 1, Brown L 1, Hockaday 1, Jones 1, Mohan 1, Norton 1, own goals 3.
Coca Cola Cup (2): Atkinson 1, Hockaday 1.
FA Cup (2): Atkinson 1, Norton 1.

Fettis 20	Hockaday 25	Hobson 17 + 4	Mail 38 + 1	Lund 11	Warren 35 + 1	Stoker 5 + 1	Atkinson 44 + 2	Hunter 19 + 7	Windass 40 + 1	Jenkinson 25 + 1	France 9 + 17	Norton 45	Heard 3 + 1	Allison 7 + 4	Calvert 5 + 2	Williams 4	Mohan 5	Young 4	Wilcox 28 + 1	Edeson — + 2	Miller 20 + 5	Carruthers 13	Wilson 26	Abbott 27	Brown 20 + 3	Jones 11 + 1	Stowe — + 1	Match No.
1	2	3	4	5	6	7	8	9	10	11	12																	1
1	2	3	4	5	6		8	9	10	11	12	7																2
1	2	5	4	9	6		8		10	*11*	12	7	3	14														3
1	2	5	4	9	6		8	12	10		11	7	3															4
1	2	5	4	9	6		8	11	10		12	7	*3*		14													5
1	2	5			6		8	9	10	11	3	7		4														6
1	2	5			6		8	9	10	11	3	7	12	4														7
1	*2*	5			6	14	8	9	10	11	12	7		4	3													8
1	5	12			2	4	8		10	11		7				3	6	9										9
1	5				2	4	8	12	10	11		7				3	6	9										10
1	2		4		6		8		10	11		7				3	5		*9*		12	14						11
1	2	12	4				8	9	10	11		7					6			*3*	5	14						12
1	2		4	5	3		8	9	10	11	12	7					6											13
1	2	5			6	4	8	12	10	11		7									3	9						14
1	2	5			6		8	12	10	11		7		4							3	9						15
	2	5			6	14	8		10	11	12	7		*4*							3	9		1				16
	2		4				8	9	10	11		7							5		3	6		1				17
	2		4				8	9	10	11	12	7							5		3	6		1				18
	2		4				8		10	11	6	7							5		3	9		1				19
	2		4		6		8				11	7							5		3	9		1	10			20
	2		4		6		8				11	7		12					5		3	9		1	10			21
	2	14	4		6		8	12			11	7							5		*3*	9		1	10			22
	2		4				8	12		14	11	7							5		*3*	9		1	10	6		23
	2	3	4				8		10			7							5			9		1	6	11		24
	2	3	4	11			8		10			7							5			9		1	6			25
	2	*3*	4	11			8	12	10			7							5			9		1	6	14		26
	2		4	9			8		10	11		7							5		12			1	6	3		27
	4			9	6		11		10			2							5		3			1	8	7		28
	4			9	6		11	12	10			2							5		3			1	8	7		29
	4			9	6		11		10		12	2							5		*3*			1	8	7		30
	4						8		10	11	12	2							5		3			1	6	7	9	31
	4						8		10	11	12	2							5		3			1	6	7	9	32
	4			9			8		10	11	12	2							5		3			1	6	7		33
	12		4		11		*8*	9				2		5	10						3			1	6	7	14	34
	4		3				8	9				2		5	11									1	6	7	10	35
	4	3					8		10		12	2		11					5					1	6	7	9	36
	12	4	3				8	11	10			2		14					5					1	6	7	*9*	37
	3	4			11		8	9	10		12	2		14					5					1	6	7		38
1	4			8			3	9	10			2							5						6	7	11	39
1	4		*8*				3	9	10	12		2							5		14				6	7	11	40
1	4		8				3	9	10	12	*2*			5							14				6	7	11	41
1	4		8				3	9	10	11		2							5		12				6	7		42
1	4		*8*				3	9	10	11		2							5		12				6	7	14	43
	4		8		11				10	12		2		14					5		3			1	6	*7*	9	44
	4		*8*		14	9			10		7	2							5		3			1	6	12	11	45
	4		8		11				10	12		2		9					5		3			1	6	14	*7*	46

Coca Cola Cup	First Round	Rotherham U (h)	2-2
		(a)	0-1
FA Cup	First Round	Darlington (a)	2-1
	Second Round	Rotherham U (a)	0-1

HULL CITY

Player and Position	Ht	Wt	Date	Birth Place	Source	Clubs	League App	Gls
Goalkeepers								
David Cleminshaw‡	6 1	12 09	1 11 70	South Cave	Trainee	Hull C	—	—
Alan Fettis	6 1	11 04	1 2 71	Newtonards	Ards	Hull C	63	—
Steve Wilson	5 11	11 00	24 4 74	Hull	Trainee	Hull C	31	—
Defenders								
Neil Allison	6 2	11 10	20 10 73	Hull	Trainee	Hull C	19	—
Pat Heard†	5 10	11 00	17 3 60	Hull	Apprentice	Everton	11	—
						Aston Villa	24	2
						Sheffield W	25	3
						Newcastle U	34	2
						Middlesbrough	25	2
						Hull C	80	5
						Rotherham U	44	7
						Cardiff C	46	4
						Hull C	4	
Gary Hobson	6 2	12 10	12 11 72	North Ferriby	Trainee	Hull C	41	—
David Hockaday*	5 9	11 02	9 11 57	Billingham	Amateur	Blackpool	147	24
						Swindon T	245	6
						Hull C	72	2
						Stoke C (loan)	7	—
David Mail	5 11	11 12	12 9 62	Bristol	Apprentice	Aston VIlla	—	—
						Blackburn R	206	4
						Hull C	112	2
Robert Millar	6 0	11 10	3 11 72	Manchester	Trainee	Oldham Ath	—	—
						Hull C	25	—
Russell Wilcox	6 0	11 10	25 3 64	Hemsworth	Apprentice	Doncaster R	1	—
						Cambridge U. Northampton T	138	9
						Frickley Ath. Hull C	100	7
Midfield								
Greg Abbott	5 9	10 07	14 12 63	Coventry	Apprentice	Coventry C	—	—
						Bradford C	281	38
						Halifax T	28	1
					Guiseley	Hull C	27	1
Linton Brown	5 9	11 00	12 4 68	Driffield	Guiseley	Halifax T	3	—
						Hull C	23	1
Darren Cairns*	5 10	11 02	1 9 74	Glasgow	Trainee	Hull C	—	—
David Norton	5 7	11 03	3 3 65	Cannock	Apprentice	Aston Villa	44	2
						Notts Co	27	1
						Rochdale (loan)	9	—
						Hull C (loan)	15	—
						Hull C	90	3
Gareth Stoker*	5 9	10 03	22 2 73	Bishop Auckland	Leeds U	Hull C	30	2
Dean Stowe§	5 9	11 02	27 3 75	Burnley	Trainee	Hull C	1	—
Lee Warren	6 0	11 13	28 2 69	Manchester	Trainee	Leeds U	—	—
						Rochdale	31	1
						Hull C	120	1
						Lincoln C (loan)	3	1
Dean Windass	5 9	12 03	1 4 69	Hull		Hull C	73	13
Forwards								
Graeme Atkinson	5 10	10 02	11 11 71	Hull	Trainee	Hull C	100	15
Mark Calvert*	5 9	11 05	11 9 70	Consett	Trainee	Hull C	30	1
Matthew Edeson§	5 10	11 00	11 8 76	Beverley	Trainee	Hull C	2	—
Darren France*	6 0	14 02	8 8 67	Hull	North Ferriby	Hull C	43	7
Paul Hunter*	6 0	12 09	30 8 68	Kirkcaldy	Leven Royal Colts	East Fife	164	56
						Hull C	68	11

HULL CITY

Colours: Black and amber striped shirts, black shorts, amber stockings. **Change colours:** All white with black and amber edging.

Foundation: The enthusiasts who formed Hull City in 1904 were brave men indeed. More than that they were audacious for they immediately put the club on the map in this Rugby League fortress by obtaining a three-year agreement with the Hull Rugby League club to rent their ground! They had obtained quite a number of conversions to the dribbling code, before the Rugby League forbade the use of any of their club grounds by Association Football clubs. By that time, Hull City were well away having entered the FA Cup in their initial season and the Football League, Second Division after only a year.

First Football League game: 2 September, 1905, Division 2, v Barnsley (h) W 4-1 – Spendiff; Langley, Jones; Martin, Robinson, Gordon (2); Rushton, Spence (1), Wilson (1), Howe, Raisbeck.

Did you know: The nearest Hull City came to achieving Division 1 status was in 1909–10 when they finished third, one point behind the champions Manchester City and level on points with Oldham Athletic and Derby County. They needed one point for promotion at Oldham but lost 3-0.

Managers (and Secretary-Managers)
James Ramster 1904–05*, Ambrose Langley 1905–13, Harry Chapman 1913–14, Fred Stringer 1914–16, David Menzies 1916–21, Percy Lewis 1921–23, Bill McCracken 1923–31, Haydn Green 1931–34, John Hill 1934–36, David Menzies 1936, Ernest Blackburn 1936–46, Major Frank Buckley 1946–48, Raich Carter 1948–51, Bob Jackson 1952–55, Bob Brocklebank 1955–61, Cliff Britton 1961–70 (continued as GM to 1971), Terry Neill 1970–74, John Kaye 1974–77, Bobby Collins 1977–78, Ken Houghton 1978–79, Mike Smith 1979–82, Bobby Brown 1982, Colin Appleton 1982–84, Brian Horton 1984–88, Eddie Gray 1988–89, Colin Appleton 1989, Stan Ternent 1989–91, Terry Dolan February 1991–.

Player and Position	Ht	Wt	Birth Date	Birth Place	Source	Clubs	League App	Gls
David Jones	6 4	13 10	3 7 64	Harrow		Chelsea	—	—
						Bury	1	—
						Leyton Orient	2	—
						Burnley	4	—
						Ipswich T	—	—
						Doncaster R	40	14
						Bury	9	—
						Hull C	12	1

Trainees
Beddard, Elliot J; Cass, Jamie M; Edeson, Matthew K; Fisher, Steven L; Hopkin, Matthew C; Houghton, Nicholas N; Kirk, Wayne K; Knight, Simon; Lobley, Hayden S; Lowthorpe, Andrew; Mitchell, Alexander S; Mulligan, Stephen T; Said, Lee S; Shirtliffe, Mark A; Stead, Nathan D; Stowe, Dean D.

Associated Schoolboys
Benson, Paul J; Cobley, Stephen; Fewings, Paul J; Henderson, Carl S; Hunnaball, Richard L; Ogle, Gareth D; Pridmore, Lee C; Stead, Matthew R; Tolhurst, Adrian P.

Associated Schoolboys who have accepted the club's offer of a Traineeship/Contract
Armstrong, Gary; Doughty, Mark J; Knight, Paul M; Plant, Ian; Skewis, Darren A.

IPSWICH TOWN 1992–93 *Back row (left to right):* Geraint Williams, Simon Milton, Gavin Johnson, Neil Thompson, Steve Whitton, Eddie Youds, Adam Tanner, David Lowe, Lee Honeywood. *Centre row:* Gary Thompson, Steve Palmer, Phil Whelan, Craig Forrest, Declan Devine, Jason Winters, David Gregory, Neil Gregory, Lee Durrant. *Front row:* Mick Stockwell, Frank Yallop, Paul Goddard, David Linighan, Jason Dozzell, Chris Kiwomya, Glenn Pennyfather.

FA Premier

IPSWICH TOWN

Portman Road, Ipswich, Suffolk IP1 2DA. Telephone Ipswich (0473) 219211 (4 lines). Ticket office: (0473) 221133. Sales & Marketing Dept: (0473) 212202.

Ground capacity: 23,000.

Record attendance: 38,010 v Leeds U, FA Cup 6th rd, 8 March 1975.

Record receipts: £105,950 v AZ 67 Alkmaar, UEFA Cup Final 1st leg, 6 May 1981.

Pitch measurements: 112yd × 70yd.

Chairman: J. Kerr MBE.

President: P. M. Cobbold. *Vice-President:* J. M. Sangster.

Directors: H. R. Smith, K. H. Brightwell, J. Kerridge, D. Sheepshanks, P. M. Cobbold.

Team Manager: Mick McGiven. *Manager:* John Lyall. *Assistant Manager:* Charlie Woods. *Reserve Coach:* Bryan Klug. *Youth Team Coach:* Peter Trevivian. *Reserve Coach:*

Physio: D. Bingham.

Secretary: David C. Rose.

Commercial Manager: Mike Noye.

Year Formed: 1878. *Turned Professional:* 1936. *Ltd Co.:* 1936.

Club Nickname: 'Blues' or 'Town'.

Record League Victory: 7–0 v Portsmouth, Division 2, 7 November 1964 – Thorburn; Smith, McNeil; Baxter, Bolton, Thompson; Broadfoot (1), Hegan (2), Baker (1), Leadbetter, Brogan (3). 7–0 v Southampton, Division 1, 2 February 1974 – Sivell; Burley, Mills (1), Morris, Hunter, Beattie (1), Hamilton (2), Viljoen, Johnson, Whymark (2), Lambert (1) (Woods). 7–0 v WBA, Division 1, 6 November 1976 – Sivell; Burley, Mills, Talbot, Hunter, Beattie (1), Osborne, Wark (1), Mariner (1) (Bertschin), Whymark (4), Woods.

Record Cup Victory: 10–0 v Floriana, European Cup, Prel. rd, 25 September 1962 – Bailey; Malcolm, Compton; Baxter, Laurel, Elsworthy (1); Stephenson, Moran (2), Crawford (5), Phillips (2), Blackwood.

Record Defeat: 1–10 v Fulham, Division 1, 26 December 1963.

Most League Points (2 for a win): 64, Division 3 (S), 1953–54 and 1955–56.

Most League Points (3 for a win): 84, Division 1, 1991–92.

Most League Goals: 106, Division 3 (S), 1955–56.

Highest League Scorer in Season: Ted Phillips, 41, Division 3 (S), 1956–57.

Most League Goals in Total Aggregate: Ray Crawford, 203, 1958–63 and 1966–69.

Most Capped Player: Allan Hunter, 47 (53), Northern Ireland.

Most League Appearances: Mick Mills, 591, 1966–82.

Record Transfer Fee Received: £800,000 from Sheffield U for Brian Gayle, September 1991.

Record Transfer Fee Paid: £650,000 to Derby Co for Geraint Williams, July 1992.

Football League Record: 1938 Elected to Division 3 (S); 1954–55 Division 2; 1955–57 Division 3 (S); 1957–61 Division 2; 1961–64 Division 1; 1964–68 Division 2; 1968–86 Division 1; 1986–92 Division 2; 1992– FA Premier League.

Honours: Football League: Division 1 – Champions 1961–62; Runners-up 1980–81, 1981–82; Division 2 – Champions 1960–61, 1967–68, 1991–92; Division 3 (S) – Champions 1953–54, 1956–57. *FA Cup:* Winners 1977–78. *Football League Cup:* best season: Semi-final 1981–82, 1984–85, *Texaco Cup:* 1972–73. **European Competitions:** *European Cup:* 1962–63. *European Cup-Winners' Cup:* 1978–79. *UEFA Cup:* 1973–74, 1974–75, 1975–76, 1977–78, 1979–80, 1980–81 (winners), 1981–82, 1982–83.

IPSWICH TOWN 1992—93 LEAGUE RECORD

Match No.	Date	Venue	Opponents	Result	H/T Score	Lg. Pos.	Goalscorers	Attendance
1	Aug 15	H	Aston Villa	D	1-1	1-0	—	Johnson	16,818
2	18	A	Wimbledon	W	1-0	1-0	—	Johnson	4954
3	22	A	Manchester U	D	1-1	0-0	9	Kiwomya	31,704
4	25	H	Liverpool	D	2-2	0-1	—	Dozzell, Kiwomya	20,109
5	30	H	Tottenham H	D	1-1	1-1	—	Wark	20,100
6	Sept 1	A	Middlesbrough	D	2-2	1-0	—	Wark, Goddard	14,255
7	5	A	QPR	D	0-0	0-0	13		12,806
8	12	H	Wimbledon	W	2-1	1-1	7	Stockwell 2	13,333
9	19	A	Oldham Ath	L	2-4	0-1	8	Wark, Thompson	11,150
10	26	H	Sheffield U	D	0-0	0-0	10		16,353
11	Oct 3	H	Leeds U	W	4-2	3-0	8	Kiwomya, Wark 2 (1 pen), Dozzell	21,200
12	17	A	Chelsea	L	1-2	0-1	10	Whitton	16,707
13	24	H	Crystal Palace	D	2-2	0-0	11	Dozzell 2	17,861
14	31	A	Nottingham F	W	1-0	1-0	8	Dozzell	21,411
15	Nov 7	H	Southampton	D	0-0	0-0	9		15,722
16	21	A	Sheffield W	D	1-1	0-1	10	Kiwomya	24,270
17	28	H	Everton	W	1-0	0-0	10	Johnson	18,034
18	Dec 5	A	Coventry C	D	2-2	1-1	8	Kiwomya, Whitton (pen)	11,294
19	12	H	Manchester C	W	3-1	0-1	6	Stockwell, Johnson, Goddard	16,833
20	21	A	Norwich C	W	2-0	0-0	—	Kiwomya, Thompson	20,032
21	26	A	Arsenal	D	0-0	0-0	6		26,198
22	28	H	Blackburn R	W	2-1	0-0	5	Guentchev, Kiwomya	21,431
23	Jan 9	H	Oldham Ath	L	1-2	0-1	5	Kiwomya	15,025
24	16	A	Sheffield U	L	0-3	0-1	5		16,758
25	27	H	Tottenham H	W	2-0	0-0	—	Yallop, Guentchev	23,738
26	30	H	Manchester U	W	2-1	1-0	4	Kiwomya, Yallop	22,068
27	Feb 6	A	Aston Villa	L	0-2	0-2	5		25,395
28	9	H	QPR	D	1-1	1-0	—	Thompson	17,354
29	20	A	Liverpool	D	0-0	0-0	5		36,680
30	27	A	Leeds U	L	0-1	0-0	7		28,848
31	Mar 2	H	Middlesbrough	L	0-1	0-1	—		15,430
32	10	H	Sheffield W	L	0-1	0-0	—		16,538
33	13	A	Southampton	L	3-4	2-1	11	Linighan, Goddard, Kiwomya	15,428
34	20	H	Coventry C	D	0-0	0-0	14		16,698
35	24	A	Everton	L	0-3	0-1	—		15,638
36	Apr 3	A	Manchester C	L	1-3	1-0	16	Johnson	20,680
37	6	H	Chelsea	D	1-1	1-0	—	Guentchev	17,444
38	10	H	Arsenal	L	1-2	1-1	17	Wark (pen)	20,358
39	12	A	Blackburn R	L	1-2	0-2	17	Milton	14,071
40	19	H	Norwich C	W	3-1	1-1	—	Dozzell 2, Stockwell	21,081
41	May 1	A	Crystal Palace	L	1-3	1-2	17	Gregory	18,881
42	8	H	Nottingham F	W	2-1	1-0	16	Milton, Whitton (pen)	22,093

Final League Position: 16

GOALSCORERS

League (50): Kiwomya 10, Dozzell 7, Wark 6 (2 pens), Johnson 5, Stockwell 4, Goddard 3, Guentchev 3, Thompson 3, Whitton 3 (2 pens), Milton 2, Yallop 2, Gregory 1, Linighan 1.
Coca Cola Cup (11): Kiwomya 6, Johnson 2, Thompson 1, Whitton 1 (pen), own goal 1.
FA Cup (11): Guentchev 5, Dozzell 2, Kiwomya 1, Thompson 1, Wark 1, Whitton 1.

Forrest 11	Whelan 28 + 4	Thompson 31	Stockwell 38 + 1	Wark 36 + 1	Linighan 42	Williams 37	Goddard 19 + 6	Johnson 39 + 1	Dozzell 41	Kiwomya 38	Youds 10 + 6	Milton 7 + 5	Pennyfather 2 + 2	Yallop 5 + 1	Baker 30 + 1	Whitton 20 + 4	Palmer 4 + 3	Gregory 1 + 2	Bozinoski 3 + 6	Guentchev 19 + 2	Petterson 1	Match No.
1	2	3	4	5	6	7	8	9	10	11	12	14										1
1	2	3	4	5	6	7	8	9	10	11		12										2
1	2	3	4	5	6	7	8	9	10	11	12	14										3
1	2	3	4	5	6	7	8	9	10	11		12										4
1	2	3	4	5	6	7	8	9	10	11		12										5
1	2	3	4	5	6	7	8	9	10		11											6
1	2	3	4	5	6	7	8	9	10		11		12	14								7
1	2	3	4	5	6	7		9	10			8	11									8
1	2	3	4	5	6			9	10	11	7	8										9
1	2	3	4	5	6		8	9	10	11	7		12									10
1	2	3	4	5	6	7	8	9	10	11												11
	2	3	4	5	6	7	8	9	10	11					1	12	14					12
		3	4	5	6	7	8	2	10	11					1	9			12			13
	2	3	4	5	6	7		9	10	11					1				12	8		14
		3	4	5	6	7	12	2	10	11					1	9				8		15
	2	3	4		6	7	8	5	10	11					1	9						16
	2	3	4		6	7	8	5	10	11					1	9	12					17
	2	3	4	5	6		8	7	10	11	12				1	9			14			18
	2	3	4	5	6		8	7	10		12				1	9			11			19
	12	3	4	5	6	7	8	2	10	11					1	9						20
	12	3	4	5	6	7	8	2	10	11					1	9			14			21
		3	4	5	6	7		2	10	11					1	9				8		22
		3	4	5	6	7	12	2	10	11					1	9				8		23
	5	3	4		6	7		2	10	11	12				1	9			14	8		24
	5	3			6	4		2	10	11				7	1				9	8		25
	5	3	12	14	6	4		2	10	11				7	1				9	8		26
	2	3	4	5	6	7	12		10	11					1	9				8		27
		3	4	5	6	7		2	10	11					1	9			12	8		28
		3	4	5	6	7		2	10	11					1	9				8		29
		3	4	5	6	7	12	2	10	11					1	9				8		30
	14	3	4	5	6	7	12			11			2		1	9			10	8		31
	7		4	5	6		12	2	10	11			3	14	1	9				8		32
	3		4	5	6		9	2	10	11				7	1	12				8		33
	3		4	5	6	7	9	2	10	11					1	12				8		34
	3		4	5	6	7	9	2	10	11	12				1					8		35
	2		4	5	6	7	12	3	10	11			9		1				14	8		36
			4	5	6	7		3	10	11			2	9	1				12	8		37
				5	6	4		3	10	11			2	9	1	7				8		38
	5				6	4		3	10	11			2	9	1	7			12	8		39
			8	5	6	4		3	10	11			2	9	1	7						40
	3		4	5	6	7		10	11					9	1	12	8	2		14		41
	14		4	5	6	7		3	10	11			2	9			8	12			1	42

Coca Cola Cup	Second Round	Wigan Ath (a)	2-2
		(h)	4-0
	Third Round	Portsmouth (a)	1-0
	Fourth Round	Aston Villa (a)	2-2
		(h)	1-0
	Fifth Round	Sheffield W (h)	1-1
		(a)	0-1
FA Cup	Third Round	Plymouth Arg (h)	3-1
	Fourth Round	Tranmere R (a)	2-1
	Fifth Round	Grimsby T (h)	4-0
	Sixth Round	Arsenal (h)	2-4

IPSWICH TOWN

Player and Position	Ht	Wt	Date	Birth Place	Source	Clubs	League App	Gls
Goalkeepers								
Clive Baker	5 9	11 00	14 3 59	North Walsham	Amateur	Norwich C	4	—
						Barnsley	291	—
						Coventry C	—	—
						Ipswich T	31	—
Ron Fearon	6 0	11 12	19 11 60	Romford	QPR	Reading	61	—
					Sutton	Ipswich T	28	—
						Brighton (loan)	7	—
						Leyton Orient	—	—
						Ipswich T	—	—
						Walsall (loan)	1	—
Craig Forrest	6 5	14 00	20 9 67	Vancouver	Apprentice	Ipswich T	173	—
						Colchester U (loan)	11	—
Jason Winters*	6 0	11 08	15 9 71	Oatham	Trainee	Chelsea	—	—
						Ipswich T	—	—
Defenders								
Lee Honeywood	5 8	10 10	3 8 71	Chelmsford	Trainee	Ipswich T	—	—
Gavin Johnson	5 11	11 12	10 10 70	Eye	Trainee	Ipswich T	99	10
David Linighan	6 2	13 00	9 1 65	Hartlepool	Local	Hartlepool U	91	5
						Leeds U (loan)	—	—
						Derby Co	—	—
						Shrewsbury T	65	1
						Ipswich T	205	9
Neil Thompson	5 11	13 08	21 10 63	Beverley	Nottingham F	Hull C	31	—
					Scarborough	Scarborough	87	15
						Ipswich T	159	18
John Wark	5 11	12 12	4 8 57	Glasgow	Apprentice	Ipswich T	296	94
						Liverpool	70	28
						Ipswich T	89	23
						Middlesbrough	32	2
						Ipswich T	74	9
Phil Whelan	6 4	14 01	7 8 72	Stockport		Ipswich T	40	2
Frank Yallop	5 11	12 00	4 4 64	Watford	Apprentice	Ipswich T	261	6
Edward Youds	6 1	13 03	3 5 70	Liverpool	Trainee	Everton	8	—
						Cardiff C (loan)	1	—
						Wrexham (loan)	20	2
						Ipswich T	17	—
Midfield								
Andy Bernal	5 10	12 05	16 7 66	Canberra		Ipswich T	9	—
Vlado Bozinoski	5 10	11 03	30 3 64	Macedonia	Sporting Lisbon	Ipswich T	9	—
Jason Dozzell	6 1	12 13	9 12 67	Ipswich	School	Ipswich T	332	52
Lee Durrant	5 10	11 07	18 12 73	Gt Yarmouth	Trainee	Ipswich T	—	—
David Gregory	5 11	11 10	23 1 70	Sudbury	Trainee	Ipswich T	31	2
Simon Milton	5 10	11 05	23 8 63	London	Bury St	Ipswich T	161	36
					Edmunds	Exeter C (loan)	2	3
						Torquay U (loan)	4	1
Steve Palmer	6 1	12 13	31 3 68	Brighton	Cambridge University	Ipswich T	58	1
Mick Stockwell	5 9	11 04	14 2 65	Chelmsford	Apprentice	Ipswich T	258	19
Adam Tanner	6 0	12 01	25 10 73	Maldon	Trainee	Ipswich T	—	—
Geraint Williams	5 7	10 06	5 1 62	Treorchy	Apprentice	Bristol R	141	8
						Derby Co	277	9
						Ipswich T	37	—

IPSWICH TOWN

Colours: Blue shirts, white sleeves, white shorts, blue stockings. **Change colours:** Red and black striped shirts, black shorts, red and black stockings.

Foundation: Considering that Ipswich Town only reached the Football League in 1938, many people outside of East Anglia may be surprised to learn that this club was formed at a meeting held in the Town Hall as far back as 1878 when Mr. T. C. Cobbold, MP, was voted president. Originally it was the Ipswich Association FC to distinguish it from the older Ipswich Football Club which played rugby. These two amalgamated in 1888 and the handling game was dropped in 1893.

First Football League game: 27 August, 1938, Division 3(S), v Southend U (h) W 4-2 – Burns; Dale, Parry; Perrett, Fillingham, McLuckie; Williams, Davies (1), Jones (2), Alsop (1), Little.

Did you know: Ipswich Town turned professional in 1936 but too late to be granted exemption from the early rounds of the FA Cup. They ran up a total of 39 goals including an 11-0 win over Cromer.

Managers (and Secretary-Managers)
Mick O'Brien 1936–37, Scott Duncan 1937–55 (continued as secretary), Alf Ramsey 1955–63, Jackie Milburn 1963–64, Bill McGarry 1964–68, Bobby Robson 1969–82, Bobby Ferguson 1982–87, Johnny Duncan 1987–90, John Lyall May 1990– .

Player and Position	Ht	Wt	Date	Birth Place	Source	Clubs	League App	Gls
Forwards								
Paul Goddard	5 7	12 00	12 10 59	Harlington	Apprentice	QPR	70	23
						West Ham U	170	54
						Newcastle U	61	19
						Derby Co	49	15
						Millwall	20	1
						Ipswich T	68	13
Neil Gregory	5 11	11 10	7 10 72	Zambia	Trainee	Ipswich T	—	—
Bontcho Guentchev	5 10	11 07	7 7 64	Bulgaria	Sporting Lisbon	Ipswich T	21	3
Chris Kiwomya	5 10	10 12	2 12 69	Huddersfield		Ipswich T	173	43
Gary Thompson	6 0	11 04	7 9 72	Ipswich		Ipswich T	—	—
Steve Whitton	6 1	13 06	4 12 60	East Ham	Apprentice	Coventry C	74	21
						West Ham U	39	6
						Birmingham C (loan)	8	2
						Birmingham C	95	28
						Sheffield W	32	4
						Ipswich T	77	14

Trainees
Connell, Graham; Cotterell, Leo S; Dolby, Gavin P; Eason, Jeremy J; Mansfield, Graham P; Morgan, Philip J; Mortley, Peter R; Norfolk, Lee R; Pirie, David W; Powley, Darren L. W; Scowcroft, James B; Theodorou, Theodoros; Vaughan, Anthony J; Weston, Kenneth; Weston, Matthew.

Associated Schoolboys
Bell, Leon C; Brown, Wayne L; Clarke, Alex R; Dyer, Kieron; Elsworth, Patrick D; Gibbs, Carl P; Keeble, Christopher; May, Robert D; Miller, Marc P; Miller, Thomas W; Milligan, Kieran J; Naylor, Richard A; Pearson, Craig D; Theobald, David J; Tolhurst, James J; Vickery, Barry; Wolton, Dominic J; Woolsey, Jeffrey A; Wright, Richard I.

Associated Schoolboys who have accepted the club's offer of a Traineeship/Contract
Coates, Scott L; Eaton, Daniel J; Ellis, Kevin E; Graham, Stephen; Hood, Paul; Portrey, Simon D; Travers, Benjamin.

LEEDS UNITED 1992–93 *Back row (left to right):* Chris Whyte, Gary McAllister, John Lukic, Lee Chapman, Mervyn Day, Jon Newsome, David Wetherall. *Centre row:* Alan Sutton (Physio), Mel Sterland, Steve Hodge, David Rocastle, Chris Fairclough, Carl Shutt, Eric Cantona, Michael Hennigan (Assistant Manager). *Front row:* Scott Sellars, Gary Speed, Tony Dorigo, Howard Wilkinson (Manager), Gordon Strachan, David Batty, Rod Wallace.

FA Premier

LEEDS UNITED

Elland Road, Leeds LS11 0ES. Telephone Leeds (0532) 716037 (4 lines). Ticket Office: (0532) 710710. Fax: (0532) 720370. Clubcall: 0898 121181.

Ground capacity: 43,000.

Record attendance: 57,892 v Sunderland, FA Cup 5th rd (replay), 15 March 1967.

Record receipts: £291,549 v Manchester U, Rumbelows Cup semi-final 2nd leg, 24 February 1991.

Pitch measurements: 117yd × 72yd.

President: The Right Hon The Earl of Harewood LLD.

Chairman: L. Silver OBE.

Directors: P. J. Gillman, W. J. Fotherby, J. W. G. Marjason, G. M. Holmes, R. Barker, P. Risdale, K. J. Woolmer, E. Carlile, R. Feldman, A. Hudson, M. Bedford.

Manager: Howard Wilkinson. *Assistant Manager:* Mike Hennigan.

Company Secretary: Nigel Pleasants.

Coaches: Paul Hart, Peter Gunby.

Physios: Alan Sutton, Geoff Ladley.

Commercial Manager: Bob Baldwin.

Year Formed: 1919, as Leeds United after disbandment (by FA order) of Leeds City (formed in 1904). *Turned Professional:* 1920. *Ltd Co.:* 1920.

Club Nickname: 'United'.

Record League Victory: 8–0 v Leicester C, Division 1, 7 April 1934 – Moore; George Milburn, Jack Milburn; Edwards, Hart, Copping; Mahon (2), Firth (2), Duggan (2), Furness (2), Cochrane.

Record Cup Victory: 10–0 v Lyn (Oslo), European Cup, 1st rd 1st leg, 17 September 1969 – Sprake; Reaney, Cooper, Bremner (2), Charlton, Hunter, Madeley, Clarke (2), Jones (3), Giles (2) (Bates), O'Grady (1).

Record Defeat: 1–8 v Stoke C, Division 1, 27 August 1934.

Most League Points (2 for a win): 67, Division 1, 1968–69.

Most League Points (3 for a win): 85, Division 2, 1989–90.

Most League Goals: 98, Division 2, 1927–28.

Highest League Scorer in Season: John Charles, 42, Division 2, 1953–54.

Most League Goals in Total Aggregate: Peter Lorimer, 168, 1965–79 and 1983–86.

Most Capped Player: Billy Bremner, 54, Scotland.

Most League Appearances: Jack Charlton, 629, 1953–73.

Record Transfer Fee Received: £1,200,000 from Manchester U for Eric Cantona, November 1992.

Record Transfer Fee Paid: £2,000,000 to Arsenal for David Rocastle, July 1992.

Football League Record: 1920 Elected to Division 2; 1924–27 Division 1; 1927–28 Division 2; 1928–31 Division 1; 1931–32 Division 2; 1932–47 Division 1; 1947–56 Division 2; 1956–60 Division 1; 1960–64 Division 2; 1964–82 Division 1; 1982–90 Division 2; 1990–92 Division 1; 1992– FA Premier Division.

Honours: Football League: Division 1 – Champions 1968–69, 1973–74, 1991–92; Runners-up 1964–65, 1965–66, 1969–70, 1970–71, 1971–72; Division 2 – Champions 1923–24, 1963–64, 1989–90; Runners-up 1927–28, 1931–32, 1955–56. *FA Cup:* Winners 1972; Runners-up 1965, 1970, 1973. *Football League Cup:* Winners 1967–68. **European Competitions:** *European Cup:* 1969–70, 1974–75 (runners-up), 1992–93. *European Cup-Winners' Cup:* 1972–73 (runners-up). *European Fairs Cup:* 1965–66, 1966–67 (runners-up), 1967–68 (winners), 1968–69, 1970–71 (winners). *UEFA Cup:* 1971–72, 1973–74, 1979–80.

LEEDS UNITED 1992—93 LEAGUE RECORD

Match No.	Date	Venue	Opponents	Result	H/T Score	Lg. Pos.	Goalscorers	Atten dance
1	Aug 15	H	Wimbledon	W 2-1	1-0	—	Chapman 2	25,795
2	19	A	Aston Villa	D 1-1	0-0	—	Speed	29,151
3	22	A	Middlesbrough	L 1-4	0-2	10	Cantona	18,649
4	25	H	Tottenham H	W 5-0	3-0	—	Wallace Rod, Cantona 3, Chapman	28,218
5	29	H	Liverpool	D 2-2	1-1	7	McAllister, Chapman	29,597
6	Sept 1	A	Oldham Ath	D 2-2	0-0	—	Cantona 2	13,848
7	6	A	Manchester U	L 0-2	0-2	—		31,296
8	13	H	Aston Villa	D 1-1	0-1	—	Hodge	27,817
9	19	A	Southampton	D 1-1	0-1	12	Speed	16,229
10	26	H	Everton	W 2-0	0-0	8	McAllister (pen), Chapman	27,915
11	Oct 3	A	Ipswich T	L 2-4	0-3	10	Chapman, Speed	21,200
12	17	H	Sheffield U	W 3-1	1-0	8	Chapman, Speed, Whyte	29,706
13	24	A	QPR	L 1-2	0-0	10	Strachan	19,326
14	31	H	Coventry C	D 2-2	0-1	12	Chapman, Fairclough	28,018
15	Nov 7	A	Manchester C	L 0-4	0-2	13		27,255
16	21	H	Arsenal	W 3-0	0-0	12	Fairclough, Chapman, McAllister	30,516
17	29	A	Chelsea	L 0-1	0-0	—		24,345
18	Dec 5	H	Nottingham F	L 1-4	0-1	15	Speed	29,364
19	12	H	Sheffield W	W 3-1	1-1	14	Speed, Chapman, Varadi	29,770
20	20	A	Crystal Palace	L 0-1	0-1	—		14,462
21	26	A	Blackburn R	L 1-3	1-2	16	McAllister	19,910
22	28	H	Norwich C	D 0-0	0-0	16		30,282
23	Jan 9	H	Southampton	W 2-1	0-1	13	Chapman, Speed	26,071
24	16	A	Everton	L 0-2	0-1	15		21,031
25	30	A	Middlesbrough	W 3-0	0-0	14	Strandli, Batty, Fairclough	30,344
26	Feb 6	A	Wimbledon	L 0-1	0-0	15		6704
27	8	H	Manchester U	D 0-0	0-0	—		34,166
28	13	H	Oldham Ath	W 2-0	1-0	14	McAllister (pen), Chapman	27,654
29	20	A	Tottenham H	L 0-4	0-2	16		32,040
30	24	A	Arsenal	D 0-0	0-0	—		21,061
31	27	H	Ipswich T	W 1-0	0-0	13	Dorigo (pen)	28,848
32	Mar 13	H	Manchester C	W 1-0	1-0	16	Rocastle	30,840
33	21	H	Nottingham F	D 1-1	1-1	—	Wallace Rod	25,148
34	24	H	Chelsea	D 1-1	1-0	—	Wetherall	28,135
35	Apr 6	A	Sheffield U	L 1-2	1-1	—	Strandli	20,562
36	10	H	Blackburn R	W 5-2	2-0	16	Strachan 3 (2 pens), Wallace Rod, Chapman	31,791
37	14	A	Norwich C	L 2-4	1-3	—	Chapman, Wallace Rod	18,613
38	17	H	Crystal Palace	D 0-0	0-0	18		27,545
39	21	A	Liverpool	L 0-2	0-0	—		34,992
40	May 1	H	QPR	D 1-1	0-1	16	Hodge	31,408
41	4	A	Sheffield W	D 1-1	1-0	—	King (og)	26,855
42	8	A	Coventry C	D 3-3	1-2	17	Wallace Rod 3	19,591

Final League Position: 17

GOALSCORERS

League (57): Chapman 14, Speed 7, Rod Wallace 7, Cantona 6, McAllister 5 (2 pens), Strachan 4 (2 pens), Fairclough 3, Hodge 2, Strandli 2, Batty 1, Dorigo 1 (pen), Rocastle 1, Varadi 1, Wetherall 1, Whyte 1, own goal 1.
Coca Cola Cup (7): Chapman 2, McAllister 1, Shutt 1, Speed 1, Strachan 1, Rod Wallace 1.
FA Cup (8): Speed 3, McAllister 2, Chapman 1, Shutt 1, own goal 1.

Lukic 39	Newsome 30 + 7	Dorigo 33	Batty 30	Fairclough 29 + 1	Whyte 34	Cantona 12 + 1	Wallace Rod 31 + 1	Chapman 36 + 4	McAllister 32	Speed 39	Strachan 25 + 6	Hodge 9 + 14	Sellars 6 + 1	Wetherall 13	Shutt 6 + 8	Rocastle 11 + 7	Day 2	Wallace Ray 5 + 1	Varadi 2 + 2	Sterland 3	Strandli 5 + 5	Bowman 3 + 1	Kerslake 8	Forrester 5 + 1	Kerr 3 + 2	Tinkler 5 + 2	Sharp 4	Beeney 1	Whelan 1	Match No.
1	2	3	4	5	6	7	8	9	10	11	12	14																		1
1	2	3	4	5	6	7	8	9	10	11	12	14																		2
1	2	3	4	5	6	7	8	9	10	11	12	14																		3
1	2	3	4	5	6	7	8	9	10	11																				4
1	2	3	4	5	6	7	8	9	10	11	12	14																		5
1	2	3	4	5	6	7	8	9	10	11			12																	6
1	2	3	4	5	6	7	8	9	10	11	12	14																		7
1	2		4	5	6	7		9	10	11	8	12	3																	8
1		3	4	5	6			9	10	11	7		8	12		2	14													9
1		3	4	5	6		8	9	10	11	7			2	12															10
1		3	4	5	6		8	9	10	11	7			2		12														11
1	2	3	4	5	6		8	9	10	11	7			12																12
1	2	3	4	5	6		8	9	10	11	7			12	14															13
1	2	3	4	5	6	12	8	9	10	11	7				14															14
	2			5	6		8	9	12	10	11	7	4			3	1													15
1	2	3		5	6		8	9	10	11	7			12		4														16
1	2	3		5	6		8	9	10	11	7					4														17
1	2	3		5			8	9	10	11	7	14			12	4	6													18
1	2	3		5	6		8	9	10	11	7	14				4	12													19
1	2	3		5	6		8	9	10	11	7	14				4	12													20
1	12	3	4	5	6			9	10	11	7				8								2							21
1	12	3	4	5				9	10	11	7		6		8								2							22
1	12	3		5			4	9	10	11	7		6	8	14								2							23
	2	3	4	14	6	12		9	10	11	7		5	8			1													24
1		3	4	5	6			9	10	11	7		2	8	14								12							25
1	5	3	4		6			9	10	11			2			12	7						8	14						26
1	5	3	4		6			9	10	11	14		2	8									12	7						27
1	5	3	4		6		8	9	10	11	14		2	12									7							28
1	5	3	4		6		8	9	10	11	7		14										12	2						29
1	14	3	4	2	6		8	12	10	11	7		5										9							30
1	2	3	4	5			8	12		11	7		6			10							9							31
1	14	3	4	5			8	12		11	10		6	7									9		2					32
1	6	3	4				8	9		11	10		5	7				2	12											33
1	6	3	4				8	9		11	12	10	5	7				14	2											34
1			6						10	11	7	12	5					9	2	8	3	4								35
1	12			5	6		8	9		11	7							2	10	3	4									36
1	12			5	6		8	9		11	7	14						2	10	3	4									37
1	6						8	9	10	11	7		5					2	4	12	3									38
1	5				6		8	9		11	7		10					2		3										39
1	5		4		6		8	9		10			7	2		12		11		14	3									40
1	5		4		6		8	9		10				2				12	11	3	7									41
	5	3	4		6		8	9		10			7	14				2		12	11			1						42

Coca Cola Cup	Second Round	Scunthorpe U (h)	4-1
		(a)	2-2
	Third Round	Watford (a)	1-2
FA Cup	Third Round	Charlton Ath (h)	1-1
		(a)	3-1
	Fourth Round	Arsenal (a)	2-2
		(h)	2-3

LEEDS UNITED

Player and Position	Ht	Wt	Date	Birth Place	Source	Clubs	League App	Gls
Goalkeepers								
Mark Beeney	6 4	14 07	30 12 67	Pembury		Gillingham	2	—
						Maidstone U	50	—
						Aldershot (loan)	7	—
						Brighton & HA	69	—
						Leeds U	1	—
Scott Cousin			31 1 75	Leeds	Trainee	Leeds U	—	—
Mervyn Day*	6 2	15 01	26 6 55	Chelmsford	Apprentice	West Ham U	194	—
						Orient	170	—
						Aston Villa	30	—
						Leeds U	227	—
						Coventry C (loan)	—	—
						Luton T (loan)	4	—
						Sheffield U (loan)	1	—
John Lukic	6 4	13 13	11 12 60	Chesterfield	Apprentice	Leeds U	146	—
						Arsenal	223	—
						Leeds U	119	—
Paul Pettinger			1 10 75	Sheffield	Barnsley	Leeds U	—	—
Defenders								
Robert Bowman			21 11 75	Durham	Trainee	Leeds U	4	—
Andrew Couzens			4 6 75	Shipley	Trainee	Leeds U	—	—
Tony Dorigo	5 10	10 09	31 12 65	Australia	Apprentice	Aston Villa	111	1
						Chelsea	146	11
						Leeds U	71	4
Chris Fairclough	5 11	11 02	12 4 64	Nottingham	Apprentice	Nottingham F	107	1
						Tottenham H	60	5
						Leeds U	148	17
Dylan Kerr	5 11	12 05	14 1 67	Valetta	Arcadia Shepherds	Leeds U	13	—
						Doncaster R (loan)	7	1
						Blackpool (loan)	12	1
John McClelland (To St Johnstone August 1992)	6 2	13 02	7 12 55	Belfast	Portadown Bangor	Cardiff C	4	1
						Mansfield T	125	8
						Rangers	96	4
						Watford	184	3
						Leeds U	24	—
						Watford (loan)	1	—
						Notts Co (loan)	6	—
Jon Newsome	6 2	13 11	6 9 70	Sheffield	Trainee	Sheffield W	7	—
						Leeds U	47	2
Gary O'Hara			13 12 73	Belfast	Trainee	Leeds U	—	—
Mel Sterland	6 0	13 05	1 10 61	Sheffield	Apprentice	Sheffield W	279	37
						Rangers	9	3
						Leeds U	114	16
Ray Wallace	5 6	10 02	2 10 69	Lewisham	Trainee	Southampton	35	—
						Leeds U	6	—
						Swansea C (loan)	2	—
David Wetherall	6 3	12 00	14 3 71	Sheffield	School	Sheffield W	—	—
						Leeds U	14	1
Chris Whyte	6 1	11 10	2 9 61	London	Amateur	Arsenal	90	8
						Crystal Palace (loan)	13	—
					Los Angeles R	WBA	84	7
						Leeds U	113	5
Russell Wigley‡			9 1 72	Cardiff	Trainee	Leeds U	—	—
Midfield								
David Batty	5 7	10 07	2 12 68	Leeds	Trainee	Leeds U	202	4
Mark Ford			10 10 75	Pontefract	Trainee	Leeds U	—	—
Richard Hepworth‡			8 1 74	Pontefract	Trainee	Leeds U	—	—
Steve Hodge	5 8	9 11	25 10 62	Nottingham	Apprentice	Nottingham F	123	30
						Aston Villa	53	12
						Tottenham H	45	7
						Nottingham F	82	20
						Leeds U	46	9
Garry Kelly			9 7 74	Drogheda	Home Farm	Leeds U	2	—
David Kerslake	5 8	11 00	19 6 66	London	Apprentice	QPR	58	6
						Swindon T	135	1
						Leeds U	8	—

LEEDS UNITED

Colours: All white. **Change colours:** All yellow.

Foundation: Immediately the Leeds City club (founded in 1904) was wound up by the FA in October 1919, following allegations of illegal payments to players, a meeting was called by a Leeds solicitor, Mr. Alf Masser, at which Leeds United was formed. They joined the Midland League playing their first game in that competition in November 1919. It was in this same month that the new club had discussions with the directors of a virtually bankrupt Huddersfield Town who wanted to move to Leeds in an amalgamation. But Huddersfield survived even that crisis.

First Football League game: 28 August, 1920, Division 2, v Port Vale (a) L 0-2 – Down; Duffield, Tillotson; Musgrove, Baker, Walton; Mason, Goldthorpe, Thompson, Lyon, Best.

Did you know: Two of the FA National School 1991 graduates Jamie Forrester and Kevin Sharp spent a year in France with Auxerre, returned joining Leeds United and making their bow in the FA Premier League and helping the club win the FA Youth Cup.

Managers (and Secretary-Managers)
Dick Ray 1919–20, Arthur Fairclough 1920–27, Dick Ray 1927–35, Bill Hampson 1935–47, Willis Edwards 1947–48, Major Frank Buckley 1948–53, Raich Carter 1953–58, Bill Lambton 1958–59, Jack Taylor 1959–61, Don Revie 1961–74, Brian Clough 1974, Jimmy Armfield 1974–78, Jock Stein 1978, Jimmy Adamson 1978–80, Allan Clarke 1980–82, Eddie Gray 1982–85, Billy Bremner 1985–88, Howard Wilkinson October 1988–   .

Player and Position	Ht	Wt	Birth Date	Birth Place	Source	Clubs	League App	Gls
Gary McAllister	6 1	10 11	25 12 64	Motherwell	Fir Park BC	Motherwell	59	6
						Leicester C	201	47
						Leeds U	112	12
Kevin Sharp			19 9 74	Canada	Auxerre	Leeds U	4	—
Matthew Smithard			13 6 76	Leeds*	Trainee	Leeds U	—	—
Gary Speed	5 9	10 06	8 9 69	Hawarden	Trainee	Leeds U	144	24
Gordon Strachan	5 6	10 06	9 2 57	Edinburgh		Dundee	60	13
						Aberdeen	183	55
						Manchester U	160	33
						Leeds U	158	34
Mark Tinkler			24 10 74	Bishop Auckland	Trainee	Leeds U	7	—

Forwards

Player and Position	Ht	Wt	Birth Date	Birth Place	Source	Clubs	League App	Gls
Lee Chapman	6 2	13 00	5 12 59	Lincoln	Amateur	Stoke C	99	34
						Plymouth Arg (loan)	4	—
						Arsenal	23	4
						Sunderland	15	3
						Sheffield W	149	63
					Niort	Nottingham F	48	15
						Leeds U	137	63
Jamie Forrester			1 11 74	Bradford	Auxerre	Leeds U	6	—
Damian Henderson*			12 5 73	Leeds	Trainee	Leeds U	—	—
Ryan Nicholls			10 5 73	Cardiff	Trainee	Leeds U	—	—
Patrick O'Connell‡			7 10 73	Dublin	Trainee	Leeds U	—	—
David Rocastle	5 9	11 12	2 5 67	Lewisham	Apprentice	Arsenal	218	24
						Leeds U	18	1
Carl Shutt	5 10	11 13	10 10 61	Sheffield	Spalding U	Sheffield W	40	16
						Bristol C	46	10
						Leeds U	79	17
Frank Strandli‡			16 5 72	Norway	IK Start	Leeds U	10	2
Rodney Wallace	5 7	10 01	2 10 69	Lewisham	Trainee	Southampton	128	45
						Leeds U	66	18
Noel Whelan			30 12 74	Leeds	Trainee	Leeds U	1	—

Trainees
Atkinson, Richard; Byrne, Alexander; Connor, David M; Daly, Kevin; Hill, Stephen; Hoyle, Michael S; Littlewood, Martin; Lynam, Gary M; Oliver, Simon; Tobin, Steven.

Associated Schoolboys
Brown, Matthew; Davies, Lawrence; Fidler, Richard M; Gill, Andrew; Heath, Stephen D; Jackson, Mark G; Jenkins, Lee; McCulloch, Andrew J; McDonald, Philip J; Morgan, Simon R; Murfin, Andrew J; Owen, Alun H; Shaw, James; Shepherd, Paul; Trower, Kevin J; Utley, Darren.

Associated Schoolboys who have accepted the club's offer of a Traineeship/Contract
Blunt, Jason J; Cross, Graham; Fawell, Nicholas; Marks, Jamie; Wharton, Paul W; Willetts, Harvey A.

LEICESTER CITY 1992–93   Back row (left to right): Ashley Ward, Jimmy Willis, Colin Gordon, Steve Walsh, Carl Muggleton, Kevin Poole, Russell Hoult, Tony James, Michael Trotter, Gary Coatsworth, Richard Smith.
Centre row: Neil Lewis, Colin Gibson, Lewis Mogg, Gary Mills, Paul Fitzpatrick, Ian Ormondroyd, David Oldfield, Steve Thompson, Nicky Platnauer, Colin Hill.
Front row: David Lowe, Simon Grayson, Warren Haughton, Allan Evans (Coach), Brian Little (Manager), John Gregory (Coach), Steve Holden, Mike Whitlow, Phil Gee.

Division 1   **LEICESTER CITY**

City Stadium, Filbert St, Leicester LE2 7FL. Telephone Leicester (0533) 555000. Fax (0533) 470585. Ticket line: 0891 121028. Clubcall: 0891 121185. Marketing: (0533) 854000. Shop: (0533) 559455.

Ground capacity: 24,000.

Record attendance: 47,298 v Tottenham H, FA Cup 5th rd, 18 February 1928.

Record receipts: £179,912 v Nottingham F, Zenith Data Systems Cup, Northern semi-final, 12 February 1992.

Pitch measurements: 112yd × 75yd.

President: K. R. Brigstock.

Chairman: Martin George. *Vice-Chairman:* Tom Smeaton.

Directors: J. M. Elsom FCA, R. W. Parker, J. E. Sharp, T. W. Shipman, W. K. Shooter FCA.

Manager: Brian Little. *Coaches:* Allan Evans, John Gregory. *Youth coach:* Steve Hunt.

General Secretary: Alan Bennett.

Physio: Alan Smith. *PRO:* Alan Birchenall. *Press Officer:* Paul Mace.

Director of Marketing: Barrie Pierpoint. *Sales & Marketing Manager:* Richard Hughes. *Business Development Manager:* Trevor Dempsey. *Commercial Manager:* Peter Hill.

Year Formed: 1884.

Club Nickname: 'Fiberts' or 'Foxes'.

Previous Grounds: 1884, Victoria Park; 1887, Belgrave Road; 1888, Victoria Park; 1891, Filbert Street.

Previous Name: 1884–1919, Leicester Fosse.

Record League Victory: 10–0 v Portsmouth, Division 1, 20 October 1928 – McLaren; Black, Brown; Findlay, Carr, Watson; Adcock, Hine (3), Chandler (6), Lochhead, Barry (1).

Record Cup Victory: 8–1 v Coventry C (away), League Cup, 5th rd, 1 December 1964 – Banks; Sjoberg, Norman (2); Roberts, King, McDerment; Hodgson (2), Cross, Goodfellow, Gibson (1), Stringfellow (2). (1 og).

Record Defeat: 0–12 (as Leicester Fosse) v Nottingham F, Division 1, 21 April 1909.

Most League Points (2 for a win): 61, Division 2, 1956–57.

Most League Points (3 for a win): 77, Division 2, 1991–92.

Most League Goals: 109, Division 2, 1956–57.

Highest League Scorer in Season: Arthur Rowley, 44, Division 2, 1956–57.

Most League Goals in Total Aggregate: Arthur Chandler, 259, 1923–35.

Most Capped Player: John O'Neill, 39, Northern Ireland.

Most League Appearances: Adam Black, 528, 1920–35.

Record Transfer Fee Received: £1,350,000 from Derby Co for Paul Kitson, March 1992.

Record Transfer Fee Paid: £500,000 to Everton for Wayne Clarke, July 1989.

Football League Record: 1894 Elected to Division 2; 1908–09 Division 1; 1909–25 Division 2; 1925–35 Division 1; 1935–37 Division 2; 1937–39 Division 1; 1946–54 Division 2; 1954–55 Division 1; 1955–57 Division 2; 1957–69 Division 1; 1969–71 Division 2; 1971–78 Division 1; 1978–80 Division 2; 1980–81 Division 1; 1981–83 Division 2; 1983–87 Division 1; 1987–92 Division 2; 1992– Division 1.

Honours: Football League: Division 1 – Runners-up 1928–29; Division 2 – Champions 1924–25, 1936–37, 1953–54, 1956–57, 1970–71, 1979–80; Runners-up 1907–08. *FA Cup:* Runners-up 1949, 1961, 1963, 1969. *Football League Cup:* Winners 1964; Runners-up 1965. **European Competitions:** *European Cup-Winners' Cup:* 1961–62.

LEICESTER CITY 1992—93 LEAGUE RECORD

Match No.	Date	Venue	Opponents	Result		H/T Score	Lg. Pos.	Goalscorers	Attendance
1	Aug 15	H	Luton T	W	2-1	1-1	—	Walsh, Whitlow	17,428
2	18	A	Wolverhampton W	L	0-3	0-2	—		15,821
3	22	A	Notts Co	D	1-1	1-0	9	Gee	10,501
4	26	H	Derby Co	W	3-2	2-1	—	Gee 2, Thompson	17,739
5	29	H	Portsmouth	W	1-0	1-0	3	Davison	14,780
6	Sept 5	A	Southend U	L	1-3	1-2	6	Gee	5119
7	13	H	Wolverhampton W	D	0-0	0-0	—		12,965
8	19	H	Brentford	D	0-0	0-0	7		12,972
9	26	H	Watford	W	3-0	1-0	4	Davison, Lowe, Ormondroyd	8715
10	Oct 3	H	Barnsley	W	2-1	0-1	6	Grayson, Davison	12,290
11	10	A	Birmingham C	W	2-0	1-0	4	Davison, Joachim	13,443
12	18	H	Peterborough U	L	0-2	0-2	—		10,952
13	24	A	Bristol C	L	1-2	1-0	7	Davison	10,408
14	31	H	Newcastle U	W	2-1	2-0	3	Lowe, Davison	19,687
15	Nov 4	A	Charlton Ath	L	0-2	0-0	—		4107
16	7	H	Tranmere R	L	0-1	0-0	9		13,538
17	15	A	Sunderland	W	2-1	1-1	—	Joachim 2	14,945
18	21	H	Cambridge U	D	2-2	1-1	7	Thompson 2 (1 pen)	12,175
19	28	H	Bristol R	L	0-1	0-1	9		12,848
20	Dec 5	A	Grimsby T	W	3-1	2-0	7	Oldfield 2, Ormondroyd	7488
21	13	A	Oxford U	D	0-0	0-0	—		7949
22	20	H	Swindon T	W	4-2	3-0	—	Oldfield, Lowe 2, Joachim	15,088
23	28	A	Millwall	L	0-2	0-1	6		12,230
24	Jan 9	A	Brentford	W	3-1	1-1	6	Walsh, Thompson 2	8517
25	16	H	Watford	W	5-2	3-0	5	Philpott 2, Walsh, Lowe, Joachim	12,854
26	23	H	Notts Co	D	1-1	1-0	6	Joachim	15,716
27	30	H	West Ham U	L	1-2	1-1	6	Lowe	18,838
28	Feb 6	A	Luton T	L	0-2	0-1	8		9140
29	20	A	Portsmouth	D	1-1	0-0	9	Philpott	14,160
30	24	A	Derby Co	L	0-2	0-1	—		17,507
31	28	H	Birmingham C	W	2-1	1-1	—	Walsh, Lowe	10,284
32	Mar 6	A	Barnsley	W	3-2	1-1	7	Coatsworth 2, Walsh	9452
33	10	H	Sunderland	W	3-2	2-2	—	Walsh 2, Lowe	15,609
34	13	A	Tranmere R	W	3-2	1-1	6	Walsh, Thompson, Lowe	9680
35	20	H	Grimsby T	W	3-0	3-0	6	Walsh, Groves (og), Oldfield	15,930
36	23	A	Cambridge U	W	3-1	0-0	—	Joachim, Lowe 2	6836
37	27	H	Charlton Ath	W	3-1	2-0	5	Joachim, Walsh 2	17,290
38	Apr 3	A	Bristol R	D	0-0	0-0	6		5270
39	7	H	Oxford U	W	2-1	1-1	—	Thompson (pen), Walsh	16,611
40	11	A	West Ham U	L	0-3	0-2	—		13,951
41	14	A	Millwall	W	3-0	1-0	—	Agnew, Thompson, Oldfield	19,711
42	17	A	Swindon T	D	1-1	1-0	5	Walsh	15,428
43	20	H	Southend U	W	4-1	1-0	—	Joachim 2, Edwards (og), Walsh	18,003
44	24	A	Peterborough U	L	0-3	0-2	5		15,445
45	May 1	H	Bristol C	D	0-0	0-0	5		19,294
46	9	A	Newcastle U	L	1-7	0-6	—	Walsh	30,129

Final League Position: 6

GOALSCORERS

League (71): Walsh 15, Joachim 10, Lowe 11, Thompson 8 (2 pens), Davison 6, Oldfield 5, Gee 4, Philpott 3, Coatsworth 2, Ormondroyd 2, Agnew 1, Grayson 1, Whitlow 1, own goals 2.
Coca Cola Cup (4): Davison 1, Joachim 1, Lowe 1, Thompson 1.
FA Cup (3): Joachim 1, Oldfield 1, Thompson 1 (pen).

Muggleton 17	Mills 42 + 1	Whitlow 23 + 1	Smith 44	Walsh 40	Hill 46	Oldfield 44	Thompson 44	Davison 21 + 4	Ormondroyd 17 + 9	Gee 11 + 7	Gordon — + 3	Grayson 14 + 10	Fitzpatrick — + 1	Hoult 10	Lewis 2 + 5	Lowe 27 + 5	Trotter 1	Gibson 5 + 4	Joachim 25 + 1	Poole 19	Platnauer 6	Philpott 27	James 2 + 14	Agnew 9	Coatsworth 10	Match No.
1	2	3	4	5	6	7	8	9	10	11	12															1
1	2	3	4	5	6	7	8	9	10	11																2
1	2	3	4	5	6	7	8	9	10	11																3
1	2	3	4	5	6	7	8	9	10	11		12														4
1	2	3	4	5	6	7	8	9	10	*11*		12	14													5
1	2	3	4		6	7	8	9	10	11				5												6
	2	3	4		6	7	8	9	10	11				5	1	12										7
	2	3	4	5	6	*7*	8	9	10	11				1	12	14										8
	2	3	4	5	6		8	9	10			14		1		11	7	*12*								9
	2		4	5	6	7	8	9	10			3		1	12				11							10
	2	3	4	5	6	7	8	9	10			14	12	1					*11*							11
		3	4	5	6	*7*	8	9	10			14	12	2		1			11							12
		3	4	5	6	7	8	9	10			12	2	1	14				*11*							13
	2		4	5	6	7	*8*	9	14	11		12				10				1	3					14
	2		4	5	6	7		9	12	11		8				10				1	3					15
	2		4	5	6	7	8	9	14	*11*		12				10				1	3					16
	2		4	5	6	7	8		9			11				12			10	1	3					17
	2		4		6	7	8	12	9					5	14	11			10	1	3					18
	2		4		6	7	8	9	10					5	12					1	3	11				19
	2		4	5	6		8	9	14			3				10		12	7	1		11				20
	2		4	5	6		8	9	12			3				10			7	1		11				21
	2	3	4	5	6	7	8	12								10			9	1		11				22
	2		4	5	6	7	8	12				3				10			9	1		11				23
	2	3	4	5	6	7	8									10			9	1		11				24
	2	3	4	5	6	7	8									10			9	1		11				25
	2	*4*	4	5	6	7	8					14		1		10		12	9			11				26
	2		4	5	6	7	8						14	1		10		3	*9*			11	12			27
	2	3	4	5	6	7	8					14		1		10		12	9			11				28
1	2			5	6	7	8	9								10					3	4	11			29
1	2			5	6	*7*	8	9	12				14			10					3	4	11			30
1	7		4	5	6		8									10			3			11	12	9	2	31
1			4	5	6	7	8	14								*10*			3			11	12	9	2	32
1	12		4	5	6	7	8	14								10			3			11		*9*	2	33
1	3		4	5	6	7	8	14				9				10						*11*	12		2	34
1	3		4	5	6	7	8					9				10						11	12		2	35
1	8		4	5	6	7						14			3	10			9			11	12		*2*	36
1	3		4	5	6	7	8									10			9			11	12		2	37
1	3		4	5	6	7	8					14				10			*9*			11	12		2	38
1	3		4	5	6	7	8								14	10			9			*11*	12		2	39
	3	14	4	5	6	7	8									10			9	1		*11*	12		2	40
	2	3	4	5	6	7	8									10				1		11		9		41
	2	3	4	5	6	7	8					14				10				1		11	12	9		42
	2	3	4	5	6	7	8					14				10				1		11	12	*9*		43
	2	3	4	5	6	7	8					14				10				1		*11*	12	9		44
	2	3	4	5	6	7	8								14	10			9	1		11	12			45
	2	3	4	5	6	7	8					12	14		11	10			9	1						46

Coca Cola Cup	Second Round	Peterborough U (h)	2-0
		(a)	1-2
	Third Round	Sheffield W (a)	1-7
FA Cup	Third Round	Barnsley (h)	2-2
		(a)	1-1

LEICESTER CITY

Player and Position	Ht	Wt	Date	Birth Place	Source	Clubs	League App	Gls
Goalkeepers								
Russell Hoult	6 3	14 01	22 11 72	Leicester	Trainee	Leicester C	10	—
						Lincoln C (loan)	2	—
						Blackpool (loan)	—	—
Carl Muggleton	6 2	13 07	13 9 68	Leicester	Apprentice	Leicester C	46	—
						Chesterfield (loan)	17	—
						Blackpool (loan)	2	—
						Hartlepool U (loan)	8	—
						Stockport Co (loan)	4	—
						Liverpool (loan)	—	—
Kevin Poole	5 10	12 06	21 7 63	Bromsgrove	Apprentice	Aston Villa	28	—
						Northampton T (loan)	3	—
						Middlesbrough	34	—
						Hartlepool U (loan)	12	—
						Leicester C	61	—
Defenders								
Ian Blyth			21 10 74	Coventry	Trainee	Leicester C	—	—
Gary Coatsworth	6 0	13 02	7 10 68	Sunderland		Barnsley	6	—
						Darlington	22	2
						Leicester C	13	2
Colin Gibson*	5 8	11 01	6 4 60	Bridport	Apprentice	Aston Villa	185	10
						Manchester U	79	9
						Port Vale (loan)	6	2
						Leicester C	44	4
Simon Grayson	5 11	12 13	16 12 69	Ripon	Trainee	Leeds U	2	—
						Leicester C	37	1
Colin Hill	5 11	12 08	12 11 63	Hillingdon	Apprentice	Arsenal	46	1
						Brighton (loan)	—	—
					Maritimo	Colchester U	69	—
						Sheffield U	82	1
						Leicester C (loan)	10	—
						Leicester C	46	—
Tony James	6 3	14 02	27 6 67	Sheffield	Gainsborough T	Lincoln C	29	—
						Leicester C	98	10
Neil Lewis	5 7	10 09	28 6 74	Wolverhampton	Trainee	Leicester C	7	—
Richard Smith	5 11	12 10	3 10 70	Leicester	Trainee	Leicester C	77	1
						Cambridge U (loan)	4	—
Steve Walsh	6 2	13 13	3 11 64	Fulwood	Local	Wigan Ath	126	4
						Leicester C	235	37
Mike Whitlow	5 11	12 03	13 1 68	Northwich	Witton Alb	Leeds U	77	4
						Leicester C	29	1
Jimmy Willis	6 0	12 02	12 7 68	Liverpool	Blackburn R	Halifax T	—	—
						Stockport Co	10	—
						Darlington	90	6
						Leicester C	10	—
						Bradford C (loan)	9	1
Midfield								
Steve Agnew	5 8	11 10	9 11 65	Shipley	Apprentice	Barnsley	194	29
						Blackburn R	2	—
						Portsmouth (loan)	5	—
						Leicester C	9	1
Warren Haughton	5 7	10 02	13 9 73	Birmingham	Trainee	Leicester C	—	—
Ally Mauchlen (To Hearts August 1992)	5 8	13 07	29 6 60	Kilwinning	Irvine Meadow	Kilmarnock	120	10
						Motherwell	76	4
						Leicester C	239	11
						Leeds U (loan)	—	—
David Oldfield	5 11	13 02	30 5 68	Perth, Australia	Apprentice	Luton T	29	4
						Manchester C	26	6
						Leicester C	147	21
Ian Thompson			17 2 75	Leicester	Trainee	Leicester C	—	—
Steve Thompson	5 10	12 00	2 11 64	Oldham	Apprentice	Bolton W	335	49
						Luton T	5	—
						Leicester C	78	11
Michael Trotter	6 0	12 12	27 10 69	Hartlepool	Trainee	Middlesbrough	—	—
						Doncaster R (loan)	3	—
						Darlington	29	2
						Leicester C	3	—
Darren Williams*	5 10	10 05	15 12 68	Birmingham	Trainee	Leicester C	10	2
						Lincoln C (loan)	9	—
						Chesterfield (loan)	5	1
Forwards								
Bobby Davison	5 9	11 09	17 7 59	South Shields	Seaham CW	Huddersfield T	2	—
						Halifax T	63	29
						Derby Co	206	83
						Leeds U	91	31

LEICESTER CITY

Colours: All blue. **Change colours:** All white.

Foundation: In 1884 a number of young footballers who were mostly old boys of Wyggeston School, held a meeting at a house on the Roman Fosse Way and formed Leicester Fosse FC. They collected 9d (less than 4p) towards the cost of a ball, plus the same amount for membership. Their first professional, Harry Webb from Stafford Rangers, was signed in 1888 for 2s 6d (12p) per week, plus travelling expenses.

First Football League game: 1 September, 1894, Division 2, v Grimsby T (a) L 3-4 – Thraves; Smith, Bailey; Seymour, Brown, Henrys; Hill, Hughes, McArthur (1), Skea (2), Priestman.

Did you know: Billy Frame's career with Leicester City spanned the Second World War and he made 220 peacetime appearances in the League and the same number in wartime matches as a full-back.

Managers (and Secretary-Managers)
William Clark 1896–97, George Johnson 1898–1907*, James Blessington 1907–09, Andy Aitken 1909–11, J. W. Bartlett 1912–14, Peter Hodge 1919–26, William Orr 1926–32, Peter Hodge 1932–34, Andy Lochhead 1934–36, Frank Womack 1936–39, Tom Bromilow 1939–45, Tom Mather 1945–46, Johnny Duncan 1946–49, Norman Bullock 1949–55, David Halliday 1955–58, Matt Gillies 1959–68, Frank O'Farrell 1968–71, Jimmy Bloomfield 1971–77, Frank McLintock 1977–78, Jock Wallace 1978–82, Gordon Milne 1982–86, Bryan Hamilton 1986–87, David Pleat 1987–91, Brian Little May 1991

Player and Position	Ht	Wt	Birth Date	Birth Place	Source	Clubs	League App	Gls
						Derby Co (loan)	10	8
						Sheffield U (loan)	11	4
						Leicester C	25	6
Phil Gee	6 0	12 01	19 12 64	Pelsall	Gresley R	Derby Co	124	26
						Leicester C	32	6
Colin Gordon‡	6 1	12 12	17 1 63	Stourbridge	Oldbury U	Swindon T	72	33
						Wimbledon	3	—
						Gillingham (loan)	4	2
						Reading	24	9
						Bristol C (loan)	8	4
						Fulham	17	2
						Birmingham C	26	3
						Hereford U (loan)	6	—
						Walsall (loan)	6	1
						Bristol R (loan)	4	—
						Leicester C	24	5
Julian Joachim	5 6	11 10	20 9 74	Peterborough	Trainee	Leicester C	26	10
David Lowe	5 10	11 10	30 8 65	Liverpool	Apprentice	Wigan Ath	188	40
						Ipswich T	134	37
						Port Vale (loan)	9	2
						Leicester C	32	11
Gary Mills	5 9	11 10	11 11 61	Northampton	Apprentice	Nottingham F	58	8
					Seattle S	Derby Co	18	1
					Seattle S	Nottingham F	79	4
						Notts Co	75	8
						Leicester C	176	15
Lewis Mogg*	5 6	11 06	2 5 74	Melton Mowbray	Trainee	Leicester C	—	—
Ian Ormondroyd	6 4	13 05	22 9 64	Bradford	Thackley	Bradford C	87	20
						Oldham Ath (loan)	10	1
						Aston Villa	56	6
						Derby Co	25	8
						Leicester C	40	3
Lee Philpott	5 9	12 00	21 2 70	Barnet	Trainee	Peterborough U	4	—
						Cambridge U	134	17
						Leicester C	27	3

Trainees
Aston, Keith A; Bedder, Mathew J; Bunting, Nathan J; Clay, Richard D; Clines, James R; Crane, Adrian P; Eustace, Scott D; Finney, Nicki D. J; Halford, Dean C; Hings, Ryan J; Maisey, Neil K; McMahon, Sam K; Murphy, Gerald J; Stone, Richard B. N; Warner, Timothy V.

Associated Schoolboys
Arcos-Diaz, Miguel; Austen, Jonathan; Battle, Gary S; Bott, Adam M; Butcher, Gareth; Campbell, Stuart; Davis, Brendan S; Dear, Stephen P; Farrell, Lee; Heskey, Emile; Johnson, Colin; Kew, Adam; King, Neil I; Mason, James D; Mathew, Carl; Middleton, Carl; Oakes, Stefan T; Oram, Kevin F; Quincey, Lee P; Tilbury, Stephen J; Wilson, Stuart K.

Associated Schoolboys who have accepted the club's offer of a Traineeship/Contract
Clowes, Gavin; Hallam, Craig D; James, Scott; Poole, Richard J.

LEYTON ORIENT 1992–93 *Back row (left to right):* Robert Taylor, Mark Cooper, Paul Heald, Chris Turner, Keith Day, Sam Kitchen.

Centre row: Geoff Pike (Coach), Bernie Dixson (Chief Scout/Youth Development Officer), Mark Warren, Simon Livett, Chris Zoricich, Warren Hackett, Adrian Whitbread, Greg Berry, Andy Jones, Barry Lakin, Mick Pentney (Kit Manager), Andy Taylor (Physio).

Front row: Mickey Tomlinson, Danny Carter, Kenny Achampong, Peter Eustace (Manager), Frank Clark (Managing Director), Kevin Hales, Steve Okai, Dominic Ludden.

Division 2   **LEYTON ORIENT**

Leyton Stadium, Brisbane Road, Leyton, London E10 5NE.
Telephone 081–539 2223/4. Fax 081–539 4390. Clubcall: 0898
121150.

Ground capacity: 18,869 (7,171 seats).

Record attendance: 34,345 v West Ham U, FA Cup 4th rd,
25 January 1964.

Record receipts: £87,867.92 v West Ham U, FA Cup 3rd rd,
10 January 1987.

Pitch measurements: 110yd × 80yd.

Chairman: T. Wood OBE.

Directors: A. Pincus, D. L. Weinrabe, H. Linney, V. Marsh.

Team Manager: Peter Eustace. *Assistant Manager:* Chris Turner. *Physio:* A. Taylor.

Secretary: Miss Carol Stokes. *Asst. Sec.:* Mrs Sue Tilling. *Commercial Manager:* Frank
Woolf.

Year Formed: 1881. *Turned Professional:* 1903. *Ltd Co.:* 1906.

Club Nickname: 'The O's'.

Previous Names: 1881–86, Glyn Cricket and Football Club; 1886–88, Eagle Football Club;
1888–98, Orient Football Club; 1898–1946, Clapton Orient; 1946–66, Leyton Orient; 1966–
87, Orient.

Previous Grounds: Glyn Road, 1884–96; Whittles Athletic Ground, 1896–1900; Millfields
Road, 1900–30; Lea Bridge Road, 1930–37.

Record League Victory: 8–0 v Crystal Palace, Division 3 (S), 12 November 1955 – Welton;
Lee, Earl; Blizzard, Aldous, McKnight; White (1), Facey (3), Burgess (2), Heckman,
Hartburn (2). 8–0 v Rochdale, Division 4, 20 October 1987 – Wells; Howard, Dickenson
(1), Smalley (1), Day, Hull, Hales (2), Castle (Sussex), Shinners (2), Godfrey (Harvey),
Comfort (2). 8–0 v Colchester U, Division 4, 15 October 1988 – Wells; Howard, Dickenson,
Hales (1p), Day (1). Sitton (1), Baker (1), Ward, Hull (3). Juryeff, Comfort (1).

Record Cup Victory: 9–2 v Chester, League Cup, 3rd rd, 15 October 1962 – Robertson;
Charlton, Taylor; Gibbs, Bishop, Lea; Deeley (1), Waites (3), Dunmore (2), Graham (3),
Wedge.

Record Defeat: 0–8 v Aston Villa, FA Cup 4th rd, 30 January 1929.

Most League Points (2 for a win): 66, Division 3 (S), 1955–56.

Most League Points (3 for a win): 75, Division 4, 1988–89.

Most League Goals: 106, Division 3 (S), 1955–56.

Highest League Scorer in Season: Tom Johnston, 35, Division 2, 1957–58.

Most League Goals in Total Aggregate: Tom Johnston, 121, 1956–58, 1959–61.

Most Capped Player: John Chiedozie, 8 (10), Nigeria.

Most League Appearances: Peter Allen, 432, 1965–78.

Record Transfer Fee Received: £600,000 from Notts Co for John Chiedozie, August 1981.

Record Transfer Fee Paid: £175,000 to Wigan Ath for Paul Beesley, October 1989.

Football League Record: 1905 Elected to Division 2; 1929–56 Division 3 (S); 1956–62
Division 2; 1962–63 Division 1; 1963–66 Division 2; 1966–70 Division 3; 1970–82 Division
2; 1982–85 Division 3; 1985–89 Division 4; 1989–92 Division 3; 1992– Division 2.

Honours: Football League: Division 1 best season: 22nd, 1962–63; Division 2 – Runners-up
1961–62; Division 3 – Champions 1969–70; Division 3 (S) – Champions 1955–56; Runners-
up 1954–55. *FA Cup:* Semi-final 1977–78. *Football League Cup:* best season: 5th rd, 1963.

LEYTON ORIENT 1992—93 LEAGUE RECORD

Match No.	Date		Venue	Opponents	Result		H/T Score	Lg. Pos.	Goalscorers	Attendance
1	Aug	15	H	Brighton & HA	W	3-2	1-0	—	Zoricich, Jones 2	5614
2		22	A	Reading	D	1-1	1-1	3	Day	4207
3		29	H	Blackpool	W	1-0	1-0	3	Howard	4310
4	Sept	1	H	Huddersfield T	W	4-1	1-0	—	Ludden, Jones 2, Taylor	3765
5		5	A	Plymouth Arg	L	0-2	0-1	6		7319
6		12	H	Chester C	W	4-3	1-1	2	Taylor 2, Hales (pen), Jones	4158
7		15	A	Hartlepool U	W	2-0	1-0	—	Taylor 2	3129
8		19	A	Exeter C	L	0-1	0-0	4		2788
9		26	H	Hull C	D	0-0	0-0	4		4951
10	Oct	3	H	Bolton W	W	1-0	0-0	2	Okai	3946
11		10	A	Stoke C	L	1-2	0-0	3	Otto	12,640
12		17	H	Bournemouth	W	1-0	0-0	1	Otto	4528
13		24	A	Bradford C	L	0-1	0-0	5		7235
14		31	H	Swansea C	W	4-2	2-0	3	Taylor 2, Cooper 2	5683
15	Nov	3	A	Port Vale	L	0-2	0-0	—		7387
16		7	H	WBA	W	2-0	0-0	4	Taylor, Kitchen	8640
17		21	A	Wigan Ath	L	1-3	0-2	5	Cooper	1806
18		28	H	Mansfield T	W	5-1	3-0	2	Taylor, Howard 3 (1 pen), Cooper	4557
19	Dec	12	A	Burnley	L	0-2	0-1	5		8882
20		18	H	Preston NE	W	3-1	1-0	—	Flynn (og), Jones, Cooper	3436
21		26	H	Fulham	D	0-0	0-0	3		8431
22		28	A	Stockport Co	D	1-1	0-1	3	Taylor	6368
23	Jan	2	A	Chester C	W	3-1	0-1	2	Jones, Harvey, Cooper	2510
24		9	H	Hartlepool U	D	0-0	0-0	3		5539
25		16	A	Hull C	D	0-0	0-0	3		3897
26		23	H	Exeter C	W	5-0	2-0	2	Jones, Taylor 3, Carter	5247
27		26	A	Blackpool	L	1-3	0-3	—	Gore (og)	3164
28		30	H	Reading	L	1-2	0-1	3	Howard	5466
29	Feb	6	A	Brighton & HA	W	3-1	2-0	3	Otto 3	7850
30		13	H	Plymouth Arg	W	2-0	1-0	4	Achampong, Otto	5804
31		20	A	Huddersfield T	D	1-1	1-0	3	Bellamy	5112
32		27	H	Stoke C	W	1-0	1-0	3	Cooper	10,798
33	Mar	6	A	Bolton W	L	0-1	0-0	5		7763
34		9	H	Rotherham U	D	1-1	1-0	—	Bellamy	4401
35		13	A	WBA	L	0-2	0-0	5		15,023
36		20	H	Port Vale	L	0-1	0-0	6		5950
37		23	A	Mansfield T	L	0-3	0-0	—		2774
38		27	H	Wigan Ath	L	1-2	1-1	7	Carter	4104
39	Apr	3	A	Rotherham U	D	1-1	0-0	7	Taylor	3083
40		6	H	Burnley	W	3-2	3-1	—	Harvey, Bellamy, Whitbread	4236
41		10	A	Fulham	L	0-1	0-0	7		5976
42		12	H	Stockport Co	W	3-0	3-0	6	Lakin, Carter, Bellamy	4654
43		17	A	Preston NE	W	4-1	3-0	6	Harvey, Lakin, Taylor 2	5890
44		24	A	Bournemouth	L	0-3	0-2	8		4595
45	May	1	H	Bradford C	W	4-2	1-0	7	Otto, Taylor 2, Harvey	5504
46		8	A	Swansea C	W	1-0	1-0	7	Otto	6543

Final League Position: 7

GOALSCORERS

League (69): Taylor 18, Jones 8, Otto 8, Cooper 7, Howard 5 (1 pen), Bellamy 4, Harvey 4, Carter 3, Lakin 2, Achampong 1, Day 1, Hales 1 (pen), Kitchen 1, Ludden 1, Okai 1, Whitbread 1, Zoricich 1, own goals 2.
Coca Cola Cup (2): Cooper 1, Tomlinson 1.
FA Cup (5): Cooper 2, Howard 1, Jones 1, Whitbread 1.

Turner 17	Zoricich 10 + 2	Howard 41	Hales 29	Day 7 + 3	Whitbread 36	Tomlinson 3 + 5	Livett 16 + 7	Jones 24 + 5	Cooper 20 + 8	Okai 5 + 8	Ryan 18 + 2	Achampong 19 + 6	Kitchen 28 + 4	Taylor 36 + 3	Ludden 21 + 3	Bellamy 38 + 1	Otto 18 + 5	Carter 26 + 3	Heald 26	Warren 14	Harvey 19 + 2	Benstock 8 + 1	Hackett 16 + 1	Lakin 8 + 1	Newell 3	Match No.
1	2	3	4	5	6	*7*	8	9	10	11	12	14														1
1		3	4	5	6	7	*8*	9	10	11	14		2	12												2
1	*2*	3	4	5	6		8	9	10	11		7		12	14											3
1	2	3	4	5	6		8	9				7	12	10	*11*											4
1	2	3	4	5	6	14	8	9				7	12	10	*11*											5
1	2	3	4		6	*11*	8		9	12		7		5	10	14										6
1		3	4		6		8	9	12	11	7	2	10	5												7
1		3	4		6	14	*8*	9	12	11	7	5	10	2												8
1	14	3	4		6			9	8	12	11	5	*10*	2	7											9
1		3	4		6		9	14	12	11	8	5	10	2	7											10
1	14	3	4		6		9	12	*11*	8	5	10	2	7												11
1	10	3	4		6		9	12	11	8	5	2	7													12
1	10	3	4		6	12	9	11		8	5	2	7													13
1	10	3	4		6	12	14	11		*8*	5	7	2	9												14
1	7	3	4	2	6	14	8	9	11	12	5	10														15
1		3	4	6	12	9		11	10	8	5	7	2													16
1		3	4	12	6	*9*	14	11	10	8	5	7	2													17
		3	4		6	10		11		8	5	7	2	12		1	9									18
6		3	4			10	8	11		5	7	14	2	12		1	*9*									19
		3	4	*6*		10	11			5	7	9	8	1	2	12			14							20
		3	*4*			10	11	14	5	7	2	8	6	1	9	12										21
		3				8	11	4	5	7	6	2	12	1	9	10										22
		3				8	10	5	7	6	2	12	4	1	9	11										23
		3				8	10	12	5	*7*	6	2	4	1	9	11										24
		3	12			11	8	10	5		6	*2*	4	1	9	7										25
		3				8		5	10	6	2	12	4	1	9	11	*7*									26
		3				7	8	5	10	6	2	12	4	1	9	11										27
		3				7	*8*	14	5	10	6	2	12	4	1	9	11									28
		3	12	5				14	7		6	2	10	4	1	9	*11*	8								29
		3		5			11	14	7	*8*	6	2	10	4	1	9		12								30
		3		5			11		7	8	6	2	10	4	1			12	9							31
		3		5			11		7		12	6	2	10	4	1		8	9							32
				5	14				4	7	12	11	6	2	10		1	3	8	9						33
		3		5					7	12		11	2	10	4	1		6	8	9						34
		3		5					7	12		11	6	2	10	4	1		8	9						35
		3		5				14	7	6	12	11		2	10	4	1		8	9						36
				5				12	7	8	3	11	6	2	10	4	1		9							37
	6			5				10	7		4	11	3	2		9	1	8								38
	6			5	12	14					4	11	3	*2*		9	1	*8*		10	7					39
	6			5	12						4	11	3	2		9	1	8		10	7					40
	4	6		5				12				11	3	2		9	1	8		10	7					41
	4	6		5		12	14					11		2		9	1		8	3	10	7				42
	4	6		5		12	14					11		2		9	*1*		8	3	10	7				43
	4	6	5				14					11		2	12	9		*8*	3	10	7	1				44
	3	6		5				11	12			2	10	9		8			4	7	1					45
	3			5		12		14				*11*	6	2	10	9		8		4	7	1				46

Coca Cola Cup	First Round	Millwall (h)	2-2
		(a)	0-3
FA Cup	First Round	Dagenham & Redbge (a)	5-4
	Second Round	Reading (a)	0-3

LEYTON ORIENT

Player and Position	Ht	Wt	Date	Birth Place	Source	Clubs	League App	Gls
Goalkeepers								
Paul Heald	6 2	12 05	20 8 68	Wath-on-Dearne	Trainee	Sheffield U	—	—
						Leyton Orient	131	—
						Coventry C (loan)	2	—
						Crystal Palace (loan)	—	—
Paul Newell	6 1	11 05	23 2 69	Greenwich	Trainee	Southend U	15	—
						Leyton Orient	21	—
						Colchester U (loan)	14	—
George O'Hanlon*			9 12 72	Dublin	Trainee	Leyton Orient	—	—
Chris Turner	5 11	11 12	15 9 58	Sheffield	Apprentice	Sheffield W	91	—
						Lincoln C (loan)	5	—
						Sunderland	195	—
						Manchester U	64	—
						Sheffield W	75	—
						Leeds U (loan)	2	—
						Leyton Orient	51	—
Defenders								
Gary Bellamy	6 2	11 05	4 7 62	Worksop	Apprentice	Chesterfield	184	7
						Wolverhampton W	136	9
						Cardiff (loan)	9	—
						Leyton Orient	39	4
Danny Benstock			10 7 70	London	Barking	Leyton Orient	9	—
Keith Day*	6 1	11 00	29 11 62	Grays	Aveley	Colchester U	113	12
						Leyton Orient	192	9
Warren Hackett	5 9	11 12	16 12 71	Newham	Tottenham H	Leyton Orient	39	—
Kevin Hales*	5 7	10 04	13 1 61	Dartford	Apprentice	Chelsea	20	2
						Leyton Orient	300	23
Terry Howard	6 1	11 07	26 2 66	Stepney	Apprentice	Chelsea	6	—
						C Palace (loan)	4	—
						Chester C (loan)	2	—
						Leyton Orient	276	28
Sam Kitchen			11 6 67	Germany	Frickley Ath	Leyton Orient	32	1
Mark O'Neill‡	5 8	10 12	4 10 72	Dublin	Trainee	Leyton Orient	—	—
Adrian Whitbread	6 2	11 13	22 10 71	Epping	Trainee	Leyton Orient	125	2
Chris Zoricich‡	5 11	11 10	3 5 69	New Zealand		Leyton Orient	62	1
Midfield								
Kenny Achampong*	5 9	11 01	26 6 66	London	Apprentice	Fulham	81	15
						West Ham U (loan)	—	—
						Charlton Ath	10	—
						Leyton Orient	83	7
Danny Carter	5 11	11 12	29 6 69	Hackney	Billericay	Leyton Orient	123	15
Barry Lakin			19 9 73	Dartford	Trainee	Leyton Orient	9	2
Simon Livett	5 10	12 02	8 1 69	Newham	Trainee	West Ham U	1	—
						Leyton Orient	23	—
Dominic Ludden			30 3 74	Basildon	Trainee	Leyton Orient	24	1
Stephen Okai			3 12 73	Ghana	Schoolboy	Leyton Orient	14	2
Ricky Otto	5 10	11 00	9 11 67	London	Dartford	Leyton Orient	56	13
Brett Patience*			12 10 73	London	Trainee	Leyton Orient	—	—
Vaughan Ryan	5 8	10 12	2 9 68	Westminster		Wimbledon	82	3
						Sheffield U (loan)	3	—
						Leyton Orient	20	—
Keith Sharman‡	6 2	12 00	6 11 71	London	Trainee	Leyton Orient	—	—
Michael Tomlinson	5 9	11 00	15 9 72	Lambeth	Trainee	Leyton Orient	10	1
Mark Warren			12 11 74	Clapton	Trainee	Leyton Orient	15	—

LEYTON ORIENT

Colours: Red shirts with white pinstripe, white shorts, red stockings. **Change colours:** White shirts with blue pinstripe, blue shorts, blue stockings.

Foundation: There is some doubt about the foundation of Leyton Orient, and, indeed, some confusion with clubs like Leyton and Clapton over their early history. As regards the foundation, the most favoured version is that Leyton Orient was formed originally by members of Homerton Theological College who established Glyn Cricket Club in 1881 and then carried on through the following winter playing football. Eventually many employees of the Orient Shipping Line became involved and so the name Orient was chosen in 1888.

First Football League game: 2 September, 1905, Division 2, v Leicester Fosse (a) L 1-2 – Butler; Holmes, Codling; Lamberton, Boden, Boyle; Kingaby (1), Wootten, Leigh, Evenson, Bourne.

Did you know: Orient became the first Football League club to have two Nigerian internationals on their staff when John Chiedozie and Tunji Banjo were included in the African Nations Cup games in 1980.

Managers (and Secretary-Managers)
Sam Omerod 1905–06, Ike Ivenson 1906, Billy Holmes 1907–22, Peter Proudfoot 1922–29, Arthur Grimsdell 1929–30, Peter Proudfoot 1930–31, Jimmy Seed 1931–33, David Pratt 1933–34, Peter Proudfoot 1935–39, Tom Halsey 1939–39, Billy Wright 1939–45, Billy Hall 1945, Billy Wright 1945–46, Charlie Hewitt 1946–48, Neil McBain 1948–49, Alec Stock 1949–56, 1956–58, 1958–59, Johnny Carey 1961–63, Benny Fenton 1963–64, Dave Sexton 1965, Dick Graham 1966–68, Jimmy Bloomfield 1968–71, George Petchey 1971–77, Jimmy Bloomfield 1977–81, Paul Went 1981, Ken Knighton 1981, Frank Clark May 1982–91 (MD), Peter Eustace July 1991–.

Player and Position	Ht	Wt	Date	Birth Place	Source	Clubs	League App	Gls
Forwards								
Paul Cobb*	5 6	10 02	13 12 72	Thurrock	Purfleet	Leyton Orient	5	—
Mark Cooper	6 2	13 04	5 4 67	Cambridge	Apprentice	Cambridge U	71	17
						Tottenham H	—	—
						Shrewsbury T	6	2
						Gillingham	49	11
						Leyton Orient	121	37
Lee Harvey*	5 11	11 07	21 12 66	Harlow	Local	Leyton Orient	184	23
Andy Jones	5 11	13 06	9 1 63	Wrexham	Rhyl	Port Vale	90	49
						Charlton Ath	66	15
						Port Vale (loan)	17	3
						Bristol C (loan)	4	1
						Bournemouth	40	8
						Leyton Orient	59	13
Robert Taylor	6 0	11 07	30 4 71	Norwich	Trainee	Norwich C	—	—
						Leyton Orient (loan)	3	1
						Birmingham C	—	—
						Leyton Orient	50	19
David Thompson*			9 9 73	Islington	Trainee	Leyton Orient	—	—

Trainees
Beckett, Nathan J; Bird, Robert J; Collinson, David J; Denny, Neil R; Fowler, Lee P; Gamble, Bradley D; McDermott, Dean P; Munyenya, Daniel N; Pallecaros, George; Quinn, John P; Ramage, Andrew W; Rolls, George E; Sweetman, Nicholas E; Wedlock, Grant.

Associated Schoolboys
Blogg, James D; Doe, Steven R; Haynes, Jason D; Honeyball, Scott R; Jones, Anthony S; Martin, Gary D; Nash, Daniel T; Pike, David A; Shearer, Lee S; Skinner, Keith R; Sopp, Darryl J; Sugg, Darren W; Weir, Andrew J.

Associated Schoolboys who have accepted the club's offer of a Traineeship/Contract
Loomes, Jody D; Pipal, Joseph; Purse, Darren J.

LINCOLN CITY 1992–93 *Back row (left to right):* Paul Dobson, Paul Ward, Jason Kabia, John Schofield, David Puttnam, Dean West, David Clarke.
Third row: Graham Bressington, Sean Dunphy, Gary West, James Morgan, Ian Bowling, Jason Lee, Matt Carmichael, Kevin Finney, Grant Brown, Anthony Lormor.
Second row: Darren Chapman, Simon Whittle, Matt Carbon, Stuart Donnelly, Keith Alexander (Youth Team Coach), Steve Thompson (Manager), Neil McDiarmid (Physio), Robin Spencer, Steve Parkinson.
Front row: Ben Dixon, Ian Wright, Chris Rawlinson, Ashley Irlam, Kasi Oseni, Darren Huckerby, Richard Charles, Steve Williams, Jamie Gilliatt.

Division 3   **LINCOLN CITY**

Sincil Bank, Lincoln LN5 8LD. Telephone Lincoln (0522) 522224 and 510263. Fax: (0522) 520564. Executive Club: (0522) 532634. Centre spot: (0522) 536438.

Ground capacity: 12,461.

Record attendance: 23,196 v Derby Co, League Cup 4th rd, 15 November 1967.

Record receipts: £34,843.30 v Tottenham H, Milk Cup 2nd rd, 26 October 1983.

Pitch measurements: 110yd × 75yd.

Hon. Life Presidents: V. C. Withers, D. W. L. Bocock.

President: H. Dove.

Chairman: K. J. Reames. *Vice-chairman:* G. R. Davey (and Managing).

Directors: M. B. Pryor, H. C. Sills, J. Hicks.

Hon. Consultant Surgeon: Mr Brian Smith. *Hon. Club Doctor:* Nick Huntley.

Secretary: G. R. Davey.

Manager: Keith Alexander. *Physio:* Neil McDiarmid GRAD DIP (Phys), MCSP, SRP.

Year Formed: 1883. *Turned Professional:* 1892. *Ltd Co.:* 1892.

Club Nickname: 'The Red Imps'.

Previous Grounds: 1883, John O'Gaunt's; 1894, Sincil Bank.

Record League Victory: 11–1 v Crewe Alex, Division 3 (N), 29 September 1951 – Jones; Green (1p), Varney; Wright, Emery, Grummett (1); Troops (1), Garvey, Graver (6), Whittle (1), Johnson (1).

Record Cup Victory: 8–1 v Bromley, FA Cup, 2nd rd, 10 December 1938 – McPhail; Hartshorne, Corbett; Bean, Leach, Whyte (1); Hancock, Wilson (1), Ponting (3), Deacon (1), Clare (2).

Record Defeat: 3–11 v Manchester C, Division 2, 23 March 1895.

Most League Points (2 for a win): 74, Division 4, 1975–76.

Most League Points (3 for a win): 77, Division 3, 1981–82.

Most League Goals: 121, Division 3 (N), 1951–52.

Highest League Scorer in Season: Allan Hall, 42, Division 3 (N), 1931–32.

Most League Goals in Total Aggregate: Andy Graver, 144, 1950–55 and 1958–61.

Most Capped Player: David Pugh, 3 (7), Wales and George Moulson, 3, Eire.

Most League Appearances: Tony Emery, 402, 1946–59.

Record Transfer Fee Received: £250,000 plus increments from Blackburn R for Matt Dickins, March 1992.

Record Transfer Fee Paid: £60,000 to Southampton for Gordon Hobson, September 1988, £60,000 to Sheffield U for Alan Roberts, October 1989, and £60,000 to Leicester C for Grant Brown, January 1990.

Football League Record: 1892 Founder member of Division 2. Remained in Division 2 until 1920 when they failed re-election but also missed seasons 1908–09 and 1911–12 when not re-elected. 1921–32 Division 3 (N); 1932–34 Division 2; 1934–48 Division 3 (N); 1948–49 Division 2; 1949–52 Division 3 (N); 1952–61 Division 2; 1961–62 Division 3; 1962–76 Division 4; 1976–79 Division 3; 1979–81 Division 4; 1981–86 Division 3; 1986–87 Division 4; 1987–88 GM Vauxhall Conference; 1988–92 Division 4; 1992– Division 3.

Honours: *Football League:* Divison 2 best season: 5th, 1901–02; Division 3 (N) – Champions 1931–32, 1947–48, 1951–52; Runners-up 1927–28, 1930–31, 1936–37; Division 4 – Champions 1975–76; Runners-up 1980–81. *FA Cup:* best season: 1st rd of Second Series (5th rd equivalent), 1886–87, 2nd rd (5th rd equivalent), 1889–90, 1901–02. *Football League Cup:* best season: 4th rd, 1967–68. GM Vauxhall Conference Champions – 1987–88.

LINCOLN CITY 1992—93 LEAGUE RECORD

Match No.	Date		Venue	Opponents	Result		H/T Score	Lg. Pos.	Goalscorers	Attendance
1	Aug	15	A	Colchester U	L	1-2	1-2	—	West D	4131
2		22	H	York C	L	0-1	0-1	22		3032
3		29	A	Carlisle U	L	0-2	0-0	22		4023
4	Sept	1	A	Hereford U	W	2-0	2-0	—	Lee, Clarke	1403
5		5	H	Scunthorpe U	W	1-0	0-0	13	Lee	3764
6		12	H	Halifax T	W	2-1	1-0	7	Carmichael, Lee	2689
7		18	A	Doncaster R	D	0-0	0-0	—		2936
8		26	A	Shrewsbury T	L	0-1	0-0	13		2746
9	Oct	3	A	Northampton T	W	2-0	0-0	10	Clarke, Kabia	1922
10		10	H	Walsall	L	0-2	0-2	13		3095
11		17	A	Bury	W	2-1	1-0	10	Costello, Lee	2208
12		24	H	Barnet	W	4-1	2-1	7	Costello, Bressington (pen), Phillips (og), Lee	2955
13		31	A	Darlington	W	3-1	3-0	6	Costello 2, Lee	2051
14	Nov	3	A	Scarborough	W	1-0	0-0	—	Dunphy	2084
15		7	H	Wrexham	D	0-0	0-0	4		3699
16		21	A	Crewe Alex	W	2-1	0-1	3	Carmichael, Smith	3208
17		28	H	Gillingham	D	1-1	1-0	3	Baraclough	3175
18	Dec	19	A	Rochdale	L	1-5	0-2	4	Matthews	1793
19		28	H	Cardiff C	W	3-2	0-0	6	Puttnam, Matthews, West D	4359
20	Jan	16	A	Shrewsbury T	L	2-3	1-2	9	Bressington (pen), Matthews	2506
21		23	H	Doncaster R	W	2-1	0-0	7	Costello 2	3269
22		26	H	Carlisle U	W	2-1	0-0	—	Lee, Smith	2947
23		30	A	York C	L	0-2	0-1	6		3948
24	Feb	6	H	Colchester U	D	1-1	0-0	8	Bressington	3380
25		13	A	Scunthorpe U	D	1-1	0-1	8	Bressington (pen)	3748
26		16	A	Halifax T	L	1-2	1-2	—	West	1260
27		20	A	Hereford U	W	2-0	1-0	7	Matthews 2	2875
28		27	H	Walsall	W	2-1	2-1	6	Baraclough, Lee	3345
29	Mar	2	A	Chesterfield	L	1-2	0-1	—	Matthews	2842
30		6	H	Northampton T	W	2-0	2-0	6	Baraclough (pen), Matthews	3328
31		9	H	Torquay U	D	2-2	1-1	—	Matthews, Baraclough (pen)	2781
32		13	A	Wrexham	L	0-2	0-0	6		5246
33		20	H	Scarborough	W	3-0	0-0	5	Baraclough (pen), Lee, Matthews	3725
34		23	A	Gillingham	L	1-3	0-0	—	Matthews	2906
35		27	A	Crewe Alex	D	1-1	1-1	6	Carmichael	4235
36	Apr	10	H	Chesterfield	D	1-1	1-0	9	Lee	4271
37		12	A	Cardiff C	L	1-3	0-2	9	Matthews	11,257
38		17	H	Rochdale	L	1-2	1-0	9	Lee	2922
39		20	A	Torquay U	W	2-1	1-1	—	Carmichael, Smith	3688
40		24	H	Bury	L	1-2	1-0	9	Puttnam	3651
41	May	1	A	Barnet	D	1-1	0-0	9	Lee	4422
42		8	H	Darlington	W	2-0	2-0	8	Costello, Brown	3107

Final League Position: 8

GOALSCORERS

League (57): Lee 12, Matthews 11, Costello 7, Baraclough 5 (3 pens), Bressington 4 (3 pens), Carmichael 4, Smith 3, West 3, Clarke 2, Puttnam 2, Brown 1, Dunphy 1, Kabia 1, own goal 1.
Coca Cola Cup: (6): Bressington 2, Carmichael 1, Dunphy 1, Finney 1, Puttnam 1.
FA Cup (1): Costello 1.

Bowling 15	West D 12 + 7	Clarke 30 + 1	Bressington 25 + 3	Carmichael 41	Brown 40	Schofield 32 + 8	Ward 1	Lee 36 + 5	Kabia 7 + 6	Puttnam 37	Alexander — + 7	Finney 10 + 4	Baraclough 34 + 2	McParland 3 + 1	Dunphy 29 + 2	Smith 28 + 5	Pollitt 27	Costello 22 + 5	Matthews 21 + 3	Parkinson — + 2	Yates 10 + 4	Dixon 1 + 1	Carbon 1	Match No.
1	2	3	4	5	6	7	8	9	10	11	12	14												1
1	2	3	8	5	6	7		9	10			14	4	11	12									2
1	2		8	3	6	7		9	12			14	4	11	10	5								3
1		3	8	2	6	7		9	11			14	4	12	10	5								4
1		3	8	4	6	7		9	11			12			10	5	2							5
1		3	8	4	6	7		9	10	11			14		12	5	2							6
1		3	8	4	6	7		9	10	11	12					5	2							7
		3	8	4	6	7		9	12	11						5	2	1	10					8
		3	8	4	6	7		9	12	11			2			5		1	10					9
		3	8	4	6	7		9		11			2			5	12	1	10					10
		3	8	4	6	7		9	12	11			2			5	14	1	10					11
		3	8	4	6	7		9	12	11			2			5	14	1	10					12
1		3	8	4	6	7		9	12	11			2			5	14		10					13
1		3	8	4	6	7		9		11			2			5			10					14
1	12	3	8	4	6	7		9	10	11			2			5	14							15
1	12		8	4	6	7		9		11			3			5	2		10					16
1		3	8	4	6	12		9		11			7			5	2		10					17
1	12	3			6	7		9		11			4		8	5	2		10	14				18
	7	3			6	12		9		11			4		8	5	2	1	10	14				19
		3	8	4	6	2		9		11			12		7	5		1	10	14				20
	7	3	8	5	6	12		14		11			4				2	1	10		9			21
	7	3	8	5	6	12		14		11			4				2	1	10		9			22
14		3	8	5	6	12		9		11			4				2	1	10		7			23
	7	3	8	5	6			12		11			4				2	1	10		9			24
	14		8	5	6	7		9		11			12		3		2	1	10		4			25
			8	5	6	7		9					4		3		2	1	10	11	12			26
	7	3		5	6			12		11			4		10		2	1	9		8			27
	7	3		5	6	14		9		11			12		8		2	1	10		4			28
		3			6	7		9		11					8	5	2	1	10		4			29
	7			5	6	14		9		11					8	3	2	1	10		4		12	30
	7			5	6	14		9		11			8		3	12	2	1	10		4			31
14		3		5	6	7		9		11					8	12	2	1	10		4			32
		3	4		6	7		9		11					8	5	2	1	12	10	14			33
		3	4		6	7		9		11					8	5	2	1	12	10	14			34
		3		4	6	7		9		11					8	5	2	1	10	12				35
		3	8	4	6	7		9		11						5	2	1	12	10	14			36
			4		6	2		9		11					3	5	7	1	12	10	8			37
	14		4		6	7		9		11					3	5	2	1	12	10	8			38
	12		4		6	7		9		11					3	5	2	1	10		8			39
	12		4		6	2		9		11					3	5		1	7	10	8			40
1	14		8	4	6	7		12		11					3	5	2		10		9			41
1	14	3			6	7				10			2			5		8	9	12	11		4	42

Coca Cola Cup	First Round	Doncaster R (a)	3-0
		(h)	1-1
	Second Round	Crystal Palace (a)	1-3
		(h)	1-1
FA Cup	First Round	Stafford R (h)	0-0
		(a)	1-2

LINCOLN CITY

Player and Position	Ht	Wt	Date	Birth Place	Source	Clubs	League App	Gls
Goalkeepers								
Ian Bowling	6 3	14 08	27 7 65	Sheffield	Gainsborough T	Lincoln C	59	—
						Hartlepool U (loan)	1	—
						Bradford C (loan)	7	—
Michael Pollitt	6 4	14 00	29 2 72	Bolton	Trainee	Manchester U	—	—
						Oldham Ath (loan)	—	—
						Bury	—	—
						Lincoln C	27	—
Defenders								
Graham Bressington	6 0	12 00	8 7 66	Eton	Wycombe W	Lincoln C	141	7
Grant Brown	6 0	11 12	19 11 69	Sunderland	Trainee	Leicester C	14	—
						Lincoln C	143	5
Matthew Carbon	6 2	11 13	8 6 75	Nottingham	Trainee	Lincoln C	1	—
Sean Dunphy	6 3	13 05	5 11 70	Rotherham	Trainee	Barnsley	6	—
						Lincoln C	36	2
Dean West*	5 10	11 07	5 12 72	Wakefield	Leeds U	Lincoln C	52	7
Gary West‡	6 2	13 02	25 8 64	Scunthorpe	Apprentice	Sheffield U	75	1
						Lincoln C	83	4
						Gillingham	52	3
						Port Vale	17	1
						Lincoln C (loan)	3	—
						Gillingham (loan)	1	—
						Lincoln C	18	1
						Walsall (loan)	9	1
Midfield								
Ian Baraclough	6 1	12 00	4 12 70	Leicester	Trainee	Leicester C	—	—
						Wigan Ath (loan)	9	2
						Grimsby T (loan)	4	—
						Grimsby T	1	—
						Lincoln C	36	5
David Clarke*	5 10	11 00	3 12 64	Nottingham	Apprentice	Notts Co	123	7
						Lincoln C	140	8
Kevin Finney*	6 0	12 00	19 10 69	Newcastle-under-Lyme	Apprentice	Port Vale	29	1
						Lincoln C	37	2
Steve Parkinson§	5 11	11 11	27 8 74	Lincoln	Trainee	Lincoln C	2	—
David Puttnam	5 10	11 09	3 2 67	Leicester	Leicester U	Leicester C	7	—
						Lincoln C	142	15
Jon Schofield	5 11	11 03	16 5 65	Barnsley	Gainsborough T	Lincoln C	179	8
Paul Ward*	5 11	12 05	15 9 63	Sedgefield	Apprentice	Chelsea	—	—
						Middlesbrough	76	1
						Darlington	124	9
						Leyton Orient	31	1
						Scunthorpe U	55	6
						Lincoln C	39	—
Forwards								
Keith Alexander†	6 4	13 06	14 11 58	Nottingham	Barnet	Grimsby T	83	26
						Stockport Co	11	—
						Lincoln C	45	4
Matt Carmichael	6 2	11 07	13 5 64	Singapore	Army	Lincoln C	133	18
Peter Costello	6 0	12 00	31 10 69	Halifax	Trainee	Bradford C	20	2
						Rochdale	34	10
						Peterborough U	8	—
						Lincoln C (loan)	3	—
						Lincoln C	27	7
Ben Dixon	6 1	11 00	16 9 74	Lincoln	Trainee	Lincoln C	5	—

LINCOLN CITY

Colours: Red and white striped shirts, black shorts, red stockings with white trim. **Change colours:** Jade shirts, black shorts, jade stockings.

Foundation: Although there was a Lincoln club as far back as 1861, the present organisation was formed in 1883 winning the Lincolnshire Senior Cup in only their fourth season. They were Founder members of the Midland League in 1889 and that competition's first champions.

First Football League game: 3 September, 1892, Division 2, v Sheffield U (a) L 2-4 – W. Gresham; Coulton, Neill; Shaw, Mettam, Moore; Smallman, Irving (1), Cameron (1), Kelly, J. Gresham.

Did you know: On 16 September 1935, Alf Horne the Lincoln City captain converted three penalties against Stockport County in a Division 3 (N) fixture in a 3-0 win.

Managers (and Secretary-Managers)
David Calderhead 1900–07, John Henry Strawson 1907–14 (had been secretary), George Fraser 1919–21, David Calderhead Jnr. 1921–24, Horace Henshall 1924–27, Harry Parkes 1927–36, Joe McClelland 1936–46, Bill Anderson 1946–65 (GM to 1966), Roy Chapman 1965–66, Ron Gray 1966–70, Bert Loxley 1970–71, David Herd 1971–72, Graham Taylor 1972–77, George Kerr 1977–78, Willie Bell 1977–78, Colin Murphy 1978–85, John Pickering 1985, George Kerr 1985–87, Peter Daniel 1987, Colin Murphy 1987–90, Allan Clarke 1990, Steve Thompson November 1990–93, Keith Alexander April 1993–.

Player and Position	Ht	Wt	Date	Birth Place	Source	Clubs	League App	Gls
Jason Kabia*	5 11	12 00	28 5 69	Sutton in Ashfield	Oakham United	Lincoln C	28	4
						Doncaster R (loan)	5	—
Jason Lee	6 3	13 08	9 5 71	Newham	Trainee	Charlton Ath	1	—
						Stockport Co (loan)	2	—
						Lincoln C	93	21
Tony Lormor*	6 1	12 03	29 10 70	Ashington	Trainee	Newcastle U	8	3
						Norwich C (loan)	—	—
						Lincoln C	90	29
Neil Matthews	6 0	12 12	19 9 66	Grimsby		Grimsby T	11	1
						Scunthorpe U (loan)	1	—
						Halifax T (loan)	9	2
						Bolton W (loan)	1	—
						Halifax T	105	29
						Stockport Co	43	15
						Halifax T (loan)	3	—
						Lincoln C	24	11
Paul Smith	5 10	10 09	9 11 64	Rotherham	Apprentice	Sheffield U	36	1
						Stockport Co (loan)	7	5
						Port Vale	44	7
						Lincoln C	179	27

Trainees
Chapman, Darren; Charles, Richard; Donnelly, Stuart; Hackett, Lee; Morgan, James; Parkinson, Steven; Whittle, Simon.

**Non-Contract
Alexander, Keith.

Associated Schoolboys
Bartlett, Darren S; Brown, Kevin; Clawson, Graham P; Davis, Matthew D; Dixon, Andrew S; Gresham, Robert K; Hyde, Christopher R; Taylor, Ben; Whitlam, Mark A; Wilkins, Adam L.

Associated Schoolboys who have accepted the club's offer of a Traineeship/Contract
Coles, Christopher J; Rawlinson, Christopher; Sewell, Steven J; Williams, Steven R.

**Non-Contract Players who are retained must be re-signed before they are eligible to play in League matches.

302

LIVERPOOL 1992-93 *Back row (left to right):* Jan Molby, Nicky Tanner, Mike Hooper, David James, Bruce Grobbelaar, Mark Walters, Rob Jones.
Centre row: Ronnie Moran, David Burrows, Michael Thomas, Istvan Kozma, Barry Venison, Ronny Rosenthal, Ray Houghton, Steve McManaman, Phil Boersma, Roy Evans.
Front row: Mike Marsh, Dean Saunders, Steve Nicol, Graeme Souness (Manager), Mark Wright, Ian Rush, Ronnie Whelan.

FA Premier

LIVERPOOL

Anfield Road, Liverpool 4. Telephone 051–263 2361. Clubcall: 0898 121184. Ticket and Match Information: 051–260 9999 (24-hour service) or 051–260 8680 (office hours) Credit Card bookings.

Ground Capacity: 45,054.

Record attendance: 61,905 v Wolverhampton W, FA Cup 4th rd, 2 February 1952.

Record receipts: £342,000 v Genoa, UEFA Cup, 4th rd 2nd leg, 18 March 1992.

Pitch measurements: 110yd × 75yd.

Chairman: D. R. Moores.

Directors: Sir J. W. Smith CBE, JP, DL, HON. LLD, J. T. Cross, N. White FSCA, T. D. Smith, P. B. Robinson, T. Saunders.

Vice-presidents: C. J. Hill, H. E. Roberts, W. D. Corkish FCA, R. Paisley OBE, HON MSC.

Team Manager: Graeme Souness. *Assistant Manager:* Roy Evans. *Coach:* Ron Moran.

Chief Executive/General Secretary: Peter Robinson. *Commercial Manager:* M. L. Turner.

Year Formed: 1892. *Turned Professional:* 1892. *Ltd Co.:* 1892.

Club Nickname: 'Reds' or 'Pool'.

Record League Victory: 10–1 v Rotherham T, Division 2, 18 February 1896 – Storer; Goldie, Wilkie; McCarthy, McQueen, Holmes; McVean (3), Ross (2), Allan (4), Becton (1), Bradshaw.

Record Cup Victory: 11–0 v Stromsgodset Drammen, ECWC 1st rd 1st leg, 17 September 1974 – Clemence; Smith (1), Lindsay (1p), Thompson (2), Cormack (1), Hughes (1), Boersma (2), Hall, Heighway (1), Kennedy (1), Callaghan (1).

Record Defeat: 1–9 v Birmingham C, Division 2, 11 December 1954.

Most League Points (2 for a win): 68, Division 1, 1978–79.

Most League Points (3 for a win): 90, Division 1, 1987–88.

Most League Goals: 106, Division 2, 1895–96.

Highest League Scorer in Season: Roger Hunt, 41, Division 2, 1961–62.

Most League Goals in Total Aggregate: Roger Hunt, 245, 1959–69.

Most Capped Player: Emlyn Hughes, 59 (62), England.

Most League Appearances: Ian Callaghan, 640, 1960–78.

Record Transfer Fee Received: £3,200,000 from Juventus for Ian Rush, June 1986.

Record Transfer Fee Paid: £2,900,000 to Derby Co for Dean Saunders, July 1991.

Football League Record: 1893 Elected to Division 2; 1894–95 Division 1; 1895–96 Division 2; 1896–1904 Division 1; 1904–05 Division 2; 1905–54 Division 1; 1954–62 Division 2; 1962–92 Division 1; 1992– FA Premier Division.

Honours: Football League: Division 1 – Champions 1900–01, 1905–06, 1921–22, 1922–23, 1946–47, 1963–64, 1965–66, 1972–73, 1975–76, 1976–77, 1978–79, 1979–80, 1981–82, 1982–83, 1983–84, 1985–86, 1987–88, 1989–90 (Liverpool have a record number of 18 League Championship wins); Runners-up 1898–99, 1909–10, 1968–69, 1973–74, 1974–75, 1977–78, 1984–85, 1986–87, 1988–89, 1990–91; Division 2 – Champions 1893–94, 1895–96, 1904–05, 1961–62. *FA Cup:* Winners 1965, 1974, 1986, 1989, 1992; Runners-up 1914, 1950, 1971, 1977, 1988; *Football League Cup:* Winners 1981, 1982, 1983, 1984; Runners-up 1977–78, 1986–87. *League Super Cup:* Winners 1985–86. **European Competitions:** *European Cup:* 1964–65, 1966–67, 1973–74, 1976–77 (winners), 1977–78 (winners), 1978–79, 1979–80, 1980–81 (winners), 1981–82, 1982–83, 1983–84 (winners), 1984–85 (runners-up); *European Cup-Winners' Cup:* 1965–66 (runners-up), 1971–72, 1974–75, 1992–93; *European Fairs Cup:* 1967–68, 1968–69, 1969–70, 1970–71; *UEFA Cup:* 1972–73 (winners), 1975–76 (winners), 1991–92; *Super Cup:* 1977 (winners), 1978, 1984; *World Club Championship:* 1981 (runners-up).

LIVERPOOL 1992—93 LEAGUE RECORD

Match No.	Date		Venue	Opponents	Result		H/T Score	Lg. Pos.	Goalscorers	Atten dance
1	Aug	16	A	Nottingham F	L	0-1	0-1	—		20,038
2		19	H	Sheffield U	W	2-1	1-1	—	Walters, Stewart	33,107
3		23	H	Arsenal	L	0-2	0-0	—		34,961
4		25	A	Ipswich T	D	2-2	1-0	—	Walters, Molby (pen)	20,109
5		29	A	Leeds U	D	2-2	1-1	16	Whelan, Molby (pen)	29,597
6	Sept	1	H	Southampton	D	1-1	0-0	—	Wright	30,024
7		5	H	Chelsea	W	2-1	1-0	14	Saunders, Redknapp	34,199
8		12	A	Sheffield U	L	0-1	0-1	15		20,632
9		19	A	Aston Villa	L	2-4	1-1	17	Walters, Rosenthal	37,863
10		26	H	Wimbledon	L	2-3	2-2	19	Molby (pen), McManaman	29,574
11	Oct	3	H	Sheffield W	W	1-0	0-0	15	Hutchison	35,785
12		18	A	Manchester U	D	2-2	2-0	—	Hutchison, Rush	33,243
13		25	A	Norwich C	W	4-1	2-1	—	Thomas, Hutchison, Burrows, Walters (pen)	36,318
14		31	A	Tottenham H	L	0-2	0-0	14		32,917
15	Nov	7	H	Middlesbrough	W	4-1	3-1	11	Rosenthal 2, McManaman, Rush	34,974
16		23	A	QPR	W	1-0	0-0	—	Rosenthal	21,056
17		28	H	Crystal Palace	W	5-0	3-0	8	McManaman 2, Marsh, Rosenthal, Hutchison	36,380
18	Dec	7	A	Everton	L	1-2	0-0	—	Wright	35,826
19		13	H	Blackburn R	W	2-1	0-0	—	Walters 2	43,668
20		19	A	Coventry C	L	1-5	0-1	10	Redknapp	19,779
21		28	H	Manchester C	D	1-1	0-1	11	Rush	43,037
22	Jan	9	H	Aston Villa	L	1-2	1-0	11	Barnes	40,826
23		16	A	Wimbledon	L	0-2	0-1	12		11,294
24		31	A	Arsenal	W	1-0	0-0	—	Barnes (pen)	27,580
25	Feb	6	H	Nottingham F	D	0-0	0-0	12		40,463
26		10	A	Chelsea	D	0-0	0-0	—		20,981
27		13	A	Southampton	L	1-2	0-1	15	Hutchison	17,216
28		20	H	Ipswich T	D	0-0	0-0	15		36,680
29		27	A	Sheffield W	D	1-1	1-0	15	Hutchison	33,964
30	Mar	6	H	Manchester U	L	1-2	0-1	15	Rush	44,374
31		10	H	QPR	W	1-0	0-0	—	Rush	30,370
32		13	A	Middlesbrough	W	2-1	1-1	14	Hutchison, Rush	22,463
33		20	H	Everton	W	1-0	0-0	13	Rosenthal	44,619
34		23	A	Crystal Palace	D	1-1	0-0	—	Rush	18,688
35	Apr	3	A	Blackburn R	L	1-4	0-3	13	Rush	15,032
36		10	H	Oldham Ath	W	1-0	0-0	13	Rush	36,129
37		12	A	Manchester C	D	1-1	0-1	12	Rush	28,098
38		17	H	Coventry C	W	4-0	2-0	8	Walters 3 (1 pen), Burrows	33,328
39		21	H	Leeds U	W	2-0	0-0	—	Barnes, Walters (pen)	34,992
40	May	1	A	Norwich C	L	0-1	0-0	7		20,610
41		5	A	Oldham Ath	L	2-3	1-3	—	Rush 2	15,381
42		8	H	Tottenham H	W	6-2	2-0	5	Rush 2, Barnes 2, Harkness, Walters (pen)	43,385

Final League Position: 6

GOALSCORERS

League (62):Rush 14, Walters 11 (4 pens), Hutchison 7, Rosenthal 6, Barnes 5 (1 pen), McManaman 4, Molby 3 (3 pens), Burrows 2, Redknapp 2, Wright 2, Harkness 1, Marsh 1, Saunders 1, Stewart 1, Thomas 1, Whelan 1.
Coca Cola Cup (13): Marsh 3 (3 pens), Hutchison 2, McManaman 2, Walters 2, Redknapp 1, Rosenthal 1, Rush 1, Wright 1.
FA Cup (2): Rush 1, own goal 1.

Match No.	James 29	Tanner 2 + 2	Burrows 29 + 1	Nicol 32	Whelan 17	Wright 32 + 1	Saunders 6	Stewart 21 + 3	Rush 31 + 1	Walters 26 + 8	Thomas 6 + 2	McManaman 27 + 4	Rosenthal 16 + 11	Jones R 30	Molby 8 + 2	Marsh 22 + 6	Harkness 9 + 1	Redknapp 27 + 2	Piechnik 15 + 1	Hutchison 27 + 4	Grobbelaar 5	Kozma — + 1	Hooper 8 + 1	Barnes 26 + 1	Bjornebye 11
1	1	2	3	4	5	6	7	8	9	10	11	12	14												
2	1		3	4	5	6	7	8		10	11	9	12	2											
3	1	8	3		5	6	7		10	11	9	12	2	4	14										
4	1		3		5	6	7	8	9	11		12		2	10	4									
5	1		3		5	6	7	8	9	12			2	10	14	4	11								
6	1		3		5	6		9	11	12	7		2	10		4	8								
7	1		3		5	6	7		9	12	11		2	10		4	8								
8	1		3	4	5	6		8	9	11		7		12	14	2	10								
9	1		3	4		6			11		7		10	8		5	2	9							
10			3			6			11		8	7	10	2		5	4	9	1	12					
11			3	4				8	9	11		7	12	2	10	5	6	1							
12	14		3	4					9		12	7	11	10	2	8	5	6	1						
13			3	4		12				8	11	7	9	2		10	5	6	1						
14	1	14	3		5		12	9	8	11	7			2		10	4	6							
15			3	4		11	9			7	10			2		8	5	6	1						
16			3	4		9				7	11	10		2		8	5	6		1			12		
17			3	4		12				7	9	11		2		8	5	6		1			10		
18			4	3		12	14			7	9	11		2		8	5	6		1			10		
19			4	3		9	12			7	6	11		2		8	5			1			10		
20					6			7	9	11		3		2		8	5	12		1			10	4	
21			4						9	11	7	3		2		8	5			1			10	6	
22						4	14	11	7	9	3			2		8	5	12		1			10	6	
23	1			6	4		7	12	3			2	14	8	5	9							10	11	
24	1		4	5	11	9		7	3			2	8	12									10	6	
25	1		4	5	11	9	12	7	3			2	8										10	6	
26	1		4	5	11	9		7	8	3		2		12									10	6	
27	1		4	5	11	9		7		3		2	12	8									10	6	
28	1		4	5	11	9	12	7		3	14	2		8									10	6	
29	1		4	5	11		9	7		3	12	2		8									10	6	
30	1	14	4	5	11	12	9	7		3		2		8									10	6	
31	1	11	4	6	5	9			7	12	3	2		8									10		
32	1	2	4	6	5	9	12		7	11	3			14	8								10		
33	1	2	4	6	5	9	11		7	12	14	3		8									10		
34	1	2	4	6		9	11	12	7		5	3		8									10		
35	1	3	4	6		9	11	12	7		2	5		8									10		
36	1	3	4	6	5	9	11		7	12	2			8									10		
37	1	3	4	6	5	9	11		7		2	12		8									10		
38	1	3	4	6	5	7	9	11		12	2			8									10		
39	1	3	4	6	5	7	9	11			2			8									10		
40	1	3	4		5	7	9	11		12	2			6	8			14					10		
41	1	3	4		5	7	9	11		12	2			6	14	8							10		
42			3	4		5		9	11		2			7	6		8	1					10		

Coca Cola Cup	Second Round	Chesterfield (h)		4-4
		(a)		4-1
	Third Round	Sheffield U (a)		0-0
		(h)		3-0
	Fourth Round	Crystal Palace (h)		1-1
		(a)		1-2
FA Cup	Third Round	Bolton W (a)		2-2
		(h)		0-2

LIVERPOOL

Player and Position	Ht	Wt	Date	Birth Place	Source	Clubs	League App	Gls
Goalkeepers								
Daniel Embleton	5 11	11 04	27 3 75	Liverpool	Trainee	Liverpool	—	—
Bruce Grobbelaar	6 1	13 00	6 10 57	Durban	Vancouver Whitecaps	Crewe Alex	24	1
					Vancouver Whitecaps	Liverpool	411	—
						Stoke C (loan)	4	—
Michael Hooper	6 2	13 05	10 2 64	Bristol		Bristol C	1	—
						Wrexham (loan)	20	—
						Wrexham	14	—
						Liverpool	51	—
						Leicester C (loan)	14	—
David James	6 4	14 13	1 8 70	Welwyn	Trainee	Watford	89	—
						Liverpool	29	—
Defenders								
Stig Inge Bjornebye	5 10	11 09	11 12 69	Norway	Rosenborg	Liverpool	11	—
Lee Bryden	5 11	11 00	15 11 74	Stockton	Trainee	Liverpool	—	—
David Burrows	5 10	11 08	25 10 68	Dudley	Apprentice	WBA	46	1
						Liverpool	142	3
Rob Jones	5 8	11 00	5 11 71	Wrexham	Trainee	Crewe Alex	75	2
						Liverpool	58	—
Rodney McAree	5 7	10 02	19 8 74	Dungannon	Trainee	Liverpool	—	—
Dominic Matteo	6 1	11 10	28 4 74	Dumfries	Trainee	Liverpool	—	—
Torben Piechnik	6 0	12 04	21 5 63	Copenhagen	Copenhagen	Liverpool	16	—
John Scott	5 8	10 09	9 3 75	Aberdeen	Trainee	Liverpool	—	—
Nick Tanner	6 2	13 07	24 5 65	Bristol	Mangotsfield	Bristol R	107	3
						Liverpool	40	1
						Norwich C (loan)	6	—
						Swindon T (loan)	7	—
Tom White*	5 8	11 08	6 11 74	Auckland NZ		Liverpool	—	—
Mark Wright	6 2	13 03	1 8 63	Dorchester	Amateur	Oxford U	10	—
						Southampton	170	7
						Derby Co	144	10
						Liverpool	54	2
Midfield								
Phil Charnock	5 11	11 02	14 2 75	Southport	Trainee	Liverpool	—	—
Ian Frodsham	5 09	11 00	22 12 75	Liverpool	Trainee	Liverpool	—	—
Stuart Gelling*	5 7	10 04	8 9 73	Liverpool	Trainee	Liverpool	—	—
Steve Harkness	5 10	11 02	27 8 71	Carlisle	Trainee	Carlisle U	13	—
						Liverpool	21	1
Craig Johnston	5 8	10 13	8 12 60	South Africa	Lake McQuarrie	Middlesbrough	64	16
						Liverpool	190	30
Marc Kenny*	5 11	11 00	17 9 73	Dublin	Trainee	Liverpool	—	—
Istvan Kozma	5 9	12 00	3 12 64	Paszto, Hungary	Bordeaux	Dunfermline Ath	90	8
						Liverpool	6	—
Jan Molby	6 1	14 07	4 7 63	Kolding	Ajax	Liverpool	193	40
Ashley Neal	6 00	11 10	16 12 74	Liverpool	Trainee	Liverpool	—	—
Terry Nestor	5 10	11 04	22 10 74	Warrington	Trainee	Liverpool	—	—
Steve Nicol	5 10	12 00	11 12 61	Irvine	Ayr U BC	Ayr U	70	7
						Liverpool	308	35
Paul O'Donnell	5 10	11 03	6 10 75	Limerick	Trainee	Liverpool	—	—
Scott Paterson	5 11	12 00	13 5 72	Aberdeen	Cove Rangers	Liverpool	—	—
Jamie Redknapp	6 0	12 00	25 6 73	Barton on Sea	Trainee	Bournemouth	13	—
						Liverpool	35	3
Mark Stalker	5 10	11 05	24 9 74	Liverpool	Trainee	Liverpool	—	—

LIVERPOOL

Colours: All red with white markings. **Change colours:** Racing green with white markings.

Foundation: But for a dispute between Everton FC and their landlord at Anfield in 1892, there may never have been a Liverpool club. This dispute persuaded the majority of Evertonians to quit Anfield for Goodison Park, leaving the landlord, Mr. John Houlding, to form a new club. He originally tried to retain the name "Everton" but when this failed, he founded Liverpool Association FC on 15 March, 1892.

First Football League game: 2 September, 1893, Division 2, v Middlesbrough Ironopolis (a) W 2-0 – McOwen; Hannah, McLean; Henderson, McQue (1), McBride; Gordon, McVean (1), M. McQueen, Stott, H. McQueen.

Did you know: On 26 December 1981 Liverpool lost 3-1 at home to Manchester City and were 12th in Division 1 with 24 points from 17 games. But they lost only twice in the remaining 25 matches to achieve their 13th championship title.

Managers (and Secretary-Managers)
W. E. Barclay 1892–96, Tom Watson 1896–1915, David Ashworth 1920–22, Matt McQueen 1923–28, George Patterson 1928–36 (continued as secretary), George Kay 1936–51, Don Welsh 1951–56, Phil Taylor 1956–59, Bill Shankly 1959–74, Bob Paisley 1974–83, Joe Fagan 1983–85, Kenny Dalglish 1985–91, Graeme Souness April 1991–.

Player and Position	Ht	Wt	Birth Date	Birth Place	Source	Clubs	League App	Gls
Michael Thomas	5 9	12 06	24 8 67	Lambeth	Apprentice	Arsenal	163	24
						Portsmouth (loan)	3	—
						Liverpool	25	4
Ronnie Whelan	5 9	10 13	25 9 61	Dublin	Home Farm	Liverpool	339	45
Forwards								
John Barnes	5 11	12 07	7 11 63	Jamaica	Sudbury Court	Watford	233	65
						Liverpool	179	67
Tony Cousins*	5 9	11 10	25 8 69	Dublin	Dundalk	Liverpool	—	—
						Hereford U (loan)	3	—
Robbie Fowler	5 9	11 08	9 4 75	Liverpool	Trainee	Liverpool	—	—
Don Hutchison	6 2	11 08	9 5 71	Gateshead	Trainee	Hartlepool U	24	2
						Liverpool	34	7
Lee Jones	5 8	10 08	29 5 73	Wrexham	Trainee	Wrexham	39	10
						Liverpool	—	—
Steve McManaman	6 0	10 06	11 2 72	Liverpool	School	Liverpool	63	9
Mike Marsh	5 8	11 00	21 7 69	Liverpool	Kirkby T	Liverpool	67	1
Ronny Rosenthal	5 11	12 00	11 10 63	Haifa	Standard Liege	Luton T (loan)	—	—
						Liverpool (loan)	8	7
						Liverpool	63	14
Ian Rush	6 0	12 06	20 10 61	St. Asaph	Apprentice	Chester	34	14
						Liverpool	224	139
						Juventus	29	7
						Liverpool	147	59
Paul Stewart	5 11	11 03	7 10 64	Manchester	Apprentice	Blackpool	201	56
						Manchester C	51	26
						Tottenham H	131	28
						Liverpool	24	1
Mark Walters	5 9	11 08	12 1 61	Birmingham	Apprentice	Aston Villa	181	39
						Rangers	106	32
						Liverpool	59	14

Trainees
Dennis, Wayne A; Fallon, Sean P. F; Jones, Stuart J; Li, Christian; Morris, Stephen; Robinson, Paul J; Snape, Paul F.

**Non-Contract
Robinson, David J.

Associated Schoolboys
Brazier, Philip; Carragher, James L; Cassidy, Jamie; Cooling, Michael J; Hawkings, David T; Larmour, David J; Lyonette, Paul M; Moore, Michael A; Newby, Jon P. R; Prior, Lee J; Proctor, Paul; Quinn, Mark P; Quinn, Stuart; Roberts, Gareth W; Stannard, John F; Thompson, David A.

Associated Schoolboys who have accepted the club's offer of a Traineeship/Contract
Brenchley, Scott A; Brunskill, Iain R; Clegg, David L; Harris, Andrew D. D; Kinney, Westley M; Wilkinson, Martin D; Wyke, Stanley.

LUTON TOWN 1992–93   *Back row (left to right):* Darren Salton, Jamie Campbell, Des Linton, Alec Chamberlain, Marvin Johnson, Jurgen Sommer, David Greene, John Dreyer, Chris Kamara.
Centre row: John Moore (Coach), Julian James, Paul Telfer, Tim Allpress, Kurt Nogan, Richard Harvey, Trevor Peake, Brian Owen (Physio).
Front row: Steve Claridge, Phil Gray, David Pleat (Manager), Ceri Hughes, Jason Rees, Scott Oakes.

Division 1   LUTON TOWN

Kenilworth Road Stadium, 1 Maple Rd, Luton, Beds. LU4 8AW.
Telephone, Offices: Luton (0582) 411622; Ticket Office: (0582)
416976. Credit Hotline (0582) 30748 (24 hrs); Banqueting:
(0582) 411526. Special Loupe system for deaf and blind in our
handicapped area. Soccer Line 0839 664466.

Ground capacity: 13,449.

Record attendance: 30,069 v Blackpool, FA Cup 6th rd replay,
4 March 1959.

Record receipts: £77,000 v Oxford U, Littlewoods Cup semi-
final, 28 February 1988.

Pitch measurements: 110yd × 72yd.

President: E. Pearson.

Chairman: R. J. Smith. *Managing Director:* D. A. Kohler.

Secretary: J. K. Smylie.

Directors: P. Collins, E. S. Pearson, H. Richardson, N. Terry.

Commercial Manager: Andy King.

Manager: David Pleat. *Assistant Manager:* John Moore.

Reserve team coach: Wayne Turner. *Youth team coach:* Terry Westley.

Physio: Andy McDade.

Year Formed: 1885. *Turned Professional:* 1890. *Ltd Co.:* 1897.

Club Nickname: 'The Hatters'.

Previous Grounds: 1885, Excelsior, Dallow Lane; 1897, Dunstable Road; 1905, Kenilworth
Road.

Record League Victory: 12–0 v Bristol R, Division 3 (S), 13 April 1936 – Dolman; Mackey,
Smith; Finlayson, Nelson, Godfrey; Rich, Martin (1), Payne (10), Roberts (1), Stephenson.

Record Cup Victory: 9–0 v Clapton, FA Cup, 1st rd (replay after abandoned game), 30
November 1927 – Abbott; Kingham, Graham; Black, Rennie, Fraser; Pointon, Yardley (4),
Reid (2), Woods (1), Dennis (2).

Record Defeat: 0–9 v Small Heath, Division 2, 12 November 1898.

Most League Points (2 for a win): 66, Division 4, 1967–68.

Most League Points (3 for a win): 88, Division 2, 1981–82.

Most League Goals: 103, Division 3 (S), 1936–37.

Highest League Scorer in Season: Joe Payne, 55, Division 3 (S), 1936–37.

Most League Goals in Total Aggregate: Gordon Turner, 243, 1949–64.

Most Capped Player: Mal Donaghy, 58 (84), Northern Ireland.

Most League Appearances: Bob Morton, 494, 1948–64.

Record Transfer Fee Received: £1,500,000 from Nottingham F for Kingsley Black, August
1991.

Record Transfer Fee Paid: £850,000 to Odense for Lars Elstrup, August 1989.

Football League Record: 1897 Elected to Division 2; 1900 Failed re-election; 1920 Division
3; 1921–37 Division 3 (S); 1937–55 Division 2; 1955–60 Division 1; 1960–63 Division 2;
1963–65 Division 3; 1965–68 Division 4; 1968–70 Division 3; 1970–74 Division 2; 1974–75
Division 1; 1975–82 Division 2; 1982– Division 1.

Honours: Football League: Division 1 best season: 7th, 1986–87; Division 2 – Champions
1981–82; Runners-up 1954–55, 1973–74; Division 3 – Runners-up 1969–70; Division 4 –
Champions 1967–68; Division 3 (S) – Champions 1936–37; Runners-up 1935–36. *FA Cup:*
Runners-up 1959. *Football League Cup:* Winners 1987–88; Runners-up 1988–89. *Simod
Cup:* Runners-up 1988.

LUTON TOWN 1992—93 LEAGUE RECORD

Match No.	Date		Venue	Opponents	Result		H/T Score	Lg. Pos.	Goalscorers	Atten dance
1	Aug 15	A		Leicester C	L	1-2	1-1	—	Campbell	17,428
2		22	H	Bristol C	L	0-3	0-1	22		7926
3		29	A	Charlton Ath	D	0-0	0-0	21		6302
4	Sept	2	A	Newcastle U	L	0-2	0-2	—		27,054
5		5	H	Tranmere R	D	3-3	2-3	23	Claridge, Linton, Oakes	6801
6		13	A	Brentford	W	2-1	0-0	—	James, Gray	7310
7		19	H	Birmingham C	D	1-1	0-0	21	Claridge (pen)	8481
8		26	A	Notts Co	D	0-0	0-0	21		5992
9	Oct	3	H	Portsmouth	L	1-4	1-3	22	Dreyer	7954
10		10	A	Barnsley	L	0-3	0-3	23		5261
11		17	H	Derby Co	L	1-3	0-1	23	Johnson	8848
12		24	A	Peterborough U	W	3-2	3-1	22	Gray 2, Telfer	7125
13		31	H	Southend U	D	2-2	2-0	22	James, Gray	7256
14	Nov	3	A	Cambridge U	D	3-3	1-0	—	Oakes, Gray 2	5716
15		7	H	Grimsby T	L	1-4	0-3	22	Gray	6928
16		14	A	Oxford U	L	0-4	0-2	22		5760
17		21	H	Millwall	D	1-1	1-0	23	Gray	8371
18		29	H	Watford	W	2-0	0-0	—	Benjamin, Oakes	8341
19	Dec	5	A	Bristol R	L	0-2	0-2	22		6245
20		12	A	Wolverhampton W	W	2-1	1-1	19	Gray 2	13,932
21		19	H	Sunderland	D	0-0	0-0	20		8286
22		28	A	West Ham U	D	2-2	0-0	20	Hughes, Dreyer	18,786
23	Jan	9	A	Birmingham C	L	1-2	1-1	22	Hughes	9601
24		16	H	Notts Co	D	0-0	0-0	22		6729
25		27	H	Newcastle U	D	0-0	0-0	—		10,237
26		30	A	Bristol C	D	0-0	0-0	24		8877
27	Feb	6	H	Leicester C	W	2-0	1-0	21	Johnson, Gray	9140
28		9	H	Brentford	D	0-0	0-0	—		7248
29		13	A	Tranmere R	W	2-0	1-0	19	Gray, Johnson	8723
30		20	H	Charlton Ath	W	1-0	0-0	19	Gray	8443
31		27	H	Barnsley	D	2-2	1-0	19	Dixon, Gray (pen)	7595
32	Mar	6	A	Portsmouth	L	1-2	1-1	20	Gray	10,457
33		9	H	Oxford U	W	3-1	1-1	—	Preece, Gray, Oakes	6687
34		13	A	Grimsby T	L	1-3	0-1	18	Gray	5193
35		17	H	Swindon T	D	0-0	0-0	—		8902
36		20	H	Bristol R	D	1-1	0-0	17	Maddison (og)	7717
37		24	A	Millwall	L	0-1	0-1	—		8286
38		27	H	Cambridge U	W	2-0	1-0	17	Dixon, Oakes	8077
39	Apr	3	A	Watford	D	0-0	0-0	17		10,656
40		7	H	Wolverhampton W	D	1-1	0-0	—	Gray	7948
41		10	A	Swindon T	L	0-1	0-0	21		10,934
42		13	H	West Ham U	W	2-0	0-0	—	Gray (pen), Williams	10,959
43		17	A	Sunderland	D	2-2	0-1	16	Preece, Telfer	16,493
44		24	A	Derby Co	D	1-1	1-0	17	Preece	13,741
45	May	1	H	Peterborough U	D	0-0	0-0	17		10,011
46		8	A	Southend U	L	1-2	1-2	20	Dixon	11,042

Final League Position: 20

GOALSCORERS

League (48): Gray 19 (2 pens), Oakes 5, Dixon 3, Johnson 3, Preece 3, Claridge 2 (1 pen), Dreyer 2, Hughes 2, James 2, Telfer 2, Benjamin 1, Campbell 1, Linton 1, Williams 1, own goal 1.
Coca Cola Cup (4): Claridge 3, Preece 1.
FA Cup (3): Gray 1, Hughes 1, Telfer 1.

Petterson 14	Linton 17 + 3	James 43	Kamara 21	Peake 40	Dreyer 38	Oakes 25 + 19	Hughes 26 + 3	Gray 45	Preece 43	Campbell 2 + 7	Claridge 15 + 1	Johnson 38 + 2	Rees 29 + 3	Salton 15	Matthew 3 + 2	Telfer 30 + 2	Chamberlain 32	Benjamin 5 + 5	Williams 7 + 15	Dixon 16 + 1	Greene 1	Harvey 1	Match No.
1	2	3	4	5	6	7	8	9	10	11	12												1
1	2	3	4	5	6	12	8	9	10	11	7	14											2
1	2	3	4	5	6	12	8	9	10	11	7												3
1	2	3	4	5	6	12	8	9	10	11	7												4
1	2	3	4	5	6	12	8	9	10	11	7												5
1	2	3	4	5	6	7	8	9	10	11													6
1	2	3	4	5	6	12	8	9	10	11	7	14											7
1	2	3	4	5	6	12	8	9	10	11	7	14											8
1	2	3	4	5	6	12	8	9	10	11	7	14											9
1	2	3	4	5	6	12	8	9	10	11	7	14											10
1	2	3	4	5	6	12	8	9	10	11	7												11
1	2	3	4	5	6	12	8	9	10	11	7												12
1	2	3	4	5	6	12	8	9	10	11	7												13
1	2	3	4	5	6	7	8	9	10	11													14
1	2	3	4	5	6	12	8	9	10	11	7	14											15
1	2	3	4	5	6	12	8	9	10	11	7												16
	2	3		5	6	12	8	9	10	11		14	4			7	1						17
	2	3		5	6	12	8	9	10	11			4			7	1						18
14	2	3		5	6	12	8	9	10	11			4			7	1						19
14	2	3		5	6	12	8	9	10	11			4			7	1						20
14	2	3		5	6	12	8	9	10	11			4			7	1						21
	2	3		5	6	12	8	9	10	11		14	4			7	1						22
	2	3		5	6	12	8	9	10	11			4			7	1						23
	2	3		5	6	12	8	9	10	11		14	4			7	1						24
	2	3		5	6	12	8	9	10	11		14	4			7	1						25
	2	3		5	6	12	8	9	10	11		14	4			7	1						26
	2	3		5	6	12	8	9	10	11		14	4			7	1						27
	2	3		5	6		8	9	10	11			4			7	1						28
	2	3		5	6	12	8	9	10	11			4			7	1						29
	2	3		5	6		8	9	10	11			4			7	1						30
	2	3		5	6	12	8	9	10	11			4			7	1						31
	2	3		5	6	12	8	9	10	11		14	4			7	1						32
	2	3		5	6	12	8	9	10	11			4			7	1						33
	2	3		5	6	12	8	9	10	11		14	4			7	1						34
	2	3		5	6	12	8	9	10	11		14	4			7	1						35
	2	3		5	6	12	8	9	10	11			4			7	1						36
	2	3		5	6	12	8	9	10	11		14	4			7	1						37
	2	3		5	6		8	9	10	11			4			7	1						38
	2	3		5	6	12	8	9	10	11			4			7	1						39
	2	3		5	6	12	8	9	10	11		14	4			7	1						40
	2	3		5	6	12	8	9	10	11			4			7	1						41
	2	3		5	6	12	8	9	10	11		14	4			7	1						42
	2	3		5	6	12	8	9	10	11		14	4			7	1						43
	2	3		5	6		8	9	10	11			4			7	1						44
	2	3		5	6	12	8	9	10	11			4			7	1						45
	2	3		5	6	12	8	9	10	11		14	4			7	1						46

Coca Cola Cup	Second Round	Plymouth Arg (h)	2-2
		(a)	2-3
FA Cup	Third Round	Bristol C (h)	2-0
	Fourth Round	Derby Co (h)	1-5

LUTON TOWN

Player and Position	Ht	Wt	Date	Birth Place	Source	Clubs	League App	Gls
Goalkeepers								
Alec Chamberlain*	6 2	13 01	20 6 64	March		Ipswich T	—	—
						Colchester U	184	—
						Everton	—	—
						Tranmere R (loan)	15	—
						Luton T	138	—
						Chelsea (loan)	—	—
Andrew Petterson	6 1	14 10	26 9 69	Fremantle		Luton T	14	—
						Swindon T (loan)	—	—
						Ipswich T (loan)	—	—
						Ipswich T (loan)	1	—
Jurgen Sommer	6 4	15 12	27 2 64	New York		Luton T	—	—
						Brighton (loan)	1	—
						Torquay U (loan)	10	—
Defenders								
Tim Allpress*	6 0	12 00	27 1 71	Hitchin	Trainee	Luton T	1	—
						Preston NE (loan)	9	—
John Dreyer	6 1	11 06	11 6 63	Alnwick	Wallingford T	Oxford U	60	2
						Torquay U (loan)	5	—
						Fulham (loan)	12	2
						Luton T	174	10
David Greene	6 2	13 05	26 10 73	Luton	Trainee	Luton T	1	—
Richard Harvey	5 10	11 10	17 4 69	Letchworth	Apprentice	Luton T	105	2
						Blackpool (loan)	5	—
Marvin Johnson	6 0	12 03	29 10 68	Wembley	Apprentice	Luton T	103	3
Des Linton	6 1	13 02	5 9 71	Birmingham	Trainee	Leicester C	11	—
						Luton T	23	1
Trevor Peake	6 0	12 10	10 2 57	Nuneaton	Nuneaton Bor	Lincoln C	171	7
						Coventry C	278	6
						Luton T	78	—
Midfield								
Ceri Hughes	5 10	11 05	26 2 71	Pontypridd	Trainee	Luton T	65	3
Julian James	5 10	11 10	22 3 70	Tring	Trainee	Luton T	112	6
						Preston NE (loan)	6	—
Chris Kamara	6 1	12 00	25 12 57	Middlesbrough	Apprentice	Portsmouth	63	7
						Swindon T	147	21
						Portsmouth	11	—
						Brentford	152	28
						Swindon T	87	6
						Stoke C	60	5
						Leeds U	20	1
						Luton T	49	—
						Sheffield U (loan)	8	—
						Middlesbrough (loan)	5	—
David Preece	5 6	11 05	28 5 63	Bridgnorth	Apprentice	Walsall	111	5
						Luton T	265	12
Jason Rees	5 5	9 10	22 12 69	Pontypridd	Trainee	Luton T	72	—
Aaron Skelton	5 10	11 05	22 11 74	Welwyn Garden	Trainee	Luton T	—	—
Paul Telfer	5 9	11 06	21 10 71	Edinburgh	Trainee	Luton T	53	3
Anthony Thorpe			10 4 74	Leicester		Luton T	—	—
Forwards								
Ian Benjamin	5 11	13 01	11 12 61	Nottingham	Apprentice	Sheffield U	5	3
						WBA	2	—
						Notts Co	—	—
						Peterborough U	80	14

LUTON TOWN

Colours: White shirts with royal blue and orange stripe on collar, sleeves and waist, royal blue shorts with white and orange trim, white stockings with royal blue and orange turnover. **Change colours:** Royal blue shirts with white and orange trim, white shorts with royal blue and orange trim, royal blue stockings with white and orange turnover.

Foundation: Formed by an amalgamation of two leading local clubs, Wanderers and Excelsior a works team, at a meeting in Luton Town Hall in April 1885. The Wanderers had three months earlier changed their name to Luton Town Wanderers and did not take too kindly to the formation of another Town club but were talked around at this meeting. Wanderers had already appeared in the FA Cup and the new club entered in its inaugural season.

First Football League game: 4 September, 1897, Division 2, v Leicester Fosse (a) D 1–1 – Williams; McCartney, McEwen; Davies, Stewart, Docherty; Gallacher, Coupar, Birch, McInnes, Ekins (1).

Did you know: On 20 February 1993, Luton Town equalled a 70 year old club record by completing seven matches without conceding goal after beating Charlton Athletic 1-0 in a Division 1 match.

Managers (and Secretary-Managers)
Charlie Green 1901–28*, George Thomson 1925, John McCartney 1927–29, George Kay 1929–31, Harold Wightman 1931–35, Ted Liddell 1936–38, Neil McBain 1938–39, George Martin 1939–47, Dally Duncan 1947–58, Syd Owen 1959–60, Sam Bartram 1960–62, Bill Harvey 1962–64, George Martin 1965–66, Allan Brown 1966–68, Alec Stock 1968–72, Harry Haslam 1972–78, David Pleat 1978–86, John Moore 1986–87, Ray Harford 1987–89, Jim Ryan 1900–91, David Pleat June 1991–.

Player and Position	Ht	Wt	Date	Birth Place	Source	Clubs	League App	Gls
						Northampton T	150	59
						Cambridge U	25	2
						Chester C	22	2
						Exeter C	32	4
						Southend U	122	33
						Luton T	10	1
Jamie Campbell	6 1	11 03	21 10 72	Birmingham	Trainee	Luton T	20	1
Steve Flain*			24 11 73	Herts	Welwyn Garden C	Luton T	—	—
Philip Gray	5 10	12 03	2 10 68	Belfast	Apprentice	Tottenham H	9	—
						Barnsley (loan)	3	—
						Fulham (loan)	3	—
						Luton T	59	22
John Hartson	5 11	11 13	5 4 75	Swansea	Trainee	Luton T	—	—
Paul Murray*	5 10	11 00	12 10 73	Henley	Trainee	Luton T	—	—
Scott Oakes	5 11	11 04	5 8 72	Leicester	Trainee	Leicester C	3	—
						Luton T	65	7
Darren Salton	6 2	13 00	16 3 72	Edinburgh	Trainee	Luton T	18	—
Martin Williams	5 9	11 12	12 7 73	Luton	Leicester C	Luton T	23	1

Trainees
Brittain, Vincent J; Butler, Neal C; Campbell, Lee A; Gibb, Darren W; Jukes, Andrew; Kuntz, Trevor P. J; McDonagh, Patrick; Philip, Richard W; Rioch, Gregor J; Ryan, Neil; Simpson, Gary J; Woolgar, Matthew.

**Non-Contract
Gentle, Justin.

Associated Schoolboys
Childs, Christopher; Curtin, Mark D; Delegate, Gavin C; Douglas, Stuart A; Edgeworth, Paul T; Flinn, Gary; Hartwig, Scott; Jenner, Roger A; Johnson, Simon K; Jones, Ian; Kester, Alan; Linnell, Craig R; Mumford, Peter M; Quince, Jason; Thomas, Ricky; Webb, Nicholas M.

Associated Schoolboys who have accepted the club's offer of a Traineeship/Contract
Davis, Kelvin G; Goodridge, Steven J; Issott, Gary D; McLaren, Paul A; Palmer, Stephen; Power, Daniel J; Woodford, Jamie.

**Non-Contract Players who are retained must be re-signed before they are eligible to play in League matches.

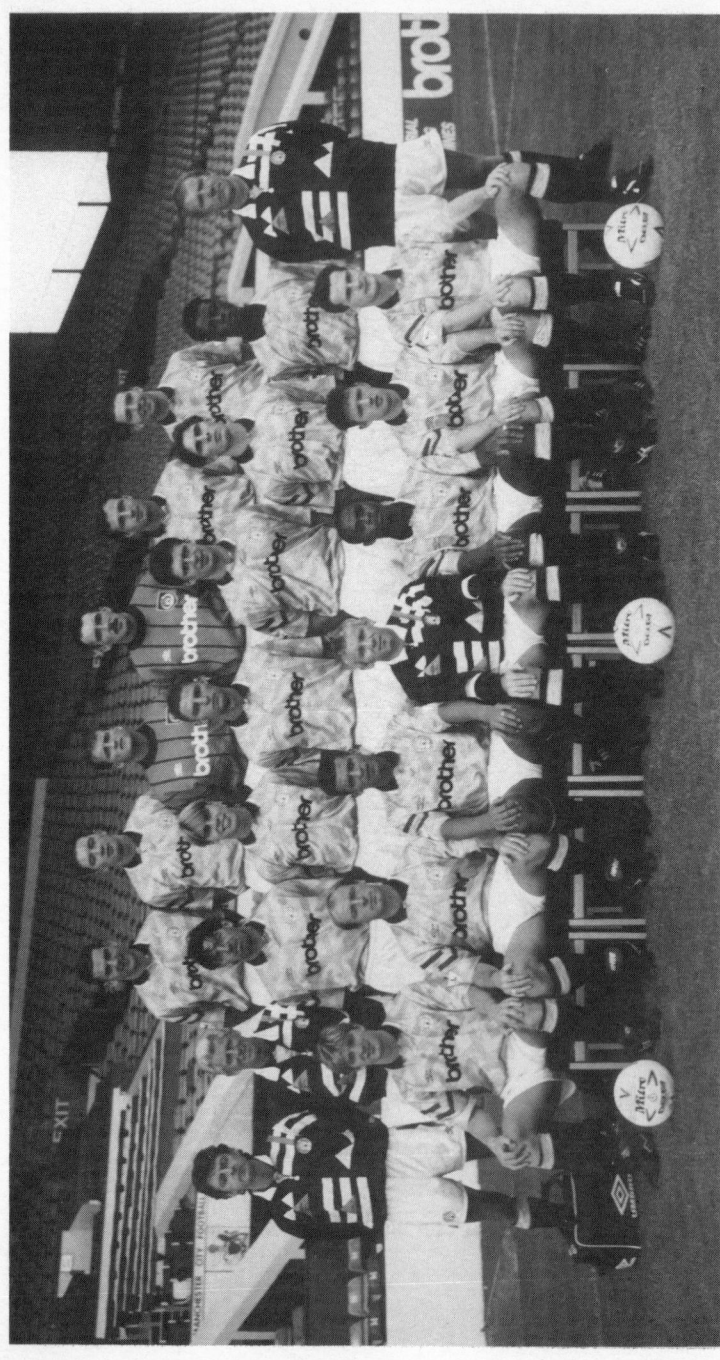

MANCHESTER CITY 1992–93 *Back row (left to right):* David White, David Brightwell, Martyn Margetson, Tony Coton, Andy Hill, Mark Brennan. *Centre row:* Eamonn Salmon (Physio), Tony Book (First Team Coach), Rick Holden, Garry Flitcroft, Michel Vonk, Niall Quinn, Paul Lake, Adrian Mike, Sam Ellis (Assistant Manager), Peter Reid (Player/Manager), Fitzroy Simpson, Michael Quigley, Mike Sheron. *Front row:* Ian Brightwell, Steve McMahon, Keith Curle, Peter Reid (Player/Manager), Fitzroy Simpson, Michael Quigley, Mike Sheron. (*Picture courtesy of Manchester Evening News*)

FA Premier

MANCHESTER CITY

Maine Road, Moss Side, Manchester M14 7WN. Telephone 061–226 1191/2. Ticket Office: 061–226 2224. Dial-a-Seat: 061–227 9229. Development Office: 061–226 3143. Clubcall: 0891 121191. Ticketcall: 0891 121591.

Ground capacity: 39,800.

Record attendance: 84,569 v Stoke C, FA Cup 6th rd, 3 March 1934 (British record for any game outside London or Glasgow).

Record receipts: £469,419 Manchester U v Oldham Ath, FA Cup semi-final, 8 April 1990.

Pitch measurements: 118yd × 76yd.

Chairman: P. J. Swales. *Vice-charman:* F. Pye. *Directors:* I. L. G. Niven, C. B. Muir OBE, A. Thomas, G. Doyle, W. A. Miles, B. Turnbull, J. Greibach.

General Secretary: J. B. Halford. *Commercial Manager:* P. Critchley.

General Manager: Jimmy Frizzell. *Player-manager:* Peter Reid. *First team coach:* Tony Book. *Assistant Manager:* Sam Ellis. *Physio:* Eamonn Salmon.

Year Formed: 1887 as Ardwick FC; 1894 as Manchester City.

Turned Professional: 1887 as Ardwick FC. *Ltd Co.:* 1894. *Club Nickname:* Blues The Citizens.

Previous Names: 1887–94, Ardwick FC (formed through the amalgamation of West Gorton and Gorton Athletic, the latter having been formed in 1880).

Previous Grounds: 1880–81, Clowes Street; 1881–82, Kirkmanshulme Cricket Ground; 1882–84, Queens Road; 1884–87, Pink Bank Lane; 1887–1923, Hyde Road (1894–1923, as City); 1923, Maine Road.

Record League Victory: 10–1 Huddersfield T, Division 2, 7 November 1987 – Nixon; Gidman, Hinchcliffe, Clements, Lake, Redmond, White (3), Stewart (3), Adcock (3), McNab (1) Simpson.

Record Cup Victory: 10–1 v Swindon T, FA Cup, 4th rd, 29 January 1930 – Barber; Felton, McCloy; Barrass, Cowan, Heinemann; Toseland, Marshall (5), Tait (3), Johnson (1), Brook (1).

Record Defeat: 1–9 v Everton, Division 1, 3 September 1906.

Most League Points (2 for a win): 62, Division 2, 1946–47.

Most League Points (3 for a win): 82, Division 2, 1988–89.

Most League Goals: 108, Division 2, 1926–27.

Highest League Scorer in Season: Tommy Johnson, 38, Division 1, 1928–29.

Most League Goals in Total Aggregate: Tommy Johnson, 158, 1919–30.

Most Capped Player: Colin Bell, 48, England.

Most League Appearances: Alan Oakes, 565, 1959–76.

Record Transfer Fee Received: £1,700,000 from Tottenham H for Paul Stewart, June 1988.

Record Transfer Fee Paid: £2,500,000 to Wimbledon for Keith Curle, August 1991.

Football League Record: 1892 Ardwick elected founder member of Division 2; 1894 Newly-formed Manchester C elected to Division 2; Division 1 1899–1902, 1903–09, 1910–26, 1928–38, 1947–50, 1951–63, 1966–83, 1985–87, 1989–92; Division 2 1902–03, 1909–10, 1926–28, 1938–47, 1950–51, 1963–66, 1983–85, 1987–89; 1992– FA Premier League.

Honours: Football League: Division 1 – Champions 1936–37, 1967–68; Runners-up 1903–04, 1920–21, 1976–77; Division 2 – Champions 1898–99, 1902–03, 1909–10, 1927–28, 1946–47, 1965–66; Runners-up 1895–96, 1950–51, 1987–88. *FA Cup:* Winners 1904, 1934, 1956, 1969; Runners-up 1926, 1933, 1955, 1981. *Football League Cup:* Winners 1970, 1976; Runners-up 1973–74. **European Competitions:** *European Cup:* 1968–69. *European Cup-Winners' Cup:* 1969–70 (winners), 1970–71. *UEFA Cup:* 1972–73, 1976–77, 1977–78, 1978–79.

MANCHESTER CITY 1992—93 LEAGUE RECORD

Match No.	Date	Venue	Opponents		Result	H/T Score	Lg. Pos.	Goalscorers	Atten dance
1	Aug 17	H	QPR	D	1-1	1-0	—	White	24,471
2	19	A	Middlesbrough	L	0-2	0-2	—		15,369
3	22	A	Blackburn R	L	0-1	0-0	19		19,433
4	26	H	Norwich C	W	3-1	1-0	—	White 2, McMahon	23,182
5	29	H	Oldham Ath	D	3-3	3-3	15	Quinn, Vonk, White	27,288
6	Sept 1	H	Wimbledon	W	1-0	0-0	—	White	4714
7	5	A	Sheffield W	W	3-0	1-0	5	White 2, Vonk	27,169
8	12	H	Middlesbrough	L	0-1	0-1	8		25,244
9	20	H	Chelsea	L	0-1	0-1	—		22,420
10	28	A	Arsenal	L	0-1	0-1	—		21,504
11	Oct 3	H	Nottingham F	D	2-2	1-0	12	Holden, Simpson	22,571
12	17	A	Crystal Palace	D	0-0	0-0	14		14,005
13	24	H	Southampton	W	1-0	0-0	12	Sheron	20,089
14	31	A	Everton	W	3-1	2-0	9	Sheron 2, White	20,242
15	Nov 7	H	Leeds U	W	4-0	2-0	7	Sheron, White, Hill, Brightwell I	27,255
16	21	A	Coventry C	W	3-2	0-1	6	Sheron, Quinn, Curle (pen)	14,590
17	28	A	Tottenham H	L	0-1	0-0	7		25,496
18	Dec 6	A	Manchester U	L	1-2	0-1	—	Quinn	35,408
19	12	A	Ipswich T	L	1-3	1-0	11	Flitcroft	16,833
20	19	H	Aston Villa	D	1-1	0-1	11	Flitcroft	23,525
21	26	H	Sheffield U	W	2-0	1-0	9	White 2	27,455
22	28	A	Liverpool	D	1-1	1-0	10	Quinn	43,037
23	Jan 9	A	Chelsea	W	4-2	2-0	8	White, Sheron 2, Sinclair (og)	15,939
24	16	H	Arsenal	L	0-1	0-0	9		25,041
25	26	A	Oldham Ath	W	1-0	0-0	—	Quinn	14,903
26	30	H	Blackburn R	W	3-2	1-2	6	Sheron, Curle (pen), White	29,122
27	Feb 6	A	QPR	D	1-1	0-0	7	Sheron	13,003
28	20	A	Norwich C	L	1-2	0-2	10	Sheron	16,386
29	23	H	Sheffield W	L	1-2	0-0	—	Quinn	23,619
30	27	A	Nottingham F	W	2-0	1-0	9	White, Flitcroft	25,956
31	Mar 10	H	Coventry C	W	1-0	1-0	—	Flitcroft	20,092
32	13	A	Leeds U	L	0-1	0-1	7		30,840
33	20	H	Manchester U	D	1-1	0-0	7	Quinn	37,136
34	24	A	Tottenham H	L	1-3	0-2	—	Sheron	27,247
35	Apr 3	H	Ipswich T	W	3-1	0-1	5	Quinn, Holden, Vonk	20,680
36	9	A	Sheffield U	D	1-1	1-0	—	Pemberton (og)	18,231
37	12	H	Liverpool	D	1-1	1-0	8	Flitcroft	28,098
38	18	A	Aston Villa	L	1-3	1-0	—	Quinn	33,108
39	21	H	Wimbledon	D	1-1	0-0	—	Holden	19,524
40	May 1	A	Southampton	W	1-0	1-0	5	White	11,830
41	5	H	Crystal Palace	D	0-0	0-0	—		21,167
42	8	H	Everton	L	2-5	1-3	8	White, Curle (pen)	25,180

Final League Position: 9

GOALSCORERS

League (56): White 16, Sheron 11, Quinn 9, Flitcroft 5, Curle 3 (3 pens), Holden 3, Vonk 3, Brightwell I 1, Hill 1, McMahon 1, Simpson 1, own goals 2.
Coca Cola Cup (2): Holden 1, own goal 1.
FA Cup (11): Sheron 3, White 3, Flitcroft 1, Holden 1, Phelan 1, Quinn 1, Vonk 1.

Coton 40	Hill 23 + 1	Brightwell I 21	Simpson 27 + 2	Curle 39	Vonk 26	White 42	Lake 2	Quinn 39	Holden 40 + 1	McMahon 24 + 3	Sheron 33 + 5	Phelan 37	Reid 14 + 6	Flitcroft 28 + 4	Mike 1 + 2	Brightwell D 4 + 4	Ranson 17	Ingebritsen 2 + 5	Dibble 1 + 1	Quigley 1 + 4	Kerr — + 1	Margetson 1	Match No.
1	2	3	4	5	6	7	8	9	10	11	12												1
1	2	3	4	5	6	7	8	9	10	11	12												2
1	2	3	4	5	6	7		9	10	11	8												3
1		2	4	5	6	7		9	10	11	8	3											4
1		2	4	5	6	7		9	10	11	8	3	12	14									5
1		2	10	5	6	7		9	11	12		3	4	8									6
1		2	10	5	6	7		11	12	9		3	4	8									7
1		2	10	5	6	7		11		9		3	4	8	12								8
1	6	2	10	5		7		11		9		3	4	8	12								9
1	6	2	10	5		7		9	11	12		3	4	8									10
1	6	2	10	5		7		9	11	4	8	3	12										11
1	6	2	10	5		7		9	11	4		3		8									12
1	6	2	10	5		7		9	11	4	8	3											13
1	6	2	10	5		7		9	11	4	8	3	12	14									14
1	6	2	10	5		7		9	11	4	8	3											15
1	6	2	10	5		7		9	11	4	8	3			12								16
1	6		10	5		7		9	11	4	8	3			12	2							17
1	6	2	10	5		7		9	11	4	8	3	12	14									18
1	6	2		5		7		9	11	4	12	3		8	10								19
1	6	2		5		7		9	11	4	12	3		8	10								20
1	6	2		5		7		9	11	4	8	3			10								21
1	6	2		5		7		9	11	4	8	3	12		10								22
1				5		7		9	11	4	8	3			10	6	2						23
1	4			5		7		9	11		8	3			10	6	2						24
1		6		5		7		9	11	4	8	3			10		2						25
1	10			5	6	7		9	11	4	8	3					2	12					26
	10			5	6	7		9	11	4	8	3	14				2	12	1				27
1	12			5	6	7		9	11		8	3			10		2	4		14			28
1	3			5	6	7		9			8	10	11	12			2	4					29
1	5		4		6	7		9	11		8	3			10		2	12					30
1	2		4	5	6	7		9	11		8	3			10								31
1	2		4	5	6	7		9	11	12		3			10	8							32
1	2			5	6	7		9	11		8	3	4		10								33
1	2			5	6	7		9	11		8	3	4		10			12		14			34
1				5	6	7		9	11		8	3	4		10		2	12					35
1					6	7		9	11		8	3	4		10		2	5					36
1				5	6	7		9	11		8	3	4		10		2	12		14			37
1	8			5	6	7		9	11			3	4		10	12	2						38
1	11			5	6	7		9	14		8	3	4		10	12	2						39
1	12			5	6	7		9	11	4	8	3			10		2						40
1				5	6	7		9	11	4	8	3			10		2			12			41
	12			5	6	7		9	11	4	8	3			10		2	14				1	42

Coca Cola Cup	Second Round	Bristol R (h)	0-0
		(a)	2-1
	Third Round	Tottenham H (h)	0-1
FA Cup	Third Round	Reading (h)	1-1
		(a)	4-0
	Fourth Round	QPR (a)	2-1
	Fifth Round	Barnsley (h)	2-0
	Sixth Round	Tottenham H (h)	2-4

MANCHESTER CITY

Player and Position	Ht	Wt	Date	Birth Place	Source	Clubs	League App	Gls
Goalkeepers								
Tony Coton	6 2	13 07	19 5 61	Tamworth	Mile Oak	Birmingham C	94	—
						Hereford U (loan)	—	—
						Watford	233	—
						Manchester C	110	—
Andy Dibble	6 2	13 07	8 5 65	Cwmbran	Apprentice	Cardiff C	62	—
						Luton T	30	—
						Sunderland (loan)	12	—
						Huddersfield T (loan)	5	—
						Manchester C	76	—
						Aberdeen (loan)	5	—
						Middlesbrough (loan)	19	—
						Bolton W (loan)	13	—
						WBA (loan)	9	—
						Oldham Ath (loan)	—	—
Martyn Margetson	6 0	13 10	8 9 71	West Glamorgan	Trainee	Manchester C	6	—
Defenders								
Keith Curle	6 0	12 07	14 11 63	Bristol	Apprentice	Bristol R	32	4
						Torquay U	16	5
						Bristol C	121	1
						Reading	40	—
						Wimbledon	93	3
						Manchester C	79	8
Richard Edghill	5 9	10 01	23 9 74	Oldham	Trainee	Manchester C	—	—
Gary Flitcroft	5 11	11 08	6 11 72	Bolton	Trainee	Manchester C	32	5
						Bury (loan)	12	—
John Foster	5 10	11 01	19 9 73	Manchester	Trainee	Manchester C	—	—
Andy Hill	5 10	12 00	20 1 65	Maltby	Apprentice	Manchester U	—	—
						Bury	264	10
						Manchester C	68	6
Kare Ingebritsen	5 7	10 03	11 11 65	Rosenborg	Rosenborg	Manchester C	7	—
Terry Phelan	5 8	10 00	16 3 67	Manchester		Leeds U	14	—
						Swansea C	45	—
						Wimbledon	159	1
						Manchester C	37	—
Ray Ranson*	5 9	11 12	12 6 60	St. Helens	Apprentice	Manchester C	183	1
						Birmingham C	137	—
						Newcastle U	83	1
						Manchester C	17	—
Michael Vonk	6 3	13 03	28 10 68	Holland	SVV/Dordrecht	Manchester C	35	3
Midfield								
David Brightwell	6 1	13 05	7 1 71	Lutterworth	Trainee	Manchester C	12	—
						Chester C (loan)	6	—
Ian Brightwell	5 10	11 07	9 4 68	Lutterworth	Congleton T	Manchester C	197	16
Joseph Harkin			9 12 75	Derry	Trainee	Manchester C	—	—
Sean Harkin*			3 12 73	Birmingham	Trainee	Manchester C	—	—
Rick Holden	5 11	12 07	9 9 64	Skipton		Burnley	1	—
						Halifax T	67	12
						Watford	42	8
						Oldham Ath	129	19
						Manchester C	41	3
David Kerr	5 11	11 00	6 9 74	Dumfries	Trainee	Manchester C	1	—
Paul Lake	6 0	12 02	28 10 68	Manchester	Trainee	Manchester C	110	7
Nicholas Limber	5 9	11 01	23 1 74	Doncaster	Trainee	Doncaster R	13	1
						Manchester C	—	—
						Peterborough U (loan)	2	—
Steve Lomas	6 0	12 08	18 1 74	Hanover	Trainee	Manchester C	—	—

MANCHESTER CITY

Colours: Sky blue shirts, white shorts, sky blue stockings. **Change colours:** Purple shirts with candy-stripe, purple shorts, purple stockings with white top.

Foundation: Manchester City was formed as a Limited Company in 1894 after their predecessors Ardwick had been forced into bankruptcy. However, many historians like to trace the club's lineage as far back as 1880 when St. Mark's Church, West Gorton added a football section to their cricket club. They amalgamated with Gorton Athletic in 1884 as Gorton FC. Because of a change of ground they became Ardwick in 1887.

First Football League game: 3 September, 1892, Division 2, v Bootle (h) W 7-0 – Douglas; McVickers, Robson; Middleton, Russell, Hopkins; Davies (3), Morris (2), Angus (1), Weir (1), Milarvie.

Did you know: On 14 June 1947 Manchester City completed their final game of an extended season, prolonged because of bad weather, against already-relegated Newport County. George Smith scored all five City goals in a 5-1 win to equal an individual club scoring record.

Managers (and Secretary-Managers)
Joshua Parlby 1893–95*, Sam Omerod 1895–1902, Tom Maley 1902–06, Harry Newbould 1906–12, Ernest Magnall 1912–24, David Ashworth 1924–25, Peter Hodge 1926–32, Wilf Wild 1932–46 (continued as secretary to 1950), Sam Cowan 1946–47, John "Jock" Thomson 1947–50, Leslie McDowall 1950–63, George Poyser 1963–65, Joe Mercer 1965–71 (continued as GM to 1972), Malcolm Allison 1972–73, Johnny Hart 1973, Ron Saunders 1973–74, Tony Book 1974–79, Malcolm Allison 1979–80, John Bond 1980–83, John Benson 1983, Billy McNeill 1983–86, Jimmy Frizzell 1986–87 (continued as GM), Mel Machin 1987–89, Howard Kendall 1990, Peter Reid November 1990–.

Player and Position	Ht	Wt	Birth Date	Birth Place	Source	Clubs	League App	Gls
Steve McMahon	5 9	11 08	20 8 61	Liverpool	Apprentice	Everton	100	11
						Aston Villa	75	7
						Liverpool	204	29
						Manchester C	45	1
Mike Quigley	5 6	9 04	2 10 70	Manchester	Trainee	Manchester C	10	—
Peter Reid	5 8	10 07	20 6 56	Huyton	Apprentice	Bolton W	225	23
						Everton	159	8
						QPR	29	1
						Manchester C	99	1
Mike Sheron	5 9	11 03	11 1 72	Liverpool	Trainee	Manchester C	67	18
						Bury (loan)	5	1
Fitzroy Simpson	5 8	10 07	26 2 70	Trowbridge	Trainee	Swindon T	105	9
						Manchester C	40	2
Garry Sliney*	5 10	12 03	2 9 73	Dublin		Manchester C	—	—
Scott Thomas	5 9	10 08	30 10 74	Bury	Trainee	Manchester C	—	—
Greg Thomson	5 10	10 10	13 9 75	Edinburgh	Trainee	Manchester C	—	—
Forwards								
Chris Beech			5 11 75	Congleton	Trainee	Manchester C	—	—
Stephen Finney	5 10	12 00	31 10 73	Hexham	Trainee	Preston NE	6	1
						Manchester C	—	—
Michael Hughes (To Strasbourg July 1992)	5 6	10 08	2 8 71	Larne	Carrick R	Manchester C	26	1
Adie Mike	6 0	11 06	16 11 73	Manchester	Trainee	Manchester C	5	1
						Bury (loan)	7	1
Niall Quinn	6 3	13 10	6 10 66	Dublin		Arsenal	67	14
						Manchester C	121	45
David White	6 1	12 09	30 10 67	Manchester		Manchester C	269	78

Trainees
Bentley, James G; Ingram, Rae; Lydiate, Joseph L; McDowell, Stephen A; McHugh, Darren R; Owen, Phillip J. G; Riches, Nevin; Roe, David; Sharpe, John J; Turner, David E; Walker, David A.

**Non-Contract
Whitleg, James.

Associated Schoolboys
Bailey, Alan; Barrass, Nathan C; Blore, Darren L; Brisco, Neil A; Callaghan, Anthony S; Crooks, Lee R; Freeborn, John G; Greenacre, Christopher M; Harris, Samuel R; Jagielka, Stephen; Morley, David T; Morley, Neal T; Muir, Alex; Rothwell, Neil A; Rowlands, Aled J. R; Smith, Steven J; Whitley, Jeffrey; Wills, David J.

Associated Schoolboys who have accepted the club's offer of a Traineeship/Contract
Brennan, Steven J; Brown, Michael R; Evans, Gareth J; Kielty, Gerrard T; McDonnell, John M; Morgan, Matthew A; Samuel, Gavin; Smith, Ian R; Tarpey, Gerard E.

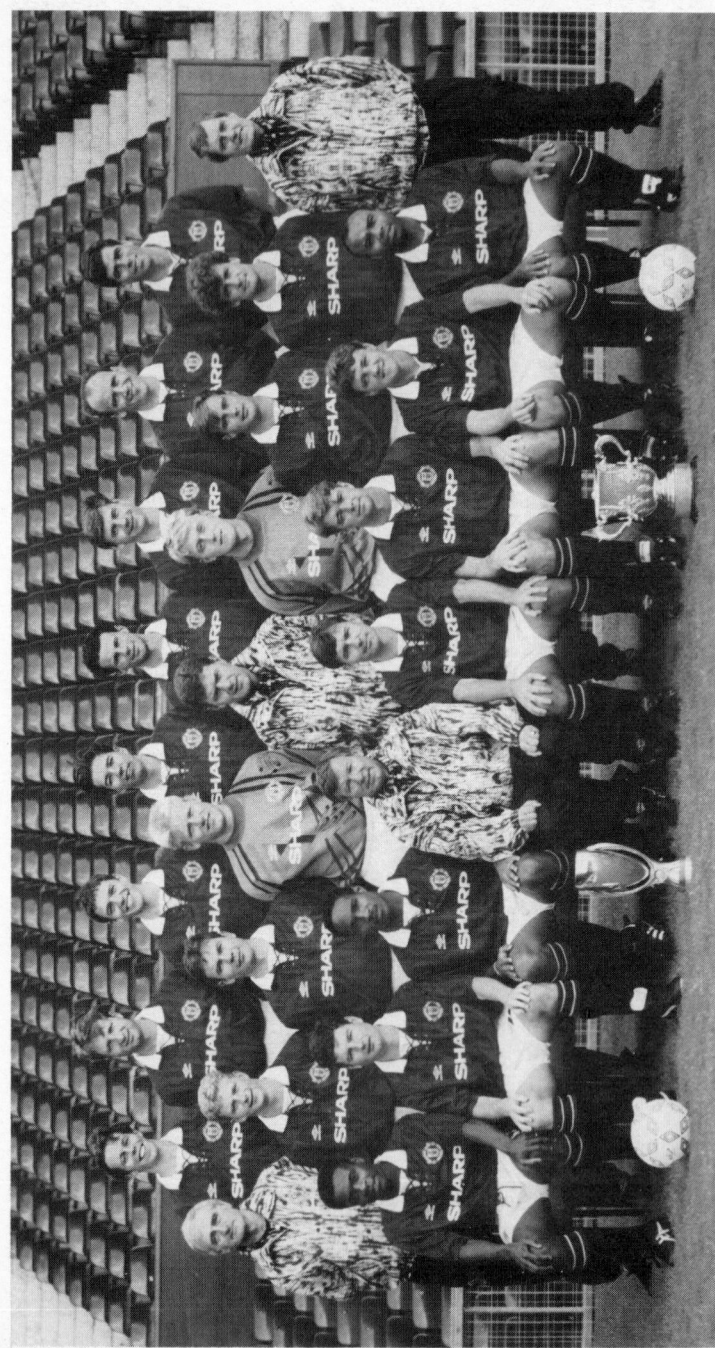

MANCHESTER UNITED 1992-93 *Back row (left to right):* Russell Beardsmore, Lee Martin, Lee Sharpe, Darren Ferguson, Ryan Giggs, Andrei Kanchelskis, Mike Phelan, Neil Webb.
Centre row: Jim McGregor (Physio), Mark Robins, Brian McClair, Brian Kidd (Assistant Manager), Peter Schmeichel, Gary Walsh (Assistant Manager), Clayton Blackmore, Mark Hughes, Norman Davies (Kit Manager).
Front row: Paul Parker, Denis Irwin, Paul Ince, Alex Ferguson (Manager), Bryan Robson (Manager), Gary Pallister, Steve Bruce, Danny Wallace.

FA Premier   **MANCHESTER UNITED**

Old Trafford, Manchester M16 0RA. Telephone 061–872 1661. Fax 061–876 5502. Ticket and Match Information: 061–872 0199. Membership enquiries: 061–872 5208. Souvenir shop: 061–872 3398.

Ground capacity: 45,000.

Record attendance: 76,962 Wolverhampton W v Grimsby T, FA Cup semi-final. 25 March 1939.

Club record: 70,504 v Aston Villa, Division 1, 27 December 1920.

Record receipts: £432,345.80 v Legia Warsaw, European Cup-Winners Cup semi-final, 24 April 1991.

Pitch measurements: 116yd × 76yd.

President: Sir Matt Busby CBE, KCSG. *Vice-presidents:* J. A. Gibson, W. A. Young, J. G. Gulliver, R. L. Edwards. *Chairman/Chief Executive:* C. M. Edwards. *Directors:* J. M. Edelson, R. Charlton CBE, E. M. Watkins LL.M., A. M. Midani, R. L. Olive, R. P. Launders. *Manager:* Alex Ferguson. *Assistant Manager:* Brian Kidd. *Secretary:* Kenneth Merrett. *Commercial Manager:* D. A. McGregor. *Physio:* Jim McGregor.

Year Formed: 1878 as Newton Heath LYR; 1902, Manchester United.

Turned Professional: 1885. *Ltd Co.:* 1907.

Previous Name: Newton Heath, 1880–1902.

Club Nickname: 'Red Devils'.

Previous Grounds: 1880–93, North Road, Monsall Road; 1893, Bank Street; 1910, Old Trafford (played at Maine Road 1941–49).

Record League Victory: 10–1 v Wolverhampton W, Division 1, 15 October 1892 – Warner; Mitchell, Clements; Perrins, Stewart (3), Erentz; Farman (1), Hood (1), Donaldson (3), Carson (1), Hendry (1).

Record Cup Victory: 10–0 v RSC Anderlecht, European Cup, Prel. rd (2nd leg), 26 September 1956 – Wood; Foulkes Byrne; Colman, Jones, Edwards; Berry (1), Whelan (2), Taylor (3), Viollet (4), Pegg.

Record Defeat: 0–7 v Blackburn R, Division 1, 10 April 1926 and v Aston Villa, Division 1, 27 December 1930 and v Wolverhampton W. Division 2, 26 December 1931.

Most League Points (2 for a win): 64, Division 1, 1956–57.

Most League Points (3 for a win): 84, FA Premier League, 1992–93.

Most League Goals: 103, Division 1, 1956–57 and 1958–59.

Highest League Scorer in Season: Dennis Viollet, 32, 1959–60.

Most League Goals in Total Aggregate: Bobby Charlton, 199, 1956–73.

Most Capped Player: Bobby Charlton, 106, England.

Most League Appearances: Bobby Charlton, 606, 1956–73.

Record Transfer Fee Received: £1,800,000 from Barcelona for Mark Hughes, August 1986.

Record Transfer Fee Paid: £2,300,000 to Middlesbrough for Gary Pallister, August 1989.

Football League Record: 1892 Newton Heath elected to Division 1; 1894–1906 Division 2; 1906–22 Division 1; 1922–25 Division 2; 1925–31 Division 1; 1931–36 Division 2; 1936–37 Division 1; 1937–38 Division 2; 1938–74 Division 1; 1974–75 Division 2; 1975–92 Division 1; 1992– FA Premier League.

Honours: *FA Premier League:* – Champions 1992–93. *Football League:* Division 1 – Champions 1907–8, 1910–11, 1951–52, 1955–56, 1956–57, 1964–65, 1966–67, Runners-up 1946–47, 1947–48, 1948–49, 1950–51, 1958–59, 1963–64, 1967–68, 1979–80, 1987–88, 1991–92. Division 2 – Champions 1935–36, 1974–75; Runners-up 1896–97, 1905–06, 1924–25, 1937–38. *FA Cup:* Winners 1909, 1948, 1963, 1977, 1983, 1985, 1990; Runners-up 1957, 1958, 1976, 1979. *Football League Cup:* Winners 1991–92, 1982–83 (Runners-up), 1990–91 (Runners-up). **European Competitions:** *European Cup:* 1956–57 (s-f), 1957–58 (s-f), 1965–66 (s-f), 1967–68 (winners), 1968–69 (s-f). *European Cup-Winners' Cup:* 1963–64, 1977–78, 1983–84, 1990–91 (winners). 1991–92. *European Fairs Cup:* 1964–65. *UEFA Cup:* 1976–77, 1980–81, 1982–83, 1984–85, 1992–93. *Super Cup:* 1991 (winners).

MANCHESTER UNITED 1992—93 LEAGUE RECORD

Match No.	Date	Venue	Opponents	Result		H/T Score	Lg. Pos.	Goalscorers	Atten dance
1	Aug 15	A	Sheffield U	L	1-2	0-1	—	Hughes	28,070
2	19	H	Everton	L	0-3	0-1	—		31,901
3	22	H	Ipswich T	D	1-1	0-0	20	Irwin	31,704
4	24	A	Southampton	W	1-0	0-0	—	Dublin	15,623
5	29	A	Nottingham F	W	2-0	1-0	8	Hughes, Giggs	19,694
6	Sept 2	H	Crystal Palace	W	1-0	0-0	—	Hughes	29,736
7	6	H	Leeds U	W	2-0	2-0	—	Kanchelskis, Bruce	31,296
8	12	A	Everton	W	2-0	1-0	3	McClair, Bruce (pen)	30,002
9	19	A	Tottenham H	D	1-1	1-0	4	Giggs	33,296
10	26	H	QPR	D	0-0	0-0	4		33,287
11	Oct 3	A	Middlesbrough	D	1-1	1-0	6	Bruce (pen)	24,172
12	18	H	Liverpool	D	2-2	0-2	—	Hughes 2	33,243
13	24	A	Blackburn R	D	0-0	0-0	7		20,305
14	31	H	Wimbledon	L	0-1	0-0	7		32,622
15	Nov 7	A	Aston Villa	L	0-1	0-1	10		39,063
16	21	H	Oldham Ath	W	3-0	3-0	8	McClair, Hughes	33,497
17	28	A	Arsenal	W	1-0	1-0	5	Hughes	29,739
18	Dec 6	H	Manchester C	W	2-1	1-0	—	Ince, Hughes	35,408
19	12	H	Norwich C	W	1-0	0-0	3	Hughes	34,500
20	19	A	Chelsea	D	1-1	0-0	4	Cantona	34,464
21	26	A	Sheffield W	D	3-3	0-2	3	McClair 2, Cantona	37,708
22	28	H	Coventry C	W	5-0	2-0	2	Giggs, Hughes, Cantona (pen), Sharpe, Irwin	36,025
23	Jan 9	H	Tottenham H	W	4-1	1-0	1	Cantona, Irwin, McClair, Parker	35,648
24	18	A	QPR	W	3-1	2-1	—	Ince, Giggs, Kanchelskis	21,117
25	27	H	Nottingham F	W	2-0	0-0	—	Ince, Hughes	36,085
26	30	A	Ipswich T	L	1-2	0-1	2	McClair	22,068
27	Feb 6	H	Sheffield U	W	2-1	0-1	1	McClair, Cantona	36,156
28	8	A	Leeds U	D	0-0	0-0	—		34,166
29	20	H	Southampton	W	2-1	0-0	2	Giggs 2	36,257
30	27	H	Middlesbrough	W	3-0	1-0	2	Giggs, Irwin, Cantona	36,251
31	Mar 6	A	Liverpool	W	2-1	1-0	1	Hughes, McClair	44,374
32	9	A	Oldham Ath	L	0-1	0-1	—		17,106
33	14	H	Aston Villa	D	1-1	0-0	—	Hughes	36,163
34	20	A	Manchester C	D	1-1	0-0	2	Cantona	37,136
35	24	A	Arsenal	D	0-0	0-0	—		37,301
36	Apr 5	A	Norwich C	W	3-1	3-0	—	Giggs, Kanchelskis, Cantona	20,582
37	10	H	Sheffield W	W	2-1	0-0	1	Bruce 2	40,102
38	12	A	Coventry C	W	1-0	1-0	1	Irwin	24,429
39	17	H	Chelsea	W	3-0	2-0	1	Hughes, Clarke (og), Cantona	40,139
40	21	A	Crystal Palace	W	2-0	0-0	—	Hughes, Ince	30,115
41	May 3	H	Blackburn R	W	3-1	1-1	—	Giggs, Ince, Pallister	40,447
42	9	A	Wimbledon	W	2-1	0-0	—	Ince, Robson	30,115

Final League Position: 1

GOALSCORERS

League (67): Hughes 15, Cantona 9 (1 pen), Giggs 9, McClair 9, Ince 6, Bruce 5 (2 pens), Irwin 5, Kanchelskis 3, Dublin 1, Pallister 1, Parker 1, Robson 1, Sharpe 1, own goal 1.
Coca Cola Cup (2): Hughes 1, Wallace 1.
FA Cup (4): Giggs 2, Gillespie 1, Phelan 1.

Schmeichel 42	Irwin 40	Blackmore 12 + 2	Bruce 42	Ferguson 15	Pallister 42	Kanchelskis 14 + 13	Ince 41	McClair 41 + 1	Hughes 41	Giggs 40 + 1	Phelan 5 + 6	Dublin 3 + 4	Webb — + 1	Wallace — + 2	Robson 5 + 9	Parker 31	Sharpe 27	Butt — + 1	Cantona 21 + 1	Match No.
1	2	3	4	5	6	7	8	9	10	11	12	14								1
1	2	3	4	5	6	7	8	9	10	11	12	14								2
1	2	3	4	5	6	7		9	10	11	8	12	14							3
1		3	4	5	6		8	9	10	11	2	7								4
1	3	14	4	5	6	12	8	9	10	11	2	7								5
1	3	2	4	5	6	12	8	9	10	11		7								6
1	3	2	4	5	6	7	8	9	10	11										7
1	2	3	4	5	6	7	8	9	10	11										8
1	2	3	4	5	6	7	8	9	10	11				12						9
1	2	3	4	5	6	7	8	9	10	11				12						10
1	2	7	4	5	6	12	8	9	10	11	3			14						11
1	3	12	4	5	6	7	8	9	10	11						2				12
1	3	7	4	5	6	12	8	9	10	11						2				13
1		3	4	5	6	7	8	9	10	11					12	2				14
1		3	4	5	6		8	12	10	11					7	2	9			15
1		3	4		6		8	9	10	11	12				7	2	5	14		16
1		3	4		6		8	9	10	11					7	2	5			17
1		3	4		6		8	9	10	11					7	2	5		12	18
1		3	4		6		8	9	10	11						2	5		7	19
1		3	4		6	12	8	9	10						5	2	11		7	20
1		3	4		6	12	8	9	10	11						2	5		7	21
1		3	4		6	12	8	9	10	11		14				2	5		7	22
1		3	4		6	12	8	9	10	11		14				2	5		7	23
1		3	4		6	7	8	9	10	11					12	2	5			24
1		3	4		6		8	9	10	11						2	5		7	25
1		3	4		6	12	8	9	10	11						2	5		7	26
1		3	4		6	12	8	9	10	11						2	5		7	27
1		3	4		6	12	8	9	10	11						2	5		7	28
1		3	4		6		8	9	10	11						2	5		7	29
1		3	4		6		8	9	10	11						2	5		7	30
1		3	4		6	7	8	9	10	11						2	5			31
1		3	4		6	7	8	9	10	11					12	2	5			32
1		3	4		6		8	9	10	11						2	5		7	33
1		3	4		6		8	9	10	11						2	5		7	34
1		3	4		6		8	9	10	11					12	2	5		7	35
1		3	4		6	10	8	9		11					12	2	5		7	36
1		3	4		6		8	9	10	11					12	2	5		7	37
1		3	4		6		8	9	10	11					12	2	5		7	38
1		3	4		6	14	8	9	10	11					12	2	5		7	39
1		3	4		6	5	8	9	10	11					12	2			7	40
1		3	4		6	14	8	9	10	11					12	2	5		7	41
1		3	4		6		8	9	10	12					7	2	5		11	42

Coca Cola Cup	Second Round	Brighton & HA (a)	1-1
		(h)	1-0
	Third Round	Aston Villa (a)	0-1
FA Cup	Third Round	Bury (h)	2-0
	Fourth Round	Brighton & HA (h)	1-0
	Fifth Round	Sheffield U (a)	1-2

MANCHESTER UNITED

Player and Position	Ht	Wt	Date	Birth Place	Source	Clubs	League App	Gls
Goalkeepers								
Kevin Pilkington	6 0	12 00	5 3 74	Hitchin	Trainee	Manchester U	—	—
Peter Schmeichel	6 4	13 06	18 11 68	Glodsone	Brondby	Manchester U	82	—
Les Sealey	6 1	13 06	29 9 57	Bethnal Green	Apprentice	Coventry C	158	—
						Luton T	207	—
						Plymouth Arg (loan)	6	—
						Manchester U (loan)	2	—
						Manchester U	31	—
						Aston Villa	18	—
						Coventry C (loan)	2	—
						Birmingham C (loan)	12	—
						Manchester U	—	—
Gary Walsh	6 1	13 01	21 3 68	Wigan		Manchester U	37	—
						Airdrie (loan)	3	—
Ian Wilkinson*	5 11	12 00	2 7 73	Warrington	Trainee	Manchester U	—	—
Defenders								
Steve Bruce	6 0	12 6	31 12 60	Newcastle	Apprentice	Gillingham	205	29
						Norwich C	141	14
						Manchester U	203	30
Brian Carey	6 3	11 13	31 5 68	Cork	Cork C	Manchester U	—	—
						Wrexham (loan)	3	—
						Wrexham (loan)	13	1
Chris Casper	5 11	10 09	28 4 75	Burnley	Trainee	Manchester U	—	—
Denis Irwin	5 8	11 00	31 70 65	Cork	Apprentice	Leeds U	72	1
						Oldham Ath	167	4
						Manchester U	112	9
Patrick McGibbon	6 0	11 07	6 9 73	Lurgan	Portadown	Manchester U	—	—
Lee Martin	5 11	11 05	5 2 68	Hyde		Manchester U	72	1
Colin Murdock	6 1	12 00	2 7 75	Ballymena	Trainee	Manchester U	—	—
Gary Neville	5 10	11 04	18 2 75	Bury	Trainee	Manchester U	—	—
John O'Kane	5 10	11 04	15 11 74	Nottingham	Trainee	Manchester U	—	—
Gary Pallister	6 4	13 04	30 6 65	Ramsgate		Middlesbrough	156	5
						Darlington (loan)	7	—
						Manchester U	153	5
Paul Parker	5 7	10 13	4 4 64	Essex	Apprentice	Fulham	153	2
						QPR	125	1
						Manchester U	57	1
Mike Phelan	5 11	11 01	24 9 62	Nelson	Apprentice	Burnley	168	9
						Norwich C	156	9
						Manchester U	100	2
George Switzer*	5 6	9 10	13 10 73	Salford	Trainee	Manchester U	—	—
Neil Whitworth	6 2	12 06	12 4 72	Ince	Trainee	Wigan Ath	2	—
						Manchester U	1	—
						Preston NE (loan)	6	—
						Barnsley (loan)	11	—
Midfield								
Russell Beardsmore*	5 6	8 10	28 9 68	Wigan	Apprentice	Manchester U	56	4
						Blackburn R (loan)	2	—
David Beckham	5 11	10 09	2 5 75	Leytonstone	Trainee	Manchester U	—	—
Clayton Blackmore	5 9	11 06	23 9 64	Neath	Apprentice	Manchester U	186	19
Nicky Butt	5 10	11 00	21 1 75	Manchester	Trainee	Manchester U	1	—
Simon Davies	5 11	10 02	23 4 74	Winsford	Trainee	Manchester U	—	—
Adrian Doherty*	5 8	10 06	10 6 73	Strabane	School	Manchester U	—	—
Darren Ferguson	5 10	10 04	9 2 72	Glasgow	Trainee	Manchester U	24	—
Paul Ince	5 10	11 07	21 10 67	Ilford	Trainee	West Ham U	72	7
						Manchester U	131	12
Andrei Kanchelskis	5 10	12 04	23 1 69	Kirowgrad	Donezts	Manchester U	62	8
Craig Lawton	5 7	10 03	5 1 72	Mancot	Trainee	Manchester U	—	—
Bryan Robson	5 10	11 11	11 1 57	Chester-le-Street	Apprentice	WBA	197	39
						Manchester U	330	73
Lee Sharpe	5 11	11 04	25 7 71	Halesowen	Trainee	Torquay U	14	3
						Manchester U	104	5
Kieran Toal (To Motherwell March 1993)	5 8	11 01	14 12 71	Manchester	Trainee	Manchester U	—	—

MANCHESTER UNITED

Colours: Red shirts, white shorts, black stockings. **Change colours:** Black shirts, black shorts, black stockings.

Foundation: Manchester United was formed as comparatively recently as 1902 after their predecessors, Newton Heath, went bankrupt. However, it is usual to give the date of the club's foundation as 1878 when employees of the Lancashire and Yorkshire Railway Company formed Newton Heath L and YR. Cricket and Football Club. They won the Manchester Cup in 1886 and as Newton Heath FC were admitted to the Second Division in 1892.

First Football League game: 3 September, 1892, Division 1, v Blackburn R (a) L 3-4 – Warner; Clements, Brown; Perrins, Stewart, Erentz; Farman (1), Coupar (1), Donaldson (1), Carson, Mathieson.

Did you know: During 1967–68, Manchester United reported an average League attendance of 57,549 in Division 1. Though they finished runners-up in the championship, they won the European Cup.

Managers (and Secretary-Managers)
Ernest Magnall 1900–12, John Robson 1914–21, John Chapman 1921–26, Clarence Hildrith 1926–27, Herbert Bamlett 1927–31, Walter Crickmer 1931–32, Scott Duncan 1932–37, Jimmy Porter 1938–44, Walter Crickmer 1944–45*, Matt Busby 1945–69 (continued as GM then Director), Wilf McGuinness 1969–70, Frank O'Farrell 1971–72, Tommy Docherty 1972–77, Dave Sexton 1977–81, Ron Atkinson 1981–86, Alex Ferguson November 1986– .

Player and Position	Ht	Wt	Birth Date	Birth Place	Source	Clubs	League App	Gls
Forwards								
Raphael Burke‡	5 8	10 07	3 7 74	Bristol	Trainee	Manchester U	—	—
Eric Cantona	6 1	12 10	24 5 66	Paris	Nimes	Auxerre	13	2
						Martigues	—	—
						Auxerre	68	21
						Marseille	22	5
						Bordeaux	11	6
						Montpellier	33	10
						Marseille	18	8
						Leeds U	28	9
						Manchester U	22	9
Dion Dublin	6 0	12 04	22 4 69	Leicester		Norwich C	—	—
						Cambridge U	156	52
						Manchester U	7	1
Ryan Giggs	5 11	10 10	29 11 73	Cardiff	School	Manchester U	81	14
Keith Gillespie	5 9	11 00	18 2 75	Larne	Trainee	Manchester U	—	—
Mark Hughes	5 9	11 12	1 11 63	Wrexham	Apprentice	Manchester U	89	37
					Barcelona, Bayern Munich	Manchester U	186	63
Richard Irving	5 8	10 07	10 9 75	Halifax	Forward	Manchester U	—	—
Brian McClair	5 9	12 00	8 12 63	Bellshill	Apprentice	Aston Villa		
						Motherwell	39	15
						Celtic	145	99
						Manchester U	235	79
Colin McKee	5 10	11 00	22 8 73	Glasgow	Trainee	Manchester U		
						Bury (loan)	2	—
Giuliano Maiorana*	5 9	11 08	18 4 69	Cambridge	Histon	Manchester U	7	—
Paul Scholes	5 8	10 07	16 11 74	Salford	Trainee	Manchester U	—	—
Colin Telford‡			14 1 74	Belfast	Trainee	Manchester U	—	—
Ben Thornley	5 8	10 07	21 4 75	Bury	Trainee	Manchester U	—	—
Danny Wallace	5 4	10 04	21 1 64	London	Apprentice	Southampton	255	64
						Manchester U	47	6
						Millwall (loan)	3	—

Trainees
Appleton, Michael A; Barnes, Lee M; Brown, Karl D; Cooke, Terence J; Dean, Craig; Flash, Richard G; Hart, Ian M; Johnson, David A; McDonald, Robert F; Marsh, Paul J; Monaghan, Matthew S; O'Keefe, Paul G; Parkin, Daniel J; Pierce, David E; Rawlinson, Mark D; Riley, Steven; Roberts, Joseph E; Ryan, Mark; Savage, Robert W; Twynham, Gary S; Westwood, Ashley M; Whittam, Philip R.

Associated Schoolboys
Brickhill, Gary; Brightwell, Stuart; Byers, James A; Crossland, Mark D; Duncan, Andrew; Fitzpatrick, Lee G; Macken, Jonathan P; Marsh, Neil D; Maxon, Heath R; McGlinchey, Brian; Michael, James D; Millard, Ross J; Mulryne, Philip P; Phillips, Jonathan J; Phillips, Paul D; Quinn, Stephen; Smith, Thomas E; Trees, Robert V; Twiss, Michael J; Wallwork, Ronald; Watson, Richard; Wheeler, Adam; Wood, Jamie.

Associated Schoolboys who have accepted the club's offer of a Traineeship/Contract
Gardner, David S; Gibson, Paul R; Hall, Danny; Hall, Stephen; Heckingbottom, Paul; Hudson, Vincent J; Lyons, Paul; Mustoe, Neil; Neville, Philip J.

MANSFIELD TOWN 1992-93 *Back row (left to right):* Greg Fee, Steve Wilkinson, Nicky Clarke, Darren Ward, Andy Beasley, Jason Pearcey, Kevin Gray, Paul Holland.
Centre row: Dennis Pettit (Physio), Kevin Randall (Youth Team Coach), Paul McLoughlin, Chris Withe, Ian Stringfellow, Gary Castledine, Alex Sykes, Wayne Davison, Nicky Roddis, Paul Fleming, Steve Parkin, John Newman (Chief Scout).
Front row: Kevin Noteman, Phil Stant, Steve Charles, George Foster (Manager), Bill Dearden (Assistant Manager), Gary Ford, Wayne Fairclough, Steve Spooner.

Division 3   **MANSFIELD TOWN**

Field Mill Ground, Quarry Lane, Mansfield. Telepone Manfield (0623) 23567. Commercial Office/Shop: 0623 658070. Fax: 0623 25014

Ground capacity: 10,468.

Record attendance: 24,467 v Nottingham F, FA Cup 3rd rd, 10 January 1953.

Record receipts: £46,915 v Sheffield W, FA Cup 3rd rd, 5 January 1991.

Pitch measurements: 115yd × 70yd.

Chairman: J. W. Pratt. *Vice-chairman:*

Directors: G. Hall (Managing), J. A. Brown, A. H. Bostock.

Player-manager: George Foster. *Assistant Manager/Coach:* Bill Dearden.

Physio: Dennis Pettitt. *Community Scheme Organiser:* D. Bentley Tel: 0623 25197.

Secretary: J. D. Eaton. *Commercial Manager:* J. Slater.

Year Formed: 1910. *Turned Professional:* 1910. *Ltd Co.:* 1921.

Previous Name: Mansfield Wesleyans 1891–1910.

Club Nickname: 'The Stags'.

Record League Victory: 9–2 v Rotherham U, Division 3 (N), 27 December 1932 – Wilson; Anthony, England; Davies, S. Robinson, Slack; Prior, Broom, Readman (3), Hoyland (3), Bowater (3).

Record Cup Victory: 8–0 v Scarborough (away), FA Cup, 1st rd, 22 November 1952 – Bramley; Chessell, Bradley; Field, Plummer, Lewis; Scott, Fox (3), Marron (2), Sid Watson (1), Adam (2).

Record Defeat: 1–8 v Walsall, Division 3 (N), 19 January 1933.

Most League Points (2 for a win): 68, Division 4, 1974–75.

Most League Points (3 for a win): 81, Division 4, 1985–86.

Most League Goals: 108, Division 4, 1962–63.

Highest League Scorer in Season: Ted Harston, 55, Division 3 (N), 1936–37.

Most League Goals in Total Aggregate: Harry Johnson, 104, 1931–36.

Most Capped Player: John McClelland, 6 (53), Northern Ireland.

Most League Appearances: Rod Arnold, 440, 1970–83.

Record Transfer Fee Received: £500,000 from Middlesbrough for Simon Coleman, September 1989.

Record Transfer Fee Paid: £80,000 to Leicester C for Steve Wilkinson, September 1989.

Football League Record: 1931 Elected to Division 3 (S); 1932–37 Division 3 (N); 1937–47 Division 3 (S); 1947–58 Division 3 (N); 1958–60 Division 3; 1960–63 Division 4; 1963–72 Division 3; 1972–75 Division 4; 1975–77 Division 3; 1977–78 Division 2; 1978–80 Division 3; 1980–86 Division 4; 1986–91 Division 3; 1991–92 Division 4; 1992–93 Division 2; 1993–Division 3.

Honours: Football League: Division 2 best season: 21st, 1977–78; Division 3 – Champions 1976–77; Division 4 – Champions 1974–75; Division 3 (N) – Runners-up 1950–51. *FA Cup:* best season: 6th rd, 1968–69. *Football League Cup:* best season: 5th rd, 1975–76. *Freight Rover Trophy:* Winners 1986–87.

MANSFIELD TOWN 1992—93 LEAGUE RECORD

Match No.	Date		Venue	Opponents	Result		H/T Score	Lg. Pos.	Goalscorers	Atten dance
1	Aug 15		H	Plymouth Arg	D	0-0	0-0	—		4166
2		22	A	Swansea C	L	0-4	0-1	21		2792
3		29	H	Fulham	L	2-3	0-1	22	Stant 2 (1 pen)	3228
4	Sept	1	H	Bournemouth	L	0-2	0-1	—		3031
5		5	A	Blackpool	D	1-1	0-1	23	Castledine	4322
6		12	H	Bradford C	W	5-2	3-2	17	Holland, Charles (pen), Stringfellow, Fee 2	3545
7		15	A	Chester C	W	2-1	1-1	—	Fee (pen), Stant	3326
8		19	A	Burnley	L	0-1	0-1	16		8613
9		26	H	Stoke C	L	0-4	0-3	20		6828
10	Oct	3	A	Wigan Ath	L	0-2	0-1	22		1644
11		10	H	Stockport Co	W	2-0	0-0	19	Walker, Wilkinson	3836
12		17	A	Exeter C	L	0-2	0-2	21		2820
13		24	H	Preston NE	D	2-2	1-1	21	Stant, Withe	3047
14		31	A	Rotherham U	L	0-2	0-1	21		5030
15	Nov	3	H	Hull C	W	3-1	0-0	—	Withe, Stant, McCord	3038
16		7	A	Huddersfield T	L	1-2	1-2	20	Stant	4933
17		28	A	Leyton Orient	L	1-5	0-3	21	Spooner	4557
18	Dec	5	A	Fulham	D	0-0	0-0	21		3285
19		12	H	Brighton & HA	L	1-3	0-1	21	Noteman (pen)	2869
20		20	A	WBA	L	0-2	0-0	—		13,134
21		28	H	Reading	D	1-1	1-0	21	Ford	3043
22	Jan	2	A	Bradford C	D	0-0	0-0	21		6940
23		9	H	Chester C	W	2-0	0-0	21	Withe, Noteman	2659
24		16	A	Stoke C	L	0-4	0-2	21		14,643
25		23	H	Burnley	D	1-1	0-1	21	Charles	3991
26		30	H	Swansea C	D	3-3	3-1	22	Wilkinson, Holland, Stringfellow	2641
27	Feb	6	A	Plymouth Arg	L	2-3	1-0	22	Wilkinson 2	4630
28		13	H	Blackpool	D	2-2	1-1	22	Wilkinson, Charles (pen)	3593
29		16	H	Hartlepool U	W	2-0	0-0	—	Wilkinson, Stringfellow	2655
30		20	A	Bournemouth	L	1-4	0-3	22	Wilkinson	3987
31		26	A	Stockport Co	W	1-0	0-0	—	Stringfellow	5307
32	Mar	6	H	Wigan Ath	W	2-0	0-0	21	Wilkinson, Castledine	3024
33		9	A	Bolton W	L	1-2	1-1	—	Noteman	6557
34		13	H	Huddersfield T	L	1-2	1-0	22	Noteman	3987
35		20	A	Hull C	L	0-1	0-1	23		3551
36		23	H	Leyton Orient	W	3-0	0-0	—	McLoughlin 2, Withe	2774
37		27	A	Hartlepool U	W	1-0	0-0	21	Castledine	2292
38	Apr	3	H	Bolton W	D	1-1	1-0	22	Wilkinson	5366
39		7	A	Brighton & HA	L	1-3	0-2	—	Wilkinson	4731
40		10	H	Port Vale	L	0-1	0-0	22		5078
41		12	A	Reading	L	1-3	1-1	22	Fairclough	4904
42		17	H	WBA	L	0-3	0-2	22		6659
43		24	H	Exeter C	D	0-0	0-0	22		2527
44		27	A	Port Vale	L	0-3	0-2	—		9996
45	May	1	A	Preston NE	W	5-1	2-1	22	Clarke, Holland, McLoughlin, Wilkinson, Stringfellow	5889
46		8	H	Rotherham U	L	1-3	0-1	22	McLoughlin	3833

Final League Position: 22

GOALSCORERS

League (52): Wilkinson 11, Stant 6 (1 pen), Stringfellow 5, McLoughlin 4, Noteman 4 (1 pen), Withe 4, Castledine 3, Charles 3 (2 pens), Fee 3 (1 pen), Holland 3, Clarke 1, Fairclough 1, Ford 1, McCord 1, Spooner 1, Walker 1.
Coca Cola Cup (1): Stant 1.
FA Cup (1): Fairclough 1.

Pearcey 33	Parkin 16	Charles 22 + 1	Spooner 12 + 3	Gray 31 + 2	Holland 39	Ford 37	Fairclough 32 + 1	Stant 17	Wilkinson 35 + 8	Withe 44 + 1	McLoughlin 20 + 6	McCord 11	Castledine 23 + 5	Clarke 9 + 3	Stringfellow 26 + 4	Fee 7 + 3	Noteman 15 + 9	Walker 22	Peer 10	Foster 10	Rowbotham 4	Ward 13	Hodson 17	Wilson — + 4	Perkins 1 + 4	Match No.
1	2	3	4	5	6	7	8	9	10	11	12															1
1	2	3	14	5	6	7	8	9	10	11	12	_4_														2
1	2	11		5		7	8	9	3	10			4	6	12											3
1	2	11		5	6	7	_8_	9	4	3	10		14	12												4
1	_2_	11		5	6	7	8	9	3	10			14	12	4											5
1		3				4	7		9	12		2	10		_11_	6	8	5	14							6
1		3	8			4	7		9	12		2	10		11	6		5	14							7
1		11	2			4	7	9	12	3	10		8			6		5								8
1	2	3				7	4	9	12	14	10		8		5	11	6									9
1	2	11				4	7	9	12	3	10		8			6		5								10
1	2	11	4			7		9	10	3			8		5	6										11
1	2	11	4			7		9	10	3			8	12	5	6										12
1	2		8	11		7	12	9	10	3			4	6	5											13
1	2	11	8		6	7		9	10	3			4		5											14
1	2	11			6	7		9	10	3			4	8	5											15
1	2	11	14		6	7		9	10	3			4	8	12			5								16
1	2		6	12	4	7	11	9	10	3			_8_					5	14							17
1	2			4	6	7	8		10	3			11		9			5								18
1	2		6	11	4	7	8		10	3					9	12		5								19
1					6		8		3	11	10				9			5	2	4	7					20
1					6		8	9	3	11	10				12			5	2	4	7					21
1	5				6		8		3	11	12				9			10	2	4	7					22
1	12			5	6	7	8		3	11					9			10	2	4						23
1				5	6		8	9	3		12				10	11			2	4	7					24
1	11	14			6	7	8		3		12				9			10	5	2	4					25
1	11				6	7	8	9	3				10	4	12			5	2							26
1	11	12			6		8	9	3			10	7	14				5	2		_4_					27
1	11				6	7	8	9	3				10	4				5	2							28
	11				6	7	8	9	3				10	4	12			5	2			1				29
	11				6	7	8	9	3			14	12	10				5		4		1	2			30
					6	7	8	9	3		12		10	4	5	11						1	2			31
			5		6	7	8	9	3		12		10	4		11						1	2			32
			5		6	7	8	9	3		12		10	4		11						1	2			33
					6	7	8	9	3		12		10	4		11		5				1	2			34
					6		8	9	3		7		10	4		11		5				1	2		12	35
			5		6		8	9	3		7		10	4		11						1	2			36
		11		5	6		8	9	3		7		10	4								1	2	12		37
		11		5	6		8	9	3		7		10	4	12							1	2			38
		11		5	6		8	9	3		7		10	4	12							1	2			39
1		11		5	6		8	9	3		7		10	_4_	12								2	14		40
1		11		5	6		8	9	3		7		10	4									2	14	12	41
1				5	6	7	8	9	3				10	11	4	_12_							2	14		42
1				5	6	7	8	9	3				10	11	12	_4_							2			43
1				5	6	7	8	9	3				10	12	11	_4_							2			44
				5		7	8	9	10		12			4	11	6						1	2	3		45
				5		7	8	_9_	3				10	4	11	6						1	2	14	12	46

Coca Cola Cup	First Round	Newcastle U (a)		1-2
		(h)		0-0
FA Cup	First Round	Shrewsbury T (a)		1-3

MANSFIELD TOWN

Player and Position	Ht	Wt	Date	Birth Place	Source	Clubs	League App	Gls
Goalkeepers								
Andy Beasley*	6 2	13 02	5 2 64	Sedgley	Apprentice	Luton T.	—	—
						Mansfield T (loan)	—	—
						Gillingham (loan)	—	—
						Mansfield T	94	—
						Peterborough U (loan)	7	—
						Scarborough (loan)	4	—
						Bristol R (loan)	1	—
Jason Pearcey	6 1	13 06	2 7 71	Leamington Spa	Trainee	Mansfield T	65	—
Darren Ward	5 11	12 09	11 5 74	Worksop	Trainee	Mansfield T	13	—
Defenders								
Martin Clark (To Partick T)	5 9	10 11	13 10 68	Uddington	Hamilton A	Clyde	51	2
						Nottingham F	—	—
						Falkirk (loan)	3	1
						Mansfield T (loan)	14	1
						Mansfield T	33	—
Nicky Clarke	5 11	13 11	20 8 67	Walsall	Apprentice	Wolverhampton W	81	1
						Mansfield T	28	2
						Chesterfield (loan)	7	—
Wayne Fairclough	5 10	12 02	27 4 68	Nottingham	Apprentice	Notts Co	71	—
						Mansfield T	112	10
Greg Fee*	6 1	13 02	24 6 64	Halifax		Bradford C	7	—
					Boston UH	Sheffield W	26	—
						Preston NE (loan)	15	—
						Northampton T (loan)	1	—
						Leyton Orient (loan)	5	—
						Mansfield T	54	7
						Chesterfield (loan)	10	—
Paul Fleming*	5 7	11 08	6 9 67	Halifax		Halifax T	139	1
						Mansfield T	38	—
George Foster*	5 10	11 02	26 9 56	Plymouth	Apprentice	Plymouth Arg	212	6
						Torquay U (loan)	6	3
						Exeter C (loan)	28	—
						Derby Co	30	—
						Mansfield T	373	—
Simeon Hodson	5 10	11 06	5 3 66	Lincoln	Apprentice	Notts Co	27	—
						Charlton Ath	5	—
						Lincoln C	56	—
						Newport Co	34	1
						WBA	83	—
						Doncaster R	15	—
						Mansfield T	17	—
Steve Parkin	5 6	11 07	7 11 65	Mansfield	Apprentice	Stoke C	113	5
						WBA	48	2
						Mansfield T	16	—
Chris Perkins	5 11	10 09	9 1 74	Nottingham	Trainee	Mansfield T	5	—
Alan Walker	6 2	12 11	17 12 59	Mossley	Telford U	Lincoln C	75	4
						Millwall	92	8
						Gillingham	151	7
						Plymouth Arg	2	1
						Mansfield T	22	1
Chris Withe*	5 10	11 12	25 9 62	Liverpool	Apprentice	Newcastle U	2	—
						Bradford C	143	2
						Notts Co	80	3
						Bury	31	1
						Chester C (loan)	2	—
						Mansfield T (loan)	11	—
						Mansfield T	65	5
Midfield								
Wayne Davidson	5 9	11 00	7 12 68	Wallsend		Mansfield T	—	—

MANSFIELD TOWN

Colours: Amber shirts with blue trim, blue shorts, amber stockings. **Change colours:** Green shirt, white shorts, white stockings.

Foundation: Many records give the date of Mansfield Town's formation as 1905. But the present club did not come into being until 1910 when the Mansfield Wesleyans (formed 1891) and playing in the Notts and District League, decided to spread their wings and changed their name to Mansfield Town, joining the new Central Alliance in 1911.

First Football League game: 29 August, 1931, Division 3(S), v Swindon T (h) W 3-2 – Wilson; Clifford, England; Wake, Davis, Blackburn; Gilhespy, Readman (1), Johnson, Broom (2), Baxter.

Did you know: Ted Harston made a successful debut for Mansfield Town on 19 October 1935, scoring a hat-trick in the first seven minutes of play, though Southport drew with them 3-3.

Managers (and Secretary-Managers)
John Baynes 1922–25, Ted Davison 1926–28, Jack Hickling 1928–33, Henry Martin 1933–35, Charlie Bell 1935, Harold Wightman 1936, Harold Parkes 1936–38, Jack Poole 1938–44, Lloyd Barke 1944–45, Roy Goodall 1945–49, Freddie Steele 1949–51, George Jobey 1952–53, Stan Mercer 1953–55, Charlie Mitten 1956–58, Sam Weaver 1958–60, Raich Carter 1960–63, Tommy Cummings 1963–67, Tommy Eggleston 1967–70, Jock Basford 1970–71, Danny Williams 1971–74, Dave Smith 1974–76, Peter Morris 1976–78, Billy Bingham 1978–79, Mick Jones 1979–81, Stuart Boam 1981–83, Ian Greaves 1983–89, George Foster February 1989–.

Player and Position	Ht	Wt	Date	Birth Place	Source	Clubs	League App	Gls
Gary Ford*	5 8	12 05	8 2 61	York	Apprentice	York C	366	52
						Leicester C	16	2
						Port Vale	75	12
						Walsall (loan)	13	2
						Mansfield T	88	6
Kevin Gray	6 0	13 08	7 1 72	Sheffield	Trainee	Mansfield T	99	1
Paul Holland	5 11	12 05	8 7 73	Lincoln	School	Mansfield T	78	9
Nick Roddis*	5 8	11 07	18 2 73	Rotherham	Trainee	Nottingham F	—	—
						Mansfield T	—	—
Forwards								
Gary Castledine	5 8	11 04	27 3 70	Dumfries		Mansfield T	35	3
Paul McLoughlin	5 10	11 11	23 12 63	Bristol	Bristol C	Cardiff C	49	4
					Gisborne C	Hereford U	74	14
						Wolverhampton W	28	4
						Walsall (loan)	9	4
						York C (loan)	1	—
						Mansfield T	38	7
Kevin Noteman	5 10	11 12	15 10 69	Preston	Trainee	Leeds U	1	—
						Doncaster R	106	20
						Mansfield T	30	4
Ian Stringfellow	5 9	11 04	8 5 69	Nottingham	Apprentice	Mansfield T	153	25
						Blackpool (loan)	3	1
Alex Sykes	5 4	11 07	2 4 74	Mansfield	School	Mansfield T	—	—
Steve Wilkinson	6 0	11 02	1 9 68	Lincoln	Apprentice	Leicester C	9	1
						Rochdale (loan)	—	—
						Crewe Alex (loan)	5	2
						Mansfield T	149	51
Lee Wilson†			23 5 72	Mansfield		Mansfield T	4	—

Trainees
Baines, Michael; Crookes, Dominic; Doughty, Stephen; Foster, Stephen; Johnson, Carl; Kerry, Christopher B; Langton, Mark; Marrows, Dean; Morgan, James K; Sears, Wayne S; Smith, Dean; Timons, Christopher; Wilkinson, Lee A; Wood, Mark J.

**Non-Contract
Wilson, Lee.

Associated Schoolboys
Baughan, Russell M; Burley, Dean A; Clarke, Darrell J; Hopley, Dean C; Johnson, Craig A; Sisson, Michael A; Spink, Neil D; Storer, David J; Winter, David M; Wright, Darren.

Associated Schoolboys who have accepted the club's offer of a Traineeship/Contract
Musson, Robert J; Stark, Wayne R; Williams, Michael J.

**Non-Contract Players who are retained must be re-signed before they are eligible to play in League matches.

MIDDLESBROUGH 1992-93 *Back row (left to right):* Jimmy Phillips, Derek Whyte, Paul Wilkinson, Nicky Mohan, Willie Falconer, Jamie Pollock, Robbie Mustoe.
Centre row: Chris Morris, Jon Gittens, Curtis Fleming, Ian Ironside, Steve Pears, Andy Peake, Tommy Wright, Mark Nile (Physio).
Front row: Gary Parkinson, Mark Proctor, Lennie Lawrence (Manager), Alan Kernaghan, John Pickering (First Team Coach), Bernie Slaven, John Hendrie.

Division 1   MIDDLESBROUGH

Ayresome Park, Middlesbrough, Cleveland TS1 4PB. Telephone Middlesbrough (0642) 819659. Commercial Dept. (0642) 826664. Ticket office: (0642) 815996. Fax (0642) 820244. Clubcall: 0891 121181.

Ground capacity; 26,629.

Record attendance: 53,596 v Newcastle U, Division 1, 27 December 1949.

Record receipts: £200,351 v Newcastle U, Coca Cola Cup 2nd rd 2nd leg, 7 October 1992.

Pitch measurements: 114yd × 74yd.

Directors: R. Corbidge, G. Fordy, S. Gibson, M. C. Henderson.

Chief Executive/Secretary: Keith Lamb.

Manager: Lennie Lawrence. *Assistant Manager:* John Pickering.

Physio: Mark Nile.

Youth Development Officer: Ron Bone.

Press & PR Consultant: Clive Armitage.

Year Formed: 1876. *Turned Professional:* 1889; became amateur 1892, and professional again, 1899. *Ltd Co:* 1892.

Club Nickname: 'The Boro'.

Previous Grounds: 1877, Old Archery Ground, Linthorpe Road; 1903, Ayresome Park.

Record League Victory: 9–0 v Brighton & HA, Division 2, 23 August 1958 – Taylor; Bilcliff, Robinson; Harris (2 pens), Phillips, Walley; Day, McLean, Clough (5), Peacock (2), Holliday.

Record Cup Victory: 9–3 v Goole T, FA Cup, 1st rd, 9 January 1915 – Williamson; Haworth, Weir; Davidson, Cook, Malcolm; Wilson, Carr (3), Elliott (3), Tinsley (3), Davies.

Record Defeat: 0–9 v Blackburn R, Division 2, 6 November 1954.

Most League Points (2 for a win): 65, Division 2, 1973–74.

Most League Points (3 for a win): 94, Division 3, 1986–87.

Most League Goals: 122, Division 2, 1926–27.

Highest League Scorer in Season: George Camsell, 59, Division 2, 1926–27 (Second Division record).

Most League Goals in Total Aggregate: George Camsell, 326, 1925–39.

Most Capped Player: Wilf Mannion, 26, England.

Most League Appearances: Tim Williamson, 563, 1902–23.

Record Transfer Fee Received: £2,300,000 from Manchester United for Gary Pallister, August 1989.

Record Transfer Fee Paid: £900,000 to Celtic for Derek Whyte, August 1992.

Football League Record: 1899 Elected to Division 2; 1902–24 Division 1; 1924–27 Division 2; 1927–28 Division 1; 1928–29 Division 2; 1929–54 Division 1; 1954–66 Division 2; 1966–67 Division 3; 1967–74 Division 2; 1974–82 Division 1; 1982–86 Division 2; 1986–87 Division 3; 1987–88 Division 2; 1988–89 Division 1; 1989–92 Division 2; 1992–93 FA Premier League; 1993– Division 1.

Honours: Football League: Division 1 best season: 3rd, 1913–14. Division 2 – Champions 1926–27, 1928–29, 1973–74; Runners-up 1901–02, 1991–92. Division 3 – Runners-up 1966–67, 1986–87. *FA Cup:* best season: 6th rd, 1935–36, 1946–47, 1969–70, 1974–75, 1976–77, 1977–78; old last eight 1900–01, 1903–04. *Football League Cup:* Semi-final 1975–76. *Amateur Cup:* Winners 1895, 1898, *Anglo-Scottish Cup:* Winners 1975–76.

MIDDLESBROUGH 1992—93 LEAGUE RECORD

Match No.	Date		Venue	Opponents		Result	H/T Score	Lg. Pos.	Goalscorers	Atten dance
1	Aug	15	A	Coventry City	L	1-2	0-1	—	Wilkinson	12,681
2		19	H	Manchester City	W	2-0	2-0	—	Slaven 2	15,369
3		22	H	Leeds U	W	4-1	2-0	5	Wilkinson 2, Wright, Hendrie	18,649
4		29	A	Southampton	L	1-2	0-0	9	Wilkinson	13,003
5	Sept	1	A	Ipswich T	D	2-2	0-1	—	Kernaghan, Wilkinson	14,255
6		5	H	Sheffield U	W	2-0	1-0	6	Falconer, Wright	15,179
7		12	A	Manchester C	W	1-0	1-0	6	Flitcroft (og)	25,244
8		19	A	QPR	D	3-3	1-0	6	Kernaghan, Wright, Falconer	12,272
9		26	H	Aston Villa	L	2-3	0-1	7	Slaven, McGrath (og)	20,905
10	Oct	3	A	Manchester U	D	1-1	0-1	9	Slaven	24,172
11		17	A	Tottenham H	D	2-2	2-0	9	Mustoe, Wilkinson	24,735
12		21	A	Nottingham F	L	0-1	0-0	—		17,846
13		24	H	Sheffield W	D	1-1	1-1	9	Wilkinson	18,414
14		31	A	Norwich C	D	1-1	0-0	11	Wilkinson	14,499
15	Nov	7	A	Liverpool	L	1-4	1-3	12	Phillips (pen)	34,974
16		21	H	Wimbledon	W	2-0	0-0	11	Hendrie, Morris	14,524
17		28	A	Oldham Ath	L	1-4	1-3	14	Falconer	12,401
18	Dec	5	H	Blackburn R	W	3-2	0-1	12	Hendrie 3	20,096
19		11	H	Chelsea	D	0-0	0-0	—		15,599
20		19	A	Arsenal	D	1-1	1-0	12	Seaman (og)	23,197
21		26	A	Everton	D	2-2	0-0	12	Hignett 2	24,391
22		28	H	Crystal Palace	L	0-1	0-0	13		21,123
23	Jan	9	H	QPR	L	0-1	0-0	14		15,616
24		17	A	Aston Villa	L	1-5	0-3	—	Hignett	19,977
25		26	H	Southampton	W	2-1	1-0	—	Mohan, Wilkinson	13,918
26		30	A	Leeds U	L	0-3	0-0	16		30,344
27	Feb	6	A	Coventry C	L	0-2	0-0	18		14,008
28		9	A	Sheffield U	L	0-2	0-1	—		15,184
29		20	H	Nottingham F	L	1-2	0-0	19	Phillips	15,639
30		27	A	Manchester U	L	0-3	0-1	21		36,251
31	Mar	2	A	Ipswich T	W	1-0	1-0	—	Wilkinson	15,430
32		9	A	Wimbledon	L	0-2	0-1	—		5821
33		13	H	Liverpool	L	1-2	1-1	20	Nicol (og)	22,463
34		20	A	Blackburn R	D	1-1	1-1	20	Hendrie	14,041
35		22	H	Oldham Ath	L	2-3	0-2	—	Mohan, Hignett	12,290
36	Apr	3	A	Chelsea	L	0-4	0-0	22		13,043
37		6	H	Arsenal	W	1-0	1-0	—	Hendrie	12,726
38		10	H	Everton	L	1-2	0-1	21	Wilkinson	16,627
39		12	A	Crystal Palace	L	1-4	0-0	22	Wilkinson	15,123
40		20	H	Tottenham H	W	3-0	2-0	—	Wright 2, Wilkinson	14,472
41	May	1	A	Sheffield W	W	3-2	2-0	20	Falconer, Pollock, Hendrie	25,949
42		8	H	Norwich C	D	3-3	1-1	21	Falconer, Wilkinson, Hendrie	15,155

Final League Position: 21

GOALSCORERS

League (54): Wilkinson 14, Hendrie 9, Falconer 5, Wright 5, Hignett 4, Slaven 4, Kernaghan 2, Mohan 2, Phillips 2 (1 pen), Morris 1, Mustoe 1, Pollock 1, own goals 4.
Coca Cola Cup (1): Wilkinson 1.
FA Cup (3): Falconer 2, Wright 1.

Pears 26	Morris 22 + 3	Phillips 40	Kernaghan 22	Whyte 34 + 1	Peake 33	Wright 34 + 2	Mustoe 21 + 2	Wilkinson 41	Hendrie 31 + 1	Falconer 22 + 6	Slaven 13 + 5	Ironside 11 + 1	Pollock 17 + 5	Parkinson 4	Horne 3 + 1	Gittens 13	Proctor 6 + 5	Fleming 22 + 2	Kavanagh 6 + 4	Hignett 18 + 3	Mohan 18	Kamara 3 + 2	Marshall — + 3	Moore — + 2	Collett 2	Match No.
1	2	3	4	5	6	7	8	9	10	11	12															1
	2	3	4	5	6	10	12	9	11	8	7	1														2
	2	3	4	5	6	10	12	9	11	8	7	1	14													3
	2	3	4	5	6	10	11	9		8	7	1														4
		3	4	5	6	10	11	9		8	7	1			2	12										5
	2	3	4	5	6	10	11	9		8	7				1											6
	2	3	4	5	6	10	7	9	11	8					1											7
	2	3	4	5		10	11	9	7	8	12		6		1											8
	2	3	4	5	6	11	8	9			7	1	10													9
	2	3		5	6	11	8	9		12	7	1	10	4												10
1	2	3	4	5		10	8	9					7			6	11	12								11
1	2	3	4	5		10		9					7			6	11	12	8							12
1	2	3	4			11		9					7			6	8	5	10							13
1	12	3	4	5		7		9	11	8						6	10	2								14
1	14	3	4	5		7		9	11	8	12					6	10	2								15
1	11	3		5		6		9	10	7			8			4	12	2	14							16
1				5		11	4	9		7			12	3		6	10	2	14	8						17
1		3		5	8	11	6	9	7					12			14	2		10	4					18
1		3		5	8	11		9	7					6				2	12	10	4					19
1		3		5	8	11		9		7	12			6			14	2		10	4					20
1		3		5	8	11		9	7	12				6				2		10	4					21
1		3		5	8	11		9	7	12				6			14	2		10	4					22
1		3			8	10		9	11	12				6		5		2		7	4					23
1		3	4		8	10		9	11	6			14			5			7	12	2					24
1	4	3				10	7	9	11	6			8					2			5					25
1	4	3				10	7	9	11	6			8					2		12	5					26
1	2	3				10	12	9	11	6	7		14			5				8	4					27
1			4	10		9			7	14	8	3		6	12	2		11	5							28
1	14	3	4		6	11		9		7			2	5			12	8	10							29
1	2	3		4	6	11	8	9	7	12						5	10									30
	2	3	4	6	5	11	8	9	7	12	1						10									31
1	2	3	4	6	5	11	8	9	7	10	12															32
	2	3		6	5	12	8	9	7	10		1						11	4							33
	2	3		6	5	7	8	9	11	10	1							4	12							34
		3		6	5	11	8	9	7	10	1					2		12	4	14						35
		3	5	6		11	8	9	7	10	1					2		4				12				36
1		3	4		6		9	7		10						2	8	11	5							37
1		3	4	12	6		9	7		10						2	8	11	5	14						38
1		3	5		10		9	7		8						2	11	4	6							39
1		3	4	5	6	8	9	7		10						2	11									40
	5	3		6	10	11		9	7	12		8				2	4		14	1						41
	3	4	5	6		11	9	7	8							2	10		12	14	1					42

Coca Cola Cup	Second Round	Newcastle U (a)	0-0
		(h)	1-3
FA Cup	Third Round	Chelsea (h)	2-1
	Fourth Round	Nottingham F (a)	1-1
		(h)	0-3

MIDDLESBROUGH

Player and Position	Ht	Wt	Date	Birth Place	Source	Clubs	League App	Gls
Goalkeepers								
Andy Collett	5 11	12 00	28 10 73	Middlesbrough	Trainee	Middlesbrough	2	—
Ian Ironside	6 2	13 00	8 3 64	Sheffield	N. Ferriby U	Scarborough	88	—
						Middlesbrough	13	—
						Scarborough (loan)	7	—
Steve Pears	6 0	12 11	22 1 62	Brandon	Apprentice	Manchester U	4	—
						Middlesbrough (loan)	12	—
						Middlesbrough	276	—
Ben Roberts			22 6 75	Bishop Auckland	Trainee	Middlesbrough	—	—
Defenders								
Michael Barron			22 12 74	Chester le Street	Trainee	Middlesbrough	—	—
Anthony Cole‡			18 9 72	Gateshead	Trainee	Middlesbrough	—	—
Curtis Fleming	5 8	11 04	8 10 68	Manchester	St Patrick's Ath	Swindon T	—	—
					St Patrick's Ath	Middlesbrough	52	—
Jon Gittens*	6 0	12 06	22 1 64	Moseley	Paget R	Southampton	18	—
						Swindon T	126	6
						Southampton	19	—
						Middlesbrough (loan)	12	1
						Middlesbrough	13	—
Alan Kernaghan	6 2	13 00	25 4 67	Otley	Apprentice	Middlesbrough	206	15
						Charlton Ath (loan)	13	—
Robert Lake†			13 10 71	Stockton	Trainee	Middlesbrough	—	—
Richard Liburd			26 9 73	Nottingham	Eastwood T	Middlesbrough	—	—
Nicky Mohan	6 2	12 00	6 10 70	Middlesbrough	Trainee	Middlesbrough	73	4
						Hull C (loan)	5	1
Chris Morris	5 10	10 08	24 12 63	Newquay		Sheffield W	74	1
						Celtic	163	8
						Middlesbrough	25	1
Michael Oliver			2 8 75	Cleveland	Trainee	Middlesbrough	—	—
Jimmy Phillips	6 0	12 00	8 2 66	Bolton	Apprentice	Bolton W	108	2
						Rangers	25	—
						Oxford U	79	8
						Middlesbrough	139	6
Mark Taylor			8 11 74	Saltburn	Trainee	Middlesbrough	—	—
Andrew Todd	5 10	10 11	21 9 74	Derby	Trainee	Middlesbrough	—	—
Derek Whyte	5 11	11 05	31 8 68	Glasgow	Celtic BC	Celtic	216	7
						Middlesbrough	35	—
Midfield								
Willie Falconer	6 1	11 09	5 4 66	Aberdeen	Lewis U	Aberdeen	77	13
						Watford	98	12
						Middlesbrough	53	10
Craig Hignett	5 10	11 00	12 1 70	Whiston		Crewe Alex	121	42
						Middlesbrough	21	4
Graham Kavanagh	5 10	11 00	3 12 73	Dublin	Home Farm	Middlesbrough	10	—
Alan Moore	5 10	11 00	25 11 74	Dublin	Rivermount	Middlesbrough	2	—
Robbie Mustoe	5 10	10 08	28 8 68	Oxford		Oxford U	91	10
						Middlesbrough	94	7
Andy Payton (To Celtic August 1992)	5 9	10 06	23 10 66	Burnley	Apprentice	Hull C	144	55
						Middlesbrough	19	3
Andy Peake	5 10	12 00	1 11 61	Market Harborough	Apprentice	Leicester C	147	13
						Grimsby T	39	4
						Charlton Ath	177	5
						Middlesbrough	56	—
Jamie Pollock	6 0	11 12	16 2 74	Stockton	Trainee	Middlesbrough	49	2

MIDDLESBROUGH

Colours: Red shirts, white shorts, red stockings. **Change colours:** White shirts, black shorts, black stockings.

Foundation: The story of how the idea of a Middlesbrough football club was first mooted at a tripe supper at the Corporation Hotel in 1875 is well known locally. But the club was formally established at a meeting in the Talbot Hotel the following year and is one of the oldest clubs in the North East.

First Football League game: 2 September, 1899, Division 2, v Lincoln C (a) L 0-3 – Smith; Shaw, Ramsey; Allport, McNally, McCracken; Wanless, Longstaffe, Gettins, Page, Pugh.

Did you know: In 1973–74, Middlesbrough finished 15 points ahead of their nearest rivals in winning the Division 2 championship, the highest margin produced by a title-winning team in the Football League under the two points for a win system.

Managers (and Secretary-Managers)
John Robson 1899–1905, Alex Massie 1905–06, Andy Aitken 1906–09, J. Gunter 1908–10*, Andy Walker 1910–11, Tom McIntosh 1911–19, James Howie 1920–23, Herbert Bamlett 1923–26, Peter McWilliam 1927–34, Wilf Gillow 1934–44, David Jack 1944–52, Walter Rowley 1952–54, Bob Dennison 1954–63, Raich Carter 1963–66, Stan Anderson 1966–73, Jack Charlton 1973–77, John Neal 1977–81, Bobby Murdoch 1981–82, Malcolm Allison 1982–84, Willie Maddren 1984–86, Bruce Rioch 1986–90, Colin Todd 1990–91, Lennie Lawrence July 1991–.

Player and Position	Ht	Wt	Date	Birth Place	Source	Clubs	League App	Gls
Mark Proctor*	5 10	11 13	30 1 61	Middlesbrough	Apprentice	Middlesbrough	109	12
						Nottingham F	64	5
						Sunderland (loan)	5	—
						Sunderland	112	19
						Sheffield W	59	4
						Middlesbrough	120	6
						Tranmere R (loan)	13	1
Philip Stamp			12 12 75	Middlesbrough	Trainee	Middlesbrough	—	
Forwards								
Paul Forrester			3 11 72	Edinburgh		Middlesbrough	—	—
John Hendrie	5 7	11 07	24 10 63	Lennoxtown	Apprentice	Coventry C	21	2
						Hereford U (loan)	6	—
						Bradford C	173	46
						Newcastle U	34	4
						Leeds U	27	5
						Middlesbrough	111	15
Neil Illman			29 4 75	Doncaster	Trainee	Middlesbrough	—	—
Paul Wilkinson	6 0	11 09	30 10 64	Louth	Apprentice	Grimsby T	71	27
						Everton	31	7
						Nottingham F	34	5
						Watford	134	52
						Middlesbrough	87	29
Tommy Wright	5 7	9 10	10 1 66	Dunfermline	Apprentice	Leeds U	81	24
						Oldham Ath	112	23
						Leicester C	129	22
						Middlesbrough	36	5

Trainees
Agiadis, Nicholas; Creamer, Christopher P; Dwyer, Paul J; Johnson, Ian; Maddick, Kevin A; McGargle, Stephen; McKinlay, David; Norton, Paul.

**Non-Contract
Lake, Robert M; McDowell, Roddy.

Associated Schoolboys
Cosgrove, Antony; Cummings, Peter; Fielding, Kyle W; Harrison, Paul; Howarth, Andrew J; Knight, Robert G; Lloyd, Gary P; Payne, Lee J; Rose, Richard; Slater, Darren.

Associated Schoolboys who have accepted the club's offer of a Traineeship/Contract
Mills, Andrew D; Richardson, Paul; Skingsley, Ross A; Summerbell, Mark; Ward, Richard T.

**Non-Contract Players who are retained must be re-signed before they are eligible to play in League matches.

338

MILLWALL 1992–93 *Back row (left to right):* Paul Holsgrove, Etienne Verveer, Keith Stevens, Chris Armstrong, Mark Foran, John McGlashan, Tony McCarthy, Paul Stephenson, Tony Dolby.
Centre row: Keith Johnstone (Physio), Paul Manning, John McGinlay, Jon Goodman, Brian Horne, Aidan Davison, John Donegan, Kasey Keller, Carl Emberson, Ken Cunningham, Brian Lee, John Humphrey, Peter Melville (Physio).
Front row: Andy May, Andy Roberts, Ian Bogie, Alex Ray, Mick McCarthy (Player/Manager), Ian Evans (First Team Coach), Phil Barber, Colin Cooper, Ian Dawes, Malcom Allen.
(Photograph: Tom Morris)

Division 1   **MILLWALL**

The Den, Zampa Road, Bermondsey SE16 3LH. Telephone 071–232 1222. Ticket Office: 071–231 9999. Fax: 071–231 3663.

Ground capacity: 20,000.

Record Attendance: 48,672 v Derby Co, FA Cup 5th rd, 20 February 1937.

Record Receipts: £106,839 v West Ham U, Division 2, 10 November 1990.

Pitch measurements: 115yd × 73yd.

President: Lord Mellish of Bermondsey.

Chairman: Reg Burr. *Vice-chairman:* Peter Mead. *Directors:* Brian Mitchell, Jeff Burnige, Cllr. David Sullivan.

Chief Executive Secretary: Graham Hortop. *Assistant Secretary:* Yvonne Haines.

Player-Manager: Mick McCarthy. *First team coach:* Ian Evans.

Reserve team coach: Ian McDonald. *Youth team coach:* Tom Walley. *Chief Scout:* Ron Howard. *Youth Development Officer:* Allen Batsford. *Physios:* Peter Melville, Keith Johnstone. *Hon. Medical Officer:* Dr. Daniel Baron.

Sales & Promotions Manager: Mike Sullivan. *Commercial Manager:* Billy Neil.

Year Formed: 1885. *Turned Professional:* 1893. *Ltd Co.:* 1894.

Previous Names: 1885, Millwall Rovers; 1889, Millwall Athletic.

Club Nickname: 'The Lions'.

Previous Grounds: 1885, Glengall Road, Millwall; 1886, Back of 'Lord Nelson'; 1890, East Ferry Road; 1901, North Greenwich; 1910, The Den, Cold Blow Lane; 1993, The Den, Bermondsey.

Record League Victory: 9–1 v Torquay U, Division 3 (S), 29 August 1927 – Lansdale; Tilling, Hill; Amos, Bryant (3), Graham; Chance, Hawkins (3), Landells (1), Phillips (2), Black. 9–1 v Coventry C, Division 3 (S), 19 November 1927 – Lansdale; Fort, Hill; Amos, Collins (1), Graham; Chance, Landells (4), Cock (2), Phillips (2), Black.

Record Cup Victory: 7–0 v Gateshead, FA Cup, 2nd rd, 12 December 1936 – Yuill; Ted Smith, Inns; Brolly, Hancock, Forsyth; Thomas (1), Mangnall (1), Ken Burditt (2), McCartney (2), Thorogood (1).

Record Defeat: 1–9 v Aston Villa, FA Cup 4th rd, 28 January 1946.

Most League Points (2 for a win): 65, Division 3 (S), 1927–28 and Division 3, 1965–66.

Most League Points (3 for a win): 90, Division 3, 1984–85.

Most League Goals: 127, Division 3 (S), 1927–28.

Highest League Scorer in Season: Richard Parker, 37, Division 3 (S), 1926–27.

Most League Goals in Total Aggregate: Teddy Sheringham, 93, 1984–91.

Most Capped Player: Eamonn Dunphy, 22 (23), Eire.

Most League Appearances: Barry Kitchener, 523, 1967–82.

Record Transfer Fee Received: £2,000,000 from Nottingham F for Teddy Sheringham, July 1991.

Record Transfer Fee Paid: £800,000 to Derby Co for Paul Goddard, December 1989.

Football League Record: 1920 Original Members of Division 3; 1921 Division 3 (S); 1928–34 Division 2; 1934–38 Division 3 (S); 1938–48 Division 2; 1948–58 Division 3 (S); 1958–62 Division 4; 1962–64 Division 3; 1964–65 Division 4; 1965–66 Division 3; 1966–75 Division 2; 1975–76 Division 3; 1976–79 Division 2; 1979–85 Division 3; 1985–88 Division 2; 1988–90 Division 1; 1990–92 Division 2; 1992– Division 1.

Honours: Football League: Division 1 best season: 7th 1992–93; Division 2 – Champions 1987–88; Division 3 (S) – Champions 1927–28, 1937–38; Runners-up 1952–53; Division 3 – Runners-up 1965–66, 1984–85; Division 4 – Champions 1961–62; Runners-up 1964–65. *FA Cup:* Semi-final 1900, 1903, 1937 (first Division 3 side to reach semi-final). *Football League Cup:* best season: 5th rd, 1973–74, 1976–77. *Football League Trophy:* Winners 1982–83.

MILLWALL 1992—93 LEAGUE RECORD

Match No.	Date	Venue	Opponents	Result	H/T Score	Lg. Pos.	Goalscorers	Atten dance
1	Aug 15	A	Watford	L	1-3	1-2	—	McGinlay	9745
2	22	H	Oxford U	W	3-1	2-0	12	Rae, Armstrong, Allen	6746
3	29	A	Barnsley	D	0-0	0-0	12		4795
4	Sept 5	H	Swindon T	W	2-1	0-1	10	McGinlay, Goodman	8091
5	12	H	Birmingham C	D	0-0	0-0	10		8581
6	15	H	Peterborough U	D	0-0	0-0	—		5619
7	19	H	Notts Co	W	6-0	1-0	5	Goodman, Allen 2, Barber 2, Dolby	6689
8	26	A	Brentford	D	1-1	0-1	6	Allen	8823
9	Oct 3	A	Sunderland	L	0-2	0-0	9		14,871
10	10	H	Cambridge U	D	2-2	2-2	11	Allen, Goodman	7096
11	18	A	Charlton Ath	W	2-0	1-0	—	Rae, Moralee	7527
12	25	H	Wolverhampton W	W	2-0	0-0	—	Cooper, Moralee	6814
13	31	A	Bristol R	L	0-1	0-0	8		5378
14	Nov 4	H	Bristol C	W	4-1	4-1	—	Cooper, Allen, May, Moralee	5934
15	7	A	Derby Co	W	2-1	0-1	5	Moralee, Rae	17,087
16	15	H	West Ham U	W	2-1	1-0	—	Allen (pen), Barber	12,445
17	21	A	Luton T	D	1-1	0-1	5	Byrne	8371
18	28	A	Portsmouth	L	0-1	0-1	6		12,445
19	Dec 5	H	Southend U	D	1-1	1-1	6	Barber	7928
20	12	H	Grimsby T	W	2-1	1-0	4	Moralee 2	6900
21	20	A	Newcastle U	D	1-1	1-0	—	Moralee	26,089
22	26	A	Tranmere R	D	1-1	0-1	4	Goodman	13,118
23	28	H	Leicester C	W	2-0	1-0	4	Moralee, Goodman	12,230
24	Jan 9	A	Notts Co	W	2-1	0-1	3	Moralee, Goodman	6148
25	17	H	Brentford	W	6-1	3-0	—	Rae, Goodman 2, Cooper, Moralee 2	7571
26	27	H	Peterborough U	W	4-0	2-0	—	Barber, McCarthy, Rae, Goodman	8732
27	30	A	Oxford U	L	0-3	0-1	3		7474
28	Feb 6	H	Watford	W	5-2	4-0	3	Moralee 2, Rae, Cooper, Goodman	8847
29	9	A	Birmingham C	D	0-0	0-0	—		8504
30	13	H	Swindon T	L	0-3	0-1	3		10,544
31	20	H	Barnsley	L	0-4	0-3	3		8034
32	27	A	Cambridge U	D	1-1	1-0	3	Allen	5144
33	Mar 6	H	Sunderland	D	0-0	0-0	5		8761
34	9	A	Bristol C	W	1-0	1-0	—	Barber	8771
35	13	H	Derby Co	W	1-0	0-0	5	Allen (pen)	9365
36	21	A	Southend U	D	3-3	3-1	—	Barber, Stevens, Goodman	3840
37	24	H	Luton T	W	1-0	1-0	—	Moralee	8286
38	28	H	West Ham U	D	2-2	1-2	—	Moralee, Stevens	15,723
39	Apr 3	H	Portsmouth	D	1-1	0-1	5	Kerr	12,921
40	6	A	Grimsby T	L	0-1	0-0	—		4445
41	10	A	Tranmere R	D	0-0	0-0	6		9392
42	14	A	Leicester C	L	0-3	0-1	—		19,711
43	17	H	Newcastle U	L	1-2	1-0	7	Barber	14,262
44	24	H	Charlton Ath	W	1-0	1-0	7	Goodman	10,159
45	May 1	A	Wolverhampton W	L	1-3	0-3	7	Allen	12,054
46	8	H	Bristol R	L	0-3	0-1	7		15,821

Final League Position: 7

GOALSCORERS

League (65): Moralee 15, Goodman 12, Allen 10 (2 pens), Barber 8, Rae 6, Cooper 4, McGinlay 2, Stevens 2, Armstrong 1, Byrne 1, Dolby 1, Kerr 1, McCarthy 1, May 1.
Coca Cola Cup (7): Allen 2, Roberts 2, Armstrong 1, Stevens 1, own goal 1.
FA Cup (0).

Appearances and goals grid (League). Player column headings show total appearances (+ substitute appearances). Numbers in each row are the shirt numbers worn in that match; italic numbers indicate substitute appearances/goals as printed.

Davison 1	Cunningham 37	Dawes 46	May 34 + 1	Cooper 41	Stevens 31	Roberts 41 + 4	McGinlay 6 + 1	Allen 30 + 11	Armstrong 3	Barber 46	Stephenson — + 5	Rae 23 + 7	Keller 45	Goodman 29 + 6	Bogie 20 + 2	Holsgrove 3 + 8	Dolby 4 + 14	Moralee 31 + 6	Byrne 11 + 2	McCarthy T 6 + 1	McLeary 4 + 2	Kerr 1 + 5	Maguire 9	Gaynor — + 3	Wallace 3	Kennedy — + 1	Manning 1	Verveer — + 1	Match No.
1	2	3	4	5	6	7	8	9	10	11	12	14																	1
	2	3	4	5	6	7	8	9	10	11		14	1	12															2
	2	3		5	6	7	8	10		11	12	4	1	9															3
	2	3		5	6	7	8			11	12		1	9	4	10	14												4
	2	3	4	5	6	7	8	9		11			1	10				12											5
	2	3	4	5	6	7	8	9		11			1	10				14	12										6
	2	3	4	5	6	7	12	9		11			1	10				14	8										7
	2	3	4	5	6	7		9		11			1	10					8										8
	2	3	4	5	6	7		9		11			1	10				14	8	12									9
	2	3	4	5	6	7		9		11		14	1	10					8	12									10
	2	3	4	5		7		9		11		6	1	10	12			8											11
	2	3	4	5		7		9		11		6	1	10	14	12		8											12
	2	3	4	5		7		9		11		6	1	10	12			8	14										13
	2	3	4	5		7		9		11		6	1	14	12			8	10										14
	2	3	4	5		7		9		11		6	1	14	12			8	10										15
	2	3	4	5	6			9		11		7	1	14	12			8	10										16
	2	3	4	5	6	12		9		11		7	1	8	10														17
	2	3	4	5	6	12		9		11		7	1	14	8	10													18
	2	3	4	5	6	7		9		11		14	1	12	8	10													19
	2	3	4	5	6	7		14		11			1	9	12	8	10												20
	2	3	4	5	6	7	12			11		14	1	10	9	8													21
	2	3	4	5	6	7	12			11		14	1	10	9	8													22
	2	3	4	5	6	7	12			11			1	10	9	8													23
	2	3	4	5	6	7	12			11			1	10	9	8													24
		3	4	5	6	7	12			11		2	1	10	9	14	8												25
		3	4			7	12			11		2	1	10	9	14	8				5	6							26
		3	4			7	12			11		2	1	10	9	14	8				5	6							27
		3	4	5	6	7	12			11		2	1	10	9	8													28
		3	4	5	6	7				11		2	1	10	9	8					12								29
		3	4	5	6	7	12			11			1	10	9	2	8				14								30
		3	4	5	6	7	12			11		14	1	10	9	8					2								31
	2	3	4	5	6	7	8			11		14	1	9				12	10										32
	2	3	4	5	6	7	8			11		14	1	9				12	10										33
	2	3		5	6	7		9		11		4	1	8				14	12	10									34
	2	3	4	5	6	14		9		11		7	1	8				12	10										35
	2	3		5	6	7				11			1	9	8	4		10	12	14									36
	2	3		5	6	4		9		11		7	1	8				10					12						37
	2	3		5	6	4		9		11		7	1	8				10					12	7	14				38
	2	3		5		4		9		11			1	14				10				6	12	7	8				39
		3	2			4				11			1	14				10			6	5	9	7	12	8			40
	2	3	4			14		9		11		7	1	8				10			5		12	6					41
	2	3	4					9		11		7	1	10				14	8		5		12	6					42
	2	3		5		4		9		11		7	1	10				14				6	12	8					43
	2	3		5		4		9		11		7	1	10				8				6	12						44
	2	3	12	5		4		9		11		7	1	10				14	8			6							45
		3		5		4		9		11		7	1	10				14	8			6		2				12	46

Coca Cola Cup	First Round	Leyton Orient (a)	2-2
		(h)	3-0
	Second Round	Arsenal (a)	1-1
		(h)	1-1
FA Cup	Third Round	Southend U (a)	0-1

MILLWALL

Player and Position	Ht	Wt	Date	Birth Place	Source	Clubs	League App	Gls
Goalkeepers								
Aidan Davison	6 2	13 11	11 5 68	Sedgefield	Billingham Syn	Notts Co	1	—
						Leyton Orient (loan)	—	—
						Bury	—	—
						Chester C (loan)	—	—
						Blackpool (loan)	—	—
						Millwall	34	—
John Donegan‡	6 0	13 01	19 5 71	Cork	Killkenny	Millwall	—	—
Carl Emberson	6 1	13 11	13 7 73	Epsom	Trainee	Millwall	—	—
						Colchester U (loan)	13	—
Kasey Keller	6 1	13 07	27 11 69	Washington	Portland Univ	Millwall	46	—
Defenders								
Mark Beard			8 10 74	Roehampton	Trainee	Millwall	—	—
Colin Cooper	5 11	11 05	28 2 67	Durham		Middlesbrough	188	6
						Millwall	77	6
Ken Cunningham	6 0	11 08	28 6 71	Dublin		Millwall	82	—
Ian Dawes	5 10	11 10	22 2 63	Croydon	Apprentice	QPR	229	3
						Millwall	190	5
Mark Foran	6 4	13 12	30 10 73	Aldershot	Trainee	Millwall	—	—
Brian Lee‡	5 11	11 00	24 9 73	Greenwich	Trainee	Millwall	—	—
Mick McCarthy	6 2	13 12	7 2 59	Barnsley	Apprentice	Barnsley	272	7
						Manchester C	140	2
						Celtic	48	—
					Lyon	Millwall	35	2
Tony McCarthy	6 1	12 03	9 11 69	Dublin	Shelbourne	Millwall	7	1
Alan McLeary‡	6 0	11 11	6 10 64	London	Apprentice	Millwall	307	5
						Sheffield U (loan)	3	—
						Wimbledon (loan)	4	—
Matthew Middleton			22 1 75	Lambeth	Trainee	Millwall	—	—
Keith Stevens	6 0	12 10	21 6 64	Merton	Apprentice	Millwall	346	6
Ben Thatcher			30 11 75	Swindon		Millwall	—	—
Midfield								
Ian Bogie	5 7	12 00	6 12 67	Newcastle	Apprentice	Newcastle U	14	—
						Preston NE	79	12
						Millwall	47	—
Daniel Chapman			21 11 74	Deptford	Trainee	Millwall	—	—
James Connor			22 8 74	Middlesbrough		Millwall	—	—
Paul Holsgrove	6 2	12 11	26 8 69	Wellington	Trainee	Aldershot	3	—
						Wimbledon (loan)	—	—
						WBA (loan)	—	—
					Wokingham	Luton T	2	—
					Heracles	Millwall	11	—
Gavin Maguire	5 10	11 08	24 11 67	Hammersmith	Apprentice	QPR	40	—
						Portsmouth	91	—
						Newcastle U (loan)	3	—
						Millwall	9	—
Paul Manning	5 8	10 12	21 1 74	Lewisham	Trainee	Millwall	1	—
Andy May	5 8	11 10	26 2 64	Bury	Apprentice	Manchester C	150	8
						Huddersfield T	114	5
						Bolton W (loan)	10	2
						Bristol C	90	4
						Millwall	35	1
Geoffrey Pitcher			15 8 75	Sutton	Trainee	Millwall	—	—
Alex Rae	5 9	11 05	30 9 69	Glasgow	Bishopbriggs	Falkirk	83	20
						Millwall	107	27
Andy Roberts	5 10	13 00	20 3 74	Dartford	Trainee	Millwall	52	—
Etienne Verveer	5 11	11 12	22 9 67	Surinam	Chur	Millwall	26	2

MILLWALL

Colours: Blue shirts, white shorts, blue stockings. **Change colours:** Yellow shirts, black shorts, black stockings.

Foundation: Formed in 1885 as Millwall Rovers by employees of Morton & Co, a jam and marmalade factory in West Ferry Road. The founders were predominantly Scotsmen. Their first headquarters was the The Islanders pub in Tooke Street, Millwall. Their first trophy was the East End Cup in 1887.

First Football League game: 28 August, 1920, Division 3, v Bristol R (h) W 2-0 – Lansdale; Fort, Hodge; Voisey (1), Riddell, McAlpine; Waterall, Travers, Broad (1), Sutherland, Dempsey.

Did you know: In three successive seasons Millwall finished in 14th place in Division 2 with 39 points. In 1928–29 they won 16 and drew seven of their 42 matches, in 1929–30 won 12 and drew 15, while in 1930–31 they again won 16 and drew seven.

Managers (and Secretary-Managers)
Willie Henderson 1894–95*, John Beveridge 1895–1907* (continued as secretary until 1915), Fred Kidd 1907–08, George Saunders 1908–09, Herbert Lipsham 1913–19, Robert Hunter 1919–33, Bill McCracken 1933–36, Charlie Hewitt 1936–40, Bill Voisey 1940–44, Jack Cock 1944–48, Charlie Hewitt 1948–56, Ron Gray 1956–57, Jimmy Seed 1958–59, Reg Smith 1959–61, Ron Gray 1961–63, Billy Gray 1963–66, Benny Fenton 1966–74, Gordon Jago 1974–77, George Petchey 1978–80, Peter Anderson 1980–82, George Graham 1982–86, John Docherty 1986–90, Bob Pearson 1990, Bruce Rioch April 1990–92, Mick McCarthy March 1992–.

Forwards

Name				Birthplace	Previous	Clubs	Apps	Goals
Malcolm Allen	5 8	11 10	21 3 67	Dioniolen	Apprentice	Watford	39	5
						Aston Villa (loan)	4	—
						Norwich C	35	8
						Millwall	81	24
Philip Barber	5 11	12 12	10 6 65	Tring	Aylesbury	Crystal Palace	234	35
						Millwall	75	12
John Byrne	5 11	13 01	1 2 61	Manchester	Apprentice	York C	175	55
						QPR	126	30
					Le Havre	Brighton	51	14
						Sunderland	33	8
						Millwall	13	1
						Brighton (loan)	7	2
Tony Dolby	5 10	12 02	16 4 74	Greenwich	Trainee	Millwall	18	1
Tommy Gaynor*	6 1	13 02	29 1 63	Limerick	Limerick	Doncaster R	33	7
						Nottingham F	57	10
						Newcastle U (loan)	4	1
						Millwall	3	—
Jon Goodman	5 11	12 11	2 6 71	Walthamstow	Bromley	Millwall	75	20
John Humphrey*	5 11	12 09	2 7 69	Guildford	Leatherhead	Millwall	—	—
						Exeter C (loan)	2	—
Mark Kennedy†	5 11	11 09	15 5 76	Dublin	Trainee	Millwall	1	—
John Kerr	5 8	11 05	6 3 65	Toronto	Harrow Borough	Portsmouth	4	—
						Peterborough U (loan)	10	1
					San Diego Sockers	Millwall	6	1
Jamie Moralee	5 11	11 05	2 12 71	Wandsworth	Trainee	Crystal Palace	6	—
						Millwall	37	15
Romano Sion‡			9 6 71	Surinam		Millwall	—	—
Jermaine Wright			21 10 75	Greenwich	Trainee	Millwall	—	—

Trainees
Franics, Dean; Gordon, Neville; Irving, Paul R; Knight, Glen J; Luckett, Colin A; Morgan, Vaughan A; Smith, Brett R; Walley, Simon J; Wietecha, David.

**Non-Contract
Kennedy, Mark.

Associated Schoolboys
Aris, Steven; Bishop, Joe; Canoville, Dean; Dann, James; Dillon, Spencer; Dillon, Warren; Godbold, Marc; Hirst, Matthew; Hope, Stephen J; Jackson, Stephen R; Johnson, Steven L; Jones, Michael; Kelly, Steven; Keown, Darren; O'Neil, Phil; Sole, Salvatore; Stevens, Shaun; Taylor, Paul S; Woolterton, Toby.

Associated Schoolboys who have accepted the club's offer of a Traineeship/Contract
Ham, Nathan G; Hatcher, Kevin T; Jones, Steven; Morey, Robert B.

**Non-Contract Players who are retained must be re-signed before they are eligible to play in League matches.

NEWCASTLE UNITED 1992–93 *Back row (left to right):* David Roche, Andy Hunt, Alan Neilson, Darron McDonough, Rob Elliott, Matty Appleby, Barry Venison, David Kelly, Mick Quinn, Peter Garland, John Watson, Phil Mason.

Centre row: Derek Fazackerley (Coach), Colin Suggett (Coach), Pavel Srnicek, Bjorn Kristensen, Peter Cormack, Liam O'Brien, Stephen Howey, Stephen Watson, Kevin Scott, Alan Thompson, Tommy Wright, Derek Wright (Physio), Chris Guthrie (Kit Man).

Front row: Mark Stimson, Kevin Sheedy, Franz Carr, Kevin Brock, Lee Clark, Terry McDermott (Assistant Manager), Kevin Keegan (Manager), Brian Kilcline, Gavin Peacock, Ray Ranson, Paul Bracewell, John Beresford.

FA Premier

NEWCASTLE UNITED

St James' Park, Newcastle-upon-Tyne NE1 4ST. Telephone 091–232 8361. Promotions: 091–230 2861. Commercial Dept: 091–232 0406. Ticket Office Hotline: 091–261 1571. Club Shop: 091–261 6357. Club Shop Answering Service: 091–232 4080. Football in the Community Scheme: 091–261 9715. Conference and Banqueting: 091–222 1860. Club Fax: 091–232 9875. Clubcall: 0898 121590. Clubcall Ticket Line: 0898 121190.

Ground capacity: 37,029.

Record attendance: 68,386 v Chelsea, Division 1, 3 Sept 1930.

Record receipts: £157,153 v Sunderland, Division 2 play-off, semi-final, 16 May 1990.

Pitch measurements: 110yd × 73yd.

President: T. L. Bennett.

Chairman: Sir John Hall.

Vice-chairman: W. F. Shepherd. *Chief Executive:* A. O. Fletcher.

Directors: D. S. Hall, R. Jones.

Manager: Kevin Keegan. *Assistant Manager:* Terry McDermott.

Coaches: Colin Suggett and Derek Fazackerley. *Physio:* Derek Wright.

General Manager/Secretary: R. Cushing.

Assistant Secretary: K. Slater. *Commercial Manager:*

Year Formed: 1881. *Turned Professional:* 1889. *Ltd Co.:* 1890.

Club Nickname: 'Magpies'.

Previous Names: Stanley 1881; Newcastle East End 1882–1892.

Previous Grounds: South Byker, 1881; Chillingham Road, Heaton, 1886 to 1892.

Record League Victory: 13–0 v Newport Co, Division 2, 5 October 1946 – Garbutt; Cowell, Graham; Harvey, Brennan, Wright; Milburn (2), Bentley (1), Wayman (4), Shackleton (6), Pearson.

Record Cup Victory: 9–0 v Southport (at Hillsborough) FA Cup, 4th rd, 1 February 1932 – McInroy; Nelson, Fairhurst; McKenzie, Davidson, Weaver (1); Boyd (1), Jimmy Richardson (3), Cape (2), McMenemy (1), Lang (1).

Record Defeat: 0–9 v Burton Wanderers, Division 2, 15 April 1895.

Most League Points (2 for a win): 57, Division 2, 1964–65.

Most League Points (3 for a win): 96, Division 1, 1992–93.

Most League Goals: 98, Division 1, 1951–52.

Highest League Scorer in Season: Hughie Gallacher, 36, Division 1, 1926–27.

Most League Goals in Total Aggregate: Jackie Milburn, 178, 1946–57.

Most Capped Player: Alf McMichael, 40, Northern Ireland.

Most League Appearances: Jim Lawrence, 432, 1904–22.

Record Transfer Fee Received: £2,000,000 from Tottenham H for Paul Gascoigne, July 1988.

Record Transfer Fee Paid: £1,750,000 to Bristol C for Andy Cole, March 1993.

Football League Record: 1893 Elected to Division 2; 1898–1934 Division 1; 1934–48 Division 2; 1948–61 Division 1; 1961–65 Division 2; 1965–78 Division 1; 1978–84 Division 2; 1984–89 Division 1; 1989–92 Division 2; 1992–93 Division 1; 1993– FA Premier League.

Honours: Football League: Division 1 – Champions 1904–05, 1906–07, 1908–09, 1926–27, 1992–93; Division 2 – Champions 1964–65; Runners-up 1897–98, 1947–48. *FA Cup:* Winners 1910, 1924, 1932, 1951, 1952, 1955; Runners-up 1905, 1906, 1908, 1911, 1974. *Football League Cup:* Runners-up 1975–76. *Texaco Cup:* Winners 1973–74, 1974–75. **European Competitions:** *European Fairs Cup:* 1968–69 (winners), 1969–70, 1970–71 *UEFA Cup:* 1977–78. *Anglo-Italian Cup:* Winners 1973.

NEWCASTLE UNITED 1992—93 LEAGUE RECORD

Match No.	Date		Venue	Opponents		Result	H/T Score	Lg. Pos.	Goalscorers	Attendance
1	Aug	15	H	Southend U	W	3-2	2-0	—	Bracewell, Prior (og), Clark	28,545
2		22	A	Derby Co	W	2-1	0-0	4	Peacock, Clark	17,522
3		29	H	West Ham U	W	2-0	2-0	4	Peacock, Kelly	29,855
4	Sept	2	H	Luton T	W	2-0	2-0	—	Clark, Kelly	27,054
5		5	A	Bristol R	W	2-1	1-1	2	Sheedy, O'Brien	7487
6		12	H	Portsmouth	W	3-1	2-0	1	Quinn 2, Kelly	29,885
7		19	H	Bristol C	W	5-0	2-0	1	O'Brien, Peacock 2 (2 pens), Carr, Brock	29,465
8		26	A	Peterborough U	W	1-0	0-0	1	Sheedy	14,487
9	Oct	4	A	Brentford	W	2-1	1-0	—	Kelly, Peacock	10,131
10		10	H	Tranmere R	W	1-0	1-0	1	Kelly	30,137
11		18	A	Sunderland	W	2-1	1-0	—	Brock, O'Brien	28,098
12		24	H	Grimsby T	L	0-1	0-0	1		30,088
13		31	A	Leicester C	L	1-2	0-2	1	O'Brien	19,687
14	Nov	4	A	Birmingham C	W	3-2	3-2	—	Peacock, Scott, Matthewson (og)	14,376
15		8	H	Swindon T	D	0-0	0-0	—		28,091
16		14	A	Charlton Ath	W	3-1	2-0	1	Peacock 2, Howey	12,945
17		21	H	Watford	W	2-0	0-0	1	Peacock, Lee	28,871
18		28	H	Cambridge U	W	4-1	1-0	1	Kelly 3 (1 pen), Peacock	27,991
19	Dec	5	A	Notts Co	W	2-0	0-0	1	Sheedy, Peacock	14,840
20		13	A	Barnsley	L	0-1	0-0	—		13,263
21		20	H	Millwall	D	1-1	0-1	—	Kelly (pen)	26,089
22		26	H	Wolverhampton W	W	2-1	1-1	1	Kelly 2	30,137
23		28	A	Oxford U	L	2-4	2-3	1	O'Brien, Clark	9293
24	Jan	9	A	Bristol C	W	2-1	2-1	1	Kelly, Scott	15,446
25		16	H	Peterborough U	W	3-0	1-0	1	Lee 2, Kelly	29,155
26		20	A	Southend U	D	1-1	1-1	—	Peacock	8246
27		27	A	Luton T	D	0-0	0-0	—		10,237
28		31	H	Derby Co	D	1-1	0-1	—	O'Brien	27,285
29	Feb	9	A	Portsmouth	L	0-2	0-2	—		21,028
30		21	A	West Ham U	D	0-0	0-0	—		24,159
31		24	A	Bristol R	D	0-0	0-0	—		29,372
32		28	A	Tranmere R	W	3-0	2-0	—	Lee 2, Kelly	13,082
33	Mar	6	H	Brentford	W	5-1	1-0	1	Kelly, Bracewell, Clark 2, Lee	30,006
34		10	H	Charlton Ath	D	2-2	2-1	—	Lee, Kelly	29,582
35		13	A	Swindon T	L	1-2	1-0	1	Kelly	17,574
36		20	A	Notts Co	W	4-0	1-0	1	Lee, Kelly 2, Cole	30,029
37		23	A	Watford	L	0-1	0-0	—		11,634
38		28	H	Birmingham C	D	2-2	0-2	—	Cole, Lee	27,087
39	Apr	3	A	Cambridge U	W	3-0	1-0	1	Howey, Kelly, Cole	7925
40		7	H	Barnsley	W	6-0	2-0	—	Cole 3, Clark, Beresford (pen), Sellars	29,460
41		10	H	Wolverhampton W	L	0-1	0-0	1		17,244
42		17	A	Millwall	W	2-1	0-1	1	Clark, Cole	14,262
43		25	H	Sunderland	W	1-0	1-0	—	Sellars	30,364
44	May	4	A	Grimsby T	W	2-0	0-0	—	Cole, Kelly	14,402
45		6	H	Oxford U	W	2-1	0-0	—	Clark, Cole	29,438
46		9	H	Leicester C	W	7-1	6-0	—	Cole 3, Lee, Kelly 3	30,129

Final League Position: 1

GOALSCORERS

League (92): Kelly 24 (2 pens), Cole 12, Peacock 12 (2 pens), Lee 10, Clark 9, O'Brien 6, Sheedy 3, Bracewell 2, Brock 2, Howey 2, Quinn 2, Scott 2, Sellars 2, Beresford 1 (pen), Carr 1, own goals 2.
Coca Cola Cup (6): Kelly 2, Peacock 2, Lee 1, O'Brien 1.
FA Cup (7): Lee 2, Peacock 2, Clark 1, Kelly 1, Sheedy 1.

Wright 14	Venison 44	Beresford 42	Bracewell 19 + 6	Kilcline 7 + 12	Howey 41	Watson 1 + 1	Peacock 29 + 3	Kelly 45	Clark 46	Sheedy 23 + 1	Scott 45	Carr 8 + 2	Ranson 3	O'Brien 33	Quinn 4 + 1	Thompson 1 + 1	Brock 4 + 3	Lee 36	Neilson 2 + 1	Srnicek 32	Stimson 1 + 1	Robinson 2 + 7	Sellars 13	Cole 11 + 1	Match No.
1	2	3	4	5	6	7	8	9	10	11															1
1	2	3	5	4			8	9	10	11	6	7													2
1	2				6		8	9	10	11	5	7	3	4											3
1	2				6		8	9	10	11	5	7	3	4											4
1	2		14	12	6		8	9	10	11	5	7	3	4											5
1	2	3			6			9	10	11	5	7		4	8	12									6
1	2	3			6		8	9	10	11	5	7		4	12	14									7
1	2	3			6			9	10	11	5			4	8	12		7							8
1	2	3			6		8	9	10	11	5			4				7							9
1	2	3			6		8	9	10		5			4	11			7							10
1	2	3			6		8	9	10		5			4	11			7							11
1	2	3	14	12	6		8		10		5			4	9	11		7							12
1		3		12	6		8	9	10	11	5			4				7	2						13
1	2	3		12	6		8	9	10	11	5	7		4	14										14
	2	3			6		8	9	10	11	5	7		4						1					15
	2	3	11		6		8	9	10		5			4				7		1					16
	2	3	11	12	6		8	9	10		5	14		4				7		1					17
	2	3			6		8	9	10		5			4	11			7		1					18
	2	3			6		8	9	10		5			4				7		1					19
	2	3			6		8	9	10	11	5			4				7		1					20
	2	3	8	12	6			9	10	11	5	14		4				7		1					21
	2				6		8	9	10	11	5			4				7	3	1					22
	2	3		12	6		8	9	10	11	5			4				7		1					23
	2	3	12		6		8	9	10	11	5			4				7		1					24
	2	3	12		6		8	9	10	11	5			4				7		1					25
	2	3			6		8	9	10		5			4	11			7		1					26
	2	3	11		6		8	9	10		5			4				7		1					27
	2	3	14	12	6		8	9	10	11	5			4				7		1					28
	2	3	11	5			8	9	10	12	6			4				7		1					29
	2	3			6		8	9	10	11	5			4				7		1					30
	2	3			6	12	8	9	10	11	5			4				7		1					31
	2	3	14	12	6		8	9	10	11	5			4				7		1					32
	2	3	8		6			9	10		5			4				7	12	1	11				33
		3	8		6			9	10		5			4				7		1	12	2	11		34
	2	3	8		6			9	10		5			4				7		1			11	12	35
	2	3	4		6		12	9	10		5							7		1		14	11	8	36
	2	3	4		6			9	10		5							7		1		12	11	8	37
	2	3	4		6			9	10		5							7		1			11	8	38
	2	3	4		6			9	10		5							7		1		12	11	8	39
	2	3	4	12	6			9	10		5							7		1		14	11	8	40
	2	3	4	12	6			9	10		5							7		1		14	11	8	41
	2	3	4		6			9	10		5							7		1		12	11	8	42
	2	3	4		6			9	10		5							7		1			11	8	43
	2	3	4		6			9	10		5							7		1			11	8	44
	2	3	4		6		12	9	10		5							7		1		14	11	8	45
	2	3	14		6		12	9	10		5							7		1		4	11	8	46

Coca Cola Cup	First Round	Mansfield T (h)		2-1
		(a)		0-0
	Second Round	Middlesbrough (h)		0-0
		(a)		3-1
	Third Round	Chelsea (a)		1-2
FA Cup	Third Round	Port Vale (h)		4-0
	Fourth Round	Rotherham U (a)		1-1
		(h)		2-0
	Fifth Round	Blackburn R (a)		0-1

NEWCASTLE UNITED

Player and Position	Ht	Wt	Date	Birth Place	Source	Clubs	League App	Gls
Goalkeepers								
Pavel Srnicek	6 2	14 09	10 3 68	Ostrava	Banik Ostrava	Newcastle U	52	—
Tommy Wright	6 1	13 05	29 8 63	Belfast	Linfield	Newcastle U	70	—
						Hull C (loan)	6	—
Defenders								
Matthew Appleby	5 10	11 02	16 4 72	Middlesbrough	Trainee	Newcastle U	19	—
Peter Cormack	6 0	11 05	8 6 74	Liverpool	Hutcheson Vale	Meadowbank T	2	—
						Newcastle U	—	—
Robbie Elliott	5 10	10 13	25 12 73	Newcastle	Trainee	Newcastle U	15	—
Brian Kilcline	6 2	12 00	7 5 62	Nottingham	Apprentice	Notts Co	158	9
						Coventry C	173	28
						Oldham Ath	8	—
						Newcastle U	31	—
Darron McDonough	5 11	12 12	7 11 62	Antwerp	Apprentice	Oldham Ath	183	14
						Luton T	105	5
						Newcastle U	3	—
Phillip Mason‡	5 6	10 07	3 12 71	Consett	Trainee	Newcastle U	—	—
Nathan Murray			10 9 75	South Shields	Trainee	Newcastle U	—	—
Alan Neilson	5 11	11 07	26 9 72	Wegburg	Trainee	Newcastle U	22	1
David Roche	5 11	12 01	13 12 70	Newcastle	Trainee	Newcastle U	36	—
						Peterborough U (loan)	4	—
Kevin Scott	6 2	11 06	17 12 66	Easington		Newcastle U	209	8
Mark Stimson	5 11	11 00	27 12 67	Plaistow	Trainee	Tottenham H	2	—
						Leyton Orient (loan)	10	—
						Gillingham (loan)	18	—
						Newcastle U	86	2
						Portsmouth (loan)	4	—
Barry Venison	5 10	11 09	16 8 64	Consett	Apprentice	Sunderland	173	2
						Liverpool	110	1
						Newcastle U	44	—
Steve Watson	6 0	12 07	1 4 74	North Shields	Trainee	Newcastle U	54	1
Midfield								
John Beresford	5 5	10 04	4 9 66	Sheffield	Apprentice	Manchester C	—	—
						Barnsley	88	5
						Portsmouth	107	8
						Newcastle U	42	1
Paul Bracewell	5 8	10 09	19 7 62	Stoke	Apprentice	Stoke C	129	5
						Sunderland	38	4
						Everton	95	7
						Sunderland	113	2
						Newcastle U	25	2
Kevin Brock	5 9	10 12	9 9 62	Middleton Stoney	Apprentice	Oxford U	246	26
						QPR	40	2
						Newcastle U	145	15
Lee Clark	5 7	11 07	27 10 72	Wallsend	Trainee	Newcastle U	94	16
Steve Howey	6 1	10 05	26 10 71	Sunderland	Trainee	Newcastle U	74	3
Liam O'Brien	6 1	13 03	5 9 64	Dublin	Shamrock R	Manchester U	31	2
						Newcastle U	145	19
Gavin Peacock	5 8	11 08	18 11 67	Kent		QPR	17	1
						Gillingham	70	11
						Bournemouth	56	8
						Newcastle U	105	35
Mark Robinson	5 9	11 08	21 11 68	Manchester	Trainee	WBA	2	—
						Barnsley	137	6
						Newcastle U	9	—

NEWCASTLE UNITED

Colours: Black and white striped shirts, black shorts, black stockings. **Change colours:** All blue.

Foundation: It stemmed from a newly formed club called Stanley in 1881. In October 1882 they changed their name to Newcastle East End to avoid confusion with Stanley in Co. Durham. Shortly afterwards another club Rosewood merged with them. Newcastle West End had been formed in August 1882 and they played on a ground which is now St. James' Park. In 1889, West End went out of existence after a bad run and the remaining committee men invited East End to move to St. James' Park. They accepted and at a meeting in Bath Lane Hall in 1892, changed their name to Newcastle United.

First Football League game: 2 September, 1893, Division 2, v Royal Arsenal (a) D 2-2 – Ramsay; Jeffery, Miller; Crielly, Graham, McKane; Bowman, Crate (1), Thompson, Sorley (1), Wallace. Graham and not Crate scored according to some reports.

Did you know: Newcastle United set a club record of ten straight wins at the start of the 1992–93 season. This doubled the number of victories previously achieved at the beginning of 1908–09.

Managers (and Secretary-Managers)
Frank Watt 1895–32 (continued as secretary to 1932), Andy Cunningham 1930–35, Tom Mather 1935–39, Stan Seymour 1939–47 (Hon-manager), George Martin 1947–50, Stan Seymour 1950–54 (Hon-manager), Duggie Livingstone 1954–56, Stan Seymour (Hon-manager 1956–58), Charlie Mitten 1958–61, Norman Smith 1961–62, Joe Harvey 1962–75, Gordon Lee 1975–77, Richard Dinnis 1977, Bill McGarry 1977–80, Arthur Cox 1980–84, Jack Charlton 1984, Willie McFaul 1985–88, Jim Smith 1988–91, Ossie Ardiles 1991–92, Kevin Keegan February 1992–.

Player and Position	Ht	Wt	Date	Birth Place	Source	Clubs	League App	Gls
Scott Sellars	5 7	9 10	27 11 65	Sheffield	Apprentice	Leeds U	76	12
						Blackburn R	202	35
						Leeds U	7	—
						Newcastle U	13	2
Kevin Sheedy*	5 9	10 11	21 10 59	Builth Wells	Apprentice	Hereford U	51	4
						Liverpool	3	—
						Everton	274	67
						Newcastle U	37	4
Alan Thompson	6 0	12 05	22 12 73	Newcastle	Trainee	Newcastle U	16	—
John Watson*	5 9	10 10	14 4 74	South Shields	Trainee	Newcastle U	1	—
Forwards								
Andrew Cole	5 11	11 02	15 10 71	Nottingham	Trainee	Arsenal	1	—
						Fulham (loan)	13	3
						Bristol C (loan)	12	8
						Bristol C	29	12
						Newcastle U	12	12
Andy Hunt	6 0	11 07	9 6 70	Thurrock	Kettering T	Newcastle U	43	11
						WBA (loan)	10	9
David Kelly	5 11	11 03	25 11 65	Birmingham	Alvechurch	Walsall	147	63
						West Ham U	41	7
						Leicester C	66	22
						Newcastle U	70	35
Robert Lee	5 10	11 13	1 2 66	West Ham	Hornchurch	Charlton Ath	298	59
						Newcastle U	36	10

Trainees
Alderson, Richard; Anderson, Daniel L; Appleby, Richard D; Christie, Gary S; Finley, Robin; Geddes, Paul A; Greenwood, Thomas P; Kirkham, Peter J; Stokoe, Graham L; Walton, Simon S.

Associated Schoolboys
Aiston, Sam J; Barrett, Paul D; Brayson, Paul; Garrity, James K; Gibson, Barry J; Gibson, David E; Lawson, Alexander; Main, Paul; Rushworth, John; Turner, Ross.

Associated Schoolboys who have accepted the club's offer of a Traineeship/Contract
Baldwin, Shaun T; Keen, Peter A; McAlindon, Gareth E; McGivern, Josheph C; Pepper, Graham A; Pouton, Alan; Thornton, Mark D.

NORTHAMPTON TOWN 1992–93 *Back row (left to right):* Martin Aldridge, Scott Stackman, Simon Stancombe, James Wareing, Richard Preston, Nigel Reed, Mark Tero.
Third row: Paul Curtis (Youth Coach), Mark Parsons, Craig Adams, Terry Angus, Barry Richardson, Steve Brown, Michael Bell, Sean Parker, Brian Knight (Youth Coach), Russell Lewis (Community Officer).
Second row: Lee Colkin, Jason Burnham, Stuart Beavon, Phil Chard (Manager), Kevin Wilkin, Steve Terry, Morrys Scott.
Front row: Martin Scott, Ricky Bulzis, Paul Lamb, Stuart Knight, Damion Willoughby, Steve Justin, Jim Benton.
(Photograph: Pete Norton).

Division 3   **NORTHAMPTON TOWN**

County Ground, Abington Avenue, Northampton NN1 4PS.
Telephone Northampton (0604) 234100.. Fax (0604) 604176.
Commercial Dept: (0604) 234100. Information Line: 0839
664477.

Ground capacity: 9107.

Record attendance: 24,523 v Fulham, Division 1, 23 April 1966.

Record receipts: £47,292.40 v Coventry C, FA Cup 3rd rd, 6
January 1990.

Pitch measurements: 112yd × 75yd.

Chairman: B. J. Ward.

Company Secretary: Philip Mark Hough.

Player-Manager: Phil Chard.

Physio: Dennis Casey. *Managerial Consultant:* J. Barnwell.

Year Formed: 1897. *Turned Professional:* 1901. *Ltd Co.:* 1901.

Club Nickname: 'The Cobblers'.

Record League Victory: 10–0 v Walsall, Division 3 (S), 5 November 1927 – Hammond;
Watson, Jeffs; Allen, Brett, Odell; Daley, Smith (3), Loasby (3), Hoten (1), Wells (3).

Record Cup Victory: 10–0 v Sutton T FA Cup pr rd, 7 December 1907 – Cooch; Drennan,
Lloyd Davies, Tirrell (1), McCartney, Hickleton, Badenock (3), Platt (3), Lowe (1),
Chapman (2), McDiarmid.

Record Defeat: 0–11 v Southampton, Southern League, 28 December 1901.

Most League Points (2 for a win): 68, Division 4, 1975–76.

Most League Points (3 for a win): 99, Division 4, 1986–87.

Most League Goals: 109, Division 3, 1962–63 and Division 3 (S), 1952–53.

Highest League Scorer in Season: Cliff Holton, 36, Division 3, 1961–62.

Most League Goals in Total Aggregate: Jack English, 135, 1947–60.

Most Capped Player: E. Lloyd Davies, 12 (16), Wales.

Most League Appearances: Tommy Fowler, 521, 1946–61.

Record Transfer Fee Received: £265,000 from Watford for Richard Hill, July 1987.

Record Transfer Fee Paid: £85,000 to Manchester C for Tony Adcock, January 1988.

Football League Record: 1920 Original Member of Division 3; 1921 Division 3 (S); 1958–61
Division 4; 1961–63 Division 3; 1963–65 Division 2; 1965–66 Division 1; 1966–67 Division
2; 1967–69 Division 3; 1969–76 Division 4; 1976–77 Division 3; 1977–87 Division 4; 1987–
90 Division 3; 1990–92 Division 4; 1992– Division 3.

Honours: Football League: Division 1 best season: 21st, 1965–66; Division 2 – Runners-up
1964–65; Division 3 – Champions 1962–63; Division 3 (S) – Runners-up 1927–28, 1949–50;
Division 4 – Champions 1986–87; Runners-up 1975–76. *FA Cup:* best season: 5th rd, 1933–
34, 1949–50, 1969–70. *Football League Cup:* best season: 5th rd, 1964–65, 1966–67.

352

NORTHAMPTON TOWN 1992—93 LEAGUE RECORD

Match No.	Date		Venue	Opponents	Result		H/T Score	Lg. Pos.	Goalscorers	Atten dance
1	Aug	15	A	Gillingham	W	3-2	2-1	—	Brown, Scott, Chard	3863
2		28	A	Crewe Alex	L	2-3	0-2	—	Brown, Terry	3603
3	Sept	1	A	Cardiff C	L	1-2	1-0	—	Brown	7494
4		6	H	Hereford U	D	1-1	0-0	—	Beavon (pen)	2668
5		12	H	Scunthorpe U	W	1-0	0-0	10	Wilkin	1835
6		15	A	Barnet	L	0-3	0-0	—		2885
7		19	A	Torquay U	L	0-1	0-1	18		2393
8		26	H	Halifax T	L	2-5	0-2	20	Wilkin, Brown	2021
9	Oct	3	H	Lincoln C	L	0-2	0-0	22		1922
10		10	A	Scarborough	L	2-4	1-0	21	Terry, Aldridge	1539
11		13	H	Chesterfield	L	0-1	0-1	—		1922
12		17	H	Doncaster R	L	0-1	0-0	21		2137
13		24	A	Wrexham	W	1-0	1-0	21	Bell	3099
14		31	H	Shrewsbury T	D	0-0	0-0	21		2731
15	Nov	3	H	Darlington	L	1-2	0-1	—	Wilkin	1991
16		21	H	York C	W	4-3	3-2	21	Angus, Curtis, Terry, Chard	2812
17		28	A	Carlisle U	L	0-2	0-1	22		3603
18	Dec	12	A	Bury	D	3-3	1-3	21	McParland, Terry, Bell	1954
19		26	H	Colchester U	W	1-0	1-0	21	McParland	4861
20		28	A	Walsall	L	0-2	0-1	21		5080
21	Jan	8	A	Barnet	D	1-1	0-0	—	Wilkin	4266
22		16	A	Halifax T	D	2-2	0-0	21	Harmon, McParland	1323
23		23	H	Torquay U	L	0-1	0-0	21		3082
24		26	H	Crewe Alex	L	0-2	0-2	—		2510
25		30	A	Chesterfield	W	3-1	1-0	20	Chard, Terry, Scott	3031
26	Feb	6	H	Gillingham	D	2-2	1-2	20	Brown, Bell	3812
27		13	A	Hereford U	L	2-3	1-1	20	Young, Chard	2352
28		19	H	Cardiff C	L	1-2	0-0	—	Brown (pen)	4519
29		27	H	Scarborough	L	1-3	1-1	22	Bell	2451
30	Mar	6	A	Lincoln C	L	0-2	0-2	22		3328
31		9	A	Rochdale	W	3-0	3-0	—	Chard, Brown, Young	1446
32		20	A	Darlington	L	1-3	0-0	22	Bell	2106
33		23	H	Carlisle U	W	2-0	2-0	—	Gavin, Angus	2561
34		26	A	York C	L	1-2	1-0	—	Gavin	3334
35		30	A	Scunthorpe U	L	0-5	0-3	—		2307
36	Apr	2	H	Rochdale	W	1-0	0-0	—	Brown	2965
37		6	H	Bury	W	1-0	0-0	—	Hawke	2878
38		12	H	Walsall	D	0-0	0-0	20		4177
39		20	A	Colchester U	L	0-2	0-0	—		3519
40		24	A	Doncaster R	D	2-2	2-2	19	Brown, Aldridge	2111
41		27	A	Wrexham	L	0-2	0-2	—		7504
42	May	8	A	Shrewsbury T	W	3-2	0-2	20	Chard, Gavin 2	6612

Final League Position: 20

GOALSCORERS

League (48): Brown 9 (1 pen), Chard 6, Bell 5, Terry 5, Gavin 4, Wilkin 4, McParland 3, Aldridge 2, Angus 2, Scott 2, Young 2, Beavon 1 (pen), Curtis 1, Harmon 1, Hawke 1.
Coca Cola Cup (1): Terry 1.
FA Cup (8): Brown 2, Wilkin 2, Bell 1, Chard 1, McParland 1, Terry 1.

Richardson 42	Parker 4	Burnham 28 + 3	Beavon 21 + 3	Angus 36 + 1	Terry 42	Bell 34 + 5	Scott 10 + 7	Lamb 2 + 1	Brown 38	Wilkin 34 + 7	Chard 29 + 5	Parsons 19	Colkin 12 + 1	Benton 2 + 3	Curtis 22	Aldridge 7 + 2	Harmon 22 + 3	McParland 11	Young 7 + 1	Tisdale 5	Gavin 13 + 1	Holmes 6	Gillard 9	Hawke 7	Fox — + 1	Match No.
1	2	3	4	5	6	7	8	9	10	11	12															1
1		3	4	5	6	7	8	9	10	11	12	2														2
1		3	4	5	6	7	9		10	11	12	2			8											3
1	12		4	5	6	7	9		10	11	3	2			8											4
1	9	7	4	5	6		12		10	11	3	2			8											5
1	9	7	4	5	6		12	14	10	11	3	2			*8*											6
1	9	7	4	5	6		12	14	10	11	3	2			*8*											7
1		7	4	5	6	12	9	14	10	11	*3*	2			8											8
1		7	4	5	6	8	12		10	11	3				2	9										9
1		7	4	5	6	8			10	11	*3*		14	12	2	9										10
1		7	4	5	6	8		14	10	11	*3*			12	2	9										11
1		7	4	5	6	8	12		10	11	3				2	9										12
1		7		5	6	11			10	8	12	3			2		4						9			13
1		7	12	5	6				10	8	11	3			2		4						9			14
1		7		5	6				10	11	8	3			2		4						9			15
1		7	3	5	6		9		10	8	11				2		4									16
1		7	3	5	6		9		10	8	11		12		2		4									17
1		7	3	5	6	12	14		10		*8*	9			2		4	11								18
1		7		5	6		9		10		8	3			2		4	11								19
1		7		5	6		9		10		8	3			2		4	11								20
1		7		5	6		9		10		8	3			2		4	11								21
1		7		5	6		9	12	10		8	2			3		4	11								22
1		7		5	6		9	8	10		12	2			3		4	11								23
1		7	14	5	6		9	8	10		12	2			3		*4*	11								24
1		7	2	5	6		9	8	10	11		3					4									25
1			12	5	6		9	8	10	11		3			2		4				7					26
1		7		5	6		9	3	10		12		14		2		4	11	8							27
1		7		5	6		9		10		12	3			2	14	4	11	8							28
1		*7*		5	6		9		10		12	3			2	14	4	11	8							29
1		7	12	5	6		9		10				14		2		4	11	8		3					30
1		7		5	6		9		10						2		4	11	8		3					31
1				5	6	7			10		12				2		4	11				8	9	3		32
1	4			5	6	7			10		12				2			11				8	9	3		33
1				5	6	7			10		12				2		4	11				8	9	3		34
1			12	5	6	7			10						2		4	11				8	9	3	14	35
1				5	6	7			10	11					2		4					8	9	3		36
1				5	6	7			10	11					2		4					8	9	3		37
1				5	6	7			10		12				2		4	11				8	9	3		38
1				5	6	7			10		12				2		4	11				8	9	3		39
1			12	5	6	7			10						2		4	11				8	9	3		40
1		3		5	6	7			10						2		4	11				8	9			41
1				5	6	7			10						2		4	11			12	8	9	3		42

Coca Cola Cup	First Round	Gillingham (a)		1-2
		(h)		0-2
FA Cup	First Round	Fulham (h)		3-1
	Second Round	Bath C (a)		2-2
		(h)		3-0
	Third Round	Rotherham U (h)		0-1

NORTHAMPTON TOWN

Player and Position	Ht	Wt	Date	Birth Place	Source	Clubs	League App	Gls
Goalkeepers								
Barry Richardson	6 0	12 00	5 8 69	Willington Key	Trainee	Sunderland	—	—
						Scunthorpe U	—	—
						Scarborough	30	—
						Northampton T	69	—
Defenders								
Terry Angus*	5 11	12 00	14 1 66	Coventry	VS Rugby	Northampton T	116	6
James Benton§			9 4 75	Wexford	Trainee	Northampton T	10	1
Jason Burnham	5 10	11 07	8 5 73	Mansfield	Notts County	Northampton T	71	2
Lee Colkin	5 11	12 00	15 7 74	Nuneaton	Trainee	Northampton T	16	—
Paul Curtis†			1 7 63	London	Corby	Northampton T	22	1
Matthew Fox‡	6 0	13 00	13 7 71	Birmingham	Trainee	Birmingham C	14	—
						Northampton T	1	—
Ken Gillard	5 9	11 08	30 4 72	Dublin	Trainee	Luton T	—	—
						Northampton T	9	—
Sean Parker‡	5 10	11 11	23 8 73	Newcastle	Trainee	Northampton T	10	—
Mark Parsons§			24 2 75	Luton		Northampton T	32	—
Steve Terry	6 1	13 05	14 6 62	Clapton	Apprentice	Watford	160	14
						Hull C	62	4
						Northampton T	142	16
Midfield								
Stuart Beavon*	5 6	10 04	30 11 58	Wolverhampton	Apprentice	Tottenham H	4	—
						Notts Co (loan)	6	—
						Reading	396	44
						Northampton T	98	14
Michael Bell	5 8	10 04	15 11 71	Newcastle	Trainee	Northampton T	103	9
Phil Chard	5 8	11 03	16 10 60	Corby	Nottingham F	Peterborough U	172	18
						Northampton T	115	27
						Wolverhampton W	34	5
						Northampton T	135	18
Darren Harmon	5 5	9 12	30 1 73	Northampton	Trainee	Notts Co	—	—
						Shrewsbury T	6	2
						Northampton T	25	1
Micky Holmes‡	5 8	10 12	9 9 65	Blackpool		Bradford C	5	—
						Burnley	—	—
						Wolverhampton W	83	13
						Huddersfield T	7	—
						Cambridge U	11	—
						Rochdale	54	7
						Torquay U	40	3
						Carlisle U	34	4
						Northampton T	6	—
Paul Lamb§			12 9 74	Plumstead	Trainee	Northampton T	3	—
Forwards								
Martin Aldridge§			6 12 74	Northampton	Trainee	Northampton T	14	2
Steve Brown	5 9	10 12	6 7 66	Northampton		Northampton T	—	—
					Irthlingborough D	Northampton T	134	15
Pat Gavin‡	6 0	12 00	5 6 67	Hammersmith	Hanwell T	Gillingham	13	7
						Leicester C	3	—
						Gillingham (loan)	34	1
						Peterborough U	23	5
						Barnet	—	—
						Northampton T	14	4

NORTHAMPTON TOWN

Colours: Maroon shirts, white shorts, maroon stockings. **Change colours:** White shirts, maroon shorts, white stockings.

Foundation: Formed in 1897 by school teachers connected with the Northampton and District Elementary Schools' Association, they survived a financial crisis at the end of their first year when they were £675 in the red and became members of the Midland League – a fast move indeed for a new club. They achieved Southern League membership in 1901.

First Football League game: 28 August, 1920, Division 3, v Grimsby T (a) L 0-2 – Thorpe; Sproston, Hewison; Jobey, Tomkins, Pease; Whitworth, Lockett, Thomas, Freeman, MacKechnie.

Did you know: Sharing the County Ground with Northamptonshire County Cricket Club, Northampton Town have problems at the beginning and end of the season. In 1963, the year of the big freeze, the ground switched to football twice after cricket started. But Town still won the Division 3 title.

Managers (and Secretary-Managers)
Arthur Jones 1897–1907*, Herbert Chapman 1907–12, Walter Bull 1912–13, Fred Lessons 1913–19, Bob Hewison 1920–25, Jack Tresadern 1925–30, Jack English 1931–35, Syd Puddefoot 1935–37, Warney Cresswell 1937–39, Tom Smith 1939–49, Bob Dennison 1949–54, Dave Smith 1954–59, David Bowen 1959–67, Tony Marchi 1967–68, Ron Flowers 1968–69, Dave Bowen 1969–72 (continued as GM and secretary to 1985 when joined the board), Billy Baxter 1972–73, Bill Dodgin Jnr 1973–76, Pat Crerand 1976–77, Bill Dodgin Jnr 1977, John Petts 1977–78, Mike Keen 1978–79, Clive Walker 1979–80, Bill Dodgin Jnr 1980–82, Clive Walker 1982–84, Tony Barton 1984–85, Graham Carr 1985–90, Theo Foley 1990–92, Phil Chard April 1992–.

Player and Position	Ht	Wt	Birth Date	Birth Place	Source	Clubs	League App	Gls
Ian McParland‡	5 8	10 08	4 10 61	Edinburgh	Ormiston Primrose	Notts Co	221	69
						Hull C	47	7
						Walsall	11	6
						Dunfermline Ath	16	2
						Lincoln C	4	—
						Northampton T	11	3
Morrys Scott‡	6 3	12 06	17 12 70	Swansea	Trainee Colchester U	Cardiff C	9	—
						Southend U	—	—
						Plymouth Arg	6	—
						Northampton T	17	2
Kevin Wilkin			1 1 67	Cambridge	Cambridge C	Northampton T	50	6
Stuart Young*	5 11	12 00	16 12 72	Hull	Arsenal	Hull C	19	2
						Northampton T	8	2

Trainees
Adams, Craig J; Aldridge, Martin J; Benton, James; Bulzis, Riccardo; Justin, Steven M; Lamb, Paul D; Parsons, Mark C; Preddie, Delroy E; Preston, Richard J; Reed, Nigel J; Scott, Martin A; Stockman, Harry S; Willoughby, Damian.

**Non-Contract
Curtis, Paul.

**Non-Contract Players who are retained must be re-signed before they are eligible to play in League matches.

NORWICH CITY 1992–93   *Back row (left to right):* Darren Beckford, Colin Woodthorpe, Ian Culverhouse, Bryan Gunn, Chris Sutton, Mark Walton, Rob Newman, John Polston, Andy Johnson. *Centre row:* Tim Sheppard (Physio). Sean Collins, Tim Wooding, Jason Minett, Daryl Sutch, Paul Blades, Gary Megson, David Smith, David Phillips, Lee Power, John Faulkner (Reserve Team Manager).
Front row: Ian Crook, Jeremy Goss, Ian Butterworth, Mike Walker (Manger), John Deehan (Assistant Manager), Ruel Fox, Mark Bowen, Robert Ullathorne.

FA Premier

NORWICH CITY

Carrow Road, Norwich NR1 1JE. Telephone Norwich (0603) 612131. Fax (0603) 665510. Box Office: (0603) 761661. Clubcall: 0898 121144. Match Information Line: 0898 121514.

Ground capacity: 20,639.

Record attendance: 43,984 v Leicester C, FA Cup 6th rd, 30 March 1963.

Record receipts: £173,570 v Nottingham F, FA Cup 6th rd, 9 March 1991.

Pitch measurements: 114yd × 74yd.

President: G. C. Watling.

Chairman: Robert T. Chase JP. *Vice-chairman:* J. A. Jones.

NORWICH CITY FC

Directors: B. W. Lockwood, G. A. Paterson.

Manager: Mike Walker. *Assistant Manager:* John Deehan. *Reserve team coach:* John Faulkner.

Commercial Manager: Ray Cossey.

Physio: Tim Sheppard MCSP, SRP.

Secretary: A. R. W. Neville.

Year Formed: 1902. *Turned Professional:* 1905. *Ltd Co.:* 1905.

Club Nickname: 'The Canaries'.

Previous Grounds: 1902, Newmarket Road; 1908–35, The Nest, Rosary Road.

Record League Victory: 10–2 v Coventry C, Division 3 (S), 15 March 1930 – Jarvie; Hannah, Graham; Brown, O'Brien, Lochhead (1); Porter (1), Anderson, Hunt (5), Scott (2), Slicer (1).

Record Cup Victory: 8–0 v Sutton U, FA Cup, 4th rd, 28 January 1989 – Gunn; Culverhouse, Bowen, Butterworth, Linighan, Townsend (Crook), Gordon, Fleck (3), Allen (4), Phelan, Putney (1).

Record Defeat: 2–10 v Swindon T, Southern League, 5 September 1908.

Most League Points (2 for a win): 64, Division 3 (S), 1950–51.

Most League Points (3 for a win): 84, Division 2, 1985–86.

Most League Goals: 99, Division 3 (S), 1952–53.

Highest League Scorer in Season: Ralph Hunt, 31. Division 3 (S), 1955–56.

Most League Goals in Total Aggregate: Johnny Gavin, 122, 1945–54, 1955–58.

Most Capped Player: David Phillips, 24 (46), Wales.

Most League Appearances: Ron Ashman, 592, 1947–64.

Record Transfer Fee Received: £2,100,000 from Chelsea for Robert Fleck, July 1992.

Record Transfer Fee Paid: £925,000 to Port Vale for Darren Beckford, June 1991.

Football League Record: 1920 Original Member of Division 3; 1921 Division 3 (S): 1934–39 Division 2; 1946–58 Division 3 (S); 1958–60 Division 3; 1960–72 Division 2; 1972–74 Division 1; 1974–75 Division 2; 1975–81 Division 1; 1981–82 Division 2; 1982–85 Division 1; 1985–86 Division 2; 1986–92 Division 1; 1992– FA Premier League.

Honours: Football League: Division 1 best season: 4th, 1988–89; Division 2 – Champions 1971–72, 1985–86. Division 3 (S) – Champions 1933–34; Division 3 – Runners-up 1959–60. *FA Cup:* Semi-finals 1959, 1989, 1992. *Football League Cup:* Winners 1962, 1985; Runners-up 1973, 1975.

NORWICH CITY 1992—93 LEAGUE RECORD

Match No.	Date	Venue	Opponents	Result	H/T Score	Lg. Pos.	Goalscorers	Attendance
1	Aug 15	A	Arsenal	W 4-2	0-2	—	Robins 2, Phillips, Fox	24,030
2	19	H	Chelsea	W 2-1	0-1	—	Phillips, Robins	15,164
3	22	H	Everton	D 1-1	0-0	2	Fox	14,150
4	26	A	Manchester C	L 1-3	0-1	—	Megson	23,182
5	29	A	Crystal Palace	W 2-1	1-1	3	Power, Phillips	12,033
6	31	H	Nottingham F	W 3-1	1-1	—	Crook, Power, Phillips	14,104
7	Sept 5	H	Southampton	W 1-0	0-0	1	Robins	12,452
8	12	A	Chelsea	W 3-2	0-2	1	Robins 2, Phillips	16,880
9	19	H	Sheffield W	W 1-0	1-0	1	Newman	13,367
10	26	A	Coventry C	D 1-1	1-1	1	Crook	16,436
11	Oct 3	A	Blackburn R	L 1-7	1-4	2	Newman	16,312
12	17	H	QPR	W 2-1	0-0	1	Bowen (pen), Sutton	16,009
13	25	A	Liverpool	L 1-4	1-2	—	Butterworth	36,318
14	31	H	Middlesbrough	D 1-1	0-0	2	Sutch	14,499
15	Nov 9	A	Oldham Ath	W 3-2	2-2	—	Robins 3	11,081
16	21	H	Sheffield U	W 2-1	0-0	1	Beesley (og), Robins	14,874
17	28	A	Aston Villa	W 3-2	2-1	1	Phillips, Beckford, Sutch	28,837
18	Dec 5	H	Wimbledon	W 2-1	0-0	1	Robins, Phillips	14,161
19	12	A	Manchester U	L 0-1	0-0	1		34,500
20	21	A	Ipswich T	L 0-2	0-0	—		20,032
21	26	H	Tottenham H	D 0-0	0-0	1		19,413
22	28	A	Leeds U	D 0-0	0-0	1		30,282
23	Jan 10	A	Sheffield W	L 0-1	0-1	—		23,360
24	16	A	Coventry C	D 1-1	1-0	1	Sutton	13,613
25	27	H	Crystal Palace	W 4-2	2-2	—	Power 2, Sutton, Goss	13,543
26	30	A	Everton	W 1-0	1-0	1	Sutton	20,301
27	Feb 10	A	Southampton	L 0-3	0-2	—		12,969
28	20	H	Manchester C	W 2-1	2-0	3	Robins, Power	16,386
29	28	H	Blackburn R	D 0-0	0-0	—		15,821
30	Mar 3	H	Arsenal	D 1-1	1-0	—	Fox	14,802
31	6	A	QPR	L 1-3	1-2	3	Robins	13,892
32	10	A	Sheffield U	W 1-0	0-0	—	Fox	15,583
33	13	H	Oldham Ath	W 1-0	1-0	3	Henry (og)	19,597
34	17	A	Nottingham F	W 3-0	1-0	—	Robins, Power, Crook	20,799
35	20	A	Wimbledon	L 0-3	0-2	3		10,875
36	24	H	Aston Villa	W 1-0	0-0	—	Polston	19,528
37	Apr 5	H	Manchester U	L 1-3	0-3	—	Robins	20,582
38	9	A	Tottenham H	L 1-5	0-2	—	Ekoku	31,425
39	14	H	Leeds U	W 4-2	3-1	—	Sutton 3, Phillips (pen)	18,613
40	19	A	Ipswich T	L 1-3	1-1	—	Sutton	21,081
41	May 1	H	Liverpool	W 1-0	0-0	3	Phillips (pen)	20,610
42	8	A	Middlesbrough	D 3-3	1-1	3	Ekoku 2, Johnson	15,155

Final League Position: 3

GOALSCORERS

League (61): Robins 15, Phillips 9 (2 pens), Sutton 8, Power 6, Fox 4, Crook 3, Ekoku 3, Newman 2, Sutch 2, Beckford 1, Bowen 1 (pen), Butterworth 1, Goss 1, Johnson 1, Megson 1, Polston 1, own goals 2.
Coca Cola Cup (4): Sutton 2, Goss 1, Robins 1.
FA Cup (1): Beckford 1.

Gunn 42	Culverhouse 41	Bowen 42	Butterworth 26	Polston 34	Megson 20 + 3	Fox 32 + 2	Newman 16 + 2	Sutton 32 + 6	Goss 25	Phillips 42	Robins 34 + 3	Crook 32 + 2	Power 11 + 7	Woodthorpe 5 + 2	Sutch 14 + 8	Beckford 7 + 1	Johnson 1 + 1	Smith 5 + 1	Minett — + 1	Ekoku 1 + 3	Match No.
1	2	3	4	5	6	7	8	9	10	11	12	14									1
1	2	3	4	5	6	7	8	12	10	11	9										2
1	2	3	4		6	7	8	5	10	11	9	12	14								3
1	2	3	4		6	7	12	5	8	11	9	10			14						4
1	2	3	4		6		8	5	10	11		7	9		12						5
1	2	3	4		6		8	5	10	11		7	9								6
1	2	3	4		6		8	5	10	11	12	7	9								7
1	2	3		4	6		8	5	10	11	9	7			12						8
1	2	3	4		6		8	5	10	11	9	7									9
1	2	3	4				8	5	10	11	9	7			6						10
1	2	3	4				8	5	10	11	9	7	12		6						11
1	2	3	4	5				11	10	8	9	7	12		6						12
1	2	3	4	5	14	6		11	10	8	9	7	12								13
1		3	4	5	14	8	2		10	11	9	7	6		12						14
1	2	3	4	5				10	12	11	9	7	6		8						15
1	2	3	4	5				10		11	9	7	6		8						16
1	2	3	4	5				10	12	11	9	7	6		8						17
1	2	3	4	5	14			10	12	11	9	7	6		8						18
1	2	3	4	5	14			10	12	11	9	7	6		8						19
1	2	3	4	5		7	10	14	12	11	9		6		8						20
1	2	3		5	6	10	4	8		11	9	7									21
1	2	3		5	6	10	4	8		11	9	7			12						22
1	2	3	4	5	6	10				11	9	7	8		12						23
1	2	3	4	5		10		9	6	11		7	14	12	8						24
1	2	3	4	5	6	10		9	7	11					8						25
1	2	3	4	5	6	10		9	7	11	12				8						26
1	2	3	4	5	6	10		7		11	9		8		12						27
1	2	3	4	5	6	10		7		11	9		8		12	14					28
1	2	3		5		10	4			11	9	8	7			6					29
1	2	3		5		10	4			11	9	8	7			6					30
1	2	3				10	4			11	9	7	8	5		6	12				31
1	2	3		5		10	4			11	9	7	8			6	12				32
1	2	3		5		10	4			11	9	7	12		8	6					33
1	2	3		5		10	4			11	9	7	12		8	6					34
1	2	3		5		10	4			11	9	7	12		8	6					35
1	2	3		5	6	10		4	8	11	9	7			12						36
1	2	3		5	6	10		4	8	11	9	7							12		37
1	2	3		5	6	10		4	8	11	9	7							12		38
1	2	3	4	5		10		8	6	11	9	7									39
1	2	3	4	5		10		8	6	11	9	7									40
1	2	3		5	14	10	4	8	6	11	9	7							12		41
1	2	3		5		10	4		8	11		7					6			9	42

Coca Cola Cup	Second Round	Carlisle U (a)	2-2
		(h)	2-0
	Third Round	Blackburn R (a)	0-2
FA Cup	Third Round	Coventry C (h)	1-0
	Fourth Round	Tottenham H (h)	0-2

NORWICH CITY

Player and Position	Ht	Wt	Date	Birth Place	Source	Clubs	League App	Gls
Goalkeepers								
Bryan Gunn	6 2	13 13	22 12 63	Thurso	Invergordon BC	Aberdeen	15	—
						Norwich C	242	—
Mark Walton	6 2	13 13	1 6 69	Merthyr	Swansea C	Luton T	—	—
						Colchester U	40	—
						Norwich C	22	—
Defenders								
Mark Bowen	5 8	11 13	7 12 63	Neath	Apprentice	Tottenham H	17	2
						Norwich C	212	15
Ian Butterworth	6 1	12 10	25 1 65	Crewe	Apprentice	Coventry C	90	—
						Nottingham F	27	—
						Norwich C	210	4
Ian Culverhouse	5 10	11 02	22 9 64	Bishop's Stortford	Apprentice	Tottenham H	2	—
						Norwich C	254	—
Rob Newman	6 0	13 00	13 12 63	Bradford-on-Avon	Apprentice	Bristol C	394	52
						Norwich C	59	9
Mark Peters*	6 0	11 03	6 7 72	St Asaph	Trainee	Manchester C	—	—
						Norwich C	—	—
John Polston	5 11	11 03	10 6 68	London	Apprentice	Tottenham H	24	1
						Norwich C	80	6
Robert Ullathorne	5 8	10 00	11 10 71	Wakefield	Trainee	Norwich C	22	3
Tim Wooding*	6 00	12 00	5 7 73	Wellingborough	Trainee	Norwich C	—	—
Colin Woodthorpe	5 11	11 08	13 1 69	Ellesmere Pt	Apprentice	Chester C	155	6
						Norwich C	23	1
Midfield								
Sean Collins‡	5 8	11 00	1 1 74	Belfast	Trainee	Norwich C	—	—
Ian Crook	5 8	10 06	18 1 63	Romford	Apprentice	Tottenham H	20	1
						Norwich C	204	14
Ruel Fox	5 6	10 00	14 1 68	Ipswich	Apprentice	Norwich C	147	15
Jeremy Goss	5 9	10 09	11 5 65	Cyprus	Amateur	Norwich C	113	5
Andrew Johnson	5 11	11 06	2 5 74	Bath	Trainee	Norwich C	4	1
Gary Megson	5 10	12 00	2 5 59	Manchester	Apprentice	Plymouth Arg	78	10
						Everton	22	2
						Sheffield W	123	13
						Nottingham F	—	—
						Newcastle U	24	1
						Sheffield W	110	12
						Manchester C	82	2
						Norwich C	23	1
Jason Minett*	5 10	10 02	12 8 71	Peterborough	Trainee	Norwich C	3	—
						Exeter C (loan)	12	—
David Phillips	5 10	11 02	29 7 63	Wegberg	Apprentice	Plymouth Arg	73	15
						Manchester C	81	13
						Coventry C	100	8
						Norwich C	152	18
David Smith	5 9	11 12	26 12 70	Liverpool	Trainee	Norwich C	11	—
Daryl Sutch	6 0	12 00	11 9 71	Lowestoft	Trainee	Norwich C	35	2
Forwards								
Adeola Akinbiyi	6 1	11 09	10 10 74	Hackney	Trainee	Norwich C	—	—
Jamie Cureton	5 8	10 05	28 8 75	Bristol	Trainee	Norwich C	—	—
Darren Eadie	5 7	10 00	10 6 75	Chippenham	Trainee	Norwich C	—	—
Efan Ekoku	6 1	12 00	8 6 67	Manchester	Sutton U	Bournemouth	62	21
						Norwich C	4	3

Colours: Yellow shirts, green trim, green shorts, yellow trim, yellow stockings. **Change colours:** All white with blackcurrant trim.

Foundation: Formed in 1902, largely through the initiative of two local schoolmasters who called a meeting at the Criterion Cafe, they were shocked by an FA Commission which in 1904 declared the club professional and ejected them from the FA Amateur Cup. However, this only served to strengthen their determination. New officials were appointed and a professional club established at a meeting in the Agricultural Hall in March 1905.

First Football League game: 28 August, 1920, Division 3, v Plymouth A (a) D 1-1 – Skermer; Gray, Gadsden; Wilkinson, Addy, Martin; Laxton, Kidger, Parker, Whitham (1), Dobson.

Did you know: Norwich City fielded an unchanged team in the first 23 matches of the 1950–51 season in Division 3 (S). They used 20players that season, seven of them contributing only 22 of a possible 506 appearances.

Managers (and Secretary-Managers)
John Bowman 1905–07, James McEwen 1907–08, Arthur Turner 1909–10, Bert Stansfield 1910–15, Major Frank Buckley 1919–20, Charles O'Hagan 1920–21, Albert Gosnell 1921–26, Bert Stansfield 1926, Cecil Potter 1926–29, James Kerr 1929–33, Tom Parker 1933–37, Bob Young 1937–39, Jimmy Jewell 1939, Bob Young 1939–45, Cyril Spiers 1946–47, Duggie Lochhead 1945–50, Norman Low 1950–55, Tom Parker 1955–57, Archie Macaulay 1957–61, Willie Reid 1961–62, George Swindin 1962, Ron Ashman 1962–66, Lol Morgan 1966–69, Ron Saunders 1969–73, John Bond 1973–80, Ken Brown 1980–87, Dave Stringer December 1987–92, Mike Walker June 1992–.

Player and Position	Ht	Wt	Birth Date	Birth Place	Source	Clubs	League App	Gls
Lee Power	5 11	11 02	30 6 72	Lewisham	Trainee	Norwich C	39	10
						Charlton Ath (loan)	5	—
Mark Robins	5 7	10 04	22 12 69	Ashton-under-Lyme.	Apprentice	Manchester U	48	11
						Norwich C	37	15
Chris Sutton	6 3	12 01	10 3 73	Nottingham	Trainee	Norwich C	61	10

Trainees
Brace, Deryn P. J; Carey, Shaun P; Crowfoot, Darren, L; Ewins, Scott R; Gibb, Alistair S; Harrington, Justin D; Kreft, Stacey J; Liffen, Neil J; Marshall, Andrew J; Mellon, Richard C; Oldbury, Marcus J; Roberts, Glyn S; Simpson, James R; Snowling, Scott; Weston, Gary W; Wright, Jonathan.

Associated Schoolboys
Baines, Wesley; Collins, Darren J; Coote, Adrian; Dibble, Anthony J; Hobbs, Paul G; Jones, Owen R; Morgan, Ryan S; Shore, James A; Wilson, Che C. A.

Associated Schoolboys who have accepted the club's offer of a Traineeship/Contract
Carus, Joshua M. E; Levin, Gavin B; Morgan, Christian W; Woodman, Clayton K.

NOTTINGHAM FOREST 1992–93 *Back row (left to right):* Roy Keane, Ian Woan, Steve Chettle, Carl Tiler, Terry Wilson, Raymond McKinnon, Tommy Gaynor, Cary Charles.
Centre row: Ron Fenton (Assistant Manager), Archie Gemmill (Coach), Liam O'Kane (Coach), Andrew Marriott, Edward Sheringham, Kingsley Black, Mark Crossley, Graham Lyas (Physio), Alan Hill (Chief Scout).
Front row: Nigel Clough, Scot Gemmill, Lee Glover, Brian Clough (Manager), Stuart Pearce, Brian Laws, Gary Crosby.

Division 1   NOTTINGHAM FOREST

City Ground, Nottingham NG2 5FJ. Telephone Nottingham (0602) 822202. Fax (0602) 455581. Information Desk: 821122. Commercial Manager: 820444. Commercial office fax (0602) 818095. Ticket office: (0602) 813801. Souvenir shop: (0602) 822664.

Ground capacity: 28,264 (22,931 seats).

Record attendance: 49,945 v Manchester U, Division 1, 28 October 1967.

Record receipts: £236,593 v Middlesbrough, FA Cup 4th rd, 23 January 1993.

Pitch measurements: 115yd × 78yd.

Chairman: F. Reacher. *Vice-chairman:* I. I. Korn.

Directors: F. Reacher, I. I. Korn, J. F. Hickling.

Manager: Frank Clark. *Assistant Manager:* Ron Fenton.

Secretary: P. White. *Commercial Manager:* Dave Pullan.

Coach: Liam O'Kane. *Physio:* G. Lyas.

Year Formed: 1865. *Turned Professional:* 1889. *Ltd Co.:* 1982.

Club Nickname: 'Reds'.

Previous Grounds: 1865, Forest Racecourse; 1879, The Meadows; 1880, Trent Bridge Cricket Ground; 1882, Parkside, Lenton; 1885, Gregory, Lenton; 1890, Town Ground; 1898, City Ground.

Record League Victory: 12–0 v Leicester Fosse, Division 1, 12 April 1909 – Iremonger; Dudley, Maltby; Hughes (1), Needham, Armstrong; Hooper (3), Marrison, West (3), Morris (2), Spouncer (3 incl. 1p).

Record Cup Victory: 14–0 v Clapton (away), FA Cup, 1st rd, 17 January 1891 – Brown; Earp, Scott; A. Smith, Russell, Jeacock; McCallum (2), 'Tich' Smith (1), Higgins (5), Lindley (4), Shaw (2).

Record Defeat: 1–9 v Blackburn R, Division 2, 10 April 1937.

Most League Points (2 for a win): 70, Division 3 (S), 1950–51.

Most League Points (3 for a win): 74, Division 1, 1983–84.

Most League Goals: 110, Division 3 (S), 1950–51.

Highest League Scorer in Season: Wally Ardron, 36, Division 3 (S), 1950–51.

Most League Goals in Total Aggregate: Grenville Morris, 199, 1898–1913.

Most Capped Player: Stuart Pearce, 53, England

Most League Appearances: Bob McKinlay, 614, 1951–70.

Record Transfer Fee Received: £2,100,000 from Tottenham H for Teddy Sheringham, August 1992.

Record Transfer Fee Paid: £2,000,000 to Millwall for Teddy Sheringham, July 1991 and £2,000,000 to Southend U for Stan Collymore, June 1992.

Football League Record: 1892 Elected to Division 1; 1906–07 Division 2; 1907–11 Division 1; 1911–22 Division 2; 1922–25 Division 1; 1925–49 Division 2; 1949–51 Division 3 (S); 1951–57 Division 2; 1957–72 Division 1; 1972–77 Division 2; 1977–92 Division 1; 1992–93 FA Premier League; 1993– Division 1.

Honours: Football League: Division 1 – Champions 1977–78; Runners-up 1966–67, 1978–79; Division 2 – Champions 1906–07, 1921–22; Runners-up 1956–57; Division 3 (S) – Champions 1950–51. *FA Cup:* Winners 1898, 1959; Runners-up 1991. *Anglo-Scottish Cup:* Winners 1976–77; *Football League Cup:* Winners 1977–78, 1978–79, 1988–89, 1989–90; Runners-up 1979–80. *Simod Cup:* Winners 1989. *Zenith Data Systems Cup:* Winners 1991–92. **European Competitions:** *Fairs Cup:* 1961–62, 1967–68. *European Cup:* 1978–79 (winners), 1979–80 (winners), 1980–81. *Super Cup:* 1979–80 (winners), 1980–81 (runners-up). *World Club Championship:* 1980–81 (runners-up). *UEFA Cup:* 1983–84, 1984–85.

NOTTINGHAM FOREST 1992—93 LEAGUE RECORD

Match No.	Date	Venue	Opponents	Result		H/T Score	Lg. Pos.	Goalscorers	Atten dance
1	Aug 16	H	Liverpool	W	1-0	1-0	—	Sheringham	20,038
2	19	A	Sheffield W	L	0-2	0-1	—		29,623
3	22	A	Oldham Ath	L	3-5	0-3	15	Pearce (pen), Bannister 2	11,632
4	29	H	Manchester U	L	0-2	0-1	20		19,694
5	31	A	Norwich C	L	1-3	1-1	—	Clough	14,104
6	Sept 5	A	Blackburn R	L	1-4	1-1	22	Bannister	16,180
7	12	H	Sheffield W	L	1-2	0-1	22	Bannister	19,420
8	21	H	Coventry C	D	1-1	0-1	—	Clough	17,553
9	26	A	Chelsea	D	0-0	0-0	22		19,760
10	Oct 3	A	Manchester C	D	2-2	0-1	22	McKinnon, Pearce	22,571
11	17	H	Arsenal	L	0-1	0-1	22		24,862
12	21	H	Middlesbrough	W	1-0	0-0	—	Black	17,846
13	24	A	Sheffield U	D	0-0	0-0	22		19,152
14	31	H	Ipswich T	L	0-1	0-1	22		21,411
15	Nov 7	H	Everton	L	0-1	0-0	22		20,941
16	21	A	Crystal Palace	D	1-1	0-1	22	Bannister	15,330
17	28	H	Southampton	L	1-2	1-1	22	Clough	19,942
18	Dec 5	A	Leeds U	W	4-1	1-0	22	Clough, Keane 2, Black	29,364
19	12	A	Aston Villa	L	1-2	1-1	22	Keane	29,015
20	20	H	Wimbledon	D	1-1	1-1	—	Clough	19,326
21	28	A	Tottenham H	L	1-2	0-1	22	Gemmill	32,118
22	Jan 9	A	Coventry C	W	1-0	0-0	22	Woan	15,264
23	16	H	Chelsea	W	3-0	1-0	22	Bannister 2, Orlygsson	23,249
24	27	A	Manchester U	L	0-2	0-0	—		36,085
25	30	H	Oldham Ath	W	2-0	1-0	21	Woan 2	21,240
26	Feb 6	A	Liverpool	D	0-0	0-0	21		40,463
27	20	A	Middlesbrough	W	2-1	0-0	20	Clough, Stone	15,639
28	24	A	QPR	W	1-0	0-0	—	Crosby	22,436
29	27	H	Manchester C	L	0-2	0-1	19		25,956
30	Mar 3	H	Crystal Palace	D	1-1	1-1	—	Keane	20,603
31	13	A	Everton	L	0-3	0-3	21		21,271
32	17	A	Norwich C	L	0-3	0-1	—		20,799
33	21	H	Leeds U	D	1-1	1-1	—	Clough (pen)	25,148
34	24	A	Southampton	W	2-1	2-0	—	Clough, Keane	18,005
35	Apr 4	H	Aston Villa	L	0-1	0-0	—		26,742
36	7	H	Blackburn R	L	1-3	0-1	—	Clough (pen)	20,467
37	10	A	QPR	L	3-4	1-2	22	Bannister, Black 2	15,815
38	12	H	Tottenham H	W	2-1	2-1	21	Black, Rosario	25,682
39	17	A	Wimbledon	L	0-1	0-1	21		9358
40	21	H	Arsenal	D	1-1	0-0	—	Keane	19,024
41	May 1	H	Sheffield U	L	0-2	0-1	22		26,752
42	8	A	Ipswich T	L	1-2	0-1	22	Clough (pen)	22,093

Final League Position: 22

GOALSCORERS

League (41): Clough 10 (3 pens), Bannister 8, Keane 6, Black 5, Woan 3, Pearce 2 (1 pen), Crosby 1, Gemmill 1, McKinnon 1, Orlygsson 1, Rosario 1, Sheringham 1, Stone 1.
Coca Cola Cup (8): Orlygsson 2, Bannister 1, Black 1, Clough 1, Keane 1, Woan 1, own goal 1.
FA Cup (6): Webb 2, Bannister 1, Clough 1, Keane 1, Woan 1.

Crossley 37	Laws 32 + 1	Pearce 23	Wilson 5	Chettle 30	Keane 40	Crosby 20 + 3	Gemmill 33	Clough 42	Sheringham 3	Woan 27 + 1	Black 19 + 5	Bannister 27 + 4	Orlygsson 15 + 5	Tiler 37	McKinnon 5 + 1	Charles 14	Glover 9 + 5	Webb 9	Williams 9	Stone 11 + 1	Rosario 10	Marriott 5	Match No.
1	2	3	4	5	6	7	8	9	10	11	12												1
1	2	3	4	5	6	7	8	9	10	11													2
1	2	3	4	5	6	7	8	9	*10*	11	12		14										3
1	2	3	4	5	6	7	8	9		11	10												4
1	2	3	4	5	6		8	9		11	10	7											5
1	2	3		5	6	11	8	9		10		7	4										6
1	2	3		5	6	7	8	9		11	10		4	12									7
1	2	3			6	7	8	9				10	11	5	4								8
1	2	3			6	7	8	9				10	11	5	4								9
1	2	3			6	7	8	9				10	11	5	4								10
1		3			6	7	8	9			12	10	11	5	4	2							11
1		3		4	6	7	8	9		11	10			5	12	2							12
1		3		4	6	7	8	9		11		10		5		2							13
1	2	3		4	6	7	8	9		11	12			5			10						14
1	2	3		4	6		8	9		11		7		5			10						15
1	2	3		4	6		8	9		11		7		5			10						16
1	2	3		4	6		8	9		11		7		5	12		10						17
1	2	3		4	6		8	9		11	12	7	14	5			*10*						18
1	2	3		4	6		8	9		11	12	7		5			10						19
1	2	3		4	6	7	8	9		11				5			10						20
1	2	3		4	6	7	8	9		11	12			5			10						21
1	2	3		4	6		8	9		11		7		5			10						22
1	2	3		4	6		8	9		11		7		5	12		10						23
1	2	3		4	*6*	14	8	9		11		7		5	12		10	3					24
1	2			4	6		8	9		11		7		5			10	3					25
1	2			4	6		8	9		11	10	7		5				3					26
1		3			6		8	9		11	10	7		5		2				4			27
1		3			6	7	8	9		11	10			5		2				4			28
1	12	3			6	7	8	9		11				5		2	10			4			29
1		3		4	6	7	8	9		11	12			5		2	10						30
1		3		4	6	7		9		11	10			5	8	2	12						31
1		3		4	6	7		9		11	12	*10*	14	5		2		8					32
1		3			6		8	9		11		7		5		2				4	10		33
1		*3*			6		8	9		11		7		5	12	2				4	10		34
1		3			6		8	9		11		7		5	12	2				4	10		35
1		3			6		8	9		11		7		5		2				4	10		36
1					6		8	9		11		7		5		2		3		4	10		37
	2				6		8	9		11		7		5	12			3		4	10	1	38
	2				6		8	9		11		7		5	12			3		4	10	1	39
	2				6		8	9		11		7		5	12			3		4	10	1	40
	2			4	6		8	9		11		7		5				3			10	1	41
	2			4	6		8	9		11		7		5	12			3			10	1	42

Coca Cola Cup	Second Round	Stockport Co (a)	3-2	
		(h)	2-1	
	Third Round	Crewe Alex (a)	1-0	
	Fourth Round	Tottenham H (h)	2-0	
	Fifth Round	Arsenal (a)	0-2	
FA Cup	Third Round	Southampton (h)	2-1	
	Fourth Round	Middlesbrough (h)	1-1	
		(a)	3-0	
	Fifth Round	Arsenal (a)	0-2	

NOTTINGHAM FOREST

Player and Position	Ht	Wt	Date	Birth Place	Source	Clubs	League App	Gls
Goalkeepers								
Mark Crossley	6 0	13 09	16 6 69	Barnsley		Nottingham F	121	—
						Manchester U (loan)	—	—
Christian Davies‡	6 01	12 09	18 11 74	Essex	Trainee	Nottingham F	—	—
Andrew Marriott	6 0	12 07	11 10 70	Nottingham	Trainee	Arsenal	—	—
						Nottingham F	11	—
						WBA (loan)	3	—
						Blackburn R (loan)	2	—
						Colchester U (loan)	10	—
						Burnley (loan)	15	—
Mark Statham	6 2	12 02	11 11 75	Barnsley	Trainee	Nottingham F	—	—
Defenders								
Steve Blatherwick	6 1	12 12	20 9 73	Nottingham	Notts Co	Nottingham F	—	—
Craig Boardman*	6 0	11 08	30 11 70	Barnsley	Trainee	Nottingham F	—	—
Gary Bowyer*	6 0	12 13	22 6 71	Manchester		Hereford U	14	2
						Nottingham F	—	—
Ray Byrne	6 1	11 02	4 7 72	Newry	Newry	Nottingham F	—	—
Gary Charles	5 9	10 13	13 4 70	London		Nottingham F	56	1
						Leicester C (loan)	8	—
Steve Chettle	6 1	12 00	27 9 68	Nottingham	Apprentice	Nottingham F	169	6
Nathan Drury	6 0	11 02	15 1 76	Leeds	Trainee	Nottingham F	—	—
Cuan Forrest‡	5 10	11 10	26 3 74	Zimbabwe	Trainee	Nottingham F	—	—
Paul Haywood	5 11	10 02	4 10 75	Barnsley	Trainee	Nottingham F	—	—
Danny Hinshelwood	5 9	10 11	4 12 75	Bromley	Trainee	Nottingham F	—	—
Chris Hope‡	6 0	11 01	14 11 72	Sheffield	Darlington	Nottingham F	—	—
Ian Kilford	5 10	10 05	6 10 73	Bristol	Trainee	Nottingham F	—	—
Brian Laws	5 10	11 05	14 10 61	Wallsend	Apprentice	Burnley	125	12
						Huddersfield T	56	1
						Middlesbrough	107	12
						Nottingham F	140	4
Ray McKinnon	5 8	9 11	5 8 70	Dundee	S Form	Dundee U	53	6
						Nottingham F	6	1
Stuart Pearce	5 10	12 09	24 4 62	London	Wealdstone	Coventry C	51	4
						Nottingham F	259	41
Richard Smith	5 11	11 10	24 1 74	Lichfield	Trainee	Nottingham F	—	—
Carl Tiler	6 2	13 00	11 2 70	Sheffield	Trainee	Barnsley	71	3
						Nottingham F	63	1
Des Walker (To Sampdoria May 1992)	5 10	11 05	26 11 65	Hackney	Apprentice	Nottingham F	264	1
Vance Warner	5 11	11 05	3 9 74	Leeds	Trainee	Nottingham F	—	—
Brett Williams	5 10	11 12	19 3 68	Dudley	Apprentice	Nottingham F	43	—
						Stockport Co (loan)	2	—
						Northampton T (loan)	4	—
						Hereford U (loan)	14	—
						Oxford U (loan)	7	—
Dale Wright	6 00	12 05	21 12 74	Middlesbrough	Trainee	Nottingham F	—	—
Midfield								
Craig Armstrong	5 11	12 04	23 5 75	South Shields	Trainee	Nottingham F	—	—
Kingsley Black	5 8	10 11	22 6 68	Luton	School	Luton T	127	26
						Nottingham F	49	9
Gary Crosby	5 7	9 11	8 5 64	Sleaford	Lincoln U Grantham	Lincoln C	7	—
						Nottingham F	146	12
John Finnigan	5 8	10 05	29 3 76	Wakefield	Trainee	Nottingham F	—	—
Scot Gemmill	5 10	10 01	2 1 71	Paisley	School	Nottingham F	76	9
Neil Glasser‡	5 09	11 03	17 10 74	Johannesbury	Trainee	Nottingham F	—	—

NOTTINGHAM FOREST

Colours: Red shirts, white shorts, red stockings. **Change colours:** White shirts, black shorts, white stockings.

Foundation: One of the oldest football clubs in the world, Nottingham Forest was formed at a meeting in the Clinton Arms in 1865. Known originally as the Forest Football Club, the game which first drew the founders together was "shinney" a form of hockey. When they determined to change to football in 1865, one of their first moves was to buy a set of red caps to wear on the field.

First Football League game: 3 September, 1892, Division 1, v Everton (a) D 2-2 – Brown; Earp, Scott; Hamilton, A. Smith, McCracken; McCallum, W. Smith, Higgins (2), Pike, McInnes.

Did you know: After only 21 matches in European competition, Nottingham Forest could claim to have won two major honours: The European Cup on their 15th game and the Super Cup after 21.

Managers (and Secretary-Managers)
Harry Radford 1889–97*, Harry Haslam 1897–1909*, Fred Earp 1909–12, Bob Masters 1912–25, John Baynes 1925–29, Stan Hardy 1930–31, Noel Watson 1931–36, Harold Wightman 1936–39, Billy Walker 1939–60, Andy Beattie 1960–63, John Carey 1963–68, Matt Gillies 1969–72, Dave Mackay 1972, Allan Brown 1973–75, Brian Clough 1975–93, Frank Clark June 1993–.

Player and Position	Ht	Wt	Birth Date	Birth Place	Source	Clubs	League App	Gls
Stephen Howe	5 7	10 04	6 11 73	Annitsford	Trainee	Nottingham F	—	—
Roy Keane	5 10	11 03	10 8 71	Cork	Cobh Ramblers	Nottingham F	114	22
Thorvaldur Orlygsson*	5 11	10 08	2 8 66	Odense	FC Akureyri	Nottingham F	37	2
Steven Stone	5 9	11 03	20 8 71	Gateshead	Trainee	Nottingham F	13	1
Lee Stratford	5 10	10 08	11 11 75	Barnsley	Trainee	Nottingham F	—	—
Justin Walker	5 10	11 08	6 9 75	Nottingham	Trainee	Nottingham F	—	—
Neil Webb	6 0	13 07	30 7 63	Reading	Apprentice	Reading	72	22
						Portsmouth	123	34
						Nottingham F	146	47
						Manchester U	75	8
						Nottingham F	9	—
Terry Wilson*	6 0	10 10	8 2 69	Broxburn	Apprentice	Nottingham F	105	9
						Newcastle U (loan)	2	—
Ian Woan	5 10	11 09	14 12 67	Wirrall	Runcorn	Nottingham F	61	11
Forwards								
Gary Bannister*	5 10	11 08	22 7 60	Warrington	Apprentice	Coventry C	22	3
						Sheffield W	118	55
						QPR	136	56
						Coventry C	43	11
						WBA	72	18
						Oxford U (loan)	10	2
						Nottingham F	31	8
Nigel Clough	5 9	11 04	19 3 66	Sunderland	ACT Hunters	Nottingham F	311	101
Lee Glover	5 10	12 01	24 4 70	Kettering	Trainee	Nottingham F	58	4
						Leicester C (loan)	5	1
						Barnsley (loan)	8	—
						Luton T (loan)	1	—
Stephen Guinan	6 1	12 12	24 12 75	Birmingham	Trainee	Nottingham F	—	—
Luke Hughes	5 10	10 04	17 9 75	Sunderland	Trainee	Nottingham F	—	—
Jason Kaminsky			5 12 73	Leicester	Trainee	Nottingham F	1	—
Paul McGregor	5 10	10 04	17 12 74	Liverpool	Trainee	Nottingham F	—	—
Lee Marshall	5 9	9 12	1 8 75	Nottingham	Trainee	Nottingham F	—	—
Carl Rookyard	5 9	10 05	3 9 75	Burton on Trent	Trainee	Nottingham F	—	—
Robert Rosario	6 3	12 01	4 3 66	Hammersmith	Hillingdon Bor	Norwich C	126	18
						Wolverhampton W (loan)	2	1
						Coventry C	59	8
						Nottingham F	10	1

Associated Schoolboys
Adams, Stephen; Archer, Paul; Atkinson, Craig; Clark, Cameron; Clifford, Mark; Cooper, David M; Cowling, Lee; Dawson, Andrew; Dilnot, John; Gash, Ben; George, Daniel; Inwood, Dale; Melton, Stephen; Morgan, Ian; O'Neill, Shane; Orr, Stephen; Poole, Darren; Priest, Christen; Redden, Damion; Simpson, Mark; Turner, Barry; Turner, Darren; Waddley, Kevin; Wood, Matthew; Ziccardi, Mariano.

Associated Schoolboys who have accepted the club's offer of a Traineeship/Contract
Gilmore, Craig; Mendum, Craig; Thom, Stuart P; Walley, Mark; Watkins, Darren; Wilson, Ross E; Woolford, Stephen.

NOTTS COUNTY 1992-93 *Back row (left to right):* Gavin Worboys, Richard Walker, Andy Williams, Meindert Dijkstra, Kevin Wilson, Michael Johnson, Rob Matthews, Chris Short, Paul Harding, Paul Cox, Steve Slawson, Mark Wells.

Centre row: Dave Lawson (Physio), Paul Devlin, Richard Dryden, Charlie Palmer, Dean Yates, James Walker, Bob Catlin, Steve Cherry, Craig Short, Alan Paris, Don O'Riordan, Tommy Gallagher, Mick Jones (Assistant Manager).

Front row: Dave Smith, Tony Agana, Phil Turner, Derek Pavis (Chairman), Neil Warnock (Manager), Mark Draper, Kevin Bartlett, Dean Thomas.
(Photograph: Empics)

Division 1   **NOTTS COUNTY**

County Ground, Meadow Lane, Nottingham NG2 3HJ. Telephone Nottingham (0602) 861155. Ticket office: (0602) 850632. Clubline: 0891 888684. Football in the Community: 863656. County '75: 864718. Supporters Club: 866802.

Ground capacity: 18,781.

Record attendance: 47,310 v York C, FA Cup 6th rd, 12 March 1955.

Record receipts: £124,539.10 v Manchester C, FA Cup 6th rd, 16 February 1991.

Pitch measurements: 114yd × 74yd.

Chairman: D. C. Pavis. *Vice-chairman:* J. Mounteney.

Directors: W. A. Hopcroft, D. Ward, F. Sherwood.

Manager: Mick Walker. *Assistant Manager:* Russell Slade. *Commerical Manager:* Elaine Howes.

Coach: Wayne Jones. *Chief Executive:* N. E. Hook MCIM. AMLD. *Physio:* David Lawson.

Year Formed: 1862 *(see Foundation).*

Turned Professional: 1885. *Ltd Co.:* 1888.

Club Nickname: 'Magpies'.

Previous Grounds: 1862, The Park; 1864, The Meadows; 1877, Beeston Cricket Ground; 1880, Castle Ground; 1883, Trent Bridge; 1910, Meadow Lane.

Record League Victory: 11–1 v Newport C, Division 3 (S), 15 January 1949 – Smith; Southwell, Purvis; Gannon, Baxter, Adamson; Houghton (1), Sewell (4), Lawton (4), Pimbley, Johnston (2).

Record Cup Victory: 15–0 v Rotherham T (at Trent Bridge), FA Cup, 1st rd, 24 October 1885 – Sherwin; Snook, H. T. Moore; Dobson (1), Emmett (1), Chapman; Gunn (1), Albert Moore (2), Jackson (3), Daft (2), Cursham (4). (1 og).

Record Defeat: 1–9 v Blackburn R, Division 1, 16 November, 1889 and v Aston Villa, Division 1, 29 September, 1888 and v Portsmouth, Division 2, 9 April, 1927.

Most League Points (2 for a win): 69, Division 4, 1970–71.

Most League Points (3 for a win): 87, Division 3, 1989–90.

Most League Goals: 107, Division 4, 1959–60.

Highest League Scorer in Season: Tom Keetley, 39, Division 3 (S), 1930–31.

Most League Goals in Total Aggregate: Les Bradd, 124, 1967–78.

Most Capped Player: Harry Cursham, 8, England, Martin O'Neill, 8 (64), Northern Ireland, Kevin Wilson, 8 (33), Northern Ireland.

Most League Appearances: Albert Iremonger, 564, 1904–26.

Record Transfer Fee Received: £2,500,000 from Derby Co for Craig Short, September 1992.

Record Transfer Fee Paid: £685,000 to Sheffield U for Tony Agana, November 1991.

Football League Record: 1888 Founder Member of the Football League; 1893–97 Division 2; 1897–1913 Division 1; 1913–14 Division 2; 1914–20 Division 1; 1920–23 Division 2; 1923–26 Division 1; 1926–30 Division 2; 1930–31 Division 3 (S); 1931–35 Division 2; 1935–50 Division 3 (S); 1950–58 Division 2; 1958–59 Division 3; 1959–60 Division 4; 1960–64 Division 3; 1964–71 Division 4; 1971–73 Division 3; 1973–81 Division 2; 1981–84 Division 1; 1984–85 Division 2; 1985–90 Division 3; 1990–91 Division 2; 1991– Division 1.

Honours: Football League: Division 1 best season: 3rd, 1890–91, 1900–01; Division 2 – Champions 1896–97, 1913–14, 1922–23; Runners-up 1894–95, 1980–81; Division 3 (S) – Champions 1930–31, 1949–50; Runners-up 1936–37; Division 3 – Runners-up 1972-73; Division 4 – Champions 1970–71; Runners-up 1959–60. *FA Cup:* Winners 1893–94; Runners-up 1890–91. *Football League Cup:* best season: 5th rd, 1963–64, 1972–73, 1975–76.

NOTTS COUNTY 1992—93 LEAGUE RECORD

Match No.	Date		Venue	Opponents	Result		H/T Score	Lg. Pos.	Goalscorers	Atten- dance
1	Aug	16	A	Birmingham C	L	0-1	0-1	—		10,614
2		22	H	Leicester C	D	1-1	0-1	18	Smith D (pen)	10,501
3		25	H	Watford	L	1-2	1-1	—	Slawson	6274
4		29	A	Peterborough U	W	3-1	1-1	11	Smith D, Wilson, Williams	6670
5	Sept	5	H	Barnsley	L	1-3	0-3	17	Short Craig	6205
6		12	A	Watford	W	3-1	1-1	12	Draper, Lund, Slawson	7077
7		19	A	Millwall	L	0-6	0-1	16		6689
8		26	H	Luton T	D	0-0	0-0	17		5992
9		29	A	Tranmere R	L	1-3	0-2	—	Murphy	5403
10	Oct	3	A	Bristol R	D	3-3	2-3	17	Bartlett, Smith D, O'Riordan	5031
11		10	H	Grimsby T	W	1-0	1-0	14	Lund	6442
12		17	A	Swindon T	L	1-5	0-2	16	Thomas	7589
13		24	H	Oxford U	D	1-1	0-1	17	Turner P	5226
14		31	A	Sunderland	D	2-2	0-1	18	Short Chris, Slawson	15,473
15	Nov	3	H	Derby Co	L	0-2	0-2	—		15,267
16		7	A	West Ham U	L	0-2	0-1	21		12,345
17		14	H	Wolverhampton W	D	2-2	0-1	20	Bartlett 2	8494
18		21	A	Southend U	L	1-3	0-2	21	Bartlett	3219
19		28	A	Bristol C	L	0-1	0-0	21		9065
20	Dec	5	H	Newcastle U	L	0-2	0-0	23		14,840
21		12	A	Cambridge U	W	1-0	1-0	22	Turner R	5037
22		19	A	Portsmouth	D	0-0	0-0	22		8943
23		28	H	Brentford	D	1-1	1-1	23	Agana	6892
24	Jan	9	H	Millwall	L	1-2	1-0	24	Thomas	6148
25		16	H	Luton T	D	0-0	0-0	24		6729
26		23	A	Leicester C	D	1-1	0-1	24	Draper	15,716
27		26	H	Tranmere R	W	5-1	3-0	—	Matthews, Smith 2 (1 pen), Agana, Draper	5642
28		30	A	Charlton Ath	L	1-2	0-0	23	Draper	8337
29	Feb	6	H	Birmingham C	W	3-1	2-0	19	Smith (pen), Matthews, Bartlett	8550
30		21	A	Peterborough U	W	1-0	1-0	—	Smith (pen)	7468
31		27	A	Grimsby T	D	3-3	2-1	21	Devlin, Draper, Lund	5871
32	Mar	6	H	Bristol R	W	3-0	1-0	19	Draper 2, Devlin	6445
33		9	A	Wolverhampton W	L	0-3	0-0	—		11,482
34		13	H	West Ham U	W	1-0	0-0	17	Walker	10,272
35		16	A	Barnsley	D	0-0	0-0	—		6372
36		20	A	Newcastle U	L	0-4	0-1	19		30,029
37		23	H	Southend U	W	4-0	1-0	—	Lund, Cox, Draper 2	6109
38	Apr	3	H	Bristol C	D	0-0	0-0	18		6633
39		6	A	Cambridge U	L	0-3	0-1	—		4583
40		10	H	Charlton Ath	W	2-0	0-0	15	Thomas, Draper	6206
41		12	A	Brentford	D	2-2	1-1	16	Devlin, Walker	8045
42		17	H	Portsmouth	L	0-1	0-0	17		11,014
43		24	T	Swindon T	D	1-1	1-1	19	Reeves	8382
44	May	1	A	Oxford U	D	1-1	1-1	20	Walker	6171
45		5	A	Derby Co	L	0-2	0-0	—		13,326
46		8	H	Sunderland	W	3-1	3-0	17	Reeves, Smith D, Draper	14,417

Final League Position: 17

GOALSCORERS

League (55): Draper 11, Smith D 8 (4 pens), Bartlett 5, Lund 4, Devlin 3, Slawson 3, Thomas 3, Walker 3, Agana 2, Matthews 2, Reeves 2, Cox 1, Murphy 1, O'Riordan 1, Chris Short 1, Craig Short 1, Turner P 1, Turner R 1, Williams 1, Wilson 1.
Coca Cola Cup (6): Lund 2, Agana 1, Draper 1, O'Riordan 1, Robinson 1.
FA Cup (0).

Cherry 44	Palmer 30 + 1	Thomas 36 + 1	Craig Short 3	Johnson 37	O'Riordan 15 + 2	Draper 44	Williams 17 + 5	Agana 23 + 6	Matthews 5 + 3	Smith D 37	Wilson 23 + 9	Harding — + 1	Dijkstra 11	Slawson 9 + 11	Turner P 17 + 3	Catlin 2	Chris Short 30 + 1	Murphy 3 + 5	Lund 26 + 2	Robinson 1	Devlin 28 + 4	Smith M 4 + 1	Bartlett 11 + 5	Turner R 7 + 1	Dryden 2	Cox 21	Walker 12	Reeves 8 + 1	Wells — + 1	Match No.
1	2	3	4	5	6	*7*	8	9	10	11	12	14																		1
1	2		4	5	6	7	8	9		*11*	12						3	10	14											2
1	2			5	6	7	8	9		11	12						3	10	4											3
	2		4		6	7	8		11		9						3	10	12	1	5									4
	2	14	4		6	7			11		9						*5*	10	8	1	3	12								5
1	2			6	7				11	10							5	12	8		3	4	9							6
1		3		6	7				11	10							2	12	8		4	9	5							7
1	5	3	4	6	7				11								10	8			2	9	12							8
1		3	4	6	7				11								8				2	5	9	10						9
1		3	5	6	7				*11*								8				2	12	9	14	4	10				10
1	2	3		5	6	7											8				9	11	4	10						11
1	*2*	3		5	6	7											12	8			14	9	11	4	10					12
1	4	3		5	6	7	8	10									12				2		9	11						13
1	4	3		5		7	6	10		11							12	8			2		9							14
1	4	3		5		7	6	10									11	8			2		9	12						15
1	4	3		5	10	6											11	8			2		9	7	12					16
1	4	3		5	6		10			14							11	*8*			2		9	7	12					17
1	4	3		*6*	7	8											12				2	14	9	11		10	5			18
1	2	4		*6*	14	8		9		11	7			3	12											10	5			19
1	2	4			14	7		9		11	*8*			3	12		6									10	5			20
1	6	4			7	14	9			11	8			*3*			2		12							10	5			21
1	2	4			7	6	9			11	8			3								12	10				5			22
1	6	4			7		9			11	8			3			2									10	5			23
1	6	*4*				7	9	12	11		8						2	14				3	10	5						24
1	5	4	6		7	2	9	12	11	10							8										3			25
1		4	6			8	9	12	11	10							2				7					3	5			26
1	6	4	3		8		9	10	11	12							2				7					5				27
1	6	4	3		8	14	9	10	11	12							2				7					*5*				28
1	6		3		8	4	9	10	11								2				7	12				5				29
1	6		3		8	4	9	7	11								2				10	12				5				30
1	6	4		3		8	12	9	11								2				7	10				5				31
1	6	4		3		8		9	11								2				7	10	12			5				32
1	6	4		3		8	14		11	12							2				7	*10*	9			5				33
1		4	3		8	10		11	9								2				7	12				5	6			34
1		4	3		8	2		9		11							7				10					5	6			35
1		*3*		8	14		11	9	12								2				7	10				5	6			36
1		4	3		8		11	9	12								2	*7*			10		14			5	6			37
1		4	3		8	12		11	*9*								2	7			10					5	6	14		38
1	14	4		*3*	8	12		11									2	7			10					5	6	9		39
1	*2*	4	3		8		7		11	14	12										10					5	6	9		40
1		4	3		8	*7*		11	2	14											10					5	6	9	12	41
1		4	3		8	7		11	14								*2*	12			10					5	6	9		42
1		3		8	12		11	4						2							7					5	6	9		43
1		3		8	12		11	4					2						*7*						5	6	9			44
1		3		8	12		11	*4*					2	14					7				10		5	6	9			45
1	6	3		8	12		11	4					2					7			10				5		9			46

Coca Cola Cup	Second Round	Wolverhampton W (h)	3-2	
		(a)	1-0	
	Third Round	Cambridge U (h)	2-3	
FA Cup	Third Round	Sunderland (h)	0-2	

NOTTS COUNTY

Player and Position	Ht	Wt	Date	Birth Place	Source	Clubs	League App	Gls
Goalkeepers								
Bob Catlin	6 2	14 00	22 6 65	London	Marconi	Notts Co	2	—
						Birmingham C (loan)	8	—
Steve Cherry	6 1	13 00	5 8 60	Nottingham	Apprentice	Derby Co	77	—
						Port Vale (loan)	4	—
						Walsall	71	—
						Plymouth Arg	73	—
						Chesterfield (loan)	10	—
						Notts Co	196	—
Paul Dolan	6 4	13 05	16 4 66	Ottawa	Vancouver W	Notts Co	—	—
James Walker*	5 11	11 00	9 7 73	Mansfield	Trainee	Notts Co	—	—
Defenders								
Paul Cox	5 11	11 12	1 1 72	Nottingham	Trainee	Notts Co	22	1
Meindert Dijkstra	5 11	12 00	28 2 67	Eindhoven	Willem II	Notts Co	11	—
Tommy Gallagher	5 10	10 08	25 8 74	Nottingham	Trainee	Notts Co	—	—
Michael Johnson	5 11	11 00	4 7 73	Nottingham	Trainee	Notts Co	42	—
Shaun Murphy	6 0	12 00	5 11 70	Sydney	Perth Italia	Notts Co	8	1
Charlie Palmer	6 0	12 03	10 7 63	Aylesbury	Apprentice	Watford	10	1
						Derby Co	51	2
						Hull C	70	1
						Notts Co	160	6
Alan Paris	6 0	11 10	15 8 64	Slough	Slough T	Watford		
						Peterborough U	137	2
						Leicester C	88	3
						Notts Co	42	1
David Robinson	6 0	13 00	14 1 65	Cleveland		Hartlepool U	66	1
						Halifax T	72	1
						Peterborough U	95	9
						Notts Co	1	—
Paul Sherlock	5 11	11 05	17 11 73	Wigan	Trainee	Notts Co	—	—
Chris Short	5 10	12 02	9 5 70	Munster		Scarborough	43	1
						Manchester U (loan)	—	—
						Notts Co	73	2
Mark Smith	6 2	13 11	21 3 60	Sheffield	Apprentice	Sheffield W	282	16
						Plymouth Arg	82	6
						Barnsley	104	10
						Notts Co	5	—
						Chesterfield (loan)	6	1
						Huddersfield T (loan)	5	—
						Port Vale (loan)	6	—
Dean Thomas	5 10	11 08	19 12 61	Bedworth	Nuneaton Borough Fortuna Dusseldorf	Wimbledon	57	8
						Northampton T	74	11
						Notts Co	127	8
Richard Walker	6 0	12 00	9 11 71	Derby	Trainee	Notts Co	12	3
Dean Yates	6 1	12 00	26 10 67	Leicester	Apprentice	Notts Co	292	33
Midfield								
Mark Draper	5 10	11 00	11 11 70	Derby	Trainee	Notts Co	178	27
Paul Harding	5 9	12 05	6 3 64	Mitcham	Barnet	Notts Co	54	1
Gary Patterson*	5 11	11 05	27 11 72	Newcastle	Trainee	Notts Co	—	—
Darren Saunders*	5 6	10 10	19 10 73	Nottingham	Trainee	Notts Co	—	—
Michael Simpson	5 9	10 08	28 2 74	Nottingham	Trainee	Notts Co	—	—
Eddie Snook	5 7	10 01	18 10 68	Washington	Apprentice	Notts Co	—	—
Phil Turner	5 9	10 13	12 2 62	Sheffield	Apprentice	Lincoln C	241	19
						Grimsby T	62	8
						Leicester C	24	2
						Notts Co	147	11
Robert Turner	6 3	14 01	18 9 66	Durham	Apprentice	Huddersfield T	1	—
						Cardiff C	39	8
						Hartlepool U (loan)	7	1
						Bristol R	26	2
						Wimbledon	10	—
						Bristol C	52	12
						Plymouth Arg	66	17
						Notts Co	8	1
						Shrewsbury T (loan)	9	—
Richard Ward*	5 8	11 00	17 11 73	Scarborough	Trainee	Notts Co	—	—
Mark Wells	5 9	10 10	15 10 71	Leicester	Trainee	Notts Co	2	—
Andy Williams	6 0	11 09	29 7 62	Birmingham	Solihull B	Coventry C	9	—
						Rotherham U	87	13
						Leeds U	46	3
						Port Vale (loan)	5	—
						Notts Co	37	2

NOTTS COUNTY

Colours: Black and white striped shirts, black shorts, white stockings. **Change colours:** All turquoise.

Foundation: For many years the foundation date of the Football League's oldest club was given as 1862 and the club celebrated its centenary in 1962. However, the researches of Keith Warsop have since shown that the club was on a very haphazard basis at that time, playing little more than practice matches. The meeting which put it on a firm footing was held at the George IV Hotel in December 1864, when they became known as the Notts Football Club.

First Football League game: 15 September, 1888, Football League, v Everton (a) L 1-2 – Holland; Guttridge, McLean; Brown, Warburton, Shelton; Hodder, Harker, Jardine, Moore (1), Wardle.

Did you know: The first player to score a hat-trick in an FA Cup final was Jimmy Logan of Notts County in 1894 during a 4-1 win. Two of his goals came in a three-minute spell in the second half.

Managers (and Secretary-Managers)
Edwin Browne 1883–93*, Tom Featherstone 1893*, Tom Harris 1893–13*, Albert Fisher 1913–27, Horace Henshall 1927–34, Charlie Jones 1934–35, David Pratt 1935, Percy Smith 1935–36, Jimmy McMullan 1936–37, Harry Parkes 1938–39, Tony Towers 1939–42, Frank Womack 1942–43, Major Frank Buckley 1944–46, Arthur Stollery 1946–49, Eric Houghton 1949–53, George Poyser 1953–57, Tommy Lawton 1957–58, Frank Hill 1958–61, Tim Coleman 1961–63, Eddie Lowe 1963–65, Tim Coleman 1965–66, Jack Burkitt 1966–67, Andy Beattie (GM 1967), Billy Gray 1967–68, Jimmy Sirrel 1969–75, Ron Fenton 1975–77, Jimmy Sirrel 1978–82 (continues as GM to 1984), Howard Wilkinson 1982–83, Larry Lloyd 1983–84, Richie Barker 1984–85, Jimmy Sirrel 1985–87, John Barnwell 1987–88, Neil Warnock 1989–93, Mick Walker January 1993–.

Player and Position	Ht	Wt	Birth Date	Place	Source	Clubs	League App	Gls
Forwards								
Tony Agana	6 0	12 02	2 10 63	London	Weymouth	Watford	15	1
						Sheffield U	118	42
						Notts C	13	1
						Leeds U (loan)	2	—
						Notts Co	29	2
Paul Devlin	5 8	10 05	14 4 72	Birmingham	Stafford R	Notts Co	34	3
Philip Hill	5 8	11 00	14 6 74	Scarborough	Trainee	Notts Co	—	—
Gary Lund	6 0	11 00	13 9 64	Grimsby	School	Grimsby T	60	24
						Lincoln C	44	13
						Notts Co	179	46
						Hull C (loan)	11	3
Rob Matthews	6 0	12 05	14 10 70	Slough	Loughborough Univ	Notts Co	13	5
David Reeves	6 0	11 05	19 11 67	Birkenhead	Heswall	Sheffield W	17	2
						Scunthorpe U (loan)	4	2
						Scunthorpe U (loan)	6	4
						Burnley (loan)	16	8
						Bolton W	134	29
						Notts Co	9	2
Stephen Slawson	6 0	12 06	13 11 72	Nottingham	Trainee	Notts Co	33	4
						Burnley (loan)	5	2
David Smith	5 11	12 00	25 6 61	Sidcup	Welling U	Gillingham	104	10
						Bristol C	97	10
						Plymouth Arg	18	2
						Notts Co	37	8
Kevin Wilson	5 7	10 10	18 4 61	Banbury	Banbury U	Derby Co	122	30
						Ipswich T	98	34
						Chelsea	152	42
						Notts Co	40	2
Gavin Worboys	6 0	11 00	14 7 74	Doncaster	Trainee	Doncaster R	7	2
						Notts Co	—	—

Trainees
Dodson, Matthew J; Galloway, Michael A; Henry, Alvin M; Horseman, Brian G; King, Jon M; Lawley, Edward W. H; Lewis, Gavin; Ludlow, Lee; Malpass, Jody; Marshall, Daniel J; Muir, James M; Needham, Benjamin D; Ridgeway, Ian D; Rigby, Malcolm R; Smith, Paul A; Wells, Iain D.

Associated Schoolboys
Barke, Christopher P; Brearley, Richard; Bryan, Courtney; Derry, Shaun P; Eaton, Jamie; Fitzgerald, Louis; Folwell, John A; Gare, Darren; Heightonth, Henry P; Hennessy, Simon; Hurst, Liam J. J; Marshall, Jamie; Marston, Marvin A; Mitchell, Paul; Moroziuk, Stefan; Russell, Matthew L; Shepperson, Timothy J; Spray, Gary R; Syms, Gareth; Wilkes, Timothy C; Wilson, Scott R.

Associated Schoolboys who have accepted the club's offer of a Traineeship/Contract
Burke, Anthony G; Chadbourne, Martyn; Hunt, James M; Pearson, Christopher D.

OLDHAM ATHLETIC 1992-93 *Back row (left to right):* Niel Tolson, Richard Jobson, Ian Marshall, Jon Hallworth, Paul Gerrard, John Keeley, Ian Olney, Paul Moulden, Willie Donachie. *Centre row:* Bill Urmson (Coach), Andy Holden (Coach), Gunnar Halle, Roger Palmer, Paul Bernard, Neil McDonald, Andy Ritchie, Steve Redmond, Neil Adams, Ronnie Evans (Assistant Physio), Ian Liversedge (Physio). *Front row:* Craig Fleming, Graeme Sharp, Mike Milligan, Joe Royle (Manager), Andy Barlow, Nick Henry, Neil Pointon.

FA Premier   **OLDHAM ATHLETIC**

Boundary Park, Oldham. Telephone 061–624 4972. Ticket office: 0898 121582. Commercial Dept: 061–652 0966. Clubcall: 0898 121142.

Ground capacity: 17,004 (seats 11,414 seats, 5590 standing).

Record attendance: 47,671 v Sheffield W, FA Cup 4th rd. 25 January 1930.

Record receipts: £129,365 v Manchester U, FA Premier League, 9 March 1993.

Pitch measurements: 110yd × 74yd.

President: R. Schofield.

Chairman & Chief Executive: I. H. Stott, *Vice-chairman:* D. A. Brierley.

Directors: G. T. Butterworth, R. Adams, D. R. Taylor, P. Chadwick, J. Slevin, N. Holden.

Manager: Joe Royle.

Secretary: Terry Cale. *Commercial Manager:* Alan Hardy.

Coach: Willie Donachie. *Physio:* Ian Liversedge.

Year Formed: 1895. *Turned Professional:* 1899. *Ltd Co.:* 1906.

Previous Name: 1895, Pine Villa; 1899, Oldham Athletic.

Club Nickname: 'The Latics'.

Previous Ground: Sheepfoot Lane; 1905, Boundary Park.

Record League Victory: 11–0 v Southport, Division 4, 26 December 1962 – Hollands; Branagan, Marshall; McCall, Williams, Scott; Ledger (1), Johnstone, Lister (6), Colquhoun (1), Whitaker (3).

Record Cup Victory: 10–1 v Lytham, FA Cup, 1st rd, 28 November 1925 – Gray; Wynne, Grundy; Adlam, Heaton, Naylor (1), Douglas, Pynegar (2), Ormston (2), Barnes (3), Watson (2).

Record Defeat: 4–13 v Tranmere R, Division 3 (N), 26 December 1935.

Most League Points (2 for a win): 62, Division 3, 1973–74.

Most League Points (3 for a win): 88, Division 2, 1990–91.

Most League Goals: 95, Division 4, 1962–63.

Highest League Scorer in Season: Tom Davis, 33, Division 3 (N), 1936–37.

Most League Goals in Total Aggregate: Roger Palmer, 141, 1980–92.

Most Capped Player: Albert Gray, 9 (24), Wales.

Most League Appearances: Ian Wood, 525, 1966–80.

Record Transfer Fee Received: £1,700,000 from Aston Villa for Earl Barrett, February 1992.

Record Transfer Fee Paid: £700,000 to Aston Villa for Ian Olney, June 1992.

Football League Record: 1907 Elected to Division 2; 1910–23 Division 1; 1923–35 Division 2; 1935–53 Division 3 (N); 1953–54 Division 2; 1954–58 Division 3 (N); 1958–63 Division 4; 1963–69 Division 3; 1969–71 Division 4; 1971–74 Division 3; 1974–91 Division 2; 1991–92 Division 1; 1992– FA Premier League.

Honours: Football League: Division 1 – Runners-up 1914–15; Division 2 – Champions 1990–91; Runners-up 1909–10; Division 3 (N) – Champions 1952–53; Division 3 – Champions 1973–74; Division 4 – Runners-up 1962–63. *FA Cup:* Semi-final 1913, 1990. *Football League Cup:* Runners-up 1990.

OLDHAM ATHLETIC 1992—93 LEAGUE RECORD

Match No.	Date		Venue	Opponents	Result		H/T Score	Lg. Pos.	Goalscorers	Atten dance
1	Aug	15	A	Chelsea	D	1-1	0-0	—	Henry	20,699
2		19	H	Crystal Palace	D	1-1	1-0	—	Sharp	11,063
3		22	H	Nottingham F	W	5-3	3-0	7	Adams, Sharp, Henry, Halle, Bernard	11,632
4		26	A	Arsenal	L	0-2	0-2	—		20,796
5		29	A	Manchester C	D	3-3	3-3	13	Jobson, Milligan, Halle	27,288
6	Sept	1	H	Leeds U	D	2-2	0-0	—	Olney 2	13,848
7		5	H	Coventry C	L	0-1	0-0	16		11,254
8		12	A	Crystal Palace	D	2-2	1-0	17	Olney, Sharp	11,224
9		19	H	Ipswich T	W	4-2	1-0	11	Marshall, Sharp, Halle, Henry	11,150
10		26	A	Blackburn R	L	0-2	0-1	14		18,393
11	Oct	4	H	Everton	W	1-0	1-0	—	Jobson	13,013
12		17	A	Sheffield W	L	1-2	1-2	13	Milligan	24,485
13		24	A	Aston Villa	D	1-1	1-0	14	Olney	13,457
14		31	A	Southampton	L	0-1	0-0	16		10,827
15	Nov	9	H	Norwich C	L	2-3	2-2	—	Sharp, Marshall	11,081
16		21	A	Manchester U	L	0-3	0-3	19		33,497
17		28	H	Middlesbrough	W	4-1	3-1	17	Halle, Pointon, Sharp, Adams	12,401
18	Dec	5	A	QPR	L	2-3	1-2	17	Adams, Olney	11,804
19		12	A	Wimbledon	L	2-5	0-3	20	Brennan, Milligan	3386
20		19	A	Tottenham H	W	2-1	1-0	18	Sharp, Olney	11,735
21	Jan	9	A	Ipswich T	W	2-1	1-0	18	Brennan, Bernard	15,025
22		16	A	Blackburn R	L	0-1	0-0	21		13,742
23		23	A	Coventry C	L	0-3	0-3	21		10,544
24		26	H	Manchester C	L	0-1	0-0	—		14,903
25		30	A	Nottingham F	L	0-2	0-1	22		21,240
26	Feb	6	H	Chelsea	W	3-1	1-0	20	Henry, Adams, Brennan	11,772
27		13	A	Leeds U	L	0-2	0-1	21		27,654
28		20	H	Arsenal	L	0-1	0-0	22		12,311
29		22	A	Sheffield U	L	0-2	0-1	—		14,628
30		27	A	Everton	D	2-2	1-0	22	Adams 2 (1 pen)	18,025
31	Mar	9	H	Manchester U	W	1-0	1-0	—	Adams	17,106
32		13	A	Norwich C	L	0-1	0-1	22		19,597
33		20	H	QPR	D	2-2	1-0	21	Henry, Adams	10,946
34		22	A	Middlesbrough	W	3-2	2-0	—	Bernard, Olney, Ritchie	12,290
35	Apr	3	H	Wimbledon	W	6-2	3-0	19	Fashanu (og), Bernard, Olney 2, Adams, Beckford	11,606
36		7	H	Sheffield W	D	1-1	1-0	—	Pointon	12,312
37		10	A	Liverpool	L	0-1	0-0	20		36,129
38		13	A	Sheffield U	D	1-1	1-1	—	Ritchie	14,795
39		17	A	Tottenham H	L	1-4	1-0	20	Beckford	26,663
40	May	2	A	Aston Villa	W	1-0	1-0	—	Henry	37,247
41		5	H	Liverpool	W	3-2	3-1	—	Beckford, Olney 2	15,381
42		8	H	Southampton	W	4-3	2-1	19	Pointon, Olney, Ritchie, Halle	14,597

Final League Position: 19

GOALSCORERS

League (63): Olney 12, Adams 9 (1 pen), Sharp 7, Henry 6, Halle 5, Bernard 4, Beckford 3, Brennan 3, Milligan 3, Pointon 3, Ritchie 3, Jobson 2, Marshall 2, own goal 1.
Coca Cola Cup (2): Bernard 1, Henry 1.
FA Cup (2): Bernard 1, Olney 1.

Hallworth 16	Redmond 28 + 3	Barlow 6	Henry 32	Jobson 40	Marshall 26 + 1	Halle 41	Palmer 5 + 12	Sharp 20 + 1	Milligan 42	Bernard 32 + 1	Tolson — + 3	Pointon 34	Adams 26 + 6	Olney 32 + 2	McDonald 2 + 2	Keeley 1	Brennan 14	Gerrard 25	Fleming 23 + 1	Ritchie 10 + 2	Moulden 1 + 3	Beckford 6 + 1	Keizerweerd — + 1	Match No.
1	2	3	4	5	6	7	8	9	10	11	12													1
1	2		4	5	6	7	8	9	10	11		3												2
1	2		4	5	6	7	12	9	10	8		3	11											3
1	2		4	5	6	7		9	10	8		3	11	12										4
1	2			5	6	7		9	10	4		3	11	8										5
1	2			5	6	7	12	9	10	4		3	11	8										6
1	2		4	5	6	7	12	9	10	11		3	14	8										7
1	2		4	5	6	7		9	10	11		3	12	8										8
1	2		4	5	6	7		9	10	11		3		8										9
1	2			5	6	4		9	10	11		3	7	8										10
1	2		4	5	6	7		9	10	11		3		8										11
1	6	7	4	5			2	9	10	11		3	12	8										12
1	6		4	5	8		2	9	10	11		3		7	12									13
1	6		4	5	8	7		9	10	11		3	12		2									14
1	6		4	5	8		2	9	10	11		3	12	7										15
1	6		4	5	8		2	9	10			3	11	12	7									16
	6		4	5			2	9	10			3	7	8		1	11							17
	6		4	5			2	12	9	10		3	7	8			11	1						18
	6		4	5			2	12	9	10		3	7	8			11	1	14					19
		3		5			2	9	10	4			7	8			11	1	6					20
14	3	7		5		9	2	12	10	4				8			11	1	6					21
11				5	9	2			10	4		3	7	8				1	6					22
11				5	9	2	7		10	4		3	12	8				1	6					23
				5	6	2	7		10	4			11	8				1	3	9	12			24
				5	6	2	7		10			3	11	8				9	1	4	12			25
	5		4		6	3			10				7	8			11	1	2	9				26
	5		4		6	3	12		10				7	14	8		11	1	2	9				27
			4	5	6	3			10				7	8			11	1	2	9	12			28
	6		4	5	9		12		10				14	3	7		11	1	2			8		29
	6		4	5	9		3	12	10					7			11	1	2			8	14	30
12			4	5			2		10	8		3	7	9			11	1	6					31
14			4	5			2	12	10	8		3	7	9			11	1	6					32
			4	5	8		2	12	10	14		3	7	9			11	1	6					33
			4	5			2		10	11		3	7	9				1	6	8				34
			4	5			2		10	11		3	7	9				1	6	8		12		35
			4	5			2		10	11		3	7	9				1	6			8		36
			4	5			2		10	11		3	7	9	12			1	6			8	14	37
			4	5			2	12	10	11		3	7					1	6	8		9		38
			4	5			2	12	10	11		3	7					1	6	8		9		39
		7	4	5			2		10	11		3		8				1	6			9		40
		7	4	5			2		10	11		3		8				1	6	12		9		41
		7	4	5	12		2		10	11		3		9				1	6			8		42

Coca Cola Cup	Second Round	Exeter C (a)		1-0
		(h)		0-0
	Third Round	Swindon T (a)		1-0
	Fourth Round	Cambridge U (a)		0-1
FA Cup	Third Round	Tranmere R (h)		2-2
		(a)		0-3

OLDHAM ATHLETIC

Player and Position	Ht	Wt	Date	Birth Place	Source	Clubs	League App	Gls
Goalkeepers								
Paul Gerrard	6 1	12 06	22 1 73	Heywood	Trainee	Oldham Ath	25	—
Jon Hallworth	6 1	14 03	26 10 65	Stockport	School	Ipswich T	45	—
						Swindon T (loan)	—	—
						Fulham (loan)	—	—
						Bristol R (loan)	2	—
						Oldham Ath	134	—
John Keeley	6 1	14 02	27 7 61	Plaistow	Apprentice	Southend U	54	—
					Chelmsford C	Brighton	138	—
						Oldham Ath	2	—
						Oxford U (loan)	6	—
						Reading (loan)	6	—
						Chester C (loan)	4	—
Defenders								
Andy Barlow	5 9	11 01	24 11 65	Oldham		Oldham Ath	253	5
Willie Donachie	5 9	11 05	5 10 51	Glasgow	Juniors	Manchester C	351	2
					Portland T	Norwich C	11	—
					Portland T	Burnley	60	3
						Oldham Ath	169	3
Craig Fleming	6 0	11 07	6 10 71	Calder	Trainee	Halifax T	57	—
						Oldham Ath	56	1
David Hall			19 10 73	Manchester	Trainee	Oldham Ath	—	—
Gunnar Halle	5 11	11 02	11 8 65	Oslo	Lillestrom	Oldham Ath	68	5
Andy Holden	6 1	13 10	14 9 62	Flint	Rhyl	Chester C	100	17
						Wigan Ath	49	4
						Oldham Ath	21	4
Richard Jobson	6 1	13 05	9 5 63	Hull	Burton Alb	Watford	28	4
						Hull C	221	17
						Oldham Ath	120	5
Richard Lockley*			2 6 74	Oldham	Trainee	Oldham Ath	—	—
Chris Makin	5 11	11 00	8 5 73	Manchester	Trainee	Oldham Ath	—	—
						Wigan Ath (loan)	15	2
Neil Pointon	5 10	11 00	28 11 64	Church Warsop	Apprentice	Scunthorpe U	159	2
						Everton	102	5
						Manchester C	74	2
						Oldham Ath	34	3
Steven Redmond	5 11	12 13	2 11 67	Liverpool	Apprentice	Manchester C	235	7
						Oldham Ath	31	—
Midfield								
Paul Bernard	5 11	11 08	30 12 72	Edinburgh	Trainee	Oldham Ath	56	10
Mark Brennan	5 10	10 13	4 10 65	Rossendale	Apprentice	Ipswich T	168	19
						Middlesbrough	65	6
						Manchester C	29	6
						Oldham Ath	14	3
Nick Henry	5 6	9 08	21 2 69	Liverpool	Trainee	Oldham Ath	181	16
Neil McDonald	5 11	11 04	2 11 65	Wallsend	Wallsend BC	Newcastle U	180	24
						Everton	90	4
						Oldham Ath	21	1
Mike Milligan	5 8	11 00	20 2 67	Manchester		Oldham Ath	162	17
						Everton	17	1
						Oldham Ath	78	6
Gregory Wilson*			11 11 72	Ashton-u-Lyne	Trainee	Oldham Ath	—	—
Forwards								
Neil Adams	5 7	10 06	23 11 65	Stoke	Local	Stoke C	32	4
						Everton	20	—
						Oldham Ath (loan)	9	—
						Oldham Ath	116	23

OLDHAM ATHLETIC

Colours: All blue with red piping. **Change colours:** Red and white shirts, white shorts, white stockings.

Foundation: It was in 1895 that John Garland, the landlord of the Featherstall and Junction Hotel, decided to form a football club. As Pine Villa they played in the Oldham Junior League. In 1899 the local professional club Oldham County, went out of existence and one of the liquidators persuaded Pine Villa to take over their ground at Sheepfoot Lane and change their name to Oldham Athletic.

First Football League game: 9 September, 1907, Division 2, v Stoke (a) W 3-1 – Hewitson; Hodson, Hamilton; Fay, Walders, Wilson; Ward, W. Dodds (1), Newton (1), Hancock, Swarbrick (1).

Did you know: Oldham Athletic were still seeking their first win of the season after eight games in 1947–48, having scored only five goals, when they won 6-0 at Darlington in a Division 3 (N) match.

Managers (and Secretary-Managers)
David Ashworth 1906–14, Herbert Bamlett 1914–21, Charlie Roberts 1921–22, David Ashworth 1923–24, Bob Mellor 1924–27, Andy Wilson 1927–32, Jimmy McMullan 1933–34, Bob Mellor 1934–45 (continued as secretary to 1953), Frank Womack 1945–47, Billy Wootton 1947–50, George Hardwick 1950–56, Ted Goodier 1956–58, Norman Dodgin 1958–60, Jack Rowley 1960–63, Les McDowall 1963–65, Gordon Hurst 1965–66, Jimmy McIlroy 1966–68, Jack Rowley 1968–69, Jimmy Frizzell 1970–82, Joe Royle July 1982–.

Player and Position	Ht	Wt	Date	Birth Place	Source	Clubs	League App	Gls
Darren Beckford	6 1	11 01	12 5 67	Manchester	Apprentice	Manchester C	11	—
						Bury (loan)	12	5
						Port Vale (loan)	11	4
						Port Vale	167	68
						Norwich C	38	8
						Oldham Ath	7	3
Orfeo Keizerweerd*	5 8	10 11	21 11 68		Rodez	Oldham Ath	1	—
Ian Marshall	6 1	12 12	20 3 66	Oxford	Apprentice	Everton	15	1
						Oldham Ath	170	36
Ian Olney	6 1	11 00	17 12 69	Luton	Trainee	Aston Villa	88	16
						Oldham Ath	34	12
Roger Palmer*	5 10	11 00	30 1 59	Manchester	Apprentice	Manchester C	31	9
						Oldham Ath	458	141
Andy Ritchie	5 10	11 11	28 11 60	Manchester	Apprentice	Manchester U	33	13
						Brighton	89	23
						Leeds U	136	40
						Oldham Ath	162	69
Graeme Sharp	6 1	11 09	16 10 60	Glasgow	Eastercraigs	Dumbarton	40	17
						Everton	322	111
						Oldham Ath	63	19
Neil Tolson	6 1	10 07	25 10 73	Wordley	Trainee	Walsall	9	1
						Oldham Ath	3	—

Trainees
Adams, Christian; Berry, Matthew; Boden, Liam T; Booth, Matthew J; Eyre, John R; Feltham, Paul D; Frost, John A; Graham, Richard E; Gray, Ian J; Hilton, Robert C; Hoolickin, Anthony P; Knapman, Stephen C; Lane, Steven; McGregor, Barry J; Pemberton, Martin C; Price, Stephen J; Rickers, Paul S; Serrant, Carl; Speak, Matthew I; Woods, Andrew N.

Associated Schoolboys
Agg, Nathan; Allott, Mark S; Brown, David A; Darnborough, Lee; Hill, Phillip A; Holt, Andrew; Hughes, Andrew J; Jablonski, Mark P; Levendis, Andrew; Mather, Gregg R; McNiven, David J; McNiven, Scott A; Meehan, Andrew T; O'Donavan, Jonathon; Richardson, Lloyd M; Stott, Lee; Thorp, Matthew C.

Associated Schoolboys who have accepted the club's offer of a Traineeship/Contract
Beresford, David; Evans, Richard; Gorman, Darren A; Kay, Simon P; Quinn, Dean S; Smith, Howard.

OXFORD UNITED 1992–93 *Back row (left to right):* Paul Wanless, Mark Druce, Steve Tavinor, Nick Cusack, Paul Kee, Andrew Wallbridge, Ken Veysey, David Collins, Jon Narbett, Robert Mutchell, Joey Beauchamp.

Centre row: Peter Rhoades-Brown (Football in the Community Officer), Steve McClaren (Reserve and Youth Team Coach), John Clinkard (Physio), Keith Holmes, Garry Smart, Chris Allen, Tristan Didcock, John Durnin, Matthew Keeble, David Moss (Coach), Maurice Evans (General Manager), Malcolm Elias (Youth Development Officer).

Front row: Les Robinson, Mickey Lewis, David Penney, Jim Magilton, Brian Horton (Manager), Andrew Melville, Ceri Evans, Mike Ford, Les Phillips.

Division 1 OXFORD UNITED

OXFORD UNITED F.C.

Manor Ground, Headington, Oxford. Telephone Oxford (0865) 61503. Supporters Club: (0865) 63063. Clubcall (information): 0898 121029. Clubcall (match commentary) 0898 121172. Fax: (0865) 741820.

Ground capacity: 11,071.

Record attendance: 22,750 v Preston NE, FA Cup 6th rd, 29 February 1964.

Record receipts: £71,304 v Aston Villa, Milk Cup semi-final, 12 March 1986.

Pitch measurements: 110yd × 75yd.

President: The Duke of Marlborough.

Directors: K. A. Cox (managing), D. M. Clitheroe, G. E. Coppock, P. L. Lowe, T. J. Midgley (environmental).

Manager: Brian Horton. *Coach:* David Moss. *Physio:* John Clinkard.

Directors: K. A. Cox (managing), D. M. Clitheroe, G. E. Coppock, P. L. Lowe, T. J. Midgley (environmental).

Secretary: Mick Brown. *Promotions manager:* Mark Shanahan.

Year Formed: 1893. *Turned Professional:* 1949. *Ltd Co.:* 1949.

Club Nickname: 'The U's'.

Previous Names: 1893, Headington; 1894, Headington United; 1960, Oxford United.

Previous Grounds: 1893–94 Headington Quarry; 1894–98 Wootten's Field; 1898–1902 Sandy Lane Ground; 1902–09 Britannia Field; 1909–10 Sandy Lane; 1910–14 Quarry Recreation Ground; 1914–22 Sandy Lane; 1922–25 The Paddock Manor Road; 1925– Manor Ground.

Record League Victory: 7–0 v Barrow, Division 4, 19 December 1964 – Fearnley; Beavon, Quartermann; Ron Atkinson (1), Kyle, Jones; Morris, Booth (3), Willey (1), Graham Atkinson (1), Harrington (1).

Record Cup Victory: 6–0 v Gillingham, League Cup, 2nd rd (1st leg), 24 September 1986 – Judge; Langan, Trewick, Phillips (Brock), Briggs, Shotton, Houghton (1), Aldridge (4 incl. 1p), Charles (Leworthy), Hebberd, Slatter. (1 og).

Record Defeat: 0–6 v Liverpool, Division 1, 22 March 1986.

Most League Points (2 for a win): 61, Division 4, 1964–65.

Most League Points (3 for a win): 95, Division 3, 1983–84.

Most League Goals: 91, Division 3, 1983–84.

Highest League Scorer in Season: John Aldridge, 30, Division 2, 1984–85.

Most League Goals in Total Aggregate: Graham Atkinson, 77, 1962–73.

Most Capped Player: Jim Magilton, 15, Northern Ireland.

Most League Appearances: John Shuker, 478, 1962–77.

Record Transfer Fee Received: £1,190,000 from Derby Co for Dean Saunders, October 1988.

Record Transfer Fee Paid: £285,000 to Gillingham for Colin Greenall, February 1988.

Football League Record: 1962 Elected to Division 4; 1965–68 Division 3; 1968–76 Division 2; 1976–84 Division 3; 1984–85 Division 2; 1985–88 Division 1; 1988–92 Division 2; 1992– Division 1.

Honours: Football League: Division 1 best season: 18th, 1985–86, 1986–87; Division 2 – Champions 1984–85; Division 3 – Champions 1967–68, 1983–84; Division 4 – Promoted 1964–65 (4th). *FA Cup:* best season: 6th rd, 1963–64 (record for 4th Division club). *Football League Cup:* Winners 1985–86.

OXFORD UNITED 1992—93 LEAGUE RECORD

Match No.	Date		Venue	Opponents		Result	H/T Score	Lg. Pos.	Goalscorers	Atten dance
1	Aug	15	H	Bristol R	W	2-1	2-0	—	Penney (pen), Beauchamp	7333
2		22	A	Millwall	L	1-3	0-2	14	Penney	6746
3		29	H	Wolverhampton W	D	0-0	0-0	14		7592
4	Sept	5	A	Grimsby T	D	1-1	0-0	15	Durnin	4546
5		12	H	Sunderland	L	0-1	0-1	20		6003
6		15	H	Cambridge U	W	3-0	1-0	—	Magilton (pen), Allen, Penney	3785
7		20	A	Swindon T	D	2-2	0-1	—	Melville, Penney	7717
8		26	H	Tranmere R	L	1-2	0-1	13	Magilton	4683
9	Oct	3	H	Birmingham C	D	0-0	0-0	15		7096
10		11	A	Derby Co	W	1-0	0-0	—	Durnin	14,249
11		17	H	Barnsley	D	0-0	0-0	14		4422
12		24	A	Notts Co	D	1-1	1-0	16	Cusack	5226
13		31	H	Watford	D	1-1	0-1	16	Magilton (pen)	6234
14	Nov	3	H	Portsmouth	D	5-5	2-4	—	Penney, Magilton 2 (1 pen), Durnin, Allen	5490
15		7	A	Southend U	W	3-0	3-0	15	Durnin 2, Penney	3356
16		14	H	Luton T	W	4-0	2-0	13	Durnin 4	5760
17		21	A	West Ham U	L	3-5	1-3	13	Durnin, Magilton, Melville	11,842
18		28	A	Brentford	L	0-1	0-1	15		8017
19	Dec	13	H	Leicester C	D	0-0	0-0	—		7949
20		19	A	Charlton Ath	D	1-1	1-0	16	Ford	7287
21		26	A	Bristol C	D	1-1	1-1	16	Beauchamp	10,737
22		28	H	Newcastle U	W	4-2	3-2	16	Durnin, Cusack, Magilton 2 (1 pen)	9293
23	Jan	9	A	Swindon T	L	0-1	0-1	16		9146
24		15	A	Tranmere R	L	0-4	0-2	—		8317
25		23	A	Cambridge U	D	2-2	2-2	16	Ford 2	4536
26		30	H	Millwall	W	3-0	1-0	15	Magilton (pen), Beauchamp 2	7474
27	Feb	6	A	Bristol R	W	1-0	0-0	13	Melville	5593
28		9	A	Sunderland	L	0-2	0-2	—		13,314
29		20	A	Wolverhampton W	W	1-0	1-0	12	Beauchamp	12,791
30		23	H	Grimsby T	L	0-1	0-0	—		4944
31		27	H	Derby Co	L	0-1	0-0	15		7456
32	Mar	6	A	Birmingham C	L	0-1	0-1	15		11,104
33		9	A	Luton T	L	1-3	1-1	—	Cusack	6687
34		13	H	Southend U	L	0-1	0-0	16		4576
35		20	H	Peterborough U	D	1-1	1-1	16	Beauchamp	6316
36		23	H	West Ham U	W	1-0	0-0	—	Melville	9506
37		27	A	Portsmouth	L	0-3	0-0	16		14,648
38	Apr	3	H	Brentford	L	0-2	0-1	19		5466
39		7	A	Leicester C	L	1-2	1-1	—	Ford	16,611
40		10	H	Bristol C	W	2-0	1-0	16	Druce, Beauchamp	6145
41		17	H	Charlton Ath	L	0-1	0-1	21		5121
42		20	H	Peterborough U	W	2-1	2-0	—	Magilton (pen), Melville	4525
43		24	A	Barnsley	W	1-0	1-0	15	Melville	5523
44	May	1	H	Notts Co	D	1-1	1-1	15	Magilton	6171
45		6	A	Newcastle U	L	1-2	0-0	—	Cusack	29,438
46		8	A	Watford	W	1-0	1-0	14	Allen	8127

Final League Position: 14

GOALSCORERS

League (53): Durnin 11, Magilton 11 (6 pens), Beauchamp 7, Melville 6, Penney 6 (1 pen), Cusack 4, Ford 4, Allen 3, Druce 1.
Coca Cola Cup (5): Allen 2, Cusack 2, Beauchamp 1.
FA Cup (3): Beauchamp 1, Cusack 1, Magilton 1 (pen).

Kee 11	Smart 41	Ford 43 + 1	Collins 12 + 1	Evans 41	Melville 44	Phillips 9 + 2	Beauchamp 44	Cusack 30 + 9	Penney 23 + 10	Durnin 34 + 3	Allen 18 + 13	Lewis 40 + 1	Magilton 40	Reece 35	Robinson 14 + 2	Narbett 12 + 2	Wanless 5 + 2	Varadi 3 + 2	Jackson 1	Keeble 1	Druce 3 + 1	Murphy 2	Match No.
1	2	3	4	5	6	7	8	9	10	11													1
1	2	3	4	5	6	7	8	9	10	11	12	14											2
1	2	3		5	6		8	9	10	11	12	4	7										3
1	2	3		5	6		8	9	10	11	12	4	7										4
1	2	3		5	6		8	9	12	10	11	4	7										5
1	2	3	12	5	6		8		9	10	11	4	7										6
1	2	3		5	6	12	8		9	10	11	4	7										7
1	2		3	5	6	12	8	14	9	10	11	4	7										8
	2	3	11	5	6	7	8		9	10	12	4		1									9
	2	3		5	6	11	8	9	10			4	7	1									10
	2	3		5	6	11	8	9	10			4	7	1									11
	2	3		5	6	11	8	9	10			4	7	1	12								12
	2	3		5	6	11	8	9	10		12	4	7	1									13
	2	3		5	6		8	12	9	10	11	4	7	1	14								14
	2	3		5	6		8	9	10	11		4	7	1	12								15
	2	3		5	6		8	12	9	10	11	4	7	1									16
	2	3		5	6		8	12	9	10	11	4	7	1									17
	2	3		5	6		8	12	9	10	11	4	7	1									18
	2	3		5	6		8	10	9	11		4	7	1	12								19
	2	3		5	6		8	10	9	11		4	7	1									20
	2	3		5	6		8	10	9	11	12	4	7	1									21
	2			5	6		8	9	10	11		4	7	1	3								22
	2	14		5	6		8	9	12	10	11	4	7	1	3								23
	2	3		5	6		8	9	12	11	14	4	7	1	10								24
	2	3		5	6		8	9	10			4	7	1	11	12							25
	2	3		5	6		8		10			4	7	1	11		9						26
	2	3		5	6		8	12	10			4	7	1	11		9						27
	2	3		5	6		8	12	10		14	4	7	1	11		9						28
	2	3		5	6		8	9	10			4	7	1	11	12							29
	2	3		5			8	9	12	10	14	4	7	1	11		6						30
	2	3		5	6		8	9	10	12	14	4	7	1	11								31
	2	3		5	6		8	9	10	12	14	4	7	1	11								32
	2	3		5	6		8	9	10			4	7	1	11								33
		3	4	5			8	9	12				7	1	2	11	6	10					34
		3	4	5	6		8	9	10				7	1	2	11							35
		3		5	6	7	8	9	10			4		1	2	11							36
		3	4	5	6		8	9	10	11			7	1	2								37
		3	4	5	6		8	9	10	12	11		7	1	2	14							38
1	2	3	4	5	6		8	9					7		11					10			39
1	2	3	4	5	6		8	9			12		7		11						10		40
1	2	3	4	5	6		8	9			12		7		11				14		10		41
	2	3		5	6		8		10	11		4	7	1				9					42
	2	3		5	6		8	14	12	10	11	4	7	1				9					43
	2	3		5	6		8	12	10			4	7	1	11			9					44
	2	3		5	6		8	14	12	11		4	7	1				9			10		45
	2	3		5	6		8	14		11	12	4	7	1				9			10		46

Coca Cola Cup	First Round	Swansea C (h)	3-0
		(a)	0-1
	Second Round	Aston Villa (h)	1-2
		(a)	1-2
FA Cup	Third Round	Swansea C (a)	1-1
		(h)	2-2

OXFORD UNITED

Player and Position	Ht	Wt	Date	Birth Place	Source	Clubs	League App	Gls
Goalkeepers								
Paul Kee	6 3	12 05	8 11 69	Belfast	Ards	Oxford U	53	—
Paul Reece	5 11	12 07	16 7 68	Nottingham	Kettering T	Grimsby T	54	—
						Doncaster R	1	—
						Oxford U	35	—
Ken Veysey*	5 11	11 08	8 6 67	Hackney	Arsenal	Torquay U	72	—
						Oxford U	57	—
						Sheffield U (loan)	—	—
Defenders								
David Collins	6 1	12 10	30 10 71	Dublin	Trainee	Liverpool	—	—
						Wigan Ath (loan)	9	—
						Oxford U	13	—
Ceri Evans	6 1	14 02	2 10 63	Christchurch	Otago Univ	Oxford U	116	3
Mike Ford	6 0	11 02	9 2 66	Bristol	Apprentice Devizes	Leicester C	—	—
						Cardiff C	145	13
						Oxford U	122	9
Darren Jackson	6 1	12 08	24 9 71	Bristol	Trainee	Oxford U	12	—
						Reading (loan)	5	—
Andy Melville	6 0	12 00	29 11 68	Swansea	School	Swansea C	175	22
						Oxford U	135	13
Robert Mutchell	5 10	11 02	2 1 74	Solihull	Trainee	Oxford U	—	—
Les Robinson	5 8	11 01	1 3 67	Mansfield	Local	Mansfield T	15	—
						Stockport Co	67	3
						Doncaster R	82	12
						Oxford U	87	—
Gary Smart	5 9	11 03	29 4 64	Totnes	Wokingham	Oxford U	152	—
Steve Tavinor	5 10	11 06	28 1 74	Oxford	Trainee	Oxford U	—	—
Andy Wallbridge	6 0	12 00	14 11 73	Croydon	Trainee	Oxford U	—	—
Midfield								
Tristan Didcock	5 9	10 00	19 9 73	Chipping Norton	Trainee	Oxford U	—	—
Robert Ford			22 9 74	Oxford	Trainee	Oxford U	—	—
Mickey Lewis	5 6	10 10	15 2 65	Birmingham	School	WBA	24	—
						Derby Co	43	1
						Oxford U	196	6
Steve McClaren	5 7	9 04	3 5 61	Fulford	Apprentice	Hull C	178	16
						Derby Co	25	—
						Lincoln C (loan)	8	—
						Bristol C	61	2
						Oxford U	33	—
Jim Magilton	5 10	12 07	6 5 69	Belfast	Apprentice	Liverpool	—	—
						Oxford U	121	29
Jon Narbett	5 10	10 08	21 11 68	Birmingham	Apprentice	Shrewsbury T	26	3
						Hereford U	149	31
						Leicester C (loan)		
						Oxford U	14	—
Les Phillips*	5 8	10 06	7 1 63	Lambeth	Apprentice	Birmingham C	44	3
						Oxford U	179	9
Paul Wanless	6 1	13 04	14 12 73	Banbury	Trainee	Oxford U	13	—
Forwards								
Chris Allen	5 11	12 02	18 11 72	Oxford	Trainee	Oxford U	45	4
Joe Beauchamp	5 11	11 10	13 3 71	Oxford	Trainee	Oxford U	79	14
						Swansea C (loan)	5	2

OXFORD UNITED

Colours: Gold shirts with blue sleeves, blue shorts, gold stockings. **Change colours:** Red and blue mix shirts, red shorts, red stockings.

Foundation: There had been an Oxford United club around the time of World War I but only in the Oxfordshire Thursday League and there is no connection with the modern club which began as Headington in 1893, adding "United" a later. Playing first on Quarry Fields and subsequently Wootten's Fields, they owe much to a Dr. Hitchings for their early development.

First Football League game: 18 August, 1962, Division 4, v Barrow (a) L 2-3 – Medlock; Beavon, Quartermain; R. Atkinson, Kyle, Jones; Knight, G. Atkinson (1), Houghton (1), Cornwell, Colfar.

Did you know: When known as Headington United, Oxford met Millwall, the first Football League club they had been drawn against in the FA Cup, for a Second Round tie on 12 December 1953. After a 3-3 draw at The Den, Headington won the replay 1-0 with a Ken Smith goal.

Managers (and Secretary-Managers)
Harry Thompson 1949–58 (Player Manager 1949-51), Arthur Turner 1959–69 (continued as GM to 1972), Ron Saunders 1969, George Summers 1969–75, Mike Brown 1975–79, Bill Asprey 1979–80, Ian Greaves 1980–82, Jim Smith 1982–85, Maurice Evans 1985–88, Mark Lawrenson 1988, Brian Horton October 1988– .

Player and Position	Ht	Wt	Birth Date	Birth Place	Source	Clubs	League App	Gls
Nicky Cusack	6 0	11 13	24 12 65	Rotherham	Alvechurch	Leicester C	16	1
						Peterborough U	44	10
						Motherwell	77	17
						Darlington	21	6
						Oxford U	39	4
Mark Druce	5 11	11 11	3 3 74	Oxford	Trainee	Oxford U	6	1
John Durnin	5 10	11 04	18 8 65	Bootle	Waterloo Dock	Liverpool	—	—
						WBA (loan)	5	2
						Oxford U	161	44
Keith Holmes	5 10	10 10	4 3 74	Oxford	Trainee	Oxford U	—	—
Matthew Keeble	5 9	10 00	8 9 72	Chipping Norton		Oxford U	1	—
Matt McDonnell‡	5 10	10 10	10 4 71	Reading	Trainee	Oxford U	—	—
Matthew Murphy			20 8 71	Northampton	Corby	Oxford U	2	—
David Penney	5 8	10 07	17 8 64	Wakefield	Pontefract	Derby Co	19	—
						Oxford U	94	13
						Swansea C (loan)	12	3

Trainees
Bayliss, Gary J; Border, Benjamin J; Conneely, Michael; Forinton, Howard L; Girolami, Adriano U; Godfrey, Russell L; Goodall, Grant S; Greig, Neil J; Hillman, Stephen J; Maciak, Jason; Maisey, Darren; Morrissey, Terence; Stevens, Greg R; Turner, Simon J; Watts, Darren W.

Associated Schoolboys
Bowen, Jamie; Concannon, Ian D; Deacon, Tom; Gardner, John W; Goodwin, Richard; Hammond, Paul J; Hawrot, Lee J; Hayter, Jonathon R; McGregor, Marc R; Moodey, Jonathan J; Powell, Paul; Redknap, Benjamin M; Robertson, Andrew; Smith, Kirk A; Smith, Lee J; Stanway, Mark R; Tregurtha, David M; Wells, Nicholas K; Wilsdon, Christian J; Wilson, Neil A.

Associated Schoolboys who have accepted the club's offer of a Traineeship/Contract
Bastable, Gary J; Byles, Paul J; Cullip, Daniel; Foster, Dale; Gordon, Ian P; Mann, Alan S; Stirling, Leon W.

PETERBOROUGH UNITED 1992–93 *Back row (left to right):* Darren Bradshaw, Tony Adcock, Pat Gavin, David Robinson, Lee Howarth, Steve Welsh, Marcus Ebdon. *Centre row:* Gerry McElhinney (Youth Team Manager), Hamish Curtis, Peter Costello, Ken Charlery, Fred Barber, Ian Bennett, Ronnie Robinson, Chris White, Noel Luke, Keith Oakes (Team Physio). *Front row:* Worrell Sterling, Gary Cooper, Bil Harvey (Club Physio), Lil Fuccillo (Assistant Manager), Chris Turner (Manager), Mick Halsall, Jason O'Connor, Bobby Barnes.

Division 1   **PETERBOROUGH UNITED**

London Road Ground, Peterborough PE2 8AL. Telephone Peterborough (0733) 63947. Fax 0733 557210.

Ground capacity: 20,500.

Record attendance: 30,096 v Swansea T, FA Cup 5th rd, 20 February 1965.

Record receipts: £51,315 v Brighton & HA, 5th rd, 15 February 1986.

Pitch measurements: 112yd × 75yd.

Chairman: Chris Turner. *Vice-chairman:* A. H. Hand.

Directors: S. Reilly, P. Sagar. *Company Secretary:* A. H. Hand.

General Manager:

Manager: Lil Fuccillo. *Assistant Manager:* Keith Oakes. *Coach:* Mick Halsall.

Secretary: Miss Caroline Hand.

Physio: Keith Oakes.

Commercial Manager: Michael Vincent.

Year Formed: 1934. *Turned Professional:* 1934. *Ltd Co.:* 1934.

Club Nickname: 'The Posh'.

Record League Victory: 8–1 v Oldham Ath, Division 4, 26 November 1969 – Drewery; Potts, Noble; Conmy, Wile, Wright; Moss (1), Price (3), Hall (4), Halliday, Robson.

Record Cup Victory: 6–0 v Redditch, FA Cup, 1st rd (replay), 22 November 1971 – Drewery; Carmichael, Brookes; Oakes, Turner, Wright; Conmy, Price (1), Hall (2), Barker (2), Robson (1).

Record Defeat: 1–8 v Northampton T, FA Cup 2nd rd (2nd replay), 18 December, 1946.

Most League Points (2 for a win): 66, Division 4, 1960–61.

Most League Points (3 for a win): 82, Division 4, 1981–82.

Most League Goals: 134, Division 4, 1960–61.

Highest League Scorer in Season: Terry Bly, 52, Division 4, 1960–61.

Most League Goals in Total Aggregate: Jim Hall, 122, 1967–75.

Most Capped Player: Tony Millington, 8 (21), Wales.

Most League Appearances: Tommy Robson, 482, 1968–81.

Record Transfer Fee Received: £400,000 from Notts Co for David Robinson, October 1992.

Record Transfer Fee Paid: £100,000 to Halifax T for David Robinson, July 1989 and to Millwall for John McGlashan, February 1993.

Football League Record: 1960 Elected to Division 4; 1961–68 Division 3, when they were demoted for financial irregularities; 1968–74 Division 4; 1974–79 Division 3; 1979–91 Division 4; 1991–92 Division 3; 1992– Division 1.

Honours: Football League: Division 3 best season: promotion through play-offs 1991–92; Division 4 – Champions 1960–61, 1973–74. *FA Cup:* best season: 6th rd, 1965. *Football League Cup:* Semi-final 1966.

PETERBOROUGH UNITED 1992—93 LEAGUE RECORD

Match No.	Date	Venue	Opponents	Result	H/T Score	Lg. Pos.	Goalscorers	Atten dance
1	Aug 15	H	Derby Co	W 1-0	0-0	—	Charlery	9955
2	22	A	Southend U	W 1-0	0-0	6	Adcock	4651
3	29	H	Notts Co	L 1-3	1-1	9	Barnes	6670
4	Sept 5	A	Wolverhampton W	L 3-4	1-2	12	Halsall, Charlery, Sterling	14,532
5	12	H	West Ham U	L 1-3	1-3	17	Adcock	10,657
6	15	H	Millwall	D 0-0	0-0	—		5619
7	19	A	Barnsley	W 2-1	1-0	9	Adcock, Sterling	5275
8	26	H	Newcastle U	L 0-1	0-0	11		14,487
9	Oct 3	A	Grimsby T	W 3-1	2-0	10	Adcock, Charlery, Sterling	5208
10	10	H	Brentford	D 0-0	0-0	13		5818
11	18	A	Leicester C	W 2-0	2-0	—	Philliskirk, Sterling	10,952
12	24	H	Luton T	L 2-3	1-3	13	Cooper, Adcock	7125
13	30	A	Tranmere R	D 1-1	1-0	—	Ebdon	8068
14	Nov 3	A	Watford	W 2-1	1-0	—	Philliskirk 2	7016
15	7	H	Sunderland	W 5-2	1-0	8	Adcock 2, Philliskirk, Cooper, Iorfa	8193
16	21	H	Bristol R	D 1-1	0-0	11	Adcock	6120
17	29	H	Swindon T	D 3-3	2-1	—	Adcock 2, Taylor (og)	5976
18	Dec 12	H	Portsmouth	D 1-1	1-0	13	Philliskirk	6516
19	19	A	Bristol C	W 1-0	1-0	11	Welsh	7309
20	28	H	Charlton Ath	D 1-1	1-1	13	Philliskirk	8931
21	Jan 9	H	Barnsley	D 1-1	1-0	14	Cooper (pen)	6008
22	16	A	Newcastle U	L 0-3	0-1	15		29,155
23	22	A	Birmingham C	L 0-2	0-2	—		10,277
24	27	A	Millwall	L 0-4	0-2	—		8732
25	30	H	Southend U	W 1-0	1-0	13	Philliskirk	6180
26	Feb 6	A	Derby Co	W 3-2	2-2	11	Curtis, Philliskirk, Adcock	16,062
27	9	A	West Ham U	L 1-2	1-2	—	Ebdon	12,537
28	13	H	Wolverhampton W	L 2-3	1-1	12	Halsall, Adcock	9195
29	21	A	Notts Co	L 0-1	0-1	—		7468
30	27	A	Brentford	W 1-0	1-0	13	Philliskirk	6337
31	Mar 6	H	Grimsby T	W 1-0	1-0	12	Adcock	6657
32	9	A	Birmingham C	W 2-1	1-1	—	Holmes (og), Barnes	7600
33	13	A	Sunderland	L 0-3	0-0	12		18,372
34	16	A	Cambridge U	D 2-2	0-2	—	Adcock 2	8077
35	20	H	Oxford U	D 1-1	1-1	10	Sterling	6316
36	24	A	Bristol R	L 1-3	0-2	—	Sterling	4855
37	27	H	Watford	D 0-0	0-0	13		7631
38	Apr 3	A	Swindon T	L 0-1	0-0	13		10,314
39	6	A	Portsmouth	L 0-4	0-3	—		15,093
40	10	H	Cambridge U	W 1-0	1-0	13	Sterling	10,235
41	12	A	Charlton Ath	W 1-0	0-0	10	Sterling	6721
42	17	H	Bristol C	D 1-1	0-0	13	Barnes	5169
43	20	A	Oxford U	L 1-2	0-2	—	Philliskirk	4525
44	24	H	Leicester C	W 3-0	2-0	10	Philliskirk, Adcock, Ebdon	15,445
45	May 1	A	Luton T	D 0-0	0-0	10		10,011
46	8	H	Tranmere R	D 1-1	1-1	10	Ebdon	8189

Final League Position: 10

GOALSCORERS

League (55): Adcock 16, Philliskirk 11, Sterling 8, Ebdon 4, Barnes 3, Charlery 3, Cooper 3 (1 pen), Halsall 2, Curtis 1, Iorfa 1, Welsh 1, own goals 2.
Coca Cola Cup (8): Charlery 3, Adcock 2, Cooper 1 (pen), Costello 1, Halsall 1.
FA Cup (4): Sterling 2, Adcock 1, Philliskirk 1.

Bennett 46	Luke 22 + 6	Robinson R 20	Cooper 35	Howarth 26 + 4	Welsh 45	Sterling 43 + 1	Ebdon 28	Adcock 44 + 1	Charley 10	Barnes 22 + 4	Bradshaw 32 + 2	White 3 + 2	Halsall 25	Robinson D 1	Costello — + 2	Ingram — + 1	Gavin — + 1	Curtis 8 + 3	Limber 2	Philliskirk 31 + 1	Retallick 2 + 3	Iorfa 3 + 23	Roche 4	Spearing 21 + 1	Tuttle 7	McGlashan 18	Greenman 8 + 1	Match No.
1	2	3	4	5	6	7	8	9	10	11	12																	1
1	2	3	4	5	6	7	8	9	10	11																		2
1	2	3	4	5	6	7	8	9	10	11																		3
1		3	14		6	7	8	9	10	11		2	4	5	12													4
1	2	3		5	6	7	8	9	10	11			4		12													5
1	2	3		5	6	7	8	9	10	*11*		12	4		14													6
1		3		5	6	7	8	9	10	11		2	4															7
1	12	3		5	6	7	8	9	10	*11*		2	4		14													8
1	2	3	8	5	6	7		9	10	11			4		12													9
1	2		8	5	6	7		9	10	*11*		12	4		14			3										10
1	2		8	5	6	7		9		11			4					3		10		12						11
1	2	3	8	5	6	7		9		11			4							10		12						12
1	14	3	8	5	6	7	11	*9*			*2*		4							10		12						13
1		3	8	5	6	7	11	9			2		4							10								14
1	14	3	8	5	6	7	11	9			*2*		4							10		12						15
1		3	8	5	6	7	11	9			2		4							10		12						16
1	14	3	8	5	6	*7*	11	9			2		4							10		12						17
1	2	3	8		6	7	11	9			5		4							10								18
1	2	3	8		6	7	11	9			5		4							10								19
1	2	3	8		6	7	11	9			5		4							10		12						20
1	2	3	8		6	7		9			5		4							10		12	11					21
1	2	3			6	7		9		8	5		4							10	14	12	*11*					22
1	2		8		6	7		9					4							10		12	11	3	5			23
1	2		8		6	*7*		9		14			4							10		12	11	3	*5*			24
1	2				6	7	12				5		4					11		10	14	9		3		8		25
1	2				6	*7*		9			5		4					11		10		12		3		8		26
1	2		14		*6*	7		9			5		4					11		10		12		3		8		27
1	14				6	7		9		12	2		4					11		10				3	5	8		28
1			4		6	7	11	9			2									10		12		3	5	8		29
1			4		6	7		9			2							11		10				3	5	8		30
1			4		6	7		9			2							11		10		12		3	5	8		31
1	14		4		6	7		9		12	2							11		10				3	*5*	8		32
1	5		4		6	7		9		12	2							11		10				3		8		33
1	5		4	14	6	7		9		*11*	2									10		12		3		8		34
1	5		4		6	7		9			2							11		10		12		3		8		35
1			4	5	6	7		9			2							11		10		12		3		8		36
1			4	14	6	*7*		9			2							11		10		12		3		8	5	37
1		3	4		6	7		9			*2*							11		10		12	14			8	5	38
1			4	5	6	7	10	9		11	2											12		3		8		39
1		3	4		6	7	10	9		11	2											12				8	5	40
1			4		6	7	10	9		11	2											12		3		8	5	41
1			4	9	6	7	8			11	2									10		12		3			5	42
1			4		6	7	10	9		11	2											12		3		8	5	43
1			4	5	6	7	10	9			2							11				12		3		8		44
1			4	5	6	7	10	9			2							11				12		3		8		45
1			4	5	6	*7*	10	9		14	2											12		3		8	11	46

Coca Cola Cup	First Round	Barnet (h)	4-0
		(a)	2-2
	Second Round	Leicester C (a)	0-2
		(h)	2-1
FA Cup	First Round	Kingstonian (a)	1-1
		(h)	1-0
	Second Round	Plymouth Arg (a)	2-3

PETERBOROUGH UNITED

Player and Position	Ht	Wt	Date	Birth Place	Source	Clubs	League App	Gls
Goalkeepers								
Fred Barber	5 10	12 00	26 8 63	Ferryhill	Apprentice	Darlington	135	—
						Everton	—	—
						Walsall	153	—
						Peterborough U (loan)	6	—
						Chester (loan)	8	—
						Blackpool (loan)	2	—
						Peterborough U	39	—
						Colchester U (loan)	10	—
						Chesterfield (loan)	—	—
Ian Bennett	6 0	12 00	10 10 71	Worksop	Newcastle U	Peterborough U	53	—
Defenders								
Gary Cooper	5 8	11 03	20 11 65	Edgware	Fisher Ath	Maidstone U	60	7
						Peterborough U	74	8
Chris Greenman	5 10	11 06	22 12 68	Bristol	School	Coventry C	6	—
						Peterborough U	9	—
Lee Howarth	6 1	12 06	3 1 68	Bolton	Chorley	Peterborough U	37	—
Ronnie Robinson	5 9	11 05	22 10 66	Sunderland		Ipswich T	—	—
					Vaux Breweries	Leeds U	27	—
						Doncaster R	78	5
						WBA	1	—
						Rotherham U	86	2
						Peterborough U	47	—
Tony Spearing	5 9	10 12	7 10 64	Romford	Apprentice	Norwich C	69	—
						Stoke C (loan)	9	—
						Oxford U (loan)	5	—
						Leicester C	73	1
						Plymouth Arg	35	—
						Peterborough U	22	—
Steve Welsh	6 0	12 03	19 4 68	Glasgow	Army	Cambridge U	1	—
						Peterborough U	87	1
Midfield								
Darren Bradshaw	5 11	11 04	19 3 67	Sheffield	Matlock T	Chesterfield	18	—
						York C	59	3
						Newcastle U	38	—
						Peterborough	34	—
Andy Curtist	5 10	11 07	2 12 72	Doncaster	Trainee	York C	12	—
						Peterborough U	11	1
Marcus Ebdon	5 9	11 00	17 10 70	Pontypool	Trainee	Everton	—	—
						Peterborough U	43	6
Mick Halsall	5 10	11 04	21 7 61	Bootle	Apprentice	Liverpool	—	—
						Birmingham C	36	3
						Carlisle U	92	11
						Grimsby T	12	—
						Peterborough U	248	28
Graham Retallickt	5 10	11 13	8 2 70	Cambridge	Histon	Peterborough U	5	—
Worrell Sterling	5 7	10 11	8 6 65	Bethnal Green	Apprentice	Watford	94	14
						Peterborough U	193	29
Forwards								
Tony Adcock	5 11	11 09	27 2 63	Bethnal Green	Apprentice	Colchester U	210	98
						Manchester C	15	5
						Northampton T	72	30
						Bradford C	38	6
						Northampton T	35	10
						Peterborough U	69	23

PETERBOROUGH UNITED

Colours: Royal blue shirts, white shorts, blue stockings. **Change colours:** Green shirts, white shorts, green stockings.

Foundation: The old Peterborough & Fletton club, founded in 1923, was suspended by the FA during season 1932–33 and disbanded. Local enthusiasts determined to carry on and in 1934 a new professional club Peterborough United was formed and entered the Midland League the following year.

First Football League game: 20 August, 1960, Division 4, v Wrexham (h) W 3-0 – Walls; Stafford, Walker; Rayner, Rigby, Norris; Halls, Emery (1), Bly (1), Smith, McNamee (1).

Did you know: Not all Peterborough's giant-killing has been in the years long past. In 1991–92 they defeated Aldershot, Wimbledon, Newcastle United and Liverpool in the League Cup before losing to Middlesbrough.

Managers (and Secretary-Managers)
Jock Porter 1934–36, Fred Taylor 1936–37, Vic Poulter 1937–38, Sam Madden 1938–48, Jack Blood 1948–50, Bob Gurney 1950–52, Jack Fairbrother 1952–54, George Swindin 1954–58, Jimmy Hagan 1958–62, Jack Fairbrother 1962–64, Gordon Clark 1964–67, Norman Rigby 1967–69, Jim Iley 1969–72, Noel Cantwell 1972–77, John Barnwell 1977–78, Billy Hails 1978–79, Peter Morris 1979–82, Martin Wilkinson 1982–83, John Wile 1983–86, Noel Cantwell 1986–88 (continued as GM), Mick Jones 1988–89, Mark Lawrenson 1989–90, Chris Turner 1991–92, Lil Fuccillo December 1992–.

Player and Position	Ht	Wt	Date	Birth Place	Source	Clubs	League App	Gls
Bobby Barnes	5 7	10 09	17 12 62	Kingston	Apprentice	West Ham	43	5
						Scunthorpe U (loan)	6	—
						Aldershot	49	26
						Swindon T	45	13
						Bournemouth	14	—
						Northampton T	98	37
						Peterborough U	41	8
Dominic Iorfa	6 1	12 12	1 10 68	Lagos	Antwerp	QPR	8	—
						Peterborough U	26	1
John McGlashan	6 1	12 00	3 6 67	Dundee	Dundee Violet	Montrose	68	11
						Millwall	16	—
						Cambridge U (loan)	1	—
						Fulham (loan)	5	1
						Peterborough U	18	—
Tony Philliskirk	6 1	12 02	10 2 65	Sunderland	Amateur	Sheffield U	80	20
						Rotherham U (loan)	6	1
						Oldham Ath	10	1
						Preston NE	14	6
						Bolton W	141	51
						Peterborough U	32	11

Trainees
Brown, Paul J; Dawson, James P; Fuff, Glen B; Giggs, Matthew K; Judge, Kevin A; Stanhope, Andrew P; Wilson, Simon R.

**Non-Contract
Curtis, Andrew; Edey, Darren; Retallick, Graham J; Taylor, Robin G.

Associated Schoolboys
Coleman, Andrew D; Curtis, Jason F; Jarvis, Darren P; Knowles, Christopher J.

**Non-Contract Players who are retained must be re-signed before they are eligible to play in League matches.

PLYMOUTH ARGYLE 1992–93 *Back row (left to right)*: Adrian Burrows, Kevin Nugent, Michael Evans, Dave Regis, Ray Newland, Robbie Turner, Andrew Morrison, Steve Morgan.
Centre row: Paul Adcock, Steve Jones, Tony Spearing, Kevin Hodges, Mark Fiore, Mark Cload, Marc Edworthy, Darren Garner, Martin Barlow.
Front row: Warren Joyce, Dwight Marshall, Gary Poole, John McGovern (Assistant Manager), Peter Shilton (Manager), Gordon Nisbet (Reserve Team Manager), Steve McCall, Steve Castle, Nicky Marker.

Division 2 **PLYMOUTH ARGYLE**

Home Park, Plymouth, Devon PL2 3DQ. Telephone Plymouth (0752) 562561–2–3. Marketing Department: 0752 569597. Lottery Shop: 561041. Pilgrim Shop: 0752 558292. Fax 0752 606167.

Ground capacity: 19,620.

Record attendance: 43,596 v Aston Villa, Division 2, 10 October 1936.

Record receipts: £96,989.57 v Derby Co, FA Cup 6th rd, 10 March 1984.

Pitch measurements: 112yd × 75yd.

President: S. J. Rendell.

Chairman: D. McCauley.

Directors: P. Bloom, G. Jasper, I. Jones, D. Angilley.

Manager: Peter Shilton. *Assistant Manager:* John McGovern.

Secretary: Michael Holladay. *Commercial Manager:* Peter Friend.

Physio: Paul Sumner.

Year Formed: 1886. *Turned Professional:* 1903. *Ltd Co.:* 1903.

Club Nickname: 'The Pilgrims'.

Previous Name: 1886–1903, Argyle Athletic Club.

Record League Victory: 8–1 v Millwall, Division 2, 16 January 1932 – Harper; Roberts, Titmuss; Mackay, Pullan, Reed; Grozier, Bowden (2), Vidler (3), Leslie (1), Black (1). (1 og).

Record Cup Victory: 6–0 v Corby T, FA Cup, 3rd rd, 22 January 1966 – Leiper; Book, Baird; Williams, Nelson, Newman; Jones (1), Jackson (1), Bickle (3), Piper (1), Jennings.

Record Defeat: 0–9 v Stoke C, Division 2, 17 December 1960.

Most League Points (2 for a win): 68, Division 3 (S), 1929–30.

Most League Points (3 for a win): 87, Division 3, 1985–86.

Most League Goals: 107, Division 3 (S), 1925–26 and 1951–52.

Highest League Scorer in Season: Jack Cock, 32, Division 3 (S), 1925–26.

Most League Goals in Total Aggregate: Sammy Black, 180, 1924–38.

Most Capped Player: Moses Russell, 20 (23), Wales.

Most League Appearances: Kevin Hodges, 530, 1978–92.

Record Transfer Fee Received: £500,000 from Blackburn R for Nicky Marker, September 1992.

Record Transfer Fee Paid: £200,000 to Hartlepool U for Paul Dalton, May 1992.

Football League Record: 1920 Original Member of Division 3; 1921–30 Division 3 (S); 1930–50 Division 2; 1950–52 Division 3 (S); 1952–56 Division 2; 1956–58 Division 3 (S); 1958–59 Division 3; 1959–68 Division 2; 1968–75 Division 3; 1975–77 Division 2; 1977–86 Division 3; 1986– Division 2.

Honours: Football League: Division 2 best season: 4th, 1931–32, 1952–53; Division 3 (S) – Champions 1929–30, 1951–52; Runners-up 1921–22, 1922–23, 1923–24, 1924–25, 1925–26, 1926–27 (record of six consecutive years); Division 3 – Champions 1958–59; Runners-up 1974–75, 1985–86. *FA Cup:* best season: semi-final 1983–84. *Football League Cup:* Semi-final 1965, 1974.

PLYMOUTH ARGYLE 1992—93 LEAGUE RECORD

Match No.	Date	Venue	Opponents	Result	H/T Score	Lg. Pos.	Goalscorers	Atten dance
1	Aug 15	A	Mansfield T	D	0-0	0-0	—	4166
2	22	H	Bradford C	W	3-0	1-0	4	Poole, Skinner, Marshall	6504
3	28	A	Hull C	L	0-2	0-0	—	4194
4	Sept 5	A	Leyton Orient	W	2-0	1-0	12	Marker, Adcock	7319
5	12	H	Stoke C	D	1-1	0-1	13	Walker	8208
6	15	A	Huddersfield T	L	1-2	1-1	—	Marker	4411
7	19	A	Fulham	L	1-3	0-0	18	Adcock	5439
8	26	H	Bolton W	W	2-1	2-0	16	Regis, Nugent	6829
9	29	A	Burnley	D	0-0	0-0	—		8676
10	Oct 3	A	Preston NE	W	2-1	2-1	10	Joyce, Regis	4401
11	10	H	Chester C	W	2-0	1-0	8	Poole 2 (2 pens)	7182
12	17	A	Port Vale	L	0-4	0-2	11		6584
13	24	H	Wigan Ath	W	2-0	2-0	8	Joyce, Castle	5967
14	31	A	Reading	L	0-3	0-1	11		5088
15	Nov 3	A	Swansea C	D	0-0	0-0	—		5430
16	7	H	Rotherham U	W	2-1	1-0	10	Hutchings (og), Nugent	6519
17	20	A	Stockport Co	L	0-3	0-0	—		5377
18	28	H	Bournemouth	W	2-1	1-0	9	Boardman, Nugent	6408
19	Dec 12	H	Hartlepool U	D	2-2	2-1	11	Nugent, Castle	5996
20	19	A	Brighton & HA	L	1-2	0-1	12	Nugent	5872
21	26	A	Exeter C	L	0-2	0-1	14		6534
22	28	H	WBA	D	0-0	0-0	14		11,370
23	Jan 16	A	Bolton W	L	1-3	1-3	16	Dalton	8256
24	23	H	Fulham	D	1-1	0-0	14	Castle (pen)	5703
25	26	H	Hull C	D	0-0	0-0	—		4612
26	30	A	Bradford C	D	0-0	0-0	15		5528
27	Feb 6	H	Mansfield T	W	3-2	0-1	15	Nugent 3	4630
28	13	A	Leyton Orient	L	0-2	0-1	15		5804
29	20	A	Burnley	L	1-2	1-1	16	Nugent	5905
30	27	A	Chester C	W	2-1	0-0	15	Butler (og), Hodges L	2163
31	Mar 6	H	Preston NE	W	4-0	3-0	15	Hodges L, Leonard (og), Castle, Evans	5201
32	9	H	Blackpool	W	2-1	1-0	—	Poole (pen), Castle	5959
33	13	A	Rotherham U	D	2-2	1-1	13	Dalton, Nugent	4276
34	20	A	Swansea C	L	0-1	0-1	13		6233
35	23	A	Bournemouth	W	3-1	0-0	—	Castle, Dalton 2	4150
36	27	A	Stockport Co	L	3-4	2-2	13	Nugent, Dalton 2	6132
37	30	H	Huddersfield T	L	1-3	1-1	—	Dalton	4986
38	Apr 3	H	Blackpool	D	1-1	0-1	13	Castle	4397
39	5	A	Hartlepool U	L	0-1	0-0	—		1822
40	10	H	Exeter C	L	0-3	0-1	14		9391
41	12	A	WBA	W	5-2	2-1	14	Castle 3, Dalton, Barlow	16,130
42	17	A	Brighton & HA	W	3-2	2-1	14	Castle, Burrows, McCall	4924
43	24	H	Port Vale	L	0-1	0-1	14		5563
44	28	A	Stoke C	L	0-1	0-1	—		19,718
45	May 1	A	Wigan Ath	W	2-0	1-0	14	Dalton, Morgan S	1432
46	8	H	Reading	D	2-2	2-1	14	Poole (pen), Joyce	5137

Final League Position: 14

GOALSCORERS

League (59): Castle 11 (1 pen), Nugent 11, Dalton 9, Poole 5 (4 pens), Joyce 3, Adcock 2, Hodges L 2, Marker 2, Regis 2, Barlow 1, Boardman 1, Burrows 1, Evans 1, McCall 1, Marshall 1, Morgan S 1, Skinner 1, Walker 1, own goals 3.
Coca Cola Cup (11): Regis 3, Dalton 2, Nugent 2, Poole 2 (1 pen), Joyce 1, Marker 1.
FA Cup (7): Marshall 3, Castle 2, Dalton 2.

Shilton 23	Poole 39	McCall 35	Burrows 20	Marker 7	Morrison 29	Joyce 28 + 2	Garner 8 + 2	Nugent 45	Marshall 21 + 3	Evans 16 + 7	Hodges K 2 + 2	Fiore — + 1	Skinner 12 + 1	Spearing 5	Morgan S 35 + 1	Walker 2	Adcock 2 + 7	Kite 2	Edworthy 14 + 1	Regis 7	Barlow 17 + 7	Hill 36	Dalton 30 + 2	Castle 31	Turner 2	Newland 21	Dryden 5	Boardman 2	Crocker 1 + 3	Hodges L 6 + 1	Morgan J 3	Match No.
1	2	3	4	5	6	7	8	9	10	11	12	14																				1
1	2	3	5	6	4	7		9	10	11			8																			2
1	2	11	5	6	4	8	12	9	10	14			7		3																	3
1	2	11		6	4	8		9	10				7		3		5	12														4
	2	8		6	4			9	10	11			7		3		5	12	1													5
	2	11	5	6				9	10				7		3			12	1	4	8											6
1	2	6	5			11		9	12				7		3		8		4	10	14											7
1	2	11	5		8			9					7		3			12	10	6	4											8
1	6	11	5		8			9					7		3				2	10	4											9
1		11	5	8	6			9					7		3				2	10	4											10
1	6		5	8				12					7		3		9		2	10	11	4	14									11
1	3	8	5	6				9	12				7						2	10	4	11										12
1	7		5	6				9	10						3				2	12	4	11	8									13
1	7		5	6				9	10						3				2		4	11	8									14
1	2		5	6				9	10				7		3						4		8	11								15
1	2		5	6				9	10			7		12	3						4		8	11								16
	2		5					7	9	10					12				6		4	11	8			1	3					17
	2	5						7	9	10					6						4		8			1	3	11				18
	2	5					6	9	10						3				7		4	11	8			1						19
	2	5		6		7		9	10				12						14		4	11	8			1	3					20
1		5			6	11		9	10						3	12			7	2			8			4						21
1			5	6				9	10			7		11					2	14	4	12	8			3						22
1	2		5	6		9		7	10						3				12		4	11	8									23
1	2		5		6	9		7	10						3						4	11	8									24
1	2		5	6		9		7	10						3	12					4	11	8									25
1	2	6	5	7		9		10							3						4	11	8									26
	2	7	5	6		9		10							3						4	11	8			1		12				27
	2	10	5		6	9									3				7		4	11	8			1		12				28
	2	7	5			9									3				6	12	4	11	8			1			10			29
	2	7	6	5		9									3						4	11	8			1				10		30
	2	6	5	12		9		14							3					7	4	11	8			1				10		31
	2	6	5			9	12								3					7	4	11	8			1				10		32
	2	3	6	5		9	12								4					7		11	8			1				10		33
	2	6	5			9	12								3					7	4	11	8			1				10		34
	2	3	5			9	12								6					7	4	11	8			1				10		35
	2	3	5			12	9	10							6					7	4	11	8			1			14			36
	2	3	5		14		9	10							6	12				7	4	11	8			1						37
	2	3	5		7		9	10							6						4	11	8			1						38
	2	3	5		7		9	10							6	12					4	11	8			1						39
	2	3	5			7	9	12							6					14	4	11	8			1		10				40
	2	3	5				9	10							6					7	4	11	8			1						41
	2	6	5			9	10								3				4	7		11	8			1						42
1	2	6	5			9	10								3					7	4	11	8						12			43
1	2	3			6	9	10							5	7						4	11								8		44
1	2	3			6	9	10							5	7						4	11								8		45
	2	3	5		6	9	10								4					7		11				1				8		46

Coca Cola Cup	First Round	WBA (a)	0-1
		(h)	2-0
	Second Round	Luton T (a)	2-2
		(h)	3-2
	Third Round	Scarborough (h)	3-3
		(a)	1-2
FA Cup	First Round	Dorking (a)	3-2
	Second Round	Peterborough U (h)	3-2
	Third Round	Ipswich T (a)	1-3

PLYMOUTH ARGYLE

Player and Position	Ht	Wt	Date	Birth Place	Source	Clubs	League App	Gls
Goalkeepers								
Ray Newland	6 1	12 01	19 7 71	Liverpool	Everton	Plymouth Arg	21	—
Peter Shilton†	6 0	14 00	18 9 49	Leicester	Apprentice	Leicester C	286	1
						Stoke C	110	—
						Nottingham F	202	—
						Southampton	188	—
						Derby Co	175	—
						Plymouth Arg	30	—
Defenders								
Adrian Burrows	5 11	11 12	16 1 59	Sutton	Local	Mansfield T	78	5
						Northampton T	88	4
						Plymouth Arg	255	14
						Southend U (loan)	6	—
Keith Hill	6 0	11 03	17 5 69	Bolton	Apprentice	Blackburn R	96	3
						Plymouth Arg	36	—
Steve Morgan	5 11	13 00	19 9 68	Oldham	Apprentice	Blackpool	144	10
						Plymouth Arg	121	6
Gary Poole	6 0	11 00	11 9 67	Stratford	Arsenal	Tottenham H	—	—
						Cambridge U	43	—
					Barnet	Barnet	40	2
						Plymouth Arg	39	5
Midfield								
Martin Barlow	5 7	10 03	25 6 71	Barnstable	Trainee	Plymouth Arg	84	5
Steve Castle	5 11	12 05	17 5 66	Barkingside	Apprentice	Orient	243	55
						Plymouth Arg	31	11
Mark Clode*	5 6	9 06	24 2 73	Plymouth	Trainee	Plymouth Arg	—	—
Paul Dalton	5 11	11 07	25 4 67	Middlesbrough	Brandon	Manchester U	—	—
						Hartlepool U	151	37
						Plymouth Arg	32	9
Mark Edworthy	5 7	9 08	24 12 72	Barnstaple	Trainee	Plymouth Arg	30	—
Mark Fiore‡	5 10	11 10	18 11 69	Southwark	Trainee	Wimbledon	1	—
						Plymouth Arg	83	8
Darren Garner	5 6	10 01	10 12 71	Plymouth	Trainee	Plymouth Arg	27	1
Warren Joyce	5 9	11 11	20 1 65	Oldham	Local	Bolton W	184	17
						Preston NE	177	34
						Plymouth Arg	30	3
Steve McCall	5 11	12 06	15 10 60	Carlisle	Apprentice	Ipswich T	257	7
						Sheffield W	29	2
						Carlisle U (loan)	6	—
						Plymouth Arg	44	2
Jamie Morgan§	5 11	11 00	1 10 75	Plymouth	Trainee	Plymouth Arg	3	—
Andy Morrison	5 11	12 00	30 7 70	Inverness	Trainee	Plymouth Arg	113	6
Forwards								
Paul Adcock*	5 8	10 02	2 5 72	Ilminster	Trainee	Plymouth Arg	21	2
Paul Boardman	6 0	11 02	6 11 67	Tottenham		Plymouth Arg	2	1
Marcus Crocker§	5 10	11 05	8 10 74	Plymouth	Trainee	Plymouth Arg	4	—
Mike Evans	6 0	11 02	1 1 73	Plymouth	Trainee	Plymouth Arg	40	1
						Blackburn R (loan)	—	—
Stephen Jones*			11 3 74	Plymouth	Trainee	Plymouth Arg	1	—
Dwight Marshall	5 7	10 10	3 10 65	Jamaica	Grays Ath	Plymouth Arg	68	15
						Middlesbrough (loan)	3	—

PLYMOUTH ARGYLE

Colours: Green and white striped shirts, black shorts, black stockings. **Change colours:** White shirts, green trim, white shorts, green trim, white stockings, green trim.

Foundation: The Plymouth Argyle Association Football Club developed out of the Argyle Athletic club which was formed in 1886 at a meeting in Argyle Terrace, Mutley. Plymouth was a rugby stronghold, but servicemen brought soccer to the town and it spread quickly. At first Argyle Athletic Club played both soccer and rugby in colours of green and black. The rugby section was eventually disbanded, and after a number of exhibition games had satisfied the locals of the feasibility of running a professional club, Plymouth Argyle was formed in 1903.

First Football League game: 28 August, 1920, Division 3, v Norwich C (h) D 1-1 – Craig; Russell, Atterbury; Logan, Dickinson, Forbes; Kirkpatrick, Jack, Bowler, Heeps (1), Dixon.

Did you know: In March 1973, Plymouth Argyle beat the Brazilian team Santos 3-2 in a friendly at Home Park. One of the visitors' goals was scored by Edson Arantes do Nascimento (Pele).

Managers (and Secretary-Managers)
Frank Brettell 1903–05, Bob Jack 1905–06, Bill Fullerton 1906–07, Bob Jack 1910–38, Jack Tresadern 1938–47, Jimmy Rae 1948–55, Jack Rowley 1955–60, Neil Dougall 1961, Ellis Stuttard 1961–63, Andy Beattie 1963–64, Malcolm Allison 1964–65, Derek Ufton 1965–68, Billy Bingham 1968–70, Ellis Stuttard 1970–72, Tony Waiters 1972–77, Mike Kelly 1977–78, Malcolm Allison 1978–79, Bobby Saxton 1979–81, Bobby Moncur 1981–83, Johnny Hore 1983–84, Dave Smith 1984–88, Ken Brown 1988–90, David Kemp 1990–92, Peter Shilton March 1992–.

Player and Position	Ht	Wt	Date	Birth Place	Source	Clubs	League App	Gls
Kevin Nugent	6 1	12 04	10 4 69	Edmonton	Trainee	Leyton Orient	94	20
						Cork C (loan)	—	—
						Plymouth Arg	49	11
Craig Skinner	5 8	11 00	21 10 70	Bury	Trainee	Blackburn R	16	—
						Plymouth Arg	13	1

Trainees
Albery, Matthew D; Balfour, Dax; Crocker, Marcus A; Davey, Joseph L; Draper, Ryan J; Hutchinson, James; Jones, Gerrard; Morgan, James A; O'Hagan, Daniel A. N; Rutkowski, Yan M; Sullivan, Martyn G; Twiddy, Christopher.

**Non-Contract
Shilton, Peter L.

Associated Schoolboys
Atkinson, David J; Beswetherick, Jonathan B; Francis, Kevin; Garland, Philip L; Hardy, Nicholas W; Henwood, Mark D; Hoare, Steven J; Hobbs, Peter C; Hobbs, Wayne K; Hockley, Wayne; King, Simon; Lockyer, Adam J; Mallett, David J; Martin, Paul; Morgan, Stuart J; Neno, Richard J; Newberry, Philip J; Nicholls, Keir C; Platt, David J; Richardson, Dominic K; Sammels, David H. J; Shilton, Sam; Sullivan, Craig D; Thomas, Christopher M; Thompson, Mark R; Tucker, Lee A; Williams, Jeremy J.

Associated Schoolboys who have accepted the club's offer of a Traineeship/Contract
Dawe, Simon.

**Non-Contract Players who are retained must be re-signed before they are eligible to play in League matches.

PORTSMOUTH 1992–93   *Back row (left to right):* Mark Chamberlain, Guy Whittingham, Darryl Powell, Mark Kelly, Warren Aspinall, Ray Daniel.
Centre row: Mike Bailey (Reserve Team Coach), Gordon Neave (Kit Man), Lee Russell, Chris Burns, Colin Clarke, Alan Knight, Guy Butters, Kit Symons, Shaun Gale, Neil Sillett (Physio), Kenny Todd (Youth Team Manager).
Front row: Warren Neill, Steve Wigley, Alan McLoughlin, Andy Awford, Gavin Maguire, Graham Paddon (Assistant Manager), Jim Smith (Manager), Martin Kuhl (Manager), Stuart Doling, Micky Ross, Shaun Murray, Paul Walsh.

Division 1　　　　　　　　　　　　**PORTSMOUTH**

Fratton Park, Frogmore Rd, Portsmouth PO4 8RA. Telephone Portsmouth (0705) 731204. Fax (0705) 734129. Commercial Dept: (0705) 827111. Ticket Office: (0705) 750825. Lottery Office: (0705) 825016. Clubcall: 0898 338383.

Ground capacity: 26,452.

Record attendance: 51,385 v Derby Co, FA Cup 6th rd, 26 February 1949.

Record receipts: £208,000 v Nottingham F, FA Cup 6th rd, 7 March 1992.

Pitch measurements: 116yd × 73yd.

Chairman: J. A. Gregory. *Vice-chairman:* D. K. Deacon.

Directors: M. H. Gregory, D. K. Deacon, B. Henson, P. Britten.

Team Manager: Jim Smith. *Coach:* Graham Paddon.

Club Secretary: P. Weld. *Marketing Manager:* Julie Baker.

Physio: N. Sillett. *Youth Team Coach:* K. Todd.

Year Formed: 1898. *Turned Professional:* 1898. *Ltd Co.:* 1898.

Club Nickname: 'Pompey'.

Record League Victory: 9–1 v Notts Co, Division 2, 9 April 1927 – McPhail; Clifford, Ted Smith; Reg Davies (1), Foxall, Moffat; Forward (1), Mackie (2), Haines (3), Watson, Cook (2).

Record Cup Victory: 7–0 v Stockport Co, FA Cup, 3rd rd, 8 January 1949 – Butler; Rookes, Ferrier; Scoular, Flewin, Dickinson; Harris (3), Barlow, Clarke (2), Phillips (2), Froggatt.

Record Defeat: 0–10 v Leicester C, Division 1, 20 October 1928.

Most League Points (2 for a win): 65, Division 3, 1961–62.

Most League Points (3 for a win): 91, Division 3, 1982–83.

Most League Goals: 91, Division 4, 1979–80.

Highest League Scorer in Season: Guy Whittingham, 42, Division 1, 1992–93.

Most League Goals in Total Aggregate: Peter Harris, 194, 1946–60.

Most Capped Player: Jimmy Dickinson, 48, England.

Most League Appearances: Jimmy Dickinson, 764, 1946–65.

Record Transfer Fee Received: £2,000,000 from Tottenham H for Darren Anderton, May 1992.

Record Transfer Fee Paid: £450,000 to QPR for Colin Clarke, June 1990.

Football League Record: 1920 Original Member of Division 3; 1921 Division 3 (S); 1924–27 Division 2; 1927–59 Division 1; 1959–61 Division 2; 1961–62 Division 3; 1962–76 Division 2; 1976–78 Division 3; 1978–80 Division 4; 1980–83 Division 3; 1983–87 Division 2; 1987–88 Division 1; 1988–92 Division 2; 1992– Division 1.

Honours: Football League: Division 1 – Champions 1948–49, 1949–50; Division 2 – Runners-up 1926–27, 1986–87; Division 3 (S) – Champions 1923–24; Division 3 – Champions 1961–62, 1982–83. *FA Cup:* Winners 1939; Runners-up 1929, 1934. *Football League Cup:* best season: 5th rd, 1960–61, 1985–86.

PORTSMOUTH 1992—93 LEAGUE RECORD

Match No.	Date		Venue	Opponents	Result	H/T Score	Lg. Pos.	Goalscorers	Attendance
1	Aug	15	A	Bristol C	D 3-3	2-2	—	Whittingham 3	15,301
2		22	H	Barnsley	W 1-0	0-0	8	Whittingham	11,473
3		29	A	Leicester C	L 0-1	0-1	13		14,780
4	Sept	1	A	Brentford	L 1-4	1-1	—	Symons	8471
5		5	H	Birmingham C	W 4-0	1-0	7	Daniel, Walsh, Kuhl, Whittingham	12,152
6		12	A	Newcastle U	L 1-3	0-2	11	Whittingham	29,885
7		18	A	Southend U	D 0-0	0-0	—		5267
8		27	H	West Ham U	L 0-1	0-1	—		12,158
9	Oct	3	H	Luton T	W 4-1	3-1	11	Whittingham 3, Clarke	7954
10		10	H	Swindon T	W 3-1	2-0	10	McLoughlin, Whittingham, Chamberlain	12,442
11		17	A	Wolverhampton W	D 1-1	1-0	9	Whittingham	14,750
12		24	H	Sunderland	W 2-0	2-0	9	Whittingham, Burns	10,689
13		31	A	Grimsby T	L 0-3	0-1	11		5708
14	Nov	3	A	Oxford U	D 5-5	4-2	—	McLoughlin, Whittingham 2, Evans (og), Chamberlain	5490
15		7	H	Cambridge U	W 3-0	1-0	10	McLoughlin, Whittingham 2	8956
16		14	A	Watford	D 0-0	0-0	12		8714
17		21	H	Tranmere R	W 4-0	3-0	8	McLoughlin, Whittingham, Walsh, Daniel	9982
18		28	H	Millwall	W 1-0	1-0	7	McLoughlin	12,445
19	Dec	5	A	Charlton Ath	L 0-1	0-1	8		8337
20		12	A	Peterborough U	D 1-1	0-1	9	Whittingham	6516
21		19	H	Notts Co	D 0-0	0-0	8		8943
22		26	H	Bristol R	W 4-1	2-1	6	Whittingham 4	14,288
23		28	A	Derby Co	W 4-2	1-1	5	Whittingham 2, McLoughlin 2	21,478
24	Jan	9	H	Southend U	W 2-0	1-0	4	Whittingham, Walsh	9717
25		16	A	West Ham U	L 0-2	0-1	6		18,127
26		23	H	Brentford	W 1-0	0-0	5	Aspinall (pen)	10,267
27		30	A	Barnsley	D 1-1	0-0	5	Whittingham	6551
28	Feb	6	H	Bristol C	L 2-3	1-1	5	Walsh, Whittingham	10,675
29		9	H	Newcastle U	W 2-0	2-0	—	Whittingham, Symons	21,028
30		13	A	Birmingham C	W 3-2	1-0	4	McLoughlin, Whittingham 2	10,935
31		20	H	Leicester C	D 1-1	0-0	4	Walsh	14,160
32		27	A	Swindon T	L 0-1	0-0	5		14,077
33	Mar	6	H	Luton T	W 2-1	1-1	4	Whittingham, Aspinall (pen)	10,457
34		9	H	Watford	W 1-0	0-0	—	Chamberlain	10,716
35		13	A	Cambridge U	W 1-0	1-0	4	Clayton (og)	5975
36		20	H	Charlton Ath	W 1-0	1-0	3	Whittingham	12,854
37		23	A	Tranmere R	W 2-0	0-0	—	Whittingham 2 (1 pen)	7472
38		27	H	Oxford U	W 3-0	0-0	2	Robinson (og), McLoughlin, Whittingham	14,648
39	Apr	3	A	Millwall	D 1-1	1-0	3	Chamberlain	12,921
40		6	H	Peterborough U	W 4-0	3-0	—	Whittingham 3, Butters	15,093
41		10	A	Bristol R	W 2-1	1-0	2	Kristensen, Whittingham	5377
42		12	H	Derby Co	W 3-0	2-0	2	Whittingham, Walsh 2	23,805
43		17	A	Notts Co	W 1-0	0-0	2	Walsh	11,014
44		24	H	Wolverhampton W	W 2-0	0-0	1	Daniel, Walsh	23,074
45	May	1	A	Sunderland	L 1-4	0-1	2	Whittingham	21,309
46		8	H	Grimsby T	W 2-1	0-1	3	Daniel, Whittingham	24,955

Final League Position: 3

GOALSCORERS

League (80): Whittingham 42 (1 pen), McLoughlin 9, Walsh 9, Chamberlain 4, Daniel 4, Aspinall 2 (2 pens), Symons 2, Burns 1, Butters 1, Clarke 1, Kristensen 1, Kuhl 1, own goals 3.
Coca Cola Cup (6): McLoughlin 2, Whittingham 2, Clarke 1, Murray 1.
FA Cup (0).

Knight 46	Awford 44	Powell 4 + 19	McLoughlin 46	Symons 41	Russell 12 + 2	Neill 28	Chamberlain 37 + 4	Walsh 37 + 6	Whittingham 46	Burns 28 + 4	Clarke 11 + 8	Doling 2 + 4	Daniel 40	Kuhl 3	Murray 2 + 5	Aspinall 19 + 8	Maguire 18 + 3	Agnew 3 + 2	Stimson 3 + 1	Butters 13 + 2	Price 13	Lawrence — + 12	Kristensen 10	Match No.
1	2	3	4	5	6	7	8	9	10	11	12		14											1
1	2		4	5	6	7	12	9	10	11	8		3											2
1	2	8	4	5	6	7	14	9	10	11	12		*3*											3
1	2	14	4	5	6	7	8	9	10	11	12		*3*											4
1	2	14	4	5		7	6	9	10	11	12		3	8										5
1	2	*9*	4	5		7			10	11	12	6	3	8	14									6
1	2	14	4	5		7		9	*10*		12		3	8		11	6							7
1	2	14	4	5		7		12	10		9		3	8		*11*	6							8
1	2		4	5		7	14	*8*	10	12	9		3			6	11							9
1	2		*4*	5		7	8	12	10	14	9		*3*			6	11							10
1	2		4	5		7	8	12	10		9		3			6	11							11
1		14	4	5		7	8	12	10	2	9		3			*6*	11							12
1	*2*		4	5		7	*8*	12	10	14	9		3			6	11							13
1	2	14	4	5		7	8	*9*	10	6	12		3				11							14
1	2	14	4	5		7	*8*	9	10	6	12		3				11							15
1	2		4	5		7	8	9	10	6			3				11							16
1	2		4	5		7	*8*	9	10	6	12		3				11	14						17
1	2	14	4			7	8		10	6	9		*3*			12	11	5						18
1	2		4	5		7	8	12	10	14	9		*3*			11	6							19
1	2		4	5		7	8	9	10	6	11	12	3											20
1	2	14	4	5	7		9	10	6	11	8		3											21
1	2		4	5	7		8	9	10	6	12		*3*			11	14							22
1	2	12	4	5	7		8	9	10	6	11		3											23
1	2		4	5		7	8	9	10	6			3			11								24
1	2	12	4	5		*7*	8	9	10	6			3			11	14							25
1		12	4	5	*7*		8	9	10	6			3		2	11	14							26
1	*2*	12	4	5			9	10	6				3			11	8	14	7					27
1	2	12	4	5	14	8	9	10	6				3			*11*			7					28
1	2	12	4	5		8	9	10	6				3			*11*	14		7					29
1	2	12	4	5		8	9	10	6				3			11			7					30
1	2	12	4	5	11	8	*9*	10	6		14		3						7					31
1	2	12	*4*	5	11	8	9	10	6				3				14		7					32
1	2	8	4	5	14	12	9	10	*6*				3			11			7					33
1	2		4		3	8	9	10	6	11	5									12	7				34
1	2	12	4	8	9	10	6	*11*	5										3	7	14			35
1	2		4	5	8	*9*	10	6	12										3	7	14	11		36
1	2		4	*8*	9	10	6	12	5										3	7	14	11		37
1	2		4	8	9	10	6	12	5										3	7	14	11		38
1	2		4	5	11	8	*9*	10	6	12									3	*7*	14			39
1	2		*4*	5	8	9	10	6	12										3	7	14	11		40
1	2		4	5	7	8	*9*	10	6	12									3	14	11			41
1	2		4	5	7	8	*9*	10	6	12									3	14	11			42
1	2		4	5	7	8	9	*10*	6	12									3	14	11			43
1	2		4	5	*7*	8	9	10	6										3	12	11			44
1	2		4	5	*7*	8	9	10	6	12									3	14	11			45
1	*2*		4	5	7	8	9	10	6	12									3	14	11			46

Coca Cola Cup	Second Round	Blackpool (a)	4-0
		(h)	2-0
	Third Round	Ipswich T (h)	0-1
FA Cup	Third Round	Brighton & HA (a)	0-1

PORTSMOUTH

Player and Position	Ht	Wt	Date	Birth Place	Source	Clubs	League App	Gls
Goalkeepers								
Brian Horne	5 11	13 13	5 10 67	Billericay	Apprentice	Millwall	163	—
						Watford (loan)	—	—
						Middlesbrough (loan)	4	—
						Stoke C (loan)	1	—
						Portsmouth	—	—
Alan Knight	6 0	13 00	3 6 61	Balham	Apprentice	Portsmouth	492	—
Defenders								
Andy Awford	5 9	11 09	14 7 72	Worcester	Worcester C	Portsmouth	107	—
Guy Butters	6 3	13 00	30 10 69	Hillingdon	Trainee	Tottenham H	35	1
						Southend U (loan)	16	3
						Portsmouth	71	3
Shaun Gale	6 0	11 06	8 10 69	Reading	Trainee	Portsmouth	3	—
Bjorn Kristensen	6 1	12 05	10 10 63	Malling	Aarhus	Newcastle U	80	4
						Bristol C (loan)	4	—
						Portsmouth	10	1
Warren Neill	5 9	11 05	21 11 62	Acton	Apprentice	QPR	181	3
						Portsmouth	176	—
Chris Price	5 7	10 02	30 3 60	Hereford	Apprentice	Hereford U	330	27
						Blackburn R	83	11
						Aston Villa	110	2
						Blackburn R	19	3
						Portsmouth	13	—
Lee Russell	5 11	11 04	3 9 69	Southampton	Trainee	Portsmouth	47	1
Kit Symons	6 1	10 10	8 3 71	Basingstoke	Trainee	Portsmouth	91	3
Midfield								
Chris Burns	6 0	12 00	9 11 67	Manchester	Cheltenham T	Portsmouth	78	9
Ray Daniel	5 8	11 09	10 12 64	Luton	Apprentice	Luton T	22	4
						Gillingham (loan)	5	—
						Hull C	58	3
						Cardiff C	56	1
						Portsmouth	62	4
Stuart Doling	5 6	10 06	28 10 72	Newport, IOW	Trainee	Portsmouth	19	2
Alan McLoughlin	5 8	10 00	20 4 67	Manchester	Local	Manchester U	—	—
						Swindon T	9	—
						Torquay U	24	4
						Swindon T	97	19
						Southampton	24	1
						Aston Villa (loan)	—	—
						Portsmouth	60	11
Christian Owen‡	5 6	10 00	27 2 74	Swansea	Trainee	Portsmouth	—	—
Forwards								
Warren Aspinall	5 8	10 6	13 9 67	Wigan	Apprentice	Wigan Ath	10	1
						Everton	7	—
						Wigan Ath (loan)	41	21
						Aston Villa	44	14
						Portsmouth	127	21
Mark Chamberlain	5 9	10 07	19 11 61	Stoke	Apprentice	Port Vale	96	17
						Stoke C	112	17
						Sheffield W	66	8
						Portsmouth	148	19
Colin Clarke	6 0	13 06	30 10 62	Newry	Apprentice	Ipswich T	—	—
						Peterborough	82	18
						Gillingham (loan)	8	1
						Tranmere R	45	22
						Bournemouth	46	26

PORTSMOUTH

Colours: Blue shirts, white shorts, red stockings. **Change colours:** red and black halved shirts, red shorts, red stockings.

Foundation: At a meeting held in his High Street, Portsmouth offices in 1898, solicitor Alderman J. E. Pink and five other business and professional men agreed to buy some ground close to Goldsmith Avenue for £4,950 which they developed into Fratton Park in record breaking time. A team of professionals was signed up by manager Frank Brettell and entry to the Southern League obtained for the new club's September 1899 kick-off.

First Football League game: 28 August, 1920, Division 3, v Swansea T (h) W 3-0 – Robson; Probert, Potts; Abbott, Harwood, Turner; Thompson, Stringfellow (1), Reid (1), James (1), Beedie.

Did you know: Portsmouth goalkeeper Ernie Butler was the club's only ever-present player in their consecutive League Championship successes of 1948–49 and 1949–50. Though born in Portsmouth he had been signed from Bath City in 1938.

Managers (and Secretary-Managers)
Frank Brettell 1898–1901, Bob Blyth 1901–04, Richard Bonney 1905–08, Bob Brown 1911–20, John McCartney 1920–27, Jack Tinn 1927–47, Bob Jackson 1947–52, Eddie Lever 1952–58, Freddie Cox 1958–61, George Smith 1961–70, Ron Tindall 1970–73 (GM to 1974), John Mortimore 1973–74, Ian St. John 1974–77, Jimmy Dickinson 1977–79, Frank Burrows 1979–82, Bobby Campbell 1982–84, Alan Ball 1984–89, John Gregory 1989–90, Frank Burrows 1990–1991, Jim Smith May 1991–.

Player and Position	Ht	Wt	Birth Date	Birth Place	Source	Clubs	League App	League Gls
						Southampton	82	36
						Bournemouth (loan)	4	2
						QPR	46	11
						Portsmouth	85	18
Paul Hall	5 9	10 02	3 7 72	Manchester	Trainee	Torquay U	93	1
						Portsmouth	—	—
Mark Kelly	5 8	9 10	27 11 69	Sutton		Portsmouth	49	2
						Tottenham H (loan)	—	—
George Lawrence†	5 10	12 02	14 9 62	London	Apprentice	Southampton	10	1
						Oxford U (loan)	15	4
						Oxford U	63	21
						Southampton	68	11
						Millwall	28	4
						Bournemouth	75	5
					Weymouth	Portsmouth	12	—
Shaun Murray	5 8	11 02	7 2 70	Newcastle	Trainee	Tottenham H	—	—
						Portsmouth	34	1
Darryl Powell	6 0	12 03	15 1 71	Lambeth	Trainee	Portsmouth	70	6
Mike Ross	5 6	9 13	2 9 71	Southampton		Portsmouth	4	—
Paul Walsh	5 7	10 08	1 10 62	Plumstead	Apprentice	Charlton Ath	87	24
						Luton T	80	24
						Liverpool	77	25
						Tottenham H	128	19
						QPR (loan)	2	—
						Portsmouth	43	9
Guy Whittingham	5 10	11 12	10 11 64	Evesham	Yeovil	Portsmouth	160	88
Steve Wigley*	5 9	10 05	15 10 61	Ashton	Curzon Ashton	Nottingham F	82	2
						Sheffield U	28	1
						Birmingham C	87	4
						Portsmouth	120	12
Roy Young	5 9	11 00	28 10 73	Romsey	Trainee	Portsmouth	—	—

Trainees
Anderton, Ryan J; Birmingham, Michael J; Bromige, Glyn J; Burton, Nicholas J; Cunningham, Aaron M; Flahavan, Aaron A; Gardner, Christopher D; Green, Barry J; Hussey, Matthew R; Igoe, Samuel G; Mosedale, Anthony J; Ogburn, Mark; Pearson, Dylan; Rowe, David J; Stewart, Paul T; Sutton, Graham W.

Associated Schoolboys
Ahmet, Jason J; Barker, Daniel T; Bundy, Scott D; Burrows, Marc P; Clarke, Jonathon M; Crotty, Anthony M; Dines, Stephen; Elliott, Paul M; Guile, Neil R; Hawley, Jonathan A; Janes, Neil M; Lee, Deryck A; Marshall, John P; Orsborn, Steven C; O'Rourke, Sean A; Page, Christopher M; Porter, Daniel J; Ramsay, Peter E; Silence, Scott; Thompson, Mark; Wearn, Sean R; Wheeler, Mark A; Williams, Adam L; Willsher, Matthew J; Woodley, Simon P.

Associated Schoolboys who have accepted the club's offer of a Traineeship/Contract
Burden, Steven L; Burton, Deon J; Spake, Daniel; Waterman, David G.

404

PORT VALE 1992-93 *Back row (from left to right):* Robin van der Laan, Michael Harrison, Neil Aspin, Richard Clark, Ian Taylor, Keith Houchen, Peter Swan, Chris Gillard, Simon Mills, Dean Glover.
Centre row: John Rudge (Manager), Jim Boyce (Physio), Nicky Cross, Ray Walker, Bradley Sandeman, Martin Foyle, Ian Miller (Youth Team Coach), Bobby Downes (First Team Coach).
Front row: Trevor Wood, Chris Sulley, Andy Porter, John Jeffers, Kevin Kent, Paul Kerr, Paul Musselwhite.

Division 2 **PORT VALE**

Vale Park, Burslem, Stoke-on-Trent. Telephone Stoke-on-Trent (0782) 814134. Commercial Dept: (0782) 835524. Clubcall: 0898 121636. Fax: 834981. Commercial Fax (0782) 836875. Valiant Leisure shop: (0782) 818718.

Ground capacity: 22,359.

Record attendance: 50,000 v Aston Villa, FA Cup 5th rd, 20 February 1960.

Record receipts: £170,022 v Liverpool, Rumbelows Cup 3rd rd replay, 20 November 1991.

Pitch measurements: 116yd × 76yd.

President: J. Burgess.

Chairman: W. T. Bell TECH. ENG, MIMI.

Directors: N. C. Tizley, I. McPherson, A. Belfield (vice-chairman).

Manager: John Rudge. *Secretary:* Eddie Harrison. *Commercial Executive:* Jake Roberts.

Coach: Bobby Downes. *Physio:* J. Joyce MCSP, SRP, GRAD.DIP (Phys). *Medical Officer:* Dr. G. Gardner MB, CHB. *Stadium manager:* F. W. Lodey. *Groundsman:* R. Fairbanks. *Community scheme officer:* Jim Cooper (0782 575594).

Year Formed: 1876. *Turned Professional:* 1885. *Ltd Co.:* 1911.

Club Nickname: 'Valiants'.

Previous Name: Burslem Port Vale; became Port Vale, 1911.

Previous Grounds: 1876, Limekin Lane, Longport; 1881, Westport; 1884, Moorland Road, Burslem; 1886, Athletic Ground, Cobridge; 1913, Recreation Ground, Hanley; 1950, Vale Park.

Record League Victory: 9–1 v Chesterfield, Division 2, 24 September 1932 – Leckie; Shenton, Poyser; Sherlock, Round, Jones; McGrath, Mills, Littlewood (6), Kirkham (2), Morton (1).

Record Cup Victory: 7–1 v Irthlingborough (away), FA Cup, 1st rd, 12 January 1907 – Matthews; Dunn, Hamilton; Eardley, Baddeley, Holyhead; Carter, Dodds (2), Beats, Mountford (2), Coxon (3).

Record Defeat: 0–10 v Sheffield U, Division 2, 10 December 1892 and v Notts Co, Division 2, 26 February 1895.

Most League Points (2 for a win): 69, Division 3 (N), 1953–54.

Most League Points (3 for a win): 89, Division 2, 1992–93.

Most League Goals: 110, Division 4, 1958–59.

Highest League Scorer in Season: Wilf Kirkham 38, Division 2, 1926–27.

Most League Goals in Total Aggregate: Wilf Kirkham, 154, 1923–29, 1931–33.

Most Capped Player: Sammy Morgan, 7 (18), Northern Ireland.

Most League Appearances: Roy Sproson, 761, 1950–72.

Record Transfer Fee Received: £925,000 from Norwich C for Darren Beckford, June 1991.

Record Transfer Fee Paid: £375,000 from Oxford U for Martin Foyle, June 1991.

Football League Record: 1892 Original Member of Division 2, Failed re-election in 1896; Re-elected 1898; Resigned 1907; Returned in Oct, 1919, when they took over the fixtures of Leeds City; 1929–30 Division 3 (N); 1930–36 Division 2; 1936–38 Division 3 (N); 1938–52 Division 3 (S); 1952–54 Division 3 (N); 1954–57 Division 3 (S); 1957–58 Division 3 (S); 1958–59 Division 4; 1959–65 Division 3; 1965–70 Division 4; 1970–78 Division 3; 1978–83 Division 4; 1983–84 Division 3; 1984–86 Division 4; 1986–89 Division 3; 1989– Division 2.

Honours: Football League: Division 2 best season: 3rd, 1992–93; Division 3 (N) – Champions 1929–30, 1953–54; Runners-up 1952–53; Division 4 – Champions 1958–59; Promoted 1969–70 (4th). *FA Cup:* Semi-final 1954, when in Division 3. *Football League Cup:* never past 2nd rd. *Autoglass Trophy:* Winners: 1992–93.

PORT VALE 1992—93 LEAGUE RECORD

Match No.	Date	Venue	Opponents	Result	H/T Score	Lg. Pos.	Goalscorers	Attendance
1	Aug 15	H	Fulham	D	0-0	0-0	—	6746
2	22	A	Bournemouth	L	1-2	0-1	20	Taylor	4825
3	29	H	Stockport Co	D	0-0	0-0	19		6340
4	Sept 1	H	Rotherham U	W	4-2	3-1	—	Taylor, Jeffers, Swan, Van der Laan	5370
5	5	A	Swansea C	L	0-2	0-0	14		3868
6	12	H	Exeter C	D	2-2	1-1	15	Taylor, Kelly (og)	5642
7	15	A	Burnley	D	1-1	0-0	—	Houchen	8556
8	19	A	Hartlepool U	D	1-1	0-1	17	Walker (pen)	2871
9	26	H	Chester C	W	2-0	0-0	14	Bartlett, Walker	6392
10	Oct 3	H	Brighton & HA	W	3-1	1-1	13	Cross, Walker (pen), Houchen	5731
11	10	A	WBA	W	1-0	0-0	12	Taylor	17,512
12	17	A	Plymouth Arg	W	4-0	2-0	8	Sandeman, Glover, Taylor, Houchen	6584
13	24	A	Stoke C	L	1-2	0-0	9	Kerr	24,500
14	31	H	Blackpool	W	2-1	0-0	9	Taylor, Walker	7057
15	Nov 3	H	Leyton Orient	W	2-0	0-0	—	Taylor, Kerr	7387
16	7	A	Bolton W	D	1-1	1-0	5	Winstanley (og)	7349
17	21	H	Hull C	D	1-1	0-1	7	Taylor	6202
18	28	A	Huddersfield T	W	2-1	1-1	6	Walker, Foyle	5822
19	Dec 12	A	Preston NE	W	5-2	1-1	3	Cross, Van der Laan, Taylor, Porter, Foyle	6038
20	19	H	Wigan Ath	D	2-2	1-1	3	Walker, Van der Laan	6647
21	28	A	Bradford C	L	2-3	0-0	7	Glover, Taylor	8018
22	Jan 9	H	Burnley	W	3-0	1-0	5	Taylor, Cross, Swan	8815
23	16	A	Chester C	W	2-1	0-1	4	Foyle, Kerr	4367
24	30	H	Bournemouth	W	3-0	2-0	4	Cross 2, Houchen	6834
25	Feb 6	A	Fulham	W	2-1	1-1	4	Taylor, Kerr	4905
26	9	H	Hartlepool U	W	2-0	0-0	—	Taylor, Jeffers	6629
27	13	A	Swansea C	W	2-0	1-0	2	Cross, Houchen	7191
28	16	A	Stockport Co	L	0-2	0-1	—		7449
29	20	A	Rotherham U	L	1-4	1-3	2	Sulley	5545
30	27	H	WBA	W	2-1	0-1	2	Cross, Foyle	13,291
31	Mar 6	A	Brighton & HA	W	2-0	0-0	2	Glover, Kent	7294
32	10	A	Reading	L	0-1	0-0	—		4873
33	13	H	Bolton W	D	0-0	0-0	2		11,055
34	20	A	Leyton Orient	W	1-0	0-0	2	Walker	5950
35	23	A	Huddersfield T	W	1-0	1-0	—	Van der Laan	7747
36	27	A	Hull C	W	1-0	0-0	2	Walker	4558
37	31	H	Stoke C	L	0-2	0-1	—		20,373
38	Apr 3	H	Reading	W	3-1	1-1	2	Houchen, Cross, Walker (pen)	7099
39	6	A	Preston NE	D	2-2	0-2	—	Cross, Kerr	8271
40	10	A	Mansfield T	W	1-0	0-0	2	Kerr	5078
41	13	H	Bradford C	L	1-2	1-0	—	Cross	8743
42	17	A	Wigan Ath	W	4-0	1-0	2	Slaven, Kerr (pen), Van der Laan, Cross	3743
43	24	A	Plymouth Arg	W	1-0	1-0	2	Cross	5563
44	27	H	Mansfield T	W	3-0	2-0	—	Kerr 2, Taylor	9996
45	May 4	A	Exeter C	D	1-1	0-0	—	Kerr (pen)	3219
46	8	A	Blackpool	W	4-2	1-2	3	Van der Laan, Kerr, Slaven, Taylor	9295

Final League Position: 3

GOALSCORERS

League (79): Taylor 15, Cross 12, Kerr 11 (2 pens), Walker 9 (3 pens), Houchen 6, Van der Laan 6, Foyle 4, Glover 3, Jeffers 2, Slaven 2, Swan 2, Bartlett 1, Kent 1, Porter 1, Sandeman 1, Sulley 1, own goals 2.
Coca Cola Cup (2): Foyle 1, Taylor 1.
FA Cup (7): Foyle 3, Porter 1, Swan 1, Taylor 1, Van der Laan 1.

Wood 5	Mills 3	Sulley 40	Walker 34 + 1	Aspin 35	Glover 39	Kent 21 + 6	Van der Laan 29 + 9	Foyle 10 + 6	Kerr 34 + 4	Taylor 41	Houchen 26 + 2	Sandeman 20 + 2	Swan 38	Jeffers 15 + 11	Cross 33 + 5	Bartlett 5	Musselwhite 41	Porter 12 + 5	Smith 6	Billing 10 + 2	Slaven 9 + 1	Mathie — + 3	Match No.
1	2	3	4	5	6	7	8	9	10	11	12												1
1	2	3	4	5	6	12	8	9	7	11	10	14											2
1		3	4		6		8		10	11	9		2	5	7	12							3
1		3	4		6		8		10	11	9		2	5	7	12							4
1		3	4		6		8		10	11			2	5	7	12	9						5
		3	4		6		8		10	11	9		2	5	7		1						6
		3	4	2	6				10	11	12			5	7	9	1	8					7
		3	4	7	6				10	11	12	14	2	5	9		1	8					8
		3	4		6		8		10	11	9	14	2	5	7	12	1						9
		3	4	7	6		8	12	10	11	9		2	5			1						10
		3	4	7	6		8		10	11	9		2	5			1						11
		3	4	7	6		8		10	11	9		2	5			1						12
		3	4	7	6		8	12	10	11	9		2	5			1						13
		3	4	7	6		8	12	10	11	9		2	5			1						14
		3	4	7	6		8		10	11	9		2	5			1						15
		3	4	7	6		8	12	10	11	9		2	5			1						16
		3	4	7	6		8	12	10	11	9	14	2	5			1						17
		3	4		6			12	10	11	9		2	5	7		1	8					18
	2	3	4		6				10	11	9			5	7		1	8					19
		3	4	5	6			12	10	11	9	14	2		7		1	8					20
		3	4	5	6	7		12	10	11	9	14	2				1	8					21
		3	4		6		8	12	10	11	9		2	5	7		1						22
		3	4	7	6		8	12	10	11	9	14	2	5			1						23
		3	4				8	12	10	11	9	14	2	5	7		1		6				24
		3	4	2		7	8	12	10	11	9			5			1		6				25
		3	4	2		7	8		10	11	9	14		5			1	12	6				26
		3	4	2		7	8		10	11	9			5			1		6				27
		3	4	2				12	10	11	9	14		5	7		1	8	6				28
		3	4	2		7	8	12	10	11	9	14		5			1		6				29
		3	4	2	6	7	8	12	10	11	9						1			5			30
		3	4	2	6	7	8	12	10	11	9						1			5			31
		3	4	2	6	7	8	12	10	11	9						1			5			32
	14	3	4	2	6	7	8	12	10	11	9						1			5			33
		3	4	2	6		8	9	10	11							1	12		5	7		34
		3	4	2	6		8	9	10	11							1			5	7		35
		3	4	2	6		8	9	10	11		14		5			1	12			7		36
		3	4	2	6		8	9	10	11		14		5			1	12			7		37
		3	4	2	6	7	8		10	11	9			5			1	12					38
		3	4	2	6	7	8		10	11	9			5			1	12					39
		3	4	2	6	7	8		10	11	9			5			1	12					40
		3	4	2	6	7	8		10	11	9			5			1	12				14	41
			4	2	6		8		10	11	9			5			1			3	7		42
			4	2	6		8	12	10	11	9			5			1			3	14	7	43
			4	2	6		8	12	10	11	9	14		5			1			3	7		44
		3		2	6		8	12	10	11	9	14		5			1			4	7		45
		3	4	2	6		8	9	10	11							1	12		5	7		46

Coca Cola Cup	First Round	Bolton W (a)	1-2
		(h)	1-1
FA Cup	First Round	Stoke C (a)	0-0
		(h)	3-1
	Second Round	Altrincham (a)	4-1
	Third Round	Newcastle U (a)	0-4

PORT VALE

Player and Position	Ht	Wt	Date	Birth Place	Source	Clubs	League App	Gls
Goalkeepers								
Paul Musselwhite	6 2	12 07	22 12 68	Portsmouth		Portsmouth	—	—
						Scunthorpe U	132	—
						Port Vale	41	—
Trevor Wood	5 11	13 00	3 11 68	Jersey	Apprentice	Brighton	—	—
						Port Vale	42	—
Defenders								
Neil Aspin	6 0	12 3	12 4 65	Gateshead	Apprentice	Leeds U	207	5
						Port Vale	160	1
Richard Clark*	5 10	11 00	12 9 73	Bristol	Cheltenham T	Port Vale	—	—
Chris Gillard*	5 11	12 06	30 9 73	Burton	Trainee	Port Vale	—	—
Dean Glover	5 10	11 13	29 12 63	West Bromwich	Apprentice	Aston Villa	23	—
						Sheffield U (loan)	10	—
						Middlesbrough	50	5
						Port Vale	192	9
Gareth Griffiths	6 4	14 00	10 4 70	Winsford	Rhyl	Port Vale	—	—
Darren Hughes	5 11	10 11	6 10 65	Prescot	Apprentice	Everton	3	—
						Shrewsbury T	37	1
						Brighton	26	2
						Port Vale	184	4
Simon Mills	5 8	11 04	16 8 64	Sheffield	Apprentice	Sheffield W	5	—
						York C	99	5
						Port Vale	184	8
Dean Stokes			23 5 70	Birmingham	Halesowen	Port Vale	—	—
Chris Sulley*	5 8	10 00	3 12 59	Camberwell	Apprentice	Chelsea	—	—
						Bournemouth	206	3
						Dundee U	7	—
						Blackburn R	134	3
						Port Vale	40	1
Midfield								
Andy Porter	5 9	11 02	17 9 68	Manchester	Trainee	Port Vale	146	4
Bradley Sandeman	5 10	10 08	24 2 70	Northampton	Trainee	Northampton T	58	3
						Maidstone U	57	8
						Port Vale	22	1
Ian Taylor	6 1	12 00	4 6 68	Birmingham	Moor Green	Port Vale	41	15
Ray Walker	5 10	11 12	28 9 63	North Shields	Apprentice	Aston Villa	23	—
						Port Vale (loan)	15	1
						Port Vale	276	32
Forwards								
Nicky Cross	5 9	11 12	7 2 61	Birmingham	Apprentice	WBA	105	15
						Walsall	109	45
						Leicester C	58	15
						Port Vale	107	27
Martin Foyle	5 10	11 02	2 5 63	Salisbury	Amateur	Southampton	12	1
						Blackburn R (loan)	—	—
						Aldershot	98	35
						Oxford U	126	36
						Port Vale	59	15
Michael Harrison	6 1	12 02	19 1 73	Cannock	Trainee	Port Vale	—	—
Keith Houchen*	6 2	12 08	25 7 60	Middlesbrough	Chesterfield	Hartlepool U	170	65
						Orient	76	20
						York C	67	19
						Scunthorpe U	9	3
						Coventry C	54	7
						Hibernian	57	11
						Port Vale	49	10

PORT VALE

Colours: White shirts, black shorts, black and white stockings. **Change colours:** All yellow.

Foundation: Formed in 1876 as Port Vale, adopting the prefix 'Burslem' in 1884 upon moving to that part of the city. It was dropped in 1911.

First Football League game: 3 September, 1892, Division 2, v Small Heath (a) L 1-5 – Frail; Clutton, Elson; Farrington, McCrindle, Delves; Walker, Scarratt, Bliss (1), Jones. (Only 10 men).

Did you know: When Port Vale beat Liverpool 4-3 on 8 April 1955 in a Division 2 match, all four Vale goals were scored by Cyril Done, a former Anfield player.

Managers (and Secretary-Managers)
Sam Gleaves 1896–1905*, Tom Clare 1905–11, A. S. Walker 1911–12, H. Myatt 1912–14, Tom Holford 1919–24 (continued as trainer), Joe Schofield 1924–30, Tom Morgan 1930–32, Tom Holford 1932–35, Warney Cresswell 1936–37, Tom Morgan 1937–38, Billy Frith 1945–46, Gordon Hodgson 1946–51, Ivor Powell 1951, Freddie Steele 1951–57, Norman Low 1957–62, Freddie Steele 1962–65, Jackie Mudie 1965–67, Sir Stanley Matthews (GM) 1965–68, Gordon Lee 1968–74, Roy Sproson 1974–77, Colin Harper 1977, Bobby Smith 1977–78, Dennis Butler 1978–79, Alan Bloor 1979, John McGrath 1980–83, John Rudge March 1984–.

Player and Position	Ht	Wt	Date	Birth Place	Source	Clubs	League App	Gls
John Jeffers	5 10	11 10	5 10 68	Liverpool	Trainee	Liverpool	—	—
						Port Vale	145	8
Kevin Kent	5 11	11 00	19 3 65	Stoke	Apprentice	WBA	2	—
						Newport Co	33	1
						Mansfield T	229	36
						Port Vale	61	1
Paul Kerr	5 8	11 03	9 6 64	Portsmouth	Apprentice	Aston Villa	24	3
						Middlesbrough	125	13
						Millwall	44	14
						Port Vale	38	11
Alex Mathie (on loan from Morton)	5 10	10 07	20 12 68	Bathgate		Port Vale	3	—
Bernie Slaven	5 11	12 00	13 11 60	Paisley		Morton	22	1
						Airdrie	2	—
						Queen of the South	2	—
						Albion R	42	27
						Middlesbrough	307	118
						Port Vale	10	2
Peter Swan	6 0	12 00	29 9 66	Leeds	Local	Leeds U	49	11
						Hull C	80	24
						Port Vale	71	5
Robin Van der Laan	5 11	12 05	5 9 68	Schiedam	Wageningen	Port Vale	99	15

Trainees
Abbey, Paul A; Allum, Christopher D; Brammeld, Craig G; Brown, Christopher E; Byrne, Paul T; Carvell, Matthew J; Corden, Simon W; Day, Myles A. J; Heron, Derek J; Hickey, Benjamin J; Hughes, Simon D; Johnson, Mark; McCarthy, Anthony M; Morris, Adam J; Sheard, Timothy D; Stirk, Mark A.

Associated Schoolboys
Brown, Mark; Cowley, Robert W; Davis, Neal N; Edge, Paul S; Heth, Dominic; Morrell, Neal; Wilson, Kenneth J.

Associated Schoolboys who have accepted the club's offer of a Traineeship/Contract
Burton, Matthew; Cunningham, Dean; Patrick, Matthew.

410

PRESTON NORTH END 1992-93 *Back row (left to right):* Sam Allardyce (Youth Team Coach), Gary McCullough, Adam Critchley, David Flitcroft, Colin Greenall, David Christie, Ronnie Jepson, Mike Flynn, Ryan Kidd, Steven Finney, David Eaves, Simon Burton, Craig Moylon, Walter Joyce (Assistant Manager).

Front row: Martin James, Jason Kerfoot, Les Cartwright, Lee Ashcroft, John Bagnall, Les Chapman (Manager), Simon Farnworth, John Tinkler, Lee Fowler, Graham Shaw, Johnathan Davidson.

Division 3 **PRESTON NORTH END**

Deepdale, Preston PR1 6RU. Telephone Preston (0772) 795919 (club). (0772) 795465 (Commercial). (0772) 704275 (Community office). Fax (0772) 653266 (club). (0772) 703800 (Commercial).

Ground capacity: 17,200.

Record attendance: 42,684 v Arsenal, Division 1, 23 April 1938.

Record receipts: £68,650 v Sheffield W, FA Cup 3rd rd, 4 January 1992.

Pitch measurements: 110yd × 71yd. (Artificial surface.)

President: Tom Finney OBE, JP.

Vice President: T. C. Nicholson JP, FCIOB.

Chairman: Keith W. Leeming.

Directors: M. J. Woodhouse (snr) (vice-chairman), J. T. Garratt, E. Griffith BVSC, MRCVS (Company Secretary), D. Shaw, J. E. Starkie LL.B (Lond), M. J. Woodhouse (jnr).

Manager: John Beck. *Asst. Manager:* Gary Peters.

Chief Executive: Paul Agnew. *Assistant secretary:* Mrs Audrey Shaw. *Physio:* Roy Johnson.

Year Formed: 1881. *Turned Professional:* 1885. *Ltd Co.:* 1893.

Club Nicknames: 'The Lilywhites' or 'North End'.

Record League Victory: 10–0 v Stoke, Division 1, 14 September 1889 – Trainer; Howarth, Holmes; Kelso, Russell (1), Graham; Gordon, Jimmy Ross (2), Nick Ross (3), Thomson (2), Drummond (2).

Record Cup Victory: 26–0 v Hyde, FA Cup, 1st rd, 15 October 1887 – Addision; Howarth, Nick Ross; Russell (1), Thomson (5), Graham (1); Gordon (5), Jimmy Ross (8), John Goodall (1), Dewhurst (3), Drummond (2).

Record Defeat: 0–7 v Blackool, Division 1, 1 May 1948.

Most League Points (2 for a win): 61, Division 3, 1970–71.

Most League Points (3 for a win): 90, Division 4, 1986–87.

Most League Goals: 100, Division 2, 1927–28 and Division 1, 1957–58.

Highest League Scorer in Season: Ted Harper, 37, Division 2, 1932–33.

Most League Goals in Total Aggregate: Tom Finney, 187, 1946–60.

Most Capped Player: Tom Finney, 76, England.

Most League Appearances: Alan Kelly, 447, 1961–75.

Record Transfer Fee Received: £765,000 from Manchester C for Michael Robinson, June 1979.

Record Transfer Fee Paid: £125,000 to Norwich C for Mike Flynn, December 1989.

Football League Record: 1888 Founder Member of League; 1901–04 Division 2; 1904–12 Division 1; 1912–13 Division 2; 1913–14 Division 1; 1914–15 Division 2; 1919–25 Division 1; 1925–34 Division 2; 1934–49 Division 1; 1949–51 Division 2; 1951–61 Division 1; 1961–70 Division 2; 1970–71 Division 3; 1971–74 Division 2; 1974–78 Division 3; 1978–81 Division 2; 1981–85 Division 3; 1985–87 Division 4; 1987–92 Division 3; 1992–93 Division 2; 1993– Division 3.

Honours: Football League: Division 1 – Champions 1888–89 (first champions), 1889–90; Runners-up 1890–91, 1891–92, 1892–93, 1905–06, 1952–53, 1957–58; Division 2 – Champions 1903–04, 1912–13, 1950–51; Runners-up 1914–15, 1933–34; Division 3 – Champions 1970–71; Division 4 – Runners-up 1986–87. *FA Cup:* Winners 1889, 1938; Runners-up 1888, 1922, 1937, 1954, 1964. *Double Performed:* 1888–89. *Football League Cup:* best season: 4th rd, 1963, 1966, 1972, 1981.

PRESTON NORTH END 1992—93 LEAGUE RECORD

Match No.	Date	Venue	Opponents	Result	H/T Score	Lg. Pos.	Goalscorers	Atten dance
1	Aug 15	H	Bournemouth	D	1-1	0-1	—	Ellis	4756
2	22	A	Fulham	L	1-2	0-1	18	Ellis	3641
3	29	H	Chester C	W	4-3	1-2	10	Cartwright, Flynn, Ashcroft, Leonard	4471
4	Sept 5	A	Brighton & HA	L	0-2	0-0	17		6026
5	12	H	Burnley	W	2-0	0-0	14	Tinkler, Ashcroft	7209
6	15	A	Hull C	W	4-2	1-2	—	Ellis 2, Ashcroft, Cartwright	4463
7	19	A	Bradford C	L	0-4	0-1	13		5882
8	26	H	Hartlepool U	L	0-2	0-1	17		4347
9	Oct 3	H	Plymouth Arg	L	1-2	1-2	18	Davidson	4401
10	10	A	Blackpool	W	3-2	2-1	16	Ellis 3	7631
11	17	H	Stoke C	L	1-2	0-2	17	Callaghan	8138
12	20	H	Reading	W	2-0	2-0	—	Flitcroft, Ashcroft (pen)	3329
13	24	A	Mansfield T	D	2-2	1-1	14	James, Fowler L	3047
14	31	H	Bolton W	D	2-2	2-0	15	James, Cartwright	7013
15	Nov 3	A	Stockport Co	L	0-3	0-1	—		4860
16	7	H	Wigan Ath	W	2-0	1-0	14	Callaghan, James	4442
17	21	A	Rotherham U	L	0-1	0-0	16		4246
18	28	H	WBA	D	1-1	1-0	15	Ellis	6306
19	Dec 12	H	Port Vale	L	2-5	1-1	17	James, Ashcroft (pen)	6038
20	18	A	Leyton Orient	L	1-3	0-1	—	Ashcroft	3436
21	28	H	Exeter C	D	2-2	2-1	19	Garnett, Norbury	5796
22	Jan 9	H	Hull C	L	1-2	1-1	19	Garnett	4719
23	16	A	Hartlepool U	D	0-0	0-0	20		2682
24	23	H	Bradford C	W	3-2	3-1	19	Norbury, James, Ellis	5155
25	26	A	Chester C	W	4-2	1-1	—	Norbury, Flynn, Ellis, Flitcroft	2901
26	30	H	Fulham	L	1-2	1-0	18	Ellis	5858
27	Feb 6	A	Bournemouth	L	1-2	0-2	19	Tinkler	3601
28	13	A	Brighton & HA	W	1-0	0-0	18	Norbury	4334
29	16	A	Burnley	L	0-2	0-1	—		12,648
30	20	A	Reading	L	0-4	0-1	18		3543
31	27	H	Blackpool	D	3-3	1-1	18	Ellis 2, Fowler L	10,403
32	Mar 6	A	Plymouth Arg	L	0-4	0-3	19		5201
33	9	H	Swansea C	L	1-3	0-3	—	Norbury	4396
34	12	A	Wigan Ath	W	3-2	2-1	—	Norbury, Burton 2	3562
35	17	A	Huddersfield T	L	0-1	0-0	—		4915
36	20	H	Stockport Co	L	2-3	1-1	19	Ellis 2	5255
37	24	A	WBA	L	2-3	1-2	—	Ellis, Ashcroft	13,270
38	27	H	Rotherham U	W	5-2	2-0	19	Norbury 2, Ellis 3	4859
39	Apr 6	A	Port Vale	D	2-2	2-0	—	Ellis, Watson	8271
40	10	H	Huddersfield T	W	2-1	1-0	20	Watson, Ellis	7647
41	12	A	Exeter C	W	1-0	0-0	16	Watson	3410
42	17	H	Leyton Orient	L	1-4	0-3	19	Burton	5890
43	24	A	Stoke C	L	0-1	0-0	21		18,334
44	27	A	Swansea C	L	0-2	0-0	—		6933
45	May 1	H	Mansfield T	L	1-5	1-2	21	Ellis	5889
46	8	A	Bolton W	L	0-1	0-0	21		21,270

Final League Position: 21

GOALSCORERS

League (65): Ellis 22, Norbury 8, Ashcroft 7 (2 pens), James 5, Burton 3, Cartwright 3, Watson 3, Callaghan 2, Flitcroft 2, Flynn 2, Fowler L 2, Garnett 2, Tinkler 2, Davidson 1, Leonard 1.
Coca Cola Cup (2): Ellis 1, Tinkler 1.
FA Cup (5): Callaghan 1, Davidson 1, Ellis 1, Fowler L 1, Graham 1.

Farnworth 35	Davidson 18 + 3	Fowler L 29 + 3	Tinkler 22 + 2	Flynn 35	Callaghan 33 + 2	Ashcroft 37 + 2	Cartwright 33 + 1	Leonard 19 + 3	Ellis 34 + 1	James 22 + 3	Eaves 1 + 3	Flitcroft 4 + 4	Christie 1 + 1	Burton 17 + 4	Finney 1 + 3	Kidd 13 + 2	Graham 8	Allardyce S 1 + 2	Taylor 4	Siddall 1	Garnett 10	Moylon — + 1	Lucas 26	Ainsworth 26	Norbury 21	Johnstone 10	Greenall 20	Fowler J 5 + 1	Whalley 14	Watson 6 + 2	Allardyce C — + 1	Match No.
1	2	3	4	5	6	7	8	9	10	11																						1
1	2	3	4	5	6	7	8	9	10	*11*	12	14																				2
1	2	3	*4*	5	6	7	8	9	10	11				14	12																	3
1	2	3		5	6	7	8	9	10	14		4			*11*	12																4
1	2	3	4	5	*6*	7	8	9	10	11		14			12																	5
1	2	3	4	5	6	7	8	9	10	11																						6
1	2	3	4	5	6	7	8	9	10	11				12																		7
1	2	3	4	5	6	7	8	9	10	11			12																			8
1	2	3	4	5	6	7	8	9	10	11																						9
1	2	*3*	4	5	6	7	8	9	10	11				12	14																	10
1	2	3	4	5	6	7	8	9	10	11				12																		11
1	12	3	4	5	11	7	2	9	10				8	6																		12
1	12	3	4	5	10	7	2	*9*		11						6	8	14														13
1	12	3	4	5	8		2		10	11						6	7	9														14
1	3	6	4	5	8		*2*		10	11	12					7	14	9														15
1	3	6		5	4	7	2		10	11							8	9														16
1	3	6		5	4	7	2			11					12		8	9	10													17
1	3	6	7	5	4	9	2		10	11							8															18
	2	3		5	4	9			10	11			8				7				1		6									19
1	3	*2*		5	4				10	11	12		8				9		7				6	14								20
1	2			5	4	7								11									6	3	8		9					21
1	12	2		5	4	7								11	10								6	3	8		9					22
1	11			5	4	7	2							10									6	3	8		9					23
1		2		5	4	7							10	11									6	3	8		9					24
1		*2*		5	4	7							10	11	14	12							6	3	8		9					25
	12				4	7	2		10	11			5								1		6	3	8		9					26
	11	4				7	2		10					12							1		6	3	8		9	5				27
	12	2		5		7			10					11							1		6	3	8		9	4				28
	3	*2*		5	12	7		14	10					11							1		6	4	8		9					29
	3			5	12	11	2	14	10												1		6	4	8	7	9					30
	8			5	4	11									10						1		6	3		7	9		2			31
				5	12	7								11	10						1		6	3	8		9		2	4	14	32
1			7	5	11									10									6	3	8		9		2	4		33
			7	5	11								12	10									6	3	8		9		2	4		34
			7	5	8								12	11	10								6	3			9		2	4		35
				5	8									11	10	7							6	3			9		2	4		36
1				5	8									11	10	7							6	3			9		2	4		37
1					11	7								10	8	5							6	3					2	4		38
1					11	7								10	*8*	5							6	3			9	12	2	4	14	39
1					11	7								10	8	5							6	3			9		2	4		40
1	12				11	7								10	8	5							6	3			9		2	4		41
1					11	7								10	8	5							6	3			9		2	4		42
1	12				11	7	2	8						10		5							6	3		4	9					43
1					11		2	14						10	8	5							6	3		7	9	12		4		44
1	3				12									10	11	5							6		8	7	9		2	4		45
1	7				11		2							10		5							6	3	8		9	12		4		46

Coca Cola Cup	First Round	Stoke C (h)	2-1
		(a)	0-4
FA Cup	First Round	Bradford C (a)	1-1
		(h)	4-5

PRESTON NORTH END

Player and Position	Ht	Wt	Date	Birth Place	Source	Clubs	League App	Gls
Goalkeepers								
Simon Farnworth	6 0	11 13	28 10 63	Chorley	Apprentice	Bolton W	113	—
						Stockport Co (loan)	10	—
						Tranmere R (loan)	7	—
						Bury	105	—
						Preston NE	81	—
Glenn Johnstone	6 3	14 07	5 6 67	Kenya	Lancaster C	Preston NE	10	—
Barry Siddall‡	6 1	14 02	12 9 54	Ellesmere Port	Apprentice	Bolton W	137	—
						Sunderland	167	—
						Darlington (loan)	8	—
						Port Vale	81	—
						Blackpool (loan)	7	—
						Stoke C	20	—
						Tranmere R (loan)	12	—
						Manchester C (loan)	6	—
						Blackpool	110	—
						Stockport Co	21	—
						Hartlepool U	11	—
						WBA	—	—
						Carlisle U	24	—
						Chester C	9	—
						Preston NE	1	—
Defenders								
Craig Allardyce§	6 2	13 06	9 6 75	Bolton	Trainee	Preston NE	1	—
Sam Allardyce†	6 2	14 00	19 10 54	Dudley	Apprentice	Bolton W	184	21
						Sunderland	25	2
						Millwall	63	2
						Coventry C	28	1
						Huddersfield T	37	
						Bolton W	14	—
						Preston NE	90	2
						WBA	1	—
					Ireland	Preston NE	3	—
Aaron Callaghan	5 11	11 02	8 10 66	Dublin	Apprentice	Stoke C	7	—
						Crewe Alex (loan)	8	—
						Oldham Ath	16	2
						Crewe Alex	158	6
						Preston NE	35	2
Adam Critchley‡	5 11	12 00	12 10 73	Wegber	Trainee	Preston NE	—	—
Jonathan Davidson	5 8	11 11	1 3 70	Cheadle	Trainee	Derby Co	12	2
						Preston NE	21	1
						Chesterfield (loan)	1	—
Colin Greenall*	5 10	11 06	30 12 63	Billinge	Apprentice	Blackpool	183	9
						Gillingham	62	4
						Oxford U	67	2
						Bury (loan)	3	—
						Bury	68	5
						Preston NE	29	1
Ryan Kidd	6 0	11 07	6 10 71	Heywood	Trainee	Port Vale	1	—
						Preston NE	15	—
Craig Moylon*	5 10	10 10	16 10 72	Munster	Trainee	Preston NE	1	—
Midfield								
Lee Cartwright	5 8	10 06	19 9 72	Rawtenstall	Trainee	Preston NE	81	8
Richard Lucas	5 10	11 04	22 9 70	Sheffield	Trainee	Sheffield U	10	—
						Preston NE	26	—
Kevin Magee	5 10	11 04	10 4 71	Bangour	Armadale T	Partick T	11	—
						Preston NE	—	—
Paul Sixsmith‡	5 10	10 12	22 9 71	Bolton	Trainee	Manchester U	—	—
						Preston NE	—	—

PRESTON NORTH END

Colours: White shirts, navy blue shorts, navy blue stockings. **Change colours:** Yellow and blue shirts, white shorts, white stockings.

Foundation: North End Cricket and Rugby Club which was formed in 1863, indulged in most sports before taking up soccer in about 1879. In 1881 they decided to stick to football to the exclusion of other sports and even a 16–0 drubbing by Blackburn Rovers in an invitation game at Deepdale, a few weeks after taking this decision, did not deter them for they immediately became affiliated to the Lancashire FA.

First Football League game: 8 September, 1888, Football League, v Burnley (h) W 5-2 – Trainer; Haworth, Holmes; Robertson, W. Graham, J. Graham; Gordon (1), Ross (2), Goodall, Dewhurst (2), Drummond.

Did you know: Preston fielded an unchanged team during their 1953–54 FA Cup run when they had five Englishmen, five Scots and an Australian born centre-half in Joe Marston. Charlie Wayman scored in every round.

Managers (and Secretary-Managers)
Charlie Parker 1906–15, Vincent Hayes 1919–23, Jim Lawrence 1923–25, Frank Richards 1925–27, Alex Gibson 1927–31, Lincoln Hayes 1931–1932 (run by committee 1932–36), Tommy Muirhead 1936–37, (run by committee 1937–49), Will Scott 1949–53, Scot Symon 1953–54, Frank Hill 1954–56, Cliff Britton 1956–61, Jimmy Milne 1961–68, Bobby Seith 1968–70, Alan Ball Sr 1970–73, Bobby Charlton 1973–75, Harry Catterick 1975–77, Nobby Stiles 1977–81, Tommy Docherty 1981, Gordon Lee 1981–83, Alan Kelly 1983–85, Tommy Booth 1985–86, Brian Kidd 1986, John McGrath 1986–90, Les Chapman 1990–92, John Beck December 1992–.

John Tinkler	5 8	11 07	24 8 68	Trimdon		Hartlepool U	170	7
						Preston NE	24	2
Neil Whalley	6 0	12 09	29 10 65	Liverpool	Warrington T	Preston NE	14	—
Forwards								
Gareth Ainsworth	5 9	11 09	10 5 73	Blackburn	Blackburn R	Preston NE	5	—
						Cambridge U	4	1
						Preston NE	26	—
Lee Ashcroft	5 10	11 00	7 9 72	Preston	Trainee	Preston NE	91	13
Simon Burton	5 10	10 04	29 12 73	Bolton	Trainee	Preston NE	21	3
David Eaves*	5 11	11 07	13 2 73	Blackpool	Trainee	Preston NE	7	—
Tony Ellis	5 11	11 00	20 10 64	Salford	Northwich Vic	Oldham Ath	8	—
						Preston NE	86	26
						Stoke C	77	19
						Preston NE	35	22
David Flitcroft	6 0	13 09	14 1 74	Bolton	Trainee	Preston NE	8	2
Lee Fowler	5 8	11 07	26 1 69	Nottingham	Trainee	Stoke C	49	—
						Preston NE	32	2
Mark Leonard	5 11	11 10	27 9 62	St Helens	Witton Albion	Everton	—	—
						Tranmere R (loan)	7	—
						Crewe Alex	54	15
						Stockport Co	73	24
						Bradford C	157	29
						Rochdale	9	1
						Preston NE	22	1
Mike Norbury	6 1	11 10	22 1 69	Hemsworth	Bridlington	Cambridge U	26	3
						Preston NE	21	8
Liam Watson	5 11	11 10	21 5 70	Liverpool	Warrington T	Preston NE	8	3

Trainees
Allardyce, Craig S; Banks, Andrew M; Brandes, Christopher M; England, Kieran J; Farragher, Kieran T; Hall, Andrew B; Heavey, Paul A; Holland, Christopher J; Ilse, Thomas W. S; Linford, Paul R; McCullough, Gary; Parkinson, Stuart G; Raywood, Matthew; Rimmer, Christopher E; Sheridan, Brian J; Squires, James A.

**Non-Contract
Allardyce, Samuel; Bamber, Lee E.

Associated Schoolboys
Almond, Timothy J; Barnes, Stephen W; Bolton, James L; Bolton, Michael R. D; Dean, Paul M; Haworth, Robert A; Hayton, Kyle; Keenan, Christopher J; Lucas, David A; McKenna, Paul S; Price, James R; Roberts, Gary P; Smith, Kevin J; Stanley, Ian; Stewart, Simon D. S; Webb, Daniel.

Associated Schoolboys who have accepted the club's offer of a Traineeship/Contract
Arnold, Lee; Browick, Christopher S; Brooks, Gilbert I; Calligan, John K; Kilbane, Kevin D; McMenemy, Paul J.

**Non-Contract Players who are retained must be re-signed before they are eligible to play in League matches.

416

QUEENS PARK RANGERS 1992–93 *Back row (left to right):* Leslie Ferdinand, Stephen Gallen, Garry Thompson, Michael Meaker, Jan Stejskal, Tony Witter, Alan McDonald, Peter Caldwell, Karl Ready, Darren Peacock, Danny Maddix, Gary Penrice.

Centre row: Des Bulpin (Youth Team Manager), Ron Berry (Kit Manager), Ian Holloway, Dennis Bailey, David McEnroe, Maurice Doyle, Bradley Allen, Tony Roberts, Andy Tillson, Alan McCarthy, Douglas Freedman, Gary Waddock, Roger Cross (Reserve Team Manager), Les Boyle (Youth Team Physio), Brian Morris (Physio).

Front row: Clive Wilson, David Bardsley, Rufus Brevett, Andy Sinton, Ray Wilkins, Frank Sibley (Assistant Manager), Gerry Francis (Manager), Simon Barker, Darren Finlay, Andrew Impey, Justin Channing, Robert Herrera.

FA Premier   QUEENS PARK RANGERS

South Africa Road, W12 7PA. Telephone 081–743 0262. Box Office: 081–749 5744 (24 hour information service 081 749 7798). Supporters Club: 081–749 6771. Club Shop: 081–749 6862. Marketing: 081–740 8737.

Ground capacity: 21,700 (17,000 covered).

Record attendance: 35,353 v Leeds U, Division 1, 27 April 1974.

Record receipts: £213,274 v Arsenal, FA Premier League, 2 September 1992.

Pitch measurements: 112yd × 72yd.

Chairman: R. C. Thompson.

Directors: (Corporate): R. B. Copus (Club); P. D. Ellis, A. Ingham, A. Ellis.

Manager: Gerry Francis. *Assistant Manager/Coach:* Frank Sibley.

Secretary: Miss S. F. Marson. *Marketing Executive: Lynne Davie.*

Reserve Team Coach: Roger Cross.

Physio: Brian Morris.

Year Formed: 1885 *(see Foundation).* *Turned Professional:* 1898. *Ltd Co.:* 1899.

Club Nicknames: 'Rangers' or 'Rs'. *Previous Name:* 1885–87, St Jude's.

Previous Grounds: 1885 *(see Foundation),* Welford's Fields; 1888–99; London Scottish Ground, Brondesbury, Home Farm, Kensal Rise Green, Gun Club Wormwood Scrubs, Kilburn Cricket Ground; 1899, Kensal Rise Athletic Ground; 1901, Latimer Road, Notting Hill; 1904, Agricultural Society, Park Royal; 1907, Park Royal Ground; 1917, Loftus Road; 1931, White City; 1933, Loftus Road; 1962, White City; 1963, Loftus Road.

Record League Victory: 9–2 v Tranmere R, Division 3, 3 December 1960 – Drinkwater; Woods, Ingham; Keen, Rutter, Angell; Lazarus (2), Bedford (2), Evans (2), Andrews (1), Clark (2).

Record Cup Victory: 8–1 v Bristol R (away), FA Cup, 1st rd, 27 November 1937 – Gilfillan; Smith, Jefferson; Lowe, James, March; Cape, Mallett, Cheetham (3), Fitzgerald (3) Bott (2). 8–1 v Crewe Alex, Milk Cup, 1st rd, 3 October 1983 – Hucker; Neill, Dawes, Waddock (1), McDonald (1), Fenwick, Micklewhite (1), Stewart (1), Allen (1), Stainrod (3), Gregory.

Record Defeat: 1–8 v Mansfield T, Division 3, 15 March 1965 and v Manchester U, Division 1, 19 March 1969.

Most League Points (2 for a win): 67, Division 3, 1966–67.

Most League Points (3 for a win): 85, Division 2, 1982–83.

Most League Goals: 111, Division 3, 1961–62.

Highest League Scorer in Season: George Goddard, 37, Division 3 (S), 1929–30.

Most League Goals in Total Aggregate: George Goddard, 172, 1926–34.

Most Capped Player: Don Givens, 26 (56), Eire.

Most League Appearances: Tony Ingham, 519, 1950–63.

Record Transfer Fee Received: £1,300,000 from Arsenal for David Seaman, May 1990.

Record Transfer Fee Paid: £1,000,000 to Luton T for Roy Wegerle, December 1989.

Football League Record: 1920 Original Members of Division 3; 1921–48 Division 3 (S); 1948–52 Division 2; 1952–58 Division 3 (S); 1958–67 Division 3; 1967–68 Division 2; 1968–69 Division 1; 1969–73 Division 2; 1973–79 Division 1; 1979–83 Division 2; 1983–92 Division 1; 1992– FA Premier League.

Honours: Football League: Division 1 – Runners-up 1975–76; Division 2 – Champions 1982–83; Runners-up 1967–68, 1972–73; Division 3 (S) – Champions 1947–48; Runners-up 1946–47; Division 3 – Champions 1966–67. *FA Cup:* Runners-up 1982. *Football League Cup:* Winners 1966–67; Runners-up 1985–86. (In 1966–67 won Division 3 and Football League Cup). **European Competition:** *UEFA Cup:* 1976–77, 1984–85.

QUEENS PARK RANGERS 1992—93 LEAGUE RECORD

Match No.	Date		Venue	Opponents	Result		H/T Score	Lg. Pos.	Goalscorers	Atten dance
1	Aug	17	A	Manchester C	D	1-1	0-1	—	Sinton	24,471
2		19	H	Southampton	W	3-1	0-1	—	Ferdinand 2, Bardsley	10,639
3		22	H	Sheffield U	W	3-2	2-1	3	Ferdinand, Barker, Bailey	10,925
4		26	A	Coventry C	W	1-0	1-0	—	Impey	13,563
5		29	A	Chelsea	L	0-1	0-0	2		22,910
6	Sept	2	H	Arsenal	D	0-0	0-0	—		20,868
7		5	H	Ipswich T	D	0-0	0-0	4		12,806
8		12	A	Southampton	W	2-1	0-1	4	Sinton, Channing	14,125
9		19	H	Middlesbrough	D	3-3	0-1	5	Ferdinand, Penrice, Sinton (pen)	12,272
10		26	A	Manchester U	D	0-0	0-0	5		33,287
11	Oct	3	H	Tottenham H	W	4-1	0-1	4	Holloway, Wilkins, Penrice 2	19,845
12		17	A	Norwich C	L	1-2	0-0	4	Allen	16,009
13		24	H	Leeds U	W	2-1	0-0	3	Bardsley, Ferdinand	19,326
14	Nov	1	A	Aston Villa	L	0-2	0-1	—		20,140
15		7	A	Wimbledon	W	2-0	2-0	5	Allen, Wilkins	6771
16		23	H	Liverpool	L	0-1	0-0	—		21,056
17		28	A	Blackburn R	L	0-1	0-1	6		15,850
18	Dec	5	H	Oldham Ath	W	3-2	2-1	5	Ferdinand 2, Penrice	11,804
19		12	H	Crystal Palace	L	1-3	1-0	7	Penrice	14,571
20		19	A	Sheffield W	L	0-1	0-1	9		23,164
21		28	H	Everton	W	4-2	1-0	7	Sinton 3, Penrice	14,802
22	Jan	9	A	Middlesbrough	W	1-0	0-0	6	Ferdinand	15,616
23		18	H	Manchester U	L	1-3	1-2	—	Allen	21,117
24		27	A	Chelsea	D	1-1	0-0	—	Allen	15,806
25		30	A	Sheffield U	W	2-1	1-0	7	Allen, Holloway	16,366
26	Feb	6	H	Manchester C	D	1-1	0-0	8	Wilson (pen)	13,003
27		9	A	Ipswich T	D	1-1	0-1	—	White	17,354
28		20	H	Coventry C	W	2-0	2-0	4	Pearce (og), Peacock	12,453
29		24	H	Nottingham F	L	0-1	0-0	—		22,436
30		27	A	Tottenham H	L	2-3	0-2	6	Peacock, White	32,341
31	Mar	6	H	Norwich C	W	3-1	2-1	4	Ferdinand 2, Wilson	13,892
32		10	A	Liverpool	L	0-1	0-0	—		30,370
33		13	H	Wimbledon	L	1-2	1-1	5	Ferdinand	12,270
34		20	A	Oldham Ath	D	2-2	0-1	5	Allen, Sinton	10,946
35		24	H	Blackburn R	L	0-3	0-1	—		10,677
36	Apr	3	H	Crystal Palace	D	1-1	1-0	8	Allen	14,705
37		10	H	Nottingham F	W	4-3	2-1	5	Ferdinand 3, Wilson (pen)	15,815
38		12	A	Everton	W	5-3	2-1	5	Impey, Ferdinand 3, Bardsley	19,057
39	May	1	A	Leeds U	D	1-1	1-0	6	Ferdinand	31,408
40		4	A	Arsenal	D	0-0	0-0	—		18,817
41		9	H	Aston Villa	W	2-1	0-1	—	Ferdinand, Allen	18,904
42		11	H	Sheffield W	W	3-1	2-0	—	Allen 2, Ferdinand	12,177

Final League Position: 5

GOALSCORERS

League (63): Ferdinand 20, Allen 10, Sinton 7 (1 pen), Penrice 6, Bardsley 3, Wilson 3 (2 pens), Holloway 2, Impey 2, Peacock 2, White 2, Wilkins 2, Bailey 1, Barker 1, Channing 1, own goal 1.
Coca Cola Cup (5): Ferdinand 2, Allen 1, Bailey 1, Peacock 1.
FA Cup (4): Ferdinand 2, Holloway 1, Penrice 1.

Stejskal 14 + 1	Bardsley 40	Wilson 41	Wilkins 27	Peacock 35 + 3	McDonald 39	Impey 39 + 1	Holloway 23 + 1	Ferdinand 37	Bailey 13 + 2	Sinton 36	Thompson — + 4	Roberts 28	Barker 21 + 4	Penrice 10 + 5	Channing 2	Maddix 9 + 5	Brevett 14 + 1	Allen 21 + 4	White 3 + 4	Doyle 5	Ready 2 + 1	Meaker 3	Match No.
1	2	3	4	5	6	7	8	9	10	11	12												1
	2	3	4	5	6	7	8	9	10	11	12	1											2
1	2	3	4	5	6		8	9	10	11	12		7										3
1	2	3	4	5	6	7		9	10	11			8	12									4
1	2	3	4	5	6	7		9	10	11			8	12									5
	2	3	4	5	6	7		9	10	11		1	8	12									6
1	2	3	4	5	6	7		9	10	11			8	12									7
1		3	4	5	6	7		9		11			8	10		2	12						8
1		3	4	5	6	7	14	9		11			8	10		2	12						9
1	2		4	5		7	8	9		11			12	10		6	3						10
1	2	3	4	5	6	7	8	9		11						10							11
1	2	3	4	5	6	7	8	9		11				*10*		12	14						12
1	2	3	4	5	6	7	8	9		11	12					10							13
	2	3	4	5	6	7	8	9	12			1	11			10							14
	2	3	4	5	6	7	8	9		11		1				10							15
	2	3	4	5	6	7	8	9		11		1				10							16
1	2	3	4	5	6	7	8	9	10	11	12												17
1	2	3	4	5	6	7	8	9		*11*				10		12	14						18
1	2	3	4	5	6	7	8	9		11						10							19
	2	3	4	5	6	7	8	9		11		1		12		10							20
	2	3	4	5	6		8	9		11		1	7			10							21
	2		4	5	6	7		9		11		1	8	*10*		12	3	14					22
	2	3		5	6	7	8	10	11	12		1	4					9					23
	2	7			6	11	8	9				1	4			5	3	10	12				24
	2	7	12		6	11	8	9				1	4			5	3	10					25
	2	7			6		8	9		11		1	4			5	3	10					26
	2	7	12		6		8	9		11		1				5	3	10	14	*4*			27
	2	7			6		8	9		11		1	4				3	10		5			28
	2	7		5			8	9	12	11		1	4			6	3	10					29
	2	7		5	6	12		9		11		1	4			8	3	10					30
	2	7			6		8	9				1				5	3	12	10	4	11		31
	2	8	12		6	7		9				1				5	3	10		4	11		32
14	2		8	5	6	7		9				*1*					3	10	12	4	11		33
	2	3		5	6	7	8	9		11		1				10				4	12		34
	2		4		6	7	8	9		11		1					3	10		5			35
	2		4	5	6	7	8	9		11		1					3	10	12				36
	2	3	4	5	6	7	8	9		11		1				10							37
	2	3	4	5	6	7	8	9		11		1		12		10							38
	2	3	4	5	6	7		9		11		1	8			10							39
	2	3	4	5	6	7		9		11		1	8	12		10							40
	2	3	4	5	6	7		9		11		1	8			10							41
	2	3	4	5	6	7		9		11		1	8			10							42

Coca Cola Cup	Second Round	Grimsby T (h)	2-1
		(a)	1-2
	Third Round	Bury (a)	2-0
	Fourth Round	Sheffield W (a)	0-4
FA Cup	Third Round	Swindon T (h)	3-0
	Fourth Round	Manchester C (h)	1-2

QUEENS PARK RANGERS

Player and Position	Ht	Wt	Date	Birth Place	Source	Clubs	League App	Gls
Goalkeepers								
Peter Caldwell	6 1	13 00	5 6 72	Dorchester	Trainee	QPR	—	—
Tony Roberts	6 0	12 00	4 8 69	Bangor	Trainee	QPR	47	—
Jan Stejskal	6 3	12 00	15 1 62	Czechoslovakia	Sparta Prague	QPR	82	—
Defenders								
David Bardsley	5 10	11 00	11 9 64	Manchester	Apprentice	Blackpool	45	—
						Watford	100	7
						Oxford U	74	7
						QPR	150	4
Rufus Brevett	5 8	11 00	24 9 69	Derby	Trainee	Doncaster R	109	3
						QPR	32	—
Darren Finlay	5 4	10 00	19 12 73	Belfast	Trainee	QPR	—	—
Stephen Gallen	6 00	12 00	21 11 73	London	Trainee	QPR	—	—
Roberto Herrera	5 7	10 06	12 6 70	Torbay	Trainee	QPR	6	—
						Torquay U (loan)	11	—
						Torquay U (loan)	5	—
Brian Law‡	6 2	11 12	1 1 70	Merthyr	Apprentice	QPR	20	—
Alan McCarthy	5 11	12 10	11 1 72	London	Trainee	QPR	5	—
Alan McDonald	6 2	12 07	12 10 63	Belfast	Apprentice	QPR	286	8
						Charlton Ath (loan)	9	—
Danny Maddix	5 10	11 07	11 10 67	Ashford	Apprentice	Tottenham H	—	—
						Southend U (loan)	2	—
						QPR	139	6
Darren Peacock	6 2	12 06	3 2 68	Bristol	Apprentice	Newport Co	28	—
						Hereford U	59	4
						QPR	96	3
Karl Ready	6 1	12 00	14 8 72	Neath		QPR	4	—
Tony Witter	6 1	12 07	12 8 65	London	Grays Ath	Crystal Palace	—	—
						QPR	—	—
						Millwall (loan)	—	—
						Plymouth Arg (loan)	3	1
Midfield								
Simon Barker	5 9	11 00	4 11 64	Farnworth	Apprentice	Blackburn R	182	35
						QPR	147	12
Brian Croft	5 9	10 10	27 9 67	Chester		Chester C	59	3
						Cambridge U	17	2
						Chester C	114	3
						QPR	—	—
Ian Holloway	5 8	10 10	12 3 63	Kingswood	Apprentice	Bristol R	111	14
						Wimbledon	19	2
						Brentford (loan)	13	2
						Brentford	16	—
						Torquay U (loan)	6	—
						Bristol R	179	26
						QPR	64	2
David McEnroe*	5 8	10 10	19 8 72	Dublin	Trainee	QPR	—	—
Michael Meaker	5 11	11 05	18 8 71	Greenford	Trainee	QPR	12	—
						Plymouth Arg (loan)	4	—
Andy Sinton	5 8	10 10	19 3 66	Newcastle	Apprentice	Cambridge U	93	13
						Brentford	149	28
						QPR	160	22
Ray Wilkins	5 8	11 02	14 9 56	Hillingdon	Apprentice	Chelsea	179	30
						Manchester U	160	7
						AC Milan	73	2
					Paris St Germain	Rangers	70	2
						QPR	115	6
Clive Wilson	5 7	10 00	13 11 61	Manchester	Local	Manchester C	98	9
						Chester (loan)	21	2
						Chelsea	81	5
						Manchester C (loan)	11	—
						QPR	94	7
Forwards								
Bradley Allen	5 7	10 00	13 9 71	Harold Wood	School	QPR	47	17

QUEENS PARK RANGERS

Colours: Blue and white hooped shirts, white shorts, white stockings. **Change colours:** Red and black hooped shirts, black shorts, black stockings with 4 red bands at top.

Foundation: There is an element of doubt about the date of the foundation of this club, but it is believed that in either 1885 or 1886 it was formed through the amalgamation of Christchurch Rangers and St. Jude's Institute FC. The leading light was George Wodehouse, whose family maintained a connection with the club until comparatively recent times. Most of the players came from the Queen's Park district so this name was adopted after a year as St. Jude's Institute.

First Football League game: 28 August, 1920, Division 3, v Watford (h) L 1-2 – Price; Blackman, Wingrove; McGovern, Grant, O'Brien; Faulkner, Birch (1), Smith, Gregory, Middlemiss.

Did you know: Queens Park Rangers became the first Football League club to install an artificial surface in 1981–82. The Rangers manager Terry Venables had ten years earlier written a novel with Gordon Williams called *They used to play on grass*.

Managers (and Secretary-Managers)
James Cowan 1906–13, James Howie 1913–20, Ted Liddell 1920–24, Will Wood 1924–25 (had been secretary since 1903), Bob Hewison 1925–30, John Bowman 1930–31, Archie Mitchell 1931–33, Mick O'Brien 1933–35, Billy Birrell 1935–39, Ted Vizard 1939–44, Dave Mangnall 1944–52, Jack Taylor 1952–59, Alec Stock 1959–65 (GM to 1968), Jimmy Andrews 1965, Bill Dodgin Jnr 1968, Tommy Docherty 1968, Les Allen 1969–70, Gordon Jago 1971–74, Dave Sexton 1974–77, Frank Sibley 1977–78, Steve Burtenshaw 1978–79, Tommy Docherty 1979–80, Terry Venables 1980–84, Gordon Jago 1984, Alan Mullery 1984, Frank Sibley 1984–85, Jim Smith 1985–88, Trevor Francis 1988–90, Don Howe 1990–91, Gerry Francis June 1991–.

Player and Position	Ht	Wt	Birth Date	Birth Place	Source	Clubs	League App	Gls
Dennis Bailey	5 10	11 06	13 11 65	Lambeth	Farnborough T	Crystal Palace	5	1
						Bristol R (loan)	17	9
						Birmingham C	75	23
						Bristol R (loan)	6	1
						QPR	39	10
Marvin Bryan	6 0	12 02	2 8 75	Paddington	Trainee	QPR	—	—
Maurice Doyle	5 8	10 07	17 10 69	Ellesmere Port	Trainee	Crewe Alex	8	2
						QPR	5	—
						Crewe Alex (loan)	7	2
						Wolverhampton W (loan)	—	—
Les Ferdinand	5 11	13 05	18 12 66	London	Hayes	QPR	90	40
						Brentford (loan)	3	—
						Besiktas (loan)	—	—
Doug Freedman	5 9	11 00	21 1 74	Glasgow	Trainee	QPR	—	—
Kevin Gallen	5 11	12 03	21 9 75	Hammersmith	Trainee	QPR	—	—
Andrew Impey	5 8	10 06	13 9 71	Hammersmith	Yeading	QPR	53	2
Gary Penrice	5 8	10 06	23 3 64	Bristol	Bristol C	Bristol R	188	54
						Watford	43	18
						Aston Villa	20	1
						QPR	34	9
Garry Thompson*	6 1	14 00	7 10 59	Birmingham	Apprentice	Coventry C	134	38
						WBA	91	39
						Sheffield W	36	7
						Aston Villa	60	17
						Watford	34	8
						Crystal Palace	20	3
						QPR	19	1
Devon White	6 3	14 00	2 3 64	Nottingham	Arnold T Boston U	Lincoln C	29	4
						Bristol R	202	53
						Cambridge U	22	4
						QPR	7	2

Trainees
Brazier, Matthew R; Challis, Trevor M; Cross, John R; Dichio, Daniele S. E; Dickinson, Steven D; Goodwin, Lee; Goodwin, Paul A; Graham, Mark R; Millard, Martyn L. D; Pratt, Benjamin K.

Associated Schoolboys
Bruce, Paul M; Camilleri, Colin F; Fleming, Hayden V; Gibb, Christopher A; Harris, Jonathan; Hodges, Kevin; Holloway, Grant J; Holman, Lee C; Mitchell, Terrence F; Morrish, Luke; Motton, Mathew P. J; Nile, David A; Nuttall, Steven R; Perry, Mark J; Quashie, Nigel F; Webster, Philip J.

Associated Schoolboys who have accepted the club's offer of a Traineeship/Contract
Hurst, Richard A; Mahoney-Johnson, Michael A; McCarthy, Billy; Monteath, Jonathan; Plummer, Christopher S; Power, Graeme R; White, Dene; Wood, Kristian J.

READING 1992–93 *Back row (left to right):* Colin Lee (First Team Coach), Tom Jones, Phil Parkinson, Jeff Hopkins, Steve Francis, Jimmy Quinn, Adrian Williams, Kevin Dillon, Scott Taylor, John Haselden (Physio).

Front row: Michael Gilkes, Mark Holzman, Keith McPherson, Mark McGhee (Manager), Stuart Lovell, Steve Richardson, Mick Gooding.

Division 2

READING

READING F.C. 1871 ©

Elm Park, Norfolk Road, Reading. Telephone Reading (0734) 507878.

Ground capacity: 13,200.

Record attendance: 33,042 v Brentford, FA Cup 5th rd, 19 February 1927.

Record receipts: £70,693.79 v Arsenal, FA Cup 3rd rd, 10 January 1987.

Pitch measurements: 112yd × 77yd.

Life President: J. H. Brooks.

Chairman: John Madejski. *Managing Director:* M. J. Lewis.

Directors: G. Denton.

Manager: Mark McGhee.

Coach: Colin Lee. *Youth development officer:*

Physio: John Haselden.

Commercial Manager: Kevin Girdler.

Secretary: Jayne E. Hill.

Year Formed: 1871. *Turned Professional:* 1895. *Ltd Co.:* 1895.

Club Nickname: 'The Royals'.

Previous Grounds: 1871, Reading Recreation; Reading Cricket Ground; 1882, Coley Park; 1889, Caversham Cricket Ground; 1896, Elm Park.

Record League Victory: 10–2 v Crystal Palace, Division 3 (S), 4 September 1946 – Groves; Glidden, Gulliver; McKenna, Ratcliffe, Young; Chitty, Maurice Edelston (3), McPhee (4), Barney (1), Deverell (2).

Record Cup Victory: 6–0 v Leyton, FA Cup, 2nd rd, 12 December 1925 – Duckworth; Eggo, McConnell; Wilson, Messer, Evans; Smith (2), Braithwaite (1), Davey (1), Tinsley, Robson (2).

Record Defeat: 0–18 v Preston NE, FA Cup 1st rd, 1893–94.

Most League Points (2 for a win): 65, Division 4, 1978–79.

Most League Points (3 for a win): 94, Division 3, 1985–86.

Most League Goals: 112, Division 3 (S), 1951–52.

Highest League Scorer in Season: Ronnie Blackman, 39, Division 3 (S), 1951–52.

Most League Goals in Total Aggregate: Ronnie Blackman, 158, 1947–54.

Most Capped Player: Billy McConnell, 8, Northern Ireland.

Most League Appearances: Martin Hicks, 500, 1978–91.

Record Transfer Fee Received: £500,000 from Wimbledon for Keith Curle, October 1988.

Record Transfer Fee Paid: £250,000 to Leicester C for Steve Moran, November 1987 and £250,000 to Huddersfield T for Craig Maskell, August 1990.

Football League Record: 1920 Original Member of Division 3; 1921–26 Division 3 (S); 1926–31 Division 2; 1931–58 Division 3 (S); 1958–71 Division 3; 1971–76 Division 4; 1976–77 Division 3; 1977–79 Division 4; 1979–83 Division 3; 1983–84 Division 4; 1984–86 Division 3; 1986–88 Division 2; 1988–92 Division 3; 1992– Division 2.

Honours: Football League: Division 2 best season: 13th, 1986–87; Division 3 – Champions 1985–86. Division 3 (S) – Champions 1925–26; Runners-up 1931–32, 1934–35, 1948–49, 1951–52; Division 4 – Champions 1978–79. *FA Cup:* Semi-final 1927. *Football League Cup:* best season: 4th rd, 1965, 1966, 1978. *Simod Cup:* Winners 1987–88.

READING 1992—93 LEAGUE RECORD

Match No.	Date		Venue	Opponents	Result		H/T Score	Lg. Pos.	Goalscorers	Atten dance
1	Aug	15	A	Hartlepool U	D	1-1	0-0		Quinn	4149
2		22	H	Leyton Orient	D	1-1	1-1	16	McGhee	4207
3		29	A	Bolton W	L	1-2	0-1	18	Williams	4877
4	Sept	5	H	Hull C	L	1-2	1-1	22	Taylor	3465
5		9	A	WBA	L	0-3	0-1	—		13,164
6		16	H	Rotherham U	W	3-1	0-0	—	Quinn 2, Gilkes	2481
7		19	H	Wigan Ath	W	4-0	2-0	15	Quinn 2, Gilkes, Gooding	3084
8		26	A	Brighton & HA	W	1-0	1-0	13	Lovell	7341
9	Oct	2	H	Fulham	W	3-0	2-0	—	Lovell, Quinn, Gilkes	7204
10		10	A	Huddersfield T	D	0-0	0-0	13		5281
11		17	H	Bradford C	D	1-1	0-0	13	Gilkes	4348
12		20	A	Preston NE	L	0-2	0-2	—		3329
13		24	A	Swansea C	L	1-2	0-1	16	Williams	5317
14	Nov	31	H	Plymouth Arg	W	3-0	1-0	12	Jones, Quinn, McPherson	5088
15		3	A	Burnley	D	1-1	1-1	—	McGhee	8382
16		7	H	Blackpool	D	0-0	0-0	15		4163
17		21	A	Bournemouth	D	1-1	0-0	15	Gilkes	4418
18		28	H	Exeter C	L	2-3	1-2	16	Quinn, Parkinson	4015
19	Dec	12	A	Chester C	W	3-0	1-0	15	Gilkes 2, Lambert	2011
20		19	A	Stockport Co	L	2-4	1-1	15	Gilkes, Moody	3832
21		26	H	Stoke C	L	0-1	0-1	16		7269
22		28	A	Mansfield T	D	1-1	0-1	16	Lambert	3043
23	Jan	9	A	Rotherham U	L	2-3	0-3	18	Quinn 2	4492
24		16	H	Brighton & HA	W	3-0	2-0	18	Taylor 2, Gooding	4400
25		23	A	Wigan Ath	D	1-1	0-1	15	Lambert	1860
26		27	H	Bolton W	L	1-2	1-1	—	Williams	4640
27		30	A	Leyton Orient	W	2-1	1-0	14	Dillon, Parkinson	5466
28	Feb	6	A	Hartlepool U	W	2-0	0-0	12	Williams, Quinn	3431
29		13	A	Hull C	D	1-1	0-0	13	Gray	3593
30		20	H	Preston NE	W	4-0	1-0	12	Taylor, Gilkes, Gray, Quinn	3543
31		27	H	Huddersfield T	W	2-1	2-0	11	Gray, Gilkes	3948
32	Mar	6	A	Fulham	D	0-0	0-0	10		4818
33		10	H	Port Vale	W	1-0	0-0	—	Hopkins	4873
34		13	A	Blackpool	W	1-0	0-0	8	Quinn	4160
35		20	H	Burnley	W	1-0	0-0	8	Gilkes	6398
36		23	A	Exeter C	D	0-0	0-0	—		2874
37		27	H	Bournemouth	W	3-2	2-0	6	Lovell 2, Quinn	5978
38	Apr	3	A	Port Vale	L	1-3	1-1	6	Quinn	7099
39		7	H	Chester C	W	1-0	0-0	—	Parkinson	3754
40		10	A	Stoke C	L	0-2	0-1	8		16,919
41		12	H	Mansfield T	W	3-1	1-1	7	Lovell, Gooding, Taylor	4904
42		16	A	Stockport Co	D	2-2	0-1	—	Quinn (pen), Lovell	5001
43		21	H	WBA	D	1-1	1-1	—	Parkinson	8026
44		24	A	Bradford C	L	0-3	0-1	10		7042
45	May	1	H	Swansea C	W	2-0	2-0	9	Quinn (pen), Lovell	6922
46		8	A	Plymouth Arg	D	2-2	1-2	8	Lovell, Gilkes	5137

Final League Position: 8

GOALSCORERS

League (66): Quinn 17 (2 pens), Gilkes 12, Lovell 8, Taylor 5, Parkinson 4, Williams 4, Gooding 3, Gray 3, Lambert 3, McGhee 2, Dillon 1, Hopkins 1, Jones 1, McPherson 1, Moody 1.
Coca Cola Cup (2): Quinn 1, Williams 1.
FA Cup (5): Quinn 3 (1 pen), Parkinson 1, Taylor 1.

Francis 34	Jones 21	Richardson 11 + 4	McPherson 44	Williams 30 + 1	Parkinson 38 + 1	Taylor 30 + 2	Dillon 40	Quinn 42	McGhee 9 + 4	Barkus 4 + 5	Lovell 18 + 4	Hopkins 36	Gooding 38 + 2	Gilkes 38	Hislop 12	Lambert 9 + 18	Bass 5	Gray 8 + 3	Moody 5	McCance 1	Viveash 5	Holzman 12 + 4	Jackson 5	McDonald 11	Match No.
1	2	3	4	5	6	7	8	9	10	11	12														1
1	11	3	4	5	6	*7*	*8*	9	10	12				2	14										2
1	11	3	4	5	6		8	9	10					2	7										3
1	11	3	4	5	6		8	9	10	12				2	7										4
	11		4	5	6	10	8	9	12	7			3	2		1									5
	11	2	4	5	6		8	9	12			10	3		7	1	14								6
	11		4	5	6		8	9				10	3	2	7	1	12								7
	11	12	4	5			8	9				10	3	2	7	1	6								8
	11		4	5	6		8	9				10	3	2	7	1									9
	11	12	4	5	6		8	9				*10*	3	2	7	1	14								10
	11	12	4	5	6		8	9				*10*	3	2	7	1	14								11
	11		4	5	6		8	9				10	3	2	7	1	12								12
	11	9	4	5	6	14	*8*		12			10	3	2	7	1									13
	11	5	4		6		8	9	10				3	2	7	1	12								14
1	11	5	4		6		8	9	10				3	2	7		12								15
1	11	12	4	5	6		8	9	10				3	2	7										16
	11		4	5	6		8	9					3	2	7	1	10								17
	11	8	4	5	6			9	12				3	2	7	1	14	*10*							18
1	11	2	4		6		8						3	5	7	10		9							19
1	11		4	5	6		8						3	2	7	10		9							20
1	11	2	4	5	6		8		12				3	14	7	10		9							21
1			4		6	3	8	9		7				2				11	10	5					22
1			4	5		12	8	9		*7*				2				11	10			3	6		23
1			4	5	10	11	8	9						2	7							3	6		24
1			4	5	10	11	8	9						2	7	12						3	6		25
1			*4*	5	14	11	8	9	12					2	7			10				3	6		26
1				5	10	11	8	9						2	4	7						3	6		27
1				5	6	11	8	9					3	7		12		10				2	4		28
1	5				6	11	8	9					2	3	7	12		10					4		29
1			4		6	11	8	9					5	2	7	12		10					3		30
1			4		6	11	8	9	12				5	2	7			10					3		31
1			4		6	11	8	9					5	2	7							3	10		32
1			4		6	11	8	9					5	3	7			10						2	33
1			4	14	6	11	8	9					5	3	7	12		10						2	34
1			4	*6*		11	8	9					5	3	7	12		10					14	2	35
1			4			11	8	9					5	3	7	12	6	10						2	36
1			4		6	11	8	9	10				5	3	7	12							14	*2*	37
1			4		6	11	8	9	10				5	3	7	12							14	*2*	38
1			4		6	3	8	9	10				5		7		11					12		2	39
1			4		6	11	8	9	10				5		7	12	14						3	2	40
1			4		6	11		9	10				5	3	7							8		2	41
1			4	7	6	11		9	12		10	5	3									8		2	42
1			4	5	6	11	8	9	12		10		3	7										2	43
1			4	5	6	11		9	12		10	8	3	7										2	44
1			4	5	6		8	9	7			10		3			11	12						2	45
1			4	5	6	11	8	9				10		3	7	12								2	46

Coca Cola Cup	Second Round	Watford (a)	2-2
		(h)	0-2
FA Cup	First Round	Birmingham C (h)	1-0
	Second Round	Leyton Orient (h)	3-0
	Third Round	Manchester C (a)	1-1
		(h)	0-4

READING

Player and Position	Ht	Wt	Date	Birth Place	Source	Clubs	League App	Gls
Goalkeepers								
Steve Francis	5 11	11 05	29 5 64	Billericay	Apprentice	Chelsea	71	—
						Reading	216	—
Neil Hislop	6 6	12 02	22 2 69	London		Reading	12	—
Daniel Honey*	6 2	13 00	2 4 73	Ascot	Trainee	Reading	—	—
Defenders								
Stuart Dennis*			5 3 74	Reading		Reading	—	—
Mark Holzman	5 7	10 07	22 2 73	Bracknell	Trainee	Reading	32	1
Jeff Hopkins	6 0	12 12	14 4 64	Swansea	Apprentice	Fulham	219	4
						Crystal Palace	70	2
						Plymouth Arg (loan)	8	—
						Bristol R	6	—
						Reading	36	1
Graham Kemp*			21 6 68	Birmingham	Redditch	Reading	—	—
Daren McCance	6 0	10 12	13 9 73	Consett	Trainee	Reading	1	—
Keith McPherson	5 11	10 11	11 9 63	Greenwich	Apprentice	West Ham U	1	—
						Cambridge U (loan)	11	1
						Northampton T	182	8
						Reading	134	5
Steve Richardson*	5 5	10 03	11 2 62	Slough	Apprentice	Southampton	—	—
						Reading	380	3
Adrian Williams	5 10	11 00	16 8 71	Reading	Trainee	Reading	102	10
Midfield								
Kevin Dillon	6 0	12 07	18 12 59	Sunderland	Apprentice	Birmingham C	186	15
						Portsmouth	215	45
						Newcastle U	62	—
						Reading	69	6
Tommy Jones	5 10	11 07	7 10 64	Aldershot	Weymouth	Aberdeen	28	3
						Swindon T	168	12
						Reading	21	1
Stuart Lovell	5 10	10 06	9 1 72	Sydney	Trainee	Reading	76	14
Philip Parkinson	6 0	11 06	1 12 67	Chorley	Apprentice	Southampton	—	—
						Bury	145	5
						Reading	39	4
Scott Taylor	5 9	11 00	23 11 70	Portsmouth	Trainee	Reading	125	10
Forwards								
Lea Barkus	5 6	9 13	7 12 74	Reading	Trainee	Reading	15	1
David Bass§	6 0	11 04	29 11 74	Frimley	Trainee	Reading	8	—
Andrew Deaner			8 6 73			Reading	—	—
Michael Gilkes	5 8	10 02	20 7 65	Hackney		Reading	238	32
						Chelsea (loan)	1	—
						Southampton (loan)	6	—
Mick Gooding	5 7	10 13	12 4 59	Newcastle	Bishop Auckland	Rotherham U	102	10
						Chesterfield	12	—
						Rotherham U	156	33
						Peterborough U	47	21
						Wolverhampton W	44	4
						Reading	151	16
Andy Gray	5 6	10 10	25 10 73	Southampton		Reading	12	3
James Lambert	5 7	10 04	14 9 73	Henley	School	Reading	27	3

READING

Colours: Navy and white hooped shirts, white shorts, white stockings. **Change colours:** Yellow and navy blue hooped shirts, blue shorts, blue stockings.

Foundation: Reading was formed as far back as 1871 at a public meeting held at the Bridge Street Rooms. They first entered the FA Cup as early as 1877 when they amalgamated with the Reading Hornets. The club was further strengthened in 1889 when Earley FC joined them. They were the first winners of the Berks and Bucks Cup in 1878–79.

First Football League game: 28 August, 1920, Division 3, v Newport C (a) W 1-0 – Crawford; Smith, Horler; Christie, Mavin, Getgood; Spence, Weston, Yarnell, Bailey (1), Andrews.

Did you know: Steve Hetzke was Reading's youngest debutant at 16 years, 191 days on 18 December 1971. He also wore all but the No. 8 shirt during his service and was nominated emergency goalkeeper in 1974–75, though not called upon.

Managers (and Secretary-Managers)
Thomas Sefton 1897–1901*, James Sharp 1901–02, Harry Matthews 1902–20, Harry Marshall 1920–22, Arthur Chadwick 1923–25, H. S. Bray 1925–26 (secretary only since 1922 and 26–35), Andrew Wylie 1926–31, Joe Smith 1931–35, Billy Butler 1935–39, John Cochrane 1939, Joe Edelston 1939–47, Ted Drake 1947–52, Jack Smith 1952–55, Harry Johnston 1955–63, Roy Bentley 1963–69, Jack Mansell 1969–71, Charlie Hurley 1972–77, Maurice Evans 1977–84, Ian Branfoot 1984–89, Ian Porterfield 1989–91, Mark McGhee May 1991–.

Player and Position	Ht	Wt	Birth Date	Birth Place	Source	Clubs	League App	League Gls
Mark McGhee†	5 10	12 00	25 5 57	Glasgow	Apprentice	Bristol C	—	—
						Morton	64	37
						Newcastle U	28	5
						Aberdeen	164	63
						SV Hamburg	30	7
						Celtic	88	27
						Newcastle U	67	24
						Reading	45	7
Jimmy Quinn	6 0	12 07	18 11 59	Belfast	Oswestry T	Swindon T	49	10
						Blackburn R	71	17
						Swindon T	64	30
						Leicester C	31	6
						Bradford C	35	14
						West Ham U	47	18
						Bournemouth	43	19
						Reading	42	17

Trainees
Bass, David; Brown, Philip R; Champion, Marc G; Dean, Richard A; Embery, John A; Holzman, Gary R; Humphries, Steven P; Kent, Aron R; Minor, David J; Montgomery, Noel T; Mukabaa, Anthony G; Sharp, James; Thorpe, Michael S; Timothy, David.

**Non-Contract
McGhee, Mark.

Associated Schoolboys
Dugdale, Andrew; Frith, Alastair S; Gibbs, Jason D; Jones, Matthew; Jones, Russell; Kostiw, Richard; Lynch, Glen S; Oleinik, Gary J; Richards, Scott; Szymonik, Ben.

Associated Schoolboys who have accepted the club's offer of a Traineeship/Contract
Caswell, James R; Curran, James M; Jenkins, Steven D; Jupp, Peter R; Murphy, Michael J; Simpson, Derek F; Stowell, Mathew D; Wilkinson, Robert H.

**Non-Contract Players who are retained must be re-signed before they are eligible to play in League matches.

ROCHDALE 1992-93 *Back row (left to right):* Phil Stock (Physio), Andy Milner, Jon Bowden, Alan Reeves, Kevin Rose, Paul Butler, Tony Brown, John Ryan, Jimmy Robson (Youth Team Manager).
Centre row: Andy Thackeray, Mark Payne, Andy Flounders, Mick Docherty (Assistant Manager), Dave Sutton (Manager), Steve Whitehall, Jimmy Graham, Shaun Reid.
Front row: Jason Anders, Andy Howard, Carl Parker.

Spotland, Sandy Lane, Rochdale OL11 5DS. Telephone Rochdale (0706) 44648. Fax: 0706 48466

Ground capacity: 5600.

Record attendance: 24,231 v Notts Co, FA Cup 2nd rd, 10 December 1949.

Record receipts: £46,000 v Burnley, Division 4, 5 May 1992.

Pitch measurements: 114yd × 76yd.

President: Mrs L. Stoney.

Chairman: D. F. Kilpatrick. ***Vice-chairman:*** G. Morris.

Directors: G. R. Brierley, T. Butterworth, C. Dunphy, M. Mace, J. Marsh, G. Morris.

Manager: Dave Sutton.

Secretary: Keith Clegg. ***Coach:*** Mick Docherty. ***Commercial Manager:*** S. Walmsley. ***Advertising & Sponsorship Manager:*** L. Duckworth.

Physio: P. Stock. ***Coach:*** J. Lee.

Year Formed: 1907. ***Turned Professional:*** 1907. ***Ltd Co.:*** 1910.

Club Nickname: 'The Dale'.

Record League Victory: 8–1 v Chesterfield, Division 3 (N), 18 December 1926 – Hill; Brown, Ward; Hillhouse, Parkes, Braidwood; Hughes, Bertram, Whitehurst (5), Schofield (2), Martin (1).

Record Cup Victory: 8–2 v Crook T, FA Cup, 1st rd, 26 November 1927 – Moody; Hopkins, Ward; Braidwood, Parkes, Barker; Tompkinson, Clennell (3) Whitehurst (4), Hall, Martin (1).

Record Defeat: 0–8 v Wrexham, Division 3 (N), 28 December 1929, 0–8 v Leyton Orient, Division 4, 20 October 1987, and 1–9 v Tranmere R, Division 3 (N), 25 December 1931.

Most League Points (2 for a win): 62, Division 3 (N), 1923–24.

Most League Points (3 for a win): 67, Division 4, 1991–92.

Most League Goals: 105, Division 3 (N), 1926–27.

Highest League Scorer in Season: Albert Whitehurst, 44, Division 3 (N), 1926–27.

Most League Goals in Total Aggregate: Reg Jenkins, 119, 1964–73.

Most Capped Player: None.

Most League Appearances: Graham Smith, 317, 1966–74.

Record Transfer Fee Received: £200,000 from Bristol C for Keith Welch, July 1991.

Record Transfer Fee Paid: £80,000 to Scunthorpe U for Andy Flounders, August 1991.

Football League Record: 1921 Elected to Division 3 (N); 1958–59 Division 3; 1959–69 Division 4; 1969–74 Division 3; 1974–92 Division 4; 1992– Division 3.

Football League: Division 3 best season: 9th, 1969–70; Division 3 (N) – Runners-up 1923–24, 1926–27. *FA Cup:* best season: 5th rd, 1989–90. *Football League Cup:* Runners-up 1962 (record for 4th Division club).

ROCHDALE 1992—93 LEAGUE RECORD

Match No.	Date		Venue	Opponents	Result		H/T Score	Lg. Pos.	Goalscorers	Atten dance
1	Aug	15	H	Halifax T	L	2-3	0-1	—	Flounders, Milner	2497
2		22	A	Wrexham	L	1-3	0-1	18	Whitehall	2661
3		29	H	Scarborough	W	3-0	3-0	12	Whitehall 2, Thackeray	1585
4	Sept	5	A	Shrewsbury T	W	2-1	1-0	10	Milner, Whitehall	2547
5		15	H	Gillingham	D	1-1	1-0	—	Payne (pen)	1879
6		19	H	Darlington	W	3-1	0-1	9	Whitehall, Reeves, Bowden	1854
7		26	A	Hereford U	D	1-1	0-0	10	Jones	1834
8	Oct	3	A	Cardiff C	D	1-1	1-1	11	Payne (pen)	6161
9		10	H	Carlisle U	D	2-2	1-2	9	Whitehall 2	2543
10		17	A	York C	L	0-3	0-1	15		4161
11		24	A	Walsall	W	4-3	2-1	11	Whitehall, Milner, Payne, Flounders	1834
12		31	A	Chesterfield	W	3-2	1-0	8	Bowden 2, Anders	3094
13	Nov	3	A	Torquay U	W	2-0	1-0	—	Whitehall, Reid	2064
14		7	H	Crewe Alex	L	0-1	0-0	9		3058
15		21	A	Colchester U	D	4-4	2-2	8	Payne (pen), Milner, Flounders 2 (1 pen)	3172
16		28	H	Doncaster R	D	1-1	0-0	10	Flounders (pen)	2094
17	Dec	12	A	Barnet	L	0-2	0-1	10		2778
18		19	H	Lincoln C	W	5-1	2-0	9	Flounders 3, Whitehall, Howard	1793
19		26	H	Scunthorpe U	W	2-0	2-0	5	Whitehall, Flounders	3043
20	Jan	2	A	Doncaster R	D	1-1	0-1	9	Payne	2559
21		8	A	Gillingham	L	2-4	1-1	—	Thackeray, Payne (pen)	3052
22		16	A	Hereford U	L	1-3	1-1	11	Reid	1751
23		23	A	Darlington	W	4-0	3-0	10	Flounders 2, Whitehall 2	1710
24		30	H	Wrexham	L	1-2	1-1	10	Mulrain	4500
25	Feb	6	A	Halifax T	W	3-2	2-2	9	Butler, Reid (pen), Mulrain	1906
26		13	A	Shrewsbury T	W	2-0	1-0	9	Reeves 2	2446
27		20	A	Scarborough	D	1-1	1-1	9	Page	1765
28		27	A	Carlisle U	L	0-3	0-1	11		3021
29	Mar	6	A	Cardiff C	L	1-2	0-1	12	Bowden	2831
30		9	H	Northampton T	L	0-3	0-3	—		1446
31		12	A	Crewe Alex	D	1-1	0-0	—	Thackeray	3515
32		16	A	Bury	D	2-2	0-0	—	Thackeray 2	3315
33		20	H	Torquay U	W	1-0	1-0	12	Saunders (og)	1594
34		27	H	Colchester U	W	5-2	2-2	11	Jones, Howard, Whitehall, Thackeray, Bowden	1783
35	Apr	2	A	Northampton T	L	0-1	0-0	—		2965
36		6	H	Barnet	L	0-1	0-0	—		1661
37		10	A	Scunthorpe U	L	1-5	0-3	13	Reid	2926
38		13	H	Bury	L	1-2	0-0	—	Flounders	2905
39		17	A	Lincoln C	W	2-1	0-1	12	Bowden 2	2922
40		24	H	York C	W	1-0	0-0	12	Bowden	3920
41	May	1	A	Walsall	L	1-3	1-2	12	Flounders	4118
42		8	H	Chesterfield	W	2-1	0-0	11	Flounders, Butler	1544

Final League Position: 11

GOALSCORERS

League (70): Flounders 14 (2 pens), Whitehall 14, Bowden 8, Payne 6 (4 pens), Thackeray 6, Milner 4, Reid 4 (1 pen), Reeves 3, Butler 2, Howard 2, Jones 2, Mulrain 2, Anders 1, Page 1, own goal 1.
Coca Cola Cup (2): Reeves 1, Ryan 1.
FA Cup (2): Reid 1, Whitehall 1.

Rose 40	Thackeray 41	Graham 37 + 1	Reid 40	Brown 4 + 1	Bowden 31 + 4	Ryan 25 + 1	Payne 26 + 2	Flounders 31 + 1	Whitehall 41 + 1	Milner 17 + 1	Reeves 40 + 1	Ashurst 1	Parker 4 + 6	Howard 4 + 11	Jones 28 + 1	Anders 2 + 13	Butler 14 + 2	Beever — + 1	Mulrain 3 + 3	Doyle 18	Clarke 2	Snowden 8 + 5	Page 3 + 1	Luke 2 + 1	Match No.
1	2	3	4	5	6	7	8	9	10	11	12														1
1	2	3	8	4	11	7	6	9	12	14	5	10													2
1	2	3	4		6	7	8	9	*10*	11	5		12	14											3
1	2	3	4		9	7	8		10	11	5			12	6										4
1	2	3	4		9	7	8		10	11	5				6										5
1	2	3	4		9	7	8	12	10	11	5				6										6
1	2	3	4			7	8	*9*	10	11	5			12	6	14									7
1	2	3	4		*9*	7	8		10	11	5			12	6	14									8
1	2	3	4	12		7	8	*9*	10	11	5					14	6								9
1	2	3	4	6	12	7	8	9	10	*11*	5					14									10
1	2	3	4			7	8	9	10	11	5				6										11
1	2	3	4			7	8	9	10	11	5			12	6										12
1	2	3	*4*		7	6	8	9	10	11	5		14	12											13
1	2	3	4		7	6	8	9	10	11	5			12											14
1	2	3	4		7	6	*8*	9	10	11	5		14	12											15
1	2	3	4			7	6	8	9	*10*	5			11	12	14									16
1	2		4		11	7	8	9	10		5			3	6				12						17
1	2		4		7	3	8	9	11	10	5			14	12	6									18
1	2		4		7	3	8	9	11	10	5			12	6										19
1	2	12	4		7	3	8	9	11	10	5				6										20
1	2	11	4		7	3	8	*9*	10		5			14	12	6									21
1	2		4		11	7	8	9	10		5			3	12	6									22
1	2	11	4			7	8	9	10		5			3	6				12						23
1	*2*	11	4			7	8	9	10		5			3	6	14			12						24
1		3	4		9	7			10		5				6	2				11	8				25
	2	3	4		12	7		9	10		5				6					8	11	1	14		26
	2	3	4		12	7			10		5				6					8	11	1	14	*9*	27
1	2	3	4		8	7			10		5				6						11	12	9		28
1	2	3	4			7	*8*		10		5				6	12					11	14	9		29
1	2	3	4		9				10		5				6	7				8		11	12		30
1	2	3	4			7			10		5				6	12	9			8		11			31
1	2	3	4			7			10		5				6	11	9			8					32
1	2	3	4			7		9	10		5				6					8		11			33
1	2	3		*12*				9	10		5			7	6	14	4			11			8		34
1	2	3	4		12			9	10		5			*7*	6	14	8			11					35
1	2	3	4					9	10		5			12			8			11		7	6		36
1	2	3	4					9	10		5			12	6		*8*			11		7	14		37
1	2	3	4	8	12			9	10		5				6					11		7			38
1	2	3		8	*4*			9	10		5			14	6	12				11		7			39
1	2	3	4	8	14			9	10		5			12	6					11		7			40
1	2	3	4	8				9	10		5			12	6					11		7			41
1	2	3	4	8				9	10	7	5				6					11		12			42

Coca Cola Cup	First Round	Crewe Alex (a)	1-4
		(h)	1-2
FA Cup	First Round	Blackpool (a)	1-1
		(h)	1-0
	Second Round	Bolton W (a)	0-4

ROCHDALE

Player and Position	Ht	Wt	Date	Birth Place	Source	Clubs	League App	Gls
Goalkeepers								
Kevin Rose*	6 1	13 03	23 11 60	Evesham	Ledbury T	Lincoln C	—	—
					Ledbury T	Hereford U	268	—
						Bolton W	10	—
						Halifax T (loan)	—	—
						Carlisle U (loan)	11	—
						Rochdale (loan)	3	—
						Rochdale (loan)	28	—
						Rochdale	40	—
Defenders								
Jack Ashurst‡	6 0	12 04	12 10 54	Coatbridge	Apprentice	Sunderland	140	4
						Blackpool	53	3
						Carlisle U	194	2
						Leeds U	89	1
						Doncaster R	73	1
					Bridlington	Doncaster R	66	1
						Rochdale	1	—
Tony Brown*	6 2	12 07	17 9 58	Bradford	Thackley	Leeds U	24	1
						Doncaster R (loan)	14	—
						Doncaster R	73	2
						Scunthorpe U	54	2
						Rochdale	114	—
Paul Butler	6 2	13 00	2 11 72	Bradford	Trainee	Rochdale	43	2
Jimmy Graham	5 11	11 00	15 11 69	Glasgow	Trainee	Bradford C	7	—
						Rochdale (loan)	11	—
						Rochdale	97	1
Alex Jones	6 2	12 08	27 11 64	Blackburn	Apprentice	Oldham Ath	9	—
						Stockport Co (loan)	3	—
						Preston NE	101	3
						Carlisle U	62	4
						Rochdale	13	—
						Motherwell	12	1
						Rochdale	29	2
Alan Reeves	6 0	12 00	19 11 67	Birkenhead		Norwich C	—	—
						Gillingham (loan)	18	—
						Chester C	40	2
						Rochdale	75	6
John Ryan	5 10	11 07	18 2 62	Ashton	Apprentice	Oldham Ath	77	8
						Newcastle U	28	1
						Sheffield W	8	1
						Oldham Ath	23	—
						Mansfield T	62	1
						Chesterfield	82	6
						Rochdale	58	2
Jason Smart+	6 0	12 10	15 2 69	Rochdale	Trainee	Rochdale	117	4
						Crewe Alex	89	2
						Rochdale	—	—
Midfield								
Jon Bowden	6 10	11 07	21 1 63	Stockport	Local	Oldham Ath	82	5
						Port Vale	70	7
						Wrexham	147	20
						Rochdale	66	14
Steve Doyle	5 9	11 01	2 6 58	Neath	Apprentice	Preston NE	197	8
						Huddersfield T	161	6
						Sunderland	100	2
						Hull C	47	2
						Rochdale	76	—
Andy Howard	5 6	10 02	15 3 72	Southport	Liverpool	Blackpool	—	—
					Fleetwood	Rochdale	15	2

ROCHDALE

Colours: Blue/white trim. **Change colours:** Yellow and black.

Foundation: Considering the love of rugby in their area, it is not surprising that Rochdale had difficulty in establishing an Association Football club. The earlier Rochdale Town club formed in 1900 went out of existence in 1907 when the present club was immediately established and joined the Manchester League, before graduating to the Lancashire Combination in 1908.

First Football League game: 27 August, 1921, Division 3(N), v Accrington Stanley (h) W 6-3 – Crabtree; Nuttall, Sheehan; Hill, Farrer, Yarwood; Hoad, Sandiford, Dennison (2), Owens (3), Carney (1).

Did you know: Rochdale centre-forward Tom Tippett scored six goals in a Division 3 (N) game at Hartlepools on Easter Monday 1930. He was a native of Newcastle.

Managers (and Secretary-Managers)

Billy Bradshaw 1920, (run by committee 1920–22), Tom Wilson 1922–23, Jack Peart 1923–30, Will Cameron 1930–31, Herbert Hopkinson 1932–34, Billy Smith 1934–35, Ernest Nixon 1935–37, Sam Jennings 1937–38, Ted Goodier 1938–52, Jack Warner 1952–53, Harry Catterick 1953–58, Jack Marshall 1958–60, Tony Collins 1960–68, Bob Stokoe 1967–68, Len Richley 1968–70, Dick Conner 1970–73, Walter Joyce 1973–76, Brian Green 1976–77, Mike Ferguson 1977–78, Doug Collins 1979, Bob Stokoe 1979–80, Peter Madden 1980–83, Jimmy Greenhoff 1983–84, Vic Halom 1984–86, Eddie Gray 1986–88, Danny Bergara 1988–89, Terry Dolan 1989–91, Dave Sutton February 1991–.

Player and Position	Ht	Wt	Birth Date	Birth Place	Source	Clubs	League App	Gls
Noel Luke‡	5 11	10 11	28 12 64	Birmingham	School	WBA	9	1
						Mansfield T	50	9
						Peterborough U	277	27
						Rochdale	3	—
Carl Parker*	6 0	12 00	25 3 71	Burnley	Rossendale United	Rochdale	16	1
Mark Payne*	5 9	11 09	3 8 60	Cheltenham	Cambuur	Stockport Co	87	16
						Rochdale	62	8
Shaun Reid	5 8	11 10	13 10 65	Huyton	Local	Rochdale	133	4
						Preston NE (loan)	3	—
						York C	106	7
						Rochdale	40	4
Trevor Snowden	5 8	11 00	4 10 73	Sunderland	Seaham Red Star	Rochdale	13	—
Andy Thackeray	5 9	11 00	13 2 68	Huddersfield		Manchester C	—	—
						Huddersfield T	2	—
						Newport Co	54	4
						Wrexham	152	14
						Rochdale	41	6
Forwards								
Jason Anders	5 10	10 06	13 3 74	Rochdale	Trainee	Rochdale	17	1
Anthony Beever§	6 0	12 05	18 9 74	Huddersfield	Trainee	Rochdale	1	—
Andy Flounders	5 11	11 06	13 12 63	Hull	Apprentice	Hull C	159	54
						Scunthorpe U	196	87
						Rochdale	74	31
						Rotherham U (loan)	6	2
Andy Milner	5 11	11 07	10 2 67	Kendal	Netherfield	Manchester C	—	—
						Rochdale	102	23
Steve Mulrain	5 10	11 07	23 10 72	Lambeth	Trainee	Leeds U	—	—
						Rochdale	6	2
Steve Whitehall	5 9	10 11	8 12 66	Bromborough	Southport	Rochdale	76	22

Trainees
Beever, Anthony M; Brown, Richard A; Clayton, Michael; Crowe, Asa A; Emmett, Martin; Fishwick, Alexander J; McCartney, William; McCormick, Matthew P; Murray, William A; Walsh, Lee; Wilkinson, Adam.

**Non-Contract
Nixon, Craig G; Smart, Jason.

Associated Schoolboys
Chadwick, Gavin R. D; Ross, Jason; Swettenham, Andrew B; Taylor, Jamie L.

**Non-Contract Players who are retained must be re-signed before they are eligible to play in League matches.

434

ROTHERHAM UNITED 1992–93 *Back row (left to right):* Michael Ridenton, Tony Cunningham, Neil Richardson, Nicky Law, Billy Mercer, Matthew Clarke, Nigel Johnson, Jason Rockett, Shaun Goater, Leonard Curtis.

Centre row: Billy Russell (Youth Team Coach), Des Hazel, Jonathan Howard, Ian Banks, John Breckin (Assistant Manager), Ally Pickering , Steven Gleeson, Don Page, Ian Bailey (Physio).

Front row: Andy Taylor, Mark Todd, Chris Hutchings, Phil Henson (Manager), Shaun Goodwin, Dean Barrick, Ian Hathaway.

Division 2   **ROTHERHAM UNITED**

Millmoor Ground, Rotherham. Telephone Rotherham (0709) 562434. Fax (0709) 563336.

Ground Capacity: 13,037.

Record attendance: 25,000 v Sheffield U, Division 2, 13 December 1952 and v Sheffield W, Division 2, 26 January 1952.

Record receipts: £79,155 v Newcastle U, FA Cup 4th rd, 23 January 1993.

Pitch measurements. 115yd × 75yd.

President: Sir J. Layden.

Chairman: K. F. Booth.

Directors: R. Hull (Vice-chairman), C. A. Luckock, J. A. Webb.

Manager: Phil Henson. *Asst. Manager:* John Breckin. *Physio:* Ian Bailey.

Secretary: N. Darnill.

Commercial Manager: D. Nicholls.

Year Formed: 1884. *Turned Professional:* 1905. *Ltd Co.:* 1920.

Club Nickname: 'The Merry Millers'.

Previous Names: 1884, Thornhill United; 1905, Rotherham County; 1925, amalgamated with Rotherham Town under Rotherham United.

Previous Ground: Red House Ground; 1907, Millmoor.

Record League Victory: 8–0 v Oldham Ath, Division 3 (N), 26 May 1947 – Warnes; Selkirk, Ibbotson; Edwards, Horace Williams, Danny Williams; Wilson (2), Shaw (1), Ardron (3), Guest (1), Hainsworth (1).

Record Cup Victory: 6–0 v Spennymoor U, FA Cup, 2nd rd, 17 December 1977 – McAlister; Forrest, Breckin, Womble, Stancliffe, Green, Finney, Phillips (3), Gwyther (2) (Smith), Goodfellow, Crawford (1). 6–0 v Wolverhampton W, FA Cup, 1st rd, 16 November 1985 – O'Hanlon; Forrest, Dungworth, Gooding (1), Smith (1), Pickering, Birch (2), Emerson, Tynan (1), Simmons (1), Pugh.

Record Defeat: 1–11 v Bradford C, Division 3 (N), 25 August 1928.

Most League Points (2 for a win): 71, Division 3 (N), 1950–51.

Most League Points (3 for a win): 82, Division 4, 1988–89.

Most League Goals: 114, Division 3 (N), 1946–47.

Highest League Scorer in Season: Wally Ardron, 38, Division 3 (N), 1946–47.

Most League Goals in Total Aggregate: Gladstone Guest, 130, 1946–56.

Most Capped Player: Harold Millership, 6, Wales.

Most League Appearances: Danny Williams, 459, 1946–62.

Record Transfer Fee Received: £200,000 from Bristol C for Martin Scott, December 1990.

Record Transfer Fee Paid: £100,000 to Cardiff C for Ronnie Moore, August 1980.

Football League Record: 1893 Rotherham Town elected to Division 2; 1896 Failed re-election; 1919 Rotherham County elected to Division 2; 1923–51 Division 3 (N); 1951–68 Division 2; 1968–73 Division 3; 1973–75 Division 4; 1975–81 Division 3; 1981–83 Division 2; 1983–88 Division 3; 1988–89 Division 4; 1989–91 Division 3; 1991–92 Division 4; 1992– Division 2.

Honours: Football League: Division 2 best season: 3rd, 1954–55 (equal points with champions and runners-up); Division 3 – Champions 1980–81; Division 3 (N) – Champions 1950–51; Runners-up 1946–47, 1947–48, 1948–49; Division 4 – Champions 1988–89; Runners-up 1991–92. *FA Cup:* best season: 5th rd, 1953, 1968. *Football League Cup:* Runners-up 1961.

ROTHERHAM UNITED 1992—93 LEAGUE RECORD

Match No.	Date	Venue	Opponents	Result	H/T Score	Lg. Pos.	Goalscorers	Atten dance
1	Aug 15	A	Exeter C	W 2-0	0-0	—	Goater, Cunningham	3362
2	22	H	Hartlepool U	D 0-0	0-0	6		4355
3	29	A	Burnley	D 1-1	0-0	8	Cunningham	9684
4	Sept 1	A	Port Vale	L 2-4	1-3	—	Goodwin, Todd	5370
5	5	H	Wigan Ath	L 2-3	1-1	13	Todd (pen), Goater	3806
6	12	H	Bolton W	W 2-1	1-0	12	Goater 2	5227
7	16	A	Reading	L 1-3	0-0	—	Goater	2481
8	19	A	Hull C	W 1-0	0-0	10	Barrick	4780
9	26	H	Blackpool	W 3-2	1-1	9	Cunningham, Hazel, Banks	4408
10	Oct 3	H	Huddersfield T	W 1-0	0-0	7	Goater	5459
11	10	A	Bournemouth	D 0-0	0-0	7		4761
12	17	H	Brighton & HA	W 1-0	1-0	6	Cunningham	4404
13	24	A	WBA	D 2-2	2-2	7	Todd 2 (1 pen)	13,170
14	31	H	Mansfield T	W 2-0	1-0	6	Currie, Banks	5030
15	Nov 3	A	Chester C	D 3-3	2-2	—	Barrick 2, Hazel	4188
16	7	A	Plymouth Arg	L 1-2	0-1	8	Currie	6519
17	21	H	Preston NE	W 1-0	0-0	6	Pickering	4246
18	28	A	Bradford C	W 3-0	2-0	3	Hazel, Barrick, Banks	9004
19	Dec 12	H	Fulham	W 1-0	1-0	2	Johnson	3629
20	18	H	Swansea C	D 0-0	0-0	—		4600
21	28	A	Stoke C	L 0-2	0-1	5		21,714
22	Jan 9	H	Reading	W 3-2	3-0	4	Howard, Cunningham 2 (1 pen)	4492
23	16	A	Blackpool	L 0-2	0-0	5		6144
24	26	H	Burnley	L 0-1	0-0	—		4989
25	30	A	Hartlepool U	W 2-0	1-0	5	Johnson, Wilder	3992
26	Feb 6	H	Exeter C	D 1-1	1-0	6	Goater	4210
27	9	H	Hull C	L 0-1	0-1	—		3660
28	13	A	Wigan Ath	D 1-1	0-1	6	Page	1902
29	20	H	Port Vale	W 4-1	3-1	6	Wilder (pen), Flounders 2, Howard	5545
30	26	H	Bournemouth	L 1-2	0-0	—	Wilder (pen)	4401
31	Mar 2	H	Stockport Co	L 0-2	0-2	—		4280
32	6	A	Huddersfield T	D 1-1	0-0	8	Varadi	5235
33	9	A	Leyton Orient	D 1-1	0-1	—	Hazel	4401
34	13	H	Plymouth Arg	D 2-2	1-1	9	Morrison (og), Wilder (pen)	4276
35	19	A	Chester C	W 2-1	0-0	—	Varadi, Wilder	2265
36	23	H	Bradford C	W 2-0	1-0	—	Varadi 2 (1 pen)	4447
37	27	A	Preston NE	L 2-5	0-2	8	Banks, Wilder	4859
38	30	A	Bolton W	L 0-2	0-1	—		7985
39	Apr 3	H	Leyton Orient	D 1-1	0-0	8	Hazel	3083
40	6	H	Fulham	D 1-1	0-1	—	Page	3065
41	9	A	Stockport Co	D 2-2	2-2	—	Banks, Law	5440
42	12	H	Stoke C	L 0-2	0-1	10		9021
43	17	A	Swansea C	L 0-2	0-0	11		4658
44	24	A	Brighton & HA	W 2-1	0-0	11	Wilder (pen), Hazel	7841
45	May 1	H	WBA	L 0-2	0-0	12		8059
46	8	A	Mansfield T	W 3-1	1-0	11	Law, Hazel, Wilder (pen)	3833

Final League Position: 11

GOALSCORERS

League (60): Wilder 8 (5 pens), Goater 7, Hazel 7, Cunningham 6 (1 pen), Banks 5, Barrick 4, Todd 4 (2 pens), Varadi 4 (1 pen) Currie 2, Flounders 2, Howard 2, Johnson 2, Law 2, Page 2, Goodwin 1, Pickering 1, own goals 1.
Coca Cola Cup (4): Todd 2 (1 pen), Banks 1, Goater 1.
FA Cup (7): Cunningham 2, Goodwin 2, Howard 2, Johnson 1.

Mercer 36	Wilder 31 + 1	Hutchings 30	Banks 45	Johnson 31	Law 44	Goodwin 28 + 2	Todd 16	Cunningham 31 + 2	Goater 20 + 3	Barrick 45 + 1	Page 11 + 13	Hazel 31 + 5	Taylor 6 + 1	Pickering 38	Richardson 8 + 6	Currie 5	Kite 1	Howard 12 + 5	Campbell — + 1	Clarke 9	Flounders 6	Buckley 2 + 2	Gridelet 9	Varadi 11	Marginson — + 1	Match No.
1	2	3	4	5	6	7	8	9	10	11	12															1
1	2	3	4	5	6	7	8	9	10	11	12	14														2
1	2		4	5	6	7	8	9	10	11			3													3
1	2		4	5	6	7	8	9	10	11	12		3													4
1	2	3	4	5	6	7	8	9	10	11	12															5
1	2	3	4	5	6		8	9	10	11			7													6
1	2	3	4	5	6		8	9	10	11			7													7
1	2	3	4	5	6		8	9	10	11	12		7													8
1		3	4	5	6		8	9	10	11	12		7	2	14											9
1		3	4	5	6		8	9	10	11	12		7	2												10
1		3	4	5	6		8	9	10	11	12		7	2												11
1		3	4	5	6		8	9		11	12		7	2				10								12
		3	4	5	6	12	8	9		11			7	2			1	10								13
1		3	4	5	6		8	9		11			7	2				10								14
1		3	4	5	6	12	8	9		11			7	2	14			10								15
1		3	4	5	6		8	9		11			7	2	12			10								16
1		3	4	5	6	8		9		11			7	2				10								17
1		3	4	5	6	8		9		11			7	2				10	12							18
1		3	4	5	6	8		9		11	12		7	2	14			10								19
1		3	4	5	6	8		9	12	11			7	2				10								20
1		3	4	5	6	8		9	12	11			7	2				10								21
1		3	4	5	6	8		9	7	11				2				10								22
1	12	3	4	5	6	8		9	7	11				2				10								23
1	7	3	4	5	6	8		9	10	11	12			2												24
1	7	3	4	5	6	8			10	11				2							9					25
	7	3	4	5	6	8		12	10	11				2						1	9					26
	7	3	4	5		8			10	11	12	14		2	6					1	9					27
	7	3	4	5	6	8			10	11	9		12	2						1						28
1	7	3	4	5	6	8			10	11				2				12			9					29
1	7	3	4	5	6	8				11			14	2				10			9	12				30
1	7		4	5		8				11		14	3	2	6			10			9	12				31
		3	4	5		8					12		7	2						1	9	11	6	10		32
		3	4	5		8				11			7	2				12		1	9		6	10		33
		3	4	5						11			7	2	14			12		1	9	8	6	10		34
		3	4	5		8		9		11			7	2						1			6	10		35
		3	4	5		8		9		11			7	2						1			6	10		36
		3	4	5		8		9	10	11			7	2				12		1			6			37
1		3	4	5		8		9	10	11			7	2	14			12					6			38
1		3	4	5		8		9	12	11			7	2	6									10		39
1		3	4	5		8		9		11			7	2	6									10		40
1		3	4	5		8		9		11	12		7	2	6									10		41
1			4	5		8		9		11	12	3	7	2	6									10		42
1			4	5		8		9	10	11		3	7	2	6										12	43
1		3	4	5		8		9	10	11			7	2	6											44
1		3	4	5				9	10	11	12		7	2	6								8			45
1		3	4	5		8		9		11			7	2	6									10		46

Coca Cola Cup	First Round	Hull C (a)	2-2
		(h)	1-0
	Second Round	Everton (h)	1-0
		(a)	0-3
FA Cup	First Round	Walsall (h)	4-0
	Second Round	Hull C (h)	1-0
	Third Round	Northampton T (a)	1-0
	Fourth Round	Newcastle U (h)	1-1
		(a)	0-2

ROTHERHAM UNITED

Player and Position	Ht	Wt	Date	Birth Place	Source	Clubs	League App	Gls
Goalkeepers								
Matthew Clarke	6 3	11 07	3 11 73	Sheffield	Trainee	Rotherham U	9	—
William Mercer	6 1	13 05	22 5 69	Liverpool	Trainee	Liverpool	—	—
						Rotherham U	86	—
Defenders								
Len Curtis	5 11	13 00	2 1 73	Dublin	Leeds U	Rotherham U	—	—
Chris Hutchings	5 10	11 06	5 7 57	Winchester	Harrow Bor	Chelsea	87	3
						Brighton	153	4
						Huddersfield T	110	10
						Walsall	40	—
						Rotherham U	71	4
Nigel Johnson	6 2	13 13	23 6 64	Rotherham	Apprentice	Rotherham U	89	1
						Nottingham F (loan)	—	—
						Manchester C	4	—
						Rotherham U	175	9
Nicky Law	6 1	12 07	8 9 61	London	Apprentice	Arsenal	—	—
						Barnsley	114	1
						Blackpool	66	1
						Plymouth Arg	38	5
						Notts Co	47	4
						Scarborough (loan)	12	—
						Rotherham U	118	4
Ally Pickering	5 11	11 01	22 6 67	Manchester	Buxton	Rotherham U	76	1
Neil Richardson	5 11	13 02	3 3 68	Sunderland	Brandon U	Rotherham U	50	4
Michael Ridenton‡	6 0	11 11	23 8 68	New Zealand	Mount Wellington	Rotherham U	—	—
Billy Russell	5 10	11 03	14 9 59	Glasgow	Apprentice Celtic	Everton	—	—
						Doncaster R	244	15
						Scunthorpe U	117	7
						Rotherham U	104	2
Andy Taylor*	5 8	10 13	19 1 73	Rawmarsh	Trainee	Rotherham U	18	—
Chris Wilder	5 11	11 02	23 9 67	Wortley	Apprentice	Southampton	—	—
						Sheffield U	93	1
						Walsall (loan)	4	—
						Charlton Ath (loan)	1	—
						Charlton Ath (loan)	2	—
						Leyton Orient (loan)	16	1
						Rotherham U	32	8
Midfield								
Ian Banks	5 10	13 07	9 1 61	Mexborough	Apprentice	Barnsley	164	37
						Leicester C	93	14
						Huddersfield T	78	17
						Bradford C	30	3
						WBA	4	—
						Barnsley	96	7
						Rotherham U	45	5
Dean Barrick	5 8	11 07	30 9 69	Hemsworth	Trainee	Sheffield W	11	2
						Rotherham U	99	7
Steven Gleeson*	5 8	10 05	18 10 73	Manchester	Trainee	Rotherham U	—	—
Shaun Goodwin	5 8	10 11	14 6 69	Rotherham	Trainee	Rotherham U	185	19
Desmond Hazel	5 11	10 13	15 7 67	Bradford	Apprentice	Sheffield W	6	—
						Grimsby T (loan)	9	2
						Rotherham U	188	26
Karl Marginson	6 0	11 00	11 11 70	Manchester		Rotherham U	1	—
Jason Rockett*	5 11	12 00	26 9 69	London		Rotherham U	—	—
Mark Todd	5 8	10 04	4 12 67	Belfast	Trainee	Manchester U	—	—
						Sheffield U	70	5
						Wolverhampton W (loan)	7	—
						Rotherham U	39	6
Forwards								
John Buckley	5 9	11 00	10 5 62	Glasgow	Celtic	Partick T	45	5
						Doncaster R	84	11
						Leeds U	10	1
						Leicester C (loan)	5	—

ROTHERHAM UNITED

Colours: Red shirts, white shorts, red stockings. **Change colours:** White shirts with black collar, black shorts with red and white trim, black stockings with red and white tops.

Foundation: This club traces its history back to the formation of Thornhill United in 1878 (reformed 1884). They changed their name to Rotherham County in 1905. Confusion exists because of the existence of the Rotherham Town club (founded c. 1885) and in the Football League as early as 1893 but this club was not the one previously mentioned. The Town amalgamated with Rotherham County to form Rotherham United in 1925.

First Football League game: 2 September, 1893, Division 2, Rotherham T v Lincoln C (a) D 1-1 – McKay; Thickett, Watson; Barr, Brown, Broadhead; Longden, Cutts, Leatherbarrow, McCormick, Pickering. 1 o.g. 30 August, 1919, Division 2, Rotherham C v Nottingham F (h) W 2-0 – Branston; Alton, Baines; Bailey, Coe, Stanton; Lee (1), Cawley (1), Glennon, Lees, Lamb.

Did you know: Herbert John Emery, a Welshman, saved nine out of ten penalties he faced keeping goal for Rotherham United's first and second teams in 1929–30.

Managers (and Secretary-Managers)
Billy Heald 1925–29 (secretary only for long spell), Stanley Davies 1929–30, Billy Heald 1930–33, Reg Freeman 1934–52, Andy Smailes 1952–58, Tom Johnston 1958–62, Danny Williams 1962–65, Jack Mansell 1965–67, Tommy Docherty 1967–68, Jimmy McAnearney 1968–73, Jimmy McGuigan 1973–79, Ian Porterfield 1979–81, Emlyn Hughes 1981–83, George Kerr 1983–85, Norman Hunter 1985–87, Dave Cusack 1987–88, Billy McEwan 1988–91, Phil Henson January 1991–.

Player and Position	Ht	Wt	Birth Date	Birth Place	Source	Clubs	League App	Gls
						Doncaster R (loan)	6	—
						Rotherham U	105	13
						Partick Th	26	5
						Scunthorpe U	43	8
						Rotherham U	4	—
Tony Cunningham*	6 1	13 13	12 11 57	Jamaica	Stourbridge	Lincoln C	123	32
						Barnsley	42	11
						Sheffield W	28	5
						Manchester C	18	1
						Newcastle U	47	4
						Blackpool	71	17
						Bury	58	17
						Bolton W	9	4
						Rotherham U	69	24
Shaun Goater	6 1	12 00	25 2 70	Bermuda		Manchester C	—	—
						Rotherham U	81	20
Ian Hathaway*	5 6	11 04	22 8 68	Worsley	Bedworth U	Mansfield T	44	2
						Rotherham U	13	1
Jonathan Howard	6 0	12 02	7 10 71	Sheffield	Trainee	Rotherham U	28	5
Don Page	5 10	11 03	18 1 64	Manchester	Runcorn	Wigan Ath	74	15
						Rotherham U	55	13
						Rochdale (loan)	4	1
Imre Varadi	5 10	12 00	8 7 59	Paddington	Letchworth GC	Sheffield U	10	4
						Everton	26	6
						Newcastle U	81	39
						Sheffield W	76	33
						WBA	32	9
						Manchester C	65	26
						Sheffield W	22	3
						Leeds U	26	5
						Luton T (loan)	6	1
						Oxford U (loan)	5	—
						Rotherham U	11	4

Trainees
Barnard, Mark; Bennett, Paul S; Breckin, Ian; Bunting, James R. S; Dolby, Christopher J; Green, Paul W; Handbury, Lee A; Heaton, Simon; Hilton, Christopher; Hinshelwood, Shane; Hoe, Michael J; Hurst, Paul M; Jarvis, Steven M; Smith, Scott D; Varney, Paul; Wood, Marcus.

**Non-Contract
Ingham, Gary.

Associated Schoolboys
Ashcroft, Richard G; Davis, Ashley R; Davis, Craig; Duffy, Stewart; Egan, Jonathan C; Evans, Darren; Flynn, Richard; Garlick, Richard P; Hempsey, Scott A; Heppenstall, Michael; Hopson, Gavin J; Hunte, Anthony S; Jenkinson, Matthew; King, Matthew A; Melbourne, Andrew M; Melvin, Michael B; Nixon, Dean M; Parkin, Philip D; Partridge, Paul G; Piletto, Simon D; Portman, Robert D; Riley, Matthew M; Roberts, Martin J; Roberts, Trevor F; Thornton, Jamie D.

Associated Schoolboys who have accepted the club's offer of a Traineeship/Contract
Ayrton, Matthew R; Colley, Chad; Duffty, Cary H; Haran, Mark P; Hogg, Stuart S; Thomas, Steven M; Wake, Ryan; Wilkinson, Damian D.

**Non-Contract Players who are retained must be re-signed before they are eligible to play in League matches.

SCARBOROUGH 1992–93   *Back row (left to right):* Ian Kerr (Football in the Community), Aidan Murphy, Andrew Mockler, Roger McKenzie, Lee Hirst, Mark Evans, Stuart Ford, Chris Curran, Kyle Lightbourne, Brendan Ormsby, Darren Edmonds, Lee Barrow.
Centre row: Gary Himsworth, Chris Lee, Darren Foreman, Phil Chambers (Coach), Ray McHale (Manager), Tommy Mooney, Simon Thompson, Owen McGee, John Ashdjian.
Front row: Mark Jules, Paul Mudd.

Division 3   SCARBOROUGH

The McCain Stadium, Seamer Road, Scarborough YO12 4HF. Telephone (0723) 375094. Fax (0723) 378733.

Ground capacity: 7176.

Record Attendance: 11,130 v Luton T, FA Cup 3rd rd, 8 January 1938. Football League: 7314 v Wolverhampton W, Division 4, 15 August 1987.

Record receipts: £37,609.50 v Arsenal, Coca Cola Cup 4th rd, 6 January 1993.

Pitch measurements: 120yd × 75yd.

President and Chief Executive: John Birley.

Chairman: G. Richmond.

Directors: J. W. Fawcett, B. Connolly, M. Bramham.

Manager: Phil Chambers. *Assistant Manager:*

Administrator: Miss H. Crinnion. *Secretary:* Shaun Harvey.

Assistant Secretary: Miss S. B. Wright.

Commercial Manager: Shirley Nettleton. *Physio:* K. Warner.

Year Formed: 1879. *Turned Professional:* 1926. *Ltd Co.:* 1933.

Club Nickname: 'The Boro'.

Previous Grounds: 1879–87, Scarborough Cricket Ground; 1887–98, Recreation Ground; 1898– Athletic Ground.

Record League Victory: 4–0 v Bolton W, Division 4, 29 August 1987 – Blackwell; McJannet, Thompson, Bennyworth (Walker), Richards (1) (Cook), Kendall, Hamill (1), Moss, McHale, Mell (1), Graham. (1 og). 4–0 v Newport Co (away), Division 4, 12 April 1988 – Ironside; McJannet, Thompson, Kamara, Richards (1), Short (1), Adams (Cook 1), Brook, Outhart (1), Russell, Graham.

Record Cup Victory: 6–0 v Rhyl Ath, FA Cup, 1st rd, 29 November 1930 – Turner; Severn, Belton; Maskell, Robinson, Wallis; Small (1), Rand (2), Palfreman (2), A. D. Hill (1), Mickman.

Record Defeat: 1–16 v Southbank, Northern League, 15 November 1919.

Most League Points (3 for a win): 77, Division 4, 1988–89.

Most League Goals: 69, Division 4, 1990–91.

Highest League Scorer in Season: Darren Foreman, 27, Division 4, 1992–93.

Most League Goals in Total Aggregate: Darren Foreman, 34, 1991–93.

Most Capped Player: None.

Most League Appearances: Steve Richards, 119, 1987–90.

Record Transfer Fee Received: £240,000 from Notts Co for Chris Short, September 1990.

Record Transfer Fee Paid: £102,000 to Leicester C for Martin Russell, March 1989.

Football League Record: Promoted to Division 4 1987; 1992– Division 3.

Honours: Football League: Division 4 best season: 5th, 1988–89. *FA Cup:* best seasons: 3rd rd, 1931, 1938, 1976, 1978. *Football League Cup:* best season: 4th rd 1993. *FA Trophy:* Winners 1973, 1976, 1977. *GM Vauxhall Conference:* Winners 1987.

SCARBOROUGH 1992—93 LEAGUE RECORD

Match No.	Date	Venue	Opponents	Result	H/T Score	Lg. Pos.	Goalscorers	Attendance
1	Aug 15	A	Hereford U	D 1-1	1-1	—	Foreman	1836
2	22	H	Crewe Alex	W 1-0	0-0	7	Ashdjian	1829
3	29	A	Rochdale	L 0-3	0-3	11		1585
4	Sept 5	H	Gillingham	D 1-1	1-0	16	Hirst	1412
5	12	H	Torquay U	W 1-0	0-0	8	Foreman (pen)	1300
6	15	A	Shrewsbury T	L 0-2	0-1	—		1527
7	19	A	Halifax T	W 4-3	3-1	8	Lee, Jules, Foreman 2	1230
8	26	H	Doncaster R	D 1-1	1-1	9	Ashdjian	1859
9	Oct 3	A	Bury	W 2-0	1-0	7	Jules, Foreman	2048
10	10	H	Northampton T	W 4-2	0-1	5	Foreman 3, Mudd	1539
11	17	A	Darlington	W 3-2	1-1	3	Foreman, Ashdjian, Jules	2474
12	24	H	Chesterfield	D 2-2	0-1	5	Foreman, Hirst	1797
13	31	A	Carlisle U	D 2-2	1-0	4	Foreman, Ashdjian	3150
14	Nov 3	H	Lincoln C	L 0-1	0-0	—		2084
15	7	A	Walsall	L 1-2	0-1	8	Wheeler, Foreman	3001
16	28	H	Scunthorpe U	W 2-1	0-1	6	Jules, Foreman	2807
17	Dec 12	A	Wrexham	L 1-4	0-1	8	Foreman	2238
18	19	H	York C	W 4-2	3-0	6	Foreman 3, Mooney	3892
19	29	A	Colchester U	L 0-1	0-1	—		3640
20	Jan 2	A	Torquay U	W 3-1	1-0	8	Curran, Foreman, Mooney	2109
21	16	A	Doncaster R	L 3-4	1-2	10	Mooney, Curran, Mockler	2009
22	23	H	Halifax T	W 2-0	1-0	8	Mooney 2	1552
23	30	A	Crewe Alex	W 3-2	2-1	7	Foreman, Lightbourne, Mooney	3067
24	Feb 6	A	Hereford U	W 2-0	1-0	6	Lightbourne, Mooney	1467
25	13	A	Gillingham	L 1-3	1-2	7	Foreman	3022
26	20	H	Rochdale	D 1-1	1-1	8	Foreman	1765
27	27	A	Northampton T	W 3-1	1-1	8	Foreman, Ormsby, Jules	2451
28	Mar 6	H	Bury	L 1-3	0-2	9	Charles (pen)	2189
29	9	A	Cardiff C	L 0-1	0-1	—		8583
30	13	H	Walsall	W 4-1	0-1	9	Foreman 2, Mooney, Lightbourne	1681
31	20	A	Lincoln C	L 0-3	0-0	10		3725
32	23	H	Scunthorpe U	L 1-2	1-2	—	Charles (pen)	2007
33	30	H	Barnet	D 2-2	1-1	—	Horsefield, Foreman	2301
34	Apr 3	H	Cardiff C	L 1-3	1-2	12	Charles (pen)	2223
35	6	H	Wrexham	D 1-1	0-1	—	Ashdjian	1861
36	10	A	Barnet	L 1-3	0-2	11	Foreman	3118
37	13	H	Colchester U	L 0-1	0-1	—		1803
38	17	A	York C	L 0-1	0-1	14		5993
39	20	H	Shrewsbury T	L 1-2	1-1	—	Mooney	1325
40	24	H	Darlington	L 0-3	0-2	14		1733
41	May 1	A	Chesterfield	W 3-0	1-0	14	Jules 2, Foreman	2271
42	8	H	Carlisle U	D 2-2	0-1	13	Himsworth, Jules	2948

Final League Position: 13

GOALSCORERS

League (66): Foreman 27 (1 pen), Mooney 9, Jules 8, Ashdjian 5, Charles 3 (3 pens), Lightbourne 3, Curran 2, Hirst 2, Himsworth 1, Horsefield 1, Lee 1, Mockler 1, Mudd 1, Ormsby 1, Wheeler 1.
Coca Cola Cup (16): Mooney 5, Foreman 2, Hirst 2, Lee 2, Ashdjian 1, Curran 1, Jules 1, Mockler 1, own goal 1.
FA Cup (1): Mockler 1.

Evans 20	Barrow 11	Mudd 38	Lee 26 + 2	Hirst 35 + 1	Curran 32	Thompson 34 + 3	Himsworth 27 + 6	Mooney 39 + 1	Foreman 41 + 1	Jules 27 + 9	Ashdjian 20 + 8	Murphy 7 + 1	Edmonds — + 1	Ford 22	Swales 2 + 1	Ormsby 15 + 1	Mockler 8 + 2	McKenzie — + 1	Wheeler 2 + 5	McGee 13 + 3	Lightbourne 11 + 8	Toman 6	Charles 16	Hargreaves 2 + 1	Horsefield 6	James — + 6	Cawthorn 2 + 1	Match No.
1	2	3	4	5	6	7	8	9	10	11	12	14																1
1	2	3	4	5	6	7		9	10	11	12	8																2
1	2	3	4	5	6	7		9	10	11	12	8	14															3
1	2	3	4	5	6	7		9	10	11		8																4
	2		4	5	6	7		9	10	11	12	8		1	3	14												5
1	2		4	5	6	7		9	10	14	12	8			3	11												6
1		3	4	5	6	2	12	9	10	11	7	8					14											7
1	6	3	4	5		2	12	9	10	11	7	8					14											8
		3	4	5	6	2	8	9	10	11	7			1			12											9
		3	4	5	6	2	8	9	10	11	7			1			12											10
		3	4	5	6	2	8	9	10	11	7			1			12											11
		3	4	5	6	2	8	9	10	11	7			1			12											12
1		3	4	5	6	2	8	9	10	11	7						12											13
1		3	4	5	6	2	8	9	10	12	7						11											14
1		3	4	5	6	2	8	12	10	11	7									9	14							15
		3		5	6	2	8	9	10	11				1		4	7											16
	3	14	5	6		2	8	9	10	11	12			1		4	7											17
		3	4	5	6	2	8	9	10	11	7			1						14	12							18
		3	4	5	6	2	8	9	10	11	7			1						14	12							19
			4		6	2	8	9	10	12	7			1		5				3	11							20
		3	4	14	6			9	10	7	12			1		5	8			2	11							21
	2	3	4		6			9	10	7	12			1		5	8				11							22
	2	3	4		6	14	12	9	10	7				1		5	8				11							23
	2	3	4		6	14	12	9	10	7				1		5	8				11							24
	2	3	4		6	14	7	9	10	12				1		5	8				11							25
		4			6	2	8	9	10	3	7			1		5	12				11							26
		3			6	2	8	9	10	11				1		5				12			4	7				27
		3			6	2	14	9	10	11				1		5				12			4	7	8			28
1		3			6	2	8	9	10	14						5				12			4	7	11			29
1		3	14		6	2	8	9	10							5				11			4	7	12			30
1		3	8		6	2	12	9	10	14						5				11			4	7				31
1		3			6	2	8	9	10	12						5				11			4	7				32
1		3			6	2	11	9	10		7					5				12			4		8	14		33
		3		5	6			9	10		7			1		4				2	12		8		11	14		34
		3	4	5	6			9	10		7			1						2			8		11	12		35
		3		5	6	14	4	9	10		7			1						2	11		8		12			36
		3		5	6	9	4	10			7			1						2	12		11		14			37
1		3		5	6	11	4	9	10	12	7									2			8					38
1		3		5	6	8	4	9	10	11										2			7					39
1		3		5	6	8	4	9	10	11										2			7			12		40
1		6		5	2	4		9	12	11										3			8		10	7		41
1		6		5	2	4		10	9						12					3			8		11	14	7	42

Coca Cola Cup	First Round	Bradford C (h)	3-0
		(a)	5-3
	Second Round	Coventry (a)	0-2
		(h)	3-0
	Third Round	Plymouth Arg (a)	3-3
		(h)	2-1
	Fourth Round	Arsenal (h)	0-1
FA Cup	First Round	Burnley (a)	1-2

SCARBOROUGH

Player and Position	Ht	Wt	Date	Birth Place	Source	Clubs	League App	Gls
Goalkeepers								
Mark Evans	6 0	11 08	24 8 70	Leeds	Trainee	Bradford C	12	—
						Scarborough	20	—
Stuart Ford*	5 11	11 13	20 7 71	Sheffield	Trainee	Rotherham U	5	—
						Scarborough (loan)	6	—
						Scarborough	22	—
Defenders								
Lee Hirst‡	6 2	12 07	26 1 69	Sheffield		Scarborough	108	6
Lutel James‡	5 5	10 00	2 6 72			Scarborough	6	—
Owen McGee	5 5	10 08	29 4 70	Teesside	Trainee	Middlesbrough	21	1
						Scarborough	24	
Adrian Meyer*	6 0	14 00	22 9 70	Bristol	Trainee	Scarborough	65	8
Paul Mudd	5 8	11 02	13 11 70	Hull	Trainee	Hull C	1	—
						Scarborough	98	2
Brendan Ormsby‡	5 11	11 12	1 10 60	Birmingham	Apprentice	Aston Villa	117	4
						Leeds U	46	5
						Shrewsbury T (loan)	1	—
						Doncaster R	78	7
						Scarborough	16	1
Steve Swales	5 8	10 00	26 12 73	Whitby	Trainee	Scarborough	7	—
Midfield								
Paul Cawthorn§	5 6	10 00	26 5 75	Pontefract	Trainee	Scarborough	3	—
Steve Charles	5 9	10 07	10 5 60	Sheffield	Sheffield Univ	Sheffield U	123	10
						Wrexham	113	37
						Mansfield T	237	39
						Scunthorpe U (loan)	4	—
						Scarborough	16	3
Martin Gill			7 9 73	Sunderland	Hartlepool U	Scarborough	—	—
Geoff Horsefield	5 10	10 07	1 11 73	Barnsley		Scarborough	6	1
Chris Lee*	5 10	11 07	18 6 71	Halifax	Trainee	Bradford C	—	—
						Rochdale	26	2
						Scarborough	78	3
Andrew Mockler	5 11	11 13	18 11 70	Stockton	Trainee	Arsenal	—	—
						Scarborough	68	10
Aidan Murphy	5 10	11 03	17 9 67	Manchester	Apprentice	Manchester U	—	—
						Lincoln C (loan)	2	—
						Oldham Ath (loan)	—	—
						Crewe Alex	113	13
						Scarborough	8	—
Forwards								
John Ashdjian	5 10	10 07	13 9 72	Hackney	Northampton T	Scarborough	60	14
Steve Carter	5 8	12 00	13 4 72	Sunderland	Manchester U	Scarborough	37	3
Chris Curran	6 1	12 06	6 1 71	Manchester	Trainee	Crewe Alex	5	—
						Scarborough	40	4
Darren Foreman	5 10	10 08	12 2 68	Southampton		Barnsley	47	8
						Crewe Alex	23	4
						Scarborough	80	34
Gary Himsworth*	5 7	9 08	19 12 69	Appleton	Trainee	York C	88	8
						Scarborough	92	6
Mark Jules	5 10	11 01	5 9 71	Bradford	Trainee	Bradford C	—	—
						Scarborough	77	16
Kyle Lightbourne	6 2	11 00	29 9 68	Bermuda		Scarborough	19	3
Roger McKenzie‡	6 2	11 00	27 1 73	Sheffield	Trainee	Doncaster R	17	1
						Scarborough	1	—

SCARBOROUGH

Colours: Red shirts, white shorts, red stockings. **Change colours:** Yellow shirts, blue shorts, yellow stockings.

Foundation: Scarborough came into being as early as 1879 when they were formed by members of the town's cricket club and went under the name of Scarborough Cricketers' FC with home games played on the North Marine Road Cricket Ground.

First Football League game: 15 August, 1987, Division 4, v Wolverhampton W (h) D 2-2 – Blackwell; McJannet, Thompson, Bennyworth, Richards, Kendall, Hamill, Moss, McHale (1), Mell (1), Graham.

Did you know: Colin Appleton, a former Scarborough player, joined the club again as player-coach in 1969 and in ten years helped them to three FA Trophy successes.

Managers (and Secretary-Managers)
B. Chapman 1945–47*, George Hall 1946–47, Harold Taylor 1947–48, Frank Taylor 1948–50, A. C. Bell (Director & Hon. TM) 1950–53, Reg Halton 1953–54, Charles Robson (Hon. TM) 1954–57, George Higgins 1957–58, Andy Smailes 1959–61, Eddie Brown 1961–64, Albert Franks 1964–65, Stuart Myers 1965–66, Graham Shaw 1968–69, Colin Appleton 1969–73, Ken Houghton 1974–75, Colin Appleton 1975–81, Jimmy McAnearney 1981–82, John Cottam 1982–84, Harry Dunn 1984–86, Neil Warnock 1986–88, Colin Morris 1989, Ray McHale 1989–93, Phil Chambers April 1993–.

Player and Position	Ht	Wt	Date	Birth Place	Source	Clubs	League App	Gls
Tommy Mooney	5 10	12 05	11 8 71	Teesside North	Trainee	Aston Villa	—	—
						Scarborough	107	30
Simon Thompson	5 9	10 06	27 2 70	Sheffield	Trainee	Rotherham U	28	—
						Scarborough	60	3

Trainees
Brooks, Duncan G; Cawthorn, Paul J; Harper, Lee J; Howe, Christopher G; Hudson, Andrew; Pallant, Sean; Watt, Craig R.

446

SCUNTHORPE UNITED 1992–93 *Back row (left to right):* Paul McCullagh, David Hill, Mark Samways, Dean Martin, Graham Alexander.
Centre row: Phil McLoughlin, Jason White, Matthew Elliott, Bill Green (Manager), David Moore (Assistant Manager), Ian Helliwell, Stuart Hicks, David Cowling (Youth Team Coach).
Front row: Andrew Stevenson, Tony Daws, Paul Longden, Joe Joyce, John Buckley, Samuel Goodacre, Glenn Humphries.

Division 3   **SCUNTHORPE UNITED**

Glanford Park, Scunthorpe, South Humberside. Telephone Scunthorpe (0724) 848077. Fax (0724) 857986.

Ground capacity: 9183.

Record attendance: Old Showground: 23,935 v Portsmouth, FA Cup 4th rd, 30 January 1954. Glanford Park: 8775 v Rotherham U, Division 4, 1 May 1989.

Record receipts: £44,481.50 v Leeds U, Rumbelows Cup 2nd rd lst leg, 24 September 1991.

Pitch measurements: 110yd × 71yd.

President: Sir Reginald Sheffield, Bt.

Vice-presidents: I. T. Botham, G. Johnson, A. Harvey, G. J. Alston, R. Ashman.

Chairman: T. E. Belton.

Vice-chairman: D. M. Fletton.

Directors: J. B. Borrill, C. Plumtree, B. Collen.

Manager: Richard Money. *Coach:* C. Morris. *Physio:* David Moore.

Chief Executive/Secretary: A. D. Rowing. *Commercial Manager:* A. D. Rowing.

Year Formed: 1899. *Turned Professional:* 1912. *Ltd Co.:* 1912.

Club Nickname: 'The Iron'.

Previous Names: Amalgamated with Brumby Hall: North Lindsey United to become Scunthorpe & Lindsey United, 1910; dropped '& Lindsey' in 1958.

Previous ground: Old Showground to 1988.

Record League Victory: 8–1 v Luton T, Division 3, 24 April 1965 – Sidebottom; Horstead, Hemstead; Smith, Neale, Lindsey; Bramley (1), Scott, Thomas (5), Mahy (1), Wilson (1).

Record Cup Victory: 9–0 v Boston U, FA Cup, 1st rd, 21 November 1953 – Malan; Hubbard, Brownsword; Sharpe, White, Bushby; Mosby (1), Haigh (3), Whitfield (2), Gregory (1), Mervyn Jones (2).

Record Defeat: 0–8 v Carlisle U, Division 3 (N), 25 December 1952.

Most League Points (2 for a win): 66, Division 3 (N), 1956–57, 1957–58.

Most League Points (3 for a win): 83, Division 4, 1982–83.

Most League Goals: 88, Division 3 (N), 1957–58.

Highest League Scorer in Season: Barrie Thomas, 31, Division 2, 1961–62.

Most League Goals in Total Aggregate: Steve Cammack, 110, 1979–81, 1981–86.

Most Capped Player: None.

Most League Appearances: Jack Brownsword, 595, 1950–65.

Record Transfer Fee Received: £350,000 from Aston Villa for Neil Cox, February 1991.

Record Transfer Fee Paid: £80,000 to York City for Ian Helliwell, August 1991.

Football League Record: 1950 Elected to Division 3 (N); 1958–64 Division 2; 1964–68 Division 3; 1968–72 Division 4; 1972–73 Division 3; 1973–83 Division 4; 1983–84 Division 3; 1984–92 Division 4; 1992– Division 3.

Honours: Football League: Division 2 best season: 4th, 1961–62; Division 3 (N) – Champions 1957–58. *FA Cup:* best season: 5th rd, 1957–58, 1969–70. *Football League Cup:* never past 3rd rd.

SCUNTHORPE UNITED 1992—93 LEAGUE RECORD

Match No.	Date	Venue	Opponents	Result	H/T Score	Lg. Pos.	Goalscorers	Attendance
1	Aug 22	A	Halifax T	D 0-0	0-0	14		1793
2	29	H	Shrewsbury T	D 1-1	1-0	19	Alexander	3438
3	Sept 1	H	Walsall	W 2-0	1-0	—	Elliott, Helliwell	2828
4	5	A	Lincoln C	L 0-1	0-0	15		3764
5	12	A	Northampton T	L 0-1	0-0	20		1835
6	19	H	Crewe Alex	D 3-3	2-1	22	Goodacre, Humphries, Daws (pen)	2995
7	26	A	Carlisle U	W 2-0	1-0	16	Helliwell 2	4772
8	Oct 3	A	Chesterfield	W 2-1	1-1	12	Goodacre, White	3552
9	10	H	York C	L 1-2	1-1	16	White	4114
10	17	A	Barnet	L 0-3	0-1	17		2924
11	24	H	Colchester U	W 3-1	2-1	15	Daws, Martin, Helliwell	2473
12	31	A	Cardiff C	L 0-3	0-1	15		6027
13	Nov 3	A	Wrexham	W 2-0	1-0	—	Stevenson, Buckley	2930
14	7	H	Doncaster R	L 0-1	0-0	14		4451
15	21	A	Torquay U	W 1-0	0-0	12	Helliwell	1860
16	28	H	Scarborough	L 1-2	1-0	14	McCullagh	2807
17	Dec 12	H	Hereford U	W 3-1	1-1	12	Alexander, Elliott 2	1970
18	19	A	Darlington	D 2-2	0-1	13	White 2	1801
19	26	A	Rochdale	L 0-2	0-2	14		3043
20	28	H	Gillingham	D 2-2	0-1	12	Daws 2 (1 pen)	2835
21	Jan 16	H	Carlisle U	D 0-0	0-0	16		2570
22	26	A	Shrewsbury T	L 1-2	1-0	—	Helliwell	2190
23	30	H	Halifax T	W 4-1	3-0	15	Helliwell 2, Martin, Buckley	2460
24	Feb 13	A	Lincoln C	D 1-1	1-0	15	Stevenson	3748
25	20	A	Walsall	L 2-3	0-1	15	Stevenson, Helliwell	2935
26	27	A	York C	L 1-5	0-2	16	Farrell	2990
27	Mar 6	A	Chesterfield	L 0-1	0-1	17		2725
28	9	H	Bury	W 2-0	0-0	—	Alexander, Platnauer	2589
29	13	A	Doncaster R	W 1-0	0-0	15	Elliott	2760
30	20	H	Wrexham	D 0-0	0-0	14		3282
31	23	A	Scarborough	W 2-1	2-1	—	White, Alexander	2007
32	27	H	Torquay U	D 2-2	1-1	14	Alexander, Elliott	2568
33	30	H	Northampton T	W 5-0	3-0		Elliott, Goodacre 2, Helliwell, Thompstone	2307
34	Apr 3	A	Bury	D 0-0	0-0	14		2509
35	6	A	Hereford U	D 2-2	1-0	—	Helliwell, Goodacre	1740
36	10	H	Rochdale	W 5-1	3-0	12	Helliwell, Goodacre 2, Platnauer, Martin	2926
37	12	A	Gillingham	D 1-1	1-1	11	Thompstone	3859
38	17	A	Darlington	L 1-3	1-1	13	Goodacre	2774
39	20	A	Crewe Alex	L 0-1	0-1	—		3006
40	24	H	Barnet	W 2-0	1-0	13	Goodacre, Helliwell	2810
41	May 1	A	Colchester U	L 0-1	0-1	13		3421
42	8	H	Cardiff C	L 0-3	0-2	14		7407

Final League Position: 14

GOALSCORERS

League (57): Helliwell 13, Goodacre 9, Elliott 6, Alexander 5, White 5, Daws 4 (2 pens), Martin 3, Stevenson 3, Buckley 2, Platnauer 2, Thompstone 2, Farrell 1, Humphries 1, McCullagh 1.
Coca Cola Cup (6): Helliwell 4, Alexander 1, Daws 1.
FA Cup (1): Buckley 1.

Samways 31	Stevenson 25	Longden 20	Hill 19	Elliott 39	Humphries 29 + 1	Martin 38	Alexander 41	Daws 21 + 3	Buckley 13 + 2	Helliwell 40 + 1	White 27 + 10	Whitehead 8	Goodacre 13 + 8	Greaves 9 + 6	Broddle 5	McCullagh 5	Ryan 1	Joyce 30	Charles 4	Farrell 4 + 1	Duffy 4	Constable 2 + 5	Crisp 6 + 2	Platnauer 14	Foy 1 + 2	Thompstone 10 + 1	Wilmott 3	Maxwell — + 2	Match No.
1	2	3	4	5	6	7	8	9	10	11	12																		1
1	2	3	4	5	6	7	8	9	10	11																			2
1	2	3	4	5	6	7	8	9		11	10																		3
	2	3	4	5	6	7	8	9		11	10	1																	4
	2	3	*4*	5	6	7	8	9		11	10	1	12	14															5
	2	3		5	6	7	8	9		11	12	1	*10*	14		4													6
	2	3		5		7	8			11	9	1	10		4	6													7
	2	3		5			8	12		11	9	1	10	7	4	6													8
	2	3		5			8	12	14	11	9	1	10	7	*4*	6													9
	2	3		5		7	8	12	14	11	9	1	10	*4*		6													10
		6	3	5		4	8	7	10	11	9	1						2											11
1		6	3	5		4	8	7	*10*	11	9		12	14				2											12
1		6	3	5		4	8	9	10	11		7						2											13
1		6	3	5		4	8	9	10	11	12		14	*7*				*2*											14
1		3		5	6		4	9		11	10			*7*				2				8							15
1		3		5	6	8	4	9	10	11	12							2				7							16
1		3		5	6		4	9		11			10	7				2				8							17
1		6	3	5		7	4	9		11	10							2				8							18
1		6	3	5	8	7	4	9		11	10							2											19
1		6	3	5	12	7	4	9	10	11	8							2											20
1		3		5	6	4	10	11	7	9	8		12					2											21
1		3		5	6	10	4	8	*7*	9	12		14					2					11						22
1		3		5	6	*10*	4	8	7	9	12		14					2					11						23
1		3			6	4	10		7	9	8							2					11	5	12				24
1		3			6	4	10		7	9	8							2					11	5	12				25
1		3		5	*6*	4	*7*			9	8		14					2				12	10	11					26
1		3		5	6	4	7	11		9	8		12					2								10			27
1		11		5	6	4	7	9		8	12							2								10	3		28
1		11		5	6	4	7	9		8	12							2								10	3		29
1		11		5	6	4		9		8								2								10	3	7	30
1		11		5	6	4	7	9		8								2								10	3		31
1	3	11		5	6	4	7	9		8			14					2								10		12	32
		11		5	6	4	7	9		8								2					12	3		10	1		33
		11		5	6	4	7	9		8								2					12	3		10	1		34
		11		5	6		7	9	12	8								2	4	14				3		10	1		35
1		11		5	6	4	7	9	12	8								2		14				3		10			36
1		11		5	6	4	*7*	9	12	8								2						3		10			37
1		11		5	6	4	*7*	9	12	8								*2*						3	14	10			38
1		11		5	6	4	*7*	12	9	8								2						3		10			39
1		11			4	7	9	6		8	5							2	12					3		10			40
1				5	4	7	8	9		6								2	*11*					3	14	10		12	41
1		11		5	*6*	4	7	9		8								2						3		10		12	42

Coca Cola Cup	First Round	Darlington (a)	1-1
		(h)	2-0
	Second Round	Leeds U (a)	1-4
		(h)	2-2
FA Cup	First Round	Huddersfield T (h)	0-0
		(a)	1-2

SCUNTHORPE UNITED

Player and Position	Ht	Wt	Date	Birth Place	Source	Clubs	League App	Gls
Goalkeepers								
Mark Samways	6 2	13 10	11 11 68	Doncaster	Trainee	Doncaster R	121	—
						Scunthorpe U (loan)	8	—
						Scunthorpe U	31	—
Richard Wilmott†	6 4	13 07	29 8 69		Stevenage	Scunthorpe U	3	—
Defenders								
Graham Alexander	5 10	11 08	10 10 71	Coventry	Trainee	Scunthorpe U	78	10
Darrell Duffy*	6 0	12 04	18 1 71	Birmingham	Trainee	Aston Villa	1	—
					Moor Green	Scunthorpe U	4	—
Paul Ellender	6 1	12 07	21 10 74	Scunthorpe	Trainee	Scunthorpe U	—	—
Matthew Elliott	6 3	14 05	1 11 68	Surrey	Epsom & Ewell	Charlton Ath	—	—
						Torquay U	124	15
						Scunthorpe U (loan)	8	1
						Scunthorpe U	39	6
Glenn Humphries*	6 0	12 10	11 8 64	Hull	Apprentice	Doncaster R	180	8
						Lincoln C (loan)	9	—
						Bristol C	85	—
						Scunthorpe U	72	5
Joe Joyce	5 10	11 07	18 3 61	Consett	School	Barnsley	334	4
						Scunthorpe U	91	2
Paul Longden	5 7	11 00	28 9 62	Wakefield	Apprentice	Barnsley	5	—
						Scunthorpe U	368	—
Paul McCullagh	5 11	11 04	6 2 74	Brigg	Trainee	Scunthorpe U	5	1
Nicky Platnauer*	5 11	12 10	10 6 61	Leicester	Bedford T	Bristol R	24	7
						Coventry C	44	6
						Birmingham C	28	2
						Reading (loan)	7	—
						Cardiff C	115	6
						Notts Co	57	1
						Port Vale (loan)	14	—
						Leicester C	35	—
						Scunthorpe U	14	2
Tim Ryan			10 12 74	Stockport	Trainee	Scunthorpe U	1	—
Midfield								
Julian Broddle (on loan from Partick T)	5 9	11 07	1 11 64	Laughton		Scunthorpe U	5	—
Shaun Constable†	5 11	12 00	21 3 68	Maidstone		Scunthorpe U	7	—
David Foy	6 1	12 00	20 10 72	Coventry	Trainee	Birmingham C	3	—
						Scunthorpe U	3	—
Steve Greaves*	5 9	11 09	17 1 70	London	Trainee	Fulham	1	—
						Waterford (loan)	—	—
						Brighton (loan)	—	—
						Preston NE	2	—
						Ipswich T	—	—
						Scunthorpe U	15	—
David Hill	5 11	12 04	6 6 66	Nottingham	Local	Scunthorpe U	140	10
						Ipswich T	61	—
						Scunthorpe U	65	6
James McNeil			1 10 74	Scunthorpe	Trainee	Scunthorpe U	—	—
Dean Martin	5 11	11 10	9 9 67	Halifax	Local	Halifax T	153	7
						Scunthorpe U	75	5
Andy Stevenson*	6 0	13 05	29 9 67	Scunthorpe	School	Scunthorpe U	103	4
						Doncaster R (loan)	1	—
Ian Thompstone	6 1	13 02	17 1 71	Manchester	Trainee	Manchester C	1	1
						Oldham Ath	—	—
						Exeter C	15	3
						Halifax T	31	9
						Scunthorpe U	11	2

SCUNTHORPE UNITED

Colours: Sky blue shirts with two claret rings on sleeves, white collar, white shorts with claret stripe, white stockings with claret and blue bar. **Change colours:** White shirts with claret brush stroke, claret shorts with sky blue stripe, sky blue stockings with claret and white bar.

Foundation: The year of foundation for Scunthorpe United has often been quoted as 1910, but the club can trace its history back to 1899 when Brumby Hall FC, who played on the Old Showground, consolidated their position by amalgamating with some other clubs and changing their name to Scunthorpe United. The year 1910 was when that club amalgamated with North Lindsey United as Scunthorpe and Lindsey United. The link is Mr. W. T. Lockwood whose chairmanship covers both years.

First Football League game: 19 August, 1950, Division 3(N), v Shrewsbury T (h) D 0-0 – Thompson; Barker, Brownsword; Allen, Taylor, McCormick; Mosby, Payne, Gorin, Rees, Boyes.

Did you know: The first occasion that BBC television cameras visited the Old Show Ground was for an FA Cup third round tie against Tottenham Hotspur on 12 January 1952. A then record crowd of 22,625 saw Spurs win 3-0.

Managers (and Secretary-Managers)
Harry Allcock 1915–53*, Tom Crilly 1936–37, Bernard Harper 1946–48, Leslie Jones 1950–51, Bill Corkhill 1952–56, Ron Suart 1956–58, Tony McShane 1959, Bill Lambton 1959, Frank Soo 1959–60, Dick Duckworth 1960–64, Fred Goodwin 1964–66, Ron Ashman 1967–73, Ron Bradley 1973–74, Dick Rooks 1974–76, Ron Ashman 1976–81, John Duncan 1981–83, Allan Clarke 1983–84, Frank Barlow 1984–87, Mick Buxton 1987–91, Bill Green 1991–93, Richard Money January 1993–.

Player and Position	Ht	Wt	Date	Birth Place	Source	Clubs	League App	Gls
Forwards								
Sam Goodacre	5 7	10 12	1 12 70	Sheffield	School	Sheffield W	—	—
						Scunthorpe U	21	9
Ian Helliwell	6 3	14 02	7 11 62	Rotherham	Matlock T	York C	160	40
						Scunthorpe U	80	22
Jason Maxwell*	6 0	12 10	1 9 72			Scunthorpe U	2	—
Jason White	6 0	12 10	19 10 71	Meriden	Derby Co	Scunthorpe U	59	16

Trainees
Collom, Delme G; Housham, Steven J; Hughes, Richard G; Jakins, Wayne J; Jones, Daniel K; Nixon, Gary L; Raspin, William R; Sansam, Christian.

**Non-Contract
Constable, Shaun D; Moore, David; Wilmot, Richard G.

Associated Schoolboys
McKay, Alan M; Muir, Jamie; Smith, Ian M; Trown, Glyn G; Wallace, Scott G.

**Non-Contract Players who are retained must be re-signed before they are eligible to play in League matches.

SHEFFIELD UNITED 1992–93 *Back row (left to right):* John Pemberton, Paul Rogers, Mike Lake, Jamie Hoyland, Brian Gayle, Mel Rees, Brian Deane, Glyn Hodges, Paul Beesley, Alan Cork, Ian Bryson.

Centre row: Derek French (Physio), Dane Whitehouse, Carl Bradshaw, David Barnes, Simon Tracey, Nathan Peel, Alan Kelly, Charlie Hartfield, Kevin Gage, John Gannon, Geoff Taylor (Assistant Manager).

Front row: Brian Marwood, Tom Cowan, Andy Cale (Sports Psychologist), John Reed, Dave Bassett (Manager), Richard Lucas, John Greaves (Kit Man), Mitch Ward, Adrian Littlejohn.

FA Premier

SHEFFIELD UNITED

Bramall Lane Ground, Sheffield S2 4SU. Telephone Sheffield (0742) 738955. Bladesline (recorded message): 0898 888650.

Ground capacity: 32,000 (22,000 sheets).

Record attendance: 68,287 v Leeds U, FA Cup 5th rd, 15 February 1936.

Record receipts: £261,758 v Manchester U, FA Cup 5th rd, 14 February 1993.

Pitch measurements: 110yd × 72yd.

Chairman/Chief Executive: D. Dooley.

Directors: L. Brealey, K. McCabe, G. Proctor, A. Laver.

Team Manager: Dave Bassett. *Team Coach:* Geoff Taylor. *Youth Coach:* Keith Mincher.

Assistant Manager: *Physio:* Derek French.

Secretary: D. Capper AFA. *Commercial Manager:* Andy R. Daykin.

Youth Development Officer: John Dungworth.

Community Programme Organiser: Tony Currie, Tel: 769314.

Year Formed: 1889. *Turned Professional:* 1889. *Ltd Co.:* 1899.

Club Nickname: 'The Blades'.

Record League Victory: 10–0 v Burslem Port Vale (away), Division 2, 10 December 1892 – Howlett; Witham, Lilley; Howell, Hendry, Needham; Drummond (1), Wallace (1), Hammond (4), Davies (2), Watson (2).

Record Cup Victory: 5–0 v Newcastle U (away), FA Cup, 1st rd, 10 January 1914 – Gough; Cook, English; Brelsford, Howley, Sturgess; Simmons (2), Gillespie (1), Kitchen (1), Fazackerley, Revill (1). 5–0 v Corinthians, FA Cup, 1st rd, 10 January 1925 – Sutcliffe; Cook, Milton; Longworth, King, Green; Partridge, Boyle (1), Johnson 4), Gillespie, Tunstall. 5–0 v Barrow, FA Cup, 3rd rd, 7 January 1956 – Burgin; Coldwell, Mason; Fountain, Johnson, Iley; Hawksworth (1), Hoyland (2), Howitt, Wragg (1), Grainger (1).

Record Defeat: 0–13 v Bolton W, FA Cup 2nd rd, 1 February 1890.

Most League Points (2 for a win): 60, Division 2, 1952–53.

Most League Points (3 for a win): 96, Division 4, 1981–82.

Most League Goals: 102, Division 1, 1925–26.

Highest League Scorer in Season: Jimmy Dunne, 41, Division 1, 1930–31.

Most League Goals in Total Aggregate: Harry Johnson, 205, 1919–30.

Most Capped Player: Billy Gillespie, 25, Northern Ireland.

Most League Appearances: Joe Shaw, 629, 1948–66.

Record Transfer Fee Received: £750,000 from Notts Co for Tony Agana, November 1991.

Record Transfer Fee Paid: £700,000 to Ipswich T for Brian Gayle, September 1991.

Football League Record: 1892 Elected to Division 2; 1893–1934 Division 1; 1934–39 Division 2; 1946–49 Division 1; 1949–53 Division 2; 1953–56 Division 1; 1956–61 Division 2; 1961–68 Division 1; 1968–71 Division 2; 1971–76 Division 1; 1976–79 Division 2; 1979–81 Division 3; 1981–82 Division 4; 1982–84 Division 3; 1984–88 Division 2; 1988–89 Division 3; 1989–90 Division 2; 1990–92 Division 1; 1992– FA Premier Division.

Honours: Football League: Division 1 – Champions 1897–98; Runners-up 1896–97, 1899–1900; Division 2 – Champions 1952–53; Runners-up 1892–93, 1938–39, 1960–61, 1970–71, 1989–90; Division 4 – Champions 1981–82. *FA Cup:* Winners 1899, 1902, 1915, 1925; Runners-up 1901, 1936. *Football League Cup:* best season: 5th rd, 1961–62, 1966–67, 1971–72.

454

SHEFFIELD UNITED 1992—93 LEAGUE RECORD

Match No.	Date	Venue	Opponents	Result	H/T Score	Lg. Pos.	Goalscorers	Attendance
1	Aug 15	H	Manchester U	W 2-1	1-0	—	Deane 2 (1 pen)	28,070
2	19	A	Liverpool	L 1-2	1-1	—	Deane	33,107
3	22	A	QPR	L 2-3	1-2	14	Cork, Deane	10,925
4	25	H	Wimbledon	D 2-2	0-1	—	Beesley, Hodges	15,463
5	29	H	Aston Villa	L 0-2	0-1	19		18,773
6	Sept 2	A	Tottenham H	L 0-2	0-1	—		21,332
7	5	A	Middlesbrough	L 0-2	0-1	21		15,179
8	12	H	Liverpool	W 1-0	1-0	18	Littlejohn	20,632
9	19	A	Arsenal	D 1-1	0-0	19	Whitehouse	19,105
10	26	A	Ipswich T	D 0-0	0-0	20		16,353
11	Oct 3	H	Southampton	W 2-0	2-0	16	Whitehouse, Littlejohn	15,842
12	17	A	Leeds U	L 1-3	0-1	17	Beesley	29,706
13	24	H	Nottingham F	D 0-0	0-0	17		19,152
14	31	A	Chelsea	W 2-1	1-1	15	Littlejohn, Deane	13,763
15	Nov 8	H	Sheffield W	D 1-1	0-0	—	Littlejohn	30,039
16	21	A	Norwich C	L 1-2	0-0	16	Cork	14,874
17	28	A	Coventry C	D 1-1	1-1	18	Pearce (og)	15,625
18	Dec 5	A	Crystal Palace	L 0-2	0-1	18		12,361
19	12	H	Everton	W 1-0	1-0	16	Littlejohn	16,266
20	19	A	Blackburn R	L 0-1	0-1	19		16,057
21	26	A	Manchester C	L 0-2	0-1	20		27,455
22	Jan 9	A	Arsenal	D 1-1	0-1	20	Littlejohn	23,818
23	16	H	Ipswich T	W 3-0	1-0	19	Deane 3	16,758
24	27	A	Aston Villa	L 1-3	0-0	—	Deane	20,266
25	30	H	QPR	L 1-2	0-1	20	Hoyland	16,366
26	Feb 6	A	Manchester U	L 1-2	1-0	22	Carr	36,156
27	9	H	Middlesbrough	W 2-0	1-0	—	Carr, Deane	15,184
28	20	A	Wimbledon	L 0-2	0-2	21		3979
29	22	A	Oldham Ath	W 2-0	1-0	—	Gannon, Littlejohn	14,628
30	27	A	Southampton	L 2-3	1-3	20	Gayle, Bryson	13,814
31	Mar 2	H	Tottenham H	W 6-0	4-0	—	Carr, Gray (og), Bryson 2, Deane, Rogers	16,654
32	10	H	Norwich C	L 0-1	0-0	—		15,583
33	20	H	Crystal Palace	L 0-1	0-1	19		18,857
34	24	A	Coventry C	W 3-1	0-1	—	Whitehouse, Deane, Littlejohn	12,993
35	Apr 6	A	Leeds U	W 2-1	1-1	—	Rogers, Deane	20,562
36	9	H	Manchester C	D 1-1	0-1	—	Deane	18,231
37	13	A	Oldham Ath	D 1-1	1-1	—	Hoyland	14,795
38	17	H	Blackburn R	L 1-3	1-1	19	Hodges	18,186
39	21	A	Sheffield W	D 1-1	1-0	—	Deane	38,688
40	May 1	A	Nottingham F	W 2-0	1-0	19	Hodges, Gayle	26,752
41	4	A	Everton	W 2-0	2-0	—	Bradshaw, Hodges	15,197
42	8	H	Chelsea	W 4-2	3-0	14	Scott, Rogers, Whitehouse 2	24,850

Final League Position: 14

GOALSCORERS

League (54): Deane 15 (1 pen), Littlejohn 8, Whitehouse 5, Hodges 4, Bryson 3, Carr 3, Rogers 3, Beesley 2, Cork 2, Gayle 2, Hoyland 2, Bradshaw 1, Gannon 1, Scott 1, own goals 2.
Coca Cola Cup (5): Deane 2, Bradshaw 1, Rogers 1, Whitehouse 1.
FA Cup (12): Deane 3, Cork 2, Hodges 2, Ward 2, Beesley 1, Hoyland 1, Littlejohn 1.

Tracey 10	Gage 27	Barnes 13	Gannon 26 + 1	Beesley 39	McLeary 3	Bradshaw 24 + 8	Lake 6	Cork 11 + 16	Deane 41	Hodges 28 + 3	Bryson 9 + 7	Hartfield 12 + 5	Littlejohn 18 + 9	Cowan 21	Gayle 31	Ward 22 + 4	Rogers 26 + 1	Kelly 32 + 1	Whitehouse 14	Hoyland 15 + 7	Pemberton 19	Kamara 6 + 2	Carr 8	Scott 1 + 1	Match No.
1	2	3	*4*	5	6	7	8	9	10	11	12	14													1
1	2	3	4	5	6	7	8	12	10	11	9	14													2
1	2	3	4	5	*6*		8	9	10	11	7	14	12												3
1	2				6	12	8	9	10	11	7	4		3	5										4
1	2		4		6	12	*8*	9	10	11			14	3	5	7									5
1	2		4		6			12	10	*11*	7		9	3	5		8		14						6
1	2	3	4		6	7		9	10	11	12	14			5		8								7
1	2		4		6	7		12	10		14		9	3	5	8	*11*								8
	2		4		6	7			10				9	3	5		8	1	11						9
	2		4		6	*7*		12	10		14		9	3	5		8	1	11						10
	2		4		6	7			10				9	3	5	12	8	1	11						11
			4		6	7		11	10		12			9	3	5	2	8	1						12
1			4		6	7			10	12	11		9	3	5	2		8							13
1	2		4		6				10	11			9	3	5	7	8	12							14
	2		4		6	11			10	12			9	3	5	7	8	1							15
	2		4		6			12	10	11	9		3		7	8	1		5	14					16
			4		6	2		9	10	11		12	3		7	8	1		5	14					17
7		3	4		6	*2*		12	10	11		14			8	1		9	5						18
	2	3	4		6			12	10	*11*		9			7	8	1	14	5						19
	2	3	*4*		6	7			10	11		14			12	8	1	9	5						20
		3	4		6	9		12	*10*	11					7	8	1	14	5	2					21
	2	3	4		6			12	10	11		9			*8*	1	14	5	7						22
	2	3			6			9	10	11	12			5		1	4			7	8				23
	2	3			6	14		12	10	11		8		5		1	4		9	*7*					24
	2	3			6	7			10	11		9		5	12	1	4	8							25
					6	14		12	10		9	11		3	5	2	1	4		*8*	7				26
					6	14		12	10	11		8	9	3	5	2	1	4			*7*				27
			4		*6*			12	10	14			11	3	5	2	8	1	9		*7*				28
			12		6	7			10		9	8	11	3	5	2	1	4							29
			4		6	14	7	9	10		12		11	3	5	2	1	*8*							30
	2	*3*						12	10	11	9	8			5	14	1		4	6		7			31
	2					14			10	11	9	8	12		5	3	1		4	6		*7*			32
		4				14		10				8	7	2	5	11	9	1	3	12	6				33
	2	4						9	10			12	3	5	11		1	8	14	6		*7*			34
	2	4	8			7		12	10	11					5		9	1	3		6				35
	2	4	8			7		12	10	11					5		9	1	3		6				36
		3				7			10	9				5	2	8	1	11		4	6				37
	2		3			7			10	9	12			5	14	8	1	*11*		4	6				38
		3				7			10	9		4		5	2	8	1	11		6			12		39
		3				7			10	9		4	12	5	2	8	1	11		6					40
		3				7			10	9		4		5	2	8	1	11		6					41
		5				7			10			4	12	3		2	8	1	11	14	6		9		42

Coca Cola Cup	Second Round	Bristol C (a)		1-2
		(h)		4-1
	Third Round	Liverpool (h)		0-0
		(a)		0-3
FA Cup	Third Round	Burnley (h)		2-2
		(a)		4-2
	Fourth Round	Hartlepool U (h)		1-0
	Fifth Round	Manchester U (h)		2-1
	Sixth Round	Blackburn R (a)		0-0
		(h)		2-2
	Semi-Final at Wembley	Sheffield W		1-2

SHEFFIELD UNITED

Player and Position	Ht	Wt	Date	Birth Place	Source	Clubs	League App	Gls
Goalkeepers								
Alan Kelly	6 2	12 05	11 8 68	Preston		Preston NE	142	—
						Sheffield U	33	—
Phil Kite	6 1	14 07	26 10 62	Bristol	Apprentice	Bristol R	96	—
						Tottenham H (loan)	—	—
						Southampton	4	—
						Middlesbrough (loan)	2	—
						Gillingham	70	—
						Bournemouth	7	—
						Sheffield U	11	—
						Mansfield T (loan)	11	—
						Plymouth Arg (loan)	2	—
						Rotherham U (loan)	1	—
						Crewe Alex (loan)	5	—
						Stockport Co (loan)	5	—
Jim Leighton (on loan from Dundee)	6 1	12 09	24 7 58	Johnstone		Sheffield U	—	—
Mel Rees (Deceased)	6 2	12 02	25 1 67	Cardiff	Trainee	Cardiff C	31	—
						Watford	3	—
						Crewe Alex (loan)	6	—
						Southampton (loan)	—	—
						Leyton Orient (loan)	9	—
						WBA	18	—
						Norwich C (loan)	—	—
						Sheffield U	8	—
						Chesterfield (loan)	—	—
Simon Tracey	6 0	12 00	9 12 67	Woolwich	Apprentice	Wimbledon	1	—
						Sheffield U	123	—
Defenders								
David Barnes	5 10	11 01	16 11 61	London	Apprentice	Coventry C	9	—
						Ipswich T	17	—
						Wolves	88	4
						Aldershot	69	1
						Sheffield U	80	1
Paul Beesley	6 1	11 11	21 7 65	Wigan	Marine	Wigan Ath	155	3
						Leyton Orient	32	1
						Sheffield U	116	5
Tom Cowan	5 8	10 08	28 8 69	Bellshill	Netherdale BC	Clyde	16	2
						Rangers	12	—
						Sheffield U	41	—
Ashley Fickling	5 10	11 08	15 11 72	Sheffield	Trainee	Sheffield U	—	—
						Darlington (loan)	14	—
Kevin Gage	5 9	11 02	21 4 64	Chiswick	Apprentice	Wimbledon	168	15
						Aston Villa	115	8
						Sheffield U	49	2
Brian Gayle	6 1	12 07	6 3 65	London		Wimbledon	83	3
						Manchester C	55	3
						Ipswich T	58	4
						Sheffield U	64	5
Charles Hartfield	6 0	12 02	4 9 71	London	Trainee	Arsenal	—	—
						Sheffield U	24	—
Shane Kent*	5 9	10 04	30 8 74	Auckland	Trainee	Sheffield U	—	—
John Pemberton	5 11	12 03	18 11 64	Oldham	Chadderton	Rochdale	1	—
						Crewe Alex	121	1
						Crystal Palace	78	2
						Sheffield U	60	—
David Walton	6 2	13 04	10 4 73	Bedlingham	Trainee	Sheffield U	—	—
Mitch Ward	5 8	10 12	18 6 71	Sheffield	Trainee	Sheffield U	36	2
						Crewe Alex (loan)	4	1
Midfield								
Ian Bryson	5 11	11 11	26 11 62	Kilmarnock		Kilmarnock	215	40
						Sheffield U	155	36
Franz Carr	5 7	10 12	24 9 66	Preston	Apprentice	Blackburn R	—	—
						Nottingham F	131	17
						Sheffield W (loan)	12	—
						West Ham U (loan)	3	—
						Newcastle U	25	3
						Sheffield U	8	3
Matthew Cherrill*	5 10	11 12	10 10 73	Sheffield	Trainee	Sheffield U	—	—
John Gannon	5 8	10 10	18 12 66	Wimbledon	Apprentice	Wimbledon	16	2
						Crewe Alex (loan)	15	—
						Sheffield U (loan)	16	1
						Sheffield U	120	5
Jamie Hoyland	6 0	12 08	23 1 66	Sheffield	Apprentice	Manchester C	2	—
						Bury	172	35
						Sheffield U	69	6

SHEFFIELD UNITED

Colours: Broad red/white striped shirts, white shorts, red stripe at side, white stockings with red trim.
Change colours: Navy shirts with purple & green diagonal stripe, navy blue shorts, navy stockings with purple & green trim.

Foundation: In March 1889, Yorkshire County Cricket Club formed Sheffield United six days after an FA Cup semi-final between Preston North End and West Bromwich Albion had finally convinced Charles Stokes, a member of the cricket club, that the formation of a professional football club would prove successful at Bramall Lane. The United's first secretary, Mr. J. B. Wostinholm was also secretary of the cricket club.

First Football League game: 3 September, 1892, Division 2, v Lincoln C (h) W 4-2 – Lilley; Witham, Cain; Howell, Hendry, Needham (1); Wallace, Dobson, Hammond (3), Davies, Drummond.

Did you know: Brian Deane scored the first goal in the FA Premier League in just over four minutes of Sheffield United's 2-1 win over Manchester United on 15 August 1992. He scored the second after 50 minutes from a penalty.

Managers (and Secretary-Managers)
J. B. Wostinholm 1889–1899*, John Nicholson 1899–1932, Ted Davison 1932–52, Reg Freeman 1952–55, Joe Mercer 1955–58, Johnny Harris 1959–68 (continued as GM to 1970), Arthur Rowley 1968–69, Johnny Harris (GM resumed TM duties) 1969–73, Ken Furphy 1973–75, Jimmy Sirrel 1975–77, Harry Haslam 1978–81, Martin Peters 1981, Ian Porterfield 1981–86, Billy McEwan 1986–88, Dave Bassett January 1988– .

Player and Position	Ht	Wt	Birth Date	Birth Place	Source	Clubs	League App	Gls
Paul Rogers	6 0	12 05	21 3 65	Portsmouth	Sutton U	Sheffield U	40	3
Andy Scott	6 1	11 05	2 8 72	Epsom	Sutton U	Sheffield U	2	1
Dane Whitehouse	5 9	10 13	14 10 70	Sheffield	Trainee	Sheffield U	69	13
Forwards								
Carl Bradshaw	6 0	11 00	2 10 68	Sheffield	Apprentice	Sheffield W	32	4
						Barnsley (loan)	6	1
						Manchester C	5	—
						Sheffield U	107	7
David Brocklehurst	5 10	10 08	7 3 74	Chesterfield	Trainee	Sheffield U	—	—
Alan Cork	6 0	12 00	4 3 59	Derby	Amateur	Derby C	—	—
						Lincoln C (loan)	5	—
						Wimbledon	430	145
						Sheffield U	35	4
Brian Deane	6 3	12 07	7 2 68	Leeds	Apprentice	Doncaster R	66	12
						Sheffield U	197	83
Peter Duffield	5 6	10 07	4 2 69	Middlesbrough		Middlesbrough	—	—
						Sheffield U	58	14
						Halifax T (loan)	12	6
						Rotherham U (loan)	17	4
						Blackpool (loan)	5	1
						Bournemouth (loan)	—	—
						Stockport Co (loan)	7	4
						Crewe Alex (loan)	2	—
Glyn Hodges	6 0	12 03	30 4 63	Streatham	Apprentice	Wimbledon	232	49
						Newcastle U	7	—
						Watford	86	15
						Crystal Palace	7	—
						Sheffield U	69	10
Adrian Littlejohn	5 10	10 04	26 9 70	Wolverhampton	WBA	Walsall	44	1
						Sheffield U	34	8
Nathan Peel	6 1	12 07	17 5 72	Blackburn	Trainee	Preston NE	10	1
						Sheffield U	1	—
						Halifax T (loan)	3	—
John Reed	5 10	10 11	27 8 72	Rotherham	Trainee	Sheffield U	1	—
						Scarborough (loan)	14	6
						Scarborough (loan)	6	—
						Darlington (loan)	10	2

Trainees
Anane, David O; Anthony, Graham J; Battersby, Tony; Butterfield, Timothy; Cope, Steven; Dickerson, Ian; Foreman, Matthew; Innes, Lee M; Kennedy, Steven; Letts, Simon C; Myhill, Craig; Pearson, Gregg; Tee, Jason K; Thomson, Martin; Wainwright, Danny; Wainwright, Lee; Zivkovic, Barry L.

Associated Schoolboys
Bettney, Christopher J; Capper, David A; Crump, Andrew J; Davies, Kevin J; Del Colle, Nicholas; Dyer, Liam D; Green, Jonathan M; Hawes, Steven R; Henderson, Dean; Hobson, Daniel D; Hocking, Matthew J; Laidlaw, James R; Litten, Thomas N; Metcalf, Ian R; Quinn, Anthony J; Sampey, Mark P; Simpson, Andrew J; Spooner, Daniel; Summerell, Stewart D; Taylor, James A; Vine, Darren M; Wood, Paul J.

Associated Schoolboys who have accepted the club's offer of a Traineeship/Contract
Andison, Gary P; Beech, Neil A; Collins, Eric; Dickman, Lewis L; Evans, Thomas R; Hill, Matthew D; Holt, Craig; Pearson, Gary; Powell, Craig I; Quinn, Wayne R; Rixon, James; Storey, Brett B; Thorpe, Andrew.

SHEFFIELD WEDNESDAY 1992–93 *Back row (left to right)*: David Johnson, Peter Shirtliff, Kevin Pressman, Viv Anderson, Paul Warhurst, Chris Woods, Julian Watts, Carlton Palmer. *Centre row*: Richie Barker (Assistant Manager), Phil King, John Harkes, Gordon Watson, Chris Bart-Williams, Roland Nilsson, Nigel Worthington, Chris Waddle, Nigel Jemson, Alan Smith (Physio). *Front row*: John Sheridan, Danny Wilson, Nigel Pearson, Trevor Francis (Manager), David Hirst, Graham Hyde, Mark Bright.

FA Premier   **SHEFFIELD WEDNESDAY**

Hillsborough, Sheffield, S6 1SW. Telephone Sheffield (0742) 343122. Box Office: Sheffield 337233. Clubcall: 0898 121186.

Ground capacity: 41,237.

Record attendance: 72,841 v Manchester C, FA Cup 5th rd, 17 February 1934.

Record receipts: £533,918 Sunderland v Norwich C, FA Cup semi-final, 5 April 1992.

Pitch measurements: 115yd × 75yd.

Chairman: D. G. Richards. *Vice-chairman:* K. T. Addy.

Directors: C. Woodward, E. Barron, G. K. Hulley, R. M. Grierson FCA, J. Ashton MP.

Manager: Trevor Francis. *Assistant Manager:* Richie Barker.

Physio: A. Smith.

Secretary: G. H. Mackrell FCCA. *Commercial Manager:*

Year Formed: 1867 (fifth oldest League club).

Turned Professional: 1887. *Ltd Co.:* 1899.

Former Names: The Wednesday until 1929.

Club Nickname: 'The Owls'.

Previous Grounds: 1867, Highfield; 1869, Myrtle Road; 1877, Sheaf House; 1887, Olive Grove; 1899, Owlerton (since 1912 known as Hillsborough). Some games were played at Endcliffe in the 1880s. Until 1895 Bramall Lane was used for some games.

Record League Victory: 9–1 v Birmingham, Division 1, 13 December 1930 – Brown; Walker, Blenkinsop; Strange, Leach, Wilson; Hooper (3), Seed (2), Ball (2), Burgess (1), Rimmer (1).

Record Cup Victory: 12–0 v Halliwell, FA Cup, 1st rd, 17 January 1891 – Smith; Thompson, Brayshaw; Harry Brandon (1), Betts, Cawley (2); Winterbottom, Mumford (2), Bob Brandon (1), Woolhouse (5), Ingram (1).

Record Defeat: 0–10 v Aston Villa, Division 1, 5 October 1912.

Most League Points (2 for a win): 62, Division 2, 1958–59.

Most League Points (3 for a win): 88, Division 2, 1983–84.

Most League Goals: 106, Division 2, 1958–59.

Highest League Scorer in Season: Derek Dooley, 46, Division 2, 1951–52.

Most League Goals in Total Aggregate: Andy Wilson, 199, 1900–20.

Most Capped Player: Nigel Worthington, 44, Northern Ireland.

Most League Appearances: Andy Wilson, 502, 1900–20.

Record Transfer Fee Received: £1,750,000 from Real Sociedad for Dalian Atkinson, July 1990.

Record Transfer Fee Paid: £1,200,000 to Rangers for Chris Woods, August 1991.

Football League Record: 1892 Elected to Division 1; 1899–1900 Division 2; 1900–20 Division 1; 1920–26 Division 2; 1926–37 Division 1; 1937–50 Division 2; 1950–51 Division 1; 1951–52 Division 2; 1952–55 Division 1; 1955–56 Division 2; 1956–58 Division 1; 1958–59 Division 2; 1959–70 Division 1; 1970–75 Division 2; 1975–80 Division 3; 1980–84 Division 2; 1984–90 Division 1; 1990–91 Division 2; 1991–92 Division 1; 1992– FA Premier League.

Honours: Football League: Division 1 – Champions 1902–03, 1903–04, 1928–29, 1929–30; Runners-up 1960–61; Division 2 – Champions 1899–1900, 1925–26, 1951–52, 1955–56, 1958–59; Runners-up 1949–50, 1983–84. *FA Cup:* Winners 1896, 1907, 1935; Runners-up 1890, 1966, 1993. *Football League Cup:* Winners 1990–91; Runners-up 1992–93. **European Competitions:** *Fairs Cup:* 1961–62, 1963–64, 1992–93.

SHEFFIELD WEDNESDAY 1992—93 LEAGUE RECORD

Match No.	Date	Venue	Opponents	Result	H/T Score	Lg. Pos.	Goalscorers	Atten dance
1	Aug 15	A	Everton	D	1-1	1-1	—	Pearson	27,687
2	19	H	Nottingham F	W	2-0	1-0	—	Hirst 2	29,623
3	22	H	Chelsea	D	3-3	2-0	8	Hirst 2 (1 pen), Wilson	26,338
4	25	A	Crystal Palace	D	1-1	0-1	—	Williams P	14,005
5	29	A	Arsenal	L	1-2	1-2	10	Hirst	23,389
6	Sept 2	H	Coventry C	L	1-2	0-1	—	Bart-Williams	22,874
7	5	H	Manchester C	L	0-3	0-1	17		27,169
8	12	A	Nottingham F	W	2-1	1-0	14	Warhurst, Hyde	19,420
9	19	H	Norwich C	L	0-1	0-1	16		13,367
10	27	H	Tottenham H	W	2-0	2-0	—	Bright, Anderson	24,895
11	Oct 3	A	Liverpool	L	0-1	0-0	13		35,785
12	17	H	Oldham Ath	W	2-1	2-1	12	Palmer, Bright	24,485
13	24	A	Middlesbrough	D	1-1	1-1	13	Bright	18,414
14	31	H	Blackburn R	D	0-0	0-0	13		31,044
15	Nov 8	A	Sheffield U	D	1-1	0-0	—	Hirst	30,039
16	21	H	Ipswich T	D	1-1	1-0	14	Thompson (og)	24,270
17	28	A	Wimbledon	D	1-1	0-1	15	Bart-Williams	5740
18	Dec 5	A	Aston Villa	L	1-2	1-1	16	Bright	29,964
19	12	A	Leeds U	L	1-3	1-1	17	Nilsson	29,770
20	19	H	QPR	W	1-0	1-0	15	Bright	23,164
21	26	H	Manchester U	D	3-3	2-0	14	Hirst, Bright, Sheridan	37,708
22	28	A	Southampton	W	2-1	1-0	14	Sheridan (pen), Hirst	17,426
23	Jan 10	H	Norwich C	W	1-0	1-0	—	Worthington	23,360
24	16	A	Tottenham H	W	2-0	0-0	10	Bright, Hirst	25,702
25	30	A	Chelsea	W	2-0	1-0	9	Warhurst, Harkes	16,261
26	Feb 6	H	Everton	W	3-1	2-0	9	Warhurst, Harkes, Waddle	24,979
27	20	H	Crystal Palace	W	2-1	1-0	6	Warhurst, Wilson	26,459
28	23	A	Manchester C	W	2-1	0-0	—	Anderson, Warhurst	23,619
29	27	A	Liverpool	D	1-1	0-1	4	Anderson	33,964
30	Mar 3	H	Coventry C	L	0-1	0-1	—		13,806
31	10	A	Ipswich T	W	1-0	0-0	—	Hirst	16,538
32	20	A	Aston Villa	L	0-2	0-1	4		38,024
33	24	H	Wimbledon	D	1-1	0-0	—	Bright	20,918
34	Apr 7	A	Oldham Ath	D	1-1	0-1	—	Watson	12,312
35	10	A	Manchester U	L	1-2	0-0	8	Sheridan (pen)	40,102
36	12	H	Southampton	W	5-2	2-0	6	Bright, Bart-Williams 3, King	26,183
37	21	H	Sheffield U	D	1-1	0-1	—	Warhurst	38,688
38	May 1	A	Middlesbrough	L	2-3	0-2	10	Bart-Williams, Morris (og)	25,949
39	4	H	Leeds U	D	1-1	0-1	—	Hirst	26,855
40	6	H	Arsenal	W	1-0	1-0	—	Bright	23,645
41	8	A	Blackburn R	L	0-1	0-0	6		14,956
42	11	A	QPR	L	1-3	0-2	—	Bright	12,177

Final League Position: 7

GOALSCORERS

League (55): Bright 11, Hirst 11 (1 pen), Bart-Williams 6, Warhurst 6, Anderson 3, Sheridan 3 (2 pens), Harkes 2, Wilson 2, Hyde 1, King 1, Nilsson 1, Palmer 1, Pearson 1, Waddle 1, Watson 1, Williams P 1, Worthington 1, own goals 2.
Coca Cola Cup (25): Bright 6, Warhurst 4, Hirst 3, Watson 3, Harkes 2, Sheridan 2, Bart-Williams 1, Nilsson 1, Palmer 1, Wilson 1, Worthington 1.
FA Cup (13): Warhurst 5, Bright 3, Waddle 2, Harkes 1, Hirst 1, Sheridan 1 (pen).

Woods 39	Nilsson 32	King 11 + 1	Palmer 33 + 1	Pearson 13 + 3	Warhurst 25 + 4	Waddle 32 + 1	Hyde 14 + 6	Hirst 22	Williams P 7	Worthington 40	Watson 4 + 7	Bart-Williams 21 + 13	Wilson 21 + 5	Harkes 23 + 6	Francis 23 + 4	Shirtliff 20	Jemson 5 + 8	Anderson 24 + 2	Bright 28 + 2	Sheridan 25	Jones 9	Watts 2 + 2	Stewart 6	Pressman 3	Williams M 2 + 1	Match No.
1	2	3	4	5	6	7	8	9	10	11	12	14														1
1	2	3	4	5	6			9	10	11		8	7	12												2
1	2	3	4	5	6			9	10	11		8	14	7	12											3
1		3	4	5	2		8	9	10	11			12	7				6								4
1	2			5	3	4	9	10	11			8	7	12				6	14							5
1	2				4	5	3	9	10	11		8	14	12				6	7							6
1	2				4	5	6	9	10	11		7	8	12		3	14									7
1					4			6	8	7		11	12	10	14	2		5		3	9					8
1		4	12					8		3		10	7			2	11	5	14	6	9					9
1	7				4			8		3		11	10	12		2		5		6	9					10
1	7				4	11		8		3		14	12	10		2		5		6	9					11
1					4		2		8	3	9	12	10	14	7			5		6	11					12
1					4	5		8	11	3		12	7	10		2				6	9					13
1				5	4			8		3	9		7			2		6	10	11						14
1	2		12	5	4			8		3	9		7					6	10	11						15
1	2			5	4		6	8		3	9		7				12		10	11						16
1	2						6	8		3	9		7		4		12		5	11						17
1	2				4		6	8		3	9	12	7		14			5	10	11						18
1	2			5	4		6	8		3	9		7				12		10	11						19
1	2				4		6	8		3	9	12	7					5	10	11						20
1	2				4			8		3	9		7	12				6	5	10	11					21
1	2				4			8		3	9		7					6	5	10	11					22
1	2		12					8		3	9		14	7	4			6		10	11					23
1	2		12	5			8		7	3	9				4			6		10	11					24
1	2		12		4			9	8	3		14	7	10			6	5		11						25
1	2		12		4			9	8	3		14	7				6	5	10	11						26
1	2				4			9	8	3			7	10			6	5	12	11						27
1	2				4			9	8	3			7	10	12		6	5	14	11						28
1	2				4			9	8	3		12	7				6	5	14	10	11					29
1	2				4		9	8		3			7				12	6	10	11		5	14			30
1	2					7		9		3		12			14		8	6	10	11		5	4			31
1	2				4		9	8		3		12	7					6	10	11			5			32
1	2				4			8		3	9		7				12	6	10	11		5	14			33
1	2	14					8	7		3		11	12			5		6	10		9		4			34
1	2	9			4			8		3		11	7		14		12	6	10			5				35
		3				7		11	10						4		12	6	9		8	2	5	1	14	36
1	2				4		6	8	14	3	9	12						5	10	11	7					37
1	2				4			8		3	9	12	7			5		6	10	11						38
1	2	3	12		4			8			9	11	7	10	14			5			6					39
		3	12		4							10			14	2		5	9	11		8	6	1	7	40
1	2				4			8	14	3	9	12	7			5		6	10	11						41
	2	3	12					8				10			14			6	9	11	4	5		1	7	42

Coca Cola Cup

	Second Round	Hartlepool U (h)	3-0
		(a)	2-2
	Third Round	Leicester C (h)	7-1
	Fourth Round	QPR (h)	4-0
	Fifth Round	Ipswich T (a)	1-1
		(h)	1-0
	Semi-Final	Blackburn R (a)	4-2
		(h)	2-1
	Final at Wembley	Arsenal	1-2
FA Cup	Third Round	Cambridge U (a)	2-1
	Fourth Round	Sunderland (h)	1-0
	Fifth Round	Southend U (h)	2-0
	Sixth Round	Derby Co (a)	3-3
		(h)	1-0
	Semi-Final at Wembley	Sheffield U	2-1
	Final at Wembley	Arsenal	1-1
	Replay		1-2

SHEFFIELD WEDNESDAY

Player and Position	Ht	Wt	Birth Date	Place	Source	Clubs	League App	Gls
Goalkeepers								
Lance Key	6 2	14 13	13 5 68	Kettering	Histon	Sheffield W	—	—
						York C (loan)	—	—
Kevin Pressman	6 1	14 02	6 11 67	Fareham	Apprentice	Sheffield W	62	—
						Stoke C (loan)	4	—
Paul Robinson*			2 1 74	Scarborough	Trainee	Sheffield W	—	—
Chris Woods	6 2	14 05	14 11 59	Boston	Apprentice	Nottingham F	—	—
						QPR	63	—
						Norwich C (loan)	10	—
						Norwich C	206	—
						Rangers	173	—
						Sheffield W	80	—
Defenders								
Viv Anderson	6 0	12 02	29 8 56	Nottingham	Apprentice	Nottingham F	328	15
						Arsenal	120	9
						Manchester U	54	2
						Sheffield W	70	8
David Faulkner			8 10 75	Sheffield	Trainee	Sheffield W	—	—
Jonathan Flint*			27 10 73	Sutton in Ashfield	Trainee	Sheffield W	—	—
Phil King	5 8	13 00	28 12 67	Bristol	Apprentice	Exeter C	27	—
						Torquay U	24	3
						Swindon T	116	4
						Sheffield W	119	2
Brian Linighan			2 11 73	Hartlepool	Trainee	Sheffield W	—	—
John Linighan			2 11 73	Hartlepool	Trainee	Sheffield W	—	—
Roland Nilsson	5 10	12 00	27 11 63	Helsingborg	IFK Gothenburg	Sheffield W	113	2
Carlton Palmer	6 2	12 04	5 12 65	West Bromwich	Trainee	WBA	121	4
						Sheffield W	168	9
Nigel Pearson	6 1	14 11	21 8 63	Nottingham	Heanor T	Shrewsbury T	153	5
						Sheffield W	175	14
Peter Shirtliff	6 0	13 03	6 4 61	Barnsley	Apprentice	Sheffield W	188	4
						Charlton Ath	103	7
						Sheffield W	104	4
Simon Stewart	6 1	12 00	1 11 73	Leeds	Trainee	Sheffield W	6	—
Paul Warhurst	6 1	12 07	26 9 69	Stockport	Trainee	Manchester C	—	—
						Oldham Ath	67	2
						Sheffield W	62	6
Julian Watts	6 3	12 01	17 3 71	Sheffield		Rotherham U	20	1
						Sheffield W	4	—
						Shrewsbury T (loan)	9	—
Nigel Worthington	5 11	12 05	4 11 61	Ballymena	Ballymena U	Notts Co	67	4
						Sheffield W	307	11
Midfield								
Chris Bart-Williams	5 11	11 00	16 6 74	Freetown	Trainee	Leyton Orient	36	2
						Sheffield W	49	6
Leroy Chambers	5 10	11 12	25 10 72	Sheffield	Trainee	Sheffield W	—	—
Ian Frank*			19 9 73	Sheffield	Trainee	Sheffield W	—	—
John Harkes	5 10	11 10	8 3 67	New Jersey	USSF	Sheffield W	81	7
Graham Hyde	5 7	11 07	10 11 70	Doncaster	Trainee	Sheffield W	33	1
Ryan Jones	6 1	13 10	23 7 73	Sheffield	Trainee	Sheffield W	9	—
John Sheridan	5 9	12 00	1 10 64	Manchester	Local	Leeds U	230	47
						Nottingham F	—	—
						Sheffield W	122	21
Ronald Simpson			12 3 74	Easington	Trainee	Sheffield W	—	—
Mike Williams	5 10	11 02	21 11 69	Bradford	Maltby	Sheffield W	3	—
						Halifax T (loan)	9	1
Danny Wilson	5 6	11 00	1 1 60	Wigan	Wigan Ath	Bury	90	8
						Chesterfield	100	13
						Nottingham F	10	1

SHEFFIELD WEDNESDAY

Colours: Blue and white striped shirts, blue shorts, blue stockings. **Change colours:** All black with yellow and grey trim.

Foundation: Sheffield, being one of the principal centres of early Association Football, this club was formed as long ago as 1867 by the Sheffield Wednesday Cricket Club (formed 1825) and their colours from the start were blue and white. The inaugural meeting was held at the Adelphi Hotel and the original committee included Charles Stokes who was subsequently a founder member of Sheffield United.

First Football League game: 3 September, 1892, Division 1, v Notts C (A) W 1-0 – Allan; T. Brandon (1), Mumford; Hall, Betts, H. Brandon; Spiksley, Brady, Davis, R.N. Brown, Dunlop.

Did you know: When Sheffield Wednesday successfully defended their Division 1 title in 1929–30, they won with ten points to spare, scored 105 goals and conceded 57.

Managers (and Secretary-Managers)
Arthur Dickinson 1891–1920*, Robert Brown 1920–33, Billy Walker 1933–37, Jimmy McMullan 1937–42, Eric Taylor 1942–58 (continued as GM to 1974), Harry Catterick 1958–61, Vic Buckingham 1961–64, Alan Brown 1964–68, Jack Marshall 1968–69, Danny Williams 1969–71, Derek Dooley 1971–73, Steve Burtenshaw 1974–75, Len Ashurst 1975–77, Jackie Charlton 1977–83, Howard Wilkinson 1983–88, Peter Eustace 1988–89, Ron Atkinson 1989–91, Trevor Francis June 1991–.

Name	Ht	Wt	Birth date	Birthplace	Source	Club	Apps	Gls
						Scunthorpe U (loan)	6	3
						Brighton	135	33
						Luton T	110	24
						Sheffield W	98	11
Jeremy Wright*			3 10 73	Dewsbury	Trainee	Sheffield W	—	—
Forwards								
Mark Bright	6 0	13 00	6 6 62	Stoke	Leek T	Port Vale	29	10
						Leicester C	42	6
						Crystal Palace	227	92
						Sheffield W	30	11
Richard Curzon*			6 9 73	Mansfield	Trainee	Sheffield W	—	—
Trevor Francis†	5 10	11 07	19 4 54	Plymouth	Apprentice	Birmingham C	271	115
					Detroit E	Birmingham C	9	3
						Nottingham F	20	6
					Detroit E	Nottingham F	50	22
						Manchester C	26	12
						Sampdoria	68	17
						Atalanta	21	1
						Rangers	18	—
						QPR	32	12
						Sheffield W	75	5
Damien Hill*			7 6 74	Leicester	Trainee	Sheffield W	—	—
David Hirst	5 11	13 01	7 12 67	Barnsley	Apprentice	Barnsley	28	9
						Sheffield W	211	83
Nigel Jemson	5 10	12 10	10 8 69	Preston	Trainee	Preston NE	32	8
						Nottingham F	47	13
						Bolton W (loan)	5	—
						Preston NE (loan)	9	2
						Sheffield W	33	4
David Johnson	6 2	14 03	29 10 70	Rother Valley	Trainee	Sheffield W	6	—
						Hartlepool U (loan)	7	2
						Hartlepool U (loan)	3	—
Michael Rowntree			18 11 73	Hartlepool	Trainee	Sheffield W	—	—
Chris Waddle	6 2	12 13	14 12 60	Hepworth	Tow Law T	Newcastle U	170	46
						Tottenham H	138	33
						Marseille	107	22
						Sheffield W	33	1
Gordon Watson	5 7	13 03	20 3 71	Kent	Trainee	Charlton Ath	31	7
						Sheffield W	20	1

Trainees
Briscoe, Lee S; Burkill, Matthew J; Burrows, Marc L; Carter, Simon T; Guest, Mark A; Holmes, Darren P; Jacks, Daniel M.

Associated Schoolboys
Bowler, Martin S; Cadet, Ryan L; Gallagher, Richard; Harrison, Andrew J; Humphreys, Ritchie J; Kirkpatrick, Matthew R; Kotylo, Krystof J; Milley, Christopher; Pringle, Alan J; Sharman, Samuel J; Simpkins, James M; Thirlwell, Paul; Thorpe, Steven M; Waring, Phillip; Woods, Stuart M.

Associated Schoolboys who have accepted the club's offer of a Traineeship/Contract
Bailey, Gavin J; Barker, Richard I; Brown, Steven M; Ludlam, Craig; McVeigh, Michael B; Pass, Steven D; Sgargill, Jonathan M; Sykes, Paul K.

464

SHREWSBURY TOWN 1992–93 *Back row (left to right):* John Bond (Manager), Kevin Summerfield, O'Neill Donaldson, Tommy Lynch, Neil Lyne, Paul Edwards, Steve McKenzie, Dean Spink, Howard Clark, Mark Blake, John Brough, Richard Pratley (Youth Team Coach).
Front row: Fred Davies (Assistant Manager), Mark S. Williams, Mark Smith, Carl Griffiths, Mark Taylor, Pat O'Toole, Darren Harmon, Graeme Worsley, Malcolm Musgrove (Physio/Coach).

Division 3   SHREWSBURY TOWN

Gay Meadow, Shrewsbury. Telephone Shrewsbury (0743) 360111. Commercial Dept: 56316. Clubcall: 0898 121194.

Ground capacity: 7500.

Record attendance: 18,917 v Walsall, Division 3, 26 April 1961.

Record receipts: £36,240 v Ipswich T, FA Cup 5th rd, 13 February 1982.

Pitch measurements: 116yd × 76yd.

President: *Vice-president:* Dr J. Millard Bryson.

Chairman: K. R. Woodhouse.

Directors: F. C. G. Fry, R. Bailey (vice-chairman), M. J. Starkey, G. W. Nelson, W. H. Richards.

Manager: John Bond. *Commercial Manager:* M. Thomas.

Physio: Malcolm Musgrove. *Coach:* Fred Davies.

Secretary: M. J. Starkey.

Club Nickname: 'Town' or 'Shrews'.

Year Formed: 1886. *Turned Professional:* 1905 (approx). *Ltd Co.:* 1936.

Previous Ground: Old Shrewsbury Racecourse.

Record League Victory: 7–0 v Swindon T, Division 3 (S), 6 May 1955 – McBride; Bannister, Keech; Wallace, Maloney, Candlin; Price, O'Donnell (1), Weigh (4), Russell, McCue (2).

Record Cup Victory: 7–1 v Banbury Spencer, FA Cup, 1st rd, 4 November 1961 – Gibson; Walters, Skeech; Wallace, Pountney, Harley; Kenning (2), Pragg, Starkey (1), Rowley (2), McLaughlin (2).

Record Defeat: 1–8 v Norwich C, Division 3 (S), 1952–53 and v Coventry C, Division 3, 22 October 1963.

Most League Points (2 for a win): 62, Division 4, 1974–75.

Most League Points (3 for a win): 65, Division 2, 1984–85.

Most League Goals: 101, Division 4, 1958–59.

Highest League Scorer in Season: Arthur Rowley, 38, Division 4, 1958–59.

Most League Goals in Total Aggregate: Arthur Rowley, 152, 1958–65 (thus completing his League record of 434 goals).

Most Capped Player: Jimmy McLaughlin, 5 (12), Northern Ireland and Bernard McNally, 5, Northern Ireland.

Most League Appearances: Colin Griffin, 406, 1975–89.

Record Transfer Fee Received: £385,000 from WBA for Bernard McNally, July 1989.

Record Transfer Fee Paid: £100,000 to Aldershot for John Dungworth, November 1979 and £100,000 to Southampton for Mark Blake, August 1990.

Football League Record: 1950 Elected to Division 3 (N); 1951–58 Division 3 (S); 1958–59 Division 4; 1959–74 Division 3; 1974–75 Division 4; 1975–79 Division 3; 1979–89 Division 2; 1989– Division 3.

Honours: Football League: Division 2 best season: 8th, 1983–84, 1984–85; Division 3 – Champions 1978–79; Division 4 – Runners-up 1974–5. *FA Cup:* best season: 6th rd, 1978–79, 1981–82. *Football League Cup:* Semi-final 1961. *Welsh Cup:* Winners 1891, 1938, 1977, 1979, 1984, 1985; Runners-up 1931, 1948, 1980.

SHREWSBURY TOWN 1992—93 LEAGUE RECORD

Match No.	Date	Venue	Opponents	Result	H/T Score	Lg. Pos.	Goalscorers	Attendance
1	Aug 15	A	York C	L 0-2	0-1	—		2414
2	22	H	Doncaster R	W 2-1	1-1	13	Summerield, Griffiths	1867
3	29	A	Scunthorpe U	D 1-1	0-1	9	Taylor	3438
4	Sept 1	A	Colchester U	W 2-0	1-0	—	Griffiths, Brough	3530
5	5	H	Rochdale	L 1-2	0-1	8	Haylock	2547
6	12	A	Wrexham	L 0-2	0-0	13		4265
7	15	H	Scarborough	W 2-0	1-0	—	Griffiths, Lyne	1527
8	19	H	Bury	W 2-0	2-0	5	Griffiths 2 (1 pen)	2307
9	26	A	Lincoln C	W 1-0	0-0	3	Barham	2746
10	Oct 3	A	Barnet	D 2-2	2-0	3	Griffiths, Summerfield	2913
11	10	H	Darlington	L 1-2	0-1	6	Griffiths	2829
12	17	A	Chesterfield	W 4-2	1-2	4	Taylor, Griffiths 2, Lyne	3207
13	24	H	Cardiff C	W 3-2	2-1	3	Griffiths 3	4161
14	31	A	Northampton T	D 0-0	0-0	3		2731
15	Nov 3	H	Halifax T	W 1-0	1-0	—	O'Toole	2704
16	21	H	Walsall	L 0-3	0-3	5		4353
17	Dec 12	H	Gillingham	W 2-1	1-0	12	Griffiths 2 (1 pen)	2442
18	20	A	Torquay U	L 0-1	0-1	—		1960
19	26	A	Hereford U	D 1-1	0-0	4	Worsley	3287
20	28	H	Crewe Alex	W 4-1	1-0	4	Taylor, Brown, Lyne, Griffiths	4789
21	Jan 2	H	Wrexham	L 0-1	0-0	5		6179
22	16	H	Lincoln C	W 3-2	2-1	4	Spink, Summerfield, Taylor	2506
23	26	H	Scunthorpe U	W 2-1	0-1	—	Lynch, Griffiths	2190
24	29	A	Doncaster R	W 1-0	1-0	—	Summerfield	2227
25	Feb 6	H	York C	D 1-1	0-1	5	Taylor	3532
26	13	A	Rochdale	L 0-2	0-1	5		2446
27	20	H	Colchester U	W 4-3	1-0	5	Griffiths 2, Smith M, English (og)	2653
28	27	A	Darlington	W 2-0	1-0	5	Griffiths 2	1422
29	Mar 6	H	Barnet	W 1-0	1-0	5	Kinnaird	4518
30	9	A	Carlisle U	L 0-1	0-0	—		4022
31	20	A	Halifax T	D 1-1	0-1	6	Blake	3872
32	27	A	Walsall	D 1-1	0-0	7	Griffiths	5573
33	30	A	Bury	D 0-0	0-0	—		2976
34	Apr 3	A	Carlisle U	L 2-3	1-1	6	Williams M S, Summerfield	3100
35	6	A	Gillingham	L 0-1	0-1	—		3086
36	10	H	Hereford U	D 1-1	1-1	8	Griffiths	3604
37	12	A	Crewe Alex	D 2-2	0-1	7	Griffiths 2	4215
38	17	H	Torquay U	L 0-1	0-1	8		3082
39	20	A	Scarborough	W 2-1	1-1	—	Summerfield, Griffiths	1325
40	24	H	Chesterfield	D 2-2	1-1	8	Worsley, Griffiths (pen)	3473
41	May 1	A	Cardiff C	L 1-2	1-1	8	Summerfield	17,253
42	8	H	Northampton T	L 2-3	2-0	9	Lynch, Griffiths	6612

Final League Position: 9

GOALSCORERS

League (57): Griffiths 27 (3 pens), Summerfield 7, Taylor 5, Lyne 3, Lynch 2, Worsley 2, Barham 1, Blake 1, Brough 1, Brown 1, Haylock 1, Kinnaird 1, O'Toole 1, Smith 1, Spink 1, Williams MS 1, own goal 1.
Coca Cola Cup (2): Griffiths 1, Smith 1.
FA Cup (5): Griffiths 2, Lyne 1, Summerfield 1, Williams L 1.

Edwards 42	Worsley 20 + 8	Clark 30 + 3	Evans P 3 + 1	Spink 22 + 1	Blake 32	Taylor 42	Summerfield 34 + 1	Brough 6 + 8	Hodges 1	Lyne 18 + 2	Griffiths 41 + 1	Williams M S 26 + 2	Smith N 2	O'Toole 2 + 6	Lynch 39	Barham 7 + 1	Haylock 16 + 2	Smith M 31	Harmon — + 1	Williams L 2 + 1	Watts 9	Brown 17	MacKenzie 3 + 5	Kinnaird 4	Brooks 1	Piggott 3 + 1	Turner 9	Seabury — + 1	Williams M — + 2	Evans J — + 1	Match No.
1	2	3	4	5	6	7	8	9	10	11	12																	14			1
1	2			5	3	6	8	10		11	9	4	7	12																	2
1	2	14		5	6	4	8	12		11	10	9	7		3																3
1	2			5	6	4	8	7		11	10	9			3																4
1	2			5	6	4	8	7		11	10	9			3	12	14														5
1		4	9	5	3		8	12		11	10	6			7	2															6
1	8			5	6	4		11		10					3	7	2	9	12												7
1	12	8		5	6	4				11	10				3	7	2	9											14		8
1	12	8		5	6	4				11	10			14	3	7	2	9													9
1	12	8		5	6	4				11	14		10		3	7	2	9													10
1	8			5	6	4				11	12		10		3	7	2	9													11
1	8			5	6	4				11	9		10		3	7	2														12
1	12	8		5	6	4				11	9		10		3		2	7													13
1	12	8	7	5	6	4				11	9		10		3		2														14
1	8			5	6	4		7			9	10	12		11	3	2														15
1	12	8		5	6	4		11		9			10		14	3	2	7													16
1	2	8		5	6	4		12		11	10				3			9	7												17
1	2	8			4	5	12			11	10	6			9	3				14	7										18
1	2				4	8				9	10	5			3			11					6	7							19
1	2	12			4	8				9	10	5			3			11					6	7							20
1	2	8			4					9	10	5			3			11					6	7							21
1	12		9		6	4	8			10					3	2	11						5	7				14			22
1					6	4	8			10		5			9		2	11					3	7							23
1					6	4	8			10		5			9		2	11					3	7	12						24
1	7	8			6	4				10		5			9		2	11					3		12						25
1	14				6	4	8	12		10					9		2	5					3			7	11				26
1	2	12			6	4	8	9		10		5			14	3		11								7					27
1	2	9			6	4	8			10		5			3			11								7					28
1		2			6	4	8			10		5			3			11							12	7	9				29
1		2			6	4	8	12		10		5			3	14	11									7	9				30
1		2			6	4	8			10		5		14	3		11									7	12	9			31
1		2			6	4				10		5		14	3		11								7	8	12	9			32
1	2		6			4	8			10		5			3		11								7		9				33
1	9	2	6			4	8			10		5		12	3		11								7						34
1	2	12	6			4	8			10		5			3		11								7		9				35
1	2		6			4	8	12		10		5			3		11								7		9				36
1	2	6				4	8			10		5			3		11								7		9				37
1	6	2				4	8	12		10		5			3		11								7		9	14			38
1	7	2	6			4	8			10		5			3		11										9				39
1	7	2	6			4	8	12		10		5			3		11										9				40
1	7	2	6			4	8			10		3					11						5	12			9				41
1	12	2	6			4	8			10		3					11						5	7			9				42

Coca Cola Cup	First Round	Wigan Ath (h)	1-2
		(a)	1-0
FA Cup	First Round	Mansfield T (h)	3-1
	Second Round	Burnley (a)	1-1
		(h)	1-2

SHREWSBURY TOWN

Player and Position	Ht	Wt	Date	Birth Place	Source	Clubs	League App	Gls
Goalkeepers								
Paul Edwards	5 11	11 05	22 2 65	Liverpool	St. Helens T	Crewe Alex	29	—
						Shrewsbury T	42	—
Ron Green‡	6 2	14 00	3 10 56	Birmingham	Alvechurch	Walsall	163	—
						WBA (loan)	—	—
						Shrewsbury T	19	—
						Bristol R (loan)	18	—
						Bristol R	38	—
						Scunthorpe U	78	—
						Wimbledon	4	—
						Shrewsbury T (loan)	17	—
						Manchester C (loan)	—	—
						Walsall	67	—
					Local	Colchester U	4	—
						Cambridge U	—	—
						Shrewsbury T	—	—
Defenders								
Mark Blake	6 1	12 08	19 12 67	Portsmouth	Apprentice	Southampton	18	2
						Colchester U (loan)	4	1
						Shrewsbury T (loan)	10	—
						Shrewsbury T	117	3
Howard Clark*	5 11	11 01	19 9 68	Coventry	Apprentice	Coventry C	20	1
						Darlington (loan)	5	—
						Shrewsbury T	56	—
Paul Haylock*	5 9	11 10	24 3 63	Lowestoft	Apprentice	Norwich C	155	3
						Gillingham	152	—
						Maidstone U	48	1
						Shrewsbury T	18	1
Kevin Thelwell‡	5 10	12 00	27 10 73	Winsford	Trainee	Shrewsbury T	—	—
Mark S Williams	6 0	13 00	28 9 70	Cheshire	Newtown	Shrewsbury T	31	1
Graeme Worsley*	5 10	11 02	4 1 69	Liverpool	Bootle	Shrewsbury T	105	4
Midfield								
Mark Barham‡	5 7	11 00	12 7 62	Folkestone	Apprentice	Norwich C	177	23
						Huddersfield T	27	1
						Middlesbrough	4	—
						WBA	4	—
						Brighton	73	8
						Shrewsbury T	8	1
Jason Evans*	5 7	11 05	22 1 74	Cambridge	Trainee	Shrewsbury T	1	—
Paul Evans§	5 6	10 08	1 9 74	Oswestry	Trainee	Shrewsbury T	6	—
David Hodges‡	5 9	10 02	17 1 70	Hereford		Mansfield T	85	7
						Torquay U	16	—
						Shrewsbury T	1	—
Tommy Lynch	6 0	12 06	10 10 64	Limerick	Limerick	Sunderland	4	—
						Shrewsbury T	140	6
Steve MacKenzie	5 11	12 05	23 11 61	Romford	Apprentice	Crystal Palace	—	—
						Manchester C	58	8
						WBA	148	23
						Charlton Ath	100	7
						Sheffield W	15	2
						Shrewsbury T	21	1
Pat O'Toole*	5 7	11 00	2 1 65	Dublin	Shelbourne	Leicester C	—	—
						Exeter C	6	—
						Shrewsbury T	46	1
Kevin Seabury	5 9	11 06	24 11 73	Shrewsbury	Trainee	Shrewsbury T	1	—
Mark Smith	5 9	10 04	16 12 64	Bellshill	St Mirren BC	Queen's Park	82	7
						Celtic	6	—
						Dunfermline Ath	53	6
						Stoke C (loan)	2	—
						Nottingham F	—	—
						Reading (loan)	3	—
						Shrewsbury T	31	1
Nigel Smith‡	5 7	10 04	21 12 69	Leeds	Leeds U	Burnley	13	—
						Bury	34	3
						Shrewsbury T	2	—

SHREWSBURY TOWN

Colours: Amber/blue trim shirts, blue shorts, amber stockings, blue trim. **Change colours:** Red shirts, white shorts, red stockings.

Foundation: Shrewsbury School having provided a number of the early England and Wales internationals it is not surprising that there was a Town club as early as 1876 which won the Birmingham Senior Cup in 1879. However, the present Shrewsbury Town club was formed in 1886 and won the Welsh FA Cup as early as 1891.

First Football League game: 19 August, 1950, Division 3(N), v Scunthorpe U (a) D 0-0 – Eggleston; Fisher, Lewis; Wheatley, Depear, Robinson; Griffin, Hope, Jackson, Brown, Barker.

Did you know: Arthur Rowley overhauled Dixie Dean's record of 379 League goals on 29 April 1961 when he scored his 380th in a game for Shrewsbury Town against Bradford City.

Managers (and Secretary-Managers)
W. Adams 1905–12*, A. Weston 1912–34*, Jack Roscamp 1934–35, Sam Ramsey 1935–36, Ted Bousted 1936–40, Leslie Knighton 1945–49, Harry Chapman 1949–50, Sammy Crooks 1950–54, Walter Rowley 1955–57, Harry Potts 1957–58, Johnny Spuhler 1958, Arthur Rowley 1958–68, Harry Gregg 1968–72, Maurice Evans 1972–73, Alan Durban 1974–78, Richie Barker 1978, Graham Turner 1978–84, Chic Bates 1984–87, Ian McNeill 1987–90, Asa Hartford 1990–91, John Bond January 1991–.

Player and Position	Ht	Wt	Birth Date	Birth Place	Source	Clubs	League App	Gls
Kevin Summerfield	5 11	11 00	7 1 59	Walsall	Apprentice	WBA	9	4
						Birmingham C	5	1
						Walsall	54	17
						Cardiff C	10	1
						Plymouth Arg	139	26
						Exeter C (loan)	4	—
						Shrewsbury T	111	19
Mark Taylor	5 8	11 08	22 2 66	Walsall	Local	Walsall	113	4
						Sheffield W	9	—
						Shrewsbury T (loan)	19	2
						Shrewsbury T	71	7
Forwards								
Chris Brooks‡	5 10	11 10	6 6 72	Sutton-in-Ashfield	Luton T	Shrewsbury T	1	—
John Brough	6 1	12 07	8 1 73	Heanor	Trainee	Notts Co	—	—
						Shrewsbury T	14	1
Mike Brown	5 9	10 12	8 2 68	Birmingham	Apprentice	Shrewsbury T	190	9
						Bolton W	33	3
						Shrewsbury T	17	1
O'Neill Donaldson*	6 0	11 04	24 11 69	Birmingham	Hinckley	Shrewsbury T	19	2
Carl Griffiths	5 9	10 06	15 7 71	Coventry	Trainee	Shrewsbury T	134	49
Paul Kinnaird (To St Johnstone March 1993)	5 8	10 10	1 11 66	Glasgow	Apprentice	Norwich C	—	—
						Dundee U	18	—
						Motherwell	34	—
						St Mirren	57	4
						Partick T	33	3
						Shrewsbury T	4	1
Gary Piggott*	5 11	12 02	1 4 69	Warley	Dudley T	WBA	5	—
						Shrewsbury T	4	—
Dean Spink	5 11	13 08	22 1 67	Birmingham	Halesowen	Aston Villa	—	—
						Scarborough (loan)	3	2
						Bury (loan)	6	1
						Shrewsbury T	119	13
Mark Williams*	5 10	12 07	10 12 73	Bangor	Trainee	Shrewsbury T	3	—

Trainees
Brown, Romilly L; Davies, Ashley J; Evans, Paul D; Evans, Paul S; Jenkins, Sam B; King, Nathan P; Mulvey, James R; Parfitt, Mark; Reed, Ian P; Simpson, Paul D; Taylor, Steven D; Yates, Jason J.

**Non-Contract
Brookman, Nicholas A.

Associated Schoolboys
Archer, Darren; Caroll, Adam; Edwards, John C. A; Green, Adam B; Holgate, Christopher; James, Paul C; Pemberton, Stephen; Stephens, Philip P; Thomas, Vaughan L; Wood, James D; Woods, David; Woods, Simon.

Associated Schoolboys who have accepted the club's offer of a Traineeship/Contract
Crosling, Carl I; Martin, Lee.

**Non-Contract Players who are retained must be re-signed before they are eligible to play in League matches.

470

SOUTHAMPTON 1992–93 *Back row (left to right):* Jason Dodd, Jeff Kenna, Francis Benali, Neil Maddison, Tommy Widdrington, David Lee.
Centre row: Lew Chatterley (First Team Coach), David Speedie, Richard Hall, Tim Flowers, Kerry Dixon, Ian Andrews, Iain Dowie, Matthew le Tissier, Don Taylor (Physio).
Front row: Stuart Gray, Micky Adams, Glenn Cockerill, Ian Branfoot (Manager), Kevin Moore, Steve Wood, Terry Hurlock.

FA Premier   **SOUTHAMPTON**

The Dell, Milton Road, Southampton SO9 4XX. Telephone Southampton (0703) 220505. Fax 0703 330360. Ticket enquiries: (0703) 228575.

Ground capacity: 19,000.

Record attendance: 31,044 v Manchester U, Division 1, 8 October 1969.

Record receipts: £156,493 v Norwich C, FA Cup 6th rd, 7 March 1992.

Pitch measurements: 110yd × 72yd.

Chairman: F. G. L. Askham FCA.

Vice-Chairman: K. St. J. Wiseman.

Directors: I. L. Gordon, B. H. D. Hunt, M. R. Richards FCA.

President: J. Corbett. *Vice-president:* E. T. Bates.

Manager: Ian Branfoot. *Assistant Manager:* John Mortimore.

Coach: Lew Chatterley. *Physio:* Don Taylor.

Secretary: Brian Truscott. *Commercial Manager:* Bob Russell.

Year Formed: 1885. *Turned Professional:* 1894. *Ltd Co.:* 1897.

Club Nickname: 'The Saints'.

Previous Name: Southampton St Mary's until 1885.

Previous Grounds: 1885, Antelope Ground; 1897, County Cricket Ground; 1898, The Dell.

Record League Victory: 9–3 v Wolverhampton W, Division 2, 18 September 1965 – Godfrey; Jones, Williams; Walker, Knapp, Huxford; Paine (2), O'Brien (1), Melia, Chivers (4), Sydenham (2).

Record Cup Victory: 7–1 v Ipswich T, FA Cup, 3rd rd, 7 January 1961 – Reynolds; Davies, Traynor; Conner, Page, Huxford; Paine (1), O'Brien (3 incl. 1p), Reeves, Mulgrew (2), Penk (1).

Record Defeat: 0–8 v Tottenham H, Division 2, 28 March 1936 and v Everton, Division 1, 20 November 1971.

Most League Points (2 for a win): 61, Division 3 (S), 1921–22 and Division 3, 1959–60.

Most League Points (3 for a win): 77, Division 1, 1983–84.

Most League Goals: 112, Division 3 (S), 1957–58.

Highest League Scorer in Season: Derek Reeves, 39, Division 3, 1959–60.

Most League Goals in Total Aggregate: Mike Channon, 185, 1966–77, 1979–82.

Most Capped Player: Peter Shilton, 49 (125), England.

Most League Appearances: Terry Paine, 713, 1956–74.

Record Transfer Fee Received: £3,300,000 from Blackburn R for Alan Shearer, July 1992.

Record Transfer Fee Paid: £1,000,000 to Swindon T for Alan McLoughlin, December 1990.

Football League Record: 1920 Original Member of Division 3; 1921–22 Division 3 (S); 1922–53 Division 2; 1953–58 Division 3 (S); 1958–60 Division 3; 1960–66 Division 2; 1966–74 Division 1; 1974–78 Division 2; 1978–92 Division 1; 1992– FA Premier League.

Honours: Football League: Division 1 – Runners-up 1983–84; Division 2 – Runners-up 1965–66, 1977–78; Division 3 (S) – Champions 1921–22; Runners-up 1920–21; Division 3 – Champions 1959–60. *FA Cup:* Winners 1975–76; Runners-up 1900, 1902. *Football League Cup:* Runners-up 1978–79. *Zenith Data Systems Cup:* Runners-up 1991–92. **European Competitions:** *European Fairs Cup:* 1969–70. *UEFA Cup:* 1971–72, 1981–82, 1982–83, 1984–85. *European Cup-Winners' Cup:* 1976–77.

SOUTHAMPTON 1992—93 LEAGUE RECORD

Match No.	Date		Venue	Opponents	Result		H/T Score	Lg. Pos.	Goalscorers	Atten dance
1	Aug	15	H	Tottenham H	D	0-0	0-0	—		19,654
2		19	A	QPR	L	1-3	1-0	—	Le Tissier	10,639
3		22	A	Aston Villa	D	1-1	0-0	17	Adams	17,894
4		24	H	Manchester U	L	0-1	0-0	—		15,623
5		29	H	Middlesbrough	W	2-1	0-0	17	Le Tissier (pen), Banger	13,003
6	Sept	1	A	Liverpool	D	1-1	0-0	—	Dixon	30,024
7		5	A	Norwich C	L	0-1	0-0	18		12,452
8		12	H	QPR	L	1-2	1-0	19	Le Tissier	14,125
9		19	H	Leeds U	D	1-1	1-0	20	Groves	16,229
10		26	A	Crystal Palace	W	2-1	1-0	15	Dowie 2	13,829
11	Oct	3	A	Sheffield U	L	0-2	0-2	18		15,842
12		17	H	Wimbledon	D	2-2	0-0	18	Dowie, Groves	11,221
13		24	A	Manchester C	L	0-1	0-0	19		20,089
14		31	H	Oldham Ath	W	1-0	0-0	19	Hall	10,827
15	Nov	7	A	Ipswich T	D	0-0	0-0	19		15,722
16		22	A	Blackburn R	D	1-1	1-1	—	Le Tissier	16,626
17		28	H	Nottingham F	W	2-1	1-1	16	Le Tissier, Adams	19,942
18	Dec	5	H	Arsenal	W	2-0	1-0	13	Maddison, Dowie	17,286
19		12	H	Coventry C	D	2-2	1-2	15	Maddison, Dowie	12,306
20		19	A	Everton	L	1-2	1-2	16	Le Tissier	14,051
21		26	A	Chelsea	D	1-1	1-0	15	Dowie	18,344
22		28	H	Sheffield W	L	1-2	0-1	17	Monkou	17,426
23	Jan	9	A	Leeds U	L	1-2	1-0	19	Dixon	26,071
24		16	H	Crystal Palace	W	1-0	0-0	17	Maddison	13,397
25		26	A	Middlesbrough	L	1-2	0-1	—	Le Tissier	13,918
26		30	H	Aston Villa	W	2-0	1-0	15	Banger, Dowie	19,087
27	Feb	7	A	Tottenham H	L	2-4	1-0	—	Dowie, Hall	20,098
28		10	H	Norwich C	W	3-0	2-0	—	Hall, Adams, Banger	12,969
29		13	H	Liverpool	W	2-1	1-0	12	Maddison, Banger	17,216
30		20	A	Manchester U	L	1-2	0-0	14	Banger	36,257
31		27	H	Sheffield U	W	3-2	3-1	12	Moore, Kenna, Dowie	13,814
32	Mar	6	A	Wimbledon	W	2-1	1-1	11	Le Tissier, Moore	4534
33		9	A	Blackburn R	D	0-0	0-0	—		13,556
34		13	H	Ipswich T	W	4-3	1-2	9	Hall, Le Tissier 2 (1 pen), Kenna	15,428
35		20	A	Arsenal	L	3-4	2-3	10	Dowie, Adams, Le Tissier	24,149
36		24	H	Nottingham F	L	1-2	0-2	—	Le Tissier	18,005
37	Apr	3	A	Coventry C	L	0-2	0-1	14		10,463
38		10	H	Chelsea	W	1-0	0-0	14	Banger	15,135
39		12	A	Sheffield W	L	2-5	0-2	14	Dodd, Dowie	26,183
40		17	H	Everton	D	0-0	0-0	14		16,911
41	May	1	H	Manchester C	L	0-1	0-1	15		11,830
42		8	A	Oldham Ath	L	3-4	1-2	18	Le Tissier 3	14,597

Final League Position: 18

GOALSCORERS

League (54): Le Tissier 15 (2 pens), Dowie 11, Banger 6, Adams 4, Hall 4, Maddison 4, Dixon 2, Groves 2, Kenna 2, Moore 2, Dodd 1, Monkou 1.
Coca Cola Cup (3): Le Tissier 2 (1 pen), Dowie 1.
FA Cup (1): Le Tissier 1.

Flowers 42	Dodd 27 + 3	Adams 38	Hurlock 30	Hall 28	Wood 4	Le Tissier 40	Cockerill 21 + 2	Dixon 8 + 1	Speedie 11	Benali 31 + 2	Moore 18	Dowie 34 + 2	Kenna 27 + 2	Monkou 33	Lee — + 1	Maddison 33 + 4	Groves 13 + 2	Banger 10 + 17	Widdrington 11 + 1	Moody 2 + 1	Powell — + 2	Bound 1 + 2	Bartlett — + 1	Allan — + 1	Match No.
1	2	3	4	5	6	7	8	9	10	11															1
1	2	3	4		6	7	8	9	10	11	5	12	14												2
1		3	4	5		7	8	9	10	11	6	12	2												3
1		3	4				8	9	7	11	6	10	2	5		12									4
1	2	3	4			7		9	10		6			5		8	11	12							5
1	2	3	4			7		9	10	11	6			5		8									6
1	2		4			7			10		3	6	9	5		8	11								7
1	2		4			7			10		3	6	9	5		8	11	12							8
1	2		4	5		7		9	10		3	6	14	11	12	8									9
1	2	11				7			10		3	6	9	5		12	8		4						10
1	2	11				7	8	4			3	6	9	5		10	12								11
1	2	11	4		6		8				3	10		5		12	7		9	14					12
1	2	11	4		6	7	8				3	10		5		12		9	14						13
1		3	4	5		7	8			11		10	2	6		9									14
1		3	4	5		7	8			11		9	2	6		10									15
1		3	4	5		7	8			11		10	2	6		9	12								16
1		3	4	5		7	8			11		9	2	6		10	12								17
1		3	4	5		7	8			11		9	2	6		10	12	14							18
1		3	4	5	6	7				11		9	2			10	8								19
1	14	3	4	5		7	12			11		9	2	6		10	8								20
1	12	3	4	5		7				11		9	2	6		10	8								21
1	8	3	4	5		7				11		9	2	6		10	12								22
1		3	4	5		7	8	9		11			2	6		10	12								23
1	2	3	4	5		7	8	9						6		10	11	12							24
1	2	3	4	5		7						8	6	9		10	11	12							25
1	2	3	4	5		7				11		6	9			10	8								26
1	2	3	4	5		7				11		9		6		10	8								27
1	8	3		5		7				11		9	2	6		10	12		4						28
1	8	3		5		7				11		9	2	6		10	12		4						29
1	8	3		5		7				11		9	2	6		10	12		4						30
1	8	3		5		7						9	2	6		10	11		4						31
1	11	3		5		7	8					9	2	6		10	12		4						32
1	11	3		5		7	8					9	2	6		10	12		4		14				33
1	11	3		5		7	12					9	2	6		10	8		4						34
1	14	3	4	5		7	8			11		9	2	6		10	12								35
1		3	4	5		7	12			11		9	2	6		10	8								36
1	8	3	4	5		7				11		9	2	6		10	12								37
1	11	3	4	5		7						9	2	6		10	8	12							38
1	11	3		5		7	8			14		9	2	6		10	12		4						39
1		3	4	5		7	8						2	6		10	11	9	14	12					40
1		3				7	8					9	2	6		10	11		4			5	12	14	41
1		3		5		7	8				12	9	2	6		10	11		4						42

Coca Cola Cup	Second Round	Gillingham (a)	0-0
		(h)	3-0
	Third Round	Crystal Palace (h)	0-2
FA Cup	Third Round	Nottingham F (a)	1-2

SOUTHAMPTON

Player and Position	Ht	Wt	Date	Birth Place	Source	Clubs	League App	Gls
Goalkeepers								
Ian Andrews	6 2	12 13	1 11 64	Nottingham	Apprentice	Leicester C	126	—
						Swindon T (loan)	1	—
						Celtic	5	—
						Leeds U (loan)	1	—
						Southampton	5	—
Tim Flowers	6 2	14 01	3 2 67	Kenilworth	Apprentice	Wolverhampton W	63	—
						Southampton (loan)	—	—
						Southampton	180	—
						Swindon T (loan)	2	—
						Swindon T (loan)	5	—
Russell Meara‡	5 9	11 04	17 7 74	London	Trainee	Southampton	—	—
Defenders								
Mick Adams	5 8	11 03	8 11 61	Sheffield	Apprentice	Gillingham	92	5
						Coventry C	90	9
						Leeds U	73	2
						Southampton	125	7
Derek Allan	6 0	10 13	24 12 74	Irving	Ayr United BC	Ayr U	5	—
						Southampton	1	—
Matthew Bound	6 2	13 12	9 11 72	Trowbridge	Trainee	Southampton	4	—
Aleksey Cherednik*	5 9	11 07	12 12 60	USSR	Dnepr	Southampton	23	—
Jason Dodd	5 10	11 13	2 11 70	Bath		Southampton	99	1
Gary Ferguson	5 11	11 08	16 9 74	Belfast	Reading	Southampton	—	—
Stuart Gray	5 10	11 09	19 4 60	Withernsea	Local	Nottingham F	49	3
						Bolton W (loan)	10	—
						Barnsley	120	23
						Aston Villa	106	9
						Southampton	12	—
Richard Hall	6 2	13 01	14 3 72	Ipswich	Trainee	Scunthorpe U	22	3
						Southampton	55	7
Jeff Kenna	5 11	11 09	27 8 70	Dublin	Trainee	Southampton	45	2
Kenneth Monkou	6 3	14 05	29 11 64	Surinam	Feyenoord	Chelsea	94	2
						Southampton	33	1
Kevin Moore	6 0	13 00	29 4 58	Grimsby	Local	Grimsby T	400	27
						Oldham Ath	13	1
						Southampton	134	10
						Bristol R (loan)	7	—
						Bristol R (loan)	4	1
Stephen Roast‡	5 6	9 04	19 9 72	London	Trainee	Southampton	—	—
Steve Wood	6 1	12 04	2 2 63	Bracknell	Apprentice	Reading	219	9
						Millwall	110	—
						Southampton	19	—
Midfield								
Neal Bartlett§	5 10	12 00	7 4 75	Southampton	Trainee	Southampton	1	—
Glenn Cockerill	5 10	12 03	25 8 59	Grimsby	Louth U	Lincoln C	71	10
						Swindon T	26	1
						Lincoln C	115	25
						Sheffield U	62	10
						Southampton	273	32
David Hughes	5 9	10 10	30 12 72	St Albans	Trainee	Southampton	—	—
Terry Hurlock	5 9	13 03	22 9 58	Hackney	Leytonstone/ Ilford	Brentford	220	18
						Reading	29	—
						Millwall	104	8
						Rangers	29	2
						Southampton	59	—
Neil McKilligan‡	5 10	10 08	2 1 74	Falkirk	Trainee	Southampton	—	—
Neil Maddison	5 10	10 07	2 10 69	Darlington	Trainee	Southampton	54	6

SOUTHAMPTON

Colours: Red and white striped shirts, black shorts, black stockings. **Change colours:** Turquoise/royal blue striped shirts, turquoise shorts, royal blue stockings.

Foundation: Formed largely by players from the Deanery FC, which had been established by school teachers in 1880. Most of the founders were connected with the young men's association of St. Mary's Church. At the inaugural meeting held in November 1885 the club was named Southampton St. Mary's and the church's curate was elected president.

First Football League game: 28 August, 1920, Division 3, v Gillingham (a) D 1-1 – Allen; Parker, Titmuss; Shelley, Campbell, Turner; Barratt, Dominy (1), Rawlings, Moore, Foxall.

Did you know: Since the formation of the Football League in 1888, Southampton can claim to have made more appearances in the latter stages of the FA Cup than any other club before entering the League, reaching the last eight in 1899, 1905, 1906 and 1908, the semi-finals in 1898 and the finals of 1900 and 1902.

Managers (and Secretary-Managers)
Cecil Knight 1894–95*, Charles Robson 1895–97, E. Arnfield 1897–1911* (continued as secretary), George Swift 1911–12, E. Arnfield 1912–19, Jimmy McIntyre 1919–24, Arthur Chadwick 1925–31, George Kay 1931–36, George Gross 1936–37, Tom Parker 1937–43, J. R. Sarjantson stepped down from the board to act as secretary-manager 1943–47 with the next two listed being team managers during this period), Arthur Dominy 1943–46, Bill Dodgin Snr 1946–49, Sid Cann 1949–51, George Roughton 1952–55, Ted Bates 1955–73, Lawrie McMenemy 1973–85, Chris Nicholl 1985–91, Ian Branfoot June 1991–.

Player and Position	Ht	Wt	Date	Birth Place	Source	Clubs	League App	Gls
Paul Sheerin	5 10	10 13	28 8 74	Edinburgh	Whitehill Welfare	Alloa Southampton	— —	— —
Martin Thomas	5 8	10 08	12 9 73	Lyndhurst	Trainee	Southampton	—	—
Paul Tisdale	5 9	10 08	14 1 73	Malta	School	Southampton Northampton T (loan)	5	—
Tommy Widdrington	5 10	11 07	21 11 71	Newcastle	Trainee	Southampton Wigan Ath (loan)	15 6	—

Forwards

Player and Position	Ht	Wt	Date	Birth Place	Source	Clubs	League App	Gls
Nicky Banger	5 9	10 11	25 2 71	Southampton	Trainee	Southampton	37	6
Francis Benali	5 10	11 00	30 12 68	Southampton	Apprentice	Southampton	101	—
Frankie Bennett	5 8	11 11	3 1 69	Birmingham	Halesowen	Southampton	—	—
Kerry Dixon	6 0	14 01	24 7 61	Luton	Dunstable	Reading Chelsea Southampton Luton T (loan)	116 335 9 17	51 147 2 3
Iain Dowie	6 1	13 07	9 1 65	Hatfield	Hendon	Luton T Fulham (loan) West Ham U Southampton	66 5 12 66	16 1 4 20
Perry Groves	5 10	12 08	19 4 65	London	Apprentice	Colchester U Arsenal Southampton	156 156 15	26 21 2
Matthew Le Tissier	6 1	12 10	14 10 68	Guernsey	Trainee	Southampton	213	75
Callum McDonald‡	5 8	10 10	21 9 73	Stirling	Trainee	Southampton	—	—
Paul Moody	6 3	14 03	13 6 67	Portsmouth	Waterlooville	Southampton Reading (loan)	7 5	— 1
Lee Powell	5 5	9 00	2 6 73	Newport	Trainee	Southampton	6	—

Trainees
Allen, Peter; Barlett, Neal; Cleeve, Anthony G; Doherty, Kevin T; Elliott, Lee; Hamill, Rory; Harper, Paul; Hopper, Neil; McNally, Aron A; Murphy, Kevin; Pickering, Christopher; Robinson, Matthew R; Rowe, Richard M; Winstanley, James.

Associated Schoolboys
Basham, Steven; Carbery, Thomas; Care, Simon J; Carter, John; Collar, Stuart; Conaty, Steven; Coxon, Jordan D; Davis, Neil; Flahavan, Darryl J; Gulliver, Ross; Hayward, Daniel; Hazlehurst, Daniel R; Homer, Gareth; McAllister, Craig; Phillips, Sam; Pickersgill, Gavin; Piper, David; Roberts, Daniel; Skinner, Darren M; Smith, Christopher G; Spedding, Duncan; Warner, Philip; Williams, Andrew P.

Associated Schoolboys who have accepted the club's offer of a Traineeship/Contract
Blamey, Nathan; Carr, Neil; Cole, James; Everest, Anthony D; Jansen, Nicholas J; Joseph, Urias; Liney, Andrew; Phillips, Daniel.

SOUTHEND UNITED 1992–93 *Back row (left to right):* Chris Powell, John Cornwell, Paul Sansome, Danny Sains, Spencer Prior, Andy Sussex, Ian Benjamin. *Centre row:* Alan Raw (Physio), Steve Tilson, Scott Ashenden, Christian Hyslop, Francisco Cagigao, Simon Royce, Mark Hall, Mel Capleton, Steven Brown, Kevin O'Callaghan, Steven Helfer, Adam Locke, Danny Greaves (Coach).
Front row: Keith Jones, Paul Smith, Bob Houghton (Assistant Manager), David Martin, Colin Murphy (Manager), Brett Angell, Andy Ansah.

Division 1 **SOUTHEND UNITED**

Roots Hall Football Ground, Victoria Avenue, Southend-on-Sea SS2 6NQ. Telephone Southend (0702) 340707. Fax 0702 330164. Commercial Dept: (0702) 332113. Soccerline: 0898 700279. Ticket office: 0702 435602. Shop: 0702 435067. Infoline: 0839 664443.

Ground capacity: 13,515 (seats 5977, standing 7538).

Record attendance: 31,090 v Liverpool FA Cup 3rd rd, 10 January 1979.

Record receipts: £83,999 v West Ham U, Division 1, 7 April 1993.

Pitch measurements: 110yd × 74yd. *President:* N. J. Woodcock.

Chairman and Managing Director: V. T. Jobson. *Vice-chairman and Chief Executive:* J. W. Adams. *Secretary:* J. W. Adams.

Directors: J. Bridge, D. M. Markscheffel, R. J. Osborne (Company Secretary), W. R. Kelleway, B. R. Gunner. *Associate Director:* W. E. Parsons.

Manager: Barry Fry. *Assistant Manager:* Edwin Stein. *Player-coach:* David Howell *Youth Team Coach:* Danny Greaves. *Physio:* Alan Raw. *Commercial Manager:* John Carter. *Stadium Manager:* R. Davy Jnr. *Club Nickname:* 'The Blues or The Shrimpers'.

Year Formed: 1906. *Turned Professional:* 1906. *Ltd Co.:* 1919.

Previous Grounds: 1906, Roots Hall, Prittlewell; 1920, Kursaal; 1934, Southend Stadium; 1955, Roots Hall Football Ground.

Record League Victory: 9–2 v Newport Co, Division 3 (S), 5 September 1936 – McKenzie; Nelson, Everest (1); Deacon, Turner, Carr; Bolan, Lane (1), Goddard (4), Dickinson (2), Oswald (1).

Record Cup Victory: 10–1 v Golders Green, FA Cup, 1st rd, 24 November 1934 – Moore; Morfitt, Kelly; Mackay, Joe Wilson, Carr (1); Lane (1), Johnson (5), Cheesmuir (2), Deacon (1), Oswald. 10–1 v Brentwood, FA Cup, 2nd rd, 7 December 1968 – Roberts; Bentley, Birks; McMillan (1) Beesley, Kurila; Clayton, Chisnall, Moore (4), Best (5), Hamilton. 10–1 v Aldershot, Leyland Daf Cup, Pr rd, 6 November 1990 – Sansome; Austin, Powell, Cornwell, Prior (1), Tilson (3), Cawley, Butler, Ansah (1), Benjamin (1), Angell (4).

Record Defeat: 1–9 v Brighton & HA, Division 3, 27 November 1965.

Most League Points (2 for a win): 67, Division 4, 1980–81.

Most League Points (3 for a win): 85, Division 3, 1990–91.

Most League Goals: 92, Division 3 (S), 1950–51.

Highest League Scorer in Season: Jim Shankly, 31, 1928–29 and Sammy McCrory, 1957–58, both in Division 3 (S).

Most League Goals in Total Aggregate: Roy Hollis, 122, 1953–60.

Most Capped Player: George Mackenzie, 9, Eire.

Most League Appearances: Sandy Anderson, 451, 1950–63.

Record Transfer Fee Received: £2,000,000 from Nottingham F for Stan Collymore, June 1993.

Record Transfer Fee Paid: £250,000 to Plymouth Arg for Gary Poole, June 1993.

Football League Record: 1920 Original Member of Division 3; 1921–58 Division 3 (S); 1958–66 Division 3; 1966–72 Division 4; 1972–76 Division 3; 1976–78 Division 4; 1978–80 Division 3; 1980–81 Division 4; 1981–84 Division 3; 1984–87 Division 4; 1987–89 Division 3; 1989–90 Division 4; 1990–91 Division 3; 1991–92 Division 2; 1992– Division 1.

Honours: Football League: Best season: 18th, Division 1, 1992–93. Division 3 – Runners-up 1990–91; Division 4 – Champions 1980–81; Runners-up 1971–72, 1977–78. *FA Cup:* best season: old 3rd rd, 1920–21, 5th rd, 1925–26, 1951–52, 1975–76, 1992–93. *Football League Cup:* never past 3rd rd.

SOUTHEND UNITED 1992—93 LEAGUE RECORD

Match No.	Date		Venue	Opponents	Result	H/T Score	Lg. Pos.	Goalscorers	Atten dance
1	Aug	15	A	Newcastle U	L 2-3	0-2	—	Martin, Benjamin	28,545
2		22	H	Peterborough U	L 0-1	0-0	19		4651
3		29	A	Brentford	L 1-2	1-1	23	Benjamin	6431
4	Sept	1	A	Birmingham C	L 0-2	0-1	—		8234
5		5	H	Leicester C	W 3-1	2-1	21	Benjamin 2 (1 pen), Ansah	5119
6		12	H	Bristol C	W 1-0	0-0	16	Benjamin	9515
7		18	H	Portsmouth	D 0-0	0-0	—		5267
8		26	A	Derby Co	L 0-2	0-0	20		15,172
9	Oct	3	A	Charlton Ath	D 1-1	0-0	20	Ansah	6399
10		10	H	Wolverhampton W	D 1-1	1-1	20	Benjamin (pen)	5498
11		17	A	Grimsby T	L 0-1	0-0	22		4117
12		25	H	Cambridge U	D 1-1	0-1	—	Ansah	3810
13		31	A	Luton T	D 2-2	0-2	23	Powell, O'Callaghan	7256
14	Nov	3	A	Tranmere R	L 0-3	0-2	—		5870
15		7	H	Oxford U	L 0-3	0-3	23		3356
16		14	A	Swindon T	L 2-3	1-3	23	Benjamin, Cornwell	7777
17		21	H	Notts Co	W 3-1	2-0	22	Brown, Collymore 2	3219
18		28	H	Sunderland	L 0-1	0-0	22		4584
19	Dec	5	A	Millwall	D 1-1	1-1	24	Cornwell	7928
20		12	A	West Ham U	L 0-2	0-1	24		15,739
21		19	H	Barnsley	W 3-0	1-0	24	Powell, Collymore 2	3629
22		26	H	Watford	L 1-2	1-0	24	Sussex (pen)	5769
23		28	A	Bristol R	W 2-0	0-0	21	Brown, Collymore	7707
24	Jan	9	A	Portsmouth	L 0-2	0-1	23		9717
25		16	H	Derby Co	D 0-0	0-0	23		4243
26		20	H	Newcastle U	D 1-1	1-1	—	Sussex (pen)	8246
27		27	H	Birmingham C	W 4-0	3-0	—	Sussex, Collymore, Tilson, Scully	4065
28		30	A	Peterborough U	L 0-1	0-1	22		6180
29	Feb	10	A	Bristol C	D 1-1	1-1	—	Collymore	3086
30		21	H	Brentford	W 3-0	1-0	—	Jones, Collymore, Ansah	4123
31		27	A	Wolverhampton W	D 1-1	0-0	22	Ansah	11,563
32	Mar	6	H	Charlton Ath	L 0-2	0-0	23		5804
33		10	H	Swindon T	D 1-1	0-0	—	Scully	4371
34		13	A	Oxford U	W 1-0	0-0	22	Collymore	4576
35		21	H	Millwall	D 3-3	1-3	—	Collymore, Tilson 2	3840
36		23	A	Notts Co	L 0-4	0-1	—		6109
37		26	H	Tranmere R	L 1-2	1-1	—	Ansah	4147
38	Apr	3	A	Sunderland	W 4-2	1-2	23	Collymore, Scully, Ansah, Angell	15,071
39		7	H	West Ham U	W 1-0	1-0	—	Angell	12,813
40		10	A	Watford	D 0-0	0-0	22		7198
41		14	H	Bristol R	W 3-0	0-0	—	Angell, Collymore 2	6154
42		17	H	Barnsley	L 1-3	1-1	19	Collymore	3855
43		20	A	Leicester C	L 1-4	0-1	—	Angell	18,003
44		23	H	Grimsby T	W 1-0	0-0	—	Collymore	5807
45	May	1	A	Cambridge U	L 1-3	0-2	19	Cornwell	7137
46		8	H	Luton T	W 2-1	2-1	18	Sussex, Angell	11,042

Final League Position: 18

GOALSCORERS

League (54): Collymore 15, Ansah 7, Benjamin 7 (2 pens), Angell 5, Sussex 4 (2 pens), Cornwell 3, Scully 3, Tilson 3, Brown 2, Powell 2, Jones 1, Martin 1, O'Callaghan 1.
Coca Cola Cup (1): Benjamin 1.
FA Cup (3): Collymore 3.

Sansome 43	Cornwell 36 + 3	Powell 42	Jones 29	Scully 41 + 1	Prior 45	Locke 26 + 1	Martin 26	Sussex 18 + 5	Benjamin 16	Ansah 28 + 2	O'Callaghan 8 + 5	Tilson 26 + 5	Edwards 41	Parkinson 6	Brown 10	Ashenden 4 + 1	Hyslop 4 + 2	Collymore 30	Cagigao — +1	Hall 3 + 6	Angell 13	Smith 8	Southon — +1	Royce 3	Match No.
1	2	3	4	5	6	7	8	9	10	11	12	14													1
1	2	3	4	5	6		8	9	10	7	12	11													2
1	2	3	4	5	6	11	8	9	10	7	12														3
1	4	3		5	6		9	8		10		7	11	2											4
1	4	3		5	6		9	8		10		7	11	2											5
1	4	3		5	6		9	8		10		7	11	2											6
1	4	3		5	6		9	8		10		7	11	2											7
1	4	3		5	6		9	8		10		7	11	2											8
1	4	3		5	6		9	8		10		7	11	2											9
1	4	3		5	6		9	8		10		7	11		2										10
1	4	3			6		9	8		10	11	7	5	2											11
1	4	3			6		9	8		10	7	11	5	2											12
1	4	3	14		6		9	8		10	12	7	11	5	2										13
1	4	3			6		9	8		10	12	7	11	5	2										14
1	4	3			6		9	8		10	12	7	11	5	2										15
1	4	3		5	6	7	8	12		10			2		9	11									16
1	4			5	6	7	8						2		9	11	3	10							17
1	4			5	6	7	8	12					2		9	11	3	10	14						18
1	4	3		5	6	7	8			11			2		9			10							19
1	4	3		5	6	7	8			11			2		9			10							20
1	4	3	11	5	6	7	8						2		9			10							21
1	4	3	11	5	6		8	12				7	2		9			10							22
1	4	3	7	5	6		8			11			2		9			10							23
1	4	3	11	5	6	7	8						2		9	12		10							24
1	4	3	11	5	6	7	8	9					2					10							25
1	4	3	11	5	6	7	9	8					2					10							26
1	4	3	11	5		7	9	8				6	2			14	10	12							27
1	4	3	11	5	6	7	9	12		8			2			14	10								28
1	4			9	5	6						7	8	2		3	10		11						29
1	4	3	9	5	6		8					7	2				10		11						30
1	4	3	9	5	6		8					7	2				10		11						31
1	4	3	9	5	6		8	7			12		2				10		11						32
1	4	3	7	5	6		8	9		11			2				10								33
1	4	3	7	5	6		11						2	9			10		8	12					34
1		3	7	5	6	4		9		11			2				10	12	8						35
1	4	3	7	5	6		8	9		11			2				10								36
1	2	3	4	5	6	12	8			7	9						10		11						37
1		3	4	5	6			7		9	2						10		11	8					38
		3	4	5	6			7		9	2						10		11	8	1				39
1	14	3	4	5	6			11		7							10	12	9	8					40
1		3	4	5	6		14	7		9	2						10	12	11	8					41
1			4	5	6		14	7		9	2				3	10		12	11	8					42
1	14	3	4	5	6		8	12		7			2		10				9	11					43
		3	4	5	6		14		12	9	2						10		7	11	8		1		44
	14	3	4	5	6		8		7	9	2						10		12	11		1			45
1		3	4	5	6		8			9	2				10					7	11				46

Coca Cola Cup	Second Round	Derby Co (h)	1-0
		(a)	0-7
FA Cup	Third Round	Millwall (h)	1-0
	Fourth Round	Huddersfield T (a)	2-1
	Fifth Round	Sheffield W (a)	0-2

SOUTHEND UNITED

Player and Position	Ht	Wt	Date	Birth Place	Source	Clubs	League App	Gls
Goalkeepers								
Mel Capleton*	5 11	12 00	24 10 73	London	Trainee	Southend U	—	—
Simon Royce	6 2	11 07	9 9 71	Forest Gate	Heybridge Swifts	Southend U	4	—
Paul Sansome	6 0	13 07	6 10 61	N. Addington	Crystal Palace	Millwall	156	—
						Southend U	230	—
Defenders								
Christian Hyslop	5 11	11 07	14 6 72	Watford	Trainee	Southend U	19	—
Chris Powell	5 8	11 03	8 9 69	Lambeth		Crystal Palace	3	—
						Aldershot (loan)	11	—
						Southend U	131	3
Spencer Prior	6 1	12 09	22 4 71	Rochford	Trainee	Southend U	135	3
Daniel Sains*	6 1	12 02	24 3 74	London	Trainee	Southend U	—	—
Pat Scully	6 1	13 02	23 6 70	Dublin		Arsenal	—	—
						Preston NE (loan)	13	1
						Northampton T (loan)	15	—
						Southend U	107	6
Midfield								
Scott Ashenden*	6 0	11 00	3 2 74	Basildon	Trainee	Southend U	5	—
John Cornwell	6 4	13 00	13 10 64	Bethnal Green	Apprentice	Orient	202	35
						Newcastle U	33	1
						Swindon T	25	—
						Southend U	101	5
Andy Edwards	6 2	13 06	17 9 71	Epping	Trainee	Southend U	61	1
Mark Hall	5 6	10 12	13 1 73	London	Tottenham H	Southend U	12	—
Keith Jones	5 9	11 02	14 10 64	Dulwich	Apprentice	Chelsea	52	7
						Brentford	169	13
						Southend U	63	6
Adam Locke	5 10	12 02	20 8 70	Croydon	Trainee	Crystal Palace	—	—
						Southend U	65	4
David Martin*	6 1	13 01	25 4 63	East Ham	Apprentice	Millwall	140	6
						Wimbledon	35	3
						Southend U	221	19
Kevin O'Callaghan*	5 8	11 00	19 10 61	London	Apprentice	Millwall	20	3
						Ipswich T	115	3
						Portsmouth	87	16
						Millwall	76	14
						Southend U	21	1
Paul Smith*	5 11	14 00	18 9 71	Lenham	Trainee	Southend U	20	1
Jamie Southon§	5 9	11 09	13 10 74	Hornchurch	Trainee	Southend U	1	—
Forwards								
Brett Angell	6 2	13 12	20 8 68	Marlborough	Cheltenham T	Derby Co	—	—
						Stockport Co	70	28
						Southend U	98	41
Andy Ansah	5 10	11 01	19 3 69	Lewisham	Crystal Palace	Brentford	8	2
						Southend U	117	26
Steve Brown*	5 11	11 10	6 12 73	Southend	Trainee	Southend U	10	2
Francisco Cagigao*	5 9	12 00	10 11 69	London	Barcelona	Southend U	1	—
Stan Collymore	6 2	14 00	22 1 71	Stone	Stafford R	Crystal Palace	20	1
						Southend U	30	15
Jae Martin	5 11	11 00	5 2 76	London	Trainee	Southend U	—	—

SOUTHEND UNITED

Colours: Blue shirts, yellow trim, blue shorts, blue trim, blue stockings. **Change colours:** All yellow.

Foundation: The leading club in Southend around the turn of the century was Southend Athletic, but they were an amateur concern. Southend United was a more ambitious professional club when they were founded in 1906, employing Bob Jack as secretary-manager and immediately joining the Second Division of the Southern League.

First Football League game: 28 August, 1920, Division 3, v Brighton & HA (a) W 2-0 – Capper; Reid, Newton; Wileman, Henderson, Martin; Nicholls, Nuttall, Fairclough (2), Myers, Dorsett.

Did you know: In 1921–22 top scorer for Southend United was left-back Jimmy Evans with ten penalties. He was capped three times for Wales that season.

Managers (and Secretary-Managers)
Bob Jack 1906–10, George Molyneux 1910–11, O. M. Howard 1911–12, Joe Bradshaw 1912–19, Ned Liddell 1919–20, Tom Mather 1920–21, Ted Birnie 1921–34, David Jack 1934–40, Harry Warren 1946–56, Eddie Perry 1956–60, Frank Broome 1960, Ted Fenton 1961–65, Alvan Williams 1965–67, Ernie Shepherd 1967–69, Geoff Hudson 1969–70, Arthur Rowley 1970–76, Dave Smith 1976–83, Peter Morris 1983–84, Bobby Moore 1984–86, Dave Webb 1986–87, Dick Bate 1987, Paul Clark 1987–88, Dave Webb (GM) 1988–92, Colin Murphy 1992–93, Barry Fry April 1993–.

Player and Position	Ht	Wt	Birth Date	Birth Place	Source	Clubs	League App	Gls
Andy Sussex	6 0	13 11	23 11 64	Enfield	Apprentice	Orient	144	17
						Crewe Alex	102	24
						Southend U	38	7
Steve Tilson	5 11	12 05	27 7 66	Essex	Burnham	Southend U	147	20

Trainees
Baxter, Scott A; Gonzaque, Michael G; Hoddle, Mark D; Holman, Matthias T; Kinnear, Anthony D; Longman, Kenneth G; McGlew, Neil; O'Meara, Lee P; Perkins, Declan O; Rowbury, Neil P; Scott, Daniel L; Southon, Jamie P; Stone, Damon T; Thake, Ben.

Associated Schoolboys who have accepted the club's offer of a Traineeship/Contract
Nesling, Jon.

STOCKPORT COUNTY 1992–93   *Back row (left to right)*: Andy Preece, Alan Finley, David Redfern, Neil Edwards, Tony Barras, Jim Carstairs.
Centre row: John Sainty (Assistant Manager), John Muir, Martin McDonald, David Miller, Neil Matthews, Peter Ward, James Gannon, Paul Wheeler, David Jones (First Team Coach).
Front row: Rodger Wylde (Physio), Kevin Francis, Chris Beaumont, Darren Knowles, Danny Bergara (Manager), David Frain, Lee Todd, Paul Williams.

Division 2   **STOCKPORT COUNTY**

Edgeley Park, Hardcastle Road, Stockport, Cheshire SK3 9DD.
Telephone 061–480 8888. Clubcall: 0898 121638. Promotions
Office: 061–480 8117.

Ground capacity: 9720.

Record attendance: 27,833 v Liverpool, FA Cup 5th rd,
11 February 1950.

Record receipts: £50,152 v Stoke C, Division 2, 3 April 1993.

Pitch measurements: 110yd × 72yd.

Hon. Vice-presidents: Mike Yarwood OBE, Freddie Pye,
Andrew Barlow.

Chairman: B. Elwood. *Vice-chairman:* G. White.

Directors: M. Baker, B. Taylor, M. H. Rains, D. Jolley, V. Snell.

Chief Executive/Secretary: Dave Coxon.

Manager: Danny Bergara. *Assistant. Manager:* John Sainty.

Coach: *Physio:* Rodger Wylde.

Assistant Secretary: Andrea Welborn. *Commercial Manager:* John Rutter. *Marketing
Manager and programme editor:* Steve Bellis.

Year Formed: 1883. *Turned Professional:* 1891. *Ltd Co.:* 1908.

Club Nicknames: 'County' or 'Hatters'.

Previous Names: Heaton Norris Rovers, 1883–88; Heaton Norris, 1888–90.

Previous Grounds: 1883 Heaton Norris Recreation Ground; 1884 Heaton Norris Wanderers
Cricket Ground; 1885 Chorlton's Farm, Chorlton's Lane; 1886 Heaton Norris Cricket
Ground; 1887 Wilkes' Field, Belmont Street; 1889 Nursery Inn, Green Lane; 1902 Edgeley
Park.

Record League Victory: 13–0 v Halifax T, Division 3 (N), 6 January 1934 – McGann;
Vincent (1p), Jenkinson; Robinson, Stevens, Len Jones; Foulkes (1), Hill (3), Lythgoe (2),
Stevenson (2), Downes (4).

Record Cup Victory: 6–2 v West Auckland T (away), FA Cup, 1st rd, 14 November 1959 –
Lea; Betts (1), Webb; Murray, Hodder, Porteous; Wilson (1), Holland, Guy (2), Ritchie (1),
Davock (1).

Record Defeat: 1–8 v Chesterfield, Division 2, 19 April 1902.

Most League Points (2 for a win): 64, Division 4, 1966–67.

Most League Points (3 for a win): 82, Division 4, 1990–91.

Most League Goals: 115, Division 3 (N), 1933–34.

Highest League Scorer in Season: Alf Lythgoe, 46, Division 3 (N), 1933–34.

Most League Goals in Total Aggregate: Jack Connor, 132, 1951–56.

Most Capped Player: Harry Hardy, 1, England.

Most League Appearances: Andy Thorpe, 489, 1978–86, 1988–92.

Record Transfer Fee Received: £250,000 from WBA for Paul A. Williams, March 1991.

Record Transfer Fee Paid: £125,000 to Preston NE for Mike Flynn, March 1993.

Football League Record: 1900 Elected to Division 2; 1904 Failed re-election; 1905–21
Division 2; 1921–22 Division 3 (N); 1922–26 Division 2; 1926–37 Division 3 (N); 1937–38
Division 2; 1938–58 Division 3 (N); 1958–59 Division 3; 1959–67 Division 4; 1967–70
Division 3; 1970–91 Division 4; 1991–92 Division 3; 1992– Division 2.

Honours: Football League: Division 2 best season: 10th, 1905–06; Division 3 (N) –
Champions 1921–22, 1936–37; Runners-up 1928–29, 1929-30; Division 4 – Champions
1966–67; Runners-up 1990–91. *FA Cup:* best season: 5th rd, 1935, 1950. *Football League
Cup:* best season: 4th rd, 1972–73. *Autoglass Trophy:* Runners-up 1991–92, 1992–93.

STOCKPORT COUNTY 1992—93 LEAGUE RECORD

Match No.	Date		Venue	Opponents	Result		H/T Score	Lg. Pos.	Goalscorers	Atten dance
1	Aug	15	A	Wigan Ath	W	2-1	1-0	—	Beaumont 2	3360
2		22	H	Burnley	W	2-1	1-0	2	Gannon (pen), Francis	4953
3		29	A	Port Vale	D	0-0	0-0	5		6340
4	Sept	2	A	WBA	L	0-3	0-3	—		12,305
5		5	H	Exeter C	D	2-2	0-1	9	Finley, Gannon	3759
6		12	H	Hull C	W	5-3	4-2	7	Muir, Beaumont 2, Francis 2	4216
7		15	A	Bradford C	W	3-2	0-0	—	Muir, Francis, Beaumont	5070
8		19	A	Chester C	W	3-0	0-0	2	Francis, Muir, Beaumont	3627
9		25	H	Fulham	D	0-0	0-0	—		4755
10	Oct	3	H	Swansea C	D	1-1	0-0	3	Ward	4943
11		10	A	Mansfield T	L	0-2	0-0	4		3836
12		16	H	Blackpool	D	0-0	0-0	—		5680
13		24	A	Bournemouth	L	0-1	0-0	11		4058
14		30	H	Huddersfield T	W	5-0	1-0	—	Preece 2, Ward, Francis 2	5405
15	Nov	3	H	Preston NE	W	3-0	1-0	—	Francis, Preece, Beaumont	4860
16		7	A	Brighton & HA	L	0-2	0-1	6		5742
17		20	H	Plymouth Arg	W	3-0	0-0	—	Francis 2, Preece	5377
18		28	A	Hartlepool U	L	2-3	0-1	7	Preece, Francis	2814
19	Dec	19	A	Reading	W	4-2	1-1	5	Gannon 2, Preece, Francis	3832
20		28	H	Leyton Orient	D	1-1	1-0	10	Beaumont	6368
21	Jan	9	H	Bradford C	D	2-2	1-0	10	Francis, Duxbury L (og)	4999
22		16	H	Fulham	L	1-2	0-1	10	Gannon (pen)	3516
23		22	H	Chester C	W	2-0	2-0	—	Francis, Williams B	4427
24		30	A	Burnley	D	1-1	0-0	9	Beaumont	11,229
25	Feb	5	H	Wigan Ath	W	3-0	0-0	—	Francis 2, Beaumont	4799
26		9	H	Bolton W	W	2-0	1-0	—	Preece, Francis	7363
27		13	A	Exeter C	D	2-2	2-1	5	Williams P A, Beaumont	2795
28		16	H	Port Vale	W	2-0	1-0	—	Preece, Beaumont	7449
29		20	H	WBA	W	5-1	1-1	5	Gannon 2, Francis, Carstairs, Williams P A	7181
30		26	H	Mansfield T	L	0-1	0-0	—		5307
31	Mar	2	A	Rotherham U	W	2-0	2-0	—	Beaumont, Francis	4280
32		5	A	Swansea C	D	2-2	0-2	—	Gannon (pen), Francis	4755
33		9	A	Stoke C	L	1-2	0-0	—	Francis	17,484
34		13	H	Brighton & HA	D	0-0	0-0	4		5298
35		20	A	Preston NE	W	3-2	1-1	3	Duffield 2, Gannon (pen)	5255
36		23	H	Hartlepool U	W	4-1	0-0	—	Francis, Beaumont, Duffield 2	4154
37		27	A	Plymouth Arg	W	4-3	2-2	3	Williams P, Francis 3	6132
38	Apr	3	H	Stoke C	D	1-1	0-1	3	Ward	9402
39		6	A	Bolton W	L	1-2	0-1	—	Francis	13,773
40		9	H	Rotherham U	D	2-2	2-2	—	Francis 2	5440
41		12	A	Leyton Orient	L	0-3	0-3	5		4654
42		16	H	Reading	D	2-2	1-0	—	Gannon 2	5001
43		24	A	Blackpool	L	0-2	0-1	5		7205
44		27	A	Hull C	W	2-0	0-0	—	Miller, Gannon	4079
45	May	1	H	Bournemouth	D	0-0	0-0	5		5446
46		8	A	Huddersfield T	L	1-2	1-1	6	Williams P A	7673

Final League Position: 6

GOALSCORERS

League (81): Francis 28, Beaumont 14, Gannon 12 (4 pens), Preece 8, Duffield 4, Muir 3, Ward 3, Williams PA 3, Carstairs 1, Finley 1, Miller 1, Williams B 1, Williams P 1, own goal 1.
Coca Cola Cup (6): Beaumont 2, Francis 2, Carstairs 1, Gannon 1.
FA Cup (6): Francis 2, McCord 1, Preece 1, Todd 1, Williams B 1.

Edwards 35	Knowles 10 + 1	Todd 36 + 3	Frain 37 + 4	Williams B 22	Finley 22	Gannon 46	Ward 35	Francis 41 + 1	Beaumont 44	Preece 23 + 6	Muir 7 + 2	Carstairs 13 + 1	Matthews 1 + 4	Miller 36 + 1	Masefield 7	Williams P 24 + 2	Wallace 5 + 3	Redfern 6	Barras 12 + 2	McCord 4 + 4	Wheeler — + 1	Williams P A 6 + 10	Ryan 3 + 1	Connelly 7	Duffield 6 + 1	James 4 + 4	Kite 5	Flynn 9 + 1	Match No.
1	2	3	4	5	6	7	8	9	10	11	12																		1
1	2	3	4	5	6	7	8	9	10	11																			2
1	2	3	4	5	6	7		9	10	11		8																	3
1	2	3	4	5	6	7		9	10	14		8	11	12															4
1	2	3	4		6	7		9	10	11		8		5															5
1	12		4		6	7		9	10	14	11	8				5	2	3											6
1		3	4	5	6	7		9	10		11	8				5	2												7
1		3		4	6	7		9	10	14	11	8	12			5	2												8
1	14	3	4		6	7		9	10		11	8	12			5	2												9
1			4		6		7	8	9	10		11				5	2	3											10
1		3	4		6	7	8	9	10		11					5	2	12											11
1	2	3	4		6	7	8	9	10	12						5	11												12
		3	4	6		7	8	12	10	9		14				5	2	11	1										13
	2	3	4	6	5	7	8	9	10	11	12						1												14
	2	3	4	6	5	7	8	9	10	11							1												15
	2	3	4	6	5	7	8	9	10		11					12	1	14											16
	2		4	6		7	8	9	10	11			12			3	1	5											17
	2	3	4	6		7		9	10	11			12	8			1	5											18
1		2		6		7	8	9	10	11		3		4			5												19
1		2	4	6		7	8	9	10	11		3					5	12											20
1		2		6		7	8	9	10	11			4	3			5	12	14										21
1		2	14	6		7	8		10	11			4	3			5	12		9									22
1		2	4	6		7	8	9	10	11			5	3				12											23
1		2	4	6		7	8	9	10	11			5	3															24
1		2	4	6		7	8	9	10	11			5	3															25
1		2	4	6		7	8	9	10	11			5	3				12											26
1		2	4	6		7	8		10	11			5	3				9											27
1		2	4		6	7	8		10	11			5	3		14	12	9											28
1		2		6		7		9	10	11		8	5	3			4	12											29
1		2	14	6		7		9	10	12		8	5	3			4	11											30
1		2	4			7	8	9	10				5	3			6	11	12										31
1		2	4			7	8	9	10				5	3			6	11	12										32
1		2	4			7	8	9	10	11			5	3			6		12										33
1		2	4			7	8	9		11			5	3	14		6		12	10									34
1			4		6	7	8	9	10				5	3								2	11						35
1			4		6	7	8	9	10				5	3								2	11	12					36
			4		6	7	8	9	10				5	3								2	11	12	1	14			37
			4			7	8	9	10				5	3						12		2	11	14	1	6			38
	14		4			7	8	9	10				5	3		6				12			11	1	2				39
			4			7	8	9	10				5	3						12		2		11	1	6			40
	12					4	8	9	10				5	3								2	7	11	1	6			41
1		2	4			7	8	9				3	5	14						10		11		12		6			42
1			4			7	8	9	10			3	5	14		6				12		2	11			8			43
1		2			6	7	8	9	10				5		3					11			12			4			44
1		2	14		6	7	8	9	10	12			5		3								11			4			45
1		2	12		6	7	8		10	11			5		3					9						4			46

Coca Cola Cup	First Round	Chester C (h)	1-1
		(a)	2-1
	Second Round	Nottingham F (h)	2-3
		(a)	1-2
FA Cup	First Round	York C (a)	3-1
	Second Round	Macclesfield (a)	2-0
	Third Round	Derby Co (a)	1-2

STOCKPORT COUNTY

Player and Position	Ht	Wt	Date	Birth Place	Source	Clubs	League App	Gls
Goalkeepers								
Neil Edwards	5 8	11 02	5 12 70	Aberdare	Trainee	Leeds U	—	—
						Huddersfield T (loan)	—	—
						Stockport Co	74	—
David Redfern*	6 2	13 12	8 11 62	Sheffield	School	Sheffield W	—	—
						Doncaster R (loan)	—	—
						Rochdale (loan)	19	—
						Rochdale	68	—
					Gainsborough T	Stockport Co	48	—
Defenders								
Jim Carstairs	6 0	12 05	29 1 71	St. Andrews	Trainee	Arsenal	—	—
						Brentford (loan)	8	—
						Cambridge U	—	—
						Stockport C	34	1
Sean Connelly	5 10	11 10	26 6 70	Sheffield	Hallam	Stockport Co	7	—
Alan Finley	6 3	14 03	10 12 67	Liverpool	Marine	Shrewsbury T	63	2
						Stockport Co	59	5
						Carlisle U (loan)	1	—
Mike Flynn	6 0	11 00	23 2 69	Oldham	Trainee	Oldham Ath	40	1
						Norwich C	—	—
						Preston NE	136	7
						Stockport Co	10	—
Jim Gannon	6 2	13 00	7 9 68	London	Dundalk	Sheffield U	—	—
						Halifax T (loan)	2	—
						Stockport Co	137	35
Bill Williams	5 10	12 11	7 10 60	Rochdale	Local	Rochdale	95	2
						Stockport Co	104	1
						Manchester C	1	—
						Stockport Co	140	6
Midfield								
Martin James	5 10	11 07	18 5 71	Formby	Trainee	Preston NE	98	11
						Stockport Co	8	—
Darren Knowles*	5 6	10 01	8 10 70	Sheffield	Trainee	Sheffield U	—	—
						Stockport Co	63	—
Brian McCord	5 10	11 06	24 8 68	Derby	Apprentice	Derby Co	5	—
						Barnsley	43	2
						Mansfield T (loan)	11	1
						Stockport Co	8	—
Martin McDonald*			4 12 73	Irvine		Stockport Co	—	—
David Miller	5 11	11 12	8 1 64	Burnley	Apprentice	Burnley	32	3
						Crewe Alex (loan)	3	—
						Tranmere R	29	1
						Preston NE	58	2
						Burnley (loan)	4	—
						Carlisle U	109	7
						Stockport Co	40	1
Andy Preece	6 1	12 00	27 3 67	Evesham		Northampton T	1	—
					Worcester C.	Wrexham	51	7
						Stockport Co	54	21
Darren Ryan	5 10	11 00	3 7 72	Oswestry	Trainee	Shrewsbury T	4	—
						Chester C	17	2
						Stockport Co	4	—
Michael Wallace	5 8	10 02	5 10 70	Farnworth	Trainee	Manchester C	—	—
						Stockport Co	8	—
Forwards								
Tony Barras	6 0	12 03	29 3 71	Teesside	Trainee	Hartlepool U	12	—
						Stockport Co	96	5

STOCKPORT COUNTY

Colours: Royal blue shirts with red/white pattern, white shorts, white stockings. **Change colours:** White shirts with red/blue horizontal pattern, blue shorts, blue stockings.

Foundation: Formed at a meeting held at Wellington Road South by members of Wycliffe Congregational Chapel in 1883, they called themselves Heaton Norris Rovers until changing to Stockport County in 1890, a year before joining the Football Combination.

First Football League game: 1 September, 1900, Division 2, v Leicester Fosse (a) D 2-2 – Moores; Earp, Wainwright; Pickford, Limond, Harvey; Stansfield, Smith (1), Patterson, Foster, Betteley (1).

Did you know: On 25 April 1981, Stockport County arrived at Bury for a Division 4 match minus three snowbound players. They played the first half with nine men and when they succeeded in completing a full side afterwards, managed to win 1-0.

Managers (and Secretary-Managers)
Fred Stewart 1894–1911, Harry Lewis 1911–14, David Ashworth 1914–19, Albert Williams 1919–24, Fred Scotchbrook 1924–26, Lincoln Hyde 1926–31, Andrew Wilson 1932–33, Fred Westgarth 1934–36, Bob Kelly 1936–38, George Hunt 1938–39, Bob Marshall 1939–49, Andy Beattie 1949–52, Dick Duckworth 1952–56, Billy Moir 1956–60, Reg Flewin 1960–63, Trevor Porteous 1963–65, Bert Trautmann (GM) 1965–66, Eddie Quigley (TM) 1965–66, Jimmy Meadows 1966–69, Wally Galbraith 1969–70, Matt Woods 1970–71, Brian Doyle 1972–74, Jimmy Meadows 1974–75, Roy Chapman 1975–76, Eddie Quigley 1976–77, Alan Thompson 1977–78, Mike Summerbee 1978–79, Jimmy McGuigan 1979–82, Eric Webster 1982–85, Colin Murphy 1985, Les Chapman 1985–86, Jimmy Melia 1986, Colin Murphy 1986–87, Asa Hartford 1987–89, Danny Bergara April 1989–.

Player and Position	Ht	Wt	Birth Date	Birth Place	Source	Clubs	League App	Gls
Chris Beaumont	5 11	11 07	5 12 65	Sheffield	Denaby	Rochdale	34	7
						Stockport Co	145	36
David Frain	5 8	10 05	11 10 62	Sheffield	Rowlinson YC	Sheffield U	44	5
						Rochdale	42	12
						Stockport Co	152	9
Kevin Francis	6 7	15 08	6 12 67	Moseley	Mile Oak R	Derby Co	10	—
						Stockport Co	90	48
John Muir*	6 2	14 06	26 4 63	Sedgley	Dudley T	Doncaster R	75	18
						Stockport Co	13	3
						Torquay U (loan)	12	—
Lee Todd	5 5	10 03	7 3 72	Hartlepool	Hartlepool U	Stockport Co	72	—
Peter Ward	6 0	11 10	15 10 64	Durham	Chester-le-Street	Huddersfield T	37	2
						Rochdale	84	10
						Stockport Co	79	4
Paul Williams	5 7	10 00	11 9 69	Leicester	Trainee	Leicester C	—	—
						Stockport Co	70	4
Paul A Williams	6 3	14 06	8 9 63	Sheffield	Nuneaton	Preston NE	1	—
						Newport Co	26	3
						Sheffield U	8	—
						Hartlepool U	8	—
						Stockport Co	24	14
						WBA	44	5
						Coventry C (loan)	2	—
						Stockport Co	16	3

Trainees
Leigh, Malcolm; McCauley, Andrew; Radcliffe, Robert T; Ryan, Mark D; Warburton, Richard J; Wright, Paul F.

488

STOKE CITY 1992-93 *Back row (left to right):* Alex McLeish, Tony Gallimore, Carl Beeston, Vince Overson, Ian Wright, Ian Cranson, Marcus Jones, Adrian Potts, Lee Sandford, Mark Devlin.
Centre row: Matthew Wileman, Chris Male, David Kevan, Tony Kelly, John Butler, Peter Fox, Ronnie Sinclair, Mark Reid, Gareth Jennings, Danny Martin, Tony Green, Keith Long.
Front row: Robert Brunton, Gary Pick, Paul Ware, Paul Rennie, Mark Stein, Mike Macari, Steve Foley, Kevin Russell, Graham Harbey, Jason Percival.

Division 1

STOKE CITY

Victoria Ground, Stoke-on-Trent. Telephone Stoke-on-Trent (0782) 413511. Commercial Dept: (0782) 45840. Soccerline Information: 0898 700278. Football in the Community: 0782 744347.

Ground capacity: 25,409.

Record attendance: 51,380 v Arsenal, Division 1, 29 March 1937.

Record receipts: £97,000 v Liverpool, FA Cup 3rd rd, 9 January 1988.

Pitch measurements: 116yd × 75yd.

Vice-president: J. A. M. Humphries.

Chairman: P. Coates. *Vice-chairman:* K. A. Humphreys.

Directors: R. C. Lee, P. J. Wright, R. D. Kenyon.

Manager: Lou Macari. *Assistant Manager:* Chic Bates.

Physio: Richard Gray.

Secretary: M. J. Potts.

Sales & Marketing Manager: M. J. Cullerton.

Year Formed: 1863 *(see Foundation).

Turned Professional: 1885. *Ltd Co.:* 1908.

Club Nickname: 'The Potters'.

Previous Name: Stoke.

Previous Grounds: 1875, Sweeting's Field; 1878, Victoria Ground (previously known as the Athletic Club Ground).

Record League Victory: 10–3 v WBA, Division 1, 4 February 1937 – Doug Westland; Brigham, Harbot; Tutin, Turner (1p), Kirton; Matthews, Antonio (2), Freddie Steele (5), Jimmy Westland, Johnson (2).

Record Cup Victory: 7–1 v Burnley, FA Cup, 2nd rd (replay), 20 February 1896 – Clawley; Clare, Eccles; Turner, Grewe, Robertson; Willie Maxwell, Dickson, A. Maxwell (3), Hyslop (4), Schofield.

Record Defeat: 0–10 v Preston NE, Division 1, 14 September 1889.

Most League Points (2 for a win): 63, Division 3 (N), 1926–27.

Most League Points (3 for a win): 93, Division 2, 1992–93.

Most League Goals: 92, Division 3 (N), 1926–27.

Highest League Scorer in Season: Freddie Steele, 33, Division 1, 1936–37.

Most League Goals in Total Aggregate: Freddie Steele, 142, 1934–49.

Most Capped Player: Gordon Banks, 36 (73), England.

Most League Appearances: Eric Skeels, 506, 1958–76.

Record Transfer Fee Received: £750,000 from Everton for Peter Beagrie, October 1989.

Record Transfer Fee Paid: £480,000 to Sheffield W for Ian Cranson, July 1989.

Football League Record: 1888 Founder Member of Football League; 1890 Not re-elected; 1891 Re-elected; relegated in 1907, and after one year in Division 2, resigned for financial reasons; 1919 re-elected to Division 2; 1922–23 Division 1; 1923–26 Division 2; 1926–27 Division 3 (N); 1927–33 Division 2; 1933–53 Division 1; 1953–63 Division 2; 1963–77 Division 1; 1977–79 Division 2; 1979–85 Division 1; 1985–90 Division 2; 1990–92 Division 3; 1992–93 Division 2; 1993– Division 1.

Honours: Football League: Division 1 best season: 4th, 1935–36, 1946–47; Division 2 – Champions 1932–33, 1962–63, 1992–93; Runners-up 1921–22; Promoted 1978–79 (3rd); Division 3 (N) – Champions 1926–27. *FA Cup:* Semi-finals 1899, 1971, 1972. *Football League Cup:* Winners 1971–72. *Autoglass Trophy:* Winners: 1992. **European Competitions:** *UEFA Cup:* 1972–73, 1974–75.

STOKE CITY 1992—93 LEAGUE RECORD

Match No.	Date		Venue	Opponents	Result		H/T Score	Lg. Pos.	Goalscorers	Atten dance
1	Aug	15	A	Hull C	L	0-1	0-0	—		9088
2		22	H	Wigan Ath	W	2-1	1-0	14	Biggins, Foley	12,902
3		29	A	Exeter C	D	2-2	2-1	13	Stein 2	4106
4	Sept	2	A	Bradford C	L	1-3	1-1	—	Stein	5959
5		5	H	Bolton W	D	0-0	0-0	15		14,252
6		12	A	Plymouth Arg	D	1-1	1-0	16	Stein	8208
7		16	H	Brighton & HA	D	1-1	1-0	—	Sandford	10,867
8		19	H	WBA	W	4-3	1-1	14	Foley, Russell 2, Cranson	18,764
9		26	A	Mansfield T	W	4-0	3-0	11	Stein 2, Ware, Biggins	6828
10	Oct	3	A	Chester C	D	1-1	0-0	11	Beeston	5237
11		10	H	Leyton Orient	W	2-1	0-0	10	Stein 2	12,640
12		17	A	Preston NE	W	2-1	2-0	7	Butler, Sandford	8138
13		24	H	Port Vale	W	2-1	0-0	4	Cranson, Stein (pen)	24,500
14		31	A	Burnley	W	2-0	2-0	2	Shaw 2	16,667
15	Nov	3	A	Fulham	D	0-0	0-0	—		5903
16		7	H	Bournemouth	W	2-0	0-0	2	Stein 2 (1 pen)	15,146
17		21	A	Blackpool	W	3-1	2-1	1	Russell 2, Stein	8028
18		28	H	Swansea C	W	2-1	0-0	1	Shaw, Stein (pen)	13,867
19	Dec	12	H	Huddersfield T	W	3-0	0-0	1	Ware 2, Cranson	13,377
20		19	A	Hartlepool U	W	2-1	1-0	1	Regis, Gleghorn	4021
21		26	A	Reading	W	1-0	1-0	1	Regis	7269
22		28	H	Rotherham U	W	2-0	1-0	1	Beeston, Foley	21,714
23	Jan	9	A	Brighton & HA	D	2-2	0-0	1	Stein, Foley	8622
24		16	H	Mansfield T	W	4-0	2-0	1	Russell, Gray (og), Regis, Overson	14,643
25		23	A	WBA	W	2-1	1-1	1	Gleghorn, Stein	29,341
26		27	H	Exeter C	D	1-1	1-1	—	Regis	14,181
27		30	A	Wigan Ath	D	1-1	1-1	1	Beeston	4775
28	Feb	6	H	Hull C	W	3-0	2-0	1	Ware, Foley, Stein	15,391
29		20	H	Bradford C	W	1-0	0-0	1	Kevan	16,494
30		27	H	Leyton Orient	L	0-1	0-1	1		10,798
31	Mar	6	H	Chester C	W	4-0	2-0	1	Stein 2, Shaw, Foley	14,534
32		9	H	Stockport Co	W	2-1	0-0	—	Stein, Gleghorn	17,484
33		13	A	Bournemouth	D	1-1	0-0	1	Stein (pen)	7129
34		20	A	Fulham	W	1-0	0-0	1	Stein (pen)	17,935
35		23	A	Swansea C	W	2-1	0-1	—	Gleghorn, Foley	8366
36		27	H	Blackpool	L	0-1	0-0	1		17,918
37		31	A	Port Vale	W	2-0	1-0	—	Stein, Gleghorn	20,373
38	Apr	3	A	Stockport Co	D	1-1	1-0	1	Regis	9402
39		7	A	Huddersfield T	L	0-1	0-1	—		11,089
40		10	H	Reading	W	2-0	1-0	1	Shaw, Gleghorn	16,919
41		12	A	Rotherham U	W	2-0	1-0	1	Stein 2	9021
42		17	A	Hartlepool U	L	0-1	0-1	1		17,363
43		24	H	Preston NE	W	1-0	0-0	1	Stein	18,334
44		28	H	Plymouth Arg	W	1-0	1-0	—	Gleghorn	19,718
45	May	4	A	Bolton W	L	0-1	0-1	—		19,238
46		8	H	Burnley	D	1-1	0-1	1	Stein	21,840

Final League Position: 1

GOALSCORERS

League (73): Stein 26 (5 pens), Foley 7, Gleghorn 7, Regis 5, Russell 5, Shaw 5, Ware 4, Beeston 3, Cranson 3, Biggins 2, Sandford 2, Butler 1, Kevan 1, Overson 1, own goal 1.
Coca Cola Cup (8): Stein 4, Biggins 2, Overson 1, Shaw 1.
FA Cup (1): Sandford 1.

Sinclair 29	Butler 44	Harbey 16 + 1	Cranson 45	Overson 43	Sandford 42	Foley 44	Ware 21 + 7	Stein 46	Kelly 2 + 5	Russell 30 + 10	Shaw 20 + 9	Devlin 3	Biggins 8	Kevan 13 + 2	Wright 1	Parks 2	Beeston 25 + 2	Horne 1	Fox 10	Gleghorn 34	Regis 16 + 9	Hockaday 7	Grobbelaar 4	Match No.
1	2	3	4	5	6	7	8	9	10	11	12													1
1	2	3	4	5	6	7		9		11		8	10											2
1	2	3	4	5	6	7		9		11		8	10	12										3
1	2	3	4	5		7		9	6	11	12	8	10											4
1	2	3	4	5	6	7	8	9		11			10	12										5
1	2	3	4	5		7	8	9	12	11	10		6											6
1	2	3	4	5	6	7	8	9	12	11	10													7
	2	3	4	5	6	7	8	9		11	10					1								8
	2	3	4	5	6	7	8	9	12	11	10			14		1								9
	2	3	4	5	6	7	8	9	10	11					1									10
	2	3	4	5	6	7	8	9	12	10	11								1					11
1	2	3	4	5	6	7	8	9	12	10	11													12
1	2		4	5	6	7	8	9	12	10	11									3				13
1	2	7	4	5	6		8	9	12	10	11									3				14
1	2	3	4	5		7	8	9	12	10	11									6				15
1	2		4	5	3	7		9		8	10						11			6	12			16
1	2		4	5	3	7		9		8	10						11			6	12			17
1	2		4	5	3	7	12	9		8	10						11			6				18
1	2	14	4	5	3	7	12	9		8	10						11			6				19
1	2		4	5	3	7	11	9		8	12									6	10			20
1	2		4	5	3	7		9		8							11			6	10			21
1	2		4	5	3	7		9		8							11			6	10			22
1	2		4	5	3	7	11	9		8	12									6	10			23
1	2	3	4	5		7	11	9		8										6	10			24
1	2		4	5	3	7		9		8	12						11			6	10			25
1	2		4	5	3	7		9		8	12						11			6	10			26
1	2		4	5	3	7		9		8							11			6	10			27
1	2	3	4	5		7	11	9		8	10									6				28
1	2		4	5	3	7		9		8	10						11			6	12			29
1	2		4	5	3		11	9		8	10			7						6	12			30
1			4	5	3	7	14	9		8	10			2			11			6	12			31
1			4	5	3	7		9		8	10						11			6	2			32
1	2		4	5		7	14	9		8	10						11			6	12	3		33
	2		4	5		7	14	9		8	10						11		1	6	12	3		34
	2			5	3	7		9		8	12			4			11		1	6	10			35
	2		4	5	3	7		9		8	12						11		1	6	10			36
	2		4	5	3	7	11	9	14	8	12								1	6	10			37
	2		4	5	3	7		9		8							11		1	6	10			38
	2		4	5	3	7		9	12	8							11		1	6	10			39
	2		4	5	3	7	14	9	12	10	8						11		1	6				40
	2		4	5	3	7	12	9		8									1	6	10	11		41
	2		4	5	3	7	11	9	14	8	12								1	6	10			42
	2		4	5	3	7	11	9		10	8									6			1	43
	2		4	5	3	7	11	9	14	10	8									6	12		1	44
	2		4	5	3	7		9		8	12									6	10	11	1	45
	2		4	5	3	7		9	14	10	8									6	12	11	1	46

Coca Cola Cup	First Round	Preston NE (a)	1-2
		(h)	4-0
	Second Round	Cambridge U (a)	2-2
		(h)	1-2
FA Cup	First Round	Port Vale (h)	0-0
		(a)	1-3

STOKE CITY

Player and Position	Ht	Wt	Date	Birth Place	Source	Clubs	League App	Gls
Goalkeepers								
Peter Fox‡	5 10	12 04	5 7 57	Scunthorpe	Apprentice	Sheffield W	49	—
						West Ham U (loan)	—	—
						Barnsley (loan)	1	—
						Stoke C	409	—
						Wrexham (loan)	—	—
Tony Parks (To Falkirk October 1992)	5 11	10 08	26 1 63	Hackney	Apprentice	Tottenham H	37	—
						Oxford U (loan)	5	—
						Gillingham (loan)	2	—
						Brentford	71	—
						QPR (loan)	—	—
						Fulham	2	—
						West Ham U	6	—
						Stoke C	2	—
Ron Sinclair	5 10	11 13	19 11 64	Stirling	Apprentice	Nottingham F	—	—
						Wrexham (loan)	11	—
						Derby Co (loan)	—	—
						Sheffield U (loan)	—	—
						Leeds U (loan)	—	—
						Leeds U	8	—
						Halifax T (loan)	4	—
						Halifax T (loan)	10	—
						Bristol C	44	—
						Walsall (loan)	10	—
						Stoke C	55	—
Defenders								
Robert Brunton†			5 9 73	Dublin	Belvedere	Stoke C	—	—
John Butler	5 11	11 07	7 2 62	Liverpool	Prescot Cables	Wigan Ath	245	15
						Stoke C	186	7
Ian Cranson	6 0	13 04	2 7 64	Easington	Apprentice	Ipswich T	131	5
						Sheffield W	30	—
						Stoke C	112	7
Tony Green†	5 10	10 04	30 4 74	Newcastle	Trainee	Stoke C	—	—
Graham Harbey	5 8	11 08	29 8 64	Chesterfield	Apprentice	Derby Co	40	1
						Ipswich T	59	1
						WBA	97	2
						Stoke C	17	—
Alex McLeish‡	5 9	11 06	3 9 73	Stoke	Trainee	Stoke C	—	—
Vince Overson	6 0	14 10	15 5 62	Kettering	Apprentice	Burnley	211	6
						Birmingham C	182	3
						Stoke C	78	4
Paul Rennie	5 9	11 04	26 10 71	Nantwich	Trainee	Crewe Alex	2	—
						Stoke C	4	—
Lee Sandford	6 1	12 02	22 4 68	Basingstoke	Apprentice	Portsmouth	72	1
						Stoke C	135	6
Matthew Wileman‡	5 9	11 00	24 1 74	Nuneaton	Trainee	Stoke C	—	—
Ian Wright	6 1	12 08	10 3 72	Lichfield	Trainee	Stoke C	6	—
Midfield								
Carl Beeston	5 9	12 04	30 6 67	Stoke	Apprentice	Stoke C	186	12
Mark Devlin	5 10	11 04	18 1 73	Irvine	Trainee	Stoke C	24	2
Steve Foley	5 7	11 03	4 10 62	Liverpool	Apprentice	Liverpool	—	—
						Fulham (loan)	3	—
						Grimsby T	31	2
						Sheffield U	66	14
						Swindon T	151	23
						Stoke C	64	8
Tony Gallimore	5 10	11 10	21 2 72	Crewe	Trainee	Stoke C	11	—
						Carlisle U (loan)	16	—
						Carlisle U (loan)	8	1
Nigel Gleghorn	6 0	13 04	12 8 62	Seaham	Seaham Red Star	Ipswich T	66	11
						Manchester C	34	7
						Birmingham C	142	33
						Stoke C	34	7
Gareth Jennings‡	5 10	11 12	16 12 73	Nuneaton	Trainee	Stoke C	—	—
David Kevan	5 8	10 12	31 8 68	Wigtown	Apprentice	Notts Co	89	3
						Cardiff C (loan)	7	—
						Stoke C	80	2
						Maidstone U (loan)	3	—
Keith Long†	5 9	10 00	14 11 73	Dublin	St Josephs Boys	Stoke C	—	—
Michael Macari			4 2 73	Kilwinning	Trainee	West Ham U	—	—
						Stoke C	—	—
Chris Male‡	5 9	11 09	16 6 72	Portsmouth		Stoke C	—	—
Jason Percival†	5 7	10 11	20 9 73	Nuneaton	Trainee	Stoke C	—	—
Gary Pick	5 8	11 08	9 7 71	Leicester	Leicester U	Stoke C	—	—

STOKE CITY

Colours: Red and white striped shirts, white shorts, red stockings. **Change colours:** All purple with white trim.

Foundation: The date of the formation of this club has long been in doubt. The year 1863 was claimed, but more recent research by Wade Martin has uncovered nothing earlier than 1868, when a couple of Old Carthusians, who were apprentices at the local works of the old North Staffordshire Railway Company, met with some others from that works, to form Stoke Ramblers. It should also be noted that the old Stoke club went bankrupt in 1908 when a new club was formed.

First Football League game: 8 September, 1888, Football League, v WBA (h) L 0-2 – Rowley; Clare, Underwood; Ramsey, Shutt, Smith; Sayer, McSkimming, Staton, Edge, Tunnicliffe.

Did you know: Stoke City established a club record 25 League games unbeaten from 5 September 1992 until 27 February 1993, winning 17 and drawing eight games.

Managers (and Secretary-Managers)
Tom Slaney 1874–83*, Walter Cox 1883–84*, Harry Lockett 1884–90, Joseph Bradshaw 1890–92, Arthur Reeves 1892–95, William Rowley 1895–97, H. D. Austerberry 1897–1908, A. J. Barker 1908–14, Peter Hodge 1914–15, Joe Schofield 1915–19, Arthur Shallcross 1919–23, John "Jock" Rutherford 1923, Tom Mather 1923–35, Bob McGrory 1935–52, Frank Taylor 1952–60, Tony Waddington 1960–77, George Eastham 1977–78, Alan A'Court 1978, Alan Durban 1978–81, Richie Barker 1981–83, Bill Asprey 1984–85, Mick Mills 1985–89, Alan Ball 1989–91, Lou Macari May 1991–.

Player and Position	Ht	Wt	Birth Date	Birth Place	Source	Clubs	League App	Gls
Ernie Tapai	5 7	10 05	14 2 67	Melbourne	Adelaide C	Stoke C	—	—
Paul Ware	5 9	11 05	7 11 70	Congleton	Trainee	Stoke C	114	10
Forwards								
Marcus Jones‡	6 2	13 00	24 6 74	Wolverhampton	Trainee	Stoke C	—	—
Tony Kelly	5 9	11 06	14 2 66	Meridan		Bristol C	6	1
					St Albans C	Stoke C	58	5
						Hull C (loan)	6	1
						Cardiff C (loan)	5	1
Steven Leslie			6 2 76	Dumfries		Stoke C	—	—
James Mulligan	5 7	10 12	21 4 74	Dublin	Trainee	Stoke C	—	—
Dave Regis	6 1	13 08	3 3 64	Paddington	Barnet	Notts Co	46	15
						Plymouth Arg	31	4
						Bournemouth (loan)	6	2
						Stoke C	25	5
Kevin Russell	5 8	10 12	6 12 66	Portsmouth	Brighton	Portsmouth	4	1
						Wrexham	84	43
						Leicester C	43	10
						Peterborough U (loan)	7	3
						Cardiff C (loan)	3	—
						Hereford U (loan)	3	1
						Stoke C (loan)	5	1
						Stoke C	40	5
Graham Shaw	5 8	10 05	7 6 67	Stoke	Apprentice	Stoke C	99	18
						Preston NE	121	29
						Stoke C	29	5
Mark Stein	5 6	11 02	28 1 66	S. Africa		Luton T	54	19
						Aldershot (loan)	2	1
						QPR	33	4
						Oxford U	82	18
						Stoke C	82	42

Trainees
Allerton, Daniel J; Ayres, Timothy; Bailey, Mark; Blair, Scott; Burke, Robert E; Davies, Stephen M; Holden, Mark C; Jukes, Paul W; Lacey, John P; Lovelock, Owen J; Mills, Andrew J; Moseley, Christopher K; Stokes, Lee F; Winstone, Simon J.

**Non-Contract
Brunton, Robert A. M; Green, Anthony J; Long, Keith D; Percival, Jason C; Reid, Mark.

Associated Schoolboys
Barratt, Richard J; Carter, Richard; Flynn, Barry J; Kelly, Stuart; Watson, David; Worth, Matthew J.

Associated Schoolboys who have accepted the club's offer of a Traineeship/Contract
Birch, Mark; Callan, Aidan J; Hawkes, Marc J; Woods, Stephen.

**Non-Contract Players who are retained must be re-signed before they are eligible to play in League matches.

494

SUNDERLAND 1992–93 *Back row (left to right):* Anthony Smith, Ian Patterson, Richard Ord, Terry Butcher, Thomas Hauser, Gordon Armstrong, Ian Samson, Anton Rogan, Gary Owers, Don Goodman, John Byrne.

Centre row: Malcolm Crosby (Manager), Bobby Ferguson (Assistant Manager), John Colquhoun, Brian Mooney, Gareth Cronin, Anthony Robinson, Tony Norman, Tim Carter, Peter Davenport, Shaun Cunnington, John Kay, Gary Bennett, Jim Morrow (Youth Development Officer), Roger Jones (Reserve Team Coach).

Front row: Steve Smelt (Physio), Paul Williams, Craig Russell, Wayne Walls, Brian Atkinson, Keiron Brady, Kevin Ball, Michael Gray, David Rush, Steven Brodie, Warren Hawke, Martin Gray, John Trigg (Youth Team Coach).

Division 1 SUNDERLAND

Roker Park Ground, Sunderland. Telephone Sunderland 091–514 0332. Fax 091 5145854. Commercial Dept: 091–567 2275.

Ground capacity: 29,234.

Record attendance: 75,118 v Derby Co, FA Cup 6th rd replay, 8 March 1933.

Record receipts: £186,000 v Tottenham H, Division 1, 28 August 1990.

Pitch measurements: 113yd × 74yd.

Chairman: R. S. Murray FCCA.

Deputy chairman: G. S. Wood.

Directors: J. G. Wood, J. R. Featherstone, G. Davidson.

Manager: Terry Butcher.

General Manager/Secretary: G. Davidson FCA.

Chief Coach: Bobby Ferguson. *Reserve team coach:* Roger Jones. *Physio:* Steve Smelt. *Youth development officer:* J. Morrow. *Youth team coach:* Jonathan Trigg. *Commercial Manager:* Alec King.

Year Formed: 1879. *Turned Professional:* 1886. *Ltd Co.:* 1906.

Club Nickname: 'Rokermen'.

Previous Name: 1879–80, Sunderland and District Teacher's AFC.

Previous Grounds: 1879, Blue House Field, Hendon; 1882, Groves Field, Ashbrooke; 1883, Horatio Street; 1884, Abbs Field, Fulwell; 1886, Newcastle Road; 1898, Roker Park.

Record League Victory: 9–1 v Newcastle U (away), Division 1, 5 December 1908 – Roose; Forster, Melton; Daykin, Thomson, Low; Mordue, Hogg (4), Brown, Holley (3), Bridgett (2).

Record Cup Victory: 11–1 v Fairfield, FA Cup, 1st rd, 2 February 1895 – Doig; McNeill, Johnston; Dunlop, McCreadie (1), Wilson; Gillespie (1), Millar (5), Campbell, Hannah (3), Scott (1).

Record Defeat: 0–8 v West Ham U, Division 1, 19 October 1968 and v Watford, Division 1, 25 September 1982.

Most League Points (2 for a win): 61, Division 2, 1963–64.

Most League Points (3 for a win): 93, Division 3, 1987–88.

Most League Goals: 109, Division 1, 1935–36.

Highest League Scorer in Season: Dave Halliday, 43, Division 1, 1928–29.

Most League Goals in Total Aggregate: Charlie Buchan, 209, 1911–25.

Most Capped Player: Martin Harvey, 34, Northern Ireland.

Most League Appearances: Jim Montgomery, 537, 1962–77.

Record Transfer Fee Received: £1,500,000 from Crystal Palace for Marco Gabbiadini, September 1991.

Record Transfer Fee Paid: £900,000 to WBA for Don Goodman, December 1991.

Football League Record: 1890 Elected to Division 1; 1958–64 Division 2; 1964–70 Division 1; 1970–76 Division 2; 1976–77 Division 1; 1977–80 Division 2; 1980–85 Division 1; 1985–87 Division 2; 1987–88 Division 3; 1988–90 Division 2; 1990–91 Division 1; 1991–92 Division 2; 1992– Division 1.

Honours: Football League: Division 1 – Champions 1891–92, 1892–93, 1894–95, 1901–02, 1912–13, 1935–36; Runners-up 1893–94; 1897–98, 1900–01, 1922–23, 1934–35; Division 2 – Champions 1975–76; Runners-up 1963–64, 1979–80; Division 3 – Champions 1987–88. *FA Cup:* Winners 1937, 1973; Runners-up 1913, 1992. *Football League Cup:* Runners-up 1984–85. **European Competitions:** *Cup-Winners' Cup:* 1973–74.

SUNDERLAND 1992—93 LEAGUE RECORD

Match No.	Date	Venue	Opponents	Result	H/T Score	Lg. Pos.	Goalscorers	Atten dance
1	Aug 15	A	Swindon T	L	0-1	0-0	—	11,094
2	22	H	Tranmere R	W	1-0	0-0	16	Cunnington	16,667
3	29	A	Bristol C	D	0-0	0-0	15		14,076
4	Sept 5	H	Charlton Ath	L	0-2	0-0	19		17,954
5	12	A	Oxford U	W	1-0	1-0	14	Rush	6003
6	19	A	Cambridge U	L	1-2	0-1	20	Rush	5383
7	26	H	Bristol R	D	1-1	0-1	19	Byrne	15,593
8	29	A	Watford	L	1-2	0-0	—	Goodman	6263
9	Oct 3	H	Millwall	W	2-0	0-0	14	Goodman 2	14,871
10	11	A	West Ham U	L	0-6	0-3	—		10,326
11	18	H	Newcastle U	L	1-2	0-1	—	Armstrong	28,098
12	24	A	Portsmouth	L	0-2	0-2	20		10,689
13	31	H	Notts Co	D	2-2	1-0	21	Owers, Ball	15,473
14	Nov 3	H	Wolverhampton W	W	2-0	1-0	—	Cunnington, Goodman	15,144
15	7	A	Peterborough U	L	2-5	0-1	20	Davenport (pen), Rush	8193
16	15	H	Leicester C	L	1-2	1-1	—	Davenport	14,945
17	21	A	Derby Co	W	1-0	1-0	20	Goodman	17,581
18	28	A	Southend U	W	1-0	0-0	18	Sampson	4584
19	Dec 5	H	Barnsley	W	2-1	2-0	17	Gray Michael, Cunnington	17,395
20	12	A	Brentford	L	1-3	1-1	17	Cunnington	16,972
21	19	A	Luton T	D	0-0	0-0	18		8286
22	28	H	Grimsby T	W	2-0	1-0	17	Goodman, Rush	20,771
23	Jan 9	H	Cambridge U	D	3-3	2-1	17	Mooney, Rush, Atkinson	16,778
24	16	A	Bristol R	D	2-2	2-1	16	Rush, Cunnington	6140
25	27	H	Watford	L	1-2	0-1	—	Ball	14,703
26	Feb 6	H	Swindon T	L	0-1	0-0	18		17,234
27	9	H	Oxford U	W	2-0	2-0	—	Goodman (pen), Gray Michael	13,314
28	13	A	Charlton Ath	W	1-0	0-0	17	Goodman (pen)	8151
29	20	H	Bristol C	D	0-0	0-0	17		17,122
30	27	H	West Ham U	D	0-0	0-0	16		19,068
31	Mar 6	A	Millwall	D	0-0	0-0	16		8761
32	10	A	Leicester C	L	2-3	2-2	—	Goodman, Armstrong	15,609
33	13	H	Peterborough U	W	3-0	0-0	15	Davenport, Goodman, Cunnington	18,372
34	16	A	Birmingham C	L	0-1	0-0	—		10,934
35	21	A	Barnsley	L	0-2	0-1	—		7278
36	24	H	Derby Co	W	1-0	0-0	—	Cunnington	17,246
37	27	A	Wolverhampton W	L	1-2	1-1	15	Harford	12,731
38	Apr 3	H	Southend U	L	2-4	2-1	15	Harford, Goodman	15,071
39	6	A	Brentford	D	1-1	0-1	—	Goodman	9302
40	10	H	Birmingham C	L	1-2	1-1	18	Davenport	16,382
41	12	A	Grimsby T	L	0-1	0-0	20		8090
42	17	H	Luton T	D	2-2	1-0	18	Goodman 2	16,493
43	25	A	Newcastle U	L	0-1	0-1	—		30,364
44	May 1	H	Portsmouth	W	4-1	1-0	18	Goodman 2 (2 pens), Gray Martin, Armstrong	21,309
45	4	A	Tranmere R	L	1-2	1-1	—	Atkinson	9685
46	8	A	Notts Co	L	1-3	0-3	21	Ball	14,417

Final League Position: 21

GOALSCORERS

League (50): Goodman 16 (4 pens), Cunnington 7, Rush 6, Davenport 4 (1 pen), Armstrong 3, Ball 3, Atkinson 2, Michael Gray 2, Harford 2, Byrne 1, Martin Gray 1, Mooney 1, Owers 1, Sampson 1.
Coca Cola Cup (3): Ball 1, Butcher 1, Davenport 1.
FA Cup (2): Cunnington 1, Goodman 1.

Match No.	Norman 33	Ball 43	Bennett 14 + 1	Butcher 37 + 1	Smith 7	Owers 33	Cunnington 38 + 1	Goodman 41	Colquhoun 12 + 8	Byrne 6	Atkinson 31 + 5	Davenport 20 + 14	Armstrong 41 + 4	Carter 13	Kay 36	Ord 21 + 3	Rogan 12 + 1	Rush 12 + 6	Martin Gray 9 + 3	Sampson 4 + 1	Michael Gray 23 + 4	Mooney 10 + 2	Hawke — + 2	Harford 10 + 1	Howey — + 1
1	1	2	3	4	5	6	7	8	9	10	11	12	14												
2		6		5	3	4	7		9	10		12	14	1	2	11									
3		6	9	5		4	7	8		10		12		1	2	11	3								
4		6	9	5		4	7	8	12	10			14	1	2	11	3								
5		6	9	5		4	7	8				12	11	1	2		3	10							
6		6	9	5		4	7	8	14			12	11	1	2	3		10							
7		6		5		4	7	8	9		10	12	11	1	2		3								
8		6	14	5		4	7	8	9		10	12	11	1	2		3								
9		6		5		4	7	8	9			12	11	1	2		3	10							
10		6		5		4	7	8	9			14	11	1	2		3	12	10						
11		6		5		4	7	8	9		10	12	11	1	2		3								
12		6				4	7	8	9		10	12	11	1	2	5	3	14							
13	1	6				4	7	8	9		10		11		2	5	3								
14		6				4	7	8	9		10		11	1	2	5	3								
15		6	14			4	7	8	9		10		11	1	2	5	3	12							
16	1	6	14	5		4	7	8	9		10		11		2		3	12							
17	1	6		5		4	7	8	9		10		11		2		3	12	14						
18	1			5		4	7		9		10	12	11		2	6	3	8	14						
19	1	6		5			7	8	9		10	12	11		2	4	3		14						
20	1	6		5			7				10		11		2			12	9	4	3	8			
21	1	6		5			7		9				11		2			10	12	4	3	8			
22	1	6		5			7	8				12	11		2	4		10			3	9			
23	1	6		5			7	8				12	11		2	4		10			3	9			
24	1	6		5			7	8				12	11		2	4		10			3	9	14		
25	1	6		5		4	7	8				12	11		2			10			3	9			
26	1	6		5		4			9			12	11		2			10	7	8	3				
27	1	6		5		4		8	9				11		2			10	7		3		12		
28	1	6		5		4		8	9				11		2			10	7		3		12		
29	1	6		5		4		8	9				11		2			10	7	14	3		12		
30	1	6		5		4		8	9			12	11		2			10	7		3				
31	1	6		5		4	7	8	9				11		2			10			3		12		
32	1	6		5		4	7	8	9			12	11		2			10			3				
33	1	6		5		4	7	8	9		10	12	11		2						3				
34	1	6		5		4	7	8	9		10		11		2						3				
35	1	6	2	5		4	7	8			10	12	11								3		14	9	
36	1	6	2	5		4	7	8			10		11						12		3			9	
37	1	6		5		4	7	8			10		11		2						3			9	
38	1	6		5		4	7	8			10		11			2					3			9	
39	1	6		5		4	7	8			10		11			2					3			9	
40	1	6		5		4	7	8			10	12	11			2					3			9	
41	1	6		5		4	7	8			10		11			2		12			3			9	
42	1	6		5		4	7	8			10	12	11			2					3			9	
43	1	6		5		4	7	8			10	12	11			2				14	3			9	
44	1	6		5		4	7	8	9		10	12	11			2					3				14
45	1	6		5		4	7	8	9		10		11			2					3			12	
46	1	6	2	5		4	7	8			10	12	11							14	3			9	

Coca Cola Cup	First Round	Huddersfield T (h)	2-3
		(a)	1-0
FA Cup	Third Round	Notts Co (a)	2-0
	Fourth Round	Sheffield W (a)	0-1

SUNDERLAND

Player and Position	Ht	Wt	Date	Birth Place	Source	Clubs	League App	Gls
Goalkeepers								
Tim Carter	6 2	13 11	5 10 67	Bristol	Apprentice	Bristol R	47	—
						Newport Co (loan)	1	—
						Carlisle U (loan)	4	—
						Sunderland	37	—
						Bristol C (loan)	3	—
						Birmingham C (loan)	2	—
Tony Norman	6 2	13 10	24 2 58	Mancot	Amateur	Burnley	—	—
						Hull C	372	—
						Sunderland	166	—
Defenders								
Kevin Ball	5 9	12 00	12 11 64	Hastings	Apprentice	Portsmouth	105	4
						Sunderland	109	7
Gary Bennett	6 1	12 01	4 12 61	Manchester	Amateur	Manchester C	—	—
						Cardiff C	87	11
						Sunderland	311	23
Terry Butcher	6 4	14 00	28 12 58	Singapore	Amateur	Ipswich T	271	16
						Rangers	127	9
						Coventry C	6	—
						Sunderland	38	—
Gareth Cronin			18 2 75	Cork	Trainee	Sunderland	—	—
Shaun Cunnington	5 10	11 07	4 1 66	Bourne	Bourne T	Wrexham	199	12
						Grimsby T	182	13
						Sunderland	39	7
Michael Gray			3 8 74	Sunderland	Trainee	Sunderland	27	2
John Kay	5 10	11 06	29 1 64	Sunderland	Apprentice	Arsenal	14	—
						Wimbledon	63	2
						Middlesbrough (loan)	8	—
						Sunderland	196	—
Richard Ord	6 2	12 08	3 3 70	Easington	Trainee	Sunderland	93	2
						York C (loan)	3	—
Ian Patterson*	6 2	13 00	4 4 73	Chatham	Trainee	Sunderland	—	—
Anthony Robinson			5 10 73	Sunderland	Trainee	Sunderland	—	—
Anton Rogan	5 11	12 06	25 3 66	Belfast	Distillery	Celtic	127	4
						Sunderland	46	1
Ian Sampson	6 2	12 08	14 11 68	Wakefield	Goole T	Sunderland	13	1
Tony Smith	5 10	11 04	21 9 71	Sunderland	Trainee	Sunderland	18	—
						Hartlepool U (loan)	5	—
Wayne Walls*	5 10	11 12	23 7 72	Sunderland	Trainee	Sunderland	—	—
Midfield								
Gordon Armstrong	6 0	11 10	15 7 67	Newcastle	Apprentice	Sunderland	307	47
Brian Atkinson	5 10	12 00	19 1 71	Darlington	Trainee	Sunderland	88	4
Kieron Brady*	5 9	11 13	17 9 71	Glasgow	Trainee	Sunderland	33	7
						Doncaster R (loan)	4	3
Martin Gray	5 9	10 11	17 8 71	Stockton	Trainee	Sunderland	13	1
						Aldershot (loan)	5	—
Warren Hawke*	5 10	10 11	20 9 70	Durham	Trainee	Sunderland	25	1
						Chesterfield (loan)	7	1
						Carlisle U (loan)	8	2
						Northampton T (loan)	7	1
Brian Mooney*	5 10	11 02	2 2 66	Dublin	Home Farm	Liverpool	—	—
						Wrexham (loan)	9	2
						Preston NE	128	20
						Sheffield W (loan)	—	—
						Sunderland	27	1
						Burnley (loan)	6	—
Gary Owers	5 10	11 10	3 10 68	Newcastle	Apprentice	Sunderland	219	22
Paul Williams*	6 0	12 02	25 9 70	Liverpool	Trainee	Sunderland	9	—
						Swansea C (loan)	12	1

SUNDERLAND

Colours: Red and white striped shirts, black shorts, red stockings, white turnover. **Change colours:** White shirts, blue and green sleeves, navy blue shorts, white stockings, navy blue trim.

Foundation: A Scottish schoolmaster named James Allan, working at Hendon Boarding School, took the initiative in the foundation of Sunderland in 1879 when they were formed as The Sunderland and District Teachers' Association FC at a meeting in the Adults School, Norfolk Street. Because of financial difficulties, they quickly allowed members from outside the teaching profession and so became Sunderland AFC in October 1880.

First Football League game: 13 September, 1890, Football League, v Burnley (h) L 2-3 – Kirtley; Porteous, Oliver; Wilson, Auld, Gibson; Spence (1), Miller, Campbell (1), Scott, D. Hannah.

Did you know: Sunderland played their first game at Roker Park on 10 September 1898 and beat Liverpool 1-0. Attendances that season averaged 13,863.

Managers (and Secretary-Managers)
Tom Watson 1888–96, Bob Campbell 1896–99, Alex Mackie 1899–1905, Bob Kyle 1905–28, Johnny Cochrane 1928–39, Bill Murray 1939–57, Alan Brown 1957–64, George Hardwick 1964–65, Ian McColl 1965–68, Alan Brown 1968–72, Bob Stokoe 1972–76, Jimmy Adamson 1976–78, Ken Knighton 1979–81, Alan Durban 1981–84, Len Ashurst 1984–85, Lawrie McMenemy 1985–87, Denis Smith 1987–91, Malcolm Crosby 1992–93, Terry Butcher February 1993–.

Player and Position	Ht	Wt	Birth Date	Birth Place	Source	Clubs	League App	Gls
Forwards								
Stephen Brodie	5 10	11 00	14 1 73	Sunderland	Trainee	Sunderland	—	—
John Colquhoun	5 7	11 00	14 7 63	Stirling	Grangemouth Inter	Stirling Albion	104	45
						Celtic	32	4
						Hearts	231	54
						Millwall	27	3
						Sunderland	20	—
Peter Davenport*	5 10	11 06	24 3 61	Birkenhead	Everton	Nottingham F	118	54
						Manchester U	92	22
						Middlesbrough	59	7
						Sunderland	99	15
Don Goodman	5 10	11 10	9 5 66	Leeds	School	Bradford C	70	14
						WBA	158	60
						Sunderland	63	27
Mick Harford	6 3	14 05	12 2 59	Sunderland	Lambton St BC	Lincoln C	115	41
						Newcastle U	19	4
						Bristol C	30	11
						Birmingham C	92	25
						Luton T	139	57
						Derby Co	58	15
						Luton T	29	12
						Chelsea	28	9
						Sunderland	11	2
Thomas Hauser (To Cambuur October 1992)	6 3	12 06	10 4 65	West Germany	Berne OB	Sunderland	53	9
Lee Howey	6 2	13 09	1 4 69	Sunderland	AC Hemptinne	Sunderland	1	
Colin Pascoe	5 9	10 00	9 4 65	Port Talbot	Apprentice	Swansea C	174	39
						Sunderland	126	22
						Swansea C (loan)	15	4
David Rush	5 11	10 10	15 5 71	Sunderland	Trainee	Sunderland	54	12
						Hartlepool U (loan)	8	2
Craig Russell			4 2 74	South Shields	Trainee	Sunderland	4	—
Martin Smith			13 11 74	Sunderland	Trainee	Sunderland	—	—

Trainees
Beary, Daniel M; Carmichael, Barry; Gate, Paul W; Harding, Alan; Manners, Andrew C; McGee, Dean; Musgrave, Sean; Piggott, Craig; Preece, David; Waldock, John A.

Associated Schoolboys
Bell, Russell; Brown, Mark; Clark, Lee; Coultard, David; Logan, Lee; McPake, Christopher; Norton, Peter; Parker, Neal; Richardson, Paul; Simpson, Neil.

Associated Schoolboys who have accepted the club's offer of a Traineeship/Contract
Berrisford, Adrian C; Brumwell, Philip; Forster, Lee C; Mawson, David; Pickering, Steven; Smith, Stephen, Stoddart, Neil.

SWANSEA CITY 1992–93   *Back row (left to right):* Tony Cullen, Reuben Agboola, Colin Pascoe, Des Lyttle, Russell Coughlin.
Centre row: Stephen Jenkins, John Ford, Andy McFarlane, Steve McMahon, Mark Harris, Colin West, Keith Walker.
Front row: Paul Wimbleton, Shaun Chapple, Roger Freestone, John Cornforth, James Heeps, Jason Bowen, Andrew Legg.

Division 2   **SWANSEA CITY**

Vetch Field, Swansea SA1 3SU. Telephone Swansea (0792) 474114. Fax: (0792) 646120. Club shop: 33 William St, Swansea SA1 3QS.

Ground capacity: 16,540.

Record attendance: 32,796 v Arsenal, FA Cup 4th rd, 17 February 1968.

Record receipts: £36,477.42 v Liverpool, Division 1, 18 September 1982.

Pitch measurements: 112yd × 74yd.

President: I. C. Pursey MBE.

Chairman: D. J. Sharpe.

Directors: D. G. Hammond FCA, MBIM (Vice-chairman), M. Griffiths.

Chief Executive: Robin Sharpe.

Team Manager: Frank Burrows. *Assistant Manager:* Bobby Smith.

Youth Team Manager: Jimmy Rimmer. *Physio:* Mike Davenport.

Commercial and Marketing Manager: John Gwilt. *Programme Editor:* Major Reg Pike.

Year Formed: 1912. *Turned Professional:* 1912. *Ltd Co.:* 1912.

Secretary: George Taylor.

Previous Name: Swansea Town until February 1970.

Club Nickname: 'The Swans'.

Record League Victory: 8–0 v Hartlepool U, Division 4, 1 April 1978 – Barber; Evans, Bartley, Lally (1) (Morris), May, Bruton, Kevin Moore, Robbie James (3 incl. 1p), Curtis (3), Toshack (1), Chappell.

Record Cup Victory: 12–0 v Sliema W (Malta), ECWC 1st rd 1st leg, 15 September 1982 – Davies; Marustik, Hadziabdic (1), Irwin (1), Kennedy, Rajkovic (1), Loveridge (2) (Leighton James), Robbie James, Charles (2), Stevenson (1), Latchford (1) (Walsh (3)).

Record Defeat: 0–8 v Liverpool, FA Cup 3rd rd, 9 January 1990.

Most League Points (2 for a win): 62, Division 3 (S), 1948–49.

Most League Points (3 for a win): 73, Division 2, 1992–93.

Most League Goals: 90, Division 2, 1956–57.

Highest League Scorer in Season: Cyril Pearce, 35, Division 2, 1931–32.

Most League Goals in Total Aggregate: Ivor Allchurch, 166, 1949–58, 1965–68.

Most Capped Player: Ivor Allchurch, 42 (68), Wales.

Most League Appearances: Wilfred Milne, 585, 1919–37.

Record Transfer Fee Received: £370,000 from Leeds U for Alan Curtis, May 1979.

Record Transfer Fee Paid: £340,000 to Liverpool for Colin Irwin, August 1981.

Football League Record: 1920 Original Member of Division 3; 1921–25 Division 3 (S); 1925–47 Division 2; 1947–49 Division 3 (S); 1949–65 Division 2; 1965–67 Division 3; 1967–70 Division 4; 1970–73 Division 3; 1973–78 Division 4; 1978–79 Division 3; 1979–81 Division 2; 1981–83 Division 1; 1983–84 Division 2; 1984–86 Division 3; 1986–88 Division 4; 1988–92 Division 3; 1992– Division 2.

Honours: Football League: Division 1 best season: 6th, 1981–82; Division 2 – Promoted 1980–81 (3rd); Division 3 (S) – Champions 1924–25, 1948–49; Division 3 – Promoted 1978–79 (3rd); Division 4 – Promoted 1969–70 (3rd), 1977–78 (3rd). *FA Cup:* Semi-finals 1926, 1964. *Football League Cup:* best season: 4th rd, 1964–65, 1976–77. *Welsh Cup:* Winners 9 times; Runners-up 8 times. **European Competitions:** *European Cup-Winners' Cup:* 1961–62, 1966–67, 1981–82, 1982–83, 1983–84, 1989–90, 1991–92.

SWANSEA CITY 1992—93 LEAGUE RECORD

Match No.	Date		Venue	Opponents	Result		H/T Score	Lg. Pos.	Goalscorers	Attendance
1	Aug	15	A	Burnley	L	0-1	0-0	—		10,913
2		22	H	Mansfield T	W	4-0	1-0	9	Pascoe, Cornforth, Legg, Gray (og)	2792
3		29	A	Wigan Ath	W	3-2	2-0	6	Harris, Ford, Cornforth	1565
4	Sept	1	A	Hull C	L	0-1	0-0	—		4408
5		5	H	Port Vale	W	2-0	0-0	8	West 2 (1 pen)	3868
6		12	H	Blackpool	W	3-0	2-0	5	West, Pascoe, Legg	3861
7		15	A	Fulham	D	1-1	0-1	—	Cornforth	4268
8		19	A	Huddersfield T	W	2-1	0-0	3	West, Legg	4839
9		26	H	Bradford C	D	1-1	1-1	3	West (pen)	4781
10	Oct	3	A	Stockport Co	D	1-1	0-0	5	Cullen	4943
11		10	H	Exeter C	D	0-0	0-0	5		4439
12		17	A	Hartlepool U	W	1-0	0-0	3	Harris	4175
13		24	H	Reading	W	2-1	1-0	1	Cornforth, Harris	5317
14		31	A	Leyton Orient	L	2-4	0-2	5	Pascoe, Cullen	5683
15	Nov	3	H	Plymouth Arg	D	0-0	0-0	—		5430
16		7	A	Chester C	L	2-3	1-2	7	Pascoe, Legg	2861
17		20	H	Brighton & HA	L	0-1	0-0	—		4645
18		28	A	Stoke C	L	1-2	0-0	12	Cullen	13,867
19	Dec	12	H	WBA	D	0-0	0-0	13		5610
20		18	A	Rotherham U	D	0-0	0-0	—		4600
21		26	H	Bournemouth	W	2-0	0-0	11	West, Legg	4995
22		28	H	Bolton W	L	1-2	1-1	11	West	7220
23	Jan	5	A	Blackpool	D	0-0	0-0	—		3417
24		9	H	Fulham	D	2-2	1-0	11	Wimbleton, West	5048
25		16	A	Bradford C	D	0-0	0-0	12		5551
26		30	A	Mansfield T	D	3-3	1-3	12	West, McFarlane, Ford	2641
27	Feb	5	H	Burnley	D	1-1	1-0	—	Bowen	4973
28		13	A	Port Vale	L	0-2	0-1	14		7191
29		20	H	Hull C	W	1-0	1-0	13	McFarlane	2656
30		27	A	Exeter C	W	2-0	0-0	13	Lyttle, West	3146
31	Mar	5	H	Stockport Co	D	2-2	2-0	—	Bowen, West (pen)	4755
32		9	A	Preston NE	W	3-1	3-0	—	West (pen), Bowen 2	4396
33		13	H	Chester C	W	4-2	2-1	11	Bowen 3, Legg	4056
34		20	A	Plymouth Arg	W	1-0	1-0	10	Bowen	6233
35		23	H	Stoke C	L	1-2	1-0	—	Legg	8366
36		27	A	Brighton & HA	W	2-0	1-0	10	Legg, Bowen	7558
37	Apr	7	A	WBA	L	0-3	0-2	—		13,401
38		10	H	Bournemouth	W	2-1	1-0	11	Legg, Bowen	5101
39		12	A	Bolton W	L	1-3	1-0	11	Ford	10,854
40		17	H	Rotherham U	W	2-0	0-0	10	McFarlane, Cornforth	4658
41		20	H	Huddersfield T	W	3-0	1-0	—	Legg, Harris, Walker	5190
42		24	H	Hartlepool U	W	3-0	1-0	7	Legg, Walker, McFarlane	5310
43		27	H	Preston NE	W	2-0	0-0	—	Harris, McFarlane	6933
44	May	1	A	Reading	L	0-2	0-2	6		6922
45		4	H	Wigan Ath	W	2-1	0-1	—	Coughlin, Legg	7361
46		8	H	Leyton Orient	L	0-1	0-1	5		6543

Final League Position: 5

GOALSCORERS

League (65): Legg 12, West 12 (4 pens), Bowen 10, Cornforth 5, Harris 5, McFarlane 5, Pascoe 4, Cullen 3, Ford 3, Walker 2, Coughlin 1, Lyttle 1, Wimbleton 1, own goal 1.
Coca Cola Cup (1): McFarlane 1.
FA Cup (8): Legg 2, West 2, Bowen 1, Cornforth 1, Cullen 1, Wimbleton 1.

Freestone 46	Lyttle 46	Jenkins 29 + 4	Walker 42	Harris 42	Coughlin 38 + 1	Cullen 20 + 7	Pascoe 15	McFarlane 17 + 7	Cornforth 44	Legg 46	Bowen 23 + 15	Ford 36 + 7	Agboola 6 + 1	West 29 + 4	Connor 3	Wimbleton 10 + 5	Chapple 4	Hayes 8 + 7	McMahon 2	Match No.
1	2	3	4	5	6	7	8	9	10	11	12	14								1
1	2			5	6	7	8	9	10	11		3		4						2
1	2	8		5	6	7		9	10	11	12	3		4	14					3
1	2			5	6	7	8	9	10	11	12	3		4						4
1	2		4	5	6	7	8		10	11	12	3	14	9						5
1	2		4	5	6	7	8		10	11	12	3		9						6
1	2		4	5	6	12	8		10	11		7	3	9						7
1	2		4	5	6	12	8		10	11		7	3	9						8
1	2		4	5	6	12	8		10	11		7	3	9						9
1	2		4	5	6	7	8		10	11	12	3		9						10
1	2		4	5	6	7	8		10	11		3		9						11
1	2		4	5	6	7	8		10	11	12	3		9						12
1	2		4	5	6	7	8		10	11		3		9						13
1	2	14	4	5	6	7	8		10	11	12	3		9						14
1	2	12	4	5	6	7	8		10	11		3		9						15
1	2	14		5	6	7	8		10	11	12	3	4	9						16
1	2	3			6			12	10	11	7	5	4	9	8					17
1	2	3		5		7		12	10	11	6	14	4	9	8					18
1	2		4	5	6	7			10	11	12	3		9	8					19
1	2	3	4	5	6	7			10	11	12			9	8					20
1	2	3	4	5		7			10	11	12			9	8					21
1	2	3	4	5		7	14		10	11	12	6		9	8					22
1	2	3	4	5	6	7				11	12			9	8	10				23
1	2	3	4	5	6				10	11	12	14		9	8	7				24
1	2	3	4	5					10	11	12			9	8	6	7			25
1	2	3	4	5				12	10	11		14		9	8	6	7			26
1	2	3	4	5					10	11	8	12		9		6	7			27
1	2	3	4	5				14	10	11	12	6		9	8		7			28
1	2	12	4	5	6		8		10	11	7	3		9						29
1	2	3	4	5			8	12	10	11		7	6	9						30
1	2	3	4	5			8	12	10	11		7	6	9						31
1	2	3	4	5			8	12	10	11		7	6	9						32
1	2	3	4				8		10	11		7	6	9					5	33
1	2	3	4				8		10	11		7	6			12		9	5	34
1	2	3	4	5			8	9	10	11		7	6			12		14		35
1	2	3	4	5			8	9		11		7	6			10				36
1	2	3	4	5			8	9	10	11		7	6			12		14		37
1	2	3	4	5			8	9	10	11		7	6			12		14		38
1	2	3	4	5			12	9	10	11		7	6			8		14		39
1	2	3	4	5	6			9	10	11		7	8			12				40
1	2	3	4	5			8	9	10	11		7	6			12				41
1	2	3	4	5		12	8	9	10	11		7	6					14		42
1	2	3	4	5			8	9	10	11		7	6							43
1	2	3	4	5		12	8	9	10	11		7	6					14		44
1	2	3	4	5		12	8	9	10	11		7		14		6				45
1	2	3	4	5	8		7	9	10	11	12			14		6				46

Coca Cola Cup	First Round	Oxford U (a)	0-3
		(h)	1-0
FA Cup	Second Round	Exeter C (a)	5-2
	Third Round	Oxford U (h)	1-1
		(a)	2-2
	Fourth Round	Grimsby T (h)	0-0
		(a)	0-2

SWANSEA CITY

Player and Position	Ht	Wt	Date	Birth Place	Source	Clubs	League App	Gls
Goalkeepers								
Roger Freestone	6 2	12 03	19 8 68	Newport		Newport Co	13	—
						Chelsea	42	—
						Swansea C (loan)	14	—
						Hereford U (loan)	8	—
						Swansea C	88	—
Jimmy Heeps*			16 5 71	Luton	Trainee	Swansea C	1	—
Defenders								
Reuben Agboola*	5 10	11 09	30 5 62	London	Apprentice	Southampton	90	—
						Sunderland	140	—
						Charlton Ath (loan)	1	—
						Port Vale (loan)	9	—
						Swansea C	28	—
John Cornforth	6 1	12 08	7 10 67	Whitley Bay	Apprentice	Sunderland	32	2
						Doncaster R (loan)	7	3
						Shrewsbury T (loan)	3	—
						Lincoln C (loan)	9	1
						Swansea C	61	5
Mark Harris	6 1	12 05	15 7 63	Reading	Wokingham	Crystal Palace	2	—
						Burnley (loan)	4	—
						Swansea C	168	11
Steve Jenkins	5 10	11 02	16 7 72	Merthyr	Trainee	Swansea C	68	—
Des Lyttle	5 9	12 00	24 9 71	Wolverhampton	Worcester C	Swansea C	46	1
Steven McMahon*	6 4	14 03	22 4 70	Glasgow	Ferguslie	Swansea C	2	—
Midfield								
Jason Bowen	5 6	10 07	24 8 72	Merthyr	Trainee	Swansea C	52	10
Shaun Chapple	5 11	12 03	14 2 73	Swansea	Trainee	Swansea C	25	2
Russell Coughlin	5 8	11 12	15 2 60	Swansea	Apprentice	Manchester C	—	—
						Blackburn R	24	—
						Carlisle U	130	13
						Plymouth Arg	131	18
						Blackpool	102	8
						Shrewsbury T (loan)	5	—
						Swansea C	101	2
John Ford	6 1	13 01	12 4 68	Birmingham	Cradley T	Swansea C	87	3
Andy Legg	5 8	10 07	28 7 66	Neath	Briton Ferry	Swansea C	163	29
Keith Walker	6 0	11 09	17 4 66	Edinburgh	ICI Juveniles	Stirling Albion	91	17
						St Mirren	43	6
						Swansea C	111	3
Paul Wimbleton*	5 8	10 12	13 11 64	Havant	Apprentice	Portsmouth	10	—
						Cardiff C	119	17
						Bristol C	16	2
						Shrewsbury T	34	1
						Maidstone U (loan)	2	1
						Exeter C	36	4
						Swansea C	15	1
Forwards								
Tony Cullen*	5 6	11 07	30 9 69	Newcastle	Local	Sunderland	29	—
						Carlisle U (loan)	2	1
						Rotherham U (loan)	3	1
						Bury (loan)	4	—
						Swansea C	27	3
Martin Hayes	5 10	11 12	21 3 66	Walthamstow	Apprentice	Arsenal	102	26
						Celtic	7	—
						Wimbledon (loan)	2	—
						Swansea C	15	—

SWANSEA CITY

Colours: White shirts, white shorts, black stockings. **Change colours:** All yellow.

Foundation: The earliest Association Football in Wales was played in the Northern part of the country and no international took place in the South until 1894, when a local paper still thought it necessary to publish an outline of the rules and an illustration of the pitch markings. There had been an earlier Swansea club, but this has no connection with Swansea Town (now City) formed at a public meeting in June 1912.

First Football League game: 28 August, 1920, Division 3, v Portsmouth (a) L 0-3 – Crumley; Robson, Evans; Smith, Holdsworth, Williams; Hole, I. Jones, Edmundson, Rigsby, Spottiswood.

Did you know: Swansea defeated Real Madrid 3-0 during a close season tour of Spain and Portugal in 1927. They were the second British club to win there after Nelson in 1923.

Managers (and Secretary-Managers)
Walter Whittaker 1912–14, William Bartlett 1914–15, Joe Bradshaw 1919–26, Jimmy Thomson 1927–31, Neil Harris 1934–39, Haydn Green 1939–47, Bill McCandless 1947–55, Ron Burgess 1955–58, Trevor Morris 1958–65, Glyn Davies 1965–66, Billy Lucas 1967–69, Roy Bentley 1969–72, Harry Gregg 1972–75, Harry Griffiths 1975–77, John Toshack 1978–83 (resigned October re-appointed in December) 1983–84, Colin Appleton 1984, John Bond 1984–85, Tommy Hutchison 1985–86, Terry Yorath 1986–89, Ian Evans 1989–90, Terry Yorath 1990–91, Frank Burrows March 1991–.

Player and Position	Ht	Wt	Date	Birth Place	Source	Clubs	League App	Gls
Andy McFarlane	6 3	12 06	30 11 66	Wolverhampton	Cradley T	Portsmouth	2	—
						Swansea C	24	5
Darren Perrett†	5 9	11 06	29 12 69	Cardiff	Cheltenham T	Swansea C	—	—
Colin West	6 0	13 11	13 11 62	Wallsend	Apprentice	Sunderland	102	21
						Watford	45	20
						Rangers	10	2
						Sheffield W	45	8
						WBA	73	22
						Port Vale (loan)	5	1
						Swansea C	33	12

Trainees
Barnhouse, David J; Coates, Jonathan S; Edwards, Christian; Elsey, Kristian G; Evans, Ian D; Hole, Steven T; Jones, Andrew P; Martin, Gareth E; Miles, Benjamin D; Moran, Lee; Rickard, Jamie M; Savage, Christopher J; Savage, Robert T; Thomas, David J; Williams, Steven S;

**Non-Contract
Perrett, Darren J.

Associated Schoolboys
Creeden, Kevin M; Cunningham, John L; Dent, Paul R. J; Grey, Jonathan R; Harris, Gareth; Jenkins, David M; John, Carl M; Jones, Lee E; Jones, Mathew; Lewis, Huw A. W; Llewellyn, Lee; O;Leary, Kristian; Synnock, Steven M.

**Non-Contract Players who are retained must be re-signed before they are eligible to play in League matches.

506

SWINDON TOWN 1992-93 *Back row (left to right):* John Moncur, Darren Hall, Fraser Digby, Paul Hunt, Nicky Hammond, David Bennett, Craig Maskell, Steve White.
Centre row: John Trollope (Youth Team Manager), Ross MacLaren, Nicky Summerbee, Colin Calderwood, Shaun Taylor, Adrian Viveash, David Mitchell, Andrew Thomson, Kevin Horlock.
Andy Rowland (Reserve Team Coach).
Front row: Kevin Morris (Physio), Martin Ling, David Kerslake, Wayne O'Sullivan, Glenn Hoddle (Team Manager), John Gorman (Assistant Manager), Paul Bodin, Shaun Close, Micky Hazard,
Eddie Buckley (Kit Manager).

FA Premier

SWINDON TOWN

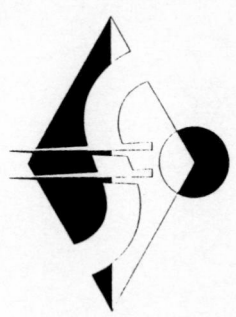

SWINDON TOWN FC

County Ground, Swindon, Wiltshire SN1 2ED. Telephone Swindon (0793) 430430. Fax: 0793 536170. Clubcall: 0898 121640.

Ground capacity: 18,152.

Record attendance: 32,000 v Arsenal, FA Cup 3rd rd, 15 January 1972.

Record receipts: £101,221 v Aston Villa, FA Cup 5th rd, 16 February 1992.

Pitch measurements: 114yd × 72yd.

President: C. J. Green.

Chairman: R. V. Hardman. *Vice-chairman:* L J. M. Spearman.

Directors: P. T. Archer, Sir Seton Willis Bt, C. J. Puffett, J. R. Hunt (Associate).

Manager: John Gorman. *Assistant. Manager:* David Hay.

Coach: Andy Rowland. *Physio:* Kevin Morris.

Secretary: Jon Pollard. *Youth Team Manager:* John Trollope.

Commercial Manager: Janet Garrett.

Year Formed: 1881 *(see Foundation).* **Turned Professional:** 1894. *Ltd Co.:* 1894.

Club Nickname: 'Robins'.

Previous Ground: 1881–96, The Croft.

Record League Victory: 9–1 v Luton T, Division 3 (S), 28 August 1920 – Nash; Kay, Macconachie; Langford, Hawley, Wareing; Jefferson (1), Fleming (4), Rogers, Batty (2), Davies (1). (1 og).

Record Cup Victory: 10–1 v Farnham U Breweries (away), FA Cup, 1st rd (replay), 28 November 1925 – Nash; Dickenson, Weston, Archer, Bew, Adey; Denyer (2), Wall (1), Richardson (4), Johnson (3), Davies.

Record Defeat: 1–10 v Manchester C, FA Cup 4th rd (replay), 25 January 1930.

Most League Points (2 for a win): 64, Division 3, 1968–69.

Most League Points (3 for a win): 102, Division 4, 1985–86 (League record).

Most League Goals: 100, Division 3 (S), 1926–27.

Highest League Scorer in Season: Harry Morris, 47, Division 3 (S), 1926–27.

Most League Goals in Total Aggregate: Harry Morris, 216, 1926–33.

Most Capped Player: Rod Thomas, 30 (50), Wales.

Most League Appearances: John Trollope, 770, 1960–80.

Record Transfer Fee Received: £1,000,000 from Southampton for Alan McLoughlin, December 1990.

Record Transfer Fee Paid: £250,000 to Huddersfield T for Duncan Shearer, June 1988.

Football League Record: 1920 Original Member of Division 3; 1921–58 Division 3 (S); 1958–63 Division 3; 1963–65 Division 2; 1965–69 Division 3; 1969–74 Division 2; 1974–82 Division 3; 1982–86 Division 4; 1986–87 Division 3; 1987–92 Division 2; 1992–93 Division 1; 1993– FA Premier League.

Honours: Football League: Division 1 best season: promotion through play-offs 1992–93; Division 3 – Runners-up 1962–63, 1968–69; Division 4 – Champions 1985–86 (with record 102 points). *FA Cup:* Semi-finals 1910, 1912. *Football League Cup:* Winners 1968–69. *Anglo-Italian Cup:* Winners 1970.

SWINDON TOWN 1992—93 LEAGUE RECORD

Match No.	Date	Venue	Opponents	Result		H/T Score	Lg. Pos.	Goalscorers	Atten dance
1	Aug 15	H	Sunderland	W	1-0	0-0	—	Hoddle	11,094
2	19	A	Bristol R	W	4-3	3-1	—	Taylor, Mitchell 2, Bodin (pen)	6150
3	22	A	Wolverhampton W	D	2-2	1-1	3	Maskell, Taylor	15,493
4	29	H	Cambridge U	W	4-1	2-0	2	Taylor, Maskell 3 (1 pen)	8134
5	Sept 5	A	Millwall	L	1-2	1-0	5	Maskell	8091
6	12	H	Bristol R	D	2-2	1-0	5	Mitchell, Maskell	10,006
7	20	H	Oxford U	D	2-2	1-0	—	Ling, Taylor	7717
8	26	A	Charlton Ath	L	0-2	0-1	8		6742
9	29	H	Grimsby T	W	1-0	1-0	—	Maskell	5759
10	Oct 3	H	Watford	W	3-1	0-1	4	Maskell 2, Taylor	7723
11	10	A	Portsmouth	L	1-3	0-2	5	White	12,442
12	17	H	Notts Co	W	5-1	2-0	5	Ling, Mitchell, Summerbee, Moncur, Horlock	7589
13	24	A	West Ham U	W	1-0	0-0	2	Maskell	17,842
14	31	H	Barnsley	W	1-0	1-0	2	Maskell (pen)	7784
15	Nov 3	H	Brentford	L	0-2	0-2	—		7832
16	8	A	Newcastle U	D	0-0	0-0	—		28,091
17	14	H	Southend U	W	3-2	3-1	2	Maskell 2, Ling	7777
18	21	A	Bristol C	D	2-2	1-1	2	Maskell, Summerbee	14,066
19	29	A	Peterborough U	D	3-3	1-2	—	Taylor 2, Maskell	5976
20	Dec 6	H	Derby Co	L	2-4	0-2	—	Hazard, Maskell	8924
21	20	A	Leicester C	L	2-4	0-3	—	Hazard, Maskell	15,088
22	Jan 9	A	Oxford U	W	1-0	1-0	7	White	9146
23	12	H	Birmingham C	D	0-0	0-0	—		14,398
24	16	H	Charlton Ath	D	2-2	2-2	7	Summerbee, Calderwood	8605
25	26	A	Grimsby T	L	1-2	0-1	—	Bodin	5207
26	30	H	Wolverhampton W	W	1-0	0-0	7	Bodin	10,812
27	Feb 6	A	Sunderland	W	1-0	0-0	6	Bodin	17,234
28	13	H	Millwall	W	3-0	1-0	6	White, Bodin, Taylor	10,544
29	20	A	Cambridge U	L	0-1	0-0	6		5437
30	23	H	Tranmere R	W	2-0	1-0	—	Mitchell 2	10,059
31	27	A	Portsmouth	W	1-0	0-0	4	Bodin	14,077
32	Mar 6	A	Watford	W	4-0	3-0	3	White 3, Mitchell	8791
33	10	A	Southend U	D	1-1	0-0	—	White	4371
34	13	H	Newcastle U	W	2-1	0-1	3	Bodin (pen), Calderwood	17,574
35	17	A	Luton T	D	0-0	0-0	—		8902
36	21	A	Derby Co	L	1-2	0-0	—	Taylor	12,166
37	24	H	Bristol C	W	2-1	1-0	—	Marwood, Bodin (pen)	13,157
38	27	A	Brentford	D	0-0	0-0	4		10,197
39	Apr 3	H	Peterborough U	W	1-0	0-0	4	Bodin	10,314
40	6	A	Tranmere R	L	1-3	1-0	—	Mitchell	8335
41	10	H	Luton T	W	1-0	0-0	4	Bodin	10,934
42	12	A	Birmingham C	W	6-4	1-2	4	Taylor, Maskell 2, Mitchell 3	17,903
43	17	H	Leicester C	D	1-1	0-1	4	Taylor	15,428
44	24	A	Notts Co	D	1-1	1-1	4	Bodin (pen)	8382
45	May 2	H	West Ham U	L	1-3	0-1	—	Hazard	17,004
46	8	A	Barnsley	L	0-1	0-1	5		6031

Final League Position: 5

GOALSCORERS

League (74): Maskell 19 (2 pens), Bodin 11 (4 pens), Mitchell 11, Taylor 11, White 7, Hazard 3, Ling 3, Summerbee 3, Calderwood 2, Hoddle 1, Horlock 1, Marwood 1, Moncur 1.
Coca Cola Cup (9): Mitchell 3, White 2, Hoddle 1, Ling 1, Maskell 1, Taylor 1.
FA Cup (0).

Digby 33	Summerbee 36 + 3	Bodin 34 + 1	Hoddle 41 + 1	Calderwood 46	Taylor 46	Hazard 30 + 2	Moncur 11 + 3	Maskell 32 + 1	Ling 43	Mitchell 37 + 4	Close 1 + 6	White 20 + 14	Kerslake 30 + 1	Hammond 13	Horlock 13 + 1	Hunt 3 + 2	Gray 3	MacLaren 22	Viveash 5	Marwood 6 + 5	Hamon 1 + 1	Match No.
1	2	3	4	5	6	7	8	9	10	11	12											1
1	2	3	4	5	6	7	8	9	10	11		12	14									2
1	2	3	4	5	6	7	8	9		11			10									3
1		3	4	5	6	7	8	9	10	11			2									4
1		3	4	5	6	7	8	9	10	11		12	2									5
1	7	3	4	5	6		8	9	10	11			2									6
1		3	4	5	6	7	8	9	10	11			2									7
1	14	3	4	5	6	7	8	9	10	11		12	2									8
		3	4	5	6	7	8	9	10	11			2	1								9
	8	3	4	5	6	7		9	10	11		12	2	1								10
	8	3	4	5	6	7		9	10	11		12	2	1	14							11
	8		4	5	6	7	14	9	10	11		12	2	1	3							12
			4	5	6	7	8	9	10	11		12	2	1	3							13
	8		4	5	6	7		9	10	11		12	2	1	3							14
	8		4	5	6	7		9	10	11		12	2	1	3							15
	8		4	5	6	7		9	10	11		12	2	1	3							16
	8		4	5	6	7		9	10	11			2	1	3	12						17
	8		4	5	6	7		9	10	11		12	2	1	3							18
	8		4	5	6	7		9	10	11			2	1	3							19
	8		4	5	6	7	14	9	10	11		12	2	1	3							20
	11	14	4	5	6	7	8	9	10			12	2	1	3							21
1		3	4	5	6	7		9	10			11	2					8				22
1		3	4	5	6	7		9	12			11	2			10		8				23
1	4	3		5	6	7		9	12			11	2			10		8				24
1	14	3	4	5	6	7		9	10	12		11	2					8				25
1	14	3	4	5	6	7		9	10	12		11	2					8				26
1	7	3	4	5	6			10	9			11	2					8				27
1	7	3	4	5	6			10	9			11	2					8				28
1	7	3	4	5	6			9	10	12		11	2					8				29
1	7	3	4	5	6			10	9			11	2					8				30
1	7	3	4	5	6			10	9			11	2					8				31
1	7	3	4	5	6			10	9			11	2					8				32
1	2	3		5	6			10	9			11				7		8	4			33
1	2	3		5	6			10	9			11				7		8	4	12		34
1	2	3		5	6			10	9			11				7		8	4	12		35
1	2	3	14	5	6			10	9	12		11						8	4	7		36
1	2	3	4	5	6			10	9	12		11				14		8	7			37
1	2	3	4	5	6			10	9	12		11						8	7			38
1	2	3	4	5	6			10	9			11						8	7			39
1	2	3	4	5	6	14		10	9	12		11						8	7			40
1	2	3	4	5	6	14		9	10			11						8		7	12	41
1	2	3	4	5	6	7		11	10	9								8				42
1	2	3	4	5	6	7		11	10	9								8	12			43
1	2	3	4	5	6	7		11	10	9	12							8				44
1	2		4	5	6	7	12	10	9			11						8		3	14	45
1	2		4	5	6	7	14	9	10								3	8	12	11		46

Coca Cola Cup	Second Round	Torquay U (a)	6-0
		(h)	3-2
	Third Round	Oldham Ath (h)	0-1
FA Cup	Third Round	QPR (a)	0-3

SWINDON TOWN

Player and Position	Ht	Wt	Date	Birth Place	Source	Clubs	League App	Gls
Goalkeepers								
Fraser Digby	6 1	12 12	23 4 67	Sheffield	Apprentice	Manchester U	—	—
						Oldham Ath (loan)	—	—
						Swindon T (loan)	—	—
						Swindon T	256	—
						Manchester U (loan)	—	—
Nicky Hammond	6 0	11 13	7 9 67	Hornchurch	Apprentice	Arsenal	—	—
						Bristol R (loan)	3	—
						Peterborough U (loan)	—	—
						Aberdeen (loan)	—	—
						Swindon T	47	—
Defenders								
Colin Calderwood	6 0	12 00	20 1 65	Stranraer	Amateur	Mansfield T	100	1
						Swindon T	330	20
Darren Hall*	5 10	11 06	3 1 73	Grays	Trainee	Swindon T	—	—
Kevin Horlock	6 0	12 00	1 11 72	Bexley	Trainee	West Ham U	—	—
						Swindon T	14	1
Lee Middleton	5 9	11 09	10 9 70	Nuneaton	Trainee	Coventry C	2	—
						Swindon T	—	—
Edwin Murray	5 11	12 00	31 8 73	Redbridge	Trainee	Swindon T	1	—
Wayne O'Sullivan	5 8	10 06	25 2 74	Akrotiri	Trainee	Swindon T	—	—
Shaun Taylor	6 1	13 00	26 3 63	Plymouth	Bideford	Exeter C	200	16
						Swindon T	88	15
Andrew Thomson	6 3	13 08	28 3 74	Swindon	Trainee	Swindon T	—	—
Midfield								
Austin Berkley	5 9	10 10	28 1 73	Dartford	Trainee	Gillingham	3	—
						Swindon T	—	—
Paul Bodin	6 0	13 01	13 9 64	Cardiff	Chelsea	Newport Co	—	—
						Cardiff C	57	3
					Bath C	Newport Co	6	1
						Swindon T	93	9
						Crystal Palace	9	—
						Newcastle U (loan)	6	—
						Swindon T	56	13
Mike Hazard	5 7	10 05	5 2 60	Sunderland	Apprentice	Tottenham H	91	13
						Chelsea	81	9
						Portsmouth	8	1
						Swindon T	110	17
Glenn Hoddle	6 0	11 06	27 10 57	Hayes	Apprentice	Tottenham	377	88
					Monaco	Chelsea	—	—
						Swindon T	64	1
Ross MacLaren	5 10	12 12	14 4 62	Edinburgh	Glasgow	Shrewsbury T	161	18
					Rangers	Derby Co	122	4
						Swindon T	182	9
Brian Marwood†	5 7	11 06	5 2 60	Seaham Harbour	Apprentice	Hull C	158	51
						Sheffield W	128	27
						Arsenal	52	16
						Sheffield U	22	3
						Middlesbrough (loan)	3	—
						Swindon T	11	1
John Moncur	5 7	9 10	22 9 66	Stepney	Apprentice	Tottenham H	21	1
						Cambridge U (loan)	4	—
						Doncaster R (loan)	4	—
						Portsmouth (loan)	7	—
						Brentford (loan)	5	1
						Ipswich T (loan)	6	—
						Nottingham F (loan)	—	—
						Swindon T	17	1
Marcus Phillips	5 11	11 07	17 10 73	Bradford on Avon	Trainee	Swindon T	—	—
Forwards								
Dave Bennett*	5 9	10 07	11 7 59	Manchester	Amateur	Manchester C	52	9
						Cardiff C	77	18
						Coventry C	172	25
						Sheffield W	28	—

SWINDON TOWN

Colours: All red. **Change colours:** Yellow shirts with green trim, sky blue shorts, white stockings.

Foundation: It is generally accepted that Swindon Town came into being in 1881, although there is no firm evidence that the club's founder, Rev. William Pitt, captain of the Spartans (an offshoot of a cricket club) changed his club's name to Swindon Town before 1883, when the Spartans amalgamated with St. Mark's Young Men's Friendly Society.

First Football League game: 28 August, 1920, Division 3, v Luton T (h) W 9-1 – Nash; Kay, Macconachie; Langford, Hawley, Wareing; Jefferson (1), Fleming (4), Rogers, Batty (2), Davies (1). 1 o.g.

Did you know: When they won the 1969 League Cup, Swindon were refused a place in the Fairs Cup because they were still in Division 3. Instead they won the newly-organised Anglo-Italian Cup, beating Napoli 3-0 in the final in Italy.

Managers (and Secretary-Managers)
Sam Allen 1902–33, Ted Vizard 1933–39, Neil Harris 1939–41, Louis Page 1945–53, Maurice Lindley 1953–55, Bert Head 1956–65, Danny Williams 1965–69, Fred Ford 1969–71, Dave Mackay 1971–72, Les Allen 1972–74, Danny Williams 1974–78, Bobby Smith 1978–80, John Trollope 1980–83, Ken Beamish 1983–84, Lou Macari 1984–89, Ossie Ardiles 1989–91, Glenn Hoddle 1991–93, John Gorman June 1993–.

Player and Position	Ht	Wt	Birth Date	Birth Place	Source	Clubs	League App	Gls
						Swindon T	1	—
						Shrewsbury T (loan)	2	2
Shaun Close*	5 8	10 01	8 9 66	Islington	Trainee	Tottenham H	9	—
						Bournemouth	39	8
						Swindon T	44	1
Chris Hamon	6 1	13 07	27 4 70	Jersey	St Peter	Swindon T	2	—
Steven Heffer‡	6 1	12 00	11 1 73	Southend	West Ham U	Southend U	—	—
						Swindon T	—	—
Paul Hunt*	5 5	10 02	8 10 71	Swindon	Trainee	Swindon T	11	—
Martin Ling	5 7	9 12	15 7 66	West Ham	Apprentice	Exeter C	116	14
						Swindon T	2	—
						Southend U	138	31
						Mansfield T (loan)	3	—
						Swindon T (loan)	1	—
						Swindon T	64	6
Craig Maskell	5 10	11 04	10 4 68	Aldershot	Apprentice	Southampton	6	1
						Swindon T (loan)	—	—
						Huddersfield T	87	43
						Reading	72	26
						Swindon T	33	19
David Mitchell	6 1	12 07	13 6 62	Glasgow		Rangers	26	6
					Feyenoord	Chelsea	7	—
						Newcastle U (loan)	2	1
						Swindon T	68	16
Ollie Morah*	5 11	13 02	3 9 72	Islington	Trainee	Tottenham H	—	—
						Hereford U (loan)	2	—
						Swindon T	—	—
Nicky Summerbee	5 11	11 08	26 8 71	Altrincham	Trainee	Swindon T	74	3
Adrian Viveash	6 1	11 12	30 9 69	Swindon	Trainee	Swindon T	40	1
						Reading (loan)	5	—
Steve White	5 10	11 04	2 1 59	Chipping Sodbury	Mangotsfield U	Bristol R	50	20
						Luton T	72	25
						Charlton Ath	29	12
						Lincoln C (loan)	3	—
						Luton T (loan)	4	—
						Bristol R	101	24
						Swindon T	238	83

Trainees
Cook, Shane; Elsey, David J; French, Robert J. D; James, Stuart E; Kearns, Andrew S; Lane, Steven J; Luwero, Stephen; O'Driscoll, Mark A; Phillips, James A; Phillips, Kevin M; Pitman, Jamie R; Reeves, Stephen J; Worrall, Benjamin J.

**Non-Contract
Marwood, Brian.

Associated Schoolboys
Gee, David G; Harvey, Iain D; Jay, Christopher R; Little, Paul D; Mifsud, Justin A; Robbins, Sean M; Rutter, Thomas; Smith; Adam J; Souter, Ryan J; Wimble, Shaun.

Associated Schoolboys who have accepted the club's offer of a Traineeship/Contract
Hamblin, Christopher P; Holloway, Jonathan S; Jordon, Mark J; Medcroft, Scott J; Thorne, Gary R.

**Non-Contract Players who are retained must be re-signed before they are eligible to play in League matches.

TORQUAY UNITED 1992-93   *Back row (left to right):* Arron Davis, Paul Hall, Neil Sang, Adrian Foster, Scott Colcombe, Duane Darby.
Centre row: Bruce Stuckey (Reserve Manager), Paul Trollope, Wes Saunders, Matthew Lowe, Dave Walters, Matthew Gardiner, Darren Moore, John James (Chief Scout).
Front row: Jeff Franklin, Chris Curran, Justin Fashanu (Assistant Manager), Paul Compton (Manager), Norman Medhurst (Physio), Chris Myers, Sean Joyce.
(Photograph: Colin Bratcher)

Division 3

TORQUAY UNITED

Plainmoor Ground, Torquay, Devon TQ1 3PS. Telephone Torquay (0803) 328666/7. Clubcall: 0898 121641. Fax: 0803 323976.

Ground capacity: 6455.

Record attendance: 21,908 v Huddersfield T, FA Cup 4th rd, 29 January 1955.

Record receipts: £26,205 v Exeter C, Division 3, 1 January 1992.

Pitch measurements: 112yd × 74yd.

President: A. J. Boyce.

Chairman/Managing Director: M. Bateson. *Vice-Chairman:* M. Benney.

Directors: D. Turner, Mrs S. Bateson.

Player-Manager: Don O'Riordan. *Physio:* Norman Medhurst.

Company Secretary: Miss H. Kindeleit.

Secretary General Manager: D. F. Turner. *Lottery Administrators:* C. Munslow and A. Sandford. *Commercial Manager:* D. Turner.

Year Formed: 1898. *Turned Professional:* 1921. *Ltd Co.:* 1921.

Previous Name: 1910, Torquay Town; 1921, Torquay United,

Nickname: 'The Gulls'.

Previous Grounds: 1898, Teignmouth Road; 1901, Torquay Recreation Ground; 1905, Cricket Field Road; 1907–10, Torquay Cricket Ground.

Record League Victory: 9–0 v Swindon T, Division 3 (S), 8 March 1952 – George Webber; Topping, Ralph Calland; Brown, Eric Webber, Towers; Shaw (1), Marchant (1), Northcott (2), Collins (3), Edds (2).

Record Cup Victory: 7–1 v Northampton T, FA Cup, 1st rd, 14 November 1959 – Gill; Penford, Downs; Bettany, George Northcott, Rawson; Baxter, Cox, Tommy Northcott (1), Bond (3), Pym (3).

Record Defeat: 2–10 v Fulham, Division 3 (S), 7 September 1931 and v Luton T, Division 3 (S), 2 September 1933.

Most League Points (2 for a win): 60, Division 4, 1959–60.

Most League Points (3 for a win): 77, Division 4, 1987–88.

Most League Goals: 89, Division 3 (S), 1956–57.

Highest League Scorer in Season: Sammy Collins, 40, Division 3 (S), 1955–56.

Most League Goals in Total Aggregate: Sammy Collins, 204, 1948–58.

Most Capped Player: None.

Most League Appearances: Dennis Lewis, 443, 1947–59.

Record Transfer Fee Received: £180,000 from Manchester U for Lee Sharpe, May 1988.

Record Transfer Fee Paid: £60,000 to Dundee for Wes Saunders, July 1990.

Football League Record: 1927 Elected to Division 3 (S); 1958–60 Division 4; 1960–62 Division 3; 1962–66 Division 4; 1966–72 Division 3; 1972–91 Division 4; 1991– Division 3.

Honours: Football League: Division 3 best season: 4th, 1967–68; Division 3 (S) – Runners-up 1956–57; Division 4 – Promoted 1959–60 (3rd), 1965–66 (3rd), 1990–91 (Play-offs). *FA Cup:* best season: 4th rd, 1949, 1955, 1971, 1983, 1990. *Football League Cup:* never past 3rd rd. *Sherpa Van Trophy:* Runners-up 1989.

514

TORQUAY UNITED 1992—93 LEAGUE RECORD

Match No.	Date		Venue	Opponents	Result		H/T Score	Lg. Pos.	Goalscorers	Attendance
1	Aug	15	A	Crewe Alex	L	2-4	0-2	—	Fashanu, Darby	3096
2		29	A	Doncaster R	W	3-2	0-2	15	Fashanu, Myers, Darby	1969
3	Sept	1	A	York C	L	1-2	1-1	—	Darby	3365
4		5	H	Cardiff C	W	2-1	1-0	11	Fashanu, Darby	2939
5		12	H	Scarborough	L	0-1	0-0	17		1300
6		15	H	Wrexham	D	1-1	0-1	—	Darby	2093
7		19	H	Northampton T	W	1-0	1-0	11	Foster	2393
8		26	A	Bury	L	0-2	0-1	12		2199
9	Oct	2	A	Darlington	L	1-4	1-0	—	Joyce	1423
10		10	H	Chesterfield	D	2-2	0-1	18	Joyce, Foster	2354
11		17	A	Hereford U	L	1-3	1-2	18	Colcombe	1780
12		24	H	Carlisle U	L	0-2	0-1	19		1960
13		31	A	Gillingham	W	2-0	0-0	18	Foster 2	3067
14	Nov	3	H	Rochdale	L	0-2	0-1	—		2064
15		7	A	Halifax T	W	2-0	2-0	17	Foster, Fashanu	1651
16		21	H	Scunthorpe U	L	0-1	0-0	19		1860
17	Dec	11	A	Colchester U	L	0-2	0-2	—		2774
18		20	H	Shrewsbury T	W	1-0	1-0	—	Joyce	1960
19		26	H	Walsall	L	0-1	0-1	19		3010
20		28	A	Barnet	L	4-5	1-0	19	Huxford (og), Foster, Trollope, Darby	3891
21	Jan	2	H	Scarborough	L	1-3	0-1	19	Johnson	2109
22		9	A	Wrexham	L	2-4	0-1	19	Darby 2	5465
23		16	H	Bury	L	0-1	0-0	20		1796
24		23	A	Northampton T	W	1-0	0-0	20	Fashanu	3082
25		26	H	Doncaster R	L	1-2	0-1	—	Foster	1771
26	Feb	6	H	Crewe Alex	L	1-2	0-1	21	Darby	1931
27		13	A	Cardiff C	L	0-4	0-1	22		7771
28		20	H	York C	W	1-0	0-0	20	Kelly	3119
29		27	A	Chesterfield	L	0-1	0-0	20		2657
30	Mar	6	H	Darlington	L	0-2	0-1	20		3147
31		9	A	Lincoln C	D	2-2	1-1	—	Foster, Sale	2781
32		13	H	Halifax T	W	2-0	0-0	18	Kelly (pen), Trollope	3345
33		20	A	Rochdale	L	0-1	0-1	19		1594
34		27	A	Scunthorpe U	D	2-2	1-1	20	Moore, Sale	2568
35	Apr	6	H	Colchester U	D	2-2	0-1	—	Barrow, Hodges	2915
36		10	A	Walsall	D	2-2	1-0	22	Barrow, Moore	3541
37		13	H	Barnet	L	0-1	0-0	—		4090
38		17	A	Shrewsbury T	W	1-0	1-0	22	Darby	3082
39		20	H	Lincoln C	L	1-2	1-1	—	Darby	3688
40		24	H	Hereford U	D	0-0	0-0	21		3414
41	May	1	A	Carlisle U	W	1-0	0-0	20	Darby	2689
42		8	H	Gillingham	W	2-1	0-1	19	Foster, Kelly (pen)	4645

Final League Position: 19

GOALSCORERS
League (45): Darby 12, Foster 9, Fashanu 5, Joyce 3, Kelly 3 (2 pens), Barrow 2, Moore 2, Sale 2, Trollope 2, Colcombe 1, Hodges 1, Johnson 1, Myers 1, own goal 1.
Coca Cola Cup (9): Saunders 3 (1 pen), Fashanu 2, Foster 2, Darby 1, Myers 1.
FA Cup (2): Foster 1, Herd 1.

Walter 1	Davies 1 + 2	Davis 11 + 1	Saunders 6	Moore 30 + 1	Joyce 26 + 1	Hall 27 + 1	Foster 23 + 13	Fashanu 20	Myers 28	Trollope 33 + 3	Darby 20 + 14	Lowe 13	Curran 33 + 1	Colcombe 20 + 4	Ginter 1	Salman 20	Gardiner 5 + 2	Compton — + 2	Herrera 5	Sommer 10	Johnson 9	Herd 5 + 2	Lewis 9	Hodges 7 + 1	Stamps 1 + 1	Blackwell 18	Kelly 18	Hayrettin 3 + 1	O'Riordan 16	Muir 7 + 5	Barrow 15	Chapman 6 + 2	Sale 10 + 1	Hancox 5 + 2	Match No.
1	2	3	4	5	6	7	8	9	10	*11*	12			14																					1
		3	4	5	6	7		9	10	11	8	1	2																						2
	14	3	4	5	6	7	12	9	10	11	8	1	*2*																						3
	14		4	5	6	7	12	9	10	11	8	1	*2*	3																					4
	14		*4*	5		7	12	9	10	11	8	1	2	3	6																				5
				5	6	7	12	9	10	11	8	1	2	3		4																			6
				5	6	7		9	10	11	8	1	2	3		4																			7
				5	6	7		9	10	11	8	1	2	3		4	12																		8
				5	6	7	8	9	10	11	12	1	4	3			2	14																	9
		11		5	6	7	8	9	10			1	2	3		4																			10
		11		*5*	6	7	8	9	10	14	12	1	2	3		4																			11
	2		14		6	7	12	9	10		8	1	5	11		4			3																12
					6	7	11	9	10		8		5			4	2		3	1															13
					6	7	11	9	10	*8*	12		5	14		4	2		3	1															14
				12		7	11	9	10	8			5	14		4	2	*3*		1	6														15
						7	11	9	10				6			4	12	*2*	3	1	5	8													16
		3		5		7	8		10				9			11					1	4	12	2	6										17
		3				7	12	9	10		8		5			11					1	4	6	2											18
		3				7	14	12	9	10	8		5			11					1	4	6	*2*											19
		3				7	2	8	9	10	14	12	5			11					1	4	*6*												20
		3			*6*	7	9		10	14	8		5			11					1	4		2 12											21
					6	7	8	9	10	11	12		14			5					1	4	*2*	3											22
					4	6	7	9		8			5			12					11	2		1		3 10									23
				5	6	7	8	9		11 12		1				4						2				3 10									24
					6	7	8	9		11 12			5	14		2						1				3 10									25
				5		7	8		10	9			11			2 12						4	*6*	1		3 14									26
				5	6	7	8		10 12		1		11			2								3		4 9									27
				5	6	7		10 12	1		11		2										1	3		4 9	2 8								28
				5	6	*7* 12		8 14		11			1	3		4								1	3		4 9	2 10							29
				5	6	7	8		10				11										1	3		4	*9*	2 12 14							30
				5		11			7 10			8	3										1	6		4 12	2		9						31
				5		11			7			8	3										1	6		4 10	2 12	9							32
			5			11			7			8	3										1	6		4 12	2 *10*	9 14							33
				5		12			*7* 14			8	3										10	1	6	4	2	9 11							34
				5					7 14			8	3										10	1	6	4 12	2	*9* 11							35
				5					7 12			8	*3*										10	1	6	4	2	9 11							36
				5					*7* 14			8											3	1	6	4 12	2	9 11							37
				5		12			10 *7* 11			8	3										6	1		4	2	9							38
				5		11			7			8	3										1	6		4 14	2	*9* 6							39
				5					10 7 11			3											1	8		4	2 6	9 12							40
				5		12			10 7 11			8											1	3		4 9	2 6								41
				5		12			*10* 7 11			8											14 1	3		4 9	2 6								42

Coca Cola Cup First Round Hereford U (a) 2-2
      (h) 5-0
    Second Round Swindon T (h) 0-6
      (a) 2-3
FA Cup First Round Yeovil (h) 2-5

TORQUAY UNITED

Player and Position	Ht	Wt	Date	Birth Place	Source	Clubs	League App	Gls
Goalkeepers								
Kevin Blackwell*	5 11	12 10	21 12 58	Luton	Barnet	Scarborough	44	—
						Notts Co	—	—
						Torquay U	18	—
Matthew Lowe	6 0	12 10	25 2 74	Birmingham	Trainee	Torquay U	20	—
David Walter*	6 3	13 03	3 9 64	Barnstaple	Bideford T	Exeter C	44	—
						Plymouth Arg (loan)	—	—
						Plymouth Arg	15	—
						Torquay U	1	—
Defenders								
Lee Barrow	5 10	13 00	1 5 73	Belper	Trainee	Notts Co	—	—
						Scarborough	11	—
						Torquay U	15	2
Paul Compton*	6 1	13 01	6 6 61	Stroud	Trowbridge T	Bournemouth	64	—
						Aldershot	13	—
						Torquay U	95	4
					Youth Development Officer	Torquay U	21	—
Chris Curran	5 11	11 09	17 9 71	Birmingham	Trainee	Torquay U	65	—
Andy Davies*	6 0	11 06	6 6 72	Wolverhampton	Trainee	Torquay U	13	—
						Hartlepool U	7	—
						Torquay U	3	—
Aaron Davis*	5 8	11 00	11 2 72	London		Torquay U	24	—
Matthew Gardiner*	5 4	10 10	28 3 74	Birmingham	Trainee	Torquay U	7	—
Ian Johnson*	6 2	13 08	14 2 69	Newcastle	Whitley Bay	Torquay U	9	1
Tom Kelly	5 9	12 05	28 3 64	Bellshill	Hibs	Hartlepool U	15	—
						Torquay U	120	—
						York C	35	2
						Exeter C	88	9
						Torquay U	18	3
Dudley Lewis*	5 11	10 10	17 11 62	Swansea	Apprentice	Swansea C	230	2
						Huddersfield T	34	—
						Halifax T (loan)	11	—
						Wrexham	9	—
						Halifax T	13	—
						Torquay U	9	—
Darren Moore	6 2	15 00	22 4 74	Birmingham	Trainee	Torquay U	36	3
Danis Salman*	5 10	12 02	12 3 60	Cyprus	Apprentice	Brentford	325	8
						Millwall	93	4
						Plymouth Arg	74	4
						Peterborough U (loan)	1	—
						Torquay U	20	—
Wes Saunders‡	6 0	11 11	23 2 63	Sunderland	School	Newcastle U	79	—
						Bradford C (loan)	4	—
						Carlisle U	97	11
						Dundee	50	2
						Torquay U	61	6
Midfield								
Scott Colcombe	5 6	10 00	15 12 71	West Bromwich	Trainee	WBA	—	—
						Torquay U	52	1
Tony Ginter§			6 11 74	Plymouth	Trainee	Torquay U	1	—
Richard Hancox			14 10 70	Stourbridge	Stourbridge S	Torquay U	7	—
Stuart Herd‡			25 2 74	Tittensor	Norwich C	Torquay U	7	—
Kevin Hodges	5 8	10 08	12 6 60	Bridport	Apprentice	Plymouth Arg	530	81
						Torquay U (loan)	3	—
						Torquay U	8	1
Sean Joyce*	5 8	10 05	15 2 67	Doncaster		Doncaster R	41	1
						Exeter C (loan)	1	—
						Torquay U	158	15
Chris Myers	5 10	11 10	1 4 69	Yeovil	Apprentice local	Torquay U	9	—
						Torquay U	96	7
Don O'Riordan	6 0	12 08	14 5 57	Dublin	Apprentice	Derby Co	6	1
						Doncaster R (loan)	2	—

TORQUAY UNITED

Colours: Yellow and navy hooped shirts, navy shorts, yellow stockings. **Change colours:** Blue shirts, white shorts, blue stockings.

Foundation: The idea of establishing a Torquay club was agreed by old boys of Torquay College and Torbay College, while sitting in Princess Gardens listening to the band. A proper meeting was subsequently held at Tor Abbey Hotel at which officers were elected. This was in 1898 and the club's first competition was the Eastern League (later known as the East Devon League).

First Football League game: 27 August, 1927, Division 3(S), v Exeter C (h) D 1-1 – Millsom; Cook, Smith; Wellock, Wragg, Connor, Mackey, Turner (1), Jones, McGovern, Thomson.

Did you know: In August 1956 Sammy Collins scored the fastest penalty awarded in a Football League match after ten seconds of the match with Walsall in Division 3 (S).

Managers (and Secretary-Managers)
Percy Mackrill 1927–29, A. H. Hoskins 1929*, Frank Womack 1929–32, Frank Brown 1932–38, Alf Steward 1938–40, Billy Butler 1945–46, Jack Butler 1946–47, John McNeil 1947–50, Bob John 1950, Alex Massie 1950–51, Eric Webber 1951–65, Frank O'Farrell 1965–68, Alan Brown 1969–71, Jack Edwards 1971–73, Malcolm Musgrove 1973–76, Mike Green 1977–81, Frank O'Farrell 1981–82 (continued as GM to 1983), Bruch Rioch 1982–84, Dave Webb 1984–85, John Sims 1985, Stuart Morgan 1985–87, Cyril Knowles 1987–89, Dave Smith 1989–91, John Impey 1991–92, Ivan Golac 1992, Paul Compton 1992–93, Don O'Riordan March 1993–.

Player and Position	Ht	Wt	Birth Date	Birth Place	Source	Clubs	League App	Gls
					Tulsa	Preston NE	158	8
						Carlisle U	84	18
						Middlesbrough	41	2
						Grimsby T	86	14
						Notts Co	109	5
						Mansfield T (loan)	6	—
						Torquay U	16	—
Paul Trollope	6 0	12 02	3 6 72	Swindon	Trainee	Swindon T	—	—
						Torquay U (loan)	10	—
						Torquay U	36	2
Forwards								
Gary Chapman*	5 8	11 07	1 5 64	Bradford	Local	Bradford C	5	—
						Notts Co	25	4
						Mansfield T (loan)	6	—
						Exeter C	24	5
						Torquay U	8	—
Duane Darby	5 11	12 06	17 10 73	West Midlands	Trainee	Torquay U	48	14
Justin Fashanu (To Airdrie February 1993)	6 1	13 01	19 2 61	Kensington	Apprentice	Norwich C	90	35
						Nottingham F	32	3
						Southampton	9	3
						Nottingham F	—	—
						Notts Co	64	20
						Brighton	16	2
					Edmonton	Manchester C	2	—
						West Ham U	2	—
						Leyton Orient	5	—
					Toronto B	Newcastle U	—	—
						Torquay U	41	15
Adrian Foster	5 9	11 00	20 7 71	Kidderminster	Trainee	WBA	27	2
						Torquay U	36	9
Mark Loram‡	6 0	12 00	13 8 67	Brixham	Brixham	Torquay U	52	8
						QPR (loan)	—	—
						QPR	—	—
						Torquay U (loan)	13	4
						Torquay U	196	36
						Stockport Co (loan)	4	—
						Exeter C (loan)	3	—
Mark Sale	6 5	13 08	27 2 72	Burton-on-Trent	Trainee	Stoke C	2	—
						Cambridge U	—	—
						Birmingham C	21	—
						Torquay U	11	2

Trainees
Anbany, Simon J; Ginter, Anthony P; Hardy, Paul A; Laight, Ellis, S; Lockyer, Mark J; Maloney, Shaun M; Manton, Neil R; Stacey, Steven J; Stamps, Scott; White, Richard J; Winteridge, Graham.

Associated Schoolboys
Aggett, Neil R. P; Cox, David J; Dawes, Christian L; Duckett, John W; Male, Neil J; McFarlane, Francis; Nickson, Adam; Nickson, Carl; Shannon, Michael J.

Associated Schoolboys who have accepted the club's offer of a Traineeship/Contract
Head, Kevin; Setter, Lee T; Willis, Lee.

518

TOTTENHAM HOTSPUR 1992–93 *Back row (left to right):* Jason Cundy, Darren Anderton, Peter Beadle, Ian Walker, David Tuttle, Erik Thorstvedt, Steve Sedgley, David Howells, Ian Hendon.
Centre row: John Sheridan (Physio), Dave Butler (Physio), Scott Houghton, Andy Gray, Gordon Durie, Nayim, Vinny Samways, Paul Moran, Keith Waldon (Reserve Team Manager), Roy Reyland (Kit Manager).
Front row: Doug Livermore (Coach), Justin Edinburgh, Paul Allen, Neil Ruddock, Gary Mabbutt, Dean Austin, Terry Fenwick, John Hendry, Ray Clemence (Coach).
(Photograph: Action Images)

FA Premier   **TOTTENHAM HOTSPUR**

748 High Rd, Tottenham, London N17. Telephone 081–808 6666. Commercial Dept: 081–808 0281. Recorded information: 0898 100515. Additional recorded information: 081 880 3377. Dial-a-seat: 081–808 3030. Telex: 24739 and 295261. Spurs Line: 0898 100500. Fax: 081–885 1951.

Ground capacity: 32,786.

Record attendance: 75,038 v Sunderland, FA Cup 6th rd, 5 March 1938.

Record receipts: £336,702 v Manchester U, Division 1, 28 September 1991.

Pitch measurements: 110yd × 73yd.

Directors: A. M. Sugar (Chairman), A. G. Berry (Deputy Chairman). *Vice-presidents:* F. P. Sinclair, N. Soloman.

Manager: Ossie Ardiles. *Assistant Manager:* Steve Perryman MBE. *First Team Coach/Chief Scout:* Doug Livermore. *Coach:* Chris Hughton. *Physios:* John Sheridan and Dave Butler. *Secretary:* Peter Barnes. *Commercial Manager:* Mike Rollo. *PRO:* John Fennelly.

Year Formed: 1882. *Turned Professional:* 1895. *Ltd Co.:* 1898.

Club Nickname: 'Spurs'.

Previous Name: 1882–85, Hotspur Football Club.

Previous Grounds: 1882, Tottenham Marshes; 1885, Northumberland Park; 1898, White Hart Lane.

Record League Victory: 9–0 v Bristol R, Division 2, 22 October 1977 – Davies; Naylor, Holmes, Hoddle (1), McAllister, Perryman, Pratt, McNab, Morris (3), Lee (4), Taylor (1).

Record Cup Victory: 13–2 v Crewe Alex, FA Cup, 4th rd (replay), 3 February 1960 – Brown; Hills, Henry; Blanchflower, Norman, Mackay; White, Harmer (1), Smith (4), Allen (5), Jones (3 incl. 1p).

Record Defeat: 0–7 v Liverpool, Division 1, 2 September 1978.

Most League Points (2 for a win): 70, Division 2, 1919–20.

Most League Points (3 for a win): 77, Division 1, 1984–85.

Most League Goals: 115, Division 1, 1960–61.

Highest League Scorer in Season: Jimmy Greaves, 37, Division 1, 1962–63.

Most League Goals in Total Aggregate: Jimmy Greaves, 220, 1961–70.

Most Capped Player: Pat Jennings, 74 (119), Northern Ireland.

Most League Appearances: Steve Perryman, 655, 1969–86.

Record Transfer Fee Received: £5,500,000 from Lazio for Paul Gascoigne, May 1992.

Record Transfer Fee Paid: £2,200,000 to Chelsea for Gordon Durie, August 1991.

Football League Record: 1908 Elected to Division 2; 1909–15 Division 1; 1919–20 Division 2; 1920–28 Division 1; 1928–33 Division 2; 1933–35 Division 1; 1935–50 Division 2; 1950–77 Division 1; 1977–78 Division 2; 1978–92 Division 1; 1992– FA Premier League.

Honours: Football League: Division 1 – Champions 1950–51, 1960–61; Runners-up 1921–22, 1951–52, 1956–57, 1962–63; Division 2 – Champions 1919–20, 1949–50; Runners-up 1908–09, 1932–33; Promoted 1977–78 (3rd). *FA Cup:* Winners 1901 (as non-League club), 1921, 1961, 1962, 1967, 1981, 1982, 1991 (8 wins stands as the record); Runners-up 1986–87. *Football League Cup:* Winners 1970–71, 1972–73; Runners-up 1981–82. **European Competitions:** *European Cup:* 1961–62. *European Cup-Winners' Cup:* 1962–63 (winners), 1963–64, 1967–68, 1981–82 (runners-up), 1982–83, 1991–92. *UEFA Cup:* 1971–72 (winners), 1972–73, 1973–74 (runners-up), 1983–84 (winners), 1984–85.

TOTTENHAM HOTSPUR 1992—93 LEAGUE RECORD

Match No.	Date	Venue	Opponents	Result	H/T Score	Lg. Pos.	Goalscorers	Atten dance
1	Aug 15	A	Southampton	D	0-0	0-0	—	19,654
2	19	H	Coventry C	L	0-2	0-2	—	24,388
3	22	H	Crystal Palace	D	2-2	1-1	18	Durie, Sedgley	25,237
4	25	A	Leeds U	L	0-5	0-3	—	28,218
5	30	A	Ipswich T	D	1-1	1-1	—	Cundy	20,100
6	Sept 2	H	Sheffield U	W	2-0	1-0	—	Sheringham, Durie	21,332
7	5	H	Everton	W	2-1	0-1	15	Allen, Turner	26,503
8	14	A	Coventry C	L	0-1	0-0	—		15,348
9	19	H	Manchester U	D	1-1	0-1	14	Durie	33,296
10	27	A	Sheffield W	L	0-2	0-2	—		24,895
11	Oct 3	A	QPR	L	1-4	1-0	19	Sheringham	19,845
12	17	H	Middlesbrough	D	2-2	0-2	19	Sheringham (pen), Barmby	24,735
13	25	A	Wimbledon	D	1-1	0-1	—	Barmby	8628
14	31	H	Liverpool	W	2-0	0-0	17	Nayim, Ruddock	32,917
15	Nov 7	A	Blackburn R	W	2-0	0-0	14	Howells, Sheringham (pen)	17,305
16	21	A	Aston Villa	D	0-0	0-0	15		32,852
17	28	A	Manchester C	W	1-0	0-0	12	Phelan (og)	25,496
18	Dec 5	H	Chelsea	L	1-2	0-0	14	Campbell	31,540
19	12	H	Arsenal	W	1-0	1-0	13	Allen	33,707
20	19	A	Oldham Ath	L	1-2	0-1	13	Sheringham	11,735
21	26	A	Norwich C	D	0-0	0-0	13		19,413
22	28	H	Nottingham F	W	2-1	1-0	12	Barmby, Mabbutt	32,118
23	Jan 9	A	Manchester U	L	1-4	0-1	12	Barmby	35,648
24	16	H	Sheffield W	L	0-2	0-0	14		25,702
25	27	H	Ipswich T	L	0-2	0-0	—		23,738
26	30	A	Crystal Palace	W	3-1	3-0	13	Sheringham 2, Gray	20,937
27	Feb 6	H	Southampton	W	4-2	0-1	—	Sheringham 2, Barmby, Anderton	20,098
28	10	A	Everton	W	2-1	1-1	—	Mabbutt, Allen	16,164
29	20	H	Leeds U	W	4-0	2-0	9	Sheringham 3 (1 pen), Ruddock	32,040
30	27	H	QPR	W	3-2	2-0	8	Sheringham 2, Anderton	32,341
31	Mar 2	A	Sheffield U	L	0-6	0-4	—		16,654
32	10	A	Aston Villa	D	0-0	0-0	—		37,727
33	20	A	Chelsea	D	1-1	1-0	11	Sheringham (pen)	25,157
34	24	H	Manchester C	W	3-1	2-0	—	Anderton, Nayim, Turner	27,247
35	Apr 9	H	Norwich C	W	5-1	2-0	—	Ruddock, Sheringham 2, Barmby, Nayim	31,425
36	12	A	Nottingham F	L	1-2	1-2	9	Sedgley	25,682
37	17	H	Oldham Ath	W	4-1	0-1	6	Sheringham 2 (2 pens), Anderton, Turner	26,663
38	20	A	Middlesbrough	L	0-3	0-2	—		14,472
39	May 1	H	Wimbledon	D	1-1	1-0	9	Anderton	24,473
40	5	H	Blackburn R	L	1-2	0-1	—	Anderton	23,097
41	8	A	Liverpool	L	2-6	0-2	11	Sheringham, Sedgley	43,385
42	11	A	Arsenal	W	3-1	1-0	—	Sheringham, Hendry 2	26,393

Final League Position: 8

GOALSCORERS

League (60): Sheringham 21 (6 pens), Anderton 6, Barmby 6, Allen 3, Durie 3, Nayim 3, Ruddock 3, Sedgley 3, Turner 3, Hendry 2, Mabbutt 2, Campbell 1, Cundy 1, Gray 1, Howells 1, own goal 1.
Coca Cola Cup (8): Sheringham 3 (1 pen), Anderton 1, Durie 1, Samways 1, Turner 1, Watson 1.
FA Cup (14): Sheringham 4, Barmby 3, Nayim 3, Samways 2, Anderton 1, Sedgley 1.

Walker 17	Fenwick 3 + 2	Edinburgh 31 + 1	Howells 16 + 2	Cundy 13 + 2	Ruddock 38	Turner 7 + 11	Durie 17	Samways 34	Anderton 32 + 2	Allen 38	Gray 9 + 8	Thorstvedt 25 + 2	Sedgley 20 + 2	Tuttle 4 + 1	Hendry 2 + 3	Austin 33 + 1	Sheringham 38	Van Den Hauwe 13 + 5	Barmby 17 + 5	Watson 4 + 1	Nayim 15 + 3	Mabbutt 29	Moran — + 3	Campbell — + 1	Bergsson — + 5	Nethercott 3 + 2	Hill 2 + 2	Dearden — + 1	Hodges — + 4	McDonald 2	Match No.
1	2	3	4	5	6	7	8	9	10	11	12																				1
1	2	3	4	5	6	7	8	9	10	11	12	14																			2
	2	3			6		8	9	10	11	12	1	4	5	7	14															3
		3	4	5	6		8	9	10	11		1			7	2															4
1		3		5	6		8	9	7	11	12		4			2	10														5
1				5	6	14	8	9	7	11	12		4			2	10	3													6
1				5	6	12	8	9	7	11			4			2	10	3													7
1				5	6	12	8	9	7	11			4		14	2	10	3													8
1				5	6		8	9	7	11	12		4		14	2	10	3													9
1	14		4	5	6			9	7	11						2	10	3	12			8									10
1	14	2		5	6	12		9	7	11			4				10	3				8									11
1	2		4		6		8	9	7	11			5				10	3	12			14									12
1	2		4		6	7	8			11			14			3	10		12		9	5									13
	2		12		6	14	8		7	11		1	4			3	10				9	5									14
	2		4		6	7	8			11		1				3	10				9	5									15
	2		4	14	6	7	8			11		1				3	10		12		9	5									16
	2		4	14	6	7				11		1				3	10		8		9	5	12								17
		3	4	12	6	7				11		1				2	10		8		9	5	14								18
		3	4		6	7	8			11		1				2	10		12		9	5									19
		3	4		6	7	8			11		1				2	10		12		9	5									20
		3	4		6	7		9		11		1				2	10					8			5	12					21
		3	4		6	7		9		11		1				2	10					8			5	12	14				22
		3	4	12	6	7		9		11		1				2	10					8			5		14				23
		3	4		6	7		9		11		1			12	2	10					8			5	14					24
		3	4	12	6		8	9		11		1				2	10	14	7			5									25
		3	4		6	7		9		11		1		8		2	10	12				5									26
		3	4		6	7		9		11	12	1				2	10	14	8			5									27
		3	4		6	7		9		11		1		8		2	10	14			12	5									28
		3	4		6	7		9		11	12	1				2	10	14	8			5									29
		3	4		6	7		9	7	11		1				2	10		8		12	5									30
			4		6			9	7	11	12	1			14	2	10	3	8			5									31
		3		12	6			9		11		1			7	2	10					8			5						32
		3			6	11		9	4			1				2	10				7	8			14	5	12				33
			4	12	6			9		11		1			7	2	10	3				8			5	14					34
		3	4	12	6			9		11		1			7	2	10				4	8			5		14				35
		3	4	12	6			9		11		1			7	2	10				4	8			5				14		36
1		3	4	12	6			9		11					7	2	10					8			5						37
1	14	3	4	12	6			9		11					7	2	10					8			5						38
1			4		6	8		9		11	12				7		10	3				5			2		14				39
1			4		6	8		9		11					7		10	3				5			2	12	14				40
1					6			9		11					7		10	3	8			5			12	4	14			2	41
1					6			9		11					7	8	10	3				5				4			12	2	42

Coca Cola Cup	Second Round	Brentford (h)	3-1
		(a)	4-2
	Third Round	Manchester C (a)	1-0
	Fourth Round	Nottingham F (a)	0-2
FA Cup	Third Round	Marlow (a)	5-1
	Fourth Round	Norwich C (a)	2-0
	Fifth Round	Wimbledon (h)	3-2
	Sixth Round	Manchester C (a)	4-2
	Semi-Final at Wembley	Arsenal	0-1

TOTTENHAM HOTSPUR

Player and Position	Ht	Wt	Date	Birth Place	Source	Clubs	League App	Gls
Goalkeepers								
Chris Day	6 0	12 00	28 7 74	Whipps Cross	Trainee	Tottenham H	—	—
Kevin Dearden	5 11	12 08	8 3 70	Luton	Trainee	Tottenham H	1	—
						Cambridge U (loan)	15	—
						Hartlepool U (loan)	10	—
						Oxford U (loan)	—	—
						Swindon T (loan)	1	—
						Peterborough U (loan)	7	—
						Hull C (loan)	3	—
						Rochdale (loan)	2	—
						Birmingham C (loan)	12	—
						Portsmouth (loan)	—	—
Michael Heath*	5 9	11 00	7 2 74	Hull	Trainee	Tottenham H	—	—
Erik Thorstvedt	6 4	14 03	28 10 62	Stavanger	IFK Gothenburg	Tottenham H	140	—
Ian Walker	6 1	11 09	31 10 71	Watford	Trainee	Tottenham H	36	—
						Oxford U (loan)	2	—
						Ipswich T (loan)	—	—
Defenders								
Dean Austin	6 0	12 04	26 4 70	Hemel Hempstead	St. Albans C	Southend U	96	2
						Tottenham H	34	—
Gudni Bergsson	6 01	12 03	21 7 65	Iceland	Valur	Tottenham H	71	2
Sol Campbell	6 0	12 00	18 9 74	Newham	Trainee	Tottenham H	1	1
David Culverhouse	6 0	11 06	9 9 73	Harlow	Trainee	Tottenham H	—	—
Jason Cundy	6 1	13 07	12 11 69	Wimbledon	Trainee	Chelsea	41	1
						Tottenham H (loan)	10	—
						Tottenham H	15	1
Justin Edinburgh	5 10	11 08	18 12 69	Brentwood	Trainee	Southend U	37	—
						Tottenham H (loan)	—	—
						Tottenham H	71	1
Terry Fenwick*	5 10	11 12	17 11 59	Camden, Co. Durham	Apprentice	Crystal Palace	70	—
						QPR	256	33
						Tottenham H	93	8
						Leicester C (loan)	8	1
Ian Hendon	6 0	12 10	5 12 71	Ilford	Trainee	Tottenham H	4	—
						Portsmouth (loan)	4	—
						Leyton Orient (loan)	6	—
						Barnsley (loan)	6	—
Gary Mabbutt	5 9	12 09	23 8 61	Bristol	Apprentice	Bristol R	131	10
						Tottenham H	368	27
David McDonald	5 11	11 07	2 1 71	Dublin	Trainee	Tottenham H	2	—
						Gillingham (loan)	10	—
						Bradford C (loan)	7	—
						Reading (loan)	11	—
Andrew Marlowe‡	5 7	11 02	25 9 73	Birmingham	Trainee	Tottenham H	—	—
Stuart Nethercott	6 0	12 04	21 3 73	Chadwell Heath	Trainee	Tottenham H	5	—
						Maidstone U (loan)	13	1
						Barnet (loan)	3	—
Neil Ruddock	6 2	12 06	9 5 68	London	Apprentice	Millwall	—	—
						Tottenham H	9	—
						Millwall	2	1
						Southampton	107	9
						Tottenham H	38	3
David Tuttle	5 9	12 10	6 2 72	Reading	Trainee	Tottenham H	13	—
						Peterborough U (loan)	7	—
Pat Van Den Hauwe	5 11	11 10	16 12 60	Dendermonde	Apprentice	Birmingham C	123	1
						Everton	135	2
						Tottenham H	116	—
Neil Young	5 8	11 03	31 8 73	Harlow	Trainee	Tottenham H	—	—

TOTTENHAM HOTSPUR

Colours: White shirts, navy blue shorts, white stockings. **Change colours:** All yellow or all sky blue.

Foundation: The Hotspur Football Club was formed from an older cricket club in 1882. Most of the founders were old boys St. John's Presbyterian School and Tottenham Grammar School. The Casey brothers were well to the fore as the family provided the club's first goalposts (painted blue and white) and their first ball. They soon adopted the local YMCA as their meeing place, but after a couple of moves settled at the Red House, which is still their headquarters, although now known simply as 748 High Road.

First Football League game: 1 September, 1908, Division 2, v Wolverhampton W (h) W 3-0 – Hewitson; Coquet, Burton; Morris (1), Steel (D), Darnell; Walton, Woodward (2), Macfarlane, R. Steel, Middlemiss.

Did you know: Tottenham Hotspur forward Andy Turner became the youngest scorer in the Premier League when he was on the mark against Everton on 5 September 1992 at the age of 17 years, 166 days.

Managers (and Secretary-Managers)
Frank Brettell 1898–99, John Cameron 1899–1906, Fred Kirkham 1907–08, Peter McWilliam 1912–27, Billy Minter 1927–29, Percy Smith 1930–35, Jack Tresadern 1935–38, Peter McWilliam 1938–42, Arthur Turner 1942–46, Joe Hulme 1946–49, Arthur Rowe 1949–55, Jimmy Anderson 1955–58, Bill Nicholson 1958–74, Terry Neill 1974–76, Keith Burkinshaw 1976–84, Peter Shreeves 1984–86, David Pleat 1986–87, Terry Venables 1987–91, Peter Shreeves 1991–92, Ossie Ardiles June 1993–.

Player and Position	Ht	Wt	Date	Birth Place	Source	Clubs	League App	Gls
Midfield								
Paul Allen	5 7	10 10	28 8 62	Aveley	Apprentice	West Ham U	152	6
						Tottenham H	291	23
Darren Caskey	5 8	11 09	21 8 74	Basildon	Trainee	Tottenham H	—	—
Paul Gascoigne (To Lazio May 1992)	5 10	11 07	27 5 67	Gateshead	Apprentice	Newcastle U	92	21
						Tottenham H	92	19
Andy Gray	5 11	13 03	22 2 64	Lambeth	Dulwich H	Crystal Palace	98	27
						Aston Villa	37	4
						QPR	11	2
						Crystal Palace	90	12
						Tottenham H (loan)	14	1
						Tottenham H	17	1
						Swindon T (loan)	3	—
Danny Hill	5 9	11 00	1 10 74	Edmonton	Trainee	Tottenham H	4	—
Scott Houghton	5 5	11 06	22 10 71	Hitchin	Trainee	Tottenham H	10	2
						Ipswich T (loan)	8	1
						Cambridge U (loan)	—	—
						Gillingham (loan)	3	—
						Charlton Ath (loan)	6	—
Greg Howell*	5 9	11 02	26 3 73	Swindon	Trainee	Tottenham H	—	—
Nayim (Mohamed Ali Amar) (To Zaragoza May 1993)	5 8	11 08	5 11 66	Morocco	Barcelona	Tottenham H	112	11
Vinny Samways	5 8	11 00	27 10 68	Bethnal Green	Apprentice	Tottenham H	154	8
Steve Sedgley	6 1	13 03	26 5 68	Enfield	Apprentice	Coventry C	84	3
						Tottenham H	122	3
Kevin Watson	5 9	12 06	3 1 74	Hackney	Trainee	Tottenham H	5	—
Forwards								
Darren Anderton	6 1	11 12 00	3 3 72	Southampton	Trainee	Portsmouth	62	7
						Tottenham H	34	6

Continued on page 585

Trainees
Anderson, Ijah M; Binks, Spencer C; Brady, Gary; Carr, Stephen; Clapham, James R; Foot, Daniel F; Grogan, Darren M; Haynes, Junior L. A; Hudson, William G; Hurst, Glynn; Knott, Gareth R; Landon, Christopher S; Le Bihan, Neil E. R; McDougald, David E. J; Quy, Andrew J; Reynolds, Christopher C; Simpson, Robert A; Slade, Steven A; Townley, Leon.

Associated Schoolboys
Adams, Kieren C; Allen, Robert P; Allen, Rory W; Arber, Mark A; Barnes, Ben C; Box, Richard, D; Bunn, James T; Carlisle, Jason A; Clemence, Stephen N; Davies, Darren J; Devor, Damian M; Evans, James M; Fortune, Quinton; Gower, Mark; Janney, Mark; Laycock, Wayne D; McVeigh, Paul; Outram, Ross P; Shave, Arran L; Thompson, Neil P; Wilkinson, Jeffrey M; Winston, Samuel A.

Associated Schoolboys who have accepted the club's offer of a Traineeship/Contract
Brown, Simon J; Callcut, Dean E; Gain, Peter T; Gosnell, Darren S; Maher, Kevin A; Spencer, Simon D; Williams, Richard I; Wormull, Simon J.

524

TRANMERE ROVERS 1992–93 *Back row (left to right):* Alan Morgan, Mike Foster, Ged Brannan, Dave Higgins, John McGreal, Ian Nolan, Kenny Irons, John Morrissey, Tony Thomas. *Centre row:* Norman Wilson (Secretary), Kenny Jones (Physio), Neil McNab, Steve Vickers, Graham Branch, Chris Malkin, Eric Nixon, Danny Coyne, John Aldridge, Ronnie Moore (Coach), Ray Mathias (Reserves), Warwick Rimmer (Youth Development Officer). *Front row:* Shaun Garnett, Steve Cooper, Ian Muir, Steve Mungall, John King (Manager), Mike Smith, Mark Hughes, Dave Martindale, Tony Draper.

Division 1   **TRANMERE ROVERS**

Prenton Park, Prenton Road West, Birkenhead. Telephone 051–608 3677. Fax 051 608 4385. Commercial/Cashline 051–608 0371. Valley Road Training Centre: 051–652 2578. Shop: 051–608 0438.

Ground capacity: 17,500.

Record attendance: 24,424 v Stoke C, FA Cup 4th rd, 5 February 1972.

Record receipts: £70,077 v Liverpool, 8 August 1991.

Pitch measurements: 112yd × 71yd.

President: H. B. Thomas.

Chairman: P. R. Johnson. *Vice-chairman and Chief Executive:* F. D. Corfe.

Directors: A. J. Adams BDS, G. E. H. Jones LLB, F. J. Williams, J. J. Holsgrove FCA, G. A. Higham MSC TECH LRSC, M INST PI.

Secretary: Norman Wilson FAAI. *Commercial Manager:* Nigel Coates.

Development Manager: Nobby Abbott.

Manager: John King. *Trainer:* Kenny Jones.

Youth Development Manager: Warwick Rimmer.

Coach: Ronnie Moore. *Physio:* Alec McLellan.

Year Formed: 1884. *Turned Professional:* 1912. *Ltd Co.:* 1920.

Previous Name: Belmont AFC, 1884–85.

Club Nickname: 'The Rovers'.

Previous Grounds: 1884, Steeles Field; 1887, Ravenshaws Field/Old Prenton Park; 1912, Prenton Park.

Record League Victory: 13–4 v Oldham Ath, Division 3 (N), 26 December 1935 – Gray; Platt, Fairhurst; McLaren, Newton, Spencer; Eden, MacDonald (1), Bell (9), Woodward (2), Urmson (1).

Record Cup Victory: 13–0 v Oswestry U, FA Cup 2nd pr rd, 10 October 1914 – Ashcroft; Stevenson, Bullough, Hancock, Taylor, Holden (1), Moreton (1), Cunningham (2), Smith (5), Leck (3), Gould (1).

Record Defeat: 1–9 v Tottenham H, FA Cup 3rd rd (replay), 14 January 1953.

Most League Points (2 for a win): 60, Division 4, 1964–65.

Most League Points (3 for a win): 80, Division 4, 1988–89 and Division 3, 1989–90.

Most League Goals: 111, Division 3 (N), 1930–31.

Highest League Scorer in Season: Bunny Bell, 35, Division 3 (N), 1933–34.

Most League Goals in Total Aggregate: Ian Muir, 125, 1985–93.

Most Capped Player: John Aldridge, 15 (54), Republic of Ireland.

Most League Appearances: Harold Bell, 595, 1946–64 (incl. League record 401 consecutive appearances).

Record Transfer Fee Received: £120,000 from Cardiff C for Ronnie Moore, February 1979.

Record Transfer Fee Paid: £350,000 to Celtic for Tommy Coyne, March 1993.

Football League Record: 1921 Original Member of Division 3 (N): 1938–39 Division 2; 1946–58 Division 3 (N); 1958–61 Division 3; 1961–67 Division 4; 1967–75 Division 3; 1975–76 Division 4; 1976–79 Division 3; 1979–89 Division 4; 1989–91 Division 3; 1991–92 Division 2; 1992– Division 1.

Honours: *Football League* Division 1 best season: 4th, 1992–93; Division 3 (N) – Champions 1937–38; Promotion to 3rd Division: 1966–67, 1975–76; Division 4 – Runners-up 1988–89. *FA Cup:* best season: 5th rd, 1967–68. *Football League Cup:* best season: 4th rd, 1961, 1982, 1989, 1990. *Welsh Cup:* Winners 1935; Runners-up 1934. *Leyland Daf Cup:* Winners 1990; Runners-up 1991.

TRANMERE ROVERS 1992—93 LEAGUE RECORD

Match No.	Date	Venue	Opponents	Result	H/T Score	Lg. Pos.	Goalscorers	Atten dance
1	Aug 15	H	Cambridge U	W 2-0	0-0	—	Aldridge, Malkin	5248
2	22	A	Sunderland	L 0-1	0-0	15		16,667
3	28	H	Bristol R	W 2-1	0-1	—	Muir, Garnett	5458
4	Sept 5	A	Luton T	D 3-3	3-2	9	Aldridge, Muir, Nevin	6801
5	12	H	Grimsby T	D 1-1	1-0	9	Nevin	5330
6	18	H	Charlton Ath	D 0-0	0-0	—		6055
7	26	A	Oxford U	W 2-1	1-0	9	Morrissey, Nevin	4683
8	29	H	Notts Co	W 3-1	2-0	—	Mungall, Aldridge, Brannan	5403
9	Oct 3	H	Bristol C	W 3-0	1-0	5	Aldridge 2 (1 pen), Nevin	5975
10	10	A	Newcastle U	L 0-1	0-1	6		30,137
11	17	H	Birmingham C	W 4-0	1-0	6	Aldridge 2 (1 pen), Mungall, Irons	7901
12	24	A	Watford	L 2-3	2-2	6	Morrissey, Dublin (og)	6937
13	30	H	Peterborough U	D 1-1	0-1	—	Malkin	8068
14	Nov 3	H	Southend U	W 3-0	2-0	—	Morrissey, Aldridge, McNab	5870
15	7	A	Leicester C	W 1-0	0-0	2	Nevin	13,538
16	14	H	Brentford	W 3-2	0-2	3	Irons, Nevin 2	7852
17	21	A	Portsmouth	L 0-4	0-3	3		9982
18	28	A	Derby Co	W 2-1	0-1	2	Aldridge 2	15,665
19	Dec 4	H	West Ham U	W 5-2	1-1	—	Aldridge 3, Irons, Malkin	11,782
20	19	H	Wolverhampton W	W 3-0	1-0	2	Aldridge 3	9758
21	26	H	Millwall	D 1-1	1-0	2	Morrissey	13,118
22	28	A	Barnsley	L 1-3	0-2	2	Mungall	8204
23	Jan 9	A	Charlton Ath	D 2-2	1-1	2	Aldridge, Nevin	8337
24	15	H	Oxford U	W 4-0	2-0	—	Higgins, Aldridge 2 (1 pen), Smart (og)	8317
25	26	A	Notts Co	L 1-5	0-3	—	Higgins	5642
26	Feb 6	A	Cambridge U	W 1-0	0-0	4	McNab	4802
27	13	H	Luton T	L 0-2	0-1	5		8723
28	20	A	Bristol R	L 0-1	0-1	5		5135
29	23	A	Swindon T	L 0-2	0-1	—		10,059
30	28	H	Newcastle U	L 0-3	0-2	—		13,082
31	Mar 6	A	Bristol C	W 3-1	2-0	6	Malkin 2, Nevin	8810
32	9	A	Brentford	W 1-0	0-0	—	Nevin	7993
33	13	H	Leicester C	L 2-3	1-1	7	Morrissey, Malkin	9680
34	16	A	Grimsby T	D 0-0	0-0	—		5686
35	20	A	West Ham U	L 0-2	0-0	7		16,369
36	23	H	Portsmouth	L 0-2	0-0	—		7472
37	26	A	Southend U	W 2-1	1-1	—	Martindale, Coyne T	4147
38	Apr 2	H	Derby Co	W 2-1	1-1	—	Nevin 2	7774
39	6	H	Swindon T	W 3-1	0-1	—	Irons 3	8335
40	10	A	Millwall	D 0-0	0-0	7		9392
41	12	A	Barnsley	W 2-1	1-0	5	Higgins, Irons	6436
42	17	A	Wolverhampton W	W 2-0	2-0	6	Higgins, Proctor	13,060
43	24	A	Birmingham C	D 0-0	0-0	6		14,600
44	May 1	H	Watford	W 2-1	1-0	6	Aldridge 2 (1 pen)	8315
45	4	A	Sunderland	W 2-1	1-1	—	Martindale, Nevin	9685
46	8	A	Peterborough U	D 1-1	1-1	4	Malkin	8189

Final League Position: 4

GOALSCORERS

League (72): Aldridge 21 (4 pens), Nevin 13, Irons 7, Malkin 7, Morrissey 5, Higgins 4, Mungall 3, McNab 2, Martindale 2, Muir 2, Brannan 1, Coyne T 1, Garnett 1, Proctor 1, own goals 2.
Coca Cola Cup (3): Aldridge 2, Garnett 1.
FA Cup (6): Morrissey 2, Nevin 2, Aldridge 1 (pen), Vickers 1.

Nixon 45	Brannan 38	Nolan 14	Irons 40+2	Hughes 7+4	Garnett 5	Morrissey 42+1	Aldridge 29+1	Malkin 35+1	Martindale 18+8	Thomas 16	Nevin 43	McNab 30+1	Muir 7+4	Vickers 42	Mungall 29+6	Higgins 40	Cooper 3+3	Coyne T 9+3	Branch —+3	Proctor 13	Coyne D 1	Match No.
1	2	3	4	5	6	7	8	9	10	11												1
1	2	3	4	5	6	12	8	9		11	7	10										2
1	2	3	4	5	6	7	8		12	11	9	10										3
1	2	3	4	5		7	8	9			11	10		6								4
1	2	3	4	5		7	8	9	12		11	10		6	14							5
1	3		4			7	8	9	12		11	10		6	5	2						6
1	3					7	8	9	4		11	10		6	5	2						7
1	3					7	8	9	4		11	10		6	5	2						8
1	3					7	8	9	4		11	10		6	5	2						9
1	3	14				7	8	9	4		11	10	12	6	5	2						10
1	3		4			7	8				11	10		6	5	2	9					11
1	3		4	12		7	8				11	10		6	5	2	9					12
1	3		4	2		7	8	9			11	10		6	5							13
1	3		4			7	8	9			11	10		6	5	2						14
1	3		4	10		7	8	9			11			6	5	2						15
1	3		4	12		7	8	9			11	10		6	5	2						16
1	3		4			7	8	9			11	10		6	5	2						17
1	3		4			7	8	9	11			10		6	5	2						18
1	3		4			7	8	9	12		11	10		6	5	2						19
1	3		4			7	8	9	11			10		6	5	2						20
1	3		4	6		7	8	12			11	10	9		5	2						21
1	3		4			7	8				11	10	9	6	5	2						22
1		4	3			7	8	9	12		11	10		6	5	2						23
1		3	4			7	8	9	12		11	10		6	5	2						24
1		3	4			7		9	12		11	8	10	6	5	2		14				25
1		3	4			7		9	8		11	10	12	6	5	2						26
1		3	4			7	8	9	14		11	10	12	6	5	2						27
1		3	4			7	8	9	14		11	10	12	6	5	2						28
1		3	4			7		9	8		11	10	12	6	5	2						29
1	3	12	14			7		9	4		11	8	10	6	5	2						30
1	3		4	12		7		9	8		11	10		6	5	2						31
1	3		4			7		9	11		8	10		6	5	2						32
1	3		4			7		9	11	8	5			6		2	10	12				33
1	3		4			7		9	11	10				6		2	8			5		34
1			4			7		9	11	10				6	3	2	8	12		5		35
1	4	3				7		14	11	10				6		2	8	9	12	5		36
1	3	8				7		4	11	10				6		2		9		5		37
1	3		4			7		8	11	10				6	12	2		9		5		38
1	3		4			7		8	11	10				6	12	2		9		5		39
1	3		4				9	8	11	10				6	7	2				5		40
1	3		4			7	9	8	11	10				6	12	2	14			5		41
1	3		4			7	8		11	10				6		2		9		5		42
1	3		4			7	12	8	11	10				6		2		9		5		43
1	3		4			7	8	9	11	10				6	12	2	14			5		44
1	3	11	4				8	9	7	10				6	12	2	14			5		45
	3	11	4				8	9	7	10				6		2				5	1	46

Coca Cola Cup	First Round	Blackpool (h)	3-0
		(a)	0-4
FA Cup	Third Round	Oldham Ath (a)	2-2
		(h)	3-0
	Fourth Round	Ipswich T (h)	1-2

TRANMERE ROVERS

Player and Position	Ht	Wt	Date	Birth Place	Source	Clubs	League App	Gls
Goalkeepers								
Danny Coyne	6 0	13 00	27 8 73	St Asaph	Trainee	Tranmere R	1	—
Eric Nixon	6 2	14 03	4 10 62	Manchester	Curzon Ashton	Manchester C	58	—
						Wolverhampton W (loan)	16	—
						Bradford C (loan)	3	—
						Southampton (loan)	4	—
						Carlisle U (loan)	16	—
						Tranmere R (loan)	8	—
						Tranmere R	225	—
Defenders								
Ged Brannan	6 0	13 03	15 1 72	Liverpool	Trainee	Tranmere R	74	3
Tony Draper*	5 5	10 00	29 11 73	Liverpool	Trainee	Tranmere R	—	—
Mike Foster*	5 9	11 06	24 9 73	Portmadoc		Tranmere R	—	—
Dave Higgins	6 0	11 00	19 8 61	Liverpool	Eagle	Tranmere R	28	—
					S. Liverpool, Caernarforn	Tranmere R	227	10
Mark Hughes	6 0	12 08	3 2 62	Port Talbot	Apprentice	Bristol R	74	3
						Torquay U (loan)	9	1
						Swansea C	12	—
						Bristol C	22	—
						Tranmere R	258	9
John McGreal	5 11	10 08	2 6 72	Birkenhead	Trainee	Tranmere R	3	—
Steve Mungall	5 8	11 05	22 5 58	Bellshill		Motherwell	20	—
						Tranmere R	468	12
Ian Nolan	6 0	11 10	9 7 70	Liverpool	Marine	Tranmere R	48	1
Tony Thomas	5 11	12 05	12 7 71	Liverpool	Trainee	Tranmere R	130	10
Steve Vickers	6 2	12 00	13 10 67	Bishop Auckland	Spennymoor U	Tranmere R	300	11
Midfield								
Shaun Garnett	6 2	11 00	22 11 69	Wallasey	Trainee	Tranmere R	34	2
						Chester C (loan)	9	—
						Preston NE (loan)	10	2
						Wigan Ath (loan)	13	1
Neil McNab*	5 7	11 00	4 6 57	Greenock		Morton	14	—
						Tottenham H	72	3
						Bolton W	35	4
						Brighton	103	4
						Leeds U (loan)	5	—
						Portsmouth (loan)	—	—
						Manchester C	221	16
						Tranmere R	105	6
						Huddersfield T (loan)	11	—
Dave Martindale	5 11	11 10	9 4 64	Liverpool	Caernarfon	Tranmere R	153	9
John Morrissey	5 8	11 09	8 3 65	Liverpool	Apprentice	Everton	1	—
						Wolverhampton W	10	1
						Tranmere R	301	43
Forwards								
John Aldridge	5 11	11 10	18 9 58	Liverpool	South Liverpool	Newport Co	170	69
						Oxford U	114	72
						Liverpool	83	50
						Real Sociedad	63	33
						Tranmere R	73	43
Graham Branch	6 2	13 00	12 2 72	Heswall	Heswall Ath	Tranmere R	7	—
						Bury (loan)	4	1

TRANMERE ROVERS

Colours: All white. **Change colours:** Green shirts, navy blue shorts and stockings.

Foundation: Formed in 1884 as Belmont they adopted their present title the following year and eventually joined their first league, the West Lancashire League in 1889–90, the same year as their first success in the Wirral Challenge Cup. The club almost folded in 1899–1900 when all the players left en bloc to join a rival club, but they survived the crisis and went from strength to strength winning the 'Combination' title in 1907–08 and the Lancashire Combination in 1913–14. They joined the Football League in 1921 from the Central League.

First Football League game: 27 August 1921, Division 3(N), v Crewe Alex (h) W 4-1 – Bradshaw; Grainger, Stuart (1); Campbell, Milnes (1), Heslop; Moreton, Groves (1), Hyam, Ford (1), Hughes.

Did you know: Tranmere Rovers playing at home to Hereford United on 20 January 1978, made their first team change of the season in their 29th match, for a post-war record sequence of an unaltered line-up.

Managers (and Secretary-Managers)
Bert Cooke 1912–35, Jackie Carr 1935–36, Jim Knowles 1936–39, Bill Ridding 1939–45, Ernie Blackburn 1946–55, Noel Kelly 1955–57, Peter Farrell 1957–60, Walter Galbraith 1961, Dave Russell 1961–69, Jackie Wright 1969–72, Ron Yeats 1972–75, John King 1975–80, Bryan Hamilton 1980–85, Frank Worthington 1985–87, Ronnie Moore 1987, John King April 1987–.

Player and Position	Ht	Wt	Birth Date	Birth Place	Source	Clubs	League App	Gls
Steve Cooper	5 11	10 12	22 6 64	Birmingham		Birmingham C	—	—
						Halifax T (loan)	7	1
						Mansfield T (loan)	—	—
						Newport Co	38	11
						Plymouth Arg	73	15
						Barnsley	77	13
						Tranmere R	32	3
						Peterborough U (loan)	9	—
						Wigan Ath (loan)	4	—
Tommy Coyne	5 11	12 00	14 11 62	Glasgow	Hillwood BC	Clydebank	80	37
						Dundee U	52	8
						Dundee	89	51
						Celtic	105	43
						Tranmere R	12	1
Kenny Irons	5 9	11 00	4 11 70	Liverpool	Trainee	Tranmere R	120	20
Chris Malkin	6 0	10 12	4 6 67	Bebington	Overpool	Tranmere R	161	36
Alan Morgan	5 10	11 00	2 11 73	Aberystwyth	Trainee	Tranmere R	—	—
Ian Muir	5 8	11 00	5 5 63	Coventry	Apprentice	QPR	2	2
						Burnley (loan)	2	1
						Birmingham C	1	—
						Brighton	4	—
						Swindon T (loan)	2	—
						Tranmere R	279	125
Pat Nevin	5 6	11 09	6 9 63	Glasgow	Gartcosh U	Clyde	73	17
						Chelsea	193	36
						Everton	109	16
						Tranmere R (loan)	8	—
						Tranmere R	43	13
Mike Smith*	5 10	11 06	28 9 73	Liverpool	Trainee	Tranmere R	—	—

Trainees
Allen, Gavin; Bate, Christopher J; Cassidy, Thomas S; Edwards, Michael; Evans, John D; Gerard, Robbie; Johnson, Philip; Jones, Gary S; Jones, Martin W; Kenworthy, Jonathan R; McCullach, Edward; Moore, Ian R; Parkinson, Mark R; Rogers, David R; Smith, Paul; Watt, Simon C.

Associated Schoolboys
Blundell, Greg; Burns, Brian; Ellis, James; Fearns, Terry; Fitzsimmons, Jamie L; Hardie, Greg; Hazlehurst, Ian J; Jones, Paul N; Lampkin, Ricky J; Lepts, Damien A; Love, Barrie; Quayle, Mark L; Runacas, Matthew; Tynan, Paul S; Walker, Danny; Webster, Christopher R; Williams, Robert H.

Associated Schoolboys who have accepted the club's offer of a Traineeship/Contract
Davies, Philip A; Hammond, John E; McKenna, David; Smith, Stephen P.

WALSALL 1992–93   *Back row (left to right):* Tom Bradley (Physio), Scott Ollerenshaw, Kevin MacDonald, Colin Methven, Steve O'Hara, Mark Gayle, Jonathan Norris, Wayne Clarke, Dean Smith, Stuart Ryder, Charlie Ntamark, Eric McManus.

Front row: Chris Marsh, Mick Cecere, Richard Brown, Chris Demetrios, David Edwards, Kenny Hibbitt (Manager), Rod McDonald, Steve Winter, Richard Knight, Derek Statham, Wayne Williams.

Division 3 **WALSALL**

Bescot Stadium, Bescot Cresent, Walsall WS1 4SA. Telephone Walsall (0922) 22791. Commercial Dept: (0922) 30696. Clubcall: 0898 121104.

Ground capacity: 10,400.

Record attendance: 10,628 B International, England v Switzerland, 20 May 1991.

Record receipts: £50,926.50 v Watford, FA Cup 5th rd, 2nd replay, 2 March 1987 (at Fellows Park); £42,401 v Aston Villa, Friendly, 18 August 1990.

Pitch measurements: 113yd × 73yd.

President: .

Chairman: J. W. Bonsor.

Directors: M. N. Lloyd, K. R. Whalley, C. Welch.

Manager: Kenny Hibbitt. *General Manager:* Paul Taylor. *Coach:* Kevin MacDonald.

Physio: T. Bradley.

Secretary/Commercial Manager: Roy Whalley.

Year Formed: 1888. *Turned Professional:* 1888. *Ltd Co.:* 1921.

Club Nickname: 'The Saddlers'.

Previous Names: Walsall Swifts (founded 1877) and Walsall Town (founded 1879) amalgamated in 1888 and were known as Walsall Town Swifts until 1895.

Previous Grounds: Fellows Park to 1990.

Record League Victory: 10–0 v Darwen, Division 2, 4 March 1899 – Tennent; E. Peers (1), Davies; Hickinbotham, Jenkyns, Taggart; Dean (3), Vail (2), Aston (4), Martin, Griffin.

Record Cup Victory: 6–1 v Leytonstone (away), FA Cup, 1st rd, 30 November 1946 – Lewis; Netley, Skidmore; Crutchley, Foulkes, Newman; Maund (1), Talbot, Darby (1), Wilshaw (2), Davies (2). 6–1 v Margate, FA Cup, 1st rd (replay), 24 November 1955 – Davies; Haddington, Vinall; Dorman, McPherson, Crook; Morris, Walsh (3), Richards (2), McLaren (1), Moore.

Record Defeat: 0–12 v Small Heath, 17 December 1892 and v Darwen, 26 December 1896, both Division 2.

Most League Points (2 for a win): 65, Division 4, 1959–60.

Most League Points (3 for a win): 82, Division 3, 1987–88.

Most League Goals: 102, Division 4, 1959–60.

Highest League Scorer in Season: Gilbert Alsop, 40, Division 3 (N), 1933–34 and 1934–35.

Most League Goals in Total Aggregate: Tony Richards, 184, 1954–63, and Colin Taylor, 184, 1958–63, 1964–68, 1969–73.

Most Capped Player: Mick Kearns, 15 (18), Eire.

Most League Appearances: Colin Harrison, 467, 1964–82.

Record Transfer Fee Received: £600,000 from West Ham U for David Kelly, July 1988.

Record Transfer Fee Paid: £175,000 to Birmingham C for Alan Buckley, June 1979.

Football League Record: 1892 Elected to Division 2; 1895 Failed re-election; 1896–1901 Division 2; 1901 Failed re-election; 1921 Original Member of Division 3 (N); 1927–31 Division 3 (S); 1931–36 Division 3 (N); 1936–58 Division 3 (S); 1958–60 Division 4; 1960–61 Division 3; 1961–63 Division 2; 1963–79 Division 3; 1979–80 Division 4; 1980–88 Division 3; 1988–89 Division 2; 1989–90 Division 3; 1990–92 Division 4; 1992– Division 3.

Honours: Football League: Division 2 best season: 6th, 1898–99; Division 3 – Runners-up 1960–61; Division 4 – Champions 1959–60; Runners-up 1979–80. *FA Cup:* best season: 5th rd, 1939, 1975, 1978, and last 16 1888–89. *Football League Cup:* Semi-final 1983–84.

WALSALL 1992—93 LEAGUE RECORD

Match No.	Date		Venue	Opponents	Result		H/T Score	Lg. Pos.	Goalscorers	Atten dance
1	Aug	15	A	Carlisle U	W	4-3	1-1	—	Oghani (og), Clarke, Marsh, McDonald	4199
2		22	H	Cardiff C	L	2-3	0-2	8	Ntamark, O'Hara	4611
3		29	A	Hereford U	W	3-1	2-1	4	McDonald, Clarke 2 (1 pen)	2895
4	Sept	1	A	Scunthorpe U	L	0-2	0-1	—		2828
5		5	H	York C	W	3-1	1-1	4	Ollerenshaw, Clarke, Marsh	3574
6		12	A	Colchester U	L	1-3	0-2	6	Ntamark	3218
7		15	H	Bury	W	4-3	0-2	—	Clarke 3, West	3097
8		26	A	Gillingham	W	1-0	0-0	4	Ollerenshaw	2821
9	Oct	10	A	Lincoln C	W	2-0	2-0	4	Cecere 2	3095
10		17	H	Halifax T	L	1-2	0-1	6	Clarke (pen)	3867
11		24	A	Rochdale	L	3-4	1-2	8	McDonald, Whitehall (og), Cecere	1834
12		31	H	Doncaster R	W	3-1	1-0	7	McDonald, Clarke, Cecere	3525
13	Nov	3	A	Barnet	L	0-3	0-2	—		2623
14		7	H	Scarborough	W	3-2	1-0	6	Evans (og), Demetrios, Cecere	3001
15		21	A	Shrewsbury T	W	3-0	3-0	4	MacDonald, Clarke (pen), Cecere	4353
16		28	H	Wrexham	D	1-1	1-0	4	Cecere	3519
17	Dec	12	H	Darlington	D	2-2	0-2	5	MacDonald, Clarke	3002
18		26	A	Torquay U	W	1-0	1-0	3	Smith	3010
19		28	H	Northampton T	W	2-0	1-0	3	Reece, Clarke (pen)	5080
20	Jan	2	A	Colchester U	L	1-3	0-2	4	Clarke	3669
21		9	A	Bury	L	1-2	1-1	4	Clarke	2421
22		16	H	Gillingham	D	1-1	0-0	5	Ollerenshaw	3253
23		23	A	Wrexham	L	1-3	1-1	6	Ollerenshaw	5324
24		26	H	Hereford U	D	1-1	0-0	—	Ntamark	2719
25		30	A	Cardiff C	L	1-2	1-2	8	McDonald	9012
26	Feb	6	H	Carlisle U	W	2-1	1-0	7	Clarke, Cecere	2817
27		13	A	York C	W	1-0	1-0	6	Williams	3467
28		20	H	Scunthorpe U	W	3-2	1-0	6	Clarke 2, McDonald	2935
29		27	H	Lincoln C	L	1-2	1-2	7	Cecere	3345
30	Mar	9	H	Chesterfield	W	3-2	1-1	—	Clarke, McDonald, Knight	2884
31		13	A	Scarborough	L	1-4	1-0	7	MacDonald	1681
32		20	A	Barnet	W	2-0	1-0	7	McDonald 2	3418
33		27	H	Shrewsbury T	D	1-1	0-0	8	Clarke	5573
34	Apr	3	A	Chesterfield	L	1-2	1-1	9	Cecere	3278
35		6	A	Darlington	W	2-1	1-0	—	Kelly, O'Connor	1739
36		10	H	Torquay U	D	2-2	0-1	5	McDonald, Clarke	3541
37		12	A	Northampton T	D	0-0	0-0	5		4177
38		17	H	Crewe Alex	W	1-0	1-0	5	Cecere	4643
39		24	A	Halifax T	W	4-0	1-0	6	Cecere 3, McDonald	2829
40		27	A	Crewe Alex	W	1-0	1-0	—	Ntamark	4549
41	May	1	H	Rochdale	W	3-1	2-1	5	Clarke, McDonald, Marsh	4118
42		8	A	Doncaster R	W	3-0	0-0	5	Cecere 2, Kelly	2900

Final League Position: 5

GOALSCORERS

League (76): Clarke 21 (4 pens), Cecere 16, McDonald 12, Ntamark 4, Ollerenshaw 4, MacDonald 3, Marsh 3, Kelly 2, Demetrios 1, Knight 1, O'Connor 1, O'Hara 1, Reece 1, Smith 1, West 1, Williams 1, own goals 3.
Coca Cola Cup (2): Clarke 1, McDonald 1.
FA Cup (0).

Gayle 41	Williams 14	Statham 18 + 3	MacDonald 28 + 5	O'Hara 22 + 4	Smith 39 + 3	Ntamark 40 + 1	Clarke 39	Marsh 29 + 4	Cecere 33 + 6	McDonald 39	Ollerenshaw 8 + 12	Demetrios 3 + 4	West 9	Edwards 3 + 2	Winter 1 + 1	Knight 26 + 1	Parker — + 1	Ryder 20 + 2	Methven 23	Reece 9	Fearon 1	McManus — + 1	O'Connor 10	Kelly 7 + 3	Match No.
1	2	3	4	5	6	7	8	9	10	11	12														1
1	2	3	4	5	6	7	8	9	12	11	10														2
1	2	3	4	5	6	7	8	9	12	11	*10*	14													3
1	2	3	4	5	*6*	7	8	9	12	11	10	14													4
1	2	3	4	12	6	7	8	9		11	*10*		5	14											5
1	2	3	4		6	7	8	9		11	10		5	12											6
1	2	3		4	6	7	8	9	12	11	10		5												7
1	2	3		4	6	7	8	9		11	12		5	10											8
1	2	3	14	4	6	7	8	9	5	11	12			10											9
1	2	3		4	6	14	8	9	5	11	12		7	10											10
1	2	*3*	10	4	6	7		9	8	11	12		5	14											11
1		*3*	10	4	6	7	8	9	2	11	12		5			14									12
1	2		10	4	6	7		9	8	11		3	5		12	14									13
1			10	4	12	7	8	9	2	11		3	5			6									14
1		10			6	7	8	9	2	11						5		4	3						15
1		10			6	7	8	9	2	11	12					5		4	3						16
1		10			6	7	8	9	2	11						5		4	3						17
1		10			6	7	8	9	2	11						5		4	3						18
1	12	10			6	7	8	9	2	11						5	14	4	3						19
1	12	10			6	7	8	9	2	11						5		4	3						20
1		10	11		6	7	8	9	2							5		4	3						21
1		10	11		6	7	8	9	2		12					5		4	3						22
1		3	10	14			8	9	12	11	7			*2*		6		4	5						23
1		3	10	14	6		8	9	12	11	7			2		5	*4*								24
1		10	7	4	5	8	9	3	11	12	14			2		6									25
			7	4	5	8	9	10	11		3			2		6					1				26
1	2		7	4	5	8	9	10	11									6	3						27
1	2		7	4	5	8	9	10	11	12								6	3						28
1		14	7	4	5	8	9	10	11	12				2				6	3						29
1	3	9	7	4	5	8		10	11					2				6							30
1	*3*	9	7	4	5	8		10	11	12	14			2				6							31
1		9	7	4	5	8		10	11					2				6	3			12			32
1		7	4	5	8		9		11					2				6	3				10	12	33
1			4	5	8		9		11					2				6	3				10	7	34
1			4	5	8		9		11					2				6	3				10	7	35
1		12	4	5	8		9		11					*2*				6	3				10	7	36
1		12	14	4	5	8	*9*		11					2				6	3				10	*7*	37
1		12	14	4	5	8	9		11					2				6	3				*10*	7	38
1		7		4	5	8	12	9	11					2				6	3				10	14	39
1	6	14		4	9	12	8		11					2				5	*3*				10	7	40
1		7	3	4	5	8	12	9	11					2				6					10	14	41
1	14	7		4	5	8	12	9	11					*2*				6					10	3	42

Coca Cola Cup	First Round	Bournemouth (h)		1-1
		(a)		1-0
	Second Round	Chelsea (h)		0-3
		(a)		0-1
FA Cup	First Round	Rotherham U (a)		0-4

WALSALL

Player and Position	Ht	Wt	Date	Birth Place	Source	Clubs	League App	Gls
Goalkeepers								
Mark Gayle	6 0	12 00	21 10 69	Bromsgrove	Trainee	Leicester C	—	—
						Blackpool	—	—
					Worcester C	Walsall	65	—
Defenders								
Richard Knight	5 9	10 13	31 8 74	Burton	Trainee	Walsall	27	1
Colin Methven*	6 2	12 07	10 12 55	India	Leven Royals	East Fife	144	14
						Wigan Ath	296	21
						Blackpool	173	11
						Carlisle U (loan)	12	—
						Walsall	97	3
Steve O'Hara	6 1	12 02	21 2 71	Lanark	Trainee	Walsall	101	4
Stuart Ryder	6 0	12 01	6 11 73	Sutton Coldfield	Trainee	Walsall	22	—
Dean Smith	6 0	12 01	19 3 71	West Bromwich	Trainee	Walsall	106	1
Derek Statham*	5 5	11 05	24 3 59	Wolverhampton	Apprentice	WBA	299	8
						Southampton	64	2
						Stoke C	41	1
						Walsall	50	
Wayne Williams*	5 11	11 09	17 11 63	Delford	Apprentice	Shrewsbury T	221	7
						Northampton T	55	1
						Walsall	56	1
Midfield								
Chris Demetrios‡	5 8	11 01	26 10 73	Dudley	Trainee	Walsall	7	1
David Edwards	5 10	10 08	13 1 74	Bridgnorth	Trainee	Walsall	27	1
Kevin MacDonald	6 1	12 06	22 12 60	Inverness	Inverness Caley	Leicester C	138	8
						Liverpool	40	1
						Leicester C (loan)	3	—
						Rangers (loan)	3	—
						Coventry C	31	—
						Cardiff C (loan)	8	—
						Walsall	53	6
Steven McManus§	5 11	11 07	8 3 75	Nottingham	Trainee	Walsall	1	—
Chris Marsh	5 10	12 11	14 1 70	Dudley	Trainee	Walsall	118	6
Charlie Ntamark	5 8	11 12	22 7 64	Cameroon		Walsall	124	10
Steven Winter	5 7	10 03	26 10 73	Bristol	Trainee	Walsall	18	—
Forwards								
Michele Cecere	6 0	11 04	4 1 68	Chester	Apprentice	Oldham Ath	52	8
						Huddersfield T	54	8
						Stockport Co (loan)	1	—
						Walsall	106	30
Wayne Clarke	6 0	11 08	28 2 61	Wolverhampton	Apprentice	Wolverhampton W	148	30
						Birmingham C	92	38
						Everton	57	18
						Leicester C	11	1
						Manchester C	21	2
						Shrewsbury T (loan)	7	6
						Stoke C (loan)	9	3
						Wolverhampton W (loan)	1	—
						Walsall	39	21
Rod McDonald	5 10	12 07	20 3 67	London	Colne Dynamoes	Walsall	114	35
Scott Ollerenshaw*	5 10	11 07	9 2 68	Sydney	Sydney Olympic	Walsall	20	4
Richard Parker†	6 1	12 02	6 7 73	Wolverhampton	Trainee	Walsall	1	—

WALSALL

Colours: Red shirts, red shorts, black stockings. **Change colours:** Black and white striped shirts, white shorts, white stockings.

Foundation: Two of the leading clubs around Walsall in the 1880s were Walsall Swifts (formed 1877) and Walsall Town (formed 1879). The Swifts were winners of the Birmingham Senior Cup in 1881, while the Town reached the 4th round (5th round modern equivalent) of the FA Cup in 1883. These clubs amalgamated as Walsall Town Swifts in 1888, becoming simply Walsall in 1895.

First Football League game: 3 September, 1892, Division 2, v Darwen (h) L 1-2 – Hawkins; Withington, Pinches; Robinson, Whitrick, Forsyth; Marshall, Holmes, Turner, Gray (1), Pangbourn.

Did you know: Walsall's giant-killing cup performances against Arsenal are well documented: 1933 FA Cup and 1983 League Cup, but when both teams were in Division 2 before the turn of the century, Walsall won six and drew three of 14 League meetings.

Managers (and Secretary-Managers)
H. Smallwood 1888–91*, A. G. Burton 1891–93, J. H. Robinson 1893–95, C. H. Ailso 1895–96*, A. E. Parsloe 1896–97*, L. Ford 1897–98*, G. Hughes 1898–99*, L. Ford 1899–1901*, J. E. Shutt 1908–13*, Haydn Price 1914–20, Joe Burchell 1920–26, David Ashworth 1926–27, Jack Torrance 1927–28, James Kerr 1928–29, S. Scholey 1929–30, Peter O'Rourke 1930–32, G. W. Slade 1932–34, Andy Wilson 1934–37, Tommy Lowes 1937–44, Harry Hibbs 1944–51, Tony McPhee 1951, Brough Fletcher 1952–53, Major Frank Buckley 1953–55, John Love 1955–57, Billy Moore 1957–64, Alf Wood 1964, Reg Shaw 1964–68, Dick Graham 1968, Ron Lewin 1968–69, Billy Moore 1969–72, John Smith 1972–73, Doug Fraser 1973–77, Dave Mackay 1977–78, Alan Ashman 1978, Frank Sibley 1979, Alan Buckley 1979–86, Neil Martin (joint manager with Buckley) 1981–82, Tommy Coakley 1986–88, John Barnwell 1989–90, Kenny Hibbitt May 1990–   .

Trainees
Blackwood, Ian C; Butler, Martin N; Forrester, Matthew; Gardner, Richard B; Hodgson, Craig B; Instone, Wayne A; Jones, Mark; Lake, Stuart; McManus, Steven; Norman, Karl M; Parker, Paul J; Pickett, James A; Power, Andrew J; Thomas, Matthew A; Vaughan, Stephen A; Westwood, John T.

**Non-Contract
Haman, Gary; Parker, Richard J; Winter, Steven D.

Associated Schoolboys
Bagnall, Mark G; Baldwin, David J; Bentley, Gavin; Blakeley, Andrew P; Brant, Gavin J; Davies, Stuart J; Derry, Leighton W; Edwards, Gavin D; Faulkner, Richard S; Mitchell, Wayne A; Peach, Richard F; Tarbuck, Wayne M; Webb, Neal.

Associated Schoolboys who have accepted the club's offer of a Traineeship/Contract
Baker, James A; Mathews, Stuart J; Rollo, James; Smith, Christopher G.

**Non-Contract Players who are retained must be re-signed before they are eligible to play in League matches.

536

WATFORD 1992–93 *Back row (left to right):* Ken Brooks (Kit Manager), Alex Inglethorpe, Julian Alsford, Barry Ashby, Steve Butler, Andy Kennedy, Jason Soloman, Jason Drysdale, Trevor Putney, Billy Hails (Physio).

Centre row: Kenny Jackett (Youth Team Manager), Perry Suckling, Luther Blissett, Darren Bazeley, Richard Johnson, David Holdsworth, Paul Furlong, Joe Gallen, Gerard Lavin, Simon Sheppard, Stuart Murdoch (Reserve Team Manager).

Front row: James Meara, Gary Porter, Daniel Nwaokolo, Lee Nogan, Nigel Gibbs, Peter Taylor (Assistant Manager), Steve Perryman (Manager), Joe McLaughlin, Keith Dublin, Andy Hessenthaler, Rod Thomas, David Byrne.

Division 1   **WATFORD**

Vicarage Road Stadium, Watford WD1 8ER. Telephone Watford (0923) 230933. Fax 0923 239759. Hornet Hotline 0898 121030. Ticket Office: 220393. Club shop: 220847. Catering: 221457. Junior Hornets Club: 53836. Marketing: 225761.

Ground capacity: 20,000.

Record attendance: 34,099 v Manchester U, FA Cup 4th rd (replay), 3 February 1969.

Record receipts: £115,000 v Leeds U, Coca Cola Cup 3rd rd, 10 November 1992.

Pitch measurements: 115yd × 75yd.

Life President: Elton John.

Chairman: Jack Petchey. *Vice-chairman:* G. A. Smith.

Directors: G. S. Lawson Rogers, C. D. Lissack, Dr. S. R. Timperley PHD, M. Winwood.

Chief Executive: Eddie Plumley FAAI.

Team Manager: Glenn Roeder. *Assistant Manager:* Phil Holder.

Reserve Team Coach: Stuart Murdoch. *Youth Team Coach:* Kenny Jackett. *Physio:* Billy Hails.

Director of Marketing: Brian Blower. *Public Relations Manager:* Ed Coan.

Year Formed: 1891*(see Foundation).* *Turned Professional:* 1897. *Ltd Co.:* 1909.

Club Nickname: 'The Hornets'.

Previous Name: West Herts.

Previous Ground: 1899, Cassio Road; 1922, Vicarage Road.

Record League Victory: 8–0 v Sunderland, Division 1, 25 September 1982 – Sherwood; Rice, Rostron, Taylor, Terry, Bolton, Callaghan (2), Blissett (4), Jenkins (2), Jackett, Barnes.

Record Cup Victory: 10–1 v Lowestoft T, FA Cup, 1st rd, 27 November 1926 – Yates; Prior, Fletcher (1); F. Smith, 'Bert' Smith, Strain; Stephenson, Warner (3), Edmonds (2), Swan (2), Daniels (1). (1 og).

Record Defeat: 0–10 v Wolverhampton W, FA Cup 1st rd (replay), 13 January 1912.

Most League Points (2 for a win): 71, Division 4, 1977–78.

Most League Points (3 for a win): 80, Division 2, 1981–82.

Most League Goals: 92, Division 4, 1959–60.

Highest League Scorer in Season: Cliff Holton, 42, Division 4, 1959–60.

Most League Goals in Total Aggregate: Luther Blissett, 158, 1976–83, 1984–88, 1991–92.

Most Capped Player: John Barnes, 31 (73), England and Kenny Jackett, 31, Wales.

Most League Appearances: Luther Blissett, 415, 1976–83, 1984–88, 1991–92.

Record Transfer Fee Received: £1,000,000 from AC Milan for Luther Blissett, July 1983, from Manchester C for Tony Coton, July 1990, from Aston Villa for Gary Penrice, March 1991 and from Liverpool for David James, July 1992.

Record Transfer Fee Paid: £550,000 to AC Milan for Luther Blissett, August 1984.

Football League Record: 1920 Original Member of Division 3; 1921–58 Division 3 (S); 1958–60 Division 4; 1960–69 Division 3; 1969–72 Division 2; 1972–75 Division 3; 1975–78 Division 4; 1978–79 Division 3; 1979–82 Division 2; 1982–88 Division 1; 1988–92 Division 2; 1992– Division 1.

Honours: Football League: Division 1 – Runners-up 1982–83; Division 2 – Runners-up 1981–82; Division 3 – Champions 1968–69; Runners-up 1978–79; Division 4 – Champions 1977–78; Promoted 1959–60 (4th). *FA Cup:* Runners-up 1984. *Football League Cup:* Semi-final 1978–79. **European Competitions:** *UEFA Cup:* 1983–84.

548

WATFORD 1992—93 LEAGUE RECORD

Match No.	Date		Venue	Opponents	Result		H/T Score	Lg. Pos.	Goalscorers	Attendance
1	Aug	15	H	Millwall	W	3-1	2-1	—	Drysdale (pen), Nogan, Bazeley	9745
2		22	A	Grimsby T	L	2-3	2-2	11	Furlong, Dublin	4772
3		25	A	Notts Co	W	2-1	1-1	—	Drysdale, Furlong	6274
4		29	H	Derby Co	D	0-0	0-0	6		9809
5	Sept	5	A	West Ham U	L	1-2	0-0	8	Furlong	11,921
6		12	H	Notts Co	L	1-3	1-1	13	Drysdale	7077
7		19	A	Wolverhampton W	D	2-2	1-1	11	Furlong, Nogan	13,497
8		26	H	Leicester C	L	0-3	0-1	14		8715
9		29	H	Sunderland	W	2-1	0-0	—	Hessenthaler 2	6263
10	Oct	3	A	Swindon T	L	1-3	1-0	12	Furlong	7723
11		10	H	Bristol R	W	4-2	2-1	9	Drysdale (pen), Furlong, Nogan 2	7624
12		17	A	Brentford	D	1-1	0-1	8	Nogan	8490
13		24	H	Tranmere R	W	3-2	2-2	8	Furlong 2, Charlery	6937
14		31	A	Oxford U	D	1-1	1-0	9	Furlong	6234
15	Nov	3	H	Peterborough U	L	1-2	0-1	—	Charlery	7016
16		7	A	Barnsley	W	1-0	0-0	11	Hessenthaler	6193
17		14	H	Portsmouth	D	0-0	0-0	14		8714
18		21	H	Newcastle U	L	0-2	0-0	14		28,871
19		29	A	Luton T	L	0-2	0-0	—		8341
20	Dec	5	H	Bristol C	D	0-0	0-0	15		6746
21		13	H	Charlton Ath	D	1-1	0-1	—	Charlery	6541
22		19	A	Birmingham C	D	2-2	1-0	15	Furlong 2	7182
23		26	A	Southend U	W	2-1	0-1	14	Soloman, Charlery	5769
24		28	H	Cambridge U	D	2-2	2-0	14	Charlery, Willis	8147
25	Jan	9	H	Wolverhampton W	W	3-1	1-0	13	Furlong 2, Nogan	6845
26		16	A	Leicester C	L	2-5	0-3	13	Soloman, Nogan	12,854
27		27	A	Sunderland	W	2-1	1-0	—	Willis, Furlong	14,703
28		30	H	Grimsby T	L	2-3	1-0	11	Furlong, Nogan	6613
29	Feb	6	A	Millwall	L	2-5	0-4	12	Furlong, Nogan	8847
30		13	H	West Ham U	L	1-2	0-1	14	Charlery	13,115
31		20	A	Derby Co	W	2-1	2-0	11	Charlery, Furlong	15,190
32		27	A	Bristol R	W	3-0	1-0	12	Charlery 2, Nogan	5702
33	Mar	6	H	Swindon T	L	0-4	0-3	13		8791
34		9	A	Portsmouth	L	0-1	0-0	—		10,716
35		13	H	Barnsley	L	1-2	0-1	14	Furlong	5785
36		20	A	Bristol C	L	1-2	1-1	14	Charlery	8265
37		23	H	Newcastle U	W	1-0	0-0	—	Furlong	11,634
38		27	A	Peterborough U	D	0-0	0-0	14		7631
39	Apr	3	H	Luton T	D	0-0	0-0	14		10,656
40		6	A	Charlton Ath	L	1-3	1-2	—	Leaburn (og)	6462
41		10	H	Southend U	D	0-0	0-0	14		7198
42		13	A	Cambridge U	D	1-1	1-0	—	Nogan	5106
43		17	H	Birmingham C	W	1-0	1-0	14	Charlery	9186
44		24	H	Brentford	W	1-0	1-0	14	Drysdale (pen)	9045
45	May	1	A	Tranmere R	L	1-2	0-1	14	Drysdale (pen)	8315
46		8	H	Oxford U	L	0-1	0-1	16		8127

Final League Position: 16

GOALSCORERS

League (57): Furlong 19, Charlery 11, Nogan 11, Drysdale 6 (4 pens), Hessenthaler 3, Soloman 2, Willis 2, Bazeley 1, Dublin 1, own goal 1.
Coca Cola Cup (7): Furlong 3, Drysdale 2 (1 pen), Holdsworth 1, Lavin 1.
FA Cup (1): Nogan 1.

Suckling 37	Gibbs 7	Drysdale 37 + 2	Dublin 46	Holdsworth 38 + 1	Ashby 33 + 2	Hessenthaler 45	Nogan 40 + 2	Furlong 41	Soloman 34 + 2	Bazeley 10 + 12	Porter 25 + 8	Butler 2 + 7	Putney 16 + 8	Lavin 24 + 4	Thomas 1	Alsford 2 + 3	Willis 28 + 4	Charlery 30 + 2	Johnson — + 1	Sheppard 5	Waugh 4	Dyer — + 2	Meara 1 + 1	Match No.
1	2	3	4	5	6	7	8	*9*	10	11	12	14												1
1	2	3	4	5	6	7	8	9		11	10	12												2
1	2	3	4	5	6	7	8	9		11				10										3
1	2	3	4	5	6	7	8	9		11	10	12	14											4
1	2	3	4	5	6	7	8	9		11	12	14		*10*										5
1	2	3	4	5	6	7	*8*	9		11	10	12	14											6
1		3	4	5	6	7	8	9		11				10			2							7
1	*3*		4	5	6	7	8	9		11	12	8	14	10			2							8
1		3	4	5	6	7	8	9		11				10			2							9
1		3	4	5	6	*7*	8	9		11	12	14		10			2							10
1		3	4	5	6	7	8	9		11	12						2	10						11
1		3	4	5	6	7	8	9		11	12						2	10	14					12
1	2	3	4	5		7	8	9		11	12			*6*				10						13
1	2	3	4	5		7	8	9		11	12			6				10						14
1	2	3	4	5	6	7	8	9		11	12	14						10						15
1		3	4	5	6	7	8	*9*	10	11	12	14					2							16
1		3	4	5	6	7	*8*	9	10	11	12	14					2							17
1		3	4	5	6	7	*8*	9	10	11	12	14					2							18
1		3	4	5	6	7	8	9	10	11	12						2							19
1		3	4	5	6	7	8	9	10	11	12	14					*2*							20
1		3	4	5		7	8	9		11	12			6			2	10						21
1		3	4			7	8	9		11	12			6			2	10						22
1		3	4	5		7	8	9		11				6			2	10						23
1		3	4			7	8	9		11	12			6			2	10						24
		3	4	5		7	8	9		11	12			6			2	10		1				25
		3	4	5		7	8	9		*11*	12	14		6			2	10		1				26
		3	4	5		7	8	9		11				6			2	10		1				27
		3	4	5		7	8	9		11				6			2	10		1				28
		3	4	*5*		7	8	9		11	12	14		6			2	10		1				29
1		3	4	5		7	*8*	9		11	12	14		6			2	10						30
1		3	4	5		7	8	9		11				6			2	10						31
1		3	4	5		7	8	9		11	12	14		6			2	*10*						32
1		3	4	5		7	8	9		11	12	14		6			2	10						33
1		3	4	5		7	8	9		11	12	14		6			2	10						34
1		3	4	5	6	7	8	9		11	12	14					2	*10*						35
1		3	4	5	6	7	8	9		11	12	14					2	10						36
		3	4	5	6	7	8	9		11	12						2	10	1					37
		3	4	5	*6*	7	8	9		11	12						2	10	1					38
		3	4	5	6	7	8	9	10	11	12						2		1					39
		3	4	5	*6*	7	8	9	10	11	12	14					2		1					40
1	12	3	4	5	6	7	8	9	10	11							2							41
1	12	3	4	5	6	7	8	9		11							2	10						42
1		3	4	5	6	7	8	9		11							2	*10*				12		43
1		3	4	5	6	7	8	9		11							2	10						44
1		3	4	5	6	7	8	9		11							2	10				12		45
1		3	4	5	6	7	8	9		11	12						*2*	10				14	6	46

Coca Cola Cup	Second Round	Reading (h)	2-2
		(a)	2-0
	Third Round	Leeds U (h)	2-1
	Fourth Round	Blackburn R (a)	1-6
FA Cup	Third Round	Wolverhampton W (h)	1-4

WATFORD

Player and Position	Ht	Wt	Date	Birth Place	Source	Clubs	League App	Gls
Goalkeepers								
Simon Sheppard	6 4	14 03	7 8 73	Clevedon	Trainee	Watford	5	—
Perry Suckling	6 2	13 02	12 10 65	Leyton	Apprentice	Coventry C	27	—
						Manchester C	39	—
						Crystal Palace	59	—
						West Ham U (loan)	6	—
						Brentford (loan)	8	—
						Watford	37	—
Keith Waugh*	6 1	13 00	27 10 56	Sunderland	Apprentice	Sunderland	—	—
						Peterborough U	195	—
						Sheffield U	99	—
						Bristol C (loan)	3	—
						Cambridge U (loan)	4	—
						Bristol C	167	—
						Coventry C	1	—
						Watford	7	—
Defenders								
Julian Alsford	6 2	12 11	24 12 72	Poole		Watford	5	—
Barry Ashby	6 2	12 03	21 11 70	London	Trainee	Watford	97	1
Jason Drysdale	5 10	12 00	17 11 70	Bristol	Trainee	Watford	126	11
Keith Dublin	6 0	12 10	29 1 66	Wycombe	Apprentice	Chelsea	51	—
						Brighton	132	5
						Watford	135	1
Nigel Gibbs	5 7	11 01	20 11 65	St Albans	Apprentice	Watford	271	3
David Holdsworth	6 1	12 04	8 11 68	London	Trainee	Watford	164	8
Craig McIntosh			30 6 75	Watford	Trainee	Watford	—	—
Joe McLaughlin (To Falkirk September 1992)	6 1	12 00	2 6 60	Greenock	School	Morton	134	3
						Chelsea	220	5
						Charlton Ath	31	—
						Watford	46	2
Danny Nwaokolo	5 11	11 10	11 10 73	London	Trainee	Watford	—	—
Robert Page			3 9 74	Llwyn	Trainee	Watford	—	—
Jason Soloman	6 0	11 10	6 10 70	Welwyn	Trainee	Watford	73	2
Roger Willis	6 1	11 06	17 6 67	Sheffield		Grimsby T	9	—
					Barnet	Barnet	44	13
						Watford	32	2
Midfield								
Andy Hessenthaler	5 7	11 00	17 8 65	Gravesend	Redbridge Forest	Watford	80	4
Richard Johnson	5 10	11 13	27 4 74	Kurri, Kurri	Trainee	Watford	3	—
Gerard Lavin	5 9	10 07	5 2 74	Corby	Trainee	Watford	29	—
Jim Meara	5 7	10 06	7 10 72	London	Trainee	Watford	2	—
Gary Porter	5 6	10 06	6 3 66	Sunderland	Apprentice	Watford	281	34
Trevor Putney	5 9	11 08	11 2 61	Harold Hill	Brentwood & W	Ipswich T	103	8
						Norwich C	82	9
						Middlesbrough	48	1
						Watford	52	2
John White			9 9 74	Honiton	Trainee	Watford	—	—
Forwards								
Darren Bazeley	5 10	10 09	5 10 72	Northampton	Trainee	Watford	64	7
Luther Blissett*	5 10	12 03	1 2 58	W. Indies	Juniors	Watford	246	95
						AC Milan	30	5
						Watford	127	44
						Bournemouth	121	56
						Watford	42	10
						WBA (loan)	3	1

WATFORD

Colours: Yellow shirts, black shorts, black stockings. **Change colours:** Navy/white (striped design) shirts, white shorts, white stockings.

Foundation: Tracing this club's foundation proves difficult. Nowadays it is suggested that Watford was formed as Watford Rovers in 1891. Another version is that Watford Rovers were not forerunners of the present club whose history began in 1898 with the amalgamation of West Herts and Watford St. Mary's.

First Football League game: 28 August, 1920, Division 3, v QPR (a) W 2-1 – Williams; Horseman, F. Gregory; Bacon, Toone, Wilkinson; Bassett, Ronald (1), Hoddinott, White (1), Waterall.

Did you know: Watford achieved the most impressive turn round of fortune over two legs of a League Cup tie in defeating Southampton. In 1980–81 they lost 4-0 in the first leg at Southampton, but won the second leg 7-1 after extra time.

Managers (and Secretary-Managers)
John Goodall 1903–10, Harry Kent 1910–26, Fred Pagnam 1926–29, Neil McBain 1929–37, Bill Findlay 1938–47, Jack Bray 1947–48, Eddie Hapgood 1948–50, Ron Gray 1950–51, Haydn Green 1951–52, Len Goulden 1952–55 (GM to 1956), Johnny Paton 1955–56, Neil McBain 1956–59, Ron Burgess 1959–63, Bill McGarry 1963–64, Ken Furphy 1964–71, George Kirby 1971–73, Mike Keen 1973–77, Graham Taylor 1977–87, Dave Bassett 1987–88, Steve Harrison 1988–90, Colin Lee 1990, Steve Perryman November 1990–.

Player and Position	Ht	Wt	Date	Birth Place	Source	Clubs	League App	Gls
David Byrne (To St Johnstone January 1993)	5 8	10 09	5 3 61	London	Kingstonian	Gillingham	23	3
						Millwall	63	6
						Cambridge U (loan)	4	—
						Blackburn R (loan)	4	—
						Plymouth Arg	59	2
						Bristol R (loan)	2	—
						Watford	17	2
						Reading (loan)	7	2
						Fulham (loan)	5	—
Ken Charlery	6 1	12 07	28 11 64	Stepney	Beckton U	Maidstone U	59	11
						Peterborough U	51	19
						Watford	32	11
Bruce Dyer			13 4 75	Ilford	Trainee	Watford	2	—
Paul Furlong	6 0	12 11	1 1 68	London	Enfield	Coventry C	37	4
						Watford	41	19
Joe Gallen*	5 11	11 08	2 9 72	Hammersmith	Trainee	Watford	—	—
						Exeter C (loan)	6	—
Alex Inglethorpe	5 10	11 07	14 11 71	Epsom	School	Watford	3	—
Lee Nogan	5 10	11 00	21 5 69	Cardiff	Apprentice	Oxford U	64	10
						Brentford (loan)	11	2
						Southend U (loan)	6	1
						Watford	65	16
Kevin Slinn			2 9 74	Northampton	Trainee	Watford	—	—
Rod Thomas*	5 6	10 10	10 10 70	London	Trainee	Watford	84	9
						Gillingham (loan)	8	1

Trainees
Birch, Terry; Boachie, Nana; Gould, Darran; Hutchins, Neil; Parkin, Steven C; Simpson, Colin R; Vier, Matthew P; Walters, Scott; Willingham, Lee R.

Associated Schoolboys
Andrews, Wayne M; Belgrave, Kevin; Buoy, Nicholas; Carter, John A; Donald, Neil G. M; Easton, Clint; Grieves, Daniel; Grime, Dominic R; Grime, Nicholas G; Jennings, Paul; Johnson, Andrew; Johnson, Christopher; Moody, Tom; Morrissey, Robert E; Palmer, Glenn S; Pluck, Colin I; Rogers, David A; Rooney, Mark J; Sargent, David G; Smith, Dean W.

Associated Schoolboys who have accepted the club's offer of a Traineeship/Contract
Allen, Mark J; Calderhead, Robert; Connolly, David; Fitzgerald, Gary; Marshall, Robert.

542

WEST BROMWICH ALBION 1992-93. *Back row (left to right):* Ian Hamilton, Carl Heggs, Paul Raven, Stuart Naylor, Gary Strodder, Daryl Burgess, Bob Taylor.
Centre row: Danny Thomas, Simon Hodson, Roy Hunter, Wayne Fereday, Darren Bradley, Steve Lilwall, Dennis Mortimer.
Front row: Bernard McNally, Gary Robson, Kwame Ampadu, Keith Burkinshaw, Ossie Ardiles, Craig Shakespeare, Stacy Coldicott, Gary Hackett.

Division 1   **WEST BROMWICH ALBION**

The Hawthorns, West Bromwich B71 4LF. Telephone 021–525 8888 (all Depts). Fax: 021–553 6634.

Ground capacity: 31,700 (10,865 seats).

Record attendance: 64,815 v Arsenal, FA Cup 6th rd, 6 March 1937.

Record receipts: £174,235.95 v Stoke C, Div 2, 23 January 1993.

Pitch measurements: 115yd × 75yd.

President: Sir F. A. Millichip. *Vice-president:* John G. Silk LL.B (Lond).

Chairman: T. J. Summers. *Vice-chairman:* A. B. Hale.

Directors: J. W. Brandrick, A. B. Hale, C. M. Stapleton, B. Hurst, T. K. Guy.

Manager: Keith Burkinshaw. *Assistant Manager:* Dennis Mortimer. *Reserve team coach:* John Trewick.

Physio: Danny Thomas. *Secretary:* Dr. J. J. Evans BA, PHD. (Wales).

Club Statistician: Tony Matthews. *Commercial Manager:* Tom Cardall.

Year Formed: 1879. *Turned Professional:* 1885. *Ltd Co.:* 1892.

Previous Name: 1879–81, West Bromwich Strollers.

Club Nicknames: 'Throstles', 'Baggies', 'Albion'.

Previous Grounds: 1879, Coopers Hill; 1879, Dartmouth Park; 1881, Bunns Field, Walsall Street; 1882, Four Acres (Dartmouth Cricket Club); 1885, Stoney Lane; 1900, The Hawthorns.

Record League Victory: 12–0 v Darwen, Division 1, 4 April 1892 – Reader; Horton, McCulloch; Reynolds (2), Perry, Groves; Bassett (3), McLeod, Nicholls (1), Pearson (4), Geddes (1). (1 og).

Record Cup Victory: 10–1 v Chatham (away), FA Cup, 3rd rd, 2 March 1889 – Roberts; Horton, Green; Timmins (1), Charles Perry, Horton; Bassett (2), Perry (1), Bayliss (2), Pearson, Wilson (3). (1 og).

Record Defeat: 3–10 v Stoke C, Division 1, 4 February 1937.

Most League Points (2 for a win): 60, Division 1, 1919–20.

Most League Points (3 for a win): 85, Division 2, 1992–93.

Most League Goals: 105, Division 2, 1929–30.

Highest League Scorer in Season: William 'Ginger' Richardson, 39, Division 1, 1935–36.

Most League Goals in Total Aggregate: Tony Brown, 218, 1963–79.

Most Capped Player: Stuart Williams, 33 (43), Wales.

Most League Appearances: Tony Brown, 574, 1963–80.

Record Transfer Fee Received: £1,500,000 from Manchester U for Bryan Robson, October 1981.

Record Transfer Fee Paid: £748,000 to Manchester C for Peter Barnes, July 1979.

Football League Record: 1888 Founder Member of Football League; 1901–02 Division 2; 1902–04 Division 1; 1904–11 Division 2; 1911–27 Division 1; 1927–31 Division 2; 1931–38 Division 1; 1938–49 Division 2; 1949–73 Division 1; 1973–76 Division 2; 1976–86 Division 1; 1986–91 Division 2; 1991–92 Division 3; 1992–93 Division 2; 1933– Division 1.

Honours: Football League: Division 1 – Champions 1919–20; Runners-up 1924–25, 1953–54; Division 2 – Champions 1901–02, 1910–11; Runners-up 1930–31, 1948–49; Promoted to Division 1 1975–76 (3rd). *FA Cup:* Winners 1888, 1892, 1931, 1954, 1968; Runners-up 1886, 1887, 1895, 1912, 1935. *Football League Cup:* Winners 1965–66; Runners-up 1966–67, 1969–70. **European Competitions:** *European Cup-Winners' Cup:* 1968–69; *European Fairs Cup:* 1966–67; *UEFA Cup:* 1978–79, 1979–80, 1981–82.

WEST BROMWICH ALBION 1992—93 LEAGUE RECORD

Match No.	Date	Venue	Opponents	Result	H/T Score	Lg. Pos.	Goalscorers	Attendance
1	Aug 15	H	Blackpool	W 3-1	2-1	—	Taylor 2, McNally	16,527
2	22	A	Huddersfield T	W 1-0	1-0	1	Garner	7947
3	29	H	Bournemouth	W 2-1	1-0	1	Taylor, Shakespeare (pen)	12,563
4	Sept 2	H	Stockport Co	W 3-0	3-0	—	Garner 2, Hamilton	12,305
5	5	A	Fulham	D 1-1	1-0	1	Taylor	9143
6	9	H	Reading	W 3-0	1-0	—	Garner, Taylor, Shakespeare	13,164
7	15	A	Bolton W	W 2-0	0-0	—	Taylor 2	8531
8	19	A	Stoke C	L 3-4	1-1	1	Taylor 2, Garner	18,764
9	26	H	Exeter C	W 2-0	1-0	1	Hamilton, McNally	14,676
10	Oct 3	A	Burnley	L 1-2	0-1	1	Garner	14,796
11	10	H	Port Vale	L 0-1	0-0	1		17,512
12	17	A	Wigan Ath	L 0-1	0-1	2		4408
13	24	H	Rotherham U	D 2-2	2-2	3	Taylor, Donovan	13,170
14	31	A	Hull C	W 2-1	1-0	1	Garner, Bradley	5443
15	Nov 3	H	Hartlepool U	W 3-1	1-1	—	Taylor, Blissett, Robson	13,046
16	7	A	Leyton Orient	L 0-2	0-0	3		8640
17	21	H	Bradford C	D 1-1	1-1	3	Raven	15,416
18	28	A	Preston NE	D 1-1	0-1	4	Robson	6306
19	Dec 12	A	Swansea C	D 0-0	0-0	4		5610
20	20	H	Mansfield T	W 2-0	0-0	—	McNally, Dickens	13,134
21	26	H	Chester C	W 2-0	1-0		Raven 2	15,209
22	28	A	Plymouth Arg	D 0-0	0-0	2		11,370
23	Jan 9	H	Bolton W	W 3-1	1-1	2	Hamilton, Strodder, Taylor	14,581
24	16	A	Exeter C	W 3-2	0-1	2	Heggs, Hackett, Hamilton (pen)	5437
25	23	H	Stoke C	L 1-2	1-1	3	Taylor	29,341
26	26	A	Bournemouth	W 1-0	1-0	—	Speedie	5687
27	30	H	Huddersfield T	D 2-2	0-0	2	Donovan, Speedie	13,667
28	Feb 6	A	Blackpool	L 1-2	1-1	2	Taylor	9386
29	13	H	Fulham	W 4-0	2-0	3	Taylor (pen), Hamilton, Mellon, Fereday	12,859
30	20	A	Stockport Co	L 1-5	1-1	4	Taylor	7181
31	27	A	Port Vale	L 1-2	1-0	4	Hamilton	13,291
32	Mar 6	H	Burnley	W 2-0	1-0	4	Garner, Taylor	15,722
33	10	A	Brighton & HA	L 1-3	0-0	—	Taylor (pen)	7440
34	13	H	Leyton Orient	W 2-0	0-0	3	Burgess, Donovan	15,023
35	20	A	Hartlepool U	D 2-2	1-1	4	Hamilton, Raven	4174
36	24	H	Preston NE	W 3-2	2-1	—	Taylor 2, Mellon	13,270
37	28	A	Bradford C	D 2-2	1-1	—	Taylor (pen), Hunt	6627
38	Apr 3	H	Brighton & HA	W 3-1	0-0	4	Hunt 3	13,002
39	7	H	Swansea C	W 3-0	2-0	—	Taylor 2, Hunt	13,401
40	10	A	Chester C	W 3-1	1-0	3	Hunt, Raven, Donovan	4812
41	12	A	Plymouth Arg	L 2-5	1-2	4	Taylor, Donovan	16,130
42	17	A	Mansfield T	W 3-0	2-0	3	Hunt, Taylor, Heggs	6659
43	21	A	Reading	D 1-1	1-1	—	Taylor	8026
44	24	H	Wigan Ath	W 5-1	1-1	3	Taylor 2, Mellon, Donovan, Raven	14,867
45	May 1	A	Rotherham U	W 2-0	0-0	4	Raven, Taylor	8059
46	8	H	Hull C	W 3-1	1-0	4	Taylor, Hunt 2	20,122

Final League Position: 4

GOALSCORERS

League (88): Taylor 30 (3 pens), Hunt 9, Garner 8, Hamilton 7 (1 pen), Raven 7, Donovan 6, McNally 3, Mellon 3, Heggs 2, Robson 2, Shakespeare 2 (1 pen), Speedie 2, Blissett 1, Bradley 1, Burgess 1, Dickens 1, Fereday 1, Hackett 1, Strodder 1.
Coca Cola Cup (1): Taylor 1.
FA Cup (11): Donovan 3, Taylor 3, Bradley 1, Hamilton 1, McNally 1, Raven 1, Robson 1.

Naylor 32	Fereday 13 + 3	Lilwall 44	Hunter 1	Strodder 26 + 3	Shakespeare 12 + 2	Garner 21 + 4	Hamilton 46	Taylor 46	McNally 39 + 1	Robson 16 + 6	Hodson 1 + 1	Bradley 41 + 1	Ampadu 1 + 9	Hackett 4 + 6	Raven 43 + 1	Coldicott 10 + 4	Heggs — + 17	Donovan 30 + 2	Blissett 3	Burgess 17 + 1	Reid 10 + 5	Dickens 3	Speedie 7	Lange 14	Mellon 15 + 2	Hunt 9 + 1	Darton 2	Match No.
1	2	3	4	5	6	7	8	9	10	11	12																	1
1		3		5	6	7	8	9	10	11					4	12		2										2
1	2	3		5	6	10	8	9				11			4	14	7	12										3
1		3		5		7	8	9	10			11			4	6		2										4
1		3		5	12	7	8	9	10			11			4	6		2										5
1		3		5	6	7	8	9				11			4	10		2										6
1		3		5	6	7	8	9	10	11					4	12		2	14									7
1	14	3			6	7	8	9	10	11					4	12		5	2									8
1	2	3			6	7	8	9	10	11					4	12		5	14									9
1	2	3			6	7	8	9	10	11					4	12		5	14									10
1	2	3			6	7	8	9	10	11					4	12		5	14									11
1		3			6		8	9	10			11			4	12	7	5	2									12
1		3			14	6	8	9	10						4	12	7	5	2	11								13
1	14	3			6	7	8	9	10		12	11			4			5	2									14
1	2	3			6	7	8	9	10		12				4			5		11	14							15
1		3			6		8	9	10						4		7	5	2	11								16
1		3			6	7	8	9	10						4			5	2	11								17
1	14	3			6	7	8	9	10		12				4			5	2	11								18
1		3			6	7	8	9	10		12				4			5			2	11						19
1		3			6		8	9	10						4		7	5			2	11						20
1		3			6	12	8	9	10	14					4		7	5			2	11						21
1		3			6		8	9	10			11		14	4	12	7	5	2									22
1	2	3			6		8	9	10		12				4	14	7	5		11								23
1	2	3			6		8	9	10		12				4	14	7	5		11								24
1	2	3			6		8	9	10						4	12	14	5		11			7					25
1	2	3			6		8	9	10						4	11		5			12		7					26
	2	3			6		8	9	10						4	12	14	5		11			7		1			27
1	2	3			6		8	9	10						4	12		5		11			7					28
1	2	3			6		8	9	10						4		14	5		11			7		12			29
1		3			6		8	9	10		2				4	12		5		11			7					30
1		3			6		8	9			2				4	12	14	5		11			7			10		31
1		3				7	8	9							4	11		5	2	6	12					10		32
1		3				7	8	9							4	11	14	5	2	6	12					10		33
		3			12	7	8	9							4	11		5		6	2				1	10		34
		3			12	7	8	9							4	11	14	5		6	2				1	10		35
		3				7	8	9							4	11	14	5	2	6	12				1	10		36
		3				7	8	9	10						4	11		5		6	2			14	1	12		37
		3			14		8	9							4	11		5	2	6	12		7		1	10		38
		3			14		8	9							4	11		5	2	6	12		7		1	10		39
		3					8	9							4	11	14	5	2	6	12		7		1	10		40
		3					8	9							4	11	14	5	2	6	12		7		1	10		41
		3					8	9			12				4	11	14	5	2	6			7		1	10		42
		3					8	9							4	11	14	5	2	6	12		7		1	10		43
		3					8	9							4	11		5	2	6	12		7		1	10		44
		3					8	9							4	11	14	5	2	6	12		7		1	10		45
		3					8	9							4	11		5	2	6			7		1	10		46

Coca Cola Cup	First Round	Plymouth Arg (h)	1-0
		(a)	0-2
FA Cup	First Round	Aylesbury (h)	8-0
	Second Round	Wycombe W (a)	2-2
		(h)	1-0
	Third Round	West Ham U (h)	0-2

WEST BROMWICH ALBION

Player and Position	Ht	Wt	Date	Birth Place	Source	Clubs	League App	Gls
Goalkeepers								
Tony Lange	6 0	12 09	10 12 64	London	Apprentice	Charlton Ath	12	—
						Aldershot (loan)	7	—
						Aldershot	125	—
						Wolverhampton W	8	—
						Aldershot (loan)	2	—
						Torquay U (loan)	1	—
						Portsmouth (loan)	—	—
						WBA	14	—
Stuart Naylor	6 4	12 02	6 12 62	Wetherby	Yorkshire A	Lincoln C	49	—
						Peterborough U (loan)	8	—
						Crewe Alex (loan)	38	—
						Crewe Alex (loan)	17	—
						WBA	266	—
Defenders								
Darren Bradley	5 7	11 12	24 11 65	Birmingham	Apprentice	Aston Villa	20	—
						WBA	214	7
Daryl Burgess	5 11	12 03	20 4 71	Birmingham	Trainee	WBA	113	3
Stacy Coldicott	5 11	11 02	29 4 74	Worcester	Trainee	WBA	14	—
Scott Darton			27 3 75	Ipswich	Trainee	WBA	2	—
Steve Lilwall	5 11	12 00	5 2 70	Solihull	Kidderminster H	WBA	44	—
Matthew Nelson*	5 8	10 04	15 4 74	Bilston	Trainee	WBA	—	—
Paul Raven	6 0	12 03	28 7 70	Salisbury	School	Doncaster R	52	4
						WBA	74	8
						Doncaster R (loan)	7	—
Nicky Reid	5 10	12 00	30 10 60	Ormston	Apprentice	Manchester C	217	2
						Blackburn R	174	9
						Bristol C (loan)	4	—
						WBA	15	—
Marc Sinfield*	6 2	13 06	24 3 74	Herts	Trainee	WBA	—	—
Gary Strodder	6 1	12 06	1 4 65	Leeds	Apprentice	Lincoln C	132	6
						West Ham U	65	2
						WBA	100	5
Midfield								
Wayne Fereday	5 9	11 08	16 6 63	Warley	Apprentice	QPR	197	21
						Newcastle U	33	—
						Bournemouth	23	—
						WBA	38	3
Alex Grace‡	5 7	10 10	20 3 74	Dumbarton	Trainee	WBA	—	—
Roy Hunter	5 9	11 00	29 10 73	Cleveland		WBA	7	1
Bernard McNally	5 7	10 12	17 2 63	Shrewsbury	Apprentice	Shrewsbury T	282	23
						WBA	127	10
Michael Mellon	5 8	11 03	18 3 72	Paisley	Trainee	Bristol C	35	1
						WBA	17	3
Gary Robson*	5 7	10 12 -	6 7 65	Durham	Apprentice	WBA	218	28
Craig Shakespeare	5 10	12 05	26 10 63	Birmingham	Apprentice	Walsall	284	45
						Sheffield W	17	—
						WBA	112	12
Forwards								
Kwame Ampadu	5 10	10 13	20 12 70	Bradford	Trainee	Arsenal	2	—
						Plymouth Arg (loan)	6	1
						WBA (loan)	7	1
						WBA	31	3

WEST BROMWICH ALBION

Colours: Navy blue and white striped shirts, white shorts, blue and white stockings. **Change colours:** Green & yellow striped shirts, green shorts, yellow stockings.

Foundation: There is a well known story that when employees of Salter's Spring Works in West Bromwich decided to form a football club in 1879, they had to send someone to the nearby Association Football stronghold of Wednesbury to purchase a football. A weekly subscription of 2d (less than 1p) was imposed and the name of the new club was West Bromwich Strollers.

First Football League game: 8 September, 1888, Football League, v Stoke (a) W 2-0 – Roberts; J. Horton, Green; E. Horton, Perry, Bayliss; Bassett, Woodhall (1), Hendry, Pearson, Wilson (1).

Did you know: West Bromwich Albion were the first British club to win a match in the then Soviet Union. In June 1957 they drew 1-1 with Zenit Leningrad, beat Dynamo Tbilisi 3-0 and CSKA Moscow 4-2.

Managers (and Secretary-Managers)
Louis Ford 1890–92*, Henry Jackson 1892–94*, Edward Stephenson 1894–95*, Clement Keys 1895–96*, Frank Heaven 1896–1902*, Fred Everiss 1902–48, Jack Smith 1948–52, Jesse Carver 1952, Vic Buckingham 1953–59, Gordon Clark 1959–61, Archie Macaulay 1961–63, Jimmy Hagan 1963–67, Alan Ashman 1967–71, Don Howe 1971–75, Johnny Giles 1975–77, Ronnie Allen 1977, Ron Atkinson 1978–81, Ronnie Allen 1981–82, Ron Wylie 1982–84, Johnny Giles 1984–85, Ron Saunders 1986–87, Ron Atkinson 1987–88, Brian Talbot 1988–91, Bobby Gould 1991–92, Ossie Ardiles 1992–93, Keith Burkinshaw June 1993–.

Player and Position	Ht	Wt	Date	Birth Place	Source	Clubs	League App	Gls
Kevin Donovan	5 7	10 10	17 12 71	Halifax	Trainee	Huddersfield T	20	1
						Halifax T (loan)	6	—
						WBA	32	6
Simon Garner	5 9	11 12	23 11 59	Boston	Apprentice	Blackburn R	484	168
						WBA	25	8
Gary Hackett	5 7	11 03	11 10 62	Stourbridge	Bromsgrove R	Shrewsbury T	150	17
						Aberdeen	15	—
						Stoke C	73	7
						WBA	44	3
Ian Hamilton	5 9	11 03	14 12 67	Stevenage	Apprentice	Southampton	—	—
						Cambridge U	24	1
						Scunthorpe U	145	18
						WBA	46	7
Kirk Hammond‡	6 0	13 00	6 12 72	Ipswich	Trainee	WBA	—	—
Carl Heggs	6 0	11 08	11 10 70	Leicester	Paget R	WBA	20	2
James McCue			29 6 75	Glasgow	Trainee	WBA	—	—
Bob Taylor	5 10	11 09	3 2 67	Horden	Horden CW	Leeds U	42	9
						Bristol C	106	50
						WBA	65	38

Trainees
Annan, Tony; Coll, Damien M; Davies, David; Germaine, Gary; Godfrey, Christopher P; Harnett, David R; Harris, Lee P; Harris, Richard J; Hicks, Daniel; Leonard, Matthew; Love, Brett A; Marshall, Daniel P; Owen, Darren L; Skitt, Craig; West, Simon J.

Associated Schoolboys
Boughton, Carl; Cattell, Mark P; Cleverley, Jay; Cornfield, James; Dobson, Ryan A; Enever, Richard; Hughes, Andrew W; Jackson, David C; Knight, Lee K; Lyon, Gary S; Morris, Mark; O'Brien, Scott; Tranter, Carl; Turner, Brendon; Williams, Richard; Wills, James D.

Associated Schoolboys who have accepted the club's offer of a Traineeship/Contract
Costigan, Glyn B; Cresswell, Mark A; Cutler, Neil A; Dew, Robert A; Simmonds, Robert J; Taylor, Stuart G.

548

WEST HAM UNITED 1992–93 *Back row (left to right):* Tim Breacker, Tony Gale, Steven Banks, Alvin Martin, Mitchell Thomas, Ludek Miklosko, Colin Foster, Martin Allen.
Centre row: Trevor Morley, Simon Clarke, Kenny Brown, George Parris, Steve Potts, Matthew Rush, Clive Allen.
Front row: Kevin Keen, Mark Robson, Dean Martin, Julian Dicks, Ian Bishop, Peter Butler, Matthew Holmes.

FA Premier

WEST HAM UNITED

Boleyn Ground, Green Street, Upton Park, London E13.
Telephone 081 472–2740. General: 081 472–5756. Fax 081 471–
2997. Membership Office: 081 552 7640. Commercial: 081 475–
0555. Hammer Line: 081 472–3322. Dial-a-seat: 081 472–2422.
Football in the Community: 0898 121165 Clubcall.

Ground capacity: 22,503.

Record attendance: 42,322 v Tottenham H, Division 1,
17 October 1970.

Record receipts: £146,074 v Tottenham H, League Cup 5th rd,
27 January 1987.

Pitch measurements: 112yd × 72yd.

Chairman: T. W. Brown FCIS, ATII, FCCA. *Vice-chairman:* M. W.
Cearns ACIB.

Directors: L. C. Cearns, W. F. Cearns, C. J. Warner, P. J. Storrie (managing).

Manager: Billy Bonds MBE. *Assistant Manager:* Harry Redknapp. *Coaches:* Paul Hilton,
Tony Carr. *Physio:* John Green BSC (hons) MCSP, SRP.

Secretary: Tom Finn. *Commercial Manager:* Peter Storrie.

Year Formed: 1895. *Turned Professional:* 1900. *Ltd Co.:* 1900.

Previous Name: Thames Ironworks FC, 1895–1900.

Club Nickname: 'The Hammers'.

Previous Ground: Memorial Recreation Ground, Canning Town: 1904 Boleyn Ground.

Record League Victory: 8–0 v Rotherham U, Division 2, 8 March 1958 – Gregory; Bond,
Wright; Malcolm, Brown, Lansdowne; Grice, Smith (2), Keeble (2), Dick (4), Musgrove. 8–
0 v Sunderland, Division 1, 19 October 1968 – Ferguson; Bonds, Charles; Peters,
Stephenson, Moore (1); Redknapp, Boyce, Brooking (1), Hurst (6), Sissons.

Record Cup Victory: 10–0 v Bury, League Cup, 2nd rd (2nd leg), 25 October 1983 – Parkes;
Stewart (1), Walford, Bonds (Orr), Martin (1), Devonshire (2), Allen, Cottee (4),
Swindlehurst, Brooking (2), Pike.

Record Defeat: 2–8 v Blackburn R, Division 1, 26 December 1963.

Most League Points (2 for a win): 66, Division 2, 1980–81.

Most League Points (3 for a win): 88, Division 1, 1992–93.

Most League Goals: 101, Division 2, 1957–58.

Highest League Scorer in Season: Vic Watson, 41, Division 1, 1929–30.

Most League Goals in Total Aggregate: Vic Watson, 306, 1920–35.

Most Capped Player: Bobby Moore, 108, England.

Most League Appearances: Billy Bonds, 663, 1967–88.

Record Transfer Fee Received: £2,000,000 from Everton for Tony Cottee, July 1988.

Record Transfer Fee Paid: £1,200,000 to Celtic for Frank McAvennie, March 1989.

Football League Record: 1919 Elected to Division 2; 1923–32 Division 1; 1932–58 Division
2; 1958–78 Division 1; 1978–81 Division 2; 1981–89 Division 1; 1989–91 Division 2; 1991–
93 Division 1; 1993– FA Premier League.

Honours: Football League: Division 1 best season: 3rd, 1985–86; Division 2 – Champions
1957–58, 1980–81; Runners-up 1922–23, 1990–91. *FA Cup:* Winners 1964, 1975, 1980;
Runners-up 1922–23. *Football League Cup:* Runners-up 1966, 1981. **European
Competitions:** *European Cup-Winners' Cup:* 1964–65 (winners), 1965–66, 1975–76 (runners-
up), 1980–81.

WEST HAM UNITED 1992—93 LEAGUE RECORD

Match No.	Date	Venue	Opponents	Result	H/T Score	Lg. Pos.	Goalscorers	Atten dance
1	Aug 16	A	Barnsley	W 1-0	1-0	—	Allen C	6791
2	22	H	Charlton Ath	L 0-1	0-1	17		17,054
3	29	A	Newcastle U	L 0-2	0-2	19		29,855
4	Sept 5	H	Watford	W 2-1	0-0	13	Allen M, Allen C	11,921
5	12	H	Peterborough U	W 3-1	3-1	7	Morley, Allen M, Keen	10,657
6	15	A	Bristol C	W 5-1	3-0	—	Robson, Morley 2, Allen C 2	14,130
7	20	H	Derby Co	D 1-1	0-1	—	Morley	11,493
8	27	A	Portsmouth	W 1-0	1-0	—	Allen C	12,158
9	Oct 4	A	Wolverhampton W	D 0-0	0-0	—		14,391
10	11	H	Sunderland	W 6-0	3-0	—	Keen, Morley, Allen M, Martin, Robson 2	10,326
11	17	A	Bristol R	W 4-0	3-0	2	Morley, Dicks (pen), Keen, Allen C	6187
12	24	H	Swindon T	L 0-1	0-0	3		17,842
13	31	A	Cambridge U	L 1-2	0-1	4	Morley	7214
14	Nov 3	A	Grimsby T	D 1-1	0-0	—	Morley	9119
15	7	H	Notts Co	W 2-0	1-0	4	Allen C, Morley	12,345
16	15	A	Millwall	L 1-2	0-1	—	Robson	12,445
17	21	H	Oxford U	W 5-3	3-1	4	Allen C, Breacker, Dicks 2, Morley	11,842
18	28	H	Birmingham C	W 3-1	1-1	3	Allen C 2, Morley	15,004
19	Dec 4	A	Tranmere R	L 2-5	1-1	—	Morley, Allen C	11,782
20	12	H	Southend U	W 2-0	1-0	3	Morley, Allen C	15,739
21	20	A	Brentford	D 0-0	0-0	—		11,912
22	26	A	Charlton Ath	D 1-1	1-0	3	Dicks	8337
23	28	H	Luton T	D 2-2	0-0	3	Dicks (pen), Breacker	18,786
24	Jan 10	A	Derby Co	W 2-0	2-0	—	Robson, Morley	13,737
25	16	H	Portsmouth	W 2-0	1-0	3	Morley, Foster	18,127
26	27	H	Bristol C	W 2-0	0-0	—	Morley, Robson	12,118
27	30	A	Leicester C	W 2-1	1-1	2	Robson, Gale	18,838
28	Feb 6	H	Barnsley	D 1-1	1-1	2	Jones	14,101
29	9	H	Peterborough U	W 2-1	2-1	—	Butler, Jones	12,537
30	13	A	Watford	W 2-1	1-0	2	Robson, Keen	13,115
31	21	H	Newcastle U	D 0-0	0-0	—		24,159
32	27	A	Sunderland	D 0-0	0-0	2		19,068
33	Mar 6	H	Wolverhampton W	W 3-1	0-0	2	Morley, Dicks (pen), Mountfield (og)	24,679
34	9	H	Grimsby T	W 2-1	2-0	—	Dicks 2	13,170
35	13	A	Notts Co	L 0-1	0-0	2		10,272
36	20	H	Tranmere R	W 2-0	0-0	2	Dicks 2 (2 pens)	16,369
37	23	A	Oxford U	L 0-1	0-0	—		9506
38	28	H	Millwall	D 2-2	2-1	—	Keen, Morley	15,723
39	Apr 3	A	Birmingham C	W 2-1	0-1	2	Brown, Bishop	19,053
40	7	A	Southend U	L 0-1	0-1	—		12,813
41	11	H	Leicester C	W 3-0	2-0	3	Speedie 2, Keen	13,951
42	13	A	Luton T	L 0-2	0-0	—		10,959
43	17	H	Brentford	W 4-0	1-0	3	Butler, Keen, Morley, Allen M	16,522
44	24	H	Bristol R	W 2-1	0-0	3	Dicks (pen), Speedie	16,682
45	May 2	A	Swindon T	W 3-1	1-0	—	Morley, Allen C, Brown	17,004
46	8	H	Cambridge U	W 2-0	0-0	2	Speedie, Allen C	27,399

Final League Position: 2

GOALSCORERS

League (81): Morley 20, Allen C 14, Dicks 11 (6 pens), Robson 8, Keen 7, Allen M 4, Speedie 4, Breacker 2, Brown 2, Butler 2, Jones 2, Bishop 1, Foster 1, Gale 1, Martin 1, own goal 1.
Coca Cola Cup (0).
FA Cup (3): Allen C 1, Morley 1 (pen), Robson 1.

Miklosko 46	Breacker 39	Dicks 34	Potts 46	Martin A 23	Parris 10 + 6	Bishop 15 + 7	Butler 39	Small 5 + 4	Allen C 25 + 2	Keen 46	Robson 41 + 3	Gale 21 + 2	Holmes 6 + 12	Allen M 33 + 1	Morley 41	Thomas 3	Brown 13 + 2	Clarke — + 1	Foster 3 + 3	Bunbury 2 + 2	Jones 4 + 2	Speedie 11	Match No.
1	2	3	4	5	6	7	8	9	*10*	11	12	14											1
1	2	3	4	5	6	*7*	8	9	10	11	12												2
1	2	3	4	5		7	8	12	10	11				6	9								3
1	2	3	4	5	12		8		10	11	*7*			6	9								4
1	2		4	5			8	12	10	11	7			6	9		3						5
1	2		4	5			8	12	10	11	*7*			6	9		3						6
1	2		4	5			8	12	10	11	*7*			6	9		3						7
1	2	3	4	5			8		10	11	7		12	6	9								8
1	2	3	4	5			8		*10*	11	7	14	12	6	9								9
1	2	3	4	5			8		10	11	7			6	9								10
1	2	3	4	5			8		10	11	7			6	9								11
1	2		4	5	3		8		10	11	7			6	9								12
1	2		4	5	3		8		10	11	7			6	9								13
1	2		4	5	3		8		10	11	*7*		12	6	9								14
1	2		4	5			8		10	11	7			6	9		3						15
1	2		4	5	6				10	11	7		8		9		3		12				16
1	2	3	4	5	6				10	11	7		8		9		12						17
1	2	3	4		6	12			10	11	7		8		9		5						18
1	2	3	4	5	6	12			10	11	7		*8*		9		14						19
1	2	3	4	5	6	12			10	11	7		8		9								20
1	2	3	4	5			8		10	11	7			6	9				12				21
1	2	3	4	5			6		10	11	7		8		9				12				22
1	2	3	4	5			8		10	11	7			6	9								23
1	2	3	4	5	12		8		10	11	7			6	9				14				24
1	2	3	4		12		8		*10*	11	7		14	6	9		5						25
1	2		4		12		8			11	7	5	14	6	9		3		*10*				26
1	2		4		12		8			11	7	5	10	6	9		3		14				27
1	2	3	4				8			11	7	5		6	9				10				28
1	2	3	4				8			11	7	5	12	6	9				10				29
1	2	3	4			14	8			11	7	5	12	6	9				*10*				30
1		3	4			10	8			11	7	5		6	9		2		12				31
1		3	4		14	6	8			11	7	5	12		9		2		*10*				32
1		3	4			6	8		10	11	7	5	12		9		2						33
1		3	4			12	8		10	11	7	5		6	9		2						34
1		3	4			12	8		10	11	7	5		6	9		2						35
1		3	4				8			11	7	5	12	6	10		2					9	36
1		3	4				8			11	12	5	7	6	10		2					9	37
1	2		4			6	8			11	7	5			10		3					9	38
1	2		4			6	8			11	7	5	12				3		14		*10*	9	39
1	2	3	4			6	8			11	7	5							10			9	40
1	2	3	4			6	8			11	7	5		10								9	41
1	2	3	4				8			11		5	12	7	10							9	42
1	2	3	4				8			11	7	5		6	10							9	43
1	2	3	4			12	8			11	7	5		6	10							9	44
1	2	3	4			6	8		12	11	7	5		*10*			14					9	45
1	2	3	4			6	8		12	11	7	5		14	10							*9*	46

Coca Cola Cup	Second Round	Crewe Alex (h)	0-0
		(a)	0-2
FA Cup	Third Round	WBA (a)	2-0
	Fourth Round	Barnsley (a)	1-4

WEST HAM UNITED

Player and Position	Ht	Wt	Date	Birth Place	Source	Clubs	League App	Gls
Goalkeepers								
Steven Banks*	5 11	11 04	9 2 72	Hillingdon	Trainee	West Ham U	—	—
Ludek Miklosko	6 5	14 00	9 12 61	Ostrava	Banik Ostrava	West Ham U	146	—
Defenders								
Michael Basham	5 10	11 12	27 9 73	Barking	Trainee	West Ham U	—	—
Tim Breacker	5 11	13 00	2 7 65	Bicester		Luton T	210	3
						West Ham U	97	5
Kenny Brown	5 8	11 06	11 7 67	Barking	Apprentice	Norwich C	25	—
						Plymouth Arg	126	4
						West Ham U	42	5
Julian Dicks	5 10	13 00	8 8 68	Bristol	Apprentice	Birmingham C	89	1
						West Ham U	152	29
Colin Foster	6 4	14 01	16 7 64	Chislehurst	Apprentice	Orient	174	10
						Nottingham F	72	5
						West Ham U	88	5
Tony Gale	6 1	13 07	19 11 59	London	Apprentice	Fulham	277	19
						West Ham U	268	5
Paul Marquis	6 1	12 00	29 8 72	Enfield	Trainee	West Ham U	—	—
Alvin Martin	6 1	13 07	29 7 58	Bootle	Apprentice	West Ham U	424	25
Steven Potts	5 7	10 11	7 5 67	Hartford (USA)	Apprentice	West Ham U	195	1
Mitchell Thomas	6 2	12 00	2 10 64	Luton	Apprentice	Luton T	107	1
						Tottenham H	157	6
						West Ham U	38	3
David White‡			31 3 74	Thurrock	Trainee	West Ham U	—	—
Midfield								
Martin Allen	5 10	11 00	14 8 65	Reading	School	QPR	136	16
						West Ham U	132	16
Ian Bishop	5 9	10 12	29 5 65	Liverpool	Apprentice	Everton	1	—
						Crewe Alex (loan)	4	—
						Carlisle U	132	14
						Bournemouth	44	2
						Manchester C	19	2
						West Ham U	120	8
Peter Butler	5 9	11 02	27 8 66	Halifax	Apprentice	Huddersfield T	5	—
						Cambridge U (loan)	14	1
						Bury	11	—
						Cambridge U	55	9
						Southend U	142	9
						Huddersfield T (loan)	7	—
						West Ham U	39	2
Matthew Holland	5 9	11 00	11 4 74	Bury	Trainee	West Ham U	—	—
Kevin Keen	5 8	11 00	25 2 67	Amersham	Apprentice	West Ham U	219	21
Matthew Rush	5 11	12 10	6 8 71	Dalston	Trainee	West Ham U	15	2
						Cambridge U (loan)	10	—
Danny Williamson	5 10	11 06	5 12 73	London	Trainee	West Ham U	—	—
Forwards								
Clive Allen	5 10	12 03	20 5 61	London	Apprentice	QPR	49	32
						Arsenal	—	—
						Crystal Palace	25	9
						QPR	87	40
						Tottenham H	105	60
					Bordeaux	Manchester C	53	16
						Chelsea	16	7
						West Ham U	31	15

WEST HAM UNITED

Colours: Claret shirts, white shorts, white stockings. **Change colours:** Blue shirts, blue shorts, blue stockings.

Foundation: Thames Ironworks FC was formed by employees of this shipbuilding yard in 1895 and entered the FA Cup in their initial season at Chatham and the London League in their second. Short of funds, the club was wound up in June 1900 and relaunched a month later as West Ham United. Connection with the Ironworks was not finally broken until four years later.

First Football League game: 30 August, 1919, Division 2, v Lincoln City (h) D 1-1 – Hufton; Cope, Lee; Lane, Fenwick, McCrae; D. Smith, Moyes (1), Puddefoot, Morris, Bradshaw.

Did you know: West Ham United were the first British club to recommence fixtures against teams from the Central European powers after the First World War. In 1923 they won two and drew two of a four-match tour of Austria-Hungary.

Managers (and Secretary-Managers)
Syd King 1902–32, Charlie Paynter 1932–50, Ted Fenton 1950–61, Ron Greenwood 1961–74 (continued as GM to 1977), John Lyall 1974–89, Lou Macari 1989–90, Billy Bonds February 1990–.

Player and Position	Ht	Wt	Birth Date	Birth Place	Source	Clubs	League App	Gls
Alex Bunbury	5 10	11 00	18 6 67	British Guyana	Montreal Supra	West Ham U	4	—
Simon Clarke*	5 11	11 02	23 9 71	Chelmsford	Trainee	West Ham U	3	—
Matt Holmes	5 7	10 07	1 8 69	Luton	Trainee	Bournemouth	114	8
						Cardiff C (loan)	1	—
						West Ham U	18	—
Steve Jones	5 11	12 00	17 3 70	Cambridge	Billericay	West Ham U	6	2
Dean Martin	5 8	10 06	31 8 72	London	Fisher Ath	West Ham U	2	—
						Colchester U (loan)	8	2
Trevor Morley	5 11	12 01	20 3 61	Nottingham	Nuneaton	Northampton T	107	39
						Manchester C	72	18
						West Ham U	122	44
John Purdie*	5 10	11 00	28 12 72	Newham	Trainee	West Ham U	—	—
Tony Richards*			17 9 73	Newham	Trainee	West Ham U	—	—
Mark Robson	5 7	10 05	22 5 69	Newham	Trainee	Exeter C	26	7
						Tottenham H	8	—
						Reading (loan)	7	—
						Watford (loan)	1	—
						Plymouth Arg (loan)	7	—
						Exeter C (loan)	8	1
						West Ham U	44	8
Stuart Slater (To Celtic August 1992)	5 9	10 04	27 3 69	Sudbury	Apprentice	West Ham U	141	11
Mike Small	6 1	13 05	2 3 62	Birmingham		Luton T	3	—
					Twente, Standard Liege	Peterborough U	4	1
					Go Ahead	Brighton	39	15
					Eagles/PAOK Salonika	West Ham U	49	13
Paul Whitmarsh	5 8	10 12	18 9 73	London	Trainee	West Ham U	—	—

Trainees
Bates, Jonathon P; Canham, Scott W; Currie, Darren P; Geraghty, Jason W; Johnson, Roy J; Peat, Martin D; Rose, Christopher A; Victory, Jamie C; Waters, Gary J.

**Non-Contract
Pratt, David J.

Associated Schoolboys
Campbell, Paul I; Clements, Mathew C; Farrell, Kevin J; Ferdinand, Rio G; Foley, Westley A; Hodges, Lee L; Keith, Joseph R; Moore, Jason M; Omoyimni, Emmanuel; Partridge, David W; Strain, Anthony M; Walton, David G. J; Wraight, Gary P.

Associated Schoolboys who have accepted the club's offer of a Traineeship/Contract
Blaney, Steven D; Browne, Anthony; John, Jerome L; Josceyline, Wayne; Maeer, Darren J; Moore, Scott; Oakley, Warren N; Richardson, Stuart J; Shipp, Daniel A.

**Non-Contract Players who are retained must be re-signed before they are eligible to play in League matches.

WIGAN ATHLETIC 1992–93 *Back row (left to right):* John Robertson, Joe Parkinson, Alan Johnson, Tony Pennock, Nigel Adkins, John Doolan, Steve Appleton, Phil Daley.
Centre row: David Crompton, Neill Rimmer, Allen Tankard, Andy Pilling, Gary Powell, Gary Worthington, Phil Jones, Paul Gray, Alex Cribley.
Front row: Bryan Griffiths, Steve Nugent, Dave Philpotts, Kevin Langley, Bryan Hamilton, Chris Sharratt, Andy Roberts.

Division 3   **WIGAN ATHLETIC**

Springfield Park, Wigan. Telephone Wigan (0942) 44433. Commercial Dept: (0942) 43067. Latics Clubcall 0891 121655. Fax 0942 494654.

Ground capacity: 9538.

Record attendance: 27,500 v Hereford U, 12 December 1953.

Record receipts: £40,577 v Leeds U, FA Cup 6th rd, 15 March 1987.

Pitch measurements: 114yd × 72yd.

President: T. Hitchen.

Chairman: S. Gage. *Vice-chairman:*

Directors: J. A. Bennett, J. D. Fillingham, S. Jackson, P. F. Spencer, N. Bitel, P. Connors.

Vice-president: J. H. Farrimond.

Secretary: *Marketing Manager:* B. Eccles.

Manager: Kenny Swain. *Physio:* Alex Cribley. *Safety officer:* D. Stott. *Groundsman:* D. Pinch.

Year Formed: 1932.

Club Nickname: 'The Latics'.

Record League Victory: 7–2 v Scunthorpe U (away), Division 4, 12 March 1982 – Tunks; McMahon, Glenn, Wignall, Cribley, Methven (1), O'Keefe, Barrow (1), Bradd (3), Houghton (2), Evans.

Record Cup Victory: 6–0 v Carlisle U (away), FA Cup, 1st rd, 24 November 1934 – Caunce; Robinson, Talbot; Paterson, Watson, Tufnell; Armes (2), Robson (1), Roberts (2), Felton, Scott (1).

Record Defeat: 1–6 v Bristol R, Division 3, 3 March 1990.

Most League Points (2 for a win): 55, Division 4, 1978–79 and 1979–80.

Most League Points (3 for a win): 91, Division 4, 1981–82.

Most League Goals: 80, Division 4, 1981–82.

Highest League Scorer in Season: Warren Aspinall, 21, Division 3, 1985–86.

Most League Goals in Total Aggregate: Peter Houghton, 62, 1978–84.

Most Capped Player: None.

Most League Appearances: Colin Methven, 296, 1979–86.

Record Transfer Fee Received: £329,000 from Coventry C for Peter Atherton, August 1991.

Record Transfer Fee Paid: £65,000 to Everton for Eamon O'Keefe, January 1982.

Football League Record: 1978 Elected to Division 4; 1982 –92 Division 3; 1992–93 Division 2; 1993– Division 3.

Honours: Football League: Best season in Division 3: 4th, 1985–86, 1986–87; Division 4 – Promoted (3rd) 1981–82. *FA Cup:* 6th rd 1986–87. *Football League Cup:* best season: 4th rd, 1981–82. *Freight Rover Trophy:* Winners 1984–85.

WIGAN ATHLETIC 1992—93 LEAGUE RECORD

Match No.	Date		Venue	Opponents	Result		H/T Score	Lg. Pos.	Goalscorers	Atten dance
1	Aug	15	H	Stockport Co	L	1-2	0-1	—	Griffiths	3360
2		22	A	Stoke C	L	1-2	0-1	22	Griffiths	12,902
3		29	H	Swansea C	L	2-3	0-2	23	Griffiths 2 (1 pen)	1565
4	Sept	1	H	Fulham	L	1-3	1-3	—	Daley	1591
5		5	A	Rotherham U	W	3-2	1-1	20	Griffiths 2 (1 pen), Daley	3806
6		11	H	Hartlepool U	D	2-2	1-1	—	Makin, Johnson	2073
7		15	A	Exeter C	D	0-0	0-0	—		2393
8		19	A	Reading	L	0-4	0-2	22		3084
9		26	H	Burnley	D	1-1	0-0	22	Griffiths	4032
10	Oct	3	H	Mansfield T	W	2-0	1-0	19	Griffiths 2	1644
11		10	A	Brighton & HA	L	0-1	0-1	20		5784
12		17	H	WBA	W	1-0	1-0	19	Makin	4408
13		24	A	Plymouth Arg	L	0-2	0-2	20		5967
14		31	H	Bournemouth	D	0-0	0-0	19		1803
15	Nov	3	H	Bradford C	L	1-2	0-1	—	Pilling	2070
16		7	A	Preston NE	L	0-2	0-1	22		4442
17		21	H	Leyton Orient	W	3-1	2-0	20	Tankard, Daley 2	1806
18		28	A	Chester C	W	2-1	0-1	20	Griffiths, Pilling	2395
19	Dec	12	H	Blackpool	W	2-1	0-0	20	Powell, Daley	2492
20		19	A	Port Vale	D	2-2	1-1	19	Pilling, Griffiths	6647
21		26	A	Bolton W	L	1-2	1-0	19	Powell	11,493
22	Jan	9	H	Exeter C	L	0-1	0-0	20		1882
23		16	A	Burnley	W	1-0	0-0	19	Griffiths (pen)	9154
24		23	H	Reading	D	1-1	1-0	20	Powell	1860
25		30	H	Stoke C	D	1-1	1-1	20	Pilling	4775
26	Feb	5	A	Stockport Co	L	0-3	0-0	—		4799
27		13	H	Rotherham U	D	1-1	1-0	21	Sharratt	1902
28		16	H	Huddersfield T	W	1-0	1-0	—	Brolly	2474
29		20	A	Fulham	L	0-1	0-0	20		3502
30		27	H	Brighton & HA	L	1-2	0-1	21	Skipper	2033
31	Mar	2	A	Hartlepool U	D	0-0	0-0	—		1791
32		6	A	Mansfield T	L	0-2	0-0	22		3024
33		9	A	Hull C	D	0-0	0-0	—		3394
34		12	H	Preston NE	L	2-3	1-2	—	Powell 2	3562
35		20	A	Bradford C	L	1-2	0-0	21	Robertson	4748
36		23	H	Chester C	L	1-2	0-2	—	Appleton	1861
37		27	A	Leyton Orient	W	2-1	1-1	22	Garnett, Powell	4104
38	Apr	3	H	Hull C	W	2-0	2-0	23	White 2	1872
39		6	A	Blackpool	L	1-2	1-0	—	Griffiths	5096
40		10	H	Bolton W	L	0-2	0-0	23		5408
41		12	A	Huddersfield T	L	1-2	0-1	23	Sharratt	6822
42		17	H	Port Vale	L	0-4	0-1	23		3743
43		24	A	WBA	L	1-5	1-1	23	Daley	14,867
44	May	1	H	Plymouth Arg	L	0-2	0-1	23		1432
45		4	A	Swansea C	L	1-2	1-0	—	Sharratt	7361
46		8	A	Bournemouth	D	0-0	0-0	23		3838

Final League Position: 23

GOALSCORERS

League (43): Griffiths 13 (3 pens), Daley 6, Powell 6, Pilling 4, Sharratt 3, Makin 2, White 2, Appleton 1, Brolly 1, Garnett 1, Johnson 1, Robertson 1, Skipper 1, Tankard 1.
Coca Cola Cup (4): Daley 1, Johnson 1, Tankard 1, Worthington 1.
FA Cup (4): Griffiths 1 (pen), Powell 1, own goals 2.

Adkins 38	Parkinson 13	Tankard 39 + 2	Johnson 36	Doolan 16 + 1	Langley 40	Jones 25 + 2	Pilling 27 + 4	Daley 31	Worthington 7 + 3	Griffiths 43 + 1	Powell 22 + 14	Robertson 21 + 3	Sharratt 11 + 9	Appleton 24 + 5	Wilson 5	Makin 14 + 1	Skipper 32	Pennock 8	Nugent 5 + 4	Cooper 4	Woods 12 + 1	Connelly 7	Brolly 2	Garnett 13	White 10	Ogden 1 + 1	Rimmer — + 1	Match No.
1	2	3	4	5	6	7	8	9	10	11	12																	1
1	2	3		5	6	7		9	10	11	8		4	12	14													2
1				5	6	7		9	10	11	8		4			2	3											3
1	2	3	4	5	6	7		9	10	11	12		8				14											4
1	2		4	5	6			9		11	10		8	12		7	3											5
1	2		4	5	6			9		11	10		8	12		7	3											6
1	2	12	4	5	6			9		11	10		8			7	3											7
1	2	12	4	5	6			9	14	11	10		8			7	3											8
1	2	3	4	5		7		9	12	11	10		8				6											9
1	2	3	4	5		7		9		11	10		8				6											10
1		3	4	5	6	7		9	11	10	8		12				2											11
1	2	3	4		6	7	12	9	10	11		8					5											12
1	2		4		6	7	12	9	10	11	14	8		5			3											13
1	2		4		6	7	10	9		11		8		5			3											14
1	2	3	4		6	7	10	9		11	12					8	5											15
1		3	4		6	7	10	9		11	8		12			2	5											16
1		3	4		6		10	9		11	8	5				2	7											17
1		3	4		6		10	9		11	8	5	12	2			7											18
1		3	4		6	2	10	9		11	8	5		12			7											19
		3	4		6		10	9		11	8	5		2			7	1	12									20
		3	4	2	6		10		14	11	8	5		12			7	1		9								21
1		3	4	14	6		9			11	12	5		2			7			10	8							22
1		3	4		6		5			11	8			2			7			10	9							23
1		3	4		6		5			11	8			2			7			10	9							24
1		3	4		6	9	5			11	8	12	2				7				10							25
1		3	4		6	9	5			11		8	12	2			7				10							26
1		3	4		6	9	5			11	14	8	2				7		12		10							27
1		3	4		6	9	5				14		8	12			7			10	2	11						28
1		3	4		6		5				14	8	9				7		12	10	2	11						29
1		3			6		9			11	12	8	5				7			10	2		4					30
		3			6	10	9			11		8	5				7	1			2		4					31
		3			10	6	9			11	14	8	5				7	1	12		2		4					32
		3	6	12			9	11		10	5						7	1			8	2	4					33
		3	6	12	14		9	11		10	5						7	1			8	2	4					34
		3	6	5	8	9		11	10	4	12	2					7	1			14							35
		3	6	5		9		11		10	2						7	1			8		4					36
1		3		6	5	8	9	11	14	12	2						7							4	10			37
1		3	4		5	8	9	11		12	2						7							6	10			38
1		3	4		5	8	9	11		12	2						7							6	10			39
1		3	4		5	8	9	11	14	12	2						7							6	10			40
1		3	4	6			9	11	8	12	2						7							5	10			41
1		3	4	6	12		9	11			2						7	8						5	10			42
1		3	4	8	6		2	9	14	12							7	10						5	11			43
1		3	4	2	6		5			11		10					7	9								8		44
1		3	4	2	6		5			11		10					7	9								8	12	45
1	11	4	2	6			5			10							7	9								8	3 12	46

Coca Cola Cup	First Round	Shrewsbury T (a)		2-1
		(h)		0-1
	Second Round	Ipswich T (h)		2-2
		(a)		0-4
FA Cup	First Round	Carlisle U (h)		3-1
	Second Round	Bury (h)		1-1
		(a)		0-1

WIGAN ATHLETIC

Player and Position	Ht	Wt	Date	Birth Place	Source	Clubs	League App	Gls
Goalkeepers								
Nigel Adkins*	5 11	13 04	11 3 65	Birkenhead	Apprentice	Tranmere R	86	—
						Wigan Ath	155	—
Tony Pennock	5 11	10 09	10 4 71	Swansea	School	Stockport Co	—	—
						Wigan Ath (loan)	2	—
						Wigan Ath	8	—
Defenders								
Steve Appleton*	5 11	10 09	27 7 73	Liverpool	Trainee	Wigan Ath	48	1
Alan Johnson	5 11	11 12	19 2 71	Ince	Trainee	Wigan Ath	164	12
Philip Jones*	5 8	10 09	1 12 69	Liverpool	Trainee	Everton	1	—
						Blackpool (loan)	6	—
						Wigan Ath	88	2
Paul Kirwan‡	5 9	10 12	18 7 74	Billinge	Trainee	Wigan Ath	—	—
Neil Ogden§	5 10	10 04	29 11 75	Billinge	Trainee	Wigan Ath	2	—
Joe Parkinson	5 11	12 02	11 6 71	Eccles	Trainee	Wigan Ath	119	6
John Robertson	6 2	13 02	8 1 74	Liverpool	Trainee	Wigan Ath	24	1
Peter Skipper	6 0	13 08	11 4 58	Hull	Local	Hull C	23	2
						Scunthorpe U (loan)	1	—
						Darlington	91	4
						Hull C	265	17
						Oldham Ath	27	1
						Walsall	81	2
						Wrexham	2	—
						Wigan Ath	18	—
					Stafford R	Wigan Ath	32	1
Greg Strong	6 2	11 12	5 9 75	Bolton	Trainee	Wigan Ath	—	—
Allen Tankard	5 10	11 07	21 5 69	Fleet	Trainee	Southampton	5	—
						Wigan Ath	209	4
Midfield								
Richard Brolly‡	6 0	11 03	5 10 69	York	Illinois Univ	Wigan Ath	2	1
Dino Connelly	5 9	10 08	6 1 70	Glasgow	Celtic BC	Arsenal	—	—
						Barnsley	13	—
						Wigan Ath (loan)	12	2
						Carlisle U (loan)	3	—
						Wigan Ath	7	—
John Doolan	5 10	10 12	10 11 68	South Liverpool	Knowsley U	Wigan Ath	19	—
Kevin Langley	6 1	10 03	24 5 64	St. Helens	Apprentice	Wigan Ath	160	6
						Everton	16	2
						Manchester C (loan)	9	—
						Manchester C	—	—
						Chester C (loan)	9	—
						Birmingham C	76	2
						Wigan Ath	124	4
Andy Pilling*	5 10	11 04	30 6 69	Wigan	Trainee	Preston NE	1	—
						Wigan Ath	156	20
Neill Rimmer	5 6	10 03	13 11 67	Liverpool	Apprentice	Everton	1	—
						Ipswich T	22	3
						Wigan Ath	107	6
Ian Wilson‡	5 6	11 10	27 3 58	Aberdeen	Elgin C	Leicester C	285	17
						Everton	34	1
					Besiktas	Derby Co	11	—
						Bury	24	1
						Wigan Ath	5	—
Forwards								
Philip Daley	6 2	12 09	12 4 67	Walton	Newton	Wigan Ath	143	36
Julian Dowe	6 1	12 04	9 9 75	Manchester	Trainee	Wigan Ath	—	—

WIGAN ATHLETIC

Colours: Black and blue striped shirts, black shorts with blue and white trim, black stockings with blue turnover. **Change colours:** Mixed red, black and white shirts, red shorts with black trim, red stockings with black turnover.

Foundation: Following the demise of Wigan Borough and their resignation from the Football League in 1931, a public meeting was called in Wigan at the Queen's Hall in May 1932 at which a new club Wigan Athletic, was founded in the hope of carrying on in the Football League. With this in mind, they bought Springfield Park for £2,250, but failed to gain admission to the Football League until 46 years later.

First Football League game: 19 August, 1978, Division 4, v Hereford U (a) D 0-0 – Brown; Hinnigan, Gore, Gillibrand, Ward, Davids, Corrigan, Purdie, Houghton, Wilkie, Wright.

Did you know: Wigan Athletic were losing 3-0 at home to Port Vale in a Division 4 match on 13 April 1979 when they scored five goals in 25 minutes to win 5-3.

Managers (and Secretary-Managers)
Charlie Spencer 1932–37, Jimmy Milne 1946–47, Bob Pryde 1949–52, Ted Goodier 1952–54, Walter Crook 1954–55, Ron Suart 1955–56, Billy Cooke 1956, Sam Barkas 1957, Trevor Hitchen 1957–58, Malcolm Barrass 1958–59, Jimmy Shirley 1959, Pat Murphy 1959–60, Allenby Chilton 1960, Johnny Ball 1961–63, Allan Brown 1963–66, Alf Craig 1966–67, Harry Leyland 1967–68, Alan Saunders 1968, Ian McNeill 1968–70, Gordon Milne 1970–72, Les Rigby 1972–74, Brian Tiler 1974–76, Ian McNeill 1976–81, Larry Lloyd 1981–83, Harry McNally 1983–85, Bryan Hamilton 1985–86, Ray Mathias 1986–89, Bryan Hamilton 1989–93, Dave Philpotts 1993, Kenny Swain May 1993–.

Player and Position	Ht	Wt	Birth Date	Birth Place	Source	Clubs	League App	Gls
Paul Gray*	5 9	11 08	28 1 70	Portsmouth	Trainee	Luton T	7	1
						Wigan Ath	5	—
Brian Griffiths	5 9	11 00	26 1 65	Prescot	St Helens T	Wigan Ath	189	44
Stephen Nugent*	5 10	12 06	7 5 73	Wigan	Trainee	Wigan Ath	13	—
Gary Powell*	5 10	10 02	2 4 69	Holylake	Trainee	Everton	—	—
						Lincoln C (loan)	11	—
						Scunthorpe U (loan)	4	1
						Wigan Ath (loan)	14	4
						Wigan Ath	70	13
Chris Sharratt*	5 7	11 04	13 8 70	West Kirby	Stalybridge	Wigan Ath	24	3
Winston White*	5 10	10 12	26 10 58	Leicester	Apprentice	Leicester C	12	1
						Hereford U	175	21
						Chesterfield	1	—
						Port Vale	1	—
						Stockport Co	4	—
						Bury	125	11
						Rochdale (loan)	4	—
						Colchester U	65	8
						Burnley	104	14
						WBA	16	1
						Bury	2	—
						Carlisle U	6	—
						Doncaster R	4	2
						Wigan Ath	10	2
Gary Worthington*	5 10	10 05	10 11 66	Cleethorpes	Apprentice	Manchester U	—	—
						Huddersfield T	—	—
						Darlington	40	15
						Wrexham	72	18
						Wigan Ath	63	20

Trainees
Brooks, Matthew L; Carragher, Mathew; Dixon, Stephen; Gallagher, Andrew N; Gallagher, Simon K; Greenwood, Carl; Harrison, Anthony; Kelly, Damian P; O'Brien, Stephen J; Ogden, Neil; Peoples, Martin P; Saint, Darren.

Associated Schoolboys
Chisnall, Robert G; Fitzhenry, Neil; Green, Paul R; Hogg, Russell S; Jones, Paul A; Just, Paul G; Livesey, Stephen J; Millet, Michael P; Moss, Ian D; Scott, Anthony; Traynor, Stuart G; Tyrrell, Kevin M; Weston, Steven M.

Associated Schoolboys who have accepted the club's offer of a Traineeship/Contract
Dowds, Scott K; McAteer, Michael; Newton, Steven J; O'Hara, Terence.

WIMBLEDON 1992–93   *Back row (left to right):* Joe Dillon (Assistant Kit Manager), Neal Ardley, Chris Perry, Paul Miller, Dean Blackwell, Neil Sullivan, Leighton Allen, Hans Segers, Stewart Castledine, Aidan Newhouse, Brian McAllister, Warren Barton, Ron Stuart (Chief Scout).

Centre row: Syd Neal (Kit Manager), Peter Fear, Steve Talboys, Scott Fitzgerald, Carlton Fairweather, John Scales, Steve Anthrobus, Lawrie Sanchez, John Fashanu, Dean Holdsworth, Roger Joseph, Steve Cotterill, Paul Jennings, Vaughan Ryan, Roger Smith (Youth Development Officer).

Front row: Ernie Tippett (Youth Team Manager), Grant Payne, Paul McGee, Gerald Dobbs, Terry Burton (Assistant Manager), Robbie Earle, Gary Elkins, Joe Kinnear (Manager), Terry Gibson, Andy Clarke, Brian Sparrow (Reserve Team Manager), Justin Skinner, Lee Fiori, Steve Allen (Physio).

FA Premier

WIMBLEDON

Selhurst Park, South Norwood, London SE25 6PY. Telephone 081 771 2233. Box Office 081 771 8841. Fax 081 768 0640.

Ground capacity: 29,215.

Record attendance: 30,115 v Manchester U, FA Premier League, 9 May 1993.

Record receipts: £303,797 v Manchester U, FA Premier League, 9 May 1993.

Pitch measurements: 110yd × 74yd.

Chairman: S. G. Reed. *Vice-chairman:* J. Lelliott.

Managing Director: S. Hammam.

Directors: P. Cork, P. R. Cooper, N. N. Hammam.

Chief Executive: David Barnard.

Manager: Joe Kinnear. *Assistant manager:* Terry Burton. *Physio:* Steve Allen.

Secretary: Steve Rooke. *Commercial Manager:* Reg Davis.

Year Formed: 1889. *Turned Professional:* 1964. *Ltd Co.:* 1964.

Previous Name: Wimbledon Old Centrals, 1899–1905.

Previous Ground: Plough Lane.

Club Nickname: 'The Dons'.

Record League Victory: 6–0 v Newport C, Division 3, 3 September 1983 – Beasant; Peters, Winterburn, Galliers, Morris, Hatter, Evans (2), Ketteridge (1), Cork (3 incl. 1p), Downes, Hodges (Driver).

Record Cup Victory: 7–2 v Windsor & Eton, FA Cup, 1st rd, 22 November 1980 – Beasant; Jones, Armstrong, Galliers, Mick Smith (2), Cunningham (1), Ketteridge, Hodges, Leslie, Cork (1), Hubbick (3).

Record Defeat: 0–8 v Everton, League Cup 2nd rd, 29 August 1978.

Most League Points (2 for a win): 61, Division 4, 1978–79.

Most League Points (3 for a win): 98, Division 4, 1982–83.

Most League Goals: 97, Division 3, 1983–84.

Highest League Scorer in Season: Alan Cork, 29, 1983–84.

Most League Goals in Total Aggregate: Alan Cork, 145, 1977–92.

Most Capped Player: Terry Phelan, 8 (15), Republic of Ireland.

Most League Appearances: Alan Cork, 430, 1977–92.

Record Transfer Fee Received: £2,500,000 from Manchester C for Keith Curle, August 1991.

Record Transfer Fee Paid: £775,000 to Port Vale for Robbie Earle, July 1991.

Football League Record: 1977 Elected to Division 4; 1979–80 Division 3; 1980–81 Division 4; 1981–82 Division 3; 1982–83 Division 4; 1983–84 Division 3; 1984–86 Division 2; 1986–92 Division 1; 1992– FA Premier League.

Honours: Football League: Division 1 best season: 6th, 1986–87; Division 3 – Runners-up 1983–84; Division 4 – Champions 1982–83. *FA Cup:* Winners 1987–88. *Football League Cup:* best season: 4th rd, 1979–80, 1983–84, 1988–89. *League Group Cup:* Runners-up 1981–82.

WIMBLEDON 1992—93 LEAGUE RECORD

Match No.	Date		Venue	Opponents	Result	H/T Score	Lg. Pos.	Goalscorers	Attendance
1	Aug 15	A		Leeds U	L 1-2	0-1	—	Barton	25,795
2	18	H		Ipswich T	L 0-1	0-1	—		4954
3	22	H		Coventry C	L 1-2	0-1	22	Holdsworth	3759
4	25	A		Sheffield U	D 2-2	1-0	—	Barton, Holdsworth	15,463
5	29	A		Everton	D 0-0	0-0	21		18,118
6	Sept 1	H		Manchester C	L 0-1	0-0	—		4714
7	5	H		Arsenal	W 3-2	1-1	19	Sanchez, Fashanu, Earle	12,906
8	12	A		Ipswich T	L 1-2	1-1	20	Holdsworth	13,333
9	19	H		Blackburn R	D 1-1	1-1	21	Ardley	6117
10	Oct 26	A		Liverpool	W 3-2	2-2	17	Fashanu, Earle 2	29,574
11	3	H		Aston Villa	L 2-3	1-2	21	Newhouse, Clarke	6849
12	17	A		Southampton	D 2-2	0-0	20	Cotterill 2	11,221
13	25	H		Tottenham H	D 1-1	1-0	—	Gibson	8628
14	31	A		Manchester U	W 1-0	0-0	18	Sanchez	32,622
15	Nov 7	H		QPR	L 0-2	0-2	20		6771
16	21	A		Middlesbrough	L 0-2	0-0	20		14,524
17	28	H		Sheffield W	D 1-1	0-1	20	Jones (pen)	5740
18	Dec 5	A		Norwich C	L 1-2	0-0	20	Sanchez	14,161
19	12	H		Oldham Ath	W 5-2	3-0	19	Ardley 2, Holdsworth 2, Clarke	3386
20	20	A		Nottingham F	D 1-1	1-1	—	Clarke	19,326
21	26	A		Crystal Palace	L 0-2	0-2	21		16,825
22	28	H		Chelsea	D 0-0	0-0	21		14,687
23	Jan 9	A		Blackburn R	D 0-0	0-0	21		14,504
24	16	H		Liverpool	W 2-0	1-0	20	Fashanu (pen), Cotterill	11,294
25	26	H		Everton	L 1-3	0-0	—	Fashanu	3039
26	30	A		Coventry C	W 2-0	1-0	18	Holdsworth, Clarke	11,774
27	Feb 6	H		Leeds U	W 1-0	0-0	17	Holdsworth	6704
28	10	A		Arsenal	W 1-0	1-0	—	Holdsworth	18,253
29	20	H		Sheffield U	W 2-0	2-0	13	Fashanu, Dobbs	3979
30	27	A		Aston Villa	L 0-1	0-0	16		34,496
31	Mar 6	H		Southampton	L 1-2	1-1	16	Holdsworth	4534
32	9	H		Middlesbrough	W 2-0	1-0	—	Scales, Holdsworth	5821
33	13	A		QPR	W 2-1	1-1	15	Fashanu, Earle	12,270
34	20	H		Norwich C	W 3-0	2-0	12	Holdsworth 2, Ardley	10,875
35	24	A		Sheffield W	D 1-1	0-0	—	Holdsworth	20,918
36	Apr 3	A		Oldham Ath	L 2-6	0-3	12	Holdsworth 2	11,606
37	9	H		Crystal Palace	W 4-0	2-0	—	Earle 2, Holdsworth 2	12,275
38	12	A		Chelsea	L 2-4	0-1	13	Holdsworth, Sanchez	13,138
39	17	H		Nottingham F	W 1-0	1-0	11	Clarke	9358
40	21	A		Manchester C	D 1-1	0-0	—	Miller	19,524
41	May 1	A		Tottenham H	D 1-1	0-1	11	Earle	24,473
42	9	H		Manchester U	L 1-2	0-0	—	Holdsworth	30,115

Final League Position: 12

GOALSCORERS

League (56): Holdsworth 19, Earle 7, Fashanu 6 (1 pen), Clarke 5, Ardley 4, Sanchez 4, Cotterill 3, Barton 2, Dobbs 1, Gibson 1, Jones 1 (pen), Miller 1, Newhouse 1, Scales 1.
Coca Cola Cup (3): Ardley 1, Fashanu 1, Jones 1.
FA Cup (5): Cotterill 1, Dobbs 1, Earle 1, Elkins 1, Fashanu 1.

Segers 41	Joseph 31 + 1	Elkins 17 + 1	Barton 23	Scales 32	Fitzgerald 18 + 2	Miller 11 + 8	Earle 42	Holdsworth 34 + 2	Sanchez 23 + 4	Clarke 23 + 10	Blackwell 19 + 5	Dobbs 16 + 3	Berry 2 + 1	Anthrobus 4 + 1	McAllister 26 + 1	Fashanu 27 + 2	Gibson 6 + 2	Ardley 24 + 2	Jones 27	Skinner 1	Newhouse — + 1	Sullivan 1	McLeary 4	Cotterill 4 + 3	McGee 1 + 2	Talboys 3 + 4	Fear 2 + 2	Match No.
1	2	3	4	5	6	7	8	9	10	*11*	12	14																1
1	*2*	3	4		6	7	8	9	10	12	5	14	11															2
1	2	3	4		6	14	8	9	10	12	5	*7*		11														3
1		14	4		6	2	8	*9*	10	12	5	*7*		11	3													4
1			4		6	2	8	9	10	12	5	*7*		11	3													5
1			4		6	*7*	8	11	10	12	5		2	3	9													6
1			4			6	8	7	10	11	5		12	*3*	9	2	14											7
1	*3*		2	6	12	14	8	10		11	5			9	7		4											8
1		3	2	5	12		8	10		11	6			9		7	4											9
1		2	5	6	14		8	10	12	11				9		*7*	4	3										10
1		3	2	5	6	4	8		10	11				9	7		12											11
	3		2		6	7	8		11					9		4				1	5	10						12
1	3		2		6		8	12		11			14	9	*7*	4				5	10							13
1	3		2			8	9	10	12			11	6	7		4			5									14
1	3		2			8	9	*10*	12			11	6	7		4			5	14								15
1	3		2	5		12	8	9		*10*		6	7		4				14	11								16
1	3		2	5		11	8	9	10	7			6	12	4													17
1	3		5		11	8	*9*	10	7			6	12	14	4						2							18
1	3		5			8	9	10	11	7			6		2	4												19
1	3		5	14		8	9		11	7		6	12	2	4						10							20
1	*3*		5		8	2	10	11	*7*			6	9	14	4						12							21
1	2		5	14		8	10	*11*	6			3	9	*7*	4						12							22
1	2	3	5		8	10	11	6	7			9		4														23
1	2	3	5		8	12	10	*11*	6			9	7		4				14									24
1	2	3	5		8	11	10	12	6			9	7	4														25
1	2		5		8	10	11	6	12			3	9	7	4													26
1	2	6	5		*8*	10	4	12		11			3	9	7						14							27
1	2	3	5	6	8	10			11			9	7		4					12								28
1	2	3	5		8	10	11				6	9	7	4														29
1	2	3	5		8	12		11			6	9	7	4					10									30
1	2	3	5		8	10	11				6	9	7	4														31
1	2	3	5		8	10	11		12		6	9	7	4														32
1	2	3	5		8	10	12		11		6	9	*7*	4														33
1	2	3	5		8	10			11		6	9	7	4														34
1	2	*3*	5		8	10	12	14	11		6	9	7	4														35
1	2		5		8	10	4	6	11			9	7						12		3							36
1	2	3	5	6	14	8	10	4	*11*	12	9			7														37
1	2	3	5	6	14	8	10	4	*11*	12	9			7														38
1		2	5	6	9	8	10	*4*	11	12		3	7						14									39
1		2	5	6	7	8		11			3	9		4				12	10									40
1		2	5	6		8	*10*	12	11		3	9	7	4				14										41
1	12		2	5	6		8	10		11		3	9	*7*	4													42

Coca Cola Cup	Second Round	Bolton W (a)	3-1
		(h)	0-1
	Third Round	Everton (a)	0-0
		(h)	0-1
FA Cup	Third Round	Everton (h)	0-0
		(a)	2-1
	Fourth Round	Aston Villa (a)	1-1
		(h)	0-0
	Fifth Round	Tottenham H (a)	2-3

WIMBLEDON

Player and Position	Ht	Wt	Date	Birth Place	Source	Clubs	League App	Gls
Goalkeepers								
Hans Segers	5 11	12 12	30 10 61	Eindhoven	PSV Eindhoven	Nottingham F	58	—
						Stoke C (loan)	1	—
						Sheffield U (loan)	10	—
						Dunfermline Ath (loan)	4	—
						Wimbledon	190	—
Neil Sullivan	6 0	12 01	24 2 70	Sutton	Trainee	Wimbledon	3	—
						Crystal Palace (loan)	1	—
Defenders								
Warren Barton	6 0	11 00	19 3 69	London	Leytonstone/ Ilford	Maidstone U	42	—
						Wimbledon	102	6
Dean Blackwell	6 1	12 10	5 12 69	London	Trainee	Wimbledon	66	1
						Plymouth Arg (loan)	7	—
Gerald Dobbs	5 8	11 07	24 1 71	London	Trainee	Wimbledon	23	1
Peter Fear	5 10	11 05	10 9 73	London	Trainee	Wimbledon	4	—
Scott Fitzgerald	6 0	12 02	13 8 69	London	Trainee	Wimbledon	57	1
Paul Jennings*	5 10	11 00	16 6 74	London	Trainee	Wimbledon	—	—
Roger Joseph	5 11	11 10	24 12 65	Paddington	Juniors	Brentford	104	2
						Wimbledon	146	—
Brian McAllister	5 11	12 05	30 11 70	Glasgow	Trainee	Wimbledon	40	—
						Plymouth Arg (loan)	8	—
Chris Perry	5 9	11 01	26 4 73	London	Trainee	Wimbledon	—	—
John Scales	6 2	12 07	4 7 66	Harrogate		Leeds U	—	—
						Bristol R	72	2
						Wimbledon	200	11
Justin Skinner	5 7	11 00	17 9 72	London	Trainee	Wimbledon	1	—
Midfield								
Stewart Castledine	6 0	12 00	22 1 73	London	Trainee	Wimbledon	2	—
Gary Elkins	5 09	11 12	4 5 66	Wallingford	Apprentice	Fulham	104	2
						Exeter C (loan)	5	—
						Wimbledon	46	1
Lee Fiori*	5 8	10 06	12 12 73	London		Wimbledon	—	—
Vinny Jones	5 11	11 10	5 1 65	Watford	Wealdstone	Wimbledon	77	9
						Leeds U	46	5
						Sheffield U	35	2
						Chelsea	42	4
						Wimbledon	27	1
Jamie McCarthy	5 10	11 07	14 8 73	London	Trainee	Wimbledon	—	—
Aidan Newhouse	6 2	13 05	23 5 72	Wallasey	Trainee	Chester C	44	6
						Wimbledon	23	2
Lawrie Sanchez	5 11	12 00	22 10 59	Lambeth	Thatcham	Reading	262	28
						Wimbledon	255	31
Steve Talboys	5 11	11 10	18 9 66	Bristol	Gloucester C	Wimbledon	7	—
Forwards								
Leighton Allen	6 0	11 02	22 1 73	Brighton	Trainee	Wimbledon	—	—
Steve Anthrobus	6 2	12 13	10 11 68	Lewisham		Millwall	21	4
						Southend U (loan)	—	—
						Wimbledon	28	—
Neil Ardley	5 9	12 02	1 9 72	Epsom	Trainee	Wimbledon	35	4
Greg Berry	5 10	12 00	5 3 71	Essex	East Thurrock	Leyton Orient	80	14
						Wimbledon	3	—
Andy Clarke	5 10	11 07	22 7 67	London	Barnet	Wimbledon	79	11

WIMBLEDON

Colours: Blue shirts yellow trim, blue shorts yellow trim, blue stockings yellow trim. **Change colours:** All red.

Foundation: Old boys from Central School formed this club as Wimbledon Old Centrals in 1889. Their earliest successes were in the Clapham League before switching to the Southern Suburban League in 1902.

First Football League game: 20 August, 1978, Division 4, v Halifax T (h) D 3-3 – Guy; Bryant (1), Galvin, Donaldson, Aitken, Davies, Galliers, Smith, Connell (1), Holmes, Leslie (1).

Did you know: Wimbledon's Plough Lane ground was requisitioned during the Second World War by the National Fire Service, but the club was able to resume playing there from 1945–46.

Managers (and Secretary-Managers)
Les Henley 1955–71, Mike Everitt 1971–73, Dick Graham 1973–74, Allen Batsford 1974–78, Dario Gradi 1978–81, Dave Bassett 1981–87, Bobby Gould 1987–90, Ray Harford 1990–91, Peter Withe 1991, Joe Kinnear January 1992–.

Player and Position	Ht	Wt	Date	Birth Place	Source	Clubs	League App	Gls
Steve Cotterill	6 1	12 05	20 7 64	Cheltenham	Burton A	Wimbledon	17	6
						Brighton (loan)	11	4
Robbie Earle	5 9	10 10	27 1 65	Newcastle, Staffs.	Stoke C	Port Vale	294	77
						Wimbledon	82	21
Carlton Fairweather*	5 11	11 00	22 9 61	London	Tooting & Mitcham	Wimbledon	138	26
John Fashanu	6 1	11 12	18 9 63	Kensington	Cambridge U	Norwich C	7	1
						Crystal Palace (loan)	1	—
						Lincoln C	36	10
						Millwall	50	12
						Wimbledon	240	96
Terry Gibson*	5 5	10 00	23 12 62	Walthamstow	Apprentice	Tottenham H	18	4
						Coventry C	98	43
						Manchester U	23	1
						Wimbledon	86	22
						Swindon T (loan)	9	1
Dean Holdsworth	5 11	11 13	8 11 68	London	Trainee	Watford	16	3
						Carlisle U (loan)	4	1
						Port Vale (loan)	6	2
						Swansea C (loan)	5	1
						Brentford (loan)	7	1
						Brentford	110	53
						Wimbledon	36	19
Paul McGee	5 6	9 10	17 5 68	Dublin	Bohemians	Colchester U	3	—
						Wimbledon	60	9
Paul Miller	6 0	11 00	31 1 68	Bisley	Trainee	Wimbledon	80	10
						Newport Co (loan)	6	2
						Bristol C (loan)	3	—
Grant Payne	5 9	11 04	25 12 75	Woking	Trainee	Wimbledon	—	—

Trainees
Brooker, Daniel P; Cable, Marc B; Cunningham, Jason; Di'Rubbo, Franco; Fairbairn, Neil; Fell, Gavin A; Finegan, Leon G; Fleming, Shaun A; John, Vincent; Lingley, Peter C; Mosley, David; Stephenson, Paul; Swift, Kieron, Thomas, Mark L.

Associated Schoolboys
Cooper, Grant; Cort, Carl E. R; Courtney, Lee; Enifer, Dean H; Futcher, Andrew R; Gardner, James; Hawkins, Peter S; Longman, Luke; McCormack, Francis, O'Neill, Daniel H; Summers, Robert R.

Associated Schoolboys who have accepted the club's offer of a Traineeship/Contract
Board, Kevin J. F; Cobb, Simon P; Evell, Jason J; Griffiths, Leonard W; Hodges, Daniel W; Laidlaw, Iain L; Mumford, Steven B; Owusu, Clement; Piper, Leonard H.

WOLVERHAMPTON WANDERERS 1992-93   *Back row (left to right):* Paul Cook, Mark Venus, Darren Roberts, Mike Stowell, Shane Westley, Paul Jones, Derek Mountfield, Darren Simkin, Lawrie Madden.
Centre row: Steve Bull, Andy Mutch, Robbie Dennison, Mark Burke, Tim Steele, Mark Rankine, Tom Bennett, James Kelly.
Front row: Andy Thompson, Keith Downing, Gary Pendrey, Graham Turner, Paul Darby, Paul Birch, Kevin Ashley.

Division 1 WOLVERHAMPTON WANDERERS

Molineux Grounds, Wolverhampton WV1 4QR. Telephone Admin office: Wolverhampton (0902) 712181; lottery shop: (0902) 27524. Commercial Office: (0902) 23166. Ticket office: 0902 25899. Fax 0902 24612.

Ground capacity: 23,258.

Record attendance: 61,315 v Liverpool, FA Cup 5th rd, 11 February 1939.

Record receipts: £114,574 v Bolton W, FA Cup 4th rd, 24 January 1993.

Pitch measurements: 116yd × 74yd.

President: Sir Jack Hayward.

Chairman: Jonathan Hayward.

Directors: Jack Harris, Billy Wright, John Harris, Nic Stones, Keith Pearson ACIS.

Team Manager: Graham Turner.

Coaches: Gary Pendrey, Chris Evans and Robert Kelly. *Physio:* Paul Darby.

Chief Executive:

Secretary: Keith Pearson ACIS. *Commercial Manager:* Gary Leaver.

Year Formed: 1877*(see Foundation).* *Turned Professional:* 1888. *Ltd Co.:* 1982.

Club Nickname: 'Wolves'.

Previous Grounds: 1877, Goldthorn Hill; 1879, John Harper's Field; 1881, Dudley Road; 1889, Molineux.

Previous Names: 1880, St Luke's, Blakenhall combined with Blakenhall Wanderers to become Wolverhampton Wanderers (1923) Ltd until 1982.

Record League Victory: 10–1 v Leicester C, Division 1, 15 April 1938 – Sidlow; Morris, Dowen; Galley, Cullis, Gardiner; Maguire (1), Horace Wright, Westcott (4), Jones (1), Dorsett (4).

Record Cup Victory: 14–0 v Cresswell's Brewery, FA Cup, 2nd rd, 13 November 1886 – I. Griffiths; Baugh, Mason; Pearson, Allen (1), Lowder; Hunter (4), Knight (2), Brodie (4), B. Griffiths (2), Wood. Plus one goal 'scrambled through'.

Record Defeat: 1–10 v Newton Heath, Division 1, 15 October 1892.

Most League Points (2 for a win): 64, Division 1, 1957–58.

Most League Points (3 for a win): 92, Division 4, 1988–89.

Most League Goals: 115, Division 2, 1931–32.

Highest League Scorer in Season: Dennis Westcott, 38, Division 1, 1946–47.

Most League Goals in Total Aggregate: Steve Bull, 171, 1986–93.

Most Capped Player: Billy Wright, 105, England (70 consecutive).

Most League Appearances: Derek Parkin, 501, 1967–82.

Record Transfer Fee Received: £1,150,000 from Manchester C for Steve Daley, September 1979.

Record Transfer Fee Paid: £1,175,000 to Aston Villa for Andy Gray, September 1979.

Football League Record: 1888 Founder Member of Football League: 1906–23 Division 2; 1923–24 Division 3 (N); 1924–32 Division 2; 1932–65 Division 1; 1965–67 Division 2; 1967–76 Division 1; 1976–77 Division 2; 1977–82 Division 1; 1982–83 Division 2; 1983–84 Division 1; 1984–85 Division 2; 1985–86 Division 3; 1986–88 Division 4; 1988–89 Division 3; 1989–92 Division 2; 1992– Division 1.

Honours: Football League: Division 1 – Champions 1953–54, 1957–58, 1958–59; Runners-up 1937–38, 1938–39, 1949–50, 1954–55, 1959–60; Division 2 – Champions 1931–32, 1976–77; Runners-up 1966–67, 1982–83; Division 3 (N) – Champions 1923–24; Division 3 – Champions 1988–89; Division 4 – Champions 1987–88. *FA Cup:* Winners 1893, 1908, 1949, 1960; Runners-up 1889, 1896, 1921, 1939. *Football League Cup:* Winners 1973–74, 1979–80. *Texaco Cup:* 1970–71. *Sherpa Van Trophy:* Winners 1988. **European Competitions:** *European Cup:* 1958–59, 1959–60. *European Cup-Winners' Cup:* 1960–61. *UEFA Cup:* 1971–72 (runners-up), 1973–74, 1974–75, 1980–81.

WOLVERHAMPTON WANDERERS 1992—93 LEAGUE RECORD

Match No.	Date		Venue	Opponents	Result		H/T Score	Lg. Pos.	Goalscorers	Atten dance
1	Aug	15	A	Brentford	W	2-0	0-0	—	Dennison, Bull	9069
2		18	H	Leicester C	W	3-0	2-0	—	Bull, Mutch, Birch (pen)	15,821
3		22	H	Swindon T	D	2-2	1-1	2	Mutch, Downing	15,493
4		29	A	Oxford U	D	0-0	0-0	5		7592
5	Sept	1	A	Barnsley	W	1-0	1-0	—	Birch	6906
6		5	H	Peterborough U	W	4-3	2-1	3	Bull, Burke, Mutch 2	14,532
7		13	A	Leicester C	D	0-0	0-0	—		12,965
8		19	H	Watford	D	2-2	1-1	3	Bull 2	13,497
9		27	A	Birmingham C	W	4-0	4-0	—	Roberts 3, Downing	14,391
10	Oct	4	H	West Ham U	D	0-0	0-0	—		14,391
11		10	A	Southend U	D	1-1	1-1	3	Mutch	5498
12		17	H	Portsmouth	D	1-1	0-1	3	Birch	14,750
13		25	A	Millwall	L	0-2	0-0	—		6814
14		31	H	Derby Co	L	0-2	0-1	6		17,270
15	Nov	3	A	Sunderland	L	0-2	0-1	—		15,144
16		7	H	Bristol R	W	5-1	2-1	7	Dennison, Bull 2, Burke 2	12,163
17		14	A	Notts Co	D	2-2	1-0	5	Dennison, Bull	8494
18		22	H	Charlton Ath	W	2-1	1-1	—	Burke, Roberts	10,593
19		28	H	Grimsby T	W	2-1	2-0	5	Mountfield, Burke	14,240
20	Dec	5	A	Cambridge U	D	1-1	0-0	5	Bull	6429
21		12	H	Luton T	L	1-2	1-1	6	Blades	13,932
22		19	A	Tranmere R	L	0-3	0-1	6		9758
23		26	A	Newcastle U	L	1-2	1-1	9	Cook	30,137
24		28	H	Bristol C	D	0-0	0-0	7		16,419
25	Jan	9	A	Watford	L	1-3	0-1	9	Mountfield	6845
26		17	H	Birmingham C	W	2-1	0-1	—	Burke, Mutch	13,560
27		27	H	Barnsley	W	1-0	0-0	—	Mutch	11,342
28		30	A	Swindon T	L	0-1	0-0	10		10,812
29	Feb	6	A	Brentford	L	1-2	0-0	10	Mutch	12,361
30		13	A	Peterborough U	W	3-2	1-1	8	Burke, Phrilliskirk (og), Roberts	9195
31		20	H	Oxford U	L	0-1	0-1	8		12,791
32		27	H	Southend U	D	1-1	0-0	9	Bull	11,563
33	Mar	6	A	West Ham U	L	1-3	0-0	11	Bull	24,679
34		9	H	Notts Co	W	3-0	0-0	—	Bull 2, Johnson (og)	11,482
35		13	A	Bristol R	D	1-1	1-0	11	Bull	5982
36		20	H	Cambridge U	L	1-2	0-1	12	Bull	11,473
37		23	A	Charlton Ath	W	1-0	0-0	—	Dennison	7852
38		27	H	Sunderland	W	2-1	1-1	8	Dennison, Sampson (og)	12,731
39	Apr	3	A	Grimsby T	L	0-1	0-0	9		5080
40		7	A	Luton T	D	1-1	0-0	—	Bull	7948
41		10	A	Newcastle U	W	1-0	0-0	9	Mutch	17,244
42		12	A	Bristol C	L	0-1	0-0	9		11,756
43		17	H	Tranmere R	L	0-2	0-2	10		13,060
44		24	A	Portsmouth	L	0-2	0-0	11		23,074
45	May	1	H	Millwall	W	3-1	3-0	9	Burke, Bradbury 2	12,054
46		8	A	Derby Co	L	0-2	0-0	11		15,083

Final League Position: 11

GOALSCORERS

League (57): Bull 16, Mutch 9, Burke 8, Dennison 5, Roberts 5, Birch 3 (1 pen), Bradbury 2, Downing 2, Mountfield 2, Blades 1, Cook 1, own goals 3.
Coca Cola Cup (2): Bull 1, Cook 1 (pen).
FA Cup (4): Bull 1, Downing 1, Mutch 1, own goal 1.

Stowell 26	Ashley 28	Thompson 15 + 5	Downing 30 + 1	Westley 6 + 2	Blades 38 + 2	Birch 27 + 1	Cook 44	Bull 36	Mutch 34 + 5	Dennison 31 + 6	Edwards 33 + 2	Madden 19 + 5	Roberts 12 + 9	Burke 27 + 5	Mountfield 34 + 2	Bennett — + 1	Rankine 23 + 4	Jones 16	Venus 12	Taylor — + 1	Beasant 4	Steele 1 + 3	Simkin 7	Bradbury 2	Turner 1	Match No.
1	2	3	4	5	6	7	8	9	10	11																1
1	2	3	4	5	6	7	8	9	10	11																2
1	2	3	4	5	6	7	8	9	10	11	12															3
1	2	3	4	5	6	7	8	9	10	*11*		12	14													4
1	2		4	12	6	7			9	10	11	*3*	5	14	8											5
1	*2*	14	4	12	6	7	8	9	10			3	5		11											6
1	2		4	5		7	8	9	10			3			11		6	12								7
1	2		4	5		7	8	9	10	12		3		14	6		11									8
1	2	14	4			7	8	9		12	*3*	5	10		6		11									9
1	2		4		6	7	8	9	12	3		10	5		11											10
1	2		4		6	7	8	9	10	12	3		5		11											11
1	2		4		6	7	8	9	10	12	3		5		11											12
1	2		4		6	7	8	9	10	12	3		5		11											13
1	2		*4*		6	7	8	9	10	11	3	12	5	14												14
	2				6	7	8	9	10	11	3	12	5					4	1							15
	2				6	7	8	9	10	11	3	12	4					5	1							16
	2				6	7	8	9		11	3	10	4				12	5	1							17
	2				6	7	8	9		11	3	10	4					5	1							18
	2				6	7	8	9		11	3	10	4					5	1							19
	2	12			6	7	8	9		11	3	10	4					5	1							20
	2	11			6	7	8	9			3	12	10				4	5	1							21
	2	7			6		8	9			3	10					4	5	1	11	12					22
	2	10			14		8	9	12		3				6		4	*5*		7	1	11				23
	2	7			6		8	9	12		3	5			4		10				1	11				24
		3	7		6	11	8	9	10		2		12	5	4				1							25
		7		11	8	9	10	12	3	6		2	5		4					1						26
		7	14		8	9	10	11	3	6	12	2	5		*4*					1						27
		7	2		8	9	10	11	3	6	12		4	5						1						28
		7	2		8	9	10	11	3	6		4	5	12						1						29
		7	2		8		10	11	3	6	9	4	5		1							12				30
		2			8		10	11	3	6	9	4	5	12	1							7				31
		2			8	9	10	11	3	6		4	5		7	1										32
1		10			2		8	9	12	11		6		4	5	7	3									33
1		10	5		2		8	9	12	11	3	6		4		7										34
1		3	5		2		8	9	10	11		6		4	12	7										35
1	5	14			2		8	9	10	*11*	3	6		4	12	7										36
1	6	14			2	4	8		10	11	3		9	12	5		7									37
1	6	3			2	4	8		10	11		9	12	5		7										38
1	6		8		2	4		9	10	11		5	7	3												39
1	12	4			6		8	9	10	11		5	7	3										2		40
1	9	4			6		8		10	11	12	5	7	3										2		41
1	9	4			6	14	8		10	11	12	5	*7*	3										2		42
1	9				7	*8*			10	11	14	6	12	4	5		3							2		43
1	9					8			10	11	*7*	6	12	4	5		3				14	2				44
	9		5			8			10	11	3	12	4				1	6				2	7			45
	9		5			8			10		3	12	4				1	6			14	2	7	11		46

Coca Cola Cup	Second Round	Notts Co (a)	2-3
		(h)	0-1
FA Cup	Third Round	Watford (a)	4-1
	Fourth Round	Bolton W (h)	0-2

WOLVERHAMPTON WANDERERS

Player and Position	Ht	Wt	Date	Birth Place	Source	Clubs	League App	Gls
Goalkeepers								
Andy Debont	6 2	15 06	7 2 74	Wolverhampton	Trainee	Wolverhampton W	—	—
Paul Jones	6 3	14 00	18 4 67	Chirk	Kidderminster H	Wolverhampton W	16	—
Mike Stowell	6 2	11 10	19 4 65	Preston	Leyland Motors	Preston NE	—	—
						Everton	—	—
						Chester C (loan)	14	—
						York C (loan)	6	—
						Manchester C (loan)	14	—
						Port Vale (loan)	7	—
						Wolverhampton W (loan)	7	—
						Preston NE (loan)	2	—
						Wolverhampton W	111	—
Defenders								
Kevin Ashley	5 7	10 04	31 12 68	Birmingham	Apprentice	Birmingham C	57	1
						Wolverhampton W	88	1
Tom Bennett	5 11	11 08	12 12 69	Falkirk	Trainee	Aston Villa	—	—
						Wolverhampton W	97	2
Paul Blades	6 0	10 12	5 1 65	Peterborough	Apprentice	Derby Co	166	1
						Norwich C	47	—
						Wolverhampton W	40	1
Danny Collier	6 3	12 08	15 1 74	Eccles	Trainee	Wolverhampton W	—	—
Paul R Edwards	5 11	11 00	25 12 63	Birkenhead	Altrincham	Crewe Alex	86	6
						Coventry C	36	—
						Wolverhampton W	35	—
Rob Hindmarch*	6 1	13 04	27 4 61	Stannington	Apprentice	Sunderland	115	2
						Portsmouth (loan)	2	—
						Derby Co	164	9
						Wolverhampton W	40	2
John Howard	6 2	13 02	2 4 74	Stafford	Trainee	Wolverhampton W	—	—
Lawrie Madden*	5 11	13 01	28 9 55	London	Arsenal Manchester Univ	Mansfield T	10	—
						Charlton Ath	113	7
						Millwall	47	2
						Sheffield W	212	2
						Leicester C (loan)	3	—
						Wolverhampton W	67	1
Derek Mountfield	6 1	12 07	2 11 62	Liverpool	Apprentice	Tranmere R	26	1
						Everton	106	19
						Aston Villa	90	9
						Wolverhampton W	64	3
Darren Simkin	6 0	12 00	24 3 70	Walsall	Blakenhall	Wolverhampton W	7	—
Mark Venus	6 0	11 08	6 4 67	Hartlepool		Hartlepool U	4	—
						Leicester C	61	1
						Wolverhampton W	147	3
Midfield								
Paul Birch	5 6	10 04	20 11 62	West Bromwich	Apprentice	Aston Villa	173	16
						Wolverhampton W	93	13
Paul Cook	5 11	10 10	22 2 67	Liverpool		Wigan Ath	83	14
						Norwich C	6	—
						Wolverhampton W	157	17
Keith Downing*	5 8	11 00	23 7 65	Oldbury	Mile Oak R	Notts Co	23	1
						Wolverhampton W	191	8
Jimmy Kelly	5 7	11 10	14 2 73	Liverpool	Trainee	Wrexham	21	—
						Wolverhampton W	3	—
						Walsall (loan)	10	2
Mark Rankine	5 10	11 01	30 9 69	Doncaster	Trainee	Doncaster R	164	20
						Wolverhampton W	42	1

WOLVERHAMPTON WANDERERS

Colours: Gold shirts, black shorts, gold stockings. **Change colours:** All sky blue.

Foundation: Another club where precise details of information are confused, due in part to the existence of an earlier Wolverhampton club which played rugby. However, it is now considered likely that it came into being in 1879 when players from St. Luke's (founded 1877) and Goldthorn (founded 1876) broke away to form Wolverhampton Wanderers Association FC.

First Football League game: 8 September, 1888, Football League, v Aston Villa (h) D 1-1 – Baynton; Baugh, Mason; Fletcher, Allen, Lowder; Hunter, Cooper, Anderson, White, Cannon. Scorer – Cox o.g.

Did you know: Wolves became the first Football League club to win the championship of all four divisions when taking the Division 3 title in 1988–89.

Managers (and Secretary-Managers)
George Worrall 1877–85*, John Addenbrooke 1885–1922, George Jobey 1922–24, Albert Hoskins 1924–26 (had been secretary since 1922), Fred Scotchbrook 1926–27, Major Frank Buckley 1927–44, Ted Vizard 1944–48, Stan Cullis 1948–64, Andy Beattie 1964–65, Ronnie Allen 1966–68, Bill McGarry 1968–76, Sammy Chung 1976–78, John Barnwell 1978–81, Ian Greaves 1982, Graham Hawkins 1982–84, Tommy Docherty 1984–85, Bill McGarry 1985, Sammy Chapman 1985–86, Brian Little 1986, Graham Turner October 1986–.

Player and Position	Ht	Wt	Birth Date	Birth Place	Source	Clubs	League App	League Gls
Andy Thompson	5 4	10 06	9 11 67	Carnock	Apprentice	WBA	24	1
						Wolverhampton W	231	23
Mark Turner	6 0	11 01	4 10 72	Bebbington	Trainee	Wolverhampton W	1	—
Forwards								
Shaun Bradbury	5 10	11 00	11 2 74	Birmingham	Trainee	Wolverhampton W	2	2
Steve Bull	5 11	11 04	28 3 65	Tipton	Apprentice	WBA	4	2
						Wolverhampton W	283	171
Mark Burke	5 10	11 08	12 2 69	Solihull	Apprentice	Aston Villa	7	—
						Middlesbrough	57	6
						Darlington (loan)	5	1
						Ipswich T (loan)	—	—
						Wolverhampton W	56	10
Robert Dennison	5 7	11 00	30 4 63	Banbridge	Glenavon	WBA	16	1
						Wolverhampton W	243	33
Lee Mills	6 1	12 11	10 7 70	Mexborough	Stocksbridge	Wolverhampton W	—	—
Andy Mutch	5 10	11 00	28 12 63	Liverpool	Southport	Wolverhampton W	289	97
Darren Roberts	6 0	12 10	12 10 69	Birmingham	Burton Alb	Wolverhampton W	21	5
Tim Steele*	5 9	11 00	1 2 67	Coventry	Apprentice	Shrewsbury T	61	5
						Wolverhampton W	75	7
						Stoke C (loan)	7	1
Colin Taylor*	6 0	12 07	25 12 71	Liverpool	Trainee	Wolverhampton W	19	2
						Wigan Ath (loan)	7	2
						Preston NE (loan)	4	—
						Doncaster R (loan)	2	—

Trainees
Barnett, Jason V; Bowers, Kevin T; Dale, David A; Eades, Gary J; Graham, Iain J; Gregory, Alan; Hanbury, Jay P; Humphrey, Paul B; Innes, Michael P; Jackson, Grant S; Macbeth, Andrew M; Nicholls, Alan; Phillips, Richard W; Pearce, Stephen; Shaw, Darren R; Smith, James J. A; Smith, Jason J; Voice, Scott H; Walker, Steven J.

Associated Schoolboys
Biddle, Steven J; Davis, Paul; Harper, Lee N; Hayward, Brett; Hind, Barry; Holmes, Martin L; Leadbitter, Richard P; Murphy, Leroy; Sawyers, Robert; Smith, Darryl C; Wilson, Christopher J.

Associated Schoolboys who have accepted the club's offer of a Traineeship/Contract
Bytheway, Matthew; Mahon, Gavin; Westwood, Christopher J.

WREXHAM 1992-93 *Back row (left to right):* Jonathan Cross, Kevin Jones, Craig Knight, Barry Jones, Tony Humes, John Paskin, Mark Sertori, Karl Connolly, Gary Bennett, Mickey Thomas.
Centre row: Mike Rigg (Community Scheme Organiser), Cliff Sear (Youth Development Officer), Stephen Pugh, Richard Laughton, Steve Watkin, Ken Hughes, Mark Morris, Scott Williams, Simon Betts, David Brammer, Joey Jones (Coach), Steve Wade (Physio).
Front row: Kieron Durkan, Phil Myddleton, Wayne Phillips, Richard McNeil, Brian Flynn (Manager), Kevin Reeves (Assistant Manager), Phil Hardy, Mel Pejic, Gareth Owen, Dave Esdaille.

Division 2   **WREXHAM**

Racecourse Ground, Mold Road, Wrexham. Telephone Wrexham (0978) 262129. Fax 0978 357821. Commercial Dept: (0978) 352536. Clubcall: 0898 121642.

Ground capacity: 11,881.

Record attendance: 34,445 v Manchester U, FA Cup 4th rd, 26 January 1957.

Record receipts: £126,012 v West Ham U, FA Cup 4th rd, 4 February 1992.

Pitch measurements: 111yd × 71yd.

President: G. Mytton.

Chairman: W. P. Griffiths.

Managing Director: D. L. Rhodes.

Directors: C. Griffiths, S. Mackreth, G. Paletta, B. Williams (vice-chairman).

Manager: Brian Flynn. *Assistant Manager:* Kevin Reeves.

Secretary: D. L. Rhodes. *Player-coach:* Joey Jones.

Commercial Manager: P. Stokes. *Physio:* Steve Wade.

Year Formed: 1873 (oldest club in Wales).

Turned Professional: 1912. *Ltd Co.:* 1912.

Previous Ground: Acton Park.

Club Nickname: 'Robins'.

Record League Victory: 10–1 v Hartlepools, Division 4, 3 March 1962 – Keelan; Peter Jones, McGavan; Tecwyn Jones, Fox, Ken Barnes; Ron Barnes (3), Bennion (1), Davies (3), Ambler (3), Ron Roberts.

Record Cup Victory: 6–0 v Gateshead, FA Cup, 1st rd, 20 November 1976 – Lloyd; Evans, Whittle, Davis, Roberts, Thomas (Hill), Shinton (3 incl. 1p), Sutton, Ashcroft (2), Lee (1), Griffiths. 6–0 v Charlton Ath, FA Cup, 3rd rd, 5 January 1980 – Davies; Darracott, Kenworthy, Davis, Jones (Hill), Fox, Vinter (3), Sutton, Edwards (1), McNeil (2), Carrodus.

Record Defeat: 0–9 v Brentford, Division 3, 15 October 1963.

Most League Points (2 for a win): 61, Division 4, 1969–70 and Division 3, 1977–78.

Most League Points (3 for a win): 80, Division 3, 1992–93.

Most League Goals: 106, Division 3 (N), 1932–33.

Highest League Scorer in Season: Tom Bamford, 44, Division 3 (N), 1933–34.

Most League Goals in Total Aggregate: Tom Bamford, 175, 1928–34.

Most Capped Player: Dai Davies, 28 (51), Wales.

Most League Appearances: Arfon Griffiths, 592, 1959–61, 1962–79.

Record Transfer Fee Received: £300,000 from Manchester U for Mickey Thomas, November 1978, from Manchester C for Bobby Shinton, July 1979 and from Liverpool for Lee Jones, March 1992.

Record Transfer Fee Paid: £210,000 to Liverpool for Joey Jones, October 1978.

Football League Record: 1921 Original Member of Division 3 (N); 1958–60 Division 3; 1960–62 Division 4; 1962–64 Division 3; 1964–70 Division 4; 1970–78 Division 3; 1978–82 Division 2; 1982–83 Division 3; 1983–92 Division 4; 1992– Division 3.

Honours: Football League: Division 2 best season: 15th, 1978–79; Division 3 – Champions 1977–78; Division 3 (N) – Runners-up 1932–33; Division 4 – Runners-up 1969–70. *FA Cup:* best season: 6th rd, 1973–74, 1977–78. *Football League Cup:* best season: 5th rd, 1961, 1978. *Welsh Cup:* Winners 21 times. Runners-up 19 times. Record number of victories and appearances in finals. **European Competition:** *European Cup-Winners' Cup:* 1972–73, 1975–76, 1978–79, 1979–80, 1984–85, 1986–87, 1990–91.

WREXHAM 1992—93 LEAGUE RECORD

Match No.	Date	Venue	Opponents	Result	H/T Score	Lg. Pos.	Goalscorers	Attendance
1	Aug 22	H	Rochdale	W	3-1	1-0	10	Owen, Jones, Cross	2661
2	29	A	York C	L	0-4	0-2	17		2554
3	Sept 1	A	Gillingham	L	1-4	0-3	—	Watkin	2503
4	5	H	Doncaster R	D	1-1	1-1	19	Connolly	2389
5	12	H	Shrewsbury T	W	2-0	0-0	11	Paskin 2	4265
6	15	A	Torquay U	D	1-1	1-0	—	Connolly	2093
7	26	H	Barnet	L	2-3	1-2	17	Bennett, Thomas	3078
8	Oct 3	A	Hereford U	D	1-1	0-0	17	Connolly	2916
9	10	H	Bury	W	4-2	1-0	14	Bennett 3, Taylor	2829
10	17	A	Carlisle U	W	2-0	0-0	12	Paskin 2	3520
11	24	H	Northampton T	L	0-1	0-1	14		3099
12	30	A	Colchester U	W	4-2	2-1	—	Bennett 2, Jones, Connolly	4423
13	Nov 3	H	Scunthorpe U	L	0-2	0-1	—		2930
14	7	A	Lincoln C	D	0-0	0-0	12		3699
15	21	H	Halifax T	D	1-1	1-0	13	Connolly	1873
16	28	A	Walsall	D	1-1	0-1	13	Bennett	3519
17	Dec 12	H	Scarborough	W	4-1	1-0	11	Bennett 2, Lake, Watkin	2238
18	18	A	Cardiff C	W	2-1	1-1	—	Cross 2	6832
19	26	A	Crewe Alex	W	1-0	0-0	6	Bennett	4481
20	28	H	Chesterfield	W	5-4	2-1	5	Watkin 2, Lake, Bennett, Cash (og)	5339
21	Jan 2	A	Shrewsbury T	W	1-0	0-0	3	Watkin	6179
22	9	H	Torquay U	W	4-2	1-0	3	Bennett, Lake, Cross 2	5465
23	16	A	Barnet	L	1-3	1-3	3	Paskin	4079
24	23	H	Walsall	W	3-1	1-1	3	Watkin 2 (1 pen), Paskin	5324
25	26	H	York C	W	3-0	0-0	—	Connolly, Watkin 2	6894
26	30	A	Rochdale	W	2-1	1-1	2	Owen, Watkin	4500
27	Feb 13	A	Doncaster R	D	1-1	0-1	3	Lake	2693
28	20	H	Gillingham	W	2-0	0-0	3	Paskin, Bennett (pen)	4415
29	27	A	Bury	L	1-3	0-2	3	Watkin	4550
30	Mar 6	H	Hereford U	W	2-0	2-0	3	Cross, Bennett	5280
31	9	A	Darlington	D	1-1	0-1	—	Pejic	1597
32	13	H	Lincoln C	W	2-0	0-0	4	Connolly, Owen	5246
33	20	A	Scunthorpe U	D	0-0	0-0	3		3282
34	26	A	Halifax T	W	1-0	0-0	—	Watkin	3920
35	Apr 2	H	Darlington	D	1-1	1-1	—	Watkin	6972
36	6	A	Scarborough	D	1-1	1-0	—	Cross	1861
37	10	H	Crewe Alex	W	2-0	2-0	4	Taylor, Watkin	8164
38	12	A	Chesterfield	W	3-2	1-1	4	Connolly, Lake, Watkin	5385
39	17	H	Cardiff C	L	0-2	0-2	4		10,852
40	24	H	Carlisle U	W	3-1	2-1	4	Pejic, Watkin, Paskin	5912
41	27	A	Northampton T	W	2-0	2-0	—	Bennett 2 (1 pen)	7504
42	May 8	H	Colchester U	W	4-3	2-0	2	Connolly, Betts (og), Watkin 2	9705

Final League Position: 2

GOALSCORERS

League (75): Watkin 18 (1 pen), Bennett 16 (2 pens), Connolly 9, Paskin 8, Cross 7, Lake 5, Owen 3, Jones B 2, Pejic 2, Taylor 2, Thomas 1, own goals 2.
Coca Cola Cup (4): Bennett 2, Pejic 1, own goal 1.
FA Cup (1): Bennett 1.

Hughes 8	Jones B 42	Hardy 32	Phillips 14 + 1	Humes 38	Pejic 39	Watkin 31 + 2	Owen 38 + 3	Connolly 40 + 2	Paskin 10 + 9	Cross 34 + 3	Sertori 10 + 2	Bennett 34 + 1	Taylor 13 + 6	Williams 1	Thomas 8	Durkan — + 1	Morris 34	Pugh 1 + 2	Brammer 1 + 1	Esdaille 4	Jones K 3	Flynn 1 + 1	Lake 25 + 1	Case 1 + 3	Match No.
1	2	3	4	5	6	7	8	9	10	11	12														1
1	2	3	4	5	6		8	9	10	14	12	7	11												2
1	2	3		5	4	9	8	12	10	11	6	7													3
1	2			5	4	10	8	9	12	3	6	7		11											4
1	2		4	5	6		8	9	11	3		7			10										5
1	2		4	5	6	12	8	9	11	3	10	7			14										6
1	2		4	5	3		8	9	11			6	7		12		10								7
	2		4	5	6		8	9		3		7	11		10		1	12							8
	2		4	5	6			9		3		7	11		10		1			8					9
	2		4	5	6	14	9	12		3		7	11		10		1			8					10
	2		4	5	6	14	9	11		3		7	12		10		1			8					11
		5		3			8	9			6	7	11		10		1			4	2			12	12
	2			5		12	8	9			6	7	11		10		1					4			13
	2	3		5	4		8	9			6	7	11				1		10						14
	2	3	4	5	6	10	8	9		11		7					1								15
	2	3	4	5	6	10	14	9		11		7	12				1						8		16
	2	3		5	6	10	4	12		11		7	9				1						8		17
	2	3		5	6	10	4	9		11		7					1						8		18
	2	3		5	6	10	4	9		11		7					1						8		19
	2	3		5	6	10	4	9		11		7					1						8		20
	2	3		5	6	10	4	9		11		7					1						8		21
	2	3		5	6	10	4	9		11		7					1						8		22
1	2	3	14		6	10	4	9				7	11	5			12						8		23
	2	3		5	6	10	4	9	12	11		7					1						8		24
	2	3		5	6	10	4	9				7	11				1						8		25
	2	3	7	5	6	10	4	9		11							1	8					12		26
	2	3		5	6	10	4	9	12	11		7					1						8		27
	2	3		5	6	10	4	9	12	11		7					1						8		28
	2	3			6	10	4	9		14	5	7					1	12	11				8		29
	5	3			6	10	4	9		11		7	12				1		2				8		30
	2	3		5	6	10	4	9		11		7	12				1						8		31
	2	3		5	6	10	4	9	12			7	11				1						8		32
	2	3		5	6	10	4	9	12	14		7	11				1						8		33
	2	3		5	6	10	4	9		11		7					1						8		34
	2	3		5		10	4	9	12	11	6	7					1						8		35
	2	3		5	6	10	4	9	7	11			12				1						8	14	36
	2	3		5	6	10	4	9		11		7					1						8		37
	2	3		5	6	10	4	9		11		7					1						8	12	38
	2	3		5	6	10	4	9		11	12	7					1						8		39
	2	3		5	6	10	4	9	12	11		7					1						8		40
	2	3		5	6	10	4	9		11		7					1						8		41
	2	3		5	6	10	4	9		11		7					1						8	12	42

Coca Cola Cup	First Round	Bury (h)	1-1
		(a)	3-4
FA Cup	First Round	Crewe Alex (a)	1-6

WREXHAM

Player and Position	Ht	Wt	Date	Birth Place	Source	Clubs	League App	Gls
Goalkeepers								
Ken Hughes*	6 0	11 06	9 1 66	Barmouth		Crystal Palace	—	—
						Shrewsbury T	74	—
						Wrexham	8	—
Mark Morris	6 0	12 00	1 8 68	Chester		Wrexham	97	—
Defenders								
Phil Hardy	5 8	11 00	9 4 73	Chester		Wrexham	107	—
Tony Humes	5 11	11 00	19 3 66	Blyth	Apprentice	Ipswich T	120	10
						Wrexham	46	—
Barry Jones	5 10	11 02	20 6 70	Prescot	Prescot T	Liverpool	— —	—
						Wrexham	42	2
Kevin Jones	5 10	11 00	16 2 74	Wrexham	Trainee	Wrexham	4	—
Craig Knight	6 1	12 00	24 10 73	Wrexham	Trainee	Wrexham	1	—
Phil Myddleton	5 8	10 12	22 12 72	St Asaph	Trainee	Wrexham	—	—
Mel Pejic	5 9	10 13	27 4 59	Chesterton	Local	Stoke C	1	—
						Hereford U	412	14
						Wrexham	46	2
Mark Sertori	6 1	13 00	1 9 67	Manchester		Stockport Co	4	—
						Lincoln C	50	9
						Wrexham	95	2
Scott Williams§	6 0	11 00	7 8 74	Bangor	Trainee	Wrexham	1	—
Midfield								
David Brammer§	5 9	10 05	28 2 75	Bromborough	Trainee	Wrexham	2	—
Jimmy Case*	5 9	12 08	18 5 54	Liverpool	South Liverpool	Liverpool	186	23
						Brighton	127	10
						Southampton	215	10
						Bournemouth	40	1
						Halifax T	21	2
						Wrexham	4	—
Karl Connolly	5 11	11 02	9 2 70	Prescot	Napoli (Liverpool Sunday League)	Wrexham	78	17
Jonathan Cross	5 10	11 04	2 3 75	Wallasey	Trainee	Wrexham	43	7
Kieron Durkan	5 10	11 05	1 12 73	Chester	Trainee	Wrexham	2	—
Brian Flynn*	5 4	10 00	12 10 55	Port Talbot	Apprentice	Burnley	120	8
						Leeds U	154	11
						Burnley (loan)	2	—
						Burnley	80	11
						Cardiff C	32	—
						Doncaster R	27	—
						Bury	19	—
					Limerick	Doncaster R	24	1
						Wrexham	100	5
Michael Lake	6 1	12 11	6 11 66	Manchester	Macclesfield T	Sheffield U	35	4
						Wrexham	26	5
Gareth Owen	5 7	11 10	21 10 71	Chester	Trainee	Wrexham	117	12
Wayne Phillips	5 10	11 00	15 12 70	Bangor	Trainee	Wrexham	78	3
Mark Taylor	5 7	11 00	20 11 64	Hartlepool	Local	Hartlepool U	47	4
						Crewe Alex (loan)	3	—
						Blackpool	100	40
						Cardiff C (loan)	6	3
						Wrexham	28	2

WREXHAM

Colours: Red shirts, white shorts, red stockings. **Change colours:** White shirts, red shorts, white stockings.

Foundation: The oldest club still in existence in Wales, Wrexham was founded in 1873 by a group of local businessmen initially to play a 17-a-side game against the Provincial Insurance team. By 1875 their team formation was reduced to 11 men and a year later they were among the founders of the Welsh FA.

First Football League game: 27 August, 1921, Division 3(N), v Hartlepools U (h) L 0-2 – Godding; Ellis, Simpson; Matthias, Foster, Griffiths; Burton, Goode, Cotton, Edwards, Lloyd.

Did you know: Wrexham were losing 2-0 to Halifax Town in a Division 3 (N) match on 10 September 1932 with 15 minutes remaining, only to recover and win 5-2.

Managers (and Secretary-Managers)
Ted Robinson 1912–25* (continued as secretary to 1930), Charlie Hewitt 1925–29, Jack Baynes 1929–31, Ernest Blackburn 1932–36, Jimmy Logan 1937–38, Arthur Cowell 1938, Tom Morgan 1938–40, Tom Williams 1940–49, Les McDowall 1949–50, Peter Jackson 1951–54, Cliff Lloyd 1954–57, John Love 1957–59, Billy Morris 1960–61, Ken Barnes 1961–65, Billy Morris 1965, Jack Rowley 1966–67, Alvan Williams 1967–68, John Neal 1968–77, Arfon Griffiths 1977–81, Mel Sutton 1981–82, Bobby Roberts 1982–85, Dixie McNeil 1985–89, Brian Flynn November 1989–.

Player and Position	Ht	Wt	Birth Date	Birth Place	Source	Clubs	League App	League Gls
Mickey Thomas*	5 6	10 07	7 7 54	Mochdre	Amateur	Wrexham	230	33
						Manchester U	90	11
						Everton	10	—
						Brighton	20	—
						Stoke C	57	14
						Chelsea	44	9
						WBA	20	—
						Derby Co (loan)	9	—
					Wichita W	Shrewsbury T	40	1
						Leeds U	3	—
						Stoke C (loan)	5	—
						Stoke C	38	7
						Wrexham	34	2
Forwards								
Gary Bennett	5 11	12 00	20 9 63	Liverpool	Local	Wigan Ath	20	3
						Chester C	126	36
						Southend U	42	6
						Chester C	80	15
						Wrexham	35	16
John Paskin	6 2	12 05	1 2 62	Capetown	Seiko	WBA	25	5
						Wolverhampton W	34	3
						Stockport Co (loan)	5	1
						Birmingham C (loan)	10	3
						Shrewsbury T (loan)	1	—
						Wrexham	36	11
Stephen Pugh	5 10	11 00	27 11 73	Bangor	Trainee	Wrexham	3	—
Steve Watkin	5 10	10 05	16 6 71	Wrexham	School	Wrexham	70	27

Trainees
Barnes, Richard I; Brammer, David; Burke, Damian P. W; Carroll, Matthew; Coulthard, Christopher; Dixon, Kenneth J; Hughes, Bryan; Jones, Scott L; Merola, Anthony; Morgan, Steven J; Oldfield, Damon M; Pritchard, Andrew; Roberts, Paul; Roden, Damian J; Sadler, Philip A; Williams, Christopher; Williams, Scott J.

**Non-Contract
Jones, Hugh R.

Associated Schoolboys
Acott, Lee; Clays, Warren M; Davey, Richard W; Davies, Andrew M; Davies, Stephen; McGrath, Martin G; Morris, Robert I; Owens, Robert; Roberts, Neil W; Roberts, Ryland; Rock, Stuart; Williams, Gavin P; Wilson, Gareth E.

Associated Schoolboys who have accepted the club's offer of a Traineeship/Contract
Bignall, Michael; Coady, Lewis; Cody, Michael D; Edwards, Arwel R; Futcher, Stephen A; Jones, Paul P; McGregor, Mark D. T; Rawlins, Richard.

**Non-Contract Players who are retained must be re-signed before they are eligible to play in League matches.

WYCOMBE WANDERERS 1992–93 *Back row (left to right):* Matt Crossley, Keith Scott, Paul Hyde, Jason Cousins, Gary Smith.
Centre row: John Rearden (Assistant Manager), Jim Melvin (Youth Team Coach), Dave Carroll, Simon Stapleton, Trevor Roffey, Chuck Moussaddik, Keith Ryan, Andy Kerr, Paul Franklin
(Coach), Dave Jones (Physio).
Front row: John Deakin, Steve Thompson, Mark West, Glyn Creaser, Steve Guppy, Martin O'Neill (Manager), Ty Gooden, Dennis Greene, Kim Casey, Simon Hutchinson, Gavin Covington.

Division 3   WYCOMBE WANDERERS

Adams Park, Hillbottom Road, Sands, High Wycombe HP12 4HJ. Telephone 0494 472100. Fax: 0494 527633. Information Line 0891 446855.

Ground Capacity: 7188.

Record attendance: 7230 v Slough T, GM Vauxhall Conference, 23 March 1993.

Record receipts: £27,695.00 v Slough T, GM Vauxhall Conference, 23 March 1993.

Pitch measurements: 115 × 75yd.

Chairman: I. L. Beeks.

Directors: G. Peart, G. Richards, B. Lee, G. Cox, A. Parry, A. Thibault.

Founded 1884

Manager: Martin O'Neill. *Assistant Manager:* John Reardon. *Secretary:* John Goldsworthy. *Coach:* Paul Franklin. *Physio:* Dave Jones. *Commercial Manager:* Mike Phillips/Mark Austin.

Year Formed: 1884. *Club Nickname:* The Blues. *Previous Ground:* Loakes Park.

Record Transfer Fee Received: £30,000.00 from Lincoln City for Keith Scott, March 1991.

Record Transfer Fee Paid: £25,000 to Barnet for Nicky Evans, January 1991.

Players: Goalkeepers: Paul Hyde, 7.4.63 Hayes, ex-Hayes; Chuck Moussaddik, 23.2.70 Morocco, Wimbledon.

Defenders: Jason Cousins, 4.10.70 Hayes, Brentford; Glyn Creaser, 1.9.59 London, Barnet; Matt Crossley, 18.3.68 Basingstoke, Newbury; Andy Kerr, 7.4.66 West Bromwich, Telford; Anton Vircavs, 28.3.61 Oxford, Cheltenham; Geoff Cooper, 27.12.60 Kingston, Barnet.

Midfield: David Carroll, 20.9.66 Paisley, Ruislip Manor; Keith Ryan, 25.6.70 Northampton, Berkhamsted; Simon Stapleton, 10.12.68 Oxford, Bristol R; Hakan Hayrettin, 4.2.70 London, Barnet; Steve Thompson, 12.1.63 Plymouth, Slough.

Forwards: Kim Casey, 31.3.61 Birmingham, Cheltenham; Ty Gooden, 23.10.72 Canvey Island, Arsenal; Dennis Greene, 14.4.65 London, Chelmsford; Steve Guppy, 29.3.69 Winchester, Southampton; Simon Hutchinson, 24.9.69 Sheffield, Eastwood T; Tim Langford, 12.9.65 Kingswinford, Telford; Keith Scott, 10.6.67 London, Lincoln C; Mark West, 12.2.66 High Wycombe, Reading.

Colours: Light & dark blue quartered shirts, navy blue shorts, sky blue stockings.

Change colours: All yellow.

580

YORK CITY 1992–93 *Back row (left to right):* Paul Atkin, Steve Tutill, Paul Stancliffe, Chris Marples, Dean Kiely, Ray Warburton, John Borthwick, Darren Tilley.
Centre row: Alan Little (Coach), Paul Barnes, Jon McCarthy, Phil Crosby, Andy McMillan, Gary Swann, Glenn Naylor, Nigel Pepper, Ian Blackstone, Geoff Miller (Physio).
Front row: Andy Smith, Wayne Hall, Tony Barratt, John Ward (Manager), Tony Canham, Steve Bushell, Craig Hall.

Division 2 **YORK CITY**

Bootham Crescent, York. Telephone York 0904 624447. Fax 0904 631457

Ground capacity: 12,547.

Record attendance: 28,123 v Huddersfield T, FA Cup 6th rd, 5 March 1938.

Record receipts: £38,054 v Liverpool, FA Cup 5th rd, 15 February 1986.

Pitch measurements: 115yd × 74yd.

Chairman: D. M. Craig OBE, JP, BSC, FICE, FI, MUN E, FCI ARB, M CONS E

Directors: B. A. Houghton, C. Webb, E. B. Swallow, J. E. H. Quickfall FCA.

Manager: Alan Little. *Assistant Manager:*

Secretary: Keith Usher. *Commercial Manager:* Mrs Sheila Smith.

Physio: Jeff Miller.

Hon. Orthopaedic Surgeon: Mr Peter De Boer MA, FRCS. *Medical Officer:* Dr R. Porter.

Year Formed: 1922. *Turned Professional:* 1922. *Ltd Co.:* 1922.

Club Nickname: 'Minstermen'.

Previous Ground: 1922, Fulfordgate; 1932, Bootham Crescent.

Record League Victory: 9–1 v Southport, Division 3 (N), 2 February 1957 – Forgan; Phillips, Howe; Brown (1), Cairney, Mollatt; Hill, Bottom (4 incl. 1p), Wilkinson (2), Wragg (1), Fenton (1).

Record Cup Victory: 6–0 v South Shields (away), FA Cup, 1st rd, 16 November 1968 – Widdowson; Baker (1p), Richardson; Carr, Jackson, Burrows; Taylor, Ross (3), MacDougall (2), Hodgson, Boyer.

Record Defeat: 0–12 v Chester, Division 3 (N), 1 February 1936.

Most League Points (2 for a win): 62, Division 4, 1964–65.

Most League Points (3 for a win): 101, Division 4, 1983–84.

Most League Goals: 96, Division 4, 1983–84.

Highest League Scorer in Season: Bill Fenton, 31, Division 3 (N), 1951–52; Arthur Bottom, 31, Division 3 (N), 1954–55 and 1955–56.

Most League Goals in Total Aggregate: Norman Wilkinson, 125, 1954–66.

Most Capped Player: Peter Scott, 7 (10), Northern Ireland.

Most League Appearances: Barry Jackson, 481, 1958–70.

Record Transfer Fee Received: £100,000 from Carlisle U for Gordon Staniforth, October 1979, and from QPR for John Byrne, October 1985.

Record Transfer Fee Paid: £50,000 to Aldershot for Dale Banton, November 1984 and £50,000 to Stoke C for Paul Barnes, July 1992.

Football League Record: 1929 Elected to Division 3 (N); 1958–59 Division 4; 1959–60 Division 3; 1960–65 Division 4; 1965–66 Division 3; 1966–71 Division 4; 1971–74 Division 3; 1974–76 Division 2; 1976–77 Division 3; 1977–84 Division 4; 1984–88 Division 3; 1988–92 Division 4; 1992–93 Division 3; 1993– Division 2.

Honours: Football League: Division 2 best season: 15th, 1974–75; Division 3 – Promoted 1973–74 (3rd); Division 4 – Champions 1983–84. *FA Cup:* Semi-finals 1955, when in Division 3. *Football League Cup:* best season: 5th rd, 1962.

YORK CITY 1992—93 LEAGUE RECORD

Match No.	Date		Venue	Opponents	Result		H/T Score	Lg. Pos.	Goalscorers	Attendance
1	Aug	15	H	Shrewsbury T	W	2-0	1-0	—	Warburton, Barnes	2414
2		22	A	Lincoln C	W	1-0	1-0	3	Barnes	3032
3		29	H	Wrexham	W	4-0	2-0	1	Blackstone, Pepper (pen), Borthwick, Barnes	2554
4	Sept	1	H	Torquay U	W	2-1	1-1	—	Pepper (pen), Warburton	3365
5		5	A	Walsall	L	1-3	1-1	1	Warburton	3574
6		12	A	Carlisle U	W	2-1	1-0	1	Pepper (pen), McCarthy	5355
7		15	H	Hereford U	W	4-2	1-0	—	Borthwick 2, Blackstone, McCarthy	3672
8		19	H	Colchester U	W	2-0	1-0	1	Blackstone 2	3820
9		25	A	Darlington	W	1-0	0-0	—	Blackstone	3787
10	Oct	3	H	Doncaster R	D	1-1	0-0	1	Pepper (pen)	4611
11		10	A	Scunthorpe U	W	2-1	1-1	1	McCarthy, Pepper (pen)	4114
12		17	H	Rochdale	W	3-0	1-0	1	Barnes, Borthwick 2	4161
13		31	A	Bury	D	1-1	1-0	—	Borthwick	2763
14	Nov	7	H	Barnet	W	2-0	1-0	1	Barnes, Pepper (pen)	6425
15		21	A	Northampton T	L	3-4	2-3	1	Hall, Blackstone 2	2812
16		28	H	Crewe Alex	W	3-1	2-0	1	Atkin 2, Blackstone	4190
17	Dec	12	H	Chesterfield	D	0-0	0-0	2		3382
18		19	A	Scarborough	L	2-4	0-3	1	Barnes, Canham	3892
19		26	A	Cardiff C	D	3-3	0-3	1	Blackstone 2, Barnes	10,411
20		29	H	Halifax T	D	1-1	1-0	—	Barnes	4068
21	Jan	9	A	Hereford U	D	1-1	1-1	2	Borthwick	1975
22		16	H	Darlington	D	0-0	0-0	2		3563
23		19	A	Carlisle U	D	2-2	1-0	—	Borthwick, Barnes	3071
24		22	A	Colchester U	D	0-0	0-0	—		4528
25		26	A	Wrexham	L	0-3	0-0	—		6894
26		30	H	Lincoln C	W	2-0	1-0	3	Stancliffe, Canham	3948
27	Feb	6	A	Shrewsbury T	D	1-1	1-0	2	Canham	3532
28		13	H	Walsall	L	0-1	0-1	4		3467
29		20	A	Torquay U	L	0-1	0-0	4		3119
30		27	H	Scunthorpe U	W	5-1	2-0	4	Barnes 4, Blackstone	2990
31	Mar	5	A	Doncaster R	W	1-0	0-0	—	Blackstone	3188
32		9	H	Gillingham	D	1-1	1-0	—	Barnes	3327
33		13	A	Barnet	W	5-1	2-1	3	Barnes 3, Blackstone, Barnett (og)	4985
34		20	H	Bury	L	1-2	0-1	4	McCarthy	3985
35		23	A	Crewe Alex	L	1-3	1-2	—	McCarthy	3381
36		26	H	Northampton T	W	2-1	0-1	—	Canham, Blackstone	3334
37	Apr	2	A	Gillingham	W	4-1	2-1	—	Blackstone, Barnes 2, McCarthy	3912
38		6	A	Chesterfield	D	1-1	0-1	—	Barnes	3850
39		10	A	Cardiff C	W	3-1	2-0	3	McCarthy, Blackstone, Pepper	6568
40		12	A	Halifax T	W	1-0	0-0	2	Barnes	3983
41		17	H	Scarborough	W	1-0	1-0	2	Pepper (pen)	5993
42		24	A	Rochdale	L	0-1	0-0	3		3920

Final League Position: 4

GOALSCORERS

League (72): Barnes 21, Blackstone 16, Borthwick 8, Pepper 8 (7 pens), McCarthy 7, Canham 4, Warburton 3, Atkin 2, Hall 1, Stancliffe 1, own goal 1.
Coca Cola Cup (0).
FA Cup (1): Canham 1.

Kiely 40	McMillan 42	Hall 42	Pepper 34	Stancliffe 41	Warburton 9 + 1	McCarthy 42	Borthwick 28 + 5	Barnes 40	Swann 38	Blackstone 37 + 2	Canham 16 + 13	Atkin 28 + 3	Barratt 4 + 6	Tutill 6 + 2	Jordan — + 1	Marples 2	Bushell 8	Tilley 4 + 2	Naylor 1 + 3	Match No.
1	2	3	4	5	6	7	8	9	10	11	12									1
1	2	3	4	5	6	7	8	9	10	11	12									2
1	2	3	4	5	6	7	8	9	10	11	12									3
1	2	3	4	5	6	7	8	9	10	11										4
1	2	3	4	5	6	7	8	9	10	11	12									5
1	2	3	4	5	6	7	8	9	10	11	12									6
1	2	3	4	5	6	7	8	9	10	11										7
1	2	3	4	5	6	7	8	9	10	11										8
1	2	3	4	5	6	7	8	9	10	11	12									9
1	2	3	4	5		7	8	9	10	11		6								10
1	2	3	*4*	5		7	8	9	10	11	12	6	14							11
1	2	3	*4*	5		7	8	9	10	11	12	6		14						12
1	2	3	4	5		7	8	9	10	11	12	6								13
1	2	3	4	5		7	8	9	10	11	12	6								14
	2	3		5		7	8	9	10	11		6				1	4			15
	2	3		5		7	8	9	10	11	12	6				1	4			16
1	2	3		5	12	7	8	9	10	11		6					4			17
1	2	3	4	5		7	8	9	10	*11*	12	6	14							18
1	2	3	4	5		7	8	9	10	11		6								19
1	2	3	4	5		7	8	9	10	11		6			12					20
1	2	3	4	5		7	8	9	10	11	12	6								21
1	2	3	4	5		7	8	9	10	11	12	6								22
1	2	3	4	5		7	8	9	10	11	12	6								23
1	2	3	4	5		7	8	9	10	11		6							12	24
1	2	3	4	5		7	8	9	10	11		6							12	25
1	2	3	4	5		7		*9*	14	11	12	6					10	8		26
1	2	3	4	5		7		9		11	12	6					10	8		27
1	2	3	4	5		7		9		11	12	6					10	8	14	28
1	2	3	4			7				11	12	6	14	5			10	*8*	9	29
1	2	3	4	5		7	8	9	10	11		6								30
1	2	3	4	5		7	8	9	10	11	12	6								31
1	2	3	4	5		7	8	9	10	11	12	6								32
1	2	3	4	5		7		9	10	11	8	6								33
1	2	3	4	5		7	12	9	10	11	8	6	14							34
1	2	3		5		7		9	10	11	8	6					4			35
1	2	3		5		7		9	10	11	8	6					4			36
1	2	3		5		7		9	10	11	8	6					4			37
1	2	3		5		7	12	9	10	*11*	8	6					4		14	38
1	2	3	4	5		7	12	9	10	11	8	6								39
1	2	3	4	5		7		9	10	11	8	6								40
1	2	3	4	5		7	12	9	10	11	8	6								41
1	2	3		5		7	12	9	10	11	8	6					4			42

Coca Cola Cup	First Round	Chesterfield (a)	0-2
		(h)	0-0
FA Cup	First Round	Stockport Co (h)	1-3

YORK CITY

Player and Position	Ht	Wt	Date	Birth Place	Source	Clubs	League App	Gls
Goalkeepers								
Dean Kiely	6 0	12 08	10 10 70	Manchester	WBA	Coventry C	—	—
						Ipswich T (loan)	—	—
						York C (loan)	—	—
						York C	78	—
Glen Livingstone	6 2	14 01	13 10 72	Birmingham	Trainee	Aston Villa	—	—
						York C	—	—
Defenders								
Paul Atkin	6 0	12 11	3 9 69	Nottingham	Trainee	Notts Co	—	—
						Bury	21	1
						York C	64	3
Tony Barratt	5 8	11 01	18 10 65	Salford	Billingham T	Grimsby T	22	—
					Billingham T	Hartlepool U	98	4
						York C	118	8
Robert Ellis	6 1	13 07	6 10 73	York	Trainee	York C	—	—
Andy McMillan	5 11	11 04	22 6 68	Bloemfontein		York C	177	2
Paul Stancliffe	6 2	13 05	5 5 58	Sheffield	Apprentice	Rotherham U	285	8
						Sheffield U	278	12
						Rotherham U (loan)	5	—
						Wolverhampton W	17	—
						York C	59	2
Steve Tutill	6 0	12 02	1 10 69	Derwent	Trainee	York C	174	2
Ray Warburton	6 0	12 09	7 10 67	Rotherham	Apprentice	Rotherham U	4	—
						York C	84	9
Midfield								
Steve Bushell	5 9	11 00	28 12 72	Manchester	Trainee	York C	39	—
Tony Canham	5 8	11 05	8 6 60	Leeds	Harrogate Railway	York C	276	52
Craig Hall	5 7	10 00	7 5 74	Oldham	Trainee	York C	—	—
Wayne Hall	5 9	10 04	25 10 68	Rotherham	Darlington	York C	154	8
Scott Jordan	5 10	11 02	19 7 75	Newcastle	Trainee	York C	1	—
Graeme Murty	5 10	11 05	13 11 74	Middlesbrough	Trainee	York C	—	—
Nigel Pepper	5 10	11 05	25 4 68	Rotherham	Apprentice	Rotherham U	45	1
						York C	108	15
Andy Smith*	5 10	11 05	9 4 74	Oldham	Trainee	York C	—	—
Gary Swann	5 11	11 13	11 4 62	York	Apprentice	Hull C	186	9
						Preston NE	199	37
						York C	38	—
Forwards								
Paul Barnes	5 10	12 09	16 11 67	Leicester	Apprentice	Notts Co	53	14
						Stoke C	24	3
						Chesterfield (loan)	1	—
						York C	40	21
Ian Blackstone	6 0	13 00	7 8 64	Harrogate	Harrogate T	York C	97	30
John Borthwick*	6 1	12 05	24 3 64	Hartlepool	Local	Hartlepool U	117	15
						Darlington	75	15
						York C	33	8
Jon McCarthy	5 10	11 01	18 8 70	Middlesbrough		Hartlepool U	1	—
					Shepshed	York C	111	15
Glenn Naylor	5 11	11 02	11 8 72	York	Trainee	York C	46	13
Darren Tilley*	6 2	13 07	15 3 67	Bristol	Yate T	York C	21	—

YORK CITY

Colours: Red shirts, blue shorts, red stockings. **Change colours:** White shirts, red shorts, blue stockings.
Foundation: Although there was a York City club formed in 1903 by a soccer enthusiast from Darlington, this has no connection with the modern club because it went out of existence during World War I. Unlike many others of that period who restarted in 1919, York City did not re-form until 1922 and the tendency now is to ignore the modern club's pre-1922 existence.
First Football League game: 31 August, 1929, Division 3(N), v Wigan Borough (a) W 2-0 – Farmery; Archibald, Johnson; Beck, Davis, Thompson; Evans, Gardner, Cowie (1), Smailes, Stockhill (1).
Did you know: Jack Pinder, one of the members of York City's original staff when they entered the League in 1929, remained an active player until the end of 1947–48.
Managers (and Secretary-Managers)
Bill Sherrington 1924–60 (was secretary for most of this time but virtually secretary-manager for a long pre-war spell), John Collier 1929–36, Tom Mitchell 1936–50, Dick Duckworth 1950–52, Charlie Spencer 1952–53, Jimmy McCormick 1953–54, Sam Bartram 1956–60, Tom Lockie 1960–67, Joe Shaw 1967–68, Tom Johnston 1968–75, Wilf McGuinness 1975–77, Charlie Wright 1977–80, Barry Lyons 1980–81, Denis Smith 1982–87, Bobby Saxton 1987–88, John Bird 1988–91, John Ward 1991–93, Alan Little March 1993–.

Trainees
Bowker, Andrew J; Davison, Jamie; Dooley, Eammon G; Falk, Darren L; Gosling, Michael J; Harris, Raymond M; Medforth, Lee; Mennell, Nicholas; Mockler, Paul F; Roberts, Steven; Simpson, Elliott; Tomlinson, Lea R; Vincent, Paul R; Warrington, Andrew.

Associated Schoolboys
Cresswell, Richard P. W; Culkin, Nicholas; Grice, Paul; Jones, Simon D; Mace, Richard; Minett; Alex J. R; Murr, Michael; O'Hara, Daniel; Ranson, David; Rich, Oliver C; Robinson, Wesley K; Tate, Christopher.

Associated Schoolboys who have accepted the club's offer of a Traineeship/Contract
Osborne, Wayne; Watkinson, Mark; Williams, Darren.

Tottenham Hotspur *Players continued from page 523*

Name			DOB	Birthplace	Source	Club	Apps	Gls
Nick Barmby	5 6	11 04	11 2 74	Hull	Trainee	Tottenham H	22	6
Peter Beadle	6 0	11 12	13 5 72	London	Trainee	Gillingham	67	14
						Tottenham H	—	—
						Bournemouth (loan)	9	2
Gordon Durie	6 0	12 00	6 12 65	Paisley	Hill of Beath H	East Fife	81	26
						Hibernian	47	14
						Chelsea	123	51
						Tottenham H	48	10
John Hendry	5 11	10 06	6 1 70	Glasgow	Hillington YC	Dundee	2	—
						Forfar Ath (loan)	10	6
						Tottenham H	14	5
						Charlton Ath (loan)	5	1
Lee Hodges	5 9	11 06	4 9 73	Epping	Trainee	Tottenham H	4	—
						Plymouth Arg (loan)	7	2
David Howells	5 11	11 10	15 12 67	Guildford	Trainee	Tottenham H	152	15
Gary Lineker (To Grampus Eight May 1992)	5 9	11 10	30 11 60	Leicester	Apprentice	Leicester C	194	95
						Everton	41	30
						Barcelona	99	44
						Tottenham H	105	67
Gerard McMahon	5 11	11 00	29 12 73	Belfast	Glenavon	Tottenham H	—	—
Paul Mahorn	5 8	11 06	13 8 73	Whipps Cross	Trainee	Tottenham H	—	—
Jeffrey Minton	5 5	11 07	28 12 73	Hackney	Trainee	Tottenham H	2	1
Paul Moran	5 10	11 00	22 5 68	Enfield	Trainee	Tottenham H	31	2
						Portsmouth (loan)	3	—
						Leicester C (loan)	10	1
						Newcastle U (loan)	1	—
						Southend U (loan)	1	—
						Cambridge U (loan)	—	—
Anthony Potts*	5 8	11 09	24 10 72	Erith	Trainee	Tottenham H	—	—
Stephen Robinson	5 9	11 00	10 12 74	Lisburn	Trainee	Tottenham H	—	—
Teddy Sheringham	6 0	12 05	2 4 66	Highams Park	Apprentice	Millwall	220	93
						Aldershot (loan)	5	—
						Nottingham F	42	14
						Tottenham H	38	21
Andy Turner	5 9	11 00	23 3 75	Woolwich	Trainee	Tottenham H	18	3

END OF SEASON PLAY-OFFS 1992–93

Whatever the moral attitudes surrounding the play-offs there is no doubt that the introduction of these test matches has coincided with increased interest in the League season. Moreover the three finals at Wembley produced nearly 150,000 spectators.

The First Division final attracted 73,802 on Bank Holiday Monday and saw a dramatic match in which Swindon almost threw away a 3–0 lead before scoring a late penalty winner.

Swindon had started their semi-final well enough beating Tranmere 3–1 after taking a 2–0 lead in the opening three minutes. They led the seond leg match 1–0 after 28 minutes but were 2–1 down after just over an hour.

Craig Maskell made it 2–2 in the 81st minute before Kenny Irons gave Rovers some hope with a penalty two minutes later. But it was not to be.

In the other semi-final, Portsmouth had to play without the suspended Paul Walsh and Guy Butters, sent off in a crucial 4–1 defeat at Sunderland. They trailed to a late Julian Joachim goal at Leicester and though Butters returned for the second leg, Pompey missed Walsh and the free-scoring Guy Whittingham had little support up front in the 2–2 draw.

Stockport County were also handicapped by the absence of their leading scorer Kevin Francis through suspension. They could only manage a 1–1 draw at home to Port Vale in the Second Division semi-final and were beaten away 1–0 by an 84th minute goal from Martin Foyle.

Vale met West Bromwich in the final, Albion having beaten Swansea City 3–2 on aggregate after losing the first leg in Wales 2–1 when Andy McFarlane scored for both teams. At the Hawthorns, a crowd of 26,025 saw Andy Hunt and Ian Hamilton score in the first 19 minutes. Swansea had Colin West (ex-Albion) sent off in the 77th minute.

At Wembley, it was Hunt who broke the deadlock in the 66th minute before Ossie Ardiles' team went on to win 3–0 before an enthusiastic crowd of 53,471.

In the Third Division, the encounters between Crewe Alexandra and Walsall produced 12 goals as both defences seemed incapable of holding their respective opposing attacks. In this regard Crewe were slightly more reliable and ran out 9–3 aggregate winners. Tony Naylor, who had set a club individual record in the season of five goals in one game, scored five including a hat-trick in the away leg.

This tie was in sharp contrast to the Bury v York City affair which was decided by one goal, Gary Swann scoring in the 60th minute of the second leg to divide the teams and give City manager Alan Little the chance of a Wembley final along with his brother Brian, manager of Leicester.

Alan Little had more good fortune in the final, however, but again after Swann had put his team in front in extra time, Crewe equalised through a Dave McKearney penalty and it required the unsatisfactory penalty shoot-out to gain promotion for York.

There was no consoling Leicester of course. It was their second successive play-off failure at Wembley and the sixth defeat between the twin towers overall.

Swindon T (3) 3 *(Vickers (og), Mitchell, Maskell)*
Tranmere R (0) 1 *(Morrissey)* 14,230
Swindon T: Digby; Summerbee, Bodin, Hoddle, Calderwood, Taylor, Moncur (Hazard), MacLaren, Mitchell, Ling, Maskell (White).
Tranmere R: Nixon; Higgins, Brannan, Irons, Proctor, Vickers, Morrissey, Aldridge, Malkin, Nevin (Coyne), Nolan.

DIVISION 2

Stockport Co (1) 1 *(Gannon (pen))*
Port Vale (1) 1 *(Glover)* 7856
Stockport Co: Edwards; Todd, Wallace, Flynn, Williams B, Finley, Gannon (Miller), Ward, Williams PA, Beaumont, Ryan (Duffield).
Port Vale: Musselwhite; Aspin, Sulley (Kent), Billing, Glover, Slaven, Van der Laan, Foyle, Kerr, Taylor.

Swansea C (0) 2 *(McFarlane, Hayes)*
WBA (0) 1 *(McFarlane (og))* 13,917
Swansea C: Freestone; Lyttle, Jenkins, Walker, Harris, Hayes, Cullen (West), Coughlin, McFarlane, Cornforth (Ford), Legg.
WBA: Lange; McNally, Lilwall, Bradley, Raven, Burgess, Hunt (Heggs), Hamilton, Taylor, Mellon (Reid), Donovan.

DIVISION 3

Bury (0) 0
York C (0) 0 6620
Bury: Kelly; Ward, Stanislaus, Hughes, Valentine, Knill, Adekola (Lyons), Rigby, Reid, Stevens, Robinson.
York C: Kiely; McMillan, Hall, Pepper, Stancliffe, Atkin, McCarthy, Canham, Barnes, Swann, Blackstone.

Crewe Alex (2) 5 *(Naylor 2, Clarkson, Edwards, Ward)*
Walsall (1) 1 *(Cecere)* 6198
Crewe Alex: Smith M: McKearney, Smith S, Evans, Wilson, Whalley, Ward, Naylor, Clarkson, Walters (Lennon), Edwards (Woodward).
Walsall: Gayle; Knight (Marsh), Kelly, Smith, Ntamark, Ryder, MacDonald, Methven (Clarke), Cecere, O'Connor, McDonald.

Semi-finals, First Leg

16 MAY
DIVISION 1
Leicester C (0) 1 *(Joachim)*
Portsmouth (0) 0 24,538
Leicester C: Poole; Mills, Whitlow, Smith, Walsh, Hill, Oldfield, Thompson, Gee, Gibson (Grayson), Philpott (Joachim).
Portsmouth: Knight; Awford, Price, McLoughlin, Symons, Daniel, Neill, Chamberlain (Burns), Powell (Lawrence), Whittingham, Kristensen.

Semi-finals, Second Leg

19 MAY
DIVISION 1
Portsmouth (0) 2 *(McLoughlin, Kristensen)*
Leicester C (0) 2 *(Ormondroyd, Thompson)* 25,438
Portsmouth: Knight; Awford, Butters, McLoughlin, Symons, Daniel, Neill (Powell), Price (Hall), Lawrence, Whittingham, Kristensen.
Leicester C: Poole; Mills, Whitlow, Smith, Walsh, Hill, Oldfield, Thompson, Joachim, Ormondroyd, Agnew (Gibson).

Tranmere R (1) 3 *(Proctor, Nevin, Irons (pen))*
Swindon T (1) 2 *(Moncur, Maskell)*   16,083
Tranmere R: Nixon; Higgins, Brannan, Irons, Proctor, Vickers, Morrissey, Aldridge, Malkin, Nevin, Nolan (Coyne).
Swindon T: Digby; Summerbee, Bodin, Hoddle, Calderwood, Taylor, Moncur, MacLaren, Mitchell, Ling, White (Maskell).

DIVISION 2

Port Vale (0) 1 *(Foyle)*
Stockport Co (0) 0   12,689
Port Vale: Musselwhite; Aspin, Kent, Porter, Billing, Glover, Slaven, Van der Laan, Foyle, Kerr, Taylor.
Stockport Co: Edwards; Todd, Wallace, Flynn, Miller, Williams B, Gannon, Ward, Williams PA, Beaumont, Ryan.

WBA (2) 2 *(Hunt, Hamilton)*
Swansea C (0) 0   26,025
WBA: Lange; McNally, Lilwall, Bradley, Raven, Strodder, Hunt, Hamilton, Taylor, Mellon, Donovan.
Swansea C: Freestone; Lyttle, Jenkins, Walker, Harris, Hayes (West), Cullen, Coughlin, McFarlane, Cornforth (Ford), Legg.

DIVISION 3

Walsall (1) 2 *(Clarke, O'Connor)*
Crewe Alex (2) 4 *(Naylor 3, Ward)*   7398
Walsall: Gayle; Marsh, Kelly, Smith, Ntamark, Ryder, MacDonald (Statham), Clarke, Cecere, O'Connor, McDonald (Ollerenshaw).
Crewe Alex: Smith M; McKearney, Smith S, Evans, Wilson (Woodward), Whalley, Ward, Naylor, Lennon, Walters (Clark), Edwards.

York C (0) 1 *(Swann)*
Bury (0) 0   9206
York C: Kiely; McMillan, Hall, Pepper, Stancliffe, Atkin, McCarthy, Canham, Barnes, Swann, Blackstone (Borthwick).

Bury: Kelly; Ward, Stanislaus, Hughes, Valentine, Knill, Adekola (Lyons), Rigby, Reid, Stevens, Robinson.

Finals (at Wembley)

29 MAY
DIVISION 3
Crewe Alex (0) 1 *(McKearney (pen))*
York C (0) 1 *(Swann)*   22,416
Crewe Alex: Smith M; McKearney, Smith S, Evans, Carr, Whalley, Ward, Naylor, Lennon, Walters (Clarkson), Edwards (Woodward).
York C: Kiely; McMillan, Hall, Pepper, Stancliffe (Tutill), Atkin, McCarthy, Canham, Barnes, Swann, Blackstone.
aet; York C won 5-3 on penalties

30 MAY
DIVISION 2
Port Vale (0) 0
WBA (0) 3 *(Hunt, Reid, Donovan)*   53,471
Port Vale: Musselwhite; Aspin, Kent (Billing), Porter, Swan, Glover, Slaven, Van der Laan (Cross), Foyle, Kerr, Taylor.
WBA: Lange; Reid, Lilwall, Bradley, Raven, Strodder, Hunt (Garner), Hamilton, Taylor, McNally, Donovan.

31 MAY
DIVISION 1
Leicester C (0) 3 *(Joachim, Walsh, Thompson)*
Swindon T (1) 4 *(Hoddle, Maskell, Taylor, Bodin (pen))*   73,802
Leicester C: Poole; Mills, Whitlow, Smith, Walsh, Hill, Oldfield, Thompson, Joachim, Agnew, Philpott.
Swindon T: Digby; Summerbee, Bodin, Hoddle, Calderwood, Taylor, Moncur (Hazard), MacLaren, Mitchell, Ling, Maskell (White).

Paul Bodin converts from the penalty spot past Leicester City goalkeeper Kevin Poole, ensuring Swindon Town of a place in the Premier League. (Colorsport)

FA PREMIER LEAGUE

		P	W	D	L	F	A	W	D	L	F	A	Pts	GD
			Home			*Goals*		*Away*			*Goals*			
1	Manchester U	42	14	5	2	39	14	10	7	4	28	17	84	+36
2	Aston Villa	42	13	5	3	36	16	8	6	7	21	24	74	+17
3	Norwich City	42	13	6	2	31	19	8	3	10	30	46	72	−4
4	Blackburn R	42	13	4	4	38	18	7	7	7	30	28	71	+22
5	QPR	42	11	5	5	41	32	6	7	8	22	23	63	+8
6	Liverpool	42	13	4	4	41	18	3	7	11	21	37	59	+7
7	Sheffield W	42	9	8	4	34	26	6	6	9	21	25	59	+4
8	Tottenham H	42	11	5	5	40	25	5	6	10	20	41	59	−6
9	Manchester C	42	7	8	6	30	25	8	4	9	26	26	57	+5
10	Arsenal	42	8	6	7	25	20	7	5	9	15	18	56	+2
11	Chelsea	42	9	7	5	29	22	5	7	9	22	32	56	−3
12	Wimbledon	42	9	4	8	32	23	5	8	8	24	32	54	+1
13	Everton	42	7	6	8	26	27	8	2	11	27	28	53	−2
14	Sheffield U	42	10	6	5	33	19	4	4	13	21	34	52	+1
15	Coventry C	42	7	4	10	29	28	6	9	6	23	29	52	−5
16	Ipswich T	42	8	9	4	29	22	4	7	10	21	33	52	−5
17	Leeds U	42	12	8	1	40	17	0	7	14	17	45	51	−5
18	Southampton	42	10	6	5	30	21	3	5	13	24	40	50	−7
19	Oldham Ath	42	10	6	5	43	30	3	4	14	20	44	49	−11
20	Crystal Palace	42	6	9	6	27	25	5	7	9	21	36	49	−13
21	Middlesbrough	42	8	5	8	33	27	3	6	12	21	48	44	−21
22	Nottingham F	42	6	4	11	17	25	4	6	11	24	37	40	−21

BARCLAYS LEAGUE

DIVISION ONE

		P	W	D	L	F	A	W	D	L	F	A	PTS	GLS
			Home			*Goals*		*Away*			*Goals*			
1	Newcastle U	46	16	6	1	58	15	13	3	7	34	23	96	(92)
2	West Ham U	46	16	5	2	50	17	10	5	8	31	24	88	(81)
3	Portsmouth	46	19	2	2	48	9	7	8	8	32	37	88	(80)
4	Tranmere R	46	15	4	4	48	24	8	6	9	24	32	79	(72)
5	Swindon T	46	15	5	3	41	23	6	8	9	33	36	76	(74)
6	Leicester C	46	14	5	4	43	24	8	5	10	28	40	76	(71)
7	Millwall	46	14	6	3	46	21	4	10	9	19	32	70	(65)
8	Derby Co	46	11	2	10	40	33	8	7	8	28	24	66	(68)
9	Grimsby T	46	12	6	5	33	25	7	1	15	25	32	64	(58)
10	Peterborough U	46	7	11	5	30	26	9	3	11	25	37	62	(55)
11	Wolverhampton W	46	11	6	6	37	26	5	7	11	20	30	61	(57)
12	Charlton Ath	46	10	8	5	28	19	6	5	12	21	27	61	(49)
13	Barnsley	46	12	4	7	29	19	5	5	13	27	41	60	(56)
14	Oxford U	46	8	7	8	29	21	6	7	10	24	35	56	(53)
15	Bristol C	46	10	7	6	29	25	4	7	12	20	42	56	(49)
16	Watford	46	8	7	8	27	30	6	6	11	30	41	55	(57)
17	Notts Co	46	10	7	6	33	21	2	9	12	22	49	52	(55)
18	Southend U	46	9	8	6	33	22	4	5	14	21	42	52	(54)
19	Birmingham C	46	10	4	9	30	32	3	8	12	20	40	51	(50)
20	Luton T	46	6	13	4	26	26	4	8	11	22	36	51	(48)
21	Sunderland	46	9	6	8	34	28	4	5	14	16	36	50	(50)
22	Brentford	46	7	6	10	28	30	6	4	13	24	41	49	(52)
23	Cambridge U	46	8	6	9	29	32	3	10	10	19	37	49	(48)
24	Bristol R	46	6	6	11	30	42	4	5	14	25	45	41	(55)

DIVISION TWO

		P	Home W	D	L	Goals F	A	Away W	D	L	Goals F	A	PTS	GLS
1	Stoke C	46	17	4	2	41	13	10	8	5	32	21	93	(73)
2	Bolton W	46	18	2	3	48	14	9	7	7	32	27	90	(80)
3	Port Vale	46	14	7	2	44	17	12	4	7	35	27	89	(79)
4	WBA	46	17	3	3	56	22	8	7	8	32	32	85	(88)
5	Swansea C	46	12	7	4	38	17	8	6	9	27	30	73	(65)
6	Stockport Co	46	11	11	1	47	18	8	4	11	34	39	72	(81)
7	Leyton Orient	46	16	4	3	49	20	5	5	13	20	33	72	(69)
8	Reading	46	14	4	5	44	20	4	11	8	22	31	69	(66)
9	Brighton & HA	46	13	4	6	36	24	7	5	11	27	35	69	(63)
10	Bradford C	46	12	5	6	36	24	6	9	8	33	43	68	(69)
11	Rotherham U	46	9	7	7	30	27	8	7	8	30	33	65	(60)
12	Fulham	46	9	9	5	28	22	7	8	8	29	33	65	(57)
13	Burnley	46	11	8	4	38	21	4	8	11	19	38	61	(57)
14	Plymouth Arg	46	11	6	6	38	28	5	6	12	21	36	60	(59)
15	Huddersfield T	46	10	6	7	30	22	7	3	13	24	39	60	(54)
16	Hartlepool U	46	8	6	9	19	23	6	6	11	23	37	54	(42)
17	AFC Bournemouth	46	7	10	6	28	24	5	7	11	17	28	53	(45)
18	Blackpool	46	9	9	5	40	30	3	6	14	23	45	51	(63)
19	Exeter C	46	5	8	10	26	30	6	9	8	28	39	50	(54)
20	Hull C	46	9	5	9	28	26	4	6	13	18	43	50	(46)
21	Preston NE	46	8	5	10	41	47	5	3	15	24	47	47	(65)
22	Mansfield T	46	7	8	8	34	34	4	3	16	18	46	44	(52)
23	Wigan Ath	46	6	6	11	26	34	4	5	14	17	38	41	(43)
24	Chester C	46	6	2	15	30	47	2	3	18	19	55	29	(49)

DIVISION THREE

		P	Home W	D	L	Goals F	A	Away W	D	L	Goals F	A	PTS	GLS
1	Cardiff C	42	13	7	1	42	20	12	1	8	35	27	83	(77)
2	Wrexham	42	14	3	4	48	26	9	8	4	27	26	80	(75)
3	Barnet	42	16	4	1	45	19	7	6	8	21	29	79	(66)
4	York C	42	13	6	2	41	15	8	6	7	31	30	75	(66)
5	Walsall	42	11	6	4	42	31	11	1	9	34	30	73	(76)
6	Crewe Alex	42	13	3	5	47	23	8	4	9	28	33	70	(75)
7	Bury	42	10	7	4	36	19	8	2	11	27	36	63	(63)
8	Lincoln C	42	10	6	5	31	20	8	3	10	26	33	63	(57)
9	Shrewsbury T	42	11	3	7	36	30	6	8	7	21	22	62	(57)
10	Colchester U	42	13	3	5	38	26	5	2	14	29	50	59	(67)
11	Rochdale	42	10	3	8	38	29	6	7	8	32	41	58	(70)
12	Chesterfield	42	11	3	7	32	28	4	8	9	27	35	56	(59)
13	Scarborough	42	7	7	7	32	30	8	2	11	34	41	54	(66)
14	Scunthorpe U	42	8	7	6	38	25	6	5	10	19	29	54	(57)
15	Darlington	42	5	6	10	23	31	7	8	6	25	22	50	(48)
16	Doncaster R	42	6	5	10	22	28	5	9	7	20	29	47	(42)
17	Hereford U	42	7	9	5	31	27	3	6	12	16	33	45	(47)
18	Carlisle U	42	7	5	9	29	27	4	6	11	22	38	44	(51)
19	Torquay U	42	6	4	11	18	26	6	3	12	27	41	43	(45)
20	Northampton T	42	6	5	10	19	28	5	3	13	29	46	41	(48)
21	Gillingham	42	9	4	8	32	28	0	9	12	16	36	40	(48)
22	Halifax T	42	3	5	13	20	35	6	4	11	25	33	36	(45)

FOOTBALL LEAGUE 1888–89 to 1992–93

FA PREMIER LEAGUE
Maximum points: 126

	First	Pts	Second	Pts	Third	Pts
1992–93	Manchester U	84	Aston Villa	74	Norwich C	72

FIRST DIVISION
Maximum points: 138

1992–93	Newcastle U	96	West Ham U	88	Portsmouth††	88

SECOND DIVISION
Maximum points: 138

1992–93	Stoke C	93	Bolton W	90	Port Vale††	89

THIRD DIVISION
Maximum points: 126

1992–93	Cardiff C	83	Wrexham	80	Barnet	79

†† *Not promoted after play-offs.*

FOOTBALL LEAGUE

	First	Pts	Second	Pts	Third	Pts
1888–89a	Preston NE	40	Aston Villa	29	Wolverhampton W	28
1889–90a	Preston NE	33	Everton	31	Blackburn R	27
1890–91a	Everton	29	Preston NE	27	Notts Co	26
1891–92b	Sunderland	42	Preston NE	37	Bolton W	36

FIRST DIVISION to 1991–92
Maximum points: a 44; b 52; c 60; d 68; e 76; f 84; g 126; h 120; k 114.

	First	Pts	Second	Pts	Third	Pts
1892–93c	Sunderland	48	Preston NE	37	Everton	36
1893–94c	Aston Villa	44	Sunderland	38	Derby Co	36
1894–95c	Sunderland	47	Everton	42	Aston Villa	39
1895–96c	Aston Villa	45	Derby Co	41	Everton	39
1896–97c	Aston Villa	47	Sheffield U*	36	Derby Co	36
1897–98c	Sheffield U	42	Sunderland	37	Wolverhampton W*	35
1898–99d	Aston Villa	45	Liverpool	43	Burnley	39
1899–1900d	Aston Villa	50	Sheffield U	48	Sunderland	41
1900–01d	Liverpool	45	Sunderland	43	Notts Co	40
1901–02d	Sunderland	44	Everton	41	Newcastle U	37
1902–03d	The Wednesday	42	Aston Villa*	41	Sunderland	41
1903–04d	The Wednesday	47	Manchester C	44	Everton	43
1904–05d	Newcastle U	48	Everton	47	Manchester C	46
1905–06e	Liverpool	51	Preston NE	47	The Wednesday	44
1906–07e	Newcastle U	51	Bristol C	48	Everton*	45
1907–08e	Manchester U	52	Aston Villa*	43	Manchester C	43
1908–09e	Newcastle U	53	Everton	46	Sunderland	44
1909–10e	Aston Villa	53	Liverpool	48	Blackburn R*	45
1910–11e	Manchester U	52	Aston Villa	51	Sunderland*	45
1911–12e	Blackburn R	49	Everton	46	Newcastle U	44
1912–13e	Sunderland	54	Aston Villa	50	Sheffield W	49
1913–14e	Blackburn R	51	Aston Villa	44	Middlesbrough*	43
1914–15e	Everton	46	Oldham Ath	45	Blackburn R*	43
1919–20f	WBA	60	Burnley	51	Chelsea	49
1920–21f	Burnley	59	Manchester C	54	Bolton W	52
1921–22f	Liverpool	57	Tottenham H	51	Burnley	49
1922–23f	Liverpool	60	Sunderland	54	Huddersfield T	53
1923–24f	Huddersfield T*	57	Cardiff C	57	Sunderland	53
1924–25f	Huddersfield T	58	WBA	56	Bolton W	55
1925–26f	Huddersfield T	57	Arsenal	52	Sunderland	48
1926–27f	Newcastle U	56	Huddersfield T	51	Sunderland	49
1927–28f	Everton	53	Huddersfield T	51	Leicester C	48
1928–29f	Sheffield W	52	Leicester C	51	Aston Villa	50
1929–30f	Sheffield W	60	Derby Co	50	Manchester C*	47
1930–31f	Arsenal	66	Aston Villa	59	Sheffield W	52
1931–32f	Everton	56	Arsenal	54	Sheffield W	50
1932–33f	Arsenal	58	Aston Villa	54	Sheffield W	51
1933–34f	Arsenal	59	Huddersfield T	56	Tottenham H	49
1934–35f	Arsenal	58	Sunderland	54	Sheffield W	49
1935–36f	Sunderland	56	Derby Co*	48	Huddersfield T	48
1936–37f	Manchester C	57	Charlton Ath	54	Arsenal	52
1937–38f	Arsenal	52	Wolverhampton W	51	Preston NE	49
1938–39f	Everton	59	Wolverhampton W	55	Charlton Ath	50
1946–47f	Liverpool	57	Manchester U*	56	Wolverhampton W	56
1947–48f	Arsenal	59	Manchester U*	52	Burnley	52
1948–49f	Portsmouth	58	Manchester U*	53	Derby Co	53
1949–50f	Portsmouth*	53	Wolverhampton W	53	Sunderland	52

* *Won or placed on goal average.*

591

	First	Pts	Second	Pts	Third	Pts
1950–51f	Tottenham H	60	Manchester U	56	Blackpool	50
1951–52f	Manchester U	57	Tottenham H*	53	Arsenal	53
1952–53f	Arsenal*	54	Preston NE	54	Wolverhampton W	51
1953–54f	Wolverhampton W	57	WBA	53	Huddersfield T	51
1954–55f	Chelsea	52	Wolverhampton W*	48	Portsmouth*	48
1955–56f	Manchester U	60	Blackpool*	49	Wolverhampton W	49
1956–57f	Manchester U	64	Tottenham H*	56	Preston NE	56
1957–58f	Wolverhampton W	64	Preston NE	59	Tottenham H	51
1958–59f	Wolverhampton W	61	Manchester U	55	Arsenal*	50
1959–60f	Burnley	55	Wolverhampton W	54	Tottenham H	53
1960–61f	Tottenham H	66	Sheffield W	58	Wolverhampton W	57
1961–62f	Ipswich T	56	Burnley	53	Tottenham H	52
1962–63f	Everton	61	Tottenham H	55	Burnley	54
1963–64f	Liverpool	57	Manchester U	53	Everton	52
1964–65f	Manchester U*	61	Leeds U	61	Chelsea	56
1965–66f	Liverpool	61	Leeds U*	55	Burnley	55
1966–67f	Manchester U	60	Nottingham F*	56	Tottenham H	56
1967–68f	Manchester C	58	Manchester U	56	Liverpool	55
1968–69f	Leeds U	67	Liverpool	61	Everton	57
1969–70f	Everton	66	Leeds U	57	Chelsea	55
1970–71f	Arsenal	65	Leeds U	64	Tottenham H*	52
1971–72f	Derby Co	58	Leeds U*	57	Liverpool*	57
1972–73f	Liverpool	60	Arsenal	57	Leeds U	53
1973–74f	Leeds U	62	Liverpool	57	Derby Co	48
1974–75f	Derby Co	53	Liverpool*	51	Ipswich T	57
1975–76f	Liverpool	60	QPR	59	Manchester U	56
1976–77f	Liverpool	57	Manchester C	56	Ipswich T	52
1977–78f	Nottingham F	64	Liverpool	57	Everton	55
1978–79f	Liverpool	68	Nottingham F	60	WBA	59
1979–80f	Liverpool	60	Manchester U	58	Ipswich T	53
1980–81f	Aston Villa	60	Ipswich T	56	Arsenal	53
1981–82g	Liverpool	87	Ipswich T	83	Manchester U	78
1982–83g	Liverpool	82	Watford	71	Manchester U	70
1983–84g	Liverpool	80	Southampton	77	Nottingham F*	74
1984–85g	Everton	90	Liverpool*	77	Tottenham H	77
1985–86g	Liverpool	88	Everton	86	West Ham U	84
1986–87g	Everton	86	Liverpool	77	Tottenham H	71
1987–88h	Liverpool	90	Manchester U	81	Nottingham F	73
1988–89k	Arsenal*	76	Liverpool	76	Nottingham F	64
1989–90k	Liverpool	79	Aston Villa	70	Tottenham H	63
1990–91k	Arsenal†	83	Liverpool	76	Crystal Palace	69
1991–92g	Leeds U	82	Manchester U	78	Sheffield W	75

No official competition during 1915–19 and 1939–46.
† 2 pts deducted

SECOND DIVISION to 1991–92
Maximum points: a 44; b 56; c 60; d 68; e 76; f 84; g 126; h 132; k 138.

	First	Pts	Second	Pts	Third	Pts
1892–93a	Small Heath	36	Sheffield U	35	Darwen	30
1893–94b	Liverpool	50	Small Heath	42	Notts Co	39
1894–95c	Bury	48	Notts Co	39	Newton Heath*	38
1895–96c	Liverpool*	46	Manchester C	46	Grimsby T*	42
1896–97c	Notts Co	42	Newton Heath	39	Grimsby T	38
1897–98c	Burnley	48	Newcastle U	45	Manchester C	39
1898–99d	Manchester C	52	Glossop NE	46	Leicester Fosse	45
1899–1900d	The Wednesday	54	Bolton W	52	Small Heath	46
1900–01d	Grimsby T	49	Small Heath	48	Burnley	44
1901–02d	WBA	55	Middlesbrough	51	Preston NE*	42
1902–03d	Manchester C	54	Small Heath	51	Woolwich A	48
1903–04d	Preston NE	50	Woolwich A	49	Manchester U	48
1904–05d	Liverpool	58	Bolton W	56	Manchester U	53
1905–06e	Bristol C	66	Manchester U	62	Chelsea	53
1906–07e	Nottingham F	60	Chelsea	57	Leicester Fosse	48
1907–08e	Bradford C	54	Leicester Fosse	52	Oldham Ath	50
1908–09e	Bolton W	52	Tottenham H*	51	WBA	51
1909–10e	Manchester C	54	Oldham Ath*	53	Hull C*	53
1910–11e	WBA	53	Bolton W	51	Chelsea	49
1911–12e	Derby Co*	54	Chelsea	54	Burnley	52
1912–13e	Preston NE	53	Burnley	50	Birmingham	46
1913–14e	Notts Co	53	Bradford PA*	49	Woolwich A	49
1914–15e	Derby Co	53	Preston NE	50	Barnsley	47
1919–20f	Tottenham H	70	Huddersfield T	64	Birmingham	56
1920–21f	Birmingham*	58	Cardiff C	58	Bristol C	51
1921–22f	Nottingham F	56	Stoke C*	52	Barnsley	52
1922–23f	West Ham U*	51	Leicester C	51		
1922–23f	Notts Co	53	West Ham U*	51	Leicester C	51
1923–24f	Leeds U	54	Bury*	51	Derby Co	51
1924–25f	Leicester C	59	Manchester U	57	Derby Co	55
1925–26f	Sheffield W	60	Derby Co	57	Chelsea	52
1926–27f	Middlesbrough	62	Portsmouth*	54	Manchester C	54
1927–28f	Manchester C	59	Leeds U	57	Chelsea	54
1928–29f	Middlesbrough	55	Grimsby T	53	Bradford*	48
1929–30f	Blackpool	58	Chelsea	55	Oldham Ath	53

Won or placed on goal average/goal difference.

592

	First	Pts	Second	Pts	Third	Pts
1930–31f	Everton	61	WBA	54	Tottenham H	51
1931–32f	Wolverhampton W	56	Leeds U	54	Stoke C	52
1932–33f	Stoke C	56	Tottenham H	55	Fulham	50
1933–34f	Grimsby T	59	Preston NE	52	Bolton W*	51
1934–35f	Brentford	61	Bolton W*	56	West Ham U	56
1935–36f	Manchester U	56	Charlton Ath	55	Sheffield U*	52
1936–37f	Leicester C	56	Blackpool	55	Bury	52
1937–38f	Aston Villa	57	Manchester U*	53	Sheffield U	53
1938–39f	Blackburn R	55	Sheffield U	54	Sheffield W	53
1946–47f	Manchester C	62	Burnley	58	Birmingham C	55
1947–48f	Birmingham C	59	Newcastle U	56	Southampton	52
1948–49f	Fulham	57	WBA	56	Southampton	55
1949–50f	Tottenham H	61	Sheffield W*	52	Sheffield U*	52
1950–51f	Preston NE	57	Manchester C	52	Cardiff C	50
1951–52f	Sheffield W	53	Cardiff C*	51	Birmingham C	51
1952–53f	Sheffield U	60	Huddersfield T	58	Luton T	52
1953–54f	Leicester C*	56	Everton	56	Blackburn R	55
1954–55f	Birmingham C*	54	Luton T*	54	Rotherham U	54
1955–56f	Sheffield W	55	Leeds U	52	Liverpool*	48
1956–57f	Leicester C	61	Nottingham F	54	Liverpool	53
1957–58f	West Ham U	57	Blackburn R	56	Charlton Ath	55
1958–59f	Sheffield W	62	Fulham	60	Sheffield U*	53
1959–60f	Aston Villa	59	Cardiff C	58	Liverpool*	50
1960–61f	Ipswich T	59	Sheffield U	58	Liverpool	52
1961–62f	Liverpool	62	Leyton O	54	Sunderland	53
1962–63f	Stoke C	53	Chelsea*	52	Sunderland	52
1963–64f	Leeds U	63	Sunderland	61	Preston NE	56
1964–65f	Newcastle U	57	Northampton T	56	Bolton W	50
1965–66f	Manchester C	59	Southampton	54	Coventry C	53
1966–67f	Coventry C	59	Wolverhampton W	58	Carlisle U	52
1967–68f	Ipswich T	59	QPR*	58	Blackpool	58
1968–69f	Derby Co	63	Crystal Palace	56	Charlton Ath	50
1969–70f	Huddersfield T	60	Blackpool	53	Leicester C	51
1970–71f	Leicester C	59	Sheffield U	56	Cardiff C*	53
1971–72f	Norwich C	57	Birmingham C	56	Millwall	55
1972–73f	Burnley	62	QPR	61	Aston Villa	50
1973–74f	Middlesbrough	65	Luton T	50	Carlisle U	49
1974–75f	Manchester U	61	Aston Villa	58	Norwich C	53
1975–76f	Sunderland	56	Bristol C*	53	WBA	53
1976–77f	Wolverhampton W	57	Chelsea	55	Nottingham F	52
1977–78f	Bolton W	58	Southampton	57	Tottenham H*	56
1978–79f	Crystal Palace	57	Brighton*	56	Stoke C	56
1979–80f	Leicester C	55	Sunderland	54	Birmingham C*	53
1980–81f	West Ham U	66	Notts Co	53	Swansea C*	50
1981–82g	Luton T	88	Watford	80	Norwich C	71
1982–83g	QPR	85	Wolverhampton W	75	Leicester C	70
1983–84g	Chelsea*	88	Sheffield W	88	Newcastle U	80
1984–85g	Oxford U	84	Birmingham C	82	Manchester C	74
1985–86g	Norwich C	84	Charlton Ath	77	Wimbledon	76
1986–87g	Derby Co	84	Portsmouth	78	Oldham Ath††	75
1987–88h	Millwall	82	Aston Villa*	78	Middlesbrough	78
1988–89k	Chelsea	99	Manchester C	82	Crystal Palace	81
1989–90k	Leeds U*	85	Sheffield U	85	Newcastle U††	80
1990–91k	Oldham Ath	88	West Ham U	87	Sheffield W	82
1991–92k	Ipswich T	84	Middlesbrough	80	Derby Co	78

No competition during 1915–19 and 1939–46.
††Not promoted after play-offs.

THIRD DIVISION to 1991–92
Maximum points: 92; 138 from 1981–82.

	First	Pts	Second	Pts	Third	Pts
1958–59	Plymouth Arg	62	Hull C	61	Brentford*	57
1959–60	Southampton	61	Norwich C	59	Shrewsbury T*	52
1960–61	Bury	68	Walsall	62	QPR	60
1961–62	Portsmouth	65	Grimsby T	62	Bournemouth*	59
1962–63	Northampton T	62	Swindon T	58	Port Vale	54
1963–64	Coventry C*	60	Crystal Palace	60	Watford	58
1964–65	Carlisle U	60	Bristol C*	59	Mansfield T	59
1965–66	Hull C	69	Millwall	65	QPR	57
1966–67	QPR	67	Middlesbrough	55	Watford	54
1967–68	Oxford U	57	Bury	56	Shrewsbury T	55
1968–69	Watford*	64	Swindon T	64	Luton T	61
1969–70	Orient	62	Luton T	60	Bristol R	56
1970–71	Preston NE	61	Fulham	60	Halifax T	56
1971–72	Aston Villa	70	Brighton	65	Bournemouth*	62
1972–73	Bolton W	61	Notts Co	57	Blackburn R	55
1973–74	Oldham Ath	62	Bristol R*	61	York C	61
1974–75	Blackburn R	60	Plymouth Arg	59	Charlton Ath	55
1975–76	Hereford U	63	Cardiff C	57	Millwall	56
1976–77	Mansfield T	64	Brighton & HA	61	Crystal Palace*	59
1977–78	Wrexham	61	Cambridge U	58	Preston NE*	56
1978–79	Shrewsbury T	61	Watford*	60	Swansea C	60

* Won or placed on goal average/goal difference.

	First	Pts	Second	Pts	Third	Pts
1979–80	Grimsby T	62	Blackburn R	59	Sheffield W	58
1980–81	Rotherham U	61	Barnsley*	59	Charlton Ath	59
1981–82	Burnley*	80	Carlisle U	80	Fulham	78
1982–83	Portsmouth	91	Cardiff C	86	Huddersfield T	82
1983–84	Oxford U	95	Wimbledon	87	Sheffield U*	83
1984–85	Bradford C	94	Millwall	90	Hull C	87
1985–86	Reading	94	Plymouth Arg	87	Derby Co	84
1986–87	Bournemouth	97	Middlesbrough	94	Swindon T	87
1987–88	Sunderland	93	Brighton & HA	84	Walsall	82
1988–89	Wolverhampton W	92	Sheffield U	84	Port Vale	84
1989–90	Bristol R	93	Bristol C	91	Notts Co	87
1990–91	Cambridge U	86	Southend U	85	Grimsby T*	83
1991–92	Brentford	82	Birmingham C	81	Huddersfield T	78

FOURTH DIVISION (1958–1992)

Maximum points: 92; 138 from 1981–82.

	First	Pts	Second	Pts	Third	Pts	Fourth	Pts
1958–59	Port Vale	64	Coventry C*	60	York C	60	Shrewsbury T	58
1959–60	Walsall	65	Notts Co*	60	Torquay U	60	Watford	57
1960–61	Peterborough U	66	Crystal Palace	64	Northampton T*	60	Bradford PA	60
1961–62†	Millwalh	56	Colchester U	55	Wrexham	53	Carlisle U	52
1962–63	Brentford	62	Oldham Ath*	59	Crewe Alex	59	Mansfield T*	57
1963–64	Gillingham*	60	Carlisle U	60	Workington T	59	Exeter C	58
1964–65	Brighton	63	Millwall*	62	York C	62	Oxford U	61
1965–66	Doncaster R*	59	Darlington	59	Torquay U	58	Colchester U*	56
1966–67	Stockport Co	64	Southport*	59	Barrow	59	Tranmere R	58
1967–68	Luton T	66	Barnsley	61	Hartlepools U	60	Crewe Alex	58
1968–69	Doncaster R	59	Halifax T	57	Rochdale*	56	Bradford C	56
1969–70	Chesterfield	64	Wrexham	61	Swansea C	60	Port Vale	59
1970–71	Notts Co	69	Bournemouth	60	Oldham Ath	59	York C	56
1971–72	Grimsby T	63	Southend U	60	Brentford	59	Scunthorpe U	57
1972–73	Southport	62	Hereford U	58	Cambridge U	57	Aldershot*	56
1973–74	Peterborough U	65	Gillingham	62	Colchester U	60	Bury	59
1974–75	Mansfield T	68	Shrewsbury T	62	Rotherham U	59	Chester*	57
1975–76	Lincoln C	74	Northampton T	68	Reading	60	Tranmere R	58
1976–77	Cambridge U	65	Exeter C	62	Colchester U*	59	Bradford C	59
1977–78	Watford	71	Southend U	60	Swansea C*	56	Brentford	56
1978–79	Reading	65	Grimsby T*	61	Wimbledon*	61	Barnsley	61
1979–80	Huddersfield T	66	Walsall	64	Newport Co	61	Portsmouth*	60
1980–81	Southend U	67	Lincoln C	65	Doncaster R	56	Wimbledon	55
1981–82	Sheffield U	96	Bradford C*	91	Wigan Ath	91	AFC Bournemouth	88
1982–83	Wimbledon	98	Hull C	90	Port Vale	88	Scunthorpe U	83
1983–84	York C	101	Doncaster R	85	Reading*	82	Bristol C	82
1984–85	Chesterfield	91	Blackpool	86	Darlington	85	Bury	84
1985–86	Swindon T	102	Chester C	84	Mansfield T	81	Port Vale	79
1986–87	Northampton T	99	Preston NE	90	Soqthend U	80	Wolverhampton W††	79
1987–88	Wolverhampton W	90	Cardiff C	85	Bolton W	78	Scunthorpe U††	77
1988–89	Rotherham U	82	Tranmere R	80	Crewe Alex	78	Scunthorpe U††	77
1989–90	Exeter C	89	Grimsby T	79	Southend U	75	Stockport Co††	74
1990–91	Darlington	83	Stockport Co*	82	Hartlepool U	82	Peterborough U	80
1991–92†*	Burnley	80	Rotherham U*	77	Mansfield T	77	Blackpool	76

†*Maximum points:* 88 owing to Accrington Stanley's resignation.   ††*Not promoted after play-offs.*
†**Maximum points:* 126 owing to Aldershot being expelled.

THIRD DIVISION—SOUTH (1920–1958)

Maximum points: a 84; b 92.

	First	Pts	Second	Pts	Third	Pts
1920–21a	Crystal Palace	59	Southampton	54	QPR	53
1921–22a	Southampton*	61	Plymouth Arg	61	Portsmouth	53
1922–23a	Bristol C	59	Plymouth Arg*	53	Swansea T	53
1923–24a	Portsmouth	59	Plymouth Arg	55	Millwall	54
1924–25a	Swansea T	57	Plymouth Arg	56	Bristol C	53
1925–26a	Reading	57	Plymouth Arg	56	Millwall	53
1926–27a	Bristol C	62	Plymouth Arg	60	Millwall	56
1927–28a	Millwall	65	Northampton T	55	Plymouth Arg	53
1928–29a	Charlton Ath*	54	Crystal Palace	54	Northampton T*	52
1929–30a	Plymouth Arg	68	Brentford	61	QPR	51
1930–31a	Notts Co	59	Crystal Palace	51	Brentford	50
1931–32a	Fulham	57	Reading	55	Southend U	53
1932–33a	Brentford	62	Exeter C	58	Norwich C	57
1933–34a	Norwich C	61	Coventry C*	54	Reading*	54
1934–35a	Charlton Ath	61	Reading	53	Coventry C	51
1935–36a	Coventry C	57	Luton T	56	Reading	54
1936–37a	Luton T	58	Notts Co	56	Brighton	53
1937–38a	Millwall	56	Bristol C	55	QPR*	53
1938–39a	Newport Co	55	Crystal Palace	52	Brighton	49
1939–46	Competition cancelled owing to war.					
1946–47a	Cardiff C	66	QPR	57	Bristol C	51
1947–48a	QPR	61	Bournemouth	57	Walsall	51
1948–49a	Swansea T	62	Reading	55	Bournemouth	52
1949–50a	Notts Co	58	Northampton T*	51	Southend U	51

* Won or placed on goal average.

	First	Pts	Second	Pts	Third	Pts
1950–51b	Nottingham F	70	Norwich C	64	Reading*	57
1951–52b	Plymouth Arg	66	Reading*	61	Norwich C	61
1952–53b	Bristol R	64	Millwall*	62	Northampton T	62
1953–54b	Ipswich T	64	Brighton	61	Bristol C	56
1954–55b	Bristol C	70	Leyton O	61	Southampton	59
1955–56b	Leyton O	66	Brighton	65	Ipswich T	64
1956–57b	Ipswich T*	59	Torquay U	59	Colchester U	58
1957–58b	Brighton	60	Brentford*	58	Plymouth Arg	58

THIRD DIVISION—NORTH (1921–1958)
Maximum points: a 76; b 84; c 80; d 92.

	First	Pts	Second	Pts	Third	Pts
1921–22a	Stockport Co	56	Darlington*	50	Grimsby T	50
1922–23a	Nelson	51	Bradford PA	47	Walsall	46
1923–24b	Wolverhampton W	63	Rochdale	62	Chesterfield	54
1924–25b	Darlington	58	Nelson*	53	New Brighton	53
1925–26b	Grimsby T	61	Bradford PA	60	Rochdale	59
1926–27b	Stoke C	63	Rochdale	58	Bradford PA	55
1927–28b	Bradford PA	63	Lincoln C	55	Stockport Co	54
1928–29g	Bradford C	63	Stockport Co	62	Wrexham	52
1929–30b	Port Vale	67	Stockport Co	63	Darlington*	50
1930–31b	Chesterfield	58	Lincoln C	57	Wrexham*	54
1931–32c	Lincoln C*	57	Gateshead	57	Chester	50
1932–33b	Hull C	59	Wrexham	57	Stockport Co	54
1933–34b	Barnsley	62	Chesterfield	61	Stockport Co	59
1934–35b	Doncaster R	57	Halifax T	55	Chester	54
1935–36b	Chesterfield	60	Chester*	55	Tranmere R	55
1936–37b	Stockport Co	60	Lincoln C	57	Chester	53
1937–38b	Tranmere R	56	Doncaster R	54	Hull C	53
1938–39b	Barnsley	67	Doncaster R	56	Bradford C	52
1939–46	Competition cancelled owing to war.					
1946–47b	Doncaster R	72	Rotherham U	60	Chester	56
1947–48b	Lincoln C	60	Rotherham U	59	Wrexham	50
1948–49b	Hull C	65	Rotherham U	62	Doncaster R	50
1949–50b	Doncaster R	55	Gateshead	53	Rochdale*	51
1950–51d	Rotherham U	71	Mansfield T	64	Carlisle U	62
1951–52d	Lincoln C	69	Grimsby T	66	Stockport Co	59
1952–53d	Oldham Ath	59	Port Vale	58	Wrexham	56
1953–54d	Port Vale	69	Barnsley	58	Scunthorpe U	57
1954–55d	Barnsley	65	Accrington S	61	Scunthorpe U*	58
1955–56d	Grimsby T	68	Derby Co	63	Accrington S	59
1956–57d	Derby Co	63	Hartlepool U	59	Accrington S*	58
1957–58d	Scunthorpe U	66	Accrington S	59	Bradford C	57

* Won or placed on goal average.

PROMOTED AFTER PLAY-OFFS
(Not accounted for in previous section)

1986–87   Aldershot to Division 3.
1987–88   Swansea C to Divison 3.
1988–89   Leyton O to Division 3.
1989–90   Cambridge U to Division 3; Notts Co to Division 2; Sunderland to Division 1.
1990–91   Notts Co to Division 1; Tranmere R to Division 2; Torquay U to Division 3.
1991–92   Blackburn R to Premier League; Peterborough U to Division 1.
1992–93   Swindon T to Premier League; WBA to Division 1; York C to Division 2.

LEAGUE TITLE WINS

FA PREMIER LEAGUE – Manchester U 1.

LEAGUE DIVISION 1 – Liverpool 18, Arsenal 10, Everton 9, Manchester U 7, Aston Villa 7, Sunderland 6, Newcastle U 5, Sheffield W 4, Huddersfield T 3, Leeds U 3, Wolverhampton W 3, Blackburn R 2, Portsmouth 2, Preston NE 2, Burnley 2, Manchester C 2, Tottenham H 2, Derby Co 2, Chelsea 1, Sheffield U 1, WBA 1, Ipswich T 1, Nottingham F 1 each.

LEAGUE DIVISION 2 – Leicester C 6, Manchester C 6, Sheffield W 5, Birmingham C (one as Small Heath) 4, Derby Co 4, Liverpool 4, Ipswich T 3, Leeds U 3, Notts Co 3, Preston NE 3, Middlesbrough 3, Stoke C 3, Grimsby T 2, Norwich C 2, Nottingham F 2, Tottenham H 2, WBA 2, Aston Villa 2, Burnley 2, Chelsea 2, Manchester U 2, West Ham U 2, Wolverhampton W 2, Bolton W 2, Huddersfield T, Bristol C, Brentford, Bury, Bradford C, Everton, Fulham, Sheffield U, Newcastle U, Coventry C, Blackpool, Blackburn R, Sunderland, Crystal Palace, Luton T, QPR, Oxford U, Millwall, Oldham Ath 1 each.

LEAGUE DIVISION 3 – Portsmouth 2, Oxford U 2, Plymouth Arg, Southampton, Bury, Northampton T, Coventry C, Carlisle U, Hull C, QPR, Watford, Leyton O, Preston NE, Aston Villa, Bolton W, Oldham Ath, Blackburn R, Hereford U, Mansfield T, Wrexham, Shrewsbury T, Grimsby T, Rotherham U, Burnley, Bradford C, Bournemouth, Reading, Sunderland, Wolverhampton W, Bristol R, Cambridge U, Brentford, Cardiff C 1 each.

LEAGUE DIVISION 4 – Chesterfield 2, Doncaster R 2, Peterborough U 2, Port Vale, Walsall, Millwall, Brentford, Gillingham, Brighton, Stockport Co, Luton T, Notts Co, Grimsby T, Southport, Mansfield T, Lincoln C, Cambridge U, Watford, Reading, Huddersfield T, Southend U, Sheffield U, Wimbledon, York C, Swindon T, Northampton T, Wolverhampton W, Rotherham U, Exeter C, Darlington, Burnley 1 each.

To 1957–58

DIVISION 3 (South) – Bristol C 3; Charlton Ath, Ipswich T, Millwall, Notts Co, Plymouth Arg, Swansea T 2 each; Brentford, Bristol R, Cardiff C, Crystal Palace, Coventry C, Fulham, Leyton O, Luton T, Newport Co, Nottingham F, Norwich C, Portsmouth, QPR, Reading, Southampton, Brighton 1 each.

DIVISION 3 (North) – Barnsley, Doncaster R, Lincoln C 3 each; Chesterfield, Grimsby T, Hull C, Port Vale, Stockport Co 2 each; Bradford PA, Bradford C, Darlington, Derby Co, Nelson, Oldham Ath, Rotherham U, Stoke C, Tranmere R, Wolverhampton W, Scunthorpe U 1 each.

RELEGATED CLUBS

1891–92 League extended. Newton Heath, Sheffield W and Nottingham F admitted. *Second Division formed* including Darwen.

1892–93 In Test matches, Sheffield U and Darwen won promotion in place of Notts Co and Accrington S.

1893–94 In Tests, Liverpool and Small Heath won promotion. Newton Heath and Darwen relegated.

1894–95 After Tests, Bury promoted, Liverpool relegated.

1895–96 After Tests, Liverpool promoted, Small Heath relegated.

1896–97 After Tests, Notts Co promoted, Burnley relegated.

1897–98 Test system abolished after success of Stoke C and Burnley. League extended. Blackburn R and Newcastle U elected to First Division. *Automatic promotion and relegation introduced.*

FA PREMIER LEAGUE TO DIVISION 1

1992–93 Crystal Palace, Middlesbrough, Nottingham Forest

DIVISION 1 TO DIVISION 2

1898–99 Bolton W and Sheffield W
1899–1900 Burnley and Glossop
1900–01 Preston NE and WBA
1901–02 Small Heath and Manchester C
1902–03 Grimsby T and Bolton W
1903–04 Liverpool and WBA
1904–05 League extended. Bury and Notts Co, two bottom clubs in First Division, re-elected.
1905–06 Nottingham F and Wolverhampton W
1906–07 Derby Co and Stoke C
1907–08 Bolton W and Birmingham C
1908–09 Manchester C and Leicester Fosse
1909–10 Bolton W and Chelsea
1910–11 Bristol C and Nottingham F
1911–12 Preston NE and Bury
1912–13 Notts Co and Woolwich Arsenal
1913–14 Preston NE and Derby Co
1914–15 Tottenham H and Chelsea*
1919–20 Notts Co and Sheffield W
1920–21 Derby Co and Bradford PA
1921–22 Bradford C and Manchester U
1922–23 Stoke C and Oldham Ath
1923–24 Chelsea and Middlesbrough
1924–25 Preston NE and Nottingham F
1925–26 Manchester C and Notts Co
1926–27 Leeds U and WBA
1927–28 Tottenham H and Middlesbrough
1928–29 Bury and Cardiff C
1929–30 Burnley and Everton
1930–31 Leeds U and Manchester U
1931–32 Grimsby T and West Ham U
1932–33 Bolton W and Blackpool
1933–34 Newcastle U and Sheffield U
1934–35 Leicester C and Tottenham H
1935–36 Aston Villa and Blackburn R
1936–37 Manchester U and Sheffield W
1937–38 Manchester C and WBA
1938–39 Birmingham C and Leicester C
1946–47 Brentford and Leeds U
1947–48 Blackburn R and Grimsby T
1948–49 Preston NE and Sheffield U
1949–50 Manchester C and Birmingham C
1950–51 Sheffield W and Everton

1951–52 Huddersfield and Fulham
1952–53 Stoke C and Derby Co
1953–54 Middlesbrough and Liverpool
1954–55 Leicester C and Sheffield W
1955–56 Huddersfield and Sheffield U
1956–57 Charlton Ath and Cardiff C
1957–58 Sheffield W and Sunderland
1958–59 Portsmouth and Aston Villa
1959–60 Luton T and Leeds U
1960–61 Preston NE and Newcastle U
1961–62 Chelsea and Cardiff C
1962–63 Majchester C and Leyton O
1963–64 Bolton W and Ipswich T
1964–65 Wolverhampton W and Birmingham C
1965–66 Northampton T and Blackburn R
1966–67 Aston Villa and Blackpool
1967–68 Fulham and Sheffield U
1968–69 Leicester C and QPR
1969–70 Sunderland and Sheffield W
1970–71 Burnley and Blackpool
1971–72 Huddersfield T and Nottingham F
1972–73 Crystal Palace and WBA
1973–74 Southampton, Manchester U, Norwich C
1974–75 Luton T, Chelsea, Carlisle U
1975–76 Wolverhampton W, Burnley, Sheffield U
1976–77 Sunderland, Stoke C, Tottenham H
1977–78 West Ham U, Newcastle U, Leicester C
1978–79 QPR, Birmingham C, Chelsea
1979–80 Bristol C, Derby Co, Bolton W
1980–81 Norwich C, Leicester C, Crystal Palace
1981–82 Leeds U, Wolverhampton W, Middlesbrough
1982–83 Manchester C, Swansea C, Brighton & HA
1983–84 Birmingham C, Notts Co, Wolverhampton W
1984–85 Norwich C, Sunderland, Stoke C
1985–86 Ipswich T, Birmingham C, WBA
1986–87 Leicester C, Manchester C, Aston Villa
1987–88 Chelsea**, Portsmouth, Watford, Oxford U
1988–89 Middlesbrough, West Ham U, Newcastle U
1989–90 Sheffield W, Charlton Ath, Millwall
1990–91 Sunderland and Derby Co
1991–92 Luton T, Notts Co, West Ham U
1992–93 Brentford, Cambridge U, Bristol R

**Relegated after play-offs.*
Subsequently re-elected to Division 1 when League was extended after the War.

DIVISION 2 TO DIVISION 3

1920–21 Stockport Co
1921–22 Bradford and Bristol C
1922–23 Rotherham C and Wolverhampton W
1923–24 Nelson and Bristol C
1924–25 Crystal Palace and Coventry C
1925–26 Stoke C and Stockport Co
1926–27 Darlington and Bradford C
1927–28 Fulham and South Shields
1928–29 Port Vale and Clapton O
1929–30 Hull C and Notts Co
1930–31 Reading and Cardiff C
1931–32 Barnsley and Bristol C
1932–33 Chesterfield and Charlton Ath
1933–34 Millwall and Lincoln C
1934–35 Oldham Ath and Notts Co

1935–36 Port Vale and Hull C
1936–37 Doncaster R and Bradford C
1937–38 Barnsley and Stockport Co
1938–39 Norwich C and Tranmere R
1946–47 Swansea T and Newport Co
1947–48 Doncaster R and Millwall
1948–49 Nottingham F and Lincoln C
1949–50 Plymouth Arg and Bradford
1950–51 Grimsby T and Chesterfield
1951–52 Coventry C and QPR
1952–53 Southampton and Barnsley
1953–54 Brentford and Oldham Ath
1954–55 Ipswich T and Derby Co
1955–56 Plymouth Arg and Hull C
1956–57 Port Vale and Bury

1957–58 Doncaster R and Notts Co	1975–76 Oxford U, York C, Portsmouth
1958–59 Barnsley and Grimsby T	1976–77 Carlisle U, Plymouth Arg, Hereford U
1959–60 Bristol C and Hull C	1977–78 Blackpool, Mansfield T, Hull C
1960–61 Lincoln C and Portsmouth	1978–79 Sheffield U, Millwall, Blackburn R
1961–62 Brighton & HA and Bristol R	1979–80 Fulham, Burnley, Charlton Ath
1962–63 Walsall and Luton T	1980–81 Preston NE, Bristol C, Bristol R
1963–64 Grimsby T and Scunthorpe U	1981–82 Cardiff C, Wrexham, Orient
1964–65 Swindon T and Swansea T	1982–83 Rotherham U, Burnley, Bolton W
1965–66 Middlesbrough and Leyton O	1983–84 Derby Co, Swansea C, Cambridge U
1966–67 Northampton T and Bury	1984–85 Notts Co, Cardiff C, Wolverhampton W
1967–68 Plymouth Arg and Rotherham U	1985–86 Carlisle U, Middlesbrough, Fulham
1968–69 Fulham and Bury	1986–87 Sunderland**, Grimsby T, Brighton & HA
1969–70 Preston NE and Aston Villa	1987–88 Huddersfield T, Reading, Sheffield U**
1970–71 Blackburn R and Bolton W	1988–89 Shrewsbury T, Birmingham C, Walsall
1971–72 Charlton Ath and Watford	1989–90 Bournemouth, Bradford, Stoke C
1972–73 Huddersfield T and Brighton & HA	1990–91 WBA and Hull C
1973–74 Crystal Palace, Preston NE, Swindon T	1991–92 Plymouth Arg, Brighton & HA, Port Vale
1974–75 Millwall, Cardiff C, Sheffield W	1992–93 Preston NE, Mansfield T, Wigan Ath, Chester C

DIVISION 3 TO DIVISION 4

1958–59 Rochdale, Notts Co, Doncaster R and Stockport	1973–74 Cambridge U, Shrewsbury T, Southport, Rochdale
1959–60 Accrington S, Wrexham, Mansfield T and York C	1974–75 AFC Bournemouth, Tranmere R, Watford, Huddersfield T
1960–61 Chesterfield, Colchester U, Bradford C and Tranmere R	1975–76 Aldershot, Colchester U, Southend U, Halifax T
1961–62 Newport Co, Brentford, Lincoln C and Torquay U	1976–77 Reading, Northampton T, Grimsby T, York C
1962–63 Bradford PA, Brighton, Carlisle U and Halifax T	1977–78 Port Vale, Bradford C, Hereford U, Portsmouth
1963–64 Millwall, Crewe Alex, Wrexham and Notts Co	1978–79 Peterborough U, Walsall, Tranmere R, Lincoln C
1964–65 Luton T, Port Vale, Colchester U and Barnsley	1979–80 Bury, Southend U, Mansfield T, Wimbledon
1965–66 Southend U, Exeter C, Brentford and York C	1980–81 Sheffield U, Colchester U, Blackpool, Hull C
1966–67 Doncaster R, Workington, Darlington and Swansea T	1981–82 Wimbledon, Swindon T, Bristol C, Chester
1967–68 Scunthorpe U, Colchester U, Grimsby T and Peterborough U (demoted)	1982–83 Reading, Wrexham, Doncaster R, Chesterfield
1968–69 Oldham Ath, Crewe Alex, Hartlepool and Northampton	1983–84 Scunthorpe U, Southend U, Port Vale, Exeter C
1969–70 Bournemouth, Southport, Barrow, Stockport Co	1984–85 Burnley, Orient, Preston NE, Cambridge U
1970–71 Reading, Bury, Doncaster R, Gillingham	1985–86 Lincoln C, Cardiff C, Wolverhampton W, Swansea C
1971–72 Mansfield T, Barnsley, Torquay U, Bradford C	1986–87 Bolton W**, Carlisle U, Darlington, Newport Co
1972–73 Rotherham U, Brentford, Swansea C, Scunthorpe U	1987–88 Doncaster R, York C, Grimsby T, Rotherham U**
	1988–89 Southend U, Chesterfield, Gillingham, Aldershot
	1989–90 Cardiff C, Northampton T, Blackpool, Walsall
	1990–91 Crewe Alex, Rotherham U, Mansfield T
	1991–92 Bury, Shrewsbury T, Torquay U, Darlington

** *Relegated after play-offs.*

APPLICATIONS FOR RE-ELECTION

FOURTH DIVISION

Eleven: Hartlepool U.
Seven: Crewe Alex.
Six: Barrow (lost League place to Hereford U 1972), Halifax T, Rochdale, Southport (lost League place to Wigan Ath 1978), York C.
Five: Chester C, Darlington, Lincoln C, Stockport Co, Workington (lost League place to Wimbledon 1977).
Four: Bradford PA (lost League place to Cambridge U 1970), Newport Co, Northampton T.
Three: Doncaster R, Hereford U.
Two: Bradford C, Exeter C, Oldham Ath, Scunthorpe U, Torquay U.
One: Aldershot, Colchester U, Gateshead (lost League place to Peterborough U 1960), Grimsby T, Swansea C, Tranmere R, Wrexham, Blackpool, Cambridge U, Preston NE.
Accrington S resigned and Oxford U were elected 1962.
Port Vale were forced to re-apply following expulsion in 1968.

THIRD DIVISIONS NORTH & SOUTH

Seven: Walsall.
Six: Exeter C, Halifax T, Newport Co.
Five: Accrington S, Barrow, Gillingham, New Brighton, Southport.
Four: Rochdale, Norwich C.
Three: Crystal Palace, Crewe Alex, Darlington, Hartlepool U, Merthyr T, Swindon T.
Two: Aberdare Ath, Aldershot, Ashington, Bournemouth, Brentford, Chester, Colchester U, Durham C, Millwall, Nelson, QPR, Rotherham U, Southend U, Tranmere R, Watford, Workington.
One: Bradford C, Bradford PA, Brighton, Bristol R, Cardiff C, Carlisle U, Charlton Ath, Gateshead, Grimsby T, Mansfield T, Shrewsbury T, Torquay U, York C.

LEAGUE STATUS FROM 1986–87

RELEGATED FROM LEAGUE	PROMOTED TO LEAGUE
1986–87 Lincoln C	Scarborough
1987–88 Newport Co	Lincoln C
1988–89 Darlington	Maidstone U
1989–90 Colchester U	Darlington
1990–91 —	Barnet
1991–92 —	Colchester U
1992–93 Halifax T	Wycombe W

LEADING GOALSCORERS 1992–93

	League	FA Cup	Coca Cola Cup	Other Cups	Total
FA PREMIER LEAGUE					
Teddy Sheringham *(Tottenham Hotspur)(Including 1 for Nottingham Forest)*	22	4	3	0	29
Ian Wright *(Arsenal)*	15	10	6	0	31
Mick Quinn *(Coventry City)(Including 2 League and 3 Coca Cola Cup for Newcastle United)*	19	0	3	0	22
Les Ferdinand *(QPR)*	20	2	2	0	24
Alan Shearer *(Blackburn Rovers)*	16	0	6	0	22
Ian Rush *(Liverpool)*	14	1	1	5	21
Mike Newell *(Blackburn Rvoers)*	13	5	3	0	21
Brian Deane *(Sheffield United)*	15	3	2	0	20
Mark Bright *(Sheffield Wednesday)(Including 1 for Crystal Palace)*	12	3	6	0	21
David White *(Manchester City)*	16	3	0	0	19
Lee Chapman *(Leeds United)*	14	1	2	1	18
Dean Holdsworth *(Wimbledon)*	19	0	0	0	19
Matthew Le Tissier *(Southampton)*	15	1	2	0	18
Eric Cantona *(Manchester United)(Including 6 League and 2 European Cup for Leeds United)*	15	0	0	2	17
Mark Hughes *(Manchester United)*	15	0	1	0	16
Dean Saunders *(Aston Villa)(Including 1 for Liverpool)*	14	2	2	0	18
DIVISION 1					
Guy Whittingham *(Portsmouth)*	42	0	2	3	47
Gary Blissett *(Brentford)*	21	0	4	4	29
Andy Cole *(Newcastle United)(Including 12 League, 3 Coca Cola and 1 Anglo-Italian for Bristol City)*	24	0	3	1	28
John Aldridge *(Tranmere Rovers)*	21	1	2	2	26
David Kelly *(Newcastle United)*	21	1	2	1	25
Craig Maskell *(Swindon Town)*	19	0	1	4	24
Paul Kitson *(Derby County)*	17	1	1	4	23
Trevor Morley *(West Ham United)*	20	1	0	1	22
Paul Furlong *(Watford)*	19	0	3	0	22
Paul Gray *(Luton Town)*	19	1	0	0	20
Tony Adcock *(Peterborough United)*	16	1	2	0	19
Steve Bull *(Wolverhampton Wanderers)*	16	1	1	1	19
Marco Gabbiadini *(Derby County)*	9	2	2	6	19
Stan Collymore *(Southend United)*	15	3	0	0	18
DIVISION 2					
Bob Taylor *(West Bromwich Albion)*	30	3	1	3	37
Kevin Francis *(Stockport County)*	28	2	2	6	38
Mark Stein *(Stoke City)*	26	0	4	3	33
Andy Walker *(Bolton Wanderers)*	26	4	1	2	33
Tony Ellis *(Preston North End)*	22	1	1	1	25
Sean McCarthy *(Bradford City)*	17	2	1	5	25
Jimmy Quinn *(Reading)*	17	3	1	2	23
Kurt Nogan *(Brighton & HA)*	20	0	0	2	22
Adrian Heath *(Burnely)*	19	3	0	0	22
John McGinlay *(Bolton Wanderers)*	16	5	0	1	22
Stuart Rimmer *(Chester City)*	20	0	0	0	20
Paul Jewell *(Bradford City)*	16	2	1	0	19
Ian Taylor *(Port Vale)*	15	1	1	2	19
Robert Taylor *(Leyton Orient)*	18	0	0	0	18
David Eyres *(Blackpool)*	16	0	1	2	19
DIVISION 3					
Darren Foreman *(Scarborough)*	27	0	2	2	31
Carl Griffiths *(Shrewsbury Town)*	27	2	1	1	31
Wayne Clarke *(Walsall)*	21	0	1	2	24
Andy Barnes *(York City)*	21	0	0	0	21
Gary Bennett *(Wrexham)*	16	1	2	2	21
Steve Watkin *(Wrexham)*	18	0	0	2	20
Tony Naylor *(Crewe Alexandra)*	16	2	2	5	25
Gary Bull *(Barnet)*	17	0	2	0	19
Phil Stant *(Cardiff City)(Including 6 League and 1 Coca Cola for Mansfield Town)*	17	0	1	1	19
Michele Cecere *(Walsall)*	16	0	0	2	18
Ian Helliwell *(Scunthorpe United)*	13	0	4	0	17
Ian Blackstone *(York City)*	16	0	0	0	16
George Oghani *(Carlisle United)*	15	0	1	0	16
Phil Clarkson *(Crewe Alexandra)*	13	2	1	1	17
Tommy Mooney *(Scarborough)*	9	0	5	2	16

N.B. Because of the wide-range of competitions included, players in the above lists are not in any specific order. The other matches refer to European games, the play-offs, Autoglass Trophy and Anglo-Italian Trophy.

FA CHARITY SHIELD WINNERS 1908–92

1908	Manchester U v QPR	4-0 after 1-1 draw
1909	Newcastle U v Northampton T	2-0
1910	Brighton v Aston Villa	1-0
1911	Manchester U v Swindon T	8-4
1912	Blackburn R v QPR	2-1
1913	Professionals v Amateurs	7-2
1919	WBA v Tottenham H	2-0
1920	Tottenham H v Burnley	2-0
1921	Huddersfield T v Liverpool	1-0
1922	Not played	
1923	Professionals v Amateurs	2-0
1924	Professionals v Amateurs	3-1
1925	Amateurs v Professionals	6-1
1926	Amateurs v Professionals	6-3
1927	Cardiff C v Corinthians	2-1
1928	Everton v Blackburn R	2-1
1929	Professionals v Amateurs	3-0
1930	Arsenal v Sheffield W	2-1
1931	Arsenal v WBA	1-0
1932	Everton v Newcastle U	5-3
1933	Arsenal v Everton	3-0
1934	Arsenal v Manchester C	4-0
1935	Sheffield W v Arsenal	1-0
1936	Sunderland v Arsenal	2-1
1937	Manchester C v Sunderland	2-0
1938	Arsenal v Preston NE	2-1
1948	Arsenal v Manchester U	4-3
1949	Portsmouth v Wolverhampton W	1-1*
1950	World Cup Team v Canadian Touring Team	4-2
1951	Tottenham H v Newcastle U	2-1
1952	Manchester U v Newcastle U	4-2
1953	Arsenal v Blackpool	3-1
1954	Wolverhampton W v WBA	4-4*
1955	Chelsea v Newcastle U	3-0
1956	Manchester U v Manchester C	1-0
1957	Manchester U v Aston Villa	4-0
1958	Bolton W v Wolverhampton W	4-1
1959	Wolverhampton W v Nottingham F	3-1
1960	Burnley v Wolverhampton W	2-2*
1961	Tottenham H v FA XI	3-2
1962	Tottenham H v Ipswich T	5-1
1963	Everton v Manchester U	4-0
1964	Liverpool v West Ham U	2-2*
1965	Manchester U v Liverpool	2-2*
1966	Liverpool v Everton	1-0
1967	Manchester U v Tottenham H	3-3*
1968	Manchester C v WBA	6-1
1969	Leeds U v Manchester C	2-1
1970	Everton v Chelsea	2-1
1971	Leicester C v Liverpool	1-0
1972	Manchester C v Aston Villa	1-0
1973	Burnley v Manchester C	1-0
1974	Liverpool† v Leeds U	1-1
1975	Derby Co v West Ham U	2-0
1976	Liverpool v Southampton	1-0
1977	Liverpool v Manchester U	0-0*
1978	Nottingham F v Ipswich T	5-0
1979	Liverpool v Arsenal	3-1
1980	Liverpool v West Ham U	1-0
1981	Aston Villa v Tottenham H	2-2*
1982	Liverpool v Tottenham H	1-0
1983	Manchester U v Liverpool	2-0
1984	Everton v Liverpool	1-0
1985	Everton v Manchester U	2-0
1986	Everton v Liverpool	1-1*
1987	Everton v Coventry C	1-0
1988	Liverpool v Wimbledon	2-1
1989	Liverpool v Arsenal	1-0
1990	Liverpool v Manchester U	1-1*
1991	Arsenal v Tottenham H	0-0*

Each club retained shield for six months. † Won on penalties.

FA CHARITY SHIELD 1992

Leeds U (2) 4, Liverpool (1) 3
At Wembley, 8 August 1992, attendance 61,291

Leeds U: Lukic; Newsome (Strachan), Dorigo, Batty, Fairclough, Whyte, Cantona, Rodney Wallace, Chapman (Hodge), McAllister, Speed.

Scorers: Cantona 3, Dorigo.

Liverpool: Grobbelaar; Tanner, Burrows, Marsh (Hutchison), Whelan, Wright, Saunders, Stewart, Rush, Rosenthal (Kozma), Walters.

Scorers: Rush, Saunders, Strachan (og).

TRANSFERS 1992–93

	From	*To*	*Fee*
May 1992			
27 Gray, Andrew. A	Crystal Palace	Tottenham Hotspur	£700,000
21 Hobson, Paul J.	St Albans City	Enfield	undisclosed
20 Holmes P	Torquay United	Birmingham City	£40,000
28 Jeffrey, Michael R.	Bolton Wanderers	Doncaster Rovers	£20,000
20 Joyce, Warren G.	Preston North End	Plymouth Argyle	£160,000
27 Olney, Ian D.	Aston Villa	Oldham Athletic	£700,000
27 Pembridge, Mark	Luton Town	Derby County	£1,250,000
20 Taylor, Ian	Moor Green	Port Vale	£15,000
Temporary transfers			
1 Day, Mervyn R.	Leeds United	Sheffield United	
4 Day, Mervyn R.	Sheffield United	Leeds United (transfer back)	
1 Sullivan, Neil	Wimbledon	Crystal Palace	
6 Varadi, Imre	Luton Town	Leeds United (transfer back)	
20 Arnott, Andrew J.	Gillingham	Manchester United	
20 Swan, Adrian	Darlington	Leicester City	
June 1992			
3 Anderton, Darren R.	Portsmouth	Tottenham Hotspur	£2,000,000
3 Austin, Dean B.	Southend United	Tottenham Hotspur	£375,000
22 Barrows, Nigel J.	Stourbridge	Hednesford Town	undisclosed
3 Beadle, Peter C.	Gillingham	Tottenham Hotspur	£300,000
16 Bracewell, Paul W.	Sunderland	Newcastle United	£250,000
9 Castle, Stephen C.	Leyton Orient	Plymouth Argyle	£195,000
4 Cross, Ryan	Plymouth Argyle	Hartlepool United	Exchange
5 Dalton, Paul	Hartlepool United	Plymouth Argyle	Exchange
19 Elliott, Matthew S.	Torquay United	Scunthorpe United	£50,000
19 Fishenden, Paul	Wokingham Town	Crawley Town	undisclosed
29 Golley, Mark A.	Welling United	Sutton United	undisclosed
15 Hackett, Brendan	Telford United	Halesowen Town	undisclosed
30 Hallam, Mark	Leicester United	Boston United	undisclosed
10 Hamilton, Ian R.	Scunthorpe United	West Bromwich Albion	£170,000
18 Hine, Mark	Scunthorpe United	Doncaster Rovers	Exchange
10 Lilwall, Stephen	Kidderminster Harriers	West Bromwich Albion	£5000
25 McCarthy, Anthony P.	Shelbourne	Millwall	£100,000
18 May, Andrew M.	Bristol City	Millwall	Exchange
26 O'Connor, Martin J.	Bromsgrove Rovers	Crystal Palace	£25,000
11 O'Neill, Daren S.	Wokingham Town	Crawley Town	undisclosed
25 Patterson, Darren J.	Wigan Athletic	Crystal Palace	£225,000
19 Rouse, Shaun	Rangers	Bristol City	Free
17 Samways, Mark	Doncaster Rovers	Scunthorpe United	£20,000 + player
8 Thomas, Paul D.	Newport (IOW)	Waterlooville	undisclosed
13 Thompson, David	Millwall	Bristol City	Exchange
11 Thompson, David J.	Wokingham Town	Crawley Town	undisclosed
5 Walsh, Paul A.	Tottenham Hotspur	Portsmouth	£400,000
17 Wassall, Darren P	Nottingham Forest	Derby County	£600,000
July 1992			
21 Babb, Philip A.	Bradford City	Coventry City	£500,000
15 Barnes, Paul L.	Stoke City	York City	£50,000
2 Beresford, John	Portsmouth	Newcastle United	£650,000
3 Brooks, Christopher	Ilkeston Town	Luton Town	undisclosed
3 Carroll, Mathew P.	Kidderminster Harriers	Sutton Coldfield Town	undisclosed
17 Carty, Paul	Nuneaton Borough	VS Rugby	undisclosed
29 Claridge, Stephen E.	Cambridge United	Luton Town	£160,000
17 Clark, Martin J.	Mansfield Town	Partick Thistle	Free
22 Coates, Neil R.	Dorchester Town	Yeovil Town	undisclosed
21 Cole, Andrew	Arsenal	Bristol City	£500,000
10 Colquhoun, John	Millwall	Sunderland	£220,000
25 Coombe, Mark A.	Salisbury	Dorchester Town	undisclosed
2 Cundy, Jason V.	Chelsea	Tottenham Hotspur	£800,000
20 Cunnington, Shaun G.	Grimsby Town	Sunderland	£650,000
16 Cusack, Nicholas J.	Darlington	Oxford United	£95,000
17 Davidson, Jonathan S	Derby County	Preston North End	£50,000
22 Dixon, Kerry M.	Chelsea	Southampton	£575,000
22 Furlong, Paul A.	Coventry City	Watford	£250,000
27 Gittens, Jon	Southampton	Middlesbrough	£200,000
30 Gosney, Andrew	Portsmouth	Birmingham City	£35,000
29 Gould, Jonathan A.	West Bromwich Albion	Coventry City	£7500
6 Harbey, Graham K.	West Bromwich Albion	Stoke City	£80,000
14 Hardyman, Paul G. T.	Sunderland	Bristol Rovers	£160,000
31 Hill, Colin F.	Sheffield United	Leicester City	£200,000
29 Horne, Barry	Southampton	Everton	£675,000

	From	To	Fee
28 Houghton, Raymond J.	Liverpool	Aston Villa	£900,000
13 Hurst, Mark D.	Grantham Town	Leicester United	undisclosed
6 James, David	Watford	Liverpool	£1,000,000
22 Jones, Murray L.	Grimsby Town	Brentford	£75,000
3 Jones, Tom	Swindon Town	Reading	Exchange
10 Kerr, Paul A.	Millwall	Port Vale	£200,000
28 Lowe, David A.	Ipswich Town	Leicester City	£250,000
20 Makel, Lee	Newcastle United	Blackburn Rovers	£160,000
3 Maskell, Craig D.	Reading	Swindon Town	Exchange
17 Massey, Stuart A.	Sutton United	Crystal Palace	£20,000
17 McKenna, John	Boston United	Dagenham & Redbridge	undisclosed
13 Morrell Peter A.	Dorchester Town	Wimborne Town	undisclosed
23 Musselwhite, Paul S.	Scunthorpe United	Port Vale	£20,000
1 Narbett, Jonathan V.	Hereford United	Oxford United	£65,000
10 Parkinson, Philip J.	Bury	Reading	£37,500
22 Quinn, James M.	AFC Bournemouth	Reading	£55,000
21 Reid, Paul R.	Leicester City	Bradford City	£25,000
20 Ripley, Stuart E	Middlesbrough	Blackburn Rovers	£1,300,000
20 Rosegreen Mark A.	VS Rugby	Nuneaton Borough	undisclosed
23 Ruddock, Neil	Southampton	Tottenham Hotspur	£750,000
3 Russell, Andrew	Woking	Kingstonian	undisclosed
16 Russell, Kevin J.	Leicester City	Stoke City	£95,000
29 Sellars, Scott	Blackburn Rovers	Leeds United	£950,000
27 Shearer, Alan	Southampton	Blackburn Rovers	£3,300,000
10 Smith, David A.	Plymouth Argyle	Notts County	£150,000
27 Speedie, David R.	Blackburn Rovers	Southampton	£400,000
29 Stewart, Paul A.	Tottenham Hotspur	Liverpool	£2,300,000
31 Sulley, Christopher S.	Blackburn Rovers	Port Vale	Free
15 Thackeray, Andrew J.	Wrexham	Rochdale	£15,000
31 Venison, Barry	Liverpool	Newcastle United	£250,000
29 Wilmot, Rhys J.	Plymouth Argyle	Grimsby Town	£87,500
15 Williams,David G.	Derby County	Ipswich Town	£650,000
9 Williams, John	Swansea City	Coventry City	£250,000
22 Wright, Thomas E.	Leicester City	Middlesbrough	£650,000

Temporary transfers

	From	To	
29 Bailey, Danny S.	Reading	Fulham	
14 Bennett, Michael R.	Wimbledon	Brentford	
23 Duffield, Peter	Sheffield United	Blackpool	
13 Holdsworth, Dean C.	Brentford	Wimbledon	
24 Kelly, Alan T.	Preston North End	Sheffield United	
14 Kruszynski, Zbigniew	Wimbledon	Brentford	
23 McLeary, Alan T.	Millwall	Sheffield United	
30 Morah, Olisa H.	Tottenham Hotspur	Swindon Town	
24 Pascoe, Colin J.	Sunderland	Swansea City	
30 Wilder, Christopher J.	Sheffield United	Rotherham United	

August 1992

	From	To	
20 Alleyne Xavier J.	Leatherhead	Crawley Town	undisclosed
10 Bennett, Michael R.	Wimbledon	Brentford	£60,000
28 Beresford, Marlon	Sheffield Wednesday	Burnley	undisclosed
14 Berry, Gregory J.	Leyton Orient	Wimbledon	£250,000
26 Brazil, Derek M.	Manchester United	Cardiff City	£85,000
20 Brindley, Christopher P.	Telford United	Kidderminster Harriers	undisclosed
19 Burnett, Wayne	Leyton Orient	Blackburn Rovers	£80,000
7 Butler, Peter J. F.	Southend United	West Ham United	£120,000
14 Callaghan, Aaron J.	Crewe Alexandra	Preston North End	undisclosed
11 Campbell, Stephen A.	Redditch United	Atherstone United	undisclosed
17 Carroll, Robert	Yeovil Town	Woking	undisclosed
13 Collins, Paul	Fisher Athletic	Welling United	undisclosed
11 Cormack, Lee D.	Basingstoke Town	Waterlooville	undisclosed
21 Crawley, Ian S.	VS Rugby	Tamworth	undisclosed
20 Croft, Brian	Chester City	Queens Park Rangers	£60,000
12 Davison, Robert	Leeds United	Leicester City	£50,000
14 Daws, Nicholas J.	Altrincham	Bury	undisclosed
7 Dear, Andrew M.	Kingstonian	Hayes	undisclosed
17 Dent, Nicholas W.	Poole Town	Dover Athletic	undisclosed
13 Donaghy, Malachy M.	Manchester United	Chelsea	£150,000
7 Dublin, Dion	Cambridge United	Manchester United	£1,000,000
14 Ellis, Anthony	Stoke City	Preston North End	£50,000
15 Elmes, Richard M.	Havant Town	Newport (IOW)	undisclosed
13 Fleck, Robert	Norwich City	Chelsea	£2,100,000
3 Fletcher, Steven M.	Hartlepool United	AFC Bournemouth	£30,000
12 Francis, John A.	Burnley	Cambridge United	£95,000
6 Garner, Simon	Blackburn Rovers	West Bromwich Albion	£30,000
5 Graham, Jon	Kettering Town	Boston United	undisclosed
12 Groves, Paul	Blackpool	Grimsby Town	£150,000
24 Groves, Perry	Arsenal	Southampton	£750,000

	From	To	Fee
13 Harford, Michael G.	Luton Town	Chelsea	£300,000
6 Holden, Richard W.	Oldham Athletic	Manchester City	£900,000
10 Holdsworth, Dean C.	Brentford	Wimbledon	£720,000
19 Holmes, Matthew J. E.	AFC Bournemouth	West Ham United	£40,000
14 Horlock, Kevin	West Ham United	Swindon Town	undisclosed
28 Hulme, Timothy J.	Crawley Town	Sittingbourne	undisclosed
6 Huxford, Richard	Kettering Town	Barnet	Exchange
14 James, Robert M.	Bradford City	Cardiff City	Free
6 Jepson, Ronald F.	Preston North End	Exeter City	£60,000
20 Kelly, Alan T.	Preston North End	Sheffield United	£150,000
27 Kelly, Anthony J.	Unattached	Hayes	undisclosed
11 Kitchen, David E.	Frickley Athletic	Leyton Orient	undisclosed
10 Kruszynski, Zbigniew	Wimbledon	Brentford	£60,000
14 Leonard, Mark A.	Rochdale	Preston North End	undisclosed
6 McFarlane, Andrew A.	Portsmouth	Swansea City	£20,000
4 Megson, Gary J.	Manchester City	Norwich City	Free
13 Mendonca, Clive P.	Sheffield United	Grimsby Town	£85,000
21 Monkou, Kenneth J.	Chelsea	Southampton	£750,000
21 Nevin, Patrick K. F.	Everton	Tranmere Rovers	£250,000
6 Nuttell, Michael J.	Boston United	Kettering Town	undisclosed
14 Pennock, Adrian	Norwich City	AFC Bournemouth	£35,000
25 Phelan, Terry	Wimbledon	Manchester City	£2,500,000
7 Pointon, Neil G.	Manchester City	Oldham Athletic	Exchange
7 Redmond, Stephen	Manchester City	Oldham Athletic	£150,000
21 Reid, Andrew M.	Altrincham	Bury	undisclosed
24 Richardson, Nicholas J.	Halifax Town	Cardiff City	£35,000
14 Robins, Mark G.	Manchester United	Norwich City	£800,000
4 Rocastle, David C.	Arsenal	Leeds United	£2,000,000
28 Rogers, Anthony K.	Dover Athletic	Chelmsford City	undisclosed
14 Ryan, Vaughan W.	Wimbledon	Leyton Orient	Exchange
12 Shaw, Graham P.	Preston North End	Stoke City	Exchange
28 Sheringham, Teddy	Nottingham Forest	Tottenham Hotspur	£2,100,000
14 Slater, Stuart	West Ham United	Celtic	£1,500,000
28 Wilder, Christopher J.	Sheffield United	Rotherham United	£50,000

Temporary transfers

21 Baraclough, Ian R.	Grimsby Town	Lincoln City
10 Bennett, Michael R.	Brentford	Wimbledon (transfer back)
14 Blades, Paul A.	Norwich City	Wolverhampton Wanderers
10 Brazil, Derek M.	Manchester United	Cardiff City
27 Connelly, Dean	Barnsley	Carlisle United
13 Cotterill, Stephen	Wimbledon	Brighton & Hove Albion
6 Dearden, Kevin C.	Tottenham Hotspur	Portsmouth
28 Dobson, Paul	Lincoln City	Darlington
21 Duffield, Peter	Sheffield United	Blackpool
13 Edwards, Paul R.	Coventry City	Wolverhampton Wanderers
10 Hicks, Stuart J.	Scunthorpe United	Doncaster Rovers
28 Horne, Brian	Millwall	Middlesbrough
28 Hoyle, Colin R.	Barnsley	Bradford City
27 Juryeff, Ian M.	Halifax Town	Darlington
28 Keeley, John H.	Oldham Athletic	Chester City
10 Kruszynski, Zbigniew	Brentford	Wimbledon (transfer back)
14 Lund, Gary J.	Notts County	Hull City
28 Makin, Christopher	Oldham Athletic	Wigan Athletic
13 McCord, Brian J.	Barnsley	Mansfield Town
28 McDonald, David H.	Tottenham Hotspur	Bradford City
14 Moulden, Paul A.	Oldham Athletic	Brighton & Hove Albion
12 Newell, Paul C.	Leyton Orient	Colchester United
13 Regis, David	Plymouth Argyle	AFC Bournemouth
13 Richardson, Nicholas J.	Halifax Town	Cardiff City
21 Skinner, Craig R.	Blackburn Rovers	Plymouth Argyle

September 1992

	From	To	Fee
1 Armstrong, Christopher	Millwall	Crystal Palace	£1,000,000
7 Barness, Anthony	Charlton Athletic	Chelsea	£350,000
11 Bright, Mark A.	Crystal Palace	Sheffield Wednesday	£375,000 + exchange
19 Coe, John Ryan	VS Rugby	Rushden & Diamonds	undisclosed
23 Costello, Peter	Peterborough United	Lincoln City	£15,000
29 Dobson, Paul	Lincoln City	Darlington	undisclosed
1 Friel, George P.	Woking	Slough Town	undisclosed
22 Hill, Keith J.	Blackburn Rovers	Plymouth Argyle	Exchange + cash
5 James, Simon	Havant Town	Waterlooville	undisclosed
10 Jones, Vincent P.	Chelsea	Wimbledon	£700,000
29 Juryeff, Ian M.	Halifax Town	Darlington	Free
22 Kennedy, Andrew J.	Watford	Brighton & Hove Albion	£40,000
25 Kuhl, Martin	Portsmouth	Derby County	£650,000
22 Lee, Robert M.	Charlton Athletic	Newcastle United	£700,000
24 Marker, Nicholas R.	Plymouth Argyle	Blackburn Rovers	£250,000 + exchange

	From	To	Fee
11 McLaughlin, Joseph	Watford	Falkirk	£70,000
22 Massey, Andrew D.	Redditch United	Shepshed Albion	undisclosed
30 McGinlay, John	Millwall	Bolton Wanderers	£125,000
1 Moralee, Jamie D.	Crystal Palace	Millwall	Free
18 Olner, Paul	Atherstone United	VS Rugby	undisclosed
15 Robinson, David A.	Peterborough United	Notts County	£350,000
15 Robinson, John R. C.	Brighton & Hove Albion	Charlton Athletic	£75,000
10 Saunders, Dean N.	Liverpool	Aston Villa	£2,300,000
16 Short, Craig J.	Notts County	Derby County	£2,500,000
22 Skinner, Craig R.	Blackburn Rovers	Plymouth Argyle	Exchange
11 Williams, Paul A.	Sheffield Wednesday	Crystal Palace	+ exchange

Temporary transfers

3 Bartlett, Kevin F.	Notts County	Port Vale
10 Bellamy, Gary	Wolverhampton Wanderers	Leyton Orient
18 Broddle, Julian	St Mirren	Scunthorpe United
18 Browning, Marcus T.	Bristol Rovers	Hereford United
11 Cairns, Darren	Hull City	Ards
18 Chamberlain, Alec F. R.	Luton Town	Chelsea
25 Evans, Michael J.	Plymouth Argyle	Blackburn Rovers
4 Fox, Peter D.	Stoke City	Linfield
12 Heald, Paul A.	Leyton Orient	Crystal Palace
17 Houghton, Scott A.	Tottenham Hotspur	Cambridge United
4 Jones, Alexander	Motherwell	Rochdale
9 Keeley, John H.	Chester City	Oldham Athletic (transfer back)
9 Kite, Philip D.	Sheffield United	Plymouth Argyle
18 Kite, Philip D.	Plymouth Argyle	Sheffield United (transfer back)
17 Loram, Mark J.	Torquay United	Exeter City
28 Makin, Christopher	Oldham Athletic	Wigan Athletic
25 Matthew, Damian	Chelsea	Luton Town
26 Mohan, Nicholas	Middlesbrough	Hull City
11 Mooney, Brian J.	Sunderland	Burnley
17 Moran, Paul	Tottenham Hotspur	Cambridge United
17 Peyton, Gerald J.	Everton	Brentford
24 Pollitt, Michael F.	Bury	Lincoln City
3 Proudlock, Paul	Carlisle United	Hartlepool United
17 Reid, Nicholas S.	Blackburn Rovers	Bristol City
1 Robinson, Philip J.	Notts County	Huddersfield Town
17 Stringfellow, Ian R.	Mansfield Town	Blackpool
15 Tillson, Andrew	Queens Park Rangers	Grimsby Town
30 Wallace, Michael	Manchester City	Stockport County
4 West, Gary	Lincoln City	Walsall
4 Whitehead, Philip M.	Barnsley	Scunthorpe United
17 Williams, Gareth J.	Barnsley	Hull City

October 1992

23 Baraclough, Ian R.	Grimsby Town	Lincoln City	undisclosed
1 Biggins, Wayne	Stoke City	Barnsley	£200,000
2 Blades, Paul A.	Norwich City	Wolverhampton Wanderers	£325,000
26 Byrne, John F.	Sunderland	Millwall	£250,000
15 Charley, Kenneth L.	Peterborough United	Watford	£350,000
1 Donovan, Kevin	Huddersfield Town	West Bromwich Albion	£25,000
21 Danzey, Michael J.	St Albans City	Cambridge United	undisclosed
22 Eaton, Jason	Gloucester City	Cheltenham Town	undisclosed
13 Edwards, Paul R.	Coventry City	Wolverhampton Wanderers	£100,000
23 Gleghorn, Nigel W.	Birmingham City	Stoke City	£100,000
23 Harmon, Darren J.	Shrewsbury Town	Northampton Town	undisclosed
9 Hicks, Stuart J.	Scunthorpe United	Doncaster Rovers	Free
2 Hoyle, Colin R.	Barnsley	Bradford City	undisclosed
16 Joseph, Antone E.	Kidderminster Harriers	Hednesford Town	undisclosed
30 Millar, Robert J.	Oldham Athletic	Hull City	undisclosed
13 Niblett, Nigel	VS Rugby	Telford United	undisclosed
19 Philliskirk, Anthony	Bolton Wanderers	Peterborough United	£85,000
23 Regis, David	Plymouth Argyle	Stoke City	£100,000
2 Smith, Mark C.	Barnsley	Notts County	£70,000
28 Walker, Gary	Radcliffe Borough	Buxton	undisclosed
30 Westley, Shane L. M.	Wolverhampton Wanderers	Brentford	£100,000
5 Willis, Roger C.	Barnet	Watford	£175,000

Temporary transfers

24 Beasant, David	Chelsea	Grimsby Town
23 Blissett, Luther L.	Watford	West Bromwich Albion
23 Brady, Kieron	Sunderland	Doncaster Rovers
5 Burns, Philip	Airdrieonians	Portsmouth
31 Carruthers, Martin G.	Aston Villa	Hull City
24 Channing, Justin A.	Queens Park Rangers	Bristol Rovers
15 Currie, David N.	Barnsley	Rotherham United
2 Dewhurst, Robert M.	Blackburn Rovers	Huddersfield Town

		From	*To*	*Fee*
14	Emberson, Carl W.	Millwall	Rotherham United	
25	Evans, Michael	Plymouth Argyle	Blackburn Rovers	
2	Evans, Richard W.	Bristol Rovers	Exeter City	
1	Garnett, Shaun M.	Tranmere Rovers	Chester City	
24	Graham, Deniol W. T.	Barnsley	Preston North End	
30	Harvey, Richard G.	Luton Town	Blackpool	
9	Hawke, Warren R.	Sunderland	Carlisle United	
24	Herrera, Roberto	Queens Park Rangers	Torquay United	
17	Holden, Steven A.	Leicester City	Carlisle United	
2	Horne, Brian	Millwall	Stoke City	
30	Kelly, Anthony O. N.	Stoke City	Cardiff City	
24	Kite, Philip D.	Sheffield United	Rotherham United	
29	Kite, Philip D.	Rotherham United	Sheffield United (transfer back)	
9	Limber, Nicholas	Manchester City	Peterborough United	
16	McLeary, Alan	Millwall	Wimbledon	
17	Moore, Kevin T.	Southampton	Bristol Rovers	
23	Morgan, Nicholas	Bristol City	AFC Bournemouth	
10	Parkinson, Gary	Middlesbrough	Southend United	
17	Philliskirk, Tony	Bolton Wanderers	Peterborough United	
2	Sealey, Leslie J.	Aston Villa	Birmingham City	
17	Smith, Kevan	Darlington	Hereford United	
31	Sommer, Jurgen P.	Luton Town	Torquay United	
23	Speedie, David R.	Southampton	Birmingham City	
31	Taylor, Colin D.	Wolverhampton Wanderers	Preston North End	
2	Wheeler, Paul	Stockport County	Scarborough	
23	Williams, Paul A.	West Bromwich Albion	Coventry City	

November 1992

		From	*To*	*Fee*
19	Allon, Joseph B.	Chelsea	Brentford	£275,000
17	Bellamy, Gary	Wolverhampton Wanderers	Leyton Orient	£30,000
20	Benjamin, Ian T.	Southend United	Luton Town	£50,000
24	Brennan, Mark R.	Manchester City	Oldham Athletic	undisclosed
27	Cantona, Eric	Leeds United	Manchester United	£1,200,000
20	Claridge, Stephen E.	Luton Town	Cambridge United	£190,000
20	Cooper, Mark N.	Birmingham City	Fulham	£40,000
20	Hallam, Mark	Boston United	Hednesford Town	undisclosed
27	Hignett, Craig J.	Crewe Alexandra	Middlesbrough	£500,000
3	Ireland, Simon P.	Huddersfield Town	Blackburn Rovers	200,000
24	Jenkins, Michael G.	Havant Town	Waterlooville	undisclosed
16	Jones, Stephen G.	Billericay Town	West Ham United	£22,000
3	Morah, Olisa H.	Tottenham Hotspur	Swindon Town	Free
5	Nelson, Stephen E.	Telford United	Burton Albion	undisclosed
24	Philpott, Lee	Cambridge United	Leicester City	£350,000
7	Reid, Nicholas S.	Blackburn Rovers	West Bromwich Albion	Free
3	Robinson, Philip J.	Notts County	Huddersfield Town	undisclosed
13	Smart, Erskine	Enfield	St Albans City	undisclosed
5	Tillson, Andrew	Queens Park Rangers	Bristol Rovers	£275,000
5	Waddock, Gary P.	Queens Park Rangers	Bristol Rovers	£100,000
23	Webb, Neil J.	Manchester United	Nottingham Forest	£800,000

Temporary transfers

		From	*To*
21	Agnew, Stephen M.	Blackburn Rovers	Portsmouth
11	Bellamy, Gary	Wolverhampton Wanderers	Leyton Orient
20	Branch, Graham	Tranmere Rovers	Bury
5	Browning, Marcus T.	Hereford United	Bristol Rovers (transfer back)
20	Charles, Stephen	Mansfield Town	Scunthorpe United
20	Collymore, Stanley V.	Crystal Palace	Southend United
20	Connor, Terence F.	Bristol City	Swansea City
27	Cousins, Anthony J.	Liverpool	Hereford United
27	Dewhurst, Robert M.	Huddersfield Town	Blackburn Rovers (transfer back)
4	Digby, Fraser C.	Swindon Town	Manchester United
18	Dryden, Richard A.	Notts County	Plymouth Argyle
27	Fee, Gregory P.	Mansfield Town	Chesterfield
26	Fickling, Ashley	Sheffield United	Darlington
29	Horne, Brian	Millwall	Sunderland
20	Johnson, David A.	Sheffield Wednesday	Hartlepool United
13	Kamara, Christopher	Luton Town	Sheffield United
21	Keeley, John H.	Oldham Athletic	Chester City
26	Keeley, John H.	Chester City	Oldham Athletic (transfer back)
27	Kite, Philip D.	Sheffield United	Crewe Alexandra
20	Kristensen, Bjorn	Newcastle United	Bristol City
26	Lake, Michael C.	Sheffield United	Wrexham
20	Lancashire, Graham	Burnley	Halifax Town
2	Lee, David	Southampton	Bolton Wanderers
13	Livingstone, Glen	Aston Villa	York City
25	Makin, Christopher	Wigan Athletic	Oldham Athletic (transfer back)
5	O'Hanlon, George T.	Leyton Orient	Swindon Town
19	Quinn, Michael	Newcastle United	Coventry City

	From	*To*	*Fee*
20 Reece, Andrew J.	Bristol Rovers	Walsall	
21 Sonner, Daniel J.	Burnley	Bury	
21 Stephenson, Paul	Millwall	Gillingham	
21 Turner, Robert P.	Plymouth Argyle	Notts County	
21 Ward, Ashley S.	Leicester City	Blackpool	
19 Whitehead, Philip M.	Barnsley	Bradford City	
8 Williams, Lee	Aston Villa	Shrewsbury Town	

December 1992

23 Ainsworth, Gareth	Cambridge United	Preston North End	Free
24 Benstock, Danny	Barking	Leyton Orient	undisclosed
23 Butler, Stephen	Watford	Cambridge United	£75,000
4 Came, Mark R.	Bolton Wanderers	Chester City	undisclosed
21 Collymore, Stanley V.	Crystal Palace	Southend United	£100,000
18 Garland, Peter J.	Newcastle United	Charlton Athletic	undisclosed
7 Hodges, Kevin	Plymouth Argyle	Torquay United	Free
24 Horne, Brian S.	Millwall	Portsmouth	Free
1 Jones, Alexander	Motherwell	Rochdale	£35,000
30 Lee, David M.	Southampton	Bolton Wanderers	£200,000
15 Livingstone, Glen	Aston Villa	York City	Free
23 Norbury, Michael S.	Cambridge United	Preston North End	£32,500
22 Quinn, Michael	Newcastle United	Coventry City	£250,000
1 Scott, Andrew	Sutton United	Sheffield United	undisclosed
8 Stant, Philip	Mansfield Town	Cardiff City	£100,000
11 Taylor, Justin S.	Tamworth	Redditch United	undisclosed
23 Turner, Robert P.	Plymouth Argyle	Notts County	£90,000
23 Wallace, Michael	Manchester City	Stockport County	Free
1 Ward, Ashley S.	Leicester City	Crewe Alexandra	£80,000

Temporary transfers

21 Brooks, Shaun	AFC Bournemouth	Stockport County	
23 Brown, Michael A.	Bolton Wanderers	Shrewsbury Town	
18 Butler, Stephen	Watford	AFC Bournemouth	
23 Butler, Stephen	AFC Bournemouth	Watford (transfer back)	
24 Cooper, Stephen B.	Tranmere Rovers	Wigan Athletic	
10 Dickens, Alan W.	Chelsea	West Bromwich Albion	
30 Digby, Fraser	Manchester United	Swindon Town (transfer back)	
17 Emberson, Carl W.	Millwall	Colchester United	
17 Finley, Alan J.	Stockport County	Carlisle United	
17 Gallen, Joseph M.	Watford	Exeter City	
11 Garnett, Shaun M.	Tranmere Rovers	Preston North End	
23 Gray, Andrew A.	Tottenham Hotspur	Swindon Town	
18 Harrison, Lee D.	Charlton Athletic	Fulham	
17 Houghton, Scott A.	Tottenham Hotspur	Gillingham	
31 Jenkins, Iain	Everton	Bradford City	
24 Lucas, Richard	Sheffield United	Preston North End	
17 Marples, Christopher	York City	Chesterfield	
31 Martin, Dean	West Ham United	Colchester United	
17 Matthews, Neil	Stockport County	Lincoln City	
11 McGlashan, John	Millwall	Fulham	
9 Moody, Paul	Southampton	Reading	
18 Peer, Dean	Birmingham City	Mansfield Town	
4 Power, Lee M.	Norwich City	Charlton Athletic	
18 Rowbotham, Darren	Birmingham City	Mansfield Town	
10 Stimson, Mark	Newcastle United	Portsmouth	
29 Talia, Frank	Blackburn Rovers	Hartlepool United	
30 Veysey, Kenneth J.	Oxford United	Sheffield United	
1 Ward, Ashley S.	Blackpool	Leicester City (transfer back)	
18 Watts, Julian	Sheffield Wednesday	Shrewsbury Town	
23 Williams, Lee	Shrewsbury Town	Aston Villa (transfer back)	
18 Williams, Michael A.	Sheffield Wednesday	Halifax Town	

January 1993

7 Baker, David P.	Motherwell	Gillingham	£40,000
15 Blackwell, Kevin P.	Notts County	Torquay United	Free
7 Channing, Justin A.	Queens Park Rangers	Bristol Rovers	£250,000
6 Hayes, Martin	Celtic	Swansea City	Free
14 Kelly, Thomas J.	Exeter City	Torquay United	Free
15 Lyne, Neil G.	Shrewsbury Town	Cambridge United	£75,000
8 May, Leroy A.	Tividale	Hereford United	Free
27 McGlashan, John	Millwall	Peterborough United	£75,000
15 Murray, Paul G.	Burnley	Berwick Rangers	Free
29 Price, Christopher J.	Blackburn Rovers	Portsmouth	£50,000
25 Ryan, Darren T.	Chester City	Stockport County	Exchange
19 Watkins, Dale A.	Grantham Town	Rushden & Diamonds	undisclosed
25 Wheeler, Paul	Stockport County	Chester City	Exchange
26 White, Devon W.	Cambridge United	Queens Park Rangers	£100,000
11 Williams, Paul A.	West Bromwich Albion	Stockport County	£25,000

	From	*To*	*Fee*
Temporary transfers			
22 Allpress, Timothy J.	Luton Town	Boston United	
12 Beasant, David	Chelsea	Wolverhampton Wanderers	
12 Carr, Franz A.	Newcastle United	Sheffield United	
22 Dickins, Matthew J.	Blackburn Rovers	Blackpool	
15 Donowa, Brian L.	Birmingham City	Burnley	
12 Dryden, Richard A.	Plymouth Argyle	Notts County (transfer back)	
15 Duffield, Peter	Sheffield United	Crewe Alexandra	
25 Farrell, David	Aston Villa	Scunthorpe United	
28 Gallen, Joseph M.	Watford	Shamrock Rovers	
15 Hayrettin, Hakan	Barnet	Torquay United	
25 Kabia, Jason	Lincoln City	Doncaster Rovers	
13 Kite, Philip D.	Crewe Alexandra	Sheffield United (transfer back)	
25 Lund, Gary J.	Notts County	Hull City	
15 McGlashan, John	Millwall	Cambridge United	
26 McGlashan, John	Cambridge United	Millwall (transfer back)	
8 McKee, Colin	Manchester United	Bury	
15 Maddison, Lee	Bristol Rovers	Bath City	
22 Mortimer, Paul H.	Crystal Palace	Brentford	
6 Ranson, Raymond	Newcastle United	Manchester City	
8 Roche, David	Newcastle United	Peterborough United	
8 Rowland, Keith	AFC Bournemouth	Coventry City	
8 Smith, David	Coventry City	AFC Bournemouth	
25 Smith, Mark C.	Notts County	Port Vale	
21 Speedie, David R.	Birmingham City	Southampton (transfer back)	
21 Speedie, David R.	Southampton	West Bromwich Albion	
29 Thomas, Martin R.	Birmingham City	Aston Villa	
21 Tuttle, David P.	Tottenham Hotspur	Peterborough United	
21 Varadi, Imre	Leeds United	Oxford United	
13 Veysey, Kenneth J.	Sheffield United	Oxford United (transfer back)	
4 Viveash, Adrian L.	Swindon Town	Reading	
15 White, Christopher	Peterborough United	Doncaster Rovers	
15 Williams, David P.	Burnley	Crewe Alexandra	
8 Woods, Raymond G.	Coventry City	Wigan Athletic	
February 1993			
9 Agnew Stephen M.	Blackburn Rovers	Leicester City	£250,000
24 Bennett, Frank	Halesowen Town	Southampton	£7500
5 Bradder, Gary V.	VS Rugby	Nuneaton Borough	undisclosed
25 Buckley, John W.	Scunthorpe United	Rotherham United	£20,000
19 Chapman, Gary A.	Exeter City	Torquay United	Free
26 Charles, Stephen	Mansfield Town	Scarborough	undisclosed
5 Fashanu, Justin	Torquay United	Airdrieonians	undisclosed
19 Greeno, Michael P.	Fareham Town	Havant Town	undisclosed
25 Harriman, Lee J.	Hinckley Town	VS Rugby	undisclosed
24 Holden, Steven A.	Leicester City	Carlisle United	Free
11 Jordan, David	Ashford Town	Margate	undisclosed
4 Keown, Martin R.	Everton	Arsenal	£2,000,000
25 Lucas, Richard	Sheffield United	Preston North End	£40,000
1 Marples, Christopher	York City	Chesterfield	Free
26 Masefield, Paul D.	Stockport County	Doncaster Rovers	undisclosed
17 Matthews, Neil	Stockport County	Lincoln City	£20,000
11 Mellon, Michael J.	Bristol City	West Bromwich Albion	£75,000
12 Murphy, Matthew S.	Corby Town	Oxford United	undisclosed
4 Sansom, Kenneth	Coventry City	Everton	Free
5 Watson, Andrew	Carlisle United	Blackpool	£55,000
1 Wilson, Paul A.	Halifax Town	Burnley	undisclosed
26 Young, Stuart R.Hull City	Northampton Town		undisclosed
Temporary transfers			
25 Alexander, Timothy M.	Barnet	Woking	
1 Barber, Frederick	Peterborough United	Chesterfield	
9 Beasant, David	Wolverhampton Wanderers	Chelsea (transfer back)	
26 Billing, Peter G.	Coventry City	Port Vale	
9 Brooks, Christopher	Luton Town	Shrewsbury Town	
26 Burgess, David J.	Blackpool	Carlisle United	
25 Clarke, Nicholas J.	Mansfield Town	Chesterfield	
12 Clarke, Timothy J.	Huddersfield Town	Rochdale	
26 Clarke, Timothy J.	Rochdale	Huddersfield Town (transfer back)	
2 Cooper, Geoffrey	Barnet	Welling United	
5 Dobson, Paul	Darlington	Gateshead	
19 Dixon, Kerry M.	Southampton	Luton Town	
25 Fee, Gregory P.	Chesterfield	Mansfield Town (transfer back)	
17 Flounders, Andrew J.	Rochdale	Rotherham United	
19 Fowler, John A.	Cambridge United	Preston North End	
26 Garnett, Shaun M.	Tranmere Rovers	Wigan Athletic	
19 Gilzean, Ian R.	Dundee	Doncaster Rovers	

	From	*To*	*Fee*
26 Hodges, Lee L.	Tottenham Hotspur	Plymouth Argyle	
26 Houghton, Scott A.	Tottenham Hotspur	Charlton Athletic	
4 Jackson, Darren W.	Oxford United	Reading	
19 Kamara, Christopher	Luton Town	Middlesbrough	
24 Lake, Michael	Wrexham	Sheffield United (transfer back)	
11 McIntyre, James	Bristol City	Exeter City	
12 Manning, Paul J.	Millwall	Farnborough Town	
8 Muir, Johnny G.	Stockport County	Torquay United	
19 Mulligan, James	Stoke City	Macclesfield Town	
17 Page, Donald R.	Rotherham United	Rochdale	
3 Peel, Nathan J.	Sheffield United	Halifax Town	
6 Pennyfather, Glenn J.	Ipswich Town	Bristol City	
5 Ritchie, Paul M.	Dundee	Gillingham	
12 Slawson, Stephen M.	Notts County	Burnley	
25 Smark, Mark C.	Notts County	Huddersfield Town	
1 Sommer, Jurgen P.	Luton Town	Kettering Town	
26 Taylor, Colin D.	Wolverhampton Wanderers	Doncaster Rovers	
12 Thompson, Leslie A.	Burnley	Wycombe Wanderers	
12 Tisdale, Paul R.	Southampton	Northampton Town	
25 Toman, James A.	Darlington	Scarborough	
16 Watts, Julian	Shrewsbury Town	Sheffield Wednesday (transfer back)	
4 Williamson, Daniel A.	West Ham United	Farnborough Town	
26 Wilson, Darren A.	Bury	Cliftonville	
19 Yates, Mark J.	Burnley	Lincoln City	
5 Young, Stuart R.	Hull City	Northampton Town	

March 1993

	From	*To*	*Fee*
25 Bartlett, Kevin F.	Notts County	Cambridge United	£60,000
25 Beckford, Darren R.	Norwich City	Oldham Athletic	£300,000
8 Brown, Michael A.	Bolton Wanderers	Shrewsbury Town	undisclosed
19 Buzaglo, Timothy J.	Woking	Marlow	undisclosed
30 Byrne, Alan	Solihull Borough	Nuneaton Borough	undisclosed
12 Cole, Andrew	Bristol City	Newcastle United	£1,750,000
12 Coyne, Thomas	Celtic	Tranmere Rovers	£350,000
26 Daws, Anthony	Scunthorpe United	Grimsby Town	£50,000
5 Dobson, Paul	Darlington	Gateshead	Free
19 Dryden, Richard A.	Notts County	Birmingham City	£165,000
25 Ekoku, Efangwu	AFC Bournemouth	Norwich City	£765,000
25 Flynn, Michael A.	Preston North End	Stockport County	£125,000
19 Foy, David L.	Birmingham City	Scunthorpe United	Free
26 Francis, John A.	Cambridge United	Burnley	£70,000
23 Gallacher, Kevin W.	Coventry City	Blackburn Rovers	£1,500,000
25 Greenman, Christopher	Coventry City	Peterborough United	Free
25 Hall, Paul A.	Torquay United	Portsmouth	£100,000
19 Harford, Michael G.	Chelsea	Sunderland	£250,000
12 Hiley, Scott	Exeter City	Birmingham City	£100,000
18 Holmes, Paul	Birmingham City	Everton	£100,000
12 Hurst, Mark D.	Leicester United	Gresley Rovers	undisclosed
16 James, Martin J.	Preston North End	Stockport County	£50,000
12 Jenkinson, Leigh	Hull City	Coventry City	£300,000
11 Kerslake, David	Swindon Town	Leeds United	£500,000
26 Kristensen, Bjorn	Newcastle United	Portsmouth	£120,000
3 Lake, Michael C.	Sheffield United	Wrexham	£60,000
25 Le Saux, Graeme P.	Chelsea	Blackburn Rovers	Exchange
25 Liburn, Richard	Eastwood Town	Middlesbrough	undisclosed
23 Livingstone, Stephen	Blackburn Rovers	Chelsea	Exchange
25 Maguire, Gavin T.	Portsmouth	Millwall	£115,000
12 Moulden, Paul A.	Oldham Athletic	Birmingham City	£150,000
11 Parris, George M.	West Ham United	Birmingham City	£150,000
12 Pennyfather, Glenn J.	Ipswich Town	Bristol City	£80,000
24 Pickering, Nicholas	Darlington	Burnley	£15,000
8 Platnauer, Nicholas R.	Leicester City	Scunthorpe United	Free
25 Reeves, David	Bolton Wanderers	Notts County	£80,000
11 Rennie, David	Birmingham City	Coventry City	Exchange
9 Robinson, Mark J.	Barnsley	Newcastle United	£450,000
2 Rosario, Robert M.	Coventry City	Nottingham Forest	£400,000
18 Sale, Mark D.	Birmingham City	Torquay United	£10,000
22 Saville, Andrew V.	Hartlepool United	Birmingham City	£155,000
9 Sellars, Scott	Leeds United	Newcastle United	£700,000
25 Shail, Mark E. D.	Yeovil Town	Bristol City	£45,000
19 Slaven, Bernard	Middlesbrough	Port Vale	Free
11 Smith, David	Coventry City	Birmingham City	Exchange
19 Smith, Gary J.	Sutton Coldfield Town	Worcester City	undisclosed
4 Stephenson, Paul	Millwall	Brentford	£30,000
24 Storer, Stuart J.	Bolton Wanderers	Exeter City	£25,000
25 Thompstone, Ian P.	Halifax Town	Scunthorpe United	£15,000
22 Tinnion, Brian	Bradford City	Bristol City	£180,000
5 Varadi, Imre	Leeds United	Rotherham United	Free

		From	To	Fee
23	Vircavs, Anton	Cheltenham Town	Wycombe Wanderers	undisclosed
23	Wegerle, Roy C.	Blackburn Rovers	Coventry City	£1,000,000

Temporary transfers

25	Aylott, Trevor	Gillingham	Wycombe Wanderers	
25	Banks, Steven	West Ham United	Gillingham	
19	Barber, Frederick	Peterborough United	Colchester United	
25	Bartlett, Kevin F.	Notts County	Peterborough United	
25	Bartlett, Kevin F.	Peterborough United	Notts County (transfer back)	
25	Beadle, Peter C.	Tottenham Hotspur	AFC Bournemouth	
25	Beasley, Andrew	Mansfield Town	Bristol Rovers	
25	Bowling, Ian	Lincoln City	Bradford City	
5	Brain, Simon	Hereford United	Bromsgrove Rovers	
25	Byrne, John F.	Millwall	Brighton & Hove Albion	
5	Catlin, Robert	Notts County	Birmingham City	
25	Cooper, Mark N.	Fulham	Huddersfield Town	
3	Crisp, Richard I.	Aston Villa	Scunthorpe United	
25	Davidson, Jonathan S.	Preston North End	Chesterfield	
18	Digweed, Perry M.	Brighton & Hove Albion	Wimbledon	
24	Donowa, Brian L.	Birmingham City	Crystal Palace	
19	Duffield, Peter	Sheffield United	Stockport County	
25	Ellison, Anthony L.	Darlington	Hartlepool United	
18	Emberson, Carl W.	Millwall	Slough Town	
19	Emmett, Darren	Bury	Altrincham	
11	Farrell, David	Scunthorpe United	Aston Villa (transfer back)	
25	Fitzpatrick, Paul J.	Birmingham City	Bury	
23	Fox, Peter D.	Stoke City	Wrexham	
25	Gallimore, Anthony	Stoke City	Carlisle United	
19	Gardner, Stephen G.	Bury	Witton Albion	
19	Gillard, Kenneth J.	Luton Town	Northampton Town	
25	Gorton, Andrew	Bury	Altrincham	
17	Greenhalgh, Lawrence	Bury	Cliftonville	
5	Gridelet, Philip R.	Barnsley	Rotherham United	
17	Grobbelaar, Bruce D.	Liverpool	Stoke City	
4	Hargreaves, Christian	Grimsby Town	Scarborough	
19	Hawke, Warren R.	Sunderland	Northampton Town	
17	Hendon, Ian M.	Tottenham Hotspur	Barnsley	
23	Hitchcock, Kevin	Chelsea	West Ham United	
8	Hockaday, David	Hull City	Stoke City	
25	Hunt, Andrew	Newcastle United	West Bromwich Albion	
25	Kamara, Christopher	Middlesbrough	Luton Town (transfer back)	
25	Kelly, James	Wolverhampton Wanderers	Walsall	
25	Kelly, Paul	Fulham	Woking	
25	Kite, Philip D.	Sheffield United	Stockport County	
19	Kristensen, Bjorn	Newcastle United	Portsmouth	
19	Lambert, Matthew R.	Bury	Witton Albion	
25	Lim, Harvey C.	Gillingham	Kettering Town	
6	McDonald, David H.	Tottenham Hotspur	Reading	
25	Marshall, Dwight W.	Plymouth Argyle	Middlesbrough	
30	Mathie, Alexander M.	Morton	Port Vale	
25	Mike, Adrian R.	Manchester City	Bury	
19	Minett, Jason	Norwich City	Exeter City	
19	Mulligan, James	Macclesfield Town	Stoke City (transfer back)	
19	Mulligan, James	Stoke City	Telford United	
24	O'Connor, Martin J.	Crystal Palace	Walsall	
25	Peters, Robert	Brentford	Woking	
22	Pickering, Nicholas	Darlington	Burnley	
15	Proctor, Mark G.	Middlesbrough	Tranmere Rovers	
19	Reed, John P.	Sheffield United	Darlington	
25	Rowbotham, Darren	Birmingham City	Hereford United	
12	Rush, Matthew J.	West Ham United	Cambridge United	
5	Sale, Mark D.	Birmingham City	Torquay United	
25	Smith, Mark C.	Notts County	Chesterfield	
25	Sommer, Jurgen P.	Kettering Town	Luton Town (transfer back)	
19	Speedie, David R.	West Bromwich Albion	Southampton (transfer back)	
19	Speedie, David R.	Southampton	West Ham United	
24	Thomas, Martin R.	Birmingham City	Crystal Palace	
25	Turner, Robert P.	Notts County	Shrewsbury Town	
25	Wallace, David L.	Manchester United	Millwall	
25	Williams, Wayne	Walsall	Kidderminster Harriers	
25	Williams, William J.	Cardiff City	Yeovil Town	
15	Williamson, Daniel A.	Farnborough Town	West Ham United (transfer back)	

April 1993

22	Beeney, Mark R.	Brighton & Hove Albion	Leeds United	350,000
8	Carr, Franz A.	Newcastle United	Sheffield United	undisclosed
20	Gillard, Kenneth J.	Luton Town	Northampton Town	undisclosed

608

Temporary transfers

20 Broddle, Julian	Partick Thistle	Preston North End
24 Digweed, Perry M.	Wimbledon	Brighton & Hove Albion (transfer back)
13 Fowler, John A.	Preston North End	Cambridge United (transfer back)
2 Fox, Peter D.	Wrexham	Stoke City (transfer back)
8 Gridelet, Philip R.	Rotherham United	Barnsley (transfer back)
2 Grobbelaar, Bruce D.	Stoke City	Liverpool (transfer back)
29 Kee, Paul	Oxford United	Wimbledon
13 Thomas, Martin R.	Crystal Palace	Birmingham City (transfer back)

May 1993

17 Brown, Ian	Chelmsford City	Bristol City	undisclosed
21 Jules, Mark A.	Scarborough	Chesterfield	undisclosed
14 Miller, Kevin	Exeter City	Birmingham City	undisclosed

FOOTBALL LEAGUE COMPETITION ATTENDANCES

SEASON 1992–1993

ANGLO-ITALIAN CUP

(Games played in England only)

	Attendances	Matches	Average
Preliminary round	97,055	24	4,044
International stage	84,090	16	5,256
Semi-finals	19,561	2	9,781
Final	37,024	1	37,024
Totals	237,730	43	5,529

COCA-COLA CUP

	Attendances	Matches	Average
Round one	229,049	56	4,090
Round two	577,067	64	9,017
Round three	285,924	20	14,296
Round four	176,497	11	16,045
Round five	113,064	5	22,613
Semi finals	102,423	4	25,606
Final	74,007	1	74,007
Total	1,558,031	161	9,677

AUTOGLASS TROPHY

	Attendances	Matches	Average
Round one	85,736	42	2,041
Round two	52,814	16	3,301
Area quarter-finals	38,133	8	4,766
Area semi-finals	34,816	4	8,704
Area finals	26,377	4	6,594
Final	35,885	1	35,885
Total	273,761	75	3,650

LEAGUE ATTENDANCES SINCE 1946–47

Season	Matches	Total	Div. 1	Div. 2	Div. 3 (S)	Div. 3 (N)
1946–47	1848	35,604,606	15,005,316	11,071,572	5,664,004	3,863,714
1947–48	1848	40,259,130	16,732,341	12,286,350	6,653,610	4,586,829
1948–49	1848	41,271,414	17,914,667	11,353,237	6,998,429	5,005,081
1949–50	1848	40,517,865	17,278,625	11,694,158	7,104,155	4,440,927
1950–51	2028	39,584,967	16,679,454	10,780,580	7,367,884	4,757,109
1951–52	2028	39,015,866	16,110,322	11,066,189	6,958,927	4,880,428
1952–53	2028	37,149,966	16,050,278	9,686,654	6,704,299	4,708,735
1953–54	2028	36,174,590	16,154,915	9,510,053	6,311,508	4,198,114
1954–55	2028	34,133,103	15,087,221	8,988,794	5,996,017	4,051,071
1955–56	2028	33,150,809	14,108,961	9,080,002	5,692,479	4,269,367
1956–57	2028	32,744,405	13,803,037	8,718,162	5,622,189	4,601,017
1957–58	2028	33,562,208	14,468,652	8,663,712	6,097,183	4,332,661

Season	Matches	Total	Div. 1	Div. 2	Div. 3	Div. 4
1958–59	2028	33,610,985	14,727,691	8,641,997	5,946,600	4,276,697
1959–60	2028	32,538,611	14,391,227	8,399,627	5,739,707	4,008,050
1960–61	2028	28,619,754	12,926,948	7,033,936	4,784,256	3,874,614
1961–62	2015	27,979,902	12,061,194	7,453,089	5,199,106	3,266,513
1962–63	2028	28,885,852	12,490,239	7,792,770	5,341,362	3,261,481
1963–64	2028	28,535,022	12,486,626	7,594,158	5,419,157	3,035,081
1964–65	2028	27,641,168	12,708,752	6,984,104	4,436,245	3,512,067
1965–66	2028	27,206,980	12,480,644	6,914,757	4,779,150	3,032,429
1966–67	2028	28,902,596	14,242,957	7,253,819	4,421,172	2,984,648
1967–68	2028	30,107,298	15,289,410	7,450,410	4,013,087	3,354,391
1968–69	2028	29,382,172	14,584,851	7,382,390	4,339,656	3,075,275
1969–70	2028	29,600,972	14,868,754	7,581,728	4,223,761	2,926,729
1970–71	2028	28,194,146	13,954,337	7,098,265	4,377,213	2,764,331
1971–72	2028	28,700,729	14,484,603	6,769,308	4,697,392	2,749,426
1972–73	2028	25,448,642	13,998,154	5,631,730	3,737,252	2,081,506
1973–74	2027	24,982,203	13,070,991	6,326,108	3,421,624	2,163,480
1974–75	2028	25,577,977	12,613,178	6,955,970	4,086,145	1,992,684
1975–76	2028	24,896,053	13,089,861	5,798,405	3,948,449	2,059,338
1976–77	2028	26,182,800	13,647,585	6,250,597	4,152,218	2,132,400
1977–78	2028	25,392,872	13,255,677	6,474,763	3,332,042	2,330,390
1978–79	2028	24,540,627	12,704,549	6,153,223	3,374,558	2,308,297
1979–80	2028	24,623,975	12,163,002	6,112,025	3,999,328	2,349,620
1980–81	2028	21,907,569	11,392,894	5,175,442	3,637,854	1,701,379
1981–82	2028	20,006,961	10,420,793	4,750,463	2,836,915	1,998,790
1982–83	2028	18,766,158	9,295,613	4,974,937	2,943,568	1,552,040
1983–84	2028	18,358,631	8,711,448	5,359,757	2,729,942	1,557,484
1984–85	2028	17,849,835	9,761,404	4,030,823	2,667,008	1,390,600
1985–86	2028	16,488,577	9,037,854	3,551,968	2,490,481	1,408,274
1986–87	2028	17,379,218	9,144,676	4,168,131	2,350,970	1,715,441
1987–88	2030	17,959,732	8,094,571	5,341,599	2,751,275	1,772,287
1988–89	2036	18,464,192	7,809,993	5,887,805	3,035,327	1,791,067
1989–90	2036	19,445,442	7,883,039	6,867,674	2,803,551	1,891,178
1990–91	2036	19,508,202	8,618,709	6,285,068	2,835,759	1,768,666
1991–92	2064*	20,487,273	9,989,160	5,809,787	2,993,352	1,694,974
1992–93	2028	20,657,327	9,759,809†	5,874,017	3,483,073	1,540,428

This is the first time since the war that attendances have risen for seven consecutive seasons.

Figures include matches played by Aldershot.

†FA Premier League.

LEAGUE ATTENDANCES 1992–93

PREMIER LEAGUE STATISTICS

	Average Gate			Season 1992/93	
	1991/92	1992/93	+/–%	Highest	Lowest
Arsenal	31,905	24,403	–23.5	29,740	18,253
Aston Villa	24,818	29,594	+19.2	39,063	17,120
Blackburn Rovers	13,251	16,246	+22.6	20,305	13,556
Chelsea	18,684	18,787	+0.6	25,157	12,739
Coventry City	13,876	14,951	+7.7	24,410	10,455
Crystal Palace	17,618	15,748	–10.6	30,115	11,224
Everton	23,148	20,445	–11.7	35,827	14,023
Ipswich Town	14,274	18,223	+27.7	22,007	14,053
Leeds United	29,459	29,250	–0.7	34,166	25,774
Liverpool	34,799	37,004	+6.3	44,619	29,574
Manchester City	27,690	24,698	–10.8	37,136	19,524
Manchester United	44,984	35,152	–21.9	40,693	29,736
Middlesbrough	14,703	16,724	+13.7	22,463	12,290
Norwich City	13,858	16,154	+16.6	20,610	12,452
Nottingham Forest	23,721	21,910	–7.6	26,752	17,553
Oldham Athletic	15,087	12,859	–14.8	17,106	10,946
Queens Park Rangers	13,592	15,015	+10.5	21,056	10,677
Sheffield United	22,097	18,801	–14.9	30,039	14,628
Sheffield Wednesday	29,560	27,263	–7.8	38,668	20,918
Southampton	14,070	15,382	+9.3	19,654	10,827
Tottenham Hotspur	27,761	27,740	–0.1	33,709	20,098
Wimbledon	6,905	8,4(5	+21.7	30,115	3,039

BARCLAYS LEAGUE: DIVISION ONE STATISTICS

	Average Gate			Season 1992/93	
	1991/92	1992/93	+/–%	Highest	Lowest
Barnsley	7,508	6,415	–14.6	13,263	3,855
Birmingham City	12,400	12,328	–0.6	22,234	6,807
Brentford	7,156	8,476	+18.4	11,912	6,334
Bristol City	11,479	11,004	–4.1	21,854	6,755
Bristol Rovers	5,850	5,745	–1.8	7,714	3,921
Cambridge United	7.078	5,545	–21.7	8,077	3,896
Charlton Athletic	6,786	7,005	+3.2	12,945	4,205
Derby County	14,664	15,020	+2.4	21,478	12,166
Grimsby Town	6,921	6,088	+12.0	14,402	4,117
Leicester City	15,202	15,362	+1.1	19,687	10,284
Luton Town	9,715	8,212	–15.5	10,959	6,687
Millwall	7,921	9,188	+16.0	15,821	5,924
Newcastle United	21,148	29,018	+37.2	30,360	26,136
Notts County	10,987	8,151	–25.8	14,841	5,037
Oxford United	5,671	6,356	+12.1	9,499	3,785
Peterborough United	6,279	8,064	+28.4	15,517	5,169
Portsmouth	11,789	13,706	+16.3	24,955	8,943
Southend United	6,733	5,396	–19.9	12,813	2,651
Sunderland	18,390	17,258	–6.2	28,098	13,314
Swindon Town	10,009	10,715	+7.1	17,936	6,090
Tranmere Rovers	8,845	8,071	–8.8	13,118	5,248
Watford	8,511	8,275	–2.8	13,115	5,785
West Ham United	21,342	16,001	–25.0	27,399	10,326
Wolverhampton Wanderers	13,743	13,598	–1.1	17,270	10,593

BARCLAYS LEAGUE: DIVISION TWO STATISTICS

| | Average Gate | | | Season 1992/93 | |
	1991/92	1992/93	+/−%	Highest	Lowest
AFC Bournemouth	5,471	4,454	−18.6	7,129	2,829
Blackpool	4,335	5,501	+26.9	9,386	3,164
Bolton Wanderers	6,030	9,062	+50.3	21,720	4,136
Bradford City	6,115	6,581	+7.6	10,235	3,900
Brighton & Hove Albion	8,002	6,710	−16.1	8,741	4,731
Burnley	10,521	10,537	+0.2	16,667	7,332
Chester City	1,857	2,992	+61.1	5,237	1,614
Exeter City	3,627	3,275	−9.7	6,534	2,393
Fulham	4,492	4,736	+5.4	9,143	3,285
Hartlepool United	3,201	3,144	−1.8	4,396	1,791
Huddersfield Town	7,540	5,918	−21.5	11,089	3,563
Hull City	4,115	4,672	+13.5	9,088	3,167
Leyton Orient	4,460	5,377	+20.6	10,800	3,436
Mansfield Town	3,803	3,730	−19.2	6,820	2,527
Plymouth Argyle	6,739	6,377	−5.4	11,370	4,612
Port Vale	7,382	8,092	+9.6	20,373	5,370
Preston North End	4,722	5,689	+20.5	10,403	3,330
Reading	3,841	4,782	+24.5	8,026	2,491
Rotherham United	4,750	4,769	+0.4	9,021	3,050
Stockport County	4,896	5,504	+12.4	9,402	3,759
Stoke City	13,007	16,579	+27.5	24,334	10,854
Swansea City	3,367	5,199	+54.4	8,366	2,656
West Bromwich Albion	12,711	15,161	+19.3	29,341	12,305
Wigan Athletic	2,862	2,598	−9.2	5,403	1,432

BARCLAYS LEAGUE: DIVISION THREE STATISTICS

| | Average Gate | | | Season 1992/93 | |
	1991/92	1992/93	+/−%	Highest	Lowest
Barnet	3,643	3,429	−5.9	4,985	2,623
Bury	2,901	2,670	−8.0	4,550	1,739
Cardiff City	6,195	8,560	+38.2	17,253	4,348
Carlisle United	2,554	3,611	+41.4	5,357	2,527
Chesterfield	3,439	3,213	−6.6	5,452	2,271
Colchester United	3,514	3,777	+7.5	5,609	2,774
Crewe Alexandra	3,733	3,455	−7.4	4,549	2,671
Darlington	2,904	1,960	−32.5	3,787	1,366
Doncaster Rovers	2,058	2,411	+17.2	3,350	1,719
Gillingham	3,135	3,301	+5.3	6,985	2,043
Halifax Town	1,633	2,231	+36.6	7,451	1,230
Hereford United	2,735	2,211	−19.2	4,039	1,401
Lincoln City	2,822	3,331	+18.0	4,359	2,689
Northampton Town	2,789	3,234	+16.0	7,504	1,922
Rochdale	2,784	2,312	−17.0	4,500	1,446
Scarborough	1,677	1,929	+15.0	3,863	1,300
Scunthorpe United	3,189	3,147	−1.3	7,407	1,970
Shrewsbury Town	3,456	3,411	−1.3	7,278	1,527
Torquay United	2,734	2,695	−1.4	4,645	1,771
Walsall	3,367	3,628	+7.8	5,573	2,719
Wrexham	2,608	4,987	+91.2	10,852	1,893
York City	2,506	3,946	+57.5	6,568	2,443

LEAGUE CUP FINALISTS 1961–93

Played as a two-leg final until 1966. All subsequent finals at Wembley.

Year	Winners	Runners-up	Score
1961	Aston Villa	Rotherham U	0-2, 3)0 (aet)
1962	Norwich C	Rochdale	3-0, 1-0
1963	Birmingham C	Aston Villa	3-1, 0-0
1964	Leicester C	Stoke C	1-1, 3-2
1965	Chelsea	Leicester C	3-2, 0-0
1966	WBA	West Ham U	1-2, 4-1
1967	QPR	WBA	3-2
1968	Leeds U	Arsenal	1-0
1969	Swindon T	Arsenal	3-1 (aet)
1970	Manchester C	WBA	2-1 (aet)
1971	Tottenham H	Aston Villa	2-0
1972	Stoke C	Chelsea	2-1
1973	Tottenham H	Norwich C	1-0
1974	Wolverhampton W	Manchester C	2-1
1975	Aston Villa	Norwich C	1-0
1976	Manchester C	Newcastle U	2-1
1977	Aston Villa	Everton	0-0, 1-1 (aet), 3-2 (aet)
1978	Nottingham F	Liverpool	0-0 (aet), 1-0
1979	Nottingham F	Southampton	3-2
1980	Wolverhampton W	Nottingham F	1-0
1981	Liverpool	West Ham U	1-1 (aet), 2-1

MILK CUP

Year	Winners	Runners-up	Score
1982	Liverpool	Tottenham H	3-1 (aet)
1983	Liverpool	Manchester U	2-1 (aet)
1984	Liverpool	Everton	0-0 (aet), 1-0
1985	Norwich C	Sunderland	1-0
1986	Oxford U	QPR	3-0

LITTLEWOODS CUP

Year	Winners	Runners-up	Score
1987	Arsenal	Liverpool	2-1
1988	Luton T	Arsenal	3-2
1989	Nottingham F	Luton T	3-1
1990	Nottingham F	Oldham Ath	1-0

RUMBELOWS LEAGUE CUP

Year	Winners	Runners-up	Score
1991	Sheffield W	Manchester U	1-0
1992	Manchester U	Nottingham F	1-0

COCA COLA CUP

Year	Winners	Runners-up	Score
1993	Arsenal	Sheffield W	2-1

LEAGUE CUP WINS
Liverpool 4, Nottingham F 4, Aston Villa 3, Arsenal 2, Manchester C 2, Norwich C 2, Tottenham H, Wolverhampton W 2, Birmingham C 1, Chelsea 1, Leeds U 1, Leicester C 1, Luton T 1, Manchester U 1, Oxford U 1, QPR 1, Sheffield W 1, Stoke C 1, Swindon T 1, WBA 1.

APPEARANCES IN FINALS
Liverpool 6, Nottingham F 6, Arsenal 5, Aston Villa 5, Norwich C 4, Manchester C 3, Manchester U 3, Tottenham H 3, WBA 3, Chelsea 2, Everton 2, Leicester C 2, Luton T 2, QPR 2, Sheffield W 2, Stoke C 2, West Ham U 2, Wolverhampton W 2, Birmingham C 1, Leeds U 1, Newcastle U 1, Oldham Ath 1, Oxford U 1, Rochdale 1, Rotherham U 1, Southampton 1, Sunderland 1, Swindon T 1.

APPEARANCES IN SEMI-FINALS
Aston Villa 8, Liverpool 8, Tottenham H 8, Arsenal 7, West Ham U 7, Manchester U 6, Nottingham F 6, Chelsea 5, Manchester C 5, Norwich C 5, Leeds U 4, WBA 4, Burnley 3, Everton 3, QPR 3, Wolverhampton W 3, Birmingham C 2, Blackburn R 2, Bristol C 2, Coventry C 2, Ipswich T 2, Leicester C 2, Luton T 2, Middlesbrough 2, Oxford U 2, Plymouth Arg 2, Sheffield W 2, Southampton 2, Stoke C 2, Sunderland 2, Swindon T 2, Blackpool 1, Bolton W 1, Bury 1, Cardiff C 1, Carlisle U 1, Chester C 1, Crystal Palace 1, Derby Co 1, Huddersfield T 1, Newcastle U 1, Oldham Ath 1, Peterborough U 1, Rochdale 1, Rotherham U 1, Shrewsbury T 1, Walsall 1, Watford 1.

LEAGUE CUP FINALISTS 1961–92

1960–61 ROTHERHAM UNITED Ironside; Perry, Morgan, Lambert, Madden, Waterhouse, Webster, Weston, Houghton, Kirkman, Bambridge. *Scorers:* Webster, Kirkman.

2–0 ASTON VILLA Sims; Lynn, Lee, Crowe, Dugdale, Deakin, McEwan, Thomson, Brown, Wylie, McParland.
ASTON VILLA Sidebottom; Neal, Lee, Crowe, Dugdale, Deakin, McEwan, O'Neill, McParland, Thomson, Burrows. *Scorers:* O'Neill, Burrows, McParland.

3–0 ROTHERHAM UNITED Ironside; Perry, Morgan, Lambert, Madden, Waterhouse, Webster, Weston,
aet Houghton, Kirkman, Bambridge. **Aston Villa won on aggregate 3–2.**

1961–62 ROCHDALE Burgin; Milburn, Winton, Bodell, Aspden, Thompson, Wragg, Hepton, Bimpson, Cairns, Whitaker.

0–3 NORWICH CITY Kennon; McCrohan, Ashman, Burton, Butler, Mullett, Mannion, Lythgoe, Scott, Hill, Punton. *Scorers:* Lythgoe 2, Punton.
NORWICH CITY Kennon; McCrohan, Ashman, Burton, Butler, Mullett, Mannion, Lythgoe, Scott, Hill, Punton. *Scorer:* Hill.

1–0 ROCHDALE Burgin; Milburn, Winton, Bodell, Aspden, Thompson, Whyke, Richardson, Bimpson, Cairns, Whitaker. **Norwich City won on aggregate 4–0.**

1962–63 BIRMINGHAM CITY Schofield; Lynn, Green, Hennessey, Smith, Beard, Hellawell, Bloomfield, Harris, Leek, Auld. *Scorers:* Leek 2, Bloomfield.

3–1 ASTON VILLA Sims; Fraser, Aitken, Crowe, Sleeuwenhoek, Lee, Baker, Graham, Thomson, Wylie, Burrows. *Scorer:* Thomson.
ASTON VILLA Chatterley took the place of Sleeuwenhoek.

0–0 BIRMINGHAM CITY No change in team. **Birmingham City won on aggregate 3–1.**

1963–64 STOKE CITY Leslie; Asprey, Allen, Palmer, Kinnell, Skeels, Dobing, Viollet, Ritchie, McIlroy, Bebbington. *Scorer:* Bebbington.

1–1 LEICESTER CITY Banks; Sjoberg, Appleton, Dougan, King, Cross, Riley, Heath, Keyworth, Gibson, Stringfellow. *Scorer:* Gibson.
LEICESTER CITY Banks; Sjoberg, Norman, Cross, King, Appleton, Riley, Gibson, Keyworth, Sweenie, Stringfellow. *Scorers:* Stringfellow, Gibson, Riley.

3–2 STOKE CITY Irvine; Asprey, Allen, Palmer, Kinnell, Skeels, Dobing, Viollet, Ritchie, McIlroy, Bebbington. *Scorers:* Viollet, Kinnell. **Leicester City won on aggregate 4–3.**

1964–65 CHELSEA Bonetti; Hinton, Harris, Hollins, Young, Boyle, Murray, Graham, McCreadie, Venables, Tambling. *Scorers:* Tambling, Venables (pen), McCreadie.

3–2 LEICESTER CITY Banks; Sjoberg, Norman, Chalmers, King, Appleton, Hodgson, Cross, Goodfellow, Gibson, Sweenie. *Scorers:* Appleton, Goodfellow.
LEICESTER CITY Banks; Walker, Norman, Roberts, Sjoberg, Appleton, Hodgson, Cross, Goodfellow, Gibson, Stringfellow.

0–0 CHELSEA Bonetti; Hinton, McCreadie, Harris, Mortimore, Upton, Murray, Boyle, Bridges, Venables, Tambling. **Chelsea won on aggregate 3–2.**

1965–66 WEST HAM UNITED Standen; Burnett, Burkett, Peters, Brown, Moore, Brabrook, Boyce, Byrne, Hurst, Dear. *Scorers:* Moore, Byrne.

2–1 WEST BROMWICH ALBION Potter; Cram, Fairfax, Fraser, Campbell, Williams, Brown, Astle, Kaye, Lovett, Clark. *Scorer:* Astle.
WEST BROMWICH ALBION Potter; Cram, Fairfax, Fraser, Campbell, Williams, Brown, Astle, Kaye, Hope, Clark. *Scorers:* Kaye, Brown, Clark, Williams.

4–1 WEST HAM UNITED Standen; Burnett, Peters, Bovington, Brown, Moore, Brabrook, Boyce, Byrne, Hurst, Sissons. *Scorer:* Peters. **West Bromwich Albion won on aggregate 5–3.**

1966–67 QUEEN'S PARK RANGERS Springett; Hazell, Langley, Sibley, Hunt, Keen, Lazarus, Sanderson, Allen, Marsh, Morgan R. *Scorers:* Morgan R, Marsh, Lazarus.

3–2 WEST BROMWICH ALBION Sheppard; Cram, Williams, Collard, Clarke D, Fraser, Brown, Astle, Kaye, Hope, Clark C. *Scorer:* C Clark 2.

1967–68 LEEDS UNITED Sprake; Reaney, Cooper, Bremner, Charlton, Hunter, Greenhoff, Lorimer, Madeley, Giles, Gray (Belfitt). *Scorer:* Cooper.

1–0 ARSENAL Furnell; Storey, McNab, McLintock, Simpson, Ure, Radford, Jenkins, Graham, Sammels, Armstrong.

1968–69 SWINDON TOWN Downsborough; Thomas, Trollope, Butler, Burrows, Harland, Heath, Smart, Smith, Noble (Penman), Rogers. *Scorers:* Smart, Rogers 2.

3–1 ARSENAL Wilson; Storey, McNab, McLintock, Ure, Simpson (Graham), Radford, Sammels, Court, Gould, Armstrong. *Scorer:* Gould.

1969–70 MANCHESTER CITY Corrigan; Book, Mann, Doyle, Booth, Oakes, Heslop, Bell, Summerbee (Bowyer), Lee, Pardoe. *Scorers:* Doyle, Pardoe.

2–1 WEST BROMWICH ALBION Osborne; Fraser, Wilson, Brown, Talbut, Kaye, Cantello, Suggett, Astle, Hartford (Krzywicki), Hope. *Scorer:* Astle.

1970–71 TOTTENHAM HOTSPUR Jennings; Kinnear, Knowles, Mullery, Collins, Beal, Gilzean, Perryman, Chivers, Peters, Neighbour. *Scorer:* Chivers 2.

2–0 ASTON VILLA Dunn; Bradley, Aitken, Godfrey, Turnbull, Tiler, McMahon, Rioch, Lochhead, Hamilton, Anderson.

1971–72 STOKE CITY Banks; Marsh, Pejic, Bernard, Smith, Bloor, Conroy, Greenhoff (Mahoney), Ritchie, Dobing, Eastham. *Scorers:* Conroy, Eastham.

   2–1 CHELSEA Bonetti; Mulligan (Baldwin), Harris, Hollins, Dempsey, Webb, Cooke, Osgood, Hudson, Houseman. *Scorer:* Osgood.

1972–73 TOTTENHAM HOTSPUR Jennings; Kinnear, Knowles, Pratt (Coates), England, Beal, Gilzean, Perryman, Chivers, Peters, Pearce. *Scorer:* Coates.

   1–0 NORWICH CITY Keelan; Payne, Butler, Stringer, Forbes, Briggs, Livermore, Blair (Howard), Cross, Paddon, Anderson.

1973–74 WOLVERHAMPTON WANDERERS Pierce; Palmer, Parkin, Bailey, Munro, McAlle, Sunderland, Hibbitt, Richards, Dougan, Wagstaffe (Powell). *Scorers:* Hibbitt, Richards.

   2–1 MANCHESTER CITY MacRae; Pardoe, Donachie, Doyle, Booth, Towers, Summerbee, Bell, Lee, Law, Marsh. *Scorer:* Bell.

1974–75 ASTON VILLA Cumbes; Robson, Aitken, Ross, Nicholl, McDonald, Graydon, Little, Leonard, Hamilton, Carrodus. *Scorer:* Graydon.

   1–0 NORWICH CITY Keelan; Machin, Sullivan, Morris, Forbes, Stringer, Miller, MacDougall, Boyer, Suggett, Powell.

1975–76 MANCHESTER CITY Corrigan; Keegan, Donachie, Doyle, Watson, Oakes, Barnes, Booth, Royle, Hartford, Tueart. *Scorers:* Barnes, Tueart.

   2–1 NEWCASTLE UNITED Mahoney; Nattrass, Kennedy, Barrowclough, Keeley, Howard, Burns, Cassidy, Macdonald, Gowling, Craig. *Scorer:* Gowling.

1976–77 ASTON VILLA Burridge; Gidman, Robson, Phillips, Nicholl, Mortimer, Deehan, Little, Gray, Cropley, Carrodus.

   0–0 EVERTON Lawson; Jones, Darracott, Lyons, McNaught, King, Hamilton, Dobson, Latchford, McKenzie, Goodlass. *First replay (at Hillsborough)*

R: 1–1 ASTON VILLA Burridge; Gidman, Robson, Phillips, Nicholl, Mortimer, Deehan, Little, Gray, Cowans, **aet** Carrodus. *Scorer:* Kenyon og.

   EVERTON Lawson; Bernard, Darracott, Lyons, McNaught, King, Hamilton (Pearson), Kenyon, Latchford, McKenzie, Goodlass. *Scorer:* Latchford. *Second replay (at Old Trafford, Manchester)*

R: 3–2 ASTON VILLA Burridge; Gidman (Smith), Robson, Phillips, Nicholl, Mortimer, Graydon, Little, Deehan, **aet** Cropley, Cowans. *Scorers:* Little 2, Nicholl.

   EVERTON Lawson; Robinson, Darracott, Lyons, McNaught, King, Hamilton, Dobson, Latchford, Pearson (Seargeant), Goodlass. *Scorers:* Latchford, Lyons.

1977–78 NOTTINGHAM FOREST Woods; Anderson, Clark, McGovern (O'Hare), Lloyd, Burns, O'Neill, Bowyer, Withe, Woodcock, Robertson.

   0–0 LIVERPOOL Clemence; Neal, Smith, Thompson, Kennedy (Fairclough), Hughes, Dalglish, Case, **aet** Heighway, McDermott, Callaghan. *Replay (at Old Trafford, Manchester)*

R: 1–0 NOTTINGHAM FOREST Woods; Anderson, Clark, O'Hare, Lloyd, Burns, O'Neill, Bowyer, Withe, Woodcock, Robertson. *Scorer:* Robertson (pen).

   LIVERPOOL Clemence; Neal, Smith, Thompson, Kennedy, Hughes, Dalglish, Case (Fairclough), Heighway, McDermott, Callaghan.

1978–79 NOTTINGHAM FOREST Shilton; Barrett, Clark, McGovern, Lloyd, Needham, O'Neill, Gemmill, Birtles, Woodcock, Robertson. *Scorers:* Birtles 2, Woodcock.

   3–2 SOUTHAMPTON Gennoe; Golac, Peach, Williams, Nicholl, Waldron, Ball, Boyer, Hayes (Sealy), Holmes, Curran. *Scorers:* Peach, Holmes.

1979–80 WOLVERHAMPTON WANDERERS Bradshaw; Palmer, Parkin, Daniel, Berry, Hughes, Carr, Hibbitt, Gray, Richards, Eves. *Scorer:* Gray.

   1–0 NOTTINGHAM FOREST Shilton; Anderson, Gray, McGovern, Needham, Burns, O'Neill, Bowyer, Birtles, Francis, Robertson.

1980–81 LIVERPOOL Clemence; Neal, Kennedy A, Irwin, Kennedy R, Hansen, Dalglish, Lee, Heighway (Case), McDermott, Souness. *Scorer:* Kennedy A.

   1–1 WEST HAM UNITED Parkes; Stewart, Lampard, Bonds, Martin, Devonshire, Neighbour, Goddard **aet** (Pearson), Cross, Brooking, Pike. *Scorer:* Stewart (pen). *Replay (at Villa Park)*

R: 2–1 LIVERPOOL Clemence; Neal, Kennedy A, Thompson, Kennedy R, Hansen, Dalglish, Lee, Rush, McDermott, Case. *Scorers:* Dalglish, Hansen.

   WEST HAM UNITED Parkes; Stewart, Lampard, Bonds, Martin, Devonshire, Neighbour, Goddard, Cross, Brooking, Pike (Pearson). *Scorer:* Goddard.

1981–82 LIVERPOOL Grobbelaar; Neal, Kennedy, Thompson A, Whelan, Lawrenson, Dalglish, Lee, Rush, McDermott (Johnson), Souness. *Scorers:* Whelan 2, Rush.

   3–1 TOTTENHAM HOTSPUR Clemence; Hughton, Miller, Price, Hazard (Villa), Perryman, Ardiles, **aet** Archibald, Galvin, Hoddle, Crooks. *Scorer:* Archibald.

1982–83 LIVERPOOL Grobbelaar; Neal, Kennedy, Lawrenson, Whelan, Hansen, Dalglish, Lee, Rush, Johnston (Fairclough), Souness. *Scorers:* Kennedy, Whelan.

   2–1 MANCHESTER UNITED Bailey; Duxbury, Albiston, Moses, Moran (Macari), McQueen, Wilkins, **aet** Muhren, Stapleton, Whiteside, Coppell. *Scorer:* Whiteside.

1983–84 LIVERPOOL Grobbelaar; Neal, Kennedy, Lawrenson, Whelan, Hansen, Dalglish, Lee, Rush, Johnston (Robinson), Souness.

   0–0 EVERTON Southall; Stevens, Bailey, Ratcliffe, Mountfield, Reid, Irvine, Heath, Sharp, Richardson, **aet** Sheedy (Harper).

R: **1–0** LIVERPOOL   Grobbelaar; Neal, Kennedy, Lawrenson, Whelan, Hansen, Dalglish, Lee, Rush, Johnston, Souness. *Scorer:* Souness.
EVERTON   Southall; Stevens, Bailey, Ratcliffe, Mountfield, Reid, Irvine (King), Heath, Sharp, Richardson, Harper.   *Replay (at Maine Road, Manchester)*

1984–85 NORWICH CITY   Woods; Haylock, Van Wyk, Bruce, Mendham, Watson, Barham, Channon, Deehan, Hartford, Donowa. *Scorer:* Chisholm (og).
1–0 SUNDERLAND   Turner; Venison, Pickering, Bennett, Chisholm, Corner (Gayle), Daniel, Wallace, Hodgson, Berry, Walker.

1985–86 OXFORD UNITED   Judge; Langan, Trewick, Phillips, Briggs, Shotton, Houghton, Aldridge, Charles, Hebberd, Brock. *Scorers:* Hebberd, Houghton, Charles.
3–0 QUEEN'S PARK RANGERS   Barron; McDonald, Dawes, Neill, Wicks, Fenwick, Allen (Rosenoir), James, Bannister, Byrne, Robinson.

1986–87 ARSENAL   Lukic; Anderson, Sansom, Williams, O'Leary, Adams, Rocastle, Davis, Quinn (Groves), Nicholas, Hayes (Thomas). *Scorer:* Nicholas 2.
2–1 LIVERPOOL   Grobbelaar; Gillespie, Venison, Spackman, Whelan, Hansen, Walsh (Dalglish), Johnston, Rush, Molby, McMahon (Wark). *Scorer:* Rush.

1987–88 LUTON TOWN   Dibble; Breacker, Johnson, Hill, Foster, Donaghy, Wilson, Stein B, Harford (Stein M), Preece (Grimes). *Scorers:* Stein B 2, Wilson.
3–2 ARSENAL   Lukic; Winterburn, Sansom, Thomas, Caesar, Adams, Rocastle, Davis, Smith, Groves (Hayes), Richardson. *Scorers:* Hayes, Smith.

1988–89 NOTTINGHAM FOREST   Sutton; Laws, Pearce, Walker, Wilson, Hodge, Gaynor, Webb, Clough, Chapman, Parker. *Scorers:* Clough 2 (1 pen), Webb.
3–1 LUTON TOWN   Sealey; Breacker, Grimes (McDonough), Preece, Foster, Beaumont, Wilson, Wegerle, Harford, Hill, Black. *Scorer:* Harford.

1989–90 NOTTINGHAM FOREST   Sutton; Laws, Pearce, Walker, Chettle, Hodge, Crosby, Parker, Clough, Jemson, Carr. *Scorer:* Jemson.
1–0 OLDHAM ATHLETIC   Rhodes; Irwin, Barlow, Henry, Barrett, Warhurst, Adams, Ritchie, Bunn (Palmer), Milligan, Holden R.

1990–91 SHEFFIELD WEDNESDAY   Turner; Nilsson, King, Harkes (Madden), Shirtliff, Pearson, Wilson, Sheridan, Hirst, Williams, Worthington. *Scorer:* Sheridan.
1–0 MANCHESTER UNITED   Sealey; Irwin, Blackmore, Bruce, Webb (Phelan), Pallister, Robson, Ince, McClair, Hughes, Sharpe.

1991–92 MANCHESTER UNITED   Schmeichel; Parker, Irwin, Bruce, Phelan, Pallister, Kanchehskis (Sharpe), Ince, McClair, Hughes, Giggs. *Scorer:* McClair.
1–0 NOTTINGHAM FOREST   Marriott; Charles (Laws), Williams, Walker, Wassall, Keane, Crosby, Gemmill, Clough, Sheringham, Black.

Steve Morrow celebrates Arsenal's winning goal at 2-1 in the Coca Cola Cup Final against Sheffield Wednesday. Unfortunately he was injured after the match, when his captain Tony Adams dropped him onto his shoulder while attempting to lift him off the ground. (Colorsport)

COCA COLA CUP 1992-93

FIRST ROUND FIRST LEG

18 AUG

Bolton W (2) 2 *(Stubbs, Green)*
Port Vale (0) 1 *(Foyle)* 3282
Bolton W: Branagan; Brown P, Burke, Darby, Seagraves, Winstanley, Green, Stubbs, Walker (Reeves), Philliskirk, Patterson.
Port Vale: Wood; Mills, Sulley, Walker, Aspin, Glover (Sandeman), Kent, Van der Laan, Foyle, Kerr, Taylor.

Cardiff C (1) 1 *(Dale)*
Bristol C (0) 0 7708
Cardiff C: Grew; James, Searle, Millar, Perry, Brazil, Ramsey, Griffith, Pike (Gibbins), Dale, Blake.
Bristol C: Welch; Mitchell, Scott, Thompson, Bryant, Edwards, Mellon, Dziekanowski, Rosenior, Cole, Shelton.

Carlisle U (2) 4 *(Gabbiadini 2, Barnsley (pen), Watson)*
Burnley (0) 1 *(Sonner)* 4066
Carlisle U: O'Hanlon; Williams, Thorpe, Holmes (Walsh), Walling (Arnold), Barnsley, Gabbiadini, Davey, Oghani, Watson, Edmondson.
Burnley: Williams; Measham, Jakub, Randall, Pender, Farrell, Penney, Yates, Painter (Sonner), Conroy, Harper.

Chesterfield (0) 2 *(Morris, Norris)*
York C (0) 0 2080
Chesterfield: Leonard; Lemon, Carr, Williams, Brien, McGugan, Cash, Norris, Morris, Lancaster, Hebberd.
York C: Kiely; McMillan, Hall, Pepper, Stancliffe, Warburton, McCarthy, Borthwick (Blackstone), Barnes, Swann, Canham.

Colchester U (0) 1 *(English)*
Brighton & HA (0) 1 *(Wilkins)* 3817
Colchester U: Newell; Donald, Roberts, Kinsella, English, Oxbrow, Devereux, Bennett, McDonough, Grainger, Smith.
Brighton & HA: Beeney; Chivers, Chapman, Wilkins, Bissett, Foster, Robinson, Funnell, Edwards, Codner, Walker.

Crewe Alex (3) 4 *(Hignett, Harvey, Clarkson, Naylor)*
Rochdale (0) 1 *(Reeves)* 2558
Crewe Alex: Greygoose; McKearney, Jackson, Wilson, Hughes, Smith, Hignett, Naylor (Garvey), Clarkson, Harvey (Whalley), Walters.
Rochdale: Rose; Thackeray, Graham, Brown, Reeves, Payne, Ryan, Reid, Flounders, Milner, Bowden.

Darlington (0) 1 *(Mardenborough)*
Scunthorpe U (0) 1 *(Helliwell)* 1489
Darlington: Prudhoe; Hinchley, Dowson, Gaughan, Parkin, O'Shaughnessy, Pickering, Toman (Bell), Ellison (Shaw), Dobie, Mardenborough.
Scunthorpe U: Samways; McCullagh, Longden, Hill, Elliott, Humphries, Martin, Alexander, Daws, Buckley, Helliwell.

Doncaster R (0) 0
Lincoln C (2) 3 *(Finney, Bressington, Carmichael)*
2507
Doncaster R: Crichton; Douglas, Prindiville (Crosby), Hine, Richards, Hicks, Quinlan, Gormley (Hewitt), Heritage, Jeffrey, Hodder.
Lincoln C: Bowling; West D (Alexander), Clarke, Bressington, Carmichael, Brown, Schofield, Ward (Dunphy), Lee, Kabia, Finney.

Exeter C (0) 0
Birmingham C (0) 0 3030
Exeter C: Miller; Hiley, Cooper, Williams, Bond, Whiston, Collins, Harris, Jepson, Moran (Dolan), Brown.
Birmingham C: Gosney; Clarkson, Frain, Rennie, Mardon, Rogers, Donowa, Tait, Sale (Rodgerson), Gleghorn, Sturridge.

Fulham (0) 0
Brentford (1) 2 *(Booker, Blissett)* 5067
Fulham: Stannard; Morgan, Pike, Ferney (Baah), Nebbeling, Thomas, Hails, Marshall, Farrell, Eckhardt, Kelly.
Brentford: Benstead; Statham, Hughton, Millen, Bates, Ratcliffe, Bennett, Booker, Godfrey (Jones), Blissett (Gayle), Smillie.

Gillingham (1) 2 *(Crown, Lovell)*
Northampton T (0) 1 *(Terry)* 2245
Gillingham: Barrett; Green, Palmer, Butler, Breen, Smith, Clark, Lovell (Arnott), Crown, O'Connor, Henry.
Northampton T: Richardson; Parker, Burnham, Beavon, Angus, Terry, Bell, Lamb, Scott, Brown, Wilkin (Chard).

Halifax T (0) 1 *(Megson)*
Hartlepool U (1) 2 *(MacPhail, Johnrose)* 1370
Halifax T: Bracey; Megson, Wilson, Lucketti, Thompstone, Bradley, Matthews, Case, Thomas, Juryeff (Greenwood), Hildersley.
Hartlepool U: Hodge; Cross R, Cross P, Tait, MacPhail, Emerson, Johnrose, Olsson, Saville, Honour, Gallagher (Southall).

Hereford U (2) 2 *(Pickard 2)*
Torquay U (0) 2 *(Fashanu, Darby)* 1201
Hereford U: Judge; Fry, Downs, Jones, Devine, Theodosiou, Hall, Anderson, Brain, Pickard, Wade.
Torquay U: Lowe; Curran (Colcombe), Davis, Saunders, Davies, Joyce, Hall, Foster (Darby), Fashanu, Myers, Trollope.

Hull C (1) 2 *(Atkinson, Hockaday)*
Rotherham U (1) 2 *(Banks, Todd)* 3226
Hull C: Fettis; Hockaday, Hobson, Mail, Allison, Warren, Stoker (France), Atkinson, Hunter, Windass, Jenkinson.
Rotherham U: Mercer; Wilder, Hutchings, Banks, Johnson, Law, Goodwin, Todd, Cunningham, Goater, Barrick.

Leyton Orient (1) 2 *(Tomlinson, Cooper)*
Millwall (0) 2 *(Roberts, Stevens)*   4939
Leyton Orient: Turner; Kitchen, Howard, Hales, Day, Whitbread, Tomlinson, Livett, Jones, Cooper (Ryan), Okai (Achampong).
Millwall: Davison; Cunningham, Dawes, May, Cooper, Stevens, Roberts, McGinlay, Allen, Armstrong, Barber.

Oxford U (1) 3 *(Cusack, Allen 2)*
Swansea C (0) 0   3582
Oxford U: Kee; Smart, Ford, Collins (Lewis), Evans, Melville, Phillips, Beauchamp, Cusack (Allen), Penney, Durnin.
Swansea C: Freestone; Lyttle, Ford, Agboola, Harris, Coughlin, Cullen, Pascoe, McFarlane, Cornforth, Legg.

Peterborough U (2) 4 *(Adcock 2, Charlery, Costello)*
Barnet (0) 0   2770
Peterborough U: Bennett; Luke, Bradshaw, Cooper, Howarth, Welsh, Sterling, Ebdon, Adcock, Charlery, Barnes (Costello).
Barnet: Phillips; Huxford (Hayrettin), Cooper, Bodley, Howell, Horton (Hoddle), Lowe, Carter, Bull, Payne, Showler.

Preston NE (1) 2 *(Tinkler, Ellis)*
Stoke C (1) 1 *(Stein)*   5581
Preston NE: Farnworth; Davidson, Fowler, Tinkler, Flynn, Callaghan, Ashcroft, Cartwright, Leonard, Ellis, James.
Stoke C: Sinclair; Butler, Harbey, Cranson, Overson, Sandford, Foley, Ware (Kelly), Stein, Shaw, Russell.

Shrewsbury T (0) 1 *(Griffiths)*
Wigan Ath (1) 2 *(Daley, Tankard)*   1337
Shrewsbury T: Edwards; Worsley, Lynch, Evans, Spink, Blake, Taylor, Summerfield, Brough, Hodges (Griffiths), Lyne.
Wigan Ath: Adkins; Parkinson, Tankard, Robertson, Doolan, Langley, Jones, Pilling (Powell), Daley, Worthington, Griffiths.

Stockport Co (1) 1 *(Gannon)*
Chester C (0) 1 *(Comstive)*   2785
Stockport Co: Edwards; Knowles, Todd, Frain, Miller, Finley, Gannon, Carstairs (Muir), Francis, Beaumont, Preece.
Chester C: Stewart; Preece, Comstive, Butler, Abel (Whelan), Lightfoot, Thompson, Ryan, Rimmer, Bishop, Pugh.

Sunderland (0) 2 *(Butcher, Ball)*
Huddersfield T (2) 3 *(Starbuck, Parsley, Roberts)*   10,726
Sunderland: Norman; Kay, Smith, Owers, Butcher, Ball, Cunnington, Goodman, Colquhoun (Davenport), Byrne, Ord (Armstrong).
Huddersfield T: Clarke; Parsley, Charlton, Marsden, Bright, Jackson, Barnett, O'Regan, Roberts, Starbuck, Onuora.

Wrexham (0) 1 *(Pejic)*
Bury (0) 1 *(Hulme)*   2847
Wrexham: Hughes; Jones, Hardy, Phillips, Humes, Pejic, Watkin, Owen, Connolly (Sertori), Thomas (Esdaille), Cross.
Bury: Kelly; Anderson, Robertson, Hughes (Daws), Valentine, Knill, Lyons (Hulme), Robinson, Stevens, Kearney, Scott.

Grimsby T (1) 1 *(Mendonca)*
Barnsley (1) 1 *(Redfearn)*   3927
Grimsby T: Wilmot; McDermott, Jobling, Rodger, Agnew, Dobbin, Watson, Gilbert, Rees (Groves), Mendonca, Woods.
Barnsley: Butler; Robinson, Taggart, Bishop, Fleming, Bullimore, Liddell, Rammell, Pearson, Redfearn, Archdeacon.

Newcastle U (1) 2 *(Peacock 2)*
Mansfield T (0) 1 *(Stant)*   14,083
Newcastle U: Wright; Venison, Beresford, Howey, Kilcline, Scott, Brock (Carr), Peacock, Kelly (Quinn), Clark, Sheedy.
Mansfield T: Pearcey; Parkin, Withe, Spooner, Gray, Holland, Ford, Fairclough, Stant, Wilkinson, Charles.

Scarborough (2) 3 *(Mooney, Lee, Oliver (og))*
Bradford C (0) 0   2089
Scarborough: Evans; Barrow, Mudd, Lee, Hirst, Curran, Thompson, Murphy, Mooney (Ashdjian), Foreman (McKenzie), Jules.
Bradford C: Pearce; Duxbury M, Heseltine (Margerison), Duxbury L, Blake, Oliver, Jewell, McCarthy, Torpey, Tinnion, Reid.

Tranmere R (0) 3 *(Aldridge 2, Garnett)*
Blackpool (0) 0   3719
Tranmere R: Nixon; Brannan, Nolan, Irons, Hughes, Garnett, Morrissey (Muir), Aldridge, Malkin, Martindale (Branch), Thomas.
Blackpool: McIlhargey (Bonner); Burgess, Murphy, Horner, Briggs, Thornber, Rodwell, Sinclair, Robinson (Duffield), Garner, Eyres.

Walsall (1) 1 *(Clarke)*
Bournemouth (0) 1 *(Morris)*   3001
Walsall: Gayle; Williams, Statham, MacDonald (Methven), O'Hara, Smith, Ntamark, Clarke, Marsh, Cecere, McDonald (Ollerenshaw).
Bournemouth: Bartram; Pennock, Morrell, Watson, Morris, Scott, Mean (Mundee), O'Driscoll, Fletcher, McGorry, Rowland.

WBA (1) 1 *(Taylor)*
Plymouth Arg (0) 0   8264
WBA: Naylor; Hodson, Lilwall, Bradley, Strodder, Shakespeare, Garner, Hamilton, Taylor (Ampadu), McNally, Robson.
Plymouth Arg: Shilton; Poole, Spearing, Morrison, Burrows, Marker, Joyce, McCall, Nugent, Marshall, Evans.

618

FIRST ROUND SECOND LEG

25 AUG

Barnet (1) 2 *(Bull 2 (2 pens))*
Peterborough U (1) 2 *(Cooper (pen), Charlery)* 1789
Barnet: Phillips; Huxford, Cooper, Hoddle (Lowe), Barnett, Horton, Willis, Carter, Bull, Payne, Hunt (Lynch).
Peterborough U: Bennett; Luke, Robinson R, Cooper, Howarth, Welsh, Sorrell (White), Ebdon, Costello (Ingram), Charlery, Barnes.
Peterborough U won 6-2 on aggregate.

Barnsley (0) 1 *(Liddell)*
Grimsby T (1) 1 *(Mendonca)* 4636
Barnsley: Butler; Robinson, Taggart, Bishop, Fleming, Bullimore (Graham), Liddell, Rammell (Currie), Pearson, Redfearn, Archdeacon.
Grimsby T: Wilmot; McDermott, Jobling, Handyside, Agnew, Dobbin, Watson, Smith, Groves, Mendonca, Woods (Hargreaves).
aet; Grimsby T won 5-3 on penalties.

Birmingham C (0) 1 *(Sale)*
Exeter C (2) 4 *(Dolan 2, Kelly, Hodge)* 5715
Birmingham C: Gosney; Clarkson, Frain, Peer (Rowbotham), Rogers, Mardon, Donowa, Tait, Sale, Gleghorn, Rodgerson.
Exeter C: Miller; Hiley, Cooper, Kelly, Brown, Whiston, Collins, Harris, Dolan (Chapman), Jepson, Hodge.
Exeter C won 5-2 on aggregate.

Blackpool (0) 4 *(Garnett (og), Murphy, Robinson, Eyres)*
Tranmere R (0) 0 2734
Blackpool: Martin; Burgess, Murphy, Horner, Briggs, Thornber, Rodwell, Sinclair, Robinson, Garner, Eyres.
Tranmere R: Nixon; Brannan (Morrissey), Nolan, Irons, Hughes, Garnett, Nevin, Aldridge, Malkin (Muir), McNab, Thomas.
Blackpool won 4-3 on aggregate.

Bournemouth (0) 0
Walsall (0) 1 *(McDonald)* 3567
Bournemouth: Bartram; Pennock, Morrell, Watson, Morris, Scott (Cooke), Mean, O'Driscoll, Fletcher, McGorry, Rowland.
Walsall: Gayle; Williams, Statham, Methven (MacDonald), O'Hara, Smith (Cecere), Ntamark, Clarke, Marsh, Ollerenshaw, McDonald.
Walsall won 2-1 on aggregate.

Brentford (0) 2 *(Bates, Blissett)*
Fulham (0) 0 4806
Brentford: Benstead; Statham, Hughton, Millen, Bates, Ratcliffe (Godfrey), Bennett, Booker, Jones (Gayle), Blissett, Smillie.
Fulham: Stannard; Morgan, Pike, Ferney, Nebbeling (Onwere), Thomas, Hails, Marshall, Farrell, Eckhardt, Baah.
Brentford won 4-0 on aggregate.

Bristol C (3) 5 *(Cole 3, Rosenior, Allison)*
Cardiff C (0) 1 *(Dale)* 9801
Bristol C: Welch; Mitchell, Scott, Thompson, Bryant, Aizlewood, Mellon, Dziekanowski, Rosenior (Allison), Cole, Shelton (Harrison).
Cardiff C: Grew; James, Searle, Millar, Perry, Brazil, Gibbins, Galloway (Baddeley), Bird, Dale, Blake.
Bristol C won 5-2 on aggregate.

Burnley (0) 1 *(Pender)*
Carlisle U (1) 1 *(Oghani)* 5524
Burnley: Williams; Measham, Jakub, Randall, Pender, Farrell, Penney (Thompson), Deary, Clayton (Heath), Conroy, Painter.
Carlisle U: O'Hanlon; Williams, Thorpe, Holmes, Walling, Barnsley, Gabbiadini, Davey, Oghani, Watson, Edmondson.
Carlisle U won 5-2 on aggregate.

Bury (1) 4 *(Valentine 2, Kearney, Robinson)*
Wrexham (1) 3 *(Reid (og), Bennett 2)* 2193
Bury: Kelly; Anderson, Robertson (Greenhalgh), Reid, Valentine, Daws, Lyons, Robinson, Hulme, Kearney, Scott (Stevens).
Wrexham: Hughes; Jones, Hardy, Phillips, Humes, Pejic, Bennett, Owen, Connolly, Paskin, Taylor (Cross).
Bury won 5-4 on aggregate.

Chester C (0) 1 *(Bishop)*
Stockport Co (1) 2 *(Beaumont, Carstairs)* 4505
Chester C: Stewart (Morton); Preece, Comstive, Pugh, Abel, Lightfoot, Whelan, Thompson, Rimmer, Bishop, Ryan (Goodwin).
Stockport Co: Edwards; Knowles, Todd, Frain, Miller, Finley, Gannon, Carstairs, Francis, Beaumont (Matthews), Preece.
Stockport Co won 3-2 on aggregate.

Hartlepool U (2) 3 *(Johnrose 2, Southall)*
Halifax T (2) 2 *(Thomas, Lucketti)* 2191
Hartlepool U: Hodge; Cross R, Cross P, Tait, MacPhail, Olsson, Johnrose, Emerson, Saville, Honour, Southall.
Halifax T: Bracey; Megson, Wilson, Lucketti, Lewis, Bradley, Matthews, German, Thomas, Greenwood, Hildersley (Thompstone).
Hartlepool U won 5-3 on aggregate.

Lincoln C (0) 1 *(Dunphy)*
Doncaster R (1) 1 *(Hewitt)* 1996
Lincoln C: Bowling; West D, Clarke (Alexander), Finney, Carmichael, Dunphy, Schofield, Bressington, Lee, McParland (Kabia), Baraclough.
Doncaster R: Crichton; Douglas, Prindiville, Crosby, Richards, Hicks, Hewitt, Hine (Gormley), Heritage (Quinlan), Jeffrey, Rowe.
Lincoln C won 4-1 on aggregate.

Mansfield T (0) 0
Newcastle U (0) 0 6725
Mansfield T: Pearcey; Parkin, Withe, Castledine, Gray, Holland (Wilkinson), Ford, Fairclough, Stant, McLoughlin, Charles.
Newcastle U: Wright; Venison, Ranson, Howey, Kilcline, Scott, Carr, Peacock, Kelly, Clark, Sheedy.
Newcastle U won 2-1 on aggregate.

Plymouth Arg (1) 2 *(Marker, Poole (pen))*
WBA (0) 0   7866
Plymouth Arg: Shilton; Poole, Spearing, Morrison, Burrows, Marker, Joyce, McCall, Nugent, Marshall, Evans.
WBA: Naylor; Hodson (Coldicott), Lilwall, Bradley, Strodder, Shakespeare, Garner, Hamilton, Taylor, Raven, Robson.
Plymouth Arg won 2-1 on aggregate.

Port Vale (1) 1 *(Taylor)*
Bolton W (1) 1 *(Walker)*   4850
Port Vale: Wood; Sandeman, Sulley, Walker, Swan, Glover, Jeffers, Van der Laan (Houchen), Foyle, Kerr, Taylor.
Bolton W: Branagan; Brown P, Burke, Darby, Seagraves, Winstanley, Green, Stubbs, Walker, Philliskirk (Brown M), Patterson.
Bolton W won 3-2 on aggregate.

Rochdale (1) 1 *(Ryan)*
Crewe Alex (0) 2 *(Garvey, Hignett)*   1302
Rochdale: Rose; Thackeray, Graham, Reid, Reeves, Ashurst (Brown), Ryan, Payne, Flounders, Howard (Whitehall), Milner.
Crewe Alex: Greygoose; McKearney, Annan, Wilson, Hughes, Macauley, Garvey, Mettioui (Hignett), Clarkson (Smith), Harvey, Walters.
Crewe Alex won 6-2 on aggregate.

Rotherham U (1) 1 *(Todd (pen))*
Hull C (0) 0   3565
Rotherham U: Mercer; Wilder, Taylor, Banks (Hazel), Johnson, Law, Goodwin, Todd, Cunningham, Goater, Barrick.
Hull C: Fettis; Hockaday, Hobson, Mail, Allison, Warren (France), Norton, Atkinson, Hunter, Windass, Jenkinson.
Rotherham U won 3-2 on aggregate.

Scunthorpe U (2) 2 *(Daws, Alexander)*
Darlington (0) 0   2299
Scunthorpe U: Samways; Stevenson, Longden, Hill, Elliott, Humphries, Martin, Alexander, Daws, Buckley, Helliwell.
Darlington: Prudhoe; Hinchley, Ball, Gaughan, Parkin, Shaw, Mardenborough, Toman, O'Shaughnessy, Dobie, Tupling (Dowson).
Scunthorpe U won 3-1 on aggregate.

Swansea C (1) 1 *(McFarlane)*
Oxford U (0) 0   2256
Swansea C: Freestone; Lyttle, Ford, Agboola, Harris, Coughlin, Cullen (Jenkins), Pascoe, McFarlane (West), Cornforth, Legg.
Oxford U: Kee; Smart, Ford, Lewis, Evans, Melville, Magilton, Beauchamp, Cusack, Penney, Narbett.
Oxford U won 3-1 on aggregate.

Torquay U (2) 5 *(Fashanu, Foster, Saunders 3 (1 pen))*
Hereford U (0) 0   2140
Torquay U: Perks; Curran, Colcombe, Saunders, Moore (Davis), Joyce, Hall, Foster, Fashanu (Darby), Myers, Trollope.
Hereford U: Judge; Fry (Nicholson), Downs, Jones, Devine, Theodosiou, Hall, Anderson, Brain, Pickard, Davies.
Torquay U won 7-2 on aggregate.

Wigan Ath (0) 0
Shrewsbury T (1) 1 *(Smith)*   1380
Wigan Ath: Adkins; Parkinson (Appleton), Tankard, Robertson, Doolan, Langley, Jones, Powell, Daley, Worthington, Griffiths (Sharratt).
Shrewsbury T: Edwards; Worsley, Lynch, Taylor, Spink, Blake, Smith (Evans), Summerfield, Williams MS, Griffiths, Lyne (Brough).
aet; Wigan Ath won on away goals.

York C (0) 0
Chesterfield (0) 0   2336
York C: Kiely; McMillan (Naylor), Hall, Pepper, Tutill, Warburton, McCarthy, Borthwick, Barnes, Swann, Blackstone.
Chesterfield: Leonard; Lemon, Carr, Williams, Brien, McGugan, Cash, Norris, Morris, Lancaster, Hebberd.
Chesterfield won 2-0 on aggregate.

26 AUG

Bradford C (2) 3 *(Reid, Jewell, McCarthy)*
Scarborough (3) 5 *(Hirst, Lee, Foreman, Mooney 2)*   2894
Bradford C: Tomlinson; Margerison, Heseltine, Duxbury L, Blake, Oliver, Jewell, Partridge (McCarthy), Torpey (McHugh), Tinnion, Reid.
Scarborough: Evans; Barrow, Mudd, Lee, Hirst, Curran, Thompson, Mooney, Murphy, Foreman (Ashdjian), Jules.
Scarborough won 8-3 on aggregate.

Brighton & HA (0) 1 *(Wilkins)*
Colchester U (0) 0   4125
Brighton & HA: Beeney; Chivers, Chapman, Wilkins, Crumplin, Foster, Robinson, Funnell, Edwards (Wosahlo), Codner (Wilkinson), Walker.
Colchester U: Newell; Donald (Abrahams), Roberts, Kinsella, English, Oxbrow, Cook, Bennett, McDonough, Hazel, Smith.
Brighton & HA won 2-1 on aggregate.

Huddersfield T (0) 0
Sunderland (0) 1 *(Davenport)*   6737
Huddersfield T: Clarke; Parsley, Charlton, Marsden, Wright, Jackson, O'Regan, Barnett, Roberts, Starbuck, Onuora.
Sunderland: Carter; Kay, Smith (Armstrong), Owers, Butcher, Ball, Cunnington, Goodman, Colquhoun (Davenport), Byrne, Ord.
aet; Huddersfield T won on away goals.

Millwall (2) 3 *(Armstrong, Allen 2)*
Leyton Orient (0) 0   5444
Millwall: Keller; Cunningham, Dawes, Rae, Cooper, Stevens, Roberts, McGinlay, Allen (Goodman), Armstrong, Barber (Holsgrove).
Leyton Orient: Turner; Achampong, Howard, Hales, Day, Whitbread, Tomlinson, Livett (Taylor), Jones, Cooper, Ryan.
Millwall won 5-2 on aggregate.

620

Stoke C (0) 4 *(Stein, Overson, Biggins 2)*
Preston NE (0) 0   9745
Stoke C: Sinclair; Butler, Harbey, Cranson, Overson, Sandford (Kelly), Foley, Devlin, Stein (Shaw), Biggins, Russell.
Preston NE: Farnworth; Davidson (Flitcroft), Fowler, Tinkler, Flynn, Callaghan, Ashcroft, Cartwright, Leonard, Ellis (Eaves), James.
aet; Stoke C won 5-2 on aggregate.

9 SEPT

Northampton T (0) 0
Gillingham (0) 2 *(Crown, Aylott)*   2390
Northampton T: Richardson; Parsons, Chard, Beavon, Angus, Terry, Bell (Aldridge), Colkin, Scott (Burnham), Brown, Wilkin.
Gillingham: Lim; Green, Henry, Butler, Breen, Smith, Clark, Crown, Aylott (Forster), O'Connor (Carpenter), Lovell.
Gillingham won 4-1 on aggregate.

SECOND ROUND FIRST LEG

21 SEPT

Tottenham H (1) 3 *(Sheringham, Watson, Durie)*
Brentford (0) 1 *(Blissett)*   19,365
Tottenham H: Walker; Tuttle, Van Den Hauwe, Watson (Edinburgh), Cundy, Ruddock, Sedgley, Durie, Anderton (Minton), Sheringham, Allen.
Brentford: Bayes; Statham, Hughton, Millen, Bates, Ratcliffe (Booker) (Godfrey), Luscombe, Kruszynski, Gayle, Blissett, Smillie.

22 SEPT

Arsenal (0) 1 *(Campbell)*
Millwall (0) 1 *(Roberts)*   20,940
Arsenal: Seaman; Dixon, Winterburn, Hillier, Bould, Adams, Parlour, Wright, Smith, Merson, Limpar (Campbell).
Millwall: Keller; Cunningham, Dawes, May, Cooper, Stevens, Roberts, Dolby (McGinlay), Allen, Goodman, Barber.

Bolton W (0) 1 *(Stubbs)*
Wimbledon (2) 3 *(Fashanu, Ardley, Jones)*   5049
Bolton W: Branagan; Brown P, Burke, Kelly, Came, Winstanley, Green, Stubbs, Walker, Philliskirk, Patterson.
Wimbledon: Segers; Barton, Elkins (Miller), Jones, Scales, Fitzgerald, Ardley, Earle, Fashanu, Holdsworth, Clarke.

Bristol C (2) 2 *(Edwards, Scott (pen))*
Sheffield U (1) 1 *(Rogers)*   6922
Bristol C: Welch; Mitchell, Scott, Thompson, Bryant, Edwards, Connor (Harrison), Dziekanowski, Allison, Mellon, Shelton.
Sheffield U: Kelly; Gage, Cowan (Hartfield), Gannon, Gale, Beesley, Bradshaw, Rogers, Cork (Bryson), Deane, Hodges.

Bury (0) 0
Charlton Ath (0) 0   2393
Bury: Kelly; Kearney, Stanislaus, Daws, Valentine, Knill, Lyons, Robinson, Reid, Mauge, Ward.
Charlton Ath: Bolder; Pitcher, Minto, Pardew, Webster, Balmer, Bacon, Bumstead, Leaburn, Nelson (Dyer), Walsh.

Cambridge U (1) 2 *(Philpott, Chapple)*
Stoke C (1) 2 *(Stein 2)*   3428
Cambridge U: Sheffield; Fensome, Kimble, Dennis (Fowler), Chapple, Daish, Rowett, Leadbitter, Raynor, Cheetham (Francis), Philpott.
Stoke C: Parks; Butler, Harbey, Cranson, Overson, Sandford, Foley, Ware, Stein, Biggins, Russell.

Carlisle U (1) 2 *(Barnsley (pen), Edmondson)*
Norwich C (0) 2 *(Robins, Goss)*   10,328
Carlisle U: O'Hanlon; Williams, Thorpe, Holmes, Walling, Barnsley, Gabbiadini, Davey, Oghani (Sendall), Watson, Edmondson.
Norwich C: Gunn; Culverhouse, Bowen, Polston, Sutton, Sutch, Crook, Newman, Robins, Goss, Phillips.

Crystal Palace (1) 3 *(Southgate, Salako, McGoldrick)*
Lincoln C (0) 1 *(Bressington)*   6947
Crystal Palace: Martyn; Humphrey, Sinnott, Southgate, Young, Osborn, Williams, Coleman, Collymore (Ndah), Salako, McGoldrick.
Lincoln C: Bowling; Smith, Clarke, Carmichael, Dunphy, Brown, Schofield, Bressington, Lee, Baraclough (Finney), Puttnam (Kabia).

Exeter C (0) 0
Oldham Ath (0) 1 *(Henry)*   4375
Exeter C: Miller; Hiley, Cook, Kelly, Brown, Whiston, Cooper, Harris, Dolan, Loram (Collins), Hodge.
Oldham Ath: Hallworth; Redmond, Pointon, Henry, Jobson, Marshall, Adams, Olney, Sharp, Milligan, Bernard.

Leeds U (2) 4 *(Strachan, Chapman, Speed, Shutt)*
Scunthorpe U (0) 1 *(Helliwell)*   10,113
Leeds U: Lukic; Wetherall, Dorigo (Hodge), Batty, Sellars (Rocastle), Whyte, Strachan, Shutt, Chapman, McAllister, Speed.
Scunthorpe U: Whitehead; Stevenson, Longden, Broddle, Elliott, McCullagh, Martin, Alexander, Daws, Goodacre, Helliwell.

Liverpool (0) 4 *(Rosenthal, Hutchison, Walters, Wright)*
Chesterfield (2) 4 *(Norris 2, Lancaster 2)* 12,533
Liverpool: James; Marsh, Burrows, Tanner, Redknapp, Wright, Rosenthal, Charnock (Kozma), Hutchison, Molby, Walters.
Chesterfield: Leonard; Lemon, Carr, Williams, Brien, Rogers, Cash, Norris (Turnbull), Morris, Lancaster (Kennedy), Hebberd.

Notts Co (3) 3 *(Lund 2, Robinson)*
Wolverhampton W (1) 2 *(Bull, Cook (pen))* 4197
Notts Co: Cherry; Short, Thomas, Johnson, Robinson, O'Riordan, Draper, Turner, Lund, Slawson, Smith.
Wolverhampton W: Stowell; Ashley, Edwards, Downing, Madden, Mountfield, Birch, Cook, Bull, Mutch, Rankine (Dennison).

Watford (1) 2 *(Furlong 2)*
Reading (1) 2 *(Quinn, Williams)* 4036
Watford: Suckling; Lavin, Drysdale, Dublin, Holdsworth, Ashby, Hessenthaler, Nogan, Furlong, Putney, Soloman (Butler).
Reading: Hislop; Gooding, Hopkins, McPherson, Williams, Parkinson, Gilkes, Dillon, Quinn, Lovell, Jones.

Wigan Ath (0) 2 *(Johnson, Worthington)*
Ipswich T (1) 2 *(Johnson, Robertson (og))* 2684
Wigan Ath: Adkins; Parkinson, Tankard, Johnson, Doolan, Langley (Worthington), Jones, Robertson, Daley, Powell, Griffiths.
Ipswich T: Forrest; Whelan, Thompson, Stockwell, Wark, Linighan, Youds, Pennyfather, Johnson, Dozzell, Kiwomya.

23 SEPT

Blackpool (0) 0
Portsmouth (0) 4 *(Clarke, McLoughlin 2, Murray)*
4422
Blackpool: Martin; Davies, Murphy, Horner, Briggs, Thornber, Rodwell, Sinclair, Stringfellow (Robinson), Leitch (Mitchell), Eyres.
Portsmouth: Knight; Awford, Daniel (Powell), McLoughlin, Symons, Aspinall, Neill, Doling, Clarke, Whittingham, Murray.

Brighton & HA (0) 1 *(Edwards)*
Manchester U (1) 1 *(Wallace)* 16,649
Brighton & HA: Beeney; Chivers, Chapman, Wilkins, McCarthy, Foster, Crumplin, Edwards, Kennedy, Codner, Walker.
Manchester U: Walsh; Irwin, Martin, Bruce, Webb, Pallister, Kanchelskis (Beckham), Ince, McClair, Hughes, Wallace.

Coventry C (0) 2 *(Borrows (pen), Ndlovu)*
Scarborough (0) 0 5993
Coventry C: Ogrizovic; Borrows, Sansom, Atherton, Pearce, Ndlovu, McGrath, Hurst, Babb, Gallacher, Williams.
Scarborough: Evans; Thompson, Mudd, Lee, Hirst, Curran, Ashdjian, Murphy, Mooney, Foreman (Mockler), Jules (Himsworth).

Gillingham (0) 0
Southampton (0) 0 7488
Gillingham: Barrett; Green, Henry, Butler, Breen, Smith, Clark, Forster (Dempsey), Aylott, O'Connor, Lovell.
Southampton: Flowers; Dodd, Benali, Hurlock, Monkou, Moore, Le Tissier, Banger, Dixon, Speedie, Adams.

Huddersfield T (0) 1 *(Onuora)*
Blackburn R (0) 1 *(Shearer)* 11,071
Huddersfield T: Elliott; Parsley, Charlton, Donovan, Dyson, Jackson, Barnett, O'Regan, Roberts, Billy, Onuora.
Blackburn R: Mimms; May, Dobson (Newell), Sherwood, Hendry, Moran, Price, Atkins, Shearer, Wegerle, Wright.

Leicester C (0) 2 *(Lowe, Thompson)*
Peterborough U (0) 0 10,366
Leicester C: Hoult; Mills, Whitlow, Smith, Walsh, Hill, Trotter, Thompson, Davison, Ormondroyd, Gee (Lowe).
Peterborough U: Bennett; White, Robinson, Halsall, Howarth, Welsh, Sterling, Ebdon, Adcock, Charlery, Barnes (Gavin).

Luton T (1) 2 *(Claridge 2)*
Plymouth Arg (0) 2 *(Regis 2)* 3702
Luton T: Petterson; Linton, James, Salton (Rees), Peake, Johnson (Campbell), Claridge, Kamara, Gray, Preece, Oakes.
Plymouth Arg: Shilton; Poole, Morgan, Hill, Morrison, Edworthy, Skinner, Joyce, Nugent, Regis, McCall.

Manchester C (0) 0
Bristol R (0) 0 9967
Manchester C: Coton; Brightwell I, Phelan, Reid, Curle, Hill, White, Flitcroft, Quinn, Simpson, Holden.
Bristol R: Parkin; Alexander, Twentyman, Yates, Maddison, Wilson (Reece), Cross, Skinner, Taylor, Stewart, Hardyman.

Newcastle U (0) 0
Middlesbrough (0) 0 25,814
Newcastle U: Wright; Venison, Beresford, O'Brien, Scott, Howey, Lee (Carr), Quinn, Kelly, Clark, Sheedy.
Middlesbrough: Ironside; Morris, Phillips, Kernaghan, Whyte, Pollock, Hendrie, Falconer (Slaven), Wilkinson, Wright, Mustoe.

Oxford U (0) 1 *(Beauchamp)*
Aston Villa (0) 2 *(McGrath, Teale)* 8837
Oxford U: Kee; Smart, Collins, Lewis, Evans, Melville, Magilton, Beauchamp, Penney, Durnin, Allen.
Aston Villa: Spink; Barrett, Staunton, Teale, McGrath, Richardson, Houghton, Parker, Saunders, Atkinson (Yorke), Froggatt.

QPR (1) 2 *(Ferdinand 2)*
Grimsby T (0) 1 *(Watson)* 7275
QPR: Roberts; Channing, Brevett, Wilkins, Peacock, Maddix, Impey, Holloway, Ferdinand, Bailey (Penrice), Sinton.
Grimsby T: Wilmot; McDermott, Croft, Rodger, Handyside, Dobbin, Watson, Gilbert, Rees (Mendonca), Groves, Woods.

Rotherham U (1) 1 *(Goater)*
Everton (0) 0 7736
Rotherham U: Mercer; Pickering, Hutchings, Banks (Goodwin), Johnson, Law, Hazel, Todd, Cunningham (Page), Goater, Barrick.
Everton: Southall; Harper, Hinchcliffe, Ebbrell, Watson, Ablett, Jackson (Beagrie), Horne, Barlow (Unsworth), Cottee, Radosavljevic.

Sheffield W (0) 3 *(Watson, Bright, Wilson)*
Hartlepool U (0) 0 10,112
Sheffield W: Pressman; Harkes, Worthington, Palmer, Shirtliff, Francis, Wilson, Waddle, Bright, Bart-Williams, Watson.
Hartlepool U: Hodge; Cross R, Cross P, Tait, MacPhail, Emerson, Johnrose, Olsson, Saville, Nobbs, Gallacher (Wratten).

Southend U (0) 1 *(Benjamin)*
Derby Co (0) 0   2492
Southend U: Sansome; Edwards, Powell, Cornwell, Scully, Prior, Ansah, Martin, Locke, Benjamin, O'Callaghan.
Derby Co: Sutton; Comyn, Forsyth, Short, Wasall, Pembridge, Johnson, Coleman, Kitson, Gabbiadini, Simpson.

Stockport Co (1) 2 *(Francis 2)*
Nottingham F (1) 3 *(Bannister, Clough, Orlygsson)*
                                                      7964
Stockport Co: Edwards; Masefield (Knowles), Todd, Frain, Miller, Finley, Gannon, Carstairs, Francis, Beaumont, Muir.
Nottingham F: Crossley; Laws, Pearce, McKinnon, Tiler, Keane, Crosby, Gemmill, Clough, Bannister, Orlygsson.

Torquay U (0) 0
Swindon T (3) 6 *(Maskell, Mitchell 2, Ling, Taylor, White)*   3560
Torquay U: Lowe; Curran, Colcombe, Salman, Moore, Joyce, Hall, Darby (Ginter), Foster, Myers, Trollope.
Swindon T: Digby; Kerslake, Bodin, Hoddle (White), Calderwood, Taylor, Hazard, Moncur (Summerbee), Maskell, Ling, Mitchell.

Walsall (0) 0
Chelsea (2) 3 *(Wise, Newton, Townsend)*   5510
Walsall: Gayle; Williams, Statham, O'Hara, West, Smith, Ntamark, Clarke, Marsh, Ollerenshaw (Edwards), McDonald.
Chelsea: Hitchcock; Stuart, Sinclair, Townsend, Lee, Donaghy, Newton, Fleck, Harford, Spackman, Wise.

West Ham U (0) 0
Crewe Alex (0) 0   6981
West Ham U: Miklosko; Breacker, Thomas, Potts, Martin, Allen M, Robson, Butler, Morley, Allen C, Keen (Small).
Crewe Alex: Greygoose; McKearney, Whalley, Wilson, Carr, Macauley, Gardiner, Garvey, Clarkson (Naylor), Harvey (Hughes), Walters.

SECOND ROUND SECOND LEG

6 OCT

Blackburn R (1) 4 *(Shearer 2, Wegerle, Newell)*
Huddersfield T (0) 3 *(Barnett, Roberts, Ireland)* 15,038
Blackburn R: Mimms; Brown, Wright, Sherwood, Hendry, Wegerle, Ripley (Wilcox), Atkins (Moran), Shearer, Newell, Cowans.
Huddersfield T: Elliott; Parsley, Charlton, Lampkin, Wright, Dyson (Starbuck), Barnett, O'Regan, Roberts, Robinson (Billy), Ireland.
aet; Blackburn R won 5-4 on aggregate.

Chesterfield (1) 1 *(Hebberd)*
Liverpool (3) 4 *(Hutchison, Redknapp, Walters, Rush)*
                                                     10,632
Chesterfield: Leonard; Lemon, Carr, Williams, Brien, Rogers, Cash, Norris, Morris (Turnbull), Lancaster, Hebberd.
Liverpool: Grobbelaar; Marsh, Burrows, Nicol, Piechnik, Hutchison, McManaman, Rosenthal, Rush, Redknapp, Walters.
Liverpool won 8-5 on aggregate.

Grimsby T (0) 2 *(Watson, Woods)*
QPR (0) 1 *(Bailey)*   8443
Grimsby T: Wilmot; Ford (Watson), Croft, Rodger, Lever, Dobbin, Childs, Gilbert, Groves, Mendonca (Rees), Woods.
QPR: Stejskal; Bardsley, Wilson, Peacock, McDonald, Holloway, Impey, Wilkins, Bailey, Penrice (Thompson), Sinton.
aet; QPR won 6-5 on penalties.

Hartlepool U (0) 2 *(Saville (pen), Johnrose)*
Sheffield W (1) 2 *(Bright, Warhurst)*   4667
Hartlepool U: Hodge; Cross R, Cross P, Tait, MacPhail, Emerson, Johnrose, Olsson, Saville, Nobbs, Honour.
Sheffield W: Pressman; Anderson, Worthington, Palmer, Shirtliff, Pearson, Wilson, Waddle (Bart-Williams), Bright, Warhurst, Hyde.
Sheffield W won 5-2 on aggregate.

Ipswich T (2) 4 *(Johnson, Kiwomya 3)*
Wigan Ath (0) 0   7305
Ipswich T: Forrest; Whelan (Youds), Thompson, Stockwell, Wark, Linighan, Williams, Goddard, Johnson, Dozzell, Kiwomya.
Wigan Ath: Adkins; Parkinson (Wilson), Tankard, Johnson, Doolan, Langley, Jones, Robertson, Daley, Powell (Worthington), Griffiths.
Ipswich T won 6-2 on aggregate.

Lincoln C (1) 1 *(Puttnam)*
Crystal Palace (1) 1 *(Southgate)*   6255
Lincoln C: Pollitt; Baraclough, Clarke, Carmichael (Smith), Dunphy, Brown, Schofield, Bressington, Lee, Kabia (Alexander), Puttnam.
Crystal Palace: Martyn; Humphrey, Sinnott, Southgate, Young, Osborn, Williams, Coleman, Thomas (Collymore), Salako, McGoldrick.
Crystal Palace won 4-2 on aggregate.

Peterborough U (2) 2 *(Halsall, Charlery)*
Leicester C (1) 1 *(Joachim)*   6936
Peterborough U: Bennett; Luke, Robinson R (White), Halsall, Howarth, Welsh, Sterling, Cooper, Adcock, Charlery, Barnes (Curtis).
Leicester C: Hoult; Mills, Grayson, Smith, Walsh, Hill, Oldfield, Thompson, Davison, Ormondroyd, Joachim (Gee).
Leicester C won 3-2 on aggregate.

Plymouth Arg (1) 3 *(Nugent, Poole, Regis)*
Luton T (0) 2 *(Claridge, Preece)*   8946
Plymouth Arg: Shilton; Edworthy, Spearing, Hill, Morrison, Poole, Skinner, Joyce, Nugent (Adcock), Regis, Garner.
Luton T: Petterson; Linton, James (Oakes), Salton, Peake (Dreyer), Johnson, Claridge, Kamara, Gray, Preece, Rees.
Plymouth Arg won 5-4 on aggregate.

Portsmouth (1) 2 *(Whittingham 2)*
Blackpool (0) 0 3096
Portsmouth: Knight; Awford, Daniel, Chamberlain, Symons, Aspinall (Doling), Neill (Butters), Walsh, Burns, Whittingham, Maguire.
Blackpool: McIlhargey; Murphy (Bonner), Stoneman, Horner, Briggs, Gore, Rodwell, Sinclair, Robinson (Stringfellow), Gouck, Eyres.
Portsmouth won 6-0 on aggregate.

Swindon T (3) 3 *(Hoddle, White, Mitchell)*
Torquay U (0) 2 *(Myers, Foster)* 3293
Swindon T: Hammond; Kerslake, Horlock, Hoddle, Calderwood, Taylor, Hazard (Phillips), Summerbee, White, Ling (Close), Mitchell.
Torquay U: Lowe; Gardiner, Colcombe, Curran, Davies, Joyce, Hall, Darby (Foster), Fashanu, Myers (Trollope), Davis.
Swindon T won 9-2 on aggregate.

Wimbledon (0) 0
Bolton W (0) 1 *(Philliskirk)* 1987
Wimbledon: Segers; Barton, Elkins, Miller, Scales, Fitzgerald, Ardley (Talboys), Newhouse (Joseph), Clarke, Holdsworth, Sanchez.
Bolton W: Branagan; Spooner, Oliver, Darby, Lydiate, Winstanley, Green, Fisher, Philliskirk, Stubbs, Patterson.
Wimbledon won 3-2 on aggregate.

7 OCT

Aston Villa (1) 2 *(Atkinson, Richardson)*
Oxford U (0) 1 *(Cusack)* 19,808
Aston Villa: Spink; Barrett, Staunton, Teale, Ehiogu, Richardson, Houghton, Parker, Saunders, Atkinson, Yorke.
Oxford U: Reece; Smart, Collins (Allen), Lewis, Evans, Melville, Phillips, Cusack, Penney, Durnin, Ford.
Aston Villa won 4-2 on aggregate.

Brentford (1) 2 *(Blissett, Millen)* 11,445
Tottenham H (2) 4 *(Anderton, Sheringham 2 (1 pen), Turner)*
Brentford: Bayes; Statham, Hughton, Millen, Bates, Ratcliffe, Luscombe (Bennett), Chalmers (Manuel), Gayle, Blissett, Smillie.
Tottenham H: Walker; Edinburgh, Van Den Hauwe, Samways (Austin), Tuttle, Ruddock, Sedgley, Barmby (Turner), Anderton, Sheringham, Allen.
Tottenham H won 4-2 on aggregate.

Bristol R (0) 1 *(Reece)*
Manchester C (0) 2 *(Maddison (og), Holden)* 7823
Bristol R: Parkin; Alexander, Twentyman, Yates, Maddison (Saunders), Wilson, Mehew, Reece, Taylor, Stewart, Hardyman (Cross).
Manchester C: Coton; Brightwell I, Phelan, McMahon (Reid), Curle, Hill, White, Sheron (Flitcroft), Quinn, Simpson, Holden.
aet; Manchester C won 2-1 on aggregate).

Charlton Ath (0) 0
Bury (0) 1 *(Hulme)* 2083
Charlton Ath: Bolder; Balmer, Minto, Pardew, Webster, Pitcher, Leaburn, Bumstead, Warden (Grant), Nelson, Walsh (Primus).
Bury: Kelly; Ward, Scott, Daws, Valentine, Knill, Mauge, Robinson, Hulme, Kearney, Reid.
Bury won 1-0 on aggregate.

Chelsea (0) 1 *(Fleck (pen)*
Walsall (0) 0 7646
Chelsea: Hitchcock; Hall, Sinclair, Townsend, Lee, Newton, Stuart, Fleck, Harford (Spencer), Spackman (Barnard), Wise.
Walsall: Gayle; Williams, Cecere, O'Hara, West, Smith, Ntamark, Clarke (Ollerenshaw), Marsh, Edwards, McDonald.
Chelsea won 4-0 on aggregate.

Crewe Alex (0) 2 *(Naylor, Hignett)*
West Ham U (0) 0 5427
Crewe Alex: Greygoose; McKearney, Whalley, Wilson, Carr, Macauley, Hignett, Naylor, Clarkson (Garvey), Harvey (Gardiner), Walters.
West Ham U: Miklosko; Breacker, Dicks, Potts, Martin, Allen M, Robson, Butler, Morley, Allen C, Keen.
Crewe Alex won 2-0 on aggregate.

Derby Co (3) 7 *(Kitson, Martin (og), Gabbiadini 2, Simpson 2, Johnson)*
Southend U (0) 0 13,328
Derby Co: Sutton; Comyn, Forsyth, Short (Coleman), Wassall, Pembridge, Johnson, Kuhl (Goulooze), Kitson, Gabbiadini, Simpson.
Southend U: Sansome; Cornwell, Powell, Jones, Scully, Prior, Locke, Martin, Sussex, Benjamin, O'Callaghan.
Derby Co won 7-1 on aggregate.

Everton (2) 3 *(Rideout 2, Cottee (pen))*
Rotherham U (0) 0 10,302
Everton: Southall; Hinchcliffe, Unsworth, Kenny, Watson, Ablett, Warzycha, Horne (Moore), Rideout (Johnston), Cottee, Beagrie.
Rotherham U: Mercer; Pickering, Hutchings, Banks (Richardson), Johnson, Law, Hazel, Todd, Cunningham, Goater (Page), Barrick.
Everton won 3-1 on aggregate.

Manchester U (1) 1 *(Hughes)*
Brighton & HA (0) 0 25,405
Manchester U: Schmeichel; Parker, Irwin, Bruce, Kanchelskis, Pallister, Robson, Ince, McClair, Hughes, Giggs.
Brighton & HA: Beeney; Chivers, Chapman, Wilkins, McCarthy, Foster, Crumplin, Edwards (Funnell), Kennedy, Codner, Walker.
Manchester U won 2-1 on aggregate.

Middlesbrough (0) 1 *(Wilkinson)*
Newcastle U (1) 3 *(Kelly 2, O'Brien)* 24,390
Middlesbrough: Ironside; Morris, Phillips, Kernaghan, Whyte, Peake (Gittens), Slaven, Mustoe, Wilkinson, Wright, Hendrie (Pollock).
Newcastle U: Wright; Venison, Beresford, O'Brien, Scott, Howey, Lee, Peacock, Kelly, Clark, Sheedy (Quinn).
Newcastle U won 3-1 on aggregate.

Millwall (1) 1 *(Dixon (og))*
Arsenal (1) 1 *(Campbell)*   18,500
Millwall: Keller; Cunningham, Dawes, May (Rae), Cooper, Stevens, Roberts, Dolby (Moralee), Allen, Goodman, Barber.
Arsenal: Seaman; Dixon, Winterburn, Hillier, Bould, Adams, Jensen, Wright, Smith, Merson (Parlour), Campbell.
aet; Arsenal won 3-1 on penalties.

Norwich C (0) 2 *(Sutton 2)*
Carlisle U (0) 0   8489
Norwich C: Walton; Culverhouse, Bowen, Butterworth, Polston, Sutch, Crook, Newman, Robins, Goss, Sutton.
Carlisle U: O'Hanlon; Williams, Thorpe, Holmes (McCreery), Barnsley, Edmondson, Sendall, Davey, Oghani, Watson, Potts.
Norwich C won 4-2 on aggregate.

Nottingham F (1) 2 *(Black, Gannon (og))*
Stockport Co (1) 1 *(Beaumont)*   15,573
Nottingham F: Crossley; Laws, Pearce, Chettle, Tiler, Keane, Crosby, Gemmill, Clough, Bannister, Black.
Stockport Co: Edwards; Masefield (Knowles), Todd, Frain, Miller, Williams B, Gannon, Ward, Francis (Preece), Beaumont, Muir.
Nottingham F won 5-3 on aggregate.

Oldham Ath (0) 0
Exeter C (0) 0   6269
Oldham Ath: Hallworth; Fleming, Pointon, Henry, Jobson, Redmond, Marshall (Adams), Olney, Sharp, Milligan, Bernard.
Exeter C: Miller; Hiley, Cook, Kelly, Brown, Whiston, Cooper, Harris, Jepson, Loram (Dolan), Hodge.
Oldham Ath won 1-0 on aggregate.

Reading (0) 0
Watford (1) 2 *(Drysdale, Lavin)*   7386
Reading: Hislop; Gooding, Hopkins, McPherson, Williams, Parkinson, Gilkes, Dillon, Quinn, Taylor (Lambert), Jones.
Watford: Suckling; Lavin, Drysdale, Dublin, Holdsworth, Porter (Bazeley), Hessenthaler, Nogan, Butler, Putney, Soloman.
Watford won 4-2 on aggregate.

Scarborough (0) 3 *(Mooney, Foreman, Hirst)*
Coventry C (0) 0   2633
Scarborough: Ford; Thompson, Mudd, Lee, Hirst, Curran, Ashdjian (Wheeler), Himsworth, Mooney, Foreman, Jules.
Coventry C: Ogrizovic; Borrows, Sansom, Atherton, Pearce, Smith, McGrath, Babb, Rosario (Fleming), Gallacher, Williams.
Scarborough won 3-2 on aggregate.

Sheffield U (2) 4 *(Whitehouse, Bradshaw, Deane 2)*
Bristol C (1) 1 *(Cole)*   7588
Sheffield U: Kelly; Ward, Cowan, Gannon, Gayle, Beesley, Bradshaw, Rogers, Littlejohn, Deane, Whitehouse (Cork).
Bristol C: Welch; Mitchell, Scott, Thompson, Osman, Edwards, Harrison, Rosenior (Dziekanowski), Allison, Cole, Shelton (Gavin).
Sheffield U won 5-3 on aggregate.

Southampton (1) 3 *(Dowie, Le Tissier 2 (1 pen))*
Gillingham (0) 0   6764
Southampton: Flowers; Dodd, Adams, Hurlock, Monkou, Wood, Le Tissier, Cockerill (Benali), Dixon, Dowie, Groves.
Gillingham: Barrett; Carpenter, Henry, Butler, Breen, Smith, Clark, Dunne (Forster), Arnott, O'Connor (Eeles), Lovell.
Southampton won 3-0 on aggregate.

Stoke C (0) 1 *(Shaw)*
Cambridge U (1) 2 *(Fowler, Francis)*   10,732
Stoke C: Horne; Butler, Harbey, Cranson, Wright (Devlin), Sandford, Foley, Ware, Stein, Shaw, Beeston.
Cambridge U: Sheffield; Clayton, Kimble, Rowett, Chapple (Fowler), Daish, Raynor, Leadbitter, White, Cheetham (Francis), Philpott.
Cambridge U won 4-3 on aggregate.

Wolverhampton W (0) 0
Notts Co (0) 1 *(O'Riordan)*   11,146
Wolverhampton W: Stowell; Ashley, Edwards, Downing, Mountfield, Blades (Roberts), Birch, Cook (Dennison), Bull, Mutch, Rankine.
Notts Co: Cherry; Palmer, Thomas, Smith, Johnson, O'Riordan, Draper, Turner, Lund, Bartlett (Murphy), Devlin.
Notts Co won 4-2 on aggregate.

27 OCT

Scunthorpe U (2) 2 *(Helliwell 2)*
Leeds U (1) 2 *(Wallace, Chapman)*   7419
Scunthorpe U: Whitehead; Joyce, Longden, Greaves, Elliott, Stevenson, Daws, Alexander, White, Buckley (Goodacre), Helliwell.
Leeds U: Lukic; Newsome, Kerr, Batty, Fairclough, Wetherall, Strachan (Sellars) (Whyte), Rodney Wallace, Chapman, McAllister, Speed.
Leeds U won 6-3 on aggregate.

THIRD ROUND

Bury (0) 0
QPR (0) 2 *(Peacock, Allen)*   4680
Bury: Kelly; Anderson, Robertson (Reid), Daws, Valentine, Knill, Mauge (Lyons), Robinson, Hulme, Hughes, Stevens.
QPR: Roberts; Bardsley, Wilson, Wilkins, Peacock, McDonald, Barker, Holloway, Ferdinand, Allen, Sinton (Thompson).

Notts Co (0) 0 *(Draper, Agana)*
Cambridge U (1) 3 *(Clayton, Danzey, White)*   3742
Notts Co: Cherry; Short (Wilson), Thomas, Palmer, Walker, Turner, Draper, Williams, Lund, Agana, Devlin.
Cambridge U: Sheffield; Fensome, Kimble, Raynor, Heathcote, O'Shea, Rowett, Danzey (Fowler), White, Clayton (Ainsworth), Philpott.

Plymouth Arg (0) 3 *(Dalton, Joyce, Nugent)*
Scarborough (1) 3 *(Curran, Jules, Ashdjian)* 8619
Plymouth Arg: Shilton; Poole, Spearing, Edworthy, Morrison, Castle, Skinner (Barlow), Joyce, Nugent, Marshall, Dalton.
Scarborough: Evans; Thompson, Mudd, Lee, Hirst, Curran, Ashdjian, Himsworth, Mooney, Foreman, Jules (Wheeler).

Portsmouth (0) 0
Ipswich T (1) 1 *(Thompson)* 10,773
Portsmouth: Knight; Awford, Daniel, McLoughlin, Symons, Aspinall (Walsh), Neill, Chamberlain, Clarke, Whittingham, Maguire.
Ipswich T: Baker; Johnson, Thompson, Stockwell, Wark, Linighan, Williams, Goddard (Gregory), Whitton, Dozzell, Kiwomya.

Sheffield W (2) 7 *(Hirst, Worthington, Bright 2, Watson 2, Bart-Williams)*
Leicester C (0) 1 *(Davison)* 17,326
Sheffield W: Woods; Harkes, Worthington, Palmer, Pearson, Anderson, Wilson, Waddle, Hirst (Watson), Bright, Sheridan (Bart-Williams).
Leicester C: Hoult; Mills (Lowe), Platnauer, Smith, Walsh, Hill, Oldfield, Thompson, Davison, Ormondroyd (Grayson), Gee.

Swindon T (0) 0
Oldham Ath (0) 1 *(Bernard)* 8811
Swindon T: Hammond; Kerslake, Horlock, Hoddle, Calderwood, Taylor, Hazard, Summerbee, Maskell, Ling (White), Mitchell.
Oldham Ath: Hallworth; McDonald, Pointon, Henry, Jobson, Redmond, Adams, Marshall, Sharp, Milligan, Bernard.

28 OCT

Aston Villa (0) 1 *(Saunders)*
Manchester U (0) 0 35,964
Aston Villa: Spink; Barrett, Staunton, Teale, McGrath, Richardson, Houghton, Parker, Saunders, Atkinson, Yorke.
Manchester U: Schmeichel; Parker, Irwin (Kanchelskis), Bruce, Ferguson, Pallister, Blackmore, Ince, McClair, Hughes, Giggs.

Blackburn R (1) 2 *(Shearer, May)*
Norwich C (0) 0 14,216
Blackburn R: Mimms; May, Wright, Sherwood, Hendry, Dobson, Ripley (Makel), Atkins, Shearer, Newell, Wilcox.
Norwich C: Gunn; Culverhouse (Fox), Bowen, Butterworth, Polston, Sutch, Crook, Phillips, Newman, Goss (Robins), Sutton.

Chelsea (0) 2 *(Sinclair, Harford)*
Newcastle U (0) 1 *(Lee)* 30,193
Chelsea: Hitchcock; Hall, Sinclair, Townsend, Lee, Donaghy, Stuart (Le Saux), Fleck, Harford, Newton, Wise.
Newcastle U: Wright; Nielson, Beresford, O'Brien, Scott, Howey, Lee, Peacock, Quinn, Clark, Brock.

Crewe Alex (0) 0
Nottingham F (0) 1 *(Orlygsson)* 7042
Crewe Alex: Greygoose; McKearney, Smith (Clarkson), Wilson, Carr, Macauley, Hignett, Naylor, Edwards, Lennon (Gardiner), Walters.
Nottingham F: Crossley; Charles (Chettle), Pearce, Keane, Tiler, Orlygsson, Crosby, Gemmill, Clough, Glover, Black.

Derby Co (0) 1 *(Simpson (pen))*
Arsenal (0) 1 *(Campbell)* 22,208
Derby Co: Sutton; Comyn, Forsyth, Short, Wassall, Pembridge, Johnson, Kuhl, Kitson, Gabbiadini, Simpson.
Arsenal: Seaman; Lydersen, Morrow, Hillier, Bould, Adams, Jensen, Campbell, Smith, Merson, Limpar.

Everton (0) 0
Wimbledon (0) 0 9541
Everton: Southall; Jackson, Ablett, Kenny, Watson, Keown, Warzycha (Hinchcliffe), Beardsley (Barlow), Rideout, Horne, Beagrie.
Wimbledon: Segers; Barton, Joseph, Jones, McLeary, McAllister, Gibson, Earle, Fashanu (Holdsworth), Dobbs, Anthrobus.

Manchester C (0) 0
Tottenham H (1) 1 *(Samways)* 18,399
Manchester C: Coton; Brightwell I, Phelan, McMahon, Curle, Hill, White, Sheron, Quinn, Simpson, Holden.
Tottenham H: Thorstvedt; Edinburgh, Austin, Samways (Turner), Mabbutt, Ruddock, Sedgley, Barmby, Nayim (Howells), Sheringham, Allen.

Sheffield U (0) 0
Liverpool (0) 0 17,856
Sheffield U: Tracey; Gage, Cowan, Gannon, Gayle, Beesley, Bradshaw (Cork), Rogers, Littlejohn, Deane, Bryson (Hodges).
Liverpool: Grobbelaar; Marsh, Burrows, Piechnik (Tanner), Wright, Hutchison, McManaman, Walters, Rush, Redknapp, Thomas.

Southampton (0) 0
Crystal Palace (2) 2 *(McGoldrick, Salako)* 9060
Southampton: Flowers; Dodd, Adams, Hurlock (Widdrington), Hall, Monkou, Le Tissier, Cockerill, Maddison, Dowie, Groves (Benali).
Crystal Palace: Martyn; Shaw, Sinnott, Southgate, Young, Thorn, Osborn, Williams, Coleman, Salako, McGoldrick.

10 NOV

Watford (0) 2 *(Holdsworth, Drysdale (pen))*
Leeds U (0) 1 *(McAllister)* 18,035
Watford: Suckling; Putney, Drysdale, Dublin, Holdsworth, Ashby, Hessenthaler, Nogan (Butler), Furlong, Porter, Lavin.
Leeds U: Lukic; Newsome (Rocastle), Kerr, Rodney Wallace, Fairclough, Whyte, Strachan, Cantona, Chapman, McAllister, Speed.

THIRD ROUND REPLAYS

Wimbledon (0) 0
Everton (0) 1 *(Beardsley)*   3686
Wimbledon: Segers; Barton, Joseph, Jones, McLeary, McAllister, Gibson, Earle, Holdsworth, Dobbs (Fashanu), Clarke.
Everton: Southall; Jackson (Hinchcliffe), Ablett, Snodin, Watson, Keown, Harper, Beardsley, Rideout, Horne, Ebbrell (Warzycha).

11 NOV

Liverpool (2) 3 *(McManaman 2, Marsh (pen))*
Sheffield U (0) 0   17,654
Liverpool: Hooper; Marsh, Burrows, Nicol, Piechnik, Hutchison, McManaman, Redknapp, Rush, Walters (Wright), Stewart (Jones R).
Sheffield U: Kelly; Gage, Barnes, Gannon, Gayle, Beesley, Bradshaw (Hoyland), Rogers, Littlejohn (Bryson), Deane, Hodges.

Scarborough (0) 2 *(Mooney, Mockler)*
Plymouth Arg (1) 1 *(Dalton)*   3466
Scarborough: Ford; Thompson, Mudd, Lee, Hirst, Curran, McGee (Mockler), Himsworth, Mooney, Foreman, Wheeler.
Plymouth Arg: Shilton; Poole, Morgan, Hill, Morrison, Joyce, Evans (Garner), Castle, Nugent, Marshall (Edworthy), Dalton.

1 DEC

Arsenal (2) 2 *(Wright, Campbell)*
Derby Co (1) 1 *(Pembridge (pen))*   24,587
Arsenal: Seaman; Dixon, Morrow, Hillier, Bould, Adams, Parlour, Wright, Campbell, Merson, Flatts.
Derby Co: Sutton; Comyn (Williams), Forsyth, Short, Coleman, Pembridge, Johnson, Kuhl, Kitson, Gabbiadini, McMinn (Micklewhite).

FOURTH ROUND

Cambridge U (1) 1 *(Rowett)*
Oldham Ath (0) 0   5488
Cambridge U: Vaughan; Fensome, Kimble, Raynor, Heathcote, O'Shea, Francis, Rowett (Cheetham), White, Clayton, Leadbitter.
Oldham Ath: Keeley; Halle, Pointon, Henry, Jobson, Redmond, Adams, Olney, Sharp, Milligan, Brennan (Palmer).

Liverpool (0) 1 *(Marsh (pen))*
Crystal Palace (0) 1 *(Coleman)*   18,525
Liverpool: Hooper; Marsh, Burrows (Wright), Nicol, Piechnik, Hutchison, McManaman, Redknapp, Stewart, Barnes, Jones R.
Crystal Palace: Martyn; Humphrey, Shaw, Southgate, Young, Thorn, Osborn, Ndah, Coleman, Bowry, McGoldrick.

2 DEC

Aston Villa (0) 2 *(Atkinson, Saunders)*
Ipswich T (0) 2 *(Kiwomya 2)*   21,545
Aston Villa: Spink; Barrett, Staunton, Kubicki, McGrath, Richardson, Houghton (Regis), Parker (Cox), Saunders, Atkinson, Small.
Ipswich T: Baker; Whelan, Thompson, Stockwell, Wark, Linighan, Johnson, Goddard (Youds), Whitton, Dozzell, Kiwomya.

Everton (2) 2 *(Beardsley, Barlow)*
Chelsea (1) 2 *(Harford, Stuart)*   14,457
Everton: Southall; Harper, Ablett, Snodin, Watson, Keown, Kenny, Beardsley, Barlow, Johnston (Cottee), Hinchcliffe (Horne).
Chelsea: Hitchcock; Hall (Le Saux), Sinclair, Townsend, Lee, Donaghy, Stuart, Fleck, Harford, Newton, Wise.

Nottingham F (1) 2 *(Woan, Keane)*
Tottenham H (0) 0   22,312
Nottingham F: Crossley; Laws, Pearce, Chettle, Tiler, Keane, Black, Gemmill, Clough, Glover, Woan (Bannister).
Tottenham H: Thorstvedt; Edinburgh, Austin, Samways, Mabbutt, Ruddock, Cundy, Durie (Barmby), Nayim, Sheringham, Allen (Watson).

Sheffield W (2) 4 *(Bright, Hirst, Palmer, Nilsson)*
QPR (0) 0   17,161
Sheffield W: Woods; Nilsson, Worthington, Palmer (Bart-Williams), Anderson, Warhurst, Harkes, Waddle, Hirst, Bright (Watson), Sheridan.
QPR: Stejskal; Bardsley, Wilson, Wilkins (Allen), Peacock, McDonald, Impey, Holloway, Ferdinand, Penrice, Sinton.

9 DEC

Blackburn R (2) 6 *(Atkins, Shearer 2, Newell 2, Wegerle)*
Watford (0) 1 *(Furlong)*   13,187
Blackburn R: Mimms; May, Wright, Atkins, Hendry, Dobson, Ripley (Wegerle), Cowans (Makel), Shearer, Newell, Wilcox.
Watford: Suckling; Putney, Drysdale, Dublin, Holdsworth, Bazeley, Hessenthaler, Nogan, Furlong, Porter, Lavin.

FOURTH ROUND REPLAYS

15 DEC

Ipswich T (0) 1 *(Kiwomya)*
Aston Villa (0) 0   19,196
Ipswich T: Baker; Whelan, Thompson, Stockwell, Wark, Linighan, Johnson, Goddard (Williams), Whitton, Dozzell, Kiwomya.
Aston Villa: Spink; Barrett, Staunton, Teale, McGrath, Richardson, Houghton, Parker (Breitkreutz), Saunders, Regis (Yorke), Cox.

16 DEC

Chelsea (1) 1 *(Townsend)*
Everton (0) 0   19,496
Chelsea: Hitchcock; Hall, Sinclair, Townsend, Lee, Donaghy, Stuart, Fleck, Le Saux, Newton, Wise.
Everton: Southall; Harper (Jenkins), Ablett, Kenny, Watson, Keown, Warzycha (Barlow), Beardsley, Rideout, Horne, Beagrie.

Crystal Palace (1) 2 *(Watts, Thorn)*
Liverpool (1) 1 *(Marsh (pen)) aet*   16,622
Crystal Palace: Martyn; Humphrey, Shaw, Southgate, Young, Thorn, Osborn, Bowry, Rodger, Watts (Ndah) (Sinnott), McGoldrick.
Liverpool: Hooper; Marsh, Jones R (Tanner), Nicol, Piechnik, Stewart, McManaman (Rosenthal), Redknapp, Rush, Barnes, Walters.

19 JAN

Ipswich T (0) 1 *(Whitton (pen))*
Sheffield W (0) 1 *(Sheridan)*   19,374
Ipswich T: Baker; Johnson (Bozinoski), Thompson,
Williams, Wark, Linighan, Yallop (Whelan), Guent-
chev, Whitton, Dozzell, Kiwomya.
Sheffield W: Woods; Warhurst, Worthington, Harkes,
Pearson, Shirtliff, Wilson, Waddle, Hirst (Bart-Wil-
liams), Bright, Sheridan.

FIFTH ROUND REPLAY

3 FEB

Sheffield W (0) 1 *(Warhurst)*
Ipswich T (0) 0   26,328
Sheffield W: Woods; Nilsson, Worthington, Palmer,
Harkes, Shirtliff, Wilson, Waddle, Warhurst, Bart-
Williams (Pearson), Sheridan.
Ipswich T: Baker; Johnson, Thompson, Williams,
Whelan, Linighan, Yallop, Guentchev (Wark), Bozi-
noski (Stockwell), Dozzell, Kiwomya.

SEMI-FINAL FIRST LEG

7 FEB

Crystal Palace (0) 1 *(Osborn (pen))*
Arsenal (2) 3 *(Wright (pen), Smith 2)*   26,508
Crystal Palace: Martyn; Sinnott (Watts), Shaw, Col-
eman, Young, Thorn, Osborn, Thomas, Bowry,
Rodger, McGoldrick.
Arsenal: Seaman; Dixon, Winterburn, Hillier, Linig-
han, Adams, Selley, Wright (Morrow), Smith, Mer-
son, Campbell.

10 FEB

Blackburn R (2) 2 *(Wegerle, Palmer (og))*
Sheffield W (4) 4 *(Harkes, Sheridan, Warhurst 2)* 17,283
Blackburn R: Mimms; Berg, Wright, Sherwood
(May), Hendry, Andersson, Ripley (Atkins), Cowans,
Wegerle, Newell, Wilcox. *Sheffield W:* Woods; Nils-
son, Worthington, Palmer, Harkes, Shirtliff, Wilson,
Waddle, Warhurst, Bart-Williams (Pearson) (Jem-
son), Sheridan.

SEMI-FINAL SECOND LEG

10 MAR

Arsenal (2) 2 *(Linighan, Wright)*
Crystal Palace (0) 0   28,584
Arsenal: Seaman; Dixon, Winterburn (Hillier), Davis,
Linighan, Adams, Carter, Wright, Smith (Campbell),
Merson, Morrow.
Crystal Palace: Martyn; Humphrey, Southgate, Col-
eman, Young, Gordon, Osborn, Thomas, Watts
(Ndah), Rodger, McGoldrick.
Arsenal won 5-1 on aggregate.

FOURTH ROUND

6 JAN

Scarborough (0) 0
Arsenal (0) 1 *(Winterburn)*   6261
Scarborough: Ford; Thompson, McGee, Lee,
Ormsby, Curran, Ashdjian, Himsworth, Mooney,
Foreman, Lightbourne (Jules).

Arsenal: Seaman; Dixon, Winterburn, Hillier, Bould,
Adams, O'Leary, Wright, Smith, Merson (Campbell),
Limpar.

FIFTH ROUND

Blackburn R (0) 3 *(Newell 2, Wegerle)*
Cambridge U (0) 2 *(Clayton, Heathcote)*   14,165
Blackburn R: Mimms; May, Wright, Sherwood,
Hendry, Moran, Ripley, Cowans (Atkins), Shearer
(Wegerle), Newell, Wilcox.
Cambridge U: Vaughan; Fensome, Kimble, Raynor,
Heathcote, O'Shea, Francis, Rowett (Dennis), White,
Clayton, Leadbitter.

Crystal Palace (2) 3 *(Coleman, Ndah, Watts)*
Chelsea (1) 1 *(Townsend)*   28,510
Crystal Palace: Martyn; Humphrey, Bowry, Col-
eman, Young, Thorn, Ndah, Thomas, Watts (Gor-
don), Rodger, McGoldrick.
Chelsea: Hitchcock; Clarke, Sinclair, Townsend, Lee,
Donaghy, Stuart, Fleck (Spencer), Harford, Newton,
Myers (Le Saux).

12 JAN

Arsenal (0) 2 *(Wright 2)*
Nottingham F (0) 0   25,600
Arsenal: Seaman; Dixon, Winterburn, Hillier, Linig-
han, Adams, Jensen, Wright, Smith, Merson, Limpar
(Campbell).
Nottingham F: Crossley; Laws, Pearce, Chettle, Tiler,
Keane, Black (Stone), Gemmill, Clough, Wilson
(Orlygsson), Woan.

14 MAR

Sheffield W (0) 2 *(Hirst, Bright)*
Blackburn R (1) 1 *(Andersson)*   30,048
Sheffield W: Woods; Nilsson, King (Hirst), Palmer,
Hyde, Andersson, Wilson, Waddle, Warhurst, Bright,
Sheridan (Stewart).
Blackburn R: Mimms; May, Berg, Sherwood, Hendry,
Atkins, Ripley, Andersson (Brown), Livingstone
(Wegerle), Newell, Wilcox.
Sheffield W won 6-3 on aggregate.

FINAL at Wembley

18 APR

Arsenal (1) 2 *(Merson, Morrow)*
Sheffield W (1) 1 *(Harkes)*   74,007
Arsenal: Seaman; O'Leary, Winterburn, Parlour,
Adams, Linighan, Morrow, Merson, Wright, Camp-
bell, Davis.
Sheffield W: Woods; Nilsson, King (Hyde), Palmer,
Anderson, Harkes, Wilson (Hirst), Waddle, War-
hurst, Bright, Sheridan.
Referee: A.Gunn (Sussex).

LEAGUE CUP ATTENDANCES

Totals

Season	Attendances	Games	Average
1960/61	1,204,580	112	10,755
1961/62	1,030,534	104	9,909
1962/63	1,029,893	102	10,097
1963/64	945,265	104	9,089
1964/65	962,802	98	9,825
1965/66	1,205,876	106	11,376
1966/67	1,394,553	118	11,818
1967/68	1,671,326	110	15,194
1968/69	2,064,647	118	17,497
1969/70	2,299,819	122	18,851
1970/71	2,035,315	116	17,546
1971/72	2,397,154	123	19,489
1972/73	1,935,474	120	16,129
1973/74	1,722,629	132	13,050
1974/75	1,901,094	127	14,969
1975/76	1,841,735	140	13,155
1976/77	2,236,636	147	15,215
1977/78	2,038,295	148	13,772
1978/79	1,825,643	139	13,134
1979/80	2,322,866	169	13,745
1980/81	2,051,576	161	12,743
1981/82	1,880,682	161	11,681
1982/83	1,679,756	160	10,498
1983/84	1,900,491	168	11,312
1984/85	1,876,429	167	11,236
1985/86	1,579,916	163	9,693
1986/87	1,531,498	157	9,755
1987/88	1,539,253	158	9,742
1988/89	1,552,780	162	9,585
1989/90	1,836,916	168	10,934
1990/91	1,675,496	159	10,538
1991/92	1,622,337	164	9,892

THE FOOTBALL TRUST
Helping the game

During the past year, the Football Trust has received over £36m to support the game at all levels. The Government contributes some £23m annually from the 1990 Budget reduction in pool betting duty, and a further £13m is donated by the pools companies Littlewoods, Vernons and Zetters from their Spotting-the-Ball competition.

The Trust's main task is to assist the professional game to fund capital works in line with the recommendations of the Taylor Report. Trust grants have been awarded to England and Scottish League clubs for major projects including new stadia and stands, and seating and roofing initiatives. Last season the following awards were made:

		£
Ayr United	Replacement Seating Main Stand	12,750
Blackburn Rovers	New Stand at the Blackburn End	500,000
Bristol City	New North Stand	1,350,000
Burnley	New Stand at the Beehole End	750,000
Cardiff City	Seats/cover for the Popular Bank & Canton Stand	200,000
Celtic	Seating in Main Stand (upper tier)	36,750
Charlton Athletic	Redevelopment of The Valley	55,000
Chelsea	New North Stand	1,860,000
Coventry City	New East Stand & cover for North Stand	1,800,000
Cowdenbeath	Replacement of Seats in the Main Stand	184,000
Dundee United	Redevelopment of East Stand	500,000
Everton	New Stand at the Park End	1,300,000
Hartlepool United	760 Seats for the Rink End Stand	16,200
Heart of Midlothian	Redevelopment of Tynecastle	2,000,000
Huddersfield Town	New Kirklees Stadium	1,500,000
Leicester City	Main Stand redevelopments	1,800,000
Newcastle United	New stand at the Leazes End	2,000,000
Partick Thistle	New East Stand	1,500,000
Queens Park Rangers	South Africa Stand redevelopments	327,727
	Seating in the School End	300,000
Scarborough	Cover for Seamer Road End	150,000
Swansea City	Seating and cover for the North Bank	500,000
Swindon Town	New South Stand	800,000
Torquay United	New covered terrace at the Popular End	225,000
Tottenham Hotspur	Cover & Seating in the North Stand	1,200,000
Tranmere Rovers	New Stand at the Bebington Kop End	1,300,000
Watford	Phase One — Vicarage Road redevelopments	1,500,000
West Ham United	New South Stand	2,000,000
Wolves	New South Bank Stand	500,000

The Trust also awards grants to enable clubs to complete important safety work and facility improvements. Initiatives include facilities for people with disabilities, family enclosures, new toilets, and anti-hooligan measures such as closed circuit television, stewarding and transport improvements.

Last season, the Trust paid out over £7.6m towards improving the safety and comfort of supporters throughout England and Scotland, bringing the Trust's total support for safety and improvement work to some £69m. A further £2m was awarded in grant aid to assist clubs with policing and stewarding costs, and £629,000 towards anti-hooligan measures including the installation and upgrading of CCTV at English and Scottish League grounds.

The remainder of the Trust's income is allocated to projects for the general benefit of the game in the Pyramid and at grass roots level. Grants have been made towards essential safety work at non-league clubs and for pitch and dressing room improvements. The Trust has also continued to support the dual use of educational facilities, artificial floodlights pitches, hard surface play areas, charitable playing fields' organisations, youth and community groups and the supply of kit to junior teams.

JEWSON'S FAMILY INVOLVEMENT

For the second consecutive year the awards from the scheme funded by Jewsons, the East Anglian based builders merchants, and the People Sunday People newspaper, boosted the efforts of Football League clubs in improving their facilities.

More than £5,500,000 has been paid out since the scheme started in 1991 and the plan is for it to continue for at least one more season. Top award for the year under review went to west London club Brentford who collected £25,000 for their efforts in providing better facilities for their fans and integrating more with the local community.

Ironically their performances on the field did not match their attention to spectator comfort and they were demoted at the end of the season despite nearly doubling their average home attendance to 8,482, since the 1987 season.

At Griffin Park, 1,740 places have been set aside for Family, Junior Bees enclosures and community promotions though the latter are free tickets for standing at matches.

Excellence awards also went to Huddersfield Town, in Division Two, and Walsall in Division Three.

Wolverhampton Wanderers, Leyton Orient and Lincoln City each were given a £5,000 award as divisional winners for their facilities for their disabled fans while Notts County, AFC Bournemouth and Crewe Alexandra collected cheques for £5,000 each as divisional winners in the Progress section for their efforts in improving their facilities.

One crucial group of people in the smooth running of any sporting contest are the groundsmen., And in the past year their efforts have been recognised with a special award which embraces both the Premier and Football Leagues.

The 92 clubs were split into three regions — Northern, Midlands and Southern — and there was a winner from the clubs of each division, plus a regional one, making 16 awards in all.

The overall winner was Bill Pilbeam, of Wolverhampton Wanderers, who received a total of awards worth £1,200 for keeping the condition of Molineux top class.

Other award Winners were:-

REGIONAL — Northern; Douglas Rose (Everton), Steve Millard (Sunderland), Gary Kent (Chester), Graham Colby (Scunthorpe). Southern: Steve Braddock (Arsenal), Colin Powell (Charlton Athletic), Charles Hasler (Leyton Orient), Bill File (Gillingham). Midlands: Tony Eden (Aston Villa), Bill Corby (Rotherham United), Roger Johnson (Walsall). DIVISIONAL — D. Rose, C. Hasler, B File. OVERALL (Regional and Divisional) AWARDS: Bill Pilbeam (Wolverhampton Wanderers).

The firm have also extended their sponsorship to allow clubs a discount on materials for improving the facilities at their grounds.

Certainly the scheme is to be applauded as it goes a positive way towards the day when all soccer stadia are all-seater and the freezing days of being soaked at uncovered grounds are a thing of the past.

TREVOR WILLIAMSON

ANGLO-ITALIAN CUP

PRELIMINARY ROUND

1 SEPT

Bristol C (0) 1 *(Shelton)*
Watford (0) 0   3588
Bristol C: Welch; Mitchell, Scott, Thompson, Bryant, Edwards, Mellon, Dziekanowski, Rosenior (Allison), Cole (Harrison), Shelton.
Watford: Suckling; Gibbs, Drysdale, Dublin, Soloman, Ashby, Putney (Lavin), Butler, Furlong, Porter, Bazeley (Nogan).

Cambridge U (0) 1 *(Philpott)*
Sunderland (1) 1 *(Armstrong)*   2199
Cambridge U: Vaughan; Heathcote, Kimble, Raynor, Chapple, Daish, Rowett, Leadbitter (Francis), Norbury, Cheetham, Philpott.
Sunderland: Carter; Kay, Rogan, Martin Gray, Bennett, Ball, Armstrong, Goodman, Colquhoun, Davenport (Owers), Ord.

Oxford U (0) 1 *(Magilton)*
Swindon T (2) 3 *(Maskell, Summerbee, Berkley)* 4069
Oxford U: Kee; Smart, Ford, Lewis, Evans, Melville, Magilton, Beauchamp, Cusack (Allen), Penney, Durnin.
Swindon T: Digby; O'Sullivan, Bodin, Hunt, Calderwood, Viveash, Summerbee, Close, Maskell (White), Ling, Berkley.

Peterborough U (0) 0
Tranmere R (0) 0   1954
Peterborough U: Bennett; White, Robinson R, Halsall, Robinson D, Welsh, Ingram (Adcock), Ebdon, Costello, Charlery, Barnes.
Tranmere R: Nixon; Brannan, Nolan, Irons, McNab, Garnett, Morrissey, Aldridge, Nevin, Muir, Thomas (Mungall).

2 SEPT

Derby Co (2) 4 *(Williams, Pembridge, Simpson, Gabbiadini)*
Notts Co (2) 2 *(Short, O'Riordan)*   6767
Derby Co: Sutton; Kavanagh, Forsyth, Pembridge, Coleman, Wassall, McMinn (Gabbiadini), Kitson, Johnson, Williams, Simpson.
Notts Co: Catlin; Chris Short (Gallagher), Thomas, Craig Short (Walker), Johnson, O'Riordan, Draper, Turner, Wilson, Slawson, Smith.

Leicester C (3) 4 *(Davison 2, Gee 2)*
Grimsby T (0) 0   4112
Leicester C: Muggleton; Mills, Whitlow (Fitzpatrick), Smith, Grayson, Hill, Oldfield (Trotter), Thompson, Davison, Ormondroyd, Gee.
Grimsby T: Wilmot; McDermott, Jobling, Handyside, Agnew, Dobbin (Childs), Watson, Smith (Hargreaves), Groves, Mendonca, Woods.

Millwall (1) 1 *(Cunningham)*
Charlton Ath (0) 2 *(Barness, Pardew)*   3975
Millwall: Keller; Cunningham, Holsgrove, Rae (Dolby), Cooper, McLeary, Roberts, McGinlay, Goodman, Bogie, Stephenson.
Charlton Ath: Bolder; Balmer, Minto, Pardew, Webster, Gatting, Lee, Bumstead (Barness), Dyer, Nelson (Leaburn), Walsh.

West Ham U (1) 2 *(Dicks 2)*
Bristol R (0) 2 *(Stewart 2)*   4809
West Ham U: Banks; Potts, Dicks, Gale, Martin, Allen M, Robson (Rush), Butler, Morley, Allen C, Keen.
Bristol R: Parkin; Alexander, Twentyman, Yates, Hardyman, Maddison (Clark), Cross, Skinner, Taylor, Stewart, Pounder (Browning).

15 SEPT

Charlton Ath (0) 1 *(Leaburn)*
Portsmouth (2) 3 *(Aspinall, Whittingham, Clarke)*
                                                    1853
Charlton Ath: Bolder; Balmer, Minto, Pardew, Pitcher, Gatting, Robinson (Dyer), Bacon, Leaburn, Nelson, Walsh.
Portsmouth: Knight; Awford, Russell (Butters), Aspinall, Symonds, Murray, Neill, Kuhl (Doling), Clarke, Whittingham, Powell.

Notts Co (0) 1 *(Palmer)*
Barnsley (0) 1 *(O'Connell)*   2115
Notts Co: Cherry; Palmer, Dijkstra (Thomas), Johnson, Murphy, O'Riordan, Draper, Turner, Lund, Wilson (Slawson), Smith.
Barnsley: Butler; Smith, Taggart, Bishop, Fleming, Burton, Liddell, Rammell, Pearson, Redfearn, Archdeacon (O'Connell).

Sunderland (0) 0
Birmingham C (1) 1 *(Sale)*   5871
Sunderland: Carter; Williams (Martin Gray), Rogan, Atkinson, Bennett, Ball, Cunnington, Goodman, Rush (Davenport), Armstrong, Ord.
Birmingham C: Gosney; Clarkson, Frain, Hicks, Rogers, Matthewson, Donowa, Tait, Sale, Gleghorn, Rowbotham.

Tranmere R (0) 2 *(Aldridge 2 (1 pen))*
Wolverhampton W (1) 1 *(Birch (pen))*   3361
Tranmere R: Nixon; Higgins, Brannan, Irons, Mungall, Vickers, Morrissey, Aldridge, Malkin (Cooper), McNab, Nevin.
Wolverhampton W: Stowell; Ashley, Edwards, Downing (Dennison), Westley, Mountfield, Birch, Cook, Bull, Roberts, Rankine.

Watford (0) 0
Luton T (0) 0   5197
Watford: Suckling; Lavin, Drysdale, Dublin, Holdsworth, Putney (Nogan), Hessenthaler, Bazeley (Butler), Furlong, Thomas, Soloman.
Luton T: Petterson; Linton, James, Salton, Peake, Johnson, Claridge (Oakes), Kamara, Gray (Campbell), Preece, Rees.

16 SEPT

Bristol R (1) 3 *(Stewart (pen), Saunders, Hardyman)*
Southend U (0) 0   3007
Bristol R: Parkin; Alexander, Twentyman, Yates, Maddison, Wilson, Pounder (Saunders), Skinner, Taylor, Stewart, Hardyman.
Southend U: Sansome; Edwards, Powell, Cornwell, Scully (Smith), Prior, Locke, Martin, Sussex, Brown, Jones.

Grimsby T (1) 2 *(Rees, Groves)*
Newcastle U (2) 2 *(Quinn, Kelly)*   2159
Grimsby T: Wilmot; Futcher, Croft, Tillson, Handyside, Dobbin, Watson (Childs), Gilbert, Rees (Hargreaves), Groves, Woods.
Newcastle U: Srnicek; Venison, Beresford, Kilcline, Scott, Howey, Kristensen, Quinn, Kelly, Clark, Brock.

Swindon T (0) 1 *(Mitchell)*
Brentford (1) 2 *(Gayle, Godfrey)*   3819
Swindon T: Digby; Kerslake, Bodin, Summerbee, Calderwood, Taylor, Hazard, Moncur, Maskell (White), Ling, Mitchell.
Brentford: Bayes; Statham, Hughton, Millen, Bates, Ratcliffe, Bennett, Kruszynski, Gayle, Blissett (Godfrey), Luscombe.

29 SEPT

Barnsley (1) 1 *(Taggart)*
Derby Co (1) 2 *(Pembridge, Goulooze)*   3960
Barnsley: Butler; Robinson M, Robinson J, Bishop, Taggart, Burton, Liddell (Currie), O'Connell, Rammell, Redfearn (Godfrey), Archdeacon.
Derby Co: Sutton; Comyn, Forsyth, Coleman, Wassall, Pembridge, Johnson, Goulooze (Kavanagh), Kitson, Gabbiadini (Hayward), Simpson.

Birmingham C (1) 3 *(Gleghorn, Frain, Sale)*
Cambridge U (2) 3 *(Philpott, Raynor, White)*   3102
Birmingham C: Thomas; Clarkson, Frain, Matthewson, Hicks, Rogers, Rogerson, Tait (Sale), Donowa, Gleghorn, Sturridge (Rowbotham).
Canbridge U: Sheffield; Fensome, Kimble, Dennis, Chapple, Daish, Raynor, Leadbitter, White, Cheetham, Philpott.

Brentford (0) 2 *(Ratcliffe, Blissett)*
Oxford U (0) 0   2607
Brentford: Peyton; Statham, Hughton, Millen, Bates, Ratcliffe, Luscombe (Gayle), Manuel (Buckle), Godfrey, Blissett, Smillie.
Oxford U: Kee; Smart, Collins, Lewis, Evans, Melville, Phillips (Allen), Beauchamp, Penney (Cusack), Durnin, Narbett.

Luton T (0) 1 *(Claridge)*
Bristol C (0) 1 *(Allison)*   2538
Luton T: Petterson; Linton, James, Salton, Matthew (Preece), Dreyer, Claridge, Kamara, Gray, Campbell (Oakes), Rees.
Bristol C: Welch; Mitchell, Scott, Thompson, Bryant, Edwards, Mellon, Dziekanowski (Bent), Allison, Harrison (McIntyre), Reid.

Portsmouth (0) 1 *(Whittingham)*
Millwall (1) 1 *(Rae)*   2535
Portsmouth: Knight; Awford, Powell (Murray), McLoughlin, Symons, Aspinall, Chamberlain, Walsh, Clarke, Whittingham, Burns (Maguire).
Millwall: Davison; Cunningham, Dawes (Manning), Holsgrove, McCarthy M, Roberts, Stephenson, Rae, Bogie, Moralee, Sion.

30 SEPT

Newcastle U (2) 4 *(Brock, Quinn 2 (1 pen), Sheedy)*
Leicester C (0) 0   14,046
Newcastle U: Srnicek; Kristensen, Stimson, O'Brien (Appleby M), Kilcline, Neilson, Brock, Quinn, Kelly (Garland), Thompson, Sheedy.
Leicester C: Hoult; Mills, Whitlow, Smith, Walsh, Hill, Grayson, Thompson, Davison (Gordon), Ormondroyd, Lowe.

Southend U (0) 0
West Ham U (2) 3 *(Morley, Dicks (pen), Holmes)*
                                                        6482
Southend U: Sansome; Edwards, Powell, Cornwell, Scully, Prior, Ansah, Jones, Locke, Sussex, Tilson.
West Ham U: Miklosko; Breacker, Dicks, Potts, Martin, Allen M, Robson, Holmes, Morley, Allen C, Keen.

Wolverhampton W (1) 2 *(Taylor, Bull)*
Peterborough U (0) 0   3091
Wolverhampton W: Jones; Ashley, Thompson, Downing (Burke), Madden, Mountfield, Birch, Cook, Bull, Taylor (Roberts), Dennison.
Peterborough U: Bennett; Luke, Robinson R, Cooper, Howarth, Welsh, Tomlinson, Ebdon (White), Gavin (Dunn), Nogan, Curtis.

INTERNATIONAL STAGE

Group A

11 NOV

Ascoli (0) 1 *(Bierhoff)*
Brentford (2) 3 *(Bates, Gayle, Blissett)*   1000
Ascoli: Bizzarri; Pascucci, Di Rocco, Pierleoni, Fusco, Bosi (Cacciatori), Bianchi (Bierhoff), Troglio, Spinelli, Gioffi, Pierantozzi.
Brentford: Peyton; Statham, Hughton, Millen, Bates, Chalmers, Bennett, Manuel, Gayle, Blissett (Jones), Luscombe (Godfrey).

Birmingham C (0) 1 *(Cooper)*
Bari (0) 0   4970
Birmingham C: Sealey; Tait (Donowa), Potter, Rogers, Frain, Matthewson, Rodgerson, Gayle (Peschisolido), Speedie, Cooper, Sturridge.
Bari: Taglialatela; Brambati, Sassarini (Jarni), Parente (Terracenere), Montanari, Progna, Laureri, Cucchi, Capocchiano, Barone, Caggianelli.

Lucchese (1) 1 *(Venison (og))*
Newcastle U (0) 1 *(Kristensen)* 744
Lucchese: Quironi; Di Francesco, Vignini, Delli Carri, Monaco (Bianchi), Baraldi, Di Stefano (Baldini), Giusti, Paci, Russo, Rastelli.
Newcastle U: Srnicek; Venison, Beresford, Bracewell, Kilcline, Howey, Carr (Quinn), Peacock, Kristensen (Brock), Clark, Sheedy.

Portsmouth (1) 2 *(Walsh, Symons)*
Cesena (0) 0 4752
Portsmouth: Knight; Awford, Daniel, McLoughlin (Doling), Symons, Aspinall, Russell, Chamberlain (Wigley), Walsh, Whittingham, Burns.
Cesena: Dadina; Barcella, Scugugia (Polvepapi), Piraccini, Marin, Jozic, Gautieri, Piangerelli, Lerda (Destro), Masolini, Pazzaglia.

Brentford (0) 1 *(Allon)*
Lucchese (0) 0 4339
Brentford: Peyton; Statham, Hughton, Millen, Bates, Ratcliffe, Smillie (Bennett), Chalmers, Allon, Blissett, Luscombe (Manuel).
Lucchese: Quironi; Costi, Bettarini, Delli Carri, Giusti, Baraldi, Di Francesco, Bianchi, Lugnan (Dolcetti), Russo, Rastelli.

Newcastle U (0) 0
Ascoli (0) 1 *(Bierhoff)* 9789
Newcastle U: Srnicek; Venison, Neilson, O'Brien, Kilcline, Scott, Watson S (Carr), Hunt (Ranson), Kelly, Thompson, Sheedy.
Ascoli: Bizzarri; Mancini, Pascucci, Cacciatori, Fusco, Bosi, Pierantozzi (Perozzi), Cioffi, Bierhoff, Menolascina, Spinelli, (Carbone).

Group B

Bristol C (0) 0
Cosenza (0) 2 *(Negri, Signorelli)* 3644
Bristol C: Welch; Bryant, Scott, Thompson, Edwards, Osman (Mellon), Harrison, Shelton (Dziekanowski), Rosenior, Cole, Gavin.
Cosenza: Graziani; Balleri, Marino, Napoli, Napolitano, Bia, Statuto (Altomare), Signorelli, Negri, De Rosa, Oliva (Fiore).

Cremonese (0) 2 *(Florjancic 2)*
West Ham U (0) 0 2100
Cremonese: Violini; Gualco, Castagna, Cristiani, Montorfano, Pedroni, Giandebiaggi, Ferraroni (Nicolini), Dezotti (Tentoni), Lombardini, Florjancic.
West Ham U: Miklosko; Brown, Dicks, Potts, Martin, Allen M, Robson, Parris (Keen), Morley, Allen C, Holmes.

Derby Co (2) 3 *(Johnson, Forsyth, Pembridge)*
Pisa (0) 0 8059
Derby Co: Sutton; Comyn, Forsyth, Coleman, Wassall, Pembridge, Johnson, Williams, McMinn, Gabbiadini, Simpson.
Pisa: Ciucci; Chamot, Fasce, Fimognari, Lampugnani, Larsen, Rotella, Fiorentini (Gallaccio), Scarafoni (Polidori), Rocci, Vieri.

Reggiana (0) 0
Tranmere R (0) 0 2251
Reggiana: Bucci; Corrado, Parlato, Monti, Dominissini, Francesconi, Sacchetti (Falco), Vivani, Pacione (De Falco), Zannoni, Morello.
Tranmere R: Nixon; Higgins, Brannan, Irons, Mungall, Vickers, Morrissey, Aldridge, Malkin (Muir), McNab, Nevin.

Group B

Cosenza (0) 0
Derby Co (3) 3 *(Comyn, Kitson, Gabbiadini)* 4263
Cosenza: Graziani; Balleri, Marino, Napoli (Losacco), Bia, Gazzaneo, Monza (Signorelli), De Rosa, Negri, Fabris, Statuto.
Derby Co: Sutton; Comyn, Forsyth, Coleman, Wassall (Kavanagh), Pembridge, Johnson, Williams, Kitson, Gabbiadini, McMinn.

Pisa (4) 4 *(Rocco, Scarafoni, Bosco, Vieri)*
Bristol C (2) 3 *(Edwards, Shelton, Scott (pen))* 1500
Pisa: Berti; Lampugnani, Fasce, Bosco, Susic, Cristallini (Fimognari), Rotella, Gallaccio, Scarafoni, Rocco, Vieri (Polidori).
Bristol C: Welch; Harrison, Scott, Thompson, Bryant, Mellon, Shelton, Dziekanowski, Allison, Cole (Bent), Edwards (Rouse).

Tranmere R (1) 1 *(Malkin)*
Cremonese (1) 2 *(Florjancic, Verdelli)* 5727
Tranmere R: Nixon; Higgins (Hughes), Brannan, Irons, Mungall, Vickers, Morrissey, Aldridge, Malkin (Muir), McNab, Nevin.
Cremonese: Violini; Gualco, Montorfano, Castagna, Colonnese, Verdelli, Lombardini, Ferraroni, Tentoni (Nicolini), Maspero (Giandebiaggi), Florjancic.

West Ham U (0) 2 *(Allen C 2)*
Reggiana (0) 0 6872
West Ham U: Miklosko; Breacker, Dicks, Potts, Martin, Allen M, Robson, Holmes, Morley, Allen C, Keen.
Reggiana: Bucci; Parlato, Zanutta, Monti, Sgarbossa, Francesconi, Sacchetti, Vivani, Morello (Accardi), Picasso, Zannoni.

Group A

24 NOV

Bari (0) 3 *(Caggianelli, Alessio, Capocchiano)*
Portsmouth (0) 0 800
Bari: Taglialatela; Calcaterra (Civero), Sassarini, Terracenere, Loseto, Consagra, Laureri, Cucchi, Capocchiano, Alessio (Barone), Caggianelli.
Portsmouth: Knight; Awford, Daniel (Russell), Agnew, Symons, Burns, Neill, Chamberlain, Clarke, Whittingham, Maguire (Powell).

Group A

2 DEC

Cesena (0) 1 *(Hubner (pen))*
Birmingham C (0) 2 *(Frain (pen), Sturridge)* 2090
Cesena: Dadina; Marin, Scugugia (Piangerelli), Medri, Barcella, Pepi, Pazzaglia, Leoni (Gautieri), Hubner, Masolini, Salvetti.
Birmingham C: Thomas; Clarkson, Potter, Tait, Frain, Rogers, Rowbotham (Peer), Gayle, Sturridge, Sale, Rodgerson.

634

8 DEC

Bari (2) 3 *(Capocchiano 2, Tovalieri)*
Newcastle U (0) 0   2000
Bari: Taglialatela; Calcaterra, Rizzardi, Terracenere
Barone), Loseto, Montanari, Lauteri (Caggianelli),
Cucchi, Capocchiano, Alessio, Tovalieri.
Newcastle U: Srnicek; Appleby M, Stimson, Watson
S, Kilcline, Howey, Carr, Appleby R, Hunt (Watson
J), Thompson, Sheedy (Roche).

Birmingham C (1) 1 *(Sturridge)*
Ascoli (1) 1 *(D'Ainzara)*   3963
Birmingham C: Sealey; Clarkson, Potter, Fenwick,
Frain, Matthewson, Rodgerson, Tait, Speedie, Sale
(Donowa), Sturridge.
Ascoli: Bizzarri; Mancini, Pergolizzi, Cacciatori, Pas-
cucci, Cavaliere, Menolascina (Benetti), Troglio, Bier-
hoff, Cioffi, (Zaini), D'Ainzara.

Cesena (0) 0
Brentford (0) 1 *(Allon)*   450
Cesena: Dadina; Destro, Scugugia, Piraccini (Polver-
ari), Marin, Jozic, Piangerelli, Teodorani (Giovani),
Pazzaglia, Masolini, Hubner.
Brentford: Benstead; Statham, Hughton, Millen,
Bates, Ratcliffe, Allon (Godfrey), Manuel, Gayle
(Luscombe), Blissett, Bennett.

Portsmouth (0) 2 *(Powell 2)*
Lucchese (1) 1 *(Paci)*   2363
Portsmouth: Knight; Awford, Powell, McLoughlin
(Ross), Suymons, Burns, Neill, Doling, Walsh, Aspi-
nall, Maguire (Butters).
Lucchese: Quironi; Ansaldi, Bettarini (Giusti), Delli
Carri, Monaco, Baraldi, Di Francesco, Marta, Paci
(Bianchi), Dolcetti, Rastelli.

Group B

Bristol C (1) 1 *(Allison)*
Reggiana (1) 2 *(Pacione, Accardi)*   2281
Bristol C: Welch; Mitchell, Scott, Atteveld (Thomp-
son), Bryant, Edwards, Mellon, Dziekanowski, Rose-
nior, Allison, Gavin.
Reggiana: Sardini; Corrado, Parlato, Monti, Domi-
nissini, Accardi, Falco, Scienza, Pacione (Morello),
Picasso, Del Falco.

Cosenza (0) 0
West Ham U (1) 1 *(Allen C)*   2500
Cosenza: Graziani; Balleri, Compagno, Marino
(Actomare), Napolitano, Losacco, Signorelli (Viscig-
lia), De Rosa, Fabris, Negri, Gazzaneo.
West Ham U: Miklosko; Breacker, Dicks, Potts, Mar-
tin, Allen M, Rush, Parris, Jones, Allen C (Foster),
Keen (Brown).

Derby Co (1) 1 *(Kitson)*
Cremonese (3) 3 *(Florjancic 2, Wassall (og))* 7050
Derby Co: Sutton; Goulooze (Kavanagh), Forsyth,
Coleman, Wassall, Pembridge, McMinn (Hayward),
Williams, Kitson, Gabbiadini, Simpson.
Cremonese: Turci; Castagna, Pedroni, Cristiani (Pian-
toni), Colonesse, Verdelli, Giandebiaggi, Ferraroni,
Dezotti, Maspero, Florjancic (Pessotto).

Pisa (0) 0
Tranmere R (0) 1 *(Irons)*   750
Pisa: Berti; Lampugnani, Chamot, Fimognari, Susic,
Fasce (Gallaccio), Rotella, Rocco, Vieri, Cristallini,
Polidori.
Tranmere R: Nixon; Higgins (McGreal), Brannan,
Irons, Mungall, Hughes, Morrissey, Cooper (Malkin),
Martindale, Muir, Nevin.

Group A

16 DEC

Ascoli (1) 1 *(Bierhoff)*
Portsmouth (0) 2 *(Whittingham, Aspinall)* 500
Ascoli: Bizzarri; Mancini, Pascucci, Zanoncelli, Fusco,
Cavaliere (Bosi), Menolascina, Cioffi (Troglio), Bier-
hoff, Zaini, Pierantozzi.
Portsmouth: Knight; Awford, Butters, McLoughlin
(Murray), Symons, Burns, Aspinall, Agnew, Clarke,
Whittingham (Ross), Powell.

Brentford (1) 2 *(Godfrey, Luscombe)*
Bari (0) 1 *(Capocchiano)*   4554
Brentford: Benstead; Statham, Godfrey, Luscombe,
Bates, Chalmers, Bennett, Manuel, Allon, Blissett,
Gayle.
Bari: Taglialatela; Civero, Rizzardi (Sassarini), Andri-
sani, Loseto, Montanari, Laureri, Alessio, Protti, Bar-
one, Tovarieri (Capocchiano).

Lucchese (2) 3 *(Bettari, Paci, Rastelli)*
Birmingham C (0) 0   139
Lucchese: Mancini; Baldini, Ansaldi, Delli Carri,
Monaco, Baraldi, Russo, Bianchi, Paci (Rastelli),
Dolcetti (Di Stefano), Bettarini.
Birmingham C: Sealey; Clarkson, Potter, Rennie,
Hicks, Matthewson, Rodgerson, Gayle, Rowbotham,
Tait, Peschisolido.

Newcastle U (1) 2 *(Peacock 2)*
Cesena (1) 2 *(Hubner, Pazzaglia)*   4609
Newcastle U: Wright; Appleby M, Neilson, O'Brien,
Bracewell, Howey (Kristensen), Carr, Peacock, Kelly,
Clark, Appleby R (Watson S).
Cesena: Dadina; Destro, Piangerelli, Leoni (Ceccar-
elli), Scugugia (Pepi), Medri, Teodorani, Masolini,
Pazzaglia, Lantignotti, Hubner.

Group B

Cremonese (0) 2 *(Florjancic 2)*
Bristol C (0) 2 *(Cole, Rosenior)*   535
Cremonese: Violini (Razzetti); Piantoni; Lucarelli,
Castagna, Colonnese (Bruzzano), Pedroni, Mariani,
Ferraroni, Florjancic, Pessotto, Lombardini.
Bristol C: Welch; Harrison, Scott, Mitchell, Osman,
Shelton (Mellon), Bent, Dziekanowski (Rouse), Rose-
nior, Cole, Gavin.

Reggiana (0) 0
Derby Co (3) 3 *(Kitson, Pembridge, Gabbiadini)* 598
Reggiana: Bucci; Mozzini (Corrado), Parlato, Monti,
Dominissini, Accardi, Cherubini, Vivani, Pacione,
Picasso, Sacchetti (Falco).
Derby Co: Taylor; Kavanagh, Forsyth, Comyn, Col-
eman, Pembridge, Johnson (Simpson), Hayward, Kit-
son (Micklewhite), Gabbiadini, McMinn.

Tranmere R (2) 2 *(Irons, Morrissey)*
Cosenza (0) 1 *(Signorelli)* 3659
Tranmere R: Nixon; Hughes, Brannan, Irons, Mungall, Vickers, Morrissey, Aldridge, Malkin, McNab, Martindale.
Cosenza: Graziani; Losacco (Balleri), Compagno, De Rosa, Napolitano, Marino, Monza, Signorelli, Oliva (Negri), Fabris, Gazzaneo.

West Ham U (0) 0
Pisa (0) 0 7123
West Ham U: Miklosko; Breacker, Dicks, Potts, Martin, Allen M, Rush, Bishop, Bunbury, Allen C, Keen.
Pisa: Berti; Luciano, Chamot, Bosco, Susic, Fasce, Rotella, Fimognari, Rocco, Cristallini, Polidori.

SEMI-FINAL FIRST LEG

27 JAN

Brentford (2) 3 *(Allon 3)*
Derby Co (3) 4 *(Patterson 2, Gabbiadini, Kitson)* 5227
Brentford: Benstead; Bennett, Mortimer, Millen, Statham, Manuel, Allon, Chalmers (Gayle), Godfrey, Blissett, Luscombe (Buckle).
Derby Co: Sutton; Kavanagh, Forsyth, Coleman, Wassall, Pembridge, Johnson, Comyn, Kitson, Gabbiadini, Patterson.

3 FEB

Cremonese (2) 4 *(Nicolini, Florjancic, Tentoni, Lombardini)*
Bari (1) 1 *(Verdelli (og))* 2599
Cremonese: Turci; Giandebiaggi, Pedroni, Cristiani (Castagna), Colonnese, Verdelli, Lombardini, Nicolini, Tentoni (Bruzzano), Maspero, Florjancic.
Bari: Biato (Taglialatela); Brambati, Laureri, Andrisani, Civero (Loseto), Consagra, Parente, Alessio, Caggianelli, Barone, Di Muri.

SEMI-FINAL SECOND LEG

Derby Co (1) 1 *(Gabbiadini)*
Brentford (0) 2 *(Blissett 2)* 14,494
Derby Co: Sutton; Kavanagh, Forsyth, Coleman, Comyn, Pembridge, Johnson, McMinn (Williams), Kitson, Gabbiadini (Micklewhite), Patterson.
Brentford: Benstead; Statham, Mortimer, Millen, Bates, Manuel (Buckle), Allon, Bennett, Godfrey, Blissett, Gayle (Luscombe).

17 FEB

Bari (2) 2 *(Jarni, Cucchi)*
Cremonese (1) 2 *(Dezotti 2)* 898
Bari: Biato; Calcaterra (Loseto), Di Muri (Cucchi), Terracenere, Montanari, Consagra, Laureri, Andrisani, Protti, Jarni, Capocchiano.
Cremonese: Turci; Montorfano, Pedroni, Ferraroni, Colonnese, Verdelli, Castagna, Nicolini, Dezotti, Maspero (Lombardini), Florjancic.

FINAL (at Wembley)

27 MAR

Cremonese (1) 3 *(Verdelli, Maspero (pen), Tentoni)*
Derby Co (1) 1 *(Gabbiadini)* 37,024
Cremonese: Turci; Gualco, Pedroni, Cristiani, Colonnese, Verdelli, Giandebiaggi, Nicolini, Tentoni (Montorfano), Maspero, Florjancic (Dezotti).
Derby Co: Taylor; Patterson, Forsyth, Nicholson, Coleman, Pembridge, Micklewhite, Goulooze (Hayward), Kitson, Gabbiadini, Johnson (Simpson).
Referee: J.Velasquez (Spain).

AUTOGLASS TROPHY 1992-93

FIRST ROUND

1 DEC

Colchester U (1) 1 *(Grainger (pen))*
Northampton T (1) 2 *(Beavon (pen), Brown)* 1454
Colchester U: Green; Donald, Grainger, Devereux, Oxbrow, English, Hazel (Bennett), Roberts (Kinsella), McDonough, McGavin, Smith.
Northampton T: Richardson; Curtis, Beavon, Harmon, Angus, Terry, Burnham, Wilkin, Bell (Benton), Brown, McParland.

Doncaster R (0) 2 *(Prindiville, Hine)*
York C (0) 1 *(Canham)* 1419
Doncaster R: Crichton; Hine, Prindiville, Reddish, Richards, Hicks, Hewitt, Hodson, Morrow, Heritage, Gormley.
York C: Marples; McMillan, Hall, Bushell, Stancliffe, Atkin, McCarthy, Borthwick, Barnes, Swann, Blackstone (Canham).

Halifax T (0) 0
Bradford C (2) 4 *(McCarthy 2, Tinnion, Torpey)* 1434
Halifax T: Bracey; Megson, Wilson, Lucketti, Thompstone, Bradley, Matthews, German, Patterson, Lancashire (Barr), Hardy.
Bradford C: Whitehead; Hoyle (Richards), Williams, Duxbury M, Oliver, Heseltine, Torpey, Lawford, McCarthy, Tinnion (McHugh), Reid.

Leyton Orient (3) 4 *(Achampong, Day, Cooper, Livett)*
Gillingham (1) 1 *(Aylott)* 1667
Leyton Orient: Heald; Bellamy, Howard, Hales, Kitchen, Whitbread (Day), Jones, Achampong, Warren, Livett, Cooper.
Gillingham: Lim; Green, Palmer, Roeder (Hunt), Hague, Smith (Watson), Stephenson, O'Connor, Aylott, Henry, Dempsey.

Lincoln C (0) 0
Rotherham U (1) 1 *(Cunningham)* 1066
Lincoln C: Bowling; Smith, Clarke, Carmichael (Schofield), Dunphy, Brown, Baraclough, Bressington, Lee, Costello (Kabia), Puttnam.
Rotherham U: Mercer; Pickering, Hutchings, Banks, Johnson, Law, Hazel, Goodwin, Cunningham, Howard, Barrick.

Preston NE (0) 1 *(Ellis)*
Blackpool (1) 1 *(Eyres)* 2852
Preston NE: Farnworth; Cartwright, Davidson, Callaghan, Flynn, Eaves, Tinkler, Graham, Ashcroft, Ellis, James.
Blackpool: Martin; Burgess, Murphy, Horner, Briggs, Stoneman, Rodwell, Sinclair, Mitchell (Robinson), Bonner, Eyres.

Reading (0) 1 *(Gilkes)*
Brighton & HA (1) 1 *(Wilkinson)* 1209
Reading: Hislop; Gooding (Taylor), Richardson, McPherson, Williams, Hopkins (Parkinson), Gilkes, Dillon, Quinn, Lambert, Jones.
Brighton & HA: Beeney; Chivers, Chapman, Wilkins, McCarthy, Bissett, Crumplin, Kennedy, Edwards, Codner, Wilkinson.

Rochdale (0) 0
Bolton W (0) 0 1348
Rochdale: Rose; Thackeray, Graham, Reid, Reeves, Jones, Ryan, Parker, Flounders, Bowden (Payne), Whitehall.
Bolton W: Branagan; Brown P, Burke, Lee, Seagraves, Winstanley, Green (Roscoe), Kelly, Walker, McGinlay, Patterson.

Shrewsbury T (0) 1 *(Griffiths)*
Cardiff C (1) 3 *(Millar, Richardson, Dale)* 936
Shrewsbury T: Edwards; Haylock (Worsley), Lynch, Taylor, Spink, Blake, Williams L (O'Toole), Clark, Smith, Griffiths, Summerfield.
Cardiff C: Ward; James, Searle, Millar, Perry, Brazil, Ramsey, Richardson, Pike, Dale, Blake.

5 DEC

Chester C (0) 0
Chesterfield (1) 1 *(Williams)* 1276
Chester C: Stewart; Preece, Albiston, Butler, Came, Lightfoot, Thompson (Kelly), Ryan, Morton, Barrow, Comstive.
Chesterfield: Leonard; Lemon, Carr, Whitehead, Brien, Rogers, Hebberd, Williams, Lancaster (Morris), Turnbull, Kennedy.

Scarborough (1) 4 *(Jules, Curran, Mooney, Mockler)*
Carlisle U (0) 0 943
Scarborough: Ford; Thompson (Lee), Mudd, Mockler, Hirst, Curran, McGee, Himsworth, Mooney (Ashdjian), Foreman, Jules.
Carlisle U: O'Hanlon; Williams, Dalziel, Holden, Walsh, Davey, Proudlock, Edmondson, Hawke, Arnold (Oghani), Thorpe.

8 DEC

Blackpool (2) 3 *(Gouck 2, Eyres)*
Wigan Ath (1) 2 *(Griffiths, Daley)* 1658
Blackpool: Martin; Burgess, Murphy, Horner, Briggs, Stoneman, Rodwell (Davies), Sinclair, Mitchell, Gouck, Eyres.
Wigan Ath: Adkins; Appleton, Tankard, Kirwan, Robertson, Langley, Skipper, Powell (Sharratt), Daley, Pilling, Griffiths.

Bolton W (0) 1 *(McGinlay)*
Bury (1) 1 *(Sonner)* 3278
Bolton W: Branagan; Brown P (Stubbs), Burke, McAteer, Lydiate, Winstanley, Green, Lee, Walker, McGinlay, Patterson.
Bury: Kelly; Hughes, Reid, Daws, Valentine, Knill, Lyons, Sonner, Hulme, Mauge, Branch.

Cardiff C (1) 3 *(Ramsey (pen), Stant, Dale)*
Hereford U (1) 2 *(Pickard 2)* 3246
Cardiff C: Ward; James, Searle, Millar, Perry, Brazil, Ramsey, Richardson, Stant, Dale, Blake.
Hereford U: Judge; Titterton, Downs, Davies, Theodosiou, Anderson, Hall, Jones, Pickard, Cousins, Nicholson.

Chesterfield (0) 0
Stockport Co (1) 3 *(Francis 2, Preece)* 1956
Chesterfield: Leonard; Lemon, Carr, Whitehead, Brien, Cash, Hebberd, Williams, Lancaster, Turnbull (Morris), Kennedy.
Stockport Co: Edwards; Todd, Carstairs, Frain, Barras, Williams B, Gannon, McCord, Francis, Beaumont (Wallace), Preece.

Crewe Alex (0) 0
Wrexham (0) 3 *(Bennett 2, Preece)* 1577
Crewe Alex: Kite; McKearney, Annan, Wilson, Carr, Macauley, Harvey, Naylor (Clarkson), Ward, Whalley (Gardiner), Lyons.
Wrexham: Morris; Jones, Hardy, Owen, Humes, Pejic, Bennett, Lake, Taylor, Watkin, Cross.

Exeter C (2) 5 *(Moran 3 (1 pen), Collins, Dolan)*
Torquay U (0) 0 2118
Exeter C: Miller; Hiley, Cook, Bailey, Daniels, Whiston, Collins, Kelly (Redwood), Moran, Dolan, Hodge.
Torquay U: Sommer; Lewis, Curran (Joyce), Johnson, Moore, Hodges, Colcombe (Darby), Trollope, Fashanu, Myers, Foster.

Gillingham (1) 3 *(Henry 2, O'Connor)*
Fulham (1) 3 *(Baah, Farrell, Eckhardt)* 1085
Gillingham: Barrett; Green, Palmer, Hague, Joseph, Smith (Watson), Stephenson, O'Connor, Aylott, Henry, Dempsey.
Fulham: Gough; Newson, Pike, Eckhardt, Cooper, Baah, Hails, Marshall, Farrell, Tierling (Tucker), Onwere.

Hartlepool U (3) 4 *(Olsson, Johnson, Honour, Saville)*
Scarborough (0) 1 *(Foreman)* 1193
Hartlepool U: Hodge; Cross R, Cross P, McGuckin, MacPhail, Emerson (Southall), Johnrose, Olsson, Saville, Honour, Johnson (Peverell).
Scarborough: Ford; Thompson, Mudd, Mockler (Lee), Hirst, Curran, McGee (Horsefield), Himsworth, Ashdjian, Foreman, Jules.

Rotherham U (1) 3 *(Barrick, Cunningham, Hazel)*
Scunthorpe U (0) 1 *(Goodacre)* 1634
Rotherham U: Mercer; Pickering, Hutchings, Banks, Johnson, Law, Hazel, Campbell (Richardson), Cunningham, Howard (Page), Barrick.
Scunthorpe U: Samways; McCullagh, Longden, Alexander, Elliott, Martin, Greaves (White), Charles, Daws, Goodacre, Helliwell.

Walsall (1) 2 *(McDonald, Clarke)*
Mansfield T (0) 0 1837
Walsall: Gayle; Cecere, Reece, Methven, Knight, Smith, Ntamark, Clarke (O'Hara), Marsh, MacDonald, McDonald.
Mansfield T: Pearcey; Parkin, Withe, Spooner (Gray), Walker, Holland, Ford, Fairclough, Stringfellow, Wilkinson, Castledine (Noteman).

York C (0) 0
Hull C (0) 0 2253
York C: Kiely; McMillan, Hall, Bushell, Stancliffe, Atkin, McCarthy, Borthwick (Naylor), Tilley, Swann, Blackstone.
Hull C: Wilson; Hockaday, Miller, Mail, Wilcox, Carruthers, Norton, Atkinson (Stoker), France, Windass, Jenkinson.

9 DEC

Bradford C (0) 0
Huddersfield T (0) 0 1638
Bradford C: Whitehead; Duxbury M, Williams (Richards), Duxbury L, Blake, Hoyle, McHugh, Heseltine, McCarthy, Torpey (Lawford), Reid.
Huddersfield T: Clarke; Parsley, Charlton, Mooney, Mitchell, Jackson, Barnett, O'Regan, Roberts, Dunn, Stuart (Billy).

Brighton & HA (3) 3 *(Wilkinson, Walker, Nogan)*
Bournemouth (2) 2 *(Morgan, Mundee)* 1607
Brighton & HA: Beeney; Munday, Gallacher, Wilkins, McCarthy, Bissett, Wilkinson, Nogan, Edwards, Codner, Walker.
Bournemouth: Bartram; Pennock, Masters, Morris, Watson, McGorry, Wood, Shearer, Mundee, Morgan, Mean.

Northampton T (0) 2 *(McParland, Scott)*
Barnet (0) 1 *(Curtis (og))* 1591
Northampton T: Richardson; Curtis, Beavon, Harmon, Angus, Terry, Burnham, Wilkin (Bell), Benton, Brown (Scott), McParland.
Barnet: Phillips; Huxford (Carter), Cooper, Bodley, Barnett, Hunt (Hayrettin), Payne, Stein, Bull, Lowe, Showler.

14 DEC

Scunthorpe U (1) 2 *(Clarke (og), Alexander)*
Lincoln C (0) 2 *(Costello, Carmichael)* 1263
Scunthorpe U: Samways; Joyce, Longden, Alexander, Elliott, Martin, Greaves (Stevenson), Charles, Daws, Whie, Helliwell.
Lincoln C: Bowling; Smith, Clarke, Finney, Carmichael, Carbon (West D), Schofield, Baraclough, Lee, Costello, Puttnam.

15 DEC

Carlisle U (0) 2 *(Arnold, Proudlock)*
Hartlepool U (0) 0 859
Carlisle U: O'Hanlon; Williams, Dalziel, Holden, Walling, Davey, Proudlock, Walsh, Sendall, Holmes, Arnold.
Hartlepool U: Hodge; Cross R, Cross P, Gilchrist, MacPhail, Emerson, Johnrose, Olsson, Saville, Honour, Johnson (Peverell).

Fulham (0) 2 *(Eckhardt, Tierling)*
Leyton Orient (1) 2 *(Jones 2)* 1276
Fulham: Stannard; Newson, Pike, Eckhardt, Cooper, Thomas (Kelly P), Hails, Marshall, Farrell (Tierling), McGlashan, Baah.
Leyton Orient: Heald; Bellamy, Ludden, Hales, Kitchen, Lakin, Carter (Zoricich), Jones, Warren, Otto (Tomlinson), Cooper.

Huddersfield T (1) 5 *(Dunn 3, Roberts 2)*
Halifax T (0) 0   1236
Huddersfield T: Clarke; Parsley, Charlton, Mooney
(Starbuck), Mitchell, Jackson, Barnett, O'Regan,
Roberts, Dunn, Stuart (Wright).
Halifax T: Bracey; Barr, Wilson, German, Lucketti,
Bradley (Lancaster), Patterson, Peake, Thompstone,
Greenwood, Hildersley.

Hull C (0) 2 *(Norton, Abbott)*
Doncaster R (1) 1 *(Crosby)*   1716
Hull C: Wilson; Hockaday, Miller, Mail, Wilcox,
France (Warren), Norton, Atkinson, Carruthers,
Windass (Abbott), Jenkinson.
Doncaster R: Crichton; Hine (Douglas), Prindiville,
Reddish, Richards, Crosby, Hewitt, Hodson, Morrow
(Heritage), Falana, Gormley.

Stockport Co (0) 2 *(Preece 2)*
Chester C (0) 0   2064
Stockport Co: Edwards; Todd, Carstairs, Frain
(Wheeler), Barras, Miller (Fitzsimons), Gannon,
Ward, Francis, Beaumont, Preece.
Chester C: Stewart; Whelan, Albiston, Butler (Abel),
Came, Lightfoot, Barrow (Ryan), Kelly, Morton,
Bishop, Pugh.

Wrexham (0) 0
Stoke C (2) 2 *(Russell, Ware)*   3974
Wrexham: Morris, Jones, Hardy, Owen, Humes,
Pejic, Bennett, Lake, Durkan (Connolly), Watkin,
Cross.
Stoke C: Sinclair; Butler, Sandford, Cranson,
Overson, Gleghorn, Foley, Russell, Stein, Regis
(Harbey), Ware.

21 DEC

Barnet (3) 4 *(Evans, Carter, Stein, Hunt)*
Colchester U (0) 2 *(Ball, Cook)*   1193
Barnet: Phillips; Huxford, Cooper, Bodley, Barnett
(Hayrettin), Horton (Wilson), Payne, Carter, Stein,
Evans, Hunt.
Colchester U: Monk; Betts, Phillips (Donald),
Roberts, Partner, Ball, Cook, Bennett, Abrahams,
McGavin, Smith.

22 DEC

Hereford U (2) 2 *(Cousins, Hall)*
Shrewsbury T (0) 1 *(Lynch)*   662
Hereford U: Judge; Fry, Downs, Davies, Titterton,
Anderson, Hall, Jones, Pickard (Brain), Cousins,
Nicholson.
Shrewsbury T: Edwards; Worsley, Watts,
Summerfield, Williams MS, Lynch, Brough (Yates),
Clark, Lyne, Smith, Williams L.

5 JAN

Bournemouth (0) 1 *(Ekoku)*
Reading (1) 1 *(Viveash)*   1218
Bournemouth: Bartram; Pennock, Masters, Morris
(Murray), Watson, Mean (Scott), Wood, Shearer,
McGorry, Ekoku, Mundee.
Reading: Hislop; Gooding, Viveash, McPherson,
Williams, Parkinson, Barkus (Lambert), Holzman,
Quinn, Moody, Taylor.

Plymouth Arg (0) 1 *(Marshall)*
Exeter C (0) 1 *(Cook)*   3761
Plymouth Arg: Shilton; Edworthy, Dryden, Hill
(Spearing), Morrison, Joyce, McCall, Castle, Nugent,
Marshall, Dalton.
Exeter C: Miller; Hiley, Cook, Bailey, Daniels
(Phillips), Whiston, Brown, Kelly, Moran, Gallen,
Tonge (Cooper).

WBA (1) 4 *(Donovan, Hamilton, Taylor (pen),
Heggs)*
Walsall (0) 0   6702
WBA: Lange; Fereday, Darton, Bradley, Raven,
Shakespeare (Hamilton), Hackett, Donovan, Taylor,
Dickens (Heggs), Robson.
Walsall: Gayle; Cecere, Reece, Methven, Knight,
Smith, Ntamark, Clarke, Marsh, Statham,
McDonald.

6 JAN

Stoke C (2) 2 *(Stein, Regis)*
Crewe Alex (0) 2 *(Evans, Gardiner)*   9714
Stoke C: Sinclair; Butler, Sandford (Tapai), Cranson,
Overson, Gleghorn, Foley, Russell, Stein (Shaw),
Regis, Ware.
Crewe Alex: Kite; McKearney, Whalley, Wilson,
Carr, Jackson (Smith), Harvey, Clarkson, Evans,
Gardiner, Walters (Lyons).

Wigan Ath (1) 2 *(Skipper, Pilling)*
Preston NE (1) 1 *(Norbury)*   1932
Wigan Ath: Pennock; Appleton, Tankard, Johnson,
Robertson, Langley, Skipper, Powell (Worthington),
Pilling, Cooper, Griffiths.
Preston NE: Farnworth; Davidson, Lucas, Callaghan,
Flynn, Garnett, Ashcroft (Flitcroft), Ainsworth,
Norbury, Finney, Burton (James).

12 JAN

Bury (1) 1 *(Stevens)*
Rochdale (0) 2 *(Thackeray 2)*   1215
Bury: Kelly; Kearney, Stanislaus, Daws, Valentine,
Knill, Lyons (McKee), Stevens, Rigby, Mauge (Reid),
Ward.
Rochdale: Rose; Parker, Beever (Thackeray), Reid,
Reeves, Jones, Ryan, Payne, Bowden, Whitehall,
Howard.

Mansfield T (0) 0
WBA (0) 1 *(Taylor)*   2356
Mansfield T: Pearcey; Peer, Withe, Spooner,
Wilkinson, Gray, Ford, Holland, Stringfellow,
Noteman (Castledine), Fairclough.
WBA: Lange; Coldicott (Hamilton), Darton, Sinfield,
Raven, Shakespeare, Hackett, Hunter, Taylor
(McCue), Heggs, Donovan.

*Darlington, Burnley, Port Vale, Swansea C received
byes.*

SECOND ROUND

Hull C (0) 0
Chesterfield (0) 1 *(Hebberd)* 1833
Hull C: Wilson; Brown, Hunter, Mail, Wilcox, Abbott, Norton, Atkinson, Carruthers, Windass, Jenkinson (France).
Chesterfield: Goldring; Lemon, Carr, Hebberd, Rogers, Brien, Cash, Williams (Morris), Lancaster, Dyche, Kennedy.

Port Vale (1) 4 *(Foyle, Glover 2 (1 pen), Taylor)*
Fulham (1) 3 *(Pike, Eckhardt, Hails) aet* 3581
Port Vale: Musselwhite; Sandeman, Sulley, Walker, Swan, Glover, Kerr (Kent), Aspin, Cross (Van der Laan), Foyle, Taylor.
Fulham: Harrison; Newson, Pike, Eckhardt, Ferney (Tierling), Thomas, Cooper, Marshall, Hails, Baah (Kelly P), Onwere.

Scarborough (1) 3 *(Foreman, Mooney, Jules)*
Bradford C (3) 4 *(McHugh, McCarthy 3)* 740
Scarborough: Ford; Barrow (Hirst), McGee, Lee, Ormsby, Curran, Ashdjian (Lightbourne), Himsworth, Mooney, Foreman, Jules.
Bradford C: Whitehead; Duxbury M, Jenkins, Duxbury L, Blake, Oliver, Jewell, Hoyle, McCarthy, McHugh, Reid.

Stockport Co (1) 1 *(Preece)*
Hartlepool U (0) 0 2383
Stockport Co: Edwards; Todd, Williams P, Frain, Barras, Gannon, Miller, Ward, Williams PA, McCord (Beaumont), Preece.
Hartlepool U: Talia; Cross R, Cross P, Gilchrist, MacPhail, Emerson, Johnrose, Olsson, Saville, Honour, Southall (Gallacher).

Leyton Orient (1) 4 *(Carter, Harvey, Jones, Howard)*
Wrexham (1) 1 *(Watkin)* 1513
Leyton Orient: Heald; Bellamy, Howard, Carter (Day), Kitchen, Ludden, Taylor (Otto), Jones, Warren, Benstock, Harvey.
Wrexham: Morris; Jones (Phillips), Hardy, Owen, Sertori, Pejic, Bennett (Paskin), Lake, Connolly, Watkin, Cross.

18 JAN

Brighton & HA (1) 4 *(Walker, Nogan, Chivers, Kennedy)*
Walsall (0) 2 *(Ollerenshaw, Cecere) aet* 1577
Brighton & HA: Beeney; Chivers, Chapman, Wilkins, Foster, McCarthy, Crumplin (Codner), Kennedy, Nogan, Munday, Walker.
Walsall: Gayle; Knight, Statham, Methven, Williams, Smith (Ryder), Ollerenshaw (Parker), Reece, Marsh, Cecere, MacDonald.

Blackpool (1) 1 *(Gouck)*
Burnley (0) 3 *(Conroy 2, Farrell)* 2979
Blackpool: Martin; Davies, Thornber, Horner, Briggs, Gore, Leitch (Bonner), Sinclair, Bamber, Gouck, Eyres.
Burnley: Beresford; Measham, Jakub, Davis, Pender, Deary, Donowa, Randall (Farrell), Eli, Conroy, Harper.

Cardiff C (1) 1 *(Blake)*
Swansea C (0) 2 *(Legg, Hayes) aet* 13,516
Cardiff C: Ward; James, Searle, Matthews, Perry, Ratcliffe, Ramsey (Brazil), Richardson, Stant, Blake, Griffiths (Bird).
Swansea C: Freestone; Lyttle, Jenkins (Ford), Walker, Harris, Chapple, Hayes, Wimbleton (McFarlane), West, Cornforth, Legg.

Darlington (1) 3 *(Mardenborough, Dobie 2)*
Bolton W (3) 4 *(Walker 2, Lee, Kelly) aet* 1265
Darlington: Prudhoe; Fickling, Pickering, Gregan, Parkin, O'Shaughnessy, Mardenborough, Toman (Gaughan), Juryeff (Isaacs), Dobie, Dowson.
Bolton W: Branagan, Brown P, Burke, Lee, Seagraves, Winstanley, Green (Storer), Kelly, Walker (Reeves), McGinlay, Patterson.

Northampton T (0) 4 *(McParland 2, Scott, Bell)*
Hereford U (0) 0 1962
Northampton T: Richardson; Parsons, Curtis, Harmon, Angus, Terry, Burnham, Scott, Bell, Brown (Beavon), McParland (Wilkin).
Hereford U: Judge; Fry, Devine, Downs, Titterton, Anderson, Hall, Jones, Pickard (Theodosiou), Brain, Nicholson (May).

Rochdale (0) 0
Scunthorpe U (0) 0 1046
Rochdale: Rose; Thackeray, Parker, Reid (Graham), Reeves, Jones, Ryan, Payne, Flounders (Howard), Whitehall, Bowden.
Scunthorpe U: Samways; Joyce, Stevenson, Martin, Elliott, Humphries, Alexander, Daws, Helliwell (White), Greaves, Buckley.
Abandoned 87 minutes; floodlight failure.

Rotherham U (3) 3 *(Goodwin, Cunningham, Hazel)*
Wigan Ath (2) 3 *(Powell 2, Johnson)* 1704
Rotherham U: Mercer; Pickering, Hutchings, Banks, Johnson, Law, Hazel (Howard), Goodwin (Wilder), Cunningham, Goater, Barrick.
Wigan Ath: Adkins; Appleton, Tankard, Johnson, Pilling (Sharratt), Langley, Skipper, Powell, Woods, Cooper, Griffiths (Brolly).
aet; Wigan Ath won 5-4 on penalties.

20 JAN

Huddersfield T (2) 3 *(Barnett, Dunn, O'Regan (pen))*
Doncaster R (0) 0 1535
Huddersfield T: Elliott; Parsley, Charlton, Robinson, Wright, Jackson, Barnett, O'Regan, Roberts, Dunn (Starbuck), Onuora.
Doncaster R: Crichton; Rowe (Crosby), Prindiville, White C (Bennett), Richards, Hicks, Hewitt, White W, Douglas, Jeffrey, Gormley.

Stoke C (1) 4 *(Foley 3, Gleghorn)*
Barnet (0) 1 *(Carter)* 8892
Stoke C: Sinclair; Butler, Harbey, Wright, Overson, Gleghorn, Foley, Russell, Stein, Regis (Shaw), Beeston.
Barnet: Phillips; Stein E (Huxford), Naylor, Bodley, Barnett, Horton, Payne, Stein B (Carter), Bull, Evans, Hunt.

2 FEB

FIRST ROUND

Torquay U (0) 2 *(Hall, Hodges)*
Plymouth Arg (1) 1 *(Marshall)*　　　　2423
Torquay U: Blackwell; Gardiner, Davis, Lewis, Moore, Hodges, Hall, Foster, Darby, Trollope, Colcombe.
Plymouth Arg: Shilton; McCall (Poole), Morgan, Hill, Morrison, Burrows (Adcock), Joyce, Castle, Nugent, Marshall, Dalton.

SECOND ROUND

Rochdale (1) 1 *(Graham)*
Scunthorpe U (1) 2 *(Daws 2)*　　　　1312
Rochdale: Rose; Parker (Butler), Graham, Doyle, Reeves, Jones, Ryan, Mulrain, Flounders, Whitehall, Howard (Anders).
Scunthorpe U: Samways; Joyce, Stevenson, Martin, Elliott, Humphries, Buckley, Daws, Helliwell, Alexander, Farrell.

AREA QUARTER-FINALS

Bradford C (1) 3 *(Williams 3 (1 pen))*
Stockport Co (3) 4 *(Ward 2, Francis 2)*　　2790
Bradford C: Whitehead; Williams, Heseltine, Duxbury L, Blake (Stapleton), Oliver, Jewell, Duxbury M, Torpey, McHugh, Reid.
Stockport Co: Edwards; Todd, Williams P, Frain, Miller, Williams B, Gannon, Ward, Francis, Beaumont, Preece.

Chesterfield (2) 3 *(Lancaster 3 (1 pen))*
Burnley (0) 0　　　　3314
Chesterfield: Barber; Dyche, Carr, Hebberd, Brien, Rogers, Cash (Fee), Norris, Lancaster, Turnbull (Morris), Kennedy.
Burnley: Beresford; Measham, Jakub, Davis, Pender, Deary, Donowa (Monington), Farrell, Heath, Conroy, Harper.

Huddersfield T (2) 3 *(Roberts, Stubbs (og), Stuart)*
Bolton W (0) 0　　　　2996
Huddersfield T: Elliott; Parsley, Charlton, Dunn (Onuora), Dyson, Jackson, Barnett, O'Regan, Roberts, Starbuck, Stuart.
Bolton W: Branagan; Brown P, Burke, Lee, Seagraves, Stubbs, Storer, Kelly (McAteer), Walker, McGinlay, Patterson (Darby).

Port Vale (2) 4 *(Swan, Smith, Kerr, Walker)*
Northampton T (1) 2 *(Scott, Chard)*　　4834
Port Vale: Musselwhite; Sandeman (Kent), Sulley, Walker, Swan, Smith, Jeffers, Kerr, Cross, Houchen, Taylor.
Northampton T: Richardson; Beavon, Curtis, Harmon, Angus, Terry, Burnham, Scott, Bell, Chard (Parsons), Wilkin.

SECOND ROUND

9 FEB

Exeter C (0) 2 *(Hodge, Tonge)*
Reading (0) 2 *(Quinn 2)*　　　　1677
Exeter C: Miller; Hiley, Cooper, Bailey, Daniels, Brown, Harris, Tonge (Taylor), Jepson, Dolan, Hodge.
Reading: Francis; Holzman (Lambert), Hopkins, Jackson, Williams, Parkinson, Gooding, Dillon, Quinn, Gray, Taylor.
aet; Exeter C won 4-2 on penalties.

WBA (0) 2 *(Donovan 2)*
Torquay U (1) 1 *(Muir)*　　　　5216
WBA: Lange; Fereday, Darton, Hackett (Heggs), Hunter (Coldicott), Strodder, Speedie, Hamilton, Taylor, McNally, Donovan.
Torquay U: Blackwell (Darby); Salman, Johnson (Trollope), Lewis, Moore, Hodges, Hall, Foster, Muir, Joyce, Colcombe.

AREA QUARTER-FINALS

Wigan Ath (1) 2 *(Langley, Sharratt)*
Scunthorpe U (0) 1 *(Humphries (pen))*　　1512
Wigan Ath: Adkins; Appleton, Tankard, Johnson, Pilling, Langley, Skipper, Sharratt, Jones, Woods, Griffiths.
Scunthorpe U: Samways; Joyce, Stevenson, Alexander, Martin, Humphries, Buckley (McCullagh), White, Helliwell, Daws (Greaves), Farrell.

16 FEB

Swansea C (0) 1 *(West (pen))*
Leyton Orient (0) 0　　　　3339
Swansea C: Freestone; Lyttle, Jenkins (Coughlin), Walker, Harris, Ford, McFarlane, Bowen, West, Cornforth, Legg.
Leyton Orient: Heald; Bellamy, Howard, Carter, Whitbread, Ludden, Ryan, Achampong, Hackett, Otto, Cooper.

17 FEB

Stoke C (0) 2 *(Stein 2)*
WBA (0) 1 *(Taylor)*　　　　17,568
Stoke C: Sinclair; Butler, Harbey, Cranson, Sandford, Gleghorn, Ware, Russell (Regis), Stein, Kevan, Shaw.
WBA: Naylor; Fereday (Robson), Lilwall, Bradley, Raven, Strodder, Speedie, Hamilton, Taylor, Shakespeare, Donovan.

17 FEB

Brighton & HA (0) 0
Exeter C (0) 1 *(Daniels)*　　　　1875
Brighton & HA: Beeney; Munday, Chapman, Wilkins, McCarthy, Foster, Crumplin (Kennedy), Edwards, Nogan, Codner, Walker.
Exeter C: Miller; Hiley, Cooper, Bailey, Daniels, Redwood, Tonge, Taylor, Dolan, McIntyre, Hodge.

SOUTH SEMI-FINAL

23 FEB

Swansea C (1) 2 *(Daniels (og), Legg)*
Exeter C (2) 3 *(Dolan, McIntyre, Jepson) aet* 4971
Swansea C: Freestone; Lyttle, Jenkins, Walker,
Harris, Ford (Hayes), Coughlin, Bowen, West
(McFarlane), Cornforth, Legg.
Exeter C: Miller; Hiley, Cook, Bailey, Daniels,
Brown, Taylor (Tonge), McIntyre, Jepson, Dolan,
Hodge.

NORTH SEMI-FINALS

Stockport Co (1) 2 *(Williams PA, Francis)*
Chesterfield (1) 1 *(Morris)* 4613
Stockport Co: Edwards; Williams B, Williams P,
McCord, Miller, Finley, Gannon, Carstairs, Francis,
Beaumont, Williams PA.
Chesterfield: Barber; Rogers, Carr, Fee, Brien,
Whitehead, Morris, Williams (Norris), Lancaster,
Turnbull, Hebberd.

Wigan Ath (2) 5 *(Woods 3, Griffiths, Daley)*
Huddersfield T (0) 2 *(Roberts, Starbuck)* 2978
Wigan Ath: Adkins; Connelly, Tankard, Johnson
(Pilling), Appleton, Langley, Skipper, Sharratt, Daley
(Powell), Woods, Griffiths.
Huddersfield T: Elliott; Parsley, Charlton, Robinson,
Dyson, Onuora (Dunn), Barnett, O'Regan, Roberts,
Starbuck, Stuart.

SOUTH SEMI-FINAL

3 MAR

Stoke C (0) 0
Port Vale (0) 1 *(Van der Laan)* 22,267
Stoke C: Sinclair; Butler, Sandford, Cranson,
Overson, Gleghorn, Foley (Russell), Ware, Shaw,
Stein, Beeston.
Port Vale: Musselwhite; Aspin, Sulley, Van der Laan,
Billing, Glover, Kent, Kerr, Cross, Foyle (Porter),
Taylor.

AREA FINALS First Leg

16 MAR

Port Vale (1) 2 *(Kerr (pen), Taylor)*
Exeter C (1) 1 *(Bailey)* 8866
Port Vale: Musselwhite; Kent, Sulley, Walker, Swan,
Glover, Kerr (Houchen), Van der Laan, Cross,
Jeffers, Taylor.
Exeter C: Miller; Brown, Cook (Tonge), Bailey,
Daniels, Whiston, Redwood, McIntyre, Jepson,
Moran (Dolan), Hodge.

Wigan Ath (1) 2 *(Daley, Griffiths)*
Stockport Co (0) 1 *(Gannon)* 4136
Wigan Ath: Pennock; Connelly (Sharratt), Tankard,
Johnson, (Robertson), Jones, Langley, Skipper,
Woods, Daley, Powell, Griffiths.
Stockport Co: Edwards; Knowles (Wallace), Williams
P (Carstairs), Frain, Miller, Finley, Gannon, Ward,
Francis, Todd, Williams PA.

AREA FINALS Second Leg

20 APR

Stockport Co (1) 2 *(Ward, Francis)*
Wigan Ath (0) 0 6315
Stockport Co: Edwards; Todd, Carstairs, Frain,
Miller, Barras, Gannon, Ward (Williams P), Francis,
Beaumont, Duffield.
Wigan Ath: Adkins; Appleton, Tankard, Pilling
(O'Brien), Robertson (Sharratt), Langley, Skipper,
Doolan, Daley, Nugent, Griffiths.
(Stockport Co won 3-2 on aggregate)

21 APR

Exeter C (0) 1 *(Minett)*
Port Vale (0) 1 *(Slaven)* 7060
Exeter C: Miller; Harris, McIntyre, Bailey, Daniels,
Brown, Bond, Minett, Moran (Phillips), Dolan,
Hodge.
Port Vale: Musselwhite; Aspin, Porter, Kent, Swan,
Glover, Slaven, Van der Laan, Cross (Foyle), Kerr,
Taylor.
(Port Vale won 3-2 on aggregate)

FINAL at Wembley

22 MAY

Port Vale (2) 2 *(Kerr, Slaven)*
Stockport Co (0) 1 *(Francis)* 35,885
Port Vale: Musselwhite; Aspin, Kent, Porter, Swan,
Glover, Slaven, Van der Laan (Billing), Foyle, Kerr,
Taylor.
Stockport Co: Edwards; Todd, Wallace, Finley,
Miller, Williams B, Gannon, Ward, Francis,
Beaumont (Preece), Duffield.
Referee: D. Elleray (Harrow).

FA CUP FINALS 1872–1993

1872 and 1874–92	Kennington Oval	1911	Replay at Old Trafford
1873	Lillie Bridge	1912	Replay at Bramall Lane
1886	Replay at Derby (Racecourse Ground)		
1893	Fallowfield, Manchester	1915	Old Trafford, Manchester
1894	Everton	1920–22	Stamford Bridge
1895–1914	Crystal Palace	1923 to date	Wembley
1901	Replay at Bolton	1970	Replay at Old Trafford
1910	Replay at Everton	1981	Replay at Wembley

Year	Winners	Runners-up	Score
1872	Wanderers	Royal Engineers	1-0
1873	Wanderers	Oxford University	2-0
1874	Oxford University	Royal Engineers	2-0
1875	Royal Engineers	Old Etonians	2-0 (after 1-1 draw aet)
1876	Wanderers	Old Etonians	3-0 (after 1-1 draw aet)
1877	Wanderers	Oxford University	2-1 (aet)
1878	Wanderers*	Royal Engineers	3-1
1879	Old Etonians	Clapham R	1-0
1880	Clapham R	Oxford University	1-0
1881	Old Carthusians	Old Etonians	3-0
1882	Old Etonians	Blackburn R	1-0
1883	Blackburn Olympic	Old Etonians	2-1 (aet)
1884	Blackburn R	Queen's Park, Glasgow	2-1
1885	Blackburn R	Queen's Park, Glasgow	2-0
1886	Blackburn R†	WBA	2-0 (after 0-0 draw)
1887	Aston Villa	WBA	2-0
1888	WBA	Preston NE	2-1
1889	Preston NE	Wolverhampton W	3-0
1890	Blackburn R	Sheffield W	6-1
1891	Blackburn R	Notts Co	3-1
1892	WBA	Aston Villa	3-0
1893	Wolverhampton W	Everton	1-0
1894	Notts Co	Bolton W	4-1
1895	Aston Villa	WBA	1-0
1896	Sheffield W	Wolverhampton W	2-1
1897	Aston Villa	Everton	3-2
1898	Nottingham F	Derby Co	3-1
1899	Sheffield U	Derby Co	4-1
1900	Bury	Southampton	4-0
1901	Tottenham H	Sheffield U	3-1 (after 2-2 draw)
1902	Sheffield U	Southampton	2-1 (after 1-1 draw)
1903	Bury	Derby Co	6-0
1904	Manchester C	Bolton W	1-0
1905	Aston Villa	Newcastle U	2-0
1906	Everton	Newcastle U	1-0
1907	Sheffield W	Everton	2-1
1908	Wolverhampton W	Newcastle U	3-1
1909	Manchester U	Bristol C	1-0
1910	Newcastle U	Barnsley	2-0 (after 1-1 draw)
1911	Bradford C	Newcastle U	1-0 (after 0-0 draw)
1912	Barnsley	WBA	1-0 (aet, after 0-0 draw)
1913	Aston Villa	Sunderland	1-0
1914	Burnley	Liverpool	1-0
1915	Sheffield U	Chelsea	3-0
1920	Aston Villa	Huddersfield T	1-0 (aet)
1921	Tottenham H	Wolverhampton W	1-0
1922	Huddersfield T	Preston NE	1-0
1923	Bolton W	West Ham U	2-0
1924	Newcastle U	Aston Villa	2-0
1925	Sheffield U	Cardiff C	1-0
1926	Bolton W	Manchester C	1-0
1927	Cardiff C	Arsenal	1-0
1928	Blackburn R	Huddersfield T	3-1
1929	Bolton W	Portsmouth	2-0
1930	Arsenal	Huddersfield T	2-0
1931	WBA	Birmingham	2-1
1932	Newcastle U	Arsenal	2-1
1933	Everton	Manchester C	3-0
1934	Manchester C	Portsmouth	2-1
1935	Sheffield W	WBA	4-2
1936	Arsenal	Sheffield U	1-0
1937	Sunderland	Preston NE	3-1
1938	Preston NE	Huddersfield T	1-0 (aet)
1939	Portsmouth	Wolverhampton W	4-1
1946	Derby Co	Charlton Ath	4-1 (aet)
1947	Charlton Ath	Burnley	1-0 (aet)
1948	Manchester U	Blackpool	4-2
1949	Wolverhampton W	Leicester C	3-1
1950	Arsenal	Liverpool	2-0
1951	Newcastle U	Blackpool	2-0
1952	Newcastle U	Arsenal	1-0

Year	Winners	Runners-up	Score
1953	Blackpool	Bolton W	4-3
1954	WBA	Preston NE	3-2
1955	Newcastle U	Manchester C	3-1
1956	Manchester C	Birmingham C	3-1
1957	Aston Villa	Manchester U	2-1
1958	Bolton W	Manchester U	2-0
1959	Nottingham F	Luton T	2-1
1960	Wolverhampton W	Blackburn R	3-0
1961	Tottenham H	Leicester C	2-0
1962	Tottenham H	Burnley	3-1
1963	Manchester U	Leicester C	3-1
1964	West Ham U	Preston NE	3-2
1965	Liverpool	Leeds U	2-1 (aet)
1966	Everton	Sheffield W	3-2
1967	Tottenham H	Chelsea	2-1
1968	WBA	Everton	1-0 (aet)
1969	Manchester C	Leicester C	1-0
1970	Chelsea	Leeds U	2-1 (aet)
	(after 2-2 draw, after extra time, at Wembley)		
1971	Arsenal	Liverpool	2-1 (aet)
1972	Leeds U	Arsenal	1-0
1973	Sunderland	Leeds U	1-0
1974	Liverpool	Newcastle U	3-0
1975	West Ham U	Fulham	2-0
1976	Southampton	Manchester U	1-0
1977	Manchester U	Liverpool	2-1
1978	Ipswich T	Arsenal	1-0
1979	Arsenal	Manchester U	3-2
1980	West Ham U	Arsenal	1-0
1981	Tottenham H	Manchester C	3-2
	(after 1-1 draw, after extra time, at Wembley)		
1982	Tottenham H	QPR	1-0
	(after 1-1 draw, after extra time, at Wembley)		
1983	Manchester U	Brighton & HA	4-0
	(after 2-2 draw, after extra time, at Wembley)		
1984	Everton	Watford	2-0
1985	Manchester U	Everton	1-0 (aet)
1986	Liverpool	Everton	3-1
1987	Coventry C	Tottenham H	3-2 (aet)
1988	Wimbledon	Liverpool	1-0
1989	Liverpool	Everton	3-2 (aet)
1990	Manchester U	Crystal Palace	1-0
	(after 3-3 draw, after extra time, at Wembley)		
1991	Tottenham H	Nottingham F	2-1 (aet)
1992	Liverpool	Sunderland	2-0
1993	Arsenal	Sheffield W	2-1 (aet)
	(after 1-1 draw, after extra time, at Wembley)		

* Won outright, but restored to the Football Association.
† A special trophy was awarded for third consecutive win.

FA CUP WINS

Tottenham H 8, Aston Villa 7, Manchester U 7, Arsenal 6, Blackburn R 6, Newcastle U 6, Liverpool 5, The Wanderers 5, WBA 5, Bolton W 4, Everton 4, Manchester C 4, Sheffield U 4, Wolverhampton W 4, Sheffield W 3, West Ham U 3, Bury 2, Nottingham F 2, Old Etonians 2, Preston NE 2, Sunderland 2, Barnsley 1, Blackburn Olympic 1, Blackpool 1, Bradford C 1, Burnley 1, Cardiff C 1, Charlton Ath 1, Chelsea 1, Clapham R 1, Coventry C 1, Derby Co 1, Huddersfield T 1, Ipswich T 1, Leeds U 1, Notts Co 1, Old Carthusians 1, Oxford University 1, Portsmouth 1, Royal Engineers 1, Southampton 1, Wimbledon 1.

APPEARANCES IN FINALS

Arsenal 12, Everton 11, Manchester U 11, Newcastle U 11, WBA 10, Liverpool 10, Aston Villa 9, Tottenham H 9, Blackburn R 8, Manchester C 8, Wolverhampton W 8, Bolton W 7, Preston NE 7, Old Etonians 6, Sheffield U 6, Sheffield W 6, Huddersfield T 5, *The Wanderers 5, Derby Co 4, Leeds U 4, Leicester C 4, Oxford University 4, Royal Engineers 4, Sunderland 4, West Ham U 4, Blackpool 3, Burnley 3, Chelsea 3, Nottingham F 3, Portsmouth 3, Southampton 3, Barnsley 2, Birmingham C 2, *Bury 2, Cardiff C 2, Charlton Ath 2, Clapham R 2, Notts Co 2, Queen's Park (Glasgow) 2, *Blackburn Olympic 1, *Bradford C 1, Brighton & HA 1, Bristol C 1, *Coventry C 1, Crystal Palace 1, Fulham 1, *Ipswich T 1, Luton T 1, *Old Carthusians 1, QPR 1, Watford 1, *Wimbledon 1.

* Denotes undefeated.

APPEARANCES IN SEMI-FINALS

Everton 22, Liverpool 19, WBA 19, Arsenal 18, Manchester U 18, Aston Villa 17, Blackburn R 16, Sheffield W 16, Tottenham H 14, Derby Co 13, Newcastle U 13, Wolverhampton W 13, Bolton W 12, Nottingham F 12, Sheffield U 11, Sunderland 11, Chelsea 10, Manchester C 10, Preston NE 10, Southampton 10, Birmingham C 9, Burnley 8, Leeds U 8, Huddersfield T 7, Leicester C 7, Old Etonians 6, Oxford University 6, West Ham U 6, Fulham 5, Notts Co 5, Portsmouth 5, The Wanderers 5, Queen's Park (Glasgow) 4, Royal Engineers 4, Blackpool 3, Cardiff C 3, Clapham R 3, Ipswich T 3, Luton T 3, Millwall 3, Norwich C 3, Old Carthusians 3, Stoke C 3, The Swifts 3, Watford 3, Barnsley 2, Blackburn Olympic 2, Bristol C 2, Bury 2, Charlton Ath 2, Crystal Palace (professional club) 2, Grimsby T 2, Oldham Ath 2, Swansea T 2, Swindon T 2, Bradford C 1, Brighton & HA 1, Cambridge University 1, Coventry C 1, Crewe Alex 1, Crystal Palace (amateur club) 1, Darwen 1, Derby Junction 1, Glasgow R 1, Hull C 1, Marlow 1, Old Harrovians 1, Orient 1, Plymouth Arg 1, Port Vale 1, QPR 1, Reading 1, Shropshire W 1, Wimbledon 1, York C 1.

FA CUP FINALISTS 1872-1992

R: replay; aet: after extra time.

1871-72 THE WANDERERS R. de C. Welch; C. W. Alcock, M. P. Betts, A. G. Bonsor, E. E. Bowen, W. P. Crake, T. C. Hooman, E. Lubbock, A. C. Thompson, R. W. S. Vidal, C. H. R. Wollaston. (In alphabetical order.) *Scorer:* 'A. H. Chequer' (M. P. Betts).

1-0 ROYAL ENGINEERS Capt. Marindin; Capt. Merriman, Lieut. Addison; Lieut. Creswell, Lieut. Mitchell, Lieut. Renny-Tailyour; Lieut. Rich, Lieut. Goodwyn, Lieut. Muirhead, Lieut. Cotter, Lieut. Bogle.

1872-73 THE WANDERERS E. E. Bowen; C. M. Thompson, R. de C. Welch; Hon. A. F. Kinnaird, L. S. Howell, C. H. R. Wollaston; J. R. Sturgiss, Rev. H. H. Stewart, W. S. Kenyon-Slaney, R. K. Kingsford, A. G. Bonsor. *Scorers:* Kinnaird, Wollaston.

2-0 OXFORD UNIVERSITY A. Kirke-Smith; A. J. Leach, C. C. Mackarness; F. H. Birley; C. J. Longman, F. B. Chappell-Maddison; H. B. Cixon, W. B. Paton, R. W. S. Vidal, W. E. Sumner, C. J. Ottaway.

1873-74 OXFORD UNIVERSITY C. E. B. Neapean; C. C. Mackarness, F. H. Birley; F. T. Green, R. W. S. Vidal, C. J. Ottaway; R. H. Benson, F. J. Patton, W. S. Rawson, F. B. Chappell-Maddison, Rev. A. H. Johnson. *Scorers:* Mackarness, Patton.

2-0 ROYAL ENGINEERS Capt. Merriman; Major Marindin, Lieut. G. W. Addison; Lieut. G. C. Onslow, Lieut. H. G. Oliver, Lieut. T. Digby; Lieut. H. W. Renny-Tailyour, Lieut. H. E. Rawson, Lieut. J. E. Blackman, Lieut. A. K. Wood, Lieut. P. G. von Donop.

1874-75 ROYAL ENGINEERS Capt. Merriman; Lieut. G. H. Sim, Lieut. G. C. Onslow; Lieut. R. M. Ruck, Lieut. P. G. von Donop, Lieut. C. K. Wood; Lieut. H. E. Rawson, Lieut. R. H. Stafford, Capt. H. W. Renny-Tailyour, Lieut. Mein, Lieut. C. Wingfield Stratford. *Scorers:* (First match) Renny-Tailyour; (Second match) Renny-Tailyour, Stafford.

1-1 OLD ETONIANS Capt. E. H. Drummond-Moray; M. Farrer, E. Lubbock; F. H. Wilson, Hon. A. F.
aet Kinnaird, J. H. Stronge; F. J. Patton, C. E. Farmer, A. G. Bonsor, A. Lubbock, T. Hammond. (C. J.
R:2-0 Ottaway, W. S. Kenyon-Slaney, R. H. Benson and A. G. Thompson took part in the first match in place of A. Lubbock, T. Hammond, M. Farrer and Capt. E. H. Drummond-Moray.) *Scorer:* Bonsor.

1875-76 THE WANDERERS W. D. O. Greig; A. Stratford, W. Lindsay; F. B. C. Maddison, F. H. Birley, C. H. R. Wollaston; H. Heron, F. Heron, J. H. Edwards, J. Kenrick, T. Hughes. *Scorers:* (First match) Edwards; (Second match) Wollaston, Hughes 2.

1-1 OLD ETONIANS Q. Hogg; E. Lubbock, Hon. E. Lyttelton; M. G. Faner, Hon. A. F. Kinnaird, J. H.
aet Stronge; W. S. Kenyon-Slaney, Hon. A. Lyttelton, J. R. Sturgis, A. G. Bonsor, H. P. Allene. (C. Meysey,
R:3-0 A. C. Thompson and J. E. C. Welldon took part in the first match in place of J. H. Stronge, M. G. Faner and E. Lubbock.) *Scorer:* Bonsor.

1876-77 THE WANDERERS Hon. A. F. Kinnaird; W. Lindsay, A. Stratford; F. H. Birley, C. A. Denton, F. T. Green; H. Heron, T. Hughes, J. Kenrick, H. Wace, C. H. R. Wollaston. *Scorers:* Heron, Kenrick.

2-1 OXFORD UNIVERSITY E. H. Allington; J. Bain, O. R. Dunnell; J. H. Savory, A. H. Todd, E. W.
aet Waddington; P. H. Fernandez, A. F. Hills, H. S. Otter, E. H. Parry, W. S. Rawson. *Scorer:* Kinnaird (og).

1877-78 THE WANDERERS J. Kirkpatrick; A. Stratford, W. Lindsay; Hon. A. F. Kinnaird, F. T. Green, C. H. R. Wollaston; H. Heron, J. G. Wylie, H. Wace, C. A. Denton, J. Kenrick. *Scorers:* Kenrick 2, opponent own goal.

3-1 ROYAL ENGINEERS L. B. Friend; J. H. Cowan, W. J. Morris; C. B. Mayne, F. C. Heath, C. E. Haynes; M. Lindsay, R. B. Hedley, F. G. Bond, H. H. Barnet, O. E. Ruck. *Scorer:* unknown.

1878-79 OLD ETONIANS J. P. Hawtrey; E. Christian, L. Bury; Hon. A. F. Kinnaird, E. Lubbock, C. J. Clerke; N. Pares, H. C. Goodhart, H. Whitfield, J. B. T. Chevallier, H. Beaufoy. *Scorer:* Clerke.

1-0 CLAPHAM ROVERS R. H. Birkett; R. A. Ogilvie, E. Field; N. C. Bailey, J. F. M. Prinsep, F. L. Rawson; A. J. Stanley, S. W. Scott, H. S. Bevington, E. F. Growse, C. Keith-Falconer.

1879-80 CLAPHAM ROVERS R. H. Birkett; R. A. Ogilvie, E. Field; A. Weston, N. C. Bailey, H. Brougham; A. J. Stanley, F. Barry, F. J. Sparks, C. A. Lloyd-Jones, E. A. Ram. *Scorer:* Lloyd-Jones.

1-0 OXFORD UNIVERSITY P. C. Parr; C. W. Wilson, C. J. S. King; F. A. H. Phillips, B. Rogers, R. T. Heygate; G. B. Childs, J. Eyre, F. D. Crowdy, E. H. Hill, J. B. Lubbock.

1880-81 OLD CARTHUSIANS L. F. Gillett; W. H. Norris, E. G. Colvin; J. F. M. Prinsep, A. J. Vintcent, W. E. Hansell; L. M. Richards, W. R. Page, E. G. Wyngard, E. H. Parry, A. H. Todd. *Scorers:* Wyngard, Parry, Todd.

3-0 OLD ETONIANS J. F. P. Rawlinson; C. W. Foley, C. H. French; Hon. A. F. Kinnaird, R. B. Farrer, J. B. T. Chevallier; W. J. Anderson, H. C. Goodhart, R. H. Macaulay, H. Whitfield, P. C. Novelli.

1881-82 OLD ETONIANS J. F. P. Rawlinson; T. H. French, P. J. de Paravicini; Hon. A. F. Kinnaird, C. W. Foley, P. C. Novelli; A. T. R. Dunn, R. H. Macaulay, H. C. Goodhart, W. J. Anderson, J. B. T. Chevallier. *Scorer:* Anderson.

1-0 BLACKBURN ROVERS R. Howarth; H. McIntyre, F. Suter; H. Sharples, F. W. Hargreaves, J. Duckworth; J. Douglas, T. Strachan, J. Brown, G. Avery, J. Hargreaves.

1882-83 BLACKBURN OLYMPIC T. Hacking; J. T. Ward, S. A. Warburton; T. Gibson, W. Astley, J. Hunter; T. Dewhurst, A. Matthews, G. Wilson, J. Costley, J. Yates. *Scorers:* Costley, Matthews.

2-1 OLD ETONIANS J. F. P. Rawlinson, T. H. French, P. J. de Paravicini; Hon. A. F. Kinnaird, C. W.
aet Foley, J. B. T. Chevallier; W. J. Anderson, R. H. Macaulay, H. C. Goodhart, A. T. B. Dunn, H. W. Bainbridge. *Scorer:* Goodhart.

1883-84 BLACKBURN ROVERS H. J. Arthur; J. Beverley, F. Suter; H. McIntyre, J. Hargreaves, J. H. Forrest; J. M. Lofthouse, J. Douglas, J. Sowerbutts, J. Inglis, J. Brown. *Scorers:* Brown, Forrest.

2-1 QUEEN'S PARK G. Gillespie; W. Arnott, J. MacDonald; C. Campbell, J. J. Gow, W. Anderson; W. W. Watt, Dr Smith, W. Harrower, D. S. Allan, R. M. Christie. *Scorer:* Christie.

1884-85 BLACKBURN ROVERS H. J. Arthur; R. G. Turner, F. Suter; H. McIntyre, G. Haworth, J. H. Forrest; J. M. Lofthouse, J. Douglas, J. Brown, H. E. Fecitt, J. Sowerbutts. *Scorers:* Forrest, Brown.

2-0 QUEEN'S PARK G. Gillespie; W. Arnott, W. Macleod; C. Campbell, J. MacDonald, A. Hamilton; W. Anderson, W. Sellar, W. Gray, N. McWhannel, D. S. Allan.

1885-86 BLACKBURN ROVERS H. J. Arthur; Turner, Suter; Douglas, Forrest, McIntyre; Walton, Strachan, Brown, Fecitt, J. Sowerbutts. (Heyes played in the first match at the Oval, but Walton took his place in the
0-0 replay.) *Scorers:* Brown, Sowerbutts.

R:2-0 WEST BROMWICH ALBION Roberts; H. Green, H. Bell; Horton, Perry, Timmins; Woodhall, T. Green, Bayliss, Loach, G. Bell.
1886–87 ASTON VILLA Warner; Coulton, Simmonds; Yates, Dawson, Burton; Davis, Brown, Hunter, Vaughton, Hodgetts. *Scorers:* Hunter, Hodgetts.
2-0 WEST BROMWICH ALBION Roberts; H. Green, Aldridge; Horton, Perry, Timmins; Woodhall, T. Green, Bayliss, Paddock, Pearson.
1887–88 WEST BROMWICH ALBION Roberts; Aldridge, Green; Horton, Perry, Timmins; Bassett, Woodhall, Bayliss, Wilson, Pearson. *Scorers:* Woodhall, Bayliss.
2-1 PRESTON NORTH END Dr R. H. Mills-Roberts; Howarth, N. J. Ross; Holmes, Russell, Graham; Gordon, J. Ross, J. Goodall, F. Dewhurst, Drummond. *Scorer:* Goodall.
1888–89 PRESTON NORTH END Dr R. H. Mills-Roberts; Howarth, Holmes; Drummond, Russell, Graham; Gordon, Ross, J. Goodall, F. Dewhurst, Thompson. *Scorers:* Dewhurst, Ross, Thompson.
3-0 WOLVERHAMPTON WANDERERS Baynton; Baugh, Mason; Fletcher, Allen, Lowder; Hunter, Wykes, Broodie, Wood, Knight.
1889–90 BLACKBURN ROVERS J. K. Horne; Southworth (Jas.), Forbes; Barton, Dewar, Forrest; Lofthouse, Campbell, Southworth (John), Walton, Townley. *Scorers:* Dewar, Southworth (John), Lofthouse, Townley 3.
6-1 SHEFFIELD WEDNESDAY Smith (J.); Brayshaw, H. Morley; Dungworth, Betts, Waller; Ingram, Woodhouse, Bennett, Mumford, Cawley. *Scorer:* Bennett.
1890–91 BLACKBURN ROVERS Pennington; Brandon, J. Forbes; Barton, Dewar, Forrest; Lofthouse, Walton, Southworth (John), Hall, Townley. *Scorers:* Dewar, Southworth, Townley.
3-1 NOTTS COUNTY Thraves; Ferguson, Hendry; H. Osborne, Calderhead, Shelton; A. McGregor, McInnes, Oswald, Locker, H. B. Daft. *Scorer:* Oswald.
1891–92 WEST BROMWICH ALBION Reader; Nicholson, McCulloch; Reynolds, Perry, Groves; Bassett, McLeod, Nicholls, Pearson, Geddes. *Scorers:* Geddes, Nicholls, Reynolds.
3-0 ASTON VILLA Warner; Evans, Cox; H. Devey, Cowan, Baird; Athersmith, J. Devey, Dickson, Campbell, Hodgetts.
1892–93 WOLVERHAMPTON WANDERERS Rose; Baugh, Swift; Malpass, Allen, Kinsey; R. Topham, Wykes, Butcher, Wood, Griffin. *Scorer:* Allen.
1-0 EVERTON Williams; Howarth, Kelso; Stewart, Holt, Boyle; Latta, Gordon, Maxwell, Chadwick, Milward.
1893–94 NOTTS COUNTY Toone; Harper, Hendry; Bramley, Calderhead, A. Shelton; Watson, Donnelly, Logan, Bruce, H. B. Daft. *Scorers:* Watson, Logan 3.
4-1 BOLTON WANDERERS Sutcliffe; Somerville, Jones; Gardiner, Paton, Hughes; Dickinson, Wilson, Tannahill, Bentley, Cassidy. *Scorer:* Cassidy.
1894–95 ASTON VILLA Wilkes; Spencer, Welford; Reynolds, Cowan (Jas.), Russell; Athersmith, Chatt, J. Devey, Hodgetts, S. Smith. *Scorer:* Devey.
1-0 WEST BROMWICH ALBION Reader; Williams, Horton; Taggart, Higgins, T. Perry; Bassett, McLeod, Richards, Hutchinson, Banks.
1895–96 SHEFFIELD WEDNESDAY Massey; Earp, Langley; H. Brandon, Crawshaw, Petrie; Brash, Brady, L. Bell, Davis, Spiksley. *Scorer:* Spiksley 2.
2-1 WOLVERHAMPTON WANDERERS Tennant; Baugh, Dunn; Owen, Malpass, Griffiths; Tonks, Henderson, Beats, Wood, Black. *Scorer:* Black.
1896–97 ASTON VILLA Whitehouse; Spencer, Evans; Reynolds, Cowan (Jas.), Crabtree; Athersmith, J. Devey, Campbell, Wheldon, Cowan (John). *Scorers:* Campbell, Wheldon, Crabtree.
3-2 EVERTON Menham; Meecham, Storrier; Boyle, Holt, Stewart; Taylor, Bell, Hartley, Chadwick, Milward. *Scorers:* Boyle, Bell.
1897–98 NOTTINGHAM FOREST Allsop; Richie, Scott; Forman (Frank), McPherson, Wragg; McInnes, Richards, Benbow, Capes, Spouncer. *Scorers:* Capes 2, McPherson.
3-1 DERBY COUNTY Fryer; Methven, Leiper; Cox, A. Goodall, Turner; J. Goodall, Bloomer. Boag, Stevenson, McOueen. *Scorer:* Bloomer.
1898–99 SHEFFIELD UNITED Foulke; Thickett, Boyle; Johnson, Morren, Needham; Bennett, Beers, Hedley, Almond, Priest. *Scorers:* Bennett, Beers, Almond, Priest.
4-1 DERBY COUNTY Fryer; Methven, Staley; Cox, Paterson, May; Arkesden, Bloomer, Boag, McDonald, Allen. *Scorer:* Boag.
1899– BURY Thompson; Darrock, Davidson; Pray, Leeming, Ross; Richards, Wood, McLuckie, Sagar, Plant.
1900 *Scorers:* McLuckie 2, Wood, Plant.
4-0 SOUTHAMPTON Robinson; Meehan, Durber; Meston, Chadwick, Petrie; Turner, Yates, Farrell, Wood, Milward.
1900–01 TOTTENHAM HOTSPUR Clawley; Erentz, Tait; Norris, Hughes, Jones; Smith, Cameron, Brown, Copeland, Kirwan. *Scorers:* (First match) Brown 2; (Second match) Cameron, Smith, Brown.
2-2 SHEFFIELD UNITED Foulke; Thickett, Boyle; Johnson, Morren, Needham; Bennett, Field, Hedley, *R*:3-1 Priest, Lipsham. *Scorers:* (First match) Bennett, Priest; (Second match) Priest.
1901–02 SHEFFIELD UNITED Foulke; Thickett, Boyle; Needham, Wilkinson, Johnson; Barnes, Common, Hedley, Priest, Lipsham. (Bennett was injured in the first match and Barnes took his place in the replay.) *Scorers:* (First match) Common; (Second match) Hedley, Barnes.
1-1 SOUTHAMPTON Robinson; C. B. Fry, Molyneux; Meston, Bowman, Lee; A. Turner, Wood, Brown, *R*:2-1 Chadwick, J. Turner. *Scorers:* (First match) Wood; (Second match) Brown.
1902–03 BURY Monteith; Lindsey, McEwen; Johnson, Thorpe, Ross; Richards, Wood, Sagar, Leeming, Plant. *Scorers:* Ross, Sagar, Leeming 2, Wood, Plant.
6-0 DERBY COUNTY Fryer; Methven, Morris; Warren, A. Goodall, May; Warrington, York, Boag, Richards, Davis.
1903–04 MANCHESTER CITY Hillman; McMahon, Burgess; Frost, Hynds, S. B. Ashworth; Meredith, Livingstone, Gillespie, A. Turnbull, Booth. *Scorer:* Meredith.
1-0 BOLTON WANDERERS D. Davies; Brown, Struthers; Clifford, Greenhaigh, Freebairn; Stokes, Marsh, Yenson, White, Taylor.
1904–05 ASTON VILLA George; Spencer, Miles; Pearson, Leake, Windmill; Brawn, Garratty, Hampton, Bache, Hall. *Scorer:* Hampton 2.
2-0 NEWCASTLE UNTED Lawrence; McCombie, Carr; Gardner, Aitken, McWilliam; Rutherford, Howie, Appleyard, Veitch, Gosnell.

1905–06 EVERTON Scott; W. Balmer, Crelly; Makepeace, Taylor, Abbott; Sharp, Bolton, Young, Settle, H. P. Hardman. *Scorer:* Young.
1-0 NEWCASTLE UNITED Lawrence; McCombie, Carr; Gardner, Aitken, McWilliam; Rutherford, Howie, Veitch, Orr, Gosnell.
1906–07 SHEFFIELD WEDNESDAY Lyall; Layton, Burton; Brittleton, Crawshaw, Bartlett; Chapman, Bradshaw, Wilson, Stewart, Simpson. *Scorers:* Stewart, Simpson.
2-1 EVERTON Scott; W. Balmer, R. Balmer; Makepeace, Taylor, Abbott; Sharp, Bolton, Young, Settle, H. P. Hardman. *Scorer:* Sharp.
1907–08 WOLVERHAMPTON WANDERERS Lunn; Jones, Collins; Rev. K. R. G. Hunt, Wooldridge, Bishop; Harrison, Shelton, Hedley, Radford, Pedley. *Scorers:* Hunt, Hedley, Harrison.
3-1 NEWCASTLE UNITED Lawrence; McCracken, Pudan; Gardner, Veitch, McWilliam; Rutherford, Howie, Appleyard, Speedie, Wilson. *Scorer:* Howie.
1908–09 MANCHESTER UNITED Moger; Stacey, Hayes; Duckworth, Roberts, Bell; Meredith, Halse, J. Turnbull, A. Turnbull, Wall. *Scorer:* A. Turnbull.
1-0 BRISTOL CITY Clay; Annan, Cottle; Hanlin, Wedlock, Spear; Staniforth, Hardy, Gilligan, Burton, Hilton.
1909–10 NEWCASTLE UNITED Lawrence; McCracken, Carr; Veitch, Low, McWilliam; Rutherford, Howie, Shepherd, Higgins, Wilson. (Whitson was injured in the first match and Carr took his place in the replay.) *Scorers:* (First match) Rutherford; (Second match) Shepherd 2 (1 pen).
1-1 BARNSLEY Mearns; Downs, Ness; Glendinning, Boyle, Utley; Bartrop, Gadsby, Lillycrop, Tuffnell, R:2-0 Forman. *Scorer:* (First match) Tuffnell.
1910–11 BRADFORD CITY Mellors; Campbell, Taylor; Robinson, Torrance, McDonald; Logan, Spiers, O'Rourke, Devine, Thompson. (Gildea played centre-half in the first match.) *Scorer:* Spiers.
0-0 NEWCASTLE UNITED Lawrence; McCracken, Whitson; Veitch, Low, Willis; Rutherford, Jobey, R:1-0 Stewart, Higgins, Wilson.
1911–12 BARNSLEY Cooper; Downs, Taylor; Glendinning, Bratley, Utley; Bartrop, Tuffnell, Lillycrop, Travers, 0-0 Moore. *Scorer:* Tuffnell.
R:1-0 WEST BROMWICH ALBION Pearson; Cook, Pennington; Baddeley, Buck, McNeal; Jephcott, Wright, aet Pailor, Bowser, Shearman.
1912–13 ASTON VILLA Hardy; Lyons, Weston; Barber, Harrop, Leach; Wallace, Halse, Hampton, C. Stephenson, Bache. *Scorer:* Barber.
1-0 SUNDERLAND Butler; Gladwin, Ness; Cuggy, Thompson, Low; Mordue, Buchan, Richardson, Holley, Martin.
1913–14 BURNLEY Sewell; Bamford, Taylor; Halley, Boyle, Watson; Nesbit, Lindley, Freeman, Hodgson, Mosscrop. *Scorer:* Freeman.
1-0 LIVERPOOL Campbell; Longworth, Pursell; Fairfoul, Ferguson, McKinlay; Sheldon, Metcalf, Miller, Lacey, Nicholl.
1914–15 SHEFFIELD UNITED Gough; Cook, English; Sturgess, Brelsford, Utley; Simmons, Fazackerley, Kitchen, Masterman, Evans. *Scorers:* Simmons, Fazackerley, Kitchen.
3-0 CHELSEA Molyneux; Bettridge, Harrow; Taylor, Logan, Walker; Ford, Halse, Thompson, Croal, McNeil.
1919–20 ASTON VILLA Hardy; Smart, Weston; Ducat, Barson, Moss; Wallace, Kirton, Walker, C. Stephenson, Dorrell. *Scorer:* Kirton.
1-0 HUDDERSFIELD TOWN Mutch; Wood, Bullock; Slade, Wilson, Watson; Richardson, Mann, Taylor, aet Swan, Islip.
1920–21 TOTTENHAM HOTSPUR Hunter; Clay, McDonald; Smith, Walters, Grimsdell; Banks, Seed, Cantrell, Bliss, Dimmock. *Scorer:* Dimmock.
1-0 WOLVERHAMPTON WANDERERS George; Woodward, Marshall; Gregory, Hodnet, Riley; Lea, Burrill, Edmonds, Potts, Brooks.
1921–22 HUDDERSFIELD TOWN Mutch; Wood, Wadsworth; Slade, Wilson, Watson; Richardson, Mann, Islip, Stephenson, W. H. Smith. *Scorer:* Smith (pen).
1-0 PRESTON NORTH END J. F. Mitchell; Hamilton, Doolan; Duxbury, McCall, Williamson; Rawlings, Jefferis, Roberts, Woodhouse, Quinn.
1922–23 BOLTON WANDERERS Pym; Haworth, Finney; Nuttall, Seddon, Jennings; Butler, Jack, J. R. Smith, J. Smith, Vizard. *Scorers:* Jack, J. R. Smith.
2-0 WEST HAM UNITED Hufton; Henderson, Young; Bishop, Kay, Tresadern, Richards, Brown, V. Watson, Moore, Ruffell.
1923–24 NEWCASTLE UNITED Bradley; Hampson, Hudspeth; Mooney, Spencer, Gibson; Low, Cowan, Harris, McDonald, Seymour. *Scorers:* Harris, Seymour.
2-0 ASTON VILLA Jackson; Smart, Mort; Moss, Dr V. E. Milne, Blackburn; York, Kirton, Capewell, Walker, Dorrell.
1924–25 SHEFFIELD UNITED Sutcliffe; Cook, Milton; Pantling, King, Green; Mercer, Boyle, Johnson, Gillespie, Tunstall. *Scorer:* Tunstall.
1-0 CARDIFF CITY Farquharson; Nelson, Blair; Wake, Keenor, Hardy; W. Davies, Gill, Nicholson, Beadles, J. Evans.
1925–26 BOLTON WANDERERS Pym; Haworth, Greenhalgh; Nuttall, Seddon, Jennings; Butler, Jack, J. R. Smith, J. Smith, Vizard. *Scorer:* Jack.
1-0 MANCHESTER CITY Goodchild; Cookson, McCloy; Pringle, Cowan, McMullan; Austin, Browell, Roberts, Johnson, Hicks.
1926–27 CARDIFF CITY Farquharson; Nelson, Watson; Keenor, Sloan, Hardy; Curtis, Irving, Ferguson, I. Davies, McLachlan. *Scorer:* Ferguson.
1-0 ARSENAL Lewis; Parker, Kennedy; Baker, Butler, John; Hulme, Buchan, Brain, Blyth, Hoar.
1927–28 BLACKBURN ROVERS Crawford; Hutton, Jones; Healless, Rankin, Campbell; Thornewell, Puddefoot, Roscamp, McLean, Rigby. *Scorers:* Roscamp 2, McLean.
3-1 HUDDERSFIELD TOWN Mercer; Goodall, Barkas; Redfern, Wilson, Steele; A. Jackson, Kelly, Brown, Stephenson, W. H. Smith. *Scorer:* Jackson.
1928–29 BOLTON WANDERERS Pym; Haworth, Finney; Kean, Seddon, Nuttall; Butler, McClelland, Blackmore, Gibson, W. Cook. *Scorers:* Butler, Blackmore.
2-0 PORTSMOUTH Gilfillan; Mackie, Bell; Nichol, McIlwaine, Thackeray; Forward, J. Smith, Weddle, Watson, F. Cook.

1929–30 ARSENAL Preedy; Parker, Hapgood; Baker, Seddon, John; Hulme, Jack, Lambert, James, Bastin. *Scorers:* James, Lambert.
2-0 HUDDERSFIELD TOWN Turner; Goodall, Spence; Naylor, Wilson, Campbell; A. Jackson, Kelly, Davies, Raw, W. H. Smith.
1930–31 WEST BROMWICH ALBION Pearson; Shaw, Trentham; Magee, W. Richardson, Edwards; Glidden, Carter, W. G. Richardson, Sandford, Wood. *Scorer:* W. G. Richardson 2.
2-1 BIRMINGHAM Hibbs; Liddell, Barkas; Cringan, Morrall, Leslie; Briggs, Crosbie, Bradford, Gregg, Curtis. *Scorer:* Bradford.
1931–32 NEWCASTLE UNITED McInroy; Nelson, Fairhurst; McKenzie, Davidson, Weaver; Boyd, Richardson, Allen, McMenemy, Lang. *Scorer:* Allen 2.
2-1 ARSENAL Moss; Parker, Hapgood; C. Jones, Roberts, Male; Hulme, Jack, Lambert, Bastin, John. *Scorer:* John.
1932–33 EVERTON Sagar; Cook, Cresswell; Britton, White, Thomson; Geldard, Dunn, Dean, Johnson, Stein. *Scorers:* Stein, Dean, Dunn.
3-0 MANCHESTER CITY Langford; Cann, Dale; Busby, Cowan, Bray; Toseland, Marshall, Herd, McMullan, Brook.
1933–34 MANCHESTER CITY Swift; Barnett, Dale; Busby, Cowan, Bray; Toseland, Marshall, Tilson, Herd, Brook. *Scorer:* Tilson 2.
2-1 PORTSMOUTH Gilfillan; Mackie, W. Smith; Nichol, Allen, Thackeray; Worrall, J. Smith, Weddle, Easson, Rutherford. *Scorer:* Rutherford.
1934–35 SHEFFIELD WEDNESDAY Brown; Nibloe, Catlin; Sharp, Millership, Burrows; Hooper, Surtees, Palethorpe, Starling, Rimmer. *Scorers:* Rimmer 2, Palethorpe, Hooper.
4-2 WEST BROMWICH ALBION Pearson; Shaw, Trentham; Murphy, W. Richardson, Edwards; Glidden, Carter, W. G. Richardson, Sandford, Boyes. *Scorers:* Boyes, Sandford.
1935–36 ARSENAL Wilson; Male, Hapgood; Crayston, Roberts, Copping; Hulme, Bowden, Drake, James, Bastin. *Scorer:* Drake.
1-0 SHEFFIELD UNITED Smith; Hooper, Wilkinson; Jackson, Johnson, McPherson; Barton, Barclay, Dodds, Pickering, Williams.
1936–37 SUNDERLAND Mapson; Gorman, Hall; Thomson, Johnson, McNab; Duns, Carter, Gurney, Gallacher, Burbanks. *Scorers:* Gurney, Carter, Burbanks.
3-1 PRESTON NORTH END Burns; Gallimore, A. Beattie; Shankly, Tremelling, Milne; Dougal, Beresford, F. O'Donnell, Fagan, H. O'Donnell. *Scorer:* F. O'Donnell.
1937–38 PRESTON NORTH END Holdcroft; Gallimore, A. Beattie; Shankly, Smith, Batey; Watmough, Mutch, Maxwell, R. Beattie, H. O'Donnell. *Scorer:* Mutch (pen).
1-0 HUDDERSFIELD TOWN Hesford; Craig, Mountford; Willingham, Young, Boot; Hulme, Isaac,
aet McFadyen, Barclay, Beasley.
1938–39 PORTSMOUTH Walker; Morgan, Rochford; Guthrie, Rowe, Wharton; Worrall, McAlinden, Anderson, Barlow, Parker. *Scorers:* Parker 2, Barlow, Anderson.
4-1 WOLVERHAMPTON WANDERERS Scott; Morris, Taylor; Galley, Cullis, Gardiner; Burton, McIntosh, Westcott, Dorsett, Maguire. *Scorer:* Dorsett.
1945–46 DERBY COUNTY Woodley; Nicholas, Howe; Bullions, Leuty, Musson; Harrison, Carter, Stamps, Doherty, Duncan. *Scorers:* H. Turner (og), Doherty, Stamps 2.
4-1 CHARLTON ATHLETIC Bartram; Phipps, Shreeve; H. Turner, Oakes, Johnson; Fell, Brown, A. A.
aet Turner, Welsh, Duffy. *Scorer:* H. Turner.
1946–47 CHARLTON ATHLETIC Bartram; Croker, Shreeve; Johnson, Phipps, Whittaker; Hurst, Dawson, W. Robinson, Welsh, Duffy. *Scorer:* Duffy.
1-0 BURNLEY Strong; Woodruff, Mather; Attwell, Brown, Bray; Chew, Morris, Harrison, Potts, F. P.
aet Kippax.
1947–48 MANCHESTER UNITED Crompton; Carey, Aston; Anderson, Chilton, Cockburn; Delaney, Morris, Rowley, Pearson, Mitten. *Scorers:* Rowley 2, Pearson, Anderson.
4-2 BLACKPOOL Robinson; Shimwell, Crosland; Johnston, Hayward, Kelly; Matthews, Munro, Mortensen, Dick, Rickett. *Scorers:* Shimwell (pen), Mortensen.
1948–49 WOLVERHAMPTON WANDERERS Williams; Pritchard, Springthorpe; W. Crook, Shorthouse, Wright; Hancock, Smyth, Pye, Dunn, Mullen. *Scorers:* Pye 2, Smyth.
3-1 LEICESTER CITY Bradley; Jelly, Scott; W. Harrison, Plummer, King; Griffiths, Lee, J. Harrison, Chisholm, Adam. *Scorer:* Griffiths.
1949–50 ARSENAL Swindin; Scott, Barnes; Forbes, L. Compton, Mercer; Cox, Logie, Goring, Lewis, D. Compton. *Scorer:* Lewis 2.
2-0 LIVERPOOL Sidlow; Lambert, Spicer; Taylor, Hughes, Jones; Payne, Baron, Stubbins, Fagan, Liddell.
1950–51 NEWCASTLE UNITED Fairbrother; Cowell, Corbett; Harvey, Brennan, Crowe; Walker, Taylor, Milburn, G. Robledo, Mitchell. *Scorer:* Milburn 2.
2-0 BLACKPOOL Farm; Shimwell, Garrett; Johnston, Hayward, Kelly; Matthews, Mudie, Mortensen; W. J. Slater, Perry.
1951–52 NEWCASTLE UNITED Simpson; Cowell, McMichael; Harvey, Brennan, E. Robledo; Walker, Foulkes, Milburn, G. Robledo, Mitchell. *Scorer:* G. Robledo.
1-0 ARSENAL Swindin; Barnes, L. Smith; Forbes, Daniel, Mercer; Cox, Logie, Holton, Lishman, Roper.
1952–53 BLACKPOOL Farm; Shimwell, Garrett; Fenton, Johnston, Robinson; Matthews, Taylor, Mortensen, Mudie, Perry. *Scorers:* Mortensen 3, Perry.
4-3 BOLTON WANDERERS Hanson; Ball, R. Banks; Wheeler, Barass, Bell; Holden, Moir, Lofthouse, Hassall, Langton. *Scorers:* Lofthouse, Moir, Bell.
1953–54 WEST BROMWICH ALBION Sanders; Kennedy, Millard; Dudley, Dugdale, Barlow; Griffin, Ryan, Allen, Nicholls, Lee. *Scorers:* Allen 2 (1 pen), Griffin.
3-2 PRESTON NORTH END Thompson; Cunningham, Walton; Docherty, Marston, Forbes; Finney, Foster, Wayman, Baxter, Morrison. *Scorers:* Morrison, Wayman.
1954–55 NEWCASTLE UNITED Simpson; Cowell, Batty; Scoular, Stokoe, Casey; White, Milburn, Keeble, Hannah, Mitchell. *Scorers:* Milburn, Mitchell, Hannah.
3-1 MANCHESTER CITY Trautmann; Meadows, Little; Barnes, Ewing, Paul; Spurdle, Hayes, Revie, Johnstone, Fagan. *Scorer:* Johnstone.

648

1955–56 MANCHESTER CITY   Trautmann; Leivers, Little; Barnes, Ewing, Paul; Johnstone, Hayes, Revie, Dyson, Clarke. *Scorers:* Hayes, Dyson, Johnstone.
3–1 BIRMINGHAM CITY   Merrick; Hall, Green; Newman, Smith, Boyd; Astall, Kinsey, Brown, Murphy, Govan. *Scorer:* Kinsey.
1956–57 ASTON VILLA   Sims; Lynn, Aldis; Crowther, Dugdale, Saward; Smith, Sewell, Myerscough, Dixon, McParland. *Scorer:* McParland 2.
2–1 MANCHESTER UNITED   Wood; Foulkes, Byrne; Colman, J. Blanchflower, Edwards; Berry, Whelan, T. Taylor, R. Charlton, Pegg. *Scorer:* Taylor.
1957–58 BOLTON WANDERERS   Hopkinson; Hartle, Banks; Hennin, Higgins, Edwards; Birch, Stevens, Lofthouse, Parry, Holden. *Scorer:* Lofthouse 2.
2–0 MANCHESTER UNITED   Gregg; Foulkes, Greaves; Goodwin, Cope, Crowther; Dawson, E. Taylor, R. Charlton, Viollet, Webster.
1958–59 NOTTINGHAM FOREST   Thomson; Whare, McDonald; Whitefoot, McKinlay, Burkitt; Dwight, Quigley, Wilson, Gray, Imlach. *Scorers:* Dwight, Wilson.
2–1 LUTON TOWN   Baynham; McNally, Hawkes; Groves, Owen, Pacey; Bingham, Brown, Morton, Cummins, Gregory. *Scorer:* Pacey.
1959–60 WOLVERHAMPTON WANDERERS   Finlayson; Showell, Harris; Clamp, Slater, Flowers; Deeley, Stobart, Murray, Broadbent, Horne. *Scorers:* McGrath (og), Deeley 2.
3–0 BLACKBURN ROVERS   Leyland; Bray, Whelan; Clayton, Woods, McGrath; Bimpson, Dobing, Dougan, Douglas, McLeod.
1960–61 TOTTENHAM HOTSPUR   Brown; Baker, Henry; D. Blanchflower, Norman, Mackay; Jones, White, Smith, Allen, Dyson. *Scorers:* Smith, Dyson.
2–0 LEICESTER CITY   Banks; Chalmers, Norman; McLintock, King, Appleton; Riley, Walsh, McIlmoyle, Keyworth, Cheesebrough.
1961–62 TOTTENHAM HOTSPUR   Brown; Baker, Henry; D. Blanchflower, Norman, Mackay; Medwin, White, Smith, Greaves, Jones. *Scorers:* Greaves, Smith, Blanchflower (pen).
3–1 BURNLEY   Blacklaw; Angus, Elder; Adamson, Cummings, Miller; Connelly, McIlroy, Pointer, Robson, Harris. *Scorer:* Robson.
1962–63 MANCHESTER UNITED   Gaskell; Dunne, Cantwell; Crerand, Foulkes, Setters; Giles, Quixall, Herd, Law, R. Charlton. *Scorers:* Herd 2, Law.
3–1 LEICESTER CITY   Banks; Sjoberg, Norman; McLintock, King, Appleton; Riley, Cross, Keyworth, Gibson, Stringfellow. *Scorer:* Keyworth.
1963–64 WEST HAM UNITED   Standen; Bond, Burkett; Bovington, Brown, Moore; Brabrook, Boyce, Byrne, Hurst, Sissons. *Scorers:* Sissons, Hurst, Boyce.
3–2 PRESTON NORTH END   Kelly; Ross, Smith; Lawton, Singleton, Kendall; Wilson, Ashworth, Dawson, Spavin, Holden. *Scorers:* Holden, Dawson.
1964–65 LIVERPOOL   Lawrence; Lawler, Byrne; Strong, Yeats, Stevenson; Callaghan, Hunt, St John, Smith, Thompson. *Scorers:* Hunt, St John.
2–1 LEEDS UNITED   Sprake; Reaney, Bell; Bremner, J. Charlton, Hunter; Giles, Storrie, Peacock, Collins,
aet Johanneson. *Scorer:* Bremner.
1965–66 EVERTON   West; Wright, Wilson; Gabriel, Labone, Harris; Scott, Trebilcock, Young, Harvey, Temple. *Scorers:* Trebilcock 2, Temple.
3–2 SHEFFIELD WEDNESDAY   Springett; Smith, Megson; Eustace, Ellis, Young; Pugh, Fantham, McCalliog, Ford, Quinn. *Scorers:* McCalliog, Ford.
1966–67 TOTTENHAM HOTSPUR   Jennings; Kinnear, Knowles; Mullery, England, Mackay; Robertson, Greaves, Gilzean, Venables, Saul. *Scorers:* Robertson, Saul.
2–1 CHELSEA   Bonetti; A. Harris, McCreadie; Hollins, Hinton, R. Harris; Cooke, Baldwin, Hateley, Tambling, Boyle. *Scorer:* Tambling.
1967–68 WEST BROMWICH ALBION   Osborne; Fraser, Williams; Brown, Talbut, Kaye (Clarke); Lovett, Collard, Astle, Hope, Clark. *Scorer:* Astle.
1–0 EVERTON   West; Wright, Wilson; Kendall, Labone, Harvey; Husband, Ball, Royle, Hurst,
aet Morrissey.
1968–69 MANCHESTER CITY   Dowd; Book, Pardoe; Doyle, Booth, Oakes; Summerbee, Bell, Lee, Young, Coleman. *Scorer:* Young.
1–0 LEICESTER CITY   Shilton; Rodrigues, Nish; Roberts, Woollett, Cross; Fern, Gibson, Lochhead, Clarke, Glover (Manley).
1969–70 CHELSEA   Bonetti; Webb, McCreadie; Hollins, Dempsey, R. Harris (Hinton); Baldwin, Houseman, Osgood, Hutchinson, Cooke. *Scorers:* Houseman, Hutchinson.
2–2 LEEDS UNITED   Sprake; Madeley, Cooper; Bremner, J. Charlton, Hunter; Lorimer, Clarke, Jones, Giles,
aet E. Gray. *Scorers:* Charlton, Jones.
Replay (at Old Trafford, Manchester)
R:2–1 CHELSEA   Bonetti; R. Harris, McCreadie; Hollins, Dempsey, Webb; Baldwin, Cooke, Osgood (Hinton),
aet Hutchinson, Houseman. *Scorers:* Osgood, Webb.
LEEDS UNITED   Harvey; Madeley, Cooper; Bremner, J. Charlton, Hunter; Lorimer, Clarke, Jones, Giles, E. Gray. *Scorer:* Jones.
1970–71 ARSENAL   Wilson; Rice, McNab; Storey (Kelly), McLintock, Simpson; Armstrong, Graham, Radford, Kennedy, George. *Scorers:* Kelly, George.
2–1 LIVERPOOL   Clemence; Lawler, Lindsay; Smith, Lloyd, Hughes; Callaghan, Evans (Thompson), Heigh-
aet way, Toshack, Hall. *Scorer:* Heighway.
1971–72 LEEDS UNITED   Harvey; Reaney, Madeley; Bremner, J. Charlton, Hunter; Lorimer, Clarke, Jones, Giles, E. Gray. *Scorer:* Clarke.
1–0 ARSENAL   Barnett; Rice, McNab; Storey, McLintock, Simpson; Armstrong, Ball, George, Radford (Kennedy), Graham.
1972–73 SUNDERLAND   Montgomery; Malone, Guthrie; Horswill, Watson, Pitt; Kerr, Hughes, Halom, Porterfield, Tueart. *Scorer:* Porterfield.
1–0 LEEDS UNITED   Harvey; Reaney, Cherry; Bremner, Madeley, Hunter; Lorimer, Clarke, Jones, Giles, E. Gray (Yorath).
1973–74 LIVERPOOL   Clemence; Smith, Lindsay, Thompson, Cormack, Hughes, Keegan, Hall, Heighway,

Toshack, Callaghan. *Scorers:* Keegan 2, Heighway.
3-0 NEWCASTLE UNITED McFaul; Clark, Kennedy, McDermott, Howard, Moncur, Smith (Gibb), Cassidy, Macdonald, Tudor, Hibbitt.
1974–75 WEST HAM UNITED Day; McDowell, T. Taylor, Lock, Lampard, Bonds, Paddon, Brooking, Jennings, A. Taylor, Holland. *Scorer:* A. Taylor 2.
2-0 FULHAM Mellor; Cutbush, Lacy, Moore, Fraser, Mullery, Conway, Slough, Mitchell, Busby, Barrett.
1975–76 SOUTHAMPTON Turner; Rodrigues, Peach, Holmes, Blyth, Steele, Gilchrist, Channon, Osgood, McCalliog, Stokes. *Scorer:* Stokes.
1-0 MANCHESTER UNITED Stepney; Forsyth, Houston, Daly, Greenhoff, Buchan, Coppell, McIlroy, Pearson, Macari, Hill (McCreery).
1976–77 MANCHESTER UNITED Stepney; Nicholl, Albiston, McIlroy, B. Greenhoff, Buchan, Coppell, J. Greenhoff, Pearson, Macari, Hill (McCreery). *Scorers:* Pearson, J. Greenhoff.
2-1 LIVERPOOL Clemence; Neal, Jones, Smith, Kennedy, Hughes, Keegan, Case, Heighway, Johnson (Callaghan), McDermott. *Scorer:* Case.
1977–78 IPSWICH TOWN Cooper; Burley, Mills, Osborne (Lambert), Hunter, Beattie, Talbot, Wark, Mariner, Geddis, Woods. *Scorer:* Osborne.
1-0 ARSENAL Jennings; Rice, Nelson, Price, Young, O'Leary, Brady (Rix), Hudson, Macdonald, Stapleton, Sunderland.
1978–79 ARSENAL Jennings; Rice, Nelson, Talbot, O'Leary, Young, Brady, Sunderland, Stapleton, Price (Walford), Rix. *Scorers:* Talbot, Stapleton, Sunderland.
3-2 MANCHESTER UNITED Bailey; Nicholl, Albiston, McIlroy, McQueen, Buchan, Coppell, J. Greenhoff, Jordan, Macari, Thomas. *Scorers:* McQueen, McIlroy.
1979–80 WEST HAM UNITED Parkes; Stewart, Lampard, Bonds, Martin, Devonshire, Allen, Pearson, Cross, Brooking, Pike. *Scorer:* Brooking.
1-0 ARSENAL Jennings; Rice, Devine (Nelson), Talbot, O'Leary, Young, Brady, Sunderland, Stapleton, Price, Rix
1980–81 TOTTENHAM HOTSPUR Aleksic; Hughton, Miller, Roberts, Perryman, Villa (Brooke), Ardiles, Archibald, Galvin, Hoddle, Crooks. *Scorer:* Hutchison (og).
1-1 MANCHESTER CITY Corrigan; Ranson, McDonald, Reid, Power, Caton, Bennett, Gow, MacKenzie, **aet** Hutchison (Henry), Reeves. *Scorer:* Hutchison.
R:3-2 TOTTENHAM HOTSPUR Aleksic; Hughton, Miller, Roberts, Perryman, Villa, Ardiles, Archibald, Galvin, Hoddle, Crooks. *Scorers:* Villa 2, Crooks.
MANCHESTER CITY Corrigan; Ranson, McDonald (Tueart), Caton, Reid, Gow, Power, MacKenzie, Reeves, Bennett, Hutchison. *Scorers:* MacKenzie, Reeves (pen).
1981–82 TOTTENHAM HOTSPUR Clemence; Hughton, Miller, Price, Hazard (Brooke), Perryman, Roberts, Archibald, Galvin, Hoddle, Crooks. *Scorer:* Hoddle.
1-1 QPR Hucker; Fenwick, Gillard, Waddock, Hazell, Roeder, Currie, Flanagan, Allen (Micklewhite), Stain-**aet** rod, Gregory. *Scorer:* Fenwick.
R:1-0 TOTTENHAM HOTSPUR Clemence; Hughton, Miller, Price, Hazard (Brooke), Perryman, Roberts, Archibald, Galvin, Hoddle, Crooks. *Scorer:* Hoddle (pen).
QPR Hucker; Fenwick, Gillard, Waddock, Hazell, Neill, Currie, Flanagan, Micklewhite (Burke), Stainrod, Gregory.
1982–83 MANCHESTER UNITED Bailey; Duxbury, Moran, McQueen, Albiston, Davies, Wilkins, Robson, Muhren, Stapleton, Whiteside. *Scorers:* Stapleton, Wilkins.
2-2 BRIGHTON & HOVE ALBION Moseley; Ramsey (Ryan), Stevens, Gatting, Pearce, Smillie, Case, **aet** Grealish, Howlett, Robinson, Smith. *Scorers:* Smith, Stevens.
R:4-0 MANCHESTER UNITED Bailey; Duxbury, Albiston, Wilkins, Moran, McQueen, Robson, Muhren, Stapleton, Whiteside, Davies. *Scorers:* Robson 2, Whiteside, Muhren (pen).
BRIGHTON & HOVE ALBION Moseley; Gatting, Pearce, Grealish, Foster, Stevens, Case, Howlett, Robinson, Smith, Smillie.
1983–84 EVERTON Southall; Stevens, Bailey, Ratcliffe, Mountfield, Reid, Steven, Heath, Sharp, Gray, Richardson. *Scorers:* Sharp, Gray.
2-0 WATFORD Sherwood; Bardsley, Price (Atkinson), Taylor, Terry, Sinnott, Callaghan, Johnston, Reilly, Jackett, Barnes.
1984–85 MANCHESTER UNITED Bailey; Gidman, Albiston (Duxbury), Whiteside, McGrath, Moran, Robson, Strachan, Hughes, Stapleton, Olsen. *Scorer:* Whiteside.
1-0 EVERTON Southall; Stevens, Van den Hauwe, Ratcliffe, Mountfield, Reid, Steven, Gray, Sharp, Brace-**aet** well, Sheedy.
1985–86 LIVERPOOL Grobbelaar; Lawrenson, Beglin, Nicol, Whelan, Hansen, Dalglish, Johnston, Rush, Molby, MacDonald. *Scorers:* Rush 2, Johnston.
3-1 EVERTON Mimms; Stevens (Heath), Van Den Hauwe, Ratcliffe, Mountfield, Reid, Steven, Lineker, Sharp, Bracewell, Sheedy. *Scorer:* Lineker.
1986–87 COVENTRY CITY Ogrizovic; Phillips, Downs, McGrath, Kilcline (Rodger), Peake, Bennett, Gynn, Regis, Houchen, Pickering. *Scorers:* Bennett, Houchen, Mabbutt (og).
3-2 TOTTENHAM HOTSPUR Clemence; Hughton (Claesen), M. Thomas, Hodge, Gough, Mabbutt, C. **aet** Allen, P. Allen, Waddle, Hoddle, Ardiles (Stevens). *Scorers:* C. Allen, Kilcline (og).
1987–88 WIMBLEDON Beasant; Goodyear, Phelan, Jones, Young, Thorn, Gibson (Scales), Cork (Cunningham), Fashanu, Sanchez, Wise. *Scorer:* Sanchez.
1-0 LIVERPOOL Grobbelaar; Gillespie, Ablett, Nicol, Spackman (Molby), Hansen, Beardsley, Aldridge (Johnston), Houghton, Barnes, McMahon.
1988–89 LIVERPOOL Grobbelaar; Ablett, Staunton (Venison), Nicol, Whelan, Hansen, Beardsley, Aldridge (Rush), Houghton, Barnes, McMahon. *Scorers:* Aldridge, Rush 2.
3-2 EVERTON Southall; McDonald, Van Den Hauwe, Ratcliffe, Watson, Bracewell (McCall), Nevin, Steven, **aet** Sharp, Cottee, Sheedy (Wilson). *Scorer:* McCall 2.
1989–90 MANCHESTER UNITED Leighton; Ince, Martin (Blackmore), Bruce, Phelan, Pallister (Robins), Robson, Webb, McClair, Hughes, Wallace. *Scorers:* Robson, Hughes 2.
3-3 CRYSTAL PALACE Martyn; Pemberton, Shaw, Gray (Madden), O'Reilly, Thorn, Barber (Wright), **aet** Thomas, Bright, Salako, Pardew. *Scorers:* O'Reilly, Wright 2.

650

*R:*1–0 MANCHESTER UNITED Sealey; Ince, Martin, Bruce, Phelan, Pallister, Robson, Webb, McClair, Hughes, Wallace, *Scorer:* Martin.
CRYSTAL PALACE Martyn; Pemberton, Shaw, Gray, O'Reilly, Thorn, Barber (Wright), Thomas, Bright, Salako (Madden), Pardew.

1990–91 TOTTENHAM HOTSPUR Thorstvedt; Edinburgh, Van Den Hauwe, Sedgley, Howells, Mabbutt, Stewart,
2-1 Gascoigne (Nayim), Samways (Walsh), Lineker, Allen. *Scorers:* Stewart, Walker (og).
aet NOTTINGHAM FOREST Crossley; Charles, Pearce, Walker, Chettle, Keane, Crosby, Parker, Clough, Glover (Laws), Woan (Hodge). *Scorer:* Pearce.

1991–92 LIVERPOOL Grobbelaar; Jones R, Burrows, Nicol, Molby, Wright, Saunders, Houghton, Rush, McManaman, Thomas. *Scorers:* Thomas, Rush.
2-0 SUNDERLAND Norman; Owers, Ball, Bennett, Rogan, Rush (Hardyman), Bracewell, Davenport, Armstrong, Byrne, Atkinson (Hawke).

Andy Linighan heads the injury-time winning goal for Arsenal in the 1993 FA Cup Final against Sheffield Wednesday. (Colorsport)

FA CUP 1992–93

PRELIMINARY AND QUALIFYING ROUNDS

Preliminary Round

Hebburn v Annfield Plain	1-1, 1-5
Easington Colliery v Shotton Comrades	2-1
Newcastle Blue Star v Whickham	0-0, 2-0
Workington v West Auckland Town	3-2
Bamber Bridge v Prudhoe East End	4-0
Shildon v Blackpool (wren) Rovers	2-0
Peterlee Newton v Evenwood Town	1-0
Willington v Whitby Town	1-5
Ferryhill Athletic v Spennymoor United	2-3
Esh Winning v Alnwick Town	0-0, 1-2
Armthorpe Welfare v Brandon United	2-0
Darlington CB v Consett	0-1
Chester-le-Street Town v Billingham Town	0-1
Ossett Town v Dunston FB	1-2
Horden CW v Darwen	1-1, 0-5
Crook Town v Norton & Stockton Acients	0-3
Northallerton Town v Langley Park	6-1
South Bank v Bedlington Terriers	5-0
Yorkshire Amateur v Seaham Red Star	1-3
St Helens Town v Tow Law Town	3-2
Eccleshill United v Harworth CI	3-2
Washington v Stockton	1-3
(at Stockton)	
Salford City v North Ferriby United	0-1
Chadderton v Lancaster City	2-1
Ashton United v Garforth Town	1-2
Formby v Bootle	1-2
Irlam Town v Atherton LR	1-2
Sheffield v Rossendale United	2-2, 2-1
Great Harwood Town v Prescot	2-1
Thackley v Radcliffe Borough	2-1
Harrogate Town v Louth United	4-3
Bradford Park Avenue v Burscough	1-1, 2-1
Warrington Town v Skelmersdale United	6-1
Mickleover RBL v Belper Town	0-2
Clitheroe v Immingham Town	2-1
Flixton v Worksop Town	1-1, 0-3
Hucknall Town v Grantham Town	2-1
Arnold Town v Liversedge	4-0
(at Kimberley Town)	
Congleton Town v Eastwood Town	2-0
Denaby United v Heanor Town	2-5
Nantwich Town v Maltby MW	1-1, 3-2
Ilkeston Town v Harrogate RA	7-0
West Midlands Police v Bridgnorth Town	5-2
Halesowen Harriers v Wednesfield	2-2, 3-2
Bedworth United v Walsall Wood	1-0
Lye Town v Barwell	1-1, 3-1
(first game at Dudley Town)	
Alfreton Town v Oakham United	2-1
Bilston Town v Newcastle Town	1-3
Pelsall Villa v Oldbury United	0-0, 4-4, 1-0
Gresley Rovers v Highgate United	4-2
Hinckley Town v Willenhall Town	1-1, 1-2
Nuneaton Borough v Boldmere St Michaels	2-1
Raunds Town v Rocester	2-2, 4-3
Leicester United v Dudley Town	3-0
Stratford Town v Hinckley Athletic	6-2
Stewart & Lloyds v Evesham United	4-2
Northampton Spencer v Rushall Olympic	1-1, 2-3
Sutton Coldfield Town v West Bromwich Town	
	0-0, 2-0
Sandwell Borough v Malvern Town	4-0
Boston v Banbury United	4-1
Histon v Long Buckby	1-2
Stourport Swifts v Stourbridge	0-5
Rushden & Diamonds v Desborough Town	2-0
Bourne Town v Peterborough City	3-2
Hitchin Town v Chatteris Town	3-1
Eynesbury Rovers v Milton Keynes Borough	4-5
Wisbech Town v Wellingborough Town	10-0

Cheshunt v Spalding United	0-0, 5-0
Letchworth Garden City v Haverhill Rovers	1-1, 4-3
Chalfont St Peter v Hoddesdon Town	1-0
March Town United v Braintree Town	1-3
Purfleet v Great Yarmouth Town	4-1
Harwich & Parkeston v Leighton Town	3-3, 0-2
Watton United v Burnham Ramblers	1-0
Brook House v Aveley	1-1, 0-1
Rainham Town v Mirrless Blackstone	2-0
Haringey Borough v Bury Town	5-2
Norwich United v Edgware Town	1-0
Gorleston v Clapton	5-2
Biggleswade Town v Barking	1-3
(at Langford)	
Leyton v Felixstowe Town	5-4
Tilbury v Collier Row	3-2
Sudbury Town v Saffron Walden Town	6-1
Newmarket Town v Langford	4-0
Royston Town v Potton United	1-2
Waltham Abbey v Halstead Town	1-1, 4-3
(first game at Halstead)	
Wealdstone v Tiptree United	2-1
Flackwell Heath v Walthamstow Pennant	2-0
Witham Town v Wingate & Finchley	4-3
Ware v Stowmarket Town	1-2
Ruislip Manor v Hornchurch	1-0
Rayners Lane v Ashford Town (Middx)	2-2, 1-0
Basildon United v Tring Town	1-0
Uxbridge v Southall	4-2
Fisher Athletic v Brightlingsea United	2-1
(at Brightlingsea)	
Harefield United v Barkingside	0-1
Burnham v Canvey Island	1-0
(at Windsor & Eton)	
Wembley v Welwyn Garden City	5-0
Viking Sports v Bishop's Stortford	0-1
Molesey v Northwood	3-1
Kingsbury Town v Oakwood	4-3
East Thurrock United v Chipstead	1-0
Beckenham Town v Feltham & Hounslow Borough	
	2-0
Redhill v Boreham Wood	1-5
Metropolitan Police v Ford United	0-0, 2-0
Three Bridges v Alma Swanley	0-3
Lewes v Leatherhead	1-0
Haywards Heath Town v Bedfont	0-1
Wick v Ashford Town	1-1, 1-3
Deal Town v Epsom & Ewell	3-0
Portfield v Faversham Town	2-4
Merstham v Malden Vale	0-0, 1-3
Whyteleafe v Pagham	5-1
Croydon Athletic v Arundel	7-3
Banstead Athletic v Eastbourne United	2-1
Dorking w.o Hythe Town withdrew	
Herne Bay v Camberley Town	3-3, 3-2
Walton & Hersham v Peacehaven & Telscombe	2-1
Egham Town v Selsey	2-1
Sheppey United v Croydon	0-1
Worthing v Chatham Town	8-0
Canterbury City v Bracknell Town	4-1
Hailsham Town v Steyning Town	3-1
Tunbridge Wells v Margate	0-4
Worthing United v Langney Sports	1-4
Corinthian v Cove	1-0
Lancing v Littlehampton Town	2-3
Whitehawk v Chichester City	5-2, 3-1
(after a protest from Chichester that extra time should not have been played a replay was ordered)	
Totton v Havant Town	0-1
Whitstable Town v Sittingbourne	1-2
Horsham YMCA v Eastbourne Town	4-3
Ryde Sports v Southwick	1-2

Poole Town v Abingdon United	0-1
Shoreham v Witney Town	0-3
Sholing Sports v Bemerton Heath Harlequins	1-2
Andover v Ringmer	5-0
Fleet Town v Abingdon Town	1-2
Eastleigh v Newport (IW)	1-2
Oxford City v Devizes Town	2-3
Wimborne Town v Bournemouth	1-1, 3-1
Welton Rovers v Hungerford Town	4-1
Petersfield United v Chippenham Town	0-1
Gosport Borough v Calne Town	0-4
Westbury United v Thatcham Town	0-5
Shortwood United v Brockenhurst	0-4
Minehead v Lymington	2-2, 1-2
Melksham Town v Swanage Town & Herston	1-5
Paulton Rovers v Bristol Manor Farm	0-2
Cinderford Town v Newbury Town	3-0
Forest Green Rovers v Barnstaple Town	4-2
Taunton Town v Barri	0-3
Dawlish Town v Newport AFC	0-3
Clevedon Town v Yate Town	4-1
St Blazey v Falmouth Town	1-4
Ilfracombe Town v Truro City	3-4
Exmouth Town v Elmore	1-2
Torrington v Bideford	1-0

First Qualifying Round

Annfield Plain v Newcastle Blue Star	0-1
Durham City v Bishop Auckland	1-1, 2-5
Penrith v Blyth Spartans	1-2
Easington Colliery v Workington	1-1, 0-1
Bamber Bridge v Peterlee Newton	1-1, 2-0
Spennymoor United v Gretna	4-0
Gateshead v Billingham Synthonia	3-1
Shildon v Whitby Town	0-2
Alnwick Town v Consett	0-0, 0-2
Ossett Albion v Netherfield	1-3
Murton v Guisborough Town	1-2
Armthorpe Welfare v Billingham Town	2-2, 0-2
Dunston FB v Norton & Stockton Acients	7-0
South Bank w.o North Shields withdrew	
Fleetwood Town v Guiseley	3-2
Darwen v Northallerton Town	1-6
Seaham Red Star v Eccleshill United	3-2
Maine Road v Morecambe	2-1
Chorley v Knowsley United	1-1, 1-2
St Helens Town v Stockton	3-4
North Ferriby United v Garforth Town	1-0
Brigg Town v Bridlington Town	2-1
Southport v Buxton	0-0, 2-1
Chadderton v Bootle	3-0
Atherton LR v Great Harwood Town	1-1, 2-1
Caernarfon Town v Colwyn Bay	1-4
Altrincham v Curzon Ashton	3-0
Sheffield v Thackley	3-1
(at Thackley)	
Harrogate Town v Warrington Town	1-2
Stocksbridge Park Steels v Stalybridge Celtic	0-4
Hyde United v Accrington Stanley	1-5
Bradford Park Avenue v Belper Town	2-0
Clitheroe v Hucknall Town	1-3
Glossop North End v Macclesfield Town	0-1
Goole Town v Horwich RMI	0-1
Worksop Town v Arnold Town	5-3
Congleton Town v Nantwich Town	0-0, 1-2
Blakenall v Droylsden	4-3
Marine v Emley	5-0
Heanor Town v Ilkeston Town	2-1
West Midlands Police v Bedworth United	1-2
Alfreton Town v Stafford Rangers	0-0, 0-3
Frickley Athletic v Lincoln United	0-0, 1-0
Halesowen Harriers v Lye Town	2-1
Newcastle Town v Gresley Rovers	0-1
Paget Rangers v Gainsborough Trinity	1-3
Mossley v Borrowash Victoria	0-0, 1-0
Pelsall Villa v Willenhall Town	1-0
Nuneaton Borough v Leicester United	3-1
Rothwell Town v Matlock Town	0-2
Northwich Victoria v Winsford United	4-1
Raunds Town v Stratford Town	0-0, 2-1

Stewart & Lloyds v Sutton Coldfield Town	1-3
Racing Club Warwick v Eastwood Hanley	0-2
Leek Town v Burton Albion	3-2
Rushall Olympic v Sandwell Borough	3-0
Boston v Stourbridge	3-4
Arlesey Town v Shepshed Albion	0-1
Hednesford Town v Tamworth	1-1, 4-2
Long Buckby v Rushden & Diamonds	0-1
Bourne Town v Milton Keynes Borough	3-2
Barton Rovers v Moor Green	2-3
VS Rugby w.o Alvechurch withdrew	
Hitchin Town v Wisbech Town	4-2
Cheshunt v Chalfont St Peter	1-0
Hemel Hempstead v Solihull Borough	1-2
Chasetown v Redditch United	1-0
Letchworth Garden City v Braintree Town	0-4
Purfleet v Watton United	6-1
Rainham Town v Corby Town	0-1
Boston United v Kings Lynn	2-1
Leighton Town v Aveley	2-4
Haringey Borough v Gorleston	0-0, 0-1
Leyton v Lowestoft Town	4-2
Heybridge Swifts v Cambridge City	2-4
Norwich United v Barking	2-1
Tilbury v Newmarket Town	1-1, 0-1
Waltham Abbey v Baldock Town	2-3
(at Baldock)	
Chelmsford City v Grays Athletic	0-0, 1-2
Sudbury Town v Potton United	3-2
Wealdstone v Witham Town	2-1
Kempston Rovers v Wivenhoe Town	3-4
Dagenham & Redbridge v Billericay Town	1-1, 4-1
Flackwell Heath v Stowmarket Town	0-5
Ruislip Manor v Basildon United	3-1
Fisher Athletic v Stevenage Borough	1-7
(at Stevenage)	
St Albans City v Brimsdown Rovers	3-1
Rayners Lane v Uxbridge	1-1, 1-0
Barkingside v Wembley	1-3
Slade Green w.o Harlow Town withdrew	
Hertford Town v Hendon	0-2
Burnham v Bishop's Stortford	3-2
(at Windsor & Eton)	
Molesey v East Thurrock United	4-2
Boreham Wood v Chesham United	2-2, 1-9
Harrow Borough v Berkhamsted Town	0-2
Kingsbury Town v Beckenham Town	2-3
Metropolitan Police v Lewes	2-1
Corinthian-Casuals v Slough Town	1-1, 3-4
Staines Town v Yeading	0-3
Alma Swanley v Bedfont	1-0
Ashford Town v Faversham Town	1-1, 2-0
Whyteleafe v Windsor & Eton	1-3
Dartford withdrew, Horsham w.o	
Deal Town v Malden Vale	4-0
Croydon Athletic v Dorking	1-2
Walton & Hersham v Wokingham Town	2-0
Tonbridge v Dover Athletic	0-0, 1-2
Banstead Athletic v Herne Bay	4-1
Egham Town v Worthing	1-1, 1-7
Hailsham Town v Bromley	2-3
Burgess Hill Town v Hastings Town	0-2
Croydon v Canterbury City	1-0
Margate v Corinthian	0-0, 1-1, 0-4
Chertsey Town v Gravesend & Northfleet	3-2
Kingstonian v Dulwich Hamlet	4-0
Langney Sports v Littlehampton Town	3-1
Whitehawk v Sittingbourne	0-1
Fareham Town v Tooting & Mitcham	2-0
Carshalton Athletic v Erith & Belvedere	1-2
Havant Town v Horsham YMCA	2-1
Southwick v Witney Town	2-5
Andover v Hampton	0-6
Bognor Regis Town v Romsey Town	9-2
Abingdon United v Bemerton Heath Harlequins	0-5
Abingdon Town v Devizes Town	4-0
Buckingham Town v Maidenhead United	1-1, 1-2
Thame United v Bashley	2-3
Newport (IW) v Wimborne Town	2-3
Welton Rovers v Calne Town	1-4

Brockenhurst v Basingstoke Town	1-0
Salisbury v Trowbridge Town	6-2
Chippenham Town v Thatcham Town	1-2
Lymington v Bristol Manor Town	3-3, 2-0
(replay at Keynsham)	
Mangotsfield United v Dorchester Town	0-1
Waterlooville v Cheltenham Town	0-0, 0-2
Swanage Town & Herston v Cinderford Town	1-2
Forest Green Rovers v Newport AFC	1-2
Frome Town v Worcester City	1-2
Gloucester City v Weston-super-Mare	2-3
Barri v Clevedon Town	1-3
Falmouth Town v Elmore	2-0
Glastonbury v Bath City	0-4
Weymouth v Saltash United	1-0
Truro City v Torrington	2-0

Second Qualifying Round

Newcastle Blue Star v Bishop Auckland	0-1
Blyth Spartans v Workington	6-0
Bamber Bridge v Spennymoor United	0-4
Gateshead v Whitby Town	5-2
Consett v Netherfield	1-1 (abandoned,fog), 3-4
Guisborough Town v Billingham Town	3-0
Dunston FB v South Bank	2-0
Fleetwood Town v Northallerton Town	1-2
Seaham Red Star v Maine Road	1-1, 1-1, 5-0
Knowsley United v Stockton	0-2
North Ferriby United v Brigg Town	0-2
Southport v Chadderton	2-0
Atherton LR v Colwyn Bay	1-2
Altrincham v Sheffield	3-1
Warrington Town v Stalybridge Celtic	0-3
Accrington Stanley v Bradford Park Avenue	2-0
Hucknall Town v Macclesfield Town	1-1, 1-3
Horwich RMI v Worksop Town	1-1, 5-1
Nantwich Town v Blakenall	1-0
Marine v Heanor Town	2-0
Bedworth United v Stafford Rangers	1-1, 0-1
Frickley Athletic v Halesowen Harriers	8-2
Gresley Rovers v Gainsborough Trinity	1-4
Mossley v Pelsall Villa	1-2
Nuneaton Borough v Matlock Town	2-1
Northwich Victoria v Raunds Town	0-2
Sutton Coldfield Town v Eastwood Hanley	2-1
Leek Town v Rushall Olympic	0-1
Stourbridge v Shepshed Albion	0-0, 2-4
Hednesford Town v Rushden & Diamonds	4-1
Bourne Town v Moor Green	4-8
VS Rugby v Hitchin Town	3-0
Cheshunt v Solihull Borough	0-0, 0-4
Chasetown v Braintree Town	0-2
Purfleet v Corby Town	2-2, 0-1
Boston United v Aveley	1-2
Gorleston v Leyton	1-2
Cambridge City v Norwich United	6-1
Newmarket Town v Baldock Town	2-2, 6-2
Grays Athletic v Sudbury Town	1-0
Wealdstone v Wivenhoe Town	1-1, 2-0
Dagenham & Redbridge v Stowmarket Town	6-1
Ruislip Manor v Stevenage Borough	1-3
St Albans City v Rayners Lane	1-3
Wembley v Slade Green	3-2
Hendon v Burnham	6-0
Molesey v Chesham United	0-4
Berkhamsted Town v Beckenham Town	0-0, 1-0
Metropolitan Police v Slough Town	0-1
Yeading v Alma Swanley	7-1
Ashford Town v Windsor & Eton	2-2, 3-2
Horsham v Deal Town	1-6
Dorking v Walton & Hersham	4-2
Dover Athletic v Banstead Athletic	0-0, 2-1
Worthing v Bromley	2-1
Hastings Town v Canterbury City	1-2
Margate v Chertsey Town	1-4
Kingstonian v Langney Sports	2-2, 1-1, 3-1
Sittingbourne v Fareham Town	3-2
Erith & Belvedere v Havant Town	1-1, 4-5
Witney Town v Hampton	3-1

Bognor Regis Town v Bemerton Heath Harlequins	
	1-1, 2-2, 1-1, 0-1
Abingdon Town v Maidenhead United	2-0
Bashley v Wimborne Town	3-1
Calne Town v Brockenhurst	0-1
Salisbury v Thatcham Town	4-0
Lymington v Dorchester Town	1-1, 4-2
Cheltenham Town v Cinderford Town	3-0
Newport AFC v Worcester City	3-0
Weston-super-Mare v Clevedon Town	0-4
Falmouth Town v Bath City	0-3
Weymouth v Truro City	3-2

Third Qualifying Round

Bishop Auckland v Blyth Spartans	1-3
Spennymoor United v Gateshead	0-7
Netherfield v Guisborough Town	4-1
Dunston FB v Northallerton Town	0-3
Seaham Red Star v Stockton	1-2
Brigg Town v Southport	0-1
Colwyn Bay v Altrincham	3-3, 1-1, 1-3
Stalybridge Celtic v Accrington Stanley	1-2
Macclesfield Town v Horwich RMI	1-0
Nantwich Town v Marine	0-1
Stafford Rangers v Frickley Athletic	3-0
Gainsborough Trinity v Pelsall Villa	4-2
Nuneaton Borough v Raunds Town	4-0
Sutton Coldfield Town v Rushall Olympic	0-0, 1-1, 2-1
Shepshed Albion v Hednesford Town	1-2
Moor Green v VS Rugby	1-2
Solihull Borough v Braintree Town	4-1
Corby Town v Aveley	4-1
Leyton v Cambridge City	3-0
Newmarket Town v Grays Athletic	1-0
Wealdstone v Dagenham & Redbridge	1-6
Stevenage Borough v St Albans City	3-3, 1-2
Wembley v Hendon	1-0
Chesham United v Berkhamsted Town	3-0
Slough Town v Yeading	2-1
Ashford Town v Deal Town	3-1
Dorking v Dover Athletic	1-0
Worthing v Canterbury City	3-1
Chertsey Town v Kingstonian	1-3
Sittingbourne v Havant Town	3-2
Witney Town v Bemerton Heath Harlequins	1-0
Abingdon Town v Bashley	4-2
Brockenhurst v Salisbury	1-3
Lymington v Cheltenham Town	0-1
Newport AFC v Clevedon Town	1-1, 1-1, 4-2
Bath City v Weymouth	2-0

Fourth Qualifying Round

Barrow v Southport	0-0, 2-3
Gateshead v Whitley Bay	3-0
Blyth Spartans v Stockton	1-1, 2-1
Gainsborough Trinity v Altrincham	0-2
Accrington Stanley v Northallerton Town	3-1
Runcorn v Marine	1-4
Netherfield v Macclesfield Town	1-1, 0-5
Wembley v Nuneaton Borough	1-1, 0-0, 1-2
Stafford Rangers v Bromsgrove Rovers	3-0
Kettering Town v Corby Town	2-1
Hednesford Town v Dagenham & Redbridge	1-3
Enfield v Aylesbury United	0-0, 1-2
Halesowen Town v VS Rugby	1-2
Sutton Coldfield Town v Leyton	6-1
Telford United v St Albans City	1-2
Newmarket Town v Hayes	0-2
Kidderminster Harriers v Atherstone United	2-0
Solihull Borough v Chesham United	3-1
Kingstonian v Welling United	2-1
Crawley Town v Yeovil Town	1-2
Ashford Town v Slough Town	1-2
Tiverton Town v Bath City	0-0 1-2
Cheltenham Town v Worthing	3-2
Sittingbourne v Marlow	1-1, 1-2
Witney Town v Salisbury	1-2
Newport AFC v Sutton United	1-4
Farnborough Town v Dorking	1-1, 0-2
Abingdon Town v Merthyr Tydfil	0-0, 1-2

FA CUP 1992–93

COMPETITION PROPER

FIRST ROUND

14 NOV

Accrington S (1) 3 *(Beck 3)*
Gateshead (1) 2 *(Lamb, Bell)* 2270
Accrington S: Collings; Clark, Lampkin, Owen, Blackman, Hoskin, Collins, Cooper, Hughes, Beck, Lutkevitch (Burns).
Gateshead: Smith; Higgins, Holliday, Wrightson (Corner), McDowell, Elliott, Farrey, Cooke, Askew (Farnaby), Bell, Lamb.

Blackpool (1) 1 *(Mitchell)*
Rochdale (1) 1 *(Whitehall)* 4069
Blackpool: Martin; Burgess, Mercer, Horner, Briggs, Bonner (Robinson), Rodwell, Sinclair, Mitchell (Leitch), Gouck, Eyres.
Rochdale: Rose; Thackeray, Graham, Reid, Reeves, Ryan, Bowden, Payne, Flounders (Parker), Whitehall, Milner.

Blyth S (1) 1 *(Howie)*
Southport (1) 2 *(Haw, Withers)* 2136
Blyth S: Gardner; Liddle (Walker), Hayes, Mason, Raffell, Teesdale, Howie, Peattie, Pyle, Middleton (Nicholl), Plaskett.
Southport: Moore; McDonald, Fuller, Mooney, Goulding, Schofield, Senior, Brennan, Haw, Baines, Withers.

Bolton W (1) 2 *(Reeves, Walker)*
Sutton Cd (0) 1 *(Dale)* 5345
Bolton W: Branagan; Spooner, Burke (Kelly), Lydiate, Seagraves, Winstanley, Green, Stubbs, Walker, Reeves, Patterson.
Sutton Cd: Belford; Ling, Cowdrill, Sturgeon, Whittingham, Hadland, Carroll (Biddle), Whitehouse, Hunt, Dale, Clarke.

Bournemouth (0) 0
Barnet (0) 0 4688
Bournemouth: Bartram; O'Driscoll, Morrell, Morris, Watson, Shearer, Wood, Mundee, Lovell, Scott, Rowland (Masters).
Barnet: Phillips; Huxford, Naylor, Howell, Barnett, Horton, Payne, Carter, Bull, Lowe (Hoddle), Stein (Showler).

Bradford C (0) 1 *(Jewell)*
Preston NE (0) 1 *(Fowler)* 8553
Bradford C: Tomlinson; Heseltine, Oliver, Duxbury L, Blake, Jackson (Lawford), Hoyle, Jewell, McCarthy, Tinnion, Duxbury M.
Preston NE: Farnworth; Cartwright, Davidson, Callaghan, Flynn, Fowler, Ashcroft, Graham, Allardyce, Ellis (Finney), James.

Brighton & HA (1) 2 *(Kennedy, Codner)*
Hayes (0) 0 5879
Brighton & HA: Beeney; Chivers, Chapman, Wilkins, McCarthy, Foster, Crumplin, Kennedy, Edwards, Codner, Walker.
Hayes: Chatfield; Kelly W, Brown, Deer (Cuffie), Pedlar, Wingfield, Marshall, Walton (Baker), Pearce, Stevens, Kelly T.

Burnley (1) 2 *(Conroy, Curran (og))*
Scarborough (0) 1 *(Mockler)* 8359
Burnley: Beresford; Measham, Jakub, Davis, Pender, Farrell, Penney, Deary, Heath, Conroy, Harper.
Scarborough: Ford; Thompson, Mudd, Lee (McGee), Hirst, Curran, Mockler, Himsworth, Mooney, Foreman, Wheeler (Jules).

Bury (1) 2 *(Knill (pen), Robinson (pen))*
Witton Alb (0) 0 2682
Bury: Kelly; Anderson, Kearney, Daws, Valentine, Knill, Hughes, Robinson, Hulme, Reid, Stevens (Lyons).
Witton Alb: Mason; Senior, Coathup, McNelis, Connor, Lillis, Thomas, Rose (Alford), Gallagher, Burke, Adams.

Cardiff C (2) 2 *(Millar, Blake)*
Bath C (1) 3 *(Withey, Gill, Vernon)* 4506
Cardiff C: Ward; Gibbins (Perry), Searle, James, Matthews, Brazil, Ramsey, Griffith (Pike), Blake, Dale, Millar.
Bath C: Mogg; Palmer, Dicks, Smart (Vernon), Crowley, Cousins, Banks, Weston, Withey, Boyle, Gill.

Chester C (1) 1 *(Ryan)*
Altrincham (0) 1 *(Comstive (og))* 4033
Chester C: Stewart; Preece, Comstive, Whelan, Abel, Lightfoot, Thompson, Ryan (Goodwin), Rimmer, Barrow, Pugh.
Altrincham: Paladino; Woodhead, Freeman, France, Sidderley, Green, Saunders (Bradshaw), Ogley, Harris, Carmody, Rudge.

Colchester U (2) 4 *(Sorrell, Bennett 2, Ball)*
Slough T (0) 0 3848
Colchester U: Greene; Sorrell, Roberts, Kinsella, Cawley, English, Ball, Bennett, McDonough (Oxbrow), McGavin, Smith.
Slough T: Bunting; Whitby, Pluckrose, Briley, Foran, Anderson, Hazell, Scott, Sayer, McKinnon, Fiore.

Crewe Alex (2) 6 *(Hignett 4, McKearney 2)*
Wrexham (0) 1 *(Bennett)* 5556
Crewe Alex: Greygoose; McKearney, Whalley, Wilson, Carr, Macauley, Hignett, Naylor, Clarkson, Lennon (Harvey).
Wrexham: Morris; Jones B, Hardy, Phillips, Humes, Sertori, Bennett, Esdaille (Owen), Connelly, Thomas, Taylor (Watkin).

655

Dagenham & Redbridge (3) 4 *(Broom, Connor, Butterworth, Cavell)*
Leyton Orient (2) 5 *(Howard, Whitbread, Cooper 2, Jones)* 5300
Dagenham & Redbridge: McKenna; Shirtliff (Kimble), Watts, Pamphlett, Connor, Broom, Owers (Georgiou), Butterworth, Cavell, Nuttell, Blackford.
Leyton Orient: Turner; Bellamy, Howard, Hales (Jones), Kitchen, Whitbread, Taylor, Achampong, Livett, Ryan, Cooper.

Darlington (0) 1 *(Dobie)*
Hull C (0) 2 *(Atkinson, Norton)* 3132
Darlington: Prudhoe; Tupling, Ball, Gaughan, Parkin, O'Shaughnessy, Gregan, Pickering, Juryeff, Dobie, Mardenborough (Isaacs) (Ellison).
Hull C: Wilson; Hockaday, Miller, Mail, Wilcox, France, Norton, Atkinson, Hunter, Windass, Jenkinson.

Doncaster R (1) 1 *(Quinlan)*
Hartlepool U (0) 2 *(Johnrose, Saville (pen))* 4513
Doncaster R: Crichton; Morrow, Prindiville, Reddish, Richards, Hicks, Hewitt, Hodson, Heritage (Hine), Quinlan, Gormley.
Hartlepool U: Hodge; Cross R, Cross P, Tait, MacPhail, Emerson, Johnrose, Olsson, Saville, Honour, Wratten.

Exeter C (1) 1 *(Moran)*
Kidderminster H (0) 0 3082
Exeter C: Miller; Hiley, Cook, Bond, Brown, Whiston, Collins (Harris), Kelly, Jepson, Moran, Hodge.
Kidderminster H: Steadman; Benton, McGrath, Weir, Brindley, Forsyth, Deakin, Grainger, Davies (Hadley), Palmer, Hansen (Wilcox).

Gillingham (2) 3 *(Clark, Crown, Forster)*
Kettering T (1) 2 *(Brown, Hill (pen))* 3962
Gillingham: Barrett; Green, Martin, Butler, Carpenter (O'Connor), Smith, Clark, Crown, Arnott, Forster, Dempsey.
Kettering T: Beasley (Docker); Reed, Gernon, Nicol, Smalley, Stebbing, Brown, Donald, Riley, Murphy, Hill.

Kingstonian (1) 1 *(Russell)*
Peterborough U (0) 1 *(Adcock)* 5000
Kingstonian: Blake; Cowler, Finch, Russell, Broderick, Kempton, Harlow, Parr, Barham (Brathwaite), Vines, Cherry (Sheldrick).
Peterborough U: Bennett; Robinson, Bradshaw (Luke), Halsall, Howarth, Welsh, Sterling, Cooper, Adcock, Philliskirk, Ebdon (Iorfa).

Lincoln C (0) 0
Stafford R (0) 0 3380
Lincoln C: Bowling; Baraclough (Smith), Clarke, Carmichael, Dunphy, Brown, Schofield, Bressington, Lee, Costello, Puttnam.
Stafford R: Price; Pearson, Bradshaw, Simpson, Essex, Berry, Wood, Jones, Callaghan, Palgrave, Clayton.

Macclesfield T (0) 0
Chesterfield (0) 0 3063
Macclesfield T: Farrelly S; Shepherd, Bimson, Edwards, Kendall, Sorvel, Askey, Timmons, Lambert, Mitchell, Leicester.
Chesterfield: Leonard; Lemon, Carr, Williams, Brien, Rogers, Cash, Morris, Lancaster, Turnbull, Kennedy.

Marine (3) 4 *(Ward, Gautrey, Rowland, Camden)*
Halifax T (0) 1 *(German)* 1892
Marine: O'Brien; Ward, Johnson, Roche, Draper, Gautrey (McDonough), Murray, Rowlands, Ross, Camden (Grant), Dawson.
Halifax T: Bracey; Lewis, Wilson, Lucketti, Thompstone, Bradley (Megson), Matthews, Case, Thomas, Paterson, Peake (German).

Marlow (1) 3 *(Lay, Watkins, Glasgow)*
Salisbury (2) 3 *(Loveridge, Sanders, Fletcher)* 940
Marlow: Ellis; George (Blackman), Mikurenda (Ferguson), Stone, Hubbick, Dell, Lay, Regan, Watkins, Davies, Glasgow.
Salisbury: Simpkins; Payne, Green, Loveridge, Emms, Fletcher, Gomersall, Shaw, Sanders, Chalk, Bale.

Northampton T (2) 3 *(Wilkin, Brown, Terry)*
Fulham (0) 1 *(Farrell)* 4823
Northampton T: Richardson; Curtis, Beavon, Harmon, Angus, Terry, Burnham, Wilkin, Bell, Brown, Chard.
Fulham: Stannard; Morgan, Pike, Eckhardt, Nebbeling (Newson), Thomas, Hails, Marshall, Farrell, Tierling, Lewis (Onwere).

Rotherham U (2) 4 *(Goodwin 2, Cunningham, Howard)*
Walsall (0) 0 4201
Rotherham U: Mercer; Pickering, Hutchings, Banks, Johnson, Law, Hazel, Goodwin, Cunningham, Howard, Barrick.
Walsall: Gayle; Cecere, Demetrios (O'Hara), Methven, West, Williams, Ntamark, Clarke (Ollerenshaw), Marsh, MacDonald, McDonald.

Scunthorpe U (0) 0
Huddersfield T (0) 0 4312
Scunthorpe U: Samways; McCullagh, Longden, Alexander, Elliott, Stevenson, Greaves, White, Daws, Buckley (Humphries), Helliwell.
Huddersfield T: Clarke; Dyson, Charlton, Robinson, Parsley, Jackson, Barnett, Stuart (Onuora), Booth, Wright, Starbuck.

Shrewsbury T (2) 3 *(Summerfield, Lyne, Williams L)*
Mansfield T (1) 1 *(Fairclough)* 3355
Shrewsbury T: Edwards; Haylock, Worsley, Taylor, Spink, Blake, Williams L, O'Toole, Lyne, Griffiths, Summerfield.
Mansfield T: Pearcey; Parkin, Withe, Holland, Walker, Gray, Fairclough, Castledine, Stant, Wilkinson, Ford.

Solihull (2) 2 *(Canning, Carter)*
VS Rugby (1) 2 *(Bufton, Green)* 1395
Solihull: Houghton; Byrne (Hawker), Latchford, Boxall, Dyson, Ollis, Mulders, Tuohy, Canning, Carter, Burton.
VS Rugby: Martin; Sweeney, Hardwick, Fitzpatrick, Olner, Redgate, Smith, Bradder, Bufton (Warner), Shearer, Green.

St Albans C (0) 1 *(Duffield (pen))*
Cheltenham T (0) 2 *(Willetts (pen), Purdie)* 3189
St Albans C: Westwood; Smart (Brett), Risley, Dowie, Price, Cockram, Duffield, Gurney, Clark, Williams, King.
Cheltenham T: Nicholls; Howells, Willetts, Brown, Vircavs, Tucker, Lovell, Smith N, Smith J, Bloomer, Hirons (Purdie),

Sutton U (1) 1 *(Quail)*
Hereford U (1) 2 *(Pickard, Barton (og))* 2749
Sutton U: Fearon; Gates, Barton, Golley N, Costello, Golley M (Browne), Byrne, Quail, Feltham (Evans), Thomas, Scott.
Hereford U: Judge; Fry, Downs, Davies, Devine, Rowbotham, Hall, Jones, Pickard, Brain, Nicholson.

Torquay U (0) 2 *(Foster, Herd)*
Yeovil T (1) 5 *(Wilson, Spencer, Batty 3 (2 pens))* 3453
Torquay U: Lowe; Gardiner, Colcombe, Salman (Joyce), Moore, Curran, Hall, Trollope (Herd), Fashanu, Myers, Foster.
Yeovil T: Coles; Coates, Sherwood, Shail, Ferns, Cooper (Wallace), Sanderson, Batty, Wilson (Nevin), Spencer, Harrower.

WBA (4) 8 *(Donovan 3, McNally, Taylor, Robson, Raven, Hamilton)*
Aylesbury U (0) 0 12,337
WBA: Naylor; Burgess (Coldicott), Lilwall, Bradley, Raven, Strodder, Garner (Robson), Hamilton, Taylor, McNally, Donovan.
Aylesbury U: Garner; Day, Collins, Grenfell, Mason, Cassidy (Tomlinson), Robinson, Ashby, Lawford (Jones), Sansom, Heath.

Wigan Ath (3) 3 *(Williams (og), Dalziel (og), Powell)*
Carlisle U (1) 1 *(Arnold)* 2963
Wigan Ath: Adkins; Appleton, Tankard, Johnson, Robertson, Langley, Jones (Kirwan), Powell, Daley, Pilling, Griffiths.
Carlisle U: O'Hanlon; Williams, Dalziel, Holden, McCreery (Arnold), Heron, Proudlock, Edmondson, Sendall, Watson, Thorpe.

Woking (1) 3 *(Clement, Biggins, Carroll)*
Nuneaton (1) 2 *(Bullock, Culpin)* 3280
Woking: Batty; Clement, Nugent, Baron, Wye L, Wye S, Fielder, Biggins, Steele (Fleming), Senior, Puckett (Carroll).
Nuneaton: Manuel; Wade, Tarry, Bullock, Ridding, Cottrill, Simpson, Culpin, Rosegreen, Mogford, Symonds.

Wycombe W (2) 3 *(Scott, Carroll, Stapleton)*
Merthyr T (1) 1 *(Rogers)* 4322
Wycombe W: Hyde; Cousins, Crossley, Kerr, Creaser, Hutchinson, Carroll, Casey, Stapleton, Scott, Guppy.
Merthyr T: Morris; Williams M, James, Boyle, Abraham, Rogers, Beattie, Davies, D'Auria, Coates, Williams C.

York C (0) 1 *(Canham)*
Stockport Co (0) 3 *(Todd, Francis 2)* 5640
York C: Marples; McMillan, Hall, Jordan, Stancliffe, Atkin, McCarthy, Borthwick, Barnes, Swann, Canham.
Stockport Co: Redfern; Todd, Williams P, Frain, Barras, Williams B, Gannon (Miller), Ward, Francis, Beaumont, Preece.

15 NOV

Dorking (1) 2 *(Grainger, Lunn)*
Plymouth Arg (1) 3 *(Dalton 2, Marshall)* 3200
Dorking: Orkney; Bird, Rains (Thornton), Welch, Marriner, Tutt, Robson, Grainger, Lunn, Hanlan, Anderson.
Plymouth Arg: Newland; Poole, Morgan, Hill, Morrison, Joyce, Adcock, Castle, Nugent, Marshall, Dalton.

Reading (1) 1 *(Quinn)*
Birmingham C (0) 0 7667
Reading: Francis; Gooding, Hopkins, McPherson, Williams, Parkinson, Gilkes, Dillon, Quinn, Lambert (Lovell), Jones.
Birmingham C: Thomas; Holmes, Potter (Rogers), Cooper (Peschisolido), Hicks, Matthewson, Rodgerson, Gayle, Frain, Tait, Sturridge.

16 NOV

Stoke C (0) 0
Port Vale (0) 0 24,500
Stoke C: Sinclair; Butler, Sandford, Cranson, Overson, Gleghorn, Foley, Russell, Stein, Shaw, Beeston.
Port Vale: Musselwhite; Sandeman, Sulley, Walker, Swan, Glover, Aspin, Kerr (Jeffers), Cross (Foyle), Houchen, Taylor.

FIRST ROUND REPLAYS

24 NOV

Port Vale (2) 3 *(Foyle 2, Porter)*
Stoke C (1) 1 *(Sandford)* 19,810
Port Vale: Musselwhite; Sandeman, Sulley, Walker, Swan, Glover, Aspin (Jeffers), Porter, Cross, Foyle, Taylor.
Stoke C: Sinclair; Butler, Sandford, Cranson, Overson, Gleghorn, Foley, Russell, Stein, Shaw (Regis), Beeston.

25 NOV

Altrincham (0) 2 *(Harris, Freeman)*
Chester C (0) 0 3000
Altrincham: Paladino; Woodhead, Freeman, France, Sidderley, Ogley, Saunders, Harris, Green (Bradshaw), Carmody, Rudge.
Chester C: Stewart; Preece, Comstive, Kelly (Ryan), Abel, Lightfoot, Thompson (Morton), Butler, Rimmer, Barrow, Pugh.

Barnet (0) 1 *(Carter)*
Bournemouth (2) 2 *(Lovell, Mundee)*   3731
Barnet: Phillips; Huxford, Naylor, Bodley, Howell, Horton, Payne, Stein, Bull, Lowe (Carter), Showler (Hunt).
Bournemouth: Bartram; Mundee, Morrell, Morris, Watson, Pennock, O'Driscoll, McGorry (Murray), Lovell (Masters), Wood, Rowland.

Chesterfield (1) 2 *(Turnbull, Williams (pen))*
Macclesfield T (1) 2 *(Mitchell 2)*   4143
Chesterfield: Leonard; Lemon, Carr, Williams, Brien, Rogers, Hebberd, Morris, Lancaster, Turnbull, Kennedy.
Macclesfield T: Farrelly S; Shepherd, Bimson, Edwards, Kendall, McMahon, Askey, Timmons (Farrelly M), Lambert, Mitchell, Leicester.
aet; Macclesfield T won 3-2 on penalties.

Huddersfield T (1) 2 *(Barnett 2)*
Scunthorpe U (0) 1 *(Buckley) aet*   4841
Huddersfield T: Clarke; Parsley, Charlton, Robinson, Dyson, Jackson, Barnett, Onuora, Roberts, Wright, Starbuck.
Scunthorpe U: Samways; McCullagh, Longden, Alexander, Elliott, Humphries, Greaves (Buckley), Martin, Daws, White, Helliwell.

Peterborough U (3) 9 *(Philliskirk 5, Adcock 2, Cooper, Harlow (og))*
Kingstonian (0) 1 *(Finch)*   5307
Peterborough U: Bennett; Bradshaw, Robinson, Iorfa, Welsh, Howarth, Sterling (Barnes), Adcock, Philliskirk, Cooper, Ebdon.
Kingstonian: Blake (Shelford); Finch, Lewis, Eriemo, Broderick, Kempton, Harlow, Barham (Gbogindo), Cherry, Brathwaite, Parr.
(Match ordered to be replayed by FA; coin thrown from crowd struck Blake who had to be taken off in 55th minute.)

Preston NE (1) 4 *(Graham, Ellis, Davidson, Callaghan)*
Bradford C (3) 5 *(McCarthy 2, Blake, Tinnion (pen), Jewell)*   7905
Preston NE: Farnworth; Cartwright, Davidson, Callaghan, Flynn, Fowler, Ashcroft, Graham, Allardyce (Tinkler), Ellis, James.
Bradford C: Tomlinson; Heseltine, Williams, Duxbury L, Blake, Hoyle, Jewell, Oliver, McCarthy, Tinnion, Duxbury M.

Rochdale (0) 1 *(Reid)*
Blackpool (0) 0 *aet*   3408
Rochdale: Rose; Thackeray, Graham, Reid, Reeves, Ryan, Bowden, Payne, Flounders, Whitehall, Milner (Anders) (Parker).
Blackpool: Martin; Burgess, Murphy, Horner, Briggs, Stoneman, Rodwell, Sinclair, Bonner, Gouck, Eyres.

VS Rugby (0) 2 *(Green, Smith)*
Solihull (1) 1 *(Canning (pen)) aet*   1289
VS Rugby: Martin; Sweeney, McGinty T, Fitzpatrick, Olner, Redgate, Smith, Bradder, Carty, Shearer (Hardwick), Green.
Solihull: Houghton; Pinner, Latchford, Mulders, Dyson, Ollis, Hawker, Tuohy (Attwood), Canning (Bertschin), Carter, Burton.

Stafford R (1) 2 *(Boughey, Bradshaw)*
Lincoln C (0) 1 *(Costello)*   2209
Stafford R: Price; Circuit, Bradshaw, Wood, Essex, Berry, Boughey, Griffiths, Clayton, Palgrave, Callaghan (Jones).
Lincoln C: Bowling; Smith, Baraclough, Carmichael (Kabia), Dunphy (Clarke), Brown, Schofield, Bressington, Lee, Costello, Puttnam.

4 DEC

Peterborough U (0) 1 *(Sterling)*
Kingstonian (0) 0   behind closed doors
Peterborough U: Bennett; Bradshaw, Robinson, Halsall, Howarth (Luke), Welsh, Sterling, Cooper, Adcock, Philliskirk, Ebdon.
Kingstonian: Blake; Finch, Cowler, Eriemo, Broderick, Kempton, Harlow, Sheldrick (Cherry), Vines, Brathwaite, Parr.

5 DEC

Salisbury (1) 2 *(Chalk, Sanders)*
Marlow (0) 2 *(Hannigan, Glasgow)*   1854
Salisbury: Simpkins; Payne, Green, Loveridge, Emms, Fletcher, Hobson (Gomersall), Shaw, Sanders, Chalk, Bale (Maskell).
Marlow: Lester; Ferguson, Mikurenda, Stone (Glasgow), Hannigan, Hubbick, Lay, Regan, Watkins, Bushay (Franks), Caesar.
aet; Marlow won 4-3 on penalties.

Swansea C received a bye to the Second Round.

SECOND ROUND

Accrington S (0) 1 *(Cooper)*
Crewe Alex (2) 6 *(Carr, Naylor 2, Whalley 2, Clarkson)*   10,801
Accrington S: Collings; Clark, Lampkin (Schofield), Owen, Johnstone, Burns (McCluskie), Collins, Cooper, Hughes, Beck, Hoskin.
Crewe Alex: Kite; Lennon, Whalley, Wilson, Carr, Macauley, Harvey, Naylor (Clarkson), Evans, Gardiner (Annan), Walters.

Altrincham (0) 1 *(Dyson)*
Port Vale (2) 4 *(Swan, Foyle, Taylor, Van der Laan)*   3859
Altrincham: Paladino; Woodhead, Freeman, France, Sidderley, Ogley, Saunders (Hayde), Harris, Bradshaw, Carmody, Rudge (Dyson).
Port Vale: Musselwhite; Mills, Sulley, Walker, Swan, Van der Laan, Jeffers, Porter, Cross, Foyle, Taylor.

Bolton W (1) 4 *(McAteer, McGinlay 2, Walker)*
Rochdale (0) 0   6876
Bolton W: Branagan; Brown P, Burke, McAteer, Seagraves, Winstanley, Green, Kelly, Walker, McGinlay, Patterson (Reeves).
Rochdale: Rose; Thackeray, Graham, Reid, Reeves, Jones, Ryan, Payne (Howard), Flounders, Bowden, Whitehall.

Brighton & HA (1) 1 *(Kennedy)*
Woking (0) 1 *(Wye S)* 9208
Brighton & HA: Beeney; Chivers, Chapman (Wilkinson), Wilkins, McCarthy, Bissett, Crumplin (Nogan), Kennedy, Edwards, Codner, Walker.
Woking: Batty; Clement, Wye L, Nugent, Alexander, Wye S, Fleming, Biggins, Senior, Puckett (Carroll), Fielder.

Burnley (0) 1 *(Conroy)*
Shrewsbury T (0) 1 *(Griffiths)* 10,038
Burnley: Beresford; Measham, Jakub, Davis, Pender, Farrell (Conroy), Penney, Deary, Heath (Randall), Eli, Harper.
Shrewsbury T: Edwards; Worsley, Lynch, Taylor, Spink, Blake, Williams M, Clark, Smith, Griffiths, Summerfield.

Cheltenham T (0) 1 *(Warren)*
Bournemouth (1) 1 *(Shearer)* 4100
Cheltenham T: Nicholls; Howells, Willetts, Brown, Vircays, Tucker (Warren), Lovell, Smith N, Smith J, Purdie, Bloomer.
Bournemouth: Bartram; Pennock, Morrell, Morris, Watson, O'Driscoll, Wood, Shearer, McGorry, Morgan (Mundee), Rowland.

Exeter C (0) 1 *(Dolan)*
Swansea C (1) 2 *(Cornforth, Jenkins)* 3889
Exeter C: Miller; Hiley, Cook, Redwood (Moran), Bond, Whiston, Collins, Tonge (Dolan), Jepson, Kelly, Hodge.
Swansea C: Freestone; Lyttle, Jenkins, Agboola, Harris, Coughlin, Cullen, Wimbleton (Ford), West, Cornforth, Legg.
Abandoned 86 mins–floodlight failure.

Gillingham (1) 1 *(Crown)*
Colchester U (0) 1 *(McGavin)* 5319
Gillingham: Barrett; Green, Martin, Butler, Breen, Smith, Clark, Crown, Arnott, Forster (O'Connor), Dempsey (Henry).
Colchester U: Green; Grainger, Roberts, Kinsella, Cawley, English, Cook, Sorrell, McDonough, McGavin, Smith.

Macclesfield T (0) 0
Stockport Co (1) 2 *(Preece, Williams B)* 5700
Macclesfield T: Farrelly S; Shepherd, Bimson (Farrelly M), Edwards, Kendall, McMahon, Askey, Timmons, Lambert, Mitchell (Sorvel), Leicester.
Stockport Co: Redfern; Todd, Williams P (Miller), Frain, Barras, Williams B, Gannon, Carstairs, Francis, Beaumont, Preece.

Marine (2) 3 *(Murray 2, Gautrey)*
Stafford R (0) 2 *(Berry (pen), Palgrave)* 1965
Marine: O'Brien; Ward, Johnson, Roche (McDonough), Draper, Gautrey, Murray, Rowlands, Ross, Camden (Grant), Dawson.
Stafford R: Price; Circuit, Bradshaw, Henry, Essex, Berry, Boughey (Wood), Griffiths, Callaghan (Hemmings), Palgrave, Clayton.

Reading (2) 3 *(Quinn 2 (1 pen), Parkinson)*
Leyton Orient (0) 0 7213
Reading: Francis; Taylor (Gooding), Hopkins, McPherson, Williams, Parkinson, Gilkes, Dillon, Quinn, Lambert (Lovell), Jones.
Leyton Orient: Heald; Bellamy, Howard, Hales, Kitchen, Day, Taylor, Achampong (Otto), Warren, Livett, Cooper.

Rotherham U (0) 1 *(Cunningham)*
Hull C (0) 0 6118
Rotherham U: Mercer; Pickering, Hutchings, Banks, Johnson, Law, Hazel, Goodwin, Cunningham, Howard, Barrick.
Hull C: Wilson; Hockaday, Miller, Mail, Wilcox, France, Norton, Atkinson, Young (Warren), Windass, Jenkinson.

Yeovil T (0) 0
Hereford U (0) 0 8085
Yeovil T: Coles; Coates, Sherwood, Shail, Ferns, Batty, Sanderson (Hughes), Wallace, Wilson, Spencer (Nevin), Dobbins.
Hereford U: Judge; Fry (Nicholson), Downs, Davies, Theodosiou, Titterton, Hall, Brain (Devine), Pickard, Anderson, Cousins.

6 DEC

Bath C (0) 2 *(Smart, Randall)*
Northampton T (0) 2 *(Brown, Chard)* 3626
Bath C: Mogg; Palmer (Singleton), Dicks, Gill, Crowley, Cousins, Banks, Weston (Randall), Withey, Smart, Vernon.
Northampton T: Richardson; Curtis, Beavon, Harmon, Angus, Terry, Burnham, Wilkin (Chard), Bell, Brown, McParland.

Bradford C (0) 0
Huddersfield T (1) 2 *(Dunn, O'Regan (pen))* 10,606
Bradford C: Tomlinson; Duxbury M, Williams, Duxbury L, Blake (Heseltine), Hoyle, Jewell, Oliver, McCarthy, Tinnion (Torpey), Reid.
Huddersfield T: Clarke; Parsley, Charlton, Robinson, Mitchell, Jackson, Barnett, O'Regan, Roberts, Dunn, Stuart.

Hartlepool U (0) 4 *(Peverell, Saville 3)*
Southport (0) 0 4171
Hartlepool U: Hodge; Cross R, Cross P, McGuckin, MacPhail, Emerson (Wratten), Johnrose, Olsson, Saville, Honour, Peverell (Southall).
Southport: Moore; McDonald, Fuller, Mooney, Goulding, Schofield, Walmsley (Baines), Brennan, Haw, Gamble (Senior), Withers.

Wycombe W (0) 2 *(Creaser, Thompson)*
WBA (2) 2 *(Bradley, Taylor)* 6904
Wycombe W: Hyde; Cousins, Crossley, Hutchinson, Creaser, Thompson, Carroll, Casey (Greene), Stapleton, Scott, Guppy.
WBA: Naylor; Reid, Lilwall, Bradley (Williams), Raven, Strodder, Garner, Hamilton, Taylor, McNally, Robson (Donovan).

9 DEC

Plymouth Arg (2) 3 *(Marshall 2, Castle)*
Peterborough U (0) 2 *(Philliskirk, Sterling)* 6057
Plymouth Arg: Newland; Poole, Morgan, Hill, Burrows, Garner, Barlow, Castle, Nugent, Marshall, Dalton.
Peterborough U: Bennett; Bradshaw, Robinson, Halsall, Luke, Welsh, Sterling, Iorfa (Barnes), Adcock, Philliskirk, Ebdon.

VS Rugby (0) 0
Marlow (0) 0 2258
VS Rugby: Martin; Sweeney, McGinty T, Fitzpatrick, Olner, Redgate, Smith, Bradder, Hardwick (Warner), Shearer, Green.
Marlow: Lester; Ferguson, Mikurenda, Glasgow (Franks), Hubbick, Hannigan, Lay, Regan, Watkins, Bushay, Caesar (George).

15 DEC

Exeter C (1) 2 *(Moran, Cook)*
Swansea C (2) 5 *(West, Legg, Wimbleton, Cullen, Bowen)* 2941
Exeter C: Miller; Hiley, Cook, Williams, Daniels, Bond, Tonge, Kelly, Moran, Chapman, Hodge.
Swansea C: Freestone; Lyttle, Jenkins, Walker, Harris, Coughlin, Cullen (Bowen), Wimbleton (Ford), West, Cornforth, Legg.

Wigan Ath (0) 1 *(Griffiths (pen))*
Bury (1) 1 *(Hulme)* 3764
Wigan Ath: Adkins; Appleton, Tankard, Johnson, Robertson, Langley, Kirwan (Sharratt), Powell, Daley, Pilling, Griffiths.
Bury: Kelly; Anderson, Hughes, Daws, Valentine, Knill, Lyons, Sonner, Hulme, Reid, Mauge.

SECOND ROUND REPLAYS

Northampton T (0) 3 *(McParland, Wilkin, Bell)*
Bath C (0) 0 4106
Northampton T: Richardson; Curtis, Beavon, Chard, Angus, Terry, Burnham, Wilkin, Bell, Brown, McParland.
Bath C: Mogg; Singleton, Dicks, Ricketts (Vernon), Crowley, Cousins, Banks, Gill, Withey, Smart, Randall.

Shrewsbury T (0) 1 *(Griffiths)*
Burnley (0) 2 *(Pender, Conroy)* 5671
Shrewsbury T: Edwards; Worsley, Lynch, Taylor, Spink, Williams M, Summerfield, Clark, Smith (O'Toole), Griffiths (Williams L), Lyne.
Burnley: Beresford; Measham, Jakub (Monington), Davis, Pender, Farrell (Eli), Penney, Deary, Heath, Conroy, Harper.

WBA (0) 1 *(Taylor)*
Wycombe W (0) 0 17,640
WBA Naylor; Reid, Lilwall, Bradley, Raven, Strodder, Donovan, Hamilton, Taylor, McNally, Robson (Heggs).
Wycombe W: Hyde; Cousins, Crossley, Kerr, Creaser, Thompson, Carroll, Buckle (Hutchison), Stapleton, Scott, Guppy.

16 DEC

Bournemouth (1) 3 *(Mundee, McGorry, Morgan)*
Cheltenham T (0) 0 5100
Bournemouth: Bartram; Pennock, Masters, Morris, Watson, McGorry, Wood, Shearer, Mundee, Morgan, O'Driscoll.
Cheltenham T: Churchward; Howells, Willetts, Brown, Vircavs, Tucker, Lovell (Ring), Smith N, Smith J, Warren (Iddles), Bloomer.

Colchester U (0) 2 *(Ball 2)*
Gillingham (3) 3 *(Forster, Arnott, Henry (pen))* 4440
Colchester U: Green; Grainger, Roberts, Kinsella, Ball, English, Cook (Betts), Sorrell (Bennett), McDonough, McGavin, Smith.
Gillingham: Barrett; Henry, Martin, Butler, Breen, Smith, Clark, Forster (Aylott), Arnott, O'Connor, Dempsey (Palmer).

Hereford U (0) 1 *(Pickard)*
Yeovil T (1) 2 *(Sanderson, Coates)* 6031
Hereford U: Judge; Titterton, Downs, Devine, Theodosiou, Cousins, Hall, Jones (Anderson), Pickard, Brain (Fry), Nicholson.
Yeovil T: Coles; Dobbins, Sherwood, Shail, Ferns, Cooper (Coates), Sanderson, Batty, Wilson, Spencer, Harrower.

Marlow (0) 2 *(Bushay, Watkins)*
VS Rugby (0) 0 1904
Marlow: Lester; Franks, Ferguson, Hubbick, Stone, Dell, Lay, Glasgow (Caesar), Watkins, Bushay (Regan), Hannigan.
VS Rugby: Martin; Sweeney, McGinty, Fitzpatrick, Olner, Redgate, Smith (Warner), Bradder (Bufton), Hardwick, Shearer, Green.

Woking (1) 1 *(Senior)*
Brighton & HA (1) 2 *(Codner, Crumplin)* 5870
Woking: Batty; Fleming, Wye L, Brown K, Alexander, Wye S, Brown D, Biggins, Senior, Puckett (Buzaglo), Fielder.
Brighton & HA: Beeney; Chivers, Chapman, Wilkins, McCarthy, Bissett, Wilkinson (Crumplin), Kennedy, Nogan, Codner, Walker.

2 JAN

Bury (0) 1 *(Mauge)*
Wigan Ath (0) 0 5136
Bury: Kelly; Kearney, Stanislaus, Daws, Gardner, Knill, Lyons (Stevens), Sonner, Hulme, Mauge, Ward.
Wigan Ath: Pennock; Appleton, Tankard, Johnson, Robertson, Langley, Pilling, Powell (Kirwan), Sharratt, Worthington (Nugent), Griffiths.

THIRD ROUND

Aston Villa (1) 1 *(Cox)*
Bristol R (0) 1 *(Browning)* 27,040
Aston Villa: Spink; Barrett, Staunton (Cox), Teale, McGrath, Richardson, Houghton, Parker, Saunders, Yorke (Regis), Froggatt.
Bristol R: Kelly; Alexander, Tillson, Yates, Hardyman, Evans, Browning, Stewart (Mehew), Taylor, Saunders, Waddock.

Blackburn R (0) 3 *(Ripley 2, Newell)*
Bournemouth (1) 1 *(Ekoku)*   13,773
Blackburn R: Mimms; May, Wright, Atkins (Sherwood), Hendry, Marker, Ripley, Cowans, Wegerle, Newell, Wilcox.
Bournemouth: Bartram; Pennock, Masters, Morris, Watson, McGorry, Wood, Shearer, O'Driscoll, Ekoku, Mundee.

Brentford (0) 0
Grimsby T (1) 2 *(Mendonca, Dobbin)*   6880
Brentford: Benstead; Statham, Bennett, Chalmers, Westley, Gayle, Allon, Manuel, Luscombe, Blissett, Smillie.
Grimsby T: Wilmot; Ford, Agnew, Futcher, Rodger, Dobbin, Watson (Jobling), Gilbert, Groves, Mendonca, Rees (Smith).

Brighton & HA (1) 1 *(Edwards)*
Portsmouth (0) 0   17,851
Brighton & HA: Beeney; Chivers, Gallacher, Wilkins, Foster, Bissett, Crumplin, Kennedy, Nogan, Codner, Edwards (Funnell).
Portsmouth: Knight; Awford, Daniel, McLoughlin, Symons, Burns, Russell (Ross), Chamberlain, Walsh (Murray), Powell, Aspinall.

Derby Co (1) 2 *(Short, Miller (og))*
Stockport Co (0) 1 *(McCord)*   17,960
Derby Co: Sutton; Kavanagh, Forsyth, Short, Wassall, Pembridge, Johnson, Kuhl, Kitson (McMinn), Gabbiadini (Simpson), Williams.
Stockport Co: Edwards; Todd, Williams P, Miller, Barras, Williams B, Gannon (Frain), Ward, Francis, Beaumont, Preece (McCord).

Gillingham (0) 0
Huddersfield T (0) 0   5413
Gillingham: Lim; Green, Palmer, Butler, Breen, Carpenter, Clark, O'Connor, Arnott, Henry, Eeles.
Huddersfield T: Elliott; Parsley, Charlton, Robinson, Mitchell, Jackson, Barnett, O'Regan, Roberts, Dunn, Onuora.

Hartlepool U (0) 1 *(Saville (pen))*
Crystal Palace (0) 0   6721
Hartlepool U: Jones; Cross R, Cross P, Gilchrist, MacPhail, Emerson, Johnrose, Olsson, Saville, Honour, Southall.
Crystal Palace: Martyn; Humphrey, Shaw, Coleman, Young, Bowry, Osborn, Thomas, Armstrong, Rodger, McGoldrick.

Leeds U (0) 1 *(Speed)*
Charlton Ath (0) 1 *(Nelson)*   21,827
Leeds U: Lukic; Sterland (Newsome), Dorigo, Batty (Rodney Wallace), Fairclough, Wetherall, Strachan, Shutt, Chapman, McAllister, Speed.
Charlton Ath: Bolder; Pitcher, Minto, Bumstead (Grant), Webster, Balmer, Robinson, Leaburn, Garland, Nelson, Walsh.

Manchester C (0) 1 *(Sheron)*
Reading (1) 1 *(Taylor)*   20,523
Manchester C: Coton; Brightwell I (Brightwell D), Phelan, McMahon, Curle, Hill, White, Sheron, Quinn, Flitcroft, Holden.
Reading: Francis; Gooding, Hopkins, McPherson, Williams, Parkinson, Gilkes, Holzman, Quinn, Lambert, Taylor.

Marlow (0) 1 *(Lay) at White Hart Lane*
Tottenham H (2) 5 *(Sheringham, Barmby 2, Samways 2)*   26,636
Marlow: Lester; Franks (Regan), Ferguson, Hubbick, Stone, Dell, Lay, Caesar (Glasgow), Watkins, Bushay, Hannigan.
Tottenham H: Thorstvedt; Austin, Edinburgh, Samways (Anderton), Mabbutt, Ruddock, Howells, Barmby, Nayim, Sheringham, Allen (Watson).

Newcastle U (0) 4 *(Peacock 2, Lee, Sheedy)*
Port Vale (0) 0   29,873
Newcastle U: Srnicek; Venison, Beresford, O'Brien, Scott (Kilcline), Howey, Lee, Peacock, Kelly (Bracewell), Clark, Sheedy.
Port Vale: Musselwhite; Sandeman, Sulley, Walker, Swan, Glover, Jeffers, Aspin, Cross (Van der Laan), Foyle, Taylor.

Oldham Ath (0) 2 *(Olney, Bernard)*
Tranmere R (2) 2 *(Aldridge (pen), Nevin)* 13,389
Oldham Ath: Gerrard; Halle, Barlow, Bernard, Jobson, Fleming, Adams, Olney, Sharp, Milligan, Brennan.
Tranmere R: Nixon; Hughes, Brannan (Martindale), Irons, Mungall, Vickers, Morrissey, Aldridge, Malkin, McNab, Nevin.

Sheffield U (0) 2 *(Hodges, Beesley)*
Burnley (2) 2 *(Heath 2)*   23,041
Sheffield U: Kelly; Gage, Barnes, Gannon (Hoyland), Pemberton, Beesley, Bradshaw (Deane), Rogers, Littlejohn, Cork, Hodges.
Burnley: Beresford; Measham, Jakub, Davis, Pender, Farrell, Painter, Randall, Heath, Conroy, Harper.

Swansea C (0) 1 *(West)*
Oxford U (0) 1 *(Cusack)*   6985
Swansea C: Freestone; Lyttle, Jenkins, Walker, Harris, Coughlin, Cullen, Wimbleton, West, Cornforth (Bowen), Legg.
Oxford U: Reece; Smart, Robinson, Lewis, Evans, Melville, Magilton, Beauchamp, Cusack, Durnin, Allen.

Watford (1) 1 *(Nogan)*   12,363
Wolverhampton W (1) 4 *(Holdsworth (og), Downing, Mutch, Bull)*
Watford: Suckling; Soloman, Drysdale, Dublin, Holdsworth, Willis, Putney, Nogan, Furlong, Charlery, Lavin.
Wolverhampton W: Jones; Madden, Edwards, Rankine, Mountfield, Blades, Downing, Cook, Bull, Mutch, Venus (Birch).

WBA (0) 0
West Ham U (2) 2 *(Allen C, Robson)*   25,896
WBA: Naylor; Shakespeare (Fereday), Lilwall, Bradley, Raven, Strodder, Garner, Hamilton, Taylor, McNally, Donovan (Hackett).
West Ham U: Miklosko; Breacker, Dicks, Potts, Martin, Allen M, Robson, Butler, Morley, Allen C, Keen.

Wimbledon (0) 0
Everton (0) 0   7818
Wimbledon: Segers; Joseph, McAllister, Jones, Scales, Blackwell, Miller (Berry), Earle, Fashanu, Sanchez, Clarke.
Everton: Southall; Jackson, Ablett, Snodin (Horne), Watson, Keown, Harper (Barlow), Beardsley, Rideout, Kenny, Ebbrell.

Yeovil T (0) 1 *(Batty (pen))*
Arsenal (2) 3 *(Wright 3)*   8612
Yeovil T: Coles; Dobbins, Sherwood, Wallace, Ferns, Cooper (Coates), Sanderson, Batty, Wilson (Nevin), Spencer, Harrower.
Arsenal: Seaman; Dixon, Winterburn, Hillier, Bould, Adams, O'Leary, Wright, Smith, Merson, Limpar.

3 JAN

Bolton W (2) 2 *(McGinlay, Seagraves)*
Liverpool (0) 2 *(Winstanley (og), Rush)*   21,502
Bolton W: Branagan; Brown P, Burke, Lee, Seagraves, Winstanley, Green, Kelly, Walker, McGinlay, Patterson.
Liverpool: Hooper; Marsh, Jones, Nicol, Piechnik, Bjornebye, McManaman, Hutchison, Rush, Barnes, Thomas (Rosenthal).

Nottingham F (2) 2 *(Keane, Webb)*
Southampton (1) 1 *(Le Tissier)*   13,592
Nottingham F: Crossley; Laws, Pearce, Chettle, Tiler, Keane, Crosby, Gemmill, Clough, Webb, Woan.
Southampton: Flowers; Kenna (Groves), Adams, Dodd, Hall, Monkou, Le Tissier, Cockerill, Dixon, Maddison, Benali (Banger).

4 JAN

QPR (3) 3 *(Ferdinand 2, Penrice)*
Swindon T (0) 0   12,106
QPR: Roberts; Bardsley, Wilson, Wilkins, Peacock, McDonald, Barker, Holloway, Ferdinand, Penrice (Impey), Sinton.
Swindon T: Hammond; Kerslake, Bodin, Hoddle, Mitchell, Taylor, Hazard, Horlock (Summerbee), Maskell (Murray), Ling, White.

5 JAN

Manchester U (1) 2 *(Phelan, Gillespie)*
Bury (0) 0   30,668
Manchester U: Schmeichel; Parker, Irwin (Blackmore), Bruce, Sharpe, Pallister, Cantona, Gillespie, McClair (Robson), Hughes, Phelan.
Bury: Kelly; Kearney, Stanislaus, Daws, Gardner, Knill, Lyons, Sonner (Stevens), Hulme, Mauge, Ward.

12 JAN

Crewe Alex (3) 3 *(McKearney (pen), Edwards, Clarkson)*
Marine (0) 1 *(Johnson)*   4036
Crewe Alex: Greygoose; McKearney (Garvey), Whalley, Wilson, Carr, Hughes, Harvey, Clarkson, Evans, Gardiner, Edwards.
Marine: O'Brien; Ward, Johnson, Roche, Proctor, Gautrey, Murray (Grant), Rowlands, Ross, Camden, Dawson (McDonough).

Ipswich T (1) 3 *(Thompson, Dozzell, Whitton)*
Plymouth Arg (1) 1 *(Castle)*   12,803
Ipswich T: Baker; Johnson, Thompson, Stockwell, Wark (Youds), Whelan, Williams, Guentchev, Whitton, Dozzell, Kiwomya.
Plymouth Arg: Shilton; McCall, Morgan, Hill, Morrison, Joyce, Skinner (Marshall), Castle, Nugent, Evans, Dalton.

Northampton T (0) 0
Rotherham U (0) 1 *(Howard)*   7256
Northampton T: Richardson; Parsons, Curtis, Harmon, Angus, Terry, Burnham, Wilkin (Scott), Bell, Brown, McParland.
Rotherham U: Mercer; Pickering, Hutchings, Banks, Johnson, Law, Goater, Goodwin, Cunningham (Wilder), Howard, Barrick.

Notts Co (0) 0
Sunderland (1) 2 *(Cunningham, Goodman)*   8522
Notts Co: Cherry; Short, Dryden, Thomas, Turner, Palmer, Williams, Wilson, Agana (Lund), Matthews, Smith D (Slawson).
Sunderland: Norman; Kay, Atkinson, Ord, Butcher, Ball, Cunnington, Mooney (Davenport), Goodman, Rush, Armstrong.

THIRD ROUND REPLAYS

Burnley (1) 2 *(Heath, Monington)*
Sheffield U (3) 4 *(Deane 3, Littlejohn)*   19,061
Burnley: Beresford; Measham, Jakub, Davis, Pender, Farrell (Eli), Harper, Randall, Heath, Conroy, Monington.
Sheffield U: Kelly; Gage, Barnes, Hoyland, Gayle, Beesley, Cork, Rogers, Littlejohn, Deane, Hodges (Bradshaw).

Everton (0) 1 *(Watson)*
Wimbledon (1) 2 *(Fashanu, Earle)*   15,293
Everton: Kearton; Jackson, Ablett, Snodin (Warzycha), Watson, Keown, Radosavljevic, Beardsley, Barlow, Kenny (Harper), Ebbrell.
Wimbledon: Segers; Joseph, Elkins, Cotterill, Scales, Blackwell, Ardley, Earle, Fashanu, Sanchez, Clarke (Talboys).

Oxford U (0) 2 *(Magilton (pen), Beauchamp)*
Swansea C (0) 2 *(Cornforth, Legg)*   4707
Oxford U: Reece; Smart, Ford, Lewis, Evans, Melville, Magilton, Beauchamp, Cusack (Penney), Durnin, Allen.
Swansea C: Freestone; Lyttle, Jenkins, Walker, Harris, Coughlin (Ford), Bowen, Wimbleton (McFarlane), West, Cornforth, Legg.
aet; Swansea C won 5-4 on penalties.

Tranmere R (1) 3 *(Vickers, Morrissey 2)*
Oldham Ath (0) 0   12,525
Tranmere R: Nixon; Higgins, Nolan, Irons, Mungall, Vickers, Morrissey, Aldridge, Malkin, McNab, Nevin.
Oldham Ath: Gerrard; Halle, Barlow, Bernard, Jobson, Fleming, Henry (Redmond), Olney, Marshall, Milligan, Brennan (Sharp).

THIRD ROUND

13 JAN

Cambridge U (0) 1 *(Heathcote)*
Sheffield W (0) 2 *(Harkes, Bright)* 7754
Cambridge U: Vaughan; Fensome, Kimble, Raynor, Heathcote, O'Shea, White (Rowett), Claridge, Butler, Clayton, Leadbitter (Francis).
Sheffield W: Woods; Nilsson, Worthington, Harkes, Pearson, Shirtliff, Wilson, Waddle, Hirst (Warhurst), Bright, Sheridan.

Leicester C (0) 2 *(Thompson (pen), Oldfield)*
Barnsley (1) 2 *(Whitlow (og), Redfearn)* 19,137
Leicester C: Poole; Mills, Whitlow, Smith, Walsh, Hill, Oldfield, Thompson, Joachim, Ormondroyd (Lowe), Philpott.
Barnsley: Butler; Robinson M, Fleming, Bishop, Taggart, O'Connell, Biggins (Pearson), Rammell, Currie, Redfearn, Archdeacon.

Middlesbrough (0) 2 *(Wright, Falconer)*
Chelsea (0) 1 *(Mohan (og))* 16,776
Middlesbrough: Pears; Fleming (Pollock), Phillips, Mohan, Gittens, Kavanagh (Proctor), Hendrie, Peake, Wilkinson, Falconer, Wright.
Chelsea: Hitchcock; Clarke (Spencer), Sinclair, Townsend, Lee (Burley), Donaghy, Stuart, Fleck, Harford, Newton, Le Saux.

Norwich C (0) 1 *(Beckford)*
Coventry C (0) 0 15,301
Norwich C: Gunn; Culverhouse, Bowen, Butterworth, Polston, Megson (Goss), Crook, Beckford, Sutton, Fox, Phillips.
Coventry C: Ogrizovic; Borrows, Babb, Atherton, Pearce, Ndlovu, McGrath (Busst), Williams, Rosario, Quinn (Gynn), Gallacher.

Southend U (1) 1 *(Collymore)*
Millwall (0) 0 8028
Southend U: Sansome; Edwards, Powell, Cornwell, Scully, Prior, Locke, Sussex, Martin (Brown), Collymore, Jones.
Millwall: Keller; Rae, Dawes, May, Cooper, Stevens, Roberts, Moralee, Bogie (Holsgrove), Goodman (Allen), Barber.

THIRD ROUND REPLAYS

Charlton Ath (0) 1 *(Pitcher (pen))*
Leeds U (1) 3 *(Speed, Garland (og), McAllister)* 8337
Charlton Ath: Bolder; Pitcher, Gatting, Pardew (Grant), Webster, Balmer, Robinson, Leaburn, Garland, Nelson, Walsh.
Leeds U: Day; Sterland (Fairclough), Dorigo, Rodney Wallace (Rocastle), Wetherall, Whyte, Strachan, Shutt, Chapman, McAllister, Speed.

Huddersfield T (1) 2 *(Robinson, Dunn)*
Gillingham (0) 1 *(Green (pen))* 5144
Huddersfield T: Elliott; Parsley, Charlton, Robinson, Mitchell, Jackson, Barnett, O'Regan, Roberts, Dunn, Onuora.
Gillingham: Barrett; Green, Palmer, Butler, Breen, Smith, Clark, O'Connor, Arnott, Carpenter, Eeles.

Liverpool (0) 0
Bolton W (1) 2 *(McGinlay, Walker)* 34,790
Liverpool: Hooper; Marsh, Jones, Stewart, Piechnik, Bjornebye, Walters, Redknapp, Rosenthal, Barnes, Thomas (Hutchison).
Bolton W: Branagan; Brown P, Burke, Lee, Seagraves, Winstanley, Green, Kelly, Walker, McGinlay, Patterson.

Reading (0) 0
Manchester C (2) 4 *(Sheron, Holden, Flitcroft, Quinn)* 12,065
Reading: Francis; Gooding, Hopkins (Lovell), McPherson, Williams, Holzman, Gilkes, Dillon, Quinn, Lambert (Barkus), Taylor.
Manchester C: Coton; Simpson, Phelan, Reid (Vonk), Curle, Brightwell D, White, Sheron, Quinn, Flitcroft, Holden.

THIRD ROUND

19 JAN

Luton T (1) 2 *(Gray, Hughes)*
Bristol C (0) 0 6094
Luton T: Chamberlain; Dreyer, James, Johnson (Harvey), Hughes, Peake, Telfer, Benjamin (Oakes), Rees, Gray, Preece.
Bristol C: Welch; Harrison, Scott, Llewellyn, Bryant, Osman, Shelton, Mellon (Rosenior), Allison, Cole, Gavin (Aizlewood).

THIRD ROUND REPLAYS

20 JAN

Barnsley (0) 1 *(Archdeacon)*
Leicester C (1) 1 *(Joachim)* 15,238
Barnsley: Butler; Robinson M, Fleming (Pearson), Bishop, Taggart, O'Connell, Biggins, Rammell (Bullimore), Currie, Redfearn, Archdeacon.
Leicester C: Poole; Mills, Whitlow (Gibson), Smith, Walsh, Hill (Ormondroyd), Oldfield, Thompson, Joachim, Lowe, Philpott.
aet; Barnsley won 5-4 on penalties.

Bristol R (0) 0
Aston Villa (1) 3 *(Saunders 2, Houghton)* 8880
Bristol R: Kelly; Jones, Clark, Yates, Hardyman, Evans (Twentyman), Browning, Waddock, Stewart, Taylor, Saunders.
Aston Villa: Spink; Barrett, Staunton, Teale, McGrath, Richardson, Houghton, Parker (Froggatt), Saunders, Yorke (Regis), Cox.

FOURTH ROUND

23 JAN

Aston Villa (1) 1 *(Yorke)*
Wimbledon (1) 1 *(Elkins)* 21,088
Aston Villa: Spink; Barrett, Staunton, Teale, McGrath, Richardson, Houghton, Parker, Saunders, Yorke, Froggatt.
Wimbledon: Segers; Joseph, Elkins, Jones, Scales, Blackwell, Ardley, Earle, Fashanu, Sanchez, Cotterill (Holdsworth).

Crewe Alex (0) 0
Blackburn R (1) 3 *(Wegerle, Newell, Moran)*   7054
Crewe Alex: Greygoose; Annan, Smith (Duffield), Wilson, Macauley, Hughes, Harvey, Whalley, Clarkson (Evans), Gardiner, Edwards.
Blackburn R: Mimms; May, Wright (Atkins), Sherwood, Hendry, Moran, Ripley, Cowans, Wegerle, Newell, Wilcox.

Huddersfield T (1) 1 *(Mitchell)*
Southend U (1) 2 *(Collymore 2)*   7961
Huddersfield T: Elliott; Parsley, Charlton, Robinson, Mitchell, Jackson, Barnett (Wright), O'Regan, Roberts, Dunn (Starbuck), Onuora.
Southend U: Sansome; Edwards, Powell, Cornwell, Scully, Prior, Locke, Sussex, Martin, Collymore, Jones.

Luton T (1) 1 *(Telfer)*
Derby Co (3) 5 *(Short, Pembridge 3, Gabbiadini)* 9170
Luton T: Chamberlain; Dreyer, James, Johnson, Hughes, Peake, Telfer, Benjamin (Harvey), Rees (Oakes), Gray, Preece.
Derby Co: Sutton; Kavanagh, Forsyth, Short, Wassall, Pembridge, Johnson, Kuhl, Kitson, Gabbiadini, Goulooze (Micklewhite).

Manchester U (0) 1 *(Giggs)*
Brighton & HA (0) 0   33,610
Manchester U: Schmeichel; Parker, Irwin, Bruce, Sharpe, Pallister, Wallace (Gillespie), Ince, McClair, Phelan, Giggs.
Brighton & HA: Beeney; Chivers, Chapman, Wilkins, Foster, Bissett, Munday, Kennedy (Edwards), Nogan, Codner, Walker.

Nottingham F (0) 1 *(Webb)*
Middlesbrough (1) 1 *(Falconer)*   22,296
Nottingham F: Crossley; Laws, Pearce, Chettle, Tiler, Keane, Bannister, Gemmill, Clough, Webb, Woan.
Middlesbrough: Pears; Fleming, Phillips, Morris, Mohan, Falconer, Wright, Pollock, Wilkinson, Peake, Hendrie.

QPR (0) 1 *(Holloway)*
Manchester C (0) 2 *(White, Vonk)*   18,652
QPR: Roberts; Bardsley, Brevett, Barker, Maddix, McDonald, Wilson, Holloway, Ferdinand, Allen, Sinton (Bailey).
Manchester C: Coton; Ranson, Phelan, McMahon, Vonk, Simpson, White, Sheron, Quinn, Flitcroft, Holden.

Rotherham U (0) 1 *(Johnson)*
Newcastle U (1) 1 *(Lee)*   13,405
Rotherham U: Mercer; Pickering, Hutchings, Banks, Johnson, Law, Hazel (Wilder), Goodwin, Cunningham, Goater, Barrick.
Newcastle U: Srnicek; Venison, Beresford, O'Brien, Scott, Howey, Lee, Peacock, Kelly, Clark, Bracewell.

Sheffield U (0) 1 *(Cork)*
Hartlepool U (0) 0   20,074
Sheffield U: Kelly; Gage, Barnes, Hoyland, Gayle, Beesley, Carr (Ward), Rogers, Cork, Deane, Hodges (Bryson).
Hartlepool U: Jones; Cross R, Cross P, Gilchrist, MacPhail, Tait, Johnrose, Southall, Saville, Honour, Gallacher (Peverell).

Tranmere R (1) 1 *(Nevin)*
Ipswich T (0) 2 *(Dozzell, Guentchev)*   13,683
Tranmere R: Nixon; Higgins, Nolan, Irons, Mungall (Hughes), Vickers, Morrissey, McNab, Malkin, Muir (Martindale), Nevin.
Ipswich T: Baker; Johnson, Thompson, Williams, Wark, Linighan, Yallop, Guentchev (Whelan), Whitton, Dozzell, Kiwomya.

24 JAN

Barnsley (2) 4 *(Rammell 3, Redfearn)*
West Ham U (0) 1 *(Morley (pen))*   13,716
Barnsley: Butler; Gridelet, Fleming, Bishop, Taggart, O'Connell, Biggins (Pearson), Rammell, Currie, Redfearn, Archdeacon.
West Ham U: Miklosko; Breacker, Brown, Potts, Foster, Allen M, Robson (Bunbury), Butler, Morley, Holmes, Keen.

Norwich C (0) 0
Tottenham H (1) 2 *(Sheringham 2)*   15,003
Norwich C: Gunn; Culverhouse, Bowen, Butterworth, Polston, Megson, Goss (Power), Beckford, Sutton, Fox, Phillips.
Tottenham H: Thorstvedt; Austin, Edinbugh, Samways, Mabbutt, Ruddock, Barmby, Durie (Howells), Anderton, Sheringham, Allen.

Sheffield W (0) 1 *(Bright)*
Sunderland (0) 0   33,422
Sheffield W: Woods; Nilsson, Worthington, Harkes, Pearson (Palmer), Shirtliff, Wilson, Waddle, Watson (Bart-Williams), Bright, Sheridan.
Sunderland: Norman; Kay, Michael Gray, Atkinson, Butcher, Ball, Cunnington, Davenport, Mooney (Owers), Rush, Armstrong.

Wolverhampton W (0) 0
Bolton W (2) 2 *(Green, McGinlay)*   19,120
Wolverhampton W: Beasant; Burke, Edwards, Rankine, Mountfield, Madden, Downing, Cook, Bull, Mutch, Dennison.
Bolton W: Branagan; Brown P, Burke, Lee, Seagraves, Winstanley, Green, Kelly, Walker (Reeves), McGinlay, Patterson.

25 JAN

Arsenal (0) 2 *(Parlour, Merson)*
Leeds U (2) 2 *(Speed, Chapman)*   26,516
Arsenal: Seaman; Dixon, Winterburn, Hillier, Linighan, Adams, Jensen (Carter), Campbell, Smith, Merson, Parlour.
Leeds U: Lukic; Wetherall, Dorigo, Batty, Fairclough, Whyte, Strachan, Shutt, Chapman (Rodney Wallace), McAllister (Rocastle), Speed.

2 FEB

Swansea C (0) 0
Grimsby T (0) 0   8307
Swansea C: Freestone; Lyttle, Jenkins, Walker, Harris, Chapple (McFarlane), Hayes, Wimbleton (Ford), West, Cornforth, Legg.
Grimsby T: Wilmot; McDermott, Agnew (Croft), Futcher, Rodger, Dobbin, Childs, Gilbert (Smith), Groves, Mendonca, Rees.

FOURTH ROUND REPLAYS

3 FEB

Leeds U (0) 2 *(Shutt, McAllister)*
Arsenal (0) 3 *(Smith, Wright 2) aet*   26,449
Leeds U: Lukic; Fairclough (Rodney Wallace),
Dorigo, Batty, Wetherall, Whyte, Strachan
(Rocastle), Shutt, Chapman, McAllister, Speed.
Arsenal: Seaman; Dixon, Winterburn (O'Leary),
Selley, Linighan, Adams, Morrow, Wright, Smith,
Merson, Parlour (Campbell).

Middlesbrough (0) 0
Nottingham F (2) 3 *(Bannister, Clough, Woan)* 20,514
Middlesbrough: Pears; Fleming, Phillips, Morris,
Mohan, Falconer, Wright, Pollock (Kavanagh),
Wilkinson, Peake (Slaven), Hendrie.
Nottingham F: Crossley; Laws, Williams, Chettle,
Tiler, Keane, Bannister, Gemmill, Clough, Webb,
Woan.

Newcastle U (0) 2 *(Kelly, Clark)*
Rotherham U (0) 0   29,005
Newcastle U: Srnicek; Venison, Beresford, O'Brien,
Scott, Howey (Kilcline), Lee, Peacock (Sheedy),
Kelly, Clark, Bracewell.
Rotherham U: Mercer; Pickering, Hutchings, Banks,
Johnson, Law (Richardson), Wilder, Goodwin,
Howard, Goater, Barrick.

Wimbledon (0) 0
Aston Villa (0) 0   8048
Wimbledon: Segers; Joseph, McAllister, Jones, Scales,
Blackwell, Ardley, Earle, Fashanu, Holdsworth,
Clarke (Dobbs).
Aston Villa: Bosnich; Barrett, Staunton, Teale,
McGrath, Richardson, Houghton, Parker, Saunders,
Yorke, Cox.
aet; Wimbledon won 6-5 on penalties.

9 FEB

Grimsby T (1) 2 *(Mendonca, Gilbert)*
Swansea C (0) 0   8452
Grimsby T: Wilmot; McDermott, Agnew, Futcher,
Rodger, Dobbin, Childs, Gilbert, Groves, Mendonca,
Rees.
Swansea C: Freestone; Lyttle, Jenkins, Harris,
Walker, Ford, Hayes (Wimbleton), Bowen, West,
Cornforth, Legg (Chapple).

FIFTH ROUND

13 FEB

Arsenal (2) 2 *(Wright 2)*
Nottingham F (0) 0   27,591
Arsenal: Seaman; Dixon, Winterburn, Hillier,
Linighan, Adams, Jensen, Wright (Morrow), Selley,
Merson, Limpar (Campbell).
Nottingham F: Crossley; Laws, Pearce, Tiler, Chettle,
Keane, Bannister, Gemmill, Clough, Webb (Crosby),
Woan.

Blackburn R (0) 1 *(Wegerle)*
Newcastle U (0) 0   19,972
Blackburn R: Mimms; May, Wright, Sherwood,
Hendry, Moran, Atkins, Cowans, Wegerle, Newell,
Wilcox.
Newcastle U: Srnicek; Venison, Beresford, O'Brien,
Scott, Kilcline, Lee, Peacock, Kelly, Clark, Sheedy
(Bracewell).

Derby Co (1) 3 *(Short 2, Williams)*
Bolton W (1) 1 *(Walker)*   20,289
Derby Co: Taylor; Patterson, Forsyth, Coleman,
Short, Pembridge, Williams, Kuhl, Kitson,
Gabbiadini, Simpson.
Bolton W: Branagan; Brown P, Burke, Lee, Lydiate,
Stubbs, Storer, McAteer, Walker, McGinlay,
Patterson.

Ipswich T (1) 4 *(Guentchev 3, Wark)*
Grimsby T (0) 0   17,894
Ipswich T: Baker; Johnson (Yallop), Thompson,
Stockwell, Wark, Linighan, Williams, Guentchev,
Whitton (Bozinoski), Dozzell, Goddard.
Grimsby T: Wilmot; McDermott, Agnew, Futcher,
Rodger, Dobbin, Childs (Smith), Gilbert, Groves,
Mendonca, Rees (Croft).

Manchester C (1) 2 *(White 2)*
Barnsley (0) 0   32,807
Manchester C: Coton; Reid (Hill), Phelan, Simpson,
Curle, Vonk, White, Sheron, Quinn, Flitcroft,
Holden.
Barnsley: Butler; Robinson M, Fleming (Williams),
Bishop, Taggart, O'Connell, Currie, Rammell, Liddell
(Biggins), Redfearn, Archdeacon.

Sheffield W (1) 2 *(Warhurst 2)*
Southend U (0) 0   26,446
Sheffield W: Woods; Nilsson, Worthington, Palmer,
Harkes, Shirtliff, Wilson, Waddle, Warhurst
(Anderson), Bart-Williams (Jemson), Sheridan.
Southend U: Sansome; Edwards, Powell, Cornwell,
Scully, Prior, Ansah, Martin, Jones, Collymore,
Angell.

14 JAN

Sheffield U (2) 2 *(Hoyland, Hodges)*
Manchester U (1) 1 *(Giggs)*   27,150
Sheffield U: Kelly; Ward, Cowan, Hoyland, Gayle,
Beesley, Carr (Littlejohn), Hartfield, Bryson, Deane,
Hodges.
Manchester U: Schmeichel; Parker, Irwin, Bruce,
Sharpe, Pallister, Kanchelskis, Ince, McClair,
Hughes, Giggs.

Tottenham H (3) 3 *(Anderton, Sheringham, Barmby)*
Wimbledon (0) 2 *(Dobbs, Cotterill)*   26,594
Tottenham H: Thorstvedt; Austin, Edinburgh,
Samways, Mabbutt, Ruddock, Howells, Barmby,
Anderton, Sheringham, Allen.
Wimbledon: Segers; Joseph (Cotterill), Elkins, Jones,
Scales, McAllister, Ardley, Earle, Fashanu,
Holdsworth, Dobbs.

SIXTH ROUND

6 MAR

Blackburn R (0) 0
Sheffield U (0) 0   15,107
Blackburn R: Mimms; May, Dobson, Sherwood, Hendry, Moran, Ripley, Andersson (Atkins), Wegerle, Newell, Wilcox.
Sheffield U: Kelly; Gage, Whitehouse (Beesley), Hoyland, Gayle, Pemberton, Carr (Cork), Hartfield, Bryson, Deane, Hodges.

Ipswich T (1) 2 *(Kiwomya, Guentchev)*   22,054
Arsenal (1) 4 *(Adams, Wright (pen), Whelan (og), Campbell)*
Ipswich T: Baker; Johnson, Thompson (Goddard), Stockwell, Wark, Linighan, Williams, Guentchev, Whelan, Dozzell, Kiwomya.
Arsenal: Seaman; Dixon, Winterburn, Davis, Linighan, Adams, Carter (Hillier), Wright, Smith (Campbell), Merson, Morrow.

7 MAR

Manchester C (1) 2 *(Sheron, Phelan)*
Tottenham H (2) 4 *(Nayim 3, Sedgley)*   23,050
Manchester C: Coton; Hill, Phelan, Simpson, Curle, Vonk, White, Sheron, Quinn, Flitcroft, Holden.
Tottenham H: Thorstvedt; Austin, Edinburgh, Samways, Mabbutt, Ruddock, Sedgley, Nayim, Anderton (Turner), Sheringham, Allen.

8 MAR

Derby Co (1) 3 *(Nicholson, Gabbiadini, Kitson)*
Sheffield W (2) 3 *(Sheridan (pen), Warhurst 2)* 22,511
Derby Co: Taylor; Patterson, Forsyth, Nicholson, Short, Pembridge, Williams, Kuhl, Kitson, Gabbiadini, Johnson.
Sheffield W: Woods; Nilsson, Worthington, Palmer, Harkes (Jemson), Anderson, Wilson, Waddle, Warhurst, Bright, Sheridan (Hyde).

SIXTH ROUND REPLAYS

16 MAR

Sheffield U (0) 2 *(Ward 2)*
Blackburn R (0) 2 *(Livingstone, Newell)*   23,920
Sheffield U: Kelly; Gage (Ward), Whitehouse, Hoyland, Gayle, Pemberton, Littlejohn, Hartfield, Bryson (Beesley), Cork, Hodges.
Blackburn R: Mimms; May, Dobson, Sherwood, Hendry, Moran, Ripley, Marker, Livingstone (Wegerle), Newell, Wilcox.
aet; Sheffield U won 5-3 on penalties

17 MAR

Sheffield W (1) 1 *(Warhurst)*
Derby Co (0) 0   32,033
Sheffield W: Woods; Nilsson, Worthington, Palmer, King (Hirst), Anderson, Wilson, Waddle, Warhurst, Bright, Sheridan.
Derby Co: Taylor; Patterson (Comyn), Coleman, Nicholson, Short, Pembridge, Hayward (Stallard), Kuhl, Kitson, Gabbiadini, Johnson.

SEMI-FINALS at Wembley

3 APR

Sheffield U (1) 1 *(Cork)*
Sheffield W (1) 2 *(Waddle, Bright)*   75,364
Sheffield U: Kelly; Gage, Whitehouse, Gannon, Gayle, Pemberton, Carr, Ward (Littlejohn), Cork, Deane, Hodges (Hoyland).
Sheffield W: Woods; Nilsson, Worthington, Palmer, Harkes, Anderson, Wilson, Waddle, Warhurst (Hirst), Bright, Sheridan (Hyde).

4 APR

Arsenal (0) 1 *(Adams)*
Tottenham H (0) 0   76,263
Arsenal: Seaman; Dixon, Winterburn, Hillier, Linighan, Adams, Parlour (Smith), Wright (Morrow), Campbell, Merson, Selley.
Tottenham H: Thorstvedt; Austin, Edinburgh, Samways (Barmby), Mabbutt, Ruddock, Sedgley (Bergsson), Nayim, Anderton, Sheringham, Allen.

FINAL at Wembley

15 MAY

Arsenal (1) 1 *(Wright)*
Sheffield W (0) 1 *(Hirst)* aet   79,347
Arsenal: Seaman; Dixon, Winterburn, Davis, Linighan, Adams, Jensen, Wright (O'Leary), Campbell, Merson, Parlour (Smith).
Sheffield W: Woods; Nilsson, Worthington, Palmer, Anderson (Hyde), Warhurst, Harkes, Waddle (Bart-Williams), Hirst, Bright, Sheridan.
Referee: K. Barratt (Coventry).

FINAL REPLAY at Wembley

20 MAY

Arsenal (1) 2 *(Wright, Linighan)*
Sheffield W (0) 1 *(Waddle)* aet   62,267
Arsenal: Seaman; Dixon, Winterburn, Davis, Linighan, Adams, Jensen, Wright (O'Leary), Smith, Merson, Campbell.
Sheffield W: Woods; Nilsson (Bart-Williams), Worthington, Harkes, Palmer, Warhurst, Wilson (Hyde), Waddle, Hirst, Bright, Sheridan.
Referee: K. Barratt (Coventry).

THE SCOTTISH SEASON 1992-93

A year ago we were looking forward to the European finals. They came and went, and our team had a successful visit, both players and supporters coming away with great credit -if no medals. Before the team had time to gather its breath, the World Cup qualifiers were upon them, and early results were poor. By April of this year, what appeared to be a 'final chance' game in Lisbon ended in a highly disappointing result. Perhaps we had been expecting more miracles. This time, they were not performed. There are plenty now ready to go public on the demise of Scottish Football; many have their ideas to put forward, and many of those who have a say in the running of the game at all levels are prepared to criticize, usually at the expense of someone else. this is no place to enter that forum. All one can do is to hope that far-seeing and sensible people will come up with proper solutions to our problems, and that vested interests may perhaps play not such a large part in decisions in the interests of the national game. Then we may see our national teams able to hold their own, hopefully with Andy Roxburgh still in command.

Jim McLean is retiring as manager of Dundee United. He has achieved wonders with the club, and has taken it from the depths to a position amongst the elite. In his twenty-two years as manager there, he has instilled a spirit which has been second to none. There have been his detractors, but they look small when his record is examined. There are very many who share his disappointment in not having won the Scottish Cup; he has been so close on so many occasions. So, too, did European silverware elude him, but he gave his team a name to conjure with on the Continent: who can forget the enormous coverage he received in the Catalan press after his team had defeated Barcelona there? And they did, too, find a photograph of him in which he was almost smiling! He set himself high standards, and was disappointed when others fell from them.

Only a day or two ago the AGM of the Scottish League agreed to a new set of four divisions of ten clubs in the league, to start in 1994-95. It was passed by the smallest margin, and some clubs are clearly disturbed that they will lose contact with the clubs in the top echelon. It is up to them. It does mean that competition is going to be fierce next year in all parts of the league. The other matter of outstanding interest is which two teams will join the league. There must be a place now for the Highland League to be represented.

Rangers went to their fifth Premier success in a row, and realistically no one ever looked like matching them. They were a class above most of the rest, and if Aberdeen and Celtic on occasions looked capable of beating them on the day, then they certainly did not have the sustained capacity to hold on throughout a long season. Rangers had their magnificent run in the European Cup, and it made them somehow the more readily able to cope with the everyday vicissitudes of less prestigious encounters. The Edinburgh clubs faded in the later stages, and Dundee United were pleased to take the last place in Europe. Jim McLean's successor has a promising side now and one which should challenge for honours in the next year or two. St Johnstone finished as far up the Premier as they ever have done, and Dundee and Partick were always just about holding their heads above the surface; Motherwell had a struggle to survive, but they did, and Airdrieonians and Falkirk go down. Falkirk resolutely refused to stop playing football in an effort to grub for points; they were also winners of the Fair Play award, and it is doubly a shame that they leave the top group. Perhaps it is only for a year.

Raith Rovers had a fine league season and carried nearly all before them: they were undefeated at home, and in fact lost no game until December. Inspiring leadership both on and off the field by player/manager Jimmy Nicholl together with inspired goalscoring from Gordon Dalziel and Craig Brewster, ably supported by the rest of the team, saw them finish far ahead of the rest. Several teams battled for the second place, but late on, Dunfermline and Kilmarnock looked to be the only contenders; then a fine run by St Mirren meant that they almost sneaked in ahead; in the end, however, Dunfermline's lamentable home form led to their undoing, and Kilmarnock gratefully accepted the runners-up berth.

Cowdenbeath never left the bottom of the table and were quickly left behind. They had little success, but did have a say in the final placings when, in three consecutive fixtures late on, they beat Dunfermline and St Mirren but lost to Kilmarnock. Meadowbank Thistle and Stirling Albion were the other two contenders for relegation: Stirling Albion, now ensconced in their fine new stadium, showed some form when it mattered, and survived.

Clyde, also looking forward to the opening of their new HQ, proved the strongest team in the Second Division. There were times when they faltered, but in the end they had a little to spare; the evergreen Frank McGarvey was their top scorer. There was great interest on the final day to see if Stranraer could, for the first time ever, leave the lowest division: they came within a minute or two of promotion, but a late penalty gave Brechin City the win they needed, and the Angus team go up with Clyde. Alloa and Stenhousemuir both had

Rangers manager Walter Smith holds the League Championship trophy after another triumph for the Ibrox club.
(Colorsport)

patches of good form and could beat the best; neither side achieved a very prominent position, but each influenced the final placings.

The Cups produced the usual run of surprises. Stranraer and Brechin showed their form early with the former taking Airdrieonians out of the Skol Cup, and the latter doing the same to Hamilton. Arbroath had a highly rewarding set of cup draws at home, starting when they entertained Aberdeen (unsuccessfully) in the Skol; they took Dunfermline 3-0 in the B & Q, followed this by disposing of Morton by the same score in the Scottish Cup and then, after destroying East Fife in a replay at Bayview, having a gala occasion against Rangers at Gayfield: nearly the whole town was involved, and Rangers were merciful against a side which always tried hard. Football needs characters, and has one in the dashing and ebullient Danny McGrain who has breathed new life and energy not only into his team, but wherever he has gone. His bearded supporters have seen the team steadily coming up the table in the league as well as relishing their cup outings. Huntly had another good cup run with success against two Second Division teams before thoroughly enjoying an unsuccessful day out at Tynecastle. It is good to see Highland League success continuing in the Scottish Cup, and perhaps the more relevant just at the moment.

Of the Highland League itself, it was a shame in their centenary year that the championship should have had to be annulled. Considerable successes by some clubs had to be forgotten in the aftermath.

The new season will be upon us in next to no time. Will Rangers win everything again? Probably, but hopefully in the interests of Scottish football there will be strong competition. With places in the new four divisions at stake there will be frantic activity in all parts of the league. When the new set up is in place, will there be machinery for the bottom club in the bottom division to be replaced -perhaps by a play-off with three top contenders for a place in the League? That would give some point to the lowest reaches and ensure that each year the bottom club would not simply re-appear, Phoenix-like, at the start of each new season.

Not much has been said so far of our European results: in the Cup Winners and UEFA cups there was little to note; but that brings us to the European Cup and to Rangers, of whom little enough has been said so far. Rangers won everything on the home front; in addition, they played ten matches in Europe and lost not one of them. Their success was based on utter inability to give up when all seemed lost, on a scoring combination which had other teams in a tizzie, on a defence which was resolute and adaptable, a mid-field which worked hard all the time, and a pool of players -many of them home-reared -who could step in and fill gaps whenever injuries arose. There were many notable moments, but perhaps we may be excused for singling out the defeat of English champions Leeds, the startling come-back to make up a two-goal deficiency against Marseilles, and a thrilling goal of Ian Durrant's. The effervescent Ally McCoist bubbled along, and was almost as mobile on crutches as without them. But the captain takes responsibility for his ship: Walter Smith is a fine advertisement for his country and for his team.

ALAN ELLIOTT

ABERDEEN   Premier Division

Year Formed: 1903. *Ground & Address:* Pittodrie Stadium, Pittodrie St, Aberdeen AB2 1QH. *Telephone:* 0224 632328.
Ground Capacity: 21,655 seated: All. *Size of Pitch:* 110yd × 72yd.
Chairman: Richard M. Donald. *Secretary:* Ian J. Taggart. *Commercial Manager:* Dave Johnston.
Manager: Willie Miller. *Assist. Managers:* Drew Jarvie/Roy Aitken. *Physio:* David Wylie. *Coach:* Neil Cooper.
Managers since 1975: Ally MacLeod; Billy McNeill; Alex Ferguson; Ian Porterfield; Alex Smith and Jocky Scott; Willie
Miller. *Club Nicknames(s):* The Dons. *Previous Grounds:* None.
Record Attendance: 45,061 v Hearts, Scottish Cup 4th rd; 13 Mar, 1954.
Record Transfer Fee received: £970,000 for David Robertson to Rangers (July 1991).
Record Transfer Fee paid: £650,000 for Hans Gillhaus from PSV Eindhoven, November 1989.
Record Victory: 13-0 v Peterhead, Scottish Cup; 9 Feb, 1923.
Record Defeat: 0-8 v Celtic, Division I; 30 Jan, 1965.
Most Capped Players: Alex McLeish, 77, Scotland.
Most League Appearances: 556: Willie Miller, 1973-90.
Most League Goals in Season (Individual): 38: Benny Yorston, Division I; 1929-30.
Most Goals Overall (Individual): 199: Joe Harper.

ABERDEEN 1992—93 LEAGUE RECORD

Match No.	Date	Venue	Opponents	Result	H/T Score	Lg. Pos.	Goalscorers	Atten dance
1	Aug 1	H	Hibernian	W 3-0	0-0	—	Shearer 2, Booth	12,503
2	5	H	Celtic	D 1-1	1-1	—	Shearer	14,618
3	8	A	Falkirk	W 1-0	0-0	1	Aitken	5925
4	15	A	Motherwell	L 1-2	1-1	2	Jess	5561
5	22	H	Dundee	W 2-1	2-1	1	Shearer, Paatelainen	11,604
6	29	A	Rangers	L 1-3	1-0	5	Aitken	41,636
7	Sept 2	H	Airdrieonians	D 0-0	0-0	—		9021
8	12	A	Hearts	L 0-1	0-1	6		10,630
9	19	H	Partick T	W 2-0	0-0	5	Grant, Paatelainen	9755
10	26	A	St Johnstone	W 3-0	0-0	2	Shearer 2, Paatelainen	7320
11	Oct 3	H	Dundee U	L 0-1	0-0	5		12,936
12	7	A	Hibernian	W 3-1	0-1	—	Shearer, Jess 2	8824
13	17	H	Falkirk	W 3-1	1-1	3	Jess, Paatelainen, Booth	9016
14	31	A	Airdrieonians	W 2-1	1-1	4	Sandison (og), Shearer	3221
15	Nov 7	A	Dundee	W 2-1	0-0	3	Shearer, Richardson	6902
16	11	H	Motherwell	W 2-0	0-0	—	Shearer, Grant	8725
17	Nov 24	A	Partick T	W 7-0	1-0	—	Shearer 3, Jess, Mason, Booth, Kane	3986
18	28	H	Hearts	W 6-2	2-0	2	Irvine, Shearer 3, Mason, Booth	13,555
19	Dec 2	A	Celtic	D 2-2	2-1	—	Jess, Kane	29,122
20	5	H	St Johnstone	W 3-0	2-0	2	Irvine, Roddie, Mason	11,750
21	12	A	Dundee U	D 2-2	1-0	2	Jess, Irvine	10,394
22	19	H	Hibernian	W 2-0	0-0	2	Richardson, Booth	11,018
23	26	A	Motherwell	W 2-0	0-0	2	Irvine, Jess	7907
24	Jan 2	H	Dundee	D 0-0	0-0	2		13,201
25	16	H	Airdrieonians	W 7-0	4-0	2	Paatelainen 4, Jess, Booth, Irvine	8805
26	30	A	Falkirk	W 4-1	2-0	2	Jess 2, Shearer, Booth	6886
27	Feb 2	H	Rangers	L 0-1	0-0	—		15,055
28	13	H	Celtic	D 1-1	1-0	2	Paatelainen	14,673
29	20	A	St Johnstone	W 2-0	1-0	2	Jess, Booth	6176
30	24	H	Dundee U	D 0-0	0-0	—		12,603
31	Mar 2	H	Partick T	W 1-0	0-0	—	Paatelainen	8287
32	9	A	Hibernian	W 2-1	0-1	—	Kane, Paatelainen	7029
33	13	H	Falkirk	D 2-2	0-0	2	Roddie, Shearer	9095
34	20	A	Dundee	W 2-1	1-0	2	Paatelainen, Booth	5783
35	27	H	Motherwell	W 1-0	1-0	2	Booth	9155
36	30	A	Rangers	L 0-2	0-0	—		44,570
37	Apr 10	A	Airdrieonians	D 1-1	1-0	2	Shearer	3005
38	17	H	Hearts	W 3-2	2-0	2	Shearer, Paatelainen, Mason	9700
39	20	A	Partick T	W 3-1	2-0	2	Paatelainen 2, Kane	3445
40	May 1	A	Celtic	L 0-1	0-1	2		20,642
41	5	A	Hearts	W 2-1	1-0	—	Shearer, Paatelainen	6038
42	8	H	St Johnstone	D 1-1	1-1	2	Booth	7727
43	12	H	Rangers	W 1-0	1-0	—	Shearer	13,079
44	15	A	Dundee U	W 4-1	1-1	2	Booth 2, Gibson, Grant	9078

Final League Position: 2

Honours

League Champions: Division I 1954-55. Premier Division 1979-80, 1983-84, 1984-85; *Runners-up:* Division I 1910-11, 1936-37, 1955-56, 1970-71, 1971-72. Premier Division 1977-78, 1980-81, 1981-82, 1988-89, 1989-90, 1990-91.
Scottish Cup Winners: 1947, 1970, 1982, 1983, 1984, 1986, 1990; *Runners-up:* 1937, 1953, 1954, 1959, 1967, 1978, 1993.
League Cup Winners: 1955-56, 1976-77, 1985-86, 1989-90; *Runners-up:* 1946-47, 1978-79, 1979-80, 1987-88, 1988-89, 1992-93.
Drybrough Cup Winners: 1971, 1980.
European: *European Cup* 12 matches (1980-81, 1984-85, 1985-86); *Cup Winners Cup Winners:* 1982-83. Semi-finals 1983-84. 35 matches (1967-68, 1970-71, 1978-79, 1982-83, 1983-84, 1986-87, 1990-91); *UEFA Cup* 34 matches (*Fairs Cup:* 1968-69. *UEFA Cup:* 1971-72, 1972-73, 1973-74, 1977-78, 1979-80, 1981-82, 1987-88, 1988-89, 1989-90, 1991-92).
Club colours: Shirt, Shorts, Stockings: Red with white trim.

Goalscorers: *League (87):* Shearer 22, Paatelainen 16, Booth 13, Jess 12, Irvine 5, Kane 4, Mason 4, Grant 3, Aitken 2, Richardson 2, Roddie 2, Gibson 1, own goal 1.   *Scottish Cup (13):* Booth 6, Irvine 2, Jess 2, Paatelainen 1, Richardson 1, Shearer 1 (pen).   *Skol Cup (11):* Shearer 5, Paatelainen 3, Jess 2, Irvine 1.

Snelders T 41	Wright S 34 + 2	Winnie D 18 + 3	Aitken R 18 + 8	Irvine B 39	Smith G 40	Mason P 31 + 8	Bett J 17	Booth S 21 + 8	Shearer D 32 + 2	Paatelainen M 33	Jess E 28 + 3	Ferguson G — + 1	McKimmie S 14	Thomson S — + 2	Roddie A 1 + 10	Kane P 13 + 14	Grant B 29	McLeish A 27	Ten Caat T 11 + 4	Richardson L 28 +	Watt M 3	Connor R 5 + 1	Gibson A 1	Match No.
1	2	3	4	5	6	7	8	9	10	11	12													1
1	2	3	4	5	6	7	8	9	10	11	12													2
1	12	3	4	5	6	7			10	11	9		2											3
1	8	3	4	5	6	7			10	11	9	12	2	14										4
1	3	12	4	5	6		8		10	11	9		2	14				7						5
1	3	12	4	5	6	7			10	11	9		2	14				8						6
1	3	10	4	5	6	7				11	9		2	14				8						7
1	14	3	4	5	6	12	8		10	11	9		2					7						8
1	2	3			6	7			10	11	9				4	5		8	14					9
	2	3			6	12			10	11	9			7	4	5	14	8	1					10
1	2	3		5	6	12			10	11	9			14	4		7	8						11
1	2	3		5	6	7			10	11	9		14	12	4		8							12
1	2	3	7		6	12		14	10	11	9				4	5		8						13
1	2	3		5	6	8			10	11	9		12		4			7						14
1	2	3		5	6	12	8		10	11	9				4			7						15
1	2	3		5	6	12	8		10	11	9				4			7						16
1	2			5	6	11	8	14	10		9				12	4	3	7						17
1	2			5	6	11	8	14	10		9				12	4	3	7						18
1	2			5	6	11	8	10		9			14	12	4	3		7						19
1	2			5	6	11	8	9			10				4	3		7						20
1	2			5	6	11	8	10		9				12	4	3		7						21
1	2	14		5	6	11	8	10		9				12	4	3		7						22
1	2			5	6	11	8	10		9			14		4	3		7						23
1	2			5	6	11	8	10		9					4	3		7						24
1	2	12	5	3	8			10		11	9			14		4	6		7					25
1	2	12	5	3	11			8	10		9			14		4	6		7					26
1	2		5	3	11			8	12	10	9			14		4	6		7					27
1	2	3	8	5				14	10	11	9					4	6		7					28
	2	12	5	3	8			14	10	11	9					4	6		7	1				29
1	2		4	5	3	8		14	10	11	9						6		7					30
1	2	12	5	3	14			8	10	11	9					4	6		7					31
1	2	8	5	3				10	11				14	12	4	6	9		7					32
1	2	3	8	5				10	11				14	7	4	6	9							33
1	2		8	5	3	14		9	12	11		6				7	4		10					34
1	2			3	8	9			11			6		14	4	5	10		7					35
1	2			3	8	9		10	11			6	14	4		5	12		7					36
1	12		5	3	8	9		10	11			2	14	4		6			7					37
1			4	5	3	8		9	10	11		2	14			6	7							38
1			5	3	9	8	14	10	11			2		4			6	7					12	39
1		4	5		7	14		10	11		2	12		8			6	9				3		40
		4	5		7			9	10	11	2		8			6	12			1	3			41
1	2	12	5	6	8			9	10	11				4		14	7				3			42
1	2	12	5	6	8			9	10					4		11	7				3			43
1	2	12	5	6	8			9			14			4		7	11				3	10		44

AIRDRIEONIANS

First Division

Year Formed: 1878. *Ground & Address:* Broomfield Park, Gartlea Rd, Airdrie M16 9JL. *Telephone:* 0236 62067.
Ground Capacity: 10,250, seated: 1350. *Size of Pitch:* 112yd × 67yd.
Chairman and Secretary: George W. Peat CA. *Commercial Manager:* Dorothy Martin.
Manager: Alex MacDonald. *Assistant Manager:* John McVeigh. *Physio:* Dan Young. *Coach:* Tom McAdam.
Managers since 1975: I. McMillan; J. Stewart; R. Watson; W. Munro; A. MacLeod; D. Whiteford; G. McQueen; J. Bone.
Club Nickname(s): The Diamonds or The Waysiders. *Previous Grounds:* Mavisbank.
Record Attendance: 24,000 v Hearts, Scottish Cup; 8 Mar, 1952.
Record Transfer Fee received: £200,000 for Sandy Clark to West Ham U, May 1982.
Record Transfer Fee paid: £175,000 for Owen Coyle from Clydebank, February 1990.
Record Victory: 15-1 v Dundee Wanderers, Division II; 1 Dec, 1984.
Record Defeat: 1-11 v Hibernian, Division I; 24 Oct, 1959.
Most Capped Player: Jimmy Crapnell, 9, Scotland.
Most League Appearances: 523: Paul Jonquin, 1962-79.
Most League Goals in Season (Individual): 52, Hugh Baird, Division II, 1954-55. *Most Goals Overall (Individual):* —

AIRDRIEONIANS 1992—93 LEAGUE RECORD

Match No.	Date		Venue	Opponents	Result	H/T Score	Lg. Pos.	Goalscorers	Atten dance
1	Aug	1	A	Partick T	L 0-1	0-0	—		4483
2		4	A	Rangers	L 0-2	0-1	—		36,613
3		8	H	Dundee	D 0-0	0-0	12		2510
4		15	A	St Johnstone	L 0-3	0-2	12		3708
5		22	H	Falkirk	W 2-0	1-0	12	Honor, Lawrence	3900
6		29	H	Celtic	D 1-1	0-1	11	Boyle	12,222
7	Sept	2	A	Aberdeen	D 0-0	0-0	—		9021
8		12	H	Dundee U	L 1-2	0-1	10	Coyle	2773
9		19	A	Hibernian	D 2-2	1-1	10	Boyle 2 (1 pen)	6909
10		26	H	Hearts	W 1-0	1-0	10	Coyle	4372
11	Oct	3	A	Motherwell	L 0-2	0-0	10		4720
12		10	H	Partick T	D 2-2	1-2	9	Coyle, Jack (pen)	4204
13		17	A	Dundee	L 0-2	0-2	10		3831
14		24	A	Celtic	L 0-2	0-1	10		19,549
15		31	H	Aberdeen	L 1-2	1-1	11	Balfour	3221
16	Nov	7	A	Falkirk	L 1-5	1-2	11	Kirkwood (pen)	4715
17		14	H	St Johnstone	L 0-2	0-1	11		2550
18		21	H	Hibernian	W 2-0	0-0	11	Honor (pen), Coyle	3129
19		28	A	Dundee U	D 0-0	0-0	11		5178
20	Dec	1	H	Rangers	D 1-1	0-1	—	Boyle	9251
21		5	A	Hearts	W 3-1	1-0	11	Coyle, Jack, Lawrence	6665
22		12	H	Motherwell	L 0-2	0-0	11		3630
23		19	A	Partick T	D 1-1	0-0	10	Jack (pen)	3274
24		26	A	St Johnstone	L 0-1	0-0	11		4139
25	Jan	2	H	Falkirk	L 0-1	0-1	11		5748
26		16	A	Aberdeen	L 0-7	0-4	11		8805
27		23	H	Celtic	L 0-1	0-1	12		7473
28		30	H	Dundee	D 2-2	2-0	12	Kirkwood (pen), Smith	2203
29	Feb	6	A	Motherwell	D 0-0	0-0	12		5382
30		13	A	Rangers	D 2-2	1-2	12	Coyle 2	39,816
31		20	H	Hearts	D 0-0	0-0	12		3347
32		27	A	Hibernian	L 1-3	1-1	11	Black	5011
33	Mar	6	H	Dundee U	L 1-3	1-2	12	Fashanu	2291
34		9	H	Partick T	D 2-2	0-1	—	Honor, Coyle	3080
35		13	A	Dundee	D 1-1	0-0	12	Smith	2929
36		20	A	Falkirk	W 1-0	1-0	11	Smith	4172
37		27	H	St Johnstone	D 1-1	0-0	11	Coyle	2339
38	Apr	6	A	Celtic	L 0-4	0-2	—		10,671
39		10	H	Aberdeen	D 1-1	0-1	12	Fashanu	3005
40		17	A	Dundee U	L 0-3	0-2	12		4200
41		20	H	Hibernian	W 3-1	2-0	11	Fashanu 2, Stewart	2585
42	May	1	H	Rangers	L 0-1	0-0	12		12,514
43		8	A	Hearts	D 1-1	0-0	12	Smith	5104
44		15	H	Motherwell	L 1-2	1-2	12	Fashanu	3088

Final League Position: 12

Honours

League Champions: Division II 1902-03, 1954-55, 1973-74; *Runners-up:* Division I 1922-23, 1923-24, 1924-25, 1925-26.
First Division 1979-80, 1989-90, 1990-91. Division II 1900-01, 1946-47, 1949-50, 1965-66.
Scottish Cup Winners: 1924; *Runners-up:* 1975, 1992. *Scottish Spring Cup Winners:* 1976.
League Cup semi-finalists: 1991-92.
European: *UEFA Cup* 2 matches (1992-93).
Club colours: Shirt: White with Red diamond. Shorts: White. Stockings: Red.

Goalscorers: *League (35):* Coyle 9, Fashanu 5, Boyle 4 (1 pen), Smith 4. Honor 3 (1 pen), Jack 3 (2 pens), Kirkwood 2 (2 pens), Lawrence 2, Balfour 1, Black 1, Stewart 1.   *Scottish Cup (0).Skol Cup (2):* Conn 1, Kirkwood 1.

Martin J 43	Honor C 28 + 1	Stewart A 43	Jack P 32 + 1	Caesar G 29	Black K 33	Boyle J 36 + 4	Balfour E 26 + 1	Lawrence A 23 + 12	Coyle O 42	Conn S 4 + 10	Kidd W 30 + 1	Reid W 18 + 7	Sandison J 37 + 1	Kirkwood D 17 + 10	Smith A 20 + 14	Wilson M 2 + 2	Watson J 4 + 4	Fashanu J 16	Dick J — + 1	McCulloch W 1	Dempsey S — + 1	Match No.
1	2	3	4	5	6	7	8	9	10	11	12	14										1
1	2	3	11	5	6	7	8	9	10			12	4	14								2
1	2	3	11	5	6	7	8	9	10	14			4	12								3
1	2	3	11	5	6	7	8	14	9			10	4	12								4
1	5	3			6	7	8	10	11	9	2	14	4									5
1	11	3		5	6	7	8	9	10	14	2		4	12								6
1	11	3		5	6	7	8	9	10		2		4	12	14							7
1	2	3		5	6	7	8	10	11				4	12	9							8
1	5	3			6	7	8	11	10		2	12	4	14	9							9
1	5	3			6	7	8	10	11		2	14	4	12	9							10
1	11	3		5	6	7	8	14	10		2	12	4		9							11
1	5	3	4		6	7	8	10	11	12	2				9							12
1	5	3			6	7	8	10	11	14	2		4		9							13
1	5	3			6	7	8	9	10		2		4	11	14							14
1	5	3			6	7	8	9	10		2		4	11	14							15
1	5	3	10		6	7	8		9	12	2		4	11	14							16
1	6	3	2	10		7	11	14	5	8			4	12	9							17
1	7	3	14	5	6		8	12	10		2	11	4		9							18
1	7	3	10	5	6	14	8	12	11		2		4		9							19
1		3	10	5	6	7	8	9	14		2		4	11	12							20
1		3	10	5	6	7	8	12	9		2		4	11	14							21
1		3	10	5	6	7	8	12	9		2		4	11	14							22
1		3	10	5	6	7	8	14	9		2		4	11	12							23
1		3	10	5	6	7	8	14	9		2		4	11	12							24
1		3	11	5	6	7	8	14	10		2		4	12	9							25
1		2	5	3	8	9	10	6	7	4	11	12	14									26
1		3	6	5	2	11	10	7	4	8				12				9				27
1		3	4		7	8	10	12	2	6	11				5			9				28
1		3	4	5	6	12	10	2	7	8				11				9				29
1		3	4		6	11	10	2	7	8	12				5		9	14				30
1		3	4	5	6	11	10	2	8	7								9				31
1		3	4	5	6	14	11	10	2	8				12			7	9				32
1	14	3		5	6	7	12	11	2	8			4	10				9				33
	5	3	10		6	7	12	11	2	8			4					9		1		34
1	6	3	5		7		11	2		4	8	10		12				9				35
1	8	3	7	5	6	14	12	11	2				4	10				9				36
1	8	3	7	5	6		12	11	2				4	10				9				37
1	8	3	7	5	6	2		11	12				4	10				9				38
1	8	3	7	5	6	2		10	11				4	12				9				39
1	8	3	7	5	6	2		10	11				4	14				9				40
1	5	3	7		6	2	8	10	11				4	12	14			9				41
1	5	2	3		7	8	11	12	4				10	14	6			9				42
1	2	3	5		7	8	11	14	4				10	6	12			9				43
1		3	2		7	11	5	4	8	6			10					9			14	44

ALBION ROVERS   Second Division

Year Formed: 1882. *Ground & Address:* Cliftonhill Stadium, Main St, Coatbridge ML5 3RB. *Telephone:* 0236 432350.
Ground capacity: total: 1238, seated: 538. *Size of Pitch:* 110yd × 70yd.
Chairman: Jack McGoogan. *Secretary:* D. Forrester CA. *Commercial Manager:* Laurie Cameron. *Manager:* Tommy
Gemmell. *Assistant Manager:* —. *Physio:* Michael McBride. *Coach:* —. *Managers since 1975:* G. Caldwell; S. Goodwin;
H. Hood; J. Baker; D. Whiteford; M. Ferguson; W. Wilson; B. Rooney; A. Ritchie; T. Gemmell; D. Provan; M. Oliver; B.
McLaren; T. Gemmell. *Club Nickname(s):* The Wee Rovers. *Previous Grounds:* Cowheath Park, Meadow Park, Whifflet.
Record Attendance: 27,381 v Rangers, Scottish Cup 2nd rd; 8 Feb, 1936.
Record Transfer Fee received: £40,000 from Motherwell for Bruce Cleland.
Record Transfer Fee paid: £7000 for Gerry McTeague to Stirling Albion, September 1989.
Record Victory: 12-0 v Airdriehill, Scottish Cup; 3 Sept, 1887.
Record Defeat: 0-9 v St Johnstone, League Cup, 9 March 1946.
Most Capped Player: Jock White, 1 (2), Scotland.

ALBION ROVERS 1992—93 LEAGUE RECORD

Match No.	Date	Venue	Opponents	Result	H/T Score	Lg. Pos.	Goalscorers	Atten dance
1	Aug 8	A	Clyde	L	0-2	0-1	—	555
2	15	H	Queen's Park	W	3-2	2-0	10	Scott 2, Riley	268
3	22	A	Queen of the S	W	3-0	1-0	4	McKeown, Scott (pen), Ferguson	437
4	29	A	Brechin C	L	0-2	0-0	6		494
5	Sept 5	H	Berwick R	D	1-1	0-0	6	Ferguson	273
6	12	H	Montrose	D	2-2	1-1	6	Kerrigan 2	217
7	19	A	Stranraer	D	1-1	0-0	6	Scott	627
8	26	A	East Stirling	D	1-1	0-1	6	Ferguson	284
9	Oct 3	H	Alloa	L	0-1	0-0	10		337
10	10	A	Arbroath	L	0-2	0-2	11		508
11	17	H	Forfar Ath	W	2-1	2-1	9	Scott, Archer	288
12	24	A	Stenhousemuir	L	0-2	0-0	11		304
13	31	H	East Fife	L	0-5	0-2	12		276
14	Nov 7	H	Brechin C	L	1-4	1-2	13	Scott (pen)	259
15	14	A	Berwick R	D	1-1	0-1	13	Kelly	325
16	21	H	Stranraer	D	1-1	0-0	13	Scott (pen)	274
17	28	A	Montrose	L	1-2	1-0	13	Scott	459
18	Dec 12	H	Clyde	L	1-2	1-1	12	Scott	470
19	26	A	Alloa	L	0-4	0-0	13		508
20	Jan 2	A	Queen's Park	L	0-1	0-1	14		543
21	9	H	Queen of the S	W	2-1	1-0	12	Scott (pen), Moore	188
22	16	A	East Fife	L	0-5	0-3	12		504
23	30	H	East Stirling	D	2-2	2-0	12	Gallagher, Scott	207
24	Feb 6	A	Forfar Ath	L	2-3	1-2	14	Scott 2	519
25	13	H	Arbroath	L	0-1	0-0	14		254
26	16	H	Stenhousemuir	D	0-0	0-0	—		205
27	20	A	Alloa	L	0-1	0-1	14		403
28	27	H	Stranraer	L	1-2	0-1	14	Cadden	251
29	Mar 6	A	Montrose	D	1-1	1-0	14	Kelly	335
30	13	H	Berwick R	L	0-2	0-1	14		200
31	20	A	Queen's Park	D	1-1	0-1	14	Kerrigan	389
32	27	A	Queen of the S	L	1-3	0-1	14	Scott	283
33	Apr 3	H	East Fife	W	4-2	4-2	14	Kerrigan 4	295
34	10	A	Forfar Ath	L	2-5	1-3	14	McCaffrey, Kerrigan	557
35	17	A	Clyde	L	0-4	0-0	14		595
36	24	H	Stenhousemuir	L	0-2	0-0	14		324
37	May 1	H	Arbroath	L	1-2	0-0	14	Scott	234
38	8	A	Brechin C	L	0-2	0-1	14		483
39	15	A	East Stirling	W	1-0	0-0	14	Scott	247

Final League Position: 14

Most League Appearances: 399, Murdy Walls, 1921-36.
Most League Goals in Season (Individual): 41: Jim Renwick, Division II; 1932-33.
Most Goals Overall (Individual): 105: Bunty Weir, 1928-31.

Honours
League Champions: Division II 1933-34, Second Division 1988-89; Runners-up: Division II 1913-14, 1937-38, 1947-48.
Scottish Cup Runners-up: 1920. League Cup: —.
Club Colours: Shirt: Yellow with red trim. Shorts: Red with yellow stripes. Stockings: Yellow.

Goalscorers: League (36): Scott 16 (4 pens), Kerrigan 8, Ferguson 3, Kelly 2, Archer 1, Cadden 1, Gallagher 1, McCaffrey 1, McKeown 1, Moore 1, Riley 1. Scottish Cup (0). Skol Cup (1): Ferguson 1. B & Q Cup (0)

Guidi M 18	Walsh R 10 + 4	McKeown D 37 +	Kelly J 22	Armour N 11 +	Riley D 17 +	McBride M 31 +	Cadden S 30	Ferguson W 13 + 2	McCoy G 7 + 4	Scott M 37 + 2	Archer S 9 + 2	Hendry A 9 + 5	Moore S 19 + 2	Kerrigan S 24 + 5	McCaffrey J 29	Brown R 2 + 1	Kiernan D 3 + 1	Millar G 13 + 1	Seggie D 5 + 5	Conway M 3	Gaughan M 10 + 4	McDonald D 1	McGuigan R 1	Fraser A 1	McConnachie R 10	Pryde A 4 + 3	Gallagher J 11 + 2	Gray W 7 + 5	McAulay I 3	Andrews G 2	Pathak J 1	Jackson S 7 + 3	Houston J 11 + 1	McQuade A 3 + 4	Mirner E 8	Match No.
1	2	3	4	5	6	7	8	9	10	11	12	14																								1
1	2	3	4	5	14	7	6	9		10	11	12	8																							2
1	2	3	4	5	8	7	6	9		10	11	12		14																						3
1	2	3	4	5		7	6	9		10	11	12		14	8																					4
1	2	3	4	5		7	6	9		10	11				8		12	14																		5
1		3	4	5		7	6			10	11		9	8							2	12														6
1		3		5		7		9	12	10	11			4	8			6			2	14														7
1		3		5	12	7		9	14	10	11			4	8			6			2															8
1		3		5	6	7		9	14	10	11			4	8			12			2															9
1		3	4	14		7	6	12		10	11		9	5				8			2															10
1	2	3	4			7	6	9		10	11		8	5					14		12															11
1	2	3	4			7	6			10	11	14	9	5					12		8															12
1		3				7	6			10			11	14	5	4	12				2				8	9										13
		3	2	6		7		9		10				8	5	4		11							1	14										14
	2	3	6	4	12	7	9	14		10				5	8			11							1											15
		3	6		7	10	12	4	11	9	14	5		2				8							1											16
1			5		7		9	12	10	4	11	8		2				6							3											17
		3	2	5	6	8		10	9	11	7	4		12											1	14										18
		3				10	9	6	8	4		2	14	5											1	12	11									19
	14	6	4		7	12	10	9		8		5		2											1	3	11									20
	14	4	8		7	10	11	12		6		5		2											1	3	9									21
	12	3	4	6	7	10	9			11				2	14										1	8	5									22
1			10	7	8		9	11	4					2	5										14	6	3									23
1	12		5	6		10	9	11	14	4				2	3																	7	8			24
1	12	3			8	6	11		9					2	5										7	10	4					14				25
	8	4			6	10	11		9					2											5	3	7	12	1							26
	4	2		5	7	6	9	8	11																10	3	12	1	14							27
		3		10	12	4	11	8	9	5		2													6			1	7							28
	4	3		5	7	6	9	11	2																10	12	8	1	14							29
	4	3		8	10	11	9	2	6																14	12	5	1	7							30
		3		7	5	11	12	9	2	6															10		8	1	14	4						31
		3		8	12	5	11	10	9	6																14	2	1	7	4						32
		3		11	7	8	10	6	9	5															14		2	1		4						33
		3	4	11	7	8	10	6	9	5		14													12		2	1								34
1		3	4	12	8	10	7	9	5																6		2	11								35
	3	4	2	14	10	8	7	9	5																11		1	6								36
		3	2	4	12	8	10	7	9	11															6		1	5								37
		3	2	8	11	9	7	10	5															1	6		12	4								38
		3	6	2	7	10	12	9	5							8								1	11		14	4								39

ALLOA

Second Division

Year Formed: 1883. *Ground & Address:* Recreation Park, Clackmannan Rd, Alloa FK10 1RR. *Telephone:* 0259 722695.
Ground Capacity: total: 3100, seated: 180. *Size of Pitch:* 110yd × 75yd.
Chairman: Pat Lawlor. *Secretary:* E. G. Cameron. *Commercial Manager:* William McKie.
Manager: Billy Lamont. *Assistant Manager:* —. *Physio:* —. *Coach:* —.
Managers since 1975: H. Wilson; A. Totten; W. Garner; J. Thomson; D. Sullivan; G. Abel; B. Little; H. McCann. *Club Nickname(s):* The Wasps. *Previous Grounds:* None.
Record Attendance: 13,000 v Dunfermline Athletic, Scottish Cup 3rd rd replay; 26 Feb, 1939.
Record Transfer Fee received: £30,000 for Martin Nelson to Hamilton A (1988).
Record Transfer Fee paid: —.
Record Victory: 9-2 v Forfar Ath, Division II; 18 Mar, 1933.
Record Defeat: 0-10 v Dundee, Division II; 8 Mar, 1947: v Third Lanark, League Cup, 8 Aug, 1953.
Most Capped Player: Jock Hepburn, 1, Scotland.
Most League Appearances: —.

ALLOA 1992—93 LEAGUE RECORD

Match No.	Date		Venue	Opponents	Result	H/T Score	Lg. Pos.	Goalscorers	Atten dance
1	Aug	8	H	Berwick R	W 2-0	2-0	—	McNiven, Moffat	431
2		15	A	East Fife	L 0-2	0-1	8		624
3		22	H	Stenhousemuir	W 2-1	1-0	7	Newbigging 2 (2 pens)	517
4		29	H	Clyde	L 1-5	0-2	9	Smith	812
5	Sept	5	A	Forfar Ath	D 1-1	0-0	8	Hendry	745
6		12	H	Arbroath	L 0-2	0-1	10		459
7		19	A	East Stirling	L 2-4	0-1	12	Smith, McAvoy	372
8		26	H	Brechin C	W 3-2	1-1	10	Tait, Russell, Smith	465
9	Oct	3	A	Albion R	W 1-0	0-0	8	Newbigging (pen)	337
10		10	H	Stranraer	L 1-4	0-2	9	Hendry	509
11		17	A	Queen of the S	W 2-1	2-0	7	Moffat, Newbigging (pen)	703
12		24	H	Queen's Park	D 0-0	0-0	7		513
13		31	H	Montrose	W 4-1	2-0	5	Moffat 3, Smith	666
14	Nov	7	A	Clyde	D 1-1	1-1	5	Smith	626
15		14	H	Forfar Ath	D 1-1	1-1	6	Tait	517
16		21	H	East Stirling	W 1-0	0-0	5	Tait	372
17		28	A	Arbroath	D 0-0	0-0	4		670
18	Dec	12	A	Berwick R	D 2-2	0-1	5	McCormick, Moffat	310
19		26	H	Albion R	W 4-0	0-0	4	McCaffrey (og), Smith, Moffat, McNiven	508
20	Jan	2	H	East Fife	L 0-2	0-1	5		736
21		26	H	Montrose	W 3-0	1-0	—	Moffat, Russell, McAvoy	326
22		30	A	Brechin C	L 2-4	1-0	6	Wilcox, McCormick	496
23	Feb	2	A	Stenhousemuir	W 1-0	1-0	—	McAvoy	459
24		6	H	Queen of the S	D 2-2	2-0	5	Bennett, McCormick	450
25		9	A	Queen's Park	W 3-0	1-0	—	Smith 2, Moffat	405
26		13	A	Stranraer	W 2-1	0-1	5	Moffat, McAvoy	585
27		20	A	Albion R	W 1-0	1-0	4	Moffat	403
28		27	A	East Stirling	W 2-0	1-0	4	Crombie, Moffat	437
29	Mar	6	A	East Fife	D 2-2	0-1	4	Moffat 2	563
30		13	H	Montrose	W 3-1	2-1	4	McAvoy, Moffat, Smith	453
31		20	H	Berwick R	L 0-2	0-2	5		418
32		27	A	Brechin C	L 0-1	0-0	5		502
33	Apr	3	H	Arbroath	L 0-3	0-0	5		386
34		10	A	Queen's Park	D 2-2	1-2	6	Hendry, Wilcox	475
35		17	A	Stranraer	D 3-3	0-2	5	Hendry, Moffat 2	619
36		24	H	Clyde	D 1-1	1-0	6	Hendry	849
37	May	1	H	Stenhousemuir	L 0-2	0-2	6		424
38		8	A	Forfar Ath	D 1-1	1-1	6	Tait	441
39		15	A	Queen of the S	W 7-0	2-0	5	Tait, Lee, Moffat 2 (1 pen), McAvoy, McCormick 2	318

Final League Position: 5

Most League Goals in Season (Individual): 49: William 'Wee' Crilley, Division II; 1921-22.
Most Goals Overall (Individual): —.

Honours
League Champions: Division II 1921-22; *Runners-up:* Division II 1938-39. Second Division 1976-77, 1981-82, 1984-85, 1988-89.
Scottish Cup: —.
League Cup: —.
Club colours: Shirt: Gold with black trim. Shorts: Black. Stockings: Gold.

Goalscorers: *League (63):* Moffat 19 (1 pen), Smith 9, McAvoy 6, Hendry 5, McCormick 5, Tait 5, Newbigging 4 (4 pens), McNiven 2, Russell 2, Wilcox 2, Bennett 1, Crombie 1, Lee 1, own goal 1.   *Scottish Cup (2):* McAvoy 1, Moffat 1.   *Skol Cup (2):* McAvoy 1, Moffat 1.   *B & Q Cup (2):* McNiven 1, Wilcox 1.

Butter J 37	Newbigging W 27 + 3	McAvoy N 34 + 3	Romaines S 4 + 1	McCulloch K 25 + 1	Campbell C 33	Moffat B 35 + 1	McNiven J 31 + 1	Smith S 32 + 2	Hendry M 24 + 5	Sheerin P 7 + 2	Bennett N 30 + 3	Conroy J 1 + 2	Lee R 6	Wilcox D 31 + 1	McCormick S 9 + 9	Ramsay S 6 + 3	Tait G 18 + 2	Russell G 5 + 19	Thomson J 2	Campbell K — + 2	Gibson J 9 + 9	Crombie L 18 + 1	Herd W 3	Binnie N 2	Match No.
1	2	3	4	5	6	7	8	9	10	11	12		14												1
1	2	11			6	7	8	9	10	4				3	5	12	14								2
1	2	3			6	7	8	9	4	14	12			5	10	11									3
1	2	3		5	6		8	9	12	4			7	14	10	11									4
1	2	3		5	6	12	8	9	7	14					10	11	4								5
1	2			5	6	12	8	9	7	14				3	10	11	4								6
1	2	14	4	5	6	7		9	10					3	12	11	8								7
1	2	14	7	5		10		9	12	8	3			4			6	11							8
1	2			5	10	6	9		7	3				4			8	11							9
1	2	14		5	10	6	9	12	7	3				4			8	11							10
1	2	5	14	6	10				7	9	11			4			8	12	3						11
1	2	5		6	10	14	7	9		11				4			8	12	3						12
1	2	5		6	10	8	7	9	3					4		11	12	14							13
1	2	5		6	10	8	7	9	3					4		11	14	12							14
1	2	5		6	10	8	7	9	3					4		11	12								15
1	2	5		6	10	8	7	9	3					4		11	12		14						16
1	2	5		6	10	8	7	9	3					4		11	12		14						17
1	2	5		6	10	8	7		3					4	9	11		12							18
1	2	11		5	6	10	8	9		3				4	12		14	7							19
1	11			5	6	10	8			3				4	9	14	12		7	2					20
1	2	5		6	10	8	7		3					4	9	11	12		14						21
1	2	5		6	10	8	9		3					4	14	7	12	11							22
1		5	2	6	10	8		14	3					4	9	12	11	7							23
1	14	5	2	6		7		9	10	3				4	12	11	8								24
1	14	5	2	6	7		9	10	3					4	12	11	8								25
1	14	5	2	6	7	8	9	10	3					4	12	11									26
1	2	6		5		7	8	9	10	3				4	14	12	11								27
1	2	11		5		7	8	9	10	3				4	14	12	6								28
1	2	11		5		7	8	9	10	3				4	14	6									29
1	2	11			6	7	8	9	10	3				4	14	12	5								30
1	2	11	14		6	7	8	9	10	3				4	12	5									31
1	10			5	6	7	8	9	12	3				4	11	2									32
1	11			5	6	10	8	9		3	2	14		7	12	4									33
1	11	8	2	6	10		14	9		3				4	12		7	5							34
1	11			5	6	9	8	10		3				4	12	14		7	2						35
1	11			5	6	10		9		3				4	12	8	14	7	2						36
1	11			5	6	10	8	12	9	3				4				14	2	7					37
	2	11		5	6	9		10		3					8	14			4	7	1				38
	11			5	6	10	4	9		14				3	12	8			2	7	1				39

ARBROATH
Second Division

Year Formed: 1878. *Ground & Address:* Gayfield Park, Arbroath DD11 1QB. *Telephone:* 0241 72157.
Ground Capacity: 6488. seated: 715. *Size of Pitch:* 115yd × 71yd.
President: James King. *Secretary:* Andrew Warrington. *Commercial Manager:* David Kean.
Manager: Daniel McGrain MBE. *Assistant Manager:* Cameron Evans. *Physio:* William Shearer. *Coach:* Charles Adam.
Managers since 1975: A. Henderson; I. J. Stewart; G. Fleming; J. Bone; J. Young; W. Borthwick; M. Lawson.
Club Nickname(s): The Red Lichties. *Previous Grounds:* None.
Record Attendance: 13,510 v Rangers, Scottish Cup 3rd rd; 23 Feb, 1952.
Record Transfer Fee received: £50,000 for Mark McWalter to St Mirren (June 1987).
Record Transfer Fee paid: £20,000 for Douglas Robb from Montrose (1981).
Record Victory: 36-0 v Bon Accord, Scottish Cup 1st rd; 12 Sept, 1885.
Record Defeat: 0-8 v Kilmarnock, Division II; 3 Jan, 1949.
Most Capped Player: Ned Doig, 2 (5), Scotland.
Most League Appearances: 445: Tom Cargill, 1966-81.

ARBROATH 1992—93 LEAGUE RECORD

Match No.	Date		Venue	Opponents	Result		H/T Score	Lg. Pos.	Goalscorers	Atten dance
1	Aug	8	H	Brechin C	D	0-0	0-0	—		552
2		15	A	Forfar Ath	D	1-1	1-0	9	McNaughton	861
3		22	H	East Stirling	L	4-5	3-2	8	Macdonald, Sorbie 2, Tindal	380
4		29	H	Queen's Park	W	2-1	0-0	5	Sorbie 2	402
5	Sept	5	A	Clyde	L	0-2	0-1	9		599
6		12	A	Alloa	W	2-0	1-0	7	Godfrey, Sorbie	459
7		19	H	East Fife	L	1-3	1-1	8	Adam	564
8		26	A	Montrose	L	3-4	1-1	11	Tosh 2, Macdonald	802
9	Oct	3	A	Berwick R	L	1-5	0-1	13	Martin	396
10		10	H	Albion R	W	2-0	2-0	12	Tindal, Sorbie	508
11		17	A	Stenhousemuir	W	3-1	1-1	10	Sorbie 2, Godfrey	469
12		24	H	Queen of the S	D	0-0	0-0	9		535
13		31	H	Stranraer	L	0-1	0-0	10		554
14	Nov	7	A	Queen's Park	W	1-0	0-0	8	Sorbie	432
15		14	H	Clyde	D	1-1	0-0	8	Tosh	935
16		21	A	East Fife	W	3-1	1-1	8	Adam, Tosh 2	634
17		28	H	Alloa	D	0-0	0-0	8		670
18	Dec	12	A	Brechin C	L	0-2	0-0	9		770
19	Jan	2	H	Forfar Ath	L	2-3	0-2	10	Sorbie 2	1435
20		5	H	Berwick R	L	0-1	0-0	—		557
21		20	H	Stranraer	W	2-1	1-1	—	Sorbie, Tindal	469
22		30	A	Montrose	D	1-1	0-1	9	Sorbie	865
23	Feb	2	A	Queen of the S	W	1-0	0-0	—	McNaughton (pen)	495
24		10	H	Stenhousemuir	W	3-2	1-0	—	Buckley, Sorbie 2	535
25		13	A	Albion R	W	1-0	0-0	7	Macdonald (pen)	254
26		20	H	Brechin C	W	2-0	1-0	7	Sorbie, McNaughton	2014
27		23	A	East Stirling	W	2-1	0-0	—	Sorbie, Tindal	303
28		27	A	Queen's Park	L	1-2	0-1	7	Adam	461
29	Mar	9	A	Clyde	L	0-2	0-0	—		558
30		16	H	East Stirling	D	0-0	0-0	—		520
31		20	A	Queen of the S	W	3-2	2-1	7	Tosh, Buckley, Wright (og)	310
32		27	H	Stenhousemuir	W	2-1	2-1	7	Tosh, Buckley	621
33	Apr	3	A	Alloa	W	3-0	0-0	6	Sorbie, Tosh 2	386
34		10	H	Berwick R	W	6-0	2-0	5	Buckley 3 (1 pen), Macdonald, Sorbie, Tosh	855
35		17	A	Montrose	L	0-2	0-1	6		946
36		24	H	Stranraer	L	1-4	1-1	6	Martin	777
37	May	1	A	Albion R	W	2-1	0-0	5	Tosh 2	234
38		8	H	East Fife	W	3-0	0-0	5	Adam, Strachan, Tindal	703
39		15	H	Forfar Ath	D	0-0	0-0	6		1007

Final League Position: 6

Most League Goals in Season (Individual): 45: Dave Easson, Division II; 1958-59.
Most Goals Overall (Individual): 120: Jimmy Jack; 1966-71.

Honours
League Champions Runners-up: Division II 1934-35, 1958-59, 1967-68, 1971-72.
Scottish Cup: —.
League Cup: —.
Club colours: Shirt: Maroon with white and sky blue shoulder flashes. Shorts: White with maroon and sky blue flashes on thighs. Stockings: Maroon with white and sky blue hoop tops.

Goalscorers: *League (59):* Sorbie 19, Tosh 12, Buckley 6 (1 pen), Tindal 5, Adam 4, Macdonald 4 (1 pen), McNaughton 3 (1 pen), Godfrey 2, Martin 2, Strachan 1, own goal 1. *Scottish Cup (10):* Sorbie 3, Martin 2, Tosh 2, Macdonald 1, McNaughton 1, Tindal 1. *Skol Cup (3):* Adam 1, Macdonald 1, Tindal 1. *B & Q Cup (3):* Macdonald 1, Sorbie 1, Tosh 1.

Balfour D 5	Hamilton J 21 + 4	Martin C 32 + 2	Mitchell B 36	Farnan C 36	Boyd W 34 + 1	Tindal K 29 + 4	Adam C 28 + 1	Macdonald K 28 + 1	McNaughton B 12 + 6	Sorbie S 39	Tosh P 26 + 8	Holmes W — + 8	Godfrey P 11	Sneddon H — + 2	Harkness M 34	Florence S 28	Will B 9 + 5	Buckley G 14	Strachan J 7 + 1	Match No.
1	2	3	4	5	6	7	8	9	10	11	12	14								1
1		3	4	7	6	12	8	9	2	11	10				5					2
1		3	4	7	6	12	8	9	2	11	10	14			5					3
1		3		7	6	4	8	9	2	11	10				5	12				4
1		3	2	7	6	4	8	9	10	11	12				5	14				5
		3	2	7	6	4	8	9	14	11	10	12			5	1				6
		3	2	7	6	4	8	9		11	10	12			5	1				7
	12	3	2	7	6	4	8	9		11	10	14			5	1				8
	12	3	2	7	6	4	8	9	14	11	10				5	1				9
		3	2	7	6	4		9	14	11	8				5	1		10		10
	12	3	2	7	6	4	8	9		11		14			5	1		10		11
		3	2	7	6	4	12	9		11	8				5	1		10		12
	12	3	2	7	6	4		9		11	8	14			5	1		10		13
	10	3	2	7		4	8	9		11		14			5	1		6		14
	7	3	4	2	6	12		9	10	11		14			5	1	8			15
	7	3	4	2	6			9	10	11					5	1	8			16
	7	3	4	2	6			9	10	11					5	1	8			17
		3	4	2	6			9	10	11					5	1	8	7		18
		3	4	2	6			9	10	11	12				5	1	7	8		19
		3	4	2	6			9	10	11					5	1	7	8		20
	7	3	4	2	6			9	10	11					5	1	8			21
	7	3	4	2	6					11	12				5	1	8	9	10	22
	7	3	4		6		8		14	11	12				5	1	10	2	9	23
	7	3	5		6	4	2	9		11	12					1	8	10		24
	7	3	4	2	6			9		11	12				5	1	8	14	10	25
			4	2	6			9	10	11					5	1	8	7	3	26
		3	4	2	6			9	10	11	12				5	1	8	7		27
		3	4	2	6			9	10	11	12				5	1	8	7	14	28
	7		4		6	14		9	10	11	12				5	1	8	2	3	29
	7		4	2	6			9	10	11					5	1	8		3	30
	7		4		6			9	10	11	12				5	1	8	2	3	31
	7		4	2	6			9	10	11					5	1	8	14	3	32
	7	14	4	2	6			9		11					5	1	8	10	3	33
	7	14	4	2	6			9		11	12				5	1	8	10	3	34
	7		4	2	6			9		11	12				5	1	8	10	3	35
	7	3	4	2	6			9		11	12				5	1	8	10		36
	7	3	4	2	6				10	11					5	1	8	9		37
	7	3	4	2	6			9		11					5	1	8	10		38
	7	3	4	2	6			9		11					5	1	8	10		39

AYR UNITED

First Division

Year Formed: 1910. *Ground & Address:* Somerset Park, Tryfield Place, Ayr KA8 9NB. *Telephone:* 0292 263435.
Ground Capacity: 13,918. seated: 1450. *Size of Pitch:* 111yd × 72yd.
Chairman: D. M. MacIntyre. *Secretary:* David Quayle. *Commercial Manager:* Sandy Kerr. ·
Manager: George Burley. *Assistant Manager:* Dale Roberts. *Physio:* Andrew MacLeod.
Managers since 1975: Alex Stuart; Ally MacLeod; Willie McLean; George Caldwell; Ally MacLeod. *Club Nickname(s):*
The Honest Men. *Previous Grounds:* None.
Record Attendance: 25,225 v Rangers, Division I; 13 Sept, 1969.
Record Transfer Fee received: £300,000 for Steven Nicol to Liverpool (Oct 1981).
Record Transfer Fee paid: £50,000 for Peter Weir from St Mirren, June 1990.
Record Victory: 11-1 v Dumbarton, League Cup; 13 Aug, 1952.
Record Defeat: 0-9 in Division I v Rangers (1929); v Hearts (1931); v Third Lanark (1954).
Most Capped Player: Jim Nisbet, 3, Scotland.

AYR UNITED 1992—93 LEAGUE RECORD

Match No.	Date		Venue	Opponents	Result	H/T Score	Lg. Pos.	Goalscorers	Attendance
1	Aug	1	H	Dunfermline Ath	D	1-1	0-1	—	Mair	2588
2		4	H	Meadowbank T	L	1-2	1-1	—	Agnew	1518
3		8	A	Clydebank	D	1-1	1-1	8	Walker	757
4		15	H	Raith R	L	0-1	0-0	10		1417
5		22	H	Kilmarnock	W	2-0	0-0	9	Kennedy, Agnew	5475
6		29	A	Hamilton A	D	1-1	1-0	9	Graham	1592
7	Sept	5	H	Morton	L	0-2	0-1	11		2300
8		12	H	Cowdenbeath	L	0-1	0-0	11		1487
9		19	A	Dumbarton	W	3-0	2-0	9	Graham, Traynor, McTurk	882
10		26	A	St Mirren	L	0-2	0-1	9		3079
11	Oct	3	H	Stirling Albion	W	2-1	1-0	8	Graham 2	1580
12		10	A	Dunfermline Ath	W	3-1	2-1	8	Graham, McTurk, Traynor	3037
13		17	H	Clydebank	W	2-1	1-0	8	Traynor, Mair	1785
14		24	A	Morton	L	1-2	1-1	9	Shotton	1787
15		31	H	Hamilton A	D	0-0	0-0	8		1796
16	Nov	7	H	Raith R	D	1-1	1-0	9	Walker	2160
17		14	A	Kilmarnock	L	0-3	0-2	9		5709
18		21	H	Dumbarton	W	5-3	2-1	9	Traynor, Robertson, Mair 3	1317
19	Dec	1	A	Stirling Albion	D	0-0	0-0	—		344
20		5	H	St Mirren	W	2-0	1-0	8	Graham, Walker	2516
21		8	A	Cowdenbeath	D	2-2	2-1	—	Graham, Traynor	284
22		12	H	Dunfermline Ath	W	1-0	1-0	8	Graham	1939
23		19	A	Meadowbank T	L	0-1	0-0	8		339
24		26	H	Raith R	D	1-1	1-0	8	Mair	3119
25	Jan	2	H	Kilmarnock	L	0-1	0-0	8		8424
26		26	H	Stirling Albion	D	2-2	1-2	—	Traynor, Mair	2061
27		30	A	Clydebank	D	1-1	1-1	8	Russell	946
28	Feb	9	H	Morton	D	0-0	0-0	—		1675
29		13	H	Meadowbank T	W	1-0	1-0	7	Graham	1406
30		20	A	St Mirren	L	0-1	0-0	8		2371
31		27	A	Dumbarton	L	0-2	0-1	8		988
32	Mar	2	A	Hamilton A	W	3-1	1-0	—	Bryce, Walker, Scott	1329
33		6	H	Cowdenbeath	W	3-1	1-0	7	Bryce (pen), Traynor, Scott	1270
34		10	A	Dunfermline Ath	D	1-1	1-0	7	Bryce (pen)	2624
35		13	H	Clydebank	D	0-0	0-0	7		1713
36		20	A	Kilmarnock	D	1-1	1-1	7	Walker	5660
37		27	H	Raith R	D	0-0	0-0	7		2664
38	Apr	3	A	Morton	L	0-1	0-0	7		997
39		10	H	Hamilton A	W	1-0	0-0	7	Kennedy	1836
40		17	A	Cowdenbeath	W	1-0	0-0	7	Bryce	213
41		24	H	Dumbarton	D	0-0	0-0	7		1525
42	May	1	A	Meadowbank T	W	2-1	1-1	7	Walker, Bryce	276
43		8	H	St Mirren	D	3-3	1-0	7	Hood, McWhirter (og), Scott	3235
44		15	A	Stirling Albion	D	1-1	0-0	7	Walker	1171

Final League Position: 7

Most League Appearances: 371: Ian McAllister, 1977-90.
Most League Goals in Season (Individual): 66: Jimmy Smith, 1927-28.
Most Goals Overall (Individual): —.

Honours
League Champions: Division II 1911-12, 1912-13, 1927-28, 1936-37, 1958-59, 1965-66. Second Division 1987-88; Runners-up: Division II 1910-11, 1955-56, 1968-69.
Scottish Cup: —. League Cup: —.
B&Q Cup: Runners-up:1990-91, 1991-92.
Club colours: Shirt: White with black sleeves. Shorts: Black. Stockings: White.

Goalscorers: League (49): Graham 9, Mair 7, Traynor 7, Walker 7, Bryce 5 (2 pens), Scott 3, Agnew 2, Kennedy 2, McTurk 2, Hood 1, Robertson G 1, Russell 1, Shotton 1, own goal 1. Scottish Cup (2): Mair 1 (pen), Walker 1. Skol Cup (0). B & Q Cup (2): Walker 2

Duncan C 41	Robertson G 43+1	Agnew G 18	Furphy W 6	Howard N 24	Kennedy D 29+3	George D 37	Walker T 38+3	Graham A 30	Gardner L 2	Mair G 20+2	McTurk A 12+11	McLean P 2	McVie G 6+2	Traynor J 36	Shaw G —+5	Shotton M 35	Burley G 33	Carse J 1+5	Crews B 1+3	Burke P 4+2	McGuigan R 3+2	Spence W 3	Robertson S 4+2	McGivern S 9	Russell R 4	Allan D 5	Bryce S 14	Scott B 12+1	Hood G 12	Match No.
1	2	3	4	5	6	7	8	9	10	11	12																			1
1	2	3	4	5		6	8	9	10	11	12	7																		2
1	6	3	4		2	10	8	9		11	12		5	7																3
1	6		4	5	2	10	8	9		11		3	7	12																4
1	6	3	4	5	2	10	8	9		11				7	12															5
1	6	3	4	5	2	10	8	9		14	11			7	12															6
1	6	3		5	2	10	8	9		11				7	12	4														7
1	7	3			2	10	8	9	11		6		5	12	4															8
1	7	3		5	6		8	9		11	12			10		4	2													9
1	7	3		5	6		8	9		11	12			10		4	2													10
1	7	3			6	10	8	9		11				5		4	2	12												11
1	7	3		5		6	8	9		11				10		4	2													12
1	7	3		5		6	8	9		12	11			10		4	2	14												13
1	7	3		5		6	8	9		11				10		4	2													14
1	7	3		5		6	8	9						10		4	2	12	14	11										15
1	7		5		6	8	9			11				10		4	2	12		12			3							16
1	7		5		6	8	9			11		3	2			4		12	10	14										17
1	7		5		6	8	9			11		14	10			4	2			3										18
1	2	3		5		6	8	9		11	12			10		4				7										19
1	7	3		5		6	8	9		11				10		4	2													20
1	7	3		5		6	8	9		11				10		4	2			14										21
	7	3		5	14	6	8	9		11				10		4	2				1									22
1	7		5	3	6	8	9			11				10		4	2	12				14								23
1	7		5	14	6	8	9			11				10		4	2					3								24
1	7		5	6		12	9			11				10		4	2					3	8							25
1	12			6	7	9				11				5		4	2					3	8		10					26
1	3			7	6	12	9			11				5		4	2						8		10					27
1	3			7	6		9			11	12					4	2			14			8		10	5				28
1	3			7	6		9			11				10		4	2			14			8			5				29
1	7			10	6		9			11			14			4	2			12		3	8			5				30
1	3			7	6	8				12						4	2					9		10		5	11			31
1	3			7	6	8				12				10		4	2							5	9	11				32
1	3			12	6	8				14				10		4	2	7							9	11	5			33
	3	4	10	6	8								2					7	1					9	11	5				34
1	3			10	6	8							7			4	2	12							9	11	5			35
1	3			7	6	8							10			4	2							9	11	5				36
1	3			6	8								10			4	2	7						9	11	5				37
1	3		4	6	8								7		10		2							9	11	5				38
1	7			6	8					3	10					4	2							9	11	5				39
1	3			6	7					4	10			2			8							9	11	5				40
	2			7	6	12				3	10		4			1		8						9	11	5				41
1	3			7	6	8							10			4	2							9	11	5				42
1	7			3	6	8				14	10					4	2							9	11	5				43
1	3			7	6	8							10			4	2	11						9	12	5				44

BERWICK RANGERS Second Division

Year Formed: 1881. *Ground & Address:* Shielfield Park, Tweedmouth, Berwick-upon-Tweed TD15 2EF. *Telephone:* 0289 307424. Club 24 hour hotline 0891 800697. *Ground Capacity:* 1100. seated: 500. *Size of Pitch:* 112yd × 76yd.
Chairman: Roy McDowell. *Vice-chairman:* Tom Davidson. *Company Secretary:* Colin Walker. *Club Secretary:* Dennis McCleary.
Manager: Jim Crease. *Assistant Manager:* Tom Hendrie. *Physio/Coach:* Ian Oliver.
Managers since 1975: H. Melrose; G. Haig; W. Galbraith; D. Smith; F. Connor; J. McSherry; E. Tait; J. Thomson; J. Jefferies; J. Anderson.
Club Nickname(s): The Borderers. *Previous Grounds:* Bull Stob Close, Pier Field, Meadow Field, Union Park, Old Shielfield.
Record Attendance: 13,365 v Rangers, Scottish Cup 1st rd; 28 Jan, 1967.
Record Victory: 8-1 v Forfar Ath. Division II; 25 Dec, 1965; v Vale of Leithen, Scottish Cup; Dec, 1966.
Record Defeat: 1-9 v Hamilton A, First Division; 9 Aug, 1980.
Most Capped Player: —.

BERWICK RANGERS 1992—93 LEAGUE RECORD

Match No.	Date		Venue	Opponents	Result		H/T Score	Lg. Pos.	Goalscorers	Atten dance
1	Aug	8	A	Alloa	L	0-2	0-2	—		431
2		15	A	Stenhousemuir	W	3-1	1-0	5	Cass, Graham, Davidson	243
3		22	A	Brechin C	L	1-5	1-1	11	Graham	347
4		29	A	Montrose	W	3-1	1-1	8	Davidson 2, Scott	519
5	Sept	5	A	Albion R	D	1-1	0-0	7	Davidson	273
6		12	A	Queen of the S	L	0-1	0-0	9		475
7		19	H	Queen's Park	W	1-0	0-0	7	Fisher	432
8		26	A	East Fife	L	2-4	1-1	9	Fisher, Robertson	617
9	Oct	3	H	Arbroath	W	5-1	1-0	7	Scott 2, Cunningham 2, Waldie	396
10		10	A	Forfar Ath	L	3-5	0-3	8	Hutchinson, Graham, Irvine	599
11		17	H	East Stirling	L	2-5	1-1	11	Scott, Graham (pen)	362
12		24	H	Stranraer	L	1-2	1-0	13	Graham	326
13		31	A	Clyde	L	0-2	0-1	13		505
14	Nov	7	H	Montrose	W	3-0	0-0	12	Irvine, Scott 2	310
15		14	H	Albion R	D	1-1	1-0	10	Irvine	325
16		21	A	Queen's Park	L	0-4	0-2	12		385
17		28	H	Queen of the S	L	1-4	1-1	11	Scott	308
18	Dec	12	H	Alloa	D	2-2	1-0	11	Scott 2	310
19	Jan	2	H	Stenhousemuir	D	1-1	1-1	11	Irvine	470
20		5	A	Arbroath	W	1-0	0-0	—	Scott	557
21		16	H	Clyde	L	0-3	0-1	11		378
22		23	A	Stranraer	W	3-1	2-0	11	Cunningham, Richardson, Irvine	468
23		30	H	East Fife	W	3-0	1-0	10	Scott, Irvine, Cunningham	417
24	Feb	6	A	Brechin C	L	0-2	0-0	10		394
25		10	A	East Stirling	L	0-2	0-1	—		246
26		13	H	Forfar Ath	W	2-1	1-0	10	Graham (pen), Cunningham	352
27		20	H	Queen of the S	W	3-0	1-0	9	McGovern, Cunningham, Graham	329
28		27	A	Stenhousemuir	D	0-0	0-0	9		314
29	Mar	6	H	Clyde	L	0-1	0-0	9		482
30		13	A	Albion R	W	2-0	1-0	9	Cunningham, Irvine	200
31		20	A	Alloa	W	2-0	2-0	9	Wilson, Kane	418
32		27	H	Montrose	W	2-0	0-0	9	Graham 2 (1 pen)	369
33	Apr	3	H	Brechin C	W	2-1	2-0	9	Neil, Hall	409
34		10	A	Arbroath	L	0-6	0-2	9		855
35		17	A	Forfar Ath	W	2-0	0-0	9	Irvine, Cunningham	515
36		24	H	Queen's Park	D	1-1	0-1	9	Irvine	465
37	May	1	H	East Stirling	D	0-0	0-0	9		394
38		8	A	Stranraer	L	1-3	1-2	9	Richardson	1020
39		15	A	East Fife	W	2-1	0-0	8	Cunningham, Wilson	469

Final League Position: 8

Most League Appearances: 435;: Eric Tait, 1970-87.
Most League Goals in Season (Individual): 38: Ken Bowron, Division II; 1963-64.
Most Goals Overall (Individual): 115: Eric Tait, 1970-87.

Honours
League Champions: Second Division 1978-79.
Scottish Cup: —.
League Cup: Semi-final 1963-64.
Club colours: Shirt: Black and gold stripes. Shorts: Black, gold trim. Stockings: Gold and black.

Goalscorers: *League (56):* Scott 11, Cunningham 9, Graham 9 (3 pens), Irvine 9, Davidson 4, Fisher 2, Richardson 2, Wilson 2, Cass 1, Hall 1, Hutchinson 1, Kane 1, McGovern 1, Neil 1, Robertson 1, Waldie 1. *Scottish Cup (3):* Anderson 1, Hall 1, Richardson 1. *Skol Cup (0).* *B & Q Cup (5):* Davidson 2, Cunningham 1, Irvine 1, Scott 1.

Egan J 4	Davidson G 31	O'Donnell J 5	Brownlee P 1	Hall A 37	Thorpe B 5+2	Hendrie T 26+4	Valentine C 38	Cunningham C 28+1	Bickmore S 2+1	Graham T 38	Waldie I 3+11	Fisher W 10+2	Cass M 13	Thomson G 1	Scott D 22+5	Robertson J 10+4	Neilson D 9	Hutchinson I 12+8	Kerr D 1+3	Irvine W 28+1	Malone L 1+4	Massie K 13	Richardson S 22	Shell K 1	Anderson P 8	Wilson M 12+4	Murray P 8+4	McGovern P 2	O'Connor G 13	Kane K 11	Muir S 3+2	Neil M 6	Gibson K 5	Match No.
1	2	3	4	5	6	7	8	9	10	11	12																							1
1	6	3		4	2	8	9	*9*	12	10	14	7	5	11																				2
1	2	3		5	10	4	8	9		11	12	7	6																					3
1	7	3		5	14	2	8	11		*10*	4	6	9	12																				4
	4	*3*		5	12	2	8	11		10	7	6	9	14	1																			5
	4			5	10	2	8	11		12	7	6	9		3	1																		6
	4			5	10	2	8	11		7	6	9			3	1																		7
	4			5	10	2	8	11		7	6	9			3	1	14																	8
	4			5	2	10	11	12		7	6	9	8		1	3																		9
	4			*5*	2	7	10	11		12	6	9	8		1	3	14																	10
	5			4	*10*	11	12	14		6	9	2	1		3	8	7																	11
	5			2	*10*	9	11	14		8	6	4	1		3	12	7																	12
	4			5	2	8	*10*	11		6	9	12	1		3	7	14																	13
	4			5	2	10	14	11		9	8	3	7		1	6																		14
	4			5	2	*10*	11	9		8	3	7	1		6																			15
	5			2	10	11	14	6		9	8	3	7		12	1	4																	16
	5	2		3	4	11	*8*	9		14	10	7	12		1	6																		17
	4	8		2	3	10	11	9		7			1		6	5																		18
	4	6		2	3	8	11	9		10	7	12	1		5																			19
	8	*2*		3	10	11	12	14		7	9	1	6		5	4																		20
	4	8		2	3	10	11	14		9	7	1	6		*5*	12																		21
	4	5		2	3	10	11	9		7	1	6	8																					22
	2	8		3	10	11	14	*9*		12	7	1	6		5	4																		23
	8	2		3	11	10	9	12		7	1	6	5		4																			24
	8	14		3	10	11	9	12		7	1	6	5		4	2																	25
	2	4	12	3	11	9	14	8		1	5	7	6	*10*																				26
	5	2		3	10	11	14	7		6	8	4	9	1																				27
	4	2		3	9	11	8	7		5	6	10	1																					28
	2	8	14	3	9	11	6	7		5	12	*4*	1	10																				29
	2	4		3	10	6	12	9		5	7	1	11	8																				30
	4	2		3	9	11	14	12		10	5	*7*	1	6	8																		31
	4	5		2	3	9	11	12		10	7	1	6	8																				32
	2	4		3	9	11	14	10		5	7	1	6	12	*8*																		33
	2	4		3	11	9	10	5		7	14	1	6	12	*8*																		34
	4	8		3	9	11	10	5		14	1	6	*7*	2																			35
	4	8		3	9	11	12	14		10	5	7	*7*	1	6	2																	36
	4	8		3	9	11	10	5		12	14	1	6	*7*	2																		37
	4	8		3	9	*11*	10	5		12	14	1	6	*7*	2																		38
	4	8	12	3	9	11	14	5		*10*	1	6	*7*	2																			39

BRECHIN CITY   First Division

Year Formed: 1906. *Ground & Address:* Glebe Park, Trinity Rd, Brechin, Angus DD9 6BJ. *Telephone:* 0356 622856.
Ground Capacity: total: 3900. seated: 1518. *Size of Pitch:* 110yd × 67yd.
Chairman: Hugh Campbell Adamson. *Secretary:* George C. Johnston. *Commercial Manager:* —.
Manager: Ian Redford. *Assistant Manager:* John Young. *Physio:* Tom Gilmartin.
Managers since 1975: Charlie Dunn; Ian Stewart; Doug Houston; Ian Fleming; John Ritchie. *Club Nickname(s):* The
City. *Previous Grounds:* Nursery Park.
Record Attendance: 8122 v Aberdeen, Scottish Cup 3rd rd; 3 Feb, 1973.
Record Transfer Fee received: £100,000 for Scott Thomson to Aberdeen (1991).
Record Transfer Fee paid: £16,000 for Sandy Ross from Berwick Rangers (1991).
Record Victory: 12-1 v Thornhill, Scottish Cup 1st rd; 28 Jan, 1926.
Record Defeat: 0-10 v Airdrieonians, Albion R and Cowdenbeath, all in Division II; 1937-38.
Most Capped Player: —.

BRECHIN CITY 1992—93 LEAGUE RECORD

Match No.	Date		Venue	Opponents	Result		H/T Score	Lg. Pos.	Goalscorers	Atten dance
1	Aug	8	A	Arbroath	D	0-0	0-0	—		552
2		15	H	Montrose	W	3-1	0-1	3	Miller (pen), Ross, Hutt	740
3		22	H	Berwick R	W	5-1	1-1	1	Brand 2, Ross, Lorimer, O'Brien	347
4		29	H	Albion R	W	2-0	0-0	2	Lees, Ross	494
5	Sept	5	A	Queen of the S	D	0-0	0-0	3		563
6		12	H	Stranraer	D	1-1	0-0	3	Ross (pen)	441
7		19	A	Stenhousemuir	W	4-2	2-0	2	Lees, Ross 2, Lorimer	278
8		26	A	Alloa	L	2-3	1-1	3	Ross 2	465
9	Oct	3	H	East Stirling	W	2-1	1-0	3	Brand 2	380
10		10	A	Queen's Park	W	2-1	1-1	2	Miller 2	399
11		17	H	East Fife	W	1-0	0-0	1	Miller	506
12		24	H	Clyde	W	2-1	1-0	1	Ross, McKillop	664
13		31	A	Forfar Ath	W	1-0	1-0	1	Ross	1044
14	Nov	7	A	Albion R	W	4-1	2-1	1	Scott, Brand, Ross (pen), Miller	259
15		14	H	Queen of the S	W	3-0	2-0	1	Heggie, Ross, Scott	518
16		21	H	Stenhousemuir	D	2-2	2-1	1	Heggie, Brand	450
17		28	A	Stranraer	D	0-0	0-0	1		927
18	Dec	12	H	Arbroath	W	2-0	0-0	1	Ross 2	770
19		26	A	East Stirling	D	0-0	0-0	1		427
20	Jan	2	A	Montrose	W	2-0	1-0	1	Ross 2	1211
21		30	H	Alloa	W	4-2	0-1	1	Miller, Brand, O'Brien, Ross (pen)	496
22	Feb	2	H	Forfar Ath	L	1-2	0-1	—	Ross	932
23		6	A	Berwick R	W	2-0	0-0	1	Ross 2	394
24		9	A	East Fife	L	0-1	0-1	—		822
25		13	H	Queen's Park	W	1-0	0-0	1	Scott	497
26		20	A	Arbroath	L	0-2	0-1	1		2014
27		23	A	Clyde	W	1-0	0-0	—	O'Brien	735
28		27	H	Montrose	D	0-0	0-0	1		620
29	Mar	6	A	Queen of the S	W	2-1	0-0	1	McNeill, Heggie	417
30		13	H	Stranraer	L	0-1	0-1	1		530
31		20	A	Stenhousemuir	L	0-3	0-1	2		360
32		27	H	Alloa	W	1-0	0-0	2	Ross	502
33	Apr	3	A	Berwick R	L	1-2	0-2	2	Brand	409
34		10	H	East Stirling	W	5-0	2-0	2	Ross, Miller 2, McNeill 2	555
35		17	A	Queen's Park	L	0-1	0-1	2		468
36		24	H	Forfar Ath	L	0-1	0-0	2		830
37	May	1	A	East Fife	W	2-1	2-0	2	Brand, Ross	580
38		8	H	Albion R	W	2-0	1-0	2	McNeill, Miller	483
39		15	A	Clyde	W	2-1	1-1	2	Miller 2 (1 pen)	1435

Final League Position: 2

Most League Appearances: 459: David Watt, 1975-89.
Most League Goals in Season (Individual): 26: W. McIntosh, Division II; 1959-60.
Most Goals Overall (Individual): 131: Ian Campbell.

Honours
League Champions: Second Division 1982-83. C Division 1953-54. Second Division 1989-90. *Runners-up:* 1992-93.
Scottish Cup: —.
League Cup: —.
Club colours: Shirt, Shorts, Stockings: Red with white trimmings.

Goalscorers: *League (62):* Ross 23 (3 pens), Miller 11 (2 pens), Brand 9, McNeill 4, Heggie 3, O'Brien 3, Scott 3, Lees 2, Lorimer 2, Hutt 1, McKillop 1. *Scottish Cup (1):* Lees 1. *Skol Cup (7):* Brown 2, Miller 2, Hutt 1, Lees 1, Ross 1. *B & Q Cup (1):* Lorimer 1.

Allan R 39	McLaren P 29 + 3	Cairney H 38	Brown R 37	McKillop A 36	Hutt G 23 + 4	Lees G 17 + 9	Scott D 30	Heggie A 11 + 8	Miller M 30 + 1	O'Brien P 20 + 3	Lorimer R 29 + 3	Ross A 36 + 2	Brand R 23 + 8	Thomson N 4 + 8	Baillie R 11 + 6	Fisher D 1	Sexton P — + 1	Conway F 4 + 3	McNeill W 11	Paterson I G — + 2	Match No.
1	2	3	4	5	6	7	8	*9*	10	11	12	14									1
1	2	3	4	5	6	7	8	9	10	*11*	12	14									2
1	*2*	3	4	5			8		10	11	6	9	7	14							3
1	*2*	3	4	5			8	12	10	11	6	9	7	14							4
1	2	3	4	5			8	7	10	11	6	9	14	12							5
1		3	4	5	6	7	8		*10*	11		*2*	9	12	14						6
1	14	3	4	5	6	7		10	12	11		*2*	9		8						7
1	4	3		5	6	7		10	12	11		*2*	9	14	8						8
1	2	3	4	5			8	12	*10*	11	6	9	7	14							9
1	2	3	4	5		12	8		10	11	6	9	7								10
1	2	3	4	5		7	8		10		6	9	12						11		11
1	2	3	4	5		12	8	*11*	10		6	9	7				14				12
1	2	3	4	5	14	12	8	11	10		6	9	7								13
1	2	3	4	5		12	8	11	10		6	9	7	14							14
1	2	3	4	5		12	8	11	10		6	9	*7*	14							15
1	2	3	4	5		14	8	11	10	*9*	6		7								16
1	2	3	4	5		7	8	12	10	11	6	9									17
1	2	3	4	5		7	8		10	11	6	9									18
1	2	3	4	5		7	8	14	10	11	6	9	12								19
1	2	3	4	5			8	12	*10*	11	6	9	7	14							20
1	2	3	4	5		12	8		10	11	6	9	7	14							21
1	2	3	4	5		12	8		*10*	11	6	9	7	14							22
1		3	4	5	2		8	14	10	*11*	6	9	7								23
1		3	4	5	2		8	14	10	*11*	6	9	7								24
1		3	4	5			8	10	*7*	14	6	9	11		2						25
1		3	4	5			8	*11*	10	14	6	9	7		2			12			26
1	14	3	4	5		10	7	8			2	9	11	6							27
1	10	3	4	5	8	7			12	2	9	11	6						14		28
1	2	3	4	5	8	*7*	12		10	9			6						11		29
1	6	3	4	5	8		7		10	9	12	2						14	11		30
1	14	3	4	5	8	12	7		10	9		2						6	11		31
1		3	4	5		7	10	11		9	12	6	2				8	14			32
1		3	4	5		7	10	11		9	12	6	*2*				8	14			33
1	2	3	4	5	6	*8*		10		9	7	12	14				11				34
1	2	3	4	5	6		8	10		9	7						11				35
1	*2*	3	4	5	6	14	8	10		9	7	12					11				36
1	2		4		6	14	8	10		12	9	7	3				5	*11*			37
1	2	3			6	7	8	10		9	12	4					5	11			38
1	2	3	4		6	7	8	10		9							5	11			39

CELTIC Premier Division

Year Formed: 1888. *Ground & Address:* Celtic Park, 95 Kerrydale St, Glasgow G40 3RE. *Telephone:* 041 556 2611.
Ground Capacity: total: 51,709. *Seated:* 9000. *Size of Pitch:* 115yd × 75yd.
Chairman: J. Kevin Kelly. *Secretary:* Chris D. White, CA. *Commercial Manager:* Jim Torbett.
Manager: Liam Brady. *Assistant Manager:* Joe Jordan. *Physio:* Brian Scott. *Coaches:* Frank Connor, Tom McAdam.
Youth Development Officer: Tommy Craig. *Managers since 1975:* Jock Stein; Billy McNeill; David Hay; Billy McNeill.
Club Nickname(s): The Bhoys. *Previous Grounds:* None.
Record Attendance: 92,000 v Rangers, Division I; 1 Jan, 1938.
Record Transfer Fee received: £1,400,000 for Paul Elliott to Chelsea, July 1991.
Record Transfer Fee paid: £1,100,000 for Tony Cascarino from Aston Villa, July 1991.
Record Victory: 11-0 Dundee, Division I; 26 Oct, 1895.
Record Defeat: 0-8 v Motherwell, Division I; 30 Apr, 1937.
Most Capped Player: Danny McGrain, 62, Scotland.
Most League Appearances: 486: Billy McNeill 1957-75.
Most League Goals in Season (Individual): 50: James McGrory, Division I; 1935-36.
Most Goals Overall (Individual): 397: James McGrory; 1922-39.

Honours
League Champions: (35 times) Division I 1892-93, 1893-94, 1895-96, 1897-98, 1904-05, 1905-06, 1906-07, 1907-08, 1908-09,

CELTIC 1992—93 LEAGUE RECORD

Match No.	Date		Venue	Opponents	Result	H/T Score	Lg. Pos.	Goalscorers	Atten dance
1	Aug	1	A	Hearts	W 1-0	0-0	—	Levein (og)	18,510
2		5	A	Aberdeen	D 1-1	1-1	—	Creaney	14,618
3		8	H	Motherwell	D 1-1	0-0	4	Mowbray	24,935
4		15	H	Dundee U	W 2-0	2-0	1	Creaney 2	30,513
5		22	A	Rangers	D 1-1	0-0	2	Creaney	43,239
6		29	A	Airdrieonians	D 1-1	1-0	4	Payton	12,222
7	Sept	2	H	St Johnstone	W 3-1	1-0	—	Collins 2, Creaney	21,831
8		12	H	Hibernian	L 2-3	1-1	4	Wdowczyk, McStay	28,130
9		19	A	Falkirk	W 5-4	1-1	2	Wdowczyk (pen), Creaney 2, Payton, Collins	9678
10		26	H	Partick T	L 1-2	0-1	3	Payton	21,486
11	Oct	3	A	Dundee	W 1-0	0-0	2	Galloway	12,866
12		7	H	Hearts	D 1-1	1-1	—	Miller	26,049
13		17	A	Motherwell	W 3-1	1-1	2	Miller, Galloway (pen), Grant	10,016
14		24	H	Airdrieonians	W 2-0	1-0	2	Collins, McStay	19,549
15		31	A	St Johnstone	D 0-0	0-0	2		9783
16	Nov	7	A	Rangers	L 0-1	0-1	4		51,950
17		11	A	Dundee U	D 1-1	0-1	—	Nicholas	11,831
18		21	H	Falkirk	W 3-2	2-2	3	Mowbray, Creaney, O'Neil	15,978
19	Nov	28	A	Hibernian	W 2-1	2-0	3	O'Neil 2	12,985
20	Dec	2	A	Aberdeen	D 2-2	1-2	—	Slater, Vata	29,122
21		5	A	Partick T	W 3-2	2-1	3	Payton, Grant, Creaney	13,312
22		12	H	Dundee	W 1-0	0-0	3	Payton	16,797
23		19	A	Hearts	L 0-1	0-1	3		13,554
24		26	H	Dundee U	L 0-1	0-1	3		22,852
25	Jan	2	A	Rangers	L 0-1	0-1	3		46,039
26		23	A	Airdrieonians	W 1-0	1-0	3	Coyne	7473
27		30	H	Motherwell	D 1-1	0-0	4	McStay	18,513
28	Feb	3	H	St Johnstone	W 5-1	4-0	—	Coyne 2 (2 pens), McAvennie, Wdowczyk, Collins	12,931
29		13	A	Aberdeen	D 1-1	0-1	3	Payton	14,673
30		20	H	Partick T	D 0-0	0-0	3		15,561
31		23	A	Dundee	W 1-0	0-0	—	Payton	7221
32		27	A	Falkirk	W 3-0	0-0	3	McAvennie, Payton 2	8165
33	Mar	10	H	Hearts	W 1-0	0-0	—	Payton	16,984
34		16	H	Hibernian	W 2-1	0-0	—	Payton 2	12,178
35		20	H	Rangers	W 2-1	1-0	3	Collins, Payton	52,779
36		27	A	Dundee U	W 3-2	1-0	3	McAvennie, Galloway, Collins	12,185
37	Apr	3	A	Motherwell	L 0-2	0-2	3		10,102
38		6	H	Airdrieonians	W 4-0	2-0	—	Slater, Collins, McAvennie, Vata	10,671
39		10	A	St Johnstone	D 1-1	1-1	3	McAvennie	8609
40		17	A	Hibernian	L 1-3	0-3	3	Nicholas	11,132
41		20	H	Falkirk	W 1-0	0-0	—	McAvennie	10,151
42	May	1	H	Aberdeen	W 1-0	1-0	3	McAvennie	20,642
43		8	A	Partick T	W 1-0	1-0	3	McAvennie (pen)	9834
44		15	H	Dundee	W 2-0	0-0	3	McStay, McAvennie	19,436

Final League Position: 3

1909-10, 1913-14, 1914-15, 1915-16, 1916-17, 1918-19, 1921-22, 1925-26, 1935-36, 1937-38, 1953-54, 1965-66, 1966-67, 1967-68, 1968-69, 1969-70, 1970-71, 1971-72, 1972-73, 1973-74. Premier Division 1976-77, 1978-79, 1980-81, 1981-82, 1985-86, 1987-88. *Runners-up:* 21 times.
Scottish Cup Winners: (29 times) 1892, 1899, 1900, 1904, 1907, 1908, 1911, 1912, 1914, 1923, 1925, 1927, 1931, 1933, 1937, 1951, 1954, 1965, 1967, 1969, 1971, 1972, 1974, 1975, 1977, 1980, 1985, 1988, 1989; *Runners-up:* 16 times.
League Cup Winners: (9 times) 1956-57, 1957-58, 1965-66, 1966-67, 1967-68, 1968-69, 1969-70, 1974-75, 1982-83; *Runners-up:* 9 times.
European: *European Cup Winners:* 1966-67. 78 matches (1966-67 winners, 1967-68, 1968-69, 1969-70 runners-up, 1970-71, 1971-72 semi-finals, 1972-73, 1973-74 semi-finals, 1974-75, 1977-78, 1979-80, 1981-82, 1982-83, 1986-87, 1988-89); *Cup Winners Cup:* 35 matches (1963-64 semi-finals, 1965-66 semi-finals, 1975-76, 1980-81, 1984-85, 1985-86, 1989-90); *UEFA Cup:* 24 matches (*Fairs Cup:* 1962-63, 1964-65. *UEFA Cup:* 1976-77, 1983-84, 1987-88, 1991-92, 1992-93).
Club colours: Shirt: Green and white hoops. Shorts: White. Stockings: White.

Goalscorers: *League (68):* Payton 13, Creaney 9, McAvennie 9 (1 pen), Collins 8, McStay 4, Coyne 3 (2 pens), Galloway 3 (1 pen), O'Neil 3, Wdowczyk 3 (1 pen), Grant 2, Miller 2, Mowbray 2, Nicholas 2, Slater 2, Vata 2, own goal 1. *Scottish Cup (1):* Coyne 1. *Skol Cup (6):* Creaney 3, Payton 2, Coyne 1.

Marshall G 11	Morris C 3	Boyd T 42	Wdowczyk D 24 + 1	Mowbray A 26	Gillespie G 18	O'Neil B 11 + 6	McStay P 43	Creaney G 23 + 3	Nicholas C 12 + 4	Collins J 43	Coyne T 5 + 5	Miller J 10 + 13	Whyte D — + 1	Galloway M 29 + 1	Payton A 19 + 10	Grant P 27 + 4	McNally M 25 + 2	Slater S 37 + 2	Fulton S 3 + 3	Bonner P 33	Vata R 15 + 7	McCarrison D — + 1	McAvennie F 19	Smith B 4 + 2	McQuilken J 1	Gray S 1	Match No.
1	2	3	4	5	6	7	8	9	10	11	12	14															1
1	2	3	4	5	*6*	7	8	9	10	11	12		14														2
1	2	3	4	5	6	*7*	8	9	10	11	12	14															3
1	2	3		5	6	14	8		10	11	12	7		4	9												4
1	2			5		14	8	9		11		7		3	10	4	6	12									5
1	2	3		5			8		10	11		7		6	9	4		12									6
1	2	3		5		4	8		10	11				6	9	14	7	12									7
1	2	3		5		4	8		10	11	12			6	9		7										8
	2	3		5	6		8		10	11				9	4	14	7			1							9
		3		5	6		8		10	11	12			14	*9*	*4*	2	7		1							10
		3		5			8		10	11				6	12	4	2	9	14	1	7						11
		3		5			8		10	11		7		6	12	4	2	9		1							12
		3		5		14	8		10	11		7		*6*	12	4	2	9		1							13
		3		5			8		12	11		7		6	*10*	4	2	9		1	14						14
		3		5	6		8		10	11		7		2	12	4		9		1							15
	7	3		5	6	14	8	10	12	11				2	4	9				1							16
	7	3		5	6	14	8	10	12	11				2	4	9				1							17
	2	3		5	6	4	8	9	10	11				12		7				1	14						18
		3	6	5		4	8	9	10	11				12		7				1	14						19
		3	6	5		7	8		10	11				12	4	2	9			1	14						20
		3		5			8	12	10	11				9	4	2	7			1	6						21
	2				6		8		10	3				9	4	5	11	14		1	7	12					22
		3		5	6		8	12		11		14		9	4	2	10			1	7						23
		3		5			8		10	6	7			4	9	12	2	11		1	14						24
		3		5		14	8		10	6	7			4	*9*	12	2	11		1							25
		3		5			8	12	11	10				6		2	7			1	*4*		9				26
		3		5			8		11	10				6	12	2	7			1	4		9				27
		3		5			8	12	11	10				6	14	2	7			1	4		9				28
	2	3				4	8		11	10				6	12		5	7		1	14		9				29
	2	3				4	8		11	10				6	12		5	7		1			9				30
	2	3					8			11	12			6	10		5	7		1	4		9				31
	2	3					8			11				6	10	4	5	7		1			9				32
	2	3					8			11	12			6	10	4	5	7		1			9				33
	2	3					8			11				6	10	4	5	7		1			9				34
	2	3					8			11				6	10	4	5	7		1			9				35
	2	3					8		10	11				6		4	5	7		1	12		9				36
	2	3			6		8		10	11						4	5	7		1			9				37
	6	3					8		10	11	12					4	5	7		1	2		9	14			38
		3		5	6		8		10	11	12					4		7		1	2		9				39
		3		5	6		8		10	11	12					4		7		1	2		9	14			40
							8		10	11				6		4	7	5		1			9	2	3		41
1		3					8				12			6	10	4	7	5					9	2		11	42
1		3		14			8			11		7		6	10	4	5						9	2			43
1		3		5			8		10	11	12			6	14		7	4					9	2			44

CLYDE

First Division

Year Formed: 1878. *Ground & Address:* Douglas Park, Douglas Park Lane, Hamilton M13 0DF. *Telephone:* (Mon-Fri: 041 221 7669), (Match Days Only): 0698 286103.
Ground Capacity: total: 6500, seated: 1595. *Size of Pitch:* 110yd × 70yd.
Chairman: John F. McBeth FRICS. *Secretary:* John D. Taylor. *Commercial Manager:* John Donnelly.
Manager: Alex Smith. *Assistant Manager:* John Brownlie. *Physio:* J. Watson: *Coach:* Bill Munro.
Managers since 1975: S. Anderson; C. Brown; J. Clark. *Club Nickname(s):* The Bully Wee. *Previous Grounds:* Barrowfield & Shawfield Stadium.
Record Attendance: 52,000 v Rangers, Division I; 21 Nov, 1908.
Record Transfer Fee received: £95,000 for Pat Nevin to Chelsea (July 1983).
Record Transfer Fee paid: £14,000 for Harry Hood from Sunderland (1966).
Record Victory: 11-1 v Cowdenbeath, Division II; 6 Oct, 1951.
Record Defeat: 0-11 v Dumbarton, Scottish Cup 4th rd, 22 Nov, 1879; v Rangers, Scottish Cup 4th rd, 13 Nov, 1880.
Most Capped Player: Tommy Ring, 12, Scotland.
Most League Appearances: 428: Brian Ahern.

CLYDE 1992—93 LEAGUE RECORD

Match No.	Date		Venue	Opponents	Result	H/T Score	Lg. Pos.	Goalscorers	Attendance
1	Aug	8	H	Albion Rovers	W 2-0	1-0	—	Ronald, Clarke	555
2		15	A	East Stirling	W 2-1	1-1	1	McGarvey 2	475
3		22	H	East Fife	D 2-2	0-1	3	Thompson D, Morrison	608
4		29	A	Alloa	W 5-1	2-0	3	McGarvey, Tennant, Thomson J, Clarke, McCarron	812
5	Sept	5	H	Arbroath	W 2-0	1-0	1	Thomson J, Morrison	599
6		12	A	Queen's Park	W 6-1	3-0	1	Clarke, Tennant, McGarvey, Thompson D, Ronald, Morrison	951
7		19	H	Forfar Ath	D 0-0	0-0	1		829
8		26	H	Stenhousemuir	D 0-0	0-0	1		554
9	Oct	3	A	Queen of the S	L 1-3	0-1	2	Thomson J	763
10		10	H	Montrose	L 1-2	0-2	4	Quinn	631
11		17	A	Stranraer	D 1-1	1-1	4	Clarke	794
12		24	A	Brechin C	L 1-2	0-1	4	Strain	664
13		31	H	Berwick R	W 2-0	1-0	3	Clarke, Thompson D	505
14	Nov	7	H	Alloa	D 1-1	1-1	4	McGarvey	626
15		14	A	Arbroath	D 1-1	0-0	4	McAulay	935
16		21	H	Forfar Ath	W 4-2	4-1	3	Clarke, Thompson D, Strain, McGarvey	635
17		28	H	Queen's Park	W 4-1	2-0	3	Thompson D 2 (1 pen), McGarvey 2	676
18	Dec	12	A	Albion R	W 2-1	1-1	3	McGarvey, McCarron	470
19	Jan	2	H	East Stirling	W 5-1	3-1	3	Quinn, McAulay, McGarvey, Strain, Knox	726
20		16	A	Berwick R	W 3-0	1-0	3	McCarron, Strain, Quinn	378
21		26	A	East Fife	D 1-1	1-0	—	Strain	816
22		30	A	Stenhousemuir	W 2-0	1-0	2	Quinn, Dickson	706
23	Feb	6	A	Stranraer	D 0-0	0-0	2		827
24		13	A	Montrose	W 2-1	1-0	2	Tennant (pen), Thompson D	653
25		16	H	Queen of the S	W 2-1	2-0	—	Clarke, Knox	621
26		20	H	Queen's Park	L 2-3	2-0	2	Thompson D, Tennant (pen)	678
27		23	H	Brechin C	L 0-1	0-0	—		735
28		27	A	East Fife	W 3-2	1-0	2	McGarvey 2, McAulay	716
29	Mar	6	A	Berwick R	W 1-0	0-0	2	McGarvey	482
30		9	H	Arbroath	W 2-0	0-0	—	McGill, Strain	558
31		20	A	Stranraer	D 1-1	0-0	1	Wylde	1040
32		27	H	East Stirling	W 2-1	0-0	1	Mitchell, Knox	620
33	Apr	3	A	Stenhousemuir	L 0-3	0-1	1		584
34		10	H	Montrose	W 2-1	2-1	1	Clarke 2	596
35		17	H	Albion R	W 4-0	0-0	1	McGarvey, Morrison, McCarron, Dickson	595
36		24	A	Alloa	D 1-1	0-1	1	McCarron	849
37	May	1	H	Forfar Ath	W 3-2	2-1	1	McCarron, Morrison, McGarvey	1021
38		8	A	Queen of the S	W 3-2	2-1	1	Morrison, Clarke, McGarvey	1130
39		15	H	Brechin C	L 1-2	1-1	1	Morrison (pen)	1435

Final League Position: 1

Most League Goals in Season (Individual): 32: Bill Boyd, 1932-33.
Most Goals Overall (Individual): —.

Honours
League Champions: Division II 1904-05, 1951-52, 1956-57, 1961-62, 1972-73. Second Division 1977-78, 1981-82, 1992-93.
Runners-up: Division II 1903-04, 1905-06, 1925-26, 1963-64.
Scottish Cup Winners: 1939, 1955, 1958; Runners-up: 1910, 1912, 1949.
League Cup: —
Club colours: Shirt: White with red and black trim. Shorts: Black. Stockings: Black with red and white tops.

Goalscorers: League (77): McGarvey 16, Clarke 10, Thompson D 8 (1 pen), Morrison 7 (1 pen), McCarron 6, Strain 6, Quinn 4, Tennant 4 (2 pens), Knox 3, McAulay 3, Thomson J 3, Dickson 2, Ronald 2, McGill 1, Mitchell 1, Wylde 1. Scottish Cup (4): McCarron 2, Dickson 1, Thomson J 1. Skol Cup (5): Clarke 2, Thompson D 2, Speirs 1. B & Q Cup (1): McCheyne 1.

Howie S 39	McFarlane R 31	Tennant S 35	Wylde G 17 + 1	Knox K 37	Thomson J 36	Thompson D 19 + 4	McCheyne G 19 + 2	McGarvey F 33 + 1	Clarke S 26 + 3	Ronald P 15	Quinn K 6 + 9	Speirs C 1 + 2	Morrison S 15 + 9	Dickson J 13 + 14	McCarron J 24 + 8	Mitchell J 9 + 7	Mallan S 1 + 1	Strain B 24 + 1	McAulay J 20 + 8	Watson E 1 + 5	McGill D 7 + 2	Neill A 1	Match No.
1	2	3	4	5	6	7	8	9	10	11	12	14											1
1	2	3	4	5	6	7	8	9	10	11			12	14									2
1	2	3	4	5	6	7	8	9	10	11			12	14									3
1	2	3	4	5	6	7	8	9	10	11			12		14								4
1	2	3	4	5	6	7	8	9	10	11			12	14									5
1	2	3	4	5	6	7	8	9	10	11			12	14									6
1	2	3	4	5	6	7	8	9		11			10	12									7
1	2	3	4		6	7	8	9		11			5	10	14	12							8
1	2	3	14		6	7	5		10	11			4	9	12	8							9
1	2			5	6	7	8	9	10		12		11	14		3	4						10
1				6	5		3	9	10	7	11		4	12	8	2	14						11
1	2			5	6		3	9	10	7	11		4	14	8	12							12
1	2	3		5	6	7		9	10				12	14	11	8	4						13
1	2	3		5	6	7	12	9	10				14		11	8	4						14
1	2	3		5	6	7	8	9	10				14	11		4	12						15
1	2	3		5		7	8	9	10				14	6	12	11	4						16
1	2	3		5		7	8	9			12		10	6	11	4	14						17
1	2	3		5	6	7	8	9					14	10	12	11	4						18
1	2	3		5	6		8	9			12		7	10	14			11	4				19
1	2	3		5	6	12		9					14	8	7	10		11	4				20
1	2	3		5	6			9					8	7	10	12		11	4	14			21
1	2	3		5	6			9					8	7	10	14		11	4	12			22
1		3	2	5	6		12	9					8	7	10			11	4	14			23
1		3	2	5	6	12	8	9	10				14	7				11	4				24
1	2	3		5	6	9		12	10				14	7				11	4	8			25
1	2	3	8	5		6	10	9					14	7				11	4	12			26
1	2	3		5	6	14		9	10	7				8	12			11	4				27
1	2	3		5	6		8	9	4				14	10	11		12		7				28
1	2	3		5	6			9	10				12	4	8		14	11	7				29
1	2	3		5	6			9					14	12	4	8		11	10		7		30
1	2		3	5	6	14		9	12				10	8				11	4		7		31
1		3	2	5	6	14		9	12				10	8				11	4		7		32
1		3	2	5		7		9	10				14	12	8			11	4		6		33
1		3	2	5	6		8	9	10				12	11	14			4	7				34
1		3	4	5	6		8	9	10				2	12	7	14		11					35
1		3	4	5	6	7		9	10				2	12	8			11		14			36
1	4	3		5	6		8	9	10				2	7	11				12	14			37
1	2	3		5	6			9	10				4	7	8			11	12	14			38
1	2	3		5	6		8	10		12			4	7	11					14	9		39

CLYDEBANK

First Division

Year Formed: 1965. *Ground & Address:* Kilbowie Park, Arran Place, Clydebank G81 2PB. *Telephone:* 041 952 2887.
Ground Capacity: total: 9950. seated: All. *Size of Pitch:* 110yd × 68yd.
Chairman: C. A. Steedman. *Secretary:* I. C. Steedman. *Commercial Manager:* David Curwood.
Manager: J. S. Steedman. *Managing Director:* J. S. Steedman. *Physio:* John Jolly. *Coach:* Brian Wright.
Managers since 1975: William Munro; J. S. Steedman. *Club Nickname(s):* The Bankies. *Previous Grounds:* None.
Record Attendance: 14,900 v Hibernian, Scottish Cup 1st rd; 10 Feb, 1965.
Record Transfer Fee received: £175,000 for Owen Coyle from Airdrieonians, (Feb 1990).
Record Transfer Fee paid: £50,000 for Gerry McCabe from Clyde.
Record Victory: 8-1 Arbroath, First Division; 3 Jan 1977.
Record Defeat: 1-9 v Gala Fairydean, Scottish Cup qual rd; 15 Sept, 1965.
Most Capped Player: —.
Most League Appearances: 620: Jim Fallon; 1968-86.

CLYDEBANK 1992—93 LEAGUE RECORD

Match No.	Date	Venue	Opponents	Result	H/T Score	Lg. Pos.	Goalscorers	Atten dance
1	Aug 1	A	Cowdenbeath	D 3-3	0-1	—	Henderson, McIntosh, Flannigan C	538
2	4	A	Morton	L 1-5	1-2	—	Bryce	1154
3	8	H	Ayr U	D 1-1	1-1	9	Eadie	757
4	15	A	St Mirren	D 0-0	0-0	9		2296
5	22	H	Dumbarton	L 0-1	0-1	11		990
6	29	A	Dunfermline Ath	W 3-1	0-1	10	Eadie 2, Flannigan C	3237
7	Sept 5	H	Kilmarnock	D 1-1	0-1	8	Crawford	2119
8	12	A	Meadowbank T	L 0-1	0-1	8		300
9	19	H	Stirling Albion	W 4-1	1-0	7	Eadie 2 (1 pen), Flannigan C, Henry	704
10	26	H	Hamilton A	W 3-1	1-0	6	Henry, Flannigan C, McIntosh	876
11	Oct 3	A	Raith R	D 2-2	0-0	6	Eadie, Flannigan C	2424
12	10	H	Cowdenbeath	W 4-1	3-1	5	Flannigan C, Henry, Sweeney, Eadie	772
13	17	A	Ayr U	L 1-2	0-1	7	Flannigan C	1785
14	24	A	Kilmarnock	D 3-3	0-1	7	Harvey, Flannigan C, Eadie	3582
15	31	H	Dunfermline Ath	W 1-0	0-0	6	Harvey	1041
16	Nov 7	H	St Mirren	L 1-2	1-0	7	Henry	2133
17	14	A	Dumbarton	L 1-3	0-1	8	Wilson	1382
18	21	A	Stirling Albion	W 1-0	0-0	7	Henry	396
19	28	H	Meadowbank T	D 0-0	0-0	7		965
20	Dec 1	H	Raith R	W 3-0	1-0	—	Henry 2, McIntosh	1257
21	8	A	Hamilton A	L 0-2	0-1	—		1161
22	12	A	Cowdenbeath	W 3-1	1-1	7	Flannigan C, Eadie, Harvey	297
23	19	H	Morton	D 2-2	0-2	7	Wilson, Henry	901
24	26	A	St Mirren	L 2-3	0-0	7	Flannigan C, Eadie (pen)	2503
25	Jan 2	A	Dumbarton	W 3-1	0-0	7	Henry 2, Flannigan C	1368
26	26	A	Raith R	L 2-4	1-2	—	Flannigan C, Wilson	2016
27	30	H	Ayr U	D 1-1	1-1	7	Eadie	946
28	Feb 2	A	Dunfermline Ath	L 0-2	0-1	—		2165
29	13	A	Morton	L 0-2	0-0	8		1245
30	16	H	Kilmarnock	W 2-0	0-0	—	Harvey, Flannigan C	2049
31	20	H	Hamilton A	L 0-1	0-0	7		766
32	27	H	Stirling Albion	D 1-1	0-0	7	Eadie	636
33	Mar 9	H	Cowdenbeath	W 5-0	4-0	—	McIntosh, Sweeney, Henry, Eadie (pen), Harvey	447
34	13	A	Ayr U	D 0-0	0-0	8		1713
35	20	A	Dumbarton	W 2-0	0-0	8	Flannigan C, Hay	1035
36	27	H	St Mirren	L 0-3	0-1	8		1460
37	31	A	Meadowbank T	W 1-0	1-0	—	Eadie	249
38	Apr 3	A	Kilmarnock	L 0-6	0-4	8		3005
39	10	H	Dunfermline Ath	D 1-1	0-1	8	Flannigan C	1055
40	17	H	Meadowbank T	W 3-1	1-1	8	Flannigan C 3	474
41	24	A	Stirling Albion	W 3-2	0-1	8	Henry, Eadie 2	2301
42	May 1	H	Morton	D 2-2	1-2	8	Eadie 2 (1 pen)	726
43	8	A	Hamilton A	L 1-2	0-1	8	Eadie	1048
44	15	H	Raith R	W 4-1	1-0	8	Flannigan C 3, Eadie	1046

Final League Position: 8

Most League Goals in Season (Individual): 29: Ken Eadie, First Division, 1990-91.
Most Goals Overall (Individual): 84, Blair Millar, 1977-83.

Honours
League Champions: Second Division 1975-76; *Runners-up:* First Division 1976-77, 1984-85.
Scottish Cup: Semi-finalists 1990. *League Cup:* —.
Club colours: Shirt: White with black collar and red and black shoulder flashings. Shorts: White with red and black trim.
Stockings: White with red/black stripes.

Goalscorers: *League (71):* Flannigan C 21, Eadie 20 (4 pens), Henry 12, Harvey 5, McIntosh 4, Wilson 3, Sweeney 2, Bryce 1, Crawford 1, Hay 1, Henderson 1. *Scottish Cup (8):* Eadie 4, Flannigan C 1, Henry 1, McIntosh 1, Maher 1. *Skol Cup (0).* *B & Q Cup (1):* Flannigan C 1.

Spence W 2	Murray M 6	Crawford J 15 + 13	Smith B 2	Sweeney S 36	McIntosh M 32 + 1	Henry J 32	Jack S 42 + 1	Flannigan C 37 + 1	Bryce T 16 + 8	Henderson D 2 + 3	Maher J 33 + 1	Lansdowne A 14 + 14	Harvey P 37 + 2	Flannigan M 1 + 2	Woods S 42	Eadie K 36	Wilson K 14 + 7	Goldie P 3 + 3	Hay G 30	Barron D 23 + 4	Currie T 5	Smith L 5 + 5	Murdoch S 16	Brown T 1	Sludden J 1	Bowman G 1	Match No.
1	2	3	4	5	6	7	8	9	10	11	12	14															1
1	2	3	4	5	6		10	9	8	11	7	12	14														2
	2			5	3	7	6	10		14	4		8		1	9	11										3
4	12			5	3		6	10	7	14		8			1	9	11	2									4
4				5	3	10	8		12	14		7			1	9	11	2	6								5
4	12			5	3	8	11	14	10		2				1	9	7		6								6
	14			5	6	8	11	10		2	12				1	9	7		3	4							7
	6			5	8	11	10	12	2	14	7				1	9			3	4							8
	12			5	6	8	10	11	14	2					1	9	7		3	4							9
				5	6	8	11	10		2	7				1	9			3	4							10
	12			5	6	8	11	10		2	7				1	9	14		3	4							11
	12			5	6	8	11	10		2	7				1	9	14		3	4							12
	12			5	6	8	11	10		2	7				1	9			3	4							13
	3			5	6	8	11	10	2	14	7				1	9				4							14
	3			5	6	8	11	10		2	7	14			1	9				4							15
	3			5	6	8	11		14	2	7	10			1	9				4							16
	3			5	6	8	11	10		2	12	7			1	9	14			4							17
	12			5	3	8	11	10		2	14	7			1	9	6			4							18
				5	3	8	11	10		2	14	6			1	9	7			4							19
				5	6	8	11	10		2	7				1	9			3	4							20
				5	6	8	11	10	14	2	12	7			1	9			3	4							21
	12			5	6	8	11	10		2	7				1	9	14		3	4							22
	3			5		8	11	10		2	12	7			1	9	14		6	4							23
	3					8	11	10		2	7				1	9	14		6	4	5						24
	12			5		8	11	10		2	14				1	9	7		3	4		6					25
				5		8	6	10		7					1	9	11		3	4	2						26
	12			5	6	8	2	10		14	7				1	9	11		3	4							27
				5	3	11	10		2	8	7				1	9	14		6								28
	3			5		11	10	9	2	8	7				1		6	14					12	4			29
	3		5	12		10	11	2	8	7					1	6			14	4	9						30
	3			5		11	10	9	2	8	7				1		6	12					14	4			31
	3			5		11	10	14	2	7	8				1	9	6					12	4				32
	12			5	3	8	6	10		14	7				1	9	11		2			4					33
	6					14	10	9	2	7					1		11	5	3	4		8					34
				5		6	10	9	2	8	7				1		11	14	3	12		4					35
				5		11	9	10	2	8	7				1			12	3	14	6	4					36
				5	3	11	10	8	14	7					1	9				2	6	4					37
				5		6	10	12	2	8	7				1	9		3				4	11				38
				5		8	6	10	11	2	14	7			1	9	12				3		4				39
				5		8	11	10		2	12	7			1	9		3		6	4						40
				5		8	6	10		11	7				1	9		3		2	12	4					41
				5		8	11	10	14	2	6	7			1	9		3				4					42
	12			5	6	8	2	10		11	7				1	9		3				4					43
	3					6	8	2	10		11	7			1	9					5	4					44

COWDENBEATH Second Division

Year Formed: 1881. *Ground & Address:* Central Park, Cowdenbeath KY4 9EY. *Telephone:* 0383 511205.
Ground Capacity: total: 4778. seated: 1072. *Size of Pitch:* 110yd × 70yd.
Chairman: Gordon McDougall. *Secretary:* Tom Ogilvie. *Commercial Director:* Ian Fraser.
Manager: Andrew Harrow. *Assistant Manager/Player:* Colin Harris. *Physio:* Ian Cardle. *Coach:* —.
Managers since 1975: D. McLindon; F. Connor; P. Wilson; A. Rolland; H. Wilson; W. McCulloch; J. Clark; J. Craig; R. Campbell; J. Blackley; J. Brownlie. *Club Nickname(s):* Cowden. *Previous Grounds:* North End Park, Cowdenbeath.
Record Attendance: 25,586 v Rangers, League Cup quarter-final; 21 Sept, 1949.
Record Transfer Fee received: £12,000 for Roddy Grant from St Johnstone, (Oct 1988).
Record Transfer Fee paid: —
Record Victory: 12-0 v Johnstone, Scottish Cup 1st rd; 21 Jan, 1928.
Record Defeat: 1-11 v Clyde, Division II; 6 Oct, 1951.
Most Capped Player: Jim Paterson, 3, Scotland.
Most League Appearances: —.

COWDENBEATH 1992—93 LEAGUE RECORD

Match No.	Date		Venue	Opponents	Result		H/T Score	Lg. Pos.	Goalscorers	Atten dance
1	Aug	1	H	Clydebank	D	3-3	1-0	—	Robertson 3	538
2		5	H	Dunfermline Ath	L	2-5	1-3	—	Wright, Malone	2223
3		8	A	Stirling Albion	L	1-2	1-0	12	Condie	393
4		15	A	Hamilton A	L	0-3	0-1	12		1064
5		22	H	Meadowbank T	L	1-5	1-1	12	Syme	329
6		29	A	Morton	L	0-1	0-0	12		1446
7	Sept	5	H	Dumbarton	L	0-1	0-1	12		418
8		12	A	Ayr U	W	1-0	0-0	12	Condie	1487
9		19	H	Raith R	L	0-3	0-1	12		1974
10		26	A	Kilmarnock	L	0-3	0-1	12		2798
11	Oct	3	H	St Mirren	L	1-2	1-1	12	Wright	1022
12		10	A	Clydebank	L	1-4	1-3	12	Callaghan	772
13		17	H	Stirling Albion	D	1-1	0-0	12	Callaghan	359
14		24	A	Dumbarton	L	0-1	0-0	12		716
15		31	H	Morton	L	1-3	0-1	12	Malone	610
16	Nov	7	H	Hamilton A	L	0-3	0-2	12		444
17		14	A	Meadowbank T	L	0-2	0-1	12		273
18		21	A	Raith R	L	0-3	0-1	12		2002
19	Dec	2	A	St Mirren	L	0-5	0-1	—		1648
20		5	H	Kilmarnock	L	2-3	2-1	12	Callaghan 2	1176
21		8	H	Ayr U	D	2-2	1-2	—	Callaghan, Buckley	284
22		12	H	Clydebank	L	1-3	1-1	12	Callaghan	297
23		19	A	Dunfermline Ath	L	1-4	1-1	12	Douglas	2844
24		26	A	Hamilton A	L	0-4	0-2	12		1313
25	Jan	20	H	Meadowbank T	D	2-2	2-1	—	Henderson (pen), Condie	160
26		27	H	St Mirren	L	0-3	0-2	—		535
27	Feb	2	A	Morton	L	2-3	2-1	—	Robertson, Wright	814
28		13	H	Dunfermline Ath	L	1-2	0-1	12	Henderson	2165
29		16	A	Stirling Albion	L	1-2	0-1	—	Watt	283
30		20	A	Kilmarnock	D	1-1	0-0	12	Henderson	2928
31		23	H	Dumbarton	L	0-2	0-1	—		222
32		27	H	Raith R	L	0-2	0-1	12		1978
33	Mar	6	A	Ayr U	L	1-3	0-1	12	Robertson	1270
34		9	A	Clydebank	L	0-5	0-4	—		447
35		13	H	Stirling Albion	D	1-1	0-1	12	Herd	310
36		20	A	Meadowbank T	L	1-3	0-0	12	Henderson (pen)	179
37		27	H	Hamilton A	L	0-4	0-0	12		239
38	Apr	3	A	Dumbarton	D	0-0	0-0	12		552
39		10	H	Morton	L	0-1	0-0	12		244
40		17	H	Ayr U	L	0-1	0-0	12		213
41		24	A	Raith R	L	1-4	1-3	12	Robertson	2752
42	May	1	A	Dunfermline Ath	W	2-0	0-0	12	Callaghan 2	3105
43		8	H	Kilmarnock	L	0-3	0-1	12		2754
44		15	A	St Mirren	W	2-1	0-0	12	Callaghan, Henderson (pen)	1905

Final League Position: 12

Most League Goals in Season (Individual): 40: Willie Devlin, Division II; 1925-26.
Most Goals Overall (Individual): —.

Honours
League Champions: Division II 1913-14, 1914-15, 1938-39; *Runners-up:* Division II 1921-22, 1923-24, 1969-70. Second Division 1991-92.
Scottish Cup: —.
League Cup: —.
Club colours: Shirt: Royal blue shadow vertical stripe with white chest band. Shorts: White with blue side stripe. Stockings: Royal blue.

Goalscorers: *League (33):* Callaghan 9, Robertson 6, Henderson 5 (3 pens), Condie 3, Wright 3, Malone 2, Buckley 1, Douglas 1, Herd 1, Syme 1, Watt 1. *Scottish Cup (1):* Henderson 1 (pen). *Skol Cup (0). B & Q Cup (4):* Buckley 1, Callaghan 1, Lee 1, Malone 1.

Lamont W 23	Watt D 32+2	Robertson A 30	McGovern D 27	Archibald E 33	Irvine N 7	Wright J 28+9	Malone G 16	Condie T 25+5	Buckley G 12+7	Johnston P 3+1	Syme W 5+2	Scott C 14+5	Herd W 33+2	Lamont P 2+3	Combe A 20	Petrie E 32+1	Ferguson S 2+1	Bennett W 1	Lee I 18+1	Douglas H 28+3	Dixon A 3+14	Callaghan W 29+2	Henderson N 30	O'Hanlon S 1	Archibald A 6+1	Maratea D 4+6	Kelso M —+1	McMahon B 12	Stout D 2+1	Bowmaker K 1+1	Harris C 5	Match No.
1	2	3	4	5	6	7	8	9	10	11	12	14																				1
1	2	3	4	5	6	7	8	9	10	11			12	14																		2
			4	5	6	7	8	9	12	11				3	10	1	2		14													3
			4	5	6	7	8	9	10			14	12	3		1	2		11													4
			4		6	7	8	9	14			10	12	3		1	2		11	5												5
1			4	5	6	7	8	9	12			11	14	3			2		10													6
1	2		4	5	6		8	9	7			11	12			10			3	14												7
1	2	3	4	5		7	8	9	12			11		14		10			6													8
1	2	3		5		7	8	9				11		4			14		10	6		12										9
1	2	3		5		7	8	9	14			4							10	6		11										10
1	2	3		5		7	8	9						4	12				10			11	6									11
1	2	3		5		7		9				8		4	12				10	14		11	6									12
	2	3		5		7	8	14						4	9				10	12		11	6	1								13
		3	4	5			8	9				6				1	2		10			11	7		14							14
		3	4	5		14	8	9	11			6				1	2		10				7									15
12		3	4	5		7		9	11			6				1	2		10			14	8									16
		3	4	5		7		9	11			6				1	2		10	14		8										17
14		3	4	5		7	8	9	12			10				1	2			6						11						18
		3	4	5		14	8	9	12			10				1	2			6						11	7					19
8			4	5		14						11				1	2			6		9	7			10	3					20
8	6	4				12						11				3		1	2	5	14	9	7			10						21
8			4	5								11				3		1	2	6	14	9	7			10						22
8			4									11				3		1	2	12	5	14	9	7		10	6					23
1	2		4			12						14	11		3				8	5		9	7			10	6					24
	2	3	4	5		12			11						10	1	8			6		9	7									25
	2	3	4	5		12			11			14	10		1	8			6		9	7										26
1	2	3	4	5		11						10				8			6	14	9	7										27
1	2	3	4			11		14				10	8		5				6		9	7				12						28
1	2	3	4			11		10				8							6		9	7		5	12							29
1	2	3	4			11		9				10	8						6	12		7		14	5							30
1	2		4	5		11						10	8	3							7	9			12	6						31
1	2			5		12		11				10							8	6	14	9	7		3	4						32
1	2	3	4	5		11		14				10							6	12	9	7			8							33
1	2	3		5		11						10	8		6				12	9	7			4	14							34
	2	3		5		14						10	6	1	8				11	9	7			4								35
1	2	3		5		11						10	8		6				9	12				4	7							36
		3		5	12			8				1	2	6	14	9	11			4	7	10										37
		3		5	7			8				1	2	10	6	9			4							11						38
	2	3		5	7			1	8	10	6	14	9	12			4				11											39
1	2	3		5	7		8	10	6	9	11	4																				40
1	2	3		7		10	5	8	6	11	9	12	4	14																		41
1	2		7	10	3	5	4	6	9	8	14	11																				42
1	2		7	10	3	5	4	6	12	9	8	11																				43
	2		7	10	3	1	5	4	6	12	9	8	14	11																		44

DUMBARTON

First Division

Year Formed: 1872. *Ground & Address:* Boghead Park, Miller St, Dumbarton G82 2JA. *Telephone:* 0389 62569/67864.
Ground Capacity: total: 10,700. seated: 303. *Size of Pitch:* 110yd × 68yd.
Chairman: A. Hagen. *Secretary:* Alistair Paton.
Manager: Murdo MacLeod. *Assistant Manager:* Billy Simpson. *Physio:* Bobby McCallum. *Coaches:* —.
Managers since 1975: A. Wright; D. Wilson; S. Fallon; W. Lamont; D. Wilson; D. Whiteford; A. Totten; M. Clougherty;
R. Auld; J. George; W. Lamont. *Club Nickname(s):* The Sons. *Previous Grounds:* Broadmeadow, Ropework Lane.
Record Attendance: 18,000 v Raith Rovers, Scottish Cup; 2 Mar, 1957.
Record Transfer Fee received: £125,000 for Graeme Sharp to Everton (March 1982).
Record Transfer Fee paid: £50,000 for Charlie Gibson from Stirling Albion (1989).
Record Victory: 13-1 v Kirkintilloch Cl. 1st Rd; 1 Sept, 1888.
Record Defeat: 1-11 v Albion Rovers, Division II; 30 Jan, 1926: v Ayr United, League Cup; 13 Aug, 1952.

DUMBARTON 1992—93 LEAGUE RECORD

Match No.	Date		Venue	Opponents	Result	H/T Score	Lg. Pos.	Goalscorers	Atten dance
1	Aug	1	H	Stirling Albion	W 4-3	2-1	—	Nelson, Gilmour, McQuade 2	903
2		4	H	Kilmarnock	L 1-3	0-2	—	McQuade	2109
3		8	A	St Mirren	L 0-4	0-1	10		2363
4	Aug 15		H	Morton	L 0-1	0-0	11		1257
5		22	A	Clydebank	W 1-0	1-0	10	McQuade	990
6		29	H	Raith R	L 1-2	0-0	11	Gibson	1105
7	Sept	5	A	Cowdenbeath	W 1-0	1-0	9	Gibson	418
8		12	A	Hamilton A	L 2-3	1-2	9	Boyd, Gibson	1283
9		19	H	Ayr U	L 0-3	0-2	10		882
10		26	A	Dunfermline Ath	L 2-3	1-3	11	Docherty, Mooney	2832
11	Oct	3	H	Meadowbank T	W 3-2	1-1	10	McQuade, McAnenay, Foster	550
12		10	A	Stirling Albion	W 2-1	0-0	9	Mooney (pen), Gibson	475
13		17	H	St Mirren	W 4-2	3-1	9	Gibson, McAnenay 2, McQuade	2022
14		24	H	Cowdenbeath	W 1-0	0-0	8	McQuade	716
15		31	A	Raith R	L 1-4	1-3	9	Martin	1990
16	Nov	7	A	Morton	W 2-1	2-0	8	McQuade, Mooney	1867
17		14	H	Clydebank	W 3-1	1-0	7	Mooney, Martin, McQuade	1382
18		21	A	Ayr U	L 3-5	1-2	8	Gibson, Mooney 2	1317
19		28	A	Hamilton A	D 2-2	1-1	8	Mooney, McQuade	843
20	Dec	1	H	Meadowbank T	L 0-1	0-1	—		624
21		5	H	Dunfermline Ath	L 0-1	0-0	9		1154
22		12	H	Stirling Albion	L 0-3	0-1	9		716
23		19	A	Kilmarnock	L 0-1	0-0	9		3591
24		26	H	Morton	W 3-1	0-0	9	Meechan, McQuade, Boyd	1456
25	Jan	2	A	Clydebank	L 1-3	0-0	9	Boyd	1368
26		27	A	Meadowbank T	D 3-3	1-1	—	Boag, Mooney, Gow	244
27		30	A	St Mirren	L 1-2	0-0	9	Gibson	2453
28	Feb	6	H	Raith R	L 1-2	1-1	10	Mooney	1201
29		13	H	Kilmarnock	W 1-0	0-0	9	Mooney	2346
30		20	A	Dunfermline Ath	D 2-2	1-1	9	Foster, McAnenay	2542
31		23	A	Cowdenbeath	W 2-0	1-0	—	McAnenay, McQuade	222
32		27	H	Ayr U	W 2-0	1-0	9	Boyd, Mooney	988
33	Mar	6	A	Hamilton A	D 1-1	0-0	9	McQuade	1261
34		9	A	Stirling Albion	L 0-1	0-0	—		418
35		13	H	St Mirren	W 2-1	0-1	9	Boyd, McQuade	1558
36		20	H	Clydebank	L 0-2	0-0	9		1035
37		27	A	Morton	L 1-2	0-1	9	McAnenay	953
38	Apr	3	H	Cowdenbeath	D 0-0	0-0	9		552
39		10	A	Raith R	L 0-2	0-1	9		4893
40		17	H	Hamilton A	W 2-0	1-0	9	McQuade, Meechan	660
41		24	A	Ayr U	D 0-0	0-0	9		1525
42	May	1	A	Kilmarnock	L 0-1	0-1	9		3793
43		8	H	Dunfermline Ath	D 0-0	0-0	9		1078
44		15	A	Meadowbank T	L 1-2	1-1	9	Mooney	234

Final League Position: 9

Most Capped Player: John Lindsay, 8, Scotland; James McAulay, 8, Scotland.
Most League Appearances: 297: Andy Jardine, 1957-67.
Most Goals in Season (Individual): 38: Kenny Wilson, Division II; 1971-72.
Most Goals Overall (Individual): 169: Hughie Gallacher, 1954-62 (including C Division 1954-55).

Honours
League Champions: Division I 1890-91 (shared with Rangers), 1891-92. Division II 1910-11, 1971-72. Second Division 1991-92; Runners-up: First Division 1983-84. Division II 1907-08.
Scottish Cup Winners: 1883; Runners-up: 1881, 1882, 1887, 1891, 1897. League Cup: —.
Club colours: Shirt: Gold. Shorts: Gold. Stockings: Gold and black.

Goalscorers: League (56): McQuade 15, Mooney 12 (1 pen), Gibson 7, McAnenay 6, Boyd 5, Foster 2, Martin 2, Meechan 2, Boag 1, Docherty 1, Gilmour 1, Gow 1, Nelson 1. Scottish Cup (0). Skol Cup (0). B & Q Cup (0).

MacFarlane I 40	Gow S 38	Marsland J 37 + 1	Melvin M 42	Martin P 40	Dempsey J 3	McQuade J 38 + 2	Meechan J 27 + 7	Gibson C 36 + 6	Nelson M 9 + 9	Gilmour J 5	Willock A 1 + 7	Cowell J — + 7	McConville R 17 + 6	Boyd J 35 + 2	Wishart F 2	McAnenay M 27 + 11	Monaghan M 4	McDonald D 3	Docherty R 26 + 6	McGarvey M 1 + 3	Mooney M 27 + 7	Foster A 15 + 5	Boag J 6 + 1	Furphy W 1	Young J 3	Speirs A 1	Match No.
1	2	3	4	5	6	7	8	9	10	11			14														1
1	3	2	4	5	6	7	8	9	10	11		14	12														2
1	3	2	4	5		7	10	9	6	11		12	8	14													3
1	4	14	6	5		7		12	8	11			10			3	2		9								4
1	6	2	4	5	10	7		9	8			12				3					11						5
1	6	2	4	5		7		9	8	11			14			3					10						6
	6	8		5		7		9	14			12				10	3	2			11		1	4			7
	6	2	4	5		7		9	12				14			10	3				11		1	8			8
	4	2		5		7	12	9								10	3				11		1	6	8	14	9
1	4	2	6	5		7		9	14			12	10			3			8		11						10
1	2		4	5		7	14	9	12	6			11	8	10	3											11
1	2		4	5		7	8	12	6			14	10	11	9	3											12
1	2		4	5		7	6	9	8			10	11	14	12	3											13
1	4	2	6	5		7	8							12	10	3			11	14	9						14
1	3	2	4	5		7	6						14	10	12				11	8	9						15
1		2	4	5		7	6	9							10	3			12		8	11					16
1		2	4	5		7	6	9	14						10	3			12		8	11					17
1		2	4	5		7	6	9							10	3			12		8	11					18
1		2	4	5		7	8	9								3			12	10	11	6					19
1	6	2	4	5		7	10	12							14	3			11	8	9						20
1		2	4	5		7		9	14						10	3			12	8	11	6					21
1	3	2	4	5		7	12	9						14	10				8		11		6				22
1	6		4	5		7	8	9							12	3			10	11	14	2					23
1	6	2	4	5		7	8	9							14	3			12	10	11						24
	6	2	4	5		7	8	9							14	3			12	1	10	11					25
1	6	2	4	5		7	8	9								3			14	12	11	10					26
1	6	2	4	5				9	14							3			7	8	12	11		10			27
1		2	4	5			12	9							14	3			7	10	11	8	6				28
1	4	2	6	5		8	9									3			7	11	14	12			10		29
1	4	2	6	5	14	10	9									3			11	7	12	8					30
1	4	2	6	5		7	14	9								3			11	8	12				10		31
1	4	2	6	5		7	14	12								3			11	8	9				10		32
1	4	2	6	5		7	14	9								3			11	12	10				8		33
1	4		6	5		7	8	9								3			11	10	12		14	2			34
1		2	4	5		7	8	12								3			9	14	11				10		35
1		2	4	5		7	8	12								3			9	10	11		6	14			36
1	6	2	4	5		7	8	9								3			11	12	10	5					37
1	4	2	6	5		7	8	9								3			11	12	10						38
1	4	2	6	5		14	8	9								3			12	7	11				10		39
1	5	2	4			7	6	9							10	3			12	8	11		14				40
1	4	2	6	5		7	10	9								3			14	8	11		12				41
1	3	2	4	5		7	6	9						14	10				8		11	12					42
1	5	2	4			7	6	9	14						11	3			10	8			12				43
1	5	2	4					9	14							3			8	7	10		6	11			44

693

DUNDEE   Premier Division

Year Formed: 1893. *Ground & Address:* Dens Park, Sandeman St, Dundee DD3 7JY. *Telephone:* 0382 826104.
Ground Capacity: 16,871. seated: 11,516. *Size of Pitch:* 110yd × 70yd.
Chairman: Ron Dixon. *Secretary:* Andrew Drummond. *Marketing Manager:* June Webster.
Manager: Simon Stainrod. *Assistant Manager:* Jim Duffy. *Coach:* —.
Managers since 1975: David White; Tommy Gemmell; Donald Mackay; Archie Knox; Jocky Scott; Dave Smith; Gordon
Wallace; Iain Munro. *Club Nickname(s):* The Dark Blues or The Dee. *Previous Grounds:* Carolina Port 1893-98.
Record Attendance: 43,024 v Rangers, Scottish Cup; 1953.
Record Transfer Fee received: £500,000 for Tommy Coyne to Celtic (March 1989).
Record Transfer Fee paid: £200,000 for Jim Leighton (Feb 1992).
Record Victory: 10-0 Division II v Alloa; 9 Mar, 1947 and v Dunfermline Ath; 22 Mar, 1947.
Record Defeat: 0-11 v Celtic, Division I; 26 Oct, 1895.
Most Capped Player: Alex Hamilton, 24, Scotland.
Most League Appearances: 341: Doug Cowie 1945-61.
Most League Goals in Season (Individual): 38: Dave Halliday, Division I; 1923-24.
Most Goals Overall (Individual): 113: Alan Gilzean.

DUNDEE 1992—93 LEAGUE RECORD

Match No.	Date		Venue	Opponents	Result	H/T Score	Lg. Pos.	Goalscorers	Attendance
1	Aug	1	H	Falkirk	L 1-2	1-1	—	Rix	8914
2		4	H	St Johnstone	D 1-1	1-0	—	Dinnie	5663
3		8	A	Airdrieonians	D 0-0	0-0	8		2510
4		15	H	Rangers	W 4-3	2-2	7	Den Bieman, Gilzean, Dodds 2 (1 pen)	12,801
5	Aug	22	A	Aberdeen	L 1-2	1-2	7	Paterson	11,604
6		29	A	Partick T	L 3-6	2-2	10	Dodds 2, Gilzean	4520
7	Sept	1	H	Hearts	L 1-3	1-2	—	Dodds	5878
8		12	H	Motherwell	W 2-1	1-0	9	Dodds, Vrto	3792
9		19	A	Dundee U	W 1-0	0-0	9	Dodds (pen)	12,622
10		26	A	Hibernian	D 0-0	0-0	8		7290
11	Oct	3	H	Celtic	L 0-1	0-1	9		12,866
12		10	A	Falkirk	D 2-2	1-2	8	Den Bieman, Dodds	4818
13		17	H	Airdrieonians	W 2-0	2-0	7	McKeown, Dodds	3831
14		24	H	Partick T	L 0-2	0-1	8		5428
15		31	A	Hearts	L 0-1	0-0	8		7452
16	Nov	7	A	Aberdeen	L 1-2	0-0	8	Dodds	6902
17		11	A	Rangers	L 1-3	1-1	—	Den Bieman	37,255
18		21	H	Dundee U	L 1-3	1-1	9	Dodds	11,116
19		28	A	Motherwell	W 3-1	1-0	9	Gilzean 2, Stainrod	3534
20	Dec	2	A	St Johnstone	D 4-4	1-1	—	Pittman, Wieghorst, Dodds 2	5766
21		5	H	Hibernian	D 1-1	0-0	9	Stainrod	5467
22		12	A	Celtic	L 0-1	0-0	9		16,797
23		19	H	Falkirk	W 2-1	1-0	9	Dodds, Stainrod	6066
24		26	A	Rangers	L 1-3	0-1	9	Stainrod	13,778
25	Jan	2	A	Aberdeen	D 0-0	0-0	9		13,201
26		27	A	Partick T	L 0-2	0-1	—		2514
27		30	A	Airdrieonians	D 2-2	0-2	9	Reid (og), Paterson	2203
28	Feb	3	H	Hearts	W 1-0	0-0	—	McGowan	4182
29		13	A	St Johnstone	W 1-0	0-0	8	Stainrod	4869
30		20	A	Hibernian	W 3-1	1-0	7	Stainrod, Dow, Kiwomya	5668
31		23	H	Celtic	L 0-1	0-0	—		7221
32		27	A	Dundee U	L 0-1	0-1	8		12,140
33	Mar	6	H	Motherwell	D 1-1	1-0	7	Rix	3230
34		10	A	Falkirk	L 0-1	0-1	—		3454
35		13	A	Airdrieonians	D 1-1	0-0	8	Dodds	2929
36		20	H	Aberdeen	L 1-2	0-1	9	Stainrod	5783
37		27	A	Rangers	L 0-3	0-1	9		40,294
38	Apr	3	H	Partick T	L 0-1	0-1	10		3846
39		10	A	Hearts	D 0-0	0-0	9		6033
40		17	A	Motherwell	W 2-1	1-0	9	Ritchie, Dodds	4287
41		20	H	Dundee U	L 0-4	0-2	—		9589
42	May	1	A	St Johnstone	D 1-1	1-0	8	Ritchie	4471
43		8	H	Hibernian	W 3-1	2-0	8	Ritchie, Wieghorst, Gilzean	5115
44		15	A	Celtic	L 0-2	0-0	10		19,436

Final League Position: 10

Honours
League Champions: Division I 1961-62. First Division 1978-79, 1991-92. Division II 1946-47; *Runners-up:* Division I 1902-03, 1906-07, 1908-09, 1948-49, 1980-81.
Scottish Cup Winners: 1910; *Runners-up:* 1925, 1952, 1964.
League Cup Winners: 1951-52, 1952-53, 1973-74; *Runners-up:* 1967-68, 1980-81.
B&Q (Centenary) Cup: Winners: 1990-91.
European: *European Cup:* 1962-63 (semi-final). *Cup Winners:* 1964-65.
UEFA Cup: (Fairs Cup 1967-68 semi-final), 1971-72, 1973-74, 1974-75.
Club colours: Shirt: Dark blue with red and white trim. Shorts: White. Stockings: Blue and White.

Goalscorers: *League (48):* Dodds 16 (2 pens), Stainrod 7, Gilzean 5, Den Bieman 3, Ritchie 3, Paterson 2, Rix 2, Wieghorst 2, Dinnie 1, Dow 1, Kiwomya 1, McGowan 1, McKeown 1, Pittman 1, Vrto 1, own goal 1. *Scottish Cup (2):* Dodds 1 (pen), Wieghorst. *Skol Cup (3):* Campbell D 1, Dodds 1, McGowan 1.

Leighton J 8	Dinnie A 26	Campbell S 20	Duffy J 39	McGowan J 21	McKeown G 20	Ritchie P 17 + 2	McMartin G 2 + 1	Gilzean I 17 + 7	Dodds W 41	Rix G 12 + 2	Beedie S 8 + 6	Gallagher E 2 + 2	Den Bieman I 23 + 1	Vrto D 32	Ratcliffe K 4	Bain K 24	Campbell D 2 + 2	Paterson G 11 + 9	Stainrod S 10 + 10	McQuillan J 27 + 2	Mathers P 36	Dow A 8 + 6	Kiwomya A 11 + 10	Christie M 1 + 2	Pittman S 20	Wieghorst M 22 + 1	West C 2 + 5	McCann N 2 + 1	David L 8	Frail S 7	Armstrong L 1	Match No.
1	2	3	4	5	6	7		8	9	10	11		14																			1
1	2	3	4	5	6			12	9	10	11		8	7																		2
1	2	3	4	5	6			9	10	11	12	14	7	8																		3
1	2		4		5			9	10	11	3		7	8	6																	4
1	2				5	4			10	11	3		7	8	6		12	9	14													5
1	2		4		5	6			9	10	11		7	8	3			14	12													6
	2	6	4		5				9	10	11		7	8	3			14	12		1											7
	2	3	4		6				10	11			5					9	8	7	1											8
	2	3	4		6			12	9	10			7	8		5		11			1											9
	2	3	4		6			12	9	10			7	8		5		11			1		14									10
	2	3	4		6			12	9	10			7	8		5		11			1		14									11
	2	3	4		6			12	9	10			7	8		5		11			1		14									12
	2	3	4		6			12	10	11			7	8		5					1		9									13
	2	3	4		6			12	10	11			7	8		5					1		9									14
	2		4						10		3		9	7	8	5		12	14	11	1					6						15
	2			4	8				10				6	9	7	5			11		1				12	3						16
	2	3	4	5		11			9	10			7	8			12	14	6		1											17
	2	3	4	5		11			14	10	12		7				8	9	6		1											18
	2			5		4			9	10			8			7		12	14	11	1	6			3							19
	2			5					9	10			8			7		12	14	11	1	6			3	4						20
1	2								9	10			7	8			5	12	14	11		6			3	4						21
	2			5					9	10			7	8				14	11		1	6	12		3	4						22
	2					4		7	10				8	9			5			11	1				3	6						23
1	2			5				14	10				8	6		7		9			1		12		11	3	4					24
	2			5				9	10				12	8				14	7		1	6	11			3	4					25
		5		7				12	10		14		9	8						2	1	6	11			3	4					26
	2			5				9	10	11			7	8			6	14			1		12			3	4					27
		5		6	11	7			10				8			4		9		2	1					3	14					28
		5		7					10				8					9		2	1	14				3	4	11				29
	3	5		7					10				8			6		9		2	1	12	14				4	11				30
		5		7					10	14			8			6		9		2	1					3	4	12				31
		5		7					10				9	8		6				2	1	14	11			3	4	12				32
		5		7					10	11			8			6		9		2	1		12			3	4					33
		5		7					10	11			8			6		9		2	1	14				3	4	12				34
		5						9	10				8	11		4	14	2			1	6	12			3		7				35
		5		7					10				8	6		12	9	2			1	11				3	4					36
		5		7					10	9				6		2				1	12					3	4	11	8			37
		5	4	7					10	11				6		9		1			3	12	14					8	2			38
	3	5				11	7		14	10				6		9		1			12						4		8	2		39
	3	5				11	7		12	10				6		9		1			14						4		8	2		40
	3	5				11	7		12	10				6		9		1			14						4		8	2		41
	3	5					10	7	9					6	14			1			11						4		8	2		42
	3	5					10	7	9					6	14			1			11						4		8	2		43
	3	5					10	7	14					6				1			11	12					4		8	2	9	44

DUNDEE UNITED — Premier Division

Year Formed: 1909 (1923). *Ground & Address:* Tannadice Park, Tannadice St, Dundee DD3 7JW. *Telephone:* 0382 833166.
Ground Capacity: total: 16,868, seated: south 2217; George Fox 5149.
Size of Pitch: 110yd × 74yd.
Chairman: James Y. McLean. *Company Secretary:* Miss Priti Trivedi. *Commercial Manager:* Bobby Brown.
Manager: —. *Physio:* John Sharp. *Coach:* Paul Sturrock.
Managers since 1975: J. McLean. *Club Nickname(s):* The Terrors. *Previous Grounds:* None.
Record Attendance: 28,000 v Barcelona, Fairs Cup; 16 Nov, 1966.
Record Transfer Fee received: £900,000 for Kevin Gallacher to Coventry C (Jan 1990).
Record Transfer Fee paid: £350,000 for Michael O'Neill from Newcastle U (Aug 1989).
Record Victory: 14-0 v Nithsdale Wanderers, Scottish Cup 1st rd; 17 Jan, 1931.
Record Defeat: 1-12 v Motherwell, Division II; 23 Jan, 1954.
Most Capped Player: Maurice Malpas, 55, Scotland.
Most League Appearances: 606, Dave Narey; 1973-93.
Most Appearances in European Matches: 75, Dave Narey (record for Scottish player).
Most League Goals in Season (Individual): 41: John Coyle, Division II; 1955-56.
Most Goals Overall (Individual): 158: Peter McKay.

DUNDEE UNITED 1992—93 LEAGUE RECORD

Match No.	Date		Venue	Opponents	Result	H/T Score	Lg. Pos.	Goalscorers	Attendance
1	Aug	1	A	Motherwell	W 1-0	0-0	—	Ferguson	5037
2		4	A	Partick T	W 1-0	0-0	—	Connolly	5128
3		8	H	Hearts	D 1-1	1-0	3	Ferguson	9112
4		15	A	Celtic	L 0-2	0-2	5		30,513
5		22	H	St Johnstone	W 2-1	2-0	3	Connolly, O'Neil J	7353
6		29	H	Falkirk	W 2-0	0-0	1	Ferguson 2	6444
7	Sept	2	A	Hibernian	L 1-2	0-0	—	Connolly	7721
8		12	A	Airdrieonians	W 2-1	1-0	3	Ferguson 2	2773
9		19	H	Dundee	L 0-1	0-0	4		12,622
10		26	H	Rangers	L 0-4	0-2	6		13,759
11	Oct	3	A	Aberdeen	W 1-0	0-0	4	Ferguson	12,936
12		7	H	Motherwell	D 1-1	0-0	—	Connolly	5380
13		17	A	Hearts	L 0-1	0-0	6		8209
14		24	A	Falkirk	D 1-1	1-0	6	McInally	4473
15		31	H	Hibernian	W 1-0	0-0	6	McInally	6955
16	Nov	7	A	St Johnstone	L 0-2	0-0	6		5513
17		11	H	Celtic	D 1-1	1-0	—	Galloway (og)	11,831
18		21	A	Dundee	W 3-1	1-1	5	Bollan, Connolly, Clark	11,116
19		28	H	Airdrieonians	D 0-0	0-0	5		5178
20	Dec	1	H	Partick T	W 2-1	1-0	—	McInally, O'Neil J	5241
21		12	A	Aberdeen	D 2-2	0-1	5	Crabbe, McKinlay	10,394
22		26	A	Celtic	W 1-0	1-0	5	Ferguson	22,852
23	Jan	2	H	St Johnstone	L 1-2	0-1	5	Crabbe	10,316
24		5	A	Rangers	L 2-3	0-2	—	Welsh, Perry	40,239
25		16	H	Hibernian	L 1-2	1-1	5	McInally	5518
26		23	H	Falkirk	W 2-1	2-1	5	Crabbe, Connolly	5626
27		30	H	Hearts	L 0-1	0-0	5		7732
28	Feb	2	A	Motherwell	L 0-2	0-1	—		3783
29		13	A	Partick T	W 4-0	1-0	5	Crabbe (pen), Connolly 2, Ferguson	3846
30		20	H	Rangers	D 0-0	0-0	5		13,443
31		24	H	Aberdeen	D 0-0	0-0	—		12,603
32		27	H	Dundee	W 1-0	1-0	5	Ferguson	12,140
33	Mar	6	A	Airdrieonians	W 3-1	2-1	5	Ferguson, Connolly, Clark	2291
34		9	H	Motherwell	D 0-0	0-0	—		5134
35		13	A	Hearts	L 0-1	0-1	5		7087
36		20	A	St Johnstone	W 4-1	2-1	5	McInally, O'Neill M, Connolly, O'Neil J	4510
37		27	H	Celtic	L 2-3	0-1	5	Connolly, Ferguson	12,185
38	Apr	3	A	Falkirk	W 2-1	1-0	5	Connolly, Johnson	3599
39		13	H	Hibernian	L 0-3	0-1	—		5167
40		17	H	Airdrieonians	W 3-0	2-0	4	Dailly, Bollan, Connolly	4200
41		20	A	Dundee	W 4-0	2-0	4	Connolly, Dailly 2, Bollan	9589
42	May	1	H	Partick T	W 3-1	2-0	4	Connolly 2, O'Neill M	5590
43		8	A	Rangers	L 0-1	0-0	4		42,917
44		15	H	Aberdeen	L 1-4	1-1	4	Dailly	9078

Final League Position: 4

Honours

League Champions: Premier Division 1982-83. Division II 1924-25, 1928-29; *Runners-up:* Division II 1930-31, 1959-60.
Scottish Cup Runners-up: 1974, 1981, 1985, 1987, 1988, 1991.
League Cup Winners: 1979-80, 1980-81; *Runners-up:* 1981-82, 1984-85.
Summer Cup Runners-up: 1964-65. *Scottish War Cup Runners-up:* 1939-40.
European: European Cup: 8 matches 1983-84 (semi-finals), 1988-89; *Cup Winners Cup:* 4 matches 1974-75; *UEFA Cup Runners-up:* 1986-87. 78 matches *Fairs Cup:* 1966-67, 1969-70, 1970-71. *UEFA Cup:* 1971-72, 1975-76, 1977-78, 1978-79, 1979-80, 1980-81, 1981-82, 1982-83, 1984-85, 1985-86, 1986-87, 1987-88, 1989-90, 1990-91.
Club colours: Tangerine jersey, black shorts. Change colours: all white.

Goalscorers: *League 56:* Connolly 16, Ferguson 12, McInally 5, Crabbe 4 (1 pen), Dailly 4, Bollan 3, O'Neil J 3, Clark 2, O'Neill M 2, Johnson 1, McKinlay 1, Perry 1, Welsh 1, own goal 1. *Scottish Cup (3):* Ferguson 1, McKinlay 1, Welsh 1. *Skol Cup (11):* Connolly 3, Ferguson 2, Ferreyra 2, Johnson 2, McKinlay 1, O'Neil J 1.

Main A 43	Clark J 35 + 2	Malpas M 37	McKinlay W 36 + 1	Van Der Hoorn F 31 + 1	Narey D 27 + 1	O'Neil J 21 + 7	Johnson G 15 + 2	Cleland A 21 + 3	Ferguson D 30	Bollan G 12 + 3	Connolly P 32 + 10	McInally J 26 + 6	McLaren A 4 + 1	Ferreyra V 3 + 4	Welsh F 15	Bowman D 18 + 6	Dailly C 8 + 6	Crabbe S 22 + 5	Perry M 17 + 1	O'Neill M 22 + 3	Krivokapic M 8	Hannah D — + 5	Van De Kamp G 1	Match No.
1	2	3	4	5	6	7	8	9	10	11	12													1
1	2	3	4	5	6	7	8	9	10	*11*	12	14												2
1	2	3	4	5	6	7	8	*9*	10	11		14												3
1	2	3	4	5	6	7	8	14	10	*11*	9	12												4
1	2	3	*4*	14		7	8	9	10	11	5					6								5
1	2	3	4	5		7	8	*9*	10	12	11					6	14							6
1	2	3		5	6	7	8	9	10	11	*4*	12	14											7
1	2	3		5	6	7	8	9	10	11	4	12												8
1	2	3		5	6	7	*8*	9	10	11	4	12	14											9
1	2	3	*4*	5	6	7	8	9		11	12			14	10									10
1	2	3	7	5					11	6	10	14			4	8	9							11
1	2	3	7	5					11	12	6	10	14		4	8	9							12
1	2	3	7	5					14	12	6	10	11		4	8	9							13
1	2	3	8	5			6		10	11	9		4		7	14								14
1	2	3		5	6				10	14	4		7		9	8	11							15
1	2	3			6		12		14	4	7		9		8	10	11							16
1	9	3	8	5	6				11	10	4		14		12	7				2				17
1	9	3	8	5		7			11	10	4	6			14	12				2				18
1	9	3	8	5		7			10	11	14	6			4	12				2				19
1		3		5		7			10	11	9	4			6	8				2				20
1		3	12	5		7			10	14	4				6		9	11	8	2				21
1	12	3	7	5		8			10	14	4				6		9	11	2					22
1			7	5	12				10	3	14	4			6		9	11	8	2				23
1	14		7	5			8			3	10	4			6		9	11		2				24
1		3	8	5	2	7			12	10	4				6		9	11						25
1	5	3	8		6	7			12	10	4						9		2	11				26
1	5	3	4		6	7	8		11	10							2		9	12				27
1	5	3	8		6	7			11	10	4				14		9			2				28
1	5	3	8		6				10	11	4						7	2	9	14				29
1	5	3	8		6		12		10	11	4						7	2	9					30
1	5	3	8		6				10	11	4	12					7	2	9					31
1	5	3	8		6		12		10	11	4						7	2	9					32
1	5	3	8		6				10	11	*4*						7	2	9	14				33
1	5	3	9				12		10	11	4	6					*7*	2	8					34
1	5	3	8		6				10	11	14	4					12	7	2	9				35
1	5	3	8		6		12		10	11	4						7	2	*9*	14				36
1	5	3		6	12	8			10	11	4					14	7	2	9					37
1	5	3	4	2	6	14	8	12	10	11							7		*9*					38
	5	3	4	2	6	*8*	7	11	10	12							9		14	1				39
1		8	5		7		3	11		6	4	9	10			2		14						40
1		8	5	2	7		3	*11*	14	6	4	9	12			10								41
1		8	5	*2*	7		3	11	14	6	4	9	12			10								42
1	6	8	5	2	7		14	11	3	4	9	12	*10*											43
1	2	8	5		3		11	*7*	6	4	9	12	14	10										44

DUNFERMLINE ATHLETIC   First Division

Year Formed: 1885. *Ground & Address:* East End Park, Halbeath Rd, Dunfermline KY12 7RB. *Telephone:* 0383 724295.
Ground Capacity: total: 18,340. seated: 4020. *Size of Pitch:* 114yd × 72yd.
Chairman: C. R. Woodrow. *Secretary:* Henry W. Melrose. *Commercial Manager:* Audrey Kelly.
Manager: Bert Paton. *Assistant Manager:* Dick Campbell.
Physio: Philip Yeates, MCSP.
Managers since 1975: G. Miller; H. Melrose; P. Stanton; T. Forsyth; J. Leishman; I. Munro; J. Scott. *Club Nickname(s):*
The Pars. *Previous Grounds:* None.
Record Attendance: 27,816 v Celtic, Division I, 30 April, 1968.
Record Transfer Fee received: £200,000 for Ian McCall to Rangers (Aug 1987).
Record Transfer Fee paid: £540,000 for Istvan Kozma from Bordeaux (Sept 1989).
Record Victory: 11-2 v Stenhousemuir, Division II, 27 Sept, 1930.
Record Defeat: 1-11 v Hibernian, Scottish Cup, 3rd rd replay, 26 Oct, 1889.
Most Capped Player: Andy Wilson, 6 (12), Scotland.
Most League Appearances: 360: Bobby Robertson; 1977-88.
Most League Goals in Season (Individual): 55: Bobby Skinner, Division II, 1925-26.
Most Goals Overall (Individual): 154: Charles Dickson.

DUNFERMLINE ATHLETIC 1992—93 LEAGUE RECORD

Match No.	Date		Venue	Opponents	Result	H/T Score	Lg. Pos.	Goalscorers	Atten dance
1	Aug	1	A	Ayr U	D 1-1	1-0	—	Kennedy (og)	2588
2		5	A	Cowdenbeath	W 5-2	3-1	—	Leitch, Robertson, Davies 2, O'Boyle	2223
3		8	H	Hamilton A	W 2-1	1-1	1	Davies 2	3323
4		15	A	Kilmarnock	W 1-0	0-0	1	O'Boyle	5347
5		22	H	Raith R	L 0-1	0-0	2		6377
6		29	H	Clydebank	L 1-3	0-0	3	Leitch	3237
7	Sept	5	A	Stirling Albion	W 5-0	2-0	3	Chalmers 2, Grant, McWilliams, McCathie	1371
8		12	A	St Mirren	L 1-2	1-1	5	Chalmers	3372
9		19	H	Meadowbank T	W 3-1	1-1	4	Davies, Chalmers, McWilliams	2624
10		26	H	Dumbarton	W 3-2	3-1	3	Grant, French, Cooper	2832
11	Oct	3	A	Morton	W 1-0	1-0	3	Grant	2480
12		10	H	Ayr U	L 1-3	1-2	3	Cooper	3037
13		17	A	Hamilton A	L 1-2	0-1	4	McWilliams	2147
14		24	H	Stirling Albion	W 1-0	0-0	3	French	2388
15		31	A	Clydebank	L 0-1	0-0	5		1041
16	Nov	7	A	Kilmarnock	W 2-0	1-0	3	Williamson, French	3924
17		14	A	Raith R	L 0-1	0-0	5		5794
18		21	A	Meadowbank T	L 2-3	2-0	6	Davies, Laing	709
19		28	H	St Mirren	W 2-0	0-0	5	Laing, Leitch	3074
20	Dec	2	H	Morton	D 0-0	0-0	—		2544
21		5	A	Dumbarton	W 1-0	0-0	4	McCathie	1154
22		12	A	Ayr U	L 0-1	0-1	5		1939
23		19	H	Cowdenbeath	W 4-1	1-1	4	Chalmers, French, Davies, Moyes	2844
24		26	H	Kilmarnock	W 3-2	1-1	4	French 2, Robertson	5762
25	Jan	2	H	Raith R	D 0-0	0-0	4		10,798
26		30	H	Hamilton A	W 2-1	1-1	5	Leitch 2	2716
27	Feb	2	H	Clydebank	W 2-0	1-0	—	Chalmers, Davies	2165
28		6	A	Morton	W 1-0	1-0	4	Chalmers	1700
29		9	A	Stirling Albion	W 2-1	0-1	—	Leitch, Robertson	1023
30		13	A	Cowdenbeath	W 2-1	1-0	2	Smith, Leitch	2165
31		20	H	Dumbarton	D 2-2	1-1	2	Grant, Chalmers	2542
32		27	H	Meadowbank T	W 3-2	2-1	2	Laing, Leitch, Davies	2343
33	Mar	6	A	St Mirren	W 1-0	0-0	2	French	2695
34		10	H	Ayr U	D 1-1	0-1	—	Davies	2624
35		13	A	Hamilton A	W 2-0	0-0	2	French 2	2351
36		20	A	Raith R	L 0-2	0-0	2		6985
37		27	H	Kilmarnock	D 2-2	0-0	2	Wilson (og), Leitch	5223
38	Apr	3	H	Stirling Albion	L 0-1	0-1	2		2607
39		10	A	Clydebank	D 1-1	1-0	2	French	1055
40		17	H	St Mirren	L 1-2	1-0	3	French	3252
41		24	A	Meadowbank T	W 1-0	0-0	2	French	1384
42	May	1	H	Cowdenbeath	L 0-2	0-0	3		3105
43		8	A	Dumbarton	D 0-0	0-0	3		1078
44		15	H	Morton	L 1-2	0-1	3	Chalmers	3106

Final League Position: 3

Honours

League Champions: First Division 1988-89. Division II 1925-26. Second Division 1985-86; *Runners-up:* First Division 1986-87 Division II 1912-13, 1933-34, 1954-55, 1957-58, 1972-73. Second Division 1978-79.
Scottish Cup Winners: 1961, 1968; *Runners-up:* 1965.
League Cup Runners-up: 1949-50, 1991-92.
European: *European Cup:* —. *Cup Winners Cup:* 1961-62, 1968-69 (semi-finals). *UEFA Cup:* 1962-63, 1964-65, 1965-66, 1966-67, 1969-70 (*Fairs Cup*).
Club colours: Shirt: Black and white vertical stripes, stippled with red dots. Shorts: Black with white side panel. Stockings: White with red chevrons.

Goalscorers: *League (64):* French 12, Davies 10, Chalmers 9, Leitch 9, Grant 4, Laing 3, McWilliams 3, Robertson 3, Cooper 2, McCathie 2, O'Boyle 2, Moyes 1, Smith 1, Williamson 1, own goals 2. *Scottish Cup (1):* Chalmers 1. *Skol Cup (6):* O'Boyle 2, Davies 1, Grant 1, Leitch 1, McWilliams 1. *B & Q Cup (0).*

Hamilton L 39	Bowes M 4	Sharp R 27	McCathie N 30 + 2	Robertson C 34	Cooper N 33	McWilliams D 22 + 3	Shannon R 42	Grant R 18 + 14	Leitch S 34 + 8	Cunnington E 26 + 8	Davies W 39 + 2	O'Boyle G 3	Kelly N 4	Sinclair C 1 + 5	Laing D 11 + 2	Chalmers P 23 + 9	Reilly J — + 1	French H 36 + 2	Haro M 2	Williamson A 4 + 1	Moyes D 30	McAllister P — + 1	McNamara J 1 + 2	Smith P 16	Hillcoat J 5	Match No.
1	2	3	4	5	6	7	8	9	10	11	12															1
1		3	4	5	6		2	9	10		11					8		7								2
1		3	4	5	6	14	2	9	10	12	11					8		7								3
1		3	4	5	6	7	2	9	10		11					8		14								4
1		3	4	5	6	7	2		10		11					8	14	9								5
1		3	4	5	6	7		9	10	12	11			2		8		14								6
1		3	4	5	6	7	2	9	14	11	10					8		12								7
1		3	4	5	6	7	2	9	14	*11*	10					8		12								8
1		3			6	7	2	9	14	12	10					8		*11*		4	5					9
1		3			6	7	2	9	4	14	10					8		11	5							10
1		3	4		6	7	2	9	14	5	10					*8*		11								11
1		3	4		6	7	2	9	14	5	10					*8*		11								12
1		3	4		6	7	2	9	5	14	10	*10*				*8*		11								13
1	2	3	4		6	*7*	8	9		12	10					14		11			5					14
1	2	3		6	4			8	11	*10*			14	9		7					5					15
1		3	4		6		2	*9*	12		10			14		8	7	11			5					16
1		*3*	4		6		2	9	10	12						8	7	11		5	14					17
1		3	4	6			2			8	11	10				*9*	14	7		5						18
1		3		4	6	11	2			8		10				9		7		5		12				19
1		3		4	6	11	2			8		10				9	14	7		5		12				20
1		3	4	6		11	2			8		10				9		7		5						21
1		3	4	6			2	*11*	8	12	10					9	14	7		5						22
1		3	4	6			2	14	8	12	10					*9*	11	7		5						23
1			4	9	6		2		8	3	10					11	7	12		5						24
1			4	6	*9*		2	14	8	3	10					11	7			5						25
1				6	11	2		8	3	10						9	7			5	4					26
1			4	6			2	14	*8*	3	10					9	7			5		11				27
1			4	6			2	14	*8*	3	10					9	7			5		11				28
1			4	6	12		2	14	*8*	3	10					9	7			5		11				29
1			4	6			2	14	8	3	10					*9*	7			5		11				30
1		12		6			2	11	8	3	10					9	7			5	4					31
1			4	6			2	12	8	3	10					9	14	7		5		11				32
1		12	4	6	11		2		8	3	10						7			5	9					33
1			4	6	*6*	11	2	14	8	3	10						7			5	9					34
1			4	6		11	2	14	8	3	*10*					12	7			5	9					35
1			4	6		*11*	2	14	8	3	10						7			5	9					36
1			4	10	6	12	2	14	8	3						11	7			5	9					37
1		3	4	6		*11*	2	9	12		10					14	7			5	8					38
1		3	4	8	6		2	14	12		10					*9*	7			5	11					39
			4	10	6			2	12	8	3					14	*9*	7			5	11			1	40
			4	11	6		2		8	*3*	10					14	9	7			5				1	41
			4	11	6		2	14	8	3	10					*9*	7		5						1	42
		3	4	*6*			2		8		10					9	14	7			5		11		1	43
	2	3	4	6				8		*10*						11	12	14			5		9		1	44

EAST FIFE   Second Division

Year Formed: 1903. *Ground & Address:* Bayview Park, Methil, Fife KY8 3AG. *Telephone:* 0333 426323. *Fax:* 426376.
Ground Capacity: total: 5385. seated: 600. *Size of Pitch:* 110yd × 71yd.
Chairman: James Baxter. *Secretary:* William McPhee. *Commercial Manager:* James Bonthrone.
Manager: Alex Totten. *Assistant Manager:* Kenny Thomson. *Physio:* Bob Pender. *Coach:* David Gorman.
Managers since 1975: Frank Christie; Roy Barry; David Clarke; Gavin Murray. *Club Nickname(s):* The Fifers. *Previous
Grounds:* None.
Record Attendance: 22,515 v Raith Rovers, Division I; 2 Jan, 1950.
Record Transfer Fee received: £150,000 for Paul Hunter from Hull C (March 1990).
Record Transfer Fee paid: £70,000 for John Sludden from Kilmarnock (July 1991).
Record Victory: 13-2 v Edinburgh City, Division II; 11 Dec, 1937.
Record Defeat: 0-9 v Hearts, Division I; 5 Oct, 1957.
Most Capped Player: George Aitken, 5 (8), Scotland.
Most League Appearances: 517: David Clarke, 1968-86.

EAST FIFE 1992—93 LEAGUE RECORD

Match No.	Date	Venue	Opponents	Result	H/T Score	Lg. Pos.	Goalscorers	Atten dance
1	Aug 8	H	Stenhousemuir	D 1-1	1-0	—	Elliott	558
2	15	H	Alloa	W 2-0	1-0	4	McBride, Scott	624
3	22	A	Clyde	D 2-2	1-0	5	Sludden, Scott	608
4	29	A	Forfar Ath	L 0-3	0-2	7		803
5	Sept 5	A	Queen's Park	W 3-1	0-0	5	Beaton (pen), McBride, Scott	465
6	12	H	East Stirling	D 2-2	1-1	5	Sludden 2	528
7	19	A	Arbroath	W 3-1	1-1	5	Scott 2, Brown	564
8	26	H	Berwick R	W 4-2	1-1	4	McBride, Elliott, Scott, Sludden	617
9	Oct 3	A	Stranraer	L 1-2	0-1	5	Scott	567
10	10	A	Queen of the S	L 2-5	0-2	6	Sludden 2	715
11	17	A	Brechin C	L 0-1	0-0	6		506
12	24	H	Montrose	L 2-3	0-2	8	McBride 2	592
13	31	H	Albion R	W 5-0	2-0	6	Sludden 2, Scott 2, Hope	276
14	Nov 7	A	Forfar Ath	D 2-2	2-0	6	Scott 2	648
15	14	H	Queen's Park	W 2-1	1-0	5	McBride, Sludden	569
16	21	H	Arbroath	L 1-3	1-0	6	Burns	634
17	28	A	East Stirling	W 6-1	2-0	5	McBride, Skelligan 2, Hope 2, Allan	323
18	Dec 12	A	Stenhousemuir	L 1-3	0-1	7	Andrew	473
19	26	H	Stranraer	L 0-1	0-1	7		678
20	Jan 2	A	Alloa	W 2-0	1-0	7	Brown, Allan	736
21	16	H	Albion R	W 5-0	3-0	4	McBride 2, Skelligan 2, Andrew	504
22	23	A	Montrose	W 3-1	2-0	5	Sludden 2, Elliott	580
23	26	H	Clyde	D 1-1	0-1	—	Burns	816
24	30	A	Berwick R	L 0-3	0-1	5		417
25	Feb 9	H	Brechin C	W 1-0	1-0	—	Scott	822
26	13	A	Queen of the S	D 1-1	0-1	6	Scott	469
27	20	A	Forfar Ath	W 2-1	1-1	6	Beaton (pen), Hope	507
28	27	H	Clyde	L 2-3	0-1	6	Hope, Burns	716
29	Mar 6	H	Alloa	D 2-2	1-0	6	Brown, Beaton (pen)	563
30	13	A	Queen's Park	D 2-2	1-0	6	Burns, Sludden	406
31	20	A	East Stirling	W 3-1	0-1	6	Brown, Hope, Sludden	350
32	27	A	Stranraer	D 1-1	0-1	6	Scott	722
33	Apr 3	A	Albion R	L 2-4	2-4	7	Scott, Hope	295
34	10	H	Stenhousemuir	W 2-1	0-0	7	Skelligan, Beaton	569
35	17	A	Queen of the S	L 0-2	0-0	7		538
36	24	H	Montrose	D 0-0	0-0	7		499
37	May 1	H	Brechin C	L 1-2	0-2	8	Beaton	580
38	8	A	Arbroath	L 0-3	0-0	8		703
39	15	H	Berwick R	L 1-2	0-0	9	Scott	469

Final League Position: 9

Most League Goals in Season (Individual): 41: Jock Wood, Division II; 1926-27 and Henry Morris, Division II; 1947-48.
Most Goals Overall (Individual): 196: George Dewar (149 in League).

Honours
League Champions: Division II 1947-48; *Runners-up:* Division II 1929-30, 1970-71. Second Division 1983-84.
Scottish Cup Winners: 1938; *Runners-up:* 1927, 1950.
League Cup Winners: 1947-48, 1949-50, 1953-54.
Club colours: Shirt: Amber with black collar and cuffs. Shorts: Amber with black flashes. Stockings: Amber with 3 black stripes on top.

Goalscorers: *League (70):* Scott 16, Sludden 13, McBride 9, Hope 7, Beaton 5 (3 pens), Skelligan 5, Brown 4, Burns 4, Elliott 3, Allan 2, Andrew 2.   *Scottish Cup (5):* Skelligan 2, Brown 1, Hope 1, Sludden 1. *Skol Cup (0).*   *B & Q Cup (0).*

Moffat J 4	Bell G 19+6	Spence T 24+1	Burns W 34+3	Beaton D 35	McCracken D 10+2	Elliott D 9+13	Brown W 32+2	Scott R 26+2	Sludden J 31+1	McBride J 33+4	Hope D 33+4	Skelligan R 14+6	Burgess S 21	Taylor P H 24+2	Allan G 18+8	Charles R 32	Blyth A —+1	Andrew B 9+12	Speirs A —+1	Lennox S 8+1	Fraser A 3+3	Wilson E 3	Gibson J 1	Barron D 5	Long D 1+1	Match No.
1	2	3	4	5	6	7	8	9	10	11	12	14														1
1		6	3	4		7	8	9	10	11	14			2	5											2
1	12	6	5	4		7	8	9	10	11	14			2	3											3
1	14	6	5	4		7	8	9	10	11				2	3											4
		2	3		6	14	8	9	10	11	4			5	7	1										5
		6	3	2		7	8	9	10	11	4			5	12	1										6
	3		7	2	14		8	9	10	11	4			5	6	1										7
	3	14	7	6	12		8	9	10	11	4			5	2	1										8
	3	12	7	6			8	9	10	11	4			5	2	1	14									9
	3	6		5	12		8	9	10	7	11			2	4	1		14								10
		2	3	11	12		8	9	10	7	5			4	6	1		14								11
		2	3	4	6		8	9	10	11	12			5	14	1		7								12
		2	3	7	6	14	8	9	10	11	4			5		1		12								13
		2	7		6	12	8	9	10	11	4			5	3	1										14
		2	7		6	12	8	9	10	11	4	14		5	3	1										15
		2	7	14	6	12	8	9	10	11	4			5	3	1										16
		2	7	3	12	14	8		10	11	4			5	6	1		9								17
		2	3	6	12	14	8		10	11	7			4	5	1		9								18
		2	4	3			8	9	10	11		14		5	6	1		12			7					19
		2	7	3			8	9	10	11		14		5	6	1		12			4					20
	3	5	7		12		8		10	11	4	14		2	6	1		9								21
		2	7	3	12		8		10	11	4	14		5	6	1		9								22
		2	3	7	12		8	9	10	11	4	14		5	6	1										23
		2	4	3	12		8		10	11	7	14		5	6	1		9								24
		2	3	11			8	9	10	7	4	14		5	6	1		12								25
		2	3	4			8	9	10	11	7	14		5	6	1		12								26
	3	6			12		8		10	11	4	14		5	2	7		9					1			27
	12	6	7	4			8	9	10	11				2	5	1				14					3	28
	14	6	3	4	12		8	9	10	11	7			2	5	1										29
	12	6	3	5			8	9	10	11	4	14		2	7	1										30
		5	3	4			8	9	10	11	7	14		2	6	1										31
		5	3	4	12		8	9	10	11	7			2	6	1				14						32
		2	3	5	12			9	10	11	7	14			6	1				8				4		33
		6	3	5	12			9	10	11	7	14		2		1				8				4		34
		6	3	5	12			9	10	11	7	14		2		1				8				4		35
		6	3	5				9	10	11	7			2		1				8				4		36
	12	6	3	5				9	10	11	7	14		2		1				8				4		37
		2	3	5	6			9	10	11	7	14				1		12		8				4		38
		2	3	5	6			9	10	11	7	14				1		12		8				4		39

EAST STIRLINGSHIRE Second Division

Year Formed: 1880. *Ground & Address:* Firs Park, Firs St, Falkirk FK2 7AY. *Telephone:* 0324 23583.
Ground Capacity: total: 1880. seated: 200. *Size of Pitch:* 112yd × 72yd.
Chairman: William Laird. *Secretary:* Marshall Paterson. *Commercial Manager:* Tom Kirk.
Manager: Bobby McCulley. *Assistant Manager:* Archie Rose. *Physio:* Sandra Togneri. *Coach:* Robert Shields.
Managers since 1975: I. Ure; D. McLinden; W. P. Lamont; M. Ferguson; W. Little; D. Whiteford; D. Lawson; J. D.
Connell; A. Mackin; Dom Sullivan. *Club Nickname(s):* The Shire. *Previous Grounds:* Burnhouse, Randyford Park,
Merchiston Park, New Kilbowie Park.
Record Attendance: 12,000 v Partick T, Scottish Cup 3rd rd; 19 Feb 1921.
Record Transfer Fee received: £35,000 for Jim Docherty to Chelsea (1978).
Record Transfer Fee paid: £6,000 for Colin McKinnon from Falkirk (March 1991).
Record Victory: 11-2 v Vale of Bannock, Scottish Cup 2nd rd; 22 Sept, 1888.
Record Defeat: 1-12 v Dundee United, Division II; 13 Apr, 1936.
Most Capped Player: Humphrey Jones, 5 (14), Wales.

EAST STIRLINGSHIRE 1992—93 LEAGUE RECORD

Match No.	Date		Venue	Opponents	Result	H/T Score	Lg. Pos.	Goalscorers	Attendance
1	Aug	8	H	Montrose	L 0-2	0-0	—		314
2		15	H	Clyde	L 1-2	1-1	14	Tierney	475
3		22	A	Arbroath	W 5-4	2-3	9	Roberts 3, Walker (pen), Barclay	380
4		29	A	Queen of the S	L 1-2	1-0	11	McKinnon	289
5	Sept	5	A	Stranraer	L 1-4	1-2	13	Kemp	479
6		12	A	East Fife	D 2-2	1-1	13	Geraghty, Kemp	528
7		19	H	Alloa	W 4-2	1-0	11	Walker, Houston, Friar, Geraghty	372
8		26	H	Albion R	D 1-1	1-0	12	Walker	284
9	Oct	3	A	Brechin C	L 1-2	0-1	11	Friar	380
10		10	H	Stenhousemuir	L 3-7	0-4	13	Russell, McKinnon, Geraghty	371
11		17	A	Berwick R	W 5-2	1-1	13	Friar, Walker, Thomson, Roberts, Ross	362
12		24	H	Forfar Ath	W 1-0	1-0	12	Walker (pen)	316
13		31	A	Queen's Park	L 2-4	1-1	11	McKinnon 2	469
14	Nov	7	A	Queen of the S	W 2-1	0-0	10	Woods 2	512
15		14	H	Stranraer	L 1-2	0-2	11	Tierney	374
16		21	A	Alloa	L 0-1	0-0	11		372
17		28	H	East Fife	L 1-6	0-2	12	Tierney	323
18	Dec	12	A	Montrose	L 1-4	0-1	13	Houston	446
19		26	H	Brechin C	D 0-0	0-0	12		427
20	Jan	2	A	Clyde	L 1-5	1-3	12	Houston	726
21		23	A	Forfar Ath	L 1-5	1-2	13	Walker (pen)	371
22		30	A	Albion R	D 2-2	0-2	13	Roberts 2	207
23	Feb	2	H	Queen's Park	D 2-2	0-0	—	Tierney, Friar	274
24		10	H	Berwick R	W 2-0	1-0	—	Geraghty, Kemp	246
25		13	A	Stenhousemuir	W 2-1	1-1	12	McKinnon, Geraghty	407
26		20	A	Stranraer	D 0-0	0-0	11		443
27		23	H	Arbroath	L 1-2	0-0	—	Geraghty	303
28		27	H	Alloa	L 0-2	0-1	12		437
29	Mar	13	H	Forfar Ath	L 0-2	0-1	13		305
30		16	A	Arbroath	D 0-0	0-0	—		520
31		20	H	East Fife	L 1-3	1-0	13	Roberts	350
32		27	A	Clyde	L 1-2	0-0	13	Geraghty	620
33	Apr	3	A	Queen's Park	W 4-1	1-0	11	Craig 2, Thomson, Roberts	283
34		10	A	Brechin C	L 0-5	0-2	12		555
35		17	A	Stenhousemuir	L 0-2	0-0	13		299
36		24	H	Queen of the S	L 1-2	1-2	13	Roberts	334
37	May	1	A	Berwick R	D 0-0	0-0	13		394
38		8	H	Montrose	D 0-0	0-0	13		255
39		15	H	Albion R	L 0-1	0-0	13		247

Final League Position: 13

Most League Appearances: 379: Gordon Simpson, 1968-80.
Most League Goals in Season (Individual): 36: Malcolm Morrison, Division II; 1938-39.
Most Goals Overall (Individual): —.

Honours
League Champions: Division II 1931-32; *Runners-up:* Division II 1962-63. Second Division 1979-80.
Scottish Cup: —.
League Cup: —.
Club colours: Shirt: Black and white hoops. Shorts: Black. Stockings: Black.

Goalscorers: *League (50):* Roberts 9, Geraghty 7, Walker 6 (3 pens), McKinnon 5, Friar 4, Tierney 4, Houston 3, Kemp 3, Craig 2, Thomson 2, Woods 2, Barclay 1, Ross 1, Russell 1. *Scottish Cup (10):* Geraghty 2, McKinnon 2, Roberts 2, Barclay 1, Thomson 1, Walker 1, own goal 1. *Skol Cup (0).* *B & Q Cup (2):* Geraghty 2.

Imrie P 15	Russell G 22 + 2	Friar P 30 + 1	Ross B 34	Craig D 16	Houston P 16 + 3	McKinnon C 36	Thomson S 32 + 2	Roberts P 20 + 10	Walker D 25 + 1	Auld A 2 + 2	Barclay S 13 + 6	McMillan C 6 + 7	Tierney S 15 + 5	Mackie P — + 1	Lawson O 2	Kemp B 36	McCarter S — + 1	Geraghty M 29	Woods T 19 + 5	Watson G 22	O'Sullivan D 10 + 1	McFadyen I 2	Yates D 21	Clark R 3	McAuley I 3 + 2	Match No.
1	2	3	4	5	*6*	7	8	9	10	11	12	14														1
1	2	3	4	5	6	7	8		10	11		9	12													2
1	5	6	4	3		7	8	11	10	14	12	*2*	*9*													3
	2	5	4	3	12	7	8		10	11			14	*9*	1	6										4
	5	7	4	3	9	2	11	10	12				8		1	6	14									5
1	2	8	4	5	9	7	6	12	10							3		11								6
1		8	4	5	9	6	7	12	10							3		11	2							7
1		8	4	5	9	6	7		10							3		11	2							8
12		8	4	5	9	6	7	14	10							3		11	2	1						9
2		6	4	3	9		7	12	10							8		11	5	1						10
2	8	6			9		7	12	10							3		11	5	1	4					11
2	8	6			9		7		10							3		11	5	1	4					12
2	8	6			9		7	12	10							3		11	5	1	4					13
3	5				10	7	9	12					14			8		11	6	1	4	*2*				14
		8			6	7	9		10	2	12					3		11	5	1	4					15
		8		14	6	7		12	10				11			3		9	5	1	4	*2*				16
2		8			9	6	7	14	10				12			3		*11*	5	1	4					17
11		6				7	8		10				2			3		9		1	4		5			18
2		8			9	7	6		10							3		11	5	1	4					19
	14		4		9	7	8	12	10				2			3		11	*6*	1			5			20
		7	5		9		8	14	10				12			3		11	2	1	4		6			21
		7	4		9		8	11	10	5		14	12			3				1	2		*6*			22
		7	4		9		8		10			6	11			3			5	1	2					23
		7	4		9			2	10	14	6	12	8			3		*11*		1			5			24
		7	4		9			2	10		6		8			3		11		1			5			25
		7	4	12	9			2	10		6		8			3		11		1			5			26
		7	4		9			2	10		6		8			3		11		1			5			27
11	14	7	4		9			2	10	12	6		8			3		11		1			5			28
11		7	4				8	2	10			14	9			3		12		1			5	6		29
	2	11	4			7	8		10				9			3		12		1			5	6		30
1	2	11	4			7	8		10				9			3		12					5	6		31
1	2	11	4			7	8	12					9			3		10	6				5			32
1	2	7	4		10		8						9			3		*11*	6				5		*14*	33
1	2	7	4	6	10		8	12				9				3		11					5		14	34
1	2	6	4			7	8	12				14	9			3		11					5		*10*	35
1	2		4	6		7	8		10			14	9			3		11	12				5			36
1	2				10	7	8				6		9			3		11	4				5			37
1			4		10	7	8					14	9			3		11	2				5		*6*	38
1			4	6	10		8					2	9			3		11	12		14		5		7	39

FALKIRK

First Division

Year Formed: 1876. *Ground & Address:* Brockville Park, Hope St, Falkirk FK1 5AX. *Telephone:* 0324 24121/32487. *Fax:* 0324 612418.
Ground Capacity: total: 12,800. seated: 2661. *Size of Pitch:* 110yd × 70yd.
Chairman: C. Christie. *Secretary:* A. D. Moffat. *Commercial Manager:* Jim Hendry.
Manager: Jim Jefferies. *Assistant Manager:* Billy Brown. *Physio:* Joe Cross. *Coach:* Willie Wilson.
Managers since 1975: J. Prentice; G. Miller; W. Little; J. Hagart; A. Totten; G. Abel; W. Lamont; D. Clarke; J. Duffy.
Club Nickname(s): The Bairns. *Previous Grounds:* Randyford; Blinkbonny Grounds; Hope Street.
Record Attendance: 23,100 v Celtic, Scottish Cup 3rd rd; 21 Feb, 1953.
Record Transfer Fee received: £270,000 for Gordon Marshall to Celtic (Aug 1991).
Record Transfer Fee paid: £225,000 to Chelsea for Kevin McAllister (Aug 1991).
Record Victory: 12-1 v Laurieston, Scottish Cup 2nd rd; 23 Mar, 1893.
Record Defeat: 1-11 v Airdrieonians, Division I; 28 Apr, 1951.
Most Capped Player: Alex Parker, 14 (15), Scotland.

FALKIRK 1992—93 LEAGUE RECORD

Match No.	Date		Venue	Opponents	Result		H/T Score	Lg. Pos.	Goalscorers	Attendance
1	Aug	1	A	Dundee	W	2-1	1-1	—	Sloan, Drinkell	8914
2		5	A	Hearts	L	0-3	0-0	—		8198
3		8	H	Aberdeen	L	0-1	0-0	10		5925
4		15	H	Hibernian	W	2-1	2-0	8	May, McQueen (pen)	6024
5		22	A	Airdrieonians	L	0-2	0-1	11		3900
6		29	A	Dundee U	L	0-2	0-0	12		6444
7	Sept	5	H	Partick T	L	0-1	0-1	12		5691
8		12	A	St Johnstone	L	2-3	1-2	12	Smith, McLaughlin	4361
9		19	H	Celtic	L	4-5	1-1	12	McQueen (pen), McCall 2, May	9678
10		26	H	Motherwell	W	1-0	1-0	11	Sloan	4275
11	Oct	3	A	Rangers	L	0-4	0-2	12		40,691
12		10	H	Dundee	D	2-2	2-1	12	May, McQueen	4818
13		17	A	Aberdeen	L	1-3	1-1	12	Sloan	9016
14		24	H	Dundee U	D	1-1	0-1	12	Sloan	4473
15		31	A	Partick T	W	2-1	1-0	10	May (pen), Cadette	5535
16	Nov	7	H	Airdrieonians	W	5-1	2-1	10	Drinkell 2, Cadette, Lennox, May	4715
17		14	A	Hibernian	L	1-3	1-1	10	Lennox	7237
18		21	A	Celtic	L	2-3	2-2	10	Drinkell, McAllister	15,978
19		28	H	St Johnstone	D	2-2	1-0	10	Duffy 2	4565
20	Dec	2	H	Hearts	W	2-1	2-1	—	McCall, Drinkell	5475
21		5	A	Motherwell	L	1-3	1-1	10	Cadette	5018
22		12	H	Rangers	L	1-2	0-1	10	Wishart	11,585
23		19	A	Dundee	L	1-2	0-1	11	Cadette	6066
24		26	H	Hibernian	D	3-3	1-2	10	Cadette, Drinkell, McCall	6925
25	Jan	2	A	Airdrieonians	W	1-0	1-0	10	Duffy	5748
26		23	A	Dundee U	L	1-2	1-2	10	Duffy	5626
27		30	H	Aberdeen	L	1-4	0-2	10	McCall	6886
28	Feb	2	A	Partick T	W	4-2	2-1	—	Taylor, McAllister 2, Duffy	4690
29		9	A	Rangers	L	0-5	0-2	—		37,780
30		13	A	Hearts	L	1-3	0-0	11	Cadette	7700
31		20	H	Motherwell	L	1-3	0-2	11	McCall	4536
32		27	H	Celtic	L	0-3	0-0	12		8165
33	Mar	10	H	Dundee	W	1-0	1-0		Cadette	3454
34		13	A	Aberdeen	D	2-2	0-0	11	Drinkell, Johnston	9095
35		16	A	St Johnstone	L	0-1	0-0	—		3546
36		20	A	Airdrieonians	L	0-1	0-1	12		4172
37		27	A	Hibernian	D	1-1	1-1	12	Sloan	5168
38	Apr	3	H	Dundee U	L	1-2	0-1	12	Shaw	3599
39		10	A	Partick T	W	1-0	1-0	11	May	4677
40		17	H	St Johnstone	D	2-2	0-1	11	Sloan, Shaw	3860
41		20	A	Celtic	L	0-1	0-0	—		10,151
42	May	1	H	Hearts	W	6-0	2-0	11	Weir, Wishart, Baptie 2, Rice, Cadette	4124
43		8	A	Motherwell	L	1-2	0-1	11	Rice	8577
44		15	H	Rangers	L	1-2	1-1	11	McQueen (pen)	9288

Final League Position: 11

Most League Appearances: (post-war): John Markie, 349.
Most League Goals in Season (Individual): 43: Evelyn Morrison, Division I; 1928-29.
Most Goals Overall (Individual): Dougie Moran, 86.

Honours
League Champions: Division II 1935-36, 1969-70, 1974-75. First Division 1990-91. Second Division 1979-80; Runners-up: Division I 1907-08, 1909-10. First Division 1904-05, 1951-52, 1960-61.
Scottish Cup Winners: 1913, 1957. League Cup Runners-up: 1947-48.
Club colours: Shirt: Dark blue with white flashings. Shorts: White. Stockings: Red.

Goalscorers: League (60): Cadette 8, Drinkell 7, McCall 6, May 6 (1 pen), Sloan 6, Duffy 5, McQueen 4 (3 pens), McAllister 3, Baptie 2, Lennox 2, Rice 2, Shaw 2, Wishart 2, Johnston 1, McLaughlin 1, Smith 1, Taylor 1, Weir 1. Scottish Cup (7): May 2, Sloan 2, Cadette 1, Duffy 1, McCall 1. Skol Cup (6): Drinkell 2, McAllister 1, McQueen 1, May 1, Smith 1.

Westwater J 24	Duffy C 33 + 1	McQueen T 30	Baptie C 8 + 1	Hughes J 15	Rice B 15 + 2	McAllister K 40 + 1	May E 40 + 2	Drinkell K 33 + 2	Sloan S 21 + 8	Smith P 19	Johnston F 17 + 5	McCall I 27 + 8	Taylor A 3 + 5	Cadette R 24 + 7	Oliver N 24 + 1	McGivern S 1	McDougall G 5	Taggart C 3 + 2	McLaughlin J 8	Lennox G 17 + 3	Parks A 15	Weir D 30	Wishart F 23 + 1	MacKenzie S 2 + 1	Treanor M 3	Shaw G 4 + 2	Young K — + 1	Match No.
1	2	3	4	5	6	7	8	9	10	11	14																	1
1	2	3		5		7	6	9	10	11	4	8	14															2
1	4	3		5	6	7	8	9	10	11	14				2													3
1	4	3	10	5	6	7	8	9		11		12			2													4
1	2	3	4	5	6		8	9		11	14	10		12		7												5
					4	5	6	7	8	9	12	11	3	10	2		1	14										6
					4	5	6	7	8	9	12	11	3	10	2		1	14										7
	4				6	7	14	9	8	11	3	10			2		1					5						8
	2	3	14		6	9	7	11	4	10	8						1					5						9
	2	3			6	9	7	11	10						4		1					5	8					10
1	4	3				12	6	9	7	11	10				2							5	8					11
1	4	3				7	6	9	8	11	10				2							5	12					12
1	4	3				7	9			10	11	6	12		2							5	8					13
	5					7	6	9	8	4	3	10	12							11	1	2						14
	5					7	6	9	8	4	3	10	12	14						11	1	2						15
	3	5				7	6	9	8	4		10								11	1	2						16
	3	5				7	6	9	8	4		10								11	1	2						17
	14	3	5			7	6	9	8	4		10	12							11	1	2						18
	4	3				7	6	9	10	8										11	1	5	2					19
	4	3				7	6	9	14	10	8									11	1	5	2					20
	4	3				7	6	9	12	14	10	8								11	1	5	2					21
1	4	3				7	6	9	10	8										11		5	2					22
1	4	3				7	6	12	11	10	14	9							8			5	2					23
1	4	3				7	6	8	12	10	9									11		5	2					24
	4					7	11	8			3	10		9	6					12	1	5	2					25
	4					7	11	8	12		3	10		9	6						1	5	2					26
	4	3				7	6	8	11	12	9				2						1	5	14	10				27
	4				6	14	7	11	12	3	10	8		9							1	5	2					28
	4				6	7	11	8	14	3	10	9									1	5	2					29
	4				6	7	11	8		3	10	14		9							1	5	2					30
	2	3				7	6	8	12	14	9	10						5		11	1	4						31
1	8	3				7	6	12	9		10				2		14	5				4	11					32
1		3				6	7	11	8		10			9	4				14			5	2					33
1	6	3				7	11	8	12		10			9	4							5	2					34
1	6	3				7	11	8	12		10			9	4							5	2					35
1	8	3			6	7	11	9			10			12	4							5	2					36
1	8	3				7	9				10			12	4					11		5	2		6			37
1	8		14			7	11	9			10			3	4							5	2		6	12		38
1						6	7	11			10			3	4				8			5	2		9			39
1						6	7	11			10			3	12		14		8			5	2	4	9			40
1	8					6	7	11			10			3	12		14		4			5	2		9			41
1	11	3	8		6	7					10			9	4							5	2					42
1	11	3	8		6	7		12			10			9	4							5	2		14			43
1		3		5		6	7				10			9	4		8						2	12		11	14	44

FORFAR ATHLETIC   Second Division

Year Formed: 1885. *Ground & Address:* Station Park, Carseview Road, Forfar. *Telephone:* 0307 463576.
Ground Capacity: total: 8359. seated: 711. *Size of Pitch:* 115yd × 69yd.
Chairman: George Enston. *Secretary:* David McGregor. *Commercial Manager:* —.
Manager: Tommy Campbell. *Assistant Manager:* Brian McLaughlin. *Physio:* Andy Bell. *Coaches:* Stewart Kennedy, Tom McCallum.
Managers since 1975: Jerry Kerr; Archie Knox; Alex Rae; Doug Houston; Henry Hall; Bobby Glennie; Paul Hegarty.
Club Nickname(s): Loons. *Previous Grounds:* None.
Record Attendance: 10,780 v Rangers, Scottish Cup 2nd rd; 2 Feb, 1970.
Record Transfer Fee received: £57,000 for Craig Brewster to Raith R (July 1991).
Record Transfer Fee paid: £50,000 for Ian McPhee from Airdrieonians (1991).
Record Victory: 14-1 v Lindertis, Scottish Cup 1st rd; 1 Sept 1988.
Record Defeat: 2-12 v King's Park, Division II; 2 Jan, 1930.
Most Capped Player: —.

FORFAR ATHLETIC 1992—93 LEAGUE RECORD

Match No.	Date	Venue	Opponents	Result	H/T Score	Lg. Pos.	Goalscorers	Atten dance
1	Aug 8	H	Queen of the S	W 5-1	0-1	—	Petrie 2, McKenna, Donaldson, Winter	508
2	15	H	Arbroath	D 1-1	0-1	2	Petrie	861
3	22	A	Queen's Park	W 2-1	1-0	2	Hamill, Petrie	406
4	29	A	East Fife	W 3-0	2-0	1	McPhee, Donaldson, McKenna	803
5	Sept 5	H	Alloa	D 1-1	0-0	2	Donaldson	745
6	12	H	Stenhousemuir	W 3-1	1-1	2	Petrie 2, Winter (pen)	522
7	19	A	Clyde	D 0-0	0-0	3		829
8	26	H	Stranraer	W 4-1	2-0	2	Heddle, Winter (pen), Petrie, McPhee	522
9	Oct 3	A	Montrose	D 0-0	0-0	1		993
10	10	H	Berwick R	W 5-3	3-0	1	Petrie 3, Donaldson, McPhee	599
11	17	H	Albion R	L 1-2	1-2	2	Mearns	288
12	24	A	East Stirling	L 0-1	0-1	3		316
13	31	H	Brechin C	L 0-1	0-1	4		1044
14	Nov 7	A	East Fife	D 2-2	0-2	3	Petrie, Winter	648
15	14	A	Alloa	D 1-1	1-1	3	Petrie	517
16	21	H	Clyde	L 2-4	1-4	4	McKenna, Smith	635
17	28	A	Stenhousemuir	L 0-2	0-1	6		308
18	Dec 12	A	Queen of the S	D 1-1	0-1	6	Bingham	355
19	Jan 2	A	Arbroath	W 3-2	2-0	6	Smith, Heddle, Petrie	1435
20	19	H	Montrose	W 4-3	1-0	—	Winter, Mann, Heddle, Bingham	852
21	23	H	East Stirling	W 5-1	2-1	4	Heddle, McKenna 3, Smith	371
22	26	A	Queen's Park	W 2-0	0-0	—	Bingham, Winter (pen)	551
23	30	A	Stranraer	L 0-2	0-0	4		560
24	Feb 2	A	Brechin C	W 2-1	1-0	—	Petrie 2	932
25	6	H	Albion R	W 3-2	2-1	4	Sheridan, McCaffrey (og), Winter	519
26	13	A	Berwick R	L 1-2	0-1	4	Smith	352
27	20	H	East Fife	L 1-2	1-1	5	Petrie	507
28	27	A	Queen of the S	W 4-2	2-1	5	McKenna, Bingham, Heddle, Petrie	399
29	Mar 6	H	Stenhousemuir	W 1-0	0-0	5	Winter	441
30	13	A	East Stirling	W 2-0	1-0	5	McCafferty, McKenna	305
31	20	A	Montrose	W 3-1	2-0	4	Heddle, Bingham, Petrie	627
32	27	H	Queen's Park	D 2-2	1-1	4	McIntyre, McKenna	531
33	Apr 3	A	Stranraer	L 1-3	1-2	4	Bingham	510
34	10	H	Albion R	W 5-2	3-1	4	Smith 2, Petrie 3	557
35	17	H	Berwick R	L 0-2	0-0	4		515
36	24	A	Brechin C	W 1-0	0-0	4	McKenna	830
37	May 1	A	Clyde	L 2-3	1-2	4	Morris, Smith	1021
38	8	H	Alloa	D 1-1	1-1	4	Smith	441
39	15	A	Arbroath	D 0-0	0-0	4		1007

Final League Position: 4

Most League Appearances: 376: Alex Brash, 1974-86.
Most League Goals in Season (Individual): 45: Dave Kilgour, Division II; 1929-30.
Most Goals Overall (Individual): 124, John Clark.

Honours
League Champions: Second Division 1983-84. C Division 1948-49.
Scottish Cup: Semi-finals 1982.
League Cup: Semi-finals 1977-78.
Club colours: Shirt: Royal/sky/white geometric patterned. Shorts: White. Stockings: Royal blue.

Goalscorers: *League (74):* Petrie 21, McKenna 10, Smith 8, Winter 8 (3 pens), Bingham 6, Heddle 6, Donaldson 4, McPhee 3, Hamill 1, McCafferty 1, McIntyre 1, Mann 1, Mearns 1, Morris 1, Sheridan 1, own goal 1. *Scottish Cup (8):* Heddle 3, McIntyre 1, McKenna 1, Mearns 1, Petrie 1, own goal 1. *Skol Cup (1):* Heddle 1. *B & Q Cup (2):* Mearns 1, Winter 1.

Thomson S 39	McIntyre S 27 + 3	Hamill A 39	Morris R 23	Mann R 35	Winter G 37	McKenna I 24 + 12	McPhee I 36	Petrie S 37	Donaldson G 11	Pryde 1 1	Heddle I 37 + 1	Perry J — + 3	McAulay A 1 + 6	Mearns S 28 + 3	Price G — + 2	Byrne J 1	Sheridan J 7 + 7	Smith R 15 + 10	Glass S 1	Bingham D 20	McCafferty A 6 + 12	Cameron D 2 + 1	Hall A 2	Match No.
1	2	3	4	5	6	7	8	9 10	11 12 14															1
1	2	3	4	5	6	7	8	9 10		11	14													2
1	7	3	4	5	6 12		8	9 10		11 14		2												3
1		3	4	5	6 12		8	9 10		11		7	2 14											4
1		3	4	5	6	7	8	9 10		11	12	2												5
1		3	4	5	6	7	8	9 10		11	12	2												6
1		3	4	5	6	7	8	9 10		11		2												7
1		3	4	5	6	7	8	9 10		11 14	12	2												8
1		3	4	5	6	7	8	9		11	12	2			10									9
1		3	4	5	6	7	8	9 10		11		2 14		12										10
1	8	3	4	5	6	7		9 10		11		2			14									11
1 12	8	4	5	6	7			9 10		11		2			14	3								12
1	7	3	4	5	6 12		8	9		11		2		14 10										13
1	2	3	4	5	6	7		9		11	12	8		10 14										14
1	7	3	4	5	6 10		8	9		11		2												15
1	7	3	4	5	6 10		8	9		11		2		12										16
1	2	3	4	5 10		7	8	9		6		11		12										17
1 12	8		4	5		7	3			11		2	6	9		10 14								18
1 12	10		4	5	6		3	9		11		2		8		7 14								19
1	4	10		5	6 12		3	9		11		2		8		7								20
1	2	10		5	6	4	3	9		11		12		8		7 14								21
1	2	10		5	6	4	3	9		11		12		8		7 14								22
1	2	10		5	6	4	3	9		11		12		8		7 14								23
1		10		5	6	4	3	9		11		2		8		7 12 14								24
1	2	10		5	6	4	3	9		11				8 14		7 12								25
1	2	10			6	4	3	9		11				8 14		7 12	5							26
1	2	10			6	4	3	9		11				12 8		7	5							27
1		3		5	6	9	8 10			11		2				7 4								28
1	2	3		5	6	9	8 10			11		4		12		7 14								29
1	2	3		5	6 14		8 10			11				12 9		7 4								30
1	4	3		5	6		8 10			11				9 14		7		2						31
1	4	3	2		6 12		8 9			11				14		7 10	5							32
1	2	3			6 12		8 10			11		4		14		7 9	5							33
1	2	3		5	6 14		8 9			11		4		10		7 12								34
1	2	3		5	6		8 9			11		4		14 10		7 12								35
1	2	3		5	6 14		8 10			11		4		9		7								36
1	2	3	6	5			14	8 10		11		4		12 9		7								37
1	2	3	4	5	6 14		8 10			11		7		9										38
1	2	3	4	5	6 12		8			11				10 9		7 14								39

HAMILTON ACADEMICAL First Division

Year Formed: 1874. *Ground & Address:* Douglas Park Lane, Hamilton ML3 0DF. *Telephone:* 0698 286103. *Fax:* 0698 285422.
Ground Capacity: total: 6550. seated: 1592. *Size of Pitch:* 112yd × 73yd.
Chairman: George J. Fulston. *Secretary:* Scott A. Struthers BA. *Commercial Manager:* George Miller.
Manager: Iain Munro. *Assistant Manager:* Phil Bonnyman. *Physio:* Frank Ness: *Coach:* Colin Miller.
Managers since 1975: J. Eric Smith; Dave McParland; John Blackley; Bertie Auld; John Lambie; Jim Dempsey; John Lambie; Billy McLaren. *Club Nickname(s):* The Accies. *Previous Grounds:* Bent Farm, South Avenue, South Haugh.
Record Attendance: 28,690 v Hearts, Scottish Cup 3rd rd; 3 Mar, 1937.
Record Transfer Fee received: £110,000 for Willie Jamieson to Dundee (Jan 1990).
Record Transfer Fee paid: £60,000 for Paul Martin from Kilmarnock (Oct 1988).
Record Victory: 11-1 v Chryston, Lanarkshire Cup; 28 Nov, 1885.
Record Defeat: 1-11 v Hibernian, Division I; 6 Nov, 1965.
Most Capped Player: Colin Miller, 25 (36), Canada.

HAMILTON ACADEMICAL 1992—93 LEAGUE RECORD

Match No.	Date		Venue	Opponents	Result		H/T Score	Lg. Pos.	Goalscorers	Atten dance
1	Aug	1	H	Meadowbank T	L	1-3	0-0	—	McDonald	1518
2		5	H	St Mirren	D	0-0	0-0	—		2154
3		8	A	Dunfermline Ath	L	1-2	1-1	11	Kelly (og)	3323
4		15	H	Cowdenbeath	W	3-0	1-0	8	Cramb 2, Smith	1064
5		22	A	Stirling Albion	W	2-0	1-0	6	Miller, Smith	644
6		29	H	Ayr U	D	1-1	0-1	7	Clark	1592
7	Sept	5	A	Raith R	L	1-2	1-1	6	McDonald	2384
8		12	H	Dumbarton	W	3-2	2-1	6	Millen, Ward, Cramb	1283
9		19	A	Morton	L	1-2	0-0	6	Reid	1851
10		26	A	Clydebank	L	1-3	0-1	7	Smith	876
11	Oct	3	H	Kilmarnock	D	1-1	0-0	7	McDonald	2864
12		10	A	Meadowbank T	W	4-0	3-0	7	Smith 2, Harris 2	497
13		17	H	Dunfermline Ath	W	2-1	1-0	6	Harris, Reid	2147
14		24	H	Raith R	D	2-2	0-2	6	McDonald (pen), Harris	2418
15		31	A	Ayr U	D	0-0	0-0	7		1796
16	Nov	7	A	Cowdenbeath	W	3-0	2-0	6	McDonald, Ward, Smith	444
17		14	H	Stirling Albion	W	1-0	0-0	6	McDonald	1518
18		24	H	Morton	W	3-1	2-1	—	Smith, Miller 2	2018
19		28	A	Dumbarton	D	2-2	1-1	4	Ward, McDonald (pen)	843
20	Dec	1	A	Kilmarnock	L	0-1	0-1	—		3711
21		8	H	Clydebank	W	2-0	1-0	—	Cramb, Harris	1161
22		19	A	St Mirren	W	2-0	2-0	3	Millen, Reid	2110
23		26	H	Cowdenbeath	W	4-0	2-0	3	Clark, McDonald, Cramb, Ward	1313
24	Jan	2	A	Stirling Albion	D	0-0	0-0	3		779
25		6	H	Meadowbank T	W	2-0	0-0	—	Ward 2	1364
26		27	H	Kilmarnock	L	1-2	1-2	—	Harris	3106
27		30	A	Dunfermline Ath	L	1-2	1-1	4	Cramb	2716
28	Feb	2	A	Raith R	D	1-1	0-0	—	McDonald	2690
29		13	H	St Mirren	D	0-0	0-0	5		2593
30		20	A	Clydebank	W	1-0	0-0	5	Smith	766
31		27	A	Morton	W	2-1	1-0	5	Weir, Clark	1560
32	Mar	2	H	Ayr U	L	1-3	0-1	—	Lorimer	1329
33		6	H	Dumbarton	D	1-1	0-0	5	Clark	1261
34		10	H	Meadowbank T	W	2-1	2-1	—	Millen, McDonald (pen)	271
35		13	H	Dunfermline Ath	L	0-2	0-0	4		2351
36		20	H	Stirling Albion	W	2-0	0-0	4	Ward, Clark	1017
37		27	A	Cowdenbeath	W	4-0	0-0	3	McDonald, Ward 3	239
38	Apr	3	H	Raith R	D	2-2	1-0	4	McKee, Clark	3014
39		10	A	Ayr U	L	0-1	0-0	4		1836
40		17	A	Dumbarton	L	0-2	0-1	5		660
41		24	H	Morton	W	2-1	1-1	5	McLean, Clark	1511
42	May	1	A	St Mirren	L	1-2	0-0	5	Napier	2671
43		8	H	Clydebank	W	2-1	1-0	5	Cramb, Clark	1048
44		15	A	Kilmarnock	D	0-0	0-0	5		12,830

Final League Position: 5

Most League Appearances: 447: Rikki Ferguson, 1974-88.
Most League Goals in Season (Individual): 34: David Wilson, Division I; 1936-37.
Most Goals Overall (Individual): 246: David Wilson, 1928-39.

Honours
League Champions: First Division 1985-86, 1987-88. Division II 1903-04; *Runners-up:* Division II 1952-53, 1964-65.
Scottish Cup Runners-up: 1911, 1935. *League Cup:* Semi-finalists three times.
B&Q Cup Winners: 1991-92 and 1992-93.
Club colours: Shirt: Red and white hoops. Shorts: White. Stockings: White.

Goalscorers: League (65): McDonald 11 (3 pens), Ward 10, Clark 8, Smith 8, Cramb 7, Harris 6, Millen 3, Miller 3, Reid 3, Lorimer 1, McKee 1, McLean 1, Napier 1, Weir 1, own goal 1. *Scottish Cup (1):* Reid 1. *Skol Cup (2):* Clark 1, Smith 1. *B & Q Cup (14):* Clark 5, McDonald 3 (1 pen), Smith 2, Hillcoat 1, Reid 1, Ward 1, Weir 1.

Ferguson A 37	Hillcoat C 33	Miller C 30	Millen A 41	Weir J 37	Napier C 27 + 2	Ward K 25 + 9	McEntegart S 12 + 3	Clark G 34 + 3	Reid W 35 + 2	McDonald P 44	Smith T 22 + 6	McKee K 19 + 1	Rae G 9	McKenzie P 15 + 6	Cramb C 25 + 8	Harris C 14 + 13	McCulloch R 7	Waters M 4 + 7	Lorimer D 1 + 5	McInulty S 8 + 1	McLean C 4 + 2	Doyle P 1	Match No.
1	2	3	4	5	6	7	8	9	10	11	12												1
1	3		4	6		7		9	8	11	10	2	5										2
1		3	4	6	14	7		9	8	11	10	2	5	12									3
1	2	3		4	6	12	8		14	11	10			5	7	9							4
1	2	3	4		6	14	8	12		11	10			5	7	9							5
1	2	3	4		6		8	14		11	10			5	7	9	12						6
1	2	3	4	6		8	14			11	10			5	7	9	12						7
1		3	4	6		10		8	11	14	2	5	7	9	12								8
1	2	3	4		10	14		8	11	12				5	7	9	6						9
1	2	3	4	6	14	7		8	12	11	10		5		9								10
1	2	3	4	5	6		7	8	11	10				14	9								11
1		3	4	5	6		7	8	11	10	2			9									12
1	3		4	5	6	12		7	8	11	10	2		14	9								13
1	3		4	5	6	12		7	8	11	10	2		9									14
1	3		4	5	6	10	7		8	11	14	2		9									15
1	3		4	5	6	7	14	9	8	11	10	2		12									16
	2		4	5	3			8	6	11	10		7	14	9	1							17
1	2	3	4	5				8	6	11	10		7	9									18
1	2	3	4	5		9		8	6	11	10		7	12	14								19
1	6	3	4	5		7	8		11	10	2		12	14	9								20
1	2	3	4	5	6		10	8	11		7	9	12	14									21
1	2	3	4	5	6	7		10	8	11		9	12	14									22
1	2	3	4		6	7		10	8	11		12	9	5	14								23
1	2	3	4	5	6	7		10	8	11		9	14										24
1	2	3	4	5	6	7		10	8	11		9	14										25
1	2	3	4	5	6	7		10	8	11		12	14	9									26
1	2	3	4	5	6		10	8	11	12		9	7										27
1	2	3	4	5	6	12		7	8	11	10		9	14									28
1	2	3	4	5	6	10		8	11		9	12	7										29
1	2	3	4	5	6		8	11	10		9	12	7										30
1	2	3	4	5	6	14		7	8	11	10		9	12									31
1		3	4	5	6	12		7	8	11	10		9	2	14								32
1		3	4	5		9		7	8	11	10	2				12	14	6					33
1		3	4	5		9	14	10		11	12	2		8			7	6					34
1	6	3	4	5		9		7	8	11	10	2		12	14								35
1	4	3		5		10		6	8	11		2		12	9			14		7			36
			4		5		10		6	8	11	2		12	9		1	14		3	7		37
		6	4	5		10		7	8	11	2		9	1			3						38
		6	4	5		10		7	8	11	2		9	1	12			3	14				39
			4	5		9	10	7	8	11	2		14	1			3			6			40
			4		3	12	6	8		11	2		5	9		1	7		10				41
			4		3	12	6	8		11	2		5	9		1	7		14	10			42
1			4		2	10	6	7	8	11		12		5	9			14	3				43
1		4	6	2	10	7		8	11			5	9				12	3	14				44

HEART OF MIDLOTHIAN   Premier Division

Year Formed: 1874. *Ground & Address:* Tynecastle Park, Gorgie Rd, Edinburgh EH11 2NL. *Telephone:* 031 337 6132.
Ground Capacity: total: 25,177. seated: 11,987. *Size of Pitch:* 110yd × 74yd.
Chairman: A. Wallace Mercer. *Secretary:* L. W. Porteous. *Commercial Manager:* Charles Burnett.
Manager: Sandy Clark. *Assistant Manager:* Hugh McCann.
Physio: Alan Rae. *Coach:* —.
Managers since 1975: J. Hagart; W. Ormond; R. Moncur; T. Ford; A. MacDonald; A. MacDonald & W. Jardine; A. MacDonald; J. Jordan.
Club Nickname(s): Hearts. *Previous Grounds:* The Meadows 1874, Powderhall 1878, Old Tynecastle 1881, (Tynecastle Park, 1886).
Record Attendance: 53,396 v Rangers, Scottish Cup 3rd rd; 13 Feb, 1932.
Record Transfer Fee received: £1,300,000 for Dave McPherson from Rangers (July 1992).
Record of Transfer paid: £750,000 for Derek Ferguson to Rangers (July 1990).
Record Victory: 21-0 v Anchor, EFA Cup 1880.
Record Defeat: 1-8 v Vale of Leithen, Scottish Cup, 1888.
Most Capped Player: Bobby Walker, 29, Scotland.
Most League Appearances: 426: Henry Smith, 1981-93.

HEART OF MIDLOTHIAN 1992—93 LEAGUE RECORD

Match No.	Date		Venue	Opponents	Result		H/T Score	Lg. Pos.	Goalscorers	Atten dance
1	Aug	1	H	Celtic	L	0-1	0-0	—		18,510
2		5	H	Falkirk	W	3-0	0-0	—	Robertson 2 (1 pen), Crabbe	8198
3		8	A	Dundee U	D	1-1	0-1	5	Levein	9112
4		15	H	Partick Thistle	W	2-1	0-0	3	Mackay, Baird	7911
5		22	A	Hibernian	D	0-0	0-0	4		15,937
6		29	H	Motherwell	W	1-0	1-0	3	Berry	7285
7	Sept	1	A	Dundee	W	3-1	2-1	—	Robertson, Ferguson D, Levein	5878
8		12	H	Aberdeen	W	1-0	1-0	2	Robertson	10,630
9		19	A	Rangers	L	0-2	0-1	3		41,888
10		26	A	Airdrieonians	L	0-1	0-1	4		4372
11	Oct	3	H	St Johnstone	D	1-1	1-0	3	Robertson	7738
12		7	A	Celtic	D	1-1	1-1	—	Preston	26,049
13		17	H	Dundee U	W	1-0	0-0	4	Hogg	8209
14		24	A	Motherwell	W	3-1	1-0	3	Robertson, Martin (og), Ferguson I	5171
15		31	H	Dundee	W	1-0	0-0	3	Baird	7452
16	Nov	7	H	Hibernian	W	1-0	1-0	2	Baird	17,342
17		10	A	Partick T	D	1-1	1-0	—	McLaren	5355
18		21	H	Rangers	D	1-1	0-1	2	Baird	20,831
19		28	A	Aberdeen	L	2-6	0-2	4	Baird, Hogg	13,555
20	Dec	2	A	Falkirk	L	1-2	1-2	—	Robertson (pen)	5475
21		5	H	Airdrieonians	L	1-3	0-1	4	Baird	6665
22		12	A	St Johnstone	D	1-1	1-0	4	Ferguson I	4362
23		19	H	Celtic	W	1-0	1-0	4	Ferguson I	13,554
24		26	H	Partick T	D	1-1	0-0	4	Mackay	9922
25	Jan	2	A	Hibernian	D	0-0	0-0	4		21,657
26		20	H	St Johnstone	W	2-0	2-0	—	Robertson, Baird	5060
27		23	H	Motherwell	D	0-0	0-0	4		6610
28		30	A	Dundee U	W	1-0	0-0	3	Robertson	7732
29	Feb	3	A	Dundee	L	0-1	0-0	—		4182
30		13	H	Falkirk	W	3-1	0-0	4	McKinlay, Thomas, Taylor (og)	7700
31		20	A	Airdrieonians	D	0-0	0-0	4		3347
32		27	A	Rangers	L	1-2	0-2	4	Millar	42,128
33	Mar	10	A	Celtic	L	0-1	0-0	—		16,984
34		13	H	Dundee U	W	1-0	1-0	4	Baird	7087
35		20	H	Hibernian	W	1-0	0-0	4	Robertson	13,740
36		27	A	Partick T	D	1-1	0-1	4	Preston	4594
37	Apr	10	H	Dundee	D	0-0	0-0	4		6033
38		14	H	Rangers	L	2-3	1-1	—	Robertson, Bannon	14,622
39		17	A	Aberdeen	L	2-3	0-2	5	Levein, Ferguson I	9700
40		20	A	Motherwell	L	1-2	0-2	—	Baird	4355
41	May	1	A	Falkirk	L	0-6	0-2	5		4124
42		5	H	Aberdeen	L	1-2	0-1	—	Thomas	6038
43		8	H	Airdrieonians	D	1-1	0-0	5	Johnston	5104
44		15	A	St Johnstone	L	1-3	0-1	5	Harrison	3900

Final League Position: 5

Most League Goals in Season (Individual): 44: Barney Battles.
Most Goals Overall (Individual): 206: Jimmy Wardhaugh, 1946-59.

Honours
League Champions: Division I 1894-95, 1896-97, 1957-58, 1959-60. First Division 1979-80; *Runners-up:* Division I 1893-94, 1898-99, 1903-04, 1905-06, 1914-15, 1937-38, 1953-54, 1956-57, 1958-59, 1964-65. Premier Division 1985-86, 1987-88, 1991-92. First Division 1977-78, 1982-83.
Scottish Cup Winners: 1891, 1896, 1901, 1906, 1956; *Runners-up:* 1903, 1907, 1968, 1976, 1986.
League Cup Winners: 1954-55, 1958-59, 1959-60, 1962-63; *Runners-up:* 1961-62.
European: *European Cup* 4 matches (1958-59, 1960-61). *Cup Winners Cup:* 4 matches (1976-77). *UEFA Cup:* 32 matches (*Fairs Cup:* 1961-62, 1963-64, 1965-66. *UEFA Cup:* 1984-85, 1986-87, 1988-89, 1990-91, 1992-93.
Club colours: Shirt: Maroon. Shorts: White. Stockings: Maroon with white tops.

Goalscorers: *League (46):* Robertson 11 (2 pens), Baird 9, Ferguson I 4, Levein 3, Hogg 2, Mackay 2, Preston 2, Thomas 2, Bannon 1, Berry 1, Crabbe 1, Ferguson D 1, Harrison 1, Johnston 1, McKinlay 1, McLaren 1, Millar 1, own goals 2. *Scottish Cup (11):* Robertson 3 (1 pen), Baird 2, Boothroyd 2, Preston 2, Ferguson D 1, Snodin 1. *Skol Cup (4):* Mackay 1, McKinlay 1, McLaren 1, Robertson 1.

Smith H 25	McLaren A 34	McKinlay T 32+2	Levein C 37	Mackay G 36+1	Van De Ven P 37	Crabbe S 4+4	Mauchlen A 16+2	Baird I 34	Wright G 8+4	Bannon E 8+11	Hogg G 20+2	Robertson J 41+1	Snodin G 16+11	Ferguson D 37	Foster W 7+4	Berry N 16+1	Millar J 23+1	Preston A 19+2	Ferguson I 9+15	Walker N 18	Boothroyd A —+4	Thomas K 2+2	Harrison T 3+1	Johnston A 2	Locke G —+1	Match No.
1	2	3	4		5	6		7	8		9	10	11	12	14											1
1	2	3	4			6	14	8		9	10	11		5	7	12										2
1	2	3	4		6	12	10	9	14	11		5	7		8											3
1	2	3	4	6		11	10	9				5	7		8	12										4
1	2	3	4	5	6	12	10	9				14	7		8	11										5
1		3	4	5	6	9			14	2	7	12	8	11	10											6
1		3	4	5	6			9		2	7		8	11	10											7
1		3	4	5	6	12	10	9			2	7	14	8	11											8
1		3	4	5	6	7	10	9		12	2		14	8		11										9
1		3	4		6		9	5	12	2		7	8	11	10	14										10
1	8	3	4		6		14	9	5	12	2	7	10		11											11
1		3	4	5	6		8	9		12	2	7	10		11											12
1		3	4	5	6		9		12	2	7	14	8		10	11										13
1	2	3		5	6	9	4			7	14	8		10	11	12										14
1	2	3	4	5	6		9			7	8		10		12											15
1	2	3	4	5	6		11	9		7	14	8		10		12										16
1	2	3	4		6		5	9		7	14	8		10	11	12										17
1	2	3	4		6		9	11		7	14	8		5	10		12									18
1	2	3	4	5		9		6	7	14	8		11	10		12										19
1	2		4	5	6		9		7	3	8	14	11	10												20
	2	3	4	5	6		9		7		8		10	12	11					1						21
	2	3	4	5	6		7		8		10	11	9							1	14					22
	2	3	4	5	6		7		8	12		10	11	9						1	14					23
	2		4	5	6		12		7	3	8	9	10	11						1	14					24
	2		4	5	6	11	9		7	3	8		10	12						1						25
	2		4	5	6	10	9		7	3	8		11	12						1						26
	2		4	5	6	10	9		7	3	8	12	11							1						27
	2	14	4	5	6	10	9		7	3	8		11							1	12					28
	2		5	6		9		4	7	3	8		10	11	12					1						29
	2	3		5	6	10		14	7		8	4		11	9	1	12									30
	2	3		5	6	10	14		7		4	8	11	9	1											31
	2	3		5	6		14	12		7		8	4	10	11	9	1									32
	2	3	6	5		9	14		7		8	4	10	11	12	1										33
	2		4		14	9	6	12	5	7	3	8		10		11	1									34
	2		4	14	6		9		12	5	7	3	8		10		11	1								35
	2	14	4	5		9	8		7	3		6	10	11	12	1										36
	2	3	4	5	6		9		7		8	14	10	11	12	1										37
		3	4	5	6		9	11		7		8	2	10		1										38
		3	4	5	6		1		11	2	7	14	8	10		9		12								39
1	2		4	5		9	11	6	7	3	8		10	12												40
1	2		4	5	6		9	11		7	3	8	10		12											41
1	5	3		10	6		9		2	11	8	7					14	4								42
1	5	3	4	10		2	11	8		12		9	6	7												43
1		3		10	6		2	11	8	5		14		9	4	7	12									44

HIBERNIAN   Premier Division

Year Formed: 1875. *Ground & Address:* Easter Road Stadium, Albion Rd, Edinburgh EH7 5QG. *Telephone:* 031 661 2159.
Fax: 031 659 6488.
Ground Capacity: total: 21,889. seated: 6299. *Size of Pitch:* 112yd × 74yd.
Chairman: Douglas Cromb. *Managing Director:* —. *Secretary:* Cecil F. Graham, FIFA, MInst CM. *Commercial Manager:* Kenneth McLean.
Manager: Alex Miller. *Assistant Manager:* —.
Physio: Stewart Collie. *Coach:* Andy Watson.
Managers since 1975: Eddie Turnbull; Willie Ormond; Bertie Auld; Pat Stanton; John Blackley. *Club Nickname(s):* Hibees. *Previous Grounds:* Meadows 1875-78, Powderhall 1878-79, Mayfield 1879-80, First Easter Road 1880-92, Second Easter Road 1892-.
Record Attendance: 65,860 v Hearts, Division I; 2 Jan, 1950.
Record Transfer Fee received: £1,000,000 for Andy Goram to Rangers (June 1991).
Record Transfer Fee paid: £450,000 for Keith Wright from Dundee.
Record Victory: 22-1 v 42nd Highlanders; 3 Sept, 1881.
Record Defeat: 0-10 v Rangers; 24 Dec, 1898.
Most Capped Player: Lawrie Reilly, 38, Scotland.
Most League Appearances: 446: Arthur Duncan.

HIBERNIAN 1992—93 LEAGUE RECORD

Match No.	Date		Venue	Opponents	Result	H/T Score	Lg. Pos.	Goalscorers	Atten dance
1	Aug	1	A	Aberdeen	L 0-3	0-0	—		12,503
2		4	A	Motherwell	W 2-1	0-0	—	Wright, McGinlay	5391
3		8	H	Rangers	D 0-0	0-0	7		17,237
4		15	A	Falkirk	L 1-2	0-2	11	Tortolano	6024
5		22	H	Hearts	D 0-0	0-0	10		15,937
6		29	A	St Johnstone	D 1-1	1-0	8	McIntyre	6017
7	Sept	1	A	Dundee U	W 2-1	0-0	—	Tortolano, Jackson D (pen)	7721
8		12	A	Celtic	W 3-2	1-1	5	Wright, Jackson D (pen), Evans	28,130
9		19	H	Airdrieonians	D 2-2	1-1	6	Honor (og), Weir	6909
10		26	H	Dundee	D 0-0	0-0	5		7290
11	Oct	3	A	Partick T	D 2-2	0-1	6	Jackson D, Weir	6332
12		7	H	Aberdeen	L 1-3	1-0	—	Wright	8824
13		17	A	Rangers	L 0-1	0-0	8		40,978
14		24	H	St Johnstone	W 3-1	1-0	7	Jackson D 2, Weir	5988
15		31	A	Dundee U	L 0-1	0-0	7		6955
16	Nov	7	A	Hearts	L 0-1	0-1	7		17,342
17		14	H	Falkirk	W 3-1	1-1	7	Tortolano, Evans, Hamilton	7237
18		21	A	Airdrieonians	L 0-2	0-0	7		3129
19		28	H	Celtic	L 1-2	0-2	8	Jackson D	12,985
20	Dec	1	H	Motherwell	D 2-2	1-1	—	Wright, McGinlay	4777
21		5	A	Dundee	D 1-1	0-0	7	Jackson D	5467
22		12	H	Partick T	W 1-0	0-0	6	Jackson D (pen)	6077
23		19	A	Aberdeen	L 0-2	0-0	6		11,018
24		26	A	Falkirk	D 3-3	2-1	6	Fellenger 2, Evans	6925
25	Jan	2	H	Hearts	D 0-0	0-0	7		21,657
26		16	H	Dundee U	W 2-1	1-1	6	Jackson D, Van Der Hoorn (og)	5518
27		23	A	St Johnstone	L 0-2	0-0	7		4206
28		30	H	Rangers	L 3-4	0-1	7	McGinlay 2, Jackson D	17,447
29	Feb	13	A	Motherwell	D 0-0	0-0	7		5021
30		16	A	Partick T	W 3-0	1-0	—	McGinlay 2, Weir	3064
31		20	H	Dundee	L 1-3	0-1	6	McGinlay	5668
32		27	H	Airdrieonians	W 3-1	1-1	6	Jackson D 2, McGinlay (pen)	5011
33	Mar	9	H	Aberdeen	L 1-2	1-0	—	McGinlay	7029
34		13	A	Rangers	L 0-3	0-2	6		41,076
35		16	A	Celtic	L 1-2	0-0	—	Wright	12,178
36		20	A	Hearts	L 0-1	0-0	7		13,740
37		27	H	Falkirk	D 1-1	1-1	7	Wright	5168
38	Apr	6	H	St Johnstone	D 2-2	0-2	—	Wright, Evans	3526
39		13	A	Dundee U	W 3-0	1-0	—	Wright 3	5167
40		17	H	Celtic	W 3-1	3-0	7	Jackson D (pen), Evans, Wright	11,132
41		20	A	Airdrieonians	L 1-3	0-2	—	McGinlay	2585
42	May	1	H	Motherwell	W 1-0	0-0	6	Weir	4799
43		8	A	Dundee	L 1-3	0-2	7	Evans	5115
44		15	H	Partick T	L 0-1	0-1	7		5467

Final League Position: 7

Most League Goals in Season (Individual): 42: Joe Baker.
Most Goals Overall (Individual): 364: Gordon Smith.

Honours
League Champions: Division I 1902-03, 1947-48, 1950-51, 1951-52. First Division 1980-81. Division II 1893-94, 1894-95, 1932-33; *Runners-up:* Division I 1896-97, 1946-47, 1949-50, 1952-53, 1973-74.
Scottish Cup Winners: 1887, 1902; *Runners-up:* 1896, 1914, 1923, 1924, 1947, 1958, 1972, 1979.
League Cup Winners: 1972-73, 1991-92; *Runners-up:* 1950-51, 1968-69, 1974-75.
European: *European Cup:* 6 matches (1955-56 semi-finals). *Cup Winners Cup:* 6 matches (1972-73). *UEFA Cup:* 56 matches (*Fairs Cup:* 1960-61 semi-finals, 1961-62, 1962-63, 1965-66, 1967-68, 1968-69, 1970-71. *UEFA Cup:* 1973-74, 1974-75, 1975-76, 1976-77, 1978-79, 1992-93).
Club colours: Shirt: Green with white sleeves. Shorts: White. Stockings: Green with white trim.

Goalscorers: *League (54):* Jackson D 13 (4 pens), Wright 11, McGinlay 10 (1 pen), Evans 6, Weir 5, Tortolano 3, Fellenger 2, Hamilton 1, McIntyre 1, own goals 2. *Scottish Cup (8):* McGinlay 2, Weir 2, Wright 2, Jackson D 1, Tweed 1. *Skol Cup (5):* Evans 2, Hamilton 1, McGinlay 1, Wright 1.

Reid C 14	Orr N 20 + 1	Mitchell G 41	Beaumont D 16	McIntyre T 12	MacLeod M 26 + 5	Weir M 30 + 3	Hamilton B 39 + 2	Wright K 42	Jackson D 35 + 1	McGinlay P 40	Evans G 22 + 17	Tortolano J 16 + 5	Miller W 29 + 5	Milne C 10 + 5	Buridge J 30	Findlay W 3 + 4	Lennon D 7 + 6	Raynes S 2	McGraw M 1 + 1	Fellenger D 1 + 4	Farrell D 9 + 3	Hunter G 23	Donald G 1 + 3	Tweed S 13 + 1	Love G 1	Miller G 1	Jackson C — + 1	Match No.
1	2	3	4	5	6	7	8	9	10	11	12																	1
1	2	3	4	5	6	7	8	9	10	11	12																	2
1		4	3	5	6		8	9	10	11	12	7	2	14														3
1		4	3	5	6	14	8	9	7	11	10	12	2															4
		4	3	5		7	8	9	6	11	10	2	14	1														5
		4	3	5		7	8	9	6	11	10	2	1	14														6
		4	3	5		7	8	9	6	11	10	12	2	1	14													7
		4	3	5	6	7	8	9	10	11	12	2	14	1														8
		4	3	5	6	7	8	9	10	11		2	12	1		14												9
		3		5	12		8	9	10	11	7	6	2	1		4	14											10
			4	5	6	7	8	9	10	11		2	3	1														11
		4	3	5		7	8	9	10	11	12	2	6	1		14												12
		3		5	6	7	4	9	10	11	8	2		1														13
		3		5	6	7	4	9	10	11	8	2		1		14												14
			4	5	6	7	8	9	11	10	3	2		1		12												15
		3		5	6	7	8	9	10	11	12	14	2	1							4							16
		3			6	14	8	11	7	10		2		1						5	4	9						17
		3		10	6		8	9	7	11		2		1		14				5		4	12					18
		3		5	6	7		9	10	11	12	2		1	8						4							19
		3		5	6	7	14	9	10	11	12	2	4	1	8													20
		4	3	5		12	8	9	10	11		7	2	1								6						21
1		4	3	5	14		7	8	10	9		2	11			12	6											22
1		4	3	5		6	8	9	7	11	12	2							10	14								23
1				5		6	8	9		7	3	2	10						11	14		4	12					24
1	2	3		5	6	7	8	9	10	11												4						25
1	2	3		5	6	7	8	9	10	11	12	14										4						26
1	2	3		5	6	7	8	9	10	11	12	14										4						27
1	2	3			6	7	5	9	10	11	8		14									4						28
1		3			6	7		9	11	10	12	2							14	8		4		5				29
1		3			6	7	8	9	11	12	10	14	2									4		5				30
1		3			6	7		9	11	12	10	14	2				8					4		5				31
	2	3			6	7	8	9	10	11	12				1							4		5				32
		3		4			8	9	10	11	12		6		1	7						2		5				33
		3					8	9	10	11	12		6		1	7	14				2	4		5				34
		3				7	8	9	10	11	12	2	14		1						6	4		5				35
		3				7	8	9	6	11	10				1				12			4		5				36
		3				7	8	9	10	11		2	6		1				12			4		5				37
		3			6		8	9	10	11	14	7	2		1				12			4		5				38
		3			12		8	9	10	11	7	5	2		1						6	14	4					39
		3			12	14	8	9	10	11	7	5	2		1						6	4						40
		3			12		8	9	10	11	7	5	2		1						6	4	14					41
		3			6		8	9	10	11	7	14	2		1							4		5				42
14		3				7	8	9	12	11	10		2		1						6	4		5				43
						7	4	9	11		8		2		1						6	12		5	3	10	14	44

KILMARNOCK   Premier Division

Year Formed: 1869. *Ground & Address:* Rugby Park, Kilmarnock KA1 2DP. *Telephone:* 0563 25184.
Ground Capacity: total: 12,991. seated: 3141. *Size of Pitch:* 115yd × 75yd.
Chairman: Robert Fleeting. *Secretary:* Kevin Collins. *Commercial Manager:* Denny Martin. *Stadium Manager:* G. Hollas.
Manager: Tommy Burns. *Assistant Manager:* Billy Stark. *Physio:* Hugh Allan. *Coach:* —.
Managers since 1975: W. Fernie; D. Sneddon; J. Clunie; E. Morrison; J. Fleeting. *Club Nickname(s):* Killie. *Previous
Grounds:* Rugby Park (Dundonald Road); The Grange; Holm Quarry; Present ground since 1899.
Record Attendance: 35,995 v Rangers, Scottish Cup; 10 March, 1962.
Record Transfer Fee received: £120,000 for Davie Provan to Celtic (1978).
Record Transfer Fee paid: £100,000 for Bobby Williamson from Rotherham United (Nov 1990).
Record Victory: 11-1 v Paisley Academical, Scottish Cup; 18 Jan, 1930 (15-0 v Lanemark, Ayrshire Cup; 15 Nov, 1890).
Record Defeat: 1-9 v Celtic, Division I; 13 Aug, 1938.
Most Capped Player: Joe Nibloe, 11, Scotland.
Most League Appearances: 481: Alan Robertson, 1972-88.
Most League Goals in Season (Individual): 34: Harry 'Peerie' Cunningham 1927-28 and Andy Kerr 1960-61.
Most Goals Overall (Individual): 148: W. Culley; 1912-23.

KILMARNOCK 1992—93 LEAGUE RECORD

Match No.	Date		Venue	Opponents	Result	H/T Score	Lg. Pos.	Goalscorers	Atten dance
1	Aug	1	A	Morton	W 2-0	2-0	—	Mitchell, Jack	3274
2		4	A	Dumbarton	W 3-1	2-0	—	Paterson, Jack, Tait	2109
3		8	H	Raith R	D 1-1	0-1	2	Mitchell	4566
4		15	H	Dunfermline Ath	L 0-1	0-0	4		5347
5		22	A	Ayr U	L 0-2	0-0	7		5475
6		29	H	Meadowbank T	W 1-0	0-0	4	Campbell	2821
7	Sept	5	A	Clydebank	D 1-1	1-0	5	Williamson	2119
8		12	H	Stirling Albion	W 1-0	1-0	4	Jack	1326
9		19	H	St Mirren	L 1-2	0-1	5	Williamson (pen)	5291
10		26	H	Cowdenbeath	W 3-0	1-0	5	Williamson, Porteous, Jack	2798
11	Oct	3	A	Hamilton A	D 1-1	0-0	5	Skilling	2864
12		10	H	Morton	W 3-0	1-0	4	Burns 2, McCluskey	3991
13		17	A	Raith R	D 1-1	0-0	3	Reilly (pen)	3718
14		24	H	Clydebank	D 3-3	1-0	5	McCluskey 2, McSkimming	3582
15		31	A	Meadowbank T	D 1-1	1-0	4	McSkimming	1014
16	Nov	7	A	Dunfermline Ath	L 0-2	0-1	5		3924
17		14	H	Ayr U	W 3-0	2-0	4	McCluskey, Skilling, Traynor (og)	5709
18		21	A	St Mirren	W 1-0	1-0	3	Black (pen)	4686
19		28	H	Stirling Albion	W 1-0	1-0	2	Skilling	3526
20	Dec	1	H	Hamilton A	W 1-0	1-0	—	MacPherson	3711
21		5	A	Cowdenbeath	W 3-2	1-2	2	Jack, Reilly (pen), MacPherson	1176
22		19	H	Dumbarton	W 1-0	0-0	2	Campbell	3591
23		26	H	Dunfermline Ath	L 2-3	1-1	2	Stark, Reilly	5762
24		29	A	Morton	L 0-2	0-1	—		2958
25	Jan	2	A	Ayr U	W 1-0	0-0	2	Porteous	8424
26		16	H	Meadowbank T	W 5-0	4-0	2	Williamson, McCluskey 2, MacPherson, Porteous	3366
27		27	A	Hamilton A	W 2-1	2-1	—	Williamson, Porteous	3106
28		30	H	Raith R	W 3-0	0-0	2	Porteous 2, Stark	7003
29	Feb	13	A	Dumbarton	L 0-1	0-0	3		2346
30		16	A	Clydebank	L 0-2	0-0	—		2049
31		20	H	Cowdenbeath	D 1-1	0-0	3	Campbell	2928
32		27	H	St Mirren	W 1-0	0-0	3	McCluskey	6555
33	Mar	6	A	Stirling Albion	L 0-2	0-1	3		1327
34		9	H	Morton	D 2-2	1-0	—	Doak (og), Williamson	3407
35		13	A	Raith R	L 0-2	0-1	3		4738
36		20	H	Ayr U	D 1-1	1-1	3	Skilling	5660
37		27	A	Dunfermline Ath	D 2-2	0-0	4	Campbell, McSkimming	5223
38	Apr	3	H	Clydebank	W 6-0	4-0	3	McSkimming, McCluskey 2, MacPherson, Mitchell 2	3005
39		14	A	Meadowbank T	D 1-1	1-1	—	McSkimming	1492
40		17	H	Stirling Albion	W 3-0	1-0	2	McCluskey, Mitchell, McCarrison	3852
41		24	A	St Mirren	L 1-2	1-0	2	Mitchell	8432
42	May	1	H	Dumbarton	W 1-0	1-0	2	McCluskey	3793
43		8	A	Cowdenbeath	W 3-0	1-0	2	Stark, Crainie, MacPherson	2754
44		15	H	Hamilton A	D 0-0	0-0	2		12,830

Final League Position: 2

Honours

League Champions: Division I 1964-65. Division II 1897-98, 1898-99; *Runners-up:* Division I 1959-60, 1960-61, 1962-63, 1963-64. First Division 1975-76, 1978-79, 1981-82. Division II 1953-54, 1973-74. Second Division 1989-90.
Scottish Cup Winners: 1920, 1929; *Runners-up:* 1898, 1932, 1938, 1957, 1960.
League Cup Runners-up: 1952-53, 1960-61, 1962-63.
European: *European Cup:* 1965-66. *UEFA Cup (Fairs):* 1964-65 (semi-finals), 1969-70, 1970-71.
Club colours: Shirt: Blue and white vertical stripes. Shorts: Blue. Stockings: Blue.

Goalscorers: *League (67):* McCluskey 11, Mitchell 6, Porteous 6, Williamson 6 (1 pen), Jack 5, MacPherson 5, McSkimming 5, Campbell 4, Skilling 4, Reilly 3 (2 pens), Stark 3, Burns T 2, Black 1 (pen), Crainie 1, McCarrison 1, Paterson 1, Tait 1, own goals 2. *Scottish Cup (5):* Williamson 3, McCluskey 1, MacPherson 1. *Skol Cup (7):* Burns T 2, Campbell 1, Jack 1, McCluskey 1, McSkimming 1, Skilling 1. *B & Q Cup (4):* McCluskey 2, Burns T 1, Mitchell 1.

Geddes R 44	Burns H 9 + 1	Black T 10	Montgomerie R 42	Paterson C 21	MacPherson A 39 + 1	Porteous I 17 + 3	Skilling M 40	Jack R 11 + 7	Tait T 5	Mitchell A 26 + 6	Campbell C 13 + 11	Reilly M 18 + 1	Burns T 39	Williamson R 26 + 7	McSkimming S 35	McCluskey G 29 + 2	McStay W — + 1	Furphy W 1	Roberts M 4 + 1	Crainie D 3 + 6	Wilson T 18 + 1	Stark W 28	McCarrison D 6 + 2	Match No.
1	2	3	4	5	6	7	8	9	10	11	12													1
1	2	3	4	5	6	*7*	8	9	10	11	12	14												2
1	2	3	4	5		7	8	9	10	11				6	14									3
1	2	3	4				8	9	5	11				6	7	10	14							4
1	2	3	4				8	9	5	11	12			6	*7*	*10*	14							5
1		3	4	5	2	14	8			7	9			6	10	11								6
1		3	4	5	2		8		14	7	*9*			6	10	11	12							7
1			4	5	2		8	9		7			3	6	10	11								8
1	2		8	10	5	9	7	14					3	6	12	11	4							9
1		4		2	8	5	12	7	14				3	6	9	*11*	10							10
1		4	5	2		8	12	7					3	6	9	11	10							11
1		4	5	2	14	8	12	7					3	6	9	*11*	10							12
1		4	5	2		8		7	14				3	6	9	*11*	10							13
1		4	5	2		8		7					3	6	9	11	10							14
1		4		2	8	5	12	7					3	6	9	11	10							15
1		4		2	*8*	5	12	7					3	6	9	11	10		14					16
1		3	4		8		5			7	12		6			9			11			2	10	17
1		3	4		8		5			7			6			9			11			2	10	18
1		4		2		5	14	12	7	3	6		8	9		11			10					19
1		4			8		5	11		7	3	6			9			14			2	10		20
1		4			8		5	11		7	3	6			9						2	10		21
1		4			8		5	9		11	*7*	3	6	12					14			2	10	22
1		4			8		5	9		12	7	3	6	14				*11*				2	10	23
1		4			8		5			12	7	3	6	9	11							2	10	24
1		4			8	7	5					6	11	3	9							2	10	25
1		4			8	7	5			14		6	11	3	*9*				12			2	10	26
1		4			8	*7*	5			14		6	11	3	9							2	10	27
1		4			8	7	5					6	11	3	9							2	10	28
1		4			8	7	5			9		6	11	3					14			2	10	29
1		4		2		7	5			12	8	6	11	3					9				10	30
1	14	4			8	7	5			9	12	6	11	3								*2*	10	31
1	2		4		8		5					6	11	3	9							10	7	32
1	2		4		8	12	5			14		6	11	*3*	9							10	7	33
1	2		4		8		5					6	11	3	9							10	7	34
1	2		4	5	8	7				12		6	11	3	9							10		35
1		4	5				8			7		6	11	3	9							2	10	12	36
1		4	5	7			8			11		6	12	3	9							2	10	37
1		4	5	7			8			14	*11*	6	12	3	9							2	10	38
1		4	5	12			8			7		6	*11*	3	9							2	10	14	39
1		4	5	2			8			7		*6*		3	9				14			10	11	40
1		4	5	2			*8*			7		6	12	3	9				14			10	11	41
1		4	5	2			8			7	6			3	9				12			10	11	42
1		4	5				8			7	6			3	9				11			2	10	43
1		4	5				8		2	7	6			3	9				11			10		44

715

MEADOWBANK THISTLE Second Division

Year Formed: 1974. *Ground & Address:* Meadowbank Stadium, London Rd, Edinburgh EH7 6AE. *Telephone:* 031 661 5351.
Ground Capacity: total: 16,500. seated: 16,500. Main stand only used 7500. *Size of Pitch:* 105yd × 72yd.
Chairman: William L. Mill. *Secretary:* William P. Hunter. *Directors:* J. Bain, R. Clark, W. Hay. *Vice-chairman:* Hugh Cowan. *Commercial Manager:* W. P. Hunter.
Manager: Donald Park. *Assistant Manager:* George Mackie. *Club Doctor:* Dr M. M. Morrison. *Physio:* Arthur Duncan. *Coach:* M. McDermott.
Managers since 1975: John Bain; Alec Ness; Willie MacFarlane; Terry Christie. *Club Nickname(s):* Thistle; Wee Jags.
Previous Grounds: None.
Record Attendance: 4000 v Albion Rovers, League Cup 1st rd; 9 Sept, 1974.
Record Transfer Fee received: £115,000 for John Inglis to St Johnstone (1990).
Record Transfer Fee paid: £28,000 for Victor Kasule from Albion Rovers (1987).
Record Victory: 6-0 v Raith R, Second Division; 9 Nov, 1985.
Record Defeat: 0-8 v Hamilton A. Division II; 14 Dec, 1974.

MEADOWBANK THISTLE 1992—93 LEAGUE RECORD

Match No.	Date		Venue	Opponents	Result	H/T Score	Lg. Pos.	Goalscorers	Atten dance
1	Aug	1	A	Hamilton A	W 3-1	0-0	—	Irvine, Banks, Little	1518
2		4	A	Ayr U	W 2-1	1-1	—	Irvine, Little	1518
3		8	H	Morton	L 0-3	0-0	5		528
4		15	H	Stirling Albion	L 0-1	0-1	6		356
5		22	A	Cowdenbeath	W 5-1	1-1	4	Roseburgh, Little, Irvine 2, Coughlin	329
6		29	A	Kilmarnock	L 0-1	0-0	6		2821
7	Sept	5	H	St Mirren	L 0-2	0-0	7		1337
8		12	H	Clydebank	W 1-0	1-0	7	Roseburgh	300
9		19	A	Dunfermline Ath	L 1-3	1-1	8	Roseburgh	2624
10		26	H	Raith R	L 0-2	0-1	8		1142
11	Oct	3	A	Dumbarton	L 2-3	1-1	9	Coughlin, McLeod	550
12		10	H	Hamilton A	L 0-4	0-3	10		497
13		17	A	Morton	L 1-4	1-4	10	Rutherford	1255
14		24	A	St Mirren	D 1-1	1-0	10	Rutherford	3538
15		31	H	Kilmarnock	D 1-1	0-1	10	Wilson	1014
16	Nov	7	A	Stirling Albion	L 1-4	0-2	11	Little	389
17		14	H	Cowdenbeath	W 2-0	1-0	10	Bailey, Rutherford	273
18		21	H	Dunfermline Ath	W 3-2	0-2	10	McLeod, Wilson 2	709
19		28	A	Clydebank	D 0-0	0-0	10		965
20	Dec	1	A	Dumbarton	W 1-0	1-0	—	Wilson	624
21		5	A	Raith R	L 0-5	0-1	10		1930
22		19	H	Ayr U	W 1-0	0-0	10	Coyle	339
23	Jan	6	A	Hamilton A	L 0-2	0-0	—		1364
24		16	A	Kilmarnock	L 0-5	0-4	10		3366
25		20	A	Cowdenbeath	D 2-2	1-2	—	Bailey 2	160
26		27	H	Dumbarton	D 3-3	1-1	—	Rae, Rutherford 2	244
27		30	H	Morton	D 1-1	1-1	10	Bailey	369
28	Feb	3	H	St Mirren	L 1-2	1-0	—	Roseburgh	718
29		6	H	Stirling Albion	D 1-1	0-0	9	Kerr (og)	305
30		13	A	Ayr U	L 0-1	0-1	10		1406
31		20	H	Raith R	D 1-1	0-1	10	Bailey	988
32		27	A	Dunfermline Ath	L 2-3	1-2	10	Rae, Little	2343
33	Mar	10	H	Hamilton A	L 1-2	1-2	—	Bailey	271
34		13	A	Morton	L 0-2	0-0	11		1016
35		20	H	Cowdenbeath	W 3-1	0-0	10	Roseburgh (pen), Rutherford, Hutchison	179
36		27	A	Stirling Albion	D 2-2	0-1	10	McLeod, Roseburgh	475
37		31	H	Clydebank	L 0-1	0-1	—		249
38	Apr	3	A	St Mirren	W 2-1	1-0	10	Little 2	2619
39		14	H	Kilmarnock	D 1-1	1-1	—	Rutherford	1492
40		17	A	Clydebank	L 1-3	0-1	11	Rutherford	474
41		24	A	Dunfermline Ath	L 0-1	0-1	11		1384
42	May	1	H	Ayr U	L 1-2	1-1	11	Bailey	276
43		8	A	Raith R	L 2-3	1-1	11	Roseburgh, Rutherford	1961
44		15	H	Dumbarton	W 2-1	1-1	11	Duthie, Roseburgh	234

Final League Position: 11

Most Capped Player (under 18): I. Little.
Most League Appearances: 446: Walter Boyd, 1979-89.
Most League Goals in Season (Individual): 21: John McGachie, 1986-87. *(Team):* 69; Second Division, 1986-87.
Most Goals Overall (Individual): 64: David Roseburgh, 1986-93.

Honours
League Champions: Second Division 1986-87; *Runners-up:* Second Division 1982-83. First Division 1987-88.
Scottish Cup: —. *League Cup:* Semi-finals 1984-85.
Club colours: Shirt: Amber with black trim. Shorts: Black. Stockings: Amber.

Goalscorers: *League (51):* Rutherford 9, Roseburgh 8 (1 pen), Bailey 7, Little 7, Irvine 4, Wilson 4, McLeod 3, Coughlin 2, Rae 2, Banks 1, Coyle 1, Duthie 1, Hutchison 1, own goal 1. *Scottish Cup (1):* Rutherford 1. *Skol Cup (0).* *B & Q Cup (5):* Wilson 2, Kane 1, Logan 1, Roseburgh 1.

McQueen J 18	Coughlin J 35 + 2	Armstrong G 14	Williamson S 35	Grant D 7	Banks A 24 + 4	Wilson S 39	Ryrie B 7 + 4	Irvine W 6 + 3	Roseburgh D 35 + 2	Bailey L 29 + 1	Little I 26 + 13	Duthie M 5 + 13	McNeill W 2	Kane K 3 + 7	Young J 10 + 1	Murray M 31	Coyle M 4 + 3	Ellison S 26	Nicol A 11	Elder S 21 + 6	McLeod G 28	Rutherford P 27	Logan S — + 3	Graham T 2	Neil C 1 + 1	Scott S 1	Rae G 21	Hutchison M 13 + 3	Fleming D 3 + 1	Match No.
1	2	3	4	5	6	7	8		9	10	11	12	14																	1
1	2	3	4	5	6	8	7		9	10	11	12	14																	2
1	2	3	4	5	6	8	7		9	10	*11*	12	14																	3
1	2	3	4	5	6	8	7		9	10	11	12																		4
1	2	3	4	5	6	8	7	12	*10*	9	11			14																5
1	2	3	4	5	6	8	7		9	11	10			14																6
1	2	3	4	5	*6*				9	10	11	12		14	7	8														7
1	2	3	4		6	8	12	14	10		11				7	5	*9*													8
1	2	3	4		6	8		12	10		11			14	7	5	9													9
	2	3	4		6	8			10		7	12			11	9		1		5	14									10
	2	3	4		6				10		11	12			7	9		1		5	14	*8*								11
	2	3	4		6	8			10		12				7		1		*5*	11	9	14								12
		3	4		6	8			10	14	*7*				11		1	2		5	9	12								13
1	2	3	4		6	7			10		11				12				5		*8*	9	14							14
1	2		4		6	8			10		12			*9*	11	3				5	14	7								15
	2				6	8			10		12			9	*11*	3	1		4	14	7			5						16
	2		4		6	8				11	7					3	1		5	12	10	9								17
	2		4		6	8				11	7	12				3	1		5	10	9		14							18
			4			8				11	7	14				3	1	6	5	10	9		*2*							19
			4		6	8				11	7	14				3	1	2	5	10	9									20
12			4		6					11	*7*	14				3	1	2	5	10	9					8				21
			4		6	8				*11*	7					2	14	1	3	10	9						5			22
1			4	3	8				12	11	7					2	14		6	10	*9*						5			23
			4		6	8			12	11	7					2	1		*3*	10	9						5			24
	2		4			14			6	11	8	7				9	10	1		*3*							5	12		25
10			4	7	*11*	6	8				14					2	1			3	9						5			26
10			4		8	6	*7*	14	12					9		2	14	1		3							5	11		27
6			4		8	3	7	12	10					9		2	14		1								5	11		28
10			4		11	3	7									2		1	6	8	9						5			29
3			4		8	6		7	12							2		1		10	9						5	11		30
	2				8	6	7	10						9				1	3		4						5	11		31
	2				8	6	7	10	14									1	3		4	9					5	11		32
			4		8	14	6	7	12							2		1	3	10	9		5					11		33
6			4		8	14	3	7	10							2		1	5		*9*							11		34
3			4	14	8	6	7									2		1		10	9						5	11		35
3			4		8	6	7	12								2		1		10	9						5	11		36
3	*4*		4		8	6	7	12								2		1	14	10	9						5	11		37
			4	14	8	6	7	11								2		1	3	10	9		5					12		38
1	4			12	8	6	7									2			3	10	9						5	11		39
1	4			12	8	6	7	*11*								2			3	10	9						5	14		40
1	4			11	8	6	*7*	12								2			3	10	9						5		14	41
1	8	4			6	7										2			3	10	9						5	11		42
1	14	*4*			8	6	7	12								2				10	9						5	11	3	43
1		2			6	7		8								4				10	9						5	11	3	44

MONTROSE   Second Division

Year Formed: 1879. *Ground & Address:* Links Park, Wellington St, Montrose DD10 8QD. *Telephone:* 0674 73200.
Ground Capacity: total: 6500. seated: 268. *Size of Pitch:* 113yd × 70yd.
Chairman: Brian Keith. *Secretary:* Malcolm J. Watters. *Commercial Manager:* Allan Paul.
Manager: John Holt. *Assistant Manager:* —.
Physio: Neil Bryson. *Player/Coach:* Ross Jack.
Managers since 1975: A. Stuart; K. Cameron; R. Livingstone; S. Murray; D. D'Arcy; I. Stewart; C. McLelland; D. Rougvie; J. Leishman. *Club Nickname(s):* The Gable Endies. *Previous Grounds:* None.
Record Attendance: 8983 v Dundee, Scottish Cup 3rd rd; 17 Mar, 1973.
Record Transfer Fee received: £50,000 for Gary Murray to Hibernian (Dec 1980).
Record Transfer Fee paid: £17,500 for Jim Smith from Airdrieonians (Feb 1992).
Record Victory: 12-0 v Vale of Leithen, Scottish Cup 2nd rd; 4 Jan, 1975.
Record Defeat: 0-13 v Aberdeen; 17 Mar, 1951.
Most Capped Player: Alexander Keillor, 2 (6), Scotland.
Most League Appearances: 343: Martin Allan, 1983-93.

MONTROSE 1992—93 LEAGUE RECORD

Match No.	Date		Venue	Opponents	Result		H/T Score	Lg. Pos.	Goalscorers	Atten dance
1	Aug	8	A	East Stirling	W	2-0	0-0	—	Craib S (pen), Craib M	314
2		15	A	Brechin C	L	1-3	1-0	6	Callaghan	740
3		22	H	Stranraer	L	0-2	0-2	10		561
4		29	A	Berwick R	L	1-3	1-1	12	Fraser	519
5	Sept	5	H	Stenhousemuir	L	0-1	0-1	12		581
6		12	A	Albion R	D	2-2	1-1	11	Grant 2	217
7		19	H	Queen of the S	W	5-1	1-0	10	Grant, Fraser 2, Forsyth, Logan	511
8		26	A	Arbroath	W	4-3	1-1	8	Yeats, Fleming, Logan, Kelly	802
9	Oct	3	H	Forfar Ath	D	0-0	0-0	9		993
10		10	A	Clyde	W	2-1	2-0	7	Fraser 2	631
11		17	H	Queen's Park	L	0-2	0-2	8		705
12		24	A	East Fife	W	3-2	2-0	6	Bell (og), Grant 2	592
13		31	H	Alloa	L	1-4	0-2	9	Grant	666
14	Nov	7	A	Berwick R	L	0-3	0-0	11		310
15		14	A	Stenhousemuir	L	0-2	0-2	12		337
16		21	A	Queen of the S	W	1-0	1-0	9	Maver	389
17		28	H	Albion R	W	2-1	0-1	9	Allan, Christie	459
18	Dec	12	H	East Stirling	W	4-1	1-0	8	Nelson, Logan, Grant, Robertson	446
19	Jan	2	H	Brechin C	L	0-2	0-1	8		1211
20		9	A	Stranraer	L	1-3	1-0	9	Grant	543
21		19	A	Forfar Ath	L	3-4	0-1	—	Yeats, Craib M, Allan	852
22		23	H	East Fife	L	1-3	0-2	10	Grant	580
23		26	A	Alloa	L	0-3	0-1	—		326
24		30	H	Arbroath	D	1-1	1-0	11	Maver	865
25	Feb	6	A	Queen's Park	L	1-3	0-1	11	Yeats	357
26		13	H	Clyde	L	1-2	0-1	11	Allan (pen)	653
27		20	H	Stenhousemuir	L	1-4	1-2	12	Clouston (og)	377
28		27	A	Brechin C	D	0-0	0-0	11		620
29	Mar	6	H	Albion R	D	1-1	0-1	11	Craib S	335
30		13	A	Alloa	L	1-3	1-2	11	Grant	453
31		20	H	Forfar Ath	L	1-3	0-2	12	Logan	627
32		27	A	Berwick R	L	0-2	0-0	12		369
33	Apr	3	H	Queen of the S	L	0-1	0-0	13		408
34		10	A	Clyde	L	1-2	1-2	13	Maver	596
35		17	H	Arbroath	W	2-0	1-0	12	Craib S, Maver	946
36		24	A	East Fife	D	0-0	0-0	12		499
37	May	1	H	Stranraer	L	0-2	0-1	12		510
38		8	A	East Stirling	D	0-0	0-0	12		255
39		15	H	Queen's Park	W	3-1	1-0	12	Jack 2, Yeats	402

Final League Position: 12

Most League Goals in Season (Individual): 28: Brian Third, Division II; 1972-73.
Most Goals Overall (Individual): —.

Honours
League Champions: Second Division 1984-85, *Runners-up:* 1990-91.
Scottish Cup: Quarter-finals 1973, 1976.
League Cup: Semi-finals 1975-76.
Club colours: Shirt: Blue with white pin stripe. Shorts: White. Stockings: Red.

Goalscorers: *League (46):* Grant 10, Fraser 5, Logan 4, Maver 4, Yeats 4, Allan 3 (1 pen), Craib S 3 (1 pen), Craib M 2, Jack 2, Callaghan 1, Christie 1, Fleming 1, Forsyth 1, Kelly 1, Nelson 1, Robertson 1, own goals 2. *Scottish Cup (0). Skol Cup (0). B & Q Cup (9):* Grant 3, Fraser 2, Allan 1, Forsyth 1, Kelly 1, Logan 1.

Larter D 27	Morrison B 10 + 2	Fleming J 22	Fraser C 18	Forbes G 12	Forsyth S 14	Craib M 38	Robertson I 36	Logan A 17 + 4	Craib S 16 + 5	Dolan A 1 + 1	Callaghan W 4	Houghton G 10 + 2	Maver C 18 + 5	Smith J 28	Fotheringham J — + 1	Garden M 2	Kelly M 3 + 5	Irvine N 25	Grant D 28	Yeats C 20 + 7	McGovern P 2	Allan M 20 + 5	Smith L — + 1	Furphy W 1	Christie G 13 + 7	Kasule V 1	Moffat J 12	Nelson M 5	Masson P — + 3	Burnett C 8	Davidson G 1	Lavelle M 6 + 2	Ritchie M 5	Jack R 6	Match No.
1	2	3	4	5	6	7	8	9	10	11																									1
1	2	3		5	6	4	8	10	11			9	14	7																					2
1	12	3			6	4	2	11	9			10	8	7				5	14																3
1		3	7	6	10	4	2	8	11	12	9			5																					4
1		10	6	7	4	3	8	11				9	12	5				2	14																5
1		7	6	2	4	3	14							5				10	8	9		11													6
1		7	6	2	4	3	14	10						5					8	9		11													7
1		3		7	4	2	10						6	5				12	8	9		11													8
1		3	7	2	6	4	9	11						5				14	8			10													9
1		3	7	2	6	4	9							5				14	8	10		11													10
1		3	7			4		11				2	9	5	14			6	8	10		12													11
1		3	7	5	2	4			10			8	6					11	9	14		12													12
1		3	7	5	2	4						8	6					11	9			10													13
1	12	3	7			4						6	2	5				11	8	9	14	10													14
1	2		4	6	3		7							5					8	9		11			10		14								15
1	2	11	5	3			7												8	9	4	6			10		12								16
1	2		5	6	3		7						14						8	9	4	6			10		12	11							17
	2	3	4	5			7										11	14	8	9		10								6	1				18
	2	3	4	5	6								10						8	9		12			7					11	1				19
	2	3	4	5			8		10				14	6					9	7		11			12						1				20
	2	3	4	5			8		10				6						9	7		11			12		14				1				21
		3	4		6				10				12	5					9	8		11			7					2	1				22
		3	4						10				12	5				7	9	8		11			6					2	1				23
		3	4	5	2									7					10	9		6			11					8	1				24
		3	4	5	2									7					9	8		11			10		12			6	1				25
		3	4		6		8							5		9				10					14			11	2	7	1				26
		3	4		6		8							5		9		7		10					12			11	14	2	1				27
		3	6	7					12					5			9	11	8	10					4					2	1				28
		3	6	7										5			9	14	4	10		12			8			11		2	1				29
1		3	6	7					12					5			9	14	4	10					8			11		2					30
1		3	6										14	5			9	11	7	4		8			10			12		2					31
1		3	4						12				2	5					8	10		11			7								6	9	32
1		3	4						12				2	5				11	8	10					7								6	9	33
1		3	4				8						2	5				7	11	10		9			12							14	6		34
1		3	4				8						2	5				7	10	12					11								6	9	35
1		3	4				8						2	5				7	10	14		12			11								6	9	36
1		3	4				8						2	5				7	12	10	6	9			11										37
1		3					8						2	5				7	11	10		6			14								4	9	38
1	2	3							11					5				7	6	14		10			12							8	4	9	39

GREENOCK MORTON · First Division

Year Formed: 1874. *Ground & Address:* Cappielow Park, Sinclair St, Greenock. *Telephone:* 0475 23511.
Ground Capacity: total: 14,250. seated: 5150. *Size of Pitch:* 110yd × 71yd.
Chairman: John Wilson. *Secretary:* Mrs Jane Rankin.
Manager: Allan McGraw. *Assistant Manager:* John McMaster. *Physio:* John Tierney. *Coach:* Billy Osborne.
Managers since 1975: Joe Gilroy; Benny Rooney; Alex Miller; Tommy McLean; Willie McLean. *Club Nickname(s):* The
Ton. *Previous Grounds:* Grant Street 1874, Gravel Park 1875, Cappielow Park 1879, Ladyburn Park 1882, (Cappielow
Park 1883).
Record Attendance: 23,000 v Celtic; 1922.
Record Transfer Fee received: £350,000 for Neil Orr to West Ham U.
Record Transfer Fee paid: £150,000 for Allan Mahood from Nottingham Forest.
Record Victory: 11-0 v Carfin Shamrock, Scottish Cup 1st rd; 13 Nov, 1886.
Record Defeat: 1-10 v Port Glasgow Ath, Division II; 5 May, 1894 and v St Bernards, Division II; 14 Oct, 1933.
Most Capped Player: Jimmy Cowan, 25, Scotland.
Most League Appearances: 358: David Hayes, 1969-84.

MORTON 1992—93 LEAGUE RECORD

Match No.	Date		Venue	Opponents	Result		H/T Score	Lg. Pos.	Goalscorers	Atten dance
1	Aug	1	H	Kilmarnock	L	0-2	0-2	—		3274
2		4	H	Clydebank	W	5-1	2-1	—	Alexander, Mathie 3, Hopkin	1154
3		8	A	Meadowbank T	W	3-0	0-0	4	Alexander, Mathie, Mahood	528
4		15	A	Dumbarton	W	1-0	0-0	3	Mathie	1257
5		22	H	St Mirren	L	0-1	0-1	3		4040
6		29	H	Cowdenbeath	W	1-0	0-0	2	Alexander	1446
7	Sept	5	A	Ayr U	W	2-0	1-0	2	Johnstone, Mahood	2300
8		12	A	Raith R	L	1-2	1-1	3	Alexander	2613
9		19	H	Hamilton A	W	2-1	0-0	3	Alexander, Mahood	1851
10		26	A	Stirling Albion	D	1-1	1-1	4	McArthur	750
11	Oct	3	H	Dunfermline Ath	L	0-1	0-1	4		2480
12		10	A	Kilmarnock	L	0-3	0-1	6		3991
13		17	H	Meadowbank T	W	4-1	4-1	5	Mahood, Mathie, Johnstone, Armstrong (og)	1255
14		24	H	Ayr U	W	2-1	1-1	4	Rafferty, Lilley	1787
15		31	A	Cowdenbeath	W	3-1	1-0	3	Lilley, Mathie 2	610
16	Nov	7	H	Dumbarton	L	1-2	0-2	4	Johnstone	1867
17		14	A	St Mirren	W	3-2	1-0	3	McArthur, Alexander, McDonald	5148
18		24	A	Hamilton A	L	1-3	1-2	4	McInnes	2018
19		28	H	Raith R	L	3-4	2-1	6	Mahood 2, Tolmie	2583
20	Dec	2	A	Dunfermline Ath	D	0-0	0-0	—		2544
21		5	H	Stirling Albion	D	2-2	1-0	5	Johnstone, MacCabe	1343
22		19	A	Clydebank	D	2-2	2-0	6	Mathie 2	901
23		26	A	Dumbarton	L	1-3	0-0	6	Mathie (pen)	1456
24		29	H	Kilmarnock	W	2-0	1-0	—	Alexander, Johnstone	2958
25	Jan	2	H	St Mirren	D	1-1	0-1	6	McInnes	5170
26		30	A	Meadowbank T	D	1-1	1-1	6	McArthur	369
27	Feb	2	H	Cowdenbeath	W	3-2	1-2	—	MacCabe 3	814
28		6	H	Dunfermline Ath	L	0-1	0-1	6		1700
29		9	A	Ayr U	D	0-0	0-0	—		1675
30		13	A	Clydebank	W	2-0	0-0	6	McArthur, Lilley	1245
31		20	A	Stirling Albion	W	2-0	1-0	6	Lilley, McArthur	422
32		27	H	Hamilton A	L	1-2	0-1	6	Alexander	1560
33	Mar	6	A	Raith R	L	0-2	0-1	6		1938
34		9	A	Kilmarnock	D	2-2	0-1	—	Doak, Tolmie	3407
35		13	H	Meadowbank T	W	2-0	0-0	6	McArthur, Mathie	1016
36		20	A	St Mirren	L	0-2	0-0	6		2697
37		27	A	Dumbarton	W	2-1	1-0	6	Gahagan, Alexander	953
38	Apr	3	A	Ayr U	W	1-0	0-0	6	Johnstone	997
39		10	A	Cowdenbeath	W	1-0	0-0	5	Rafferty	244
40		17	H	Raith R	D	1-1	1-0	6	Alexander	1792
41		24	A	Hamilton A	L	1-2	1-1	6	Gahagan	1511
42	May	1	A	Clydebank	D	2-2	2-1	6	MacCabe 2	726
43		8	H	Stirling Albion	L	1-3	1-1	6	Mathie	1058
44		15	A	Dunfermline Ath	W	2-1	1-0	6	McEwan 2	3106

Final League Position: 6

Most League Goals in Season (Individual): 58: Allan McGraw, Division II; 1963-64.
Most Goals Overall (Individual): —.

Honours
League Champions: First Division 1977-78, 1983-84, 1986-87. Division II 1949-50, 1963-64, 1966-67.
Scottish Cup Winners: 1922; *Runners-up:* 1948. *League Cup Runners-up:* 1963-64.
B&Q Cup: Runners-up: 1992-93.
European: *UEFA Cup (Fairs):* 1968-69.
Club colours: Shirt: Royal blue tartan. Shorts: Royal blue. Stockings: Royal blue.

Goalscorers: *League (65):* Mathie 13 (1 pen), Alexander 10, Johnstone 6, McArthur 6, MacCabe 6, Mahood 6, Lilley 4, Gahagan 2, McEwan 2, McInnes 2, Rafferty 2, Tolmie 2, Doak 1, Hopkin 1, McDonald 1, own goal 1. *Scottish Cup (0).* *Skol Cup (2):* Alexander 1, Mathie 1. *B & Q Cup (14):* Mathie 7, Alexander 4, Lilley 1, Mahood 1, Tolmie 1.

Wylie D 44	Collins D 41	McArthur S 39	Rafferty S 31 + 7	Doak M 27 + 4	Boag J 5	Mathie A 31 + 1	Mahood A 17	Alexander R 30 +	McInnes D 40	Hopkin D 9	Lilley D 16 + 6	McDonald I 14 + 11	MacCabe D 10 + 3	Johnstone D 32	Pickering M 25 + 3	Fowler J 13 + 6	Tolmie J 14 + 7	McCahill S 23 + 1	Gahagan J 16 + 3	McGhee D 3	Thomson R 2 + 6	Sanders G — + 1	Shearer N 1	McEwan A 1 + 1	Match No.
1	2	3	4	5	6	7	8	9	10	11															1
1	2	3	4	5	6	7	8	9	10	11	12	14													2
1	2	3	4	5	6	7	8	9	10	11															3
1	2	3	4	5	6	7	8	9	10	11	12	14													4
1	2	3	4	5	6	7	8		10	11	9			12											5
1	2	3	4	5		7	8	9	10	11				6											6
1	2	3	4	5		7	8	9	10	11				6											7
1	2	3	4	5		7	8	9	10	11	12			6		14									8
1	2	3				7	8	9		11	10	4	12	6	5	14									9
1	2	3		5		7	8	9	10		11			6	4										10
1	2	3		5		7	8	9	10		11			6	4	14	12								11
1	2		4	5		7	8		10					6	11	9	3								12
1	2	11	4	5		7	8						12	6	3	10	9								13
1	2	11	4	5		7	8		10			14	12	6	3		9								14
1	2		4	5		7	8		10		11		12	6	3	14	9								15
1	2		4			7	8		10	9				6	3	14	11	5							16
1	2	8	14	5		7		9	10			4		6	3	12	11								17
1	2	8	4	5		7		9	10			12		6	3	11	14								18
1	2	12	5			7	8	9	10			4		6	3	11	14								19
1	2	3	4	5		7		9	10			12		6		8	14	11							20
1	2	10	4	5				9				8	14	6	3	12	11			7					21
1	2		4	5		7		9	10					6		8	11	3	14						22
1	2	3	14			7		9	10			4		6		8	12	5	11						23
1	2	3	4			7		9	10			14		6		8	12	5	11						24
1	2	3	4			7		9	10					6		8	12	5	11						25
1	2	11	4									14	10		9	12	8	5	3		6	7			26
1	2	11	14												9	10	4	8	5	3	7	12	6		27
1	2	3	14												9	10	4	8	5	12	7	11	6		28
1	2	11	4	12											9	10	14	8	5	3	6		7		29
1	2	11	4	12											9	10	14	8	5	3	6		7		30
1	2	11	4												9	10	8	7	6	3	5				31
1	2	8	4	5					12						9	10	11	7	6	3	14				32
1	2	10	4			7									9	11	12	6	3	8	5	14			33
1	2	3	12	5		7									10	9	4	8	11		6	14			34
1	2	3	4	5		7									10	9	12	14	8		11	6			35
1	2	8		5		7									10	9	4	3	12	6	11	14			36
1	2	8		12											9	10	7	4	6	3	5	11	14		37
1	2	8		12											9	10	7	4	6	3	5	11	14		38
1	2	8		12	6										9	10	7	4		3	5	11			39
1	2	8	4	6											9	10	7			3	5	11			40
1	2	8	4						10						7	9		3	6		5	11	14		41
1		3	4			7			10						9	5			6	11	8	14		2	42
1		3	4			7			10						9	6	2	5	11		8	14			43
1		3	4	6		7			10						2		5	9	11		8				44

MOTHERWELL   Premier Division

Year Formed: 1886. *Ground & Address:* Fir Park, Motherwell ML1 2QN. *Telephone:* 0698 261437/8/9.
Ground Capacity: total: 15,500. seated: 6500. *Size of Pitch:* 110yd × 75yd.
Chairman: John C. Chapman. *Secretary:* Alan C. Dick. *Commercial Manager:* John Swinburne.
Manager: Tommy McLean. *Assistant Manager:* Tom Forsyth. *Physio:* John Porteous. *Coach:* Cameron Murray.
Managers since 1975: Ian St. John; Willie McLean; Rodger Hynd; Ally MacLeod; David Hay; Jock Wallace; Bobby
Watson. *Club Nickname(s):* The Well. *Previous Grounds:* Roman Road, Dalziel Park.
Record Attendance: 35,632 v Rangers, Scottish Cup 4th rd replay; 12 Mar, 1952.
Record Transfer Fee received: £800,000 for Tom Boyd to Chelsea (June 1991).
Record Transfer Fee paid: £175,000 for Brian Martin from St Mirren (Oct 1991).
Record Victory: 12-1 v Dundee U, Division II; 23 Jan, 1954.
Record Defeat: 0-8 v Aberdeen, Premier Division; 26 Mar, 1979.
Most Capped Player: George Stevenson, 12, Scotland.

MOTHERWELL 1992—93 LEAGUE RECORD

Match No.	Date		Venue	Opponents	Result	H/T Score	Lg. Pos.	Goalscorers	Atten dance
1	Aug	1	H	Dundee U	L	0-1	0-0	—	5037
2		4	H	Hibernian	L	1-2	0-0	—	Kirk	5391
3		8	A	Celtic	D	1-1	0-0	11	Kirk	24,935
4		15	H	Aberdeen	W	2-1	1-1	9	Arnott, Angus	5561
5		22	A	Partick T	D	2-2	1-1	8	Ferguson, Arnott	4564
6		29	A	Hearts	L	0-1	0-1	9		7285
7	Sept	2	H	Rangers	L	1-4	0-1	—	Arnott	10,074
8		12	A	Dundee	L	1-2	0-1	11	O'Donnell	3792
9		19	H	St Johnstone	D	3-3	1-1	11	Cooper (pen), Baker, Kirk	4002
10		26	A	Falkirk	L	0-1	0-1	12		4275
11	Oct	3	H	Airdrieonians	W	2-0	0-0	11	Simpson, Kirk	4720
12		7	A	Dundee U	D	1-1	0-0	—	McCart	5380
13		17	H	Celtic	L	1-3	1-1	11	McCart	10,016
14		24	H	Hearts	L	1-3	0-1	11	Kirk	5171
15		31	H	Rangers	L	2-4	1-2	12	Angus, Martin	38,719
16	Nov	7	H	Partick T	L	0-2	0-2	12		5379
17		11	A	Aberdeen	L	0-2	0-0	—		8725
18		24	A	St Johnstone	L	0-2	0-1	—		3582
19		28	H	Dundee	L	1-3	0-1	12	Arnott	3534
20	Dec	1	A	Hibernian	D	2-2	1-1	—	Ferguson, Kirk	4777
21		5	H	Falkirk	W	3-1	1-1	12	Kirk, Martin, McGrillen	5018
22		12	A	Airdrieonians	W	2-0	0-0	12	O'Donnell, Arnott	3630
23		26	H	Aberdeen	L	0-2	0-0	12		7907
24	Jan	2	A	Partick T	W	1-0	1-0	12	Martin	6467
25		23	A	Hearts	D	0-0	0-0	11		6610
26		30	A	Celtic	D	1-1	0-0	11	Angus	18,513
27	Feb	2	H	Dundee U	W	2-0	1-0	—	Kirk, McGrillen	3783
28		6	H	Airdrieonians	D	0-0	0-0	10		5382
29		13	H	Hibernian	D	0-0	0-0	10		5021
30		20	A	Falkirk	W	3-1	0-0	10	Weir (og), McGrillen, Dolan	4536
31		23	A	Rangers	L	0-4	0-0	—		14,006
32		27	H	St Johnstone	D	1-1	1-1	10	Dolan	4278
33	Mar	6	A	Dundee	D	1-1	0-1	9	Griffin	3230
34		9	A	Dundee U	D	0-0	0-0	—		5134
35		20	H	Partick T	L	2-3	2-0	10	Kirk, McGrillen	6499
36		27	A	Aberdeen	L	0-1	0-1	10		9155
37	Apr	3	H	Celtic	W	2-0	2-0	9	Kirk, Cooper	10,102
38		10	A	Rangers	L	0-1	0-0	10		41,353
39		17	A	Dundee	L	1-2	0-1	10	McGrillen	4287
40		20	H	Hearts	W	2-1	2-0	—	O'Donnell, McGrillen	4355
41		24	A	St Johnstone	D	0-0	0-0	9		5544
42	May	1	A	Hibernian	L	0-1	0-0	10		4799
43		8	H	Falkirk	W	2-1	1-0	10	McCart, Arnott	8577
44		15	A	Airdrieonians	W	2-1	2-1	9	Graham, O'Donnell	3088

Final League Position: 9

Most League Appearances: 626: Bobby Ferrier, 1918-37.
Most League Goals in Season (Individual): 52: Willie McFadyen, Division I; 1931-32.
Most Goals Overall (Individual): 283: Hugh Ferguson, 1916-25.

Honours
League Champions: Division I 1931-32. First Division 1981-82, 1984-85. Division II 1953-54, 1968-69; *Runners-up:* Division I 1926-27, 1929-30, 1932-33, 1933-34. Division II 1894-95, 1902-03. *Scottish Cup:* 1952, 1991; *Runners-up:* 1931, 1933, 1939, 1951.
League Cup: 1950-51. *Runners-up:* 1954-55 *Scottish Summer Cup:* 1944, 1965.
Club colours: Shirt: Amber with claret hoop and trimmings. Shorts: Claret. Stockings: Amber.

Goalscorers: *League (46):* Kirk 10, Arnott 6, McGrillen 6, O'Donnell 4, Angus 3, McCart 3, Martin 3, Cooper 2 (1 pen), Dolan 2, Ferguson 2, Baker 1, Graham 1, Griffin 1, Simpson 1, own goal 1. *Scottish Cup (0).* *Skol Cup (4):* Ferguson 3, Angus 1.

Thomson W 9	Sneddon A 16	McKinnon R 35	Simpson N 12	Kromheer E 11 + 1	Nijholt L 31 + 3	Kirk S 26 + 14	Martin B 43 + 1	Arnott D 28 + 5	Angus I 25 + 6	Cooper D 42 + 1	Shepstone P 1	Ferguson I 11 + 4	McLeod J 4 + 6	Shepherd A 2 + 3	Gardner J 1 + 2	O'Donnell P 32	Philliben J 31	Baker P 5 + 4	McCart C 28 + 1	Dykstra S 35	Griffin J 24 + 1	Bryce S 1	Dolan J 15 + 10	Gourlay A — + 2	Verheul B — + 1	McGrillen P 12 + 10	Graham A 4	Match No.
1	2	3	4	5	6	7	8	9	10	11		14																1
1	2	3	4	5	6	10	8	9		11		7	14															2
1	2	3	4	5	6	7	8	9	12	11			14			10												3
1	2	3	4	5		8	6	9	10	11		7	12															4
1	2	3	4	5	6		8	9		11		7	14			10												5
1		3		5	2	14	4	9	12	11		7	8			10			6									6
1	2	3		5		12	4	9	8	11		7				10		14	6									7
1		3		5	2	12	4	9	8	11		7				10			6									8
		3		5		8	4	9	6	11		12				10				1	2	7	14					9
		3		5			8			11		12	7	14		10		9	6	1	2		4					10
		3			2	14	4		12	11		9	7			10	5		6	1			8					11
	8	3			2	7	4	9	10	11		14					5		6	1			12					12
	2	3	4			7	8	9	10	11		12					5		6	1			14					13
		3		5	2		8	9	10	11		12	7						6	1	4		14					14
	2	3		5			4		10	11		14						9	6	1			8			12	7	15
1		3		5	2	7	8	9	10	11									6		4		14			12		16
	2	3		6		12	4	9	10	11		7	14				5			1			8					17
	2	3		7	6	14	4		8	11		12				10	5	9		1								18
		3			2	7	8			11						10	5	9	6	1	4		14					19
		3			2	14	8	9		11		7				10	5		6	1	4							20
		3			2	7	8	9		11						10	5		6	1	4		12			14		21
		3	4			14	8	9		11		7	12			10	5		6	1	2							22
	2	3			12	7		9		11						10	5		6	1	4		8					23
		3	4		2	7	8	9		11		14	12			10	5		6	1								24
		3			2	12	8	9		11		7	14			10	5		6	1	4							25
		3			2	12	4		6	11		14				10	5			1	7		8				9	26
	6			7	2	14	4			11						10	5	9		1	3		8			12		27
		3			2	7	4	9		11						10	5		6	1			8			14		28
		3			2	7	4	9	12	11						10	5		6	1			8			14		29
	6	3			2	7	4	8		11		14				10	5			1						12	9	30
	6	3			2	12	4			11						10	5			1			8	14		7	9	31
		3			6	7	4			11		12					5			1	2		8	10		9		32
		3			6	12	4			11		7					5			1	2		8	10		9		33
		3				7	4	9	8	11						10	5		6	1	2		14			12		34
		3			2	7	4		12	11						10	5		6	1			8				9	35
		3			2	7	4	9	8	11						10	5		6	1			14			12		36
		3				7	4	9	8	11						10	5		6	1	2		14					37
		3			12	7	4	9	8	11						10	5		6	1	2		14					38
		3	4			7	8			11		14				10	5		6	1	2						9	39
		3			2	12	4			11		7				10	5		6	1			8			14	9	40
		3			2	12	4		14	11		7				10	5		6	1			8				9	41
		3			2	12	4	9		11		7				10	5		6	1			8			14		42
		3			2	7	4	8	12	11						10	5		6	1	14						9	43
		3				12	4	14	8							10	5		6	1	2		7			11	9	44

PARTICK THISTLE   Premier Division

Year Formed: 1876. *Ground & Address:* Firhill Park, 80 Firhill Rd, Glasgow G20 7BA. *Telephone:* 041 945 4811.
Ground Capacity: total: 19,336. seated: 2906. *Size of Pitch:* 110yd × 74yd.
Chairman: James Oliver. *Company Secretary:* Robert Reid. *Secretary:* Robert Reid. *General Commercial Manager:* Jez Moxey.
Manager: John Lambie. *Assistant Manager:* Gerry Collins. *Physio:* Harrison Stevenson.
Managers since 1975: R. Auld; P. Cormack; B. Rooney; R. Auld; D. Johnstone; W. Lamont; S. Clark. *Club Nickname(s):* The Jags. *Previous Grounds:* Jordanvale Park; Muirpark; Inchview; Meadowside Park.
Record Attendance: 49,838 v Rangers, Division I; 18 Feb, 1922.
Record Transfer Fee received: £200,000 for Mo Johnston to Watford.
Record Transfer Fee paid: £85,000 for Andy Murdoch from Celtic (Feb 1991).
Record Victory: 16-0 v Royal Albert, Scottish Cup 1st rd; 17 Jan, 1931.
Record Defeat: 0-10 v Queen's Park, Scottish Cup; 3 Dec, 1881.
Most Capped Player: Alan Rough, 51 (53), Scotland.

PARTICK THISTLE 1992—93 LEAGUE RECORD

Match No.	Date		Venue	Opponents	Result	H/T Score	Lg. Pos.	Goalscorers	Atten dance
1	Aug	1	H	Airdrieonians	W 1-0	0-0	—	Irons	4483
2		4	H	Dundee U	L 0-1	0-0	—		5128
3		3	A	St Johnstone	D 1-1	1-0	6	McGlashan	4401
4		15	A	Hearts	L 1-2	0-0	10	Britton (pen)	7911
5		22	H	Motherwell	D 2-2	1-1	9	Cameron, Shaw	4564
6		29	H	Dundee	W 6-3	2-2	6	Shaw 4 (1 pen), Paterson (og), Britton	4520
7	Sept	5	A	Falkirk	W 1-0	1-0	5	Britton	5691
8		12	H	Rangers	L 1-4	1-1	7	Shaw	18,752
9		19	A	Aberdeen	L 0-2	0-0	8		9755
10		26	A	Celtic	W 2-1	1-0	7	Shaw 2	21,486
11	Oct	3	H	Hibernian	D 2-2	1-0	7	Farningham 2	6332
12		10	A	Airdrieonians	D 2-2	2-1	6	Shaw, Cameron	4204
13		17	H	St Johnstone	W 1-0	0-0	5	Farningham	4211
14		24	A	Dundee	W 2-0	1-0	5	Jamieson, Cameron	5428
15		31	A	Falkirk	L 1-2	0-1	6	Britton	5535
16	Nov	7	A	Motherwell	W 2-0	2-0	5	Jamieson, Craig	5379
17		10	H	Hearts	D 1-1	0-1	—	Britton	5355
18		24	H	Aberdeen	L 0-7	0-1	—		3986
19		28	A	Rangers	L 0-3	0-0	6		40,939
20	Dec	1	A	Dundee U	L 1-2	0-1	—	Britton	5241
21		5	H	Celtic	L 2-3	1-2	6	Farningham 2	13,312
22		12	A	Hibernian	L 0-1	0-0	8		6077
23		19	A	Airdrieonians	D 1-1	0-0	7	Johnston	3274
24		26	A	Hearts	D 1-1	0-0	8	Britton	9922
25	Jan	2	H	Motherwell	L 0-1	0-1	8		6467
26		27	H	Dundee	W 2-0	1-0	—	Kinnaird, Britton	2514
27		30	A	St Johnstone	D 0-0	0-0	8		4555
28	Feb	2	A	Falkirk	L 2-4	1-2	—	Tierney, Shaw	4690
29		13	H	Dundee U	L 0-4	0-1	9		3846
30		16	H	Hibernian	L 0-3	0-1	—		3064
31		20	A	Celtic	D 0-0	0-0	9		15,561
32	Mar	2	A	Aberdeen	L 0-1	0-0	—		8287
33		9	A	Airdrieonians	D 2-2	1-0	—	Cameron (pen), Irons	3080
34		13	H	St Johnstone	D 1-1	0-1	9	Byrne (og)	3534
35		20	A	Motherwell	W 3-2	0-2	8	Farningham, McGlashan, Jamieson	6499
36		27	H	Hearts	D 1-1	1-0	8	Farningham	4594
37	Apr	3	A	Dundee	W 1-0	1-0	7	Cameron (pen)	3846
38		10	H	Falkirk	L 0-1	0-1	7		4677
39		17	A	Rangers	L 1-3	0-1	8	Britton	42,636
40		20	H	Aberdeen	L 1-3	0-2	—	Taylor	3445
41	May	1	A	Dundee U	L 1-3	0-2	9	Britton	5590
42		4	H	Rangers	W 3-0	1-0	—	Farningham, Tierney, Britton	9303
43		8	H	Celtic	L 0-1	0-1	9		9834
44		15	A	Hibernian	W 1-0	1-0	8	Britton	5467

Final League Position: 8

Most League Appearances: 410: Alan Rough, 1969-82.
Most League Goals in Season (Individual): 41: Alec Hair, Division I; 1926-27.
Most Goals Overall (Individual): —.

Honours
League Champions: First Division 1975-76. Division II 1896-97, 1899-1900, 1970-71; *Runners-up:* Division II 1901-02.
Scottish Cup Winners: 1921; *Runners-up:* 1930.
League Cup Winners: 1971-72; *Runners-up:* 1953-54, 1956-57, 1958-59.
European: *UEFA Cup:* 6 matches (*Fairs Cup:* 1963-64. *UEFA Cup:* 1972-73).
Club colours: Shirt: Red and yellow vertical stripes. Shorts: Black. Stockings: Black.

Goalscorers: *League (50):* Britton 12 (1 pen), Shaw 10 (1 pen), Farningham 8, Cameron 5 (2 pens), Jamieson 3, Irons 2, McGlashan 2, Tierney 2, Craig 1, Johnston 1, Kinnaird 1, Taylor 1, own goals 2. *Scottish Cup (0). Skol Cup (4):* Britton 1, Farningham 1, Kinnaird 1, Shaw 1

Nelson C 27	Law R 34	McVicar D 38	Chisholm G 8+1	Tierney G 16	Clark M 8	McWalter M 7+5	Peebles G 8+1	McGlashan C 12+10	Irons D 43	Cameron I 38+3	Shaw G 28+3	Kinnaird P 14+6	Britton G 39+1	Farningham R 35+2	McLaughlin P 22+1	Craig A 26+3	Jamieson W 26+2	Johnston S 11+4	Murdoch A 17	English I 3+10	Smith T 2	Magee K —+5	Palin L 5	Broddie J 6	Taylor A 8	McKilligan N 3+2	Docherty S —+1	Match No.
1	2	3	4	5	6	7	8	9	10	11	12		14															1
1	2	3	4	5	6		8	9	10	11	12		14															2
1	2	3	4	5	6		8	9	10	11	12	7	14															3
1	2	3		5	4			10	11	7		14	9	8	6													4
1	2	3	6	5		12	4	10	11	7			9	8														5
1	2	3	6	5			4	10	11	7			9	8	14													6
1	2	3	6	5			4	10	11	7			9	8														7
1	2	3	4					10	11	7	6		9	8	12	5	14											8
1	2	3	6				4	12	10	11	7		9	8		5	14											9
	2		4			14		10	6	7	11	9	5	3	8				1									10
1	2	3				14		10	6	7	11	9	4	5	8	12												11
1	2	3				12		10	6	7	11	9	4	8	5													12
1	2	3		6				10		7	11	9	4	8	5													13
1	2	3		6		12		10	14	7	11	9	4	8	5													14
1	2	3				14		10	6	7	11	9	4	8	5													15
		3	2					12	10	11	7	14	9	4	6	8	5	1										16
	8	3	2			14		10	11	7		9	4	6	5	1												17
			5	2		6	11	7	10	9		3	4	8	1	14												18
		3	7		11	10	12		14	9	2	6	5	4	1	8												19
		3				10	6		14	9	2	4	5	8	1	11	7											20
1	2	3				10	6	7	11	9	4		8	5	14													21
1	2	3				12		10	6	7	11	9	4	5	8													22
1	2	3		9				10	6	7	11		4	5	8		14											23
1	2	3				11	10	7		9	4	5	8	6	12	14												24
1		3				11	10		7	9	2	4	8	6	12	5												25
	2	3	5			10	6	7	11	9	4	8		1	12													26
	2	3	5			10	6	7	11	9	4	8		1	12													27
	2	3	5			12	10	6	7	11	9	4	8	14	1													28
		3	5	6	2	14	12	7	9	4	8	1				10	11											29
1	2		5	11		10	6	9		4	8	14	12						7	3								30
1	2					10	6	9	7	4	8	5		12		11	3											31
1	2	3				14	10	6	9	8	4	5	12			7	11											32
1	2	3				14	6	11	7	9	8	4	5			10												33
1	2	3				7	6	10	9	8	5	4	12	14	11													34
	2	3				10	6	11	9	8	14	5	4	1			7											35
		3				10	6	11	7	9	2	5	4	1	14		8											36
		3				10	6	11	7	2	14	9	5	4	1	12	8											37
		3				10	6	11	7	2		5	4	1	9	8	14											38
		3				10	6	11	9	2	4	7	5	12	14	8												39
	2	3				6	9	8	4	10	5	1	11	7														40
	2	3				6	10	9	8	4	7	5	1	11	12													41
1	2		5			6	10	12	9	8	3	11	4	7														42
1	2		5			12	6	10	14	9	8	3	11	4	7													43
1	3		5			12	6	10	7	9	8		4	11	2	14												44

QUEEN OF THE SOUTH   Second Division

Year Formed: 1919. *Ground & Address:* Palmerston Park, Terregles St, Dumfries DG2 9BA. *Telephone:* 0387 54853.
Ground Capacity: total: 6750. seated: 1300. *Size of Pitch:* 112yd × 72yd.
Chairman: William Jardine. *Secretary:* Mrs Doreen Alcorn. *Commercial Manager:* John Paterson.
Manager: William McLaren. *Assistant Manager:* —. *Physio:* Derek Kelly.
Managers since 1975: M. Jackson; G. Herd; A. Busby; R. Clark; M. Jackson; D. WIlson; W. McLaren; F. McGarvey; A.
MacLeod. *Club Nickname(s):* The Doonhamers. *Previous Grounds:* None.
Record Attendance: 24,500 v Hearts, Scottish Cup 3rd rd; 23 Feb, 1952.
Record Transfer Fee received: £100,000 for K. McMinn to Rangers (1985).
Record Transfer Fee paid: —.
Record Victory: 11-1 v Stranraer, Scottish Cup 1st rd; 16 Jan, 1932.
Record Defeat: 2-10 v Dundee, Division I; 1 Dec, 1962.
Most Capped Player: Billy Houliston, 3, Scotland.
Most League Appearances: 619: Allan Ball; 1962-83.

QUEEN OF THE SOUTH 1992—93 LEAGUE RECORD

Match No.	Date		Venue	Opponents	Result		H/T Score	Lg. Pos.	Goalscorers	Atten dance
1	Aug	8	A	Forfar Ath	L	1-5	1-0	—	Robertson (pen)	508
2		15	A	Stranraer	D	2-2	1-0	13	Robertson, Templeton	982
3		22	H	Albion R	L	0-3	0-1	14		437
4		29	A	East Stirling	W	2-1	0-1	10	Thomson, Sermanni	289
5	Sept	5	H	Brechin C	D	0-0	0-0	10		563
6		12	H	Berwick R	W	1-0	0-0	8	Thomson	475
7		19	A	Montrose	L	1-5	0-1	9	Thomson	511
8		26	A	Queen's Park	W	2-1	1-0	7	McGhie, McGuire D	438
9	Oct	3	H	Clyde	W	3-1	1-0	6	Thomson 2, McGuire D	763
10		10	A	East Fife	W	5-2	2-0	5	McGuire D 2, Thomson 3	715
11		17	H	Alloa	L	1-2	0-2	5	Robertson	703
12		24	A	Arbroath	D	0-0	0-0	5		535
13		31	H	Stenhousemuir	L	0-1	0-1	7		625
14	Nov	7	A	East Stirling	L	1-2	0-0	9	McFadyen (og)	512
15		14	A	Brechin C	L	0-3	0-2	9		518
16		21	H	Montrose	L	0-1	0-1	10		389
17		28	A	Berwick R	W	4-1	1-1	10	McGuire D, Thomson, McFarlane, Henderson	308
18	Dec	12	H	Forfar Ath	D	1-1	1-0	10	McFarlane	355
19	Jan	2	H	Stranraer	W	2-0	0-0	9	Henderson, McGuire J	1240
20		9	A	Albion R	L	1-2	0-1	8	McGuire J	188
21		26	A	Stenhousemuir	D	1-1	1-0	—	McGuire J	315
22		30	H	Queen's Park	W	5-2	2-0	8	Henderson, McGhie 2, Thomson 2 (1 pen)	492
23	Feb	2	H	Arbroath	L	0-1	0-0	—		495
24		6	A	Alloa	D	2-2	0-2	9	Sermanni, Thomson	450
25		13	H	East Fife	D	1-1	1-0	9	McFarlane	469
26		16	A	Clyde	L	1-2	0-2	—	Henderson	621
27		20	A	Berwick R	L	0-3	0-1	10		329
28		27	A	Forfar Ath	L	2-4	1-2	10	McGhie, Thomson	399
29	Mar	6	H	Brechin C	L	1-2	0-0	10	Rowe	417
30		13	A	Stenhousemuir	L	1-2	0-0	10	Thomson	384
31		20	H	Arbroath	L	2-3	1-2	10	Thomson 2	310
32		27	A	Albion R	W	3-1	1-0	10	Sermanni, McFarlane, Robertson	283
33	Apr	3	A	Montrose	W	1-0	0-0	10	Henderson	408
34		10	H	Stranraer	D	3-3	1-2	10	Rowe, Henderson, Thomson	1095
35		17	H	East Fife	W	2-0	0-0	10	Henderson, Thomson	538
36		24	A	East Stirling	W	2-1	2-1	10	Thomson 2	334
37	May	1	A	Queen's Park	D	1-1	1-0	10	Henderson	449
38		8	H	Clyde	L	2-3	1-2	10	Thomson, Henderson	1130
39		15	H	Alloa	L	0-7	0-2	10		318

Final League Position: 10

Most League Goals in Season (Individual): 33: Jimmy Gray, Division II; 1927-28.
Most Goals Overall (Individual): —.

Honours
League Champions: Division II 1950-51; *Runners-up:* Division II 1932-33, 1961-62, 1974-75. Second Division 1980-81, 1985-86.
Scottish Cup: —.
League Cup: —.
Club colours: Shirt: Royal blue. Shorts: White. Stockings: Royal blue with white tops.

Goalscorers: *League (57):* Thomson 21 (1 pen), Henderson 9, McGuire D 5, McFarlane 4, McGhie 4, Robertson 4 (1 pen), McGuire J 3, Sermanni 3, Rowe 2, Templeton 1, own goal 1. *Scottish Cup (4):* Henderson 2, Rowe 2. *Skol Cup (3):* Templeton 3. *B & Q Cup (4):* Rowe 2, Templeton 1, Thomson 1.

Davidson A 8	Dickson J 27+2	McFarlane A 37	Mills D 19	Hetherington K 1	Gordon S 16+6	Wright B 25	Bell A 20+4	Thomson A 38	Robertson J 15+8	McGuire J 15+1	Templeton H 1+7	McGhie W 31+3	Fraser G 6+4	Sim W 18+2	Rowe G 36	Sermanni P 27+1	McKeown B 12+1	McGuire D 19+7	Hoy D 28	Henderson D 25+1	Hair P 3	Frye J F —+1	Sharp K —+2	McCulloch D 1	Gillespie A 1	Match No.
1	2	3	4	5	6	7	8	9	10	11	12	14														1
1	2	3	4		7	10		9	11		8	12	5	6												2
1	2	8	5		14	7		9	11	10	12		4	6	3											3
1	2		5		6	7		9	11			10	3		4	8										4
1		3	5		6	7		9	11	10		2	12		4	8										5
1		3	5			7		9	10	11		2			4	6		8								6
1	14	3	5			7	12	9	11	10		2		6	4		8									7
1	12	3	5			7	8	9	11			2			4	6	10									8
	2	3	5	14			8	9	11						6	4	7	10	1							9
	5	3			2		8	9	11	12				6	14	4	7	10	1							10
	6	3			2		8	9	11	14	5				4	7	12	10	1							11
	5	3			2	11	8	9		14					4	7	6	10	1							12
	5	3			2		8	9	11		14				4	7	6	10	1	12						13
	5	3					8	9		12	2				4	7	6	11	1	10						14
	2	3	5			8		9	11	10		14			4		6	12	1	7						15
	2	3	5			8	6	9	7		12				10	4	14		1	11						16
	2	11	5	14				9					10	3	4	12	6	7	1	8						17
	6	10			2			9	12					8	3	5	7	4	1	11						18
	2			8	12	11		9	14					5	6	3	4	7	1	10						19
	2		6		12	8	11	9	14					5		3	4	7	1	10						20
	2	11				7		9	10						6	3	5	4	1	8						21
	2	11				7		9	10						6	3	5	4	12	8	1					22
	2	10	5			7		9	11						6	14	3	4	1	8						23
	2	3	6			11		9							10	5	7	4	12	1	8		14			24
			6		2			9	11						5	3	4	7	10	1	8		14			25
		10			2	4	12	9							5	3	6	7	11	1	8		14			26
		10	5			4	8	9							2	3	6	11	1					7		27
	2		6		14	7	8	9							5	3	4	10	1	11						28
	2		6		10	7	8	9	12						5	3	4	14	1	11						29
	2		6		8	7	14	9							5	3	4	11	12	1					10	30
	2		8			7	6	9							5	3	4	10	1	11						31
	7		6			5		9	12						2	3	4	8	11	1					10	32
	8		6			4		9	12						2	3	5	10	7	1	11					33
	8					4	6	9	12						2	3	5	10	7	1	11					34
	10		6			4	3	9							2	5	8		7	1	11					35
	10		5			6	8	9	12						2	3	7	4		1	11					36
	10		5			8	3	9							2	4	7	6	14	1	11					37
	10		5			4	6	9	12						2	14	3	8	7	11	1					38
	10					5	12	9	11						2	14	4	8	7	6	1				3	39

QUEEN'S PARK   Second Division

Year Formed: 1867. *Ground & Address:* Hampden Park, Mount Florida, Glasgow G42 9BA. *Telephone:* 041 632 1275.
Ground Capacity: total: 48,643. seated: 16,160. *Size of Pitch:* 115yd × 75yd.
President: Malcolm D. Mackay. *Secretary:* James C. Rutherford. *Commercial Manager:* —. *Physio:* R. C. Findlay. *Coach:*
Edward Hunter.
Coaches since 1975: D. McParland, J. Gilroy. *Club Nickname(s):* The Spiders. *Previous Grounds:* 1st Hampden
(Recreation Ground); (Titwood Park was used as an interim measure between 1st & 2nd Hampdens); 2nd Hampden
(Cathkin); 3rd Hampden.
Record Attendance: 95,772 v Rangers, Scottish Cup, 18 Jan, 1930.
Record for Ground: 149,547 Scotland v England, 1937.
Record Transfer Fee received: Not applicable due to amateur status.
Record Transfer Fee paid: Not applicable due to amateur status.
Record Victory: 16-0 v St. Peters, Scottish Cup 1st rd; 29 Aug, 1885.
Record Defeat: 0-9 v Motherwell, Division I; 26 Apr, 1930.
Most Capped Player: Walter Arnott, 15, Scotland.
Most League Appearances: 473: J. B. McAlpine.

QUEEN'S PARK 1992—93 LEAGUE RECORD

Match No.	Date		Venue	Opponents	Result	H/T Score	Lg. Pos.	Goalscorers	Atten dance
1	Aug	8	H	Stranraer	D 1-1	0-0	—	McCormick	390
2		15	A	Albion R	L 2-3	0-2	11	Greig, Caven	268
3		22	H	Forfar Ath	L 1-2	0-1	12	Caven	406
4		29	A	Arbroath	L 1-2	0-0	13	Crooks	402
5	Sept	5	H	East Fife	L 1-3	0-0	14	Mackay	465
6		12	H	Clyde	L 1-6	0-3	14	Caven	951
7		19	A	Berwick R	L 0-1	0-0	14		432
8		26	H	Queen of the S	L 1-2	0-1	14	Mills (og)	438
9	Oct	3	A	Stenhousemuir	L 0-2	0-0	14		357
10		10	H	Brechin C	L 1-2	1-1	14	Rodden	399
11		17	A	Montrose	W 2-0	2-0	14	Caven, Rodden	705
12		24	A	Alloa	D 0-0	0-0	14		513
13		31	H	East Stirling	W 4-2	1-1	14	Elder, O'Neill 2, Caven	469
14	Nov	7	A	Arbroath	L 0-1	0-0	14		432
15		14	H	East Fife	L 1-2	0-1	14	McCormick	569
16		21	H	Berwick R	W 4-0	2-0	14	Jackson, Caven 2, Stevenson	385
17		28	A	Clyde	L 1-4	0-2	14	Elder	676
18	Dec	12	A	Stranraer	D 1-1	1-1	14	Rodden	529
19		26	H	Stenhousemuir	D 2-2	0-1	14	Caven, McCormick	531
20	Jan	2	H	Albion R	W 1-0	1-0	13	Caven	543
21		26	A	Forfar Ath	L 0-2	0-0	—		551
22		30	A	Queen of the S	L 2-5	0-2	14	Rodden, Caven	492
23	Feb	2	A	East Stirling	D 2-2	0-0	—	Caven, Orr G	274
24		6	H	Montrose	W 3-1	1-0	12	Rodden 2, Stevenson	357
25		9	H	Alloa	L 0-3	0-1	—		405
26		13	A	Brechin C	L 0-1	0-0	13		497
27		20	A	Clyde	W 3-2	0-2	13	Strain (og), McCormick, Rodden	678
28		27	H	Arbroath	W 2-1	1-0	13	Graham, Rodden	461
29	Mar	6	A	Stranraer	L 2-4	0-3	13	Black, Millar	506
30		13	H	East Fife	D 2-2	0-1	12	Black, Mackay	406
31		20	H	Albion R	D 1-1	1-0	11	Mackay	389
32		27	A	Forfar Ath	D 2-2	1-1	11	Rodden, O'Neill	531
33	Apr	3	A	East Stirling	L 1-4	0-2	12	Kerr	283
34		10	A	Alloa	D 2-2	2-1	11	O'Neill, Black	475
35		17	H	Brechin C	W 1-0	1-0	11	O'Neill	468
36		24	A	Berwick R	D 1-1	1-0	11	O'Neill	465
37	May	1	H	Queen of the S	D 1-1	0-1	11	Elder	449
38		8	A	Stenhousemuir	D 0-0	0-0	11		379
39		15	A	Montrose	L 1-3	0-1	11	McCormick	402

Final League Position: 11

Most League Goals in Season (Individual): 30: William Martin, Division I; 1937-38.
Most Goals Overall (Individual): 163: J. B. McAlpine.

Honours
League Champions: Division II 1922-23. B Division 1955-56. Second Division 1980-81.
Scottish Cup Winners: 1874, 1875, 1876, 1880, 1881, 1882, 1884, 1886, 1890, 1893; *Runners-up:* 1892, 1900.
League Cup: —.
FA Cup runners-up: 1884, 1885.
Club colours: Shirt: White and black hoops. Shorts: White. Stockings: White with black hoops.

Goalscorers: *League (51):* Caven 11, Rodden 9, O'Neill 6, McCormick 5, Black 3, Elder 3, Mackay 3, Stevenson 2, Crooks 1, Graham 1, Greig 1, Jackson 1, Kerr 1, Millar 1, Orr G 1, own goals 2. *Scottish Cup (0). Skol Cup (1):* McCormick 1. *B & Q Cup (2):* Jackson 1, McCormick 1.

Moonie D 11	Callan D 12 + 1	Morris S 4 + 1	Elder G 27	Mackay M 33	Jackson D 35	Caven R 34	Orr G 33 + 2	Graham D 29 + 3	McCormick S 30 + 2	O'Neill J 19 + 8	Greig D 5 + 3	Bradley R 3 + 2	O'Brien J — + 1	Chalmers J 28	Ferguson P 1	Crooks G 3 + 5	Orr J 11	Devlin W 6	Mackenzie K 2	Millar G 5 + 15	Sneddon S 11	Rodden J 22 + 4	Stevenson C 24 + 2	Kerr G 26	Henrici G 2 + 2	Black S 4 + 5	Kavanagh J 9	McIntyre D — + 1	Bryers C — + 1	Match No.
1	2	3	4	5	6	7	8	9	10	11	12	14																		1
1	2	3	4	5	6	7	8	14	10	12	11	9																		2
1	2	3	4	5	6	7	8	9	10	12	11		14																	3
	2		4	5	8	10	7	6	11	9				1		3	14													4
	6	3	4	5	9	11	8	7	10	14				1		12	2													5
	2	12		5	9	7	8	6	10					1		4	3	11												6
1	7		4	5	9	8	2	10	11								3	6												7
1	2		4	5	8	7	3	9	12							11	10	6												8
	6		4	5	8	7	3	10	11					1		9	14	2	12											9
	6		4	5	8	7	3	9	11					1		12	2	10												10
			7	5	8	3	6	10	14					1								9	11	2	4					11
			4	5	7	3	6	10						1						14	9	12	11	8	2					12
			7	5	8	10	3	6	9					1								12	11	2	4					13
			7	5	8	10	3	6	14	9				1								12	11	2	4					14
			4	5	9	7	8	6	10	11				1								3	12	2		14				15
			7	5	9	10	14	6	11					1							3	4	12	2		8				16
			7	5	9	10	8	14	11					1							3	4	12	6	2					17
			4	6	8	9	7	11						1		12					5	10	3	2						18
			4	8	7	3	6	11	12					1			9					10	2	5		14				19
			4	5	8	7	14	6	11	12				1								10	3	2		9				20
				5	8	7	6	10	9					1			2				14	11	3	4						21
			4	5	8	10	6	14	9					1			2					11	3	7						22
			4	5	9	7	8	6	10					1								11	3	2						23
				5	9	7	8	6	10					1			2				14	11	3	4			12			24
				5	9	7	6	10						1			2				8	11	3	4						25
1				5	7	8	6	9	14	11							2				12	10	3	4						26
1				5	9	7	3	6	10	14	8											12	11	2	4					27
1				5	8	7	3	6	11	9													10	2	4	12				28
1				5	8	7	3	6	11	9							2				14	10		4		12				29
1				5	9	7	8	6	11	12								4	14				3	10	2					30
				5	9	7	6	10						1		4	12					3	8	11	2		14			31
				5	8		6	10						1		4						11	3	7	9	2				32
			4	5	9	8	6	10						1							14	11	3	7	12	2				33
1			7		9	3	6	10												8	5	11		4	14	2				34
14				5	9	7	6	11						1							2	3	4	10	8		12			35
6				5	9	7	8	11	10					1							12	2	3	4						36
				5	3	9	7	6	10	11				1								12	8	4		2				37
				5	2	7	14	6	11	9				1							3	10	12	4		8				38
				5	8	11	6	7	9					1							12	2	10	14	4		3			39

RAITH ROVERS   Premier Division

Year Formed: 1883. *Ground & Address:* Stark's Park, Pratt St, Kirkcaldy KY1 1SA. *Telephone:* 0592 263514.
Ground Capacity: total: 8500. seated: 3040. *Size of Pitch:* 113yd × 67yd.
Chairman: P. J. Campsie. *Secretary:* Mrs S. Rankin. *Commercial Manager:* P. Rodger.
Manager: James Nicholl. *Assistant Manager and Coach:* Martin Harvey. *Physio:* Gerry Docherty. *Reserve Coach:* Derek Smith.
Managers since 1975: R. Paton; A. Matthew; W. McLean; G. Wallace; R. Wilson; F. Connor. *Club Nickname(s):* Rovers.
Previous Grounds: Robbie's Park.
Record Attendance: 31,306 v Hearts, Scottish Cup 2nd rd; 7 Feb, 1953.
Record Transfer Fee received: £110,000 for Paul Sweeney to Newcaslte U (March 1989).
Record Transfer Fee paid: £70,000 for Kenny Macdonald from Airdrieonians (Oct 1989).
Record Victory: 10-1 v Coldstream, Scottish Cup 2nd rd; 13 Feb, 1954.
Record Defeat: 2-11 v Morton, Division II; 18 Mar, 1936.
Most Capped Player: David Morris, 6, Scotland.
Most League Appearances: 430: Willie McNaught.

RAITH ROVERS 1992—93 LEAGUE RECORD

Match No.	Date		Venue	Opponents	Result	H/T Score	Lg. Pos.	Goalscorers	Atten dance
1	Aug	1	H	St Mirren	W 7-0	3-0	—	Dalziel 3, Dair, Coyle, Brewster 2	2254
2		4	H	Stirling Albion	D 0-0	0-0	—		1513
3		8	A	Kilmarnock	D 1-1	1-0	3	Dalziel	4566
4		15	H	Ayr U	W 1-0	0-0	2	Brewster	1417
5		22	A	Dunfermline Ath	W 1-0	0-0	1	Thomson	6377
6		29	A	Dumbarton	W 2-1	0-0	1	Dalziel 2	1105
7	Sept	5	H	Hamilton A	W 2-1	1-1	1	Brewster, Thomson	2384
8		12	H	Morton	W 2-1	1-1	1	Dalziel, Brewster	2613
9		19	A	Cowdenbeath	W 3-0	1-0	1	Dalziel 3	1974
10		26	A	Meadowbank T	W 2-0	1-0	1	Dalziel, MacKenzie	1142
11	Oct	3	H	Clydebank	D 2-2	0-0	1	Dalziel, McStay	2424
12		10	A	St Mirren	D 1-1	1-0	1	Hetherston	6194
13		17	H	Kilmarnock	D 1-1	0-0	1	MacKenzie	3718
14		24	A	Hamilton A	D 2-2	2-0	1	Brewster, Dalziel	2418
15		31	H	Dumbarton	W 4-1	3-1	1	Dalziel 2, McStay, Nicholl	1990
16	Nov	7	A	Ayr U	D 1-1	0-0	1	Brewster	2160
17		14	H	Dunfermline Ath	W 1-0	0-0	1	Crawford	5794
18		21	H	Cowdenbeath	W 3-0	1-0	1	Hetherston, Dalziel, Nicholl	2002
19		28	A	Morton	W 4-3	1-2	1	Dalziel 2, Brewster, Hetherston	2583
20	Dec	1	A	Clydebank	L 0-3	0-1	—		1257
21		5	H	Meadowbank T	W 5-0	1-0	1	Dalziel, McStay, Nicholl, Brewster, MacKenzie	1930
22		12	H	St Mirren	W 3-1	1-0	1	McStay, Dalziel, Brewster	3211
23		26	H	Ayr U	D 1-1	0-1	1	Brewster	3119
24		29	A	Stirling Albion	W 3-0	2-0	—	Dalziel 2, Thomson	1251
25	Jan	2	A	Dunfermline Ath	D 0-0	0-0	1		10,798
26		26	H	Clydebank	W 4-2	2-1	—	Crawford, Thomson, Dalziel, Brewster	2016
27		30	A	Kilmarnock	L 0-3	0-0	1		7003
28	Feb	2	H	Hamilton A	D 1-1	0-0	—	Dalziel	2690
29		6	A	Dumbarton	W 2-1	1-1	1	Brewster, Dalziel (pen)	1201
30		13	H	Stirling Albion	W 2-0	1-0	1	Crawford, MacLeod	2103
31		20	H	Meadowbank T	D 1-1	1-0	1	Dalziel	988
32		27	A	Cowdenbeath	W 2-0	1-0	1	Cameron, Dalziel	1978
33	Mar	6	H	Morton	W 2-0	1-0	1	Dalziel, Brewster	1938
34		10	A	St Mirren	D 1-1	1-1	—	MacLeod	2700
35		13	H	Kilmarnock	W 2-0	1-0	1	Brewster, Dalziel	4738
36		20	H	Dunfermline Ath	W 2-0	0-0	1	Nicholl 2	6985
37		27	A	Ayr U	D 0-0	0-0	1		2664
38	Apr	3	A	Hamilton A	D 2-2	0-1	1	Dalziel, Brewster	3014
39		10	H	Dumbarton	W 2-0	1-0	1	Brewster 2	4893
40		17	A	Morton	D 1-1	0-1	1	Brewster	1792
41		24	H	Cowdenbeath	W 4-1	3-1	1	Brewster, Hetherston, Dalziel 2	2752
42	May	1	A	Stirling Albion	L 1-2	1-1	1	Dennis	1536
43		8	H	Meadowbank T	W 3-2	1-1	1	Brewster 2, Murray (og)	1961
44		15	A	Clydebank	L 1-4	0-1	1	McStay	1046

Final League Position: 1

Most League Goals in Season (Individual): 38: Norman Haywood, Division II; 1937-38.
Most Goals Overall (Individual): 146: Gordon Dalziel (League), 1992-93.

Honours
League Champions: First Division: 1992-93. Division II 1907-08, 1909-10 (shared), 1937-38, 1948-49; *Runners-up:* Division II 1908-09, 1926-27, 1966-67. Second Division 1975-76, 1977-78, 1986-87.
Scottish Cup Runners-up: 1913. *League Cup Runners-up:* 1948-49.
Club colours: Shirt: Navy blue, white trim. Shorts: White. Stockings: Red.

Goalscorers: *League (85):* Dalziel 32 (1 pen), Brewster 22, McStay 5, Nicholl 5, Hetherston 4, Thomson 4, Crawford 3, MacKenzie 3, MacLeod 2, Cameron 1, Coyle 1, Dair 1, Dennis 1, own goal 1. *Scottish Cup (0). Skol Cup (1):* McStay 1. *B & Q Cup (0).*

Arthur G 17	McStay J 41	MacLeod I 34 + 2	Coyle R 35	Dennis S 31	Sinclair D 25 + 7	Nicholl J 38	Dalziel G 44	Hetherston P 44	Brewster C 44	Dair J 10 + 5	MacKenzie A 5 + 18	Thomson I 26 + 8	Raeside R 10	Carson T 27	McGeachie G 29 + 1	Williamson T — + 2	Crawford S 10 + 10	Cameron C 13 + 3	Cusick J 1 + 1	Match No.
1	2	3	4	5	6	7	8	9	10	11	12	14								1
1	2	3	4	5	6	7	8	9	10	11										2
1	2	3	4	5		7	8	9	10	11	12	14	6							3
	2	3	4	5	6		8	9	10	11		7		1						4
	2	3	4	5	6		8	9	10	11	12	7		1	14					5
	2	3		5	14	4	8	9	10	11	12	7		1	6					6
	2	3		5	14	4	8	9	10	11	12	7		1	6					7
	2	3		5	12	4	8	9	10		11	7		1	6					8
	2	3		5	12	4	8	9	10		11	7		1	6					9
	2	3		5	12	4	8	9	10		11	7		1	6					10
	2	3		5		4	8	9	10		11	7		1	6	14				11
	2	3	4	5		7	8	9	10		11			1	6					12
		3	4		7	2	8	9	10		12	11	5	1	6	14				13
	2	3	4		5	7	8	9	10		12	11		1	6					14
	2	3	4	5	12	7	8	9	10		11			1	6		14			15
	2	3	4	5	12	7	8	9	10		11			1	6		14			16
	2	3	4		6	7	8	9	10		14	5		1			11			17
	2	3	4		6	7	8	9	10			5		1			11			18
	2	3	4		6	7	8	9	10		14	5		1			11			19
	2		4		6	7	8	9	10	14	12	3	5	1			11			20
	2		4		6	7	8	9	10		12	3		1	5		11			21
	2	14	4		5	7	8	9	10		12	3		1	6		11			22
	2		4		6	7	8	9	10			3		1	5		11			23
	2		4		6	7	8	9	10		12	3		1	5		11			24
	2	3	4		6	7	8	9	10		12	11		1	5		14			25
	2	3	4		5		8	9	10		12	6		1			11	7		26
	2	3	4	5	6		8	9	10		12	11		1			14	7		27
	2		4	5	6	7	8	9	10	11		3		1			14	12		28
	2	12	4	5	6	7	8	9	10		11	3		1			14			29
1		3	4	5	2		8	9	10		12				6		11	7		30
1	2	3	4	5	11		8	9	10						6			7		31
1	2	3	4	5	11		8	9	10		12				6			7		32
1	2	3	4	5	11		8	9	10		12				6		14	7		33
1	2	3	4	5	11	7	8	9	10						6					34
1	2	3	4	5	11	7	8	9	10	14					6			12		35
1	2	3	4		5	7	8	9	10		12				6			11		36
1	2	3	4	5	11	7	8	9	10		12				6					37
1	2	3	4	5		7	8	9	10						6			11		38
1	2	3	4	5		7	8	9	10	14					6		12	11		39
1	2	3		5		4	8	9	10	12					6		14	7	11	40
1	2			5		7	8	9	10	14		3	4		6			11	12	41
1	2		4	5		7	8	9	10	14		3			6			11		42
1	2			5		7	8	9	10	11		14	6	3			12	4		43
	2		4	5		7	8	9	10	11	12	3		1	6		14			44

RANGERS   Premier Division

Year Formed: 1873. *Ground & Address:* Ibrox Stadium, Edminston Drive, Glasgow G51 2XD. *Telephone:* 041 427 8500.
Ground Capacity: total: 44,500. seated: 36,500. *Size of Pitch:* 115yd × 75yd.
Chairman: David Murray. *Secretary:* R. C. Ogilvie. *Commercial Manager:* Bob Reilly.
Manager: Walter Smith. *Assistant Manager:* Archie Knox. *Physio:* Bill Collins. *Coach:* Davie Dodds. *Reserve team coaches:* John McGregor, Billy Kirkwood.
Managers since 1975: Jock Wallace; John Greig; Jock Wallace; Graeme Souness. *Club Nickname(s):* The Gers. *Previous Grounds:* Burnbank, Kinning Park.
Record Attendance: 118,567 v Celtic, Division I; 2 Jan, 1939.
Record Transfer Fee received: £5,580,000 for Trevor Steven to Marseille (Aug 1991).
Record Transfer Fee paid: £2,500,000 for Alexei Mikhailichenko from Sampdoria (June 1991).
Record Victory: 14-2 v Blairgowrie, Scottish Cup 1st rd; 20 Jan, 1934.
Record Defeat: 2-10 v Airdrieonians; 1886.
Most Capped Player: George Young, 53, Scotland.
Most League Appearances: 496: John Greig, 1962-78.
Most League Goals in Season (Individual): 44: Sam English, Division I; 1931-32.
Most Goals Overall (Individual): 233: Bob McPhail; 1927-39.

Honours
League Champions: (43 times) Division I 1890-91 (shared), 1898-99, 1899-1900, 1900-01, 1901-02, 1910-11, 1911-12, 1912-13, 1917-18, 1919-20, 1920-21, 1922-23, 1923-24, 1924-25, 1926-27, 1927-28, 1928-29, 1929-30, 1930-31, 1932-33, 1933-34, 1934-35, 1936-37, 1938-39, 1946-47, 1948-49, 1949-50, 1952-53, 1955-56, 1956-57, 1958-59, 1960-61, 1962-63, 1963-64,

RANGERS 1992—93 LEAGUE RECORD

Match No.	Date		Venue	Opponents	Result		H/T Score	Lg. Pos.	Goalscorers	Atten dance
1	Aug	1	H	St Johnstone	W	1-0	0-0	—	McCoist	38,036
2		4	H	Airdrieonians	W	2-0	1-0	—	Gordon, Hateley	36,613
3		8	A	Hibernian	D	0-0	0-0	2		17,237
4		15	A	Dundee	L	3-4	2-2	4	McCoist 2, Ferguson	12,801
5		22	H	Celtic	D	1-1	0-0	5	Durrant	43,239
6		29	H	Aberdeen	W	3-1	0-1	2	Durrant, McCoist, Mikhailichenko	41,636
7	Sept	2	A	Motherwell	W	4-1	1-0	—	Brown, McCoist 3	10,074
8		12	A	Partick T	W	4-1	1-1	1	McPherson, McCall, Gough, Hateley	18,752
9		19	H	Hearts	W	2-0	1-0	1	McCall, McCoist	41,888
10		26	A	Dundee U	W	4-0	2-0	1	Steven, Huistra 2, McCoist	13,759
11	Oct	3	H	Falkirk	W	4-0	2-0	1	McCoist 4	40,691
12		7	A	St Johnstone	W	5-1	2-1	1	Hateley, McCoist 2 (1 pen), Ferguson	9532
13		17	H	Hibernian	W	1-0	0-0	1	McCoist	40,978
14		31	H	Motherwell	W	4-2	2-1	1	McCoist 3 (1 pen), Brown	38,719
15	Nov	7	A	Celtic	W	1-0	1-0	1	Durrant	51,950
16		11	H	Dundee	W	3-1	1-1	1	McCoist 2, Hateley	37,255
17		21	A	Hearts	D	1-1	1-0	1	McCoist	20,831
18		28	H	Partick T	W	3-0	0-0	1	Steven, McSwegan, McPherson	40,939
19	Dec	1	A	Airdrieonians	D	1-1	1-0	—	Brown	9251
20		12	A	Falkirk	W	2-1	1-0	1	Hateley, McCoist	11,585
21		19	H	St Johnstone	W	2-0	0-0	1	Gough, Robertson D	37,369
22		26	A	Dundee	W	3-1	1-0	1	McCoist, Hateley 2	13,778
23	Jan	2	H	Celtic	W	1-0	1-0	1	Steven	46,039
24		5	A	Dundee U	W	3-2	2-0	1	Hateley, McCall, McCoist	40,239
25		30	A	Hibernian	W	4-3	1-0	1	Mikhailichenko 2, Steven, McCoist	17,447
26	Feb	2	A	Aberdeen	W	1-0	0-0	—	Hateley	15,055
27		9	H	Falkirk	W	5-0	2-0	—	Huistra, Hateley 2, Steven, Robertson D	37,780
28		13	H	Airdrieonians	D	2-2	2-1	1	McCoist 2	39,816
29		20	A	Dundee U	D	0-0	0-0	1		13,443
30		23	A	Motherwell	W	4-0	0-0	—	McCoist, Hateley 2, Mikhailichenko	14,006
31		27	H	Hearts	W	2-1	2-0	1	McCoist, Robertson D	42,128
32	Mar	10	A	St Johnstone	D	1-1	0-0	1	McCoist	9258
33		13	H	Hibernian	W	3-0	2-0	1	Hagen, Hateley, McCoist	41,076
34		20	A	Celtic	L	1-2	0-1	1	Hateley	52,779
35		27	H	Dundee	W	3-0	1-0	1	McCall, McCoist, Ferguson	40,294
36		30	H	Aberdeen	W	2-0	0-0	—	Ferguson, McCoist	44,570
37	Apr	10	A	Motherwell	W	1-0	0-0	1	Brown	41,353
38		14	A	Hearts	W	3-2	1-1	—	McCall, Hateley 2	14,622
39		17	H	Partick T	W	3-1	1-0	1	McSwegan 2, Hagen	42,636
40	May	1	A	Airdrieonians	W	1-0	0-0	1	McSwegan	12,514
41		4	A	Partick T	L	0-3	0-1	—		9303
42		8	H	Dundee U	W	1-0	0-0	1	Huistra	42,917
43		12	A	Aberdeen	L	0-1	0-1	—		13,079
44		15	A	Falkirk	W	2-1	1-1	1	Mikhailichenko, Hateley	9288

Final League Position: 1

1974-75. Premier Division: 1975-76, 1977-78, 1986-87, 1988-89, 1989-90, 1990-91, 1991-92, 1992-93; *Runners-up:* 23 times.
Scottish Cup Winners: (26 times) 1894, 1897, 1898, 1903, 1928, 1930, 1932, 1934, 1935, 1936, 1948, 1949, 1950, 1953, 1960, 1962, 1963, 1964, 1966, 1973, 1976, 1978, 1979, 1981, 1992, 1993; *Runners-up:* 15 times.
League Cup Winners: (18 times) 1946-47, 1948-49, 1960-61, 1961-62, 1963-64, 1964-65, 1970-71, 1975-76, 1977-78, 1978-79, 1981-82, 1983-84, 1984-85, 1986-87, 1987-88, 1988-89, 1990-91, 1992-93; *Runners-up:* 7 times.
European: *European Cup:* 69 matches (1956-57, 1957-58, 1959-60 semi-finals, 1961-62, 1963-64, 1964-65, 1975-76, 1976-77, 1978-79, 1987-88, 1989-90, 1990-91, 1992-93 final pool).
Cup Winners Cup Winners: 1971-72. 50 matches (1960-61 runners-up, 1962-63, 1966-67 runners-up, 1969-70, 1971-72 winners, 1973-74, 1977-78, 1979-80, 1981-82, 1983-84). *UEFA Cup:* 38 matches (*Fairs Cup:* 1967-68, 1968-69 semi-finals, 1970-71 *UEFA Cup*; 1982-83, 1984-85, 1985-86, 1986-87, 1988-89).
Club colours: Shirt: Royal blue with red and white trim. Shorts: White. Stockings: Red.

Goalscorers: *League (97):* McCoist 34 (2 pens), Hateley 19, McCall 5, Mikhailichenko 5, Steven 5, Brown 4, Ferguson 4, Huistra 4, McSwegan 4, Durrant 3, Robertson D 3, Gough 2, Hagen 2, McPherson 2, Gordon 1. *Scottish Cup (11):* McCoist 5 (1 pen), Hateley 2, Murray 2, Gordon 1, McPherson 1. *Skol Cup (18):* McCoist 8, Hateley 3, Durrant 1, Gordon 1, Gough 1, Huistra 1, McCall 1, Mikhailichenko 1, own goal 1.

Goram A 34	Nisbet S 10	Robertson D 39	Gough R 25	McPherson D 34	Brown J 39	Durrant I 19+11	McCall S 35+1	McCoist A 32+2	Hateley M 36+1	Huistra P 27+3	Rideout P —+1	Kuznetsov O 8+1	Gordon D 18+4	Mikhailichenko A 16+13	Steven T 24	Maxwell A 10	Ferguson I 29+1	Spackman N 2	McSwegan G 8+1	Hagen D 5+3	Robertson A —+2	Stevens G 9	Pressley S 8	Murray N 11+5	Watson S 3	Reid B 2	Robertson L 1	Match No.
1	2	3	4	5	6	7	8	9	10	11	12		14															1
1	2	3	4		6	14	8	9	10						5	7	11											2
1	2	3	4	5	6	12	8	9	10						11	14	7											3
	2	3	4	5	6	12	8	9	10					14	7	11			1									4
1		3	4	5	6	12	8	9	10	11				14	7		2											5
1		3	4	5	6	7		9		11				10			8	2										6
1		3	4	5	6	7		9		11				10			8	2										7
1		3	4	5	6	10	2	9	12	7				11			8											8
1		3	4	5	6	10	2	9		11					7		8		14									9
1	5	3			6		2	9	10	11			4		7	8			14									10
1	2	3		5	6	12	7	9	10	11			4				8											11
1	2	3		5	6	4	9	10	11				14	7			8											12
1		3	4		6	9	12	14	10	11	2		5	7			8											13
1		3		5	6	7	9		11	2	4	10			8		12											14
1		3	4	5	6	11	2	9	10	12				7	14		8											15
1		3		5	6	4	7	9	10	11				14			8	2										16
1		3		5	6	12		9	10	11				4	7		8	2										17
1		3		5	6	10			11					4	7		8	9	2									18
1		3			6	4			10				12	11	7		8	9	2	5								19
1		3		5	6	4	8	9	10				7	11			2											20
1		3	4	5		6	8	9	10	11				7			2											21
1		3	4	5		11	6	9	10				14	7		8	2											22
1		3	4	5	6	11	2		10				9	14	7		8											23
1		3	4	5	6		2	9	10	12				11	7		8											24
1		3		5	6	12	8	9	10	14			4	11	7		2											25
1		3		5	6		8	9	10				4	11	7		2											26
1		3	4		6		8	9	10	11	5			7			2											27
1		3	4			6		9	10	11	5	14	8	7			12	2										28
1		3	4	5		7	9	10	11				8				2	6										29
1		3	4	5	6	2	9	10	11				12	7			8							14				30
1	2	3		5	6	4	9	10	11				7	12			8							14				31
	2	3		5	6	12	8	9	10				11	7		1								4				32
		3		5	6	8	2	9	10				12			1	11					7	4					33
1	2	3		5	6	11	9	12	10				14	7			8							4				34
		3	4	5	6	2	9	10	11				14	7		1	8							12				35
1		3	4	5	6	2	9	10	11				14	7		1	8							12				36
		4	5	6	14	2	9	10	11					7		1	8							3				37
				6	12	2		10	11					7		1	8		9			5	4	3				38
				6	2		10						7			1	8		9	11		5	4	3				39
1		3	4	5	6	2		10	11				8	9			7											40
		4		6	8		10	11		5	7	14			1	9						2	3					41
1		3	4	5	6	10			11	2			14	8	9	7								12				42
		5	6	12		3	7	11		1	8		14	10			2					4	9					43
	3		4	8		10			7	11	1		9	12	6	2					5							44

ST JOHNSTONE
Premier Division

Year Formed: 1884. *Ground & Address:* McDiarmid Park, Crieff Road, Perth PH1 2SJ. *Telephone:* 0738 26961. *Clubcall:* 0898 121559.
Ground Capacity: total: 10,721. seated: 10,721. *Size of Pitch:* 115yd × 75yd.
Chairman: G. S. Brown. *Secretary and General Manager:* John Litster.
Manager: John McClelland. *Sales Executive:* Mrs Christine Drummond. *Physio:* J. Peacock. *Coach:* Ken Wharton.
Reserve Coach: Raymond Stewart.
Managers since 1975: J. Stewart; J. Storrie; A. Stuart; A. Rennie; I. Gibson; A. Totten. *Club Nickname(s):* Saints.
Previous Grounds: Recreation Grounds, Muirton Park.
Record Attendance: (McDiarmid Park): 10,504 v Rangers, Premier Division; 20 Oct, 1990.
Record Transfer Fee received: £400,000 for Ally McCoist to Sunderland (1982).
Record Transfer Fee paid: £285,000 for Paul Wright from Hibernian (Aug 1991).
Record Victory: 9-0 v Albion R, League Cup; 9 March, 1946.
Record Defeat: 1-10 v Third Lanark, Scottish Cup; 24 January, 1903.
Most Capped Player: Sandy McLaren, 5, Scotland.
Most League Appearances: 298: Drew Rutherford.

ST JOHNSTONE 1992—93 LEAGUE RECORD

Match No.	Date		Venue	Opponents	Result		H/I Score	Lg. Pos.	Goalscorers	Atten dance
1	Aug	1	A	Rangers	L	0-1	0-0	—		38,036
2		4	A	Dundee	D	1-1	0-1	—	Curran	5663
3		8	H	Partick T	D	1-1	0-1	9	Wright	4401
4		15	H	Airdrieonians	W	3-0	2-0	6	Curran, Torfason, Wright	3708
5		22	A	Dundee U	L	1-2	0-2	6	Torfason	7353
6		29	H	Hibernian	D	1-1	0-1	7	Wright (pen)	6017
7	Sept	2	A	Celtic	L	1-3	0-1	—	Wright	21,831
8		12	H	Falkirk	W	3-2	2-1	8	Arkins, Curran, Treanor	4361
9		19	A	Motherwell	D	3-3	1-1	7	Curran, Wright, Moore	4002
10		26	H	Aberdeen	L	0-3	0-0	9		7320
11	Oct	3	A	Hearts	D	1-1	0-1	8	Davies	7738
12		7	H	Rangers	L	1-5	1-2	—	Arkins	9532
13		17	A	Partick T	L	0-1	0-0	9		4211
14		24	A	Hibernian	L	1-3	0-1	9	Arkins	5988
15		31	H	Celtic	D	0-0	0-0	9		9783
16	Nov	7	H	Dundee U	W	2-0	0-0	9	Wright, Arkins	5513
17		14	A	Airdrieonians	W	2-0	1-0	8	Wright 2	2550
18		24	A	Motherwell	W	2-0	1-0	—	Curran, Maskrey	3582
19		28	A	Falkirk	D	2-2	0-1	7	Cherry, Curran	4565
20	Dec	2	H	Dundee	D	4-4	1-1	—	Davies, Wright 2, Maskrey	5766
21		5	A	Aberdeen	L	0-3	0-2	8		11,750
22		12	H	Hearts	D	1-1	0-1	7	Wright	4362
23		19	A	Rangers	L	0-2	0-0	8		37,369
24		26	H	Airdrieonians	W	1-0	0-0	7	Arkins	4139
25	Jan	2	A	Dundee U	W	2-1	1-0	6	Davies, Wright	10,316
26		20	A	Hearts	L	0-2	0-2	—		5060
27		23	H	Hibernian	W	2-0	0-0	6	Deas, Turner	4206
28		30	H	Partick T	D	0-0	0-0	6		4555
29	Feb	3	A	Celtic	L	1-5	0-4	—	Arkins	12,931
30		13	A	Dundee	L	0-1	0-0	6		4869
31		20	H	Aberdeen	L	0-2	0-1	8		6176
32		27	A	Motherwell	D	1-1	1-1	7	Redford	4278
33	Mar	10	H	Rangers	D	1-1	0-0	—	Wright	9258
34		13	A	Partick T	D	1-1	1-0	7	Davies	3534
35		16	H	Falkirk	W	1-0	0-0	—	Dunne	3546
36		20	H	Dundee U	L	1-4	1-2	6	Dunne	4510
37		27	A	Airdrieonians	D	1-1	0-0	6	Redford	2339
38	Apr	6	A	Hibernian	D	2-2	2-0	—	Moore, Buglione	3526
39		10	H	Celtic	D	1-1	1-1	6	Moore	8609
40		17	A	Falkirk	D	2-2	1-0	6	Curran, McGowne	3860
41		24	A	Motherwell	D	0-0	0-0	6		5544
42	May	1	H	Dundee	D	1-1	0-1	7	Wright	4471
43		8	A	Aberdeen	D	1-1	1-1	6	Torfason	7727
44		15	H	Hearts	W	3-1	1-0	6	Torfason (pen), Curran, Buglione	3900

Final League Position: 6

Most League Goals in Season (Individual): 36: Jimmy Benson, Division II; 1931-32.
Most Goals Overall (Individual): 114: John Brogan, 1977-83.

Honours
League Champions: First Division 1982-83, 1989-90. Division II 1923-24, 1959-60, 1962-63; *Runners-up:* Division II 1931-32. Second Division 1987-88.
Scottish Cup: Semi-finals 1934, 1968, 1989, 1991.
League Cup Runners-up: 1969.
European: UEFA Cup: 1971-72.
Club colours: Shirt: Royal blue with white trim. Shorts: White. Stockings: Royal blue, white trim.

Goalscorers: *League (52):* Wright 14 (1 pen), Curran 8, Arkins 6, Davies 4, Torfason 4 (1 pen), Moore 3, Buglione 2, Dunne 2, Maskrey 2, Redford 2, Cherry 1, Deas 1, McGowne 1, Treanor 1, Turner 1. *Scottish Cup (7):* Arkins 2, Wright 2, Cherry 1, Davies 1, Maskrey 1. *Skol Cup (9):* Wright 5 (1 pen), Curran 1, McAuley 1, Maskrey 1, Torfason 1.

Rhodes A 44	Treanor M 7+2	McAuley S 24+2	Baltacha S 25	Inglis J 39	McClelland J 25+1	Moore A 17+9	Davies J 33+5	Wright P 42	McGinnis G 26+1	Curran H 32+2	Cherry P 12+4	Maskrey S 3+16	Turner T 25+3	Redford I 12+4	Torfason G 9+1	McGowne K 25+1	Arkins V 24+2	Dunne L 4+4	Deas P 25	Scott P 2+1	Sweeney P 2	Byrne D 12	Kinnaird P 2+6	Cole A 7	Buglione M 6+1	Match No.
1	2	3	4	5	6	7	8	9	10	11	12	14														1
1	2	3	4	5	6	7	8	9	10	11			14	12												2
1		3	2	5	6	7	12	9	4	11			10	8	14											3
1		3	2	5	6	7		9	4	11			14	8			10									4
1		3	2	5	6	7	12	9	4	11			14	8			10									5
1		3	2	5	6		14	9	11	4			7	8	12		10									6
1	4	3	2	5	6		14	9		11	12		7	8			10									7
1	12	3		5	6	7		9	4	8		14	11			2	10									8
1		3		5	6	7	12	9	4	11			8			2	10									9
1	12	3		5	6		14	9	4	11			7	8		2	10									10
1	2	3	4	5	14	7		9	6	11	8						10	12								11
1	2	3	4	5	14	7		9	6	11	8						10	12								12
1	2	3	4	5	14	7		9	6	11	8						10									13
1	2	5	3			7	4	9	6	11		14		8			10									14
1		3	4	5	6	7		9		11			8			2	10									15
1		3	4	5	6	7		9		11			8	12		2	10									16
1		3	4	5	6	7		9		8			12	11		2	10									17
1		3	4	5	6	7		9		11			8		14	2	10									18
1		3	4	5	6	7		9		11			8		14	2	10									19
1		3	4	5		7		9		11			8		14	2	10		6							20
1		3	4	5	14	7		9		11			8			2	10		6							21
1		3		5		7		9		11		14		8		2	10		6							22
1	6		4	5		7		9		11				8		2	10		3							23
1	6		4	5		7		9		11			14	12	8	2	10		3							24
1		3	4	5		7		9		11			14	8	12	2	10		6							25
1			4	5	6	7		9					10	12	8	2	11	14	3							26
1	6		4	5		7		9		11				8		2	10		3							27
1	6		4	5		7		9		8			12	11		2	10		3							28
1	12			5	6	7		9	4	8		14				2	10		3	11						29
1	6		4	5		7		9		8		14	11	12		2	10		3							30
1	6		4	5	12	7		9		8		14		11		2	10		3							31
1	14		4	5	12	7	6	9		11						2	10		3		8					32
1			4	5		7	8	9		11					14	6	10		3	2		12				33
1			4	5		7	8	9							14	6	10		3	2		12	11			34
1			4	5		7	10	9		11						6	8		3	2					14	35
1	14		4	5		7	8	9		11						6	10		3	2		12				36
1			4	5		7	8	9		11		14				6	10		3	2		12				37
1			4	5		7	8	9		11					12				3	2			14	6	10	38
1			4	5		7	8	9		11									3	2				6	10	39
1			4	5		7	8	9		11		14							3	2				6	10	40
1			4	5		7	8	9		11									3	2		12		6	10	41
1			4	5		7	8	9		11		14			12				3	2				6	10	42
1	12	2	4	5			8	9		10				11					3				7	6	14	43
1	6	2	4		12		8	9		11					14				3				7	5	10	44

ST MIRREN   First Division

Year Formed: 1877. *Ground & Address:* St Mirren Park, Love St, Paisley PA3 2EJ. *Telephone:* 041 889 2558/041 840 1337.
Fax: 041 848 6444.
Ground Capacity: total: 16,195. seated: 6380; 5920 covered, 10,275 uncovered. *Size of Pitch:* 112yd × 73yd.
Chairman: Alan W. Marshall. *Secretary:* A. R. Craig. *Commercial/Marketing Manager:* Bill Campbell.
Manager: Jimmy Bone. *General Manager:* Jack Copland. *Physio:* Andrew Binning. *Coach:* —.
Managers since 1975: Alex Ferguson; Jim Clunie; Rikki MacFarlane; Alex Miller; Alex Smith; Tony Fitzpatrick; David
Hay. *Club Nickname(s):* The Buddies. *Previous Grounds:* Short Roods 1877-79, Thistle Park Greenhill 1879-83,
Westmarch 1883-94.
Record Attendance: 47,438 v Celtic, League Cup, 20 Aug, 1949.
Record Transfer Fee received: £850,000 for Ian Ferguson to Rangers (1988).
Record Transfer Fee paid: £400,000 for Thomas Stickroth from Bayer Uerdingen (1990).
Record Victory: 15-0 v Glasgow University, Scottish Cup 1st rd; 30 Jan, 1960.
Record Defeat: 0-9 v Rangers, Division I; 4 Dec, 1897.
Most Capped Player: Godmundor Torfason, 29, Iceland.
Most League Appearances: 351: Tony Fitzpatrick, 1973-88.

ST MIRREN 1992—93 LEAGUE RECORD

Match No.	Date		Venue	Opponents	Result	H/T Score	Lg. Pos.	Goalscorers	Atten dance
1	Aug	1	A	Raith R	L 0-7	0-3	—		2254
2		5	A	Hamilton A	D 0-0	0-0	—		2154
3		8	H	Dumbarton	W 4-0	1-0	7	Baillie, Lavety, McGill 2	2363
4		15	H	Clydebank	D 0-0	0-0	7		2296
5		22	A	Morton	W 1-0	1-0	5	Lavety	4040
6		29	A	Stirling Albion	D 0-0	0-0	5		2504
7	Sept	5	A	Meadowbank T	W 2-0	0-0	4	Lavety 2	1337
8		12	H	Dunfermline Ath	W 2-1	1-1	2	Hewitt, Gillies K	3372
9		19	A	Kilmarnock	W 2-1	1-0	2	Farrell, Elliot	5291
10		26	A	Ayr U	W 2-0	1-0	2	Farrell, Hewitt	3079
11	Oct	3	A	Cowdenbeath	W 2-1	1-1	2	McDowall, Archibald (og)	1022
12		10	H	Raith R	D 1-1	0-1	2	MacLeod (og)	6194
13		17	A	Dumbarton	L 2-4	1-3	2	McDowall, Charnley (pen)	2022
14		24	A	Meadowbank T	D 1-1	0-1	2	Elliot	3538
15		31	A	Stirling Albion	W 1-0	0-0	2	Hewitt	1073
16	Nov	7	A	Clydebank	W 2-1	0-1	2	Lavety 2	2133
17		14	H	Morton	L 2-3	0-1	2	Lambert, Elliot	5148
18		21	H	Kilmarnock	L 0-1	0-1	2		4686
19		28	A	Dunfermline Ath	L 0-2	0-0	3		3074
20	Dec	2	H	Cowdenbeath	W 5-0	1-0	—	Money (pen), McVie, Gillies R, Lavety 2	1648
21		5	A	Ayr U	L 0-2	0-1	3		2516
22		12	A	Raith R	L 1-3	0-1	3	Baillie	3211
23		19	H	Hamilton A	L 0-2	0-2	5		2110
24		26	H	Clydebank	W 3-2	0-0	5	Money (pen), Lavety, Gallagher	2503
25	Jan	2	A	Morton	D 1-1	1-0	5	Gallagher	5170
26		16	H	Stirling Albion	W 1-0	0-0	4	Elliot	1931
27		27	A	Cowdenbeath	W 3-0	2-0	—	Lavety, Gallagher 2	535
28		30	H	Dumbarton	W 2-1	0-0	3	Baillie, Hewitt	2453
29	Feb	3	A	Meadowbank T	W 2-1	0-1	—	Gallagher, Lavety	718
30		13	A	Hamilton A	D 0-0	0-0	4		2593
31		20	H	Ayr U	W 1-0	0-0	4	Lavety	2371
32		27	A	Kilmarnock	L 0-1	0-0	4		6555
33	Mar	6	H	Dunfermline Ath	L 0-1	0-0	4		2695
34		10	H	Raith R	D 1-1	1-1	—	Lavety	2700
35		13	A	Dumbarton	L 1-2	1-0	5	Baillie	1558
36		20	H	Morton	W 2-0	0-0	5	Gallagher (pen), Lavety	2697
37		27	A	Clydebank	W 3-0	1-0	5	Lavety 2, Gallagher	1460
38	Apr	3	A	Meadowbank T	L 1-2	0-1	5	McWhirter	2619
39		10	A	Stirling Albion	L 1-2	1-0	6	Gallagher	879
40		17	A	Dunfermline Ath	W 2-1	0-1	4	McDowall, Elliot	3252
41		24	H	Kilmarnock	W 2-1	0-1	4	Gallagher, Hewitt	8432
42	May	1	H	Hamilton A	W 2-1	0-0	4	Gallagher 2	2671
43		8	A	Ayr U	D 3-3	0-1	4	McIntyre, Lavety, Gallagher (pen)	3235
44		15	H	Cowdenbeath	L 1-2	0-0	4	Lavety	1905

Final League Position: 4

Most League Goals in Season (Individual): 45: Dunky Walker, Division I; 1921-22.
Most Goals Overall (Individual): 221: David McCrae, 1923-24.

Honours
League Champions: First Division 1976-77. Division II 1967-68; *Runners-up:* 1935-36.
Scottish Cup Winners: 1926, 1959, 1987. *Runners-up* 1908, 1934, 1962.
League Cup Runners-up: 1955-56.
Victory Cup: 1919-20. *Summer Cup:* 1943-44. *Anglo-Scottish Cup:* 1979-80.
European: *Cup Winners Cup:* 1987-88. *UEFA Cup:* 1980-81, 1983-84, 1985-86.
Club colours: Shirt: Black and white vertical stripes. Shorts: White with black side panel. Stockings: White with black hoop. Change colours: All red.

Goalscorers: League (62): Lavety 18, Gallagher 12 (2 pens), Elliot 5, Hewitt 5, Baillie 4, McDowall 3, Farrell 2, McGill 2, Money 2 (2 pens), Charnley 1 (pen), Gillies K 1, Gillies R 1, Lambert 1, McIntyre 1, McVie 1, McWhirter 1, own goals 2. *Scottish Cup (2):* Gallagher 1, Lavety 1. *Skol Cup (1):* Lavety 1. *B & Q Cup (1):* Charnley 1.

Money C 25	Dawson R 34	Reid M 5	Manley R 20	Baillie A 38	Charnley J 14	Elliot D 38+2	Lambert P 38+1	Torfason G 1	McGill D 6+3	Broddie J 13+1	McIntyre P 14+6	Lavety B 32+10	McLaughlin B 2	McDowall K 12+1	Fabiani R —+6	McWhirter N 34	Gillies K 8+11	Baker M 29	Cummings P 1+3	McVie G 3+3	Farrell S 15+4	Hewitt J 24+3	Fullarton J 25+1	Gillies R 2+6	Taylor S 2	Gallagher E 18+1	Fridge L 18	Beattie J 2	Bone A 2+7	Peacock J 7+1	McGrotty G —+2	Watson D 1	Paterson A 1	Hetherston B —+1	Match No.
1	2	3	4	5	6	7	8	9	10	11	12	14																							1
1	2	3	4	5		7	8		14	11		6		10		*9*																			2
1	2	3	4	5		7	8		9	11		6		10																					3
1	2	3	4	5		7	8		9	11				10		6	12																		4
1	2	3	4	5		7	8			*11*				10		9	12		6	14															5
1	2		4	5		7	8		9			10		6		11		3				12	14												6
1	2		4	5			8		14			10		6		12		3		9		7	11												7
1	2		4	5		9	8		14			10		6		7		3				12	11												8
1	2		4	5	6	11	*8*							9	12	14		3				7	10												9
1	2		4	5	6	11	8							14		9		3				7	10												10
1	2		4	5	6	14						11				9	8	3				7	10	12											11
1	2		4	5	6	11	12					14				9	8	3				7	*10*												12
1			4	5	6	11	8					14				9	2	3	12			7	10												13
1	2			5	6	11	8					14		9		4	12	3				7	10												14
1	2			5	6	12	8			11		14				4	3					7	10	9											15
1	2			5	6	7	8			11	*10*	14				4	12	3					9												16
1	2			5	6	7	8			11				9		4		3				12	10												17
1	2	3		5	6	7	8			11				9		4						14	10												18
1	2	3		5	6	7	8			11		14				4			12			9	10												19
1	2	3		5	6	11	8							9		4	7					14	10	12											20
1	2			5	6	11	8		7			14				4					9		10		3										21
1	2		6	5	7					11	12					4	14		9	8		10			3										22
1	2	3		5			8			11						4			14	12		10	6				7								23
1				5			8			11					3	4	6		14	9		10		2			7								24
1	2			5			8			11					3	4	6		14	12		*10*	9				7								25
				5			8			11				9		4		3		2		10	6			*7*	1								26
				5			8			11	12			9		4		3	14	2		10	6			*7*	1								27
				5			8			11			2	9		4	12					10	6			7	1		3	14					28
				5			8			11			2	9		4	12	3				10	6			7	1								29
				5			8			11			2	9		4						10	6			7	1		3	14					30
				5			8			11			2	9		4		3				10	6	12		7	1								31
			2	5			8			11		10		9		4	14	3					6			7	1								32
11				5			8					2		9		4	10	3	14				6	12		7	1								33
			2	5			8			11				9		4		3		10	14		6			7	1		12						34
			2	5			8			11				9		4		3		12		10	6			7	1		14						35
			2	5			8			11		12		9		4		3					6			7	1		14	10					36
			2	5			8			11		6		9		4		3				12				7	1		14	10					37
			2	5			8			11		6		9		4		3					12				1			7		*10*	14		38
			2	5								6		9		4	7	3					11	14		8	1		12	*10*					39
			2	5			11					12		9		4	7	3					6	14		8	1			10					40
			2	5						11		12		9		4	7	3				10	6			14	1				*8*				41
			2	5			8			11		12		9	*5*	4		*3*	14			10	6				1			7					42
			2	5			8			11		5		9		4	7	3				14	6				1		10	12					43
												9				4		3				10	6						7	5	8	*11*	14	1	44

STENHOUSEMUIR   Second Division

Year Formed: 1884. *Ground & Address:* Ochilview Park, Gladstone Rd, Stenhousemuir FK5 5QL. *Telephone:* 0324 562992.
Ground Capacity: total: 3480. seated: 340. *Size of Pitch:* 113yd × 78yd.
Chairman: Greig Thomson. *Secretary:* A. T. Bullock. *Commercial Manager:* John Sharp.
Manager: Terry Christie. *Assistant Manager:* Graeme Armstrong. *Physio:* Lee Campbell. *Coach:* Gordon Buchanan.
Managers since 1975: H. Glasgow; J. Black; A. Rose; W. Henderson; A. Rennie; J. Meakin; D. Lawson. *Club*
Nickname(s): The Warriors. *Previous Grounds:* Tryst Ground 1884-86, Goschen Park 1886-90.
Record Attendance: 12,500 v East Fife, Scottish Cup 4th rd; 11 Mar, 1950.
Record Transfer Fee received: £30,000 for David Beaton to Falkirk (June 1989).
Record Transfer Fee paid: £7000 to Meadowbank T for Lee Bullen (Nov 1990).
Record Victory: 9-2 v Dundee U, Division II; 19 Apr, 1937.
Record Defeat: 2-11 v Dunfermline Ath. Division II; 27 Sept, 1930.

STENHOUSEMUIR 1992—93 LEAGUE RECORD

Match No.	Date		Venue	Opponents	Result	H/T Score	Lg. Pos.	Goalscorers	Atten dance
1	Aug	8	A	East Fife	D 1-1	0-1	—	Kemp (pen)	558
2		15	H	Berwick R	L 1-3	0-1	12	Mathieson	243
3		22	A	Alloa	L 1-2	0-1	13	Mathieson	517
4		29	H	Stranraer	L 1-2	0-2	14	Bell	241
5	Sept	5	A	Montrose	W 1-0	1-0	11	Mathieson	581
6		12	A	Forfar Ath	L 1-3	1-1	12	Bell	522
7		19	H	Brechin C	L 2-4	0-2	13	Fisher, Haddow	278
8		26	A	Clyde	D 0-0	0-0	13		554
9	Oct	3	H	Queen's Park	W 2-0	0-0	12	Mathieson, Dickov	357
10		10	A	East Stirling	W 7-3	4-0	10	Mathieson 4, Dickov, Aitken, Mackie	371
11		17	H	Arbroath	L 1-3	1-1	12	Bell	469
12		24	H	Albion R	W 2-0	0-0	10	Lytwyn, Aitken	304
13		31	A	Queen of the S	W 1-0	1-0	8	Mathieson	625
14	Nov	7	A	Stranraer	D 0-0	0-0	7		578
15		14	A	Montrose	W 2-0	2-0	7	Mathieson 2	337
16		21	A	Brechin C	D 2-2	1-2	7	Lytwyn, Mathieson	450
17		28	H	Forfar Ath	W 2-0	1-0	7	Mathieson, McLafferty	308
18	Dec	12	H	East Fife	W 3-1	1-0	4	Lytwyn, Mathieson 2	473
19		26	A	Queen's Park	D 2-2	1-0	5	Mathieson, Steel	531
20	Jan	2	A	Berwick R	D 1-1	1-1	4	Haddow	470
21		26	H	Queen of the S	D 1-1	0-1	—	McLafferty	315
22		30	H	Clyde	L 0-2	0-1	7		706
23	Feb	2	A	Alloa	L 0-1	0-1	—		459
24		10	A	Arbroath	L 2-3	0-1	—	Mathieson 2	535
25		13	H	East Stirling	L 1-2	1-1	8	Mathieson	407
26		16	A	Albion R	D 0-0	0-0	—		205
27		20	A	Montrose	W 4-1	2-1	8	Steel, Mathieson, Fisher, Haddow	377
28		27	H	Berwick R	D 0-0	0-0	8		314
29	Mar	6	A	Forfar Ath	L 0-1	0-0	8		441
30		13	H	Queen of the S	W 2-1	0-0	8	Mathieson, Steel	384
31		20	H	Brechin C	W 3-0	1-0	8	Armstrong, Mathieson 2	360
32		27	A	Arbroath	L 1-2	1-2	8	Steel	621
33	Apr	3	H	Clyde	W 3-0	1-0	8	Dickov, Hallford, McCarron (og)	584
34		10	A	East Fife	L 1-2	0-0	8	Mathieson	569
35		17	H	East Stirling	W 2-0	0-0	8	Ross (og), Mathieson	299
36		24	A	Albion R	W 2-0	0-0	8	Irvine, Mathieson	324
37	May	1	A	Alloa	W 2-0	2-0	7	Irvine, Steel	424
38		8	H	Queen's Park	D 0-0	0-0	7		379
39		15	H	Stranraer	L 2-5	1-2	7	Steel, Irvine	1231

Final League Position: 7

Most Capped Player: —.
Most League Appearances: 298: Harry Cairney.
Most League Goals in Season (Individual): 32: Robert Taylor, Division II; 1925-26.
Most Goals Overall (Individual): —.

Honours
League Champions: —. *Scottish Cup:* Semi-finals 1902-03. *League Cup:* Quarter-finals 1947-48, 1960-61, 1975-76.
Club colours: Shirt: Maroon with silver stripe. Shorts: White with maroon insert. Stockings: White.

Goalscorers: *League (59):* Mathieson 26, Steel 6, Bell 3, Dickov 3, Haddow 3, Irvine 3, Lytwyn 3, Aitken 2, Fisher 2, McLafferty 2, Armstrong 1, Hallford 1, Kemp 1 (pen), Mackie 1, own goals 2. *Scottish Cup (2):* Hallford 1 (pen), Lytwyn 1. *Skol Cup (2):* Irvine 1, Steel 1. *B & Q Cup (2):* Bell 1, Mathieson 1.

Kelly C 16	Clarke J 26 + 2	Kemp B 2	Barr R 4 + 5	Prior S 6 + 1	Fisher J 36	Aitken N 23 + 1	Bell D 15 + 10	Mathieson M 39	Steel T 22 + 2	Irvine J 8 + 5	Hallford E 38 + 1	Anderson P 9 + 1	Clouston B 27 + 2	Haddow L 24 + 4	Barnstaple K 23	Tracey K 4 + 1	Reid J 1	Lytwyn C 13 + 4	Mackie P 8 + 5	Dickov S 10 + 7	Armstrong G 28	Godfrey P 19	McLafferty W 4 + 4	Logan S 22 + 1	Black K 2	Match No.
1	2	3	4	5	6	7	8	9	10	11	12															1
1	6	8	4	5	10			7	12	11	3	14	2	9												2
	2				12		11	8	10	6	3	4	7		1	5		9								3
	2				12	5	11	8	10	6	3	4	7		1	14		9								4
	2	8	14				11	7	10	6	3	4	12		1	5		9								5
	2		4				8	7	10	11	3	6	14	12	1	5		9								6
	12		4		11	2		7	9		3	6	8	10	1	5		14								7
	5		4		7	12	8	9	10	14	3	6	2		1			11								8
	4	5			11		2	6	9	14	3	8			1	7		10								9
	4			12	11		2	6	9	3	5	8	14		1	7		10								10
	4			12	11		2	6	9	3	5	8	14		1	7		10								11
	11				2		6	9		3	5	8	7		1			14	12	10	4					12
	6				2			9			3	8		11	1			10		7	4	5				13
	6				2			9			3	8		11	1			10		12	4	5	7			14
	6				2			9			3	8		11	1			10		7	4	5				15
	6				2			9			3	8		11	1			10			4	5	7			16
	6				2		14	9			3	8		11	1			10			4	5	12	7		17
	2				6			9			3	8		11	1			10			4	5	12	7		18
	6				2			9	14		3	8		11	1			10			4	5	12	7		19
	6				2		14	9		8	3			11	1			10	12		4	5	7			20
	6				2			9		11	3	8			1			10	14		4	5	12	7		21
	6				2			9			3	8		11	1			12	14		4	5	10	7		22
	14				2			9			3	8		11	1			12	6		4	5	10	7		23
	14				6		2	9			3			11	1			12	8	10	4	5	7			24
	2				6		8	9			3		14	11	1			10		7	4	5	12			25
1	5				6		2	9		11	3	8						10		12	4			7		26
1	5				6			9		11	3	8						10			4			7	2	27
1	5				6		14	9		11	3	8						10		12	4			7	2	28
1	5				6		2	9		11	14	3		8				10		12	4			7		29
1	2				12			9		11		6	3	8				10			4	5		7		30
1	5				6			9		11		8	3	2				10			4			7		31
1	5				6		12	9		11		8	3	2				10			4			7		32
1	5				6		12	9		11			3	2				10		8	4			7		33
1	5				6		2	14	9	11		12	3	8				10			4			7		34
1	8				6		2		12	9		11	3					10			4	5		7		35
1	8			2	6			9		11		12	3	14				10			4	5		7		36
1	8				6		2		12	9		11	10		3						4	5		7		37
1	8				6		2		12	9		11	10		3			14			4	5		7		38
1	8				6		2			9		11	10		3					12	4	5		7		39

STIRLING ALBION

First Division

Year Formed: 1945. *Ground & Address:* Forthbank Stadium, Springkerse Industrial Estate, Stirling FK7 7UW. *Telephone:* 0786 450399.
Chairman: Peter McKenzie. *Secretary:* David McCallum. *Commercial Manager:* —.
Manager: John Brogan. *Assistant Manager:* Jimmy Sinclair. *Physio:* George Cameron.
Managers since 1975: A. Smith; G. Peebles; J. Fleeting. *Club Nickname(s):* The Binos. *Previous Grounds:* None.
Record Attendance: 26,400 v Celtic, Scottish Cup 4th rd; 14 Mar, 1959.
Record Transfer Fee received: £70,000 for John Philliben to Doncaster R (Mar 1984).
Record Transfer Fee paid: £17,000 for Douglas Lawrie from Airdrieonians (Dec 1989).
Record Victory: 20-0 v Selkirk, Scottish Cup 1st rd; 8 Dec, 1984.
Record Defeat: 0-9 v Dundee U, Division I; 30 Dec, 1967.
Most Capped Player: —.

STIRLING ALBION 1992—93 LEAGUE RECORD

Match No.	Date		Venue	Opponents	Result	H/T Score	Lg. Pos.	Goalscorers	Atten dance
1	Aug	1	A	Dumbarton	L 3-4	1-2	—	Reilly 2, McInnes	903
2		4	A	Raith R	D 0-0	0-0	—		1513
3		8	H	Cowdenbeath	W 2-1	0-1	6	Moore, Watters	393
4		15	A	Meadowbank T	W 1-0	1-0	5	McInnes	356
5		22	H	Hamilton A	L 0-2	0-1	8		644
6		29	A	St Mirren	D 0-0	0-0	8		2504
7	Sept	5	H	Dunfermline Ath	L 0-5	0-2	10		1371
8		12	H	Kilmarnock	L 0-1	0-1	10		1326
9		19	A	Clydebank	L 1-4	0-1	11	McCallum	704
10		26	H	Morton	D 1-1	1-1	10	Mitchell	750
11	Oct	3	A	Ayr U	L 1-2	0-1	11	Watters	1580
12		10	H	Dumbarton	L 1-2	0-0	11	Lawrie	475
13		17	A	Cowdenbeath	D 1-1	0-0	11	Watters	359
14		24	A	Dunfermline Ath	L 0-1	0-0	11		2388
15		31	H	St Mirren	L 0-1	0-0	11		1073
16	Nov	7	H	Meadowbank T	W 4-1	2-0	10	Shanks, McInnes, Callaghan, Reilly	389
17		14	A	Hamilton A	L 0-1	0-0	11		1518
18		21	H	Clydebank	L 0-1	0-0	11		396
19		28	A	Kilmarnock	L 0-1	0-1	11		3526
20	Dec	1	H	Ayr U	D 0-0	0-0	—		344
21		5	A	Morton	D 2-2	0-1	11	McKenna, Callaghan	1343
22		12	A	Dumbarton	W 3-0	1-0	11	Mitchell 2 (1 pen), Lawrie	716
23		29	H	Raith R	L 0-3	0-2	—		1251
24	Jan	2	H	Hamilton A	D 0-0	0-0	11		779
25		16	A	St Mirren	L 0-1	0-0	11		1931
26		26	A	Ayr U	D 2-2	2-1	—	Watters, Pew	2061
27	Feb	6	A	Meadowbank T	D 1-1	0-0	11	Elder (og)	305
28		9	H	Dunfermline Ath	L 1-2	1-0	—	Pew	1023
29		13	A	Raith R	L 0-2	0-1	11		2103
30		16	H	Cowdenbeath	W 2-1	1-0	—	Pew, Watters (pen)	283
31		20	H	Morton	L 0-2	0-1	11		422
32		27	A	Clydebank	D 1-1	0-0	11	Watters	636
33	Mar	6	H	Kilmarnock	W 2-0	1-0	11	Watters 2 (1 pen)	1327
34		9	H	Dumbarton	W 1-0	0-0	—	McCallum	418
35		13	A	Cowdenbeath	D 1-1	1-0	10	Watters	310
36		20	A	Hamilton A	L 0-2	0-0	11		1017
37		27	A	Meadowbank T	D 2-2	1-0	11	Watters, Tait	475
38	Apr	3	A	Dunfermline Ath	W 1-0	1-0	11	Moore	2607
39		10	H	St Mirren	W 2-1	0-1	10	Moore 2	879
40		17	A	Kilmarnock	L 0-3	0-1	10		3852
41		24	H	Clydebank	L 2-3	1-0	10	Tait, Armstrong (pen)	2301
42	May	1	H	Raith R	W 2-1	1-0	10	Watson, Armstrong (pen)	1536
43		8	A	Morton	W 3-1	1-1	10	McCallum 2, McInnes	1058
44		15	H	Ayr U	D 1-1	0-0	10	Watters	1171

Final League Position: 10

Most League Appearances: 504: Matt McPhee, 1967-81.
Most League Goals in Season (Individual): 27: Joe Hughes, Division II; 1969-70.
Most Goals Overall (Individual): 129: Billy Steele, 1971-83.

Honours
League Champions: Division II 1952-53, 1957-58, 1960-61, 1964-65. Second Division 1976-77, 1990-91; *Runners-up:* Division II 1948-49, 1950-51.
Scottish Cup: —. *League Cup:* —.
Club colours: Shirt: Red with white sleeves. Shorts: White. Stockings: White.

Goalscorers: *League (44):* Watters 11 (2 pens), McCallum 4, McInnes 4, Moore 4, Mitchell 3 (1 pen), Pew 3, Reilly 3, Armstrong 2 (2 pens), Callaghan 2, Lawrie 2, Tait 2, McKenna 1, Shanks 1, Watson 1, own goal 1. *Scottish Cup (1):* McInnes. *Skol Cup (0). B & Q Cup (2):* Moore 1, Watters 1.

McGeown M 44	Mitchell C 39	Watson P 31	Shanks D 21 + 3	Lawrie D 28	Clark R 7	Reilly R 24 + 9	Moore V 28 + 3	Watters W 25 + 9	McInnes I 34 + 9	Armstrong P 42	Docherty R 3 + 4	Docherty A 7 + 17	Taylor G 4	Robertson S 9	Kerr J 26	Brown 11 + 3	McCallum M 9 + 10	McCormack J T 18	Tait T 26 + 1	Ross B 2	Dempsey J 4	Callaghan T 18 + 8	Pew D 17 + 3	McKenna A 17 + 2	Brogan J — + 1	Match No.
1	2	3	4	5	6	7	8	9	10	11	12	14														1
1	2		4		6	7	8	9	14	3	12	11			5	10										2
1	2		4	5		7	8	9	14	3	12	11			10	6										3
1	2		4	5			8	9	7	3	11	12			10	6										4
1	2		4	5			8	9	7	3	11				10	6	14	12								5
1	2	3	4	5			8	9	10	11	12	14			6	7										6
1	2	3		5		7	8	9	10	11	4	14			6	12										7
1		3	4			7		9	12	11		14	5		6		2	8	10							8
1		3	4			7		9	10	11		14			6		8	2	5			12				9
1	2	3		5			8	9	14						10	6	11					4	7			10
1	2	3	14	5		7	8	9	4						10	6						11	12			11
1	2	14		5			8	9	4	3					10	6	12					11	7			12
1	2	3	4	5			8	9		11		14			10	6		7								13
1	6	3	2	5			8	9	4	11					10		14					12	7			14
1	2	3	4	5			8	9	12	11					10	6						14	7			15
1	2	3	4				12	5	14	11					10	6						8	9			16
1	2	3		5			12	8	14	11					10	6			4			9				17
1	6	3	2			7	8	9	10	11		14	5						4			12				18
1	2	3		5		7	8		10	11	14							6	4			12	9			19
1	2	3		5		7	8		10	11	12							6	4			9	14			20
1	2	3		5			12		7	11	14	8			6				4			10	9			21
1	2	3		5			12		8	11					7			6	4			10	9			22
1	2	3		5			12	8	11			14			7			6	4			10	9			23
1	6	3		5		7			8	11		14					12	2	4			10	9			24
1	2	3		5			12	9	7	10	8				6				4			14	11			25
1	2	3		5			14	9	7	10	8				6				4			12	11			26
1		3	14	5				9	7	10					6			2	4			8	11	12		27
1		3	4	5			12		7	10					6			2	8			14	11	9		28
1		3	4				12	14	7	10					6			2		5		8	11	9		29
1	2	3	4				8		14	7	10				6				5			12	11	9		30
1	2	3	4	5			8		14	7	10				6		9	12				11				31
1	2		5			10	8	9	14	3					6		12		4			7	11			32
1	2		5			10	8	9	12	3					6		14		4			7	11			33
1	2		5			10	8	9	12	3					14		6		4			7	11			34
1	2		5			10	8	9	12	3					14		6		4			7	11			35
1	2	6	5			10	8	9	12	3					14				4			7	11			36
1	2	3		5			10	8	9	7	6				11		4									37
1	2	3					10	8	12	7	11	14			6		4					9	5			38
1	2	3					10	8	12	7	11	14			6		4					9	5			39
1	2	3					10	8	12	7	11	14			6		4					9	5			40
1	2						10	8	9	7	3	14			6		12	11	4				5			41
1	6	3		8	5			7	11	12		9			2		4					10	14			42
1	2			8	5		12	7	11						6		9	3	4			10	14			43
1	6	2		5			8	14	7	11	12				9		3	4				10				44

STRANRAER Second Division

Year Formed: 1870. *Ground & Address:* Stair Park, London Rd, Stranraer DG9 8BS. *Telephone:* 0776 3271.
Ground Capacity: total: 5000. seated: 700. *Size of Pitch:* 110yd × 70yd.
Chairman: G. F. Compton. *Secretary:* Graham Rodgers. *Commercial Manager:(contact Secretary).*
Manager: Alex McAnespie. *Physio:* Derek McHarg. *Player/Coach:* Lex Grant.
Managers since 1975: J. Hughes; N. Hood; G. Hamilton; D. Sneddon; J. Clark; R. Clark; A. McAnespie. *Club Nickname(s):* The Blues. *Previous Grounds:* None.
Record Attendance: 6500 v Rangers, Scottish Cup 1st rd; 24 Jan, 1948.
Record Transfer Fee received: £30,000 for Duncan George to Ayr Utd.
Record Transfer Fee paid: £15,000 for Colin Harkness from Kilmarnock (Aug 1989).
Record Victory: 7-0 v Brechin C, Division II; 6 Feb, 1965.
Record Defeat: 1-11 v Queen of the South, Scottish Cup 1st rd; 16 Jan, 1932.
Most Capped Player: —.

STRANRAER 1992—93 LEAGUE RECORD

Match No.	Date	Venue	Opponents	Result	H/T Score	Lg. Pos.	Goalscorers	Atten dance
1	Aug 8	A	Queen's Park	D 1-1	0-0	—	Duncan (pen)	390
2	15	H	Queen of the S	D 2-2	0-1	7	Sloan, Diver	982
3	22	A	Montrose	W 2-0	2-0	6	Sloan, Diver	561
4	29	A	Stenhousemuir	W 2-1	2-0	4	McIntyre, Diver	241
5	Sept 5	H	East Stirling	W 4-1	2-1	4	Diver, Sloan 2, Hughes	479
6	12	A	Brechin C	D 1-1	0-0	4	McIntyre	441
7	19	H	Albion R	D 1-1	0-0	4	Sloan	627
8	26	A	Forfar Ath	L 1-4	0-2	5	Diver	522
9	Oct 3	H	East Fife	W 2-1	1-0	4	Sloan, Gallagher	567
10	10	A	Alloa	W 4-1	2-0	3	Gallagher, Diver 3	509
11	17	H	Clyde	D 1-1	1-1	3	Grant	794
12	24	A	Berwick R	W 2-1	0-1	2	Duncan (pen), McLean	326
13	31	H	Arbroath	W 1-0	0-0	2	Grant	554
14	Nov 7	A	Stenhousemuir	D 0-0	0-0	2		578
15	14	A	East Stirling	W 2-1	2-0	2	Duncan, Cody	374
16	21	A	Albion R	D 1-1	0-0	2	Sloan	274
17	28	H	Brechin C	D 0-0	0-0	2		927
18	Dec 12	H	Queen's Park	D 1-1	1-1	2	Sloan	529
19	26	A	East Fife	W 1-0	1-0	2	Duncan (pen)	678
20	Jan 2	A	Queen of the S	L 0-2	0-0	2		1240
21	9	H	Montrose	W 3-1	0-1	2	Gallagher, Sloan, Diver	543
22	20	A	Arbroath	L 1-2	1-1	—	Sloan	469
23	23	H	Berwick R	L 1-3	0-2	2	Diver	468
24	30	H	Forfar Ath	W 2-0	0-0	3	Grant, Diver	560
25	Feb 6	A	Clyde	D 0-0	0-0	3		827
26	13	H	Alloa	L 1-2	1-0	3	Sloan	585
27	20	H	East Stirling	D 0-0	0-0	3		443
28	27	A	Albion R	W 2-1	1-0	3	Duncan, McLean	251
29	Mar 6	A	Queen's Park	W 4-2	3-0	3	Sloan, Grant, McLean 2	506
30	13	A	Brechin C	W 1-0	1-0	3	Brown (og)	530
31	20	H	Clyde	D 1-1	0-0	3	Grant	1040
32	27	A	East Fife	D 1-1	1-0	3	Sloan	722
33	Apr 3	A	Forfar Ath	W 3-1	2-1	3	Grant 2, Millar	510
34	10	A	Queen of the S	D 3-3	2-1	3	Sloan 2, McLean	1095
35	17	H	Alloa	D 3-3	2-0	3	Ferguson, Sloan, Duncan	619
36	24	A	Arbroath	W 4-1	1-1	3	Gallagher, Sloan 2, Grant	777
37	May 1	A	Montrose	W 2-0	1-0	3	Grant, Gallagher	510
38	8	H	Berwick R	W 3-1	2-1	3	McIntyre, Grant, Duncan (pen)	1020
39	15	A	Stenhousemuir	W 5-2	2-1	3	Sloan, Brannigan, Duncan (pen), Ferguson, Grant	1231

Final League Position: 3

Most League Appearances: 256: Ian McDonald.
Most League Goals in Season (Individual): 27: Derek Frye, Second Division; 1977-78.
Most Goals Overall (Individual): —.

Honours
League Champions: —.
Scottish Cup: —.
League Cup: —.
Qualifying Cup Winners: 1937.
Club colours: Shirt: Royal blue with amber chest band. Shorts: Royal blue. Stockings: Royal blue.

Goalscorers: *League (69):* Sloan 19, Diver 11, Grant 11, Duncan 8 (5 pens), Gallagher 5, McLean 5, McIntyre 3, Ferguson 2, Brannigan 1, Cody 1, Hughes 1, Millar 1, own goal 1.   *Scottish Cup (2):* Cody 1, Duncan 1.   *Skol Cup (3):* Cody 1, Grant 1, Sloan 1.   *B & Q Cup (3):* Diver 1, McIntyre 1, Sloan 1.

Duffy B 15	McIntyre S 26 + 1	Hughes J 37	Spittal I 15	Duncan G 35 + 4	Butler J 2	Kelly P 9 + 14	Sloan T 38	Diver D 21 + 4	Cody S 20 + 9	Love J 11 + 9	Grant A 36 + 2	Geraghty M — + 1	Brannigan K 38	McCann J 35	Evans S 6 + 4	Gallagher A 23 + 2	Ross S 24	McLean P 22 + 1	Smith A — + 2	Fraser A 1 + 2	Ferguson W 4 + 7	Millar G 11	Match No.
1	2	3	4	5	6	7	8	9	10	11	12	14											1
1	2	3	4	11	8		7	9	10		14		5	6		12							2
1	2	3	4	12		14	7	9			8		5	6	11	10							3
1	2	3	4	14		12	7	9			10		5	6	11	8							4
1	2	3	4	12			7	9	14		8		5	6	11	10							5
1	2	3	4	12			7	9			8		5	6	11	10							6
1	2	3		10			7	9	14		8		5	6	11	4							7
1	2	3	4	10			7	9	14		8		5	6	11	12							8
1	2	3	4	10		14	7		11	9	8		5	6									9
1	2	3	4	11		14	7	9	6		8		5	10		12							10
1	2	3	4				7	9	6	11	8		5	10		12							11
	2	3		6		14	7	9	10		8		5	4			1	11					12
	2	3		6		12	7	9	11		8		5	4			1	10			14		13
	2	3		6		12	7	9	11		8		5	4			1	10					14
	2	3	4				8	9	11		7		5	6			1	10			14		15
	2	3	4	14			7	9	11		8		5	6			1	10			12		16
	2	3	4			14	7		11		10		5	6		9	1	8					17
	2	3	4	11		12	7	9			8		5	6			1	10			14		18
	2	3	4	11			7	9	14		8		5	6		12	1	10					19
	2	3	4	11		14	7	9	12		8		5	6			1	10					20
	2	3	4				7	9	14	12	8		5	6		10	1	11					21
	2	3	4					9	11	12	8		5	6		10	1	7					22
	2	3		6		12	7	14	11		8		5	4		10	1				9		23
	2	3		9			8	14	11	12	10		5	4		6	1	7					24
	2	3		9			10	12	11	14	8		5	4		6	1	7					25
	2	3		9			12	10	8	11	14		5	4		6	1	7					26
	2	3		9			11	10	14		8		5	4		6	1	7				12	27
	2			9			12		8		7		5	4		6	1	11				10	28
	2			9			11	12	8		7		5	4		14	1	6			10	3	29
	2	3		9			11	12	8		7		5	4			1	10			14	6	30
	2	3		9			11	12	8		7		5	4			1	10			14	6	31
		3		9			11		8		7		5	4		6	1	10				2	32
	2			9			11	12	8		7		5	4		6	1	10			14	3	33
	2			9			11	12	8		7		5	4		6	1	10			14	3	34
	2	3		10			12	14	11	8	7		5	6			1				9	4	35
1	2	3		9		14	7			11	8		5	4		6					12	10	36
1	2	3		9			7			11	8		5	4		6						10	37
1	2	3		9			7			11	8		5	4		6						10	38
1	2	3		9			7			11	8		5	4		6		14			12	10	39

SCOTTISH LEAGUE 1992–93

Premier Division

		P	Home W	D	L	Goals F	A	Away W	D	L	Goals F	A	Pt	GD
1	Rangers	44	20	2	0	52	11	13	5	4	45	24	73	+62
2	Aberdeen	44	13	7	2	41	13	14	3	5	46	23	64	+51
3	Celtic	44	13	5	4	37	18	11	7	4	31	23	60	+27
4	Dundee U	44	8	7	7	25	27	11	2	9	31	22	47	+7
5	Hearts	44	12	6	4	26	15	3	8	11	11	20	44	−5
6	St Johnstone	44	8	10	4	29	27	2	10	10	23	39	40	−14
7	Hibernian	44	8	8	6	32	28	4	5	13	22	36	37	−10
8	Partick T	44	5	6	11	26	41	7	6	9	24	30	36	−21
9	Motherwell	44	7	4	11	27	37	4	9	9	19	25	35	−16
10	Dundee	44	7	4	11	25	34	4	8	10	23	34	34	−20
11	Falkirk	44	7	5	10	40	39	4	2	16	20	47	29	−26
12	Airdrieonians	44	4	9	9	22	27	2	8	12	13	43	29	−35

First Division

		P	Home W	D	L	Goals F	A	Away W	D	L	Goals F	A	Pt	GD
1	Raith R	44	17	5	0	54	14	8	10	4	31	27	65	+44
2	Kilmarnock	44	13	6	3	43	14	8	6	8	24	26	54	+27
3	Dunfermline Ath	44	10	5	7	33	27	12	3	7	31	20	52	+17
4	St Mirren	44	11	5	6	33	20	10	4	8	29	32	51	+10
5	Hamilton A	44	11	7	4	36	23	8	5	9	29	22	50	+20
6	Morton	44	11	3	8	36	27	8	7	7	29	29	48	+9
7	Ayr U	44	9	9	4	27	19	5	9	8	22	25	46	+5
8	Clydebank	44	10	8	4	42	22	6	5	11	29	44	45	+5
9	Dumbarton	44	10	3	9	30	30	5	4	13	26	41	37	−15
10	Stirling Albion	44	7	5	10	23	31	4	8	10	21	30	35	−17
11	Meadowbank T	44	6	6	10	23	32	5	4	13	28	48	32	−29
12	Cowdenbeath	44	0	5	17	18	55	3	2	17	15	54	13	−76

Second Division

		P	Home W	D	L	Goals F	A	Away W	D	L	Goals F	A	Pt	GD
1	Clyde	39	11	5	4	37	18	11	5	3	40	24	54	+35
2	Brechin C	39	13	3	3	37	13	10	4	6	25	19	53	+30
3	Stranraer	39	8	9	2	33	21	11	6	3	36	23	53	+25
4	Forfar Ath	39	10	5	4	47	30	8	5	7	27	24	46	+20
5	Alloa	39	8	4	7	25	28	8	8	4	38	26	44	+9
6	Arbroath	39	8	6	6	34	26	10	2	7	25	24	44	+9
7	Stenhousemuir	39	9	3	8	30	25	6	7	6	29	23	40	+11
8	Berwick R	39	8	5	6	30	25	8	2	10	26	39	39	−8
9	East Fife	39	6	6	8	32	33	8	4	7	38	31	38	+6
10	Queen of the S	39	5	4	11	27	37	7	5	7	30	35	33	−15
11	Queen's Park	39	6	6	7	29	32	2	6	12	22	41	28	−22
12	Montrose	39	5	3	12	24	35	5	4	10	22	36	27	−25
13	East Stirling	39	4	4	12	24	39	4	5	10	26	46	25	−35
14	Albion R	39	4	5	10	22	36	2	5	13	14	40	22	−40

SCOTTISH LEAGUE 1890–91 to 1992–93

*On goal average/difference. †Held jointly after indecisive play-off. ‡Won on deciding match.
††Held jointly. ¶Two points deducted for fielding ineligible player.
Competition suspended 1940–45 during war. ‡‡Two points deducted for registration irregularities.

PREMIER DIVISION

Maximum points: 72

	First	Pts	Second	Pts	Third	Pts
1975–76	Rangers	54	Celtic	48	Hibernian	43
1976–77	Celtic	55	Rangers	46	Aberdeen	43
1977–78	Rangers	55	Aberdeen	53	Dundee U	40
1978–79	Celtic	48	Rangers	45	Dundee U	44
1979–80	Aberdeen	48	Celtic	47	St Mirren	42
1980–81	Celtic	56	Aberdeen	49	Rangers*	44
1981–82	Celtic	55	Aberdeen	53	Rangers	43
1982–83	Dundee U	56	Celtic*	55	Aberdeen	55
1983–84	Aberdeen	57	Celtic	50	Dundee U	47
1984–85	Aberdeen	59	Celtic	52	Dundee U	47
1985–86	Celtic*	50	Hearts	50	Dundee U	47

Maximum points: 88

1986–87	Rangers	69	Celtic	63	Dundee U	60
1987–88	Celtic	72	Hearts	62	Rangers	60

Maximum points: 72

1988–89	Rangers	56	Aberdeen	50	Celtic	46
1989–90	Rangers	51	Aberdeen*	44	Hearts	44
1990–91	Rangers	55	Aberdeen	53	Celtic*	41

Maximum points: 88

1991–92	Rangers	72	Hearts	63	Celtic	62
1992–93	Rangers	73	Aberdeen	64	Celtic	60

FIRST DIVISION

Maximum points: 52

1975–76	Partick T	41	Kilmarnock	35	Montrose	30

Maximum points: 78

1976–77	St Mirren	62	Clydebank	58	Dundee	51
1977–78	Morton*	58	Hearts	58	Dundee	57
1978–79	Dundee	55	Kilmarnock*	54	Clydebank	54
1979–80	Hearts	53	Airdrieonians	51	Ayr U	44
1980–81	Hibernian	57	Dundee	52	St Johnstone	51
1981–82	Motherwell	61	Kilmarnock	51	Hearts	50
1982–83	St Johnstone	55	Hearts	54	Clydebank	50
1983–84	Morton	54	Dumbarton	51	Partick T	46
1984–85	Motherwell	50	Clydebank	48	Falkirk	45
1985–86	Hamilton A	56	Falkirk	45	Kilmarnock	44

Maximum points: 88

1986–87	Morton	57	Dunfermline Ath	56	Dumbarton	53
1987–88	Hamilton A	56	Meadowbank T	52	Clydebank	49

Maximum points: 78

1988–89	Dunfermline Ath	54	Falkirk	52	Clydebank	48
1989–90	St Johnstone	58	Airdrieonians	54	Clydebank	44
1990–91	Falkirk	54	Airdrieonians	53	Dundee	52

Maximum points: 88

1991–92	Dundee	58	Partick T*	57	Hamilton A	57
1992–93	Raith R	65	Kilmarnock	54	Dunfermline Ath	52

SECOND DIVISION

Maximum points: 52

1975–77	Clydebank*	40	Raith R	40	Alloa	35

Maximum points: 78

1976–77	Stirling A	55	Alloa	51	Dunfermline Ath	50
1977–78	Clyde*	53	Raith R	53	Dunfermline Ath	48
1978–79	Berwick R	54	Dunfermline Ath	52	Falkirk	50
1979–80	Falkirk	50	East Stirling	49	Forfar Ath	46
1980–81	Queen's Park	50	Queen of the S	46	Cowdenbeath	45
1981–82	Clyde	59	Alloa*	50	Arbroath	50
1982–83	Brechin C	55	Meadowbank T	54	Arbroath	49
1983–84	Forfar Ath	63	East Fife	47	Berwick R	43
1984–85	Montrose	53	Alloa	50	Dunfermline Ath	49
1985–86	Dunfermline Ath	57	Queen of the S	55	Meadowbank T	49
1986–87	Meadowbank T	55	Raith R*	52	Stirling A	52

	First	Pts	Second	Pts	Third	Pts
1987–88	Ayr U	61	St Johnstone	59	Queen's Park	51
1988–89	Albion R	50	Alloa	45	Brechin C	43
1989–90	Brechin C	49	Kilmarnock	48	Stirling A	47
1990–91	Stirling A	54	Montrose	46	Cowdenbeath	45
			Maximum points: 78			
1991–92	Dumbarton	52	Cowdenbeath	51	Alloa	50
1992–93	Clyde	54	Brechin C*	53	Stranraer	53

FIRST DIVISION to 1974–75

Maximum points: a 36; b 44; c 40; d 52; e 60; f 68; g 76; h 84.

	First	Pts	Second	Pts	Third	Pts
1890–91a††	Dumbarton	29	Rangers	29	Celtic	24
1891–92b	Dumbarton	37	Celtic	35	Hearts	30
1892–93a	Celtic	29	Rangers	28	St Mirren	23
1893–94a	Celtic	29	Hearts	26	St Bernard's	22
1894–95a	Hearts	31	Celtic	26	Rangers	21
1895–96a	Celtic	30	Rangers	26	Hibernian	24
1896–97a	Hearts	28	Hibernian	26	Rangers	25
1897–98a	Celtic	33	Rangers	29	Hibernian	22
1898–99a	Rangers	36	Hearts	26	Celtic	24
1899–1900a	Rangers	32	Celtic	25	Hibernian	24
1900–01c	Rangers	35	Celtic	29	Hibernian	25
1901–02a	Rangers	28	Celtic	26	Hearts	22
1902–03b	Hibernian	37	Dundee	31	Rangers	29
1903–04d	Third Lanark	43	Hearts	39	Rangers*	38
1904–05d	Celtic‡	41	Rangers	41	Third Lanark	35
1905–06e	Celtic	49	Hearts	43	Airdrieonians	38
1906–07f	Celtic	55	Dundee	48	Rangers	45
1907–08f	Celtic	55	Falkirk	51	Rangers	50
1908–09f	Celtic	51	Dundee	50	Clyde	48
1909–10f	Celtic	54	Falkirk	52	Rangers	46
1910–11f	Rangers	52	Aberdeen	48	Falkirk	44
1911–12f	Rangers	51	Celtic	45	Clyde	42
1912–13f	Rangers	53	Celtic	49	Hearts*	41
1913–14g	Celtic	65	Rangers	59	Hearts*	54
1914–15g	Celtic	65	Hearts	61	Rangers	50
1915–16g	Celtic	67	Rangers	56	Morton	51
1916–17g	Celtic	64	Morton	54	Rangers	53
1917–18f	Rangers	56	Celtic	55	Kilmarnock	43
1918–19f	Celtic	58	Rangers	57	Morton	47
1919–20h	Rangers	71	Celtic	68	Motherwell	57
1920–21h	Rangers	76	Celtic	66	Hearts	56
1921–22h	Celtic	67	Rangers	66	Raith R	56
1922–23g	Rangers	55	Airdrieonians	50	Celtic	46
1923–24g	Rangers	59	Airdrieonians	50	Celtic	41
1924–25g	Rangers	60	Airdrieonians	57	Hibernian	52
1925–26g	Celtic	58	Airdrieonians*	50	Hearts	50
1926–27g	Rangers	56	Motherwell	51	Celtic	49
1927–28g	Rangers	60	Celtic*	55	Motherwell	55
1928–29g	Rangers	67	Celtic	51	Motherwell	50
1929–30g	Rangers	60	Motherwell	55	Aberdeen	53
1930–31g	Rangers	60	Celtic	58	Motherwell	56
1931–32g	Motherwell	66	Rangers	61	Celtic	48
1932–33g	Rangers	62	Motherwell	59	Hearts	50
1933–34g	Rangers	66	Motherwell	62	Celtic	47
1934–35g	Rangers	55	Celtic	52	Hearts	50
1935–36g	Celtic	66	Rangers*	61	Aberdeen	61
1936–37g	Rangers	61	Aberdeen	54	Celtic	52
1937–38g	Celtic	61	Hearts	58	Rangers	49
1938–39g	Rangers	59	Celtic	48	Aberdeen	46
1946–47e	Rangers	46	Hibernian	44	Aberdeen	39
1947–48e	Hibernian	48	Rangers	46	Partick T	36
1948–49e	Rangers	46	Dundee	45	Hibernian	39
1949–50e	Rangers	50	Hibernian	49	Hearts	43
1950–51e	Hibernian	48	Rangers*	38	Dundee	38
1951–52e	Hibernian	45	Rangers	41	East Fife	37
1952–53e	Rangers*	43	Hibernian	43	East Fife	39
1953–54e	Celtic	43	Hearts	38	Partick T	35
1954–55e	Aberdeen	49	Celtic	46	Rangers	41
1955–56f	Rangers	52	Aberdeen	46	Hearts*	45
1956–57f	Rangers	55	Hearts	53	Kilmarnock	42
1957–58f	Hearts	62	Rangers	49	Celtic	46
1958–59f	Rangers	50	Hearts	48	Motherwell	44

1959–60f	Hearts	54	Kilmarnock	50	Rangers*	42
1960–61f	Rangers	51	Kilmarnock	50	Third Lanark	42
1961–62f	Dundee	54	Rangers	51	Celtic	46
1962–63f	Rangers	57	Kilmarnock	48	Partick T	46
1963–64f	Rangers	55	Kilmarnock	49	Celtic*	47
1964–65f	Kilmarnock*	50	Hearts	50	Dunfermline Ath	49
1965–66f	Celtic	57	Rangers	55	Kilmarnock	45
1966–67f	Celtic	58	Rangers	55	Clyde	46
1967–68f	Celtic	63	Rangers	61	Hibernian	45
1968–69f	Celtic	54	Rangers	49	Dunfermline Ath	45
1969–70f	Celtic	57	Rangers	45	Hibernian	44
1970–71f	Celtic	56	Aberdeen	54	St Johnstone	44
1971–72f	Celtic	60	Aberdeen	50	Rangers	44
1972–73f	Celtic	57	Rangers	56	Hibernian	45
1973–74f	Celtic	53	Hibernian	49	Rangers	48
1974–75f	Rangers	56	Hibernian	49	Celtic	45

SECOND DIVISION to 1974–75

Maximum points: a 76; b 72; c 68; d 52; e 60; f 36; g 44; h 52.

1893–94f	Hibernian	29	Cowlairs	27	Clyde	24
1894–95f	Hibernian	30	Motherwell	22	Port Glasgow	20
1895–96f	Abercorn	27	Leith Ath	23	Renton	21
1896–97f	Partick T	31	Leith Ath	27	Kilmarnock	21
1897–98f	Kilmarnock	29	Port Glasgow	25	Morton	22
1898–99f	Kilmarnock	32	Leith Ath	27	Port Glasgow	25
1899–1900f	Partick T	29	Morton	26	Port Glasgow	20
1900–01f	St Bernard's	26	Airdrieonians	23	Abercorn	21
1901–02f	Port Glasgow	32	Partick T	31	Motherwell	26
1902–03g	Airdrieonians	35	Motherwell	28	Ayr U	27
1903–04g	Hamilton A	37	Clyde	29	Ayr U	28
1904–05g	Clyde	32	Falkirk	28	Hamilton A	27
1905–06g	Leith Ath	34	Clyde	31	Albion R	27
1906–07g	St Bernard's	32	Vale of Leven*	27	Arthurlie	27
1907–08g	Raith R	30	Dumbarton	‡‡27	Ayr U	27
1908–09g	Abercorn	31	Raith R*	28	Vale of Leven	28
1909–10g‡	Leith Ath	33	Raith R	33	St Bernard's	27
1910–11g	Dumbarton	31	Ayr U	27	Albion R	25
1911–12g	Ayr U	35	Abercorn	30	Dumbarton	27
1912–13h	Ayr U	34	Dunfarmline Ath	33	East Stirling	32
1913–14g	Cowdenbeath	31	Albion R	27	Dunfermline Ath	26
1914–15h	Cowdenbeath*	37	St Bernard's*	37	Leith Ath	37
1921–22a	Alloa	60	Cowdenbeath	47	Armadale	45
1922–23a	Queen's Park	57	Clydebank	¶50	St Johnstone	¶45
1923–24a	St Johnstone	56	Cowdenbeath	55	Bathgate	44
1924–25a	Dundee U	50	Clydebank	48	Clyde	47
1925–26a	Dunfermline Ath	59	Clyde	53	Ayr U	52
1926–27a	Bo'ness	56	Raith R	49	Clydebank	45
1927–28a	Ayr U	54	Third Lanark	45	King's Park	44
1928–29b	Dundee U	51	Morton	50	Arbroath	47
1929–30a	Leith Ath*	57	East Fife	57	Albion R	54
1930–31a	Third Lanark	61	Dundee U	50	Dunfermline Ath	47
1931–32a	East Stirling*	55	St Johnstone	55	Raith Rovers*	46
1932–33c	Hibernian	54	Queen of the S	49	Dunfermline Ath	47
1933–34c	Albion R	45	Dunfermline Ath*	44	Arbroath	44
1934–35c	Third Lanark	52	Arbroath	50	St Bernard's	47
1935–36c	Falkirk	59	St Mirren	52	Morton	48
1936–37c	Ayr U	54	Morton	51	St Bernard's	48
1937–38c	Raith R	59	Albion R	48	Airdrieonians	47
1938–39c	Cowdenbeath	60	Alloa*	48	East Fife	48
1946–47d	Dundee	45	Airdrieonians	42	East Fife	31
1947–48e	East Fife	53	Albion R	42	Hamilton A	40
1948–49e	Raith R*	42	Stirling Albion	42	Airdrieonians*	41
1949–50e	Morton	47	Airdrieonians	44	St Johnstone*	36
1950–51e	Queen of the S*	45	Stirling Albion	45	Ayr U	36
1951–52e	Clyde	44	Falkirk	43	Ayr U	39
1952–53e	Stirling Albion	44	Hamilton A	43	Queen's Park	37
1953–54e	Motherwell	45	Kilmarnock	42	Third Lanark*	36
1954–55e	Airdrieonians	46	Dunfermline Ath	42	Hamilton A	39
1955–56b	Queen's Park	54	Ayr U	51	St Johnstone	49
1956–57b	Clyde	64	Third Lanark	51	Cowdenbeath	45
1957–58b	Stirling Albion	55	Dunfermline Ath	53	Arbroath	47
1958–59b	Ayr U	60	Arbroath	51	Stenhousemuir	40
1959–60b	St Johnstone	53	Dundee U	50	Queen of the S	49

748

1960–61b	Stirling Albion	55	Falkirk	54	Stenhousemuir	50
1961–62b	Clyde	54	Queen of the S	53	Morton	441
1962–63b	St Johnstone	55	East Stirling	49	Morton	48
1963–64b	Morton	67	Clyde	53	Arbroath	46
1964–65b	Stirling Albion	59	Hamilton A	50	Queen of the S	45
1965–66b	Ayr U	53	Airdrieonians	50	Queen of the S	49
1966–67b	Morton	69	Raith R	58	Arbroath	57
1967–68b	St Mirren	62	Arbroath	53	East Fife	40
1968–69b	Motherwell	64	Ayr U	53	East Fife*	47
1969–70b	Falkirk	56	Cowdenbeath	55	Queen of the S	50
1970–71b	Partick T	56	East Fife	51	Arbroath	46
1971–72b	Dumbarton*	52	Arbroath	52	Stirling Albion	50
1972–73b	Clyde	56	Dumfermline Ath	52	Raith R*	47
1973–74b	Airdrieonians	60	Kilmarnock	59	Hamilton A	55
1974–75a	Falkirk	54	Queen of the S	53	Montrose	53

Elected to First Division: 1894 Clyde; 1897 Partick T; 1899 Kilmarnock; 1900 Partick T; 1902 Partick T; 1903 Airdrieonians; 1905 Falkirk, Aberdeen and Hamilton A; 1906 Clyde; 1910 Raith R; 1913 Ayr U.

RELEGATED FROM PREMIER DIVISION

1975–76 Dundee, St Johnstone
1976–77 Hearts, Kilmarnock
1977–78 Ayr U, Clydebank
1978–79 Hearts, Motherwell
1979–80 Dundee, Hibernian
1980–81 Kilmarnock, Hearts
1981–82 Partick T, Airdrieonians
1982–83 Morton, Kilmarnock
1983–84 St Johnstone, Motherwell
1984–85 Dumbarton, Morton
1985–86 *No relegation due to League reorganization*
1986–87 Clydebank, Hamilton A
1987–88 Falkirk, Dunfermline Ath, Morton
1988–89 Hamilton A
1989–90 Dundee
1990–91 None
1991–92 St Mirren, Dunfermline Ath
1992–93 Falkirk, Airdrieonians

RELEGATED FROM DIVISION 1

1975–76 Dunfermline Ath, Clyde
1976–77 Raith R, Falkirk
1977–78 Alloa Ath, East Fife
1978–79 Montrose, Queen of the S
1979–80 Arbroath, Clyde
1980–81 Stirling A, Berwick R
1981–82 East Stirling, Queen of the S
1982–83 Dunfermline Ath, Queen's Park
1983–84 Raith R, Alloa
1984–85 Meadowbank T, St Johnstone
1985–86 Ayr U, Alloa
1986–87 Brechin C, Montrose
1987–88 East Fife, Dumbarton
1988–89 Kilmarnock, Queen of the S
1989–90 Albion R, Alloa
1990–91 Clyde, Brechin C
1991–92 Montrose, Forfar Ath
1992–93 Meadowbank T, Cowdenbeath

RELEGATED FROM DIVISION 1 (TO 1973–74)

1921–22 *Queen's Park, Dumbarton, Clydebank
1922–23 Albion R, Alloa Ath
1923–24 Clyde, Clydebank
1924–25 Third Lanark, Ayr U
1925–26 Raith R, Clydebank
1926–27 Morton, Dundee U
1927–28 Dunfermline Ath, Bo'ness
1928–29 Third Lanark, Raith R
1929–30 St Johnstone, Dundee U
1930–31 Hibernian, East Fife
1931–32 Dundee U, Leith Ath
1932–33 Morton, East Stirling
1933–34 Third Lanark, Cowdenbeath
1934–35 St Mirren, Falkirk
1935–36 Airdrieonians, Ayr U
1936–37 Dunfermline Ath, Albion R
1937–38 Dundee, Morton
1938–39 Queen's Park, Raith R
1946–47 Kilmarnock, Hamilton A
1947–48 Airdrieonians, Queen's Park
1948–49 Morton, Albion R
1949–50 Queen of the S, Stirling Albion
1950–51 Clyde, Falkirk

1951–52 Morton, Stirling Albion
1952–53 Motherwell, Third Lanark
1953–54 Airdrieonians, Hamilton A
1954–55 No clubs relegated
1955–56 Stirling Albion, Clyde
1956–57 Dunfermline Ath, Ayr U
1957–58 East Fife, Queen's Park
1958–59 Queen of the S, Falkirk
1959–60 Arbroath, Stirling Albion
1960–61 Ayr U, Clyde
1961–62 St Johnstone, Stirling Albion
1962–63 Clyde, Raith R
1963–64 Queen of the S, East Stirling
1964–65 Airdrieonians, Third Lanark
1965–66 Morton, Hamilton A
1966–67 St Mirren, Ayr U
1967–68 Motherwell, Stirling Albion
1968–69 Falkirk, Arbroath
1969–70 Raith R, Partick T
1970–71 St Mirren, Cowdenbeath
1971–72 Clyde, Dunfermline Ath
1972–73 Kilmarnock, Airdrieonians
1973–74 East Fife, Falkirk

*Season 1921–22 – only 1 club promoted, 3 clubs relegated.

Scottish League championship wins: Rangers 43, Celtic 35, Aberdeen 4, Hearts 4, Hibernian 4, Dumbarton 2, Dundee 1, Dundee United 1, Kilmarnock 1, Motherwell 1, Third Lanark 1.

The Scottish Football League was reconstructed into three divisions at the end of the 1974–75 season, so the usual relegation statistics do not apply. Further reorganization took place at the end of the 1985–86 season. From 1986–87, the Premier and First Division had 12 teams each. The Second Division remains at 14. From 1988–89, the Premier Division reverted to 10 teams, and the First Division to 14 teams but in 1991–92 the Premier and First Division reverted to 12.

SCOTTISH LEAGUE SKOL CUP FINALS 1946–93

Season	Winners	Runners-up	Score
1946–47	Rangers	Aberdeen	4-0
1947–48	East Fife	Falkirk	4-1 after 0-0 draw
1948–49	Rangers	Raith R	2-0
1949–50	East Fife	Dunfermline Ath	3-0
1950–51	Motherwell	Hibernian	3-0
1951–52	Dundee	Rangers	3-2
1952–53	Dundee	Kilmarnock	2-0
1953–54	East Fife	Partick T	3-2
1954–55	Hearts	Motherwell	4-2
1955–56	Aberdeen	St Mirren	2-1
1956–57	Celtic	Partick T	3-0 after 0-0 draw
1957–58	Celtic	Rangers	7-1
1958–59	Hearts	Partick T	5-1
1959–60	Hearts	Third Lanark	2-1
1960–61	Rangers	Kilmarnock	2-0
1961–62	Rangers	Hearts	3-1 after 1-1 draw
1962–63	Hearts	Kilmarnock	1-0
1963–64	Rangers	Morton	5-0
1964–65	Rangers	Celtic	2-1
1965–66	Celtic	Rangers	2-1
1966–67	Celtic	Rangers	1-0
1967–68	Celtic	Dundee	5-3
1968–69	Celtic	Hibernian	6-2
1969–70	Celtic	St Johnstone	1-0
1970–71	Rangers	Celtic	1-0
1971–72	Partick T	Celtic	4-1
1972–73	Hibernian	Celtic	2-1
1973–74	Dundee	Celtic	1-0
1974–75	Celtic	Hibernian	6-3
1975–76	Rangers	Celtic	1-0
1976–77	Aberdeen	Celtic	2-1
1977–78	Rangers	Celtic	2-1
1978–79	Rangers	Aberdeen	2-1
1979–80	Dundee U	Aberdeen	3-0 after 0-0 draw
1980–81	Dundee U	Dundee	3-0
1981–82	Rangers	Dundee U	2-1
1982–83	Celtic	Rangers	2-1
1983–84	Rangers	Celtic	3-2
1984–85	Rangers	Dundee U	1-0
1985–86	Aberdeen	Hibernian	3-0
1986–87	Rangers	Celtic	2-1
1987–88	Rangers	Aberdeen	3-3
		(Rangers won 5-3 on penalties)	
1988–89	Rangers	Aberdeen	3-2
1989–90	Aberdeen	Rangers	2-1
1990–91	Rangers	Celtic	2-1
1991–92	Hibernian	Dunfermline Ath	2-0
1992–93	Rangers	Aberdeen	2-1

SCOTTISH LEAGUE CUP WINS

Rangers 18, Celtic 9, Hearts 4, Aberdeen 4, Dundee 3, East Fife 3, Dundee U 2, Hibernian 2, Motherwell 1, Partick T 1.

APPEARANCES IN FINALS

Rangers 24, Celtic 20, Aberdeen 10, Hibernian 6, Dundee 5, Hearts 5, Dundee U 4, Partick T 4, East Fife 3, Kilmarnock 3, Dunfermline Ath 2, Motherwell 2, Falkirk 1, Morton 1, Raith R 1, St Johnstone 1, St Mirren 1, Third Lanark 1.

SKOL CUP 1992–93

FIRST ROUND

1 AUG

East Stirling (0) 0
Alloa (1) 1 *(Moffat)*   386
East Stirling: Imrie; McMillan, Russell, Ross, Craig, Houston, McKinnon, Ferguson (Thomson), Roberts (Barclay), Walker, Auld
Alloa: Butter; Newbigging, Lee, Sheerin, McCulloch, Campbell C, Moffat, McNiven, Smith (Conroy), Hendry, McAvoy

Stenhousemuir (2) 2 *(Irvine, Steel)*
Arbroath (1) 3 *(Adam, Tindal, Macdonald)*   375
Stenhousemuir: Kelly; Clouston, Hallford, Anderson, Prior, Fisher, Kemp, Steel (Bell), McCallum (Haddow), Mathieson, Irvine
Arbroath: Balfour; Hamilton, Martin, Mitchell, Farnan, Boyd, Tindal (Holmes), Adam, Macdonald (Tosh), McNaughton, Sorbie

Stranraer (0) 0
East Fife (0) 0 *aet*   474
Stranraer: Duffy; McCann, Hughes, Spittal, Gallagher, Evans, Kelly (Duncan), Sloan, Diver, Cody (Grant), Love
East Fife: Charles; Taylor, Spence, Burns, Bell, McCracken, Elliott, Brown, Scott, Sludden, McBride (Hope)
(Stranraer won 5-4 on penalties)

4 AUG

Brechin C (1) 2 *(Brown, Miller)*
Albion R (1) 1 *(Ferguson)*   408
Brechin C: Allan; McLaren, Cairney, Brown, McKillop, Paterson, Lees, Hutt, Heggie, Miller, O'Brien
Albion R: Guidi; Walsh, McKeown, Kelly, Armour, Riley, McBride, Cadden, Ferguson, McCoy, Scott (Moore)

Queen's Park (0) 1 *(McCormick)*
Clyde (3) 3 *(Thompson D, Clarke 2)*   886
Queen's Park: Moonie; Callan, Morris, Elder, Mackay, Jackson (Orr J), Graham, Caven, Orr G, McCormick, O'Neill
Clyde: Howie; McFarlane, Tennant, Wylde, Knox, Thomson J, Thompson D, McCheyne (Quinn), McGarvey, Clarke, Morrison (Ronald)

Queen of the S (1) 3 *(Templeton 3)*
Berwick R (0) 0   637
Queen of the S: Davidson; Dickson, Sim, Templeton, Hetherington, Mills, Wright, Gordon, Thomson, Bell, Robertson
Berwick R: Massie; Davidson, O'Donnell, Brownlee, Hall, Thorpe, Cass, Valentine, Cunningham (Fisher), Bickmore, Graham

SECOND ROUND

11 AUG

Airdrieonians (2) 2 *(Conn, Kirkwood)*
Stranraer (1) 3 *(Cody, Sloan, Grant) aet*   1494
Airdrieonians: Martin; Jack (Reid), Stewart, Sandison, Caesar (Watson), Black, Boyle, Balfour, Conn, Coyle, Kirkwood
Stranraer: Duffy; McIntyre (Gallagher), Hughes, Spittal, Brannigan, McCann, Sloan, Cody, Diver (Grant), Evans, Duncan

Alloa (1) 1 *(McAvoy)*
St Johnstone (1) 3 *(Curran, Wright 2)*   1178
Alloa: Butter; Newbigging, Lee, Sheerin, Wilcox, Campbell, Moffat, McNiven (Ramsay), Smith, Hendry, McAvoy (Bennett)
St Johnstone: Rhodes; Baltacha, McAuley, McGinnis, Inglis,Davies (Cherry) Moore (Maskrey), Turner, Wright, Torfason, Curran

Brechin C (1) 4 *(Hutt, Ross, Miller, Lees)*
Hamilton A (1) 2 *(Clark, Smith)*   502
Brechin C: Allan; McLaren, Cairney, Brown, McKillop, Hutt, Lees, Scott, Heggie (Ross), Miller, O'Brien (Lorimer)
Hamilton A: Ferguson; Harris, Miller, Millen, Rae (Hillcoat), Weir, Ward, Reid, Clark (McEntegart), Smith, McDonald

Dumbarton (0) 0 *at Hampden Park*
Rangers (2) 5 *(Durrant, Gordon, Hateley, McCoist, Mikhailichenko)*   11090
Dumbarton: MacFarlane; Marsland, Boyd, Gow, Martin, Melvin, McQuade, Nelson (Meechan), Gibson, McConville, Cowell (Willock)
Rangers: Maxwell; Nisbet, Robertson D, Gough, McPherson, Durrant, Gordon, McCall (Brown), McCoist (Rideout), Hateley, Mikhailichenko

Dundee U (4) 6 *(Johnson 2, Connolly 2, McKinlay, Ferreyra)*
Queen of the S (0) 0   4512
Dundee U: Main; Clark, Malpas, McKinlay (McInally), Van Der Hoorn, Narey, O'Neil J, Johnson, Cleland, Connolly (Ferreyra)
Queen of the S: Davidson; Dickson, McFarlane, Mills, McGhie, Gordon (Fraser), Wright, Bell, Thomson, Templeton, Robertson

Meadowbank T (0) 0
Dundee (1) 3 *(Dodds, McGowan, Campbell D)*   867
Meadowbank T: McQueen; Coughlin (Hutchison), Armstrong, Williamson, Grant, Duthie, Ryrie, Wilson, Irvine, Roseburgh, Little (McNeill)
Dundee: Leighton; Dinnie, Beedie, Duffy, McGowan (Bain), McKeown, Den Bieman, Vrto, Gilzean (Campbell D), Dodds, Rix

Morton (1) 2 *(Mathie, Alexander)*
Kilmarnock (0) 3 *(Jack, Burns T 2) aet* 3454
Morton: Wylie; Collins, McArthur, Rafferty (McDonald), Doak, Boag, Mathie (Lilley), Mahood, Alexander, McInnes, Hopkin
Kilmarnock: Geddes; Burns H, Black, Montgomerie, Paterson (Campbell), Burns T, Porteous (Williamson), Skilling, Jack, Tait, Mitchell

Motherwell (1) 4 *(Angus, Ferguson 3)*
Clyde (1) 2 *(Thompson D, Speirs)* 3030
Motherwell: Thomson; Sneddon, McKinnon, Simpson, Martin, Nijholt (Ferguson), Kirk, McLeod (Shepstone), Arnott, Angus, Cooper
Clyde: Howie; McFarlane, Tennant, Wylde, Speirs, Thomson J (Morrison), Thompson D, Knox, McGarvey (Quinn), Clarke, Ronald

Partick T (0) 2 *(Farningham, Kinnaird)*
Ayr U (0) 0 2600
Partick T: Nelson; Law, McVicar, Peebles (Kinnaird), Tierney, Clark, Britton, Farningham, McGlashan (Shaw), Irons, Cameron
Ayr U: Duncan; Kennedy, Agnew, Furphy, McVie, Robertson, Traynor, McTurk, Walker, McLean (Fraser), Mair

12 AUG

Arbroath (0) 0
Aberdeen (1) 4 *(Paatelainan 2, Shearer, Jess)* 4130
Arbroath: Balfour; Hamilton (Holmes), Martin, Mitchell, Godfrey, Boyd, Farnan, Adam, Macdonald, Tosh (McNaughton), Sorbie
Aberdeen: Snelders; McKimmie, Winnie, Aitken (Thomson), Irvine, Smith, Mason, Bett (Wright), Jess, Shearer, Paatelainen

Falkirk (0) 4 *(Drinkell, Smith, May, McAllister)*
Forfar Ath (0) 1 *(Heddle)* 2403
Falkirk: Westwater; Johnston, McQueen, Duffy, Hughes, Rice (May), McAllister, McCall, Drinkell, Sloan (Baptie), Smith
Forfar Ath: Thomson; McIntyre (Pryde), Hamill, Morris, Mann, Winter, McKenna (Perry), McPhee, Petrie, Donaldson, Heddle

Hearts (0) 1 *(McLaren)*
Clydebank (0) 0 5758
Hearts: Smith; McLaren, McKinlay, Levein, Hogg, Mackay (Foster), Robertson, Ferguson D, Baird, Wright G, Crabbe
Clydebank: Woods; Murray, McIntosh, Goldie, Sweeney, Jack, Henry (Flannigan C), Harvey, Eadie, Bryce, Wilson (Henderson)

Hibernian (2) 4 *(Evans 2, Hamilton, McGinlay)*
Raith R (0) 1 *(McStay)* 7267
Hibernian: Reid; Miller, Mitchell, Orr, Beaumont, MacLeod, Weir (Tortolano), Hamilton, Wright, Evans, McGinlay
Raith R: Arthur; McStay, MacLeod, Coyle (Cameron), Raeside, Nicholl, Thomson (Mackenzie), Dalziel, Hetherston, Brewster, Dair

Montrose (0) 0
Dunfermline Ath (4) 6 *(O'Boyle 2, Leitch, Grant, McWilliams, Davies)* 1955
Montrose: Larter; Forsyth, Fleming, Craib M, Smith, Forbes, Fraser (Maver), Robertson, Logan, Callaghan, Craib S
Dunfermline Ath: Hamilton; Shannon (Cunnington), Sharp, McCathie, Robertson, Cooper (Laing), McWilliams, O'Boyle, Grant R, Leitch, Davies

St Mirren (1) 1 *(Lavety)*
Cowdenbeath (0) 0 1888
St Mirren: Money; Dawson (McDonald), Reid, Manley, Baillie, Beattie, Elliot, Lambert, McGill (McLaughlin), Lavety, Broddle
Cowdenbeath: Combe; Petrie, Herd, Bennett, Archibald, Ferguson, Wright, Malone, Condie, Lamont P (Buckley), Johnston (Syme)

Stirling Albion (0) 0 *at Hampden Park*
Celtic (0) 3 *(Coyne, Creaney 2)* 7630
Stirling Albion: McGeown; Mitchell, Armstrong, Shanks, Clark, Kerr, McInnes (Brown), Moore, Watters, Robertson S (Docherty A), Docherty R
Celtic: Marshall; McNally, Boyd, Galloway, Mowbray, Wdowczyk, O'Neil, Fulton (Grant), Creaney, Nicholas (Coyne), Collins

THIRD ROUND

18 AUG

Dundee U (1) 3 *(Ferguson 2, O'Neil J)*
St Mirren (0) 0 5586
Dundee U: Main; Clark, Malpas, McInally, Van Der Hoorn, Krivokapic (Preston), O'Neil J, Johnson, Cleland, Ferguson, Connolly (Ferreyra)
St Mirren: Money; Dawson, Reid, Manley, Baillie, Fabiani (McGill), Elliot, Lambert, McDowall, Beattie (Lavety), Broddle

Kilmarnock (1) 3 *(McSkimming, McCluskey, Skilling)*
Hibernian (0) 1 *(Wright) aet* 7495
Kilmarnock: Geddes; Burns H, Black, Montgomerie, Tait, Burns T, Williamson (McCluskey), Skilling, Jack, McSkimming (Campbell), Mitchell
Hibernian: Reid; Miller, Mitchell, Orr, Beaumont, Milne (Evans), Weir, Hamilton (McIntyre), Wright, Jackson, McGinlay

19 AUG

Aberdeen (0) 1 *(Paatelainen)*
Dunfermline Ath (0) 0 *aet* 10791
Aberdeen: Snelders; McKimmie, Wright, Aitken (Thomson), Irvine, Smith, Mason (Kane), Bett, Jess, Shearer, Paatelainen
Dunfermline Ath: Hamilton; Shannon (Laing), Sharp, McCathie, Robertson, Cooper, McWilliams, O'Boyle (Cunnington), Grant, Leitch, Davies

752

Brechin C (0) 1 *(Brown)*
Hearts (0) 2 *(McKinlay, Robertson) aet*   1903
Brechin C: Allan; McLaren, Cairney, Brown, McKillop, Hutt, Lees, Scott (Lorimer), Heggie (O'Brien), Miller, Ross
Hearts: Smith; McLaren, McKinlay, Levein, Hogg, Mackay, Robertson, Ferguson D (Snodin), Baird (Crabbe), Mauchlen, Foster

Celtic (1) 1 *(Payton)*
Dundee (0) 0   30849
Celtic: Marshall; O'Neil, Boyd, Grant, Mowbray (Slater), McNally, Miller, McStay, Payton, Creaney (Fulton), Collins
Dundee: Leighton; Dinnie, Beedie, Duffy, McGowan, Ratcliffe, Den Bieman, Vrto, Gilzean, Dodds, Rix (Campbell D)

Motherwell (0) 0
Falkirk (1) 1 *(Drinkell)*   5510
Motherwell: Thomson; Nijholt, McKinnon, Simpson (Angus), Kromheer, Martin, Arnott, Kirk, Baker (Ferguson), O'Donnell, Cooper
Falkirk: Westwater; Oliver, McQueen, Baptie, Hughes, Rice, McAllister, May, Drinkell, McCall, Smith

St Johnstone (2) 2 *(Wright, McAuley)*
Partick T (2) 2 *(Britton, Shaw) aet*   4716
St Johnstone: Rhodes; Baltacha, McAuley, McGinnis, Inglis, McClelland, Moore, Turner (Davies), Wright, Torfason (Maskrey), Curran
Partick T: Nelson; Law, McVicar, Clark (Kinnaird), Tierney, McLaughlin (McWalter), Shaw, Farningham, Britton, Irons, Cameron
(St Johnstone won 4-3 on penalties)

Stranraer (0) 0
Rangers (3) 5 *(Hateley 2, McCoist 3)*   4430
Stranraer: Duffy; McIntyre, Hughes, Spittal, Brannigan, McCann, Sloan, Gallagher, Diver, Evans, Duncan (Grant)
Rangers: Goram; Murray, Robertson D, Gough, McPherson, Ferguson, Durrant, McCall (Brown), McCoist, Hateley, Huistra

QUARTER FINALS

25 AUG

Kilmarnock (0) 1 *(Campbell)*
St Johnstone (0) 3 *(Torfason, Maskrey, Wright)* 8293
Kilmarnock: Geddes; Burns H (Campbell), Black, Montgomerie, Paterson, Burns T, Mitchell, Tait, Jack, McCluskey (Williamson), McSkimming
St Johnstone: Rhodes; Baltacha, McAuley, McGinnis (Cherry), Inglis, McClelland, Maskrey, Turner, Wright, Torfason (Redford), Curran

26 AUG

Dundee U (0) 2 *(Ferreyra, Connolly)*
Rangers (0) 3 *(McCoist, Gough, Huistra) aet* 15716
Dundee U: Main; Clark, Malpas, McInally, Van Der Hoorn, Narey, O'Neil J, Johnson, Cleland (Welsh), Ferreyra (Preston), Connolly

Rangers: Goram; Spackman, Robertson D, Gough, McPherson, Brown, Durrant, Ferguson, McCoist, McSwegan (Steven), Huistra

Falkirk (1) 1 *(McQueen)*
Aberdeen (2) 4 *(Shearer 3, Irvine)*   8022
Falkirk: Westwater; Oliver (Cadette), McQueen, Duffy, Hughes, Rice, McAllister, May, Drinkell, Baptie, Smith (McCall)
Aberdeen: Snelders; McKimmie, Wright, Aitken, Irvine, Smith, Mason, Bett (Thomson), Jess, Shearer, Winnie

Hearts (1) 1 *(Mackay)*
Celtic (1) 2 *(Payton, Creaney)*   21502
Hearts: Smith; Hogg, McKinlay (Snodin), Levein, Mackay, Van de Ven, Robertson, Ferguson D, Crabbe, Mauchlen (Berry), Foster
Celtic: Marshall; Boyd, Wdowczyk, Grant, Mowbray, Galloway, O'Neil, McStay, Payton (Slater), Creaney, Collins

SEMI-FINALS

22 SEPT at Hampden Park

St Johnstone (0) 1 *(Wright [pen])*
Rangers (2) 3 *(McCoist 3)*   30062
St Johnstone: Rhodes; McGowne, Redford, McGinnis, Inglis, McClelland, Moore (Maskrey), Turner, Wright, Arkins, Curran
Rangers: Goram; McCall, Robertson D, Gough (Nisbet), McPherson, Brown, Durrant, Ferguson, McCoist, Hateley, Huistra

Sept 23 at Hampden Park

Celtic (0) 0
Aberdeen (1) 1 *(Jess)*   40618
Celtic: Bonner; Boyd, Wdowczyk (McNally), Grant, Galloway, Gillespie (Miller), Slater, McStay, Payton, Creaney, Collins
Aberdeen: Snelders; Wright, Winnie, Grant, McLeish, Smith, Mason, Aitken, Jess, Shearer (Richardson), Paatelainen

FINAL

Oct 25 at Hampden Park

Rangers (1) 2 *(McCall, Smith [og])*
Aberdeen (0) 1 *(Shearer) aet*   45298
Rangers: Goram; McCall, Robertson D, Gough (Mikhailichenko), McPherson, Brown, Steven (Gordon), Ferguson, McCoist, Hateley, Durrant
Aberdeen: Snelders; Wright, Winnie, Grant, McLeish, Smith, Aitken (Richardson), Bett (Booth), Jess, Shearer, Paatelainen
Referee: D D Hope (Erskine)

SCOTTISH CUP FINALS 1874–1993

Year	Winners	Runners-up	Score
1874	Queen's Park	Clydesdale	2-0
1875	Queen's Park	Renton	3-0
1876	Queen's Park	Third Lanark	2-0 after 1-1 draw
1877	Vale of Leven	Rangers	3-2 after 0-0 and 1-1 draws
1878	Vale of Leven	Third Lanark	1-0
1879	Vale of Leven*	Rangers	
1880	Queen's Park	Thornlibank	3-0
1881	Queen's Park†	Dumbarton	3-1
1882	Queen's Park	Dumbarton	4-1 after 2-2 draw
1883	Dumbarton	Vale of Leven	2-1 after 2-2 draw
1884	Queen's Park‡	Vale of Leven	
1885	Renton	Vale of Leven	3-1 after 0-0 draw
1886	Queen's Park	Renton	3-1
1887	Hibernian	Dumbarton	2-1
1888	Renton	Cambuslang	6-1
1889	Third Lanark§	Celtic	2-1
1890	Queen's Park	Vale of Leven	2-1 after 1-1 draw
1891	Hearts	Dumbarton	1-0
1892	Celtic¶	Queen's Park	5-1
1893	Queen's Park	Celtic	2-1
1894	Rangers	Celtic	3-1
1895	St Bernard's	Renton	2-1
1896	Hearts	Hibernian	3-1
1897	Rangers	Dumbarton	5-1
1898	Rangers	Kilmarnock	2-0
1899	Celtic	Rangers	2-0
1900	Celtic	Queen's Park	4-3
1901	Hearts	Celtic	4-3
1902	Hibernian	Celtic	1-0
1903	Rangers	Hearts	2-0 after 1-1 and 0-0 draws
1904	Celtic	Rangers	3-2
1905	Third Lanark	Rangers	3-1 after 0-0 draw
1906	Hearts	Third Lanark	1-0
1907	Celtic	Hearts	3-0
1908	Celtic	St Mirren	5-1
1909	●●		
1910	Dundee	Clyde	2-1 after 2-2 and 0-0 draws
1911	Celtic	Hamilton A	2-0 after 0-0 draw
1912	Celtic	Clyde	2-0
1913	Falkirk	Raith R	2-0
1914	Celtic	Hibernian	4-1 after 0-0 draw
1920	Kilmarnock	Albion R	3-2
1921	Partick T	Rangers	1-0
1922	Morton	Rangers	1-0
1923	Celtic	Hibernian	1-0
1924	Airdrieonians	Hibernian	2-0
1925	Celtic	Dundee	2-1
1926	St Mirren	Celtic	2-0
1927	Celtic	East Fife	3-1
1928	Rangers	Celtic	4-0
1929	Kilmarnock	Rangers	2-0
1930	Rangers	Partick T	2-1 after 0-0 draw
1931	Celtic	Motherwell	4-2 after 2-2 draw
1932	Rangers	Kilmarnock	3-0 after 1-1 draw
1933	Celtic	Motherwell	1-0
1934	Rangers	St Mirren	5-0
1935	Rangers	Hamilton A	2-1
1936	Rangers	Third Lanark	1-0
1937	Celtic	Aberdeen	2-1
1938	East Fife	Kilmarnock	4-2 after 1-1 draw
1939	Clyde	Motherwell	4-0
1947	Aberdeen	Hibernian	2-1
1948	Rangers	Morton	1-0 after 1-1 draw
1949	Rangers	Clyde	4-1
1950	Rangers	East Fife	3-0
1951	Celtic	Motherwell	1-0
1952	Motherwell	Dundee	4-0
1953	Rangers	Aberdeen	1-0 after 1-1 draw
1954	Celtic	Aberdeen	2-1
1955	Clyde	Celtic	1-0 after 1-1 draw
1956	Hearts	Celtic	3-1
1957	Falkirk	Kilmarnock	2-1 after 1-1 draw
1958	Clyde	Hibernian	1-0
1959	St Mirren	Aberdeen	3-1
1960	Rangers	Kilmarnock	2-0
1961	Dunfermline Ath	Celtic	2-0 after 0-0 draw
1962	Rangers	St Mirren	2-0
1963	Rangers	Celtic	3-0 after 1-1 draw
1964	Rangers	Dundee	3-1

Year	Winners	Runners-up	Score
1965	Celtic	Dunfermline Ath	3-2
1966	Rangers	Celtic	1-0 after 0-0 draw
1967	Celtic	Aberdeen	2-0
1968	Dunfermline Ath	Hearts	3-1
1969	Celtic	Rangers	4-0
1970	Aberdeen	Celtic	3-1
1971	Celtic	Rangers	2-1 after 1-1 draw
1972	Celtic	Hibernian	6-1
1973	Rangers	Celtic	3-2
1974	Celtic	Dundee U	3-0
1975	Celtic	Airdrieonians	3-1
1976	Rangers	Hearts	3-1
1977	Celtic	Rangers	1-0
1978	Rangers	Aberdeen	2-1
1979	Rangers	Hibernian	3-2 after 0-0 and 0-0 draws
1980	Celtic	Rangers	1-0
1981	Rangers	Dundee U	4-1 after 0-0 draw
1982	Aberdeen	Rangers	4-1 (aet)
1983	Aberdeen	Rangers	1-0 (aet)
1984	Aberdeen	Celtic	2-1 (aet)
1985	Celtic	Dundee U	2-1
1986	Aberdeen	Hearts	3-0
1987	St Mirren	Dundee U	1-0 (aet)
1988	Celtic	Dundee U	2-1
1989	Celtic	Rangers	1-0
1990	Aberdeen	Celtic	0-0 (aet)
		(Aberdeen won 9-8 on penalties)	
1991	Motherwell	Dundee U	4-3 (aet)
1992	Rangers	Airdrieonians	2-1
1993	Rangers	Aberdeen	2-1

*Vale of Leven awarded cup, Rangers failing to appear for replay after 1-1 draw.
†After Dumbarton protested the first game, which Queen's Park won 2-1.
‡Queen's Park awarded cup, Vale of Leven failing to appear.
§Replay by order of Scottish FA because of playing conditions in first match, won 3-0 by Third Lanark.
¶After mutually protested game which Celtic won 1-0.
●●Owing to riot, the cup was withheld after two drawn games – Celtic 2-1, Rangers 2-1.

SCOTTISH CUP WINS

Celtic 29, Rangers 26, Queen's Park 10, Aberdeen 7, Hearts 5, Clyde 3, St Mirren 3, Vale of Leven 3, Dunfermline Ath 2, Falkirk 2, Hibernian 2, Kilmarnock 2, Motherwell 2, Renton 2, Third Lanark 2, Airdrieonians 1, Dumbartor 1, Dundee 1, East Fife 1, Morton 1, Partick Th 1, St Bernard's 1.

APPEARANCES IN FINAL

Celtic 46, Rangers 42, Aberdeen 14, Queen's Park 12, Hearts 10, Hibernian 10, Kilmarnock 7, Vale of Leven 7, Clyde 6, Dumbarton 6, St Mirren 6, Third Lanark 6, Dundee U 6, Motherwell 6, Renton 5, Dundee 4, Dunfermline Ath 3, East Fife 3, Airdrieonians 2, Falkirk 2, Hamilton A 2, Morton 2, Partick Th 2, Albion R 1, Cambuslang 1, Clydesdale 1, Raith R 1, St Bernard's 1 Thornlibank 1.

SCOTTISH CUP 1992–93

FIRST ROUND

5 DEC

Huntly (2) 4 *(Thomson 3, Copland)*
Stranraer (0) 2 *(Duncan, Cody)* 1400
Huntly: Gardiner; Walker K, McGinlay, Murphy,
Rougvie, Selbie, Stewart, Copland (De Barros),
Thomson, Whyte (Walker C), Dunsire
Stranraer: Ross; McIntyre (Diver), Hughes, Duncan,
Brannigan, McCann, Grant, Sloan, Fraser, McLean,
Cody (Spittal)

Inverness T (1) 3 *(MacDonald T 2, Bell)*
Civil Service Strollers (0) 1 *(Givven)* 682
Inverness T: Calder; MacDonald S, Stevenson,
Wilson, Milroy, Murphy, MacDonald A, MacDonald
T, Polworth, Bell, MacLean
Civil Service Strollers: Mackintosh; Leslie, McKinlay
(Davies), Wood, Chambers, Burns, Scott, Temple
(McPhee), Keenan, McGhee, Givven

Queen of the S (1) 3 *(Rowe 2, Henderson)*
Spartans (0) 0 550
Queen of the S: Hoy; Dickson, Sim, McKeown,
Rowe, McFarlane, Sermanni, Fraser, Thomson,
McGuire J, Henderson
Spartans: Houston F; Finlay, Lynch, Carrick,
Lennox, McKeating, Smith (McDaide), Thomson,
Govan, Houston T (Galbraith), McKinnon

Queen's Park (0) 0
Clyde (1) 1 *(McCarron* 1205
Queen's Park: Chalmers; Sneddon, Stevenson, Elder,
Mackay, Orr G, Jackson, Graham (Kerr), Rodden,
Caven, Crooks (Devlin)
Clyde: Howie; McFarlane, Tennant, McAulay
(Thomson J), Knox, Mitchell (Quinn), Thompson D,
McCheyne, McGarvey, McCarron, Strain

8 DEC

Cove R (1) 2 *(Stephen 2)*
Peterhead (0) 0 1000
Cove R: MacLean; Forbes, Whyte, Morland,
Paterson, Cormack, Yule, Baxter, Stephen, Murphy,
Megginson
Peterhead: Tait; Watson, King (Brown), Madden,
McCarron, Gerrard, Campbell (Fraser), Emslie,
McGachie, Wilson, Mackintosh

Forfar Ath (0) 5 *(Mearns, McKenna, Petrie, Cadden
(og), Heddle)*
Albion R (0) 0 404
Forfar Ath: Thomson; Mearns, McPhee, Morris,
Mann, Byrne, McKenna, McIntyre, Petrie (Smith),
Hamill (Cameron), Heddle
Albion R: McConnachie; Millar, Gallagher,
McKeown, Kelly (Archer), Gaughan, McBride
(McCoy), Cadden, Moore, Ferguson, Hendry

SECOND ROUND

19 DEC

Clyde (0) 3 *(Thomson, McCarron, Dickson)* at
Douglas Park
Brechin C (1) 1 *(Lees)* 813
Clyde: Howie; McFarlane, Tennant, McAulay, Knox,
Thomson J, Dickson, Mitchell (Morrison),
McGarvey, McCarron, Strain (Quinn)

Brechin C: Allan; McLaren, Cairney, Brown,
Paterson, Lorimer, Lees, Scott, Ross, Miller, Brand
(Fisher)

Cove R (1) 2 *(Stephen, Cormack)*
Montrose (0) 0 1100
Cove R: MacLean; Forbes, Whyte, Morland,
Paterson, Cormack (Park), Yule, Baxter, Stephen
(Lavelle), Murphy, Megginson
Montrose: Moffat; Morrison, Robertson, Craib M,
Fraser, Fleming, Maver (Craib S), Irvine, Grant,
Logan (Allan), Yeats

East Fife (1) 1 *(Hope)*
Alloa (0) 1 *(Moffat)* 829
East Fife: Charles; Bell, Beaton, Allan (Skelligan),
Burgess, Taylor, Brown, Hope, Scott, Sludden,
McBride
Alloa: Butter; Newbigging (Russell), Bennett, Wilcox,
McCulloch, Campbell, Gibson, McNiven,
McCormick (Smith), Moffat, McAvoy

Gala Fairydean (1) 1 *(Lothian)*
Arbroath (1) 1 *(McNaughton)* 553
Gala Fairydean: Cairns; Henry, Main, Jones, Frizzel,
Neil Collins (Potts), Whitehead, Norman Collins,
Lothian, Kerr (Hunter), D'Acrosa
Arbroath: Harkness; Tindal, Martin, Mitchell, Boyd,
Farnan, Will, Hamilton, McNaughton, Tosh
(Macdonald), Sorbie

Vale of Leithen (0) 2 *(Hogarth, Ross)*
East Stirling (1) 2 *(McKinnon, Walker)* 200
Vale of Leithen: McDermott; Finlayson, Ross,
Shearer, McNaughton, Nisbet (Rathie), Thorpe,
Mitchell, Hogarth, Gray (Brown), Selkirk
East Stirling: Watson; Ross, Friar, Houston, Woods,
Thomson, McKinnon, Kemp, Barclay, Walker,
Geraghty

26 DEC

Inverness T (0) 0
Berwick R (0) 1 *(Anderson)* 1558
Inverness T: Calder; Wilson (Murphy), Stevenson,
Sweeney, Milroy, Masson (Bremner), MacDonald A,
MacDonald T, Polworth, Bell, MacLean
Berwick R: Massie; Hendrie, Valentine, Davidson,
Anderson, Richardson, Irvine, Hall, Scott,
Cunningham, Graham

28 DEC

Stenhousemuir (0) 2 *(Lytwyn, Hallford (pen))*
Forfar Ath (0) 3 *(McIntyre, Heddle 2)* 750
Stenhousemuir: Barnstaple; Aitken, Hallford,
Armstrong, Godfrey, Fisher, Logan, Clouston
(McLafferty), Mathieson, Lytwyn, Haddow
Forfar Ath: Thomson; Mearns, McPhee, Morris,
Mann, Winter, Bingham, McIntyre (McCafferty),
McKenna (Smith), Hamill, Heddle

4 JAN

Huntly (2) 2 *(Copland, Rougvie)*
Queen of the S (0) 1 *(Henderson)* 3000
Huntly: Gardiner; Walker K, Grant, Murphy,
Rougvie, Selbie, Walker C (De Barros), Copland,
Thomson, Whyte (Paterson), Dunsire

Queen of the S: Hoy; Dickson, Sim, Rowe, McGhie, Fraser (Templeton), Sermanni, McFarlane, McGuire J (Gordon), Henderson, Robertson

SECOND ROUND REPLAYS
28 DEC

Alloa (0) 1 *(McAvoy)*
East Fife (0) 1 *(Brown)* 1131
Alloa: Butter; Russell (Newbigging), Bennett, Wilcox, McCulloch, Campbell, Gibson, McNiven, McCormick (Tait), Moffat, McAvoy
East Fife: Charles; Bell, Allan (Andrew), Beaton, Burgess, Taylor, Hope, Burns, Brown, Sludden, McBride (Elliott)
aet; East Fife won 6-5 on penalties

Arbroath (0) 2 *(Macdonald, Tindal)*
Gala Fairydean (0) 0 1119
Arbroath: Harkness; Tindal, Martin, Mitchell, Boyd, Farnan, Will, Hamilton, McNaughton (Tosh), Macdonald, Sorbie
Gala Fairydean: Cairns; Henry, Loughran, Jones, Frizzel, Hunter, Kerr (Notman), Neil Collins, Whitehead (Main), Norman Collins, Lothian

East Stirling (1) 3 *(Roberts 2, Geraghty)*
Vale of Leithen (0) 2 *(Hogarth, Selkirk) aet* 514
East Stirling: Watson; Ross, Kemp, Barclay, Woods, Thomson (Friar), McKinnon, Houston, Roberts, Walker (Tierney), Geraghty
Vale of Leithen: McDermott; Finlayson, Ross, Shearer (Brown), McNaughton, Nisbet, Thorpe, Rathie (McCulloch), Hogarth, Gray, Selkirk

THIRD ROUND
9 JAN

Aberdeen (1) 4 *(Booth 3, Irvine)*
Hamilton A (1) 1 *(Reid)* 10,800
Aberdeen: Snelders; Wright, Winnie (Smith), Grant, Irvine, McLeish, Richardson, Bett (Mason), Jess, Booth, Paatelainen
Hamilton A: Ferguson; Hillcoat, Miller, Millen, Weir, Napier (Cramb), Ward, Reid, Harris, Clark, McDonald

Airdrieonians (0) 0
Clydebank (0) 0 2500
Airdrieonians: Martin; Kidd, Stewart, Sandison, Caesar, Black, Boyle, Balfour (Kirkwood), Watson (Smith), Coyle, Jack
Clydebank: Woods; Murdoch, Hay, Barron, Sweeney, Jack, Harvey, Henry, Eadie, Flannigan C, Wilson (McIntosh)

Arbroath (0) 3 *(Sorbie 3)*
Morton (0) 0 1517
Arbroath: Harkness; Tindal, Martin, Mitchell, Boyd, Farnan, Will, Florence, Adam, Macdonald, Sorbie
Morton: Wylie; Collins, Pickering, Rafferty, McCahill, Johnstone, Mathie, Tolmie (McDonald), Alexander (Fowler), McInnes, Gahagan

Clyde (0) 0
Celtic (0) 0 7000
Clyde: Howie; McFarlane, Tennant, McAulay, Knox, Thomson J, Dickson (Quinn), Morrison (McCheyne), McGarvey, McCarron, Strain

Celtic: Bonner; Grant, Boyd, Wdowczyk (Coyne), McNally, Galloway, O'Neil (Miller), McStay, Creaney, Slater, Collins

Cove R (O) 2 *(Megginson, Lavelle)*
East Stirling (1) 2 *(Thomson, Barclay)* 1000
Cove R: MacLean; Park, Whyte, Morland, Paterson, Cormack (McLennan), Yule, Baxter, Stephen (Lavelle), Murphy, Megginson
East Stirling: Watson; Woods, Ross, Barclay, Yates, Kemp (Friar), McKinnon, Houston, Geraghty, Walker, Thomson

Dundee U (1) 3 *(McKinlay, Welsh, Ferguson)*
Meadowbank T (1) 1 *(Rutherford)* 5263
Dundee U: Main; Perry, Malpas, McInally, Van Der Hoorn, Welsh, McLaren (Cleland), McKinlay, Crabbe (Connolly), Ferguson, O'Neil J
Meadowbank T: Ellison; Murray, Elder (Roseburgh), Williamson, Rae, Banks, Little, Wilson, Rutherford, McLeod, Bailey (Coyle)

Dunfermline Ath (0) 1 *(Chalmers)*
Ayr U (2) 2 *(Mair (pen), Walker)* 3814
Dunfermline Ath: Hamilton; Shannon, Cunnington (Grant), McCathie, Moyes, Williamson, French, Leitch (McWilliams), Robertson, Davies, Chalmers
Ayr U: Duncan; Burley, Robertson S, Shotton, Howard, George, Robertson G (Kennedy), Walker, Graham (McTurk), Traynor, Mair

Hearts (4) 6 *(Baird, Ferguson D, Snodin, Robertson, Boothroyd 2)*
Huntly (0) 0 9520
Hearts: Walker; McLaren, Snodin, Levein, Mackay, Van De Ven, Robertson, Ferguson D (Boothroyd), Baird, Mauchlen, Preston (Foster)
Huntly: Gardiner; Walker K (Grant), McGinlay, Murphy, Rougvie, Selbie, Stewart, Copland, Thomson, Whyte (Walker C), De Barros

Hibernian (3) 5 *(Jackson, McGinlay, Weir 2, Wright)*
St Mirren (0) 2 *(Lavety, Gallagher)* 7997
Hibernian: Reid; Orr, Mitchell, Hunter, McIntyre, MacLeod, Weir (Fellenger), Hamilton, Wright, Jackson (Evans), McGinlay
St Mirren: Fridge; Manley (Elliot), Broddle, McWhirter, Baillie, Fullarton, Gallagher, Lambert, McIntyre, Hewitt, Farrell (Lavety)

Kilmarnock (2) 5 *(Williamson 3, McCluskey, MacPherson)*
Raith R (0) 0 7309
Kilmarnock: Geddes; Wilson, McSkimming, Montgomerie, Skilling, Burns T (Crainie), Porteous, MacPherson, McCluskey, Stark, Williamson (Campbell)
Raith R: Carson (Crawford); McStay, MacLeod, Coyle (Raeside), Sinclair, McGeachie, Mackenzie, Dalziel, Hetherston, Brewster, Thomson

Motherwell (0) 0
Rangers (1) 2 *(McCoist 2)* 14,314
Motherwell: Dykstra; Nijholt, McKinnon (Angus), Martin, Philliben, McCart, Kirk (Ferguson), Simpson, Arnott, Kromheer, Cooper
Rangers: Goram; Nisbet, Robertson D, Gordon, McPherson, Brown, Steven, McCall, McCoist, Hateley, Mikhailichenko

Partick T (0) 0
Cowdenbeath (0) 1 *(Henderson (pen))*   3265
Partick T: Nelson; Law, McVicar (English), McLaughlin, Jamieson, Kinnaird, Shaw, Johnston (Cameron), Britton, Irons, Magee
Cowdenbeath: Lamont W; Watt, Robertson, McGovern, Douglas, Herd, Henderson, Petrie, Callaghan, Maratea, Condie (Wright)

St Johnstone (3) 6 *(Wright 2, Cherry, Arkins 2, Maskrey)*
Forfar Ath (0) 0   3970
St Johnstone: Rhodes; McGowne, Deas, McClelland (Maskrey), Inglis, Baltacha (McGinnis), Davies, Cherry, Wright, Arkins, Curran
Forfar Ath: Thomson; Mearns, McPhee, Morris (McIntyre), Mann, Winter, Bingham, McKenna (Smith), Petrie, Hamill, Heddle

Stirling Albion (0) 1 *(McInnes)*
East Fife (2) 2 *(Skelligan 2)*   1091
Stirling Albion: McGeown; McCormack, Watson, Tait, Lawrie, Mitchell, Reilly, McInnes, McKenna (McCallum), Callaghan (Docherty A), Armstrong
East Fife: Charles; Bell, Spence, Skelligan, Burgess (Andrew), Taylor, Burns, Hope, Brown, Sludden (Scott), Allan

10 JAN

Dundee (0) 2 *(Wieghorst, Dodds (pen))*
Dumbarton (0) 0   4290
Dundee: Mathers; McQuillan, Pittman, Wieghorst, Duffy (McGowan), Dow, Bain, Vrto, Stainrod, Dodds, Campbell D (Den Bieman)
Dumbarton: MacFarlane; Marsland, Boyd (McConville), Melvin, Martin, Gow, McQuade, Boag (Meechan), Mooney, Nelson, McAnenay

27 JAN

Falkirk (2) 5 *(Sloan 2, McCall, May, Cadette)*
Berwick R (1) 2 *(Richardson, Hall)*   4500
Falkirk: Parks; Wishart, McQueen, Duffy, Weir, May (Rice), McAllister, Drinkell (Lennox), Cadette, McCall, Sloan
Berwick R: Massie; Hendrie (Hutchinson), Valentine, Davidson, Anderson, Richardson, Irvine, Hall, Scott (Waldie), Cunningham, Graham

THIRD ROUND REPLAYS

19 JAN

Clydebank (1) 2 *(Eadie 2)*
Airdrieonians (0) 0   1979
Clydebank: Woods; Barron, Hay, Murdoch, Sweeney, Jack, Harvey, Henry, Eadie, Flannigan C, Wilson
Airdrieonians: Martin; Boyle, Jack, Sandison, Honor (Watson), Reid, Kirkwood, Balfour, Smith, Coyle, Lawrence (Conn)

20 JAN

Celtic (1) 1 *(Coyne)*
Clyde (0) 0   16,559
Celtic: Bonner; McNally, Boyd, Slater, Galloway, Gillespie, Miller (Grant), McStay, Payton (Creaney), Coyne, Collins
Clyde: Howie; McFarlane, Tennant, McAulay, Knox, Thomson J, Quinn (McCheyne), Morrison, McGarvey (Dickson), McCarron, Strain

25 JAN

East Stirling (2) 2 *(McKinnon, Morland (og))*
Cove R (0) 1 *(Stephen (pen))*   802
East Stirling: Watson; O'Sullivan, Kemp, Ross, Barclay, Yates, Friar, McKinnon, Houston, Walker (Tierney), Geraghty
Cove R: MacLean; Baxter, Whyte, Morland, Paterson, Cormack, Megginson, Yule, Stephen (McLennan), Murphy, Lavelle

FOURTH ROUND

6 FEB

Arbroath (0) 0
East Fife (0) 0   2984
Arbroath: Harkness; Tindal (Tosh), Martin, Mitchell, Boyd, Farnan, Hamilton, Florence, Will, Macdonald (Buckley), Sorbie
East Fife: Charles; Bell, Allan (Elliott), Skelligan, Burgess, Taylor, Burns, Hope, Andrew (Scott), Sludden, Beaton

Ayr U (0) 0
Rangers (1) 2 *(McCoist, Gordon)*   13,176
Ayr U: Duncan; Burley, Robertson, Shotton, Traynor (Howard), George, Kennedy, McGivern, Graham, Russell, Mair
Rangers: Goram; Stevens, Robertson D, Gordon, Nisbet, Brown, Steven, McCall, McCoist, Hateley, Mikhailichenko (Huistra)

Cowdenbeath (0) 0
Hibernian (0) 0   4509
Cowdenbeath: Lamont W; Watt, Robertson, McGovern, Archibald E, Douglas, Henderson, Petrie (Herd), Callaghan, Scott, Condie (Wright)
Hibernian: Reid; Orr, Mitchell, Hunter, McIntyre, MacLeod (Miller), Weir, Hamilton, Wright, Jackson, McGinlay

Falkirk (1) 2 *(Duffy, May)*
Celtic (0) 0   13,012
Falkirk: Parks; Wishart, Johnston, Duffy, Weir, Hughes, McAllister (Sloan), Drinkell, Cadette, McCall, May
Celtic: Bonner; McNally, Boyd, Vata (Grant), Wdowczyk, Galloway, Slater, McStay, McAvennie (Payton), Coyne, Collins

Hearts (1) 2 *(Baird, Robertson)*
Dundee (0) 0   12,021
Hearts: Walker; McLaren, McKinlay, Levein, Mackay, Van De Ven, Robertson D, Baird (Bannon), Mauchlen, Ferguson I (Boothroyd)
Dundee: Mathers; McQuillan, Pittman (Kiwomya), Dinnie (Den Bieman), Duffy, McGowan, Bain, Vrto, Paterson, Dodds, West

Kilmarnock (0) 0
St Johnstone (0) 0   9278
Kilmarnock: Geddes; Wilson, McSkimming, Montgomerie, Skilling, Burns T, Porteous (Campbell), MacPherson, Crainie (Mitchell), Stark, Williamson
St Johnstone: Rhodes; McGowne, Deas, Cherry, Inglis, McClelland, Davies, Curran, Wright, Arkins, Moore (Maskrey)

7 FEB

Aberdeen (0) 2 *(Jess 2)*
Dundee U (0) 0   14,500
Aberdeen: Snelders; Wright, Smith, Grant, Irvine,
McLeish, Richardson, Mason (Booth), Jess, Shearer
(Aitken), Paatelainen
Dundee U: Main; Clark, Malpas, Bowman, Perry,
Narey, McKinlay, Johnson (Connolly), Dailly,
Crabbe, Bollan

East Stirling (1) 1 *(Geraghty)*
Clydebank (1) 2 *(Eadie, Flannigan C)*   1177
East Stirling: Watson; Woods (McMillan), Kemp,
Ross, Yates, Barclay, Friar, McKinnon, Houston,
Roberts, Geraghty (Tierney)
Clydebank: Woods; Maher, Crawford, Murdoch,
Sweeney, Hay, Harvey, Jack, Eadie, Flannigan C,
Wilson (Lansdowne)

FOURTH ROUND REPLAYS

10 FEB

Hibernian (1) 1 *(McGinlay)*
Cowdenbeath (0) 0   8701
Hibernian: Reid; Orr, Mitchell, Hunter, McIntyre,
MacLeod, Weir, Hamilton, Wright, Evans, McGinlay
Cowdenbeath: Lamont W; Watt (Petrie), Robertson,
McGovern, Archibald E, Douglas, Henderson
(Condie), Herd, Callaghan, Scott, Wright

St Johnstone (0) 1 *(Davies)*
Kilmarnock (0) 0 *aet*   7144
St Johnstone: Rhodes; McGowne, Deas, Cherry
(McGinnis), Inglis, McClelland, Davies, Curran,
Wright, Arkins, Moore (Maskrey)
Kilmarnock: Geddes; Wilson, McSkimming,
Montgomerie, Skilling, Burns T, Porteous,
MacPherson, McCluskey (Mitchell), Stark,
Williamson

16 FEB

East Fife (1) 1 *(Sludden)*
Arbroath (1) 4 *(Tosh 2, Martin 2)*   3722
East Fife: Charles; Bell (Elliott), Spence, Burns,
Burgess, Taylor, Hope, Beaton, Scott (Andrew),
Sludden, McBride
Arbroath: Harkness; Tindal, Martin, Mitchell, Boyd,
Farnan, Hamilton (Will), Florence, Macdonald
(McNaughton), Tosh, Sorbie

QUARTER-FINALS

6 MAR

Aberdeen (1) 1 *(Shearer (pen))*
Clydebank (0) 1 *(McIntosh)*   11,300
Aberdeen: Snelders; Wright, Smith, Grant, Irvine,
McLeish, Richardson, Aitken, Jess (Booth), Shearer
(Ten Caat), Paatelainen
Clydebank: Woods; Maher, Hay (Crawford),
Murdoch, Sweeney, McIntosh, Harvey, Henry
(Lansdowne), Eadie, Flannigan C, Jack

Arbroath (0) 0
Rangers (2) 3 *(Hateley, Murray, McCoist (pen))* 6488
Arbroath: Harkness; Tindal (Will), Martin, Mitchell,
Boyd, Farnan, Hamilton, Florence, Macdonald
(Buckley), Adam, Sorbie

Rangers: Maxwell; Nisbet, Robertson D, Murray,
McPherson, Brown, Mikhailichenko (Durrant),
McCall, McCoist, Hateley, Huistra (McSwegan)

Hearts (1) 2 *(Preston, Robertson (pen))*
Falkirk (0) 0   12,721
Hearts: Walker; McLaren, McKinlay, Berry,
Mackay, Wright, Robertson (Thomas), Ferguson D,
Baird, Mauchlen (Bannon), Preston
Falkirk: Westwater; Oliver, McQueen, Duffy, Weir,
Rice, McAllister, Lennox, Drinkell, May, Sloan
(Taggart)

Hibernian (1) 2 *(Tweed, Wright)*
St Johnstone (0) 0   10,785
Hibernian: Burridge; Orr, Mitchell, Hunter, Tweed,
MacLeod, Lennon, Hamilton, Wright, Jackson
(Evans), McGinlay
St Johnstone: Rhodes; McGowne (Moore), Sweeney
(McGinnis), Deas, Redford, McClelland, Davies,
Inglis, Wright, Arkins, Turner

QUARTER-FINAL REPLAY

16 MAR

Clydebank (1) 3 *(Eadie, Maher, Henry)*
Aberdeen (2) 4 *(Irvine, Paatelainen, Booth 2)* 8000
Clydebank: Woods; Maher, Hay, Murdoch, Sweeney,
McIntosh, Harvey, Henry, Eadie, Flannigan C, Jack
Aberdeen: Snelders; Wright, McKimmie, Grant,
Irvine, McLeish, Kane, Aitken, Booth, Ten Caat,
Paatelainen

SEMI-FINALS

3 APR at Tynecastle Park

Hibernian (0) 0
Aberdeen (0) 1 *(Booth)*   21,413
Hibernian: Burridge; Miller, Mitchell, Hunter, Tweed,
MacLeod (Evans), Lennon, Hamilton (Orr), Wright,
Jackson, McGinlay
Aberdeen: Snelders; McKimmie, Smith, Aitken (Ten
Caat), Irvine, McLeish, Richardson, Mason, Booth
(Shearer), Kane, Paatelainen

At Celtic Park

Rangers (0) 2 *(McPherson, McCoist)*
Hearts 0 1 *(Preston)*   41738
Rangers: Goram; McCall, Robertson D, Gough,
McPherson, Brown, Steven, Ferguson, McCoist,
Hateley, Hagen (Durrant)
Hearts: Walker; McLaren, McKinlay, Levein,
Mackay, Van De Ven, Robertson, Ferguson D
(Snodin), Baird, Millar, Preston (Ferguson I)

FINAL

29 MAY at Celtic Park

Rangers (2) 2 *(Murray, Hateley)*
Aberdeen (0) 1 *(Richardson)*   50715
Rangers: Goram; McCall, Robertson D, Gough,
McPherson, Brown, Murray, Ferguson, Durrant,
Hateley, Huistra (Pressley)
Aberdeen: Snelders; McKimmie, Wright (Smith),
Grant, Irvine, McLeish, Richardson, Mason, Booth,
Shearer (Jess), Paatelainen
Referee: J McCluskey (Stewarton)

B & Q CUP 1992–93

FIRST ROUND

29 SEPT

Ayr U (1) 2 *(Walker 2)*
St Mirren (0) 1 *(Charnley)* 2360
Ayr U: Duncan; Burley, McVie, Shotton, Howard, Kennedy, Robertson G. Walker, Graham, Traynor, Mair (McTurk)
St Mirren: Fridge; Farrell, Baker, Manley (Dawson), Baillie, Fabiani, Gillies, Lambert (Charnley), McGill, Hewitt, Elliot

Berwick R (1) 2 *(Cunningham, Davidson)*
East Stirling (0) 2 *(Geraghty 2) aet* 333
Berwick R: Neilson; Hendrie, Robertson, Davidson, Hall, Cass, Hutchinson (Kerr), Valentine, Scott, Cunningham (Waldie), Graham
East Stirling: Imrie; Woods, Kemp, Ross, Craig, McKinnon, Thomson, Friar, Houston, Walker, Geraghty
(Berwick R won 5-4 on penalties)

Dumbarton (0) O
Hamilton A (1) 3 *(Clark, McDonald, Reid)* 634
Dumbarton: McFarlane; Marsland (Cowell), Foster (Willock), McDonald, Martin, Melvin, McQuade, Nelson, Gibson, Meechan, Docherty
Hamilton A: Ferguson; Hillcoat, Miller, Millen, Weir, Napier, Clark, Reid, Harris (Cramb), Smith (Ward), McDonald

Forfar Ath (0) 2 *(Mearns, Winter)*
Morton (4) 5 *(Mathie 3, Alexander, Mahood)* 652
Forfar Ath: Thomson; Cameron (Byrne), Hamill, Morris, Mann, Winter, Mearns, McPhee (McAulay), Petrie, McKenna, Heddle
Morton: Wylie; Collins, McArthur, Pickering, Doak, Johnstone, Mathie (Lilley), Mahood, Alexander, McInnes, McDonald (Fowler)

Kilmarnock (2) 2 *(McCluskey, Mitchell)*
Clyde (0) 1 *(McCheyne)* 2686
Kilmarnock: Geddes; MacPherson, Reilly, Montgomerie, Skilling, Roberts, Mitchell, Porteous, Williamson, McCluskey (Campbell), McSkimming
Clyde: Howie; McFarlane, McCheyne, Wylde (Ronald), Strain, Thomson J, Thompson D, Mitchell, Dickson, Clarke (Morrison), McCarron

Queen's Park (2) 2 *(Jackson, McCormick)*
Montrose (2) 3 *(Fraser 2, Kelly) aet* 302
Queen's Park: Chalmers; Sneddon (Millar), Graham, Elder, Mackay, Callan, Caven, Jackson, McCormick, Mackenzie (Greig), Crooks
Montrose: Larter; Forsyth, Fleming, Craib M, Smith, Robertson, Fraser, Yeats, Kelly, Logan, Irvine

Stenhousemuir (0) 2 *(Bell, Mathieson)*
Cowdenbeath (3) 4 *(Callaghan, Lee, Malone, Buckley)* 329
Stenhousemuir: Barnstaple; Clouston, Hallford, Barr, Clarke (Prior), Aitken, Fisher, Bell, Mathieson, Steel, Dickov (Irvine)
Cowdenbeath: Lamont W; Watt, Robertson (Buckley), Herd, Archibald, Henderson, Wright, Malone, Condie, Lee, Callaghan (Syme)

Stranraer (2) 3 *(Sloan, Diver, McIntyre)*
Alloa (1) 2 *(McNiven, Wilcox)* 469
Stranraer: Ross; McIntyre, Hughes, Spittal, Brannigan, Duncan (Gallagher), Sloan, Grant, Diver, Cody (Evans), Love
Alloa: Binnie; Newbigging, Bennett, Wilcox, McCulloch, McNiven, Sheerin, Mackay (Russell), Moffat, Smith, Hendry

6 OCT

Arbroath (2) 3 *(Macdonald, Tosh, Sorbie)*
Dunfermline Ath (0) 0 706
Arbroath: Harkness; Mitchell, Martin, Tindal, Godfrey, Boyd, Farnan, Tosh, Macdonald, Florence, Sorbie
Dunfermline Ath: Hamilton; Bowes, Cunnington, McCathie, Robertson (Kelly) Williamson, McNamara, Chalmers (Laing), French, Leitch, Sinclair

7 OCT

Meadowbank T (0) 1 *(Logan)*
East Fife (0) 0 *aet* 272
Meadowbank T: Ellison; Nicol, Banks, Armstrong, McLeod, Williamson, Wilson, Elder (Logan), Young, Little (McNeill), Roseburgh
East Fife: Charles; Taylor (Elliott), Beaton, Allan, Burgess (Skelligan), Burns, McBride, Brown, Scott, Sludden, Hope

SECOND ROUND

20 OCT

Albion R (0) 0
Hamilton A (1) 2 *(Smith, McDonald [pen])* 559
Albion R: Guidi; Walsh, McKeown, Armour (Seggie), McCaffrey, Cadden, McBride, Gaughan, Kerrigan, Scott, Archer
Hamilton A: Ferguson; McKee, Hillcoat, Millen, Weir, Napier, Clark, McEntegart, Harris (McKenzie), Smith (Ward), McDonald

Berwick R (1) 1 *(Scott)*
Arbroath (0) 0 346
Berwick R: Neilson; Hendrie, Hutchinson, Robertson, Hall, Cass, Fisher, Irvine, Scott, Cunningham (Valentine), Graham
Arbroath: Harkness; Mitchell, Martin, Tindal, Godfrey, Holmes (Tosh), Farnan (Boyd), Hamilton, Macdonald, Florence, Sorbie

Brechin C (1) 1 *(Lorimer)*
Morton (2) 2 *(Mathie, Tolmie)* 518
Brechin C: Allan; McLaren, Cairney, Brown, McKillop, Lorimer (Hutt), Lees, Scott, Ross, Miller, Brand (Heggie)
Morton: Wylie; Collins, Pickering, Rafferty, Doak, Johnstone, Mathie, Mahood, Tolmie (Lilley), Fowler (McDonald), McArthur

Cowdenbeath (0) 0
Montrose (2) 4 *(Grant 2, Logan, Allan)* 282
Cowdenbeath: O'Hanlon; Watt, Robertson, McGovern, Archibald, Douglas, Henderson, Malone, Lamont P (Condie), Lee (Herd), Callaghan
Montrose: Larter; Forsyth, Fleming, Forbes, Smith, Craib M (Allan), Fraser, Maver, Grant, Logan, Irvine

Kilmarnock (1) 1 *(McCluskey)*
Ayr U (0) 0 7122
Kilmarnock: Geddes; MacPherson, Reilly, Montgomerie, Paterson, Burns T, Mitchell, Skilling, Williamson, McCluskey (Campbell), McSkimming
Ayr U: Duncan; Burley, Agnew, Shotton, Howard, George, Robertson, Walker, Graham, Traynor, Fraser (Carse)

Raith R (0) 0
Meadowbank T (0) 0 *aet* 1203
Raith R: Arthur; McStay, MacLeod, Nicholl, Herrick, Coyle (Young), Williamson, Cameron (Crawford), Mackenzie, Brewster, Dair
Meadowbank T: McQueen; Nicol, Murray, Williamson, Elder (Roseburgh), Banks, Little, Wilson, Rutherford, McLeod, Kane (Bailey)
(Meadowbank T won 4-2 on penalties)

Stirling Albion (1) 2 *(Watters, Moore)*
Clydebank (0) 1 *(Flannigan C)* 315
Stirling Albion: McGeown; Shanks, Watson, Callaghan, Lawrie, Mitchell, McInnes (Docherty A), Moore, Watters (Brown), McKenna, Armstrong
Clydebank: Woods; Maher, Hay (Crawford), Barron, Sweeney, McIntosh, Harvey (Lansdowne), Henry, Eadie, Flannigan C, Jack

Stranraer (0) 0
Queen of the S (1) 2 *(Rowe, Templeton)* 1004
Stranraer: Ross; Hughes, Love, Duncan, Brannigan, Gallagher, Sloan, Grant, Diver, Evans, Kelly
Queen of the S: Hoy; Gordon, McFarlane, Rowe, Dickson, McKeown, Sermanni, Bell, Thomson (Templeton), McGuire D, Robertson

QUARTER-FINALS

27 OCT

Stirling Albion (0) 0
Montrose (0) 1 *(Grant)* 432
Stirling Albion: Robertson SA: Shanks, Watson, McInnes (Callaghan), Lawrie, Mitchell, McKenna, Moore, Watters, Robertson S, Armstrong
Montrose: Larter; Forsyth, Fleming, Craib M, Forbes, Smith, Fraser (Yeats), Maver, Grant, Logan (Allan), Irvine

28 OCT

Hamilton A (3) 5 *(Clark 2, Weir, Ward, Smith)*
Berwick R (1) 2 *(Irvine, Davidson)* 1235
Hamilton A: Ferguson; McKee, Hillcoat, Millen, Weir, McEntegart, Ward, Reid (Waters), Harris (Smith), Clark, McDonald

Berwick R: Neilson; Hendrie, Hutchinson, Davidson, Hall, Cass, Irvine, Robertson (Valentine), Scott, Cunningham (Malone), Graham

Kilmarnock (0) 1 *(Burns T)*
Morton (0) 2 *(Mathie, Lilley)* 4956
Kilmarnock: Geddes; MacPherson, Reilly, Montgomerie, Furphy, Burns T, Mitchell, Skilling, Williamson, McCluskey, McSkimming (Jack)
Morton: Wylie; Collins, Pickering, Rafferty, Doak, Johnstone, Mathie, Mahood, Tolmie (Fowler), McInnes, Lilley

Meadowbank T (2) 3 *(Wilson, Roseburgh, Kane)*
Queen of the S (1) 2 *(Thomson, Rowe)* 616
Meadowbank T: McQueen; Coughlin, Murray, McLeod, Nicol, Banks, Little (Duthie), Wilson, Rutherford, Roseburgh, Kane
Queen of the S: Hoy; Gordon (Wright), McFarlane, Rowe, Dickson, McKeown, Sermanni (Templeton), Bell, Thomson, Henderson, McGuire D

SEMI-FINALS

10 NOV

Morton (1) 3 *(Mathie 2, Alexander)*
Montrose (1) 1 *(Forsyth)* *aet* 2840
Morton: Wylie; Collins, Pickering, Rafferty, Doak, Johnstone, Mathie, Mahood, Little (Alexander), McInnes, Tolmie (McDonald)
Montrose: Larter; Morrison, Fleming (Houghton), Forsyth, Forbes, Craib M, Maver, Irvine, Grant, Yeats, Logan (Kelly)

11 NOV

Hamilton A (0) 1 *(McDonald)*
Meadowbank T (1) 1 *(Wilson)* *aet* 1590
Hamilton A: Ferguson; Hillcoat, Napier, Millen, Weir, Reid, Ward, Clark, Harris, Smith, McDonald
Meadowbank T: Ellison; Coughlin, Murray, Nicol, Graham (Elder), Banks, McLeod, Wilson, Rutherford, Roseburgh, Bailey (Little)
(Hamilton A won 2-1 on penalties)

FINAL

13 DEC at Love Street, Paisley

Hamilton A (2) 3 *(Clark 2, Hillcoat)*
Morton (1) 2 *(Alexander 2)* 7391
Hamilton A: Ferguson; Hillcoat, Miller, Millen, Weir, Napier, Waters (McKenzie), Harris, Cramb (Ward), Clark, McDonald
Morton: Wylie; Collins, Pickering, Rafferty, Doak, Johnstone, Mathie, Mahood (Gahagan), Alexander, McInnes, Tolmie
Referee: J.J.Timmons (Kilwinning)

WELSH FOOTBALL 1992-93

KONICA LEAGUE OF WALES 1992-93

	P	W	D	L	F	A	Pts
Cwmbran	38	26	9	3	69	22	87
Inter Cardiff	38	26	5	7	79	36	83
Aberystwyth Town	38	25	3	10	85	49	78
Ebbw Vale	38	19	9	10	76	61	66
Bangor City	38	19	7	12	77	58	64
Holywell Town	38	17	8	13	65	48	59
Conwy United	38	16	9	13	51	51	57
Connah's Quay Nomads	38	17	4	17	66	67	55
Porthmadog	38	14	11	13	61	49	53
Haverfordwest County	38	16	5	17	66	66	53
Caersws	38	14	10	14	64	60	52
Afan Lido	38	14	10	14	64	65	52
Mold Alexandra	38	16	4	18	63	69	48*
Llanelli	38	11	8	19	49	64	41
Maesteg Park Athletic	38	9	13	16	52	59	40
Flint Town United	38	11	6	21	47	67	39
Briton Ferry Athletic	38	10	9	19	61	87	39
Newtown	38	9	9	20	55	87	36
Llanidloes Town	38	7	9	22	48	93	30
Abergavenny Thursdays	38	7	7	24	36	76	28

*3 points deducted

KONICA LEAGUE CUP

Group One

	P	W	D	L	F	A	Pts
Caersws	8	6	1	1	22	11	19
Bangor City	8	5	1	2	18	14	16
Porthmadog	8	4	0	4	14	13	12
Conwy United	8	3	1	4	14	16	10
Llanidloes Town	8	0	1	7	12	26	1

Group Two

	P	W	D	L	F	A	Pts
Newtown	8	5	2	1	17	7	17
Flint Town United	8	4	1	3	13	13	13
Connah's Quay Nomads	8	3	3	2	15	14	12
Holywell Town	8	2	1	5	12	17	7
Mold Alexandra	8	2	1	5	10	15	7

Group Three

	P	W	D	L	F	A	Pts
Maesteg Park Athletic	8	3	4	1	19	11	13
Ebbw Vale	8	3	4	1	20	14	13
Cwmbran Town	8	3	2	3	14	17	11
Inter Cardiff	8	3	1	4	11	14	10
Abergavenny Thursdays	8	1	3	4	8	16	6

Group Four

	P	W	D	L	F	A	Pts
Afan Lido	8	5	2	1	15	7	17
Haverfordwest County	8	4	1	3	15	10	13
Llanelli	8	3	2	3	10	14	11
Aberystwyth Town	8	2	3	3	13	10	9
Briton Ferry Athletic	8	1	2	5	10	22	5

SEMI-FINALS: Newtown 0 Caersws 1 (at Newtown)
Afan Lido 2 Maesteg Park Athletic 0 (at Afan Lido)
FINAL: Afan Lido 1, Caersws 1 (at Aberystwyth) (Caersws won on penalties aet)

THE ABACUS LEAGUE

Division One

	P	W	D	L	F	A	Pts
Ton Pentre	26	22	1	3	71	20	67
Brecon	26	17	4	5	74	40	55
Pontypridd	26	14	9	3	53	23	51
Caldicot	26	14	4	8	50	31	46
Aberaman	26	13	3	10	54	47	42
Ammanford	26	11	7	8	38	44	40
Pembroke Boro	26	11	3	12	46	51	36
Cardiff Civil Service	26	11	2	13	40	36	35
Port Talbot	26	10	4	12	48	49	34

	P	W	D	L	F	A	Pts
Morriston	26	9	5	12	46	66	32
Caerleon	26	8	2	16	36	54	26
Blaenrhondda	26	6	5	15	32	50	23
Bridgend	26	6	5	15	38	58	23
Ferndale	26	2	2	22	19	76	8

Division Two

	P	W	D	L	F	A	Pts
AFC Porth	26	20	4	2	81	25	64
Caerau	26	16	5	5	61	30	53
Llanwern	26	15	6	5	43	22	51
Risca	26	15	4	7	44	29	49
Carmarthen	26	10	8	8	51	43	38
Taffs Well	26	11	5	10	48	42	38
Skewen	26	11	2	13	46	48	35
B P	26	9	8	9	35	41	35
Tonyrefail	26	7	9	10	38	42	30
Garw	26	6	8	12	40	55	26
Fields Pk/Pontllanfraith	26	7	4	15	33	43	25
Cardiff Corries**	26	7	7	12	33	69	25
Newport YMCA	26	6	3	17	37	64	21
Seven Sisters	26	4	3	19	24	61	15

Division Three

	P	W	D	L	F	A	Pts
Treowen	26	21	4	1	61	14	67
Pontyclun	26	16	5	5	58	32	53
Milford	26	15	2	9	74	36	47
Penrhiwceiber	26	13	8	5	57	44	47
Cardiff Institute HE	26	11	6	9	63	49	39
Panteg	26	10	8	8	44	39	38
Pontardawe	26	9	9	8	46	44	36
Goytre	26	11	3	12	48	49	36
Pontlottyn	26	7	9	10	35	44	30
Abercynon	26	7	8	11	35	47	29
AFC Tondu	26	6	8	12	43	60	26
Treharris	26	6	5	15	40	51	23
S W Constabulary	26	4	8	14	34	63	20
Trelewis	26	3	3	20	27	93	12

**3 Points Deducted
Cyril Rogers Cup: Pembroke Boro 1 v Penrhiwceiber Rangers 0

MANWEB CYMRU ALLIANCE

	P	W	D	L	F	A	Pts
Llansantffraid	28	23	3	2	89	34	72
Welshpool Town	28	21	2	5	92	34	65
Rhyl	28	20	4	4	74	22	64
Wrexham	28	19	4	5	81	34	61
Lex XI	28	14	8	6	60	42	50
Carno	28	9	11	8	44	56	38
Cefn Druids	28	10	5	13	46	41	35
Penryncoch	28	10	5	13	56	71	35
Ruthin Town	28	9	7	12	43	58	34
Rhos Aelwyd	28	7	6	15	37	67	27
Knighton Town	28	7	6	15	48	82	27
Mostyn	28	7	3	18	35	64	24
Rhayader	28	6	5	17	32	66	23
Gresford Ath	28	6	1	21	36	16	19
Brymbo	28	3	8	17	40	66	17

League Cup: Rhyl 5 Gresford Athletic 1 (at Brymbo)

RICHARDS THE BUILDERS MID-WALES LEAGUE

	P	W	D	L	F	A	Pts
Machynlleth	36	28	2	6	116	51	86
Morda Utd	36	26	4	6	85	36	82
Llandrindod	36	22	4	10	108	57	70
Talgarth	36	19	10	7	80	50	67
Waterloo Rovers	36	21	4	11	80	63	67
Caersws Res	36	21	2	13	82	57	65
Aberystwyth Res	36	19	8	9	70	59	65
Vale of Arrow	36	18	10	8	77	49	64
Berriew	36	19	5	12	68	44	62

Newtown Res	36	14	7	15	71	57	49
Penparcau	36	14	6	16	86	75	48
Kington	36	13	7	16	77	84	46
Clun Valley	36	8	11	17	31	58	35
Builth Wells	36	8	9	19	48	79	33
Presteigne S A	36	7	10	19	53	93	31
Knighton Res	36	8	7	21	50	99	31
Penrhyncoch Res	36	5	8	23	38	107	23
U C W	36	5	7	24	47	96	22
Llanidloes Res	36	3	7	26	44	97	16

SEALINK WELSH ALLIANCE

	P	W	D	L	F	A	Pts
Cemaes Bay	32	23	6	3	113	30	75
Llanfairpwll	32	22	4	6	73	42	70
Llangefni Town	32	21	6	5	97	45	69
Pilkingtons	32	18	6	8	78	57	60
Rhydymwyn	32	16	4	12	58	46	52
Nefyn Utd	32	13	8	11	61	64	47
Loco Llanberis	32	11	12	9	71	68	45
Bangor City	32	13	6	13	61	57	45
Nantlle Vale	32	12	6	14	74	79	42
Llanrwst Utd	32	11	5	16	58	82	38
Llandyrnog Utd	32	9	7	16	50	71	34
Connahs Quay No	32	9	6	17	47	84	33

Y Felinheli	32	7	10	15	52	64	31
Conwy Utd	32	6	5	21	49	78	23
Rhyl Utd	32	5	4	23	48	103	19
Penmaenmawr Ph	32	3	5	24	33	104	14

READ CONSTRUCTION
WELSH NATIONAL LEAGUE
(WREXHAM AREA)

Premier Division

	P	W	D	L	F	A	Pts
Penley	26	15	7	4	63	36	52
Buckley	26	16	3	7	59	37	51
New Broughton	26	13	9	4	56	29	48
Llay Welfare	26	14	6	6	60	39	48
Marchwiel	26	14	5	7	61	43	47
Lex XI Res	26	12	5	9	46	40	41
Chirk A A A	26	11	6	9	51	41	39
Pen-y-Cae	26	10	7	9	60	54	37
Llay R B L	26	8	6	12	49	46	30
Ruthin T Res	26	7	8	11	37	45	29
Overton	26	8	1	17	36	60	25
Corwen	26	6	6	14	41	66	24
Treuddyn	26	6	2	18	49	90	20
Castell AC	26	3	7	16	30	69	16

ALLBRIGHT BITTER WELSH CUP 1992–93

Preliminary Round

Abbey Life v British Aerospace	2-2, 1-2
(at Mostyn FC)	
Buckley v Ruthin Town	0-3
Cardiff Inst H E v Treowen Stars	0-6
Carmarthen Town v Pontyclun	3-2
Llandrindod Wells v Builth Wells	0-2
Llay Welfare v Penley	1-0
(at Brymbo FC)	
Nantlle Vale v Nefyn United	0-1
Overton Athletic v Rhos Aelwyd	1-2
Panteg v Skewen Athletic	3-2
Penparcau v Newcastle Emlyn	6-1
Pontardawe Athletic v Porthcawl Town	0-1
Rockwell v New Broughton	2-4
(at New Broughton FC)	
South Wales Constabulary v Tonyrefail Welfare	0-2
Trelewis Welfare v Abercynon Athletic	0-2

First Round

Aberaman Athletic v Risca United	1-2
AFC Porth v Panteg	5-1
Ammanford Town v Porthcawl Town	2-2, 0-1
Bala Town v Llay Royal British Legion	
(withdrawn)	
BP Llandarcy v Abercynon Athletic	1-1, 0-2
Bridgend Town v Caerleon	1-1, 0-3
British Aerospace v Marchwiel Villa	3-0
Brymbo v New Broughton	3-2
Caldicot Town v Tonyrefail Welfare	2-0
Cardiff Civil Service v Treowen Stars	4-3
Cemaes Bay v Locomotive Llanberis	3-2
Chirk AAA v Cefn Druids	1-3
CPD Felinheli v Nefyn United	3-2
Ferndale Athletic v Ton Pentre	0-2
Fields Park Pontllanfraith v Cardiff Corinthians	0-0, 0-1
Goytre United v Brecon Corinthians	1-4
Knighton Town v Penparcau	4-2
Lex XI v Penycae	3-0
Llandyrnog United v Mostyn	0-4
Llanfairpwll v Llanrwst United	3-0
Llangefni Town v Llandudno	3-4
Llay Welfare v Ruthin Town	0-1
Llansantffraid v Presteigne St Andrews	8-0
Morda United v Penrhyncoch	4-0
Morriston Town v Caerau	2-2, 0-3
Pembroke Borough v Newport YMCA	6-2
Pontlottyn Blast Furnace v Llanwern	1-2
Rhayader Town v Carno	0-1

Rhos Aelwyd v Gresford Athletic	2-2, 0-2
Rhyl v Pilkingtons'	3-0
Seven Sisters v Carmarthen Town	0-3
(at Carmarthen Town FC)	
Taffs Well v Port Talbot Athletic	1-5
Welshpool Town v Builth Wells	10-1

Second Round

Aberystwyth Town v Knighton Town	6-0
AFC Porth v Cardiff Civil Service	3-1
Bangor City v Mostyn	7-1
BP Llandarcy v Cardiff Corinthians	0-1
Brecon Corinthians v Ton Pentre	0-3
British Aerospace v Llay Royal British Legion	2-2, 1-2
Briton Ferry Athletic v Caldicot Town	4-1
Caerau v Afan Lido	5-1
Caersws v Kidderminster Harriers	2-2, 3-4
Carno v Morda United	4-3
Cefn Druids v Connah's Quay Nomads	1-2
Conwy United v Holywell Town	1-0
Cwmbran Town v Merthyr Tydfil	0-1
Ebbw Vale v Abergavenny Thursdays	3-1
Haverfordwest County v Pembroke Borough	2-0
Inter Cardiff v Porthcawl Town	5-1
Lex XI v Gresford Athletic	0-1
Llanfairpwll v Llandudno	2-4
Llansantffraid v Welshpool Town	5-1
Llanwern v Llanelli	1-5
Mold Alexandra v Brymbo	1-0
Newtown v Llanidloes Town	0-2
Port Talbot Athletic v Carmarthen Town	3-0
Porthmadog v Cemaes Bay	2-7
Rhyl v CPD Felinheli	6-0
Risca United v Caerleon	3-2
Ruthin Town v Flint Town United	0-1

Third Round

AFC Porth v Llanelli	2-0
Briton Ferry Athletic v Aberystwyth Town	2-6
Caerau v Ebbw Vale	4-3
Cemaes Bay v Carno	2-1
Connah's Quay Nomads v Conwy United	4-2
Haverfordwest County v Cardiff Corinthians	5-1
Hereford United v Flint Town United	6-0
Kidderminster Harriers v Bangor City	2-2, 1-2
Llandudno v Llay Royal British Legion	1-0
Llanidloes Town v Wrexham	0-3
Llansantffraid v Mold Alexandra	1-1, 2-1
Maesteg Park Athletic v Inter Cardiff	5-1

Merthyr Tydfil v Swansea City	2-0
Port Talbot Athletic v Risca United	0-0, 2-0
Rhyl v Gresford Athletic	3-1
Ton Pentre v Cardiff City	0-2

Fourth Round

Aberystwyth Town v AFC Porth	1-2
Caerau v Cardiff City	0-9
(at Cardiff City FC)	
Cemaes Bay v Connah's Quay Nomads	0-1
Haverfordwest County v Rhyl	0-2
Hereford United v Wrexham	2-3
Llansantffraid v Llandudno	2-1

Maesteg Park Athletic v Port Talbot Athletic	3-0
Merthyr Tydfil v Bangor City	3-2

Fifth Round

AFC Porth v Connah's Quay Nomads	1-3
Cardiff City v Maesteg Park Athletic	4-0
Llansantffraid v Rhyl	0-4
Wrexham v Merthyr Tydfil	1-0

Semi-Finals

Cardiff City v Wrexham	2-0
Wrexham v Cardiff City	1-0
Rhyl v Connah's Quay Nomads	2-0
Connah's Quay Nomads v Rhyl	1-0

FINAL: CARDIFF CITY 5, RHYL 0

(at National Stadium, Cardiff, 16 May 1993) Att: 16,443

Cardiff City: Ward; James, Searle, Brazil (Pike), Perry, Millar (Dale), Ramsey, Richardson, Stant, Blake, Griffith
Rhyl: Lichfield; Lee, Jones R, Espley, Lacey, Jones S, Cross (Norman), Congerton, McMullen, Taylor (Marriott), Jones A
Referee: W Burge (Tonypandy)

WELSH INTERMEDIATE CUP 1992–93

First Round

Abbey Life v British Aerospace	1-0
Abertillery Town v Grange Harlequins	2-3
Berriew v Builth Wells	1-0
Bettws v Ragged School	0-2
British Steel (Port Talbot) v North End	1-2
Bryntirion Athletic v Llwydcoed Welfare	0-3
Buckley v Llay Welfare	2-0
Chepstow Town v Christchurch	2-1
Corwen Amateurs v Rhos Aelwyd	1-0
Dinas Powys v Grange Albion	1-1
(Grange Albion won on penalties aet)	
Hoover Sports v Llantwit Fardre	4-2
Lisvane Hornets v Croesyceiliog	3-5
Llandrindod Wells v Newcastle Emlyn	4-2
Llangeinor v Port Tennant Colts	2-1
Llanrug United v Blaenau Amateurs	2-3
Llay Royal British Legion v Ruthin Town	0-1
Maltsters v Kenfig Hill	1-1, 1-3
Montgomery Town v Presteigne St Andrews	2-3
Nefyn United v Nantlle Vale	3-3, 3-1 *(aet)*
Newport Corinthians v Hirwaun Welfare	1-1, 2-3
Overton Athletic v Penycae	1-3
Pencoed v Porthcawl Town	0-5
Rhayader Town v Penparcau	5-1
Rhydymwyn v Mochdre	5-0
Rockwell v New Broughton	1-5
Tongwynlais v Cilfynydd	2-0
Tredomen v Undy United	5-1
Waterloo Rovers v Morda United	1-3

Second Round

Berriew v Llansantffraid	1-1, 2-4
Blaenau Amateurs v Llanrwst United	3-3, 0-4
Blaenrhondda v AFC Tondu	2-0
Brecon Corinthians v Tonyrefail Welfare	3-0
Brymbo v New Broughton	3-3, 3-1
Buckley v Chirk AAA	0-1
Cardiff Corinthians v North End	3-3, 3-1
Carno v Morda United	1-1, 1-2
Chepstow Town v Ton Pentre	0-1
Corwen Amateurs v Lex XI	1-2
Ferndale Athletic v Morriston Town	0-3
Fields Park Pontllanfraith v Tongwynlais	1-1, 0-2
Grange Harlequins v Risca United	2-3
Gresford Athletic v Abbey Life	1-0
Hirwaun Welfare v Kenfig Hill	3-4
(at Kenfig Hill)	
Llandyrnog United v Llandudno	1-5
Llangeinor v Grange Albion	5-3
Llwydcoed Welfare v Port Talbot Athletic	1-3
Locomotive Llanberis v Cemaes Bay	1-7
Mostyn v Rhydymwyn	1-1, 3-1
Nefyn United v Llanfairpwll	2-2, 2-5
Penrhyncoch v Knighton town	2-0
Penycae v Marchweil Villa	5-2
Pontyclun v Treharris Athletic	0-1

Ragged School v Carmarthen Town	4-0
Rhayader Town v Presteigne St Andrews	2-3
Ruthin Town v Cefn Druids	4-0
Skewen Athletic v Porthcawl Town	2-3
Taffs Well v Pontypridd Town	0-1
Tredomen v Hoover Sports	1-4
Trelewis Welfare v Croesyceiliog	3-2
Welshpool Town v Llandrindod Wells	8-1

Third Round

Bridgend Town v Hoover Sports	1-0
CPD Felinheli v Llanrwst United	3-3, 2-1
Cemaes Bay v Llandudno	4-0

Fourth Round

Blaenrhondda v Pontypridd Town	2-1
Brymbo v CPD Felinheli	0-2
Cemaes Bay v Welshpool Town	1-5
Lex XI v Chirk AAA	5-0
Llanfairpwll v Mostyn	4-0
Llangefni Town v Penrhyncoch	2-1
Morda United v Penycae	3-1
Morristown Town v Risca United	0-2
Porthcawl Town v Port Talbot Athletic	1-1, 0-6
Presteigne St Andrews v Gresford Athletic	0-9
Ragged School v Bridgend Town	2-5
Ruthin Town v Llansantffraid	0-1 *(aet)*
Tongwynlais v Llangeinor	0-4
Ton Pentre v Cardiff Corinthians	2-0
Treharris Athletic v Brecon Corinthians	0-2
Trelewis Welfare v Kenfig Hill	1-5

Fifth Round

CPD Felinheli v Bridgend Town	3-2
Gresford Athletic v Brecon Corinthians	2-2
(Brecon Corinthians won on penalties aet	
Kenfig Hill v Llanfairpwll	1-2
Lex XI v Llangefni Town	1-1, 3-2
Llangeinor v Risca United	2-2, 2-3
Llansantffraid v Blaenrhondda	2-1
Ton Pentre v Port Talbot Athletic	1-2
Welshpool Town v Morda United	0-0, 2-1

Sixth Round

CPD Felinheli v Llansantffraid	2-5
Port Talbot Athletic v Brecon Corinthians	1-2
Risca United v Lex XI	1-1, 0-2
Welshpool Town v Llanfairpwll	2-1

Semi-Finals

Brecon Corinthians v Welshpool Town	2-1
(at Rhayader Town FC)	
Llansantffraid v Lex XI	3-2
(at Cefn Druids FC)	

Final

Brecon Corinthians v Llansantffraid	0-3 *(aet)*
(at Victoria Avenue, Llanidloes Town FC)	

NORTHERN IRISH FOOTBALL 1992–93

It has been a year of dramatic change in Northern Ireland football with the planned introduction of promotion and relegation from the 1994–95 season, continued increased sponsorship at domestic and international level and a new name on the Bass Irish Cup.

Internationally the situation was something of a curate's egg — an unlucky 1-0 home defeat by European champions Denmark, a disastrous 3-0 humiliation by the Republic of Ireland at Lansdowne Road, the expected loss to Spain in Seville and then collecting six points from away games with Albania, Lithuania and Latvia.

Manager Billy Bingham, who retires in December after 12 highly successful years, still clings to the hope, alas somewhat forlorn, that qualification can be achieved from the fascinating seven-nation Group Three series for the USA 94 finals. "I expect the pacesetters will drop some silly points, and, if we continue to win, there is every chance we can make it. We are not dead yet," he said.

Trophies were spread throughout the competitions with no team dominating although Bangor's 20-year-old midfielder Paul Byrne, transferred to Glasgow Celtic for £70,000, made a clean sweep of the Player of the Year awards from the Football Writers' Association and the PFA.

Bangor won the Irish Cup for the first time in its history with a second replay victory over near neighbours Ards and they also took the Wilkinson Sword League Cup. This, unquestionably, was their greatest ever season. Their Cup Final saga, however, with Ards was so long drawn out that the Irish FA have decided to have extra time in the first game, and, if a second is necessary, to play it to a finish.

Linfield, under manager Trevor Anderson, appointed in October, won the Smirnoff Irish League championship and entered European football after four years' absence; Crusaders were pipped on the post but qualified for the UEFA Cup; Portadown won the TNT Gold Cup and the Budweiser Cup but failed in their European quest.

There were six managerial departures — John Flanagan (Bangor), Colin O'Neill (Coleraine), Jim Platt (Ballyclare Comrades), Billy Sinclair (Cliftonville), Eric Bowyer (Linfield) and Tommy Jackson (Glentoran); Sinclair and Bowyer joined Coleraine; Platt went into Swedish football as a coach and former Northern Ireland midfielder Tommy Cassidy (Newcastle United) took over at the Oval.

MALCOLM BRODIE

SMIRNOFF IRISH LEAGUE CHAMPIONSHIP FINAL TABLE

	P	W	D	L	F	A	Pts
Linfield	30	20	6	4	49	15	66
Crusaders	30	21	3	6	53	27	66
Bangor	30	20	4	6	61	32	64
Portadown	30	18	9	3	70	26	63
Distillery	30	20	2	8	61	36	62
Glenavon	30	14	6	10	48	36	48
Glentoran	30	13	8	9	70	40	47
Ards	30	12	9	9	45	45	45
Carrick	30	12	2	16	50	73	38
Ballymena	30	10	6	14	41	51	36
Cliftonville	30	10	3	17	42	48	33
Omagh	30	9	5	16	38	57	32
Larne	30	9	3	18	41	59	30
Newry	30	5	5	20	30	72	20
Coleraine	30	5	3	22	28	63	18
Ballyclare	30	2	6	22	28	75	12

Note: This was the first time the championship had been decided on goal difference.

BUDWEISER CUP FINAL

Portadown 3 Ballymena United 1 *(at Windsor Park, December 15, 1992)*
Portadown: Keenan; Major, Murray, Bell, Strain, Stewart, Cunningham, Russell, Cowan, Fraser, Davidson.
Ballymena United: Grant; Carlisle, Heron, Fullerton (Ritchie), Magill, Young, Burn, Connolly, Speak, Hardy, Candlish.
Referee: D. Magill (Belfast).
Scorers: Portadown — Russell, Fraser; Ballymena United — Candlish.
Attendance: 2700.

Semi-finals

Ards 2 Portadown 4
Ballymena Utd 0 Distillery 0 *(aet — Ballymena won 4-2 on pens)*

Previous Winners: 1988: Glentoran, 1989: Glenavon, 1990: Glentoran, 1991: Portadown, 1992: Omagh Town

IRISH LEAGUE CHAMPIONSHIP WINNERS

Year	Winner	Year	Winner	Year	Winner	Year	Winner	Year	Winner
1891	Linfield	1910	Cliftonville	1934	Linfield	1961	Linfield	1981	Glentoran
1892	Linfield	1911	Linfield	1935	Linfield	1962	Linfield	1982	Linfield
1893	Linfield	1912	Glentoran	1936	Belfast Celtic	1963	Distillery	1983	Linfield
1894	Glentoran	1913	Glentoran	1937	Belfast Celtic	1964	Glentoran	1984	Linfield
1895	Linfield	1914	Linfield	1938	Belfast Celtic	1965	Derry City	1985	Linfield
1896	Distillery	1915	Belfast Celtic	1939	Belfast Celtic	1966	Linfield	1986	Linfield
1897	Glentoran	1920	Belfast Celtic	1940	Belfast Celtic	1967	Glentoran	1987	Linfield
1898	Linfield	1921	Glentoran	1948	Belfast Celtic	1968	Glentoran	1988	Glentoran
1899	Distillery	1922	Linfield	1949	Linfield	1969	Linfield	1989	Linfield
1900	Belfast Celtic	1923	Linfield	1950	Linfield	1970	Glentoran	1990	Portadown
1901	Distillery	1924	Queen's Island	1951	Glentoran	1971	Linfield	1991	Portadown
1902	Linfield	1925	Glentoran	1952	Glenavon	1972	Glentoran	1992	Glentoran
1903	Distillery	1926	Belfast Celtic	1953	Glentoran	1973	Crusaders	1993	Linfield
1904	Linfield	1927	Belfast Celtic	1954	Linfield	1974	Coleraine		
1905	Glentoran	1928	Belfast Celtic	1955	Linfield	1975	Linfield		
1906	Cliftonville/	1929	Belfast Celtic	1956	Linfield	1976	Crusaders		
	Distillery	1930	Linfield	1957	Glentoran	1977	Glentoran		
1907	Linfield	1931	Glentoran	1958	Ards	1978	Linfield		
1908	Linfield	1932	Linfield	1959	Linfield	1979	Linfield		
1909	Linfield	1933	Belfast Celtic	1960	Glenavon	1980	Linfield		

ULSTER CUP

SECTIONAL TABLES

Section A	P	W	D	L	F	A	Pts
Bangor	3	3	0	0	7	3	9
Omagh T	3	2	0	1	8	6	6
Glentoran	3	1	0	2	6	7	3
Carrick	3	0	0	3	4	7	0

Section B	P	W	D	L	F	A	Pts
Ards	3	3	0	0	11	1	9
Portadown	3	2	0	1	7	3	6
Ballymena	3	1	0	2	2	9	3
Distillery	3	0	0	3	0	7	0

Section C	P	W	D	L	F	A	Pts
Linfield	3	2	1	0	6	4	7
Crusaders	3	2	0	1	12	5	6
Newry	3	0	0	3	3	10	0

Section D	P	W	D	L	F	A	Pts
Glenavon	3	2	1	0	6	1	7
Coleraine	3	1	2	0	5	3	5
Cliftonville	3	1	0	2	5	5	3
Larne	3	0	2	2	1	8	1

Winners

1949	Linfield	1958	Distillery	1967	Linfield	1976	Glentoran	1985	Coleraine
1950	Larne	1959	Glenavon	1968	Coleraine	1977	Linfield	1986	Coleraine
1951	Glentoran	1960	Linfield	1969	Coleraine	1978	Linfield	1987	Larne
1952		1961	Ballymena U	1970	Linfield	1979	Linfield	1988	Glentoran
1953	Glentoran	1962	Linfield	1971	Linfield	1980	Ballymena U	1989	Glentoran
1954	Crusaders	1963	Crusaders	1972	Coleraine	1981	Glentoran	1990	Portadown
1955	Glenavon	1964	Linfield	1973	Ards	1982	Glentoran	1991	Bangor
1956	Linfield	1965	Coleraine	1974	Linfield	1983	Glentoran	1992	Linfield
1957	Linfield	1966	Glentoran	1975	Coleraine	1984	Linfield		

ULSTER CUP FINAL

Linfield 2 Ards 0 (HT 2-0) *(at The Oval, September 23, 1992)*
Linfield: Fox; Crothers, Dornan, Doherty, McConnell, Beatty, McCoosh, Johnston, Hunter (J Magee), Campbell (Curry), Bailie.
Ards: Smith; Campbell, Morrison, Mitchell, Jeffrey, Bustard, Davies (McDonald), Cairns (Walker), M Magee, Erskine, Beattie.
Referee: A. Snoddy (Carryduff).
Scorers: Linfield — Campbell, Johnston.
Attendance: 5000.
Note: Competition was not sponsored, but Wilkinson Sword commercially backed the semi-finals and final.

Quarter-finals
Bangor 0, Portadown 0 (aet) *(Portadown won 3-2 on pens)*
Ards 1, Omagh Town 1 (aet) *(Ards won 3-1 on pens)*
Linfield 1, Coleraine 0
Glenavon 3, Crusaders 2

Semi-finals
Ards 1, Glenavon 0 *(September 1, Windsor Park)*
Portadown 2, Linfield 3 *(September 2, Oval)*

TNT GOLD CUP FINAL

Section A	P	W	D	L	F	A	Pts
Glenavon	3	2	1	0	7	3	7
Glentoran	3	2	0	1	7	3	6
Ards	3	1	1	1	4	4	4
Ballyclare	3	0	0	3	0	8	0

Section B	P	W	D	L	F	A	Pts
Portadown	3	2	1	0	6	2	7
Cliftonville	3	1	2	0	5	2	5
Newry	3	0	2	1	2	4	2
Omagh	3	0	1	2	2	7	1

Section C	P	W	D	L	F	A	Pts
Distillery	3	2	0	1	6	7	6
Bangor	3	1	1	1	7	4	4
Coleraine	3	1	1	1	2	4	4
Linfield	3	0	2	1	2	3	2

Section D	P	W	D	L	F	A	Pts
Crusaders	3	2	1	0	3	1	7
Ballymena	3	2	0	1	7	2	6
Larne	3	1	1	1	3	4	4
Carrick	3	0	0	3	2	8	0

Portadown 1 Cliftonville 0 (HT 1-0) *(at Windsor Park, Belfast, November 11, 1992)*
Portadown: Keenan; Major, Murray, Bell, Strain, Stewart, Casey, Russell, Cowan, Fraser, Davidson.
Cliftonville: Rice, Nutt, McCreadie, Tabb, Donnelly, McGurnaghan, Cunningham (O'Kane), McFadden (Stitt), Drake, Breslin, McCaw.
Referee: F. McDonald (Newry).
Scorer: Portadown — Nutt (og).
Attendance: 5100.

Quarter-finals
Glenavon 1, Cliftonville 2
Distillery 0, Ballymena 2
Crusaders 1, Bangor 5
Portadown 1, Glentoran 0

Semi-finals
Cliftonville 2, Ballymena Utd 1 *(Windsor Park, October 27)*
Portadown 4, Bangor 0 *(The Oval, October 28)*

IRISH CUP FINALS (from 1946–47)

1946–47	Belfast Celtic 1, Glentoran 0	1963–64	Derry City 2, Glentoran 0
1947–48	Linfield 3, Coleraine 0	1964–65	Coleraine 2, Glenavon 1
1948–49	Derry City 3, Glentoran 1	1965–66	Glentoran 2, Linfield 0
1949–50	Linfield 2, Distillery 1	1966–67	Crusaders 3, Glentoran 1
1950–51	Glentoran 3, Ballymena U 1	1967–68	Crusaders 2, Linfield 0
1951–52	Ards 1, Glentoran 0	1968–69	Ards 4, Distillery 2
1952–53	Linfield 5, Coleraine 0	1969–70	Linfield 2, Ballymena U 1
1953–54	Derry City 1, Glentoran 0	1970–71	Distillery 3, Derry City 0
1954–55	Dundela 3, Glenavon 0	1971–72	Coleraine 2, Portadown 1
1955–56	Distillery 1, Glentoran 0	1972–73	Glentoran 3, Linfield 2
1956–57	Glenavon 2, Derry City 0	1973–74	Ards 2, Ballymena U 1
1957–58	Ballymena U 2, Linfield 0	1974–75	Coleraine 1:0:1,
1958–59	Glenavon 2, Ballymena U 0		Linfield 1:0:0
1959–60	Linfield 5, Ards 1	1975–76	Carrick Rangers 2, Linfield 1
1960–61	Glenavon 5, Linfield 1	1976–77	Coleraine 4, Linfield 1
1961–62	Linfield 4, Portadown 0	1977–78	Linfield 3, Ballymena U 1
1962–63	Linfield 2, Distillery 1	1978–79	Cliftonville 3, Portadown 2

1979–80	Linfield 2, Crusaders 0
1980–81	Ballymena U 1, Glenavon 0
1981–82	Linfield 2, Coleraine 1
1982–83	Glentoran 1:2, Linfield 1:1
1983–84	Ballymena U 4,
	Carrick Rangers 1
1984–85	Glentoran 1:1, Linfield 1:0
1985–86	Glentoran 2, Coleraine 1
1986–87	Glentoran 1, Larne 0
1987–88	Glentoran 1, Glenavon 0
1988–89	Ballymena U 1, Larne 0
1989–90	Glentoran 3, Portadown 0
1990–91	Portadown 2, Glenavon 1
1991–92	Glenavon 2, Linfield 1
1992–93	Bangor 1:1:1, Ards 1:1:0

BASS IRISH CUP 1992–93

First Round

Armoy Utd v H & W Welders	1-3
Culleybackey v Downshire YM	1-4
Killymoon Rangers v Magherafelt Sky Blues	0-1
Abbey Villa v Ballynahinch Utd	7-2
Dromore Amateurs v Ballymacash Rangers	2-3
Armagh City v AFC	2-2, 5-4
Annagh Utd v Dungiven	3-2
1st Bangor v Seapatrick	3-1
UU Jordanstown v Civil Service	0-0, 1-5
UU Coleraine v Tandragee Rovers	1-1, 1-1
(UUC won 5-4 on pens)	
Annalong Swifts v Connor	4-4, 1-2
Richhill v Barn Utd	1-5
1st Liverpool v Wellington Rec	6-0
Comber Rec v Dervock Utd	4-1
Institute v Northern Telecom	0-0, 0-2
Hanover v Shorts	0-2
Roe Valley v Bessbrook Utd	2-1
Southend Utd v ECC	4-5
Glebe Rangers v Dromara Village	3-2
Portglenone v Macosquin	2-5
Portstewart v Saintfield Utd	0-0, 3-8
Bridgend v Oxford Utd Stars	1-2
Scarva Rangers v Drummond Utd	2-3
Ards Rangers v Orangefield OB	5-2

Second Round

Bangor Amateurs v Macosquin	2-4
Saintfield Utd v Connor	3-3, 3-6
Civil Service v 1st Bangor	0-2
1st Shankhill NISC v Killyleagh	2-3
Shorts v H & W Welders	1-6
Northern Telecom v Magherafelt Sky Blues	0-2
Glebe Rangers v Ards Rangers	1-3
ECC v East Belfast	3-2
Donard Hospital v Ballymacash Rangers	3-0
H & W Sports v Oxford Utd Stars	2-1
Drummond Utd v Downshire YM	2-0
Abbey Villa v Larne Tech OB	4-1
Barn Utd v Rathfriland Rangers	5-3
Comber Rec v UU Coleraine	1-0
Roe Valley v Annagh Utd	2-0
Sirocco Works v 1st Liverpool	4-1
Armagh City v Cookstown Royals	6-4
Islandmagee v Queens University	4-2

Third Round

Islandmagee v Barn Utd	1-0
Abbey Villa v Comber Rec	1-3
Sirocco Works v Armagh City	1-2
Macosquin v Drummond Utd	3-0
Roe Valley v 1st Bangor	4-0
Killyleagh YC v H & W Sports	8-4
Ards Rangers v Connor	2-0
Donard Hospital v Magherafelt Sky Blues	4-3
ECC v H & W Welders	2-5

Fourth Round

Dundela v Moyola Park	3-1
Banbridge Town v Ards Rangers	2-1
Park v Brantwood	1-2
Ballymoney Utd v Armagh City	5-6
Crumlin Utd v Limavady Utd	0-2
Kilmore Rec v Roe Valley	0-0, 1-5
Ballinamallard Utd v FC Enkalon	4-1
British Telecom v Tobermore Utd	1-0
Chimney Corner v Comber Rec	1-1, 3-2
Loughgall v Crewe Utd	4-1
Coagh Utd v Macosquin	2-0
H & W Welders v Donard Hospital	6-1
Dunmurry Rec v Donegal Celtic	1-1, 1-3
Drumaness Mills v Islandmagee	2-1
RUC v Killyleagh YC	2-1
Dungannon Swifts v Cookstown Utd	1-1, 2-1

Fifth Round

Larne v Crusaders	2-2, 0-1
Glenavon v Ballymena Utd	0-3
RUC v Armagh City	2-3
Brantwood v Donegal Celtic	2-0
Limavady Utd v Roe Valley	3-0
Coagh Utd v Dungannon Swifts	2-1
Ballyclare Comrades v Banbridge Town	2-0
Distillery v British Telecom	6-0
Linfield v Coleraine	6-1
Cliftonville v H & W Welders	1-0
Dundela v Newry Town	2-2, 1-1
(Newry won 5-3 on pens)	
Glentoran v Portadown	0-0, 0-1
Chimney Corner v Drumaness Mills	0-1
Omagh Town v Ballinamallard Utd	3-0
Carrick Rangers v Bangor	2-4
Ards v Loughgall Utd	3-0

Sixth Round

Bangor v Armagh City	2-0
Brantwood v Glentoran	0-1
Cliftonville v Ballymena Utd	2-0
Coagh Utd v Larne	1-8
Distillery v Ballyclare Comrades	1-1, 2-1
Drumaness Mills v Ards	0-4
Dundela v Limavady Utd	3-2
Linfield v Omagh Town	1-1, 0-3

Quarter-finals

Linfield v Bangor	1-2
Ards v Distillery	0-0, 1-4
Dundela v Glentoran	1-2
Larne v Cliftonville	1-1, 0-2

Semi-finals

Ards v Cliftonville *(Oval, April 2)*	3-2
Bangor v Glentoran *(Windsor Park, April 3)*	3-1

BASS IRISH CUP FINAL

First Match

Ards 1 Bangor 1 *(at Windsor Park, May 1, 1993)*
Ards: Vance; McDonald, Leeman, Mitchell, Jeffrey, Bustard, Beattie, Connell, Erskine, McCourt, Davies.
Bangor: Eachus; Canning, Glendinning, Muldoon (Surgeon), Brown, O'Connor, Hill, Magee (McCreadie), McCallan, Byrne, McEvoy.
Referee: A. Snoddy (Carryduff).
Scorers: Ards — McCourt; Bangor — Glendinning.
Attendance: 8500.

First Replay

Ards 1 Bangor 1 *(aet)* *(at Windsor Park, May 8, 1993)* Ards: Vance, McDonald, Leeman, Mitchell, Jeffrey, Bustard, Beattie (Kavanagh), Connell, Erskine, McCourt, Davies (Campbell).
Bangor: Eachus; Canning, Glendinning, Hill, Brown, O'Connor, Surgeon, McCreadie (Magee), McCallan, Byrne, McEvoy (Muldoon).
Referee: A. Snoddy (Carryduff).
Scorers: Ards — Erskine; Bangor — Glendinning.
Attendance: 6000.

Second Replay

Bangor 1 Ards 0 *(at Windsor Park, May 11, 1993)*
Ards: Vance; McDonald, Leeman, Mitchell, Jeffrey, Bustard, Beattie (Kavanagh), Connell, Erskine, McCourt, Davies (Campbell).
Bangor: Eachus; Canning, Glendinning, Muldoon, Brown, O'Connor, Hill, McCreadie, McCallan (Magee), Byrne, McEvoy.
Referee: A. Snoddy (Carryduff).
Scorer: Bangor — Byrne.
Attendance: 5000.
NOTE: This was the first time Bangor, formed in 1918, had won the cup.

INTERNATIONAL DIRECTORY

The latest available information has been given regarding numbers of clubs and players registered with FIFA, the world governing body. Where known, official colours are listed. With European countries, League tables show a number of signs. * indicates relegated teams, + play-offs, *+ relegated after play-offs. In Yugoslavia, drawn matches result in penalty shoot-outs, the winners receiving a point.

There are 178 FIFA members. In addition Azerbaijan and Moldova are associate members of UEFA and will be able to join FIFA in 1994. Kazakhstan, Kyrgyzstan, Tajikistan, Turkmenistan and Uzbekistan may become associate members of AFC and consequently apply for FIFA membership in 1994. The four home countries, England, Scotland, Northern Ireland and Wales, are dealt with elsewhere in the Yearbook; but basic details appear in this directory.

EUROPE

ALBANIA

Federation Albanaise De Football, Rruga Dervish Hima Nr. 31, Tirana.
Founded: 1930; *Number of Clubs:* 49; *Number of Players:* 5,192; *National Colours:* Red shirts, black shorts, red stockings.
Telephone: 355–42/2 78 77; *Cable:* ALBSPORT TIRANA; *Telex:* 2228 BFSSH sb. *Fax:* 355–42/2 78 77.

International matches 1992

Greece (h) 1-0, Spain (a) 0-3, Eire (a) 0-2, Lithuania (h) 1-0, N. Ireland (a) 0-3, Latvia (h) 1-1.

League Championship wins (1945–92)

Dinamo Tirana 15; Partizani Tirana 15; 17 Nentori 8; Vllaznia 7; Flamurtari 1; Labinoti 1.

Cup wins (1948–92)

Partizani Tirana 13; Dinamo Tirana 12; 17 Nentori 6; Vllaznia 5; Flamurtari 2; Labinoti 1; Elbasan 1.

Final League Table 1992–93

	P	W	D	L	F	A	Pts
Partizani	30	17	9	4	53	22	43
Teuta	30	15	8	7	32	21	38
Besa	30	14	9	7	42	22	37
Vllaznia	30	15	7	8	44	26	37
Elbasan	30	12	7	11	36	32	31
Dinamo	30	10	9	11	32	33	29
Apolonia	30	9	10	11	41	43	28
Lushnia	30	10	8	12	30	35	28
Albpetrol	30	10	8	12	38	48	28
Laci	30	11	6	13	26	37	28
SK Tirana	30	7	13	10	24	28	27
Sopoti	30	9	9	12	36	41	27
Flamurtari	30	8	11	11	28	34	27
Kastrioti*	30	8	10	12	29	32	26
Tomori*	30	11	3	16	28	53	25
Pogradeci*	30	8	5	17	26	38	21

Top scorer: Dosti (Partizani) 21
Cup Final: Partizani 1, Albpetrol 0

ARMENIA

Football Federation of Armenia, 9, Abovian Str. 375001 Erevan, Armenia.
Number of Clubs: 956; *Number of Players:* 12,055.
Telephone: 885–52 7582, 885–52 7014, 885–52 7974; *Telex:* 885–52 3376. ; *Fax:* 885–52 3376.

League Champions 1992–93

Shirak Gyumri.

Cup winners 1992–93

Ararat Erevan.

AUSTRIA

Oesterreichischer Fussball-Bund, Wiener Stadion, Sektor A/F, Meierestrasse, A-1020 Wien.
Founded: 1904; *Number of Clubs:* 2,081; *Number of Players:* 253,576; *National Colours:* White shirts, black shorts, black stockings.
Telephone: 0043-1-217 18; *Cable:* FOOTBALL WIEN; *Telex:* 111919 OEFB A; *Fax:* 0043-1-218 16 32.

International matches 1992

Hungary (a) 1-2, Lithuania (h) 4-0, Wales (h) 1-1, Poland (h) 2-4, Holland (a) 2-3, Czechoslovakia (a) 2-2, Portugal (h) 1-1, France (a) 0-2, Israel (h) 5-2, Germany (a) 0-0.

League Championship wins (1912–92)

Rapid Vienna 29; FK Austria 22; Admira-Energie-Wacker (prev. Sportklub Admira & Admira-Energie) 8; First Vienna 6; Tirol-Svarowski-Innsbruck (prev. Wacker Innsbruck) 7; Wiener Sportklub 3; FAC 1; Hakoah 1; Linz ASK 1; Wacker Vienna 1; WAF 1; Voest Linz 1.

Cup wins (1919–92)

FK Austria 24; Rapid Vienna 13; TS Innsbruck (prev. Wacker Innsbruck) 7; Admira-Energie-Wacker (prev. Sportklub Admira & Admira-Energie) 5; First Vienna 3; Linz ASK 1; Wacker Vienna 1; WAF 1; Wiener Sportklub 1; Graz 1; Stockerau 1.

Qualifying Table 1992–93

	P	W	D	L	F	A	Pts
FK Austria	22	13	4	5	48	24	30
Austria Salzburg	22	11	7	4	45	27	29
Tirol	22	10	8	4	45	22	26
Rapid	22	9	8	5	34	26	26
Admira Wacker	22	11	3	8	47	33	25
Wiener SC	22	10	5	7	30	34	25
St Polten	22	6	10	6	34	37	22
Vorwaerts	22	8	6	8	30	34	22
Modling	22	8	3	11	39	41	22
Linz	22	4	6	12	21	46	14
Stahl Linz	22	3	6	13	20	43	12
Sturm Graz	22	3	6	13	23	49	12

Final table 1992–93

	P	W	D	L	F	A	Pts
FK Austria	36	22	6	8	81	35	36
Austria Salzburg	36	20	10	6	69	33	36
Admira Wacker	36	17	6	13	72	54	28
Rapid	36	15	10	11	53	51	27
Tirol	36	14	12	10	63	43	26
St Polten	36	9	16	11	51	61	23
Wiener SC	36	14	8	14	47	67	23
Vorwaerts	36	10	9	17	37	53	18

Promotion/Relegation

	P	W	D	L	F	A	Pts
Modling	14	11	2	1	26	6	24
Sturm Graz	14	8	2	4	26	12	18
Linz	14	5	6	3	11	8	16
Graz AK	14	4	7	3	20	13	15
Leoben	14	3	5	6	14	18	11
Stahl Linz	14	3	4	7	12	16	10
Ried	14	4	1	9	14	26	9
Favoritner	14	3	3	8	10	34	9

Modling and Sturm Graz promoted to a ten team First Division.
Top scorer: Danek (Tirol) 24
Cup Final: Tirol 3, Rapid Vienna 1

BELARUS

Football Federation of Belarus, 8–2 Kyrov Str. 220600 Minsk, Belarus.
Founded: 1992; Number of Players: 120,000.
Telephone: 172–27 2920, 172–27 2325; *Telex:* 252175 athlet su; *Fax:* 172–27 6184.

International matches 1992

Ukraine (h) 1-1.

BELGIUM

Union Royale Belge Des Societes De Football; Eturl, Association, Rue De La Loi 43, Boite 1, B-1040 Bruxelles.
Founded: 1895; *Number of Clubs:* 2,120; *Number of Players:* 390,468; *National Colours:* Red shirts with tri-coloured trim, red shorts, red stockings with trim.
Telephone: 32 2 477 1211; *Cable:* UBSFA BRUXELLES; *Telex:* 23257 BVBFBF B; *Fax:* 32 2 2147 82391.

International matches 1992

Tunisia (a) 1-2, France (a) 3-3, Cyprus (h) 1-0, Faeroes (a) 3-0, Czechoslovakia (a) 2-1, Romania (h) 1-0, Wales (h) 2-0.

League Championship wins (1896–1992)

Anderlecht 22; Union St Gilloise 11; FC Brugge 9; Standard Liege 8; Beerschot 7; RC Brussels 6; FC Liège 5; Daring Brussels 4; Antwerp 4; Mechelen 4; Lierse SK 3; SV Brugge 3; Beveren 2; RWD Molenbeek 1.

Cup wins (1954–92)

Anderlecht 7; FC Brugge 5; Standard Liege 5; Beerschot 2; Waterschei 2; Beveren 2; Gent 2; Antwerp 2; Lierse SK 1; Racing Doornik 1; Waregem 1; SV Brugge 1; Mechelen 1; FC Liège 1.

Final League Table 1992–93

	P	W	D	L	F	A	Pts
Anderlecht	34	26	6	2	80	24	58
Standard Liege	34	18	9	7	69	43	45
Mechelen	34	18	6	10	53	33	42
Waregem	34	17	8	9	78	45	42
Antwerp	34	17	7	10	61	42	41
FC Brugge	34	16	8	10	49	32	40
Charleroi	34	16	8	10	58	46	40
Beveren	34	15	7	12	47	42	37
Gent	34	12	10	12	51	51	34
Lierse	34	12	7	15	41	51	31
RWD Molenbeek	34	10	11	13	39	45	31
CS Brugge	34	9	10	15	65	73	28
Liege	34	10	8	16	48	71	28
Ekeren	34	10	7	17	57	67	27
Genk	34	8	11	15	37	50	27
Lommel	34	9	4	21	42	79	22
Lokeren*	34	4	12	18	32	58	20
Boom*	34	6	7	21	40	95	19

Top scorer: Weber (CS Brugge) 31
Cup Final: Standard Liege 2, Charleroi 0

BULGARIA

Bulgarian Football Union, Gotcho Gopin 19, 1000 Sofia.
Founded: 1923; *Number of Clubs:* 376; *Number of Players:* 48,240; *National Colours:* White shirts, green shorts, red stockings.
Telephone: 87 74 90; *Cable:* BULFUTBOL; *Telex:* 23145 BFS BG; *Fax:* 87 74 90.

International matches 1992

Switzerland (a) 2-0, Finland (a) 3-0, Mexico (h) 1-1, Tu7rkey (a) 2-3, France (h) 2-0, Sweden (a) 0-2, Portugal (a) 1-2, Israel (a) 2-0.

League Championship wins (1925–92)

CSKA Sofia 27; Levski Sofia 17; Slavia Sofia 6; Vladislav Varna 3; Lokomotiv Sofia 3; Trakia Plovdiv 2; AS 23 Sofia 1; Botev Plovdiv 1; SC Sofia 1; Sokol Varna 1; Spartak Plovdiv 1; Tichka Varna 1; ZSZ Sofia 1; Beroe Stara Zagora 1; Etur 1.

Cup wins (1946–92)

Levski Sofia 17; CSKA Sofia 14; Slavia Sofia 6; Loko motiv Sofia 3; Botev Plovdiv 1; Spartak Plovdiv 1; Spartak Sofia 1; Marek Stanke 1; Trakia Plovdiv 1; Spartak Varna 1; Sliven 1.

Final League Table 1992–93

	P	W	D	L	F	A	Pts
Levski Sofia	30	22	6	2	76	28	50
CSKA Sofia	30	17	8	5	66	31	42
Botev Plovdiv	30	16	6	8	53	33	38
Lokomotiv Plovdiv	30	16	5	9	57	29	37
Lokomotiv Sofia	30	11	13	6	52	39	35
Etur	30	13	9	8	37	36	35
Pirin	30	12	8	10	31	33	32
Lokomotiv Gorna	30	11	9	10	35	36	31
Tschernomoretz	30	11	8	11	33	31	30
Beroe	30	10	8	12	29	35	28
Yantra	30	10	6	14	38	51	26
Spartak Varna	30	8	8	14	30	48	24
Dobroudja	30	9	4	17	31	56	22
Slavia Sofia	30	8	5	17	39	56	21
Haskovo*	30	6	6	18	33	64	18
Sliven*	30	6	1	23	26	57	13

Top scorer: Guetov (Levski Sofia) 26
Cup Final: CSKA Sofia 1, Botev Plovdiv 0

CROATIA

Croatian Football Federation, Illica 21/11, CRO-41000 Zagreb, Croatia.
Telephone: 841/42 46 47, 841/42 4642. *Fax:* 841/42 46 39.

International matches 1992

Australia (a) 0-1, Australia (a) 1-3, Australia (a) 0-0, Mexico (h) 3-0.

Final League Table 1992–93

	P	W	D	L	F	A	Pts
Zagreb	30	21	7	2	84	27	49
Hajduk Split	30	15	11	4	52	27	42
Zagreb	30	15	10	5	51	28	40
Rijeka	30	14	11	4	41	24	39
Vinkoveci	30	11	9	10	31	30	31
Osijek	30	11	7	12	40	42	29
Varteks	30	10	9	11	38	47	29
Istra Pola	30	12	4	14	32	35	28
Inker	30	9	9	12	35	31	27
Segesta Sisak	30	10	5	15	31	44	25
Pazinka Pisino	30	7	11	12	20	28	25
Zadar	30	9	7	14	30	48	25
Radnik	30	9	7	14	30	52	25
Dubrovnik	30	9	7	14	24	37	25
Belisce*	30	8	9	13	34	50	25
Sibenik*	30	4	8	18	21	45	16

Top scorer: Vlaovic (Croatia Zagreb) 15
Cup Final: Hajduk Split 4,1, Croatia Zagreb 1,2

CYPRUS

Cyprus Football Association, Stasinos Str. 1, Engomi 152, P.O. Box 5071, Nicosia.
Founded: 1934; *Number of Clubs:* 85; *Number o f Players:* 6,000; *National Colours:* Sky blue shirts, white shorts, blue and white stockings.
Telephone: (2) 44 53 41, 44 53 42, 45 99 59; *Cable:* FOOTBALL NICOSIA; *Telex:* 3880 FOOTBALL CY; *Fax:* (2) 47 25 44.

International matches 1992

Israel (a) 1-2, Greece (h) 1-3, Belgium (a) 0-1, Faeroes (a) 2-0, Greece (a) 3-2, Malta (h) 3-0, Wales (h) 0-1, Slovenia (h) 1-1, Romania (h) 1-4.

League Championship wins (1935–92)

Omonia 17; Apoel 6; Anorthosis 6; AEL 5; EPA 3; Olympiakos 3; Pezoporikos 2; Ch etin Kayal 1; Trast 1; Apollon 1.

Cup wins (1935–92)

Apoel 13; Omonia 9; AEL 6; EPA 5; Anorthosis 4; Apollon 4; Trast 3; Chetin Kayal 2; Olympiakos 1; Pezoporikos 1; Salamina 1.

Final League Table 1992–93

	P	W	D	L	F	A	Pts
Omonia	26	18	5	3	75	30	59
Apollon	26	17	6	3	66	25	57
Salamina	26	15	3	8	44	28	48
Apoel	26	12	7	7	52	39	43
Anorthosis	26	11	6	9	32	33	39
Pezoporikos	26	8	10	8	46	39	34
AEL	26	9	16	11	42	40	33
Paralimni	26	10	3	13	46	48	33
Ethnikos	26	10	3	13	46	49	33
EPA	26	8	8	10	40	48	32
Olympiakos	26	8	7	11	34	52	31
Evagoras+	26	8	6	12	39	45	30
Aris*	26	8	6	12	33	52	30
Apop*	26	1	2	23	17	84	5

Top scorer: Scepovic (Apollon) 25
Cup Final: Apoel 4, Apollon 1

RCS -Representation of Czechs and Slovaks (formerly CZECHOSLOVAKIA)

Ceskoslovensky Fotbalovy Svaz, Na Porici 12, 11530 Praha 1.
Founded: 1906; *Number of Clubs:* 5,930; *Number of Players:* 375,380; *National Colours:* Red shirts, white shorts, blue stockings.
Telephone: 225836/2350065; *Cable:* SPORTSVAZ PRAHA; *Telex:* 122650 CSTV C.

International matches 1992

Egypt (a) 0-2, England (h) 2-2, Germany (h) 1-1, Poland (a) 0-1, Austria (h) 2-2, Belgium (h) 1-2, Faeroes (h) 4-0, Romania (a) 1-1.

League Championship wins (1926–92)

Sparta Prague 21; Slavia Prague 12; Dukla Prague (prev. UDA) 11; Slovan Bratislava 7; Spartak Trnava 5; Banik Ostrava 3; Inter-Bratislava 1; Spartak Hradec Kralove 1; Viktoria Zizkov 1; Zbrojovka Brno 1; Bohemians 1; Vitkovice 1.

Cup wins (1991–92)

Dukla Prague 8; Sparta Prague 8; Slovan Bratislava 5; Spartak Trnava 4; Banik Ostrava 3; Lokomotiv Kosice 3; TJ Gottwaldov 1; Dunajska Streda 1.

Final League Table 1992–93

	P	W	D	L	F	A	Pts
Sparta Prague	30	23	2	5	66	24	48
Slavia Prague	30	18	7	5	70	28	43
Slovan Bratislava	30	17	4	7	61	30	42
Dunaskja	30	16	5	9	46	36	37
Sigma Olomouc	30	14	7	9	44	38	35
Inter Bratislava	30	14	3	13	46	42	31
Brno	30	13	5	12	40	51	31
Banik Ostrava	30	10	11	9	47	38	31
Tatran Presov	30	9	8	13	42	40	28
Hradec Kralove	30	10	7	13	32	36	27
Vitkovice	30	9	9	12	30	44	27
Nitra	30	6	13	10	27	38	25
Budejovice	30	9	5	16	36	39	23
Bohemians	30	5	9	16	23	53	19
Dukla Prague	30	7	5	18	38	74	19
Spartak Trnava	30	3	10	17	24	60	16

Six Slovak clubs will play in the Slovak First Division next season. The championship of the Czech Republic will have sixteen teams, nine from the Czechoslovakian First Division and seven promoted teams. Bohemians will be relegated.
Top scorer: Dubrovsky (Slovan Bratislava) 24
Czech Cup Final: Sparta Prague 2, Brno 0
Slovak Cup Final: Kosice 0, Dunaskja 0
Kosice won 5-4 on penalties
Czechoslovakian Cup Final: Kosice 5, Sparta Prague 1

DENMARK

Dansk Boldspil Union, Ved Amagerbanen 15, DK-2300, Copenhagen S.
Founded: 1889; *Number of Clubs:* 1,555; *Number of Players:* 268,517; *National Colours:* Red shirts, white shorts, red stockings.
Telephone: (45) 3195 0511; *Cable:* DANSKBOLDSPIL COPENHAGEN; *Telex:* 15545 DBU DK; *Fax:* (45) 3195 0588.

International matches 1992

Turkey (a) 1-2, Norway (h) 1-0, CIS (h) 1-1, England (n) 0-0, Sweden (n) 0-1, France (n) 2-1, Holland (n) 2-2, Germany (n) 2-0, Latvia (a) 0-0, Germany (h) 1-2, Lithuania (a) 0-0, Eire (h) 0-0, N. Ireland (a) 1-0.

League Championship wins (1913–91)

KB Copenhagen 15; B 93 Copenhagen 9; AB (Akademisk) 9; B 1903 Copenhagen 7; Frem 6; Esbjerg BK 5; Vejle BK 5; AGF Aarhus 5; Brondby 4; Hvidovre 3; Odense BK 3; B 1909 Odense 2; Koge BK 2; Lyngby 2; FC Copenhagen 1.

Cup wins (1955–91)

Aarhus GF 8; Vejle BK 6; Randers Freja 3; Lyngby 3; OB Odense 3; B1909 Odense 2; Aalborg BK 2; Esbjerg BK 2; Frem 2; B 1903 Copenhagen 2; B 93 Copenhagen 1; KB Copenhagen 1; Vanlose 1; Hvidovre 1; B1913 Odense 1; Brondby 1.

Final League Table 1992–93

	P	W	D	L	F	A	Pts
FC Copenhagen	14	8	3	3	31	23	32
Odense	14	8	3	3	19	15	31
Brondby	14	8	3	3	29	16	30
Aalborg	14	5	5	4	24	22	20
Silkeborg	14	4	5	5	17	17	23
Aarhus	14	4	4	3	24	29	21
Lyngby	14	4	2	8	22	22	18
Naestved	14	1	4	9	16	36	14

Top scorer: Moller (Aalborg) 22
Cup Final: Odense 2, Aalborg 0

ENGLAND

The Football Association, 16 Lancaster Gate, London W2 3LW*K Founded:* 1863; *Number of Clubs:* 42,000; *Number of Players:* 2,250,000; *National Colours:* White shirts, navy blue shorts, white stockings.
Telephone: 071/262 4542; *Cable:* FOOTBALL ASSOCIATION LONDON W2; *Telex:* 261110; *Fax:* 071/402 0486.

ESTONIA

Estonian Football Association, Refati PST 1-376, 20 0103 Tallinn.
Number of Clubs: 40; *Number of Players:* 12,000.
Telephone: 142–23 8253; *Telex:* 173236 Sport; *Fax:* 142–23 8387.

International matches 1992

Slovenia (h) 1-1, Latvia (a) 1-2, Lithuania (a) 1-1, Switzerland (h) 0-6, Malta (a) 0-0.

FAEROE ISLANDS

Fotboltssamband Foroya, The Faeroes' Football Assn., Gundalur, P.O. Box 1028, FR-110, Torshavn.
Founded: 1979; *Number of Clubs:* 16; *Number of Players:* 1,014.
Telephone: 298 12606; *Telex:* 81332 ITROTT FA; *Fax:* 298 12421.

International matches 1992

Romania (a) 0-7, Norway (a) 0-2, Belgium (h) 0-3, Cyprus (h) 0-2, Israel (h) 1-1, Wales (a) 0-6, Czechoslovakia (a) 0-4.

Final League Table 1992

	P	W	D	L	F	A	Pts
B68	18	11	5	2	35	18	27
GI	18	11	3	4	33	20	25
HB	18	8	7	3	35	21	23
KI	18	7	8	3	30	17	22
TB	17	8	4	5	28	27	20
B36	18	5	8	5	30	30	18
VB	18	4	9	5	20	24	17
B71	17	2	7	8	25	29	11
SIF*	18	3	5	10	27	41	11
NSI*	18	1	2	15	14	50	4

Top scorer: Justinussen (GI) 14
Cup Final: HB 1, KI 0

FINLAND

Suomen Palloliitto Finlands Bollfoerbund, Kuparitie 1, P.O. Box 29, SF-00441 Helsinki.
Founded: 1907; *Number of Clubs:* 1,135; *Number of Players:* 66,100; *National Colours:* White shirts, blue shorts, white stockings.
Telephone: 90-56 26 233; *Cable:* SUOMIFOTBOLL HELSINKI; *Tele x:* 1001438 SPL SF; *Fax:* 5626413.

International matches 1992

Turkey (a) 1-1, Scotland (a) 1-1, Brazil (a) 1-3, Bulgaria (h) 0-3, England (h) 1-2, Poland (h) 0-0, Sweden (h) 0-1, Tunisia (a) 1-1, France (a) 1-2.

League Championship wins (1949–91)

Helsinki JK 9; Turun Palloseura 5; Kuopion Palloseura 5; Valkeakosken Haka 4; Kuusysi 4; Lahden Reipas 3; Ilves-Kissat 2; IF Kamraterna 2; Kotkan TP 2; OPS Oulu 2; Torun Pyrkivä 1; IF Kronohagens 1; Helsinki PS 1; Kokkolan PV 1; IF Kamraterna 1; Vasa 1.

Cup wins (1955–91)

Valkeakosken Haka 9; Lahden Reipas 7; Kotkan TP 4; Helsinki JK 3; Mikkelin 2; Kuusysi 2; Kuopion Palloseura 2; Ilves Tampere 2; IFK Abo 1; Drott 1; Helsinki PS 1; Pallo-Peikot 1; Rovaniemi PS 1; TPS Turku 1; MyPa 1.

Final League Table 1992

	P	W	D	L	F	A	Pts
HJK Helsinki	33	20	6	7	59	35	66
Kuusysi	33	19	6	8	61	38	63
Jazz Pori	33	18	9	6	62	42	63
MyPa	33	16	8	9	57	29	56
Jaro	33	14	8	11	49	37	50
Haka	33	15	5	13	42	51	50
Rops Rovaniemi	33	12	6	15	55	49	42
TPS Turku	33	9	8	16	29	45	35
Ilves	33	10	5	18	43	54	35
MP Mikkeli	33	10	3	20	34	60	33
Oulu*	33	9	5	19	42	68	32
Kups*	33	8	7	18	33	56	31

Top scorer: Antonio (Jazz Pori) 21
Cup Final: MyPa 2, Jaro 0

FRANCE

Federation Francaise De Football, 60 Bis A venue D'Iena, F-75783 Paris, Cedex 16.
Founded: 1919; *Number of Clubs:* 21,629; *Number of Players:* 1,692,205; *National Colours:* Blue shirts, white shorts, red stockings.
Telephone: 44 31 73 00; *Cable:* CEFI PARIS 034; *Telex:* 640000; *Fax:* (1) 4720 8296.

International matches 1992

England (a) 0-2, Belgium (h) 3-3, Switzerland (a) 1-2, Holland (h) 1-1, Sweden (n) 1-1, England (n) 0-0, Denmark (n) 1-2, Brazil (h) 0-2, Bulgaria (a) 0-2, Austria (h) 2-0, Finland (h) 2-1.

League Championship wins (1933–92)

Saint Etienne 10; Olympique Marseille 8; Stade de Reims 6; Nantes 6; AS Monaco 5; OGC Nice 4; Girondins Bordeaux 4; Lille OSC 3; FC Sete 2; Sochaux 2; Racing Club Paris 1 Roubaix-Tourcoing 1; Strasbourg 1; Paris St Germain 1.

Cup wins (1918–92)

Olympique Marseille 10; Saint Etienne 6; Lille OSC 5; Racing Club Paris 5; Red Star 5; AS Monaco 5; Olympique Lyon 4; Girondins Bordeaux 3; CAS Genereaux 2; Nancy 2; OGC Nice 2; Racing Club Strasbourg 2; Sedan 2; FC Sete 2; Stade de Reims 2; SO Montpellier 2; Stade Rennes 2; Paris St Germain 2; AS Cannes 1; Club Français 1; Excelsior Roubaix 1; Le Havre 1; Olympique de Pantin 1; CA Paris 1; Sochaux 1; Toulouse 1; Bastia 1; Nantes 1; Metz 1.

Final League Table 1992–93

	P	W	D	L	F	A	Pts
Marseille	38	23	9	6	72	36	55
Paris St Germain	38	20	11	7	61	29	51
Monaco	38	21	9	8	56	29	51
Bordeaux	38	18	12	8	42	25	48
Nantes	38	17	11	10	54	39	45
Auxerre	38	18	7	13	57	44	43
St Etienne	38	13	17	8	34	26	43
Strasbourg	38	12	16	10	58	57	40
Lens	38	12	16	10	36	41	40
Montpellier	38	12	12	14	36	41	36
Caen	38	13	9	16	54	54	35
Metz	38	11	13	14	44	45	35
Toulouse	38	9	16	13	36	45	34
Lyon	38	9	15	14	40	45	33
Le Havre	38	11	11	16	42	53	33
Sochaux	38	11	10	17	33	50	32
Lille	38	7	16	15	26	48	30
Valenciennes+	38	9	11	18	42	57	29
Toulon*	38	6	13	19	31	57	25
Nimes*	38	3	16	19	32	66	22

Top scorer: Boksic (Marseille) 23
Cup Final: Paris St Germain 3, Nantes 0

GEORGIA

Football Federation of Georgia, 5 Shota Iamanidze Str, Tbillisi 380012, Georgia.
Founded: 1992; Number of Clubs: 4050. *Number of Players:* 115,000.
Telephone: 8832–34 0744; *Telex:* 8832–96 0820. *Fax:* 00431–1602 9695 (Austria).

GERMANY

Deutsche Fussball-Bund, Otto-Fleck-Schneise 6, Postfach 710265, D-6000, Frankfurt (Main) 71.
Founded: 1900; *Number of Clubs:* 26,760; *Number of Players:* 5,260,320; *National Colours:* White shirts, black shorts, white stockings.
Telephone: (069) 67 880; *Cable:* FUSSBALL FRANKFURT; *Telex:* 4 168 15; *Fax:* (69) 67 88 266.

International matches 1992

Italy (a) 0-1, Czechoslovakia (a) 1-1, Turkey (h) 1-0, N. Ireland (h) 1-1, CIS (h) 1-1, Scotland (n) 2-0, Holland (n) 1-3, Sweden (n) 3-2, Denmark (n) 0-2, Denmark (a) 2-1, Mexico (h) 1-1, Austria (h) 0-0, Brazil (a) 1-3, Uruguay (a) 4-1.

League Championship wins (1903–92)

Bayern Munich 12; IFC Nuremberg 9; Schalke 04 7; SV Hamburg 6; Borussia Moenchengladbach 5; VfB Stuttgart 4; VfB Leipzig 3; Sp Vgg Furth 3; Borussia Dortmund 3; IFC Cologne 3; IFC Kaiserslautern 3; Werder Bremen 3; Viktoria Berlin 2; Hertha Berlin 2; Hanover 96 2; Dresden SC 2; Munich 1860 1; Union Berlin 1; FC Freiburg 1; Phoenix Karlsruhe 1; Karlsruher FV 1; Holsten Kiel 1; Fortuna Dusseldorf 1; Rapid Vienna 1; VfB Mannheim 1; Rot-Weiss Essen 1; Eintracht Frankfurt 1; Eintracht Brunswick 1.

Cup wins (1935–92)

Bayern Munich 8; IFC Cologne 4; Eintracht Frankfurt 4; IFC Nuremberg 3; SV Hamburg 3; Dresden SC 2; Fortuna Dusseldorf 2; Karlsruhe SC 2; Munich 1860 2; Schalke 04 2; VfB Stuttgart 2; Borussia Moenchengladbach 2; Borussia Dortmund 2; Werder Bremen 2; First Vienna 1; VfB Leipzig 1; Kickers Offenbach 1; Rapid Vienna 1; Rot-Weiss Essen 1; SW Essen 1; Bayer Uerdin gen 1; IFC Kaiserslautern 1; Hannover 96 1; Leverkusen 1.

Final League Table 1992–93

	P	W	D	L	F	A	Pts
Werder Bremen	34	19	10	5	63	30	48
Bayern Munich	34	18	11	5	74	45	47
Eintracht	34	15	12	7	56	39	42
Borussia Dortmund	34	18	5	11	61	43	41
Leverkusen	34	14	12	8	64	45	40
Karlsruhe	34	14	11	9	60	54	39
Stuttgart	34	12	12	10	56	50	36
Kaiserslautern	34	13	9	12	50	40	35
Moenchengladbach	34	13	9	12	59	59	35
Schalke	34	11	12	11	42	43	35
Hamburg	34	8	15	11	42	44	31
Cologne	34	12	4	18	41	51	28
Nuremberg	34	10	8	16	30	47	28
Wattenschied	34	10	8	16	46	67	28
Dynamo Dresden	34	7	13	14	32	49	27
Bochum*	34	8	10	16	45	52	26
Uerdingen*	34	7	10	17	35	64	24
Sarrebrucken*	34	5	13	16	37	71	23

Top scorer: Yeboah (Eintracht) 20
Kirsten (Leverkusen) 20
Cup Final: Leverkusen 1, Hertha Berlin 0

GREECE

Federation Hellenique De Football, Singrou Avenue 137, Athens.
Founded: 1926; *Number of Clubs:* 4,050; *Number of Players:* 180,000; *National Colours:* White shirts, blue shorts, white stocking s.
Telephone: 9338850; *Cable:* FOOTBALL ATHENES; *Telex:* 215328; *Fax:* 9359666.

International matches 1992

Albania (a) 0-1, Romania (h) 1-0, Cyprus (a) 3-1, Iceland (h) 1-0, Cyprus (h) 2-3, Iceland (a) 1-0, Hungary (h) 0-0.

League Championship wins (1928–92)

Olympiakos 25; Panathinaikos 16; AEK Athens 10; Aris Salonika 3; PAOK Salonika 2; Larissa 1.

Cup wins (1932–92)

Olympiakos 20; Panathinaikos 14; AEK Athen s 9; PAOK Salonika 2; Aris Salonika 1; Ethnikos 1; Iraklis 1; Panionios 1; Kastoria 1; Larissa 1; Ofi Crete 1.

Final League Table 1992–93

	P	W	D	L	F	A	Pts
AEK Athens	34	24	6	4	78	27	78
Panathinaikos	34	24	5	5	85	21	77
Olympiakos	34	20	8	6	68	31	68
Ofi Crete	34	19	9	6	64	32	66
PAOK Salonika	34	17	6	11	52	38	57
Iraklis	34	16	8	10	51	41	56
Larissa	34	11	10	13	36	42	43
Xanthi	34	11	9	14	56	66	42
Aris Salonika	34	12	6	16	40	50	42
Panachaiki	34	10	9	15	41	50	39
Athinaikos	34	9	12	13	27	37	39
Apollon	34	10	7	17	27	49	37
Doxa Drama	34	9	9	16	34	57	36
Kalamaria	34	9	8	17	38	60	35
Edessaikos	34	9	8	17	38	60	35
Pierikos*	34	9	7	18	35	62	34
Ionikos*	34	9	6	19	33	49	33
Korinthos*	34	6	9	19	28	65	27

Top scorer: Dimitriadis (AEK Athens) 33
Cup Final: Panathinaikos 1, Olympiakos 0

HOLLAND

Koninklijke Nederlandsche Voetbalbond, Woudenbergseweg 56, Postbus 515, NL-3700 AM, Zeist.
Founded: 1889; *Number of Clubs:* 3,097; *Number of Players:* 962,397; *National Colours:* Orange shirts, white shorts, orange stockings.
Telephone: 3429 9211/1268; *Cable:* VOETBAL ZEIST; *Telex:* 40497; *Fax:* 03439 1397.

International matches 1992

Portugal (a) 0-2, Yugoslavia (h) 2-0, Austria (h) 3-2, Wales (h) 4-0, France (a) 1-1, Scotland (n) 1-0, CIS (n) 0-0, Germany (n) 3-1, Denmark (n) 2-2, Italy (h) 2-3, Norway (a) 1-2, Turkey (a) 3-1.

League Championship wins (1898–1992)

Ajax Amsterdam 23; Feyenoord 14; PSV Eindhoven 13; HVV The Hague 8; Sparta Rotterdam 6; Go Ahead Deventer 4; HBS The Hague 3; Willem II Tilburg 3; RCH Haarlem 2; RAP 2; Heracles 2; ADO The Hague 2; Quick The Hague 1; BVV Schiedam 1; NAC Breda 1; Eindhoven 1; Enschede 1; Volewijckers Amsterdam 1; Limburgia 1; Rapid JC Haarlem 1; DOS Utrecht 1; DWS Amsterdam 1; Haarlem 1; Be Quick Groningen 1; SVV Schiedam 1; AZ 67 Alkmaar 1.

Cup wins (1899–1992)

Ajax Amsterdam 12; Feyenoord 8; PSV Eindhoven 7; Quick The Hague 4; AZ 67 Alkemaar 3; Rotterdam 3; DFC 2; Fortuna Geleen 2; Haarlem 2; HBS The Hague 2; RCH 2; VOC 2; Wageningen 2; Willem II Tilburg 2; FC Den Haag 2; Concordia Rotterdam 1; CVV 1; Eindhoven 1; HVV The Hague 1; Longa 1; Quick Nijmegen 1; RAP 1; Roermond 1; Schoten 1; Velocitas Breda 1; Velocitas Gr oningen 1; VSV 1; VUC 1; VVV Groningen 1; ZFC 1; NAC Breda 1; Twente Enschede 1; Utrecht 1.

Final League Table 1992–93

	P	W	D	L	F	A	Pts
Feyenoord	34	22	9	3	82	32	53
PSV Eindhoven	34	22	7	5	81	34	51
Ajax	34	20	9	5	87	30	49
Vitesse	34	16	14	4	58	29	46
Twente	34	17	8	9	64	39	42
Volendam	34	12	13	9	51	34	37
Maastricht	34	15	7	12	49	47	37
Utrecht	34	12	11	11	44	40	35
RKC Waalwijk	34	12	9	13	49	57	33
Willem II	34	12	8	14	41	38	32
Roda	34	11	7	16	51	59	29
Groningen	34	9	11	14	31	49	29
Sparta	34	8	11	15	36	65	27
Cambuur	34	6	13	15	39	58	25
Go Ahead	34	8	9	17	36	64	25
Fortuna Sittard*	34	7	7	20	34	76	21
Den Bosch*	34	6	9	19	35	79	21
Dordrecht*	34	5	10	19	30	66	20

Top scorer: Bergkamp (Ajax) 26
Cup Final: Ajax 6, Heerenveen 2

HUNGARY

Magyar Labdarugo Szovetseg, Hungarian Football Federation, Nepkoztarsasag Utja 47, H-1061 Budapest VI.
Founded: 1901; *Number of Clubs:* 1944; *Number of Players* 95,986; *National Colours:* Red shirts, white shorts, green stockings.
Telephone: 36-1-1255 817, 36-1-1420 704; 36-1-1425 103, 36-1-1421 556; *Cable:* MLSZ BUDAPEST; *Telex:* 225782 MLSZ H; *Fa x:* 36-1-1425 103.

International matches 1992

Austria (h) 2-1, Ukraine (a) 3-1, England (h) 0-1, Sweden (a) 1-2, Iceland (h) 1-2, Ukraine (h) 2-1, Luxembourg (a) 3-0, Israel (h) 0-0, Qatar (a) 4-1, Qatar (a) 1-1, Greece (a) 0-0.

League Championship wins (1901–92)

Ferencvaros (prev. FRC) 24; MTK-VM Budapest (prev. Hungaria, Bastay and Vörös Lobogo) 19; Ujpest Dozsa 19; Honved 13; Vasas Budapest 6; Csepel 3; Raba Györ (prev. Vasas Györ) 3; BTC 2; Nagy varad 1.

Cup wins (1910–92)

Farencvaros (prev. FRC) 16; MTK-VM Budapest (prev. Hungaria, Bastay and Vörös Lobogo) 9; Ujpest Dozsa 8; Raba Györ (prev. Vasas Györ) 4; Vasas Budapest 3; Honved 3; Diösgyör 2; Bocskai 1; III Ker 1; Kispesti AC 1; Soroksar 1; Szolnoki MAV 1; Siofok Banyasz 1; Bekescsaba 1; Pecs 1.
Cup not regularly held until 1964K

Final League Table 1992–93

	P	W	D	L	F	A	Pts
Honved Kispest	30	19	5	6	59	28	43
Vac	30	17	8	5	48	28	42
Ferencvaros	30	19	3	8	49	27	41
MTK	30	14	8	8	59	27	36
Bekescsaba	30	12	12	6	42	31	36
Videoton	30	15	5	10	42	34	35
Csepel	30	12	6	12	29	37	30
Siofok	30	11	7	12	36	39	29
Raba Gyor	30	10	9	11	38	43	29
Vasas	30	7	13	10	31	33	27
Pecs	30	10	7	13	35	39	27
BVSC	30	10	6	14	32	37	26
Diosgyor	30	7	9	14	26	45	23
Ujpest Dozsa	30	4	12	14	29	45	20
Nyiregyhaza	30	3	12	15	17	39	18
Veszprem	30	6	6	18	25	54	18

Top scorer: Repasi (Vac) 16
Cup Final: Ferencvaros 1,1, Haladas 1,1
Ferencvaros won 5-3 on penalties.

ICELAND

Knattspyrnusamband Island, P.O. Box 8511, 128 Reykjavik.
Founded: 1929; *Number of Clubs:* 73; *Number of Players:* 23,673; *National Colours:* Blue shirts, white short s, blue stockings.
Telephone: 84 444; *Cable* KSI REYKJAVIK; *Telex:* 2314 ISI IS; *Fax:* 1 68 97 66.

International matches 1992

Malta (a) 1-0, Israel (a) 2-2, Greece (a) 0-1, Hungary (a) 2-1, Israel (h) 0-2, Greece (h) 0-1, Russia (a) 0-1.

League Championship wins (1912–91)

R 20; Valur 19; Fram 18; IA Akranes 13; Vikingur 5; IBK Keflavik 3; IBV Vestmann 2; KA Akureyri 1.

Cup wins (1960–91)

Valur 8; R 7; Fram 7; IA Akranes 5; IBV Vestmann 3 ; IBA Akureyri 1; Vikingur 1; IBK Keflavik 1.

Final League Table 1992

	P	W	D	L	F	A	Pts
IA Akranes	18	12	4	2	40	19	40
KR	18	11	4	3	41	17	37
Thor	18	11	4	3	41	17	37
Valur	18	10	5	3	30	14	35
Fram	18	9	4	5	33	27	31
FH	18	5	6	7	24	29	21
Vikingur	18	5	4	9	25	33	19
IBV	18	5	1	12	23	44	16
UBK*	18	4	3	11	14	30	15
KA*	18	3	4	11	18	33	13

Top scorer: Gunnlauggson (IA Akranes) 15
Cup Final: Valur 5, KA 2

REPUBLIC OF IRELAND

The Football Association of Ireland, (Cumann Peile Na H-Eireann), 80 Merrion Square, South Dublin 2.
Founded: 1921; *Number of Clubs:* 3,190; *Number of Players:* 124,615; *National Colours:* Green shirts, white shorts, green stockings.
Telephone: 76 68 64; *Cable:* SOCCER DUBLIN; *Telex:* 913967 FAI EI; *Fax:* (01) 610 931.

International matches 1992

Wales (h) 0-1, Switzerland (h) 2-1, USA (h) 4-1, Albania (h) 2-0, USA (a) 1-3, Italy (a) 0-2, Portugal (h) 2-0, Latvia (h) 4-0, Denmark (a) 0-0, Spain (a) 0-0.

League Championship wins (1922–92)

Shamrock Rovers 14; Dundalk 8; Shelbourne 8; Bohemians 7; Waterford 6; Cork United 5; Drumcondra 5; St Patrick's Athletic 4; St James's Gate 2; Cork Athletic 2; Sligo Rovers 2; Limerick 2; Athlone Town 2; Dolphin 1; Cork Hibernians 1; Cork Celtic 1; Derry City 1, Cork City 1.

Cup wins (1922–92)

Shamrock Rovers 24; Dundalk 8; Drumcondra 5; Bohemians 5; Shelbourne 3; Cork Athletic 2; Cork United 2; St James's Gate 2; St Patrick's Athletic 2; Cork Hibernians 2; Limerick 2; Waterford 2; Alton United 1; Athlone Town 2; Cork 1; Fordsons 1; Transport 1; Finn Harps 1; Home Farm 1; Sligo 1; UCD 1; Derry City 1; Bray Wanderers 1; Galway United 1.

Qualifying Table 1992–93

	P	W	D	L	F	A	Pts
Bohemians	22	10	10	2	37	12	30
Cork City	22	12	5	5	36	25	29
Derry City	22	9	10	3	17	12	28
Shelbourne	22	10	7	5	42	24	27
Dundalk	22	8	10	4	29	24	26
Limerick City	22	6	11	5	24	18	23
St Patrick's Ath	22	5	13	4	19	17	23
Shamrock Rovers	22	6	6	10	33	27	18
Drogheda U	22	3	11	8	20	32	17
Sligo Rovers	22	4	9	9	10	25	17
Bray Wanderers	22	2	9	11	13	35	13
Waterford U	22	5	3	14	22	51	13

Final Round

	P	W	D	L	F	A	Pts
Bohemians	32	13	14	5	46	19	40
Shelbourne	32	15	10	7	53	29	40
Cork City	32	16	8	8	47	34	40
Dundalk	32	13	13	6	35	28	39
Derry City	32	11	15	6	26	23	37
Limerick City	32	6	15	11	27	31	27

Title Round

	P	W	D	L	F	A	Pts
Shelbourne	4	1	2	1	3	3	4
Bohemians	4	1	2	1	2	2	4
Cork City	4	1	2	1	2	2	4

Play-offs: Cork City 1, Bohemians 0; Cork City 3, Shelbourne 2; Bohemians 2, Shelbourne 1. Cork City champions.

Promotion/Relegation

	P	W	D	L	F	A	Pts
St Patrick's Ath	32	7	16	9	27	27	30
Shamrock Rovers	32	8	12	12	39	35	28
Drogheda U	32	7	13	12	29	41	27
Waterford U*	32	10	7	15	34	59	27
Sligo Rovers*	32	6	14	12	16	32	26
Bray Wanderers*	32	5	13	14	19	40	23

Top scorer: Pat Morley (Cork City) 21
Cup Final: Shelbourne 1, Dundalk 0

ISRAEL

Israel Football Association, 12 Carlibach Street, P.O. Box 20188, Tel Aviv 61201.
Founded: 1928; *Number of Clubs:* 544; *Number of Players:* 30,449; *National Colours:* White shirts, blue shorts, white stockings.
Telephone: 56 10 888; *Cable:* CADUREGEL TEL AVIV; *Telex:* 361353 FA; *Fax:* 03 5610838.

International matches 1992

CIS (h) 1-2, Cyprus (h) 2-1, Iceland (h) 2-2, Faeroes (a) 1-1, Iceland (a) 2-0, Poland (a) 1-1, Hungary (a) 0-0, Austria (a) 2-5, Sweden (h) 1-3, Bulgaria (h) 0-2.

ITALY

Federazione Italiana Giuoco Calcio, Via Gregorio Allegri 14, C.P. 2450, 1-00198, Roma.
Founded: 1898; *Number of Clubs:* 20,961; *Number of Players:* 1,420,160; *National Colours:* Blue shirts, white shorts, blue stockings, white trim.
Telephone: 84 911; *Cable:* FEDERCALCIO ROMA; *Telex:* 611438 CALCIO; *Fax:* 06 849 1239. K

International matches 1992

San Marino (h) 4-0, Germany (h) 1-0, Portual (h) 0-0, Eire (h) 2-0, USA (a) 1-1, Holland (a) 3-2, Switzerland (h) 2-2, Scotland (a) 0-0, Malta (a) 2-1.

League Championship wins (1898–1992)

Juventus 22; Inter-Milan 13; AC Milan 13; Genoa 9; Torino 8; Pro Vercelli 7; Bologna 7; Fiorentina 2; Napoli 2; AS Roma 2; Casale 1; Novese 1; Cagliari 1; Lazio 1; Verona 1; Sampdoria 1.

Cup wins (1922–92)

Juventus 8; AS Roma 8; Torino 4; Fiorentina 4; AC Milan 4; Inter-Milan 3; Napoli 3; Sampdoria 3; Bologna 2; Atalanta 1; Genoa 1; Lazio 1; Vado 1; Venezia 1; Parma 1.

Final League Table 1992–93

	P	W	D	L	F	A	Pts
AC Milan	34	18	14	2	65	32	50
Internazionale	34	17	12	5	59	36	46
Parma	34	16	9	9	47	34	41
Juventus	34	15	9	10	59	47	39
Lazio	34	13	12	9	65	51	38
Cagliari	34	14	9	11	45	33	37
Sampdoria	34	12	12	10	50	48	36
Atalanta	34	14	8	12	42	44	36
Torino	34	9	17	8	38	39	35
Roma	34	8	17	9	42	39	33
Napoli	34	10	12	12	49	50	32
Foggia	34	10	12	12	38	53	32
Genoa	34	7	17	10	41	55	31
Fiorentina*	34	8	14	12	53	56	30
Udinese+	34	10	10	14	42	48	30
Brescia*	34	9	12	13	36	44	30
Ancona*	34	6	7	21	40	73	19
Pescara*	34	6	5	23	45	74	17

Top scorer: Signori (Lazio) 26
Cup Final: Torino 3,2, Roma 0,5

LATVIA

Latvian Football Federation, 1a, E. Melngaila Str.; LV 1010 Riga.
Founded: ????; *Number of Clubs:* 250; *Number of Players:* 5000.
National Colours: Carmine red shirts, white shorts, carmine red stockings.
Telephone: 7-0132-333429; *Telex:* 161183 ritm su; *Fax:* 7-0132-284412.
Twelve teams in championship. *Cable:* Melngaila Str. 1a, LV 1010 Riga.

International matches 1992

Romania (a) 0-2, Malta (a) 0-1, Estonia (h) 2-1, Lithuania (h) 2-3, Lithuania (h) 1-2, Denmark (h) 0-0, Eire (a) 0-4, Spain (h) 0-0, Lithuania (a) 1-1, Albania (a) 1-1, Poland (a) 0-1, Spain (a) 0-5.

LIECHTENSTEIN

Liechtensteiner Fussball-Verband, Am schragen Weg 17, Postfach 165, 9490 Vaduz.
Founded: 1933; *Number of Clubs:* 7; *Number of Players:* 1,247; *National Colours:* Blue & red shirts, red shorts, blue stockings.
Telephone: 41–75/233 24 28; *Cable:*
FUSSBALLVERBAND VADUZ; *Telex:* 889 261; *Fax:* 41–75/233 24 30.

No International matches 1992
Liechtenstein has no national league. Teams compete in Swiss regional leagues.

LITHUANIA

Lithuanian Football Federation, 6, Zemaites Street, 232675 Vilnius. Championship of 14 teams.
Number of Clubs: 20; *Number of Players:* 16,600.
Telephone: 22-261713; *Telex:* 261118 LSK SU; *Fax:* 122-661223.

International matches 1992
Austria (a) 0-4, N. Ireland (a) 2-2, Albania (a) 0-1, Estonia (h) 1-1, Latvia (a) 3-2, Latvia (a) 2-1, Denmark (h) 0-0, Latvia (h) 1-1.

LUXEMBOURG

Federation Luxembourgeoise De Football, (F.L.F.), 50, Rue De Strasbourg, L-2560, Luxembourg.
Founded: 1908; *Number of Clubs:* 126; *Number of Players:* 21,684; *National Colours:* Red shirts, white shorts, blue stockings.
Telephone: 48 86 65; *Cable:* FOOTBALL LUXEMBOURG; *Telex:* 2426 FLF LU; *Fax:* 400 201.

International matches 1992
Turkey (h) 2-3, Hungary (h) 0-3, Russia (a) 0-2.

League Championship wins (1910–92)
Jeunesse Esch 21; Spora Luxembourg 11; Stade Dudelange 10; Red Boys Differdange 6; Avenir Beggen 6; US Hollerich-Bonnevoie 5; Fola Esch 5; US Luxembourg 5; Aris Bonnevoie 3; Progres Niedercor 3.

Cup wins (1922–92)
Red Boys Differdange 16; Jeunesse Esch 9; US Luxembourg 9; Spora Luxembourg 8; Avenir Beggen 5; Stade Dudelange 4; Progres Niedercorn 4; Fola Esch 3; Alliance Dudelange 2; US Rumelange 2; Aris Bonnevoie 1; US Dudelange 1; Jeunesse Hautchar age 1; National Schiffige 1; Racing Luxembourg 1; SC Tetange 1; Hesperange 1.

Qualifying Table

	P	W	D	L	F	A	Pts
Union	18	10	5	3	44	17	25
Avenir Beggen	18	9	6	3	33	17	25
Jeunesse Esch	18	10	4	4	31	16	24
Grevenmacher	18	7	7	4	32	20	21
Dudelange	18	6	6	6	19	22	18
Fola Esch	18	6	5	7	28	27	17
Spora	18	6	5	7	23	30	17
Aris	18	5	5	8	30	32	15
Red Boys	18	4	6	8	25	40	13
Ettelbruck*	18	1	3	14	11	52	5

Final Table 1992–93

	P	W	D	L	F	A	Pts
Avenir Beggen	10	7	2	1	31	14	28.5
Union	10	7	1	2	27	10	27.5
Jeunesse Esch	10	4	3	3	23	23	23
Grevenmacher	10	3	3	4	12	20	20.5
Dudelange	10	4	1	5	19	21	18
Fola Esch	10	0	0	10	6	30	8.5

Top scorer: Krings (Avenir Beggen) 23
Cup Final: Avenir Beggen 5, Dudelange 2

MALTA

Malta Football Association, 280 St. Paul Street, Valletta.
Founded: 1900; *Number of Clubs:* 252; *Number of Players:* 5,544; *National Colours:* Red shirts, white shorts, red stockings.
Telephone: 22 26 97; *Cable:* FOOTBALL MALTA VALLETTA; *Telex:* 1752 MALFA MW; *Fax:* 24 51 36.

International matches 1992
Iceland (h) 1-0, Latvia (h) 1-0, Cyprus (a) 0-3, Estonia (h) 0-0, Switzerland (a) 0-3, Italy (h) 1-2.

League Championship wins (1910–92)
Floriana 25; Sliema Wanderers 22; Valletta 14; Hibernians 6; Hamrun Spartans 6; Rabat Ajax 2; St George's 1; KOMR 1.

Cup wins (1935–92)
Sliema Wanderers 17; Floriana 17; Valletta 6; Hamrun Spartans 6; Hibernians 5; Gzira United 1; Melita 1; Zurrieq 1; Rabat Ajax 1.

Final League Table 1992–93

	P	W	D	L	F	A	Pts
Floriana	18	13	3	2	35	13	29
Hamrun Spartans	18	11	2	5	46	23	24
Valletta	18	10	4	4	32	23	24
St Andrew's	18	9	4	5	43	30	22
Hibernians	18	9	3	6	45	30	21
Sliema Wanderers	18	6	3	9	26	31	15
Rabat Ajax	18	6	3	9	30	38	15
Birkirkara	18	5	3	10	22	37	13
St George's	18	3	4	11	18	44	10
Mellieha	18	2	3	13	14	42	7

Top Scorer: Zacchau (Hibernians) 22
Cup Final: Floriana 5, Sliema Wanderers 0

NORTHERN IRELAND

Irish Football Association Ltd, 20 Windsor Avenue, Belfast BT9 6EG.
Founded: 1880; *Number of Clubs:* 1,555; *Number of Players:* 24,558; *National Colours:* Green shirts, white shorts, green stockings.
Telephone: (0232) 66 94 58; *Cable:* FOOTBALL BELFAST; *Telex:* 747317; *Fax:* (0232) 667620.

NORWAY

Norges Fotballforbund Ullevaal Stadion, Postboks 3823, Ulleval Hageby, 0805 Oslo 8.
Founded: 1902; *Number of Clubs:* 1,810; *Number of Players:* 300,000; *National Colours:* Red shirts, white shorts, blue & white stockings.
Telephone: 47–22/95 10 00; *Cable*
FOTBALLFORBUND OSLO; *Telex:* 71722 NFF N; *Fax:* 47–22/95 10 10.

International matches 1992

Egypt (a) 0-0, Bermuda (a) 3-1, Denmark (a) 0-1, Faeroes (h) 2-0, Scotland (h) 0-0, Sweden (h) 2-2, San Marino (h) 10-0, Holland (h) 2-1, San Marino (a) 2-0, England (a) 1-1, Hong Kong (a) 3-3.

League Championship wins (1938–91)

Fredrikstad 9; Viking Stavanger 8; Lillestroem 6; Rosenborg Trondheim 6; Valerengen 4; Larvik Turn 3; Brann Bergen 2; Lyn Oslo 2; IK Start 2; Friedig 1; Fram 1; Skeid Oslo 1; Strömsgodset Drammen 1; Moss 1.

Cup wins (1902–91)

Odds Bk, Skien 11; Fredrikstad 10; Lyn Oslo 8; Skeid Oslo 8; Sarpsborg FK 6; Brann Bergen 5; Rosenborg Trondheim 5; Orn F Horten 4; Lillestroem 4; Viking Stavanger 4; Strömsgodset Drammen 4; Frigg 3; Mjondalens F 3; Mercantile 2; Grane Nordstrand 1; Kvik Halden 1; Sparta 1; Gjovik 1; Bodo-Glimt 1; Valerengen 1; Moss 1; Tromso 1; Byrne 1.
(Until 1937 the cup-winners were regarded as champions.)K

Final League Table 1992–93

	P	W	D	L	F	A	Pts
Rosenborg	22	14	4	4	58	19	45
Kongsvinger	22	12	4	6	43	27	40
Start	22	11	6	5	38	28	39
Lillestrom	22	11	5	6	48	28	38
Lyn	22	11	4	7	33	29	37
Molde	22	11	3	8	30	30	36
Brann	22	4	12	6	26	30	24
Tromso	22	6	6	10	22	37	24
Viking	22	4	9	9	25	34	21
Hamark	22	5	5	12	30	46	20
Sogndal*	22	5	5	12	30	56	20
Mjondalen*	22	5	3	14	20	42	18

Top scorer: Kaasa (Kongsvinger) 17
Cup Final: Rosenborg 3, Lillestrom 0

POLAND

Federation Polonaise De Foot-Ball, Al. Ujazdowskie 22, 00-478 Warszawa.
Founded: 1923; *Number of Clubs:* 5,881; *Number of Players:* 317,442; *National Colours:* White shirts, red shorts, white & red stockings.
Telephone: 48-22-28 93 44; 48-22-28 58 21; *Cable:* PEZETPEEN WARSZAWA; *Telex:* 825320 PZPN PL; *Fax:* 48 22 219175.

International matches 1992

Sweden (a) 0-5, Austria (a) 4-2, Czechoslovakia (h) 1-0, Guatemala (a) 2-2, Finland (a) 0-0, Israel (h) 1-1, Turkey (h) 1-0, Holland (a) 2-2, Latvia (h) 1-0, Argentina (a) 0-2, Uruguay (a) 1-0.

League Championship wins (1921–92)

Gornik Zabrze 14; Ruch Chorzow 13; Wisla Krakow 6; Lech Poznan 5; Pogon Lwow 4; Legia Warsaw 4; Cracovia 3; Warta Poznan 2; Polonia Bytom 2; Stal Mielec 2; Widzew Lodz 2; Garbarnia Krakow 1; Polonia Warsaw 1; LKS Lodz 1; Slask Wroclaw 1; Szombierki Bytom 1; Zaglebie Lubin 1.

Cup wins (1951–92)

Legia Warsaw 9; Gornik Zabrze 6; Zaglebie Sosnowiec 4; Lech Poznan 3; GKS Katowice 3; Ruch Chorzow 2; Slask Wroclaw 2; Gwardia Warsaw 1; LKS Lodz 1; Polonia Warsaw 1; Wisla Krakow 1; Stal Rzeszow 1; Arka Gdynia 1; Lechia Gdansk 1; Widzew Lodz 1; Miedz Legnica 1.

Final League Table 1992–93

	P	W	D	L	F	A	Pts
Legia	34	21	7	6	55	26	49
LKS Lodz	34	19	11	4	60	33	49
Lech Poznan	34	17	13	4	70	29	47
Ruch	34	19	6	9	52	27	44
Widzew	34	16	11	7	60	42	43
Stal	34	12	15	7	41	28	39
Pogon	34	15	9	10	33	33	39
Katowice	34	13	11	10	52	36	37
Gornik Zabrze	34	11	13	10	43	39	35
Wisla	34	12	10	12	49	44	34
Siarka	34	11	9	14	39	42	31
Bydgoszcz	34	12	6	16	39	56	30
Zaglebie Lubin	34	10	10	14	48	41	30
Hutnik	34	8	13	13	40	46	29
Slask	34	9	5	20	33	74	23
Bytom	34	8	7	19	31	59	23
Olimpia*	34	7	7	20	28	56	21
Bialystok*	34	2	5	27	28	91	9

Points deducted from Legia and LKS Lodz for alleged match-fixing. Lech Poznan declared champions.
Top scorer: Podbrozny (Lech) 25
Sliwowski (Legia) 25
Cup Final: Katowice 1, Ruch 1
Katowice won 5-4 on penalties.

PORTUGAL

Federacao Portuguesa De Futebol, Praca De Alegria N.25, Apartado 21.100, P-1128, Lisboa Codex.
Founded: 1914; *Number of Clubs:* 204; *Number of Players:* 79,235; *National Colours:* Red shirts, white shorts, red stockings.
Telephone: 328207/08/09; *Cable:* FUTEBOL LISBOA; *Telex:* 13489 FPF P; *Fax:* 346 7231.

International matches 1992

Spain (h) 0-0, Holland (h) 2-0, Italy (a) 0-0, USA (a) 0-1, Eire (a) 0-2, Austria (a) 1-1, Scotland (a) 0-0, Bulgaria (h) 2-1.

League Championship wins (1935–92)

Benfica 29; Sporting Lisbon 16; FC Porto 13; Belenenses 1.

Cup wins (1939–92)

Benfica 22; Sporting Lisbon 11; FC Porto 7; Boavista 4; Belenenses 3; Vitoria Setubal 2; Academica Coimbra 1; Leixoes Porto 1; Sporting Braga 1; Amadora 1.

Final League Table 1992–93

	P	W	D	L	F	A	Pts
Porto	34	24	6	4	59	17	54
Benfica	34	22	8	4	60	18	52
Sporting	34	17	11	6	59	30	45
Boavista	34	14	11	9	46	34	39
Maritimo	34	15	7	12	56	48	37
Farense	34	11	13	10	41	36	35
Belenenses	34	11	12	11	42	40	34
Beira Mar	34	10	12	12	24	33	32
Gil Vicente	34	12	7	15	34	42	31
Pacos Ferreira	34	10	11	13	35	44	31
Guimaraes	34	14	3	17	41	53	31
Braga	34	12	6	16	33	34	30
Estoril	34	9	12	13	29	41	30
Famalicao	34	10	10	14	29	48	30
Salgueiros	34	10	9	15	28	44	29
Tirsense*	34	10	8	16	27	37	28
Espinho*	34	9	10	15	38	55	28
Chaves*	34	4	8	22	34	61	16

Top scorer: Cadete (Sporting) ??
Cup Final: Benfica 5, Boavista 2

ROMANIA

Federatia Romana De Fotbal, Vasile Conta 16, Bucharest 70130.
Founded: 1908; *Number of Clubs:* 414; *Number of Players:* 22,920; *National Colours:* Yellow shirts, blue shorts, red stockings.
Telephone: 10 70 90; *Cable:* SPORTROM BUCURESTI-FOTBAL; *Telex:* 11180; *Fax:* 11 70 75 and 11 98 69K

International matches 1992

Greece (a) 0-1, Latvia (h) 2-0, Faeroes (h) 7-0, Wales (h) 5-1, Mexico (h) 2-0, Belgium (a) 0-1, Czechoslovakia (h) 1-1, Cyprus (a) 4-1.

League Championship wins (1910–92)

Steaua Bucharest (prev. CCA) 15; Dinamo Bucharest 14; Venus Bucharest 8, Chinezul Timisoara 6; UT Arad 6; Ripensia Temesvar 4; Uni Craiova 4; Petrolul Ploesti 3; Olimpia Bucharest 2; Colentina Bucharest 2; Arges Pitesti 2; ICO Oradea 2; Soc RA Bucharest 1; Prahova Ploesti 1; Coltea Brasov 1; Juventus Bucharest 1; Metalochimia Resita 1; Ploesti United 1; Unirea Tricolor 1; Rapid Bucharest 1.

Cup wins (1934–92)

Steaua Bucharest (prev. CCA) 17; Rapid Bucharest 9; Dinamo Bucharest 7; Un i Craiova 6; UT Arad 2; Ripensia Temesvar 2; Politehnica Timisoara 2; ICO Oradeo 1; Metalochimia Resita 1; Petrolul Ploesti 1; Stinta Cluj 1; CFR Turnu Severin 1; Chimia Rannicu Vilcea 1; Jiul Petroseni 1; Progresul Bucharest 1; Progresul Oradea 1.

Final League Table 1992–93

	P	W	D	L	F	A	Pts
Steaua	34	25	7	2	84	22	57
Dinamo	34	23	7	4	82	40	53
Uni Craiova	34	15	9	10	40	33	39
Gloria	34	15	5	14	45	41	35
Elect. Craiova	34	13	9	12	35	32	35
Sportul	34	13	8	13	40	43	34
Inter Sibiu	34	11	11	12	40	46	33
Farul	34	14	4	16	57	66	32
Otelul	34	13	6	15	40	49	32
Cluj	34	14	2	18	43	51	30
Brasov	34	12	6	16	36	45	30
Timisoara	34	8	13	13	34	46	29
Braila	34	10	9	15	36	51	29
Progresul	34	9	11	14	38	53	29
Petrolul	34	12	3	19	47	50	27
Bacau*	34	8	9	17	24	44	25
Resita*	34	9	3	22	34	73	21

Top scorer: Dumitrescu (Steaua) 24
Cup Final: Uni Craiova 2, Braila 0

RUSSIA (formerly USSR)

Football Union of Russia; Luzhnetskaya Naberezyhnaja, 8. SU-119270 Moscow. Telephone: 952–01 0834; *Telex:* 411 287 priz su; *Fax:* 952–01 1303; New space up-link fax: 7–502/220 2037.
Founded: 1992; *Number of Clubs:* 43,700; *Number of Players:* 2,170,000.

International matches 1992

Mexico (h) 2-0, Iceland (h) 1-0, Luxembourg (h) 2-0.

League Championship wins (1945–92)

Dynamo Kiev 13; Spartak Moscow 13; Dynamo Moscow 11; CSKA Moscow 7; Torpedo Moscow 3; Dynamo Tbilisi 2; Dnepr Dnepropetrovsk 2; Saria Voroshilovgrad 1; Ararat Erevan 1; Dynamo Minsk 1; Zenit Leningrad 1.

Cup wins (1936–92)

Dynamo Kiev 10; Spartak Moscow 10; Torpedo Moscow 7; Dynamo Moscow 6; CSKA Moscow 5; Donetsk Shaktyor 4; Lokomotiv Moscow 2; Dynamo Tbilisi 2; Ararat Erevan 2; Karpaty Lvov 1; SKA Rostov 1; Zenit Leningrad 1; Metallist Kharkov 1; Dnepr 1.

Qualifying Table 1992–93

Group A

	P	W	D	L	F	A	Pts
Dynamo Moscow	18	10	4	4	35	16	24
Lokomotiv Moscow	18	9	6	3	23	14	24
Vladikavkaz	18	9	5	4	31	18	23
CSKA Moscow	18	9	5	4	29	20	23
Kamyshine	18	8	5	5	20	17	21
Ekaterinbourg	18	8	3	7	28	29	19
Nakhodka	18	7	4	7	24	25	18
Voronezh	18	4	6	8	10	19	14
Dynamo Stavropol	18	4	1	13	14	31	9
Tyumen	18	2	1	15	11	36	5

Group B

	P	W	D	L	F	A	Pts
Spartak Moscow	18	11	6	1	35	9	28
Asmaral Moscow	18	11	4	3	34	21	26
Novgorod	18	7	9	2	16	11	23
Rostov	18	7	6	5	20	17	20
Samara	18	5	8	5	12	19	18
Torpedo Moscow	18	7	3	8	20	20	17
Volgograd	18	6	4	8	23	19	16
St Petersburg	18	4	6	8	21	35	14
Krasnodar	18	3	6	9	19	30	12
Yaroslav	18	1	4	13	11	30	6

Final Table

	P	W	D	L	F	A	Pts
Spartak Moscow	14	10	4	0	36	12	24
Vladikavkaz	14	7	3	4	26	20	17
Dynamo Moscow	14	6	4	4	26	21	16
Lokomotiv Moscow	14	5	5	4	14	15	15
CSKA Moscow	14	5	4	5	25	19	14
Novgorod	14	2	7	5	10	18	11
Asmaral Moscow	14	3	3	8	17	36	9
Rostov	14	1	4	9	3	16	6

Top scorer: Kasumov (Spartak Moscow) 16
Cup Final: Torpedo Moscow 1, CSKA Moscow 1
Torpedo Moscow won 5-4 on penalties

Promotion/Relegation

	P	W	D	L	F	A	Pts
Ekaterinbourg	22	12	6	4	40	21	30
Kamyshine	22	12	4	6	23	13	28
Torpedo Moscow	22	12	4	6	27	17	28
Volgograd	22	11	4	7	35	22	26
Nakhodka	22	10	5	7	26	26	25
Samara	22	9	7	6	22	16	25
Dynamo Stavropol	22	10	4	8	27	23	24
St Petersburg*	22	9	6	7	30	25	24
Voronezh*	22	9	4	9	17	17	22
Krasnodar*	22	4	6	12	16	35	14
Yaroslav*	22	3	5	14	19	34	11
Tyumen*	22	3	1	18	16	49	7

SAN MARINO

Federazione Sammarinese Giuoco Calcio, Viale Campo dei Giudei, 14; 47031-Rep. San Marino.
Founded: 1931; *Number of Clubs:* 17; *Number of Players:* 1,033; *Colours:* Blue and white.
Telephone: 549–99 05 15/99 05 40; *Cable:* FEDERCALCIO SAN MARINO; *Telex:* 0505 284 cosmar so; *Fax:* 549 992348.

International matches 1992

Italy (a) 0-4, Norway (a) 0-10, Norway (h) 0-2, Turkey (a) 1-4.

SCOTLAND

The Scottish Football Association Ltd, 6 Park Gardens, Glasgow G3 7YF.
Founded: 1873; *Number of Clubs:* 6,148; *Number of Players:* 135,474; *National Colours:* Dark blue shirt s, white shorts, red stockings.
Telephone: 41 332 6372; *Cable:* EXECUTIVE GLASGOW; *Telex:* 778904 SFA G; *Fax:* 41 332 7559.

SLOVENIA

Nogometna Zveza Slovenije, dunajska 47/V, P.P. 90, 61109 Ljubljana, Slovenia.
Founded: 1992; *Number of Clubs:* 232; *Number of Players:* 15,048.
Telephone: 861–31 1888. *Fax:* 861–30 2337.

International matches 1992

Estonia (a) 1-1, Cyprus (a) 1-1.

Final League Table 1992–93

	P	W	D	L	F	A	Pts
Olimpija Ljubljana	34	22	8	4	94	20	52
Branik Maribor	34	18	12	4	49	19	48
Mura	34	19	8	7	60	28	46
Ljubljana	34	16	8	10	44	34	40
Naklo	34	15	10	9	54	47	40
Kompas	34	14	10	10	38	33	38
Studio	34	13	12	9	35	30	38
Koper	34	11	13	10	40	44	35
Rudar	34	13	7	14	45	52	33
Publikum	34	12	8	14	37	47	32
Slovan Mavrica	34	9	13	12	45	43	31
Gorica	34	11	9	14	39	46	31
Isola	34	10	10	14	45	45	30
Potrosnik	34	12	5	17	51	62	29
Zagorje*	34	10	8	16	29	40	28
Steklar*	34	4	14	16	33	72	22
Zeleznicar*	34	6	8	20	30	62	20
Nafta*	34	6	7	21	30	64	19

Top scorer: Udovic (Slovan Mavrica) 25
Cup Final: Olimpija Ljubljana 2, Publikum 1

SPAIN

Real Federacion Espanola De Futbol, Calle Alberto Bosch 13, Apartado Postal 347, E-28014 Madrid.
Founded: 1913; *Number of Clubs:* 10,240; *Number of Players:* 408,135; *National Colours:* Red shirts, dark blue shorts, black stockings, yellow trim.
Telephone: 420 13 62; *Cable:* FUTBOL MADRID; *Telex:* 42420 RFEF; *Fax:* 420 20 94.

International matches 1992

Portugal (a) 0-0, CIS (h) 1-1, USA (h) 2-0, Albania (h) 3-0, England (h) 1-0, Latvia (a) 0-0, N. Ireland (a) 0-0, Eire (h) 0-0, Latvia (h) 5-0.

League Championship wins (1945–92)

Real Madrid 25; Barcelona 13; Atleti co Madrid 8; Athletic Bilbao 8; Valencia 4; Real Sociedad 2; Real Betis 1; Seville 1.

Cup wins (1902–92)

Athletic Bilbao 23; Barcelona 22; Real Madrid 17; Atletico Madrid 8; Valencia 5; Real Union de Irun 3; Seville 3; Real Zaragoza 2; Espanol 2; Arenas 1; Ciclista Sebastian 1; Racing de Irun 1; Vizcaya Bilbao 1; Real Betis 1; Real Sociedad 1.

Final League Table 1992–93

	P	W	D	L	F	A	Pts
Barcelona	38	25	8	5	87	34	58
Real Madrid	38	24	9	5	75	28	57
La Coruna	38	22	10	6	67	33	54
Valencia	38	19	10	9	60	33	48
Tenerife	38	15	14	9	59	47	44
Atletico Madrid	38	16	11	11	52	42	43
Seville	38	17	9	12	46	44	43
Athletic Bilbao	38	17	6	15	53	49	40
Zaragoza	38	11	13	14	37	52	35
Osasuna	38	12	10	16	42	41	34
Celta	38	9	16	13	25	32	34
Real Sociadad	38	13	8	17	46	59	34
Sporting Gijon	38	11	12	15	38	57	34
Rayo Vallecano	38	8	17	13	40	49	33
Logrones	38	11	11	16	32	48	33
Oviedo	38	11	10	17	42	52	32
Albacete	38	11	9	18	54	59	31
Espanol	38	9	11	18	40	56	29
Cadiz*	38	5	12	21	30	70	22
Burgos*	38	4	14	20	29	69	22

Top scorer: Bebeto (La Coruna) 30
Cup Final: Real Madrid 2, Zaragoza 0

SWEDEN

Svenska Fotbollfoer bundet, Box 1216, S-17123 Solna.
Founded: 1904; *Number of Clubs:* 3,250; *Number of Players:* 485,000; *National Colours:* Yellow shirts, blue shorts, yellow and blue stockings.
Telephone: 8-735 0900; *Cable:* FOOTBALL-S; *Telex:* 17711 FOTBOLL S; *Fax:* 8-27 51 47.

International matches 1992

Australia (a) 0-0, Australia (a) 0-1, Australia (a) 0-1, Tunisia (a) 1-0, Poland (h) 5-0, Hungary (h) 2-1, France (h) 1-1, Denmark (h) 1-0, England (h) 2-1, Germany (h) 2-3, Norway (a) 2-2, Finland (a) 1-0, Bulgaria (h) 2-0, Israel (a) 3-1.

League Championship wins (1896–1991)

Oergryte IS Gothenburg 14; Malmo FF 13; IFK Gothenburg 13; IFK Norrköping 12; AIK Stockholm 9; Djurgaarden 8; GAIS Gothenburg 6; IF Halsingborg 5; Boras IF Elfsborg 4; Oster Vaxjo 4; Halmstad 2; Atvidaberg 2; IFK Ekilstune 1; IF Gavic Brynas 1; IF Gothenburg 1; Fassbergs 1; Norrköping IK Sleipner 1.

Cup wins (1941–91)

Malmo FF 13; IFK Norrköping 5; AIK Stockholm 4; IFK Gothenburg 4; Atvidaberg 2; Kalmar 2; GAIS Gothenburg 13; IF Halsingborg 1; Raa 1; Landskrona 1; Oster Vaxjo 1; Djurgaarden 1; Degerfors 1.

Qualifying Table 1992–93

	P	W	D	L	F	A	Pts
Norrkoping	18	10	4	4	38	23	34
Osters	18	8	5	5	36	29	29
Trelleborg	18	7	7	4	20	20	28
AIK	18	7	6	5	24	18	27
Malmo	18	7	5	6	22	16	26
IFK Gothenburg	18	7	2	9	25	24	23
Djurgaarden*	18	6	5	7	26	32	23
Orebro	18	4	8	6	17	23	20
Frolunda*	18	4	6	8	22	27	18
GAIS Gothenburg	18	4	4	10	14	32	16

Final Table

	P	W	D	L	F	A	Pts
AIK	10	6	2	2	23	11	34
Norrkoping	10	4	2	4	14	18	32
Osters	10	4	3	3	18	17	30
Trelleborg	10	4	0	6	23	29	26
IFK Gothenburg	10	4	1	5	17	17	25
Malmo	10	3	2	5	11	14	24

Top scorer: Eklund (Osters) 16
Cup Final: Degefors 3, Landskrona 0

SWITZERLAND

Schweizerisher Fussballverband. Haus des Schweizer Fussballs, Worbstrasse 48, 3074 Muri/BE. Mailing Address: PO Box 3000 Bern 15.
Founded: 1895; *Number of Clubs:* 1,473; *Number of Players:* 185,286; *National Colours:* Red shirts, white shorts, red stockings.
Telephone: 41–31/950 81 11; *Cable:* SWISSFOOT BERNE; *Telex:* 912910; *Fax:* 41–31/950 81 81.

International matches 1992

UAE (a) 2-0, Eire (a) 1-2, Bulgaria (h) 0-2, France (h) 2-1, Estonia (a) 6-0, Scotland (h) 3-1, Italy (a) 2-2, Malta (h) 3-0.

League Championship wins (1898–1992)

Grasshoppers 22; Servette 15; Young Boys Berne 11; FC Zurich 9; FC Basle 8; Lausanne 7; La Chaux-de-Fonds 3; FC Lugano 3; Winterthur 3; FX Aarau 3; Neuchatel Xamax 2; FC Anglo-American 1; St Gallen 1; FC Brühl 1; Cantonal-Neuchatel 1; Biel 1; Bellinzona 1; FC Etoile Le Chaux-de-Fonds 1; Lucerne 1; Sion 1.

Cup wins (1926–92)

Grasshoppers 17; Lausan ne 7; La Chaux-de-Fonds 6; Young Boys Berne 6; Servette 6; FC Sion 6; FC Basle 5; FC Zurich 5; Lucerne 2; FC Lugano 2; FC Granges 1; St Gallen 1; Urania Geneva 1; Young Fellows Zurich 1; Aarau.

Qualifying Table 1992–93

	P	W	D	L	F	A	Pts
Young Boys	22	11	6	5	44	30	28
Servette	22	10	7	5	32	18	27
Sion	22	8	10	4	28	21	26
Lausanne	22	7	10	5	28	21	24
Aarau	22	9	6	7	20	34	24
Zurich	22	8	7	7	21	22	23
Neuchatel Xamax	22	6	10	6	30	26	22
Lugano	22	7	8	7	29	28	22
Grasshoppers	22	5	11	6	27	27	21
St Gallen	22	4	10	8	21	28	18
Chiasso	22	5	6	11	15	26	16
Bulle	22	4	5	13	18	42	13

Final Table

	P	W	D	L	F	A	Pts
Aarau	14	9	4	1	21	7	34
Young Boys	14	5	4	5	15	15	28
Lugano	14	7	2	5	21	14	27
Servette	14	5	3	6	16	19	27
Zurich	14	5	4	5	13	14	26
Neuchatel Xamax	14	4	5	5	16	16	24
Sion	14	4	3	7	17	22	24
Lausanne	14	3	3	8	11	23	21

Top scorer: Anderson (Sion) 20
Cup Final: Lugano 4, Grasshoppers 1

Promotion/Relegation
Group A

	P	W	D	L	F	A	Pts
Grasshoppers	14	10	2	2	42	6	22
Lucerne	14	10	2	2	30	6	22
Bulle	14	8	3	3	28	20	19
Basle	14	7	4	3	25	17	18
Delemont	14	4	2	8	14	28	10
Chenois	14	4	1	9	9	29	9
Locarno	14	3	1	10	16	31	7
Wil	14	1	3	10	7	32	5

Group B

	P	W	D	L	F	A	Pts
Yverdon	14	9	3	2	32	21	21
Kriens	14	9	3	2	22	15	21
St Gallen	14	10	0	4	34	12	20
Schaffhausen	14	8	1	5	22	16	17
Chiasso	14	7	2	5	22	15	16
Winterthur	14	2	3	9	12	28	7
Etoile Carouge	14	3	0	11	14	33	6
Granges	14	1	2	11	8	26	4

TURKEY

Federation Turque De Football, Konur Sokak No. 10, Ankara Kizilay.
Founded: 1923; *Number of Clubs:* 230; *Number of Players:* 64,521; *National Colours:* White shirts, white shorts, red and white stockings.
Telephone: 1259182/1259189; *Cable:* FUTBOLSPOR ANKARA; *Telex:* 46308; *Fax:* (4) 117 1090.

International matches 1992

Finland (h) 1-1, Luxembourg (a) 3-2, Denmark (h) 2-1, Germany (a) 0-1, Bulgaria (h) 3-2, Poland (a) 0-1, San Marino (h) 4-1, England (a) 0-4, Holland (h) 1-3.

League Championship wins (1960–92)

Fenerbahce 12; Besiktas 9; Galatasaray 9; Trabzonspor 6.

Cup wins (1963–92)

Galatasaray 10; Fenerbahce 4; Besiktas 4; Trabzonspor 4; Goztepe Izmir 2; Atay Ismir 2; Ankaragucu 2; Eskisehirspor 1; Bursapor 1; Genclerbirligi 1; Sakaryaspor 1.

Final League Table 1992–93

	P	W	D	L	F	A	Pts
Galatasaray	30	20	6	4	74	21	66
Besiktas	30	19	9	2	68	23	66
Trabzonspor	30	17	9	4	57	27	60
Kocaelispor	30	17	8	5	56	30	59
Fenerbahce	30	18	4	8	75	41	58
Bursaspor	30	12	6	21	42	42	42
Altay	30	11	4	15	34	40	37
Ankaragucu	30	11	4	15	40	59	37
Sariyer	30	10	5	15	39	45	35
Genclerbirligi	30	9	8	13	41	56	35
Gaziantep	30	10	5	15	40	56	35
Kayseri	30	7	11	12	26	39	32
Karsiyaka	30	7	9	14	36	54	30
Bakirkoy*	30	8	5	17	36	48	29
Aydin*	30	6	9	15	22	50	27
Konya*	30	2	10	18	29	84	16

Top scorer: Tanju (Fenerbahce) 27
Cup Final: Galatasaray 1,2, Besiktas 0,2

UKRAINE

Football Federation of Ukraine, 42, Kuybysheva Street, 252023 Kiev 23, Ukraine.
Founded: 1992; *Number of Teams:* 30,460; *Number of Players:* 757,758.
Telephone: 044/220 1344, 044/220 1300; *Telex:* 161866. *Fax:* 044/220 1294, 044/220 1344; 044/228 4135 (Dynamo Kiev).

International matches 1992

Hungary (h) 1-3, USA (a) 0-0, Hungary (a) 1-2, Belarus (a) 1-1.

Final League Table

	P	W	D	L	F	A	Pts
Dynamo Kiev	30	18	8	4	59	14	44
Dnepr	30	18	8	4	75	28	44
Chernomorets	30	17	4	9	43	31	38
Shakhtjor	30	11	12	7	44	32	34
Metallist	30	12	7	11	37	34	31
Karpaty	30	10	10	10	37	38	30
Metallurg	30	10	9	11	38	35	29
Kryvbas	30	8	11	11	27	40	27
Kremin	30	8	11	11	23	40	27
Bukovina	30	9	8	13	27	32	26
Tavria	30	11	4	15	37	39	26
Volyn	30	10	6	14	37	54	26
Nyva	30	8	9	13	22	25	25
Torpedo	30	9	7	14	32	36	25
Veres	30	9	6	15	29	39	24
Zorya	30	10	4	16	26	46	24

Cup Final: Dynamo Kiev 2, Karpaty 1

CIS (formerly USSR)

International matches 1992

USA (a) 1-0, El Salvador (a) 3-0, USA (a) 1-2, Israel (a) 2-1, Spain (a) 1-1, England (h) 2-2, Denmark (a) 1-1, Germany (n) 1-1, Holland (a) 0-0, Scotland (a) 0-3.

WALES

The Football Association of Wales Limited, Plymouth Chambers, 3 Westgate Street, Cardiff.
Founded: 1876; *Number of Clubs:* 2,326; *Number of Players:* 53,926; *National Colours:* All red. *Telephone:* 0222 372325; *Telex:* 497 363 FAW G.

YUGOSLAVIA

Yugoslav Football Association, P.O. Box 263, Terazij e 35, 11000 Beograd.
Founded: 1919; *Number of Clubs:* 6,532; *Number of Players:* 229,024; *National Colours:* Blue shirts, white shorts, red stockings.

Telephone: 333-433 and 11/334-253; *Cable:* JUGOFUDBAL BEOGRAD; *Telex:* 11666 FSJ YU; *Fax:* 0038-11-33 34 33.

International matches 1992

Holland (a) 0-2.

League Championship wins (1923–92)

Red Star Belgrade 19; Partizan Belgrade 12; Hajduk Split 9; Gradjanski Zagreb; BSK Belgrade 5; Dynamo Zagreb 4; Jugoslavija Belgrade 2; Concordia Zagreb 2; FC Sarajevo 2; Vojvodina Novi Sad 2; HASK Zagreb 1; Zeljeznicar 1.

Cup wins (1947–92)

Red Star Belgrade 13; Hajduk Split 9; Dynamo Zagreb 8; Partizan Belgrade 6; BSK Belgrade 2; OFK Belgrade 2; Rejeka 2; Velez Mostar 2; Vardar Skopje 1; Borac Banjaluka 1.

Final League Table 1992–93

	P	W	D	L	F	A	Pts
Partizan Belgrade	36	31	3	2	103	20	65
Red Star Belgrade	36	19	13	4	70	25	51
Vojvodina	36	19	8	9	72	17	46
Zemun	36	16	8	12	62	48	40
Rad	36	13	13	10	47	35	39
Napredak	36	13	12	11	44	58	38
Radnicki Nis	36	15	7	14	40	36	37
Hajduk Kula	36	12	12	12	34	35	36
Proleter	36	15	6	15	43	45	36
Buducnost	36	14	8	14	44	48	36
OFK Belgrade	36	9	17	10	38	54	35
Becej	36	12	9	15	50	44	33
OFK Kinda	36	11	9	16	38	58	31
Mogren	36	12	7	17	46	52	31
Sutjeska	36	11	7	18	46	67	29
Radnicki B	36	11	7	18	44	62	29
Spartak	36	7	12	17	31	57	26
Borac	36	5	13	18	35	64	23
Pristina	36	7	9	20	32	64	23

Top scorer: Mihajlovic (Vojvodina) 22
Drobrnjak (Red Star Belgrade) 22
Cup Final: Red Star Belgrade 1,0, Partizan Belgrade 0,1
Red Star won 5-4 on penalties.

SOUTH AMERICA

ARGENTINA

Asociacion Del Futbol Argentina, Viamonte 1366/76, 1053 Buenos Aires.
Founded: 1893; *Number of Clubs:* 3,035; *Number of Players:* 306,365; *National Colours:* Blue & white shirts, black shorts, white stockings.
Telephone: 40-4276; *Cable:* FUTBOL BUENOS AIRES; *Telex:* 17848 afa ar; *Fax:* 953 3469 AFA.

BOLIVIA

Federacion Boliviana De Futbol, Av. 16 De Julio No. N. 0782, Casilla No. 474, Cochabamba.
Founded: 1925; *Number of Clubs:* 305; *Number of Players:* 15,290; *National Colours:* Green shirts, white shorts, green stockings.
Telephone: 4-5064; *Cable:* FEDFUTBOL COCHABAMBA; *Telex:* 6239 FEDBOL; *Fax:* 4-7951.

BRAZIL

Confederacao Brasileira De Futebol, Rua Da Alfandega, 70, P.O. Box 1078, 20.070 Rio De Janeiro.
Founded: 1914; *Number of C lubs:* 12,987; *Number of Players:* 551,358; *National Colours:* Yellow shirts, blue shorts, white stockings, green trim.
Telephone: 221/5937; *Cable:* DESPORTOS RIO DE JANEIRO; *Telex:* 2121509 CBDS BR; *Fax:* (021) 252 9294.

CHILE

Federacion De Futbol De Chile, Calle Erasmo Escala No. 1822, Casilla No. 3733, Santiago De Chile.
Founded: 1895; *Number of Clubs:* 4,598; *Number of Players:* 609,724; *National C olours:* Red shirts, blue shorts, white stockings.
Telephone: 696 5381; *Cable:* FEDFUTBOL SANTIAGO DE CHILE; *Telex:* 440474 FEBOL CZ; *Fax:* 698 7082.

COLOMBIA

Presidencia: Federacion Colombiana De Futbol, Calle 20 Norte No. 4 N-56, Barrio Versalles, Cali.
Founded: 1925; *Number of Clubs:* 3,685; *Number of Players:* 188,050; *National Colours:* Red shirts, blue shorts, tricolour stockings.
Telephone: 923/614 697 and 616 258; *Fax:* 923/689 599.

ECUADOR

Federacion Ecuatoriana De Futbol, Calle Jose Mascote 1.103 (Piso 2), Luque, Casilla 7447, Guayaquil.
Founded: 1925; *Number of Clubs:* 170; *Number of Players:* 15,700; *National Colours:* Yellow shirts, blue shorts, red stockings.
Telephone: 37 16 74; *Cable:* ECUAFUTBOL GUAYAQUIL; *Telex:* 42970 FEECFU ED; *Fax:* (593-4) 373-320.

PARAGUAY

Liga Paraguaya De Futbol, Estadio De Sajonia, Calles Mayor Martinez Y Alejo Garcia, Asuncion.
Founded: 1906; *Number of Clubs:* 1,500; *Number of Players:* 140,000; *National Colours:* Red & white shirts, blue shorts, blue stockings.
Telephone: 81743; *Telex:* 627 PY FUTBOL; *Fax:* 595 21 81743.

PERU

Federacion Peruana De Futbol, Estadio Nacional/Puerto No. 4, Calle Jose Diaz, Lima.
Founded: 1922; *Number of Clubs:* 10,000; *Number of Players:* 325,650; *National Colours:* White shirts, red trim, white shorts, white stockings.
Telephone: 32 05 17; *Cable* FEPEFUTBOL LIMA; *Telex:* 20066 FEPEFUT PE.

URUGUAY

Asociacion Uruguaya De Futbol, Guayabo 1531, Montevideo.
Founded: 1900; *Number of Clubs:* 1,091; *Number of Players:* 134,310; *National Colours:* Light blue shirts, black shorts, black stockings.
Telephone: 40 71 01/06; *Cable:* FUTBOL MONTEVIDEO; *Telex:* AUF UY 22607.

VENEZUELA

Federacion Venezolana De Futbol, Avda Este Estadio Nacional, El Paraiso Apdo. Postal 14160, Candelaria, Caracas.
Founded: 1926; *Number of Clubs:* 1,753; *Number of Players:* 63,175; *National Colours:* Magenta shirts, white shorts, white stockings.
Telephone: 461 80 10; *Cable:* FEVEFUTBOL CARACAS; *Telex:* 26 140 FVFCS VC.

ASIA

AFGHANISTAN

The Football Federation of National Olympic Committee, Kabul.
Founded: 1922; *Number of Clubs:* 30; *Number of Players:* 3,300; *National Colours:* White shirts, white shorts, white stockings.
Telephone: 20579; *Cable:* OLYMPIC KABUL.

BAHRAIN

Bahrain Football Association, P.O. Box 5464, Bahrain.
Founded: 1951; *Number of Clubs:* 25; *Number of Players:* 2,030; *National Colours:* White shirts, red shorts, white stockings.
Telephone: 72 95 63; *Cable:* BAHKORA BAHRAIN; *Telex:* 9040 FAB BN; *Fax:* 729361.

BANGLADESH

Bangladesh Football Federation, Stadium, Dhaka 2.
Founded: 1972; *Number of Clubs:* 1,265; *Number of Players:* 30,385; *National Colours:* Orange shirts, white shorts, green stockings.
Telephone: 23 60 72/23 59 28; *Cable:* FOOTBALFED DHAKA; *Telex:* 642460 BHL BJ. *Fax:* 880–2/86 47 69.

BRUNEI

Brunei Amateur Football Association, P.O. Box 2010, Bandar Seri Begawan 1920, Brunei Darussalam.
Founded: 1959; *Number of Clubs:* 22; *Number of Players:* 830; *National Colours:* Gold shirts, black shorts, gold stockings.
Telephone: 673-02-24 22 83, 24 31 71; *Cable:* BAFA BRUNEI; *Telex:* dirwyas BU 2575 Attn: BAFA; *Fax:* 673-02-24 23 00.

BURMA (now Myanmar)

Myanmar Football Federation, Aung San Memorial St adium, Kandawgalay Post Office, Yangon.
Founded: 1947; *Number of Clubs:* 600; *Number of Players:* 21,000; *National Colours:* Red shirts, white shorts, red stockings.
Telephone: 75 249; *Cable:* YANGON MYANMAR; *Telex:* 21218 BRCROS BRN.

CHINA PR

Football Association of The People's Republic of China, 9 Tiyuguan Road, Beijing.
Founded: 1924; *Number of Clubs:* 1,045; *Number of Players:* 2,250,000; *Nati onal Colours:* Red shirts, white shorts, red stockings.
Telephone: 01/701 70 18; *Cable:* SPORTSCHINE BEIJING; *Telex:* 22034 ACSF CN; *Fax:* 01/511 25 33.

HONG KONG

The Hong Kong Football Association Ltd, 55 Fat Kwong Street, Homantin, Kowloon, Hong Kong.
Founded: 1914; *Number of Clubs:* 69; *Number of Players:* 3,274; *National Colours:* Red shirts, white shorts, red stockings.
Telephone: 3-712 9122-5; *Cable:* FOOTBALL HONG KONG; *Telex:* 40518 FAHKG HX; *Fax:* 3-760 4303.

INDIA

All India Football Federation, Netaji Indoor Stadium, Eden Gardens, Calcutta 700 021.
Founded: 1937; *Number of Clubs:* 2,000; *Number of Players:* 56,000; *National Colours:* Light blue shirts, white shorts, dark blue stockings.
Telephone: 28 8484; *Cable:* SOCCER CALCUTTA; *Telex:* 212216 MCPL IN.

INDONESIA

All Indonesia Footbal l Federation, Main Stadium
Senayan, Gate VII, P.O. Box 2305, Jakarta.
Founded: 1930; *Number of Clubs:* 2,880; *Number of
Players:* 97,000; *National Colours:* Red shirts, white
shorts, red stockings.
Telephone: 581541/584386; *Cable:* PSSI JAKARTA;
Telex: 65739 as; *Fax:* (021) 584386.

IRAN

Football Federation of The Islamic Republic of Iran, Ave
Varzandeh No. 10, P.O. Box 11/1642, Tehran.
Founded: 1920; *Number of Clubs:* 6,326; *Number of
Players:* 306,000; *National Colours:* Green shirts, white
shorts, red stockings.
Telephone: (021) 825534; *Cable:* FOOTBALL IRAN
TEHRAN; *Telex:* 212691 VARZ IR.

IRAQ

Iraqi Football Association, Youth City, P.O. Box 484,
Baghdad.
Founded: 1948; *Number of Clubs:* 155; *Number of
Players:* 4,400; *National Colours:* White shirts, white
shorts, white stockings.
Telephone : 772 8430; *Cable:* BALL BAGHDAD; *Telex:*
214074 IRFA IK; *Fax:* 772 84 24.

JAPAN

The Football Association of Japan, 1-1-1 Jinnan,
Shibuya-Ku, Tokyo.
Founded: 1921; *Number of Clubs:* 13,047; *Number of
Players:* 358,989; *National Colours:* Blue shirts, white
shorts, blue stockings.
Telephone: 03-481-2311; *Cable:* SOCCERJAPAN
TOKYO; *Telex:* 2422975 FOTJPN J; *Fax:* 81 3 481
0976.

JORDAN

Jordan Football Association, P.O. Box 1954, Amman.
Founded: 1949; *Number of Clubs:* 98; *Nu mber of
Players:* 4,305; *National Colours:* White shirts, white
shorts, white stockings.
Telephone: 009626-62 4481, or 62 59 93; *Cable:*
JORDAN FOOTBALL ASSOCIATION AM; *Telex:*
22415 FOBALL JO. *Fax:* 009626-62 4454.

KAMPUCHEA

Federation Khmere De Football Association, C.P. 101,
Complex Sportif National, Phnom-Penh.
Founded: 1933; *Number of Clubs:* 30; *Number of Players:*
650; *National Colours:* Red shirts, wh ite shorts, red
stockings.
Telephone: 22 469; *Cable:* FKFA PHNOMPENH.

KOREA, NORTH

*Football Association of The Democratic People's Rep. of
Korea,* Munsin-Dong 2, Dongdaewon Distr, Pyongyang.
Founded: 1928; *Number of Clubs:* 90; *Number of Players:*
3,420; *National Colours:* Red shirts, white shorts, red
stockings.
Telephone: 6-3998; *Cable:* DPR KOREA FOOTBALL
PYONGYANG; *Telex:* 5472 KP; *Fax:* 850-2/81 4 4 03.

KOREA, SOUTH

Korea Football Association, 110-39, Kyeonji-Dong,
Chongro-Ku, Seoul.
Founded: 1928; *Number of Clubs:* 476; *Number of
Players:* 2,047; *National Colours:* Red shirts, red shorts,
red stockings.
Telephone: 02-733-6764; *Cable:* FOOTBALLKOREA
SEOUL; *Telex:* KFASEL K 25373; *Fax:* 02 735 2755.

KUWAIT

Kuwait Football Association, Udailiyya, BL. 4, Al-Ittihad
St, P.O. Box 2029 (Safat), 13021 Safat.
Founded: 1952; *Number of Clubs:* 14 (senior); *Number of
Players:* 1,526; *National Colours:* Blue shirts, white
shorts, blue stockings.
Telephone: 00965/255 58 51 or 255 58 39; *Cable:*
FOOTKUWAIT; *Telex:* FOOTKUW 22600 KT; *Fax:*
00965/256 37 37.

LAOS

Federation De Foot-Ball Lao, c/o Dir. Des Sports,
Education, Physique Et Artistique, Vientiane.
Founded: 1951; *Number of Clubs:* 76; *Number of Play
ers:* 2,060; *National Colours:* Red shirts, white shorts,
blue stockings.
Telephone: 27 41; *Cable:* FOOTBALL VIENTIANE.

LEBANON

Federation Libanaise De Football Association, P.O. Box
4732, Omar Ibn Khattab Street, Beirut.
Founded: 1933; *Number of Clubs:* 105; *Number of
Players:* 8,125; *National Colours:* Red shirts, white
shorts, red stockings.
Telephone: (1) 30 07 60; *Cable:* FOOTBALL BEIRUT;
Telex: 23001 ALABAL.

MACAO

Associacao De Futebol De Macau (AFM), P.O. Box 920,
Macau.
Founded: 1939; *Number of Clubs:* 52; *Number of Players:*
800; *National Colours:* Green shirts, white shorts, green
and white stockings.
Telephone: 71 996 (559315); *Cable:* FOOTBALL
MACAU.

MALDIVES REPUBLIC

Football Association of Maldives, Attn. Mr. Bandhu
Ahamed Saleem, Sports Division, Male.
Founded: 1986; *Number of Clubs:* ; *Number of Players:* ;
National Colours: Green shirts, white shorts, green and
white stockings.
Telephone: 3432; *Telex:* 77039 MINHOM MF; *Fax:*
(960) 32 47 39.

MALAYSIA

Football Association of Malaysia, Wisma Fam, Tingkat
4, Jalan SS5A/9, Kelana Jaya, 47301 Petaling, Jaya
Selangor.
Founded: 1933; *Number of Clubs:* 450; *Number of
Players:* 11,250; *National Colours:* Black and gold shirts,
white shorts, black and gold stockings.
Telephone: 03-776 3766; *Cable:* FOOTBALL
PETALING JAYA SELANGO; *Telex:* FAM PJ MA
36701; *Fax:* 03-775 7984.

782

NEPAL

All-Nepal Football Association, Dasharath Rangashala, Tripureshwor, Kathmandu.
Founded: 1951; *Number of Clubs:* 85; *Number of Players:* 2,550; *National Colours:* Red shirts, blue shorts, blue and white stockings.
Telephone: 2-15 703; *Cable:* ANFA KATHMANDU; *Telex:* 2390 NSC NP.

OMAN

Oman Football Association, P.O. Box 6462, Ruwi-Muscat.
Founded: 1978; *Number of Clubs:* 47; *Number of Players:* 2,340; *National Colours:* White shirts, red shorts, white stockings.
Telephone: 70 78 85; *Cable:* FOOTBALL MUSCAT; *Telex:* 3760 FOOTBALL ON; *Fax:* 707829.

PAKISTAN

Pakistan Football Federation, General Secretary, 43 Rettigon Road, Lahore, Pakistan.
Founded: 1948; *Number of Clubs:* 882; *Number of Players:* 21,000; *National Colours:* Green shirts, white shorts, green stockings.
Telephone: 92 42/23 33 48 or 21 06 38; *Cable:* FOOTBALL QUETTA; *Telex:* 47643 PFF PK; *Fax:* 92 42/23 72 97.

PHILIPPINES

Philippine Football Federation, Room 207, Administration Building, Rizal Memorial Sports Complex, Vito Cruz, Metro Manila.
Founded: 1907; *Number of Clubs:* 650; *Number of Players:* 45,000; *National Colours:* Blue shirts, white shorts, blue stockings.
Telephone: 58 83 17; *Cable:* FOOTBALL MANILA; Telex: 63539 ANSCOR PN.

QATAR

Qatar Football Association, P.O. Box 5333, Doha.
Founded: 1960; *Number o Clubs:* 8 (senior); *Number of Players:* 1,380; *National Colours:* White shirts, maroon shorts, white stockings.
Telephone: 351641, 454444; *Cable:* FOOTQATAR DOHA; *Telex:* 47 49 QATFOT DH; *Fax:* (0974) 411660.

SAUDI ARABIA

Saudi Arabian Football Federation, North Al-Morabbaa Quarter, P.O. Box 5844, Riyadh 11432.
Founded: 1959; *Number of Clubs:* 120; *Number of Players:* 9,600; *National Colours:* White shirts, white shorts, white stockings.
Telephone: 402 2699; *Cable:* KORA RIYADH; *Telex:* 404300 SAFOTB SJ; *Fax:* 01 402 1276.

SINGAPORE

Football Association of Singapore, Jal an Besar Stadium, Tyrwhitt Road, Singapore 0820.
Founded: 1892; *Number of Clubs:* 250; *Number of Players:* 8,000; *National Colours:* Sky blue shirts, sky blue shorts, sky blue stockings.
Telephone: 293 1477; *Cable:* SOCCER SINGAPORE; *Telex:* SINFA RS 37683.

SRI LANKA

Football Federation of Sri Lanka, No. 2, Old Grand Stand, Race Course Reid Avenue, Colombo 7.
Founded: 1939; *Number of Clubs:* 600; *Number o f Players:* 18,825; *National Colours:* Maroon shirts, white shorts, white stockings.
Telephone: 596179; *Cable:* SOCCER COLOMBO; *Telex:* 21537 METALIX CE; *Fax:* 94-1-580721.

SYRIA

Association Arabe Syrienne De Football, General Sport Fed. Building, October Stadium, Damascus Baremke.
Founded: 1936; *Number of Clubs:* 102; *Number of Players:* 30,600; *National Colours:* White shirts, white shorts, white stocking s.
Telephone: 33 15 11; *Cable:* FOOTBALL DAMASCUS; *Telex:* HOTECH 41 19 35.

THAILAND

The Football Association of Thailand, c/o National Stadium, Rama I Road, Bangkok.
Founded: 1916; *Number of Clubs:* 168; *Number of Players:* 15,000; *National Colours:* Crimson shirts, white shorts, crimson stockings.
Telephone: 02 214 1058; *Cable:* FOOTBALL BANGKOK; *Telex:* 20211 FAT TH; *Fax:* 2154494.

UNITED ARAB EMIRATES

United Arab Emirates Football Association, Post Box 5458, Dubai.
Founded: 1971; *Number of Clubs:* 23 (senior); *Number of Players:* 1,787; *National Colours:* White shirts, white shorts, white stockings.
Telephone: 245 636; *Cable:* FOOTBALL EMIRATES DUBAI; *Telex:* 47623 UAEFA EM; *Fax:* 245 559.

VIETNAM

Association De Football De La Republique Du Viet-Nam, No. 36, Boulevard Tran-Phu, Hanoi. *Fo unded:* 1962; *Number of Clubs:* 55 (senior); *Number of Players:* 16,000; *National Colours:* Red shirts, white shorts, red stockings.
Telephone: 5/48 67; *Cable:* AFBVN, 36, TRAN-PHU-HANOI.

YEMEN

Yemen Football Association, P.O. Box 908, Sana'a.
Founded: 1962; *Number of Clubs:* 26; *Number of Players:* 1750; *National Colours:* Green.
Telephone: 00967/2/215720. *Telex:* 2710 YOUTH YE

CONCACAF

ANTIGUA

The Antigua Football Association, P.O. Box 773, St. Johns.
Founded: 1928; *Number of Clubs:* 60; *Number of Players:* 1,008; *National Colours:* Gold shirts, black shorts, black stockings.
Telephone: 809 462 3945; *Cable:* AFA ANTIGUA; *Telex:* 2177 SIDAN AK; *Fax:* 809 462 2649.

BAHAMAS

Bahamas Football Association, P.O. Box N 8434, Nassau, N.P.
Founded: 1967; *Num ber of Clubs:* 14; *Number of Players:* 700; *National Colours:* Yellow shirts, black shorts, yellow stockings.
Telephone: 809 32 47099; *Cable:* BAHSOCA NASSAU; *Fax:* 809 324 6484.

BARBADOS

Barbados Football Association, P.O. Box 833E, Bridgetown.
Founded: 1910; *Number of Clubs:* 92; *Number of Players:* 1,100; *National Colours:* Royal blue shirts, gold shorts, royal blue stockings.
Telphone: 809 424 4 413; *Cable:* FOOTBALL BRIDGETOWN; *Telex:* 2306 SHAMROCK WB; *Fax:* (809) 436 0130.

BELIZE

Belize National Football Association, P.O. Box 1742, Belize City.
Founded: 1986; *National Colours:* Blue shirts, red & white trim, white shorts, blue stockings.
Telephone: 08-2609 or 08 2637; 02 77031 32; 08-2200; *Telex:* 102 FOREIGN BZ.

BERMUDA

The Bermuda Football Association, P.O. Box HM 745, Hamilton 5 HM CX.
Founded: 1928; *Number of Clubs:* 30; *Number of Players:* 1,947; *National Colours:* Blue shirts, white shorts, white stockings.
Telephone: (809) 295 2199; *Cable:* FOOTBALL BERMUDA; *Telex:* 3441 BFA BA; *Fax:* (809) 295 0773.

CANADA

The Canadian Soccer Association, 1600 James Naismith Drive, Gloucester, Ont. K1B 5N4.
Founded: 1912; *Number of Clubs:* 1,600; *Number of Players:* 224,290; *National Colours:* R ed shirts, red shorts, red stockings.
Telephone: (613) 748-5667; *Cable:* SOCCANADA OTTAWA; *Telex:* 053-3350; *Fax:* (613) 745-1938.

CAYMAN ISLANDS

Cayman Islands Football Association, PO Box 178, Georgetown, Grand Cayman, Cayman Islands W1.
Number of Clubs: 25; *Number of Players:* 875.
Telephone: 809-949 4733, 809-949 8228. *Fax:* 809-949 8738.

COSTA RICA

Federacion Costarricense De Futbol, Calle 40-Ave, CTLI, San Jose.
Founded: 1921; *Number of Clubs:* 431; *Number of Players:* 12,429; *National Colours:* Red shirts, blue shorts, white stockings.
Telephone: 22 15 44; *Cable:* FEDEFUTBOL SAN JOSE; *Telex:* 3394 DIDER CR.

CUBA

Asociacion De Futbol De Cuba, c/o Comite Olimpico Cubano, Calle 13 No. 601, Esq. C. Vedado, La Habana, ZP 4.
Founded: 1924; *Number of Clubs:* 70; *Number of Players:* 12,900; *National Colours:* White shirts, blue shorts, white stockings.
Telephone: 40 35 81; *Cable:* FOOTBALL HABANA; *Telex:* 511332 INDER CU.

DOMINICAN REPUBLIC

Federacion Dominicana de Futbol, Apartado De Correos No. 1953, Santo Domingo.
Founded: 1953; *Number of Clubs:* 128; *Number of Players:* 10,706; *National Colours:* Blue shirts, white shorts, red stockings.
Telephone: 542-6923. *Cable:* FEDOFUTBOL SANTO DOMINGO.

EL SALVADOR

Federacion Salvadorena De Futbol, Av. Jm. Delgado, Col. Escalon, Centro Espanol, Apartado 1029, San Salvador.
Founded: 1936; *Number of Clubs:* 944; *Number of Players:* 21,294; *National Colours:* Blue shirts, bl ue shorts, blue stockings.
Telephone: 23 73 62; *Cable:* FESFUT SAN SALVADOR; *Telex:* 20484 FESFUT SAL.

GRENADA

Grenada Football Association, P.O. Box 326, St. Juilles Street St. George's.
Founded: 1924; *Number of Clubs:* 15; *Number of Players:* 200; *National Colours:* Green & yellow shirts, red shorts, green & yellow stockings.
Telephone: 1-809/440 1986; *Cable:* GRENBALL GRENADA; *Telex:* 3431 CW BUR; *Fax:* 1-809/440 1986.

GUATEMALA

Federacion Nacional De Futbol De Guatemala C.A., Apartado Postal No. 1809, Guatemala C.A.
Founded: 1933; *Number of Clubs:* 1,611; *Number of Players:* 43,516; *National Colours:* White/blue diagonal striped shirts, blue shorts, white stockings.
Telephone: 362211; *Cable:* FEDFUTBOL GUATEMALA.

GUYANA

Guyana Football Association, P.O. Box 10727 Georgetown.
Founded: 1902; *Number of Clubs:* 103; *Number of Players:* 1,665; *National Colours:* Green & yellow shirts, black shorts, white & green stockings.
Telephone: 02-59458/9; *Cable:* FOOTBALL GUYANA; *Telex:* 2266 RICEBRD GY; *Fax:* (005922) 52169.

HAITI

Federation Haitienne De Football, Stade Sylvio-Cator, Port-Au-Prince.
Founded: 1904; *Number of Clubs:* 40; *Number of Players:* 4,000; *National Colours:* R ed shirts, black shorts, red stockings.
Telephone: 2/3237; *Cable:* FEDHAFOOB PORT-AU-PRINCE.

HONDURAS

Federacion Nacional Autonoma De Futbol De Honduras, Apartado Postal 827, Costa Oeste Del Est. Nac, Tegucigalpa, De. C.
Founded: 1951; *Number of Clubs:* 1,050; *Number of Players:* 15,300; *National Colours:* Blue shirts, blue shorts, blue stockings.
Telephone: 32-1897; *Cable* FENAFUTH TEGUCIGALPA; *Telex:* 1209 F ENEFUTH; *Fax:* 31 14 28.

784

JAMAICA

Jamaica Football Federation, Room 9, National Stadium, Kingston 6.
Founded: 1910; *Number of Clubs:* 266; *Number of Players:* 45,200; *National Colours:* Green shirts, black shorts, green & gold stockings.
Cable: FOOTBALL JAMAICA KINGSTON.

MEXICO

Federacion Mexicana De Futbol Asociacion, A.C., Abraham Gonzales 74, C.P. 06600, Col. Juarez, Mexico 6, D.F.
Founded: 1927; *Number of Clu bs:* 77 (senior); *Number of Players:* 1,402,270; *National Colours:* Green shirts, white shorts, green stockings.
Telephone: 566 21 55; *Cable:* MEXFUTBOL MEXICO; *Telex:* 1771678 MSUTME; *Fax:* (915) 566 7580.

NETHERLANDS ANTILLES

Nederlands Antiliaanse Voetbal Unie, P.O. Box 341, Curacao, N.A.
Founded: 1921; *Number of Clubs:* 85; *Number of Players:* 4,500; *National Colours:* white shirts, white shorts, red stockings.
Telephone: ; *Cable:* NAVU CURACAO; *Telex:* 1046 ennia na; *Fax:* (599-9) 611173 ennia caribe.

NICARAGUA

Federacion Nicaraguense De Futbol, Inst. Nicaraguense De Deportes, Apartado Postal 976 0 383, Managua.
Founded: 1968; *Number of Clubs:* 31; *Number of Players:* 160 (senior); *National Colours:* Blue shirts, blue shorts, blue stockings.
Telephone: 505 2/66 41 34; *Cable:* FEDEFOOT MANAG UA; *Telex:* 2156 IND NK.

PANAMA

Federacion Nacional De Futbol De Panama, Apdo 1436, Balboa, Ancon., Panama.
Founded: 1937; *Number of Clubs:* 65; *Number of Players:* 4,225; *National Colours:* Red & white shirts, blue shorts, red stockings.
Telephone: 27–0454, 27–0448; *Cable:* PANAOLIMPIC PANAMA; *Telex:* 2534 INDE PG; *Fax:* 27–0460.

PUERTO RICO

Federacion Puertorriquena De Futbol, Coliseo Roberto Clemen te, P.O. Box 4355, Hato Rey, 00919-4355.
Founded: 1940; *Number of Clubs:* 175; *Number of Players:* 4,200; *National Colurs:* White & red shirts, blue shorts, white & blue stockings.
Telephone: 766 1461; *Cable:* BORIKENFPF; *Telex:* 3450296; *Fax:* 8660489, 764-2025.

ST KITTS AND NEVIS

St Kitts and Nevis Football Association, P.O. Box 465, Basseterre, St Kitts, West Indies.
Number of Clubs: 36; *Number of Players:* 600.
Telephone: 809–465 2521, 809–465 4086; *Fax:* 809–465 550/1042.

SURINAM

Surinaamse Voetbal Bond, Cultuuruinlaan 7, P.O. Box 1223, Paramaribo.
Founded: 1920; *Number of Clubs:* 168; *Number of Players:* 4,430; *National Colours:* Red shirts, white shorts, white stockings.
Telephone: 73112; *Cable:* SVB Paramaribo.

TRINIDAD AND TOBAGO

Trinidad & Tobago Football Association, Cor. Duke & Scott-Bushe Street, Port of Spain, Trinidad, P.O. Box 400.
Founded: 1906; *Number of Clubs:* 124; *Number of Players:* 5,050; *National Colours:* Red shirts, black shorts, red stockings.
Telephone: 624 5183. *Cable:* TRAFA PORT OF SP AIN; *Telex:* 22652 TRAFA; *Fax:* 627-7661.

USA

United States Soccer Federation, 1750 East Boulder Street, Colorado Springs, CO 80909.
Founded: 1913; *Number of Clubs:* 7,000; *Number of Players:* 1,411,500; *National Colours:* White shirts, blue shorts, red stockings.
Telephone: (719) 578-4678; *Cable:* SOCCERUSA COLORADOSPRINGS; *Telex:* 450024 US SOCCER FED; *Fax:* (719) 578-4636.
Recent additions; ARUBA, SA NTA LUCIA, ST. VINCENT and the GRENADINES.

OCEANIA

AUSTRALIA

Australian Soccer Federation, First Floor, 2325 Frederick Street, Rockdale, NSW 2216.
Founded: 1961; *Number of Clubs:* 6,816; *Number of Players:* 433,957; *National Colours:* Gold shirts, green shorts, white stockings.
Telephone: 29 7026; *Cable:* FOOTBALL SYDNEY; *Telex:* AA 170512; *Fax:* 02 296 556.

FIJI

Fiji Football Association, Mr. J. D. Maharaj, Hon. Secretary Government Bldgs, P.O.B. 2514 Suva.
Founded: 1946; *Number of Clubs:* 140; *Number of Players:* 21,300; *National Colours:* White shirts, black shorts, black stockings.
Telephone: 300453; *Cable:* FOOTSOCCER SUVA; *Telex:* 2366 FJ; *Fax:* 304642.

NEW ZEALAND

New Zealand Football Association, Inc., P.O. Box 62-532, Central Park, Green Lane, Auckland 6.
Founded: 1891; *Number of Clubs:* 312; *Number of Players:* 52,969; *National Colours:* White shirts, black shorts, white stockings.
Telephone: 0-9-525-6120; *Fax:* 0-9-525-6123.

PAPUA-NEW-GUINEA

Papua New Guinea Football (Soccer) Association Inc., P.O. Box 1716, Boroko.
Founded: 1962; *Number of Clubs:* 350; *Number of Players:* 8,250; *National Colours:* Red shirts, black shorts, red stockings.
Telephone: 25 41 09; *Telex:* TOTOTRA NE 2343 6.

WESTERN SAMOA

Western Samoa Football (Soccer) Association, Min. of Youth, Sports Culture, Private Bag, Apia.
Founded: 1986; *National Colours:* Blue shirts, white shorts, blue and white stockings.
Telephone: 23315; *Telex:* 230 SAMGAMES SX.

Recent additions: SOLOMON ISLANDS, TAHITI and VANUATU. The Solomon Islands are situated in the South Pacific to the south-east of Papua New Guinea. There are 4,000 registered players. Vanuatu was formerly known as the New Hebrides and is a double chain of islands to the south-east of the Solomons. *Colours:* Gold and black.

AFRICA

ALGERIA

Federation Algerienne De Futbol, Route Ahmed Ouaked, Boite Postale No. 39, Alger Dely Ibrahim.
Founded: 1962; *Number of Clubs:* 780; *Number of Players:* 58,567; *National Colours:* Green shirts, white shorts, red stockings.
Telephone: 213/365 947 and 365 948; *Cable:* FAFOOT ALGER; *Telex:* 6 1378. *Fax:* 213/366 181.

ANGOLA

Federation Angolaise De Football, B.P. 3449, Luanda.
Founded: 1977; *Number of Clubs:* 276; *Number of Players:* 4,269; *National Colours:* Red shirts, black shorts, red stockings.
Telephone: 338635/338233; *Cable:* FUTANGOLA; *Telex:* 4072 CIAM AN.

BENIN

Federation Beninoise De Football, B.P. 965, Cotonou.
Founded: 1968; *Number of Clubs:* 117; *Number of Players:* 6,700; *Nati onal Colours:* Green shirts, green shorts, green stockings.
Telephone: 33 05 37; *Cable:* FEBEFOOT COTONOU;K*Telex:* 5033 BIMEX COTONOU; *Fax:* 30 02 14.

BOTSWANA

Botswana Football Association, P.O. Box 1396, Gabarone.
Founded: 1976; *National Colours:* Sky blue shirts, white shorts, sky blue stockings. *Cable:* BOTSBALL GABARONE; *Telex:* 2977 BD; *Fax:* (267) 372 911.

BURKINA FASO

Federation Burkinabe De F oot-Ball, B.P. 57, Ouagadougou.
Founded: 1960; *Number of Clubs:* 57; *Number of Players:* 4,672; *National Colours:* Black shirts, white shorts, red stockings.
Telephone: 33 58 20; *Cable:* FEDEFOOT OUAGADOUGOU.

BURUNDI

Federation De Football Du Burundi, B.P. 3426, Bujumbura.
Founded: 1948; *Number of Clubs:* 132; *Number of Players:* 3,930; *National Colours:* Red shirts, white shorts, green stockings.
Telephone: 2 3078; *Cable:* FFB BUJA.

CAMEROON

Federation Camerounaise De Football, B.P. 1116, Yaounde.
Founded: 1960; *Number of Clubs:* 200; *Number of Players:* 9,328; *National Colours:* Green shirts, red shorts, yellow stockings.
Telephone: 22 25 38; *Cable:* FECAFOOT YAOUNDE; *Telex:* JEUNESPO 8568 KNK

CAPE VERDE ISLANDS

Federacao Cabo-Verdiana De Futebol, C.P. 234, PRAIA.
Founded: 1986; *National Colours:* Green shirts, green shorts, green stockings.
Telephone: 611362; *Cable:* FCF-CV; *Telex:* 6030 MICDE-CV.

CENTRAL AFRICAN REPUBLIC

Federation Centrafricaine De Football, B.P. 344, Bangui.
Founded: 1937; *Number of Clubs:* 256; *Number of Players:* 7,200; *National Colours:* Grey & blue shirts, white shorts, red stockings.
Telephone: 2141; *Cable:* FOOTBANGUI BANGUI.

CONGO

Federation Co ngolaise De Football, B.P. 4041, Brazzaville.
Founded: 1962; *Number of Clubs:* 250; *Number of Players:* 5,940; *National Colours:* Red shirts, red shorts, white stockings.
Telephone: 81 51 01; *Cable:* FECOFOOT BRAZZAVILLE; *Telex:* 5210 KG.

EGYPT

Egyptian Football Association, 5, Shareh Gabalaya, Guezira, Al Borg Post Office, Cairo.
Founded: 1921; *Number of Clubs:* 247; *Number of Players:* 19,735; *National Colours:* Red shirts, white shorts, black stockings.
Telephone: 340 1793; *Cable:* KORA CAIRO; *Telex:* 23504 KORA.

ETHIOPIA

Ethiopia Football Federation, Addis Ababa Stadium, P.O. Box 1080, Addis Ababa.
Founded: 1943; *Number of Clubs:* 767; *Number of Players:* 20,594; *National Colours:* Green shirts, yellow shorts, red stockings.
Telephone: 51 44 53 and 51 43 21. *Cable:* FOOTBALL ADDIS ABABA; *Telex:* 21377 NESCO ET.

GABON

Federation Gabonaise De Football, B.P. 181, Libreville.
Founded: 1962; *Number of Clubs:* 320; *Number of Players:* 10,000; *National Colours:* Blue shirts, white shorts, white stockings.
Telephone: 72 22 37; *Cable:* FEGAFOOT LIBREVILLE; *Telex:* 5642 GO.

GAMBIA

Gambia Football Association, P.O. Box 523, Banjul.
Founded: 1952; *Number of Clubs:* 30; *Number of Playe rs:* 860; *National Colours:* White & red shirts, white shorts, white stockings.
Telephone: 958 35; *Cable:* SPORTS GAMBIA BANJUL; *Fax:* GNOSC 220/96270.

GHANA

Ghana Football Association, P.O. Box 1272, Accra.
Founded: 1957; *Number of Clubs:* 347; *Number of Players:* 11,275; *National Colours:* White shirts, white shorts, white stockings.
Telephone: 63 924/7; *Cable:* GFA, ACCRA; *Telex:* 25 19 SPORTS GH.

GUINEA

Federation Guineenne De Football, P.O. Box 3645, Conakry.
Founded: 1959; *Number of Clubs:* 351; *Number of Players:* 10,000; *National Colours:* Red shirts, yellow shorts, green stockings.
Telephone: 445041; *Cable:* GUINEFOOT CONAKRY; *Telex:* 22302 MJ.

GUINEA-BISSAU

Federacao De Football Da Guinea-Bissau, Apartado 375, 1035 Bissau-Codex, Rua 4 no 10c.
Founded: 1986; *National Colours:*
cf1 Green shirts, green shorts, green stockings.
Telephone: 21 25 45; *Cable:* FUTEBOL BISSAU; *Telex:* PAIGC 230 BI.

GUINEA, EQUATORIAL

Federacion Ecuatoguineana De Futbol, Malabo.
Founded: 1986; *National Colours:* All red.
Telephone: 2732; *Cable:* FEGUIFUT/MALABO.

IVORY COAST

Federation Ivoirienne De Football, Stade Felix Houphouet Boigny, B.P. 1202, Abidjan.
Founded: 1960; *Number of Clubs:* 84 (senior); *Number of Players:* 3,655; *National Colours:* Orange shirts, white shorts, green stockings.
Telephone: 22 22 82; *Cable:* FIF ABIDJAN; *Telex:* 22722 FIF CI.

KENYA

Kenya Football Federation, Nyayo National Stadium, P.O. Box 40234, Nairobi.
Founded: 1960; *Number of Clubs:* 351; *Number of Players:* 8,880; *National Colours:* Red shirts, red shorts, red stockings.
Telephone: 340382/339761/9 ; *Cable:* KEFF NAIROBI; *Telex:* 25784 KFF.

LESOTHO

Lesotho Sports Council, P.O. Box 138, Maseru 100.
Founded: 1932; *Number of Clubs:* 88; *Number of Players:* 2,076; *National Colours:* White shirts, blue shorts, white stockings.
Telephone: 311 291 MASERU; *Cable:* LIPAPALI MASERU; *Telex:* 4493.

LIBERIA

The Liberia Football Association, P.O. Box 1066, Monrovia.
Founded: 1962; *National Col ours:* Blue & white shirts, white shorts, blue & white stockings.
Telephone: 22 21 77; *Cable:* LIBFOTASS MONROVIA; *Telex:* 44220 EXM LBR. *Fax:* 231–735 003.

LIBYA

Libyan Arab Jamahiriya Football Federation, P.O. Box 5137, Tripoli.
Founded: 1963; *Number o Clubs:* 89; *Number of Players:* 2,941; *National Colours:* Green shirts, white shorts, green stockings.
Telephone: 46 610; *Telex:* 20896 KURATP LY. *Fax:* 218-21/607 016.

MADAGASCAR

Federatio n Malagasy De Football, c/o Comite Nat. De Coordination De Football, B.P. 4409, Antananarivo 101.
Founded: 1961; *Number of Clubs:* 775; *Number of Players:* 23,536; *National Colours:* Red shirts, white shorts, green stockings.
Telephone: 21373; *Telex:* 22264.

MALAWI

Football Association of Malawi, P.O. Box 865, Blantyre.
Founded: 1966; *Number of Clubs:* 465; *Number of Players:* 12,500; *National Colour s:* Red shirts, red shorts, red stockings.
Telephone: 636686; *Cable:* FOOTBALL BLANTYRE; *Telex:* 4526 SPORTS MI. *Fax:* 265/63 69 41.

MALI

Federation Malienne De Football, Stade Mamdou Konate, B.P. 1020, Bamako.
Founded: 1960; *Number of Clubs:* 128; *Number of Players:* 5,480; *National Colours:* Green shirts, yellow shorts, red stockings.
Telephone: 22 41 52; *Cable:* MALIFOOT BAMAKO; Telex: 0985 1200/1202.

MAURITANIA

Federation De Foot-Ball De La Rep. Isl. De Mauritanie, B.P. 566, Nouakshott.
Founded: 1961; *Number of Clubs:* 59; *Number of Players:* 1,930; *National Colours:* Green and yellow shirts, blue shorts, green stockings.
Telephone: 536 09; *Cable:* FOOTRIM NOUAKSHOTT.

MAURITIUS

Mauritius Football Association, Chancery House, 14 Lislet Geoffroy Street, (2nd Floor, Nos. 303.305), Port Louis.
Founded: 1952; *Number of Club s:* 397; *Number of Players:* 29,375; *National Colours:* Red shirts, white shorts, red stockings.
Telephone: 212 1418, 212 5771; *Cable:* MFA PORT LOUIS; *Telex:* 4427 MSA IW; *Fax:* (230) 208 41 00.

MOROCCO

Federation Royale Marocaine De Football, Av. Ibn Sina, C.N.S. Bellevue, B.P. 51, Rabat.
Founded: 1955; *Number of Clubs:* 350; *Number of Players:* 19,768; *National Colours:* Red shirts, green shorts, red stockings.
Telephone: 67 27 06/08 or 67 26 07; *Cable:* FERMAFOOT RABAT; *Telex:* 32940 FERMFOOT M. *Fax:* 67 10 70K

MOZAMBIQUE

Federacao Mocambicana De Futebol, Av. Samora
Machel, 11-2, Caixa Postal 1467, Maputo.
Founded: 1978; *Number of Clubs:* 144; *National Colours:*
Red shirts, red shorts, red stockings.
Telephone: 26 475; *Cable:* MOCAMBOLA MAPUTO;
Telex: 6-221/2.

NAMIBIA

Namibia Football Federation, 18 Curt von Francois Str.
PO Box 1345, Windhoek 2000; Namibia. *Fax:* 061-22
4454.
Number of Clubs: 244; *Number of Players:* 7320.

NIGER

Federation Niger ienne De Football, Stade National
Niamey, B.P. 10299, Niamey.
Founded: 1967; *Number of Clubs:* 64; *Number of Players:*
1,525; *National Colours:* Orange shirts, white shorts,
green stockings.
Telephone: 73 31 97; *Cable:* FEDERFOOT NIGER
NIAMEY.
Telex: (975) 5527 or 5349. *Fax:* (00227) 73 55 12.

NIGERIA

Nigeria Football Association National Sports Commission,
National Stadium, P.O. Box 466, Lagos.
Founded: 1 945; *Number of Clubs:* 326; *Number of
Players:* 80,190; *National Colours:* Green shirts, white
shorts, green stockings.
Telephone: 234-1-83 52 65; *Cable:* FOOTBALL LAGOS;
Telex: 26570 NFA NG; *Fax:* 63 22 39 m Lagos.

RWANDA

Federation Rwandaise De Foot-Ball Amateur, B.P. 2000,
Kigali.
Founded: 1972; *Number of Clubs:* 167; *National Colours:*
Red shirts, red shorts, red stockings.
Telephone: 75811 ext. 223; *Cable:* MIJENCOOP
KIGALI; *Telex:* 22504 PUBLIC RW; *Fax:* (250) 76574.

SENEGAL

Federation Senegalaise De Football, Stade De L'Amitie,
Route De L'Aeroport De Yoff, Dakar.
Founded: 1960; *Number of Clubs:* 75 (senior); *Number of
Players:* 3,977; *National Colours:* Green shirts, yellow
shorts, red stockings.
Telephone: 25 00 57; *Cable:* SENEFOOT DAKAR.

SEYCHELLES

Seychelles Football Federation, P.O. Box 580, Mont
Fleuri, Victoria.
Founded: 1986; *National Colours:* Green shirts, yellow
shorts, red stockings.
Telephone: 24 126; *Telex:* 2271 SZ; *Fax:* 23 518.

ST. THOMAS AND PRINCIPE

Federation Santomense De Fut., P.O. Box 42, Sao Tome.
Founded: 1986; *National Colours:* Green shirts, green
shorts, green stockings.
Telephone: 22320; *Telex:* 213 PUBLICO STP.

SIERRA LEONE

Sierra Leone Amateur Footbal l Association, S. Stevens
Stadium, Brookfields, P.O. Box 672, Freetown.
Founded: 1967; *Number of Clubs:* 104; *National Colours:*
Players: 8,120; *National Colours:* Green shirts, white
shorts, blue stockings.
Telephone: 41872; *Cable:* SLAFA FREETOWN; *Telex:*
3210 BOOTH SL.

SOMALIA

Somali Football Federation, Ministry of Sports, C.P. 247,
Mogadishu.
Founded: 1951; *Number of Clubs:* 46 (senior); *Number of
Players :* 1,150; *National Colours:* Sky blue shirts, white
shorts, white stockings.
Telephone: 22 273; *Cable:* SOMALIA FOOTBALL
MOGADISHU; *Telex:* 3061 SONOC SM.

SOUTH AFRICA

South African Football Association, First National Bank
Stadium, Nasrec; PO Box 910, Johannesburg 2000;
South Africa.
Number of Teams: 51,944; *Number of Players:* 1,039,880.
Telephone: 011-494 3522; *Fax:* 011-494 3447.

SUDAN

Sudan Football Association, P.O. Box 437, Khartoum.
Founded: 1936; *Number of Clubs:* 750; *Number of
Players:* 42,200; *National Colours:* White shirts, white
shorts, white stockings.
Telephone: 76 633; *Cable:* ALKOURA, KHARTOUM;
Telex: 23007 KOR SD.

SWAZILAND

National Football Association of Swaziland, P.O. Box
641, Mbabane.
Founded: 1976; *Number of Clubs:* 136; *National Colours:*
Blue and gold shirts, white shorts, blue and gold
stockings.
Telephone: 46 852; *Telex:* 2245 EXP WD.

TANZANIA

Football Association of Tanzania, P.O. Box 1574, Dar Es
Salaam.
Founded: 1930; *Number of Clubs:* 51; *National Colours:*
Yellow shirts, yellow shorts, yellow stockings.
Telephone: 32 334; *Cable:* FAT DAR ES SALAAM.

TOGO

Federation Togolaise De Football, C.P. 5, Lome.
Founded: 1960; *Number of Clubs:* 144; *Number of
Players:* 4,346; *National Colours:* Red shirts, white
shorts, red stockings.
Telephone: 21 26 98; *Cable:* TOGOFOOT LOME; *Telex:*
5015 CNOT TG. *Fax:* (228) 221 314.

TUNISIA

Federation Tunisienne De Football, 20 Rue Bilal, El-
Menzah VI, Tunis 1004.
Found ed: 1957; *Number of Clubs:* 215; *Number of
Players:* 18,300; *National Colours:* Red shirts, white
shorts, red stockings.
Telephone: 23 33 03, 23 35 44; *Cable:* FOOTBALL
TUNIS; *Telex:* 14783 FTFOOT TN.

UGANDA

Federation of Uganda Football Associations, P.O. Box 10475, Kampala.
Founded: 1924; *Number of Clubs:* 400; *Number of Players:* 1,518; *National Colours:* Yellow shirts, black shorts, yellow stock ings.
Telephone: 256 41/25 6021; *Cable:* FUFA KAMPALA; *Telex:* 61272; *Fax:* 256 41/24 55 80.

ZAIRE

Federation Zairoise De Football-Association, Via Agence Zairoise de Presse, Brussels.
Founded: 1919; *Number of Clubs:* 3,800; *Number of Players:* 64,627; *National Colours:* Green shirts, yellow shorts, yellow stockings. *Cable:* FEZAFA KINSHASA; *Telex:* 63915. *Fax:* 87–11/5065 55.

ZAMBIA

Football Association of Zambi a, P.O. Box 33474, Lusaka.
Founded: 1929; *Number of Clubs:* 20 (senior); *Number of Players:* 4,100; *National Colours:* Green shirts, white shorts, black stockings.
Telephone: 21 11 45; *Cable:* FOOTBALL LUSAKA; *Telex:* 40204.

ZIMBABWE

Zimbabwe Football Association, P.O. Box 8343, Causeway, Harare.
Founded: 1965; *National Colours:* White shirts, black shorts, black stockings.
Telephone: 79 12 75/6/7; *Cable:* SOCCER HARARE; *Telex:* 22299 SOCCER ZW; *Fax:* 793 320.
Other addition: CHAD (readmitted).

EUROPEAN FOOTBALL CHAMPIONSHIP

(formerly EUROPEAN NATIONS' CUP)

Year	Winners		Runners-up		Venue
1960	USSR	2	Yugoslavia	1	Paris
1964	Spain	2	USSR	1	Madrid
1968	Italy	2	Yugoslavia	0	Rome
	After 1-1 draw				
1972	West Germany	3	USSR	0	Brussels
1976	Czechoslovakia	2	West Germany	2	Belgrade
	(Czechoslovakia won on penalties)				
1980	West Germany	2	Belgium	1	Rome
1984	France	2	Spain	0	Paris
1988	Holland	2	USSR	0	Munich
1992	Denmark	2	Germany	0	Gothenburg

EUROPEAN NATIONS' CUP 1958–60

Preliminary Round

Eire 2, Czechoslovakia 0
Czechoslovakia 4, Eire 0

First Round

France 7, Greece 1
Greece 1, France 1
USSR 3, Hungary 1
Hungary 0, USSR 1
Romania 3, Turkey 0
Turkey 2, Romania 0
Norway 0, Austria 1
Austria 5, Norway 2
Yugoslavia 2, Bulgaria 0
Bulgaria 1, Yugoslavia 1
Portugal 3, East Germany 2
East Germany 0, Portugal 2
Denmark 2, Czechoslovakia 2
Czechoslovakia 5, Denmark 1
Poland 2, Spain 4
Spain 3, Poland 0

Quarter-finals

Portugal 2, Yugoslavia 1
Yugoslavia 5, Portugal 1
France 5, Austria 2
Austria 2, France 4
Romania 0, Czechoslovakia 2
Czechoslovakia 3, Romania 0
USSR w.o. Spain withdrew

Semi-finals

Yugoslavia 5, France 4 (in Paris)
USSR 3, Czechoslovakia 0 (in Marseilles)

Third Place Match (Marseilles)

Czechoslovakia 2, France 0

Final (Paris, 10 July 1960, 17,966)

USSR (0) 2, Yugoslavia (1) 1 after extra time

USSR: Yachin; Tchekeli, Kroutikov; Voinov, Maslenkin, Netto; Metreveli, Ivanov, Ponedelnik, Bubukin, Meshki.
Yugoslavia: Vidinic; Durkovic, Jusufi; Zanetic, Miladinovic, Perusic; Sekularac, Jerkovic, Galic, Matus, Kostic.
Scorers: Metreveli, Ponedelnik for USSR; Netto og for Yugoslavia.

EUROPEAN NATIONS' CUP 1962–64

First Round

Spain 6, Romania 0
Romania 3, Spain 1
Poland 0, Northern Ireland 2

Northern Ireland 2, Poland 0
Denmark 6, Malta 1
Malta 1, Denmark 3
Eire 4, Iceland 2
Iceland 1, Eire 1
Greece withdrew against Albania
East Germany 2, Czechoslovakia 1
Czechoslovakia 1, East Germany 1
Hungary 3, Wales 1
Wales 1, Hungary 1
Italy 6, Turkey 0
Turkey 0, Italy 1
Holland 3, Switzerland 1
Switzerland 1, Holland 1
Norway 0, Sweden 2
Sweden 1, Norway 1
Yugoslavia 3, Belgium 2
Belgium 0, Yugoslavia 1
Bulgaria 3, Portugal 1
Portugal 3, Bulgaria 1
Bulgaria 1, Portugal 0
England 1, France 1
France 5, England 2

Second Round

Spain 1, Northern Ireland 1
Northern Ireland 0, Spain 1
Denmark 4, Albania 0
Albania 1, Denmark 0
Austria 0, Eire 0
Eire 3, Austria 2
East Germany 1, Hungary 2
Hungary 3, East Germany 3
USSR 2, Italy 0
Italy 1, USSR 1
Holland 1, Luxembourg 1
Luxembourg 2, Holland 1
Yugoslavia 0, Sweden 0
Sweden 3, Yugoslavia 2
Bulgaria 1, France 0
France 3, Bulgaria 1

Quarter-finals

Luxembourg 2, Denmark 2
Denmark 3, Luxembourg 3
Denmark 1, Luxembourg 0
Spain 5, Eire 1
Eire 0, Spain 2
France 1, Hungary 3
Hungary 2, France 1
Sweden 1, USSR 1
USSR 3, Sweden 1

Semi-finals

USSR 3, Denmark 0 (in Barcelona)
Spain 2, Hungary 1 (in Madrid)

Third Place Match (Barcelona)

Hungary 3, Denmark 1 after extra time

Final (Madrid, 21 June 1964, 120,000)

Spain (1) 2, USSR (1) 1

Spain: Iribar; Rivilla, Calleja; Fuste, Olivella, Zoco; Amancio, Pereda, Marcellino, Suarez, Lapetra.
USSR: Yachin; Chustikov, Mudrik, Voronin, Shesternjev, Anitchkin; Chislenko, Ivanov, Ponedelnik, Kornaev, Khusainov.
Scorers: Pereda, Marcellino for Spain; Khusainov for USSR.

EUROPEAN CHAMPIONSHIP 1966–68

Group 1
Eire 0, Spain 0
Eire 2, Turkey 1
Spain 2, Eire 0
Turkey 0, Spain 0
Turkey 2, Eire 1
Eire 0, Czechoslovakia 2
Spain 2, Turkey 0
Czechoslovakia 1, Spain 0
Spain 2, Czechoslovakia 1
Czechoslovakia 3, Turkey 0
Turkey 0, Czechoslovakia 0
Czechoslovakia 1, Eire 2

Group 2
Norway 0, Bulgaria 0
Portugal 1, Sweden 2
Bulgaria 4, Norway 2
Sweden 1, Portugal 1
Norway 1, Portugal 2
Sweden 0, Bulgaria 2
Norway 3, Sweden 1
Sweden 5, Norway 2
Bulgaria 3, Sweden 0
Portugal 2, Norway 1
Bulgaria 1, Portugal 0
Portugal 0, Bulgaria 0

Group 3
Finland 0, Austria 0
Austria 2, Finland 1
Greece 2, Finland 1
Greece 4, Austria 1
Finland 1, Greece 1
Austria 1, USSR 0
USSR 4, Austria 3
Greece 0, USSR 1
USSR 2, Finland 0
Austria 1, Greece 1
Finland 2, USSR 5
USSR 4, Greece 0

Group 4
Albania 0, Yugoslavia 2
West Germany 6, Albania 0
Yugoslavia 1, West Germany 0
West Germany 3, Yugoslavia 1
Yugoslavia 4, Albania 0
Albania 0, West Germany 0

Group 5
Holland 2, Hungary 2
Hungary 6, Denmark 0
Holland 2, Denmark 0
East Germany 4, Holland 3
Hungary 2, Holland 1
Denmark 0, Hungary 2
Denmark 1, East Germany 1
Holland 1, East Germany 0
Hungary 3, East Germany 1
Denmark 3, Holland 2
East Germany 3, Denmark 2
East Germany 1, Hungary 0

Group 6
Cyprus 1, Romania 5
Romania 4, Switzerland 2
Italy 3, Romania 1
Cyprus 0, Italy 2
Romania 7, Cyprus 0

Switzerland 7, Romania 1
Italy 5, Cyprus 0
Switzerland 5, Cyprus 0
Switzerland 2, Italy 2
Italy 4, Switzerland 0
Cyprus 2, Switzerland 1
Romania 0, Italy 1

Group 7
Poland 4, Luxembourg 0
France 2, Poland 1
Luxembourg 0, France 3
Luxembourg 0, Bulgaria 5
Luxembourg 0, Poland 0
Poland 3, Belgium 1
Belgium 2, France 1
Poland 1, France 4
Belgium 2, Poland 4
France 1, Belgium 1
Belgium 3, Luxembourg 0
France 3, Luxembourg 1

Group 8
Northern Ireland 0, England 2
Wales 1, Scotland 1
England 5, Wales 1
Scotland 2, Northern Ireland 1
Northern Ireland 0 Wales 0
England 2, Scotland 3
Wales 0, England 3
Northern Ireland 1, Scotland 0
England 2, Northern Ireland 0
Scotland 3, Wales 2
Scotland 1, England 1
Wales 2, Northern Ireland 0

Quarter-finals
England 1, Spain 0
Spain 1, England 2
Bulgaria 3, Italy 2
Italy, 2, Bulgaria 0
France 1, Yugoslavia 1
Yugoslavia 5, France 1
Hungary 2, USSR 0
USSR 3, Hungary 0

Semi-finals
Yugoslavia 1, England 0 (in Florence)
Italy 0, USSR 0 (Italy won toss) (in Naples)

Third Place Match (Rome)
England 2, USSR 0

Final (Rome, 8 June 1968, 60,000)
Italy (0) 1, Yugoslavia (1) 1
Italy: Zoff; Burgnich, Facchetti; Ferrini, Guarneri,
Castano; Domenghini, Juliano, Anastasi, Lodetti,
Prati.
Yugoslavia: Pantelic; Fazlagic, Damjanovic; Pavlovic,
Paunovic, Holcer; Petkovic, Acimovic, Musemic,
Trivic, Dzajic.
Scorers: Domenghini for Italy; Dzajic for Yugoslavia.

Final Replay (Rome, 10 June 1968, 75,000)
Italy (2) 2, Yugoslavia (0) 0
Italy: Zoff; Burgnich, Facchetti; Rosato, Guarneri,
Salvadore; Domenghini, Mazzola, Anastasi, De Sisti,
Riva.
Yugoslavia: Pantelic; Fazlagic, Damjanovic, Pavlovic,
Paunovic, Holcer; Hosic, Acimovic, Musemic, Trivic,
Dzajic.
Scorers: Riva, Anastasi for Italy.

EUROPEAN CHAMPIONSHIP 1970–72

Group 1

Czechoslovakia 1, Finland 1
Romania 3, Finland 0
Wales 0, Romania 0
Wales 1, Czechoslovakia 3
Finland 0, Wales 1
Czechoslovakia 1, Romania 0
Finland 0, Czechoslovakia 4
Finland 0, Romania 4
Wales 3, Finland 0
Czechoslovakia 1, Wales 0
Romania 2, Czechoslovakia 1
Romania 2, Wales 0

Group 2

Norway 1, Hungary 3
France 3, Norway 1
Bulgaria 1, Norway 1
Hungary 1, France 1
Bulgaria 3, Hungary 0
Norway 1, Bulgaria 4
Norway 1, France 3
Hungary 2, Bulgaria 0
France 0, Hungary 2
Hungary 4, Norway 0
France 2, Bulgaria 1
Bulgaria 2, France 1

Group 3

Greece 0, Switzerland 1
Malta 1, Switzerland 2
Malta 0, England 1
England 3, Greece 0
Switzerland 5, Malta 0
England 5, Malta 0
Malta 1, Greece 1
Switzerland 1, Greece 0
Greece 2, Malta 0
Switzerland 2, England 3
England 1, Switzerland 1
Greece 0, England 2

Group 4

Spain 3, Northern Ireland 0
Cyprus 0, Northern Ireland 3
Northern Ireland 5, Cyprus 0
Cyprus 1, USSR 3
Cyprus 0, Spain 2
USSR 2, Spain 1
USSR 6, Cyprus 1
USSR 1, Northern Ireland 0
Northern Ireland 1, USSR 1
Spain 0, USSR 0
Spain 7, Cyprus 0
Northern Ireland 1, Spain 1

Group 5

Denmark 0, Portugal 1
Scotland 1, Denmark 0
Belgium 2, Denmark 0
Belgium 3, Scotland 0
Belgium 3, Portugal 0
Portugal 2, Scotland 0
Denmark 1, Scotland 0
Portugal 5, Denmark 0
Denmark 1, Belgium 2
Scotland 2, Portugal 1
Scotland 1, Belgium 0
Portugal 1, Belgium 1

Group 6

Eire 1, Sweden 1
Sweden 1, Eire 0
Austria 1, Italy 2
Italy 3, Eire 0
Eire 1, Italy 2
Eire 1, Austria 4
Sweden 1, Austria 0
Sweden 0, Italy 0
Austria 1, Sweden 0
Italy 3, Sweden 0
Austria 6, Eire 0
Italy 2, Austria 2

Group 7

Holland 1, Yugoslavia 1
East Germany 1, Holland 0
Luxembourg 0, East Germany 5
Yugoslavia 2, Holland 0
East Germany 2, Luxembourg 1
Luxembourg 0, Yugoslavia 2
Holland 6, Luxembourg 0
East Germany 1, Yugoslavia 2
Holland 3, East Germany 2
Yugoslavia 0, East Germany 0
Yugoslavia 0, Luxembourg 0
Luxembourg 0, Holland 8

Group 8

Poland 3, Albania 0
West Germany 1, Turkey 1
Turkey 2, Albania 1
Albania 0, West Germany 1
Turkey 0, West Germany 3
Albania 1, Poland 1
West Germany 2, Albania 0
Poland 5, Turkey 1
Poland 1, West Germany 3
Albania 3, Turkey 0
West Germany 0, Poland 0
Turkey 1, Poland 0

Quarter-finals

England 1, West Germany 3
Italy 0, Belgium 0
Hungary 1, Romania 1
Yugoslavia 0, USSR 0
West Germany 0, England 0
Belgium 2, Italy 1
USSR 3, Yugoslavia 0
Romania 2, Hungary 2
Play-off: Hungary 2, Romania 1

Semi-finals

USSR 1, Hungary 0 (in Brussels)
West Germany 2, Belgium 1 (in Antwerp)

Third Place Match (Liège)

Belgium 2, Hungary 1

Final (Brussels, 18 June 1972, 43,437)

West Germany (1) 3, USSR (0) 0

West Germany: Maier; Hottges, Schwarzenbeck, Beckenbauer, Breitner, Hoeness, Wimmer, Netzer, Heynckes, Müller, Kremers.
USSR: Rudakov; Dzodzuashvili, Khurtsilava, Kaplichny, Istomin, Troshkin, Kolotov, Baidachni, Konkov (Dolmatov), Banishevski (Kozinkievits), Onishenko.
Scorers: Müller 2, Wimmer for West Germany.

EUROPEAN CHAMPIONSHIP 1974–76

Group 1

England 3, Czechoslovakia 0
England 0, Portugal 0
England 5, Cyprus 0
Czechoslovakia 4, Cyprus 0
Czechoslovakia 5, Portugal 0

Cyprus 0, England 1
Cyprus 0, Portugal 2
Czechoslovakia 2, England 1
Portugal 1, Czechoslovakia 1
Portugal 1, England 1
Cyprus 0, Czechoslovakia 3
Portugal 1, Cyprus 0

Group 2

Austria 2, Wales 1
Luxembourg 2, Hungary 4
Wales 2, Hungary 0
Wales 5, Luxembourg 0
Luxembourg 1, Austria 2
Austria 0, Hungary 0
Hungary 1, Wales 2
Luxembourg 1, Wales 3
Hungary 2, Austria 1
Austria 6, Luxembourg 2
Hungary 8, Luxembourg 1
Wales 1, Austria 0

Group 3

Norway 2, Northern Ireland 1
Yugoslavia 3, Norway 1
Sweden 0, Northern Ireland 2
Northern Ireland 1, Yugoslavia 0
Sweden 1, Yugoslavia 2
Norway 1, Yugoslavia 3
Sweden 3, Norway 1
Norway 0, Sweden 2
Northern Ireland 1, Sweden 2
Yugoslavia 3, Sweden 0
Northern Ireland 3, Norway 0
Yugoslavia 1, Northern Ireland 0

Group 4

Denmark 1, Spain 2
Denmark 0, Romania 0
Scotland 1, Spain 2
Spain 1, Scotland 1
Spain 1, Romania 1
Romania 6, Denmark 1
Romania 1, Scotland 1
Denmark 0, Scotland 1
Spain 2, Denmark 0
Scotland 3, Denmark 1
Romania 2, Spain 2
Scotland 1, Romania 1

Group 5

Finland 1, Poland 2
Finland 1, Holland 3
Poland 3, Finland 0
Holland 3, Italy 1
Italy 0, Poland 0
Finland 0, Italy 1
Holland 4, Finland 1
Poland 4, Holland 1
Italy 0, Finland 0
Holland 3, Poland 0
Poland 0, Italy 0
Italy 1, Holland 0

Group 6

Eire 3, USSR 0
Turkey 1, Eire 1
Turkey 2, Switzerland 1
USSR 3, Turkey 0
Switzerland 1, Turkey 1
Eire 2, Switzerland 1
USSR 2, Eire 1
Switzerland 1, Eire 0
Switzerland 0, USSR 1
Eire 4, Turkey 0
USSR 4, Switzerland 1
Turkey 1, USSR 0

Group 7

Iceland 0, Belgium 2
East Germany 1, Iceland 1
Belgium 2, France 1
France 2, East Germany 2
East Germany 0, Belgium 0
Iceland 0, France 0
Iceland 2, East Germany 1
France 3, Iceland 0
Belgium 1, Iceland 0
Belgium 1, East Germany 2
East Germany 2, France 1
France 0, Belgium 0

Group 8

Bulgaria 3, Greece 3
Greece 2, West Germany 2
Greece 2, Bulgaria 1
Malta 0, West Germany 1
Malta 2, Greece 0
Bulgaria 1, West Germany 1
Greece 4, Malta 0
Bulgaria 5, Malta 0
West Germany 1, Greece 1
West Germany 1, Bulgaria 0
Malta 0, Bulgaria 2
West Germany 8, Malta 0

Quarter-finals

Spain 1, West Germany 1
Yugoslavia 2, Wales 0
Czechoslovakia 2, USSR 0
Holland 5, Belgium 0
West Germany 2, Spain 0
USSR 2, Czechoslovakia 2
Wales 1, Yugoslavia 1
Belgium 1, Holland 2

Semi-finals

Czechoslovakia 3, Holland 1 after extra time (in Zagreb)
West Germany 4, Yugoslavia 2 after extra time (in Belgrade)

Third Place Match (Zagreb)

Holland 3, Yugoslavia 2 after extra time

Final (Belgrade, 20 June 1976, 45,000)

Czechoslovakia (2) 2, West Germany (1) 2 (aet)
(*Czechoslovakia won 5-3 on penalties*)
Czechoslovakia: Viktor; Dobias (Vesely F), Pivarnik, Ondrus, Capkovic, Gogh, Moder, Panenka, Svehlic (Jurkemik), Masny, Nehoda.
West Germany: Maier; Vogts, Beckenbauer, Schwarzenbeck, Dietz, Bonhof, Wimmer (Flohe), Müller D, Beer (Bongartz), Hoeness, Holzenbein.
Scorers: Svehlic, Dobias for Czechoslovakia; Müller, Holzenbein for West Germany.

EUROPEAN CHAMPIONSHIP 1978–80

Group 1

Denmark 3, Eire 3
Denmark 3, England 4
Eire 0, Northern Ireland 0
Denmark 2, Bulgaria 2
Eire 1, England 1
Northern Ireland 2, Denmark 1
Bulgaria 0, Northern Ireland 2
England 4, Northern Ireland 0
Northern Ireland 2, Bulgaria 0
Eire 2, Denmark 0
Bulgaria 1, Eire 0
Denmark 4, Northern Ireland 0
Bulgaria 0, England 3
England 1, Denmark 0

Eire 3, Bulgaria 0
Northern Ireland 1, England 5
Bulgaria 3, Denmark 0
Northern Ireland 1, Eire 0
England 2, Bulgaria 0
England 2, Eire 0

Group 2

Norway 0, Austria 2
Belgium 1, Norway 1
Austria 3, Scotland 2
Portugal 1, Belgium 1
Scotland 3, Norway 2
Austria 1, Portugal 2
Portugal 1, Scotland 0
Belgium 1, Austria 1
Austria 0, Belgium 0
Norway 0, Portugal 1
Norway 0, Scotland 4
Austria 4, Norway 0
Norway 1, Belgium 2
Belgium 2, Portugal 0
Scotland 1, Austria 1
Portugal 3, Norway 1
Belgium 2, Scotland 0
Portugal 1, Austria 2
Scotland 1, Belgium 3
Scotland 4, Portugal 1

Group 3

Yugoslavia 1, Spain 2
Romania 3, Yugoslavia 2
Spain 1, Romania 0
Spain 5, Cyprus 0
Cyprus 0, Yugoslavia 3
Romania 2, Spain 2
Cyprus 1, Romania 1
Spain 0, Yugoslavia 1
Yugoslavia 2, Romania 1
Yugoslavia 5, Cyprus 0
Romania 2, Cyprus 0
Cyprus 1, Spain 3

Group 4

Iceland 0, Poland 2
Holland 3, Iceland 0
East Germany 3, Iceland 1
Switzerland 1, Holland 3
Holland 3, East Germany 0
Poland 2, Switzerland 0
Holland 3, Switzerland 0
East Germany 2, Poland 1
Poland 2, Holland 0
Switzerland 0, East Germany 2
Switzerland 2, Iceland 0
Iceland 1, Switzerland 2
Iceland 0, Holland 4
Switzerland 0, Poland 2
Iceland 0, East Germany 3
Poland 1, East Germany 1
Poland 2, Iceland 0
East Germany 5, Switzerland 2
Holland 1, Portugal 1
East Germany 2, Holland 3

Group 5

France 2, Sweden 2
Sweden 1, Czechoslovakia 3
Luxembourg 1, France 3
France 3, Luxembourg 0
Czechoslovakia 2, France 0
Luxembourg 0, Czechoslovakia 3
Sweden 3, Luxembourg 0
Sweden 1, France 3
Czechoslovakia 4, Sweden 1
Luxembourg 1, Sweden 1
France 2, Czechoslovakia 0
Czechoslovakia 4, Luxembourg 0

Group 6

Finland 3, Greece 0
Finland 2, Hungary 1
USSR 2, Greece 0
Hungary 2, USSR 0
Greece 8, Finland 1
Greece 4, Hungary 1
Hungary 0, Greece 0
USSR 2, Hungary 2
Finland 1, USSR 1
Greece 1, USSR 0
Hungary 3, Finland 1
USSR 2, Finland 2

Group 7

Wales 7, Malta 0
Wales 1, Turkey 0
Malta 0, West Germany 0
Turkey 2, Malta 1
Turkey 0, West Germany 0
Wales 0, West Germany 2
Malta 0, Wales 2
West Germany 5, Wales 1
Malta 1, Turkey 2
Turkey 1, Wales 0
West Germany 2, Turkey 0
West Germany 8, Malta 0

Final Tournament
Group 1

West Germany 1, Czechoslovakia 0
Greece 0, Holland 1
West Germany 3, Holland 2
Czechoslovakia 3, Greece 1
Czechoslovakia 1, Holland 1
West Germany 0, Greece 0

Group 2

Belgium 1, England 1
Spain 0, Italy 0
Spain 1, Belgium 2
Italy 1, England 0
England 2, Spain 1
Italy 0, Belgium 0

Third Place Match (Naples)

Italy 1, Czechoslovakia 1 after extra time
(*Czechoslovakia won 9-8 on penalties*)

Final (Rome, 22 June 1980, 47,864)

West Germany (1) 2, Belgium (0) 1

West Germany: Schumacher; Briegel, Forster K,
Dietz, Schuster, Rummenigge, Hrubesch, Müller,
Aloffs, Stielike, Kaltz.
Belgium: Pfaff; Gerets, Millecamps, Meeuws,
Renquin, Cools, Van der Eycken, Van Moer,
Mommens, Van der Elst, Ceulemans.
Scorers: Hrubesch 2 for West Germany; Van der
Eycken for Belgium.

EUROPEAN CHAMPIONSHIP 1982–84

Group 1

Belgium 3, Switzerland 0
Scotland 2, East Germany 0
Switzerland 2, Scotland 0
Belgium 3, Scotland 2
East Germany 1, Belgium 2
Scotland 2, Switzerland 2
Belgium 2, East Germany 1
Switzerland 0, East Germany 0
East Germany 3, Switzerland 0
Scotland 1, Belgium 1
Switzerland 3, Belgium 1
East Germany 2, Scotland 1

Group 2

Finland 2, Poland 3
Finland 0, Portugal 2
Portugal 2, Poland 1
USSR 2, Finland 0
Poland 1, Finland 1
USSR 5, Portugal 0
Poland 1, USSR 1
Finland 0, USSR 0
Portugal 5, Finland 0
USSR 2, Poland 0
Poland 0, Portugal 1
Portugal 1, USSR 0

Group 3

Denmark 2, England 2
Luxembourg 0, Greece 2
Luxembourg 1, Denmark 2
Greece 0, England 3
England 9, Luxembourg 0
Luxembourg 2, Hungary 6
England 0, Greece 0
Hungary 6, Luxembourg 2
Denmark 1, Greece 0
England 2, Hungary 0
Hungary 2, Greece 3
Denmark 3, Hungary 1
England 0, Denmark 1
Denmark 6, Luxembourg 0
Hungary 0, England 3
Hungary 1, Denmark 0
Greece 0, Denmark 2
Luxembourg 0, England 4
Greece 2, Hungary 2
Greece 1, Luxembourg 0

Group 4

Wales 1, Norway 0
Norway 3, Yugoslavia 1
Bulgaria 2, Norway 2
Bulgaria 0, Yugoslavia 1
Yugoslavia 4, Wales 4
Wales 1, Bulgaria 0
Norway 1, Bulgaria 2
Norway 0, Wales 0
Yugoslavia 2, Norway 1
Bulgaria 1, Wales 0
Wales 1, Yugoslavia 1
Yugoslavia 3, Bulgaria 2

Group 5

Romania 3, Cyprus 1
Romania 2, Sweden 0
Czechoslovakia 2, Sweden 2
Cyprus 0, Sweden 1
Italy 2, Czechoslovakia 2
Italy 0, Romania 0
Cyprus 1, Italy 1
Cyprus 1, Czechoslovakia 1
Czechoslovakia 6, Cyprus 0
Romania 1, Italy 0
Sweden 5, Cyprus 0
Romania 0, Czechoslovakia 1
Sweden 2, Italy 0
Sweden 0, Romania 1
Sweden 1, Czechoslovakia 0
Italy 0, Sweden 3
Cyprus 0, Romania 1
Czechoslovakia 2, Italy 0
Czechoslovakia 1, Romania 1
Italy 3, Cyprus 1

Group 6

Austria 5, Albania 0
Austria 2, Northern Ireland 0
Turkey 1, Albania 0
Austria 4, Turkey 0
Northern Ireland 1, West Germany 0
Albania 0, Northern Ireland 0
Albania 1, West Germany 2
Northern Ireland 2, Turkey 1
Turkey 0, West Germany 3
Austria 0, West Germany 0
Northern Ireland 1, Albania 0
Albania 1, Turkey 1
Albania 1, Austria 2
Northern Ireland 3, Austria 1
West Germany 3, Austria 0
Turkey 1, Northern Ireland 0
West Germany 5, Turkey 1
Turkey 3, Austria 1
West Germany 0, Northern Ireland 1
West Germany 2, Albania 1

Group 7

Malta 2, Iceland 1
Iceland 1, Holland 1
Holland 2, Eire 1
Eire 2, Iceland 0
Spain 1, Iceland 0
Eire 3, Spain 3
Malta 0, Holland 6
Spain 1, Holland 0
Malta 0, Eire 1
Spain 2, Eire 0
Malta 2, Spain 3
Iceland 0, Spain 1
Iceland 1, Malta 0
Holland 3, Iceland 0
Iceland 0, Eire 3
Eire 2, Holland 3
Holland 2, Spain 1
Eire 8, Malta 0
Holland 5, Malta 0
Spain 12, Malta 1

Final Tournament

Group 1

France 1, Denmark 0
Belgium 2, Yugoslavia 0
France 5, Belgium 0
Denmark 5, Yugoslavia 0
France 3, Yugoslavia 2
Denmark 3, Belgium 2

Group 2

West Germany 0, Portugal 0
Spain 1, Romania 1
Spain 1, Portugal 1
West Germany 2, Romania 1
West Germany 0, Spain 1
Portugal 1, Romania 0

Semi-finals

France 3, Portugal 2
Denmark 1, Spain 1 after extra time
(*Spain won 5-4 on penalties*)

Final (Paris, 27 June 1984, 48,000)

France (0) 2, Spain (0) 0

France: Bats; Battiston (Amoros), Le Roux, Bossis, Domergue, Giresse, Platini, Tigana, Fernandez, Lacombe (Genghini), Bellone.
Spain: Arconada; Urquiaga, Salva (Roberto), Gallego, Camacho, Francisco, Julio Alberto (Sarabia), Senor, Victor, Carrasco, Santillana.
Scorers: Platini, Bellone for France.

EUROPEAN CHAMPIONSHIP 1986–88

Group 1

Romania 4, Austria 0
Austria 3, Albania 0
Spain 1, Romania 0
Albania 1, Spain 2
Romania 5, Albania 1

Austria 2, Spain 3
Albania 0, Austria 1
Romania 3, Spain 1
Spain 2, Austria 0
Albania 0, Romania 1
Spain 5, Albania 0
Austria 0, Romania 0

Group 2

Sweden 2, Switzerland 0
Portugal 1, Sweden 1
Switzerland 1, Portugal 1
Italy 3, Switzerland 2
Malta 0, Sweden 5
Malta 0, Italy 2
Italy 5, Malta 0
Portugal 0, Italy 1
Portugal 2, Malta 2
Switzerland 4, Malta 1
Sweden 1, Malta 0
Sweden 1, Italy 0
Switzerland 1, Sweden 1
Sweden 0, Portugal 1
Switzerland 0, Italy 0
Portugal 0, Switzerland 0
Italy 2, Sweden 1
Malta 1, Switzerland 1
Italy 3, Portugal 0
Malta 0, Portugal 1

Group 3

Iceland 0, France 0
Iceland 1, USSR 1
Norway 0, East Germany 0
France 0, USSR 2
USSR 4, Norway 0
East Germany 2, Iceland 0
East Germany 0, France 0
France 2, Iceland 0
USSR 2, East Germany 0
Norway 0, USSR 1
Iceland 0, East Germany 6
Norway 2, France 0
USSR 1, France 1
Iceland 2, Norway 1
Norway 0, Iceland 1
East Germany 1, USSR 1
France 1, Norway 1
USSR 2, Iceland 0
East Germany 3, Norway 1
France 0, East Germany 1

Group 4

England 3, Northern Ireland 0
Yugoslavia 4, Turkey 0
England 2, Yugoslavia 0
Turkey 0, Northern Ireland 0
Northern Ireland 0, England 2
Northern Ireland 1, Yugoslavia 2
Turkey 0, England 0
Yugoslavia 3, Northern Ireland 0
England 8, Turkey 0
Yugoslavia 1, England 4
Northern Ireland 1, Turkey 0
Turkey 2, Yugoslavia 3

Group 5

Hungary 0, Holland 1
Poland 2, Greece 1
Greece 2, Hungary 1
Holland 0, Poland 0
Cyprus 2, Greece 4
Cyprus 0, Holland 2
Greece 3, Cyprus 1
Cyprus 0, Hungary 1
Holland 1, Greece 1
Poland 0, Cyprus 0
Greece 1, Poland 0

Holland 2, Hungary 0
Hungary 5, Poland 3
Poland 3, Hungary 2
Hungary 3, Greece 0
Poland 0, Holland 2
Holland 8, Cyprus 0
Cyprus 0, Poland 1
Hungary 1, Cyprus 0
Holland 4, Cyprus 0
Greece 0, Holland 3

Group 6

Finland 1, Wales 1
Czechoslovakia 3, Finland 0
Denmark 1, Finland 0
Czechoslovakia 0, Denmark 0
Wales 4, Finland 0
Finland 0, Denmark 1
Wales 1, Czechoslovakia 0
Denmark 1, Czechoslovakia 1
Wales 1, Denmark 0
Finland 3, Czechoslovakia 0
Denmark 1, Wales 0
Czechoslovakia 2, Wales 0

Group 7

Scotland 0, Bulgaria 0
Belgium 2, Eire 2
Luxembourg 0, Belgium 6
Eire 0, Scotland 0
Scotland 3, Luxembourg 0
Belgium 1, Bulgaria 1
Scotland 0, Eire 1
Belgium 4, Scotland 1
Bulgaria 2, Eire 1
Eire 0, Belgium 0
Luxembourg 1, Bulgaria 4
Bulgaria 3, Luxembourg 0
Luxembourg 0, Eire 2
Eire 2, Luxembourg 1
Bulgaria 2, Belgium 0
Scotland 2, Belgium 0
Eire 2, Bulgaria 0
Belgium 3, Luxembourg 0
Bulgaria 0, Scotland 1
Luxembourg 0, Scotland 0

Final Tournament

Group 1

West Germany 1, Italy 1
Spain 3, Denmark 2
West Germany 2, Denmark 0
Italy 1, Spain 0
West Germany 2, Spain 0
Italy 2, Denmark 0

Group 2

England 0, Eire 1
Holland 0, USSR 1
Holland 3, England 1
Eire 1, USSR 1
England 1, USSR 3
Holland 1, Eire 0

Semi-finals

West Germany 1, Holland 2
USSR 2, Italy 0

Final (Munich, 25 June 1988, 72,308)

Holland (1) 2, USSR (0) 0

Holland: Van Breukelen; Van Aerle, Van Tiggelen, Wouters, Koeman R, Rijkaard, Vanenburg, Gullit, Van Basten, Muhren, Koeman E.
USSR: Dassayev; Khidiatulin, Aleinikov, Mikhailichenko, Litovchenko, Demianenko, Belanov, Gotsmanov (Baltacha 68), Protasov (Pasulko 71), Zavarov, Rats.
Scorers: Gullit, Van Basten for Holland.

EUROPEAN CHAMPIONSHIP 1990–92

Group 1
Iceland 2, Albania 0
Iceland 1, France 2
Czechoslovakia 1, Iceland 0
Spain 2, Iceland 1
France 2, Czechoslovakia 1
Czechoslovakia 3, Spain 2
Albania 0, France 1
Spain 9, Albania 0
France 3, Spain 1
France 5, Albania 0
Albania 0, Czechoslovakia 2
Albania 1, Iceland 0
Iceland 0, Czechoslovakia 1
Czechoslovakia 1, France 2
Iceland 2, Spain 0
Spain 1, France 2
Czechoslovakia 2, Albania 1
Spain 2, Czechoslovakia 1
France 3, Iceland 1
Albania v Spain not played

Group 2
Switzerland 2, Bulgaria 0
Scotland 2, Romania 1
Romania 0, Bulgaria 3
Scotland 2, Switzerland 1
Bulgaria 1, Scotland 1
San Marino 0, Switzerland 4
Romania 6, San Marino 0
Scotland 1, Bulgaria 1
San Marino 1, Romania 3
Switzerland 0, Romania 0
Bulgaria 2, Switzerland 3
San Marino 0, Scotland 2
San Marino 0, Bulgaria 3
Switzerland 7, San Marino 0
Switzerland 2, Scotland 2
Bulgaria 4, San Marino 0
Romania 1, Scotland 0
Romania 1, Switzerland 0
Scotland 4, San Marino 0
Bulgaria 1, Romania 1

Group 3
USSR 2, Norway 0
Norway 0, Hungary 0
Hungary 1, Italy 1
Hungary 4, Cyprus 2
Italy 0, USSR 0
Cyprus 0, Norway 3
Cyprus 0, Italy 4
Cyprus 0, Hungary 2
Hungary 0, USSR 1
Italy 3, Hungary 1
Norway 3, Cyprus 0
USSR 4, Cyprus 0
Norway 2, Italy 1
Norway 0, USSR 1
USSR 2, Hungary 2
USSR 0, Italy 0
Hungary 0, Norway 0
Italy 1, Norway 1
Cyprus 0, USSR 3
Italy 2, Cyprus 0

Group 4
Northern Ireland 0, Yugoslavia 2
Faeroes 1, Austria 0
Denmark 4, Faeroes 1
Northern Ireland 1, Denmark 1
Yugoslavia 4, Austria 1
Denmark 0, Yugoslavia 2
Austria 0, Northern Ireland 0

Yugoslavia 4, Northern Ireland 1
Yugoslavia 1, Denmark 2
Northern Ireland 1, Faeroes 1
Yugoslavia 7, Faeroes 0
Austria 3, Faeroes 0
Denmark 2, Austria 1
Faeroes 0, Northern Ireland 5
Faeroes 0, Denmark 4
Austria 0, Denmark 3
Faeroes 0, Yugoslavia 2
Northern Ireland 2, Austria 1
Denmark 2, Northern Ireland 1
Austria 0, Yugoslavia 2

Group 5
Wales 3, Belgium 1
Luxembourg 2, Germany 3
Luxembourg 0, Wales 1
Belgium 3, Luxembourg 0
Belgium 1, Wales 1
Germany 1, Belgium 0
Wales 1, Germany 0
Luxembourg 0, Belgium 2
Germany 4, Wales 1
Wales 1, Luxembourg 0
Belgium 0, Germany 1
Germany 4, Luxembourg 0

Group 6
Finland 0, Portugal 0
Portugal 1, Holland 0
Greece 4, Malta 0
Holland 2, Greece 0
Malta 1, Finland 1
Malta 0, Holland 8
Greece 3, Portugal 2
Malta 0, Portugal 1
Portugal 5, Malta 0
Holland 1, Malta 0
Holland 2, Finland 0
Finland 2, Malta 0
Finland 1, Holland 1
Portugal 1, Finland 0
Finland 1, Greece 1
Holland 1, Portugal 0
Greece 2, Finland 0
Portugal 1, Greece 0
Greece 0, Holland 2
Malta 1, Greece 1

Group 7
England 2, Poland 0
Eire 5, Turkey 0
Eire 1, England 1
Turkey 0, Poland 1
England 1, Eire 1
Poland 3, Turkey 0
Eire 0, Poland 0
Turkey 0, England 1
Poland 3, Eire 3
England 1, Turkey 0
Turkey 1, Eire 3
Poland 1, England 1

Final Tournament
Group 1
Sweden 1, France 1
Denmark 0, England 0
England 0, France 0
Sweden 1, Denmark 0
Denmark 2, France 1
Sweden 2, England 1

Group 2
CIS (formerly USSR) 1, Germany 1
Holland 1, Scotland 0

Holland 0, CIS 0
Scotland 0, Germany 2
Scotland 3, CIS 0
Holland 3, Germany 1

Semi-finals
Sweden 2, Germany 3
Denmark 2, Holland 2 aet
Denmark won 5-4 on penalties

Final (in Gothenburg, 26 June 1992, 37,800)
Denmark (1) 2, Germany (0) 0
Denmark: Schmeichel; Sivebaek (Christiansen), Nielsen K, Olsen L, Christofte, Jensen, Povlsen, Laudrup, Piechnik, Larsen, Vilfort.
Germany: Illgner; Reuter, Brehme, Kohler, Buchwald, Hässler, Riedle, Helmer, Sammer (Doll), Effenberg (Thon), Klinsmann.
Scorers: Jensen, Vilfort for Denmark.

THE WORLD CUP 1930–90

Year	Winners		Runners-up		Venue	Attendance	Referee
1930	Uruguay	4	Argentina	2	Montevideo	90,000	Langenus (B)
1934	Italy	2	Czechoslovakia	1	Rome	50,000	Eklind (Se)
	(after extra time)						
1938	Italy	4	Hungary	2	Paris	45,000	Capdeville (F)
1950	Uruguay	2	Brazil	1	Rio de Janeiro	199,854	Reader (E)
1954	West Germany	3	Hungary	2	Berne	60,000	Ling (E)
1958	Brazil	5	Sweden	2	Stockholm	49,737	Guigue (F)
1962	Brazil	3	Czechoslovakia	1	Santiago	68,679	Latychev (USSR)
1966	England	4	West Germany	2	Wembley	93,802	Dienst (Sw)
	(after extra time)						
1970	Brazil	4	Italy	1	Mexico City	107,412	Glockner (EG)
1974	West Germany	2	Holland	1	Munich	77,833	Taylor (E)
1978	Argentina	3	Holland	1	Buenos Aires	77,000	Gonella (I)
	(after extra time)						
1982	Italy	3	West Germany	1	Madrid	90,080	Coelho (Br)
1986	Argentina	3	West Germany	2	Mexico City	114,580	Filho (Br)
1990	West Germany	1	Argentina	0	Rome	73,603	Codesal (Mex)

GOALSCORING AND ATTENDANCES IN WORLD CUP FINAL ROUNDS

	Matches	Goals (avge)	Attendance (avge)
1930, Uruguay	18	70 (3.8)	434,500 (24,138)
1934, Italy	17	70 (4.1)	395,000 (23,235)
1938, France	18	84 (4.6)	483,000 (26,833)
1950, Brazil	22	88 (4.0)	1,337,000 (60,772)
1954, Switzerland	26	140 (5.3)	943,000 (36,270)
1958, Sweden	35	126 (3.6)	868,000 (24,800)
1962, Chile	32	89 (2.7)	776,000 (24,250)
1966, England	32	89 (2.7)	1,614,677 (50,458)
1970, Mexico	32	95 (2.9)	1,673,975 (52,311)
1974, West Germany	38	97 (2.5)	1,774,022 (46,684)
1978, Argentina	38	102 (2.6)	1,610,215 (42,374)
1982, Spain	52	146 (2.8)	1,766,277 (33,967)
1986, Mexico	52	132 (2.5)	2,199,941 (42,307)
1990, Italy	52	115 (2.21)	2,510,686* (48,282)

1994 FIFA WORLD CUP

WORLD CUP VENUES USA 1994

Giants Stadium
New York/New Jersey
East Rutherford, New Jersey
Capacity: 76,891
Record attendance: 77,691 New York Cosmos v Fort Lauderdale 14 August 1977
Average July temperature 29.7°C

Robert F Kennedy Memorial Stadium
Washington D.C.
Washington (near Capitol)
Capacity: 56,500
Record attendance: 56,500 (for American football team Washington Redskins)
Average July temperature 31°C

The Citrus Bowl
Orlando, Florida
Orlando, mile west of town centre
Capacity: 70,188
Record attendance: 70,000 (annual Citrus Bowl final)
Average July temperature 26.7°C

Foxboro Stadium
Boston, Massachusetts
Situated between Boston and Providence
Capacity: 61,000
Record attendance: 59,828 (for American football team New England Patriots)
Average July temperature 27.6°C

Pontiac Silverdome
Detroit, Michigan
Pontiac, Michigan
Capacity: 72,794
Record attendance: 82,000 (American football Super Bowl)
Average July temperature 28.3°C

Soldier Field
Chicago, Illinois
On Michigan Lake
Capacity: 66,814
Record attendance: 67,475 (American football team Chicago Bears)
Average July temperature 28.5°C

The Cotton Bowl
Dallas, Texas
Centre of Dallas Fair Park
Capacity: 72,000
Record attendance: 72,000 (American collegiate football)
Average July temperature 36.5°C

The Rose Bowl
Los Angeles, California
Pasadena, outside Los Angeles
Capacity: 102,083
Record attendance: 101,799 (Olympic Soccer final France
  v Brazil 11 August 1984)
Average July temperature 28.3°C

Stanford Stadium
San Francisco, California
Palo Alto, south of San Francisco
Capacity: 86,019
Record attendance: 84,059 (American football Super
  Bowl)
Average July temperature 21°C

1994 FIFA WORLD CUP FIXTURES

Group 1
 5. 9.93 Estonia v Portugal
 8. 9.93 Scotland v Switzerland
22. 9.93 Estonia v Italy
13.10.93 Italy v Scotland
13.10.93 Portugal v Switzerland
10.11.93 Portugal v Estonia
17.11.93 Italy v Portugal
17.11.93 Malta v Scotland
17.11.93 Switzerland v Estonia

Group 2
 8. 9.93 England v Poland
22. 9.93 Norway v Poland
22. 9.93 San Marino v Holland
13.10.93 Holland v England
13.10.93 Poland v Norway
27.10.93 Turkey v Poland
10.11.93 Turkey v Norway
16.11.93 San Marino v England
17.11.93 Poland v Holland

Group 3
25. 8.93 Denmark v Lithuania
 8. 9.93 Albania v Denmark
 8. 9.93 Northern Ireland v Latvia
 8. 9.93 Republic of Ireland v Lithuania
22. 9.93 Albania v Spain
13.10.93 Denmark v Northern Ireland
13.10.93 Republic of Ireland v Spain
17.11.93 Northern Ireland v Republic of Ireland
17.11.93 Spain v Denmark

Group 4
 8. 9.93 Wales v Czechoslovakia
 8. 9.93 Faeroes v Romania
13.10.93 Romania v Belgium
13.10.93 Wales v Cyprus
27.10.93 Czechoslovakia v Cyprus
17.11.93 Belgium v Czechoslovakia
17.11.93 Wales v Romania

Group 5
22. 8.93 Yugoslavia v Iceland
 8. 9.93 Hungary v CIS
 8. 9.93 Iceland v Luxembourg
 6.10.93 CIS v Yugoslavia
12.10.93 Luxembourg v Greece
27.10.93 Greece v Yugoslavia
27.10.93 Hungary v Luxembourg
17.11.93 Greece v CIS
17.11.93 Yugoslavia v Hungary

Group 6
22. 8.93 Sweden v France
25. 8.93 Austria v Finland
 8. 9.93 Bulgaria v Sweden
 8. 9.93 Finland v France
13.10.93 Bulgaria v Austria
13.10.93 France v Israel
13.10.93 Sweden v Finland
27.10.93 Israel v Austria
10.11.93 Austria v Sweden
10.11.93 Israel v Finland
17.11.93 France v Bulgaria

Group A (Argentina, Colombia, Paraguay, Peru)
 1. 8.93 Colombia v Paraguay
 1. 8.93 Peru v Argentina
 8. 8.93 Paraguay v Argentina
 8. 8.93 Peru v Colombia
15. 8.93 Colombia v Argentina
15. 8.93 Paraguay v Peru
22. 8.93 Argentina v Peru
22. 8.93 Paraguay v Colombia
29. 8.93 Argentina v Paraguay
29. 8.93 Colombia v Peru
 5. 9.93 Argentina v Colombia
 5. 9.93 Peru v Paraguay

Group B (Brazil, Uruguay, Ecuador, Bolivia, Venezuela)
18. 7.93 Ecuador v Brazil
18. 7.93 Venezuela v Bolivia
25. 7.93 Bolivia v Brazil
25. 7.93 Venezuela v Uruguay
 1. 8.93 Uruguay v Ecuador
 1. 8.93 Venezuela v Brazil
 8. 8.93 Bolivia v Uruguay
 8. 8.93 Ecuador v Venezuela
15. 8.93 Bolivia v Ecuador
15. 8.93 Uruguay v Brazil
22. 8.93 Bolivia v Venezuela
22. 8.93 Brazil v Ecuador
29. 8.93 Brazil v Bolivia
29. 8.93 Uruguay v Venezuela
 5. 9.93 Brazil v Venezuela
 5. 9.93 Ecuador v Uruguay
12. 9.93 Uruguay v Bolivia
12. 9.93 Venezuela v Ecuador
19. 9.93 Brazil v Uruguay
19. 9.93 Ecuador v Bolivia

WORLD CUP 1994

Europe

Group 1

Tallinn, 16 August 1992, 3000

Estonia (0) 0
Switzerland (2) 6 *(Chapuisat 23, 68, Bregy 29, Knup 46, Ohrel 66, Sforza 84)*
Estonia: Poom; Hepner, Kaljend, Kallaste T, Lindmaa (Veensalu 78), Kristal, Olumets, Linnunae, Kallaste R, Reim, Pustov (Kirs 64).
Switzerland: Pascolo; Egli, Geiger, Hottiger, Rothenbuhler, Bregy, Sutter B (Bonvin 79), Ohrel, Sforza, Chapuisat, Knup.

Berne, 9 September 1992, 10,000

Switzerland (1) 3 *(Knup 2, 71, Bregy 81)*
Scotland (1) 1 *(McCoist)*
Switzerland: Pascolo; Hottiger, Quentin, Egli, Geiger, Bregy (Piffaretti 89), Sutter A, Ohrel, Knup (Sutter B 86), Sforza, Chapuisat.
Scotland: Goram; Gough, Malpas, McCall, Boyd (Gallacher 75), McPherson, Durie, McAllister, McCoist, McStay, McClair (Durrant 57).

Cagliari, 14 October 1992, 34,000

Italy (0) 2 *(Roberto Baggio 83, Eranio 89)*
Switzerland (2) 2 *(Ohrel 17, Chapuisat 21)*
Italy: Marchegiani; Tassotti, Di Chiara, Eranio, Costacurta, Lanna, Lentini, Donadoni (Albertini 71), Vialli, Roberto Baggio, Evani (Bianchi 48).
Switzerland: Pascolo; Hottiger, Quentin, Egli, Geiger, Bregy, Sutter A, Ohrel (Piffaretti 56), Knup (Sutter B 89), Sforza, Chapuisat.

Ibrox, 14 October 1992, 22,583

Scotland (0) 0
Portugal (0) 0
Scotland: Goram; Malpas, Boyd, McCall, Whyte, Levein, Gallacher (McClair 33), McStay, McCoist, McAllister, Collins (Durrant 71).
Portugal: Vitor Baia; Joao Pinto I, Helder, Veloso, Fernando Couto, Oceano, Vitor Paneira, Semedo (Figo 53), Domingos, Futre, Andre.

Valletta, 25 October 1992, 8000

Malta (0) 0
Estonia (0) 0
Malta: Cluett; Gregory (Suda 78), Vella S, Galea, Brincat, Buttigieg, Busuttil, Vella R, Zerafa (Saliba 78), Laferla, Sultana.
Estonia: Poom; Kaljend, Hepner, Prins, Kallaste T, Ratnikov, Olumets, Pustov (Rayala 75), Kirs, Reim, Kallaste R.

Ibrox, 18 November 1992, 33,029

Scotland (0) 0
Italy (0) 0
Scotland: Goram; McPherson, Malpas, McStay, McLaren, Whyte, Durie (Jess 71), McAllister, McCoist, Durrant (Robertson 88), Boyd.
Italy: Pagliuca; Mannini, Di Chiara (Costacurta 7), Maldini, Baresi, Lentini, Albertini, Eranio, Bianchi, Signori (Donadoni 46), Roberto Baggio.

Berne, 18 November 1992, 14,200

Switzerland (2) 3 *(Bickel 2, Sforza 42, Chapuisat 89)*
Malta (0) 0
Switzerland: Pascolo; Hottiger, Geiger, Egli, Rothenbuhler, Bickel (Bonvin 82), Bregy, Sforza, Sutter A, Knup (Turkyilmaz 75), Chapuisat.
Malta: Cluett; Buttigieg, Buhagiar, Galea (Camilleri E 17), Vella S, Brincat, Gregory, Camilleri J, Saliba, Vella R (Scerri 75), Busuttil.

Valletta, 19 December 1992, 15,000

Malta (0) 1 *(Gregory 85)*
Italy (0) 2 *(Vialli 59, Signori 62)*
Malta: Cluett; Vella S, Buhagiar (Camilleri J 46), Galea, Brincat, Buttigieg, Busuttil, Saliba (Vella R 73), Gregory, Laferla, Scerri.
Italy: Pagliuca; Maldini, Di Chiara (Bianchi 46), Baresi, Costacurta, Eranio, Albertini, Donadoni (Simone 58), Evani, Vialli, Signori.

Valletta, 24 January 1993, 10,000

Malta (0) 0
Portugal (0) 1 *(Rui Aguas 56)*
Malta: Cluett; Vella S, Galea, Brincat, Buhagiar, Buttigieg, Vella R (Suda 75), Busuttil, Gregory, Laferla, Scerri (Degiorgio 65).
Portugal: Vitor Baia; Joao Pinto I, Veloso, Fernando Couto, Cristovao, Cruz, Vitor Paneira (Joao Pinto II 56), Samedo (Jaime Magalhaes 75), Oliveira, Rui Aguas, Figo.

Ibrox, 17 February 1993, 35,490

Scotland (1) 3 *(McCoist 15, 68, Nevin 84)*
Malta (0) 0
Scotland: Goram; McPherson (Robertson 64), Boyd, McStay, McLeich, McLaren, Nevin, McAllister (Ferguson 73), McCoist, Collins, Jess.
Malta: Cluett; Vella S, Buhagiar (Camilleri E 83), Galea, Brincat, Buttigieg, Busuttil, Saliba, Camilleri J, Laferla, Sultana (Vella R 74).

Oporto, 24 February 1993, 70,000

Portugal (0) 1 *(Couto 57)*
Italy (2) 3 *(Roberto Baggio 2, Casiraghi 24, Dino Baggio 75)*
Portugal: Vitor Baia; Joao Pinto I, Helder (Rui Barros 35), Mendes, Fernando Couto, Oceano, Semedo, Figo, Domingos, Futre, Carlos Xavier (Rui Aguas 46).
Italy: Pagliuca; Tassotti, Maldini, Di Chiara, Costacurta, Vierchowod, Fuser, Albertini, Casiraghi (Lentini 26), Roberto Baggio (Mancini 85), Signori.

Palermo, 24 March 1993, 35,000

Italy (2) 6 *(Dino Baggio 19, Signori 38, Vierchowod 48, Mancini 59, 89, Maldini 73)*
Malta (0) 1 *(Busuttil 68 (pen))*
Italy: Pagliuca (Marchegiani 80); Porrini, Maldini, Dino Baggio, Vierchowod, Baresi, Fuser, Albertini, Melli, Mancini, Signori.
Malta: Cluett; Vella S, Zerafa, Galea, Saliba, Laferla, Busuttil, Vella R, Gregory (Delia 57), Degiorgio (Suda 73), Scerri.

800

Berne, 3l March 1993, 31,200

Switzerland (1) 1 *(Chapuisat 39)*

Portugal (1) 1 *(Semedo 44)*

Switzerland: Pascolo; Hottiger, Herr, Geiger, Rothenbuhler, Ohrel, Bregy, Sforza, Sutter A, Knup (Bonvin 46), Chapuisat.
Portugal: Vitor Baia; Peixe, Oceano, Jorge Costa, Semedo (Mendes 50), Abel Xavier, Rui Costa, Sousa, Figo (Rui Barros 68), Futre, Rui Aguas.

Trieste, 14 April 1993, 33,000

Italy (1) 2 *(Roberto Baggio 21, Signori 86)*

Estonia (0) 0

Italy: Pagliuca; Porrini (Mannini 46), Di Chiara, Dino Baggio (Di Mauro 68), Vierchowod, Baresi, Fuser, Albertini, Melli, Roberto Baggio, Signori.
Estonia: Poom; Kallaste R, Lensalu, Prins, Kaljend, Kallaste T, Borisov, Kristal, Reim (Olumets 89), Ratnikov, Pustov (Rajala 83).

Valletta, 17 April 1993, 8000

Malta (0) 0

Switzerland (1) 2 *(Ohrel 31, Turkyilmaz 89)*

Malta: Cluett; Vella S, Brincat, Galea, Buhagiar, Busuttil, Buttigieg, Camilleri J (Delia 46), Saliba (Carabott 46), Laferla, Scerri.
Switzerland: Pascolo; Hottiger, Herr, Geiger, Rothenbuhler (Sylvestre 50), Henchoz, Sforza, Sutter A, Ohreil, Grassi, Bonvin (Turkyilmaz 60).

Lisbon, 28 April 1993, 28,000

Portugal (2) 5 *(Rui Barros 5, 70, Cadete 45, 72, Futre 67)*

Scotland (0) 0

Portugal: Vitor Baia; Abel Xavier, Jorge Costa, Rui Costa (Veloso 53), Fernando Couto, Oceano, Rui Barros, Sousa, Semedo, Futre, Cadete (Domingos 81).
Scotland: Goram; Gough, McInally, McPherson, McKimmie, Levein (Nevin 60), McStay, McCall, McCoist, Collins (Durrant 75), Gallacher.

Berne, 1 May 1993, 31,000

Switzerland (0) 1 *(Hottiger 55)*

Italy (0) 0

Switzerland: Pascolo; Hottiger, Geiger, Herr, Quentin, Bregy, Ohrel, Sforza, Sutter A, Knup (Grassi 76), Chapuisat.
Italy: Pagliuca; Mannini, Baresi, Vierchowod, Maldini, Fuser, Zoratto (Lentini 64), Dino Baggio, Signori, Mancini (Di Mauro 46), Roberto Baggio.

Tallinn, 12 May 1993, 14,000

Estonia (0) 0

Malta (1) 1 *(Laferla 16)*

Estonia: Poom; Kallaste R (Bragin 75), Hepner, Prins, Kaljend, Kallaste T, Borisov, Kristal, Reim, Ratnikov (Olumets 20), Pustov.
Malta: Cluett; Vella S, Buhagiar, Saliba, Brincat, Buttigieg, Gregory (Delia 77), Vella R, Carabott (Sultana 46), Laferla, Camilleri J.

Tallinn, 19 May 1993, 5100

Estonia (0) 0

Scotland (1) 3 *(Gallacher 43, Collins 59, Booth 73)*

Estonia: Poom; Kallaste R, Lensalu, Prins, Kaljend, Kallaste T, Borisov, Kristal (Hepner 46), Reim, Veensalu (Pustov 76), Bragin.

Scotland: Gunn; Wright (McLaren 80), Boyd, McStay, Hendry, Irvine, Gallacher, Bowman, Robertson (Booth 61), McClair, Collins.

Aberdeen, 2 June 1993, 14,309

Scotland (2) 3 *(McClair 16, Nevin 27, 72 (pen))*

Estonia (0) 1 *(Bragin 57)*

Scotland: Gunn; McLaren (Robertson 72), Boyd, McStay, Hendry, Irvine, Gallacher, Ferguson (Booth 55), McClair, Collins, Nevin.
Estonia: Poom; Kallaste R, Lensalu (Bragin 46), Prins, Kaljend, Kallaste T, Borisov, Kristal, Reim, Olumets (Veensalu 73), Rajala.

Oporto, 19 June 1993, 7000

Portugal (3) 4 *(Nogueira 2, Rui Costa 9, Joao Pinto II 23, Cadete 87)*

Malta (0) 0

Portugal: Vitor Baia; Nogueira (Figo 70), Fernando Couto, Oceano, Abel Xavier, Semedo, Sousa, Rui Costa, Joao Pinto II, Cadete, Domingos (Rui Aguas 46).
Malta: Cluett; Vella S, Buhagiar, Delia, Cauchi, Buttigieg, Saliba, Gregory, Camilleri J (Scerri 66), Laferla, Zerafa (Vella R 41).

Group 1

	P	W	D	L	F	A	Pts
Switzerland	7	5	2	0	18	4	12
Italy	7	4	2	1	15	6	10
Portugal	6	3	2	1	12	4	8
Scotland	7	3	2	2	10	9	8
Malta	9	1	1	7	3	21	3
Estonia	6	0	1	5	1	15	1

Group 2

Oslo, 9 September 1992, 6511

Norway (4) 10 *(Rekdal 5, 79, Halle 6, 51, 69, Sorloth 15, 21, Nilsen 46, 67, Mykland 74)*

San Marino (0) 0

Norway: Thorstvedt; Pedersen T, Bratseth, Nilsen R, Halle, Mykland, Rekdal, Leonhardsen (Ingebritsen 57), Jakobsen JI, Sorloth (Fjortoft 75), Flo.
San Marino: Benedettini; Guerra, Gobbi, Canti, Gennari, Mazza M, Bonini, Francini (Matteoni 70), Manzaroli P, Mazza P, Pasolini W (Muccioli B 46).

Oslo, 23 September 1992, 19,998

Norway (1) 2 *(Rekdal 9 (pen), Sorloth 78)*

Holland (1) 1 *(Bergkamp 10)*

Norway: Thorstvedt; Nilsen R, Pedersen T, Bratseth, Bjornebye, Halle (Strandli 60), Mykland, Ingebritsen, Rekdal, Sorloth (Flo 81), Jakobsen JI.
Holland: Menzo; Koeman, Blind, Silooy, De Boer F, Van't Schip (Taument 81), Wouters (Kieft 85), Rijkaard, Rob Witschge, Bergkamp, Van Basten.

Poznan, 23 September 1992, 11,000

Poland (1) 1 *(Waldoch 33)*

Turkey (0) 0

Poland: Bako; Rzepa, Szewczyk, Lesiak, Waldoch, Czachowski, Brzeczek, Warzycha R, Araszkiewicz (Kowalczyk 61), Kosecki (Fedoruk 64), Juskowiak.
Turkey: Hayrettin; Recep (Aykut 74), Bulent, Gokhan, Ogun, Tugay, Hami, Riza, Hakan, Oguz (Mehmet 64), Orhan.

Serravalle, 7 October 1992, 1187

San Marino (0) 0
Norway (2) 2 *(Jakobsen JI 7, Flo 19)*
San Marino: Benedettini; Guerra, Gobbi, Gennari, Bonini, Francini (Muccioli B 84), Manzaroli, Mazza M, Matteoni, Zanotti, Mazza P (Bacciocchi 25).
Norway: Thorstvedt; Bratseth, Nilsen R, Pedersen T, Halle (Bjornebye 46), Jakobsen JI, Leonhardsen (Ingebritsen 68), Mykland, Rekdal, Flo, Sorloth.

Wembley, 14 October 1992, 51,441

England (0) 1 *(Platt 55)*
Norway (0) 1 *(Rekdal 76)*
England: Woods; Dixon (Palmer 89), Walker, Adams, Pearce, Batty, Ince, Platt, Gascoigne, Wright (Merson 69), Shearer.
Norway: Thorstvedt; Nilsen R, Bratseth, Pedersen T (Berg 19), Bjornebye, Halle, Jakobsen JI, Ingebritsen, Mykland (Flo 78), Rekdal, Sorloth.

Rotterdam, 14 October 1992, 13,000

Holland (1) 2 *(Van Vossen 43, 46)*
Poland (2) 2 *(Kosecki 18, Kowalczyk 20)*
Holland: Menzo; Van Aerle, Koeman, Rijkaard (Fraser 80), Jonk, Wouters, Numan (Vanenburg 39), Rob Witschge, Bergkamp, Van Basten, Van Vossen.
Poland: Bako; Lesiak, Szewczyk, Kozminski, Adamczuk, Czachowski (Rzepa 39), Brzeczek, Kowalczyk (Smolarek 67), Warzycha R, Kosecki, Ziober.

Ankara, 28 October 1992, 35,000

Turkey (1) 4 *(Hakan 37, 89, Orhan 87, Hami 90)*
San Marino (0) 0
Turkey: Hayrettin; Riza (Mehmet 73), Bulent, Gokhan, Ogun, Orhan, Okan, Ridvan, Hakan, Oguz, Aykut (Hami 46).
San Marino: Benedettini; Gobbi, Gennari, Della Valle (Bizocchi 60), Matteoni, Guerra, Manzaroli, Mazza P, Bacciocchi, Bonini, Francini (Zanotti 80).

Wembley, 18 November 1992, 42,984

England (2) 4 *(Gascoigne 16, 61, Shearer 28, Pearce 60)*
Turkey (0) 0
England: Woods; Dixon, Pearce, Palmer, Walker, Adams, Platt, Gascoigne, Shearer, Wright I, Ince.
Turkey: Hayrettin; Recep, Bulent, Gokhan, Ogun, Orhan, Hami (Riza 69), Unal, Mehmet (Ugur 46), Oguz, Hakan.

Istanbul, 16 December 1992, 15,000

Turkey (0) 1 *(Feyyaz 60)*
Holland (0) 3 *(Van Vossen 57, 87, Gullit 59)*
Turkey: Hayrettin; Recep, Bulent, Gokhan, Ogun, Unal (Hami 77), Oguz, Tugay, Orhan, Saffet (Feyyaz 46), Hakan.
Holland: De Goey; Silooy, Koeman, Jonk (De Boer F 65), Rijkaard, Wouters, Rob Witschge, Gullit, Viscaal, Winter (Numan 76), Van Vossen.

Wembley, 17 February 1993, 51,154

England (2) 6 *(Platt 13, 24, 67, 83, Palmer 76, Ferdinand 86)*
San Marino (0) 0
England: Woods; Dixon, Walker, Adams, Dorigo, Gascoigne, Batty, Platt, Palmer, Ferdinand, Barnes.

San Marino: Benedettini; Muccioli B, Zanotti, Mazza M, Gennari, Canti, Guerra, Manzaroli, Bacciocchi (Mazza P 63), Bonini, Francini (Matteoni 80).

Utrecht, 24 February 1993, 14,000

Holland (2) 3 *(Overmars 4, Rob Witschge 37, 57)*
Turkey (1) 1 *(Feyyaz 36 (pen))*
Holland: De Goey; Silooy, De Kock, Koeman, Rob Witschge, Wouters (Winter 74), Jonk, Bergkamp, Van Vossen (De Boer F 46), Gullit, Overmars.
Turkey: Engin; Recep, Bulent, Gokhan, Ali, Tugay (Serhat 78), Feyyaz (Saffet 61), Unal, Hakan, Oguz, Orhan.

Serravalle, 10 March 1993, 957

San Marino (0) 0
Turkey (0) 0
San Marino: Benedettini (Muccioli S 9); Canti, Gennari, Zanotti, Valentini, Guerra, Manzaroli, Mazza M (Matteoni 61), Mazza P, Bacciocchi, Francini.
Turkey: Engin; Serhat (Hami 62), Bulent, Ali, Ogun, Tugay, Aykut, Unal, Mehmet, Saffet, Orhan.

Utrecht, 24 March 1993, 17,000

Holland (2) 6 *(Van den Brom 2, Canti (og) 29, De Wolf 52, 85, De Boer R 68 (pen), Van Vossen 78)*
San Marino (0) 0
Holland: De Goey; De Wolf, De Boer F, Winter, Rob Witschge, Wouters, Overmars, Meyer, Eykelkamp (De Boer R 46), Van den Brom, Blinker (Van Vossen 67).
San Marino: Muccioli S; Canti, Gennari, Matteoni (Zanotti 22), Valentini, Guerra, Manzaroli, Mazza M, Bacciocchi, Bonini, Francini.

Izmir, 31 March 1993, 60,000

Turkey (0) 0
England (2) 2 *(Platt 6, Gascoigne 44)*
Turkey: Engin (Hayrettin 42); Recep (Hami 69), Ogun, Ali, Tugay, Bulent, Feyyaz, Unal, Mehmet, Oguz, Orhan.
England: Woods; Dixon (Clough 46), Sinton, Palmer, Walker, Adams, Platt, Gascoigne, Barnes, Wright I (Sharpe 84), Ince.

Wembley, 28 April 1993, 73,163

England (2) 2 *(Barnes 2, Platt 23)*
Holland (1) 2 *(Bergkamp 34, Van Vossen 85 (pen))*
England: Woods; Dixon, Walker, Adams, Keown, Ince, Gascoigne (Merson 46), Palmer, Barnes, Platt, Ferdinand.
Holland: De Goey; Blind, De Boer F, Rijkaard, Winter, Wouters, Rob Witschge, Gullit (Van Vossen 69), Bergkamp, Bosman (De Wolf 46), Overmars.

Oslo, 28 April 1993, 21,530

Norway (2) 3 *(Rekdal 14, Fjortoft 17, Jakobsen JI 55)*
Turkey (0) 1 *(Feyyaz 57)*
Norway: Rossbach; Halle, Pedersen T, Bratseth, Bjornebye, Flo, Mykland (Nilsen R 82), Rekdal, Leonhardsen (Ingebritsen 30), Jakobsen JI, Fjortoft.
Turkey: Hayrettin; Recep, Ogun, Sedat, Serhat, Bulent, Feyyaz, Unal, Mehmet (Hamza 81), Hakan (Hami 66), Orhan.

Lodz, 28 April 1993, 10,000

Poland (0) 1 *(Furtok 68)*
San Marino (0) 0

Poland: Klak; Czachowski, Szewczyk, Kozminski, Waldoch, Brzeczek, Pisz, Juskowiak (Staniek 66), Furtok, Kosecki, Ziober.
San Marino: Benedettini; Canti, Gennari, Zanotti (Francini 79), Gobbi, Valentini, Manzaroli, Della Valle, Mazza M, Bonini (Mazza P 70), Bacciocchi.

Serravalle, 19 May 1993, 1500

San Marino (0) 0
Poland (0) 3 *(Lesniak 52, 80, Warzycha K 56)*

San Marino: Benedettini; Canti, Gennari, Zanotti, Gobbi, Valentini, Manzaroli, Francini (Muccioli B 60), Mazza M, Bonini, Bacciocchi (Mazza P 72).
Poland: Matysek; Czachowski, Brzeczek, Szewczyk, Rudy, Lesniak, Szierczewski, Warzycha K, Furtok (Staniek 82), Kosecki, Ziober.

Chorzow, 29 May 1993, 60,000

Poland (1) 1 *(Adamczuk 34)*
England (0) 1 *(Wright I 84)*

Poland: Bako; Czachowski, Szewczyk, Kozminski, Lesiak, Brzeczek (Jalocha 84), Szierczewski, Adamczuk, Furtok, Kosecki, Lesniak (Wegrzyn 75).
England: Woods; Bardsley, Dorigo, Palmer (Wright I 72), Walker, Adams, Platt, Gascoigne (Clough 79), Sheringham, Barnes, Ince.

Oslo, 2 June 1993, 22,250

Norway (1) 2 *(Leonhardsen 42, Bohinen 48)*
England (0) 0

Norway: Thorstvedt; Halle, Pedersen T, Bratseth (Nilsen R 82), Bjornebye, Flo, Mykland, Leonhardsen, Fjortoft (Sorloth 57), Rekdal, Bohinen.
England: Woods; Dixon, Pallister, Palmer, Walker (Clough 63), Adams, Platt, Gascoigne, Ferdinand, Sheringham (Wright I 46), Sharpe.

Rotterdam, 9 June 1993, 40,000

Holland (0) 0
Norway (0) 0

Hollnd: De Goey; Van Gobbel (Winter 81), Rijkaard, Koeman, De Boer F, Wouters, Overmars, Jonk, Bosman (Van Vossen 46), Bergkamp, Blinker.
Norway: Thorstvedt; Johnsen (Brendesaether 85), Pedersen T, Bratseth, Bjornebye (Nilsen R 46), Flo, Mykland, Leonhardsen, Fjortoft, Rekdal, Bohinen.

Group 2

	P	W	D	L	F	A	Pts
Norway	7	5	2	0	20	3	12
England	7	3	3	1	16	6	9
Holland	7	3	3	1	17	8	9
Poland	5	3	2	0	8	3	8
Turkey	8	1	1	6	7	17	3
San Marino	8	0	1	7	1	32	1

Group 3

Seville, 22 April 1992, 10,000

Spain (1) 3 *(Michel 2, 66 (pen), Hierro 87)*
Albania (0) 0

Spain: Zubizarreta; Abelardo, Nando, Giner, Michel (Eusebio 85), Amor, Hierro, Vizcaino, Manolo (Bakero 53), Butragueno, Goicoechea.

Albania: Strakosha (Dani 69); Josa (Peqini 55), Kola B, Lekbello, Aya, Abazi, Kushta, Barballushi, Millo, Kola A, Demollari.

Windsor Park, 28 April 1992, 4500

Northern Ireland (2) 2 *(Wilson 13, Taggart 16)*
Lithuania (1) 2 *Narberkovas 41, Fridrikas 48)*

Northern Ireland: Fettis; Donaghy (Fleming 46), Taggart, McDonald, Worthington, Black, Magilton, Wilson, Hughes, Quinn, Dowie (Rogan 80).
Lithuania: Martinkenas; Buzmakovas, Mika, Janonis, Mazeikis, Tautkas, Urbonas, Fridrikas (Zhuta 90), Narbekovas, Baranauskas, Ivanauskas (Danisevicius 89).

Dublin, 26 May 1992, 29,727

Republic of Ireland (0) 2 *(Aldridge 60, McGrath 80)*
Albania (0) 0

Republic of Ireland: Bonner; Irwin, Staunton, O'Leary, McGrath, Townsend, Keane, Houghton, Quinn, Aldridge (Coyne 83), Sheedy (McCarthy 52).
Albania: Dani; Zmijani, Qendro (Pali 71), Peqini, Vata, Abazi, Kushta, Vasi, Rraklli, Zola A (Sokoll 80), Demollari.

Tirana, 3 June 1992, 15,000

Albania (0) 1 *(Abazi 77)*
Lithuania (0) 0

Albania: Dani; Zmijani, Peqini, Lekbello, Vata, Abazi, Kushta, Milori (Rrafi 46), Millo (Fortuzi 89), Vasi, Demollari.
Lithuania: Martinkenas; Buzmakovas, Sukristovas, Mazeikis, Tomas, Danisevicius, Baranauskas, Tautkas (Zhuta 82), Urbonas, Ramelis (Zdanicius 52), Kvitkauskas.

Riga, 12 August 1992, 2000

Latvia (1) 1 *(Linards 15)*
Lithuania (0) 2 *(Poderis 65, Tereskinas 86)*

Latvia: Karavayev; Ivanovs, Sprogis (Zeminskis 65), Gnedois, Glazovs (Teplovs 46), Popkovs, Shevljakovs, Alexeyenko, Semionovs, Linards, Stradins.
Lithuania: Martinkenas; Buzmakovas, Janonis, Sukristovas (Poderis 56), Vainoras, Mazeikis, Baltusnikas, Baranauskas, Narbekovas (Tereskinas 2), Fridrikas, Ivanauskas.

Riga, 26 August 1992, 10,000

Latvia (0) 0
Denmark (0) 0

Latvia: Karavayev; Shevljakovs, Alexeyenko, Ivanovs, Gnedois, Popkovs (Astafjevs 65), Sprogis, Stradins, Yeliseyevs, Linards (Bulders 86), Glazovs.
Denmark: Schmeichel; Sivebaek (Elstrup 46), Olsen, Piechnik, Christofte, Heintze, Vilfort, Jensen, Laudrup B, Povlsen, Christensen.

Dublin, 9 September 1992, 32,000

Republic of Ireland (1) 4 *(Sheedy 30, Aldridge 59, 82 (pen), 86)*
Latvia (0) 0

Republic of Ireland: Bonner; Irwin, Staunton, Kernaghan, McGrath, Townsend, Keane, Whelan, Quinn (Coyne 61), Aldridge, Sheedy (Phelan 76).
Latvia: Igochine; Astafjevs, Alexeyenko, Bulders, Gnedois, Popkovs (Semionovs 63), Sprogis, Abzinovs (Sidorovs 36), Yeliseyevs, Linards, Glazovs.

Windsor Park, 9 September 1992, 8000

Northern Ireland (3) 3 *(Clarke, Wilson, Magilton)*
Albania (0) 0
Northern Ireland: Wright; Fleming, Worthington, Taggart, McDonald, Donaghy, Wilson, Magilton, Clarke (O'Neill M 77), Dowie, Hughes.
Albania: Strakosha; Zmijani, Peqini, Lekbello, Vata, Abazi, Kushta, Milori (Bilali 69), Millo, Kepa, Rraklli.

Riga, 23 September 1992, 60,000

Latvia (0) 0
Spain (0) 0
Latvia: Karavayev; Shevljakovs, Alexeyenko, Ivanovs, Gnedois, Popkovs (Astafjevs 70), Sprogis, Stradins, Bulders (Gilis 81), Linards, Glazovs.
Spain: Zubizarreta; Ferrer, Toni, Solozabal, Lopez, Vizcaino, Goicoechea, Fonseca (Alfonso 72), Bakero, Martin Vazquez, Alvaro (Amor 59).

Vilnius, 23 September 1992, 9500

Lithuania (0) 0
Denmark (0) 0
Lithuania: Martinkenas; Mazeikis, Sukristovas, Baltusnikas, Buzmakovas, Pankratjevas, Zhuta (Poderis 87), Zdanicius, Tereskinas, Baranauskas, Olshanskis.
Denmark: Schmeichel; Olsen, Piechnik, Sivebaek, Christofte, Larsen, Jensen, Vilfort, Laudrup B, Elstrup, Christensen (Moller 80).

Copenhagen, 14 October 1992, 40,100

Denmark (0) 0
Republic of Ireland (0) 0
Denmark: Schmeichel; Olsen, Piechnik, Sivebaek, Heintze, Rieper, Jensen, Vilfort, Larsen, Laudrup B, Povlsen (Christensen 77).
Republic of Ireland: Bonner; Irwin, Phelan, Moran, Kernaghan, Keane, Townsend, Houghton (Kelly 73), Quinn, Aldridge, McGoldrick.

Windsor Park, 14 October 1992, 9500

Northern Ireland (0) 0
Spain (0) 0
Northern Ireland: Wright; Fleming, Worthington, Taggart, McDonald, Donaghy, Black (Morrow 61), Wilson, Clarke, Quinn, Hughes.
Spain: Zubizarreta; Ferrer, Toni, Solozabal, Lopez, Hierro, Amor, Michel, Claudio (Guardiola 63), Martin Vazquez, Manolo (Alfonso 60).

Vilnius, 28 October 1992, 5000

Lithuania (0) 1 *(Fridrikas 85)*
Latvia (1) 1 *(Linards 44)*
Lithuania: Martinkenas; Buzmakovas, Baltusnikas, Tumasonis (Zhuta 61), Tereskinas, Sukristovas, Baranauskas, Ivanauskas, Pankratjevas, Fridrikas, Zdanicius (Vainoras 68).
Latvia: Karavayev; Astafjevs, Alexeyenko, Ivanovs, Gnedois, Popkovs (Jemeljanovs 74), Sprogis, Stradins, Bulders, Linards, Glazovs.

Tirana, 11 Novembr 1992, 3500

Albania (0) 1 *(Kepa 67)*
Latvia (1) 1 *(Alexeyenko 3)*
Albania: Strakosha; Zmijani, Lekbello, Vata, Peqini, Demollari, Fortuzi, Kacaj, Rraklli, Kushta (Prenja 67) (Bisha 74), Kepa.

Latvia: Karavayev; Gnedois, Sprogis, Bulders, Ivanovs, Glazovs (Popkovs 46), Shevljakovs, Alexeyenko, Stradins, Linards, Astafjevs.

Windsor Park, 18 November 1992, 11,000

Northern Ireland (0) 0
Denmark (0) 1 *(Larsen 51)*
Northern Ireland: Fettis; Fleming, Taggart, McDonald, Worthington, Donaghy, Magilton, Wilson (Black), Hughes, Clarke (Gray), Quinn.
Denmark: Schmeichel; Sivebaek (Kjeldberg 46), Rieper, Olsen, Heintze, Vilfort, Jensen, Larsen (Goldbaek 73), Povlsen, Laudrup B, Elstrup.

Seville, 18 November 1992, 33,000

Spain (0) 0
Republic of Ireland (0) 0
Spain: Zubizarreta; Ferrer, Goicoechea, Solozabal, Lopez, Hierro, Salinas (Bakero 52), Michel, Butragueno (Beguiristain 60), Martin Vazquez, Amor.
Republic of Ireland: Bonner; Irwin, Phelan, Moran, Keane, Townsend, McGrath, Houghton, Staunton, Aldridge, Quinn.

Seville, 16 December 1992, 24,500

Spain (0) 5 *(Bakero 49, Guardiola 51, Alfonso 79, Beguiristain 81, 82)*
Latvia (0) 0
Spain: Zubizarreta; Ferrer, Toni, Solozabal, Vizcaino, Amor, Claudio (Alfonso 55), Guardiola, Bakero (Martin Vazquez 62), Kiki, Beguiristain.
Latvia: Karavayev; Erglis, Alexeyendo, Ivanovs, Astafjevs, Popkovs, Gilis, Stradins, Bulders, Linards, Glazovs.

Tirana, 17 February 1993, 12,000

Albania (0) 1 *(Rrakli 89)*
Northern Ireland (0) 2 *(Magilton 14, McDonald 38)*
Albania: Kapliani; Zmijani (Peqini 46), Kacaj, Bano, Vata, Bazgo, Lekbello (Shulku 46), Fortuzi, Abazi, Rraklli, Demollari.
Northern Ireland: Wright; Fleming, Morrow, Taggart, Magilton, McDonald, Donaghy, Gray, Dowie (Quinn 73), O'Neill, Black.

Seville, 24 February 1993, 21,000

Spain (3) 5 *(Cristobal 5, Bakero 13, Beguiristain 18, Christiansen 86, Aldana 89)*
Lithuania (0) 0
Spain: Zubizarreta; Ferrer, Lasa, Alkorta, Giner, Cristobal, Guardiola, Guerrero (Aldana 59), Salinas (Christiansen 69), Bakero, Beguiristain.
Lithuania: Martinkenas; Buzmakovas, Vainoras, Mazeikis, Janonis, Sukristovas, Baranauskas, Ivanauskas, Tereskinas (Zhuta 69), Fridrikas, Zdanicius.

Copenhagen, 31 March 1993, 40,272

Denmark (1) 1 *(Povlsen 20)*
Spain (0) 0
Denmark: Schmeichel; Olsen, Rieper, Kjeldbjerg, Vilfort, Jensen, Larsen (Hansen 76), Nielsen B, Laudrup B (Tofting 86), Elstrup, Povlsen.
Spain: Zubizarreta; Cristobal, Ferrer, Fernando, Alkorta, Toni (Goicoechea 55), Amor, Guardiola (Nadal 46), Beguiristain, Aldana, Salinas.

Dublin, 31 March 1993, 33,000

Republic of Ireland (3) 3 *(Townsend 20, Quinn 22, Staunton 28)*

Northern Ireland (0) 0

Republic of Ireland: Bonner; Irwin, Phelan, McGrath, Moran, Keane, Townsend, Houghton, Quinn (McGoldrick 84), Coyne (Cascarino 78), Staunton.
Northern Ireland: Wright; Donaghy, Worthington, Taggart, McDonald, Morrow, Magilton (Quinn 51), O'Neill M (Black 74), Dowie, Gray, Hughes.

Copenhagen, 14 April 1993, 29,088

Denmark (1) 2 *(Vilfort 23, Strudal 76)*

Latvia (0) 0

Denmark: Schmeichel; Nielsen S, Rieper, Olsen, Kjeldbjerg, Goldbaek, Jensen (Larsen 61), Vilfort, Pingel (Strudal 70), Elstrup, Laudrup B.
Latvia: Karavayev; Gnedois, Shevljakovs, Ivanovs, Zemlinskis, Erglis, Glazovs, Astafjevs, Zelberlins (Gilis 46), Linards, Stradins (Bulders 64).

Vilnius, 14 April 1993, 12,000

Lithuania (2) 3 *(Baltusnikas 20, Sukristovas 25, Baranauskas 63)*

Albania (0) 1 *(Demollari 86)*

Lithuania: Martinkenas (Stauce 60); Ziukas, Baltusnikas, Mazeikis, Kalvaitis, Apanavicius (Slekys 63), Baranauskas, Sukristovas, Poderis, Kirilovas, Zdanicius.
Albania: Kapilani; Dema, Shulku, Bano, Taho, Ocelli, Kushta, Peqini, Dalipi (Dosti 46), Fortuzi, Demollari.

Dublin, 28 April 1993, 33,000

Republic of Ireland (0) 1 *(Quinn 75)*

Denmark (1) 1 *(Vilfort 27)*

Republic of Ireland: Bonner; Irwin, McGoldrick, McGrath, Kernaghan, Keane, Townsend, Houghton, Quinn, Aldridge (Cascarino 62), Staunton.
Denmark: Schmeichel; Nielsen S, Rieper, Olsen, Kjeldbjerg, Hansen F, Jensen, Vilfort, Pingel (Kristensen 60), Elstrup, Laudrup B.

Seville, 28 April 1993, 20,000

Spain (3) 3 *(Salinas 21, 26, Hierro 41)*

Northern Ireland (1) 1 *(Wilson 11)*

Spain: Zubizarreta; Ferrer, Fernando, Toni, Alkorta, Hierro, Guerrero, Adolfo, Beguiristain (Bakero 76), Salinas, Claudio (Kiki 59).
Northern Ireland: Wright, Fleming, Worthington, Donaghy, Taggart, McDonald, Black (Dennison 73), Wilson, O'Neill M (Dowie 73), Gray, Hughes.

Riga, 15 May 1993, 1810

Latvia (0) 0

Albania (0) 0

Latvia: Lajzans; Ergils, Shevljakovs, Ivanovs, Gnedois, Popkovs, Troickis, Astafjevs (Semionovs 46), Zelberlins (Sharando 62), Linards, Gorjacilovs.
Albania: Nailbani; Ocelli, Bano, Shala, Vata, Skulkju, Kushta, Zalla (Kapedani 88), Pequini, Milori, Fortuzi (Daliji 77).

Vilnius, 25 May 1993, 4000

Lithuania (0) 0

Northern Ireland (1) 1 *(Dowie 8)*

Lithuania: Martinkenas; Baltusnikas, Buzmakovas (Vichka 68), Mazeikis, Zhukas, Lushanskis (Shlenskis 46), Baranauskas, Sukristovas, Kirilovas, Fridrikas, Zdanicius.

Northern Ireland: Wright; Fleming, Taggart, McDonald, Worthington, Donaghy, Magilton, O'Neill, Wilson, Hughes, Dowie.

Tirana, 26 May 1993, 10,000

Albania (1) 1 *(Kushta 7)*

Republic of Ireland (1) 2 *(Staunton 13, Cascarino 77)*

Albania: Musta; Zmijani (Fortuzi 58), Shulku, Shala, Vata, Lekbello, Kushta, Pequini, Rraklli (Bozgo 76), Milori, Demollari.
Republic of Ireland: Bonner, Irwin, Phelan, Kernaghan, Moran, Keane, Townsend, Houghton, Quinn, Aldridge (Cascarino 76), Staunton.

Vilnius, 2 June 1993, 7000

Lithuania (0) 0

Spain (0) 2 *(Guerrero 73, 77)*

Lithuania: Martinkenas; Zhutkas, Baltusnikas, Mazeikis, Buzmakovas, Olsanskis, Baranauskas, Sukristovas, Kirilovas, Fridrikas (Zdanicius 54), Skarbalius.
Spain: Zubizarreta; Ferrer, Lasa (Beguiristain 62), Alkorta, Fernando, Hierro, Salinas (Quique Estebaranz 54), Nadal, Claudio, Guerrero, Amor.

Copenhagen, 2 June 1993, 39,504

Denmark (4) 4 *(Jensen 11, Pingel 20, 40, Moller 28)*

Albania (0) 0

Denmark: Schmeichel; Nielsen S, Rieper, Olsen, Kjeldberg, Larsen M, Jensen (Goldbaek 83), Vilfort, Pingel, Moller (Johansen 64), Laudrup B.
Albania: Musta; Fortuzi (Zala 83), Zmijani, Shulku, Ocelli, Pequini, Bano, Demollari (Bozgo 17), Kushta, Vata, Rraklli.

Riga, 2 June 1993, 2000

Latvia (0) 1 *(Linards 55)*

Northern Ireland (2) 2 *(Magilton 4, Taggart 15)*

Latvia: Karavayev; Erglis, Shevljakovs, Ivanovs, Gnedois, Popkovs, Sarando (Yeliseyevs 46), Astafjevs, Zelberlins (Babicevs 63), Linards, Gorjacilovs.
Northern Ireland: Wright; Fleming, McDonald, Taggart, Worthington, O'Neill (Quinn 85), Magilton, Donaghy, Wilson, Hughes, Dowie.

Riga, 9 June 1993, 7000

Latvia (0) 0

Republic of Ireland (2) 2 *(Aldridge 14, McGrath 42)*

Latvia: Karavayev; Erglis, Shevljakovs, Astafjevs, Ivanovs, Gnedois, Popkovs, Bulders, Babicevs (Yeliseyevs 46), Sharando (Gorjacilovs 54), Linards.
Republic of Ireland: Bonner; Irwin, Kernaghan, McGrath, Phelan, Houghton, Townsend, Keane, Staunton, Aldridge (Sheridan 80), Quinn (Cascarino 74).

Vilnius, 16 June 1993, 6000

Lithuania (0) 0

Republic of Ireland (1) 1 *(Staunton 38)*

Lithuania: Martinkenas; Zhukas, Baltusnikas, Mazeikis, Buzmakovas, Skarbalius (Zdanicius 46), Baranauskas, Urbonas (Ramelis 67), Stumprys, Kirilovas, Slekys.
Republic of Ireland: Bonner; Irwin, Phelan, McGrath, Kernaghan, Keane, Townsend, Houghton, Quinn, Aldridge (Whelan 76), Staunton.

Group 3

	P	W	D	L	F	A	Pts
Republic of Ireland	9	6	3	0	14	2	15
Spain	9	5	3	1	18	2	13
Denmark	8	4	4	0	9	1	12
Northern Ireland	9	4	2	3	11	10	10
Lithuania	10	2	3	5	8	15	7
Latvia	11	0	5	6	4	19	5
Albania	10	1	2	7	5	20	4

Group 4

Brussels, 22 April 1992, 18,000

Belgium (1) 1 *(Wilmots 24)*
Cyprus (0) 0
Belgium: Preud'homme; Albert, Grun, Van der Elst, Emmers, Scifo, Walem, Boffin (Borkelmans 82), Wilmots (Hofmans 75), Degryse, Oliveira.
Cyprus: Christofi; Costa, Pittas, Constantinou C, Nicolau, Yiangudakis, Ioannou, Larku (Constantinou G 88), Sotiriou, Papavasiliou, Hadjilukas (Panayi 70).

Bucharest, 6 May 1992, 10,000

Romania (5) 7 *(Balint 4, 40, 78, Hagi 14, Lacatus 28 (pen), Lupescu 44, Pana 55)*
Faeroes (0) 0
Romania: Stelea; Petrescu, Mihali, Popescu, Munteanu, Pana, Balint, Lupescu (Cheregi 78), Hagi, Lacatus (Gane 63), Rotariu.
Faeroes: Knudsen; Jakobsen, Hansen T, Danielsen, Justinussen, Morkore A, Jarnskor (Nielsen T 50), Dam (Jonsson 60), Hansen A, Reynheim, Muller.

Bucharest, 20 May 1992, 23,000

Romania (5) 5 *(Hagi 5, 35, Lupescu 7, 24, Balint 31)*
Wales (0) 1 *(Rush 50)*
Romania: Stelea; Petrescu, Mihali, Belodedici, Munteanu, Sabau (Timofte I 80), Popescu, Lupescu, Hagi (Gerstenmaier 71), Lacatus, Balint.
Wales: Southall; Phillips, Bowen (Blackmore 71), Aizlewood, Melville, Horne, Speed, Pembridge (Giggs 59), Hughes, Rush, Saunders.

Toftir, 3 June 1992, 5156

Faeroes (0) 0
Belgium (1) 3 *(Albert 30, Wilmots 65,71)*
Faeroes: Johannesen; Jakobsen, Hansen T, Danielsen, Jonsson T (Jensen 71), Morkore A (Justinussen 83), Nielsen T, Dam, Hansen A, Reynheim, Muller.
Belgium: Preud'homme: Staelens, Grun, Albert, Emmers, Boffin (Versavel 75), Van der Elst, Denil, Degryse, Scifo, Oliveira (Wilmots 65).

Toftir, 16 June 1992, 4500

Faeroes (0) 0
Cyprus (1) 2 *(Sotiriu 30, Papavasiliu 58)*
Faeroes: Johannesen; Jakobsen, Hansen T, Danielsen, Jonsson, Morkore A, Hansen A, Nielsen (Jarnskor 62), Rasmussen, Reynheim, Muller (Jensen 66).
Cyprus: Christofi; Costa (Larku 46), Pittas, Constantinou C, Nicolau, Yiangudakis, Ioannou, Charalambous, Savidis, Sotiriou (Panayi 84), Papavasiliou.

Prague, 2 September 1992, 9000

Czechoslovakia (0) 1 *(Kadlec 77)*
Belgium (1) 2 *(Chovanec (og) 44, Czerniatynski 83)*
Czechoslovakia: Stejskal; Chovanec, Glonek, Kadlec, Mistr, Nemecek, Kubik (Hapal 65), Nemec, Kula K (Dubovsky 77), Skuhravy, Moravcik.

Belgium: Preud'homme; Emmers, Medved, Albert, Smidts, Grum, Scifo, Van der Elst, Staelens (Dauwen 87), Czerniatynski, Degryse (Wilmots 66).

Cardiff, 9 September 1992, 7000

Wales (3) 6 *(Rush 5, 64, 89, Saunders 28, Bowen 37, Blackmore 71)*
Faeroes (0) 0
Wales: Southall; Phillips, Bowen (Giggs 66), Symons, Young, Blackmore, Horne, Saunders, Rush, Hughes, Speed.
Faeroes: Knudsen; Jakobsen, Hansen T, Danielsen, Hansen O, Morkore A, Simonsen, Dam (Justinussen 56), Jonsson, Reynheim, Muller.

Kosice, 23 September 1992, 17,000

Czechoslovakia (1) 4 *(Nemecek 24, Kuka 85, 87, Dubovsky 89 (pen))*
Faeroes (0) 0
Czechoslovakia: Stejskal; Glonek, Suchoparek, Novotny, Mistr (Latal 82), Moravcik, Nemecek, Dubovsky, Nemec, Hapal (Timko 68), Kuka.
Faeroes: Knudsen; Jakobsen, Johannesen, Hansen T, Justinussen, Simonsen, Dam, Hansen O (Morkore A 58), Jonsson, Reynheim, Muller (Arge 81).

Brussels, 14 October 1992, 21,000

Belgium (1) 1 *(Smidts 27)*
Romania (0) 0
Belgium: Preud'homme; Medved, Albert, Grun, Smidts, Boffin, Staelens, Van der Elst, Scifo, Degryse, Czerniatynski (Wilmots 69).
Romania: Stelea; Petrescu, Selymes, Mihali, Lupescu, Belodedici, Nunteanu, Sabau, Dumitrescu (Badea 78), Lacatus, Hagi.

Nicosia, 14 October 1992, 15,000

Cyprus (0) 0
Wales (0) 1 *(Hughes 51)*
Cyprus: Christofi M; Costa, Pittas (Hadjilukas 71), Constantinou, Nicolau, Yiangudakis, Ioannou D, Charalambous, Sotiriou (Ioannou Y 59), Papavasiliou, Savidis.
Wales: Southall; Phillips, Bowen, Blackmore, Young, Symons, Horne, Saunders, Rush, Hughes, Speed.

Bucharest, 14 November 1992, 30,000

Romania (0) 1 *(Dumitrescu 48)*
Czechoslovakia (0) 1 *(Nemecek 79 (pen))*
Romania: Stelea; Petrescu, Belodedici, Mihali, Munteanu, Sabau, Lupescu (Timofte D 78), Hagi, Dumitrescu, Lacatus, Hanganu (Vladoiu 66).
Czechoslovakia: Kouba; Novotny, Glonek, Suchoparek, Hapal, Latal, Nemecek, Moravcik, Nemec (Frydek 15), Siegl, Skuhravy (Kuka P 37).

Brussels, 18 November 1992, 21,000

Belgium (0) 2 *(Staelens 53, Degryse 58)*
Wales (0) 0
Belgium: Preud'homme; Medved, Grun, Albert, Smidts, Staelens (Wilmots 82), Van der Elst, Boffin, Degryse, Scifo, Czerniatynski (Nilis 46).
Wales: Southall; Phillips, Bowen (Giggs 60), Blackmore, Young, Symons, Horne, Saunders, Rush, Hughes, Speed (Pembridge 80).

806

Larnaca, 29 November 1992, 3000

Cyprus (1) 1 *(Pittas 39 (pen))*
Romania (2) 4 *(Popescu 4, Raducioiu 36, Hagi 73, Hanganu 86)*

Cyprus: Christofi M; Kalotheu, Pittas, Constantinou C, Ioannou D, Yiangudakis, Andreou (Hadjilukas 25), Christofi P, Ioannou Y (Sotiriou 62), Papavasiliou, Savidis.
Romania: Stelea; Petrescu, Belodedici, Mihali, Lupescu, Popescu, Lacatus, Dumitrescu, Raducioiu (Hanganu 58), Hagi, Munteanu.

Nicosia, 13 February 1993, 3000

Cyprus (0) 0
Belgium (2) 3 *(Scifo 2, 4, Albert 87)*

Cyprus: Oniferu; Costa, Ioannou Y, Constantinou, Kalotheu (Sotiriou 70), Pittas, Savidis, Yiangudakis (Charalambous 60), Papavasiliou, Christofi, Ioannou D.
Belgium: Preud'homme; Medved, Grun, Albert, Smidts, Staelens, Scifo (Goossens 87), Van der Elst, Boffin, Degryse, Nilis (Czerniatynski 75).

Limassol, 24 March 1993, 3000

Cyprus (0) 1 *(Sotiriou 47)*
Czechoslovakia (1) 1 *(Moravcik 33)*

Cyprus: Ioannou Y; Costa, Pittas, Ioannou D, Christofi E, Yiangudakis, Xiuruppas (Panayi 86), Charalambous, Sotiriou, Papavasiliou (Larku 71), Savidis.
Czechoslovakia: Kouba; Novotny, Suchoparek (Berger 74), Vrabec, Glonek, Nemecek, Nemec, Hapal (Latal 46), Kuka P, Skuhravy, Moravcik.

Cardiff, 31 March 1993, 27,002

Wales (2) 2 *(Giggs 18, Rush 39)*
Belgium (0) 0

Wales: Southall; Horne, Bodin, Aizlewood, Young, Ratcliffe, Saunders, Speed (Phillips 88), Rush, Hughes, Giggs (Bowen 89).
Belgium: Preud'homme; Medved (Oliveira 46), Grun, Albert, Smidts, Staelens, Van der Elst, Boffin, Degryse, Scifo, Czerniatynski (Severeyns 67).

Bucharest, 14 April 1993, 30,000

Romania (1) 2 *(Dumitrescu 33, 55)*
Cyprus (1) 1 *(Sotiriu 23)*

Romania: Stelea; Petrescu, Selymes, Sandoi, Belodedici, Munteanu, Lacatus (Stinga 78), Sabau, Ceausila (Predatu 64), Hagi, Dumitrescu.
Cyprus: Petridis; Kalotheu, Pittas, Constantinou, Christofi, Yiangudakis, Charalambous (Xiuruppas 78), Larku, Sotiriou, Papavasiliou, Savidis (Panayi 89).

Limassol, 25 April 1993, 4000

Cyprus (2) 3 *(Xiuruppas 7, Sotiriou 43, Ioannou Y 75)*
Faeroes (0) 1 *(Arge 82)*

Cyprus: Petridis; Charalambous, Christofi, Pittas, Constantinou C, Yiangudakis, Larku, Xiuruppas (Ioannou 65), Papavasiliou, Sotiriou (Hadjilukas 76), Savidis.
Faeroes: Knudsen; Jakobsen, Johannesen, Morkore K, Justinussen, Morkore A, Faero (Nielsen 46), Olsen, Reynheim (Arge 54), Hansen, Jonsson.

Ostrava, 28 April 1993, 16,000

Czechoslovakia (1) 1 *(Latal 41)*
Wales (1) 1 *(Hughes 31)*

Czechoslovakia: Kouba; Glonek (Bejbl 66), Kadlec, Novotny, Vrabec, Latal, Nemec (Dubovsky 79), Kubik, Nemecek, Kuka P, Luhovy.

Wales: Southall; Phillips, Bodin (Bowen 52), Melville, Symons, Blackmore, Horne, Saunders, Rush, Hughes, Giggs.

Brussels, 22 May 1993, 20,641

Belgium (1) 3 *(Wilmots 32, 75, Scifo 50 (pen))*
Faeroes (0) 0

Belgium: Preud'homme; Smidts (Oliveira 76), Emmers, Grun, Staelens, Boffin, Van der Elst, Degryse, Wilmots, Scifo, Nilis.
Faeroes: Knudsen; Jakobsen, Olsen, Morkore K (Reynatugvu 89), Justinussen, Morkore A, Dam, Hansen A, Nielsen T, Arge (Rasmussen 87), Reynheim.

Kosice, 2 June 1993, 15,000

Czechoslovakia (2) 5 *(Vrabec 13, Latal 37, Dubovsky 58, 83, 89)*
Romania (1) 2 *(Raducioiu 26, 55)*

Czechoslovakia: Kouba; Suchoparek, Novotny, Vrabec, Latal, Moravcik, Nemecek, Kubik (Nemec 46), Dubovsky, Kuka P (Glonek 81), Skuhravy.
Romania: Lung; Belodedici, Prodan (Hanganu 77), Popescu, Munteanu, Sabau, Hagi, Lupescu, Dumitrescu, Lacatus (Pandaru 65), Raducioiu.

Toftir, 6 June 1993, 4209

Faeroes (0) 0
Wales (2) 3 *(Saunders 22, Young 31, Rush 69)*

Faeroes: Knudsen; Jakobsen, Hansen T, Johannesen, Justinussen, Reynatugvu (Ramussen 49), Nielsen T, Dam, Hansen A, Reynheim (Mohr 59), Arge.
Wales: Southall; Phillips, Bodin, Aizlewood, Young (Melville 49), Symons, Horne, Saunders, Rush, Hughes (Speed 75), Giggs.

Toftir, 16 June 1993, 1000

Faeroes (0) 0
Czechoslovakia (3) 3 *(Hasek 3, Postulka 38,44)*

Faeroes: Knudsen; Justinussen R (Rasmussen 68), Johannesen, Jakobsen (Hansen T 70), Morkore K, Justinussen A, Morkore A, Reynatugvu, Hansen A, Dam, Nielsen.
Czechoslovakia: Kouba; Suchoparek, Hasek, Repka, Latal, Nemecek, Dubovsky, Postulka, Berger, Kuka P (Kinder 54), Moravcik (Kubik 81).

Group 4

	P	W	D	L	F	A	Pts
Belgium	8	7	0	1	15	3	14
Romania	7	4	1	2	21	10	9
Czechoslovakia	7	3	3	1	16	7	9
Wales	7	4	1	2	14	8	9
Cyprus	8	2	1	5	8	13	5
Faeroes	9	0	0	9	1	34	0

Group 5

Yugoslavia excluded due to UN sanctions.
Athens, 13 May 1992, 10,000

Greece (1) 1 *(Sofanidis 28)*
Iceland (0) 0

Greece: Papadopoulos; Apostolakis, Kalitzakis, Manolas, Nsibonas, Tsaluhidis Y, Tsaluhidis G, Sofianidis, Tursunidis (Noblias 77), Alexandria, Tsiantakis (Borbokis 60).
Iceland: Kristinsson B; Jonsson Kr, Marteinsson (Magnusson 74), Vaisson, Bergsson, Jonsson K, Gudjohnsen, Bjarnasson, Gretarsson, Sverrisson, Kristinsson R.

Budapest, 3 June 1992, 10,000

Hungary (1) 1 *(Kiprich 3)*
Iceland (0) 2 *(Orlygsson 51, Magnusson 73)*
Hungary: Petry; Telek, Kovacs E, Lorincz, Simon, Limperger, Pisont (Balog 78), Vincze (Eszenyi 54), Keller, Kiprich, Kovacs K.
Iceland: Kristinsson B; Gretarsson S (Magnusson 64), Bergsson, Orlygsson, Kristinsson R, Gretarsson A, Valsson, Jonsson Kr, Jonsson K (Bragason 80), Bjarnasson, Marteinsson.

Luxembourg, 9 September 1992, 3000

Luxembourg (0) 0
Hungary (1) 3 *(Detari 16, Kovacs K 52, 79)*
Luxembourg: Van Rijswijck; Bossi, Wolf, Petry, Birsens, Girres, Hellers, Weis, Salbene (Holtz 58), Langers, Malget (Thill 80).
Hungary: Petry; Nagy T, Disztl L, Keller, Lorincz, Limperger (Telek 65), Kiprich, Balog, Pisont (Bognar G 81), Detari, Kovacs K.

Reykjavik, 7 October 1992, 6350

Iceland (0) 0
Greece (0) 1 *(Tsaluhidis 61)*
Iceland: Kristinsson B; Bergsson, Jonsson Kr, Gudjohnsen, Marteinsson (Margeirsson 29), Kristinsson R, Bjarnasson (Hakonarsson 71), Gretarsson A, Orlygsson, Gretarsson S, Sverrisson.
Greece: Mirtsos; Apostolakis, Kalitsodakis, Manolas, Kalitzakis, Papaioannou (Mitropoulos 55), Tsiantakis, Tsaluhidis, Dimitriadis (Francheskos 69), Noblias, Donis.

Moscow, 14 October 1992, 13,000

Russia (0) 1 *(Yuran 64)*
Iceland (0) 0
Russia: Cherchesov; Khlestov, Onopko, Kolotovkin, Shalimov, Dobrovolski, Karpin, Lediakhov (Tatarchuk 46), Yuran (Kolivanov 76), Kiriakov.
Iceland: Kristinsson B; Marteinsson, Jonsson Kr, Valsson, Gretarsson A, Kristinsson R (Hakonarsson 88), Bergsson, Orlygsson, Margeirsson, Gudjohnsen (Bjarnasson 76), Gretarsson S.

28 October 1992, 1750

Russia (2) 2 *(Yuran 4, Radchenko 23)*
Luxembourg (0) 0
Russia: Cherchesov; Khlestov, Onopko, Kulkov, Karpin, Shalimov, Dobrovolski, Mostovoi, Radchenko (Tatarchuk 80), Kiriakov (Borodyuk 63), Yuran.
Luxembourg: Van Rijswijck; Birsens, Bossi, Wolf, Hellers, Girres, Salbene (Thill 77), Weis, Holtz (Groff 53), Langers, Malget.

Salonika, 11 November 1992, 40,000

Greece (0) 0
Hungary (0) 0
Greece: Mirtsos; Apostolakis, Pahaturidis, Manolas, Kolitsidakis, Tsaluhidis, Mitropoulos, Nioblias, Dimitriadis (Valtsis 46), Tursunidis, Tsiantakis (Franceskos 63).
Hungary: Petry; Disztl L, Limperger, Lorincz, Nagy, Urban, Lipcsei, Kiprich (Salloi 32), Meszaros (Paling 78), Balog, Kovacs K.

Athens, 17 February 1993, 40,000

Greece (1) 4 *(Dimitriadis 30 (pen), Mitropoulos 65)*
Luxembourg (0) 0
Greece: Minou; Manolas, Apostolakis, Kalitzakis, Tsaluhidis, Noblias, Tsiantakis, Dimitriadis, Donis (Mitropoulos 58), Franceskos (Karapialis 56), Karataidis.
Luxembourg: Koch; Petry, Wolf, Bossi, Birsens, Salbene, Hellers, Weis, Groff (Scuto 67), Malget, Langers.

Budapest, 31 March 1993, 30,000

Hungary (0) 0
Greece (0) 1 *(Apostolakis 70)*
Hungary: Petry; Telek, Csabo, Disztl L (Nagy T 36), Pisont (Balog 71), Urban, Detari, Eszenyi, Duro, Kiprich, Kovacs K.
Greece: Minou; Manolas, Kalitzakis, Kolitsidakis, Tsiantakis, Apostolakis, Mitropoulos, Nioblias, Tsaluhidis, Maragos (Antoniou 63), Mahias (Franceskos 82).

Luxembourg, 14 April 1993, 3000

Luxembourg (0) 0
Russia (1) 4 *(Kiriakov 12, 46, Shalimov 57, Kulkov 90)*
Luxembourg: Koch; Petry, Bossi, Birsens, Wolf, Salbene (Scuto 80), Hellers, Weis, Groff, Malget, Morocutti (Thill 60).
Russia: Cherchesov; Onopko, Gorlukovich, Ivanov, Shalimov, Kolivanov, Dobrovolski, Korneyev (Kulkov 60), Kanchelskis, Yuran, Kiriakov (Popov 75).

Moscow, 28 April 1993, 30,000

Russia (0) 3 *(Kanchelskis 55, Kolivanov 60, Yuran 86)*
Hungary (0) 0
Russia: Kharine; Gorlukovich, Ivanov A, Onopko, Kanchelskis, Shalimov, Dobrovolski, Korneyev (Kulkov 57), Kolivanov, Yuran, Kiriakov (Mostovoi 72).
Hungary: Petry; Telek, Nagy T, Lorincz, Pisont, Marton, Detari, Balog (Vincze 64), Duro (Banfi 64), Kovacs K, Csabi.

Luxembourg, 20 May 1993, 2000

Luxembourg (0) 1 *(Birgisson (og) 70)*
Iceland (1) 1 *(Gudjohnsen 40)*
Luxembourg: Van Rijswijck; Ferron (Carboni 64), Petry, Birsens, Wolf, Holtz, Salbene, Hellers, Groff (Scuto 50), Langers, Malget.
Iceland: Kristinsson B; Birgisson, Bergsson, Jonsson Kr, Orlygsson, Kristinsson R, Gretarsson A, Ingolfsson (Martinsson 82), Gudjohnsen, Gunnlaugsson (Thordarsson 56), Sverrisson.

Moscow, 23 May 1993, 40,000

Russia (0) 1 *(Dobrovolski 75 (pen))*
Greece (1) 1 *(Mitropoulos 45)*
Russia: Kharine; Gorlukovich, Onopko, Ivanov A, Kanchelskis, Shalimov, Dobrovolski, Kulkov (Tatarchuk 62), Kolivanov, Yuran, Kiriakov.
Greece: Minou; Apostolakis, Kolitsidakis, Manolas, Kalitzakis, Tsaluhidis, Marangos, Nioblias, Mahias (Antoniou 82), Mitropoulos (Karapialis 64), Tsiantakis.

Reykjavik, 2 June 1993, 3096

Iceland (1) 1 *(Sverrisson 26)*
Russia (1) 1 *(Kiriakov 38)*
Iceland: Kristinsson B; Bergsson, Birgisson, Jonsson Kr, Dervic, Stefansson, Thordarsson, Kristinsson R (Gretarsson A 78), Gudjohnsen, Sverrisson (Ingolfsson 83), Gunnlaugsson.
Russia: Kharine; Gorlukovich, Onopko, Kulkov, Ivanov, Kanchelskis, Dobrovolski, Tatarchuk (Korneyev 63), Kolivanov, Yuran (Lediakhov 75), Kiriakov.

Reykjavik, 16 June 1993, 5000

Iceland (1) 2 *(Sverrisson 13, Gudjohnsen 77)*
Hungary (0) 0
Iceland: Kristinsson B; Bjarnsson, Bergsson, Jonsson Kr, Dervic, Thordarsson, Kristinsson R, Stefansson (Gretarsson A 64), Gudlaugsson, Gudjohnsen, Sverrisson.
Hungary: Petry; Simon, Telek, Lorincz, Urban, Pisont, Marton, Balog, Kerezturi, Orosz (Hamon 64), Mamar (Salloi 80).

Russia and Greece qualified for finals in USA

Group 5

	P	W	D	L	F	A	Pts
Russia	6	4	2	0	12	2	10
Greece	6	4	2	0	6	1	10
Iceland	7	2	2	3	6	6	6
Hungary	6	1	1	4	4	8	3
Luxembourg	5	0	1	4	1	12	1

Group 6

Helsinki, 14 May 1992, 10,000

Finland (0) 0
Bulgaria (2) 3 *(Balakov 16, Kostadinov 25, 85)*
Finland: Huttunen; Petaja, Holmgren, Heikkinen, Eriksson, Rinne (Huhtamaki 76), Litmanen, Myyry, Jarvinen, Vanhala (Tegelberg 60), Tarkkio.
Bulgaria: Mikhailov; Ivanov, Tzvetanov, Illiev, Hubchev, Sirakov, Yankov, Stoichkov (Yordanov 69), Penev, Balakov, Kostadinov.

Sofia, 9 September 1992, 45,000

Bulgaria (2) 2 *(Stoichkov 21 (pen), Balakov 29)*
France (0) 0
Bulgaria: Mikhailov; Kiriakov, Ivanov T, Tzvetanov, Iliev N, Yankov, Kostadinov E (Yordanov 75), Stoichkov, Penev (Stoilov 76), Sirakov, Balakov.
France: Martini; Fournier, Petit, Boli, Roche, Casoni, Deschamps, Sauzee, Papin, Ginola, Vahirua (Durand 61).

Helsinki, 9 September 1992, 13,617

Finland (0) 0
Sweden (0) 1 *(Ingesson 77 (pen))*
Finland: Laukkanen; Hjelm, Tarkkio (Tauriainen 72), Ukkonen, Litmanen, Myyry (Vanhala 85), Paatelainen, Jarvinen, Holmgren, Kanerva, Remes.
Sweden: Ravelli (Eriksson L 88); Andersson P, Bjorklund, Erlingmark, Ljung, Ingesson, Limpar, Pettersson (Ekstrom 62), Schwarz, Thern, Dahlin.

Stockholm, 7 October 1992, 20,625

Sweden (0) 2 *(Dahlin 56, Pettersson 76)*
Bulgaria (0) 0
Sweden: Eriksson L; Erlingmark, Andersson P, Bjorklund, Ljung, Limpar, Thern, Schwarz, Pettersson, Ingesson, Dahlin (Andersson K 87).

Bulgaria: Mikhailov; Mladenov D, Kiriakov, Ivanov T, Tzvetanov, Kostadinov E (Yordanov 83), Sirakov, Stoilov, Yankov, Balakov, Penev.

Paris, 14 October 1992, 39,186

France (1) 2 *(Papin 3, Cantona 77)*
Austria (0) 0
France: Martini; Sauzee, Boli, Casoni, Deschamps, Sassus, Fournier (Gnako 63), Durand, Gravelaine (Vahirua 73), Papin, Cantona.
Austria: Wohlfahrt; Feiersinger, Streiter, Zsak, Wazinger, Stoger (Pfeifenberger 84), Artner, Herzog, Baur, Schinkels (Ogris 46), Polster.

Vienna, 28 October 1992, 20,000

Austria (2) 6 *(Herzog 41, 46, Polster 49, Stoger 56, Ogris 87)*
Israel (0) 2 *(Zohar 57, 77)*
Austria: Wohlfahrt; Zsak, Streiter (Baur 71), Wazinger, Prosenik, Stoger, Artner, Herzog, Schinkels (Flogel 76), Ogris, Polster.
Israel: Ginzburg; Ben-Shimon, Yeuda, Harazi, Cohen Av (Berkovich 52), Zohar, Klinger, Hazan, Nimny, Rosenthal, Tikva (Drieks 78).

Tel Aviv, 11 November 1992, 40,000

Israel (1) 1 *(Banin 42)*
Sweden (1) 3 *(Limpar 37, Dahlin 58, Ingesson 74)*
Israel: Ginzburg; Cohen Avi, Harazi (Berkovich 61), Hazan, Ben-Shimon, Klinger, Banin, Nimny, Revivo (Tikva 70), Zohar, Rosenthal.
Sweden: Ravelli; Nilsson R, Andersson P, Bjorklund, Ljung, Limpar, Rehn, Ingesson, Thern, Dahlin (Ekstrom 82), Brolin (Landberg 87).

Paris, 14 November 1992, 30,000

France (2) 2 *(Papin 17, Cantona 31)*
Finland (0) 1 *(Jarvinen 54)*
France: Martini; Roche, Boli, Casoni, Durand (Karembeu 71), Sauzee, Deschamps, Lizarazu, Papin, Cantona, Gravelaine (Vahirua 78).
Finland: Laukkanen; Holmgren, Kanerva, Ukkonen, Petaja (Kinnunen 85), Hjelm, Litmanen, Myyry, Jarvinen, Tarkkio, Paatelainen (Tauriainen 23).

Tel Aviv, 2 December 1992, 15,000

Israel (0) 0
Bulgaria (0) 2 *(Sirakov 55, Penev 83)*
Israel: Ginzburg; Halfon, Hillel, Shelach, Ben-Shimon, Klinger, Banin, Mizrachi (Hazan 80), Berkovich (Harazi 84), Revivo, Rosenthal.
Bulgaria: Mikhailov; Kiriakov, Ivanov, Bezinski, Iliev N, Yankov, Kostadinov E, Stoichkov, Penev, Sirakov, Yordanov (Iskrenov 89).

Tel Aviv, 17 February 1993, 29,000

Israel (0) 0
France (1) 4 *(Cantona 28, Blanc 62, 84, Roche 89)*
Israel: Ginzburg; Halfon, Hazan, Herazi A, Hillel, Atar (Drieks 56), Banin, Nimny, Herazi R, Rosenthal.
France: Lama; Boli, Roche, Blanc, Lizarazu (Loko 82), Deschamps, Sauzee, Le Guen, Ginoli (Petit 63), Papin, Cantona.

Vienna, 27 March 1993, 37,500

Austria (0) 0

France (0) 1 *(Papin 58)*

Austria: Wohlfahrt; Pecl, Zsak, Artner, Feiersinger, Cerny, Kuhbauer, Schinkels (Ogris 71), Herzog, Polster, Pfeifenberger.
France: Lama; Angloma, Roche, Blanc, Petit, Lizarazu, Deschamps, Le Guen, Sauzee (Martins 87), Papin, Gravelaine (Loko 71).

Vienna, 14 April 1993, 19,500

Austria (2) 3 *(Pfeifenberger 11, Kuhbauer 25, Polster 89)*

Bulgaria (0) 1 *(Ivanov 54)*

Austria: Wohlfahrt; Streiter, Pecl, Zsak, Feiersinger, Kuhbauer (Cerny 86), Lainer, Baur, Polster, Herzog, Pfeifenberger (Ogris 68).
Bulgaria: Mikhailov; Dochev (Lechkov 73), Ivanov, Iliev N, Bezinski (Iskrenov 82), Yankov, Kostadinov E, Kiriakov, Balakov, Stoichkov, Penev.

Paris, 28 April 1993, 43,000

France (1) 2 *(Cantona 42 (pen), 82)*

Sweden (1) 1 *(Dahlin 14)*

France: Lama; Angloma, Petit, Boli, Blanc, Le Guen, Deschamps, Sauzee, Ginola (Vahirua 46), Martins (Lizarazu 89), Cantona.
Sweden: Ravelli; Nilsson R, Andersson P, Bjorklund, Ljung, Rehn, Thern (Kamark 27), Brolin, Schwarz, Ingesson, Dahlin (Pettersson 65).

Sofia, 28 April 1993, 35,000

Bulgaria (2) 2 *(Stoichkov 14, Yankov 43)*

Finland (0) 0

Bulgaria: Mikhailov; Kiriakov, Rakov, Markov (Besinski 89), Yankov, Lechkov, Kostadinov E (Iskrenov 56), Stoichkov, Penev, Sirakov, Balakov.
Finland: Jakonen; Kinnunen, Kanerva, Heikkinen, Holmgren, Suominen, Litmanen, Lindberg, Hjelm, Paatelainen, Petaja (Rajamaki 62).

Sofia, 12 May 1993, 25,000

Bulgaria (1) 2 *(Stoichkov 35 (pen), Sirakov 60)*

Israel (0) 2 *(Harazi R 52, Rosenthal 53)*

Bulgaria: Mikhailov; Kiriakov, Ratkov, Markov, Ivanov, Lechkov (Borimirov 65), Balakov, Sirakov, Iskrenov (Yankov 37), Penev, Stoichkov.
Israel: Ginzburg; Halfon, Hillel, Hazan, Shelach, Klinger, Banin, Schwarz, Rosenthal, Harazi R (Atar 88), Ohana (Harazi A 89).

Pori, 13 May 1993, 13,682

Finland (2) 3 *(Paatelainen 17, Rajamaki 20, Hjelm 50)*

Austria (0) 1 *(Zisser 89)*

Finland: Jakonen; Heikkinen, Kanerva, Holmgren (Lindberg 60), Kuinunen, Petaja, Rajamaki, Hjelm, Suominen, Litmanen, Paatelainen (Grunholm 76).
Austria: Wohlfahrt; Streiter, Zsak (Cerny 60), Zisser, Baur, Kuhbauer, Herzog, Artner, Lainer, Ogris, Polster (Stoger 58).

Stockholm, 19 May 1993, 27,800

Sweden (0) 1 *(Eriksson 50)*

Austria (0) 0

Sweden: Ravelli; Nilsson R, Eriksson J, Bjorklund, Ljung, Rehn, Schwarz, Brolin, Ingesson, Ekstrom (Zetterberg 80), Dahlin (Eklund 87).

Austria: Wohlfahrt; Streiter, Pecl, Lainer, Stoger, Baur, Herzog (Janeschitz 62), Artner, Feiersinger, Ogris, Pfeifenberger.

Stockholm, 2 June 1993, 22,000

Sweden (2) 5 *(Brolin 17, 41, 65, Zetterberg 55, Landberg 89)*

Israel (0) 0

Sweden: Ravelli; Nilsson R, Eriksson J, Bjorklund, Ljung, Rehn (Landberg 74), Andersson P, Zetterberg, Ingesson, Brolin, Dahlin.
Israel: Ginzburg; Halfon, Hillel, Klinger, Shelach, Bruomer, Ohana (Revivo 65), Hazan, Schwarz, Harazi R, Rosenthal (Harazi A 46).

Lahti, 16 June 1993, 4620

Finland (0) 0

Israel (0) 0

Finland: Jakonen; Kinnunen (Lindberg 84), Holmgren, Kanerva, Heikkinen, Petaja, Suominen, Litmanen, Rajamaki, Paatelainen, Gronholm (Ruhanan 75).
Israel: Ginzburg; Klinger, Halfon, Bruomer, Shelach, Asalem, Hazan, Schwarz, Banin, Harazi R (Atar 89), Ohana.

Group 6

	P	W	D	L	F	A	Pts
Sweden	6	5	0	1	13	3	10
France	6	5	0	1	11	4	10
Bulgaria	7	4	1	2	12	7	9
Austria	6	2	0	4	9	10	4
Finland	6	1	1	4	4	9	3
Israel	7	0	2	5	5	21	2

Concacaf

Pre-preliminary round
Dominican Republic 1, Puerto Rico 2
Puerto Rico 1, Dominican Republic 1
St Lucia 1, St Vincent 0
St Vincent 3, St Lucia 1

Preliminary round
Bermuda 1, Haiti 0
Haiti 2, Bermuda 1
Jamaica 2, Puerto Rico 1
Puerto Rico 0, Jamaica 3
Cuba withdrew, St Vicent w.o
Netherlands Antilles 1, Antigua 1
Antigua 3, Netherlands Antilles 0
Guyana 1, Surinam 2
Surinam 1, Guyana 1
Barbados 1, Trinidad & Tobago 2
Trinidad & Tobago 3, Barbados 0

First round
Central Region
Guatemala 0, Honduras 0
Honduras 2, Guatemala 0
Panama 1, Costa Rica 0
Costa Rica 5, Panama 1
Nicaragua 0, El Salvador 5
El Salvador 5, Nicaragua 1

Caribbean Region
Surinam 0, St Vincent 0
St Vincent 2, Surinam 1
Antigua 0, Bermuda 3
Bermuda 2, Antigua 1
Trinidad & Tobago 1, Jamaica 2
Jamaica 1, Trinidad & Tobago 1

Second round

Group A
Costa Rica 2, Honduras 3
St Vincent 0, Mexico 4
Mexico 2, Honduras 0
St Vincent 0, Costa Rica 1
Mexico 4, Costa Rica 0
St Vincent 0, Honduras 4
Honduras 4, St Vincent 0
Costa Rica 2, Mexico 0
Honduras 2, Costa Rica 1
Mexico 11, St Vincent 0
Costa Rica 5, St Vincent 0
Honduras 1, Mexico 1

Group B
Bermuda 1, El Salvador 0
Jamaica 1, Canada 1
Bermuda 1, Jamaica 1
El Salvador 1, Canada 1
Canada 1, Jamaica 0
El Salvador 4, Bermuda 1
Canada 2, El Salvador 3
Jamaica 3, Bermuda 2
Canada 4, Bermuda 2
Jamaica 0, El Salvador 2
Bermuda 0, Canada 0
El Salvador 2, Jamaica 1

Third Round
Honduras 2, Canada 2
El Salvador 2, Mexico 1
Canada 2, El Salvador 0
Mexico 3, Honduras 0
Canada 3, Honduras 1
Mexico 3, El Salvador 1
Honduras 2, El Salvador 0
Mexico 4, Canada 0
Honduras 1, Mexico 4
El Salvador 1, Canada 2
Canada 1, Mexico 2
El Salvador 2, Honduras 1
Mexico qualified for finals in USA

Oceania

Group 1
Solomon Islands 1, Tahiti 1
Solomon Islands 1, Australia 2
Tahiti 0, Australia 3
Australia 2, Tahiti 0
Australia 1, Solomon Islands 1
Tahiti 4, Solomon Islands 2

Group 2
New Zealand 3, Fiji 0
Vanuatu 1, New Zealand 4
New Zealand 8, Vanuatu 0
Fiji 3, Vanuatu 0
Fiji 0, New Zealand 0
Vanuatu 0, Fiji 3

Second Round
New Zealand 0, Australia 1
Australia 3, New Zealand 0

Africa

First Round
Group A
Algeria 3, Burundi 1
Burundi 1, Ghana 0
Ghana 2, Algeria 0
Burundi 0, Algeria 0
Ghana 1, Burundi 0
Algeria 2, Ghana 1
Uganda withdrew

Group B
Zaire 4, Liberia 2
Cameroon 5, Swaziland 0
Swaziland 1, Zaire 0
Zaire 1, Cameroon 2
Swaziland 0, Cameroon 0
Zaire v Swaziland not played
Cameroon 0, Zaire 0
Liberia withdrew

Group C
Zimbabwe 1, Togo 0
Egypt 1, Angola 0
Togo 1, Egypt 4
Zimbabwe 2, Egypt 1
Angola 1, Zimbabwe 1
Togo 1, Zimbabwe 2
Angola 0, Egypt 0
Egypt 3, Togo 0
Zimbabwe 2, Angola 1
Angola v Togo not played
Egypt 0, Zimbabwe 0
Togo 0, Angola 1

Group D
Nigeria 4, South Africa 0
South Africa 1, Congo 0
Congo 0, Nigeria 1
South Africa 0, Nigeria 0
Congo 0, South Africa 1
Nigeria 2, Congo 0
Libya withdrew

Group E
Ivory Coast 6, Botswana 0
Niger 0, Ivory Coast 0
Botswana 0, Niger 1
Botswana 0, Ivory Coast 0
Ivory Coast 1, Niger 0
Niger 2, Botswana 1
Sudan withdrew

Group F
Morocco 5, Ethiopia 0
Tunisia 5, Benin 1
Benin 0, Morocco 1
Ethiopia 0, Tunisia 0
Ethiopia 3, Benin 1
Tunisia 1, Morocco 1
Benin 0, Tunisia 5
Ethiopia 0, Morocco 1
Morocco 5, Benin 0
Tunisia 3, Ethiopia 0
Benin 1, Ethiopia 0
Morocco 0, Tunisia 0

Group G
Gabon 3, Mozambique 1
Mozambique 0, Senegal 1
Gabon 3, Senegal 2
Mozambique 1, Gabon 1
Senegal 6, Mozambique 1
Senegal 1, Gabon 0
Mauritania withdrew

Group H
Madagascar 3, Namibia 0
Zambia 2, Tanzania 0
Tanzania 0, Madagascar 0
Namibia 0, Zambia 4
Tanzania 2, Namibia 1
Madagascar 2, Zambia 0
Tanzania 1, Zambia 1
Namibia 0, Madagascar 1
Zambia 4, Namibia 0
Zambia 3, Madagascar 1
Tanzania withdrew

Group I
Guinea 4, Kenya 0
Kenya 2, Guinea 0
Mali and Gambia withdrew

Second round
Group A
Algeria 1, Ivory Coast 1
Ivory Coast 2, Nigeria 1

Group B
Morocco 1, Senegal 0

Group C
Cameroon 3, Guinea 1
Guinea 3, Zimbabwe 0

Asia

First round
Group A
China, Iraq, Jordan, Yemen, Pakistan
Jordan 1, Yemen 1
Pakistan 0, China 5
Jordan 1, Iraq 1
Yeman 5, Pakistan 1
Iraq 6, Yemen 1
Jordan 0, China 3
Iraq 8, Pakistan 0
Yemen 1, China 0
Iraq 1, China 0
Jordan 3, Pakistan 1
China 3, Pakistan 0
Yemen 1, Jordan 1
Iraq 4, Jordan 0
Yemen 3, Pakistan 0
China 4, Jordan 1
Iraq 3, Yemen 0
Iraq 4, Pakistan 0
China 1, Yemen 0
Pakistan 5, Jordan 0
China 2, Iraq 1

Group B
Iran, Syria, Oman, Taiwan, Myanmar (withdrew)
Syria 2, Taiwan 0
Iran 0, Oman 0

Group C
Korea DPR 3, Vietnam 0
Qatar 3, Indonesia 1
Korea DPR 2, Singapore 1
Qatar 4, Vietnam 0
Korea DPR 4, Indonesia 0
Vietnam 2, Singapore 3
Qatar 4, Singapore 1
Vietnam 1, Indonesia 0
Indonesia 0, Singapore 2
Qatar 1, Korea DPR 2
Indonesia 1, Qatar 4
Vietnam 0, Korea DPR 1
Singapore 1, Korea DPR 3

Vietnam 0, Qatar 4
Indonesia 1, Korea DPR 2
Singapore 1, Vietnam 0
Indonesia 2, Vietnam 1
Singapore 1, Qatar 0
Korea DPR 2, Qatar 2
Singapore 2, Indonesia 1

Group D
Hong Kong 2, Bahrain 1
Lebanon 2, India 2
Bahrain 0, Korea Rep 0
Lebanon 2, Hong Kong 2
India 1, Hong Kong 2
Lebanon 0, Korea Rep 1
India 0, Korea Rep 3
Lebanon 0, Bahrain 0
Bahrain 2, India 1
Hong Kong 0, Korea Rep 3
Korea Rep 4, Hong Kong 1
Bahrain 3, India 0
Korea Rep 2, Lebanon 0
Korea Rep 7, India 0
Lebanon 2, Hong Kong 1
Lebanon 2, India 1
Bahrain 3, Hong Kong 0
Korea Rep 3, Bahrain 0
India 3, Hong Kong 1

Group E
Macao 0, Saudi Arabia 6
Malaysia 1, Kuwait 1
Macao 1, Kuwait 10
Malaysia 1, Saudi Arabia 1
Kuwait 0, Saudi Arabia 0
Malaysia 9, Macao 0
Kuwait 2, Malaysia 0
Saudi Arabia 8, Macao 0
Kuwait 8, Macao 0
Saudi Arabia 3, Malaysia 0
Macao 0, Malaysia 5
Saudi Arabia 2, Kuwait 0

Group F
Japan 1, Thailand 0
Sri Lanka 0, UAE 4
Japan 8, Bangladesh 0
Thailand 1, Sri Lanka 0
Sri Lanka 0, Bangladesh 1
UAE 1, Thailand 0
Japan 5, Sri Lanka 0
UAE 1, Bangladesh 0
Japan 2, UAE 0
Thailand 4, Bangladesh 1
Thailand 0, Japan 1
UAE 3, Sri Lanka 0
Bangladesh 1, Japan 4
Thailand 1, UAE 2
Bangladesh 0, UAE 7
Sri Lanka 0, Thailand 3
Bangladesh 1, Thailand 4
Sri Lanka 0, Japan 6
Bangladesh 3, Sri Lanka 0
UAE 1, Japan 1

BRITISH AND IRISH INTERNATIONAL RESULTS 1872–1993

BRITISH INTERNATIONAL CHAMPIONSHIP 1883–1984

Year	Champions	Pts	Year	Champions	Pts	Year	Champions	Pts
1883–84	Scotland	6	1920–21	Scotland	6	1956–57	England	5
1884–85	Scotland	5	1921–22	Scotland	4	1957–58	{ England	4
1885–86	{ England	5	1922–23	Scotland	5		{ N. Ireland	4
	{ Scotland	5	1923–24	Wales	6	1958–59	{ N. Ireland	4
1886–87	Scotland	6	1924–25	Scotland	6		{ England	4
1887–88	England	6	1925–26	Scotland	6	1959–60	{ England	4
1888–89	Scotland	5	1926–27	{ Scotland	4		{ Scotland	4
1889–90	{ Scotland	5		{ England	4		{ Wales	4
	{ England	5	1927–28	Wales	5	1960–61	England	6
1890–91	England	6	1928–29	Scotland	6	1961–62	Scotland	6
1891–92	England	6	1929–30	England	6	1962–63	Scotland	6
1892–93	England	6	1930–31	{ Scotland	4	1963–64	{ Scotland	4
1893–94	Scotland	5		{ England	4		{ England	4
1894–95	England	5	1931–32	England	6		{ N. Ireland	4
1895–96	Scotland	5	1932–33	Wales	5	1964–65	England	5
1896–97	Scotland	5	1933–34	Wales	5	1965–66	England	5
1897–98	England	6	1934–35	{ England	4	1966–67	Scotland	5
1898–99	England	6		{ Scotland	4	1967–68	England	5
1899–1900	Scotland	6	1935–36	Scotland	4	1968–69	England	6
1900–01	England	5	1936–37	Wales	6	1969–70	{ England	4
1901–02	Scotland	5	1937–38	England	4		{ Scotland	4
1902–03	{ England	4	1938–39	{ England	4		{ Wales	4
	{ Ireland	4		{ Scotland	4	1970–71	England	5
	{ Scotland	4		{ Wales	4	1971–72	{ England	4
1903–04	England	5	1946–47	England	5		{ Scotland	4
1904–05	England	5	1947–48	England	5	1972–73	England	6
1905–06	{ England	4	1948–49	Scotland	6	1973–74	{ England	4
	{ Scotland	4	1949–50	England	6		{ Scotland	4
1906–07	Wales	5	1950–51	Scotland	6	1974–75	England	4
1907–08	{ Scotland	5	1951–52	{ Wales	5	1975–76	Scotland	6
	{ England	5		{ England	5	1976–77	Scotland	5
1908–09	England	6	1952–53	{ England	4	1977–78	England	6
1909–10	Scotland	4		{ Scotland	4	1978–79	England	5
1910–11	England	5	1953–54	England	6	1979–80	N. Ireland	5
1911–12	{ England	5	1954–55	England	6	1980–81	*Not completed*	
	{ Scotland	5	1955–56	{ England	3	1981–82	England	6
1912–13	England	4		{ Scotland	3	1982–83	England	5
1913–14	Ireland	5		{ Wales	3	1983–84	N. Ireland	3
1919–20	Wales	4		{ N. Ireland	3			

Note: In the results that follow, wc = World Cup, ec = European Championship. For Ireland, read Northern Ireland from 1921.

ENGLAND v SCOTLAND

Played: 107; England won 43, Scotland won 40, Drawn 24. *Goals:* England 188, Scotland 168.

Year	Venue	E	S	Year	Venue	E	S	Year	Venue	E	S
1872	Glasgow	0	0	1879	Kennington Oval	5	4	1886	Glasgow	1	1
1873	Kennington Oval	4	2	1880	Glasgow	4	5	1887	Blackburn	2	3
1874	Glasgow	1	2	1881	Kennington Oval	1	6	1888	Glasgow	5	0
1875	Kennington Oval	2	2	1882	Glasgow	1	5	1889	Kennington Oval	2	3
1876	Glasgow	0	3	1883	Sheffield	2	3	1890	Glasgow	1	1
1877	Kennington Oval	1	3	1884	Glasgow	0	1	1891	Blackburn	2	1
1878	Glasgow	2	7	1885	Kennington Oval	1	1	1892	Glasgow	4	1

Year	Venue	E	S		Year	Venue	E	S		Year	Venue	E	S
1893	Richmond	5	2		1927	Glasgow	2	1		1963	Wembley	1	2
1894	Glasgow	2	2		1928	Wembley	1	5		1964	Glasgow	0	1
1895	Everton	3	0		1929	Glasgow	0	1		1965	Wembley	2	2
1896	Glasgow	1	2		1930	Wembley	5	2		1966	Glasgow	4	3
1897	Crystal Palace	1	2		1931	Glasgow	0	2		EC1967	Wembley	2	3
1898	Glasgow	3	1		1932	Wembley	3	0		EC1968	Glasgow	1	1
1899	Birmingham	2	1		1933	Glasgow	1	2		1969	Wembley	4	1
1900	Glasgow	1	4		1934	Wembley	3	0		1970	Glasgow	0	0
1901	Crystal Palace	2	2		1935	Glasgow	0	2		1971	Wembley	3	1
1902	Birmingham	2	2		1936	Wembley	1	1		1972	Glasgow	1	0
1903	Sheffield	1	2		1937	Glasgow	1	3		1973	Glasgow	5	0
1904	Glasgow	1	0		1938	Wembley	0	1		1974	Wembley	0	2
1905	Crystal Palace	1	0		1939	Glasgow	2	1		1975	Wembley	5	1
1906	Glasgow	1	2		1947	Wembley	1	1		1976	Glasgow	1	2
1907	Newcastle	1	1		1948	Glasgow	2	0		1977	Wembley	1	2
1908	Glasgow	1	1		1949	Wembley	1	3		1978	Glasgow	1	0
1909	Crystal Palace	2	0		wc1950	Glasgow	1	0		1979	Wembley	3	1
1910	Glasgow	0	2		1951	Wembley	2	3		1980	Glasgow	2	0
1911	Everton	1	1		1952	Glasgow	2	1		1981	Wembley	0	1
1912	Glasgow	1	1		1953	Wembley	2	2		1982	Glasgow	1	0
1913	Chelsea	1	0		wc1954	Glasgow	4	2		1983	Wembley	2	0
1914	Glasgow	1	3		1955	Wembley	7	2		1984	Glasgow	1	1
1920	Sheffield	5	4		1956	Glasgow	1	1		1985	Glasgow	0	1
1921	Glasgow	0	3		1957	Wembley	2	1		1986	Wembley	2	1
1922	Aston Villa	0	1		1958	Glasgow	4	0		1987	Glasgow	0	0
1923	Glasgow	2	2		1959	Wembley	1	0		1988	Wembley	1	0
1924	Wembley	1	1		1960	Glasgow	1	1		1989	Glasgow	2	0
1925	Glasgow	0	2		1961	Wembley	9	3					
1926	Manchester	0	1		1962	Glasgow	0	2					

ENGLAND v WALES

Played: 97; England won 62, Wales won 14, Drawn 21. *Goals:* England 239, Scotland 90.

Year	Venue	E	W		Year	Venue	E	W		Year	Venue	E	W
1879	Kennington Oval	2	1		1911	Millwall	3	0		1955	Cardiff	1	2
1880	Wrexham	3	2		1912	Wrexham	2	0		1956	Wembley	3	1
1881	Blackburn	0	1		1913	Bristol	4	3		1957	Cardiff	4	0
1882	Wrexham	3	5		1914	Cardiff	2	0		1958	Aston Villa	2	2
1883	Kennington Oval	5	0		1920	Highbury	1	2		1959	Cardiff	1	1
1884	Wrexham	4	0		1921	Cardiff	0	0		1960	Wembley	5	1
1885	Blackburn	1	1		1922	Liverpool	1	0		1961	Cardiff	1	1
1886	Wrexham	3	1		1923	Cardiff	2	2		1962	Wembley	4	0
1887	Kennington Oval	4	0		1924	Blackburn	1	2		1963	Cardiff	4	0
1888	Crewe	5	1		1925	Swansea	2	1		1964	Wembley	2	1
1889	Stoke	4	1		1926	Crystal Palace	1	3		1965	Cardiff	0	0
1890	Wrexham	3	1		1927	Wrexham	3	3		EC1966	Wembley	5	1
1891	Sunderland	4	1		1927	Burnley	1	2		EC1967	Cardiff	3	0
1892	Wrexham	2	0		1928	Swansea	3	2		1969	Wembley	2	1
1893	Stoke	6	0		1929	Chelsea	6	0		1970	Cardiff	1	1
1894	Wrexham	5	1		1930	Wrexham	4	0		1971	Wembley	0	0
1894	Queen's Club, Kensington	1	1		1931	Liverpool	3	1		wc1972	Cardiff	3	0
1896	Cardiff	9	1		1932	Wrexham	0	0		wc1973	Wembley	1	1
1897	Sheffield	4	0		1933	Newcastle	1	2		1973	Wembley	3	0
1898	Wrexham	3	0		1934	Cardiff	4	0		1974	Cardiff	2	0
1899	Bristol	4	0		1935	Wolverhampton	1	2		1975	Wembley	2	2
1900	Cardiff	1	1		1936	Cardiff	1	2		1976	Wrexham	2	1
1901	Newcastle	6	0		1937	Middlesbrough	2	1		1976	Cardiff	1	0
1902	Wrexham	0	0		1938	Cardiff	2	4		1977	Wembley	0	1
1903	Portsmouth	2	1		1946	Manchester	3	0		1978	Cardiff	3	1
1904	Wrexham	2	2		1947	Cardiff	3	0		1979	Wembley	0	0
1905	Liverpool	3	1		1948	Aston Villa	1	0		1980	Wrexham	1	4
1906	Cardiff	1	0		wc1949	Cardiff	4	1		1981	Wembley	0	0
1907	Fulham	1	1		1950	Sunderland	4	2		1982	Cardiff	1	0
1908	Wrexham	7	1		1951	Cardiff	1	1		1983	Wembley	2	1
1909	Nottingham	2	0		1952	Wembley	5	2		1984	Wrexham	0	1
1910	Cardiff	1	0		wc1953	Cardiff	4	1					
					1954	Wembley	3	2					

ENGLAND v IRELAND

Played: 96; England won 74, Ireland won 6, Drawn 16. *Goals:* England 319, Ireland 80.

Year	Venue	E	I	Year	Venue	E	I	Year	Venue	E	I
1882	Belfast	13	0	1914	Middlesbrough	0	3	1957	Wembley	2	3
1883	Liverpool	7	0	1919	Belfast	1	1	1958	Belfast	3	3
1884	Belfast	8	1	1920	Sunderland	2	0	1959	Wembley	2	1
1885	Manchester	4	0	1921	Belfast	1	1	1960	Belfast	5	2
1886	Belfast	6	1	1922	West Bromwich	2	0	1961	Wembley	1	1
1887	Sheffield	7	0	1923	Belfast	1	2	1962	Belfast	3	1
1888	Belfast	5	1	1924	Everton	3	1	1963	Wembley	8	3
1889	Everton	6	1	1925	Belfast	0	0	1964	Belfast	4	3
1890	Belfast	9	1	1926	Liverpool	3	3	1965	Wembley	2	1
1891	Wolverhampton	6	1	1927	Belfast	0	2	EC1966	Belfast	2	0
1892	Belfast	2	0	1928	Everton	2	1	EC1967	Wembley	2	0
1893	Birmingham	6	1	1929	Belfast	3	0	1969	Belfast	3	1
1894	Belfast	2	2	1930	Sheffield	5	1	1970	Wembley	3	1
1895	Derby	9	0	1931	Belfast	6	2	1971	Belfast	1	0
1896	Belfast	2	0	1932	Blackpool	1	0	1972	Wembley	0	1
1897	Nottingham	6	0	1933	Belfast	3	0	1973	Everton	2	1
1898	Belfast	3	2	1935	Everton	2	1	1974	Wembley	1	0
1899	Sunderland	13	2	1935	Belfast	3	1	1975	Belfast	0	0
1900	Dublin	2	0	1936	Stoke	3	1	1976	Wembley	4	0
1901	Southampton	3	0	1937	Belfast	5	1	1977	Belfast	2	1
1902	Belfast	1	0	1938	Manchester	7	0	1978	Wembley	1	0
1903	Wolverhampton	4	0	1946	Belfast	7	2	EC1979	Wembley	4	0
1904	Belfast	3	1	1947	Everton	2	2	1979	Belfast	2	0
1905	Middlesbrough	1	1	1948	Belfast	6	2	EC1979	Belfast	5	1
1906	Belfast	5	0	wc1949	Manchester	9	2	1980	Wembley	1	1
1907	Everton	1	0	1950	Belfast	4	1	1982	Wembley	4	0
1908	Belfast	3	1	1951	Aston Villa	2	0	1983	Belfast	0	0
1909	Bradford	4	0	1952	Belfast	2	2	1984	Wembley	1	0
1910	Belfast	1	1	wc1953	Everton	3	1	wc1985	Belfast	1	0
1911	Derby	2	1	1954	Belfast	2	0	wc1985	Wembley	0	0
1912	Dublin	6	1	1955	Wembley	3	0	EC1986	Wembley	3	0
1913	Belfast	1	2	1956	Belfast	1	1	EC1987	Belfast	2	0

SCOTLAND v WALES

Played: 101; Scotland won 60, Wales won 18, Drawn 23. *Goals:* Scotland 238, Wales 111.

Year	Venue	S	W	Year	Venue	S	W	Year	Venue	S	W
1876	Glasgow	4	0	1910	Kilmarnock	1	0	1955	Glasgow	2	0
1877	Wrexham	2	0	1911	Cardiff	2	2	1956	Cardiff	2	2
1878	Glasgow	9	0	1912	Tynecastle	1	0	1957	Glasgow	1	1
1879	Wrexham	3	0	1913	Wrexham	0	0	1958	Cardiff	3	0
1880	Glasgow	5	1	1914	Glasgow	0	0	1959	Glasgow	1	1
1881	Wrexham	5	1	1920	Cardiff	1	1	1960	Cardiff	0	2
1882	Glasgow	5	0	1921	Aberdeen	2	1	1961	Glasgow	2	0
1883	Wrexham	4	1	1922	Wrexham	1	2	1962	Cardiff	3	2
1884	Glasgow	4	1	1923	Paisley	2	0	1963	Glasgow	2	1
1885	Wrexham	8	1	1924	Cardiff	0	2	1964	Cardiff	2	3
1886	Glasgow	4	1	1925	Tynecastle	3	1	EC1965	Glasgow	4	1
1887	Wrexham	2	0	1926	Cardiff	3	0	EC1966	Cardiff	1	1
1888	Edinburgh	5	1	1927	Glasgow	3	0	1967	Glasgow	3	2
1889	Wrexham	0	0	1928	Wrexham	2	2	1969	Wrexham	5	3
1890	Paisley	5	0	1929	Glasgow	4	2	1970	Glasgow	0	0
1891	Wrexham	4	3	1930	Cardiff	4	2	1971	Cardiff	0	0
1892	Edinburgh	6	1	1931	Glasgow	1	1	1972	Glasgow	1	0
1893	Wrexham	8	0	1932	Wrexham	3	2	1973	Wrexham	2	0
1894	Kilmarnock	5	2	1933	Edinburgh	2	5	1974	Glasgow	2	0
1895	Wrexham	2	2	1934	Cardiff	2	3	1975	Cardiff	2	2
1896	Dundee	4	0	1935	Aberdeen	3	2	1976	Glasgow	3	1
1897	Wrexham	2	2	1936	Cardiff	1	1	wc1977	Glasgow	1	0
1898	Motherwell	5	2	1937	Dundee	1	2	1977	Wrexham	0	0
1899	Wrexham	6	0	1938	Cardiff	1	2	wc1977	Liverpool	2	0
1900	Aberdeen	5	2	1939	Edinburgh	3	2	1978	Glasgow	1	1
1901	Wrexham	1	1	1946	Wrexham	1	3	1979	Cardiff	0	3
1902	Greenock	5	1	1947	Glasgow	1	2	1980	Glasgow	1	0
1903	Cardiff	1	0	wc1948	Cardiff	3	1	1981	Swansea	0	2
1904	Dundee	1	1	1949	Glasgow	2	0	1982	Glasgow	1	0
1905	Wrexham	1	3	1950	Cardiff	3	1	1983	Cardiff	2	0
1906	Edinburgh	0	2	1951	Glasgow	0	1	1984	Glasgow	2	1
1907	Wrexham	0	1	wc1952	Cardiff	2	1	wc1985	Glasgow	0	1
1908	Dundee	2	1	1953	Glasgow	3	3	wc1985	Cardiff	1	1
1909	Wrexham	2	3	1954	Cardiff	1	0				

SCOTLAND v IRELAND

Played: 91; Scotland won 60, Ireland won 15, Drawn 16. *Goals:* Scotland 253, Ireland 81.

Year	Venue	S	I	Year	Venue	S	I	Year	Venue	S	I
1884	Belfast	5	0	1920	Glasgow	3	0	1957	Belfast	1	1
1885	Glasgow	8	2	1921	Belfast	2	0	1958	Glasgow	2	2
1886	Belfast	7	2	1922	Glasgow	2	1	1959	Belfast	4	0
1887	Glasgow	4	1	1923	Belfast	1	0	1960	Glasgow	5	2
1888	Belfast	10	2	1924	Glasgow	2	0	1961	Belfast	6	1
1889	Glasgow	7	0	1925	Belfast	3	0	1962	Glasgow	5	1
1890	Belfast	4	1	1926	Glasgow	4	0	1963	Belfast	1	2
1891	Glasgow	2	1	1927	Belfast	2	0	1964	Glasgow	3	2
1892	Belfast	3	2	1928	Glasgow	0	1	1965	Belfast	2	3
1893	Glasgow	6	1	1929	Belfast	7	3	1966	Glasgow	2	1
1894	Belfast	2	1	1930	Glasgow	3	1	1967	Belfast	0	1
1895	Glasgow	3	1	1931	Belfast	0	0	1969	Glasgow	1	1
1896	Belfast	3	3	1932	Glasgow	3	1	1970	Belfast	1	0
1897	Glasgow	5	1	1933	Belfast	4	0	1971	Glasgow	0	1
1898	Belfast	3	0	1934	Glasgow	1	2	1972	Glasgow	2	0
1899	Glasgow	9	1	1935	Belfast	1	2	1973	Glasgow	1	2
1900	Belfast	3	0	1936	Edinburgh	2	1	1974	Glasgow	0	1
1901	Glasgow	11	0	1937	Belfast	3	1	1975	Glasgow	3	0
1902	Belfast	5	1	1938	Aberdeen	1	1	1976	Glasgow	3	0
1903	Glasgow	0	2	1939	Belfast	2	0	1977	Glasgow	3	0
1904	Dublin	1	1	1946	Glasgow	0	0	1978	Glasgow	1	1
1905	Glasgow	4	0	1947	Belfast	0	2	1979	Glasgow	1	0
1906	Dublin	1	0	1948	Glasgow	3	2	1980	Belfast	0	1
1907	Glasgow	3	0	1949	Belfast	8	2	wc1981	Glasgow	1	1
1908	Dublin	5	0	1950	Glasgow	6	1	1981	Glasgow	2	0
1909	Glasgow	5	0	1951	Belfast	3	0	wc1981	Belfast	0	0
1910	Belfast	0	1	1952	Glasgow	1	1	1982	Belfast	1	1
1911	Glasgow	2	0	1953	Belfast	3	1	1983	Glasgow	0	0
1912	Belfast	4	1	1954	Glasgow	2	2	1984	Belfast	0	2
1913	Dublin	2	1	1955	Belfast	1	2	1992	Glasgow	1	0
1914	Belfast	1	1	1956	Glasgow	1	0				

WALES v IRELAND

Played: 90; Wales won 42, Ireland won 27, Drawn 21. *Goals:* Wales 181, Ireland 126.

Year	Venue	W	I	Year	Venue	W	I	Year	Venue	W	I
1882	Wrexham	7	1	1912	Cardiff	2	3	wc1954	Wrexham	1	2
1883	Belfast	1	1	1913	Belfast	1	0	1955	Belfast	3	2
1884	Wrexham	6	0	1914	Wrexham	1	2	1956	Cardiff	1	1
1885	Belfast	8	2	1920	Belfast	2	2	1957	Belfast	0	0
1886	Wrexham	5	0	1921	Swansea	2	1	1958	Cardiff	1	1
1887	Belfast	1	4	1922	Belfast	1	1	1959	Belfast	1	4
1888	Wrexham	11	0	1923	Wrexham	0	3	1960	Wrexham	3	2
1889	Belfast	3	1	1924	Belfast	1	0	1961	Belfast	5	1
1890	Shrewsbury	5	2	1925	Wrexham	0	0	1962	Cardiff	4	0
1891	Belfast	2	7	1926	Belfast	0	3	1963	Belfast	4	1
1892	Bangor	1	1	1927	Cardiff	2	2	1964	Cardiff	2	3
1893	Belfast	3	4	1928	Belfast	2	1	1965	Belfast	5	0
1894	Swansea	4	1	1929	Wrexham	2	2	1966	Cardiff	1	4
1895	Belfast	2	2	1930	Belfast	0	7	EC1967	Belfast	0	0
1896	Wrexham	6	1	1931	Wrexham	3	2	EC1968	Wrexham	2	0
1897	Belfast	3	4	1932	Belfast	0	4	1969	Belfast	0	0
1898	Llandudno	0	1	1933	Wrexham	4	1	1970	Swansea	1	0
1899	Belfast	0	1	1934	Belfast	1	1	1971	Belfast	0	1
1900	Llandudno	2	0	1935	Wrexham	3	1	1972	Wrexham	0	0
1901	Belfast	1	0	1936	Belfast	2	3	1973	Everton	0	1
1902	Cardiff	0	3	1937	Wrexham	4	1	1974	Wrexham	1	0
1903	Belfast	0	2	1938	Belfast	0	1	1975	Belfast	0	1
1904	Bangor	0	1	1939	Wrexham	3	1	1976	Swansea	1	0
1905	Belfast	2	2	1947	Belfast	1	2	1977	Belfast	1	1
1906	Wrexham	4	4	1948	Wrexham	2	0	1978	Wrexham	1	0
1907	Belfast	3	2	1949	Belfast	2	0	1979	Belfast	1	1
1908	Aberdare	0	1	wc1950	Wrexham	0	0	1980	Cardiff	0	1
1909	Belfast	3	2	1951	Belfast	2	1	1982	Wrexham	3	0
1910	Wrexham	4	1	1952	Swansea	3	0	1983	Belfast	1	0
1911	Belfast	2	1	1953	Belfast	3	2	1984	Swansea	1	1

OTHER BRITISH INTERNATIONAL RESULTS 1908–1993
ENGLAND

v ALBANIA

			E	A
wc1989	8 Mar	Tirana	2	0
wc1989	26 Apr	Wembley	5	0

v ARGENTINA

			E	A
1951	9 May	Wembley	2	1
1953	17 May	Buenos Aires	0	0
(abandoned after 21 mins)				
wc1962	2 June	Rancagua	3	1
1964	6 June	Rio de Janeiro	0	1
wc1966	23 July	Wembley	1	0
1974	22 May	Wembley	2	2
1977	12 June	Buenos Aires	1	1
1980	13 May	Wembley	3	1
wc1986	22 June	Mexico City	1	2
1991	25 May	Wembley	2	2

v AUSTRALIA

			E	A
1980	31 May	Sydney	2	1
1983	11 June	Sydney	0	0
1983	15 June	Brisbane	1	0
1983	18 June	Melbourne	1	1
1991	1 June	Sydney	1	0

v AUSTRIA

			E	A
1908	6 June	Vienna	6	1
1908	8 June	Vienna	11	1
1909	1 June	Vienna	8	1
1930	14 May	Vienna	0	0
1932	7 Dec	Chelsea	4	3
1936	6 May	Vienna	1	2
1951	28 Nov	Wembley	2	2
1952	25 May	Vienna	3	2
wc1958	15 June	Boras	2	2
1961	27 May	Vienna	1	3
1962	4 Apr	Wembley	3	1
1965	20 Oct	Wembley	2	3
1967	27 May	Vienna	1	0
1973	26 Sept	Wembley	7	0
1979	13 June	Vienna	3	4

v BELGIUM

			E	B
1921	21 May	Brussels	2	0
1923	19 Mar	Highbury	6	1
1923	1 Nov	Antwerp	2	2
1924	8 Dec	West Bromwich	4	0
1926	24 May	Antwerp	5	3
1927	11 May	Brussels	9	1
1928	19 May	Antwerp	3	1
1929	11 May	Brussels	5	1
1931	16 May	Brussels	4	1
1936	9 May	Brussels	2	3
1947	21 Sept	Brussels	5	2
1950	18 May	Brussels	4	1
1952	26 Nov	Wembley	5	0
wc1954	17 June	Basle	4	4*
1964	21 Oct	Wembley	2	2
1970	25 Feb	Brussels	3	1
EC1980	12 June	Turin	1	1
wc1990	27 June	Bologna	1	0*

After extra time

v BOHEMIA

			E	B
1908	13 June	Prague	4	0

v BRAZIL

			E	B
1956	9 May	Wembley	4	2
wc1958	11 June	Gothenburg	0	0
1959	13 May	Rio de Janeiro	0	2
wc1962	10 June	Vina del Mar	1	3
1963	8 May	Wembley	1	1

			E	B
1964	30 May	Rio de Janeiro	1	5
1969	12 June	Rio de Janeiro	1	2
wc1970	7 June	Guadalajara	0	1
1976	23 May	Los Angeles	0	1
1977	8 June	Rio de Janeiro	0	0
1978	19 Apr	Wembley	1	1
1981	12 May	Wembley	0	1
1984	10 June	Rio de Janeiro	2	0
1987	19 May	Wembley	1	1
1990	28 Mar	Wembley	1	0
1992	17 May	Wembley	1	1
1993	13 June	Washington	1	1

v BULGARIA

			E	B
wc1962	7 June	Rancagua	0	0
1968	11 Dec	Wembley	1	1
1974	1 June	Sofia	1	0
EC1979	6 June	Sofia	3	0
EC1979	22 Nov	Wembley	2	0

v CAMEROON

			E	C
wc1990	1 July	Naples	3	2*
1991	6 Feb	Wembley	2	0

v CANADA

			E	C
1986	24 May	Burnaby	1	0

v CHILE

			E	C
wc1950	25 June	Rio de Janeiro	2	0
1953	24 May	Santiago	2	1
1984	17 June	Santiago	0	0
1989	23 May	Wembley	0	0

v CIS

			E	C
1992	29 Apr	Moscow	2	2

v COLOMBIA

			E	C
1970	20 May	Bogota	4	0
1988	24 May	Wembley	1	1

v CYPRUS

			E	C
EC1975	16 Apr	Wembley	5	0
EC1975	11 May	Limassol	1	0

v CZECHOSLOVAKIA

			E	C
1934	16 May	Prague	1	2
1937	1 Dec	Tottenham	5	4
1963	29 May	Bratislava	4	2
1966	2 Nov	Wembley	0	0
wc1970	11 June	Guadalajara	1	0
1973	27 May	Prague	1	1
EC1974	30 Oct	Wembley	3	0
EC1975	30 Oct	Bratislava	1	2
1978	29 Nov	Wembley	1	0
wc1982	20 June	Bilbao	2	0
1990	25 Apr	Wembley	4	2
1992	25 Mar	Prague	2	2

v DENMARK

			E	D
1948	26 Sept	Copenhagen	0	0
1955	2 Oct	Copenhagen	5	1
wc1956	5 Dec	Wolverhampton	5	2
wc1957	15 May	Copenhagen	4	1
1966	3 July	Copenhagen	2	0
EC1978	20 Sept	Copenhagen	4	3
EC1979	12 Sept	Wembley	1	0
EC1982	22 Sept	Copenhagen	2	2
EC1983	21 Sept	Wembley	0	1
1988	14 Sept	Wembley	1	0
1989	7 June	Copenhagen	1	1

			E	D
1990	15 May	Wembley	1	0
EC1992	11 June	Malmo	0	0

v ECUADOR

			E	Ec
1970	24 May	Quito	2	0

v EGYPT

			E	Eg
1986	29 Jan	Cairo	4	0
wc1990	21 June	Cagliari	1	0

v FIFA

			E	FIFA
1938	26 Oct	Highbury	3	0
1953	21 Oct	Wembley	4	4
1963	23 Oct	Wembley	2	1

v FINLAND

			E	F
1937	20 May	Helsinki	8	0
1956	20 May	Helsinki	5	1
1966	26 June	Helsinki	3	0
wc1976	13 Juje	Helsinki	4	1
wc1976	13 Oct	Wembley	2	1
1982	3 June	Helsinki	4	1
wc1984	17 Oct	Wembley	5	0
wc1985	22 May	Helsinki	1	1
1992	3 June	Helsinki	2	1

v FRANCE

			E	F
1923	10 May	Paris	4	1
1924	17 May	Paris	3	1
1925	21 May	Paris	3	2
1927	26 May	Paris	6	0
1928	17 May	Paris	5	1
1929	9 May	Paris	4	1
1931	14 May	Paris	2	5
1933	6 Dec	Tottenham	4	1
1938	26 May	Paris	4	2
1947	3 May	Highbury	3	0
1949	22 May	Paris	3	1
1951	3 Oct	Highbury	2	2
1955	15 May	Paris	0	1
1957	27 Nov	Wembley	4	0
EC1962	3 Oct	Sheffield	1	1
EC1963	27 Feb	Paris	2	5
wc1966	20 July	Wembley	2	0
1969	12 Mar	Wembley	5	0
wc1982	16 June	Bilbao	3	1
1984	29 Feb	Paris	0	2
1992	19 Feb	Wembley	2	0
EC1992	14 June	Malmo	0	0

v GERMANY

			E	G
1930	10 May	Berlin	3	3
1935	4 Dec	Tottenham	3	0
1938	14 May	Berlin	6	3
1991	11 Sept	Wembley	0	1
1993	19 June	Detroit	1	2

v EAST GERMANY

			E	EG
1963	2 June	Leipzig	2	1
1970	25 Nov	Wembley	3	1
1974	29 May	Leipzig	1	1
1984	12 Sept	Wembley	1	0

v WEST GERMANY

			E	WG
1954	1 Dec	Wembley	3	1
1956	26 May	Berlin	3	1
1965	12 May	Nuremberg	1	0
1966	23 Feb	Wembley	1	0
wc1966	30 July	Wembley	4	2*
1968	1 June	Hanover	0	1
wc1970	14 June	Leon	2	3*
EC1972	29 Apr	Wembley	1	3
EC1972	13 May	Berlin	0	0
1975	12 Mar	Wembley	2	0

			E	WG
1978	22 Feb	Munich	1	2
wc1982	29 June	Madrid	0	0
1982	13 Oct	Wembley	1	2
1985	12 June	Mexico City	3	0
1987	9 Sept	Dusseldorf	1	3
wc1990	4 July	Turin	1	1*

*After extra time

v GREECE

			E	G
EC1971	21 Apr	Wembley	3	0
EC1971	1 Dec	Athens	2	0
EC1982	17 Nov	Athens	3	0
EC1983	30 Mar	Wembhey	0	0
1989	8 Feb	Athens	2	1

v HOLLAND

			E	N
1935	18 May	Amsterdam	1	0
1946	27 Nov	Huddersfield	8	2
1964	9 Dec	Amsterdam	1	1
1969	5 Nov	Amsterdam	1	0
1970	14 Jun	Wembley	0	0
1977	9 Feb	Wembley	0	2
1982	25 May	Wembley	2	0
1988	23 Mar	Wembley	2	2
EC1988	15 June	Dusseldorf	1	3
wc1990	16 June	Cagliari	0	0
wc1993	28 Apr	Wembley	2	2

v HUNGARY

			E	H
1908	10 June	Budapest	7	0
1909	29 May	Budapest	4	2
1909	31 May	Budapest	8	2
1934	10 May	Budapest	1	2
1936	2 Dec	Highbury	6	2
1953	25 Nov	Wembley	3	6
1954	23 May	Budapest	1	7
1960	22 May	Budapest	0	2
wc1962	31 May	Rancagua	1	2
1965	5 May	Wembley	1	0
1978	24 May	Wembley	4	1
wc1981	6 June	Budapest	3	1
wc1982	18 Nov	Wembley	1	0
EC1983	27 Apr	Wembley	2	0
EC1983	12 Oct	Budapest	3	0
1988	27 Apr	Budapest	0	0
1990	12 Sept	Wembley	1	0
1992	12 May	Budapest	1	0

v ICELAND

			E	I
1982	2 June	Reykjavik	1	1

v REPUBLIC OF IRELAND

			E	RI
1946	30 Sept	Dublin	1	0
1949	21 Sept	Everton	0	2
wc1957	8 May	Wembley	5	1
wc1957	19 May	Dublin	1	1
1964	24 May	Dublin	3	1
1976	8 Sept	Wembley	1	1
EC1978	25 Oct	Dublin	1	1
EC1980	6 Feb	Wembley	2	0
1985	26 Mar	Wembley	2	1
EC1988	12 June	Stuttgart	0	1
wc1990	11 June	Cagliari	1	1
EC1990	14 Nov	Dublin	1	1
EC1991	27 Mar	Dublin	1	1

v ISRAEL

			E	I
1986	26 Feb	Ramat Gan	2	1
1988	17 Feb	Tel Aviv	0	0

v ITALY

			E	I
1933	13 May	Rome	1	1
1934	14 Nov	Highbury	3	2
1939	13 May	Milan	2	2

			E	I
1948	16 May	Turin	4	0
1949	30 Nov	Tottenham	2	0
1952	18 May	Florence	1	1
1959	6 May	Wembley	2	2
1961	24 May	Rome	3	2
1973	14 June	Turin	0	2
1973	14 Nov	Wembley	0	1
1976	28 May	New York	3	2
wc1976	17 Nov	Rome	0	2
wc1977	16 Nov	Wembley	2	0
ec1980	15 June	Turin	0	1
1985	6 June	Mexico City	1	2
1989	15 Nov	Wembley	0	0
wc1990	7 July	Bari	1	2

		v KUWAIT	E	K
wc1982	25 June	Bilbao	1	0

		v LUXEMBOURG	E	L
1927	21 May	Luxembourg	5	2
wc1960	19 Oct	Luxembourg	9	0
wc1961	28 Sept	Highbury	4	1
wc1977	30 Mar	Wembley	5	0
wc1977	12 Oct	Luxembourg	2	0
ec1982	15 Dec	Wembley	9	0
ec1983	16 Nov	Luxembourg	4	0

		v MALAYSIA	E	M
1991	12 June	Kuala Lumpur	4	2

		v MALTA	E	M
ec1971	3 Feb	Valletta	1	0
ec1971	12 May	Wembley	5	0

		v MEXICO	E	M
1959	24 May	Mexico City	1	2
1961	10 May	Wembley	8	0
wc1966	16 July	Wembley	2	0
1969	1 June	Mexico City	0	0
1985	9 June	Mexico City	0	1
1986	17 May	Los Angeles	3	0

		v MOROCCO	E	M
wc1986	6 June	Monterrey	0	0

		v NEW ZEALAND	E	NZ
1991	3 June	Auckland	1	0
1991	8 June	Wellington	2	0

		v NORWAY	E	N
1937	14 May	Oslo	6	0
1938	9 Nov	Newcastle	4	0
1949	18 May	Oslo	4	1
1966	29 June	Oslo	6	1
wc1980	10 Sept	Wembley	4	0
wc1981	9 Sept	Oslo	1	2
wc1992	14 Oct	Wembley	1	1
wc1993	2 June	Oslo	0	2

		v PARAGUAY	E	P
wc1986	18 June	Mexico City	3	0

		v PERU	E	P
1959	17 May	Lima	1	4
1962	20 May	Lima	4	0

		v POLAND	E	P
1966	5 Jan	Everton	1	1
1966	5 July	Chorzow	1	0
wc1973	6 Jqne	Chorzow	0	2
wc1973	17 Oct	Wembley	1	1
wc1986	11 June	Monterrey	3	0
wc1989	3 June	Wembley	3	0
wc1989	11 Oct	Katowice	0	0

			E	P
ec1990	17 Oct	Wembley	2	0
wc1991	13 Nov	Poznan	1	1
wc1993	29 May	Katowice	1	1

		v PORTUGAL	E	P
1947	25 May	Lisbon	10	0
1950	14 May	Lisbon	5	3
1951	19 May	Everton	5	2
1955	22 May	Oporto	1	3
1958	7 May	Wembley	2	1
wc1961	21 May	Lisbon	1	1
wc1961	25 Oct	Wembley	2	0
1964	17 May	Lisbon	4	3
1964	4 June	São Paulo	1	1
wc1966	26 July	Wembley	2	1
1969	10 Dec	Wembley	1	0
1974	3 Apr	Lisbon	0	0
ec1974	20 Nov	Wembley	0	0
ec1975	19 Nov	Lisbon	1	1
wc1986	3 June	Monterrey	0	1

		v ROMANIA	E	R
1939	24 May	Bucharest	2	0
1968	6 Nov	Bucharest	0	0
1969	15 Jan	Wembley	1	1
wc1970	2 June	Guadalajara	1	0
wc1980	15 Oct	Bucharest	1	2
wc1981	29 April	Wembley	0	0
wc1985	1 May	Bucharest	0	0
wc1985	11 Sept	Wembley	1	1

		v SAN MARINO	E	SM
wc1992	17 Feb	Wembley	6	0

		v SAUDI ARABIA	E	SA
1988	16 Nov	Riyadh	1	1

		v SPAIN	E	S
1929	15 May	Madrid	3	4
1931	9 Dec	Highbury	7	1
wc1950	2 July	Rio de Janeiro	0	1
1955	18 May	Madrid	1	1
1955	30 Nov	Wembley	4	1
1960	15 May	Madrid	0	3
1960	26 Oct	Wembley	4	2
1965	8 Dec	Madrid	2	0
1967	24 May	Wembley	2	0
ec1968	3 Apr	Wembley	1	0
ec1968	8 May	Madrid	2	1
1980	26 Mar	Barcelona	2	0
ec1980	18 June	Naples	2	1
1981	25 Mar	Wembley	1	2
wc1982	5 July	Madrid	0	0
1987	18 Feb	Madrid	4	2
1992	9 Sept	Santander	0	1

		v SWEDEN	E	S
1923	21 May	Stockholm	4	2
1923	24 May	Stockholm	3	1
1937	17 May	Stockholm	4	0
1947	19 Nov	Highbury	4	2
1949	13 May	Stockholm	1	3
1956	16 May	Stockholm	0	0
1959	28 Oct	Wembley	2	3
1965	16 May	Gothenburg	2	1
1968	22 May	Wembley	3	1
1979	10 June	Stockholm	0	0
1986	10 Sept	Stockholm	0	1
wc1988	19 Oct	Wembley	0	0
wc1989	6 Sept	Stockholm	0	0
ec1992	17 June	Stockholm	1	2

v SWITZERLAND		E	S
1933	20 May Berne	4	0
1938	21 May Zurich	1	2
1947	18 May Zurich	0	1
1948	2 Dec Highbury	6	0
1952	28 May Zurich	3	0
wc1954	20 June Berne	2	0
1962	9 May Wembley	3	1
1963	5 June Basle	8	1
EC1971	13 Oct Basle	3	2
EC1971	10 Nov Wembley	1	1
1975	3 Sept Basle	2	1
1977	7 Sept Wembley	0	0
wc1980	19 Nov Wembley	2	1
wc1981	30 May Basle	1	2
1988	28 May Lausanne	1	0

v TUNISIA		E	T
1990	2 June Tunis	1	1

v TURKEY		E	T
wc1984	14 Nov Istanbul	8	0
wc1985	16 Oct Wembley	5	0
EC1987	29 Apr Izmir	0	0
EC1987	14 Oct Wembley	8	0
EC1991	1 May Izmir	1	0
EC1991	16 Oct Wembley	1	0
wc1992	18 Nov Wembley	4	0
wc1993	31 Mar Izmir	2	0

v URUGUAY		E	U
1953	31 May Montevideo	1	2
wc1954	26 June Basle	2	4
1964	6 May Wembley	2	1
wc1966	11 July Wembley	0	0
1969	8 June Montevideo	2	1
1977	15 June Montevideo	0	0
1984	13 June Montevideo	0	2
1990	22 May Wembley	1	2

v USA		E	USA
wc1950	29 June Belo Horizonte	0	1
1953	8 June New York	6	3
1959	28 May Los Angeles	8	1
1964	27 May New York	10	0
1985	16 Juje Los Angeles	5	0
1993	9 June Foxboro	0	2

v USSR		E	USSR
1958	18 May Moscow	1	1
wc1958	8 June Gothenburg	2	2
wc1958	17 June Gothenburg	0	1
1958	22 Oct Wembley	5	0
1967	6 Dec Wembley	2	2
EC1968	8 June Rome	2	0
1973	10 June Moscow	2	1
1984	2 June Wembley	0	2
1986	26 Mar Tbilisi	1	0
EC1988	18 June Frankfurt	1	3
1991	21 May Wembley	3	1

v YUGOSLAVIA		E	Y
1939	18 May Belgrade	1	2
1950	22 Nov Highbury	2	2
1954	16 May Belgrade	0	1
1956	28 Nov Wembley	3	0
1958	11 May Belgrade	0	5
1960	11 May Wembley	3	3
1965	9 May Belgrade	1	1
1966	4 May Wembley	2	0
EC1968	5 June Florence	0	1
1972	11 Oct Wembley	1	1
1974	5 June Belgrade	2	2
EC1986	12 Nov Wembley	2	0
EC1987	11 Nov Belgrade	4	1
1989	13 Dec Wembley	2	1

SCOTLAND

v ARGENTINA		S	A
1977	18 June Buenos Aires	1	1
1979	2 June Glasgow	1	3
1990	28 Mar Glasgow	1	0

v AUSTRALIA		S	A
wc1985	20 Nov Glasgow	2	0
wc1985	4 Dec Melbourne	0	0

v AUSTRIA		S	A
1931	16 May Vienna	0	5
1933	29 Nov Glasgow	2	2
1937	9 May Vienna	1	1
1950	13 Dec Glasgow	0	1
1951	27 May Vienna	0	4
wc1954	16 June Zurich	0	1
1955	19 May Vienna	4	1
1956	2 May Glasgow	1	1
1960	29 May Vienna	1	4
1963	8 May Glasgow	4	1
(abandoned after 79 mins)			
wc1968	6 Nov Glasgow	2	1
wc1969	5 Nov Vienna	0	2
EC1978	20 Sept Vienna	2	3
EC1979	17 Oct Glasgow	1	1

v BELGIUM		S	B
1947	18 May Brussels	1	2
1948	28 Apr Glasgow	2	0
1951	20 May Brussels	5	0
EC1971	3 Feb Liège	0	3
EC1971	10 Nov Aberdeen	1	0

		S	B
1974	2 June Brussels	1	2
EC1979	21 Nov Brussels	0	2
EC1979	19 Dec Glasgow	1	3
EC1982	15 Dec Brussels	2	3
EC1983	12 Oct Glasgow	1	1
EC1987	1 Apr Brussels	1	4
EC1987	14 Oct Glasgow	2	0

v BRAZIL		S	B
1966	25 June Glasgow	1	1
1972	5 July Rio de Janeiro	0	1
1973	30 June Glasgow	0	1
wc1974	18 June Frankfurt	0	0
1977	23 June Rio de Janeiro	0	2
wc1982	18 June Seville	1	4
1987	26 May Glasgow	0	2
wc1990	20 June Turin	0	1

v BULGARIA		S	B
1978	22 Feb Glasgow	2	1
EC1986	10 Sept Glasgow	0	0
EC1987	11 Nov Sofia	1	0
EC1990	14 Nov Sofia	1	1
EC1991	27 Mar Glasgow	1	1

v CANADA		S	C
1983	12 June Vancouver	2	0
1983	16 June Edmonton	3	0
1983	20 June Toronto	2	0
1992	21 May Toronto	3	1

820

v CHILE		S	C
1977	15 June Santiago	4	2
1989	30 May Glasgow	2	0

v CIS		S	C
EC1992	18 June Norrkoping	3	0

v COLOMBIA		S	C
1988	17 May Glasgow	0	0

v COSTA RICA		S	CR
WC1990	11 June Genoa	0	1

v CYPRUS		S	C
WC1968	17 Dec Nicosia	5	0
WC1969	11 May Glasgow	8	0
WC1989	8 Feb Limassol	3	2
WC1989	26 Apr Glasgow	2	1

v CZECHOSLOVAKIA		S	C
1937	22 May Prague	3	1
1937	8 Dec Glasgow	5	0
WC1961	14 May Bratislava	0	4
WC1961	26 Sept Glasgow	3	2
WC1961	29 Nov Brussels	2	4*
1972	2 July Porto Alegre	0	0
WC1973	26 Sept Glasgow	2	1
WC1973	17 Oct Prague	0	1
WC1976	13 Oct Prague	0	2
WC1977	21 Sept Glasgow	3	1

*After extra time

v DENMARK		S	D
1951	12 May Glasgow	3	1
1952	25 May Copenhagen	2	1
1968	16 Oct Copenhagen	1	0
EC1970	11 Nov Glasgow	1	0
EC1971	9 June Copenhagen	0	1
WC1972	18 Oct Copenhagen	4	1
WC1972	15 Nov Glasgow	2	0
EC1975	3 Sept Copenhagen	1	0
EC1975	29 Oct Glasgow	3	1
WC1986	4 June Nezahualcayotl	0	1

v EGYPT		S	E
1990	16 May Aberdeen	1	3

v ESTONIA		S	E
WC1993	19 May Tallinn	3	0
WC1993	2 June Aberdeen	3	1

v FINLAND		S	F
1954	25 May Helsinki	2	1
WC1964	21 Oct Glasgow	3	1
WC1965	27 May Helsinki	2	1
1976	8 Sept Glasgow	6	0
1992	25 Mar Glasgow	1	1

v FRANCE		S	F
1930	18 May Paris	2	0
1932	8 May Paris	3	1
1948	23 May Paris	0	3
1949	27 Apr Glasgow	2	0
1950	27 May Paris	1	0
1951	16 May Glasgow	1	0
WC1958	15 June Orebro	1	2
1984	1 June Marseilles	0	2
WC1989	8 Mar Glasgow	2	0
WC1989	11 Oct Paris	0	3

v GERMANY		S	G
1929	1 June Berlin	1	1
1936	14 Oct Glasgow	2	0
EC1992	15 June Norrkoping	0	2
1993	24 Mar Glasgow	0	1

v EAST GERMANY		S	EG
1974	30 Oct Glasgow	3	0
1977	7 Sept East Berlin	0	1
EC1982	13 Oct Glasgow	2	0
EC1983	16 Nov Halle	1	2
1985	16 Oct Glasgow	0	0
1990	25 Apr Glasgow	0	1

v WEST GERMANY		S	WG
1957	22 May Stuttgart	3	1
1959	6 May Glasgow	3	2
1964	12 May Hanover	2	2
WC1969	16 Apr Glasgow	1	1
WC1969	22 Oct Hamburg	2	3
1973	14 Nov Glasgow	1	1
1974	27 Mar Frankfurt	1	2
WC1986	8 June Queretaro	1	2

v HOLLAND		S	N
1929	4 June Amsterdam	2	0
1938	21 May Amsterdam	3	1
1959	27 May Amsterdam	2	1
1966	11 May Glasgow	0	3
1968	30 May Amsterdam	0	0
1971	1 Dec Rotterdam	1	2
WC1978	11 June Mendoza	3	2
1982	23 Mar Glasgow	2	1
1986	29 Apr Eindhoven	0	0
EC1992	12 June Gothenburg	0	1

v HUNGARY		S	H
1938	7 Dec Glasgow	3	1
1954	8 Dec Glasgow	2	4
1955	29 May Budapest	1	3
1958	7 May Glasgow	1	1
1960	5 June Budapest	3	3
1980	31 May Budapest	1	3
1987	9 Sept Glasgow	2	0

v ICELAND		S	I
WC1984	17 Oct Glasgow	3	0
WC1985	28 May Reykjavik	1	0

v IRAN		S	I
WC1978	7 June Cordoba	1	1

v REPUBLIC OF IRELAND		S	RI
WC1961	3 May Glasgow	4	1
WC1961	7 May Dublin	3	0
1963	9 June Dublin	0	1
1969	21 Sept Dublin	1	1
EC1986	15 Oct Dublin	0	0
EC1987	18 Feb Glasgow	0	1

v ISRAEL		S	I
WC1981	25 Feb Tel Aviv	1	0
WC1981	28 Apr Glasgow	3	1
1986	28 Jan Tel Aviv	1	0

v ITALY		S	I
1931	20 May Rome	0	3
WC1965	9 Nov Glasgow	1	0
WC1965	7 Dec Naples	0	3
1988	22 Dec Perugia	0	2
WC1992	18 Nov Glasgow	0	0

v LUXEMBOURG		S	L
1947	24 May Luxembourg	6	0
EC1986	12 Nov Glasgow	3	0
EC1987	2 Dec Esch	0	0

v MALTA		S	M
1988	22 Mar Valletta	1	1
1990	28 May Valletta	2	1
WC1993	17 Feb Glasgow	3	0

		NEW ZEALAND	S	NZ
wc1982	15 June	Malaga	5	2

		v NORWAY	S	N
1929	28 May	Oslo	7	3
1954	5 May	Glasgow	1	0
1954	19 May	Oslo	1	1
1963	4 June	Bergen	3	4
1963	7 Nov	Glasgow	6	1
1974	6 June	Oslo	2	1
EC1978	25 Oct	Glasgow	3	2
EC1979	7 June	Oslo	4	0
wc1988	14 Sept	Oslo	2	1
wc1989	15 Nov	Glasgow	1	1
1992	3 June	Oslo	0	0

		v PARAGUAY	S	P
wc1958	11 June	Norrkoping	2	3

		v PERU	S	P
1972	26 Apr	Glasgow	2	0
wc1978	3 June	Cordoba	1	3
1979	12 Sept	Glasgow	1	1

		v POLAND	S	P
1958	1 June	Warsaw	2	1
1960	4 June	Glasgow	2	3
wc1965	23 May	Chorzow	1	1
wc1965	13 Oct	Glasgow	1	2
1980	28 May	Poznan	0	1
1990	19 May	Glasgow	1	1

		v PORTUGAL	S	P
1950	21 May	Lisbon	2	2
1955	4 May	Glasgow	3	0
1959	3 June	Lisbon	0	1
1966	18 June	Glasgow	0	1
EC1971	21 Apr	Lisbon	0	2
EC1971	13 Oct	Glasgow	2	1
1975	13 May	Glasgow	1	0
EC1978	29 Nov	Lisbon	0	1
EC1980	26 Mar	Glasgow	4	1
wc1980	15 Oct	Glasgow	0	0
wc1981	18 Nov	Lisbon	1	2
wc1992	14 Oct	Glasgow	0	0
wc1993	28 Apr	Lisbon	0	5

		v ROMANIA	S	R
EC1975	1 June	Bucharest	1	1
EC1975	17 Dec	Glasgow	1	1
1986	26 Mar	Glasgow	3	0
EC1990	12 Sept	Glasgow	2	1
EC1991	16 Oct	Bucharest	0	1

		v SAN MARINO	S	SM
EC1991	1 May	Serravalle	2	0
EC1991	13 Nov	Glasgow	4	0

		v SAUDI ARABIA	S	SA
1988	17 Feb	Riyadh	2	2

		v SPAIN	S	Sp
wc1957	8 May	Glasgow	4	2
wc1957	26 May	Madrid	1	4

			S	Sp
1963	13 June	Madrid	6	2
1965	8 May	Glasgow	0	0
EC1974	20 Nov	Glasgow	1	2
EC1975	5 Feb	Valencia	1	1
1982	24 Feb	Valencia	0	3
wc1984	14 Nov	Glasgow	3	1
wc1985	27 Feb	Seville	0	1
1988	27 Apr	Madrid	0	0

		v SWEDEN	S	Sw
1952	30 May	Stockholm	1	3
1953	6 May	Glasgow	1	2
1975	16 Apr	Gothenburg	1	1
1977	27 Apr	Glasgow	3	1
wc1980	10 Sept	Stockholm	1	0
wc1981	9 Sept	Glasgow	2	0
wc1990	16 June	Genoa	2	1

		v SWITZERLAND	S	Sw
1931	24 May	Geneva	3	2
1948	17 May	Berne	1	2
1950	26 Apr	Glasgow	3	1
wc1957	19 May	Basle	2	1
wc1957	6 Nov	Glasgow	3	2
1973	22 June	Berne	0	1
1976	7 Apr	Glasgow	1	0
EC1982	17 Nov	Berne	0	2
EC1983	30 May	Glasgow	2	2
EC1990	17 Oct	Glasgow	2	1
EC1991	11 Sept	Berne	2	2
wc1992	9 Sept	Berne	1	3

		v TURKEY	S	T
1960	8 June	Ankara	2	4

		v URUGUAY	S	U
wc1954	19 June	Basle	0	7
1962	2 May	Glasgow	2	3
1983	21 Sept	Glasgow	2	0
wc1986	13 June	Nezahualcoyotl	0	0

		v USA	S	USA
1952	30 Apr	Glasgow	6	0
1992	17 May	Denver	1	0

		v USSR	S	USSR
1967	10 May	Glasgow	0	2
1971	14 June	Moscow	0	1
wc1982	22 June	Malaga	2	2
1991	6 Feb	Glasgow	0	1

		v YUGOSLAVIA	S	Y
1955	15 May	Belgrade	2	2
1956	21 Nov	Glasgow	2	0
wc1958	8 June	Vasteras	1	1
1972	29 June	Belo Horizonte	2	2
wc1974	22 June	Frankfurt	1	1
1984	12 Sept	Glasgow	6	1
wc1988	19 Oct	Glasgow	1	1
wc1989	6 Sept	Zagreb	1	3

		v ZAIRE	S	Z
wc1974	14 June	Dortmund	2	0

WALES

		v ARGENTINA	W	A
1992	3 June	Tokyo	0	1

		v AUSTRIA	W	A
1954	9 May	Vienna	0	2
EC1955	23 Nov	Wrexham	1	2
EC1974	4 Sept	Vienna	1	2

			W	A
1975	19 Nov	Wrexham	1	0
1992	29 Apr	Vienna	1	1

		v BELGIUM	W	B
1949	22 May	Liège	1	3
1949	23 Nov	Cardiff	5	1

			W	B
EC1990	17 Oct	Cardiff	3	1
EC1991	27 Mar	Brussels	1	1
WC1992	18 Nov	Brussels	0	2
WC1993	31 Mar	Cardiff	2	0

v BRAZIL			W	B
WC1958	19 June	Gothenburg	0	1
1962	12 May	Rio de Janeiro	1	3
1962	16 May	São Paulo	1	3
1966	14 May	Rio de Janeiro	1	3
1966	18 May	Belo Horizonte	0	1
1983	12 June	Cardiff	1	1
1991	11 Sept	Cardiff	1	0

v BULGARIA			W	B
EC1983	27 Apr	Wrexham	1	0
EC1983	16 Nov	Sofia	0	1

v CANADA			W	C
1986	10 May	Toronto	0	2
1986	20 May	Vancouver	3	0

v CHILE			W	C
1966	22 May	Santiago	0	2

v COSTA RICA			W	CR
1990	20 May	Cardiff	1	0

v CYPRUS			W	C
WC1992	14 Oct	Limassol	1	0

v CZECHOSLOVAKIA			W	C
WC1957	1 May	Cardiff	1	0
WC1957	26 May	Prague	0	2
EC1971	21 Apr	Swansea	1	3
EC1971	27 Oct	Prague	0	1
WC1977	30 Mar	Wrexham	3	0
WC1977	16 Nov	Prague	0	1
WC1980	19 Nov	Cardiff	1	0
WC1981	9 Sept	Prague	0	2
EC1987	29 Apr	Wrexham	1	1
EC1987	11 Nov	Prague	0	2
WC1993	28 Apr	Ostrava	1	1

v DENMARK			W	D
WC1964	21 Oct	Copenhagen	0	1
WC1965	1 Dec	Wrexham	4	2
EC1987	9 Sept	Cardiff	1	0
EC1987	14 Oct	Copenhagen	0	1
1990	11 Sept	Copenhagen	0	1

v FINLAND			W	F
EC1971	26 May	Helsinki	1	0
EC1971	13 Oct	Swansea	3	0
EC1987	10 Sept	Helsinki	1	1
EC1987	1 Apr	Wrexham	4	0
WC1988	19 Oct	Swansea	2	2
WC1989	6 Sept	Helsinki	0	1

v FAEROES			W	F
WC1992	9 Sept	Cardiff	6	0
WC1993	6 June	Toftir	3	0

v FRANCE			W	F
1933	25 May	Paris	1	1
1939	20 May	Paris	1	2
1953	14 May	Paris	1	6
1982	2 June	Toulouse	1	0

v EAST GERMANY			W	EG
WC1957	19 May	Leipzig	1	2
WC1957	25 Sept	Cardiff	4	1
WC1969	16 Apr	Dresden	1	2
WC1969	22 Oct	Cardiff	1	3

v WEST GERMANY			W	WG
1968	8 May	Cardiff	1	1
1969	26 Mar	Frankfurt	1	1
1976	6 Oct	Cardiff	0	2
1977	14 Dec	Dortmund	1	1
EC1979	2 May	Wrexham	0	2
EC1979	17 Oct	Cologne	1	5
WC1989	31 May	Cardiff	0	0
WC1989	15 Nov	Cologne	1	2
EC1991	5 June	Cardiff	1	0
EC1991	16 Oct	Nuremberg	1	4

v GREECE			W	G
WC1964	9 Dec	Athens	0	2
WC1965	17 Mar	Cardiff	4	1

v HOLLAND			W	H
WC1988	14 Sept	Amsterdam	0	1
WC1989	11 Oct	Wrexham	1	2
1992	30 May	Utrecht	0	4

v HUNGARY			W	H
WC1958	8 June	Sanviken	1	1
WC1958	17 June	Stockholm	2	1
1961	28 May	Budapest	2	3
EC1962	7 Nov	Budapesp	1	3
EC1963	20 Mar	Cardiff	1	1
EC1974	30 Oct	Cardiff	2	0
EC1975	16 Apr	Budapest	2	1
1985	16 Oct	Cardiff	0	3

v ICELAND			W	I
WC1980	2 June	Reykjavik	4	0
WC1981	14 Oct	Swansea	2	2
WC1984	12 Sept	Reykjavik	0	1
WC1984	14 Nov	Cardiff	2	1
1991	1 May	Cardiff	1	0

v IRAN			W	I
1978	18 Apr	Teheran	1	0

v REPUBLIC OF IRELAND			W	RI
1960	28 Sept	Dublin	3	2
1979	11 Sept	Swansea	2	1
1981	24 Feb	Dublin	3	1
1986	26 Mar	Dublin	1	0
1990	28 Mar	Dublin	0	1
1991	6 Feb	Wrexham	0	3
1992	19 Feb	Dublin	1	0
1993	17 Feb	Dublin	1	2

v ISRAEL			W	I
WC1958	15 Jan	Tel Aviv	2	0
WC1958	5 Feb	Cardiff	2	0
1984	10 June	Tel Aviv	0	0
1989	8 Feb	Tel Aviv	3	3

v ITALY			W	I
1965	1 May	Florence	1	4
WC1968	23 Oct	Cardiff	0	1
WC1969	4 Nov	Rome	1	4
1988	4 June	Brescia	1	0

v JAPAN			W	J
1992	7 June	Matsuyama	1	0

v KUWAIT			W	K
1977	6 Sept	Wrexham	0	0
1977	20 Sept	Kuwait	0	0

v LUXEMBOURG			W	L
EC1974	20 Nov	Swansea	5	0
EC1975	1 May	Luxembourg	3	1
EC1990	14 Nov	Luxembourg	1	0
EC1991	13 Nov	Cardiff	1	0

v MALTA		W	M
EC1978	25 Oct Wrexham	7	0
EC1979	2 June Valletta	2	0
1988	1 June Valletta	3	2

v MEXICO		W	M
WC1958	11 June Stockholm	1	1
1962	22 May Mexico City	1	2

v NORWAY		W	M
EC1982	22 Sept Swansea	1	0
EC1983	21 Sept Oslo	0	0
1984	6 June Trondheim	0	1
1985	26 Feb Wrexham	1	1
1985	5 June Bergen	2	4

v POLAND		W	P
WC1973	28 Mar Cardiff	2	0
WC1973	26 Sept Katowice	0	3
1991	29 May Radom	0	0

v PORTUGAL		W	P
1949	15 May Lisbon	2	3
1951	12 May Cardiff	2	1

v ROMANIA		W	R
EC1970	11 Nov Cardiff	0	0
EC1971	24 Nov Bucharest	0	2
1983	12 Oct Wrexham	5	0
1992	20 May Bucharest	1	5

v SAUDI ARABIA		W	SA
1986	25 Feb Dahran	2	1

v SPAIN		W	S
WC1961	19 Apr Cardiff	1	2
WC1961	18 May Madrid	1	1
1982	24 Mar Valencia	1	1
WC1984	17 Oct Seville	0	3
WC1985	30 Apr Wrexham	3	0

v SWEDEN		W	S
WC1958	15 June Stockholm	0	0
1988	27 Apr Stockholm	1	4
1989	26 Apr Wrexham	0	2
1990	25 Apr Stockholm	2	4

v SWITZERLAND		W	S
1949	26 May Berne	0	4
1951	16 May Wrexham	3	2

v TURKEY		W	T
EC1978	29 Nov Wrexham	1	0
EC1979	21 Nov Izmir	0	1
WC1980	15 Oct Cardiff	4	0
WC1981	25 Mar Ankara	1	0

v REST OF UNITED KINGDOM			
		W	UK
1951	5 Dec Cardiff	3	2
1969	28 July Cardiff	0	1

v URUGUAY		W	U
1986	21 Apr Wrexham	0	0

v USSR		W	USSR
WC1965	30 May Moscow	1	2
WC1965	27 Oct Cardiff	2	1
WC1981	30 May Wrexham	0	0
WC1981	18 Nov Tbilisi	0	3
1987	18 Feb Swansea	0	0

v YUGOSLAVIA		W	Y
1953	21 May Belgrade	2	5
1954	22 Nov Cardiff	1	3
EC1976	24 Apr Zagreb	0	2
EC1976	22 May Cardiff	1	1
EC1982	15 Dec Titograd	4	4
EC1983	14 Dec Cardiff	1	1
1988	23 Mar Swansea	1	2

NORTHERN IRELAND

v ALBANIA		NI	A
WC1965	7 May Belfast	4	1
WC1965	24 Nov Tirana	1	1
EC1982	15 Dec Tirana	0	0
EC1983	27 Apr Belfast	1	0
WC1992	9 Sept Belfast	3	0
WC1993	17 Feb Tirana	2	1

v ALGERIA		NI	A
WC1986	3 June Guadalajara	1	1

v ARGENTINA		NI	A
WC1958	11 June Halmstad	1	3

v AUSTRALIA		NI	A
1980	11 June Sydney	2	1
1980	15 June Melbourne	1	1
1980	18 June Adelaide	2	1

v AUSTRIA		NI	A
WC1982	1 July Madrid	2	2
EC1982	13 Oct Vienna	0	2
EC1983	21 Sept Belfast	3	1
EC1990	14 Nov Vienna	0	0
EC1991	16 Oct Belfast	2	1

v BELGIUM		NI	B
WC1976	10 Nov Liège	0	2
WC1977	16 Nov Belfast	3	0

v BRAZIL		NI	B
WC1986	12 June Guadalajara	0	3

v BULGARIA		NI	B
WC1972	18 Oct Sofia	0	3
WC1973	26 Sept Sheffield	0	0
EC1978	29 Nov Sofia	2	0
EC1979	2 May Belfast	2	0

v CHILE		NI	C
1989	26 May Belfast	0	1

v CYPRUS		NI	C
EC1971	3 Feb Nicosia	3	0
EC1971	21 Apr Belfast	5	0
WC1973	14 Feb Nicosia	0	1
WC1973	8 May London	3	0

v CZECHOSLOVAKIA		NI	C
WC1958	8 June Halmstad	1	0
WC1958	17 June Malmo	2	1*

*After extra time

v DENMARK		NI	D
EC1978	25 Oct Belfast	2	1
EC1979	6 June Copenhagen	0	4
1986	26 Mar Belfast	1	1
EC1990	17 Oct Belfast	1	1
EC1991	13 Nov Odense	1	2
WC1992	18 Nov Belfast	0	1

v FAEROES		NI	F
EC1991	1 May Belfast	1	1
EC1991	11 Sept Landsrona	5	0

v FINLAND			NI	F
wc1984	27 May	Pori	0	1
wc1984	14 Nov	Belfast	2	1

v FRANCE			NI	F
1951	12 May	Belfast	2	2
1952	11 Nov	Paris	1	3
wc1958	19 June	Norrkoping	0	4
1982	24 Mar	Paris	0	4
wc1982	4 July	Madrid	1	4
1986	26 Feb	Paris	0	0
1988	27 Apr	Belfast	0	0

v GERMANY			NI	G
1992	2 June	Bremen	1	1

v WEST GERMANY			NI	WG
wc1958	15 June	Malmo	2	2
wc1960	26 Oct	Belfast	3	4
wc1961	10 May	Hamburg	1	2
1966	7 May	Belfast	0	2
1977	27 Apr	Cologne	0	5
EC1982	17 Nov	Belfast	1	0
EC1983	16 Nov	Hamburg	1	0

v GREECE			NI	G
wc1961	3 May	Athens	1	2
wc1961	17 Oct	Belfast	2	0
1988	17 Feb	Athens	2	3

v HOLLAND			NI	N
1962	9 May	Rotterdam	0	4
wc1965	17 Mar	Belfast	2	1
wc1965	7 Apr	Rotterdam	0	0
wc1976	13 Oct	Rotterdam	2	2
wc1977	12 Oct	Belfast	0	1

v HONDURAS			NI	H
wc1982	21 June	Zaragoza	1	1

v HUNGARY			NI	H
wc1988	19 Oct	Budapest	0	1
wc1989	6 Sept	Belfast	1	2

v ICELAND			NI	I
wc1977	11 June	Reykjavik	0	1
wc1977	21 Sept	Belfast	2	0

v REPUBLIC OF IRELAND			NI	RI
EC1978	20 Sept	Bublin	0	0
EC1979	21 Nov	Belfast	1	0
wc1988	14 Sept	Belfast	0	0
wc1989	11 Oct	Dublin	0	3
wc1993	31 Mar	Dublin	0	3

v ISRAEL			NI	I
1968	10 Sept	Jaffa	3	2
1976	3 Mar	Tel Aviv	1	1
wc1980	26 Mar	Tel Aviv	0	0
wc1981	18 Nov	Belfast	1	0
1984	16 Oct	Belfast	3	0
1987	18 Feb	Tel Aviv	1	1

v ITALY			NI	I
wc1957	25 Apr	Rome	0	1
1957	4 Dec	Belfast	2	2
wc1958	15 Jan	Belfast	2	1
1961	25 Apr	Bologna	2	3

v LATVIA			NI	L
wc1993	2 June	Riga	2	1

v LITHUANIA			NI	L
wc1992	28 Apr	Belfast	2	2
wc1993	25 May	Vilnius	1	0

v MALTA			NI	M
1988	21 May	Belfast	3	0
wc1989	26 Apr	Valletta	2	0

v MEXICO			NI	M
1966	22 June	Belfast	4	1

v MOROCCO			NI	M
1986	23 Apr	Belfast	2	1

v NORWAY			NI	N
EC1974	4 Sept	Oslo	1	2
EC1975	29 Oct	Belfast	3	0
1990	27 Mar	Belfast	2	3

v POLAND			NI	P
EC1962	10 Oct	Katowice	2	0
EC1962	28 Nov	Belfast	2	0
1988	23 Mar	Belfast	1	1
1991	5 Feb	Belfast	3	1

v PORTUGAL			NI	P
wc1957	16 Jan	Lisbon	1	1
wc1957	1 May	Belfast	3	0
wc1973	28 Mar	Coventry	1	1
wc1973	14 Nov	Lisbon	1	1
wc1980	19 Nov	Lisbon	0	1
wc1981	29 Apr	Belfast	1	0

v ROMANIA			NI	R
wc1984	12 Sept	Belfast	3	2
wc1985	16 Oct	Bucharest	1	0

v SPAIN			NI	S
1958	15 Oct	Madrid	2	6
1963	30 May	Bilbao	1	1
1963	30 Oct	Belfast	0	1
EC1970	11 Nov	Seville	0	3
EC1972	16 Feb	Hull	1	1
wc1982	25 June	Valencia	1	0
1985	27 Mar	Palma	0	0
wc1986	7 June	Guadalajara	1	2
wc1988	21 Dec	Seville	0	4
wc1989	8 Feb	Belfast	0	2
wc1992	14 Oct	Belfast	0	0
wc1993	28 Apr	Seville	1	3

v SWEDEN			NI	S
EC1974	30 Oct	Solna	2	0
EC1975	3 Sept	Belfast	1	2
wc1980	15 Oct	Belfast	3	0
wc1981	3 June	Solna	0	1

v SWITZERLAND			NI	S
wc1964	14 Oct	Belfast	1	0
wc1964	14 Nov	Lausanne	1	2

v TURKEY			NI	T
wc1968	23 Oct	Belfast	4	1
wc1968	11 Dec	Istanbul	3	0
EC1983	30 Mar	Belfast	2	1
EC1983	12 Oct	Ankara	0	1
wc1985	1 May	Belfast	2	0
wc1985	11 Sept	Izmir	0	0
EC1986	12 Nov	Izmir 0	0	
EC1987	11 Nov	Belfast	1	0

v URUGUAY			NI	U
1964	29 Apr	Belfast	3	0
1990	18 May	Belfast	1	0

v USSR			NI	USSR
wc1969	19 Sept	Belfast	0	0
wc1969	22 Oct	Moscow	0	2

			NI	USSR
EC1971	22 Sept	Moscow	0	1
EC1971	13 Oct	Belfast	1	1

v YUGOSLAVIA			NI	Y
EC1975	16 Mar	Belfast	1	0
EC1975	19 Nov	Belgrade	0	1

			NI	Y
wc1982	17 June	Zaragoza	0	0
EC1987	29 Apr	Belfast	1	2
EC1987	14 Oct	Sarajevo	0	3
EC1990	12 Sept	Belfast	0	2
EC1991	27 Mar	Belgrade	1	4

REPUBLIC OF IRELAND

v ALBANIA			RI	A
wc1992	26 May	Dublin	2	0
wc1993	26 May	Tirana	2	1

v ALGERIA			RI	A
1982	28 Apr	Algiers	0	2

v ARGENTINA			RI	A
1951	13 May	Dublin	0	1
1979	29 May	Dublin	0	0*
1980	16 May	Dublin	0	1

* Not considered a full international

v AUSTRIA			RI	A
1952	7 May	Vienna	0	6
1953	25 Mar	Dublin	4	0
1958	14 Mar	Vienna	1	3
1962	8 Apr	Dublin	2	3
EC1963	25 Sept	Vienna	0	0
EC1963	13 Oct	Dublin	3	2
1966	22 May	Vienna	0	1
1968	10 Nov	Dublin	2	2
EC1971	30 May	Dublin	1	4
EC1971	10 Oct	Linz	0	6

v BELGIUM			RI	B
1928	12 Feb	Liège	4	2
1929	30 Apr	Dublin	4	0
1930	11 May	Brussels	3	1
wc1934	25 Feb	Dublin	4	4
1949	24 Apr	Dublin	0	2
1950	10 May	Brussels	1	5
1965	24 Mar	Dublin	0	2
1966	25 May	Liège	3	2
wc1980	15 Oct	Dublin	1	1
wc1981	25 Mar	Brussels	0	1
EC1986	10 Sept	Brussels	2	2
EC1987	29 Apr	Dublin	0	0

v BRAZIL			RI	B
1974	5 May	Rio de Janeiro	1	2
1982	27 May	Uberlandia	0	7
1987	23 May	Dublin	1	0

v BULGARIA			RI	B
wc1977	1 June	Sofia	1	2
wc1977	12 Oct	Dublin	0	0
EC1979	19 May	Sofia	0	1
EC1979	17 Oct	Dublin	3	0
EC1987	1 Apr	Sofia	1	2
wc1987	14 Oct	Dublin	2	0

v CHILE			RI	C
1960	30 Mar	Dublin	2	0
1972	21 June	Recife	1	2
1974	12 May	Santiago	2	1
1982	22 May	Santiago	0	1
1991	22 May	Dublin	1	1

v CHINA			RI	C
1984	3 June	Sapporo	1	0

v CYPRUS			RI	C
wc1980	26 Mar	Nicosia	3	2
wc1980	19 Nov	Dublin	6	0

v CZECHOSLOVAKIA			RI	C
1938	18 May	Prague	2	2
EC1959	5 Apr	Dublin	2	0
EC1959	10 May	Bratislava	0	4
wc1961	8 Oct	Dublin	1	3
wc1961	29 Oct	Prague	1	7
EC1967	21 May	Dublin	0	2
EC1967	22 Nov	Prague	2	1
wc1969	4 May	Dublin	1	2
wc1969	7 Oct	Prague	0	3
1979	26 Sept	Prague	1	4
1981	29 Apr	Dublin	3	1
1986	27 May	Reykjavik	1	0

v DENMARK			RI	D
wc1956	3 Oct	Dublin	2	1
wc1957	2 Oct	Copenhagen	2	0
wc1968	4 Dec	Dublin	1	1
(abandoned after 51 mins)				
wc1969	27 May	Copenhagen	0	2
wc1969	15 Oct	Dublin	1	1
EC1978	24 May	Copenhagen	3	3
EC1979	2 May	Dublin	2	0
wc1984	14 Nov	Copenhagen	0	3
wc1985	13 Nov	Dublin	1	4
wc1992	14 Oct	Copenhagen	0	0
wc1993	28 Apr	Dublin	1	1

v ECUADOR			RI	E
1972	19 June	Natal	3	2

v EGYPT			RI	E
wc1990	17 June	Palermo	0	0

v ENGLAND			RI	E
1946	30 Sept	Dublin	0	1
1949	21 Sept	Everton	2	0
wc1957	8 May	Wembley	1	5
wc1957	19 May	Dublin	1	1
1964	24 May	Dublin	1	3
1976	8 Sept	Wembley	1	1
EC1978	25 Oct	Dublin	1	1
EC1980	6 Feb	Wembley	0	2
1985	26 Mar	Wembley	1	2
EC1988	12 June	Stuttgart	1	0
wc1990	11 June	Cagliari	1	1
EC1990	14 Nov	Dublin	1	1
EC1991	27 Mar	Wembley	1	1

v FINLAND			RI	F
wc1949	8 Sept	Dublin	3	0
wc1949	9 Oct	Helsinki	1	1
1990	16 May	Dublin	1	1

v FRANCE			RI	F
1937	23 May	Paris	2	0
1952	16 Nov	Dublin	1	1
wc1953	4 Oct	Dublin	3	5
wc1953	25 Nov	Paris	0	1
wc1972	15 Nov	Dublin	2	1
wc1973	19 May	Paris	1	1
wc1976	17 Nov	Paris	0	2
wc1977	30 Mar	Dublin	1	0
wc1980	28 Oct	Paris	0	2
wc1981	14 Oct	Dublin	3	2
1989	7 Feb	Dublin	0	0

v GERMANY		RI	G
1935	8 May Dortmund	1	3
1936	17 Oct Dublin	5	2
1939	23 May Bremen	1	1

v WEST GERMANY		RI	WG
1951	17 Oct Dublin	3	2
1952	4 May Cologne	0	3
1955	28 May Hamburg	1	2
1956	25 Nov Dublin	3	0
1960	11 May Dusseldorf	1	0
1966	4 May Dublin	0	4
1970	9 May Berlin	1	2
1975	1 Mar Dublin	1	0†
1979	22 May Dublin	1	3
1981	21 May Bremen	0	3†
1989	6 Sept Dublin	1	1

†v West Germany 'B'

v HOLLAND		RI	N
1932	8 May Amsterdam	2	0
1934	8 Apr Amsterdam	2	5
1935	8 Dec Dublin	3	5
1955	1 May Dublin	1	0
1956	10 May Rotterdam	4	1
wc1980	10 Sept Dublin	2	1
wc1981	9 Sept Rotterdam	2	2
EC1982	22 Sept Rotterdam	1	2
EC1983	12 Oct Dublin	2	3
EC1988	18 June Gelsenkirchen	0	1
wc1990	21 June Palermo	1	1
1991	11 Sept Gyor	2	1

v HUNGARY		RI	H
1934	15 Dec Dublin	2	4
1936	3 May Budapest	3	3
1936	6 Dec Dublin	2	3
1939	19 Mar Cork	2	2
1939	18 May Budapest	2	2
wc1969	8 June Dublin	1	2
wc1969	5 Nov Budapest	0	4
wc1989	8 Mar Budapest	0	2
wc1989	4 June Dublin	2	0
1991	11 Sept Gyor	2	1

v ICELAND		RI	I
EC1962	12 Aug Dublin	4	2
EC1962	2 Sept Reykjavik	1	1
EC1982	13 Oct Dublin	2	0
EC1983	21 Sept Reykjavik	3	0
1986	25 May Reykjavik	2	1

v IRAN		RI	I
1972	18 June Recife	2	1

v N. IRELAND		RI	NI
EC1978	20 Sept Dublin	0	0
EC1979	21 Nov Belfast	0	1
wc1988	14 Sept Balfast	0	0
wc1989	11 Oct Dublin	3	0
wc1993	31 Mar Dublin	3	0

v ISRAEL		RI	I
1984	4 Apr Tel Aviv	0	3
1985	27 May Tel Aviv	0	0
1987	10 Nov Dublin	5	0

v ITALY		RI	I
1926	21 Mar Turin	0	3
1927	23 Apr Dublin	1	2
EC1970	8 Dec Rome	0	3
EC1971	10 May Dublin	1	2
1985	5 Feb Dublin	1	2
wc1990	30 June Rome	0	1
1992	4 June Foxboro	0	2

v LATVIA		RI	L
wc1992	9 Sept Dublin	4	0
wc1993	2 June Riga	2	1

v LITHUANIA		RI	L
wc1993	16 June Vilnius	1	0

v LUXEMBOURG		RI	I
1936	9 May Luxembourg	5	1
wc1953	28 Oct Dublin	4	0
wc1954	7 Mar Luxembourg	1	0
EC1987	28 May Luxembourg	2	0
EC1987	9 Sept Dublin	2	1

v MALTA		RI	M
EC1983	30 Mar Valletta	1	0
EC1983	16 Nov Dublin	8	0
wc1989	28 May Dublin	2	0
wc1989	15 Nov Valletta	2	0
1990	2 June Valletta	3	0

v MEXICO		RI	M
1984	8 Aug Dublin	0	0

v MOROCCO		RI	M
1990	12 Sept Dublin	1	0

v NORWAY		RI	N
wc1937	10 Oct Oslo	2	3
wc1937	7 Nov Dublin	3	3
1950	26 Nov Dublin	2	2
1951	30 May Oslo	3	2
1954	8 Nov Dublin	2	1
1955	25 May Oslo	3	1
1960	6 Nov Dublin	3	1
1964	13 May Oslo	4	1
1973	6 June Oslo	1	1
1976	24 Mar Dublin	3	0
1978	21 May Oslo	0	0
wc1984	17 Oct Oslo	0	1
wc1985	1 May Dublin	0	0
1988	1 June Oslo	0	0

v POLAND		RI	P
1938	22 May Warsaw	0	6
1938	13 Nov Dublin	3	2
1958	11 May Katowice	2	2
1958	5 Oct Dublin	2	2
1964	10 May Cracow	1	3
1964	25 Oct Dublin	3	2
1968	15 May Dublin	2	2
1968	30 Oct Katowice	0	1
1970	6 May Dublin	1	2
1970	23 Sept Dublin	0	2
1973	16 May Wroclaw	0	2
1973	21 Oct Dublin	1	0
1976	26 May Posjan	2	0
1977	24 Apr Dublin	0	0
1978	12 Apr Lodz	0	3
1981	23 May Bydgoszcz	0	3
1984	23 May Dublin	0	0
1986	12 Nov Warsaw	0	1
1988	22 May Dublin	3	1
EC1991	1 May Dublin	0	0
EC1991	16 Oct Poznan	3	3

v PORTUGAL		RI	P
1946	16 June Lisbon	1	3
1947	4 May Dublin	0	2
1948	23 May Lisbon	0	2
1949	22 May Dublin	1	0
1972	25 June Recife	1	2
1992	7 June Boston	2	0

v ROMANIA

			RI	R
1988	23 Mar	Dublin	2	0
wc1990	25 June	Genoa	0	0*

v SCOTLAND

			RI	S
wc1961	3 May	Glasgow	1	4
wc1961	7 May	Dublin	0	3
1963	9 June	Dublin	1	0
1969	21 Sept	Dublin	1	1
EC1986	15 Oct	Dublin	0	0
EC1987	18 Feb	Glasgow	1	0

v SPAIN

			RI	S
1931	26 Apr	Barcelona	1	1
1931	13 Dec	Barcelona	0	5
1946	23 June	Madrid	1	0
1947	2 Mar	Dublin	3	2
1948	30 May	Barcelona	1	2
1949	12 June	Dublin	1	4
1952	1 June	Madrid	0	6
1955	27 Nov	Dublin	2	2
EC1964	11 Mar	Seville	1	5
EC1964	8 Apr	Dublin	0	2
wc1965	5 May	Dublin	1	0
wc1965	27 Oct	Seville	1	4
wc1965	10 Nov	Paris	0	1
EC1966	23 Oct	Dublin	0	0
EC1966	7 Dec	Valencia	0	2
1977	9 Feb	Dublin	0	1
EC1982	17 Nov	Dublin	3	3
EC1983	27 Apr	Zaragoza	0	2
wc1985	26 May	Cork	0	0
wc1988	16 Nov	Seville	0	2
wc1989	26 Apr	Dublin	1	0
wc1992	18 Nov	Seville	0	0

v SWEDEN

			RI	S
wc1949	2 June	Stockholm	1	3
wc1949	13 Nov	Dublin	1	3
1959	1 Nov	Dublin	3	2
1960	18 May	Malmo	1	4
EC1970	14 Oct	Dublin	1	1
EC1970	28 Oct	Malmo	0	1

v SWITZERLAND

			RI	S
1935	5 May	Basle	0	1
1936	17 Mar	Dublin	1	0
1937	17 May	Berne	1	0
1938	18 Sept	Dublin	4	0
1948	5 Dec	Dublin	0	1
EC1975	11 May	Dublin	2	1
EC1975	21 May	Berne	0	1
1980	30 Apr	Dublin	2	0
wc1985	2 June	Dublin	3	0
wc1985	11 Sept	Berne	0	0
1992	25 Mar	Dublin	2	1

v TRINIDAD & TOBAGO

			RI	TT
1982	30 May	Port of Spain	1	2

v TUNISIA

			RI	T
1988	19 Oct	Dublin	4	0

v TURKEY

			RI	T
EC1966	16 Nov	Dublin	2	1
EC1967	22 Feb	Ankara	1	2
EC1974	20 Nov	Izmir	1	1
EC1975	29 Oct	Dublin	4	0
1976	13 Oct	Ankara	3	3
1978	5 Apr	Dublin	4	2
1990	26 May	Izmir	0	0
EC1990	17 Oct	Dublin	5	0
EC1991	13 Nov	Istanbul	3	1

v URUGUAY

			RI	U
1974	8 May	Montevideo	0	2
1986	23 Apr	Dublin	1	1

v USA

			RI	USA
1979	29 Oct	Dublin	3	2
1991	1 June	Boston	1	1
1992	29 Apr	Dublin	4	1
1992	30 May	Washington	1	3

v USSR

			RI	USSR
wc1972	18 Oct	Dublin	1	2
wc1973	13 May	Moscow	0	1
EC1974	30 Oct	Dublin	3	0
EC1975	18 May	Kiev	1	2
wc1984	12 Sept	Dublin	1	0
wc1985	16 Oct	Moscow	0	2
EC1988	15 June	Hanover	1	1
1990	25 Apr	Dublin	1	0

v WALES

			RI	W
1960	28 Sept	Dublin	2	3
1979	11 Sept	Swansea	1	2
1981	24 Feb	Dublin	1	3
1986	26 Mar	Dublin	0	1
1990	28 Mar	Dublin	1	0
1991	6 Feb	Wrexham	3	0
1992	19 Feb	Dublin	0	1
1993	17 Feb	Dublin	2	1

v YUGOSLAVIA

			RI	Y
1955	19 Sept	Dublin	1	4
1988	27 Apr	Dublin	2	0

INTERNATIONAL APPEARANCES

This is a list of full international appearances by Englishmen, Irishmen, Scotsmen and Welshmen in matches against the Home Countries and against foreign nations. It does not include unofficial matches against Commonwealth and Empire countries. The year indicated refers to the season; ie 1993 is the 1992-93 season. Explanatory code for matches played by all five countries: A represents Austria; Alb, Albania; Alg, Algeria; Arg, Argentina; Aus, Australia; B, Bohemia; Bel, Belgium; Br, Brazil; Bul, Bulgaria; C,CIS; Ca, Canada; Cam, Cameroon; Ch, Chile; Chn, China; Co, Colombia; Cr, Costa Rica; Cy, Cyprus; Cz, Czechoslovakia; D, Denmark; E, England; Ec, Ecuador; Ei, Eire; EG, East Germany; Eg, Egypt; Es, Estonia; F, France; Fa, Faeroes; Fi, Finland; G, Germany; Gr, Greece; H, Hungary; Ho, Holland; Hon, Honduras; I, Italy; Ic, Iceland; Ir, Iran; Is, Israel; J,Japan; K, Kuwait; L, Luxembourg; La, Latvia; M, Mexico; Ma, Malta; Mal, Malaysia; Mor, Morocco; N, Norway; Ni, Northern Ireland; Nz, New Zealand; P, Portugal; Para, Paraguay; Pe, Peru; Pol, Poland; R, Romania; R of E, Rest of Europe; R of UK, Rest of United Kingdom; R of W, Rest of World; S.Ar, Saudi Arabia; S, Scotland; Se, Sweden; Sm, San Marino; Sp, Spain; Sw, Switzerland; T, Turkey; Tr, Trinidad & Tobago; Tun, Tunisia; U, Uruguay; US, United States of America; USSR, Soviet Union; W, Wales; WG, West Germany; Y, Yugoslavia; Z, Zaire.
As at June 1993.

ENGLAND

Abbott, W. (Everton), 1902 v W (1)

A'Court, A. (Liverpool), 1958 v Ni, Br, A, USSR; 1959 v W (5)

Adams, T. A. (Arsenal), 1987 v Sp, T, Br; 1988 v WG, T, Y, Ho, H, S, Co, Sw, Ei, Ho, USSR; 1989 v D, Se, S.Ar.; 1991 v Ei (2); 1993 v N, T, Sm, T, Ho, Pol, N (26)

Adcock, H. (Leicester C), 1929 v F, Bel, Sp; 1930 v Ni, W (5)

Alcock, C. W. (Wanderers), 1875 v S (1)

Alderson, J. T. (C Palace), 1923 v F (1)

Aldridge, A. (WBA), 1888 v Ni; (with Walsall Town Swifts), 1889 v Ni (2)

Allen, A. (Stoke C) 1960 v Se, W, Ni (3)

Allen, A. (Aston Villa), 1888 v Ni (1)

Allen, C. (QPR), 1984 v Br (sub), U, Ch; (with Tottenham H), 1987 v T; 1988 v Is (5)

Allen, H. (Wolverhampton W), 1888 v S, W, Ni; 1889 v S; 1890 v S (5)

Allen, J. P. (Portsmouth), 1934 v Ni, W (2)

Allen, R. (WBA), 1952 v Sw; 1954 v Y, S; 1955 v WG, W (5)

Alsford, W. J. (Tottenham H), 1935 v S (1)

Amos, A. (Old Carthusians), 1885 v S; 1886 v W (2)

Anderson, R. D. (Old Etonians), 1879 v W (1)

Anderson, S. (Sunderland), 1962, v A, S (2)

Anderson, V. (Nottingham F), 1979 v Cz, Se; 1980 v Bul, Sp; 1981 v N, R, W, S; 1982 v Ni, Ic; 1984 v Ni; (with Arsenal), 1985 v T, Ni, Ei, R, Fi, S, M, US; 1986 v USSR, M; 1987 v Se, Ni (2), Y, Sp, T; (with Manchester U), 1988 v WG, H, Co (30)

Angus, J. (Burnley), 1961 v A (1)

Armfield, J. C. (Blackpool), 1959 v Br, Pe, M, US; 1960 v Y, Sp, H, S; 1961 v L, P, Sp, M, I, A, W, Ni, S; 1962 v A, Sw, Pe, W, Ni, S, L, P, H, Arg, Bul, Br; 1963 v F (2), Br, EG, Sw, Ni, W, S; 1964 v R of W, W, Ni, S; 1966 v Y, Fi (43)

Armitage, G. H. (Charlton Ath), 1926 v Ni (1)

Armstrong, D. (Middlesbrough), 1980 v Aus; (with Southampton), 1983 v WG; 1984 v W (3)

Armstrong, K. (Chelsea), 1955 v S (1)

Arnold, J. (Fulham), 1933 v S (1)

Arthur, J. W. H. (Blackburn R), 1885 v S, W, Ni; 1886 v S, W; 1887 v W, Ni (7)

Ashcroft, J. (Woolwich Arsenal), 1906 v Ni, W, S (3)

Ashmore, G. S. (WBA), 1926 v Bel (1)

Ashton, C. T. (Corinthians), 1926 v Ni (1)

Ashurst, W. (Notts Co), 1923 v Se (2); 1925 v S, W, Bel (5)

Astall, G. (Birmingham C), 1956 v Fi, WG (2)

Astle, J. (WBA), 1969 v W; 1970 v S, P, Br (sub), Cz (5)

Aston, J. (Manchester U), 1949 v S, W, D, Sw, Se, N, F; 1950 v S, W, Ni, Ei, I, P, Bel, Ch, US; 1951 v Ni (17)

Athersmith, W. C. (Aston Villa), 1892 v Ni, 1897 v S, W, Ni; 1898 v S, W, Ni; 1899 v S, W, Ni; 1900 v S, W (12)

Atyeo, P. J. W. (Bristol C), 1956 v Br, Se, Sp; 1957 v D, Ei (2) (6)

Austin, S. W. (Manchester C), 1926 v Ni (1)

Bach, P. (Sunderland), 1899 v Ni (1)

Bache, J. W. (Aston Villa), 1903 v W; 1904 v W, Ni; 1905 v S; 1907 v Ni; 1910 v Ni; 1911 v S (7)

Baddeley, T. (Wolverhampton W), 1903 v S, Ni; 1904 v S, W, Ni (5)

Bagshaw, J. J. (Derby Co), 1920 v Ni (1)

Bailey, G. R. (Manchester U), 1985 v Ei, M (2)

Bailey, H. P. (Leicester Fosse), 1908 v W, A (2), H, B (5)

Bailey, M. A. (Charlton Ath), 1964 v US; 1965 v W (2)

Bailey, N. C. (Clapham Rovers), 1878 v S; 1879 v S, W; 1880 v S; 1881 v S; 1882 v S, W; 1883 v S, W; 1884 v S, W, Ni; 1885 v S, W, Ni; 1886 v S, W; 1887 v S, W (19)

Baily, E. F. (Tottenham H), 1950 v Sp; 1951 v Y, Ni, W; 1952 v A (2), Sw, W; 1953 v Ni (9)

Bain, J. (Oxford University), 1887 v S (1)

Baker, A. (Arsenal), 1928 v W (1)

Baker, B. H. (Everton), 1921 v Bel; (with Chelsea), 1926 v Ni (2)

Baker, J. H. (Hibernian), 1960 v Y, Sp, H, Ni, S; (with Arsenal) 1966 v Sp, Pol, Ni (8)

Ball, A. J. (Blackpool), 1965 v Y, WG, Se; 1966 v S, Sp, Fi, D, U, Arg, P, WG (2), Pol (2); (with Everton), 1967 v W, S, Ni, A, Cz, Sp; 1968 v W, S, USSR, Sp (2), Y, WG; 1969 v Ni, W, S, R (2), M, Br, U; 1970 v P, Co, Ec, R, Br, Cz (sub), WG, W, S, Bel; 1971 v Ma, EG, Gr, Ma (sub), Ni, S; 1972 v Sw, Gr; (with Arsenal) WG (2), S; 1973 v W (3), Y, S (2), Cz, Ni, Pol; 1974 v P (sub); 1975 v WG, Cy (2), Ni, W, S (72)

Ball, J. (Bury), 1928 v Ni (1)

Balmer, W. (Everton), 1905 v Ni (1)

Bamber, J. (Liverpool), 1921 v W (1)

Bambridge, A. L. (Swifts), 1881 v W; 1883 v W; 1884 v Ni (3)

Bambridge, E. C. (Swifts), 1879 v S; 1880 v S; 1881 v S; 1882 v S, W, Ni; 1883 v W; 1884 v S, W, Ni; 1885 v S, W, Ni; 1886 v S, W; 1887 v S, W, Ni (18)

Bambridge, E. H. (Swifts), 1876 v S (1)

Banks, G. (Leicester C), 1963 v S, Br, Cz, EG; 1964 v W, Ni, S, R of W, U, P (2), US, Arg; 1965 v Ni, S, H, Y, WG, Se; 1966 v Ni, S, Sp, Pol (2), Y, Fi, U, M, F, Arg, P; 1967 v Ni, W, S, Cz; (with Stoke C), 1968 v W, Ni, S, USSR (2), Sp, WG, Y; 1969 v Ni, S, R (2), F, U, Br; 1970 v W, Ni, S, Ho, Bel, Co, Ec, R, Br, Cz; 1971 v Gr, Ma (2), Ni, S; 1972 v Sw, Gr, WG (2), W, S (73)

Banks, H. E. (Millwall), 1901 v Ni (1)

Banks, T. (Bolton W), 1958 v USSR (3), Br, A; 1959 v Ni (6)

Bannister, W. (Burnley), 1901 v W; (with Bolton W), 1902 v Ni (2)

Barclay, R. (Sheffield U), 1932 v S; 1933 v Ni; 1936 v S (3)

Bardsley, D. J. (QPR), 1993 v Sp (sub), Pol (2)

Barham, M. (Norwich C), 1983 v Aus (2) (2)

Barkas, S. (Manchester C), 1936 v Bel; 1937 v S; 1938 v W, Ni, Cz (5)

Barker, J. (Derby Co), 1935 v I, Ho, S, W, Ni; 1936 v G, A, S, W, Ni; 1937 v W (11)

Barker, R. (Herts Rangers), 1872 v S (1)

Barker, R. R. (Casuals), 1895 v W (1)

Barlow, R. J. (WBA), 1955 v Ni (1)

Barnes, J. (Watford), 1983 v Ni (sub), Aus (sub), Aus (2); 1984 v D, L (sub), F (sub), S, USSR, Br, U, Ch; 1985 v EG, Fi, T, Ni, R, Fi, S, I (sub), M, WG (sub), US (sub); 1986 v R (sub), Is (sub), M (sub), Ca (sub), Arg (sub); 1987 v Se, T (sub), Br; (with Liverpool), 1988 v WG, T, Y, Is, Ho, S, Co, Sw, Ei, Ho, USSR; 1989 v Se, Gr, Alb, Pol, D; 1990 v Se, I, Br, D, U, Tun, Ei, Ho, Eg, Bel, Cam; 1991 v H, Cam, Ei, T, USSR, Arg; 1992 v Cz, Fi; 1993 v Sm, T, Ho, Pol, US, G (73)

Barnes, P. S. (Manchester C), 1978 v I, WG, Br, W, S, H; 1979 v D, Ei, Cz, Ni (2), S, Bul, A; (with WBA), 1980 v D, W; 1981 v Sp (sub), Br, W, Sw (sub); (with Leeds U), 1982 v N (sub), Ho (sub) (22)

Barnet, H. H. (Royal Engineers), 1882 v Ni (1)

Barrass, M. W. (Bolton W), 1952 v W, Ni; 1953 v S (3)

Barrett, A. F. (Fulham), 1930 v Ni (1)

Barrett, E. D. (Oldham Ath), 1991 v Nz; 1993 v Br, G (3)

Barrett, J. W. (West Ham U), 1929 v Ni (1)

Barry, L. (Leicester C), 1928 v F, Bel; 1929 v F, Bel, Sp (5)

Barson, F. (Aston Villa), 1920 v W (1)

Barton, J. (Blackburn R), 1890 v Ni (1)

Barton, P. H. (Birmingham), 1921 v Bel; 1922 v Ni; 1923 v F; 1924 v Bel, S, W; 1925 v Ni (7)

Bassett, W. I. (WBA), 1888 v Ni, 1889 v S, W; 1890 v S, W; 1891 v S, Ni; 1892 v S; 1893 v S, W; 1894 v S; 1895 v S, Ni; 1896 v S, W, Ni (16)

Bastard, S. R. (Upton Park), 1880 v S (1)

Bastin, C. S. (Arsenal), 1932 v W; 1933 v I, Sw; 1934 v S, Ni, W, H, Cz; 1935 v S, Ni, I; 1936 v S, W, G, A; 1937 v W, Ni; 1938 v S, G, Sw, F (21)

Batty, D. (Leeds U), 1991 v USSR (sub), Arg, Aus, Nz, Mal; 1992 v G, T, H (sub), F, Se; 1993 v N, Sm, US, Br (14)

Baugh, R. (Stafford Road), 1886 v Ni; (with Wolverhampton W) 1890 v Ni (2)

Bayliss, A. E. J. M. (WBA), 1891 v Ni (1)

Baynham, R. L. (Luton T), 1956 v Ni, D, Sp (3)

Beardsley, P. A. (Newcastle U), 1986 v Eg (sub), Is, USSR, M, Ca (sub), P (sub), Pol, Para, Arg; 1987 v Ni (2), Y, Sp, Br, S; (with Liverpool), 1988 v WG, T, Y, Is, Ho, H, S, Co, Sw, Ei, Ho; 1989 v D, Se, Gr (sub), Alb (sub + 1), Pol, D; 1990 v Se, Pol, I, Br, U (sub), Tun (sub), Ei, Eg (sub), Cam (sub), WG, I; 1991 v Pol (sub), Ei (2), USSR (sub) (49)

Beasant, D. J. (Chelsea), 1990 v I (sub), Y (sub) (2)

Beasley, A. (Huddersfield T), 1939 v S (1)

Beats, W. E. (Wolverhampton W), 1901 v W; 1902 v S (2)

Beattie, T. K. (Ipswich T), 1975 v Cy (2), S; 1976 v Sw, P; 1977 v Fi, I (sub), Ho; 1978 v L (sub) (9)

Becton, F. (Preston NE), 1895 v Ni; (with Liverpool), 1897 v W (2)

Bedford, H. (Blackpool), 1923 v Se; 1925 v Ni (2)

Bell, C. (Manchester C), 1968 v Se, WG; 1969 v W, Bul, F, U, Br; 1970 v Ni (sub), Ho (2), P, Br (sub), Cz, WG (sub); 1972 v Gr, WG (2), W, Ni, S; 1973 v W (3), Y, S (2), Ni, Cz, Pol; 1974 v A, Pol, I, W, Ni, S, Arg, EG, Bul, Y; 1975 v Cz, P, WG, Cy (2), Ni, S; 1976 v Sw, Cy (48)

Bennett, W. (Sheffield U), 1901 v S, W (2)

Benson, R. W. (Sheffield U), 1913 v Ni (1)

Bentley, R. T. F. (Chelsea), 1949 v Se; 1950 v S, P, Bel, Ch, USA; 1953 v W, Bel; 1955 v W, WG, Sp, P (12)

Beresford, J. (Aston Villa), 1934 v Cz (1)

Berry, A. (Oxford University), 1909 v Ni (1)

Berry, J. J. (Manchester U), 1953 v Arg, Ch, U; 1956 v Se (4)

Bestall, J. G. (Grimsby T), 1935 v Ni (1)

Betmead, H. A. (Grimsby T), 1937 v Fi (1)

Betts, M. P. (Old Harrovians), 1877 v S (1)

Betts, W. (Sheffield W), 1889 v W (1)

Beverley, J. (Blackburn R), 1884 v S, W, Ni (3)

Birkett, R. H. (Clapham Rovers), 1879 v S (1)

Birkett, R. J. E. (Middlesbrough), 1936 v Ni (1)

Birley, F. H. (Oxford University), 1874 v S; (with Wanderers), 1875 v S (2)

Birtles, G. (Nottingham F), 1980 v Arg (sub), I; 1981 v R (3)

Bishop, S. M. (Leicester C), 1927 v S, Bel, L, F (4)

Blackburn, F. (Blackburn R), 1901 v S; 1902 v Ni; 1904 v S (3)

Blackburn, G. F. (Aston Villa), 1924 v F (1)

Blenkinsop, E. (Sheffield W), 1928 v F, Bel; 1929 v S, W, Ni, F, Bel, Sp; 1930 v S, W, Ni, G, A; 1931 v S, W, Ni, F, Bel; 1932 v S, W, Ni, Sp; 1933 v S, W, Ni, A (26)

Bliss, H. (Tottenham H), 1921 v S (1)

Blissett, L. (Watford), 1983 v WG (sub), L, W, Gr (sub), H, Ni, S (sub), Aus (1 + 1 sub); (with AC Milan), 1984 v D (sub), H, W (sub), S, USSR (14)

Blockley, J. P. (Arsenal), 1973 v Y (1)

Bloomer, S. (Derby Co), 1895 v S, Ni; 1896 v W, Ni; 1897 v S, W, Ni; 1898 v S; 1899 v S, W, Ni; 1900 v S; 1901 v S, W; 1902 v S, W, Ni; 1904 v S; 1905 v S, W, Ni; (with Middlesbrough), 1907 v S, W (23)

Blunstone, F. (Chelsea), 1955 v W, S, F, P; 1957 v Y (5)

Bond, R. (Preston NE), 1905 v Ni, W; 1906 v S, W, Ni; (with Bradford C), 1910 v S, W, Ni (8)

Bonetti, P. P. (Chelsea), 1966 v D; 1967 v Sp, A; 1968 v Sp; 1970 v Ho, P, WG (7)

Bonsor, A. G. (Wanderers), 1873 v S; 1875 v S (2)

Booth, F. (Manchester C), 1905 v Ni (1)

Booth, T. (Blackburn R), 1898 v W; (with Everton), 1903 v S (2)

Bowden, E. R. (Arsenal), 1935 v W, I; 1936 v W, Ni, A; 1937 v H (6)

Bower, A. G. (Corinthians), 1924 v Ni, Bel; 1925 v W, Bel; 1927 v W (5)

Bowers, J. W. (Derby Co), 1934 v S, Ni, W (3)

Bowles, S. (QPR), 1974 v P, W, Ni; 1977 v I, Ho (5)

Bowser, S. (WBA), 1920 v Ni (1)

Boyer, P. J. (Norwich C), 1976 v W (1)

Boyes, W. (WBA), 1935 v Ho; (with Everton), 1939 v W, R of E (3)

Boyle, T. W. (Burnley), 1913 v Ni (1)

Brabrook, P. (Chelsea), 1958 v USSR; 1959 v Ni; 1960 v Sp (3)

Bracewell, P. W. (Everton), 1985 v WG (sub), US; 1986 v Ni (3)

Bradford, G. R. W. (Bristol R), 1956 v D (1)

Bradford, J. (Birmingham), 1924 v Ni; 1925 v Bel; 1928 v S; 1929 v Ni, W, F, Sp; 1930 v S, Ni, G, A; 1931 v W (12)

Bradley, W. (Manchester U), 1959 v I, US, M (sub) (3)

Bradshaw, F. (Sheffield W), 1908 v A (1)

Bradshaw, T. H. (Liverpool), 1897 v Ni (1)

Bradshaw, W. (Blackburn R), 1910 v W, Ni; 1912 v Ni; 1913 v W (4)

Brann, G. (Swifts), 1886 v S, W; 1891 v W (3)

Brawn, W. F. (Aston Villa), 1904 v W, Ni (2)

Bray, J. (Manchester C), 1935 v W; 1936 v S, W, Ni, G; 1937 v S (6)

Brayshaw, E. (Sheffield W), 1887 v Ni (1)

Bridges, B. J. (Chelsea), 1965 v S, H, Y; 1966 v A (4)

Bridgett, A. (Sunderland), 1905 v S; 1908 v S, A (2), H, B; 1909 v Ni, W, H (2), A (11)

Brindle, T. (Darwen), 1880 v S, W (2)

Brittleton, J. T. (Sheffield W), 1912 v S, W, Ni; 1913 v S; 1914 v W (5)

Britton, C. S. (Everton), 1935 v S, W, Ni, I; 1937 v S, Ni, H, N, Se (9)

Broadbent, P. F. (Wolverhampton W), 1958 v USSR; 1959 v S, W, Ni, I, Br; 1960 v S (7)

Broadis, I. A. (Manchester C), 1952 v S, A, I; 1953 v S, Arg, Ch, U, US; (with Newcastle U), 1954 v S, H, Y, Bel, Sw, U (14)

Brockbank, J. (Cambridge University), 1872 v S (1)

Brodie, J. B. (Wolverhampton W), 1889 v S, Ni; 1891 v Ni (3)

Bromilow, T. G. (Liverpool), 1921 v W; 1922 v S, W; 1923 v Bel; 1926 v Ni (5)

Bromley-Davenport, W. E. (Oxford University), 1884 v S, W (2)

Brook, E. F. (Manchester C), 1930 v Ni; 1933 v Sw: 1934 v S, W, Ni, F, H, Cz; 1935 v S, W, Ni, I; 1936 v S, W, Ni; 1937 v H; 1938 v W, Ni (18)

Brooking, T. D. (West Ham U), 1974 v P, Arg, EG, Bul, Y; 1975 v Cz (sub), P; 1976 v P, W, Br, I, Fi; 1977 v Ei, Fi, I, Ho, Ni, W; 1978 v I, WG, W, S (sub), H; 1979 v D, Ei, Ni, W (sub), S, Bul, Se (sub), A; 1980 v D, Ni, Arg (sub), W, Ni, S, Bel, Sp; 1981 v Sw, Sp, R, H; 1982 v H, S, Fi, Sp (sub) (47)

Brooks, J. (Tottenham H), 1957 v W, Y, D (3)

Broome, F. H. (Aston Villa), 1938 v G, Sw, F; 1939 v N, I, R, Y (7)

Brown, A. (Aston Villa), 1882 v S, W, Ni (3)

Brown, A. S. (Sheffield U), 1904 v W; 1906 v Ni (2)

Brown, A. (WBA), 1971 v W (1)

Brown, G. (Huddersfield T), 1927 v S, W, Ni, Bel, L, F; 1928 v W; 1929 v S; (with Aston Villa), 1933 v W (9)

Brown, J. (Blackburn R), 1881 v W; 1882 v Ni; 1885 v S, W, Ni (5)

Brown, J. H. (Sheffield W), 1927 v S, W, Bel, L, F; 1930 v Ni (6)

Brown, K. (West Ham U), 1960 v Ni (1)

Brown, W. (West Ham U), 1924 v Bel (1)

Bruton, J. (Burnley), 1928 v F, Bel; 1929 v S (3)

Bryant, W. I. (Clapton), 1925 v F (1)

Buchan, C. M. (Sunderland), 1913 v Ni; 1920 v W; 1921 v W, Bel; 1923 v F; 1924 v S (6)

Buchanan, W. S. (Clapham R), 1876 v S (1)

Buckley, F. C. (Derby Co), 1914 v Ni (1)

Bull, S. G. (Wolverhampton W), 1989 v S (sub), D (sub); 1990 v Y, Cz, D (sub), U (sub), Tun (sub), Ei (sub), Ho (sub), Eg, Bel (sub); 1991 v H, Pol (13)

Bullock, F. E. (Huddersfield T), 1921 v Ni (1)

Bullock, N. (Bury), 1923 v Bel; 1926 v W; 1927 v Ni (3)

Burgess, H. (Manchester C), 1904 v S, W, Ni; 1906 v S (4)

Burgess, H. (Sheffield W), 1931 v S, Ni, F, Bel (4)

Burnup, C. J. (Cambridge University), 1896 v S (1)

Burrows, H. (Sheffield W), 1934 v H, Cz; 1935 v Ho (3)

Burton, F. E. (Nottingham F), 1889 v Ni (1)

Bury, L. (Cambridge University), 1877 v S; (with Old Etonians), 1879 v W (2)

Butcher, T. (Ipswich T), 1980 v Aus; 1981 v Sp; 1982 v W, S, F, Cz, WG, Sp; 1983 v D, WG, L, W, Gr, H, Ni, S, Aus (3); 1984 v D, H, L, F, Ni; 1985 v EG, Fi, T, Ni, Ei, R, Fi, S, I, WG, US; 1986 v Is, USSR, S, M, Ca, P, Mor, Pol, Para, Arg; (with Rangers), 1987 v Se, Ni (2), Y, Sp, Br, S; 1988 v T, Y; 1989 v D, Se, Gr, Alb (2), Ch, S, Pol, D; 1990 v Se, Pol, I, Y, Br, Cz, D, U, Tun, Ei, Ho, Bel, Cam, WG (77)

Butler, J. D. (Arsenal), 1925 v Bel (1)

Butler, W. (Bolton W), 1924 v S (1)

Byrne, G. (Liverpool), 1963 v S; 1966 v N (2)

Byrne, J. J. (C Palace), 1962 v Ni; (with West Ham U), 1963 v Sw; 1964 v S, U, P (2), Ei, Br, Arg; 1965 v W, S (11)

Byrne, R. W. (Manchester U), 1954 v S, H, Y, Bel, Sw, U; 1955 v S, W, Ni, WG, F, Sp, P; 1956 v S, W, Ni, Br, Se, Fi, WG, D, Sp; 1957 v S, W, Ni, Y, D (2), Ei (2); 1958 v W, Ni, F (33)

Callaghan, I. R. (Liverpool), 1966 v Fi, F; 1978 v Sw, L (4)

Calvey, J. (Nottingham F), 1902 v Ni (1)

Campbell, A. F. (Blackburn R), 1929 v W, Ni; (with Huddersfield T), 1931 v W, S, Ni; 1932 v W, Ni, Sp (8)

Camsell, G. H. (Middlesbrough), 1929 v F, Bel; 1930 v Ni, W; 1934 v F; 1936 v S, G, A, Bel (9)

Capes, A. J. (Stoke C), 1903 v S (1)

Carr, J. (Middlesbrough), 1920 v Ni; 1923 v W (2)

Carr, J. (Newcastle U), 1905 v Ni; 1907 v Ni (2)

Carr, W. H. (Owlerton, Sheffield), 1875 v S (1)

Carter, H. S. (Sunderland), 1934 v S, H; 1936 v G; 1937 v S, Ni, H; (with Derby Co), 1947 v S, W, Ni, Ei, Ho, F, Sw (13)

Carter, J. H. (WBA), 1926 v Bel; 1929 v Bel, Sp (3)

Catlin, A. E. (Sheffield W), 1937 v W, Ni, H, N, Se (5)

Chadwick, A. (Southampton), 1900 v S, W (2)

Chadwick, E. (Everton), 1891 v S, W; 1892 v S; 1893 v S; 1894 v S; 1896 v Ni; 1897 v S (7)

Chamberlain, M (Stoke C), 1983 v L (sub); 1984 v D (sub), S, USSR, Br, U, Ch; 1985 v Fi (sub) (8)

Chambers, H. (Liverpool), 1921 v S, W, Bel; 1923 v S, W, Ni, Bel; 1924 v Ni (8)

Channon, M. R. (Southampton), 1973 v Y, S (2), Ni, W, Cz, USSR, I; 1974 v A, Pol, I, P, W, Ni, S, Arg, EG, Bul, Y; 1975 v Cz, P, WG, Cy (2), Ni (sub), W, S; 1976 v Sw, Cz, P, W, Ni, S, Br, I, Fi; 1977 v Fi, I, L, Ni, W, S, Br (sub), Arg, U; (with Manchester C), 1978 v Sw (46)

Charles, G. A. (Nottingham F), 1991 v Nz, Mal (2)

Charlton, J. (Leeds U), 1965 v S, H, Y, WG, Se; 1966 v W, Ni, S, A, Sp, Pol (2), WG (2), Y, Fi, D, U, M, F, Arg, P; 1967 v W, S, Ni, Cz; 1968 v W, Sp; 1969 v W, R, F; 1970 v Ho (2), P, Cz (35)

Charlton, R. (Manchester U), 1958 v S, P, Y; 1959 v S, W, Ni, USSR, I, Br, Pe, M, US; 1960 v W, S, Se, Y, Sp, H; 1961 v W, S, L, P, Sp, M, I, A; 1962 v W, Ni, S, A, Sw, Pe, L, P, H, Arg, Bul, Br; 1963 v S, F, Br, Cz, EG, Sw; 1964 v S, Ni, R of W, U, P, Ei, Br, Arg, US (sub); 1965 v Ni, S, Ho; 1966 v W, Ni, S, A, Sp, WG (2), Y, Fi, N, Pol, U, M, F, Arg, P; 1967 v Ni, W, S, Cz; 1968 v W, Ni, S, USSR (2), Sp (2), Se, Y; 1969 v S, W, Ni, R (2), Bul, M, Br; 1970 v W, Ni, Ho (2), P, Co, Ec, Cz, R, Br, WG (106)

Charnley, R. O. (Blackpool), 1963 v F (1)

Charsley, C. C. (Small Heath), 1893 v Ni (1)

Chedgzoy, S. (Everton), 1920 v W; 1921 v W, S, Ni; 1922 v Ni; 1923 v S; 1924 v W; 1925 v Ni (8)

Chenery, C. J. (C Palace), 1872 v S; 1873 v S; 1874 v S (3)

Cherry, T. J. (Leeds U), 1976 v W, S (subs), Br, Fi; 1977 v Ei, I, L, Ni, S (subs), Br, Arg, U; 1978 v Sw, L, I, Br, W; 1979 v Cz, W, Se; 1980 v Ei, Arg (sub), W, Ni, S, Aus, Sp (sub) (27)

Chilton, A. (Manchester U), 1951 v Ni; 1952 v F (2)

Chippendale, H. (Blackburn R), 1894 v Ni (1)

Chivers, M. (Tottenham H), 1971 v Ma (2), Gr, Ni, S; 1972 v Sw (1+1 sub), Gr, WG (2), Ni (sub), S; 1973 v W (3), S (2), Ni, Cz, Pol, USSR, I; 1974 v A, Pol (24)

Christian, E. (Old Etonians), 1879 v S (1)

Clamp, E. (Wolverhampton W), 1958 v USSR (2), Br, A (4)

Clapton, D. R. (Arsenal), 1959 v W (1)

Clare, T. (Stoke C), 1889 v Ni; 1892 v Ni; 1893 v W; 1894 v S (4)

Clarke, A. J. (Leeds U), 1970 v Cz; 1971 v EG, Ma, Ni, W (sub), S (sub); 1973 v S (2), W, Cz, Pol, USSR, I; 1974 v A, Pol, I; 1975 v P; 1976 v Cz, P (sub) (19)

Clarke, H. A. (Tottenham H), 1954 v S (1)

Clay, T. (Tottenham H), 1920 v W; 1922 v W, S, Ni (4)

Clayton, R. (Blackburn R), 1956 v Ni, Br, Se, Fi, WG, Sp; 1957 v S, W, Ni, Y, D (2), Ei (2); 1958 v S, W, Ni, F, P, Y, USSR; 1959 v S, W, Ni, USSR, I, Br, Pe, M, US; 1960 v W, Ni, S, Se, Y (35)

Clegg, J. C. (Sheffield W), 1872 v S (1)

Clegg, W. E. (Sheffield W), 1873 v S; (with Sheffield Albion), 1879 v W (2)

Clemence, R. N. (Liverpool), 1973 v W (2); 1974 v EG, Bul, Y; 1975 v Cz, P, WG, Cy, Ni, W, S; 1976 v Sw, Cz, P, W (2), Ni, S, Br, Fi; 1977 v Ei, Fi, I, Ho, L, S, Br, Arg, U; 1978 v Sw, L, I, WG, Ni, S; 1979 v D, Ei, Ni (2), S, Bul, A (sub); 1980 v D, Bul, Ei, Arg, W, S, Bel, Sp; 1981 v R, Sp, Br, Sw, H; (with Tottenham H), 1982 v N, Ni, Fi; 1983 v L; 1984 v L (61)

Clement, D. T. (QPR), 1976 v W (sub+1), I; 1977 v I, Ho (5)

Clough, B. H. (Middlesbrough), 1960 v W, Se (2)

Clough, N. H. (Nottingham F), 1989 v Ch; 1991 v Arg (sub), Aus, Mal; 1992 v F, Cz, C; 1993 v Sp, T (sub), Pol (sub), N (sub), US, Br, G (14)

Coates, R. (Burnley), 1970 v Ni; 1971 v Gr (sub); (with Tottenham H), Ma, W (4)

Cobbold, W. N. (Cambridge University), 1883 v S, Ni; 1885 v S, Ni; 1886 v S, W; (with Old Carthusians), 1887 v S, W, Ni (9)

Cock, J. G. (Huddersfield T), 1920 v Ni; (with Chelsea), v S (2)

Cockburn, H. (Manchester U), 1947 v W, Ni, Ei; 1948 v S, I; 1949 v S, Ni, D, Sw, Se; 1951 v Arg, P; 1952 v F (13)

Cohen, G. R. (Fulham), 1964 v U, P, Ei, US, Br; 1965 v W, S, Ni, Bel, H, Ho, Y, WG, Se; 1966 v W, S, Ni, A, Sp, Pol (2), WG (2), N, D, U, M, F, Arg, P; 1967 v W, S, Ni, Cz, Sp; 1968 v W, Ni (37)

Coleclough, H. (C Palace), 1914 v W (1)

Coleman, E. H. (Dulwich Hamlet), 1921 v W (1)

Coleman, J. (Woolwich Arsenal), 1907 v Ni (1)

Common, A. (Sheffield U), 1904 v W, Ni; (with Middlesbrough), 1906 v W (3)

Compton, L. H. (Arsenal), 1951 v W, Y (2)

Conlin, J. (Bradford C), 1906 v S (1)

Connelly, J. M. (Burnley), 1960 v W, N, S, Se; 1962 v W, A, Sw, P; 1963 v W, F; (with Manchester U), 1965 v H, Y, Se; 1966 v W, Ni, S, A, N, D, U (20)

Cook, T. E. R. (Brighton), 1925 v W (1)

Cooper, N. C. (Cambridge University), 1893 v Ni (1)

Cooper, T. (Derby Co), 1928 v Ni; 1929 v W, Ni, S, F, Bel, Sp; 1931 v F; 1932 v W, Sp; 1933 v S; 1934 v S, H, Cz; 1935 v W (15)

Cooper, T. (Leeds U), 1969 v W, S, F, M; 1970 v Ho, Bel, Co, Ec, R, Cz, Br, WG; 1971 v EG, Ma, Ni, W, S; 1972 v Sw (2); 1975 v P (20)

Coppell, S. J. (Manchester U), 1978 v I, WG, Br, W, Ni, S, H; 1979 v D, Ei, Cz, Ni (2), W (sub), S, Bul, A; 1980 v D, Ni, Ei (sub), Sp, Arg, W, S, Bel, I; 1981 v R (sub), Sw, R, Br, W, S, Sw, H; 1982 v H, S, Fi, F, Cz, K, WG; 1983 v L, Gr (42)

Copping, W. (Leeds U), 1933 v I, Sw; 1934 v S, Ni, W, F; (with Arsenal), 1935 v Ni, I; 1936 v A, Bel; 1937 v N, Se, Fi; 1938 v S, W, Ni, Cz; 1939 v W, R of E; (with Leeds U), R (20)

Corbett, B. O. (Corinthians), 1901 v W (1)

Corbett, R. (Old Malvernians), 1903 v W (1)

Corbett, W. S. (Birmingham), 1908 v A, H, B (3)

Corrigan, J. T. (Manchester C), 1978 v I (sub); Br; 1979 v W; 1980 v Ni, Aus; 1981 v W, S; 1982 v W, Ic (9)

Cottee, A. R. (West Ham U), 1987 v Se (sub), Ni (sub); 1988 v H (sub); (with Everton) 1989 v D (sub), Se (sub), Ch (sub), S (7)

Cotterill, G. H. (Cambridge University), 1891 v Ni; (with Old Brightonians), 1892 v W; 1893 v S, Ni (4)

Cottle, J. R. (Bristol C), 1909 v Ni (1)

Cowan, S. (Manchester C), 1926 v Bel; 1930 v A; 1931 v Bel (3)

Cowans, G. (Aston Villa), 1983 v W, H, Ni, S, Aus (3); (with Bari), 1986 v Eg, USSR; (with Aston Villa), 1991 v Ei (10)

Cowell, A. (Blackburn R), 1910 v Ni (1)

Cox, J. (Liverpool), 1901 v Ni; 1902 v S; 1903 v S (3)

Cox, J. D. (Derby Co), 1892 v Ni (1)

Crabtree, J. W. (Burnley), 1894 v Ni; 1895 v Ni, S; (with Aston Villa), 1896 v W, S, Ni; 1899 v S, W, Ni; 1900 v S, W, Ni; 1901 v W; 1902 v W (14)

Crawford, J. F. (Chelsea), 1931 v S (1)

Crawford, R. (Ipswich T), 1962 v Ni, A (2)

Crawshaw, T. H. (Sheffield W), 1895 v Ni; 1896 v S, W, Ni; 1897 v S, W, Ni; 1901 v Ni; 1904 v W, Ni (10)

Crayston, W. J. (Arsenal), 1936 v S, W, G, A, Bel; 1938 v W, Ni, Cz (8)

Creek, F. N. S. (Corinthians), 1923 v F (1)

Cresswell, W. (South Shields), 1921 v W; (with Sunderland), 1923 v F; 1924 v Bel; 1925 v Ni; 1926 v W; 1927 v Ni; (with Everton), 1930 v Ni (7)

Crompton, R. (Blackburn R), 1902 v S, W, Ni; 1903 v S, W; 1904 v S, W, Ni; 1906 v S, W, Ni; 1907 v S, W, Ni; 1908 v S, W, Ni, A (2), H, B; 1909 v S, W, Ni, F (2), A; 1910 v S, W; 1911 v S, W, Ni; 1912 v S, W, Ni; 1913 v S, W, Ni; 1914 v S, W, Ni (41)

Crooks, S. D. (Derby Co), 1930 v S, G, A; 1931 v S, W, Ni, F, Bel; 1932 v S, W, Ni, Sp; 1933 v Ni, W, A; 1934 v S, Ni, W, F, H, Cz; 1935 v Ni; 1936 v S, W; 1937 v W, H (26)

Crowe, C. (Wolverhampton W), 1963 v F (1)

Cuggy, F. (Sunderland), 1913 v Ni; 1914 v Ni (2)

Cullis, S. (Wolverhampton W), 1938 v S, W, Ni, F, Cz; 1939 v S, Ni, R of E, N, I, R, Y (12)

Cunliffe, A. (Blackburn R), 1933 v Ni, W (2)

Cunliffe, D. (Portsmouth), 1900 v Ni (1)

Cunliffe, J. N. (Everton), 1936 v Bel (1)

Cunningham, L. (WBA), 1979 v W, Se, A (sub); (with Real Madrid), 1980 v Ei, Sp (sub); 1981 v R (sub) (6)

Curle, K. (Manchester C), 1992 v C (sub), H, D (3)

Currey, E. S. (Oxford University), 1890 v S, W (2)

Currie, A. W. (Sheffield U), 1972 v Ni; 1973 v USSR, I; 1974 v A, Pol, I; 1976 v Sw; (with Leeds U), 1978 v Br, W (sub), Ni, S, H (sub); 1979 v Cz, Ni (2), W, Se (17)

Cursham, A. W. (Notts Co), 1876 v S; 1877 v S; 1878 v S; 1879 v W; 1883 v S, W (6)

Cursham, H. A. (Notts Co), 1880 v W; 1882 v S, W, Ni; 1883 v S, W, Ni; 1884 v Ni (8)

Daft, H. B. (Notts Co), 1889 v Ni; 1890 v S, W; 1891 v Ni; 1892 v Ni (5)

Daley, A. M. (Aston Villa), 1992 v Pol (sub), C, H, Br, Fi (sub), D (sub), Se (7)

Danks, T. (Nottingham F), 1885 v S (1)

Davenport, P. (Nottingham F), 1985 v Ei (sub) (1)

Davenport, J. K. (Bolton W), 1885 v W; 1890 v Ni (2)

Davis, G. (Derby Co), 1904 v W, Ni (2)

Davis, H. (Sheffield W), 1903 v S, W, Ni (3)

Davison, J. E. (Sheffield W), 1922 v W (1)

Dawson, J. (Burnley), 1922 v S, Ni (2)

Day, S. H. (Old Malvernians), 1906 v Ni, W, S (3)

Dean, W. R. (Everton), 1927 v S, W, F, Bel, L; 1928 v S, W, Ni, F, Bel; 1929 v S, W, Ni; 1931 v S; 1932 v Sp; 1933 v Ni (16)

Deane, B. C. (Sheffield U), 1991 v Nz (sub + 1); 1993 v Sp (sub) (3)

Deeley, N. V. (Wolverhampton W), 1959 v Br, Pe (2)

Devey, J. H. G. (Aston Villa), 1892 v Ni; 1894 v Ni (2)

Devonshire, A. (West Ham U), 1980 v Aus (sub), Ni; 1982 v Ho, Ic; 1983 v WG, W, Gr; 1984 v L (8)

Dewhurst, F. (Preston NE), 1886 v W, Ni; 1887 v S, W, Ni; 1888 v S, W, Ni; 1889 v W (9)

Dewhurst, G. P. (Liverpool Ramblers), 1895 v W (1)

Dickinson, J. W. (Portsmouth), 1949 v N, F; 1950 v S, W, Ei, P, Bel, Ch, US, Sp; 1951 v Ni, W, Y; 1952 v W, Ni, S, A (2), I, Sw; 1953 v W, Ni, S, Bel, Arg, Ch, U, US; 1954 v W, Ni, S, R of E, H (2), Y, Bel, Sw, U; 1955 v Sp, P; 1956 v W, Ni, S, D, Sp; 1957 v W, Y, D (48)

Dimmock, J. H. (Tottenham H), 1921 v S; 1926 v W, Bel (3)

Ditchburn, E. G. (Tottenham H), 1949 v Sw, Se; 1953 v US; 1957 v W, Y, D (6)

Dix, R. W. (Derby Co), 1939 v N (1)

Dixon, J. A. (Notts Co), 1885 v W (1)

Dixon, K. M. (Chelsea), 1985 v M (sub), WG, US; 1986 v Ni, Is, M (sub), Pol (sub); 1987 v Se (8)

Dixon, L. M. (Arsenal), 1990 v Cz; 1991 v H, Pol, Ei (2), Cam, T, Arg; 1992 v G, T, Pol, Cz (sub); 1993 v Sp, N, T, Sm, T, Ho, N, US (20)

Dobson, A. T. C. (Notts Co), 1882 v Ni; 1884 v S, W, Ni (4)

Dobson, C. F. (Notts Co), 1886 v Ni (1)

Dobson, J. M. (Burnley), 1974 v P, EG, Bul, Y; (with Everton), 1975 v Cz (5)

Doggart, A. G. (Corinthians), 1924 v Bel (1)

Dorigo, A. R. (Chelsea), 1990 v Y (sub), Cz (sub), D (sub), I; 1991 v H (sub), USSR; (with Leeds U), 1992 v G, Cz (sub), H, Br; 1993 v Sm, Pol, US, Br (14)

Dorrell, A. R. (Aston Villa), 1925 v W, Bel, F; 1926 v Ni (4)

Douglas, B. (Blackburn R), 1958 v S, W, Ni, F, P, Y, USSR (2), Br, A; 1959 v S, USSR; 1960 v Y, H; 1961 v Ni, W, S, L, P, Sp, M, I, A; 1962 v W, Ni, S, Pe, L, P, H, Arg, Bul, Br; 1963 v S, Br, Sw (36)

Downs, R. W. (Everton), 1921 v Ni (1)

Doyle, M. (Manchester C), 1976 v W, S (sub), Br, I; 1977 v Ho (5)

Drake, E. J. (Arsenal), 1935 v Ni, I; 1936 v W; 1937 v H; 1938 v F (5)

Ducat, A. (Woolwich Arsenal), 1910 v S, W, Ni; (with Aston Villa), 1920 v S, W; 1921 v Ni (6)

Dunn, A. T. B. (Cambridge University), 1883 v Ni; 1884 v Ni; (with Old Etonians), 1892 v S, W (4)

Duxbury, M. (Manchester U), 1984 v L, F, W, S, USSR, Br, U, Ch; 1985 v EG, Fi (10)

Earle, S. G. J. (Clapton), 1924 v F; (with West Ham U), 1928 v Ni (2)

Eastham, G. (Arsenal), 1963 v Br, Cz, EG; 1964 v W, Ni, S, R of W, U, P, Ei, US, Br, Arg; 1965 v H, WG, Se; 1966 v Sp, Pol, D (19)

Eastham, G. R. (Bolton W), 1935 v Ho (1)

Eckersley, W. (Blackburn R), 1950 v Sp; 1951 v S, Y, Arg, P; 1952 v A (2), Sw; 1953 v Ni, Arg, Ch, U, US; 1954 v W, Ni, R of E, H (17)

Edwards, D. (Manchester U), 1955 v S, F, Sp, P; 1956 v S, Br, Se, Fi, WG; 1957 v S, Ni, Ei (2), D (2); 1958 v W, Ni, F (18)

Edwards, J. H. (Shropshire Wanderers), 1874 v S (1)

Edwards, W. (Leeds U), 1926 v S, W; 1927 v W, Ni, S, F, Bel, L; 1928 v S, F, Bel; 1929 v S, W, Ni; 1930 v W, Ni (16)

Ellerington, W. (Southampton), 1949 v N, F (2)

Elliott, G. W. (Middlesbrough), 1913 v Ni; 1914 v Ni; 1920 v W (3)

Elliott, W. H. (Burnley), 1952 v I, A; 1953 v Ni, W, Bel (5)

Evans, R. E. (Sheffield U), 1911 v S, W, Ni; 1912 v W (4)

Ewer, F. H. (Casuals), 1924 v F; 1925 v Bel (2)

Fairclough, P. (Old Foresters), 1878 v S (1)

Fairhurst, D. (Newcastle U), 1934 v F (1)

Fantham, J. (Sheffield W), 1962 v L (1)

Fashanu, J. (Wimbledon), 1989 v Ch, S (2)

Felton, W. (Sheffield W), 1925 v F (1)

Fenton, M. (Middlesbrough), 1938 v S (1)

Fenwick, T. (QPR), 1984 v W (sub), S, USSR, Br, U, Ch; 1985 v Fi, S, M, US; 1986 v R, T, Ni, Eg, M, P, Mor, Pol, Arg; (with Tottenham H), 1988 v Is (sub) (20)

Ferdinand, L. (QPR), 1993 v Sm, Ho, N, US (4)

Field, E. (Clapham Rovers), 1876 v S; 1881 v S (2)

Finney, T. (Preston NE), 1947 v W, Ni, Ei, Ho, F, P; 1948 v S, W, Ni, Bel, Se, I; 1949 v S, W, Ni, Se, N, F; 1950 v S, W, Ni, Ei, I, P, Bel, Ch, US, Sp; 1951 v S, Arg, P; 1952 v W, Ni, S, F, I, Sw, A; 1953 v W, Ni, S, Bel, Arg, Ch, U, US; 1954 v W, S, Bel, Sw, U, H, Y; 1955 v WG; 1956 v S, W, Ni, D, Sp; 1957 v S, W, Y, D (2), Ei (2); 1958 v S, W, S, F, P, Y, USSR (2); 1959 v Ni, USSR (76)

Fleming, H. J. (Swindon T), 1909 v S, H (2); 1910 v W, Ni; 1911 v W, Ni; 1912 v Ni; 1913 v S, W; 1914 v S (11)

Fletcher, A. (Wolverhampton W), 1889 v W; 1890 v W (2)

Flowers, R. (Wolverhampton W), 1955 v F; 1959 v S, W, I, Br, Pe, US, M (sub); 1960 v W, Ni, S, Se, Y, Sp, H; 1961 v Ni, W, S, L, P, Sp, M, I, A; 1962 v W, Ni, S, A, Sw, Pe, L, P, H, Arg, Bul, Br; 1963 v Ni, W, S, F (2), Sw; 1964 v Ei, US, P; 1965 v W, Ho, WG; 1966 v N (49)

Flowers, T. D. (Southampton), 1993 v Br (1)

Forman, Frank (Nottingham F), 1898 v S, Ni; 1899 v S, W, Ni; 1901 v S; 1902 v S, Ni; 1903 v W (9)

Forman, F. R. (Nottingham F), 1899 v S, W, Ni (3)

Forrest, J. H. (Blackburn R), 1884 v W; 1885 v S, W, Ni; 1886 v S, W; 1887 v S, W, Ni; 1889 v S; 1890 v Ni (11)

Fort, J. (Millwall), 1921 v Bel (1)

Foster, R. E. (Oxford University), 1900 v W; (with Corinthians), 1901 v W, Ni, S; 1902 v W (5)

Foster, S. (Brighton & HA), 1982 v Ni, Ho, K (3)

Foulke, W. J. (Sheffield U), 1897 v W (1)

Foulkes, W. A. (Manchester U), 1955 v Ni (1)

Fox, F. S. (Millwall), 1925 v F (1)

Francis, G. C. J. (QPR), 1975 v Cz, P, W, S; 1976 v Sw, Cz, P, W, Ni, S, Br, Fi (12)

Francis, T. (Birmingham C), 1977 v Ho, L, S, Br; 1978 v Sw, L, I (sub), WG (sub), Br, W, S, H; (with Nottingham F), 1979 v Bul (sub), Se, A (sub); 1980 v Ni, Bul, Sp; 1981 v Sp, R, S (sub), Sw; (with Manchester C), 1982 v N, Ni, W, S (sub), Fi (sub), F, Cz, K, WG, Sp; (with Sampdoria), 1983 v D, Gr, H, Ni, S, Aus (3); 1984 v D, Ni, USSR; 1985 v EG (sub), T (sub), Ni (sub), R, Fi, S, I, M; 1986 v S (52)

Franklin, C. F. (Stoke C), 1947 v S, W, Ni, Ei, Ho, F, Sw, P; 1948 v S, W, Ni, Bel, Se, I; 1949 v S, W, Ni, D, Sw, N, F, Se; 1950 v W, S, Ni, Ei, I (27)

Freeman, B. C. (Everton), 1909 v S, W; (with Burnley), 1912 v S, W, Ni (5)

Froggatt, J. (Portsmouth), 1950 v Ni, I; 1951 v S; 1952 v S, A (2), I, Sw; 1953 v Ni, W, S, Bel, US (13)

Froggatt, R. (Sheffield W), 1953 v W, S, Bel, US (4)

Fry, C. B. (Corinthians), 1901 v Ni (1)

Furness, W. I. (Leeds U), 1933 v I (1)

Galley, T. (Wolverhampton W), 1937 v N, Se (2)

Gardner, T. (Aston Villa), 1934 v Cz; 1935 v Ho (2)

Garfield, B. (WBA), 1898 v Ni (1)

Garratty, W. (Aston Villa), 1903 v W (1)

Garrett, T. (Blackpool), 1952 v S, I; 1954 v W (3)

Gascoigne, P. J. (Tottenham H), 1989 v D (sub), S.Ar (sub), Alb (sub), Ch, S (sub); 1990 v Se (sub), Br (sub), Cz, D, U, Tun, Ei, Ho, Eg, Bel, Cam, WG; 1991 v H, Pol, Cam; (with Lazio), 1993 v N, T, Sm, T, Ho, Pol, N (27)

Gates, E. (Ipswich T), 1981 v N, R (2)

Gay, L. H. (Cambridge University), 1893 v S; (with Old Brightonians), 1894 v S, W (3)

Geary, F. (Everton), 1890 v Ni; 1891 v S (2)

Geaves, R. L. (Clapham Rovers), 1875 v S (1)

Gee, C. W. (Everton), 1932 v W, Sp; 1937 v Ni (3)

Geldard, A. (Everton), 1933 v I, Sw; 1935 v S; 1938 v Ni (4)

George, C. (Derby Co), 1977 v Ei (1)

George, W. (Aston Villa), 1902 v S, W, Ni (3)

Gibbins, W. V. T. (Clapton), 1924 v F; 1925 v F (2)

Gidman, J. (Aston Villa), 1977 v L (1)

Gillard, I. T. (QPR), 1975 v WG, W; 1976 v Cz (3)

Gilliat, W. E. (Old Carthusians), 1893 v Ni (1)

Goddard, P. (West Ham U), 1982 v Ic (sub) (1)

Goodall, F. R. (Huddersfield T), 1926 v S; 1927 v S, F, Bel, L; 1928 v S, W, F, Bel; 1930 v S, G, A; 1931 v S, W, Ni, Bel; 1932 v Ni; 1933 v W, Ni, A, I, Sw; 1934 v W, Ni, F (25)

Goodall, J. (Preston NE), 1888 v S, W; 1889 v S, W; (with Derby Co), 1891 v S, W; 1892 v S; 1893 v W; 1894 v S; 1895 v S, Ni; 1896 v S, W; 1898 v W (14)

Goodhart, H. C. (Old Etonians), 1883 v S, W, Ni (3)

Goodwyn, A. G. (Royal Engineers), 1873 v S (1)

Goodyer, A. C. (Nottingham F), 1879 v S (1)

Gosling, R. C. (Old Etonians), 1892 v W; 1893 v S; 1894 v W; 1895 v W, S (5)

Gosnell, A. A. (Newcastle U), 1906 v Ni (1)

Gough, H. C. (Sheffield U), 1921 v S (1)

Goulden, L. A. (West Ham U), 1937 v Se, N; 1938 v W, Ni, Cz, G, Sw, F; 1939 v S, W, R of E, I, R, Y (14)

Graham, L. (Millwall), 1925 v S, W (2)

Graham, T. (Nottingham F), 1931 v F; 1932 v Ni (2)

Grainger, C. (Sheffield U), 1956 v Br, Se, Fi, WG; 1957 v W, Ni; (with Sunderland), 1957 v S (7)

Gray, A. A. (C Palace), 1992 v Pol (1)

Greaves, J. (Chelsea), 1959 v Pe, M, US; 1960 v W, Se, Y, Sp; 1961 v Ni, W, S, L, P, Sp, I, A; (with Tottenham H), 1962 v S, Sw, Pe, H, Arg, Bul, Br; 1963 v Ni, W, S, F (2), Br, Cz, Sw; 1964 v W, Ni, R of W, P (2), Ei, Br, U, Arg; 1965 v Ni, S, Bel, Ho, H, Y; 1966 v W, A, Y, N, D, Pol, U, M, F; 1967 v S, Sp, A (57)

Green, F. T. (Wanderers), 1876 v S (1)

Green, G. H. (Sheffield U), 1925 v F; 1926 v S, Bel, W; 1927 v W, Ni; 1928 v F, Bel (8)

Greenhalgh, E. H. (Notts Co), 1872 v S; 1873 v S (2)

Greenhoff, B. (Manchester U), 1976 v W, Ni; 1977 v Ei, Fi, I, Ho, Ni, W, S, Br, Arg, U; 1978 v Br, W, Ni, S (sub), H (sub); (with Leeds U), 1980 v Aus (sub) (18)

Greenwood, D. H. (Blackburn R), 1882 v S, Ni (2)

Gregory, J. (QPR), 1983 v Aus (3); 1984 v D, H, W (6)

Grimsdell, A. (Tottenham H), 1920 v S, W; 1921 v S, Ni; 1923 v W, Ni (6)

Grosvenor, A. T. (Birmingham), 1934 v Ni, W, F (3)

Gunn, N. (Notts Co), 1884 v S, W (2)

Gurney, R. (Sunderland), 1935 v S (1)

Hacking, J. (Oldham Ath), 1929 v S, W, Ni (3)

Hadley, N. (WBA), 1903 v Ni (1)

Hagan, J. (Sheffield U), 1949 v D (1)

Haines, J. T. W. (WBA), 1949 v Sw (1)

Hall, A. E. (Aston Villa), 1910 v Ni (1)

Hall, G. W. (Tottenham H), 1934 v F; 1938 v S, W, Ni, Cz; 1939 v S, Ni, R of E, I, Y (10)

Hall, J. (Birmingham C), 1956 v S, W, Ni, Br, Se, Fi, WG, D, Sp; 1957 v S, W, Ni, Y, D (2), Ei (2) (17)

Halse, H. J. (Manchester U), 1909 v A (1)

Hammond, H. E. D. (Oxford University), 1889 v S (1)

Hampson, J. (Blackpool), 1931 v Ni, W; 1933 v A (3)

Hampton, H. (Aston Villa), 1913 v S, W; 1914 v S, W (4)

Hancocks, J. (Wolverhampton H), 1949 v Sw; 1950 v W; 1951 v Y (3)

Hapgood, E. (Arsenal), 1933 v I, Sw; 1934 v S, Ni, W, H, Cz; 1935 v S, Ni, W, I, Ho; 1936 v S, Ni, W, G, A, Bel; 1937 v Fi; 1938 v S, G, Sw, F; 1939 v S, W, Ni, R of E, N, I, Y (30)

Hardinge, H. T. W. (Sheffield U), 1910 v S (1)

Hardman, H. P. (Everton), 1905 v W; 1907 v S, Ni; 1908 v W (4)

Hardwick, G. F. M. (Middlesbrough), 1947 v S, W, Ni, Ei, Ho, F, Sw, P; 1948 v S, W, Ni, Bel, Se (13)

Hardy, H. (Stockport Co), 1925 v Bel (1)

Hardy, S. (Liverpool), 1907 v S, W, Ni; 1908 v S; 1909 v S, W, Ni, H (2), A; 1910 v S, W, Ni; 1912 v Ni; (with Aston Villa), 1913 v S; 1914 v Ni, W, S; 1920 v S, W, Ni (21)

Harford, M. G. (Luton T), 1988 v Is (sub); 1989 v D (2)

Hargreaves, F. W. (Blackburn R), 1880 v W; 1881 v W; 1882 v Ni (3)

Hargreaves, J. (Blackburn R), 1881 v S, W (2)

Harper, E. C. (Blackburn R), 1926 v S (1)

Harris, G. (Burnley), 1966 v Pol (1)

Harris, P. P. (Portsmouth), 1950 v Ei; 1954 v H (2)

Harris, S. S. (Cambridge University), 1904 v S; (with Old Westminsters), 1905 v Ni; W; 1906 v S, W, Ni (6)

Harrison, A. H. (Old Westminsters), 1893 v S, Ni (2)

Harrison, G. (Everton), 1921 v Bel; 1922 v Ni (2)

Harrow, J. H. (Chelsea), 1923 v Ni, Se (2)

Hart, E. (Leeds U), 1929 v W; 1930 v W, Ni; 1933 v S, A; 1934 v S, H, Cz (8)

Hartley, F. (Oxford C), 1923 v F (1)

Harvey, A. (Wednesbury Strollers), 1881 v W (1)

Harvey, J. C. (Everton), 1971 v Ma (1)

Hassall, H. W. (Huddersfield T), 1951 v S, Arg, P; 1952 v F; (with Bolton W), 1954 v Ni (5)

Hateley, M. (Portsmouth), 1984 v USSR (sub), Br, U, Ch; (with AC Milan), 1985 v EG (sub), Fi, Ni, Ei, Fi, S, I, M; 1986 v R, T, Eg, S, M, Ca, P, Mor, Para (sub); 1987 v T (sub), Br (sub), S; (with Monaco), 1988 v WG (sub), Ho (sub), H (sub), Co (sub), Ei (sub), Ho (sub), USSR (sub); (with Rangers), 1992 v Cz (32)

Haworth, G. (Accrington), 1887 v Ni, W, S; 1888 v S; 1890 v S (5)

Hawtrey, J. P. (Old Etonians), 1881 v S, W (2)

Hawkes, R. M. (Luton T), 1907 v Ni; 1908 v A (2), H, B (5)

Haygarth, E. B. (Swifts), 1875 v S (1)

Haynes, J. N. (Fulham), 1955 v Ni; 1956 v S, Ni, Br, Se, Fi, WG, Sp; 1957 v W, Y, D, Ei (2); 1958 v W, Ni, S, P, Y, USSR (3), Br, A; 1959 v S, Ni, USSR, I, Br, Pe, M, US; 1960 v Ni, Y, Sp, H; 1961 v Ni, W, S, L, P, Sp, M, I, A; 1962 v W, Ni, S, A, Sw, Pe, P, H, Arg, Bul, Br (56)

Healless, H. (Blackburn R), 1925 v Ni; 1928 v S (2)

Hector, K. J. (Derby Co), 1974 v Pol (sub), I (sub) (2)

Hedley, G. A. (Sheffield U), 1901 v Ni (1)

Hegan, K. E. (Corinthians), 1923 v Bel, F; 1924 v Ni, Bel (4)

Hellawell, M. S. (Birmingham C), 1963 v Ni, F (2)

Henfrey, A. G. (Cambridge University), 1891 v Ni; (with Corinthians), 1892 v W; 1895 v W; 1896 v S, W (5)

Henry, R. P. (Tottenham H), 1963 v F (1)

Heron, F. (Wanderers), 1876 v S (1)

Heron, G. H. H. (Uxbridge), 1873 v S; 1874 v S; (with Wanderers), 1875 v S; 1876 v S; 1878 v S (5)

Hibbert, W. (Bury), 1910 v S (1)

Hibbs, H. E. (Birmingham), 1930 v S, W, A, G; 1931 v S, W, Ni; 1932 v W, Ni, Sp; 1933 v S, W, Ni, A, I, Sw; 1934 v Ni, W, F; 1935 v S, W, Ni, Ho; 1936 v G, W (25)

Hill, F. (Bolton W), 1963 v Ni, W (2)

Hill, G. A. (Manchester U), 1976 v I; 1977 v Ei (sub), Fi (sub), L; 1978 v Sw (sub), L (6)

Hill, J. H. (Burnley), 1925 v W; 1926 v S; 1927 v S, Ni, Bel, F; 1928 v Ni, W; (with Newcastle U), 1929 v F, Bel, Sp (11)

Hill, R. (Luton T), 1983 v D (sub), WG; 1986 v Eg (sub) (3)

Hill, R. H. (Millwall), 1926 v Bel (1)

Hillman, J. (Burnley), 1899 v Ni (1)

Hills, A. F. (Old Harrovians), 1879 v S (1)

Hilsdon, G. R. (Chelsea), 1907 v Ni; 1908 v S, W, Ni, A, H, B; 1909 v Ni (8)

Hine, E. W. (Leicester C), 1929 v W, Ni; 1930 v W, Ni; 1932 v W, Ni (6)

Hinton, A. T. (Wolverhampton W), 1963 v F; (with Nottingham F), 1965 v W, Bel (3)

Hirst, D. E. (Sheffield W), 1991 v Aus, Nz (sub); 1992 v F (3)

Hitchens, G. A. (Aston Villa), 1961 v M, I, A; (with Inter-Milan), 1962 v Sw, Pe, H, Br (7)

Hobbis, H. H. F. (Charlton Ath), 1936 v A, Bel (2)

Hoddle, G. (Tottenham H), 1980 v Bul, W, Aus, Sp; 1981 v Sp, W, S; 1982 v N, Ni, W, Ic, Cz (sub), K; 1983 v L (sub), Ni, S; 1984 v H, L, F; 1985 v Ei (sub), S, I (sub), M, WG, US; 1986 v R, T, Ni, Is, USSR, S, M, Ca, P, Mor, Pol, Para, Arg; 1987 v Se, Ni, Y, Sp, T, S; (with Monaco), 1988 v WG, T (sub), Y (sub), Ho (sub), H (sub), Co (sub), Ei (sub), Ho, USSR (53)

Hodge, S. B. (Aston Villa), 1986 v USSR (sub), S, Ca, P (sub), Mor (sub), Pol, Para, Arg; 1987 v Se, Ni, Y; (with Tottenham H), Sp. Ni, T, S; (with Nottingham F), 1989 v D; 1990 v I (sub), Y (sub), Cz, D, U, Tun; 1991 v Cam (sub), T (sub) (24)

Hodgetts, D. (Aston Villa), 1888 v S, W, Ni; 1892 v S, Ni; 1894 v Ni (6)

Hodgkinson, A. (Sheffield U), 1957 v S, Ei (2), D; 1961 v W (5)

Hodgson, G. (Liverpool), 1931 v S, Ni, W (3)

Hodkinson, J. (Blackburn R), 1913 v W, S; 1920 v Ni (3)

Hogg, W. (Sunderland), 1902 v S, W, Ni (3)

Holdcroft, G. H. (Preston NE), 1937 v W, Ni (2)

Holden, A. D. (Bolton W), 1959 v S, I, Br, Pe, M (5)

Holden, G. H. (Wednesday OA), 1881 v S; 1884 v S, W, Ni (4)

Holden-White, C. (Corinthians), 1888 v W, S (2)

Holford, T. (Stoke), 1903 v Ni (1)

Holley, G. H. (Sunderland), 1909 v S, W, H (2), A; 1910 v W; 1912 v S, W, NI; 1913 v S (10)

Holliday, E. (Middlesbrough), 1960 v W, Ni, Se (3)

Hollins, J. W. (Chelsea), 1967 v Sp (1)

Holmes, R. (Preston NE), 1888 v Ni; 1891 v S; 1892 v S; 1893 v S, W; 1894 v Ni; 1895 v Ni (7)

Holt, J. (Everton), 1890 v W; 1891 v S, W; 1892 v S, Ni; 1893 v S; 1894 v S, Ni; 1895 v S; (with Reading), 1900 v Ni (10)

Hopkinson, E. (Bolton W), 1958 v W, Ni, S, F, P, Y; 1959 v S, I, Br, Pe, M, US; 1960 v W, Se (14)

Hossack, A. H. (Corinthians), 1892 v W; 1894 v W (2)

Houghton, W. E. (Aston Villa), 1931 v Ni, W, F, Bel; 1932 v S, Ni; 1933 v A (7)

Houlker, A. E. (Blackburn R), 1902 v S; (with Portsmouth), 1903 v S, W; (with Southampton), 1906 v W, Ni (5)

Howarth, R. H. (Preston NE), 1887 v Ni; 1888 v S, W; 1891 v S; (with Everton), 1894 v Ni (5)

Howe, D. (WBA), 1958 v S, W, Ni, F, P, Y, USSR (3), Br, A; 1959 v S, W, Ni, USSR, I, Br, Pe, M, US; 1960 v W, Ni, Se (23)

Howe, J. R. (Derby Co), 1948 v I; 1949 v S, Ni (3)

Howell, L. S. (Wanderers), 1873 v S (1)

Howell, R. (Sheffield U), 1895 v Ni; (with Liverpool) 1899 v S (2)

Hudson, A. A. (Stoke C), 1975 v WG, Cy (2)

Hudson, J. (Sheffield), 1883 v Ni (1)

Hudspeth, F. C. (Newcastle U), 1926 v Ni (1)

Hufton, A. E. (West Ham U), 1924 v Bel; 1928 v S, Ni; 1929 v F, Bel, Sp (6)

Hughes, E. W. (Liverpool), 1970 v W, Ni, S, Ho, P, Bel; 1971 v EG, Ma (2), Gr, W; 1972 v Sw, Gr, WG (2), W, Ni, S; 1973 v W (3), S (2), Pol, USSR, I; 1974 v A, Pol, I, W, Ni, S, Arg, EG, Bul, Y; 1975 v Cz, P, Cy (sub); Ni; 1977 v I, L, W, S, Br, Arg, U; 1978 v Sw, I, I, WG, Ni, S, H; 1979 v D, Ei, Ni, W, Se; (with Wolverhampton W), 1980 v Sp (sub), Ni, S (sub) (62)

Hughes, L. (Liverpool), 1950 v Ch, US, Sp (3)

Hulme, J. H. A. (Arsenal), 1927 v S, Bel, F; 1928 v S, Ni, W; 1929 v Ni, W; 1933 v S (9)

Humphreys, P. (Notts Co), 1903 v S (1)

Hunt, G. S. (Tottenham H), 1933 v I, Sw, S (3)

Hunt, Rev K. R. G. (Leyton), 1911 v S, W (2)

Hunt, R. (Liverpool), 1962 v A; 1963 v EG; 1964 v S, US, P; 1965 v W; 1966 v S, Sp, Pol (2), WG (2), Fi, N, U, M, F, Arg, P; 1967 v Ni, W, Cz, Sp, A; 1968 v W, Ni, USSR (2), Sp (2), Se, Y; 1969 v R (2) (34)

Hunt, S. (WBA), 1984 v S (sub), USSR (sub) (2)

Hunter, J. (Sheffield Heeley), 1878 v S; 1880 v S, W; 1881 v S, W; 1882 v S, W (7)

Hunter, N. (Leeds U), 1966 v WG, Y, Fi, Sp (sub); 1967 v A; 1968 v Sp, Se, Y, WG, USSR; 1969 v R, W; 1970 v Ho, WG (sub); 1971 v Ma; 1972 v WG (2), W, Ni, S; 1973 v W (2) USSR (sub); 1974 v A, Pol, Ni (sub), S; 1975 v Cz (28)

Hurst, G. C. (West Ham U), 1966 v S, WG (2), Y, Fi, D, Arg, P; 1967 v Ni, W, S, Cz, Sp, A; 1968 v W, Ni, S, Se (sub), WG, USSR (2); 1969 v Ni, S, R (2), Bul, F, M, U, Br; 1970 v W, Ni, S, Ho (1 + 1 sub), Bel, Co, Ec, R, Br, WG; 1971 v EG, Gr, W, S; 1972 v Sw (2), Gr, WG (49)

Ince, P. E. C. (Manchester U), 1993 v Sp, N, T (2), Ho, Pol, US, Br, G (9)

Iremonger, J. (Nottingham F), 1901 v S; 1902 v Ni (2)

Jack, D. N. B. (Bolton W), 1924 v S, W; 1928 v F, Bel; (with Arsenal), 1930 v S, G, A; 1933 v W, A (9)

Jackson, E. (Oxford University), 1891 v W (1)

Jarrett, B. G. (Cambridge University), 1876 v S; 1877 v S; 1878 v S (3)

Jefferis, F. (Everton), 1912 v S, W (2)

Jezzard, B. A. G. (Fulham), 1954 v H; 1956 v Ni (2)

Johnson, D. E. (Ipswich T), 1975 v W, S; 1976 v Sw; (with Liverpool), 1980 v Ei, Arg, Ni, S, Bel (8)

Johnson, E. (Saltley College), 1880 v W; (with Stoke C), 1884 v Ni (2)

Johnson, J. A. (Stoke C), 1937 v N, Se, Fi, S, Ni (5)

Johnson, T. C. F. (Manchester C), 1926 v Bel; 1930 v W; (with Everton), 1932 v S, Sp; 1933 v Ni (5)

Johnson, W. H. (Sheffield U), 1900 v S, W, Ni; 1903 v S, W, Ni (6)

Johnston, H. (Blackpool), 1947 v S, Ho; 1951 v S; 1953 v Arg, Ch, U, US; 1954 v W, Ni, H (10)

Jones, A. (Walsall Swifts), 1882 v S, W; (with Great Lever), 1883 v S (3)

Jones, H. (Blackburn R), 1927 v S, Bel, L, F; 1928 v S, Ni (6)

Jones, H. (Nottingham F), 1923 v F (1)

Jones, M. D. (Sheffield U), 1965 v WG, Se; (with Leeds U), 1970 v Ho (3)

Jones, R. (Liverpool), 1992 v F (1)

Jones, W. (Bristol C), 1901 v Ni (1)

Jones, W. H. (Liverpool), 1950 v P, Bel (2)

Joy, B. (Casuals), 1936 v Bel (1)

Kail, E. I. L. (Dulwich Hamlet), 1929 v F, Bel, Sp (3)

Kay, A. H. (Everton), 1963 v Sw (1)

Kean, F. W. (Sheffield W), 1923 v S, Bel; 1924 v W; 1925 v Ni; 1926 v Ni, Bel; 1927 v L; (with Bolton W), 1929 v F, Sp (9)

Keegan, J. K. (Liverpool), 1973 v W (2); 1974 v W, Ni, Arg, EG, Bul, Y; 1975 v Cz, WG, Cy (2), Ni, S; 1976 v Sw, Cz, P, W (2), Ni, S, Br, Fi; 1977 v Ei, Fi, I, Ho, L; (with SV Hamburg), W, Br, Arg, U; 1978 v Sw, I, WG, Br, H; 1979 v D, Ei, Cz, Ni, W, S, Bul, Se, A; 1980 v D, Ni, Ei, Sp (2), Arg, Bel, I; (with Southampton), 1981 v Sp, Sw, H; 1982 v N, H, Ni, S, Fi, Sp (sub) (63)

Keen, E. R. L. (Derby Co), 1933 v A; 1937 v W, Ni, H (4)

Kelly, R. (Burnley), 1920 v S; 1921 v S, W, Ni; 1922 v S, W; 1923 v S; 1924 v Ni; 1925 v W, Ni, S; (with Sunderland), 1926 v W; (with Huddersfield T), 1927 v L; 1928 v S (14)

Kennedy, A. (Liverpool), 1984 v Ni, W (2)

Martin, A. (West Ham U), 1981 v Br, S (sub); 1982 v H, Fi; 1983 v Gr, L, W, Gr, H; 1984 v H, L, W; 1985 v Ni; 1986 v Is, Ca, Para; 1987 v Se (17)

Martin, H. (Sunderland), 1914 v Ni (1)

Martyn, A. N. (C Palace), 1992 v C (sub), H; 1993 v G (3)

Marwood, B. (Arsenal), 1989 v S.Ar (sub) (1)

Maskrey, H. M. (Derby Co), 1908 v Ni (1)

Mason, C. (Wolverhampton W), 1887 v Ni; 1888 v W; 1890 v Ni (3)

Matthews, R. D. (Coventry C), 1956 v S, Br, Se, WG; 1957 v Ni (5)

Matthews, S. (Stoke C), 1935 v W, I; 1936 v G; 1937 v S; 1938 v S, W, Cz, G, Sw, F; 1939 v S, W, Ni, R of E, N, I, Y; 1947 v S; (with Blackpool), 1947 v Sw, P; 1948 v S, W, Ni, Bel, I; 1949 v S, W, Ni, D, Sw; 1950 v Sp; 1951 v Ni, S; 1954 v Ni, R of E, H, Bel, U; 1955 v Ni, W, S, F, WG, Sp, P; 1956 v W, Br; 1957 v S, W, Ni, Y, D (2), Ei (54)

Matthews, V. (Sheffield U), 1928 v F, Bel (2)

Maynard, W. J. (1st Surrey Rifles), 1872 v S; 1876 v S (2)

Meadows, J. (Manchester C), 1955 v S (1)

Medley, L. D. (Tottenham H), 1951 v Y, W; 1952 v F, A, W, Ni (6)

Meehan, T. (Chelsea), 1924 v Ni (1)

Melia, J. (Liverpool), 1963 v S, Sw (2)

Mercer, D. W. (Sheffield U), 1923 v Ni, Bel (2)

Mercer, J. (Everton), 1939 v S, Ni, I, R, Y (5)

Merrick, G. H. (Birmingham C), 1952 v Ni, S, A (2), I, Sw; 1953 v Ni, W, S, Bel, Arg, Ch, U; 1954 v W, Ni, S, R of E, H (2), Y, Bel, Sw, U (23)

Merson, P. C. (Arsenal), 1992 v G (sub), Cz, H, Br (sub), Fi (sub), D, Se (sub); 1993 v Sp (sub), N (sub), Ho (sub), Br (sub), G (12)

Metcalfe, V. (Huddersfield T), 1951 v Arg, P (2)

Mew, J. W. (Manchester U), 1921 v Ni (1)

Middleditch, B. (Corinthians), 1897 v Ni (1)

Milburn, J. E. T. (Newcastle U), 1949 v S, W, Ni, Sw; 1950 v W, P, Bel, Sp; 1951 v W, Arg, P; 1952 v F; 1956 v D (13)

Miller, B. G. (Burnley), 1961 v A (1)

Miller, H. S. (Charlton Ath), 1923 v Se (1)

Mills, G. R. (Chelsea), 1938 v W, Ni, Cz (3)

Mills, M. D. (Ipswich T), 1973 v Y; 1976 v W (2), Ni, S, Br, I (sub), Fi; 1977 v Fi (sub), I, Ni, W, S; 1978 v WG, Br, W, Ni, S, H; 1979 v D, Ei, Ni (2), S, Bul, A; 1980 v D, Ni, Sp (2); 1981 v Sw (2), H; 1982 v N, H, S, Fi, F, Cz, K, WG, Sp (42)

Milne, G. (Liverpool), 1963 v Br, Cz, EG; 1964 v W, Ni, S, R of W, U, P, Ei, Br, Arg; 1965 v Ni, Bel (14)

Milton, C. A. (Arsenal), 1952 v A (1)

Milward, A. (Everton), 1891 v S, W; 1897 v S, W (4)

Mitchell, C. (Upton Park), 1880 v W; 1881 v S; 1883 v S, W; 1885 v W (5)

Mitchell, J. F. (Manchester C), 1925 v Ni (1)

Moffat, H. (Oldham Ath), 1913 v W (1)

Molyneux, G. (Southampton), 1902 v S; 1903 v S, W, Ni (4)

Moon, W. R. (Old Westminsters), 1888 v S, W; 1889 v S, W; 1890 v S, W; 1891 v S (7)

Moore, H. T. (Notts Co), 1883 v Ni; 1885 v W (2)

Moore, J. (Derby Co), 1923 v Se (1)

Moore, R. F. (West Ham U), 1962 v Pe, H, Arg, Bul, Br; 1963 v W, Ni, S, F (2), Br, Cz, EG, Sw; 1964 v W, Ni, S, R of W, U, P (2), Ei, Br, Arg; 1965 v Ni, S, Bel, H, Y, WG, Se; 1966 v W, Ni, S, A, Sp, Pol (2), WG (2), N, D, U, M, F, Arg, P; 1967 v W, Ni, S, Cz, Sp, A; 1968 v W, Ni, S, USSR (2), Sp (2), Se, Y, WG; 1969 v Ni, W, S, R, Bul, F, M, U, Br; 1970 v W, Ni, S, Ho, P, Bel, Co, Ec, R, Br, Cz, WG; 1971 v EG, Gr, Ma, Ni, S; 1972 v Sw (2), Gr, WG (2); 1973 v W (3), Y, S (2), Ni, Cz, Pol, USSR, I; 1974 v I (108)

Moore, W. G. B. (West Ham U), 1923 v Se (1)

Mordue, J. (Sunderland), 1912 v Ni; 1913 v Ni (2)

Morice, C. J. (Barnes), 1872 v S (1)

Morley, A. (Aston Villa), 1982 v H (sub), Ni, W, Ic; 1983 v D, Gr (6)

Morley, H. (Notts Co), 1910 v Ni (1)

Morren, T. (Sheffield U), 1898 v Ni (1)

Morris, F. (WBA), 1920 v S; 1921 v Ni (2)

Morris, J. (Derby Co), 1949 v N, F; 1950 v Ei (3)

Morris, W. W. (Wolverhampton W), 1939 v S, Ni, R (3)

Morse, H. (Notts Co), 1879 v S (1)

Mort, T. (Aston Villa), 1924 v W, F; 1926 v S (3)

Morten, A. (C Palace), 1873 v S (1)

Mortensen, S. H. (Blackpool), 1947 v P; 1948 v W, S, Ni, Bel, Se, I; 1949 v S, W, Ni, Se, N; 1950 v S, W, Ni, I, P, Bel, Ch, US, Sp; 1951 v S, Arg; 1954 v R of E, H (25)

Morton, J. R. (West Ham U), 1938 v Cz (1)

Mosforth, W. (Sheffield W), 1877 v S; (with Sheffield Albion), 1878 v S; 1879 v S, W; 1880 v S, W; (with Sheffield U), 1881 v W; 1882 v S, W (9)

Moss, F. (Arsenal), 1934 v S, H, Cz; 1935 v I (4)

Moss, F. (Aston Villa), 1922 v S, Ni; 1923 v Ni; 1924 v S, Bel (5)

Mosscrop, E. (Burnley), 1914 v S, W (2)

Mozley, B. (Derby Co), 1950 v W, Ni, Ei (3)

Mullen, J. (Wolverhampton W), 1947 v S; 1949 v N, F; 1950 v Bel (sub), Ch, US; 1954 v W, Ni, S, R of E, Y, Sw (12)

Mullery, A. P. (Tottenham H), 1965 v Ho; 1967 v Sp, A; 1968 v W, Ni, S, USSR, Sp (2), Se, Y; 1969 v Ni, S, R, Bul, F, M, U, Br; 1970 v W, Ni, S (sub), Ho (sub), Bel, P, Co, Ec, R, Cz, WG, Br; 1971 v Ma, EG, Gr; 1972 v Sw (35)

Neal, P. G. (Liverpool), 1976 v W, I; 1977 v W, S, Br, Arg, U; 1978 v Sw, I, WG, Ni, S, H; 1979 v D, Ei, Ni (2), S, Bul, A; 1980 v D, Ni, Sp, Arg, W, Bel, I; 1981 v R, Sw, Sp, Br, H; 1982 v N, H, W, Ho, Ic, F (sub), K; 1983 v D, Gr, L, W, Gr, H, Ni, S, Aus (2); 1984 v D (50)

Needham, E. (Sheffield U), 1894 v S; 1895 v S; 1897 v S, W, Ni; 1898 v S, W; 1899 v S, W, Ni; 1900 v S, Ni; 1901 v S, W, Ni; 1902 v W (16)

Newton, K. R. (Blackburn R), 1966 v S, WG; 1967 v Sp, A; 1968 v W, S, Sp, Se, Y, WG; 1969 v Ni, W, S, R, Bul, M, U, Br, F; (with Everton), 1970 v Ni, S, Ho, Co, Ec, R, Cz, WG (27)

Nicholls, J. (WBA), 1954 v S, Y (2)

Nicholson, W. E. (Tottenham H), 1951 v P (1)

Nish, D. J. (Derby Co), 1973 v Ni; 1974 v P, W, Ni, S (5)

Norman, M. (Tottenham H), 1962 v Pe, H, Arg, Bul, Br; 1963 v S, F, Br, Cz, EG; 1964 v W, Ni, S, R of W, U, P (2), US, Br, Arg; 1965 v Ni, Bel, Ho (23)

Nuttall, H. (Bolton W), 1928 v W, Ni; 1929 v S (3)

Oakley, W. J. (Oxford University), 1895 v W; 1896 v S, W, Ni; (with Corinthians), 1897 v S, W, Ni; 1898 v S, W, Ni; 1900 v S, W, Ni; 1901 v S, W, Ni (16)

O'Dowd, J. P. (Chelsea), 1932 v S; 1933 v Ni, Sw (3)

O'Grady, M. (Huddersfield T), 1963 v Ni; (with Leeds U), 1969 v F (2)

Ogilvie, R. A. M. M. (Clapham R), 1874 v S (1)

Oliver, L. F. (Fulham), 1929 v Bel (1)

Olney, B. A. (Aston Villa), 1928 v F, Bel (2)

Osborne, F. R. (Fulham), 1923 v Ni, F; (with Tottenham H), 1925 v Bel; 1926 v Bel (4)

Osborne, R. (Leicester C), 1928 v W (1)

Osgood, P. L. (Chelsea), 1970 v Bel, R (sub), Cz (sub); 1974 v I (4)

Osman, R. (Ipswich T), 1980 v Aus; 1981 v Sp, R, Sw; 1982 v N, Ic; 1983 v D, Aus (3); 1984 v D (11)

Ottaway, C. J. (Oxford University), 1872 v S; 1874 v S (2)

Owen, J. R. B. (Sheffield), 1874 v S (1)

Owen, S. W. (Luton T), 1954 v H, Y, Bel (3)

Page, L. A. (Burnley), 1927 v S, W, Bel, L, F; 1928 v W, Ni (7)

Paine, T. L. (Southampton), 1963 v Cz, EG; 1964 v W, Ni, S, R of W, U, US, P; 1965 v Ni, H, Y, WG, Se; 1966 v W, A, Y, N, M (19)

Pallister, G. A. (Middlesbrough), 1988 v H; 1989 v S.Ar; (with Manchester U), 1991 v Cam (sub), T; 1992 v G; 1993 v N, US, Br, G (9)

Palmer, C. L. (Sheffield W), 1992 v C, H, Br, Fi (sub), D, F, Se; 1993 v Sp (sub), N (sub), T, Sm, T, Ho, Pol, N, US, Br (sub) (17)

Pantling, H. H. (Sheffield U), 1924 v Ni (1)

Paravacini, P. J. de (Cambridge University), 1883 v S, W, Ni (3)

Parker, P. A. (QPR), 1989 v Alb (sub), Ch, D; 1990 v Y, U, Ho, Eg, Bel, Cam, WG, I; 1991 v H, Pol, USSR, Aus, Nz; (with Manchester U), 1992 v G; (17)

Parker, T. R. (Southampton), 1925 v F (1)

Parkes, P. B. (QPR), 1974 v P (1)

Parkinson, J. (Liverpool), 1910 v S, W (2)

Parr, P. C. (Oxford University), 1882 v W (1)

Parry, E. H. (Old Carthusians), 1879 v W; 1882 v W, S (3)

Parry, R. A. (Bolton W), 1960 v Ni, S (2)

Patchitt, B. C. A. (Corinthians), 1923 v Se (2) (2)

Pawson, F. W. (Cambridge University), 1883 v Ni; (with Swifts), 1885 v Ni (2)

Payne, J. (Luton T), 1937 v Fi (1)

Peacock, A. (Middlesbrough), 1962 v Arg, Bul; 1963 v Ni, W; (with Leeds U), 1966 v W, Ni (6)

Peacock, J. (Middlesbrough), 1929 v F, Bel, Sp (3)

Pearce, S. (Nottingham F), 1987 v Br, S; 1988 v WG (sub), Is, H; 1989 v D, Se, S.Ar, Gr, Alb (2), Ch, S, Pol, D; 1990 v Se v Se, Pol, I, Y, Br, Cz, D, U, Tun, Ei, Ho, Eg, Bel, Cam, WG; 1991 v H, Pol, Ei (2), Cam, T, Arg, Aus, Nz (2), Mal; 1992 v T, Pol, F, Cz, Br (sub), Fi, D, F, Se; 1993 v Sp, N, T (53)

Pearson, H. F. (WBA), 1932 v S (1)

Pearson, J. H. (Crewe Alex), 1892 v Ni (1)

Pearson, J. S. (Manchester U), 1976 v W, Ni, S, Br, Fi; 1977 v Ei, Ho (sub), W, S, Br, Arg, U; 1978 v I (sub), WG, Ni (15)

Pearson, S. C. (Manchester U), 1948 v S; 1949 v S, Ni; 1950 v Ni, I; 1951 v P; 1952 v S, I (8)

Pease, W. H. (Middlesbrough), 1927 v W (1)

Pegg, D. (Manchester U), 1957 v Ei (1)

Pejic, M. (Stoke C), 1974 v P, W, Ni, S (4)

Pelly, F. R. (Old Foresters), 1893 v Ni; 1894 v S, W (3)

Pennington, J. (WBA), 1907 v S, W; 1908 v S, W, Ni, A; 1909 v S, W, H (2), A; 1910 v S, W; 1911 v S, W, Ni; 1912 v S, W, Ni; 1913 v S, W; 1914 v S, Ni; 1920 v S, W (25)

Pentland, F. B. (Middlesbrough), 1909 v S, W, H (2), A (5)

Perry, C. (WBA), 1890 v Ni; 1891 v Ni; 1893 v W (3)

Perry, T. (WBA), 1898 v W (1)

Perry, W. (Blackpool), 1956 v Ni, S, Sp (3)

Perryman, S. (Tottenham H), 1982 v Ic (sub) (1)

Peters, M. (West Ham U), 1966 v Y, Fi, Pol, M, F, Arg, P, WG; 1967 v Ni, W, S, Cz; 1968 v W, Ni, S, USSR (2), Sp (2), Se, Y; 1969 v Ni, S, R, Bul, F, M, U, Br; 1970 v Ho (2), P (sub), Bel; (with Tottenham H), W, Ni, S, Co, Ec, R, Br, Cz, WG; 1971 v EG, Gr, Ma (2), Ni, W, S; 1972 v Sw, Gr, WG (1+1 sub), Ni (sub); 1973 v S (2), Ni, W, Cz, Pol, USSR, I; 1974 v A, Pol, I, P, S (67)

Phelan, M. C. (Manchester U), 1990 v I (sub) (1)

Phillips, L. H. (Portsmouth), 1952 v Ni; 1955 v W, WG (3)

Pickering, F. (Everton), 1964 v US; 1965 v Ni, Bel (3)

Pickering, J. (Sheffield U), 1933 v S (1)

Pickering, N. (Sunderland), 1983 v Aus (1)

Pike, T. M. (Cambridge University), 1886 v Ni (1)

Pilkington, B. (Burnley), 1955 v Ni (1)

Plant, J. (Bury), 1900 v S (1)

Platt, D. (Aston Villa), 1990 v I (sub), Y (sub), Br, D (sub), Tun (sub), Ho (sub), Eg (sub), Bel (sub), Cam,

WG, I; 1991 v H, Pol, Ei (2), T, USSR, Arg, Aus, Nz (2), Mal; (with Bari), 1992 v G, T, Pol, Cz, C, Br, Fi, D, F, Se; (with Juventus), 1993 v Sp, N, T, Sm, T, Ho, Pol, N, Br (sub), G (42)

Plum, S. L. (Charlton Ath), 1923 v F (1)

Pointer, R. (Burnley), 1962 v W, L, P (3)

Porteous, T. S. (Sunderland), 1891 v W (1)

Priest, A. E. (Sheffield U), 1900 v Ni (1)

Prinsep, J. F. M. (Clapham Rovers), 1879 v S (1)

Puddefoot, S. C. (Blackburn R), 1926 v S, Ni (2)

Pye, J. (Wolverhampton W), 1950 v Ei (1)

Pym, R. H. (Bolton W), 1925 v S, W; 1926 v W (3)

Quantrill, A. (Derby Co), 1920 v S, W; 1921 v W, Ni (4)

Quixall, A. (Sheffield W), 1954 v W, Ni, R of E; 1955 v Sp, P (sub) (5)

Radford, J. (Arsenal), 1969 v R; 1972 v Sw (sub) (2)

Raikes, G. B. (Oxford University), 1895 v W; 1896 v W, Ni, S (4)

Ramsey, A. E. (Southampton), 1949 v Sw; (with Tottenham H), 1950 v S, I, P, Bel, Ch, US, Sp; 1951 v S, Ni, W, Y, Arg, P; 1952 v S, W, Ni, F, A (2), I, Sw; 1953 v Ni, W, S, Bel, Arg, Ch, U, US; 1954 v R of E, H (32)

Rawlings, A. (Preston NE), 1921 v Bel (1)

Rawlings, W. E. (Southampton), 1922 v S, W (2)

Rawlinson, J. F. P. (Cambridge University), 1882 v Ni (1)

Rawson, H. E. (Royal Engineers), 1875 v S (1)

Rawson, W. S. (Oxford University), 1875 v S; 1877 v S (2)

Read, A. (Tufnell Park), 1921 v Bel (1)

Reader, J. (WBA), 1894 v Ni (1)

Reaney, P. (Leeds U), 1969 v Bul (sub); 1970 v P; 1971 v Ma (3)

Reeves, K. (Norwich C), 1980 v Bul; (with Manchester C), Ni (2)

Regis, C. (WBA), 1982 v Ni (sub), W (sub), Ic; 1983 v WG; (with Coventry C), 1988 v T (sub) (5)

Reid, P. (Everton), 1985 v M (sub), WG, US (sub); 1986 v R, S (sub), Ca (sub), Pol, Para, Arg; 1987 v Br; 1988 v WG, Y (sub), Sw (sub) (13)

Revie, D. G. (Manchester C), 1955 v Ni, S, F; 1956 v W, D; 1957 v Ni (6)

Reynolds, J. (WBA), 1892 v S; 1893 v S, W; (with Aston Villa), 1894 v S, Ni; 1895 v S; 1897 v S, W (8)

Richards, C. H. (Nottingham F), 1898 v Ni (1)

Richards, G. H. (Derby Co), 1909 v A (1)

Richards, J. P. (Wolverhampton W), 1973 v Ni (1)

Richardson, J. R. (Newcastle U), 1933 v I, Sw (2)

Richardson, W. G. (WBA), 1935 v Ho (1)

Rickaby, S. (WBA), 1954 v Ni (1)

Rigby, A. (Blackburn R), 1927 v S, Bel, L, F; 1928 v W (5)

Rimmer, E. J. (Sheffield W), 1930 v S, G, A; 1932 v Sp (4)

Rimmer, J. J. (Arsenal), 1976 v I (1)

Rix, G. (Arsenal), 1981 v N, R, Sw (sub), Br, W, S; 1982 v Ho (sub), Fi (sub), F, Cz, K, WG, Sp; 1983 v D, WG (sub), Gr (sub); 1984 v Ni (17)

Robb, G. (Tottenham H), 1954 v H (1)

Roberts, C. (Manchester U), 1905 v Ni, W, S (3)

Roberts, F. (Manchester C), 1925 v S, W, Bel, F (4)

Roberts, G. (Tottenham H), 1983 v Ni, S; 1984 v F, Ni, S, USSR (6)

Roberts, H. (Arsenal), 1931 v S (1)

Roberts, H. (Millwall), 1931 v Bel (1)

Roberts, R. (WBA), 1887 v S; 1888 v Ni; 1890 v Ni (3)

Roberts, W. T. (Preston NE), 1924 v W, Bel (2)

Robinson, J. (Sheffield W), 1937 v Fi; 1938 v G, Sw; 1939 v W (4)

Robinson, J. W. (Derby Co), 1897 v S, Ni; (with New Brighton Tower), 1898 v S, W, Ni; (with Southampton), 1899 v W, S; 1900 v S, W, Ni; 1901 v Ni (11)

Robson, B. (WBA), 1980 v Ei, Aus; 1981 v N, R, Sw, Sp, R, Br, W, S, Sw, H; 1982 v N; (with Manchester U), H, Ni, W, Ho, S, Fi, F, Cz, WG, Sp; 1983 v D, Gr, L, S;

1984 v H, L, F, Ni, S, USSR, Br, U, Ch; 1985 v EG, Fi, T, Ei, R, Fi, S, M, I, WG, US; 1986 v R, T, Is, M, P, Mor; 1987 v Ni (2), Sp, T, Br, S; 1988 v T, Y, Ho, H, S, Co, Sw, Ei, Ho, USSR; 1989 v S, Se, S.Ar, Gr, Alb (2), Ch, S, Pol, D; 1990 v Pol, I, Y, Cz, U, Tun, Ei, Ho; 1991 v Cam, Ei; 1992 v T (90)

Robson, R. (WBA), 1958 v F, USSR (2), Br, A; 1960 v Sp, H; 1961 v Ni, W, S, L, P, Sp, M, I; 1962 v W, Ni, Sw, L, P (20)

Rocastle, D. (Arsenal), 1989 v D, S.Ar, Gr, Alb (2), Pol (sub), D; 1990 v Se (sub), Pol, Y, D (sub); 1992 v Pol, Cz, Br (sub) (14)

Rose, W. C. (Wolverhampton W), 1884 v S, W, Ni; (with Preston NE), 1886 v Ni; (with Wolverhampton W), 1891 v Ni (5)

Rostron, T. (Darwen), 1881 v S, W (2)

Rowe, A. (Tottenham H), 1934 v F (1)

Rowley, J. F. (Manchester U), 1949 v Sw, Se, F; 1950 v Ni, I; 1952 v S (6)

Rowley, W. (Stoke C), 1889 v Ni; 1892 v Ni (2)

Royle, J. (Everton), 1971 v Ma; 1973 v Y; (with Manchester C), 1976 v Ni (sub), I; 1977 v Fi, L (6)

Ruddlesdin, H. (Sheffield W), 1904 v W, Ni; 1905 v S (3)

Ruffell, J. W. (West Ham U), 1926 v S; 1927 v Ni; 1929 v S, W, Ni; 1930 v W (6)

Russell, B. B. (Royal Engineers), 1883 v W (1)

Rutherford, J. (Newcastle U), 1904 v S; 1907 v S, Ni, W; 1908 v S, Ni, W, A (2), H, B (11)

Sadler, D. (Manchester U), 1968 v Ni, USSR; 1970 v Ec (sub); 1971 v EG (4)

Sagar, C. (Bury), 1900 v Ni; 1902 v W (2)

Sagar, E. (Everton), 1936 v S, Ni, A, Bel (4)

Salako, J. A. (C Palace), 1991 v Aus (sub), Nz (sub + 1), Mal; 1992 v G (5)

Sandford, E. A. (WBA), 1933 v W (1)

Sandilands, R. R. (Old Westminsters), 1892 v W; 1893 v Ni; 1894 v W; 1895 v W; 1896 v W (5)

Sands, J. (Nottingham F), 1880 v W (1)

Sansom, K. (C Palace), 1979 v W; 1980 v Bul, Ei, Arg, W (sub), Ni, S, Bel, I; (with Arsenal), 1981 v N, R, Sw, Sp, R, Br, W, S, Sw; 1982 v Ni, W, Ho, S, Fi, F, Cz, WG, Sp; 1983 v D, WG, Gr, L, Gr, H, Ni, S; 1984 v D, H, L, F, S, USSR, Br, U, Ch; 1985 v EG, Fi, T, Ni, Ei, R, M, S, I, M, WG, US; 1986 v R, T, Ni, Eg, Is, USSR, S, M, Ca, P, Mor, Pol, Para, Arg; 1987 v Se, Ni (2), Y, Sp, T; 1988 v WG, T, Y, Ho, S, Co, Sw, Ei, Ho, USSR (86)

Saunders, F. E. (Swifts), 1888 v W (1)

Savage, A. H. (C Palace), 1876 v S (1)

Sayer, J. (Stoke C), 1887 v Ni (1)

Scattergood, E. (Derby Co), 1913 v W (1)

Schofield, J. (Stoke C), 1892 v W; 1893 v W; 1895 v Ni (3)

Scott, L. (Arsenal), 1947 v S, W, Ni, Ei, Ho, F, Sw, P; 1948 v S, W, Ni, Bel, Se, I; 1949 v W, Ni, D (17)

Scott, W. R. (Brentford), 1937 v W (1)

Seaman, D. A. (QPR), 1989 v S.Ar, D (sub); 1990 v Cz (sub); (with Arsenal), 1991 v Cam, Ei, T, Arg; 1992 v Cz, H (sub) (9)

Seddon, J. (Bolton W), 1923 v F, Se (2); 1924 v Bel; 1927 v W; 1929 v S (6)

Seed, J. M. (Tottenham H), 1921 v Bel: 1923 v W, Ni, Bel; 1925 v S (5)

Settle, J. (Bury), 1899 v S, W, Ni; (with Everton), 1902 v S, Ni; 1903 v Ni (6)

Sewell, J. (Sheffield W), 1952 v Ni, A, Sw; 1953 v Ni; 1954 v H (2) (6)

Sewell, W. R. (Blackburn R), 1924 v W (1)

Shackleton, L. F. (Sunderland), 1949 v W, D; 1950 v W; 1955 v W, WG (5)

Sharp, J. (Everton), 1903 v Ni; 1905 v S (2)

Sharpe, L. S. (Manchester U), 1991 v Ei (sub); 1993 v T (sub), N, US, Br, G (6)

Shaw, G. E. (WBA), 1932 v S (1)

Shaw, G. L. (Sheffield U), 1959 v S, W, USSR, I; 1963 v W (5)

Shea, D. (Blackburn R), 1914 v W, Ni (2)

Shearer, A. (Southampton), 1992 v F, C, F; (with Blackburn R), 1993 v Sp, N, T (6)

Shellito, K. J. (Chelsea), 1963 v Cz (1)

Shelton A. (Notts Co), 1889 v Ni; 1890 v S, W; 1891 v S, W; 1892 v S (6)

Shelton, C. (Notts Rangers), 1888 v Ni (1)

Shepherd, A. (Bolton W), 1906 v S; (with Newcastle U), 1911 v Ni (2)

Sheringham, E. P. (Tottenham H), 1993 v Pol, N (2)

Shilton, P. L. (Leicester C), 1971 v EG, W; 1972 v Sw, Ni; 1973 v Y, S (2), Ni, W, Cz, Pol, USSR, I; 1974 v A, Pol, I, W, Ni, S, Arg; (with Stoke C), 1975 v Cy; 1977 v Ni, W; (with Nottingham F), 1978 v W, H; 1979 v Cz, Se, A; 1980 v Ni, Sp, I; 1981 v N, Sw, R; 1982 v H, Ho, S, F, Cz, K, WG, Sp; (with Southampton), 1983 v D, WG, Gr, W, Gr, H, Ni, S, Aus (3); 1984 v D, H, F, Ni, W, S, USSR, Br, U, Ch; 1985 v EG, Fi, T, Ni, R, Fi, S, I, WG; 1986 v R, T, Ni, Eg, Is, USSR, S, M, Ca, P, Mor, Pol, Para, Arg; 1987 v Se, Ni (2), Sp, Br; (with Derby Co), 1988 v WG, T, Y, Ho, S, Co, Sw, Ei, Ho; 1989 v D, Se, Gr, Alb (2), Ch, S, Pol, D; 1990 v Se, Pol, I, Y, Br, Cz, D, U, Tun, Ei, Ho, Eg, Bel, Cam, WG, I (125)

Shimwell, E. (Blackpool), 1949 v Se (1)

Shutt, G. (Stoke C), 1886 v Ni (1)

Silcock, J. (Manchester U), 1921 v S, W; 1923 v Se (3)

Sillett, R. P. (Chelsea), 1955 v F, Sp, P (3)

Simms, E. (Luton T), 1922 v Ni (1)

Simpson, J. (Blackburn R), 1911 v S, W, Ni; 1912 v S, W, Ni; 1913 v S; 1914 v W (8)

Sinton, A. (QPR), 1992 v Pol, C, H (sub), Br, F, Se; 1993 v Sp, T, Br, G (10)

Slater, W. J. (Wolverhampton W), 1955 v W, WG; 1958 v S, P, Y, USSR (3), Br, A; 1959 v USSR; 1960 v S (12)

Smalley, T. (Wolverhampton W), 1937 v W (1)

Smart, T. (Aston Villa), 1921 v S; 1924 v S, W; 1926 v Ni; 1930 v W (5)

Smith, A. (Nottingham F), 1891 v S, W; 1893 v Ni (3)

Smith, A. K. (Oxford University), 1872 v S (1)

Smith, A. M. (Arsenal), 1989 v S.Ar (sub), Gr, Alb (sub), Pol (sub); 1991 v T, USSR, Arg; 1992 v G, T, Pol (sub), H (sub), D, Se (sub) (13)

Smith, B. (Tottenham H), 1921 v S; 1922 v W (2)

Smith, C. E. (C Palace), 1876 v S (1)

Smith, G. O. (Oxford University), 1893 v Ni; 1894 v W, S; 1895 v W; 1896 v Ni, W, S; (with Old Carthusians), 1897 v Ni, W, S; 1898 v Ni, W, S; (with Corinthians), 1899 v Ni, W, S; 1899 v Ni, W, S; 1901 v S (20)

Smith, H. (Reading), 1905 v W, S; 1906 v W, Ni (4)

Smith, J. (WBA), 1920 v Ni; 1923 v Ni (2)

Smith, Joe (Bolton W), 1913 v Ni; 1914 v S, W; 1920 v W, Ni (5)

Smith, J. C. R. (Millwall), 1939 v Ni, N (2)

Smith, J. W. (Portsmouth), 1932 v Ni, W, Sp (3)

Smith, Leslie (Brentford), 1939 v R (1)

Smith, Lionel (Arsenal), 1951 v W; 1952 v W, Ni; 1953 v W, S, Bel (6)

Smith, R. A. (Tottenham H), 1961 v Ni, W, S, L, P, Sp; 1962 v S; 1963 v S, F, Br, Cz, EG; 1964 v W, Ni, R of W (15)

Smith, S. (Aston Villa), 1895 v S (1)

Smith, S. C. (Leicester C), 1936 v Ni (1)

Smith, T. (Birmingham C), 1960 v W, Se (2)

Smith, T. (Liverpool), 1971 v W (1)

Smith, W. H. (Huddersfield T), 1922 v W, S; 1928 v S (3)

Sorby, T. H. (Thursday Wanderers, Sheffield), 1879 v W (1)

Southworth, J. (Blackburn R), 1889 v W; 1891 v W; 1892 v S (3)

Sparks, F. J. (Herts Rangers), 1879 v S; (with Clapham Rovers), 1880 v S, W (3)

Spence, J. W. (Manchester U), 1926 v Bel; 1927 v Ni (2)

Spence, R. (Chelsea), 1936 v A, Bel (2)

Spencer, C. W. (Newcastle U), 1924 v S; 1925 v W (2)

Spencer, H. (Aston Villa), 1897 v S, W; 1900 v W; 1903 v Ni; 1905 v W, S (6)

Spiksley, F. (Sheffield W), 1893 v S, W; 1894 v S, Ni; 1896 v Ni; 1898 v S, W (7)

Spilsbury, B. W. (Cambridge University), 1885 v Ni; 1886 v Ni, S (3)

Spink, N. (Aston Villa), 1983 v Aus (sub) (1)

Spouncer, W. A. (Nottingham F), 1900 v W (1)

Springett, R. D. G. (Sheffield W), 1960 v Ni, S, Y, Sp, H; 1961 v Ni, S, L, P, Sp, M, I, A; 1962 v W, Ni, S, A, Sw, Pe, L, P, H, Arg, Bul, Br; 1963 v Ni, W, F (2); Sw; 1966 v W, A, N (33)

Sproston, B. (Leeds U), 1937 v W; 1938 v S, W, Ni, Cz, G, Sw, F; (with Tottenham H), 1939 v W, R of E; (with Manchester C), N (11)

Squire, R. T. (Cambridge University), 1886 v S, W, Ni (3)

Stanbrough, M. H. (Old Carthusians), 1895 v W (1)

Staniforth, R. (Huddersfield T), 1954 v S, H, Y, Bel, Sw, U; 1955 v W, WG (8)

Starling, R. W. (Sheffield W), 1933 v S; (with Aston Villa), 1937 v S (2)

Statham, D. (WBA), 1983 v W, Aus (2) (3)

Steele, F. C. (Stoke C), 1937 v S, W, Ni, N, Se, Fi (6)

Stein, B. (Luton T), 1984 v F (1)

Stephenson, C. (Huddersfield T), 1924 v W (1)

Stephenson, G. T. (Derby Co), 1928 v F, Bel; (with Sheffield W), 1931 v F (3)

Stephenson, J. E. (Leeds U), 1938 v S; 1939 v Ni (2)

Stepney, A. C. (Manchester U), 1968 v Se (1)

Sterland, M. (Sheffield W), 1989 v S.Ar (1)

Steven, T. M. (Everton), 1985 v Ni, Ei, R, Fi, I, US (sub); 1986 v T (sub), Eg, USSR (sub), M (sub), Pol, Para, Arg; 1987 v Se, Y (sub), Sp (sub); 1988 v T, Y, Ho, H, S, Sw, Ho, USSR; 1989 v S; (with Rangers), 1990 v Cz, Cam (sub), WG (sub); I; 1991 v Cam; (with Marseille); 1992 v G, C, Br, Fi, D, F (36)

Stevens, G. A. (Tottenham H), 1985 v Fi (sub), T (sub), Ni; 1986 v S (sub), M (sub), Mor (sub), Para (sub) (7)

Stevens, M. G. (Everton), 1985 v I, WG; 1986 v R, T, Ni, Eg, Is, S, Ca, P, Mor, Pol, Para, Arg; 1987 v Br, S; 1988 v T, Y, Is, Ho, H (sub), S, Sw, Ei, Ho, USSR; (with Rangers), 1989 v D, Se, Gr, Alb (2), S, Pol; 1990 v Se, Pol, I, Br, D, Tun, Ei, I; 1991 v USSR; 1992 v C, H, Br, Fi (46)

Stewart, J. (Sheffield W), 1907 v S, W; (with Newcastle U), 1911 v S (3)

Stewart, P. A. (Tottenham H), 1992 v G (sub), Cz (sub), C (sub) (3)

Stiles, N. P. (Manchester U), 1965 v S, H, Y, Se; 1966 v W, Ni, S, A, Sp, Pol (2), WG (2), N, D, U, M, F, Arg, P; 1967 v Ni, W, S, Cz; 1968 v USSR; 1969 v R; 1970 v Ni, S (28)

Stoker, J. (Birmingham), 1933 v W; 1934 v S, H (3)

Storer, H. (Derby Co), 1924 v F; 1928 v Ni (2)

Storey, P. E. (Arsenal), 1971 v Gr, Ni, S; 1972 v Sw, WG, W, Ni, S; 1973 v W (3), Y, S (2), Ni, Cz, Pol, USSR, I (19)

Storey-Moore, I. (Nottingham F), 1970 v Ho (1)

Strange, A. H. (Sheffield W), 1930 v S, A, G; 1931 v S, W, Ni, F, Bel; 1932 v S, W, Ni, Sp; 1933 v S, Ni, A, I, Sw; 1934 v Ni, W, F (20)

Stratford, A. H. (Wanderers), 1874 v S (1)

Streten, B. (Luton T), 1950 v Ni (1)

Sturgess, A. (Sheffield U), 1911 v Ni; 1914 v S (2)

Summerbee, M. G. (Manchester C), 1968 v S, Sp, WG; 1972 v Sw, WG (sub), W, Ni; 1973 v USSR (sub) (8)

Sunderland, A. (Arsenal), 1980 v Aus (1)

Sutcliffe, J. W. (Bolton W), 1893 v W; 1895 v S, Ni; 1901 v S; (with Millwall), 1903 v W (5)

Swan, P. (Sheffield W), 1960 v Y, Sp, H; 1961 v Ni, W, S, L, P, Sp, M, I, A; 1962 v W, Ni, S, A, Sw, L, P (19)

Swepstone, H. A. (Pilgrims), 1880 v S; 1882 v S, W; 1883 v S, W, Ni (6)

Swift, F. V. (Manchester C), 1947 v S, W, Ni, Ei, Ho, F, Sw, P; 1948 v S, W, Ni, Bel, Se, I; 1949 v S, W, Ni, D, N (19)

Tait, G. (Birmingham Excelsior), 1881 v W (1)

Talbot, B. (Ipswich T), 1977 v Ni (sub), S, Br, Arg, U; (with Arsenal), 1980 v Aus (6)

Tambling, R. V. (Chelsea), 1963 v W, F; 1966 v Y (3)

Tate, J. T. (Aston Villa), 1931 v F, Bel; 1933 v W (3)

Taylor, E. (Blackpool), 1954 v H (1)

Taylor, E. H. (Huddersfield T), 1923 v S, W, Ni, Bel; 1924 v S, Ni, F; 1926 v S (8)

Taylor, J. G. (Fulham), 1951 v Arg, P (2)

Taylor, P. H. (Liverpool), 1948 v W, Ni, Se (3)

Taylor, P. J. (C Palace), 1976 v W (sub + 1), Ni, S (4)

Taylor, T. (Manchester U), 1953 v Arg, Ch, U; 1954 v Bel, Sw; 1956 v S, Br, Se, Fi, WG; 1957 v Ni, Y (sub), D (2), Ei (2); 1958 v W, Ni, F (19)

Temple, D. W. (Everton), 1965 v WG (1)

Thickett, H. (Sheffield U), 1899 v S, W (2)

Thomas, D. (Coventry C), 1983 v Aus (1 + 1 sub) (2)

Thomas, D. (QPR), 1975 v Cz (sub), P, Cy (sub + 1), W, S (sub); 1976 v Cz (sub), P (sub) (8)

Thomas, G. R. (C Palace), 1991 v T, USSR, Arg, Aus, Nz (2), Mal; 1992 v Pol, F (9)

Thomas, M. L. (Arsenal), 1989 v S.Ar; 1990 v Y (2)

Thompson, P. (Liverpool), 1964 v P (2), Ei, US, Br, Arg; 1965 v Ni, W, S, Bel, Ho; 1966 v Ni; 1968 v Ni, WG; 1970 v S, Ho (sub) (16)

Thompson, P. B. (Liverpool), 1976 v W (2), Ni, S, Br, I, Fi; 1977 v Fi; 1979 v Ei (sub), Cz, Ni, S, Bul, Se (sub), A; 1980 v D, Ni, Bul, Ei, Sp (2), Arg, W, S, Bel, I; 1981 v N, R, H; 1982 v N, H, W, Ho, S, Fi, F, Cz, K, WG, Sp; 1983 v WG, Gr (42)

Thompson T. (Aston Villa), 1952 v W; (with Preston NE), 1957 v S (2)

Thomson, R. A. (Wolverhampton W), 1964 v Ni, US, P, Arg; 1965 v Bel, Ho, Ni, W (8)

Thornewell, G. (Derby Co), 1923 v Se (2); 1924 v F; 1925 v F (4)

Thornley, I. (Manchester C), 1907 v W (1)

Tilson, S. F. (Manchester C), 1934 v H, Cz; 1935 v W; 1936 v Ni (4)

Titmuss, F. (Southampton), 1922 v W; 1923 v W (2)

Todd, C. (Derby Co), 1972 v Ni; 1974 v P, W, Ni, S, Arg, EG, Bul, Y; 1975 v P (sub), WG, Cy (2), Ni, W, S; 1976 v Sw, Cz, P, Ni, S, Br, Fi; 1977 v Ei, Fi, Ho (sub), Ni (27)

Toone, G. (Notts Co), 1892 v S, W (2)

Topham, A. G. (Casuals), 1894 v W (1)

Topham, R. (Wolverhampton W), 1893 v Ni; (with Casuals) 1894 v W (2)

Towers, M. A. (Sunderland), 1976 v W, Ni (sub), I (3)

Townley, W. J. (Blackburn R), 1889 v W; 1890 v Ni (2)

Townrow, J. E. (Clapton Orient), 1925 v S; 1926 v W (2)

Tremelling, D. R. (Birmingham), 1928 v W (1)

Tresadern, J. (West Ham U), 1923 v S, Se (2)

Tueart, D. (Manchester C), 1975 v Cy (sub), Ni; 1977 v Fi, Ni, W (sub), S (sub) (6)

Tunstall, F. E. (Sheffield U), 1923 v S; 1924 v S, W, Ni, F; 1925 v Ni, S (7)

Turnbull, R. J. (Bradford), 1920 v Ni (1)

Turner, A. (Southampton), 1900 v Ni; 1901 v Ni (2)

Turner, H. (Huddersfield T), 1931 v F, Bel (2)

Turner, J. A. (Bolton W), 1893 v W; (with Stoke C) 1895 v Ni; (with Derby Co) 1898 v Ni (3)

Tweedy, G. J. (Grimsby T), 1937 v H (1)

Ufton, D. G. (Charlton Ath), 1954 v R of E (1)

Underwood A. (Stoke C), 1891 v Ni; 1892 v Ni (2)

Urwin, T. (Middlesbrough), 1923 v Se (2); 1924 v Bel; (with Newcastle U), 1926 v W (4)

Utley, G. (Barnsley), 1913 v Ni (1)

Vaughton, O. H. (Aston Villa), 1882 v S, W, Ni; 1884 v S, W (5)

Veitch, C. C. M. (Newcastle U), 1906 v S, W, Ni; 1907 v S, W; 1909 v W (6)

Veitch, J. G. (Old Westminsters), 1894 v W (1)

Venables, T. F. (Chelsea), 1965 v Ho, Bel (2)

Vidal, R. W. S. (Oxford University), 1873 v S (1)

Viljoen, C. (Ipswich T), 1975 v Ni, W (2)

Viollet, D. S. (Manchester U), 1960 v H; 1962 v L (2)

Von Donop (Royal Engineers), 1873 v S; 1875 v S (2)

Wace, H. (Wanderers), 1878 v S; 1879 v S, W (3)

Waddle, C. R. (Newcastle U), 1985 v Ei, R (sub), Fi (sub), S (sub), I, M (sub), WG, US; (with Tottenham H), 1986 v R, T, Ni, Is, USSR, S, M, Ca, P, Mor, Pol (sub), Arg (sub); 1987 v Se (sub), Ni (2), Y, Sp, T, Br, S; 1988 v WG, Is, H, S (sub), Co, Sw (sub), Ei, Ho (sub); 1989 v Se, S.Ar, Alb (2), Ch, S, Pol, D (sub); (with Marseille), 1990 v Se, Pol, I, Y, Br, D, U, Tun, Ei, Ho, Eg, Bel, Cam, WG, I (sub); 1991 v H (sub), Pol (sub); 1992 v T (62)

Wadsworth, S. J. (Huddersfield T), 1922 v S; 1923 v S, Bel; 1924 v S, Ni; 1925 v S, Ni; 1926 v W; 1927 v Ni (9)

Wainscoat, W. R. (Leeds U), 1929 v S (1)

Waiters, A. K. (Blackpool), 1964 v Ei, Br; 1965 v W, Bel, Ho (5)

Walker, D. S. (Nottingham F), 1989 v D (sub), Se (sub), Gr, Alb (2), Ch, S, Pol, D; 1990 v Se, Pol, I, Y, Br, Cz, D, U, Tun, Ei, Ho, Eg, Bel, Cam, WG, I; 1991 v H, Pol, Ei (2), Cam, T, Arg, Aus, Nz (2), Mal; 1992 v T, Pol, F, Cz, C, H, Br, Fi, D, F, Se; (with Sampdoria), 1993 v Sp, N, T, Sm, T, Ho, Pol, N, US (sub), Br, G (58)

Walden, F. I. (Tottenham H), 1914 v S; 1922 v W (2)

Walker, W. H. (Aston Villa), 1921 v Ni; 1922 v Ni, W, S; 1923 v Se (2); 1924 v S; 1925 v Ni, W, S, Bel, F; 1926 v Ni, W, S; 1927 v Ni, W; 1933 v A (18)

Wall, G. (Manchester U), 1907 v W; 1908 v Ni; 1909 v S; 1910 v W, S; 1912 v S; 1913 v Ni (7)

Wallace, C. W. (Aston Villa), 1913 v W; 1914 v Ni; 1920 v S (3)

Wallace, D. L. (Southampton), 1986 v Eg (1)

Walsh, P. (Luton T), 1983 v Aus (2 + 1 sub); 1984 v F, W (5)

Walters, A. M. (Cambridge University), 1885 v S, N; 1886 v S; 1887 v S, W; (with Old Carthusians), 1889 v S, W; 1890 v S, W (9)

Walters, K. M. (Rangers), 1991 v Nz (1)

Walters, P. M. (Oxford University), 1885 v S, Ni; (with Old Carthusians), 1886 v S, W, Ni; 1887 v S, W; 1888 v S, Ni; 1889 v S, W; 1890 v S, W (13)

Walton, N. (Blackburn R), 1890 v Ni (1)

Ward, J. T. (Blackburn Olympic), 1885 v W (1)

Ward, P. (Brighton & HA), 1980 v Aus (sub) (1)

Ward, T. V. (Derby Co), 1948 v Bel; 1949 v W (2)

Waring, T. (Aston Villa), 1931 v F, Bel; 1932 v S, W, Ni (5)

Warner, C. (Upton Park), 1878 v S (1)

Warren, B. (Derby Co), 1906 v S, W, Ni; 1907 v S, W, Ni; 1908 v S, W, Ni, A (2), H, B; (with Chelsea), 1909 v S, Ni, W, H (2), A; 1911 v S, Ni, W (22)

Waterfield, G. S. (Burnley), 1927 v W (1)

Watson, D. (Norwich C), 1984 v Br, U, Ch; 1985 v M, US (sub); 1986 v S; (with Everton), 1987 v Ni; 1988 v Is, Ho, S, Sw (sub), USSR (12)

Watson, D. V. (Sunderland), 1974 v P, S (sub), Arg, EG, Bul, Y; 1975 v Cz, P, WG, Cy (2), Ni, W, S; (with Manchester C), 1976 v Sw, Cz (sub), P; 1977 v Ho, L, Ni, W, S, Br, Arg, U; 1978 v Sw, L, I, WG, Br, W, Ni,

S, H; 1979 v D, Ei, Cz, Ni (2), W, S, Bul, Se, A; (with Werder Bremen), 1980 v D; (with Southampton), Ni, Bul, Ei, Sp (2), Arg, Ni, S, Bel, I; 1981 v N, R, Sw, R, W, S, Sw, H; (with Stoke C), 1982 v Ni, Ic (65)

Watson, V. M. (West Ham U), 1923 v W, S; 1930 v S, G, A (5)

Watson, W. (Burnley), 1913 v S; 1914 v Ni; 1920 v Ni (3)

Watson, W. (Sunderland), 1950 v Ni, I; 1951 v W, Y (4)

Weaver, S. (Newcastle U), 1932 v S, 1933 v S, Ni (3)

Webb, G. W. (West Ham U), 1911 v S, W (2)

Webb, N. J. (Nottingham F), 1988 v WG (sub), T, Y, Is, Ho, S, Sw, Ei, USSR (sub); 1989 v D, Se, Gr, Alb (2), Ch, S, Pol, D; (with Manchester U), 1990 v Se, I (sub); 1992 v F, H, Br (sub), Fi, D (sub), Se (26)

Webster, M. (Middlesbrough), 1930 v S, A, G (3)

Wedlock, W. J. (Bristol C), 1907 v S, Ni, W; 1908 v S, Ni, W, A (2), H, B; 1909 v S, W, Ni, H (2), A; 1910 v S, W, Ni; 1911 v S, W, Ni; 1912 v S, W, Ni; 1914 v W (26)

Weir, D. (Bolton W), 1889 v S, Ni (2)

Welch, R. de C. (Wanderers), 1872 v S; (with Harrow Chequers), 1874 v S (2)

Weller, K. (Leicester C), 1974 v W, Ni, S, Arg (4)

Welsh, D. (Charlton Ath), 1938 v G, Sw; 1939 v R (3)

West, G. (Everton), 1969 v W, Bul, M (3)

Westwood, R. W. (Bolton W), 1935 v S, W, Ho; 1936 v Ni, G; 1937 v W (6)

Whateley, O. (Aston Villa), 1883 v S, Ni (2)

Wheeler, J. E. (Bolton W), 1955 v Ni (1)

Wheldon, G. F. (Aston Villa), 1897 v Ni; 1898 v S, W, Ni (4)

White, D. (Manchester C), 1993 v Sp (1)

White, T. A. (Everton), 1933 v I (1)

Whitehead, J. (Accrington), 1893 v W; (with Blackburn R), 1894 v Ni (2)

Whitfeld, H. (Old Etonians), 1879 v W (1)

Whitham, M. (Sheffield U), 1892 v Ni (1)

Whitworth, S. (Leicester C), 1975 v WG, Cy, Ni, W, S; 1976 v Sw, P (7)

Whymark, T. J. (Ipswich T), 1978 v L (sub) (1)

Widdowson, S. W. (Nottingham F), 1880 v S (1)

Wignall, F. (Nottingham F), 1965 v W, Ho (2)

Wilkes, A. (Aston Villa), 1901 v S, W; 1902 v S, W, Ni (5)

Wilkins, R. G. (Chelsea), 1976 v I; 1977 v Ei, Fi, Ni, Br, Arg, U; 1978 v Sw (sub), L, I, WG, W, Ni, S, H; 1979 v D, Ei, Cz, Ni, W, S, Bul, Se (sub), A; (with Manchester U), 1980 v D, Ni, Bul, Sp (2), Arg, W (sub), Ni, S, Bel, I; 1981 v Sp (sub), R, Br, W, S, Sw, H (sub); 1982 v Ni, W, Ho, S, Fi, F, Cz, K, WG, Sp; 1983 v D, WG; 1984 v D, Ni, W, S, USSR, Br, U, Ch; (with AC Milan), 1985 v EG, Fi, T, Ni, Ei, R, Fi, S, I, M; 1986 v T, Ni, Is, Eg, USSR, S, M, Ca, P, Mor; 1987 v Se, Y (sub) (84)

Wilkinson, B. (Sheffield U), 1904 v S (1)

Wilkinson, L. R. (Oxford University), 1891 v W (1)

Williams, B. F. (Wolverhampton W), 1949 v F; 1950 v S, W, Ei, I, P, Bel, Ch, US, Sp; 1951 v Ni, W, S, Y, Arg, P; 1952 v W, F; 1955 v S, W, G, F, Sp, P; 1956 v W (24)

Williams, O. (Clapton Orient), 1923 v W, Ni (2)

Williams, S. (Southampton), 1983 v Aus (1 + 1 sub); 1984 v F; 1985 v EG, Fi, T (6)

Williams, W. (WBA), 1897 v Ni; 1898 v W, Ni, S; 1899 v W, Ni (6)

Williamson, E. C. (Arsenal), 1923 v Se (2) (2)

Williamson, R. G. (Middlesbrough), 1905 v Ni; 1911 v Ni, S, W; 1912 v S, W; 1913 v Ni (7)

Willingham, C. K. (Huddersfield T), 1937 v Fi; 1938 v S, G, Sw, F; 1939 v S, W, Ni, R of E, N, I, Y (12)

Willis, A. (Tottenham H), 1952 v F (1)

Wilshaw, D. J. (Wolverhampton W), 1954 v W, Sw, U; 1955 v S, F, Sp, P; 1956 v W, Ni, Fi, WG; 1957 v Ni (12)

Wilson, C. P. (Hendon), 1884 v S, W (2)

Wilson, C. W. (Oxford University), 1879 v W; 1881 v S (2)

Wilson, G. (Sheffield W), 1921 v S, W, Bel; 1922 v S, Ni; 1923 v S, W, Ni, Bel; 1924 v W, Ni, F (12)

Wilson, G. P. (Corinthians), 1900 v S, W (2)

Wilson, R. (Huddersfield T), 1960 v S, Y, Sp, H; 1962 v W, Ni, S, A, Sw, Pe, P, H, Arg, Bul, Br; 1963 v Ni, F, Br, Cz, EG, Sw; 1964 v W, S, R of W, U, P (2), Ei, Br, Arg; (with Everton), 1965 v S, H, Y, WG, Se; 1966 v WG (sub), W, Ni, A, Sp, Pol (2), Y, Fi, D, U, M, F, Arg, P, WG; 1967 v Ni, W, S, Cz, A; 1968 v Ni, S, USSR (2), Sp (2), Y (63)

Wilson, T. (Huddersfield T), 1928 v S (1)

Winckworth, W. N. (Old Westminsters), 1892 v W; 1893 v Ni (2)

Windridge, J. E. (Chelsea), 1908 v S, W, Ni, A (2), H, B; 1909 v Ni (8)

Wingfield-Stratford, C. V. (Royal Engineers), 1877 v S (1)

Winterburn, N. (Arsenal), 1990 v I (sub); 1993 v G (sub) (2)

Wise, D. F. (Chelsea), 1991 v T, USSR, Aus (sub), Nz (2) (5)

Withe, P. (Aston Villa), 1981 v Br, W, S; 1982 v N (sub), W, Ic; 1983 v H, Ni, S; 1984 v H (sub); 1985 v T (11)

Wollaston, C. H. R. (Wanderers), 1874 v S; 1875 v S; 1877 v S; 1880 v S (4)

Wolstenholme, S. (Everton), 1904 v S; (with Blackburn R), 1905 v W, Ni (3)

Wood, H. (Wolverhampton W), 1890 v S, W; 1896 v S (3)

Wood, R. E. (Manchester U), 1955 v Ni, W; 1956 v Fi (3)

Woodcock, A. S. (Nottingham F), 1978 v Ni; 1979 v Ei (sub), Cz, Bul (sub), Se; 1980 v Ni; (with Cologne), Bul, Ei, Sp (2), Arg, Bel, I; 1981 v N, R, Sw, R, W (sub), S; 1982 v Ni (sub), Ho, Fi (sub), WG (sub), Sp; (with Arsenal), 1983 v WG (sub), Gr, L, Gr; 1984 v L, F (sub), Ni, W, S, Br, U (sub); 1985 v EG, Fi, T, Ni; 1986 v R (sub), T (sub), Is (sub) (42)

Woodger, G. (Oldham Ath), 1911 v Ni (1)

Woodhall, G. (WBA), 1888 v S, W (2)

Woodley, V. R. (Chelsea), 1937 v S, N, Se, Fi; 1938 v S, W, Ni, Cz, G, Sw, F; 1939 v S, W, Ni, R of E, N, I, R, Y (19)

Woods, C. C. E. (Norwich C), 1985 v US; 1986 v Eg (sub), Is (sub), Ca (sub); (with Rangers), 1987 v Y, Sp (sub), Ni (sub), T, S; 1988 v Is, H, Sw (sub), USSR; 1989 v D (sub); 1990 v Br (sub), D (sub); 1991 v H, Pol, Ei, USSR, Aus, Nz (2), Mal; (with Sheffield W), 1992 v G, T, Pol, F, C, Br, Fi, D, F, Se; 1993 v Sp, N, T, Sm, T, Ho, Pol, N, US (43)

Woodward, V. J. (Tottenham H), 1903 v S, W, Ni; 1904 v S, Ni; 1905 v S, W, Ni; 1907 v S; 1908 v S, W, Ni, A (2), H, B; 1909 v W, Ni, H (2), A; (with Chelsea), 1910 v Ni; 1911 v W (23)

Woosnam, M. (Manchester C), 1922 v W (1)

Worrall, F. (Portsmouth), 1935 v Ho; 1937 v Ni (2)

Worthington, F. S. (Leicester C), 1974 v Ni (sub), S, Arg, EG, Bul, Y; 1975 v Cz, P (sub) (8)

Wreford-Brown, C. (Oxford University), 1889 v Ni; (with Old Carthusians), 1894 v W; 1895 v W; 1898 v S (4)

Wright, E, G. D. (Cambridge University), 1906 v W (1)

Wright, I. E. (C Palace), 1991 v Cam, Ei (sub), USSR, Nz; (with Arsenal), 1992 v N (sub); 1993 v N, T (2), Pol (sub), N (sub), US (sub), Br, G (sub) (13)

Wright, J. D. (Newcastle U), 1939 v N (1)

Wright, M. (Southampton), 1984 v W; 1985 v EG, Fi, T, Ei, R, I, WG; 1986 v R, T, Ni, Eg, USSR; 1987 v Y, Ni, S; (with Derby Co), 1988 v Is, Ho (sub), Co, Sw, Ei, Ho; 1990 v Cz (sub), Tun (sub), Ho, Eg, Bel, Cam, WG, I; 1991 v H, Pol, Ei (2), Cam, USSR, Arg, Aus, Nz, Mal; (with Liverpool), 1992 v F, Fi; 1993 v Sp (43)

Wright, T. J. (Everton), 1968 v USSR; 1969 v R (2), M (sub), U, Br; 1970 v W, Ho, Bel, R (sub), Br (11)

Wright, W. A. (Wolverhampton W), 1947 v S, W, Ni, Ei, Ho, F, Sw, P; 1948 v S, W, Ni, Bel, Se, I; 1949 v S, W, Ni, D, Sw, Se, N, F; 1950 v S, W, Ni, Ei, I, P, Bel, Ch, US, Sp; 1951 v Ni, S, Arg; 1952 v W, Ni, S, F, A (2), I, Sw; 1953 v Ni, W, S, Bel, Arg, Ch, U, US; 1954 v W, Ni, S, R of E, H (2), Y, Bel, Sw, U; 1955 v W, Ni, S, WG, F, Sp, P; 1956 v Ni, W, S, Br, Se, Fi, WG, D, Sp; 1957 v S, W, Ni, Y, D (2), Ei (2); 1958 v W, Ni, S, P, Y, USSR (3), Br, A, F; 1959 v W, Ni, S, USSR, I, Br, Pe, M, US (105)

Wylie, J. G. (Wanderers), 1878 v S (1)

Yates, J. (Burnley), 1889 v Ni (1)

York, R. E. (Aston Villa), 1922 v S; 1926 v S (2)

Young, A. (Huddersfield T), 1933 v W; 1937 v S, H, N, Se; 1938 v G, Sw, F; 1939 v W (9)

Young, G. M. (Sheffield W), 1965 v W (1)

R. E. Evans also played for Wales against E, Ni, S; J. Reynolds also played for Ireland against E, W, S.

NORTHERN IRELAND

Aherne, T. (Belfast C), 1947 v E; 1948 v S; 1949 v W; (with Luton T), 1950 v W (4)

Alexander, A. (Cliftonville), 1895 v S (1)

Allen, C. A. (Cliftonville), 1936 v E (1)

Allen, J. (Limavady), 1887 v E (1)

Anderson, T. (Manchester U), 1973 v Cy, E, S, W; 1974 v Bul, P; (with Swindon T), 1975 v S (sub); 1976 v Is; 1977 v Ho, Bel, WG, E, S, W, Ic; 1978 v Ic, Ho, Bel; (with Peterborough U), S, E, W; 1979 v D (sub) (22)

Anderson, W. (Linfield), 1898 v W, E, S; 1899 v S (4)

Andrews, W. (Glentoran), 1908 v S; (with Grimsby T), 1913 v E, S (3)

Armstrong, G. (Tottenham H), 1977 v WG, E, W (sub), Ic (sub); 1978 v Bel, S, E, W; 1979 v Ei, D, Bul, E, Bul, E, S, W, D; 1980 v E, Ei, Is, S, E, W, Aus (3); 1981 v Se; (with Watford), P, S, P, S, Se; 1982 v S, Is, E, F, W, Y, Hon, Sp, A, F; 1983 v A, T, Alb, S, E, W; (with Real Mallorca), 1984 v A, WG, E, W, Fi; 1985 v R, Fi, E, Sp; (with WBA), 1986 v T, R (sub), E (sub), F (sub); (with Chesterfield), D (sub), Br (sub) (63)

Baird, G. (Distillery), 1896 v S, E, W (3)

Baird, H. (Huddersfield T), 1939 v E (1)

Balfe, J. (Shelbourne), 1909 v E; 1910 v W (2)

Bambrick, J. (Linfield), 1929 v W, S, E; 1930 v W, S, E; 1932 v W; (with Chelsea), 1935 v W; 1936 v E, S; 1938 v W (11)

Banks, S. J. (Cliftonville), 1937 v W (1)

Barr, H. H. (Linfield), 1962 v E; (with Coventry C), 1963 v E, Pol (3)

Barron, H. (Cliftonville), 1894 v E, W, S; 1895 v S; 1896 v S; 1897 v E, W (7)

Barry, H. (Bohemians), 1900 v S (1)

Baxter, R. A. (Cliftonville), 1887 v S, W (2)

Bennett, L. V. (Dublin University), 1889 v W (1)

Berry, J. (Cliftonville), 1888 v S, W; 1889 v E (3)

Best, G. (Manchester U), 1964 v W, U; 1965 v E, Ho (2), S, Sw (2), Alb; 1966 v S, E, Alb; 1967 v E; 1968 v S; 1969 v E, S, W, T; 1970 v S, E, W, USSR; 1971 v Cy (2), Sp, E, S, W; 1972 v USSR, Sp; 1973 v Bul; 1974 v P; (with Fulham), 1977 v Ho, Bel, WG; 1978 v Ic, Ho (37)

Bingham, W. L. (Sunderland), 1951 v F; 1952 v E, S, W; 1953 v E, S, F, W; 1954 v E, S, W; 1955 v E, S; 1956 v E, S, W; 1957 v E, S, W, P (2), I; 1958 v S, E, W, I (2), Arg, Cz (2), WG, F; (with Luton T), 1959 v E, S, W, Sp; 1960 v S, E, W; (with Everton), 1961 v E, S, WG (2), Gr,

I; 1962 v E, Gr; 1963 v E, S, Pol (2), Sp; (with Port Vale), 1964 v S, E, Sp (56)

Black, J. (Glentoran), 1901 v E (1)

Black, K. (Luton T), 1988 v Fr (sub), Ma (sub); 1989 v Ei, H, Sp (2), Ch (sub); 1990 v H, N, U; 1991 v Y (2), D, A, Pol, Fa; (with Nottingham F), 1992 v Fa, A, D, S, Li, G; 1993 v Sp, D (sub), Alb, Ei (sub), Sp (27)

Blair, H. (Portadown), 1931 v S; 1932 v S; (with Swansea), 1934 v S (3)

Blair, J. (Cliftonville), 1907 v W, E, S; 1908 v E, S (5)

Blair, R. V. (Oldham Ath), 1975 v Se (sub), S (sub), W; 1976 v Se, Is (5)

Blanchflower, R. D. (Barnsley), 1950 v S, W; 1951 v E, S; (with Aston Villa), F; 1952 v W; 1953 v E, S, W, F; 1954 v E, S, W; 1955 v E, S (with Tottenham H), W; 1956 v E, S, W; 1957 v E, S, W, I, P (2); 1958 v E, S, W, I (2), Cz (2), Arg, F, WG; 1959 v E, S, W, Sp; 1960 v E, S, W; 1961 v E, S, W, WG (2); 1962 v E, S, W, Gr, Ho; 1963 v E, S, Pol (2) (56)

Blanchflower, J. (Manchester U), 1954 v W; 1955 v E, S; 1956 v S, W; 1957 v S, E, P; 1958 v S, E, I (2) (12)

Bookman, L. O. (Bradford C), 1914 v W; (with Luton T), 1921 v S, W; 1922 v E (4)

Bothwell, A. W. (Ards), 1926 v S, E, W; 1927 v E, W (5)

Bowler, G. C. (Hull C), 1950 v E, S, W (3)

Boyle, P. (Sheffield U), 1901 v E; 1902 v E; 1903 v S, W; 1904 v E (5)

Braithwaite, R. S. (Linfield), 1962 v W; 1963 v P, Sp; (with Middlesbrough), 1964 v W, U; 1965 v E, S, Sw (2), Ho (10)

Breen, T. (Belfast C), 1935 v E, W; 1937 v E, S; (with Manchester U), 1937 v W; 1938 v E, S; 1939 v W, S (9)

Brennan, B. (Bohemians), 1912 v W (1)

Brennan, R. A. (Luton T), 1949 v W; (with Birmingham C), 1950 v E, S, W; (with Fulham), 1951 v E (5)

Briggs, W. R. (Manchester U), 1962 v W; (with Swansea T), 1965 v Ho (2)

Brisby, D. (Distillery), 1891 v S (1)

Brolly, T. (Millwall), 1937 v W; 1938 v W; 1939 v E, W (4)

Brookes, E. A. (Shelbourne), 1920 v S (1)

Brotherston, N. (Blackburn R), 1980 v S, E, W, Aus (3); 1981 v Se, P; 1982 v S, Is, E, F, S, W, Hon (sub), A (sub); 1983 v A (sub), WG, Alb, T, Alb, E (sub), W; 1984 v T; 1985 v Is (sub), T (27)

Brown, J. (Glenavon), 1921 v W; (with Tranmere R), 1924 v E, W (3)

Brown, J. (Wolverhampton W), 1935 v E, W; 1936 v E; (with Coventry C), 1937 v E, W; 1938 v S, W; (with Birmingham C), 1939 v E, S, W (10)

Brown, W. G. (Glenavon), 1926 v W (1)

Brown, W. M. (Limavady), 1887 v W (1)

Browne, F. (Cliftonville), 1887 v E, S, W; 1888 v E, S (5)

Browne, R. J. (Leeds U), 1936 v E, W; 1938 v E, W; 1939 v E, S (6)

Bruce, W. (Glentoran), 1961 v S; 1967 v W (2)

Buckle, H. (Cliftonville), 1882 v E (1)

Buckle, H. R. (Sunderland), 1904 v E; (with Bristol R), 1908 v W (2)

Burnett, J. (Distillery), 1894 v E, W, S; (with Glentoran), 1895 v E, W (5)

Burnison, J. (Distillery), 1901 v E, W (2)

Burnison, S. (Distillery), 1908 v E; 1910 v E, S; (with Bradford), 1911 v E, S, W; (with Distillery), 1912 v E; 1913 v W (8)

Burns, J. (Glenavon), 1923 v E (1)

Butler, M. P. (Blackpool), 1939 v W (1)

Campbell, A. C. (Crusaders), 1963 v W; 1965 v Sw (2)

Campbell, D. A. (Nottingham F), 1986 v Mor (sub), Br; 1987 v E (2), T, Y; (with Charlton Ath), 1988 v Y, T (sub), Gr (sub), Pol (sub) (10)

Campbell, J. (Cliftonville), 1896 v W; 1897 v E, S, W; (with Distillery), 1898 v E, S, W; (with Cliftonville), 1899 v E; 1900 v E, S; 1901 v S, W; 1902 v S; 1903 v E; 1904 v S (15)

Campbell, J. P. (Fulham), 1951 v E, S (2)

Campbell, R. (Bradford C), 1982 v S, W (sub) (2)

Campbell, W. G. (Dundee), 1968 v S, E; 1969 v T; 1970 v S, W, USSR (6)

Carey, J. J. (Manchester U), 1947 v E, S, W; 1948 v E; 1949 v E, S, W (7)

Carroll, E. (Glenavon), 1925 v S (1)

Casey, T. (Newcastle U), 1955 v W; 1956 v W; 1957 v E, S, W, I, P (2); 1958 v WG, F; (with Portsmouth), 1959 v E, Sp (12)

Cashin, M. (Cliftonville), 1898 v S (1)

Caskey, W. (Derby Co), 1979 v Bul, E, Bul, E, D (sub); 1980 v E (sub); (with Tulsa R), 1982 v F (sub) (7)

Cassidy, T. (Newcastle U), 1971 v E (sub); 1972 v USSR (sub); 1974 v Bul (sub), S, E, W; 1975 v N; 1976 v S, E, W; 1977 v WG (sub); 1980 v E, Ei (sub), Is, S, E, W, Aus (3); (with Burnley), 1981 v Se, P; 1982 v Is, Sp (sub) (24)

Caughey, M. (Linfield), 1986 v F (sub), D (sub) (2)

Chambers, J. (Distillery), 1921 v W; (with Bury), 1928 v E, S, W; 1929 v E, S, W; 1930 v S, W; (with Nottingham F), 1932 v E, S, W (12)

Chatton, H. A. (Partick T), 1925 v E, S; 1926 v E (3)

Christian, J. (Linfield), 1889 v S (1)

Clarke, C. J. (Bournemouth), 1986 v F, D, Mor, Alg (sub), Sp, Br; (with Southampton), 1987 v E, T, Y; 1988 v Y, T, Gr, Pol, F, Ma; 1989 v Ei, H, Sp (1 + 1 sub); (with QPR), Ma, Ch; 1990 v H, Ei, N; (with Portsmouth), 1991 v Y (sub), D, A, Pol, Y (sub), Fa; 1992 v Fa, D, S, G; 1993 v Alb, Sp, D (38)

Clarke, R. (Belfast C), 1901 v E, S (2)

Cleary, J. (Glentoran), 1982 v S, W; 1983 v W (sub); 1984 v T (sub); 1985 v Is (5)

Clements, D. (Coventry C), 1965 v W, Ho; 1966 v M; 1967 v S, W; 1968 v S, E; 1969 v T (2), S, W; 1970 v S, E, W, USSR (2); 1971 v Sp, E, S, W, Cy; (with Sheffield W), 1972 v USSR (2), Sp, E, S, W; 1973 v Bul, Cy (2), P, E, S, W; (with Everton), 1974 v Bul, P, S, E, W; 1975 v N, Y, E, S, W; 1976 v Se, Y; (with New York Cosmos), E, W (48)

Clugston, J. (Cliftonville), 1888 v W; 1889 v W, S, E; 1890 v E, S; 1891 v E, W; 1892 v E, S, W; 1893 v E, S, W (14)

Cochrane, D. (Leeds U), 1939 v E, W; 1947 v E, S, W; 1948 v E, S, W; 1949 v S, W; 1950 v S, E (12)

Cochrane, M. (Distillery), 1898 v S, W, E; 1899 v E; 1900 v E, S, W; (with Leicester Fosse), 1901 v S (8)

Cochrane, T. (Coleraine), 1976 v N (sub); (with Burnley), 1978 v S (sub), E (sub), W (sub); 1979 v Ei (sub); (with Middlesbrough), D, Bul, E, Bul, E; 1980 v Is, E (sub), W (sub), Aus (1 + 2 sub); 1981 v Se (sub), P (sub), S, P, S, Se; 1982 v E (sub), F; (with Gillingham), 1984 v S, Fi (sub) (26)

Collins, F. (Celtic), 1922 v S (1)

Condy, J. (Distillery), 1882 v W; 1886 v E, S (3)

Connell, T. (Coleraine), 1978 v W (sub) (1)

Connor, J. (Glentoran), 1901 v S, E; (with Belfast C), 1905 v E, S, W; 1907 v E, S; 1908 v E, S; 1909 v W; 1911 v S, E, W (13)

Connor, M. J. (Brentford), 1903 v S, W; (with Fulham), 1904 v E (3)

Cook, W. (Celtic), 1933 v E, W, S; (with Everton), 1935 v E; 1936 v S, W; 1937 v E, S, W; 1938 v E, S, W; 1939 v E, S, W (15)

Cooke, S. (Belfast YMCA), 1889 v E; (with Cliftonville), 1890 v E, S (3)

Coulter, J. (Belfast C), 1934 v E, S, W; (with Everton), 1935 v E, S, W; 1937 v S, W; (with Grimsby T), 1938 v S, W; (with Chelmsford C), 1939 v S (11)

Cowan, J. (Newcastle U), 1970 v E (sub) (1)

Cowan, T. S. (Queen's Island), 1925 v W (1)

Coyle, F. (Coleraine), 1956 v E, S; 1957 v P; (with Nottingham F), 1958 v Arg (4)

Coyle, L. (Derry C), 1989 v Ch (sub) (1)

Coyle, R. I. (Sheffield W), 1973 v P, Cy (sub), W (sub); 1974 v Bul (sub), P (sub) (5)

Craig, A. B. (Rangers), 1908 v E, S, W; 1909 v S; (with Morton), 1912 v S, W; 1914 v E, S, W (9)

Craig, D. J. (Newcastle U), 1967 v W; 1968 v W; 1969 v T (2), E, S, W; 1970 v E, S, W, USSR; 1971 v Cy (2), Sp, S; 1972 v USSR, S (sub); 1973 v Cy (2), E, S, W; 1974 v Bul, P; 1975 v N (25)

Crawford, S. (Distillery), 1889 v E, W; (with Cliftonville), 1891 v E, S, W; 1893 v E, W (7)

Croft, T. (Queen's Island), 1924 v E (1)

Crone, R. (Distillery), 1889 v S; 1890 v E, S, W (4)

Crone, W. (Distillery), 1882 v W; 1884 v E, S, W; 1886 v E, S, W; 1887 v E; 1888 v E, W; 1889 v S; 1890 v W (12)

Crooks, W. (Manchester U), 1922 v W (1)

Crossan, E. (Blackburn R), 1950 v S; 1951 v E; 1955 v W (3)

Crossan, J. A. (Sparta-Rotterdam), 1960 v E; (with Sunderland), 1963 v W, P, Sp; 1964 v E, S, W, U, Sp; 1965 v E, S, Sw (2); (with Manchester C), W, Ho (2), Alb; 1966 v S, E, Alb, WG; 1967 v E, S; (with Middlesbrough), 1968 v S (24)

Crothers, C. (Distillery), 1907 v W (1)

Cumming, L. (Huddersfield T), 1929 v W, S; (with Oldham Ath), 1930 v E (3)

Cunningham, R. (Ulster), 1892 v S, E, W; 1893 v E (4)

Cunningham, W. E. (St Mirren), 1951 v W; 1953 v E; 1954 v S; 1955 v S; (with Leicester C), 1956 v E, S, W; 1957 v E, S, W, I, P (2); 1958 v S, W, I, Cz (2), Arg, WG, F; 1959 v E, S, W; 1960 v E, S, W; (with Dunfermline Ath), 1961 v W; 1962 v W, Ho (30)

Curran, S. (Belfast C), 1926 v S, W; 1928 v S (3)

Curran, J. J. (Glenavon), 1922 v W; (with Pontypridd), 1923 v E, S; (with Glenavon), 1924 v E (4)

Cush, W. W. (Glenavon), 1951 v E, S; 1954 v S, E; 1957 v W, I, P (2); (with Leeds U), 1958 v I (2), W, Cz (2), Arg, WG, F; 1959 v E, S, W; 1960 v E, S, W; (with Portadown), 1961 v WG, Gr; 1962 v Gr (26)

Dalton, W. (YMCA), 1888 v S; (with Linfield), 1890 v S, W; 1891 v S, W; 1892 v E, S, W; 1894 v E, S, W (11)

D'Arcy, S. D. (Chelsea), 1952 v W; 1953 v E; (with Brentford), 1953 v S, W, F (5)

Darling, J. (Linfield), 1897 v E, S; 1900 v S; 1902 v E, S, W; 1903 v E, S, W; 1905 v E, S, W; 1906 v E, S, W; 1908 v W; 1909 v E; 1910 v E, S, W; 1912 v S (21)

Davey, H. H. (Reading), 1926 v E; 1927 v E, S; 1928 v E; (with Portsmouth), 1928 v W (5)

Davis, T. L. (Oldham Ath), 1937 v E (1)

Davison, J. R. (Cliftonville), 1882 v E, S, W; 1883 v E, W; 1884 v E, W, S; 1885 v E (8)

Dennison, R. (Wolverhampton W), 1988 v F, Ma; 1989 v H, Sp Ch (sub); 1990 v Ei, U; 1991 v Y (2), A. Pol, Fa (sub); 1992 v Fa, A, D (sub); 1993 v Sp (sub) (16)

Devine, J. (Glentoran), 1990 v U (sub) (1)

Devine, W. (Limavady), 1886 v E, W; 1887 v E, W; 1888 v W (4)

Dickson, D. (Coleraine), 1970 v S (sub), W; 1973 v Cy, P (4)

Dickson, T. A. (Linfield), 1957 v S (1)

Dickson, W. (Chelsea), 1951 v W, F; 1952 v E, S, W; 1953 v E, S, W, F; (with Arsenal), 1954 v E, W; 1955 v E (12)

Diffin, W. (Belfast C), 1931 v W (1)

Dill, A. H. (Knock and Down Ath), 1882 v E, W; (with Cliftonville), 1883 v W; 1884 v E, S, W; 1885 v E, S, W (9)

Doherty, I. (Belfast C), 1901 v E (1)

Doherty, J. (Cliftonville), 1933 v E, W (2)

Doherty, L. (Linfield), 1985 v Is; 1988 v T (sub) (2)

Doherty, M. (Derry C), 1938 v S (1)

Doherty, P. D. (Blackpool), 1935 v E, W; 1936 v E, S; (with Manchester C), 1937 v E, W; 1938 v E, S; 1939 v E, W; (with Derby Co), 1947 v E; (with Huddersfield T), 1947 v W; 1948 v E, W; 1949 v S; (with Doncaster R), 1951 v S (16)

Donaghy, M. (Luton T), 1980 v S, E, W; 1981 v Sc, P, S (sub); 1982 v S, Is, E, F, S, W, Y, Hon, Sp, F; 1983 v A, WG, Alb, T, Alb. S, E, W; 1984 v A, T, WG, S, E, W, Fi; 1985 v R, Fi, E, Sp, T; 1986 v T, R, E, F, D, Mor, Alg, Sp, Br; 1987 v E (2), T, Is, Y; 1988 v Y, T, Gr, Pol, F, Ma; 1989 v Ei, H; (with Manchester U), Sp (2), Ma, Ch; 1990 v Ei, N; 1991 v Y (2), D, A, Pol, Fa; 1992 v Fa, A, D, S, Li, G; (with Chelsea), 1993 v Alb, Sp, D, Alb, Ei, Sp, Li, La (84)

Donnelly, L. (Distillery), 1913 v W (1)

Doran, J. F. (Brighton), 1921 v E; 1922 v E, W (3)

Dougan, A. D. (Portsmouth), 1958 v Cz; (with Blackburn R), 1960 v S; 1961 v E, W, I, Gr; (with Aston Villa), 1963 v S, Pol (2); (with Leicester C), 1966 v S, E, W, M, Alb, WG; 1967 v E, S; (with Wolverhampton W), 1967 v W; 1968 v S, W, Is; 1969 v T (2), E, S, W; 1970 v S, E, USSR (2); 1971 v Cy (2), Sp, E, S, W; 1972 v USSR (2), E, S, W; 1973 v Bul, Cy (43)

Douglas, J. P. (Belfast C), 1947 v E (1)

Dowd, H. O. (Glenavon), 1974 v W; (with Sheffield W), 1975 v N (sub), Se (3)

Dowie, I. (Luton T), 1990 v N (sub), U; 1991 v Y, D, A (sub), (with West Ham U), Y, Fa; (with Southampton) 1992 v Fa, A, D (sub), S (sub), Li; 1993 v Alb (2), Ei, Sp (sub), Li, La (18)

Duggan, H. A. (Leeds U), 1930 v E; 1931 v E, W; 1933 v E; 1934 v E; 1935 v S, W; 1936 v S (8)

Dunlop, G. (Linfield), 1985 v Is; 1987 v E, Y; 1990 v Ei (4)

Dunne, J. (Sheffield U), 1928 v W; 1931 v W, E; 1932 v E, S; 1933 v E, W (7)

Eames, W. L. E. (Dublin U), 1885 v E, S, W (3)

Eglinton, T. J. (Everton), 1947 v S, W; 1948 v E, S, W; 1949 v E (6)

Elder, A. R. (Burnley), 1960 v W; 1961 v S, E, W, WG (2), Gr; 1962 v E, S, Gr; 1963 v E, S, W, P (2), Sp; 1964 v W, U; 1965 v E, S, W, Sw (2), Ho (2), Alb; 1966 v E, S, W, M, Alb; 1967 v E, S, W; (with Stoke C), 1968 v E, W; 1969 v E (sub), S, W; 1970 v USSR (40)

Elleman, A. R. (Cliftonville), 1889 v W; 1890 v E (2)

Elwood, J. H. (Bradford), 1929 v W; 1930 v E (2)

Emerson, M. (Glentoran), 1920 v E, S, W; 1921 v E; 1922 v E, S; (with Burnley), 1922 v W; 1923 v E, S, W; 1924 v E (11)

English, S. (Rangers), 1933 v W, S (2)

Enright, J. (Leeds C), 1912 v S (1)

Falloon, E. (Aberdeen), 1931 v S; 1933 v S (2)

Farquharson, T. G. (Cardiff C), 1923 v S, W; 1924 v E, S, W; 1925 v E, S (7)

Farrell, P. (Distillery), 1901 v S, W (2)

Farrell, P. (Hibernian), 1938 v W (1)

Farrell, P. D. (Everton), 1947 v S, W; 1948 v E, S, W; 1949 v E, W (7)

Feeney, J. M. (Linfield), 1947 v S; (with Swansea T), 1950 v E (2)

Feeney, W. (Glentoran), 1976 v Is (1)

Ferguson, W. (Linfield), 1966 v M; 1967 v E (2)

Ferris, J. (Belfast C), 1920 v E, W; (with Chelsea), 1921 v S, E; (with Belfast C), 1928 v S (5)

Ferris, R. O. (Birmingham C), 1950 v S; 1951 v F; 1952 v S (3)

Fettis, A. (Hull C), 1992 v D, Li; 1993 v D (3)

Finney, T. (Sunderland), 1975 v N, E (sub), S, W; 1976 v N, Y, S; (with Cambridge U), 1980 v E, Is, S, E, W, Aus (2) (14)

Fitzpatrick, J. C. (Bohemians), 1896 v E, S (2)

Flack, H. (Burnley), 1929 v S (1)

Fleming, J. G. (Nottingham F), 1987 v E (2), Is, Y; 1988 v T, Gr, Pol; 1989 v Ma, Ch; (with Manchester C), 1990 v H, Ei; (with Barnsley), 1991 v Y; 1992 v Li (sub), G; 1993 v Alb, Sp, D, Alb, Sp, Li, La (21)

Forbes, G. (Limavady), 1888 v W; (with Distillery), 1891 v E, S (3)

Forde, J. T. (Ards), 1959 v Sp; 1961 v E, S, WG (4)

Foreman, T. A. (Cliftonville), 1899 v S (1)

Forsyth, J. (YMCA), 1888 v E, S (2)

Fox, W. (Ulster), 1887 v E, S (2)

Fulton, R. P. (Belfast C), 1930 v W; 1931 v E, S, W; 1932 v W, E; 1933 v E, S; 1934 v E, W, S; 1935 v E, W, S; 1936 v S, W; 1937 v E, S, W; 1938 v W (20)

Gaffikin, J. (Linfield Ath), 1890 v S, W; 1891 v S, W; 1892 v E, S, W; 1893 v E, S, W; 1894 v E, S, W; 1895 v E, W (15)

Galbraith, W. (Distillery), 1890 v W (1)

Gallagher, P. (Celtic), 1920 v E, S; 1922 v S; 1923 v S, W; 1924 v S, W; 1925 v S, W, E; (with Falkirk), 1927 v S (11)

Gallogly, C. (Huddersfield T), 1951 v E, S (2)

Gara, A. (Preston NE), 1902 v E, S, W (3)

Gardiner, A. (Cliftonville), 1930 v S, W; 1931 v S; 1932 v E, S (5)

Garrett, J. (Distillery), 1925 v W (1)

Gaston, R. (Oxford U), 1969 v Is (sub) (1)

Gaukrodger, G. (Linfield), 1895 v W (1)

Gaussen, A. W. (Moyola Park), 1884 v E, S; 1888 v E, W; 1889 v W (6)

Geary, J. (Glentoran), 1931 v S; 1932 v S (2)

Gibb, J. T. (Wellington Park) 1884 v S, W; 1885 v S, E, W; 1886 v S; 1887 v S, E, W; 1889 v S (10)

Gibb, T. J. (Cliftonville), 1936 v W (1)

Gibson W. K. (Cliftonville), 1894 v S, W, E; 1895 v S; 1897 v W; 1898 v S, W, E; 1901 v S, W, E; 1902 v S, W (13)

Gillespie, R. (Hertford), 1886 v E, S, W; 1887 v E, S, W (6)

Gillespie, W. (Sheffield U), 1913 v E, S; 1914 v E, W; 1920 v S, W; 1921 v E; 1922 v E, S, W; 1923 v E, S, W; 1924 v E, S, W; 1925 v E, S; 1926 v S, W; 1927 v E, W; 1928 v E; 1929 v E; 1931 v E (25)

Gillespie, W. (West Down), 1889 v W (1)

Goodall, A. L. (Derby Co), 1899 v S, W; 1900 v E, W; 1901 v E; 1902 v S; 1903 v E, W; (with Glossop), 1904 v E, W (10)

Goodbody, M. F. (Dublin University), 1889 v E; 1891 v W (2)

Gordon, H. (Linfield), 1891 v S; 1892 v E, S, W; 1893 v E, S, W; 1895 v E, W; 1896 v E, S (11)

Gordon, T. (Linfield), 1894 v W; 1895 v E (2)

Gorman, W. C. (Brentford), 1947 v E, S, W; 1948 v W (4)

Gowdy, J. (Glentoran), 1920 v E; (with Queen's Island), 1924 v W; (with Falkirk), 1926 v E, S; 1927 v E, S (6)

Gowdy, W. A. (Hull C), 1932 v S; (with Sheffield W), 1933 v S; (with Linfield), 1935 v E, S, W; (with Hibernian), 1936 v W (6)

Graham, W. G. L. (Doncaster R), 1951 v W, F; 1952 v E, S, W; 1953 v S, F; 1954 v E, W; 1955 v S, W; 1956 v E, S; 1959 v E (14)

Gray, P. (Luton T), 1993 v D (sub), Alb, Ei, Sp (4)

Greer, W. (QPR), 1909 v E, S, W (3)

Gregg, H. (Doncaster R), 1954 v W; 1957 v E, S, W, I, P (2); 1958 v E, I; (with Manchester U), 1958 v Cz, Arg, WG, F; 1959 v E, W; 1960 v S, E, W; 1961 v E, S; 1962 v S, Gr; 1964 v S, E (25)

Hall, G. (Distillery), 1897 v E (1)

Halligan, W. (Derby Co), 1911 v W; (with Wolverhampton W), 1912 v E (2)

Hamill, M. (Manchester U), 1912 v E; 1914 v E, S; (with Belfast C), 1920 v E, S, W; (with Manchester C), 1921 v S (7)

Hamilton, B. (Linfield), 1969 v T; 1971 v Cy (2), E, S, W; (with Ipswich T), 1972 v USSR (1 + 1 sub), Sp; 1973 v Bul, Cy (2), P, E, S, W; 1974 v Bul, S, E, W; 1975 v N, Se, Y, E; 1976 v Se, N, Y; (with Everton), Is, S, E, W; 1977 v Ho, Bel, WG, E, S, W, Ic; (with Millwall), 1978 v S, E, W; 1979 v Ei (sub); (with Swindon T), Bul (2), E, S, W, D; 1980 v Aus (2 sub) (50)

Hamilton, J. (Knock), 1882 v E, W (2)

Hamilton, R. (Distillery), 1908 v W (1)

Hamilton, R. (Rangers), 1928 v S; 1929 v E; 1930 v S, E; 1932 v S (5)

Hamilton, W. (QPR), 1978 v S (sub); (with Burnley), 1980 v S, E, W, Aus (2); 1981 v Se, P, S, P, S, Se; 1982 v S, Is, E, W, Y, Hon, Sp, A, F; 1983 v A, WG, Alb (2), S, E, W; 1984 v A, T, WG, S, E, W, Fi; (with Oxford U), 1985 v R, Sp; 1986 v Mor (sub), Alg, Sp (sub), Br (sub) (41)

Hamilton, W. D. (Dublin Association), 1885 v W (1)

Hamilton, W. J. (Dublin Association), 1885 v W (1)

Hampton, H. (Bradford C), 1911 v E, S, W; 1912 v E, W; 1913 v S, W; 1914 v E (9)

Hanna, D. R. A. (Portsmouth), 1899 v W (1)

Hanna, J. (Nottingham F), 1912 v S, W (2)

Hannon, D. J. (Bohemians), 1908 v E, S; 1911 v E, S; 1912 v W; 1913 v E (6)

Harkin, J. T. (Southport), 1968 v W; 1969 v T; (with Shrewsbury T), W (sub); 1970 v USSR; 1971 v Sp (5)

Harland, A. I. (Linfield), 1923 v E (1)

Harris, J. (Cliftonville), 1921 v W (1)

Harris, V. (Shelbourne), 1906 v E; 1907 v E, W; 1908 v E, W, S; (with Everton), 1909 v E, W, S; 1910 v E, S, W; 1911 v E, S, W; 1912 v E; 1913 v E, S; 1914 v S, W (20)

Harvey, M. (Sunderland), 1961 v I; 1962 v Ho; 1963 v W, Sp; 1964 v S, E, W, U, Sp; 1965 v E, S, W, Sw (2), Ho (2), Alb; 1966 v S, E, W, M, Alb, WG; 1967 v E, S; 1968 v E, W; 1969 v Is, T (2), E; 1970 v USSR; 1971 v Cy, W (sub) (34)

Hastings, J. (Knock), 1882 v E, W; (with Ulster), 1883 v W; 1884 v E, S; 1886 v E, S (7)

Hatton, S. (Linfield), 1963 v S, Pol (2)

Hayes, W. E. (Huddersfield T), 1938 v E, S; 1939 v E, S (4)

Healy, O. (Coleraine), 1982 v S, W, Hon (sub); (with Glentoran), 1983 v A (sub) (4)

Hegan, D. (WBA), 1970 v USSR; (with Wolverhampton W), 1972 v USSR, E, S, W; 1973 v Bul, Cy (7)

Henderson, A. W. (Ulster), 1885 v E, S, W (3)

Hewison, G. (Moyola Park), 1885 v E, S (2)

Hill, C. F. (Sheffield U), 1990 v N, U; 1991 v Pol, Y; 1992 v A, D (6)

Hill, M. J. (Norwich C), 1959 v W; 1960 v W; 1961 v WG; 1962 v S; (with Everton), 1964 v S, E, Sp (7)

Hinton, E. (Fulham), 1947 v S, W; 1948 v S, E, W; (with Millwall), 1951 v W, F (7)

Hopkins, J. (Brighton), 1926 v E (1)

Houston, J. (Linfield), 1912 v S, W; 1913 v W; (with Everton), 1913 v E, S; 1914 v S (6)

Houston, W. (Linfield), 1933 v W (1)

Houston, W. G. (Moyola Park), 1885 v E, S (2)

Hughes, M. E. (Manchester C), 1992 v D, S, Li, G; (with Strasbourg), 1993 v Alb, Sp, D, Ei, Sp, Li, La (11)

Hughes, P. (Bury), 1987 v E, T, Is (3)

Hughes, W. (Bolton W), 1951 v W (1)

Humphries, W. (Ards), 1962 v W; (with Coventry C), 1962 v Ho; 1963 v E, S, W, Pol, Sp; 1964 v S, E, Sp; 1965 v S; (with Swansea T), 1965 v W, Ho, Alb (14)

Hunter, A. (Distillery), 1905 v W; 1906 v W, E, S; (with Belfast C), 1908 v W; 1909 v W, E, S (8)

Hunter, A. (Blackburn R), 1970 v USSR; 1971 v Cy (2), E, S, W; (with Ipswich T), 1972 v USSR (2), Sp, E, S, W; 1973 v Bul, Cy (2), P, E, S, W; 1974 v Bul, S, E, W; 1975 v N, Se, Y, E, S, W; 1976 v Se, N, Y, Is, S, E, W; 1977 v Ho, Bel, WG, E, S, W, Ic; 1978 v Ic, Ho, Bel; 1979 v Ei, D, S, W, D; 1980 v E, Ei (53)

Hunter, R. J. (Cliftonville), 1884 v E, S, W (3)

Hunter, V. (Coleraine), 1962 v E; 1964 v Sp (2)

Irvine, R. J. (Linfield), 1962 v Ho; 1963 v E, S, W, Pol (2), Sp; (with Stoke C), 1965 v W (8)

Irvine, R. W. (Everton), 1922 v S; 1923 v E, W; 1924 v E, S; 1925 v E; 1926 v E; 1927 v E, W; 1928 v E, S; (with Portsmouth), 1929 v E; 1930 v S; (with Connah's Quay), 1931 v E; (with Derry C), 1932 v W (15)

Irvine, W. J. (Burnley), 1963 v W, Sp; 1965 v S, W, Sw, Ho (2), Alb; 1966 v S, E, W, M, Alb; 1967 v E, S; 1968 v E, W; (with Preston NE), 1969 v Is, T, E; (with Brighton), 1972 v E, S, W (23)

Irving, S. J. (Dundee), 1923 v S, W; 1924 v S, E, W; 1925 v S, E, W; 1926 v S, W; (with Cardiff C), 1927 v S, E, W; 1928 v S, E, W; (with Chelsea), 1929 v E; 1931 v W (18)

Jackson, T. (Everton), 1969 v Is, E, S, W; 1970 v USSR (1 + 1 sub); (with Nottingham F), 1971 v Sp; 1972 v E, S, W; 1973 v Cy, E, S, W; 1974 v Bul, P, S (sub), E (sub), W (sub); 1975 v N (sub), Se, Y, E, S, W; (with Manchester U); 1976 v Se, N, Y; 1977 v Ho, Bel, WG, E, S, W, Ic (35)

Jamison, J. (Glentoran), 1976 v N (1)

Jennings, P. A. (Watford), 1964 v W, U; (with Tottenham H), 1965 v E, S, Sw (2), Ho, Alb; 1966 v S, E, W, Alb, WG; 1967 v E, S; 1968 v S, E, W; 1969 v Is, T (2), E, S, W; 1970 v S, E, USSR (2); 1971 v Cy (2), E, S, W; 1972 v USSR, Sp, S, E, W; 1973 v Bul, Cy, P, E, S, W; 1974 v P, S, E, W; 1975 v N, Se, Y, E, S, W; 1976 v Se, N, Y, Is, S, E, W; 1977 v Ho, Bel, WG, E, S, W, Ic; (with Arsenal), 1978 v Ic, Ho, Bel; 1979 v Ei, D, Bul, E, Bul, E, S, W, D; 1980 v E, Ei, Is; 1981 v S, P, S, Se; 1982 v S, Is, E, W, Y, Hon, Sp, F; 1983 v Alb, S, E, W; 1984 v A, T, WG, S, W, Fi; 1985 v R, Fi, E, Sp, T; (with Tottenham H), 1986 v T, R, E, F, D; (with Everton), Mor; (with Tottenham H), Alg, Sp, Br (119)

Johnston, H. (Portadown), 1927 v W (1)

Johnston, R. (Old Park), 1885 v S, W (2)

Johnston, S. (Distillery), 1882 v W; 1884 v E; 1886 v E, S (4)

Johnston, S. (Linfield), 1890 v W; 1893 v S, W; 1894 v E (4)

Johnston, S. (Distillery), 1905 v W (1)

Johnston, W. C. (Glenavon), 1962 v W; (with Oldham Ath), 1966 v M (sub) (2)

Jones, J. (Linfield), 1930 v S, W; 1931 v S, W, E; 1932 v S, E; 1933 v S, E, W; 1934 v S, E, W; 1935 v S, E, W; 1936 v E, S; (with Hibernian), 1936 v W; 1937 v E, W, S; (with Glenavon), 1938 v E (23)

Jones, J. (Glenavon), 1956 v W; 1957 v E, W (3)

Jones, S. (Distillery), 1934 v E; (with Blackpool), 1934 v W (2)

Jordan, T. (Linfield), 1895 v E, W (2)

Kavanagh, P. J. (Celtic), 1930 v E (1)

Keane, T. R. (Swansea T), 1949 v S (1)

Kearns, A. (Distillery), 1900 v E, S, W; 1902 v E, S, W (6)

Kee, P. V. (Oxford U), 1990 v N; 1991 v Y (2), D, A, Pol, Fa (7)

Keith, R. M. (Newcastle U), 1958 v E, W, Cz (2), Arg, I, WG, F; 1959 v E, S, W, Sp; 1960 v S, E; 1961 v S, E, W, I, WG (2), Gr; 1962 v W, Ho (23)

Kelly, H. R. (Fulham), 1950 v E, W; (with Southampton), 1951 v E, S (4)

Kelly, J. (Glentoran), 1896 v E (1)

Kelly, J. (Derry C), 1932 v E, W; 1933 v E, W, S; 1934 v W; 1936 v E, S, W; 1937 v S, E (11)

Kelly, P. (Manchester C), 1921 v E (1)

Kelly, P. M. (Barnsley), 1950 v S (1)

Kennedy, A. L. (Arsenal), 1923 v W; 1925 v E (2)

Kernaghan, N. (Belfast C), 1936 v W; 1937 v S; 1938 v E (3)

Kirkwood, H. (Cliftonville), 1904 v W (1)

Kirwan, J. (Tottenham H), 1900 v W; 1902 v E, W; 1903 v E, S, W; 1904 v E, S, W; 1905 v E, S, W; (with Chelsea), 1906 v E, S, W; 1907 v W; (with Clyde), 1909 v S (17)

Lacey, W. (Everton), 1909 v E, S, W; 1910 v E, S, W; 1911 v E, S, W; 1912 v E; (with Liverpool), 1913 v W; 1914 v E, S, W; 1920 v E, S, W; 1921 v E, S, W; 1922 v E, S; (with New Brighton), 1925 v E (23)

Lawther, W. I. (Sunderland), 1960 v W; 1961 v I; (with Blackburn R), 1962 v S, Ho (4)

Leatham, J. (Belfast C), 1939 v W (1)

Ledwidge, J. J. (Shelbourne), 1906 v S, W (2)

Lemon, J. (Glentoran), 1886 v W; 1888 v S; (with Belfast YMCA), 1889 v W (3)

Leslie, W. (YMCA), 1887 v E (1)

Lewis, J. (Glentoran), 1899 v S, E, W; (with Distillery), 1900 v S (4)

Little, J. (Glentoran), 1898 v W (1)

Lockhart, H. (Rossall School), 1884 v W (1)

Lockhart, N. (Linfield), 1947 v E; (with Coventry C), 1950 v W; 1951 v W; 1952 v W; (with Aston Villa), 1954 v S, E; 1955 v W; 1956 v W (8)

Lowther, R. (Glentoran), 1888 v E, S (2)

Loyal, J. (Clarence), 1891 v S (1)

Lutton, R. J. (Wolverhampton W), 1970 v S, E; (with West Ham U), 1973 v Cy (sub), S (sub), W (sub); 1974 v P (6)

Lyner, D. (Glentoran), 1920 v E, W; 1922 v S, W; (with Manchester U), 1923 v E; (with Kilmarnock), 1923 v W (6)

McAdams, W. J. (Manchester C), 1954 v W; 1955 v S; 1957 v E; 1958 v S, I; (with Bolton W), 1961 v E, S, W, I, WG (2), Gr; 1962 v E, Gr; (with Leeds U), Ho (15)

McAlery, J. M. (Cliftonville), 1882 v E, W (2)

McAlinden, J. (Belfast C), 1938 v S; 1939 v S; (with Portsmouth), 1947 v E; (with Southend U), 1949 v E (4)

McAllen, J. (Linfield), 1898 v E; 1899 v E, S, W; 1900 v E, S, W; 1901 v W; 1902 v S (9)

McAlpine, W. J. (Cliftonville), 1901 v S (1)

McArthur, A. (Distillery), 1886 v W (1)

McAuley, J. L. (Huddersfield T), 1911 v E, W; 1912 v E, S; 1913 v E, S (6)

McAuley, P. (Belfast C), 1900 v S (1)

McBride, S. (Glenavon), 1991 v D (sub), Pol (sub); 1992 v Fa (sub), D (4)

McCabe, J. J. (Leeds U), 1949 v S, W; 1950 v E; 1951 v W; 1953 v W; 1954 v S (6)

McCabe, W. (Ulster), 1891 v E (1)

McCambridge, J. (Ballymena), 1930 v S, W; (with Cardiff C), 1931 v W; 1932 v E (4)

McCandless, J. (Bradford), 1912 v W; 1913 v W; 1920 v W, S; 1921 v E (5)

McCandless, W. (Linfield), 1920 v E, W; 1921 v E; (with Rangers), 1921 v W; 1922 v S; 1924 v W, S; 1925 v S; 1929 v W (9)

McCann, P. (Belfast C), 1910 v E, S, W; 1911 v E; (with Glentoran), 1911 v S; 1912 v E; 1913 v W (7)

McCashin, J. (Cliftonville), 1896 v W; 1898 v S, W; 1899 v S (4)

McCavana, W. T. (Coleraine), 1955 v S; 1956 v E, S (3)

McCaw, D. (Distillery), 1882 v E (1)

McCaw, J. H. (Linfield), 1927 v W; 1930 v S; 1931 v E, S, W (5)

McClatchey, J. (Distillery), 1886 v E, S, W (3)

McClatchey, R. (Distillery), 1895 v S (1)

McCleary, J. W. (Cliftonville), 1955 v W (1)

McCleery, W. (Linfield), 1930 v E, W; 1931 v E, S, W; 1932 v S, W; 1933 v E, W (9)

McClelland, J. (Arsenal), 1961 v W, I, WG (2), Gr; (with Fulham), M (6)

McClelland, J. (Mansfield T), 1980 v S (sub), Aus (3); 1981 v Se (sub), S; (with Rangers), S, Se; 1982 v S, W, Y, Hon, Sp, A, F; 1983 v A, WG, Alb, T, Alb, S, E, W; 1984 v A, T, WG, S, E, W, Fi; 1985 v R, Fi, Is; (with Watford), E, Sp, T; 1986 v T, F (sub); 1987 v E (2), T, Is, Y; 1988 v T, Gr, F, Ma; 1989 v Ei, H, Sp (2), Ma; (with Leeds U), 1990 v N (53)

McCluggage, A. (Bradford), 1924 v E; (with Burnley), 1927 v S, W; 1928 v S, E, W; 1929 v S, E, W; 1930 v W; 1931 v E, W (12)

McClure, G. (Cliftonville), 1907 v S, W; 1908 v E; (with Distillery), 1909 v E (4)

McConnell, E. (Cliftonville), 1904 v S, W; (with Glentoran), 1905 v S; (with Sunderland), 1906 v E; 1907 v E; 1908 v S, W; (with Sheffield W), 1909 v S, W; 1910 v S, W, E (12)

McConnell, P. (Doncaster R), 1928 v W; (with Southport), 1932 v E (2)

McConnell, W. G. (Bohemians), 1912 v W; 1913 v E, S; 1914 v E, S, W (6)

McConnell, W. H. (Reading), 1925 v W; 1926 v E, W; 1927 v E, S, W; 1928 v E, W (8)

McCourt, F. J. (Manchester C), 1952 v E, W; 1953 v E, S, W, F (6)

McCoy, J. (Distillery), 1896 v W (1)

McCoy, R. (Coleraine), 1987 v Y (sub) (1)

McCracken, R. (C Palace), 1921 v E; 1922 v E, S, W (4)

McCracken, W. (Distillery), 1902 v E, W; 1903 v E; 1904 v E, S, W; (with Newcastle U), 1905 v E, S, W; 1907 v E; 1920 v E; 1922 v E, S, W; (with Hull C), 1923 v S (15)

McCreery, D. (Manchester U), 1976 v S (sub), E, W; 1977 v Ho, Bel, WG, E, S, W, Ic; 1978 v Ic, Ho, Bel, S, E, W; 1979 v Ei, D, Bul, E, Bul, W, D; (with QPR), 1980 v E, Ei, S (sub), E (sub), W (sub), Aus (1+1 sub); 1981 v Se (sub), P (sub); (with Tulsa R), S, P, Se; 1982 v S, Is, E (sub), F, Y, Hon, Sp, A, F; (with Newcastle U), 1983 v A; 1984 v T (sub); 1985 v R, Sp (sub); 1986 v T (sub), R, E, F, D, Alg, Sp, Br; 1987 v T, E, Y; 1988 v Y; 1989 v Sp, Ma, Ch; (with Hearts), 1990 v H, Ei, N, U (67)

McCrory, S. (Southend U), 1958 v E (1)

McCullough, K. (Belfast C), 1935 v W; 1936 v E; (with Manchester C), 1936 v S; 1937 v E, S (5)

McCullough, W. J. (Arsenal), 1961 v I; 1963 v Sp; 1964 v S, E, W, U, Sp; 1965 v E, Sw; (with Millwall), 1967 v E (10)

McCurdy, C. (Linfield), 1980 v Aus (sub) (1)

McDonald, A. (QPR), 1986 v R, E, F, D, Mor, Alg, Sp, Br; 1987 v E (2), T, Is, Y; 1988 v Y, T, Pol, F, Ma; 1989 v Ei, H, Sp, Ch; 1990 v H, Ei, U; 1991 v Y, D, A, Fa; 1992 v Fa, S, Li, G; 1993 v Alb, Sp, D, Alb, Ei, Sp, Li, La (41)

McDonald, R. (Rangers), 1930 v S; 1932 v E (2)

McDonnell, J. (Bohemians), 1911 v E, S; 1912 v W; 1913 v W (4)

McElhinney, G. (Bolton W), 1984 v WG, S, E, W, Fi; 1985 v R (6)

McFaul, W. S. (Linfield), 1967 v E (sub); (with Newcastle U), 1970 v W; 1971 v Sp; 1972 v USSR; 1973 v Cy; 1974 v Bul (6)

McGarry, J. K. (Cliftonville), 1951 v W, F, S (3)

McGaughey, M. (Linfield), 1985 v Is (sub) (1)

McGee, G. (Wellington Park), 1885 v E, S, W (3)

McGrath, R. C. (Tottenham H), 1974 v S, E, W; 1975 v N; 1976 v Is (sub); 1977 v Ho; (with Manchester U), Bel, WG, E, S, W, Ic; 1978 v Ic, Ho, Bel, S, E, W; 1979 v Bul (sub), E (2 sub) (21)

McGregor, S. (Glentoran), 1921 v S (1)

McGrillen, J. (Clyde), 1924 v S; (with Belfast C), 1927 v S (2)

McGuire, E. (Distillery), 1907 v S (1)

McIlroy, H. (Cliftonville), 1906 v E (1)

McIlroy, J. (Burnley), 1952 v E, S, W; 1953 v E, S, W; 1954 v E, S, W; 1955 v E, S, W; 1956 v E, S, W; 1957 v E, S, W, I, P (2); 1958 v E, S, W, I (2), Cz (2), Arg, WG, F; 1959 v E, S, W, Sp; 1960 v E, S, W; 1961 v E, W, WG (2), Gr; 1962 v E, S, Gr, Ho; 1963 v E, S, Pol (2); (with Stoke C), 1963 v W; 1966 v S, E, Alb (55)

McIlroy, S. B. (Manchester U), 1972 v Sp, S (sub); 1974 v S, E, W; 1975 v N, Se, Y, E, S, W; 1976 v Se, N, Y, S, E, W; 1977 v Ho, Bel, E, S, W, Ic; 1978 v Ic, Ho, Bel, S, E, W; 1979 v Ei, D, Bul, E, Bul, E, S, W, D; 1980 v E, Ei, Is, S, E, W; 1981 v Se, P, S, P, S, Se; 1982 v S, Is; (with Stoke C), E, F, S, W, Y, Hon, Sp, A, F; 1983 v A, WG, Alb, T, Alb, S, E, W; 1984 v A, T, S, E, W, Fi; 1985 v Fi, E, T; (with Manchester C), 1986 v T, R, E, F, D, Mor, Alg, Sp, Br; 1987 v E (sub) (88)

McIlvenny, J. (Distillery), 1890 v E; 1891 v E (2)

McIlvenny, P. (Distillery), 1924 v W (1)

McKeag, W. (Glentoran), 1968 v S, W (2)

McKee, F. W. (Cliftonville), 1906 v S, W; (with Belfast C), 1914 v E, S, W (5)

McKelvie, H. (Glentoran), 1901 v W (1)

McKenna, J. (Huddersfield), 1950 v E, S, W; 1951 v E, S, F; 1952 v E (7)

McKenzie, H. (Distillery), 1923 v S (1)

McKenzie, R. (Airdrie), 1967 v W (1)

McKeown, H. (Linfield), 1892 v E, S, W; 1893 v S, W; 1894 v S, W (7)

McKie, H. (Cliftonville), 1895 v E, S, W (3)

McKinney, D. (Hull C), 1921 v S; (with Bradford C), 1924 v S (2)

McKinney, V. J. (Falkirk), 1966 v WG (1)

McKnight, A. (Celtic), 1988 v Y, T, Gr, Pol, F, Ma; (with West Ham U) 1989 v Ei, H, Sp (2) (10)

McKnight, J. (Preston NE), 1912 v S; (with Glentoran), 1913 v S (2)

McLaughlin, J. C. (Shrewsbury T), 1962 v E, S, W, Gr; 1963 v W; (with Swansea T), 1964 v W, U; 1965 v E, W, Sw (2); 1966 v W (12)

McLean, T. (Limavady), 1885 v S (1)

McMahon, J. (Bohemians), 1934 v S (1)

McMaster, G. (Glentoran), 1897 v E, S, W (3)

McMichael, A. (Newcastle U), 1950 v E, S; 1951 v E, S, F; 1952 v E, S, W; 1953 v E, S, W, F; 1954 v E, S, W; 1955 v E, W; 1956 v W; 1957 v E, S, W, I, P (2); 1958 v E, S, W, I (2), Cz (2), Arg, WG, F; 1959 v S, W, Sp; 1960 v E, S, W (40)

McMillan, G. (Distillery), 1903 v E; 1905 v W (2)

McMillan, S. (Manchester U), 1963 v E, S (2)

McMillen, W. S. (Manchester U), 1934 v E; 1935 v S; 1937 v S; (with Chesterfield), 1938 v S, W; 1939 v E, S (7)

McMordie, A. S. (Middlesbrough), 1969 v Is, T (2), E, S, W; 1970 v E, S, W, USSR; 1971 v Cy (2), E, S, W; 1972 v USSR, Sp, E, S, W; 1973 v Bul (21)

McMorran, E. J. (Belfast C), 1947 v E; (with Barnsley), 1951 v E, S, W; 1952 v E, S, W; 1953 v E, S, F; (with Doncaster R), 1953 v W; 1954 v E; 1956 v W; 1957 v I, P (15)

McMullan, D. (Liverpool), 1926 v E, W; 1927 v S (3)

McNally, B. A. (Shrewsbury T), 1986 v Mor; 1987 v T (sub); 1988 v Y, Gr, Ma (sub) (5)

McNinch, J. (Ballymena), 1931 v S; 1932 v S, W (3)

McParland, P. J. (Aston Villa), 1954 v W; 1955 v E, S; 1956 v E, S; 1957 v E, S, W, P; 1958 v E, S, W, I (2), Cz (2), Arg, WG, F; 1959 v E, S, W, Sp; 1960 v E, S, W; 1961 v E, S, W, I, WG (2), Gr; (with Wolverhampton W), 1962 v Ho (34)

McShane, J. (Cliftonville), 1899 v S; 1900 v E, S, W (4)

McVickers, J. (Glentoran), 1888 v E; 1889 v S (2)

McWha, W. B. R. (Knock), 1882 v E, W; (with Cliftonville), 1883 v E, W; 1884 v E; 1885 v E, W (7)

Macartney, A. (Ulster), 1903 v S, W; (with Linfield), 1904 v S, W; (with Everton), 1905 v E, S; (with Belfast C), 1907 v E, S, W; 1908 v E, S, W; (with Glentoran), 1909 v E, S, W (15)

Mackie, J. (Arsenal), 1923 v W; (with Portsmouth), 1935 v S, W (3)

Madden, O. (Norwich C), 1938 v E (1)

Magill, E. J. (Arsenal), 1962 v E, S, Gr; 1963 v E, S, W, Pol (2), Sp; 1964 v E, S, W, U, Sp; 1965 v E, S, Sw (2), Ho, Alb; 1966 v S, (with Brighton), E, Alb, W, WG, M (26)

Magilton, J. (Oxford U), 1991 v Pol, Y, Fa; 1992 v Fa, A, D, S, Li, G; 1993 v Alb, D, Alb, Ei, Li, La (15)

Maginnis, H. (Linfield), 1900 v E, S, W; 1903 v S, W; 1904 v E, S, W (8)

Maguire, E. (Distillery), 1907 v S (1)

Mahood, J. (Belfast C), 1926 v S; 1928 v E, S, W; 1929 v E, S, W; 1930 v W; (with Ballymena), 1934 v S (9)

Manderson, R. (Rangers), 1920 v W, S; 1925 v S, E; 1926 v S (5)

Mansfield, J. (Dublin Freebooters), 1901 v E (1)

Martin, C. J. (Glentoran), 1947 v S; (with Leeds U), 1948 v E, S, W; (with Aston Villa), 1949 v E; 1950 v W (6)

Martin, D. (Bo'ness), 1925 v S (1)

Martin, D. C. (Cliftonville), 1882 v E, W; 1883 v E (3)

Martin, D. K. (Belfast C), 1934 v E, S, W; 1935 v S; (with Wolverhampton), 1935 v E; 1936 v W; (with Nottingham F), 1937 v S; 1938 v E, S; 1939 v S (10)

Mathieson, A. (Luton T), 1921 v W; 1922 v E (2)

Maxwell, J. (Linfield), 1902 v W; 1903 v W, E; (with Glentoran), 1905 v W, S; (with Belfast C), 1906 v W; 1907 v S (7)

Meek, H. L. (Glentoran), 1925 v W (1)

Mehaffy, J. A. C. (Queen's Island), 1922 v W (1)

Meldon, J. (Dublin Freebooters), 1899 v S, W (2)

Mercer, H. V. A. (Linfield), 1908 v E (1)

Mercer, J. T. (Distillery), 1898 v E, S, W; 1899 v E; (with Linfield), 1902 v E, W; (with Distillery), 1903 v S, W; (with Derby Co), 1904 v E, W; 1905 v S (11)

Millar, W. (Barrow), 1932 v W; 1933 v S (2)

Miller, J. (Middlesbrough), 1929 v W, S; 1930 v E (3)

Milligan, D. (Chesterfield), 1939 v W (1)

Milne, R. G. (Linfield), 1894 v E, S, W; 1895 v E, W; 1896 v E, S, W; 1897 v E, S; 1898 v E, S, W; 1899 v E, W; 1901 v W; 1902 v E, S, W; 1903 v E, S; 1904 v E, S, W; 1906 v E, S, W (27)

Mitchell, E. J. (Cliftonville), 1933 v S; (with Glentoran), 1934 v W (2)

Mitchell, W. (Distillery), 1932 v E, W; 1933 v E, W; (with Chelsea), 1934 v S, W; 1935 v S, E; 1936 v S, E; 1937 v E, S, W; 1938 v E, S (15)

Molyneux, T. B. (Ligoniel), 1883 v E, W; (with Cliftonville), 1884 v E, W, S; 1885 v E, W; 1886 v E, W, S; 1888 v S (11)

Montgomery, F. J. (Coleraine), 1955 v E (1)

Moore, C. (Glentoran), 1949 v W (1)

Moore, J. (Linfield Ath), 1891 v E, S, W (3)

Moore, P. (Aberdeen), 1933 v E (1)

Moore, T. (Ulster), 1887 v S, W (2)

Moore, W. (Falkirk), 1923 v S (1)

Moorhead, F. W. (Dublin University), 1885 v E (1)

Moorhead, G. (Linfield), 1923 v S; 1928 v S; 1929 v S (3)

Moran, J. (Leeds C), 1912 v S (1)

Moreland, V. (Derby Co), 1979 v Bul (2 sub), E, S; 1980 v E, Ei (6)

Morgan, F. G. (Linfield), 1923 v E; (with Nottingham F), 1924 v S; 1927 v E; 1928 v E, S, W; 1929 v E (7)

Morgan, S. (Port Vale), 1972 v Sp; 1973 v Bul (sub), P, Cy, E, S, W; (with Aston Villa), 1974 v Bul, P, S, E; 1975 v Se; 1976 v Se (sub), N, Y; (with Brighton & HA), S, W (sub); (with Sparta Rotterdam), 1979 v D (18)

Morrison, J. (Linfield Ath), 1891 v E, W (2)

Morrison, T. (Glentoran), 1895 v E, S, W; (with Burnley), 1899 v W; 1900 v W; 1902 v E, S (7)

Morrogh, E. (Bohemians), 1896 v S (1)

Morrow, S. J. (Arsenal), 1990 v U (sub); 1991 v A (sub), Pol, Y; 1992 v Fa, S (sub), G (sub); 1993 v Sp (sub), Alb, Ei (10)

Morrow, W. J. (Moyola Park), 1883 v E, W; 1884 v S (3)

Muir, R. (Oldpark), 1885 v S, W (2)

Mullan, G. (Glentoran), 1983 v S, E, W, Alb (sub) (4)

Mulholland, S. (Celtic), 1906 v S, E (2)

Mulligan, J. (Manchester C), 1921 v S (1)

Murphy, J. (Bradford C), 1910 v E, S, W (3)

Murphy, N. (QPR), 1905 v E, S, W (3)

Murray, J. M. (Motherwell), 1910 v E, S; (with Sheffield W), 1910 v W (3)

Napier, R. J. (Bolton W), 1966 v WG (1)

Neill, W. J. T. (Arsenal), 1961 v I, Gr, WG; 1962 v E, S, W, Gr; 1963 v E, W, Pol, Sp; 1964 v S, E, W, U, Sp; 1965 v E, S, W, Sw, Ho (2), Alb; 1966 v S, E, W, Alb, WG, M; 1967 v S, W; 1968 v S, E; 1969 v E, S, W, Is, T (2); 1970 v S, E, W, USSR (2); (with Hull C), 1971 v Cy, Sp; 1972 v USSR (2), Sp, S, E, W; 1973 v Bul, Cy (2), P, E, S, W (59)

Nelis, P. (Nottingham F), 1923 v E (1)

Nelson, S. (Arsenal), 1970 v W, E (sub); 1971 v Cy, Sp, E, S, W; 1972 v USSR (2), Sp, E, S, W; 1973 v Bul, Cy, P; 1974 v S, E; 1975 v Se, Y; 1976 v Se, N, Is, E; 1977 v Bel (sub), WG, W, Ic; 1978 v Ic, Ho, Bel; 1979 v Ei, D, Bul, E, Bul, E, S, W, D; 1980 v E, Ei, Is; 1981 v S, P, S, Se; (with Brighton & HA), 1982 v E, S, Sp (sub), A (51)

Nicholl, C. J. (Aston Villa), 1975 v Se, Y, E, S, W; 1976 v Se, N, Y, S, E, W; 1977 v W; (with Southampton), 1978 v Bel (sub), S, E, W; 1979 v Ei, Bul, E, Bul, E, W; 1980 v Ei, Is, S, E, W, Aus (3); 1981 v Se, P, S, P, S, Se; 1982 v S, Is, E, F, W, Y, Hon, Sp, A, F; 1983 v S (sub), E, W; (with Grimsby T), 1984 v A, T (51)

Nicholl, H. (Belfast C), 1902 v E, W; 1905 v E (3)

Nicholl, J. M. (Manchester U), 1976 v Is, W (sub); 1977 v Ho, Bel, E, S, W, Ic; 1978 v Ic, Ho, Bel, S, E, W; 1979 v Ei, D, Bul, E, Bul, E, S, W, D; 1980 v E, Ei, Is, S, E, W, Aus (3); 1981 v Se, P, S, P, S, Se; 1982 v S, Is, E; (with Toronto B), F, W, Y, Hon, Sp, A, F; (with Sunderland), 1983 v A, WG, Alb, T, Alb; (with Toronto B), S, E, W; 1984 v T; (with Rangers), WG, S, E; (with Toronto B), Fi; 1985 v R; (with WBA), Fi, E, Sp, T; 1986 v T, R, E, F, Alg, Sp, Br (73)

Nicholson, J. J. (Manchester U), 1961 v S, W; 1962 v E, W, Gr, Ho; 1963 v E, S, Pol (2); (with Huddersfield T), 1965 v W, Ho (2), Alb; 1966 v S, E, W, Alb, M; 1967 v S, W; 1968 v S, E, W; 1969 v S, E, W, T (2); 1970 v S, E, W, USSR (2); 1971 v Cy (2), E, S, W; 1972 v USSR (2) (41)

Nixon, R. (Linfield), 1914 v S (1)

Nolan-Whelan, J. V. (Dublin Freebooters), 1901 v E, W; 1902 v S, W (4)

O'Brien, M. T. (QPR), 1921 v S; (with Leicester C), 1922 v S, W; 1924 v S, W; (with Hull C), 1925 v S, E, W; 1926 v W; (with Derby Co), 1927 v W (10)

O'Connell, P. (Sheffield W), 1912 v E, S; (with Hull C), 1914 v E, S, W (5)

O'Doherty, A. (Coleraine), 1970 v E, W (sub) (2)

O'Driscoll, J. F. (Swansea T), 1949 v E, S, W (3)

O'Hagan, C. (Tottenham H), 1905 v S, W; 1906 v S, W, E; (with Aberdeen), 1907 v E, S, W; 1908 v S, W; 1909 v E (11)

O'Hagan, W. (St Mirren), 1920 v E, W (2)

O'Hehir, J. C. (Bohemians), 1910 v W (1)

O'Kane, W. J. (Nottingham F), 1970 v E, W, S (sub); 1971 v Sp, E, S, W; 1972 v USSR (2); 1973 v P, Cy; 1974 v Bul, P, S, E, W; 1975 v N, Se, E, S (20)

O'Mahoney, M. T. (Bristol R), 1939 v S (1)

O'Neill, C. (Motherwell), 1989 v Ch (sub); 1990 v Ei (sub); 1991 v D (3)

O'Neill, J. (Leicester C), 1980 v Is, S, E, W, Aus (3); 1981 v P, S, P, S, Se; 1982 v S, Is, E, F, S, F (sub); 1983 v A, WG, Alb, T, Alb, S; 1984 v S (sub); 1985 v Is, Fi, E, Sp, T; 1986 v T, R, E, F, D, Mor, Alg, Sp, Br (39)

O'Neill, J. (Sunderland), 1962 v W (1)

O'Neill, M. A. (Newcastle U), 1988 v Gr, Pol, F, Ma; 1989 v Ei, H, Sp (sub), Sp (sub), Ma (sub), Ch; (with Dundee U), 1990 v H (sub), Ei; 1991 v Pol; 1992 v Fa (sub), S (sub), G (sub); 1993 v Alb (sub + 1), Ei, Sp, Li, La (22)

O'Neill, M. H. (Distillery), 1972 v USSR (sub), (with Nottingham F), Sp (sub), W (sub); 1973 v P, Cy, E, S, W; 1974 v Bul, P, E (sub), W; 1975 v Se, Y, E, S; 1976 v Y (sub); 1977 v E (sub), S; 1978 v Ic, Ho, S, E, W; 1979 v Ei, D, Bul, E, Bul, D; 1980 v Ei, Is, Aus (3); 1981 v Se, P; (with Norwich C), P, S, Se; (with Manchester C), 1982 v S; (with Norwich C), E, F, S, Y, Hon, Sp, A, F; 1983 v A, WG, Alb, T, Alb, S, E; (with Notts Co), 1984 v A, T, WG, E, W, Fi; 1985 v R, Fi (64)

O'Reilly, H. (Dublin Freebooters), 1901 v S, W; 1904 v S (3)

Parke, J. (Linfield), 1964 v S; (with Hibernian), 1964 v E, Sp; (with Sunderland), 1965 v Sw, S, W, Ho (2), Alb; 1966 v WG; 1967 v E, S; 1968 v S, E (14)

Peacock, R. (Celtic), 1952 v S; 1953 v F; 1954 v W; 1955 v E, S; 1956 v E, S; 1957 v W, I, P; 1958 v S, E, W, I (2), Arg, Cz (2), WG; 1959 v E, S, W; 1960 v S, E; 1961 v E, S, I, WG (2), Gr; (with Coleraine), 1962 v S (31)

Peden, J. (Linfield), 1887 v S, W; 1888 v W, E; 1889 v S, E; 1890 v W, S; 1891 v W, E; 1892 v W, E; 1893 v E, S, W; (with Distillery), 1896 v W, E, S; 1897 v W, S; 1898 v W, E, S; (with Linfield), 1899 v W (24)

Penney, S. (Brighton & HA), 1985 v Is; 1986 v T, R, E, F, D, Mor, Alg, Sp; 1987 v E, T, Is; 1988 v Pol, F, Ma; 1989 v Ei, Sp (17)

Percy, J. C. (Belfast YMCA), 1889 v W (1)

Platt, J. A. (Middlesbrough), 1976 v Is (sub); 1978 v S, E, W; 1980 v S, E, W, Aus (3); 1981 v Se, P; 1982 v F, S, W (sub), A; 1983 v A, WG, Alb, T; (with Ballymena U), 1984 v E, W (sub); (with Coleraine), 1986 v Mor (sub) (23)

Ponsonby, J. (Distillery), 1895 v S; 1896 v E, S, W; 1897 v E, S, W; 1899 v E (8)

Potts, R. M. C. (Cliftonville), 1883 v E, W (2)

Priestley, T. J. (Coleraine), 1933 v S; (with Chelsea), 1934 v E (2)

Pyper, Jas. (Cliftonville), 1897 v S, W; 1898 v S, E, W; 1899 v S; 1900 v E (7)

Pyper, John (Cliftonville), 1897 v E, S, W; 1899 v E, W; 1900 v E, W, S; 1902 v S (9)

Pyper, M. (Linfield), 1932 v W (1)

Quinn, J. M. (Blackburn R), 1985 v Is, Fi, E, Sp, T; 1986 v T, R, E, F, D (sub), Mor (sub); 1987 v E (sub), T; (with Swindon T), 1988 v Y (sub), T, Gr, Pol, F (sub), Ma; (with Leicester C), 1989 v Ei, H (sub), Sp (sub+1); (with Bradford C), Ma, Ch; 1990 v H, (with West Ham U), N; 1991 v Y (sub); (with Bournemouth), 1992 v Li; (with Reading), 1993 v Sp, D, Alb (sub), Ei (sub), La (sub) (34)

Rafferty, P. (Linfield), 1980 v E (sub) (1)

Ramsey, P. (Leicester C), 1984 v A, WG, S; 1985 v Is, E, Sp, T; 1986 v T, Mor; 1987 v Is, E, Y (sub); 1988 v Y; 1989 v Sp (14)

Rankine, J. (Alexander), 1883 v E, W (2)

Raper, E. O. (Dublin University), 1886 v W (1)

Rattray, D. (Avoniel), 1882 v E; 1883 v E, W (3)

Rea, B. (Glentoran), 1901 v E (1)

Redmond, J. (Cliftonville), 1884 v W (1)

Reid, G. H. (Cardiff C), 1923 v S (1)

Reid, J. (Ulster), 1883 v E; 1884 v W; 1887 v S; 1889 v W; 1890 v S, W (6)

Reid, S. E. (Derby Co), 1934 v E, W; 1936 v E (3)

Reid, W. (Hearts), 1931 v E (1)

Reilly, J. (Portsmouth), 1900 v E; 1902 v E (2)

Renneville, W. T. (Leyton), 1910 v S, E, W; (with Aston Villa), 1911 v W (4)

Reynolds, J. (Distillery), 1890 v E, W; (with Ulster), 1891 v E, S, W (5)

Reynolds, R. (Bohemians), 1905 v W (1)

Rice, P. J. (Arsenal), 1969 v Is; 1970 v USSR; 1971 v E, S, W; 1972 v USSR, Sp, E, S, W; 1973 v Bul, Cy, E, S, W; 1974 v Bul, P, S, E, W; 1975 v N, Y, E, S, W; 1976 v Se, N, Y, Is, S, E, W; 1977 v Ho, Bel, WG, E, S, Ic; 1978 v Ic, Ho, Bel; 1979 v Ei, D, E (2), S, W, D; 1980 v E (49)

Roberts, F. C. (Glentoran), 1931 v S (1)

Robinson, P. (Distillery), 1920 v S; (with Blackburn R), 1921 v W (2)

Rogan, A. (Celtic), 1988 v Y (sub), Gr, Pol (sub); 1989 v Ei (sub), H, Sp (2), Ma (sub), Ch; 1990 v H, N (sub), U; 1991 v Y (2), D, A; (with Sunderland), 1992 v Li (sub) (17)

Rollo, D. (Linfield), 1912 v W; 1913 v W; 1914 v W, E; (with Blackburn R), 1920 v S, W; 1921 v E, S, W; 1922 v E; 1923 v E; 1924 v S, W; 1925 v W; 1926 v E; 1927 v E (16)

Rosbotham, A. (Cliftonville), 1887 v E, S, W; 1888 v E, S, W; 1889 v E (7)

Ross, W. E. (Newcastle U), 1969 v Is (1)

Rowley, R. W. M. (Southampton), 1929 v S, W; 1930 v W, E; (with Tottenham H), 1931 v W; 1932 v S (6)

Russell, A. (Linfield), 1947 v E (1)

Russell, S. R. (Bradford C), 1930 v E, S; (with Derry C), 1932 v E (3)

Ryan, R. A. (WBA), 1950 v W (1)

Sanchez, L. P. (Wimbledon), 1987 v T (sub); 1989 v Sp, Ma (3)

Scott, E. (Liverpool), 1920 v S; 1921 v E, S, W; 1922 v E; 1925 v W; 1926 v E, S, W; 1927 v E, S, W; 1928 v E, S, W; 1929 v E, S, W; 1930 v E; 1931 v E; 1932 v W; 1933 v E, S, W; 1934 v E, S, W; (with Belfast C), 1935 v S; 1936 v E, S, W (31)

Scott, J. (Grimsby), 1958 v Cz, F (2)

Scott, J. E. (Cliftonville), 1901 v S (1)

Scott, L. J. (Dublin University), 1895 v S, W (2)

Scott, P. W. (Everton), 1975 v W; 1976 v Y; (with York C), Is, S, E (sub), W; 1978 v S, E, W; (with Aldershot), 1979 v S (sub) (10)

Scott, T. (Cliftonville), 1894 v E, S; 1895 v S, W; 1896 v S, E, W; 1897 v E, W; 1898 v E, S, W; 1900 v W (13)

Scott, W. (Linfield), 1903 v E, S, W; 1904 v E, S, W; (with Everton), 1905 v E, S; 1907 v E, S; 1908 v E, S, W; 1909 v E, S, W; 1910 v E, S; 1911 v E, S, W; 1912 v E; (with Leeds City), 1913 v E, S, W (25)

Scraggs, M. J. (Glentoran), 1921 v W; 1922 v E (2)

Seymour, H. C. (Bohemians), 1914 v W (1)

Seymour, J. (Cliftonville), 1907 v W; 1909 v W (2)

Shanks, T. (Woolwich Arsenal), 1903 v S; 1904 v W; (with Brentford), 1905 v E (3)

Sharkey, P. (Ipswich T), 1976 v S (1)

Sheehan, Dr G. (Bohemians), 1899 v S; 1900 v E, W (3)

Sheridan, J. (Everton), 1903 v W, E, S; 1904 v E, S; (with Stoke C), 1905 v E (6)

Sherrard, J. (Limavady), 1885 v S; 1887 v W; 1888 v W (3)

Sherrard, W. (Cliftonville), 1895 v E, W, S (3)

Sherry, J. J. (Bohemians), 1906 v E; 1907 v W (2)

Shields, J. (Southampton), 1957 v S (1)

Silo, M. (Belfast YMCA), 1888 v E (1)

Simpson, W. J. (Rangers), 1951 v W, F; 1954 v E, S; 1955 v E; 1957 v I, P; 1958 v S, E, W, I; 1959 v S (12)

Sinclair, J. (Knock), 1882 v E, W (2)

Slemin, J. C. (Bohemians), 1909 v W (1)

Sloan, A. S. (London Caledonians), 1925 v W (1)

Sloan, D. (Oxford U), 1969 v Is; 1971 v Sp (2)

Sloan, H. A. de B. (Bohemians), 1903 v E; 1904 v S; 1905 v E; 1906 v W; 1907 v E, W; 1908 v W; 1909 v S (8)

Sloan, J. W. (Arsenal), 1947 v W (1)

Sloan, T. (Cardiff C), 1926 v S, W, E; 1927 v W, S; 1928 v E, W; 1929 v E; (with Linfield), 1930 v W, S; 1931 v S (11)

Sloan, T. (Manchester U), 1979 v S, W (sub), D (sub) (3)

Small, J. (Clarence), 1887 v E (1)

Small, J. M. (Cliftonville), 1893 v E, S, W (3)

Smith, E. E. (Cardiff C), 1921 v S; 1923 v W, E; 1924 v E (4)

Smith, J. (Distillery), 1901 v S, W (2)

Smyth, R. H. (Dublin University), 1886 v W (1)

Smyth, S. (Wolverhampton W), 1948 v E, S, W; 1949 v S, W; 1950 v E, S, W; (with Stoke C), 1952 v E (9)

Smyth, W. (Distillery), 1949 v E, S; 1954 v S, E (4)

Snape, A. (Airdrie), 1920 v E (1)

Spence, D. W. (Bury), 1975 v Y, E, S, W; 1976 v Se, Is, E, W, S (sub); (with Blackpool), 1977 v Ho (sub), WG (sub), E (sub), S (sub), W (sub), Ic (sub); 1979 v Ei, D (sub), E (sub), Bul (sub), E (sub), S, W, D; 1980 v Ei; (with Southend U), Is (sub), Aus (sub); 1981 v S (sub), Se (sub); 1982 v F (sub) (29)

Spencer, S. (Distillery), 1890 v E, S; 1892 v E, S, W; 1893 v E (6)

Spiller, E. A. (Cliftonville), 1883 v E, W; 1884 v E, W, S (5)

Stanfield, O. M. (Distillery), 1887 v E, S, W; 1888 v E, S, W; 1889 v E, S, W; 1890 v E, S; 1891 v E, S, W; 1892 v E, S, W; 1893 v E; 1894 v E, S, W; 1895 v E, S; 1896 v E, S, W; 1897 v E, S, W (30)

Steele, A. (Charlton Ath), 1926 v W, S; (with Fulham), 1929 v W, S (4)

Stevenson, A. E. (Rangers), 1934 v E, S, W; (with Everton), 1935 v E, S; 1936 v S, W; 1937 v E, W; 1938 v E, W; 1939 v E, S, W; 1947 v S, W; 1948 v S (17)

Stewart, A. (Glentoran), 1967 v W; 1968 v S, E; (with Derby Co), 1968 v W; 1969 v Is, T (1 + 1 sub) (7)

Stewart, D. C. (Hull C), 1978 v Bel (1)

Stewart, I. (QPR), 1982 v F (sub); 1983 v A, WG, Alb, T, Alb, S, E, W; 1984 v A, T, WG, S, E, W, Fi; 1985 v R, Fi, Is, E, Sp, T; (with Newcastle U), 1986 v R, E, D, Mor, Alg (sub), Sp (sub), Br; 1987 v E, Is (sub) (31)

Stewart, R. H. (St Columb's Court), 1890 v E, S, W; (with Cliftonville), 1892 v E, S, W; 1893 v E, W; 1894 v E, S, W (11)

Stewart, T. C. (Linfield), 1961 v W (1)

Swan, S. (Linfield), 1899 v S (1)

Taggart, G. P. (Barnsley), 1990 v N, U; 1991 v Y, D, A, Pol, Fa; 1992 v Fa, A, D, S, Li, G; 1993 v Alb, Sp, D, Alb, Ei, Sp, Li, La (21)

Taggart, J. (Walsall), 1899 v W (1)

Thompson, F. W. (Cliftonville), 1910 v E, S, W; (with Bradford C), 1911 v E; (with Linfield), v W; 1912 v E, W; 1913 v E, S, W; (with Clyde), 1914 v E, S (12)

Thompson, J. (Belfast Ath), 1889 v S (1)

Thompson, J. (Distillery), 1897 v S (1)

Thunder, P. J. (Bohemians), 1911 v W (1)

Todd, S. J. (Burnley), 1966 v M (sub); 1967 v E; 1968 v W; 1969 v E, S, W; 1970 v S, USSR; (with Sheffield W), 1971 v Cy (2), Sp (sub) (11)

Toner, J. (Arsenal), 1922 v W; 1923 v W; 1924 v W, E; 1925 v E, S; (with St Johnstone), 1927 v E, S (8)

Torrans, R. (Linfield), 1893 v S (1)

Torrans, S. (Linfield), 1889 v S; 1890 v S, W; 1891 v S, W; 1892 v E, S, W; 1893 v E, S; 1894 v E, S, W; 1895 v E; 1896 v E, S, W; 1897 v E, S, W; 1898 v E, S; 1899 v E, W; 1901 v S, W (26)

Trainor, D. (Crusaders), 1967 v W (1)

Tully, C. P. (Celtic), 1949 v E; 1950 v E; 1952 v S; 1953 v E, S, W, F; 1954 v S; 1956 v E; 1959 v Sp (10)

Turner, E. (Cliftonville), 1896 v E, W (2)

Turner, W. (Cliftonville), 1886 v E; 1886 v S; 1888 v S (3)

Twoomey, J. F. (Leeds U), 1938 v W; 1939 v E (2)

Uprichard, W. N. M. C. (Swindon T), 1952 v E, S, W; 1953 v E, S; (with Portsmouth), 1953 v W, F; 1955 v E, S, W; 1956 v E, S, W; 1958 v S, I, Cz; 1959 v S, Sp (18)

Vernon, J. (Belfast C), 1947 v E, S; (with WBA), 1947 v W; 1948 v E, S, W; 1949 v E, S, W; 1950 v E, S; 1951 v E, S, W, F; 1952 v S, E (17)

Waddell, T. M. R. (Cliftonville), 1906 v S (1)

Walker, J. (Doncaster R), 1955 v W (1)

Walker, T. (Bury), 1911 v S (1)

Walsh, D. J. (WBA), 1947 v S, W; 1948 v E, S, W; 1949 v E, S, W; 1950 v W (9)

Walsh, W. (Manchester C), 1948 v E, S, W; 1949 v E, S (5)

Waring, R. (Distillery), 1899 v E (1)

Warren, P. (Shelbourne), 1913 v E, S (2)

Watson, J. (Ulster), 1883 v E, W; 1886 v E, S, W; 1887 v S, W; 1889 v E, W (9)

Watson, P. (Distillery), 1971 v Cy (sub) (1)

Watson, T. (Cardiff C), 1926 v S (1)

Wattle, J. (Distillery), 1899 v E (1)

Webb, C. G. (Brighton), 1909 v S, W; 1911 v S (3)

Weir, H. (Clyde), 1939 v W (1)

Welsh, E. (Carlisle U), 1966 v W, WG, M; 1967 v W (4)

Whiteside, N. (Manchester U), 1982 v Y, Hon, Sp, A, F; 1983 v WG, Alb, T; 1984 v A, T, WG, S, E, W, Fi; 1985 v R, Fi, Is, E, Sp, T; 1986 v R, E, F, D, Mor, Alg, Sp, Br; 1987 v E (2), Is, Y; 1988 v T, Pol, F; (with Everton), 1990 v H, Ei (38)

Whiteside, T. (Distillery), 1891 v E (1)

Whitfield, E. R. (Dublin University), 1886 v W (1)

Williams, J. R. (Ulster), 1886 v E, S (2)

Williams, P. A. (WBA), 1991 v Fa (sub) (1)

Williamson, J. (Cliftonville), 1890 v E; 1892 v S; 1893 v S (3)

Willigham, T. (Burnley), 1933 v W; 1934 v S (2)

Willis, G. (Linfield), 1906 v S, W; 1907 v S; 1912 v S (4)

Wilson, D. J. (Brighton & HA), 1987 v T, Is, E (sub); (with Luton T), 1988 v Y, T, Gr, Pol, F, Ma; 1989 v Ei, H, Sp, Ma, Ch; 1990 v H, Ei, N, U; (with Sheffield W), 1991 v Y, D, A, Fa; 1992 v A (sub), S (24)

Wilson, H. (Linfield), 1925 v W (1)

Wilson, K. J. (Ipswich T), 1987 v Is, E, Y; (with Chelsea), 1988 v Y, T, Gr (sub), Pol (sub), F (sub); 1989 v H (sub), Sp (2), Ma, Ch; 1990 v Ei (sub), N, U; 1991 v Y (2), A, Pol, Fa; 1992 v Fa, A, D, S; (with Notts Co), Li, G; 1993 v Alb, Sp, D, Sp, Li, La (33)

Wilson, M. (Distillery), 1884 v E, S, W (3)

Wilson, R. (Cliftonville), 1888 v W (1)

Wilson, S. J. (Glenavon), 1962 v S; 1964 v S; (with Falkirk), 1964 v E, W, U, Sp; 1965 v E, Sw; (with Dundee), 1966 v W, WG; 1967 v S; 1968 v E (12)

Wilton, J. M. (St Columb's Court), 1888 v E, W; 1889 v S, E; (with Cliftonville), 1890 v E; (with St Columb's Court), 1892 v W; 1893 v S (7)

Worthington, N. (Sheffield W), 1984 v W, Fi (sub); 1985 v Is, Sp (sub); 1986 v T, R (sub), E (sub), D, Alg, Sp; 1987 v E (2), T, Is, Y; 1988 v Y, T, Gr, Pol, F, Ma; 1989 v Ei, H, Sp, Ma; 1990 v H, Ei, U; 1991 v Y, D, A, Fa; 1992 v A, D, S, Li, G; 1993 v Alb, Sp, D, Ei, Sp, Li, La (44)

Wright, J. (Cliftonville), 1906 v E, S, W; 1907 v E, S, W (6)

Wright, T. J. (Newcastle U), 1989 v Ma, Ch; 1990 v H, U; 1992 v Fa, A, S, G; 1993 v Alb, Sp, Alb, Ei, Sp, Li, La (15)

Young, S. (Linfield), 1907 v E, S; 1908 v E, S; (with Airdrie), 1909 v E; 1912 v S; (with Linfield), 1914 v E, S, W (9)

SCOTLAND

Adams, J. (Hearts), 1889 v Ni; 1892 v W; 1893 v Ni (3)
Agnew, W. B. (Kilmarnock), 1907 v Ni; 1908 v W, Ni (3)
Aird, J. (Burnley), 1954 v N (2), A, U (4)
Aitken, A. (Newcastle U), 1901 v E; 1902 v E; 1903 v E, W; 1904 v E; 1905 v E, W; 1906 v E; (with Middlesbrough), 1907 v E, W; 1908 v E; (with Leicester Fosse), 1910 v E; 1911 v E, Ni (14)
Aitken, G. G. (East Fife), 1949 v E, F; 1950 v W, Ni, Sw; (with Sunderland), 1953 v W, Ni; 1954 v E (8)
Aitken, R. (Dumbarton), 1886 v E; 1888 v Ni (2)
Aitken, R. (Celtic), 1980 v Pe (sub), Bel, W (sub), E, Pol; 1983 v Bel, Ca (1 + 1 sub); 1984 v Bel (sub), Ni, W (sub); 1985 v E, Ic; 1986 v W, EG, Aus (2), Is, R, E, D, WG, U; 1987 v Bul, Ei (2), L, Bel, E, Br; 1988 v H, Bel, Bul, L, S.Ar, Ma, Sp, Co, E; 1989 v N, Y, I, Cy, F, Cy, E, Ch; 1990 v Y, F, N; (with Newcastle U), Arg (sub), Pol, Ma, Cr, Se, Br; (with St Mirren), 1992 v R (sub) (57)
Aitkenhead, W. A. C. (Blackburn R), 1912 v Ni (1)
Albiston, A. (Manchester U), 1982 v Ni; 1984 v U, Bel, EG, W, E; 1985 v Y, Ic, Sp (2), W; 1986 v EG, Ho, U (14)
Alexander, D. (East Stirlingshire), 1894 v W, Ni (2)
Allan, D. S. (Queen's Park), 1885 v E, W; 1886 v W (3)
Allan, G. (Liverpool), 1897 v E (1)
Allan, H. (Hearts), 1902 v W (1)
Allan, J. (Queen's Park), 1887 v E, W (2)
Allan, T. (Dundee), 1974 v WG, N (2)
Ancell, R. F. D. (Newcastle U), 1937 v W, Ni (2)
Anderson, A. (Hearts), 1933 v E; 1934 v A, E, W, Ni; 1935 v E, W, Ni; 1936 v E, W, Ni; 1937 v G, E, W, Ni, A; 1938 v E, W, Ni, Cz, Ho; 1939 v W, H (23)
Anderson, F. (Clydesdale), 1874 v E (1)
Anderson, G. (Kilmarnock), 1901 v Ni (1)
Anderson, H. A. (Raith R), 1914 v W (1)
Anderson, J. (Leicester C), 1954 v Fi (1)
Anderson, K. (Queen's Park), 1896 v Ni; 1898 v E, Ni (3)
Anderson, W. (Queen's Park), 1882 v E; 1883 v E, W; 1884 v E; 1885 v E, W (6)
Andrews, P. (Eastern), 1875 v E (1)
Archibald, A. (Rangers), 1921 v W; 1922 v W, E; 1923 v Ni; 1924 v E, W; 1931 v E; 1932 v E (8)
Archibald, S. (Aberdeen), 1980 v P (sub); (with Tottenham H), Ni, Pol, H; 1981 v Se (sub), Is, Ni, Is, Ni, E; 1982 v Ni, P, Sp (sub), Ho, Nz (sub), Br, USSR; 1983 v EG, Sw (sub), Bel; 1984 v EG, E, F; (with Barcelona), 1985 v Sp, E, Ic (sub); 1986 v WG (27)
Armstrong, M. W. (Aberdeen), 1936 v W, Ni; 1937 v G (3)
Arnott, W. (Queen's Park), 1883 v W; 1884 v E, Ni; 1885 v E, W; 1886 v E; 1887 v E, W; 1888 v E; 1889 v E; 1890 v E; 1891 v E; 1892 v E; 1893 v E (14)
Auld, J. R. (Third Lanark), 1887 v E, W; 1889 v W (3)
Auld, R. (Celtic), 1959 v H, P; 1960 v W (3)

Baird, A. (Queen's Park), 1892 v Ni; 1894 v W (2)
Baird, D. (Hearts), 1890 v Ni; 1891 v E; 1892 v W (3)
Baird, H. (Airdrieonians), 1956 v A (1)
Baird, J. C. (Vale of Leven), 1876 v E; 1878 v W; 1880 v E (3)
Baird, S. (Rangers), 1957 v Y, Sp (2), Sw, WG; 1958 v F, Ni (7)
Baird, W. U. (St Bernard), 1897 v Ni (1)
Bannon, E. (Dundee U), 1980 v Bel; 1983 v Ni, W, E, Ca; 1984 v EG; 1986 v Is, R, E, D (sub), WG (11)
Barbour, A. (Renton), 1885 v Ni (1)
Barker, J. B. (Rangers), 1893 v W; 1894 v W (2)
Barrett, F. (Dundee), 1894 v Ni; 1895 v W (2)
Battles, B. (Celtic), 1901 v E, W, Ni (3)
Battles, B. jun. (Hearts), 1931 v W (1)
Bauld, W. (Hearts), 1950 v E, Sw, P (3)

Baxter, J. C. (Rangers), 1961 v Ni, Ei (2), Cz; 1962 v Ni, W, E, Cz (2), U; 1963 v W, Ni, E, A, N, Ei, Sp; 1964 v W, E, N, WG; 1965 v W, Ni, Fi; (with Sunderland), 1966 v P, Br, Ni, W, E, I; 1967 v W, E, USSR; 1968 v W (34)
Baxter, R. D. (Middlesbrough), 1939 v E, W, H (3)
Beattie, A. (Preston NE), 1937 v E, A, Cz; 1938 v E; 1939 v W, Ni, H (7)
Beattie, R. (Preston NE), 1939 v W (1)
Begbie, I. (Hearts), 1890 v Ni; 1891 v E; 1892 v W; 1894 v E (4)
Bell, A. (Manchester U), 1912 v Ni (1)
Bell, J. (Dumbarton), 1890 v Ni; 1892 v E; (with Everton), 1896 v E; 1897 v E; 1898 v E; (with Celtic), 1899 v E, W, Ni; 1900 v E, W (10)
Bell, M. (Hearts), 1901 v W (1)
Bell, W. J. (Leeds U), 1966 v P, Br (2)
Bennett, A. (Celtic), 1904 v W; 1907 v Ni; 1908 v W; (with Rangers), 1909 v W, Ni, E; 1910 v E, W; 1911 v E, W; 1913 v Ni (11)
Bennie, R. (Airdrieonians), 1925 v W, Ni; 1926 v Ni (3)
Berry, D. (Queen's Park), 1894 v W; 1899 v W, Ni (3)
Berry, W. H. (Queen's Park), 1888 v E; 1889 v E; 1890 v E; 1891 v E (4)
Bett, J. (Rangers), 1982 v Ho; 1983 v Bel; (with Lokeren), 1984 v Bel, W, E, F; 1985 v Y, Ic, Sp (2), W, E, Ic; (with Aberdeen), 1986 v W, Is, Ho; 1987 v Bel; 1988 v H (sub); 1989 v Y; 1990 v F (sub), N, Arg, Eg, Ma, Cr (25)
Beveridge, W. W. (Glasgow University), 1879 v E, W; 1880 v W (3)
Black, A. (Hearts), 1938 v Cz, Ho; 1939 v H (3)
Black, D. (Hurlford), 1889 v Ni (1)
Black, E. (Metz), 1988 v H (sub), L (sub) (2)
Black, I. H. (Southampton), 1948 v E (1)
Blackburn, J. E. (Royal Engineers), 1873 v E (1)
Blacklaw, A. S. (Burnley), 1963 v N, Sp; 1966 v I (3)
Blackley, J. (Hibernian), 1974 v Cz, E, Bel, Z; 1976 v Sw; 1977 v W, Se (7)
Blair, D. (Clyde), 1929 v W, Ni; 1931 v E, A, I; 1932 v W, Ni; (with Aston Villa), 1933 v W (8)
Blair, J. (Sheffield W), 1920 v E, Ni; (with Cardiff C), 1921 v E; 1922 v E; 1923 v E, W, Ni; 1924 v W (8)
Blair, J. (Motherwell), 1934 v W (1)
Blair, J. A. (Blackpool), 1947 v W (1)
Blair, W. (Third Lanark), 1896 v W (1)
Blessington, J. (Celtic), 1894 v E, Ni; 1896 v E, Ni (4)
Blyth, J. A. (Coventry C), 1978 v Bul, W (2)
Bone, J. (Norwich C), 1972 v Y (sub); 1973 v D (2)
Booth, S. (Aberdeen), 1993 v G (sub), Es (2 subs) (3)
Bowie, J. (Rangers), 1920 v E, Ni (2)
Bowie, W. (Linthouse), 1891 v Ni (1)
Bowman, D. (Dundee U), 1992 v Fi, US (sub); 1993 v G, Es (4)
Bowman, G. A. (Montrose), 1892 v Ni (1)
Boyd, J. M. (Newcastle U), 1934 v Ni (1)
Boyd, R. (Mossend Swifts), 1889 v Ni; 1891 v W (2)
Boyd, T. (Motherwell), 1991 v R (sub), Sw, Bul, USSR; (with Chelsea), 1992 v Sw, R; (with Celtic), Fi, Ca, N, C; 1993 v Sw, P, I, Ma, G, Es (2) (17)
Boyd, W. G. (Clyde), 1931 v I, Sw (2)
Brackenbridge, T. (Hearts), 1888 v Ni (1)
Bradshaw, T. (Bury), 1928 v E (1)
Brand, R. (Rangers), 1961 v Ni, Cz, Ei (2); 1962 v Ni, W, Cz, U (8)
Branden, T. (Blackburn R), 1896 v E (1)
Brazil, A. (Ipswich T), 1980 v Pol (sub), H; 1982 v Sp, Ho (sub), Ni, W, E, Nz, USSR (sub); 1983 v EG, Sw, W, E (sub) (13)
Bremner, D. (Hibernian), 1976 v Sw (sub) (1)

Bremner, W. J. (Leeds U), 1965 v Sp; 1966 v E, Pol, P, Br, I (2); 1967 v W, Ni, E; 1968 v W, E; 1969 v W, E, Ni, D, A, WG, Cy (2); 1970 v Ei, WG, A; 1971 v W, E; 1972 v P, Bel, Ho, Ni, W, E, Y, Cz, Br; 1973 v D (2), E (2), Ni (sub), Sw, Br; 1974 v Cz, WG, Ni, W, E, Bel, N, Z, Br, Y; 1975 v Sp (2); 1976 v D (54)
Brennan, F. (Newcastle U), 1947 v W, Ni; 1953 v W, Ni, E; 1954 v Ni, E (7)
Breslin, B. (Hibernian), 1897 v W (1)
Brewster, G. (Everton), 1921 v E (1)
Brogan, J. (Celtic), 1971 v W, Ni, P, E (4)
Brown, A. (Middlesbrough), 1904 v E (1)
Brown, A. (St Mirren), 1890 v W; 1891 v W (2)
Brown, A. D. (East Fife), 1950 v Sw, P, F; (with Blackpool), 1952 v USA, D, Se; 1953 v W; 1954 v W, E, N (2), Fi, A, U (14)
Brown, G. C. P. (Rangers), 1931 v W; 1932 v E, W, Ni; 1933 v E; 1934 v A; 1935 v E, W; 1936 v E, W; 1937 v G, E, W, Ni, Cz; 1938 v E, W, Cz, Ho (19)
Brown, H. (Partick T), 1947 v W, Bel, L (3)
Brown, J. (Cambuslang), 1890 v W (1)
Brown, J. B. (Clyde), 1939 v W (1)
Brown, J. G. (Sheffield U), 1975 v R (1)
Brown, R. (Dumbarton), 1884 v W, Ni (2)
Brown, R. (Rangers), 1947 v Ni; 1949 v Ni; 1952 v E (3)
Brown, R. jun. (Dumbarton), 1885 v W (1)
Brown, W. D. F. (Dundee), 1958 v F; 1959 v E, W, Ni; (with Tottenham H), 1960 v W, Ni, Pol, A, H, T; 1962 v Ni, W, E, Cz; 1963 v W, Ni, E, A; 1964 v Ni, W, N; 1965 v E, Fi, Pol, Sp; 1966 v Ni, Pol, I (28)
Browning, J. (Celtic), 1914 v W (1)
Brownlie, J. (Hibernian), 1971 v USSR; 1972 v Pe, Ni, E; 1973 v D (2); 1976 v R (7)
Brownlie, J. (Third Lanark), 1909 v E, Ni; 1910 v E, W, Ni; 1911 v W, Ni; 1912 v W, Ni, E; 1913 v W, Ni, E; 1914 v W, Ni, E (16)
Bruce, D. (Vale of Leven), 1890 v W (1)
Bruce, R. F. (Middlesbrough), 1934 v A (1)
Buchan, M. M. (Aberdeen), 1972 v P (sub), Bel; (with Manchester U), W, Y, Cz, Br; 1973 v D (2), E; 1974 v WG, Ni, W, N, Br, Y; 1975 v EG, Sp, P; 1976 v D, R; 1977 v Fi, Cz, Ch, Arg, Br; 1978 v EG, W (sub), Ni, Pe, Ir, Ho; 1979 v A, N, P (34)
Buchanan, J. (Cambuslang), 1889 v Ni (1)
Buchanan, J. (Rangers), 1929 v E; 1930 v E (2)
Buchanan, P. S. (Chelsea), 1938 v Cz (1)
Buchanan, R. (Abercorn), 1891 v W (1)
Buckley, P. (Aberdeen), 1954 v N; 1955 v W, Ni (3)
Buick, A. (Hearts), 1902 v W, Ni (2)
Burley, G. (Ipswich T), 1979 v W, Ni, E, Arg, N; 1980 v P, Ni, E (sub), Pol; 1982 v W (sub), E (11)
Burns, F. (Manchester U), 1970 v A (1)
Burns, K. (Birmingham C), 1974 v WG; 1975 v EG (sub), Sp (2); 1977 v Cz (sub), W, Se, W (sub); (with Nottingham F), 1978 v Ni (sub), W, E, Pe, Ir; 1979 v N; 1980 v Pe, A, Bel; 1981 v Is, Ni, W (20)
Burns, T. (Celtic), 1981 v Ni; 1982 v Ho (sub), W; 1983 v Bel (sub), Ni, Ca (1 + 1 sub); 1988 v E (sub) (8)
Busby, M. W. (Manchester C), 1934 v W (1)

Cairns, T. (Rangers), 1920 v W; 1922 v E; 1923 v E, W; 1924 v Ni; 1925 v W, E, Ni (8)
Calderhead, D. (Queen of the South), 1889 v Ni (1)
Calderwood, R. (Cartvale), 1885 v Ni, E, W (3)
Caldow, E. (Rangers), 1957 v Sp (2), Sw, WG, E; 1958 v Ni, W, Sw, Par, H, Pol, Y, F; 1959 v E, W, Ni, WG, Ho, P; 1960 v E, W, Ni, A, H, T; 1961 v E, W, Ni, Ei (2), Cz; 1962 v Ni, W, E, Cz (2), U; 1963 v W, Ni, E (40)
Callaghan, P. (Hibernian), 1900 v Ni (1)
Callaghan, W. (Dunfermline Ath), 1970 v Ei (sub), W (2)
Cameron, J. (Rangers), 1886 v Ni (1)
Cameron, J. (Queen's Park), 1896 v Ni (1)

Cameron, J. (St Mirren), 1904 v Ni; (with Chelsea), 1909 v E (2)
Campbell, C. (Queen's Park), 1874 v E; 1876 v W; 1877 v E, W; 1878 v E; 1879 v E; 1880 v E; 1881 v E; 1882 v E, W; 1884 v E; 1885 v E; 1886 v E (13)
Campbell, H. (Renton), 1889 v W (1)
Campbell, Jas (Sheffield W), 1913 v W (1)
Campbell, J. (South Western), 1880 v W (1)
Campbell, J. (Kilmarnock), 1891 v Ni; 1892 v W (2)
Campbell, John (Celtic), 1893 v E, Ni; 1898 v E, Ni; 1900 v E, Ni; 1901 v E, W, Ni; 1902 v W, Ni; 1903 v W (12)
Campbell, John (Rangers), 1899 v E, N, Ni; 1901 v Ni (4)
Campbell, K. (Liverpool), 1920 v E, W, Ni; (with Partick T), 1921 v W, Ni; 1922 v W, Ni, E (8)
Campbell, P. (Rangers), 1878 v W; 1879 v W (2)
Campbell, P. (Morton), 1898 v W (1)
Campbell, R. (Falkirk), 1947 v Bel, L; (with Chelsea), 1950 v Sw, P, F (5)
Campbell, W. (Morton), 1947 v Ni; 1948 v E, Bel, Sw, F (5)
Carabine, J. (Third Lanark), 1938 v Ho; 1939 v E, Ni (3)
Carr, W. M. (Coventry C), 1970 v Ni, W, E; 1971 v D; 1972 v Pe; 1973 v D (sub) (6)
Cassidy, J. (Celtic), 1921 v W, Ni; 1923 v Ni; 1924 v W (4)
Chalmers, S. (Celtic), 1965 v W, Fi; 1966 v P (sub), Br; 1967 v Ni (5)
Chalmers, W. (Rangers), 1885 v Ni (1)
Chalmers, W. S. (Queen's Park), 1929 v Ni (1)
Chambers, T. (Hearts), 1894 v W (1)
Chaplin, G. D. (Dundee), 1908 v W (1)
Cheyne, A. G. (Aberdeen), 1929 v E, N, G, Ho; 1930 v F (5)
Christie, A. J. (Queen's Park), 1898 v W; 1899 v E, Ni (3)
Christie, R. M. (Queen's Park), 1884 v E (1)
Clark, J. (Celtic), 1966 v Br; 1967 v W, Ni, USSR (4)
Clark, R. B. (Aberdeen), 1968 v W, Ho; 1970 v Ni; 1971 v W, Ni, E, D, P, USSR; 1972 v Bel, Ni, W, E, Cz, Br; 1973 v D, E (17)
Clarke, S. (Chelsea), 1988 v H, Bel, Bul, S.Ar, Ma (5)
Cleland, J. (Royal Albert), 1891 v Ni (1)
Clements, R. (Leith Ath), 1891 v Ni (1)
Clunas, W. L. (Sunderland), 1924 v E; 1926 v W (2)
Collier, W. (Raith R), 1922 v W (1)
Collins, J. (Hibernian), 1988 v S.Ar; 1990 v EG, Pol (sub), Ma (sub); (with Celtic), 1991 v Sw (sub), Bul (sub); 1992 v Ni (sub), Fi; 1993 v P, Ma, G, P, Es (2) (14)
Collins, R. Y. (Celtic), 1951 v W, Ni, A; 1955 v Y, A, H; 1956 v Ni, W; 1957 v E, W, Sp (2), Sw, WG; 1958 v Ni, W, Sw, H, Pol, Y, F, Par; (with Everton), 1959 v E, W, Ni, WG, Ho, P; (with Leeds U), 1965 v E, Pol, Sp (31)
Collins, T. (Hearts), 1909 v W (1)
Colman, D. (Aberdeen), 1911 v E, W, Ni; 1913 v Ni (4)
Colquhoun, E. P. (Sheffield U), 1972 v P, Ho, Pe, Y, Cz, Br; 1973 v D (2), E (9)
Colquhoun, J. (Hearts), 1988 v S.Ar (sub) (1)
Combe, J. R. (Hibernian), 1948 v E, Bel, Sw (3)
Conn, A. (Hearts), 1956 v A (1)
Conn, A. (Tottenham H), 1975 v Ni (sub), E (2)
Connachan, E. D. (Dunfermline Ath), 1962 v Cz, U (2)
Connelly, G. (Celtic), 1974 v Cz, WG (2)
Connolly, J. (Everton), 1973 v Sw (1)
Connor, J. (Airdrieonians), 1886 v Ni (1)
Connor, J. (Sunderland), 1930 v F; 1932 v Ni; 1934 v E; 1935 v Ni (4)
Connor, R. (Dundee), 1986 v Ho; (with Aberdeen), 1988 v S.Ar (sub); 1989 v E; 1991 v R (4)
Cook, W. L. (Bolton W), 1934 v E; 1935 v W, Ni (3)
Cooke, C. (Dundee), 1966 v W, I; (with Chelsea), P, Br; 1968 v E, Ho; 1969 v W, Ni, A, WG (sub), Cy (2); 1970 v A; 1971 v Bel; 1975 v Sp, P (16)
Cooper, D. (Rangers), 1980 v Pe, A (sub); 1984 v W, E; 1985 v Y, Ic, Sp (2), W; 1986 v W (sub), EG, Aus (2),

Ho, WG (sub), U (sub); 1987 v Bul, L, Ei, Br; (with Motherwell), 1990 v N, Eg (22)

Cormack, P. B. (Hibernian), 1966 v Br; 1969 v D (sub); 1970 v Ei, WG; (with Nottingham F), 1971 v D (sub), W, P, E; 1972 v Ho (sub) (9)

Cowan, J. (Aston Villa), 1896 v E; 1897 v E; 1898 v E (3)

Cowan, J. (Morton), 1948 v Bel, Sw; F; 1949 v E, W, F; 1950 v E, W, Ni, Sw, P, F; 1951 v E, W, Ni, A (2), D, F, Bel; 1952 v Ni, W, USA, D, Se (25)

Cowan, W. D. (Newcastle U), 1924 v E (1)

Cowie, D. (Dundee), 1953 v E, Se; 1954 v Ni, W, Fi, N, A, U; 1955 v W, Ni, A, H; 1956 v W, A; 1957 v Ni, W; 1958 v H, Pol, Y, Par (20)

Cox, C. J. (Hearts), 1948 v F (1)

Cox, S. (Rangers), 1949 v E, F; 1950 v E, F, W, Ni, Sw, P; 1951 v E, D, F, Bel, A; 1952 v Ni, W, USA, D, Se; 1953 v W, Ni, E; 1954 v W, Ni, E (24)

Craig, A. (Motherwell), 1929 v N, Ho; 1932 v E (3)

Craig, J. (Celtic), 1977 v Se (sub) (1)

Craig, J. P. (Celtic), 1968 v W (1)

Craig, T. (Rangers), 1927 v Ni; 1928 v Ni; 1929 v N, G, Ho; 1930 v Ni, E, W (8)

Craig, T. B. (Newcastle U), 1976 v Sw (1)

Crapnell, J. (Airdrieonians), 1929 v E, N, G; 1930 v F; 1931 v Ni, Sw; 1932 v E, F; 1933 v Ni (9)

Crawford, D. (St Mirren), 1894 v W, Ni; 1900 v W (3)

Crawford, J. (Queen's Park), 1932 v F, Ni; 1933 v E, W, Ni (5)

Crerand, P. T. (Celtic), 1961 v Ei (2), Cz; 1962 v Ni, W, E, Cz (2), U; 1963 v W, Ni; (with Manchester U), 1964 v Ni; 1965 v E, Pol, Fi; 1966 v Pol (16)

Cringan, W. (Celtic), 1920 v W; 1922 v E, Ni; 1923 v W, E (5)

Crosbie, J. A. (Ayr U), 1920 v W; (with Birmingham), 1922 v E (2)

Croal, J. A. (Falkirk), 1913 v Ni; 1914 v E, W (3)

Cropley, A. J. (Hibernian), 1972 v P, Bel (2)

Cross, J. H. (Third Lanark), 1903 v Ni (1)

Cruickshank, J. (Hearts), 1964 v WG; 1970 v W, E; 1971 v D, Bel; 1976 v R (6)

Crum, J. (Celtic), 1936 v E; 1939 v Ni (2)

Cullen, M. J. (Luton T), 1956 v A (1)

Cumming, D. S. (Middlesbrough), 1938 v E (1)

Cumming, J. (Hearts), 1955 v E, H, P, Y; 1960 v E, Pol, A, H, T (9)

Cummings, G. (Partick T), 1935 v E; 1936 v W, Ni; (with Aston Villa), E; 1937 v G; 1938 v W, Ni, Cz; 1939 v E (9)

Cunningham, A. N. (Rangers), 1920 v Ni; 1921 v W, E; 1922 v Ni; 1923 v E, W; 1924 v E, Ni; 1926 v E, Ni; 1927 v E, W (12)

Cunningham, W. C. (Preston NE), 1954 v N (2), U, Fi, A; 1955 v W, E, H (8)

Curran, H. P. (Wolverhampton W), 1970 v A; 1971 v Ni, E, D, USSR (sub) (5)

Dalglish, K. (Celtic), 1972 v Bel (sub), Ho; 1973 v D (1 + 1 sub), E (2), W, Ni, Sw, Br; 1974 v Cz (2), WG (2), Ni, Se, P, W, Ni, E, R; 1975 v EG v D (2), R, Sw, Ni, E; 1977 v Fi, Cz, W (2), Se, Ni, E, Ch, Arg, Br; (with Liverpool), 1978 v EG, Cz, W, Bul, Ni (sub), W, E, Pe, Ir, Ho; 1979 v A, N, P, W, Ni, E, Arg, N; 1980 v Pe, A, Bel (2), P, Ni, W, E, Pol, H; 1981 v Se, P, Is; 1982 v Se, Ni, P (sub), Sp, Ho, Ni, W, E, Nz, Br (sub); 1983 v Bel, Sw; 1984 v U, Bel, EG; 1985 v Y, Ic, Sp, W; 1986 v EG, Aus, R; 1987 v Bul (sub), L (102)

Davidson, D. (Queen's Park), 1878 v W; 1879 v W; 1880 v W; 1881 v E, W (5)

Davidson, J. A. (Partick T), 1954 v N (2), A, U; 1955 v W, Ni, E, H (8)

Davidson, S. (Middlesbrough), 1921 v E (1)

Dawson, A. (Rangers), 1980 v Pol (sub), H; 1983 v Ni, Ca (2) (5)

Dawson, J. (Rangers), 1935 v Ni; 1936 v E; 1937 v G, E, W, Ni, A, Cz; 1938 v W, Ho, Ni; 1939 v E, Ni, H (14)

Deans, J. (Celtic), 1975 v EG, Sp (2)

Delaney, J. (Celtic), 1936 v W, Ni; 1937 v G, E, A, Cz; 1938 v Ni; 1939 v W, Ni; (with Manchester U), 1947 v E; 1948 v E, W, Ni (13)

Devine, A. (Falkirk), 1910 v W (1)

Dewar, G. (Dumbarton), 1888 v Ni; 1889 v E (2)

Dewar, N. (Third Lanark), 1932 v E, F; 1933 v W (3)

Dick, J. (West Ham U), 1959 v E (1)

Dickie, M. (Rangers), 1897 v Ni; 1899 v Ni; 1900 v W (3)

Dickson, W. (Dumbarton), 1888 v Ni (1)

Dickson, W. (Kilmarnock), 1970 v Ni, W, E; 1971 v D, USSR (5)

Divers, J. (Celtic), 1895 v W (1)

Divers, J. (Celtic), 1939 v Ni (1)

Docherty, T. H, (Preston NE), 1952 v W; 1953 v E, Se; 1954 v N (2), A, U; 1955 v W, E, H (2), A; 1957 v E, Y, Sp (2), Sw, WG; 1958 v Ni, W, E, Sw; (with Arsenal), 1959 v W, E, Ni (25)

Dodds, D. (Dundee U), 1984 v U (sub), Ni (2)

Dodds, J. (Celtic), 1914 v E, W, Ni (3)

Doig, J. E. (Arbroath), 1887 v Ni; 1889 v Ni; (with Sunderland), 1896 v E; 1899 v E; 1903 v E (5)

Donachie, W. (Manchester C), 1972 v Pe, Ni, E, Y, Cz, Br; 1973 v D, E, W, Ni; 1974 v Ni; 1976 v R, Ni, W, E; 1977 v Fi, Cz, W (2), Se, Ni, E, Ch, Arg, Br; 1978 v EG, W, Bul, W, E, Ir, Ho; 1979 v A, N, P (sub) (35)

Donaldson, A. (Bolton W), 1914 v E, Ni, W; 1920 v E, Ni; 1922 v Ni (6)

Donnachie, J. (Oldham Ath), 1913 v E; 1914 v E, Ni (3)

Dougall, C. (Birmingham C), 1947 v W (1)

Dougall, J. (Preston NE), 1939 v E (1)

Dougan, R. (Hearts), 1950 v Sw (1)

Douglas, A. (Chelsea), 1911 v Ni (1)

Douglas, J. (Renfrew), 1880 v W (1)

Dowds, P. (Celtic), 1892 v Ni (1)

Downie, R. (Third Lanark), 1892 v W (1)

Doyle, D. (Celtic), 1892 v E; 1893 v W; 1894 v E; 1895 v E, Ni; 1897 v E; 1898 v E, Ni (8)

Doyle, J. (Ayr U), 1976 v R (1)

Drummond, J. (Falkirk), 1892 v Ni; (with Rangers), 1894 v Ni; 1895 v Ni, E; 1896 v E, Ni; 1897 v Ni; 1898 v E; 1900 v E; 1901 v E; 1902 v E, W, Ni; 1903 v Ni (14)

Dunbar, M. (Cartvale), 1886 v Ni (1)

Duncan, A. (Hibernian), 1975 v P (sub), W, Ni, E, R; 1976 v D (sub) (6)

Duncan, D. (Derby Co), 1933 v E, W; 1934 v A, W; 1935 v E, W; 1936 v E, W, Ni; 1937 v G, E, W, Ni; 1938 v W (14)

Duncan, D. M. (East Fife), 1948 v Bel, Sw, F (3)

Duncan, J. (Alexandra Ath), 1878 v W; 1882 v W (2)

Duncan, J. (Leicester C), 1926 v W (1)

Duncanson, J. (Rangers), 1947 v Ni (1)

Dunlop, J. (St Mirren), 1890 v W (1)

Dunlop, W. (Liverpool), 1906 v E (1)

Dunn, J. (Hibernian), 1925 v W, Ni; 1927 v Ni; 1928 v Ni, E; (with Everton), 1929 v W (6)

Durie, G. S. (Chelsea), 1988 v Bul (sub); 1989 v I (sub), Cy; 1990 v Y, EG, Eg, Se; 1991 v Sw (sub), Bul (2), USSR (sub), Sm; (with Tottenham H), 1992 v Sw, R, Sm, Ni (sub), Fi, Ca, N (sub), Ho, G; 1993 v Sw, I (23)

Durrant, I. (Rangers), 1988 v H, Bel, Ma, Sp; 1989 v N (sub); 1993 v Sw (sub), P (sub), I, P (sub) (9)

Dykes, J. (Hearts), 1938 v Ho; 1939 v Ni (2)

Easson, J. F. (Portsmouth), 1931 v A, Sw; 1934 v W (3)

Ellis, J. (Mossend Swifts), 1892 v Ni (1)

Evans, A. (Aston Villa), 1982 v Ni, Ho, E, Nz (4)

Evans, R. (Celtic), 1949 v E, W, Ni, F; 1950 v W, Ni, Sw, P; 1951 v E, A; 1952 v Ni; 1953 v Se; 1954 v Ni, W, E,

(sub); 1983 v Ni, W, E, Ca (1 + 1 sub); (with Everton), 1985 v Ic (20)

Gray, D. (Rangers), 1929 v W, Ni, G, Ho; 1930 v W, E, Ni; 1931 v W; 1933 v W, Ni (10)

Gray, E. (Leeds U), 1969 v E, Cy; 1970 v WG, A; 1971 v W, Ni; 1972 v Bel, Ho; 1976 v W, E; 1977 v Fi, W (12)

Gray, F. T. (Leeds U), 1976 v Sw; 1979 v N, P, W, Ni, E, Arg (sub); (with Nottingham F), 1980 v Bel (sub); 1981 v Se, P, Is, Ni, Is, W; (with Leeds U), Ni, E; 1982 v Se, Ni, P, Sp, Ho, W, Nz, Br, USSR; 1983 v EG, Sw, Bel, Sw, W, E, Ca (32)

Gray, W. (Pollokshields Ath), 1886 v E (1)

Green, A. (Blackpool), 1971 v Bel (sub), P (sub), Ni, E; (with Newcastle U), 1972 v W, E (sub) (6)

Greig, J. (Rangers), 1964 v E, WG; 1965 v W, Ni, E, Fi (2), Sp, Pol; 1966 v Ni, W, E, Pol, I (2), P, Ho, Br; 1967 v W, Ni, E; 1968 v Ni, W, E, Ho; 1969 v W, Ni, E, D, A, WG, Cy (2); 1970 v W, E, Ei, WG, A; 1971 v D, Bel, W (sub), Ni, E; 1976 v D (44)

Groves, W. (Hibernian), 1888 v W; (with Celtic), 1889 v Ni; 1890 v E (3)

Guilliland, W. (Queen's Park), 1891 v W; 1892 v Ni; 1894 v E; 1895 v E (4)

Gunn, B. (Norwich C), 1990 v Eg; 1993 v Es (2) (3)

Haddock, H. (Clyde), 1955 v E, H (2), P, Y; 1958 v E (6)

Haddow, D. (Rangers), 1894 v E (1)

Haffey, F. (Celtic), 1960 v E; 1961 v E (2)

Hamilton, A. (Queen's Park), 1885 v E, W; 1886 v E; 1888 v E (4)

Hamilton, A. W. (Dundee), 1962 v Cz, U, W, E; 1963 v W, Ni, E, A, N, Ei; 1964 v Ni, W, E, N, WG; 1965 v Ni, W, E, Fi (2), Pol, Sp; 1966 v Pol, Ni (24)

Hamilton, G. (Aberdeen), 1947 v Ni; 1951 v Bel, A; 1954 v N (2) (5)

Hamilton, G. (Port Glasgow Ath), 1906 v Ni (1)

Hamilton, J. (Queen's Park), 1892 v W; 1893 v E, Ni (3)

Hamilton, J. (St Mirren), 1924 v Ni (1)

Hamilton, R. C. (Rangers), 1899 v E, W, Ni; 1900 v W; 1901 v E, Ni; 1902 v W, Ni; 1903 v E; 1904 v Ni; (with Dundee), 1911 v W (11)

Hamilton, T. (Hurlford), 1891 v Ni (1)

Hamilton, T. (Rangers), 1932 v E (1)

Hamilton, W. M. (Hibernian), 1965 v Fi (1)

Hannah, A. B. (Renton), 1888 v W (1)

Hannah, J. (Third Lanark), 1889 v W (1)

Hansen, A. D. (Liverpool), 1979 v W, Arg; 1980 v Bel, P; 1981 v Se, P, Is; 1982 v Se, Ni, P, Sp, Ni (sub), W, E, Nz, Br, USSR; 1983 v EG, Sw, Bel, Sw; 1985 v W (sub); 1986 v R (sub); 1987 v Ei (2), L (26)

Hansen, J. (Partick T), 1972 v Bel (sub), Y (sub) (2)

Harkness, J. D. (Queen's Park), 1927 v E, Ni; 1928 v E; (with Hearts), 1929 v W, E, Ni; 1930 v E, W; 1932 v W, F; 1934 v Ni, W (12)

Harper, J. M. (Aberdeen), 1973 v D (1 + 1 sub); (with Hibernian), 1976 v D; (with Aberdeen), 1978 v Ir (sub) (4)

Harper, W. (Hibernian), 1923 v E, Ni, W; 1924 v E, Ni, W; 1925 v E, Ni, W; (with Arsenal), 1926 v E, Ni (11)

Harris, J. (Partick T), 1921 v W, Ni (2)

Harris, N. (Newcastle U), 1924 v E (1)

Harrower, W. (Queen's Park), 1882 v E; 1884 v Ni; 1886 v W (3)

Hartford, R. A. (WBA), 1972 v Pe, W (sub), E, Y, Cz, Br; (with Manchester C), 1976 v D, R, Ni (sub); 1977 v Cz (sub), W (sub), Se, W, Ni, E, Ch, Arg, Br; 1978 v EG, Cz, W, Bul, W, E, Pe, Ir, Ho; 1979 v A, N, P, W, Ni, E, Arg, N; (with Everton), 1980 v Pe, Bel; 1981 v Ni (sub), Is, W, E; 1982 v Se; (with Manchester C), Ni, P, Sp, Ni, W, E, Br (50)

Harvey, D. (Leeds U), 1973 v D; 1974 v Cz, WG, Ni, W, E, Bel, Z, Br, Y; 1975 v EG, Sp (2); 1976 v D (2); 1977 v Fi (sub) (16)

Hastings, A. C. (Sunderland), 1936 v Ni; 1938 v Ni (2)

Haughney, M. (Celtic), 1954 v E (1)

Hay, D. (Celtic), 1970 v Ni, W, E; 1971 v D, Bel, W, P, Ni; 1972 v P, Bel, Ho; 1973 v W, Ni, E, Sw, Br; 1974 v Cz (2), WG, Ni, W, E, Bel, N, Z, Br, Y (27)

Hay, J. (Celtic), 1905 v Ni; 1909 v Ni; 1910 v W, Ni, E; 1911 v Ni, E; (with Newcastle U), 1912 v E, W; 1914 v E, Ni (11)

Hegarty, P. (Dundee U), 1979 v W, Ni, E, Arg, N (sub); 1980 v W, E; 1983 v Ni (8)

Heggie, C. (Rangers), 1886 v Ni (1)

Henderson, G. H. (Rangers), 1904 v Ni (1)

Henderson, J. G. (Portsmouth), 1953 v Se; 1954 v Ni, E, N; 1956 v W; (with Arsenal), 1959 v W, Ni (7)

Henderson, W. (Rangers), 1963 v W, Ni, E, A, N, Ei, Sp; 1964 v W, Ni, E, N, WG; 1965 v Fi, Pol, E, Sp; 1966 v Ni, W, Pol, I, Ho; 1967 v W, Ni; 1968 v Ho; 1969 v Ni, E, Cy; 1970 v Ei; 1971 v P (29)

Hendry, E. C. J. (Blackburn R), 1993 v Es (2) (2)

Hepburn, J. (Alloa Ath), 1891 v W (1)

Hepburn, R. (Ayr U), 1932 v Ni (1)

Herd, A. C. (Hearts), 1935 v Ni (1)

Herd, D. G. (Arsenal), 1959 v E, W, Ni; 1961 v E, Cz (5)

Herd, G. (Clyde), 1958 v E; 1960 v H, T; 1961 v W, Ni (5)

Herriot, J. (Birmingham C), 1969 v Ni, E, D, Cy (2), W (sub); 1970 v Ei (sub), WG (8)

Hewie, J. D. (Charlton Ath), 1956 v E, A; 1957 v E, Ni, W, Y, Sp (2), Sw, WG; 1958 v H, Pol, Y, F; 1959 v Ho, P; 1960 v Ni, W, Pol (19)

Higgins, A. (Kilmarnock), 1885 v Ni (1)

Higgins, A. (Newcastle U), 1910 v E, Ni; 1911 v E, Ni (4)

Highet, T. C. (Queen's Park), 1875 v E; 1876 v E, W; 1878 v E (4)

Hill, D. (Rangers), 1881 v E, W; 1882 v W (3)

Hill, D. A. (Third Lanark), 1906 v Ni (1)

Hill, F. R. (Aberdeen), 1930 v F; 1931 v W, Ni (3)

Hill, J. (Hearts), 1891 v E; 1892 v W (2)

Hogg, G (Hearts), 1896 v E, Ni (2)

Hogg, J. (Ayr U), 1922 v Ni (1)

Hogg, R. M. (Celtic), 1937 v Cz (1)

Holm, A. H. (Queen's Park), 1882 v W; 1883 v E, W (3)

Holt, D. D. (Hearts), 1963 v A, N, Ei, Sp; 1964 v WG (sub) (5)

Holton, J. A. (Manchester U), 1973 v W, Ni, E, Sw, Br; 1974 v Cz, WG, Ni, W, E, N, Z, Br, Y; 1975 v EG (15)

Hope, R. (WBA), 1968 v Ho; 1969 v D (2)

Houliston, W. (Queen of the South), 1949 v E, Ni, F (3)

Houston, S. M. (Manchester U), 1976 v D (1)

Howden, W. (Partick T), 1905 v Ni (1)

Howe, R. (Hamilton A), 1929 v N, Ho (2)

Howie, J. (Newcastle U), 1905 v E; 1906 v E; 1908 v E (3)

Howie, H. (Hibernian), 1949 v W (1)

Howieson, J. (St Mirren), 1927 v Ni (1)

Hughes, J. (Celtic), 1965 v Pol, Sp; 1966 v Ni, I (2); 1968 v E; 1969 v A; 1970 v Ei (8)

Hughes, W. (Sunderland), 1975 v Se (sub) (1)

Humphries, W. (Motherwell), 1952 v Se (1)

Hunter, A. (Kilmarnock), 1972 v Pe, Y; (with Celtic), 1973 v E; 1974 v Cz (4)

Hunter, J. (Dundee), 1909 v W (1)

Hunter, J. (Third Lanark), 1874 v E; (with Eastern), 1875 v E; (with Third Lanark), 1876 v E; 1877 v W (4)

Hunter, R. (St Mirren), 1890 v Ni (1)

Hunter, W. (Motherwell), 1960 v H, T; 1961 v W (3)

Husband, J. (Partick T), 1947 v W (1)

Hutchison, T. (Coventry C), 1974 v Cz (2), WG (2), Ni, W, Bel (sub), N, Z (sub); 1975 v EG, Sp (2), P, E (sub), R (sub); 1976 v D (17)

Hutton, J. (Aberdeen), 1923 v E, W, Ni; 1924 v Ni; 1926 v W, E, Ni; (with Blackburn R), 1927 v Ni; 1928 v W, Ni (10)

Hutton, J. (St Bernards), 1887 v Ni (1)

Hyslop, T. (Stoke C), 1896 v E; (with Rangers), 1897 v E (2)

Imlach, J. J. S. (Nottingham F), 1958 v H, Pol, Y, F (4)
Imrie, W. N. (St Johnstone), 1929 v N, G (2)
Inglis, J. (Kilmarnock Ath), 1884 v Ni (1)
Inglis, J. (Rangers), 1883 v E, W (2)
Irons, J. H. (Queen's Park), 1900 v W (1)
Irvine, B. (Aberdeen), 1991 v R; 1993 v G, Es (2) (4)

Jackson, A. (Cambuslang), 1886 v W; 1888 v Ni (2)
Jackson, A. (Aberdeen), 1925 v E, W, Ni; (with Huddersfield T), 1926 v E, W, Ni; 1927 v W, Ni; 1928 v E, W; 1929 v E, W, Ni; 1930 v E, W, Ni, F (17)
Jackson, C. (Rangers), 1975 v Se, P (sub), W; 1976 v D, R, Ni, W, E (8)
Jackson, J. (Partick T), 1931 v A, I, Sw; 1933 v E; (with Chelsea), 1934 v E; 1935 v E; 1936 v W, Ni (8)
Jackson, T. A. (St Mirren), 1904 v W, E, Ni; 1905 v W; 1907 v W, Ni (6)
James, A. W. (Preston NE), 1926 v W; 1928 v E; 1929 v E, Ni; (with Arsenal), 1930 v E, W, Ni; 1933 v W (8)
Jardine, A. (Rangers), 1971 v D (sub); 1972 v P, Bel, Ho; 1973 v E, Sw, Br; 1974 v Cz (2), WG (2), Ni, W, E, Bel, N, Z, Br, Y; 1975 v EG, Sp (2), Se, P, W, Ni, E; 1977 v Se (sub), Ch (sub), Br (sub); 1978 v Cz, W, Ni, Ir; 1980 v Pe, A, Bel (2) (38)
Jarvie, A. (Airdrieonians), 1971 v P (sub), Ni (sub), E (sub) (3)
Jenkinson, T. (Hearts), 1887 v Ni (1)
Jess, E. (Aberdeen), 1993 v I (sub), Ma (2)
Johnston, L. H. (Clyde), 1948 v Bel, Sw (2)
Johnston, M. (Watford), 1984 v W (sub), E (sub), F; 1985 v Y; (with Celtic), Ic, Sp (2), W; 1986 v EG; 1987 v Bul, Ei (2), L; (with Nantes), 1988 v H, Bel, L, S.Ar, Sp, Co, E; 1989 v N, Y, I, Cy, F, Cy, E, Ch (sub); (with Rangers), 1990 v F, N, EG, Pol, Ma, Cr, Se, Br; 1992 v Sw, Sm (sub) (38)
Johnston, R. (Sunderland), 1938 v Cz (1)
Johnston, W. (Rangers), 1966 v W, E, Pol, Ho; 1968 v W, E; 1969 v Ni (sub); 1970 v Ni; 1971 v D; (with WBA), 1977 v Se, W (sub), Ni, E, Ch, Arg, Br; 1978 v EG, Cz, W (2), E, Pe (22)
Johnstone, D. (Rangers), 1973 v W, Ni, E, Sw, Br; 1975 v EG, Se (sub); 1976 v Sw, Ni (sub), E (sub); 1978 v Bul (sub), Ni, W; 1980 v Bel (14)
Johnstone, J. (Abercorn), 1888 v W (1)
Johnstone, J. (Celtic), 1965 v W, Fi; 1966 v E; 1967 v W, USSR; 1968 v W; 1969 v A, WG; 1970 v E, WG; 1971 v D, E; 1972 v P, Bel, Ho, Ni, E (sub); 1974 v W, E, Bel, N; 1975 v EG, Sp (23)
Johnstone, Jas (Kilmarnock), 1894 v W (1)
Johnstone, J. A. (Hearts), 1930 v W; 1933 v W, Ni (3)
Johnstone, R. (Hibernian), 1951 v E, D, F; 1952 v Ni, E; 1953 v E, Se; 1954 v W, E, N, Fi; 1955 v Ni, H; (with Manchester C), 1955 v E; 1956 v E, Ni, W (17)
Johnstone, W. (Third Lanark), 1887 v Ni; 1889 v W; 1890 v E (3)
Jordan, J. (Leeds U), 1973 v E (sub), Sw (sub), Br; 1974 v Cz (sub + 1), WG (sub), Ni (sub), W, E, Bel, N, Z, Br, Y; 1975 v EG, Sp (2); 1976 v Ni, W, E; 1977 v Cz, W, Ni, E; 1978 v EG, Cz, W; (with Manchester U), Bul, Ni, E, Pe, Ir, Ho; 1979 v A, P, W (sub), Ni, E, N; 1980 v Bel, Ni (sub), W, E, Pol; 1981 v Is, W, E; (with AC Milan), 1982 v Se, Ho, W, E, USSR (52)

Kay, J. L. (Queen's Park), 1880 v E; 1882 v E, W; 1883 v E, W; 1884 v W (6)
Keillor, A. (Montrose), 1891 v W; 1892 v Ni; (with Dundee), 1894 v Ni; 1895 v W; 1896 v W; 1897 v W (6)
Keir, L. (Dumbarton), 1885 v W; 1886 v Ni; 1887 v E, W; 1888 v E (5)
Kelly, H. T. (Blackpool), 1952 v USA (1)

Kelly, J. (Renton), 1888 v E; (with Celtic), 1889 v E; 1890 v E; 1892 v E; 1893 v E, Ni; 1894 v W; 1896 v Ni (8)
Kelly, J. C. (Barnsley), 1949 v W, Ni (2)
Kelso, R. (Renton), 1885 v W, Ni; 1886 v W; 1887 v E, W; 1888 v E, Ni; (with Dundee), 1898 v Ni (8)
Kelso, T. (Dundee), 1914 v W (1)
Kennaway, J. (Celtic), 1934 v A (1)
Kennedy, A. (Eastern), 1875 v E; 1876 v E, W; (with Third Lanark), 1878 v E; 1882 v W; 1884 v W (6)
Kennedy, J. (Celtic), 1964 v W, E, WG; 1965 v W, Ni, Fi (6)
Kennedy, J. (Hibernian), 1897 v W (1)
Kennedy, S. (Aberdeen), 1978 v Bul, W, E, Pe, Ho; 1979 v A, P; 1982 v P (sub) (8)
Kennedy, S. (Partick T), 1905 v W (1)
Kennedy, S. (Rangers), 1975 v Se, P, W, Ni, E (5)
Ker, G. (Queen's Park), 1880 v E; 1881 v E, W; 1882 v W, E (5)
Ker, W. (Granville), 1872 v E; (with Queen's Park), 1873 v E (2)
Kerr, A. (Partick T), 1955 v A, H (2)
Kerr, P. (Hibernian), 1924 v Ni (1)
Key, G. (Hearts), 1902 v Ni (1)
Key, W. (Queen's Park), 1907 v Ni (1)
King, A. (Hearts), 1896 v E, W; (with Celtic), 1897 v Ni; 1898 v Ni; 1899 v Ni, W (6)
King, J. (Hamilton A), 1933 v Ni; 1934 v Ni (2)
King, W. S. (Queen's Park), 1929 v W (1)
Kinloch, J. D. (Partick T), 1922 v Ni (1)
Kinnaird, A. F. (Wanderers), 1873 v E (1)
Kinnear, D. (Rangers), 1938 v Cz (1)

Lambie, J. A. (Queen's Park), 1886 v Ni; 1887 v Ni; 1888 v E (3)
Lambie, W. A. (Queen's Park), 1892 v Ni; 1893 v W; 1894 v E; 1895 v E, Ni; 1896 v E, Ni; 1897 v E, Ni (9)
Lamont, D. (Pilgrims), 1885 v Ni (1)
Lang, A. (Dumbarton), 1880 v W (1)
Lang, J. J. (Clydesdale), 1876 v W; (with Third Lanark), 1878 v W (2)
Latta, A. (Dumbarton), 1888 v W; 1889 v E (2)
Law, D. (Huddersfield T), 1959 v W, Ni, Ho, P; 1960 v Ni, W; (with Manchester C), 1960 v E, Pol, A; 1961 v E, Ni; (with Torino), 1962 v Cz (2), E; (with Manchester U), 1963 v W, Ni, E, A, N, Ei, Sp; 1964 v W, E, N, WG; 1965 v W, Ni, E, Fi (2), Pol, Sp; 1966 v Ni, E, Pol; 1967 v W, E, USSR; 1968 v Ni; 1969 v Ni, A, WG; 1972 v Pe, Ni, W, E, Y, Cz, Br; (with Manchester C), 1974 v Cz (2), WG (2), Ni, Z (55)
Law, G. (Rangers), 1910 v E, Ni, W (3)
Law, T. (Chelsea), 1928 v E; 1930 v E (2)
Lawrence, J. (Newcastle U), 1911 v E (1)
Lawrence, T. (Liverpool), 1963 v Ei; 1969 v W, WG (3)
Lawson, D. (St Mirren), 1923 v E (1)
Leckie, R. (Queen's Park), 1872 v E (1)
Leggat, G. (Aberdeen), 1956 v E; 1957 v W; 1958 v Ni, H, Pol, Y, Par; (with Fulham), 1959 v E, W, Ni, WG, Ho; 1960 v E, Ni, W, Pol, A, H (18)
Leighton, J. (Aberdeen), 1983 v EG, Sw, Bel, Sw, W, E, Ca (2); 1984 v U, Bel, Ni, W, E, F; 1985 v Y, Ic, Sp (2), W, E, Ic; 1986 v W, EG, Aus (2), Is, D, WG, U; 1987 v Bul, Ei (2), L, Bel, E; 1988 v H, Bel, Bul, L, S.Ar, Ma, Sp; (with Manchester U), Co, E; 1989 v N, Cy, F, Cy, E, Ch; 1990 v Y, F, N, Arg, Ma (sub, Cr, Se, Br (58)
Lennie, W. (Aberdeen), 1908 v W, Ni (2)
Lennox, R. (Celtic), 1967 v Ni, E, USSR; 1968 v W, E; 1969 v D, A, WG, Cy (sub); 1970 v W (sub) (10)
Leslie, L. G. (Airdrieonians), 1961 v W, Ni, Ei (2), Cz (5)
Levein, C. (Hearts), 1990 v Arg, EG, Eg (sub), Pol, Ma (sub), Se; 1992 v R, Sm; 1993 v P, G, P (11)
Liddell, W. (Liverpool), 1947 v W, Ni; 1948 v E, W, Ni; 1950 v E, W, P, F; 1951 v W, Ni, E, A; 1952 v W, Ni, E,

USA, D, Sc; 1953 v W, Ni, E; 1954 v W; 1955 v P, Y, A, H; 1956 v Ni (28)

Liddle, D. (East Fife), 1931 v A, I, Sw (3)

Lindsay, D. (St Mirren), 1903 v Ni (1)

Lindsay, J. (Dumbarton), 1880 v W; 1881 v W, E; 1884 v W, E; 1885 v W, E; 1886 v E (8)

Lindsay, J. (Renton), 1888 v E; 1893 v E, Ni (3)

Linwood, A. B. (Clyde), 1950 v W (1)

Little, R. J. (Rangers), 1953 v Se (1)

Livingstone, G. T. (Manchester C), 1906 v E; (with Rangers), 1907 v W (2)

Lochhead, A. (Third Lanark), 1889 v W (1)

Logan, J. (Ayr U), 1891 v W (1)

Logan, T. (Falkirk), 1913 v Ni (1)

Logie, J. T. (Arsenal), 1953 v Ni (1)

Loney, W. (Celtic), 1910 v W, Ni (2)

Long, H. (Clyde), 1947 v Ni (1)

Longair, W. (Dundee), 1894 v Ni (1)

Lorimer, P. (Leeds U), 1970 v A (sub); 1971 v W, Ni; 1972 v Ni (sub), W, E; 1973 v D (2), E (2); 1974 v WG (sub), E, Bel, N, Z, Br, Y; 1975 v Sp (sub); 1976 v D (2), R (sub) (21)

Love, A. (Aberdeen), 1931 v A, I, Sw (3)

Low, A. (Falkirk), 1934 v Ni (1)

Low, T. P. (Rangers), 1897 v Ni (1)

Low, W. L. (Newcastle U), 1911 v E, W; 1912 v Ni; 1920 v E, Ni (5)

Lowe, J. (Cambuslang), 1891 v Ni (1)

Lowe, J. (St Bernards), 1887 v Ni (1)

Lundie, J. (Hibernian), 1886 v W (1)

Lyall, J. (Sheffield W), 1905 v E (1)

McAdam, J. (Third Lanark), 1880 v W (1)

McAllister, G. (Leicester C), 1990 v EG, Pol, Ma (sub); (with Leeds U), 1991 v R, Sw, Bul, USSR (sub), Sm; 1992 v Sw (sub), Sm, Ni, Fi (sub), US, Ca, N, Ho, G, C; 1993 v Sw, P, I, Ma (22)

McArthur, D. (Celtic), 1895 v E, Ni; 1899 v W (3)

McAtee, A. (Celtic), 1913 v W (1)

McAulay, J. (Dumbarton), 1882 v W; (with Arthurlie), 1884 v Ni (2)

McAulay, J. (Dumbarton), 1883 v E, W; 1884 v E; 1885 v E, W; 1886 v E; 1887 v E, W (8)

McAuley, R. (Rangers), 1932 v Ni, W (2)

McAvennie, F. (West Ham U), 1986 v Aus (2), D (sub), WG (sub); (with Celtic), 1988 v S.Ar (5)

McBain, E. (St Mirren), 1894 v W (1)

McBain, N. (Manchester U), 1922 v E; (with Everton), 1923 v Ni; 1924 v W (3)

McBride, J. (Celtic), 1967 v W, Ni (2)

McBride, P. (Preston NE), 1904 v E; 1906 v E; 1907 v E, W; 1908 v E; 1909 v W (6)

McCall, J. (Renton), 1886 v W; 1887 v E, W; 1888 v E; 1890 v E (5)

McCall, S. M. (Everton), 1990 v Arg, EG, Eg (sub), Pol, Ma, Cr, Se, Br; 1991 v Sw, USSR, Sm; (with Rangers), 1992 v Sw, R, Sm, US, Ca, N, Ho, G, C; 1993 v Sw, P (2) (23)

McCalliog, J. (Sheffield W), 1967 v E, USSR; 1968 v Ni; 1969 v D; (with Wolverhampton W), 1971 v P (5)

McCallum, N. (Renton), 1888 v Ni (1)

McCann, R. J. (Motherwell), 1959 v WG; 1960 v E, Ni, W; 1961 v E (5)

McCartney, W. (Hibernian), 1902 v Ni (1)

McClair, B. (Celtic), 1987 v L, Ei, E, Br (sub); (with Manchester U), 1988 v Bul, Ma (sub), Sp (sub); 1989 v N, Y, I (sub), Cy, F (sub); 1990 v N (sub), Arg (sub); 1991 v Bul (2), Sm; 1992 v Sw (sub), R, Ni, US, Ca (sub), N, Ho, G, C; 1993 v Sw, P (sub), Es (2) (30)

McClory, A. (Motherwell), 1927 v W; 1928 v Ni; 1935 v W (3)

McCloy, P. (Ayr U), 1924 v E; 1925 v E (2)

McCloy, P. (Rangers), 1973 v W, Ni, Sw, Br (4)

McCoist, A. (Rangers), 1986 v Ho; 1987 v L (sub), Ei (sub), Bel, E, Br; 1988 v H, Bel, Ma, Sp, Co, E; 1989 v Y (sub), F, Cy, E; 1990 v Y, F, N, EG (sub), Eg, Pol, Ma (sub), Cr (sub), Se (sub), Br; 1991 v R, Sw, Bul (2), USSR; 1992 v Sw, Sm, Ni, Fi (sub), US, Ca, N, Ho, G, C; 1993 v Sw, P, I, Ma, P (46)

McColl, A. (Renton), 1888 v Ni (1)

McColl, I. M. (Rangers), 1950 v E, F; 1951 v W, Ni, Bel; 1957 v E, Ni, W, Y, Sp, Sw, WG; 1958 v Ni, E (14)

McColl, R. S. (Queen's Park), 1896 v W, Ni; 1897 v Ni; 1898 v Ni; 1899 v Ni, E, W; 1900 v E, W; 1901 v E, W; (with Newcastle U), 1902 v E; (with Queen's Park), 1908 v Ni (13)

McColl, W. (Renton), 1895 v W (1)

McCombie, A. (Sunderland), 1903 v E, W; (with Newcastle U), 1905 v E, W (4)

McCorkindale, J. (Partick T), 1891 v W (1)

McCormick, R. (Abercorn), 1886 v W (1)

McCrae, D. (St Mirren), 1929 v N, G (2)

McCreadie, A. (Rangers), 1893 v W; 1894 v E (2)

McCreadie, E. G. (Chelsea), 1965 v E, Sp, Fi, Pol; 1966 v P, Ni, W, Pol, I; 1967 v E, USSR; 1968 v Ni, W, E, Ho; 1969 v W, Ni, E, D, A, WG, Cy (2) (23)

McCulloch, D. (Hearts), 1935 v W; (with Brentford), 1936 v E; 1937 v W, Ni; 1938 v Cz; (with Derby Co), 1939 v H, W (7)

MacDonald, A. (Rangers), 1976 v Sw (1)

McDonald, J. (Edinburgh University), 1886 v E (1)

McDonald, J. (Sunderland), 1956 v W, Ni (2)

MacDougall, E. J. (Norwich C) 1975 v Se, P, W, Ni, E; 1976 v D, R (sub) (7)

McDougall, J. (Liverpool), 1931 v I, A (2)

McDougall, J. (Airdrieonians), 1926 v Ni (1)

McDougall, J. (Vale of Leven), 1877 v E, W; 1878 v E; 1879 v E, W (5)

McFadyen, W. (Motherwell), 1934 v A, W (2)

Macfarlane, A. (Dundee), 1904 v W; 1906 v W; 1908 v W; 1909 v Ni; 1911 v W (5)

McFarlane, R. (Greenock Morton), 1896 v W (1)

Macfarlane, W. (Hearts), 1947 v L (1)

McGarr, E. (Aberdeen), 1970 v Ei, A (2)

McGarvey, F. P. (Liverpool), 1979 v Ni (sub), Arg; (with Celtic), 1984 v U, Bel (sub), EG (sub), Ni, W (7)

McGeoch, A. (Dumbreck), 1876 v E, W; 1877 v E, W (4)

McGhee, J. (Hibernian), 1886 v W (1)

McGhee, M. (Aberdeen), 1983 v Ca (1 + 1 sub); 1984 v Ni (sub), E (4)

McGonagle, W. (Celtic), 1933 v E; 1934 v A, E, Ni; 1935 v Ni, W (6)

McGrain, D. (Celtic), 1973 v W, Ni, E, Sw, Br; 1974 v Cz (2), WG, W (sub), E, Bel, N, Z, Br, Y; 1975 v Sp, Se, P, W, Ni, E, R; 1976 v D (2), Sw, Ni, W, E; 1977 v Fi, Cz, W (2), Se, Ni, E, Ch, Arg, Br; 1978 v EG, Cz; 1980 v Bel, P, Ni, W, E, Pol, H; 1981 v Se, P, Is, Ni, Is, W (sub), Ni, E; 1982 v Se, Sp, Ho, Ni, E, Nz, USSR (sub) (62)

McGregor, J. C. (Vale of Leven), 1877 v E, W; 1878 v E; 1880 v E (4)

McGrory, J. E. (Kilmarnock), 1965 v Ni, Fi; 1966 v P (3)

McGrory, J. (Celtic), 1928 v Ni; 1931 v E; 1932 v Ni, W; 1933 v E, Ni; 1934 v Ni (7)

McGuire, W. (Beith), 1881 v E, W (2)

McGurk, F. (Birmingham), 1934 v W (1)

McHardy, H. (Rangers), 1885 v Ni (1)

McInally, A. (Aston Villa), 1989 v Cy (sub), Ch; (with Bayern Munich), 1990 v Y (sub), F (sub), Arg, Pol (sub), Ma, Cr (8)

McInally, J. (Dundee U), 1987 v Bel, Br; 1988 v Ma (sub); 1991 v Bul (2); 1992 v US (sub), N (sub), C (sub); 1993 v G, P (10)

McInally, T. B. (Celtic), 1926 v Ni; 1927 v W (2)

McInnes, T. (Cowlairs), 1889 v Ni (1)

McIntosh, W. (Third Lanark), 1905 v Ni (1)

McIntyre, A. (Vale of Leven), 1878 v E; 1882 v E (2)

McIntyre, H. (Rangers), 1880 v W (1)

McIntyre, J. (Rangers), 1884 v W (1)

McKay, D. (Celtic), 1959 v E, WG, Ho, P; 1960 v E, Pol, A, H, T; 1961 v W, Ni; 1962 v Ni, Cz, U (sub) (14)

Mackay, D. C. (Hearts), 1957 v Sp; 1958 v F; 1959 v W, Ni; (with Tottenham H), 1959 v WG, E; 1960 v W, Ni, A, Pol, H, T; 1961 v W, Ni, E; 1963 v E, A, N; 1964 v Ni, W, N; 1966 v Ni (22)

Mackay, G. (Hearts), 1988 v Bul (sub), L (sub), S.Ar (sub), Ma (4)

McKay, J. (Blackburn R), 1924 v W (1)

McKay, R. (Newcastle U), 1928 v W (1)

McKean, R. (Rangers), 1976 v Sw (sub) (1)

McKenzie, D. (Brentford), 1938 v Ni (1)

Mackenzie, J. A. (Partick T), 1954 v W, E, N, Fi, A, U; 1955 v E, H; 1956 v A (9)

McKeown, M. (Celtic), 1889 v Ni; 1890 v E (2)

McKie, J. (East Stirling), 1898 v W (1)

McKillop, T. R. (Rangers), 1938 v Ho (1)

McKimmie, S. (Aberdeen), 1989 v E, Ch; 1990 v Arg, Eg, Cr (sub), Br; 1991 v R, Sw, Bul, Sm; 1992 v Sw, R, Ni, Fi, US, Ca (sub), N (sub), Ho, G, C; 1993 v P (21)

McKinlay, D. (Liverpool), 1922 v W, Ni (2)

McKinnon, A. (Queen's Park), 1874 v E (1)

McKinnon, R. (Rangers), 1966 v W, E, I (2), Ho, Br; 1967 v W, Ni, E; 1968 v Ni, W, E, Ho; 1969 v D, A, WG, Cy; 1970 v Ni, W, E, Ei, WG, A; 1971 v D, Bel, P, USSR, D (28)

MacKinnon, W. (Dumbarton), 1883 v E, W; 1884 v E, W (4)

McKinnon, W. W. (Queen's Park), 1872 v E; 1873 v E; 1874 v E; 1875 v E; 1876 v E, W; 1877 v E; 1878 v E; 1879 v E (9)

McLaren, A. (St Johnstone), 1929 v N, G, Ho; 1933 v W, Ni (5)

McLaren, A. (Preston NE), 1947 v E, Bel, L; 1948 v W (4)

McLaren, A. (Hearts), 1992 v US, Ca, N; 1993 v I, Ma, G, Es (sub + 1) (8)

McLaren, J. (Hibernian), 1888 v W; (with Celtic), 1889 v E; 1890 v E (3)

McLean, A. (Celtic), 1926 v W, Ni; 1927 v W, E (4)

McLean, D. (St Bernards), 1896 v W; 1897 v Ni (2)

McLean, D. (Sheffield W), 1912 v E (1)

McLean, G. (Dundee), 1968 v Ho (1)

McLean, T. (Kilmarnock), 1969 v D, Cy, W; 1970 v Ni, W; 1971 v D (6)

McLeish, A. (Aberdeen), 1980 v F, Ni, W, E, Pol, H; 1981 v Se, Is, Ni, Is, Ni, E; 1982 v Se, Sp, Ni, Br (sub); 1983 v Bel, Sw (sub), W, E, Ca (3); 1984 v U, Bel, EG, Ni, W, E, F; 1985 v Y, Ic, Sp (2), W, E, Ic; 1986 v W, EG, Aus (2), E, Ho, D; 1987 v Bel, E, Br; 1988 v Bel, Bul, L, S.Ar (sub), Ma, Sp, Co, E; 1989 v N, Y, I, Cy, F, Cy, E, Ch; 1990 v Y, F, N, Arg, EG, Eg, Cr, Se, Br; 1991 v R, Sw, USSR, Bul; 1993 v Ma (77)

McLeod, D. (Celtic), 1905 v Ni; 1906 v E, W, Ni (4)

McLeod, J. (Dumbarton), 1888 v Ni; 1889 v W; 1890 v Ni; 1892 v E; 1893 v W (5)

MacLeod, J. M. (Hibernian), 1961 v E, Ei (2), Cz (4)

MacLeod, M. (Celtic), 1985 v E (sub); 1987 v Ei, L, E, Br; (with Borussia Dortmund), 1988 v Co, E; 1989 v I, Ch; 1990 v Y, F, N (sub), Arg, EG, Pol, Se Br; (with Hibernian), 1991 v R, Sw, USSR (sub) (20)

McLeod, W. (Cowlairs), 1886 v Ni (1)

McLintock, A. (Vale of Leven), 1875 v E; 1876 v E; 1880 v E (3)

McLintock, F. (Leicester C), 1963 v N (sub), Ei, Sp; (with Arsenal), 1965 v Ni; 1967 v USSR; 1970 v Ni; 1971 v W, Ni, E (9)

McLuckie, J. S. (Manchester C), 1934 v W (1)

McMahon, A. (Celtic), 1892 v E; 1893 v E, Ni; 1894 v E; 1901 v Ni; 1902 v W (6)

McMenemy, J. (Celtic), 1905 v Ni; 1909 v Ni; 1910 v E, W; 1911 v Ni, W, E; 1912 v W; 1914 v W, Ni, E; 1920 v Ni (12)

McMenemy, J. (Motherwell), 1934 v W (1)

McMillan, J. (St Bernards), 1897 v W (1)

McMillan, I. L. (Airdrieonians), 1952 v E, USA, D; 1955 v E; 1956 v E; (with Rangers), 1961 v Cz (6)

McMillan, T. (Dumbarton), 1887 v Ni (1)

McMullan, J. (Partick T), 1920 v W; 1921 v W, Ni, E; 1924 v E, Ni; 1925 v E; 1926 v W; (with Manchester C), 1926 v E; 1927 v E, W; 1928 v E, W; 1929 v W, E, Ni (16)

McNab, A. (Morton), 1921 v E, Ni (2)

McNab, A. (Sunderland), 1937 v A; (with WBA), 1939 v E (2)

McNab, C. D. (Dundee), 1931 v E, W, A, I, Sw; 1932 v E (6)

McNab, J. S. (Liverpool), 1923 v W (1)

McNair, A. (Celtic), 1906 v W; 1907 v Ni; 1908 v E, W; 1909 v E; 1910 v W; 1912 v E, W, Ni; 1913 v E; 1914 v E, Ni; 1920 v E, W, Ni (15)

McNaught, W. (Raith R), 1951 v A, W, Ni; 1952 v E; 1955 v Ni (5)

McNeil, H. (Queen's Park), 1874 v E; 1875 v E; 1876 v E, W; 1877 v W; 1878 v E; 1879 v E, W; 1881 v E, W (10)

McNeil, M. (Rangers), 1876 v W; 1880 v E (2)

McNeill, W. (Celtic), 1961 v E, Ei (2), Cz; 1962 v Ni, E, Cz, U; 1963 v Ei, Sp; 1964 v W, E, WG; 1965 v E, Fi, Pol, Sp; 1966 v Ni, Pol; 1967 v USSR; 1968 v E; 1969 v Cy, W, E, Cy (sub); 1970 v WG; 1972 v Ni, W, E (29)

McPhail, J. (Celtic), 1950 v W; 1951 v W, Ni, A; 1954 v Ni (5)

McPhail, R. (Airdrieonians), 1927 v E; (with Rangers), 1929 v W; 1931 v E, Ni; 1932 v W, Ni, F; 1933 v E, Ni; 1934 v A, Ni; 1935 v E; 1937 v G, E, Cz; 1938 v W, Ni (17)

McPherson, D. (Kilmarnock), 1892 v Ni (1)

McPherson, D. (Hearts), 1989 v Cy, E; 1990 v N, Ma, Cr, Se, Br; 1991 v Sw, Bul (2), USSR (sub), Sm; 1992 v Sw, R, Sm, Ni, Fi, US, Ca, N, Ho, G, C; (with Rangers), 1993 v Sw, I, Ma, P (27)

McPherson, J. (Clydesdale), 1875 v E (1)

McPherson, J. (Vale of Leven), 1879 v E, W; 1880 v E; 1881 v W; 1883 v E, W; 1884 v E; 1885 v Ni (8)

McPherson, J. (Kilmarnock), 1888 v W; (with Cowlairs), 1889 v E; 1890 v Ni, E; (with Rangers), 1892 v W; 1894 v E; 1895 v E, Ni; 1897 v Ni (9)

McPherson, J. (Hearts), 1891 v E (1)

McPherson, R. (Arthurlie), 1882 v E (1)

McQueen, G. (Leeds U), 1974 v Bel; 1975 v Sp (2), P, W, Ni, E, R; 1976 v D; 1977 v Cz, W (2), Ni, E; 1978 v EG, Cz, W; (with Manchester U), Bul, Ni, W; 1979 v A, N, P, Ni, E, N; 1980 v Pe, A, Bel; 1981 v W (30)

McQueen, M. (Leith Ath), 1890 v W; 1891 v W (2)

McRorie, D. M. (Morton), 1931 v W (1)

McSpadyen, A. (Partick T), 1939 v E, H (2)

McStay, P. (Celtic), 1984 v U, Bel, EG, Ni, W, E (sub); 1985 v Y, Ic, Sp (2), W; 1986 v EG (sub), Aus, Is, U; 1987 v Bul, Ei (1 + 1 sub), L (sub), Bel, E, Br; 1988 v H, Bel, Bul, L, S.Ar, Sp, Co, E; 1989 v N, Y, I, Cy, F, Cy, E, Ch; 1990 v Y, F, N, Arg, EG (sub), Eg, Pol (sub), Ma, Cr, Se (sub), Br; 1991 v R, USSR, Bul; 1992 v Sm, Fi, US, Ca, N, Ho, G, C; 1993 v Sw, P, I, Ma, P, Es (2) (67)

McStay, W. (Celtic), 1921 v W, Ni; 1925 v E, Ni, W; 1926 v E, Ni, W; 1927 v E, Ni, W; 1928 v W, Ni (13)

McTavish, J. (Falkirk), 1910 v Ni (1)

McWhattie, G. C. (Queen's Park), 1901 v W, Ni (2)

McWilliam, P. (Newcastle U), 1905 v E; 1906 v E; 1907 v E, W; 1909 v E, W; 1910 v E; 1911 v W (8)

Macari, L. (Celtic), 1972 v W (sub), E, Y, Cz, Br; 1973 v D; (with Manchester U), E (2), W (sub), Ni (sub); 1975 v Se, P (sub), W, E (sub), R; 1977 v Ni (sub), E (sub), Ch, Arg; 1978 v EG, W, Bul, Pe (sub), Ir (24)

Macauley, A. R. (Brentford), 1947 v E; (with Arsenal), 1948 v E, W, Ni, Bel, Sw, F (7)

Madden, J. (Celtic), 1893 v W; 1895 v W (2)

Main, F. R. (Rangers), 1938 v W (1)

Main, J. (Hibernian), 1909 v Ni (1)

Maley, W. (Celtic), 1893 v E, Ni (2)

Malpas, M. (Dundee U), 1984 v F; 1985 v E, Ic; 1986 v W, Aus (2), Is, R, E, Ho, D, WG; 1987 v Bul, Ei, Bel; 1988 v Bel, Bul, L, S.Ar, Ma; 1989 v N, Y, I, Cy, F, Cy, E, Ch; 1990 v Y, F, N, Eg, Pol, Ma, Cr, Se, Br; 1991 v R, Bul (2), USSR, Sm; 1992 v Sw, R, Sm, Ni, Fi, US, Ca (sub), N, Ho, G; 1993 v Sw, P, I (55)

Marshall, G. (Celtic), 1992 v US (1)

Marshall, H. (Celtic), 1899 v W; 1900 v Ni (2)

Marshall, J. (Middlesbrough), 1921 v E, W, Ni; 1922 v E, W, Ni; (with Llanelly), 1924 v W (7)

Marshall, J. (Third Lanark), 1885 v Ni; 1886 v W; 1887 v E, W (4)

Marshall, J. (Rangers), 1932 v E; 1933 v E; 1934 v E (3)

Marshall, R. W. (Rangers), 1892 v Ni; 1894 v Ni (2)

Martin, F. (Aberdeen), 1954 v N (2), A, U; 1955 v E, H (6)

Martin, N. (Hibernian), 1965 v Fi, Pol; (with Sunderland), 1966 v I (3)

Martis, J. (Motherwell), 1961 v W (1)

Mason, J. (Third Lanark), 1949 v E, W, Ni; 1950 v Ni; 1951 v Ni, Bel, A (7)

Massie, A. (Hearts), 1932 v Ni, W, F; 1933 v Ni; 1934 v E, Ni; 1935 v E, Ni, W; 1936 v W, Ni; (with Aston Villa), 1936 v E; 1937 v G, E, W, Ni, A; 1938 v W (18)

Masson, D. S. (QPR), 1976 v Ni, W, E; 1977 v Fi, Cz, W, Ni, E, Ch, Arg, Br; 1978 v EG, Cz, W; (with Derby Co), Ni, E, Pe (17)

Mathers, D. (Partick T), 1954 v Fi (1)

Maxwell, W. S. (Stoke C), 1898 v E (1)

May, J. (Rangers), 1906 v W, Ni; 1908 v E, Ni; 1909 v W (5)

Meechan, P. (Celtic), 1896 v Ni (1)

Meiklejohn, D. D. (Rangers), 1922 v W; 1924 v W; 1925 v W, Ni, E; 1928 v W, Ni; 1929 v E, Ni; 1930 v E, Ni; 1931 v E; 1932 v W, Ni; 1934 v A (15)

Menzies, A. (Hearts), 1906 v E (1)

Mercer, R. (Hearts), 1912 v W; 1913 v Ni (2)

Middleton, R. (Cowdenbeath), 1930 v Ni (1)

Millar, A. (Hearts), 1939 v W (1)

Millar, J. (Rangers), 1897 v E; 1898 v E, W (3)

Millar, J. (Rangers), 1963 v A, Ei (2)

Miller, J. (St Mirren), 1931 v E, I, Sw; 1932 v F; 1934 v E (5)

Miller, P. (Dumbarton), 1882 v E; 1883 v E, W (3)

Miller, T. (Liverpool), 1920 v E; (with Manchester U), 1921 v E, Ni (3)

Miller, W. (Third Lanark), 1876 v E (1)

Miller, W. (Celtic), 1947 v E, W, Bel, L; 1948 v W, Ni (6)

Miller, W. (Aberdeen), 1975 v R; 1978 v Bul; 1980 v Bel, W, E, Pol, H; 1981 v Se, P, Is (sub), Ni, W, Ni, E; 1982 v Ni, P, Ho, Br, USSR; 1983 v EG, Sw (2), W, E, Ca (3); 1984 v U, Bel, EG, W, E, F; 1985 v Y, Ic, Sp (2), W, E, Ic; 1986 v W, EG, Aus (2), Is, R, E, Ho, D, WG, U; 1987 v Bul, E, Br; 1988 v H, L, S.Ar, Ma, Sp, Co, E; 1989 v N, Y; 1990 v Y, N (65)

Mills, W. (Aberdeen), 1936 v W, Ni; 1937 v W (3)

Milne, J. V. (Middlesbrough), 1938 v E; 1939 v E (2)

Mitchell, D. (Rangers), 1890 v Ni; 1892 v E; 1893 v E, Ni; 1894 v E (5)

Mitchell, J. (Kilmarnock), 1908 v Ni; 1910 v Ni, W (3)

Mitchell, R. C. (Newcastle U), 1951 v D, F (2)

Mochan, N. (Celtic), 1954 v N, A, U (3)

Moir, W. (Bolton W), 1950 v E (1)

Moncur, R. (Newcastle U), 1968 v Ho; 1970 v Ni, W, E, Ei; 1971 v D, Bel, W, P, Ni, E, D; 1972 v Pe, Ni, W, E (16)

Morgan, H. (St Mirren), 1898 v W; (with Liverpool), 1899 v E (2)

Morgan, W. (Burnley), 1968 v Ni; (with Manchester U), 1972 v Pe, Y, Cz, Br; 1973 v D (2), E (2), W, Ni, Sw, Br; 1974 v Cz (2), WG (2), Ni, Bel (sub), Br, Y (21)

Morris, D. (Raith R), 1923 v Ni; 1924 v E, Ni; 1925 v E, W, Ni (6)

Morris, H. (East Fife), 1950 v Ni (1)

Morrison, T. (St Mirren), 1927 v E (1)

Morton, A. L. (Queen's Park), 1920 v W, Ni; (with Rangers), 1921 v E; 1922 v E, W; 1923 v E, W, Ni; 1924 v E, W, Ni; 1925 v E, W, Ni; 1927 v E, Ni; 1928 v E, W, Ni; 1929 v E, W, Ni; 1930 v E, W, Ni; 1931 v E, W, Ni; 1932 v E, W, F (31)

Morton, H. A. (Kilmarnock), 1929 v G, Ho (2)

Mudie, J. K. (Blackpool), 1957 v W, Ni, E, Y, Sw, Sp (2), WG; 1958 v Ni, E, W, Sw, H, Pol, Y, Par, F (17)

Muir, W. (Dundee), 1907 v Ni (1)

Muirhead, T. A. (Rangers), 1922 v Ni; 1923 v E; 1924 v W; 1927 v Ni; 1928 v Ni; 1929 v W, Ni; 1930 v W (8)

Mulhall, G. (Aberdeen), 1960 v Ni; (with Sunderland), 1963 v Ni; 1964 v Ni (3)

Munro, A. D. (Hearts), 1937 v W, Ni; (with Blackpool), 1938 v Ho (3)

Munro, F. M. (Wolverhampton W), 1971 v Ni (sub), E (sub), D, USSR; 1975 v Se, W (sub), Ni, E, R (9)

Munro, I. (St Mirren), 1979 v Arg, N; 1980 v Pe, A, Bel, W, E (7)

Munro, N. (Abercorn), 1888 v W; 1889 v E (2)

Murdoch, J. (Motherwell), 1931 v Ni (1)

Murdoch, R. (Celtic), 1966 v W, E, I (2); 1967 v Ni; 1968 v Ni; 1969 v W, Ni, E, WG, Cy; 1970 v A (12)

Murphy, F. (Celtic), 1938 v Ho (1)

Murray, J. (Renton), 1895 v W (1)

Murray, J. (Hearts), 1958 v E, H, Pol, Y, F (5)

Murray, J. W. (Vale of Leven), 1890 v W (1)

Murray, P. (Hibernian), 1896 v Ni; 1897 v W (2)

Murray, S. (Aberdeen), 1972 v Bel (1)

Mutch, G. (Preston NE), 1938 v E (1)

Napier, C. E. (Celtic), 1932 v E; 1935 v E, W; (with Derby Co), 1937 v Ni, A (5)

Narey, D. (Dundee U), 1977 v Se (sub); 1979 v P, Ni (sub), Arg; 1980 v P, Ni, Pol, H; 1981 v W, E (sub); 1982 v Ho, W, E, Nz (sub), Br, USSR; 1983 v EG, Sw, Bel, Ni, W, E, Ca (3); 1986 v Is, R, Ho, WG, U; 1987 v Bul, E, Bel; 1989 v I, Cy (35)

Neil, R. G. (Hibernian), 1896 v W; (with Rangers), 1900 v W (2)

Neill, R. W. (Queen's Park), 1876 v W; 1877 v E, W; 1878 v W; 1880 v E (5)

Neilles, P. (Hearts), 1914 v W, Ni (2)

Nelson, J. (Cardiff C), 1925 v W, Ni; 1928 v E; 1930 v F (4)

Nevin, P. K. F. (Chelsea), 1986 v R (sub), E (sub); 1987 v L, Ei, Bel (sub); 1988 v L; (with Everton), 1989 v Cy, E; 1991 v R (sub), Bul (sub), Sm (sub); 1992 v US, G (sub), C (sub); (with Tranmere R), 1993 v Ma, P (sub), Es (17)

Niblo, T. D. (Aston Villa), 1904 v E (1)

Nibloe, J. (Kilmarnock), 1929 v E, N, Ho; 1930 v W; 1931 v E, Ni, A, I, Sw; 1932 v E, F (11)

Nicholas, C. (Celtic), 1983 v Sw, Ni, E, Ca (3); (with Arsenal), 1984 v Bel, F (sub); 1985 v Y (sub), Ic (sub), Sp (sub), W (sub); 1986 v Is, R (sub), E, D, U (sub); 1987 v Bul, E (sub); (with Aberdeen), 1989 v Cy (sub) (20)

Nicol, S. (Liverpool), 1985 v Y, Ic, Sp, W; 1986 v W, EG, Aus, E, D, WG, U; 1988 v H, Bul, S.Ar, Sp, Co, E; 1989 v N, Y, Cy, F; 1990 v Y, F; 1991 v Sw, USSR, Sm; 1992 v Sw (27)

Nisbet, J. (Ayr U), 1929 v N, G, Ho (3)

Niven, J. B. (Moffatt), 1885 v Ni (1)

O'Donnell, F. (Preston NE), 1937 v E, A, Cz; 1938 v W; (with Blackpool), E, Ho (6)
Ogilvie, D. H. (Motherwell), 1934 v A (1)
O'Hare, J. (Derby Co), 1970 v W, Ni, E; 1971 v D, Bel, W, Ni; 1972 v P, Bel, Ho (sub), Pe, Ni, W (13)
Ormond, W. E. (Hibernian), 1954 v E, N, Fi, A, U; 1959 v E (6)
O'Rourke, F. (Airdrieonians), 1907 v Ni (1)
Orr, J. (Kilmarnock), 1892 v W (1)
Orr, R. (Newcastle U), 1902 v E; 1904 v E (2)
Orr, T. (Morton), 1952 v Ni, W (2)
Orr, W. (Celtic), 1900 v Ni; 1903 v Ni; 1904 v W (3)
Orrock, R. (Falkirk), 1913 v W (1)
Oswald, J. (Third Lanark), 1889 v E; (with St Bernards), 1895 v E; (with Rangers), 1897 v W (3)

Parker, A. H. (Falkirk), 1955 v P, Y, A; 1956 v E, Ni, W, A; 1957 v Ni, W, Y; 1958 v Ni, W, E, Sw; (with Everton), Par (15)
Parlane, D. (Rangers), 1973 v W, Sw, Br; 1975 v Sp (sub), Se, P, W, Ni, E, R; 1976 v D (sub); 1977 v W (12)
Parlane, R. (Vale of Leven), 1878 v W; 1879 v E, W (3)
Paterson, G. D. (Celtic), 1939 v Ni (1)
Paterson, J. (Leicester C), 1920 v E (1)
Paterson, J. (Cowdenbeath), 1931 v A, I, Sw (3)
Paton, A. (Motherwell), 1952 v D, Se (2)
Paton, D. (St Bernards), 1896 v W (1)
Paton, M. (Dumbarton), 1883 v E; 1884 v W; 1885 v W, E; 1886 v E (5)
Paton, R. (Vale of Leven), 1879 v E, W (2)
Patrick, J. (St Mirren), 1897 v E, W (2)
Paul, H. McD. (Queen's Park), 1909 v E, W, Ni (3)
Paul, W. (Partick T), 1888 v W; 1889 v W; 1890 v W (3)
Paul, W. (Dykebar), 1891 v Ni (1)
Pearson, T. (Newcastle U), 1947 v E, Bel (2)
Penman, A. (Dundee), 1966 v Ho (1)
Pettigrew, W. (Motherwell), 1976 v Sw, Ni, W; 1977 v W (sub), Se (5)
Phillips, J. (Queen's Park), 1877 v E, W; 1878 v W (3)
Plenderleith, J. B. (Manchester C), 1961 v Ni (1)
Porteous, W. (Hearts), 1903 v Ni (1)
Pringle, C. (St Mirren), 1921 v W (1)
Provan, D. (Rangers), 1964 v Ni, N; 1966 v I (2), Ho (5)
Provan, D. (Celtic), 1980 v Bel (2 sub), P (sub), Ni (sub); 1981 v Is, W, E; 1982 v Se, P, Ni (10)
Pursell, P. (Queen's Park), 1914 v W (1)

Quinn, J. (Celtic), 1905 v Ni; 1906 v Ni, W; 1908 v Ni, E; 1909 v E; 1910 v E, Ni, W; 1912 v E, W (11)
Quinn, P. (Motherwell), 1961 v E, Ei (2); 1962 v U (4)

Rae, J. (Third Lanark), 1889 v W; 1890 v Ni (2)
Raeside, J. S. (Third Lanark), 1906 v W (1)
Raisbeck, A. G. (Liverpool), 1900 v E; 1901 v E; 1902 v E; 1903 v E, W; 1904 v E; 1906 v E; 1907 v E (8)
Rankin, G. (Vale of Leven), 1890 v Ni; 1891 v E (2)
Rankin, R. (St Mirren), 1929 v N, G, Ho (3)
Redpath, W. (Motherwell), 1949 v W, Ni; 1951 v E, D, F, Bel, A; 1952 v Ni, E (9)
Reid, J. G. (Airdrieonians), 1914 v W; 1920 v W; 1924 v Ni (3)
Reid, R. (Brentford), 1938 v E, Ni (2)
Reid, W. (Rangers), 1911 v E, W, Ni; 1912 v Ni; 1913 v E, W, Ni; 1914 v E, Ni (9)
Reilly, L. (Hibernian), 1949 v E, W, F; 1950 v W, Ni, Sw, F; 1951 v W, E, D, F, Bel, A; 1952 v Ni, W, E, USA, D, Se; 1953 v Ni, W, E, Se; 1954 v W; 1955 v H (2), P, Y, A, E; 1956 v E, W, Ni, A; 1957 v E, Ni, W, Y (38)
Rennie, H. G. (Hearts), 1900 v E, Ni; (with Hibernian), 1901 v E; 1902 v E, Ni, W; 1903 v Ni, W; 1904 v Ni; 1905 v W; 1906 v Ni; 1908 v Ni, W (13)
Renny-Tailyour, H. W. (Royal Engineers), 1873 v E (1)
Rhind, A. (Queen's Park), 1872 v E (1)

Richmond, A. (Queen's Park), 1906 v W (1)
Richmond, J. T. (Clydesdale), 1877 v E; (with Queen's Park), 1878 v E; 1882 v W (3)
Ring, T. (Clyde), 1953 v Se; 1955 v W, Ni, E, H; 1957 v E, Sp (2), Sw, WG; 1958 v Ni, Sw (12)
Rioch, B. D. (Derby Co), 1975 v P, W, Ni, E, R; 1976 v D (2), R, Ni, W, E; 1977 v Fi, Cz, W; (with Everton), W, Ni, E, Ch, Br; 1978 v Cz; (with Derby Co), Ni, E, Pe, Ho (24)
Ritchie, A. (East Stirlingshire), 1891 v W (1)
Ritchie, H. (Hibernian), 1923 v W; 1928 v Ni (2)
Ritchie, J. (Queen's Park), 1897 v W (1)
Ritchie, W. (Rangers), 1962 v U (sub) (1)
Robb, D. T. (Aberdeen), 1971 v W, E, P, D (sub), USSR (5)
Robb, W. (Rangers), 1926 v W; (with Hibernian), 1928 v W (2)
Robertson, A. (Clyde), 1955 v P, A, H; 1958 v Sw, Par (5)
Robertson, D. (Rangers), 1992 v Ni (1)
Robertson, G. (Motherwell), 1910 v W; (with Sheffield W), 1912 v W; 1913 v E, Ni (4)
Robertson, G. (Kilmarnock), 1938 v Cz (1)
Robertson, H. (Dundee), 1962 v Cz (1)
Robertson, J. (Dundee), 1931 v A, I (2)
Robertson, J. (Hearts), 1991 v R, Sw, Bul (sub), Sm (sub); 1992 v Sm, Ni (sub), Fi; 1993 v I (sub), Ma (sub), G, Es (1 + sub) (12)
Robertson, J. N. (Nottingham F), 1978 v Ni, W (sub), Ir; 1979 v P, N; 1980 v Pe, A, Bel (2), P; 1981 v Se, P, Is, Ni, Is, Ni, E; 1982 v Se, Ni (2), E (sub), Nz, Br, USSR; 1983 v EG, Sw; (with Derby Co), 1984 v U, Bel (28)
Robertson, J. G. (Tottenham H), 1965 v W (1)
Robertson, J. T. (Everton), 1898 v E; (with Southampton), 1899 v E; (with Rangers), 1900 v E, W; 1901 v W, Ni, E; 1902 v W, Ni, E; 1903 v E, W; 1904 v E, W, Ni; 1905 v W (16)
Robertson, P. (Dundee), 1903 v Ni (1)
Robertson, T. (Queen's Park), 1889 v Ni; 1890 v E; 1891 v W; 1892 v Ni (4)
Robertson, T. (Hearts), 1898 v Ni (1)
Robertson, W. (Dumbarton), 1887 v E, W (2)
Robinson, R. (Dundee), 1974 v WG (sub); 1975 v Se, Ni, R (sub) (4)
Rough, A. (Partick T), 1976 v Sw, Ni, W, E; 1977 v Fi, Cz, W (2), Se, Ni, E, Ch, Arg, Br; 1978 v Cz, W, Ni, E, Pe, Ir, Ho; 1979 v A, P, W, Arg, N; 1980 v Pe, A, Bel (2), P, W, E, Pol, H; 1981 v Se, P, Is, Ni, Is, W, E; 1982 v Se, Ni, Sp, Ho, W, E, Nz, Br, USSR; (with Hibernian), 1986 v W (sub), E (53)
Rougvie, D. (Aberdeen), 1984 v Ni (1)
Rowan, A. (Caledonian), 1880 v E; (with Queen's Park), 1882 v W (2)
Russell, D. (Hearts), 1895 v E, Ni; (with Celtic), 1897 v W; 1898 v Ni; 1901 v W, Ni (6)
Russell, J. (Cambuslang), 1890 v Ni (1)
Russell, W. F. (Airdrieonians), 1924 v W; 1925 v E (2)
Rutherford, E. (Rangers), 1948 v F (1)

St John, I. (Motherwell), 1959 v WG; 1960 v E, Ni, W, Pol, A; 1961 v E; (with Liverpool), 1962 v Ni, W, E, Cz (2), U; 1963 v W, Ni, E, N, Ei (sub), Sp; 1964 v Ni; 1965 v E (21)
Sawers, W. (Dundee), 1895 v W (1)
Scarff, P. (Celtic), 1931 v Ni (1)
Schaedler, E. (Hibernian), 1974 v WG (1)
Scott, A. S. (Rangers), 1957 v Ni, Y, WG; 1958 v W, Sw; 1959 v P; 1962 v Ni, W, E, Cz, U; (with Everton), 1964 v W, N; 1965 v Fi; 1966 v P, Br (16)
Scott, J. (Hibernian), 1966 v Ho (1)
Scott, J. (Dundee), 1971 v D (sub), USSR (2)
Scott, M. (Airdrieonians), 1898 v W (1)
Scott, R. (Airdrieonians), 1894 v Ni (1)

Scoular, J. (Portsmouth), 1951 v D, F, A; 1952 v E, USA, D, Se; 1953 v W, Ni (9)

Sellar, W. (Battlefield), 1885 v E; 1886 v E; 1887 v E, W; 1888 v E; (with Queen's Park), 1891 v E; 1892 v E; 1893 v E, Ni (9)

Semple, W. (Cambuslang), 1886 v W (1)

Shankly, W. (Preston NE), 1938 v E; 1939 v E, W, Ni, H (5)

Sharp, G. M. (Everton), 1985 v Ic; 1986 v W, Aus (2 sub), Is, R, U; 1987 v Ei; 1988 v Bel (sub), Bul, L, Ma (12)

Sharp, J. (Dundee), 1904 v W; (with Woolwich Arsenal), 1907 v W, E; 1908 v E; (with Fulham), 1909 v W (5)

Shaw, D. (Hibernian), 1947 v W, Ni; 1948 v E, Bel, Sw, F; 1949 v W, Ni (8)

Shaw, F. W. (Pollokshields Ath), 1884 v E, W (2)

Shaw, J. (Rangers), 1947 v E, Bel, L; 1948 v Ni (4)

Shearer, R. (Rangers), 1961 v E, Ei (2), Cz (4)

Sillars, D. C. (Queen's Park), 1891 v Ni; 1892 v E; 1893 v W; 1894 v E; 1895 v W (5)

Simpson, J. (Third Lanark), 1895 v E, W, Ni (3)

Simpson, J. (Rangers), 1935 v E, W, Ni; 1936 v E, W, Ni; 1937 v G, E, W, Ni, A, Cz; 1938 v W, Ni (14)

Simpson, N. (Aberdeen), 1983 v Ni; 1984 v F (sub); 1987 v E; 1988 v E (4)

Simpson, R. C. (Celtic), 1967 v E, USSR; 1968 v Ni, E; 1969 v A (5)

Sinclair, G. L. (Hearts), 1910 v Ni; 1912 v W, Ni (3)

Sinclair, J. W. E. (Leicester C), 1966 v P (1)

Skene, L. H. (Queen's Park), 1904 v W (1)

Sloan, T. (Third Lanark), 1904 v W (1)

Smellie, R. (Queen's Park), 1887 v Ni; 1888 v W; 1889 v E; 1891 v E; 1893 v E, Ni (6)

Smith, A. (Rangers), 1898 v E; 1900 v E, Ni, W; 1901 v E, Ni, W; 1902 v E, Ni, W; 1903 v E, Ni, W; 1904 v Ni; 1905 v W; 1906 v E, Ni; 1907 v W; 1911 v E, Ni (20)

Smith, D. (Aberdeen), 1966 v Ho; (with Rangers), 1968 v Ho (2)

Smith, G. (Hibernian), 1947 v E, Ni; 1948 v W, Bel, Sw, F; 1952 v E, USA; 1955 v P, Y, A, H; 1956 v E, Ni, W; 1957 v Sp (2), Sw (18)

Smith, H. G. (Hearts), 1988 v S.Ar (sub); 1992 v Ni, Ca (3)

Smith, J. (Rangers), 1935 v Ni; 1938 v Ni (2)

Smith, J. (Ayr U), 1924 v E (1)

Smith, J. (Aberdeen), 1968 v Ho (sub); (with Newcastle U), 1974 v WG, Ni (sub), W (sub) (4)

Smith, J. E. (Celtic), 1959 v H, P (2)

Smith, Jas (Queen's Park), 1872 v E (1)

Smith, John (Mauchline), 1877 v E, W; 1879 v E, W; (with Edinburgh University), 1880 v E; (with Queen's Park), 1881 v W, E; 1883 v E, W; 1884 v E (10)

Smith, N. (Rangers), 1897 v E; 1898 v W; 1899 v E, W, Ni; 1900 v E, W, Ni; 1901 v Ni, W; 1902 v E, Ni (12)

Smith, R. (Queen's Park), 1872 v E; 1873 v E (2)

Smith, T. M. (Kilmarnock), 1934 v E; (with Preston NE), 1938 v E (2)

Somers, P. (Celtic), 1905 v E, Ni; 1907 v Ni; 1909 v W (4)

Somers, W. S. (Third Lanark), 1879 v E, W; (with Queen's Park), 1880 v W (3)

Somerville, G. (Queen's Park), 1886 v E (1)

Souness, G. J. (Middlesbrough), 1975 v EG, Sp, Se; (with Liverpool), 1978 v Bul, W, E (sub), Ho; 1979 v A, N, W, Ni, E; 1980 v Pe, A, Bel, P, Ni; 1981 v P, Is (2); 1982 v Ni, P, Sp, W, E, Nz, Br, USSR; 1983 v EG, Sw, Bel, Sw, W, E, Ca (2 + 1 sub); 1984 v U, Ni, W; (with Sampdoria), 1985 v Y, Ic, Sp (2), W, E, Ic; 1986 v EG, Aus (2), R, E, D, WG (54)

Speedie, D. R. (Chelsea), 1985 v E; 1986 v W, EG (sub), Aus, E; (with Coventry C), 1989 v Y (sub), I (sub), Cy (1 + 1 sub), Ch (10)

Speedie, F. (Rangers), 1903 v E, W, Ni (3)

Speirs, J. H. (Rangers), 1908 v W (1)

Stanton, P. (Hibernian), 1966 v Ho; 1969 v Ni; 1970 v Ei, A; 1971 v D, Bel, P, USSR, D; 1972 v P, Bel, Ho, W; 1973 v W, Ni; 1974 v WG (16)

Stark, J. (Rangers), 1909 v E, Ni (2)

Steel, W. (Morton), 1947 v E, Bel, L; (with Derby Co), 1948 v F, E, W, Ni; 1949 v E, W, Ni, F; 1950 v E, W, Ni, Sw, P, F; (with Dundee), 1951 v W, Ni, E, A (2), D, F, Bel; 1952 v W; 1953 v W, E, Ni, Se (30)

Steele, D. M. (Huddersfield), 1923 v E, W, Ni (3)

Stein, C. (Rangers), 1969 v W, Ni, D, E, Cy (2); 1970 v A (sub), Ni (sub), W, E, Ei, WG; 1971 v D, USSR, Bel, D; 1972 v Cz (sub); (with Coventry C), 1973 v E (2 sub), W (sub), Ni (21)

Stephen, J. F. (Bradford), 1947 v W; 1948 v W (2)

Stevenson, G. (Motherwell), 1928 v W, Ni; 1930 v Ni, E, F; 1931 v E, W; 1932 v W, Ni; 1933 v Ni; 1934 v E; 1935 v Ni (12)

Stewart, A. (Queen's Park), 1888 v Ni; 1889 v W (2)

Stewart, A. (Third Lanark), 1894 v W (1)

Stewart, D. (Dumbarton), 1888 v Ni (1)

Stewart, D. (Queen's Park), 1893 v W; 1894 v Ni; 1897 v Ni (3)

Stewart, D. S. (Leeds U), 1978 v EG (1)

Stewart, G. (Hibernian), 1906 v W, E; (with Manchester C), 1907 v W (4)

Stewart, J. (Kilmarnock), 1977 v Ch (sub); (with Middlesbrough), 1979 v N (2)

Stewart, R. (West Ham U), 1981 v W, Ni, E; 1982 v Ni, P, W; 1984 v F; 1987 v Ei (2), L (10)

Stewart, W. E. (Queen's Park), 1898 v Ni; 1900 v Ni (2)

Storrier, D. (Celtic), 1899 v E, W, Ni (3)

Strachan, G. (Aberdeen), 1980 v Ni, W, E, Pol, H (sub); 1981 v Se, P; 1982 v Ni, P, Sp, Ho (sub), Nz, Br, USSR; 1983 v EG, Sw, Bel, Sw, Ni (sub), W, E, Ca (2 + 1 sub); 1984 v EG, Ni, E, F; (with Manchester U), 1985 v Sp (sub), E, Ic; 1986 v W, Aus, R, D, WG, U; 1987 v Bul, Ei (2); 1988 v H; 1989 v Sp; (with Leeds U), 1990 v F; 1991 v USSR, Bul, Sm; 1992 v Sw, R, Ni, Fi (50)

Sturrock, P. (Dundee U), 1981 v W (sub), Ni, E (sub); 1982 v P, Ni (sub), W (sub), E (sub); 1983 v EG (sub), Sw, Bel (sub), Ca (3); 1984 v W; 1985 v Y (sub); 1986 v Is (sub), Ho, D, U; 1987 v Bel (20)

Summers, W. (St Mirren), 1926 v E (1)

Symon, J. S. (Rangers), 1939 v H (1)

Tait, T. S. (Sunderland), 1911 v W (1)

Taylor, J. (Queen's Park), 1872 v E; 1873 v E; 1874 v E; 1875 v E; 1876 v E, W (6)

Taylor, J. D. (Dumbarton), 1892 v W; 1893 v W; 1894 v Ni; (with St Mirren), 1895 v Ni (4)

Taylor, J. (Hearts), 1892 v E (1)

Telfer, W. (Motherwell), 1933 v Ni; 1934 v Ni (2)

Telfer, W. D. (St Mirren), 1954 v W (1)

Templeton, R. (Aston Villa), 1902 v E; (with Newcastle U), 1903 v E, W; 1904 v E; (with Woolwich Arsenal), 1905 v W; (with Kilmarnock), 1908 v Ni; 1910 v E, Ni; 1912 v E, Ni; 1913 v W (11)

Thomson, A. (Arthurlie), 1886 v Ni (1)

Thomson, A. (Third Lanark), 1889 v W (1)

Thomson, A. (Airdrieonians), 1909 v Ni (1)

Thomson, A. (Celtic), 1926 v E; 1932 v F; 1933 v W (3)

Thomson, C. (Hearts), 1904 v Ni; 1905 v E, Ni, W; 1906 v W, Ni; 1907 v E, W, Ni; 1908 v E, W, Ni; (with Sunderland), 1909 v W; 1910 v E; 1911 v Ni; 1912 v E, W; 1913 v E, W; 1914 v E, Ni (21)

Thomson, C. (Sunderland), 1937 v Cz (1)

Thomson, D. (Dundee), 1920 v W (1)

Thomson, J. (Celtic), 1930 v F; 1931 v E, W, Ni (4)

Thomson, J. J. (Queen's Park), 1872 v E; 1873 v E; 1874 v E (3)

Thomson, J. R. (Everton), 1933 v W (1)

Thomson, R. (Celtic), 1932 v W (1)

Thomson, R. W. (Falkirk), 1927 v E (1)

Thomson, S. (Rangers), 1884 v W, Ni (2)

Thomson, W. (Dumbarton), 1892 v W; 1893 v W; 1898 v Ni, W (4)

Thomson, W. (Dundee), 1896 v W (1)

Thornton, R. (Rangers), 1947 v W, Ni; 1948 v E, Ni; 1949 v F; 1952 v D, Se (7)

Thomson, W. (St Mirren), 1980 v Ni; 1981 v Ni (sub+1) 1982 v P; 1983 v Ni, Ca; 1984 v EG (7)

Toner, W. (Kilmarnock), 1959 v W, Ni (2)

Townsley, T. (Falkirk), 1926 v W (1)

Troup, A. (Dundee), 1920 v E; 1921 v W, Ni; 1922 v Ni; (with Everton), 1926 v E (5)

Turnbull, E. (Hibernian), 1948 v Bel, Sw; 1951 v A; 1958 v H, Pol, Y, Par, F (8)

Turner, T. (Arthurlie), 1884 v W (1)

Turner, W. (Pollokshields Ath), 1885 v Ni; 1886 v Ni (2)

Ure, J. F. (Dundee), 1962 v W, Cz; 1963 v W, Ni, E, A, N, Sp; (with Arsenal), 1964 v Ni, N; 1968 v Ni (11)

Urquhart, D. (Hibernian), 1934 v W (1)

Vallance, T. (Rangers), 1877 v E, W; 1878 v E; 1879 v E, W; 1881 v E, W (7)

Venters, A. (Cowdenbeath), 1934 v Ni; (with Rangers), 1936 v E; 1939 v E (3)

Waddell, T. S. (Queen's Park), 1891 v Ni; 1892 v E; 1893 v E, Ni; 1895 v E, Ni (6)

Waddell, W. (Rangers), 1947 v W; 1949 v E, W, Ni, F; 1950 v E, Ni; 1951 v E, D, F, Bel, A; 1952 v Ni, W; 1954 v Ni; 1955 v W, Ni (17)

Wales, H. M. (Motherwell), 1933 v W (1)

Walker, A. (Celtic), 1988 v Co (sub) (1)

Walker, F. (Third Lanark), 1922 v W (1)

Walker, G. (St Mirren), 1930 v F; 1931 v Ni, A, Sw (4)

Walker, J. (Hearts), 1895 v Ni; 1897 v W; 1898 v Ni; (with Rangers), 1904 v W, Ni (5)

Walker, J. (Swindon T), 1911 v E, W, Ni; 1912 v E, W, Ni; 1913 v E, W, Ni (9)

Walker, N. (Hearts), 1993 v G (1)

Walker, R. (Hearts), 1900 v E, Ni; 1901 v E, W; 1902 v E, W, Ni; 1903 v E, W, Ni; 1904 v E, W, Ni; 1905 v E, W, Ni; 1906 v Ni; 1907 v E, Ni; 1908 v E, W, Ni; 1909 v E, W; 1912 v E, W, Ni; 1913 v E, W (29)

Walker, T. (Hearts), 1935 v E, W; 1936 v E, W, Ni; 1937 v G, E, W, Ni, A, Cz; 1938 v E, W, Ni, Cz, Ho; 1939 v E, W, Ni, H (20)

Walker, W. (Clyde), 1909 v Ni; 1910 v Ni (2)

Wallace, I. A. (Coventry C), 1978 v Bul (sub); 1979 v P (sub), W (3)

Wallace, W. S. B. (Hearts), 1965 v Ni; 1966 v E, Ho; (with Celtic), 1967 v E, USSR (sub); 1968 v Ni; 1969 v E (sub) (7)

Wardhaugh, J. (Hearts), 1955 v H; 1957 v Ni (2)

Wark, J. (Ipswich T), 1979 v W, Ni, E, Arg, N (sub); 1980 v Pe, A, Bel (2); 1981 v Is, Ni; 1982 v Se, Sp, Ho, Ni, Nz, Br, USSR; 1983 v EG, Sw (2), Ni, E (sub); 1984 v U, Bel, EG; (with Liverpool), E, F; 1985 v Y (29)

Watson, A. (Queen's Park), 1881 v E, W; 1882 v E (3)

Watson, J. (Sunderland), 1903 v E, W; 1904 v E; 1905 v E; (with Middlesbrough), 1909 v E, Ni (6)

Watson, J. (Motherwell), 1948 v Ni; (with Huddersfield T), 1954 v Ni (2)

Watson, J. A. K. (Rangers), 1878 v W (1)

Watson, P. R. (Blackpool), 1934 v A (1)

Watson, R. (Motherwell), 1971 v USSR (1)

Watson, W. (Falkirk), 1898 v W (1)

Watt, F. (Kilbirnie), 1889 v W, Ni; 1890 v W; 1891 v E (4)

Watt, W. W. (Queen's Park), 1887 v Ni (1)

Waugh, W. (Hearts), 1938 v Cz (1)

Weir, A. (Motherwell), 1959 v WG; 1960 v E, P, A, H, T (6)

Weir, J. (Third Lanark), 1887 v Ni (1)

Weir, J. B. (Queen's Park), 1872 v E; 1874 v E; 1875 v E; 1878 v W (4)

Weir, P. (St Mirren), 1980 v Ni, W, Pol (sub), H; (with Aberdeen), 1983 v Sw; 1984 v Ni (6)

White, John (Albion R), 1922 v W; (with Hearts), 1923 v Ni (2)

White, J. A. (Falkirk), 1959 v WG, Ho, P; 1960 v Ni; (with Tottenham H), 1960 v W, Pol, A, T; 1961 v W; 1962 v Ni, W, E, Cz (2); 1963 v W, Ni, E; 1964 v Ni, W, E, N, WG (22)

White, W. (Bolton W), 1907 v E; 1908 v E (2)

Whitelaw, J. (Vale of Leven), 1887 v Ni; 1890 v W (2)

Whyte, D. (Celtic), 1988 v Bel (sub), L; 1989 v Ch (sub); 1992 v US (sub); (with Middlesbrough), 1993 v P, I (6)

Wilson, A. (Sheffield W), 1907 v E; 1908 v E; 1912 v E; 1913 v E, W; 1914 v Ni (6)

Wilson, A. (Portsmouth), 1954 v Fi (1)

Wilson, A. N. (Dunfermline), 1920 v E, W, Ni; 1921 v E, W, Ni; (with Middlesbrough), 1922 v E, W, Ni; 1923 v E, W, Ni (12)

Wilson, D. (Queen's Park), 1900 v W (1)

Wilson, D. (Oldham Ath), 1913 v E (1)

Wilson, D. (Rangers), 1961 v E, W, Ni, Ei (2), Cz; 1962 v Ni, W, E, Cz, U; 1963 v W, E, A, N, Ei, Sp; 1964 v E, WG; 1965 v Ni, E, Fi (22)

Wilson, G. W. (Hearts), 1904 v W; 1905 v E, Ni; 1906 v W; (with Everton), 1907 v E; (with Newcastle U), 1909 v E (6)

Wilson, Hugh, (Newmilns), 1890 v W; (with Sunderland), 1897 v E; (with Third Lanark), 1902 v W; 1904 v Ni (4)

Wilson, I. A. (Leicester C), 1987 v E, Br; (with Everton), 1988 v Bel, Bul, L (5)

Wilson, J. (Vale of Leven), 1888 v W; 1889 v E; 1890 v E; 1891 v E (4)

Wilson, P. (Celtic), 1926 v Ni; 1930 v F; 1931 v Ni; 1933 v E (4)

Wilson, P. (Celtic), 1975 v Sp (sub) (1)

Wilson, R. P. (Arsenal), 1972 v P, Ho (2)

Wiseman, W. (Queen's Park), 1927 v W; 1930 v Ni (2)

Wood, G. (Everton), 1979 v Ni, E, Arg (sub); (with Arsenal), 1982 v Ni (4)

Woodburn, W. A. (Rangers), 1947 v E, Bel, L; 1948 v W, Ni; 1949 v E, F; 1950 v E, W, Ni, P, F; 1951 v E, W, Ni, A (2), D, F, Bel; 1952 v E, W, Ni, USA (24)

Wotherspoon, D. N. (Queen's Park), 1872 v E; 1873 v E (2)

Wright, K. (Hibernian), 1992 v Ni (1)

Wright, S. (Aberdeen), 1993 v G, Es (2)

Wright, T. (Sunderland), 1953 v W, Ni, E (3)

Wylie, T. G. (Rangers), 1890 v Ni (1)

Yeats, R. (Liverpool), 1965 v W; 1966 v I (2)

Yorston, B. C. (Aberdeen), 1931 v Ni (1)

Yorston, H. (Aberdeen), 1955 v W (1)

Young, A. (Hearts), 1960 v E, A (sub), H, T; 1961 v W, Ni; (with Everton), Ei; 1966 v P (8)

Young, A. (Everton), 1905 v E; 1907 v W (2)

Young, G. L. (Rangers), 1947 v E, Ni, Bel, L; 1948 v E, Ni, Bel, Sw, F; 1949 v E, W, Ni, F; 1950 v E, W, Ni, Sw, P, F; 1951 v E, W, Ni, A (2), D, F, Bel; 1952 v E, W, Ni, USA, D, Se; 1953 v W, E, Ni, Se; 1954 v Ni, W; 1955 v W, Ni, P, Y; 1956 v Ni, W, E, A; 1957 v E, Ni, W, Y, Sp, Sw (53)

Young, J. (Celtic), 1906 v Ni (1)

Younger, T. (Hibernian), 1955 v P, Y, A, H; 1956 v E, Ni, W, A; (with Liverpool), 1957 v E, Ni, W, Y, Sp (2), Sw, WG; 1958 v Ni, W, E, Sw, H, Pol, Y, Par (24)

WALES

Adams, H. (Berwyn R), 1882 v Ni, E; (with Druids), 1883 v Ni, E (4)

Aizlewood, M. (Charlton Ath), 1986 v S.Ar, Ca (2); 1987 v Fi; (with Leeds U), USSR, Fi (sub); 1988 v D (sub), Se, Ma, I; 1989 v Ho, Se (sub), WG; (with Bradford C), 1990 v Fi, WG, Ei, Cr; (with Bristol C), 1991 v D, Bel (2), L, Ei, Ic, Pol, WG; 1992 v Br, L, Ei, A, R, Ho, Arg, J; 1993 v Ei, Bel, Fa (36)

Allchurch, I. J. (Swansea T), 1951 v E, Ni, P, Sw; 1952 v E, S, Ni, R of UK; 1953 v S, E, Ni, F, Y; 1954 v S, E, Ni, A; 1955 v S, E, Ni, Y; 1956 v E, S, Ni, A; 1957 v E, S; 1958 v Ni, Is (2), H (2), M, Sw, Br; (with Newcastle U), 1959 v S, Ni; 1960 v E, S; 1961 v Ni, H, Sp (2); 1962 v E, S, Br (2), M; (with Cardiff C), 1963 v S, E, Ni, H (2); 1964 v E; 1965 v S, E, Ni, Gr, I, USSR; (with Swansea T), 1966 v USSR, E, S, D, Br (2), Ch (68)

Allchurch, L. (Swansea T), 1955 v Ni; 1956 v A; 1958 v S, Ni, EG, Is; 1959 v S; (with Sheffield U), 1962 v S, Ni, Br; 1964 v E (11)

Allen, B. W. (Coventry C), 1951 v S, E (2)

Allen, M. (Watford), 1986 v S.Ar (sub), Ca (1 + 1 sub); (with Norwich C), 1989 v Is (sub); 1990 v Ho, WG; (with Millwall), Ei, Se, Cr (sub); 1991 v L (sub), Ei (sub); 1992 v A; 1993 v Ei (sub) (13)

Arridge, S. (Bootle), 1892 v S, Ni; (with Everton), 1894 v Ni; 1895 v Ni; 1896 v E; (with New Brighton Tower), 1898 v E, Ni; 1899 v E (8)

Astley, D. J. (Charlton Ath), 1931 v Ni; (with Aston Villa), 1932 v E; 1933 v E, S, Ni; 1934 v E, S; 1935 v S; 1936 v E, Ni; (with Derby Co), 1939 v E, S; (with Blackpool), F (13)

Atherton, R. W. (Hibernian), 1899 v E, Ni; 1903 v E, S, Ni; (with Middlesbrough), 1904 v E, S, Ni; 1905 v Ni (9)

Bailiff, W. E. (Llanelly), 1913 v E, S, Ni; 1920 v Ni (4)

Baker, C. W. (Cardiff C), 1958 v M; 1960 v S, Ni; 1961 v S, E, Ei; 1962 v S (7)

Baker, W. G. (Cardiff C), 1948 v Ni (1)

Bamford, T. (Wrexham), 1931 v E, S, Ni; 1932 v Ni; 1933 v F (5)

Barnes, W. (Arsenal), 1948 v E, S, Ni; 1949 v E, S, Ni; 1950 v E, S, Ni, Bel; 1951 v E, S, Ni, P; 1952 v E, S, Ni, R of UK; 1954 v E, S; 1955 v S, Y (22)

Bartley, T. (Glossop NE), 1898 v E (1)

Bastock, A. M. (Shrewsbury), 1892 v Ni (1)

Beadles, G. H. (Cardiff C), 1925 v E, S (2)

Bell, W. S. (Shrewsbury Engineers), 1881 v E, S; (with Crewe Alex), 1886 v E, S, Ni (5)

Bennion, S. R. (Manchester U), 1926 v S; 1927 v S; 1928 v S, E, Ni; 1929 v S, E, Ni; 1930 v S; 1932 v Ni (10)

Berry, G. F. (Wolverhampton W), 1979 v WG; 1980 v Ei, WG (sub), T; (with Stoke C), 1983 v E (sub) (5)

Blackmore, C. G. (Manchester U), 1985 v N (sub); 1986 v S (sub), H (sub), S.Ar, Ei, U; 1987 v Fi (2), USSR, Cz; 1988 v D (2), Cz, Y, Se, Ma, I; 1989 v Ho, Fi, Is, WG; 1990 v F; Ho, WG, Cr; 1991 v Bel, L; 1992 v Ei (sub), A, R (sub), Ho, Arg, J; 1993 v Fa, Cy, Bel, Cz (37)

Blew, H. (Wrexham), 1899 v E, S, Ni; 1902 v S, Ni; 1903 v E, S; 1904 v E, S, Ni; 1905 v S, Ni; 1906 v E, S, Ni; 1907 v S; 1908 v E, S, Ni; 1909 v E, S; 1910 v E (22)

Boden, W. (Wrexham), 1880 v E (1)

Bodin, P. J. (Swindon T), 1990 v Cr; 1991 v D, Bel, L, Ei; (with C Palace), Bel, Ic, Pol, WG; 1992 v Br, G, L (sub); (with Swindon T), Ei (sub), Ho, Arg; 1993 v Ei, Bel, Cz, Fa (19)

Boulter, L. M. (Brentford), 1939 v Ni (1)

Bowdler, H. E. (Shrewsbury), 1893 v S (1)

Bowdler, J. C. H. (Shrewsbury), 1890 v Ni; (with Wolverhampton W), 1891 v S; 1892 v Ni; (with Shrewsbury), 1894 v E (4)

Bowen, D. L. (Arsenal), 1955 v S, Y; 1957 v Ni, Cz, EG; 1958 v E, S, Ni, EG, Is (2), H (2), M, Se, Br; 1959 v E, S, Ni (19)

Bowen, E. (Druids), 1880 v S; 1883 v S (2)

Bowen, M. R. (Tottenham H), 1986 v Ca (2 sub); (with Norwich C), 1988 v Y (sub); 1989 v Fi (sub), Is, Se, WG (sub); 1990 v Fi (sub), Ho, WG, Se; 1992 v Br (sub), G, L, Ei, A, R, Ho (sub), J; 1993 v Fa, Cy, Bel (1 + sub), Cz (sub) (24)

Bowsher, S. J. (Burnley), 1929 v Ni (1)

Boyle, T. (C Palace), 1981 v Ei, S (sub) (2)

Britten, T. J. (Parkgrove), 1878 v S; (with Presteigne), 1880 v S (2)

Brookes, S. J. (Llandudno), 1900 v E, Ni (2)

Brown, A. I. (Aberdare Ath), 1926 v Ni (1)

Bryan, T. (Oswestry), 1886 v E, Ni (2)

Buckland, T. (Bangor), 1899 v E (1)

Burgess, W. A. R. (Tottenham H), 1947 v E, S, Ni; 1948 v E, S; 1949 v E, S, Ni, P, Bel, Sw; 1950 v E, S, Ni, Bel; 1951 v S, Ni, P, Sw; 1952 v E, S, Ni, R of UK; 1953 v S, E, Ni, F, Y; 1954 v S, E, Ni, A (32)

Burke, T. (Wrexham), 1883 v E; 1884 v S; 1885 v E, S, Ni; (with Newton Heath), 1887 v E, S; 1888 v S (8)

Burnett, T. B. (Ruabon), 1877 v S (1)

Burton, A. D. (Norwich C), 1963 v Ni, H; (with Newcastle U), 1964 v E; 1969 v S, E, Ni, I, EG; 1972 v Cz (9)

Butler, J. (Chirk), 1893 v E, S, Ni (3)

Butler, W. T. (Druids), 1900 v S, Ni (2)

Cartwright, L. (Coventry C), 1974 v E (sub), S, Ni; 1976 v S (sub); 1977 v WG (sub); (with Wrexham), 1978 v Ir (sub); 1979 v Ma (7)

Carty, T. – See McCarthy – (Wrexham).

Challen, J. B. (Corinthians), 1887 v E, S; 1888 v E; (with Wellingborough GS), 1890 v E (4)

Chapman, T. (Newtown), 1894 v E, S, Ni; 1895 v S, Ni; (with Manchester C), 1896 v E; 1897 v E (7)

Charles, J. M. (Swansea C), 1981 v Cz, T (sub), S (sub), USSR (sub); 1982 v Ic; 1983 v N (sub), Y (sub), Bul (sub), S, Ni, Br; 1984 v Bul (sub); (with QPR), S (sub), S; (with Oxford U), 1985 v Ic (sub), Sp, Ic; 1986 v Ei; 1987 v Fi (19)

Charles, M. (Swansea T), 1955 v Ni; 1956 v E, S, A; 1957 v E, Ni, Cz (2), EG; 1958 v E, S, EG, Is (2), H (2), M, Se, Br; 1959 v E, S; (with Arsenal), 1961 v Ni, H, Sp (2); 1962 v E, S; (with Cardiff C), 1962 v Br, Ni; 1963 v S, H (31)

Charles, W. J. (Leeds U), 1950 v Ni; 1951 v Sw; 1953 v Ni, F, Y; 1954 v E, S, Ni, A; 1955 v S, E, Ni, Y; 1956 v E, S, A, Ni; 1957 v E, S, Ni, Cz (2), EG; (with Juventus), 1958 v Is (2), H (2) M, Se; 1960 v S; 1962 v E, Br (2), M; (with Leeds U), 1963 v S; (with Cardiff C), 1964 v S; 1965 v S, USSR (38)

Clarke, R. J. (Manchester C), 1949 v E; 1950 v S, Ni, Bel; 1951 v E, S, Ni, P, Sw; 1952 v S, E, Ni, R of UK; 1953 v S, E; 1954 v E, S, Ni; 1955 v Y, S, E; 1956 v Ni (22)

Coleman, C. (C Palace), 1992 v A (sub); 1993 v Ei (sub) (2)

Collier, D. J. (Grimsby T), 1921 v S (1)

Collins, W. S. (Llanelly), 1931 v S (1)

Conde, S. (Chirk), 1884 v E, S, Ni (3)

Cook, F. C. (Newport Co), 1925 v E, S; (with Portsmouth), 1928 v E, S; 1930 v E, S, Ni; 1932 v E (8)

Crompton, W. (Wrexham), 1931 v E, S, Ni (3)

Cross, E. A. (Wrexham), 1876 v S; 1877 v S (2)

Cross, K. (Druids), 1879 v S; 1881 v E, S (3)

Crowe, V. H. (Aston Villa), 1959 v E, Ni; 1960 v E, Ni; 1961 v S, E, Ni, Ei, H, Sp (2); 1962 v E, S, Br, M; 1963 v H (16)

Cumner, R. H. (Arsenal), 1939 v E, S, Ni (3)

Curtis, A. (Swansea C), 1976 v E, Y (sub), S, Ni, Y (sub), E; 1977 v WG, S (sub), Ni (sub); 1978 v WG, E, S; 1979 v WG, S; (with Leeds U), E, Ni, Ma; 1980 v Ei, WG, T; (with Swansea C), 1982 v Cz, Ic, USSR, Sp, E, S, Ni; 1983 v N; 1984 v R (sub); (with Southampton), S; 1985 v Sp, N (1 + 1 sub); 1986 v H; (with Cardiff C), 1987 v USSR (35)

Curtis, E. R. (Cardiff C), 1928 v S; (with Birmingham), 1932 v S; 1934 v Ni (3)

Daniel, R. W. (Arsenal), 1951 v E, Ni, P; 1952 v E, S, Ni, R of UK; 1953 v S, E, Ni, F, Y; (with Sunderland), 1954 v E, S, Ni; 1955 v E, Ni; 1957 v S, E, Ni, Cz (21)

Darvell, S. (Oxford University), 1897 v S, Ni (2)

Davies, A. (Manchester U), 1983 v Ni, Br; 1984 v E, Ni; 1985 v Ic; (with Newcastle U), 1986 v H; (with Swansea C), 1988 v Ma, I; 1989 v Ho; (with Bradford C), 1990 v Fi, Ei (11)

Davies, A. (Wrexham), 1876 v S; 1877 v S (2)

Davies, A. (Druids), 1904 v S; (with Middlesbrough), 1905 v S (2)

Davies, A. O. (Barmouth), 1885 v Ni; 1886 v E, S; (with Swifts), 1887 v E, S; 1888 v E, Ni; (with Wrexham), 1889 v S; (with Crewe Alex), 1890 v E (9)

Davies, A. T. (Shrewsbury), 1891 v Ni (1)

Davies, C. (Brecon), 1899 v Ni; (with Hereford), 1900 v Ni (2)

Davies, C. (Charlton Ath), 1972 v R (sub) (1)

Davies, D. (Bolton W), 1904 v S, Ni; 1908 v E (sub) (3)

Davies, D. C. (Brecon), 1899 v Ni; (with Hereford); 1900 v Ni (2)

Davies, D. W. (Treharris), 1912 v Ni; (with Oldham Ath), 1913 v Ni (2)

Davies, E. Lloyd (Stoke C), 1904 v E; 1907 v E, S, Ni; (with Northampton T), 1908 v S; 1909 v Ni; 1910 v Ni; 1911 v E, S; 1912 v E, S; 1913 v E, S; 1914 v Ni, E, S (16)

Davies, E. R. (Newcastle U), 1953 v S, E; 1954 v E, S; 1958 v E, EG (6)

Davies, G. (Fulham), 1980 v T, Ic; 1982 v Sp (sub), F (sub); 1983 v E, Bul, S, Ni, Br; 1984 v R (sub), S (sub), E, Ni; 1985 v Ic; (with Manchester C), 1986 v S.Ar, Ei (16)

Davies, Rev. H. (Wrexham), 1928 v Ni (1)

Davies, Idwal (Liverpool Marine), 1923 v S (1)

Davies, J. E. (Oswestry), 1885 v E (1)

Davies, Jas (Wrexham), 1878 v S (1)

Davies, John (Wrexham), 1879 v S (1)

Davies, Jos (Newton Heath), 1888 v E, S, Ni; 1889 v S; 1890 v E; (with Wolverhampton W), 1892 v E; 1893 v E (7)

Davies, Jos (Everton), 1889 v S, Ni; (with Chirk), 1891 v Ni; (with Ardwick), v E, S; (with Sheffield U), 1895 v E, S, Ni; (with Manchester C), 1896 v E; (with Millwall), 1897 v E; (with Reading), 1900 v E (11)

Davies, J. P. (Druids), 1883 v E, Ni (2)

Davies, Ll. (Wrexham), 1907 v Ni; 1910 v Ni, S, E; (with Everton), 1911 v S, Ni; 1912 v Ni, S, E; 1913 v Ni, S, E; 1914 v Ni (13)

Davies, L. S. (Cardiff C), 1922 v E, S, Ni; 1923 v E, S, Ni; 1924 v E, S, Ni; 1925 v S, Ni; 1926 v E, Ni; 1927 v E, Ni; 1928 v S, Ni, E; 1929 v S, Ni, E; 1930 v E, S (23)

Davies, O. (Wrexham), 1890 v S (1)

Davies, R. (Wrexham), 1883 v Ni; 1884 v Ni; 1885 v Ni (3)

Davies, R. (Druids), 1885 v E (1)

Davies, R. O. (Wrexham), 1892 v Ni, E (2)

Davies, R. T. (Norwich C), 1964 v Ni; 1965 v E; 1966 v Br (2), Ch; (with Southampton), 1967 v S, E, Ni; 1968 v S, Ni, WG; 1969 v S, E, Ni, I, WG, R of UK; 1970 v E, S, Ni; 1971 v Cz, S, E, Ni; 1972 v R, E, S, N; (with Portsmouth), 1974 v E (29)

Davies, R. W. (Bolton W), 1964 v E; 1965 v E, S, Ni, D, Gr, USSR; 1966 v E, S, Ni, USSR, D, Br (2), Ch (sub);

1967 v S; (with Newcastle U), E; 1968 v S, Ni, WG; 1969 v S, E, Ni, I; 1970 v EG; 1971 v R, Cz; (with Manchester C), 1972 v E, S, Ni; (with Manchester U), 1973 v E, S (sub), Ni; (with Blackpool), 1974 v Pol (34)

Davies, Stanley (Preston NE), 1920 v E, S, Ni; (with Everton), 1921 v E, S, Ni; (with WBA), 1922 v E, S, Ni; 1923 v S; 1925 v S, Ni; 1926 v S, E, Ni; 1927 v S; 1928 v S; (with Rotherham U), 1930 v Ni (18)

Davies, T. (Oswestry), 1886 v E (1)

Davies, T. (Druids), 1903 v E, Ni, S; 1904 v S (4)

Davies, W. (Wrexham), 1884 v Ni (1)

Davies, W. (Swansea T), 1924 v E, S, Ni; (with Cardiff C), 1925 v E, S, Ni; 1926 v E, S, Ni; 1927 v S; 1928 v Ni; (with Notts Co), 1929 v E, S, Ni; 1930 v E, S, Ni (17)

Davies, William (Wrexham), 1903 v Ni; 1905 v Ni; (with Blackburn R), 1908 v E, S; 1909 v E, S, Ni; 1911 v E, S, Ni; 1912 v Ni (11)

Davies, W. C. (C Palace), 1908 v S; (with WBA), 1909 v E; 1910 v S; (with C Palace), 1914 v E (4)

Davies, W. D. (Everton), 1975 v H, L, S, E, Ni; 1976 v Y (2), E, Ni; 1977 v WG, S (2), Cz, E, Ni; 1978 v K; (with Wrexham), S, Cz, WG, Ir, E, S, Ni; 1979 v Ma, T, WG, S, E, Ni, Ma; 1980 v Ei, WG, T, E, S, Ni, Ic; 1981 v T, Cz, Ei, T, S, E, USSR; (with Swansea C), 1982 v Cz, Ic, USSR, Sp, E, S, F; 1983 v Y (52)

Davies, W. H. (Oswestry), 1876 v S; 1877 v S; 1879 v E; 1880 v E (4)

Davies, W. O. (Millwall Ath), 1913 v E, S, Ni; 1914 v S, Ni (5)

Davis, G. (Wrexham), 1978 v Ir, E (sub), Ni (3)

Day, A. (Tottenham H), 1934 v Ni (1)

Deacy, N. (PSV Eindhoven), 1977 v Cz, S, E, Ni; 1978 v K (sub), S (sub), Cz (sub), WG, Ir, S (sub), Ni; (with Beringen), 1979 v T (12)

Dearson, D. J. (Birmingham), 1939 v S, Ni, F (3)

Derrett, S. C. (Cardiff C), 1969 v S, WG; 1970 v I; 1971 v Fi (4)

Dewey, F. T. (Cardiff Corinthians), 1931 v E, S (2)

Dibble, A. (Luton T), 1986 v Ca (1 + 1 sub); (with Manchester C), 1989 v Is (3)

Doughty, J. (Druids), 1886 v S; (with Newton Heath), 1887 v S, Ni; 1888 v E, S, Ni; 1889 v S; 1890 v E (8)

Doughty, R. (Newton Heath and Druids), 1888 v S, Ni (2)

Durban, A. (Derby Co), 1966 v Br (sub); 1967 v Ni; 1968 v E, S, Ni, WG; 1969 v EG, S, E, Ni, WG; 1970 v E, S, Ni, EG, I; 1971 v R, S, E, Ni, Cz, Fi; 1972 v Fi, Cz, E, S, Ni (27)

Dwyer, P. (Cardiff C), 1978 v Ir, E, S, Ni; 1979 v T, S, E, Ni, Ma (sub); 1980 v WG (10)

Edwards, C. (Wrexham), 1878 v S (1)

Edwards, G. (Birmingham C), 1947 v E, S, Ni; 1948 v E, S, Ni; (with Cardiff C), 1949 v Ni, P, Bel, Sw; 1950 v E, S (12)

Edwards, H. (Wrexham Civil Service), 1878 v S; 1880 v E; 1882 v E, S; 1883 v S; 1884 v Ni; 1887 v Ni (7)

Edwards, J. H. (Wanderers), 1876 v S (1)

Edwards, J. H. (Oswestry), 1895 v Ni; 1897 v E, Ni (3)

Edwards, J. H. (Aberystwyth), 1898 v Ni (1)

Edwards, L. T. (Charlton Ath), 1957 v Ni, EG (2)

Edwards, R. I. (Chester), 1978 v K (sub); 1979 v Ma, WG; (with Wrexham), 1980 v T (sub) (4)

Edwards, T. (Linfield), 1932 v S (1)

Egan, W. (Chirk), 1892 v S (1)

Ellis, B. (Motherwell), 1932 v E; 1933 v E, S; 1934 v S; 1936 v E; 1937 v S (6)

Ellis, E. (Nunhead), 1931 v S; (with Oswestry), E; 1932 v Ni (3)

Emanuel, W. J. (Bristol C), 1973 v E (sub), Ni (sub) (2)

England, H. M. (Blackburn R), 1962 v Ni, Br, M; 1963 v Ni, H; 1964 v S, Ni; 1965 v E, D, Gr (2), USSR, Ni, I; 1966 v E, S, Ni, USSR, D; (with Tottenham H), 1967 v S, E; 1968 v E, Ni, WG; 1969 v EG; 1970 v R of UK,

EG, E, S, Ni, I; 1971 v R; 1972 v Fi, E, S, Ni; 1973 v E (3), S; 1974 v Pol; 1975 v H, L (44)

Evans, B. C. (Swansea C), 1972 v Fi, Cz; 1973 v E (2), Pol, S; (with Hereford U), 1974 v Pol (7)

Evans, D. G. (Reading), 1926 v Ni; 1927 v Ni, E; (with Huddersfield T), 1929 v S (4)

Evans, H. P. (Cardiff C), 1922 v E, S, Ni; 1924 v E, S, Ni (6)

Evans, I. (C Palace), 1976 v A, E, Y (2), E, Ni; 1977 v WG, S (2), Cz, E, Ni; 1978 v K (13)

Evans, J. (Oswestry), 1893 v Ni; 1894 v E, Ni (3)

Evans, J. (Cardiff C), 1912 v Ni; 1913 v Ni; 1914 v S; 1920 v S, Ni; 1922 v Ni; 1923 v E, Ni (8)

Evans, J. H. (Southend U), 1922 v E, S, Ni; 1923 v S (4)

Evans, Len (Aberdare Ath), 1927 v Ni; (with Cardiff C), 1931 v E, S; (with Birmingham), 1934 v Ni (4)

Evans, M. (Oswestry), 1884 v E (1)

Evans, R. (Clapton), 1902 v Ni (1)

Evans, R. E. (Wrexham), 1906 v E, S; (with Aston Villa), Ni; 1907 v E; 1908 v E, S; (with Sheffield U), 1909 v S; 1910 v E, S, Ni (10)

Evans, R. O. (Wrexham), 1902 v Ni; 1903 v E, S, Ni; (with Blackburn R), 1908 v Ni; (with Coventry C), 1911 v E, Ni; 1912 v E, S, Ni (10)

Evans, R. S. (Swansea T), 1964 v Ni (1)

Evans, T. J. (Clapton Orient), 1927 v S; 1928 v E, S; (with Newcastle U), Ni (4)

Evans, W. (Tottenham H), 1933 v Ni; 1934 v S; 1935 v E; 1936 v E, Ni (6)

Evans, W. A. W. (Oxford University), 1876 v S; 1877 v S (2)

Evans, W. G. (Bootle), 1890 v E; 1891 v E; (with Aston Villa), 1892 v E (3)

Evelyn, E. C. (Crusaders), 1887 v E (1)

Eyton-Jones, J. A. (Wrexham), 1883 v Ni; 1884 v Ni, E, S (4)

Farmer, G. (Oswestry), 1885 v E, S (2)

Felgate, D. (Lincoln C), 1984 v R (sub) (1)

Finnigan, R. J. (Wrexham), 1930 v Ni (1)

Flynn, B. (Burnley), 1975 v L (2 sub), H (sub), S, E, Ni; 1976 v A, E, Y (2), E, Ni; 1977 v WG (sub), S (2), Cz, E, Ni; 1978 v K (2), S; (with Leeds U), Cz, WG, Ir (sub), E, S, Ni; 1979 v Ma, T, S, E, Ni, Ma; 1980 v Ei, WG, E, S, Ni, Ic; 1981 v T, Cz, Ei, T, S, E, USSR; 1982 v Cz, USSR, E, S, Ni, F; 1983 v N; (with Burnley), Y, E, Bul, S, Ni, Br; 1984 v N, R, Bul, Y, S, N, Is (66)

Ford, T. (Swansea T), 1947 v S; (with Aston Villa), 1947 v Ni; 1948 v S, Ni; 1949 v E, S, Ni, P, Bel, Sw; 1950 v E, S, Ni, Bel; 1951 v S; (with Sunderland), 1951 v E, Ni, P, Sw; 1952 v E, S, Ni, R of UK; 1953 v S, E, Ni, F, Y; (with Cardiff C), 1954 v A; 1955 v S, E, Ni, Y; 1956 v S, Ni, E, A; 1957 v S (38)

Foulkes, H. E. (WBA), 1932 v Ni (1)

Foulkes, W. I. (Newcastle U), 1952 v E, S, Ni, R of UK; 1953 v E, S, F, Y; 1954 v E, S, Ni (11)

Foulkes, W. T. (Oswestry), 1884 v Ni; 1885 v S (2)

Fowler, J. (Swansea T), 1925 v E; 1926 v E, Ni; 1927 v S; 1928 v S; 1929 v E (6)

Garner, J. (Aberystwyth), 1896 v S (1)

Giggs, R. J. (Manchester U), 1992 v G (sub), L (sub), R (sub); 1993 v Fa (sub), Bel (sub + 1), Cz, Fa (8)

Giles, D. (Swansea C), 1980 v E, S, Ni, Ic; 1981 v T, Cz, T (sub), E (sub), USSR (sub); (with C Palace), 1982 v Sp (sub); 1983 v Ni (sub), Br (12)

Gillam, S. G. (Wrexham), 1889 v S (sub), Ni; (with Shrewsbury), 1890 v E, Ni; (with Clapton), 1894 v S (5)

Glascodine, G. (Wrexham), 1879 v E (1)

Glover, E. M. (Grimsby T), 1932 v S; 1934 v Ni; 1936 v S; 1937 v E, S, Ni; 1939 v Ni (8)

Godding, G. (Wrexham), 1923 v S, Ni (2)

Godfrey, B. C. (Preston NE), 1964 v Ni; 1965 v D, I (3)

Goodwin, U. (Ruthin), 1881 v E (1)

Goss, J. (Norwich C), 1991 v Ic, Pol (sub); 1992 v A (3)

Gough, R. T. (Oswestry White Star), 1883 v S (1)

Gray, A. (Oldham Ath), 1924 v E, S, Ni; 1925 v E, S, Ni; 1926 v E, S; 1927 v S; (with Manchester C), 1928 v E, S; 1929 v E, S, Ni; (with Manchester Central), 1930 v S; (with Tranmere R), 1932 v E, S, Ni; (with Chester), 1937 v E, S, Ni; 1938 v E, S, Ni (24)

Green, A. W. (Aston Villa), 1901 v Ni; (with Notts Co), 1903 v E; 1904 v S, Ni; 1906 v Ni, E; (with Nottingham F), 1907 v E; 1908 v S (8)

Green, C. R. (Birmingham C), 1965 v USSR, I; 1966 v E, S, USSR, Br (2); 1967 v E; 1968 v E, S, Ni, WG; 1969 v S, I, Ni (sub) (15)

Green, G. H. (Charlton Ath), 1938 v Ni; 1939 v E, Ni, F (4)

Grey, Dr W. (Druids), 1876 v S; 1878 v S (2)

Griffiths, A. T. (Wrexham), 1971 v Cz (sub); 1975 v A, H (2), L (2), E, Ni; 1976 v A, E, S, E (sub), Ni, Y (2); 1977 v WG, S (17)

Griffiths, F. J. (Blackpool), 1900 v E, S (2)

Griffiths, G. (Chirk), 1887 v Ni (1)

Griffiths, J. H. (Swansea T), 1953 v Ni (1)

Griffiths, L. (Wrexham), 1902 v S (1)

Griffiths, M. W. (Leicester C), 1947 v Ni; 1949 v P, Bel; 1950 v E, S, Bel; 1951 v E, Ni, P, Sw; 1954 v A (11)

Griffiths, P. (Chirk), 1884 v E, Ni; 1888 v E; 1890 v S, Ni; 1891 v Ni (6)

Griffiths, P. H. (Everton), 1932 v S (1)

Griffiths, S. (Wrexham), 1902 v S (1)

Griffiths, T. P. (Everton), 1927 v E, Ni; 1929 v E; 1930 v E; 1931 v Ni; 1932 v Ni, S, E; (with Bolton W), 1933 v E, S, Ni; (with Middlesbrough), F; 1934 v E, S; 1935 v E, Ni; 1936 v S; (with Aston Villa), Ni; 1937 v E, S, Ni (21)

Hall, G. D. (Chelsea), 1988 v Y (sub), Ma, I; 1989 v Ho, Fi, Is; 1990 v Ei; 1991 v Ei; 1992 v A (sub) (9)

Hallam, J. (Oswestry), 1889 v E (1)

Hanford, H. (Swansea T), 1934 v Ni; 1935 v S; 1936 v E; (with Sheffield W), 1936 v Ni; 1938 v E, S; 1939 v F (7)

Harrington, A. C. (Cardiff C), 1956 v Ni; 1957 v E, S; 1958 v S, Ni, Is (2); 1961 v S, E; 1962 v E, S (11)

Harris, C. S. (Leeds U), 1976 v E, S; 1978 v WG, Ir, E, S, Ni; 1979 v Ma, T, WG, E (sub), Ma; 1980 v Ni (sub), Ic (sub); 1981 v T, Cz (sub), Ei, T, S, E, USSR; 1982 v Cz, Ic, E (sub) (24)

Harris, W. C. (Middlesbrough), 1954 v A; 1957 v EG, Cz; 1958 v E, S, EG (6)

Harrison, W. C. (Wrexham), 1899 v E; 1900 v E, S, Ni; 1901 v Ni (5)

Hayes, A. (Wrexham), 1890 v Ni; 1894 v Ni (2)

Hennessey, W. T. (Birmingham C), 1962 v Ni, Br (2); 1963 v S, E, H (2); 1964 v E, S; 1965 v S, E, D, Gr, USSR; 1966 v E, USSR; (with Nottingham F), 1966 v S, Ni, D, Br (2), Ch; 1967 v S, E; 1968 v E, S, Ni; 1969 v WG, EG, R of UK; 1970 v EG; (with Derby Co), E, S, Ni; 1972 v Fi, Cz, E, S; 1973 v E (39)

Hersee, A. M. (Bangor), 1886 v S, Ni (2)

Hersee, R. (Llandudno), 1886 v Ni (1)

Hewitt, R. (Cardiff C), 1958 v Ni, Is, Se, H, Br (5)

Hewitt, T. J. (Wrexham), 1911 v E, S, Ni; (with Chelsea), 1913 v E, S, Ni; (with South Liverpool), 1914 v E, S (8)

Heywood, D. (Druids), 1879 v E (1)

Hibbott, H. (Newtown Excelsior), 1880 v E, S; (with Newtown), 1885 v S (3)

Higham, G. G. (Oswestry), 1878 v S; 1879 v E (2)

Hill, M. R. (Ipswich T), 1972 v Cz, R (2)

Hockey, T. (Sheffield U), 1972 v Fi, R; 1973 v E (2); (with Norwich C), Pol, S, E, Ni; (with Aston Villa), 1974 v Pol (9)

Hoddinott, T. F. (Watford), 1921 v E, S (2)

Hodges, G. (Wimbledon), 1984 v N (sub), Is (sub); 1987 v USSR, Fi, Cz; (with Newcastle U), 1988 v D; (with

Watford), D (sub), Cz (sub), Se, Ma (sub), I (sub); 1990 v Se, Cr; (with Sheffield U), 1992 v Br (sub), Ei (sub), A (16)

Hodgkinson, A. V. (Southampton), 1908 v Ni (1)

Holden, A. (Chester C), 1984 v Is (sub) (1)

Hole, B. G. (Cardiff C), 1963 v Ni; 1964 v Ni; 1965 v S, E, Ni, D, Gr (2), USSR, I; 1966 v E, S, Ni, USSR, D, Br (2), Ch; (with Blackburn R), 1967 v S, E, Ni; 1968 v E, S, Ni, WG; (with Aston Villa), 1969 v I, WG, EG; 1970 v I; (with Swansea C), 1971 v R (30)

Hole, W. J. (Swansea T), 1921 v Ni; 1922 v E; 1923 v E, Ni; 1928 v E, S, Ni; 1929 v E, S (9)

Hollins, D. M. (Newcastle U), 1962 v Br (sub), M; 1963 v Ni, H; 1964 v E; 1965 v Ni, Gr, I; 1966 v S, D, Br (11)

Hopkins, I. J. (Brentford), 1935 v S, Ni; 1936 v E, Ni; 1937 v E, S, Ni; 1938 v E, Ni; 1939 v E, S, Ni (12)

Hopkins, J. (Fulham), 1983 v Ni, Br; 1984 v N, R, Bul, Y, S, E, Ni, N, Is; 1985 v Ic (1 + 1 sub), N; (with C Palace), 1990 v Ho, Cr (16)

Hopkins, M. (Tottenham H), 1956 v Ni; 1957 v Ni, S, E, Cz (2), EG; 1958 v E, S, Ni, EG, Is (2), H (2), M, Se, Br; 1959 v E, S, Ni; 1960 v E, S; 1961 v Ni, H, Sp (2); 1962 v Ni, Br (2), M; 1963 v S, Ni, H (34)

Horne, B. (Portsmouth), 1988 v D (sub), Y, Se (sub), Ma, I; 1989 v Ho, Fi, Is; (with Southampton), Se, WG; 1990 v WG (sub), Ei, Se, Cr; 1991 v D, Bel (2), L, Ei, Ic, Pol, WG; 1992 v Br, G, L, Ei, A, R, Ho, Arg, J; (with Everton), 1993 v Fa, Cy, Bel, Ei, Bel, Cz, Fa (38)

Howell, E. G. (Builth), 1888 v Ni; 1890 v E; 1891 v E (3)

Howells, R. G. (Cardiff C), 1954 v E, S (2)

Hugh, A. R. (Newport Co), 1930 v Ni (1)

Hughes, A. (Rhos), 1894 v E, S (2)

Hughes, A. (Chirk), 1907 v Ni (1)

Hughes, C. M. (Luton T), 1992 v Ho (sub) (1)

Hughes, E. (Everton), 1899 v S, Ni; (with Tottenham H), 1901 v E, S; 1902 v Ni; 1904 v E, Ni, S; 1905 v E, Ni, S; 1906 v E, Ni; 1907 v E (14)

Hughes, E. (Wrexham), 1906 v S; (with Nottingham F), 1906 v Ni; 1908 v S, E; 1910 v Ni, E, S; 1911 v Ni, E, S; (with Wrexham), 1912 v Ni, E, S; (with Manchester C), 1913 v E, S; 1914 v N (16)

Hughes, F. W. (Northwich Victoria), 1882 v E, Ni; 1883 v E, Ni, S; 1884 v S (6)

Hughes, I. (Luton T), 1951 v E, Ni, P, Sw (4)

Hughes, J. (Cambridge University), 1877 v S; (with Aberystwyth), 1879 v S (2)

Hughes, J. (Liverpool), 1905 v E, S, Ni (3)

Hughes, J. I. (Blackburn R), 1935 v Ni (1)

Hughes, L. M. (Manchester U), 1984 v E, Ni; 1985 v Ic, Sp, Ic, N, S, Sp, N; 1986 v S, H, U; (with Barcelona), 1987 v USSR, Cz; 1988 v D (2), Cz, Se, Ma, I; (with Manchester U), 1989 v Ho, Fi, Is, Se, WG; 1990 v Fi, WG, Cr; 1991 v D, Bel (2), L, Ic, Pol, WG; 1992 v Br, G, L, Ei, R, Ho, Arg, J; 1993 v Fa, Cy, Bel, Ei, Bel, Cz, Fa (50)

Hughes, P. W. (Bangor), 1887 v Ni; 1889 v Ni, E (3)

Hughes, W. (Bootle), 1891 v E; 1892 v S, Ni (3)

Hughes, W. A. (Blackburn R), 1949 v E, Ni, P, Bel, Sw (5)

Hughes, W. M. (Birmingham), 1938 v E, Ni, S; 1939 v E, Ni, S, F; 1947 v E, S, Ni (10)

Humphreys, J. V. (Everton), 1947 v Ni (1)

Humphreys, R. (Druids), 1888 v Ni (1)

Hunter, A. H. (FA of Wales Secretary), 1887 v Ni (1)

Jackett, K. (Watford), 1983 v N, Y, E, Bul, S; 1984 v N, R, Y, S, Ni, N, Is; 1985 v Ic, Sp, Ic, N, S, Sp, N; 1986 v S, H, S.Ar, Ei, Ca (2); 1987 v Fi (2); 1988 v D, Cz, Y, Se (31)

Jackson, W. (St Helens Rec), 1899 v Ni (1)

James, E. (Chirk), 1893 v E, Ni; 1894 v E, S, Ni; 1898 v S, E; 1899 v Ni (8)

James, E. G. (Blackpool), 1966 v Br (2), Ch; 1967 v Ni; 1968 v S; 1971 v Cz, S, E, Ni (9)

James, L. (Burnley), 1972 v Cz, R, S (sub); 1973 v E (3), Pol, S, Ni; 1974 v Pol, E, S, Ni; 1975 v A, H (2), L (2), S, E, Ni; 1976 v A; (with Derby Co), S, E, Y (2), Ni; 1977 v WG, S (2), Cz, E, Ni; 1978 v K (2); (with QPR), WG; (with Burnley), 1979 v T; (with Swansea C), 1980 v E, S, Ni, Ic; 1981 v T, Ei, T, S, E; 1982 v Cz, Ic, USSR, E (sub), S, Ni, F; (with Sunderland), 1983 v E (sub) (54)

James, R. M. (Swansea C), 1979 v Ma, WG (sub), S, E, Ni, Ma; 1980 v WG; 1982 v Cz (sub), Ic, Sp, E, S, Ni, F; 1983 v N, Y, E, Bul; (with Stoke C), 1984 v N, R, Bul, Y, S, E, Ni, N, Is; 1985 v Ic, Sp, Ic; (with QPR), N, S, Sp, N; 1986 v S, S.Ar, Ei, U, Ca (2); 1987 v Fi (2), USSR, Cz; (with Leicester C), 1988 v D (2); (with Swansea C), Y (47)

James, W. (West Ham U), 1931 v Ni; 1932 v Ni (2)

Jarrett, R. H. (Ruthin), 1889 v Ni; 1890 v S (2)

Jarvis, A. L. (Hull C), 1967 v S, E, Ni (3)

Jenkins, E. (Lovell's Ath), 1925 v E (1)

Jenkins, J. (Brighton), 1924 v Ni, E, S; 1925 v S, Ni; 1926 v E, S; 1927 v S (8)

Jenkins, R. W. (Rhyl), 1902 v Ni (1)

Jenkyns, C. A. L. (Small Heath), 1892 v E, S, Ni; 1895 v E; (with Woolwich Arsenal), 1896 v S; (with Newton Heath), 1897 v Ni; (with Walsall), 1898 v S, E (8)

Jennings, W. (Bolton W), 1914 v E, S; 1920 v S; 1923 v Ni, E; 1924 v E, S, Ni; 1927 v S, Ni; 1929 v S (11)

John, R. F. (Arsenal), 1923 v S, Ni; 1925 v Ni; 1926 v E; 1927 v E; 1928 v E, Ni; 1930 v E, S; 1932 v E; 1933 v F, Ni; 1935 v Ni; 1936 v S; 1937 v E (15)

John, W. R. (Walsall), 1931 v Ni; (with Stoke C), 1933 v E, S, Ni, F; 1934 v E, S; (with Preston NE), 1935 v E, S; (with Sheffield U), 1936 v E, S, Ni; (with Swansea T), 1939 v E, S (14)

Johnson, M. G. (Swansea T), 1964 v Ni (1)

Jones, A. (Port Vale), 1987 v Fi, Cz (sub); 1988 v D, (with Charlton Ath), D (sub), Cz (sub); 1990 v Hol (sub) (6)

Jones, A. F. (Oxford University), 1877 v S (1)

Jones, A. T. (Nottingham F), 1905 v E; (with Notts Co), 1906 v E (2)

Jones, Bryn (Wolverhampton W), 1935 v Ni; 1936 v E, S, Ni; 1937 v E, S, Ni; 1938 v E, S, Ni; (with Arsenal), 1939 v E, S, Ni; 1947 v S, Ni; 1948 v E; 1949 v S (17)

Jones, B. S. (Swansea T), 1963 v S, E, Ni, H (2); 1964 v S, Ni; (with Plymouth Arg), 1965 v D; (with Cardiff C), 1969 v S, E, Ni, I (sub), WG, EG, R of UK (15)

Jones, Charlie (Nottingham F), 1926 v E; 1927 v S, Ni; 1928 v E; (with Arsenal), 1930 v E, S; 1932 v E; 1933 v F (8)

Jones, Cliff (Swansea T), 1954 v A; 1956 v E, Ni, S, A; 1957 v E, S, Ni, Cz (2), EG; 1958 v EG, E, S, Is (2); (with Tottenham H), 1958 v Ni, H (2), M, Se, Br; 1959 v Ni; 1960 v E, S, Ni; 1961 v S, E, Ni, Sp, H, Ei; 1962 v E, Ni, S, Br (2), M; 1963 v S, Ni, H; 1964 v E, S, Ni; 1965 v E, S, Ni, D, Gr (2), USSR, I; 1967 v S, E; 1968 v E, S, WG; (with Fulham), 1969 v I, R of UK (59)

Jones, C. W. (Birmingham), 1935 v Ni; 1939 v F (2)

Jones, D. (Chirk), 1888 v S, Ni; (with Bolton W), 1889 v E, S, Ni; 1890 v E; 1891 v S; 1892 v Ni; 1893 v E; 1894 v E; 1895 v E; 1898 v S; (with Manchester C), 1900 v E, Ni (14)

Jones, D. E. (Norwich C), 1976 v S, E (sub); 1978 v S, Cz, WG, Ir, E; 1980 v E (8)

Jones, D. O. (Leicester C), 1934 v E, Ni; 1935 v E, S; 1936 v E, Ni; 1937 v Ni (7)

Jones, Evan (Chelsea), 1910 v S, Ni; (with Oldham Ath), 1911 v E, S; 1912 v E, S; (with Bolton W), 1914 v Ni (7)

Jones, F. R. (Bangor), 1885 v E, Ni; 1886 v S (3)

Jones, F. W. (Small Heath), 1893 v S (1)

Jones, G. P. (Wrexham), 1907 v S, Ni (2)

Jones, H. (Aberaman), 1902 v Ni (1)

866

Jones, Humphrey (Bangor), 1885 v E, Ni, S; 1886 v E, Ni, S; (with Queen's Park), 1887 v E; (with East Stirlingshire), 1889 v E, Ni; 1890 v E, S, Ni; (with Queen's Park), 1891 v E, S (14)

Jones, Ivor (Swansea T), 1920 v S, Ni; 1921 v Ni, E; 1922 v S, Ni; (with WBA), 1923 v E, Ni; 1924 v S; 1926 v Ni (10)

Jones, Jeffrey (Llandrindod Wells), 1908 v Ni; 1909 v Ni; 1910 v S (3)

Jones, J. (Druids), 1876 v S (1)

Jones, J. (Berwyn Rangers), 1883 v S, Ni; 1884 v S (3)

Jones, J. (Wrexham), 1925 v Ni (1)

Jones, J. L. (Sheffield U), 1895 v E, S, Ni; 1896 v Ni, S, E; 1897 v Ni, S, E; (with Tottenham H), 1898 v Ni, E, S; 1899 v S, Ni; 1900 v S; 1902 v E, S, Ni; 1904 v E, S, Ni (21)

Jones, J. Love (Stoke C), 1906 v S; (with Middlesbrough), 1910 v Ni (2)

Jones, J. O. (Bangor), 1901 v S, Ni (2)

Jones, J. P. (Liverpool), 1976 v A, E, S; 1977 v WG, S (2), Cz, E, Ni; 1978 v K (2), S, Cz, WG, Ir, E, S, Ni; (with Wrexham), 1979 v Ma, T, WG, S, E, Ni, Ma; 1980 v Ei, WG, T, E, S, Ni, Ic; 1981 v T, Ei, T, S, E, USSR; 1982 v Cz, Ic, USSR, Sp, E, S, Ni, F; 1983 v N; (with Chelsea), Y, E, Bul, S, Ni, Br; 1984 v N, R, Bul, Y, S, E, Ni, N, Is; 1985 v Ic, N, S, N; (with Huddersfield T), 1986 v S, H, Ei, U, Ca (2) (72)

Jones, J. T. (Stoke C), 1912 v E, S, Ni; 1913 v E, Ni; 1914 v S, Ni; 1920 v E, S, Ni; (with C Palace), 1921 v E, S; 1922 v E, S, Ni (15)

Jones, K. (Aston Villa), 1950 v S (1)

Jones, Leslie J. (Cardiff C), 1933 v F; (with Coventry C), 1935 v Ni; 1936 v S; 1937 v E, S, Ni; (with Arsenal), 1938 v E, S, Ni; 1939 v E, S (11)

Jones, P. W. (Bristol R), 1971 v Fi (1)

Jones, R. (Bangor), 1887 v S; 1889 v E; (with Crewe Alex), 1890 v E (3)

Jones, R. (Leicester Fosse), 1898 v S (1)

Jones, R. (Druids), 1899 v S (1)

Jones, R. (Bangor), 1900 v S, Ni (2)

Jones, R. (Millwall), 1906 v S, Ni (2)

Jones, R. A. (Druids), 1884 v E, Ni, S; 1885 v S (4)

Jones, R. S. (Everton), 1894 v Ni (1)

Jones, S. (Wrexham), 1887 v Ni; (with Chester), 1890 v S (2)

Jones, S. (Wrexham), 1893 v S, Ni; (with Burton Swifts), 1895 v S; 1896 v Ni; (with Druids), 1899 v E (6)

Jones, T. (Manchester U), 1926 v Ni; 1927 v E, Ni; 1930 v Ni (4)

Jones, T. D. (Aberdare), 1908 v Ni (1)

Jones, T. G. (Everton), 1938 v Ni; 1939 v E, S, Ni; 1947 v E, S; 1948 v E, S, Ni; 1949 v E, Ni, P, Bel, Sw; 1950 v E, S, Bel (17)

Jones, T. J. (Sheffield W), 1932 v Ni; 1933 v F (2)

Jones, W. E. A. (Swansea T), 1947 v E, S; (with Tottenham H), 1949 v E, S (4)

Jones, W. J. (Aberdare), 1901 v E, S, Ni; (with West Ham U), 1902 v S (4)

Jones, W. Lot (Manchester C), 1905 v E, Ni; 1906 v E, S, Ni; 1907 v E, S, Ni; 1908 v S; 1909 v E, S, Ni; 1910 v E; 1911 v E; 1913 v E, S; 1914 v S, Ni; (with Southend U), 1920 v E, Ni (20)

Jones, W. P. (Druids), 1889 v E, Ni; (with Wynstay), 1890 v S, Ni (4)

Jones, W. R. (Aberystwyth), 1897 v S (1)

Keenor, F. C. (Cardiff C), 1920 v E, Ni; 1921 v E, Ni, S; 1922 v Ni; 1923 v E, Ni, S; 1924 v E, Ni, S; 1925 v E, Ni, S; 1926 v S; 1927 v E, Ni, S; 1928 v E, Ni, S; 1929 v E, Ni, S; 1930 v E, Ni, S; 1931 v E, Ni, S; (with Crewe Alex), 1933 v S (32)

Kelly, F. C. (Wrexham), 1899 v S, Ni; (with Druids), 1902 v Ni (3)

Kelsey, A. J. (Arsenal), 1954 v Ni, A; 1955 v S, Ni, Y; 1956 v E, Ni, S, A; 1957 v E, Ni, S, Cz (2), EG; 1958 v E, S, Ni, Is (2), H (2), M, Se, Br; 1959 v E, S; 1960 v E, Ni, S; 1961 v E, Ni, S, H, Sp (2); 1962 v E, S, Ni, Br (2) (41)

Kenrick, S. L. (Druids), 1876 v S; 1877 v S; (with Oswestry), 1879 v E, S; (with Shropshire Wanderers), 1881 v E (5)

Ketley, C. F. (Druids), 1882 v Ni (1)

King, J. (Swansea T), 1955 v E (1)

Kinsey, N. (Norwich C), 1951 v Ni, P, Sw; 1952 v E; (with Birmingham C), 1954 v Ni; 1956 v E, S (7)

Knill, A. R. (Swansea C), 1989 v Ho (1)

Krzywicki, R. L. (WBA), 1970 v EG, I; (with Huddersfield T), Ni, E, S; 1971 v R, Fi; 1972 v Cz (sub) (8)

Lambert, R. (Liverpool), 1947 v S; 1948 v E; 1949 v P, Bel, Sw (5)

Latham, G. (Liverpool), 1905 v E, S; 1906 v S; 1907 v E, S, Ni; 1908 v E; 1909 v Ni; (with Southport Central), 1910 v E; (with Cardiff C), 1913 v Ni (10)

Law, B. J. (QPR), 1990 v Se (1)

Lawrence, E. (Clapton Orient), 1930 v Ni; (with Notts Co), 1932 v S (2)

Lawrence, S. (Swansea T), 1932 v Ni; 1933 v F; 1934 v S, E, Ni; 1935 v E, S; 1936 v S (8)

Lea, A. (Wrexham), 1889 v E; 1891 v S, Ni; 1893 v Ni (4)

Lea, C. (Ipswich T), 1965 v Ni, I (2)

Leary, P. (Bangor), 1889 v Ni (1)

Leek, K. (Leicester C), 1961 v S, E, Ni, H, Sp (2); (with Newcastle U), 1962 v S; (with Birmingham C), v Br (sub), M; 1963 v E; 1965 v S, Gr; (with Northampton T), 1965 v Gr (13)

Lever, A. R. (Leicester C), 1953 v S (1)

Lewis, B. (Chester), 1891 v Ni; (with Wrexham), 1892 v S, E, Ni; (with Middlesbrough), 1893 v S, E; (with Wrexham), 1894 v S, E, Ni; 1895 v S (10)

Lewis, D. (Arsenal), 1927 v E; 1928 v Ni; 1930 v E (3)

Lewis, D. (Swansea C), 1983 v Br (sub) (1)

Lewis, D. J. (Swansea T), 1933 v E, S (2)

Lewis, D. M. (Bangor), 1890 v Ni, S (2)

Lewis, J. (Bristol R), 1906 v E (1)

Lewis, J. (Cardiff C), 1926 v S (1)

Lewis, T. (Wrexham), 1881 v E, S (2)

Lewis, W. (Bangor), 1885 v E; 1886 v E, S; 1887 v E, S; 1888 v E; 1889 v E, Ni, S; (with Crewe Alex), 1890 v E; 1891 v E, S; 1892 v E, S, Ni; 1894 v E, S, Ni; (with Chester), 1895 v S, Ni, E; 1896 v E, S, Ni; (with Manchester C), 1897 v E, S; (with Chester), 1898 v Ni (27)

Lewis, W. L. (Swansea T), 1927 v E, Ni; 1928 v E, Ni; 1929 v S; (with Huddersfield T), 1930 v E (6)

Lloyd, B. W. (Wrexham), 1976 v A, E, S (3)

Lloyd, J. W. (Wrexham), 1879 v S; (with Newtown), 1885 v S (2)

Lloyd, R. A. (Ruthin), 1891 v Ni; 1895 v S (2)

Lockley, A. (Chirk), 1898 v Ni (1)

Lovell, S. (C Palace), 1982 v USSR (sub); (with Millwall), 1985 v N; 1986 v S (sub), H (sub), Ca (1 + 1 sub) (6)

Lowrie, G. (Coventry C), 1948 v E, S, Ni; (with Newcastle U), 1949 v P (4)

Lowndes, S. (Newport Co), 1983 v S (sub), Br (sub); (with Millwall), 1985 v N (sub); 1986 v S.Ar (sub), Ei, U, Ca (2); (with Barnsley), 1987 v Fi (sub); 1988 v Se (sub) (10)

Lucas, P. M. (Leyton Orient), 1962 v Ni, M; 1963 v S, E (4)

Lucas, W. H. (Swansea T), 1949 v S, Ni, P, Bel, Sw; 1950 v E; 1951 v E (7)

Lumberg, A. (Wrexham), 1929 v Ni; 1930 v E, S; (with Wolverhampton W), 1932 v S (4)

McCarthy, T. P. (Wrexham), 1899 v Ni (1)

McMillan, R. (Shrewsbury Engineers), 1881 v E, S (2)

Maguire, G. T. (Portsmouth), 1990 v Fi (sub), Ho, WG, Ei, Se; 1992 v Br (sub), G (7)

Mahoney, J. F. (Stoke C), 1968 v E; 1969 v EG; 1971 v Cz; 1973 v E (3), Pol, S, Ni; 1974 v Pol, E, S, Ni; 1975 v A, H (2), L (2), S, E, Ni; 1976 v A, Y (2), E, Ni; 1977 v WG, Cz, S, E, Ni; (with Middlesbrough), 1978 v K (2), S, Cz, Ir, E (sub), S, Ni; 1979 v WG, S, E, Ni, Ma; (with Swansea C), 1980 v Ei, WG, T (sub); 1982 v Ic, USSR; 1983 v Y, E (51)

Martin, T. J. (Newport Co), 1930 v Ni (1)

Marustik, C. (Swansea C), 1982 v Sp, E, S, Ni, F; 1983 v N (6)

Mates, J. (Chirk), 1891 v Ni; 1897 v E, S (3)

Mathews, R. W. (Liverpool), 1921 v Ni; (with Bristol C), 1923 v E; (with Bradford), 1926 v Ni (3)

Matthews, W. (Chester), 1905 v Ni; 1908 v E (2)

Matthias, J. S. (Brymbo), 1896 v S, Ni; (with Shrewsbury), 1897 v E, S; (with Wolverhampton W), 1899 v S (5)

Matthias, T. J. (Wrexham), 1914 v S, E; 1920 v Ni, S, E; 1921 v S, E, Ni; 1922 v S, E, Ni; 1923 v S (12)

Mays, A. W. (Wrexham), 1929 v Ni (1)

Medwin, T. C. (Swansea T), 1953 v Ni, F, Y; (with Tottenham H), 1957 v E, S, Ni, Cz (2), EG; 1958 v E, S, Ni, Is (2), H (2), M, Br; 1959 v E, S, Ni; 1960 v E, S, Ni; 1961 v S, Ei, E, Sp; 1963 v E, H (30)

Melville, A. K. (Swansea C), 1990 v WG, Ei, Se, Cr (sub); (with Oxford U), 1991 v Ic, Pol, WG; 1992 v Br, G, L, R, Ho, J (sub); 1993 v Cz, Fa (sub) (15)

Meredith, S. (Chirk), 1900 v S; 1901 v S, E, Ni; (with Stoke C), 1902 v E; 1903 v Ni; 1904 v E; (with Leyton), 1907 v E (8)

Meredith, W. H. (Manchester C), 1895 v E, Ni; 1896 v E, Ni; 1897 v E, Ni, S; 1898 v E, Ni; 1899 v E; 1900 v E, Ni; 1901 v E, Ni; 1902 v E, S; 1903 v E, S, Ni; 1904 v E; 1905 v E, S; (with Manchester U), 1907 v E, S, Ni; 1908 v E, Ni; 1909 v E, S, Ni; 1910 v E, S, Ni; 1911 v E, S, Ni; 1912 v E, S, Ni; 1913 v E, S, Ni; 1914 v E, S, Ni; 1920 v E, S, Ni (48)

Mielczarek, R. (Rotherham U), 1971 v Fi (1)

Millership, H. (Rotherham Co), 1920 v E, S, Ni; 1921 v E, S, Ni (6)

Millington, A. H. (WBA), 1963 v S, E, H; (with C Palace), 1965 v E, USSR; (with Peterborough U), 1966 v Ch, Br; 1967 v E, Ni; 1968 v Ni, WG; 1969 v I, EG; (with Swansea T), 1970 v E, S, Ni; 1971 v Cz, Fi; 1972 v Fi (sub), Cz, R (21)

Mills, T. J. (Clapton Orient), 1934 v E, Ni; (with Leicester C), 1935 v E, S (4)

Mills-Roberts, R. H. (St Thomas' Hospital), 1885 v E, S, Ni; 1886 v E; 1887 v E; (with Preston NE), 1888 v E, Ni; (with Llanberis), 1892 v E (8)

Moore, G. (Cardiff C), 1960 v E, S, Ni; 1961 v Ei, Sp; (with Chelsea), 1962 v Br; 1963 v Ni, H; (with Manchester U), 1964 v S, Ni; (with Northampton T), 1966 v Ni, Ch; (with Charlton Ath), 1969 v S, E, Ni, R of UK; 1970 v E, S, Ni, I; 1971 v R (21)

Morgan, J. R. (Cambridge University), 1877 v S; (with Swansea T), 1879 v S; (with Derby School Staff), 1880 v E, S; 1881 v E, S; 1882 v E, S, Ni; (with Swansea T), 1883 v E (10)

Morgan, J. T. (Wrexham), 1905 v Ni (1)

Morgan-Owen, H. (Oxford University), 1901 v E; 1902 v S; 1906 v E, Ni; (with Welshpool), 1907 v S (5)

Morgan-Owen, M. M. (Oxford University), 1897 v S, Ni; 1898 v E, S; 1899 v S; 1900 v E, S; (with Corinthians), 1903 v S; 1906 v S, E, Ni; 1907 v E (12)

Morley, E. J. (Swansea T), 1925 v E; (with Clapton Orient), 1929 v E, S, Ni (4)

Morris, A. G. (Aberystwyth), 1896 v E, Ni, S; (with Swindon C), 1897 v E; 1898 v S; (with Nottingham F), 1899 v E, S; 1903 v E, S; 1905 v E, S; 1907 v E, S; 1908 v Ni; 1910 v E, S, Ni; 1911 v E, S, Ni; 1912 v E (21)

Morris, C. (Chirk), 1900 v E, S, Ni; (with Derby Co), 1901 v E, S, Ni; 1902 v E, S; 1903 v E, S, Ni; 1904 v Ni; 1905 v E, S, Ni; 1906 v S; 1907 v S; 1908 v E, S; 1909 v E, S, Ni; 1910 v E, S, Ni; (with Huddersfield T), 1911 v E, S, Ni (28)

Morris, E. (Chirk), 1893 v E, S, Ni (3)

Morris, H. (Sheffield U), 1894 v S; (with Manchester C), 1896 v E; (with Grimsby T), 1897 v E (3)

Morris, J. (Oswestry), 1887 v S (1)

Morris, J. (Chirk), 1898 v Ni (1)

Morris, R. (Chirk), 1900 v E, Ni; 1901 v Ni; 1902 v S; (with Shrewsbury T), 1903 v E, Ni (6)

Morris, R. (Druids), 1902 v E, S; (with Newtown), Ni; (with Liverpool), 1903 v S, Ni; 1904 v E, S, Ni; (with Leeds C), 1906 v S; (with Grimsby T), 1907 v Ni; (with Plymouth Arg), 1908 v Ni (11)

Morris, S. (Birmingham), 1937 v E, S; 1938 v E, S; 1939 v F (5)

Morris, W. (Burnley), 1947 v Ni; 1949 v E; 1952 v S, Ni, R of UK (5)

Moulsdale, J. R. B. (Corinthians), 1925 v Ni (1)

Murphy, J. P. (WBA), 1933 v F, E, Ni; 1934 v E, S; 1935 v E, S, Ni; 1936 v E, S, Ni; 1937 v S, Ni; 1938 v E, S (15)

Nardiello, D. (Coventry C), 1978 v Cz, WG (sub) (2)

Neal, J. E. (Colwyn Bay), 1931 v E, S (2)

Neilson, A. B. (Newcastle U), 1992 v Ei (1)

Newnes, J. (Nelson), 1926 v Ni (1)

Newton, L. F. (Cardiff Corinthians), 1912 v Ni (1)

Nicholas, D. S. (Stoke C), 1923 v S; (with Swansea T), 1927 v E, Ni (3)

Nicholas, P. (C Palace), 1979 v S (sub), Ni (sub), Ma; 1980 v Ei, WG, T, E, S, Ni, Ic; 1981 v T, Cz, E; (with Arsenal), T, S, E, USSR; 1982 v Cz, Ic, USSR, Sp, E, S, Ni, F; 1983 v Y, Bul, S, Ni; 1984 v N, Bul, N, Is; (with C Palace), 1985 v Sp; (with Luton T), N, S, Sp, N; 1986 v S, H, S.Ar, Ei, U, Ca (2); 1987 v Fi (2) USSR, Cz; (with Aberdeen), 1988 v D (2), Cz, Y, Se; (with Chelsea), 1989 v Ho, Fi, Is, Se, WG; 1990 v Fi, Ho, WG, Ei, Se, Cr; 1991 v D (sub), Bel, L, Ei; (with Watford), Bel, Pol, WG; 1992 v L (73)

Nicholls, J. (Newport Co), 1924 v E, Ni; (with Cardiff C), 1925 v E, S (4)

Niedzwiecki, E. A. (Chelsea), 1985 v N (sub); 1988 v D (2)

Nock, W. (Newtown), 1897 v Ni (1)

Nogan, L. M. (Watford), 1992 v A (sub) (1)

Norman, A. J. (Hull C), 1986 v Ei (sub), U, Ca; 1988 v Ma, I (5)

Nurse, M. T. G. (Swansea T), 1960 v E, Ni; 1961 v S, E, H, Ni, Ei, Sp (2); (with Middlesbrough), 1963 v E, H; 1964 v S (12)

O'Callaghan, E. (Tottenham H), 1929 v Ni; 1930 v S; 1932 v S, E; 1933 v Ni, S, E; 1934 v Ni, S, E; 1935 v E (11)

Oliver, A. (Blackburn R), 1905 v E; (with Bangor), S (2)

O'Sullivan, P. A. (Brighton), 1973 v S (sub); 1976 v S; 1979 v Ma (sub) (3)

Owen, D. (Oswestry), 1879 v E (1)

Owen, E. (Ruthin Grammar School), 1884 v E, Ni, S (3)

Owen, G. (Chirk), 1888 v S; (with Newton Heath), 1889 v S, Ni; 1893 v Ni (4)

Owen, J. (Newton Heath), 1892 v E (1)

Owen, Trevor (Crewe Alex), 1899 v E, S (2)

Owen, T. (Oswestry), 1879 v E (1)

Owen, W. (Chirk), 1884 v E; 1885 v Ni; 1887 v E; 1888 v E; 1889 v E, Ni, S; 1890 v S, Ni; 1891 v E, S, Ni; 1892 v E, S; 1893 v S, Ni (16)

Owen, W. P. (Ruthin), 1880 v E, S; 1881 v E, S; 1882 v E, S, Ni; 1883 v E, S; 1884 v E, S, Ni (12)

Owens, J. (Wrexham), 1902 v S (1)

Page, M. E. (Birmingham C), 1971 v Fi; 1972 v S, Ni; 1973 v E (1+1 sub), Ni; 1974 v S, Ni; 1975 v H, L, S, E, Ni;

1976 v E, Y (2), E, Ni; 1977 v WG, S; 1978 v K (sub + 1), WG, Ir, E, S; 1979 v Ma, WG (28)

Palmer, D. (Swansea T), 1957 v Cz; 1958 v E, EG (3)

Parris, J. E. (Bradford), 1932 v Ni (1)

Parry, B. J. (Swansea T), 1951 v S (1)

Parry, C. (Everton), 1891 v E, S; 1893 v E; 1894 v E; 1895 v E, S; (with Newtown), 1896 v E, S, Ni; 1897 v Ni; 1898 v E, S, Ni (13)

Parry, E. (Liverpool), 1922 v S; 1923 v E, Ni; 1925 v Ni; 1926 v Ni (5)

Parry, M. (Liverpool), 1901 v E, S, Ni; 1902 v E, S, Ni; 1903 v E, S; 1904 v E, Ni; 1906 v E; 1908 v E, S, Ni; 1909 v E, S (16)

Parry, T. D. (Oswestry), 1900 v E, S, Ni; 1901 v E, S, Ni; 1902 v E (7)

Parry, W. (Newtown), 1895 v Ni (1)

Pascoe, C. (Swansea C), 1984 v N, Is; (with Sunderland), 1989 v Fi, Is, WG (sub); 1990 v Ho (sub), WG (sub); 1991 v Ei, Ic (sub); 1992 v Br (10)

Paul, R. (Swansea T), 1949 v E, S, Ni, P, Sw; 1950 v E, S, Ni, Bel; (with Manchester C), 1951 v S, E, Ni, P, Sw; 1952 v E, S, Ni, R of UK; 1953 v S, E, Ni, F, Y; 1954 v E, S, Ni; 1955 v S, E, Y; 1956 v E, Ni, S, A (33)

Peake, E. (Aberystwyth), 1908 v Ni; (with Liverpool), 1909 v Ni, S, E; 1910 v S, Ni; 1911 v Ni; 1912 v E; 1913 v E, Ni; 1914 v Ni (11)

Peers, E. J. (Wolverhampton W), 1914 v Ni, S, E; 1920 v E, S; 1921 v S, Ni, E; (with Port Vale), 1922 v E, S, Ni; 1923 v E (12)

Pembridge, M. A. (Luton T), 1992 v Br, Ei, R, Ho, J (sub); (with Derby Co), Bel (sub), Ei (7)

Perry, E. (Doncaster R), 1938 v E, S, Ni (3)

Phennah, E. (Civil Service), 1878 v S (1)

Phillips, C. (Wolverhampton W), 1931 v Ni; 1932 v E; 1933 v S; 1934 v E, S, Ni; 1935 v E, S, Ni; 1936 v S; (with Aston Villa), 1936 v E, Ni; 1938 v S (13)

Phillips, D. (Plymouth Arg), 1984 v E, Ni, N; (with Manchester C), 1985 v Sp, Ic, S, Sp, N; 1986 v S, H, S.Ar, Ei, U; (with Coventry C), 1987 v Fi, Cz; 1988 v D (2), Cz, Y, Se; 1989 v Se, WG; (with Norwich C), 1990 v Fi, Ho, WG, Ei, Se; 1991 v D, Bel, Ic, Pol, WG; 1992 v L, Ei, A, R, Ho (sub), Arg, J; 1993 v Fa, Cy, Bel, Ei, Bel, Cz, Fa (46)

Phillips, L. (Cardiff C), 1971 v Cz, S, E, Ni; 1972 v Cz, R, S, Ni; 1973 v E; 1974 v Pol (sub), Ni; 1975 v A; (with Aston Villa), H (2), L (2), S, E, Ni; 1976 v A, E, Y (2), E, Ni; 1977 v WG, S (2), Cz, E; 1978 v K (2), S, Cz, WG, E, S; 1979 v Ma; (with Swansea C), T, WG, S, E, Ni, Ma; 1980 v Ei, WG, T, S (sub), Ni, Ic; 1981 v T, Cz, T, S, E, USSR; (with Charlton Ath), 1982 v Cz, USSR (58)

Phillips, T. J. S. (Chelsea), 1973 v E; 1974 v E; 1975 v H (sub); 1978 v K (4)

Phoenix, H. (Wrexham), 1882 v S (1)

Poland, G. (Wrexham), 1939 v Ni, F (2)

Pontin, K. (Cardiff C), 1980 v E (sub), S (2)

Powell, A. (Leeds U), 1947 v E, S; 1948 v E, S, Ni; (with Everton), 1949 v E; 1950 v Bel; (with Birmingham C), 1951 v S (8)

Powell, D. (Wrexham), 1968 v WG; (with Sheffield U), 1969 v S, E, Ni, I, WG; 1970 v E, S, Ni, EG; 1971 v R (11)

Powell, I. V. (QPR), 1947 v E; 1948 v E, S, Ni; (with Aston Villa), 1949 v Bel; 1950 v S, Bel; 1951 v S (8)

Powell, J. (Druids), 1878 v S; 1880 v E, S; 1882 v E, S, Ni; 1883 v E, S, Ni; (with Bolton W), 1884 v E; (with Newton Heath), 1887 v E, S; 1888 v E, S, Ni (15)

Powell, Seth (WBA), 1885 v S; 1886 v E, Ni; 1891 v E, S; 1892 v E, S (7)

Price, H. (Aston Villa), 1907 v S; (with Burton U), 1908 v Ni; (with Wrexham), 1909 v S, E, Ni (5)

Price, J. (Wrexham), 1877 v S; 1878 v S; 1879 v E; 1880 v E, S; 1881 v E, S; (with Druids), 1882 v S, E, Ni; 1883 v S, Ni (12)

Price, P. (Luton T), 1980 v E, S, Ni, Ic; 1981 v T, Cz, Ei, T, S, E, USSR; (with Tottenham H), 1982 v USSR, Sp, F; 1983 v N, Y, E, Bul, S, Ni; 1984 v N, R, Bul, Y, S (sub) (25)

Pring, K. D. (Rotherham U), 1966 v Ch, D; 1967 v Ni (3)

Pritchard, H. K. (Bristol C), 1985 v N (sub) (1)

Pryce-Jones, A. W. (Newtown), 1895 v E (1)

Pryce-Jones, W. E. (Cambridge University), 1887 v S; 1888 v S, E, Ni; 1890 v Ni (5)

Pugh, A. (Rhostyllen), 1889 v S (1)

Pugh, D. H. (Wrexham), 1896 v S, Ni; 1897 v S, Ni; (with Lincoln C), 1900 v S; 1901 v S, E (7)

Pugsley, J. (Charlton Ath), 1930 v Ni (1)

Pullen, W. J. (Plymouth Arg), 1926 v E (1)

Rankmore, F. E. J. (Peterborough), 1966 v Ch (sub) (1)

Ratcliffe, K. (Everton), 1981 v Cz, Ei, T, S, E, USSR; 1982 v Cz, Ic, USSR, Sp, E; 1983 v Y, E, Bul, S, Ni, Br; 1984 v N, R, Bul, Y, S, E, Ni, N, Is; 1985 v Ic, Sp, Ic, N, S, Sp; 1986 v S, H, S.Ar, U; 1987 v Fi (2), USSR, Cz; 1988 v D (2), Cz; 1989 v Fi, Is, Se, WG; 1990 v Fi; 1991 v D, Bel (2), L, Ei, Ic, Pol, WG; 1992 v Br, G; (with Cardiff C), 1993 v Bel (59)

Rea, J. C. (Aberystwyth), 1894 v Ni, S, E; 1895 v S; 1896 v S, Ni; 1897 v S, Ni; 1898 v Ni (9)

Reece, G. I. (Sheffield U), 1966 v E, S, Ni, USSR; 1967 v S; 1969 v R of UK (sub); 1970 v I (sub); 1971 v S, E, Ni, Fi; 1972 v Fi, R, E (sub), S, Ni; (with Cardiff C), 1973 v E (sub), Ni; 1974 v Pol (sub), E, S, Ni; 1975 v A, H (2), L (2), S, Ni (29)

Reed, W. G. (Ipswich T), 1955 v S, Y (2)

Rees, A. (Birmingham C), 1984 v N (sub) (1)

Rees, J. M. (Luton T), 1992 v A (sub) (1)

Rees, R. R. (Coventry C), 1965 v S, E, Ni, D, Gr (2), I, R; 1966 v S, Ni, R, D, Br (2), Ch; 1967 v E, Ni; 1968 v E, S, Ni; (with WBA), WG; 1969 v I; (with Nottingham F), 1969 v WG, EG, S (sub), R of UK; 1970 v E, S, Ni, EG, I; 1971 v Cz, R, E (sub), Ni (sub), Fi; 1972 v Cz (sub), R (39)

Rees, W. (Cardiff C), 1949 v Ni, Bel, Sw; (with Tottenham H), 1950 v Ni (4)

Richards, A. (Barnsley), 1932 v S (1)

Richards, D. (Wolverhampton W), 1931 v Ni; 1933 v E, S, Ni; 1934 v E, S, Ni; 1935 v E, S, Ni; 1936 v S; (with Brentford), 1936 v E, Ni; 1937 v S, E; (with Birmingham), Ni; 1938 v E, S, Ni; 1939 v E, S (21)

Richards, G. (Druids), 1899 v E, S, Ni; (with Oswestry), 1903 v Ni; (with Shrewsbury), 1904 v S; 1905 v Ni (6)

Richards, R. W. (Wolverhampton W), 1920 v E, S; 1921 v Ni; 1922 v E, S; (with West Ham U), 1924 v E, S, Ni; (with Mold), 1926 v S (9)

Richards, S. V. (Cardiff C), 1947 v E (1)

Richards, W. E. (Fulham), 1933 v Ni (1)

Roach, J. (Oswestry), 1885 v Ni (1)

Robbins, W. W. (Cardiff C), 1931 v E, S; 1932 v Ni, E, S; (with WBA), 1933 v F, E, S, Ni; 1934 v S; 1936 v S (11)

Roberts, A. M. (QPR), 1993 v Ei (sub) (1)

Roberts, D. F. (Oxford U), 1973 v Pol, E (sub), Ni; 1974 v E, S; 1975 v A; (with Hull C), L, Ni; 1976 v S, Ni, Y; 1977 v E (sub), Ni; 1978 v K (1 + 1 sub), S, Ni (17)

Roberts, I. W. (Watford), 1990 v Ho; (with Huddersfield T), 1992 v A, Arg, J (4)

Roberts, Jas (Chirk), 1898 v S (1)

Roberts, Jas (Wrexham), 1913 v S, Ni (2)

Roberts, J. (Corwen), 1879 v S; 1880 v E, S; 1882 v E, S, Ni; (with Berwyn R), 1883 v E (7)

Roberts, J. (Ruthin), 1881 v S; 1882 v S (2)

Roberts, J. (Bradford C), 1906 v Ni; 1907 v Ni (2)

1894 v Ni, E; 1895 v Ni, E; 1896 v S; 1897 v Ni, S, E; 1898 v S, E; 1899 v Ni, S (20)

Turner, H. G. (Charlton Ath), 1937 v E, S, Ni; 1938 v E, S, Ni; 1939 v Ni, F (8)

Turner, J. (Wrexham), 1892 v E (1)

Turner, R. E. (Wrexham), 1891 v E, Ni (2)

Turner, W. H. (Wrexham), 1887 v E, Ni; 1890 v S; 1891 v E, S (5)

Van Den Hauwe, P. W. R. (Everton), 1985 v Sp; 1986 v S, H; 1987 v USSR, Fi, Cz; 1988 v D (2), Cz, Y, I; 1989 v Fi, Se (13)

Vaughan, Jas (Druids), 1893 v E, S, Ni; 1899 v E (4)

Vaughan, John (Oswestry), 1879 v S; 1880 v S; 1881 v E, S; 1882 v E, S, Ni; 1883 v E, S, Ni; (with Bolton W), 1884 v E (11)

Vaughan, J. O. (Rhyl), 1885 v Ni; 1886 v Ni, E, S (4)

Vaughan, N. (Newport Co), 1983 v Y (sub), Br; 1984 v N; (with Cardiff C), R, Bul, Y, Ni (sub), N, Is; 1985 v Sp (sub) (10)

Vaughan, T. (Rhyl), 1885 v E (1)

Vearncombe, G. (Cardiff C), 1958 v EG; 1961 v Ei (2)

Vernon, T. R. (Blackburn R), 1957 v Ni, Cz (2), EG; 1958 v E, S, EG, Se; 1959 v S; (with Everton), 1960 v Ni; 1961 v S, E, Ei; 1962 v Ni, Br (2), M; 1963 v S, E, H; 1964 v E, S; (with Stoke C), 1965 v Ni, Gr, I; 1966 v E, S, Ni, USSR, D; 1967 v Ni; 1968 v E (32)

Villars, A. K. (Cardiff C), 1974 v E, S, Ni (sub) (3)

Vizard, E. T. (Bolton W), 1911 v E, S, Ni; 1912 v E, S; 1913 v S; 1914 v E, Ni; 1920 v E; 1921 v E, S, Ni; 1922 v E, S; 1923 v E, Ni; 1924 v E, S, Ni; 1926 v E, S; 1927 v S (22)

Walley, J. T. (Watford), 1971 v Cz (1)

Walsh, I. (C Palace), 1980 v Ei, T, E, S, Ic; 1981 v T, Cz, Ei, T, S, E, USSR; 1982 v Cz (sub), Ic; (with Swansea C), Sp, S (sub), Ni (sub), F (18)

Ward, D. (Bristol R), 1959 v E; (with Cardiff C), 1962 v E (2)

Warner, J. (Swansea T), 1937 v E; (with Manchester U), 1939 v F (2)

Warren, F. W. (Cardiff C), 1929 v Ni; (with Middlesbrough), 1931 v Ni; 1933 v F, E; (with Hearts), 1937 v Ni; 1938 v Ni (6)

Watkins, A. E. (Leicester Fosse), 1898 v E, S; (with Aston Villa), 1900 v E, S; (with Millwall), 1904 v Ni (5)

Watkins, W. M. (Stoke C), 1902 v E; 1903 v E, S; (with Aston Villa); 1904 v E, S, Ni; (with Sunderland), 1905 v E, S, Ni; (with Stoke C), 1908 v Ni (10)

Webster, C (Manchester U), 1957 v Cz; 1958 v H, M, Br (4)

Whatley, W. J. (Tottenham H), 1939 v E, S (2)

White, P. F. (London Welsh), 1896 v Ni (1)

Wilcocks, A. R. (Oswestry), 1890 v Ni (1)

Wilding, J. (Wrexham Olympians), 1885 v E, S, Ni; 1886 v E, Ni; (with Bootle), 1887 v E; 1888 v S, Ni; (with Wrexham), 1892 v S (9)

Williams, A. L. (Wrexham), 1931 v E (1)

Williams, B. (Bristol C), 1930 v Ni (1)

Williams, B. D. (Swansea T), 1928 v Ni, E; 1930 v E, S; (with Everton), 1931 v Ni; 1932 v E; 1933 v E, S, Ni; 1935 v Ni (10)

Williams, D. G. (Derby Co), 1988 v Cz, Y, Se, Ma, I; 1989 v Ho, Is, Se, WG; 1990 v Fi, Ho; (with Ipswich T), 1993 v Ei (12)

Williams, D. M. (Norwich C), 1986 v S.Ar (sub), U, Ca (2); 1987 v Fi (5)

Williams, D. R. (Merthyr T), 1921 v E, S; (with Sheffield W), 1923 v S; 1926 v S; 1927 v E, Ni; (with Manchester U), 1929 v E, S (8)

Williams, E. (Crewe Alex), 1893 v E, S (2)

Williams, E. (Druids), 1901 v E, Ni, S; 1902 v E, Ni (5)

Williams, G. (Chirk), 1893 v S; 1894 v S; 1895 v E, S, Ni; 1898 v Ni (6)

Williams, G. E. (WBA), 1960 v Ni; 1961 v S, E, Ei; 1963 v Ni, H; 1964 v E, S, Ni; 1965 v S, E, Ni, D, Gr (2), USSR, I; 1966 v Ni, Br (2), Ch; 1967 v S, E, Ni; 1968 v Ni; 1969 v I (26)

Williams, G. G. (Swansea T), 1961 v Ni, H, Sp (2); 1962 v E (5)

Williams, G. J. J. (Cardiff C), 1951 v Sw (1)

Williams, G. O. (Wrexham), 1907 v Ni (1)

Williams, H. J. (Swansea), 1965 v Gr (2); 1972 v R (3)

Williams, H. T. (Newport Co), 1949 v Ni, Sw; (with Leeds U), 1950 v Ni; 1951 v S (4)

Williams, J. H. (Oswestry), 1884 v E (1)

Williams, J. J. (Wrexham), 1939 v F (1)

Williams, J. T. (Middlesbrough), 1925 v Ni (1)

Williams, J. W. (C Palace), 1912 v S, Ni (2)

Williams, R. (Newcastle U), 1935 v S, E (2)

Williams, R. P. (Caernarvon), 1886 v S (1)

Williams, S. G. (WBA), 1954 v A; 1955 v E, Ni; 1956 v E, S, A; 1958 v E, S, Ni, Is (2), H (2), M, Se, Br; 1959 v E, S, Ni; 1960 v E, S, Ni; 1961 v Ni, Ei, H, Sp (2); 1962 v E, S, Ni, Br (2), M; (with Southampton), 1963 v S, E, H (2); 1964 v E, S; 1965 v S, E, D; 1966 v D (43)

Williams, W. (Druids), 1876 v S; 1878 v S; (with Oswestry), 1879 v E, S; (with Druids), 1880 v E; 1881 v E, S; 1882 v E, S, Ni; 1883 v Ni (11)

Williams, W. (Northampton T), 1925 v S (1)

Witcomb, D. F. (WBA), 1947 v E, S; (with Sheffield W), 1947 v Ni (3)

Woosnam, A. P. (Leyton Orient), 1959 v S; (with West Ham U), E; 1960 v E, S, Ni; 1961 v S, E, Ni, Ei, Sp, H; 1962 v E, S, Ni, Br; (with Aston Villa), 1963 v Ni, H (17)

Woosnam, G. (Newton White Star), 1879 v S (1)

Worthington, T. (Newtown), 1894 v S (1)

Wynn, G. A. (Wrexham), 1909 v E, S, Ni; (with Manchester C), 1910 v E; 1911 v Ni; 1912 v E, S; 1913 v E, S; 1914 v E, S (11)

Wynn, W. (Chirk), 1903 v Ni (1)

Yorath, T. C. (Leeds U), 1970 v I; 1971 v S, E, Ni; 1972 v Cz, E, S, Ni; 1973 v E, Pol, S; 1974 v Pol, E, S, Ni; 1975 v A, H (2), L (2), S; 1976 v A, E, S, Y (2), E, Ni; (with Coventry C), 1977 v WG, S (2), Cz, E, Ni; 1978 v K (2), S, Cz, WG, Ir, E, S, Ni; 1979 v T, WG, S, E, Ni; (with Tottenham H), 1980 v Ei, T, E, S, Ni, Ic; 1981 v T, Cz; (with Vancouver W), Ei, T, USSR (59)

Young, E. (Wimbledon), 1990 v Cr; (with C Palace), 1991 v D, Bel (2), L, Ei; 1992 v G, L, Ei, A; 1993 v Fa, Cy, Bel, Ei, Bel, Fa (16)

REPUBLIC OF IRELAND

Aherne, T. (Belfast C), 1946 v P, Sp; (with Luton T), 1950 v Fi, E, Fi, Se, Bel; 1951 v N, Arg, N; 1952 v WG (2), A, Sp; 1953 v F; 1954 v F (16)

Aldridge, J. W. (Oxford U), 1986 v W, U, Ic, Cz; 1987 v Bel, S, Pol; (with Liverpool), S, Bul, Bel, Br, L; 1988 v Bul, Pol, N, E, USSR, Ho; 1989 v Ni, Tun, Sp, F (sub), H, Ma (sub), H; 1990 v WG; (with Real Sociedad), Ni, Ma, Fi (sub), T, E, Eg, Ho, R, I; 1991 v T, E (2), Pol; (with Tranmere R), 1992 v H (sub), T, W (sub), Sw (sub), US (sub), Alb, I, P (sub)); 1993 v La, D, Sp, D, Alb, La, Li (54)

Ambrose, P. (Shamrock R), 1955 v N, Ho; 1964 v Pol, N, E (5)

Anderson, J. (Preston NE), 1980 v Cz (sub), US (sub); 1982 v Ch, Br, Tr; (with Newcastle U), 1984 v Chn; 1986 v W, Ic, Cz; 1987 v Bul, Bel, Br, L; 1988 v R (sub), Y (sub); 1989 v Tun (16)

Andrews, P. (Bohemians), 1936 v Ho (1)

Arrigan, T. (Waterford), 1938 v N (1)

Bailham, E. (Shamrock R), 1964 v E (1)

Barber, E. (Shelbourne), 1966 v Sp; (with Birmingham C), 1966 v Bel (2)

Barry, P. (Fordsons), 1928 v Bel; 1929 v Bel (2)

Beglin, J. (Liverpool), 1984 v Chn; 1985 v M, D, I, Is, E, N, Sw; 1986 v Sw, USSR, D, W; 1987 v Bel (sub), S, Pol (15)

Bermingham, J. (Bohemians), 1929 v Bel (1)

Bermingham, P. (St James' Gate), 1935 v H (1)

Braddish, S. (Dundalk), 1978 v Pol (1)

Bonner, P. (Celtic), 1981 v Pol; 1982 v Alg; 1984 v Ma, Is, Chn; 1985 v I, Is, E, N; 1986 v U, Ic; 1987 v Bel (2), S (2), Pol, Bul, Br, L; 1988 v Bul, R, Y, N, E, USSR, Ho; 1989 v Sp, F, H, Sp, Ma, H; 1990 v WG, Ni, Ma, W, Fi, T, E, Eg, Ho, R, I; 1991 v Mor, T, E (2), W, Pol, US; 1992 v H, Pol, T, W, Sw, Alb, I; 1993 v La, D, Sp, W, Ni, D, Alb, La, Li (66)

Bradshaw, P. (St James' Gate), 1939 v Sw, Pol, H (2), G (5)

Brady, F. (Fordsons), 1926 v I; 1927 v I (2)

Brady, T. R. (QPR), 1964 v A (2), Sp (2), Pol, N (6)

Brady, W. L. (Arsenal), 1975 v USSR, T, Sw, USSR, Sw, WG; 1976 v T, N, Pol; 1977 v E, T, F (2), Sp, Bul; 1978 v Bul, N; 1979 v Ni, E, D, Bul, WG; 1980 v W, Bul, E, Cy; (with Juventus), 1981 v Ho, Bel, F, Cy, Bel; 1982 v Ho, F, Ch, Br, Tr; (with Sampdoria), 1983 v Ho, Sp, Ic, Ma; 1984 v Ic, Ho, Ma, Pol, Is; (with Internazionale), 1985 v USSR, N, D, I, E, N, Sp, Sw; 1986 v Sw, USSR, D, W; (with Ascoli), 1987 v Bel, S (2), Pol; (with West Ham U), 1988 v L, Bul; 1989 v F, H (sub), H (sub); 1990 v WG, Fi (72)

Breen, T. (Manchester U), 1937 v Sw, F; (with Shamrock R), 1947 v E, Sp, P (5)

Brennan, F. (Drumcondra), 1965 v Bel (1)

Brennan, S. A. (Manchester U), 1965 v Sp; 1966 v Sp, A, Bel; 1967 v Sp, T, Sp; 1969 v Cz, D, H; 1970 v S, Cz, D, H, Pol (sub), WG; (with Waterford), 1971 v Pol, Se, I (19)

Brown, J. (Coventry C), 1937 v Sw, F (2)

Browne, W. (Bohemians), 1964 v A, Sp, E (3)

Buckley, L. (Shamrock R), 1984 v Pol (sub); (with Waregem), 1985 v M (2)

Burke, F. (Cork), 1934 v Bel (1)

Burke, F. (Cork Ath), 1952 v WG (1)

Burke, J. (Shamrock R), 1929 v Bel (1)

Byrne, A. B. (Southampton), 1970 v D, Pol, WG; 1971 v Pol, Se (2), I (2), A; 1973 v F, USSR (sub), F, N; 1974 v Pol (14)

Byrne, D. (Shelbourne), 1929 v Bel; (with Shamrock R), 1932 v Sp; (with Coleraine), 1934 v Bel (3)

Byrne, J. (Bray Unknowns), 1928 v Bel (1)

Byrne, J. (QPR), 1985 v I, Is (sub), E (sub), Sp (sub); 1987 v S (sub), Bel (sub), Br, L (sub); 1988 v L, Bul (sub), Is, R, Y (sub), Pol (sub); (with Le Havre), 1990 v WG (sub), W, Fi, T (sub), Ma; (with Brighton & HA), 1991 v W; (with Sunderland), 1992 v T, W; (with Millwall), 1993 v W (23)

Byrne, P. (Shamrock R), 1984 v Pol, Chn; 1985 v M; 1986 v D (sub), W (sub), U (sub), Ic (sub), Cz (8)

Byrne, P. (Shelbourne), 1931 v Sp; 1932 v Ho; (with Drumcondra), 1934 v Ho (3)

Byrne, S. (Bohemians), 1931 v Sp (1)

Campbell, A. (Santander), 1985 v I (sub), Is, Sp (3)

Campbell, N. (St Patrick's Ath), 1971 v A (sub); (with Fortuna, Cologne), 1972 v Ir, Ec, Ch, P; 1973 v USSR, F (sub); 1975 v WG; 1976 v N; 1977 v Sp, Bul (sub) (11)

Cannon, H. (Bohemians), 1926 v I; 1928 v Bel (2)

Cantwell, N. (West Ham U), 1954 v L; 1956 v Sp, Ho; 1957 v D, WG, E (2); 1958 v D, Pol, A; 1959 v Pol, Cz (2); 1960 v Se, Ch, Se; 1961 v N; (with Manchester U), S (2); 1962 v Cz (2), A; 1963 v Ic (2), S; 1964 v A, Sp, E; 1965 v Pol, Sp; 1966 v Sp (2), A, Bel; 1967 v Sp, T (36)

Carey, B. P. (Manchester U), 1992 v US (sub); 1993 v W (2)

Carey, J. J. (Manchester U), 1938 v N, Cz, Pol; 1939 v Sw, Pol, H (2), G; 1946 v P, Sp; 1947 v E, Sp, P; 1948 v P, Sp; 1949 v Sw, Bel, P, Se, Sp; 1950 v Fi, E, Fi, Se; 1951 v N, Arg, N; 1953 v F, A (29)

Carolan, J. (Manchester U), 1960 v Se, Ch (2)

Carroll, B. (Shelbourne), 1949 v Bel; 1950 v Fi (2)

Carroll, T. R. (Ipswich T), 1968 v Pol; 1969 v Pol, A, D; 1970 v Cz, Pol, WG; 1971 v Se; (with Birmingham C), 1972 v Ir, Ec, Ch, P; 1973 v USSR (2), Pol, F, N (17)

Cascarino, A. G. (Gillingham), 1986 v Sw, USSR, D; (with Millwall), 1988 v Pol, N (sub), USSR (sub), Ho (sub); 1989 v Ni, Tun, Sp, F, H, Sp, Ma, H; 1990 v WG (sub), Ni, Ma; (with Aston Villa), W, Fi, T, E, Eg, Ho (sub), R (sub), I (sub); 1991 v Mor (sub), T (sub), E (2 sub), Pol (sub), Ch (sub), US; (with Celtic), 1992 v Pol, T; (with Chelsea), W, Sw, US (sub); 1993 v W, Ni (sub), D (sub), Alb (sub), La (sub) (43)

Chandler, J. (Leeds U), 1980 v Cz (sub), US (2)

Chatton, H. A. (Shelbourne), 1931 v Sp; (with Dumbarton), 1932 v Sp; (with Cork), 1934 v Ho (3)

Clarke, J. (Drogheda U), 1978 v Pol (sub) (1)

Clarke, K. (Drumcondra), 1948 v P, Sp (2)

Clarke, M. (Shamrock R), 1950 v Bel (1)

Clinton, T. J. (Everton), 1951 v N; 1954 v F, L (3)

Coad, P. (Shamrock R), 1947 v E, Sp, P; 1948 v P, Sp; 1949 v Sw, Bel, P, Se; 1951 v N (sub); 1952 v Sp (11)

Coffey, T. (Drumcondra), 1950 v Fi (1)

Colfer, M. D. (Shelbourne), 1950 v Bel; 1951 v N (2)

Collins, F. (Jacobs), 1927 v I (1)

Conmy, O. M. (Peterborough U), 1965 v Bel; 1967 v Cz; 1968 v Cz, Pol; 1970 v Cz (5)

Connolly, J. (Fordsons), 1926 v I (1)

Connolly, N. (Cork), 1937 v G (1)

Conroy, G. A. (Stoke C), 1970 v Cz, D, H, Pol, WG; 1971 v Pol, Se (2), I; 1973 v USSR, F, USSR, N; 1974 v Pol, Br, U, Ch; 1975 v T, Sw, USSR, Sw, WG (sub); 1976 v T (sub), Pol; 1977 v E, T, Pol (27)

Conway, J. P. (Fulham), 1967 v Sp, T, Sp; 1968 v Cz; 1969 v A (sub), H; 1970 v S, Cz, D, H, Pol, WG; 1971 v I, A; 1974 v U, Ch; 1975 v WG (sub); 1976 v N, Pol; (with Manchester C), 1977 v Pol (20)

Corr, P. J. (Everton), 1949 v P, Sp; 1950 v E, Se (4)

Courtney, E. (Cork U), 1946 v P (1)

Coyne, T. (Celtic), 1992 v Sw, US, Alb (sub), US (sub), I (sub), P (sub); 1993 v La (sub); (with Tranmere R), Ni (8)

Cummins, G. P. (Luton T), 1954 v L (2); 1955 v N (2), WG; 1956 v Y, Sp; 1958 v D, Pol, A; 1959 v Pol, Cz (2); 1960 v Se, Ch, WG, Se; 1961 v S (2) (19)

Cuneen, T. (Limerick), 1951 v N (1)

Curtis, D. P. (Shelbourne), 1957 v D, WG; (with Bristol C), 1957 v E (2); 1958 v D, Pol, A; (with Ipswich T), 1959 v Pol; 1960 v Se, Ch, WG, Se; 1961 v N, S; 1962 v A; 1963 v Ic; (with Exeter C), 1964 v A (17)

Cusack, S. (Limerick), 1953 v F (1)

Daish, L. S. (Cambridge U), 1992 v W (1)

Daly, G. A. (Manchester U), 1973 v Pol (sub), N; 1974 v Br (sub), U (sub); 1975 v Sw (sub), WG; 1977 v E, T, F; (with Derby Co), F, Bul; 1978 v Bul, T, D; 1979 v Ni, E, D, Bul; 1980 v Ni, E, Cy, Sw, Arg; (with Coventry C), 1981 v Ho, Bel, Cy, W, Bel, Cz, Pol (sub); 1982 v Alg,

Ch, Br, Tr; 1983 v Ho, Sp (sub), Ma (sub); 1984 v Is (sub), Ma; (with Birmingham C), 1985 v M (sub), N, Sp, Sw; 1986 v Sw; (with Shrewsbury T), U, Ic (sub), Cz (sub); 1987 v S (sub) (48)

Daly, J. (Shamrock R), 1932 v Ho; 1935 v Sw (2)

Daly, M. (Wolverhampton W), 1978 v T, Pol (2)

Daly, P. (Shamrock R), 1950 v Fi (sub) (1)

Davis, T. L. (Oldham Ath), 1937 v G, H; (with Tranmere R), 1938 v Cz, Pol (4)

Deacy, E. (Aston Villa), 1982 v Alg (sub), Ch, Br, Tr (4)

De Mange, K. J. P. P. (Liverpool), 1987 v Br (sub); (with Hull C), 1989 v Tun (sub) (2)

Dempsey, J. T. (Fulham), 1967 v Sp, Cz; 1968 v Cz, Pol; 1969 v Pol, A, D; (with Chelsea), 1969 v Cz, D; 1970 v H, WG; 1971 v Pol, Se (2), I; 1972 v A (11)

Dennehy, J. (Cork Hibernians), 1972 v Ec (sub), Ch; (with Nottingham F), 1973 v USSR (sub), Pol, F, N; 1974 v Pol (sub); 1975 v T (sub), WG (sub); (with Walsall), 1976 v Pol (sub); 1977 v Pol (sub) (11)

Desmond, P. (Middlesbrough), 1950 v Fi, E, Fi, Se (4)

Devine, J. (Arsenal), 1980 v Cz, Ni; 1981 v Cz; 1982 v Ho, Alg; 1983 v Sp, Ma; (with Norwich C), 1984 v Ic, Ho, Is; 1985 v USSR, N (12)

Donnelly, J. (Dundalk), 1935 v H, Sw, G; 1936 v Ho, Sw, H, L; 1937 v G, H; 1938 v N (10)

Donnelly, T. (Drumcondra), 1938 v N; (Shamrock R), 1939 v Sw (2)

Donovan, D. C. (Everton), 1955 v N, Ho, N, WG; 1957 v E (5)

Donovan, T. (Aston Villa), 1980 v Cz (1)

Dowdall, C. (Fordsons), 1928 v Bel; (with Barnsley), 1929 v Bel; (with Cork), 1931 v Sp (3)

Doyle, C. (Shelbourne), 1959 v Cz (1)

Doyle, D. (Shamrock R), 1926 v I (1)

Doyle, L. (Dolphin), 1932 v Sp (1)

Duffy, B. (Shamrock R), 1950 v Bel (1)

Duggan, H. A. (Leeds U), 1927 v I; 1930 v Bel; 1936 v H, L; (with Newport Co), 1938 v N (5)

Dunne, A. P. (Manchester U), 1962 v A; 1963 v Ic, S; 1964 v A, Sp, Pol, N, E; 1965 v Pol, Sp; 1966 v Sp (2), A, Bel; 1967 v Sp, T, Sp; 1969 v Pol, D, H; 1970 v H; 1971 v Se, I, A; (with Bolton W), 1974 v Br (sub), U, Ch; 1975 v T, Sw, USSR, Sw, WG; 1976 v T (33)

Dunne, J. (Sheffield U), 1930 v Bel; (with Arsenal), 1936 v Sw, H, L; (with Southampton), 1937 v Sw, F; (with Shamrock R), 1938 v N (2), Cz, Pol; 1939 v Sw, Pol, H (2), G (15)

Dunne, J. C. (Fulham), 1971 v A (1)

Dunne, L. (Manchester C), 1935 v Sw, G (2)

Dunne, P. A. J. (Manchester U), 1965 v Sp; 1966 v Sp (2), WG; 1967 v T (5)

Dunne, S. (Luton T), 1953 v F, A; 1954 v F, L; 1956 v Sp, Ho; 1957 v D, WG, E; 1958 v D, Pol, A; 1959 v Pol; 1960 v WG, Se (15)

Dunne, T. (St Patrick's Ath), 1956 v Ho; 1957 v D, WG (3)

Dunning, P. (Shelbourne), 1971 v Se, I (2)

Dunphy, E. M. (York C), 1966 v Sp; (with Millwall), 1966 v WG; 1967 v T, Sp, T, Cz; 1968 v Cz, Pol; 1969 v Pol, A, D (2), H; 1970 v D, H, Pol, WG (sub); 1971 v Pol, Se (2), I (2), A (23)

Dwyer, N. M. (West Ham U), 1960 v Se, Ch, WG, Se; (with Swansea T), 1961 v W, N, S (2); 1962 v Cz (2); 1964 v Pol (sub), N, E; 1965 v Pol (14)

Eccles, P. (Shamrock R), 1986 v U (sub) (1)

Egan, R. (Dundalk), 1929 v Bel (1)

Eglington, T. J. (Shamrock R), 1946 v P, Sp; (with Everton), 1947 v E, Sp, P; 1948 v P; 1949 v Sw, P, Se; 1951 v N, Arg; 1952 v WG (2), A, Sp; 1953 v F, A; 1954 v F, L, F; 1955 v N, Ho, WG; 1956 v Sp (24)

Ellis, P. (Bohemians), 1935 v Sw, G; 1936 v Ho, Sw, L; 1937 v G, H (7)

Fagan, E. (Shamrock R), 1973 v N (sub) (1)

Fagan, F. (Manchester C), 1955 v N; 1960 v Se; (with Derby Co), 1960 v Ch, WG, Se; 1961 v W, N, S (8)

Fagan, K. (Shamrock R), 1926 v I (1)

Fairclough, M. (Dundalk), 1982 v Ch (sub), Tr (sub) (2)

Fallon, S. (Celtic), 1951 v N; 1952 v WG (2), A, Sp; 1953 v F; 1955 v N, WG (8)

Fallon, W. J. (Notts Co), 1935 v H; 1936 v H; 1937 v H, Sw, F; 1939 v Sw, Pol; (with Sheffield W), 1939 v H, G (9)

Farquharson, T. G. (Cardiff C), 1929 v Bel; 1930 v Bel; 1931 v Sp; 1932 v Sp (4)

Farrell, P. (Hibernian), 1937 v Sw, F (2)

Farrell, P. D. (Shamrock R), 1946 v P, Sp; (with Everton), 1947 v Sp, P; 1948 v P, Sp; 1949 v Sw, P (sub), Sp; 1950 v E, Fi, Se; 1951 v Arg, N; 1952 v WG (2), A, Sp; 1953 v F, A; 1954 v F (2); 1955 v N, Ho, WG; 1956 v Y, Sp; 1957 v E (28)

Feenan, J. J. (Sunderland), 1937 v Sw, F (2)

Finucane, A. (Limerick), 1967 v T, Cz; 1969 v Cz, D, H; 1970 v S, Cz; 1971 v Se, I (1 + 1 sub); 1972 v A (11)

Fitzgerald, F. J. (Waterford), 1955 v Ho; 1956 v Ho (2)

Fitzgerald, P. J. (Leeds U), 1961 v W, N, S; (with Chester), 1962 v Cz (2) (5)

Fitzpatrick, K. (Limerick), 1970 v Cz (1)

Fitzsimons, A. G. (Middlesbrough), 1950 v Fi, Bel; 1952 v WG (2), A, Sp; 1953 v F, A; 1954 v F, L, F; 1955 v Ho, N, WG; 1956 v Y, Sp, Ho; 1957 v D, WG, E (2); 1958 v D, Pol, A; 1959 v Pol; (with Lincoln C), 1959 v Cz (26)

Flood, J. J. (Shamrock R), 1926 v I; 1929 v Bel; 1930 v Bel; 1931 v Sp; 1932 v Sp (5)

Fogarty, A. (Sunderland), 1960 v WG, Se; 1961 v S; 1962 v Cz (2); 1963 v Ic (2), S (sub); 1964 v A (2); (with Hartlepools U), Sp (11)

Foley, J. (Cork), 1934 v Bel, Ho; (with Celtic), 1935 v H, Sw, G; 1937 v G, H (7)

Foley, M. (Shelbourne), 1926 v I (1)

Foley, T. C. (Northampton T), 1964 v Sp, Pol, N; 1965 v Pol, Bel; 1966 v Sp (2), WG; 1967 v Cz (9)

Foy, T. (Shamrock R), 1938 v N; 1939 v H (2)

Fullam, J. (Preston NE), 1961 v N; (with Shamrock R), 1964 v Sp, Pol, N; 1966 v A, Bel; 1968 v Pol; 1969 v Pol, A, D; 1970 v Cz (sub) (11)

Fullam, R. (Shamrock R), 1926 v I; 1927 v I (2)

Gallagher, C. (Celtic), 1967 v T, Cz (2)

Gallagher, M. (Hibernian), 1954 v L (1)

Gallagher, P. (Falkirk), 1932 v Sp (1)

Galvin, A. (Tottenham H), 1983 v Ho, Ma; 1984 v Ho (sub), Is (sub); 1985 v M, USSR, N, D, I, N, Sp; 1986 v U, Ic, Cz; 1987 v Bel (2), S, Bul, L; (with Sheffield W), 1988 v L, Bul, R, Pol, N, E, USSR, Ho; 1989 v Sp; (with Swindon T), 1990 v WG (29)

Gannon, E. (Notts Co), 1949 v Sw; (with Sheffield W), 1949 v Bel, P, Se, Sp; 1950 v F; 1951 v N; 1952 v WG, A; 1954 v L, F; 1955 v N; (with Shelbourne), 1955 v N, WG (14)

Gannon, M. (Shelbourne), 1972 v A (1)

Gaskins, P. (Shamrock R), 1934 v Bel, Ho; 1935 v H, Sw, G; (with St James' Gate), 1938 v Cz, Pol (7)

Gavin, J. T. (Norwich C), 1950 v Fi (2); 1953 v F; 1954 v L; (with Tottenham H), 1955 v Ho, WG; (with Norwich C), 1957 v D (7)

Geoghegan, M. (St James' Gate), 1937 v G; 1938 v N (2)

Gibbons, A. (St Patrick's Ath), 1952 v WG; 1954 v L; 1956 v Y, Sp (4)

Gilbert, R. (Shamrock R), 1966 v WG (1)

Giles, C. (Doncaster R), 1951 v N (1)

Giles, M. J. (Manchester U), 1960 v Se, Ch; 1961 v W, N, S (2); 1962 v Cz (2), A; 1963 v Ic, S; (with Leeds U), 1964 v A (2), Sp (2), Pol, N, E; 1965 v Sp; 1966 v Sp (2), A, Bel; 1967 v Sp, T (2); 1969 v A, D, Cz; 1970 v S, Pol, WG; 1971 v I; 1973 v F, USSR; 1974 v Br, U, Ch; 1975

v USSR, T, Sw, USSR, Sw; (with WBA), 1976 v T; 1977 v E, T, F (2), Pol, Bul; (with Shamrock R), 1978 v Bul, T, Pol, N, D; 1979 v Ni, D, Bul, WG (59)

Givens, D. J. (Manchester U), 1969 v D, H; 1970 v S, Cz, D, H; (with Luton T), 1970 v Pol, WG; 1971 v Sc, I (2), A; 1972 v Ir, Ec, P; (with QPR), 1973 v F, USSR, Pol, F, N; 1974 v Pol, Br, U, Ch; 1975 v USSR, T, Sw, USSR, Sw, WG; 1976 v T, N, Pol; 1977 v E, T, F (2), Sp, Bul; 1978 v Bul, N, D; (with Birmingham C), 1979 v Ni (sub), E, D, Bul, WG; 1980 v US (sub), Ni (sub), Sw, Arg; 1981 v Ho, Bel, Cy (sub), W; (with Neuchatel X), 1982 v F (sub) (56)

Glen, W. (Shamrock R), 1927 v I; 1929 v Bel; 1930 v Bel; 1932 v Sp; 1936 v Ho, Sw, H, L (8)

Glynn, D. (Drumcondra), 1952 v WG; 1955 v N (2)

Godwin, T. F. (Shamrock R), 1949 v P, Se, Sp; 1950 v Fi, E; (with Leicester C), 1950 v Fi, Se, Bel; 1951 v N; (with Bournemouth), 1956 v Ho; 1957 v E; 1958 v D, Pol (13)

Golding, L. (Shamrock R), 1928 v Bel; 1930 v Bel (2)

Gorman, W. C. (Bury), 1936 v Sw, H, L; 1937 v G, H; 1938 v N, Cz, Pol; 1939 v Sw, Pol, H; (with Brentford), 1947 v E, P (13)

Grace, J. (Drumcondra), 1926 v I (1)

Grealish, A. (Orient), 1976 v N, Pol; 1978 v N, D; 1979 v Ni, E, WG; (with Luton T), 1980 v W, Cz, Bul, US, Ni, E, Cy, Sw, Arg; 1981 v Ho, Bel, F, Cy, W, Bel, Pol; (with Brighton & HA), 1982 v Ho, Alg, Ch, Br, Tr; 1983 v Ho, Sp, Ic, Sp; 1984 v Ic, Ho; (with WBA), Pol, Chn; 1985 v M, USSR, N, D, Sp (sub), Sw; 1986 v USSR, D (44)

Gregg, E. (Bohemians), 1978 v Pol, D (sub); 1979 v E (sub), D, Bul, WG; 1980 v W, Cz (8)

Griffith, R. (Walsall), 1935 v H (1)

Grimes, A. A. (Manchester U), 1978 v T, Pol, N (sub); 1980 v Bul, US, Ni, E, Cy; 1981 v Cz, Pol; 1982 v Alg; 1983 v Sp (2); (with Coventry C), 1984 v Pol, Is; (with Luton T), 1988 v L, R (17)

Hale, A. (Aston Villa), 1962 v A; (with Doncaster R), 1963 v Ic; 1964 v Sp (2); (with Waterford), 1967 v Sp; 1968 v Pol (sub); 1969 v Pol, A, D; 1970 v S, Cz; 1971 v Pol (sub); 1972 v A (sub) (13)

Hamilton, T. (Shamrock R), 1959 v Cz (2) (2)

Hand, E. K. (Portsmouth), 1969 v Cz (sub); 1970 v Pol, WG; 1971 v Pol, A; 1973 v USSR, F, USSR, Pol, F; 1974 v Pol, Br, U, Ch; 1975 v T, Sw, USSR, Sw, WG; 1976 v T (20)

Harrington, W. (Cork), 1936 v Ho, Sw, H, L (4)

Hartnett, J. B. (Middlesbrough), 1949 v Sp; 1954 v L (2)

Haverty, J. (Arsenal), 1956 v Ho; 1957 v D, WG, E (2); 1958 v D, Pol, A; 1959 v Pol; 1960 v Se, Ch; 1961 v W, N, S (2); (with Blackburn R), 1962 v Cz (2); (with Millwall), 1963 v S; 1964 v A, Sp, Pol, N, E; (with Celtic), 1965 v Pol; (with Bristol R), 1965 v Sp; (with Shelbourne), 1966 v Sp (2), WG, A, Bel; 1967 v T, Sp (32)

Hayes, A. W. P. (Southampton), 1979 v D (1)

Hayes, W. E. (Huddersfield T), 1947 v E, P (2)

Hayes, W. J. (Limerick), 1949 v Bel (1)

Healey, R. (Cardiff C), 1977 v Pol; 1980 v E (sub) (2)

Heighway, S. D. (Liverpool), 1971 v Pol, Se (2), I, A; 1973 v USSR; 1975 v USSR, T, USSR, WG; 1976 v T, N; 1977 v E, F (2), Sp, Bul; 1978 v Bul, N, D; 1979 v Ni, Bul; 1980 v Bul, US, Ni, E, Cy, Arg; 1981 v Bel, F, Cy, W, Bel; (with Minnesota K), 1982 v Ho (34)

Henderson, B. (Drumcondra), 1948 v P, Sp (2)

Hennessy, J. (Shelbourne), 1966 v Pol, Bel, Sp, WG; (with St Patrick's Ath), 1969 v A (5)

Herrick, J. (Cork Hibernians), 1972 v A, Ch (sub); (with Shamrock R), 1973 v F (sub) (3)

Higgins, J. (Birmingham C), 1951 v Arg (1)

Holmes, J. (Coventry C), 1971 v A (sub); 1973 v F, USSR, Pol, F, N; 1974 v Pol, Br; 1975 v USSR, Sw; 1976 v T,

N, Pol; 1977 v E, T, F, Sp; (with Tottenham H), F, Pol, Bul; 1978 v Bul, T, Pol, N, D; 1979 v Ni, E, D, Bul; (with Vancouver W), 1981 v W (30)

Horlacher, A. F. (Bohemians), 1930 v Bel; 1932 v Sp, Ho; 1934 v Ho (sub); 1935 v H; 1936 v Ho, Sw (7)

Houghton, R. J. (Oxford U), 1986 v W, U, Ic, Cz; 1987 v Bel (2), S (2), Pol, L; 1988 v L, Bul; (with Liverpool), Is, Y, N, E, USSR, Ho; 1989 v Ni, Tun, Sp, F, H, Sp, Ma, H; 1990 v Ni, Ma, Fi, E, Eg, Ho, R, I; 1991 v Mor, T, E (2), Pol, Ch, US; 1992 v H, Alb, US, I, P; (with Aston Villa), 1993 v D, Sp, Ni, D, Alb, La, Li (53)

Howlett, G. (Brighton & HA), 1984 v Chn (sub) (1)

Hoy, M. (Dundalk), 1938 v N; 1939 v Sw, Pol, H (2), G (6)

Hughton, C. (Tottenham H), 1980 v US, E, Sw, Arg; 1981 v Ho, Bel, F, Cy, W, Bel, Pol; 1982 v F; 1983 v Ho, Sp, Ma, Sp; 1984 v Ic, Ho, Ma; 1985 v M (sub), USSR, N, I, Is, E, Sp; 1986 v Sw, USSR, U, Ic; 1987 v Bel, Bul; 1988 v Is, Y, Pol, N, E, USSR, Ho; 1989 v Ni, F, H, Sp, Ma, H; 1990 v W (sub), USSR (sub), Fi, T (sub), Ma; 1991 v T; (with West Ham U), Ch; 1992 v T (53)

Hurley, C. J. (Millwall), 1957 v E; (with Sunderland), 1958 v D, Pol, A; 1959 v Cz (2); 1960 v Se, Ch, WG, Se; 1961 v W, N, S (2); 1962 v Cz (2), A; 1963 v Ic (2), S; 1964 v A (2), Sp (2), Pol, N; 1965 v Sp; 1966 v WG, A, Bel; 1967 v T, Sp, T, Cz; 1968 v Cz, Pol; 1969 v Pol, D, Cz, (with Bolton W), H (40)

Hutchinson, F. (Drumcondra), 1935 v Sw, G (2)

Irwin, D. J. (Manchester U), 1991 v Mor, T, W, E, Pol, US; 1992 v H, Pol, W, US, Alb, US (sub), I; 1993 v La, D, Sp, Ni, D, Alb, La, Li (21)

Jordan, D. (Wolverhampton W), 1937 v Sw, F (2)

Jordan, W. (Bohemians), 1934 v Ho; 1938 v N (2)

Kavanagh, P. J. (Celtic), 1931 v Sp; 1932 v Sp (2)

Keane, R. M. (Nottingham F), 1991 v Ch; 1992 v H, Pol, W, Sw, Alb, US; 1993 v La, D, Sp, W, Ni, D, Alb, La, Li (16)

Keane, T. R. (Swansea T), 1949 v Sw, P, Se, Sp (4)

Kearin, M. (Shamrock R), 1972 v A (1)

Kearns, F. T. (West Ham U), 1954 v L (1)

Kearns, M. (Oxford U), 1970 v Pol (sub); (with Walsall), 1974 v Pol (sub), U, Ch; 1976 v N, Pol; 1977 v E, T, F (2), Sp, Bul; 1978 v N, D; 1979 v Ni, E; (with Wolverhampton W), 1980 v US, Ni (18)

Kelly, A. T. (Sheffield U), 1993 v W (sub) (1)

Kelly, D. T. (Walsall), 1988 v Is, R, Y; (with West Ham U), 1989 v Tun (sub); (with Leicester C), 1990 v USSR, Ma; 1991 v Mor, W (sub), Ch, US; 1992 v H; (with Newcastle U), I (sub), P; 1993 v Sp (sub), Ni (15)

Kelly, J. (Derry C), 1932 v Ho; 1934 v Bel; 1936 v Sw, L (4)

Kelly, J. A. (Drumcondra), 1957 v WG, E; (with Preston NE), 1962 v A; 1963 v Ic (2), S; 1964 v A (2), Sp (2), Pol; 1965 v Bel; 1966 v A, Bel; 1967 v Sp (2), T, Cz, Pol; 1968 v Pol, Cz; 1969 v Pol, A, D, Cz, D, H; 1970 v S, D, H, Pol, WG; 1971 v Pol, Se (2), I (2), A; 1972 v Ir, Ec, Ch, P; 1973 v USSR, F, USSR, Pol, F, N (48)

Kelly, J. P. V. (Wolverhampton W), 1961 v W, N, S; 1962 v Cz (2) (5)

Kelly, M. J. (Portsmouth), 1988 v Y, Pol (sub); 1989 v Tun; 1991 v Mor (4)

Kelly, N. (Nottingham F), 1954 v L (1)

Kendrick, J. (Everton), 1927 v I; 1934 v Bel, Ho; 1936 v Ho (4)

Kennedy, M. F. (Portsmouth), 1986 v Ic, Cz (sub) (2)

Kennedy, W. (St James' Gate), 1932 v Ho; 1934 v Bel, Ho (3)

Keogh, J. (Shamrock R), 1966 v WG (sub) (1)

Keogh, S. (Shamrock R), 1959 v Pol (1)

Kernaghan, A. N. (Middlesbrough), 1993 v La, D (2), Alb, La, Li (6)

Kiernan, F. W. (Shamrock R), 1951 v Arg, N; (with Southampton), 1952 v WG (2), A (5)

Kinnear, J. P. (Tottenham H), 1967 v T; 1968 v Cz, Pol; 1969 v A; 1970 v Cz, D, H, Pol; 1971 v Se (sub), I; 1972 v Ir, Ec, Ch, P; 1973 v USSR, F; 1974 v Pol, Br, U, Ch; 1975 v USSR, T, Sw, USSR, WG; (with Brighton & HA), 1976 v T (sub) (26)

Kinsella, J. (Shelbourne), 1928 v Bel (1)

Kinsella, P. (Shamrock R), 1932 v Ho; 1938 v N (2)

Kirkland, A. (Shamrock R), 1927 v I (1)

Lacey, W. (Shelbourne), 1927 v I; 1928 v Bel; 1930 v Bel (3)

Langan, D. (Derby Co), 1978 v T, N; 1980 v Sw, Arg; (with Birmingham C), 1981 v Ho, Bel, F, Cy, W, Bel, Cz, Pol; 1982 v Ho, F; (with Oxford U), 1985 v N, Sp, Sw; 1986 v W, U; 1987 v Bel, S, Pol, Br (sub), L (sub); 1988 v L (25)

Lawler, J. F. (Fulham), 1953 v A; 1954 v L, F; 1955 v N, H, N, WG; 1956 v Y (8)

Lawlor, J. C. (Drumcondra), 1949 v Bel; (with Doncaster R), 1951 v N, Arg (3)

Lawlor, M. (Shamrock R), 1971 v Pol, Se (2), I (sub); 1973 v Pol (5)

Lawrenson, M. (Preston NE), 1977 v Pol; (with Brighton), 1978 v Bul, Pol, N (sub); 1979 v Ni, E; 1980 v E, Cy, Sw; 1981 v Ho, Bel, F, Cy, Pol; (with Liverpool), 1982 v Ho, F; 1983 v Ho, Sp, Ic, Ma, Sp; 1984 v Ic, Ho, Ma, Is; 1985 v USSR, N, D, I, E, N; 1986 v Sw, USSR, D; 1987 v Bel, S; 1988 v Bul, Is (38)

Leech, M. (Shamrock R), 1969 v Cz, D, H; 1972 v A, Ir, Ec, P; 1973 v USSR (sub) (8)

Lennon, C. (St James' Gate), 1935 v H, Sw, G (3)

Lennox, G. (Dolphin), 1931 v Sp; 1932 v Sp (2)

Lowry, D. (St Patrick's Ath), 1962 v A (sub) (1)

Lunn, R. (Dundalk), 1939 v Sw, Pol (2)

Lynch, J. (Cork Bohemians), 1934 v Bel (1)

McAlinden, J. (Portsmouth), 1946 v P, Sp (2)

McCann, J. (Shamrock R), 1957 v WG (1)

McCarthy, J. (Bohemians), 1926 v I; 1928 v Bel; 1930 v Bel (3)

McCarthy, M. (Manchester C), 1984 v Pol, Chn; 1985 v M, D, I, Is, E, Sp, Sw; 1986 v Sw, USSR, W (sub), U, Ic, Cz; 1987 v S (2), Pol, Bul, Bel, Br, L; (with Celtic), 1988 v Bul, Is, R, Y, N, E, USSR, Ho; 1989 v Ni, Tun, Sp, F, H, Sp; (with Lyon), 1990 v WG, Ni, W, USSR, Fi, T, E, Eg, Ho, R, I; (with Millwall), 1991 v Mor, T, E, US; 1992 v H, T, Alb (sub), US, I, P (57)

McCarthy, M. (Shamrock R), 1932 v Ho (1)

McConville, T. (Dundalk), 1972 v A; (with Waterford), 1973 v USSR, F, USSR, Pol, F (6)

McDonagh, Joe (Shamrock R), 1984 v Pol (sub), Ma (sub); 1985 v M (sub) (3)

McDonagh, J. (Everton), 1981 v W, Bel, Cz; (with Bolton W), 1982 v Ho, F, Ch, Br; 1983 v Ho, Sp, Ic, Ma, Sp; (with Notts Co), 1984 v Ic, Ho, Pol; 1985 v M, USSR, N, D, Sp, Sw; 1986 v Sw, USSR, D (24)

McEvoy, M. A. (Blackburn R), 1961 v S (2); 1963 v S; 1964 v A, Sp (2), Pol, N, E; 1965 v Pol, Bel, Sp; 1966 v Sp (2); 1967 v Sp, T, Cz (17)

McGee, P. (QPR), 1978 v T, N (sub), D (sub); 1979 v Ni, E, D (sub), Bul (sub); 1980 v Cz, Bul; (with Preston NE), US, Ni, Cy, Sw, Arg; 1981 v Bel (sub) (15)

McGoldrick, E. J. (C Palace), 1992 v Sw, US, I, P (sub); 1993 v D, W, Ni (sub), D (8)

McGowan, D. (West Ham U), 1949 v P, Se, Sp (3)

McGowan, J. (Cork U), 1947 v Sp (1)

McGrath, M. (Blackburn R), 1958 v A; 1959 v Pol, Cz (2); 1960 v Se, WG, Se; 1961 v W; 1962 v Cz (2); 1963 v S; 1964 v A (2), E; 1965 v Pol, Bel, Sp; 1966 v Sp; (with Bradford), 1966 v WG, A, Bel; 1967 v T (22)

McGrath, P. (Manchester U), 1985 v I (sub), Is, E, N (sub), Sw (sub); 1986 v Sw (sub), D, W, Ic, Cz; 1987 v Bel (2), S (2), Pol, Bul, Br, L; 1988 v L, Bul, Y, Pol, N, E, Ho; 1989 v Ni, F, H, Sp, Ma, H; (with Aston Villa), 1990 v WG, Ma, USSR, Fi, T, E, Eg, Ho, R, I; 1991 v E (2), W, Pol, Ch (sub), US; 1992 v Pol, T, Sw, US, Alb, US, I, P; 1993 v La, Sp, Ni, D, La, Li (61)

McGuire, W. (Bohemians), 1936 v Ho (1)

McKenzie, G. (Southend U), 1938 v N (2), Cz, Pol; 1939 v Sw, Pol, H (2), G (9)

Mackey, G. (Shamrock R), 1957 v D, WG, E (3)

McLoughlin, A. F. (Swindon T), 1990 v Ma, E (sub), Eg (sub); 1991 v Mor (sub), E (sub); (with Southampton), W, Ch (sub); 1992 v H (sub), W (sub); (with Portsmouth), US, I (sub), P; 1993 v W (13)

McLoughlin, F. (Fordsons), 1930 v Bel; (with Cork), 1932 v Sp (2)

McMillan, W. (Belfast Celtic), 1946 v P, Sp (2)

McNally, J. B. (Luton T), 1959 v Cz; 1961 v S; 1963 v Ic (3)

Macken, A. (Derby Co), 1977 v Sp (1)

Madden, O. (Cork), 1936 v H (1)

Maguire, J. (Shamrock R), 1929 v Bel (1)

Malone, G. (Shelbourne), 1949 v Bel (1)

Mancini, T. J. (QPR), 1974 v Pol, Br, U, Ch; (with Arsenal), 1975 v USSR (5)

Martin, C. (Bo'ness), 1927 v I (1)

Martin, C. J. (Glentoran), 1946 v P (sub), Sp; 1947 v E; (with Leeds U), 1947 v Sp; 1948 v P, Sp; (with Aston Villa), 1949 v Sw, Bel, P, Se, Sp; 1950 v Fi, E, Fi, Se, Bel; 1951 v Arg; 1952 v WG, A, Sp; 1954 v F (2), L; 1955 v N, Ho, N, WG; 1956 v Y, Sp, Ho (30)

Martin, M. P. (Bohemians), 1972 v A, Ir, Ec, Ch, P; 1973 v USSR; (with Manchester U), 1973 v USSR, Pol, F, N; 1974 v Pol, Br, U, Ch; 1975 v USSR, T, Sw, USSR, Sw, WG; (with WBA), 1976 v T, N, Pol; 1977 v E, T, F (2), Sp, Pol, Bul; (with Newcastle U), 1979 v D, Bul, WG; 1980 v W, Cz, Bul, US, Ni; 1981 v F, Bel, Cz; 1982 v Ho, F, Alg, Ch, Br, Tr; 1983 v Ho, Sp, Ma, Sp (51)

Meagan, M. K. (Everton), 1961 v S; 1962 v A; 1963 v Ic; 1964 v Sp; (with Huddersfield T), 1965 v Bel; 1966 v Sp (2), A, Bel; 1967 v Sp, T, Sp, T, Cz; 1968 v Cz, Pol; (with Drogheda), 1970 v S (17)

Meehan, P. (Drumcondra), 1934 v Ho (1)

Milligan, M. J. (Oldham Ath), 1992 v US (sub) (1)

Monahan, P. (Sligo R), 1935 v Sw, G (2)

Mooney, J. (Shamrock R), 1965 v Pol, Bel (2)

Moore, P. (Shamrock R), 1931 v Sp; 1932 v Ho; (with Aberdeen), 1934 v Bel, Ho; 1935 v H, G; (with Shamrock R), 1936 v Ho; 1937 v G, H (9)

Moran, K. (Manchester U), 1980 v Sw, Arg; 1981 v Bel, F, Cy, W (sub), Bel, Cz, Pol; 1982 v F, Alg; 1983 v Ic; 1984 v Ic, Ho, Ma, Is; 1985 v M; 1986 v D, Ic, Cz; 1987 v Bel (2), S (2), Pol, Bul, Br, L; 1988 v L, Bul, Is, R, Y, Pol, N, E, USSR, Ho; (with Sporting Gijon), 1989 v Ni, Sp, H, Sp, Ma, H; 1990 v Ma; (with Blackburn R), W, USSR (sub), Ma, E, Eg, Ho, R, I; 1991 v T (sub), W, E, Pol, Ch, US; 1992 v Pol, US; 1993 v D, Sp, Ni, Alb (66)

Moroney, T. (West Ham U), 1948 v Sp; 1949 v P, Se, Sp; 1950 v Fi, E, Fi, Bel; 1951 v N (2); 1952 v WG; (with Evergreen U), 1954 v F (12)

Morris, C. B. (Celtic), 1988 v Is, R, Y, Pol, N, E, USSR, Ho; 1989 v Ni, Tun, Sp, F, H (1 + 1 sub); 1990 v WG, Ni, Ma (sub), W, USSR, Fi (sub), T, E, Eg, Ho, R, I; 1991 v E; 1992 v H (sub), Pol, W, Sw, US (2), P; (with Middlesbrough), 1993 v W (35)

Moulson, C. (Lincoln C), 1936 v H, L; (with Notts Co), 1937 v H, Sw, F (5)

Moulson, G. B. (Lincoln C), 1948 v P, Sp; 1949 v Sw (3)

Mucklan, C. (Drogheda U), 1978 v Pol (1)

Muldoon, T. (Aston Villa), 1927 v I (1)

Mulligan, P. M. (Shamrock R), 1969 v Cz, D, H; 1970 v S, Cz, D; (with Chelsea), 1970 v H, Pol, WG; 1971 v Pol,

Se, I; 1972 v A, Ir, Ec, Ch, P; (with C Palace), 1973 v F, USSR, Pol, F, N; 1974 v Pol, Br, U, Ch; 1975 v USSR, T, Sw, USSR, Sw; (with WBA), 1976 v T, Pol; 1977 v E, T, F (2), Pol, Bul; 1978 v Bul, N, D; 1979 v E, D, Bul (sub), WG; (with Shamrock R), 1980 v W, Cz, Bul, US (sub) (50)

Munroe, L. (Shamrock R), 1954 v L (1)

Murphy, A. (Clyde), 1956 v Y (1)

Murphy, B. (Bohemians), 1986 v U (1)

Murphy, J. (C Palace), 1980 v W, US, Cy (3)

Murray, T. (Dundalk), 1950 v Bel (1)

Newman, W. (Shelbourne), 1969 v D (1)

Nolan, R. (Shamrock R), 1957 v D, WG, E; 1958 v Pol; 1960 v Ch, WG, Se; 1962 v Cz (2); 1963 v Ic (10)

O'Brien, F. (Philadelphia F), 1980 v Cz, E, Cy (sub), Arg (sub) (4)

O'Brien, L. (Shamrock R), 1986 v U; (with Manchester U), 1987 v Br; 1988 v Is (sub), R (sub), Y (sub), Pol (sub); 1989 v Tun; (with Newcastle U), Sp (sub); 1992 v Sw (sub); 1993 v W (10)

O'Brien, M. T. (Derby Co), 1927 v I; (with Walsall), 1929 v Bel; (with Norwich C), 1930 v Bel; (with Watford), 1932 v Ho (4)

O'Brien, R. (Notts Co), 1976 v N, Pol; 1977 v Sp, Pol (4)

O'Byrne, L. B. (Shamrock R), 1949 v Bel (1)

O'Callaghan, B. R. (Stoke C), 1979 v WG (sub); 1980 v W, US; 1981 v W; 1982 v Br, Tr (6)

O'Callaghan, K. (Ipswich T), 1981 v Cz, Pol; 1982 v Alg, Ch, Br, Tr (sub); 1983 v Sp, Ic (sub), Ma (sub), Sp (sub); 1984 v Ic, Ho, Ma; 1985 v M (sub), N (sub), D (sub), E (sub); (with Portsmouth), 1986 v Sw (sub), USSR (sub); 1987 v Br (20)

O'Connell, A. (Dundalk), 1967 v Sp; (with Bohemians), 1971 v Pol (sub) (2)

O'Connor, T. (Shamrock R), 1950 v Fi, E, Fi, Se (4)

O'Connor, T. (Fulham), 1968 v Cz; (with Dundalk), 1972 v A, Ir (sub), Ec (sub), Ch; (with Bohemians), 1973 v F (sub), Pol (sub) (7)

O'Driscoll, J. F. (Swansea T), 1949 v Sw, Bel, Se (3)

O'Driscoll, S. (Fulham), 1982 v Ch, Br, Tr (sub) (3)

O'Farrell, F. (West Ham U), 1952 v A; 1953 v A; 1954 v F; 1955 v Ho, N; 1956 v Y, Ho; (with Preston NE), 1958 v D; 1959 v Cz (9)

O'Flanagan, K. P. (Bohemians), 1938 v N, Cz, Pol; 1939 v Pol, H (2), G; (with Arsenal), 1947 v E, Sp, P (10)

O'Flanagan, M. (Bohemians), 1947 v E (1)

O'Hanlon, K. G. (Rotherham U), 1988 v Is (1)

O'Kane, P. (Bohemians), 1935 v H, Sw, G (3)

O'Keefe, E. (Everton), 1981 v W; (with Port Vale), 1984 v Chn; 1985 v M, USSR (sub), E (5)

O'Keefe, T. (Cork), 1934 v Bel; (with Waterford), 1938 v Cz, Pol (3)

O'Leary, D. (Arsenal), 1977 v E, F (2), Sp, Bul; 1978 v Bul, N, D; 1979 v E, Bul, WG; 1980 v W, Bul, Ni, E, Cy; 1981 v Ho, Cz, Pol; 1982 v Ho, F; 1983 v Ho, Ic, Sp; 1984 v Pol, Is, Chn; 1985 v USSR, N, D, Is, E (sub), N, Sp, Sw; 1986 v Sw, USSR, D, W; 1989 v Sp, Ma, H; 1990 v WG, Ni (sub), Ma, W (sub), USSR, Fi, T, Ma, R (sub); 1991 v Mor, T, E (2), Pol, Ch; 1992 v H, Pol, T, W, Sw, US, Alb, I, P; 1993 v W (67)

O'Leary, P. (Shamrock R), 1980 v Bul, US, Ni, E (sub), Cz, Arg; 1981 v Ho (7)

O'Mahoney, M. T. (Bristol R), 1938 v Cz, Pol; 1939 v Sw, Pol, H, G (6)

O'Neill, F. S. (Shamrock R), 1962 v Cz (2); 1965 v Pol, Bel, Sp; 1966 v Sp (2), WG, A; 1967 v Sp, T, Sp, T; 1969 v Pol, A, D, Cz, D (sub), H (sub); 1972 v A (20)

O'Neill, J. (Everton), 1952 v Sp; 1953 v F, A; 1954 v F, L, F; 1955 v N, Ho, N, WG; 1956 v Y, Sp; 1957 v D; 1958 v A; 1959 v Pol, Cz (2) (17)

O'Neill, J. (Preston NE), 1961 v W (1)

O'Neill, W. (Dundalk), 1936 v Ho, Sw, H, L; 1937 v G, H, Sw, F; 1938 v N; 1939 v H, G (11)

O'Regan, K. (Brighton & HA), 1984 v Ma, Pol; 1985 v M, Sp (sub) (4)

O'Reilly, J. (Brideville), 1932 v Ho; (with Aberdeen), 1934 v Bel, Ho; (with Brideville), 1936 v Ho; Sw, H, L; (with St James' Gate), 1937 v G, H, Sw, F; 1938 v N (2), Cz, Pol; 1939 v Sw, Pol, H (2), G (20)

O'Reilly, J. (Cork U), 1946 v P, Sp (2)

Peyton, G. (Fulham), 1977 v Sp (sub); 1978 v Bul, T, Pol; 1979 v D, Bul, WG; 1980 v W, Cz, Bul, E, Cy, Sw, Arg; 1981 v Ho, Bel, F, Cy; 1982 v Tr; 1985 v M (sub); 1986 v W, Cz; (with Bournemouth), 1988 v L, Pol; 1989 v Ni, Tun; 1990 v USSR, Ma; 1991 v Ch; 1992 v US (2), I (sub), P (33)

Peyton, N. (Shamrock R), 1957 v WG; (with Leeds U), 1960 v WG, Se (sub); 1961 v W; 1963 v Ic, S (6)

Phelan, T. (Wimbledon), 1992 v H, Pol (sub), T, W, Sw, US, I (sub), P; (with Manchester C), 1993 v La (sub), D, Sp, Ni, Alb, La, Li (15)

Quinn, N. J. (Arsenal), 1986 v Ic (sub), Cz; 1987 v Bul (sub); 1988 v L (sub), Bul (sub), Is, R (sub), Pol (sub), E (sub); 1989 v Tun (sub), Sp (sub), H (sub); (with Manchester C), 1990 v USSR, Ma, Eg (sub), Ho, R, I; 1991 v Mor, T, E (2) W, Pol; 1992 v H, W (sub), US, Alb, US, I (sub), P; 1993 v La, D, Sp, Ni, D, Alb, La, Li (39)

Reid, C. (Brideville), 1931 v Sp (1)

Richardson, D. J. (Shamrock R), 1972 v A (sub); (with Gillingham), 1973 v N (sub); 1980 v Cz (3)

Rigby, A. (St James' Gate), 1935 v H, Sw, G (3)

Ringstead, A. (Sheffield U), 1951 v Arg, N; 1952 v WG (2), A, Sp; 1953 v A; 1954 v F; 1955 v N; 1956 v Y, Sp, Ho; 1957 v E (2); 1958 v D, Pol, A; 1959 v Pol, Cz (2) (20)

Robinson, J. (Bohemians), 1928 v Bel; (with Dolphin), 1931 v Sp (2)

Robinson, M. (Brighton & HA), 1981 v F, Cy, Bel, Pol; 1982 v Ho, F, Alg, Ch; 1983 v Ho, Sp, Ic, Ma; (with Liverpool), 1984 v Ic, Ho, Is; 1985 v USSR, N; (with QPR), N, Sp, Sw; 1986 v D (sub), W, Cz (23)

Roche, P. J. (Shelbourne), 1972 v A; (with Manchester U), 1975 v USSR, T, Sw, USSR, Sw, WG; 1976 v T (8)

Rogers, E. (Blackburn R), 1968 v Cz, Pol; 1969 v Pol, A, D, Cz, D, H; 1970 v S, D, H; 1971 v I (2), A; (with Charlton Ath), 1972 v Ir, Ec, Ch, P; 1973 v USSR (19)

Ryan, G. (Derby Co), 1978 v T; (with Brighton & HA), 1979 v E, WG; 1980 v W, Cy (sub), Sw, Arg (sub); 1981 v F (sub), Pol (sub); 1982 v Ho, Alg (sub), Ch (sub), Tr; 1984 v Pol, Chn; 1985 v M (16)

Ryan, R. A. (WBA), 1950 v Se, Bel; 1951 v N, Arg, N; 1952 v WG (2), A, Sp; 1953 v F, A; 1954 v F, L, F; 1955 v N; (with Derby Co), 1956 v Sp (16)

Saward, P. (Millwall), 1954 v L; (with Aston Villa), 1957 v E (2); 1958 v D, Pol, A; 1959 v Pol, Cz; 1960 v Se, Ch, WG, Se; 1961 v W, N; (with Huddersfield T), 1961 v S; 1962 v A; 1963 v Ic (2) (18)

Scannell, T. (Southend U), 1954 v L (1)

Scully, P. J. (Arsenal), 1989 v Tun (sub) (1)

Sheedy, K. (Everton), 1984 v Ho (sub), Ma; 1985 v D, I, Is, Sw; 1986 v Sw, D; 1987 v S, Pol; 1988 v Is, R, Pol, E (sub), USSR; 1989 v Ni, Tun, H, Sp, Ma, H; 1990 v Ni, Ma, W (sub), USSR, Fi (sub), T, E, Eg, Ho, R, I; 1991 v W, E, Pol, Ch, US; 1992 v H, Pol, T, W; (with Newcastle U), Sw (sub), Alb; 1993 v La, W (sub) (45)

Sheridan, J. J. (Leeds U), 1988 v R, Y, Pol, N (sub); 1989 v Sp; (with Sheffield W), 1990 v W, T (sub), Ma, I (sub); 1991 v Mor (sub), T, Ch, US (sub); 1992 v H; 1993 v La (15)

Slaven, B. (Middlesbrough), 1990 v W, Fi, T (sub), Ma; 1991 v W, Pol (sub); 1993 v W (7)

Sloan, J. W. (Arsenal), 1946 v P, Sp (2)

Smyth, M. (Shamrock R), 1969 v Pol (sub) (1)

Squires, J. (Shelbourne), 1934 v Ho (1)

Stapleton, F. (Arsenal), 1977 v T, F, Sp, Bul; 1978 v Bul, N, D; 1979 v Ni, E (sub), D, WG; 1980 v W, Bul, Ni, E, Cy; 1981 v Ho, Bel, F, Cy, Bel, Cz, Pol; (with Manchester U), 1982 v Ho, F, Alg; 1983 v Ho, Sp, Ic, Ma, Sp; 1984 v Ic, Ho, Ma, Pol, Is, Chn; 1985 v N, D, I, Is, E, N, Sw; 1986 v Sw, USSR, D, U, Ic, Cz (sub); 1987 v Bel (2), S (2), Pol, Bul, L; (with Ajax), 1988 v L, Bul; (with Derby Co), R, Y, N, E, USSR, Ho; (with Le Havre), 1989 v F, Sp, Ma; (with Blackburn R), 1990 v WG, Ma (sub) (70)

Staunton, S. (Liverpool), 1989 v Tun, Sp (2), Ma, H; 1990 v WG, Ni, Ma, W, USSR, Fi, T, Ma, E, Eg, Ho, R, I; 1991 v Mor, T, E (2), W, Pol, Ch, US; (with Aston Villa), 1992 v Pol, T, Sw, US, Alb, US, I, P; 1993 v La, Sp, Ni, D, Alb, La, Li (41)

Stevenson, A. E. (Dolphin), 1932 v Ho; (with Everton), 1947 v E, Sp, P; 1948 v P, Sp; 1949 v Sw (7)

Strahan, F. (Shelbourne), 1964 v Pol, N, E; 1965 v Pol; 1966 v WG (5)

Sullivan, J. (Fordsons), 1928 v Bel (1)

Swan, M. M. G. (Drumcondra), 1960 v Se (sub) (1)

Synnott, N. (Shamrock R), 1978 v T, Pol; 1979 v Ni (3)

Thomas, P. (Waterford), 1974 v Pol, Br (2)

Townsend, A. D. (Norwich C), 1989 v F, Sp (sub), Ma (sub), H; 1990 v WG (sub), Ni, Ma, W, USSR, Fi (sub), T, Ma (sub), E, Eg, Ho, R, I; (with Chelsea), 1991 v Mor, T, E (2), W, Pol, Ch, US; 1992 v Pol, W, US, Alb, US, I; 1993 v La, D, Sp, Ni, D, Alb, La, Li (39)

Traynor, T. J. (Southampton), 1954 v L; 1962 v A; 1963 v Ic (2), S; 1964 v A (2), Sp (8)

Treacy, R. C. P. (WBA), 1966 v WG; 1967 v Sp, Cz; 1968 v Cz; (with Charlton Ath), 1968 v Pol; 1969 v Pol, Cz, D; 1970 v S, D, H (sub), Pol (sub), WG (sub); 1971 v Pol, Se (sub + 1), I, A; (with Swindon T), 1972 v Ir, Ec, Ch, P; 1973 v USSR, F, USSR, Pol, F, N; 1974 v Pol; (with Preston NE), Br; 1975 v USSR, Sw (2), WG; 1976 v T, N (sub), Pol (sub); (with WBA), 1977 v F, Pol; (with Shamrock R), 1978 v T, Pol; 1980 v Cz (sub) (42)

Tuohy, L. (Shamrock R), 1956 v Y; 1959 v Cz (2); (with Newcastle U), 1962 v A; 1963 v Ic (2); (with Shamrock R), 1964 v A; 1965 v Bel (8)

Turner, A. (Celtic), 1963 v S; 1964 v Sp (2)

Turner, C. J. (Southend U), 1936 v Sw; 1937 v G, H, Sw, F; (with West Ham U), 1938 v N (2), Cz, Pol; 1939 v H (10)

Vernon, J. (Belfast C), 1946 v P, Sp (2)

Waddock, G. (QPR), 1980 v Sw, Arg; 1981 v W, Pol (sub); 1982 v Alg; 1983 v Ic, Ma, Sp, Ho (sub); 1984 v Ic, Ho, Is; 1985 v I, Is, E, N, Sp; 1986 v USSR; (with Millwall), 1990 v USSR, T (20)

Walsh, D. J. (Linfield), 1946 v P, Sp; (with WBA), 1947 v Sp, P; 1948 v P, Sp; 1949 v Sw, P, Se, Sp; 1950 v E, Fi, Se; 1951 v N; (with Aston Villa), Arg, N; 1952 v Sp; 1953 v A; 1954 v F (2) (20)

Walsh, J. (Limerick), 1982 v Tr (1)

Walsh, M. (Blackpool), 1976 v N, Pol; 1977 v F (sub), Pol; (with Everton), 1979 v Ni (sub); (with QPR), D (sub), Bul, WG (sub); (with Porto), 1981 v Bel (sub), Cz; 1982 v Alg (sub); 1983 v Sp, Ho (sub), Sp (sub); 1984 v Ic (sub), Ma, Pol, Chn; 1985 v USSR, N (sub), D (21)

Walsh, M. (Everton), 1982 v Ch, Br, Tr; 1983 v Ic (4)

Walsh, W. (Manchester C), 1947 v E, Sp, P; 1948 v P, Sp; 1949 v Bel; 1950 v E, Se, Bel (9)

Waters, J. (Grimsby T), 1977 v T; 1980 v Ni (sub) (2)

Watters, F. (Shelbourne), 1926 v I (1)

Weir, E. (Clyde), 1939 v H (2), G (3)

Whelan, R. (St Patrick's Ath), 1964 v A, E (sub) (2)

Whelan, R. (Liverpool), 1981 v Cz (sub); 1982 v Ho (sub), F; 1983 v Ic, Ma, Sp; 1984 v Is; 1985 v USSR, N, I (sub), Is, E, N (sub), Sw (sub); 1986 v USSR (sub), W; 1987 v Bel (sub), S, Bul, Bel, Br, L; 1988 v L, Bul, Pol, N, E, USSR, Ho; 1989 v Ni, F, H, Sp, Ma; 1990 v WG, Ni, Ma, W, Ho (sub); 1991 v Mor, E; 1992 v Sw; 1993 v La, W (sub), Li (sub) (45)

Whelan, W. (Manchester U), 1956 v Ho; 1957 v D, E (2) (4)

White, J. J. (Bohemians), 1928 v Bel (1)

Whittaker, R. (Chelsea), 1959 v Cz (1)

Williams, J. (Shamrock R), 1938 v N (1)

BRITISH AND IRISH INTERNATIONAL GOALSCORERS SINCE 1872

Where two players with the same surname and initials have appeared for the same country, and one or both have scored, they have been distinguished by reference to the club which appears *first* against their name in the international appearances section (pages 812–859). Unfortunately, four of the scorers in Scotland's 10-2 victory v Ireland in 1888 are unknown, as is the scorer of one of their nine goals v Wales in March 1878.

ENGLAND

A'Court, A.	1	Carter, J. H.	4	Grainger, C.	3	Macdonald, M.	6
Adams, T. A.	4	Chadwick, E.	3	Greaves, J.	44	Mannion, W. J.	11
Adcock, H.	1	Chamberlain, M.	1	Grosvenor, A. T.	2	Mariner, P.	13
Alcock, C. W.	1	Chambers, H.	5	Gunn, W.	1	Marsh, R. W.	1
Allen, A.	3	Channon, M. R.	21			Matthews, S.	11
Allen, R.	2	Charlton, J.	6	Haines, J. T. W.	2	Matthews, V.	1
Anderson, V.	2	Charlton, R.	49	Hall, G. W.	9	McCall, J.	1
Astall, G.	1	Chenery, C. J.	1	Halse, H. J.	2	McDermott, T.	3
Athersmith, W. C.	3	Chivers, M.	13	Hampson, J.	5	Medley, L. D.	1
Atyeo, P. J. W.	5	Clarke, A. J.	10	Hampton, H.	2	Melia, J.	1
		Cobbold, W. N.	7	Hancocks, J.	2	Mercer, D. W.	1
Bache, J. W.	4	Cock, J. G.	2	Hardman, H. P.	1	Metson, P. C.	1
Bailey, N. C.	2	Common, A.	2	Harris, S. S.	2	Milburn, J. E. T.	10
Baily, E. F.	5	Connelly, J. M.	7	Hassall, H. W.	4	Miller, H. S.	1
Baker, J. H.	3	Coppell, S. J.	7	Hateley, M.	9	Mills, G. R.	3
Ball, A. J.	8	Cotterill, G. H.	2	Haynes, K. E.	4	Milward, A.	3
Bambridge, A. L.	1	Cowans, G.	2	Hegan, K. E.	4	Mitchell, C.	5
Bambridge, E. C.	12	Crawford, R.	1	Henfrey, A. G.	2	Moore, J.	1
Barclay, R.	2	Crawshaw, T. H.	1	Hilsdon, G. R.	14	Moore, R. F.	2
Barnes, J.	11	Crayston, W. J.	1	Hine, E. W.	4	Moore, W. G. B.	2
Barnes, P. S.	4	Creek, F. N. S.	1	Hirst, D. E.	1	Morren, T.	1
Barton, J.	1	Crooks, S. D.	7	Hitchens, G. A.	5	Morris, F.	1
Bassett, W. I.	7	Currey, E. S.	2	Hobbis, H. H. F.	1	Morris, J.	3
Bastin, C. S.	12	Currie, A. W.	3	Hoddle, G.	8	Mortensen, S. H.	23
Beardsley, P. A.	8	Cursham, A. W.	2	Hodgetts, D.	1	Morton, J. R.	1
Beasley, A.	1	Cursham, H. A.	5	Hodgson, G.	1	Mosforth, W.	3
Beattie, T. K.	1			Holley, G. H.	8	Mullen, J.	6
Becton, F.	2	Daft, H. B.	3	Houghton, W. E.	5	Mullery, A. P.	1
Bedford, H.	1	Davenport, J. K.	2	Howell, R.	1		
Bell, C.	9	Davis, G.	1	Hughes, E. W.	1	Neal, P. G.	5
Bentley, R. T. F.	9	Davis, H.	1	Hulme, J. H. A.	4	Needham, E.	3
Bishop, S. M.	1	Day, S. H.	2	Hunt, G. S.	1	Nicholls, J.	1
Blackburn, F.	1	Dean, W. R.	18	Hunt, R.	18	Nicholson, W. E.	1
Blissett, L.	3	Devey, J. H. G.	1	Hunter, N.	2		
Bloomer, S.	28	Dewhurst, F.	11	Hurst, G. C.	24	O'Grady, M.	3
Bond, R.	2	Dix, W. R.	1			Osborne, F. R.	3
Bonsor, A. G.	1	Dixon, K. M.	4	Jack, D. N. B.	3		
Bowden, E. R.	1	Dixon, L. M.	1	Johnson, D. E.	6	Own goals	22
Bowers, J. W.	2	Douglas, B.	11	Johnson, E.	2		
Bowles, S.	1	Drake, E. J.	6	Johnson, J. A.	2	Page, L. A.	1
Bradford, G. R. W.	1	Ducat, A.	1	Johnson, T. C. F.	5	Paine, T. L.	7
Bradford, J.	7	Dunn, A. T. B.	2	Johnson, W. H.	1	Palmer, C. L.	1
Bradley, W.	2					Parry, E. H.	1
Bradshaw, F.	3	Eastham, G.	2	Kail, E. I. L.	2	Parry, R. A.	1
Bridges, B. J.	1	Edwards, D.	5	Kay, A. H.	1	Pawson, F. W.	1
Bridgett, A.	3	Elliott, W. H.	3	Keegan, J. K.	21	Payne, J.	2
Brindle, T.	1	Evans, R. E.	1	Kelly, K.	8	Peacock, A.	3
Britton, C. S.	1			Kennedy, R.	3	Pearce, S.	3
Broadbent, P. F.	2	Ferdinand, L.	1	Kenyon-Slaney, W. S.	2	Pearson, J. S.	5
Broadis, I. A.	8	Finney, T.	30	Keown, M. R.	3	Pearson, S. C.	5
Brodie, J. B.	1	Fleming, H. J.	9	Kevan, D. T.	8	Perry, W.	2
Bromley-Davenport, W.	2	Flowers, R.	10	Kidd, B.	1	Peters, M.	20
Brook, E. F.	10	Forman, Frank	1	Kingsford, R. K.	1	Pickering, F.	5
Brooking, T. D.	5	Forman, Fred	3	Kirchen, A. J.	2	Platt, D.	20
Brooks, J.	2	Foster, R. E.	3	Kirton, W. J.	1	Pointer, R.	2
Broome, F. H.	3	Francis, G. C. J.	3				
Brown, A.	4	Francis, T.	12	Langton, R.	1	Quantrill, A.	1
Brown, A. S.	1	Freeman, B. C.	3	Latchford, R. D.	5		
Brown, G.	5	Froggatt, J.	2	Latherton, E. G.	1	Ramsay, A. E.	3
Brown, J.	3	Froggatt, R.	2	Lawler, C.	1	Revie, D. G.	4
Brown, W.	1			Lawton, T.	22	Reynolds, J.	3
Buchan, C. M.	4	Galley, T.	1	Lee, F.	10	Richardson, J. R.	2
Bull, S. G.	4	Gascoigne, P. J.	5	Lee, J.	1	Rigby, A.	3
Bullock, N.	2	Geary, F.	3	Lee, S.	2	Rimmer, E. J.	2
Burgess, H.	4	Gibbins, W. V. T.	3	Lindley, T.	15	Roberts, H.	1
Butcher, T.	3	Gilliatt, W. E.	3	Lineker, G.	48	Roberts, W. T.	4
Byrne, J. J.	8	Goddard, P.	1	Lofthouse, J. M.	3	Robinson, J.	3
		Goodall, J.	12	Lofthouse, N.	30	Robson, B.	26
Camsell, G. H.	18	Goodyer, A. C.	1	Hon. A. Lyttelton	1	Robson, R.	4
Carter, H. S.	7	Gosling, R. C.	2			Rowley, J. F.	6
		Goulden, L. A.	4	Mabbutt, G.	1	Royle, J.	2

Rutherford, J. 3
Sagar, C. 1
Sandilands, R. R. 2
Sansom, K. 1
Schofield, J. 1
Seed, J. M. 1
Settle, J. 6
Sewell, J. 3
Shackleton, L. F. 1
Sharp, J. 1
Shearer, A. 2
Shepherd, A. 2
Simpson, J. 1
Smith, A. M. 2
Smith, G. O. 12
Smith, Joe 1
Smith, J. R. 2
Smith, J. W. 4
Smith, R. 13
Smith, S. 1
Sorby, T. H. 1
Southworth, J. 3
Sparks, F. J. 3
Spence, J. W. 1
Spiksley, F. 5
Spilsbury, B. W. 5
Steele, F. C. 8
Stephenson, G. T. 2
Steven, T. M. 4
Stewart, J. 2
Stiles, N. P. 1
Storer, H. 1
Summerbee, M. G. 1

Tambling, R. V. 1
Taylor, P. J. 2
Taylor, T. 16
Thompson, P. B. 1
Thornewell, G. 1
Tilson, S. F. 6
Townley, W. J. 2
Tueart, D. 2

Vaughton, O. H. 6
Veitch, J. G. 3
Violett, D. S. 1

Waddle, C. R. 6
Walker, W. H. 9
Wall, G. 2
Wallace, D. 1
Walsh, P. 1
Waring, T. 4
Warren, B. 2
Watson, D. V. 4
Watson, V. M. 4
Webb, G. W. 1
Webb, N. 4
Wedlock, W. J. 2
Weir, D. 2
Weller, K. 1
Welsh, D. 1
Whateley, O. 2
Wheldon, G. F. 6
Whitfield, H. 1
Wignall, F. 2
Wilkes, A. 1
Wilkins, R. G. 3
Willingham, C. K. 1
Wilshaw, D. J. 10
Wilson, D. 1
Wilson, G. P. 1
Winckworth, W. N. 1
Windridge, J. E. 7
Wise, D. F. 1
Withe, P. 1
Wollaston, C. H. R. 1
Wood, H. 1
Woodcock, T. 16
Woodhall, G. 1
Woodward, V. J. 29
Worrall, F. 2
Worthington, F. S. 2
Wright, I. E. 1

Wright, M. 1
Wright, W. A. 3
Wylie, J. G. 1

Yates, J. 3

NORTHERN IRELAND

Anderson, T. 4
Armstrong, G. 12

Bambrick, J. 12
Barr, H. H. 1
Barron, H. 3
Best, G. 9
Bingham, W. L. 10
Black, K. 1
Blanchflower, D. 2
Blanchflower, J. 1
Brennan, B. 1
Brennan, R. A. 1
Brotherston, N. 3
Brown, J. 1
Browne, F. 2

Campbell, J. 1
Campbell, W. G. 1
Casey, T. 2
Caskey, W. 1
Cassidy, T. 1
Chambers, J. 3
Clarke, C. J. 13
Clements, D. 2
Cochrane, T. 1
Condy, J. 1
Connor, M. J. 1
Coulter, J. 1
Croft, T. 1
Crone, W. 1
Crossan, E. 1
Crossan, J. A. 10
Curran, S. 2
Cush, W. W. 5

Dalton, W. 6
D'Arcy, S. D. 1
Darling, J. 1
Davey, H. H. 1
Davis, T. L. 1
Dill, A. H. 1
Doherty, L. 1
Doherty, P. D. 3
Dougan, A. D. 8
Dowie, J. 2
Dunne, J. 4

Elder, A. R. 1
Emerson, W. 1
English, S. 1

Ferguson, W. 1
Ferris, J. 1
Ferris, R. O. 1
Finney, T. 2

Gaffkin, J. 5
Gara, A. 3
Gawkrodger, G. 1
Gibb, J. T. 2
Gibb, T. J. 1
Gibson, W. K. 1
Gillespie, W. 12
Goodall, A. L. 2

Halligan, W. 1
Hamill, M. 1
Hamilton, B. 4
Hamilton, W. 5
Hannon, D. J. 1
Harkin, J. T. 2
Harvey, M. 3
Hill, C. F. 1
Hughes, M. 1
Humphries, W. 1

Hunter, A. (*Distillery*) 1
Hunter, A. 1
   (*Blackburn R*)

Irvine, R. W. 3
Irvine, W. J. 8

Johnston, H. 2
Johnston, S. 2
Johnston, W. C. 1
Jones, S. 1
Jones, J. 1

Kelly, J. 4
Kernaghan, N. 2
Kirwan, J. 2

Lacey, W. 3
Lemon, J. 2
Lockhart, N. 3

Magilton, J. 4
Mahood, J. 2
Martin, D. K. 3
Maxwell, J. 7
McAdams, W. J. 7
McAllen, J. 1
McAuley, J. L. 1
McCandless, J. 3
McCaw, J. H. 1
McClelland, J. 1
McCluggage, A. 2
McCracken, W. 1
McCrory, S. 1
McCurdy, C. 1
McDonald, A. 3
McGarry, J. K. 1
McGrath, R. C. 4
McIlroy, J. 10
McIlroy, S. B. 5
McKnight, J. 2
McLaughlin, J. C. 6
McMordie, A. S. 3
McMorran, E. J. 4
McParland, P. J. 10
McWha, W. B. R. 1
Meldon, J. 1
Mercar, J. 1
Mercer, J. T. 1
Millar, W. 1
Milligan, D. 1
Milne, R. G. 2
Molyneux, T. B. 1
Moreland, V. 1
Morgan, S. 3
Morrow, W. J. 1
Murphy, N. 1

Neill, W. J. T. 2
Nelson, S. 1
Nicholl, C. J. 3
Nicholl, J. M. 2
Nicholson, J. J. 6

O'Hagan, C. 2
O'Kane, W. J. 1
O'Neill, J. 1
O'Neill, M. A. 1
O'Neill, M. H. 8
Own goals 5

Peacock, R. 2
Peden, J. 7
Penney, S. 2
Pyper, James 2
Pyper, John 1

Quinn, J. M. 6

Reynolds, J. 1
Rowley, R. W. M. 2

Sheridan, J. 2
Sherrard, J. 1

Simpson, W. J. 5
Sloan, H. A. de B. 4
Smyth, S. 5
Spence, D. W. 3
Stanfield, O. M. 9
Stevenson, A. E. 5
Stewart, I. 2

Taggart, G. P. 5
Thompson, F. W. 2
Tully, C. P. 3
Turner, E. 1

Walker, J. 1
Walsh, D. J. 5
Welsh, E. 1
Whiteside, N. 9
Whiteside, T. 1
Williams, J. R. 1
Williamson, J. 1
Wilson, D. J. 1
Wilson, K. J. 6
Wilson, S. J. 7
Wilton, J. M. 2

Young, S. 2

SCOTLAND

Aitken, R. 1
Aitkenhead, W. A. C. 2
Alexander, D. 1
Allan, D. S. 4
Allan, J. 2
Anderson, F. 1
Anderson, W. 4
Andrews, P. 1
Archibald, A. 1
Archibald, S. 4

Baird, D. 2
Baird, J. C. 2
Baird, S. 2
Bannon, E. 1
Barbour, A. 1
Barker, J. B. 4
Battles, B. Jr 1
Bauld, W. 2
Baxter, J. C. 3
Bell, J. 5
Bennett, A. 2
Berry, D. 1
Bett, J. 1
Beveridge, W. W. 1
Black, A. 3
Black, D. 1
Bone, J. 1
Booth, S. 1
Boyd, R. 1
Boyd, W. G. 1
Brackenridge, T. 1
Brand, R. 8
Brazil, A. 1
Bremner, W. J. 3
Brown, A. D. 6
Buchanan, P. S. 1
Buchanan, R. 1
Buckley, P. 1
Buick, A. 2
Burns, K. 1

Cairns, T. 1
Calderwood, R. 2
Caldow, E. 4
Campbell, C. 1
Campbell, John (*Celtic*) 5
Campbell, John 4
   (*Rangers*)
Campbell, P. 2
Campbell, R. 1
Cassidy, J. 1
Chalmers, S. 3
Chambers, T. 1
Cheyne, A. G. 4
Christie, A. J. 1

Clunas, W. L.	1
Collins, J.	3
Collins, R. Y.	10
Combe, J. R.	1
Conn, A.	1
Cooper, D.	6
Craig, J.	1
Craig, T.	1
Cunningham, A. N.	5
Curran, H. P.	1
Dalglish, K.	30
Davidson, D.	1
Davidson, J. A.	1
Delaney, J.	3
Devine, A.	1
Dewar, G.	1
Dewar, N.	4
Dickson, W.	4
Divers, J.	1
Docherty, T. H.	1
Dodds, D.	1
Donaldson, A.	1
Donnachie, J.	1
Dougall, J.	1
Drummond, J.	2
Dunbar, M.	1
Duncan, D.	7
Duncan, D. M.	1
Duncan, J.	1
Dunn, J.	1
Durie, G. S.	4
Easson, J. F.	1
Ellis, J.	1
Ferguson, J.	6
Fernie, W.	1
Fitchie, T. T.	1
Flavell, R.	2
Fleming, C.	2
Fleming, J. W.	3
Fraser, M. J. E.	4
Gallacher, H. K.	23
Gallacher, K. W.	1
Gallacher, P.	1
Galt, J. H.	1
Gemmell, T. (St Mirren)	1
Gemmell, T. (Celtic)	1
Gemmill, A.	8
Gibb, W.	1
Gibson, D. W.	3
Gibson, J. D.	2
Gibson, N.	1
Gillespie, Jas.	3
Gillick, T.	3
Gilzean, A. J.	12
Gossland, J.	2
Goudie, J.	1
Gough, C. R.	6
Gourlay, J.	1
Graham, A.	2
Graham, G.	3
Gray, A.	7
Gray, E.	3
Gray, F.	1
Greig, J.	3
Groves, W.	5
Hamilton, G.	4
Hamilton, J.	3
(Queen's Park)	
Hamilton, R. C.	14
Harper, J. M.	2
Harrower, W.	5
Hartford, R. A.	4
Heggie, C.	1
Henderson, J. G.	1
Henderson, W.	5
Herd, D. G.	4
Hewie, J. D.	2
Higgins, A.	1
(Newcastle U)	
Higgins, A. (Kilmarnock)	4
Highet, T. C.	1

Holton, J. A.	2
Houliston, W.	2
Howie, H.	1
Howie, J.	2
Hughes, J.	1
Hunter, W.	1
Hutchison, T.	1
Hutton, J.	1
Hyslop, T.	1
Imrie, W. N.	1
Jackson, A.	8
Jackson, C.	1
James, A. W.	3
Jardine, A.	1
Jenkinson, T.	1
Johnston, L. H.	1
Johnston, M.	14
Johnstone, D.	2
Johnstone, J.	4
Johnstone, Jas.	1
Johnstone, R.	9
Johnstone, W.	1
Jordan, J.	11
Kay, J. L.	5
Keillor, A.	3
Kelly, J.	1
Kelso, J.	1
Ker, G.	10
King, A.	1
King, J.	1
Kinnear, D.	1
Lambie, W. A.	5
Lang, J. J.	1
Law, D.	30
Leggat, G.	8
Lennie, W.	1
Lennnox, R.	3
Liddell, W.	6
Lindsay, J.	6
Linwood, A. B.	1
Logan, J.	1
Lorimer, P.	4
Love, A.	1
Lowe, J. (Cambuslang)	1
Lowe, J. (St Bernards)	1
Macari, L.	5
MacDougall, E. J.	3
MacLeod, M.	1
Mackay, D. C.	4
Mackay, G.	1
MacKenzie, J. A.	1
Madden, J.	5
Marshall, H.	1
Marshall, J.	1
Mason, J.	4
Massie, A.	1
Masson, D. S.	5
McAdam, J.	1
McAllister, G.	4
McAulay, J.	1
McAvennie, F.	1
McCall, J.	1
McCall, S. M.	1
McCalliog, J.	1
McCallum, N.	1
McClair, B. J.	2
McCoist, A.	15
McColl, R. S.	13
McCulloch, D.	3
McDougall, J.	4
McFarlane, A.	1
McFadyen, W.	2
McGhee, M.	2
McGregor, J. C.	1
McGrory, J.	6
McGuire, W.	1
McInally, A.	3
McInnes, T.	2
McKie, J.	2
McKimmie, S.	1
McKinnon, A.	1

McKinnon, R.	1
McKinnon, W. W.	5
McLaren, A.	4
McLaren, J.	1
McLean, A.	1
McLean, T.	1
McLintock, F.	1
McMahon, A.	6
McMenemy, J.	5
McMillan, I. L.	6
McNeil, H.	5
McNeill, W.	3
McPhail, J.	3
McPhail, R.	7
McPherson, J.	8
McPherson, R.	1
McQueen, G.	5
McStay, P.	9
Meiklejohn, D. D.	3
Millar, J.	2
Miller, T.	2
Miller, W.	1
Mitchell, R. C.	1
Morgan, W.	1
Morris, D.	1
Morris, H.	3
Morton, A. L.	5
Mudie, J. K.	9
Mulhall, G.	1
Munro, A. D.	1
Munro, N.	1
Murdoch, R.	5
Murphy, F.	1
Murray, J.	1
Napier, C. E.	3
Navey, D.	1
Neil, R. G.	2
Nevin, P. K. F.	4
Nicholas, C.	5
Nisbet, J.	2
O'Donnell, F.	2
O'Hare, J.	5
Ormond, W. E.	1
O'Rourke, F.	1
Orr, R.	1
Orr, T.	1
Oswald, J.	1
Own goals	14
Parlane, D.	1
Paul, H. McD.	2
Paul, W.	6
Pettigrew, W.	2
Provan, D.	1
Quinn, J.	7
Quinn, P.	1
Rankin, G.	2
Rankin, R.	2
Reid, W.	4
Reilly, L.	22
Renny-Tailyour, H. W.	1
Richmond, J. T.	1
Ring, T.	2
Rioch, B. D.	6
Ritchie, J.	1
Robertson, A.	2
Robertson, J.	2
Robertson, J. N.	8
Robertson, J. T.	2
Robertson, T.	1
Robertson, W.	1
Russell, D.	1
Scott, A. S.	5
Sellar, W.	4
Sharp, G.	1
Shaw, F. W.	1
Simpson, J.	1
Smith, A.	5
Smith, G.	4
Smith, J.	1
Smith, John	12

Somerville, G.	1
Souness, G. J.	3
Speedie, F.	2
St John, I.	9
Steel, W.	12
Stein, C.	10
Stevenson, G.	4
Stewart, R.	1
Stewart, W. E.	1
Strachan, G.	5
Sturrock, P.	3
Taylor, J. D.	1
Templeton, R.	1
Thomson, A.	1
Thomson, C.	4
Thomson, R.	1
Thomson, W.	1
Thornton, W.	1
Waddell, T. S.	1
Waddell, W.	6
Walker, J.	2
Walker, R.	7
Walker, T.	9
Wallace, I. A.	1
Wark, J.	7
Watson, J. A. K.	1
Watt, F.	2
Watt, W. W.	1
Weir, A.	1
Weir, J. B.	2
White, J. A.	3
Wilson, A.	2
Wilson, A. N.	13
Wilson, D.	2
(Queen's Park)	
Wilson, D. (Rangers)	9
Wilson, H.	1
Wylie, T. G.	1
Young, A.	5

WALES

Allchurch, I. J.	23
Allen, M.	3
Astley, D. J.	12
Atherton, R. W.	2
Bamford, T.	1
Barnes, W.	1
Blackmore, C. G.	1
Bodin, P. J.	3
Boulter, L. M.	1
Bowdler, J. C. H.	3
Bowen, D. L.	1
Bowen, M.	3
Boyle, T.	1
Bryan, T.	1
Burgess, W. A. R.	1
Burke, T.	1
Butler, A.	1
Chapman, T.	2
Charles, J.	1
Charles, M.	6
Charles, W. J.	15
Clarke, R. J.	5
Coleman, C.	1
Collier, D. J.	1
Cross, K.	1
Cumner, R. H.	1
Curtis, A.	6
Curtis, E. R.	3
Davies, D. W.	1
Davies, E. Lloyd	1
Davies, G.	2
Davies, L. S.	6
Davies, R. T.	8
Davies, R. W.	7
Davies, S.	5
Davies, W.	6
Davies, W. H.	1
Davies, William	5

OTHER INTERNATIONAL MATCHES 1992

January

Egypt (1) 2, Czechoslovakia (0) 0
Egypt (0) 0, Norway (0) 0
Portugal (0) 0, Spain (0) 0
USA (0) 0, CIS (0) 1
Australia (0) 0, Sweden (0) 0

February

Australia (0) 0, Sweden (0) 0
USA (1) 2, CIS (1) 1
Bermuda (1) 1, Norway (1) 3
Turkey (1) 1, Finland (0) 1
Portugal (1) 2, Holland (0) 0
Costa Rica (0) 0, USA (0) 0
Israel (1) 1, CIS (1) 2
San Marino (0) 0, Italy (2) 4
Rep of Ireland (0) 0, Wales (0) 1
Scotland (1) 1, Northern Ireland (0) 0
England (1) 2, France (0) 0
Spain (0) 1, CIS (0) 1
Tunisia (0) 1, Nigeria (0) 1
Tunisia (1) 2, Belgium (0) 1
Brazil (1) 3, USA (0) 0

March

Israel (2) 2, Cyprus (0) 1
Spain (1) 2, USA (0) 0
Mexico (1) 1, CIS (0) 1
Morocco (2) 3, USA (0) 1
Luxembourg (2) 2, Turkey (2) 3
Hungary (0) 2, Austria (1) 1
Cyprus (0) 1, Greece (2) 3
Scotland (1) 1, Finland (1) 1
Rep of Ireland (1) 2, Switzerland (1) 1
Italy (0) 1, Germany (0) 0
Holland (0) 2, Yugoslavia (0) 0
Czechoslovakia (1) 2, England (1) 2
France (2) 3, Belgium (2) 3
Poland (2) 2, Lithuania (0) 0

April

USA (2) 5, China (0) 0
Togo (0) 1, Ghana (0) 0
Turkey (1) 2, Denmark (0) 1
Romania (1) 2, Lithuania (0) 0
Israel (1) 2, Iceland (1) 2
Austria (3) 4, Lithuania (0) 0
Brazil (0) 3, Finland (1) 1
Tunisia (0) 0, Sweden (1) 1
Czechoslovakia (1) 1, Germany (1) 1
Switzerland (0) 0, Bulgaria (1) 2
Rep of Ireland (0) 4, USA (0) 1
Austria (0) 1, Wales (0) 1
Denmark (0) 1, Norway (0) 0
CIS (0) 2, England (1) 2
Uruguay (0) 1, Brazil (0) 0

May

Sweden (3) 5, Poland (0) 0
Hungary (0) 0, England (0) 1
Norway (1) 2, Faeroes (0) 0
England (0) 1, Brazil (1) 1
Austria (1) 2, Poland (2) 4
Mexico (2) 3, USA (0) 1
Canada (1) 1, Scotland (1) 3
Guatemala (1) 1, Ecuador (1) 1
Malta (1) 1, Latvia (0) 0
Switzerland (1) 2, France (1) 1
Holland (2) 3, Austria (1) 2
Sweden (2) 2, Hungary (0) 1
Norway (1) 1, Romania (0) 0
Germany (0) 1, Turkey (0) 0
Holland (2) 4, Wales (0) 0

June

Germany (1) 1, Northern Ireland (1) 1
Finland (1) 1, England (1) 2
Norway (0) 0, Scotland (0) 0
France (1) 1, Holland (1) 1
Sweden (1) 2, Colombia (0) 2
Norway (1) 1, Sweden (2) 2
Argentina (0) 2, Australia (0) 0
Uruguay (0) 2, Australia (0) 0
USA (0) 0, Ukraine (0) 0

July

Uruguay (1) 3, Ecuador (0) 1
Australia (0) 1, Croatia (0) 0
Malawi (0) 0, Zimbabwe (0) 0
Australia (2) 3, Croatia (1) 1
Honduras (1) 1, Colombia (0) 0
Malawi (0) 0, Zimbabwe (0) 0
Australia (0) 0, Croatia (0) 0
Cameroon (0) 0, Egypt (0) 1
Cameroon (0) 0, Egypt (1) 1

August

Uruguay (2) 2, Costa Rica (0) 1
Faeroes (1) 1, Israel (0) 1
Libya (0) 0, Niger (0) 0
Russia (0) 2, Mexico (0) 0
Czechoslovakia (2) 2, Austria (1) 2
Finland (0) 0, Poland (0) 0
France (0) 0, Brazil (1) 2
Norway (1) 2, Sweden (1) 2
Hungary (0) 2, Ukraine (1) 1
Romania (1) 2, Mexico (0) 0
Turkey (0) 3, Bulgaria (1) 2

September

Austria (1) 1, Portugal (0) 1
Canada (0) 0, USA (1) 2
Denmark (0) 1, Germany (0) 2
Holland (2) 2, Italy (2) 3
Poland (1) 1, Israel (1) 1
Spain (1) 1, England (0) 0
Brazil (3) 4, Costa Rica (1) 2
Hungary (0) 0, Israel (0) 0
Tunisia (1) 1, Algeria (1) 1
Uruguay (0) 0, Argentina (0) 0

October

Cyprus (0) 3, Malta (0) 0
USA (0) 0, Canada (0) 0
Germany (0) 1, Mexico (0) 1
Saudi Arabia (0) 3, USA (0) 0
Argentina (2) 4, Ivory Coast (0) 0
USA (2) 5, Ivory Coast (1) 2
Argentina (2) 3, Saudi Arabia (0) 1
Korea Rep (0) 0, United Arab Emirates (0) 0
Croatia (1) 3, Mexico (0) 0

November

Cyprus (0) 1, Slovenia (0) 1
Germany (0) 0, Austria (0) 0
Peru (0) 1, Ecuador (1) 1
Brazil (1) 1, Uruguay (1) 2
Argentina (1) 2, Poland (0) 0
Uruguay (0) 0, Poland (0) 1

December

Brazil (2) 3, Germany (0) 1
Uruguay (0) 1, Germany (1) 4

9th UEFA UNDER-21 CHAMPIONSHIP 1992–94

Group 1
Scotland 0, Portugal 0
Italy 1, Switzerland 0
Switzerland 4, Malta 0
Malta 0, Italy 1
Malta 0, Portugal 2
Scotland 3, Malta 0
Portugal 2, Italy 0
Italy 3, Malta 0
Switzerland 1, Portugal 1
Malta 1, Switzerland 4
Portugal 7, Malta 0

Group 2
San Marino 0, Norway 3
Holland 1, Poland 3
England 0, Norway 2
Turkey 4, San Marino 0
England 0, Turkey 1
Turkey 1, Holland 1
England 6, San Marino 0
Holland 0, Turkey 1
San Marino 0, Turkey 2
Holland 3, San Marino 0
Turkey 0, England 0
San Marino 0, Poland 5
Poland 1, England 4

Norway 1, England 1
Holland 2, Norway 1

Group 3
Denmark 3, Republic of Ireland 2
Albania 0, Germany 1
Spain 2, Republic of Ireland 1
Germany 1, Spain 2
Germany 4, Albania 1
Republic of Ireland 0, Germany 1
Germany 8, Republic of Ireland 0
Denmark 0, Spain 1
Denmark 1, Germany 4
Albania 1, Republic of Ireland 1
Denmark 5, Albania 0

Group 4
Belgium 1, Romania 0
Cyprus 2, Wales 4
Romania 1, Czechoslovakia 0
Belgium 3, Wales 1
Cyprus 0, Romania 2
Cyprus 0, Czechoslovakia 2
Wales 0, Belgium 0
Romania 1, Cyprus 0
Czechoslovakia 4, Romania 2

Group 5
Iceland 1, Greece 3
Russia 5, Iceland 0
Russia 2, Luxembourg 1
Greece 2, Hungary 1
Romania 1, Czechoslovakia 0
Greece 6, Luxembourg 0
Hungary 1, Greece 2
Luxembourg 0, Russia 6
Luxembourgg 1, Iceland 3
Russia 1, Greece 1
Iceland 0, Russia 1
Iceland 2, Hungary 1

Group 6
Sweden 6, Bulgaria 0
France 6, Austria 1
Austria 1, Israel 5
Israel 1, Sweden 1
Israel 1, Bulgaria 2
Israel 1, France 2
Austria 0, France 1
Austria 2, Bulgaria 0
Bulgaria 1, Israel 0
Sweden 1, Austria 1
Sweden 4, Israel 1
Finland 1, Israel 0

UEFA UNDER-18 CHAMPIONSHIP 1990–92
Final tournament in Germany

Quarter-finals
Portugal 4, Germany 0
Turkey 3, Hungary 0
England 6, Poland 1
CIS 4, Norway 4**

Fifth/Sixth place
Germany 3, Poland 2
Hungary 1, CIS 3

Semi-finals
Portugal 1**, England 1

Third place
England 1, Norway 1**

Turkey 2, Portugal 1*

*aet; **won on penalties

9th UEFA UNDER-18 CHAMPIONSHIPS
1992–93

Group 1
Belgium (2) 3, Iceland (0) 2
Iceland (1) 5, Belgium (2) 2

Group 2
Finland (1) 1, Scotland (0) 0
Scotland (0) 2, Finland (0) 1 aet

Group 3
Malta (0) 0, France (0) 0
France (2) 4, Malta (0) 0

Group 4
Albania (0) 0, Spain (2) 4
Spain (2) 3, Albania (1) 1

Group 5
Austria (2) 2, Turkey (2) 3
Turkey (0) 1, Austria (1) 1

Group 6
Cyprus (0) 0, Hungary (1) 2
Hungary (0) 5, Cyprus (1) 2

Group 7
Norway (1) 2, Germany (0) 3
Germany (0) 1, Norway (0) 1

Group 8
Czechoslovakia (0) 1, Denmark (0) 0
Denmark (1) 4, Czechoslovakia (1) 2

Group 9
Greece (2) 2, CIS (2) 2
CIS (1) 3, Greece (0) 1

Group 10
Wales (0) 0, Israel (0) 0
Wales (0), Holland (0) 1
Holland (2) 3, Israel (1) 1
Holland (1) 1, Wales (1) 1
Israel (0) 0, Holland (0) 1
Israel (1) 2, Wales (0) 2

Group 11
Romania (2) 4, Northern Ireland (1) 2
Romania (0) 1, Republic of Ireland (0) 0
Northern Ireland (0) 2, Republic of Ireland (2) 3
Republic of Ireland (0) 1, Romania (0) 1
Northern Ireland (0) 1, Romania (1) 4
Republic of Ireland (2) 3, Northern Ireland (3) 3

Group 12
Liechtenstein (0) 0, Switzerland (3) 8
Switzerland (4) 8, Liechtenstein (0) 0

Group 13
Luxembourg (0) 1, Sweden (2) 2
Luxembourg (0) 0, Portugal (2) 3
Portugal (0) 2, Sweden (0) 1

Group 14
Poland (0) 1, Bulgaria (2) 3
Bulgaria (1) 2, Poland (2) 2
Poland (1) 1, Italy (4) 5
Italy (3) 3, Bulgaria (0) 1
Italy (0) 2, Poland (0) 0
Bulgaria (0) 0, Italy (1) 2

Second Round

Group 1
Holland (1) 2, Denmark (1) 1
Denmark (0) 1, Holland (3) 3

Group 2
Portugal (1) 2, Russia (0) 1
Russia (0) 0, Portugal (0) 0

Group 3
Italy (0) 0, Hungary (1) 2
Hungary (0) 0, Italy (0) 1

Group 4
Turkey (0) 2, Switzerland (1) 1
Switzerland (0) 0, Turkey (0) 1

Group 5
Finland (3) 3, France (1) 4
France (0) 2, Finland (0) 2

Group 6
Romania (0) 0, Iceland (0) 0
Iceland (0) 0, Romania (1) 1

Group 7
Germany (0) 0, Spain (0) 0
Spain (3) 5, Germany (1) 2

(Final Tournament in England July 1993)

v France 2-0 *(Gallen, Fowler)*
England: Day; Neville, Sharp, Caskey, Casper, Campbell, Tinkler, Butt, Joachim, Forrester (Fowler), Scholes (Gallen).
v Holland 4-1 *(Fowler, Joachim 2, Gallen)*
England: Day; Neville, Sharp, Caskey, Casper, Campbell, Tinkler (Bowman), Butt, Joachim, Fowler, Gallen (Whelan).
v Spain 5-1 *(Tinkler, Fowler 3, Forrester)*
England: Day; Neville, Sharp, Caskey, Casper, Campbell, Tinkler, Butt (Scholes), Joachim, Fowler, Gallen (Forrester).
v Turkey 1-0 *(Caskey (pen))*
England: Day; Neville, Sharp, Caskey, Casper, Campbell, Tinkler, Joachim, Scholes, Fowler, Gallen (Whelan).

Group A	Group B	Final at Nottingham Forest FC
Portugal 0, Romania 0	England 2, France 0	England 1, Turkey 0 att. 23,381
Hungary 1, Turkey 1	Holland 2, Spain 3	
Portugal 2, Hungary 0	Spain 4, France 1	
Romania 0, Turkey 3	England 4, Holland 1	
Turkey 2, Portugal 0	Spain 1, England 5	
Romania 0, Hungary 1	France 1, Holland 1	

11th UEFA UNDER-16 CHAMPIONSHIP 1993

FINAL TOURNAMENT IN TURKEY

Group A
Iceland (2) 6, Northern Ireland (2) 2
Poland (1) 1, Switzerland (1) 1
Poland (1) 2, Iceland (0) 0
Switzerland (0) 1, Northern Ireland (0) 1
Northern Ireland (0) 0, Poland (0) 1
Switzerland (1) 1, Iceland (0) 0

	P	W	D	L	F	A	Pts
Poland	3	2	1	0	4	1	5
Switzerland	3	1	2	0	3	2	4
Iceland	3	1	0	2	6	5	2
Northern Ireland	3	0	1	2	3	8	1

Group B
Hungary (2) 2, Greece (0) 0
Turkey (0) 0, Spain (0) 1
Greece (0) 0, Spain (0) 1
Hungary (0) 0, Turkey (1) 1
Greece (0) 2, Turkey (0) 2
Spain (0) 1, Hungary (1) 2

	P	W	D	L	F	A	Pts
Hungary	3	2	0	1	4	2	4
Spain	3	2	0	1	3	2	4
Turkey	3	1	1	1	3	3	3
Greece	3	0	1	2	2	5	1

Group C
Belgium (0) 1, England (0) 1
Czechoslovakia (1) 2, Republic of Ireland (0) 1
Belgium (0) 0, Czechoslovakia (0) 0
England (0) 1, Republic of Ireland (0) 0
England (0) 0, Czechoslovakia (2) 2
Republic of Ireland (1) 1, Belgium (0) 2

	P	W	D	L	F	A	Pts
Czechoslovakia	3	2	1	0	4	1	5
Belgium	3	1	2	0	3	2	4
England	3	1	1	1	2	3	3
Republic of Ireland	3	0	0	3	2	5	0

Group D
France (0) 1, Russia (1) 1
Portugal (0) 1, Italy (2) 2
France (1) 3, Portugal (0) 1
Russia (0) 1, Italy (1) 2
Italy (1) 1, France (1) 1
Russia (1) 1, Portugal (1) 1

	P	W	D	L	F	A	Pts
Italy	3	2	1	0	5	3	5
France	3	1	2	0	5	3	4
Russia	3	0	2	1	3	4	2
Portugal	3	0	1	2	3	6	1

Quarter-finals
Holland (0) 0, Belgium (0) 0
Poland won on penalties
Czechoslovakia (1) 3, Switzerland (0) 0
Hungary (0) 0, France (1) 3
Italy (0) 0, Spain (0) 0
Italy won on penalties

Semi-finals
Poland (1) 2, France (0) 1 aet
Czechoslovakia (0) 0, Italy (0) 0
Italy won on penalties

Match for third place
France (1) 1, Czechoslovakia (1) 2

Final
Poland (1) 1, Italy (0) 0

OTHER BRITISH AND IRISH INTERNATIONAL MATCHES 1992–93

Santander, 9 September 1992, 22,000

Spain (1) 1 *(Fonseca)*

England (0) 0

Spain: Zubizarreta; Ferrer, Toni (Cristobal), Solozabal, Lopez, Vizcaino, Fonseca (Fernandio) Michel (Goicoechea), Bakero (Alfonso), Martin Vazquez (Alvaro), Amor.
England: Woods; Dixon (Bardsley) (Palmer), Pearce, Ince, Walker, Wright M, White (Merson), Platt, Clough, Shearer, Sinton (Deane).

Bristol, 21 October, 3360

Barclays League (2) 3 *(Maskell 2, Allen)*

Italy Serie B (0) 1 *(Maini)*

Barclays League: Wright; Kerslake, Drysdale, Futcher, Calderwood, Awford, Magilton, Allen M, Maskell (Cole), Peacock, Goodman (Stewart).
Serie B: Bucci; Tarozzi, Francesconi, Corrado, Verga, Lamacchi (Grossi), Olivares, Piubelli, Carbone (Gennari), Cristallini (Maini), Del Vecchio.

Foxboro, 9 June 1993, 37,652

USA (1) 2 *(Dooley, Lalas)*

England (0) 0

USA: Meola; Armstrong, Lapper, Doyle, Agoos, Clavijo, Dooley (Lalas), Harkes, Ramos (Jones), Wegerle, Wynalda (Stewart).
England: Woods; Dixon, Pallister, Palmer (Walker), Dorigo, Batty, Ince, Sharpe, Clough, Barnes, Ferdinand (Wright I).

Washington, 13 June 1993, 54,118

Brazil (0) 1 *(Marcio Santos 76)*

England (0) 1 *(Platt)*

Brazil: Taffarel; Jorginho, Valber, Marcio Santos, Nonato (Cafu), Luisinho (Palhinha), Dunga, Valdeir (Almir), Rai, Careca, Elivelton.

England: Flowers; Barrett, Pallister, Walker, Dorigo, Sinton Batty (Platt), Ince (Palmer), Sharpe, Wright I, Clough (Merson).

Detroit, 19 June 1993, 62,126

Germany (1) 2 *(Effenberg, Klinsmann)*

England (1) 1 *(Platt)*

Germany: Illgner; Effenberg (Zorc), Helmer, Buchwald, Moller (Sammer), Matthaus, Schulz, Ziege, Strunz, Riedle, Klinsmann.
England: Martyn; Barrett, Pallister (Keown), Walker, Sinton, Platt, Clough (Wright I), Ince, Sharpe (Winterburn), Merson, Barnes.

Dublin, 17 February 1993, 9500

Republic of Ireland: (0) 2 *(Sheedy, Coyne)*

Wales (1) 1 *(Hughes)*

Republic of Ireland: Bonner (Kelly), Morris, McGoldrick, Carey, O'Leary (Whelan) (Sheedy), Keane, O'Brien, Byrne, Cascarino (Slaven), Kelly D, McLoughlin.
Wales: Southall (Roberts), Phillips, Bodin, Aizlewood, Young (Coleman), Symons, Williams (Allen), Horne, Speed, Hughes, Pembridge.

Ibrox, 24 March 1993, 36,400

Scotland (0) 0

Germany (1) 1 *(Riedle)*

Scotland: Walker; Wright (Booth), Boyd, Levein, Irvine, McLaren, Bowman, Ferguson, Collins, McInally, Robertson.
Germany: Kopke; Zorc, Helmer, Kohler, Thon, Buchwald, Klinsmann, Hassler, Riedle, Matthaus, Doll (Effenberg).

ENGLAND UNDER-21 RESULTS 1976–93

EC UEFA Competition for Under-21 Teams

v ALBANIA

Year	Date		Venue	Eng	Alb
EC1989	Mar	7	Shkroda	2	1
EC1989	April	25	Ipswich	2	0

v BRAZIL

				Eng	B
1993	June	11	Toulon	0	0

v BULGARIA

				Eng	Bulg
EC1979	June	5	Pernik	3	1
EC1979	Nov	20	Leicester	5	0
1989	June	5	Toulon	2	3

v CZECHOSLOVAKIA

				Eng	Cz
1990	May	28	Toulon	2	1
1993	June	9	Toulon	1	1

v DENMARK

				Eng	Den
EC1978	Sept	19	Hvidovre	2	1
EC1979	Sept	11	Watford	1	0
EC1982	Sept	21	Hvidovre	4	1
EC1983	Sept	20	Norwich	4	1
EC1986	Mar	12	Copenhagen	1	0
EC1986	Mar	26	Manchester	1	1
1988	Sept	13	Watford	0	0

v EAST GERMANY

				Eng	EG
EC1980	April	16	Sheffield	1	2
EC1980	April	23	Jena	0	1

v FINLAND

				Eng	Fin
EC1977	May	26	Helsinki	1	0
EC1977	Oct	12	Hull	8	1
EC1984	Oct	16	Southampton	2	0
EC1985	May	21	Mikkeli	1	3

v FRANCE

				Eng	Fra
EC1984	Feb	28	Sheffield	6	1
EC1984	Mar	28	Rouen	1	0
1987	June	11	Toulon	0	2
EC1988	April	13	Besancon	2	4
EC1988	April	27	Highbury	2	2
1988	June	12	Toulon	2	4
1990	May	23	Toulon	7	3
1991	June	3	Toulon	1	0
1993	June	15	Toulon	1	0

v GERMANY

				Eng	G
1991	Sept	10	Scunthorpe	2	1

v GREECE

				Eng	Gre
EC1982	Nov	16	Piraeus	0	1
EC1983	Mar	29	Portsmouth	2	1
1989	Feb	7	Patras	0	1

v HOLLAND

				Eng	H
1993	Apr	27	Portsmouth	3	0

v HUNGARY

				Eng	Hun
EC1981	June	5	Keszthely	2	1
EC1981	Nov	17	Nottingham	2	0
EC1983	April	26	Newcastle	1	0
EC1983	Oct	11	Nyiregyhaza	2	0
1990	Sept	11	Southampton	3	1

v ITALY

				Eng	Italy
EC1978	Mar	8	Manchester	2	1
EC1978	April	5	Rome	0	0
EC1984	April	18	Manchester	3	1
EC1984	May	2	Florence	0	1
EC1986	April	9	Pisa	0	2
EC1986	April	23	Swindon	1	1

v ISRAEL

				Eng	Isr
1985	Feb	27	Tel Aviv	2	1

v MEXICO

				Eng	Mex
1988	June	5	Toulon	2	1
1991	May	29	Toulon	6	0

v MOROCCO

				Eng	Mor
1987	June	7	Toulon	2	0
1988	June	9	Toulon	1	0

v NORWAY

				Eng	Nor
EC1977	June	1	Bergen	2	1
EC1977	Sept	6	Brighton	6	0
1980	Sept	9	Southampton	3	0
1981	Sept	8	Drammen	0	0
EC1992	Oct	13	Peterborough	0	2
EC1993	June	1	Stavanger	1	1

v POLAND

				Eng	Pol
EC1982	Mar	17	Warsaw	2	1
EC1982	April	7	West Ham	2	2
EC1989	June	2	Plymouth	2	1
EC1989	Oct	10	Jastrzebie	3	1
EC1990	Oct	16	Tottenham	0	1
EC1993	May	28	Zdroj	4	1

v PORTUGAL

				Eng	Por
1987	June	13	Toulon	0	0
1990	May	21	Toulon	0	1
1993	June	7	Toulon	2	0

v REPUBLIC OF IRELAND

				Eng	Rep Ire
1981	Feb	25	Liverpool	1	0
1985	Mar	25	Portsmouth	3	2
1989	June	9	Toulon	0	0
EC1990	Nov	13	Cork	3	0
EC1991	Mar	26	Brentford	3	0

v ROMANIA

				Eng	Rom
EC1980	Oct	14	Ploesti	0	4
EC1981	April	28	Swindon	3	0
EC1985	April	30	Brasov	0	0
EC1985	Sept	10	Ipswich	3	0

v SAN MARINO

				Eng	SM
EC1993	Feb	16	Luton	6	0

v SENEGAL

				Eng	Sen
1989	June	7	Toulon	6	1
1991	May	27	Toulon	2	1

v SCOTLAND

				Eng	Scot
1977	April	27	Sheffield	1	0
EC1980	Feb	12	Coventry	2	1
EC1980	Mar	4	Aberdeen	0	0
EC1982	April	19	Glasgow	1	0
EC1982	April	28	Manchester	1	1
EC1988	Feb	16	Aberdeen	1	0
EC1988	Mar	22	Nottingham	1	0
1993	June	13	Toulon	1	0

v SPAIN

				Eng	Spa
EC1984	May	17	Seville	1	0
EC1984	May	24	Sheffield	2	0
1987	Feb	18	Burgos	2	1
1992	Sept	8	Burgos	1	0

v SWEDEN

				Eng	Swe
1979	June	9	Vasteras	2	1
1986	Sept	9	Ostersund	1	1
EC1988	Oct	18	Coventry	1	1
EC1989	Sept	5	Uppsala	0	1

v SWITZERLAND

				Eng	Swit
EC1980	Nov	18	Ipswich	5	0
EC1981	May	31	Neuenburg	0	0
1988	May	28	Lausanne	1	1

v USA

				Eng	USA
1989	June	11	Toulon	0	2

v TURKEY

				Eng	Tur
EC1984	Nov	13	Bursa	0	0
EC1985	Oct	15	Bristol	3	0
EC1987	April	28	Izmir	0	0
EC1987	Oct	13	Sheffield	1	1
EC1991	April	30	Izmir	2	2
EC1992	Nov	17	Orient	0	1
EC1993	Mar	30	Izmir	0	0

v USSR

				Eng	USSR
1987	June	9	Toulon	0	0
1988	June	7	Toulon	1	0
1990	May	25	Toulon	2	1
1991	May	31	Toulon	2	1

v WALES

				Eng	Wales
1976	Dec	15	Wolverhampton	0	0
1979	Feb	6	Swansea	1	0
1990	Dec	5	Tranmere	0	0

v WEST GERMANY

				Eng	WG
EC1982	Sept	21	Sheffield	3	1
EC1982	Oct	12	Bremen	2	3
1987	Sept	8	Ludenscheid	0	2

v YUGOSLAVIA

				Eng	Yugo
EC1978	April	19	Novi Sad	1	2
EC1978	May	2	Manchester	1	1
EC1986	Nov	11	Peterborough	1	1
EC1987	Nov	10	Zemun	5	1

BRITISH AND IRISH UNDER-21 TEAMS 1992—93

England Under-21 Internationals
8 Sept
Spain (0) 0
England (0) 1 *(Anderton)*   12,000
England: Walker; Hendon, Wright, Awford, Ehiogu, Whelan (Watson S), Anderton, Parlour, Bart-Williams, Clark (Sutton), Froggatt.

13 Oct
England (0) 0
Norway (1) 2 *(Strandli, Haland)*   4918
England: Walker; Hendon, Wright, Watson S (Sheron), Ehiogu, Awford, Parlour, Bart-Williams, McManaman, Clark, Heaney (Allen).

17 Nov
England (0) 0
Turkey (0) 1 *(Aydin)*   7879
England: Walker; Hendon, Minto, Imprey (Sutton), Ehiogu, Awford, Parlour (Sheron), Bart-Williams, McManaman, Allen, Heaney.

16 Feb
England (4) 6 *(Hall, Flitcroft, Anderton, Sheron, Redknapp, McManaman)*
San Marino (0) 0   7660
England: Walker; Jones (Jackson), Small, Flitcroft, Hall, Ehiogu, Anderton, Sheron (Froggatt), Cole, Redknapp, McManaman.

30 Mar
Turkey (0) 0
England (0) 0   20,000
England: Gerrard; Jackson (Whelan), Small, Sutch, Hall, Ehiogu, Kenny (Newton), Clark, Sutton, Cox, McManaman.

28 Apr
England (3) 3 *(Sheron 2, Anderton)*
Holland (0) 0   6752
England: Gerrard; Jones, Small, Jackson, Hall, Ehiogu, Flitcroft, Sheron, Sutton, Cox (Clark), Anderton.

28 May
Poland (1) 1 *(Dabrowski)*
England (2) 4 *(Hall, Cole 2, Anderton)*   4000
England: Gerrard; Ardley, Small, Jackson, Hall (Clark), Ehiogu, Cox, Sheron, Cole, Redknapp, Anderton.

1 June
Norway (0) 1 *(Ostenstad)*
England (0) 1 *(Cole)*   6840
England: Gerrard; Ardley, Small, Jackson, Cox, Ehiogu, Flitcroft, Sheron, Cole, Redknapp, Anderton.

Tournament in France
7 June
England (0) 2 *(Luis (og), Whelan)*
Portugal (0) 0
England: Gerrard; Ardley, Hall, Whelan (Sutton), Small, Flitcroft, Awford (Summerbee), Redknapp, Anderton, Allen, Sheron.

9 June
England (1) 1 *(Sheron)*
Czechoslovakia (0) 1 *(Novotny)*
England: Gerrard; Ardley, Sutton, Hall, Small, Awford, Flitcroft, Sheron, Clark (Allen), Redknapp, Anderton.

11 June
England (0) 0
Brazil (0) 0
England: Gerrard; Ardley, Awford, Hall, Small, Clark, Redknapp, Flitcroft, Anderton, Sutton, Sheron (Oakes).

14 June
England (1) 1 *(Summerbee)*
Scotland (0) 0
England: Gerrard; Ardley, Hall, Awford, Small, Clark (Summerbee), Redknapp, Flitcroft, Anderton, Sheron, Sutton.

15 June (Final)
England (0) 1 *(Flitcroft)*
France (0) 0
England: Gerrard; Ardley, Small, Awford, Hall, Sutton, Flitcroft, Sheron, Summerbee, Redknapp, Anderton.

Scotland Under-21 Internationals
8 Sept
Switzerland (1) 2 *(Christ, Meier)*
Scotland (0) 0   1200
Scotland: Reid; Wright, Bollam (Hagen), Burley, Salton (Roddie), Johnson, Barnard, O'Neil, Ferguson (Du), Dailly, Ferguson (Da).

13 Oct
Scotland (0) 0
Portugal (0) 0   2828
Scotland: Reid; Wright, Burley, Bain, O'Neil, Bernard, Bollanb, Roddie (McAuley), Johnston, Dailly (Johnson), Hagen.

18 Nov
Scotland (1) 1 *(Dailly)*
Italy (0) 2 *(Panucci, Vieri)*   6074
Scotland: Reid; Wright, Bollan, Bain, Salton, Burley, O'Neil, Bernard, Dailly, Ferguson, McLaren.

16 Feb
Scotland (1) 3 *(Booth 2, Ferguson)*
Malta (0) 0   4725
Scotland: Howie; Murray N, Deas (Dow), Wright, Bain, Bernard (McLaren), Telfer, Johnson, Ferguson (Du), Ferguson (Da), Booth.

27 Apr
Portugal (1) 2 *(Gil, Miguel)*
Scotland (1) 1 *(Booth)*   6000
Scotland: Howie; Telfer, Bollan, Burley, Bain, Barnard, Murray N, O'Donnell, Dailly, Booth, Hegan.

22 Mar
Scotland (1) 1 *(Roddie)*
Iceland (0) 1 *(Gudgonsson)*   1621
Scotland: Howie (Will); McNally, Johnston, Pressley (Skilling), Tweed (Handyside), Dow, Hagen, Murray N, Lavety (Murray R), Dailly, Roddie.

8 June
Scotland (1) 1 *(Bernard)*
Bulgaria (0) 0
Scotland: Kerr; Pressley, Bollan, Handyside, Lavin, Hannah, Bernard, Fullaton, McQuilken, Dailly, Thomas.

10 June
Scotland (1) 2 *(Bernard, Dailly)*
Mexico (0) 0
Scotland: Kerr; Pressley, Bollan, Handyside, Lavin, Hannah, Bernard, Baker, Thomas (Robertson), Dailly, Dickov (Lavety).

14 June
England (1) 1 *(Summerbee)*
Scotland (0) 0
England: Kerr; Pressley, Bolland, Handyside (Robertson), Thomas, Bernard, Baker, Dailly, McQuilken, Dickov, Lavety.

Wales Under-21 Internationals
13 Oct
Cyprus (0) 2 *(Marios, Kyriakos)*
Wales (2) 4 *(Bowen, Blake 3)*
Wales: Margetson; Neilson, Searle, Chapple, Peters, Edwards, Bowen, Owen, Blake, Jones (Bird), Hughes (Jenkins).

17 Nov
Belgium (2) 3 *(Crasson (pen), Goossens, Walem)*
Wales (1) 1 *(Jones)*
Wales: Margetson; Robinson (Pugh), Searle, Neilson, Ready, Chapple, Bowen, Owen (Hughes), Blake, Jones, Edwards.

30 Mar
Wales (0) 0
Belgium (0) 0
Wales: Margetson; Jenkins, Searle, Neilson (Pugh), Ready, Davies, Bowen, Owen, Jones, Edwards (Powell), Chapple.

27 Apr
Czechoslovakia (0) 1 *(Medved)*
Wales (1) 1 *(Blake)*
Wales: Margetson; Foster, Searle, Neilson, Davies, Peters, Hughes, Chapple, Blake, Jones, Edwards.

Republic of Ireland Internationals
13 Oct
Denmark (2) 3 *(Kristensen, Moller 2)*
Republic of Ireland (1) 2 *(Dempsey, McGrath)*
Republic of Ireland: Colgan; Byrne, Breen, Greene, Dunne, McGrath, Kinsella, Rush (Kavanagh), Dempsey, Power, Bacon (Gallen J).

17 Nov
Spain (2) 2 *(Kirko, Acosta)*
Republic of Ireland (0) 1 *(McCarthy)*
Republic of Ireland: McKenna; Broughton, Dunne, McCarthy, Greene, Kavanagh, Kinsella (Dempsey), McGrath, Rush (Kelly), Gallen J, Brady.

9 Mar
Republic of Ireland (0) 0
Germany (0) 1 *(Wuck)*
Republic of Ireland: Colgan; Gallen S, Carr, Greene, Dunne, Kinsella, McGrath, Kavanagh, Sheridan, Gallen J, Kelly.

23 Mar
Germany (3) 8 *(Lottner, Herrlich 2, Wuck, Haber, Nerlanger, Munch, Worns)*
Republic of Ireland (0) 0
Republic of Ireland: Colgan (McKenna); Kavanagh, Kinsella, Greene, Gallen S (O'Rourke), Hardy, Toal, McGrath, Sheridan, Kelly, Gallen J.

27 Apr
Republic of Ireland (0) 0
Denmark (1) 2 *(Ekelund, Sorensen-Wael)*
Republic of Ireland: Colgan; Kinsella, McCarthy (Bacon), Greene, Dunne, Kavanagh, McGrath, Sheridan, Turner, O'Connor, Power (Gallen J).

26 May
Albania (0) 1 *(Ouendo)*
Republic of Ireland (0) 1 *(Power)*
Republic of Ireland: Colgan; Purdy, (Dunne), McCarthy, Gallen S, Hardy, Bacon, Kinsella, Sheridan, Dempsey, Power (O'Connor), Kelly.

UNDER-21 APPEARANCES 1976–1993

ENGLAND

Ablett, G. (Liverpool), 1988 v Fr (1)

Adams, A. (Arsenal). 1985 v Ei, Fi; 1986 v D; 1987 v Se, Y (5)

Adams, N. (Everton), 1987 v Se (1)

Allen, B. (QPR), 1992 v H, M, Cz, F; 1993 v N (sub), T (6)

Allen, C. (QPR), 1980 v EG (sub); (with C Palace), 1981 v N, R (3)

Allen, M. (QPR), 1987 v Se (sub); 1988 v Y (sub) (2)

Allen, P. (West Ham U), 1985 v Ei, R; (with Tottenham H, 1986 v R (3)

Anderson, V. A. (Nottingham F), 1978 v I (1)

Anderton, D. R. (Tottenham H), 1993 v Sp, Sm, Ho, Pol, N (5)

Andrews, I. (Leicester C), 1987 v Se (1)

Ashcroft, L. (Preston NE), 1992 v (sub) (1)

Atherton, P. (Coventry C), 1992 v T (1)

Atkinson, B. (Sunderland), 1991 v W (sub), Sen, M, USSR (sub), F; 1992 v Pol (sub) (6)

Awford, A. T. (Portsmouth), 1993 v Sp, N, T (3)

Bailey, G. R. (Manchester U), 1979 v W, Bul; 1980 v D, S (2), EG; 1982 v N; 1983 v D, Gr; 1984 v H, F (2), I, Sp (14)

Baker, G. E. (Southampton), 1981 v N, R (2)

Barker, S. (Blackburn R), 1985 v Is (sub), Ei, R; 1986 v I (4)

Bannister, G. (Sheffield W), 1982 v Pol (1)

Barnes, J. (Watford), 1983 v D, Gr (2)

Barnes, P. S. (Manchester C), 1977 v W (sub), S, Fi, N; 1978 v N, Fi, I (2), Y (9)

Barrett, E. D. (Oldham Ath), 1990 v P, F, USSR, Cz (4)

Bart-Williams, C. G. (Sheffield W), 1993 v Sp, N, T (3)

Batty, D. (Leeds U), 1989 v Sw (sub); 1989 v Gr (sub), Bul, Sen, Ei, US; 1990 v Pol (7)

Beazeley, D. S. (Watford), 1992 v H (sub) (1)

Beagrie, P. (Sheffield U), 1988 v WG, T (2)

Beardsmore, R. (Manchester U), 1989 v Gr, Alb (sub), Pol, Bul, USA (5)

Beeston, C (Stoke C), 1988 v USSR (1)

Bertschin, K. E. (Birmingham C), 1977 v S; 1978 v Y (2)H(3)

Birtles, G. (Nottingham F), 1980 v Bul, EG (sub) (2)

Blackwell, D. R. (Wimbledon), 1991 v W, T, Sen (sub), M, USSR, F (6)

Blake, M. A. (Aston Villa), 1990 v F (sub), Cz (sub); 1991 v H, Pol, Ei (2), W; 1992 v Pol (8)

Blissett, L. L. (Watford), 1979 v W, Bul (sub), Se; 1980 v D (4)

Bracewell, P. (Stoke C), 1983 v D, Gr (1 pl 1 sub), H; 1984 v D, H, F (2), I (2), Sp (2); 1985 v T (13)Bradshaw, P. W. (Wolverhampton W), 1977 v W, S; 1978 v Fi, Y (4)

Breacker, T. (Luton C), 1986 v I (2) (2)

Brennan, M. (Ipswich T), 1987 v Y, Sp, T, Mor, F (5)

Brightwell, I. (Manchester C), 1989 v D, Alb; 1990 v Se (sub), Pol (4)

Brock, K. (Oxford U), 1984 v I, Sp (2); 1986 v I (4)

Bull, S. G. (Wolverhampton W), 1989 v Alb (2) Pol; 1990 v Se, Pol (5)

Burrows, D. (WBA), 1989 v Se (sub); (with Liverpool), Gr, Alb (2) Pol; 1990 v Se, Pol (7)

Butcher, T. I. (Ipswich T), 1979 v Se; 1980 v D, Bul, S (2), EG (2) (7)

Butters, G. (Tottenham H), 1989 v Bul, Sen (sub), Ei (sub) (3)

Butterworth, I. (Coventry C), 1985 v T, R; (with Nottingham F), 1986 v R, T, D (2), I (2) (8)

Caesar, G. (Arsenal), 1987 v Mor, USSR (sub), F (3)

Callaghan, N. (Watford), 1983 v D, Gr (sub), H (sub); 1984 v D, H, F (2), I, Sp (9)

Campbell, K. J. (Arsenal), 1991 v H, T (sub); 1992 v G, T (4)

Carr, C. (Fulham), 1985 v Ei (sub) (1)

Carr, F. (Nottingham F), 1987 v Se, Y, Sp (sub), Mor, USSR; 1988 v WG (sub), T, Y, F (9)

Caton, T. (Manchester C), 1982 v N, H (sub), Pol (2), S; 1983 v WG (2), Gr; 1984 v D, H, F (2), I (2) (14)

Chamberlain, M. (Stoke C), 1983 v Gr; 1984 v F (sub), I, Sp (4)

Chapman, L. (Stoke C), 1981 v Ei (1)

Charles, G. A. (Nottingham F), 1991 v H, W (sub), Ei; 1992 v T (4)

Chettle, S. (Nottingham F), 1988 v M, USSR, Mor, F; 1989 v D, Se, Gr, Alb (2), Bul; 1990 v Se, Pol (12)

Clark, L. R. (Newcastle U), 1992 v Cz, F; 1993 v Sp, N, T, Ho (sub), Pol (sub) (7)

Clough, N. (Nottingham F), 1986 v D (sub); 1987 v Se, Y, T, USSR, F (sub). P; 1988 v WG, T, Y, S (2), M, Mor, F (15)

Cole, A. A. (Arsenal), 1992 v H, Cz (sub), F (sub); 1993 v Sm, Pol, N (6)

Coney, D. (Fulham), 1985 v T (sub); 1986 v R; 1988 v T, WG (8)

Connor, T. (Brighton & H A), 1987 v Y (1)

Cooke, R. (Tottenham H), 1986 v D (sub) (1)

Cooper, C. (Middlesbrough), 1988 v F (2), M, USSR, Mor; 1989 v D, Se, Gr (8)

Corrigan, J. T. (Manchester C), 1978 v I (2), Y (3)

Cottee, A. (West Ham U), 1985 v Fi (sub), Is (sub), Ei, R, Fi; 1987 v Sp, P; 1988 v WG (8)

Cowans, G. S. (Aston Villa), 1979 v W, Se; 1980 v Bul, EG; 1981 v R (5)

Cox, N. J. (Aston Villa), 1993 v T, Ho, Pol, N (4)

Cranson, I. (Ipswich T), 1985 v Fi, Is, R; 1986 v R, I (5)

Crooks, G. (Stoke C), 1980 v Bul, S (2), EG (sub) (4)

Crossley, M. G. (Nottingham F), 1990 v P, USSR, Cz (3)

Cundy, J. V. (Chelsea), 1991 v Ei (2); 1992 v Pol (3)

Cunningham, L. (WBA), 1977 v S, Fi, N (sub); 1978 v N, Fi, I (6)

Curbishley, L. C. (Birmingham C), 1981 v Sw (1)

Daniel, P. W. (Hull C), 1977 v S, Fi, N; 1978 v Fi, I, Y (2) (7)

Davis, P. (Arsenal), 1982 v Pol, S; 1983 v D, Gr (1 pl 1 sub), H (sub); 1987 v T; 1988 v WG, T, Y, Fr (11)D'Avray, M. (Ipswich T), 1984 v I, Sp (sub) (2)

Deehan, J. M. (Aston Villa), 1977 v N; 1978 v N, Fi, I; 1979 v Bul, Se (sub); 1980 v D (7)

Dennis, M. E. (Birmingham C), 1980 v Bul; 1981 v N, R (3)

Dickens, A. (West Ham U), 1985 v Fi (sub) (1)

Dicks, J. (West Ham U), 1988 v Sw (sub), M, Mor, F (4)

Digby, F. (Swindon T), 1987 v Sp (sub), USSR, P; 1988 v T; 1990 v Pol (5)

Dillon, K. P. (Birmingham C), 1981 v R (1)

Dixon, K. (Chelsea), 1985 v Fi (1)

Dobson, A. (Coventry C), 1989 v Bul, Sen, Ei, US (4)

Dodd, J. R. (Southampton), 1991 v Pol, Ei, T, Sen, M, F; 1992 v G, Pol (8)

Donowa, L. (Norwich C), 1985 v Is, R (sub), Fi (sub) (3)

Dorigo, A. (Aston Villa), 1987 v Se, Sp, T, Mor, USSR, F, P; 1988 v WG, Y, S (2) (11)

Dozzell, J. (Ipswich T), 1987 v Se, Y (sub), Sp, USSR, F, P; 1989 v Se, Gr (sub); 1990 v Se (sub) (9)

Draper, M. A. (Notts Co), 1991 v Ei (sub); 1992 v G, Pol (3)

Duxbury, M. (Manchester U), 1981 v Sw (sub), Ei (sub), R (sub), Sw; 1982 v N; 1983 v WG (2) (7)

Dyson, P. I. (Coventry C), 1981 v N, R, Sw, Ei (4)

Ebbrell, J. (Everton), 1989 v Sen, Ei, US (sub); 1990 v P, F, USSR, Cz; 1991 v H, Pol, Ei, W, T; 1992 v G, T (14)
Ehiogu, U. (Aston Villa), 1992 v H, M, Cz, F; 1993 v Sp, N, T, Sm, T, Ho, Pol, N (12)
Elliott, P. (Luton T), 1985 v Fi; 1986 v T, D (3)

Fairclough, C. (Nottingham F), 1985 v T, Is, Ei; 1987 v Sp, T; (with Tottenham H), 1988 v Y, F (7)
Fairclough, D. (Liverpool), 1977 v W (1)
Fashanu, J. (Norwich C), 1980 v EG; 1981 v N (sub), R, Sw, Ei (sub), H; (with Nottingham F), 1982 v N, H, Pol. S; 1983 v WG (sub) (11)
Fenwick, T. W. (C Palace), 1981 v N, R, Sw, Ei; (with QPR), R; 1982 v N, H, S (2); 1983 v WG (2) (11)
Fereday, W. (QPR), 198.5 v T, Ei (sub). Fi; 1986 v T (sub), I (5)
Flitcroft, G. W. (Manchester C), 1993 v Sm, Hol, N (3)
Flowers, T. (Southampton), 1987 v Mor, F; 1988 v WG (sub) (3)
Forsyth, M. (Derby Co), 1988 v Sw (1)
Foster, S. (Brighton & HA), 1980 v EG (sub) (1)
Froggatt, S. J. (Aston Villa), 1993 v Sp, Sm (sub) (2)
Futcher, P. (Luton T), 1977 v W, S, Fi, N; (with Manchester C), 1978 v N, Fi, I (2), Y (2); 1979 v D (11)

Gabbiadini, M. (Sunderland), 1989 v Bul, USA (2)
Gale, A. (Fulham), 1982 v Pol (1)
Gascoigne, P. (Newcastle U), 1987 v Mo, USSR, P; 1988 v WG, Y, S (2), F (2), Sw, M, USSR (sub), Mor (13)
Gayle, H. (Birmingham C), 1984 v I, Sp (2) (3)
Gernon, T. (Ipswich T), 1983 v Gr (1)
Gerrard, P. W. (Oldham Ath), 1993 v T, Ho, Pol, N (4)
Gibbs, N. (Watford), 1987 v Mor, USSR, F, P; 1988 v T (5)
Gibson, C. (Aston Villa), 1982 v N (1)
Gilbert, W. A. (C Palace), 1979 v W, Bul; 1980 v Bul; 1981 v N, R, Sw, R, Sw, H; 1982 v N (sub), H (11)
Goddard, P. (West Ham U), 1981 v N, Sw, Ei (sub); 1982 v N (sub), Pol, S; 1983 v WG (2) (8)
Gordon, D. (Norwich C), 1987 v T (sub), Mor (sub), F, P (4)
Gray, A. (Aston Villa), 1988 v S, F (2)

Haigh, P. (Hull C), 1977 v N (sub) (1)
Hall, R. A. (Southampton), 1992 v H (sub), F; 1993 v Sm, T, Ho, Pol (6)
Hardyman, P. (Portsmouth), 1985 v Ei; 1986 v D (2)
Hateley, M. (Coventry C), 1982 v Pol, S; 1983 v Gr (2), H; (with Portsmouth), 1984 v F (2), I, Sp (2) (10)
Hayes, M. (Arsenal), 1987 v Sp, T; 1988 v F (sub) (3)
Hazell, R. J. (Wolverhampton W), 1979 v D (1)
Heaney, N. A. (Arsenal), 1992 v H, M, Cz, F; 1993 v N, T (6)
Heath, A. (Stoke C), 1981 v R, Sw, H; 1982 v N, H; (with Everton), Pol, S; 1983 v WG (8)
Hendon, I. M. (Tottenham H), 1992 v H, M, Cz, F; 1993 v Sp, N, T (7)
Hesford, I. (Blackpool), 1981 v Ei (sub), Pol (2), S (2); 1983 v WG (2) (7)
Hilaire, V. (C Palace), 1980 v Bul, S (1+1 sub), EG (2); 1981 v N, R, Sw (sub); 1982 v Pol (sub) (9)
Hillier, D. (Arsenal), 1991 v T (1)
Hinchcliffe, A. (Manchester C), 1989 v D (1)
Hinshelwood, P. A. (C Palace), 1978 v N; 1980 v EG (2)
Hirst, D. (Sheffield W), 1988 v USSR, F; 1989 v D, Bul (sub), Sen, Ei, US (7)
Hoddle, G. (Tottenham H), 1977 v W (sub); 1978 v Fi (sub), I (2), Y; 1979 v D, W, Bul; 1980 v S (2), EG (2)H(12)
Hodge, S. (Nottingham F), 1983 v Gr (sub); 1984 v D, F, I, Sp (2); (with Aston Villa), 1986 v R, T (8)
Hodgson, D. J. (Middlesbrough), 1981 v N, R (sub), Sw, Ei; 1982 v Pol; 1983 v WG (6)
Holdsworth, D. (Watford), 1989 v Gr (sub) (1)

Horne, B. (Millwall), 1989 v Gr (sub), Pol, Bul, Ei, US (5)
Hucker, P. (QPR), 1984 v I, Sp (2)

Impey, A. R. (QPR), 1993 v T (1)
Ince, P. (West Ham U), 1989 v Alb; 1990 v Se (2)

Jackson, M. A. (Everton), 1992 v H, M, Cz, F; 1993 v Sm (sub), T, Ho, Pol, N (9)
James, D. (Watford), 1991 v Ei (2), T, Sen, M, USSR, F; 1992 v G, T, Pol (10)
James, J. C. (Luton T), 1990 v F, USSR (2)
Jemson, N. B. (Nottingham F), 1991 v W (1)
Johnson, T. (Notts Co), 1991 v H (sub), Ei (sub); 1992 v G, T, Pol; (with Derby Co), M, Cz (sub) (7)
Johnston, C. P. (Middlesbrough), 1981 v N, Ei (2)
Jones, D. R. (Everton, 1977 v W (1)
Jones, C. H. (Tottenham H), 1978 v Y (sub) (1)
Jones, R. (Liverpool), 1993 v Sm, Ho (2)

Keegan, G. A. (Manchester C), 1977 v W (1)
Kenny, W. (Everton), 1993 v T (1)
Keown, M. (Aston Villa), 1987 v Sp, Mor, USSR, P; 1988 v T, S, F (2) (8)
Kerslake, D. (QPR), 1986 v T (1)
Kilcline, B. (Notts C), 1983 v D, Gr (2)
King, A. E. (Everton), 1977 v W; 1978 v Y (2)
Kitson, P. (Leicester C), 1991 v Sen (sub), M, F; 1992 v Pol; (with Derby Co), M, Cz, F (7)
Knight, A. (Portsmouth), 1983 v Gr, H (2)
Knight, I. (Sheffield W), 1987 v Se (sub), Y (2)

Lake, P. (Manchester C), 1989 v D, Alb (2), Pol; 1990 v Pol (5)
Langley, T. W. (Chelsea), 1978 v I (sub) (1)
Lee, D. J. (Chelsea), 1990 v F; 1991 v H, Pol, Ei (2), T, Sen, USSR, F; 1992 v Pol (10)
Lee, R. (Charlton Ath), 1986 v I (sub); 1987 v Se (sub) (2)
Lee, S. (Liverpool), 1981 v R, Sw, H; 1982 v S; 1983 v WG (2) (6)
Le Saux, G. (Chelsea), 1990 v P, F, USSR, Cz (4)
Lowe, D. (Ipswich T), 1988 v F, Sw (sub) (2)
Lukic, J. (Leeds U), 1981 v N, R, Ei, R, Sw, H; 1982 v H (7)
Lund, G. (Grimsby T), 1985 v T; 1986 v R, T (3)

McCall, S. H. (Ipswich T), 1981 v Sw, H; 1982 v H, S; 1983 v WG (2) (6)
McDonald, N. (Newcastle U), 1987 v Se (sub), Sp, T; 1988 v WG, Y (sub) (5)
McGrath, M. (Coventry C), 1986 v D (1)
MacKenzie, S. (WBA), 1982 v N, S (2) (3)
McLeary, A. (Millwall), 1988 v Sw (1)
McMahon, S. (Everton), 1981 v Ei; 1982 v Pol; 1983 v D, Gr (2); (with Aston Villa), 1984 v H (6)
McManaman, S. (Liverpool), 1991 v W, M (sub); 1993 v N, T, Sm, T (6)
Mabbutt, G. (Bristol R), 1982 v Pol (2), S; (with Tottenham H), 1983 v D; 1984 v F; 1986 v D, I (7)
Marriott, A. (Nottingham F), 1992 v M (1)
Martin, L. (Manchester U), 1989 v Gr (sub), Alb (sub) (2)
Martyn, N. (Bristol R), 1988 v S (sub), M, USSR, Mor, F; 1989 v D, Se, Gr, Alb (2); 1990 v Se (11)
Matthew, D. (Chelsea), 1990 v P, USSR, Cz; 1991 v Ei, M, USSR, F; 1992 v G (sub), T (9)
May, A. (Manchester C), 1986 v I (sub) (1)
Merson, P. (Arsenal), 1989 v D, Gr, Pol (sub); 1990 v Pol (4)
Middleton, J. (Nottingham F), 1977 v Fi, N; (with Derby Co), 1978 v N (3)
Miller, A. (Arsenal), 1988 v Mor (sub); 1989 v Sen; 1991 v H, Pol (4)
Mills, G. R. (Nottingham F), 1981 v R; 1982 v N (2)
Mimms, R. (Rotherham U), 1985 v Is (sub), Ei (sub); (with Everton), 1986 v I (3)
Minto, S. C. (Charlton Ath), 1991 v W; 1992 v H, M, Cz; 1993 v T (5)

Moran, S. (Southampton), 1982 v N (sub); 1984 v F (2)

Morgan, S. (Leicester C), 1987 v Se, Y (2)

Mortimer, P. (Charlton Ath), 1989 v Sen, Ei (2)

Moses, R. M. (WBA), 1981 v N (sub), Sw, Ei, R, Sw, H; 1982 v N (sub); (with Manchester U), H (8)

Mountfield, D. (Everton), 1984 v Sp (1)

Muggleton, C. D. (Leicester C), 1990 v F (1)

Mutch, A. (Wolverhampton W), 1989 v Pol (1)

Newell, M. (Luton T), 1986 v D (1+sub), I (1+sub) (4)

Newton, E. J. I. (Chelsea), 1993 v T (sub) (1)

Oldfield, D. (Luton T), 1989 v Se (1)

Olney, I. A. (Aston Villa), 1990 v P, F, USSR, Cz; 1991 v H, Pol, Ei (2), T; 1992 v Pol (sub) (10)

Ord, R. J. (Sunderland), 1991 v W, M, USSR (3)

Osman, R. C. (Ipswich T), 1979 v W (sub), Se; 1980 v D, S (2), EG (2) (7)

Owen, G. A. (Manchester C), 1977 v S, Fi, N; 1978 v N, Fi, I (2), Y; 1979 v D, W; (with WBA), Bul, Se (sub); 1980 v D, S (2), EG; 1981 v Sw, R; 1982 v N (sub), H; 1983 v WG (2) (22)

Painter, I. (Stoke C), 1986 v I (1)

Palmer, C. (Sheffield W), 1989 v Bul, Sen, Ei, US (4)

Parker, G. (Hull C), 1986 v I (2); (with Nottingham F), v F; 1987 v Se, Y (sub), Sp (6)

Parker, P. (Fulham), 1985 v Fi, T, Is (sub), Ei, R, Fi; 1986 v T, D (8)

Parkes, P. B. F. (QPR), 1979 v D (1)

Parkin, S. (Stoke C), 1987 v Sp (sub); 1988 v WG (sub), T, S (sub), F (5)

Parlour, R. (Arsenal), 1992 v H, M, Cz, F; 1993 v Sp, N, T (7)

Peach, D. S. (Southampton), 1977 v S, Fi, N; 1978 v N, I (2) (6)

Peake, A. (Leicester C), 1982 v Pol (1)

Pearce, S. (Nottingham F), 1987 v Y (1)

Pickering N. (Sunderland), 1983 v D (sub), Gr, H; 1984 v F (sub), F, I (2), Sp; 1985 v Is, R, Fi; 1986 v R, T; (with Coventry C), D, I (15)

Platt, D. (Aston Villa), 1988 v M, Mor, F (3)

Porter, G. (Watford), 1987 v Sp (sub), T, Mor, USSR, F, P (sub); 1988 v T (sub), Y, S (2), F, Sw (12)

Pressman, K. (Sheffield W), 1989 v D (sub) (1)

Proctor, M. (Middlesbrough), 1981 v Ei (sub), Sw; 1982 (with Nottingham F), v N, Pol (4)

Ramage, C. D. (Derby Co), 1991 v Pol (sub), W; 1992 v Fr (sub) (3)

Ranson, R. (Manchester C), 1980 v Bul, EG; 1981 v R (sub), R, Sw, (1+sub), H, Pol (2), S (10)

Redknapp, J. F. (Liverpool), 1993 v Sm, Pol, N (3)

Redmond, S. (Manchester C), 1988 v F (2), M, USSR, Mor, F; 1989 v D, Se, Gr, Alb (2), Pol; 1990 v Se, Pol (14)

Reeves, K. P. (Norwich C), 1978 v I, Y (2); 1979 v N, W, Bul, Sw; 1980 v D, S; (with Manchester C), EG (10)

Regis, C. (WBA), 1979 v D, Bul, Se; 1980 v S, EG; 1983 v D (6)

Reid, N. S. (Manchester C), 1981 v H (sub); 1982 v H, Pol (2), S (2) (6)

Reid, P. (Bolton W), 1977 v S, Fi, N; 1978 v Fi, I, Y (6)

Richards, J. P. (Wolverhampton W), 1977 v Fi, N (2)

Rideout, P. (Aston Villa), 1985 v Fi, Is, Ei (sub), R; (with Bari), 1986 v D (5)

Ripley, S. (Middlesbrough), 1988 v USSR, F (sub); 1989 v D (sub), Se, Gr, Alb (2); 1990 v Se (8)

Ritchie, A. (Brighton & HA), 1982 v Pol (1)

Rix, G. (Arsenal), 1978 v Fi (sub), Y; 1979 v D, Se; 1980 v D (sub), Bul, S (7)

Robins, M. G. (Manchester U), 1990 v P, F, USSR, Cz; 1991 v H (sub), Pol (6)

Robson, B. (WBA), 1979 v W, Bul (sub), Se; 1980 v D, Bul, S (2) (7)

Robson, S. (Arsenal), 1984 v I; 1985 v Fi, Is, Fi; 1986 v R, I (6)

Robson, S. (West Ham U), 1988 v S, Sw (2)

Rocastle, D. (Arsenal), 1987 v Se, Y, Sp, T; 1988 v WG, T, Y, S (2), F (2 subs), M, USSR, Mor (14)

Rodger, G. (Coventry C), 1987 v USSR, F, P; 1988 v WG (4)

Rosario, R. (Norwich C), 1987 v T (sub), Mor, F, P (sub) jy(4)Rowell, G. (Sunderland), 1977 v Fi (1)

Ruddock, N. (Southampton), 1989 v Bul (sub), Sen, Ei, US (4)

Ryan, J. (Oldham Ath), 1983 v H (1)

Samways, V. (Tottenham H), 1988 v Sw (sub); USSR, F; 1989 v D, Se (5)

Sansom, K. G. (C Palace), 1979 v D, W, Bul, Se; 1980 v S (2), EG (2) (8)

Seaman, D. (Birmingham C), 1985 v Fi, T, Is, Ei, R, Fi; 1986 v R, F, D, I (10)

Sedgley, S. (Coventry C), 1987 v USSR, F (sub), P; 1988 v F; 1989 v D (sub), Se, Gr, Alb (2), Pol; (with Tottenham H), 1990 v Se (11)

Sellars, S. (Blackburn R), 1988 v S (sub), F, Sw (3)

Sharpe, L. (Manchester U), 1989 v Gr; 1990 v P (sub), F, USSR, Cz; 1991 v H, Pol (sub), Ei (8)

Shaw, G. R. (Aston Villa), 1981 v Ei, Sw, H; 1982 v H, S; 1983 v WG (2) (7)

Shearer, A. (Southampton), 1991 v Ei (2), W, T, Sen, M, USSR, F; 1992 v G, T, Pol (11)

Shelton, G. (Sheffield W), 1985 v Fi (1)

Sheringham, T. (Millwall), 1988 v Sw (1)

Sheron, M. N. (Manchester C), 1992 v H, F; 1993 v N (sub), Sm, Ho, Pol, N (8)

Sherwood, T. A. (Norwich C), 1990 v P, F, USSR, Cz (4)

Simpson, P. (Manchester C), 1986 v D (sub); 1987 v Y, Mor, F, P (5)

Sims, S. (Leicester C), 1977 v W, S, Fi, N; 1978 v N, Fi, I (2), Y (2) (10)

Sinnott, L. (Watford), 1985 v Is (sub) (1)

Slater, S. I. (West Ham U), 1990 v P, USSR (sub), Cz (sub) (3)

Small, B. (Aston Villa), 1993 v Sm, T, Ho, Pol, N (5)

Smith, D. (Coventry C), 1988 v M, USSR (sub), Mor; 1989 v D, Se, Alb (2), Pol; 1990 v Se, Pol (10)

Smith, M. (Sheffield W), 1981 v Ei, R, Sw, H; 1982 v Pol (sub) (5)

Snodin, I. (Doncaster R), 1985 v T, Is, R, Fi (4)

Statham, B. (Tottenham H), 1988 v Sw; 1989 v D (sub), Se (3)

Statham, D. J. (WBA), 1978 v Fi, 1979 v W, Bul, Se; 1980 v D; 1983 v D (6)

Stein, B. (Luton T), 1984 v D, H, I (3)

Sterland, M. (Sheffield W), 1984 v D, H, F (2), I. Sp (2) (7)

Steven, T. (Everton), 1985 v Fi, T (2)

Stevens, G. (Brighton & HA), 1983 v H; (with Tottenham H), 1984 v H, F (1+1 sub), I (sub), Sp (1+1 sub); 1986 v I (8)

Stewart, P. (Manchester C), 1988 v F (1)

Stuart, G. C. (Chelsea), 1990 v P (sub), F, USSR, Cz; 1991 v T (sub) (5)

Suckling, P. (Coventry C), 1986 v D; (with Manchester C), 1987 v Se (sub), Y, Sp, T; (with C Palace), 1988 v S (2), F (2), Sw (10)

Sunderland, A. (Wolverhampton W), 1977 v W (1)

Sutton, C. R. (Norwich), 1993 v Sp (sub), T (sub), T, Ho (4)

Swindlehurst, D. (C Palace), 1977 v W (1)

Sutch, D. (Norwich C), 1992 v H, M, Cz; 1993 v T (4)

Talbot, B. (Ipswich T), 1977 v W (1)

Thomas, D. (Coventry C), 1981 v Ei; 1983 v WG (2), Gr, H; (with Tottenham H), v I, Sp (7)

Thomas, M. (Luton T), 1986 v T, D, I (3)

Thomas, M. (Arsenal), 1988 v Y, S, F (2), M, USSR, Mor; 1989 v Gr, Alb (2), Pol; 1990 v Se (12)

Thomas, R. E. (Watford), 1990 v P (1)

Thompson, G. L. (Coventry C), 1981 v R, Sw, H; 1982 v N, H, S (6)

Thorn, A. (Wimbledon), 1988 v WG (sub). Y, S, F, Sw (5)

Tiler, C. (Barnsley), 1990 v P, USSR, Cz; 1991 v H, Pol, Ei (2), T, Sen, USSR, F; (with Nottingham F), 1992 v G, T (13)

Venison, B. (Sunderland), 1983 v D, Gr; 1985 v Fi, T, Is, Fi; 1986 v R, T, D (2) (10)

Vinnicombe, C. (Rangers), 1991 v H (sub), Pol, Ei (2), T, Sen, M, USSR (sub), F; 1992 v G, T, Pol (12)

Waddle, C. (Newcastle U), 1985 v Fi (1)

Wallace, D. (Southampton), 1983 v Gr, H; 1984 v D, H, F (2), I, Sp (sub); 1985 v Fi, T, Is; 1986 v R, D, I (14)

Wallace, Ray (Southampton), 1989 v Bul, Sen (sub), Ei; 1990 v Se (4)

Wallace, Rod (Southampton), 1989 v Bul, Ei (sub), US; 1991 v H, Pol, Ei, T, Sen, M, USSR, F (11)

Walker, D. (Nottingham F), 1985 v Fi; 1987 v Se, T; 1988 v WG, T, S (2) (7)

Walker, I. M. (Tottenham H), 1991 v W; 1992 v H, Cz, F; 1993 v Sp, N, T, Sm (8)

Walsh, G. (Manchester U), 1988 v WG, Y (2)

Walsh, P. M. (Luton T), 1983 v D (sub), Gr (2), H (4)

Walters, K. (Aston Villa), 1984 v D (sub). H (sub); 1985 v Is, Ei, R; 1986 v R, T, D, I (sub) (9)

Ward, P. D. (Brighton & HA), 1978 v N; 1980 v EG (2)

Warhurst, P. (Oldham Ath), 1991 v H, Pol, W, Sen, M (sub), USSR, F (sub); (with Sheffield W), 1992 v G (8)

Watson, D. (Norwich C), 1984 v D, F (2), I (2), Sp (2) (7)

Watson, G. (Sheffield W), 1991 v Sen, USSR (2)

Watson, S. C. (Newcastle U), 1993 v Sp (sub), N (2)

Webb, N. (Portsmouth), 1985 v Ei; (with Nottingham F), 1986 v D (2) (3)

Whelan, P. J. (Ipswich T), 1993 v Sp, T (sub) (2)

White, D. (Manchester C), 1988 v S (2), F, USSR; 1989 v Se; 1990 v Pol (6)

Whyte, C. (Arsenal), 1982 v S (1+1 sub); 1983 v D, Gr (4)

Wicks, S. (QPR), 1982 v S (1)

Wilkins, R. C. (Chelsea), 1977 v W (1)

Wilkinson, P. (Grimsby T), 1985 v Ei, R (sub); (with Everton), 1986 v R (sub), I (4)

Williams, P. (Charlton Ath), 1989 v Bul, Sen, Ei, US (sub) (4)

Williams, P. D. (Derby Co), 1991 v Sen, M, USSR; 1992 v G, T, Pol (6)

Williams, S. C. (Southampton); 1977 v S, Fi, N; 1978 v N, I (1

pl sub), Y (2); 1979 v D, Bul, Se (sub); 1980 v D, EG (2) (14)Winterburn, N. (Wimbledon), 1986 v I (1)

Wise, D. (Wimbledon), 1988 v Sw (1)

Woodcook, A. S. (Nottingham F), 1978 v Fi, I (2)

Woods, C. C. E. (Nottingham F), 1979 v W (sub). Se; (with QPR), 1980 v Bul, EG; 1981 v Sw; (with Norwich C), 1984 v D (6)

Wright, A. G. (Blackburn), 1993 v Sp, N (2)

Wright, M. (Southampton), 1983 v Gr, H; 1984 v D, H (4)

Wright, W. (Everton), 1979 v D, W, Bul; 1980 v D, S (2) (6)

Yates, D. (Notts Co), 1989 v D (sub), Bul, Sen, Ei, US (5)

SCOTLAND

Aitken, R. (Celtic), 1977 v Cz, W, Sw; 1978 v Cz, W; 1979 v P, N (2); 1980 v Bel, E; 1984 v EG, Y (2); 1985 v WG, Ic, Sp (16)

Albiston, A. (Manchester U), 1977 v Cz, W, Sw; 1978 v Sw, Cz (5)

Archdeacon, O. (Celtic), 1987 v WG (sub) (1)

Archibald, S. (Aberdeen), 1980 v B, E (2), WG; (with Tottenham H), 1981 v D (5)

Bain, K. (Dundee), 1993 v P, I, Ma, P (4)

Baker, M. (St. Mirren), 1993 v M, E (2)

Bannon, E. J. P. (Hearts), 1979 v US, (with Chelsea), P, N (2); (with Dundee U), 1980 v Bel, WG, E (7)

Beattie, J. (St Mirren), 1992 v D, US, P, Y (4)

Beaumont, D. (Dundee U), 1985 v Ic (1)

Bell, D. (Aberdeen), 1981 v D; 1984 v Y (2)

Bernard, P. R. J. (Oldham Ath), 1992 v R (sub), D, Se (sub), US; 1993 v Sw, P, I, Ma, P, Bul, M, E (12)

Bett, J. (Rangers), 1981 v Se, D; 1982 v Se, D, I, E (2) (7)

Black, E. (Aberdeen), 1983 v EG, Sw (2), Bel; 1985 v Ic, Sp (2), Ic (8)

Blair, A. (Coventry C), 1980 v E; 1981 v Se; (with Aston Villa), 1982 v Se, D, I (5)

Bollan, G. (Dundee U), 1992 v D, G (sub), US, P, Y; 1993 v Sw, P, I, P, Bul, M, E (12)

Booth, S. (Aberdeen), 1991 v R (sub), Bul (sub pl 1), Pol, F (sub); 1992 v Sw, R, D, Se, US, P, Y; 1993 v Ma, P (14)Bowes, M. J. (Dunfermline Ath), 1992 v D (sub) (1)

Bowman, D. (Hearts), 1985 v WG (sub) (1)

Boyd, T. (Motherwell), 1987 v WG, Ei (2), Bel; 1988 v Bel (5)

Brazil, A. (Hibernian), 1978 v W (1)

Brazil, A. (Ipswich T), 1979 v N; 1980 v Bel (2), E (2), WG; 1981 v Se; 1982 v Se (8)

Brough, J. (Hearts), 1981 v D (1)

Burley, G. E. (Ipswich T), 1977 v Cz, W, Sw; 1978 v Sw, Cz (5)

Burley, C. (Chelsea), 1992 v D; 1993 v Sw, P, I, P (5)

Burns, H. (Rangers), 1985 v Sp, Ic (sub) (2)

Burns, T. (Celtic), 1977 v Cz, W, E; 1978 v Sw; 1982 v E (5)

Campbell, S. (Dundee), 1989 v N (sub), Y, F (3)

Casey, J. (Celtic), 1978 v W (1)

Christie, M. (Dundee), 1992 v D, P (sub), Y (3)

Clark, R. (Aberdeen), 1977 v Cz, W, Sw (3)

Clarke, S. (St Mirren), 1984 v Bel, EG, Y; 1985 v WG, Ic, Sp (2), Ic (8)

Cleland, A. (Dundee U), 1990 v F, N (2); 1991 v R, Sw, Bul; 1992 v Sw, R, G, Se (2) (11)

Collins, J. (Hibernian), 1988 v Bel, E; 1989 v N, Y, F; 1990 v Y, F, N (8)

Connolly, P. (Dundee U), 1991 v R (sub), Sw, Bul (3)

Connor, R. (Ayr U), 1981 v Se; 1982 v Se (2)

Cooper, D. (Clydebank), 1977 v Cz, W, Sw, E; (with Rangers), 1978 v Sw, Cz (6)

Cooper, N. (Aberdeen), 1982 v D, E (2); 1983 v Bel, EG, Sw (2); 1984 v Bel, EG, Y; 1985 v Ic, Sp, Ic (13)

Crabbe, S. (Hearts), 1990 v Y (sub), F (2)

Craig, T. (Newcastle U), 1977 v E (1)

Crainie, D. (Celtic), 1983 v Sw (sub) (1)

Creaney, G. (Celtic), 1991 v Sw, Bul (2), Pol, F; 1992 v Sw, R, G (2), Se (2) (11)

Dailly, C. (Dundee U), 1991 v R; 1992 v US, R; 1993 v Sw, P, I, Ic, P, Bul, M, E (11)

Dawson, A. (Rangers), 1979 v P, N (2); 1980 v B (2), E (2) WG (8)

Deas, P. A. (St Johnstone), 1992 v D (sub); 1993 v Ma (2)

Dennis, S. (Raith R), 1992 v Sw (1)

Dickov, P. (Arsenal), 1992 v Y; 1993 v M, E (3)

Dodds, D. (Dundee U), 1978 v W (1)

Donald, G. S. (Hibernian), 1992 v US (sub), P, Y (sub) (3)

Dow, A. (Dundee), 1993 v Ma (sub), Ic (2)

Duffy, J. (Dundee), 1987 v Ei (1)

Durie, G. S. (Chelsea), 1987 v WG, Ei, Bel; 1988 v Bel (4)

Durrant, I. (Rangers), 1987 v WG, Ei, Bel; 1988 v E (4)

Doyle, J. (Partick Th), 1981 v D, I (sub) (2)

Ferguson, D. (Rangers), 1987 v WG, Ei, Bel; 1988 v E; 1990 v Y (5)

Ferguson, D. (Dundee U), 1992 v D, G, Se (2); 1993 v Sw, Ma (6)

Ferguson, D. (Manchester U), 1992 v US, P (sub), Y; 1993 v Sw, I, Ma (6)

Ferguson, I. (Dundee), 1983 v EG (sub), Sw (sub); 1984 v Bel (sub), EG (4)

Ferguson, I. (Clyde), 1987 v WG (sub), Ei (with St Mirren), Ei, Bel; 1988 v Bel; (with Rangers), E (sub) (6)

Ferguson, R. (Hamilton A), 1977 v E (1)

Findlay, W. (Hibernian), 1991 v R, Pol, Bul (2), Pol (5)

Fitzpatrick, A. (St Mirren), 1977 v W (sub), Sw (sub), E; 1978 v Sw, Cz (5)

Flannigan, C. (Clydebank), 1993 v Ic (sub) (1)

Fleck, R. (Rangers), 1987 v WG (sub), Ei, Bel; (with Norwich C), 1988 v E (2); 1989 v Y (6)

Fridge, L. (St Mirren), 1989 v F; 1990 v Y (2)

Fullarton, J. (St. Mirren), 1993 v Bul (1)

Fulton, M. (St Mirren), 1980 v Bel, WG, E; 1981 v Se, D (sub)

Fulton, S. (Celtic), 1991 v R, Sw, Bul, Pol, F; 1992 v G (2) (7)

Gallacher, K. (Dundee U), 1987 v WG, Ei (2), Bel (sub); 1988 v E (2); 1990 v Y (7)

Galloway, M. (Hearts), 1989 v F; (with Celtic), 1990 v N (2)

Geddes, R. (Dundee), 1982 v Se, D, E (2); 1988 v E (5)

Gemmill, S. (Nottingham F), 1992 v Sw, R (sub), G (sub), Se (sub) (4)

Gillespie, G. (Coventry C), 1979 v US; 1980 v E; 1981 v D; 1982 v Se, D, I (2), E (8)

Glover, L. (Nottingham F), 1988 v Bel (sub); 1989 v N; 1990 v Y (3)

Goram, A. (Oldham Ath), 1987 v Ei (1)

Gough, C. R. (Dundee U), 1983 v EG, Sw, Bel; 1984 v Y (2) (5)

Grant, P. (Celtic), 1985 v WG, Ic, Sp; 1987 v WG, Ei (2), Bel; 1988 v Bel, E (2) (10)

Gunn, B. (Aberdeen), 1984 v EG, Y (2); 1985 v WG, Ic, Sp (2), Ic; 1990 v F (9)

Gray, S. (Aberdeen), 1987 v WG (1)

Hagen, D. (Rangers), 1992 v D (sub), US (sub), P, Y; 1993 v Sw (sub), P, Ic, P (8)

Hamilton, B. (St Mirren), 1989 v Y, F (sub); 1990 v F, N (4)

Handyside, P. (Grimsby T), 1993 v Ic (sub), Bul, M, E (4)

Hannagh, D. (Dundee U), 1993 v Bul, M (2)

Hartford, R. A. (Manchester C), 1977 v Sw (1)

Hegarty, P. (Dundee U), 1987 v WG, Bel; 1988 v E (2); 1990 v F, N (4)

Hendry, J. (Tottenham H), 1992 v D (sub) (1)

Hewitt, J. (Aberdeen), 1982 v I; 1983 v EG, Sw (2); 1984 v Bel, Y (sub) (6)

Hogg, G. (Manchester U), 1984 v Y; 1985 v WG, Ic, Sp (4)

Howie, S. (Cowdenbeath), 1993 v Ma, Ic, P (3)

Hunter, G. (Hibernian), 1987 v Ei (sub); 1988 v Bel, E (3)

Hunter, P. (East Fife), 1989 v N (sub), F (sub); 1990 v F (sub) (3)

Jardine, I. (Kilmarnock), 1979 v US (1)

Jess, E. (Aberdeen), 1990 v F (sub), N (sub); 1991 v R, Sw, Bul (2), Pol, F; 1992 v Sw, R, G (2), Se (1 + sub) (14)

Johnson, G. I. (Dundee U), 1992 v US, P, Y (3)

Johnson, I (Dundee U), 1993 v Sw, P, Ma (3)

Johnston, F. (Falkirk), 1993 v Ic (1)

Johnston, M. (Partick Th), 1984 v EG (sub); (with Watford), Y (2) (3)

Kirkwood, D. (Hearts), 1990 v Y (1)

Kerr, S. (Celtic), 1993 v Bul, M, E (3)

Lambert, P. (St Mirren), 1991 v R, Sw, Bul (2), Pol, F; 1992 v Sw, R, G (2), Se (11)

Lavety, B. (St. Mirren), 1993 v Ic, M (sub), E (3)

Lavin, G. (Watford), 1993 v Bul, M (2)

Leighton, J. (Aberdeen), 1982 v I (1)

Levein, C. (Hearts), 1985 v Sp, Ic (2)

Lindsey, J. (Motherwell), 1979 v US (1)

McAllister, G. (Leicester C), 1990 v N (1)

McAlpine, H. (Dundee U), 1983 v EG, Sw (2), Bel; 1984 v Bel (5)

McAuley, S. (St. Johnstone), 1993 v P (sub) (1)

McAvennie, F. (St Mirren), 1982 v I, E; 1985 v Is, Ei, R (5)

McBride, J. (Everton), 1981 v D (1)

McCall, S. (Bradford C), 1988 v E; (with Everton), 1990 v F (2)

McClair, B. (Celtic), 1984 v Bel (sub), EG, Y (1 pl sub); 1985 v WG, Ic, Sp, Ic (8)McCluskey, G. (Celtic), 1979 v US, P; 1980 v Bel, (2); 1982 vD,I(6)

McCoist, A. (Rangers), 1984 v Bel (1)

McCulloch, A. (Kilmarnock); 1981 v Se (1)

McCulloch, I. (Notts Co), 1982 v E (2)

MacDonald, J. (Rangers), 1980 v WG (sub); 1981 v Se; 1982 v Se (sub), L, I (2), E (2 sub) (8)

McGarvey, F. (St Mirren), 1977 v E; 1978 v Cz; (with Celtic), 1982 v D (3)

McGarvey, S. (Manchester U), 1982 v E (sub); 1983 v Bel, Sw; 1984 v Bel (4)

McGhee, M. (Aberdeen), 1981 v D (1)

McGinnis, G. (Dundee U), 1985 v Sp (1)

McInally, J. (Dundee U), 1989 v F (1)

McKimmie, S. (Aberdeen), 1985 v WG, Ic (2) (3)

McKinlay, T. (Dundee), 1984 v EG (sub); 1985 v WG, Ic, Sp (2), Ic (6)

McKinlay, W. (Dundee U), 1989 v N, Y (sub), F; 1990 v Y, F, N (6)

McKinnon, R. (Dundee U), 1991 v R, Pol (sub); 1992 v G (2), Se (2) (6)

McLaren, A, (Hearts), 1989 v F; 1990 v Y, N; 1991 v Sw, Bul, Pol, F; 1992 v R, G, Se (2) (11)

McLaren, A. (Dundee U), 1993 v I, Ma (sub) (2)

McLaughlin, A. (Morton), 1981 v D; 1982 v Se, D, I, E (2); 1983 v EG, Sw (2), Bel (10)

McLeish, A. (Aberdeen), 1978 v W; 1979 v US; 1980 v Bel, E (2); 1987 v Ei (6)

MacLeod, A. (Hibernian), 1979 v P, N (2) (3)

McLeod, J. (Dundee U), 1989 v N; 1990 v F (2)

MacLeod, M. (Dumbarton), 1979 v US; (with Celtic), P (sub), N (2); 1980 v Bel (5)

McNab, N. (Tottenham H), 1978 v W (1)

McNally, M. (Celtic), 1991 v Bul; 1993 v Ic (2)

McNichol, J. (Brentford), 1979 v P. N (2); 1980 v Bel (2), WG, E (7)

McNiven, D. (Leeds U), 1977 v Cz, W (sub), Sw (sub) (3)

McPherson, D. (Rangers), 1984 v Bel; 1985 v Sp; (with Hearts), 1989 v N, Y (4)

McQuilken, J. (Celtic), 1993 v Bul, E (2)

McStay, P. (Celtic), 1983 v EG, Sw (2); 1984 v Y (2) (5)

McWhirter, N. (St Mirren), 1991 v Bul (sub) (1)

Main, A. (Dundee U), 1988 v E; 1989 v Y; 1990 v N (3)

Malpas, M. (Dundee U), 1983 v Bel, Sw (1 + 1 sub); 1984 v Bel, EG, Y (2); 1985 v Sp (8)

May, E. (Hibernian), 1989 v Y (sub), F (2)

Melrose, J. (Partick Th), 1977 v Sw; 1979 v US, P, N (2); 1980 v Bel (sub), WG, E (8)

Miller J. (Aberdeen), 1987 v Ei (sub); 1988 v Bel; (with Celtic) E; 1989 v N, Y; 1990 v F, N (7)

Miller, W. (Aberdeen), 1978 v Sw, Cz (2)

Miller, W. (Hibernian), 1991 v R, Sw, Bul, Pol, F; 1992 v R, G (sub) (7)

Milne, R. (Dundee U), 1982 v Se (sub); 1984 v Bel, EG (3)

Money, I. C. (St Mirren), 1987 v Ei; 1988 v Bel; 1989 v N (3)

Muir, L. (Hibernian), 1977 v Cz (sub) (1)

Murray, N. (Rangers), 1993 v P (sub), Ma, Ic, P (4)

Murray, R. (Bournemouth), 1993 v Ic (sub) (1)

Narey, D. (Dundee U), 1977 v Cz, Sw; 1978 v Sw, Cz (4)

Nevin, P. (Chelsea), 1985 v WG, Ic, Sp (2), Ic (5)

Nicholas, C. (Celtic), 1981 v Se; 1982 v Se; 1983 v EG, Sw, Bel; (with Arsenal), 1984 v Y (6)

Nicol, S. (Ayr U), 1981 v Se; 1982 v Se, D; (with Liverpool), 1982 v I (2), E (2); 1983 v EG, Sw (2), Bel; 1984 v Bel, EG, Y (14)

Nisbet, S. (Rangers), 1989 v N, Y, F; 1990 v Y, F (5)

O'Donnell, P. (Motherwell), 1992 v Sw (sub), R, D, G (2), Se (1 + sub); 1993 v P (8)

O'Neil, B. (Celtic), 1992 v D, G, Se (2) (4)

O'Neil, J. (Dundee U), 1991 v Bul (sub); 1993 v Sw, P, I (7)

Orr, N. (Morton), 1978 v W (sub); 1979 v US, P, N (2); 1980 v Bel, E (7)

Parlane, D. (Rangers), 1977 v W (1)

Paterson, C. (Hibernian), 1981 v Se; 1982 v I (2)

Payne, G. (Dundee U), 1978 v Sw, Cz, W (3)

Pressley, S. (Rangers), 1993 v Ic, Bul, M, E (4)

Provan, D. (Kilmarnock), 1977 v Cz (sub) (1)

Rae, A. (Millwall), 1991 v Bul (sub pl 1), F (sub); 1992 v Sw, R, G (sub), Se (2) (8)Redford, I. (Rangers), 1981 v Se (sub); 1982 v Se, D, I (2), E (6)

Reid, B. (Rangers), 1991 v F; 1992 v D, US, P (4)

Reid, C. (Hibernian), 1993 v Sw, P, I (3)

Reid, M. (Celtic), 1982 v E; 1984 v Y (2)

Reid, R. (St Mirren), 1977 v W, Sw, E (3)

Rice, B. (Hibernian), 1985 v WG (1)

Richardson, L. (St Mirren), 1980 v WG, E (sub) (2)

Ritchie, A. (Morton), 1980 v Bel (1)

Robertson, A. (Rangers) 1991 v F (1)

Robertson, C. (Rangers), 1977 v E (sub) (1)

Robertson, D. (Aberdeen), 1987 v Ei (sub); 1988 v E (2); 1989 v N, Y; 1990 v Y, N (7)

Robertson, J. (Hearts), 1985 v WG, Ic (sub) (2)

Robertson, L. (Rangers), 1993 v M (sub), E (sub) (2)

Roddie, A. (Aberdeen), 1992 v US, P (2)

Roddie, A. (Aberdeen), 1993 v P, Ic (2)

Ross, T. W. (Arsenal), 1977 v W (1)

Russell, R. (Rangers), 1978 v W; 1980 v Bel; 1984 v Y (3)

Salton, D. B. (Luton T), 1992 v D, US, P, Y (4)

Shannon, R. (Dundee), 1987 v WG, Ei (2), Bel; 1988 v Bel, E (2) (7)

Sharp, G. (Everton), 1982 v E (1)

Sharp, R. (Dunfermline Ath), 1990 v N (sub); 1991 v R, Sw, Bul (4)

Simpson, N. (Aberdeen), 1982 v I (2), E; 1983 v EG, Sw (2), Bel; 1984 v Bel, EG, Y; 1985 v Sp (11)

Sinclair, G. (Dumbarton), 1977 v E (1)

Skilling, M. (Kilmarnock), 1993 v Ic (sub) (1)

Smith, B. M. (Celtic), 1992 v G (2), US, P, Y (5)

Smith, G. (Rangers), 1978 v W (1)

Smith, H. G. (Hearts), 1987 v WG, Bel (2)

Sneddon, A. (Celtic), 1979 v US (1)

Speedie, D. (Chelsea), 1985 v Sp (1)

Spencer, J. (Rangers), 1991 v Sw (sub), F; 1992 v Sw (3)

Stanton, P. (Hibernian), 1977 v Cz (1)

Stark, W. (Aberdeen), 1985 v Ic (1)

Stephen, R. (Dundee), 1983 v Bel (sub) (1)

Stevens, G. (Motherwell), 1977 v E (1)

Stewart, J. (Kilmarnock), 1978 v Sw, Cz; (with Middlesbrough), 1979 v P (3)

Stewart, R. (Dundee U), 1979 v P, N (2); (with West Ham U), 1980 v Bel (2), E (2), WG; 1981 v D; 1982 v I (2), E (12)

Strachan, G. (Aberdeen), 1980 v Bel (1)

Sturrock, P. (Dundee U), 1977 v Cz, W, Sw, E; 1978 v Sw, Cz; 1982 v Se, I, E (9)

Sweeney, S. (Clydebank), 1991 v R, Sw (sub), Bul (2), Pol; 1992 v Sw, R (7)

Telfer, P. (Luton T), 1993 v Ma, P (2)

Thomas, K. (Hearts), 1993 v Bul, M, E (3)

Thomson, W. (Partick Th), 1977 v E (sub); 1978 v W; (with St Mirren), 1979 v US, N (2); 1980 v Bel (2), E (2), WG (10)

Tolmie, J. (Morton), 1980 v Bel (sub) (1)

Tortolano, J. (Hibernian), 1987 v WG, Ei (2)

Tweed, S. (Hibernian), 1993 v Ic (1)

Walker, A. (Celtic), 1988 v Bel (1)

Wallace, I. (Coventry C), 1978 v Sw (1)

Walsh, C. (Nottingham F), 1984 v EG, Sw (2). Bel; 1984 v EG (5)

Wark, J. (Ipswich T), 1977 v Cz, W, Sw; 1978 v W; 1979 v P; 1980 v E (2), WG (8)

Watson, A. (Aberdeen), 1981 v Se, D; 1982 v D, I (sub) (4)

Watson, K. (Rangers), 1977 v E; 1978 v Sw (sub) (2)

Watt, M. (Aberdeen), 1991 v R, Sw, Bul (2), Pol, F; 1992 v Sw, R, G (2), Se (2) (12)

Whyte, D. (Celtic), 1987 v Ei (2), Bel; 1988 v E (2); 1989 v N, Y; 1990 v Y, N (9)

Will, J. A. (Arsenal), 1992 v D (sub), Y; 1993 v Ic (sub) (3)

Wilson, T. (St Mirren), 1983 v Sw (sub) (1)

Wilson, T. (Nottingham F), 1988 v E; 1989 v N, Y; 1990 v F (4)

Winnie, D. (St Mirren), 1988 v Bel (1)

Wright, P. (Aberdeen), 1989 v Y, F; (with QPR), 1990 v Y (sub) (3)

Wright, S. (Aberdeen), 1991 v Bul, Pol, F; 1992 v Sw, G (2), Se (2); 1993 v Sw, P, I, Ma (12)

Wright, T. (Oldham Ath), 1987 v Bel (sub) (1)

WALES

Aizlewood, M. (Luton T), 1979 v E; 1981 v Ho (2)

Balcombe, S. (Leeds Y), 1982 v F (sub) (1)

Bater, P. T. (Bristol R), 1977 v E, S (2)

Bird, A. (Cardiff C), 1993 v Cy (sub) (1)

Blackmore, C. (Manchester U), 1984 v N, Bul, Y (3)

Blake, N. (Cardiff C), 1991 v Pol (sub); 1993 v Cy, Bel, Cz (4)

Bodin, P. (Cardiff C), 1983 v Y (1)

Bowen, J. P. (Swansea C), 1993 v Cy, Bel (2) (3)

Bowen, M. (Tottenham H), 1983 v N; 1984 v Bul, Y (3)

Boyle, T. (C Palace), 1982 v F (1)

Cegielski, W. (Wrexham), 1977 v E (sub), S (2)

Chapple, S. R. (Swansea C), 1992 v R; 1993 v Cy, Bel (2), Cz (5)

Charles, J. M. (Swansea C), 1979 v E; 1981 v Ho (2)

Clark, J. (Manchester U), 1978 v S; (with Derby Co), 1979 v E (2)

Coleman, C. (Swansea C); 1990 v Pol; 1991 v E, Pol (3)

Coyne, D. (Tranmere R), 1992 v R (1)

Curtis, A. T. (Swansea C), 1977 v E (1)

Davies, A. (Manchester U), 1982 v F (2) Ho; 1983 v N, Y, Bul (6)

Davies, G. M. (Hereford U), 1993 v Bel, Cz (2)

Davies, I. C. (Norwich C), 1978 v S (sub) (1)

Deacy, N. (PSV Eindhoven), 1977 v S (1)

Dibble, A. (Cardiff C), 1983 v Bul; 1984 v N, Bul (3)

Doyle, S. C. (Preston NE), 1979 v E (sub); (with Huddersfield T), 1984 v N (2)

Dwyer, P. J. (Cardiff C), 1979 v E (1)

Ebdon, M. (Everton), 1990 v Pol; 1991 v E (2)

Edwards, R. (Bristol C.), 1991 v Pol; 1992 v R (2)

Edwards, R. I. (Chester), 1977 v S; 1978 v W; 1993 v Cy, Bel (2), Cz (6)

Evans, A. (Bristol R), 1977 v E (1)

Foster, M. G. (Tranmere R), 1993 v Cz (1)

Freestone, R. (Chelsea), 1990 v Pol (1)

Gale, D. (Swansea C), 1983 v Bul; 1984 v N (sub) (2)

Giggs, R. (Manchester U), 1991 v Pol (1)

Giles, D. C. (Cardiff C), 1977 v S; 1978 v S; (with Swansea C), 1981 v Ho; (with C. Palace), 1983 v Y (4)

Giles, P. (Cardiff C), 1982 v F (2), Ho (3)
Graham, D. (Manchester U.), 1991 v E (1)
Griffith, C. (Cardiff C), 1990 v Pol (1)
Griffiths, C. (Shrewsbury T), 1991 v Pol (sub) (1)

Hall, G. D. (Chelsea), 1990 v Pol (1)
Hodges, G. (Wimbledon), 1983 v Y (sub), Bul (sub); 1984 v N, Bul, Y (5)
Holden, A. (Chester C), 1984 v Y (sub) (1)
Hopkins, J. (Fulham), 1982 v F (sub), Ho; 1983 v N, Y, Bul (5)
Hughes, I. (Bury), 1992 v R; 1993 v Cy, Bel (sub), Cz (4)
Hughes, M. (Manchester U), 1983 v N, Y; 1984 v N. Bul, Y (5)
Hughes, W. (WBA), 1977 v E, S; 1978 v S (3)

Jackett, K. (Watford), 1981 v Ho; 1982 v F (2)
James, R. M. (Swansea C), 1977 v E, S; 1978 v S (3)
Jenkins, S. R. (Swansea C), 1993 v Cy (sub), Bel (2)
Jones, F. (Wrexham), 1981 v Ho (1)
Jones, L. (Cardiff C), 1982 v F (2), Ho (3)
Jones, P. L. (Liverpool), 1992 v R; 1993 v Cy, Bel (2), Cz (5)
Jones, V. (Bristol R), 1979 v E; 1981 v Ho (2)

Kendall, M. (Tottenham H), 1978 v S (1)

Law, B. J. (QPR), 1990 v Pol; 1991 v E (2)
Letheran, G. (Leeds U), 1977 v E, S (2)
Lewis, D. (Swansea C), 1982 v F (2), Ho; 1983 v N, Y, Bul; 1984 v N, Bul, Y (9)
Lewis, J. (Cardiff C), 1983 v N (1)
Loveridge, J. (Swansea C), 1982 v Ho; 1983 v N, Bul (3)
Lowndes, S. R. (Newport Co), 1979 v E; 1981 v Ho; (with Millwall), 1984 v Bul, Y (4)

Maddy, P. (Cardiff C), 1982 v Ho; 1983 v N (sub) (2)
Margetson, M. W. (Manchester C), 1992 v R; 1993 v Cy, Bel (2), Cz (5)
Marustik, C. (Swansea C), 1982 v F (2); 1983 v Y, Bul; 1984 v N, Bul, Y (7)
Melville, A. K. (Swansea C), 1990 v Pol; (with Oxford U), 1991 v E (2)
Micallef, C. (Cardiff C), 1982 v F, Ho; 1983 v N (3)

Nardiello, D. (Coventry C), 1978 v S (1)
Neilson, A. B. (Newcastle U), 1993 v Cy, Bel (2), Cz (4)
Nicholas, P. (C Palace), 1978 v S; 1979 v E; (with Arsenal), 1982 v F (3)
Nogan, K. (Luton T), 1990 v Pol; 1991 v E (2)
Nogan, L. (Oxford U.) 1991 v E (1)

Owen, G. (Wrexham), 1991 v E (sub), Pol; 1992 v R; 1993 v Cy, Bel (2) (6)

Pascoe, C. (Swansea C), 1983 v Bul (sub); 1984 v N (sub), Bul, Y (4)
Pembridge, M. (Luton T), 1991 v Pol (1)
Perry, J. (Cardiff C), 1990 v Pol; 1991 v E, Pol (3)
Peters, M. (Manchester C), 1992 v R; (with Norwich C), 1993 v Cy, Cz (3)
Phillips, D. (Plymouth Arg), 1984 v N, Bul, Y (3)
Phillips, L. (Swansea C), 1979 v E; (with Charlton Ath), 1983 v N (2)
Pontin, K. (Cardiff C), 1978 v S (1)
Powell, L. (Southampton), 1991 v Pol (sub); 1992 v R (sub); 1993 v Bel (sub) (3)
Price, P. (Luton T), 1981 v Ho (1)
Pugh, D. (Doncaster R), 1982 v F (2) (2)
Pugh, S. (Wrexham), 1993 v Bel (2 subs) (2)

Ratcliffe, K. (Everton), 1981 v Ho; 1982 v F (2)
Ready, K. (QPR), 1992 v R; 1993 v Bel (2) (3)
Rees, A. (Birmingham C), 1984 v N (1)
Rees, J. (Luton T), 1990 v Pol; 1991 v E, Pol (3)
Roberts, A. (QPR), 1991 v E, Pol (2)
Roberts, G. (Hull C), 1983 v Bul (1)
Roberts, J. G. (Wrexham), 1977 v E (1)
Robinson, J. (Brighton & HA), 1992 v R; (with Charlton Ath), 1993 v Bel (2)
Rush, I. (Liverpool), 1981 v Ho; 1982 v F (2)

Sayer, P. A. (Cardiff C), 1977 v E, S (2)
Searle, D. (Cardiff C), 1991 v Pol (sub); 1992 v R; 1993 v Cy, Bel (2), Cz (5)
Slatter, N. (Bristol R), 1983 v N, Y, Bul; 1984 v N, Bul, Y (6)
Speed, G. A. (Leeds U), 1990 v Pol; 1991 v E, Pol (3)
Stevenson, N. (Swansea C), 1982 v F, Ho (2)
Stevenson, W. B. (Leeds U), 1977 v E, S; 1978 v S (3)
Symons, K. (Portsmouth), 1991 v E, Pol (2)

Thomas, Martin R. (Bristol R), 1979 v E; 1981 v Ho (2)
Thomas, Mickey R. (Wrexham), 1977 v E; 1978 v S (2)
Thomas, D. G. (Leeds U), 1977 v E; 1979 v E; 1984 v N (3)
Tibbott, L. (Ipswich T), 1977 v E, S (2)

Vaughan, N. (Newport Co), 1982 v F, Ho (2)

Walsh, I. P. (C Palace), 1979 v E; (with Swansea C), 1983 v Bul (2)
Walton, M. (Norwich C.), 1991 v Pol (sub) (1)
Williams, D. (Bristol R), 1983 v Y (1)
Williams, G. (Bristol R), 1983 v Y, Bul (2)
Wilmot, R. (Arsenal), 1982 v F (2), Ho; 1983 v N, Y; 1984 v Y (6)

ENGLAND B RESULTS 1949–92

Year	Date		Venue	Eng	Alg
		v ALGIERS		Eng	Alg
1990	Dec	11	Algiers	0	0
		v AUSTRALIA		Eng	Aust
1980	Nov	17	Birmingham	1	0
		v CIS		Eng	CIS
1992	April	28	Moscow	1	1
		v CZECHOSLOVAKIA		Eng	Cz
1978	Nov	28	Prague	1	0
1990	April	24	Sunderland	2	0
1992	Mar	24	Budejovice	1	0
		v FINLAND		Eng	Fin
1949	May	15	Helsinki	4	0
		v FRANCE		Eng	Fra
1952	May	22	Le Havre	1	7
1992	Feb	18	Loftus Road	3	0
		v WEST GERMANY		Eng	WG
1954	Mar	24	Gelsenkirchen	4	0
1955	Mar	23	Sheffield	1	1
1978	Feb	21	Augsburg	2	1
		v HOLLAND		Eng	Hol
1949	May	18	Amsterdam	4	0
1950	Feb	22	Newcastle	1	0
1952	Mar	26	Amsterdam	1	0
		v ICELAND		Eng	Ice
1989	May	19	Reykjavik	2	0
1991	April	27	Watford	1	0
		v ITALY		Eng	It
1950	May	11	Milan	0	5
1989	Nov	14	Brighton	1	1
		v LUXEMBOURG		Eng	Lux
1950	May	21	Luxembourg	2	1
		v MALAYSIA		Eng	Mal
1978	May	30	Kuala Lumpur	1	1
		v MALTA		Eng	Mal
1987	Oct	14	Ta'Qali	2	0

Year	Date		Venue	Eng	NZ
		v NEW ZEALAND		Eng	NZ
1978	June	7	Christchurch	4	0
1978	June	11	Wellington	3	1
1978	June	14	Auckland	4	0
1979	Oct	15	Leyton	4	1
1984	Nov	13	Nottingham	2	0
		v NORWAY		Eng	Nor
1989	May	22	Stavanger	1	0
		v REPUBLIC OF IRELAND		Eng	RoI
1990	Mar	27	Cork	1	4
		v SCOTLAND		Eng	Scot
1953	Mar	11	Edinburgh	2	2
1954	Mar	3	Sunderland	1	1
1956	Feb	29	Dundee	2	2
1957	Feb	6	Birmingham	4	1
		v SINGAPORE		Eng	Sin
1978	June	18	Singapore	8	0
		v SPAIN		Eng	Sp
1980	Mar	26	Sunderland	1	0
1981	Mar	25	Granada	2	3
1991*	Dec	18	Castellon	1	0
*Spanish Olympic IX					
		v SWITZERLAND		Eng	Sw
1950	Jan	18	Sheffield	5	0
1954	May	22	Basle	0	2
1956	Mar	21	Southampton	4	1
1989	May	16	Winterthur	2	0
1991	May	20	Walsall	2	1
		v USA		Eng	USA
1980	Oct	14	Manchester	1	0
		v WALES		Eng	Wal
1991	Feb	5	Swansea	1	0
		v YUGOSLAVIA		Eng	Yug
1954	May	16	Ljubljana	1	2
1955	Oct	19	Manchester	5	1
1989	Dec	12	Millwall	2	1

OTHER MATCHES 1992–93

Other FA Representative matches

FA XI 2 *(Thomas, Saunders)*
Northern Premier League 3
FA XI: Mason; (Farrelly); Freeman, Johnson (Carberry), Connor, Essex, Butler, Thomas, Brown, Saunders, Rudge (Ross), Hemmings (Doherty).

FA XI 6 *(Leworthy 3, Thompson, Scott, Rogers)*
Isthmian League 1
FA XI: Hyde (Bunting); Cousins, Watts, Pamphlett (Rogers), Kerr, Thompson, Butterworth, Guppy, Leworthy, Scott (Carroll), Blackford (Golley).

FA XI 2 *(Ross 2)*
Combined Services 0
FA XI: McKenna; Shirtliff, Hatto, Thompson, Holmes, Filson, Ross, Tilly (Lamb), Cavell, Brown (Burton), Norris.

FA XI 2 *(Benbow, Hadley)*
British Students 1
FA XI: (Acton Coles); Simpson, Brighton, Richardson, Brindley, Shail, Forsyth (Hadley), Grainger (Deakin), Benbow (Webb), Palgrave, Sanderson.

Semi-Professional Internationals

England 2 *(Robbins, Leworthy)*
Wales 1
England: Price; Shirtliff, Watts, Shail, Kerr, Stapleton, Thompson, Richardson P, Robbins (Ross), Leworthy, Guppy.

England 1 *(Cavell)*
Finland 3
England: Price (Batty); Shirtliff, Watts, Hone, Conner, Butler (Collins), Webb, Richardson P, Robbins (Coleman), Cavell, Hemmings (Ross).

Highland League 2
England 2 *(Richardson P, Cavell)*
England: Price; (Batty); Hone, Watts, Richardson K, Conner, Broom, Webb (Collins), Richardson P, Ross, Cavell (Abbott), Hemmings (Butler).

International Records

MOST GOALS IN AN INTERNATIONAL

England	Malcolm Macdonald (Newcastle U) 5 goals v Cyprus, at Wembley		16.4.1975
	Willie Hall (Tottenham H) 5 goals v Ireland, at Old Trafford		16.11.1938
	G. O. Smith (Corinthians) 5 goals v Ireland, at Sunderland		18.2.1899
	Steve Bloomer (Derby Co) 5 goals* v Wales, at Cardiff		16.3.1896
	Oliver Vaughton (Aston Villa) 5 goals v Ireland, at Belfast		18.2.82
Scotland	Charles Heggie (Rangers) 5 goals v Ireland, at Belfast		20.3.1886
Ireland	Joe Bambrick (Linfield) 6 goals v Wales, at Belfast		1.2.1930
Wales	James Price (Wrexham) 4 goals v Ireland, at Wrexham		25.2.1882
	Mel Charles (Cardiff C) 4 goals v Ireland, at Cardiff		11.4.1962
	Ian Edwards (Chester) 4 goals v Malta, at Wrexham		25.10.1978

* There are conflicting reports which make it uncertain whether Bloomer scored four or five goals in this game.

MOST GOALS IN AN INTERNATIONAL CAREER

		Goals	Games
England	Bobby Charlton (Manchester U)	49	106
Scotland	Denis Law (Huddersfield T, Manchester C, Torino, Manchester U)	30	55
	Kenny Dalglish (Celtic, Liverpool)	30	102
Ireland	Colin Clarke (Bournemouth, Southampton, QPR, Portsmouth	25	60
Wales	Ian Rush (Liverpool, Juventus)	13	38
Republic of Ireland	Frank Stapleton (Arsenal, Manchester U, Ajax, Derby Co, Le Havre, Blackburn R)	20	70

HIGHEST SCORES

World Cup Match	New Zealand	13	Fiji	0		1981
European Championship	Spain	12	Malta	1		1983
Olympic Games	Denmark	17	France	1		1908
	Germany	16	USSR	0		1912
International Match	Germany	13	Finland	0		1940
	Spain	13	Bulgaria	0		1933
European Cup	Feyenoord	12	K R Reykjavik	2		1969
European Cup-Winners' Cup	Sporting Lisbon	16	Apoel Nicosia	1		1963
Fairs & UEFA Cups	Ajax	14	Red Boys	0		1984

GOALSCORING RECORDS

World Cup Final	Geoff Hurst (England) 3 goals v West Germany	1966
World Cup Final tournament	Just Fontaine (France) 13 goals	1958
Major European Cup game	Lothar Emmerich (Borussia Dortmund) v Floriana in Cup-Winners' Cup – 6 goals	1965
Career	Arthur Friedenreich (Brazil) 1329 goals	1910–30
	Pelé (Brazil) 1281 goals	*1956–78
	Franz 'Bimbo' Binder (Austria, Germany) 1006 goals	1930–50

*Pelé has since scored two goals in Testimonial matches making his total 1283.

MOST CAPPED INTERNATIONALS IN BRITISH ISLES

England	Bobby Moore	108 appearances	1962–73
Northern Ireland	Pat Jennings	119 appearances	1964–86
Scotland	Kenny Dalglish	102 appearances	1971–86
Wales	Joey Jones	72 appearances	1975–87
Republic of Ireland	Liam Brady	72 appearances	1974–90

TRANSFERS

Record British moves (UK only)

£4,000,000 Duncan Ferguson, Dundee U to Rangers, July 1993

£3,750,000 Roy Keane, Nottingham F to Manchester U, July 1993

£3,300,000 Alan Shearer, Southampton to Blackburn R, June 1992

£2,900,000 Dean Saunders, Derby Co to Liverpool, July 1991

£2,750,000 Brian Deane, Sheffield U to Leeds U, June 1993

£2,500,000 Keith Curle, Wimbledon to Manchester C, July 1991

£2,500,000 Ian Wright, Crystal Palace to Arsenal, September 1991

£2,500,000 Terry Phelan, Wimbledon to Manchester C, August 1992

£2,300,000 Gary Pallister, Middlesbrough to Manchester U, August 1989

£2,275,000 Nigel Clough, Nottingham F to Liverpool, July 1993

Other British moves

£6,500,000 David Platt, Bari to Juventus, May 1992

£5,500,000 David Platt, Aston Villa to Bari, July 1991

£5,500,000 Paul Gascoigne, Tottenham H to Lazio, May 1992

£5,200,000 David Platt, Juventus to Sampdoria, July 1993

£5,000,000 Trevor Steven, Rangers to Marseille, August 1991

£4,500,000 Chris Waddle, Tottenham H to Marseille, July 1989

£3,200,000 Ian Rush, Liverpool to Juventus, June 1987

£2,800,000 Ian Rush, Juventus to Liverpool, August 1988

£2,750,000 Gary Lineker, Everton to Barcelona, June 1986

£2,700,000 Des Walker, Sampdoria to Sheffield W, July 1993

£2,300,000 Mark Hughes, Manchester U to Barcelona, May 1986

World records

£13,000,000 Gianluigi Lentini, Torino to AC Milan, June 1992

£12,000,000 Gianluca Vialli, Sampdoria to Juventus, June 1992

£10,000,000 Jean-Pierre Papin, Marseille to AC Milan, June 1992

£8,000,000 Igor Shalimov, Foggia to Internazionalle, June 1992

FA SCHOOLS AND YOUTH GAMES 1992–93

UEFA YOUTH CHAMPIONSHIP UNDER-16

23 SEPT

Sweden 1
England 3 (*Hughes, Howell, Beresford*)
England: Cutler; Brunskill, Taylor, O'Connor, Neville, Howell, Beresford (Dennis), Clarke (Wharton), Ellis, Hughes, Cooke.

3 NOV

Holland 1
England 1 (*Howell* (*pen*))   2300
England: Cutler; Brunskill (Taylor), Neville, O'Connor, Plummer, Hughes (Cooke), Beresford, Howell, Clarke, Ellis, Spencer.

3 MAR

England 4 (*Ellis 2, Mustoe 2*)
Holland 0
England: Cutler; Neville, Taylor, O'Connor, Plummer, Howell, Beresford (Cooke), Spencer, Ellis, Mustoe (Walley), Hughes.

10 MAR

England 4 (*Plummer, Cooke 2, Walley*)
Sweden 0
England: Cutler; Neville, Taylor, O'Connor, Plummer, Howell, Cooke, Spencer, Ellis, Mustoe (Walley), Hughes (Wharton).

26 APR

Belgium 1
England 1 (*Beresford*)
England: Cutler; Neville, Taylor, O'Connor, Plummer, Howell, Beresford, Spencer (Wharton), Ellis, Mustoe (Walley), Cooke.

28 APR

Eire 0
England 1 (Walley)
England: Cutler; Neville, Hines, O'Connor, Plummer, Howell, Beresford, Wharton (Spencer), Ellis (Mustoe), Walley, Cooke.

30 APR

Czechoslovakia 2
England 0
England: Cutler; Neville, Taylor, O'Connor, Smith, Howell (Ellis), Beresford, Spencer, Walley, Mustoe, Cooke (Wharton).

GENOA TOURNAMENT UNDER-16

28 SEPT

England 1 (*Ellis*)
Spain 2
England: Cutler; Brunskill, Taylor, O'Connor, Neville, Howell, Beresford (Throp), Hughes, Clarke (White), Ellis, Pass (Lovelock).

29 SEPT

England 0
Italy 0
England: Cutler; Brunskill, Taylor, O'Connor, Neville, Howell, Beresford, Hughes (Clarke), Ellis, Pearson (Pass), Lovelock.

1 OCT

England 2 (*Clarke 2*)
Austria 1
England: Hurst; Brunskill, Taylor, O'Connor, Neville, Howell (Hughes), Beresford, Lovelock, Clarke, Throp (Ellis), Pass (White).

3 OCT

England 4 (*Ellis 3, Clarke*)
Scotland 2
England: Hurst; Brunskill, Taylor, O'Connor, Neville, Howell (Pearson), White (Lovelock), Hughes, Ellis, Clarke, Beresford.

UNDER-18

7 OCT

France 2
England 0
England: Aouf; Sulzeer Campbell, Potter, Casper, Neville, Warner, Butt, Tinkler, Ndah (Fowler), Sharp (Beckman), Eadie.

17 NOV

England 7 (*Fowler 3, Ndah, Sharp 2, Gallen*)
Switzerland 2
England: Day; Warren, Thatcher, Tinkler (Clarke), Casper, Neville, Beckham (Campbell), Sharp, Ndah (Gallen), Fowler, Eadie.

17 FEB

Spain 1
England 1 (*Ndah*)
England: Day; Warren, Stuart Campbell, Sulzeer Campbell, Casper, Neville, Beckham, Sharp, Gallen, Fowler, Ndah.

30 MAR

England 4
Denmark 2
England: Day; Sulzeer Campbell, Beckham, Tinkler, Casper, Neville, Butt, Sharp, Joachim (Gallen), Forrester, Scholes.

UNDER-19

13 OCT

England 2 (*Unsworth, Thompson*)
Egypt 1
England: Sheppard; Johnson, Unsworth, Harriott, Pearce, Hughes, Berry, Caskey, Mike, Thompson, Pollock.

17 NOV

England 2 (*Pollock, Thompson*)
Turkey 1
England: Watson D; Watson S, Unsworth, Harriott, Pearce, Myers, Pollock, Caskey, Mike (Joachim), Thompson, Butt.

16 FEB

England 0
Denmark 1
England: Sheppard; Watson S, Unsworth (Matteo), Selley, Pearce (Harriott), Hughes, Joachim, Bart-Williams (Mike), Barmby, Thompson, Caskey.

WORLD   YOUTH   CHAMPIONSHIPS (AUSTRALIA)

7 MAR

England 1 (*Pearce*)
Korea 1
England: Watson D; Watson B, Pearce, Myers, Bart-Williams, Caskey, Barmby, Pollock, Thompson, Selley (Mike), Hughes.

9 MAR

England 1 (*Bart-Williams*)
USA 0
England: Watson D; Watson S, Unsworth, Hughes, Pearce, Myers, Bart-Williams, Caskey, Barmby, Pollock, Thompson (Mike).

11 MAR

England 1 (*Joachim*)
Turkey 0
England: Watson D; Watson S, Unsworth, Pearce, Hghes, Harriott, Thompson, Caskey, Pollock, Bart-Williams, Joachim.

14 MAR

England 0
Mexico 0
England: Watson D; Watson S, Unsworth, Pearce, Hughes, Bart-Williams, Caskey, Barmby (Joachim), Pollock, Thompson, Myers (Harriott).
(England won 4-3 on penalties)

17 MAR

England 1 (*Pollock (pen)*)
Ghana 2
England: Watson D; Watson S, Unsworth (Butt), Harriott, Hughes, Pearce, Bart-Williams, Caskey, Pollock, Thompson, Joachim.

20 MAR

England 2 (*Unsworth, Joachim*)
England: Watson D; Watson S, Unsworth, Myers, Hughes, Pearce (Harriott), Bart-Williams, Caskey, Pollock, Thompson, Joachim.

WOMEN'S NATIONAL LEAGUE

Arsenal took all three major trophies in 1992–93 to emerge as the outstanding team of the season. They lost only one League game but were pushed all the way by Doncaster Belles, last season's successful Premier Division side. Understandably the matches between these two teams were closely fought affairs, Arsenal losing just away to Doncaster 2-0, while Doncaster's only other reverse was 3-2 at Wimbledon. Arsenal also defeated Doncaster 3-0 in the WFA Cup Final.

Premier Division

	P	Home W	D	L	Goals F	A	Away W	D	L	F	Goals A	GD	Pts
Arsenal	18	9	0	0	41	4	8	0	1	25	4	+58	34
Doncaster Belles	18	9	0	0	33	3	7	0	2	47	7	+70	32
Knowsley	18	6	1	2	22	13	5	0	4	15	20	+4	23
Wimbledon	18	5	1	3	17	13	4	2	3	19	24	-1	21
Red Star Southampton	18	5	1	3	26	22	2	2	5	11	19	-4	17
Ipswich Town	18	3	3	3	18	20	4	0	5	13	29	-18	17
Stanton Rangers	18	3	0	6	14	24	3	1	5	10	21	-21	13
Millwall Lionesses	18	3	0	6	9	20	0	2	7	7	21	-23	8
Maidstone Tigresses	18	1	2	6	5	22	1	2	6	3	21	-35	8
Bronte	18	1	2	6	5	20	1	1	7	11	24	-28	7

Maidstone Tigresses relegated to Division One South
Bronte relegated to Division One North

Divison One South

	P	Home W	D	L	Goals F	A	Away W	D	L	F	Goals A	GD	Pts
District Line	18	8	0	1	47	15	7	1	1	46	16	+62	31
Hassocks	18	6	2	1	30	18	6	0	3	23	20	+15	26
Town & Country	18	6	2	1	31	15	3	0	6	20	24	+12	20
Hemel Hempstead	18	6	1	2	23	14	2	3	4	15	13	+1	20
Brighton & Hove Albion	18	5	2	2	23	14	3	0	6	18	28	-1	18
Horsham	18	4	3	2	20	18	2	2	5	14	24	-8	17
Oxford	18	3	0	6	8	20	2	5	2	12	14	-14	15
Epsom & Ewell	18	3	2	4	24	23	3	0	6	20	29	-8	14
Bristol Backwell	18	3	1	5	19	22	1	2	6	12	28	-19	11
Saltdean	18	2	1	6	19	32	1	1	7	11	38	-40	8

District Line promoted to the Premier Division
Saltdean elected to compete in the play-offs, and reached the final, together with Bromley Borough, winners of the South East Region
Result of play-off final: Bromley Borough 3, Saltdean 1
Bromley Borough replace Saltdean in Division One South

Division One North

	P	Home W	D	L	Goals F	A	Away W	D	L	F	Goals A	GD	Pts
Leasowe Pacific	18	9	0	0	52	7	7	1	1	48	14	+79	33
Nottingham Argyle	18	7	0	2	41	14	7	1	1	32	9	+50	29
Abbeydale	18	7	2	0	40	7	4	1	4	22	13	+42	25
Sheffield Wednesday	18	6	0	3	40	11	3	2	4	28	18	+39	20
St Helens	18	6	0	3	35	19	3	1	5	32	30	+18	19
Wolverhampton	18	3	3	3	30	17	4	0	5	22	20	+15	17
Villa Aztecs	18	5	1	3	28	18	3	0	6	19	27	+2	17
Cowgate Kestrels	18	4	1	4	21	28	2	2	5	11	23	-19	15
Sunderland	18	3	1	5	8	40	1	0	8	11	63	-84	4
Milton Keynes	18	0	1	8	6	66	0	0	9	2	84	-142	1

Leasowe Pacific are promoted to the Premier Division
Sunderland resigned, and replaced by Luton Town, winners of the Eastern Region
Milton Region elected not to compete in the play-offs, and replaced by Kidderminster Harriers, winners of the West Midlands Region

NATIONAL LEAGUE CUP

First Round
Oxford 1, Epsom & Ewell 2
Nottingham Argyle 3, Bristol Backwell 0
Milton Keynes 0, Sunderland 8
District Line 4, Villa Aztecs 1
Arsenal 8, Hassocks 0
Town & Country 1, Saltdean 2
Sheffield Wednesday 1, Bronte 0
Wolves 3, Horsham 1
Brighton 1, Leasowe Pacific 6

Second Round
Epsom & Ewell 1, Ipswich Town 3
Wimbledon 4, Nottingham Argyle 0
Sunderland 0, District Line 5
Arsenal 9, Saltdean 0
Red Star Southampton 0, Knowsley 1

Maidstone Tigresses 2, Stanton Rangers 2
(Maidstone Tigresses won 6-5 on penalties)
Sheffield Wednesday 0, Wolves 2
Leasowe Pacific 7, Millwall Lionesses 0

Third Round
Ipswich Town 1, Wimbledon 2
District Line 1, Arsenal 5
Knowsley 2, Maidstone Tigresses 0
Wolves 1, Leasowe Pacific 3

Semi-finals
Wimbledon 2, Arsenal 4
Knowsley 5, Leasowe Pacific 4

Final
Arsenal 3, Knowsley 0

WFA CUP COMPETITION 1992–93

First Round

GROUP 1
Farnborough 11, Sutton United 0
Three Bridges 16, Buxted Rangers 3
Portsmouth 2, Gosport Borough 1
Corematch 12, Thanet Utd 0
Teynham 3, Maidstone United 0
Havant, Byes
Isle of Wight, Byes
Hassocks, Byes
Saltdean United, Byes
Brighton & Hove Albion, Byes
Horsham, Byes
Ewell & Epsom, Byes

GROUP 2
Crewkerne 3, Eastleigh 11
Bristol City 22, Bristol Rovers 1
Swansea w/o, Salisbury
Swindon 3, Frome 2
Newbury w/o, Exeter Rangers
Carterton 1, Torquay United 7
Cardiff 4, Clevedon 0
Red Vale United, Tongwynlais w/o
Truro City w/o, Corsham Town
Plymouth 4, Solent 1
Bournemouth, Byes
Bristol Backwell, Byes
Three teams qualified to the open round (4th) from these two groups

GROUP 3
Bromley Borough 6, S.E. Rangers 0
St Charles, Winchester All Stars w/o
Crystal Palace 2, Palace Eagles 3
Newham 4, Watford 6
Reading 1, Hackney 6
Yeading 0, Tottenham 4
Leyton Orient 9, Aylesbury United 0
Colliers Row 7, Walton & Hersham 0
Binfield 4, Brentford 0
Abbey Rangers, Byes
London Girls, Byes
District Line, Byes

GROUP 4
Runcorn 0, Pilkington 5
Bangor City 0, Kidderminster 6
Aston Villa 1, Tranmere Rovers 5
Bentley Tigers 0, Thame United 8
Crewe 5, Launton 1
Worcester City 6, Leek Town 8
Stockport County, Byes
Birmingham, Byes
Abbeydale Alvechurch, Byes
Villa Aztecs, Byes
Wolverhampton, Byes
Oxford United, Byes
Three teams qualified to the open round (4th) from these two groups

GROUP 5
Liverpool, Lever Club w/o
Liverpool Feds. 0, Preston Rangers 7
Atherton Laburnum 0, Ashton Limited 15
Manchester United 5, Vernon Carus 0
Broadoak w/o, Manchester City
Oldham Athletic 10, Rossendale 2
Bolton, Byes
Wigan, Byes
Rochdale, Byes
Bury, Byes
St Helens, Byes
Leasowe Pacific, Byes

GROUP 6
Cleveland 8, Bradford City 2
Oakland Rangers 2, Brighouse 5
Hull City 1, Barnsley 0
City Roses 3, Doncaster Town 8
Newcastle 11, Wiggington Grasshoppers 0
Leeds Polytechnic 0, Wakefield 7

Scarborough, Byes
Huddersfield, Byes
Cowgate Kestrels, Byes
Middlesbrough, Byes
Sunderland, Byes
Sheffield Wednesday, Byes
Three teams qualified to the open (4th) round from these two groups

GROUP 7
Sharley Park 5, Grimsby 1
Calverton, Rainworth w/o
Haigh 7, Notts County 2
Leicester 3, Sporting Kesteven 1
T.N.T. 1, Derby City 0
Nettleham, Byes
Highfield Rangers, Byes
Nottingham Argyle, Byes

GROUP 8
Luton Town 9, Beccles 1
Stevenage 1, Dunstable 9
Southend 4, Leighton Linslade 1
Chelmsford 1, Colchester United 2
Pye 3, Harlow Town 4
Norwich 6, Woodham Wanderers 0
Town & Country, Byes
Milton Keynes, Byes
Two teams qualified to the open (4th) round from these two groups

Second Round

GROUP 1
Saltdean 1, Teynham 2
Havant 3, Farnborough 1
Corematch 12, Three Bridges 1
Portsmouth 0, 0, Epsom & Ewell 0, 6
Isle of Wight 2, Horsham 9
Brighton 3, Hassocks 1

GROUP 2
Newbury 3, Torquay 1
Tongwynlais 2, Cardiff 3
Swansea 0, Swindon 3
Plymouth 5, Eastleigh 0
Bristol City 0, Bristol Backwell 5
Truro City 6, Bournemouth 0

GROUP 3
Watford 3, Tottenham 1
Colliers Row 1, Hackney 3
Winchester 1, Bromley Borough 12
Palace Eagles 0, Binfield 9
Abbey Rangers 1, Leyton Orient 11
District Line 26, London Girls 0

GROUP 4
Crewe 3, Pilkingtons 8
Kidderminster 2, Oxford United 5
Leek Town 3, Thame 0
Villa Aztecs 2, Wolverhampton 4
Tranmere Rovers 8, Birmingham 2
Abbeydale/Alvechurch 3, Stockport County 0

GROUP 5
Wigan 7, Oldham Athletic 2
Manchester United 3, Ashton 4
Bolton 0, Broadoak 6
Leasowe Pacific 6, Rochdale 0
St Helens w/o, Lever Club
Bury 2, Preston Rangers 1

GROUP 6
Wiggington 0, Doncaster Town 10
Sunderland 2, Huddersfield 4
Cowgate Kestrels 2, Hull 0
Cleveland 3, Sheffield Wednesday 9
Scarborough, Wakefield w/o
Middlesbrough 13, Brighouse 1

902

GROUP 7
Leicester City 3, 4, Sharley Park 3, 3
TNT 3, Nettleham 2
Highfield 2, Rainworth 6
Nottingham Argyle 3, Haigh 0

GROUP 8
Town & Country 11, Norwich 3
Luton 4, Harlow 0
Southend 1, Milton Keynes 2
Colchester 0, Dunstable 10

Third Round

GROUP 1
Epsom & Ewell 3, Teynham 0
Havant 0, Brighton 5
Horsham 7, Corematch 0

GROUP 2
Newbury 3, Bristol Backwell 4
Swindon 2, 3, Cardiff 2, 2
Truro City 4, Plymouth 2

GROUP 3
Tottenham 2, Bromley Borough 7
Leyton Orient 3, Binfield 2
District Line 10, Collier Row 0

GROUP 4
Pilkingtons 1, Oxford Utd 2
Abbeydale/Alvechurch 6, Tranmere Rovers 0
Leek Town 1, Wolverhampton 2

GROUP 5
Bury 1, St Helens 4
Ashton Utd 4, Wigan 5
Broadoak 0, Leasowe 8

GROUP 6
Huddersfield 0, 0, Sheffield Wednesday 0, 3
Wakefield 4, Cowgate Kestrels 6
Doncaster Town 1, Middlesbrough 2

GROUP 7
Rainworth 1, Notts Argyle 0
TNT 2, Leicester City 0

GROUP 8
Dunstable 1, Town & Country 4
Luton Town 7, Milton Keynes 0

CLUBS IN THE PREMIER DIVISION EXEMPT TO 4TH ROUND

Fourth Round
Brighton 1, Arsenal 5
Town & County 2, District Line 6
Horsham 2, Epsom & Ewell 3
Wolves 0, Red Star Southampton 4
Leasowe Pacific 4, Bristol Backwell 1
Cowgate Kestrels 2, Wimbledon 3
Rainworth 2, Oxford 0
Bromley Borough 3, Leyton Orient 0
Swindon 0 Maidstone Tigresses 4
Middlesbrough 5, Truro City 0
Wigan 3, Bronte 8
St Helens w/o, TNT
Luton Town 0, Ipswich Town 9
Stanton Rangers 3, Sheffield Wednesday 2
Abbeydale 2, Millwall Lionesses 3
Doncaster Belles w/o, Knowsley 0

Fifth Round
Arsenal 4, District Line 1
Epsom & Ewell 0, Red Star Southampton 1

Leasowe Pacific 2, Wimbledon 5
Rainworth 1, Bromley Borough 4
Maidstone Tigresses 2, Middlesbrough 0
Bronte 2, St Helens 0
Ipswich Town 3, Stanton Rangers 2
Millwall Lionesses 0, Doncaster Belles 4

Sixth Round
Arsenal 4, Red Star Southampton 1
Wimbledon 1, Bromley Borough 2
Maidstone Tigresses 1, Bronte 2
Ipswich Town 2, Doncaster Belles 5

Semi-finals
Arsenal 2, Bromley Borough 0
Bronte 1, Doncaster Belles 2

Final
Arsenal 3, Doncaster Belles 0

6th EUROPEAN CHAMPIONSHIP FOR WOMEN

Group 1
Switzerland 0, Norway 10
Belgium 0, Switzerland 0
Switzerland 0, Belgium 1
Belgium 0, Norway 0
Norway 6, Switzerland 0
Norway 8, Belgium 0

Group 2
Finland 1, Denmark 1
Denmark 4, France 1
France 0, Denmark 4
Finland 1, France 1
Denmark 5, Finland 0
France 5, Finland 1

Group 3
England 1, Scotland 0
England 4, Iceland 0
Scotland 0, Iceland 0
Iceland 2, Scotland 1
Iceland 1, England 2
Scotland 0, England 2

Group 4
Spain 0, Sweden 4
Spain 0, Republic of Ireland 1

Republic of Ireland 0, Spain 1
Sweden 1, Spain 1
Republic of Ireland 0, Sweden 1
Sweden 10, Republic of Ireland 0

Group 5
Greece 0, Romania 0
Greece 0, Holland 3
Holland 2, Greece 0
Romania 1, Greece 0
Holland 1, Romania 1
Romania 0, Holland 0

Group 6
Yugoslavia 0, Germany 3
Germany v Yugoslavia not played

Group 7
Poland 1, Czechoslovakia 2
Italy 3, Poland 1
Czechoslovakia 0, Italy 3
Czechoslovakia 3, Poland 0
Italy 2, Czechoslovakia 2
Poland 1, Italy 4

Group 8
CIS 2, Hungary 1

Bulgaria 0, Hungary 1
Hungary 0, CIS 0
Hungary 3, Bulgaria 0
CIS 3, Bulgaria 0
Bulgaria 1, CIS 2

Quarter-finals
Norway 3, Holland 0
CIS 0, Germany 7
Sweden 1, Denmark 2
Italy 3, England 2
Denmark 1, Sweden 1
England 0, Italy 3
Holland 0, Norway 3
Germany 0, CIS 0

Semi-finals
Norway 1, Denmark 0
Italy 1, Germany 1
Italy won 4-3 on penalties

Match for third place
Denmark 3, Germany 1

Final
Norway 1, Italy 0

1993 WORLD YOUTH CHAMPIONSHIP

EUROPE (*top six qualifiers from 8th UEFA Under-18 Championship*)
SOUTH AMERICA (*three qualifiers)*

GROUP A
Colombia (0) 3, Peru (0) 1
Uruguay (0) 1, Chile (0) 0
Colombia (0) 1, Chile (0) 0
Uruguay (2) 3, Peru (1) 1
Chile (0) 2, Peru (0) 0
Colombia (0) 0, Uruguay (0) 0

GROUP B
Paraguay (0) 1, Ecuador (0) 1
Brazil (0) 1, Bolivia (0) 0
Brazil (1) 2, Ecuador (0) 0
Paraguay (1) 2, Bolivia (0) 0
Brazil (0) 1, Paraguay (0) 0
Ecuador (3) 4, Bolivia (0) 1

FINAL ROUND
Brazil (0) 0, Uruguay (0) 0
Colombia (0) 0, Ecuador (0) 0
Brazil (0) 2, Ecuador (0) 0
Colombia (0) 0, Uruguay (0) 0
Colombia (0) 0, Brazil (1) 1
Uruguay (2) 3, Ecuador (0) 1

CONCACAF (*two qualifiers)*

GROUP A
Canada 4, Guadeloupe 2
Cuba 3, Guadeloupe 0
Canada 5, Cuba 1

GROUP B
Mexico 5, Netherlands Antilles 0
Jamaica 1, Honduras 2
Honduras 4, Netherlands Antilles 0
Mexico 2, Jamaica 1

Jamaica 1, Netherlands Antilles 0
Mexico 0, Honduras 0

GROUP C
USA 5, Bermuda 0
Trinidad/Tobago 0, Costa Rica 0
Costa Rica 4, Bermuda 0
USA 2, Trinidad/Tobago 0
Trinidad/Tobago 0, Bermuda 0
USA 2, Costa Rico 0

FINAL ROUND
Canada 1, Honduras 0
Mexico 3, USA 0
Honduras 0, USA 4
Canada 1, Mexico 1
Mexico 0, Honduras 0
Canada 1, USA 2

7TH OCEANIA YOUTH TOURNAMENT

Vanuatu (1) 2, Papua New Guinea (1) 1
Fiji (0) 1, New Zealand (2) 2
Papua New Guinea (0) 1, Fiji (3) 5
New Zealand (1) 1, Tahiti (0) 0
Fiji (0) 1, Tahiti (0) 3
Vanuatu (0), New Zealand (2) 3

Tahiti (0) 1, Vanuatu (0) 1
New Zealand (0) 2, Papua New Guinea (0) 0
Papua New Guinea (1) 1, Tahiti (1) 2
Vanuatu (0) 1, Fiji (3) 4
New Zealand qualified for play-off in Asia

28TH ASIAN YOUTH UNDER-19 CHAMPIONSHIP (*two qualifiers)*

GROUP A
UAE (0) 0, Iran (0) 0
India (0) 0, Japan (1) 2
Japan (1) 2, Iran (0) 0
India (0) 0, UAE (0) 3
UAE (2) 2, Japan (0) 0
Iran (0) 2, India (0) 0

GROUP B
Qatar (1) 2, Saudi Arabia (0) 0
Korea Rep (4) 8, Thailand (0) 1
New Zealand (0) 1, Korea Rep (4) 5

Thailand (0) 0, Saudi Arabia (1) 2
New Zealand (0) 0, Thailand (2) 2
Korea Rep (1) 3, Qatar (0) 1
Saudi Arabia (1) 3, New Zealand (0) 1
Thailand (2) 2, Qatar (2) 3
Saudi Arabia (3) 4, Korea Rep (0) 0
Qatar (2) 3, New Zealand (0) 0

SEMI-FINALS
UAE (0) 0, Saudi Arabia (0) 2 *aet*
Korea Rep (1) 2, Japan (0) 1

MATCH FOR 3RD PLACE
UAE (0) 0, Japan (0) 3

FINAL
Saudi Arabia (0) 2, Korea Rep (0) 0

AFRICA (*two qualifiers)*

GROUP A
Ghana 1, Mauritius 0
Cameroon 1, Nigeria 0
Mauritius 0, Nigeria 1
Cameroon 2, Ghana 0
Mauritius 2, Cameroon 1
Ghana 1, Nigeria 0

GROUP B
Egypt 0, Senegal 0
Morocco 1, Ethiopia 2
Egypt 4, Morocco 1
Ethiopia 3, Senegal 1
Egypt 1, Ethiopia 0
Senegal 1, Morocco 2

SEMI-FINALS
Cameroon 5, Ethiopia 0
Egypt 1, Ghana 3 *aet*

MATCH FOR 3RD AND PLACE
Ethiopia 0, Egypt 3

FINAL Cameroon 0, Ghana 2

FINAL TOURNAMENT IN AUSTRALIA

GROUP A
Australia (1) 2, Colombia (1) 1
Russia (2) 2, Cameroon (0) 0
Colombia (2) 3, Cameroon (2) 2
Australia (1) 3, Russia (1) 1
Colombia (0) 1, Russia (2) 3
Australia (0) 0, Cameroon (1) 2

GROUP B
Portugal (0) 0, Germany (0) 1
Uruguay (1) 1, Ghana (0) 1
Germany (1) 2, Ghana (1) 2
Portugal (1) 1, Uruguay (1) 2
Germany (0) 1, Uruguay (1) 2
Portugal (0) 0, Ghana (1) 2

GROUP C
Korea Rep (1) 1, England (0) 1
Turkey (0) 0, USA (3) 6
England (0) 1, USA (0) 0
Korea Rep (0) 1, Turkey (0) 1
England (1) 1, Turkey (0) 0
Korea Rep (1) 2, USA (1) 2

GROUP D
Mexico (1) 3, Norway (0) 0
Brazil (0) 0, Saudi Arabia (0) 0
Norway (0) 0, Saudi Arabia (0) 0
Mexico (0) 1, Brazil (1) 2
Norway (0) 0, Brazil (0) 2
Mexico (0) 2, Saudi Arabia (1) 1

QUARTER FINALS
Russia (0) 0, Ghana (0) 3
Uruguay (1) 1, Australia (0) 1
Australia won in extra time, sudden death 2-1
England (0) 0, Mexico (0) 0
England won 4-3 on penalties aet
Brazil (1) 3, USA (0) 0

SEMI-FINALS
Australia (0) 1, Brazil (2) 2
Ghana (1) 2, England (0) 0

MATCH FOR 3RD PLACE
England (1) 2, Australia (0) 1

FINAL
Ghana (1) 1, Brazil (0) 2

The things they said . . .

England manager Graham Taylor, after the 0-0 draw with Denmark in the European Championships:
"*We haven't won the game, but we haven't lost it.*" 11 June 1992

Ruud Gullit's appraisal of Scotland at the European Championships:
"*A good team with strong English character.*"

Lazio boss Dino Zoff on seeing topless pictures of an overweight Gascoigne at a nightclub:
"*I only hope it's someone else's body with his face painted on.*" July 1992

Sheffield United boss Dave Bassett, on his August Christmas party:
"*It seems we're incapable of playing until after Christmas, so we're having it before the season starts.*"

Newcastle manager Kevin Keegan:
"*Support means getting behind the team through thick and thin. Newcastle supporters have, in the last few years, been through thin and thin.*"

Halifax's despairing boss John McGrath:
"*I'm going to have to listen to offers for all my players - and the club cat Benny, who's pissed off because all the mice have died of starvation.*"

FIFA secretary-general Sepp Blatter on why football is so popular:
"*People are always kicking, young and old. Even an unborn baby is kicking.*"

Sheffield United boss Dave Bassett, after keeper Tracey is sent off at Spurs:
"*He's got the brains of a rocking-horse.*" September 1992

England boss Graham Taylor, after 'Swedes 2 Turnips 1' and 'Spanish 1 Onions 0' headlines:
"*I'm beginning to wonder what bloody vegetable grows in Norway.*"

Premier League chief executive Rick Parry:
"*The whole concept of one club, one vote is proving unworkable.*" September.

LWT's guest celebrity John Fashanu of Wimbledon commenting on the West Ham v Derby game:
"*Playing in the Premier League, we don't see a lot of the Barclays League.*"

Dave Bassett on his Sheffield United team:
"*This team is nothing like the one I had at Wimbledon - that team would have been all right against Mike Tyson.*"

Millwall community development officer Gary Stempel on the taunting of Arsenal's Ian Wright by Millwall fans:
"*It was the most venomous racial abuse I've heard for five or six years, and that was very disappointing.*"

PFA supremo Gordon Taylor on fixture congestion:
"*We're suddenly having broken legs treated as part of the game. It's becoming a 'Rollerball' game.*"

Chesterfield's Dave Lancaster, who scored two in their 4-4 draw at Anfield in the Coca-Cola Cup:
"*I thought there might be eight goals, but I never thought we would get four of them.*"

Wimbledon owner Sam Hammam on the Vinny Jones 'video nasty':
"*He [Jones] must be a mosquito brain to say that.*"

Lawrie McMenemy, England's assistant manager, after Paul Gascoigne's four-letter response to a Norwegian TV journalist:
"*Paul tends to react abruptly and often uses the wrong word. It is because he doesn't have a big vocabulary.*" October 1992

Prudential Insurance PR woman, refusing Stenhousemuir fans' request for them to sponsor a match to compensate for the TV ad that featured the score 'Stenhousemuir 1 Arbroath 7':
"*Our company only sponsor the arts. I don't think Stenhousemuir could be regarded by any stretch of the imagination as artistic.*"

George Best, when asked if, in his heyday, he was better than Paul Gascoigne:
"*It's very difficult to say, but yes.*"

Rangers striker Ally McCoist on Leeds' early goal against them at Ibrox in the European Cup:
"*The noise level when we came onto the pitch, was as loud as I've ever heard. But within a minute it was as quiet as I've ever known.*"

BBC commentator Alan Hansen on the Spartak-Liverpool game:
"*You cannot allow them [European clubs] to play an open game. If you play an open game in Europe, the Continentals will do you every time.*"

Arsenal manager George Graham, discussing the amount of football played:
"*I'm unbelievably disappointed in what's happened. They [the FA] have missed a great opportunity to promote good football - better quality, less quantity. I'll even go so far as to say we should have only one Cup competition, the FA Cup.*"

Barnet chairman Stan Flashman, on BBC Radio 5:
"*The supporters don't matter as far as I'm concerned. They just pay their entrance fee. I don't care whether they come to Barnet or not. We play good football whether they are there or not.*" November 1992

Wimbledon owner Sam Hammam:
"*When Paul Gascoigne drops his shorts, everyone calls him a prankster and no action is taken. When Vinny Jones does it, not only is he fined, but the club is as well.*"

Everton keeper Neville Southall, on his all-black strip:
"*I'm a traditionalist at heart. I don't like the ridiculous colours around today.*"

Swedish international defender Patrik Andersson, after turning down a move to Leeds:
"*If they pay peanuts, they can expect monkeys.*"

England manager Graham Taylor on saturation coverage of football on TV:
"*If I go to a match in Europe in midweek, I come back to a stack of videos and I can hardly be bothered. What's going on in Coronation Street is what I want to know ... We could get to the situation where we have only two dozen clubs playing in front of empty houses.*"

Referee Roger Milford on the penalty he gave to Wimbledon that had Sheffield Wednesday boss Trevor Francis fuming:
"*I saw Chris Woods dive across and make a save and then saw another yellow hand touch the ball. I couldn't see who it was, but my linesman confirmed it was a yellow hand.*" 28 November

FA chief executive Graham Kelly, at the trial of Gary Blissett, on the incident in which John Uzzell sustained his fractured cheek bone:
"*... an ordinary aerial challenge*" of the kind you "*could attend four matches a week and see up to 200 similar challenges.*"

1992 OLYMPICS in Spain

Qualifying tournament (European zone as Under-21 European Championship–see 1992-93 edition)

CONCACAF

First Round
Group: Caribbean Zone
Puerto Rico 0, Jamaica 3
Jamaica 2, Puerto Rico 0
Haiti 1, Cuba 1
Cuba 2, Haiti 2
Aruba 3, St Lucia 3
St Lucia 9, Aruba 0
Antigua 0, Barbados 0
Barbados 5, Antigua 0
Netherlands Antilles 0, Surinam 1
Surinam 0, Netherlands Antilles 0

Second Round
Group: Central Zone
Guatemala 2, Honduras 2
Honduras 2, Guatemala 0
Belize 0, El Salvador 2
El Salvador 3, Belize 0
Panama v Costa Rica
Costa Rica suspended for all FIFA competitions with an age limit
Group: Caribbean Zone
Barbados 0, Surinam 0
Surinam 2, Barbados 1
Trinidad & Tobago 1, Jamaica 0
Jamaica 1, Trinidad & Tobago 0
Deciding match: Trinidad & Tobago 2, Jamaica 1
St Lucia 1, Haiti 1
Haiti 2, St Lucia 1

Third Round
Group A
Surinam 1, Mexico 1
Honduras 1, Mexico 1
Mexico 0, Honduras 1
Mexico 6, Surinam 0
Honduras 2, Surinam 0
Surinam 0, Honduras 2

Group B
Canada 3, Trinidad & Tobago 0
El Salvador 3, Canada 1
Trinidad & Tobago 1, Canada 3
El Salvador 2, Trinidad & Tobago 0 by forfeit
Trinidad & Tobago failed to fulfil fixture
Trinidad & Tobago 2, El Salvador 0
Canada 4, El Salvador 0

Group C
USA 8, Haiti 0
Panama 1, USA 1
USA 7, Panama 1
Haiti 0, USA 2
Panama 2, Haiti 2
Haiti v Panama
Panama withdrew

Fourth Round
Mexico 1, USA 2
Canada 1, Mexico 1
USA 4, Honduras 3
Canada 2, Honduras 2
Honduras 3, USA 4
Mexico 4, Canada 1
Honduras 1, Canada 0
USA 3, Mexico 0
Honduras 1, Mexico 3

USA 3, Canada 1
Canada 2, USA 1
Mexico 5, Honduras 1

AFRICA

First Round
Mauritius 1, Somalia 0
Somalia 2, Mauritius 1
Mozambique 0, Swaziland 0
Swaziland 0, Mozambique 1
Ethiopia v Libya
Libya withdrew
Botswana 0, Gabon 0
Gabon 2, Botswana 1
Burkina Faso, Congo, Gambia, Mali withdrew

Second Round
Group 1
Mauritius v Zambia
Zambia suspended
Mozambique 0, Uganda 1
Uganda 3, Mozambique 1
Ethiopia v Malawi
Ethiopia withdrew
Gabon v Cameroon
Gabon suspended
Sudan 1, Egypt 2
Egypt 2, Sudan 0
Angola v Ivory Coast
Angola withdrew

Group 2
Tunisia 3, Senegal 1
Senegal 1, Tunisia 0
Algeria 0, Sierra Leone 0
Sierra Leone 1, Algeria 0
Morocco 6, Mauritania 0
Mauritania 0, Morocco 0
Liberia, Zaire withdrew; Guinea suspended

Third Round
Group 1
Egypt 3, Malawi 1
Malawi 0, Egypt 0
Uganda 1, Cameroon 2
Cameroon 2, Uganda 0
Ivory Coast withdrew

Group 2
Tunisia 3, Zimbabwe 1
Zimbabwe 5, Tunisia 2 aet
Ghana 2, Sierra Leone 1
Sierra Leone 2, Ghana 2 aet
Togo withdrew

Fourth Round
Egypt 3, Zimbabwe 0
Zimbabwe 1, Egypt 1
Cameroon 0, Morocco 0
Morocco 2, Cameroon 0
Ghana 6, Mauritius 0
Mauritius 1, Ghana 4

OCEANIA

Australia 4, Papua New Guinea 0
Australia 2, New Zealand 0
Australia 1, Fiji 0

New Zealand 4, Fiji 0
Papua New Guinea 0, Fiji 2
Papua New Guinea 0, Australia 5
New Zealand 1, Australia 2
Papua New Guinea 1, New Zealand 3
Fiji 0, Australia 3
New Zealand 4, Papua New Guinea 2
Fiji 0, New Zealand 0
Fiji 1, Papua New Guinea 1
Play-offs: Oceania/UEFA
Australia 1, Holland 1
Holland 2, Australia 2

ASIA

First Round; West/Central Asia
Group A
Qatar 2, Iran 0
Yemen 1, Pakistan 0
Iran 2, UAE 2
Yemen 1, Qatar 1
Pakistan 0, Qatar 4
UAE 2, Yemen 1
Pakistan 0, UAE 1
Yemen 1, Iran 1
Iran 5, Pakistan 0
Qatar 2, UAE 1
Iran 2, Qatar 0
Pakistan 0, Yemen 2
Qatar 3, Yemen 0
UAE 0, Iran 1
Qatar 2, Pakistan 0
Yemen 0, UAE 0
Iran 2, Yemen 1
UAE 2, Pakistan 0
Pakistan 0, Iran 6
UAE 0, Qatar 2

Group B
Oman 1, India 1
Lebanon 0, Syria 1
Oman 1, Lebanon 0
India 1, Lebanon 3
Kuwait 1, Oman 0
Lebanon 3, India 1
Syria 1, Kuwait 1
Syria 1, India 0
Lebanon 1, Kuwait 2
Oman 0, Syria 0
Syria 0, Oman 0
Kuwait 2, India 1

Group C
Bahrain 6, Sri Lanka 0
Saudi Arabia 1, Jordan 2
Bahrain 4, Jordan 0
Sir Lanka 1, Saudi Arabia 5
Bahrain 0, Saudi Arabia 2
Jordan 7, Sri Lanka 0

East Asia
Group D
Bangladesh 2, Thailand 3
Korea Rep 10, Philippines 0
Bangladesh 0, Korea Rep 6
Malaysia 5, Philippines 0
Bangladesh 0, Malaysia 1
Thailand 1, Korea Rep 2
Philippines 0, Bangladesh 8
Thailand 4, Malaysia 1
Korea Rep 0, Malaysia 0
Philippines 1, Thailand 7
Malaysia 1, Thailand 0
Philippines 0, Korea Rep 7
Malaysia 0, Korea Rep 2

Thailand 4, Bangladesh 0
Korea Rep 1, Bangladesh 0
Philippines 0, Malaysia 5
Bangladesh 3, Philippines 0
Korea Rep 2, Thailand 0
Malaysia 0, Bangladesh 1
Thailand 6, Philippines 0

Group E
Korea DPR 5, Nepal 0
Maldives 0, China 12
Nepal 0, Maldives 1
Singapore 0, Korea DPR 2
China 3, Singapore 0
Korea DPR 4, Maldives 0
Nepal 0, China 4
Maldives 1, Singapore 1
China 1, Korea DPR 1
Nepal 4, Singapore 1
China 17, Maldives 0
Nepal 0, Korea DPR 5
Korea DPR 3, Singapore 1
Maldives 1, Nepal 2
Singapore 0, China 3
Maldives 0, Korea DPR 7
China 10, Nepal 0
Singapore 4, Maldives 2
Korea DPR 0, China 1
Singapore 4, Nepal 1

Group F
Hong Kong 1, Taipei 1
Indonesia 1, Japan 2
Hong Kong 3, Japan 1
Indonesia 2, Taipei 1
Taipei 0, Japan 3
Indonesia 0, Hong Kong 0
Japan 2, Taipei 0
Hong Kong 1, Indonesia 1
Taipei 3, Indonesia 1
Japan 3, Hong Kong 0
Japan 3, Indonesia 1
Taipei 0, Hong Kong 1

Second Round
Bahrain 0, Qatar 1
Korea Rep 1, Kuwait 1
Japan 1, China 2
Bahrain 0, Korea Rep 1
China 0, Qatar 1
Kuwait 1, Japan 1
Qatar 1, Korea Rep 0
Japan 6, Bahrain 1
Kuwait 0, China 1
Bahrain 0, China 3
Korea Rep 1, Japan 0
Qatar 0, Kuwait 3
China 1, Korea Rep 3
Japan 0, Qatar 1
Kuwait 3, Bahrain 0

SOUTH AMERICA
Group A
Paraguay 1, Venezuela 0
Brazil 2, Peru 1
Brazil 1, Paraguay 0
Peru 1, Colombia 4
Brazil 0, Colombia 2
Peru 3, Venezuela 0
Colombia 4, Venezuela 0
Paraguay 7, Peru 1
Brazil 1, Venezuela 1
Paraguay 0, Colombia 0

Group B
Argentina 1, Bolivia 0
Uruguay 0, Ecuador 2
Argentina 1, Ecuador 0
Uruguay 1, Chile 0
Argentina 1, Chile 1
Ecuador 4, Bolivia 1
Chile 1, Ecuador 5
Uruguay 4, Bolivia 0
Argentina 1, Uruguay 2
Chile v Bolivia not played

Final Round
Colombia 3, Uruguay 0
Ecuador 0, Paraguay 1
Colombia 0, Paraguay 1
Ecuador 0, Uruguay 1
Colombia 1, Ecuador 1
Paraguay 0, Uruguay 0

Final Tournament in Spain
Group A
Italy 2, USA 1
Poland 2, Kuwait 0
USA 3, Kuwait 1
Italy 0, Poland 3
USA 2, Poland 2
Italy 1, Kuwait 0

Group B
Spain 4, Colombia 0
Egypt 0, Qatar 1
Colombia 1, Qatar 1
Spain 2, Egypt 0

Colombia 3, Egypt 4
Spain 2, Qatar 0

Group C
Sweden 0, Paraguay 0
Morocco 1, Korea Rep 1
Sweden 4, Morocco 0
Paraguay 0, Korea Rep 0
Sweden 1, Korea Rep 1
Paraguay 3, Morocco 1

Group D
Denmark 1, Mexico 1
Ghana 3, Australia 1
Denmark 0, Ghana 0
Mexico 1, Australia 1
Denmark 0, Australia 3
Mexico 1, Ghana 1

Quarter-finals
Spain 1, Italy 0
Poland 2, Qatar 0
Ghana 4, Paraguay 2 aet
Sweden 1, Australia 2

Semi-finals
Spain 2, Ghana 0
Poland 6, Australia 1

Third Place Match
Australia 0, Ghana 1

Final (in Barcelona)
Poland 2, Spain 3

OLYMPIC FOOTBALL

Previous medallists

1896 Athens*	1 Denmark	1932 Los Angeles		1968 Mexico City	1 Hungary
	2 Greece	no tournament			2 Bulgaria
1990 Paris*	1 Great Britain	1936 Berlin	1 Italy		3 Japan
	2 France		2 Austria	1972 Munich	1 Poland
1904 St Louis**	1 Canada		3 Norway		2 Hungary
	2 USA	1948 London	1 Sweden		3 E Germany/USSR
1908 London	1 Great Britain		2 Yugoslavia	1976 Montreal	1 East Germany
	2 Denmark		3 Denmark		2 Poland
	3 Holland	1952 Helsinki	1 Hungary		3 USSR
1912 Stockholm	1 England		2 Yugoslavia	1980 Moscow	1 Czechoslovakia
	2 Denmark		3 Sweden		2 East Germany
	3 Holland	1956 Melbourne	1 USSR		3 USSR
1920 Antwerp	1 Belgium		2 Yugoslavia	1984 Los Angeles	1 France
	2 Spain		3 Bulgaria		2 Brazil
	3 Holland	1960 Rome	1 Yugoslavia		3 Yugoslavia
1924 Paris	1 Uruguay		2 Denmark	1988 Seoul	1 USSR
	2 Switzerland		3 Hungary		2 Brazil
	3 Sweden	1964 Tokyo	1 Hungary		3 West Germany
1928 Amsterdam	1 Uruguay		2 Czechoslovakia	1992 Barcelona	1 Spain
	2 Argentina		3 East Germany		2 Poland
	3 Italy				3 Ghana

* No official tournament
** No official tournament but gold medal later awarded by IOC

EUROPEAN CUP

EUROPEAN CUP FINALS 1956–92

Year	Winners		Runners-up		Venue	Attendance	Referee
1956	Real Madrid	4	Reims	3	Paris	38,000	Ellis (E)
1957	Real Madrid	2	Fiorentina	0	Madrid	124,000	Horn (Ho)
1958	Real Madrid	3	AC Milan	2 *(aet)*	Brussels	67,000	Alsteen (Bel)
1959	Real Madrid	2	Reims	0	Stuttgart	80,000	Dutsch (WG)
1960	Real Madrid	7	Eintracht Frankfurt	3	Glasgow	135,000	Mowat (S)
1961	Benfica	3	Barcelona	2	Berne	28,000	Dienst (Sw)
1962	Benfica	5	Real Madrid	3	Amsterdam	65,000	Horn (Ho)
1963	AC Milan	2	Benfica	1	Wembley	45,000	Holland (E)
1964	Internazionale	3	Real Madrid	1	Vienna	74,000	Stoll (A)
1965	Internazionale	1	Benfica	0	Milan	80,000	Dienst (Sw)
1966	Real Madrid	2	Partizan Belgrade	1	Brussels	55,000	Kreitlein (WG)
1967	Celtic	2	Internazionale	1	Lisbon	56,000	Tschenscher (WG)
1968	Manchester U	4	Benfica	1 *(aet)*	Wembley	100,000	Lo Bello (I)
1969	AC Milan	4	Ajax	1	Madrid	50,000	Ortiz (Sp)
1970	Feyenoord	2	Celtic	1 *(aet)*	Milan	50,000	Lo Bello (I)
1971	Ajax	2	Panathinaikos	0	Wembley	90,000	Taylor (E)
1972	Ajax	2	Internazionale	0	Rotterdam	67,000	Helies (F)
1973	Ajax	1	Juventus	0	Belgrade	93,500	Guglovic (Y)
1974	Bayern Munich	1	Atletico Madrid	1	Brussels	65,000	Loraux (Bel)
Replay	Bayern Munich	4	Atletico Madrid	0	Brussels	65,000	Delcourt (Bel)
1975	Bayern Munich	2	Leeds U	0	Paris	50,000	Kitabdjian (F)
1976	Bayern Munich	1	St Etienne	0	Glasgow	54,864	Palotai (H)
1977	Liverpool	3	Moenchengladbach	1	Rome	57,000	Wurtz (F)
1978	Liverpool	1	FC Brugge	0	Wembley	92,000	Corver (Ho)
1979	Nottingham F	1	Malmo	0	Munich	57,500	Linemayr (A)
1980	Nottingham F	1	Hamburg	0	Madrid	50,000	Garrido (P)
1981	Liverpool	1	Real Madrid	0	Paris	48,360	Palotai (H)
1982	Aston Villa	1	Bayern Munich	0	Rotterdam	46,000	Konrath (F)
1983	Hamburg	1	Juventus	0	Athens	75,000	Rainea (R)
1984	Liverpool	1	Roma	1	Rome	69,693	Fredriksson (Se)
	(aet; Liverpool won 4–2 on penalties)						
1985	Juventus	1	Liverpool	0	Brussels	58,000	Daina (Sw)
1986	Steaua Bucharest	0	Barcelona	0	Seville	70,000	Vautrot (F)
	(aet; Steaua won 2–0 on penalties)						
1987	Porto	2	Bayern Munich	1	Vienna	59,000	Ponnet (Bel)
1988	PSV Eindhoven	0	Benfica	0	Stuttgart	70,000	Agnolin (I)
	(aet; PSV won 6–5 on penalties)						
1989	AC Milan	4	Steaua Bucharest	0	Barcelona	97,000	Tritschler (WG)
1990	AC Milan	1	Benfica	0	Vienna	57,500	Kohl (A)
1991	Red Star Belgrade	0	Marseille	0	Bari	56,000	Lanese (I)
	(aet; Red Star won 5–3 on penalties						
1992	Barcelona	1	Sampdoria	0 *(aet)*	Wembley	70,827	Schmidhuber (G)

Basile Boli (white shirt, second left) heads the only goal of the 1993 European Cup Final as Marseille beat AC Milan. (Colorsport)

EUROPEAN CUP 1992-93

Preliminary Round, First Leg

KI Klaksvikar (1) 1 *(Danielsen 4)*, Skonto Riga (1) 3 *(Astafiev 28, 46, Semenov 89)* 1500

Olimpija Ljubljana (0) 3 *(Ubavic 50, Topic 52, Vrabac 72)*, Norma Tallinn (0) 0 3000

Shelbourne (0) 0, Tavria Simferopol (0) 0 4000

Valletta (0) 1 *(Zerafa 75)*, Maccabi Tel Aviv (0) 2 *(Cohen 83, Nimni 88)* 3000

Preliminary Round, Second Leg

Maccabi Tel Aviv (1) 1 *(Melika 23)*, Valletta (0) 0 5000

Norma Tallinn (0) 0, Olimpija Ljubljana (1) 2 *(Zulic 27, Djuranovic 89)* 1000

Skonto Riga (2) 3 *(Yeliseyev 4, Semenov 38, Astafiev 52)*, KI Klaksvikar (0) 0 3000

Tavria Simferopol (2) 2 *(Shevchenko 8, Skeikhametov 13)*, Shelbourne (1) 1 *(Dally 41)* 16,000

First Round, First Leg

AEK Athens (1) 1 *(Alexandris 41)*, Apoel (0) 1 *(Hadjilukas 72)* 28,000

FK Austria (1) 3 *(Hasenhuttl 16, Fridrikas 82, Kogler 90)*, CSKA Sofia (0) 1 *(Shiskov 57)* 7000

Barcelona (0) 1 *(Amor 86)*, Viking Stavanger (0) 0 36,000

Glentoran (0) 0, Marseille (4) 5 *(Voller 4, Martin Vazquez 22, 29, Sauzee 42, Ferreri 85)* 8000

IFK Gothenburg (0) 2 *(Eskeleinen 72, Ekstrom 82)*, Besiktas (0) 0 5293

Kuusysi (1) 1 *(Rinne 17)*, Dinamo Bucharest (0) 0 1330

Lech Poznan (2) 2 *(Trzeciak 26, Podbrozny 41)*, Skonto Riga (0) 0 10,000

Maccabi Tel Aviv (0) 0, FC Brugge (1) 1 *(Staelens 35)* 17,000

AC Milan (2) 4 *(Van Basten 5, 49, Albertini 7, Papin 64)*, Olimpija Ljubljana (0) 0 14,300

PSV Eindhoven (2) 6 *(Koeman 24, Ellerman 36, 59, 64, Kieft 68, Numan 78)*, Zalgiris Vilnius (0) 0 13,000

Rangers (1) 2 *(Hateley 40, Huistra 67)*, Lyngby (0) 0 40,036

Sion (2) 4 *(Hottiger 17, Tulio 31, 73, Assis 76)*, Tavria Simferopol (1) 1 *(Shevchenko 84 (pen))* 8500

Slovan Bratislava (1) 4 *(Gostic 19, Dubovsky 51, 53, Morvec 83)*, Ferencvaros (0) 1 *(Lipcsei 75)* 25,000

Stuttgart (0) 3 *(Walter 62, 68, Buck 82)*, Leeds U (0) 0 38,000

Union Luxembourg (0) 1 *(Deville 63)*, FC Porto (1) 4 *(Semedo 41, Fernando Couto 47, Toni 51, Domingos 89)* 4000

Vikingur (0) 0, CSKA Moscow (0) 1 *(Korsakov 75)* 1000

First Round, Second Leg

Apoel (0) 2 *(Gogic 77, Sasulitis 84)*, AEK Athens (1) 2 *(Sabanadzovic 30, Alexandris 70)* 16,000

Besiktas (1) 2 *(Metin 25, Feyyaz 73)*, IFK Gothenburg (1) 1 *(Eskeleinen 11)* 31,400

FC Brugge (0) 3 *(Staelens 60, Verheyen 77, 85)*, Maccabi Tel Aviv (0) 0 7000 *(in Liege)*

CSKA Moscow (3) 4 *(Sergeyev 24, Korsakov 37, Grishin 44, Kolesnikov 89)*, Vikingur (0) 0 10,000

CSKA Sofia (1) 3 *(Metkov 4, Andonov 60, 72 (pen))*, FK Austria (1) 2 *(Flogel 26, Ivanauskas 68)* 8000

Dinamo Bucharest (0) 2 *(Gerstenmajer 63, Demollari 116)*, Kuusysi (0) 0 *aet* 14,000

Ferencvaros (0) 0, Slovan Bratislava (0) 0 25,500

Leeds U (2) 4 *(Speed 18, McAllister 38, Cantona 66, Chapman 80)*, Stuttgart (1) 1 *(Buck 33)* 20,457

Leeds U awarded match 3-0 on forfeit as Stuttgart included fourth foreign player

Replay: Leeds U (1) 2 *(Strachan 34, Shutt 76)*, Stuttgart (1) 1 *(Golke 40)* 10,000 *(in Barcelona)*

Lyngby (0) 0, Rangers (0) 1 *(Durrant 84)* 4273

Marseille (2) 3 *(Omam-Biyik 6, Pele 13, Boli 72)*, Glentoran (0) 0 10,000

Olimpija Ljubljana (0) 0, AC Milan (1) 3 *(Massaro 31, Rijkaard 50, Tassotti 85)* 12,000

FC Porto (3) 5 *(Kostadinov 16, 32, Toni 26, 61, Jose Carlos 67)*, Union Luxembourg (0) 0 30,000

Skonto Riga (0) 0, Lech Poznan (0) 0 3500

Tavria Simferopol (0) 1 *(Shevchenko 69 (pen))*, Sion (0) 3 *(Tulio 67, Carlos Luis 77, Domingos 88)* 10,000

Viking Stavanger (0) 0, Barcelona (0) 0 12,041

Zalgiris Vilnius (0) 0, PSV Eindhoven (2) 2 *(Numan 26, Romario 39)* 4500

Second Round, First Leg

AEK Athens (0) 1 *(Dimitriadis 53)*, PSV Eindhoven (0) 0 27,000

FC Brugge (2) 2 *(Verheyen 35, Booy 41)*, FK Austria (0) 0 16,000

CSKA Moscow (1) 1 *(Grishin 18)*, Barcelona (0) 1 *(Beguiristain 60)* 32,500

Dinamo Bucharest (0) 0, Marseille (0) 0 28,000

IFK Gothenburg (0) 1 *(Bengtsson 85)*, Lech Poznan (0) 0 8800

Rangers (2) 2 *(Lukic 21 (og), McCoist 37)*, Leeds U (1) 1 *(McAllister 1)* 44,000

Sion (0) 2 *(Orlando 55, Assis 61)*, FC Porto (0) 2 *(Semedo 80, Fernando Couto 82)* 14,800

Slovan Bratislava (0) 0, AC Milan (0) 1 *(Maldini 61)* 35,000

Second Round, Second Leg

FK Austria (0) 3 *(Zsak 49, Fridrikas 73, Ivanauskas 90)*, FC Brugge (0) 1 *(Van der Heyden 65)* 15,500

Barcelona (0) 2 *(Nadal 12, Beguiristain 31)*, CSKA Moscow (1) 3 *(Buchmanov 44, Mashkarin 56, Korsakov 60)* 63,500

Lech Poznan (0) 0, IFK Gothenburg (1) 3 *(Ekstrom 27, Nilsson 47, Mild 83)* 28,000

Leeds U (0) 1 *(Cantona 85)*, Rangers (1) 2 *(Hateley 3, McCoist 59)* 25,118

Marseille (1) 2 *(Boksic 35, 69)*, Dinamo Bucharest (0) 0 30,000

AC Milan (2) 4 *(Boban 28, Rijkaard 29, Simone 49, Papin 71)*, Slovan Bratislava (0) 0 27,500

FC Porto (0) 4 *(Jorge Costa 50, Domingos 55, Kostadinov 63, Jaime Magalhaes 87)*, Sion (0) 0 35,000

PSV Eindhoven (1) 3 *(Romario 5, 50, 84)*, AEK Athens (0) 0 21,750

Champions League

Group A

FC Brugge (1) 1 *(Amokachi 17)*, CSKA Moscow (0) 0 21,500

Rangers (0) 2 *(McSwegan 76, Hateley 82)*, Marseille (1) 2 *(Boksic 31, Voller 55)* 41,624

CSKA Moscow (0) 0, Rangers (1) 1 *(Ferguson 13)* 9000 *(in Bochum)*

Marseille (3) 3 *(Sauzee 4 (pen), Boksic 10, 26)*, FC Brugge (0) 0 30,000

FC Brugge (1) 1 *(Dziubinski 44)*, Rangers (0) 1 *(Huistra 73)* 19,000

CSKA Moscow (0) 1 *(Faizulin 55)*, Marseille (1) 1 *(Pele 27)* 20,000 *(in Berlin)*

Marseille (3) 6 *(Sauzee 4 (pen,34,48, Pele 42, Ferreri 70, Desailly 78)*, CSKA Moscow (0) 0 40,000

Rangers (1) 2 *(Durrant 40, Nisbet 71)*, FC Brugge (0) 1 *(Staelens 51)* 42,731

CSKA Moscow (1) 1 *(Sergeyev 18)*, FC Brugge (1) 2 *(Schaessens 43, Verheyen 83)* 2500 *(in Berlin)*
Marseille (1) 1 *(Sauzee 18)*, Rangers (0) 1 *(Durrant 52)* 40,000
FC Brugge (0) 0, Marseille (1) 1 *(Boksic 2)* 19,000
Rangers (0) 0, CSKA Moscow (0) 0 43,142

Final table

	P	W	D	L	F	A	Pts
Marseille	6	3	3	0	14	4	9
Rangers	6	2	4	0	7	5	8
FC Brugge	6	2	1	3	5	8	5
CSKA Moscow	6	0	2	4	2	11	2

Group B

AC Milan (1) 4 *(Van Basten 33, 53 (pen), 61, 62)*, IFK Gothenburg (0) 0 61,000
FC Porto (1) 2 *(Magalhaes 35, Jose Carlos 75)*, PSV Eindhoven (1) 2 *(Romario 43, 60)* 50,000
IFK Gothenburg (0) 1 *(Eriksson 87)*, FC Porto (0) 0 22,303

PSV Eindhoven (0) 1 *(Romario 66)*, AC Milan (1) 2 *(Rijkaard 19, Simone 62)* 27,000
PSV Eindhoven (1) 1 *(Numan 7)*, IFK Gothenburg (3) 3 *(Nilsson 19, Ekstrom 34, 44)* 27,500
FC Porto (0) 0, AC Milan (0) 1 *(Papin 71)* 55,000
IFK Gothenburg (2) 3 *(Nilsson 2, Ekstrom 44, Martinsson 48)*, PSV Eindhoven (0) 0 35,250
AC Milan (1) 1 *(Eranio 31)*, FC Porto (0) 0 67,389
IFK Gothenburg (0) 0, AC Milan (0) 1 *(Massaro 70)* 40,300
PSV Eindhoven (0) 0, FC Porto (0) 1 *(Ze Carlos 77 (pen))* 25,750
AC Milan (2) 2 *(Simone 5, 18)*, PSV Eindhoven (0) 0 50,862
FC Porto (1) 2 *(Ze Carlos 42, Timofte 56)*, IFK Gothenburg (0) 0 9000

Final table

	P	W	D	L	F	A	Pts
AC Milan	6	6	0	0	11	1	12
IFK Gothenburg	6	3	0	3	7	8	6
FC Porto	6	2	1	3	5	5	5
PSV Eindhoven	6	0	1	5	4	13	1

Final: Marseille (1) 1, AC Milan (0) 0

(in Munich, 26 May 1993, 64,400)

Marseille: Barthez; Angloma (Durand 64), Boli, Desailly, Pele, Eydelie, Sauzee, Deschamps, Di Meco, Boksic, Voller (Thomas 78). *Scorer:* Boli 43.
AC Milan: Rossi; Tassotti, Costacurta, Baresi, Maldini, Donadoni (Papin 56), Albertini, Rijkaard, Lentini, Van Basten (Eranio), Massaro.
Referee: Rothlisberger (Switzerland)

EUROPEAN CUPS DRAW 1993-94

EUROPEAN CUP
Preliminary Round
HJK Helsinki v Norma Tallinn; Ekranas v Floriana; Tofta B68 v Croatia Zagreb; Skonto Riga v Olimpija Ljubljana; Cwmbran Town v Cork City; Dynamo Tbilisi v Linfield; Avenir Beggen v Rosenborg; Partizani Tirana v Akranes; Omonia v Aarau; Zimbru Kishinev v Beitar Jerusalem.

First Round
Galatasaray v Cwmbran Town or Cork City; Werder Bremen v Dynamo Minsk; Dynamo Kiev v Barcelona; Marseille v AEK Athens; Kispest Honved v Manchester United; Rangers v Levski; AIK Stockholm v Sparta Prague; Dynamo Tbilisi or Linfield v FC Copenhagen; HJK Helsinki or Norma Tallinn v Anderlecht; Partizani Tirana or Akranes v Feyenoord; Steaua Bucharest v Tofta B68 or Croatia Zagreb; Avenir Beggen or Rosenborg v FK Austria; Porto v Ekranas or Floriana; Skonto Riga or Olimpija Ljubljana v Spartak Moscow; Omonia or Aarau v AC Milan; Lech Poznan v Zimbru Kishinev or Beitar Jerusalem.

EUROPEAN CUP-WINNERS' CUP
Preliminary Round
Karpaty Lvov v Shelbourne; RAF Jelgava v Havnar HB; Sliema Wanderers v Degerfors; Bangor v Apoel; Maccabi Haifa v Dudelange; Valur v Anjalankoski; Balzers v Albpetrol; Nikol Tallinn v Lillestrom; Kosice v Vilnius; Lugano v Neman Grodno; Odense v Publikum.

First Round
CSKA Sofia v Balzers or Albpetrol; Real Madrid v Lugano or Neman Grodno; Torpedo Moscow v Dudelange or Maccabi Haifa; Besiktas v Kosice or Vilnius; Panathinaikos v Karpaty Lvov or Shelbourne; Odense or Publikum v Arsenal; Uni Craiova v RAF Jelgava or Havnar HB; Innsbruck Tirol v Ferencvaros; Standard Liege v Cardiff City; Bangor or Apoel v Paris St Germain; Hajduk Split v Ajax; Nikol Tallinn or Lillestrom v Torino; Benfica v Katowice; Bayer Leverkusen v Zbrovjovka Brno; Sliema Wanderers or Degerfors v Parma; Valur or Anjalankoski v Aberdeen.

UEFA CUP
First Round
Twente v Bayern Munich; Bohemians v Bordeaux; Young Boys v Celtic; Aalborg v La Coruna; Norwich City v Vitesse; Hearts v Atletico Madrid; Slavia Prague v Ofi Crete; Union Luxembourg v Boavista; Norrkoping v Mechelen; Nantes v Valencia; Karlsruhe v PSV Eindhoven; FC Reykjavik v MTK Budapest; Dynamo Moscow v Eintracht Frankfurt; Kuusysi v Waregem; Crusaders v Servette; Brondby v Dundee United; Slovan Bratislava v Aston Villa; Borussia Dortmund v Spartak Vladikavkaz; Lazio v Lokomotiv Plovdiv; Osters v Kongsvinger; Admira Wacker v Dnepr; Internazionale v Rapid Bucharest; Botev Plovdiv v Olympiakos; VAC Samsung v Apollon; Kocaelispor v Sporting Lisbon; Juventus v Lokomotiv Moscow; Salzburg v Dunajska Streda; Gloria Bistrita v Maribor Branik; Tenerife v Monaco; Antwerp v Maritimo; Trabzonspor v Valetta; Dinamo Bucharest v Cagliari.

EUROPEAN CUP 1992-93 - BRITISH AND IRISH CLUBS

Preliminary Round, First Leg

19 AUG

Shelbourne (0) 0
Tavria Simferopol (0) 0   4000
Shelbourne: Byrne; Coyle, Neville, O'Doherty, Brady, Haylock, Doolin, Howlett, Rutherford, Gorman, Duffy.
Tavria Simferopol: Kolesov; Volkov, Turchenenko, Golokov, Andreev, Shevchenko (Mikhailus), Gudimaenko, Oparin, Vishnyavskas (Alibayev), Polstyanov, Voronezhki.

Preliminary Round, Second Leg

2 SEPT

Tavria Simferopol (2) 2 *(Shevchenko, Skeikhametov)*
Shelbourne (1) 1 *(Dally)*   16,000
Tavria Simferopol: Kolesov; Turchenenko, Volkov, Golovko, Voronezhki, Gudimaenko, Shevchenko, Oparin, Vishnyavskas (Novikov), Polstyanov, Skeikhametov.
Shelbourne: Byrne; Coyle, Neville, O'Doherty, Brady, Haylock (Browne), Doolin, Howlett, Rutherford, Dally, Gorman.

First Round, First Leg

16 SEPT

Glentoran (0) 0
Marseille (4) 5 *(Voller, Martin Vazquez 2, Sauzee, Ferreri)*   8000
Glentoran: Paterson; Neill, Lowry, Morrison (McCloskey), Devine, Bowers, Campbell, Mathieson, Macartney, Hillis (Jameson), Kavanagh.
Marseille: Olmeta; Angloma (Eydelie), Amoros, Boli, Sauzee, Durand (Ferreri), Casoni, Martin Vazquez, Voller, Pele, Deschamps.

Rangers (1) 2 *(Hateley, Huistra)*
Lyngby (0) 0   40,036
Rangers: Goram; McPherson, Gough, Brown, Robertson D, Ferguson, Durrant, Mikhailichenko, Hateley, McCoist, Huistra.
Lyngby: Brodersen; Risom, Gothenborg, Christiansen, Ezeugo, Larsen, Wieghorst, Nielsen M, Vilstrup (Nielsen A), Hammer, Jurgensen (Olsen).

Stuttgart (0) 3 *(Walter 2, Buck)*
Leeds U (0) 0   38,000
Stuttgart: Immel; Schneider, Frontzeck, Dubajic, Strunz (Schaefer), Buchwald, Buck, Sverisson, Walter (Knup), Gaudino, Kogl.
Leeds U: Lukic; Rocastle (Hodge), Dorigo, Batty, Fairclough, Whyte, Cantona (Shutt), Strachan, Chapman, McAllister, Speed.

First Round, Second Leg

30 SEPT

Leeds U (2) 4 *(Speed, McAllister (pen), Cantona, Chapman)*
Stuttgart (1) 1 *(Buck)*   20,457
Leeds U: Lukic; Sellars, Dorigo, Batty, Fairclough, Whyte, Strachan, Cantona, Chapman, McAllister, Speed.
Stuttgart: Immel; Schaefer, Frontzeck, Dubajic, Strunz, Buchwald, Buck, Sverisson, Walter (Knup), Gaudino (Simakic), Kogl.
Leeds awarded match 3-0 on forfeit; Stuttgart included fourth ineligible foreign player

Lyngby (0) 0
Rangers (0) 1 *(Durrant)*   4273
Lyngby: Brodersen; Larsen (Olsen), Rytter Maale, Gothenborg, Christiansen, Vilstrup, Risom, Wieghorst, Jurgensen, Nielsen M (Lykke), Kuhn.
Rangers: Goram; McCall, Robertson D, Durrant, McPherson, Brown, Steven, Ferguson, McCoist, Hateley, Huistra.

Marseille (2) 3 *(Omam-Biyik, Pele, Boli)*
Glentoran (0) 0   10,000
Marseille: Barthez; Amoros, Di Meco, Boli, Desailly, Eydelie, Thomas, Martin Vazquez, Omam-Biyik, Pele (Durand), Deschamps (Marquet).
Glentoran: Paterson; Neill, Lowry, Morrison, Devine, Bowers, Kavanagh (McCloskey), Mathieson, Macartney, Hillis, Jameson (McBride).

First Round Replay

9 OCT

Leeds U (1) 2 *(Strachan, Shutt)*
Stuttgart (1) 1 *(Golke) in Barcelona*   10,000
Leeds U: Lukic; Newsome, Dorigo, Batty, Fairclough, Whyte, Strachan, Cantona (Shutt), Chapman, McAllister, Speed.
Stuttgart: Immel; Schaefer, Frontzeck, Dubajic, Strunz (Strehmel), Buchwald, Buck, Sverisson (Knup), Walter, Golke, Kogl.

Second Round, First Leg

21 OCT

Rangers (2) 2 *(Lukic (og), McCoist)*
Leeds U (1) 1 *(McAllister)*   44,000
Rangers: Goram; McCall, Robertson D, Gough, McPherson, Brown, Steven (Huistra), Ferguson, McCoist, Hateley, Durrant.
Leeds U: Lukic; Newsome, Dorigo, Batty, Fairclough, Whyte, Strachan (Rocastle), Cantona (Rodney Wallace), Chapman, McAllister, Speed.

Second Round, Second Leg

4 NOV

Leeds U (0) 1 *(Cantona)*
Rangers (1) 2 *(Hateley, McCoist)* 25,118
Leeds U: Lukic; Newsome, Dorigo, Rocastle (Hodge), Fairclough (Rodney Wallace), Whyte, Strachan, Cantona, Chapman, McAllister, Speed.
Rangers: Goram; McCall, Robertson D, Gough, McPherson, Brown, Gordon (Mikhailichenko), Ferguson, McCoist, Hateley, Durrant.

Champions League

Group A

25 NOV

Rangers (0) 2 *(McSwegan, Hateley)*
Marseille (1) 2 *(Boksic, Voller)* 41,624
Rangers: Goram; Murray, Robertson D, Gough (Pressley), McPherson, Brown, Steven (McSwegan), McCall, Durrant, Hateley, Mikhailichenko.
Marseille: Barthez; Angloma, Di Meco, Boli, Sauzee, Desailly, Casoni, Boksic (Durand), Voller (Eydelie), Pele, Deschamps.

9 DEC

CSKA Moscow (0) 0
Rangers (1) 1 *(Ferguson) in Bochum* 9000
CSKA Moscow: Guteyev; Guschkin (Ivanov), Kolotovkin, Bystrov, Fokhin, Maliukov, Minko (Grishin), Korsakov, Sergeyev, Bushmanov, Faizulin.
Rangers: Goram; McCall, Robertson D, Durrant, McPherson, Brown, Steven, Ferguson, McCoist, Hateley, Mikhailichenko.

3 MAR

FC Brugge (1) 1 *(Dziubinski)*
Rangers (0) 1 *(Huistra)* 19,000
FC Brugge: Verlinden; Cossey (Verspaille), Van der Elst, Verheyen, Borkelmans, Dziubinski, Creve (Renier), Querter, Staelens, Booy, Amokachi.
Rangers: Goram; Nisbet (Pressley), Robertson D, Murray, McPherson, Brown, Mikhailichenko, McCall, McCoist, Hateley, Huistra.

17 MAR

Rangers (1) 2 *(Durrant, Nisbet)*
FC Brugge (0) 1 *(Staelens)* 42,731
Rangers: Goram; Nisbet, Murray, Gough, McPherson, Brown, Steven, McCall, Durrant, Hateley, Mikhailichenko.
FC Brugge: Verlinden; Disztl, Van der Elst, Verheyen, Borkelmans, Van der Heyden, Creve, Cossey, Staelens, Schaessens (Dziubinski), Amokachi.

7 APR

Marseille (1) 1 *(Sauzee)*
Rangers (0) 1 *(Durrant)* 40,000
Marseille: Barthez; Boli, Desailly, Di Meco, Angloma, Deschamps, Eydelie, Sauzee, Pele, Boksic, Voller.
Rangers: Goram; McPherson, Gough, Brown, Robertson D (Murray), Steven, McCall, Ferguson, McCoist, Durrant, Huistra (McSwegan).

21 APR

Rangers (0) 0
CSKA Moscow (0) 0 43,142
Rangers: Goram; McCall, Robertson D, Gough, McPherson, Brown, Steven (McSwegan), Ferguson, McCoist, Durrant, Huistra.
CSKA Moscow: Plotnitov; Guschkin, Mamchur, Mashkarin, Maliukov, Bushmanov, Minko, Korsakov, Antonovich, Sergeyev, Faizulin (Dudnik).

Mark Hateley celebrates after scoring for Rangers against Marseille at Ibrox. The Champions League match ended 2-2. (Action Images)

EUROPEAN CUP-WINNERS' CUP

EUROPEAN CUP-WINNERS' CUP FINALS 1961–92

Year	Winners		Runners-up		Venue	Attendance	Referee
1961	Fiorentina	2	Rangers	0 *(1st Leg)*	Glasgow	80,000	Steiner (A)
	Fiorentina	2	Rangers	1 *(2nd Leg)*	Florence	50,000	Hernadi (H)
1962	Atletico Madrid	1	Fiorentina	1	Glasgow	27,389	Wharton (S)
Replay	Atletico Madrid	3	Fiorentina	0	Stuttgart	45,000	Tschenscher (WG)
1963	Tottenham Hotspur	5	Atletico Madrid	1	Rotterdam	25,000	Van Leuwen (Ho)
1964	Sporting Lisbon	3	MTK Budapest	3 *(aet)*	Brussels	9000	Van Nuffel (Bel)
Replay	Sporting Lisbon	1	MTK Budapest	0	Antwerp	18,000	Versyp (Bel)
1965	West Ham U	2	Munich 1860	0	Wembley	100,000	Szolt (H)
1966	Borussia Dortmund	2	Liverpool	1 *(aet)*	Glasgow	41,657	Schwinte (F)
1967	Bayern Munich	1	Rangers	0 *(aet)*	Nuremberg	69,480	Lo Bello (I)
1968	AC Milan	2	Hamburg	0	Rotterdam	60,000	Ortiz (Sp)
1969	Slovan Bratislava	3	Barcelona	2	Basle	40,000	Van Ravens (Ho)
1970	Manchester C	2	Gornik Zabrze	1	Vienna	10,000	Schiller (A)
1971	Chelsea	1	Real Madrid	1 *(aet)*	Athens	42,000	Scheurer (Sw)
Replay	Chelsea	2	Real Madrid	1 *(aet)*	Athens	24,000	Bucheli (Sw)
1972	Rangers	3	Moscow Dynamo	2	Barcelona	35,000	Ortiz (Sp)
1973	AC Milan	1	Leeds U	0	Salonika	45,000	Mihas (Gr)
1974	Magdeburg	2	AC Milan	0	Rotterdam	5000	Van Gemert (Ho)
1975	Dynamo Kiev	3	Ferencvaros	0	Basle	13,000	Davidson (S)
1976	Anderlecht	4	West Ham U	2	Brussels	58,000	Wurtz (F)
1977	Hamburg	2	Anderlecht	0	Amsterdam	65,000	Partridge (E)
1978	Anderlecht	4	Austria/WAC	0	Paris	48,679	Adlinger (WG)
1979	Barcelona	4	Fortuna Dusseldorf	3 *(aet)*	Basle	58,000	Palotai (H)
1980	Valencia	0	Arsenal	0	Brussels	40,000	Christov (Cz)
	(aet; Valencia won 5-4 on penalties)						
1981	Dynamo Tbilisi	2	Carl Zeiss Jena	1	Dusseldorf	9000	Lattanzi (I)
1982	Barcelona	2	Standard Liege	1	Barcelona	100,000	Eschweiler (WG)
1983	Aberdeen	2	Real Madrid	1 *(aet)*	Gothenburg	17,804	Menegali (I)
1984	Juventus	2	Porto	1	Basle	60,000	Prokop (EG)
1985	Everton	3	Rapid Vienna	1	Rotterdam	30,000	Casarin (I)
1986	Dynamo Kiev	3	Atletico Madrid	0	Lyon	39,300	Wohrer (A)
1987	Ajax	1	Lokomotiv Leipzig	0	Athens	35,000	Agnolin (I)
1988	Mechelen	1	Ajax	0	Strasbourg	39,446	Pauly (WG)
1989	Barcelona	2	Sampdoria	0	Berne	45,000	Courtney (E)
1990	Sampdoria	2	Anderlecht	0	Gothenburg	20,103	Galler (Sw)
1991	Manchester U	2	Barcelona	1	Rotterdam	45,000	Karlsson (Se)
1992	Werder Bremen	2	Monaco	0	Lisbon	16,000	D'Elia (I)

Rudy Smidts tackles Stefano Cuoghi the Parma forward (white shirt) during the Cup-Winners Cup Final at Wembley in which Antwerp were beaten 3-1. (Action Images)

EUROPEAN CUP-WINNERS'CUP 1992-93

Preliminary Round, First Leg

Avenir Beggen (1) 1 *(Krings 1)*, B36 Torshavn (0) 0 1500

Branik Maribor (2) 4 *(Simundja 16, 30, Tarana 48, Bonkovski 76)*, Hamrun Spartans (0) 0 5000

Stromsgodset (0) 0, Hapoel Petah Tikva (0) 2 *(Bason 81, 82)* 4000

Vaduz (0) 0, Chernomoretz Odessa (1) 5 *(Tsimbalar 44, Lebed 47, Sak 53, Gousev 81, 82)* 2000

Preliminary Round, Second Leg

Chernomoretz Odessa (4) 7 *(Nikiforov 7, 44 (pen), 79, 89, Yablonski 20, Tsymbalar 24, Lebed 78)*, Vaduz (0) 1 *(Stuber 85)* 4600

Hamrun Spartans (1) 2 *(Brincat 32, 59)*, Branik Maribor (1) 1 *(Parana 37)* 1000

Hapoel Petah Tikva (1) 2 *(Levin 17, Bason 69)*, Stromsgodset (0) 0 2000

B36 Torshavn (1) 1 *(Reynheim 9)*, Avenir Beggen (1) 1 *(Krahen 28)* 665

First Round, First Leg

AIK Stockholm (0) 3 *(Simpson 51, Hallstrom 56, Yevtushenko 85)*, Aarhus (2) 3 *(Tofting 15, Christensen 36, 53)* 3976

Airdrieonians (0) 0, Sparta Prague (0) 1 *(Sopko 88)* 7000

Bohemians (0) 0, Steaua Bucharest (0) 0 4500

Branik Maribor (0) 0, Atletico Madrid (2) 3 *(Alfredo 26, Garcia 43, 56)* 5000

Cardiff C (0) 1 *(Pike 59)*, Admira Wacker (1) 1 *(Abfalterer 44)* 9624

Feyenoord (0) 1 *(Kiprich 89)*, Hapoel Petah Tikva (0) 0 15,000

Glenavon (1) 1 *(Smith 44)*, Antwerp (0) 1 *(Lehnhoff 46)* 3000

Levski Sofia (0) 2 *(Borimirov 52, Getov 70 (pen))*, Lucerne (1) 1 *(Camenzind 9)* 8000

Liverpool (3) 6 *(Stewart 4, 38, Rush 40, 50, 55, 74)*, Apollon Limassol (0) 1 *(Spoljaric 83 (pen))* 12, 769

Miedz Legnica (0) 0, Monaco (1) 1 *(Djorkaeff 3)* 6500 *(in Lubin)*

Moscow Spartak (0) 0, Avenir Beggen (0) 0 5000

Olympiakos (0) 0, Chernomoretz Odessa (1) 1 *(Sak 4)* 30,000

Parma (0) 1 *(Asprilla 48)*, Ujpest (0) 0 11,600

Trabzonspor (0) 2 *(Hami 51, 65)*, TPS Turku (0) 0 22,500

Valur (0) 0, Boavista (0) 0 400

Werder Bremen (3) 3 *(Rufer 19, 28, Bratseth 45)*, Hannover (1) 1 *(Wojcicki 26 (pen))* 17,000

First Round, Second Leg

Aarhus (0) 1 *(Harder 67)*, AIK Stockholm (1) 1 *(Simpson 20)* 9000

Admira Wacker (0) 2 *(Marschall 47, Abfalterer 70)*, Cardiff C (0) 0 4700

Apollon Limassol (0) 1 *(Spoljaric 60)*, Liverpool (0) 2 *(Rush 62, Hutchison 68)* 12,000

Antwerp (0) 1 *(Kiekens 65 (pen))*, Glenavon (0) 1 *(Farris 80)* aet 7000
Antwerp won 3-1 on penalties

Atletico Madrid (2) 6 *(Alfaro 17, Juanito 44, Sabas 58 (pen), Pizo Gomez 69, Aguilera 80, Taraba 88 (og))*, Branik Maribor (1) 1 *(Bicarcik 22)* 3000

Avenir Beggen (0) 1 *(Novak 85)*, Moscow Spartak (2) 5 *(Onopko 6, Piatnitski 9, 78, Radchenko 55, Popov 59)* 2000

Boavista (2) 3 *(Marlon 14, 81, Ricky 26)*, Valur (0) 0 15,000

Chernomoretz Odessa (0) 0, Olympiakos (2) 3 *(Mitsidonas 15, Litovchenko 27, Protasov 80)* 23,000

Hannover (2) 2 *(Daschner 29, 33)*, Werder Bremen (1) 1 *(Rufer 19 (pen))* 27, 436

Hapoel Petah Tikva (1) 2 *(Levin 2, Kakkon 50)*, Feyenoord (0) 1 *(Fraser 59)* 6000 *(at Ramat Gan)*

Lucerne (1) 1 *(Camenzind 24)*, Levski Sofia (0) 0 12,000

Monaco (0) 0, Miedz Legnica (0) 0 4000

Sparta Prague (2) 2 *(Vrabec 31, Vonasek 37)*, Airdrieonians (0) 1 *(Black 55)* 8989

Steaua Bucharest (3) 4 *(Andrasi 26, 34, Vladoiu 44, Viorel 85)*, Bohemians (0) 0 15,000

TPS Turku (1) 2 *(Kajdu 1, Lehtonen 84)*, Trabzonspor (1) 2 *(Hami 14, Orhan 60)* 2000

Ujpest (0) 1 *(Hetesi 62)*, Parma (0) 1 *(Grun 53)* 12,000

Second Round, First Leg

Aarhus (2) 3 *(Andersen 12, Christensen 19, Nielsen 89 (pen))*, Steaua Bucharest (0) 2 *(Vladoiu 64, Dumitrescu 89)* 9000

Admira Wacker (2) 2 *(Marschall 24, Bacher 41)*, Antwerp (1) 4 *(Czerniatynski 35, 73, Segers 53, Severeyens 62)* 4000

Lucerne (0) 1 *(Ruda 74)*, Feyenoord (0) 0 16, 100

Monaco (0) 0, Olympiakos (0) 1 *(Valtsis 86)* 8000

Parma (0) 0, Boavista (0) 0 15,000

Spartak Moscow (1) 4 *(Pisarev 10, Karpin 68, 82 (pen), Lediakhov 89)*, Liverpool (0) 2 *(Wright 67, McManaman 78)* 55,000

Trabzonspor (0) 0, Atletico Madrid (1) 2 *(Futre 38, Moya 60)* 20,000

Werder Bremen (0) 2 *(Neubarth 56, Rufer 81)*, Sparta Prague (2) 3 *(Sopko 25, Dvirnik 36, Vonasek 90)* 10,747

Second Round, Second Leg

Antwerp (2) 3 *(Czerniatynski 21, Severeyns 44, Van Rethy 96)*, Admira Wacker (0) 4 *(Bacher 46, Abfalterer 57, Ljung 63, 79)* aet 7000

Atletico Madrid (0) 0, Trabzonspor (0) 0 9000

Boavista (0) 0, Parma (0) 2 *(Di Chiara 11, Melli 78)* 8000

Feyenoord (2) 4 *(Taument 2, Blinker 16, Kiprich 46, 83(pen))*, Lucerne (1) 1 *(Nadig 12)* 21,000

Liverpool (0) 0, Moscow Spartak (0) 2 *(Radchenko 63, Piatnitski 89)* 37, 993

Olympiakos (0) 0, Monaco (0) 0 35,000

Sparta Prague (1) 1 *(Siegl 7)*, Werder Bremen (0) 0 35,000

Steaua Bucharest (0) 2 *(Cristescu 81, Vladoiu 89)*, Aarhus (1) 1 *(Christensen 10)* 26,000

Quarter-finals, First Leg

Antwerp (0) 0, Steaua Bucharest (0) 0 9500

Feyenoord (0) 0, Moscow Spartak (1) 1 *(Piatnitski 36)* 33, 187

Olympiakos (0) 1 *(Valtsis 64)*, Atletico Madrid (1) 1 *(Moya 10)* 55,000

Sparta Prague (0) 0, Parma (0) 0 24,900

Quarter-finals, Second Leg

Atletico Madrid (1) 3 *(Manolo 10, 57, Alfaro 67)*, Olympiakos (0) 1 *(Tsaluhidis 60)* 40,000

Moscow Spartak (1) 3 *(Karpin 7, 78, Radchenko 87)*, Feyenoord (1) 1 *(Kiprich 14)* 15,000

Parma (2) 2 *(Melli 11, Asprilla 33)*, Sparta Prague (0) 0 20,000

Steaua Bucharest (1) 1 *(Dumitrescu 19)*, Antwerp (0) 1 *(Czerniatynski 82)* 15,000

Semi-finals, First Leg

Atletico Madrid (1) 1 *(Luis Garcia 44)*, Parma (0) 2 *(Asprilla 57, 61)* 50,000

Moscow Spartak (1) 1 *(Piatnitski 36)*, Antwerp (0) 0 60,000

Continued on facing page

EUROPEAN CUP-WINNERS' CUP 1992-93 – BRITISH AND IRISH CLUBS

First Round, First Leg

15 SEPT

Airdrieonians (0) 0
Sparta Prague (0) 1 *(Sopko)* 7000
Airdrieonians: Martin; Stewart, Kidd, Sandison, Black, Boyle, Honor, Balfour, Coyle, Smith, Lawrence.
Sparta Prague: Kouba; Sopko, Hornak, Vrabec, Mistr, Bilek, Chovanec, Vonasek, Nemec, Dvisnik (Trval), Frydek (Nedved).

Glenavon (1) 1 *(Smith)*
Antwerp (1) 1 *(Lehnhoff)* 3000
Glenavon: Beck; McMullan, Scappaticci, Byrne, McKeown (McConville), Crawford, Smith, Kennedy, Ferguson, Ferris, Crowe.
Antwerp: Silvar; Emmerechts, Broeckaert, Smidts, Segers, Kiekens, Van Rethy, Van Veirdeghem, Jakovljevic, Lehnhoff, Czerniatynski (Severeyns).

16 SEPT

Bohemians (0) 0
Steaua Bucharest (0) 0 4500
Bohemians: Henderson; Byrne T, Best, Whelan, Geoghegan (Byrne P), King, Byrne A, Fenlon, Tilson, Lawless, O'Driscoll.
Steaua Bucharest: Gherasim; Panait, Pirvu, Dobos, Bacur, Iovan, Vladoiu, Dumitrescu, Viorel (Filipescu), Panduru, Stan (Sduruea).

Cardiff C (0) 1 *(Pike)*
Admira Wacker (1) 1 *(Abfalterer)* 9624
Cardiff C: Grew; Bird (Gorman), Searle, Baddeley, Abraham, Brazil, Ramsey, Griffith, Pike, Dale, Blake.
Admira Wacker: Gruber F; Dotzl, Zingler, Gruber M, Messlander, Abfalterer, Guterderer (Bacher), Artner, Tenn, Wong, Marshall.

Liverpool (3) 6 *(Stewart 2, Rush 4)*
Apollon (0) 1 *(Spoljaric(pen))* 12,769
Liverpool: James; Harkness (Charnock), Burrows, Nicol, Redknapp, Wright, Marsh, Stewart (Rosenthal), Rush, Molby, Walters.
Apollon: Christophi M; Andrellis, Pittas, Ioannou, Kenny, Yiangoudakis, Iosifides G, Spoljaric, Djoras, Christophi G (Sofocleous), Charalambous.

First Round, Second Leg

29 SEPT

Admira Wacker (0) 2 *(Marschall, Abfalterer)*
Cardiff C (0) 0 4700
Admira Wacker: Gruber F; Dotzl, Muller (Zingler), Gruber M, Nesslender, Abfalterer, Bacher, Artner, Tenn, Ljung, Marschall.
Cardiff C: Grew; James, Searle, Baddeley, Abraham (Bird), Brazil, Ramsey, Griffith, Pike, Dale, Blake.

Apollon (0) 1 *(Spoljaric)*
Liverpool (0) 2 *(Rush, Hutchison)* 12,000
Apollon: Christophi M; Andrellis, Pittas, Ioannou, Christophi G, Yiangoudakis, Iosifides G, Spoljaric, Djoras (Sofocleous), Tsolakis (Yanneris), Kenny.
Liverpool: Grobbelaar; Marsh, Burrows, Tanner, Redknapp, Hutchison, McManaman, Stewart, Rush, Molby, Walters (Harkness).

Steaua Bucharest (3) 4 *(Andrasi 2, Vladoiu, Viorel)*
Bohemians (0) 0 15,000
Steaua Bucharest: Gherasim; Panait, Pirvu, Dobos, Bacur, Fulga (Viorel), Vladoiu, Dumitrescu, Andrasi (State), Panduru, Stan.
Bohemians: Henderson; Byrne T, Geoghegan, Best, Whelan, Byrne A (King), O'Connor, O'Driscoll (Devlin), Lawless, Fenlon, Tilson.

30 SEPT

Antwerp (0) 1 *(Kiekens (pen))*
Glenavon (0) 1 *(Ferris)* 7000
Antwerp: Silvar; Kiekens, Broeckaert, Emmerechts, Smidts, Mokrim, Van Rethy (Van Veirdeghem), Segers, Severeyns, Lehnhoff, Czerniatynski (Vincent).
Glenavon: Beck; McMullan, Byrne, Scappaticci (Percy), McKeown, Kennedy, Crawford, McConville (Smith), Ferguson, Ferris, Crowe.
aet; Antwerp won 3-1 on penalties

Sparta Prague (2) 2 *(Vrabec, Vonasek)*
Airdrieonians (0) 1 *(Black)* 8989
Sparta Prague: Kouba; Sopko, Mistr, Vrabec, Hornak, Bilek, Nemec, Chovanec, Vonasek, Siegl, Dvisnik.
Airdrieonians: Martin; Kidd, Stewart, Sandison, Caesar (Kirkwood), Black, Boyle (Lawrence), Balfour, Smith, Coyle, Honor.

Second Round, First Leg

22 OCT

Spartak Moscow (1) 4 *(Pisarev, Karpin 2 (1 pen), Lediakhov)*
Liverpool (0) 2 *(Wright, McManaman)* 55,000
Spartak Moscow: Cherchesov; Khletsov, Ivanov, Pisarev, Beschastnykh (Vaseev), Chernyshov, Onopko, Karpin, Piatnitski, Lediakhov, Radchenko.
Liverpool: Grobbelaar; Marsh, Burrows, Jones (Tanner), Wright, Hutchison, McManaman, Walters, Rush (Rosenthal), Redknapp, Thomas.

Second Round, Second Leg

4 NOV

Liverpool (0) 0
Spartak Moscow (0) 2 *(Radchenko, Piatnitski)* 37,993
Liverpool: Hooper; Jones (Rosenthal), Burrows, Nicol, Wright, Hutchison, McManaman, Marsh, Rush, Redknapp, Thomas.
Spartak Moscow: Cherchesov; Khletsov, Ivanov, Pisarev (Rusajev), Beschastnykh, Chernyshov, Onopko, Karpin, Piatnitski, Lediakhov (Bakschev), Radchenko.

INTER-CITIES FAIRS & UEFA CUP

FAIRS CUP FINALS 1958–71

(Winners in italics)

Year	First Leg	Attendance	Second Leg	Attendance
1958	London 2 Barcelona 2	45,466	*Barcelona* 6 London 0	62,000
1960	Birmingham C 0 Barcelona 0	40,500	*Barcelona* 4 Birmingham C 1	70,000
1961	Birmingham C 2 Roma 2	21,005	*Roma* 2 Birmingham C 0	60,000
1962	Valencia 6 Barcelona 2	65,000	Barcelona 1 *Valencia* 1	60,000
1963	Dynamo Zagreb 1 Valencia 2	40,000	*Valencia* 2 Dynamo Zagreb 0	55,000
1964	*Zaragoza* 2 Valencia 1	50,000	(in Barcelona)	
1965	*Ferencvaros* 1 Juventus 0	25,000	(in Turin)	
1966	Barcelona 0 Zaragoza 1	70,000	Zaragoza 2 *Barcelona* 4	70,000
1967	Dynamo Zagreb 2 Leeds U 0	40,000	Leeds U 0 *Dynamo Zagreb* 0	35,604
1968	Leeds U 1 Ferencvaros 0	25,368	Ferencvaros 0 *Leeds U* 0	70,000
1969	Newcastle U 3 Ujpest Dozsa 0	60,000	Ujpest Dozsa 2 *Newcastle U* 3	37,000
1970	Anderlecht 3 Arsenal 1	37,000	*Arsenal* 3 Anderlecht 0	51,612
1971	Juventus 0 Leeds U 0 *(abandoned 51 minutes)*	42,000		
	Juventus 2 Leeds U 2	42,000	*Leeds U* 1* Juventus 1	42,483

UEFA CUP FINALS 1972–92

(Winners in italics)

Year	First Leg	Attendance	Second Leg	Attendance
1972	Wolverhampton W 1 Tottenham H 2	45,000	*Tottenham H* 1 Wolverhampton W 1	48,000
1973	Liverpool 0 Moenchengladbach 0			
	(abandoned 27 minutes)	44,967		
	Liverpool 3 Moenchengladbach 0	41,169	Moenchengladbach 0 *Liverpool* 2	35,000
1974	Tottenham H 2 Feyenoord 2	46,281	*Feyenoord* 2 Tottenham 0	68,000
1975	Moenchengladbach 0 Twente 0	45,000	Twente 1 *Moenchengladbach* 5	24,500
1976	Liverpool 3 FC Brugge 2	56,000	FC Brugge 1 *Liverpool* 1	32,000
1977	Juventus 1 Athletic Bilbao 0	75,000	Athletic Bilbao 2 *Juventus* 1*	43,000
1978	Bastia 0 PSV Eindhoven 0	15,000	*PSV Eindhoven* 3 Bastia 0	27,000
1979	Red Star Belgrade 1 Moenchengladbach 1	87,500	*Moenchengladbach* 1 Red Star Belgrade 0	45,000
1980	Moenchengladbach 3 Eintracht Frankfurt 2	25,000	*Eintracht Frankfurt* 1* Moenchengladbach 0	60,000
1981	Ipswich T 3 AZ 67 Alkmaar 0	27,532	AZ 67 Alkmaar 4 *Ipswich T* 2	28,500
1982	Gothenburg 1 Hamburg 0	42,548	Hamburg 0 *Gothenburg* 3	60,000
1983	Anderlecht 1 Benfica 0	45,000	Benfica 1 *Anderlecht* 1	80,000
1984	Anderlecht 1 Tottenham H 1	40,000	*Tottenham H* 1[1] Anderlecht 1	46,258
1985	Videoton 0 Real Madrid 3	30,000	*Real Madrid* 0 Videoton 1	98,300
1986	Real Madrid 5 Cologne 1	80,000	Cologne 2 *Real Madrid* 0	15,000
1987	Gothenburg 1 Dundee U 0	50,023	Dundee U 1 *Gothenburg* 1	20,911
1988	Espanol 3 Bayer Leverkusen 0	42,000	*Bayer Leverkusen* 3[2] Espanol 0	22,000
1989	Napoli 2 Stuttgart 1	83,000	Stuttgart 3 *Napoli* 3	67,000
1990	Juventus 3 Fiorentina 1	45,000	Fiorentina 0 *Juventus* 0	32,000
1991	Internazionale 2 Roma 0	68,887	Roma 1 *Internazionale* 0	70,901
1992	Torino 2 Ajax 2	65,377	*Ajax** 0 Torino 0	40,000

* won on away goals   [1] *Tottenham H won 4-3 on penalties aet*   [2] *Bayer Leverkusen won 3-2 on penalties aet*

Dino Baggio (Juventus, second right) scores his and his team's second goal in the UEFA Cup Final, second leg match with Borussia Dortmund. (Colorsport)

UEFA CUP 1992–93

First Round, First Leg

Benfica (2) 3 *(Vitor Paneira 43, 73, William 45 (pen))*, Belvedur Izola (0) 0 10,000

Caen (3) 3 *(Gravelaine 7, 14, Paille 37)*, Zaragoza (1) 2 *(Garcia Sanjuan 37, Pardeza 79)* 7000

Cologne (1) 2 *(Jensen 24, Ordenewitz 82)*, Celtic (0) 0 15,000

FC Copenhagen (2) 5 *(Johansen 12, 54, Uldbjerg 28, Hoyer Nielsen 69 (pen), Larsen 86)*, MP Mikkeli (0) 0 8430

Electroputere Craiova (0) 0, Panathinaikos (2) 6 *(Franceskos 4, Warzycha 40, 53, 66, Maragos 70, Kalatzis 85)* 22,000

Fenerbahce (2) 3 *(Aykut 14, 38, Tanju 55)*, Botev Plovdiv (0) 1 *(Dermeciev 51)* 12,382

Floriana (0) 0, Borussia Dortmund (1) 1 *(Rummenigge 21)* 4500

Fram (0) 0, Kaiserslautern (1) 3 *(Witeczek 29, Wegner 64, Kristinn Jonsson (og) 66)* 785

Grasshoppers (1) 1 *(Alain Sutter 37 (pen))*, Sporting Lisbon (1) 2 *(Balakov 45, Juskowiak 84)* 10,750

Hibernian (1) 2 *(Beaumont 4, McGinlay 75)*, Anderlecht (1) 2 *(Degryse 39 (pen), Van Vossen 67)* 14,213

Juventus (4) 6 *(Roberto Baggio 3, Moller 10, Vialli 42, 61, Conte 44, Torricelli 75)*, Anorthosis (0) 1 *(Kespaje 85)* 5000

GKS Katowice (0) 0, Galatasaray (0) 0 5000

Kiev Dynamo (0) 1 *(Yakovenko 46)*, Rapid (0) 0 17,000

Lokomotiv Plovdiv (1) 2 *(Sadukov 33 (pen), Vidulov 57)*, Auxerre (1) 2 *(Baticle 3, Cocard 74)* 8000

Manchester U (0) 0, Torpedo Moscow (0) 0 19,998

Mechelen (1) 2 *(Eykelkamp 30, De Boeck 63)*, Orebro (0) 1 *(Milkvist 84)* 5000

Moscow Dynamo (1) 5 *(Sklarov 34, 62, Timofeyev 46, Simotenkov 57, Tetradze 68)*, Rosenborg (0) 1 *(Loken 75)* 7250

Neuchatel Xamax (0) 2 *(Beat Sutter 51, Manfreda 52)*, Frem (2) 2 *(Mikkelsen 17, Henchoz (og) 21)* 4000

Norrkoping (0) 1 *(Blom 80)*, Torino (0) 0 8601

Paris St Germain (2) 2 *(Weah 13, 24)*, PAOK Salonika (0) 0 25,000

Politechnica Timisoara (0) 1 *(Cuc 62)*, Real Madrid (1) 1 *(Alfonso 13)* 26,000

Salzburg (0) 0, Ajax (0) 3 *(Davids 53, Overmars 65, Kreek 79)* 10,000

Sheffield W (4) 8 *(Waddle 9, Anderson 23, 29, Warhurst 31, 77, Bart-Williams 60, 81, Worthington 65)*, Spora Luxembourg (1) 1 *(Cruz 11)* 19,792

Sigma Olomouc (0) 1 *(Capka 87)*, Uni Craiova (0) 0 6129

Slavia Prague (0) 1 *(Tatarchuk 85)*, Hearts (0) 0 4594

Standard Liege (2) 5 *(Asselman 5, 44, Goossens 52, 65, Leonard 56)*, Portadown (0) 0 12,000

Vac Izzo (1) 1 *(Fuele 27)*, Groningen (0) 0 2500

Valencia (0) 0 *(Roberto 54)*, Napoli (1) 5 *(Fonseca 20, 60, 63, 87, 89)* 34,000

Vitesse (1) 3 *(Van der Brom 20, 56, Latuheru 89)*, Derry City (0) 0 10,000

Vitoria Guimaraes (2) 3 *(Kupresanin 15, 76, Barbosa 28)*, Real Sociedad (0) 0 18,000

Wacker Innsbruck (1) 1 *(Baur 36)*, Roma (3) 4 *(Giannini 17, 42, Caniggia 21, Muzzi 65)* 8500

Widzew Lodz (2) 2 *(Jozwiak 21, Koniarek 27)*, Eintracht Frankfurt (0) 2 *(Yeboah 67, Wolf 83)* 7600

First Round, Second Leg

Ajax (1) 3 *(Pettersson 26, 79, Bergkamp 49)*, Salzburg (0) 1 *(Reisinger 60)* 12,500

Anderlecht (1) 1 *(Nilis 36)*, Hibernian (1) 1 *(Jackson 15)* 25,000

Anorthosis (0) 0, Juventus (2) 4 *Ravenelli 14, Kohler 39, Casiraghi 66, 87)* 6000

Auxerre (4) 7 *(Baticle 2, 71, Cocard 11, Prunier 13, 48, Vahirua 28, Leaslandes 84)*, Botev Plovdiv (1) 1 *(Sadakov 21)* 16,000

Belvedur Izola (0) 0, Benfica (1) 5 *(Pacheco 21, 46, 66, Joao Pinto II 58, Cesar Brito 87)* 4000

Borussia Dortmund (2) 7 *(Zorc 10, Delia (og) 18, Franck 59, Rummenigge 67, Mill 72, 79, 89)*, Floriana (2) 2 *(Crawley 11, 17)* 11,790

Botev Plovdiv (2) 2 *(Iskrenov 5, Petrov 41)*, Fenerbahce (1) 2 *(Ridvan 37, 78)* 8000

Celtic (2) 3 *(McStay 35, Creaney 39, Collins 79)*, Cologne (0) 0 30,747

Derry C (0) 1 *(Mooney 60)*, Vitesse (1) 2 *(Straal 44, Laamers 65)* 5000

Eintracht Frankfurt (6) 9 *(Kruse 8, 14, 37, Yeboah 21, 22, 36, 69, Rahn 83, Bein 89)*, Widzew Lodz (0) 0 8000

Frem (3) 4 *(Haren 17, 37, Jensen 19, Thogersen 53)*, Neuchatel Xamax (1) 1 *(Manfreda 24)* 3476

Galatasaray (1) 2 *(Hakan 31, Falco 57)*, GKS Katowice (1) 1 *(Machihievski 75)* 25,000

Groningen (0) 1 *(Huizingh 55)*, Vac Izzo (1) 1 *(Fuele 43)* 5000

Hearts (3) 4 *(Mackay 10, Baird 21, Levein 42, Snodin 79)*, Slavia Prague (1) 2 *(Silhavy 14, Kuka 65)* 16,000

Kaiserslautern (1) 4 *(Kuntz 29, 84, Witeczek 55, 77)*, Fram (0) 0 23,197

MP Mikkeli (0) 1 *(Allen 63)*, FC Copenhagen (4) 5 *(Nielsen 5, Johansen 17, 32, 44, Rasmussen 82)* 971

Napoli (1) 1 *(Fonseca 7)*, Valencia (0) 0 25,000

Orebro (0) 0, Mechelen (0) 0 5085

Panathinaikos (1) 4 *(Saravakos 43, Warzycha 58, Kalatzis 67, Frantzekos 82)*, Electroputere Craiova (0) 0 8000

PAOK Salonika (0) 0, Paris St Germain (2) 2 *(Weah 15, Sassus 32)* 30,000

Abandoned 46 minutes; crowd trouble

Portadown (0) 0, Standard Liege (0) 0 2500

Rapid (3) 3 *(Mandreko 8, Fjortoft 16, 38)*, Kiev Dynamo (1) 2 *(Leonenko 44 (pen), 87)* 16,000

Real Madrid (1) 4 *(Alfonso 27, Luis Enrique 58, Esnaider 65, Michel 87)*, Politehnica Timisoara (0) 0 40,000

Real Sociedad (2) 2 *(Lumbreras 6, Miguel Angel 23)*, Vitoria Guimaraes (0) 0 19, 200

Roma (0) 1 *(Hassler 50)*, Wacker Innsbruck (0) 0 23,000

Rosenborg (1) 2 *(Ingebrigtsen 7, Loken 48)*, Moscow Dynamo (0) 0 10,218

Spora Luxembourg (1) 1 *(Cruz 20)*, Sheffield W (2) 2 *(Watson 18, Warhurst 36)* 3500

Sporting Lisbon (0) 1 *(Cadete 84)*, Grasshoppers (1) 3 *(Elber 31, 110, Magnin 83)* aet 40,000

Torino (1) 3 *(Bruno 2, Casagrande 76, Aguilera 80)*, Norrkoping (0) 0 22,500

Torpedo Moscow (0) 0, Manchester U (0) 0 aet 11, 357

Torpedo Moscow won 4-3 on penalties

Uni Craiova (1) 1 *(Gane 21)*, Sigma Olomouc (2) 2 *(Kerber 23, 42)* 15,000

Zaragoza (1) 2 *(Montanier 24, Poyet 64)*, Caen (0) 0 15,000

Second Round, First Leg

Anderlecht (2) 4 *(Nilis 23, Degryse 38, Versavel 51, Van Vossen 59)*, Kiev Dynamo (1) 2 *(Shkapenkl 20, Leonenko 53)* 20,500

Auxerre (2) 5 *(Baticle 14, 40, 80, Martins 55, Otokori 90)*, FC Copenhagen (0) 0 12,000

Benfica (1) 5 *(Yuran 42, Isias 55, 86, Pacheco 58 (pen), William 79 (pen))*, Vac Izzo (0) 1 *(Szedlaczek 82)* 30,000

Borussia Dortmund (0) 1 *(Chapuisat 70)*, Celtic (0) 0 35,803

Eintracht Frankfurt (0) 0, Galatasaray (0) 0 40,000

Fenerbahce (1) 1 *(Ismail 37)*, Sigma Olomouc (0) 0 32,195

Frem (0) 0, Zaragoza (1) 1 *(Poyet 12)* 2852

Hearts (0) 0, Standard Liege (1) 1 *(Bettagno 6)* 16, 897

Kaiserslautern (1) 3 *(Funkel 5 (pen), Marin 55, Witeczek 57)*, Sheffield W (1) 1 *(Hirst 5)* 20, 802

Napoli (0) 0, Paris St Germain (2) 2 *(Weah 15, 35)* 19,000

Panathinaikos (0) 0, Juventus (0) 1 *(Platt 68)* 75,000

Real Madrid (3) 5 *(Hierro 8, 28, 32, Zamorano 52, Michel 84 (pen))*, Torpedo Moscow (2) 2 *(Shustikov 36, Grishin 39)* 43,000

Roma (3) 3 *(Carnevale 18, Rizzitelli 25, Giannini 41)*, Grasshoppers (0) 0 35,000

Torino (0) 1 *(Timofeyev (og) 55)*, Moscow Dynamo (1) 2 *(Kasumov 44, Simutenkov 68)* 30,000

Vitesse (1) 1 *(Van der Brom 33)*, Mechelen (0) 0 9491

Vitoria Guimaraes (0) 0, Ajax (2) 3 *(Davids 1, Pettersson 38, Bergkamp 48)* 8000

Second Round, Second Leg

Ajax (1) 2 *(Bergkamp 25, Alflen 61)*, Vitoria Guimaraes (0) 1 *(Mbote 57)* 18,000

Celtic (1) 1 *(Creaney 13)*, Borussia Dortmund (0) 2 *(Chapuisat 53, Zorc 58)* 31,578

FC Copenhagen (0) 0, Auxerre (0) 2 *(Cocard 67, Bonalair 88)* 5061

Galatasaray (1) 1 *(Ugur 5)*, Eintracht Frankfurt (0) 0 32,500

Grasshoppers (1) 4 *(De Vicente 36 (pen), 68, Alain Sutter 50, Gamperle 63)*, Roma (2) 3 *(Rizzitelli 7, 87, Caniggia 30)* 9000

Juventus (0) 0, Panathinaikos (0) 0 17,500

Kiev Dynamo (0) 0, Anderlecht (1) 3 *(Van Vossen 21, Nilis 61, 69)* 40,000

Mechelen (0) 0, Vitesse (0) 1 *(Cocu 73)* 9000

Moscow Dynamo (0) 0, Torino (0) 0 4000

Paris St Germain (0) 0, Napoli (0) 0 45,000

Sheffield W (1) 2 *(Wilson 27, Sheridan 64)*, Kaiserslautern (0) 2 *(Witeczek 62, Zeyer 76)* 27,597

Sigma Olomouc (3) 7 *(Hanus 9, 90, Kerbr 12, Barborik 34, Marosi 51, Fiala 76, Vadura 80)*, Fenerbahce (1) 1 *(Aykut 38)* 10,152

Standard Liege (0) 1 *(Wilmots 62)*, Hearts (0) 0 17,000

Vac Izzo (0) 0, Benfica (1) 1 *(Schawrz 13)* 3000

Zaragoza (3) 5 *(Mateut 7, 38, 82, Seba 39, 70)*, Frem (0) 1 *(Colding 73)* 12,000

Torpedo Moscow (1) 3 *(Talalayev 11, Tishkov 62, Mudraskov 77)*, Real Madrid (1) 2 *(Zamorano 10, Hierro 56)* 6500

Third Round, First Leg

Ajax (1) 2 *(Davids 1, Jonk 83)*, Kaiserslautern (0) 0 42,000

Borussia Dortmund (3) 3 *(Chapuisat 12, Zorc 23 (pen), Povlsen 42)*, Zaragoza (0) 1 *(Franco 51)* 36,800

Moscow Dynamo (0) 2 *(Kalitvintsev 75, Dertkatch 88)*, Benfica (1) 2 *(Isaias 35, 54)* 6000

Paris St Germain (0) 0, Anderlecht (0) 0 32, 402

Roma (0) 3 *(Aldair 58, 90, Muzzi 80)*, Galatasaray (0) 1 *(Hakan 85)* 23,980

Sigma Olomouc (0) 1 *(Marosi 89)*, Juventus (1) 2 *(Moller 23, Dino Baggio 76)* 15,000

Standard Liege (1) 2 *(Goossens 9, 48)*, Auxerre (0) 2 *(Verlaat 55, Baticle 71)* 18,000

Vitesse (0) 0, Real Madrid (0) 1 *(Hierro 73)* 13,000

Third Round, Second Leg

Anderlecht (0) 1 *(Bosman 53)*, Paris St Germain (0) 1 *(Kombouare 75)* 19,000

Auxerre (0) 2 *(Baticle 71, Dutuel 82)*, Standard Liege (0) 1 *(Wilmots 88)* 19,000

Benfica (0) 2 *(Isaias 51, Yuran 58)*, Moscow Dynamo (0) 0 50,000

Galatasaray (1) 3 *(Mustafa 27, 58, Arif 75)*, Roma (1) 2 *(Caniggia 8, Hassler 47)* 30,000

Juventus (2) 5 *(Vialli 6, 50, Casiraghi 28, Moller 46, Ravanelli 69)*, Sigma Olomouc (0) 0 5000

Kaiserslautern (0) 0, Ajax (0) 1 *(Alflen 43)* 27,000

Real Madrid (1) 1 *(Zamorano 31)*, Vitesse (0) 0 36,000

Zaragoza (1) 2 *(Poyet 26, Brehme 90)*, Borussia Dortmund (0) 1 *(Chapuisat 50)* 35,000

Quarter-finals, First Leg

Auxerre (2) 4 *(Verlaat 17, Martins 43, Vahirua 82, Dutuel 89)*, Ajax (2) 2 *(Pettersson 3, Vink 44)* 18,000

Benfica (1) 2 *(Vitor Paneira 12, 76)*, Juventus (0) 1 *(Vialli 59 (pen))* 70,000

Real Madrid (2) 3 *(Butragueno 30, Zamorano 36, Michel 89)*, Paris St Germain (0) 1 *(Ginola 47)* 50,000

Roma (0) 1 *(Mihajlovic 66)*, Borussia Dortmund (0) 0 40,000

Quarter-finals, Second Leg

Ajax (0) 1 *(De Boer 61)*, Auxerre (0) 0 43,000

Borussia Dortmund (1) 2 *(Schulz 40, Sippel 46)*, Roma (0) 0 36,800

Juventus (2) 3 *(Kohler 2, Dino Baggio 45, Ravanelli 68)*, Benfica (0) 0 51,697

Paris St Germain (1) 4 *(Weah 33, Ginola 80, Valdo 87, Kombouare 90)*, Real Madrid (0) 1 *(Zamorano 89)* 45,000

Semi-finals, First Leg

Borussia Dortmund (0) 2 *(Karl 58, Zorc 87)*, Auxerre (0) 0 45,000

Juventus (0) 2 *(Roberto Baggio 3, 89)*, Paris St Germain (1) 1 *(Weah 23)* 42,793

Semi-finals, Second Leg

Auxerre (1) 2 *(Martins 6, Verlaat 71)*, Borussia Dortmund (0) 0 *aet* 18,400

Borussia Dortmund won 6-5 on penalties

Paris St Germain (0) 0, Juventus (0) 1 *(Roberto Baggio 77)* 48,000

Continued on Page 920

UEFA CUP 1992–93 – BRITISH AND IRISH CLUBS

First Round, First Leg

15 SEPT

Cologne (1) 2 *(Jensen, Ordenewitz)*
Celtic (0) 0   15,000
Cologne: Illgner; Higl, Baumann, Jensen, Heldt (Weiser), Lehmann (Sturm), Rudy, Littbarski, Flick, Steinmann, Ordenewitz.
Celtic: Marshall; Boyd, Mowbray, Gillespie, Wdowczyk, O'Neil (Grant), McStay, Galloway, Collins, Slater (Nicholas), Creaney.

Hibernian (1) 2 *(Beaumont, McGinlay)*
Anderlecht (1) 2 *(Degryse (pen), Van Vossen)* 14,213
Hibernian: Burridge; Miller, Orr, Beaumont, Mitchell, Weir, Hamilton (Evans), McGinlay, MacLeod, Wright, Jackson.
Anderlecht: De Wilde; Crasson, De Wolf, Kooiman, Albert, Emmers (Marchoul), Versavel, Van Vossen, Nilis, Degryse, Boffin.

16 SEPT

Manchester U (0) 0
Torpedo Moscow (0) 0   19,998
Manchester U: Walsh; Irwin, Martin (Neville), Bruce, Blackmore, Pallister, Kanchelskis, Webb, McClair, Hughes, Wallace.
Torpedo Moscow: Podshivalov; Filimonov, Cheltsov, Afanasyev, Vostrosablin, Shustikov (Skachenko), Grishin, Martinov, Talalayev (Ulyanov), Chuganov, Arafiev.

Sheffield W (4) 8 *(Waddle, Anderson 2, Warhurst 2, Bart-Williams 2, Worthington)*
Spora Luxembourg (1) 1 *(Cruz)*   19,792
Sheffield W: Woods; Harkes, Anderson, Palmer, Shirtliff, Warhurst (Jemson), Hyde (Wilson), Waddle, Francis, Bart-Williams, Worthington.
Spora Luxembourg: Felten; Janes, Kremer, Bei, Stange, Laera, Cardoni (Mischo), Santopietro, Cruz, Relgaud (Seyler), Chaussy.

Slavia Prague (0) 1 *(Tatarchuk)*
Hearts (0) 0   4594
Slavia Prague: Janos; Petrous, Suchoparek, Silhavy, Berger, Tatarchuk, Lerch, Penicka, Kuka, Necas, Novak.
Hearts: Smith; Hogg, Berry, Van de Ven, McKinlay, Mackay, Ferguson D, Mauchlen, Robertson (Crabbe), Baird, Foster.

Standard Liege (2) 5 *(Asselman 2, Goossens 2, Leonard)*
Portadown (0) 0   12,000
Standard Liege: Bodart; Genaux (Lashaf), Leonard, Demol, Cruz, Vervoort, Hellers, Asselman (Goossens), Betango, Vanrooy, Wilmots.
Portadown: Keenan; Major, Scappaticci, Bell, Strain, Stewart, Gorman, Russell, Casey (Surgeon), Mills (Murray), Davidson.

Vitesse (1) 3 *(Van der Brom 2, Latuheru)*
Derry C (0) 0   10,000
Vitesse: Van der Gouw; Straal, Van der Looi, Bos, Vermeulen, Laamers, Van der Brom, Eijer, Latuheru, Van Arum, Cocu.
Derry C: O'Neill; Mooney, Hutton, Roche, Curran, Gauld, Carlyle, Dunleavy, Hegarty (O'Brien), Ennis (Johnston), Kearney.

First Round, Second Leg

29 SEPT

Anderlecht (1) 1 *(Nilis)*
Hibernian (1) 1 *(Jackson)*   25,000
Anderlecht: De Wilde; Crasson, Rutjes, De Wolf, Albert, Valen, Kooiman (Versavel), Marchoul, Van Vossen, Nilis, Degryse, Boffin.
Hibernian: Burridge; Miller, Orr, Beaumont, Tortolano, Hamilton, Milne (Evans), McGinlay, MacLeod, Jackson, Wright.

Derry C (0) 1 *(Mooney)*
Vitesse (1) 2 *(Straal, Laamers)*   5000
Derry C: O'Neill; Mooney, Gauld, Curran, Hutton, Carlyle (McGinlay), Roche, Dunleavy, Kearney (McCann), Ennis, O'Brien.
Vitesse: Van der Gouw; Straal, Van der Looi, Bos, Vermeulen, Laamers, Van der Brom, Eijer, Latuheru (Roelofsen), Van Arum, Cocu.

Portadown (0) 0
Standard Liege (0) 0   2500
Portadown: Keenan; Major, Murray, Bell, Strain, Stewart, Mills, Russell, Casey, Cowan, Davidson.
Standard Liege: Bodart; Genaux, Vervoort, Demol, Leonard, Pister, Hellers, Goossens (Lashaf), Vos, Vanrooy, Wilmots.

Torpedo Moscow (0) 0
Manchester U (0) 0   11,357
Torpedo Moscow: Podshivalov; Filimonov, Cheltsov, Afanasyev, Vostrosablin (Savichev), Shustikov, Grishin, Talalayev, Arafiev, Chuganov, Pasomeyer (Ulyanov).
Manchester U: Schmeichel; Irwin, Phelan (Parker), Bruce, Webb, Pallister, Wallace (Robson), Ince, McClair, Hughes, Giggs.
aet; Torpedo Moscow won 4-3 on penalties

30 SEPT

Celtic (2) 3 *(McStay, Creaney, Collins)*
Cologne (0) 0   30,747
Celtic: Marshall; McNally, Boyd, Grant, Mowbray, Galloway, Slater (Miller), McStay, Payton (Fulton), Creaney, Collins.
Cologne: Illgner; Higl, Greiner, Baumann, Jensen, Rudy, Steinmann (Fuchs), Heldt, Keuler (Littbarski), Weiser, Ordenewitz.

920

Hearts (3) 4 *(Mackay, Baird, Levein, Snodin)*
Slavia Prague (1) 2 *(Silhavy, Kuka)*   16,000
Hearts: Smith; Hogg, McKinlay, Levein, Mackay, Van de Ven, Robertson, McLaren (Wright), Baird, Snodin, Bannon.
Slavia Prague: Janos; Petrous, Suchoparek, Silhavy, Jurasko, Tatarchuk, Binic (Berger), Penicka, Kuka, Necas (Novak), Lerch.

1 OCT

Spora Luxembourg (1) 1 *(Cruz)*
Sheffield W (2) 2 *(Watson, Warhurst)*   3500
Spora Luxembourg: Felten; Janes, Kremer, Bei (Wampach), Stange, Thomas, Laera, Seyler, Cruz, Cardonc (Santopietro), Chaussy.
Sheffield W: Pressman; Harkes, Nilsson (Waddle), Watts, Pearson, Hyde, Wilson, Williams, Warhurst (Palmer), Jemson, Watson.

Second Round, First Leg
20 OCT

Borussia Dortmund (0) 1 *(Chapuisat)*
Celtic (0) 0   35,803
Borussia Dortmund: Klos; Schmidt, Schulz, Reuter, Lusch, Zorc, Rummenigge (Poschner), Reinhardt, Povlsen, Mill (Sippel), Chapuisat.
Celtic: Bonner; McNally, Boyd, Grant, Mowbray, Gillespie, O'Neil, McStay, Slater, Creaney (Nicholas), Collins.

Kaiserslautern (1) 3 *(Funkel (pen), Marin, Witeczek)*
Sheffield W (1) 1 *(Hirst)*   20,802
Kaiserslautern: Ehrmann; Ritter, Funkel, Kadlec, Schafer, Goldbaek, Haber, Hotic, Wagner, Witeczek, Marin (Vogel).
Sheffield W: Woods; Harkes, Worthington, Palmer, Pearson, Anderson, Wilson, Waddle, Hirst, Warhurst (Watson), Hyde (Bart-Williams).

21 OCT

Hearts (0) 0
Standard Liege (1) 1 *(Bettagno)*   16,897
Hearts: Smith; Hogg, McKinlay, Levein (McLaren), Mackay, Van de Ven, Robertson, Ferguson D (Ferguson I), Baird, Snodin, Bannon.
Standard Liege: Bodart; Genaux, Vervoort, Demol, Cruz (Pister), Bettagno, Hellers, Goossens, Leonard, Vanrooy, Wilmots.

Second Round, Second Leg
3 NOV

Celtic (1) 1 *(Creaney)*
Borussia Dortmund (0) 2 *(Chapuisat, Zorc)*   31,578
Celtic: Bonner; Galloway, Mowbray, Gillespie (Miller), Boyd, Slater, McStay, Grant, Collins, Nicholas, Creaney.
Borussia Dortmund: Klos; Schmidt, Schulz, Reuter, Kutowski (Grauer), Lusch, Rummenigge (Karl), Zorc, Reinhardt, Povlsen, Chapuisat.

4 NOV

Sheffield W (1) 2 *(Wilson, Sheridan)*
Kaiserslautern (0) 2 *(Witeczek, Zeyer)*   27,597
Sheffield W: Woods; Harkes (Nilsson), Worthington, Palmer, Pearson (Bart-Williams), Anderson, Wilson, Waddle, Watson, Warhurst, Sheridan.
Kaiserslautern: Serr; Dooley, Kadlec, Ritter, Haber, Goldbaek, Hotic (Zeyer), Richter, Schafer, Witeczek (Lieberknecht), Marin.

Standard Liege (0) 1 *(Wilmots)*
Hearts (0) 0   17,000
Standard Liege: Bodart (Munaron); Genaux, Demol, Cruz, Vervoort, Leonard, Hellers, Bettagno, Goossens, Vanrooy, Wilmots.
Hearts: Smith; McLaren, Levein, Van de Ven, McKinlay, Mackay (Foster), Millar (Snodin), Mauchlen, Ferguson D, Ferguson I, Robertson.

Continued from Page 914

Semi-finals, Second Leg

Antwerp (1) 3 *(Czerniatynski 37, Jakovljevic 66, Lehnhoff 78 (pen))*, Moscow Spartak (1) 1 *(Radchenko 9)* 13,500

Parma (0) 0, Atletico Madrid (0) 1 *(Sabas 77)* 21,915

Final: Parma (2) 3, Antwerp (1) 1

(at Wembley, 12 May 1993, 37,393)

Parma: Ballotta; Benarrivo, Di Chiara, Minotti, Apolloni, Grun, Melli, Zoratto (Pin 27), Osio (Pizzi 65), Cuoghi, Brolin. *Scorers:* Minotti 10, Melli 31, Cuoghi 86.
Antwerp: Stojanovic; Kiekens, Broeckaert, Taeymans, Smidts, Jakovljevic (Van Veirdeghem), Van Rethy, Segers (Moukrim 84), Severeyns, Lehnhoff, Czerniatynski. *Scorer:* Severeyns 13.
Referee: Assenmacher (Germany).

Continued from Page 918

Final, First Leg: Borussia Dortmund (1) 1, Juventus (2) 3

(in Dortmund, 5 May 1993, 37,000)

Borussia Dortmund: Klos; Reinhardt, Franck (Mill 46), Schmidt, Grauer, Lusch, Reuter, Zorc (Karl 70), Chapuisat, Rummenigge, Poscher. *Scorer:* Rummenigge.
Juventus: Peruzzi; Carrera, De Marchi, Dino Baggio, Kohler, Julio Cesar, Conte, Marocchi, Vialli, Roberto Baggio (Di Canio 76), Moller (Galia 88). *Scorers:* Dino Baggio 26, Roberto Baggio 31,74.
Referee: Puhl (Hungary).

Final, Second Leg: Juventus (2) 3, Borussia Dortmund (0) 0

(in Turin, 19 May 1993, 62,781)

Juventus: Peruzzi; Carrera, Torricelli (Di Canio 66), De Marchi, Kohler, Julio Cesar, Galia, Dino Baggio, Vialli (Ravanelli 80), Roberto Baggio, Moller. *Scorers:* Dino Baggio 5, 42, Moller 65.
Borussia Dortmund: Klos; Reinhardt, Schmidt (Lusch 66), Schultz, Zelic, Poscher, Reuter, Karl, Sippel, Rummenigge (Franck 43), Mill.
Referee: Blankenstein (Holland).

Summary of Appearances

EUROPEAN CUP (1955–93)

English clubs
12 Liverpool
5 Manchester U
3 Nottingham F, Leeds U
2 Derby Co, Wolverhampton W, Everton, Aston Villa, Arsenal
1 Burnley, Tottenham H, Ipswich T, Manchester C

Scottish clubs
15 Celtic
14 Rangers
3 Aberdeen
2 Hearts
1 Dundee, Dundee U, Kilmarnock, Hibernian

Clubs for Northern Ireland
17 Linfield
8 Glentoran
2 Crusaders, Portadown
1 Glenavon, Ards, Distillery, Derry C, Coleraine

Clubs for Eire
7 Shamrock R, Dundalk
6 Waterford
3 Drumcondra
2 Bohemians, Limerick, Athlone T, Shelbourne
1 Cork Hibs, Cork Celtic, Derry C*, Sligo Rovers, St Patrick's Ath

Winners: Celtic 1966–67; Manchester U 1967–68; Liverpool 1976–77, 1977–78, 1980–81, 1983–84; Nottingham F 1978–79, 1979–80; Aston Villa 1981–82

Finalists: Celtic 1969–70; Leeds U 1974–75; Liverpool 1984–85

EUROPEAN CUP-WINNERS' CUP (1960–93)

English clubs
6 Tottenham H
5 Manchester U
4 West Ham U, Liverpool
2 Chelsea, Everton, Manchester C
1 Wolverhampton W, Leicester C, WBA, Leeds U, Sunderland, Southampton, Ipswich T, Arsenal

Scottish clubs
10 Rangers
7 Celtic, Aberdeen
2 Dunfermline Ath, Dundee U
1 Dundee, Hibernian, Hearts, St Mirren, Motherwell, Airdrie

Welsh clubs
13 Cardiff C
7 Wrexham, Swansea C
2 Bangor C
1 Borough U, Newport Co, Merthyr Tydfil

Clubs from Northern Ireland
7 Glentoran
4 Ballymena U, Coleraine, Glenavon
3 Crusaders
2 Ards, Linfield
1 Derry C, Distillery, Portadown, Carrick Rangers, Cliftonville

Clubs from Eire
6 Shamrock R
3 Limerick, Waterford, Dundalk, Bohemians
2 Cork Hibs, Galway U
1 Shelbourne, Cork Celtic, St Patrick's Ath, Finn Harps, Home Farm, Sligo Rovers, University College Dublin, Derry C*, Cork City, Bray Wanderers

Winners: Tottenham H 1962–63; West Ham U 1964–65; Manchester C 1969–70; Chelsea 1970–71; Rangers 1971–72; Aberdeen 1982–83; Everton 1984–85; Manchester U 1990–91

Finalists: Rangers 1960–61, 1966–67; Liverpool 1965–66; Leeds U 1972–73; West Ham U 1975–76; Arsenal 1979–80

EUROPEAN FAIRS CUP & UEFA CUP (1955–93)

English clubs
8 Leeds U, Ipswich T
7 Liverpool
6 Everton, Arsenal, Manchester U
5 Southampton, Tottenham H
4 Manchester C, Birmingham C, Newcastle U, Nottingham F, Wolverhampton W, WBA, Aston Villa
3 Chelsea, Sheffield W
2 Stoke C, Derby Co, QPR
1 Burnley, Coventry C, London Rep XI, Watford

Scottish clubs
16 Dundee U
14 Hibernian
10 Aberdeen
8 Rangers, Hearts, Celtic
5 Dunfermline Ath
4 Dundee
3 St Mirren, Kilmarnock
2 Partick Th
1 Morton, St Johnstone

Clubs from Northern Ireland
11 Glentoran
6 Coleraine
4 Linfield
3 Glenavon
2 Portadown
1 Ards, Ballymena U, Bangor

Clubs from Eire
7 Bohemians
4 Dundalk
3 Finn Harps, Shamrock R
2 Shelbourne, Drumcondra, St Patrick's Ath, Derry C*
1 Cork Hibs, Athlone T, Limerick, Drogheda U, Galway U, Cork City

Winners: Leeds U 1967–68, 1970–71; Newcastle U 1968–69; Arsenal 1969–70; Tottenham H 1971–72, 1983–84; Liverpool 1972–73, 1975–76; Ipswich T 1980–81

Finalists: London 1955–58, Birmingham C 1958–60, 1960–61; Leeds U 1966–67; Wolverhampton W 1971–72; Tottenham H 1973–74; Dundee U 1986–87

Now play in League of Ireland.

SCHOOLS FOOTBALL 1992-93

ESFA BRITISH GAS TROPHY 1992-93

FOURTH ROUND

Coventry v Hull	0-0,2-4
Leicester v E Northumberland	4-1
Dacorum v Thurrock	4-0
North Kent v North Devon	3-0
Gateshead v Kirkby Knowsley	3-4
Walsall v Sheffield	0-2
Blackpool v Doncaster	4-3
Chester v Rotherham	1-2
Bristol v North Herts	2-2, 1-4
Eastleigh v South London	0-1
St Albans v Slough	2-2, 2-1
South East Essex v Croydon	2-0
South Notts v Cannock	3-3, 2-1
Liverpool v Chorley	2-0
Poole & E Dorset v Colchester & N E Essex	0-2
Aldershot v Vale of White Horse	3-3, 1-5

FIFTH ROUND

Hull v Leicester	0-4
Dacorum v North Kent	0-4
Kirkby Knowsley v Sheffield	2-3
Blackpool v Rotherham	1-2
North Herts v South London*	0-2
St Albans v South East Essex	4-3
South Notts v Liverpool	1-1, 1-3
Colchester & N E Essex v Vale of White Horse	1-4

SIXTH ROUND

Leicester v North Kent	3-1
Sheffield v Rotherham	3-2
North Herts v St Albans	1-1, 1-2
Liverpool v Vale of White Horse	4-0

SEMI-FINALS

Leicester v Sheffield	0-2
St Albans v Liverpool	1-2

FINAL

Sheffield v Liverpool	2-2, 0-1

ESFA MARS U.19 INDIVIDUAL SCHOOLS CHAMPIONSHIP 1992-93

SECOND ROUND

Somerset v Cornwall	3-0
Wiltshire v Hampshire A	0-4
Oxfordshire A v South Glamorgan	1-0
Sussex A v Oxfordshire B	5-4
Sussex B v Essex B	7-1
Norfolk A v Bedfordshire	2-1
Suffolk B v Essex A	1-0
Surrey B v Kent B	2-0
Merseyside A v Staffordshire	2-1
S Yorkshire A v Shropshire	0-2
Hereford & Worcester v Merseyside B	1-2
Greater Manchester B v Nottinghamshire	0-0, 1-3
W Yorkshire B v Northumberland	1-1, 0-1
Humberside v Cambridgeshire	1-2
Leicestershire v Derbyshire	0-5
Durham v Cleveland	3-6

THIRD ROUND

Somerset v Hampshire A	1-2
Oxfordshire A v Sussex A	2-3
Sussex B v Norfolk	1-2
Suffolk B v Surrey B	1-3
Merseyside A v Shropshire	5-0
Merseyside B v Nottinghamshire	1-2
Northumberland A v Cambridgeshire	4-3
Derbyshire v Cleveland	1-1, 1-2

FOURTH ROUND

Hampshire A v Sussex A	2-0
Norfolk A v Surrey B	2-0
Merseyside A v Nottinghamshire	1-0
Northumberland A v Cleveland	0-3

SEMI-FINAL

Hampshire A v Norfolk A	1-1, 2-1
Merseyside A v Cleveland	1-4

FINAL

Hampshire A (Taunton's College, Southampton) v Cleveland (Longlands College, Middlesborough)	1-1

ESFA DIAMIK U.16 INDIVIDUAL SCHOOLS CHAMPIONSHIP 1992-93

SECOND ROUND

Cleveland v Northumberland	2-3
S Yorkshire A v Durham A	1-1, 0-1
Merseyside A v Lancashire B	3-3, 3-1
Staffordshire v Clwyd	8-4
Greater Manchester B v Merseyside B	2-2, 2-0
West Midlands A v Hereford & Worcestershire	2-2, 2-4
Lincolnshire A v Cumbria B	2-1
W Yorkshire B v Humberside A	0-3
Essex A v Kent B	1-5
Sussex A v Cambridgeshire	2-1
Leicestershire v Nottinghamshire	3-5
Bedfordshire v Suffolk B	2-0
Cornwall v Wiltshire	0-1
Oxfordshire v Devon B	2-2, 3-0
Dorset v Buckinghamshire	1-2
Sussex B v Inner London	0-2

THIRD ROUND

Northumberland v Durham	1-1, 1-2
Merseyside A v Staffordshire	12-1
Greater Manchester B v Hereford & Worcestershire	3-1
Lincolnshire A v Humberside	1-7
Kent B v Sussex A	7-3
Nottinghamshire v Bedfordshire	1-0
Wiltshire v Oxfordshire	3-2
Buckinghamshire v Inner London	4-0

FOURTH ROUND

Durham A v Merseyside A	3-2
Greater Manchester B v Humberside	0-0, 0-1
Kent B v Nottinghamshire	5-2
Wiltshire v Buckinghamshire	3-5

SEMI-FINALS

Durham A v Humberside	2-1
Kent B v Buckinghamshire	0-0, 0-3

FINAL

Durham A (Farringdon School, Sunderland) v Buckinghamshire (Dr Challoner's GS, Amersham)	2-2

ESFA ADIDAS U.19 COUNTY CHAMPIONSHIP 1992-93

QUARTER-FINAL

Nottinghamshire v Suffolk	1-4

SEMI-FINALS

Suffolk v South Yorkshire	0-1
Devon v Avon	3-2

FINAL

South Yorkshire v Devon	4-1

ESFA ADIDAS U.16 COUNTY CHAMPIONSHIP

SEMI-FINALS
West Midlands v Avon   1-3
Essex v South Yorkshire   2-0

FINAL
Essex v Avon   4-0

ESFA MCDONALDS INDOOR 5-A-SIDE CHAMPIONSHIP (Under 12)

SEMI-FINALS
St Benedict's School v St Paul's   2-0
Pelton Roseberry School v Ixworth School   0-0
*(Pelton qualified because of better record in preliminary
groups)*

FINAL
St Benedict's School v Pelton Roseberry School   0-0
(Trophy shared)

ESFA MONSTER MUNCH 6-A-SIDE CHAMPIONSHIP (Under 11) (at Wembley)

3RD AND 4TH PLACE PLAY-OFFS
East Boldon Junior School (Tyne and Wear) v
    Heathlands Primary School (Birmingham)   2-2

FINAL
Beacon Rise Primary School (Bristol) v Ashtree Junior
    School (Stevenage)   1-1
    (Trophy Shared)

ENGLISH SCHOOLS' F A INTERNATIONAL PROGRAMME 1992-93

UNDER 18
EIRE 2, ENGLAND 4 – Dublin, 26 February
WALES** 1, ENGLAND 1 – Merthyr, 29 March
SWITZERLAND** 2, ENGLAND 3 – Cwmbran, 31
March

ENGLAND 2, AUSTRIA 1 – Middlesbrough, 21 April
HOLLAND 3, ENGLAND 0 – Heemskerk, 5 May

***Denotes Centenary Shield Match*

CENTENARY SHIELD FINAL TABLE SEASON 1992-93

	P	W	D	L	F	A	Pts
England	2	1	1	0	4	3	3
Switzerland	2	1	0	1	4	4	2
Wales	2	0	1	1	2	3	1

VICTORY SHIELD FINAL TABLE SEASON 1992-93

	P	W	D	L	F	A	Pts
SCOTLAND	3	2	1	0	5	1	5
ENGLAND	3	2	0	1	4	3	4
N IRELAND	3	1	0	2	5	4	2
WALES	3	0	1	2	1	7	1

UNDER 15
ENGLAND 1, EIRE 0 – Reading, 13 February
ENGLAND* 1, SCOTLAND 2 – Wembley, 13 March
WALES* 1, ENGLAND 2 – Swansea, 22 March
N IRELAND* 0, ENGLAND 1 – Newtownards, 2
April
ENGLAND 0, AUSTRIA 1 – Walsall, 7 April
SWITZERLAND 2, ENGLAND 3 – Zurich, 18 May
ENGLAND 0, GERMANY 0 – Wembley, 12 June
ENGLAND 3, GERMANY 0 – Sheffield, 14 June

VICTORY SHIELD RESULTS 1992-93
SCOTLAND 3, N IRELAND 0
ENGLAND 1, SCOTLAND 2
WALES 1,ENGLAND 2
N IRELAND 0, ENGLAND 1
N IRELAND 5, WALES 0
SCOTLAND 0, WALES 0

BOODLE & DUNTHORNE INDEPENDENT SCHOOLS CUP

FIRST ROUND
Byes – St Bede's, Repton, Lancing, Aldenham.
Winchester 0, Latymer Upper 10
Chigwell 1, Bradfield 3
Alleyn's 3, Westminster 4
Malvern 0, Highgate 2
John Lyon 1, Charterhouse 5
Ardingly 6, Wellingborough 1
Forest 7, KES., Witley 1
Brentwood 4, Kimbolton 1
QEGS., Blackburn 0, Bolton 2
Manchester GS 2, Shrewsbury 3 *aet*
Bury GS 1, Wolverhampton GS 3
King's, Chester 1, Hulme GS 2 *aet*

SECOND ROUND
Hulme GS 2, Lancing 3
Forest 3, Repton 0
Charterhouse 5, Westminster 1
Highgate 1, Aldenham 0

Bolton 0, Bradfield 1
Shrewsbury 2, Latymer Upper 0
Wolverhampton GS 0, Brentwood 7
Ardingly 1, St Bede's 2

THIRD ROUND
Brentwood 0, St Bede's 2
Bradfield 1, Charterhouse 2
Forest 6, Lancing 3
Highgate 0, Shrewsbury 3

SEMI-FINALS
Shrewsbury 2, Charterhouse 4 *aet*
Forest 3, St Bede's 2

FINAL
Charterhouse 2, Forest 2 *aet*
    (Forest won on penalties)

WORLD CLUB CHAMPIONSHIP

Played annually up to 1974 and intermittently since then between the winners of the European Cup and the winners of the South American Champions Cup — known as the Copa Libertadores. In 1980 the winners were decided by one match arranged in Tokyo in February 1981 and the venue has been the same since.

1960 Real Madrid beat Penarol 0-0, 5-1	1977 Boca Juniors beat Borussia Moenchengladbach*
1961 Penarol beat Benfica 0-1, 5-0, 2-1	2-2, 3-0
1962 Santos beat Benfica 3-2, 5-2	1978 Not contested
1963 Santos beat AC Milan 2-4, 4-2, 1-0	1979 Olimpia beat Malmö* 1-0, 2-1
1964 Inter-Milan beat Independiente 0-1, 2-0, 1-0	1980 Nacional beat Nottingham Forest 1-0
1965 Inter-Milan beat Independiente 3-0, 0-0	1981 Flamengo beat Liverpool 3-0
1966 Penarol beat Real Madrid 2-0, 2-0	1982 Penarol beat Aston Villa 2-0
1967 Racing Club beat Celtic 0-1, 2-1, 1-0	1983 Gremio Porto Alegre beat SV Hamburg 2-1
1968 Estudiantes beat Manchester United 1-0, 1-1	1984 Independiente beat Liverpool 1-0
1969 AC Milan beat Estudiantes 3-0, 1-2	1985 Juventus beat Argentinos Juniors 4-2 on penalties
1970 Feyenoord beat Estudiantes 2-2, 1-0	after a 2-2 draw
1971 Nacional beat Panathinaikos* 1-1, 2-1	1986 River Plate beat Steaua Bucharest 1-0
1972 Ajax beat Independiente 1-1, 3-0	1987 FC Porto beat Penarol 2-1 after extra time
1973 Independiente beat Juventus* 1-0	1988 Nacional (Uru) beat PSV Eindhoven 7-6 on
1974 Atlético Madrid* beat Independiente 0-1, 2-0	penalties after 1-1 draw
1975 Independiente and Bayern Munich could not agree	1989 AC Milan beat Atletico Nacional (Col) 1-0 after
dates; no matches.	extra time
1976 Bayern Munich beat Cruzeiro 2-0, 0-0	1990 AC Milan beat Olimpia 3-0
	1991 Red Star Belgrade beat Colo Colo 3-0

*European Cup runners-up; winners declined to take part.

1992

12 December in Tokyo

Sao Paulo (1) 2 *(Rai 26, 79)*

Barcelona (1) 1 *(Stoichkov 13)* 80,000

Sao Paulo: Zetti; Victor, Adilson, Ronaldo, Pintado, Ronaldo Luiz, Muller, Toninho Cerezo (Dinho 83), Palinha, Rai, Cafu.
Barcelona: Zubizarreta; Ferrer, Guardiola, Koeman, Eusebio, Bakero (Goicoechea 51), Amor, Stoichkov, Laudrup, Witschge, Beguiristain (Nadal 79).
Referee: Loustau (Argentina).

EUROPEAN SUPER CUP

Played annually between the winners of the European Champions' Cup and the European Cup-Winners' Cup.

Previous Matches

1972	Ajax beat Rangers 3-1, 3-2
1973	Ajax beat AC Milan 0-1, 6-0
1974	Not contested
1975	Dynamo Kiev beat Bayern Munich 1-0, 2-0
1976	Anderlecht beat Bayern Munich 4-1, 1-2
1977	Liverpool beat Hamburg 1-1, 6-0
1978	Anderlecht beat Liverpool 3-1, 1-2
1979	Nottingham F beat Barcelona 1-0, 1-1
1980	Valencia beat Nottingham F 1-0, 1-2
1981	Not contested
1982	Aston Villa beat Barcelona 0-1, 3-0
1983	Aberdeen beat Hamburg 0-0, 2-0
1984	Juventus beat Liverpool 2-0
1985	Juventus v Everton not contested due to UEFA ban
	on English clubs
1986	Steaua Bucharest beat Dynamo Kiev 1-0
1987	FC Porto beat Real Madrid 1-0, 1-0
1988	KV Mechelen beat PSV Eindhoven 3-0, 0-1
1989	AC Milan beat Barcelona 1-1, 1-0
1990	AC Milan beat Sampdoria 1-1, 2-0
1991	Manchester U beat Red Star Belgrade 1-0

1992-93

First Leg, 10 February 1993, Bremen

Werder Bremen (0) 1 *(Allofs 88)*

Barcelona (1) 1 *(Salinas 38)* 22,098

Werder Bremen: Reck; Borowka, Bratseth, Legat, Bockenfeld, Neubarth, Votava, Herzog, Eilts, Bode (Kohn 69), Hobsch (Allofs 77).
Barcelona: Zubizarreta; Ferrer, Koeman, Eusebio, Nadal, Goicoechea, Bakero (Beguiristain 67), Amor, Salinas (Christiansen 83), Witschge, Stoichkov.
Referee: Nielsen (Denmark).

Second Leg, 10 March 1993, Barcelona

Barcelona (1) 2 *(Stoichkov 32, Goicoechea 48)*

Werder Bremen (1) 1 *(Rufer 41 (pen))* 75,000

Barcelona: Zubizarreta; Ferrer, Koeman, Eusebio, Nadal, Guardiola (Salinas 79), Bakero (Beguiristain 50), Amor, Goicoechea, Laudrup, Stoichkov.
Werder Bremen: Reck; Wolter, Borowka, Bratseth, Legat (Allofs 77), Schaaf (Gundelach 30), Eilts, Bode, Herzog, Hobsch, Rufer.
Referee: Karlsson (Sweden).

SOUTH AMERICA

COPA AMERICA
(South American Championships)

Group A
Ecuador 6, Venezuela 1
Uruguay 1, USA 0
Ecuador 2, USA 0
Uruguay 2, Venezuela 2
USA 3, Venezuela 3
Ecuador 2, Uruguay 1

	P	W	D	L	F	A	Pts
Ecuador	3	3	0	0	10	2	6
Uruguay	3	1	1	1	4	4	3
Venezuela	3	0	2	1	6	11	2
USA	3	0	1	2	3	6	1

Group B
Brazil 0, Peru 0
Paraguay 1, Chile 0
Chile 3, Brazil 2
Paraguay 1, Peru 1
Peru 1, Chile 0
Brazil 3, Paraguay 0

	P	W	D	L	F	A	Pts
Peru	3	1	2	0	2	1	4
Brazil	3	1	1	1	5	3	3
Paraguay	3	1	1	1	2	4	3
Chile	3	1	0	2	3	4	2

Group C
Colombia 2, Mexico 1
Argentina 1, Bolivia 0
Colombia 1, Bolivia 1
Mexico 1, Argentina 1
Argentina 1, Colombia 0
Mexico 0, Bolivia 0

	P	W	D	L	F	A	Pts
Argentina	3	2	1	0	3	1	5
Colombia	3	1	1	1	3	3	3
Mexico	3	0	2	1	2	3	2
Bolivia	3	0	2	1	1	2	2

Quarter-finals
Mexico 4, Peru 2
Argentina 1, Brazil 1
Ecuador 3, Paraguay 0
Colombia 1, Uruguay 1
Colombia won 5-3 on penalties

Semi-finals
Ecuador 0, Mexico 2
Argentina 0, Colombia 0
Argentina won 6-5 on penalties

Third place match
Ecuador 0, Colombia 1

Final
Argentina 2, Mexico 1

COPA LIBERTA DORES 1993
First Round
Group A

	P	W	D	L	F	A	Pts
Universitario (Per)	6	3	3	0	14	7	9
Sporting Cristal (Per)	6	3	1	2	13	9	7
Minerven (Ven)	6	1	2	3	6	12	4
Caracas (Ven)	6	1	2	3	5	10	4

Group B

	P	W	D	L	F	A	Pts
Univ Catolica (Chi)	6	3	2	1	15	8	8
Bolivar (Bol)	6	3	1	2	10	7	7
Cobreloa (Chi)	6	2	3	1	8	9	7
San Jose (Bol)	6	1	0	5	8	17	2

Group C

	P	W	D	L	F	A	Pts
Nacional (Ura)	6	3	2	1	12	6	8
Nacional (Ecu)	6	3	0	3	9	11	6
Barcelona (Ecu)	6	2	1	3	8	7	5
Bella Vista (Uru)	6	2	1	3	6	11	5

Group D

	P	W	D	L	F	A	Pts
Flamengo (Br)	6	3	1	2	9	7	7
America (Col)	6	3	1	2	12	11	7
Nacional (Col)	6	3	1	2	8	6	7
Internacional (Br)	6	0	3	3	4	9	3

Group E

	P	W	D	L	F	A	Pts
Cerro Porteno (Par)	6	2	3	1	5	4	7
Newell's Old Boys (Arg)	6	1	4	1	4	4	6
Olimpia (Par)	6	1	4	1	4	4	6
River Plate (Arg)	6	1	3	2	4	5	5

Newell's Old Boys took second place after drawing lots

Second Round First Leg
Universitario 2, Barcelona 1
Univ Catolica 2, Nacional (Col) 0
Nacional (Ura) 1, Olimpia 2
Flamengo 8, Minerven 2
Cerro Porteno 1, Cobreloa 2
Nacional (Ecu) 3, Sporting Cristal 0
America 2, Boliva 1
Newell's Old Boys 2, Sao Paulo (Br) 0

Second Leg
Barcelona 3, Universitario 0
Nacional (Col) 2, Univ Catolica 1
Olimpia 3, Nacional (Uru) 0
Minerven 0, Flamengo 1
Cobreloa 0, Cerro Porteno 2
Sporting Cristal 4, Nacional (Ecu) 0
Bolivar 1, America 1
Sao Paulo 4, Newell's Old Boys 0

Quarter-finals First Leg
Flamengo 1, Sao Paulo 1
Olimpia 1, Cerro Porteno 1
Univ Catolica 3, Barcelona 1
America 2, Sporting Cristal 2

Second Leg
Sao Paulo 2, Flemengo 0
Cerro Porteno 0, Olimpia 0
Cerro Porteno won 4-2 on penalties
Barcelona 0, Univ Catolica 1
Sporting Cristal 2, America 3

Semi-finals First Leg
Sao Paulo 1, Cerro Porteno 0
Univ Catolica 1, America 0

Semi-finals Second Leg
Cerro Porteno 0, Sao Paulo 0
America 2, Univ Catolica 2

Final First Leg
Sao Paulo 5, Univ Catolica 1

Final Second Leg
Univ Catolica 2, Sao Paulo 0

SOUTH AMERICAN SUPER CUP

First Round, First Leg
Boca Juniors 2, Estudiantes 1
Santos 1, Sao Paulo 1
Colo Colo 1, Olimpia 0
Argentinos Juniors 1, River Plate 2
Penarol 2, Nacional (Uruguay) 2
Racing 2, Independiente 1
Gremio 1, Flamengo 1
Nacional (Colombia) 1, Cruzeiro 1

First Round, Second Leg
Nacional (Uruguay) 1, Penarol 0
Estudiantes 1, Boc Juniors 0
(*Estudiantes won 4-3 on penalties*)
Olimpia 1, Colo Colo 0
(*Olimpia won 3-2 on penalties*)
River Plate 3, Argentinos Juniors 0

Racing 0, Independiente 0
Sao Paulo 4, Santos 1
Flamengo 1, Gremio 0

Second Round, First Leg
Sao Paulo 1, Olimpia 2
Cruzeiro 2, River Plate 0
Flamengo 1, Estudiantes 0
Racing w.p. Nacional (Uruguay)
(*Nacional forced to withdraw due
to players strike in Uruguay*)

Second Round, Second Leg
Olimpia 1, Sao Paulo 0
River Plate 2, Cruzeiro 0
(*Cruzeiro won 5-4 on penalties*)
Estudiantes 1, Flamengo 1

Semi-finals, First Leg
Flamengo 3, Racing 3
Olimpia 0, Cruzeiro 1

Semi-finals, Second Leg
Cruzeiro 2, Olimpia 2
Racing 1, Flamengo 0

Final First Leg
Cruzeiro 4, Racing 0

Final Second Leg
Racing 1, Cruzeiro 0

International matches 1992

Argentina
Japan (a) 1-0; Wales (a) 1-0; Australia (h) 2-0; Uruguay (a) 0-0; Ivory Coast (a) 4-0; Saudi Arabia (a) 3-1; Poland (h) 2-0.

Brazil
USA (h) 3-0; Finland (h) 3-1; Uruguay (a) 0-1; England (a) 1-1; Mexico (a) 5-0; USA (a) 1-0; France (a) 2-0; Costa Rica (h) 4-2; Uruguay (h) 1-2; Germany (h) 3-1.

Colombia
USA (a) 1-0; Mexico (a) 0-0.

Ecuador
Guatemala (a) 1-1; Costa Rica (a) 1-2; Uruguay (a) 1-3; Costa Rica (h) 1-1; Peru (a) 1-1.

Peru
Ecuador (h) 1-1.

Uruguay
Brazil (h) 1-0; Australia (h) 2-0; Ecuador (h) 3-1; Guatemala (h) 2-1; Costa Rica (h) 2-1; Argentina (h) 0-0; Brazil (a) 2-1; Poland (h) 0-1; Germany (h) 1-4.

Champions
Argentina: River Plate
Bolivia:
Brazil: Flamengo
Chile: Cobreloa
Colobia: America
Ecuador: El Nacional
Paraguay: Cerro Porteno
Peru: Universitario
Uruguay: Nacional
Venezuela: Caracas

AFRICA

1994 AFRICAN NATIONS CUP
Qualifying Tournament (Tunisia (hosts), Ivory Coast (holders) through to finals)

Preliminary Round
Lesotho 0, Botswana 0
Guinea Bissau 3, Caper Verde 1
Botswana 0, Lesotho 4
Cape Verde 0, Guinea Bissau 1

Group 1

	P	W	D	L	F	A	Pts
Gabon	4	2	2	0	5	1	6
Niger	4	2	1	1	7	5	5
Cameroon	4	1	3	0	2	0	5
Benin	4	0	0	4	2	10	0

Group 2

	P	W	D	L	F	A	Pts
Nigeria	4	2	1	1	6	1	5
Ethiopia	4	2	1	1	7	5	5
Uganda	4	1	2	1	6	6	4
Sudan	4	0	2	2	1	8	1

Group 3

	P	W	D	L	F	A	Pts
Sierra Leone	6	4	2	0			
Algeria	7	4	2	1	13	4	10
Senegal	6	3	1	2	10	5	7
Togo	6	0	4	2	1	7	4
Guinea Bissau	7	0	1	6	2	19	0

Group 4

	P	W	D	L	F	A	Pts
Zaire	2	2	0	0	5	1	4
Mozambique	2	1	0	1	3	2	2
Kenya	2	0	1	1	3	5	1
Lesotho	2	0	1	1	2	5	1

Group 5

	P	W	D	L	F	A	Pts
Zambia	4	3	1	0	6	1	7
Zimbabwe	4	2	2	0	6	2	6
South Africa	4	0	2	2	2	6	2
Mauritius	4	0	1	3	1	6	1

Group 6

	P	W	D	L	F	A	Pts
Burundi	3	1	2	0	3	2	4
Guinea	2	1	1	0	3	2	3
Congo	3	0	1	2	0	2	1
Chad withdrew							

Group 7

	P	W	D	L	F	A	Pts
Ghana	1	1	0	0	1	0	2
Liberia	1	0	0	1	0	1	0
Tanzania and Burkino Faso withdrew							

Group 8

	P	W	D	L	F	A	Pts
Egypt	4	2	1	1	4	2	5
Malawi	4	2	1	1	3	3	5
Mali	4	1	1	2	4	5	3
Morocco	4	1	1	2	2	3	3
Mauritania and Libya withdrew							
(*Competition still being played*)							

FOOTBALL AND THE LAW

The law created a running theme for football throughout the season under review. It began and ended in the courts, for situations both on and off the field of play.

The Premier League itself had surfaced from hotly contested litigation between the FA and the Football League. The Venables-Sugar Spurs clash was, in a curious way, a more spectacular re-run of share transfer litigation that took place nearly 60 years ago in London's Chancery Division of the High Court of Justice.

An attempt was made to tackle the transfer share holdings blocked by the then company's Articles of Association at a time when a successful promotion in the early 1930's was followed rapidly through injury and refusal to enter the transfer market, by a humiliating relegation notwithstanding the stalents of Arthur Rowe, Willie Hall, Willie Evans and George Hunt, at a time when the Arsenal ran riot with Highbury honours. It failed as if a warning to Terry Venables' intermediate attempts to block his sacking. That particular final contest result will not be known until after the new season has begun.

On the field no less spectacular attention was paid to the controversial evidence of the FA Chief Executive Graham Kelly in Salisbury Crown Court. He testified on behalf of Brentford's Gary Blissett, who had been charged with a serious assault on Torquay United's John Uzzell, to the effect that he attended four matches a week and saw about 200 elbow to head collisions. i.e. about 50 a match. This produced challengeable responses from the Professional Footballers Association, the Referees Association and other sources within the game. I have pointed out in more than one legal source that his evidence should have been objected to by the prosecuting barrister or the judge as inadmissible, because Kelly was not sufficiently expert to testify about the Laws of the Game (within the province of referees) or about playing techniques (a coaching domain), and even if that had been overruled, leave should have been sought to recall the referee who had penalised Blissett by way of rebutting evidence.

In parallel proceedings, Paul Elliott of Chelsea commenced a civil claim for personal injuries caused by an alleged illegal tackle by Dean Saunders when playing for Liverpool, in proceedings which are still pending and to be decided in the High Court; and that in turn gave to the disclosure that John O'Neill, who was injured on his debut for Norwich City, was suing John Fashanu and Wimbledon in proceedings begun before Paul Elliott's claim.

Against that background it was not surprising that on 6th February 1993, the 35th anniversary of the Munich Air Disaster, Old Trafford, Manchester saw the foundation of the British Association for Sport and Law, based at the only Sports Law Unit at a British University, the new Manchester Metropolitan University. Raymond Farrell, the creator of the United is the Chief Executive under the Department of Law there, headed by Peter Rayburn, with two practicising lawyers, E. Maurice Atkins, a solicitor-director of Manchester and myself representing the Bar of England and Wales, as co-founders.

In my capacity as President, I was privileged to present to the Association and Manchester United, an inscribed photograph of the United Kingdom Olympic Games Football XI, winners of the 1908 competition which included Harold Hardman, later a solicitor and chairman of Manchester United from 1951 until he died in 1965.

The first Newsletter of the newly formed Association published in July contained a timely notice by Rick Parry, the Chief Executive of the newly-formed FA Premier League:

'It is . . . wholly unrealistic to imagine that sport can exist in a vacuum, somehow isolated from the law. The promotion of a better understanding between those involved in sports and legal practitioners is surely a laudable, and wholly worthwhile, objective.'

Season 1992–93 certainly justified that message.

EDWARDS GRAYSON
President, British Association for Sport and Law

GM VAUXHALL CONFERENCE 1992–1993

Deprived of the championship on goal difference in 1991–92, Wycombe Wanderers were 15 points clear of their nearest rivals in taking the title in impressive fashion.

Slough Town, who had been as close on their heels as anyone for much of the season, faded in the latter stages and had to settle for fifth place at the end. Bromsgrove Rovers were confirmed as runners-up after a fine rally towards the run-in and Dagenham & Redbridge maintained their position to finish third. Yeovil Town were fourth after improvement in the second half of the campaign.

Wycombe were well supported at home and away. At their well-appointed Adams Park ground they averaged 4,602 spectators per game and should prove an able acquisition for the Football League.

GM VAUXHALL CONFERENCE TABLE 1992–93

		Home			Goals		Away			Goals		
	Pl	W	D	L	F	A	W	D	L	F	A	Pts
Wycombe Wanderers	42	13	5	3	46	16	11	6	4	38	21	83
Bromsgrove Rovers	42	9	7	5	35	22	9	7	5	32	27	68
Dagenham & Redbridge	42	10	5	6	48	29	9	6	6	27	18	67
Yeovil Town	42	13	5	3	42	21	5	7	9	17	28	66
Slough Town	42	12	3	6	39	28	6	8	7	21	27	65
Stafford Rangers	42	7	6	8	22	24	11	4	6	33	23	64
Bath City	42	9	8	4	29	23	6	6	9	24	23	59
Woking	42	9	2	10	30	33	8	6	7	28	29	59
Kidderminster Harriers	42	9	5	7	26	30	5	11	5	34	30	58
Altrincham	42	7	7	7	21	25	8	6	7	28	27	58
Northwich Victoria	42	5	6	10	24	29	11	2	8	44	26	56
Stalybridge Celtic	42	7	10	4	25	26	6	7	8	23	29	56
Kettering Town	42	10	5	6	36	28	4	8	9	25	35	55
Gateshead	42	9	6	6	27	19	5	4	12	26	37	52
Telford United	42	9	5	7	31	24	5	5	11	24	36	52
Merthyr Tydfil	42	4	9	8	26	37	10	1	10	25	42	52
Witton Albion	42	5	9	7	30	34	6	8	7	32	31	50
Macclesfield Town	42	7	9	5	23	20	5	4	12	17	30	49
Runcorn	42	8	3	10	32	36	5	7	9	26	40	49
Welling United	42	8	6	7	34	37	4	6	11	23	35	48
Farnborough Town	42	8	5	8	34	36	4	6	11	34	51	47
Boston United	42	5	6	10	23	31	4	7	10	27	38	40

Note: Dagenham & Redbridge deducted 1 point.

GM VAUXHALL CONFERENCE ATTENDANCES 1991·93

Aggregate 1992–93	Average Gate	% Increase	Gates over 1000	Gates over 2000	Clubs with % Increase
567,609	1,229	+1%	43%	12.5%	10

GM VAUXHALL CONFERENCE CLUB ATTENDANCES 1992–93

Club	Aggregate 1992–93	Average 1992–93	Average 1991–92	% Change
Altrincham	16,982	809	868	− 7
Bath City	13,481	642	704	− 8
Boston United	21,871	1,041	1,173	−11
Bromsgrove Rovers	30,001	1,429	836	+71
Dagenham & Redbridge	25,227	1,201	719	+67
Farnborough Town	17,287	823	975	−16
Gateshead	8,822	420	449	− 6
Kettering Town	30,543	1,454	1,857	−22
Kidderminster Harriers	30,226	1,439	1,302	+11
Macclesfield Town	13,819	658	755	−13
Merthyr Tydfil	12,647	602	650	− 7
Northwich Victoria	17,120	815	820	−
Runcorn	12,922	615	629	− 2
Slough Town	26,079	1,242	924	+34
Stafford Rangers	19,849	945	873	+ 8
Stalybridge Celtic	16,984	809	581	+39
Telford United	21,476	1,023	1,039	− 1
Welling United	19,894	947	840	+13
Witton Albion	19,095	909	913	−
Woking	41,731	1,987	1,880	+ 6
Wycombe Wanderers	96,638	4,602	3,606	+28
Yeovil Town	54,915	2,615	2,103	+24

HIGHEST CROWDS — ATTENDANCES 1992–93

7230	Wycombe Wanderers v Slough Town	23.3.93	5000	Wycombe Wanderers v Woking	6.4.93
6488	Yeovil Town v Bath City	28.12.92	4911	Woking v Wycombe Wanderers	26.12.92
6284	Wycombe Wanderers v Altrincham	17.4.93	4731	Wycombe Wanderers v Witton Albion	24.10.92
6220	Wycombe Wanderers v Runcorn	15.4.93	4569	Wycombe Wanderers v Stafford Rangers	7.11.92
5748	Wycombe Wanderers v Macclesfield Town	1.5.93	4500	Slough Town v Wycombe Wanderers	13.4.93
5495	Yeovil Town v Bromsgrove Rovers	19.12.92	5748	Wycombe Wanderers v Macclesfield Town	1.5.93
5106	Wycombe Wanderers v D'ham & Redbridge 16.2.93		5495	Yeovil Town v Bromsgrove Rovers	19.12.92

GM VAUXHALL CONFERENCE LEADING GOALSCORERS 1992–93

GMVC		FAC	VFAT	DC
32	David Leworthy *(Farnborough Town)* +	1	5	1
23	Mark Whitehouse *(Bromsgrove Rovers)* +	—	2	1
21	Malcolm O'Connor *(Northwich Victoria)* +	2	1	3
20	Keith Scott *(Wycombe Wanderers)* +	1	5	2
19	Paul Cavell *(Dagenham & Redbridge)* +	8	1	1
	Terry Robins *(Welling United)* +	1	2	1
	Andy Sayer *(Slough Town)* +	1	1	—
	Karl Thomas *(Wilson Albion)* +	—	3	—
17	Gary Abbott *(Welling United)* +	—	1	1
16	Phil Brown *(Kettering Town)* +	2	—	—
	Gary Jones *(Boston United)* +	2	5	1
	Mickey Spencer *(Yeovil Town)* +	2	1	2
15	Tony Hemmings *(Northwich Victoria)* +	1	—	4
	Alan Lamb *(Gateshead)* +	7	1	—

SPONSORSHIP AWARDS 1992–93

	Vauxhall Motors	Title Awards	Vauxhall Goals Jackpot	Vauxhall Fair Play	Drinkwise Cup	PPA	Sportscast (1992)	Total
	£	£	£	£	£	£	£	£
Altrincham	6500				200	1500	2000	10,200
Bath City	6500		250		200	1500	2000	10,450
Boston United	6500		167		200	1500	2000	10,367
Bromsgrove Rogers	6500	4000	167		200	1500	—	12,367
Dagenham & Redbridge	6500	3000	1000		750	1500	2000	14,750
Farnborough Town	6500		250	3000	200	1500	2000	13,450
Gateshead	6500				200	1500	2000	10,200
Kettering Town	6500		500		200	1500	2000	10,700
Kidderminster Harriers	6500				200	1500	2000	10,200
Macclesfield Town	6500				750	1500	2000	10,750
Merthyr Tydfil	6500				200	1500	2000	10,200
Northwich Victoria	6500		500		4000	1500	2000	14,500
Runcorn	6500		250		200	1500	2000	10,450
Slough Town	6500				200	1500	2000	10,200
Stafford Rangers	6500				200	1500	2000	10,200
Stalybridge Celtic	6500				200	1500	—	8200
Telford United	6500				200	1500	2000	10,200
Welling United	6500				200	1500	2000	10,200
Witton Albion	6500				200	1500	2000	10,200
Woking	6500				200	1500	—	8200
Wycombe Wanderers	6500	8000	750		2000	1500	2000	20,750
Yeovil Town	6500		167		200	1500	2000	10,367

HIGHEST AGGREGATE SCORES

Telford United 6-3 Farnborough Town 12.9.92
Kidderminster H. 5-3 Northwich Victoria 1.5.93
D'ham & Redbridge 4-4 Slough Town 8.2.93
Runcorn 4-4 Witton Albion 17.4.93
Boston United 3-5 Northwich Victoria 12.12.92

LARGEST HOME WINS

D'ham & Redbridge 6-1 Merthyr Tydfil 6.4.93
Farnborough Town 6-1 Gateshead 22.8.92
Kettering Town 5-0 Slough Town 3.11.92
Telford United 5-0 Merthyr Tydfil 12.4.93
Welling United 5-0 Merthyr Tydfil 21.11.92

LARGEST AWAY WINS

Stalybridge Celtic 0-6 Northwich Victoria 2.1.93
Bath City 0-5 Northwich Victoria 30.1.93
Altrincham 1-5 Stafford Rangers 30.1.93
Kidderminster H. 1-5 Farnborough Town 27.2.93
Merthyr Tydfil 1-5 Woking 24.11.92
Welling United 1-5 Northwich Victoria 20.3.93
Woking 1-5 Kidderminster H. 3.4.93

CONSECUTIVE VICTORIES

9 Wycombe Wanderers
5 Bromsgrove Rovers, Northwich Victoria, Stafford Rangers, Yeovil Town
4 Dagenham & Redbridge, Macclesfield Town, Runcorn, Slough Town, Stafford Rangers, Yeovil Town

CONSECUTIVE CONFERENCE DEFEATS

6 Northwich Victoria, Telford United
5 Boston United, Macclesfield Town, Welling United
4 Boston United, Farnborough Town, Runcorn, Stafford Rangers, Telford United, Welling United, Yeovil Town

MATCHES WITHOUT DEFEAT

10 Wycombe Wanderers (2)
9 Witton Albion
8 Altrincham, Bromsgrove Rovers (2), Kidderminster Harriers, Stafford Rangers, Yeovil Town

MATCHES WITHOUT SUCCESS

13 Witton Albion
12 Boston United
10 Macclesfield Town, Stafford Rangers
9 Merthyr Tydfil, Northwich Victoria

GM VAUXHALL CONFERENCE 1992–93

APPEARANCES AND GOALSCORERS

Altrincham
Conference Appearances: Alcide, C 2(1); Baker, W 2; Bradshaw, C 9(5); Carmody, M 32(2); Dennis, R 6; Dyson, C 16(5); Embert, D 4; Farrar, M 16; France, P 33; Freeman, C 26(6); Gorton, A 9; Green, R 13(1); Gresty, S0(1); Harris, R 34(3); Hayde, M 20(9); Hodgert, C 3; Learoyd, S 3; Lloyd, D 1; Newell, A 6; Ogley, M32(1); Paladino, J 13; Pollitt, M 6; Raymond, S 2(2); Richards, A 0(2); Rudge, S 6(1); Saunders, S33(1); Sidderley, R 33; Sharpe, P 2(3); Smith, J 22(3); Tunnacliffe, I 21; Thompson, I 5; Wilson, R6(2); Woodhead, S 36(3)
Goals (49): Freeman 8, France 7, Bradshaw 5, Tunnacliffe 5, Harris 3, Green 3, Saunders 3, Smith 3, Woodhead 3, Carmody 2, Raymond 2, Dyson 1, Emmett 1, Thompson 1, Hayde 1, Ogley 1.

Bath City
Conference Appearances: Bailey, P 1; Banks, C 41; Baverstock, R 42; Boyle, M 31; Brown, K 2; Cousins, R 33; Crowley, R 40; Dicks, G 33; Elliott, D 28; Frankland, T 1; Gill, J 39; Hedges, I 18; Jones, V 6; Maddison, L 4; Mings, A 22; Mogg, D 42; Palmer, D 19; Randall, P 28; Ricketts, T 5; Singleton, D 31; Smart, G 33; Vernon, D 26; Weston, I 27; Withey, G 33
Goals (53): Crowley 11, Vernon 7, Boyle 6, Gill 6, Mings 5, Smart 5, Withey 5, Cousins 4, Randall 1, Singleton 1, OG 2.

Boston United
Conference Appearances: Allpress, T 4; Bastock, P 42; Casey, P 26; Cavin, P 1; Chambers, S 37; Cork, D 6; Coverdale, D 7; Curtis, A 8; Curtis, H 13; Curtis, R 21; Davis, D 8; Futcher, R 2; Graham, J 25; Grayson, N 36; Hallam, M 6; Hardy, M 36; Howarth, L 7; Jones, G 32; Knight, I 10; Lee, G 25; Lister, S 7; McJannet, L 5; McKenzie, R 1; Miller, J 3; Moss, D 17; Munton, D 4; Oakes, K 1; Slack, T 10; Sorrell, T 1; Stoutt, S 23; Toone, R 2; West, G 10; White, C 9
Goals (50): Jones 16, Moss 10, Graham 7, Grayson 4, Trott 4, Hardy 2, Casey 1, Coverdale 1, Curtis, A 1, Howarth 1, Miller 1, Munton 1, Stoutt 1

Bromsgrove Rovers
Conference Appearances: Brain, S 1; Brighton, S 35; Burgher, S 11; Byrne, P 1; Carty, P 6; Cooksey, S 25; Cooper, S 15; Gray, B 33; Crisp, M 35; Daly, T 33; Davis, M 6; Grealish, T 20; Green, R 13; Hanks, C 9; Honeyfield, P 2; Oakes, M 4; Omera, S 33; Richardson, K 34; Ross, J 3; Scandrett, R 4; Shilvock, R36; Skelding, J 36; Stott, S 33; Wardle, P 31; Webb, P 42; Whitehouse, M 39; Williams, L 6.
Goals (67): Whitehouse 23, Webb 8, Crisp 7, Gray 7, Shilvock 5, Daly 4, Burgher 2, Cooper 2, Stott 2, Brain1, Brighton 1, Carty 1, Hanks 1, Omera 1, Richardson 1, Wardle 1.

Dagenham & Redbridge
Conference Appearances: Allen, G 1(1); Blackford, G 34(2); Broom, J 36(1); Butterworth, G 38(3); Cavell, P 38; Conner, S 38; DeSouza, M 3; Georgiou, G 3(2); Kimble, G 10(15); Marquis, P 6; Mayes, B 7(2); McKenna, J 40(1); Nuttall, M 29(2); Owers, A 32(1); Pamphlett, T 29; Pape, A 1; Porter, S 1; Richardson, I 9(2); Richardson, P 9(4); Shirtliff, P 32(1); Smart, L 2(1); Stebbing, G 22(3); Tomlinson, D 2; Walsh, M6(6); Warner, J 1(1); Watts, P 41.
Goals (75): Cavell 19, Blackford 11, Nuttell 8, Broom 6, Butterworth 6, Pamphlett 6, Conner 3, I Richardson3, Walsh 3, Kimble 2, P Richardson 2, Stebbing 2, DeSouza 1, Owers 1, OG 2.

Farnborough Town
Conference Appearances: Baker, S 30; Batey, P 18(2); Bell, P 3(5); Broome, B 7(2); Bye, A 36; Coleman, D 29(3); Coles, A1(1); Collins, E 11(2); Coney, D 23; Danzey, M 1; Goodsell, B 1; Holland, M 21; Holmes, D 16; Horton, J 42; Howells, G 9; Jones, M 7(2); Leworthy, D 42;

Manning, P 14; Morris, D 3; Newbery, R11(7); Power, J 26; Pratt, B 8(3); Read, S 10(8); Rogers, A 11(2); Savage, I 12(8); Taylor, M 6; Turkington, M 5(3); Wigmore, J 41; Williamson, D 4; Wilson, R 14(2).
Goals (68): Leworthy 32, Horton 9, Coney 6, Wilson 4, Coleman 3, Read 3, Wigmore 3, Bye 2, Collins 2, Baker 1, Batey 1, Newbery 1, Rogers 1.

Gateshead
Conference Appearances: Askew, W 25(12); Bell, D 32; Bond, R 2(1); Chilton, A 8(1); Cooke, J 31(2); Corner, D 26(1); Davison, W 5; Dobson, P 18; Elliott, A 2(19); Elliott, S 28(4); Farnaby, C 21(12); Farrey, M 35 (2); Guthrie, S 21(8); Halliday, B 33; Higgins, S 25(2); Johnson, W 5(6); Lamb, A 40; Lowery, A 3(4); Mason, P 1; Nicholson, G 2; Pyle, S 0(2); Roche, D 4; Smith, S 42; Stephenson, G 1; Tupling, S 13(3); Wrightson, J 37(1).
Goals (53): Lamb 15, Dobson 10, Farrey 7, Cooke 5, Farnaby 4, Askew 3, Corner 3, Higgins 3, Guthrie 2, Elliott 1.

Kettering Town
Conference Appearances: Adams, S 10; Bancroft, P 11; Barber, F 5; Beasley, A 2; Brown, P 42; Clarke, S 5; Cunningham, J 4; Curtis, A 7; Docker, I 18; Donald, W 21; Donovan, N 3; Ellis, N 3; Gavin, P 3; Gernon, I 32; Greenwood, R 4; Harris, T 9; Hill, R 13; Hodges, D 12; Hope, C 19; Howells, G 1; Humphries, S 10; Lim, H 6; Martin, D 5; McKernon, C 9; Murphy, F 13; Nicol, P 26; North, M 5; Nuttall, M 1; Oxbrow, J 5; Price, G 28; Radford, M 4; Reddish, S 6; Reece, P 6; Reed, G 21; Retallick, G 2; Riley, D 27; Roderick, M 18; Russell, G 2; Shearer, M 10; Smalley, M 23; Smith, M 1; Sommer, J 10; Sowden, S 10; Stebbing, S 5; Stringfellow, I 1; Swailes, C 5; Taylor, R 3; Tomlinson, D 8; Underwood, J 3; Whitehurst, B 4; Wood, S 26; Wright, O 19.
Goals (61): Brown 16, Riley 9, Murphy 6, Bancroft 3, Harris 3, Hill 3, Hodges 3, Hope 3, Donald 2, Donovan2, Martin 2, Docker 1, Gavin 1, Nuttall 1, Price 1, Roderick 1, Tomlinson 1, Wood 1, Wright 1, OG 1

Kidderminster Harriers
Conference Appearances: Bancroft, P 0(1); Benton, D 30(3); Brindley, C 42; Cartwright, N 8; Davis, P 30(3); Deakin, J 30(2); Forsyth, R 38; Gillett, C 6(1); Gordon, C 16; Grainger, J 32(1); Green, R 1; Hadley, D 25(3); Hanson, J3(4); Hodson, S 6; Howell, P 6; Humphreys, D 8(4); Joseph, A 1(3); McGrath, J 36(3); Palmer, L19(5); Piggott, G 3; Purdie, J 18(1); Richardson, P 4; Rogers, D 1; Steadman, D 41; Stokes, G 1(5); Sullivan, K 1; Weir, M 40; Wilcox, B 5(2); Williams, W 7; Wolsey, M 2(1); Yates, M 2.
Goals (60): Davis 11, Purdie 8, Forsyth 7, Palmer 6, Hadley 6, Grainger 6, Deakin 4, Cartwright 3, Gordon3, Benton 1, Brindley 1, Humphreys 1, McGrath 1, Weir 1, OG 1.

Macclesfield Town
Conference Appearances: Askey, J 31; Bimson, S 32; Blain, C 12(9); Bunter, S 1; Carberry, J 4(1); Dempsey, M 9(2); Doherty, M 10(9); Edwards, E 39; Farrelly, M 9(3); Farrelly, S 41; Green, A 5(2); Green, R 5; Halliday, M 1(1); Hardman, M 5(7); Johnson, P 12(3); Kendall, P 33(4); Lambert, C 24(1); Leicester, S 32(4); McMahon, J 21(5); Mitchell, R 16(13); Mulligan, J 1; O'Neill, J 4; Pickering, S0(1); Roberts, M 0(1); Shepherd, G 39; Sorvel, N 35(5); Sutton, S 1; Timmons, J 40.
Goals (40): Lambert 8, Mitchell 8, Askey 7, Blain 3, Sorvel 3, Timmons 4, Green 2, Leicester 2, Dempsey1, Farrelly 1, OG 1.

Merthyr Tydfil
Conference Appearances: Abrahams, G 7; Beattie, A 15(4); Benbow, I 14; Boyle, T 41; Chiverton, E 1; Coates, M 31(6); Cole, D11(1); D'Auria, D 39; Davies, M 34(4); Gill, C 2(2); Holtam, M 12(2); Hutchinson, T 6(3); James, R39(1); Morris, S 12; Needs, A 4(2); Rogers, K 33(4);

Trick, D 24(2); Tucker, 33(3); Wager, G 30; Webley, 14(3); Williams, C 39(1); Williams, M 35.
Goals (51): Williams 14, Coates 9, Tucker 8, Webley 5, Benbow 4, Williams 3, D'Auria 2, Rogers 2, Beattie1, Boyle 1, Needs 1, OG 1.

Northwich Victoria
Conference Appearances: Ainsworth, G 5; Bennett, M 5(2); Berryman, S 3; Bishop, J 1(1); Blain, C 6(2); Blundell, C 12(8); Boyd, C 28; Bullock, T 35; Butler, B 38; Davies, G 35(1); Donnelly, P 8(6); Easter, G 1; Hancock, M30; Hardy, N 7(1), Hemmings, T 35; Jones, M 20(5); Kidd, A 0(1); Locke, S 32(1); McGee, T 2(4); McIlroy, S 1; Nassari, D 1(1); Nixon, C 2; O'Connor, M 41; Parker, J 34(4); Paxton, D 4(11); Siddall, B 2; Simms, M 34; Smith, J 12; Stringer, J 2(1); Thelwell, K 1(1); Westray, K 24(1); Williams, J 0(1).
Goals (68): O'Connor 21, Hemmings 15, Davies 12, Butler 4, Hancock 3, Boyd 2, Parker 2, Blain 1, Donnelly 1, Hardy 1, Paxton 1, Smith 1, Westray 1, OG 3.

Runcorn
Conference Appearances: Anderson, G 37; Bates, J 26(12); Boydd, G 0(5); Brabin, G 30(3); Brady, I 25(3); Brown, J 26(7); Byrne, S 5(1); Carroll, J 14; Connor, J 16(3); Cotton, S 2(5); Donnery, A 0(2); Gallagher, M 13; Harold, I 25; Hill, G 18; Jackson, M 1; Lundon, S 10(4); McCarty, D 16; McInerny, I 11(18); McKenna, K 15; Mullen, P 6(4); Parker, N 16(20); Richards, A 1(1); Robertson, P 22; Routledge, J16; Sang, N 5(1); Shaughnessy, S 38(4); Shaw, N 2; Taylor, A 9(9); Wall, J 29(6); Wellings, B 0(3); Williams, A 26; Wilson, D 3(1).
Goals (58): McMenna 12, Shaughnessy 11, Brown 6, Brabin 5, Anderson 4, Parker 3, Connor 2, Gallagher2, McCarty 2, McInerny 2, Brady 1, Carroll 1, Cotton 1, Harold 1, Lundon 1, Sang 1, Taylor 1, Wall 1, Wilson 1,

Slough Town
Conference Appearances: Anderson, D 37; Briley, L 37; Bunting, T 40; Edwards, R 10; Emberson, C 2; Fairweather, C 7; Fielder, C 1; Fiore, M 27; Foran, M 23; Friel, G 30; Greene, D 2; Hancock, D 1; Hazel, I 39; Hemsley, S 8; Lee, B 8; Maxwell, P 3; McKinnon, P 40; Pluckrose, A 42; Quamina, M 23; Sayer, A42; Scott, S 17; Stanley, N 27; Whitby, S 37
Goals (60): Sayer 19, McKinnon 13, Fiore 7, Hazel 4, Pluckrose 3, Friel 3, Scott 2, Foran 2, Briley 2, Anderson 2, Stanley 1, Fairweather 1, OG 1

Stafford Rangers
Conference Appearances: Berry, G 29(3); Boughey, D 33(5); Bradshaw, M 41; Burr, S 23; Callaghan, N 5; Circuit, S 9(1); Clayton, P 22(8); Dawson, J 12(2); Edwards, K 2; Essex, S 40; Fisher, M 7(2); Griffiths, A 12(4); Hemming, C 29(3); Henry, A 2; Jones, M 6(1); Jones, P 34(2); Lyons, S 0(1); Mettioui, A 6; Palgrave, B 29(3); Pearson, J 16; Price, R 42; Simpson, M 37; Skipper, P 5; Whitehurst, W 2; Wood, FI9(11): **Goals (55):** Clayton 9, Boughey 7, Burr 6, Palgrave 4, Berry 4, Bradshaw 3, Essex 3, Mettioui 3, Simpson3, Dawson 2, Hemming 2, Jones, P 2, Wood 2 , Callaghan 1, Fisher 1, Griffiths 1, Henry 1 OG1

Stalybridge Celtic
Conference Appearances: Anderson, S 12; Aspinall, J 34(1); Bauress, G 30(3); Bennett, P 35(1); Blackman, R 1; Booth, K 22(2); Boyle, G 19(3); Brown, J 36(2); Bunn, F 10(2); Burrell, M 5(1); Dixon, P 33; Edmonds, N 25(3); Edwards, M 33(8); Filson, M 34(1); Higginbotham, P 5(5); Hill, J 12(4); Hughes, R 42; King, P 4(1); Kirkham, P 27(5); Morgan, S 13(4); Power, P 21(4); Priest, E 3(3); Tomlinson, D 4(1); Wood, S 2(2): **Goals (46):** Edwards 12, Kirkham 9, Power 8, Anderson 3, Bunn 3, Brown 2, Filson 2, Morgan 2, Bauress1, Dixon 1, Higginbotham 1, Priest 1, Wood 1

Telford United
Conference Appearances: Acton, D 39; Beaumont, N 29(4); Benbow, I 29(2); Bignot, M 40; Bowen, S 19; Clarke, S 14(2); Cooke, A 4(4); Fergusson, S 30; Francis,

S 23(2); Garratt, A 1(4); Grange, D 3; Green, R 16(2); Hodgin, C 5(4); Hunter, P 2; Langford, T 22; Lee, A 33; May, L 0(4); McBean, P 7(1); Moore, M 9(1); Mulligan, J 7; Myers, M 33(2); Nelson, S 8; Niblett, N 21; Ogley, M 0(4); Parrish, S 33; Pritchard, D39; Rollason, L 6(2); Wolverson, J 0(2): **Goals (55):** Fergusson 8, Benbow 7, Francis 7, Langford 6, Parrish 4, Bignot 4, Mulligan 3, Green 3, Myers3, Cooke 2, Moore 2, Hodgin 1, Beaumont 1, Clarke 1, Pritchard 1, Niblett 1, Bowen 1

Welling United
Conference Appearances: Abbott, G 42; Brown, W, 6; Clemmence, N 27(5); Collins, P 34(2); Cooper, G 5; Dennis, L 19(16); Francis, J 0(1); Glover, J 13; Harrison, L 10; Hoddy, K 18(7); Holman, M 4; Hone, M 39(20); Newman, D 12(2); Ransom, N 36(1); Reynolds, T 12; Robbins, J 42; Robinson, S 30(1); Salako, A18(2); Smith, G 22(1); Sullivan, N 5; Tivey, M 7(2); Turner, L 1; White, S 34(3); Wild, R 1; Williams, D 25
Goals (57): Robbins 19, Abbott 17, Dennis 9, White 4, Hone 2, Clemmence 1, Newman 1, Ransom 1, Salako1 OG 2

Witton Albion
Conference Appearances: Adams, S 23(2); Alford, C 23(14); Anderson, S 1(2); Bancroft, D 5(10); Bondswell, A 3; Bullock, S1(1); Burke, B 32(1); Coathup, L 39; Connor, Jim 37; Connor, Joe 8(5); Gallagher, J 26(7); Gardner, S5(1); Grant, B 5(5); Healey, J 1(1); Holt, M 6(8); Hughes, M 7; Kelly, P 3; Kilner, A 4(1); Lambert, M4; Lillis, M 33(3); Lutkevitch, M 1(2); Mason, K 29; McCarty, D 6; McCluskie, J 0(2); McNeilis, S32; Murphy, A 2(4); Paladino, G 13; Redman, I 9(3); Rose, C 22(3); Senior, S 39; Smart, J 1(1); Stewart, G 5(3); Thomas, K 37(2); Tomlinson, D 0(3): **Goals (62):** Thomas 19, Alford 12, Burke 12, Connor, Jim 3, Hughes 3, Senior 3, Lillis 2, Rose 2, Stewart 2, Bondswell 1, Kilner 1 OG 2

Woking
Conference Appearances: Alexander, T 24; Baron, T 11; Batty, L 39; Biggins, M 26; Broderick, D 3; Brown, D 29(3); Brown, K38; Bushay, A 12; Buzaglo, R 3(1); Buzaglo, T 7(7); Carroll, R 11(5); Clement, A 23(1); Coleman, D6; Fielder, C 27(1); Finch, J 1; Fleming, M 28(1); Greene, D 4(2); Honey, D 1; Horne, B 1; Joyce, T7; Kelly, P 1; Milton, S 4(3); Murphy, A 2; Nugent, R 32; Pape, A 1; Peters, R 7; Puckett, D 25(9); Roffe, G 2; Rowe, Z 1; Senior, T 26(5); Steele, S 22(7); Wye, L 17; Wye, S 18
Goals (58): Senior 11, Puckett 9, Biggins 5, Fleming 5, Steele 5, Brown, D 2, Bushay 2, Buzaglo, T 2, Carroll2, Clement 2, Milton 2, Nugent 2, Baron 1, Buzaglo, R 1, Coleman 1, Fielder 1, Greene 1, Wye, S 1, OG 1

Wycombe Wanderers
Conference Appearances: Aylott, T 3; Barrowcliff, P 1(1); Buckle, P 1(1); Carroll, D 34; Casey, K 20(5); Cooper, G 5(3); Cousins, J 39; Covington, G 1; Creaser, G 20; Crossley, M 35; Dewhurst, R 2; Gooden, T 3(1); Greene, D 9(15); Guppy, S 38; Hayrettin, H 5; Hutchinson, S 21(5); Hyde, P 40; Kerr, A 37; Langford, T 11(1); Moussaddik, C 2; Norman, A 0(1); Poole, M 0(1); Ryan, K 14(9); Scott, K 36; Sorrell, T 0(1); Stapleton, S 33; Thompson, L 7; Thompson, S 30(2); Vircavs, A 10; West, M 5(8): **Goals (84):** Scott 20, Casey 10, Carroll 7, Stapleton 7, Guppy 6, Kerr 6, Thompson 6, Hutchinson 5, Langford5, West 4, Ryan 2, Creaser 1, Dewhurst 1, Greene 1, OG 3

Yeovil Town
Conference Appearances: Batty, P 33(2); Coates, N 28(5); Coles, D 42; Cooper, R 29(2); Dang, H 1(6); Dobbins, W 17; Ferns, P34(1); Flory, N 2(1); Harrower, S 39; Hughes, M 1(2); Leonard, D 2; McPherson, M 1(3); Nevin, P12(16); Rutter, S 17(2); Sanderson, P 37(4); Shail, M 33; Sherwood, J 41; Sivell, S 0(1); Spencer, M39(1); Taylor, T 2; Wallace, A 10(6); Williams, J 7; Wilson, P 35(1)
Goals (59): Spencer 15, Wilson 13, Batty 6, Sanderson 4, Shail 4, Harrower 3, Nevin 3, Cooper 3, Wallace2, Sherwood 2, Coates 1, Dang 1, OG 2

VAUXHALL CONFERENCE: MEMBER CLUBS SEASON 1992–1993

Club: ALTRINCHAM
Colours: Red and black striped shirts, black shorts
Ground: Moss Lane, Altrincham, Cheshire WA15 8AP
Tel: 061-928 1045
Year Formed: 1903
Record Gate: 10,275 (1925 v Sunderland Boys)
Nickname: The Robins
Manager: Gerry Quinn
Secretary: Jean Baldwin

Club: BATH CITY
Colours: Black and white striped shirts, black shorts
Ground: Twerton Park, Bath BA2 1DB
Telephone: 0225 423087 and 313247
Year Formed: 1889
Record Gate: 18,020 (1960 v Brighton)
Nickname: City
Manager: Tony Ricketts
Secretary: Paul Britton

Club: BROMSGROVE ROVERS
Colours: Green and white striped shirts, black shorts
Ground: Victoria Ground, Birmingham Road, Bromsgrove, Worcs. B61 0DR
Tel: 0527 78260
Year Formed: 1885
Record Gate: 7563 (1957-58 v Worcester City)
Nickname: Rovers
Manager: Bobby Hope
Secretary: Brian Hewings

Club: DAGENHAM & REDBRIDGE
Colours: Red shirts, royal blue shorts
Ground: Victoria Road Ground, Victoria Road, Dagenham, Essex RM10 7XL
Tel: 081-592 7194, 081-593 3864
Year formed: 1992
Record gate: 5300 versus Leyton Orient (1992)
Nickname: The Daggers
Manager: John Still
Secretary: Derek Almond

Club: DOVER ATHLETIC
Colours: White shirts, black shorts
Ground: Crabble Athletic Ground, Lewisham Road, River, Dover, Kent
Tel: 0304 822373
Year formed: 1983
Record gate: 4035 versus Bromsgrove Rovers (1992)
Nickname: The Lilywhites
Manager: Chris Kinnear
Secretary: John Durrant

Club: GATESHEAD
Colours: Black & white halved shirts, black shorts
Ground: International Stadium, Neilson Road, Gateshead NE10 0EF
Telephone: 091-487 7661
Year Formed: 1977 (Reformed)
Record Gate: 20,752 (1937 v Lincoln C)
Nickname: Tynesiders
Manager: Tommy Cassidy
Secretary: Clare Tierney

Club: HALIFAX TOWN
Colours: Blue and white striped shirts, black shorts
Ground: Shay Ground, Halifax HX1 2YS
Tel: 0422 353423
Year formed: 1911
Record gate: 36,885 versus Tottenham Hotspur (1953)
Nickname: The Shaymen
Manager: Peter Wragg
Secretary: Bev Fielding (*Acting*)

Club: KETTERING TOWN
Colours: Red shirts, white shorts
Ground: Rockingham Road, Kettering, Northants NN16 9AW
Tel: 0536 83028/410815
Year Formed: 1875
Record Gate: 11,536 (1947 v Peterborough)
Nickname: The Poppies
Manager: Graham Carr
Secretary: Gerry Knowles

Club: KIDDERMINSTER HARRIERS
Colours: Red and white shirts, red shorts
Ground: Aggborough, Hoo Road, Kidderminster
Tel: 0562 823931
Year Formed: 1886
Record Gate: 9155 (1948 v Hereford)
Nickname: The Harriers
Manager: Graham Allner
Secretary: Ray Mercer

Club: MACCLESFIELD TOWN
Colours: Royal blue shirts, white shorts
Ground: Moss Rose Ground, London Road, Macclesfield, Cheshire SK11 7SP
Tel: 0625 424324
Year Formed: 1875
Record Gate: 8900 (1968 v Stockport Co)
Nickname: The Silkmen
Manager: Sammy McIlroy
Secretary: Colin Garlick

Club: MERTHYR TYDFIL
Colours: White/silver/black square shirts, black shorts
Ground: Penydarren Park, Merthyr Tydfil
Tel: 0685 384102
Year Formed: 1945
Record Gate: 21,000 (1949 v Reading)
Nickname: The Martyrs
Manager: Wynford Hopkins
Secretary: Peter Hunt

Club: NORTHWICH VICTORIA
Colours: Green and white shirts, ghite shorts
Ground: The Drill Field, Northwich, Cheshire CW9 5HN
Tel: 0606 41450
Year Formed: 1874
Record Gate: 11,290 (1949 v Witton A)
Nickname: The Vics
Manager: John Williams
Secretary: Derek Nuttall

Club: RUNCORN
Colours: Yellow shirts, green trim, green shorts
Ground: Canal Street, Runcorn, Cheshire
Tel: 0928 560076
Year Formed: 1919
Record Gate: 10,011 (1939 v Preston NE)
Nickname: The Linnets
Manager: John Carroll
Secretary: George Worrall

Club: SLOUGH TOWN
Colours: Amber shirts, navy blue shorts
Ground: Wexham Park Stadium, Wexham Road, Slough SL2 5QR
Tel: 0753 523358
Year Formed: 1890
Record Gate: 8940 (1953 v Pegasus at Dolphin Stadium); 5000 (1982 v Millwall at Wexham Stadium)
Nickname: The Rebels
Manager: John Docherty
Secretary: Richard Hayward

Club: SOUTHPORT
Colours: Old gold and black shirts, black shorts
Ground: Haig Avenue, Southport PR8 6JZ
Tel: 0704 533422
Year formed: 1881
Record gate: 20,010 versus Newcastle United (1932)
Nickname: The Sandgrounders
Manager: Brian Kettle
Secretary: Roy Morris

Club: STAFFORD RANGERS
Colours: Black and white shirts, white shorts
Ground: Marston Road, Stafford ST16 3BX
Tel: 0785 42750
Year Formed: 1876
Record Gate: 8536 (1975 v Rotherham)
Nickname: The Boro
Manager: Brendan Phillips
Secretary: Mike Hughes

Club: STALYBRIDGE CELTIC
Colours: Blue and white quartered shirts, blue shorts
Ground: Bower Ford, Mottram Road, Stalybridge, Cheshire SK15 2RT
Tel: 061-338 2828

Year Formed: 1911
Record Gate: 9753 (1922.23 v West Bromwich Albion)
Nickname: Celtic
Manager: Philip Wilson
Secretary: Martyn Torr

Club: TELFORD UNITED
Colours: White shirts, blue shorts
Ground: Bucks Head, Watling Street, Telford TF1 2NJ
Tel: 0952 223838
Year Formed: 1877
Record Gate: 13,000 (1935 v Shrewsbury)
Nickname: The Lillywhites
Manager: Gerry Daly
Secretary: Mike Ferriday

Club: WELLING UNITED
Colours: Red shirts, red shorts
Ground: Park View Road Ground, Welling, Kent
Tel: 081-301 1196
Year Formed: 1963
Record Gate: 4020 (1989 v Gillingham)
Nickname: The Wings
Manager: Terry Robbins
Secretary: Barrie Hobbins

Club: WITTON ALBION
Colours: Red and white striped shirts, black shorts
Ground: Wincham Park, Chapel Street, Wincham, Northwich, CheshireHCW9 6DA
Tel: 0606 43008
Year Formed: 1890
Record Gate: 10,000 (1948 v Northwich Victoria)
Nickname: The Albion
Manager: Mike McKenzie
Secretary: David Leather

Club: WOKING
Colours: Red and white halved shirts, white shorts
Ground: Kingfield Sports Ground, Kingfield, Woking, Surrey GU22 9AA
Tel: 0483 772470/776126
Year Formed: 1889
Record Gate: 6000 (1978.79 v Swansea)
Nickname: The Cardinals
Manager: Geoff Chapple
Secretary: Phil Ledger, JP

Club:YEOVIL TOWN
Colours: Green/white striped shirts, white shorts
Ground: Huish Park, Lufton Way, Yeovil BA22 8YF
Tel: 0935 23663
Year Formed: 1923
Record Gate: 17,200 (1949 v Sunderland)
Nickname: The Glovers
Manager: Steve Rutter
Secretary: Roger Brinsford

GM VAUXHALL CONFERENCE RESULTS 1992–93

	Alt	Bath	Bos	Brm	Dhm	Far	Gat	Ket	Kid	Mac	Mer	Nor	Run	Slo	Sta	Sly	Tel	Wel	Wit	Wok	Wyc	Yeo
Altrincham	—	1-0	1-1	2-2	1-0	2-2	0-1	3-0	2-2	1-0	0-1	0-0	0-2	1-1	1-5	0-0	0-3	2-0	2-1	1-0	0-2	1-2
Bath City	3-0	—	2-1	0-3	2-1	5-2	1-1	0-0	2-1	1-0	1-3	0-5	1-1	0-1	2-1	1-1	4-1	1-1	0-0	2-0	2-0	0-0
Boston United	1-2	1-2	—	1-2	3-1	0-0	0-2	0-1	0-3	3-0	2-0	3-5	0-0	0-1	0-1	1-1	2-2	2-1	2-2	1-0	0-3	1-0
Bromsgrove R.	4-1	1-1	2-1	—	1-2	2-2	0-2	1-1	2-2	3-0	1-2	1-2	0-0	0-1	2-3	4-0	0-0	2-2	3-2	1-2	1-0	1-0
D'ham & R'bdge	2-2	1-1	1-0	1-1	—	5-1	3-1	1-2	3-2	1-2	6-1	4-1	5-1	4-4	0-1	1-2	0-2	1-0	1-1	5-1	1-2	1-1
Farborough T.	2-5	2-1	4-0	1-1	1-4	—	6-1	3-2	2-2	1-2	2-1	0-3	2-3	1-0	1-1	1-2	0-1	3-2	1-1	0-3	0-2	2-1
Gateshead	2-0	0-4	2-2	0-0	1-1	1-0	—	1-1	1-0	1-0	4-0	0-2	4-1	1-0	0-1	0-0	0-1	1-2	3-1	1-1	0-1	4-1
Kettering Town	1-1	0-1	3-3	3-2	0-0	2-1	2-0	—	1-2	1-0	1-3	2-1	3-3	5-0	2-0	2-0	1-1	2-4	2-1	0-1	0-4	3-0
Kidderminster H.	0-1	1-0	0-2	1-0	0-1	1-5	0-0	0-0	—	2-1	1-0	5-3	2-0	1-1	0-2	2-0	2-1	2-1	0-0	1-3	1-4	1-1
Macclesfield T.	1-1	1-0	2-1	0-2	1-1	1-2	1-1	1-0	0-1	—	0-1	1-2	1-1	1-2	4-1	1-0	1-1	1-1	1-0	1-1	1-1	1-1
Merthyr Tydfil	2-2	1-1	0-3	1-1	0-2	1-3	3-0	4-3	0-1	1-2	—	3-0	0-3	0-1	0-0	1-1	4-0	1-1	0-2	1-5	1-4	1-1
Northwich Vic.	1-2	3-1	3-3	0-1	1-1	3-0	0-0	2-2	0-1	1-3	1-2	—	3-2	0-1	1-2	1-3	1-0	1-1	1-3	1-0	1-0	0-1
Runcorn	0-1	1-3	1-2	2-1	1-0	1-4	4-2	2-2	0-0	1-2	2-3	0-1	—	0-3	0-2	2-1	3-1	3-0	4-4	2-3	2-1	1-0
Slough Town	1-4	1-1	3-0	1-3	2-0	3-1	3-0	3-0	3-1	2-1	2-1	0-4	1-1	—	2-1	2-3	2-0	4-2	2-3	0-1	1-1	3-0
Stafford Rangers	0-0	3-2	0-0	3-4	0-1	2-2	2-1	2-4	0-1	1-0	0-1	1-0	0-1	1-0	—	0-0	2-1	4-3	1-1	0-0	0-1	0-1
Stalybridge C.	1-0	1-1	2-1	0-1	0-3	2-0	2-1	0-0	2-2	0-6	2-2	0-0	0-0	1-0	1-0	—	3-3	0-0	1-2	3-0	2-2	1-1
Telford United	2-1	0-0	0-1	0-1	6-3	3-1	0-1	3-1	1-0	3-1	5-0	1-0	2-1	2-1	0-0	0-2	—	1-3	0-3	3-3	2-3	1-0
Welling United	2-0	0-3	2-2	4-2	0-2	3-1	1-1	1-0	1-0	1-0	5-0	1-5	3-2	2-1	1-2	1-4	1-3	—	2-2	1-1	2-2	1-2
Witton Albion	1-1	0-0	1-2	1-1	2-2	1-1	1-3	4-2	2-2	3-1	3-1	1-3	0-3	2-1	2-5	2-0	2-1	0-1	—	1-2	2-2	1-2
Woking	0-2	0-1	3-0	0-2	1-1	4-1	0-2	3-2	1-5	4-0	0-2	1-0	4-0	1-2	0-3	2-1	3-2	1-0	1-2	—	0-3	0-0
Wycombe W'ers	0-2	2-0	3-3	4-0	1-0	1-1	2-1	1-2	1-1	4-0	4-0	1-0	5-1	1-0	2-2	4-0	4-0	3-0	2-1	0-0	—	5-1
Yeovil Town	1-0	2-1	2-1	2-2	0-3	5-2	1-3	2-1	2-2	1-1	0-1	1-1	4-0	5-1	2-0	1-1	1-0	1-0	2-0	4-1	3-0	—

DRINKWISE CUP 1992–93

First Round *(two legs)*
Altrincham 1 *(Freeman)*
Macclesfield Town 3 *(Leicester, Timmons, Farrelly)*
821

Macclesfield Town 0
Altrincham 0   449

Stafford Rangers 4 *(Simpson, Berry, Hemming, Wood)*
Bromsgrove Rovers 2 *(O'Meara, Whitehouse)*   667

Bromsgrove Rovers 2 *(Richardson, og)*
Stafford Rangers 1 *(Clayton)*   757

Northwich Victoria 2 *(O'Connor, Butler)*
Gateshead 1 *(Higgins)*   378

Gateshead 0
Northwich Victoria 2 *(Davies 2)*   132

Stalybridge Celtic 1 *(Priest)*
Kidderminster Harriers 1 *(Davies)*   554

Kidderminster Harriers 4 *(Humphreys, Palmer 2, Davies)*
Stalybridge Celtic 2 *(Kirkham 2)*   602

Yeovil Town 2 *(Spencer, Sanderson)*
Slough Town 0   1319

Slough Town 2 *(Hazel 2)*
Yeovil Town 2 *(Spencer, Dang)*   528

Woking 1 *(Puckett)*
Welling United 2 *(Abbott, Robbins)*   1363

Welling United 2 *(Dennis 2)*
Woking 2 *(Baron, Senior)*   670

Second Round
Bath City 0
Yeovil Town 0   520

Yeovil Town 1 *(Sanderson)*
Bath Cith 0   2090

Boston United 1 *(Jones)*
Dagenham & Redbridge 2 *(Butterworth, Pamphlett)*
537

Merthyr Tydfil 4 *(Williams 2, Webley, D'Auria)*
Farnborough Town 2 *(Leworthy, Read)*   404

Kidderminster Harriers 3 *(Deakin, Forsyth, Hadley)*
Kettering Town 0   624

Runcorn 2 *(Shaughnessy, Brabin)*
Northwich Victoria 3 *(Hemmings 2, Donnelly)*   600

Stafford Rangers 0
Telford United 0   631

Telford United 5 *(Clarke 3, Cooke, Green)*
Stafford Rangers 2 *(Clayton, Berry)*   625

Welling United 2 *(Smith,, Dennis)*
Wycombe Wanderers 3 *(Scott, West, Greene)*   452

Witton Albion 0
Macclesfield Town 1 *(Leicester)*   763

Quarter-finals
Dagenham & Redbridge 4 *(Conner, Butterworth, Cavell, Nuttell)*
Merthyr Tydfil 2 *(Rogers, Coates)*   525

Macclesfield Town 3 *(Lambert, Mitchell 2)*
Kidderminster Harriers 1 *(Hadley)*   203

Northwich Victoria 3 *(Locke, Hemmings 2)*
Telford United 1 *(Bowen)*   374

Yeovil Town 0
Wycombe Wanderers 1 *(Scott)*   2330

Semi-finals
Northwich Victoria 2 *(O'Connor, Paxton)*
Macclesfield Town 0   821

Macclesfield Town 1 *(McMahon)*
Northwich Victoria 1 *(O'Connor)*   422

Wycombe Wanderers 3 *(Casey, Guppy, Ryan)*
Dagenham & Redbridge 1 *(Nuttell)*   1901

Dagenham & Redbridge 0
Wycombe Wanderers 0   1247

Final First Leg
Northwich Victoria (0) 0
Wycombe Wanderers (0) 0   1005
North Victoria: Bullock; Locke, McGee (Blundell), Jones, Parker, Boyd, Westray, Hardy, Davies, O'Connor, Hemmings
Wycombe Wanderers: Hyde; Crossley, Cooper, Kerr, Vircavs, Carroll, Hayrettin, Casey (Hutchison), Aylott, Ryan, Guppy

Final Second Leg
Wycombe Wanderers (1) 2 *(Guppy, West)*
Northwich Victoria (0) 3 *(Davies 3)* aet   4264
Wycombe Wanderers: Hyde; Cousins (Ryan), Cooper, Crossley, Vircavs, Hutchinson, Carroll, Hayrettin, West (Greene), Scott, Guppy
Northwich Victoria: Bullock; Locke, Simms, Jones, Parker, Boyd, Hardy, Butler, Davies, O'Connor, Hemmings

HFS LOANS LEAGUE 1992–93

PREMIER DIVISION

	P	W	D	L	F	A	Pts
Southport	42	29	9	4	103	31	96
Winsford United	42	27	9	6	91	43	90
Morecambe	42	25	11	6	93	51	86
Marine	42	26	8	8	83	47	86
Leek Town	42	21	11	10	86	51	74
Accrington Stanley	42	20	13	9	79	45	73
Frickley Athletic	42	21	6	15	62	52	69
Barrow	42	18	11	13	71	55	65
Hyde United	42	17	13	12	87	71	64
Bishop Auckland	42	17	11	14	63	52	62
Gainsborough Trinity	42	17	8	17	63	66	59
Colwyn Bay	42	16	6	20	80	79	54
Horwich	42	14	10	18	72	79	52
Buxton	42	13	10	19	60	75	49
Matlock Town **	42	13	11	18	56	79	47
Elmey	42	13	6	23	62	91	45
Whitley Bay	42	11	8	23	57	96	41
Chorley	42	10	10	22	52	93	40
Fleetwood Town	42	10	7	25	50	77	37
Droylsden	42	10	7	25	47	84	37
Mossley	42	7	8	27	53	95	29
Goole Town	42	6	9	27	47	105	27

** Matlock Town deducted 3 points for breach of rule.

FIRST DIVISION

	P	W	D	L	F	A	Pts
Bridlington Town	40	25	11	4	84	35	86
Knowsley United	40	23	7	10	86	48	76
Ashton United	40	22	8	10	81	54	74
Guiseley	40	20	10	10	90	64	70
Warrington Town	40	19	10	11	85	57	67
Gretna	40	17	12	11	64	47	63
Curzon Ashton	40	16	15	9	69	63	63
Great Harwood Town	40	17	9	14	66	57	60
Alfreton Town	40	15	9	16	80	80	54
Harrogate Town	40	14	12	14	77	81	54
Worksop Town	40	15	9	16	66	70	54
Radcliffe Borough	40	13	14	13	66	69	53
Workington	40	13	13	14	51	61	52
Eastwood Town	40	13	11	16	49	52	50
Netherfield	40	11	14	15	68	63	47
Caernarfon Town	40	13	8	19	66	74	47
Farsley Celtic	40	12	8	20	64	77	44
Lancaster City	40	10	12	18	49	76	42
Shepshed Albion	40	9	12	19	46	66	39
Congleton Town	40	10	7	23	58	95	37
Rossendale United	40	5	5	30	50	126	20

Leading goalscorers

Lge	Cup	Tot.		Lge	Cup	Tot.	
33	12	45	John Coleman (Morecambe)	20	16	36	Liam Watson (Warrington Town)
32	12	44	Steve Haw (Southport)	27	6	33	Andy Whittaker (Netherfield)
26	15	41	Paul Beck (Accrington Stanley)	23	10	33	Chris Shaw (Ashton United)
24	13	37	Bevan Blackwood (Winsford United)	26	4	30	Peter Coyne (Radcliffe Borough)
26	8	34	Chris Camden (Peter Donnelly)	21	7	28	Graeme Jones (Bridlington Town)
23	11	34	Peter Donnelly (Colwyn Bay)	21	7	28	Gary Waller (Worksop Town)
25	8	33	Brian Ross (Marine)	20	7	27	Dave Siddell (Knowsley United)
18	12	30	Peter McCrae (Chorley)	22	4	26	Steve French (Harrogate Town)
26	-	26	Andy Graham (Hyde United)	16	10	26	Kenny Clark (Worksop Town)
24	2	26	Phil Chadwick (Hyde United)	17	7	24	David Woodcock (Bridlington Town)
18	8	26	Peter Withers (Southport)	16	8	24	Joey Dunn (Warrington Town)
22	3	25	John Brady (Barrow)	12	12	24	Keith Evans (Curzon Ashton)
21	2	23	Tony McDonald (Horwich)	20	3	23	Darren Washington (Congleton Town)
21	1	22	Stuart Lowe (Buxton)	17	6	23	Peter Smith (Great Harwood Town)
16	6	22	Bob Clarke (Emley)	12	11	23	Gavin McDonald (Warrington Town)

HFS LOANS LEAGUE CHALLENGE CUP

Qualifying Round
Curzon Ashton 5, Eastwood Town 2
Radcliffe Borough 2, Shepshed Albion 1

First Round
Alfreton Town 2, Ashton United 3
Bridlington Town 2, Guiseley 1
Gretna 3, Rossendale United 0 *(after 1-1 draw)*
Harrogate Town W/O
Knowsley United 2, Great Harwood Town 1
Lancaster City 1, Farsley Celtic 2
Netherfield 2, Congleton Town 0
Radcliffe Borough 2, Caernarfon Town 3
Workington 1, Curzon Ashton 0
Worksop Town 1, Warrington Town 3

Second Round
Bridlington Town 0, Knowsley United 1
Caernarfon Town 3, Ashton United 2
Chorley 1, Whitley Bay 3 *(after 2-2 draw)*
Colwyn Bay 6, Harrogate Town 0
Farsley Celtic 1, Winsford United 2
Gainsborough Trinity 1, Accrington Stanley 0 *(after 1-1 draw)*
Goole Town 1, Barrow 3
Gretna 3, Frickley Athletic 2
Hyde United 3, Droylsden 2
Marine 1, Morecambe 0
Matlock Town 3, Horwich 1
Mossley 1, Emley 6

Netherfield 2, Leek Town 0
Southport 4, Buxton 1
Warrington Town 1, Bishop Auckland 0
Workington 1, Fleetwood Town 0 *(after 2-2 draw)*

Third Round
Colwyn Bay 3, Emley 2 *(after 1-1 draw)*
Gainsborough Trinity 2, Barrow 1
Knowsley United 1, Gretna 2
Marine 1, Caernarfon Town 0
Netherfield 0, Matlock Town 3 *(after 2-2 draw)*
Whitley Bay 1, Warrington Town 3
Winsford United 4, Hyde United 0
Workington 2, Southport 1

Fourth Round
Gainsborough Trinity 2, Workington 4
Gretna 3, Marine 2 *(after 1-1 draw and extra-time in replay)*
Matlock Town 1, Warrington Town 2
Winsford United 3, Colwyn Bay 0

Semi-finals
Warrington Town 3,1, Gretna 2,1
Workington 0,0, Winsford United 1,1

Final
Warrington Town 1, Winsford United 1 *(at Maine Road)*
(Winsford United won 6-5 on penalties AET)

HFS LOANS LEAGUE PRESIDENT'S CUP

Final, First Leg
Winsford United 2, Southport 0

Final, Second Leg
Southport 4, Winsford United 3

HFS LOANS LEAGUE FIRST DIVISION CUP

Final, First Leg
Guiseley 1, Bridlington Town 1

Final, Second Leg
Bridlington Town 2, Guiseley 3

HFS LOANS LEAGUE—PREMIER DIVISION RESULTS 1992–93

	Accrington Stanley	Barrow	Bishop Auckland	Buxton	Chorley	Colwyn Bay	Droylsden	Emley	Fleetwood Town	Frickley Ath	Gainsborough Trinity	Goole Town	Horwich RMI	Hyde United	Leek Town	Marine	Matlock Town	Morecambe	Mossley	Southport	Whitley Bay	Winsford United
Accrington Stanley	x	2-0	0-0	0-1	0-1	1-0	3-3	0-3	0-2	3-2	0-2	0-5	2-2	2-6	3-1	2-0	1-2	2-0	0-5	2-2	1-1	2-0
Barrow	2-0	x	2-1	0-4	1-1	2-3	1-3	1-1	2-2	2-1	1-0	0-2	2-2	2-2	2-2	0-1	3-1	1-2	3-0	1-1	1-1	1-4
Bishop Auckland	0-0	4-3	x	0-3	0-0	1-2	1-1	2-3	3-0	1-1	1-0	2-1	3-1	2-3	2-0	1-5	2-1	3-1	1-0	1-4	2-0	1-3
Buxton	2-2	3-2	0-0	x	1-1	7-3	0-0	1-1	0-2	2-0	1-2	0-2	3-0	2-2	5-1	1-3	1-0	2-1	2-3	2-1	2-0	1-1
Chorley	3-1	2-1	5-0	2-3	x	1-0	2-2	2-1	1-1	2-1	1-1	0-2	2-1	4-0	3-0	1-0	3-1	2-0	1-4	7-1	2-0	0-1
Colwyn Bay	3-1	5-0	1-1	1-0	4-2	x	1-1	1-1	1-2	1-0	2-1	3-1	0-2	3-1	1-4	2-1	1-1	3-1	1-4	2-0	2-4	3-2
Droylsden	4-1	3-0	2-0	1-2	2-0	3-0	x	1-3	1-6	0-1	2-1	1-2	2-1	2-1	2-1	2-1	2-2	2-0	0-1	3-0	5-0	5-2
Emley	6-1	0-1	2-1	3-0	1-3	2-1	1-2	x	3-1	3-1	1-0	0-0	1-3	1-0	2-0	2-1	2-1	7-4	1-2	1-2	2-0	5-1
Fleetwood Town	1-0	2-0	0-1	0-3	2-1	3-1	1-1	4-3	x	1-2	1-0	0-0	2-1	3-1	4-1	2-0	0-1	4-2	2-0	5-0	0-1	2-0
Frickley Ath	1-1	1-2	0-3	2-0	1-2	0-1	2-1	2-0	1-1	x	0-1	1-3	3-1	0-0	4-0	2-0	2-1	3-0	1-2	2-1	2-2	1-1
Gainsborough Trinity	0-1	2-2	2-2	2-3	1-0	3-0	0-2	0-2	1-2	4-0	x	1-4	2-0	7-2	1-2	2-1	2-1	3-4	2-1	0-0	3-0	1-0
Goole Town	3-0	4-1	1-1	2-1	1-5	4-2	1-0	1-2	3-1	3-0	3-0	x	3-1	3-3	6-1	6-3	3-3	1-1	0-0	3-0	2-0	3-0
Horwich RMI	2-1	1-1	1-0	2-2	2-2	4-2	1-3	5-3	1-1	2-1	2-2	1-2	x	4-1	0-0	3-0	3-2	3-2	1-4	3-2	0-1	3-1
Hyde United	1-1	2-1	3-0	2-1	3-3	2-4	1-0	1-5	1-2	1-1	2-0	1-1	3-5	x	0-0	3-3	3-1	0-1	3-3	1-0	1-0	1-0
Leek Town	2-0	1-2	1-0	2-1	2-1	2-3	0-1	5-5	3-0	1-2	1-4	0-1	1-1	2-4	x	1-1	1-2	1-1	0-4	0-0	0-2	2-0
Marine	1-1	3-1	1-0	1-5	0-6	2-2	1-3	4-1	3-1	0-0	0-1	2-3	0-3	1-2	0-1	x	1-0	1-1	0-3	0-0	1-5	5-1
Matlock Town	2-0	1-0	0-1	1-1	1-1	3-1	2-0	2-2	2-3	1-0	2-4	0-4	2-4	2-0	6-0	2-2	x	2-2	0-0	3-0	2-3	0-0
Morecambe	1-1	0-3	2-2	4-1	1-2	0-1	0-1	1-2	1-2	2-0	2-3	2-8	0-1	2-2	0-0	0-3	0-6	x	1-0	1-1	0-3	2-0
Mossley	2-2	2-2	4-0	6-1	4-2	2-1	1-4	2-0	3-2	2-1	1-1	1-1	5-2	4-2	3-3	1-0	0-3	3-1	x	3-0	1-1	1-0
Southport	2-2	0-2	1-3	0-2	1-6	2-4	2-5	0-4	1-2	2-5	1-1	0-5	1-1	1-1	1-0	2-1	1-5	0-2	0-2	x	1-5	1-2
Whitley Bay	2-0	0-1	3-2	0-0	1-4	4-4	1-2	2-1	2-2	3-0	7-1	5-1	3-3	2-1	3-0	3-1	1-2	4-2	5-0	1-0	x	6-0
Winsford United	1-3	0-0	2-2	2-3	0-4	2-3	0-4	1-2	1-2	1-2	3-1	2-4	2-0	3-3	0-0	2-0	3-3	0-0	2-4	0-1	0-3	x

HFS LOANS LEAGUE—FIRST DIVISION RESULTS—SCORECHART GRID 1992–93

	Alfreton Town	Ashton United	Bridlington Town	Caernarfon Town	Congleton Town	Curzon Ashton	Eastwood Town	Farsley Celtic	Great Harwood Town	Gretna	Guiseley	Harrogate Town	Knowsley United	Lancaster City	Netherfield	Radcliffe Borough	Rossendale United	Shepshed Albion	Warrington Town	Workington	Worksop Town
Alfreton Town	x	1-2	2-3	1-0	4-1	0-1	1-2	1-3	4-0	2-3	3-5	3-2	2-1	3-2	3-3	2-2	5-3	2-1	0-3	1-1	6-2
Ashton United	6-2	x	1-1	2-0	1-2	5-1	1-4	3-1	0-0	3-0	5-2	2-1	3-0	4-0	3-0	2-1	2-0	1-1	2-1	2-1	1-0
Bridlington Town	1-4	1-3	x	0-0	5-1	1-0	2-0	1-1	3-0	1-0	2-1	3-0	2-0	0-0	2-1	4-0	6-3	5-0	1-1	0-0	1-0
Caernarfon Town	2-3	1-3	2-2	x	3-2	3-1	1-1	3-4	2-4	1-4	1-0	2-4	1-3	4-2	1-5	0-0	3-0	1-1	4-1	0-1	0-2
Congleton Town	3-2	1-0	3-3	0-2	x	0-3	0-0	1-1	1-2	0-1	1-1	3-3	1-2	1-2	0-4	1-2	6-1	1-2	2-1	0-3	1-3
Curzon Ashton	1-1	2-2	2-1	0-2	2-2	x	3-3	1-1	3-2	0-4	4-3	4-1	1-1	3-0	1-4	0-1	4-1	1-0	3-3	2-1	2-1
Eastwood Town	2-1	1-2	0-0	2-2	0-2	1-2	x	2-0	1-0	1-1	1-3	5-3	1-3	0-2	1-0	1-1	1-3	0-0	4-0	0-1	0-0
Farsley Celtic	2-3	1-1	0-2	0-4	3-2	0-1	2-0	x	1-0	3-0	1-3	0-1	1-3	3-0	1-1	1-3	7-1	2-2	1-1	1-2	2-2
Great Harwood Town	2-1	2-1	1-2	1-1	4-0	1-1	1-0	7-0	x	3-2	2-2	2-2	1-5	2-1	0-3	1-0	2-0	5-2	3-2	2-2	4-2
Gretna	2-3	3-0	1-3	4-2	5-1	0-0	2-0	3-2	2-1	x	0-1	3-2	1-2	1-2	2-1	3-3	3-0	2-1	2-0	0-0	3-0
Guiseley	1-1	4-1	2-2	3-1	5-1	3-3	3-2	3-2	2-1	0-1	x	2-3	1-2	5-0	4-2	1-1	3-2	1-1	3-2	4-3	3-1
Harrogate Town	2-2	1-1	1-5	3-0	2-1	1-5	1-1	1-6	2-3	2-0	3-2	x	1-1	2-0	1-0	2-3	3-0	1-0	2-2	1-1	1-1
Knowsley United	0-1	3-2	2-1	3-1	1-1	5-0	0-0	2-0	0-0	0-1	4-2	3-0	x	1-2	3-2	0-1	2-0	2-2	4-3	4-1	1-0
Lancaster City	1-1	1-2	2-1	0-3	1-1	0-0	1-0	1-2	0-1	0-0	1-3	1-1	1-1	x	3-3	1-5	2-0	1-1	2-2	1-3	0-1
Netherfield	1-1	1-2	1-1	1-1	1-1	2-2	3-0	0-1	2-0	1-4	1-1	1-1	2-1	3-3	x	6-1	3-2	0-0	0-1	1-2	1-1
Radcliffe Borough	3-1	0-2	0-3	1-3	1-3	1-1	1-0	2-4	5-2	0-0	0-1	4-2	1-1	2-1	3-0	x	1-1	3-0	1-1	1-1	3-3
Rossendale United	1-1	1-7	0-1	1-4	1-4	1-1	5-2	3-2	0-4	1-0	1-1	1-6	3-8	2-4	1-2	4-3	x	1-2	2-7	2-2	0-1
Shepshed Albion	1-2	3-1	3-1	3-1	0-1	1-2	0-2	1-1	1-0	0-0	0-2	3-0	0-2	2-3	0-3	2-2	2-0	x	0-3	2-2	1-0
Warrington Town	4-2	0-0	0-1	3-1	6-1	3-3	1-0	3-1	1-0	0-0	3-2	4-3	3-0	0-2	2-0	2-0	4-1	5-0	x	1-1	1-1
Workington	2-1	3-2	0-1	2-1	2-1	1-0	0-1	3-0	0-1	0-0	2-3	1-5	1-3	1-1	1-1	2-2	0-2	1-7	1-2	x	0-0
Worksop Town	3-1	0-1	0-4	1-2	6-4	0-3	0-3	2-3	1-1	2-1	1-0	0-3	1-1	6-2	5-2	4-2	5-4	4-2	1-0	3-0	x

BEAZER HOMES LEAGUES 1992–93

Premier Division

	P	W	D	L	F	A	Pts
Dover Atlantic	40	25	11	4	65	23	86
Cheltenham Town	40	21	10	9	76	40	73
Corby Town	40	20	12	8	68	43	72
Hednesford Town	40	21	7	12	72	52	70
Trowbridge Town	40	18	8	14	70	66	62
Crawley Town	40	16	12	12	68	59	60
Solihull Borough	40	17	9	14	68	59	60
Burton Albion	40	16	11	13	53	50	59
Bashley	40	18	8	14	60	60	59*
Halesown Town	40	15	11	14	67	54	56
Waterlooville	40	15	9	16	59	62	54
Chelmsford City	40	15	9	16	59	69	54
Gloucester City	40	14	11	15	66	68	53
Cambridge City	40	14	10	16	62	73	52
Atherstone United	40	13	14	13	56	60	50*
Hastings Town	40	13	11	16	50	55	50
Worcester City	40	12	9	19	45	62	45
Dorchester Town	40	12	6	22	52	74	42
Moor Green	40	10	6	24	58	79	36
V.S. Rugby	40	10	6	24	40	63	36
Weymouth	40	5	10	25	39	82	23 #

(Dartford records expunged.

Weymouth 2 points deducted.

* Atherstone United and Bashley 3 points deducted).

Midland Division

	P	W	D	L	F	A	Pts
Nuneaton Borough	42	29	5	8	102	45	92
Gresley Rovers	42	27	6	9	94	55	87
Rushden & Diamonds	42	25	10	7	85	41	85
Barri	42	26	5	11	82	49	83
Newport AFC	42	23	8	11	73	58	77
Bedworth United	42	22	8	12	72	55	74
Stourbridge	42	17	9	16	93	79	60
Sutton Coldfield TN	42	17	9	16	82	78	60
Redditch United	42	18	6	18	75	79	60
Tamworth	42	16	11	15	65	51	59
Weston Super Mare	42	17	7	18	79	86	58
Leicester United	42	16	9	17	67	67	57
Grantham Town	42	16	9	17	60	73	57
Bilston Town	42	15	10	17	74	69	55
Evesham United	42	15	8	19	67	83	53
Bridgnorth Town	42	15	7	20	61	68	52
Dudley Town	42	14	8	20	60	75	50
Yate Town	42	15	5	22	63	81	50
Forest Green Rovers	42	12	6	24	61	97	42
Hinckley Town	42	9	11	22	56	89	37*
King's Lynn	42	10	6	26	45	90	36
Racing Club Warwick	42	3	7	32	40	88	16

* (Hinckley Town 1 point deducted).

Southern Division

	P	W	D	L	F	A	Pts
Sittingbourne	42	26	12	4	102	43	90
Salisbury	42	27	7	8	87	50	88
Witney Town	42	25	9	8	77	37	84
Gravesend & Northfleet	42	25	4	13	99	63	79
Havant Town	42	23	6	13	78	55	75
Sudbury Town	42	20	11	11	89	54	71
Erith & Belvedere	42	22	5	15	73	66	71
Ashford Town	42	20	8	14	91	66	68
Braintree Town	42	20	6	16	95	65	66
Margate	42	19	7	16	65	58	64
Wealdstone	42	18	7	17	75	69	61
Buckingham Town	42	16	11	15	61	58	59
Baldock Town	42	15	9	18	59	63	54
Poole Town	42	15	7	20	61	69	52
Fareham Town	42	14	8	20	67	65	50
Burnham	42	14	8	20	53	77	50
Canterbury City	42	12	10	20	54	76	46
Newport I.O.W.	42	9	16	17	44	56	43
Fisher Athletic	42	8	9	25	38	98	33
Andover	42	7	9	26	42	99	30
Dunstable	42	5	14	23	42	92	29
Bury Town	42	8	5	29	46	119	29

LEADING GOALSCORERS

Premier Division

J. Smith (Cheltenham Town	29
R. Carter (Solihull Borough)	25
K. Bayliss (Gloucester City)	22
C. Burton (Solihull Borough)	22
P. Fishenden (Crawley Town)	22
G. Manson (Dorchester Town)	21
L. O'Connor (Hednesford Town)	21
L. Cormack (Waterlooville)	20
P. Joinson (Halesowen Town)	20
M. Murphy (Corby Town)	20
L. Ryan (Cambridge City)	20

Midland Division

E. Wright (Stourbridge)	46
P. Culpin (Nuneaton Borough)	39
D. Draper (Bedworth United)	25
D. Withers (Barri)	24
J. Baker (Bilston Town)	23
T. Hall (Stourbridge)	23
D. Watkins (Rushden & Diamonds)	23
C. Lilygreen (Newport AFC)	21
M. Twigger (Bedworth United)	21

Southern Division

S. Portway (Gravesend & Northfleet)	58
P. Smith (Sudbury Town)	34
M. Buglione (Margate)	31
S. Parnell (Sudbury Town)	27
L. McRobert (Ashford Town)	26
K. Clarke (Witney Town)	25
D. Arter (Sittingbourne)	23
J. Lillis (Sittingbourne)	18
R. Taylor (Fareham Town)	18

BEAZER HOMES SOUTHERN LEAGUE PREMIER DIVISION RESULTS 1992-93

	Atherstone United	Bashley	Burton Albion	Cambridge City	Chelmsford City	Cheltenham Town	Corby Town	Crawley Town	Dorchester Town	Dover Athletic	Gloucester City	Halesowen Town	Hastings Town	Hednesford Town	Moor Green	Solihull Borough	Trowbridge Town	VS Rugby	Waterlooville	Weymouth	Worcester City
Atherstone United	—	0-1	1-1	2-4	3-1	1-1	0-2	2-1	0-1	0-0	2-1	1-1	2-3	4-2	4-3	4-2	0-1	1-0	4-4	1-0	1-0
Bashley	2-1	—	0-1	1-1	5-3	1-3	1-1	1-3	0-2	2-1	0-3	4-3	2-1	0-1	6-1	2-0	1-1	2-0	3-0	2-0	1-0
Burton Albion	1-1	2-0	—	2-0	2-0	0-3	1-2	3-1	4-0	0-0	0-3	1-1	0-0	1-5	1-2	0-2	4-2	1-2	0-2	2-0	1-0
Cambridge City	0-3	1-1	1-0	—	3-1	0-3	1-2	6-4	3-1	1-2	6-3	0-3	2-0	3-1	4-4	1-3	3-2	2-1	2-1	3-2	0-0
Chelmsford City	2-1	2-3	1-3	1-1	—	1-1	3-4	2-1	4-2	1-1	3-1	1-0	2-0	0-2	2-0	0-0	2-2	2-0	2-2	2-2	2-0
Cheltenham Town	2-2	1-2	0-0	2-0	5-1	—	0-1	3-2	3-1	1-1	4-0	2-1	0-1	1-1	1-0	1-3	1-0	1-0	5-0	2-2	4-1
Corby Town	2-3	5-2	1-1	1-0	2-0	3-0	—	3-0	2-2	1-0	1-1	2-1	0-1	2-2	2-0	1-3	0-0	1-3	3-1	4-0	1-2
Crawley Town	1-1	3-0	2-2	0-0	3-0	0-0	2-3	—	5-1	2-1	2-1	3-0	2-1	2-2	1-1	2-1	2-0	2-0	1-1	2-2	4-0
Dorchester Town	0-1	1-0	2-1	5-0	3-0	2-0	1-1	2-3	—	0-1	1-1	3-0	0-1	2-2	0-0	1-4	1-3	0-1	2-3	0-1	2-1
Dover Athletic	2-0	3-2	3-0	5-0	1-0	0-1	2-0	0-0	3-0	—	2-0	1-0	2-1	2-1	2-0	1-0	4-0	1-0	2-0	0-1	1-1
Gloucester City	4-0	1-1	1-3	2-3	1-2	1-5	0-1	1-1	0-0	1-1	—	3-1	6-2	1-3	2-2	1-1	2-4	1-0	2-2	1-1	4-0
Halesowen Town	2-2	3-1	1-2	1-0	1-2	1-1	1-2	4-1	2-2	1-1	2-2	—	0-2	0-1	5-1	3-1	0-1	4-0	2-2	2-1	3-2
Hastings Town	0-0	0-0	3-0	1-1	1-1	2-1	1-2	2-0	3-2	1-1	2-2	1-4	—	1-2	1-0	5-1	0-1	2-1	0-2	5-2	1-1
Hednesford Town	1-1	4-1	3-0	1-1	3-2	1-0	1-0	4-2	3-1	0-1	1-2	0-3	3-2	—	5-1	0-1	2-1	2-0	3-1	1-1	1-3
Moor Green	1-1	1-2	1-4	3-5	3-1	0-2	3-3	1-0	1-2	0-1	6-0	2-0	3-0	1-2	—	0-1	2-1	1-2	0-2	3-1	2-3
Solihull Borough	5-0	0-1	2-2	0-0	1-2	1-1	0-1	2-2	1-0	1-2	1-3	2-3	1-1	3-0	3-2	—	4-0	1-0	2-1	4-2	2-1
Trowbridge Town	1-1	3-3	1-4	1-4	1-0	3-3	1-0	1-1	3-1	0-2	1-2	1-1	4-1	3-2	3-2	1-3	—	4-2	3-2	3-0	2-1
VS Rugby	1-1	2-1	0-1	2-0	0-1	0-5	1-2	1-2	4-1	1-1	0-1	1-3	1-1	1-2	2-1	3-3	2-3	—	1-0	1-1	1-0
Waterlooville	1-0	0-2	0-1	2-1	1-2	1-1	1-1	3-0	6-1	0-4	1-1	1-1	0-2	1-0	2-1	4-2	1-0	3-1	—	2-1	0-0
Weymouth	1-3	0-0	1-1	2-0	2-3	0-1	0-3	1-1	1-2	2-3	1-5	2-1	1-0	0-3	0-1	1-2	0-3	1-3	2-1	—	2-2
Worcester City	2-1	3-0	0-0	2-1	2-2	2-4	2-1	1-2	1-4	1-2	2-0	1-0	2-0	0-0	0-2	3-0	0-5	0-0	1-3	2-0	—

BEAZER HOMES SOUTHERN LEAGUE MIDLAND DIVISION RESULTS 1992–93

	Barri	Bedworth United	Bilston Town	Bridgnorth Town	Dudley Town	Evesham United	Forest Green R	Grantham Town	Gresley Rovers	Hinckley Town	King's Lynn	Leicester United	Newport AFC	Nuneaton Borough	Racing Club Warwick	Redditch United	Rushden & Diamonds	Stourbridge	Sutton Coldfield Town	Tamworth	Weston-super-Mare	Yate Town
Barri	—	1-2	2-1	1-2	3-1	3-1	2-0	0-1	1-2	1-0	2-0	3-1	4-1	1-4	3-1	0-1	2-1	0-2	3-3	2-0	3-0	3-1
Bedworth United	0-1	—	2-1	3-2	2-0	0-1	3-2	3-0	2-2	1-1	0-1	2-2	0-1	2-1	1-0	2-1	0-3	4-1	2-2	0-3	2-1	0-3
Bilston Town	1-1	1-2	—	0-3	6-2	1-0	5-0	3-1	1-0	2-2	5-2	4-2	1-1	3-4	2-1	0-2	0-1	1-0	1-1	1-1	3-1	6-3
Bridgenorth Town	2-4	0-2	0-0	—	0-0	1-0	4-1	1-0	1-4	0-1	3-0	3-0	0-1	1-2	4-2	2-1	2-2	0-6	2-3	0-0	1-1	1-1
Dudley Town	1-3	0-3	2-2	2-1	—	0-2	1-0	0-2	2-5	1-0	2-0	3-0	0-1	1-3	3-2	1-2	1-2	1-0	4-2	4-1	5-1	1-1
Evesham United	3-4	1-0	3-2	2-3	0-0	—	1-2	2-2	0-2	5-2	7-1	0-4	2-2	0-2	2-2	1-1	1-2	2-2	0-3	1-1	3-1	0-3
Forest Green R	1-6	1-2	4-1	3-2	0-2	0-3	—	2-2	0-2	1-1	0-0	3-1	1-2	2-3	4-1	1-4	1-4	1-4	4-1	1-3	4-0	2-1
Grantham Town	1-2	4-1	1-0	1-3	0-2	0-3	2-2	—	2-0	2-1	1-2	2-1	1-0	2-3	1-0	0-5	1-1	3-3	1-3	1-0	3-1	3-0
Gresley Rovers	3-1	2-2	2-0	1-2	2-0	5-0	2-1	2-3	—	1-0	2-1	2-3	3-5	0-1	3-2	4-0	2-1	2-1	1-0	3-2	4-2	3-1
Hinckley Town	1-2	2-2	3-1	1-0	6-3	1-5	1-1	2-0	1-2	—	0-2	1-2	3-4	1-5	2-0	0-2	0-0	1-1	1-1	0-0	1-2	3-1
King's Lynn	0-2	1-3	0-3	0-0	2-2	1-2	3-1	1-3	1-4	2-2	—	2-0	1-1	0-2	0-3	4-1	0-1	1-5	3-2	4-1	0-2	4-2
Leicester United	2-2	0-2	0-0	2-1	1-3	5-2	3-2	3-1	3-2	0-1	0-0	—	1-2	1-2	2-2	2-3	1-0	3-1	2-1	1-0	3-1	4-0
Newport AFC	0-0	1-3	3-1	2-0	1-0	2-3	0-0	2-0	0-0	3-1	4-1	1-1	—	0-3	3-1	0-0	1-3	2-1	2-2	3-2	0-1	3-1
Nuneaton Borough	1-3	1-1	2-1	2-1	3-0	5-1	6-1	0-1	0-2	2-1	3-0	2-0	1-1	—	3-1	8-1	1-1	1-1	1-2	1-3	1-2	4-1
Racing Club Warwick	1-0	1-3	2-3	0-2	0-0	0-1	1-2	1-2	0-2	2-2	0-1	0-0	1-2	0-2	—	0-1	1-2	2-3	1-1	0-1	2-2	0-3
Redditch United	2-4	3-1	3-1	1-2	3-3	1-2	2-0	2-0	3-0	3-0	4-2	2-2	1-3	2-3	2-1	—	2-2	2-3	2-1	2-1	2-3	2-1
Rushden & Diamonds	1-1	3-2	2-2	2-1	3-2	5-0	4-1	4-1	3-1	6-0	3-1	3-0	1-0	0-2	3-0	0-0	—	5-2	2-0	0-0	3-0	0-1
Stourbridge	1-0	1-1	0-2	4-1	0-0	4-1	6-1	3-1	2-5	2-7	1-0	4-0	1-3	0-2	6-3	0-0	2-2	—	5-1	0-3	1-0	2-2
Sutton Coldfield Town	0-3	2-1	1-2	2-3	2-1	4-1	0-1	0-1	1-1	2-1	4-1	2-1	2-4	1-3	1-0	4-2	2-0	4-3	—	0-1	3-3	5-2
Tamworth	0-1	0-1	1-1	3-2	1-2	1-2	0-0	0-0	1-1	5-0	3-0	3-4	4-3	0-0	1-0	2-1	4-1	5-2	2-1	—	0-1	3-0
Weston-super-Mare	3-1	1-4	3-1	4-2	3-0	0-2	1-3	2-2	4-4	7-2	3-0	1-1	3-0	2-1	6-1	3-4	0-2	1-5	3-3	2-1	—	2-1
Yate Town	0-1	0-3	3-2	1-0	2-5	1-0	0-2	2-2	2-3	5-0	1-0	1-0	0-2	3-1	3-0	4-0	0-3	3-2	0-3	1-1	2-0	—

BEAZER HOMES SOUTHERN LEAGUE SOUTHERN DIVISION RESULTS 1992–93

	Andover	Ashford Town	Baldock Town	Braintree Town	Buckingham Town	Burnham	Bury Town	Canterbury City	Dunstable	Erith & Belvedere	Fareham Town	Fisher Athletic	Gravesend & N	Havant Town	Margate	Newport IOW	Poole Town	Salisbury City	Sittingbourne	Sudbury Town	Wealdstone	Witney Town
Andover	—	1-1	2-1	0-5	0-2	1-2	2-0	3-3	2-2	1-1	1-4	3-0	2-2	0-1	0-0	1-4	0-1	0-5	0-3	0-3	0-2	0-5
Ashford Town	4-3	—	1-0	7-4	2-1	1-3	7-0	5-1	4-0	0-2	3-0	4-0	1-0	2-2	1-4	1-2	5-1	0-1	2-2	0-2	0-2	1-0
Baldock Town	3-2	3-3	—	1-1	2-1	1-2	2-1	5-1	1-1	3-0	0-0	6-1	2-2	2-4	0-3	1-0	4-3	0-0	1-1	0-3	3-4	1-2
Braintree Town	5-0	2-2	4-0	—	2-0	3-0	4-1	4-0	1-0	0-2	3-2	6-1	0-1	0-2	0-1	1-0	3-1	5-1	3-3	1-1	4-1	2-3
Buckingham Town	2-0	0-2	0-2	2-0	—	0-2	1-1	3-1	1-1	1-0	2-1	0-0	2-0	0-2	0-0	0-0	0-0	2-4	3-1	1-1	0-4	0-0
Burnham	1-1	2-0	3-2	1-2	0-3	—	1-2	2-2	1-1	1-0	2-1	1-2	0-5	2-1	1-3	1-1	3-0	0-0	2-3	3-2	1-3	2-6
Bury Town	1-2	1-4	0-2	0-4	2-0	2-2	—	1-1	2-1	1-0	1-4	2-3	2-7	0-0	0-5	0-2	1-4	0-3	2-3	3-2	0-4	3-2
Canterbury City	2-3	3-2	0-0	2-1	0-4	0-2	1-0	—	2-2	1-2	3-0	2-0	2-3	0-0	5-1	1-0	1-0	1-2	1-5	3-1	3-0	1-1
Dunstable	1-3	1-2	0-3	1-7	2-3	2-0	5-1	0-5	—	1-3	0-0	0-0	2-3	1-2	1-1	1-1	0-3	1-0	1-1	1-6	3-0	0-1
Erith & Belvedere	4-0	2-6	2-1	1-3	1-0	4-1	3-2	6-1	2-0	—	3-2	1-0	1-4	0-2	1-0	2-1	2-0	2-3	1-0	1-1	1-1	2-0
Fareham Town	3-0	1-2	2-0	2-2	0-0	1-0	2-0	1-2	1-1	8-0	—	1-1	3-3	1-2	1-0	2-1	1-1	1-2	1-2	1-0	5-1	2-5
Fisher Athletic	1-3	2-1	1-2	2-0	1-3	1-2	3-0	0-0	4-0	1-0	1-6	—	0-4	1-4	0-5	2-2	1-3	2-2	1-1	0-4	0-1	0-1
Gravesend & Northfleet	5-0	3-1	0-1	4-0	3-4	4-1	4-1	4-0	3-0	3-5	0-1	2-1	—	4-3	2-0	0-1	2-0	2-0	3-3	2-0	3-0	2-1
Havant Town	1-0	0-3	1-0	3-2	3-2	1-1	0-1	1-0	4-1	0-0	2-0	6-0	3-2	—	1-2	1-1	3-1	0-2	2-1	0-2	4-2	1-3
Margate	1-0	0-4	0-2	2-5	1-0	4-0	0-2	1-0	2-2	2-0	3-1	1-3	2-0	2-0	—	1-1	3-1	3-5	0-0	0-0	1-2	1-2
Newport IOW	1-1	2-1	0-0	0-0	0-1	1-0	2-2	1-1	0-0	1-2	0-0	6-0	1-2	1-2	0-0	—	0-0	4-0	0-4	1-2	1-1	0-2
Poole Town	2-1	2-1	1-3	1-2	2-2	2-1	1-2	0-0	4-1	0-2	2-0	6-0	2-3	3-2	2-1	2-3	—	4-0	0-4	3-1	1-2	1-0
Salisbury City	3-3	2-0	1-0	1-2	1-4	4-0	5-3	4-0	1-0	4-1	2-0	4-1	3-0	2-1	2-0	2-1	2-1	—	1-2	3-1	1-0	1-1
Sittingbourne	4-0	4-0	4-1	3-1	2-1	1-1	3-0	4-1	2-2	2-0	3-1	6-0	1-0	3-2	3-0	4-2	0-0	0-1	—	2-2	2-1	4-0
Sudbury Town	2-1	1-1	4-1	4-1	5-2	2-1	4-1	1-0	5-0	3-1	2-2	3-1	1-3	1-1	2-3	4-1	5-1	1-1	1-3	—	3-1	0-2
Wealdstone	5-0	2-3	0-3	2-1	3-4	1-2	3-1	3-1	2-0	2-2	4-1	2-0	3-0	1-2	1-4	0-0	2-1	4-3	2-2	0-0	—	0-1
Witney Town	1-0	2-2	1-0	3-1	2-1	2-0	0-0	1-0	2-2	2-1	1-0	3-0	7-0	1-0	1-2	5-0	2-0	1-1	0-1	1-1	1-1	—

BARCLAYS COMMERCIAL SERVICES CUP

Preliminary Round
Worcester City 0,1 Cheltenham Town 2,6
Sudbury Town 1,7, Baldock Town 0,0

First Round, First Leg
Trowbridge Town 2, Stourbridge 1
Yate Town 1, Bilston Town 1
Hednesford Town 4, King's Lynn 0
Redditch United 3, Bridgnorth Town 0
Rushden & Diamonds 4, Atherstone United 0
Wealdstone 2, Buckingham Town 5
Sutton Coldfield Town 2, Grantham Town 1
Burton Albion 0, Gresley Rovers 1
Racing Club Warwick 2, Leicester United 2
Nuneaton Borough 0, VS Rugby 0
Tamworth 0, Bedworth United 0
Corby Town 7, Hinckley Town 1
Weston-super-mare 4, Newport AFC 4
Moor Green 1, Gloucester City 0
Halesowen Town 3, Solihull Borough 1
Evesham United 1, Cheltenham Town 1
Hastings Town 1, Chelmsford City 4
Bury Town 2, Dunstable 4
Cambridge City 1, Sudbury Town 3
Burnham 2, Braintree Town 2
Salisbury 3, Havant Town 1
Fareham Town 2, Weymouth 2
Forest Green Rovers 0, Dudley Town 0
Barri 1, Witney Town 2
Poole Town 0, Andover 0
Dorchester Town 1, Bashley 1
Newport IOW 0, Waterlooville 1
Fisher Athletic 1, Crawley Town 4
Ashford Town 0, Gravesend & Northfleet 4
Erith & Belvedere w.o. Dartford withdrew
Canterbury City 1, Sittingbourne 0
Margate 2, Dover Athletic 1

First Round, Second Leg
Stourbridge 6, Trowbridge Town 2
Bilston Town 2, Yate Town 1
King's Lynn 0, Hednesford Town 1
Bridgnorth Town 0, Redditch United 1
Atherstone United 2, Rushden & Diamonds 3
Buckingham Town 1, Wealdstone 0
Grantham Town 0, Sutton Coldfield Town 2
Gresley Rovers 3, Burton Albion 2
Leicester United 4, Racing Club Warwick 0
VS Rugby 0, Nuneaton Borough 1
Bedworth United 2, Tamworth 3
Hinckley Town 0, Corby Town 6
Newport AFC 1, Weston-super-mare 4
Gloucester City 3, Moor Green 0
Solihull Borough 3, Halesowen Town 4
Cheltenham Town 1, Evesham United 2
Chelmsford City 0, Hastings Town 1
Dunstable 2, Bury Town 2

Sudbury Town 3, Cambridge City 3
Braintree Town 2, Burnham 1
Havant Town 0, Salisbury 2
Weymouth 0, Fareham Town 3
Dudley Town 2, Forest Green Rovers 2
Witney Town 2, Barri 1
Andover 0, Poole Town 1
Bashley 2, Dorchester Town 0
Waterlooville 3, Newport IOW 2
Crawley Town 5, Fisher Athletic 2
Gravesend & Northfleet 3, Ashford Town 0
Sittingbourne 3, Canterbury City 3
Dover Athletic 3, Margate 1

Second Round
Bilston Town 1,0, Stourbridge 0,2
Hednesford Town 4, Redditch United 0
Rushden & Diamonds 6, Buckingham Town 2
Sutton Coldfield Town 0,1, Gresley Rovers 0,3
Leicester United 0, Nuneaton Borough 3
Tamworth 2, Corby Town 0
Newport AFC 1,2, Gloucester City 1,3
Halesowen Town 2, Evesham United 1
Chelmsford City 2,3, Dunstable 2,1
Sudbury Town 3, Braintree Town 1
Salisbury 1, Fareham Town 0
Forest Green Rovers 0, Witney Town 1
Poole Town 1, Bashley 4
Waterlooville 2, Crawley Town 3
Gravesend & Northfleet 3, Erith & Belvedere 2
Canterbury City 1, Dover Athletic 3

Third Round
Stourbridge 2, Hednesford Town 1
Rushden & Diamonds 2, Gresley Rovers 1
Nuneaton Borough 2, Tamworth 1
Gloucester City 2,1, Halesowen Town 2,2
Chelmsford City 2,1 Sudbury Town 2,1
  (Sudbury Town won on away goals)
Salisbury 1, Witney Town 2
Bashley 1, Crawley Town 2
Dover Athletic 3, Gravesend & Northfleet 0

Fourth Round
Stourbridge 2,4, Rushden & Diamonds 2
Nuneaton Borough 0, Halesowen Town 5
Sudbury Town 4, Witney Town 1
Crawley Town 1, Dover Athletic 2

Semi-final
Stourbridge 2,2, Halesowen Town 0,3
Dover Athletic 1,1, Sudbury Town 0,2
  (Dover Athletic won on away goals)

Final
Stourbridge 2,1, Dover Athletic 0,2

DIADORA FOOTBALL LEAGUE 1992–93

Premier Division

		Home			Away			Totals			Goals		
	P	W	D	L	W	D	L	W	D	L	F	A	Pts
Chesham United	42	17	3	1	13	5	3	30	8	4	104	34	98
St Albans City	42	15	5	1	13	4	4	28	9	5	103	50	93
Enfield	42	13	1	7	12	5	4	25	6	11	94	48	81
Carshalton Athletic	42	10	7	4	12	3	6	22	10	10	96	56	76
Sutton United	42	12	5	4	6	9	6	18	14	10	74	57	68
Grays Athletic	42	13	6	2	5	5	11	18	11	13	61	64	65
Stevenage Borough	42	10	2	9	8	6	7	18	8	16	62	60	62
Harrow Borough	42	7	8	6	9	6	6	16	14	12	59	60	62
Hayes	42	7	8	6	9	5	7	16	13	13	64	59	61
Aylesbury United	42	8	5	8	10	1	10	18	6	18	70	77	60
Hendon	42	6	11	4	6	7	8	12	18	12	52	54	54
Basingstoke Town	42	7	10	4	5	7	9	12	17	13	49	45	53
Kingstonian	42	8	5	8	6	5	10	14	10	18	59	58	52
Dulwich Hamlet	42	6	5	10	6	9	6	12	14	16	52	66	50
Marlow	42	4	7	10	8	4	9	12	11	19	72	73	47
Wokingham Town	42	7	9	5	4	4	13	11	13	18	62	81	46
Bromley	42	6	4	11	5	9	7	11	13	18	51	72	46
Wivenhoe Town	42	10	2	9	3	5	13	13	7	22	41	75	46
Yeading	42	5	5	11	6	7	8	11	12	19	58	66	45
Staines Town	42	7	5	9	3	8	10	10	13	19	59	77	43
Windsor & Eton	42	3	4	14	5	3	13	8	7	27	40	90	31
Bognor Regis	42	3	5	13	2	5	14	5	10	27	46	106	25

Division One

		Home			Away			Totals			Goals		
	P	W	D	L	W	D	L	W	D	L	F	A	Pts
Hitchin Town	40	14	3	3	11	4	5	25	7	8	67	29	82
Molesey	40	12	5	3	11	6	3	23	11	6	81	38	80
Dorking	40	14	0	6	9	9	2	23	9	8	73	40	78
Purfleet	40	11	7	2	8	5	7	19	12	9	67	42	69
Bishop's Stortford	40	12	3	5	7	7	6	19	10	11	63	42	67
Abingdon Town	40	8	7	5	9	6	5	17	13	10	65	47	64
Tooting & Mitcham United	40	12	5	3	5	7	8	17	12	11	68	46	63
Billericay Town	40	12	4	4	6	2	12	18	6	16	67	61	60
Wembley	40	7	8	5	7	7	6	14	15	11	44	34	57
Walton & Hersham	40	9	5	6	5	7	8	14	12	14	58	54	54
Boreham Wood	40	5	8	7	7	6	7	12	14	14	44	43	50
Maidenhead United	40	8	8	4	2	10	8	10	18	12	45	50	48
Leyton-Wingate	40	7	7	6	4	7	9	11	14	15	56	61	47
Whyteleafe	40	8	6	6	4	4	12	12	10	18	63	71	46
Uxbridge	40	7	7	6	4	6	10	11	13	16	50	59	46
Heybridge Swifts	40	6	2	12	5	7	8	11	9	20	47	65	42
Croydon	40	7	6	7	4	3	13	11	9	20	54	82	42
Chalfont St Peter	40	5	11	4	2	6	12	7	17	16	48	70	38
Barking	40	6	5	9	4	3	13	10	8	22	42	80	38
Lewes	40	5	5	10	4	5	11	9	10	21	34	80	37
Aveley	40	4	6	10	5	1	14	9	7	24	45	87	34

Division Two

		Home			Away			Totals			Goals		
	P	W	D	L	W	D	L	W	D	L	F	A	Pts
Worthing	42	15	4	2	13	3	5	28	7	7	105	50	91
Ruislip Manor	42	14	6	1	11	6	4	25	12	5	78	33	87
Berkhamsted Town	42	13	3	5	11	5	5	24	8	10	77	55	80
Hemel Hempstead	42	15	4	2	7	8	6	22	12	8	84	52	78
Metropolitan Police	42	14	2	5	8	4	9	22	6	14	84	51	72
Malden Vale	42	11	3	7	9	6	6	20	9	13	78	54	69
Chertsey Town	42	10	2	9	10	5	6	20	7	15	84	60	67
Saffron Walden	42	11	5	5	8	5	8	19	10	13	63	49	67
Newbury Town	42	7	11	3	7	7	7	14	18	10	53	51	60
Hampton	42	10	5	6	6	6	9	16	11	15	59	59	59
Edgware Town	42	9	6	6	7	4	10	16	10	16	84	75	58
Egham Town	42	7	5	9	9	4	8	16	9	17	60	71	57
Banstead Athletic	42	9	5	7	5	8	8	14	13	15	67	52	55
Leatherhead	42	9	5	7	5	6	10	14	11	17	66	61	53
Ware	42	5	9	7	7	2	12	12	11	19	68	76	47
Witham Town	42	6	6	9	4	10	7	10	16	16	54	65	46
Tilbury	42	6	7	8	6	1	14	12	8	22	55	101	44
Barton Rovers	42	6	9	6	3	5	13	9	14	19	40	66	41
Hungerford Town	42	7	4	10	4	4	13	11	8	23	37	93	41
Rainham Town	42	4	5	12	5	5	11	9	10	23	56	80	37
Harefield United	42	4	4	13	6	3	12	10	7	25	37	72	37
Southall	42	5	2	14	2	5	14	7	7	28	43	106	28

Division Three

	P	Home W	D	L	Away W	D	L	Totals W	D	L	Goals F	A	Pts
Aldershot Town	38	14	5	0	14	3	2	28	8	2	90	35	92
Thame United	38	10	7	2	11	4	4	21	11	6	84	38	74
Collier Row	38	9	7	3	12	4	3	21	11	6	68	30	74
Leighton Town	38	11	5	3	10	5	4	21	10	7	89	47	73
Cove	38	13	2	4	8	6	5	21	8	9	69	42	71
Northwood	38	12	4	3	7	7	5	19	11	8	84	68	68
Royston Town	38	11	3	5	6	5	8	17	8	13	59	42	59
East Thurrock United	38	9	4	6	8	3	8	17	7	14	69	58	58
Kingsbury Town	38	10	4	5	5	5	9	15	9	14	62	59	54
Hertford Town	38	6	4	9	8	6	5	14	10	14	61	64	52
Flackwell Heath	38	8	5	6	7	1	11	15	6	17	82	76	51
Tring Town	38	6	6	7	7	5	8	12	11	15	59	63	47
Hornchurch	38	7	6	6	4	7	8	11	13	14	53	52	46
Horsham	38	8	3	8	4	4	11	12	7	19	63	72	43
Epsom & Ewell	38	3	7	9	7	4	8	10	11	17	52	67	41
Bracknell Town	38	3	8	8	4	5	10	7	13	18	52	94	34
Clapton	38	6	1	12	2	6	11	8	7	23	46	74	31
Camberley Town	38	2	4	13	6	3	10	8	7	23	37	72	31
Petersfield United	38	2	6	11	4	6	9	6	12	20	36	90	30
Feltham & Hounslow Borough	38	4	1	14	1	3	15	5	4	29	47	119	19

LEADING GOALSCORERS

	Premier Division	Lge	Lge. C	FMC
32	Jimmy Bolton (Carshalton Athletic)	37		3
36	Steve Clark (St. Albans City)	36		
31	Dave Pearce (Kingstonian) (inc 15 and 3 for Hayes)	27	3	1
27	Graham Westley (Aylesbury United) (inc 5 and 4 for Enfield)	23	4	
26	Darren Collins (Enfield) (inc 8 and 3 for Aylesbury United)	23	3	
24	Chris Townsend (Chesham United)	24		
	Jon Warden (Carshalton Athletic)	19	1	4
22	Winston Whittingham (Grays Athletic)	19	1	2
21	Tommy Langley (Wokingham Town)	21		
	David Lay (Marlow)	13	6	2
20	Martin Gittings (Stevenage Borough)	20		

	Division One	Lge	Lge. C	FMC
30	Mark Hynes (Whyteleafe)	30		
28	Steve Lunn (Dorking)	22		6
26	Neil Pearson (Molesey)	22	2	2
23	John Collins (Tooting & Mitcham Utd)	21	1	1
21	Michael Rose (Molesey)	18	3	
	Mark Tompkins (Tooting & Mitcham Utd)	15	3	3

		Lge	Lge. C	Amt
20	Steve Jones (Billericay Town)	18	2	
18	Marc Das (Bishop's Stortford)	17		1

	Division Two	Lge	Lge. C	Amt
29	Steve Newing (Hemel Hempstead) (inc 23 and 2 for Edgware Town)	27		2
23	Peter Skerritt (Egham Town) (inc 7 Lge goals for Chertsey Town)	23		
21	Daniel Freeman (Worthing)	19	2	
20	Andy Linsell (Hemel Hempstead)	20		
	Richard Tiltman (Worthing)	18	1	1
	Stan Blair (Malden Vale)	17	3	

	Division Three	Lge	Lge. C	Amt
33	Steve Drewe (Leighton Town)	30	1	2
31	Stephen Stairs (Aldershot Town)	27	4	
30	David Whitehead (Hertford Town)	29	1	
	Nigel Mott (Thame United)	26	3	1
28	Tony Read (Collier Row)	28		
25	Daniel Wallace (East Thurrock United)	25		
	Tony Wood (Flackwell Heath)	23	1	1

DIADORA LEAGUE PREMIER DIVISION

	Aylesbury Utd	Basingstoke	Bognor Regis	Bromley	Carshalton Ath	Chesham Utd	Dulwich Hamlet	Enfield	Grays Athletic	Harrow Borough	Hayes	Hendon	Kingstonian	Marlow	St Albans	Staines Town	Stevenage Boro	Sutton Utd	Windsor & Eton	Wivenhoe Town	Wokingham	Yeading
Aylesbury Utd	—	1-1	2-0	6-1	3-2	1-4	0-2	1-1	1-2	0-1	1-1	1-1	2-0	0-3	3-2	5-3	1-2	0-4	3-0	1-2	1-0	1-1
Basingstoke	1-2	—	0-0	1-1	0-1	2-1	2-1	4-1	4-0	0-0	0-0	1-1	0-0	0-0	4-1	0-1	0-0	1-1	3-0	1-1	5-0	0-6
Bognor Regis	4-5	1-3	—	3-2	0-6	2-0	2-2	6-2	4-1	1-2	1-2	0-2	3-4	1-5	3-0	0-0	1-1	1-1	0-1	2-0	2-2	1-4
Bromley	1-2	1-0	3-2	—	0-4	2-2	2-1	4-1	2-3	1-3	1-1	1-0	0-2	0-1	2-3	4-1	1-2	1-1	1-2	3-0	0-2	1-0
Carshalton Ath	1-0	0-0	0-4	0-4	—	1-1	1-7	2-1	2-1	1-1	1-1	3-1	3-0	3-2	3-2	2-1	3-1	2-1	1-3	3-1	1-1	1-1
Chesham Utd	2-1	2-1	6-1	2-2	5-1	—	4-0	2-1	3-2	2-2	1-0	4-0	2-1	4-3	2-2	1-0	7-1	7-0	1-0	2-1	3-1	3-0
Dulwich Hamlet	0-1	0-0	2-2	2-1	1-7	4-0	—	2-0	2-0	1-2	2-3	2-1	2-1	1-1	1-2	2-0	0-2	0-2	0-0	5-0	2-1	0-1
Enfield	3-1	4-1	6-2	4-1	2-1	2-1	2-0	—	2-1	0-1	1-0	0-2	2-2	1-4	3-0	4-1	1-0	1-0	6-0	4-0	2-1	4-1
Grays Athletic	2-1	3-2	2-1	0-2	2-2	3-2	2-0	2-1	—	2-1	2-2	0-0	1-1	1-2	1-1	1-1	2-1	1-3	0-0	2-1	2-0	3-0
Harrow Borough	2-3	0-0	2-0	3-3	2-4	0-0	2-3	0-1	0-0	—	2-0	1-1	2-0	2-5	2-1	2-2	3-1	4-3	7-1	0-0	4-1	3-0
Hayes	4-0	0-0	1-2	1-1	0-4	1-0	2-1	1-0	1-1	2-2	—	1-1	2-3	2-1	1-2	4-0	0-1	2-2	2-0	2-1	4-2	0-0
Hendon	1-1	1-1	1-0	2-2	1-2	4-0	2-1	0-2	0-1	1-1	1-1	—	1-0	0-0	2-1	1-1	1-2	1-1	3-0	1-1	1-1	3-3
Kingstonian	7-1	0-0	3-4	2-2	0-2	2-1	2-1	2-2	1-0	1-2	1-0	2-4	—	2-0	1-0	3-1	0-2	0-1	0-2	0-1	3-1	2-0
Marlow	3-4	0-0	1-2	4-0	0-5	4-3	1-1	1-4	1-1	0-0	2-1	3-0	2-0	—	5-1	5-2	2-3	1-1	2-1	5-1	3-2	1-2
St Albans	1-0	4-1	3-0	2-3	3-2	2-2	0-5	3-0	1-1	2-1	1-2	2-1	1-0	5-1	—	2-2	2-1	2-2	3-0	3-0	7-2	1-1
Staines Town	1-4	0-1	0-0	0-1	0-3	1-0	2-0	4-1	6-0	3-0	1-2	3-3	2-0	1-4	2-2	—	4-0	1-0	0-1	1-2	1-1	2-0
Stevenage Boro	1-3	0-2	1-1	3-2	3-2	7-1	0-2	1-0	6-1	0-0	2-3	4-1	1-0	2-0	3-1	1-2	—	2-2	5-2	1-0	1-1	2-0
Sutton Utd	4-0	1-0	1-1	0-1	3-1	2-1	0-2	1-0	1-1	4-3	3-1	0-2	2-0	2-1	3-0	2-4	1-0	—	0-3	3-0	2-0	2-2
Windsor & Eton	2-3	1-0	0-1	3-1	1-4	1-0	0-0	6-0	3-3	0-0	5-0	1-2	1-1	1-2	3-0	3-1	2-4	1-3	—	1-1	1-2	0-2
Wivenhoe Town	2-1	3-2	2-0	0-1	0-4	2-1	5-0	4-0	0-2	0-0	1-2	2-0	2-3	2-1	3-0	1-1	0-0	3-3	3-1	—	1-0	1-3
Wokingham	0-2	3-1	2-2	1-1	2-2	3-1	2-1	2-1	2-0	4-1	4-2	1-1	3-1	3-2	7-2	1-1	1-1	2-0	1-2	1-0	—	2-2
Yeading	2-1	1-2	1-4	0-0	1-1	3-0	0-1	4-1	3-0	3-0	0-0	3-3	2-0	1-2	1-1	2-0	2-0	2-2	0-2	1-3	2-2	—

DIADORA LEAGUE DIVISION ONE

	Abingdon Town	Aveley	Barking	Billericay T	Bishops Stort	Boreham Wood	Chalfont St P.	Croydon	Dorking	Heybridge Swts	Hitchin Town	Lewes	Leyton	Maidenhead Utd	Molesey	Purfleet	Tooting & M	Uxbridge	Walton & Hersh	Wembley	Whyteleafe
Abingdon Town	—	4-1	1-0	4-1	0-1	2-1	1-1	1-1	1-1	2-5	0-1	4-0	2-2	0-0	0-2	3-3	1-1	0-1	2-1	2-0	4-2
Aveley	1-5	—	2-2	0-2	3-0	0-2	2-2	1-3	1-3	2-2	1-1	4-0	1-3	3-3	2-3	0-2	2-2	0-0	1-4	0-1	2-1
Barking	1-0	2-1	—	1-1	4-0	1-0	3-2	1-2	0-2	1-2	0-0	1-2	3-1	1-0	0-5	0-2	0-1	1-1	1-1	1-1	0-1
Billericay T.	0-1	0-2	1-1	—	4-1	2-2	0-4	3-2	1-3	2-1	0-2	1-1	1-2	3-0	2-0	2-0	3-0	2-1	4-2	1-1	3-1
Bishops Stort	0-1	2-0	5-1	4-0	—	1-0	2-2	2-0	1-2	2-1	0-1	6-0	3-3	0-0	1-2	1-0	2-1	4-1	2-0	0-1	3-2
Boreham Wood	2-1	3-0	3-0	1-0	1-0	—	1-1	0-1	0-0	1-1	0-1	2-0	1-1	2-2	0-0	0-0	0-4	0-1	0-2	0-2	1-1
Chalfont St P.	2-2	2-2	3-0	3-2	3-2	1-1	—	1-1	2-2	0-1	0-1	4-1	2-2	1-1	1-1	2-2	2-1	0-1	0-2	2-1	1-1
Croydon	0-0	1-2	1-0	2-0	2-0	4-3	2-4	—	1-1	5-0	0-3	2-2	2-1	3-3	0-3	0-5	2-1	1-1	1-2	1-0	4-2
Dorking	0-1	4-2	7-0	2-1	1-0	0-2	4-1	2-1	—	2-1	1-0	5-0	2-3	1-0	1-2	0-1	3-1	1-0	4-0	1-3	2-3
Heybridge Swts	1-2	1-2	2-1	2-1	2-3	1-0	6-0	3-0	0-2	—	0-7	1-2	2-0	0-1	2-1	0-1	2-1	1-0	3-3	1-0	2-1
Hitchin Town	1-1	3-0	3-2	2-0	2-1	0-0	0-0	2-0	1-2	1-0	—	1-0	1-0	0-0	2-0	3-1	2-1	2-0	1-2	0-0	3-0
Lewes	0-3	0-1	1-2	2-1	2-1	0-1	1-0	2-1	1-1	1-3	0-2	—	1-0	1-0	3-5	0-1	0-2	4-4	2-2	0-3	0-2
Leyton	0-0	1-0	2-1	0-1	2-1	1-1	2-2	1-0	0-2	0-0	2-0	4-0	—	1-1	2-4	4-1	2-0	1-0	1-1	0-3	5-0
Maidenhead Utd	0-0	1-2	0-0	3-1	0-0	1-2	0-0	4-2	0-1	0-0	0-0	0-1	1-0	—	0-0	2-2	1-1	4-0	3-1	0-0	3-0
Molesey	2-1	2-1	2-0	4-1	2-0	1-0	3-2	3-1	1-1	3-0	1-2	3-1	2-0	2-0	—	2-1	2-2	3-3	2-0	1-1	5-1
Purfleet	0-1	2-1	2-0	2-2	0-1	0-0	0-0	6-0	2-2	3-1	1-2	6-1	3-0	2-0	3-2	—	1-1	3-2	0-0	2-1	1-1
Tooting & M	5-0	1-0	6-1	2-0	1-1	1-4	2-2	3-2	1-2	2-2	2-0	1-2	1-1	3-0	1-1	2-1	—	3-2	2-1	1-1	2-6
Uxbridge	0-1	4-1	2-0	3-2	1-1	3-0	2-0	0-1	3-0	2-0	2-0	1-2	1-1	3-0	0-2	0-4	0-2	—	0-0	2-3	2-0
Walton & Hersh	2-2	6-0	1-1	0-2	1-1	0-1	2-2	0-1	1-1	3-3	1-2	1-1	4-1	2-1	0-1	1-1	0-0	1-0	—	1-0	3-2
Wembley	3-2	3-1	2-2	2-0	0-1	1-2	2-1	0-1	1-1	1-1	1-1	1-1	0-2	1-2	1-2	1-3	1-0	0-0	1-1	—	0-0
Whyteleafe	0-2	3-1	2-2	0-1	1-2	1-2	3-0	3-3	2-2	2-5	1-0	4-0	4-2	5-1	1-2	1-0	1-1	1-3	2-0	0-0	—

DIADORA LEAGUE DIVISION TWO

	Worthing	Witham Town	Ware	Tilbury	Southall	Saffron Walden	Ruislip Manor	Rainham Town	Newbury Police	Met Police	Malden Vale	Leatherhead	Hungerford Town	Hemel Hempstead	Harefield Utd	Hampton	Egham Town	Edgware Town	Chertsey Town	Berkhamstead T	Barton Rovers	Banstead Ath
Banstead Ath	0-3	0-0	2-2	4-1	1-0	1-0	1-2	4-1	0-1	1-0	2-0	4-2	8-0	1-1	5-2	1-1	1-2	1-2	0-1	0-1	2-2	—
Barton Rovers	0-7	1-1	3-2	0-2	1-1	2-2	2-1	1-1	0-1	0-1	0-3	0-0	3-0	0-3	0-0	1-0	0-0	3-0	2-2	1-1	—	1-0
Berkhamstead T	1-2	0-3	2-0	3-0	6-3	3-1	1-0	2-1	2-1	1-2	1-0	2-1	2-2	1-3	1-0	6-1	1-2	3-3	4-0	—	2-0	1-1
Chertsey Town	1-2	1-1	2-3	6-1	5-0	2-3	2-1	2-4	1-1	1-3	1-3	2-1	7-2	1-0	3-0	2-1	0-3	5-1	—	5-1	4-0	1-2
Edgware Town	1-2	4-2	5-2	2-3	4-4	1-2	0-1	2-2	1-2	3-1	1-1	1-1	4-1	2-2	6-1	4-1	1-0	—	4-0	0-3	2-1	1-1
Egham Town	2-5	3-3	1-3	2-1	3-2	2-0	1-3	2-0	1-1	2-0	0-2	3-2	1-1	6-4	1-3	1-2	—	2-5	1-2	1-1	0-0	0-2
Hampton	3-0	3-0	3-1	7-0	0-2	1-0	1-1	2-0	0-0	1-3	0-3	3-7	1-0	1-1	2-2	—	2-3	1-2	1-3	0-2	2-0	0-0
Harefield Utd	0-4	1-2	1-4	2-1	0-0	0-1	0-1	2-0	2-2	0-3	0-1	0-1	0-1	1-1	—	0-1	1-0	3-3	0-2	0-0	0-2	3-2
Hemel Hempstead	0-0	0-0	1-0	1-4	4-3	3-0	1-4	4-2	3-2	0-2	2-1	1-1	3-0	—	2-2	1-0	2-0	1-2	2-1	0-1	3-0	1-1
Hungerford Town	1-1	1-3	2-1	3-0	1-0	0-1	0-0	1-4	1-0	1-0	2-1	2-1	—	1-6	1-0	0-1	0-2	2-0	1-0	0-1	2-0	0-5
Leatherhead	0-2	2-1	0-2	3-1	3-0	1-2	0-2	0-1	1-2	1-1	—	1-2	3-0	1-1	1-3	3-3	4-0	1-1	0-1	5-0	3-1	0-0
Malden Vale	2-1	3-0	4-3	5-1	2-3	2-0	1-2	1-2	1-2	3-1	2-2	1-2	5-1	3-2	2-0	1-1	1-0	5-3	0-1	3-4	2-2	3-0
Met Police	0-1	0-1	5-1	0-1	3-2	1-3	1-1	4-0	4-1	—	3-1	1-1	4-1	3-1	0-1	4-0	5-0	0-2	0-1	3-0	4-2	4-1
Newbury Town	3-1	0-1	1-1	1-3	1-0	0-4	0-0	3-2	—	3-0	2-1	2-2	0-0	2-2	0-1	3-1	0-0	1-0	2-2	0-2	2-2	1-1
Rainham Town	1-1	2-2	0-4	8-0	4-0	1-1	0-2	—	1-2	2-4	0-0	0-1	3-0	2-3	2-1	1-2	1-3	2-2	2-2	2-4	3-0	2-0
Ruislip Manor	3-2	3-2	0-3	0-1	3-0	0-2	1-1	2-1	0-2	0-0	2-2	5-0	1-0	1-0	1-0	1-1	3-2	3-1	1-0	4-0	4-0	1-1
Saffron Walden	1-2	3-0	4-0	3-0	3-0	—	1-0	0-0	1-1	1-0	0-3	1-2	1-2	1-1	3-0	1-0	2-0	2-0	2-2	2-1	2-0	0-2
Southall	2-3	2-1	1-0	0-1	—	1-1	1-1	0-4	2-3	3-6	3-3	0-2	1-1	0-7	0-3	0-1	0-2	1-0	0-5	0-2	0-3	0-3
Tilbury	4-1	2-2	1-0	—	0-0	2-2	1-2	2-1	3-0	0-1	0-3	3-2	3-4	4-4	2-2	1-1	1-1	0-4	1-3	0-3	2-1	3-2
Ware	0-0	1-1	—	1-0	2-1	1-1	1-1	1-1	4-2	1-1	2-3	1-1	2-3	2-3	0-2	2-2	2-3	4-1	0-3	0-2	2-0	2-1
Witham Town	0-3	—	1-0	2-0	7-0	1-1	2-2	1-1	1-1	2-0	2-3	2-1	2-0	0-0	6-0	0-1	1-4	1-2	1-3	1-1	2-2	2-2
Worthing	—	3-2	1-0	3-0	5-1	3-1	2-0	5-2	1-1	2-2	2-3	3-1	3-1	1-1	2-3	3-0	4-0	2-2	2-1	2-2	4-0	2-1

DIADORA LEAGUE DIVISION THREE

Home \ Away	Aldershot Town	Bracknell Town	Camberley Town	Clapton	Collier Row	Cove	East Thurrock U	Epsom & Ewell	Felt & Hounslow	Blackwell Hth	Hertford Town	Hornchurch	Horsham	Kingsbury Town	Leighton Town	Northwood	Petersfield Utd	Royston Town	Thame Utd	Tring Town
Aldershot Town	—	2-2	6-1	4-2	1-1	1-1	1-0	1-1	2-0	3-1	0-0	0-0	3-2	4-0	2-1	4-0	3-0	1-0	2-1	4-0
Bracknell Town	3-3	—	3-3	1-3	1-3	0-1	2-3	2-0	2-1	0-4	5-2	5-2	1-1	0-2	0-4	0-0	0-0	0-1	2-4	2-2
Camberley Town	1-3	3-3	—	1-0	1-0	2-1	0-3	0-1	2-1	0-2	0-2	1-2	1-3	0-1	0-3	1-4	1-1	1-1	0-2	0-4
Clapton	2-1	1-2	1-4	—	0-3	1-1	1-2	1-3	1-2	0-6	2-3	2-1	1-0	1-1	1-2	0-1	4-0	3-4	5-1	1-0
Collier Row	1-2	5-1	1-0	0-0	—	1-1	3-1	5-1	2-0	3-1	0-0	0-0	3-0	2-2	2-4	5-0	3-0	0-1	0-0	0-0
Cove	1-3	3-2	2-0	1-0	1-1	—	3-1	4-3	6-0	1-0	3-1	1-5	3-2	2-1	0-1	0-0	0-0	3-0	2-3	3-0
East Thurrock U	0-1	2-2	4-2	2-0	3-1	1-1	—	3-0	4-2	1-4	3-0	1-3	3-0	2-2	2-3	4-1	4-1	2-1	1-4	3-1
Epsom & Ewell	1-2	0-2	0-3	1-3	0-2	2-2	3-0	—	1-1	1-1	2-3	2-2	0-5	5-3	1-4	2-5	2-5	1-1	0-1	0-1
Felt & Hounslow	1-3	3-5	1-3	1-1	1-0	0-1	1-1	1-3	—	1-4	2-3	2-2	2-2	1-5	2-7	3-5	3-2	3-2	0-5	3-1
Blackwell Hth	3-6	0-4	4-0	4-1	0-4	0-3	0-1	0-0	4-1	—	3-3	1-2	2-1	1-0	2-1	2-2	2-2	1-0	1-1	2-3
Hertford Town	2-3	3-2	3-1	4-2	3-4	1-2	3-0	1-2	4-0	4-6	—	3-1	2-1	1-0	0-2	3-3	3-3	0-1	0-3	1-1
Hornchurch	1-3	2-0	0-1	0-2	0-0	0-0	1-0	0-1	3-0	5-2	0-2	—	3-0	3-1	0-0	1-1	1-1	1-2	0-1	2-0
Horsham	0-1	2-2	2-3	1-1	1-2	1-0	0-4	2-1	6-0	2-1	4-1	2-1	—	5-3	1-1	2-3	0-1	1-1	1-2	2-4
Kingsbury Town	1-0	4-0	0-0	3-0	0-2	1-3	3-2	3-3	4-1	2-1	1-2	1-1	3-0	—	5-3	1-1	3-1	1-0	1-1	1-3
Leighton Town	1-1	6-0	4-2	3-1	0-0	4-2	2-3	3-3	4-1	3-1	2-1	4-3	5-1	1-0	—	4-1	4-1	2-0	1-1	2-2
Northwood	0-3	4-3	1-0	2-0	1-3	0-1	4-1	1-0	2-2	5-4	2-5	3-3	2-3	0-0	1-1	—	1-3	1-1	2-1	3-2
Petersfield Utd	0-1	0-0	1-0	2-0	1-2	0-0	4-1	2-5	3-0	0-6	1-2	1-1	2-3	3-2	4-1	1-3	—	0-4	0-5	1-1
Royston Town	2-2	9-0	1-0	1-1	0-2	3-0	0-0	1-1	2-0	6-0	1-1	1-0	4-1	2-5	2-2	2-3	1-2	—	2-3	0-1
Thame Utd	0-2	9-0	0-1	2-1	0-3	2-3	2-0	2-0	3-1	1-0	1-1	1-0	4-1	1-0	3-2	0-2	8-0	0-0	—	0-1
Tring Town	0-2	4-1	0-1	1-1	2-0	1-6	2-2	1-2	3-1	2-0	0-0	1-1	4-1	2-3	1-1	3-3	0-2	3-1	3-1	—

DIADORA FOOTBALL LEAGUE CUP

Preliminary Round
Billericay Town 2, East Thurrock United 0
Bracknell Town 0, Banstead Athletic 3
Camberley Town 1, Edgware Town 0
Cove 3, Berkhamsted 2
Feltham & Hounslow Borough 2, Barton Rovers 1
Flackwell Heath 1, Chertsey Town 3
Hemel Hempstead 3, Lewes 1
Hertford Town 3, Southall 1
Hungerford Town 1, Metropolitan Police 5
Kingsbury Town 2, Harefield United 0
Leatherhead 1, Aldershot Town 1 (aet)
Leighton Town w/o Farnham Town
Northwood 4, Collier Row 1
Petersfield United 2, Horsham 3
Purfleet 3, Royston Town 1
Rainham Town 1, Hampton 5
Saffron Walden Town 2, Newbury Town 0
Thame United 3, Epsom & Ewell 0
Tilbury 2, Ruislip Manor 4 (aet)
Tring Town 1, Egham Town 2
Ware 1, Malden Vale 2
Witham Town 1, Clapton 0
Worthing 2, Hornchurch 0

Replay
Aldershot Town 3, Leatherhead 2

First Round
Abingdon Town 3, Camberley Town 1
Aylesbury United 4, Aveley 2
Barking 1, Wivenhoe Town 6
Basingstoke Town 3, Walton & Hersham 0
Bognor Regis Town 1, Metropolitan Police 3
Boreham Wood 4, Feltham & Hounslow Borough 1 (aet)
Chalfont St. Peter 2, Saffron Waldem Town 1
Chertsey Town 2, Egham Town 3 (aet)
Cove 0, Hayes 5
Croydon 3, Carshalton Athletic 3 (aet)
Dulwich Hamlet 1, St. Albans City 0 (aet)
    (at Tooting & Mitcham United FC)
Enfield 7, Whyteleafe 0
Grays Athletic 2, Windsor & Eton 3
Hampton 1, Dorking 0 (aet)
Harrow Borough 3, Bromley 0
Hemel Hempstead 1, Marlow 4
Hendon 7, Hertford Town 0
Horsham 2, Staines Town 4
Kingstonian 3, Malden Vale 2
Kingsbury Town 0, Aldershot Town 1
Leighton Town 2, Tooting & Mitcham United 3
Leyton 2, Chesham United 1
Maidenhead United 1, Yeading 1 (aet)
Molesey 2, Bishop's Stortford 1
Purfleet w/o Harlow Town
Ruislip Manor 3, Heybridge Swifts 0
Stevenage Borough 1, Billericay Town 2
Sutton United 2, Hitchin Town 0
Thame United 3, Wembley 1
Uxbridge 0, Northwood 1

Wokingham Town 2, Witham Town 0
Worthing 3, Banstead Athletic 1 (aet)

Replays
Carshalton Athletic 0, Croydon 1
Yeading 4, Maidenhead United 1

Second Round
Abingdon Town 3, Molesey 3 (aet)
Aldershot Town 5, Hampton 2 (aet)
Aylesbury United 3, Thame United 3 (aet)
Basingstoke Town 0, Metropolitan Police 1
Boreham Wood 2, Purfleet 0
Dulwich Hamlet 1, Worthing 3
Hayes 2, Croydon 1
Hendon 2, Ruislip Manor 1
Kingstonian 1, Billericay Town 0 (aet)
Leyton 2, Tooting & Mitcham United 3
Marlow 5, Egham Town 1
Northwood 2, Windsor & Eton 3
Staines Town 0, Yeading 1
Sutton United 4, Chalfont St. Peter 1
Wivenhoe Town 2, Harrow Borough 1
Wokingham Town 0, Enfield 1

Replays
Molesey 1, Abingdon Town 0 (aet)
Thame United 2, Aylesbury United 3 (aet)

Third Round
Aylesbury United 1, Enfield 2
Hendon 2, Aldershot Town 1
Marlow 3, Yeading 1
Metropolitan Police 1, Wivenhoe Town 2
Molesey 3, Tooting & Mitcham United 0
Sutton United 3, Boreham Wood 0
Windsor & Eton 0, Hayes 1
Worthing 1, Kingstonian 2

Fourth Round
Hendon 1, Enfield 1 (aet)
Kingstonian 0, Marlow 4
Molesey 2, Hayes 0
Wivenhoe Town 1, Sutton United 2

Replay
Enfield 2, Hendon 0

Semi-finals First Leg
Enfield 1, Molesey 0
Sutton United 0, Marlow 2

Semi-finals Second Leg
Marlow 2, Sutton United 1
    (Marlow won 4-1 on aggregate)
Molesey 5, Enfield 0
    (Molesey won 5-1 on aggregate)

Final
Marlow 2, Molesey 1
    (at Aldershot Town FC)

ISTHMIAN FOOTBALL LEAGUE FULL MEMBERS CUP

Preliminary Round
Abingdon Town 1, Basingstoke Town 2
Aveley 2, Bromley 5
Aylesbury United 2, Marlow 5
Bishop's Stortford 5, Billericay Town 0
Chesham United 1, Stevenage Borough 3
Hayes 1, Wembley 0
Heybridge Swifts 0, Wivenhoe Town 1
Molesey 2, Dulwich Hamlet 0
Sutton United 3, Lewes 1
Uxbridge 0, Harrow Borough 1
Wokingham Town 2, Chalfont St. Peter 0

First Round
Barking 0, Leyton 2
Bishop's Stortford 1, Hayes 2
Bromley 3, Maidenhead United 0
Carshalton Athletic 1, Bognor Regis Town 0
Croydon 1, Wokingham Town 2

Dorking 1, Walton & Hersham 0
Grays Athletic 2, Wivenhoe Town 0
Hendon 0, Boreham Wood 0 (aet)
    (Boreham Wood won 4-2 on penalties)
Marlow 3, St. Albans City 2
Molesey 2, Staines Town 0
Purfleet 2, Harrow Borough 1
Stevenage Borough 0, Enfield 2
Sutton United 2, Kingstonian 1
Tooting & Mitcham United 3, Basingstoke Town 1
Windsor & Eton 3, Whyteleafe 0
Yeading 1, Hitchin Town 2

Second Round
Boreham Wood 2, Hayes 4
Bromley 2, Dorking 4
    (at Dorking FC)
Enfield 1, Grays Athletic 2
Hitchin Town 1, Leyton 1 (aet)
    (Hitchin Town won 4-1 on penalties)

Marlow 2, Purfleet 3
Sutton United 2, Tooting & Mitcham United 3
Windsor & Eton 2, Molesey 1
Wokingham Town 2, Carshalton Athletic 2 (*aet*)
  (*Carshalton Athletic won 4-3 on penalties*)

Third Round
Carshalton Athletic 6, Windsor & Eton 1
Dorking 2, Hitchin Town 1 (*aet*)
Hayes 2, Grays Athletic 1

Tooting & Mitcham United 1, Purfleet 1 (*aet*)
  Tooting & Mitcham United won 4-2 on penalties)

Semi-finals
Carshalton Athletic 1, Dorking 2
Hayes 0, Tooting & Mitcham United 2

Final
Dorking 0, Tooting & Mitcham United 1
  (*at Kingstonian FC*)

ISTHMIAN LEAGUE ASSOCIATE MEMBERS TROPHY

Preliminary Round
Aldershot Town 4, Chertsey Town 1
Banstead Athletic 1, Egham Town 1 (*art*)
  (*Banstead Athletic won 5-4 on penalties*)
Barton Rovers 3, V Clapton 0
Bracknell Town 0, Newbury Town 2
East Thurrock United 1, Collier Row 0
Hemel Hempstead 2, Tring Town 4 (*aet*)
Hungerford Town 0, Hampton 1
Leighton Town 2, Flackwell Heath 1
Royston Town 3, Hornchurch 0
Saffron Walden Town 1, Ware 0

First Round
Berkhamstead Town 2, Tring Town 1
Cove 2, Banstead Athletic 3
  (*Abandoned in extra time — fog*)
Edgware Town 4, Hertford Town 1
Horsham 0, Aldershot Town 1
Leatherhead 1, Camberley Town 1 (*aet*)
  (*Leatherhead won 4-1 on penalties*)
Leighton Town 1, Barton Rovers 2
Metropolitan Police 4, Feltham & Hounslow Borough 0
Newbury Town 1, Hampton 1 (*aet*)
  (*Newbury Town won 6-5 on penalties*)
Northwood 3, East Thurrock United 1
Petersfield United 1, Malden Vale 3
Royston Town 1, Saffron Walden Town 2
Ruislip Manor 3, Rainham Town 1
Southall 3, Epsom & Ewell 2
Tilbury 1, Kingsbury Town 2
Thame United 2, Witham Town 1
Worthing 4, Harefield United 0

Replay
Banstead Athletic 0, Cove 2

Second Round
Barton Rovers 3, Ruislip Manor 0
Berkhamsted Town 0, Edgware Town 2 (*aet*)
Cove 0, Thame United 2
Kingsbury Town 4, Saffron Walden Town 3
Metropolitan Police 3, Leatherhead 2 (*aet*)
Newbury Town 3, Malden Vale 1
Southall 1, Northwood 2
Worthing 4, Aldershot Town 4 (*aet*)
  (*Worthing won 5-3 on penalties*)

Third Round
Kingsbury Town 0, Barton Rovers 1 (*aet*)
Newbury Town 3, Metropolitan Police 7
Northwood 3, Edgware Town 2
Thame United 0, Worthing 1

Semi-finals
Barton Rovers 2, Metropolitan Police 2 (*aet*)
Northwood 3, Worthing 1 (*aet*)

Replay
Metropolitan Police 1, Barton Rovers 2

Final
Barton Rovers 1, Northwood 3 (*aet*)

VAUXHALL FA CHALLENGE TROPHY 1992–93

First Qualifying Round

Spennymoor United v Brandon United	4-3
Accrington Stanley v Whitley Bay	3-1
North Shields withdrew, Easington Colliery w.o	
Peterlee Newtown v Guiseley	2-1
Chorley v Newcastle Blue Star	2-2, 1-3
Leicester United v Worksop Town	1-1, 5-1
Alvechurch withdrew, Halesowen Town w.o	
Droylsden v Winsford United	0-2
Alfreton Town v Eastwood Town	2-4
Redditch United v Caernarfon Town	0-3
Shepshed Albion v Bedworth United	1-0
Congleton Town v Grantham Town	4-2
Mossley v Dudley Town	6-2
Gainsborough Trinity v Solihull Borough	1-1, 4-4, 0-4
Moor Green v Colwyn Bay	1-1, 2-4
Chelmsford City v Hendon	1-3
Hayes v Tamworth	6-1
Stevenage Borough w.o Harlow Town withdrew	
Heybridge Swifts v Cambridge City	2-1
Corby Town v Billericay Town	1-4
Hitchin Town v Bishop's Stortford	3-1
Staines Town v Leyton	1-2
Baldock Town v Barking	4-3
Boreham Wood v Aveley	3-1
Tooting & Mitcham United v Walton & Hersham	0-1
Uxbridge v Bognor Regis Town	3-2
Ashford Town v Yeading	0-0, 2-5
Molesey v Basingstoke Town	1-3
Whyteleafe v Hastings Town	2-2, 1-1, 0-3
Croydon v Dulwich Hamlet	0-1
Fareham Town v Margate	2-2, 0-1
Andover v Abingdon Town	0-3
Carshalton Athletic v Crawley Town	1-2
Marlow v Lewes	3-2
Weymouth v Newport AFC	2-2, 1-2
Barri v Bideford	2-1
(at Bideford)	
Saltash United v Trowbridge Town	2-5
Dorchester Town v Waterlooville	3-1

Second Qualifying Round

Accrington Stanley v Easington Colliery	5-0
Seaham Red Star v Spennymoor United	2-4
Peterlee Newton v Shildon	1-1, 0-2
Workington v Newcastle Blue Star	0-2
West Auckland Town v Consett	1-1, 2-2, 1-1, 0-3
Stockton v Ferryhill Athletic	10-2
Nuneaton Borough v Congleton Town	3-1
Hednesford Town v Halesowen Town	1-2
Caernarfon Town v Goole Town	1-4
Winsford United v Buxton	0-0, 3-0
Warrington Town v Shepshed Albion	3-0
Colwyn Bay v Solihull Borough	0-1
Leicester United v Matlock Town	3-1
Mossley v Eastwood Town	3-1
Sutton Coldfield Town v Leyton	2-1
St Albans City v Hayes	3-2
Billericay Town v Stourbridge	3-4
Stevenage Borough v Chalfont St Peter	2-1
Wembley v Hitchin Town	3-1
Purfleet v Boreham Wood	3-2
Hendon v Grays Athletic	0-0, 1-2
Baldock Town v Heybridge Swifts	0-1
Basingstoke Town v Crawley Town	2-0
Abingdon Town v Marlow	2-1
Margate v Hastings Town	1-3
Yeading v Maidenhead United	2-2, 3-0
Walton & Hersham v Gravesend & Northfleet	2-0
Fisher Athletic v Canterbury City	2-2, 1-3
Uxbridge v Dulwich Hamlet	0-2
Dorchester Town v Poole Town	1-2
Trowbridge Town v Newport AFC	0-1
Barri v Weston-super-Mare	0-2

Third Qualifying Round

Fleetwood Town v Blyth Spartans	1-3
Goole Town v Bishop Auckland	0-1
Emley v Spennymoor United	2-6
Warrington Town v Stockton	5-2
Morecambe v Southport	2-2, 3-1
Horwich RMI v Winsford United	1-2
Mossley v Frickley Athletic	2-4
Guisborough Town v Shildon	2-0
Whitby Town v South Bank	2-1
Accrington Stanley v Tow Law Town	6-0
Billingham Synthonia v Consett	1-1, 6-2
Northallerton Town v Newcastle Blue Star	2-1
Nuneaton Borough v Burton Albion	0-0, 3-0
Grays Athletic v Atherstone United	2-1
Heybridge Swifts v Halesowen Town	1-0
Wealdstone v Solihull Borough	5-2
St Albans City v Purfleet	2-0
Stourbridge v Leek Town	1-4
Stafford Rangers v Wembley	1-1, 1-0
Harrow Borough v Stevenage Borough	2-2, 0-4
Sutton Coldfield Town v VS Rugby	1-1, 4-5
Chesham United v Leicester United	7-3
Slough Town v Bromley	3-1
Poole Town v Bashley	1-1, 2-2, 2-4
Newport AFC v Sutton United	1-2
Weston-super-Mare v Windsor & Eton	1-0
Basingstoke Town v Dulwich Hamlet	3-0
Abingdon Town v Dorking	2-1
Kingstonian v Canterbury City	5-0
Yeading v Walton & Hersham	3-1
Worcester City v Salisbury	2-1
Hastings Town v Wokingham Town	2-1

First Round

Spennymoor United v Boston United	1-2
Telford United v Northwich Victoria	2-1
Marine v Blyth Spartans	2-0
Hyde United v Runcorn	1-2
Warrington Town v Guisborough Town	2-1
Gateshead v Gretna	3-0
Barrow v Billingham Synthonia	0-1
Winsford United v Altrincham	1-0
Murton v Nuneaton Borough	1-2
Stalybridge Celtic v Accrington Stanley	2-0
Bishop Auckland v Leek Town	1-0
Northallerton Town v Whitby Town	3-0
Morecambe v Frickley Athletic	5-1
Macclesfield Town v Witton Albion	0-0, 0-0, 1-2
Sutton United v Woking	3-0
Basingstoke Town v Kingstonian	1-4
Yeading v Slough Town	1-1, 1-2
Welling United v Aylesbury United	2-1
Grays Athletic v Stafford Rangers	1-0
Merthyr Tydfil v Wivenhoe Town	3-0
Heybridge Swifts v Worcester City	4-0
Yeovil Town v Dagenham & Redbridge	0-0, 1-2
St Albans City v Weston-super-Mare	1-0
Dover Athletic v Hastings Town	1-1, 2-0
Kidderminster Harriers v Enfield	1-3
Wycombe Wanderers v Cheltenham Town	3-1
Stevenage Borough v Bath City	2-0
Kettering Town v Bromsgrove Rovers	0-0, 1-4
Wealdstone v Bashley	1-2
Farnborough Town v Abingdon Town	4-0
VS Rugby v Chesham United	1-6
Gloucester City received a bye	

Second Round

Farnborough Town v Enfield	4-0
Bishop Auckland v Warrington Town	0-1
St Albans City v Witton Albion	0-2
Nuneaton Borough v Marine	0-1
Northallerton Town v Bashley	1-0
Stevenage Borough v Grays Athletic	0-1
Billingham Synthonia v Winsford United	1-2

Welling United v Boston United   1-2
Gateshead v Heybridge Swifts   3-1
Kingstonian v Telford United   1-2
Morecambe v Wycombe Wanderers   1-1, 0-2
Sutton United v Slough Town   3-1
Chesham United v Dover Athletic   1-0
Bromsgrove Rovers v Dagenham & Redbridge   3-1
Gloucester City v Runcorn   3-3, 2-2, 0-0, 1-4
Stalybridge Celtic v Merthyr Tydfil   1-1, 0-1

Third Round
Telford United v Boston United   1-1, 0-4
Grays Athletic v Gateshead   1-1, 0-3
Chesham United v Sutton United   1-3
Merthyr Tydfil v Warrington Town   1-1, 2-3
Wycombe Wanderers v Bromsgrove Rovers   2-0
Witton Albion v Marine   1-0
Runcorn v Wnsford United   1-0
Northallerton Town v Farnborough Town   1-3

Fourth Round
Witton Albion v Farnborough Town   3-2
Sutton United v Warrington Town   2-1
Wycombe Wanderers v Gateshead   1-0
Boston United v Runcorn   0-2

Semi-finals
Wycombe Wanderers v Sutton United   2-3, 4-0
Runcorn v Witton Albion   2-0, 0-1

FINAL at Wembley

10 MAY

Wycombe Wanderers (2) 4 *(Cousins, Kerr, Thompson, Carroll)*

Runcorn (1) 1 *(Shaugnessy)*   32,968

Wycombe Wanderers: Hyde; Cousins, Cooper, Kerr, Crossley, Thompson, Carroll, Ryan, Hutchinson (Hayrettin), Scott, Guppy.
Runcorn: Williams; Bates, Robertson, Hill, Harold (Connor), Anderson, Brady (Parker), Brown, Shaughnessy, McKenna, Brabin.
Referee: I. Borrett (Norfolk).

FA CHALLENGE VASE 1992–93

Extra Preliminary Round

Sunderland IFG Roker v Heaton Stannington	1-0
Ponteland United v Seaton Delaval Amateurs	1-0
Newton Aycliffe v Walker	1-2
Marske United v South Shields	2-4
General Chemicals v Wythenshawe Amateurs	1-2
Poulton Victoria v Heswall	4-3
Castleton Gabriels v Ashville	2-3
Grove United v St Dominics	2-1
Atherton Collieries v Ayone	4-1
Newton (WC) v Westhoughton Town	2-1
Maghull v Blackpool Mechanics	3-1
Knypersley Victoria v Waterloo Dock	1-5
(at Waterloo Dock)	
Cheadle Town v Merseyside Police	0-1
Sutton Town v Shirebrook Colliery	1-3
Rossington Main v Priory (Eastwood)	3-5
Kimberley Town v Stocksbridge Park Steels	2-3
Liversedge v Hallam	1-2
Blidworth MW v Mickleover RBL	3-1
Tadcaster Albion v Pontefract Collieries	2-6
Selby Town v Yorkshire Amateur	3-2
Worsboro Bridge MW v Winterton Rangers	3-0
Clipstone Welfare v Hall Road Rangers	3-2
Friar Lane OB v Immingham Town	4-2
Dunkirk v Nettleham	5-3
Glasshoughton Welfare v Maltby MW	2-1
Hatfield Main v Res Parkgate	1-1, 3-1
Coleshill Town v Anstey Nomads	3-3, 2-5
Armitage v Stourport Swifts	2-0
St Andrews v Highfield Rangers	4-1
Pelsall Villa v Birstall United	5-1
Pegasus Juniors v Daventry Town	1-0
Brackley Town v Stapenhill	1-4
Eccleshall v Stewart & Lloyds	1-4
West Bromwich Town v Barwell	1-2
Westfields v Oadby Town	3-2
Lutterworth Town v Kings Heath	0-2
Mile Oak Rovers v Knowle	5-2
Cradley Town v Northfield Town	1-2
Bolehall Swifts v Holwell Sports	3-2
Pershore Town v Harrowby United	1-0
Bloxwich Town v Meir KA	1-3
Fakenham Town v Woodbridge Town	2-1
Somersham Town v Ipswich Wanderers	4-0
Downham Town v Brightlingsea United	1-1, 1-1, 3-0
Hadleigh United v Stansted	7-0
Brantham Athletic v Chatteris Town	0-1
Sawbridgeworth Town v Warboys Town	2-1
Norwich United v Cornard United	2-1
Long Sutton Athletic v Sudbury Wanderers	2-4
Ely City v St Ives Town	2-1
Totternhoe v Stotfold	2-1
Rayners Lane v Long Buckby	3-4
Harpenden Town v The 61	6-0
Hillingdon Borough v Brook House	0-5
Amersham Town v Langford	1-5
Viking Sports v London Colney	1-2
Shillington w.o Woodford Town withdrew	
Wingate & Finchley v Waltham Abbey	5-2
Beaconsfield United v Cockfosters	1-2
(at Cockfosters)	
Bowers United v Hanwell Town	1-2
Biggleswade Town v Leverstock Green	0-2
Brimsdown Rovers v Kempston Rovers	4-0
Concord Rangers v Potters Bar Town	1-4
Crowborough Athletic v West Wickham	0-1
Hartley Wintney v Deal Town	2-0
Cranleigh v Bedfont	4-0
Darenth Heathside v Petersfield United	3-2
Ash United v Broadbridge Heath	4-3
Godalming & Guildford v Slade Green	0-3
Farleigh Rovers v Cobham	1-4
(at Cobham)	
Ditton v Ramsgate	1-2
Cray Wanderers w.o Farnham Town withdrew	

Bicester Town v Brockenhurst	1-1, 0-1
BAT v Sherborne Town	3-3, 2-3
Ryde Sports v Wantage Town	1-2
Kintbury Rangers v Wollen Sports	0-2
Hamworthy United v Fleet Town	0-5
Milton United v AFC Lymington	1-2
Wotton Rovers v Bridgewater Town	0-2
Backwell United v Bishops Sutton	3-0
North Leigh v Flight Refuelling	6-2
Cirencester Town v Old Georgians	2-0
Larkhall Athletic v Cinderford Town	1-4
DRG (FP) v Brislington	2-4
Patchway v Fairford Town	1-1, 1-2
Calne Town v Tuffley Rovers	1-4
Moreton Town v Bemerton Heath Harlequins	1-2
Almondsbury Picksons v Swindon Supermarine	3-2
Truro City v Crediton United	0-1
Porthleven v Elmore	4-2

Preliminary Round

Prudhoe East End v Durham City	1-3
Cleator Moor Celtic v Annfield Plain	3-2
Esh Winning v Willington	5-1
Shotton Comrades v Norton & Stockton Ancients	3-0
Horden CW v Bedlington Terriers	0-3
Billingham Town v Ryhope CA	3-0
Walker v Pickering Town	1-1, 0-3
Langley Park v Sunderland IFG Roker	0-1
Washington v Ponteland United	0-5
(at Hebburn)	
Darlington CB v Hebburn	2-1
South Shields v Penrith	2-0
Evenwood Town v Crook Town	5-0
Lancaster City v Flixton	1-3
Waterloo Dock v Ashville	3-2
Newton (WC) v Clitheroe	0-6
Glossop North End v Rocester	2-3
St Helens Town v Maine Road	2-4
Chadderton v Prescot AFC	1-2
Atherton Collieries v Merseyside Police	1-0
Netherfield v Oldham Town	5-0
Bootle v Rossendale United	2-3
Darwen v Curzon Ashton	2-3
Maghull v Irlam Town	2-0
Formby v Atherton LR	0-2
Wythenshawe Amateurs v Burscough	1-3
Blackpool (wren) Rovers v Poulton Victoria	5-2
Ashton United v Skelmersdale United	3-3, 3-1
Grove United v Nantwich Town	1-1, 4-1
Salford City v Douglas High School OB	5-0
Louth United v Harworth CI	5-4
Glasshoughton Welfare v Selby Town	3-2
Friar Lane OB v Denaby United	3-3, 2-2, 3-0
Hinckley Town v Thackley	2-2, 1-3
Priory (Eastwood) v Oakham United	3-1
Brigg Town v Sheffield	3-0
Clipstone Welfare v Hatfield Main	4-2
Ossett Town v Rainworth MW	2-3
Borrowash Victoria v Shirebrook Colliery	2-3
Garforth Town v Eccleshill United	4-3
Dunkirk v Ilkeston Town	1-3
Heanor Town v Arnold Town	0-2
Blidworth MW v Bradford Park Avenue	1-2
Belper Town v Pontefract Collieries	4-3
Armthorpe Welfare v Hallam	4-0
Worsboro Bridge MW v Ossett Albion	1-1, 1-1, 3-3, 3-2
Stocksbridge Park Steels v Harrogate Town	4-1
Halesowen Harriers v Walsall Wood	3-0
Stratford Town v Northfield Town	2-0
Bolehall Swifts v Barwell	2-1
Mile Oak Rovers v Boldmere St Michaels	0-2
Wellingborough Town v St Andrews	0-4
Pegasus Juniors v Chasetown	4-2
Highgate United v Pelsall Villa	0-2
Armitage v Rothwell Town	1-2

Kings Heath v Stapenhill   1-4
Meir KA v Lye Town   1-1, 2-3
Bilston Town v Rushall Olympic   6-0
Rushden & Diamonds v Anstey Nomads   3-2
Racing Club Warwick v Oldbury United   1-2
Paget Rangers v Raunds Town   4-5
Pershore Town v Stewart & Lloyds   0-1
Malvern United v Sandwell Borough   1-4
Blakenall v Bridgnorth Town   3-4
Westfields v Wednesfield   1-3
Canvey Island v Peterborough City   1-0
Newmarket Town v Sawbridgeworth Town   1-2
Norwich United v Somersham Town   5-0
Chatteris Town v Boston   2-3
Soham Town Rangers v Thetford Town   6-2
Watton United v Bury Town   2-0
Desborough Town v Tiptree United   1-4
Stowmarket Town v Kings Lynn   1-2
Hadleigh United v Witham Town   6-2
Ely City v Eynesbury Rovers   1-2
Basildon United v Lowestoft Town   1-2
March Town United v Stamford Town   0-1
Histon v Gorleston   1-0
Halstead Town v Holbeach United   4-1
Sudbury Wanderers v Fakenham Town   4-1
Felixstowe Town v Mirrless Blackstone   1-2
Berkhamsted Town v Bourne Town   1-2
Downham Town v Royston Town   0-3
Kingsbury Town v Langford   2-1
Clapton v Hornchurch   3-1
Cockfosters v Haringey Borough   2-0
Leverstock Green v Brook House   0-1
Eton Manor v Hoddesdon Town   1-2
Totternhoe v Rainham Town   1-1, 1-3
Tring Town v Bracknell Town   7-0
Collier Row v Potters Bar Town   1-2
Tilbury v Cheshunt   2-1
Shillington v Feltham & Hounslow Borough   0-2
Barton Rovers v Arlesey Town   4-1
Hertford Town v Welwyn Garden City   5-0
Wootton Blue Cross v Barkingside   1-1, 1-1, 2-1
Ruislip Manor v London Colney   9-0
Milton Keynes Borough v Harpenden Town
            1-1 (abandoned, waterlogged pitch), 5-2
Hemel Hempstead v Hanwell Town   4-2
Wingate & Finchley v Ware   0-2
Flackwell Heath v Letchworth Garden City   2-1
Dunstable v Long Buckby   5-1
Brimsdown Rovers v Braintree Town   2-0
Southall v Hampton   0-8
   (at Hampton)
Cranleigh v Faversham Town   2-1
Eastbourne Town v Ringmer   2-3
Ramsgate v Egham Town   3-1
Langney Sports v Sittingbourne   0-4
Eastbourne United v Hailsham Town   0-8
Corinthian v Slade Green   2-1
Leatherhead v Alma Swanley   2-0
Steyning Town v Corinthian-Casuals   1-7
Tunbridge Wells v Three Bridges   1-1, 2-1
Chichester City v Cray Wanderers   0-3
Lancing v Chipstead   0-4
Beckenham Town v Redhill   3-2
Croydon Athletic v Greenwich Borough   1-3
Horsham v Pagham   2-1
West Wickham v Shoreham   3-4
Merstham v Horsham YMCA   3-1
Worthing United v Oakwood   1-2
Camberley Town v Haywards Heath Town   3-0
Worthing v Cove   2-0
Tonbridge v Southwick   4-1
Banstead Athletic v Whitstable Town   2-2, 1-1, 2-1
Darenth Heathside v Arundel   2-2, 1-3
Ash United v Sheppey United   1-0
Epsom & Ewell v Chatham Town   3-1
Whitehawk v Burgess Hill Town   1-2
Wick v Selsey   6-0
Ashford Town (Middx) v Havant Town   0-3
Burnham v Cobham   4-1

Hartley Whitney v Portfield   3-0
Sholing Sports v Fleet Town   1-1, 1-2
Sherborne Town v Witney Town   0-4
Thatcham Town v Brockenhurst   2-0
Westbury United v Wantage Town   3-1
Abingdon United v First Tower United   1-3
Wollen Sports v Bournemouth   2-3
Didcot Town v Eastleigh   1-2
AFC Totton v Banbury United   1-3
AFC Lymington v Swanage Town & Herston   3-1
Newbury Town v Romsey Town   6-2
Oxford City v Thame United   3-2
Minehead v Bemerton Heath Harlequins   1-2
Brislington v Cirencester Town   2-0
Bridgwater Town v Cinderford Town   2-0
North Leigh v Fairford Town   3-1
Bristol Manor Farm v Frome Town   2-1
Tuffley Rovers v Chippenham Town   1-0
Clevedon Town v Devizes Town   6-1
Backwell United v Chard Town   2-1
Almondsbury Picksons v Odd Down   4-2
Glastonbury v Melksham Town   5-3
Mangotsfield United v Wellington Town   4-1
Exmouth Town v Ilfracombe Town   1-3
Barnstaple Town v Porthleven   3-1
Crediton United v Ottery St Mary   7-0
St Blazey v Torpoint Athletic   3-1
Newquay v Liskeard Athletic   3-2
Torrington v Tiverton Town   0-2

First Round
Durham City v Evenwood Town   3-0
Sunderland IFG Roker v Esh Winning   0-1
West Allotment Celtic v Chester-le-Street Town
                                             3-3, 3-6
Cleator Moor Celtic v Ponteland United   2-2, 3-6
Alnwick Town v Dunston FB   1-1, 2-3
Pickering Town v South Shields   3-3, 1-1, 4-3
Bedlington Terriers v Eppleton CW   0-2
Shotton Comrades v Darlington CB   1-0
Whickham v Billingham Town   0-2
Prescot AFC v Salford City   0-1
Burscough v Netherfield   2-1
Rocester v Flixton   0-2
Atherton Collieries v Blackpool (wren) Rovers   4-1
Radcliffe Borough v Waterloo Dock   1-3
Atherton LR v Grove United   2-0
Curzon Ashton v Clitheroe   3-3, 1-0
Rossendale United v Ashton United   2-5
Maine Road v Maghull   3-1
Stocksbridge Park Steels v Friar Lane OB   2-0
Hucknall Town v Louth United   2-1
Arnold Town v Shirebrook Colliery   3-0
Brigg Town v Bradford Park Avenue   2-1
Garforth Town v Priory (Eastwood)   3-0
Clipstone Welfare v Glasshoughton Welfare   6-2
Belper Town v Rainworth MW   4-3
Thackley v Worsboro Bridge MW   1-2
Ilkeston Town v Lincoln United   2-2, 1-2
Harrogate RA v Armthorpe Welfare   2-1
Wednesfield v Boldmere St Michaels   3-0
Willenhall Town v Stratford Town   0-0, 0-3
Oldbury United v Lye Town   3-2
Pelsall Villa v Raunds Town   4-0
Bilston Town v Pegasus Juniors   2-1
Rothwell Town v Bolehall Swifts   4-0
Stewart & Lloyds v Stapenhill   1-2
St Andrews v Bridgnorth Town   2-2, 1-3
Rushden & Diamonds v Halesowen Harriers   3-3, 2-0
Northampton Spencer v Sandwell Borough   0-3
Watton United v Bourne Town   1-3
Halstead Town v Stamford Town   1-3
Hadleigh United v Histon   1-2
Lowestoft Town v Sudbury Wanderers   2-1
Haverhill Rovers v Sawbridgeworth Town   0-1
Mirrless Blackstone v Spalding United   2-3
Wroxham v Canvey Island   0-3
Eynesbury Rovers v Potton United   0-2
Royston Town v Tiptree United   2-2, 0-1

Norwich United v Soham Town Rangers	4-0
Boston v Kings Lynn	1-2
Ware v Milton Keynes Borough	2-3
Wootton Blue Cross v Barton Rovers	1-4
Hoddesdon Town v Hemel Hempstead	1-0
Rainham Town v Kingsbury Town	0-2
Burnham Ramblers v Potters Bar Town	3-1
Flackwell Heath v Feltham & Hounslow Borough	2-3
Ruislip Manor v Hampton	1-1, 2-1
Brimsdown Rovers v Dunstable	0-1
East Thurrock United v Clapton	2-4
Harefield United v Brook House	3-1
Ford United v Tilbury	1-0

(Ford subsequently removed from competition for playing two ineligible players.)

Leighton Town v Tring Town	1-3
Cockfosters v Hertford Town	0-4
Peacehaven & Telscombe v Herne Bay	5-1
Shoreham v Merstham	1-2
Hartley Wintney v Arundel	2-0
Corinthian-Casuals v Worthing	6-0
Greenwich Borough v Cranleigh	1-3
Burgess Hill Town v Tunbridge Wells	2-3
Erith & Belvedere v Ramsgate	2-1
Beckenham Town v Ash United	2-3
Leatherhead v Ringmer	1-0
Tonbridge v Chipstead	4-0
Sittingbourne v Camberley Town	7-0
Burnham v Corinthian	5-1
Cray Wanderers v Oakwood	2-1
Havant Town v Epsom & Ewell	1-0
Banstead Athletic v Horsham	4-3
Hailsham Town v Wick	3-2
Banbury United v Forest Green Rovers	2-2, 2-5
Fleet Town v Witney Town	0-2
Gosport Borough v Bournemouth	2-4
Thatcham Town v Newbury Town	4-2
Eastleigh v Oxford City	1-3
Westbury United v First Tower United	1-2
Bridport v AFC Lymington	0-3
Backwell United v Taunton Town	2-4
Bemerton Heath Harlequins v Brislington	2-1
Welton Rovers v Tuffley Rovers	2-0
Cinderford Town v Glastonbury	6-2
Clevedon Town v Mangotsfield United	7-1
North Leigh v Bristol Manor Farm	2-1
Shortwood United v Almondsbury Picksons	3-3, 0-3
Newquay v Dawlish Town	4-1
Barnstaple Town v Crediton United	2-1
Falmouth Town v Tiverton Town	0-3
Ilfracome Town v St Blazey	5-4

Second Round

Great Harwood Town v Bamber Bridge	2-3
Pickering Town v Billingham Town	2-2, 1-5
Bridlington Town v Eppleton CW	1-0
Chester-le-Street Town v Esh Winning	5-1
Ponteland United v Garforth Town	3-1
Shotton Comrades v Durham City	2-5
Harrogate RA v Dunston FB	0-6
Atherton Collieries v Worksboro Bridge MW	
2-2 (abandoned 90 mins),	3-3, 2-1
Waterloo Dock v Ashton United	2-6
Atherton LR v Stocksbridge Steels Park	2-2, 2-1
Knowsley United v Arnold Town	3-2
Curzon Ashton v Belper Town	3-1
Burscough v Lincoln United	3-1
Maine Road v Flixton	5-5, 1-2
Cammell Laird v Salford City	6-3
Eastwood Hanley v North Ferriby United	1-0
Newcastle Town v Brigg Town	3-4
Hucknall Town v Clipstone Welfare	0-3
Norwich United v Stamford Town	3-0
Rothwell Town v Wisbech Town	5-2
Pelsall Villa v West Midlands Police	1-1, 2-1
Bilston Town v Wednesfield	6-1
Histon v Hinckley Athletic	2-3
Rushden & Diamonds v Gresley Rovers	2-2, 1-3
Oldbury United v Stratford Town	1-2

Spalding United v Bourne Town	2-2, 1-4
Stapenhill v Bridgnorth Town	2-2, 0-7
Kings Lynn v Sandwell Borough	2-1
Harwich & Parkeston v Erith & Belvedere	2-1
Peacehaven & Telscombe v Northwood	2-1
Cray Wanderers v Merstham	1-0
Harefield United v Kingsbury Town	
2-2 (abandoned after 90 mins),	3-1
Metropolitan Police v Tilbury	0-6
Hoddesdon Town v Potton United	2-0
Great Yarmouth Town v Lowestoft Town	0-0, 0-2
Edgware Town v Barton Rovers	1-4
Hailsham Town v Clapton	4-3
Walthamstow Pennant v Tiptree United	
1-0 (ordered to be replayed),	1-0
Saffron Walden Town v Ruislip Manor	3-1
Dunstable v Buckingham Town	1-1, 3-1
Sittingbourne v Chertsey Town	4-2
Sudbury Town v Canvey Island	2-3
Tunbridge Wells v Tonbridge	3-1
Milton Keynes Borough v Tring Town	0-1
Malden Vale v Hertford Town	3-0
Burnham Ramblers v Banstead Athletic	2-3
Corinthian-Casuals v Diss Town	1-2
Burnham v Sawbridgeworth Town	3-2
Ash United v Littlehampton Town	
0-0 (aband.after 90 mins),	0-4
Newport (IW) v Thatcham Town	2-1
Cranleigh v North Leigh	3-0
Hungerford Town v Witney Town	0-3
Hartley Wintney v Bournemouth	3-1
Oxford City v Evesham United	1-2
Forest Green Rovers v Leatherhead	2-1
First Tower United v Havant Town	3-2
Yate Town v Paulton Rovers	1-2
Clevedon Town v Barnstaple Town	5-4
Wimborne Town v Almondsbury Picksons	1-4
Bemerton Heath Harlequins v Taunton Town	1-0
Welton Rovers v Ilfracombe Town	1-0
Newquay v AFC Lymington	1-0
Tiverton Town v Cinderford Town	5-1

Feltham & Hounslow Borough received a bye

Third Round

Bridgnorth Town v Atherton Collieries	4-0
Knowsley v Flixton	5-2
Hinckley Athletic v Clipstone Welfare	1-0
Bamber Bridge v Cammell Laird	1-2
Curzon Ashton v Chester-le-Street Town	7-1
Burscough v Ponteland United	1-0
Dunston FB v Billingham Town	5-1
Brigg Town v Bridlington Town	1-3
Atherton LR v Ashton United	1-2
Eastwood Hanley v Durham City	2-5
Cray Wanderers v Tring Town	2-3
Stratford Town v Bilston Town	0-2
Buckingham Town v Saffron Walden Town	3-2
Harwich & Parkeston v Banstead Athletic	0-3
Feltham & Hounslow Borough v Tunbridge Wells	1-2
Tilbury v Hoddesdon Town	2-3
Barton Rovers v Diss Town	2-1
Bourne Town v Peacehaven & Telscombe	4-4, 0-4
Norwich United v Harefield United	1-2
Burnham v Gresley Rovers	1-2
Cranleigh v Hailsham Town	1-3
Sittingbourne v Malden Vale	4-2
Walthamstow Pennant v Lowestoft Town	0-1
Littlehampton Town v Pelsall Villa	0-1
Canvey Island v Kings Lynn	1-0
Hartley Wintney v Rothwell Town	0-3
Newport (IW) v Welton Rovers	2-0
Tiverton Town v Almondsbury Picksons	2-1
First Tower United v Paulton Rovers	0-0, 1-5
Clevedon Town v Bemerton Heath Harlequins	2-1
Witney Town v Forest Green Rovers	1-2
Newquay v Evesham United	1-3

Fourth Round

Bridlington Town v Curzon Ashton	5-3
Burscough v Cammell Laird	0-1
Gresley Rovers v Bridgnorth Town	3-0
Hinckley Athletic v Pelsall Villa	2-2, 1-4
Dunston FB v Durham City	3-1
Bilston Town v Ashton United	3-0
Rothwell Town v Knowsley United	1-0
Newport (IW) v Lowestoft Town	4-1
Evesham United v Clevedon Town	
0-2 (ordered to be replayed), 1-3	
Harefield United v Canvey Island	2-2, 0-1
Peacehaven & Telscombe v Sittingbourne	4-1
Tring Town v Banstead Athletic	0-1
Buckingham Town v Paulton Rovers	4-0
Forest Green Rovers v Hailsham Town	6-5
Barton Rovers v Tiverton Town	0-4
Hoddesdon Town v Tunbridge Wells	3-1

Fifth Round

Buckingham Town v Pelsall Villa	1-0
Rothwell Town v Bridlington Town	1-2
Gresley Rovers v Peacehaven & Telscombe	1-0
Banstead Athletic v Newport (IW)	3-0
Forest Green Rovers v Tiverton Town	0-6
Dunston FB v Cammell Laird	2-1
Bilston Town v Hoddesdon Town	3-2

Canvey Island v Clevedon Town	1-0

Sixth Round

Bridlington Town v Banstead Athletic	1-0
Gresley Rovers v Dunston FB	2-0
Buckingham Town v Tiverton Town	1-4
Canvey Island v Bilston Town	2-0

Semi-finals

Bridlington Town v Gresley Rovers	2-1, 1-1
Tiverton Town v Canvey Island	2-0, 0-1

FINAL at Wembley

8 MAY

Bridlington Town (0) 0 *(Radford)*

Tiverton Town (0) 0   9061

Bridlington Town: Taylor; Brentano, McKenzie, Harvey, Bottomley, Woodcock, Grocock, Roberts, Jones, Radford (Tyrell), Parkinson.
Tiverton Town: Nott; Smith J, Saunders N, Saunders M, Short (Scott), Steele, Annunziata, Smith K, Everett, Daly, Hynds (Rogers).
Referee: R. Hart (Darlington).

FA COUNTY YOUTH CHALLENGE CUP 1992–93

First Round

North Riding v Durham	2-5
Northumberland v Liverpool	0-6
Manchester v Cheshire	2-1
Lincolnshire v Derbyshire	0-4
Worcestershire v Herefordshire	4-2
Leicestershire & Rutland v Birmingham	1-4
London v Cambridgeshire	0-1
Oxfordshire v Essex	1-7
Huntingdonshire v Bedfordshire	2-2, 4-4, 1-5
Gloucestershire v Berks & Bucks	2-1
Kent v Dorset	1-2
Royal Navy v Devon	0-4
Cornwall v Army	2-1

Second Round

Cumberland v Lancashire	3-3, 2-0
Durham v West Riding	2-0
Liverpool v Westmorland	5-2
Manchester v Sheffield & Hallamshire	2-1
Derbyshire v Staffordshire	1-5
Worcestershire v Northamptonshire	4-3
Birmingham v Shropshire	4-1
East Riding v Nottinghamshire	1-0
Cambridgeshire v Norfolk	2-1
Essex v Suffolk	1-2
Hertfordshire v Surrey	2-1
Bedfordshire v Middlesex	2-1
Gloucestershire v Hampshire	2-1

Dorset v Sussex	0-0, 1-0
Devon v Wiltshie	1-3
Cornwall v Somerset & Avon	2-5

Third Round

Liverpool v Cumberland	6-2
Durham v Manchester	4-0
East Riding v Staffordshire	3-1
Birmingham v Worcestershire	2-0
Hertfordshire v Cambridgeshire	3-1
Suffolk v Bedfordshire	1-0
Wiltshire v Gloucestershire	3-2
Dorset v Somerset & Avon	1-1, 3-1

Fourth Round

Suffolk v Dorset	3-0
Birmingham v Liverpool	1-2
Durham v Wiltshire	4-1
Hertfordshire v East Riding	2-0

Semi-finals

Liverpool v Suffolk	2-0
Durham v Hertfordshire	6-2

Final

Durham v Liverpool	4-0

FA SUNDAY CUP 1992–93

Preliminary Round

Humbledon Plains Farm v Clubmoor Nalgo	0-2
Manfast Kirkby v Green Man	4-1
Bournville Warriors v Leicester City Bus	3-5
Crawley Sports Club v Olympic Star	0-1
Lee Chapel North v Slade Celtic	2-1
Watford Labour Club v Chapel United	3-1
Hammer v Chequers (Herts)	1-4
Inter Royalle v Hamham Sunday	0-2
Lebeq Tavern v St Merton	0-1
BRSC Aidan v Reading Borough	1-5

First Round

Lynemouth v BRNESCO	1-1, 0-3
Albion Sports v Royal Oak	1-3
Almithak v Blyth Waterloo SC	1-1, 1-0
Hartlepool Lion Hotel v Nenthead	1-1, 4-1
Mayfield United withdrew, Baildon Athletic w.o	
B & A Scaffolding v Railway Hotel	1-0
Blue Union v Clubmoor Nalgo	0-3
Framwellgate Moor & Pity Me v Dudley & Weetslade	7-3
Dock v Woodlands 84	11-0
Northwood v Lion Hotel	3-4
Bolton Woods v Britannia VNC	1-2
Iron Bridge v Lobster	1-2
Mitre BS v Star Athletic	7-1
Wirral Boxers v East Levenshulme	1-3
East Bowling Unity v Croxteth & Gilmoss RBL	2-1
Littlewoods Athletic v Netherby RBL	4-1
Napoli v Whetley Lane	3-1
Chesterfield Park v Carnforth	1-4
Renbad Rovers v Manfast Kirkby	0-3
Seymour v Halewood Labour	4-1
Wednesfield Albion v Dulwich	1-2
Leicester City Bus v AD Bulwell	5-1
Altone Steels v FC Coachman	4-0
Cork & Bottle v Vanaid	0-1
Olympic Star v Ansells Stockland Star	0-1
Kenwick Dynamos v Jolly Farmers	1-2
Olton Royale v Gamlingay OB	5-1
Lee Chapel North v Inter Volante	2-3
Luton Way v Brookvale Athletic	4-3
North Lynn Sunday w.o Evergreen withdrew	
Watford Labour Club v Sandwell	1-0
St Clement's Hospital v Hundred Acre	2-1
Girton Eagles v Elliott Star (Sunday)	0-0, 2-3
Poringland Wanderers v Continental	4-2
AEL v Chequers (Herts)	2-1
Heathfield v Fryerns Community	2-0
Dereham Hobbies v Priory Sports	2-1
Collier Row Supporters v Sawston Keys	0-2
Berner United v Rolls Royce (Sunday)	2-2, 3-2
Phoenix v St Joseph's (Sth Oxhey)	0-1
Concord Rangers v Bly Spartans	1-1, 0-3
Merton Admiral v Thorn Walk Tavern	6-1
Somerset Ambury V & E v Hanham Sunday	2-1
Coach & Horses v Leyton Argyle	2-1
Broad Plain House (Sunday) v Caversham Park	1-2
Bedfont Sunday v Old Wimbledonians	5-1
Quested v ST Merton	2-1
Oxford Road Social v St Peter's	1-3
Sheerness Steel United v Northfield Rangers	1-3
Horn Park v Hove Dynamos	4-0
Poole Town Social v Reading Borough	0-2
Sartan United v Santogee 66	0-2

Second Round

Royal Oak v Mitre BS	2-1
Clubmoor Nalgo v Britannia VNC	1-1, 3-4
Seymour v Almithak	2-0
East Levenshulme v Baildon Athletic	3-3, 2-4
BRNESC v Oakenshaw	1-2
Littlewoods Athletic v Manfast Kirkby	0-2
Nicosia v Carnforth	4-0
Lobster v Hartlepool Lion Hotel	2-0

Dock v Napoli	2-3
B & A Scaffolding v Lion Hotel	2-1
A3 v Framwellgate Moor & Pity Me	4-3
Eagle Knowsley v East Bowling Unity	1-0
Dulwich v Inter Volante	2-2, 3-1
Altone Steels v Jolly Farmers	1-3
Bricklayers Sports v Vanaid	1-3
North Lynn Sunday v Marston Sports	1-2
Leicester City Bus v St Joseph's (Luton)	0-2
Olton Royale v St Clement's Hospital	4-0
Sawston Keys v Lodge Cottrell	1-2
Ansells Stockland Star v Poringland Wanderers	1-0
Ouzavich v Ford Basildon	3-1
Luton Way v Caversham Park	2-3
AEL v Dereham Hobbies	5-0
Quested v Elliott Star (Sunday)	4-1
Watford Labour Club v Theale	0-2
St Peter's v Bedfont Sunday	2-4
Heathfield v Merton Admiral	4-0
Ranelagh Sports v Northfield Rangers	4-3
Coach & Horses v Reading Borough	1-4
St Joseph's (Sth Oxhey) v Berner United	1-2
Horn Park v Somerset Ambury V & E	1-2
Santogee 66 v Bly Spartans	0-4

Third Round

Eagle Knowsley v Manfast Kirkby	2-3
B & A Scaffolding v Britannia VNC	1-0
Nicosia v Baildon Athletic	4-0
Jolly Farmers v Lobster	1-1, 1-2
Marston Sports v Royal Oak	2-1
Seymour v Napoli	0-0, 3-2
Oakenshaw v A3	6-2
St Joseph's (Luton) v Olton Royale	0-0, 1-0
Bedfont Sunday v Somerset Ambury V & E	2-2, 2-0
Lodge Cottrell v Dulwich 0-0 (abandoned 100 mins. bad light),	3-1
Berner United v Heathfield	1-3
Ansells Stockland Star v Reading Borough	1-1, 3-1
AEL v Caversham Park	1-1, 3-1
Ranelagh Sports v Vanaid	2-0
Theale v Ouzavich	5-0
Bly Spartans v Quested	2-0

Fourth Round

Seymour v Oakenshaw	5-1
Manfast Kirkby v B & A Scaffolding	1-0
Marston Sporrts v Nicosia	1-0
Lodge Cottrell v Lobster	3-1
Ranelagh Sports v Theale	2-1
St Joseph's (Luton) v Bedfont Sunday	1-2
AEL v Heathfield	1-0
Bly Spartans v Reading Borough	3-4

Fifth Round

Bedfont Sunday v Ranelagh Sports	2-1
AEL v Marston Sports	3-5
Seymour v Lodge Cottrell	3-1
Manfast Kirkby v Reading Borough	0-3

Semi-finals

Reading Borough v Seymour	0-2
Marston Sports v Bedfont Sunday	0-1

Final

Seymour v Bedfont Sunday	1-0

FA YOUTH CHALLENGE CUP 1992–93

Extra Preliminary Round

Chadderton v Marine	0-1
Huddersfield Town v Lincoln City	1-2
Chasetown v Halesowen Town	0-2
Brantham Athletic v Cambridge City	2-2, 1-3
Canvey Island v Clapton	0-5
Bracknell Town v Walton & Hersham	3-3, 1-4
Erith & Belvedere v Dulwich Hamlet	1-2
Peacehaven & Telscombe v Shoreham	5-1
Bournemouth v Dorchester Town	1-1, 1-0

Preliminary Round

Lancaster City withdrew, Hartlepool United w.o	
Billingham Synthonia w.o Stockton withdrew	
Shotton Comrades v Guisborough Town	0-4
Carlisle United v Scarborough	4-1
Burscough v Blackpool (wren) Rovers	10-0
Barrow v Rochdale	0-3
Preston North End w.o Accrington Stanley withdrew	
Wigan Athletic v Southport	7-0
Warrington Town v Bolton Wanderers	1-2
Marine v Stalybridge Celtic	3-1
Salford City v Atherton LR	5-1
Wrexham v Stockport County	1-2
Lutterworth Town w.o Halifax Town withdrew	
Lincoln City v Nottingham Forest	2-4
Mansfield Town v Grimsby Town	2-0
Hinckley Town v Burton Albion	0-2
Bilston Town v Hednesford Town	2-0
Port Vale w.o Rocester withdrew	
Pelsall Villa v Telford United	0-1
Willenhall Town v Wednesfield	2-3
Redditch United v Boldmere St Michaels	1-1, 2-6
Halesowen Town v Tamworth	4-1
Evesham United v Bedworth United	0-5
Nuneaton Borough w.o Mile Oak Rovers & Youth withdrew	
Flackwell Heath v Rothwell Town	1-3
Bromsgrove Rovers v Wootton Blue Cross	9-2
Rushden & Diamonds v Corby Town	5-0
Leighton Town v Wycombe Wanderers	0-6
Wivenhoe Town v Bishop's Stortford	4-0
Cambridge City v Harwich & Parkeston	6-2
Eynesbury Rovers v Braintree Town	4-1
Wisbech Town v Saffron Walden Town	1-1, 1-4
Brook House v Stevenage Borough	4-2
Baldock Town v Royston Town	0-3
Welwyn Garden City v Hitchin Town	2-2, 1-3
Barkingside v Bedfont	1-5
Hertfort Town v Boreham Wood	1-4
Clapton v Waltham Abbey	0-2
East Thurrock United v Beaconsfield United	6-0
Enfield v Thamesmead Town	0-0, 2-4
Eton Manor w.o Southall withdrew	
Northwood v Wembley	0-4
Uxbridge v Ruislip Manor	0-0, 1-4
Hillingdon Borough v Kingsbury Town	0-2
Staines Town v Hendon	3-0
Walton & Hersham v Marlow	0-6
Croydon v Hanwell Town	2-2, 6-2
Molesey v Hampton	2-5
Whitstable Town v Lewes	1-2
Herne Bay v Dover Athletic	0-1
Langney Sports v Margate	1-5
Oakwood v Redhill	1-2
Chipstead w.o Maidstone United withdrew	
Dulwich Hamlet v Ashford Town	3-1
Bromley v Sittingbourne	5-1
Chatham Town v Faversham Town	5-0
Worthing United v Malden Vale	2-2, 0-6
(first game at Shoreham)	
Peacehaven & Telscombe v Three Bridges	8-1
Steyning Town v Kingstonian	0-0, 1-4
Worthing v Whitehawk	9-0
Basingstoke Town v Croydon Athletic	1-3
Wick v Slough Town	2-0

Camberley Town v Farnborough Town	1-3
Maidenhead United v Wokingham Town	1-1, 1-3
Andover v Trowbridge Town	4-0
Bournemouth v Hungerford Town	0-2
Havant Town v Chippenham Town	5-2
Thatcham Town v Petersfield United	0-1
Gloucester City v Yate Town	6-1
Yeovil Town v Cheltenham Town	2-3
Weston-super-Mare v Torquay United	1-3
Frome Town v Bristol Rovers	2-4

First Qualifying Round

Carlisle United v Billingham Synthonia	9-2
Hartlepool United v Guisborough Town	4-1
Wigan Athletic v Rochdale	1-1, 1-0
Burscough v Preston North End	2-3
Stockport County v Marine	1-1, 4-2
Bolton Wanderers v Salford	5-3
Burton Albion v Nottingham Forest	1-2
Lutterworth Town v Mansfield Town	0-3
Wednesfield v Port Vale	1-6
Bilston Town v Telford United	1-1, 1-0
Nuneaton Borough v Halesowen Town	5-2
Boldmere St Michaels v Bedworth United	0-3
Wycombe Wanderers v Bromsgrove Rovers	3-1
Rothwell Town v Rushden & Diamonds	3-1
Saffron Walden Town v Cambridge City	1-1, 1-4
Wivenhoe Town v Eynesbury Rovers	4-1
Bedfont v Royston Town	2-2, 2-0
Brook House v Hitchin Town	5-4
Thamesmead Town v Waltham Abbey	1-1, 4-5
Boreham Wood v East Thurrock United	2-2, 4-1
Kingsbury Town v Wembley	0-7
Eton Manor v Ruislip Manor	2-3
Hampton v Marlow	1-2
Staines Town v Croydon	1-4
Redhill v Dover Athletic	2-1
Lewes v Margate	3-0
Chatham Town v Dulwich Hamlet	2-4
Chipstead v Bromley	2-4
Worthing v Peacehaven & Telscombe	4-4, 4-3
Malden Vale v Kingstonian	2-7
Wokingham Town v Wick	3-1
Croydon Athletic v Farnborough Town	2-3
Petersfield United v Hungerford Town	1-1, 0-6
Andover v Havant Town	1-3
Bristol Rovers v Cheltenham Town	3-0
Gloucester City v Torquay United	1-3

Second Qualifying Round

Hartlepool United v Carlisle United	0-1
Preston North End v Wigan Athletic	5-5, 2-0
Bolton Wanderers v Stockport County	0-1
Mansfield Town v Nottingham Forest	0-2
Bilston Town v Port Vale	1-2
Bedworth United v Nuneaton Borough	2-1
Rothwell Town v Wycombe Wanderers	0-5
Wivenhoe Town v Cambridge City	1-1, 2-3
Brook House v Bedfont	0-5
Boreham Wood v Waltham Abbey	2-1
Ruislip Manor v Wembley	1-4
Croydon v Marlow	4-2
Lewes v Redhill	1-1, 3-1
Bromley v Dulwich Hamlet	
1-2 (match ordered to be replayed and ended in a 1-1 draw), 2-3	
Kingstonian v Worthing	2-2, 0-4
Farnborough Town v Wokingham Town	3-2
Havant Town v Hungerford Town	2-2, 2-3
Torquay United v Bristol Rovers	2-4

First Round

Carlisle United v York City	1-1, 0-2
Stockport County v Oldham Athletic	2-2, 2-6
Burnley v Barnsley	2-2, 0-3
Blackpool v Tranmere Rovers	1-2

Rotherham United v Blackburn Rovers 2-2, 2-2, 1-2
Bradford City v Darlington   3-1
Sunderland v Preston North End   1-2
Bury v Sheffield United   1-3
Norwich City v Peterborough United   5-0
Derby County v Cambridge United   4-1
Ipswich Town v Leicester City   1-0
Nottingham Forest v Aston Villa   4-2
Northampton Town v Walsall   0-1
Stoke City v Shrewsbury Town   4-1
Scunthorpe United v Bedworth United   4-0
Kidderminster Harriers v Wolverhampton Wanderers
                                                    2-7
Luton Town v Port Vale   4-1
Whyteleafe v Fulham   1-8 (at Fulham)
Dulwich Hamlet v Carshalton Athletic   3-1
Farnborough Town v Lewes   0-1
Worthing v Sutton United   2-6
Wembley v Boreham Wood   1-1, 1-1, 0-1
St Albans City v Brighton & HA   0-4
Charlton Athletic v Gillingham   1-0
Egham Town v Cambridge City   1-2
Bedfont v Wycombe Wanderers   1-2
Epsom & Ewell v Croydon   1-0
Cardiff City v Bashley   2-2, 3-1
Hungerford Town v Swansea City   0-2
Bristol City v Bristol Rovers   4-1
Exeter City v Southampton   2-5
Swindon Town v Oxford United   3-2
AFC Bournemouth v Hereford United   6-3
Witney Town v Reading   0-4
  (at Witney)

Second Round
Barnsley v Notts County   1-3
Tranmere Rovers v Liverpool   1-6
Bradford City v Oldham Athletic   4-2
Sheffield Wednesday v Leeds United   1-2
Nottingham Forest v Middlesbrough   2-1
Manchester United v Blackburn Rovers   4-1
Preston North End v Everton   3-2
Crewe Alexandra v Stoke City   1-1, 0-1
Hull City v Manchester City   0-1
Doncaster Rovers v Sheffield United   0-2
York City v Newcastle United   2-0
Scunthorpe United v Derby County   0-0, 1-3
Chelsea v Walsall   3-0
Coventry City v Colchester United   2-1
Southend United v Arsenal   2-4
Birmingham City v Wolverhampton Wanderers
                                               4-4, 1-4
Ipswich Town v Norwich City   0-3
Boreham Wood v Queens Park Rangers   1-7
Leyton Orient v West Ham United   2-1
Watford v Tottenham Hotspur   2-3
Luton Town v West Bromwich Albion   1-2
Wycombe Wanderers v Cambridge City   2-1
Reading v Dulwich Hamlet   2-2, 2-1
Crystal Palace v Cardiff City   2-0
Bristol City v Epsom & Ewell   5-2
Brentford v Lewes   6-1
Wimbledon v Portsmouth   3-3, 2-1
Sutton United v Fulham   2-4
Swansea City v AFC Bournemouth   2-1
Swindon Town v Southampton   1-0
Millwall v Plymouth Argyle   2-2, 5-0
Charlton Athletic v Brighton & Hove Albion 1-1, 2-3

Third Round
Preston North End v Manchester City   1-1, 3-1
Derby County v Nottingham Forest   1-3
Stoke City v Leeds United   2-6

Manchester United v Notts County   3-1
West Bromwich Albion v York City   1-1, 0-2
Liverpool v Bradford City   1-1, 1-1, 3-1
Sheffield United v Wolverhampton Wanderers   4-3
Brentford v Leyton Orient   3-5
Tottenham Hotspur v Norwich City   1-2
Wycombe Wanderers v Brighton & Hove Albion
                                               1-1, 0-9
Fulham v Wimbledon   2-2, 2-3
Bristol City v Swansea City   2-1
Crystal Palace v Millwall   0-2
Chelsea v Reading   3-2
Queens Park Rangers v Coventry City
                         5-3 (at Harrow Borough)
Swindon Town v Arsenal   5-2

Fourth Round
Nottingham Forest v Preston North End   3-3, 4-3
Leeds United v Queens Park Rangers   5-1
Norwich City v Chelsea   3-2
Manchester United v Wimbledon   3-0
Sheffield United v Liverpool   0-0, 3-2
Millwall v Brighton & Hove Albion   3-0
Bristol City v Swindon Town   1-0
York City v Leyton Orient   2-0

Fifth Round
Sheffield United v Leeds United   2-2, 1-2
Bristol City v Norwich City   3-4
Manchester United v York City   5-0
Millwall v Nottingham Forest   0-0, 3-2

Semi-finals
Manchester United v Millwall   1-2, 2-0
Norwich City v Leeds United   1-4, 2-0

FINAL First Leg

10 APR

Manchester United (0) 0
Leeds United (1) 2 *(Forrester, Whelan)*   30,562
Manchester U: Whitmarsh; O'Kane, Riley, Casper,
Neville, Gillespie, Butt, Beckham (Savage), Irving
(Murdock), Scholes, Thornley.
Leeds United: Pettinger; Couzens, Sharp, Tinkler,
Daly, Bowman, Smithard, Ford, Whelan, Oliver,
Forrester.
Referee: P. Durkin (Portland).

Second Leg

13 MAY

Leeds United (2) 2 *(Forrester, Smithard)*
Manchester United (1) 1 *(Scholes (pen))*   31,037
Leeds United: Pettinger; Couzens, Sharp, Tinkler,
Daly, Bowman (Tobin), Smithard, Ford, Whelan,
Oliver (Byrne), Forrester.
Manchester United: Whitmarsh; Neville, Riley,
Casper, Neville, Gillespie, Scholes, Beckham, Irving
(Murdock), Savage, Thornley.
Referee: P. Durkin (Portland).

THE NEVILLE OVENDEN FOOTBALL COMBINATION

Division One

	P	W	D	L	F	A	Pts
Millwall	38	21	10	7	71	42	73
Chelsea	38	20	11	7	78	49	71
QPR	38	19	11	8	70	46	68
Crystal Palace	38	18	12	8	66	44	66
Southampton	38	18	10	10	56	39	64
Tottenham Hotspur	38	16	15	7	75	38	63
Oxford United	38	16	12	10	58	57	60
Watford	38	15	12	11	62	61	57
Wimbledon	38	15	10	13	60	43	55
Ipswich Town	38	16	7	15	58	62	55
Arsenal	38	12	15	11	57	46	51
Charlton Athletic	38	14	6	18	48	57	48
Luton Town	38	13	9	16	53	64	48
West Ham United	38	13	6	19	56	59	45
Norwich City	38	11	12	15	66	78	45
Swindon Town	38	10	12	16	53	60	42
Bristol City	38	8	12	18	39	60	36
Portsmouth	38	8	10	20	43	73	34
Brighton & Hove Albion	38	9	7	22	38	81	34
Fulham	38	5	7	26	28	76	22

Division Two

	P	W	D	L	F	A	Pts
Bristol Rovers	27	18	5	4	61	36	59
Swansea City	27	17	6	4	78	33	57
Birmingham City	27	14	9	4	61	42	51
AFC Bournemouth	27	10	6	11	52	44	36
Yeovil Town	27	9	6	12	48	67	33
Cheltenham Town	27	7	9	11	43	56	30
Cardiff City	27	7	8	12	48	51	29
Exeter City	27	8	4	15	45	62	28
Plymouth Argyle	27	7	6	14	51	65	27
Torquay United	27	7	3	17	30	61	24

Division Two

	P	W	D	L	F	A	Pts
Derby County	34	26	5	3	103	28	83
Everton	34	21	10	3	78	44	73
Coventry City	34	19	5	10	53	31	62
York City	34	17	8	9	48	31	59
West Bromwich Albion	34	18	5	11	54	50	59
Oldham Athletic	34	17	6	11	70	52	57
Port Vale	34	14	8	12	51	49	50
Bradford City	34	14	7	13	60	58	49
Huddersfield Town	34	15	4	15	61	56	49
Grimsby Town	34	13	7	14	51	45	46
Middlesbrough	34	14	4	16	47	53	46
Blackpool	34	13	6	15	40	55	45
Burnley	34	11	8	15	46	56	41
Mansfield Town	34	11	6	17	41	49	39
Scunthorpe United	34	10	4	20	46	64	34
Hull City	34	7	6	21	33	76	27
Wigan Athletic	34	6	5	23	25	68	23
Preston North End	34	5	6	23	43	85	21

NORTHERN LEAGUE

Division One

	P	W	D	L	F	A	Pts
Whitby Town	38	26	10	2	104	30	88
Billingham Synthonia	38	25	10	3	98	41	85
Guisborough Town	38	25	9	4	91	35	84
Blyth Spartans	38	26	4	8	83	35	82
Seaham Red Star	38	21	10	7	76	45	73
Durham City	38	21	10	7	73	51	73
Stockton	38	14	15	9	65	59	57
Murton	38	14	12	12	72	65	54
Chester-le-Street Town	38	15	8	15	82	82	53
Consett	38	15	7	16	54	56	52
Northallerton Town*	38	13	14	11	54	47	50
West Auckland Town	38	12	9	17	64	76	45
Newcastle Blue Star	38	12	6	20	64	81	42
Tow Law Town	38	11	8	19	65	73	41
Brandon United	38	11	5	22	47	81	38
Hebburn**	38	8	11	19	74	94	29
Ferryhill Athletic	38	6	10	22	51	97	28
Easington Colliery	38	6	8	24	51	94	26
Peterlee Newtown	38	3	9	26	40	105	18
South Bank*	38	3	11	24	34	95	17

* 3 points deducted

** 6 points deducted

THE PONTIN'S LEAGUE

Division One

	P	W	D	L	F	A	Pts
Aston Villa	34	21	8	5	64	32	71
Nottingham Forest	34	20	8	6	77	46	68
Blackburn Rovers	34	18	10	6	60	37	64
Leeds United	34	15	8	11	59	44	53
Bolton Wanderers	34	15	8	11	48	49	53
Manchester United	34	13	13	8	58	50	52
Liverpool	34	13	10	11	47	43	49
Sheffield Wednesday	34	13	10	11	51	48	49
Leicester City	34	12	12	10	42	38	48
Wolverhampton Wanderers	34	13	6	15	46	55	45
Notts County	34	12	8	14	56	52	44
Newcastle United	34	12	7	15	36	43	43
Sheffield United	34	10	10	14	54	59	40
Sunderland	34	11	6	17	57	57	39
Barnsley	34	9	11	14	48	58	38
Stoke City	34	8	8	18	38	56	32
Manchester City A	34	7	9	18	34	68	30
Rotherham United	34	5	6	23	29	69	21

ANSELLS MIDLAND FOOTBALL COMBINATION

Premier Division

	P	W	D	L	F	A	Pts
Armitage '90'	38	26	6	6	91	32	84
Stapenhill	38	25	4	9	105	45	79
Stratford Town	38	21	13	4	70	33	76
Pershore Town '88'	38	22	7	9	75	38	73
Sandwell Borough	38	21	8	9	89	48	71
West Midlands Police	38	20	10	8	77	39	70
Coleshill Town	38	21	6	11	63	44	69
Boldmere St Michaels	38	17	12	9	74	48	63
Bolehall Swifts	38	15	10	13	66	56	55
Knowle	38	15	10	13	70	71	55
Barwell	38	14	12	12	63	70	54
Northfield Town	38	13	12	13	58	59	51
Meir K. A.	38	9	12	17	47	60	39
Mile Oak Rovers	38	9	9	20	37	72	36
Studley B K L	38	7	14	17	39	71	35
Chelmsley Town	38	7	13	18	51	75	34
Highgate United	38	8	10	20	48	80	34
Bloxwich Town	38	5	11	22	28	74	26
Barlestone St Giles	38	5	5	28	40	104	20
Alcester Town	38	3	10	25	30	102	19

LANCASHIRE LEAGUE

Division One

	P	W	D	L	F	A	Pts
Manchester United A	30	26	1	3	122	36	79
Everton A	30	20	6	4	86	30	66
Tranmere Rovers A	30	21	3	6	74	35	66
Burnley A	30	14	9	7	67	48	51
Crewe Alexandra Reserve	30	14	8	8	78	44	50
Manchester City	30	13	9	8	48	39	48
Liverpool A	30	14	6	10	51	48	48
Bury Reserve	30	13	6	11	53	47	45
Oldham Athletic A	30	12	4	14	52	56	40
Blackpool A	30	10	4	16	56	70	34
Blackburn Rovers A	30	10	4	16	45	64	34
Morecambe Reserve	30	9	3	18	50	70	30
Bolton Wanderers A	30	6	8	16	37	71	26
Marine Reserve	30	6	7	17	37	93	25
Rochdale Reserve	30	6	2	20	36	75	22
Chester City A	30	2	6	22	26	92	12

Division Two

	P	W	D	L	F	A	Pts
Liverpool A	30	24	3	3	97	27	75
Preston North End B	30	18	7	5	102	55	61
Everton B	30	18	5	7	75	43	59
Wigan Athletic B	30	17	7	6	87	42	58
Carlisle United A	30	17	5	8	72	57	56
Manchester United B	30	15	3	12	71	46	48
Manchester City B	30	13	7	10	67	47	46
Tranmere Rovers B	30	12	10	8	52	38	46
Crewe Alexandra A	30	13	6	11	82	71	45
Burnley B	30	12	3	15	56	74	39
Blackpool B	30	11	3	16	53	68	36
Blackburn Rovers B	30	9	7	14	64	69	34
Bury A	30	6	6	18	37	77	24
Rochdale A	30	6	3	21	36	89	21
Stockport County A	30	4	6	20	45	103	18
Marine Youth	30	3	3	24	24	111	12

Division Two

	P	W	D	L	F	A	Pts
Maghull	34	21	9	4	77	26	72
Bootle	34	20	8	6	89	49	68
Oldham Town	34	20	6	8	79	47	66
Ellesmere Port Town	34	16	9	9	65	46	57
Stantondale	34	16	9	9	59	49	57
Castleton Gabriels	34	15	10	9	61	48	55
North Trafford	34	14	9	11	67	63	51
Formby	34	14	9	11	49	49	51
Atherton Collieries	34	14	7	13	63	67	49
Burnley Bank Hall	34	14	4	16	87	77	46
Westhoughton Town**	34	14	3	17	65	75	42
Cheadle Town**	34	12	7	15	44	48	40
Squires Gate	34	11	5	18	56	73	38
K Chell	34	10	8	16	52	72	38
Holker Old Boys	34	8	13	13	57	60	37
Ashton Town	34	8	8	18	51	74	32
Nelson	34	7	7	20	47	82	28
Irlam Town	34	4	5	25	47	110	17

** 3 points deducted for breach of league rule

VAUX WEARSIDE LEAGUE

Division One

	P	W	D	L	F	A	Pts
South Shields	28	20	5	3	84	36	65
Hartlepool Town	28	19	6	3	70	30	63
Silkworth	28	18	5	5	59	29	59
Jarrow Roofing	28	16	5	7	51	39	53
Marske United	28	12	11	5	55	37	47
Annfield Plain	28	11	7	10	57	58	40
Roker	28	12	3	13	54	42	39
Boldon C A	28	12	3	13	42	50	39
Cleadon S C	28	9	7	12	51	49	34
Wolviston	28	9	5	14	47	50	32
Ryhope C W	28	8	6	14	50	64	30
Newton Aycliffe	28	6	9	13	33	63	27
Cleator Moor	28	6	5	17	41	59	23
Herrington C W	28	5	6	17	36	76	21
Windscale	28	5	1	22	36	82	16

BASS NORTH WEST COUNTIES LEAGUE

Division One

	P	W	D	L	F	A	Pts
Atherton LR	42	33	7	2	75	25	106
Bamber Bridge	42	24	11	7	81	37	83
Chadderton	42	24	11	7	99	64	83
Prescot	42	20	12	10	68	44	72
Newcastle Town	42	20	8	14	70	57	68
Bradford Park Avenue	42	19	8	15	54	43	65
Clitheroe	42	17	8	17	61	40	59
St Helens Town	42	16	11	15	79	62	59
Salford City	42	15	13	14	58	61	58
Burscough	42	16	10	16	58	68	57
Flixton	42	14	15	13	50	42	57
Blackpool Rovers	42	16	9	17	66	64	57
Nantwich Town	42	14	15	13	60	60	57
Penrith	42	15	11	16	62	67	56
Bacup Borough	42	14	13	15	66	59	55
Glossop North End**	42	16	9	17	70	67	54
Darwen	42	14	10	18	54	61	52
Eastwood Hanley	42	14	10	18	45	57	52
Maine Road	42	12	9	21	55	63	45
Kidsgrove Athletic	42	9	8	25	53	94	35
Skelmersdale United	42	7	10	25	45	84	31
Blackpool Mechanics	42	2	4	36	27	137	10

** 3 points deducted for breach of league rule

THE JEWSON SOUTH-WESTERN FOOTBALL LEAGUE

	P	W	D	L	F	A	Pts
Truro City	32	23	3	6	72	28	49
Bodmin Town	32	20	6	6	84	46	46
Newquay	32	20	5	7	75	39	45
Launceston	32	17	10	5	81	41	44
St Blazey	32	14	9	9	71	65	37
Falmouth Town	32	15	6	11	77	51	36
Holsworthy	32	12	8	12	49	54	32
Tavistock	32	11	7	14	53	77	29
Mullion	32	9	10	13	51	61	28
Appledore BAAC	32	10	8	14	56	73	28
Penzance	32	10	6	16	65	69	26
Devon/Cornwall Police	32	12	5	15	61	69	26*
Porthleven	32	9	7	16	69	82	25
Wadebridge Town	32	8	9	15	49	87	25
Millbrook	32	8	8	16	50	69	24
Torpoint Athletic	32	8	8	16	44	68	23
St Austell	32	7	4	21	61	89	18

*3 points deducted

McEWANS NORTHERN ALLIANCE

Premier Division

	P	W	D	L	F	A	Pts
West Allotment	30	21	3	6	86	35	66
Seaton Delaval*	30	20	6	4	79	34	66
Carlisle	30	19	6	5	80	41	63
Morpeth	30	20	3	7	67	37	63
S Terrace	30	18	1	11	74	46	55
Walker	30	15	5	10	75	52	50
Gillford Park	30	13	9	8	72	56	48
Ponteland	30	13	6	11	71	59	45
Haltwhistle	30	12	5	13	43	41	41
Winlaton	30	12	4	14	58	64	40
Spittal	30	12	3	15	55	54	39
Heaton	30	9	4	17	49	68	31
Wark	30	8	2	20	45	79	26
Blyth KB	30	7	5	18	50	100	26
Westerhope	30	5	7	18	36	66	22
Forest Hall	30	1	1	28	24	132	4

* Seaton Delaval League Champions, after play-off

Division One

	P	W	D	L	F	A	Pts
Longbenton	30	21	4	5	105	38	67
Newbiggin	30	21	2	7	80	36	65
Benfield	30	19	3	8	84	42	60
St Columbas	30	16	6	8	63	50	54
NEI Reyrolle	30	14	7	9	76	60	49
Wylam	30	14	7	9	66	50	49
Swalwell	30	12	7	11	53	48	43
Procter & Gamble	30	11	8	11	61	59	41
Dudley	30	10	8	12	60	69	38
Percy Rovers	30	11	5	14	57	68	38
N Counties	30	10	6	14	52	74	36
New York	30	8	8	14	49	62	32
Percy Main	30	9	5	16	52	70	32
Ryton	30	7	7	16	41	69	28
Hexham	30	5	5	19	36	94	21
N Electric	30	5	5	20	48	94	20

Division Two

	P	W	D	L	F	A	Pts
Amble	30	24	3	3	132	42	75
Bohemians	30	23	3	4	101	43	72
Ashington HP	30	23	3	4	104	52	72
Shankhouse	30	20	2	8	92	46	62
Co Kitchens	30	18	3	9	119	68	57
Marden	30	16	6	8	69	48	54
Highfield	30	13	3	14	73	76	42
KOSA*	30	12	7	11	58	69	40
Swalwell CC	30	12	3	15	70	74	39
DHSS	30	10	5	15	58	87	35
Newcastle University	30	9	6	15	58	57	33
Norgas	30	8	4	18	78	100	28
Stobswood	30	7	5	18	52	106	26
Heddon	30	6	7	17	43	74	25
New Winning	30	5	3	22	73	127	18
Wallsend	30	2	1	27	32	144	7

* 3 points deducted

WEST MIDLAND (REGIONAL) LEAGUE

Premier Division

	P	W	D	L	F	A	Pts
Oldbury United	36	24	8	4	80	39	80
Chasetown	36	23	11	2	66	28	80
Paget Rangers	36	21	7	8	84	53	70
Rocester	36	20	9	7	71	41	69
Stourport Swifts	36	19	9	8	69	38	66
Ilkeston Town	36	19	8	9	73	38	65
Rushall Olympic	36	17	7	12	61	53	58
Wednesfield	36	14	10	12	58	47	52
Alvechurch	36	14	5	17	58	65	47
West Bromwich Town	36	13	6	17	54	86	45

	P	W	D	L	F	A	Pts
Pelsall Villa	36	10	12	14	60	54	42
Blakenall	36	9	13	14	57	75	40
Willenhall Town	36	12	4	20	49	69	40
Hinckley Athletic	36	11	6	19	56	68	39
Halesowen Harriers	36	8	9	19	44	62	33
Cradley Town	36	9	6	21	42	71	33
Oldswinford	36	9	6	21	39	80	33
Westfields	36	8	6	22	56	85	30
Lye Town	36	7	8	21	47	72	29

Division One

	P	W	D	L	F	A	Pts
Knypersley Victoria	36	26	3	7	105	34	81
Darlaston	36	25	6	5	69	27	81
Lichfield	36	23	6	7	75	42	75
Ettingshall HT	36	20	11	5	69	34	71
Gornal Athletic	36	17	8	11	75	52	59
Cannock Chase	36	16	4	16	50	59	52
Wolverhampton United	36	14	7	15	60	69	49
Great Wyrley	36	12	12	12	44	53	48
Tividale	36	14	5	17	76	67	47
Hill Top Rangers	36	13	8	15	58	62	47
Donnington Wood	36	12	11	13	67	77	47
Malvern Town	36	12	10	14	56	71	46
Oldbury United Reserves	36	10	13	13	52	67	43
Moxley Rangers*	36	11	11	14	48	53	41
Ludlow Town	36	10	9	17	55	78	39
Wolverhampton Casuals	36	11	5	20	57	72	38
Tipton Town	36	9	11	16	42	63	38
Gornal Sports	36	7	6	23	42	75	27
Wem Town	36	4	6	26	39	84	18

* 3 points deducted

WINSTONLEAD KENT LEAGUE

Division One

	P	W	D	L	F	A	Pts
Tonbridge	40	27	9	4	107	39	90
Herne Bay	40	26	6	8	96	44	84
Sheppey United	40	24	9	7	65	29	81
Deal Town	40	24	7	9	128	60	79
Alma Swanley	40	24	4	12	93	65	76
Chatham Town	40	19	11	10	79	52	68
Danson Furness United	40	18	13	9	58	40	67
Thamesmead Town	40	17	9	14	62	56	60
Beckenham Town	40	17	8	15	64	60	59
Whitstable Town	40	18	4	18	77	64	58
Slade Green	40	15	13	12	71	60	58
Ramsgate	40	17	5	18	78	76	56
Folkestone Invicta	40	16	5	19	78	95	53
Tunbridge Wells	40	13	6	21	66	102	45
Faversham Town	40	11	10	19	44	71	43
Greenwich Borough	40	12	5	23	49	75	41
Cray Wanderers	40	10	8	22	64	79	38
Kent Police	40	10	7	23	56	121	37
Darenth Heathside	40	9	7	24	54	104	34
Corinthian	40	6	8	26	50	95	26
Crockenhill	40	6	8	26	56	108	26

Division Two

	P	W	D	L	F	A	Pts
Dover Athletic	26	21	3	2	81	23	66
Herne Bay	26	20	2	4	78	27	62
Hastings Town	26	16	1	9	73	39	49
Beckenham Town	26	14	5	7	54	41	47
Canterbury City	26	12	5	9	62	57	41
Thamesmead Town	26	10	7	9	47	39	37
Whitstable Town	26	10	4	12	39	57	34
Tonbridge	26	9	6	11	44	49	33
Darenth Heathside	26	10	3	13	34	44	33
Folkestone Invicta	26	7	4	15	36	58	25
Chatham Town	26	7	3	16	48	59	24
Deal Town	26	6	5	15	43	66	23
Cray Wanderers	26	6	4	16	32	70	22
Ramsgate	26	4	8	14	27	69	20

GREAT MILLS LEAGUE

Premier Division

	P	W	D	L	F	A	Pts
Clevedon Town	38	34	4	0	137	23	106
Tiverton Town	38	28	8	2	134	30	92
Saltash United	38	22	8	8	98	51	74
Taunton Town	38	22	8	8	62	37	74
Mangotsfield United	38	20	8	10	89	47	68
Torrington	38	17	10	11	69	44	61
Westbury United	38	18	7	13	50	45	61
Paulton Rovers	38	15	10	13	76	51	55
Torquay United	38	16	7	15	58	62	55
Plymouth Arglye	38	15	9	14	72	64	54
Exmouth Town	38	14	9	15	47	59	51
Elmore	38	14	5	19	54	71	47
Bristol Manor Farm	38	10	13	15	49	59	43
Bideford	38	11	8	19	59	66	41
Frome Town	38	9	12	17	57	75	39
Chippenham Town	38	8	14	16	65	86	38
Minehead	38	10	8	20	59	88	38
Liskeard Athletic	38	8	9	21	61	87	33
Chard Town	38	6	3	29	37	119	21
Dawlish Town	38	2	2	34	17	186	8

First Division

	P	W	D	L	F	A	Pts
Odd Down	40	27	10	3	87	26	91
Calne Town	40	23	12	5	97	47	81
Crediton United	40	23	11	6	79	43	80
Brislington	40	22	8	10	77	41	74
Warminster Town	40	22	7	11	70	50	73
Clyst Rovers	40	18	13	9	75	48	67
Keynsham Town	40	19	10	11	66	50	67
Backwell United	40	16	14	10	68	52	62
Barnstaple Town	40	15	10	15	62	58	55
Bridport	40	14	13	13	67	66	55
Heavitree United	40	14	9	17	64	69	51
Devizes Town	40	15	6	19	61	84	51
Bishop Sutton	40	14	8	18	55	55	50
Welton Rovers	40	12	11	17	69	65	47
Wellington	40	11	14	15	53	65	47
Glastonbury	40	13	5	22	52	70	44
Larkhall Athletic	40	11	5	24	59	81	38
Ilfracombe Town	40	8	9	23	47	94	33
Ottery St Mary	40	9	5	26	53	116	32
Radstock Town	40	7	10	23	38	60	31
Melksham Town	40	6	12	22	39	98	30

JEWSON (EASTERN COUNTIES) LEAGUE

Premier Division

	P	W	D	L	F	A	Pts
Wroxham	42	32	4	6	106	36	100
Wisbech Town	42	28	6	8	109	48	90
Newmarket Town	42	27	9	6	87	37	90
Cornard United	42	22	9	11	99	68	75
Diss Town	42	24	2	16	65	52	74
Harwich & Parkeston	42	20	10	12	75	51	70
Fakenham Town	42	19	10	13	68	50	67
Norwich United	42	16	14	12	66	57	62
Felixstowe Town	42	15	12	15	66	62	57
Gorleston	42	16	9	17	64	89	57
Great Yarmouth Town	42	16	8	18	41	62	56
Tiptree United	42	15	8	19	64	76	53
Stowmarket Town	42	14	9	19	54	59	51
Haverhill Rovers	42	14	8	20	65	80	50
Halstead Town	42	14	8	20	60	83	50
Chatteris Town	42	15	4	23	64	73	49
Lowestoft Town	42	12	12	18	55	56	48
March Town United	42	13	9	20	56	67	48
Whatton United	42	12	8	22	51	84	44
Histon**	42	10	13	19	60	90	42
Brantham Athletic	42	8	12	22	47	73	36
Brightlingsea United	42	2	12	28	35	104	18

** 1 point deducted

Division One

	P	W	D	L	F	A	Pts
Sudbury Wanderers	36	26	5	5	96	37	83
Soham Town Rangers	36	24	4	8	119	45	76
Woodbridge Town	36	24	4	8	82	40	76
Hadleigh United	36	19	9	8	95	59	66
Clacton Town	36	20	6	10	78	53	66
Somersham Town	36	21	3	12	68	52	66
Cambridge City Res	36	16	7	13	104	77	55
Ely City	36	14	11	11	59	48	53
Long Sutton Athletic	36	15	8	13	69	75	53
Stanway Rovers	36	15	6	15	73	76	51
Ipswich Wanderers	36	14	6	16	63	72	48
Mildenhall Town	36	14	5	17	76	98	47
Sudbury Town Reserves	36	13	7	16	70	72	46
Warboys Town	36	10	12	14	63	72	42
King's Lynn Reserves	36	11	5	20	49	63	38
Downham Town	36	11	4	21	64	84	37
*Swaffham Town	36	12	4	20	58	97	36
Bury Town Reserves	36	6	1	29	46	122	19
Thetford Town	36	2	3	31	24	114	9

* 4 points deducted

CENTRAL MIDLANDS LEAGUE

Supreme Division

	P	W	D	L	F	A	Pts
Arnold Town	30	22	4	4	76	32	70
Heanor Town	30	22	4	4	80	42	70
Blidworth Welfare	30	18	7	5	45	22	61
Harworth CI	30	18	2	10	60	42	56
Priory (Eastwood)	30	12	11	7	47	35	47
Mickleover RBL	30	14	4	12	51	48	46
Gelding Town	30	14	3	13	64	55	45
Shirebrook Colliery	30	13	4	13	78	65	43
Louth United	30	11	7	12	60	46	40
Glapwell FC	30	11	5	14	53	60	38
Borrowash Victoria	30	11	5	14	59	71	38
Kimberley Town	30	8	8	14	43	57	32
Sheffield Aurora	30	8	6	16	48	69	30
Nettleham FC	30	7	7	16	53	76	28
Oakham United	30	4	5	21	26	64	17
Wombwell Town	30	4	4	22	28	87	16

Premier Division

	P	W	D	L	F	A	Pts
Sandiacre Town	36	31	4	1	127	24	97
Rossington FC	36	25	7	4	86	50	82
Kiveton Park	36	20	4	12	80	49	64
Norton Woodseats	36	20	2	14	79	68	62
Long Eaton United	36	19	4	13	80	58	61
Derby C & WR	36	16	11	9	65	46	59
South Normanton Athletic	36	16	10	10	62	58	58
Derby Rolls Royce	36	15	6	15	60	60	51
Askern Welfare	36	13	9	14	79	71	48
Stanton Ilkeston	36	14	4	18	61	64	46
Kilburn MW	36	13	7	16	63	81	46
Mexborough Town	36	13	6	17	61	60	45
Biwater FC	36	12	7	17	63	70	43
Newhall United	36	13	4	19	69	88	43
Radford FC	36	12	4	20	63	106	40
Blackwell MW	36	9	7	20	41	84	34
Bulwell United	36	7	10	19	63	91	31
Nuthall FC	36	8	7	21	42	79	31
Shardlow St James	36	6	7	23	40	82	25

SPARTAN FOOTBALL LEAGUE

Premier Division

	P	W	D	L	F	A	Pts
Brimsdown Rovers	42	31	4	7	99	27	97
Corinthian Casuals	42	29	5	8	98	31	92
Cheshunt	42	27	8	7	92	29	89
Willesden (Hawkeye)	42	27	8	7	102	50	89
Hanwell Town	42	27	7	8	100	50	88
St Margetsbury	42	25	5	12	93	64	80
Walthamstow Pennant	42	21	10	11	72	44	73
Cockfosters	42	21	6	15	84	65	69
St Andrews	42	15	12	15	70	85	57
Tower Hamlets	42	17	4	21	83	83	55
Croydon Athletic	42	13	15	14	72	59	54
Waltham Abbey	42	13	13	16	65	71	52
Beaconsfield United	42	14	9	19	68	85	51
Brook House	42	14	6	22	72	99	48
Haringey Borough	42	11	12	19	59	80	45
Barkingside	42	9	13	20	52	80	40
Hillingdon Borough	42	10	10	22	59	99	40
Eltham Town	42	11	6	25	50	95	39
North Greenford United	42	11	5	26	53	100	38
Amersham Town	42	8	11	23	49	93	35
Beckton United	42	9	5	28	68	117	32
Southgate Athletic	42	6	12	24	48	103	30

THE ESSEX SENIOR LEAGUE

	P	W	D	L	F	A	Pts
Canvey Island	32	23	7	2	66	20	76
Sawbridgeworth Town	32	19	7	6	82	41	64
Bowers United	32	18	9	5	56	27	63
Burnham Ramblers	32	17	6	9	80	53	57
Basildon United	32	16	7	9	65	37	55
Brentwood	32	13	9	10	58	49	48
Great Wakering Rovers	32	13	8	11	50	43	47
Ford United	32*	14	10	8	47	26	46*
Romford	32	12	9	11	48	42	45
Southend Manor	32	13	4	15	49	45	43
Concord Rangers	32	9	9	14	41	51	36
Maldon Town	32	8	10	14	45	59	34
East Ham United	32	10	4	18	46	67	34
Woodford Town	32	7	9	16	46	84	30
Eton Manor	32	7	8	17	32	75	29
Hullbridge Sports	32	7	6	19	38	70	27
Stansted	32	2	6	24	27	87	12

* 6 points deducted

PARASOL COMBINED COUNTIES

	P	W	D	L	F	A	Pts
Peppard	36	27	3	6	111	39	85
Chipstead	36	19	10	7	78	47	67
Ashford Town	36	18	13	5	67	36	67
Merstham	36	16	11	9	67	66	59
Viking Sports	36	15	10	11	67	56	55
Ash United	36	15	10	11	49	48	55
Sandhurst Town	36	14	11	11	48	52	53
Hartley Wintney	36	14	10	12	60	47	52
Godalming & G	36	14	8	14	51	61	49
Cranleigh	36	12	11	13	66	59	47
Steyning Town	36	12	8	16	55	69	44
Bedfont	36	10	13	13	51	46	43
DCA Basingstoke	36	11	8	17	50	67	42
Horley Town	36	10	12	14	60	73	41
Frimley Green	36	11	7	18	43	55	40
Farleigh Rovers	36	11	5	20	46	65	38
Cobham	36	9	10	17	54	78	37
Ditton	36	9	9	18	48	71	36
Westfield	36	6	9	21	32	68	27

NORTHERN COUNTIES EAST LEAGUE

Premier Division

	P	W	D	L	F	A	Pts
Spennymoor Utd	38	26	7	5	102	33	85
Pickering Town	38	27	4	7	90	48	85
North Ferriby Utd	38	23	7	8	90	40	76
Maltby MW	38	21	11	6	69	40	74
Thackley	38	20	7	11	62	39	67
Brigg Town	38	16	14	8	55	39	62
Denaby Utd	38	15	11	12	71	63	56
Ossett Albion	38	16	7	15	68	60	55
Eccelshill Utd	38	16	6	16	65	65	54
Winterton Rgrs	38	14	7	17	61	72	49
Ashfield Utd	38	12	11	15	69	88	47
Ossett Town	38	13	7	18	69	71	46
Belper Town	38	11	12	15	56	62	45
Liversedge	38	12	8	18	56	77	44
Sheffield	38	12	6	20	55	70	42
Stocksbridge PS	38	10	11	17	54	70	41
Pontefract Collieries	38	11	8	19	62	88	41
Glasshoughton Welfare	38	9	9	20	46	77	36
Armthorpe Welfare	38	8	8	22	49	81	32
Harrogate Railway	38	3	9	26	49	115	18

Division One

	P	W	D	L	F	A	Pts
Lincoln Utd	26	17	5	4	62	31	56
Hucknall Town	26	15	6	5	54	32	51
Hallam	26	15	5	6	50	23	50
Yorks Amateurs	26	14	3	9	42	29	45
RES Parkgate	26	12	9	5	39	38	45
Tadcaster Albion	26	12	5	9	51	43	41
Rossington Main	26	9	7	10	33	31	34
Hall Road Rgrs	26	9	6	11	48	43	33
Garforth Town	26	8	8	10	34	38	32
Worsbrough Bridge	26	7	8	11	33	48	29
Hatfield Main	26	6	6	14	40	63	24
Immingham Town	26	5	8	13	38	51	23
Brodsworth MW	26	6	4	16	41	65	22
Selby Town	26	5	4	17	34	64	19

Bradley Rgrs failed to complete their fixtures, record expunged.

SOUTH EAST COUNTIES LEAGUE

Division One

	P	W	D	L	F	A	Pts
Tottenham Hotspur	30	22	2	6	84	27	46
Millwall	30	19	6	5	81	45	44
Arsenal	30	16	6	8	65	36	38
Queens Park Rangers	30	18	1	11	81	55	37
Watford	30	14	9	7	48	37	37
Cambridge United	30	13	5	12	62	59	31
Ipswich Town	30	13	5	12	35	46	31
Chelsea	30	13	3	14	60	56	29
Charlton Athletic	30	10	9	11	54	55	29
Norwich City	30	11	4	15	54	67	26
West Ham United	30	12	2	16	57	71	26
Fulham	30	9	7	14	55	77	25
Southend United	30	8	6	16	45	62	22
Portsmouth	30	8	6	16	33	52	22
Leyton Orient	30	9	3	18	37	67	21
Gillingham	30	6	4	20	36	75	16

SPECTRE HELLENIC LEAGUE

Premier Division

	P	W	D	L	F	A	Pts
Wollen Sports	34	25	4	5	75	31	79
Milton United	34	21	7	6	67	33	70
Cirencester Town	34	20	8	6	54	28	68
Moreton Town	34	21	4	8	72	41	67
Cinderford Town	34	15	10	9	64	44	55
Almondsbury Picksons	34	15	7	12	62	50	52
Shortwood United	34	12	10	12	63	59	46
Swindon Supermarine	34	11	13	10	46	43	46
Bicester Town	34	12	9	13	45	45	45
Rayners Lane	34	13	4	17	53	63	43
Banbury United	34	10	10	14	50	66	40
Fairford Town	34	8	13	13	55	48	37
Headington Amateurs	34	10	6	18	40	67	36
Kintbury Rangers	34	9	8	17	35	51	35
Abingdon United	34	9	7	18	49	67	34
Wantage Town	34	8	8	18	47	70	32
Pegasus Juniors	34	7	9	18	52	76	30
Didcot Town	33	6	9	18	40	87	27

Division One

	P	W	D	L	F	A	Pts
Tuffley Rovers	30	25	2	3	90	24	77
North Leigh	30	21	4	5	113	43	67
Wallingford Town	30	17	9	4	84	47	60
Lambourn Sports	30	16	6	8	73	61	54
Purton	30	17	3	10	64	53	54
Kidlington	30	13	9	8	49	41	48
Yarnton	30	12	4	14	48	60	40
Cheltenham Saracens	30	12	2	16	48	47	38
Carterton Town	30	11	4	15	58	63	37
Clanfield	30	9	10	11	47	66	37
Highworth Town	30	9	6	15	48	62	33
Wootton Bassett	30	8	6	16	40	53	30
Bishops Cleeve	30	9	3	18	44	76	30
Cirencester United	30	8	4	18	41	78	28
Chipping Norton	30	7	5	18	51	82	26
Easington Sports	30	5	5	20	34	76	20

Division Two

	P	W	D	L	F	A	Pts
Wimbledon	26	19	3	4	67	26	41
Bristol City	26	16	2	8	55	35	34
Brentford	26	12	8	6	39	26	32
Luton Town	26	14	1	11	57	47	29
Brighton & Hove Albion	26	11	6	9	48	60	28
AFC Bournemouth	26	11	6	9	37	39	28
Tottenham Hotspur	26	11	5	10	48	50	27
Southampton	26	8	9	9	28	31	25
Crystal Palace	26	10	4	12	38	33	24
Oxford United	26	8	4	14	48	52	20
Swindon Town	26	7	6	13	29	45	20
Bristol Rovers	26	6	7	13	36	57	19
Colchester United	26	9	1	16	24	47	19
Reading	26	6	6	14	35	52	18

SOUTH MIDLANDS LEAGUE

Premier Division

	P	W	D	L	F	A	Pts
Oxford City	42	34	4	4	141	44	106
Brache Sparta	42	29	7	6	97	41	94
Arlesey Town	42	26	9	7	99	40	87
Wingate & Fin	42	23	11	8	84	54	80
Hatfield Town	42	21	11	10	114	71	74
Hoddesdon Town	42	21	11	10	80	48	71
Biggleswade Town	42	19	9	14	86	58	66
Shillington	42	19	9	14	63	58	66
Leverstock G	42	19	7	16	62	62	64
Harpenden Town	42	18	9	15	67	47	63
Letchworth GC	42	18	8	16	79	63	62
MK Borough	42	18	8	16	77	65	61
Potters Bar Town	42	17	9	16	81	82	60
Langford	42	14	13	15	75	63	55
Totternhoe	42	13	13	16	56	67	52
Luton Old Boys	42	15	7	20	57	75	49
Buckingham	42	11	8	23	73	103	41

Pitstone & Ivinghoe	42	11	5	26	50	99	38
Welwyn Garden City	42	9	10	23	47	88	37
The 61 FC	42	9	5	28	54	120	32
Pirton	42	4	8	30	32	115	20
New Bradwell	42	0	7	35	20	131	7

HEREFORD SPORTS UNITED COUNTIES LEAGUE

Premier Division

	P	W	D	L	F	A	Pts
Rothwell	42	30	8	4	97	28	98
Northampton Spencer	42	29	6	7	96	37	93
Raunds	42	28	6	8	93	41	90
Potton	42	26	7	9	107	56	85
Daventry	42	24	7	11	91	60	79
Cogenhoe	42	23	9	10	101	56	78
S & L Corby	42	24	6	12	97	62	78
Bourne	42	22	6	14	94	59	72
Eynesbury	42	22	6	14	92	71	72
Long Buckby	42	19	6	17	91	65	63
Boston	42	17	7	18	80	74	58
Stamford	42	18	3	21	81	76	57
Spalding	42	17	4	21	66	70	55
Newport Pagnell	42	15	9	18	65	79	54
Kempston	42	14	11	17	60	60	53
Mirrless Blackstone	42	14	8	20	69	82	50
Stotfold	42	15	3	24	90	82	48
Wootton	42	11	10	21	51	76	43
Holbeach	42	12	3	27	59	91	39
Desborough	42	5	10	27	61	127	25
Wellingborough	42	4	8	30	44	143	20
Brackley	42	0	3	39	20	210	3

Division One

	P	W	D	L	F	A	Pts
Ford Sports	34	27	3	4	134	48	84
Higham	34	22	9	3	97	28	75
Bugbrooke	34	21	4	9	78	43	67
Ramsey	34	18	10	6	76	49	64
Whitworths	34	14	8	12	68	49	50
Burton PW	34	13	11	10	60	52	50
St Ives	34	13	9	12	72	52	48
Cottingham	34	13	9	12	70	64	48
Olney	34	12	11	11	61	38	47
Thrapston	34	12	9	13	61	70	45
Peterborough City	34	13	5	16	70	78	44
Harrowby	34	11	10	13	57	60	43
O N Chenecks	34	10	11	13	69	61	41
Blisworth	34	11	7	16	51	67	40
Sharnbrook	34	11	6	17	64	74	39
British Timken	34	9	6	16	68	100	36
Irchester	34	6	6	22	58	95	24
Towcester	34	1	1	32	18	204	4

HIGHLAND LEAGUE

	P	W	D	L	F	A	Pts
Elgin City	34	24	5	5	110	35	77
Cove Rangers	34	23	4	7	78	37	73
Lossiemouth	34	21	6	7	104	54	69
Caledonian	34	21	6	7	76	41	69
Ross County	34	19	7	8	87	49	64
Huntly	34	19	5	10	96	55	62
Clachnacuddin	34	17	7	10	47	34	58
Inverness Thistle	34	17	6	11	55	50	57
Buckie Thistle	34	17	4	13	62	55	55
Fraserburgh	34	15	7	12	63	52	52
Deveronvale	34	14	4	16	57	71	46
Keith	34	12	9	13	46	59	45
Brora Rangers	34	11	8	15	72	74	41
Peterhead	34	8	10	16	61	80	34
Rothes	34	4	8	22	42	104	20
Fort William	34	5	4	25	37	89	19
Forres Mechanics	34	4	6	24	40	94	18
Nairn County	34	1	2	31	26	126	5

The result of this competition was declared null and void

AMATEUR FOOTBALL ALLIANCE
1992–93

CUP COMPETITION FINALS

Senior
Old Hamptonians v National Westminster Bank 2*:0, 2*:3

AFA Essex Senior
Duncombe Sports v Hale End Athletic   1-3

AFA Middlesex Senior
Old Cholmeleians v Winchmore Hill   0-1

AFA Surrey Senior
National Westminster Bank v Kew Association   5-0

Greenland Memorial
Liverpool Victoria v Slaughter & May   4-2

Intermediate
Franklands Village Res. v Norsemen Res.   1-4

AFA Essex Intermediate
Duncombe Sports Res. v Old Parmiterians Res.   2-1

AFA Kent Intermediate
Coutts & Co. 1st v Midland Bank Res.   2-1

AFA Middlesex Intermediate
Latymer Old Boys Res. v Old Salvatorians Res.   2-3

Junior
National Westminster Bank 3rd. v Old Stationers
3rd.   3*-1*

Minor
Old Esthameians 4th. v Old Actonians
Association 4th.   0-3

Senior Novets
Midland Bank 5th. v Old Parmiterians 5th.   1-3

Intermediate Novets
Civil Service 6th. v Old Parmiterians 6th.   0-1

Junior Novets
Old Salvatorians 9th. v Old Salvatorians 7th   2-1

Veterans
Old Fairlopians Veterans v Old Minchendenians
Veterans   0-2

Open Veterans
Old Wulfrunians Veterans v Toby Veterans   2-0

* after extra time

AFA SENIOR CUP

1st Round Proper
West Wickham 1, Glyn Old Boys 2
Carshalton 5, Old Finchleians 1
Mill Hill Village 0, Old Tiffinian 4
Old Chigwellians 6, Old Brentwoods 2
Old Esthameians 4, Old Grocers 3
Enfield Old Grammarians 2, Civil Service 1
Old Westminster Citizens 0, Old Meadonians 4
Old Bealonians 2, Old Owens 1
Old Latymerians 3, South Bank Polytechnic 4
Midland Bank 1, Southgate Olympic 0
Wandsworth Borough 1, Broomfield 2
Lloyds Bank 0, Cardinal Manning O.B. 3
Old Elizabethans 2, Old Wokingians 0
Barclays Bank 2, Old Stationers 3
Hale End Athletic 2*, Old Actonians Association 3*
Wake Green 0, Old Wilsonians 3
Kew Association 4, John Fisher Old Boys 2
Old Manorians 2, Southgate County 0
Nottsborough 5, Old Danes 1
Leyton County Old Boys 0, Old Aloysians 1
Old Parkonians 1, Old Ilseworthians 2
Tansley 4, Old Southallians 3
Old Hamptonians 5, Old Malvernian 0
Old Monovians 5, Old Cholmeleians 1
Old Grammarians 1, Old Ignatians 2
Crouch End Vampires 2, Lensbury 1
Hassocks scr, Ibis w/o
Old Parmiterians 6, Parkfield 1
Old Tollingtonians 6, Old Buckwellians 1
Silhill 1, Winchmore Hill 2
National Westminster Bank 5, Old Kingsburians 0
Old Minchendenians 2, Norsemen 3

2nd Round Proper
Old Isleworthians 6, Old Monovians 1
Old Elizabethans 1, Old Meadonians 2
Old Actionians Assn 6*, Ibis 0*
Norsemen 2, Old Chigwellians 0
Carshalton 1, Old Aloysians 2
Glyn Old Boys 2, Old Esthameians 0

* after extra time

Nottsborough 1, Old Bealonians 2
Crouch End Vampires 1*2, South Bank Polytechnic 1*0
Cardinal Manning Old Boys 2, Old Tiffinian 1
Broomfield 7, Tansley 1
Winchmore Hill 2, Old Manorians 1
Old Wilsonians 1, Old Hamptonians 3
Old Tollingtonians 2, Midland Bank 3
Old Parmiterians 4, Old Stationers 2
Kew Association 3*0, National Westminster Bank 3*2
Enfield Old Grammarians 1, Old Ignatians 2

3rd Round Proper
Winchmore Hill 3, Old Isleworthians 1
National Westminster Bank 2, Old Ignatians 1
Old Meadonians 4, Broomfield 1
Old Bealonians 2, Crouch End Vampires 9
Old Actonians Assn 0*, Norsemen 2*
Old Hamptonians 1, Old Parmiterians 0
Old Aloysians 3, Glyn Old Boys 1
Cardinal Manning Old Boys 1, Midland Bank 0

4th Round Proper
Old Hamptonians 2, Old Aloysians 0
National Westminster Bank 5, Winchmore Hill 3
Cardinal Manning Old Boys 0*1, Old Meadonians 0*2
Norsemen 1, Crouch End Vampires 0

Semi-final Results
Norsemen 2*, Old Hamptonians 3*
National Westminster Bank 4, Old Meadonians 0

AFA REPRESENTATIVE XI

v Cambridge University	Won 6-5
v Oxford University	Won 1-0
v Army FA	Lost 2-3
v Royal Navy FA	Lost 2-3
v Royal Air Force FA	Lost 1-3
v Sussex County FA	Won 4-1
v London University	Won 1-0

LONDON OLD BOYS' CUP COMPETITIONS

Senior
Glyn Old Boys v Old Westhamians   3-0

Intermediate
Chorleywood Danes Old Boys v Old Meadonians Res.
1*-4*

* after extra time

Junior
Old Meadonians 3rd. v Old Salvatorians 3rd.   1*:0, 1*:4

Minor
Chertsey Old Salesians 4th. v Old Tenisonians 4th.   0-5

Novets
City of London 5th. v Old Sinjuns 5th.   0-1

Drummond Cup
Old Parmiterians 6th v Old Tollingtonians 6th.   3-1

Nemean Cup
Glyn Old Boys 7th v Old Salvatorians 9th.   2-7

Veterans
Old Meadonians Veterans v Old Simmarians Veterans 0-3

SOUTHERN OLYMPIAN LEAGUE

SENIOR SECTION

Division One	P	W	D	L	F	A	Pts
Parkfield	18	13	4	1	45	22	30
Nottsborough	18	10	5	3	55	23	25
Old Owens	18	9	5	4	48	30	23
Old Finchleians	18	8	4	6	47	38	20
Witan	18	6	4	8	29	39	16
Old Grammarians	18	6	3	9	40	40	15
Mill Hill Village	18	5	4	9	32	41	14
Old Bealonians	18	5	4	9	26	42	14
Old Fairlopians	18	4	5	9	27	53	13
Southgate County	18	4	2	12	29	50	10

Division Two	P	W	D	L	F	A	Pts
St. Mary's College	20	13	3	4	52	26	29
Wandsworth Borough	20	12	4	4	67	31	28
Duncombe Sports	20	8	8	4	56	32	24
Academicals	20	10	4	6	44	30	24
Albanian	20	9	6	5	39	32	24
Hadley	20	10	3	7	36	30	23
Ealing Association	20	10	3	7	55	53	23
Pollygons	20	5	3	12	47	76	13
Old Monovians	20	6	1	13	26	65	13
City of London (ex Colposa)	20	5	2	13	33	48	12
Hampstead Heathens	20	3	1	16	38	70	7

Division Three	P	W	D	L	F	A	Pts
Ulysses	20	15	3	2	60	18	33
Corinthian-Casuals "A"	20	15	1	4	66	35	31
Hale End Athletic	20	13	2	5	68	27	28
Old Woodhouseians	20	14	0	6	67	43	28
Old Colfeians	20	9	4	7	43	43	22
B.B.C.	20	9	3	8	46	46	21
Pegasus (Inner Temple)	20	9	1	10	49	63	19
Westerns	20	6	4	10	34	49	16
Birkbeck College	20	4	1	15	29	55	9
Electrosport	20	3	3	14	34	75	9
Brent	20	1	2	17	19	61	4

Division Four	P	W	D	L	F	A	Pts
Honourable Artillery Company	20	17	1	2	70	28	35
Bourneside	20	15	2	3	85	25	32
London Welsh	20	14	2	4	50	35	30
Fulham Compton Old Boys	20	11	1	8	59	35	23
Centymca	20	8	4	8	34	40	20
Mayfield Athletic	20	8	2	10	48	49	18
Inland Revenue	20	8	2	10	39	40	18
London Airways	20	7	3	10	42	52	17
Economicals	20	4	2	14	38	64	10
Distillers	20	3	4	13	32	75	10
Tansley	20	3	1	16	37	91	7

Intermediate Section
Division One – 10 Teams – won by Albanian Res.
Division Two – 10 Teams – won by Parkfield Res.
Division Three – 10 Teams – won by B.B.C. Res.
Division Four – 9 Teams – won by Fulham Compton O.B. Res.

Junior Section
Division One – 10 Teams –won by Albanian 3rd. Witan 3rd.
Division Two – 10 Teams – won by Witan 3rd.
Division Three – 8 Teams – won by City of London 5th.
Division Four – 9 Teams – won by Parkfield 6th.

Minor Section
Division "A" – 10 Teams – won by Mayfield Athletic 3rd.
Division "B" – 10 Teams – won by Old Owens 4th.

Division "C" – 11 Teams – won by B.B.C. 4th.
Division "D" – 10 Teams – won by Duncombe Sports 3rd.
Division "E" – 9 Teams – won by Duncombe Sports 4th.
Division "F" – 9 Teams – won by Witan 6th.
Veterans Division – 6 Teams – won by Tansley Veterans
Senior Challenge Bowl – won by Nottsborough
Senior Challenge Shield – won by Old Grammarians
Intermediate Challenge Cup – won by Fulham Compton Old Boys Res.
Intermediate Challenge Shield – won by Parkfield Res.
Junior Challenge Cup – won by Mill Hill Village 3rd.
Junior Challenge Shield – won by Ealing Association 3rd.
Mander Cup – won by Albanian 4th.
Mander Shield – won by Academicals 4th.
Burntwood Trophy – won by Parkfield 5th.
Burntwood Shield – won by City of London 5th.
Thomas Parmiter Cup – won by Parkfield 6th.
Thomas Parmiter Shield – won by Old Finchleians 8th.
Veterans' Challenge Cup – won by City of London Veterans
Veterans' Challenge Shield – won by Corinthian-Casuals Veterans

THE ARTHUR DUNN CUP

FINAL TIE
Lancing Old Boys 1, Old Reptonians 0

ARTHURIAN LEAGUE

Premier Division	P	W	D	L	F	A	Pts
Old Etonians	16	11	0	5	42	30	22
Lancing Old Boys	16	8	6	2	35	23	22
Old Reptonians	16	9	0	7	27	27	18
Old Chigwellians	16	7	5	4	43	30	16*
Old Carthusians	16	6	4	6	33	24	16
Old Malvernians	16	6	3	7	26	24	15
Old Cholmeleians	16	4	5	7	26	27	13
Old Wellingburians	16	5	2	9	25	33	12
Old Bradfieldians	16	2	3	11	19	58	7

Division One	P	W	D	L	F	A	Pts
Old Salopians	18	15	2	1	63	23	32
Old Brentwoods	18	14	2	2	64	22	30
Old Foresters	18	12	4	2	79	31	28
Old Harrovians	18	10	1	7	61	37	21
Old Witleians	18	8	4	6	50	32	20
Old Aldenhamians	18	9	1	8	54	43	19
Old Wykehamists	18	6	0	12	31	54	12
Old Westminsters	18	4	1	13	25	76	9
Old Ardinians	18	2	1	15	29	88	5
Old Haileyburians	18	1	2	15	35	85	4

Division Two	P	W	D	L	F	A	Pts
Old Etonians Res.	16	13	2	1	51	8	28
Old Cholmeleians Res.	16	12	3	1	45	16	27
Old Carthusians Res.	16	9	1	6	47	28	19
Old Chigwellians Res.	16	7	3	6	42	33	14*
Old Foresters Res.	16	6	2	8	25	47	14
Old Reptonians Res.	16	6	1	9	34	38	13
Old Chigwellians 3rd.	16	4	6	6	32	39	11*
Old Aldenhamians Res.	16	2	3	11	25	60	7
Old Harrovians Res.	16	2	1	13	11	43	5

Division Three – 9 Teams – won by Old Salopians Res.
Division Four – 9 Teams – won by Old Wellingburian Res.
Division Five – 8 Teams – won by Old Forresters 4th.
Junior League Cup – O. Etonians Res. 4, Old Carthusians Res. 1
Derrik Moore Veterans' Cup – Old Carthusians 2, Lancing Old Boys 1

* *points deducted breach of Rule*

LONDON LEGAL LEAGUE

Division One	P	W	D	L	F	A	Pts
Slaughter & May	28	17	7	2	86	26	41
Grays Inn	26	17	6	3	100	47	40
Pegasus (Inner Temple)	26	18	4	4	55	32	40
Clifford Chance	26	13	7	6	76	51	33
Allen & Overy	26	13	6	7	91	54	32
Freshfields	26	14	3	9	82	60	31
Wilde Sapte	26	9	7	10	46	57	25
Herbert Smith	26	7	10	9	55	43	24
Linklaters & Paines	26	11	2	13	70	70	24
Cameron Markby Hewitt	26	9	5	12	59	67	23
Lovell White Durrant	26	10	2	14	50	75	22
Norton Rose	26	6	2	18	24	82	14
Titmuss Sainer & Webb	26	4	2	20	29	99	10
Macfarlanes	26	1	3	22	38	107	5

(1 Game not played)

Division Two	P	W	D	L	F	A	Pte
Nabarro Nathanson	24	19	1	4	94	34	39
Stephenson Harwood	24	15	3	6	63	42	33
Taylor Joynson Garrett	24	15	2	7	67	34	32
Gouldens	24	12	2	10	55	53	26
Simmons & Simmons	24	11	3	10	69	58	25
D.J. Freeman & Co	24	10	3	11	57	53	23
Watson Farley & Williams	24	7	9	8	40	44	23
Baker & McKenzie	24	9	4	11	34	56	22
Denton Hall	24	8	4	12	39	62	20
B.H.T. Goddard	24	5	9	10	39	55	19
Beachcroft Stanleys	24	6	6	12	39	63	18
McKenna & Co	24	7	3	14	41	67	17
Rowe & Maw	24	4	7	13	37	54	15

League Challenge Cup – Gray's Inn 3, Allen & Overy 0

Weavers Arms Cup – Freshfields 3, Taylor Joynson Garrett 1

Invitation Cup – Beachcroft Stanley 4, Titmuss Sainer & Webb 0

LONDON INSURANCE F.A.

Division One	P	W	D	L	F	A	Pts
Temple Bar	14	12	2	0	75	18	26
Colonian Mutual	14	7	4	3	47	28	18
Liverpool Victoria	14	6	3	5	45	33	15
Sun Alliance	14	7	1	6	31	32	15
Granby	14	5	2	7	33	38	12
Bardhill	14	5	1	8	24	60	11
Noble Lowndes	14	4	0	10	27	40	8
Eagle Star	14	3	1	10	25	58	7

Division Two	P	W	D	L	F	A	Pts
Bowring	16	9	3	4	54	43	21
Temple Bar Res.	16	9	3	4	51	30	21
Temple Bar 3rd.	16	9	3	4	46	31	21
Sedgwick	16	9	2	5	46	35	20
Liverpool Victoria Res.	16	8	1	7	50	49	17
Granby Res.	16	8	1	7	42	45	17
Gaflac	16	6	1	9	42	47	13
Sun Alliance Res.	16	5	1	10	40	49	11
Eagle Star Res.	16	1	1	14	25	77	3

Divison Three	P	W	D	L	F	A	Pts
Cannon Lincoln	20	19	1	0	73	14	39
Temple Bar 4th.	20	15	1	4	67	26	31
Norwich Union (London)	20	10	5	5	63	42	25
Noble Lowndes Res.	20	11	2	7	56	34	24
Sun Alliance 3rd.	20	11	2	7	53	31	24
Bowring Res.	20	7	4	9	48	53	18
Eagle Star 3rd.	20	4	6	10	53	57	14
Guardian Royal Exchange	20	5	4	11	30	45	14
Liverpool Victoria 3rd.	20	6	2	12	44	83	14
Gaflac Res.	20	4	3	13	37	75	11
Temple Bar 5th.	20	1	4	15	23	87	6

Charity Cup – Cuaco 4, Granby 1

Challenge Cup – Cuaco Res 3, Granby 1

Junior Cup – Gaflax 1*, Liverpool Victoria Res. 2*

Minor Cup – Cannon Lincoln 2, Bowring Res. 1

W.A. Jewel Memorial Trophy (5-a-Side) – Winners – Temple Bar, Runners-Up – Noble Lowndes

Sportsmanship Trophy – Noble Lowndes

Representative Matches:
Southern Olympian League 5, London Insurance F.A. 0
Bristol Insurance Institute 5, London Insurance F.A. 1
London Insurance F.A. 0, Southern Amateur League 5
London Insurance F.A. 3, Old Boys' League 5
London Banks F.A. 2, London Insurance F.A. "B" 3

LONDON BANKS F.A.

Division One	P	W	D	L	F	A	Pts
Hill Samuel Investment Management	16	11	5	0	41	18	27
Coutts & Co.	16	10	2	4	48	26	22
Credit Suisse	16	7	4	5	34	30	18
Invesco M I M	16	7	1	8	37	36	15
Kleinwort Benson	16	5	5	6	25	27	15
Salomon Brothers	16	5	5	6	29	38	15
Allied Irish Bank	16	4	5	7	26	41	13
Citibank	16	4	3	9	25	31	11
Bank of America	16	2	4	10	23	41	8

Division Two	P	W	D	L	F	A	Pts
Nikko Europe	18	15	0	3	84	33	30
Hong Kong Bank	18	13	1	4	71	37	27
Westpac Banking Corporation	18	8	4	6	45	47	20
Chemical Bank	18	9	1	8	48	39	19
Union Bank of Switzerland	18	8	2	8	40	46	18
National Westminster Bank "A"	18	4	7	7	28	41	15
Coutts & Co. Res.	18	5	5	8	25	38	15
Polytechnic	18	5	4	9	36	51	14
Morgan Stanley	18	6	1	11	40	53	13
Chase Manhattan	18	3	3	12	35	67	9

Division Three	P	W	D	L	F	A	Pts
Goldman Sachs	16	11	4	1	44	11	26
C. Hoare & Co.	16	8	5	3	35	29	21
Abbey National	16	6	6	4	30	22	18
Morgan Guaranty	16	5	6	5	29	27	16
U.C.B. Bank	16	5	5	6	20	26	15
Citibank Res.	16	4	6	6	21	29	14
National Westminster Bank "B"	16	4	4	8	23	32	12
Hill Samuel Bank	16	3	5	8	21	30	11
Bank of America Res.	16	3	5	8	19	36	11

Division Four – 9 Teams – won by United Bank of Kuwait

Challenge Cup – Midland Bank 0, Lensbury 3

Senior Cup – Coutts & Co. 0, National Westminster Bank 3rd 3

Senior Plate – Bank of America 3, Morgan Stanley 0

Minor Cup – Westpac 4, National Westminster Bank 5th. 1

Junior Cup – Union Bank of Switzerland 3, Morgan Guaranty 0

Junior Plate – Swiss Bank Corporation 1, Goldman Sachs 0

Sportsman Cup – Hill Samuel Investment Management 3, Morgan Stanley 2

Veterans' Cup – Lensbury 3, Midland Bank 0

REPRESENTATIVE TEAM RESULTS

United Banks
v Stock Exchange F.A.	Won 4-0
v Royal Marines	Drawn 4-4
v Southern Olympian League	Won 1-0
v Old Boys' League	Lost 0-2
v London University	

London Banks
v Old Boys' League "B"	Lost 0-2
v Royal Marines	Won 4-1
v London Legal League	Lost 1-4
v London Insurance	Lost 2-3

OLD BOYS' LEAGUE

Premier League	P	W	D	L	F	A	Pts
Old Meadonians	20	15	3	2	51	25	33
Old Ignatians	20	13	3	4	54	21	29
Old Tenisonians	20	8	9	3	43	30	25
Old Aloysians	20	6	8	6	36	28	20
Old Tiffinians	20	8	4	8	35	38	20
Glyn Old Boys	20	7	5	8	40	29	19
Cardinal Manning Old Boys	20	6	6	8	40	46	18
Old Wilsonians	20	5	8	7	31	46	18
Old Danes	20	5	6	9	42	56	16
Chertsey Old Salesians	20	1	10	9	24	42	12
Enfield Old Grammarians	20	3	4	13	31	66	10

Senior Division One	P	W	D	L	F	A	Pts
Old Tenisonians Res.	18	13	2	3	51	21	28
Old Hamptonians	18	10	6	2	42	20	26
Phoenix Old Boys	18	8	6	4	43	32	22
Old Suttonians	18	7	5	6	36	35	19
Old Wokingians	18	6	6	6	25	25	18
Old Salvatorians	18	6	6	6	29	35	18
Old Isleworthians	18	5	4	9	32	42	14
Latymer Old Boys	18	5	4	9	29	39	14
Old Minchendenians	18	4	5	9	32	41	13
Mill Hill County Old Boys	18	2	4	12	22	51	8

Senior Division Two	P	W	D	L	F	A	Pts
Clapham Old Xaverians	22	13	5	4	62	29	31
Old Edmontonians	22	13	3	6	62	38	29
Old Tollingtonians	22	10	7	5	50	39	27
Old Grocers	22	9	8	5	43	34	26
Old Southallians	22	10	4	8	38	39	24
Old Kingsburians	22	9	4	9	48	57	22
Old Meadonians Res.	22	8	5	9	48	40	21
Shene Old Grammarians	22	9	2	11	37	39	20
John Fisher Old Boys	22	8	3	11	43	48	19
Old Ignatians Res.	22	7	2	13	35	52	16
Old Greenfordians	22	6	4	12	31	50	16
Old Alpertonians	22	5	3	14	37	69	13

Senior Division Three	P	W	D	L	F	A	Pts
Old Vaughanians	22	18	2	2	76	23	38
Leyton County Old Boys	22	11	5	6	50	42	27
Old Wokingians	22	11	4	7	47	38	26
Old Highburians	22	12	1	9	48	40	25
Old Hamptonians Res.	22	10	5	7	47	39	25
Old Manorians	22	11	2	9	56	38	24
Phoenix Old Boys Res.	22	9	5	8	42	34	23
Old Aloysians Res.	22	10	2	10	43	54	22
Ravenscroft Old Boys	22	6	3	13	33	39	15
Old Buckwellians	22	6	3	13	34	55	15
Old Josephians	22	4	5	13	28	65	13
Enfield Old Grammarians Res.	22	4	3	15	32	69	11

Intermediate Division North – 12 Teams – won by Old Camdenians

Intermediate Division South – 12 Teams – won by Old Addeyans

Division One North – 10 Teams – won by Old Edmontonians Res.

Division One South – 11 Teams – won by Glyn Old Boys Res.

Division One West – 11 Teams – won by Old Manorians Res.

Division Two North – 11 Teams – won by Old Camdenians 3rd.

Division Two South – 11 Teams – won by Old Tiffinians Res.

Division Two West – 11 Teams – won by Old Isleworthians 3rd.

Division Three North – 9 Teams – won by Old Grocers 3rd.

Division Three South – 11 Teams – won by Clapham Old Xaverians 3rd.

Division Three West – 10 Teams – won by Old Salvatorians 4th.

Division Four North – 9 Teams – won by Old Edmontonians 4th.

Division Four South – 11 Teams – won by Chertsey Old Salesians 4th.

Division Four West – 11 Teams – won by Old Paludians Res.

Division Five North – 9 Teams – won by Old Tollingtonians 5th.

Division Five South – 10 Teams – won by Clapham Old Xaverians 4th.

Division Five West – 11 Teams – won by Old Salvatorians 6th.

Division Six North – 10 Teams – won by Latymer Old Boys 5th.

Division Six South – 11 Teams – won by Clapham Old Xaverians 5th.

Division Six West – 11 Teams – won by Cardinal Manning Old Boys 4th.

Division Seven North – 9 Teams – won by Old Egbertians 4th.

Division Seven South – 11 Teams – won by Old Sinjuns 5th.

Division Seven West – 11 Teams – won by Chorley Wood Old Boys Res.

Division Eight North – 7 Teams – won by Old Elysians 5th.

Division Eight South – 11 Teams – won by Chertsey Old Salesians 6th.

Division Eight West – 11 Teams – won by Old Hamptonians 5th.

SOUTHERN AMATEUR LEAGUE

SENIOR SECTION

First Division	P	W	D	L	F	A	Pts
National Westminster Bank	22	16	1	5	50	26	33
Crouch End Vampires	22	14	4	4	41	18	32
Old Actonians Association	22	13	5	4	47	27	31
Old Esthameians	22	10	5	7	36	24	25
Norsemen	22	9	4	9	24	34	22
West Wickman	22	8	5	9	38	35	21
South Bank Polytechnic	22	8	4	10	28	39	20
Civil Service	22	8	2	12	44	42	18
Midland Bank	22	7	3	12	28	42	17
Carshalton	22	5	7	10	28	42	17
Old Parkonians	22	6	3	13	25	39	15
Old Bromleians	22	5	3	14	23	41	13

Second Division	P	W	D	L	F	A	Pts
Lensbury	22	16	5	1	59	20	37
Winchmore Hill	22	14	5	3	53	23	33
Broomfield	22	13	6	3	53	27	32
Alexandra Park	22	13	2	7	59	43	28
Polytechnic	22	11	4	7	44	33	26
Lloyds Bank	22	7	8	7	33	27	22
Southgate Olympic	22	7	5	10	45	44	19
Old Stationers	22	5	8	9	22	31	18
Ibis	22	6	4	12	30	51	16
Kew Association	22	5	3	14	33	58	13
Barclays Bank	22	4	5	13	30	56	13
Old Salesians	22	2	3	17	31	79	7

Third Division	P	W	D	L	F	A	Pts
Old Latymerians	22	19	1	2	76	15	39
East Barnet Old Grammarians	22	16	4	2	72	25	36
Old Parmiterians	22	13	5	4	69	33	31
Cuaco	22	13	5	4	66	33	31
Old Lyonians	22	10	4	8	42	39	24
Royal Bank of Scotland	22	10	3	9	65	56	23
Brentham	22	7	9	6	41	45	23
Old Westminster Citizens	22	7	3	12	25	50	17
Bank of England	22	5	4	13	30	56	14
Merton	22	5	2	15	47	63	12
Alleyn Old Boys	22	4	2	16	27	63	10
Reigate Priory	22	1	2	19	18	100	4

Reserve Teams Section
First Division – 12 Teams – won by Old Esthameians Res.
Second Division – 12 Teams – won by National Westminster Bank Res.
Third Division – 12 Teams – won by Old Parmiterian Res.

3rd. Teams Section
First Division – 12 Teams – won by Norsemen 3rd.
Second Division – 12 Teams – won by Civil Service 3rd.
Third Division – 12 Teams – won by Old Parmiterians 3rd.

4th. Teams Section
First Division – 12 Teams – won by Polytechnic 4th.
Second Division – 12 Teams – won by Civil Service 4th.
Third Division – 12 Teams – won by Old Parmiterians 4th.

5th. Teams Section
First Division – 12 Teams – won by Midland Bank 5th.
Second Division – 11 Teams – won by Old Esthameians 5th.
Third Division – 9 Teams – won by Old Parmiterians 5th.

6th. Teams Section
First Division – 11 Teams – won by Civil Service 6th.
Second Division – 10 Teams – won by Old Actonians Associations 6th.
Third Division – 8 Teams – won by Old Parmiterians 6th.

7th. Teams Section
First Division – 10 Teams – won by Old Esthameians 7th.
Second Division – 9 Teams – won by Old Parmiterians 7th.

8th. Teams Section
First Division – 8 Teams – won by National Westminster Bank 8th.
Second Division – 7 Teams – won by Old Parmiterians 8th.

9th. & 10th. Teams Section
First Division – 12 Teams – won by Winchmore Hill 9th.

MIDLAND AMATEUR ALLIANCE

Division One	P	W	D	L	F	A	Pts
Sherwood Amateurs	22	17	1	4	88	29	35
Magdala Amateurs	22	16	1	5	89	36	33
Old Elizabethans	22	12	4	6	54	31	28
Lady Bay	22	12	3	7	52	45	27
Peoples College	22	9	6	7	49	43	24
Bassingfield	22	10	3	9	59	53	23
Tibshelf Old Boys	22	9	5	8	47	46	23
Brunts Old Boys	22	7	4	11	38	55	18
Kirton B. W.	22	5	5	12	23	51	15
Old Bemrosians	22	5	4	13	30	56	14
Nottinghamshire	22	5	4	13	28	66	14
Derbyshire Amateurs	22	2	6	14	30	76	10

Division Two	P	W	D	L	F	A	Pts
Magdala Amateurs Res.	22	18	1	3	75	28	37
Old Elizabethans Res.	22	14	3	5	70	26	31
Nottingham Spartan	22	14	3	5	80	41	31
Beeston Old Boys Assn.	22	10	3	9	55	42	23
Chilwell	22	9	5	8	41	38	23
Sherwood Amateurs Res.	22	9	4	9	46	39	22
Tibshelf Old Boys Res.	22	7	7	8	34	43	21

	P	W	D	L	F	A	Pts
Brunts Old Boys Res.	22	8	5	9	41	51	21
Nottingham Univ. Postgraduates	22	8	4	10	44	42	20
F.C. Toton	22	7	3	12	36	60	17
Nottinghamshire Res.	22	5	6	11	27	59	16
Lady Bay Res.	22	0	2	20	15	95	2

Division Three	P	W	D	L	F	A	Pte
County Nalgo	20	15	3	2	59	27	33
Ilkeston Electric	20	12	4	4	61	35	28
Woodborough United	20	10	8	2	57	40	28
W. Bridgford Casuals	20	11	5	4	60	46	27
Bassingfield Res.	20	9	3	8	67	55	21
Ilkeston Rangers	20	6	7	7	44	45	19
Monty Hind Old Boys	20	5	6	9	48	64	16
Peoples College Res.	20	5	5	10	41	44	15
Derbyshire Amateurs Res.	20	5	4	11	49	71	14
Old Elizabethans 3rd.	20	4	5	11	39	55	13
Old Bemrosians Res.	20	2	2	16	30	73	6

Division Four – 10 Teams – won by Keyworth A.F.C.
Senior Cup – 10 Teams – won by Old Elizabethans
Intermediate Cup – 10 Teams – won by Old Elizabethans Res.
Minor Cup – 10 Teams – won by Derbyshire Amateurs 3rd.
Challenge Trophy – 10 Teams – won by Magdala Amateurs
Division Two Challenge Cup – 10 Teams – won by Norringham Spartan
Division Three Challenge Cup – 10 Teams – won by County Nalgo
Division Four Challenge Cup – 10 Teams – won by Magdala Amateurs 3rd.
Supplementary Cup – 10 Teams – won by Ilkeston Rangers Res.
H.B. Poole Trophy – 10 Teams – won by Sherwood Amateurs

THE OLD BOYS' INVITATION CUP

Senior Cup – O. Esthameians 3, Owens 0
Junior Cup – O. Esthameians 2nd. 2, O. Finchleians 2nd. 1
Minor Cup – O. Esthameians 3rd. 4, O. Stationers 3rd. 3
4th. XI Cup – O. Esthameians 4th. 2, O. Stationers 5th. 0
5th. XI Cup – O. Latymerians 5th. O:WP, O. Stationers 5th., 0:LP
6th. XI Cup – O. Esthameians 6th. 2, O. Latymerians 6th. 0
7th. XI Cup – O. Esthameians 7th. 6, O. Latymerians 7th. 0
Veterans' Cup – O. Tenisonians Vets. 4, O. Stationers Vets. 2

UNIVERSITY FOOTBALL 1992–93

UNIVERSITY MATCH
(27 March 1993, at Craven Cottage, Fulham)

Oxford 1, Cambridge 1

Oxford and Cambridge shared the C. B. Fry trophy on Boat Race day. The fixture switched from December in the last few years has attracted less media attention, though ironically BBC TV cameras covered part of the game as they were on the toepath: Jimmy Hill the Fulham chairman was on hand with commentary on action replays for the goals.

COMMERCIAL UNION/UAU 1992–93

First team championship

SOUTH WEST GROUP
Bath 1, Bristol 1
Bath 4, Cranfield 2
Bath 1, Exeter 4
Bath 1, Southampton 2
Bath 0, Marjohn 3
Bristol 7, Cranfield 0
Bristol 0, Exeter 6
Bristol 0, Southampton 1
Bristol 4, Marjohn 5
Cranfield 1, Exeter 2
Cranfield 1, Southampton 8
Cranfield 1, Marjohn 5
Exeter 1, Southampton 0
Exeter 0, Marjohn 0
Marjohn 3, Southampton 1

	P	W	D	L	F	A	Pts
Exeter	5	4	1	0	13	2	9
Marjohn	5	4	1	0	15	7	9
Southampton	5	3	0	2	13	6	6
Bristol	5	1	1	3	12	13	3
Bath	5	1	2	2	7	11	3
Cranfield	5	0	0	5	5	26	0

SOUTH CENTRAL
Brunel 1, Imperial 0
Brunel 1, Kings 5
Brunel 4, Reading 2
Brunel 3, RHBNC 0
Imperial 2, Kings 2
Imperial 3, Reading 2
Imperial 3, RHBNC 2
Kings 0, Reading 2
Kings 2, RHBNC 2
Reading 2, RHBNC 1

	P	W	D	L	F	A	Pts
Brunel	4	3	0	1	9	7	6
Kings	4	2	1	1	10	6	5
Imperial	4	2	1	1	8	7	5
Reading	4	2	0	2	8	8	4
RHBNC	4	0	0	4	4	11	0

SOUTH EAST (NORTH) GROUP
Essex 0, East Anglia 1
Essex 5, QMWC 1
Essex 1, UCL 1
Essex 1, Buckingham 0
Essex 1, Middlesex 1
East Anglia 7, QMWC 0
East Anglia 6, UCL 2
East Anglia 5, Buckingham 1
East Anglia 4, Middlesex 5
QMWC 2, UCL 1
QMWC 4, Buckingham 0
QMWC 1, Middlesex 7
UCL 1, Middlesex 2
Middlesex w/o, Buckingham scr

	P	W	D	L	F	A	Pts
Middlesex	5	4	1	0	15	7	9
East Anglia	5	4	0	1	23	8	8
Essex	5	2	2	1	8	4	6
QMWC	5	2	0	3	8	20	4
UCL	5	1	1	3	7	12	3
Buckingham	5	0	0	5	2	12	0

SOUTH EAST (SOUTH) GROUP
Kent 3, City 0
Kent w/o, LSE scr
Kent 1, Surrey 2
Kent 3, Sussex 1
Kent 0, West London 5
City 1, LSE 0
City 2, Surrey 4
City 0, Sussex 4
City 0, West London 6
LSE 2, Surrey 8
LSE 1, Sussex 3
LSE 0, West London 5
Surrey 1, Sussex 1
Surrey 0, West London 7
Sussex 0, West London 3

	P	W	D	L	F	A	Pts
West London	5	5	0	0	26	0	10
Surrey	5	3	1	1	15	13	7
Kent	5	3	0	2	7	8	6
Sussex	5	2	1	2	9	8	5
City	5	1	0	4	3	17	2
LSE	5	0	0	5	3	17	0

WELSH GROUP
Aberystwyth 3, UCNW (Bangor) 0
Aberystwyth 0, UWCC 4
Aberystwyth 2, Cardiff Inst. 4
Aberystwyth 0, Glamorgan 4
Aberystwyth 0, Swansea 2
UCNW (Bangor) 0, UWCC 3
UCNW (Bangor) 0, Cardiff Inst. 2
UCNW (Bangor) 0, Glamorgan 3
UCNW (Bangor) 2, Swansea 3
UWCC 1, Cardiff Inst. 0
UWCC 5, Glamorgan 1
UWCC 2, Swansea 1
Cardiff Inst. 2, Glamorgan 1
Cardiff Inst. 2, Swansea 2
Glamorgan 0, Swansea 1

	P	W	D	L	F	A	Pts
UWCC	5	5	0	0	8	5	10
Cardiff Institute	5	3	1	1	10	6	7
Swansea	5	3	0	1	9	6	7
Glamorgan	5	2	0	3	9	8	4
Aberystwyth	5	1	0	4	5	14	2
UCNW (Bangor)	5	0	0	5	2	14	0

MIDLANDS GROUP
Loughborough 2, Nottingham 0
Loughborough 5, Warwick 0
Loughborough 1, Birmingham 2
Loughborough 3, Leicester 0
Loughborough 2, Aston 0
Loughborough 1, Bedford 1
Loughborough 3, Oxford Brookes 0
Nottingham 3, Warwick 2
Nottingham 0, Birmingham 3
Nottingham 1, Leicester 2
Nottingham 5, Aston 0
Nottingham 3, Bedford 2
Nottingham 4, Oxford Brookes 0
Warwick 1, Birmingham 5
Warwick 3, Leicester 1
Warwick 0, Aston 1

Warwick 3, Bedford 2
Warwick 0, Oxford Brookes 0
Birmingham 3, Leicester 0
Birmingham 5, Aston 0
Birmingham 2, Bedford 1
Birmingham 5, Oxford Brookes 0
Leicester 2, Aston 0
Leicester 1, Bedford 3
Leicester 1, Oxford Brookes 1
Aston 0, Bedford 8
Bedford 7, Oxford Brookes 1

	P	W	D	L	F	A	Pts
Birmingham	7	7	0	0	25	3	14
Loughborough	7	5	1	1	17	3	11
Nottingham	7	5	0	2	16	9	8
Bedford	7	3	1	3	17	10	7
Leicester	7	2	1	4	7	14	5
Warwick	7	2	1	4	9	17	5
Aston	6	1	0	5	5	14	2
Oxford Brookes	6	0	2	4	2	20	2

NORTH EAST GROUP

Newcastle 3, Sheffield 1
Newcastle 4, York 0
Newcastle 1, Hull 1
Newcastle 1, Leeds 2
Newcastle 1, Durham 1
Newcastle 3, Sunderland 1
Sheffield 1, York 1
Sheffield 4, Hull 6
Sheffield 2, Leeds 5
Sheffield 2, Durham 2
Sheffield 0, Sunderland 3

York 0, Hull 1
York 1, Leeds 5
York 2, Durham 3
York 2, Sunderland 4
Hull 2, Leeds 4
Hull 1, Durham 4
Hull 1, Sunderland 3
Leeds 2, Durham 1
Leeds 6, Sunderland 2
Durham 6, Sunderland 1

	P	W	D	L	F	A	Pts
Leeds	6	6	0	0	24	9	12
Durham	6	3	2	1	17	9	8
Newcastle	6	3	2	1	13	6	8
Sunderland	6	3	0	3	14	18	6
Hull	6	2	1	3	12	16	5
Sheffield	6	2	0	4	10	20	2
York	6	0	1	5	6	18	1

NORTH WEST GROUP

Bradford 1, UMIST 1
Bradford 0, Salford 5
Bradford 3, Keele 4
Bradford 1, Manchester 6
Bradford 3, Lancaster 3
Bradford 1, Liverpool 5
Bradford 4, Chester 4
UMIST 0, Salford 0
UMIST 4, Keele 3
UMIST 4, Manchester 5
UMIST 0, Lancaster 1
UMIST 0, Liverpool 2
UMIST 2, Chester 3
Salford 3, Keele 1

Salford 3, Manchester 4
Salford 1, Lancaster 1
Salford 0, Liverpool 3
Salford 2, Chester 3
Keele 0, Manchester 4
Keele 1, Lancaster 6
Keele 1, Liverpool 4
Keele 1, Chester 5
Manchester 5, Lancaster 0
Manchester 1, Liverpool 3
Manchester 4, Chester 1
Lancaster 3, Liverpool 1
Lancaster 1, Chester 4
Liverpool 2, Chester 1

	P	W	D	L	F	A	Pts
Manchester	7	6	0	1	25	12	12
Liverpool	7	6	0	1	20	7	12
Chester	7	4	1	2	21	16	9
Lancaster	7	3	2	2	15	15	8
Salford	7	2	2	3	14	12	6
UMIST	7	2	1	4	12	15	5
Keele	7	1	0	6	11	29	2
Bradford	7	0	2	5	13	29	2

Play-off Round
Leeds 3, Lancaster 1
Loughborough 3, Chester 0
Manchester 3, Glamorgan 1
Liverpool 2, Newcastle 0
UWCC 3, Sunderland 1
Durham 4, Nottingham 2
Brunel 0, Essex 1
Cardiff Inst. 0, Marjohn 1
West London 2, Southampton 0
Kings 3, Kent 7
Exeter 6, Imperial 1
Surrey 3, East Anglia 1
Birmingham 2, Swansea 0
Middlesex 1, Bedford 6

Challenge Round
Leeds 1, Loughborough 2
Manchester w/o
Heriot Watt 2, Liverpool 1
UWCC 0, Durham 4
Essex 0, Marjohn 2
West London 1, Kent 3
Exeter 0, Surrey 0
Surrey won on penalties 5-4
Birmingham 2, Bedford 2
Bedford won on penalties 5-4

Quarter-finals
Loughborough 6, Manchester 2
Heriot 4, Durham 0
Marjohn 2, Kent 1
Surrey 1, Bedford 3

Semi-finals
Marjohn 2, Bedford 3
Loughborough 6, Heriot Watt 1

Final (played at Walsall FC)
Bedford 1, Loughborough 5

BUSF TOURNAMENT
(UAU results only)
UAU I 3, Scotland 2
UAU I 3, London 2
UAU I 1, Wales 0
UAU II 1, N. Ireland 0
UAU II 2, Cambridge 0
UAU II 1, Oxford 3
UAU II 1, Scotland 2 (3rd/4th place)
UAU I 0, Oxford 1 (Final)

Representative matches
UAU I 3, Stoke City 1
UAU II 4, English Schools FA 3
UAU I 2, Barnsley FC 3
UAU II 1, Welsh Univs 0
UAU 2, BSSA 0
UAU 1, Irish Tech. College 1

Representative matches (Women)
UAU I 5, BSSA 1
UAU II 6, Wales 1

ADDRESSES

The Football Association: R. H. G. Kelly, F.C.I.S., 16 Lancaster Gate, London W2 3LW

Scotland: J. Farry, 6 Park Gardens, Glasgow G3 7YE. *041-332 6372*

Northern Ireland (Irish FA): D. I. Bowen, 20 Windsor Avenue, Belfast BT9 6EG. *0232-669458*

Wales: A. Evans, 3 Westgate Street, Cardiff, South Glamorgan CF1 1JF. *0222-372325*

Republic of Ireland (FA of Ireland): S. Connolly, 80 Merrion Square South, Dublin 2. *0001-766864*

International Federation (FIFA): S. Blatter, FIFA House, Hitzigweg 11, CH-8032 Zurich, Switzerland. *1-384-9595. Fax: 1-384-9696*

Union of European Football Associations: G. Aigner, PO Box 16, CH-3000 Berne 15, Switzerland. *031-321735. Fax: 031-321838.*

THE LEAGUES

The Football League: J. D. Dent, F.C.I.S., The Football League, Lytham St Annes, Lancs FY8 1JG. *0253-729421. Telex 67675*

The Scottish League: P. Donald, 188 West Regent Street, Glasgow G2 4RY. *041-248 384415*

The Irish League: H. Wallace, 87 University Street, Belfast BT7 1HP. *0232-242888*

Football League of Ireland: E. Morris, 80 Merrion Square South, Dublin 2. *0001-765120*

GM Vauxhall Conference: P. D. Hunter, 24 Barnehurst Road, Bexleyheath, Kent DA7 6EZ. *0322-521116*

Central League: D. J. Grimshaw, 118 St Stephens Road, Deepdale, Preston, Lancs PR1 6TD. *0772-795386*

North West Counties League: N. A. Rowles, 845 Liverpool Road, Peel Green, Eccles, Manchester M3O 7LJ. *061-962 4623*

Eastern Counties League: C. Lamb, 3 Land Close, Clacton, Essex CO16 8UJ

Football Combination: N. Chamberlain, 2 Vicarage Close, Old Costessey, Norwich NR8 5DL. *0603-743998*

Hellenic League: T. Cuss, 7 Blenheim Road, Kidlington, Oxford OX5 2HP. *08675-5920*

Kent League: R. Vintner, The Smithy, The Square, Chilham, Canterbury, Kent CT4 8BY

Lancashire Amateur League: R. G. Bowker, 13 Shores Green Drive, Wincham, Northwich, Cheshire CW9 6EE. *061-480 7723*

Lancashire Football League: J. W. Howarth, 465 Whalley Road, Clapton-le-Moors, Accrington, Lancs BB5 5RP. *0254-398957*

Leicestershire Senior League: P. Henwood, 450 London Road, Leicester LE2 2PP. *Leicester 704121*

London Spartan: D. Cordell, 44 Greenleas, Waltham Abbey, Essex. *Lea Valley 712428*

Manchester League: F. J. Fitzpatrick, 102 Victoria Road, Stretford, Manchester. *061-865 2726*

Midland Combination: L. W. James, 175 Barnet Lane, Kingswinford, Brierley Hill, West Midlands. *Kingswinford 3459*

Mid-Week Football League: N. A. S. Matthews, Cedar Court, Steeple Aston, Oxford. *0869-40347*

Northern Premier: R. D. Bayley, 22 Woburn Drive, Hale, Altrincham, Cheshire. *061-980 7007*

Northern Intermediate League: G. Thompson, Clegg House, 253 Pitsmoor Road, Sheffield S3 9AQ. *0742-27817*

Northern League: T. Golightly, 85 Park Road North, Chester-le-Street, Co Durham D43 3SA. *091-388-2056*

North Midlands League: G. Thompson, 7 Wren Park Close, Ridgway, Sheffield.

Peterborough and District League: M. J. Croson, 44 Storrington Way, Werrington, Peterborough, Cambs PE4 6QP.

Vauxhall League: N. Robinson, 226 Rye Lane, Peckham SE15 4NL. *081-653 3903*

Southern Amateur League: S. J. Lucas, 23 Beaufort Close, North Weald Bassett, Epping, Essex CM16 6JZ. *037882-3932*

South-East Counties League: R. A. Bailey, 10 Highlands Road, New Barnet, Herts EN5 5AB. *081-449 5131*

Southern League: D. J. Strudwick, 11 Welland Close, Durrington, Worthing, West Sussex BN13 3NR. *0903-67788*

South Midlands League: M. Mitchell, 26 Leighton Court, Dunstable, Beds LU6 1EW. *0582-67291*

South Western League: R. Lowe, Panorama, Lamerton, Tavistock, Devon PL19 8SD. *0822-61376*

United Counties League: R. Gamble, 8 Bostock Avenue, Northampton. *0604-37766*

Wearside: B. Robson, 12 Deneside, Howden-le-Wear, Crook, Co. Durham DL15 8JR. *0388-762034*

Western League: M. E. Washer, 126 Chessel Street, Bristol BS3 3DQ. *0272-638308*

The Welsh League: K. J. Tucker, 16 The Parade, Merthyr Tydfil, Mid Glamorgan CF47 0ET. *0685-723884*

West Midlands Regional League: K. H. Goodfellow, 11 Emsworth Grove, Kings Heath, Birmingham B14 6HY. *021-444 3056*

West Yorkshire League: W. Keyworth, 2 Hill Court Grove, Bramley, Yorks L13 2AP. *Pudsey 74465*

Northern Counties (East): B. Wood, 6 Restmore Avenue, Guiseley, Nr Leeds LS20 9DG. *0943-874558 (home); Bradford 29595 (9 a.m. to 5 p.m.)*

COUNTY FOOTBALL ASSOCIATIONS

Bedfordshire: P. D. Brown, 19 Lambs Close, Dunstable, LU5 4QA *0582-668013*

Berks and Bucks: W. S. Gosling, 15a London Street, Faringdon, Oxon SN7 8AG. *0367-242099*

Birmingham County: M. Pennick, County FA Offices, Rayhall Lane, Great Barr, Birmingham B43 6JE. *021-357 4278*

Cambridgeshire: R. E. Rogers, 20 Aingers Road, Histon, Cambridge CB4 4JP. *022023-2803*

Cheshire: A. Collins, The Cottage, Hartford Moss Rec Centre, Winnington, Northwich CW8 4BG.

Cornwall: J. M. Ryder, Penare, 16 Gloweth View, Truro, Cornwall TR1 3JZ.

Cumberland: R. Johnson, 72 Victoria Road, Workington, Cumbria CA14 2QT. *0900-3979*

Derbyshire: K. Compton, The Grandstand, Moorways Stadium, Moor Lane, Derby DE2 8FB. *0332-361422*

Devon County: C. Squirrel, 51a Wolborough Street, Newton Abbot, Devon TQ12 1JQ. *0626 332077*

Dorset County: P. Hough, 9 Parkstone Road, Poole, Dorset BH15 2NN. *0202-746244*

Durham: J. R. Walsh, 'Codeslaw', Ferens Park, Durham DH1 1JZ. *0385-48653*

East Riding County: D. R. Johnson, 52 Bethune Ave, Hull HU4 7EJ. *0482-641458*

Essex County: T. Alexander, 31 Mildmay Road, Chelmsford, Essex CM2 0DN. *0245-357727*

Gloucestershire: E. J. Marsh, 46 Douglas Road, Horfield, Bristol BS7 0JD. *0272-519435*

Guernsey: M. J. Le Prevost, Le Coin, Pleinmont Road, Torteval, Guernsey CI. *0481-65928*

Hampshire: R. G. Barnes, 8 Ashwood Gardens, off Winchester Road, Southampton SO9 2UA. *0703-766884*

Herefordshire: E. R. Prescott, 7 Kirkland Close, Hampton Park, Hereford HR1 1XP. *0432-51134*

Hertfordshire: R. G. Kibble, 4 The Wayside, Leverstock Green, Hemel Hempstead, Herts HP3 8NR. *0442-255918*

Huntingdonshire: M. M. Armstrong, 1 Chapel End, Great Giddings, Huntingdon. Cambs PE17 5NP. *08323-262*
Isle of Man: Mrs A. Garrett, 120 Bucks Road, Douglas, IOM. *0624-6349*
Jersey: C. Tostevin, Wellesley, Greve Dazette St Clement, Jersey JE2 6SA. *0534-24929*
Kent County: K. T. Masters, 69 Maidstone Road, Chatham, Kent ME4 6DT. *0634-43824*
Lancashire: J. Kenyon, 31a Wellington St, St John's, Blackburn, Lancs BB1 8AU. *0254-64333*
Leicestershire and Rutland: R. E. Barston, Holmes Park, Dog and Gun Lane, Whetstone, Leicester LE8 3LJ. *0533-867828*
Lincolnshire: F. S. Richardson, PO Box 26, 12 Dean Road, Lincoln LN2 4DP. *0522-24917*
Liverpool County: F. L. J. Hunter, 23 Greenfield Road, Old Swann, Liverpool L13 3EN. *051-526-9515*
London: R. S. Ashford, 4 Aldworth Grove, London SE13 6HY. *081-690 9626*
Manchester County: F. Brocklehurst, Sports Complex, Brantingham Road, Chorlton, Manchester M21 1TG. *061-881 0299*
Middlesex County: P. J. Clayton, 30 Rowland Avenue, Kenton, Harrow, Middx HA3 9AF.
Norfolk County: R. Kiddell, 39 Beaumont Road, Costessey, Norwich NR5 0HG. *0603-742421*
Northamptonshire: B. Walden, 2 Duncan Close, Red House Square, Moulton Park, Northampton NN3 1WL. *0604-670741*
North Riding County: P. Kirby, 284 Linthorpe Road, Middlesbrough TS1 3QU. *0642-224585*

Northumberland: R. E. Maughan 3, Osborne Terrace, Jesmond, Newcastle upon Tyne NE2 1NE. *091-297 0101*
Nottinghamshire: W. T. Annable, 7 Clarendon Street, Nottingham NG1 5HS. *0602-418954*
Oxfordshire: P. J. Ladbrook, 3 Wilkins Road, Cowley, Oxford OX4 2HY. *0865-775432*
Sheffield and Hallamshire: G. Thompson, Clegg House, 5 Onslow Road, Sheffield S11 7AF. *0742-670068*
Shropshire: A. W. Brett, 5 Ebnal Road, Shrewsbury SY2 6PW. *0743-56066*
Somerset & Avon (South): Mrs H. Marchment, 30 North Road, Midsomer Norton, Bath BA3 2QQ. *0761-413176*
Staffordshire: G. S. Brookes, County Showground, Weston Road, Stafford ST18 0DB. *0785-56994*
Suffolk County: W. M. Steward, 2 Millfields, Haughley, Suffolk IP14 3PU. *0449-673481*
Surrey County: A. P. Adams, 6 Lime Grove, Bellfields, Guildford GU1 1PG. *0483-68832*
Sussex County: D. M. Worsfold, County Office, Culver Road, Lancing, Sussex BN15 9AX. *0903-753547*
Westmorland: J. B. Fleming, 101, Burneside Road, Kendal, Cumbria LA9 4RZ. *0539-722915*
West Riding County: R. Carter, Unit 3, Low Mills Road, Wortley, Leeds LS12 4UY. *0532-310101*
Wiltshire: E. M. Parry, 44 Kennet Avenue, Swindon SN2 3LG. *0793-29036*
Worcestershire: M. R. Leggett Fermain, 12 Worcester Road, Eyesham, Worcs WR11 4JV. *0905-612336*

OTHER USEFUL ADDRESSES

Amateur Football Alliance: W. P. Goss, 55 Islington Park Street, London N1 1QB. *071-359 3493*
English Schools FA: M. R. Berry, 4a Eastgate Street, Stafford ST16 2NN. *0785-51142*
Oxford University: M. H. Matthews, University College, Oxford OX1 4BH.
Cambridge University: Dr A. J. Little, St Catherine's College, Cambridge CB2 1RL.
Army: Major T. C. Knight, Clayton Barracks, Aldershot, Hants GU11 2BG. *0252-24431 Ext 3571*
Royal Air Force: Group Capt P. W. Hilton, 20 Stray Walk, Harrogate, N. Yorks HG2 8HU. *0423-793573*
Royal Navy: Lt-Cdr J. Danks, R.N. Sports Office, H.M.S. Temeraire, Portsmouth, Hants PO1 4QS. *0705-822351 Ext 22671*
Universities Athletic Union: G. Gregory-Jones, Suite 36, London Fruit Exchange, Brushfield Street, London E1 6EU. *071-247 3066*
Central Council of Physical Recreation: General Secretary, 70 Brompton Road, London SW3 1HE. *071-584 6651*
British Olympic Association: 6 John Prince's Street, London W1M 0DH. *071-408 2029*
National Federation of Football Supporters' Clubs: Registered Office: A. M. Kershaw, 24 South St., Loughborough, Leics. LE11 3EG. *0509-267643* Hon. Secretary: Mark Agate, "The Stadium", 14 Coombe Close, Lordswood, Chatham, Kent ME5 8NU. *0634-863520*
National Playing Fields Association: Col R. Satterthwaite, O.B.E., 578b Catherine Place, London, SW1.
The Scottish Football Commercial Managers Association: J. E. Hillier (Chairman), c/o Keith FC Promotions Office, 60 Union Street, Keith, Banffshire, Scotland.

Professional Footballers' Association: G. Taylor, 2 Oxford Court, Bishopsgate, Off Lower Mosley Street, Manchester M2 3W2. *061-236 0575*
Referees' Association: W. J. Taylor, Cross Offices, Summerhill, Kingswinford, West Midlands DY6 9JE. *0384-288386*
Women's Football Association: Miss L. Whitehead, 448/450 Hanging Ditch, The Corn Exchange, Manchester M4 3ES. *061-832 5911*
The Association of Football League Commercial Managers: G. H. Dimbleby, Secretary WBA FC, The Hawthorns, Halford Lane, West Bromwich B71 4LF.
The Association of Football Statisticians: R. J. Spiller, 22 Bretons, Basildon, Essex SS15 5BY. *0268-416020*
The Football Programme Directory: David Stacey, 'The Beeches', 66 Southend Road, Wickford, Essex SS11 8EN.
England Football Supporters Association: Publicity Officer, David Stacey, 66 Southend Road, Wickford, Essex SS11 8EN.
The Football League Executive Staffs Association: PO Box 52, Leamington Spa, Warwickshire.
The Ninety-Two Club: 104 Gilda Crescent, Whitchurch, Bristol BS14 9LD.
The Football Trust: Second Floor, Walkden House, 10 Melton Street, London NW1 2EJ. *071-388 4504*
The Football Supporters Association: PO Box 11, Liverpool L26 1XP. *051-709-2594.*
Association of Provincial Football Supporters' Clubs in London: Tina A. Robertson, 45 Durham Avenue, Heston, Middlesex TW5 0HG. *081-843-9854*
World Association of Friends of English Football: PO Box 2221, D-30022 Hannover, Germany. *0511-885616*

OTHER AWARDS 1992-93

FOOTBALLER OF THE YEAR

The Football Writers' Association Award for the Footballer of the Year went to Chris Waddle of Sheffield Wednesday and England.

Past Winners
1947–48 Stanley Matthews (Blackpool), 1948–49 Johnny Carey (Manchester U), 1949–50 Joe Mercer (Arsenal), 1950–51 Harry Johnston (Blackpool), 1951–52 Billy Wright (Wolverhampton W), 1952–53 Nat Lofthouse (Bolton W), 1953–54 Tom Finney (Preston NE), 1954–55 Don Revie (Manchester C), 1955–56 Bert Trautmann (Manchester C), 1956–57 Tom Finney (Preston NE), 1957–58 Danny Blanchflower (Tottenham H), 1958–59 Syd Owen (Luton T), 1959–60 Bill Slater (Wolverhampton W), 1960–61 Danny Blanchflower (Tottenham H), 1961–62 Jimmy Adamson (Burnley), 1962–63 Stanley Matthews (Stoke C), 1963–64 Bobby Moore (West Ham U), 1964–65 Bobby Collins (Leeds U), 1965–66 Bobby Charlton (Manchester U), 1966–67 Jackie Charlton (Leeds U), 1967–68 George Best (Manchester U), 1968–69 Dave Mackay (Derby Co) shared with Tony Book (Manchester C), 1969–70 Billy Bremner (Leeds U), 1970–71 Frank McLintock (Arsenal), 1971–72 Gordon Banks (Stoke C), 1972–73 Pat Jennings (Tottenham H), 1973–74 Ian Callaghan (Liverpool), 1974–75 Alan Mullery (Fulham), 1975–76 Kevin Keegan (Liverpool), 1976–77 Emlyn Hughes (Liverpool), 1977–78 Kenny Burns (Nottingham F), 1978–79 Kenny Dalglish (Liverpool), 1979–80 Terry McDermott (Liverpool), 1980–81 Frans Thijssen (Ipswich T), 1981–82 Steve Perryman (Tottenham H), 1982–83 Kenny Dalglish (Liverpool), 1983–84 Ian Rush (Liverpool), 1984–85 Neville Southall (Everton), 1985–86 Gary Lineker (Everton), 1986–87 Clive Allen (Tottenham H), 1987–88 John Barnes (Liverpool), 1988–89 Steve Nicol (Liverpool), 1989–90 John Barnes (Liverpool), 1990–91 Gordon Strachan (Leeds), 1991–92 Gary Lineker (Tottenham H).

THE PFA AWARDS 1993

Player of the Year: Paul McGrath (Aston Villa).
Previous Winners: 1974 Norman Hunter (Leeds U); 1975 Colin Todd (Derby Co); 1976 Pat Jennings (Tottenham H); 1977 Andy Gray (Aston Villa); 1978 Peter Shilton (Nottingham F); 1979 Liam Brady (Arsenal); 1980 Terry McDermott (Liverpool); 1981 John Wark (Ipswich T); 1982 Kevin Keegan (Southampton); 1983 Kenny Dalglish (Liverpool); 1984 Ian Rush (Liverpool); 1985 Peter Reid (Everton); 1986 Gary Lineker (Everton); 1987 Clive Allen (Tottenham H); 1988 John Barnes (Liverpool); 1989 Mark Hughes (Manchester U); 1990 David Platt (Aston Villa); 1991 Mark Hughes (Manchester U); 1992 Gary Pallister (Manchester U).
Young Player of the Year: Ryan Giggs (Manchester U).
Previous Winners: 1974 Kevin Beattie (Ipswich T); 1975 Mervyn Day (West Ham U); 1976 Peter Barnes (Manchester C); 1977 Andy Gray (Aston Villa); 1978 Tony Woodcock (Nottingham F); 1979 Cyrille Regis (WBA); 1980 Glenn Hoddle (Tottenham H); 1981 Gary Shaw (Aston Villa); 1982 Steve Moran (Southampton); 1983 Ian Rush (Liverpool); 1984 Paul Walsh (Luton T); 1985 Mark Hughes (Manchester U); 1986 Tony Cottee (West Ham U); 1987 Tony Adams (Arsenal); 1988 Paul Gascoigne (Tottenham H); 1989 Paul Merson (Arsenal); 1990 Matthew Le Tissier (Southampton); 1991 Lee Sharpe (Manchester U); 1992 Ryan Giggs (Manchester U).
Merit Award: 1968 Manchester United team.
Previous Winners: 1974 Bobby Charlton CBE, Cliff Lloyd OBE; 1975 Dennis Law; 1976 George Eastham OBE; 1977 Jack Taylor OBE; 1978 Bill Shankly OBE; 1979 Tom Finney OBE; 1980 Sir Matt Busby CBE; 1981 John Trollope MBE; 1982 Joe Mercer OBE; 1983 Bob Paisley OBE; 1984 Bill Nicholson; 1985 Ron Greenwood; 1986 The 1966 England World Cup team, Sir Alf Ramsey, Harold Shepherdson; 1987 Sir Stanley Matthews; 1988 Billy Bonds MBE; 1989 Nat Lofthouse; 1990 Peter Shilton; 1991 Tommy Hutchison; 1992 Brian Clough.

ALEX FERGUSON TAKES BARCLAYS TOP ACCOLADE AS MANAGER OF THE YEAR IN MAN.U's ANNUS MIRABILIS

Alex Ferguson was named unopposed, by a panel of 30 leading football journalists and commentators, as Barclays Bank Manager of the Year in honour of Manchester United's historic success in the inaugural season of the FA Premier League. He received the Barclays trophy, a Silver Eagle memento and a cheque for £5,000.

Alex Ferguson pictured with the Barclays Manager of the Year award.

The presentation was made at the Barclays Bank Managers Awards Luncheon at the Savoy Hotel, London, by Mr Alastair Robinson, group vice-chairman of Barclays Bank.

This is Ferguson's 8th managerial award, following his arrival at old Trafford, in 5 years: six overall Manager of the Month awards (Jan. '89, Jan., Aug., Sept & Dec. '91 & Apr. '93) and a Special Award in 1991, the year of United's Cup-Winners Cup victory).

It is the first time in 25 years the Manager of the Year title has gone to Old Trafford: Matt Busby was the last winner in 1968, the year his side won the European Cup.

This is the sixth time a Scot has claimed the accolade in the past eight years: Kenny Dalglish in '86, '88 & '90 & George Graham in '89 & '91.

BARCLAYS BANK DIVISIONAL MANAGERS OF THE SEASON 1992–93

Kevin Keegan (Newcastle Utd.) in Barclays League Division One; *Lou Macari* (Stoke City) in Division Two; & *Eddie May* (Cardiff City) in Division Three were named by The Football League for the Barclays Bank Divisional Manager of the Season awards. Each received a Silver Eagle memento and a chegue for £1,000.

BARCLAYS BANK ACHIEVEMENT AWARD

Jim Smith of Portsmouth received the Barclays Bank Achievement Award – a Silver Eagle trophy and a cheque for £1,000 – on the vote of the League Managers Association. "The award is designed to highlight the efforts of the manager who, in the opinion of his peers, has worked wonders with the resources available to him," reads the citation.

BARCLAYS BANK SPECIAL AWARD

A special award is being struck by Barclays for Brian Clough listing, and in recognition of, his record number of 25 managerial awards in the 25 years between August '69 and May '93.

BARCLAYS BANK SERVICE TO FOOTBALL ACCOLADE

Stan Cullis, a legendary football figure as a player and manager, prinicipally with Wolverhampton Wanderers, was named for the Barclays Bank Service to Football Award by the members of IFMA (the Institute of Football Management & Administration – which includes managers, secretaries, coaches, trainers, physios, commercial managers and chief executives & directors).

Stan – born at Ellesmere Port in 1916 almost next door to his great friend, the late Joe Mercer – is the 16th winner of this accolade which comprises a silver rosebowl and a Barclays cheque for £1,000.

As a player, pre-war, Stan was described by his manager, Major Frank Buckley as "without doubt the most outstanding of the many great players who have won the Black and Gold."

Between 1937 and 1939 he won 12 international caps for England and like many of his generation was unfortunate to have his career interrupted by the war – although he played in 20 war time internationals, skippering England and the British Army.

As manager at Molineux between 1948 and 1964 he was outstanding: Wolves winning the FA Cup twice and the Football League Championship three times within the space of 12 years. Stan also pioneered floodlight football "on the box" and over 160,000 fans also came through the turnstiles to see Wolves defeat Moscow Spartak, Honved & Moscow Dynamo in those avant-garde fixtures. He spent his final six years as a manager from 1964 with Birmingham City.

BARCLAYS YOUNG EAGLE OF THE YEAR

Ryan Giggs, Manchester Utd's 19 year-old Welsh wizard, was named Barclays Young Eagle of the Year by England manager Graham Taylor and his distinguished panel. He received his prize – the Barclays Silver Eagle Trophy and a cheque for £5,000 – at 1992 the Barclays Bank Managers Awards luncheon at the Savoy Hotel in London.

THE SCOTTISH PFA AWARDS 1992

Player of the Year: Premier Division: Andy Goram (Rangers); First Division: Gordan Dalziel (Raith R); Second Division: Sandy Ross (Brechin C).

Previous Winners: 1978 Derek Johnstone (Rangers); 1979 Paul Hegarty (Dundee U); 1980 Davie Provan (Celtic); 1981 Sandy Clark (Airdrieonians); 1982 Mark McGhee (Aberdeen); 1983 Charlie Nicholas (Celtic); 1984 Willie Miller (Aberdeen); 1985 Jim Duffy (Morton); 1986 Richard Gough (Dundee U); 1987 Brian McClair (Celtic); 1988 Paul McStay (Celtic); 1989 Theo Snelders (Aberdeen); 1990 Jim Bett (Aberdeen); 1991 Paul Elliott (Celtic); Ally McCoist (Rangers).

Young Player of the Year: Eoin Jess (Aberdeen).

Previous Winners: 1978 Graeme Payne (Dundee U); 1979 Graham Stewart (Dundee U); 1980 John MacDonald (Rangers); 1981 Francis McAvennie (St Mirren); 1982 Charlie Nicholas (Celtic); 1983 Pat Nevin (Clyde); 1984 John Robertson (Hearts); 1985 Craig Levein (Hearts); 1986 Craig Levein (Hearts); 1987 Robert Fleck (Rangers); 1988 John Collins (Hibernian); 1989 Bill McKinlay (Dundee U); 1990 Scott Crabbe (Hearts); 1991 Eoin Jess (Aberdeen); 1992 Phil O'Donnell (Motherwell).

SCOTTISH FOOTBALL WRITERS' ASSOCIATION

Player of the Year 1993 – Andy Goram (Rangers)

1965 **Billy McNeill** (Celtic)
1966 **John Greig** (Rangers)
1967 **Ronnie Simpson** (Celtic)
1968 **Gordon Wallace** (Raith R)
1969 **Bobby Murdoch** (Celtic)
1970 **Pat Stanton** (Hibernian)
1971 **Martin Buchan** (Aberdeen)
1972 **Dave Smith** (Rangers)
1973 **George Connelly** (Celtic)
1974 **Scotland's World Cup Squad**
1975 **Sandy Jardine** (Rangers)
1976 **John Greig** (Rangers)
1977 **Danny McGrain** (Celtic)
1978 **Derek Johnstone** (Rangers)

1979 **Andy Ritchie** (Morton)
1980 **Gordon Strachan** (Aberdeen)
1981 **Alan Rough** (Partick Th)
1982 **Paul Sturrock** (Dundee U)
1983 **Charlie Nicholas** (Celtic)
1984 **Willie Miller** (Aberdeen)
1985 **Hamish McAlpine** (Dundee U)
1986 **Sandy Jardine** (Hearts)
1987 **Brian McClair** (Celtic)
1988 **Paul McStay** (Celtic)
1989 **Richard Gough** (Rangers)
1990 **Alex McLeish** (Aberdeen)
1991 **Maurice Malpas** (Dundee U)
1992 **Ally McCoist** (Rangers)

EUROPEAN FOOTBALLER OF THE YEAR 1992

Marco Van Basten of AC Milan and Holland received the annual *France Football* award for European Footballer of the Year and thus won the honour for the third time. He had previously taken the accolade in 1988 and 1989. But it was not a wholly happy start to 1993 for Van Basten, who suffered an ankle injury and struggled to regain his best form after lengthy absence. He was also honoured as FIFA World Player of the Year.

Past winners

1956 **Stanley Matthews** (Blackpool)
1957 **Alfredo Di Stefano** (Real Madrid)
1958 **Raymond Kopa** (Real Madrid)
1959 **Alfredo Di Stefano** (Real Madrid)
1960 **Luis Suarez** (Barcelona)
1961 **Omar Sivori** (Juventus)
1962 **Josef Masopust** (Dukla Prague)
1963 **Lev Yashin** (Moscow Dynamo)
1964 **Denis Law** (Manchester United)
1965 **Eusebio** (Benfica)
1966 **Bobby Charlton** (Manchester United)
1967 **Florian Albert** (Ferencvaros)
1968 **George Best** (Manchester United)
1969 **Gianni Rivera** (AC Milan)
1970 **Gerd Muller** (Bayern Munich)
1971 **Johan Cruyff** (Ajax)
1972 **Franz Beckenbauer** (Bayern Munich)
1973 **Johan Cruyff** (Barcelona)
1974 **Johan Cruyff** (Barcelona)
1975 **Oleg Blokhin** (Dynamo Kiev)

1976 **Franz Beckenbauer** (Bayern Munich)
1977 **Allan Simonsen** (Borussia Moenchengladbach)
1978 **Kevin Keegan** (SV Hamburg)
1979 **Kevin Keegan** (SV Hamburg)
1980 **Karl-Heinz Rummenigge** (Bayern Munich)
1981 **Karl-Heinz Rummenigge** (Bayern Munich)
1982 **Paolo Rossi** (Juventus)
1983 **Michel Platini** (Juventus)
1984 **Michel Platini** (Juventus)
1985 **Michel Platini** (Juventus)
1986 **Igor Belanov** (Dynamo Kiev)
1987 **Ruud Gullit** (AC Milan)
1988 **Marco Van Basten** (AC Milan)
1989 **Marco Van Basten** (AC Milan)
1990 **Lothar Matthaus** (Inter-Milan)
1991 **Jean-Pierre Papin** (Marseille)

BARCLAYS BANK MANAGER AWARDS 1992–93

AUGUST
Premier League – **Mike Walker** (Norwich City); *Division 1* – **Alan Curbishley/Steve Gritt** (Charlton Athletic); *Division 2* – **Ossie Ardiles** (West Bromwich Albion); *Division 3* – **John Ward** (York City).

SEPTEMBER
Premier League – **Bobby Gould** (Coventry City); *Division 1* – **Kevin Keegan** (Newcastle United); *Division 2* – **Ossie Ardiles** (West Bromwich Albion); *Division 3* – **John Ward** (York City).

OCTOBER
Premier League – **Ron Atkinson** (Aston Villa); *Division 1* – **Glenn Hoddle** (Swindon Town); *Division 2* – **Lou Macari** (Stoke City); *Division 3* – **Steve Thompson** (Lincoln City).

NOVEMBER
Premier League – **Mike Walker** (Norwich City); *Division 1* – **Kevin Keegan** (Newcastle United); *Division 2* – **Bruce Rioch** (Bolton Wanderers); *Division 3* – **David McCreery** (Carlisle United).

DECEMBER
Premier League – **Steve Coppell** (Crystal Palace); *Division 1* – **Phil Holder** (Brentford); *Division 2* – **Lou Macari** (Stoke City); *Division 3* – **Brian Flynn** (Wrexham).

JANUARY
Premier League – **Trevor Francis** (Sheffield Wed); *Division 1* – **Billy Bonds** (West Ham United); *Division 2* – **John Rudge** (Port Vale); *Division 3* – **Eddie May** (Cardiff City).

FEBRUARY
Premier League – **Doug Livermore** (Tottenham Hotspur); *Division 1* – **Glenn Hoddle** (Swindon Town) ; *Division 2* – **Tony Pulis** (AFC Bournemouth); *Division 3* – **Barry Fry** (Barnet).

MARCH
Premier League – **George Graham** (Arsenal); *Division 1* – **Brian Little** (Leicester City); *Division 2* – **Bruce Rioch** (Bolton Wanderers); *Division 3* – **Eddie May** (Cardiff City).

APRIL
Premier League – **Alex Ferguson** (Manchester United); *Division 1* – **Jim Smith** (Portsmouth); *Division 2* – **Frank Stapleton** (Bradford City); *Division 3* – **Brian Flynn** (Wrexham).

RECORDS

Major British Records

HIGHEST WINS

First-Class Match		Arbroath	36	Bon Accord	0	12 Sept 1885
		(*Scottish Cup 1st Round*)				
International Match		England	13	Ireland	0	18 Feb 1882
FA Cup		Preston NE	26	Hyde U	0	15 Oct 1887
		(*1st Round*)				
League Cup		West Ham U	10	Bury	0	25 Oct 1983
		(*2nd Round, 2nd Leg*)				
		Liverpool	10	Fulham	0	23 Sept 1986
		(*2nd Round, 1st Leg*)				
FA PREMIER LEAGUE						
	(*Home*)	Blackburn R	7	Norwich C	1	3 Oct 1992
FOOTBALL LEAGUE						
Division 1	(*Home*)	WBA	12	Darwen	0	4 April 1892
		Nottingham F	12	Leicester Fosse	0	21 April 1909
	(*Away*)	Newcastle U	1	Sunderland	9	5 Dec 1908
		Cardiff C	1	Wolverhampton W	9	3 Sept 1955
Division 2	(*Home*)	Newcastle U	13	Newport Co	0	5 Oct 1946
	(*Away*)	Burslem PV	0	Sheffield U	10	10 Dec 1892
Division 3	(*Home*)	Gillingham	10	Chesterfield	0	5 Sept 1987
	(*Away*)	Halifax T	0	Fulham	8	16 Sept 1969
Division 3(S)	(*Home*)	Luton T	12	Bristol R	0	13 April 1936
	(*Away*)	Northampton T	0	Walsall	8	2 Feb 1947
Division 3(N)	(*Home*)	Stockport Co	13	Halifax T	0	6 Jan 1934
	(*Away*)	Accrington S	0	Barnsley	9	3 Feb 1934
Division 4	(*Home*)	Oldham Ath	11	Southport	0	26 Dec 1962
	(*Away*)	Crewe Alex	1	Rotherham U	8	8 Sept 1973
Aggregate Division 3(N)		Tranmere R	13	Oldham Ath	4	26 Dec 1935
SCOTTISH LEAGUE						
Premier	(*Home*)	Aberdeen	8	Motherwell	0	26 March 1979
Division	(*Away*)	Hamilton A	0	Celtic	8	5 Nov 1988
Division 1	(*Home*)	Celtic	11	Dundee	0	26 Oct 1895
	(*Away*)	Airdrieonians	1	Hibernian	11	24 Oct 1950
Division 2	(*Home*)	Airdrieonians	15	Dundee Wanderers	1	1 Dec 1894
	(*Away*)	Alloa Ath	0	Dundee	10	8 March 1947

LEAGUE CHAMPIONSHIP HAT-TRICKS

Huddersfield T	1923–24 to 1925–26
Arsenal	1932–33 to 1934–35
Liverpool	1981–82 to 1983–84

MOST GOALS FOR IN A SEASON

		Goals	*Games*	*Season*
FA PREMIER LEAGUE				
	Blackburn R	68	42	1992–93
FOOTBALL LEAGUE				
Division 1	Aston V	128	42	1930–31
Division 2	Middlesbrough	122	42	1926–27
Division 3(S)	Millwall	127	42	1927–28
Division 3(N)	Bradford C	128	42	1928–29
Division 3	QPR	111	46	1961–62
Division 4	Peterborough U	134	46	1960–61
SCOTTISH LEAGUE				
Premier Division	Rangers	101	44	1991–92
	Dundee U	90	36	1982–83
	Celtic	90	36	1982–83
	Celtic	90	44	1986–87
Division 1	Hearts	132	34	1957–58
Division 2	Raith R	142	34	1937–38
New Division 1	Motherwell	92	39	1981–82
New Division 2	Ayr U	95	39	1987–88

FEWEST GOALS FOR IN A SEASON

FA PREMIER LEAGUE		Goals	Games	Season
	Arsenal	40	42	1992–93

FOOTBALL LEAGUE	(minimum 42 games)			
Division 1	Stoke C	24	42	1984–85
Division 2	Watford	24	42	1971–72
Division 3(S)	Crystal Palace	33	42	1950–51
Division 3(N)	Crewe Alex	32	42	1923–24
Division 3	Stockport Co	27	46	1969–70
Division 4	Crewe Alex	29	46	1981–82

SCOTTISH LEAGUE	(minimum 30 games)			
Premier Division	Hamilton A	19	36	1988–89
	Dunfermline Ath	22	44	1991–92
Division 1	Cowdenbeath	33	44	1992–93
	Ayr U	20	34	1966–67
Division 2	Lochgelly U	20	38	1923–24
New Division 1	Stirling Alb	18	39	1980–81
New Division 2	Berwick R	32	39	1987–88

MOST GOALS AGAINST IN A SEASON

FA PREMIER LEAGUE		Goals	Games	Season
	Middlesbrough	75	42	1992–93

FOOTBALL LEAGUE				
Division 1	Blackpool	125	42	1930–31
Division 2	Darwen	141	34	1898–99
Division 3(S)	Merthyr T	135	42	1929–30
Division 3(N)	Nelson	136	42	1927–28
Division 3	Accrington S	123	46	1959–60
Division 4	Hartlepools U	109	46	1959–60

SCOTTISH LEAGUE				
Premier Division	Morton	100	36	1984–85
	Morton	100	44	1987–88
Division 1	Leith Ath	137	38	1931–32
Division 2	Edinburgh C	146	38	1931–32
New Division 1	Queen of the S	99	39	1988–89
	Cowdenbeath	109	44	1992–93
New Division 2	Meadowbank T	89	39	1977–78

FEWEST GOALS AGAINST IN A SEASON

FA PREMIER LEAGUE		Goals	Games	Season
	Manchester U	31	42	1992-93

FOOTBALL LEAGUE	(minimum 42 games)			
Division 1	Liverpool	16	42	1978–79
Division 2	Manchester U	23	42	1924–25
	West Ham U	34	46	1990–91
Division 3(S)	Southampton	21	42	1921–22
Division 3(N)	Port Vale	21	46	1953–54
Division 3	Middlesbrough	30	46	1986–87
Division 4	Lincoln C	25	46	1980–81

SCOTTISH LEAGUE	(minimum 30 games)			
Premier Division	Rangers	19	36	1989–90
	Rangers	23	44	1986–87
	Celtic	23	44	1987–88
Division 1	Celtic	14	38	1913–14
Division 2	Morton	20	38	1966–67
New Division 1	Hibernian	24	39	1980–81
	Partick T	36	44	1991–92
New Division 2	St Johnstone	24	39	1987–88
	Stirling Alb	24	39	1990–91

MOST POINTS IN A SEASON

FOOTBALL LEAGUE	(under old system)	Points	Games	Season
Division 1	Liverpool	68	42	1978–79
Division 2	Tottenham H	70	42	1919–20
Division 3	Aston V	70	46	1971–72
Division 3(S)	Nottingham F	70	46	1950–51
	Bristol C	70	46	1954–55
Division 3(N)	Doncaster R	72	42	1946–47
Division 4	Lincoln C	74	46	1975–76

FA PREMIER LEAGUE

	Manchester U	84	42	1992–93

FOOTBALL LEAGUE	(three points for a win)			
Division 1	Everton	90	42	1984–85
	Liverpool	90	40	1987–88
Division 2	Chelsea	99	46	1988–89
Division 3	Bournemouth	97	46	1986–87
Division 4	Swindon T	102	46	1985–86

SCOTTISH LEAGUE				
Premier Division	Celtic	72	44	1987–88
	Aberdeen	59	36	1984–85
	Rangers	73	44	1992–93
Division 1	Rangers	76	42	1920–21
Division 2	Morton	69	38	1966–67
New Division 1	St Mirren	62	39	1976–77
	Raith R	65	44	1992–93
New Division 2	Forfar Ath	63	39	1983–84

FEWEST POINTS IN A SEASON

FA PREMIER LEAGUE		*Points*	*Games*	*Season*
	Nottingham F	40	42	1992–93
FOOTBALL LEAGUE	(minimum 34 games)			
Division 1	Stoke C	17	42	1984–85
Division 2	Doncaster R	8	34	1904–05
	Loughborough T	8	34	1899–1900
	Walsall	31	46	1988–89
Division 3	Rochdale	21	46	1973–74
	Cambridge U	21	46	1984–85
Division 3(S)	Merthyr T	21	42	1924–25 & 1929–30
	QPR	21	42	1925–26
Division 3(N)	Rochdale	11	40	1931–32
Division 4	Workington	19	46	1976–77
SCOTTISH LEAGUE	(minimum 30 games)			
Premier Division	St Johnstone	11	36	1975–76
	Morton	16	44	1987–88
Division 1	Stirling Alb	6	30	1954–55
Division 2	Edinburgh C	7	34	1936–37
New Division 1	Queen of the S	10	39	1988–89
	Cowdenbeath	13	44	1992–93
New Division 2	Berwick R	16	39	1987–88
	Stranraer	16	39	1987–88

MOST WINS IN A SEASON

FA PREMIER LEAGUE		*Wins*	*Games*	*Season*
	Manchester U	24	42	1992–93
FOOTBALL LEAGUE				
Division 1	Tottenham H	31	42	1960–61
Division 2	Tottenham H	32	42	1919–20
Division 3(S)	Millwall	30	42	1927–28
	Plymouth Arg	30	42	1929–30
	Cardiff C	30	42	1946–47
	Nottingham F	30	46	1950–51
	Bristol C	30	46	1954–55
Division 3(N)	Doncaster R	33	42	1946–47
Division 3	Aston Villa	32	46	1971–72
Division 4	Lincoln C	32	46	1975–76
	Swindon T	32	46	1985–86
SCOTTISH LEAGUE				
Premier Division	Aberdeen	27	36	1984–85
	Rangers	33	44	1991–92
	Rangers	33	44	1992–93
	Rangers	31	44	1986–87
	Celtic	31	44	1987–88
Division 1	Rangers	35	42	1920–21
Division 2	Morton	33	38	1966–67
New Division 1	Motherwell	26	39	1981–82
New Division 2	Forfar Ath	27	39	1983–84
	Ayr U	27	39	1987–88

RECORD HOME WINS IN A SEASON

Brentford won all 21 games in Division 3(S), 1929–30

UNDEFEATED AT HOME

Liverpool 85 games (63 League, 9 League Cup, 7 European, 6 FA Cup), Jan 1978–Jan 1981

RECORD AWAY WINS IN A SEASON

Doncaster R won 18 of 21 games in Division 3(N), 1946–47

FEWEST WINS IN A SEASON

FA PREMIER LEAGUE		*Wins*	*Games*	*Season*
	Nottingham F	10	42	1992–93
FOOTBALL LEAGUE				
Division 1	Stoke C	3	22	1889–90
	Woolwich Arsenal	3	38	1912–13
	Stoke C	3	42	1984–85
Division 2	Loughborough T	1	34	1899–1900
	Walsall	5	46	1988–89
Division 3(S)	Merthyr T	6	42	1929–30
	QPR	6	42	1925–26
Division 3(N)	Rochdale	4	40	1931–32
Division 3	Rochdale	2	46	1973–74
Division 4	Southport	3	46	1976–77
SCOTTISH LEAGUE				
Premier Division	St Johnstone	3	36	1975–76
	Kilmarnock	3	36	1982–83
	Morton	3	44	1987–88
Division 1	Vale of Leven	0	22	1891–92
Division 2	East Stirlingshire	1	22	1905–06
	Forfar Ath	1	38	1974–75
New Division 1	Queen of the S	2	39	1988–89
	Cowdenbeath	3	44	1992–93
New Division 2	Forfar Ath	4	26	1975–76
	Stranraer	4	39	1987–88

MOST DEFEATS IN A SEASON

FA PREMIER LEAGUE		*Defeats*	*Games*	*Season*
	Nottingham F	22	42	1992–93
FOOTBALL LEAGUE				
Division 1	Stoke C	31	42	1984–85
Division 2	Tranmere R	31	42	1938–39
Division 3	Cambridge U	33	46	1984–85
	Chester C	33	46	1992–93
Division 3(S)	Merthyr T	29	42	1924–25
	Walsall	29	46	1952–53
	Walsall	29	46	1953–54
Division 3(N)	Rochdale	33	40	1931–32
Division 4	Newport Co	33	46	1987–88
SCOTTISH LEAGUE				
Premier Division	Morton	29	36	1984–85
Division 1	St Mirren	31	42	1920–21
Division 2	Brechin C	30	36	1962–63
	Lochgelly	30	38	1923–24
New Division 1	Queen of the S	29	39	1988–89
	Cowdenbeath	34	44	1992–93
New Division 2	Berwick R	29	39	1987–88

HAT-TRICKS

Career 34 Dixie Dean (Tranmere R, Everton, Notts Co, England)
Division 1 (one season post-war) 6 Jimmy Greaves (Chelsea), 1960–61
Three for one team one match
West, Spouncer, Hooper, Nottingham F v Leicester Fosse, Division 1, 21 April 1909
Barnes, Ambler, Davies, Wrexham v Hartlepools U, Division 4, 3 March 1962
Adcock, Stewart, White, Manchester C v Huddersfield T, Division 2, 7 Nov 1987
Loasby, Smith, Wells, Northampton T v Walsall, Division 3S, 5 Nov 1927
Bowater, Hoyland, Readman, Mansfield T v Rotherham U, Division 3N, 27 Dec 1932

FEWEST DEFEATS IN A SEASON
(*Minimum 20 games*)

FA PREMIER LEAGUE		*Defeats*	*Games*	*Season*
	Manchester U	6	42	1992–93
FOOTBALL LEAGUE				
Division 1	Preston NE	0	22	1888–89
	Arsenal	1	38	1990–91
	Liverpool	2	40	1987–88
	Leeds U	2	42	1968–69
Division 2	Liverpool	0	28	1893–94
	Burnley	2	30	1897–98
	Bristol C	2	38	1905–06
	Leeds U	3	42	1963–64
	Chelsea	5	46	1988–89
Division 3	QPR	5	46	1966–67
	Bristol R	5	46	1989–90
Division 3(S)	Southampton	4	42	1921–22
	Plymouth Arg	4	42	1929–30
Division 3(N)	Port Vale	3	46	1953–54
	Doncaster R	3	42	1946–47
	Wolverhampton W	3	42	1923–24
Division 4	Lincoln C	4	46	1975–76
	Sheffield U	4	46	1981–82
	Bournemouth	4	46	1981–82
SCOTTISH LEAGUE				
Premier Division	Celtic	3	44	1987–88
Division 1	Rangers	0	18	1898–99
	Rangers	1	42	1920–21
Division 2	Clyde	1	36	1956–57
	Morton	1	36	1962–63
	St Mirren	1	36	1967–68
New Division 1	Partick T	2	26	1975–76
	St Mirren	2	39	1976–77
	Raith R	4	44	1992–93
New Division 2	Raith R	1	26	1975–76
	Clydebank	3	26	1975–76
	Forfar Ath	3	39	1983–84
	Raith R	3	39	1986–87

MOST DRAWN GAMES IN A SEASON

FA PREMIER LEAGUE		*Draws*	*Games*	*Season*
	Crystal Palace	16	42	1992–93
	Ipswich T	16	42	1992–93
FOOTBALL LEAGUE				
Division 1	Norwich C	23	42	1978–79
Division 4	Exeter C	23	46	1986–87
SCOTTISH LEAGUE				
Premier Division	Hibernian	19	44	1987–88
New Division 1	East Fife	21	44	1986–87

MOST GOALS IN A GAME

FOOTBALL LEAGUE		
Division 1	Ted Drake (Arsenal) 7 goals v Aston Villa	14 Dec 1935
	James Ross (Preston NE) 7 goals v Stoke	6 Oct 1888
Division 2	Tommy Briggs (Blackburn R) 7 goals v Bristol R	5 Feb 1955
	Neville Coleman (Stoke C) 7 goals v Lincoln C (away)	23 Feb 1957
Division 3(S)	Joe Payne (Luton T) 10 goals v Bristol R	13 April 1936
Division 3(N)	Bunny Bell (Tranmere R) 9 goals v Oldham Ath	26 Dec 1935
Division 3	Steve Earle (Fulham) 5 goals v Halifax T	16 Sept 1969
	Barrie Thomas (Scunthorpe U) 5 goals v Luton T	24 April 1965
	Keith East (Swindon T) 5 goals v Mansfield T	20 Nov 1965
	Alf Wood (Shrewsbury T) 5 goals v Blackburn R	2 Oct 1971
	Tony Caldwell (Bolton W) 5 goals v Walsall	10 Sept 1983
	Andy Jones (Port Vale) 5 goals v Newport Co	4 May 1987
	Steve Wilkinson (Mansfield T) 5 goals v Birmingham C	3 April 1990
Division 4	Bert Lister (Oldham Ath) 6 goals v Southport	26 Dec 1962
FA CUP	Ted MacDougall (Bournemouth) 9 goals v Margate (*1st Round*)	20 Nov 1971
LEAGUE CUP	Frankie Bunn (Oldham Ath) 6 goals v Scarborough	25 Oct 1989
SCOTTISH LEAGUE CUP	Jim Fraser (Ayr U) 5 goals v Dumbarton	13 Aug 1952

SCOTTISH LEAGUE

Premier Division	Paul Sturrock (Dundee U) 5 goals v Morton	17 Nov 1984
Division 1	Jimmy McGrory (Celtic) 8 goals v Dunfermline Ath	14 Sept 1928
Division 2	Owen McNally (Arthurlie) 8 goals v Armadale	1 Oct 1927
	Jim Dyet (King's Park) 8 goals v Forfar Ath	2 Jan 1930
	John Calder (Morton) 8 goals v Raith R	18 April 1936
	Norman Hayward (Raith R) 8 goals v Brechin C	20 Aug 1937
SCOTTISH CUP	John Petrie (Arbroath) 13 goals v Bon Accord (*1st Round*)	12 Sept 1885

MOST LEAGUE GOALS IN A SEASON

FOOTBALL LEAGUE		*Goals*	*Games*	*Season*
Division 1	Dixie Dean (Everton)	60	39	1927–28
Division 2	George Camsell (Middlesbrough)	59	37	1926–27
Division 3(S)	Joe Payne (Luton T)	55	39	1936–37
Division 3(N)	Ted Harston (Mansfield T)	55	41	1936–37
Division 3	Derek Reeves (Southampton)	39	46	1959–60
Division 4	Terry Bly (Peterborough U)	52	46	1960–61
FA CUP	Sandy Brown (Tottenham H)	15		1900–01
LEAGUE CUP	Clive Allen (Tottenham H)	12		1986–87

SCOTTISH LEAGUE				
Division 1	William McFadyen (Motherwell)	52	34	1931–32
Division 2	Jim Smith (Ayr U)	66	38	1927–28
Records				

MOST LEAGUE GOALS IN A CAREER

FOOTBALL LEAGUE		*Goals*	*Games*	*Season*
Arthur Rowley	WBA	4	24	1946–48
	Fulham	27	56	1948–50
	Leicester C	251	303	1950–58
	Shrewsbury T	152	236	1958–65
		434	619	

SCOTTISH LEAGUE				
Jimmy McGrory	Celtic	1	3	1922–23
	Clydebank	13	30	1923–24
	Celtic	396	375	1924–38
		410	408	

MOST CUP GOALS IN A CAREER

FA CUP
Denis Law   41   (Huddersfield T, Manchester C, Manchester U)

A CENTURY OF LEAGUE AND CUP GOALS IN CONSECUTIVE SEASONS

George Camsell	Middlesbrough	59 Lge	5 Cup	1926–27
(101 goals)		33	4	1927–28
Steve Bull	Wolverhampton W	34 Lge	18 Cup	1987–88
(102 goals)		37	13	1988–89

(Camsell's cup goals were all scored in the FA Cup; Bull had 12 in the Sherpa Van Trophy, 3 Littlewoods Cup, 3 FA Cup in 1987–88; 11 Sherpa Van Trophy, 2 Littlewoods Cup in 1988–89.)

LONGEST SEQUENCE OF CONSECUTIVE SCORING (Individual)

FOOTBALL LEAGUE RECORD		
Bill Pendergast (Chester)	15 in 12 games	1938–39

LONGEST WINNING SEQUENCE

FOOTBALL LEAGUE		*Games*	*Season*
Division 1	Everton	12	1893–94 (4) and 1894–95 (8)
Division 2	Manchester U	14	1904–05
	Bristol C	14	1905–06
	Preston NE	14	1950–51
Division 3	Reading	13	1985–86
From season's start			
Division 1	Tottenham H	11	1960–61

LONGEST WINNING SEQUENCE IN A SEASON

FOOTBALL LEAGUE		Games	Season
Division 1	Tottenham H	11	1960–61
Division 2	Manchester U	14	1904–05
Division 2	Bristol C	14	1905–06
Division 2	Preston NE	14	1950–51
SCOTTISH LEAGUE			
Division 2	Morton	23	1963–64

LONGEST UNBEATEN SEQUENCE

FOOTBALL LEAGUE		Games	Seasons
Division 1	Nottingham F	42	Nov 1977–Dec 1978

LONGEST UNBEATEN CUP SEQUENCE

Liverpool   25 rounds   League/Milk Cup   1980–84

LONGEST UNBEATEN SEQUENCE IN A SEASON

FOOTBALL LEAGUE		Games	Season
Division 1	Burnley	30	1920–21

LONGEST UNBEATEN START TO A SEASON

FOOTBALL LEAGUE		Games	Season
Division 1	Leeds U	29	1973–74
Division 1	Liverpool	29	1987–88

LONGEST SEQUENCE WITHOUT A WIN IN A SEASON

FOOTBALL LEAGUE		Games	Season
Division 2	Cambridge U	31	1983–84

LONGEST SEQUENCE WITHOUT A WIN FROM SEASON'S START

Division 1	Manchester U	12	1930–31

LONGEST SEQUENCE OF CONSECUTIVE DEFEATS

FOOTBALL LEAGUE		Games	Season
Division 2	*Darwen*	*18*	*1898–99*

GOALKEEPING RECORDS (without conceding a goal)

British record (all competitive games)
Chris Woods, Rangers, in 1196 minutes from 26 November 1986 to 31 January 1987.

Football League
Steve Death, Reading, 1103 minutes from 24 March to 18 August 1979.

PENALTIES

Most in a season (individual)		Goals	Season
Division 1 Francis Lee (Manchester C)		13	1971–72
Most awarded in one game			
Five Crystal Palace (4 – 1 scored, 3 missed) v Brighton & HA (1 scored), Div 2			1988–89
Most saved in a season			
Division 1 Paul Cooper (Ipswich T)		8 (of 10)	1979–80

MOST LEAGUE APPEARANCES

FOOTBALL LEAGUE

991 Peter Shilton (286 Leicester City, 110 Stoke City, 202 Nottingham Forest, 188 Southampton, 175 Derby County, 30 Plymouth Argyle) 1966–93
824 Terry Paine (713 Southampton, 111 Hereford United) 1957–77
795 Tommy Hutchison (165 Blackpool, 314 Coventry City, 46 Manchester City, 92 Burnley 178 Swansea City, also 68 Alloa 1965–68) 1968–91
777 Alan Oakes (565 Manchester City, 211 Chester City, 1 Port Vale) 1959–84
770 John Trollope (all for Swindon Town) 1960–80†
764 Jimmy Dickinson (all for Portsmouth) 1946–65
761 Roy Sproson (all for Port Vale) 1950–72
758 Ray Clemence (48 Scunthorpe United, 470 Liverpool, 240 Tottenham Hotspur) 1966–87
757 Pat Jennings (48 Watford, 472 Tottenham Hotspur, 237 Arsenal) 1963–86
† record for one club

Consecutive
401 Harold Bell (401 Tranmere R; 459 in all games) 1946–55

FA CUP
88 Ian Callaghan (79 Liverpool, 7 Swansea C, 2 Crewe Alex)

Most Senior Matches
1374 Peter Shilton (991 League, 86 FA Cup, 102 League Cup, 125 Internationals, 13 Under-23, 4 Football League XI, 53 others including European Cup, UEFA Cup, World Club Championship, various domestic cup competitions)

MOST FA CUP FINAL GOALS

Ian Rush (Liverpool) 5: 1986(2), 1989(2), 1992(1)

MOST LEAGUE MEDALS

Phil Neal (Liverpool) 8: 1976, 1977, 1979, 1980, 1982, 1983, 1984, 1986

OTHER RECORDS

YOUNGEST PLAYERS
Football League   Albert Geldard, 15 years 158 days, Bradford Park Avenue v Millwall, Division 2, 16.9.29; and Ken Roberts, 15 years 158 days, Wrexham v Bradford Park Avenue, Division 3N, 1.9.51
Football League scorer
   Ronnie Dix, 15 years 180 days, Bristol Rovers v Norwich City, Division 3S, 3.3.28.
Division 1
   Derek Forster, 15 years 185 days, Sunderland v Leicester City, 22.8.84.
Division 1 scorer
   Jason Dozzell, 16 years 57 days as substitute Ipswich Town v Coventry City, 4.2.84
Division 1 hat-tricks
   Alan Shearer, 17 years 240 days, Southampton v Arsenal, 9.4.88
   Jimmy Greaves, 17 years 10 months, Chelsea v Portsmouth, 25.12.57
FA Cup (any round)
   Andy Awford, 15 years 88 days as substitute Worcester City v Borehamwood, 3rd Qual. rd, 10.10.87
FA Cup proper
   Scott Endersby, 15 years 288 days, Kettering v Tilbury, 1st rd, 26.11.77
FA Cup Final
   Paul Allen, 17 years 256 days, West Ham United v Arsenal, 1980
FA Cup Final scorer
   Norman Whiteside, 18 years 18 days, Manchester United v Brighton & Hove Albion, 1983
FA Cup Final captain
   David Nish, 21 years 212 days, Leicester City v Manchester City, 1969
League Cup Final scorer
   Norman Whiteside, 17 years 324 days, Manchester United v Liverpool, 1983
League Cup Final captain
   Barry Venison, 20 years 7 months 8 days, Sunderland v Norwich City, 1985

OLDEST PLAYERS
Football League
   Neil McBain, 52 years 4 months, New Brighton v Hartlepools United, Div 3N, 15.3.47 (McBain was New Brighton's manager and had to play in an emergency)
Division 1
   Stanley Matthews, 50 years 5 days, Stoke City v Fulham, 6.2.65
FA Cup Final
   Walter Hampson, 41 years 8 months, Newcastle United v Aston Villa, 1924
FA Cup
   Billy Meredith, 49 years 8 months, Manchester City v Newcastle United, 29.3.24

SENDINGS-OFF

Season	242 (211 League, 19 FA Cup, 12 Milk Cup)	1982–83
Day	15 (3 League, 12 FA Cup*)	20 Nov 1982
	worst overall FA Cup total	
League	13	14 Dec 1985
Weekend	15	22/23 Dec 1990
FA Cup Final	Kevin Moran, Manchester U v Everton	1985
Wembley	Boris Stankovic, Yugoslavia v Sweden (Olympics)	1948
	Antonio Rattin, Argentina v England (World Cup)	1966
	Billy Bremner (Leeds U) and Kevin Keegan (Liverpool), Charity Shield	1974
	Gilbert Dresch, Luxembourg v England (World Cup)	1977
	Mike Henry, Sudbury T v Tamworth (FA Vase)	1989
Quickest	Ambrose Brown, Wrexham v Hull C (away) Div 3N: 20 secs	25 Dec 1936
Division 1	Liam O'Brien, Manchester U v Southampton (away): 85 secs	3 Jan 1987
World Cup	Jose Batista, Uruguay v Scotland, Neza, Mexico (World Cup): 55 secs	13 June 1986
Most one game	Four: Northampton T (0) v Hereford U (4) Div 3	11 Nov 1992
	Four: Crewe Alex (2) v Bradford PA (2) Div 3N	8 Jan 1955
	Four: Sheffield U (1) v Portsmouth (3) Div 2	13 Dec 1986
	Four: Port Vale (2) v Northampton T (2) Littlewoods Cup	18 Aug 1987
	Four: Brentford (2) v Mansfield T (2) Div 3	12 Dec 1987

FOOTBALL CLUB CHAPLAINCY

"Football was different in my day." "The game isn't what it was when I was young." We've all heard the comments which convince us that nostalgia isn't what it used to be! Nonetheless football has seen many changes, and one that has brought a beneficial dimension to the game is the growth of football club chaplaincy. Indeed this very publication has tracked the development in chaplaincy and the worth of such initiatives through annual articles over several years.

Chaplaincy generally is nothing new: For many years there have been chaplains in the Armed Forces, in education, and on the factory floor. There, they are now an accepted part — indeed, valued part — of the working environment. In recent years, the world of sport generally — and football in particular — has developed its own styles of chaplaincy; out of the initiatives of Rev. John Jackson who had links with Leeds Utd. in the Don Revie era, and of Rev. Mike Pusey with Aldershot in the early 1970s. There were, no doubt, other early exponents of this expression of Christian care for the local community, but now they are not isolated examples. Chaplaincy is much more widespread, far more accepted, and more openly acknowledged.

What then, is the job facing today's chaplain? Firstly, we need to kill two popular myths. He certainly isn't a modern day witchdoctor, channelling divine guidance to his particular team. There is no way in which he seeks to take credit from the vision of a board of directors; the skills of a manager; the abilities of a coach; or the talents of a player. Neither is he a football crazy nutter, who manages to live out some Freudian fantasy through chaplaincy of the local club. He's no "Rev. of the Rovers". . .

Football Club chaplaincy involves ordinary clergymen, of different church backgrounds, each with his different approach. Some are young, and able to be actively involved with the club, others are older, and adopt a more fatherly style! Some are able to give more than a whole day each week to the club, others give maybe three or four hours. Some have a deep interest in sport, others do not. But all are concerned for people. All of them care. Their point of reference is the club, not simply the team. The chaplain is available to all employees and associates of the club, not imposing himself on them, but offering his care, his experience in counselling, his spiritual insights and perspectives, his listening ear and confidentiality, as appropriate. He does not come to the club to "Bible Bash", but to serve and to care, but knows that some people, sometimes, need to talk about deeper, spiritual matters. So he is ready and willing to offer his special insights when he is asked.

Often the chaplain will have a regular time for visiting the club, when he makes contact with the employees — the administrative office; the commercial office; the club shop; the groundstaff; the management and coaching staff; the players; the YTS lads etc. Thus his face becomes known, relationships are established; and a foundation is built for situations when the chaplain's help and support might be needed. A major injury may threaten a career, or terminate it. A tragic illness may strike a family.

The pain and grief of bereavement may affect someone. One may face some deep family crisis, another is confronted with hospitalisation and surgery. One may have some deep personal problem, while some other faces a difficulty with "The Law". Yet another may find in the chaplain one to listen to a scenario that he can't talk about to anyone else at the club. All are situations where the chaplain's presence and availability can be of great benefit to those concerned.

For many years, chaplains linked up through Christians in Sport, and since 1991 one of the denominations has actually encouraged one of its ministers to work full-time specifically to develop chaplaincy in sport. Rev. John Boyers, who had 15 years' experience of sports chaplaincy with Watford F.C., and now works as Hon. Chaplain to Manchester United, spends most of his time encouraging chaplains and helping clubs who are considering starting a chaplaincy. CIS has affirmed this initiative, which now sees John employed by the newly established registered charity SCORE. He is available to help clubs and chaplains at all league levels, and can be contacted via SCORE, P.O. Box 123, Watford; or via MUFC, Old Trafford, Manchester. Other chaplains would be equally willing to share their insights on this growing work, and can be contacted via their clubs, which are listed below.

OFFICIAL CHAPLAINS TO PREMIER AND FOOTBALL LEAGUE CLUBS

Rev John Bingham — Chesterfield
Rev Richard Chewter — Exeter C
Rev Michael Lowe — Bournemouth
Rev Andrew Taggart — Torquay U
Rev David Jeans — Sheffield W
Rev Nigel Sands — Crystal Palace
Rev Graham Spencer — Leicester C
Rev Phillip Miller — Ipswich T
Rev Allen Bagshawe — Hull C
Rev David Tully — Newcastle U
Rev Derek Cleave — Bristol C
Rev Brian Rice — Hartlepool U
Rev Ken Sykes — Watford
Rev Michael Chantry — Oxford U
Rev Michael Futens — Derby C
Very Rev Brandon Jackson — Lincoln C
Rev Paul Bennett — Swindon T
Rev Ken Hawkins — Birmingham C
Rev Simon Stevenette — Bristol R

Rev Dick Syms — York City
Rev Dennis Hall — Wigan Ath
Rev William Hall — Middlesbrough
Rev Canon John Hestor — Brighton & HA
Rev Mervyn Terrett — Luton T
Rev Jim Rushton — Carlisle U
Rev Robert de Berry — Queen's Park Rangers
Rev Gary Piper — Fulham
Rev Charlie Mackenzie — Barnsley
Rev Barry Kirk — Reading
Rev Martin Short — Bradford C
Rev John Boyers — Manchester U
Rev Martin Butt — Walsall
Rev Kevin Tugwell — Cardiff C
Rev Steve Riley — Leeds U
Revs Alan Poulter and Gerald Courell — Tranmere R
Rev Mark Kichenside — Charlton Ath
Rev Owen Beament — Millwall
Rev Elwin Cockett — West Ham U

The chaplains hope that those who read this article will see the value and benefit of chaplaincy work in sport, and will take appropriate steps to spread the work where this is possible. They would also like to thank the editor of the Rothmans Yearbook for his continued support for this specialist and growing area of work.

REFEREEING AND THE REFEREES

It is often argued that refereeing is the hardest aspect of soccer. Referees come from all walks of life and usually they are recruited through contacts made by newspaper adverts, articles in club programmes or encouragement from friends. It is the numerous Referee Societies who develop the embryo referee by instructing him or her on a course and preparing them for the examination by the County Football Association. Most Referee Societies have instructors who these days have qualifications obtained from the Football Association who run one week courses for Referee Instructors. The control of referees is supervised by the Football Association Referee's Committee and their Instructional Committee are responsible for the Referee Instructors course.

A referee once qualified at the lowest class namely Class three is expected to join the Referee Society that instructed him and also to become a member of the Referees Association who help run the practical side of refereeing and produce kits, manuals and details of in-service training as well as an insurance scheme and which has a full time secretary. Each County has a County Football Association which in turn has a Referee's Secretary and the County Football Association finances courses and seminar for referees.

Progression occurs through a process of assessment for promotion by various Referee's Assessors and promotion goes from Class three onto Class two and then Class one. Referees of the appropriate age then join a supply and contributory League invariably starting on the panel as a linesman and progressing into the 'middle' as a referee. The same procedure is followed until the referee is appointed to the National League as a linesman and progresses once more into the 'centre' as a referee. National League Referees who are young enough and have good enough marks on assessment are eligible for recommendation to become FIFA officials.

Since the beginning of the 1992–1993 season the former Football League panel has been replaced by a National List run by the National Review Board which is a joint body consisting of the Football Association, the Premier League and the Football League. The Director of Refereeing is Ken Ridden based at the FA Headquarters at 16 Lancaster Gate, London W2 3LW. He is responsible for appointing referees to the Premier League and Colin Downey also of the FA is the Referee Secretary whose Committee make the various FA Cup appointments.

Full details of the National List of Referees, including dates of appointment and dates when they are expected to retire from the List are set out later. However, the list for the forthcoming season has been reduced from 90 to 81.

The age for National Referees to retire at, is 48, but subject to fitness and successful marking, referees are invited often to stay on longer. Some of the more famous names who have come off the List this year include:-

Bob Hamer, Tony Ward, Ken Redfern and former FIFA men Ray Lewis and John Martin (the most senior). Only three referees over the age of 48 are being offered an extension and they are Keith Hackett, Alan Gunn and Roger Milford (now the most senior).

Whilst the less experienced referees and most in the Football League will be assessed on each match, referees officiating on Premier League matches will not be assessed and marked by Assessors so regularly, but they will for each match be marked by the Clubs themselves in those matches in the Premier League.

Because of the recognition that the "Home Countries" of England, Scotland, Wales and Northern Ireland were the founders and original legislators of the game, they are allowed 4 votes at the annual review by FIFA of its Laws of the Game. FIFA itself retains the other 4 votes. For any change of laws or directives to be effected there has to be a three quarter majority of not less than 6 out of the 8 votes cast.

The National Review Board for Referees and Linesmen for season 1993/94 is on Page 1002.

KEN GOLDMAN

LAWS OF THE GAME

The Laws of the Game and Decisions of the International Board that follow are reproduced with the special permission of FIFA, and the text is the official text as published by FIFA.

LAW I

THE FIELD OF PLAY

The Field of Play and appurtenances shall be as shown in the following plan:

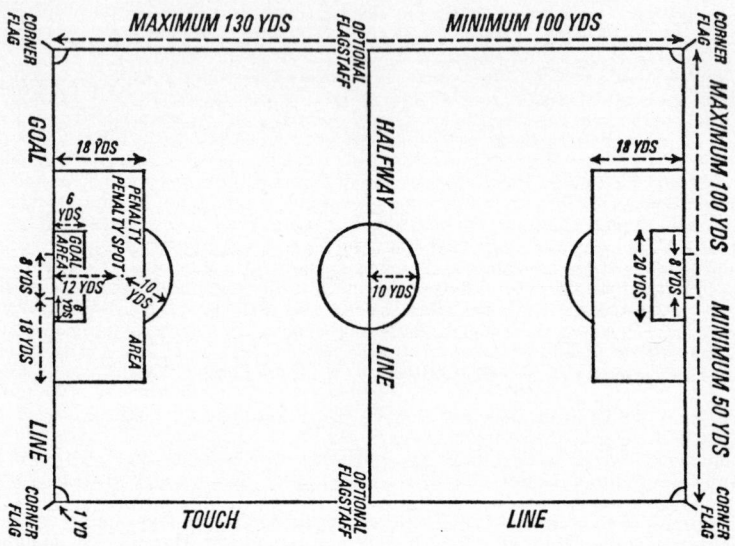

(1) **Dimensions.** The field of play shall be rectangular, its length being not more that 130 yards nor less than 100 yards, and its breadth not more than 100 yards nor less than 50 yards. (In International Matches the length shall be not more than 120 yards nor less than 110 yards and the breadth not more than 80 yards nor less than 70 yards.) The length shall in all cases exceed the breadth.

(2) **Marking.** The field of play shall be marked with distinctive lines, not more than 5 inches in width, not by a V-shaped rut, in accordance with the plan, the longer boundary lines being called the touch-lines and the shorter the goal-lines. A flag on a post not less than 5ft high and having a non-pointed top, shall be placed at each corner; a similar flag-post may be placed opposite the half-way-line on each side of the field of play, not less than 1 yard outside the touch-line. A half-way-line shall be marked out across the field of play. The centre of the field of play shall be indicated by a suitable mark and a circle with a 10 yards radius shall be marked around it.

(3) **The Goal-Area.** At each end of the field of play two lines shall be drawn at right-angles to the goal-line, 6 yards from each goal-post. These shall extend into the field of play for a distance of 6 yards and shall be joined by a line drawn parallel with the goal-line. Each of the spaces enclosed by these goal-lines and the goal-line shall be called a goal-area.

(4) **The Penalty-Area.** At each end of the field of play two lines shall be drawn at right angles to the goal-line, 18 yards from each goal-post. These shall extend into the field of play for a distance of 18 yards and shall be joined by a line drawn parallel with the goal-line. Each of the spaces enclosed by these lines and the goal-line shall be called a penalty-area. A suitable mark shall be made within each penalty area, 12 yards from the mid-point of the goal-line, measured along an undrawn line at right-angles thereto. These shall be the penalty-kick marks. From each penalty-kick mark an arc of a circle, having a radius of 10 yards, shall be drawn outside the penalty-area.

(5) **The Corner Area.** From each corner-flag post a quarter circle, having a radius of 1 yard, shall be drawn inside the field of play.

(6) **The Goals.** The goals shall be placed on the centre of each goal-line and shall consist of two upright posts, equidistant from the corner-flags and 8 yards apart (inside measurement), joined by a horizontal cross-bar the lower edge of which shall be 8ft from the ground. The width and depth

of the goal-posts and the width and depth of the cross-bars shall not exceed 5 inches (12cm). The goal-posts and the cross-bars shall have the same width.

Nets may be attached to the posts, cross-bars and ground behind the goals. They should be appropriately supported and be so placed as to allow the goal-keeper ample room.

Footnote

Goal nets. The use of nets made of hemp, jute or nylon is permitted. The nylon strings may, however, not be thinner than those made of hemp or jute.

Decisions of the International Board

(1) In International Matches the dimensions of the field of play shall be: maximum 110×75 metres; minimum 100×64 metres.

(2) National Associations must adhere strictly to these dimensions. Each National Association organising an International Match must advise the visiting Association, before the match, of the place and the dimensions of the field of play.

(3) The Board has approved this table of measurements for the laws of the Game:

130 yards	. . . 120 metres
120 yards	. . . 110
110 yards	. . . 100
100 yards	. . . 90
80 yards	. . . 75
70 yards	. . . 64
50 yards	. . . 45
18 yards	. . . 16.50
12 yards	. . . 11
10 yards	. . . 9.15
8 yards	. . . 7.32
6 yards	. . . 5.50
1 yard	. . . 1
8 feet	. . . 2.44
5 feet	. . . 1.50
28 inches	. . . 0.71
27 inches	. . . 0.68
9 inches	. . . 0.22
5 inches	. . . 0.12
$\frac{3}{4}$ inch	. . . 0.019
$\frac{1}{2}$ inch	. . . 0.0127
$\frac{3}{8}$ inch	. . . 0.010
14 ounces	. . . 396 grams
16 ounces	. . . 453 grams
15 lb/sq in	. . . 1 kg/cm^2

(4) The goal-line shall be marked the same width as the depth of the goal-posts and the cross-bar, so that the goal-line and goal-post will conform to the same interior and exterior edges.

(5) The 6 yards (for the outline of the goal-area) and the 18 yards (for the outline of the penalty-area) which have to be measured along the goal-line, must start from the inner sides of the goal-posts.

(6) The space within the inside areas of the field of play includes the width of the lines marking these areas.

(7) All Associations shall provide standard equipment, particularly in International Matches, when the laws of the Game must be complied with in every respect and especially with regard to the size of the ball and other equipment which must conform to the regulations. All cases of failure to provide standard equipment must be reported to FIFA.

(8) In a match played under the Rules of a Competition, if the cross-bar becomes displaced or broken, play shall be stopped and the match abandoned unless the cross-bar has been repaired and replaced in position or a new one provided without such being a danger to the players. A rope is not considered to be a satisfactory substitute for a cross-bar.

In a Friendly Match, by mutual consent, play may be resumed without the cross-bar provided it has been removed and no longer constitutes a danger to the players. In these circumstances, a rope may be used as a substitute for a cross-bar. If a rope is not used and the ball crosses the goal-line at a point which in the opinion of the Referee is below where the cross-bar should have been, he shall award a goal.

The game shall be restarted by the Referee dropping the ball at the place where it was when play was stopped.

(9) National Associations may specify such maximum and minimum dimensions for the cross-bars and goal-posts, within the limits laid down in Law I, as they consider appropriate.

(10) Goal-posts and cross-bars must be made of wood, metal or other approved material as decided from time to time by the International FA Board. They may be square, rectangular, round, half-round or elliptical in shape. Goal-posts and cross-bars made of other materials and in other shapes are not permitted. The goal-posts must be of white colour.

(11) 'Curtain-raisers' to International Matches should only be played following agreement on the day of the match, and taking into account the condition of the field of play, between representatives of the two Associations and the Referee (of the International Match).

(12) National Associations, particularly in International Matches, should
— restrict the number of photographers around the field of play.
— have a line ('photographers' line') marked behind the goal-lines at least 2 metres from the corner flag going through a point situated at least 3.5 metres behind the intersection of the goal-line with the line marking the goal area to a point situated at least 6 metres behind the goal-posts.
— prohibit photographers from passing over these lines.
— forbid the use of artificial lighting in the form of 'flashlights'.

LAW II – THE BALL

The ball shall be spherical; the outer casing shall be of leather or other approved materials. No material shall be used in its construction which might prove dangerous to the players.

The circumference of the ball shall not be more than 28in and not less than 27in. The weight of the ball at the start of the game shall not be more than 16oz nor less than 14oz. The pressure shall be equal to 0.6–1.1 atmosphere ($=600$–1100g/cm^2) at sea level. The ball shall not be changed during the game unless authorised by the Referee.

Decisions of the International Board

---

(1) The ball used in any match shall be considered the property of the Association or Club on whose ground the match is played, and at the close of play it must be returned to the Referee.

(2) The International Board, from time to time, shall decide what constitutes approved materials. Any approved material shall be certified as such by the International Board.

(3) The Board has approved these equivalents of the weights specified in the Law: 14 to 16 ounces = 396 to 453 grams.

(4) If the ball bursts or becomes deflated during the course of a match, the game shall be stopped and restarted by dropping the new ball at the place where the first ball became defective.

(5) If this happens during a stoppage of the game (place-kick, goal-kick, corner-kick, free-kick, penalty-kick or throw-in) the game shall be restarted accordingly.

LAW III – NUMBER OF PLAYERS

(1) A match shall be played by two teams, each consisting of not more than eleven players, one of whom shall be the goalkeeper.

(2) Substitutes may be used in any match played under the rules of an official competition under the jurisdiction of FIFA, Confederations or National Associations, subject to the following conditions:

(a) that the authority of the international association(s) or national association(s) concerned, has been obtained.

(b) that, subject to the restriction contained in the following paragraph (c), the rules of a competition shall state how many, if any, substitutes may be nominated and how many of those nominated may be used.

(c) that a team shall not be permitted to use more than two substitutes in any match, who must be chosen from not more than five players whose names may (subject to the rules of the competition) be required to be given to the referee prior to the commencement of the match.

(3) Substitutes may be used in any other match, provided that the two teams concerned reach agreement on a maximum number, not exceeding five, and that the terms of such agreement are intimated to the Referee, before the match. If the Referee is not informed, or if the teams fail to reach agreement, no more than two substitutes shall be permitted. In all cases, the substitutes must be chosen from not more than five players whose names may be required to be given to the Referee prior to the commencement of the match.

(4) Any of the other players may change places with the goalkeeper, provided that the Referee is informed before the change is made, and provided also, that the change is made during a stoppage in the game.

(5) When a goalkeeper or any other player is to be replaced by a substitute, the following conditions shall be observed.

(a) the Referee shall be informed of the proposed substitution, before it is made.

(b) the substitute shall not enter the field of play until the player he is replacing has left, and then only after having received a signal from the Referee.

(c) he shall enter the field during a stoppage in the game, and at the half-way line.

(d) a player who has been replaced shall not take any further part in the game.

(e) a substitute shall be subject to the authority and jurisdiction of the Referee whether called upon to play or not.

(f) the substitution is completed when the substitute enters the field of play, from which moment he becomes a player and the player whom he is replacing ceases to be a player.

Punishment:

(a) Play shall not be stopped for an infringement of paragraph 4. The players concerned shall be cautioned immediately the ball goes out of play.

(b) If a substitute enters the field of play without the authority of the Referee, play shall be stopped. The substitute shall be cautioned or sent off according to the circumstances. The game shall be restarted by the Referee dropping the ball at the place where it was when play was stopped, unless it was within the goal-area at that time, in which case it shall be dropped on the part of the goal-area line which runs parallel to the goal-line, at the point nearest to where the ball was when play was stopped.

(c) For any other infringement of the Law, the player concerned shall be cautioned, and if the game is stopped by the Referee, to administer the caution, it shall be restarted by an indirect free-kick, to be taken by a player of the opposing team from the place where the ball was when play was stopped. If the free-kick is awarded to a team within its own goal-area, it may be taken from any point within that half of the goal-area in which the ball was when play was stopped.

(d) If a competition's rules require the names of substitutes to be given to the Referee prior to the commencement of the match, then failure to do so will mean no substitutes can be permitted.

(1) The minimum number of players in a team is left to the discretion of National Associations.

(2) The Board is of the opinion that a match should not be considered valid if there are fewer than seven players in either of the teams.

(3) A player who has been ordered off before play begins may only be replaced by one of the named substitutes. The kick-off must not be delayed to allow the substitute to join his team.

A player who has been ordered off after play has started may not be replaced.

A named substitute who has been ordered off, either before or after play has started, may not be replaced (this decision relates only to players who are ordered off under Law XII. It does not apply to players who have infringed Law IV).

LAW IV – PLAYERS' EQUIPMENT

(1) (a) The basic compulsory equipment of a player shall consist of a jersey or shirt, shorts, stockings, shinguards and footwear.

(b) A player shall not wear anything which is dangerous to another player.

(2) Shinguards, which must be covered entirely by the stocking, shall be made of a suitable material (rubber, plastic, polyurethane or similar substance) and shall afford a reasonable degree of protection.

(3) The goalkeeper shall wear colours which distinguish him from the other players and from the Referee.

Punishment: For any infringement of this Law, the player at fault shall be sent off the field of play to adjust his equipment and he shall not return without first reporting to the Referee, who shall satisfy himself that the player's equipment is in order; the player shall only re-enter the game at a moment when the ball has ceased to be in play.

(1) In International Matches, International Competitions, International Club Competitions and friendly matches between clubs of different National Associations, the Referee, prior to the start of the game, shall inspect the players' equipment and prevent any player whose equipment does not conform to the requirements of this Law from playing until such time as it does comply. The rules of any competition may include a similar provision.

(2) If the Referee finds that a player is wearing articles not permitted by the Laws and which may constitute a danger to other players, he shall order him to take them off. If he fails to carry out the Referee's instruction, the player shall not take part in the match.

(3) A player who has been prevented from taking part in the game or a player who has been sent off the field for infringing Law IV must report to the Referee during a stoppage of the game and may not enter or re-enter the field of play unless and until the Referee has satisfied himself that the player is no longer infringing Law IV.

(4) A player who has been prevented from taking part in a game or who has been sent off because of an infringement of Law IV, and who enters or re-enters the field of play to join or rejoin his team, in breach of the conditions of Law XII(j), shall be cautioned. If the Referee stops the game to administer the caution, the game shall be restarted by an indirect free-kick, taken by a player of the opposing side, from the place where the ball was when the Referee stopped the game subject to the over-riding conditions imposed in Law XIII.

LAW V – REFEREES

A Referee shall be appointed to officiate in each game. The authority and the exercise of the powers granted to him by the Laws of the Game commence as soon as he enters the field of play.

His power of penalising shall extend to offences committed when play has been temporarily suspended, or when the ball is out of play. His decision on points of fact connected with the play shall be final, so far as the result of the game is concerned. He shall:

(a) Enforce the Laws.

(b) Refrain from penalising in cases where he is satisfied that, by doing so, he would be giving an advantage to the offending team.

(c) Keep a record of the game, act as time-keeper and allow the full or agreed time, adding thereto all time lost through accident or other cause.

(d) Have discretionary power to stop the game for any infringement of the Laws and to suspend or terminate the game whenever, by reason of the elements, interference by spectators, or other cause, he deems such stoppage necessary. In such a case he shall submit a detailed report to the competent authority, within the stipulated time, and in accordance with the provisions set up by the National Association under whose jurisdiction the match was played. Reports will be deemed to be made when received in the ordinary course of post.

(e) From the time he enters the field of play, caution any player guilty of misconduct or ungentlemanly behaviour and, if he persists, suspend him from further participation in the game. In such cases the Referee shall send the name of the offender to the competent authority, within the stipulated time, and in accordance with the provisions set up by the National Association under whose jurisdiction the match was played. Reports will be deemed to be made when received in the ordinary course of post.

(f) Allow no person other than the players and linesmen to enter the field of play without his permission.

(g) Stop the game if, in his opinion, a player has been seriously injured, have the player removed as soon as possible from the field of play, and immediately resume the game. If a player is slightly injured, the game shall not be stopped until the ball has ceased to be in play. A player who is able to go to the touch or goal-line for attention of any kind, shall not be treated on the field of play.

(h) Send off the field of play, any player who, in his opinion, is guilty of violent conduct, serious foul play, or the use of foul or abusive language.

(i) Signal for recommencement of the game after all stoppages.

(j) Decide that the ball provided for a match meets with the requirement of Law II.

Decisions of the International Board

(1) Referees in International Matches shall wear a blazer or blouse the colour of which is distinct from the colours worn by the contesting teams.

(2) Referees for International Matches will be selected from a neutral country unless the countries concerned agree to appoint their own officials.

(3) The Referee must be chosen from the official list of International Referees. This need not apply to Amateur and Youth International Matches.

(4) The Referee shall report to the appropriate authority misconduct or any misdemeanour on the part of spectators, officials, players, named substitutes or other persons which take place either on the field of play or in its vicinity at any time prior to, during, or after the match in question so that appropriate action can be taken by the authority concerned.

(5) Linesmen are assistants of the Referee. In no case shall the Referee consider the intervention of a Linesman if he himself has seen the incident and from his position on the field, is better able to judge. With this reserve, and the Linesman neutral, the Referee can consider the intervention and if the information of the Linesman applies to that phase of the game immediately before the scoring of a goal, the Referee may act thereon and cancel the goal.

(6) The Referee, however, can only reverse his first decision so long as the game has not been restarted.

(7) If the Referee has decided to apply the advantage clause and to let the game proceed, he cannot revoke his decision if the presumed advantage has not been realised, even though he has not, by any gesture, indicated his decision. This does not exempt the offending player from being dealt with by the Referee.

(8) The Laws of the Game are intended to provide that games should be played with as little interference as possible, and in this view it is the duty of Referees to penalise only deliberate breaches of the Law. Constant whistling for trifling and doubtful breaches produces bad feeling and loss of temper on the part of the players and spoils the pleasure of spectators.

(9) By para. (d) of Law V the Referee is empowered to terminate a match in the event of grave disorder, but he has no power or right to decide, in such event, that either team is disqualified and thereby the loser of the match. He must send a detailed report to the proper authority who alone has power to deal further with the matter.

(10) If a player commits two infringements of a different nature at the same time, the Referee shall punish the more serious offence.

(11) It is the duty of the Referee to act upon the information of neutral Linesmen with regard to incidents that do not come under the personal notice of the Referee.

(12) The Referee shall not allow any person to enter the field until play has stopped, and only then, if he has given him a signal to do so, nor shall he allow coaching from the boundary lines.

LAW VI – LINESMEN

Two Linesmen shall be appointed, whose duty (subject to the decision of the Referee) shall be to indicate when the ball is out of play, which side is entitled to the corner-kick, goal-kick or throw-in, and when a substitute is desired. They shall also assist the Referee to control the game in accordance with the Laws. In the event of undue interference or improper conduct by a Linesman, the Referee shall dispense with his services and arrange a substitute to be appointed. (The matter shall be reported by the Referee to the competent authority.) The Linesmen should be equipped with flags by the Club on whose ground the match is played.

Decisions of the International Board

(1) Linesmen, where neutral, shall draw the Referee's attention to any breach of the Laws of the Game of which they become aware if they consider that the Referee may not have seen it, but the Referee shall always be the judge of the decision to be taken.

(2) National Associations are advised to appoint official Referees of neutral nationality to act as Linesmen in International Matches.

(3) In International Matches, Linesmen's flags shall be of a vivid colour, bright reds and yellows. Such flags are recommended for use in all other matches.

(4) A Linesman may be subject to disciplinary action only upon a report of the Referee for unjustified interference or insufficient assistance.

LAW VII – DURATION OF THE GAME

The duration of the game shall be two equal periods of 45 minutes, unless otherwise mutually agreed upon, subject to the following: (a) Allowance shall be made in either period for all time lost through substitution, the transport from the field of injured players, time-wasting or other cause, the amount of which shall be a matter for the discretion of the Referee; (b) Time shall be extended to permit a penalty-kick being taken at or after the expiration of the normal period in either half.

At half-time the interval shall not exceed five minutes except by consent of the Referee.

Decisions of the International Board

---

(1) If a match has been stopped by the Referee, before the completion of the time specified in the rules, for any reason stated in Law V it must be replayed in full unless the rules of the competition concerned provide for the result of the match at the time of such stoppage to stand.

(2) Players have a right to an interval at half-time.

LAW VIII – THE START OF PLAY

(a) **At the beginning of the game,** choice of ends and the kick-off shall be decided by the toss of a coin. The team winning the toss shall have the option of choice of ends or the kick-off. The Referee having given a signal, the game shall be started by a player taking a place-kick (i.e. a kick at the ball while it is stationary on the ground in the centre of the field of play) into his opponents' half of the field of play. Every player shall be in his own half of the field and every player of the team opposing that of the kicker shall remain not less than 10 yards from the ball until it is kicked-off; it shall not be deemed in play until it has travelled the distance of its own circumference. The kicker shall not play the ball a second time until it has been touched or played by another player.

(b) **After a goal is scored,** the game shall be restarted in like manner by a player of the team losing the goal.

(c) **After half-time:** when restarting after half-time, ends shall be changed and the kick-off shall be taken by a player of the opposite team to that of the player who started the game.

Punishment: For any infringement of this Law, the kick-off shall be retaken, except in the case of the kicker playing the ball again before it has been touched or played by another player; for this offence, an indirect free-kick shall be taken by a player of the opposing team from the place where the infringement occurred, unless the offence is committed by a player in his opponents' goal-area, in which case the free-kick shall be taken from a point anywhere within that half of the goal-area in which the offence occurred. A goal shall not be scored direct from a kick-off.

(d) **After any other temporary suspension:** when restarting the game after a temporary suspension of play from any cause not mentioned elsewhere in these Laws, provided that immediately prior to the suspension the ball has not passed over the touch or goal-lines, the Referee shall drop the ball at the place where it was when play was suspended, unless it was within the goal area at that time, in which case it shall be dropped on that part of the goal area line which runs parallel to the goal-line, at the point nearest to where the ball was when play was stopped. It shall be deemed in play when it has touched the ground; if, however, it goes over the touch or goal-lines after it has been dropped by the Referee, but before it is touched by a player, the Referee shall again drop it. A player shall not play the ball until it has touched the ground. If this section of the Law is not complied with the Referee shall again drop the ball.

Decisions of the International Board

---

(1) If, when the Referee drops the ball, a player infringes any of the Laws before the ball has touched the ground, the player concerned shall be cautioned or sent off the field according to the seriousness of the offence, but a free-kick cannot be awarded to the opposing team because the ball was not in play at the time of the offence. The ball shall therefore be again dropped by the Referee.

(2) Kicking-off by persons other than the players competing in a match is prohibited.

LAW IX – BALL IN AND OUT OF PLAY

The ball is out of play:

(a) When it has wholly crossed the goal-line or touch-line, whether on the ground or in the air.

(b) When the game has been stopped by the Referee.

The ball is in play at all other times from the start of the match to the finish including:

(a) If it rebounds from a goal-post, cross-bar or corner-flag post into the field of play.

(b) If it rebounds off either the Referee or Linesmen when they are in the field of play.

(c) In the event of a supposed infringement of the Laws, until a decision is given.

Decisions of the International Board

---

(1) The lines belong to the area of which they are the boundaries. In consequence, the touch-lines and the goal-lines belong to the field of play.

LAW X – METHOD OF SCORING

Except as otherwise provided by these Laws, a goal is scored when the whole of the ball has passed over the goal-line, between the goal-posts and under the cross-bar, provided it has not been thrown, carried or intentionally propelled by hand or arm, by a player of the attacking side, except in the case of a goalkeeper, who is within his own penalty-area.

The team scoring the greater number of goals during a game shall be the winner; if no goals, or an equal number of goals are scored, the game shall be termed a 'draw'.

(1) Law X defines the only method according to which a match is won or drawn; no variation whatsoever can be authorised.

(2) A goal cannot in any case be allowed if the ball has been prevented by some outside agent from passing over the goal-line. If this happens in the normal course of play, other than at the taking of a penalty-kick, the game must be stopped and restarted where the ball came into contact with the interference.

(3) If, when the ball is going into goal, a spectator enters the field before it passes wholly over the goal-line, and tries to prevent a score, a goal shall be allowed if the ball goes into goal unless the spectator has made contact with the ball or has interfered with play, in which case the Referee shall stop the game and restart it by dropping the ball at the place where the contact or interference occurred.

LAW XI – OFF-SIDE

(1) A player is in an off-side position if he is nearer to his opponents' goal-line than the ball, unless:

(a) he is in his own half of the field of play, or

(b) he is not nearer to his opponents' goal-line than at least two of his opponents.

(2) A player shall only be declared off-side and penalised for being in an off-side position, if, at the moment the ball touches, or is played by, one of his team, he is, in the opinion of the Referee

(a) interfering with play or with an opponent, or

(b) seeking to gain an advantage by being in that position.

(3) A player shall not be declared off-side by the referee

(a) merely because of his being in an off-side position, or

(b) if he receives the ball, direct from a goal-kick, a corner-kick or a throw-in.

(4) If a player is declared off-side, the Referee shall award an indirect free-kick, which shall be taken by a player of the opposing team from the place where the infringement occurred, unless the offence is committed by a player in his opponents' goal-area, in which case, the free-kick shall be taken from a point anywhere within that half of the goal-area in which the offence occurred.

(1) Off-side shall not be judged at the moment the player in question receives the ball, but at the moment when the ball is passed to him by one of his own side. A player who is not in an off-side position when one of his colleagues passes the ball to him or takes a free-kick, does not therefore become off-side if he goes forward during the flight of the ball.

(2) A player who is level with the second last opponent or with the last two opponents is not in an off-side position.

LAW XII – FOULS AND MISCONDUCT

A player who intentionally commits any of the following nine offences:

(a) Kicks or attempts to kick an opponent;

(b) Trips an opponent, i.e. throwing or attempting to throw him by the use of the legs or by stooping in front of or behind him;

(c) Jumps at an opponent;

(d) Charges an opponent in a violent or dangerous manner;

(e) Charges an opponent from behind unless the latter be obstructing;

(f) Strikes or attempts to strike an opponent;

(g) Holds an opponent;

(h) Pushes an opponent;

(i) Handles the ball, i.e. carries, strikes or propels the ball with his hand or arm. (This does not apply to the goalkeeper within his own penalty-area);

shall be penalised by the award of a **direct free-kick** to be taken by the opposing side from the place where the offence occurred, unless the offence is committed by a player in his opponents' goal-area in which case, the free-kick shall be taken from a point anywhere within that half of the goal-area in which the offence occurred.

Should a player of the defending side intentionally commit one of the above nine offences within the penalty-area he shall be penalised by a **penalty-kick.**

A penalty-kick can be awarded irrespective of the position of the ball, if in play, at the time an offence within the penalty-area is committed.

A player committing any of the five following offences:

(1) Playing in a manner considered by the Referee to be dangerous, e.g. attempting to kick the ball while held by the goalkeeper.

(2) Charging fairly, i.e. with the shoulder, when the ball is not within playing distance of the players concerned and they are definitely not trying to play it.

(3) When not playing the ball, intentionally obstructing an opponent, i.e. running between the opponent and the ball, or interposing the body so as to form an obstacle to an opponent.

(4) Charging the goalkeeper except when he

(a) is holding the ball;

(b) is obstructing an opponent;

(c) has passed outside the goal-area.

(5) When playing as goalkeeper and within his own penalty-area

(a) from the moment he takes control of the ball with his hands, he takes more than four steps in any direction whilst holding, bouncing or throwing the ball in the air and catching it again, without releasing it into play, or, having released the ball into play before, during or after the four steps, he touches it again with his hands, before it has been touched or played by another player of the same team outside of the penalty-area or by a player of the opposing team either inside or outside of the penalty-area, or

(b) indulges in tactics which, in the opinion of the Referee, are designed merely to hold up the game and thus waste time and so give an unfair advantage to his own team—shall be penalised by the award of an **indirect free-kick** to be taken by the opposing side from the place where the infringement occurred, subject to the over-riding conditions imposed in Law XIII. On any occasion when a player deliberately kicks the ball to his own goalkeeper, the goalkeeper is not permitted to touch it with his hands. If, however, the goalkeeper does touch the ball with his hands, he shall be penalised by the award of an indirect free kick to be taken by the opposing team from the place where the infringement occurred, subject to the over-riding conditions of Law XIII.

A player shall be **cautioned** if:

(j) he enters or re-enters the field of play to join or rejoin his team after the game has commenced, or leaves the field of play during the progress of the game (except through accident) without, in either case, first having received a signal from the Referee showing him that he may do so. If the Referee stops the game to administer the caution the game shall be restarted by an indirect free-kick taken by a player of the opposing team from the place where the ball was when the Referee stopped the game. If the free-kick is awarded to a side within its own goal-area it may be taken from any point within the half of the goal-area in which the ball was when play was stopped. If, however, the offending player has committed a more serious offence he shall be penalised according to that section of the law he infringed.

(k) he persistently infringes the Laws of the Game;

(l) he shows by word or action, dissent from any decision given by the Referee;

(m) he is guilty of ungentlemanly conduct.

For any of these last three offences, in addition to the caution, an **indirect free-kick** shall also be awarded to the opposing side from the place where the offence occurred unless a more serious infringement of the Laws of the Game was committed. If the offence is committed by a player in his opponents' goal-area, a free-kick shall be taken from a point anywhere within that half of the goal-area in which the offence occurred.

A player shall be **sent off** the field of play, if:

(n) in the opinion of the Referee he is guilty of violent conduct or serious foul play;

(o) he uses foul or abusive language;

(p) he persists in misconduct after having received a caution.

If play be stopped by reason of a player being ordered from the field for an offence without a separate breach of the Law having been committed, the game shall be resumed by an **indirect free-kick** awarded to the opposing side from the place where the infringement occurred, subject to the over-riding conditions imposed in Law XIII.

Decisions of the International Board

(1) If the goalkeeper either intentionally strikes an opponent by throwing the ball vigorously at him or pushes him with the ball while holding it, the Referee shall award a penalty-kick, if the offence took place within the penalty-area.

(2) If a player deliberately turns his back to an opponent when he is about to be tackled, he may be charged but not in a dangerous manner.

(3) In case of body-contact in the goal-area between an attacking player and the opposing goalkeeper not in possession of the ball, the Referee, as sole judge of intention, shall stop the game if, in his opinion, the action of the attacking player was intentional, and award an indirect free-kick.

(4) If a player leans on the shoulders of another player of his own team in order to head the ball, the Referee shall stop the game, caution the player for ungentlemanly conduct and award an indirect free-kick to the opposing side.

(5) A player's obligation when joining or rejoining his team after the start of the match to 'report to the Referee' must be interpreted as meaning 'to draw the attention of the Referee from the touch-line'. The signal from the Referee shall be made by a definite gesture which makes the player understand that he may come into the field of play; it is not necessary for the Referee to wait until the game is stopped (this does not apply in respect of an infringement of Law IV), but the Referee is the sole judge of the moment in which he gives his signal of acknowledgement.

(6) The letter and spirit of Law XII do not oblige the Referee to stop a game to administer a caution. He may, if he chooses, apply the advantage. If he does apply the advantage, he shall caution the player when play stops.

(7) If a player covers up the ball without touching it in an endeavour not to have it played by an opponent, he obstructs but does not infringe Law XII para. 3 because he is already in possession of the ball and covers it for tactical reasons whilst the ball remains within playing distance. In fact, he is actually playing the ball and does not commit an infringement; in this case, the player may be charged because he is in fact playing the ball.

(8) If a player intentionally stretches his arms to obstruct an opponent and steps from one side to the other moving his arms up and down to delay his opponent, forcing him to change course, but does not make 'bodily contact' the Referee shall caution the player for ungentlemanly conduct and award an indirect free-kick.

(9) If a player intentionally obstructs the opposing goalkeeper, in an attempt to prevent him from putting the ball into play in accordance with Law XII, 5(a), the Referee shall award an indirect free-kick.

(10) If, after a Referee has awarded a free-kick a player protests violently by using abusive or foul

language and is sent off the field, the free-kick should not be taken until the player has left the field.

(11) Any player, whether he is within or outside the field of play, whose conduct is ungentlemanly or violent, whether or not it is directed towards an opponent, a colleague, the Referee, a Linesman or other person, or who uses foul or abusive language, is guilty of an offence, and shall be dealt with according to the nature of the offence committed.

(12) If, in the opinion of the Referee a goal-keeper intentionally lies on the ball longer than is necessary, he shall be penalised for ungentlemanly conduct and

(a) be cautioned and an indirect free-kick awarded to the opposing team;

(b) in case of repetition of the offence, be sent off the field.

(13) The offence of spitting at opponents, officials or other persons, or similar unseemly behaviour shall be considered as violent conduct within the meaning of section (n) of Law XII.

(14) If, when a Referee is about to caution a player, and before he has done so, the player commits another offence which merits a caution, the player shall be sent off the field of play.

Decision No (15): If, in the opinion of the referee, a player who is moving toward his opponents' goal with an obvious opportunity to score a goal is intentionally impeded by an opponent, through unlawful means, i.e. an offence punishable by a free kick (or a penalty kick), thus denying the attacking player's team the aforesaid goal-scoring opportunity, the offending player shall be sent off the field of play for serious foul play in accordance with Law XII (n).

Decision No (16): If, in the opinion of the referee, a player, other than the goalkeeper within his own penalty area, denies his opponents a goal, or an obvious goal-scoring opportunity, by intentionally handling the ball, he shall be sent off the field of play for serious foul play in accordance with Law XII (n).

Decision No (17): The International FA Board is of the opinion that a goalkeeper, in the circumstances described in Law XII 5(a), will be considered to be in control of the ball when he takes possession of the ball by touching it with any part of his hands or arms. Possession of the ball would include the goalkeeper intentionally parrying the ball, but would not include circumstances where, in the opinion of the referee, the ball rebounds accidentally from the goalkeeper, for example after he has made a save.

LAW XIII – FREE-KICK

Free-kicks shall be classified under two headings: 'Direct' (from which a goal can be scored direct against the offending side) and 'Indirect' (from which a goal cannot be scored unless the ball has been played or touched by a player other than the kicker before passing through the goal).

When a player is taking a direct or an indirect free-kick inside his own penalty-area, all of the opposing players shall be at least 10 yards (9.15m) from the ball and shall remain outside the penalty area until the ball has been kicked out of the area. The ball shall be in play immediately it has travelled the distance of its own circumference and is beyond the penalty-area. The goalkeeper shall not receive the ball into his hands, in order that he may thereafter kick it into play. If the ball is not kicked direct into play, beyond the penalty-area, the kick shall be retaken.

When a player is taking a direct or an indirect free-kick outside his own penalty-area, all of the opposing players shall be at least ten yards from the ball, until it is in play, unless they are standing on their own goal-line, between the goal-posts. The ball shall be in play when it has travelled the distance of its own circumference.

If a player of the opposing side encroaches into the penalty-area, or within ten yards of the ball, as the case may be, before a free-kick is taken, the Referee shall delay the taking of the kick, until the Law is complied with.

The ball must be stationary when a free-kick is taken, and the kicker shall not play the ball a second time, until it has been touched or played by another player.

Notwithstanding any other reference in these Laws to the point from which a free-kick is to be taken:

1. Any free-kick awarded to the defending team, within its own goal-area, may be taken from any point within the goal-area.

2. Any indirect free-kick awarded to the attacking team within its opponents' goal-area shall be taken from that part of the goal-area line which runs parallel to the goal-line, at the point nearest to where the offence was committed.

Punishment: If the kicker, after taking the free-kick, plays the ball a second time before it has been touched or played by another player an indirect free-kick shall be taken by a player of the opposing team from the spot where the infringement occurred, unless the offence is committed by a player in his opponents' goal-area, in which case the free-kick shall be taken from any point within the goal-area.

Decisions of the International Board

---

(1) In order to distinguish between a direct and indirect free-kick, the Referee, when he awards an indirect free-kick, shall indicate accordingly by raising an arm above his head. He shall keep his arm in that position until the kick has been taken and retain the signal until the ball has been played or touched by another player or goes out of play.

(2) Players who do not retire to the proper distance when a free-kick is taken must be cautioned and on any repetition be ordered off. It is particularly requested of Referees that attempts

to delay the taking of a free-kick by encroaching should be treated as serious misconduct.

(3) If, when a free-kick is being taken, any of the players dance about or gesticulate in a way calculated to distract their opponents, it shall be deemed ungentlemanly conduct for which the offender(s) shall be cautioned.

LAW XIV – PENALTY-KICK

A penalty-kick shall be taken from the penalty-mark and, when it is being taken, all players with the exception of the player taking the kick, properly identified, and the opposing goalkeeper, shall be within the field of play but outside the penalty-area, and at least 10 yards from the penalty-mark. The opposing goalkeeper must stand (without moving his feet) on his own goal-line, between the goal-posts, until the ball is kicked. The player taking the kick must kick the ball forward; he shall not play the ball a second time until it has been touched or played by another player. The ball shall be deemed in play directly it is kicked, i.e. when it has travelled the distance of its circumference. A goal may be scored directly from a penalty-kick. When a penalty-kick is being taken during the normal course of play, or when time has been extended at half-time or full-time to allow a penalty-kick to be taken or retaken, a goal shall not be nullified if, before passing between the posts and under the cross-bar, the ball touches either or both of the goal-posts or the cross-bar, or the goal-keeper, or any combination of these agencies, providing that no other infringement has occurred.

Punishment: For any infringement of this Law:

(a) by the defending team, the kick shall be retaken if a goal has not resulted.

(b) by the attacking team other than by the player taking the kick, if a goal is scored it shall be disallowed and the kick retaken.

(c) by the player taking the penalty-kick, committed after the ball is in play, a player of the opposing team shall take an indirect free-kick from the spot where the infringement occurred subject to the over-riding conditions imposed in Law XIII.

(1) When the Referee has awarded a penalty-kick, he shall not signal for it to be taken, until the players have taken up position in accordance with the Law.

(2) (a) If, after the kick has been taken, the ball is stopped in its course towards goal, by an outside agent, the kick shall be retaken.

(b) If, after the kick has been taken, the ball rebounds into play, from the goalkeeper, the cross-bar or a goal-post, and is then stopped in its course by an outside agent, the Referee shall stop play and restart it by dropping the ball at the place where it came into contact with the outside agent.

(3) (a) If, after having given the signal for a penalty-kick to be taken, the Referee sees that the goalkeeper is not in his right place on the goal-line, he shall, nevertheless, allow the kick to proceed. It shall be retaken, if a goal is not scored.

(b) If, after the Referee has given the signal for a penalty-kick to be taken, and before the ball has been kicked, the goalkeeper moves his feet, the Referee shall, nevertheless, allow the kick to proceed. It shall be retaken, if a goal is not scored.

(c) If, after the Referee has given the signal for a penalty-kick to be taken, and before the ball is in play, a player of the defending team encroaches into the penalty-area, or within 10 yards of the penalty-mark, the Referee shall, nevertheless, allow the kick to proceed. It shall be retaken, if a goal is not scored.

The player concerned shall be cautioned.

(4) (a) If, when a penalty-kick is being taken, the player taking the kick is guilty of ungentlemanly conduct, the kick, if already taken, shall be retaken, if a goal is scored.

The player concerned shall be cautioned.

(b) If, after the Referee has given the signal for a penalty-kick to be taken, and before the ball is in play, a colleague of the player taking the kick encroaches into the penalty-area or within ten yards of the penalty-mark, the Referee shall, nevertheless, allow the kick to proceed. If a goal is scored, it shall be disallowed, and the kick retaken.

The player concerned shall be cautioned.

(c) If, in the circumstances described in the foregoing paragraph, the ball rebounds into play from the goalkeeper, the cross-bar or a goal-post and a goal has not been scored, the Referee shall stop the game, caution the player and award an indirect free-kick to the opposing team from the place where the infringement occurred, subject to the over-riding conditions imposed in Law XIII.

(5) (a) If, after the referee has given the signal for a penalty-kick to be taken, and before the ball is in play, the goalkeeper moves from his position on the goal-line, or moves his feet, and a colleague of the kicker encroaches into the penalty-area or within 10 yards of the penalty mark, the kick, if taken, shall be retaken.

The colleague of the kicker shall be cautioned.

(b) If, after the Referee has given the signal for a penalty-kick to be taken, and before the ball is in play, a player of each team encroaches into the penalty area, or within 10 yards of the penalty-mark, the kick if taken, shall be retaken.

The players concerned shall be cautioned.

(6) When a match is extended, at half-time or full-time, to allow a penalty-kick to be taken or retaken, the extension shall last until the moment that the penalty-kick has been completed, i.e. until the Referee has decided whether or not a goal is scored, and the game shall terminate immediately the Referee has made his decision. After the player taking the penalty-kick has put the ball into play, no player other than the defending

goalkeeper may play or touch the ball before the kick is completed.

(7) When a penalty-kick is being taken in extended time:

(a) the provisions of all of the foregoing paragraphs, except paragraphs (2)(b) and (4)(c) shall apply in the usual way, and

(b) in the circumstances described in paragraphs (2)(b) and (4)(c) the game shall terminate immediately the ball rebounds from the goalkeeper, the cross-bar or the goal-post.

LAW XV – THROW-IN

When the whole of the ball passes over a touch-line, either on the ground or in the air, it shall be thrown in from the point where it crossed the line, in any direction, by a player of the team opposite to that of the player who last touched it. The thrower at the moment of delivering the ball must face the field of play and part of each foot shall be either on the touch-line or on the ground outside the touch-line. The thrower shall use both hands and shall deliver the ball from behind and over his head. The ball shall be in play immediately it enters the field of play, but the thrower shall not again play the ball until it has been touched or played by another player. A goal shall not be scored direct from a throw-in.

Punishment:

(a) If the ball is improperly thrown in, the throw-in shall be taken by a player of the opposing team.

(b) If the thrower plays the ball a second time before it has been touched or played by another player, an indirect free-kick shall be taken by a player of the opposing team from the place where the infringement occurred, unless the offence is committed by a player in his opponents' goal-area, in which case the free-kick shall be taken from a point anywhere within that half of the goal-area in which the offence occurred.

Decisions of the International Board

(1) If a player taking a throw-in, plays the ball a second time by handling it within the field of play before it has been touched or played by another player, the Referee shall award a direct free-kick.

(2) A player taking a throw-in must face the field of play with some part of his body.

(3) If, when a throw-in is being taken, any of the opposing players dance about or gesticulate in a way calculated to distract or impede the thrower, it shall be deemed ungentlemanly conduct for which the offender(s) shall be cautioned.

(4) A throw-in taken from any position other than the point where the ball passed over the touch-line shall be considered to have been improperly thrown.

LAW XVI – GOAL-KICK

When the whole of the ball passes over the goal-line excluding that portion between the goal-posts, either in the air or on the ground, having last been played by one of the attacking team, it shall be kicked direct into play beyond the penalty-area from any point within the goal-area, by a player of the defending team. A goalkeeper shall not receive the ball into his hands from a goal-kick in order that he may thereafter kick it into play. If the ball is not kicked beyond the penalty-area, i.e. direct into play, the kick shall be retaken. The kicker shall not play the ball a second time until it has touched—or been played by—another player. A goal shall not be scored direct from such a kick. Players of the team opposing that of the player taking the goal-kick shall remain outside the penalty-area whilst the kick is being taken.

Punishment: If a player taking a goal-kick plays the ball a second time after it has passed beyond the penalty-area, but before it has touched or been played by another player, an indirect free-kick shall be awarded to the opposing team, to be taken from the place where the infringement occurred subject to the over-riding conditions imposed in Law XIII.

Decisions of the International Board

(1) When a goal-kick has been taken and the player who has kicked the ball touches it again before it has left the penalty-area, the kick has not been taken in accordance with the Laws and must be retaken.

LAW XVII – CORNER-KICK

When the whole of the ball passes over the goal-line, excluding that portion between the goal-posts, either in the air or on the ground, having last been played by one of the defending team, a member of the attacking team shall take a corner-kick, i.e. the whole of the ball shall be placed within the quarter circle at the nearest corner-flag post, which must not be moved, and it shall be kicked from that position. A goal may be scored direct from such a kick. Players of the team opposing that of the player taking the corner-kick shall not approach within 10 yards of the ball until it is in play, i.e. it has travelled the distance of its own circumference, nor shall the kicker play the ball a second time until it has been touched or played by another player.

Punishment:

(a) If the player who takes the kick plays the ball a second time before it has been touched or played by another player, the Referee shall award an indirect free-kick to the opposing team, to be taken from the place where the infringement occurred, unless the offence is committed by a player in his opponents' goal-area, in which case the free-kick shall be taken from a point anywhere within that half of the goal-area in which the offence occurred.

(b) For any other infringement the kick shall be retaken.

STOP PRESS...
TRANSFER FEE RECORDS BROKEN

The domestic transfer fee records in England and Scotland were broken in the summer when Roy Keane moved from Nottingham Forest to Manchester United for £3.75 million and Duncan Ferguson was signed by Rangers from Dundee United for £4 million.

The transfer market appeared to be moving out of recession with several seven-figure deals completed during the close season. England's foreign legion was also involved in moves, Des Walker returning from an unhappy season in Italy and joining Sheffield Wednesday and David Platt creating something of a record in aggregate fees by a switch from Juventus to Sampdoria, Walker's former club.

Both leading domestic leagues will be under new titles. The FA Carling Premiership heralds what amounts to the second season of the Premier League while with Barclays finishing their sponsorship of the Football League, fresh backers were found in Endsleigh Insurance. By an odd coincidence, there is a hotel close to the League offices in St Annes called the Endsleigh!

But there was some domestic disquiet when referees threatened to call a strike over match fees. However, the real storm of the close season came from France where allegations of bribery hit Marseille the champions and European Cup holders.

July saw the finals of the UEFA Under-18 Championship and brought victory to England for a record ninth time in the competition. Apart from the obvious pleasing aspect of this success, attendances were excellent for the competition, considering it was out of season and even those games in which England did not compete, were well supported. This augers well for the 1996 European Championship finals which will be held in this country.

Managerial moves proved interesting. Ivan Golac, who had had a spell in charge of Torquay United, was perhaps the surprise choice to succeed Jim McLean, the long-serving boss of Dundee United. At Watford, Glenn Roeder's appointment as manager also brought Kenny Jackett as his assistant in place of Phil Holder.

In the World cup, the last continent to begin qualifying matches was South America. And there was a shock for Brazil, beaten 2-0 in Bolivia.

Barnet, who appeared to be heading for extinction, revived despite having eleven players given free transfers by the League through non-payment of wages. New chairman Stephen Glynne was able to start thinking positively after the League was unable to sustain a vote to expel the club. Thirteen clubs failed to be represented and though 38 voted in favour, one abstained and 18 voted in Barnet's favour! The League had needed 75 per cent to carry their resolution.

NATIONAL REVIEW BOARD FOR REFEREES AND LINESMEN

SEASON 1993/94 — RETIREMENT YEARS OF REFEREES AT AGE 48

	Age 52+ (1)		*Age 50+ (1)*		*Age 49+ (1)*
(81)	Milford, R.G.	(77)	Gunn, A.	(76)	Hackett, K.S.
	1993/94 (11)		*1994/5 (9)*		*1995/96 (8)*
(81)	Barratt, K.P.	(86)	Flood, W.A.	(82)	Cooper, K.
(81)	Borrett, I.J.	(87)	Foakes, P.L.	(88)	Dawson, A.
(79)	Callow, V.G.	(78)	Hill, B.	(84)	Gifford, R.B.
(90)	Frampton, D.G.	(80)	King, H.W.	(86)	Harrison, P.W.
(84)	Groves, R.G.	(85)	Lupton, K.A.	(86)	Hart, R.A.
(82)	Holbrook, T.J.	(87)	Parker, E.J.	(85)	Hemley, I.S.
(81)	Key, J.M.	(89)	Smith, A.W.	(85)	Lloyd, J.W.
(86)	Morton, K.	(84)	Vanes, P.W.	(87)	Rushton, J.
(77)	Peck, M.G.	(86)	Watson, J.L.		
(90)	Shepherd, R.				
(76)	Worrall, J.B.				
	1996/97 (8)		*(1997/98) (4)*		*1998/99 (3)*
(80)	Allison, D.B.	(85)	Ashby, G.R.	(86)	Burge, W.K.
(89)	Bigger, R.L.	(86)	Bailey, M.C.	(87)	Cooper, K.A.
(85)	Breen, K.J.	(81)	Bodenham, M.J.	(89)	Pierce, M.E.
(83)	Dilkes, L.R.	(89)	Cruikshanks, I.G.		
(88)	Pooley, G.R.				
(91)	Poulain, R.				
(88)	West, T.E.				
(86)	Wright, P.L.				
	1999/2000 (8)		*2000/2001 (4)*		*2001/2002 (6)*
(86)	Don, P.	(88)	Burns, W.C.	(88)	Alcock, P.E.
(93)	Heilbron, T.	(87)	Lodge, S.J.	(90)	Brandwood, M.J.
(87)	Kirkby, J.A.	(89)	Lunt, T.	(88)	Jones, P.
(92)	Leach, K.A	(93)	Orr, D.	(93)	Lomas, E.
(92)	Lynch, K.M.			(89)	Singh, G.
(85)	Reed, M.D.			(92)	Wolstenholme, E.K.
(88)	Wilkie, A.B.				
(86)	Wiseman, R.M.				
	2002/2003 (4)		*2003/2004 (2)*		*2004/2005 (1)*
(91)	Coddington, B.	(93)	Cain, G.	(90)	Gallagher, D.J.
(86)	Elleray, D.R.	(87)	Durkin, P.A.		
(90)	Wilkes, C.R.				
(92)	Winter, J.T.				
	2005/2006 (3)		*2006/2007 (1)*		*2007/2008 (1)*
(93)	Barry, N.S.	(93)	Holbrook, J.H.	(90)	Willard, G.S.
(87)	Danson, P.S.				
(92)	Dunn, S.W.				
			2010/2011 (1)		
		(91)	Poll, G.		

LIST OF REFEREES FOR SEASON 1993–94

Paul Alcock (S. Merstham, Surrey)
David Allison (Lancaster)
Gerald Ashby, (Worcester)
Mike Bailey, (Impington, Cambridge)
Keren Barratt, (Coventry)
Neil Barry, (Scunthorpe)
Ray Bigger, (Croydon)
Martin Bodenham, (Looe, Cornwall)
Jim Borrett, (Harleston, Norfolk)
John Brandwood, (Lichfield, Staffs.)
Kevin Breen, (Liverpool)
Keith Burge, (Tonypandy)
Billy Burns, (Scarborough)
George Cain, (Bootle)
Vic Callow, (Solihull)
Brian Coddington, (Sheffield)
Keith Cooper, (Pontypridd)
Keith Cooper, (Swindon)
Ian Cruikshanks, (Hartlepool)
Paul Danson, (Leicester)
Alan Dawson, (Jarrowe)
Roger Dilkes, (Mossley, Lancs.)
Phil Don, (Hanworth Park, Middlesex)
Steve Dunn, (Bristol)
Paul Durkin, (Portland, Dorset)
David Elleray, (Harrow)

Alan Flood, (Stockport)
Peter Foakes, (Clacton-on-Sea)
David Frampton, (Poole, Dorset)
Dermot Gallagher, (Banbury, Oxon.)
Rodger Gifford, (Llanbradach, Mid. Glam.)
Ron Groves, (Weston-Super-Mare)
Allan Gunn, (South Chailey, Sussex)
Keith Hackett, (Sheffield)
Paul Harrison, (Oldham)
Robert Hart, (Darlington)
Terry Heilbron, (Newton Aycliffe)
Ian Hemley, (Ampthill, Beds.)
Brian Hill, (Kettering)
John Holbrook (Ludlow)
Terry Holbrook, (Walsall)
Peter Jones, (Loughborough)
John Key, (Sheffield)
Howard King, (Merthyr Tydfil)
John Kirkby, (Sheffield)
Ken Leach, (Wolverhampton)
John Lloyd, (Wrexham)
Stephen Lodge, (Barnsley)
Eddie Lomas (Manchester)
Terry Lunt, (Ashton-in-Makerfield, Lancs)
Ken Lupton, (Stockton-on-Tees)
Kevin Lynch, (Lincoln)

Roger Milford, (Bristol)
Kelvin Morton, (Bury St. Edmunds)
David Orr (Iver)
Jim Parker, (Preston)
Mike Peck, (Kendal)
Micky Pierce, (Portsmouth)
Graham Poll, (Berkhamsted)
Graham Pooley, (Bishops Stortford)
Richard Poulain, (Huddersfield)
Mike Reed, (Birmingham)
Jim Rushton, (Stoke-on-Trent)
Ray Shepherd, (Leeds)
Gurnam Singh, (Wolverhampton)
Arthur Smith, (Rubery, Birmingham)
Paul Vanes, (Warley, West Midlands)
John Watson, (Whitley Bay)
Trevor West, (Hull)
Clive Wilkes, (Gloucester)
Alan Wilkie, (Chester-le-Street)
Gary Willard, (Worthing, W. Sussex)
Jeff Winter, (Middlesbrough)
Roger Wiseman (Borehamwood, Herts.)
Eddie Wolstenholme, (Blackburn)
Joe Worrall, (Warrington)
Philip Wright, (Northwich)

OBITUARIES

Archer, William (b. Scunthorpe 5.2.14; d. 17.10.92). A centre-half, who began his career with Gainsborough Trinity in the thirties, before joining Grantham. Moved on to Sheffield United during the war, for whom he made 114 appearances. He later played for Lincoln City and Doncaster Rovers, before becoming a director, then Chairman of Scunthorpe United, in the early seventies.

Ashley, Albert (b. Clowne; d. 12.92). Former Mansfield Town defender who made 69 appearances for The Stags before moving on to Sheffield Wednesday in 1935 for whom he played 106 matches.

Aston, John (b. Newport 29.7.30; d. 30.11.92). Made six appearances for his local club, Newport County, scoring once.

Atyeo, John (b. Dilton 7.2.32; d. 9.6.93). One of the few players from the lower Divisions to have represented England at full international level. A centre-forward in the old tradition, he joined Portsmouth as an amateur in 1950. But having made only two League appearances, John moved on to Bristol City in 1951, for whom he played until 1965. He made 597 League appearances for the west country club and scored 315 goals. John won six caps for England and also represented his country at Youth, Under-23 and B level, as well as being selected for The Football League.

Bailey, Roy (b. Epsom 26.5.32; d. 4.93). Roy made 118 League appearances for Crystal Palace between 1949 and 1955, before serving Ipswich Town until 1964 with great distinction. He kept goal under the managership of Alf Ramsey when the Suffolk club won the Second and First Division Championships with great style in 1961 and 1962 respectively. Father of former Manchester United and England goalkeeper, Gary.

Bakhramov, Tofik (b. 1927; d. 3.93). The General Secretary of football for his native Azerbaijan, he achieved overnight fame as the linesman who signalled that Geoff Hurst's goalbound shot in the 1966 World Cup Final had crossed the line. He refereed Peru v Morocco in the 1970 World Cup and the first leg of the 1972 UEFA Cup Final between Wolves and Tottenham.

Brown, Ben (b. 3.1.26; d. 28.9.92). Was goalkeeper in the Pegasus sides that won the 1951 and 1953 Amateur Cup Finals. Won seven caps for England as an amateur, he also represented the British Olympic team in 1952.

Bulling, James (b. West Bridgford 12.2.09; d. 13.10.92). Signed by Nottingham Forest in 1926, he moved into non league football without making a first team appearance. Joined Leicester City in 1930, then left to serve Wrexham from 1932 until 1936.

Candlin, Maurice (b. Jarrow 11.11.21; d. 31.12.92). A centre-half who saw service with Clydebank and Partick Thistle before joining Northampton Town in 1949. After 138 appearances, he moved on to Shrewsbury Town, where he played a further 69 games.

Caton, Tommy (b. Liverpool 6.10.62; d. 30.4.93). A former England Under-21 international defender, who regularly skippered his country at intermediate level, following Schoolboy and Youth recognition. He made 164 first team appearances for Manchester City between 1979 and 1983 before moving on to Arsenal, Oxford United and Charlton Athletic.

Chapman, Red (b. Shepherds Bush 7.9.21; d. 4.7.92). Made one appearance for Notts County during wartime before becoming a part-time professional with Queens Park Rangers, for whom he won a Third Division (South) Championship medal in 1947/48 and made a total of 104 appearances.

Cook, Billy (b. 1909; d. 11.12.92). A Northern Ireland international full-back, who starred for Celtic and Everton in the thirties, and won fifteen caps for his country. After hanging up his boots, he later took up coaching positions in Norway and Peru.

Cooper, Len (b. Lower Gornal 11.5.36; d. 11.92). An England Youth international who played on the left wing. He joined Wolves in 1953 but, after failing to make the first team, he moved to Walsall in 1956.

Crayston, Jack (b. Grange-over-Sands 9.10.10; d. 26.12.92). Known as 'Gentleman Jack', this elegant half-back spent 24 years at Highbury, having signed for Arsenal in 1934 for £5250 from Bradford Park Avenue. He was a member of the Championship winning sides of 1935 and 1938 and the victorious FA Cup Final team of 1936. Formerly with Barrow, Jack won 8 caps for England. After injury in 1943, he retired and became Assistant Manager at Highbury in the immediate post war years, before taking over the helm in 1956. He resigned in 1958, then managed Doncaster Rovers, where he stayed until 1961.

Croker, Ted (b. Kingston 13.2.24; d. 25.12.92). Former Secretary of the FA, who was the first professional footballer to be appointed. A one-time RAF flying instructor, he survived an air crash on the Pennines in 1945 and broke both ankles. He followed his brother Peter to Charlton Athletic in the late forties and played eight games in the 1950–51 season at centre-half. His recall to the RAF when the Korean War broke out effectively ended his full-time career. He subsequently spent three years at Headington United before a broken leg finally forced him out of the game. He then became a qualified FA coach and went into industry, setting up his own engineering business in 1960. Replaced Denis Follows in 1973 and held the post of Secretary until 1989.

Curtis, Ernie (b. Cardiff 6.7; d. 11.92). Played for Cardiff City in the 1927 FA Cup Final, before moving on to Birmingham City a year later, whom he represented in the 1931 Cup Final. Returned to Cardiff in 1933, before joining Coventry City and ending his playing career at Hartlepool in 1938. A soldier in the Royal Artillery, he was a Japanese prisoner of war for four years.

Dimbleby, Stanley (b. Killingholme 1917; d. 17.10.92). A half-back with Hull City from 1935 to 1937, where he made 21 appearances, before moving on to Grimsby Town. At Blundell Park, however, he didn't play a League game.

Dixon, Mike (b. Reading 12.,10.43; d. 30.1.93). An England Schools international goalkeeper, Mike made 112 appearances for Reading between 1962 and 1967, before moving on to Aldershot where he stayed until 1970. Became Secretary and Treasurer of Wokingham, followed by a similar post at Tilehurst.

Done, Cyril (b. Bootle 21.10.20; d. 24.2.93). A centre-forward, he joined Liverpool in 1938, scoring seven goals for the reserves in one of his early games. Stayed with Liverpool until 1952, where he won a League Championship medal in 1947, before moving on to Tranmere Rovers (61 goals in only 87 appearances), then Port Vale. He later managed Skelmersdale United.

Doyle, Brian (b. Manchester 15.7.30; d. 22.12.92). A talented full-back with Stoke City, Exeter City (100 League appearances) and Bristol Rovers, whose career spanned the years 1952–1959. He later took coaching positions in Kuwait and Finland.

Dwyer, Noel (b. Dublin 30.10.34; d. 1993). Won 14 caps for Eire and kept goal for five League clubs in a career that spanned over 12 years. Noel signed for Wolves in 1953 and went on to serve West Ham United, Swansea, Plymouth Argyle and Charlton Athletic.

Earl, Sidney (b. Norwich 1902; d. 11.92). Scored on his debut for the Canaries in 1924, he made 30 appearances for his local club. A left-half, Sid is believed to be the oldest former Norwich player.

Edwards, George (b. Great Yarmouth 1.4.18; d. 21.1.93). Was Aston Villa's top soccer during war-time football, scoring 95 goals in 121 games. After the war, he continued to be amongst the goals for Villa, scoring a further 34 in 138 games before retiring in 1950. Formerly with Norwich City.

Follon, Gerry (b. 1919; d. 9.3.93). A full-back with Dundee, he won League Cup winners medals in 1952 and 1953 and a Scottish Cup runners-up medal in 1952. Later played for St. Johnstone and was capped by the Scottish League.

Froggatt, Jack (b. Sheffield 17.11.22; d. 17.2.93). A prominent member of Pompey's title-winning teams of 1949 and 1950. He began his career as a centre-forward, but converted to outside-left and was versatile enough to play in the centre of the Pompey defence, alongside the two Jimmys — Dickinson and Scoular. Capped 13 times for England at centre-half and outside-left, but opportunities on the flank were limited, due to the wing wizardry of Tom Finney. Played 279 League games (65 goals) for Pompey, before a spell at Leicester City (143 League appearances and 18 goals) between 1954 and 1957 completed a fine career.

Granville, Norman (b. Newport 25.11.19; d. 16.12.92). A forward who played in Scotland, Northern Ireland, Wales and England, for Raith Rovers (1944/45), Cliftonville (1945), Newport County (1945) and Exeter City (1946/47), before moving on to Gillingham in 1949.

Gray, Tommy (b. 1913; d. 24.12.92). Centre-half with Morton, Dundee and Arbroath, before becoming manager of the latter in 1955. Also managed Dundee United and was assistant at St Johnstone before becoming a scout with Rangers.

Happel, Ernst (b. Vienna 29.11.25; d. 14.11.92). Won seven Championships and the domestic cup with Rapid Vienna and won 51 caps for Austria as a player. Had an equally distinguished career as a manager, taking Holland to the 1978 World Cup Finals. Among some of the many top clubs he managed were Feyenoord and Hamburg, both of whom won European Finals under his guidance. From December, 1991, until his death, he had been in charge of the Austrian national team.

Higgins, George (b. Dundee 16.6.25; d. 13.4.93). A full-back who joined Blackburn Rovers from Lochee Harp, then moved on to Bolton Wanderers in 1951 and then to Grimsby Town in 1954. George was player manager of Scarborough, before returning to Grimsby as trainer, the joined Graham Taylor at Lincoln City for a short spell as assistant manager.

Hitchen, Harry (b. Liverpool 22.10.22; d. 9.4.93). Joined New Brighton in 1946 and after 70 League games moved on to Sheffield United, whom he helped win the Second Division Championship in 1953. Ended his playing career with Bury.

Holley, Tom (b. Wolverhampton 15.11.13; d. 10.92). A dominating centre-half, he joined Sunderland, for whom his father had played, before moving on to Barnsley. He completed his playing career at Leeds United retiring, to became a journalist.

Horsfall, George (b. Australia 19.9.24; d. 29.8.92). Had two spells as a player with Southampton, sandwiched in between with one at Southend United. Following the end of his first class playing career in 1955, he became a coach at The Dell and spent a further 34 years with the club until his retirement in 1989.

Humphries, W. Wilson (b. 1.7.28; d. 22.10.92). Capped by Scotland, he was the youngest player in the Motherwell side tht won the Scottish Cup in 1952. He also played for St Mirren, Dundee United and Hamilton. He later became coach at Motherwell and Hibernian, manager at St Mirren in the early seventies, then assistant with Airdrie.

James, Joe (b. 1910; d. 1.93). Made 240 appearances in the centre of the Brentford defence between 1929 and 1946, during which period the Bees were promoted to the First Division.

Jeffrey, Robert (b. Aberdeen 24.5.20; d. 8.8.92). Signed by Derby from Aberdeen, he failed to make a League appearance for the Rams, moving on to Exeter in 1947, where he played seven times. Had a spell with Montrose and later played for Peterhead and Buckie Thistle.

Jones, Sam (b. Lurgan 14.9.11; d. 7.3.93). A Northern Ireland international who played for Distillery, Sam made his international debut in 1933 against England. Moved on to Blackpool, whom he was with until 1946.

Matthew, Andrew (b. Kirkcaldy 1932; d. 4.10.92). Joined East Fife in 1949 making 194 appearances, scoring 31 goals, and winning a League Cup medal in 1954. Signed for Rangers in 1958 and played in their title winning side of '58/59. The following season he moved on to Raith Rovers. He also had spells with Dunfermline and Cowdenbeath and was the first player to represent all four Fife senior teams.

The late Bobby Moore with Brazil's Pele after the memorable 1970 World Cup match in which England were beaten 1-0 in Guadalajara, Mexico. (Action Images)

Millar, Larry (b. ?; d. 8.92). Joined East Fife from Kings Park in 1937 and won a Scottish Cup medal with them a year later. He also played for Falkirk, Albion Rovers and St Mirren.

Mitchell, Bobby (b. Glasgow 16.8.24; d. 8.4.93). Great entertainer and a folk hero with Newcastle United fans, for whom he starred in three FA Cup Finals in the fifties. Transferred from Third Lanark in 1949 for £16,000 which, at the time, was a record fee for a winger. Nicknamed 'Bobby Dazzler' on Tyneside, he played alongside Jackie Milburn, Joe Harvey, Ernie Taylor, Jimmy Scoular, Vic Keeble and the Robledo brothers. Bobby made a total of 408 appearances for United (113 goals), won two caps for Scotland and, such was his popularity, 41,000 fans supported his testimonial match in 1961, the year he moved on to Berwick Rangers. Later, he became Player-Manager of Gateshead.

Mogford, Reg (b. Newport 12.6.19; d. 28.9.92). A forward with Newport (20 League games, 9 goals), he guested for Reading, Tottenham Hotspur and Luton Town during the war.

Moore, Bobby (b. Barking 12.4.41; d. 24.2.93). The revered former captain of England who, in 1966, led his country to their greatest triumph, victory in the World Cup Final. A defender who played the game with a great sense of fair play, combined with calm authority, he had few equals. Winner of 108 England caps, he played in over 1,000 club matches at senior level. Bobby made his debut for West Ham United in 1958 and led them to victory in the 1964 FA Cup Final, then followed that triumph with European Cup Winners' Cup success a year later. A year after England's World Cup Final win, he was awarded the OBE. He also won the Footballer of the Year award in 1963–64. Bobby joined Fulham in 1973 and, after captaining them in the 1975 FA Cup Final, ironically, against West Ham, he retired. He served Southend United between 1983 and 1986, culminating as Manager.

Morris, Henry (b. Dundee 17.12.19; d. 13.3.93). Scored 154 goals in 177 appearances for East Fife, including a goal in the 1949 League Cup Final. That same year, he won a cap for Scotland and scored in an 8-2 victory over Northern Ireland.

Murray, Ken (b. Darlington 2.4.28; d. 8.1.93). A forward, Ken joined his local club in 1950 from Bishop Auckland and scored 19 goals in 70 appearances. In 1953, he moved on to Mansfield Town and scored a further 60 goals in 138 League games. He went when on to play for Oldham, Wrexham (where he won a Welsh Cup winners medal) and Gateshead.

Neuberger Hermann (b. Saarland 12.12.19; d. 27.9.92). Vice present of FIFA, president of FIFA's organising committee and president of the German federation.

Parkin, Herbert (b. 10.4.20; d. 1.93). A full-back, who played 35 League games for Sheffield United between 1947 and 1950 and 56 matches for Chesterfield in the early fifties.

Peat, William (b. 1920; d. 24.3.93). Joined Partick Thistle in 1938 before signing for Hibernian in 1941. After the war Billy moved to St Johnstone for £4,000 and scored 31 goals in 129 matches.

Phillips, Williams (b. Maerdy 1911; d. 1.9.92). Had brief a spell as a youngster at Tottenham before joining Merthyr Tydfil, where he was spotted by Dundee in the mid-thirties. Moved to Hearts before the outbreak of war and, after guesting for a number of clubs during hostilities, he returned to Tynecastle after the war. Later played for St Johnstone and Huntly in the Highland League.

Pritchard, Roy (b. Dawley 9.5.25; d. 1.93). A full-back, who joined Wolves after the war and played over 200 games in the old gold, including the FA Cup Final victory of 1949. In 1955, he was transferred to Aston Villa, then moved on to Notts County, before ending his first class career with Port Vale.

Reed, Hugh (b. Alexandria 23.8.50; d. 11.92). A clever winger, who began his career with West Bromwich in 1967 and then, in the early seventies began his travels, taking in Plymouth, Brentford, Crewe, Huddersfield and Hartlepool.

Rees, Mel (b. Cardiff 25.1.67; d. 30.5.93). Former Welsh Youth international goalkeeper, who served Cardiff City, Watford, Crewe Alexandra, Southampton, Leyton Orient, West Bromwich Albion, Norwich City and Sheffield United. The 26-year-old died after a courageous fight against cancer.

Rogers, Alf (b. Sheffield 10.4.21; d. 28.10.92). Inside-forward for Sheffield Wednesday scoring 39 goals from 125 senior games between 1940 and 1950. Played in the promotion team of 1949–50 but his career ended prematurely with injury.

Savin, Keith (b. Oxford 5.6.29; d. 18.12.92). Keith signed for Derby County in 1950 from his local club, Oxford City. Played 65 League games at full-back for the Rams, before moving on to Mansfield Town in 1957, for whom he played 68 games. Later, he played for Nuneaton Borough and Bourne Town.

Seddon, William (b. Clapton, 28.7.01; d. 1.93). Made 75 appearances for Arsenal, including the Final of the 1930 FA Cup, when he won a winners' medal. Billy was also a member of the 1931 Championship winning side. He was transferred to Grimsby in 1932 and, after making 20 appearances, he moved on to Luton Town, where injury ended his career.

Smith, Gavin (b. Cambuslang 25.9.17; d. 10.92). A right-winger, who joined Barnsley from Dumbarton and made 257 League appearances for the Tykes, scoring 35 goals, between 1946 and 1953.

Smith, Les (b. Tamworth 16.11.21; d. 1.93). Wing-half signed by Mansfield from Bilsthorpe Colliery in November 1945. Made 35 League appearances before moving to Ilkeston Town.

Smith, Walter (b. Hilltown 1922; d. 19.9.92). Played for Scottish Schools and learnt his football with the well known Lochee Harp juniors, before playing for Dundee North End and Hibernian.

Stelling, Jack (b. Washington, Co Durham 23.1.24; d. 29.3.93). A full-back, who served Sunderland between 1946 and 1955, making 259 League appearances and scoring eight goals.

Swinscoe, Tommy (b. Mansfield 16.10.19; 2.93). Goalscoring centre-forward who joined Chesterfield in 1942 and moved to Stockport County in February 1948, scoring 30 League goals in 73 matches.

Thornhill, Dennis (b. Draycott 5.7.23; d. 8.92). Played 65 games during war-time for Wolves, before signing for Southend in 1948. After only 11 games, injury forced his premature retirement.

Traynor, Tommy (b. Bonnybridge 1943; d. 22.12.92). A winger, who spent eight years with Hearts before moving on to Dundee United in 1970. In 1974, he left to join Falkirk, then spent a season at Morton. Later, was coach at Cowdenbeath, before emigrating to Australia.

Trigg, Cyril (b. Meacham 8.4.17; d. 9.4.93). A centre-forward who played 268 games for Birmingham City and scored 67 goals for his one and only League club. Cyril won a Second Division Championsip medal in 1948.

Waddell, Willie (b. Forth 7.3.21; d. 13.10.92). A pacey, immensely skilful winger with Rangers, Willie was capped 17 times by Scotland between 1947 and 1955. He managed Kilmarnock in the mid-sixties and took over the helm at Rangers in 1969, leading the club to European Cup-Winners' Cup success in 1972. He later became General Manager at Ibrox Park.

Walker, Tommy (b. Livingston 26.5.15; d. 11.1.93). A Scottish international inside forward who won 20 caps and the respect of football fans all over Britain. Played for Hearts before and after the war, then journeyed south to sign for Chelsea in 1946, where he hit 23 goals in 97 games. Later he managed Hearts, Raith Rovers and Dunfermline, before becoming a director of Hearts. He was awarded the OBE in 1960.

Ward, Tim (b. Cheltenham 17.10.18; d. 28.1.93). Capped twice by England, this talented wing-half played a total of 238 games for Derby County, for whom he signed in 1937. In 1950, he moved to Barnsley, before becoming player-manager of Exeter City for a short period. He returned to Barnsley as manager then, in 1960, took over the helm at Grimsby Town. Two years later, Tim was in charge of Derby County, where he stayed until 1967, then spent a year as manager of Carlisle United.

Whyte, George (b. Cowdenbeath 1909; d. 23.10.92). Started out with Dunfermline, before moving to Rhyl, then Accrington Stanley. In 1931, he joined Lincoln City and made 314 appearances, scoring 31 goals.

Wilkie, Ray (b. 1941; d. 28.11.92). Formerly a player with Spennymoor United, Tow Law and West Auckland Town. Won an Amateur Cup medal with Crook Town in 1959. Managed Durham City, North Shields and Gateshead, before taking Barrow to Wembley, where they won the FA Trophy in 1990. He also led the club to promotion to the GM Vauxhall Conference.

Wilson, Hugh (b. Ballingry 1934; d. 2.9.92). Started with Hibernian as a teenager before signing for East Fife, making 20 appearances and scoring three goals. Managed Alloa and Cowdenbeath and later scouted for St Johnstone and Forfar.

Wookey, Ken (Junior) (b. Newport 30.12.46; d. 16.12.92). A centre-forward who played for his local club, County, scoring five goals in 56 League games. Went on to play for Port Vale and Workington and had latterly been manager of Shaftesbury Town. Survived by his father Ken, who was a winger with Newport, Bristol Rovers, Swansea and Ipswich between 1946 and 1950.

Wragg, Dick (b. 23.5.10; d. 6.11.92). Served for nearly 20 years as Chairman of the Football Association's International committee, he was also a life vice-president of the FA and Football League. He was a UEFA committee member, served on the League Management committee, and was on the FA Council from 1963. He became a director of Sheffield United in 1953 and was Chairman at the club between 1969 and 1974.

Wright, Douglas (b. Southend 29.4.17; d. 12.92). Began at Southend, then signed for Newcastle, for whom he made 84 appearances. In 1948, he joined Lincoln City where he stayed until 1954, making 233 League appearances, and leading them to the Third Division (North) Championship in 1952. Later, he managed Blyth Spartans. A wing-half, he played once for England — against Norway — in 1938.

James, Wyllie (b. Saltcoats 15.10.27; d. 27.6.92). Started out with Kilmarnock, then joined Southport in 1950. After 15 appearances and one goal, he signed for Wrexham, where he played a further 20 games and scored four times.

THE FA CARLING PREMIERSHIP
and
FOOTBALL LEAGUE FIXTURES 1993–94

Copyright © of The Football League Limited & The FA Premier League Limited.

Saturday 14 August 1993
FA Carling Premiership
Arsenal v Coventry C
Aston Villa v QPR
Chelsea v Blackburn R
Liverpool v Sheffield W
Manchester C v Leeds U
Newcastle U v Tottenham H
Oldham Ath v Ipswich T
Sheffield U v Swindon T
Southampton v Everton
West Ham U v Wimbledon

Football League Division 1
Barnsley v WBA
Charlton Ath v Birmingham C
Crystal Palace v Tranmere R
Derby Co v Sunderland
Grimsby T v Bolton W
Leicester C v Peterborough U
Luton T v Watford
Notts Co v Middlesbrough
Oxford U v Portsmouth
Stoke C v Millwall
Wolverhampton W v Bristol C

Football League Division 2
Barnet v Hull C
Bradford C v Brighton & HA
Brentford v Exeter C
Bristol R v AFC Bournemouth
Burnley v Port Vale
Cambridge U v Blackpool
Cardiff C v Leyton O
Hartlepool U v Fulham
Huddersfield T v Reading
Plymouth Arg v Stockport Co
Wrexham v Rotherham U
York C v Swansea C

Football League Division 3
Bury v Northampton T
Carlisle U v Wycombe W
Chester City v Doncaster R
Colchester U v Lincoln C
Darlington v Rochdale
Gillingham v Chesterfield
Hereford U v Scarborough
Mansfield T v Shrewsbury T
Preston NE v Crewe Alex
Walsall v Torquay U
Wigan Ath v Scunthorpe U

Sunday 15 August 1993
FA Carling Premiership
Norwich C v Manchester U (4.00)

Football League Division 1
Southend U v Nottingham F

Monday 16 August 1993
FA Carling Premiership
Tottenham H v Arsenal (8.00)

Tuesday 17 August 1993
FA Carling Premiership
Everton v Manchester C
Ipswich T v Southampton (7.45)
Leeds U v West Ham U (7.45)
Wimbledon v Chelsea (8.00)

Football League Division 1
Peterborough U v Barnsley (7.45)
Portsmouth v Charlton Ath (7.45)

Wednesday 18 August 1993
FA Carling Premiership
Blackburn R v Norwich C (7.45)
Coventry C v Newcastle U (7.45)
Manchester U v Sheffield U (8.00)
QPR v Liverpool (7.45)
Sheffield W v Aston Villa (7.45)
Swindon T v Oldham Ath (7.45)

Football League Division 1
Nottingham F v Derby Co

Saturday 21 August 1993
FA Carling Premiership
Blackburn R v Oldham Ath
Coventry C v West Ham U
Everton v Sheffield U
Ipswich T v Chelsea
Leeds U v Norwich C
Manchester U v Newcastle U
QPR v Southampton
Sheffield W v Arsenal
Tottenham H v Manchester C
Wimbledon v Aston Villa

Football League Division 1
Bolton W v Stoke C
Bristol C v Crystal Palace
Middlesbrough v Derby Co
Millwall v Southend U
Nottingham F v Grimsby T
Peterborough U v Notts Co
Portsmouth v Luton T
Sunderland v Charlton Ath
Tranmere R v Leicester C
Watford v Barnsley
WBA v Oxford U

Football League Division 2
AFC Bournemouth v Bradford C
Blackpool v Brentford
Brighton & HA v Hartlepool U
Exeter C v York C
Fulham v Cardiff C
Hull C v Plymouth Arg
Leyton O v Bristol R
Port Vale v Barnet
Reading v Burnley
Rotherham U v Huddersfield T
Stockport Co v Cambridge U
Swansea C v Wrexham

Football League Division 3
Chesterfield v Hereford U
Crewe Alex v Colchester U
Doncaster R v Carlisle U
Lincoln C v Darlington
Rochdale v Gillingham
Scarborough v Preston NE
Scunthorpe U v Bury
Shrewsbury T v Walsall
Torquay U v Wigan Ath
Wycombe W v Chester C

Sunday 22 August 1993
FA Carling Premiership
Swindon Town v Liverpool (4.00)

Football League Division 1
Birmingham C v Wolverhampton W

Monday 23 August 1993
FA Carling Premiership
Aston Villa v Manchester U (8.00)

Tuesday 24 August 1993
FA Carling Premiership
Arsenal v Leeds U (7.45)
Manchester C v Blackburn R (7.45)
Oldham Ath v Coventry C
Sheffield U v Wimbledon (7.45)

Football League Division 1
Barnsley v Middlesbrough (7.45)
Charlton Ath v Tranmere R (7.45)
Crystal Palace v Nottingham F (7.45)
Grimsby T v Portsmouth (7.45)
Wolverhampton W v Millwall

Wednesday 25 August 1993
FA Carling Premiership
Chelsea v QPR (7.45)
Liverpool v Tottenham H (7.45)
Newcastle U v Everton (7.45)
Norwich C v Ipswich T (7.45)
Southampton v Swindon T
West Ham U v Sheffield W (7.45)

Friday 27 August 1993
FA Carling Premiership
Manchester C v Coventry C (7.45)

Saturday 28 August 1993
FA Carling Premiership
Arsenal v Everton
Aston Villa v Tottenham H
Chelsea v Sheffield W
Liverpool v Leeds U
Norwich C v Swindon T
Oldham Ath v Wimbledon
Sheffield U v Ipswich T
Southampton v Manchester U
West Ham U v QPR

Football League Division 1
Barnsley v Birmingham C
Charlton Ath v Bolton W
Crystal Palace v Portsmouth
Derby Co v Bristol C
Grimsby T v Tranmere R
Leicester C v Millwall
Luton T v Nottingham F
Notts Co v Sunderland
Oxford U v Watford
Southend U v Peterborough U
Stoke C v WBA
Wolverhampton W v
Middlesbrough

Football League Division 2
Barnet Swansea C
Bradford C v Exeter C

Brentford v Reading
Bristol R v Fulham
Burnley v Leyton O
Cambridge U v Hull C
Cardiff C v Brighton & HA
Hartlepool U v AFC Bournemouth
Huddersfield T v Stockport Co
Plymouth Arg v Port Vale
Wrexham v Blackpool
York C v Rotherham U

Football League Division 3
Bury v Crewe Alex
Carlisle U v Rochdale
Chester C v Chesterfield
Colchester U v Northampton T
Darlington v Torquay U
Gillingham v Scarborough
Hereford U v Lincoln C
Mansfield T v Scunthorpe U
Preston NE v Shrewsbury T
Walsall v Doncaster R
Wigan Ath v Wycombe W

Sunday 29 August 1993

FA Carling Premiership
Newcastle U v Blackburn R (4.00)

Monday 30 August 1993

FA Carling Premiership
Leeds U v Oldham Ath (8.00)

Tuesday 31 August 1993

FA Carling Premiership
Everton v Aston Villa
Ipswich T v Newcastle U (7.45)
Wimbledon v Southampton (8.00)

Football League Division 1
Birmingham C v Crystal Palace
(7.45)
Bolton W v Oxford U

Football League Division 2
AFC Bournemouth v York C (7.45)
Blackpool v Plymouth Arg
Exeter C v Cardiff C
Fulham v Wrexham (7.45)
Hull C v Brentford
Leyton O v Hartlepool U (7.45)
Port Vale v Cambridge U (7.45)
Rotherham U v Burnley
Stockport Co v Bradford C
Swansea C v Huddersfield T

Football League Division 3
Chesterfield v Mansfield T
Colchester U v Shrewsbury T (7.45)
Crewe Alex v Northampton T
Darlington v Scarborough
Gillingham v Doncaster R (7.45)
Hereford U v Wycombe W
Lincoln C v Chester C
Preston NE v Bury
Rochdale v Wigan Ath
Torquay U v Carlisle U
Walsall v Scunthorpe U (7.45)

Wednesday 1 September 1993

FA Carling Premiership
Blackburn R v Arsenal (7.45)
Coventry C v Liverpool (7.45)
Manchester U v West Ham U (8.00)
QPR v Sheffield U (7.45)
Sheffield W v Norwich C (7.45)
Swindon T v Manchester C (7.45)
Tottenham H v Chelsea (7.45)

Football League Division 1
WBA v Southend U

Football League Division 2
Brighton & HA v Bristol R (7.45)
Reading v Barnet (7.45)

Saturday 4 September 1993

Football League Division 1
Birmingham C v Derby Co
Bolton W v Crystal Palace
Bristol C v Southend U
Middlesbrough v Leicester City
Millwall v Barnsley
Nottingham F v Oxford U
Peterborough U v Grimsby T
Portsmouth v Stoke C
Sunderland v Luton T
Tranmere R v Notts Co
Watford v Charlton Ath
WBA v Wolverhampton W

Football League Division 2
AFC Bournemouth v Burnley
Blackpool v Barnet
Brighton & HA v Huddersfield T
Exeter C v Hartlepool U
Fulham v Bradford C
Hull C v Bristol R
Leyton O v York C
Port Vale v Cardiff C
Reading v Cambridge U
Rotherham U v Brentford
Stockport Co v Wrexham
Swansea C v Plymouth Arg

Football League Division 3
Chesterfield v Darlington
Crewe Alex v Mansfield T
Doncaster R v Wigan Ath
Lincoln C v Preston NE
Northampton T v Walsall
Rochdale v Chester C
Scarborough v Carlisle U
Scunthorpe U v Hereford U
Shrewsbury T v Bury
Torquay U v Colchester U
Wycombe W v Gillingham

Tuesday 7 September 1993

Football League Division 1
Sunderland v Grimsby T
Watford v Wolverhampton W (7.45)

Saturday 11 September 1993

FA Carling Premiership
Arsenal v Ipswich T
Aston Villa v Coventry C
Chelsea v Manchester U
Manchester C v QPR
Norwich C v Wimbledon
Oldham Ath v Everton
Sheffield U v Tottenham H
Southampton v Leeds U
West Ham U v Swindon T

Football League Division 1
Barnsley v Nottingham F
Charlton Ath v Millwall
Crystal Palace v Sunderland
Derby Co v Peterborough U
Grimsby T v Watford
Leicester C v Birmingham C
Luton T v Bolton W
Notts Co v WBA
Oxford U v Bristol C
Southend U v Middlesbrough
Stoke C v Tranmere R
Wolverhampton W v Portsmouth

Football League Division 2
Barnet v AFC Bournemouth
Bradford C v Blackpool
Brentford v Swansea C
Bristol R v Port Vale
Burnley v Fulham
Cambridge U v Rotherham U
Cardiff C v Hull C
Hartlepool U v Stockport Co
Huddersfield T v Exeter C
Plymouth Arg v Leyton O

Wrexham v Reading
York C v Brighton & HA

Football League Division 3
Bury v Wycombe W
Carlisle U v Chesterfield
Chester C v Scunthorpe U
Colchester U v Rochdale
Darlington v Shrewsbury T
Gillingham v Torquay U
Hereford U v Northampton T
Mansfield T v Lincoln C
Preston NE v Doncaster R
Walsall v Crewe Alex
Wigan Ath v Scarborough

Sunday 12 September 1993

FA Carling Premiership
Liverpool v Blackburn R (4.00)

Monday 13 September 1993

FA Carling Premiership
Newcastle U v Sheffield W (8.00)

Tuesday 14 September 1993

Football League Division 1
Bristol C v Leicester C (7.45)
Middlesbrough v Stoke City (7.45)
Tranmere R v Luton T

Football League Division 2
Barnet v Fulham (7.45)
Brentford v Leyton O (7.45)
Burnley v Brighton & HA
Cambridge U v Swansea C (7.45)
Cardiff C v AFC Bournemouth
Hartlepool U v Blackpool
Huddersfield T v Port Vale
Plymouth Argyle v Rotherham U
(7.45)
Wrexham v Hull C
York C v Stockport Co

Wednesday 15 September 1993

Football League Division 2
Bradford C v Reading
Bristol R v Exeter C (8.00)

Friday 17 September 1993

Football League Division 3
Doncaster R v Mansfield T

Saturday 18 September 1993

FA Carling Premiership
Blackburn R v West Ham U
Coventry C v Chelsea
Everton v Liverpool
Ipswich T v Aston Villa
Leeds U v Sheffield U
QPR v Norwich City
Sheffield W v Southampton
Swindon T v Newcastle U
Tottenham H v Oldham Ath
Wimbledon v Manchester C

Football League Division 1
Birmingham C v Grimsby T
Bolton W v Leicester C
Bristol C v Charlton Ath
Middlesbrough v Luton T
Millwall v Derby Co
Nottingham F v Stoke C
Peterborough U v Oxford U
Portsmouth v Southend U
Sunderland v Wolverhampton W
Tranmere R v Barnsley
Watford v Notts Co
WBA v Crystal Palace

Football League Division 2
AFC Bournemouth v Cambridge U
Blackpool v Cardiff C
Brighton & HA v Brentford

Exeter C v Wrexham
Fulham v York C
Hull C v Huddersfield T
Leyton O v Barnet
Port Vale v Hartlepool U
Reading v Plymouth Arg
Rotherham U v Bristol R
Stockport Co v Burnley
Swansea C v Bradford C

Football League Division 3
Chesterfield v Walsall
Crewe Alex v Darlington
Lincoln C v Bury
Northampton T v Wigan Ath
Rochdale v Hereford U
Scarborough v Chester C
Scunthorpe U v Carlisle U
Shrewsbury T v Gillingham
Torquay U v Preston NE
Wycombe W v Colchester U

Sunday 19 September 1993
FA Carling Premiership
Manchester U v Arsenal (4.00)

Saturday 25 September 1993
FA Carling Premiership
Arsenal v Southampton
Blackburn R v Sheffield W
Chelsea v Liverpool
Coventry C v Leeds U
Everton v Norwich C
Manchester U v Swindon T
Newcastle U v West Ham U
Oldham Ath v Aston Villa
Sheffield U v Manchester C

Football League Division 1
Barnsley v Leicester C
Birmingham C v Luton T
Bolton W v Nottingham F
Charlton Ath v Crystal Palace
Grimsby T v Wolverhampton W
Notts Co v Derby Co
Peterborough U v Millwall
Portsmouth v Bristol C
Stoke C v Southend U
Tranmere R v Oxford U
Watford v Sunderland
WBA v Middlesbrough

Football League Division 2
Blackpool v AFC Bournemouth
Bradford C v Cambridge U
Brentford v Port Vale
Bristol R v Burnley
Cardiff C v Plymouth Arg
Exeter C v Swansea C
Hartlepool U v York C
Huddersfield T v Fulham
Leyton O v Brighton & HA
Reading v Hull C
Stockport Co v Rotherham U
Wrexham v Barnet

Football League Division 3
Chester C v Carlisle U
Colchester U v Bury
Darlington v Walsall
Gillingham v Scunthorpe U
Hereford U v Wigan Ath
Lincoln C v Northampton T
Mansfield T v Preston NE
Rochdale v Chesterfield
Scarborough v Shrewsbury T
Torquay U v Crewe Alex
Wycombe W v Doncaster R

Sunday 26 September 1993
FA Carling Premiership
Ipswich T v Tottenham H (4.00)

Monday 27 September 1993
FA Carling Premiership
Wimbledon v QPR (8.00)

Friday 1 October 1993
Football League Division 2
Swansea C v Reading

Saturday 2 October 1993
FA Carling Premiership
Aston Villa v Newcastle U
Leeds U v Wimbledon
Liverpool v Arsenal
Manchester C v Oldham Ath
Norwich C v Coventry C
QPR v Ipswich T
Sheffield W v Manchester U
Southampton v Sheffield U
Swindon T v Blackburn R
West Ham U v Chelsea

Football League Division 1
Bristol C v Bolton W
Crystal Palace v Stoke C
Derby Co v WBA
Leicester C v Notts Co
Luton T v Barnsley
Middlesbrough v Birmingham C
Millwall v Watford
Nottingham F v Portsmouth
Oxford U v Grimsby T
Southend U v Tranmere R
Sunderland v Peterborough U
Wolverhampton W v Charlton Ath

Football League Division 2
AFC Bournemouth v Stockport Co
Barnet v Bristol R
Brighton & HA v Exeter C
Burnley v Hartlepool U
Cambridge U v Brentford
Fulham v Leyton O
Hull C v Bradford C
Plymouth Arg v Huddersfield T
Port Vale v Wrexham
Rotherham U v Blackpool
York C v Cardiff C

Football League Division 3
Bury v Mansfield T
Carlisle U v Gillingham
Chesterfield v Wycombe W
Crewe Alex v Lincoln C
Doncaster R v Rochdale
Northampton T v Darlington
Preston NE v Colchester U
Scunthorpe U v Scarborough
Shrewsbury T v Torquay U
Walsall v Hereford U
Wigan Ath v Chester C

Sunday 3 October 1993
FA Carling Premiership
Tottenham H v Everton (4.00)

Saturday 9 October 1993
Football League Division 1
Barnsley v Charlton Ath
Derby Co v Luton T
Grimsby T v Southend U
Leicester C v Crystal Palace
Millwall v WBA
Notts Co v Bristol C
Oxford U v Stoke C
Peterborough U v Portsmouth
Sunderland v Birmingham C
Tranmere R v Bolton W
Watford v Middlesbrough
Wolverhampton W v Nottingham F

Football League Division 2
Brighton & HA v Stockport Co
Bristol R v Bradford C

Burnley v Plymouth Arg
Exeter C v Reading
Fulham v AFC Bournemouth
Hartlepool U v Brentford
Leyton O v Rotherham U
Port Vale v Hull C
Swansea C v Blackpool
Wrexham v Cambridge U
York C v Huddersfield T

Football League Division 3
Bury v Wigan Ath
Colchester U v Scunthorpe U
Crewe Alex v Hereford U
Darlington v Chester C
Lincoln C v Doncaster R
Mansfield T v Scarborough
Northampton T v Wycombe W
Preston NE v Chesterfield
Shrewsbury T v Carlisle U
Torquay U v Rochdale
Walsall v Gillingham

Sunday 10 October 1993
Football League Division 2
Barnet v Cardiff C (1.00)

Tuesday 12 October 1993
Football League Division 3
Northampton T v Mansfield T

Saturday 16 October 1993
FA Carling Premiership
Arsenal v Manchester C
Chelsea v Norwich C
Coventry C v Southampton
Liverpool v Oldham Ath
Manchester U v Tottenham H
Newcastle U v QPR
Sheffield W v Wimbledon
Swindon T v Everton
West Ham U v Aston Villa

Football League Division 1
Birmingham C v Watford
Bolton W v Millwall
Bristol C v Barnsley
Charlton Ath v Leicester C
Crystal Palace v Wolverhampton W
Luton T v Notts Co
Middlesbrough v Sunderland
Nottingham F v Tranmere R
Portsmouth v Derby Co
Southend U v Oxford U
Stoke C v Grimsby T
WBA v Peterborough U

Football League Division 2
AFC Bournemouth v Brighton & HA
Blackpool v Port Vale
Bradford C v Burnley
Brentford v Wrexham
Cambridge U v Hartlepool U
Cardiff C v Bristol R
Huddersfield T v Barnet
Hull C v Fulham
Plymouth Arg v York C
Reading v Leyton O
Rotherham U v Swansea C
Stockport Co v Exeter C

Football League Division 3
Carlisle U v Mansfield T
Chester C v Shrewsbury T
Chesterfield v Torquay U
Doncaster R v Bury
Gillingham v Darlington
Hereford U v Colchester U
Rochdale v Walsall
Scarborough v Crewe Alex
Scunthorpe U v Northampton T
Wigan Ath v Preston NE
Wycombe W v Lincoln C

Sunday 17 October 1993
FA Carling Premiership
Ipswich T v Leeds U (4.00)

Monday 18 October 1993
FA Carling Premiership
Blackburn R v Sheffield U (7.45)

Tuesday 19 October 1993
Football League Division 1
Bolton W v Birmingham C

Wednesday 20 October 1993
Football League Division 1
Millwall v Notts Co (7.45)

Saturday 23 October 1993
FA Carling Premiership
Aston Villa v Chelsea
Everton v Manchester U
Leeds U v Blackburn R
Manchester C v Liverpool
Norwich C v West Ham U
Oldham Ath v Arsenal
QPR v Coventry C
Sheffield U v Sheffield W
Tottenham H v Swindon T
Wimbledon v Ipswich T

Football League Division 1
Barnsley v Southend U
Derby Co v Crystal Palace
Grimsby T v Charlton Ath
Leicester C v Nottingham F
Millwall v Middlesbrough
Notts Co v Portsmouth
Oxford U v Luton T
Peterborough U v Birmingham C
Sunderland v WBA
Tranmere R v Bristol C
Watford v Bolton W
Wolverhampton W v Stoke C

Football League Division 2
Barnet v Cambridge U
Brighton & HA v Rotherham U
Bristol R v Plymouth Arg
Burnley v Huddersfield T
Exeter C v Blackpool
Fulham v Stockport Co
Hartlepool U v Bradford C
Leyton O v AFC Bournemouth
Port Vale v Reading
Swansea C v Hull C
Wrexham v Cardiff City
York C v Brentford

Football League Division 3
Bury v Hereford U
Colchester U v Wigan Ath
Crewe Alex v Gillingham
Darlington v Wycombe W
Lincoln C v Chesterfield
Mansfield T v Chester C
Northampton T v Carlisle U
Preston NE v Rochdale
Shrewsbury T v Doncaster R
Torquay U v Scunthorpe U
Walsall v Scarborough

Sunday 24 October 1993
FA Carling Premiership
Southampton v Newcastle U (4.00)

Saturday 30 October 1993
FA Carling Premiership
Arsenal v Norwich C
Blackburn R v Tottenham H
Chelsea v Oldham Ath
Ipswich T v Everton
Liverpool v Southampton
Manchester U v QPR
Newcastle U v Wimbledon

Sheffield W v Leeds U
Swindon T v Aston Villa

Football League Division 1
Birmingham C v Millwall
Bolton W v Derby Co
Bristol C v Sunderland
Charlton Ath v Oxford U
Crystal Palace v Grimsby T
Luton T v Leicester C
Middlesbrough v Peterborough U
Nottingham F v Notts Co
Portsmouth v Tranmere R
Southend U v Wolverhampton W
Stoke C v Barnsley
WBA v Watford

Football League Division 2
AFC Bournemouth v Exeter C
Blackpool v Brighton & HA
Bradford C v York C
Brentford v Barnet
Cambridge U v Burnley
Cardiff C v Hartlepool U
Huddersfield T v Bristol R
Hull C v Leyton O
Plymouth Arg v Wrexham
Reading v Fulham
Rotherham U v Port Vale
Stockport Co v Swansea C

Football League Division 3
Carlisle U v Walsall
Chester C v Torquay U
Chesterfield v Crewe Alex
Doncaster R v Northampton T
Gillingham v Colchester U
Hereford U v Preston NE
Rochdale v Lincoln C
Scarborough v Bury
Scunthorpe U v Darlington
Wigan Ath v Mansfield T
Wycombe W v Shrewsbury T

Sunday 31 October 1993
FA Carling Premiership
Coventry C v Sheffield U (4.00)

Monday 1 November 1993
FA Carling Premiership
West Ham U v Manchester C (8.00)

Football League Division 3
Doncaster R v Scunthorpe U

Tuesday 2 November 1993
Football League Division 1
Bolton W v Peterborough U
Bristol C v Birmingham C (7.45)
Charlton Ath v Derby Co (7.45)
Crystal Palace v Luton T (7.45)
Grimsby T v Leicester C (7.45)
Oxford U v Barnsley (7.45)
Portsmouth v Middlesbrough (7.45)
Tranmere R v WBA
Wolverhampton W v Notts Co

Football League Division 2
AFC Bournemouth v Port Vale
(7.45)
Blackpool v Hull C
Brentford v Cardiff C (7.45)
Cambridge U v Plymouth Arg
(7.45)
Exeter C v Fulham
Hartlepool U v Barnet
Rotherham U v Reading
Stockport Co v Leyton O
Swansea C v Burnley
York C v Bristol R

Football League Division 3
Carlisle U v Lincoln C
Chester C v Bury

Chesterfield v Wigan Ath
Darlington v Colchester U
Gillingham v Hereford U (7.45)
Rochdale v Mansfield T
Shrewsbury T v Crewe Alex
Torquay U v Northampton T
Walsall v Preston NE (7.45)
Wycombe W v Scarborough (7.45)

Wednesday 3 November 1993
Football League Division 1
Nottingham F v Millwall
Southend U v Watford (7.45)
Stoke C v Sunderland (7.45)

Football League Division 2
Bradford C v Huddersfield T
Brighton & HA v Wrexham (7.45)

Saturday 6 November 1993
FA Carling Premiership
Arsenal v Aston Villa
Coventry C v Everton
Ipswich T v Sheffield W
Leeds U v Chelsea
Liverpool v West Ham U
Oldham Ath v Newcastle U
QPR v Blackburn R
Sheffield U v Norwich C
Southampton v Tottenham H
Wimbledon v Swindon T

Football League Division 1
Barnsley v Grimsby T
Birmingham C v Nottingham F
Derby Co v Wolverhampton W
Leicester C v Southend U
Luton T v Charlton Ath
Middlesbrough v Bristol C
Millwall v Oxford U
Notts Co v Crystal Palace
Peterborough U v Tranmere R
Sunderland v Portsmouth
Watford v Stoke C
WBA v Bolton W

Football League Division 2
Barnet v Bradford C
Bristol R v Hartlepool U
Burnley v York C
Cardiff C v Stockport Co
Fulham v Brighton & HA
Huddersfield T v Cambridge U
Hull C v Rotherham U
Leyton O v Exeter C
Plymouth Arg v Brentford
Port Vale v Swansea C
Reading v Blackpool
Wrexham v AFC Bournemouth

Football League Division 3
Bury v Chesterfield
Colchester U v Walsall
Crewe Alex v Rochdale
Hereford U v Chester C
Lincoln C v Torquay U
Mansfield T v Gillingham
Northampton T v Shrewsbury T
Preston NE v Darlington
Scarborough v Doncaster R
Scunthorpe U v Wycombe W
Wigan Ath v Carlisle U

Sunday 7 November 1993
FA Carling Premiership
Manchester C v Manchester U
(4.00)

Saturday 13 November 1993
Football League Division 1
Bristol C v Millwall
Charlton Ath v Notts Co
Crystal Palace v Middlesbrough
Nottingham F v Peterborough U

Oxford U v Derby Co
Portsmouth v Watford
Southend U v Luton T
Stoke C v Leicester C
Tranmere R v Sunderland
Wolverhampton W v Barnsley

Friday 19 November 1993
Football League Division 2
Cambridge U v Cardiff C (7.45)

Saturday 20 November 1993
FA Carling Premiership
Aston Villa v Sheffield U
Blackburn R v Southampton
Chelsea v Arsenal
Everton v QPR
Manchester U v Wimbledon
Norwich C v Manchester C
Sheffield W v Coventry C
Swindon T v Ipswich T
Tottenham H v Leeds U
West Ham U v Oldham Ath

Football League Division 1
Barnsley v Crystal Palace
Birmingham C v Portsmouth
Derby Co v Grimsby T
Leicester C v Oxford U
Luton T v Wolverhampton W
Middlesbrough v Bolton W
Millwall v Tranmere R
Notts Co v Stoke C
Peterborough U v Charlton Ath
Sunderland v Southend U
Watford v Bristol C
WBA v Nottingham F

Football League Division 2
AFC Bournemouth v Hull C
Blackpool v Huddersfield T
Bradford C v Plymouth Arg
Brentford v Burnley
Brighton & HA v Reading
Exeter C v Port Vale
Hartlepool U v Wrexham
Rotherham U v Fulham
Stockport Co v Bristol R
Swansea C v Leyton O
York C v Barnet

Football League Division 3
Carlisle U v Preston NE
Chester C v Northampton T
Chesterfield v Scarborough
Darlington v Mansfield T
Doncaster R v Colchester U
Gillingham v Wigan Ath
Rochdale v Bury
Shrewsbury T v Scunthorpe U
Torquay U v Hereford U
Walsall v Lincoln C
Wycombe W v Crewe Alex

Sunday November 21 1993
FA Carling Premiership
Newcastle U v Liverpool (4.00)

Monday 22 November 1993
FA Carling Premiership
Chelsea v Manchester C (7.45)

Tuesday 23 November 1993
FA Carling Premiership
Blackburn R v Coventry C (7.45)
Everton v Leeds U

Wednesday 24 November 1993
FA Carling Premiership
Aston Villa v Southampton (7.45)
Manchester U v Ipswich T (8.00)
Newcastle U v Sheffield U (7.45)
Norwich C v Liverpool (7.45)

Sheffield W v Oldham Ath (7.45)
Swindon T v QPR (7.45)
Tottenham H v Wimbledon (7.45)
West Ham U v Arsenal (7.45)

Saturday 27 November 1993
FA Carling Premiership
Arsenal v Newcastle U
Coventry C v Manchester U
Ipswich T v Blackburn R
Leeds U v Swindon T
Manchester C v Sheffield W
Oldham Ath v Norwich C
QPR v Tottenham H
Sheffield U v Chelsea
Southampton v West Ham U
Wimbledon v Everton

Football League Division 1
Barnsley v Bolton W
Birmingham C v Tranmere R
Derby Co v Southend U
Leicester C v Wolverhampton W
Luton T v Stoke C
Middlesbrough v Charlton Ath
Millwall v Grimsby T
Notts Co v Oxford U
Peterborough U v Bristol C
Sunderland v Nottingham F
Watford v Crystal Palace
WBA v Portsmouth

Football League Division 2
Barnet v Rotherham U
Bristol R v Cambridge U
Burnley v Exeter C
Cardiff C v Bradford C
Fulham v Swansea C
Huddersfield T v Brentford
Hull C v Stockport Co
Leyton O v Blackpool
Plymouth Arg v Hartlepool U
Port Vale v Brighton & HA
Reading v AFC Bournemouth
Wrexham v York C

Football League Division 3
Bury v Darlington
Colchester U v Carlisle U
Crewe Alex v Chester C
Hereford U v Doncaster R
Lincoln C v Gillingham
Mansfield T v Walsall
Northampton T v Chesterfield
Preston NE v Wycombe W
Scarborough v Torquay U
Scunthorpe U v Rochdale
Wigan Ath v Shrewsbury T

Sunday 28 November 1993
FA Carling Premiership
Liverpool v Aston Villa (4.00)

Saturday 4 December 1993
FA Carling Premiership
Blackburn R v Chelsea
Coventry C v Arsenal
Everton v Southampton
Ipswich T v Oldham Ath
Leeds U v Manchester C
Manchester U v Norwich C
QPR v Aston Villa
Sheffield W v Liverpool
Swindon T v Sheffield U
Tottenham H v Newcastle U
Wimbledon v West Ham U

Football League Division 1
Bolton W v WBA
Bristol C v Middlesbrough
Charlton Ath v Luton T
Grimsby T v Barnsley
Nottingham F v Birmingham C
Oxford U v Millwall

Portsmouth v Sunderland
Southend U v Leicester C
Stoke C v Watford
Tranmere R v Peterborough U
Wolverhampton W v Derby Co

Sunday 5 December 1993
Football League Division 1
Crystal Palace v Notts Co

Tuesday 7 December 1993
FA Carling Premiership
Arsenal v Tottenham H (7.45)
Oldham Ath v Swindon T
Sheffield U v Manchester U (7.45)

Wednesday 8 December 1993
FA Carling Premiership
Aston Villa v Sheffield W (7.45)
Chelsea v Wimbledon (7.45)
Liverpool v QPR (7.45)
Manchester C v Everton (7.45)
Newcastle U v Coventry C (7.45)
Norwich C v Blackburn R (7.45)
Southampton v Ipswich T
West Ham U v Leeds U (7.45)

Saturday 11 December 1993
FA Carling Premiership
Arsenal v Sheffield W
Aston Villa v Wimbledon
Chelsea v Ipswich T
Liverpool v Swindon T
Manchester C v Tottenham H
Newcastle U v Manchester U
Norwich C v Leeds U
Oldham Ath v Blackburn R
Sheffield U v Everton
Southampton v QPR
West Ham U v Coventry C

Football League Division 1
Barnsley v Peterborough U
Charlton Ath v Portsmouth
Crystal Palace v Birmingham C
Derby Co v Nottingham F
Grimsby T v Sunderland
Leicester C v Bristol C
Luton T v Tranmere R
Notts Co v Millwall
Oxford U v Bolton W
Southend U v WBA
Stoke C v Middlesbrough
Wolverhampton W v Watford

Football League Division 2
Barnet v Port Vale
Bradford C v AFC Bournemouth
Brentford v Blackpool
Bristol R v Leyton O
Burnley v Reading
Cambridge U v Stockport Co
Cardiff C v Fulham
Hartlepool U v Brighton & HA
Huddersfield T v Rotherham U
Plymouth Arg v Hull C
Wrexham v Swansea C
York C v Exeter C

Football League Division 3
Bury v Scunthorpe U
Carlisle U v Doncaster R
Chester C v Wycombe W
Colchester U v Crewe Alex
Darlington v Lincon C
Gillingham v Rochdale
Hereford U v Chesterfield
Mansfield T v Northampton T
Preston NE v Scarborough
Walsall v Shrewsbury T
Wigan Ath v Torquay U

Tuesday 14 December 1993
Football League Division 3
Lincoln City v Colchester U

Friday 17 December 1993
Football League Division 2
Fulham v Hartlepool U (7.45)
Rotherham U v Wrexham
Stockport Co v Plymouth Arg

Football League Division 3
Crewe Alex v Preston NE
Doncaster R v Chester C
Shrewsbury T v Mansfield T

Saturday 18 December 1993
FA Carling Premiership
Blackburn R v Manchester C
Coventry C v Oldham Ath
Everton v Newcastle U
Ipswich T v Norwich C
Leeds U v Arsenal
Manchester U v Aston Villa
Sheffield W v West Ham U
Swindon T v Southampton
Tottenham H v Liverpool
Wimbledon v Sheffield U

Football League Division 1
Birmingham C v Charlton Ath
Bolton W v Grimsby T
Bristol C v Wolverhampton W
Middlesbrough v Notts Co
Portsmouth v Oxford U
Sunderland v Derby Co
Tranmere R v Crystal Palace
Watford v Luton T

Football League Division 2
AFC Bournemouth v Bristol R
Brighton & HA v Bradford C
Exeter C v Brentford
Hull C v Barnet
Leyton O v Cardiff C
Port Vale v Burnley
Reading v Huddersfield T
Swansea C v York C

Football League Division 3
Chesterfield v Gillingham
Northampton T v Bury
Rochdale v Darlington
Scarborough v Hereford United
Scunthorpe U v Wigan Ath
Torquay U v Walsall
Wycombe W v Carlisle U

Sunday 19 December 1993
Football League Division 1
Millwall v Stoke C
Nottingham F v Southend U
Peterborough U v Leicester C (12.00)
WBA v Barnsley

Football League Division 2
Blackpool v Cambridge U

Monday 20 December 1993
FA Carling Premiership
QPR v Chelsea (8.00)

Wednesday 22 December 1993
FA Carling Premiership
Newcastle U v Leeds U (7.45)

Sunday 26 December 1993
FA Carling Premiership
Manchester U v Blackburn R (4.00)
Sheffield U v Liverpool (12.00)
Wimbledon v Coventry C (12.00)

Football League Division 3
Rochdale v Scarborough

Monday 27 December 1993
FA Carling Premiership
Aston Villa v Manchester U
Everton v Sheffield W (7.45)
Ipswich T v West Ham U
QPR v Oldham Ath
Southampton v Chelsea
Swindon T v Arsenal
Tottenham H v Norwich C

Football League Division 1
Barnsley v Derby Co
Bolton W v Sunderland
Grimsby T v Notts Co
Leicester C v Watford (11.30)
Millwall v Portsmouth
Nottingham F v Middlesbrough
Oxford U v Crystal Palace
Peterborough U v Luton T
Southend U v Charlton Ath (12.00)
Stoke C v Birmingham C
Tranmere R v Wolverhampton W
WBA v Bristol C

Football League Division 2
AFC Bournemouth v Brentford (12.30)
Bradford C v Rotherham U
Brighton & HA v Barnet
Bristol R v Reading
Burnley v Wrexham
Cardiff C v Swansea C
Exeter C v Plymouth Arg
Fulham v Port Vale
Hartlepool U v Huddersfield T
Leyton O v Cambridge U
Stockport Co v Blackpool
York C v Hull C

Football League Division 3
Chesterfield v Doncaster R
Colchester U v Mansfield T
Crewe Alex v Wigan Ath
Darlington v Carlisle U
Gillingham v Northampton T
Hereford U v Shrewsbury T
Lincoln C v Scunthorpe U
Preston NE v Chester C
Torquay U v Wycombe W
Walsall v Bury

Tuesday 28 December 1993
FA Carling Premiership
Chelsea v Newcastle U
Coventry City v Ipswich T
Liverpool v Wimbledon
Manchester C v Southampton
West Ham U v Tottenham H

Football League Division 1
Birmingham City v WBA
Bristol C v Nottingham F
Charlton Ath v Stoke C
Derby Co v Leicester C
Middlesbrough v Tranmere R
Notts Co v Barnsley
Portsmouth v Bolton W
Sunderland v Millwall
Watford v Peterborough U
Wolverhampton W v Oxford U

Football League Division 2
Blackpool v York C
Cambridge U v Exeter C
Huddersfield T v Cardiff C
Hull C v Hartlepool U
Plymouth Arg v Fulham
Reading v Stockport Co
Rotherham U v AFC Bournemouth
Swansea C v Brighton & HA
Wrexham v Bristol R

Football League Division 3
Carlisle U v Crewe Alex
Chester C v Gillingham
Doncaster R v Darlington
Mansfield T v Hereford U
Scarborough v Colchester U
Scunthorpe U v Chesterfield
Shrewsbury T v Lincoln C
Wigan Ath v Walsall
Wycombe W v Rochdale

Wednesday 29 December 1993
FA Carling Premiership
Arsenal v Sheffield U (7.45)
Blackburn R v Everton (7.45)
Leeds U v QPR (7.45)
Norwich C v Aston Villa (7.45)
Oldham Ath v Manchester U
Sheffield W v Swindon T (7.45)

Football League Division 1
Crystal Palace v Southend U (7.45)
Luton T v Grimsby T (7.45)

Football League Division 2
Barnet v Burnley (7.45)
Brentford v Bradford C (7.45)
Port Vale v Leyton O (7.45)

Football League Division 3
Bury v Torquay U
Northampton T v Preston NE

Saturday 1 January 1994
FA Carling Premiership
Aston Villa v Blackburn R
Everton v West Ham U
Ipswich T v Liverpool
Manchester U v Leeds U
Newcastle U v Manchester C
QPR v Sheffield W
Sheffield U v Oldham Ath
Southampton v Norwich C
Swindon T v Chelsea
Tottenham H v Coventry C
Wimbledon v Arsenal

Football League Division 1
Barnsley v Portsmouth
Bolton W v Notts Co
Grimsby T v Bristol C
Leicester C v Sunderland
Millwall v Crystal Palace
Nottingham F v Charlton Ath
Oxford U v Middlesbrough
Peterborough U v Wolverhampton W
Southend U v Birmingham C
Stoke C v Derby Co
Tranmere R v Watford
WBA v Luton T

Football League Division 2
AFC Bournemouth v Plymouth Arg
Bradford C v Wrexham
Brighton & HA v Cambridge U
Bristol R v Swansea C
Burnley v Blackpool
Cardiff C v Reading
Exeter C v Hull C
Fulham v Brentford
Hartlepool U v Rotherham U
Leyton O v Huddersfield T
Stockport Co v Barnet
York C v Port Vale

Football League Division 3
Chesterfield v Shrewsbury T
Colchester U v Chester C
Crewe Alex v Doncaster R
Darlington v Wigan Ath
Gillingham v Bury
Hereford U v Carlisle U
Lincoln C v Scarborough

Preston NE v Scunthorpe U
Rochdale v Northampton T
Torquay U v Mansfield T
Walsall v Wycombe W

Monday 3 January 1994
FA Carling Premiership
Arsenal v QPR
Blackburn R v Wimbledon
Chelsea v Everton
Coventry C v Swindon T
Leeds U v Aston Villa (8.00)
Manchester C v Ipswich T
Sheffield W v Tottenham H
West Ham U v Sheffield U

Football League Division 1
Birmingham City v Oxford U
Bristol C v Stoke C
Charlton Ath v WBA
Crystal Palace v Peterborough U
Derby Co v Tranmere R
Luton T v Millwall
Middlesbrough v Grimsby T
Notts Co v Southend U
Portsmouth v Leicester C
Sunderland v Barnsley
Watford v Nottingham F
Wolverhampton W v Bolton W

Football League Division 2
Barnet v Exeter C
Blackpool v Bristol R
Brentford v Stockport Co
Cambridge U v Fulham
Huddersfield T v AFC
Bournemouth
Hull C v Burnley
Plymouth Arg v Brighton & HA
Port Vale v Bradford C
Reading v York C
Rotherham U v Cardiff C
Swansea C v Hartlepool U
Wrexham v Leyton O

Football League Division 3
Carlisle U v Torquay U
Chester C v Lincoln C
Doncaster R v Gillingham
Mansfield T v Chesterfield (11.30)
Northampton Town v Crewe Alex
Scarborough v Darlington
Scunthorpe U v Walsall
Shrewsbury T v Colchester U
Wycombe W v Hereford U

Tuesday 4 January 1994
FA Carling Premiership
Liverpool v Manchester U (7.45)
Norwich C v Newcastle U (7.45)
Oldham Ath v Southampton

Football League Division 3
Bury v Preston NE
Wigan Ath v Rochdale

Saturday 8 January 1994
Football League Division 2
AFC Bournemouth v Swansea C
Blackpool v Fulham
Bradford C v Leyton O
Brentford v Bristol R
Cambridge U v York C
Cardiff C v Burnley
Huddersfield T v Wrexham
Hull C v Brighton & HA
Plymouth Arg v Barnet
Reading v Hartlepool U
Rotherham U v Exeter C
Stockport Co v Port Vale

Football League Division 3
Carlisle U v Bury
Chester C v Walsall

Chesterfield v Colchester U
Doncaster R v Torquay U
Gillingham v Preston NE
Hereford U v Darlington
Rochdale v Shrewsbury T
Scarborough v Northampton T
Scunthorpe U v Crewe Alex
Wigan Ath v Lincoln C
Wycombe W v Mansfield T

Tuesday 11 January 1994
Football League Division 1
Luton T v Bristol C
Notts C v Birmingham C (7.45)
Oxford U v Sunderland (7.45)

Wednesday 12 January 1994
Football League Division 1
Derby Co v Watford
Leicester C v WBA (7.45)
Southend U v Bolton W
Stoke C v Peterborough U (7.45)

Friday 14 January 1994
Football League Division 2
Swansea C v Rotherham U

Saturday 15 January 1994
FA Carling Premiership
Aston Villa v West Ham U
Everton v Swindon T
Leeds U v Ipswich T
Manchester C v Arsenal
Norwich C v Chelsea
Oldham Ath v Liverpool
QPR v Newcastle U
Sheffield U v Blackburn R
Southampton v Coventry C
Tottenham H v Manchester U
Wimbledon v Sheffield W

Football League Division 1
Barnsley v Bristol C
Derby Co v Portsmouth
Grimsby T v Stoke C
Leicester C v Charlton Ath
Millwall v Bolton W
Notts Co v Luton T
Oxford U v Southend U
Peterborough U v WBA
Sunderland v Middlesbrough
Tranmere R v Nottingham F
Watford v Birmingham C
Wolverhampton W v Crystal Palace

Football League Division 2
Barnet v Huddersfield T
Brighton & HA v AFC
Bournemouth
Bristol R v Cardiff C
Burnley v Bradford C
Exeter C v Stockport Co
Fulham v Hull C
Hartlepool U v Cambridge U
Leyton O v Reading
Port Vale v Blackpool
Wrexham v Brentford
York C v Plymouth Arg

Football League Division 3
Bury v Doncaster R
Colchester U v Hereford U
Crewe Alex v Scarborough
Darlington v Gillingham
Lincoln C v Wycombe W
Mansfield T v Carlisle U
Northampton T v Scunthorpe U
Preston NE v Wigan Ath
Shrewsbury T v Chester C
Torquay U v Chesterfield
Walsall v Rochdale

Saturday 22 January 1994
FA Carling Premiership
Arsenal v Oldham Ath
Blackburn R v Leeds U
Chelsea v Aston Villa
Coventry C v QPR
Ipswich T v Wimbledon
Liverpool v Manchester C
Manchester U v Everton
Newcastle U v Southampton
Sheffield W v Sheffield U
Swindon T v Tottenham H
West Ham U v Norwich C

Football League Division 1
Birmingham C v Sunderland
Bolton W v Tranmere R
Bristol C v Notts Co
Charlton Ath v Barnsley
Crystal Palace v Leicester C
Luton T v Derby Co
Middlesbrough v Watford
Nottingham F v Wolverhampton W
Portsmouth v Peterborough U
Southend U v Grimsby T
Stoke C v Oxford U
WBA v Millwall

Football League Division 2
AFC Bournemouth v Fulham
Blackpool v Swansea C
Bradford C v Bristol R
Brentford v Hartlepool U
Cambridge U v Wrexham
Cardiff C v Barnet
Huddersfield T v York C
Hull C v Port Vale
Plymouth Arg v Burnley
Reading v Exeter C
Rotherham U v Leyton O
Stockport Co v Brighton & HA

Football League Division 3
Carlisle U v Shrewsbury T
Chester C v Darlington
Chesterfield v Preston NE
Doncaster R v Lincoln C
Gillingham v Walsall
Hereford U v Crewe Alex
Rochdale v Torquay U
Scarborough v Mansfield T
Scunthorpe U v Colchester U
Wigan Ath v Bury
Wycombe W v Northampton T

Saturday 29 January 1994
Football League Division 1
Grimsby T v WBA

Football League Division 2
Barnet v Brentford
Brighton & HA v Blackpool
Bristol R v Huddersfield T
Burnley v Cambridge U
Exeter C v AFC Bournemouth
Fulham v Reading
Hartlepool U v Cardiff C
Leyton O v Hull C
Port Vale v Rotherham U
Swansea C v Stockport Co
Wrexham v Plymouth Arg
York C v Bradford C

Football League Division 3
Bury v Scarborough
Colchester U v Gillingham
Crewe Alex v Chesterfield
Darlington v Scunthorpe U
Lincoln C v Rochdale
Mansfield T v Wigan Ath
Northampton T v Doncaster R
Preston NE v Hereford U
Shrewsbury T v Wycombe W
Torquay U v Chester C
Walsall v Carlisle U

Saturday 5 February 1994
Football League Division 1
Birmingham C v Peterborough U
Bolton W v Watford
Bristol C v Tranmere R
Charlton Ath v Grimsby T
Crystal Palace v Derby Co
Luton T v Oxford U
Middlesbrough v Millwall
Nottingham F v Leicester C
Portsmouth v Notts Co
Southend U v Barnsley
Stoke C v Wolverhampton W
WBA v Sunderland

Football League Division 2
AFC Bournemouth v Leyton O
Blackpool v Exeter C
Bradford C v Hartlepool U
Brentford v York C
Cambridge U v Barnet
Cardiff C v Wrexham
Huddersfield T v Burnley
Hull C v Swansea C
Plymouth Arg v Bristol R
Reading v Port Vale
Rotherham U v Brighton & HA
Stockport Co v Fulham

Football League Division 3
Carlisle U v Northampton T
Chester C v Mansfield T
Chesterfield v Lincoln C
Doncaster R v Shrewsbury T
Gillingham v Crewe Alex
Hereford U v Bury
Rochdale v Preston NE
Scarborough v Walsall
Scunthorpe U v Torquay U
Wigan Ath v Colchester U
Wycombe W v Darlington

Saturday 12 February 1994
FA Carling Premiership
Aston Villa v Swindon T
Everton v Ipswich T
Leeds U v Sheffield W
Manchester C v West Ham U
Norwich C v Arsenal
Oldham Ath v Chelsea
QPR v Manchester U
Sheffield U v Coventry C
Southampton v Liverpool
Tottenham H v Blackburn R
Wimbledon v Newcastle U

Football League Division 1
Barnsley v Stoke C
Derby Co v Bolton W
Grimsby T v Crystal Palace
Leicester C v Luton T
Millwall v Birmingham C
Notts Co v Nottingham F
Oxford U v Charlton Ath
Peterborough U v Middlesbrough
Sunderland v Bristol C
Tranmere R v Portsmouth
Watford v WBA
Wolverhampton W v Southend U

Football League Division 2
Barnet v Plymouth Arg
Brighton & HA v Hull C
Bristol R v Brentford
Burnley v Cardiff C
Exeter C v Rotherham U
Fulham v Blackpool
Hartlepool U v Reading
Leyton O v Bradford C
Port Vale v Stockport Co
Swansea City v AFC Bournemouth
Wrexham v Huddersfield T
York C v Cambridge U

Football League Division 3
Bury v Carlisle U
Colchester U v Chesterfield
Crewe Alex v Scunthorpe U
Darlington v Hereford U
Lincoln C v Wigan Ath
Mansfield T v Wycombe W
Northampton T v Scarborough
Preston NE v Gillingham
Shrewsbury T v Rochdale
Torquay U v Doncaster R
Walsall v Chester C

Friday 18 February 1994
Football League Division 2
Swansea C v Barnet

Saturday 19 February 1994
FA Carling Premiership
Blackburn R v Newcastle U
Coventry C v Manchester C
Everton v Arsenal
Ipswich T v Sheffield U
Leeds U v Liverpool
Manchester U v Southampton
QPR v West Ham U
Sheffield W v Chelsea
Swindon T v Norwich C
Tottenham H v Aston Villa
Wimbledon v Oldham Ath

Football League Division 1
Birmingham C v Notts Co
Bolton W v Southend U
Bristol C v Luton T
Middlesbrough v Barnsley
Millwall v Wolverhampton W
Nottingham F v Crystal Palace
Peterborough U v Stoke C
Portsmouth v Grimsby T
Sunderland v Oxford U
Tranmere R v Charlton Ath
Watford v Derby Co
WBA v Leicester C

Football League Division 2
AFC Bournemouth v Hartlepool U
Blackpool v Wrexham
Brighton & HA v Cardiff C
Exeter C v Bradford C
Fulham v Bristol R
Hull C v Cambridge U
Leyton O v Burnley
Port Vale v Plymouth Arg
Reading v Brentford
Rotherham U v York C
Stockport Co v Huddersfield T

Football League Division 3
Chesterfield v Chester C
Crewe Alex v Bury
Doncaster R v Walsall
Lincoln C v Hereford U
Northampton T v Colchester U
Rochdale v Carlisle U
Scarborough v Gillingham
Scunthorpe U v Mansfield T
Shrewsbury T v Preston NE
Torquay U v Darlington
Wycombe W v Wigan Ath

Tuesday 22 February 1994
Football League Division 1
Barnsley v Watford (7.45)
Charlton Ath v Sunderland (7.45)
Crystal Palace v Bristol C (7.45)
Grimsby T v Nottingham F (7.45)
Luton T v Portsmouth (7.45)
Notts Co v Peterborough U (7.45)
Oxford U v WBA (7.45)
Wolverhampton W v Birmingham C

Football League Division 2
Barnet v Reading (7.45)

Brentford v Hull C (7.45)
Burnley v Rotherham U
Cambridge U v Port Vale (7.45)
Cardiff C v Exeter C
Hartlepool U v Leyton O
Huddersfield T v Swansea C
Plymouth Arg v Blackpool (7.45)
Wrexham v Fulham
York C v AFC Bournemouth

Wednesday 23 February 1994
Football League Division 1
Derby Co v Middlesbrough
Leicester C v Tranmere R (7.45)
Southend U v Millwall (7.45)
Stoke C v Bolton W (7.45)

Football League Division 2
Bradford C v Stockport Co
Bristol R v Brighton & HA (8.00)

Saturday 26 February 1994
FA Carling Premiership
Arsenal v Blackburn R
Aston Villa v Everton
Chelsea v Tottenham H
Liverpool v Coventry C
Manchester C v Swindon T
Newcastle U v Ipswich T
Norwich C v Sheffield W
Oldham Ath v Leeds U
Sheffield U v QPR
Southampton v Wimbledon
West Ham U v Manchester U

Football League Division 1
Barnsley v Millwall
Charlton Ath v Watford
Crystal Palace v Bolton W
Derby Co v Birmingham C
Grimsby T v Peterborough U
Leicester C v Middlesbrough
Luton T v Sunderland
Notts Co v Tranmere R
Oxford U v Nottingham F
Southend U v Bristol C
Stoke C v Portsmouth
Wolverhampton W v WBA

Football League Division 2
Barnet v Blackpool
Bradford C v Fulham
Brentford v Rotherham U
Bristol R v Hull C
Burnley v AFC Bournemouth
Cambridge U v Reading
Cardiff C v Port Vale
Hartlepool U v Exeter C
Huddersfield T v Brighton & HA
Plymouth Arg v Swansea C
Wrexham v Stockport Co
York C v Leyton O

Football League Division 3
Bury v Shrewsbury T
Carlisle U v Scarborough
Chester C v Rochdale
Colchester U v Torquay U
Darlington v Chesterfield
Gillingham v Wycombe W
Hereford U v Scunthorpe U
Mansfield T v Crewe Alex
Preston NE v Lincoln C
Walsall v Northampton T
Wigan Ath v Doncaster R

Friday 4 March 1994
Football League Division 3
Doncaster R v Preston NE

Saturday 5 March 1994
FA Carling Premiership
Blackburn R v Liverpool
Coventry C v Aston Villa

Everton v Oldham Ath
Ipswich T v Arsenal
Leeds U v Southampton
Manchester U v Chelsea
QPR v Manchester C
Sheffield W v Newcastle U
Swindon T v West Ham U
Tottenham H v Sheffield U
Wimbledon v Norwich C

Football League Division 1
Birmingham C v Barnsley
Bolton W v Charlton Ath
Bristol C v Derby Co
Middlesbrough v Wolverhampton W
Millwall v Leicester C
Nottingham F v Luton T
Peterborough U v Southend U
Portsmouth v Crystal Palace
Sunderland v Notts Co
Tranmere R v Grimsby T
Watford v Oxford U
WBA v Stoke C

Football League Division 2
AFC Bournemouth v Barnet
Blackpool v Bradford C
Brighton & HA v York C
Exeter C v Huddersfield T
Fulham v Burnley
Hull C v Cardiff C
Leyton O v Plymouth Arg
Port Vale v Bristol R
Reading v Wrexham
Rotherham U v Cambridge U
Stockport Co v Hartlepool U
Swansea C v Brentford

Football League Division 3
Chesterfield v Carlisle U
Crewe Alex v Walsall
Lincoln C v Mansfield T
Northampton T v Hereford U
Rochdale v Colchester U
Scarborough v Wigan Athletic
Scunthorpe U v Chester C
Shrewsbury T v Darlington
Torquay U v Gillingham
Wycombe W v Bury

Saturday 12 March 1994
FA Carling Premiership
Arsenal v Manchester U
Aston Villa v Ipswich T
Chelsea v Coventry C
Liverpool v Everton
Manchester C v Wimbledon
Newcastle U v Swindon T
Norwich C v QPR
Oldham Ath v Tottenham H
Southampton v Sheffield W
West Ham U v Blackburn R

Football League Division 1
Barnsley v Tranmere R
Charlton Ath v Bristol C
Crystal Palace v WBA
Derby Co v Millwall
Grimsby T v Birmingham C
Leicester C v Bolton W
Luton T v Middlesbrough
Notts Co v Watford
Oxford U v Peterborough U
Southend U v Portsmouth
Stoke C v Nottingham F
Wolverhampton W v Sunderland

Football League Division 2
Barnet v Leyton O
Bradford C v Swansea C
Brentford v Brighton & HA
Bristol R v Rotherham U
Burnley v Stockport Co
Cambridge U v AFC Bournemouth

Cardiff C v Blackpool
Hartlepool U v Port Vale
Huddersfield T v Hull C
Plymouth Arg v Reading
Wrexham v Exeter C
York C v Fulham

Football League Division 3
Bury v Lincoln C
Carlisle U v Scunthorpe U
Chester C v Scarborough
Colchester U v Wycombe W
Darlington v Crewe Alex
Gillingham v Shrewsbury T
Hereford U v Rochdale
Mansfield T v Doncaster R
Preston NE v Torquay U
Walsall v Chesterfield
Wigan Ath v Northampton T

Sunday 13 March 1994
FA Carling Premiership
Sheffield U v Leeds U (12.00)

Tuesday 15 March 1994
Football League Division 1
Birmingham C v Leicester C (7.45)
Bolton W v Luton T
Bristol C v Oxford U (7.45)
Middlesbrough v Southend U (7.45)
Peterborough U v Derby Co (7.45)
Portsmouth v Wolverhampton W
(7.45)
Sunderland v Crystal Palace
Tranmere R v Stoke C
Watford v Grimsby T (7.45)

Football League Division 2
AFC Bournemouth v Cardiff C
(7.45)
Blackpool v Hartlepool U
Exeter C v Bristol R
Fulham v Barnet (7.45)
Hull C v Wrexham
Leyton O v Brentford (7.45)
Port Vale v Huddersfield T (7.45)
Rotherham U v Plymouth Arg
Stockport Co v York C
Swansea C v Cambridge U

Wednesday 16 March 1994
Football League Division 1
Millwall v Charlton Ath (7.45)
Nottingham F v Barnsley
WBA v Notts Co

Football League Division 2
Brighton & HA v Burnley (7.45)
Reading v Bradford C (7.45)

Saturday 19 March 1994
FA Carling Premiership
Aston Villa v Oldham Ath
Leeds U v Coventry C
Liverpool v Chelsea
Manchester C v Sheffield U
Norwich C v Everton
QPR v Wimbledon
Sheffield W v Blackburn R
Southampton v Arsenal
Swindon T v Manchester U
Tottenham H v Ipswich T
West Ham U v Newcastle U

Football League Division 1
Bristol C v Portsmouth
Crystal Palace v Charlton Ath
Derby Co v Notts Co
Leicester C v Barnsley
Luton T v Birmingham C
Middlesbrough v WBA
Millwall v Peterborough U
Nottingham F v Bolton W
Oxford U v Tranmere R

Southend U v Stoke C
Sunderland v Watford
Wolverhampton W v Grimsby T

Football League Division 2
AFC Bournemouth v Blackpool
Barnet v Wrexham
Brighton & HA v Leyton O
Burnley v Bristol R
Cambridge U v Bradford C
Fulham v Huddersfield T
Hull C v Reading
Plymouth Arg v Cardiff C
Port Vale v Brentford
Rotherham U v Stockport Co
Swansea C v Exeter C
York C v Hartlepool U

Football League Division 3
Bury v Colchester U
Carlisle U v Chester C
Chesterfield v Rochdale
Crewe Alex v Torquay U
Doncaster R v Wycombe W
Northampton T v Lincoln C
Preston NE v Mansfield T
Scunthorpe U v Gillingham
Shrewsbury T v Scarborough
Walsall v Darlington
Wigan Ath v Hereford U

Saturday 26 March 1994
FA Carling Premiership
Arsenal v Liverpool
Blackburn R v Swindon T
Chelsea v West Ham U
Coventry C v Norwich C
Everton v Tottenham H
Ipswich T v QPR
Manchester U v Sheffield W
Newcastle U v Aston Villa
Oldham Ath v Manchester C
Sheffield U v Southampton
Wimbledon v Leeds U

Football League Division 1
Barnsley v Luton T
Birmingham C v Middlesbrough
Bolton W v Bristol C
Charlton Ath v Wolverhampton W
Grimsby T v Oxford U
Notts Co v Leicester C
Peterborough U v Sunderland
Portsmouth v Nottingham F
Stoke C v Crystal Palace
Tranmere R v Southend U
Watford v Millwall
WBA v Derby Co

Football League Division 2
Blackpool v Rotherham U
Bradford City v Hull C
Brentford v Cambridge U
Bristol R v Barnet
Cardiff C v York C
Exeter C v Brighton & HA
Hartlepool U v Burnley
Huddersfield T v Plymouth Arg
Leyton O v Fulham
Reading v Swansea C
Stockport Co v AFC Bournemouth
Wrexham v Port Vale

Football League Division 3
Chester C v Wigan Ath
Colchester U v Preston NE
Darlington v Northampton T
Gillingham v Carlisle U
Hereford U v Walsall
Lincoln C v Crewe Alex
Mansfield T v Bury
Rochdale v Doncaster R
Scarborough v Scunthorpe U
Torquay U v Shrewsbury T
Wycombe W v Chesterfield

Tuesday 29 March 1994

FA Carling Premiership
Ipswich T v Manchester C (7.45)
Sheffield U v West Ham U (7.45)
Wimbledon v Blackburn R (8.00)

Football League Division 1
Barnsley v Sunderland (7.45)
Bolton W v Wolverhampton W
Grimsby T v Middlesbrough (7.45)
Oxford U v Birmingham C (7.45)
Peterborough U v Crystal Palace
Tranmere R v Derby Co

Football League Division 2
AFC Bournemouth v Huddersfield
T (7.45)
Burnley v Hull C
Cardiff C v Rotherham U
Exeter C v Barnet
Fulham v Cambridge U (7.45)
Hartlepool U v Swansea C
Leyton O v Wrexham (7.45)
Stockport Co v Brentford
York C v Reading

Wednesday 30 March 1994

FA Carling Premiership
Aston Villa v Leeds U (7.45)
Everton v Chelsea
Manchester U v Liverpool (8.00)
Newcastle U v Norwich C (7.45)
QPR v Arsenal (7.45)
Southampton v Oldham Ath
Swindon T v Coventry C (7.45)
Tottenham H v Sheffield W (7.45)

Football League Division 1
Leicester C v Portsmouth (7.45)
Millwall v Luton T (7.45)
Nottingham F v Watford
Southend U v Notts Co (7.45)
Stoke C v Bristol C (7.45)
WBA v Charlton Ath

Football League Division 2
Bradford C v Port Vale
Brighton & HA v Plymouth Arg
(7.45)
Bristol R v Blackpool (8.00)

Saturday 2 April 1994

FA Carling Premiership
Arsenal v Swindon T
Blackburn R v Manchester U
Chelsea v Southampton
Coventry C v Wimbledon
Leeds U v Newcastle U
Liverpool v Sheffield U
Manchester C v Aston Villa
Norwich C v Tottenham H
Oldham Ath v QPR
Sheffield W v Everton
West Ham U v Ipswich T

Football League Division 1
Birmingham C v Stoke C
Bristol C v WBA
Charlton Ath v Southend U
Crystal Palace v Oxford U
Derby Co v Barnsley
Luton T v Peterborough U
Middlesbrough v Nottingham F
Notts Co v Grimsby T
Portsmouth v Millwall
Sunderland v Bolton W
Watford v Leicester C
Wolverhampton W v Tranmere R

Football League Division 2
Barnet v Brighton & HA
Blackpool v Stockport Co
Brentford v AFC Bournemouth
Cambridge U v Leyton O

Huddersfield T v Hartlepool U
Hull C v York C
Plymouth Arg v Exeter C
Port Vale v Fulham
Reading v Bristol R
Rotherham U v Bradford C
Swansea C v Cardiff C
Wrexham v Burnley

Football League Division 3
Bury v Walsall
Carlisle U v Darlington
Chester C v Preston NE
Doncaster R v Chesterfield
Mansfield T v Colchester U
Northampton T v Gillingham
Scarborough v Rochdale
Scunthorpe U v Lincoln C
Shrewsbury T v Hereford U
Wigan Ath v Crewe Alex
Wycombe W v Torquay U

Monday 4 April 1994

FA Carling Premiership
Aston Villa v Norwich C
Everton v Blackburn R
Ipswich T v Coventry C
Manchester U v Oldham Ath
Newcastle U v Chelsea
QPR v Leeds U
Sheffield U v Arsenal
Southampton v Manchester C
Swindon T v Sheffield W
Tottenham H v West Ham U
Wimbledon v Liverpool

Football League Division 1
Barnsley v Portsmouth
Bolton W v Portsmouth
Grimsby T v Luton T
Nottingham F v Bristol C
Oxford U v Wolverhampton W
Stoke C v Charlton Ath
Tranmere R v Middlesbrough
WBA v Birmingham C

Football League Division 2
Bradford C v Brentford
Bristol R v Wrexham
Burnley v Barnet
Cardiff C v Huddersfield T
Exeter C v Cambridge U
Fulham v Plymouth Arg
Hartlepool U v Hull C
Leyton O v Port Vale
Stockport Co v Reading
York C v Blackpool

Football League Division 3
Chesterfield v Scunthorpe U
Colchester U v Scarborough
Crewe Alex v Carlisle U
Darlington v Doncaster R
Gillingham v Chester C
Hereford U v Mansfield T
Lincoln C v Shrewsbury T
Preston NE v Northampton T
Rochdale v Wycombe W

Tuesday 5 April 1994

Football League Division 1
Leicester C v Derby Co (7.45)
Peterborough U v Watford (7.45)

Football League Division 2
AFC Bournemouth v Rotherham U
(7.45)

Football League Division 3
Torquay U v Bury
Walsall v Wigan Ath (7.45)

Wednesday 6 April 1994

Football League Division 1
Millwall v Sunderland (7.45)
Southend U v Crystal Palace (7.45)

Football League Division 2
Brighton & HA v Swansea C (7.45)

Saturday 9 April 1994

FA Carling Premiership
Arsenal v Wimbledon
Blackburn R v Aston Villa
Chelsea v Swindon T
Coventry C v Tottenham H
Leeds U v Manchester U
Liverpool v Ipswich T
Manchester C v Newcastle U
Norwich C v Southampton
Oldham Ath v Sheffield U
Sheffield W v QPR
West Ham U v Everton

Football League Division 1
Birmingham C v Southend U
Bristol C v Grimsby T
Charlton Ath v Nottingham F
Crystal Palace v Millwall
Derby Co v Stoke C
Luton T v WBA
Middlesbrough v Oxford U
Notts Co v Bolton W
Portsmouth v Barnsley
Sunderland v Leicester C
Watford v Tranmere R
Wolverhampton W v Peterborough
U

Football League Division 2
Barnet v Stockport Co
Blackpool v Burnley
Brentford v Fulham
Cambridge U v Brighton & HA
Huddersfield T v Leyton O
Hull C v Exeter C
Plymouth Arg v AFC Bournemouth
Port Vale v York C
Reading v Cardiff C
Rotherham U v Hartlepool U
Swansea C v Bristol R
Wrexham v Bradford C

Football League Division 3
Bury v Gillingham
Carlisle U v Hereford U
Chester C v Colchester U
Doncaster R v Crewe Alex
Mansfield T v Torquay U
Northampton T v Rochdale
Scarborough v Lincoln C
Scunthorpe U v Preston NE
Shrewsbury T v Chesterfield
Wigan Ath v Darlington
Wycombe W v Walsall

Saturday 16 April 1994

FA Carling Premiership
Arsenal v Chelsea
Coventry C v Sheffield W
Ipswich T v Swindon T
Leeds U v Tottenham H
Liverpool v Newcastle U
Manchester C v Norwich C
Oldham Ath v West Ham U
QPR v Everton
Sheffield U v Aston Villa
Southampton v Blackburn R
Wimbledon v Manchester U

Football League Division 1
Barnsley v Oxford U
Birmingham C v Bristol C
Derby Co v Charlton Ath
Leicester C v Grimsby T
Luton T v Crystal Palace
Middlesbrough v Portsmouth

Millwall v Nottingham F
Notts Co v Wolverhampton W
Peterborough U v Bolton W
Sunderland v Stoke C
Watford v Southend U
WBA v Tranmere R

Football League Division 2
Barnet v Hartlepool U
Bristol R v York C
Burnley v Swansea C
Cardiff C v Brentford
Fulham v Exeter C
Hull C v Blackpool
Leyton O v Stockport Co
Plymouth Arg v Cambridge U
Port Vale v AFC Bournemouth
Reading v Rotherham U
Wrexham v Brighton & HA

Football League Division 3
Bury v Chester C
Colchester U v Darlington
Crewe Alex v Shrewsbury T
Hereford U v Gillingham
Lincoln C v Carlisle U
Mansfield T v Rochdale
Northampton T v Torquay U
Preston NE v Walsall
Scarborough v Wycombe W
Scunthorpe U v Doncaster R
Wigan Ath v Chesterfield

Sunday 17 April 1994
Football League Division 2
Huddersfield T v Bradford C (12.30)

Saturday 23 April 1994
FA Carling Premiership
Aston Villa v Arsenal
Blackburn R v QPR
Chelsea v Leeds U
Everton v Coventry C
Manchester U v Manchester C
Newcastle U v Oldham Ath
Norwich C v Sheffield U
Sheffield W v Ipswich T
Swindon T v Wimbledon
Tottenham H v Southampton
West Ham U v Liverpool

Football League Division 1
Bolton W v Middlesbrough
Bristol C v Watford
Charlton Ath v Peterborough U
Crystal Palace v Barnsley
Grimsby T v Derby Co
Nottingham F v WBA
Oxford U v Leicester C
Portsmouth v Birmingham C
Southend U v Sunderland
Stoke C v Notts Co
Tranmere R v Millwall
Wolverhampton W v Luton T

Football League Division 2
AFC Bournemouth v Wrexham
Blackpool v Reading

Bradford C v Barnet
Brentford v Plymouth Arg
Brighton & HA v Fulham
Cambridge U v Huddersfield T
Exeter C v Leyton O
Hartlepool U v Bristol R
Rotherham U v Hull C
Stockport Co v Cardiff C
Swansea C v Port Vale
York C v Burnley

Football League Division 3
Carlisle U v Wigan Ath
Chester C v Hereford U
Chesterfield v Bury
Darlington v Preston NE
Doncaster R v Scarborough
Gillingham v Mansfield T
Rochdale v Crewe Alex
Shrewsbury T v Northampton T
Torquay U v Lincoln C
Walsall v Colchester U
Wycombe W v Scunthorpe U

Saturday 30 April 1994
FA Carling Premiership
Arsenal v West Ham U
Coventry C v Blackburn R
Ipswich T v Manchester U
Leeds U v Everton
Liverpool v Norwich C
Manchester C v Chelsea
Oldham Ath v Sheffield W
QPR v Swindon T
Sheffield U v Newcastle U
Southampton v Aston Villa
Wimbledon v Tottenham H

Football League Division 1
Barnsley v Wolverhampton W
Birmingham C v Bolton W
Derby Co v Oxford U
Leicester C v Stoke C
Luton T v Southend U
Middlesbrough v Crystal Palace
Millwall v Bristol C
Notts Co v Charlton Ath
Peterborough U v Nottingham F
Sunderland v Tranmere R
Watford v Portsmouth
WBA v Grimsby T

Football League Division 2
Barnet v York C
Bristol R v Stockport Co
Burnley v Brentford
Cardiff C v Cambridge U
Fulham v Rotherham U
Huddersfield T v Blackpool
Hull C v AFC Bournemouth
Leyton O v Swansea C
Plymouth Arg v Bradford C
Port Vale v Exeter C
Reading v Brighton & HA
Wrexham v Hartlepool U

Football League Division 3
Bury v Rochdale
Colchester U v Doncaster R

Crewe Alex v Wycombe W
Hereford U v Torquay U
Lincoln C v Walsall
Mansfield T v Darlington
Northampton T v Chester C
Preston NE v Carlisle U
Scarborough v Chesterfield
Scunthorpe U v Shrewsbury T
Wigan Ath v Gillingham

Saturday 7 May 1994
FA Carling Premiership
Aston Villa v Liverpool
Blackburn R v Ipswich T
Chelsea v Sheffield U
Everton v Wimbledon
Manchester U v Coventry C
Newcastle U v Arsenal
Norwich C v Oldham Ath
Sheffield W v Manchester C
Swindon T v Leeds U
Tottenham H v QPR
West Ham U v Southampton

Football League Division 1
Bolton W v Barnsley
Bristol C v Peterborough U
Charlton Ath v Middlesbrough
Crystal Palace v Watford
Grimsby T v Millwall
Nottingham F v Sunderland
Oxford U v Notts Co
Portsmouth v WBA
Southend U v Derby Co
Stoke C v Luton T
Tranmere R v Birmingham C
Wolverhampton W v Leicester C

Football League Division 2
AFC Bournemouth v Reading
Blackpool v Leyton O
Bradford C v Cardiff C
Brentford v Huddersfield T
Brighton & HA v Port Vale
Cambridge U v Bristol R
Exeter C v Burnley
Hartlepool U v Plymouth Arg
Rotherham U v Barnet
Stockport Co v Hull City
Swansea C v Fulham
York C v Wrexham

Football League Division 3
Carlisle U v Colchester U
Chester C v Crewe Alex
Chesterfield v Northampton T
Darlington v Bury
Doncaster R v Hereford U
Gillingham v Lincoln C
Rochdale v Scunthorpe U
Shrewsbury T v Wigan Ath
Torquay U v Scarborough
Walsall v Mansfield T
Wycombe W v Preston NE

FA PREMIER LEAGUE FIXTURES 1993–94

	Arsenal	Aston Villa	Blackburn R	Chelsea	Coventry C	Everton	Ipswich T	Leeds U	Liverpool	Manchester C	Manchester U	Newcastle U	Norwich C	Oldham Ath	QPR	Sheffield U	Sheffield W	Southampton	Swindon T	Tottenham H	West Ham U	Wimbledon
Arsenal	—	6.11	26.2	16.4	14.8	28.8	11.9	24.8	26.3	16.10	12.3	27.11	30.10	22.1	3.1	29.12	11.12	25.9	2.4	7.12	30.4	9.4
Aston Villa	23.4	—	1.1	23.10	12.3	26.2	12.3	30.3	7.5	27.12	23.8	2.10	4.4	19.3	14.8	20.11	8.12	24.11	12.2	28.8	15.1	11.12
Blackburn R	1.9	9.4	—	4.12	23.11	29.12	7.5	22.1	5.3	18.12	2.4	19.2	18.8	21.8	23.4	18.10	25.9	20.11	26.3	30.10	18.9	3.1
Chelsea	20.11	22.1	14.8	—	12.3	3.1	11.12	23.4	25.9	22.1	11.9	28.12	16.10	30.10	25.8	7.5	28.8	2.4	9.4	26.2	26.3	8.12
Coventry C	4.12	5.3	30.4	18.9	—	6.11	23.12	25.9	1.9	19.2	27.11	18.8	26.3	18.12	22.1	31.10	16.4	16.10	3.1	9.4	21.8	2.4
Everton	19.2	31.8	4.4	30.3	23.4	—	12.2	23.11	18.9	17.8	23.10	18.12	25.9	5.3	20.11	31.10	27.12	4.12	15.1	26.3	1.1	7.5
Ipswich T	5.3	18.9	27.11	21.8	4.4	30.10	—	17.10	1.1	29.3	30.4	31.8	18.12	4.12	26.3	19.2	6.11	17.8	16.4	26.9	27.12	22.1
Leeds U	18.12	3.1	23.10	6.11	19.3	30.4	15.1	—	19.2	4.12	9.4	2.4	21.8	30.8	18.9	12.2	6.11	5.3	27.11	16.4	17.8	2.10
Liverpool	2.10	28.11	12.9	19.3	26.2	12.3	9.4	28.8	—	22.1	4.1	16.4	16.4	16.10	2.4	18.9	12.2	5.3	27.11	16.4	25.9	30.10
Manchester C	19.9	18.12	26.12	5.3	7.5	22.1	24.11	1.1	23.4	—	7.11	21.8	4.12	4.4	30.10	18.8	26.3	19.2	22.1	16.10	1.9	23.11
Manchester U	7.5	23.8	2.4	11.9	27.11	23.10	30.4	9.4	4.1	7.11	—	21.8	27.11	30.8	7.12	24.11	13.9	28.8	25.8	22.1	10.11	11.12
Newcastle U	12.2	2.10	19.2	28.12	18.8	18.12	31.8	2.4	16.4	21.8	21.8	—	30.3	4.4	15.1	24.11	14.8	24.10	1.1	16.10	4.12	6.11
Norwich C	23.10	4.4	18.8	16.10	26.3	25.9	18.12	21.8	16.4	16.4	1.1	27.11	—	18.9	1.9	1.9	22.1	2.1	25.8	22.1	22.1	5.3
Oldham Ath	25.9	19.3	21.8	30.10	18.12	5.3	4.12	30.8	16.10	2.10	30.8	4.4	18.9	—	27.12	24.11	4.4	18.9	24.11	18.9	20.11	19.2
QPR	30.3	14.8	23.4	25.8	22.1	20.11	26.3	18.9	2.4	11.9	7.12	15.1	1.9	27.12	—	1.9	1.1	21.8	30.4	4.1	2.4	27.9
Sheffield U	4.4	16.4	15.1	7.5	31.10	31.10	19.2	12.2	18.9	19.3	24.11	5.3	1.9	24.11	1.1	—	23.10	26.3	25.8	27.11	29.3	18.12
Sheffield W	21.8	15.1	19.3	28.8	16.4	27.12	6.11	6.11	12.2	26.3	13.9	14.8	22.1	4.4	23.10	23.10	—	18.9	29.12	22.1	3.1	25.8
Southampton	19.3	30.4	16.4	2.4	14.8	8.12	20.11	1.9	12.2	4.4	1.9	24.10	1.1	30.3	26.3	12.3	25.8	—	18.12	25.8	23.4	26.2
Swindon T	27.12	30.10	2.10	1.1	30.3	16.10	7.5	22.8	1.9	19.3	18.9	1.9	22.1	18.8	11.12	4.12	4.4	18.12	—	22.1	5.3	23.4
Tottenham H	16.8	19.2	12.3	1.9	21.8	7.5	27.12	7.5	30.3	27.12	15.1	4.12	22.1	18.9	3.1	22.1	30.3	23.4	23.10	—	28.12	11.9
West Ham U	24.11	16.10	18.12	16.10	27.11	1.1	18.12	15.1	4.12	24.11	18.9	19.3	22.1	20.11	29.3	3.1	18.12	7.5	7.5	4.4	—	14.8
Wimbledon	1.1	21.8	29.3	17.8	26.12	27.11	23.10	26.3	4.4	12.2	12.3	2.10	1.1	30.4	27.9	18.12	15.1	31.8	6.11	30.4	4.12	—

BARCLAYS LEAGUE FIXTURES 1993-94

DIVISION ONE

	Barnsley	Birmingham C	Bolton W	Bristol C	Charlton Ath	Crystal Palace	Derby Co	Grimsby T	Leicester C	Luton T	Middlesbrough	Millwall	Nottingham F	Notts Co	Oxford U	Peterborough U	Portsmouth	Southend U	Stoke C	Sunderland	Tranmere R	Watford	WBA	Wolverhampton W
Barnsley	—	28.8	5.3	7.5	16.10	22.1	23.4	2.4	4.12	19.3	2.10	19.2	4.9	16.3	28.12	2.11	17.8	9.4	5.2	30.10	3.1	18.9	21.8	19.12
Birmingham C	5.3	—	19.10	2.11	14.8	11.12	26.2	12.2	12.3	11.9	19.3	2.10	12.2	4.12	11.1	29.3	23.10	23.4	1.1	27.12	9.10	7.5	15.1	16.10
Bolton W	7.5	30.4	—	26.3	18.9	4.9	30.10	19.2	11.9	11.9	20.11	15.1	19.3	9.10	30.4	26.2	12.1	23.2	5.3	28.12	27.11	23.10	23.10	26.3
Bristol C	16.10	2.11	2.10	—	18.9	21.8	5.3	9.4	14.9	19.2	4.12	7.5	28.12	30.4	15.3	7.5	19.3	2.4	3.1	30.10	5.2	23.4	2.4	18.12
Charlton Ath	22.1	14.8	28.8	12.3	—	25.9	2.11	5.2	16.10	4.12	7.5	11.9	9.4	13.11	30.10	3.1	11.12	2.4	28.12	22.2	24.8	26.2	3.1	26.3
Crystal Palace	23.4	11.12	12.2	21.8	25.9	—	5.2	2.4	9.10	2.11	16.4	19.2	18.8	6.11	27.12	29.3	5.3	6.4	6.4	22.1	11.12	30.3	12.3	16.10
Derby Co	2.4	26.2	12.2	28.8	16.4	23.10	—	20.11	3.1	9.10	23.2	12.3	11.12	15.8	27.11	26.3	15.8	7.5	2.10	14.8	3.1	7.5	11.9	6.11
Grimsby T	4.12	12.2	14.8	9.4	5.2	16.4	2.11	—	2.11	15.1	29.12	3.1	27.11	21.8	2.10	4.9	19.2	27.11	9.10	11.12	28.12	27.12	11.9	16.10
Leicester C	19.3	11.9	12.3	11.12	16.10	2.11	28.12	2.11	—	12.2	30.10	4.9	5.3	5.2	26.3	19.12	3.1	4.12	30.4	3.1	23.2	27.12	12.1	14.8
Luton T	2.10	19.3	11.9	6.11	29.12	30.10	4.4	12.2	18.9	—	12.3	30.3	5.3	15.1	23.10	22.2	21.8	13.11	7.5	26.2	11.12	1.1	14.8	20.11
Middlesbrough	19.2	2.10	20.11	4.12	7.5	4.12	23.2	29.3	29.3	18.9	—	5.2	16.4	23.10	1.1	26.2	12.2	11.9	23.10	9.10	11.12	22.1	19.3	9.10
Millwall	4.9	12.2	19.3	11.9	19.2	11.9	16.4	26.3	5.2	30.3	28.8	—	23.10	16.10	11.12	31.8	2.10	19.12	18.9	25.9	20.11	2.10	23.4	5.2
Nottingham F	16.3	4.12	11.1	28.12	9.4	18.8	11.12	21.8	30.4	5.3	16.4	23.10	—	30.10	4.9	13.11	2.10	3.1	18.9	30.4	16.10	2.10	11.9	9.10
Notts Co	28.12	11.9	9.4	30.4	1.1	6.11	15.8	11.12	5.2	15.1	30.10	16.10	12.2	—	12.2	22.2	21.8	3.1	30.10	12.3	16.10	12.3	11.9	16.4
Oxford U	2.11	29.3	9.10	13.11	23.10	27.12	27.11	2.10	26.3	23.10	1.1	11.12	22.2	12.3	—	12.3	14.8	15.1	9.10	11.1	19.3	28.8	21.8	4.4
Peterborough U	17.8	23.10	26.2	11.1	3.1	29.3	26.3	4.9	19.12	22.2	26.2	14.8	19.3	13.11	22.1	—	12.3	2.10	12.1	2.10	26.3	4.12	12.2	16.10
Portsmouth	9.4	23.4	12.1	2.4	11.12	5.3	15.8	19.2	3.1	30.3	12.2	2.10	23.10	11.9	18.9	9.10	—	15.1	14.8	1.1	30.4	2.10	6.11	1.1
Southend U	5.2	1.1	23.2	2.4	29.12	6.4	7.5	27.11	4.12	13.11	11.9	19.12	3.1	28.8	15.1	22.1	26.2	—	25.9	18.9	4.9	26.3	16.4	30.10
Stoke C	30.10	27.12	4.9	1.1	28.12	6.4	2.10	9.10	30.4	7.5	23.10	18.9	12.1	12.1	25.9	12.1	26.2	25.9	—	19.2	16.4	11.9	23.10	5.2
Sunderland	3.1	9.10	22.1	18.12	22.2	22.1	14.8	11.12	3.1	26.2	9.10	25.9	30.4	4.4	19.2	12.2	26.3	18.9	16.4	—	30.4	19.3	23.10	18.9
Tranmere R	18.9	7.5	27.11	29.3	24.8	11.12	3.1	28.12	23.2	11.12	11.12	20.11	16.10	26.3	20.11	4.12	30.10	2.10	13.11	30.4	—	11.12	7.5	27.12
Watford	21.8	15.1	30.3	19.2	26.2	30.3	7.5	27.12	27.12	1.1	22.1	2.10	30.3	15.1	4.12	26.3	12.2	26.3	16.4	19.3	1.1	—	12.2	7.9
WBA	19.12	4.4	6.11	27.12	3.1	12.2	11.9	22.1	11.9	14.8	2.4	22.1	24.8	16.3	21.8	16.10	27.11	1.9	5.3	5.2	16.4	12.2	—	4.9
Wolverhampton	13.11	22.2	3.1	14.8	26.3	16.10	6.11	16.10	25.9	20.11	30.10	5.2	9.10	16.4	4.4	16.10	1.1	30.10	23.10	12.3	2.4	7.9	26.2	—

BARCLAYS LEAGUE FIXTURES 1993–94

DIVISION TWO

	Barnet	Blackpool	Bournemouth	Bradford C	Brentford	Brighton & HA	Bristol R	Burnley	Cambridge U	Cardiff C	Exeter C	Fulham	Hartlepool U	Huddersfield T	Hull C	Leyton O	Plymouth Arg	Port Vale	Reading	Rotherham U	Stockport Co	Swansea C	Wrexham	York City
Barnet	—	26.2	11.9	6.11	29.1	2.4	2.10	29.12	23.10	10.10	3.1	14.9	16.4	15.1	14.8	12.3	12.2	11.12	22.2	27.11	9.4	28.8	19.3	30.4
Blackpool	4.9	—	25.9	5.3	21.8	30.10	3.1	9.4	14.8	18.9	5.2	8.1	15.3	20.11	2.11	7.5	31.8	16.10	23.4	26.3	2.4	22.1	19.2	28.12
Bournemouth	5.3	19.3	—	21.8	27.12	16.10	18.12	4.9	12.3	15.3	30.10	22.1	19.2	29.3	20.11	5.2	1.1	30.3	7.5	5.4	2.10	8.1	23.4	31.8
Bradford C	23.4	11.9	11.12	—	4.4	14.8	15.3	16.10	19.3	30.10	19.2	18.12	23.10	17.4	2.10	12.2	30.4	3.1	16.3	2.4	23.2	12.3	1.1	30.10
Brentford	30.10	11.12	2.4	4.4	—	12.3	8.1	16.3	26.3	7.5	3.11	18.9	9.10	27.11	26.3	29.12	23.4	30.3	20.11	26.2	23.2	26.3	4.4	5.2
Brighton & HA	27.12	29.1	15.1	14.8	12.3	—	19.3	16.3	1.1	29.1	21.8	6.11	11.12	26.2	8.1	25.9	26.2	27.11	20.11	27.11	28.12	16.4	28.12	12.3
Bristol R	26.3	30.3	14.8	15.3	8.1	19.3	—	25.9	27.11	12.2	18.12	19.2	23.4	2.10	30.10	4.9	30.10	5.2	21.8	5.2	30.10	29.1	1.9	2.4
Burnley	4.4	1.1	26.2	15.1	16.3	30.4	25.9	—	29.1	12.2	8.1	16.3	18.9	19.2	16.3	25.9	22.1	18.12	18.9	21.8	2.4	9.10	9.4	23.4
Cambridge U	5.2	14.8	12.3	19.3	2.10	14.9	27.11	29.1	—	19.11	22.2	3.1	30.10	23.10	28.8	28.8	2.11	22.2	26.2	11.9	11.12	14.9	27.12	6.11
Cardiff C	22.1	12.3	14.9	27.11	19.2	31.8	15.3	12.2	19.11	—	22.2	21.8	18.12	28.11	6.11	28.12	18.12	19.3	26.2	9.4	23.10	12.3	23.10	2.10
Exeter C	29.3	23.10	29.1	19.2	28.8	21.8	18.12	8.1	22.2	22.2	—	2.11	16.4	27.12	15.1	3.1	4.4	27.12	30.4	1.1	6.11	25.9	27.11	16.10
Fulham	15.3	12.2	9.10	18.12	2.11	6.11	19.2	16.3	3.1	21.8	2.11	—	27.12	19.3	15.1	2.10	29.1	20.11	12.2	31.8	5.2	23.10	27.11	18.9
Hartlepool U	2.11	14.9	28.8	23.10	9.10	11.12	23.4	18.9	30.10	18.12	16.4	27.12	—	2.4	31.8	2.4	27.11	28.12	18.9	27.11	8.1	9.4	31.8	19.3
Huddersfield T	16.10	30.4	3.1	17.4	27.11	26.2	2.10	19.2	23.10	29.1	27.12	19.3	2.4	—	12.3	9.4	21.8	22.1	19.3	6.11	28.8	22.2	20.11	9.10
Hull C	18.12	16.4	30.4	2.10	26.3	8.1	30.10	16.3	28.8	23.4	31.8	27.11	31.8	12.3	—	12.3	4.4	29.1	14.8	9.10	27.11	5.2	29.3	4.4
Leyton O	18.9	27.11	23.10	12.2	4.9	25.9	4.9	25.9	28.8	28.12	3.1	2.10	2.4	9.4	12.3	—	30.10	22.1	29.12	16.10	27.11	16.4	29.3	4.9
Plymouth Arg	8.1	22.2	9.4	30.4	23.4	26.2	30.10	19.3	2.11	18.12	4.4	29.1	27.11	21.8	4.4	30.10	—	28.8	12.3	14.9	14.8	26.2	30.10	16.10
Port Vale	21.8	15.1	16.4	3.1	30.3	27.11	5.2	18.12	22.2	19.3	27.12	20.11	28.12	22.1	29.1	22.1	28.8	—	23.10	29.1	12.2	6.11	5.2	9.4
Reading	1.9	6.11	16.3	19.3	19.2	20.11	21.8	18.9	26.2	26.2	30.4	12.2	18.9	19.3	14.8	29.12	12.3	23.10	—	29.1	12.2	19.3	2.10	9.4
Rotherham U	7.5	2.10	28.12	2.4	26.2	27.11	5.2	21.8	22.2	9.4	1.1	30.11	27.11	6.11	9.10	16.10	14.9	22.1	29.1	—	19.3	16.4	14.8	25.9
Stockport Co	1.1	27.12	26.3	31.8	23.2	28.12	30.10	2.4	11.12	23.10	6.11	5.2	8.1	28.8	27.11	14.8	14.8	12.2	12.2	19.3	—	30.10	14.1	29.1
Swansea C	18.2	9.10	12.2	18.9	5.3	28.12	29.1	9.4	14.9	12.3	25.9	23.10	9.4	22.2	5.2	16.4	26.2	6.11	19.3	16.4	30.10	—	11.12	14.8
Wrexham	25.9	28.8	6.11	5.3	28.12	16.4	1.9	9.10	27.12	22.2	27.11	12.2	31.8	20.11	29.3	26.3	30.10	23.4	1.10	14.8	14.1	11.12	—	27.11
York C	20.11	4.4	22.2	29.1	23.10	11.9	23.4	12.2	6.11	8.1	26.3	12.3	19.3	9.10	27.12	26.2	15.1	9.4	29.3	15.3	19.2	14.8	7.5	—

BARCLAYS LEAGUE FIXTURES 1993-94

DIVISION THREE

	Bury	Carlisle U	Chester C	Chesterfield	Colchester U	Crewe Alex	Darlington	Doncaster R	Gillingham	Hereford U	Lincoln C	Mansfield T	Northampton T	Preston NE	Rochdale	Scarborough	Scunthorpe U	Shrewsbury T	Torquay U	Walsall	Wigan Ath	Wycombe W
Bury	—	12.2	16.4	6.11	19.3	28.8	27.11	15.1	9.4	23.10	12.3	2.10	14.8	4.1	30.4	29.1	11.12	26.2	29.12	2.4	9.10	11.9
Carlisle U	8.1	—	19.3	11.9	7.5	28.12	2.4	11.12	2.10	9.4	2.11	16.10	5.2	20.11	28.8	26.2	12.3	22.1	3.1	30.10	23.4	14.8
Chester C	2.11	25.9	—	28.8	9.4	7.5	22.1	14.8	28.12	23.4	3.1	5.2	20.11	2.4	26.2	12.3	11.9	16.10	30.10	8.1	26.3	11.12
Chesterfield	23.4	5.3	19.2	—	8.1	30.10	4.9	27.12	18.12	21.8	5.2	31.8	7.5	22.1	19.3	20.11	4.4	1.1	16.10	18.9	2.11	2.10
Colchester U	25.9	27.11	1.1	12.2	—	11.12	16.4	30.4	29.1	15.1	14.8	27.12	28.8	26.3	11.9	4.4	9.10	31.8	26.2	6.11	23.10	12.3
Crewe Alex	19.2	4.4	27.11	29.1	21.8	—	18.9	1.1	23.10	9.10	2.10	4.9	31.8	17.12	6.11	15.1	12.2	16.4	28.8	5.3	27.12	30.4
Darlington	7.5	27.12	9.10	26.2	2.11	12.3	—	4.4	15.1	12.2	11.12	20.11	30.10	23.4	14.8	31.8	29.1	11.9	28.8	25.9	1.1	23.10
Doncaster R	16.10	21.8	17.12	2.4	20.11	9.4	28.12	—	3.1	7.5	22.1	17.9	30.10	4.3	2.10	23.4	1.11	5.2	8.1	19.2	4.9	19.3
Gillingham	1.1	26.3	4.4	14.8	30.10	5.2	16.10	31.8	—	2.11	7.5	23.4	27.12	8.1	11.12	28.8	25.9	12.3	11.9	22.1	20.11	26.2
Hereford U	5.2	1.1	6.11	11.12	16.10	22.1	8.1	27.11	16.4	—	28.8	4.4	11.9	30.10	14.8	26.2	26.3	27.12	30.4	26.3	25.9	31.8
Lincoln C	18.9	16.4	31.8	23.10	14.12	26.3	21.8	9.10	27.11	19.2	—	5.3	25.9	4.9	29.1	1.1	27.12	4.4	6.11	30.4	12.2	15.1
Mansfield T	26.3	15.1	23.10	3.1	2.4	26.2	30.4	12.3	6.11	28.12	11.9	—	11.12	25.9	16.4	9.10	28.8	14.8	9.4	27.11	29.1	12.2
Northampton T	18.12	23.10	30.4	27.11	19.2	3.1	2.10	29.1	19.3	5.3	19.3	12.10	—	29.12	9.4	12.2	15.1	6.11	16.4	4.9	18.9	9.10
Preston NE	31.8	30.4	27.11	9.10	2.10	14.8	6.11	11.9	12.2	29.1	26.2	19.3	4.4	—	23.10	1.1	1.1	28.8	12.3	16.4	15.1	27.11
Rochdale	20.11	19.2	4.9	25.9	5.3	23.4	18.12	26.3	21.8	18.9	30.10	2.11	1.1	5.2	—	26.12	7.5	8.1	22.1	16.10	31.8	4.4
Scarborough	30.10	4.9	18.9	30.4	28.12	16.10	3.1	6.11	19.2	18.12	9.4	22.1	8.1	21.8	2.4	—	26.3	25.9	27.11	5.2	5.3	16.4
Scunthorpe U	21.8	18.9	5.3	28.12	22.1	8.1	30.10	16.4	19.3	4.9	2.4	19.2	16.10	9.4	27.11	2.10	—	30.4	5.2	3.1	18.12	6.11
Shrewsbury T	4.9	9.10	15.1	9.4	3.1	2.11	5.3	23.10	18.9	2.4	28.12	17.12	23.4	19.2	12.2	19.3	20.11	—	2.10	21.8	7.5	29.1
Torquay U	5.4	31.8	29.1	15.1	4.9	25.9	19.2	12.2	5.3	20.11	23.4	1.1	2.11	18.9	9.10	7.5	23.10	26.3	—	18.12	21.8	27.12
Walsall	27.12	29.1	12.2	12.3	23.4	11.9	19.3	28.8	9.10	18.12	20.11	7.5	26.2	2.11	15.1	23.10	31.8	11.12	14.8	—	5.4	1.1
Wigan Ath	22.1	6.11	21.8	16.4	5.2	2.4	9.4	26.2	30.4	19.3	8.1	30.10	12.3	2.11	4.1	11.9	14.8	17.11	11.12	18.12	—	28.8
Wycombe W	5.3	18.12	21.8	26.3	18.9	20.11	5.2	25.9	4.9	3.1	16.10	8.1	22.1	7.5	28.12	2.11	23.4	30.10	2.4	9.4	19.2	—

OTHER FIXTURES—SEASON 1993–94

August
7 Sat FA Charity Shield
14 Sat FA Premier League & Football League Season
       commences
18 Wed Coca-Cola Cup 1st Round (1st Leg)
25 Wed Coca-Cola Cup 1st Round (2nd Leg)
28 Sat FA Challenge Cup Preliminary Round

September
4 Sat FA Challenge Vase Extra Preliminary Round
7 Tues England v Poland (U-21)
       England v Romania (U-18)
8 Wed England v Poland (WC)
11 Sat FA Challenge Cup 1st Qualifying Round
       FA Youth Challenge Cup Preliminary Round*
15 Wed European Competitions 1st Round (1st Leg)
18 Sat FA Challenge Trophy—First Round Qualifying
22 Wed Coca-Cola Cup Second Round (1st Leg)
25 Sat FA Challenge Cup Second Qualifying Round
28 Tues FA XI v Herefordshire FA
29 Wed European Competitions First Round (2nd Leg)

October
2 Sat FA Challenge Vase Preliminary Round
       FA Youth Challenge Cup First Round
       Qualifying*
6 Wed Coca-Cola Cup Second Round (2nd Leg)
9 Sat FA Challenge Cup Third Round Qualifying
10 Sun FA Sunday Cup Preliminary Round (if
       required)
12 Tues Holland v England (U-21)
13 Wed Holland v England (World Cup)
       Romania v England (U-18)
16 Sat FA Challenge Trophy Second Round
       Qualifying
       FA Youth Challenge Cup Second Round
       Qualifying*
       FA County Youth Challenge Cup First
       Round*
20 Wed European Competitions Second Round (1st
       Leg)
23 Sat FA Challenge Cup Fourth Round Qualifying
27 Wed Coca-Cola Cup Third Round
       France v England (U-18)
30 Sat FA Challenge Vase First Round
31 Sun FA Sunday Cup First Round

November
3 Wed European Competitions Second Round (2nd
       Leg)
       FA XI v Southern League
13 Sat FA Challenge Cup First Round Proper
       FA Youth Challenge Cup First Round Proper*
16 Tues San Marino v England (WC)
       England v France (U-18)
       FA XI v Northern Premier League
17 Wed San Marino v England (U-21)
20 Sat FA Challenge Vase Second Round
21 Sun FA Sunday Cup Second Round
24 Wed ECL/UEFA Cup Third Round (1st Leg)
       Holland v England (U-16)
27 Sat FA Challenge Trophy Third Round Qualifying
       FA County Youth Challenge Cup Second
       Round*

December
1 Wed Coca-Cola Cup Fourth Round
4 Wed FA Challenge Cup Second Round Proper
7 Tues FA XI v Isthmian League
8 Wed ECL/UEFA Cup Third Round (2nd Leg)
       Italy v England (U-16)
11 Sat FA Challenge Vase Third Round
       FA Youth Challenge Cup Second Round
       Proper*
12 Sun FA Sunday Cup Third Round

January
8 Sat FA Challenge Cup Third Round Proper
10 Mon FA XI v British Students
11 Tues FA XI v Combined Services

12 Wed Coca-Cola Cup Fifth Round
15 Sat FA Challenge Vase Fourth Round
       FA Youth Challenge Cup Third Round
       Proper*
       FA County Youth Challenge Cup Third
       Round*
16 Sun FA Sunday Cup Fourth Round
22 Sat FA Challenge Trophy First Round Proper
29 Sat FA Challenge Cup Fourth Round Proper

February
2 Wed International date
       England v Italy (U-16)
5 Sat FA Challenge Vase Fifth Round
       FA Youth Challenge Cup Fourth Round
       Proper*
12 Sat FA Challenge Trophy Second Round Proper
13 Sun Coca-Cola Cup Semi-final (1st Leg)
       FA Sunday Cup Fifth Round
16 Wed Coca-Cola Cup Semi-final (1st Leg)
19 Sat FA Challenge Cup Fifth Round Proper
       FA County Youth Challenge Cup Fourth
       Round*
23 Wed Coca-Cola Cup Semi-final (2nd Leg)
26 Sat FA Challenge Vase Sixth Round
27 Sun Coca-Cola Semi-final (2nd Leg)

March
2 Wed ECL/ECWC and UEFA Cup Quarter-finals
       (1st Leg)
5 Sat FA Challenge Trophy Third Round Proper
       FA Youth Challenge Cup Fifth Round Proper*
9 Wed International date
       England v Holland (U-16)
12 Sat FA Challenge Cup Sixth Round Proper
16 Wed ECL/ECWC and UEFA Cup Quarter-final
       (2nd Leg)
19 Sat FA Challenge Vase Semi-final (1st Leg)
       FA County Youth Challenge Cup Semi-final*
       Anglo-Italian Cup Final—Wembley Stadium
20 Sun FA Sunday Cup Semi-final
26 Sat FA Challenge Trophy Fourth Round Proper
       FA Challenge Vase Semi-final (2nd Leg)
27 Sun Coca-Cola Cup Final
30 Wed ECL/ECWC and UEFA Cup Semi-final (1st Leg)

April
2 Sat FA Youth Challenge Cup Semi-final*
10 Sun FA Challenge Cup Semi-final
13 Wed ECL/ECWC and UEFA Cup Semi-final (2nd
       Leg)
16 Sat FA Challenge Trophy Semi-final (1st Leg)
20 Wed Germany v England (Friendly)
23 Sat FA Challenge Trophy Semi-final (2nd Leg)
27 Wed ECL Semi-final/UEFA Cup Final (1st Leg)
30 Sat FA County Youth Challenge Cup Final (fixed
       date)

May
4 Wed European Cup Winners' Cup Final
7 Sat FA Challenge Vase final—Wembley Stadium
       FA Youth Challenge Cup Final*
8 Sun FA Sunday Cup Final
11 Wed UEFA Cup Final (2nd Leg)
14 Sat FA Challenge Cup Final—Wembley Stadium
       International date
15 Sun FL Play-off Semi-final (1st Leg)
18 Web European Champion Clubs' Cup Final
       FL Ply-off Semi-final (2nd Leg)
21 Sat FA Challenge Trophy Final—Wembley
       Stadium
22 Sun International date
28 Sat FL Div 3 Play-off Final—Wembley Stadium
29 Sun FL Div 2 Play-off Final—Wembley Stadium
30 Mon FL Div 1 Play-off Final—Wembley Stadium
       Bank Holiday

June
17 Fri FIFA World Cup Finals commence
       (end 17 July)

Key
WC—FIFA World Cup — ECL – European Champions League
ECWC – European Cup Winners' Cup — * *Closing dates of rounds*
N.B. Coca-Cola dates refer to middle of week in which matches can be played. Dates for Autoglass Trophy: w/c 27 Sept,
18 Oct, 8 Nov (Round I), 29 Nov (Round 2), 10 Jan (Q-F), 7 Feb (SF), 28 Feb (Area Finals), 21 March (Area Finals), 24
April (Final)

The things they said . . .

Barnet chairman Stan Flashman to photographer before a League inquiry into alleged financial irregularities:
"If you take a picture, I'll smash that camera over your head."

Barnet manager Barry Fry, on Flashman:
"If you didn't know him, you'd think he was an absolute ignorant pig. He is, in many ways, but he does care for the club." November 1992

Barry Fry, after being sacked by Flashman for the umpteenth time:
"I'm absolutely gutted. I'm devastated. The man is a complete and utter shit." December 1992

Liverpool boss Graeme Souness after the 1-1 Coca-Cola Cup draw with Crystal Palace:
"If that's what football is about, then I'll have to look for another job. We expected a physical game, and we certainly got one."

Palace assistant manager Alan Smith:
"I don't remember Souness being a wallflower in his playing days. The side we had out couldn't maul a church choir."

Falkirk manager Jim Jefferies on Kevin Drinkell's disallowed goal against Rangers, after Richard Cadette was penalized for holding off his marker in the build-up:
"One of Cadette's strengths is holding off people with his back to goal. If that wasn't legal, nor were many of Kenny Dalglish's during his career."

Arsenal boss George Graham:"
I could not win a place in the present Arsenal team. I would be too slow."

Spurs coach Ray Clemence after a fracas between Gudni Bergsson and Forest's Stuart Pearce:
"It's very unusual for an Icelandic player to get annoyed."

Grampus 8 star Gary Lineker (on BBC TV):
"[The Premier League was] a missed opportunity. I don't think anyone is fooled. There is no difference from the old First Division. We play too much football and nothing has been done to alter that."

Hartlepool chairman Garry Gibson, after they knock Crystal Place out of the FA Cup:
"The listening bank refused to listen and the bank that likes to say 'Yes' said 'No'. Maybe they'll think again now."

BBC commentator John Motson:
"This match was settled either side of half-time."

PFA chief executive Gordon Taylor, after Vinny Jones' appeal against his 'video nasty' punishment had failed.
"If someone talks about what should not go on and is punished far heavier than someone who is carrying out the deeds, then justice is the wrong way round. If I was talking about the various ways of committing murder on TV, I could not be expected to be in more trouble than a murderer." 25 February 1993

Brian Clough, after receiving the Freedom of Nottingham:
"It's a beautiful place with lovely people. The Trent is lovely, too. I've walked on it for 18 years. Just kidding."

Sheffield United boss Dave Bassett on his directors:
"They've been loyal to me. When I came here they said there would be no money, and they've kept their promise."

Barnet manager Barry Fry's desperate cry for help as he finds that the players' pay cheques have bounced:
"Someone out there must come and get hold of Barnet and save the club." 26 March

Cardiff chairman Rick Wright, after they are held 1-1 by Barnet at Ninian Park, on handing £1,000 to the Barnet players:
"... so they can have a decent drink and a meal on the way home." 27 March

Forest fans chanting, despite having just seen Sheffield United condemn their club to the First Division after Brian Clough's last match in charge:
"Brian Clough's a football genius." 1 May

Sheffield United fans, at the same match:
"Clough for England."

England manager Graham Taylor after they let a two-goal lead slip against Holland at Wembley:
"Oh misery, misery. What's gonna become of me?" (with apologies to Buddy Holly)

Trevor Brooking, BBC TV commentator, on Les Ferdinand, after the England striker had missed a sitter against Norway:
"That's his weakness, finishing."

England manager Graham Taylor after the 1-1 draw in Poland:
"You can't play the game if your head goes, and we were running around like headless chickens."

England manager Graham Taylor a couple of days before his extraordinary team selection for the important World Cup qualifier in Norway:
"I'm taking a little more time over my selection because it's important for England - not Graham Taylor or the players, but England - that I get it right and not rush into decisions that I might regret."

Bobby Charlton, using the patriotic 'we', although he had no reason to blame himself, on England's defeat in Norway:
"We were technically naive, unprofessional in everything we did. It was a performance that really plumbed the depths."

England manager Graham Taylor on Paul Gascoigne's lack of fitness:
"I cannot allow myself to record publicly exactly what I think all his problems are. If I did, all hell would be let loose. What I find difficult is that there are people who know, but they want me or someone else to say what is wrong. However, I cannot, or will not, go all the way down the line."

England manager Graham Taylor after their defeat by the United States:
"We played them on the wrong day." 9 June 1993

1024

More bestselling non-fiction
from Headline

ROTHMANS RUGBY LEAGUE YEARBOOK 1993–94	Howes/Fletcher	£14.99
ROTHMANS RUGBY UNION YEARBOOK 1993–94	Stephen Jones	£14.99
PLAYFAIR FOOTBALL ANNUAL 1993–94	Jack Rollin	£3.99
PLAYFAIR EUROPEAN FOOTBALL ANNUAL 1993–94	Bruce Smith	£3.99
PLAYFAIR CRICKET ANNUAL 1993	Bill Frindall	£3.99
BOBBY MOORE: A TRIBUTE	David Emery	£9.99
MARTIN PIPE: THE CHAMPION TRAINER'S STORY	Martin Pipe	£5.99
HEART AND SOLE	David Sole	£5.99
DALGLISH	Stephen F Kelly	£5.99

All Headline books are available at your local bookshop or newsagent, or can be ordered direct from the publisher. Just tick the titles you want and fill in the form below. Prices and availability subject to change without notice.

Headline Book Publishing Ltd, Cash Sales Department, Bookpoint, 39 Milton Park, Abingdon, OXON, OX14 4TD, UK. If you have a credit card you may order by telephone–0235 831700.

Please enclose a cheque or postal order made payable to Bookpoint Ltd to the value of the cover price and allow the following for postage and packing:
UK & BFPO: £1.00 for the first book, 50p for the second book and 30p for each additional book ordered up to a maximum charge of £3.00.
OVERSEAS & EIRE: £2.00 for the first book, £1.00 for the second book and 50p for each additional book.

Name ....

Address ....

....

....

If you would prefer to pay by credit card, please complete:
Please debit my Visa/Access/Diner's Card/American Express (delete as applicable) card no:

Signature .... Expiry Date ....